Handbook of Attachment

Handbook of Attachment

THEORY, RESEARCH,
AND CLINICAL APPLICATIONS

Edited by

JUDE CASSIDY
PHILLIP R. SHAVER

THE GUILFORD PRESS
New York   London

© 1999 The Guilford Press
A Division of Guilford Publications, Inc.
72 Spring Street, New York, NY 10012
http://www.guilford.com

Printed in the United States of America

This book is printed on acid-free paper.

Last digit is print number: 9 8 7 6 5 4 3 2 1

Library of Congress Cataloging-in-Publication Data
Handbook of attachment : theory, research, and clinical applications /
  edited by Jude Cassidy, Phillip R. Shaver.
     p.   cm.
  Includes bibliographical references and index.
  ISBN 1-57230-087-6
  1. Attachment behavior.   2. Attachment behavior in children.
I. Cassidy, Jude.   II. Shaver, Phillip R.
BF575.A86H36   1999
155.9'2—dc21   98-53527
                                                            CIP

*With respect and gratitude
for the pioneering work
of John Bowlby and Mary Ainsworth*

About the Editors

Jude Cassidy, PhD, is Associate Professor of Psychology at the University of Maryland, College Park. Her research interests include attachment throughout the lifespan, children's peer relations, and intervention with high-risk infants. She is co-editor of the journal *Attachment and Human Development.*

Phillip R. Shaver, PhD, is Professor of Psychology at the University of California, Davis, where he recently served as department chair. His research interests include attachment processes in adult relationships, close relationships more generally, and human emotions. He is author or editor of eight books, including *In Search of Intimacy* and *Emotions, Relationships, and Health,* past editor of *Review of Personality and Social Psychology,* and former Executive Officer of the Society of Experimental Social Psychology.

Contributors

Joseph P. Allen, PhD, Department of Psychology, University of Virginia, Charlottesville, Virginia

Kathleen E. Albus, MA, Department of Psychology, University of Delaware, Newark, Delaware

Jay Belsky, PhD, Department of Human Development and Family Studies, Pennsylvania State University, University Park, Pennsylvania

Lisa J. Berlin, PhD, Research Scientist, Center for the Study of Young Children and Families, Teachers College, Columbia University, New York, New York

Kelly K. Bost, PhD, Department of Human and Community Development, University of Illinois at Urbana–Champaign, Urbana, Illinois

Inge Bretherton, PhD, Department of Child and Family Studies, University of Wisconsin, Madison, Wisconsin

Preston A. Britner, PhD, Department of Family Studies, University of Connecticut, Storrs, Connecticut

John Byng-Hall, MB, BChir, DSc (Hon.), FRCPsych, Consultant Child and Adolescent Psychiatrist, Tavistock Clinic, London, United Kingdom

Judith A. Card, PhD, Institute for Child Study, University of Maryland, College Park, Maryland

Elizabeth A. Carlson, PhD, Institute of Child Development, University of Minnesota, Minneapolis, Minnesota

Jude Cassidy, PhD, Department of Psychology, University of Maryland, College Park, Maryland

Judith A. Crowell, MD, Department of Psychiatry and Behavioral Sciences, State University of New York at Stony Brook, Stony Brook, New York

Mary Dozier, PhD, Department of Psychology, University of Delaware, Newark, Delaware

Byron Egeland, PhD, Institute of Child Development, University of Minnesota, Minneapolis, Minnesota

Judith A. Feeney, PhD, School of Psychology, University of Queensland, Brisbane, Queensland, Australia

Peter Fonagy, PhD, Sub-Department of Clinical Health Psychology, Psychoanalysis Unit, University College London, London, United Kingdom

Nathan A. Fox, PhD, Institute for Child Study, University of Maryland, College Park, Maryland

R. Chris Fraley, MA, Department of Psychology, University of California, Davis, California

Carol George, PhD, Department of Psychology, Mills College, Oakland, California

Mark T. Greenberg, PhD, Director, Prevention Research Center; College of Health and Human Development, The Pennsylvania State University, University Park, Pennsylvania

Karin Grossmann, PhD, Dipl.Psych., Department of Psychology, University of Regensburg, Regensburg, Germany

Klaus E. Grossmann, PhD, Dipl.Psych., Department of Psychology, University of Regensburg, Regensburg, Germany

Cindy Hazan, PhD, Department of Human Development, Cornell University, Ithaca, New York

Erik Hesse, PhD, Center for Child and Family Studies, Leiden University, Leiden, The Netherlands

Myron A. Hofer, MD, Department of Psychiatry, Columbia University College of Physicians and Surgeons, New York, New York

Carollee Howes, PhD, Department of Education, Graduate School of Education and Information Studies, University of California at Los Angeles, Los Angeles, California

Deborah Jacobvitz, PhD, Department of Human Ecology, University of Texas, Austin, Texas

Lee A. Kirkpatrick, PhD, Department of Psychology, College of William and Mary, Williamsburg, Virginia

Roger Kobak, PhD, Department of Psychology, University of Delaware, Newark, Delaware

Deborah Land, MA, Department of Psychology, University of Virginia, Charlottesville, Virginia

Alicia F. Lieberman, PhD, Infant–Parent Program, San Francisco General Hospital, San Francisco, California

Karlen Lyons-Ruth, PhD, Department of Psychiatry, Cambridge Hospital—Harvard Medical School, Cambridge, Massachusetts

Mary Main, PhD, Department of Psychology, University of California at Berkeley, Berkeley, California

Carol Magai, PhD, Department of Psychology, Long Island University, Brooklyn, New York

Robert S. Marvin, PhD, Department of Pediatric Medicine, University of Virginia, Charlottesville, Virginia

Jonathan J. Mohr, MS, Department of Psychology, University of Maryland, College Park, Maryland

Kristine A. Munholland, MS, Department of Child and Family Studies, University of Wisconsin, Madison, Wisconsin

Thomas G. O'Connor, PhD, Department of Child Psychiatry and Department of Psychology, Institute of Psychiatry, London, United Kingdom

H. Jonathan Polan, MD, Department of Psychiatry, Cornell University Medical College, New York, New York

Michael Rutter, MD, FRS, Social, Genetic and Developmental Psychiatry Research Centre, Institute of Psychiatry, London, United Kingdom

Abraham Sagi, MD, CPC, Department of Psychology, University of Haifa, Haifa, Israel

Phillip R. Shaver, PhD, Department of Psychology, University of California, Davis, Davis, California

Jeffry A. Simpson, PhD, Department of Psychology, Texas A & M University, College Station, Texas

Arietta Slade, PhD, Department of Clinical Psychology, City College of New York, and Parent–Infant Program, Center for Psychoanalytic Training and Research, New York, New York

Judith Solomon, PhD, Judith Wallerstein Center for the Family in Transition, Corte Madera, California

K. Chase Stovall, MA, Department of Psychology, University of Delaware, Newark, Delaware

L. Alan Sroufe, PhD, Institute of Child Development, University of Minnesota, Minneapolis, Minnesota

Stephen J. Suomi, PhD, Research Director, Laboratory of Comparative Ethology, National Institute of Child Health and Human Development, Bethesda, Maryland

Ross A. Thompson, PhD, Department of Psychology, University of Nebraska, Lincoln, Nebraska

Marinus H. van IJzendoorn, PhD, Center for Child and Family Studies, Leiden University, Leiden, The Netherlands

Brian E. Vaughn, PhD, Department of Family and Child Development, Auburn University, Auburn, Alabama

Nancy S. Weinfield, PhD, Institute of Child Development, University of Minnesota, Minneapolis, Minnesota

Charles H. Zeanah, MD, Department of Psychiatry, Tulane University School of Medicine, New Orleans, Louisiana

Debra Zeifman, PhD, Department of Psychology, Vassar College, Poughkeepsie, New York

Peter Zimmermann, PhD, Dipl.Psych., Department of Psychology, University of Regensburg, Regensburg, Germany

Preface

It seems unlikely that either John Bowlby, when he first wondered about the relation between maternal deprivation and juvenile delinquency, or Mary Ainsworth, when she answered an advertisement in a London newspaper to work as a postdoctoral researcher with Bowlby, dreamed for a moment that their theoretical efforts would spawn one of the broadest, most profound, and most creative lines of research in 20th-century psychology. But that is what happened. Anyone who today conducts a literature search on the topic of "attachment" will turn up more than 2,000 entries spread across scores of physiological, clinical, developmental, and social psychology journals; packed into numerous anthologies; and dealing with every age period from infancy to old age.

In the fields of social and emotional development, attachment theory is the most visible and empirically grounded conceptual framework. In the growing clinical literature on the effects of early parent–child relationships, including troubled and abusive relationships, attachment theory is prominent. In the rapidly expanding field of research on the close relationships of adolescents and adults—including the study of romantic, marital, or "pair-bond" relationships—attachment theory is one of the most influential approaches. Among researchers who study bereavement, Bowlby's volume on loss is a continuing source of insight and intellectual inspiration.

Moreover, attachment theory is one of the best current examples of the value of serious, coherent theorizing in psychology. It is a model of the process by which scientists move back and forth between clear conceptualizations and penetrating empirical research, with each pole of the dialectic repeatedly influencing the other over an extended period. Attachment theory today is in many respects similar to attachment theory thirty years ago, but it has become much more specific and is being extended significantly in important new directions as a result of careful and creative research. Because the theory was remarkably insightful and accurate to begin with, and because Ainsworth was such an effective researcher, the initial studies inspired by the theory were largely supportive of the theory's basic ideas but were also surprising and provocative in certain respects. The theory encountered considerable criticism at first, as any new scientific theory should. Yet the many honors accorded to Bowlby and Ainsworth toward the ends of their careers symbolize the considerable respect their work now engenders.

One problem created by the enormous literature on attachment, and by the theory's continual evolution in the light of new research, is that few scholars and researchers are familiar with the entire picture that is emerging. In order to make optimal use of the theory as a researcher, clinician, or teacher, one has to know what Bowlby and Ainsworth originally said; what subsequent research has revealed; which measures of attachment have been developed, as well as what they actually measure; and what recent theoretical and empirical developments contribute to the overall "story" of attachment relationships and personality development. The purpose of the present volume is to satisfy these important professional needs. The book will prove useful to anyone who studies attachment processes; who uses attachment theory in clinical work; or who teaches courses and seminars that touch on, or focus on, attachment. It should make an excellent single source for courses devoted to attachment theory and research.

The first section, "Overview of Attachment Theory," provides an updated primer on the theory. The first two chapters correspond roughly to the first and second volumes of Bowlby's trilogy, *Attachment and Loss:* Jude Cassidy, in Chapter 1, explains the central construct of attachment, and Roger Kobak, in Chapter 2, explains Bowlby's and Ainsworth's ideas about the emotional effects of disruption in attachment relationships. In Chapter 3, Robert Marvin and Preston Britner explain the normative development of the attachment behavioral system across the life span. Chapter 4 deals with what is perhaps the best-known part of the theory—Bowlby's and Ainsworth's conceptions of individual differences in the quality of attachment. Nancy Weinfield, Alan Sroufe, Byron Egeland, and Elizabeth Carlson summarize what has been discovered, especially in their own influential studies at the University of Minnesota, about the sequelae of early attachment patterns. In Chapter 5, Inge Bretherton and Kristine Munholland examine the concept of "internal working models," which attachment theorists since Bowlby have used to explain the coherence and continuity of attachment patterns. Although there is obviously no way to replace Bowlby's and Ainsworth's many seminal publications with one section of a single volume, the initial five chapters of this handbook will provide readers—both those new to the field and those experienced in it—with a useful theoretical base.

The second section of the volume, "Biological Perspectives," stems from Bowlby's reliance on ethology and primate research in the creation of attachment theory. Bowlby derived many of his ideas from what today might be called psychobiology and evolutionary psychology, and his borrowing from those fields has been repaid with seminal hypotheses that can be tested in studies of primates and other mammals. In Chapter 6, Jeffry Simpson shows how attachment theory fits with other midrange theories in evolutionary biology and psychology—theories that were not available when Bowlby initially formulated his theory. Just as child–parent relations made more sense when placed by Bowlby in an evolutionary, cross-species comparative framework, attachment theory itself makes more sense when placed in the context of other neo-Darwinian evolutionary theories. In Chapter 7, Jay Belsky carries this analysis further by arguing that the major attachment patterns delineated by Ainsworth (secure, avoidant, and ambivalent) may represent different evolved strategies for increasing reproductive success in particular kinds of physical and social environments.

Chapter 8 marks a shift from the broad evolutionary considerations of the previous two chapters to a review by Jonathan Polan and Myron Hofer of specific, systematic experimental studies of attachment-related behavioral and physiological processes in rats. Under these authors' high-powered analytic microscope, many remarkable details of attachment and separation responses become visible, and the notion of an attachment behavioral system becomes more complex. In Chapter 9, Stephen Suomi shows that many of Bowlby's ideas about attachment and separation processes in humans, which were strongly affected by his reading of primate research, have been tested and elaborated in more detail in recent experimental and field-observational studies of rhesus monkeys and other primates. Two of the largest contributions of this research have been to reveal the interplay of infant temperament and parenting skills in determining the long-range behavioral outcomes of parenting, and to document the intergenerational transmission of attachment orientations—a process also documented in recent studies of humans.

In Chapter 10, Brian Vaughn and Kelly Bost show that the nature and effects of temperament have been more difficult to specify in humans than in rhesus monkeys. There is still no agreement on a single definition of, or conceptual framework for characterizing, human temperament, and no clear picture of the supposed association between individuals' temperaments and the nature of their attachment relationships with particular parents or other relationship partners. Finally, Nathan Fox and Judith Card explain in Chapter 11 how researchers have attempted to use a variety of psychophysiological assessment techniques to supplement and attempt to explain behavioral indicators of attachment processes. Although promising, these techniques are not as simple or as easy to apply as many researchers might wish.

The third section of the volume, "Attachment in Infancy and Childhood," contains three chapters that are crucial for understanding much of the rest of the book. Readers of the table of contents should not infer from the relative brevity of this section that the remainder of the volume deals with something other than attachment in infancy and childhood. In fact, most of the book, like most of attachment research, deals with that broad topic. But just as the first five chapters of the volume provide a primer on the theory, the three in this section provide a rich and sophisticated overview of empirical research on patterns of attachment in infancy and childhood. In Chapter 12, Jay Belsky shows that child–parent attachment patterns need to be viewed in social and developmental context; one of a child's relationships, no matter how central, is unlikely to exist and have influences independently of other important relationships and ecological factors. Ross Thompson discusses, in Chapter 13, the complex issues that must be considered in efforts to understand why it is that infant attachment sometimes does and sometimes does not predict later functioning; he provides a detailed review of the many longitudinal studies of attachment in infancy and childhood. In Chapter 14, Judith Solomon and Carol George explain how quality of attachment has been measured in infancy and childhood. The authors show both that a complex construct has been successfully measured, with many scientific payoffs, and that much remains to be done to extend the measurement of attachment beyond infancy and to assure that it is measured in multiple, convergent ways.

The fourth section, "Attachment in Adolescence and Adulthood," contains chapters growing out of Bowlby's early contention that attachment characterizes humans "from the cradle to the grave." Chapter 15, by Joseph Allen and Deborah Land, reviews studies of attachment patterns (as measured by the Adult Attachment Interview, or AAI) and parent–child relationships in adolescence—a period in which the attached adolescent seeks increased independence from parents, while usually continuing to rely on them as a secure base. In Chapter 16, Cindy Hazan and Debra Zeifman argue that pair bonds between adult lovers and marital partners are true attachments, and that they can be best understood in terms of attachment theory. Chapter 17, by Judith Feeney, is a review of much of the recent research by personality and social psychologists that has grown out of the theoretical perspective explained by Hazan and Zeifman. Jonathan Mohr, in Chapter 18, offers the first comprehensive examination of attachment in same-sex romantic relationships. He explores the evolutionary basis of same-sex attraction and the relevance of the attachment system for same-sex relationships; he reviews research that sheds light on attachment processes in these relationships; and he shows how examination of attachment in same-sex relationships makes a unique contribution to understanding attachment processes more broadly. The remaining two chapters in this section deal with the complex measurement issues that have arisen as different kinds of researchers, with different theoretical and applied agendas, have attempted to measure attachment and attachment orientations in adolescence and adulthood. In Chapter 19, Erik Hesse provides a detailed conceptual analysis of the AAI, explaining its origins and revisions and the fascinating literature it has engendered. Chapter 20, by Judith Crowell, Chris Fraley, and Phillip Shaver, places the AAI in the context of other adult attachment measures, several of which are designed to assess patterns of attachment in close relationships other than those between children and parents.

The fifth section of the volume, "Clinical Applications of Attachment Theory and Research," contains chapters that reflect the strong roots of attachment theory in clinical psychology and psychiatry, and the contributions that the theory and associated research can now make to clinical work. Despite the fact that Bowlby—a psychiatrist and psychoanalyst who treated patients throughout his career—based his original thinking on clinical observations, and despite the fact that Ainsworth was also trained as a clinician, until recently it has been developmental and social psychologists rather than clinical psychologists who have found attachment theory and research of greatest relevance. Bowlby and Ainsworth themselves viewed their work as having important clinical applications, and both were interested in improving clinical treatment. Both were pleased, late in their careers, when clinicians increasingly found their work useful. The first three chapters of this section focus on psychopathology, and the next four examine attachment theory in relation to specific therapeutic perspectives. In Chapter 21, Mark Greenberg examines the connection between attachment and psychopathology in childhood, and in Chapter 22, Mary Dozier, Chase Stovall, and Kathleen Albus examine this connection in adulthood. The inclusion in this section of Chapter 23, Karlen Lyons-Ruth and Deborah Jacobvitz's examination of attachment disorganization, follows from recent studies of attachment and psychopathology suggesting that individuals with disorganized attachment are at particular risk for psychopathology. The chapter examines the developmental origins, correlates, and outcomes of attachment disorganization, and reviews data and theoretical models linking disorganized attachment with adult violence, trauma, and maltreatment.

Next, the contributions that attachment theory and research are making to specific forms of therapy are described. In Chapter 24, Alicia Lieberman and Charles Zeanah describe contributions to infant–parent psychotherapy and other interventions with infants and young children; in Chapter 25, Arietta Slade describes contributions, especially of findings related to the AAI, to individual psychotherapy with adults; in Chapter 27, John Byng-Hall describes contributions to family and couple therapy. Chapter 26, by Peter Fonagy, provides an overview of the complex relations between attachment theory and psychoanalytic theory, suggesting points of both substantial contact and significant divergence. These historical and theoretical considerations will help scholars and clinicians working within both frameworks to learn more readily from one another.

The final section of the volume, "Emerging Topics and Perspectives," provides a sampling of the wide array of areas into which attachment theory and research are being extended. In Chapter 28, Carol George and Judith Solomon examine caregiving behavior—the biologically based behavior (closely intertwined with attachment behavior) that Bowlby claimed must be understood in order to ensure a thorough understanding of attachment. Chapter 29 starts with the premise that caregiving is not restricted to parents, and that parents therefore are not children's only attachment figures. In this chapter, Carollee Howes examines attachment in the context of multiple caregivers, discussing criteria for identification of attachment figures, precursors and sequelae of nonmaternal attachments, and interconnections among multiple attachments. She reviews the empirical literature on children's attachments to fathers, grandparents, day care providers, teachers, foster parents, and adoptive parents. In Chapter 30, Lisa Berlin and Jude Cassidy explore several kinds of relations among relationships: the influence of infant–parent attachments on subsequent bonds, the influence of parents' other relationships on infant–parent attachments, and the concordance of attachment patterns across a caregiver's multiple children and across a child's multiple caregivers.

Chapter 31 deals with a frequently asked question about attachment processes: Are they essentially the same or importantly different across cultures? Marinus van IJzendoorn and Abraham Sagi review studies conducted around the world and show that although many of the parameter settings of the attachment behavioral system vary in understandable ways with context, the system itself is recognizably the same. In Chapter 32, Chris Fraley and Phillip Shaver revisit the issues of loss and grief that Bowlby addressed in the third volume of *Attachment and Loss*. They show that despite many interesting new issues and challenges in bereavement research, Bowlby's ideas stand up well. Chapter 33, by Klaus Grossmann, Karin Grossmann, and Peter Zimmermann, reconsiders the role of the exploratory behavioral system, as well as what Ainsworth called the "attachment–exploration balance." In Chapter 34, Carol Magai considers attachment research in conjunction with contemporary theories and research on human emotion. Lee Kirkpatrick, in Chapter 35, shows that attachment theory and research shed new light on a variety of religious phenomena. In Chapter 36, Michael Rutter and Thomas O'Connor discuss implications of attachment theory and research for public policy, especially policies concerning child care. The book concludes with an epilogue by Mary Main in which she lists important points concerning attachment theory and research, and proposes new directions for future research.

From the day Seymour Weingarten, editor-in-chief of The Guilford Press, approached us with the idea for a *Handbook of Attachment* (at the 1995 meeting of the Society for Research in Child Development, or SRCD) until the publication of the handbook (in time to appear at the 1999 meeting of the same society), many people made important contributions. Our first thanks go to the international cast of chapter authors, busy people all, who not only agreed to write for the volume but also to tailor their chapters to our specific needs. With the help of Robert Marvin, who helped outline parts of the volume on a napkin on a flight back home from the 1995 SRCD meeting, we envisioned a volume that contained the initial primer section and that covered most of the major accomplishments and new developments in the field. For an edited research volume in psychology, it is customary to allow authors to write about pretty much whatever they choose; it also isn't unusual for authors to change their assignment in midstream, away from whatever they initially agreed to do. In the case of the present volume, the authors generously agreed to accept our rough vision of the placement of their chapters in the volume as a whole, and they all delivered the kinds of chapters we had in mind, only better!

Each chapter went through two or three drafts, to assure clarity, accuracy, minimal overlap, and appropriate cross-referencing. Both of us read and commented on each chapter, as did at least one additional reviewer. We thank the following reviewers: Jay Belsky, Lisa Berlin, Preston Britner, Nathan Fox, Chris Fraley, Carol George, Mary Main, Robert Marvin, William Mason, Stephen Porges, Joanna Scheib, Ronald Seifer, Jeffry Simpson, Arietta Slade, Ross Thompson, Marinus van IJzendoorn, Brian Vaughn, and Susan Woodhouse.

We had wonderful assistance from the professionals at The Guilford Press. Seymour Weingarten helped conceptualize the book and initially "sell" it to us, and he remained incredibly supportive, patient, and enthusiastic throughout the 4-year process. Our copy editor, Marie Sprayberry, did a stellar job of improving prose that we thought we had already polished to a luster. Jeannie Tang was our multitalented production editor. Behind the scenes of any large and long effort such as this one, there are scores of other professionals who quietly do excellent work without ever meeting the beneficiaries of their labor. We thank them, sincerely, as a group.

And finally, we wish to thank each other. We were barely acquainted when the project began and haven't met face to face during the 4-year ordeal. We both became parents during those years, and both of us moved. Through e-mail, faxes, and phone calls, we kept each other encouraged and involved. Neither of us knows what it's like to be lifetime combat buddies following near-death experiences in war, but surely we have grown to know and respect each other professionally in ways that people rarely do.

JUDE CASSIDY
PHILLIP R. SHAVER

Contents

III ATTACHMENT IN INFANCY AND CHILDHOOD

IV ATTACHMENT IN ADOLESCENCE AND ADULTHOOD

V CLINICAL APPLICATIONS OF ATTACHMENT THEORY AND RESEARCH

I

OVERVIEW OF ATTACHMENT THEORY

❖

1

The Nature of the Child's Ties

❖

JUDE CASSIDY

John Bowlby's work on attachment theory can be viewed as starting shortly after his graduation from Cambridge University, with the observations he made when he worked in a home for maladjusted boys. Two boys, both of whom had suffered disruptions in their relationships with their mothers, made important impressions on him. Bowlby's more systematic retrospective examination, published over a decade later as "Forty-Four Juvenile Thieves: Their Characters and Home Life" (Bowlby, 1944), as well as the observations of others (Bender & Yarnell, 1941; Goldfarb, 1943), convinced him that major disruptions in the mother–child relationship are precursors of later psychopathology. Bowlby's observations led not only to his belief that the relationship with the mother is important for *later* functioning, but also to a belief that this relationship is of critical *immediate* importance to the child. Bowlby, along with his colleague James Robertson, observed that children experienced intense distress when separated from their mothers, even if they were fed and cared for by others. A predictable pattern emerged—one of angry protest followed by despair (Robertson & Bowlby, 1952). Bowlby came to wonder *why* the mother is so important to the child.

At the time, the two widely accepted theories that offered explanations for the child's tie to the mother were both secondary-drive theories. Psychoanalytic and social learning theorists alike proposed that the infant's relationship with the mother emerges because she feeds the infant (e.g., Freud, 1910/1957; Sears, Maccoby, & Levin, 1959), and that the pleasure experienced upon having hunger drives satisfied comes to be associated with the mother's presence in positive ways. When Bowlby was first developing attachment theory, he became aware of evidence from animal studies that seriously called this perspective into question. Lorenz (1935) noted that infant geese became attached to parents that did not feed them. Harlow (1958) observed that infant rhesus monkeys, in times of stress, preferred not the wire-mesh "mother" that provided food, but the cloth-covered "mother" that afforded contact comfort. Soon systematic observations of human infants were made, and it became evident that babies too became attached to people who did not feed them (Ainsworth, 1967; Schaffer & Emerson, 1964). Years later, Bowlby recalled that

> this [secondary-drive] theory did not seem to me to fit the facts. For example, were it true, an infant of a year or two should take readily to whomever feeds him, and this clearly is not the case. But, if the secondary drive dependency theory was inadequate, what was the alternative? (1980b, p. 650)

Because he found himself dissatisfied with traditional theories, Bowlby sought new understanding through discussion with colleagues from such fields as evolutionary biology, ethology, developmental psychology, cognitive science, and control systems theory (Bowlby, 1969/1982). He drew upon all of these fields to formulate the innovative proposition that the mechanisms underlying the infant's tie to the mother originally emerged as a result of evolutionary pressures. For Bowlby, this strikingly strong tie, evident particularly when disrupted, results not from an associational learning process (a secondary drive), but rather from a biologically based desire for proximity that arose through the process of natural selection. Bowlby (1958, 1960a, 1960b) introduced attachment theory in a series of papers, the first of which was "The Nature of the Child's Tie to His Mother." All of the major points of attachment theory were presented there in at least rudimentary form, providing, as Bretherton (1992) has noted, "the first basic blueprint of attachment theory" (p. 762). These ideas were later elaborated in Bowlby's trilogy, *Attachment and Loss* (1969/1982, 1973, 1980a).

A member of Bowlby's research team during this period of initial theoretical formulation was a developmental psychologist visiting from Canada, Mary Salter Ainsworth. Her serendipitous connection with Bowlby—a friend had shown her a newspaper advertisement for a developmental research position—proved fortunate for the development of attachment theory. Ainsworth conducted two pioneering naturalistic observation studies of mothers and infants in which she applied the ethological principles of attachment theory as a framework. One of these investigations was conducted in the early 1950s in Uganda; the other was carried out in the early 1960s in Baltimore. These inquiries provided the most extensive home observation data to date and laid the foundation for Ainsworth's contributions to attachment theory, as well as for Bowlby's continued formulations. Ainsworth later created an assessment tool, the "strange situation," that triggered the productive flowering of the empirical study of individual differences in attachment quality—the research that is largely responsible for the place of attachment theory in contemporary developmental psychology.

The present chapter summarizes Bowlby's initial ethological approach to understanding the child's tie to the mother, along with elaborations based on more recent research and theorizing. First, I discuss the biological bases of attachment, describing the evolutionary roots of attachment behavior, the attachment behavioral system and its organization, the role of context in the system's operation, the role of emotion; the role of cognition, and individual differences in attachment. Next, I examine the attachment system in relation to other behavioral systems: the exploratory, fear, sociable, and caregiving systems. Third, I consider the nature of the child's attachment bond to his or her attachment figures and how attachments differ from other affectional bonds. Finally, I discuss multiple attachments. Although Bowlby's idea that attachment is a lifespan phenomenon was present in his earliest writings (e.g., Bowlby, 1956), his principal focus was the tie to the mother during childhood, and I maintain that focus in this chapter.

BIOLOGICAL BASES OF ATTACHMENT BEHAVIOR

The most fundamental aspect of attachment theory is its focus on the biological bases of attachment behavior (Bowlby, 1958, 1969/1982). "Attachment behavior" has the predictable outcome of increasing proximity of the child to the attachment figure (usually the mother). Some attachment behaviors (smiling, vocalizing) are signaling behaviors that alert the mother to the child's interest in interaction, and thus serve to bring her to the child. Other behaviors (crying) are aversive, and bring the mother to the child to terminate them. Some (approaching and following) are active behaviors that move the child to the mother.

An Evolutionary Perspective

Bowlby proposed that during the time in which humans were evolving, when humans lived in what he called "the environment of evolutionary adaptedness," genetic selection favored attachment behaviors because they increased the likelihood of child–mother proximity, which in turn increased the likelihood of protection and provided survival advantage. In keeping with the evolutionary thinking of his time, Bowlby emphasized survival of the species in his earliest theoretical formulations. By the time he revised *Attachment* (Volume 1 of his trilogy, *Attachment and Loss*; Bowlby, 1969/1982), he noted that advances in evolutionary theory necessitated consideration of a framework within which for all behavioral systems, including attachment, "the ultimate outcome to be attained is always the survival of the genes an individual is carrying" (p. 56). For more extensive discussion of attachment and this notion of "reproductive fitness," see Simpson (Chapter 6, this volume) and Belsky (Chapter 7, this volume).

Many predictable outcomes beneficial to the child are thought to result from the child's proximity to the parent (Bowlby, 1969/1982). These include feeding, learning about the environment, and social interaction, all of which are important. But the predictable outcome of proximity thought to give particular survival advantage to the child is protection from predators. In the environment of evolutionary adaptedness, infants who were biologically predisposed to stay close to their mothers were less likely to be killed by predators. This is referred to as the "biological function" of attachment behavior: Without protection from predators, feeding is not necessary, and learning cannot take place. Because of this biological function of protection, Bowlby considered infants to be predisposed particularly to seek their parents in times of distress. In a basic Darwinian sense, then, the proclivity to seek proximity is a behavioral adaptation in the same way that a fox's white coat on the tundra is an adaptation. Within this framework, attachment is considered a normal and healthy characteristic of humans throughout the lifespan, rather than a sign of immaturity that needs to be outgrown.

The Attachment Behavioral System

Attachment behaviors are thought to be organized into an "attachment behavioral system." Bowlby (1969/1982) borrowed the concept of the behavioral system from ethology to describe a species-specific system of behaviors that leads to certain predictable outcomes, at least one of which contributes to reproductive fitness. The concept of the behavioral system involves inherent motivation. There is no need to view attachment as the by-product of any more fundamental processes or "drive." Children are thought to become attached whether their parents are meeting their physiological needs or not. This idea is supported by evidence indicating that in contrast to what secondary-drive theories lead one to expect (e.g., Freud, 1910/1957; Sears et al., 1957), attachment is not a result of associations with feeding (Ainsworth, 1967; Harlow, 1962; Schaffer & Emerson, 1964). Furthermore, findings that infants become attached even to abusive mothers (Bowlby, 1956) suggest that the system is not driven by simple pleasurable associations. Bowlby's notion of the inherent motivation of the attachment system is compatible with Piaget's (1954) formulation of the inherent motivation of the child's interest in exploration.

Central to the concept of the attachment behavioral system is that the *organization* of a variety of attachment behaviors within the individual in response to internal and external cues is what is important. Sroufe and Waters (1977) emphasized that the attachment behavioral system is

"not a set of behaviors that are constantly and uniformly operative" (p. 1185). Rather, the "functional equivalence" of behaviors is noted, with a variety of behaviors having similar meanings and serving similar functions. As Bowlby (1969/1982) noted, "whether a child moves toward a mother by running, walking, crawling, shuffling or, in the case of a thalidomide child, by rolling, is thus of very little consequence compared to the set-goal of his locomotion, namely proximity to mother" (p. 373). The behaviors chosen in a specific context are the ones the infant finds most useful at that moment. With development, the child gains access to a greater variety of ways of achieving proximity. Indeed, as Sroufe and Waters (1977) pointed out, this organizational perspective helps to explain stability within the context of both developmental and contextual changes. Thus an infant may maintain a stable internal organization of the attachment behavioral system in relation to the mother over time and across contexts, yet the specific behaviors used in the service of this organization may vary greatly. Thus, whereas a nonmobile infant may be expected to cry and reach out to the mother for contact, a mobile child may achieve the same goal of establishing contact by crawling after her.

This emphasis on the organization of the attachment behavioral system also helps explain its operation in a "goal-corrected" manner. Unlike certain reflexes that, once activated, maintain a fixed course (e.g., sneezing, rooting), the attachment behavioral system enables the individual to respond flexibly to environmental changes while attempting to attain a goal. Bowlby used the analogy of a heat-seeking missile: Once launched, the missile does not remain on a preset course; rather, it incorporates information about changes in the target's location and adjusts its trajectory accordingly. Similarly, the infant is capable of considering changes in the mother's location and behavior (as well as other environmental changes) when attempting to maintain proximity to the mother. And the flexible use of a variety of attachment behaviors, depending on the circumstances, affords the infant greater efficiency in goal-corrected responses. For instance, an infant may see the mother starting to leave in an unfamiliar environment and may desire to increase proximity to her. The infant may begin by reaching for her and then following her (changing course as she moves); if this fails, calling or crying may be initiated.

Bowlby's approach to the organization of attachment behavior involves a control systems perspective. Drawing on observations of ethologists who described instinctive behavior in animals as serving to maintain them in a certain relation with the environment for long periods of time, Bowlby proposed that a control systems approach could also be applied to attachment behavior. He described the workings of a thermostat as an example of a control system. When the room gets too cold, the thermostat activates the heater; when the desired temperature is reached, the thermostat turns the heater off. Bowlby described children as wanting to maintain a certain proximity to their mothers. When a separation becomes too great in distance or time, the attachment system becomes activated, and when sufficient proximity has been achieved, it is terminated. Bowlby (following Bretherton, 1980; see Bowlby, 1969/1982) later described the attachment system as working slightly differently from a thermostat—as being continually activated (with variations of relatively more or less activation), rather than being completely turned off at times. According to Bowlby, the goal of the child is not an object (e.g., the mother), but rather a state—a maintenance of the desired distance from the mother, depending on the circumstances. Bowlby described this idea of behavioral homeostasis as similar to the process of physiological homeostasis, whereby physiological systems (e.g., blood pressure and body temperature) are maintained within set limits. Like physiological control systems, a behavioral control system is thought to be organized within the central nervous system. According to Bowlby (1969/1982), the distinction between the two is that the latter is "one in which the set-limits concern the organism's relation to features of the environment and in which the limits are maintained by behavioral rather than physiological means" (p. 372).

The Role of Context

The child's desired degree of proximity to the parent is thought to vary under differing circumstances, and Bowlby (1969/1982) was interested in understanding how these different circumstances contribute to relative increases and decreases in activation of the attachment system. Thus he described two classes of factors that contribute to activation of the attachment system, both of which are conditions indicating danger or stress. One relates to conditions of the child (such as illness, fatigue, hunger, or pain). The other relates to conditions of the environment (such as the presence of threatening stimuli); particularly important are the location and behavior of the mother (such as her absence, withdrawal, or rejection of the child). Interaction among these causal factors can be quite complex: Sometimes only one needs to be present, and at other times several are necessary. In relation to relative deactivation of the attachment system, Bowlby made it clear that his approach had nothing in common with a model in which a behavior stops when its energy supply is depleted (e.g., Freud, 1940/1964). In Bowlby's view, attachment behavior stops in the presence of a terminating stimulus. For most distressed infants, contact with the mother is an effective terminating stimulus. Yet the nature of the stimulus that serves to terminate attachment behavior differs according to the degree of activation of the attachment system. If the attachment system is intensively activated, contact with the parent may be necessary to terminate it. If it is moderately activated, the presence or soothing voice of the parent or even of a familiar substitute caregiver may suffice. In either case, the infant is viewed as using the mother as a "safe haven" to return to in times of trouble. In sum, proximity seeking is activated when the infant receives information (from both internal and external sources) that a goal (the desired distance from the mother) is exceeded. It remains activated until the goal is achieved, and then it stops.

The Role of Emotion

According to Bowlby (1979), emotions are strongly associated with attachment:

> Many of the most intense emotions arise during the formation, the maintenance, the disruption, and the renewal of attachment relationships. The formation of a bond is described as falling in love, maintaining a bond as loving someone, and losing a partner as grieving over someone. Similarly, threat of loss arouses anxiety and actual loss gives rise to sorrow; whilst each of these situations is likely to arouse anger. The unchallenged maintenance of a bond is experienced as a source of joy. (p. 130)

It is likely that these affective responses originally resulted from evolutionary pressures. An infant predisposed to experience positive emotions in relation to an attachment and sadness with its loss may actively work to maintain attachments, which contribute in turn to the infant's enhanced reproductive fitness.

The Role of Cognition

Drawing on cognitive information theory, Bowlby (1969/1982) proposed that the organization of the attachment behavioral system involves cognitive components—specifically, mental representations of the attachment figure, the self, and the environment, all of which are largely based on experiences. (This emphasis on the importance of an individual's actual experiences was another way in which Bowlby's theory differed from that of Freud, who emphasized instead the role of internal fantasies.) Bowlby referred to these representations as "representational models" and as "internal working models." According to Bowlby, these models allow individuals to anticipate the future and make plans, thereby operating most efficiently. (There is in fact evidence that even young children are capable of using representations to make predictions about the future; Heller & Berndt, 1981.) The child is thought to rely on these models, for instance, when making decisions about which specific attachment behavior(s) to use in a specific situation with a specific person. Representational models are considered to work best when they are relatively accurate reflections of reality, and conscious processing is required to check and revise models in order to keep them up to date. Extensive discussion of these cognitive models is provided by Bretherton (1990; Bretherton & Munholland, Chapter 5, this volume) and by Main, Kaplan, and Cassidy (1985); see also Baldwin (1992) for a review of similarities between these models and a variety of constructs within the literatures on developmental, social, clinical, and cognitive psychology. Bowlby also discussed the role within the attachment system of other cognitive processes, such as object permanence, discrimination learning, nonconscious processing, selective attention and memory, and interpretative biases.

Individual Differences

In extending the biological emphasis of Bowlby's initial theorizing, Main (1990) proposed that the biologically based human tendency to become attached is paralleled by a biologically based ability to be flexible to the range of likely caregiving environments. This flexibility is thought to contribute to variations associated with quality of attachment. Whereas nearly all children become attached (even to mothers who abuse them; Bowlby, 1956), not all are *securely* attached.

Striking individual differences exist. Secure attachment occurs when a child has a mental representation of the attachment figure as available and responsive when needed. Infants are considered to be insecurely attached when they lack such a representation. Bowlby's early clinical observations led him to predict that just as feeding does not cause attachment in infants, so individual differences in feeding (e.g., breast vs. bottle feeding) do not contribute to individual differences in attachment quality. In one of his earliest writings, Bowlby (1958) predicted that the important factor is "the extent to which the mother has permitted clinging and following, and all the behavior associated with them, or has refused them" (p. 370). This prediction has since gained empirical support (e.g., Ainsworth, Blehar, Waters, & Wall, 1978; see also DeWolff & van IJzendoorn, 1997). Theoretical issues related to individual differences in attachment security are discussed in detail by Weinfield, Sroufe, Egeland, and Carlson (Chapter 4, this volume).

ATTACHMENT IN RELATION TO OTHER BEHAVIORAL SYSTEMS

The attachment behavioral system can be fully understood only in terms of its complex interplay with other biologically based behavioral systems. Bowlby highlighted two of these as being particularly related to the attachment system in young children: the exploratory behavioral system and the fear behavioral system. The activation of these other systems is related to activation of the attachment system. Activation of the fear system generally heightens activation of the attachment system. In contrast, activation of the exploratory system can, under certain circumstances, reduce activation of the attachment system. As any parent knows, providing a novel set of car keys can at least temporarily distract a baby who wants to be picked up, as long as the infant's attachment system is not intensely activated. These two behavioral systems are discussed in this section, as are the sociable and caregiving behavioral systems.

The Exploratory System

The links between the exploratory behavioral system and the attachment behavioral system are thought to be particularly intricate. According to Bowlby, the exploratory system gives survival advantage to the child by providing important information about the workings of the environment: how to use tools, build structures, obtain food, and negotiate physical obstacles. Yet unbridled exploration with no attention to potential hazards can be dangerous. The complementary yet mutually inhibiting nature of the exploratory and attachment systems is thought to have evolved to ensure that while the child is protected by maintaining proximity to attachment figures, he or she nonetheless gradually learns about the environment through exploration. According to Ainsworth (1972), "the dynamic equilibrium between these two behavioral systems is even more significant for development (and for survival) than either in isolation" (p. 118).

The framework that best captures the links between the attachment and exploratory systems is that of an infant's use of an attachment figure as a "secure base from which to explore"—a concept first described by Ainsworth (1963) and central to attachment theory (Ainsworth et al., 1978; Bowlby, 1969/1982, 1988). On the basis of her observations during the infant's first year of life, Ainsworth referred to an "attachment–exploration balance" (Ainsworth, Bell, & Stayton, 1971). Most infants balance these two behavioral systems, responding flexibly to a specific situation after assessing both the environment's characteristics and the caregiver's availability and likely behavior. For instance, when the infant experiences the environment as dangerous, exploration is unlikely. Furthermore, when the attachment system is activated (perhaps by separation from the attachment figure, illness, fatigue, or unfamiliar people and surroundings), infant exploration and play decline. Conversely, when the attachment system is not activated (e.g., when a healthy, well-rested infant is in a comfortable setting with an attachment figure nearby), exploration is enhanced. Thus, attachment, far from interfering with exploration, is viewed as fostering exploration. Bowlby (1973) described as important not only the physical presence of an attachment figure, but also the infant's belief that the attachment figure will be available if needed. A converging body of empirical work, in which maternal physical or psychological presence was experimentally manipulated, has provided compelling evidence of the theoretically predicted associations between maternal availability and infant exploration (Ainsworth & Wittig, 1969; Carr, Dabbs, & Carr, 1975; Rheingold, 1969; Sorce & Emde, 1981).

The Fear System

The fear behavioral system is also thought to be closely linked to the attachment system. For Bowlby, the biological function of the fear system, like that of the attachment system, is protection. It is biologically adaptive for children to be frightened of certain stimuli. Without such fear, survival, according to Bowlby, and reproduction, according to a modern evolutionary perspective, would be reduced. Bowlby (1973) described "natural clues to danger"—stimuli that are not *inherently* dangerous but that increase the likelihood of danger. These include darkness, loud noises, aloneness, and sudden looming movements. Because the attachment and fear systems are intertwined, so that frightened infants increase their attachment behavior, infants who find these stimuli frightening are considered more likely to seek protection and thus to survive to pass on their genes. The presence or absence of the attachment figure is thought to play an important role in the activation of an infant's fear system, such that an available and accessible attachment figure makes the infant much less susceptible to fear, and there is evidence that this is so (Morgan & Ricciuti, 1969; Sorce & Emde, 1981). In fact, even photographs of the mother can calm a fearful infant, as can "security blankets" for children who are attached to such objects (Passman & Erck, 1977; Passman & Weisberg, 1975). The fear behavioral system is discussed more extensively by Kobak (Chapter 2, this volume).

The Sociable System

A complete understanding of the attachment behavioral system rests on an understanding of its distinction from the sociable (or "affiliative") behavioral system.[1] Although Bowlby did not discuss this behavioral system as extensively as he did some others, he did point out, as have other theorists, that the sociable system is *distinct* from the attachment behavioral system. Bowlby (1969/1982) wrote,

> "Affiliation" was introduced by Murray (1938): "Under this heading are classed all manifestations of friendliness and goodwill, of the desire to do things in company with others." As such it is a much broader concept than attachment and is not intended to cover behavior that is directed towards one or a few particular figures, which is the hallmark of attachment behavior. (p. 229)

According to Ainsworth (1989), it is "reasonable to believe that there is some basic behavioral system that has evolved in social species that leads individuals to seek to maintain proximity to conspecifics, even to those to whom they are not attached or otherwise bonded, and despite the fact that wariness is likely to be evoked by those who are unfamiliar" (p. 713). Harlow and Harlow (1965) described the "peer affectional system through which infants and children interrelate . . . and develop persisting affection for each other" as an "affectional system" distinct from those involving infant and parents (p. 288). Bronson (1972) referred to affiliation as an "adaptive system" present in infancy and separate from attachment. Bretherton and Ainsworth (1974) examined the interplay among several behavioral systems in infants, including the sociable and the attachment systems, and Greenberg and Marvin (1982) examined this interplay in preschool children. Hinde (1974) described nonhuman primates' play with peers, which he identified as different from mother–child interaction, as "consum[ing] so much time and energy that it must be of crucial adaptive importance" (p. 227).

The sociable system is thus defined as the organization of the biologically based, survival-promoting tendency to be sociable with others. An important predictable outcome of activation of this system is that individuals are likely to spend at least part of their time in the company of others. Given evidence from the primate literature that individuals in the company of others are much less likely to be killed by predators (Eisenberg, 1966), it seems reasonable to assume that humans too would derive the important survival advantage of protection from associating with others. The sociable system is likely to contribute to the individual's survival and reproductive fitness in other important ways: Primates biologically predisposed to be sociable with others increase their ability to gather food, build shelter, and create warmth; they learn about the environment more efficiently; and they gain access to a group of others with whom they may eventually mate (see Huntingford, 1984, for a review). Strong evidence of the importance of the sociable system for the development of young nonhuman primates comes from several studies, most notably those of Harlow and his associates (e.g., Harlow, 1969), in which monkeys reared with their mothers but without peers were seriously hindered in their social development and could not mate or parent effectively (i.e., reproduce; see also Miller, Caul, & Mirsky, 1967).

Observations of both humans and other primates clearly show differences between the attachment and sociable systems in what activates behavior, in what terminates behavior, and in the way behaviors are organized (Bretherton & Ainsworth, 1974; Harlow, 1969; Vandell, 1980). The sociable system is most likely to be activated when the attachment system is not activated. According to Bowlby,

> A child seeks his attachment-figure when he is tired, hungry, ill, or alarmed and also when he is uncertain of that figure's whereabouts; when the attachment-figure is found he wants to remain in proximity to him or her and may want also to be held or cuddled. By contrast, a child seeks a playmate when he is in good spirits and confident of the whereabouts of his attachment-figure; when the playmate is found, moreover, the child wants to engage in playful interaction with him or her. If this analysis is right, the roles of attachment-figure and playmate are distinct. (1969/1982, p. 307)

Lewis, Young, Brooks, and Michalson (1975) interpreted their observations of pairs of one-year-olds and their mothers similarly: "Mothers are good for protection, peers for watching and playing with" (p. 56).

The Caregiving System

In one of his earliest writings, Bowlby (1956) pointed out that further understanding of attachment could be gained from examination of the mother's tie to her infant. Bowlby later (1984) wrote briefly about "parenting behavior" from a biological perspective as "like attachment behavior, . . . in some degree preprogrammed" (p. 271). He described the biologically based urge to care for and protect children, yet simultaneously viewed individual differences in the nature of parenting as emerging largely through learning. Although Bowlby wrote little about this topic, his ethological perspective, his ideas about interrelated behavioral systems, and his interest in attachment-related processes across the lifespan lend themselves readily to an elaboration of the parental side of what Bowlby (1969/1982) called the "attachment–caregiving social bond." Solomon and George (1996; George & Solomon, 1996; see also George & Solomon, Chapter 28, this volume) have filled this void, writing in detail about the "caregiving system." As George and Solomon (Chapter 28, this volume, Note 1) state, it is difficult to delineate precisely which aspects of parenting behavior should be considered part of the caregiving system. I propose that the term "caregiving system" be used to describe a subset of parental behaviors—only those behaviors designed to promote proximity and comfort when the parent perceives that the child is in real or potential danger. The chief behavior within this system is retrieval (Bowlby, 1969/1982); others include calling, reaching, grasping, restraining, following, soothing, and rocking.[2]

Just as the child's interactions with the parent involve more than the attachment system (e.g., a child may approach the father not for comfort but for play), so other parental systems may be activated during interactions with the child (Bowlby, 1969/1982). These various behavioral systems can all be viewed as enhancing the child's survival and reproductive fitness (e.g., teaching, feeding, playing). A parent may be differentially responsive to a child when each of these different parental behavioral systems is activated (e.g., sensitive when teaching or feeding, yet insensitive when the caregiving system is activated). The predominance of each of these parental behavioral systems varies considerably both across and within cultures. For instance, as Bretherton (1985) pointed out, among Mayan Indians in Mexico, mothers rarely serve as playmates for their infants but are quite available and responsive as caregivers (Brazelton, 1977; see also van IJzendoorn & Sagi, Chapter 31, this volume). Within a particular culture, one mother may be a readily available attachment figure, yet stodgy and inept in the role of playmate; another mother may be comfortable in interaction with her children only in her roles as teacher or coach when attention is focused on a task or skill, and may be uncomfortable with attachment-related interactions.

As is the case with the child's attachment system, the predictable outcome of activation of the caregiving system is parent–child proximity, and the biological function is protection of the child. In most cases, both parent and child work together to maintain a comfortable degree of proximity. If the child moves away, the parent will retrieve him or her; if the parent moves away, the child will follow or signal for the parent to return. Following Bowlby's (1969/1982) thinking, it seems likely that when the caregiving system is relatively activated, the child's attachment system can be relatively deactivated; attachment behaviors are not needed because the parent has assumed responsibility for maintaining proximity. If the caregiving system is not relatively activated, then the child's attachment system becomes activated, should the context call for it. This is one reason why the mother's leaving is particularly disturbing to a child and particularly likely to activate attachment behavior. This "dynamic equilibrium" (Bowlby, 1969/1982, p. 236) contributes to understanding the notion of the mother's providing "a secure base from which to explore." The mother's monitoring of infant–mother proximity frees the infant from such monitoring and permits greater attention to exploring. For instance, if, when visiting a new park, a mother actively follows the infant in his or her explorations, the infant is much more likely to cover a wide area than if she sits on a bench talking with friends. Empirical support for this proposition comes from a study in which the simple act of a mother's diverting her attention away from the infant to a magazine in a brief laboratory procedure reduced the quality of infant exploration (Sorce & Emde, 1981).

Yet parent and child do not always agree on what distance between them is acceptable. For example, a mother's fear system may be activated and prompt her to retrieve an infant whose activated exploratory system leads him or her to prefer to move away. Parents and their children may also differ in terms of how their priorities guide activation of their behavioral systems. For instance, when an infant's attachment system is activated in the presence of the mother, the infant's sole wish is for her to respond. Although such infant behavior is usually a powerful activating stimulus for the mother's caregiving system, the mother may choose among several competing needs and may or may not provide care (Trivers, 1974). The child's concern is immediate and focused; the mother's concerns may be more diffuse and long-range. The mother may have to leave the infant to work to support the family (in which case activation of her food-getting behavioral system has taken precedence over her caregiving system). Or she may have several children to whose needs she must attend. Main (1990) has proposed that from an evolutionary perspective, maternal insensitivity to a particular child may be useful to the mother if it maximizes the total number of surviving offspring (see also Simpson, Chapter 6, this volume, and Belsky, Chapter 7, this volume).

As is true for many behavioral systems, activation of the caregiving system results from both internal and external cues. Internal cues include presence of hormones, cultural beliefs, parental state (e.g., whether the parent is tired or sick), and activation of other parental behavioral systems (e.g., exploration, food-getting, fear). External cues include state of the environment (e.g., whether it is familiar, whether there is danger, whether others are present and who these others are), state of the infant (e.g., whether the infant is sick or tired), and behavior of the infant (e.g., whether he or she is exhibiting attachment behavior). Activation of the caregiving system has crucial implications for the infant, who cannot otherwise survive. Ethologists have suggested that infants therefore have evolved characteristics that serve to activate the caregiving system: their endearing "babyish" features (the large rounded head with the high forehead, the small nose) and their thrashing arm movements. Attachment behaviors, of course, motivate parents to respond; even aversive behaviors, such as crying, typically motivate parents to provide care in order to terminate them. Given that an infant's attachment system is activated by stimuli that indicate an increased risk of danger (e.g., loud noise, looming objects), a parent who increases proximity when a child's attachment behavior is activated increases the likelihood of being able to protect the child, should the danger prove real. Similarly, when the parent perceives or expects danger that the child does not, parental proximity also increases the likelihood of survival. Thus, it is likely that the close link between the child's attachment and fear systems is paralleled by a close link between the parent's caregiving and fear systems, such that when a parent's fear system is activated, so too is his or her caregiving system.

Fear is only one of the powerful emotions likely to be linked to the caregiving system. Just as attachment is associated with powerful emotions (Bowlby, 1979), so is the caregiving system. These emotions may in fact be as strong as any an individual experiences in his or her lifetime. The birth of a first child (which establishes the adult as a parent) is often accompanied by feelings of great joy; threats to the child are accompanied by anxiety; the death of a child brings profound grief. This intertwining of the caregiving system with intense emotions may result from selective pressures of evolution: Enhanced reproductive fitness may result when, for instance, a parent's anxiety about threats to a child prompts the parent to seek effective interventions.

The role of parental soothing as a component of the caregiving system merits consideration. Why would a parent who safely holds a crying child out of reach of a large barking dog continue to comfort the child? Why would a parent pick up a dis-

tressed child whom the parent perceives to be in no danger? What could be the role of such soothing behaviors? I propose that soothing behaviors serve, indirectly, to facilitate the parent's monitoring of potential or real dangers to the child. Parental provision of contact usually comforts a distressed child. If the child continues to be distressed for a substantial time following contact, there may be another threat of which the parent is unaware. *Through continuing attempts to soothe the child, the parent gains information about threat to the child.* The parent may not realize, for instance, that the child has a painful splinter in his or her foot. Furthermore, there are many ways in which inconsolable crying (beyond early infancy) can signal serious health problems. And a parent will not know whether crying is inconsolable unless the parent attempts to console.

Further research is needed in relation to additional aspects of the caregiving system. First, given that there are times when the child's distress does not stem from activation of his or her attachment system, research could examine whether it is best to consider parental behavior in response to such distress as part of the caregiving system. For instance, it seems plausible that a child may get upset because his or her exploratory system is frustrated, and that the child's distress prompts the mother to pick the child up and comfort him or her; it may be that the mother's behavior then contributes to the child's attachment-related expectations about the mother's likely responses to his or her distress, and thus to the formation of the child's representational model of the mother. Second, research is needed to determine how separate the caregiving system is from other parental systems, and whether it is only the caregiving system that affects the child's attachment system. Third, it is unclear whether it is best to think of a single parental caregiving system in humans or of separate maternal and paternal caregiving systems. Harlow has proposed separate maternal and paternal systems in primates (Harlow, Harlow, & Hansen, 1963). If two separate systems exist in humans, there must be considerable overlap, even though genetic, hormonal, and cultural factors may contribute to differences in the specific characteristics of these systems.[3]

THE ATTACHMENT BOND

Whereas "attachment behavior" is behavior that promotes proximity to the attachment figure, and the "attachment behavioral system" is the organization of attachment behaviors within the individual, an "attachment bond" refers to an affectional tie. Ainsworth (1989) described an attachment bond not as dyadic, but rather as characteristic of the individual, "entailing representation in the internal organization of the individual" (p. 711). Thus, this bond is not one between two people; it is instead a bond that one individual has to another individual who is perceived as stronger and wiser (e.g., the bond of an infant to the mother). A person can be attached to a person who is not in turn attached to him or her; as described below, this is usually the case with infants and their parents.[4]

The attachment bond is a specific type of a larger class of bonds that Bowlby and Ainsworth have referred to as "affectional bonds." Throughout the lifespan, individuals form a variety of different important affectional bonds that are not attachments. To make it completely clear what an attachment bond is, one needs to delineate what it is not. Ainsworth (1989) described the criteria for affectional bonds, and then the additional criterion for attachment bonds. First, an affectional bond is persistent, not transitory. Second, an affectional bond involves a specific person, a figure who is not interchangeable with anyone else. This bond reflects "the attraction that one *individual* has for another *individual*" (Bowlby, 1979, p. 67, emphasis in original). For instance, the sadness associated with the loss of a close friend is not lessened by the fact that one has other close friends. Bowlby emphasized specificity when he stated: "To complain because a child does not welcome being comforted by a kind but strange woman is as foolish as to complain that a young man deeply in love is not enthusiastic about some other good-looking girl" (1956, p. 58). Third, the relationship is emotionally significant. Fourth, the individual wishes to maintain proximity to or contact with the person. The nature and extent of the proximity/contact desired vary as a function of a variety of factors (e.g., age and state of the individual, environmental conditions). Fifth, the individual feels distress at involuntary separation from the person. Even though the individual may choose separation from the figure, the individual experiences distress when proximity is desired but prevented. In addition to these five criteria, an additional criterion exists for an attachment bond: The individual seeks security and comfort in the relationship with the person (Ainsworth, 1989). (The attachment is considered "secure" if one achieves security and "insecure" if one does not; it is the *seeking* of security that is the defining feature. See also Hinde, 1982, and Weiss, 1982.) It is this final criterion that leads to description of "parental bonds" to children and "child attachments" to parents: Parental attempts to seek security from a child are "almost always not only a sign of pathology in the parent but also a cause of it in the child" (Bowlby, 1969/1982, p. 377).

The existence of an attachment bond cannot be inferred from the presence or absence of attachment behavior. To begin with, it is important to remember that most behaviors can serve more than one behavioral system (Bretherton & Ainsworth, 1974; Sroufe & Waters, 1977). Thus, for instance, every approach does not serve the attachment system; even though approach can be an attachment behavior, it can also be an exploratory or sociable behavior. Yet it is also the case that distressed infants separated from their mothers may seek comfort from strangers (Ainsworth et al., 1978; Bretherton, 1978; Rheingold, 1969), and approach in that context is considered attachment behavior. Nonetheless, an enduring attachment bond of an infant to a stranger cannot be assumed to exist, and it is thus possible for an infant to direct attachment behavior to an individual to whom he or she is not attached. Some babies will stop crying when comforted by a stranger, but observations in the strange situation reveal that this comfort is generally not as satisfying as that provided by the mother (Ainsworth et al., 1978).

Similarly, even during a period when the child is directing no attachment behavior to the parent, the child is still attached. When, for instance, a contented child is in comfortable surroundings with the mother present, the attachment system is not likely to be activated to a level that triggers attachment behavior. Thus activation of attachment behavior is largely situational; it may or may not be present at any given time. The attachment bond, however, is considered to exist consistently over time, whether or not attachment behavior is present. Bowlby (1969/1982) pointed out that even the cessation of behavior during a long separation cannot be considered an indication that the attachment bond has ended.

The strength of attachment behaviors is sometimes mistakenly regarded as reflecting the "strength" of the attachment bond. There are striking variations in strength of activation of attachment behaviors across contexts and across children. Yet no evidence exists that these variations in themselves map onto variations in child–

mother attachment in any meaningful way. According to Ainsworth (1972),

> to equate strength of attachment with strength of attachment behavior under ordinary nonstressful circumstances would lead to the conclusion that an infant who explores when his mother is present is necessarily less attached than one who constantly seeks proximity to his mother, whereas, in fact, his freedom to explore away from her may well reflect the healthy security provided by a harmonious attachment relationship. (p. 119)

Ainsworth (1972) has described individual differences in the relationship with the attachment figure as more accurately considered to be variations in quality than in strength. Similarly, it is a mistake to label as "very attached" a young child who clings fearfully to the mother; such attachment behavior may reflect insecure attachment or secure use of the mother as a safe haven, depending on the context.

Given that the strength of attachment behaviors should not be confused with the strength of an attachment bond, is strength nonetheless a useful dimension on which to consider an attachment bond? One might assume that Bowlby's proposition that children develop "attachment hierarchies" (discussed in the following section) implies that some attachments are stronger than others. Although Bowlby himself did occasionally use this terminology—for example, "How do we understand the origin and nature of this extraordinarily strong tie between child and mother?" (Bowlby, 1988, p. 161)—such usage was relatively rare, particularly when he was comparing attachments (when doing so, he referred instead to "secure" and "insecure" attachments). Ainsworth (1982a) suggested that Hinde's (1979) notion of "penetration," as opposed to notions of either strength or intensity, may provide a more useful framework for characterizing an attachment bond. According to Hinde, penetration is a dimension of relationships that describes the centrality of one person to another's life—the extent to which a person penetrates a variety of aspects of the other person's life. Ainsworth pointed out that the concept of penetration is particularly useful when considering the changing nature of a child's attachment to the parent as the child grows older. She proposed that it may be more appropriate not to talk of the bond as becoming "weaker," but rather as characterizing a relationship that penetrates fewer aspects of the growing child's life as he or she comes to spend more time away from the parents and to develop new relationships.

For Bowlby (1969/1982), there are two important propositions about the nature of the attachment bond within the larger context of a relationship. First, the attachment bond reflects only one feature of the child's relationship with the mother: the component that deals with behavior related to the child's protection and security in time of stress. The mother not only serves as an attachment figure, but may also serve as playmate, teacher, or disciplinarian. These various roles are not incompatible, and it is possible that two or more may be filled by the same person. Thus, for example, a child may direct attachment behavior to the mother when he or she is frightened, and yet at other times may interact with her in ways relatively unrelated to attachment (e.g., play). Consequently, it would be a mistake to label as an attachment behavior a child's approach to the mother in order to engage in peekaboo. As Bretherton (1980) has noted, a behavior may serve different behavioral systems at different times, even when directed to the same individual. Yet it is important to note that even though a mother may be a frequent playmate for her 5-year-old, it does not negate the fact that this relationship is essentially characterized as an attachment relationship. Bowlby (1969/1982) summarized his position on this issue as follows:

> A parent–child relationship is by no means exclusively that of attachment–caregiving. The only justification, therefore, for referring to the bond between a child and his mother in this way is that the shared dyadic programme given top priority is one of attachment–caregiver. (p. 378)

Second, an attachment bond cannot be presumed to exist even though a relationship may contain an attachment component. As noted earlier, the fact that a 1-year-old distressed about separation from the mother will direct his or her attachment behaviors to a friendly stranger does not mean that the relationship with the stranger involves an attachment bond. This is true even in more ongoing relationships, such as relationships with peers. A child may routinely direct attachment behavior to a close friend and feel comfort in the friend's presence (particularly in a context such as the school, when a parent is not present) without that relationship's constituting an attachment bond. This is evident from the fact that the loss of such a friend usually does not have the devastating effects on the child that loss of a true attachment figure (a parent) has. Thus, even though children may at times turn to friends for comfort

(Hazan & Zeifman, 1994), these friendships need not be essentially attachment relationships.

MULTIPLE ATTACHMENTS

Bowlby stated three principal propositions about multiple attachments in infancy. First, most young infants are thought to form more than one attachment. According to Bowlby (1969/1982), "almost from the first, many children have more than one figure to whom they direct attachment behavior" (p. 304).[5] Indeed, empirical observations have revealed that the majority of children become attached to more than one familiar person during their first year (Ainsworth, 1967; Schaffer & Emerson, 1964). According to Bowlby (1969/1982), "responsiveness to crying and readiness to interact socially are amongst the most relevant variables" (p. 315) in determining who will serve as an attachment figure. In most cultures, this means that the biological parents, older siblings, grandparents, aunts, and uncles are most likely to serve as attachment figures. Generally, the mother's role as an attachment figure is clear. The father is also particularly likely to become an additional attachment figure early in the infant's life. Observational studies have revealed that fathers are competent caregivers (Belsky, Gilstrap, & Rovine, 1984) and that children use their fathers as attachment figures (Ainsworth, 1967). Ainsworth (1967) noted the special infant–father relationship that sometimes emerged in Uganda:

> It seemed to be especially to the father that these other attachments were formed, even in the cases of babies who saw their fathers relatively infrequently. One can only assume that there was some special quality in the father's interaction with his child— whether of tenderness or intense delight—which evoked in turn a strength of attachment disproportionate to the frequency of his interaction with the baby. (p. 352)

Furthermore, there is evidence that individual differences in quality of infant–father attachment are related to paternal behavior: Infants are more likely to be securely attached to fathers who have been sensitively responsive to them (Cox, Owen, Henderson, & Margand, 1992). Evidence has also emerged that siblings (Stewart & Marvin, 1984; Teti & Ablard, 1989) and day care providers (Howes, Rodning, Galluzzo, & Myers, 1988) can serve as attachment figures. In unusual and stressful situations, infants can even become attached to other infants (see Freud & Dann's [1951] observations of child survivors of a concentration camp). Howes (Chapter 29, this volume) provides an extensive discussion of multiple attachment figures.

Second, although there is usually more than one attachment figure, the potential number of attachment figures is not limitless. Bretherton (1980, p. 195) has described the infant as having a "small hierarchy of major caregivers," which is in contrast to the larger group of individuals with whom the infant has other sorts of relationships (Weinraub, Brooks, & Lewis, 1977). By the end of the first year, most infants are content (and even pleased) to approach and play with an unfamiliar friendly adult; when they are distressed, however, they strongly prefer the mother (Tracy, Lamb, & Ainsworth, 1976).

Third, although most infants have multiple attachment figures, it is important not to assume that an infant treats all attachment figures as equivalent, or that they are interchangeable; rather, an "attachment hierarchy" is thought to exist. According to Bowlby (1969/1982), "it is a mistake to suppose that a young child diffuses his attachment over many figures in such a way that he gets along with no strong attachment to anyone, and consequently without missing any particular person when that person is away" (p. 308). Bowlby proposed that this strong tendency for infants to prefer a principal attachment figure for comfort and security be termed "monotropy" (see also Ainsworth, 1964, 1982b).[6] Bowlby cited as evidence of this phenomenon the tendency of children in institutions to select, if given the opportunity, one "special" caregiver as their own (see Burlingham & Freud, 1944). Ainsworth (1982b) described responses to major separations from and losses of attachment figures as further support for the idea that a hierarchy exists: "The child would tolerate major separations from subsidiary figures with less distress than comparable separations from the principal attachment figure. Nor could the presence of several attachment figures altogether compensate for the loss of the principal attachment figure" (p. 19).[7] Also consistent with this hierarchy notion are data from observational studies of both mothers and fathers, which show that most infants prefer to seek comfort from their mothers when distressed; in the mother's absence, however, an infant is likely to seek and derive comfort and security from other attachment figures as well (Kagan, Kearsley, & Zelazo, 1978; Lamb, 1976a, 1976b, 1978; Rutter,

1981; see also Ainsworth, 1967, and Schaffer & Emerson, 1964). For a review of the relatively few experimental studies examining attachment hierarchies, and a discussion of the relevant methodological issues, see Colin (1996).

What determines the structure of an infant's attachment hierarchy? Colin (1996) has listed a likely set of contributing factors: "(1) how much time the infant spends in each figure's care; (2) the quality of care each provides, (3) each adult's emotional investment in the child, and (4) social cues" (p. 194). To this list, I would add that the repeated presence across time of the figure in the infant's life, even if each encounter is relatively brief, is likely to be important.

Why would monotropy have evolved as a tendency of human infants? Neither Bowlby nor Ainsworth addressed this question. I propose three possibilities here, all of which may operate simultaneously. The fact that there may be multiple ways in which the tendency toward monotropy contributes to infant survival and reproductive fitness increases the likelihood of its emerging through genetic selection. First, the infant's tendency to prefer a principal attachment figure may contribute to the establishment of a relationship in which that one attachment figure assumes principal responsibility for the child. Such a relationship should increase the child's likelihood of survival by helping to ensure that care of the child is not overlooked. This system seems more practical than the alternative, wherein a large number of caregivers have equal responsibility for a large number of offspring; this latter system might leave any individual child "falling between the cracks."

Second, monotropy may be most efficient for the child. When faced with danger, the child does not have to make a series of assessments and judgments about who may be most readily available, most responsive, and best suited to help. Rather, the child has a quick, automatic response to seek his or her principal attachment figure.

Third, monotropy may be the child's contribution to a process I term "reciprocal hierarchical bonding," in which the child matches an attachment heirarchy to the hierarchy of the caregiving in his or her environment. Evolutionary biologists writing on parental investment (e.g., Trivers, 1972) have suggested that adults vary in their investment in offspring largely as a function of the extent to which this investment contributes to the transmission of the adults' genes (i.e., their reproductive fitness). Following this reasoning, it should be most adaptive for the child to use as a principal attachment figure the person who, correspondingly, is most strongly bonded to him or her (i.e., the person who provides the most parental investment and has the most to gain—in terms of reproductive fitness—by the baby's healthy development). In most cases, it is the biological mother who has the greatest biological investment in the child. With the exception of an identical twin, there is no one with whom the child shares more genes than the mother (50%). Although the biological father and siblings also share 50% of their genes with a child, their investments are nonetheless considered to be less because (1) only the mother can be certain of a true (or, in the case of siblings, a truly equal) biological connection; and (2) the mother has less opportunity to produce additional offspring than fathers and siblings do. If this process of reciprocal hierarchical bonding exists, it may help explain not only monotropy, but also, in part, why the biological mother is generally the principal attachment figure.

Given the existence of multiple attachments, what is the course of their development across the lifespan? As noted earlier, two or three attachments usually develop during the infant's first year. These are usually with other family members or other people closely involved in the child's care. By middle childhood, when the child is spending more time with people outside the family, opportunities for new attachments may arise. In adolescence and young adulthood, individuals usually begin to develop attachments to sexual partners. Although attachments to parents remain throughout life, the later attachments may become the most central relationships in the individual's adult life.

When considering multiple attachments, theorists are faced with several sets of questions. One of these has to do with similarities versus differences in quality across different attachments (i.e., concordance rate). To what extent are a child's attachments to different caregivers similar? Studies examining concordance rate yield inconsistent results. Some studies reveal independence of attachment across caregivers (Belsky & Rovine, 1987; Grossmann, Grossmann, Huber, & Wartner, 1981; Main & Weston, 1981); some studies reveal similarity of attachment across caregivers (Goossens & van IJzendoorn, 1990; Steele, Steele, & Fonagy, 1996); and a meta-analysis of 11 studies revealed significant but weak concordance between attachment to mother and attachment to father (Fox, Kimmerly, & Schafer, 1991).

There are two main explanations for attachment concordance across caregivers. The first posits that attachments reveal specific infant–caregiver relationship histories, but that these histories are similar across caregivers for several reasons (e.g., parents may select mates whose capacities to serve as a secure base are similar to their own; parents may learn from each other how to parent). The second explanation is that infant characteristics, rather than a specific infant–caregiver relationship, are what determine attachment quality. In this case, the infant brings into the assessment situation traits that contribute to attachment classification no matter which caregiver is present. (See Vaughn & Bost, Chapter 10, and Berlin & Cassidy, Chapter 30, this volume, for more extensive discussions of concordance rates.)

Another question relates to the integration of multiple attachments. If a child's attachments are similar, he or she may develop a consistent set of internal working models about attachment figures, himself or herself, and relationships. Yet what if the child is faced with attachments that contribute to conflicting models? What if the child's experiences with one parent contribute to a model of the attachment figure as sensitively responsive and of the self as worthy of such care, yet negative experiences with the other parent contribute to very different models? If differing models of attachment figures eventually become integrated, how does this happen? In relation to models of the self, Bretherton (1985) asked over a decade ago: "Is an integrated internal working model of the self built from participation in a number of nonconcordant relationships" If so, how and when? Or are self models, developed in different relationships, only partially integrated or sometimes not at all?" (p. 30). Researchers have made little progress in answering these questions.

Still another question about multiple attachments relates to the issue of how these different attachments influence children's functioning. It could be that the attachment to the principal attachment figure, usually the mother, is most influential. On the other hand, it could be that one attachment is most influential in some areas and another is most influential in other areas (see van IJzendoorn & Sagi, Chapter 31, this volume). Or perhaps having at least one secure attachment, no matter who the attachment figure is, serves as a protective factor to facilitate the child's functioning across areas. Relatively little empirical work has addressed these possibilities, given that most research examining the sequelae of attachment focuses only on infant–mother attachment. The research that is available suggests that when a child is securely attached to one individual and insecurely attached to another, the child behaves more competently when the secure relationship is with the mother than when it is with the other attachment figure (Easterbrooks & Goldberg, 1987; Howes et al., 1988; Main et al., 1985; Main & Weston, 1981). These same studies indicate, however, that the most well-functioning individuals have two secure relationships, while the least competent children have none. van IJzendoorn and Sagi (Chapter 31, this volume) review the cross-cultural data and report similar evidence that multiple secure attachments enhance children's functioning; more extensive discussion of models of the influence of multiple attachments can be found in that chapter.

SUMMARY

This chapter addressed the issues that Bowlby presented in his initial ethological approach to understanding the nature of the child's tie to the mother. Bowlby's observations led him to be dissatisfied with the explanations provided by existing theories, and prompted him to consider alternative explanations. Drawing on the thinking of evolutionary biologists, cognitive scientists, control systems theorists, and developmental psychologists, he initiated what proved to be one of the earliest of the neo-Darwinian theories, tackling the problem of the ways humans evolved to master the primary task of genetic transmission: survival through infancy and childhood to reproductive age (see Simpson, Chapter 6, this volume). This chapter began with a description of the biological bases of attachment and how attachment may have evolved. Then the connection of the attachment behavioral system with other behavioral systems was described. Finally, a description of attachment and other affectional bonds was provided, and the issue of multiple attachments was discussed. Other components central to the early formulation of attachment theory are covered elsewhere in this volume: The developmental course of attachment is described by Marvin and Britner (Chapter 3) and by Hazan and Zeifman (Chapter 16); issues related to separation and loss are considered by Kobak (Chapter 2) and by Fraley and Shaver (Chapter 32); theory about individual differences in attachment quality is addressed by Weinfield et al. (Chapter 4);

and attachment-related communication and representation associated with individual differences are discussed by Bretherton and Munholland (Chapter 5).

ACKNOWLEDGMENTS

Part of this chapter was written while I was Visiting Associate Professor of Psychology at the University of Virginia. I am grateful for the support provided. The writing of this chapter was also supported by Grant No. RO1-MH50773 from the National Institute of Mental Health. Jay Belsky, Mary Main, and Phillip Shaver provided helpful comments on an earlier draft of this chapter.

NOTES

1. See Greenberg and Marvin (1982; see also Ainsworth, 1989) for discussion of the advantages of the term "sociable system" rather than "affiliative system." For data and more extensive discussion related to the interplay of the sociable system with other behavior systems, see discussions by Ainsworth et al. (1978), Bretherton (1978), Bretherton and Ainsworth (1974), Cassidy and Berlin (in press), and Greenberg and Marvin (1982).

2. This perspective differs somewhat from that of Bowlby. Bowlby (1969/1982, p. 240) described "maternal retrieval behavior" as distinct from other parenting *behavior,* with the former having the predictable outcome of proximity and the biological function of protection. It is unclear, however, what for Bowlby would constitute a behavioral *system.* The position taken here is that retrieval is the parental equivalent to child proximity seeking; it is a behavior, not a behavioral system. The relevant behavioral system would be what here is called the "caregiving system," which includes a variety of behaviors, one of which is parental retrieval of the child.

This perspective, along with Solomon and George's perspective, also differs from that proposed by Bretherton and her colleagues (Bretherton, Biringen, & Ridgeway, 1991). Their view incorporates the notion of a "parental side of attachment," in which the parent's bond to the child is considered part of the attachment system, in part because of its great emotional power.

3. Within the modern evolutionary perspective, the existence of separate maternal and paternal caregiving systems is readily understood. Both mothers and fathers are concerned with their own reproductive fitness. Yet, because mothers and fathers may differ substantially in the extent to which the survival of any one child enhances this fitness, their parenting behavior may differ. Compared to fathers, mothers have more to

gain in terms of reproductive fitness from each child for several reasons (e.g., mothers' certainty about parental status, shorter reproductive lifespan, longer interchild intervals, and greater energy expenditure per child [during pregnancy and lactation]; see Trivers, 1972).

4. Consensus is lacking about terminology related to the attachment bond. The description provided here is Ainsworth's (1989) and reflects Bowlby's most common usage. Yet in the second edition of the first volume of his trilogy, *Attachment and Loss,* Bowlby (1969/1982) described a bond as "a property of two parties," and labeled the child–parent bond as the "attachment–caregiving" bond (p. 377). In contrast to the implied notion of an "attachment relationship," Ainsworth (1982) stated:

> That there is a "relationship" between mother and child, in Hinde's (1979) sense, from the time of the infant's birth onward, and that the nature of this relationship stems from the interaction between them, is not to be gainsaid, but neither the mother-to-infant bond nor the emergent infant-to-mother attachment seems to me to comprehend all the important aspects of this relationship. (p. 24)

Bretherton (1985) also pointed out the limits of considering an attachment a "property of two parties": "A representational view of relationships . . . underscores that the two partners have, in another sense, two relationships: the relationship as mentally represented by the attached person and by the attachment figure" (p. 34). Ainsworth (personal communication, 1986) suggested that the most appropriate way to consider an "attachment relationship" is as a "shorthand" designation for "a relationship in which the attachment component is central."

5. There has been some confusion over Bowlby's position on this issue. Lamb, Thompson, Gardner, and Charnov (1985), for instance, mistakenly stated, "Bowlby was firmly convinced that infants were initially capable of forming only one attachment bond" (p. 21), when in fact from his earliest writings on (1958, 1969/1982), Bowlby described the role of multiple attachment figures. Furthermore, Bowlby (1969/1982) noted that "it has sometimes been alleged that I have expressed the view . . . that mothering "cannot be safely distributed among several figures" (Mead, 1962). No such views have been expressed by me" (p. 303).

6. Starting with his earliest writings, Bowlby (e.g., 1958) used the term "principal attachment-figure" or "mother-figure" rather than the term "mother." This usage underscored Bowlby's belief that although this figure is usually the biological mother, it is by no means necessarily so. From the beginning, Bowlby recognized that the figure's status (father, adoptive parent, grandmother, aunt, nanny) is less important than the nature of the figure's interactions with the infant.

7. One of the most moving passages of Bowlby's writing illustrates how one attachment figure can be more centrally important to a child's well-being than others:

About four weeks after mother had died, [four-year-old] Wendy complained that no one loved her. In an attempt to reassure her, father named a long list of people who did (naming those who cared for her). On this Wendy commented aptly, "But when my mommy wasn't dead I didn't need so many people—I needed just one." (Bowlby, 1980, p. 280)

REFERENCES

Ainsworth, M. D. S. (1963). The development of infant–mother interaction among the Ganda. In B. M. Foss (Ed.), *Determinants of infant behavior* (Vol. 2, pp. 67–112). New York: Wiley.

Ainsworth, M. D. S. (1964). Patterns of attachment behavior shown by the infant in interaction with his mother. *Merrill–Palmer Quarterly, 10,* 51–58.

Ainsworth, M. D. S. (1967). *Infancy in Uganda: Infant care and the growth of attachment.* Baltimore: Johns Hopkins University Press.

Ainsworth, M. D. S. (1972). Attachment and dependency: A comparison. In J. L. Gewirtz (Ed.), *Attachment and dependency* (pp. 97–137). Washington, DC: V. H. Winston.

Ainsworth, M. D. S. (1982a). *Attachment across the lifespan.* Unpublished lecture notes, University of Virginia.

Ainsworth, M. D. S. (1982b). Attachment: Retrospect and prospect. In C. M. Parkes & J. Stevenson-Hinde (Eds.), *The place of attachment in human behavior* (pp. 3–30). New York: Basic Books.

Ainsworth, M. D. S. (1989). Attachments beyond infancy. *American Psychologist, 44,* 709–716.

Ainsworth, M. D. S., Bell, S. M., & Stayton, D. J. (1971). Individual differences in Strange-Situation behavior of one-year-olds. In H. R. Schaffer (Ed.), *The origins of human social relations* (pp. 17–52). New York: Academic Press.

Ainsworth, M. D. S., Blehar, M., Waters, E., & Wall, S. (1978). *Patterns of attachment: A psychological study of the strange situation.* Hillsdale, NJ: Erlbaum.

Ainsworth, M. D. S., & Wittig, B. A. (1969). Attachment and exploratory behaviour of one-year-olds in a Strange Situation. In B. M. Foss (Ed.), *Determinants of infant behaviour* (Vol. 4, pp. 113–136). London: Methuen.

Baldwin, M. W. (1992). Relational schemas and the processing of social information. *Psychological Bulletin, 112,* 461–484.

Belsky, J., Gilstrap, B., & Rovine, M. (1984). The Pennsylvania Infant and Family Development Project: I. Stability and change in mother–infant and father–infant interaction in a family setting at one, three, and nine months. *Child Development, 55,* 692–705.

Belsky, J., & Rovine, M. (1987). Temperament and attachment security within the Strange Situation: An empirical rapprochement. *Child Development, 58,* 787–795.

Bender, L., & Yarnell, H. (1941). An observation nursery. *American Journal of Psychiatry, 97,* 1158–1174.

Bowlby, J. (1944). Forty-four juvenile thieves: Their characters and home life. *International Journal of Psycho-Analysis, 25,* 19–52, 107–127.

Bowlby, J. (1956). The growth of independence in the young child. *Royal Society of Health Journal, 76,* 587–591.

Bowlby, J. (1958). The nature of the child's tie to his mother. *International Journal of Psycho-Analysis, 39,* 350–373.

Bowlby, J. (1960a). Separation anxiety. *International Journal of Psycho-Analysis, 41,* 1–25.

Bowlby, J. (1960b). Grief and mourning in infancy. *Psychoanalytic Study of the Child, 15,* 3–39.

Bowlby, J. (1969/1982). *Attachment and loss: Vol. 1. Attachment.* New York: Basic Books.

Bowlby, J. (1973). *Attachment and loss: Vol. 2. Separation.* New York: Basic Books.

Bowlby, J. (1979). *The making and breaking of affectional bonds.* London: Tavistock.

Bowlby, J. (1980a). *Attachment and loss: Vol. 3. Loss.* New York: Basic Books.

Bowlby, J. (1980b). By ethology out of psycho-analysis: An experiment in interbreeding. *Animal Behavior, 28,* 649–656.

Bowlby, J. (1984). Caring for the young: Influences on development. In R. S. Cohen, B. J. Cohler, & S. H. Weissman (Eds.), *Parenthood: A psychodynamic perspective* (pp. 269–284). New York: Guilford Press.

Bowlby, J. (1988). *A secure base.* New York: Basic Books.

Brazelton, T. B. (1977). Implications of infant development among the Mayan Indians of Mexico. In P. H. Leiderman, S. R. Tulkin, & A. Rosenfeld (Eds.), *Culture and infancy* (pp. 151–187). New York: Academic Press.

Bretherton, I. (1978). Making friends with one-year-olds: An experimental study of infant–stranger interaction. *Merrill–Palmer Quarterly, 24,* 29–52.

Bretherton, I. (1980). Young children in stressful situations: The supporting role of attachment figures and unfamiliar caregivers. In G. V. Coelho & P. I. Ahmed (Eds.), *Uprooting and development* (pp. 179–210). New York: Plenum Press.

Bretherton, I. (1985). Attachment theory: Retrospect and prospect. In I. Bretherton & E. Waters (Eds.), Growing points of attachment theory and research. *Monographs of the Society for Research in Child Development, 50*(1–2, Serial No. 209), 3–38.

Bretherton, I. (1990). Open communication and internal working models: Their role in the development of attachment relationships. In R. A. Thompson (Ed.), *Nebraska Symposium on Motivation: Vol. 36. Socioemotional development* (pp. 59–113). Lincoln: University of Nebraska Press.

Bretherton, I. (1992). The origins of attachment theory: John Bowlby and Mary Ainsworth. *Developmental Psychology, 28,* 759–775.

Bretherton, I., & Ainsworth, M. D. S. (1974). Responses of one-year-olds to a stranger in a Strange Situation. In M. Lewis & L. A. Rosenblum (Eds.), *The origins of fear* (pp. 131–164). New York: Wiley.

Bretherton, I., Biringen, Z., & Ridgeway, D. (1991). The parental side of attachment. In K. Pillemer & K. McCartney (Eds.), *Parent–child relations through life* (pp. 1–22). Hillsdale, NJ: Erlbaum.

Bronson, G. (1972). Infants reactions to unfamiliar persons and novel objects. *Monographs of the Society for Research in Child Development, 37* (Serial No. 148).

Burlingham, D., & Freud, A. (1944). *Infants without families.* London: Allen & Unwin.

Carr, S., Dabbs, J., & Carr, T. (1975). Mother–infant attachment: The importance of the mother's visual field. *Child Development, 46,* 331–338.

Cassidy, J., & Berlin, L. J. (in press). Understanding the origins of childhood loneliness: Contributions of attachment theory. In K. J. Rotenberg & S. Hymel (Eds.), *Loneliness in childhood and adolescence.* New York: Cambridge University Press.

Colin, V. L. (1996). *Human attachment.* New York: McGraw-Hill.

Cox, M. J., Owen, M. T., Henderson, V. K., & Margand, N. A. (1992). Prediction of infant–father and infant–

mother attachment. *Developmental Psychology, 28,* 474–483.

DeWolff, M. S., & van IJzendoorn, M. H. (1997). Sensitivity and attachment: A meta-analysis on parental antecedents of infant attachment. *Child Development, 68,* 571–591.

Easterbrooks, A., & Goldberg, W. (1987). *Consequences of early family attachment patterns for later social–personality development.* Paper presented at the biennial meeting of the Society for Research in Child Development, Baltimore.

Eisenberg, J. F. (1966). The social organization of mammals. *Handbuch Zoologie, 8,* 1–92.

Fox, N. A., Kimmerly, N. L., & Schafer, W. D. (1991). Attachment to mother/attachment to father: A meta-analysis. *Child Development, 62,* 210–225.

Freud, S. (1957). Five lectures on psycho-analysis. In J. Strachey (Ed. and Trans.), *The standard edition of the complete psychological works of Sigmund Freud* (Vol. 11, pp. 3–56). London: Hogarth Press. (Original work published 1910)

Freud, S. (1964). An outline of psycho-analysis. In J. Strachey (Ed. and Trans.), *The standard edition of the complete psychological works of Sigmund Freud* (Vol. 23, pp. 139–207). London: Hogarth Press. (Original work published 1940)

Freud, A., & Dann, S. (1951). An experiment in group upbringing. *Psychoanalytic Study of the Child, 6,* 127–168.

George C., & Solomon J. (1996). Representational models of relationships: Links between caregiving and attachment. *Infant Mental Health Journal, 17,* 198–216.

Goldfarb, W. (1943). The effects of early institutional care on adolescent personality. *Journal of Experimental Education, 12,* 106–129.

Goossens, F. A., & van IJzendoorn, M. (1990). Quality of infants' attachments to professional caregivers: Relations to infant–parent attachment and daycare characteristics. *Child Development, 61,* 832–837.

Greenberg, M., & Marvin, R. S. (1982). Reactions of preschool children to an adult stranger: A behavioral systems approach. *Child Development, 53,* 481–490.

Grossmann, K. E., Grossmann, K., Huber, F., & Wartner, U. (1981). German children's behavior towards their mothers at 12 months and their fathers at 18 months in Ainsworth's Strange Situation. *International Journal of Behavioral Development, 4,* 157–181.

Harlow, H. F. (1958). The nature of love. *American Psychologist, 13,* 673.

Harlow, H. F. (1962). The development of affectional patterns in infant monkeys. In B. M. Foss (Ed.), *Determinants of infant behavior* (Vol. 1, pp. 75–88). New York: Wiley.

Harlow, H. F. (1969). Age-mate or affectional system. In D. S. Lehrman, R. A. Hinde, & E. Shaw (Eds.), *Advances in the study of behavior* (Vol. 2, pp. 334–383). New York: Academic Press.

Harlow, H. F., & Harlow, M. K. (1965). The affectional systems. In A. M. Schrier, H. F. Harlow, & F. Stollnitz (Eds.), *Behavior of non-human primates* (Vol. 2, pp. 287–334). New York: Academic Press.

Harlow, H. F., Harlow, M. K., & Hansen, E. W. (1963). The maternal affectional system of rhesus monkeys. In H. R. Rheingold (Ed.), *Maternal behavior in mammals* (pp. 254–281). New York: Wiley.

Hazan, C., & Zeifman, D. (1994). Sex and the psychological tether. *Advances in Personal Relationships, 5,* 151–177.

Heller, K. A., & Berndt, T. J. (1981). Developmental changes in the formation and organization of personality attributions. *Child Development, 52,* 683–691.

Hinde, R. A. (1974). *Biological bases of human social behavior.* New York: McGraw-Hill.

Hinde, R. A. (1979). *Towards understanding relationships.* London: Academic Press.

Hinde, R. A. (1982). Attachment: Some conceptual and biological issues. In C. M. Parkes & J. Stevenson-Hinde (Eds.), *The place of attachment in human behavior* (pp. 60–70). New York: Basic Books.

Howes, C., Rodning, C., Galluzzo, D., & Myers, I. (1988). Attachment and childcare: Relationships with mother and caregiver. *Early Childhood Research Quarterly, 3,* 403–416.

Huntingford, F. (1984). *The study of animal behavior.* London: Chapman & Hall.

Kagan, J., Kearsley, R., & Zelazo, P. (1978). *Infancy: Its place in human development.* Cambridge, MA: Harvard University Press.

Lamb, M. (1976a). Effects of stress and cohort on mother–infant and father–infant interaction. *Developmental Psychology, 12,* 435–443.

Lamb, M. (1976b). Interactions between two-year-olds and their mothers and fathers. *Psychological Reports, 38,* 447–450.

Lamb, M. (1978). Qualitative aspects of mother– and father–infant attachments. *Infant Behavior and Development, 1,* 265–275.

Lamb, M., Thompson, R. A., Gardner, W. P., & Charnov, E. L. (1985). *Infant–mother attachment.* Hillsdale, NJ: Erlbaum.

Lewis, M., Young, G., Brooks, J. & Michalson, L. (1975). The beginning of friendship. In M. Lewis & R. A. Rosenblum (Eds.), *Friendship and peer relations* (pp. 27–60). New York: Wiley.

Lorenz, K. E. (1935). Der Kumpan in der Umvelt des Vogels. In C. H. Schiller (Ed.), *Instinctive behavior.* New York: International Universities Press.

Main, M. (1990). Cross-cultural studies of attachment organization: Recent studies, changing methodologies, and the concept of conditional strategies. *Human Development, 33,* 48–61.

Main, M., Kaplan, N., & Cassidy, J. (1985). Security in infancy, childhood, and adulthood: A move to the level of representation. In I. Bretherton & E. Waters (Eds.), Growing points of attachment theory and research. *Monographs of the Society for Research in Child Development, 50* (1–2, Serial No. 209), 66–104.

Main, M., & Weston, D. (1981). The quality of the toddler's relationship to mother and to father: Related to conflict behavior and the readiness to establish new relationships. *Child Development, 52,* 932–940.

Mead, M. (1962). A cultural anthropologist's approach to maternal deprivation. In *Deprivation of maternal care: A reassessment of its effects.* Public Health Papers No. 14. Geneva: World Health Organization.

Miller, R., Caul, W., & Mirsky, I. (1967). Communication of affect between feral and socially isolated monkeys. *Journal of Personality and Social Psychology, 7,* 231–239.

Morgan, G. A., & Ricciuti, H. N. (1969). Infants' responses to strangers during the first year. In B. M. Foss (Ed.), *Determinants of infant behavior* (Vol. 4, pp. 253–272). London: Methuen.

Murray, H. A. (1938). *Explorations in personality.* New York: Oxford University Press.

Passman, R. H., & Erck, T. W. (1977, March). *Visual presentation of mothers for facilitating play in childhood: The effects of silent films of mothers.* Paper presented at the biennial meeting of the Society for Research in Child Development, New Orleans.

Passman, R. H., & Weisberg, P. (1975). Mothers and blankets as agents for promoting play and exploration by young children in a novel environment: The effects of social and nonsocial attachment objects. *Developmental Psychology, 11,* 170–177.

Piaget, J. (1954). *The construction of reality in the child.* New York: Basic Books.

Rheingold, H. (1969). The effect of a strange environment on the behavior of infants. In B. M. Foss (Ed.), *Determinants of infant behavior* (Vol. 4, pp. 137–166). London: Methuen.

Robertson, J., & Bowlby, J. (1952). Responses of young children to separation from their mothers. *Courrier of the International Children's Center, Paris, 2,* 131–140.

Rutter, M. (1981). *Maternal deprivation reassessed* (2nd ed.). New York: Penguin.

Schaffer, H. R., & Emerson, P. E. (1964). The development of social attachments in infancy. *Monographs of the Society for Research in Child Development, 29* (3, Serial No. 94), 1–77.

Sears, R. R., Maccoby, E. E., & Levin, H. (1957). *Patterns of child rearing.* Evanston, IL: Row, Peterson.

Sorce, J., & Emde, R. (1981). Mother's presence is not enough: Effect of emotional availability on infant explorations. *Developmental Psychology, 17,* 737–745.

Solomon, J., & George, C. (1996). Defining the caregiving system: Toward a theory of caregiving. *Infant Mental Health Journal, 17,* 183–197.

Sroufe, L. A., & Waters, E. (1977). Attachment as an organizational construct. *Child Development, 48,* 1184–1199.

Steele, H., Steele, M., & Fonagy, P. (1996). Associations among attachment classifications of mothers, fathers, and their infants. *Child Development, 67,* 541–555.

Stewart, R., & Marvin, R. S. (1984). Sibling relations: The role of conceptual perspective-taking in the ontogeny of sibling caregiving. *Child Development, 55,* 1322–1332.

Teti, D., & Ablard, K. (1989). Security of attachment and infant–sibling relationships. *Child Development, 60,* 1519–1528.

Tracy, L. R., Lamb, M. E., & Ainsworth, M. D. (1976). Infant approach as related to attachment. *Child Development, 47,* 571–578.

Trivers, R. L. (1972). Parental investment and sexual selection. In B. Campbell (Ed.), *Sexual selection and the descent of man, 1871–1971* (pp. 136–179). Chicago: Aldine-Atherton.

Trivers, R. L. (1974). Parent–offspring conflict. *American Zoologist, 14,* 249–264.

Vandell, D. L. (1980). Sociability with peer and mother during the first year. *Developmental Psychology, 16,* 355–361.

Weinraub, M., Brooks, J., & Lewis, M. (1977). The social network: A reconsideration of the concept of attachment. *Human Development, 20,* 31–47.

Weiss, R. S. (1982). Attachment in adult life. In C. M. Parkes & J. Stevenson-Hinde (Eds.), *The place of attachment in human behavior* (pp. 171–184). New York: Basic Books.

2

The Emotional Dynamics of Disruptions in Attachment Relationships

Implications for Theory, Research, and Clinical Intervention

❖

ROGER KOBAK

Children's reactions to separations from their parents have played a critical role in documenting the operation and regulation of the attachment system. During the 1940s and 1950s, John Bowlby and James Robertson used films of young children undergoing such separations to demonstrate the fundamental importance of the attachment relationship (Karen, 1994). These films highlighted the emotions that accompany disruptions of the attachment relationship. It was apparent to most observers that the children experienced the separations as a fundamental threat to their well-being. The films documented the significance of this threat by showing the young children's emotional reactions, including fearful expressions, angry protests, and desperate efforts to find the missing parents. The more extreme emotions of fear and anger that were immediately evident following the parents' departure eventually gave way to more subtle expressions of sadness and despair. Careful observation revealed that after a prolonged period of sadness, the infants regained some composure and became detached and less emotionally expressive. Subdued activity and a notable lack of joy or enthusiasm marked this detached stance. Much of

the impetus for Bowlby's (1969/1982) attachment theory came from his effort to account for the mechanisms and processes that organize children's reactions to separation.

Yet, despite the power of separations to illustrate the importance of attachment relationships, it soon became evident that the simple presence or absence of an attachment figure was inherently limited as a means of understanding attachment in older children and adults. The most casual observer of children could see that by 3 or 4 years of age, physical separations no longer present as serious a threat to a child, and consequently do not produce the same kinds of emotional reactions. In large part, the child's developing capacities to represent an absent parent, talk about impending separations, and plan for reunions with the parent reduce the problem posed by separations from an attachment figure. As a result, Bowlby (1973) faced a dilemma in the second volume of his *Attachment and Loss* trilogy. On the one hand, young children's responses to separations provided compelling evidence of the emotional significance of the attachment relationship. On the other hand, the lifespan and clinical implications of attachment

21

theory would be severely restricted by the assumption that a child's security is dependent upon the mere presence or absence of the attachment figure. Believing that attachment security and anxiety continue to influence the functioning of older children and adults, Bowlby had to provide a broader definition of the child's needs in the attachment relationship.

In the volume titled *Separation: Anxiety and Anger,* Bowlby (1973) introduced two theoretical ideas that are crucial to understanding attachment relationships across the lifespan. First, he emphasized that humans' capacity to forecast the future makes cognitive appraisals, or "working models," increasingly important in understanding individual differences in security and anxiety. Later attachment investigators (Bretherton, 1985; Main, Kaplan, & Cassidy, 1985) have substantially extended this emphasis on cognitive processes or working models of attachment figures. A second critical notion has received less attention from later researchers. Bowlby clearly stated that although children forecast many aspects of parents' behavior, the critical appraisal for their sense of safety and security is that their parents will be available and responsive if called upon for help. Several implications follow from Bowlby's emphasis on the availability and responsiveness of attachment figures. First, when children or adults view their attachment figures as both available and responsive, they feel secure. Second, a child's appraisal of a parent's availability and responsiveness depends not only on the physical presence or absence of the parent, but, more importantly, on expectations of parental response and the quality of parent–child communication. Third, closed communication in attachment relationships creates risk for adjustment problems, not only by increasing the child's anxiety about the parent's availability, but also by distorting the expression of attachment-related emotions such as fear, anger, and sadness.

In this chapter, I review the role of separations in the development of attachment theory, and I highlight Bowlby's theoretical contributions in the second volume of *Attachment and Loss.* I suggest that although attachment researchers have made exciting advances in understanding the cognitive processes involved in child and adult attachment, they have done so by neglecting an important aspect of Bowlby's theory. As a result, much of attachment research has become the study of internalized features of personality, rather than the study of current attachment relationships. Much of Bowlby's (1973) *Separation*

volume directs attention to the continuing importance of current attachment relationships and the role of emotional communication in maintaining the child's confidence in the availability and responsiveness of attachment figures. Similarly, Mary Ainsworth's seminal study of infant attachment (Ainsworth, Blehar, Waters, & Wall, 1978) highlights the ongoing quality of mother–infant communication as the context within which working models and attachment strategies initially develop. In reviewing Bowlby's volume on separation, I highlight this neglected aspect of Bowlby's and Ainsworth's work. Bowlby's and Ainsworth's ideas about how communication in current attachment relationships continues to influence a child's security, and about how threats to the availability and responsiveness of an attachment figure can produce dysfunctional emotional reactions, hold considerable promise for future developments in attachment research and clinical practice.

MATERNAL DEPRIVATION AND THE ORIGINS OF ATTACHMENT THEORY

During the decade following World War II, Bowlby laid much of the foundation for attachment theory. He developed his ideas in scientific and political settings that gave little recognition to the importance of a child's ties to parents. In the scientific arena, the major learning theories of child development portrayed the infant's relationship with a primary caregiver as simply a learned by-product of the drive to feed. Since the mother most often happens to be associated with feeding, the child eventually develops positive associations to her. This view implied that if a child is fed by a variety of caregivers, the relationship with mother would hold no special significance for the child. Professional child care workers of that era often maintained institutional practices that assigned little importance to the child's relationship with a parent or primary caregiver (Karen, 1994). Social workers in many industrialized countries would routinely separate young children from their mothers because the mothers were extremely poor or lacked husbands. These well-intended practices placed the physical health and well-being of the children ahead of the children's need for a primary relationship with their mothers. A similar attitude influenced hospital practice. If a young child needed to be hospitalized, it was standard policy to prevent or severely restrict parental visitation.

Beginning with his earliest work, Bowlby stressed the importance of maintaining a continuous relationship between child and mother. In a widely noted paper, Bowlby (1944) investigated the early home environments and parent–child relationships of 44 children who had been institutionalized for stealing. Social workers' reports indicated that in nearly all of these cases, the subjects had experienced highly deviant parenting marked by parental violence and emotional abuse. In several cases, a child had been blamed for a sibling's death. However, Bowlby found similar sorts of deviant parent–child relationships in a comparison group of other clinic children. The one factor that distinguished the thieves from the clinic children was evidence of prolonged separations from parents, and this difference was particularly striking among a subgroup of thieves Bowlby diagnosed as "affectionless." In many cases, the prolonged separations resulted from parental illness, death, or other family disruptions that resulted in placement of the children in foster care settings. Although many clinic children had experienced disruptions in parent–child relationships, Bowlby noted that the affectionless group had all experienced a prolonged separation after 6 months of age, and hence after they had begun to form a bond with their mothers.

In the late 1940s, Bowlby extended his investigation of the importance of the mother–child relationship by integrating research findings for a report published by the World Health Organization (WHO) on the effects of institutionalization on young children (Bowlby, 1951). Across a variety of studies from different countries, Bowlby found a similar pattern: Children who had been seriously deprived of maternal care tended to develop the same symptoms that Bowlby had identified in his "affectionless" young thieves. Institutionalized children developed into individuals who lacked feeling, had superficial relationships, and exhibited hostile or antisocial tendencies. Dorothy Burlingham and Anna Freud (1944) had reached similar conclusions, based on their work in a residential nursery for children whose parents had been unable to care for them as a result of World War II. Burlingham and Freud noted that despite extensive efforts by child care workers to develop relationships with the institutionalized children, some were nearly impossible to reach. Bowlby's conclusions from his review of research were clear. In a much-quoted phrase, he

noted that the provision of mothering is as important to a child's development as proper diet and nutrition.

The WHO report (Bowlby, 1951) signaled with unmistakable clarity the importance of the parent–child bond to the development of young children, as well as the potential emotional damage resulting from disruptions of the bond. Institutional care provided by child care experts and professionals could not substitute for the attachment bond with parents. Bowlby (cited in Karen, 1994) stated that "the services which mothers and fathers habitually render their children are so taken for granted that their magnitude is forgotten. In no other relationship do human beings place themselves so unreservedly and so continuously at the disposal of others. This holds true even for bad parents—a fact far too easily forgotten by their critics, especially critics who have never had the care of children of their own" (p. 66). The clear emphasis on the importance of the primary parent–child relationship suggested that many of the assumptions underlying child care in such institutions as hospitals, foster homes, and residential nurseries were seriously open to question. "The mothering of a child is not something which can be arranged by roster; it is a live human relationship which alters the characters of both partners" (cited in Karen, 1994, p. 66).

Claims concerning the fundamental importance of the parent–child bond stirred a great deal of controversy among a range of human service professionals responsible for child welfare (Karen, 1994). If Bowlby's claims were correct, much of then-current policy in social work training, child care agencies, and hospitals needed to be reconsidered. For the most part, these professions stressed the physical needs of children in settings where relatively little attention was paid to the emotional significance of the parent-child relationship. In sharp contrast, to a generation of professionals who felt that well-trained and educated workers could manage the care of children, Bowlby suggested that the parent–child bond provides an irreplaceable context for emotional development. Emphasizing the importance of the parent–child relationship for emotional development also stirred controversy within Bowlby's own discipline of psychiatry, where psychoanalytic theory suggested that many of children's and adults' problems are the products of internal conflicts and fantasies (Spitz, 1958). By placing so much emphasis on the adverse effects of maternal deprivation, Bowlby suggested that many childhood and adult difficulties result from a child's actual experience, as opposed to internal conflicts and fantasies. Such claims were ripe for testing and debate.

Children's Responses to Disruptions of the Attachment Bond

Notably absent from Bowlby's 1951 monograph was any theoretical understanding of the mechanisms through which maternal deprivation produced adverse effects (Bowlby, 1988). The 1950s proved to be a critical time for developing the theory and research that would lay the foundation for the attachment field. Bowlby was faced with a dual task: On the one hand, there was a lack of available theory to explain the importance of the parent–child bond; on the other hand, there was a lack of research evidence demonstrating the importance of the parent–child relationship. The literature on maternal deprivation had been largely atheoretical, and the individual studies that Bowlby reviewed were subject to alternative interpretations (Ainsworth, 1962; Rutter, 1981). Without a theory, it was difficult to conduct research that would answer critical questions about the mechanisms through which disruptions in the attachment relationship adversely affect children's emotional development.

Beginning in the late 1940s, Bowlby began a research project designed to gather the critical observations needed to understand young children's responses to separation. The hospital practices in the United Kingdom at that time provided a natural opportunity to document the effects of prolonged separations on young children. During the 1940s and 1950s parents were allowed to visit their sick children in the hospital for only 1 hour per week (Karen, 1994). For older children and their parents, this policy was manageable, but for infants, toddlers, and young children, the prolonged separation led to a substantial and largely unexplained disruption of the attachment relationship. Bowlby and his colleague James Robertson spent 4 years, 1948 to 1952, documenting and filming the effects of these separations on young children (see Robertson, 1962).

The children that Bowlby and Robertson observed ranged in age from 18 months to 4 years, and all were separated from their families in residential nurseries or hospitals for periods of a week or more. These separations consisted of both removals from the primary caregiver and placement in an unfamiliar environment in the care of a succession of unfamiliar figures. Following the children's stays in these institutions, Robertson and Bowlby continued to observe their adjustment after they returned to their families. Although there was substantial variation among the young children, Robertson and Bowlby were able to identify three phases that the children typically passed through during separations, each characterized by a particular attitude toward the missing mother figure. These phases, labeled "protest," "despair," and "detachment," were not only descriptive of Bowlby and Robertson's subjects but seemed to capture many of the descriptions of children's responses to separation provided by other observers, such as Burlingham and Freud (1944). Further evidence for these phases came from careful descriptions provided by Heinicke and Westheimer (1966).

The initial phase, protest, typically lasted from a few hours to a week or more. It began at the moment a parent prepared to leave a child at the nursery or hospital. Crying or screaming was the rule. During this phase the child signaled separation distress in a variety of ways such as crying loudly, showing anger, following the mother, pounding the door, or shaking his or her cot. Any sight or sound might produce a temporary respite, as the child eagerly checked to see whether it was a sign of the mother's return. The dominant attitude during this phase was hope that the mother would return, and the child actively attempted to regain contact with her. During this phase, efforts by alternative adults to comfort or soothe the child typically met with little success, and some children actively spurned potential caregivers. Although crying gradually subsided over several days, it commonly recurred, especially at bedtime or during the night. Searching for the missing parent often continued on a sporadic basis over a number of days. During the protest phase, the dominant emotions were fear, anger, and distress. Fear and distress signaled a child's appraisal of danger at being separated from a primary attachment figure, and anger served to mobilize the child's efforts to reestablish contact with the mother.

The phase of despair, which succeeded protest, was marked by behavior that suggested increased hopelessness about the mother's return. Although a child might continue to cry intermittently, active physical movements diminished and the child withdrew or disengaged from people in the environment. Bowlby (1973) interpreted this phase as similar to deep mourning, in that the child interpreted the separation as a loss of the attachment figure. He suggested that adults often misinterpreted the reduced activity and withdrawal as signs of the child's recovery from the distress of separation. Sadness accompanied this withdrawn state. Heinicke and Westheimer (1966) also noted that hostile behavior, directed toward another child or toward a favorite object brought from home, tended to increase over time.

A child's active turning of attention to the environment marked the final phase, detachment. In this phase, the child no longer rejected alternative caregivers, and some children even displayed sociability toward other adults or peers. The nature of this phase became most evident during reunion with the mother. A child who reached the phase of detachment showed a striking absence of joy at the mother's return; instead of enthusiastically greeting her, the detached child was likely to appear apathetic. In the Heinicke and Westheimer (1966) study, varying degrees of detachment were reported among 10 children following separations that lasted from 12 days to 21 weeks. On their initial reunion with their mothers, two of the children seemed not to recognize their mothers, and the other eight children either turned or walked away from their mothers. Children often alternated between crying and showing blank, expressionless faces. Some degree of detachment persisted following the reunions, with five of the mothers complaining that their children treated them like strangers. For many, detachment and neutrality alternated with clinging and showing fear that the mother might leave again. Observers whom the children knew from the nursery frightened the children when they visited them in their homes following the reunions.

These early efforts to document young children's distress and pain caused by separations were initially met with a great deal of disbelief and hostility from professional audiences (Karen, 1994). Because these children were too young to communicate their feelings effectively in words, it was easy for adults to downplay the significance of the mother–child separation, particularly as the children themselves moved beyond immediate protest to more subtle forms of despair and detachment. Furthermore, the distress reported by Bowlby and Robertson would have major implications for hospital policy regarding parental visitation and the degree to which nursing and pediatric staffs would have to adapt to the needs of young children and their families. Despite initial denial and criticism, Robertson persisted in documenting the effects

of separation, and during the 1950s he produced a series of films that vividly dramatize children's emotional reactions to the disruption of the attachment bond. His work, along with Bowlby's writings, would eventually alter hospital practice.

A Theoretical Explanation for Separation Distress

To many professionals and child care workers, young children's apparent distress at being separated from their parents in a well-managed hospital setting could easily be dismissed as unrealistic and immature. There was little in psychological theory to contradict these professionals. As noted earlier, the major theories of the parent–child relationship that were current in the 1950s viewed the parent–child relationship as a secondary by-product of the infant's more primary need for food. Such a perspective suggested that as long as the child receives adequate physical care, the relationship with the parent is relatively unimportant. Furthermore, existing theory suggested that separation from a parent and the distress this produces in a child should be relatively short-lived disruptions with no lasting consequences.

Bowlby viewed psychology's failure to recognize children's separation distress as a fundamental anomaly in contemporary theories of human nature. In searching for an alternative paradigm, he discovered the field of ethology, with its roots in naturalistic observation and evolutionary biology; he became particularly enthusiastic about Konrad Lorenz's observations of bonding in geese. Lorenz (1957) had demonstrated that a strong bond can develop between a mother figure and her offspring, even in a species in which the young can feed themselves. Bowlby also recognized that ethology provided new and powerful tools for reconsidering the nature of the parent–child bond. Drawing on the concept of a "behavioral system," Bowlby suggested that many of the human infant's behaviors are organized around maintaining proximity to a parent (see Cassidy, Chapter 1, this volume). Viewed in its evolutionary context, the attachment behavioral system serves the biological function of protection in species that have a prolonged period of development before reaching reproductive maturity. In those species, infants who maintain the attachment relationship are more likely to be protected and to have a distinct survival advantage.

The notion of behavioral systems also provided a way of understanding fear behaviors. The fear system is activated by what Bowlby (1973) termed "natural" clues to danger, which for humans include unfamiliarity, sudden change of stimulation, rapid or looming approach, heights, and being alone. In addition to natural clues are a variety of cultural clues that are learned through observation or association. Bowlby noted that the fear system is most likely to be activated in "compound" fear situations, in which more than one clue to danger is present. Various fear behaviors, such as avoidance, withdrawal, and attack, are well known. The goal of these behaviors is to increase distance or to eliminate the feared object.

Fear behavior and attachment behavior are often elicited together by the same set of circumstances. When a child is frightened or in pain, he or she not only wants to avoid the source of discomfort, but actively seeks a source of protection and safety. If the attachment figure is not available, the child faces a compound fear situation: Not only is the child facing danger but he or she is cut off from a critical source of protection. Both aspects of this situation elicit fear, though Bowlby sought to reserve the term "fear" for situations that alarm a child as a result of the presence of frightening stimuli, and the term "anxiety" for situations in which an attachment figure or trusted companion is absent. This makes the situation faced by the children Bowlby and Robertson observed in the residential nurseries and hospitals clearer. Not only were they alarmed at being placed in unfamiliar surroundings and cared for by unfamiliar adults; they were also anxious at not being able to gain ready access to their mothers.

Ainsworth and Wittig's (1969) naturalistic observations of mother–infant interaction illustrated the interplay among the attachment, exploration, and fear systems. In contrast to the fear system, the exploration system, whose primary function is learning, interlocks in a quite different fashion with the attachment system. In observing infants in naturalistic settings, Ainsworth noted that the presence of the mother often increased the quality of the child's play and exploration. In contrast, if the infant became distressed or the attachment system was activated, play and exploration rapidly diminished until the child had gained reassurance or comfort from the mother. Ainsworth described this interplay between the attachment and exploration systems in terms of the infant's using the mother as a "secure base" from which to explore. She noted that this balance between the attachment system, whose function is protection, and the exploration

system, whose function is learning, provides a mechanism that allows the child to learn and develop without straying too far away or remaining away for too long (Ainsworth et al., 1978).

Viewing attachment, fear, and exploration as behavioral systems allows for increased precision in understanding infants' and young children's behavior. The interplay between these systems is readily observable in Ainsworth's laboratory procedure, the strange situation. This paradigm provides an ingenious series of changing episodes that systematically alters the activation of the attachment, fear, and exploration behavioral systems. The strange situation consists of eight 3-minute episodes, beginning with an observer's introducing a mother and child to a strange laboratory playroom. During this first episode, the mother is present, and the toys in the room elicit some degree of exploration on the part of the infants. In Episode 2, the observer leaves the room, allowing the infant and mother to adjust further to the laboratory environment. Most children use their mothers' presence as a source of security and engage in exploratory play with the new toys. In Episode 3, a stranger enters, typically increasing the child's level of wariness and activating the attachment system. In Episode 4, the mother leaves the room, and the stranger tries to facilitate the infant's play with toys. This first separation tends to increase the baby's level of fear and attachment concerns about the mother's availability. As the fear and attachment systems are activated further, the level of exploration and quality of play tend to diminish. In Episode 5, the mother returns and the stranger leaves the room. Most children actively greet their mothers, and as concerns about the mothers' availability diminish, most children show increased exploration and play. In Episode 6, the mother again exits the room, leaving the baby alone. This creates a compound fear situation involving a strange environment, separation from the mother, and a natural clue to danger (being alone). As the fear system is activated, the level of attachment activation is high; many infants will actively protest this separation, making efforts to follow their mothers, crying, and showing anger. In Episode 7, the stranger reenters the room and attempts to comfort the child. The stranger has difficulty calming most children, and distress signals usually persist until Episode 8, when the mother returns to the room. In this final episode, an infant typically seeks physical contact with the mother and reassurance of her availability. As contact is reestablished, the fear system moves to a lower level of activation, and the baby typically shows a sense of increased safety and well-being.

With Ainsworth and colleagues' development of the strange situation, the study of separation had come a long way from Bowlby's early review of the maternal deprivation literature. Ainsworth had now demonstrated that a brief 20-minute laboratory paradigm using what she termed "minuscule separations" could systematically activate the attachment system and demonstrate the interrelations among the attachment, fear, and exploration behavioral systems. The interplay between attachment and exploration was strikingly supported by Ainsworth's data (Ainsworth et al., 1978). Frequency counts of exploratory locomotion, manipulation, and visual exploration during each episode of the strange situation showed that exploration peaked during Episode 2, when an infant was alone the mother, and then dramatically declined. In contrast, frequency measures of separation protest that included crying and search behavior peaked in Episode 6, when the baby was alone, while attachment behaviors measured by seeking proximity and contact showed a linear increase from Episode 2 through the reunion in Episode 8. Thus, as the attachment system became increasingly activated over the course of the eight episodes, the exploration system became increasingly deactivated. The importance of the attachment system was now apparent not only in the case of severe disruption, but in much more subtle day-to-day situations experienced by all children.

REDEFINING SEPARATIONS AS THREATS TO THE AVAILABILITY OF PARENTS

Clarifying the Set Goal of the Attachment System

Observations of children's responses to separations from their parents had provided critical evidence for the importance of the attachment relationship. As a result, it was tempting to view the primary purpose of the attachment system as the regulation and maintenance of physical proximity to the parent. This view of attachment was enormously appealing to behavioral researchers, who could easily quantify proximity seeking. Even more appealing was the notion that attachment behavior could be turned on by the absence of the parent and turned off by the presence of

the parent. Yet, by the 1970s, the limitations of using simple physical proximity or the physical presence or absence of the parent as the set goal of the attachment system were obvious to attachment theorists. Such a model did not adequately explain Ainsworth's observations of mothers and infants, and Bowlby (1973) was aware that sole reliance on physical proximity and separations would limit his efforts to extend attachment theory to older children and adults.

Ainsworth's Baltimore study of mothers and their infants had not only documented the operation of the attachment, fear, and exploration behavioral systems; of equal significance was her discovery of important individual differences in infants' responses to separations in the strange situation. The identification of "secure," "avoidant," and "ambivalent" or "resistant" patterns in the strange situation suggested that the infants entered this standardized situation with different cognitive expectations for how their parents would respond to them in times of distress. Ainsworth's detailed observations of mother–infant interaction suggested that these different expectations resulted from the infants' actual experience with their mothers during the first year of life. These expectations or "working models," of the mothers led to observable differences in how infants responded to the stress of brief separations. Thus the simple presence or absence of a parent did not provide an adequate account of these individual differences, and it was clear to Ainsworth that cognitive processes had to be incorporated into a model of how the attachment system functions.

Although Bowlby (1969/1982) initially stressed that proximity to the parent is the predictable outcome of the attachment system, he was aware that the increasing cognitive complexity that accompanies development can change with the child's capacities to maintain the attachment relationship. With the capacity to plan and to negotiate plans about separations with parents, the child could adjust his or her goals from one situation to another. "At one moment the child is determined to sit on his mother's knee and nothing else will do; at another he is content to watch her through the doorway. In ordinary circumstances, it seems clear, whatever conditions are at any one time necessary to terminate his attachment behavior become the set-goal of whatever attachment plan he adopts" (Bowlby, 1969/1982, p. 351). The notion that distal communication could serve at times to reassure the child suggested that the set goals for the attachment system are flexible and must include more than simple proximity or physical contact with the caregiver. In the first volume of the *Attachment and Loss* trilogy, however, Bowlby was less clear about how to move beyond physical proximity as the set goal of the attachment system.

Ainsworth's Emphasis on Appraisals of Availability and Responsivenes

Although separations were clearly one condition activating attachment behavior and resulting in an infant's effort to gain physical proximity to the parent, Ainsworth was clearly not satisfied with the apparent implication that the set goal of the attachment system is physical proximity to the parent. Ainsworth expressed major reservations with this "simple regulator model" of the attachment system. She and her colleagues wrote: "Overemphasis on the simple model has led many to assume that Bowlby's attachment theory defines attachment behavior rigidly and exclusively in terms of seeking literal proximity—a conception that is inadequate even when describing the attachment and attachment behavior of a 1-year-old and that is clearly misleading when attempting to comprehend the behavior of the older child or adult" (Ainsworth et al., 1978, p. 11).

Ainsworth's reservations about limiting the set goal of the attachment system to physical proximity came from several sources. If proximity were indeed the set goal, even by 1 year of age most children should respond with the same level of alarm to separations. It was clear to Ainsworth, however, that infants' responses to separations in the strange situation were influenced by other factors. For instance, infants displayed greater separation distress in the context of a strange laboratory environment than in the familiar home environment. It was also evident that infants were more distressed in the second separation episode than they were in the first. These problems disappear when separation distress is viewed as resulting from a child's *appraisal* or evaluation of the mother's departure, and not from the actual physical absence of the parent.

The importance of cognitive processes in infants' responses to separations was further highlighted by the substantial individual differences in how infants responded to the strange situation. Most notable were marked differences in reunion behavior following the second separation episode. Whereas most children actively sought contact with their mothers and were soothed by

such contact, others ignored or avoided their mothers, and still others mixed contact seeking with anger. To account for these differences, Ainsworth again relied on cognitive processes, suggesting that differences in infants' attachment behavior result from different *expectations* of how their mothers will respond. According to Ainsworth, an infant's model of a particular parent, built from previous experiences, guides the infant's expectations regarding the mother's availability and acts as an important "modifier" to the infant's set goal of proximity. Thus a child whose model leads to confident expectations concerning his or her mother's availability and responsiveness will react to a separation and subsequent reunion with open bids for contact, whereas a child who anticipates rejection will approach more cautiously or not at all.

Ainsworth's notion that appraisals and expectations organize the operation of the attachment system also explains why brief laboratory separations gradually cease to be stressful for older children. Marvin (1977), in a cross-sectional study of 2-, 3-, and 4-year-olds in the strange situation, found that whereas 2-year-olds responded to the separation episodes in much the same way as 1-year-olds, 3-year-olds showed little disturbance in the first separation episode. Although the 3-year-olds became distressed when left alone, they were more readily comforted by the stranger than were the younger children. The 4-year-olds showed even less distress, with the exception of several children who asked to go with their mothers. When the mothers, following the experimenter's instructions, refused their children's requests, the children became very distressed. These children were angry, crying, and demanding when their mothers returned. Ainsworth et al. (1978) suggested that it was not the physical separation that distressed the 4-year-olds, but their mothers' apparently arbitrary behavior.

Ainsworth's observations of infants and their mothers, and her emphasis on cognitive appraisals, plans, and working models, helped Bowlby to refine his claims about the effects of separation and maternal deprivation. Just as simple proximity seeking failed to account for children's responses to the strange situation, the simple presence or absence of the attachment figure was proving inadequate as a defining condition for attachment security. For instance, efforts to review studies of "maternal deprivation" indicated that this term was too broad and gave the mistaken impression that separations regardless of moderating conditions could create irreversible damage to a child (Ainsworth, 1962; Rutter, 1981). Although the study of separations had proved invaluable in revealing important mechanisms and showing how children cope with disruptions of the attachment bond, it was now clear that these disruptions were moderated by an increasingly complex set of appraisals and emotional processes. Claims about the consequences of separation and the set goal of the attachment system had to be substantially refined and clarified.

Bowlby's Clarification: From Physical Proximity to Availability and Responsiveness

In the second volume of *Attachment and Loss,* Bowlby refined his definition of the set goal of the attachment system. In considering the effects of separations on children, he moved toward the notion that security derives from a child's appraisal of an attachment figure's availability. In the first chapter, Bowlby stated:

> 'Presence' and 'absence' are relative terms and, unless defined, can give rise to misunderstanding. By presence is meant 'ready accessibility', by absence 'inaccessibility'. The words 'separation' and 'loss' as used in this work imply always that the subject's attachment figure is inaccessible, either temporarily (separation) or permanently (loss). (Bowlby, 1973, p. 23)

However, even "ready accessibility" is not enough to establish security for the child. Bowlby presented the case of the physically accessible but "emotionally absent" parent. To address this issue, he added a second criterion for attachment security: The child needs to experience a parent who is not only accessible but also *responsive.* This aspect of security incorporated Ainsworth's findings that it is the quality of day-to-day interactions, not just major separations, that influences infants' attachment expectations. Ainsworth's ratings of mothers' sensitivity to their infants' signals in the home showed a strong association with the confident expectation for mothers' response in the strange situation. Ainsworth viewed a mother's sensitivity to infant signals as increasing her infant's confidence in the mother's availability and responsiveness. In contrast, various nonresponsive or insensitive forms of care can undermine the infant's confidence or even lead to expectations for rejection or inconsistent response.

Establishing the set goal of the attachment system as maintaining the caregiver's accessibility and responsiveness also accounted for the three phases of children's responses to separation observed by Robertson and Bowlby. Different emotions naturally accompany a child's changing appraisals of parents' availability and play a central role in organizing a child's emotional responses. Separation distress results from the appraisal that a parent is inaccessible. This perceived threat to a parent's accessibility activates the attachment system and motivates a child to reestablish contact. Emotional reactions accompanying the appraisal of threat include fear and anger. Fear activates the attachment system and signals the child's distress. Anger results from frustrations that the child encounters in trying to regain access, and it mobilizes efforts to reestablish contact. Fear and anger are often combined in a child's protest of a parent's departure. As initial attempts to reestablish contact fail and the child's expectations for reunion are disappointed, he or she *reappraises* the situation, and frightened and angry efforts to reunite give way to sadness. Despair accompanies the recognition that protest will not succeed in reestablishing contact with the parent. Since prolonged despair and failure to reestablish contact leave the child in an intolerably painful state, the child may attempt to reduce this pain with defensive efforts to exclude information about the absent parent. Defensive detachment becomes the only available means of coping with the severe distress that the child experiences.

Moreover, defining the set goal as maintaining the caregiver's accessibility and responsiveness within comfortable limits provided an explanation for the decline of separation distress during the third and fourth years of life. As a child gains the ability to talk with an attachment figure and to understand his or her goals and plans, it becomes possible to make plans for separations that reassure the child of the attachment figure's continued accessibility and responsiveness. Because separation is no longer perceived as a threat to the caregiver's availability, separation distress declines dramatically.

The decline of separation distress does not mean that the importance of the attachment relationship declines, however. The focus on the parent's accessibility and responsiveness raised new developmental questions about how the maintenance of the attachment relationship changes with age. As a child gains an increased capacity to maintain the relationship, the nature of threats to availability also changes. Consequently, attachment theory was no longer limited to an account of young children's responses to the physical absence of their parents. The new criteria of accessibility and responsiveness allowed Bowlby (1973) to make a bolder and much broader claim: "Whether a child or adult is in a state of security, anxiety, or distress is determined in large part by the accessibility and responsiveness of his principal attachment figure" (p. 23). This claim extended the scope of attachment theory well beyond early childhood. The challenge for researchers was (and indeed still is) to move beyond the strange situation to find alternative ways of assessing older children's and adults' appraisals of their attachment figures' availability in ways that take into account their developmental stage.

Although Bowlby made the set goal of the attachment system clear in the first chapter of his 1973 volume, he did not address the critical role of cognitive appraisals in the operation of the attachment system until the third section of that book. The importance of cognitive appraisals became clear when Bowlby introduced the notion of individual differences in susceptibility to fear. He began with a clarification of the notion "caregiver responsiveness," stating that this refers to a parent's willingness to act as a comforter and protector when a child is afraid. He then provided a single term, "availability," to encompass both a caregiver's accessibility and responsiveness as the set goal of the attachment system.

With the set goal defined as caregiver "availability," three critical propositions followed that provided the scaffolding for the volume on separation:

1. When an individual is confident that an attachment figure will be available to him whenever he desires it, that person will be much less prone to either intense or chronic fear than will an individual who . . . has no such confidence.
2. Confidence in the availability of attachment, or lack of it, is built up slowly during the years of immaturity—infancy, childhood, and adolescence—and whatever expectations are developed during those years tend to persist relatively unchanged throughout the rest of life.
3. The varied expectations of the accessibility and responsiveness of attachment figures that different individuals develop during their years of immaturity are tolerably accurate reflections of the experiences those individuals have actually had. (Bowlby, 1973, p. 202)

All three of these propositions turn on the cognitive expectations or forecasts that an individual makes about the availability of his or her attachment figure. These expectations or working models become a central aspect of personality and bias how an individual will respond to frightening situations and interpret a caregiver's response. However, events that threaten the attachment figure's availability will continue to activate the attachment system. Because maintaining the attachment figure's availability remains the set goal of the attachment system, it continues to determine the individual's feelings of security and insecurity across the lifespan.

An Alternative Definition of the Set Goal: Felt Security

In 1977, Sroufe and Waters published a seminal and very influential paper titled "Attachment as an Organizational Construct." This paper highlighted the emotional processes that organize infants' behavior in the strange situation, and helped to explain how a variety of locomotive and signaling behaviors can all serve the common function of gaining access to mother. The paper also provided a compelling demonstration of how behavior needs to be interpreted according to the context and the underlying goals of the child, instead of being reduced to simple frequency counts of discrete behaviors.

The emphasis on the organization of behavior in the strange situation further emphasized the problems with proximity as the set goal of the attachment system. The concerns of Sroufe and Waters were similar to those of Ainsworth. If proximity were indeed the set goal, why should an infant be any more distressed during the second separation than during the first? Furthermore, why should distal communication with the attachment figure be reassuring to the child? Sroufe and Waters believed these questions could be addressed by specifying a set goal that makes reference to internal emotional processes, as opposed to simple distance regulation. They proposed "felt security" as the set goal of the attachment system. With felt security as the set goal, a wider range of factors could be shown to influence the activation of the attachment system, including internal cues such as mood or illness, as well as external cues such as preceding events and context.

The notion of felt security provided a useful way of talking about the operation of the attachment system in older children and adults (Cicchetti, Cummings, Greenberg, & Marvin, 1990; Kobak & Shaver, 1987). However, this concept substituted a set goal that was too broad (felt security) for a goal that had clearly been too narrow (physical proximity). There is little reason to believe that relying on an attachment figure is the only source of feeling secure. As Ainsworth (1990) pointed out, an individual can increase felt security simply by avoiding dangerous situations. The attachment relationship has little or nothing to do with this strategy or with many other strategies for maintaining felt security. Making felt security the set goal for attachment suggested that "the child plans how to become secure rather than planning for conditions that, as it turns out, make him secure" (Ainsworth, 1990, p. 474). Ainsworth's response to Sroufe and Waters led to further clarification of the set-goal of the attachment system. After reiterating that "maintenance of proximity can still be conceived as the set-goal of the attachment system, given that the definition of closeness is extended by cognitive development" (Ainsworth, 1990, p. 474), Ainsworth cited Bowlby's statement that "availability of the attachment figure is the set goal of the attachment system in older children and adults." Bowlby's definition of availability "turns on cognitive processes: (a) belief that lines of communication with the attachment figure are open, (b) that physical accessibility exists, and (c) that the attachment figure will respond if called upon for help" (Ainsworth, 1990, p. 474).

Bowlby's emphasis on availability fit with his view that attachment security derives from *appraisals of availability in current attachment relationships*. Feelings of security accompany appraisals of an attachment figure's availability, and anxiety accompanies perceived threats to availability. Although perceptions of availability are biased by past experience or internal working models, these appraisals continue to be influenced by the current behavior of the attachment figure. Thus older children and adults continue to monitor the physical accessibility and responsiveness of caregivers, although this monitoring may occur through distal forms of communication. Bowlby's and Ainsworth's focus on ongoing appraisals of availability suggests the continued need for the observational study of attachment *relationships* in older children and adults. This view is consistent with a transactional model of attachment, in which internalized aspects of personality interact with the quality of a current attachment relationship in a dynamic and reciprocal manner (Bowlby, 1973).

THREATS TO THE AVAILABILITY OF ATTACHMENT FIGURES

During childhood, adolescence, and adulthood, many individuals encounter difficulties in their relationships with parents and spouses that shake their confidence in the availability of these attachment figures. Such difficulties may fundamentally disrupt attachment relationships and dramatically reduce an individual's capacity to adapt to challenges outside the family. Just as prolonged separations were shown to have dramatic effects on the emotional life of young children, a lifespan view of attachment needs to identify situations that produce similar reactions in older children and adults. Bowlby's and Ainsworth's criteria for the availability of attachment figures provide valuable guidelines for examining attachment security in older children and adults. Threats to open communication, physical accessibility, and responsiveness may lead to anxious/insecure attachment and to many of the emotional responses that were evident in young children's responses to physical separations. The degree of threat is likely to be greatest when beliefs in all three aspects of availability are simultaneously challenged. Since both responsiveness and open communication are premised on the possibility that the attachment figure is physically accessible, threats of abandonment by or loss of an attachment figure may produce the most distress. Less severe threats may result from lack of responsiveness or emotional disengagement during communication. Threats to the availability of an attachment figure are often the source of many child and family problems that are encountered by clinicians. Much of Bowlby's 1973 volume was devoted to the types of threats that would create insecure attachment in older children and adults.

Threats to Availability in Child–Parent and Marital Relationships

The perception of physical accessibility remains the most fundamental aspect of an attachment figure's availability. The sophistication of the cognitive mapping of the attachment figure's whereabouts, the resources for seeking proximity, and the types of distal communication with the attachment figure increase dramatically with age. Yet despite these developments, the notion that if necessary the individual can reunite with the attachment figure remains a fundamental aspect of availability. Furthermore, under certain conditions, older children and adults can perceive separations as jeopardizing the availability of their attachment partners. For instance, separations in which a parent leaves in an angry or unexplained manner may disrupt a child's ability to plan for reunion and leave the child uncertain about the parents' whereabouts. Bowlby cited a research study by Newson and Newson (1968) describing how a 4-year-old had become anxious and clinging, following her father's desertion of the family 3 months earlier. The child's mother speculated that her child's difficulty with staying at day care resulted from her fear that the mother would also not come back—a speculation supported by the child's repeatedly saying to the mother, "Do you love me? You won't leave me, Mummy, will you?" (Bowlby, 1973, p. 214).

The development of verbal communication creates new possibilities both for maintaining open communication and for creating new threats to the availability of attachment figures. For instance, without actually leaving, a parent can threaten to leave or to send the child away. Such behavior is likely to occur in disciplinary contexts when the parent has become angry and exasperated with the child. For instance, Bowlby quoted a mother from the Newson and Newson (1968) study:

> I used to threaten him with the Hartley Road Boys' Home, which isn't a Home any more; and since then, I haven't been able to do it; but I can always say I shall go down town and see about it you know. And Ian says, 'Well, if I'm going with Stuart (7) it won't matter'; so I say, 'Well, you'll go to different ones—you'll go to one Home, and *you'll* go to another'. But it really got him worried, you know, and I really got him ready one day and I thought I'll take him a walk round, *as if* I was going, you know, and he really *was* worried. In fact, I had to bring him home, he started to cry. He saw I was in earnest about it—he *thought* I was, anyway. And now I've only got to threaten him. I say 'It won't take me long to get you ready.'

It is difficult to document the frequency of such statements, because many parents are ashamed to admit them to researchers. However, in his review of parenting studies, Bowlby reported that the incidence of such statements was as high as 27% in the Newson and Newson (1968) study of families in England, and 20% in a study of parents in the United States (Sears, Maccoby, & Levin, 1957).

Threats of suicide by a desperate parent may elicit even more anxiety about parental availability. In addition to the obvious threat to the physical accessibility of the parent, the child is faced with the fear of violence and with the prospect of loss. These threats often occur in the context of hostile and conflictual relations, which may further create the implication for the child that his or her angry feelings toward the parent may be responsible for the parent's desperation and despair. Bowlby noted that many children not only are exposed to threats of suicide, but may actually witness suicidal attempts. A parent may also make statements that attribute responsibility for future abandonment to the child. Statements to the child such as "You will be the death of me," or threats of abandonment that follow a child's misbehavior, are likely to confound attachment-related fears with feelings of guilt. This kind of attribution not only shakes the child's confidence in the parent's availability, but also leads directly to negative perceptions of the self.

Witnessing violence between parents may also threaten a child's confidence in the parents' availability (Davies & Cummings, 1995, 1998). The child's appraisal of marital violence is likely to include the fear that harm may come to one or both of the parents. In addition, parents who are living with constant conflict and fear are likely to have reduced capacities to attend to the child. Thus, in addition to fear of harm coming to the parents, attachment anxiety is increased by uncertainty about the parents' ability to respond to the child's distress and the lack of open communication with both parents. Even in situations with less extreme conflict, parents who become emotionally disengaged from each other and decide to separate or divorce may create fears in the child that the parents will also decide to leave the child. For the child, the notion that a parent may leave and not return creates a fundamental threat to physical accessibility. Most parents who divorce will make efforts to communicate with the child and reassure the child of their continued availability. These efforts to maintain an open line of communication and to reassure the child of the parents' responsiveness to the child's distress can substantially reduce the perceived threat and restore the child's confidence in both parents' continuing availability.

Adults may experience threats to the availability of their adult attachment figures as well. Gottman (1994) observed that distressed spouses are prone to entering into negative absorption states. These states are marked by intense negative affect in both partners and by the partners' failure to find a way of exiting from this negative state. A common self-perpetuating pattern of this type occurs when one partner rigidly pursues the other in a manner that is perceived as critical or nagging, and the partner responds by emotionally disengaging. Such disengagement can take a variety of forms: contemptuous, aloof responses, to silent stonewalling, or actual physical withdrawal from the partner. Although this disengagement can be seen as an effort to escape from a painful interaction, it paradoxically heightens the pursuing partner's efforts to engage the withdrawing partner. Each partner in this state perceives the other as behaving aversively, and both see their own efforts as legitimate attempts to reduce the distress in the relationship (Kobak, Duemmler, Burland, & Youngstrom, 1998).

From an attachment perspective, these negative absorption states are maintained by the perceived threat to the availability of the partner. The emotions accompanying an individual's appraisal that a partner is no longer available as an attachment figure and has emotionally abandoned the individual may fuel the rigid negative absorption states that mark distressed marriages. Unfortunately, fear of losing the partner or of being hurt is often mixed with defensive anger. As a result, attachment-related fears and vulnerabilities are often hidden behind cycles of blame and defense that dominate much of distressed a couple's interactions. Marital therapists are faced with the challenge of helping members of such couples access underlying attachment fears associated with appraisals that their partners are unavailable and unresponsive (Kobak, Hazan, & Ruckdeschel, 1994). Shifting from an externally focused attentional set in which a partner is viewed as primarily a source of danger to a more internally focused awareness of the fear and distress caused by the threat to the attachment relationship can be a critical step in marital therapy. When the fears that accompany perceived threats to a partner's availability are openly communicated, the high level of conflict and disengagement found in distressed marriages can be de-escalated (Johnson, 1996).

Attachment Disruptions, Communication, and Attachment Strategies

Threats to availability cannot be equated directly with disruptive events that a child or adult encounters in attachment relationships. These attachment disruptions, which include marital conflict, divorce, parental dysfunction or illness, and parent–child conflict, become threats only when the child or adult *perceives* them as jeopardizing the availability of an attachment figure. Two aspects of availability—open communication and expectations for responsiveness—play a critical role in modifying the child's or adult's appraisals of disruptive events.

Open communication can greatly reduce the extent to which disruptive events are perceived as threatening the availability of an attachment figure. For example, a parental expression of anger can be perceived by a child either as a signal that the child needs to alter his or her behavior to maintain a cooperative relationship, or as a rejection or threat of abandonment. When communication is open, parental anger is usually accompanied by an explanation that provides the child with a clear understanding of the specific source and context for the anger. This understanding allows the child to appraise the parent's concerns and to adjust his or her behavior accordingly. In contrast, a parent may express anger toward the child in hostile, critical remarks that fail to provide a clear account of the sources of the parent's frustrations. This kind of anger can easily be perceived as a potential indicator of rejection or abandonment and as a threat to a parent's (or partner's) availability. Recent research on communication processes in parent–teen relationships documents the role that open communication plays in facilitating adolescent development (Allen, Hauser, O'Connor, Bell, & Eickholt, 1996; Kobak & Duemmler, 1994).

A child's appraisal of disruptive events is also influenced by his or her expectations or working model of how the attachment figure will respond if called upon for help. These working models of the attachment figure are built from the child's previous experience with the parent at times of distress. It was these expectations that Ainsworth believed "modified" infants' appraisals of the separations they encountered in the strange situation (Ainsworth et al., 1978). Infants who had confident expectations concerning their caregivers actively sought comfort and used the parents as a safe haven following the separations. Avoidant infants, who had reason to expect rejection from their caregivers, modified their attachment behavior by avoiding the caregivers, effectively reducing anticipated conflict or rejection following the separation. Ambivalent/resistant infants, who had reason to be uncertain about their mothers' response, showed angry resistant or passive behavior that served to increase their proximity to the caregivers.

Infants who lack confidence in the responsiveness of their mothers develop avoidant or ambivalent/resistant strategies. These strategies can be viewed as organized ways of maintaining proximity to unresponsive parents (Main, 1990; Main & Weston, 1982). Ainsworth observed the secure and insecure strategies in a small sample of middle-class infants and had little cause to believe that these infants had experienced prolonged separations or abuse. As a result, there was little reason to suppose that the two insecure attachment strategies identified in the strange situation would provide a sufficient explanation of major adjustment problems associated with psychopathology (Sroufe, 1988). Instead, these strategies were ways of adapting to differing levels of parental responsiveness and provided children with a way of maintaining physical access to their attachment figures.

Bowlby's focus on threats to the availability of attachment figures may provide a more comprehensive account of the processes that contribute to insecure attachment and major adjustment problems. Rather than focusing exclusively on individual differences in attachment strategies in the strange situation or the Adult Attachment Interview (AAI), Bowlby stressed the importance of disruptive events in attachment relationships and the quality of ongoing communication. The interplay among attachment strategies, communication, and disruptive events is likely to provide much more predictive power in considering outcomes such as psychopathology. For example, an avoidant child, who lacks confidence in a parent's responsiveness, may have found ways of reducing conflict and subsequent anxiety about the parent's availability. However, if that child encounters a disruptive event—including an outburst of anger from a parent, or a more prolonged event such as marital conflict and divorce—he or she is more likely to interpret that event as a threat to the parent's availability.

Similarly, the nature of parent–child communication will also bias that child's interpretation of subsequent disruptions in attachment relationships. When lines of parent–child communication are open, disruptive events can be discussed with parents, and perceived threats to availability can be disconfirmed. Infants and toddlers lack the ability to discuss and negotiate physical separations, and as a result are much more vulnerable to perceiving physical separations as threats to the availability of their parents. Open communication continues to be an important marker of security in parent–adolescent relationships (Kobak & Cole, 1994; Kobak, Sudler, & Gamble, 1991)

and in marriages (Johnson, 1996; Kobak & Hazan, 1991).

A more comprehensive account of secure and insecure attachment must move beyond an exclusive focus on internal working models and attachment strategies. This account should include (1) current disruptions in the attachment relationship (prolonged separations, chronic conflict, marital separation, and loss); (2) the nature of communication in the attachment relationship; and (3) the attachment strategies that the child has developed to cope with parental responsiveness. The risk for psychopathology is highest when multiple factors coincide to increase the child's anxiety about his or her parent's availability. The anxiety and accompanying defensive processes that are associated with threats to availability increase the risk that attachment-related fear, anger, and sadness will be expressed in symptomatic forms.

The Special Case of Trauma and Loss

During the 1970s and 1980s, the increased awareness of child physical and sexual abuse and child neglect called attention to difficulties in attachment relationships that pose unique problems for children's adaptation. Children who are exposed to abuse or extreme forms of punishment are not only faced with threats to their attachment figures' availability; they must also manage a more profound dilemma when their attachment figures are potential sources of danger. Whereas a focus on the availability of an attachment figure assumes that the attachment relationship will serve as a source of safety, the dilemma created by abuse means that the child must also manage the possibility that the attachment figure is a source of danger. Main and Hesse (1990) noted that, placed in a situation that normally elicits attachment behavior, infants who have been unpredictably frightened by their attachment figures are caught in a conflict. Although they may display the typical secure and insecure attachment strategies, many show temporary lapses in their strategies; these are marked by fear, freezing, and disorientation. Main and Solomon (1986) developed a new classification, "disorganized/disoriented" (D), for infants showing these behaviors in the strange situation.

Initial studies of the parents of D infants pointed to a parallel form of disorganization in their discussions of loss and trauma in the AAI (Hesse, Chapter 19, this volume; Main & Goldwyn, in press). In the interview context, these adults show momentary lapses in "metacognitive monitoring" that include disorientation as to time and space, loss of monitoring of discourse, and reports of extreme behavioral reactions. These lapses can be seen as indications that aspects of the loss or trauma remain unresolved or not fully processed at a conscious level. Presumably these parents are vulnerable to similar lapses in organized behavior with their children, causing the children to perceive their parent as "frightened or frightening" (Main & Hesse, 1990).

The infant and adult disorganized classifications have been consistently linked to a variety of adjustment difficulties and to psychopathology (Lyons-Ruth & Jacobvitz, Chapter 23, this volume). During early childhood, infant D status has been associated with aggressive and externalizing symptoms (Shaw, Owens, Vondra, Keenan, & Winslow, 1996). In a 6-year longitudinal study, children who were classified as D in infancy were much more likely to develop aggressive behavior problems in pre-school and elementary school (Lyons-Ruth, 1996; Lyons-Ruth, Alpern, & Repacholi, 1993). Recent data from Sroufe and Egeland's sample of high-risk families indicate that the infant D classification predicts adjustment problems consistently from childhood and through adolescence, and that it specifically predicts dissociative symptoms (Carlson, in press). Similar patterns of maladaptation have been identified in adolescents and adults who are classified as "unresolved with respect to loss or trauma" in the AAI (Allen, Hauser, & Borman-Spurrell, 1996).

The recent work with disorganized attachment in infancy and adulthood provides important clues to the linkage between attachment and psychopathology. Symptomatic expressions of aggression, anxiety, or sadness are likely to be most evident at times when normal coping strategies break down. Similarly, parents are likely to be most frightening to their children when their unusual behavior occurs in unpredictable ways. These sorts of events not only threaten the availability of a caregiver, but also threaten a child's safety, which is fundamental to the attachment relationship.

EMOTIONAL REACTIONS TO ATTACHMENT DISRUPTIONS AND PSYCHOPATHOLOGY

States of anxiety and depression that occur during the adult years, and also psychopathic conditions, can, it

is held, be linked in a systematic way to the states of anxiety, despair, and detachment described by Burlingham and Freud.

—Bowlby (1973, pp. 4–5)

When physical separations are viewed as one example of a larger class of threats to the availability of attachment figures, observations of infants' and toddlers' emotional reactions to separation can be used to anticipate older children's and adults' responses to later threats to availability. What constitutes a threat to an attachment figure's availability may change with age, along with the capacities to manage emotional reactions. However, the core emotional reactions that accompany threats to the availability of an attachment figure remain similar across the lifespan.

Fear, Anger, and Sadness as Responses to Threats to Availability

From infancy through adulthood, specific emotions accompany an individual's appraisals of an attachment figures' availability. These emotions normally serve important motivational, self-monitoring, and communication functions for the individual (Bowlby, 1969/1982). For instance, when access to the attachment figure is jeopardized, fear takes control precedence over other activities, activates the attachment system, and leads to attachment behaviors that normally serve to reestablish access to the attachment figure. Normally, fear also serves as a communicative signal alerting the attachment figure to the child's or adult's distress and eliciting comforting responses.

Anger also plays an important role in responding to disruptions in attachment relationships. When parents are perceived as unavailable due to prolonged separation, increased anger and hostility are often observed. In a doll-play situation, Heinicke and Westheimer (1966) reported that children in a residential nursery displayed hostile themes four times as often as children living at home did. They also noted that the hostility of the separated children was frequently directed at parent dolls. Bowlby likewise reported several studies indicating that hostile behavior often continues at increased levels following a prolonged separation. Bowlby suggested that when separations are only temporary, anger can serve to (1) motivate a child to overcome obstacles to reuniting with the attachment figure and (2) communicate reproach to the attachment figure and discourage him or her from becoming unavailable in the future (Bowlby, 1973). Yet anger can easily become destructive and dysfunctional for the child when the caregiver misreads the child's anger and responds with anger or disengagment.

Sadness naturally accompanies the recognition that an attachment figure is not accessible and that efforts to reestablish contact cannot succeed. Unlike fear and anger, which are especially evident when an individual protests a threat to the attachment figure's availability, sadness tends to occur as the individual begins to accept the loss of an attachment figure. Withdrawal is the behavior that normally accompanies sadness, and this disengagement offers the individual time to accept unwelcome changes and revise working models.

Dramatic evidence that the emotions of fear, anger, and sadness persist as responses to disruptions in adult attachment relationships comes from Weiss's (1975) study of individuals who were dissolving their marriages. In studying individuals who had separated from their partners, Weiss gathered extensive descriptive information about attachment processes, with some striking parallels to the phases of separation identified by Robertson and Bowlby in young children. Weiss discovered what he termed the "persistence of attachment" in the separated spouses despite their decision to live separate lives and end their marital relationships. Many spouses reported that when they considered leaving their marriages, they become almost paralyzed with fear. The nature of separation distress was vividly depicted by one of Weiss's (1975, p. 49) subjects, who said, "When my husband left I had this panicky feeling which was out of proportion to what was really happening. I was afraid I was being abandoned. I couldn't shake the feeling." Many of the subjects had difficulty giving up hopes of restoring the relationship and regaining access to their former partners.

Weiss also found that spouses' fears were accompanied by intense anger. As one woman described it, "In separating from someone you discover in yourself things that you had never felt before in your life. That's one of the things that really freak you out. I've always used my mind to keep down anything I didn't like. And now I discover, wow, I can hate!" (Weiss, 1975, p. 98). A spouse often played on a partner's fears of separation, using threats to leave as a weapon to frighten the partner. However, as Weiss noted, such threats were a double-edged sword that only increased both partners' insecurity and fear. Together, the recurrent bouts of anger and fear were reminiscent of the protest phase identified in young children. Like adolescents who were relinquishing their parents as attachment figures but who had not replaced them with romantic partners, the adults in Weiss's studies gradually experienced loneliness. This phase mirrors the despair of young children who have given up hope of reuniting with their attachment figures. In many, it led to symptoms of depression and a perception that the world seemed "desolate of potential attachment . . . barren, silent, dead" (pp. 56–57). Similarly, feelings about self were depleted, with many subjects describing feeling empty or hollow.

Throughout the process of dissolving the marital attachment, subjects attempted to reduce the fear of separation and the despair of loneliness with defensive coping. For instance, Weiss (1975) noted; "In most marriages headed for separation the partners seem not to relinquish their attachment for one another. It would be too painful to do so, and even if they wanted to, they cannot control their feelings. But often for reasons of pride, because of hurt and anger, or from impulses toward self-protection, *they attempt to hide their attachment behind a mask of indifference*" (Weiss, 1975, p. 45; emphasis added). Despite trying to control the pain of separation by feigning indifference, many in Weiss's sample experienced breakdowns in their defenses that resulted in desperate efforts to reunite with their spouses.

Weiss's study documented the role of fear, anger, and sadness as emotional responses to disruptions in adult attachment relationships. By considering situations that threaten the availability of adults' attachment figures, he demonstrated how attachment theory can provide a guide for understanding and normalizing many of the extreme emotions that accompany threats to the availability of attachment figures in later life. His work suggests that the availability and responsiveness of attachment figures remain critical aspects of adult security and happiness. Furthermore, threats to the availability of romantic attachment figures elicit adult emotional reactions that are strikingly similar to those observed in young children's responses to separation.

Threats to Availability and Distorted Emotional Communication

When an individual has confidence in the responsiveness of his or her attachment figure and maintains open lines of communication, disruptions in physical access or perceptions of threat can be managed in ways that allow access to be regained. Open communication and secure working models go hand in hand (Bretherton, 1990, 1987; Kobak & Duemmler, 1994). Open communication depends upon the caregiver's ability to read a child's signals accurately (Crowell & Feldman, 1988), and in turn it promotes sensitivity to the infant's signals. Ainsworth and her colleagues observed that mothers of infants who would later be judged secure in the strange situation were able to manage feedings in a manner that responded to infant signals and at times required adjusting the intake of bottled and solid foods. Feeding was responsive to infants' initiatives and never forced by the mothers of secure infants (Ainsworth & Bell, 1969). In face-to-face interactions, some mothers were able to skillfully regulate pacing to establish smooth turn taking and coordination with the children's initiatives (Blehar, Lieberman, & Ainsworth, 1977). Physical contact between secure infants and their mothers was marked by a gentle and tender style that made the contact pleasurable for both mothers and infants. By the end of infancy, infants who had experienced open communication marked by sensitive care were more effective in communicating with their mothers. Grossmann, Grossmann, and Schwan (1986) also observed that infants judged secure in the strange situation engaged in more "direct communication" with their mothers, as evidenced in more eye contact, facial expression, vocalization, and showing and affective sharing of objects.

Open parent–child communication allows a child to develop secure expectations for his or her caregiver's responsiveness. These expectations result in more open and direct signaling to the parent. Secure relationships often foster a self-sustaining virtuous cycle. For instance, in relationships marked by secure working models and open communication, normal attachment disruptions often result in conversations that restore the child's confidence in the caregiver's availability. The child in such a relationship is more likely to express negative feelings associated with attachment disruptions directly. For instance, a child worrying about a mother who has an increased work schedule and who is emotionally withdrawn as a result of fights with her husband may tell the mother that he or she misses her. The mother in such a relationship is more likely to be accepting of her child's need and to be capable of acknowledging the stresses in her life in a way that reassures the child of the mother's understanding and continued availability.

Even if the child responds to attachment disruptions with indirect expressions of anger, fear, or sadness, a perceptive parent may recognize the connection between a child's angry oppositional behavior and his or her fears about perceived threats to the caregiver's availability and responsiveness. Such an understanding can in turn allow the parent to understand and respond in a more sympathetic manner to the anxious child. As a result, negative emotions serve as signals of the child's goals and needs, and open communication and confidence in caregiver responsiveness become self-maintaining features of a secure attachment relationship.

Unfortunately, more dysfunctional patterns of communication may also become self-sustaining. When negative emotions fail to restore a child's access to the attachment figure, they can rapidly become dysfunctional and contribute to a variety of problems and distorted expressions. One source of distorted communication can be traced to the detached phase of separation. This phase is characterized by an attempt to downplay attachment feelings. Bowlby viewed detachment as a defensive effort to deactivate the attachment system and thus to gain control over the painful emotions. Although this defensive detachment gives children a way of coping with anxious and angry feelings, it leads to difficulties when the children are reunited with their parents. Detached children show cool neutrality toward parents and an apparent apathy. In some cases, children may appear not to recognize their parents and show a striking absence of joy at the parent's return. Following reunions, children often alternate between crying and showing blank, expressionless faces.

When children defensively hide or distort anxious and angry feelings, parents and other observers can easily misunderstand the children's neutrality as a rebuff or lack of concern about the attachment relationship. The blank, expressionless faces described by observers of detached children can also be interpreted as general emotional disengagement. More significantly, the fear, anger, and sadness that serve to signal parents of the children's concerns are likely to be hidden by detached children and lead their parents to ignore or misunderstand their concerns. Under extreme stress, when the detached defense breaks down, anger, fear, and sadness may emerge in uncontrolled forms.

Anger resulting from disruptions in attachment relationships is especially prone to distorted expression. Bowlby (1973) described how anger as a signal of "hot displeasure" with a caregiver's lack of availability can become instead the "malice" of hatred (p. 249). Hatred and resentment toward parents may be accompanied by thoughts of wanting to harm parents, which paradoxically increase anxiety about the parents' availability. It is not uncommon for even very young children to redirect or displace anger toward other targets, such as peers. In a study of children's behavior in a day care setting, George and Main (1979) observed that children who had been physically abused by their parents were much more likely than nonabused children to attack their peers, particularly at moments when their peers were distressed. This type of hostile behavior increases the likelihood that parents will be angry at the children's misbehavior, and in turn results in further interactions that heighten the children's anxiety about their parents' availability.

Parents may also contribute to distorted communication. When children develop problematic expressions of anger, anxiety, or sadness, clinicians often encounter difficulty in getting accurate information about family interaction. Bowlby (1973) called attention to the parents' tendency to feel ashamed about the sorts of threats to availability that might account for their children's anxiety, anger, and sadness. This shame often results' in parents attempting to deny, hide, or distort the role that they may have played in their children's difficulties. These parents are acutely sensitive to any implication that difficulties in the family may be playing a role in their children's difficulties. As a result, parents are likely to omit information about attachment disruptions or actually to falsify their depictions of conflicted family relationships. A history of poor parent–child communication, and a child's lack of confidence in the availability of attachment figures, will exacerbate these problems. Not only does such a child receive little help in identifying threats to availability, but the child may suppress the memories of attachment disruptions in order to reduce painful feelings. Thus attachment-related feelings become cognitively disconnected from the family situations in which they originated.

Symptomatic Expressions of Attachment Emotions and Psychopathology

So long as current modes of perceiving and construing situations, and the feelings and actions

that ensue therefrom, are determined by emotionally significant events and experiences that have become shut away from further conscious processing, the personality will be prone to cognition, affect, and behavior maladapted to the current situation.
—BOWLBY (1988, p. 117)

When the normal emotions of fear, anger, and sadness that accompany threats to an attachment figure's availability are defensively distorted by the child and ignored or mislabeled by the parent, they are likely to be expressed in problematic forms. Attachment-related feelings of sadness and despair may become more pervasive depressive symptoms; attachment-related fears may be expressed as anxiety disorders or dissociative symptoms; and attachment-related anger may appear in aggressive and antisocial behaviors. Emotions no longer serve as signals that facilitate understanding and communication, and instead become symptoms that appear puzzling and problematic (Kobak et al., 1994).

In his volume on separation, Bowlby (1973) used childhood phobias and anxiety disorders to illustrate how attachment processes contribute to child psychopathology. Beginning with childhood anxiety disorders, Bowlby distinguished between "true phobias" (in which a child is dysfunctionally afraid of something in the environment, such as spiders or snakes) and "pseudophobias" (such as school refusal or agoraphobia). Bowlby suggested that, unlike true phobias, school refusal and agoraphobia may be better understood as resulting from the absence or feared loss of an attachment figure. Thus fear and worry about the availability of the attachment figure may result in a child's staying home to monitor the parent closely. In reviewing the clinical literature involving treatment of these cases, Bowlby found substantial evidence for attachment disruptions in the families of pseudophobic children. He identified four family patterns. In one, a parent suffers from chronic anxiety and often unconsciously comes to reverse roles with a child, using him or her as a source of safety. In such a family, the parent may often keep the child at home. In another pattern, a child fears that something dreadful may happen to a parent and stays at home to maintain a vigilant watch on the parent. In such families, parental threats of suicide or abandonment are common. The third pattern is marked by the child fearing for his or her own safety, when he or she is away from home. In yet another pattern, a parent may fear that something dreadful will happen to a child at school and may consequently work to keep the child at home. In nearly all these cases, Bowlby suggested that parents themselves may have suffered from lack of available and responsive care from their own parents. He also noted that the marital relations in the families of school-refusing children are often disturbed.

In considering agoraphobia and animal phobias in children, Bowlby was more circumspect and reported a lack of data on family interaction that made it impossible to determine the contribution of attachment fears. Although he suspected that such children may be more susceptible to fear because of anxious attachments, Bowlby left open the possibility that true phobias may develop through conditioning and avoidance learning.

Failure to understand the fundamental importance of the attachment relationship in the emotional lives of young children leads many parents and child care workers to ignore the potential impact of disturbances in attachment relationships. Bowlby believed that a great deal of psychopathology and many later difficulties emerge from this neglected aspect of children's experience. Not only separations, but also threats to the availability of attachment figures in general, leave children vulnerable to later depression, anxiety, aggression, and defensive distortions of vulnerable feelings in close relationships. Careful analysis of clinical work supports Bowlby's notion that threats to availability not only during infancy, but also during childhood, adolescence, and adulthood, continue to play a prominent role in the emergence of psychopathology (Johnson, 1996; Klerman, Weissman, Rounsaville, & Chevron, 1984; Kobak & Cole, 1994; Mufson, Moreau, Weissman, & Klerman, 1993). Yet a great deal of clinical and research work remains to be done before we fully develop the promise of Bowlby's theory.

CLINICAL AND RESEARCH IMPLICATIONS

Maintaining access to an attachment figure continues to be the set goal of the attachment system from infancy through adulthood. As the individual matures, however, access turns on the individual's cognitive appraisals of the attachment figure's availability (Ainsworth, 1990; Bowlby, 1973). Appraisals of availability (physical access, responsiveness, open lines of communication) are accompanied by feelings of security and confidence if proximity to the attachment figure can be achieved. Disruptions in attachment rela-

tionships that threaten availability result in anxious feelings, and, if confidence is not restored, in anxious/insecure attachment.

Focusing on the availability of attachment figures has critical implications for attachment researchers and clinicians. First, security from infancy through adulthood derives from *current* appraisals of attachment figures' availability. This places an emphasis on the need to assess security in the context of current attachment relationships and it suggests that attachment security from childhood through adulthood remains a relationship construct (Sroufe & Fleeson, 1986). Second, although internal working models are resistant to change and are carried forward into new relationships, these working models bias but do not determine appraisals of an attachment figure's availability. This suggests that a person may experience variability in the security of a relationship, depending on the behavior of a current attachment partner. Third, working models must be updated and revised to accommodate to new relationships (Bowlby, 1980). Consequently, attachment security results from a dynamic transaction between internal working models and the quality of current attachment relationships.

Research Implications

During the past 15 years, two new measures of attachment—the AAI (George, Kaplan, & Main, 1985) and Hazan and Shaver's (1987) self-report measure of romantic attachment styles—have led to an explosion of research on attachment in adolescence and adulthood (see Crowell, Fraley, & Shaver, Chapter 20, this volume). Both measures were designed to assess adult patterns that parallel the three patterns of infant attachment identified by Ainsworth in the strange situation. In her work with representational and discourse processes in the AAI, Mary Main has suggested that as mental life develops between infancy and adulthood, attention, feeling, and memory are organized in ways that allow the individual to preserve a particular state of mind (Main et al., 1985). This focus on the mental processes of adolescents and adults provides an account of how attachment strategies in infancy may become internalized aspects of the individual's personality. Hazan and Shaver (1987) further extended the personality model to adult attachment relationships by asking subjects how they managed closeness across their romantic relationships. The personality model of attachment tends to emphasize continuity with infant patterns of attachment and to focus exclusively on Bowlby's construct of internal working models.

What is striking about attachment research in the 1980s and 1990s is that it has almost exclusively focused on internal working models as determinants of personality and has largely neglected the study of current attachment relationships and behavior (Kobak, 1994). Most neglected is Bowlby's claim that current attachment relationships continue to be the major factor in whether a child or adult is in a secure, anxious, or distressed state. The emphasis on attachment as a relationship construct contrasts with a model suggesting that attachment security is largely determined in infancy and becomes an internalized part of personality. Although few attachment researchers explicitly endorse such a model, it implicitly informs many attachment studies. For instance, in reviewing findings linking adolescent AAI classifications to infant strange situation classification van IJzendoorn (1995) assumes that longitudinal prediction of adult (AAI) patterns of attachment from infant patterns with mothers in the strange situation is a criterion for "thorough" validation of Main and Goldwyn's AAI coding system. Such an assumption is consistent with a personality model of attachment in which individual differences in infancy determine adolescent and adult attachment patterns. In contrast, viewing attachment as a relationship construct suggests that the validity of any measure of attachment security will depend on concurrent evidence that the individual has confidence in the availability of his or her primary attachment figure.

Bowlby's theory challenges researchers to develop measures of attachment relationships of older children, adolescents, and adults that assess underlying confidence in the availability of the attachment figure. The quality of emotional communication in attachment relationships should be central in efforts to assess attachment security as a relationship construct, and it needs to be specified according to developmental level (Bretherton, 1990). By age 4 and the formation of "goal-corrected partnerships," confidence in the attachment figure is likely to be reflected in open discussion of goal conflicts, negotiation of plans, and perspective-taking communication (Kobak & Duemmler, 1994). In a secure relationship, emotions are likely to play important roles in signaling concerns and helping parent and child or romantic partners accommodate to each other. In adolescence, security of parent–

teen attachment should be reflected in a capacity of both the parent and the teen to assert autonomy and yet to maintain a sense of closeness or relatedness (Allen, Kupermine, & Bell, in press).

Once measures of attachment security in parent–child and romantic relationships are developed and validated, issues of continuity and change in developmental pathways can be more meaningfully addressed. Viewing attachment security as a relationship construct opens up important questions. At present, very little is known about the relative influence of a child's attachment security with his or her mother and father on developmental outcomes during childhood, adolescence, and adulthood (Ainsworth, 1990; Bretherton, 1985). Viewing attachment as a relationship construct also raises questions about the way in which attachment functions are transferred from parents to romantic partners during adolescence and early adulthood (Hazan & Shaver, 1994; Hazan & Zeifman, Chapter 16, this volume), and about how the relationship with the father and the marital relationship influence the child's appraisals of parental availability (Cowan, 1997; Garcia-O'Hearn, Margolin, & John, 1997). Finally, more attention to attachment security and communication in current relationships could illuminate the mechanisms that account for discontinuity in developmental pathways (Sroufe, 1997).

Clinical Implications

In studying young children's responses to separations, Bowlby gained an understanding of the emotional dynamics of the attachment system that would lead to a new understanding of later clinical problems. In his 1973 volume, he illustrated how threats to the availability of attachment figures in conjunction with defensive processes and distorted communication within the parent–child relationship can result in symptomatic expressions of fear, anger, and sadness. Clinical symptoms such as depression, anxiety, and aggression motivate individuals to seek help and account for many of the presenting problems found in clinic settings. Bowlby believed that careful assessments of family context will often reveal that behind these presenting symptoms lie basic threats to the availability of attachment figures and subsequent defensive distortions.

To understand the contribution of attachment processes to child and adult symptomatology, clinicians and researchers need to assess the emotionally significant events that have shaken individuals' confidence in the availability of their attachment figures. Interviews with family members about changes in relationships, losses experienced by family members, and marital functioning can provide clinicians with valuable information about the attachment disruptions associated with child and adolescent psychopathology. Observations of family interaction may also indicate the extent to which family communication is open and the degree to which relationships have become distressed or conflictual. Review of the history of childhood and adolescent attachment, using a format similar to George et al.'s (1985) AAI, can help clinicians identify the extent to which attachment disruptions have been processed and integrated into a coherent model of self and others.

Recent progress in identifying disorganized attachment in infants points to very important hypotheses about how more extreme forms of attachment trauma may result in a child's being frightened or terrified by a caregiver and in a breakdown of organized attachment strategies (Main & Hesse, 1990). Initial longitudinal studies of disorganized infants suggest that these children are at particular risk for later psychopathology (Carlson, in press). In these cases, clinicians may be presented with dissociative (Carlson, in press) or aggressive (Lyons-Ruth, 1996) symptoms. Research and theory suggest that clinicians need to observe family interactions carefully and to review both children's and parents' attachment histories to understand how attachment traumas have created an extreme emotional dilemma in these families.

Attachment-based treatments should focus on linking symptomatic expressions of fear and anger to disturbances in attachment relationships. In so doing, a clinician can help a child or adult experience and integrate painful experiences in order to gain control over symptoms. Parents can be helped to understand the sources of their difficulties in being available and responsive to their child. Recent innovations in marital therapy provide a prototype for how attachment theory can be used as a basis for treatment. Beginning with the well-documented negative absorption states that characterize distressed couples (Gottman, 1994), Johnson (1996) has developed exploratory techniques that help distressed partners to access attachment fears and vulnerabilities that are hidden behind angry and defensive interaction sequences. Extension of these techniques to the treatment of children and their parents offers a promising direction for at-tachment-based treatment for parent–child relationships (Kobak, et al., 1998).

CONCLUSION

In conclusion, the field of attachment has progressed substantially beyond the early studies of young children's separations. The partnership of Ainsworth and Bowlby provided a model for how theory and research can mutually inform each other: Ainsworth was guided by Bowlby's theory in nearly every aspect of her study of mothers and their infants, and her observations forced clarification and increased precision in the theory. Much of recent attachment research has suffered from a lack of theoretical perspective. As a result, methodologies such as the AAI and measures of attachment styles have dominated the field, and the personality aspects of internal working models have been stressed at the expense of understanding current attachment relationships. The limitations of this approach become most evident in the very narrow view of Ainsworth's contributions that informs recent research. Most contemporary attachment research is derived exclusively from the patterns of attachment in the strange situation and overlooks Ainsworth's study of normative development of attachment and of mother–infant communication. This exclusive focus on internal working models leads to endless reiterations of the individual differences in the strange situation, AAI, and adult attachment styles, producing little substantive advance in the study of attachment relationships. The true value of these methodologies will be realized only when working models are studied as a part of the ongoing operation of the attachment system as it functions in current relationships.

REFERENCES

Ainsworth, M. D. S. (1962). The effects of maternal deprivation: A review of findings and controversy in the context of research strategy. In *Deprivation of maternal care: A reassessment of its effects*. Geneva: World Health Organization.

Ainsworth, M. D. S. (1990). Some considerations regarding theory and assessment relevant to attachments beyond infancy. In M. T. Greenberg, D. Cicchetti, & E. M. Cummings (Eds.), *Attachment in the preschool years* (pp. 463–488). Chicago: University of Chicago Press.

Ainsworth, M. D. S., & Bell, S. M. (1969). Some contemporary patterns in the feeding situation. In A. Ambrose (Ed.), *Stimulation in early infancy* (pp. 133–170). London: Academic Press.

Ainsworth, M. D. S., Blehar, M. C., Waters, E., & Wall, S. (1978). *Patterns of attachment: A psychological study of the strange situation.* Hillsdale, NJ: Erlbaum.

Ainsworth, M. D. S., & Wittig, B. A. (1969). Attachment and exploratory behavior of one-year-olds in a strange situation. In B. M. Foss (Ed.), *Determinants of infant behaviour* (Vol. 4, pp. 129–173). London: Methuen.

Allen, J. P., Hauser, S. T., & Borman-Spurrell, E. (1996). Attachment theory as a framework for understanding sequelae of severe adolescent psychopathology: An 11-year follow-up study. *Journal of Consulting and Clinical Psychology, 64,* 254–263.

Allen, J. P., Hauser, S. T., O'Connor, T. G., Bell, K. L., & Eickholt, C. (1996). The connection of observed hostile family conflict to adolescents' developing autonomy and relatedness with parents. *Development and Psychopathology, 8,* 425–442.

Allen, J., Kuppermine, G., & Bell, K. (in press). Attachment and adolescent psychosocial functioning. *Child Development.*

Blehar, M. C., Lieberman, A. F., & Ainsworth, M. D. S. (1977). Early face-to-face interaction and its relation to later infant–mother attachment. *Child Development, 48,* 182–194.

Bowlby, J. (1944). Forty-four juvenile thieves: Their characters and home life. *International Journal of Psycho-Analysis, 25,* 19–52, 107–127.

Bowlby, J. (1951). *Maternal care and mental health* (WHO Monograph No. 2). Geneva: World Health Organization.

Bowlby, J. (1969/1982). *Attachment and loss: Vol. 1. Attachment.* New York: Basic Books.

Bowlby, J. (1973). *Attachment and loss: Vol. 2. Separation: Anxiety and anger.* New York: Basic Books.

Bowlby, J. (1980). *Attachment and loss: Vol. 3. Loss.* New York: Basic Books.

Bowlby, J. (1988). *A secure base: Parent–child attachment and healthy human development.* New York: Basic Books.

Bretherton, I. (1985). Attachment theory: Retrospect and prospect. In I. Bretherton & E. Waters (Eds.), Growing points of attachment theory and research. *Monographs of the Society for Research in Child Development, 50*(1–2, Serial No. 209), 3–35.

Bretherton, I. (1987). New perspectives on attachment relations: Security, communication, and internal working models. In J. Osofsky (Ed.), *Handbook of infant development* (2nd ed., pp. 1061–1100). New York: Wiley.

Bretherton, I. (1990). Open communication and internal working models: Their role in the development of attachment relationships. In R. A. Thompson (Ed.), *Nebraska Symposium on Motivation: Vol. 36. Socioemotional development* (pp. 57–113). Lincoln, NE: University of Nebraska Press.

Burlingham, D., & Freud, A. (1944). *Infants without families.* London: Allen & Unwin.

Carlson, E. A. (in press). A prospective longitudinal study of disorganized/disoriented attachment. *Child Development.*

Cicchetti, D., Cummings, E. M., Greenberg, M. T., & Marvin, R. S. (1990). An organizational perspective on attachment beyond infancy: Implications for theory, measurement, and research. In M. T. Greenberg, D. Cicchetti, & E. M. Cummings (Eds.), *Attachment in the preschool years* (pp. 3–50). Chicago: University of Chicago Press.

Cowan, P. (1997). Beyond meta-analysis: A plea for a family systems perspective on attachment. *Child Development, 68,* 600–603.

Crowell, J., & Feldman, S. (1988). Mothers' internal models of relationships and children's behavioral and developmental status: A study of mother–child interaction. *Child Development, 59,* 1273–1285.

Davies, P. T., & Cummings, E. M. (1995). Marital conflict and child adjustment: An emotional security hypothesis. *Psychological Bulletin, 116,* 387–411.

Davies, P. T., & Cummings, E. M. (1998). Exploring children's emotional security as a mediator of the link between marital relations and child adjustment. *Child Development, 69,* 124–139.

Garcia-O'Hearn, H., Margolin, G., & John, R. (1997). Mothers' and fathers' reports of children's reactions to naturalistic marital conflict. *Journal of the American Academy of Child and Adolescent Psychiatry, 36,* 1366–1373.

George, C., Kaplan, N., & Main, M. (1985). *Adult Attachment Interview* (2nd ed.). Unpublished manuscript, University of California at Berkeley.

George, C., & Main, M. (1979). Social interactions of young abused children: Approach, avoidance, and aggression. *Child Development, 50,* 306–318.

Gottman, J. (1994). *What predicts divorce?* Hillsdale, NJ: Erlbaum.

Grossmann, K. E., Grossmann, K., & Schwan, A. (1986). Capturing the wider view of attachment: A reanalysis of Ainsworth's Strange Situation. In C. E. Izard & P. B. Read (Eds.), *Measuring emotions in infants and children* (pp. 124–171). New York: Cambridge University Press.

Hazan, C., & Shaver, P. R. (1987). Romantic love conceptualized as an attachment process. *Journal of Personality and Social Psychology, 52,* 511–524.

Hazan, C., & Shaver, P. R. (1994). Attachment as an organizational framework for research on close relationships. *Psychological Inquiry, 5,* 1–22.

Heinicke, C., & Westheimer, I. (1966). *Brief separations.* New York: International Universities Press.

Johnson, S. (1996). *Creating connection: The practice of emotionally focused marital therapy.* New York: Brunner/Mazel.

Karen, R. (1994). *Becoming attached.* New York: Warner.

Klerman, G. L., Weissman, M. M., Rounsaville, B. J., & Chevron, E. S. (1984). *Interpersonal psychotherapy of depression.* New York: Basic Books.

Kobak, R. (1994). Adult attachment: A personality or relationship construct? Commentary on "Attachment as an organizational framework for research on close relationships." *Psychological Inquiry, 5,* 42–44.

Kobak, R., & Cole, H. (1994). Attachment and meta-monitoring: Implications for adolescent autonomy and psychopathology. In D. Cicchetti (Ed.), *Rochester Symposium on Development and Psychopathology: Vol. 5. Disorders of the self* (pp. 267–297). Rochester, NY: University of Rochester Press.

Kobak, R., & Duemmler, S. (1994). Attachment and conversation: A discourse analysis of goal-corrected partnerships. In K. Bartholomew & D. Perlman (Eds.), *Advances in personal relationships: Vol. 5. Attachment processes in adulthood* (pp. 121–149). London: Jessica Kingsley.

Kobak, R., Duemmler, S., Burland, A., & Youngstrom, E. (1998). Attachment and negative absorption states: Implications for treating distressed families. *Journal of Systemic Therapy, 17,* 80–92.

Kobak, R., & Hazan, C. (1991). Attachment in marriage: The effects of security and accuracy of working models. *Journal of Personality and Social Psychology, 60,* 861–869.

Kobak, R., Hazan, C., & Ruckdeschel, K. (1994). From symptom to signal: An attachment view of emotion in marital therapy. In S. Johnson & L. Greenberg (Eds.), *Emotions in marital therapy* (pp. 46–71). New York: Brunner/Mazel.

Kobak, R., & Shaver, P. R. (1987, June). *Strategies for maintaining felt security: Implications for adaptation and psychopathology.* Paper prepared for the Conference on Attachment and Loss in honor of John Bowlby's 80th birthday, London.

Kobak, R., Sudler, N., & Gamble, W. (1991). Attachment and depressive symptoms during adolescence: A developmental pathway analysis. *Development and Psychopathology, 3,* 461–474.

Lorenz, K. (1957). *Instinctive behavior.* New York: International Universities Press.

Lyons-Ruth, K. (1996). Attachment relationships among children with aggressive behavior problems: The role of disorganized early attachment patterns. *Journal of Consulting and Clinical Psychology, 64,* 64–73.

Lyons-Ruth, K., Alpern, L., & Repacholi, B. (1993). Disorganized infant attachment classification and maternal psychosocial problems as predictors for hostile–aggressive behavior in the preschool classroom. *Child Development, 64,* 572–585.

Main, M. (1990). Cross-cultural studies of attachment organization: Recent studies, changing methodologies, and the concept of conditional strategies. *Human Development, 33,* 48–61.

Main, M., & Goldwyn, R. (in press). *Adult attachment classification system.* Unpublished manuscript, University of California, Berkeley, CA.

Main, M., & Hesse, E. (1990). Parents' unresolved traumatic experiences are related to infant disorganized attachment status: Is frightening and/or frightened parental behavior the linking mechanism? In M. T. Greenberg, D. Cicchetti, & E. M. Cummings (Eds.), *Attachment in the preschool years* (pp. 121–160). Chicago: University of Chicago Press.

Main, M., Kaplan, N., & Cassidy, J. (1985). Security in infancy, childhood and adulthood: A move to the level of representation. In I. Bretherton & E. Waters (Eds.), Growing points of attachment theory and research. *Monographs of the Society for Research in Child Development, 50*(1–2, Serial No. 209), 66–104.

Main, M., & Solomon, J. (1986). Discovery of a new, insecure disorganized/ disoriented attachment pattern. In T. B. Brazelton & M. Yogman (Eds.), *Affective development in infancy* (pp. 95–124). Norwood, NJ: Ablex.

Main, M., & Weston, D. R. (1982). Avoidance of the attachment figure in infancy: Descriptions and interpretations. In C. Parkes & J. Stevenson-Hinde (Eds.), *The place of attachment in human behavior* (pp. 31–59). New York: Basic Books.

Marvin, R. S. (1977). An ethological–cognitive model for the attenuation of mother–child attachment behavior. In T. M. Alloway, L. Krames, & P. Pliner (Eds.), *Advances in the study of communication and affect: Vol. 3. The development of social attachments* (pp. 25–60). New York: Plenum Press.

Mufson, L., Moreau, D., Weissman, M., & Klerman, G. (1993). *Interpersonal psychotherapy for depressed adolescents.* New York: Guilford.

Newson, J., & Newson, E. (1968). *Four years old in an urban community.* Chicago: Aldine.

Robertson, J. (1962). *Hospitals and children: A parent's eye view.* New York: Gollancz.

Rutter, M. (1981). *Maternal deprivation reassessed.* Harmondsworth, England: Penguin.

Sears, R. R., Maccoby, E., & Levin, H. (1957). *Patterns of child rearing.* Evanston, IL: Row, Peterson.

Shaw, D. S., Owens, E. B., Vondra, J. I., Keenan, K., & Winslow, E. B. (1996). Early risk factors and pathways in the development of early disruptive behavior problems. *Development and Psychopathology, 8,* 679–699.

Spitz, R. (1958). Discussion of Dr. Bowlby's paper. *Psychoanalytic Study of the Child, 15,* 85–94.

Sroufe, L. A. (1988). The role of infant caregiver attachment in development. In J. Belsky & T. Neworski (Eds.), *Clinical applications of attachment* (pp. 18–40). Hillsdale, NJ: Erlbaum.

Sroufe, L. A. (1997). Psychopathology as an outcome of development. *Development and Psychopathology, 9,* 251–268.

Sroufe, L. A., & Fleeson, J. (1986). Attachment and the construction of relationships. In W. W. Hartup & Z. Rubin (Eds.), *Relationships and development* (pp. 51–71). Hillsdale, NJ: Erlbaum.

Sroufe, L. A., & Waters, E. (1977). Attachment as an organizational construct. *Child Development, 48,* 1184–1199.

van IJzendoorn, M. H. (1995). Of the way we are: On temperament, attachment, and the transmission gap: A Rejoinder to Fox (1995). *Psychological Bulletin, 117,* 411–415.

Weiss, R. S. (1975). *Marital separation: Coping with the end of a marriage and the transition to being single again.* New York: Basic Books.

3

Normative Development

The Ontogeny of Attachment

❖

ROBERT S. MARVIN
PRESTON A. BRITNER

> Whilst especially evident during early childhood, attachment behavior is held to characterize human beings from the cradle to the grave.
> —BOWLBY (1979, p. 129)

During the 1940s and 1950s, a number of studies emerged suggesting that very young children, when separated from their mothers for a considerable period of time, proceed through a series of reactions that have become known as the phases of "protest," "despair," and "detachment" (e.g., Burlingham & Freud, 1944; Heinicke & Westheimer, 1966; Robertson, 1953). These or similar reactions were so common, despite variations in familiarity of the setting or quality of care received by the youngsters, that John Bowlby (as well as others) departed from the contemporary scientific and clinical consensus and decided that it was the loss of the *specific mother figure* that was the most important factor in these reactions. It was from this beginning that Bowlby went on to develop his "ethological–control systems" theory of the infant's tie, or "attachment," to its mother or primary caregiver (Bowlby, 1958, 1969/1982, 1973, 1980). In a partnership that went on to span nearly 40 years, Bowlby and Mary Ainsworth (e.g., Ainsworth, 1967; Ainsworth, Blehar, Waters, & Wall, 1978), among others, decided to embark on a quest to answer questions such as these: Why does the young child become so distressed by the loss of the mother? What processes account for each of the three phases of loss? What *is* the bond that ties the child to the mother? What are its forms, and how do they emerge? What happens to these forms as the child matures? Do such bonds exist in the adult, and if so, in what form? And ultimately, how do we understand form and functioning "when things go wrong"?

At that point, Bowlby and his colleagues made the decision that answering those questions required a shift to the study of the early development of this bond in normally developing children and their families. They were convinced that only by understanding its normal formation and functioning would we eventually be able to understand its malfunctioning. This decision led to Ainsworth's naturalistic observational studies in Uganda and Baltimore, and to the first volume of Bowlby's trilogy on attachment. These efforts resulted in some of the most significant, and empirically and theoretically coherent, contributions to the study of children's development in the second half of this century. The theory that emerged was consistent with current theories of biology, embryology, cognitive science, and general systems theory. It was at the same time specific enough to incorporate species and cultural differences, and general enough to incorporate species and cultural similarity. It came closer than any other theory to being equally applicable to questions of normative development and of individual differences and maladaptive developmental pathways. Most of the chapters in this volume are a tribute to the power of the theory and of the methods that have both evolved from and informed the theory.

Through the mid-1970s, there was much excitement and controversy about Bowlby's theory of the ontogeny of attachment. However, by 1980 the field of attachment research had undergone a significant change: The study of individual differences had come to occupy so much of the focus that exploration of the *ontogeny* of attachment had nearly been abandoned. Ainsworth's identification of three "primary" strategies of attachment (e.g., Ainsworth et al., 1978), Main and Solomon's (1990) discovery of a "disorganized" pattern of attachment, and Main and colleagues' research on adults' attachment strategies (e.g., Main & Goldwyn, in press) have contributed enormously to our understanding of differential strategies within intimate relationships, as well as of child and adult psychopathology. The history of biology, however, demonstrates that despite some analogical similarities between immature and mature forms of an organism, any attempt to understand adaptive or maladaptive versions of the mature form without constant reference to structural transformations throughout ontogeny is doomed to failure (e.g., Bateson, 1976; Waddington, 1957). Ethological studies of behavioral development also point to the obvious but often ignored importance of survival of the individual at each developmental point. This will certainly be no less the case in the study of human attachment. It will only be through the study of individual pathways *through the course of development* that we will truly understand the origins, nature, and sequelae of this bond.

So the question becomes this: Do we already know enough about the form of the attachment behavioral system at different points in development to move so exclusively to the study of individual differences? And if not, what are the risks of not studying those changing forms? If the goal of developmental research in this area is to discover reliable and valid measures of infant behavior that predict concurrent and future outcomes, then the answer to the first question is a qualified "yes." Or if attachment behavior, and a secure attachment, are assumed to be developmental tasks only of infancy, to be superseded by

later tasks such as internal control and self-reliance (Freud, 1965), individuation (Mahler, Pine, & Bergman, 1975), autonomy (Erikson, 1950), or independent and socialized behavior (Bandura, 1978; Baumrind, 1980), it is again tempting to answer "yes." There are, however, theoretical and empirical reasons for rejecting a strong developmental-task position (Ainsworth, 1990; Cicchetti, Cummings, Greenberg, & Marvin, 1990).

Perhaps the most important reason for studying the developing forms of attachment behavior is related to common experience and to one of Bowlby's most fundamental theoretical constructs—namely, that the biological function of attachment behavior is protection of the youngster from a variety of dangers. Preschool and even older children, in our present environment as well as our "environment of evolutionary adaptedness" (Bowlby, 1969/1982), are vulnerable to a wide range of dangers. How children and their caregivers organize protective proximity and contact, and how they continue to use their caregivers as a secure base for exploration, remain as important during later periods of development as during the first year of life. Although the frequency of attachment behavior may wane across development, it remains as important when activated in a 4- or 8-year-old as it is during infancy. And how the attachment behavioral system is organized with other behavioral systems in the individual (and the caregivers), such that the person is protected while engaging in developmentally appropriate exploration or other activities, becomes a crucial question in understanding many developmental domains across the entire lifespan.

Bowlby (1969/1982) placed his theory of the development of attachment squarely within the biological, general systems, and cognitive sciences. The theory is actually an integration and elaboration of general systems theory, including especially communication and control systems theory; cognitive science, much of which itself can be considered part of systems theory; evolutionary theory; ethology and the study of primate behavior; and descriptive studies of human infants and young children interacting with their caregivers. The description of the development of attachment across the lifespan presented in this chapter combines Bowlby's theory, as originally presented; the elaboration provided by Marvin and his colleagues regarding developmental changes during the preschool years; and a brief review of contributions by others regarding possible further changes during later childhood, adolescence, and adulthood. More detailed descriptions of attachment theory as applied to adolescence and adulthood are presented in the chapters in Part IV of this volume. Reviews of the nonhuman primate literature on the bond between parent(s) and offspring, and of the crucial role played by that literature in the development of Bowlby's theory, are available in Bowlby (1969/1982), Marvin (1977, 1997), and Suomi (1995 and Chapter 9, this volume).

GENERAL SYSTEMS PERSPECTIVE

At an abstract information-theoretic level, if a system is to survive there must be certain invariants among its constituent elements, and certain invariants in its relationship with its environment (Ashby, 1952, 1956). In certain essential respects, variety must be kept within certain limits, or the system will not survive. The best-known examples in human development are the many physiological invariants. Furthermore, if a system does not have the ability to control input from the environment in a manner that keeps these essential variables with the limits required for survival, then it must be "coupled" with another system that does have the ability to keep the variety in the first system within such limits. In other words, there must be a close coupling, bond, or attachment between the two systems that serves to protect the less "self-reliant" system. This is a formal statement of Bowlby's basic thesis regarding the biological function of child–parent attachment: that it serves to protect the child from a wide range of dangers—from either internal changes or environmental inputs—that would push some essential variable(s) beyond the system's (i.e., the child's) limits of survival.

In a system that develops toward increasing self-reliance over time, this coupling can have another aspect. In many biological organisms, the protective bond has a component that facilitates the youngster's tendency to explore and learn—that is, to develop the skills necessary for self-protection through autonomous integration in the larger group. Within this protective relationship, the developing organism thus becomes progressively less and less dependent on the bond with the parent (i.e., the system with more variety) to provide that protection. Eventually, the developing organism contains the necessary variety or skills within itself, and within its cou-

pling with its larger social network, to control internal change and environmental input in ways that maintain its essential variables within the limits necessary for survival. This compound, and very complex, developmental pattern constitutes the crux of Ainsworth's (1967) concept of the child's use of the mother as a secure base for exploration. It emphasizes that at each point in development, the nature of the attachment–caregiving interactions between the youngster and his or her attachment figure(s) serves to compensate for and to complement the lack of motor, communication, and social skills on the youngster's part, such that the youngster is always protected while being afforded as much independence as possible within which to learn those skills. Finally, it suggests that at any given point in development, skills or behavior systems across developmental domains will fit together in a manner that makes adaptive sense in terms of survival at that point.

BOWLBY'S CONTROL SYSTEMS MODEL OF DEVELOPMENT

Much primate research, and an increasing amount of research on humans, indicate that this developmental pattern takes place in the context of a complex network of "affectional bonds," of which the close attachment of infant to mother is one. Ainsworth (1967) defines an affectional bond as a relatively long-enduring tie in which the partner is important as a unique, noninterchangeable individual. Harlow was one of the first to propose distinct affectional systems or bonds (Harlow & Harlow, 1965), with the explicit connotation that different bonds function to achieve different outcomes. Bowlby took this a step further in distinguishing among a number of behavioral systems, each with its own predictable outcome and biological function (see Cassidy, Chapter 1, this volume). Following on Harlow's early work, a number of distinct affectional bonds have been identified, including the attachment bond; the parent's complementary caregiving bond; the sexual pair bond; sibling/kinship bonds; and friendship bonds (Ainsworth, 1990; George & Solomon, Chapter 28, this volume; Hazan & Zeifman, Chapter 16, this volume). In our opinion, the essential contribution of Bowlby's theory is the way in which he explained these bonds in terms of the behavioral systems underlying them and the developmental changes in these behavioral systems.

Behavioral Systems

Attachment theory proposes a number of behavioral systems that are species-universal, although there may be (subtle) differences across both individuals and breeding populations (e.g., Freedman & Gorman, 1993). Each behavioral system consists of a set of interchangeable, functionally equivalent behaviors—in other words, behaviors that have the same predictable effect or outcome (Bowlby, 1969/1982). At the same time, each behavior serves more than one behavioral system. For example, locomotion serves, among others, the attachment, exploration, and wariness behavioral systems. It is for this reason that Sroufe and Waters (1977) insisted that the infant's attachment behavior can be fully understood only from an organizational perspective.

A nonexhaustive list of behavioral systems includes those related to feeding, reproduction, caregiving, attachment, exploration, sociability, and fear/wariness. Following ethological theory, Bowlby proposed that the behavior patterns associated with each of these behavioral systems have been selected through evolution because they fulfill a biological function: They help ensure the survival and reproductive success of the individual and his or her genes. The biological function of attachment behavior, and of wary behavior, is protection of the youngster from a wide range of dangers. The biological function of exploratory and sociable behavior is that of learning the skills necessary for more self-reliant survival, in terms of both individual skills and smooth integration into the social group.

Behavioral systems[1] have rules that govern the selection, activation, and termination of the behaviors as a specifiable function of the individual's internal state and the environmental context. As implied above, attachment researchers have focused on three specific behavioral systems: attachment, fear/wariness, and exploration. Ainsworth (1990) and Marvin (1997) have suggested that it is useful to think of a fourth, the sociable behavioral system, related to children's friendly interactions.

Attachment theory proposes that in normal development, the operation of these four behavioral systems is affected not only by specific environmental and organismic events. They also exhibit a complex dynamic balance among themselves (Ainsworth, 1967) that has the predictable outcome of ensuring that the youngster develops more sophisticated coping skills, but does so within the protective bond to the attachment figure(s). Specifically, when the youngster's attachment and/or wary behavior systems are minimally activated, its exploratory and/or sociable behavior systems can easily be activated. Activation of the wary system serves as a terminating condition for the exploration and/or sociable systems, and at the same time as an activating condition for the attachment behavior system. Proximity or contact with the attachment figure then often serves to minimize activation of the attachment and wariness behavioral systems, which in turn can reactivate the exploration and/or sociability systems. This is part of the underlying control system for what Ainsworth (1967) described as "using the mother as a secure base for exploration." Finally, as many mothers, fathers, babysitters, and child care providers know, a strongly activated exploration system can serve to reduce activation of the attachment system.

One can see a delightful, if somewhat disjointed, illustration of this equilibrium process in a child between the ages of 18 and 30 months who is greeted by a friendly adult stranger in the presence of the attachment figure. The child will sometimes retreat warily to the attachment figure, and from the security of that position will become interested in the stranger, make a partial approach to the stranger, retreat again to the attachment figure in wariness, and then repeat the process a number of times. Repeated oscillation through this equilibration process is analogous, in control theory terms, to having separate thermostatically controlled heating and cooling systems in a single room, with slightly different settings on their separate thermostats. There is some evidence that as the youngster develops through the preschool years, the organization among these four behavior systems changes and becomes more elaborate (e.g., Greenberg & Marvin, 1982). There is also some evidence that in young children raised in environments extremely dissimilar from the "environment of evolutionary adaptedness" (e.g., in a maltreating or institutional setting without consistent caregivers), these four behavior systems often do not exhibit this equilibrated organization, leading to what could appropriately be called a developmental disorder (e.g., Goldberg, Marvin, & Sabbagh, 1996).

Complexity of Behavioral Systems

Drawing from ethology, Bowlby (1969/1982) proposed that behavioral systems differ not only in function but also in their structural complexity. The simplest is a reflex, a highly stereotyped behavior activated by a stimulus at a specific threshold and carried to completion. A more complex behavior, called a "fixed action pattern" by the early ethologists, is also a highly stereotyped behavior activated and terminated by specific stimuli, but its threshold for activation varies according to the state of the organism, and often makes use of some proprioceptive feedback from the environment during its execution. A number of the social displays of birds and fish are of this form. Many of the basic attachment behaviors identified by Ainsworth (1967), such as grasping, crying, and smiling, can also be considered fixed action patterns.

Although quite primitive when considered in isolation, these simple behavior patterns can assume an elegant complexity when placed in the context in which they evolved—in the case of attachment behavior, the context being close proximity to a caregiver who responds with specific behaviors that complement the infant's behavior. The immediate effect of many behaviors is to bring about a change in the environment, which itself serves as an activating condition for another behavior, often forming a lengthy sequence with an eventual outcome that is necessary for the individual's survival. For example, when a hungry neonate cries, that behavior *predictably* activates the maternal behavior of picking the infant up and placing him or her at the breast. The picking up, or at least the stimulus of the breast or nipple on the infant's face, terminates the cry and activates rooting. This predictably brings the infant's mouth in contact with the nipple, which serves as a terminating condition for rooting and an activating condition for grasping the nipple with the lips. In turn, the stimulus of the nipple in the mouth activates sucking, and finally liquid in the mouth stimulates swallowing. Although the complexity and predictability of this sequence may appear purposeful, goal-directed, or (in Bowlby's terms) "goal-corrected" on the part of the infant, in fact it is not. Interruption of the sequence at any point will lead to failure of the overall sequence, unless the probable cry causes the caregiver to reactivate and correct the sequence. Instead, Bowlby referred to these behaviors as having a specified "predictable outcome," as long as the behavior is executed in an environment similar to the one in which the behavior evolved. In the case of rooting, for example, the predictable outcome of attachment behaviors more generally is proximity and/or contact with a caregiver/attachment figure. This construct of

a predictable outcome is especially important for at least two reasons. First, it allows us to understand relatively simple forms of behavior as achieving an important outcome without inferring that the youngster executed the behavior intentionally, despite the fact that the behavior sequence occurs in a predictable way. Second, it forces us to view these simple behavior patterns as taking place in a dyadic or larger context: They have little meaning if they are not described and understood in the relationship context in which they evolved.

A yet more complicated pattern of behavior is a goal-corrected pattern. Like the simpler forms of behavior, goal-corrected behaviors have activating and terminating conditions, and predictable outcomes, but they achieve these outcomes through a more sophisticated process. The process is one of choosing, from a repertoire of behaviors, specific ones that progressively bring the individual closer to achieving the goal state or "set goal." Since the original publication of the first volume of *Attachment and Loss* (Bowlby, 1969), this construct of purposeful behavior has become commonplace in the study of motor and cognitive development, and is implicit in much research in social development.

In order to engage in goal-corrected behavior, an individual must have an especially complex, dynamic, internal representation of relevant aspects of self, his or her behavior, the environment, and the object or person toward whom the behavior is directed. Bowlby used the term "internal working model" (IWM) for such a representation, but he also referred to it as a "representational model," and it is equivalent loosely to a Piagetian "scheme." IWMs are not static images, but flexible models that are used to understand and predict the organism's relations with its environment, and to construct complex sequences of behaviors (i.e., plans that can achieve specific, internally represented outcomes from a variety of beginning points). When a goal-corrected behavior sequence, such as locomoting toward the caregiver in order to make physical contact, is activated, the child continuously orients his or her behavior and selects alternative behaviors, based in part on the feedback received from the effects of the behavior. When the set goal is achieved, the perceived discrepancy between the set goal and the organism's state is reduced to zero, and the behavioral plan terminates. The theory posits that there is a logical parallel between the organization of behavior and that of the IWM. The structure of IWMs therefore can be inferred from observing the organization of behavior across situations. Although the operation of IWMs often takes place within awareness, for reasons of information-processing efficiency much takes place outside of awareness, especially as it becomes more automatic (see Bretherton & Munholland, Chapter 5, this volume).

Drawing again from the work of the ethologists, Bowlby (1982) proposed that there are variations in how behaviors, and behavioral systems, are coordinated into more complex wholes. Among them are the following:

1. Very simple behaviors can be coordinated in chain-linked sequences, with the terminating condition for one behavior serving as the activating condition for the next. This is the context for many of the complex sequences of interaction that take place between mother and infant during the first months of life.

2. There can be chains with alternative links. In this case, when one link in the chain fails to achieve an outcome that activates the next link in the chain, some other link is activated in a non-goal-corrected manner. For example, Ainsworth (1967) described how an infant of 3 months or so may look at the caregiver and smile and babble, and if that behavior does not result in contact, it is terminated and crying is activated.

3. Complex, goal-corrected behavior patterns can themselves be organized together in chain-linked sequences, with the terminating condition for the first goal-corrected pattern serving as the activating condition for the second.

4. Behavior from one behavior system alternates with that from another. Ethologists have found that these complex sequences derived from two or more conflicting behavior systems often form the basis for important social interactions and communicative signals.

5. Partially executed behaviors from one behavior system can occur simultaneously with partially executed behaviors from another, conflicting behavior system. Sensitive parents and clinicians use these cues frequently in making inferences about a child's emotional state, and again these behaviors have been found by ethologists to form the basis for many important communicative displays. An example specifically relevant to this chapter is that of coy expressions in older preschool children (see Marvin, 1997).

Whether displayed in an alternating or a simultaneous manner, conflicting behavioral tendencies have long been topics of interest to ethologists and clinicians, as cues to behavior and internal events under distress. As will be discussed below, however, they are also important for studying the elaboration of behavior systems through ontogeny.

Ontogeny of Behavioral Systems

The final step in laying the groundwork for Bowlby's model of the ontogeny of attachment is to outline the three processes that he proposed as being basic to development in general. First, in their early forms, behaviors are sometimes directed toward different objects in the environment than is the case in their mature form. Usually the range of stimuli that elicits a particular behavior becomes restricted over the course of development. Second, behavior systems that are functional early in development are often of a very simple type. Over the course of development, these simpler systems tend to be superseded by more complex, sophisticated behavior systems. This often takes the form of a simpler system's becoming incorporated into a more complex system of goal-corrected behaviors organized into plan hierarchies, with their correspondingly complex IWMs. Third, whereas some behavior systems are functional in simple form early in development, others are initially executed only partially, in a nonfunctional context, or in an inappropriate place in a behavioral sequence. In this case, the important developmental process is the integration of these nonfunctional components into functional wholes at an appropriate point in development.

One of the most important implications of this third process is that once a behavior system has become organized, it assumes some inherent stability, like other open systems (Ashby, 1956; Thelen & Ulrich, 1991). It may maintain the same organization even if it has developed along nonfunctional lines, and may persist even in the absence of the external and internal conditions in which it has developed. This part of the developmental model has clear implications for the study of developmental psychopathology. However, it also has important implications for more adaptive development, in suggesting both that there may be systemic, structurally based sensitive periods in development, and that beyond a certain point in development it may be especially difficult for a developmental process or outcome to take shape in a "normal" fashion.

THE ONTOGENY OF ATTACHMENT

Development of Attachment during the First Year of Life

Bowlby proposed that there are four phases in the development of the attachment behavioral system—the first three occurring during the first year of life, and the fourth beginning sometime around the child's third birthday.

Phase I: Orientation and Signals without Discrimination of Figure

At or very soon after birth, babies respond to stimuli in a manner that increases the likelihood of continued contact with other humans. In a complementary way, a baby's signal and motor systems are especially adept at eliciting interest and caregiving from other humans, such that proximity, physical contact, nutrition, and warmth are the predictable outcomes. In this sense, the development of the infant's attachment behavior cannot fully be understood except as taking place in the context of the complementary changes in the caregiver's behavior. Although full consideration of these caregiving behaviors and their developmental changes are beyond the scope of this chapter (but see, e.g., George & Solomon, 1996, and Chapter 28, this volume; Marvin & Britner, 1996), they are assumed at all times.

During this first phase, baby and caregiver engage in much interaction; from the perspective of the caregiver's behavior, many of these interactions are goal-corrected. From the perspective of the baby's behavior, there are predictable outcomes of the behaviors, rather than set goals. Being unable to distinguish the behavior of one person from that of another, the young infant behaves in the same way toward any two or more people who may interact with him or her in the same way. Consistent with most of the work in early cognitive development, the infant is assumed to be unable to distinguish self from other, to realize that the many different stimuli that emanate from the caregiver are organized together in that single individual, or to realize that the other exists even if not perceived by the infant. Thus, during Phase I, the infant's IWMs are extremely primitive and are probably limited to internal "on-again, off-again" experiences associated with the activation and termination of individual behaviors. In this sense, the functioning of the young infant's IWMs are no more separate from actual behaviors than in Stage I of Piaget's (1952) theory of the sensorimotor period.

At birth or very soon thereafter, every sensory system in the infant is working, and these systems continue to improve in functioning. Discrimination is relatively poor in some of them, yet there is much evidence that the sensory systems are structured so that the baby is particularly likely to respond to behavior from humans in general (Bowlby, 1969/1982).

Among the sensory systems especially important in the development of attachment behavior are the auditory and visual systems. At or soon after birth, most infants are capable of visual orientation and tracking, and are especially responsive to contour and pattern, especially if the stimulus is moving slowly. By no later than 4 weeks of age, most infants exhibit a preference for looking at the human face compared to other objects (McGraw, 1943; Wolff, 1969). And very soon after birth, infants tend to quiet and attend to soft auditory stimuli, and appear especially responsive to the human voice. During this first phase, each of these systems has its own activating and terminating conditions, and there is as yet no "internal" connection between the systems. For example, hearing a human voice does not yet activate visual search behavior.

Reaching, grasping, and clinging are also crucial attachment behaviors in all primates, and they develop relatively late in humans. It is not until after about 2 months of age that the human infant's grasp is highly developed and controlled by anything other than a reflex-like process of activation by stimulation of the palm of the hand. It is at about this same time that the visual system becomes chain-linked with the motor system in a manner allowing the infant to make ballistic-like movements toward an object in the visual field. Finally, smiling and crying are additional important attachment behaviors displaying a similar developmental course. Smiling tends to be activated, and crying terminated, in a relatively automatic way by a range of specific conditions. These conditions become increasingly selective and integrated within more complex behavior systems over the first 6 months.

Thus, at first it is largely the caregiver who maintains proximity and protects the infant, despite the fact that the newborn is equipped to be especially responsive to other humans and to elicit caregiving and affection from them. Over the course of the first weeks of life, these patterns of infant–caregiver interaction are repeated frequently. If the caregiver's initiations and responses are well attuned to the infant's behavior (i.e., if the baby's attachment behaviors are predictably terminated by the caregiver's behavior), then stable patterns of interaction are established. These reciprocal patterns of caregiver–infant behaviors ultimately minimize the frequency and intensity of such attachment behaviors as crying, and more readily elicit other behaviors, such as visual orientation and smiling. In this context the infant is seen as establishing its own behavioral and autoregulatory rhythms (e.g., Stern, 1985), so that stable internal and dyadic rhythms are becoming established at the same time.

Bowlby (1969/1982) proposed that in the environment of evolutionary adaptedness, Phase I lasts from birth to sometime between 8 and 12 weeks of age. He suggested, however, that under unfavorable conditions this phase can last much longer.

Phase II: Orientation and Signals Directed toward One or More Discriminated Figures

The shift from Phase I to Phase II is gradual, and takes place earlier with some attachment behaviors and complex attachment behavior patterns than with others (Ainsworth, 1967; Bowlby, 1969/1982). Three related issues are important in defining this transition.

First, during Phase II, there is an elaboration of simple behavior systems into more complex ones. The simple behavior systems characteristic of the Phase I infant become integrated within the infant into complex, chain-linked behavior systems. The primary focus here is on the *control* of the individual behavior systems. Whereas in Phase I the caregiver provides the conditions for terminating one behavioral link in a chain and activating the next, during Phase II the infant assumes much of this control. Many of the sensorimotor advances of the 3- to 6-month-old infant illustrate this shift in behavioral control. For example, as early as 3 months of age, perception of the bottle or breast itself serves as an activating stimulus for opening the mouth, and often bringing the hand(s) toward the mouth (Hetzer & Ripin, 1930, cited in Bowlby, 1969/1982). By 4 months the infant's visual system begins to activate the motor behavior of reaching for an object. Through a reciprocal feedback process, the infant alternates his or her gaze between the hand and the object, and then grasps the object. By 5 months the infant is so adept at this that he or she is able to reach out and grasp parts of the mother's body and clothing while being held by her, or as she is leaning over the infant. Other rsearchers have studied the same developmental elabora-

tions, using other theoretical models positing self-organization from multiple components (e.g., Piaget, 1951; Thelen & Ulrich, 1991).

The second defining issue for Phase II is the restriction of range of effective activating and terminating conditions. Bowlby proposed that as infant and caregiver repeat these sequences of interaction, and as the sequences come increasingly under the infant's control in this chain-linked fashion, there is a tendency for the activating and terminating conditions to become restricted to those that are most commonly part of the behavioral sequence (cf. Thelen & Ulrich's [1991] notion of "attractor states"). Specifically, Phase II is operationally defined in terms of the infant's differentiating between the most familiar caregivers and others in directing his or her attachment behavior.

Drawing from Ainsworth (1967), Bowlby (1969/1982) identified 13 relatively complex patterns of behavior that are differentially displayed toward one figure, usually the mother. At least 7 of these differential attachment patterns develop during Phase II, while the remainder probably emerge during Phase III. Each of the patterns can be described in terms of relatively complex, chain-linked systems of behavior, now directed primarily toward one or a few principal caregivers. The behavior patterns that develop during Phase II are differential: termination of crying; crying when the caregiver leaves; smiling; vocalization; visual–motor orientation; greeting response; and climbing and exploring.

A third and equally important component of Phase II is the infant's increasing tendency actively to initiate attachment–caregiving and sociable interactions with the principal caregiver(s). Ainsworth (1967) observed that as early as 2 months of age, and increasingly thereafter, the infants themselves were active in seeking interaction rather than passively responding to it. Thus, in at least two ways the infant of Phase II is assuming increasing responsibility for gaining and maintaining contact and interaction with attachment figure(s): initiating more of the interaction, and being able to exert more control over the interaction through the use of increasingly complex, chain-linked behaviors.

The elaboration of chain-linked behavior systems, and the infant's increasingly differential attachment and sociable behavior, may also have important implications for describing the distinct developmental pathways toward the individual differences in patterns of attachment discovered by Ainsworth (e.g., Ainsworth et al., 1978; see

Weinfield, Sroufe, Egeland, & Carlson, Chapter 4, this volume), and found to be applicable to preschoolers (Cassidy & Marvin, 1992), young school-age children (Main & Cassidy, 1988), and adults (Fonagy, Steele, & Steele, 1991; Main, Kaplan, & Cassidy, 1985). There is substantial evidence that the pathways to differential strategies of attachment begin in the first quarter of the first year of life. For example, parents of infants who are later "avoidant" tend to terminate their infants' cries less often and to hold them less during the first months of life. In such a case, the infant is left in a "painful" state for considerable periods of time. The context is then ripe for the infant eventually to develop alternative links in its behavioral chains, in which some behavior on the part of the infant terminates its distress (e.g., turning its focus in a rather forced manner to exploration). The patterns of infant–parent interaction along this developmental pathway can become stabilized through the same processes at work in the normative, eventually secure infant, leading to an avoidant strategy and a tendency for the infant to contribute to the perpetuation of the pattern. The divergent developmental pathway of the "resistant" infant develops according to an analogous process (Ainsworth, 1967; Cassidy & Berlin, 1994).

Finally, these characteristics of Phase II have implications for describing the nature of the infant's IWMs. Most importantly, the infant can increasingly differentiate his or her primary caregiver(s) from others, and in that sense "know" who the caregiver or caregivers are. However, the infant cannot yet conceive of an attachment figure as someone with a separate existence from his or her own experience. Consistent with Piaget's (1952) theory of Stages II and III of the sensorimotor period, Bowlby's theory also implies that this infant's IWMs parallel his or her chain-linked sequences of behavior: The infant's awareness has expanded to encompass the continuity represented by these relatively complex sequences, but has not yet developed to the point where he or she can use internal experimentation or manipulation of images, goals, and intentions to devise a plan for achieving a set goal.

Phase III: Maintenance of Proximity to a Discriminated Figure by Locomotion and Signals

Phase III, beginning sometime between 6 and 9 months of age, is the phase during which the infant is thought to consolidate attachment to the caregiver(s); it is characterized by a number of important motor, cognitive, and communicative changes, as well as changes in the organization among behavioral systems. Although some may consider an infant in Phase II to be attached because his or her attachment behavior is differential toward one or a few adults, it is during Phase III that most experts consider the infant to be "really" attached, due to the organizational changes in behavior.

New Attachment Behaviors. The most notable change is the onset of locomotion. As an addition to the behaviors available to its attachment system, locomotion provides the infant with a vastly increased ability to control proximity to the attachment figure, to move off to explore, and to expand his or her horizons in innumerable ways, but also to place himself or herself in significant danger. In fact, four of the six additional attachment behaviors identified by Ainsworth (1967) are based on this newly developed motor skill. These behaviors, and the earliest age at which Ainsworth observed them, are as follows: differential approach to the mother, especially on reunion or when distressed (28 weeks); differential following of the mother when she leaves the room (24 weeks); use of the mother as a secure base for exploration (making exploratory excursions from her, returning to her from time to time, and terminating exploratory behavior and attempting to regain proximity if she moves off) (28 weeks); and flight to the mother as a haven of safety when alarmed (34 weeks). Two other attachment behaviors to emerge during this same period (Ainsworth, 1967) depend less directly on locomotion, although they are often organized together with it. These are differential burying of the face (while climbing on the mother, or after an excursion away from her, burying the face in the mother's lap) (28 weeks); and differential clinging to the mother when alarmed, ill, or distressed (43 weeks). By 6 to 8 months, the baby is able to cling to the caregiver in a rather automatic way as its attention is directed elsewhere.

Information Processing and IWMs. A second and equally revolutionary change associated with the shift to Phase III is an elaboration of the infant's cognitive skills. Some of the systems mediating a child's attachment behavior and many of the earlier chain-linked behaviors become organized under the infant's intentional control. Bowlby suggested that the Phase III infant has an internal image of an end state or "set goal" that he or she would like to achieve (e.g., physical contact with the attachment figure). The infant can now operate internally on available behaviors (i.e., a plan) and select behaviors that are likely to achieve that set goal (e.g., crawling around the sofa to the mother); execute the plan; alter it as a function of feedback; and then terminate the plan when the discrepancy between the set goal and the infant's perception of his or her position is reduced to zero.

This describes, in control systems terminology, what traditional cognitive theorists have referred to as the infant's newly emerging ability to differentiate means from ends. The ability to organize attachment behavior on a goal-corrected basis also implies that the infant now has an internal image of the attachment figure that is independent of perception (object permanence). In a rather elegant longitudinal study, Bell (1970) demonstrated the parallel (in Piaget's terms, the "horizontal decalage") between the development of object permanence, person (mother) permanence, and the onset of goal-corrected proximity seeking. Consistent with the proposition that children will develop such a general-purpose skill first in relationship-based and emotionally salient contexts, Bell found that most infants developed person permanence before object permanence.

The baby's set goal in interactions with the attachment figure will vary from time to time. Sometimes the set goal will be some distance from the attachment figure while exploring the social and physical world. At other times it will be mere proximity, or nothing short of close physical contact. What "setting" a goal takes at any given time is the result of many factors, including physiological state (e.g., hunger, fatigue); the presence or absence of an alarming event in the environment; assessment of the caregiver's attention to the infant; and whether the caregiver is present, departing/absent, or returning from an absence (Bowlby, 1969/1982). It will also depend on the dyad's history of relatively stable patterns of (i.e., individual differences in) attachment–caregiving interactions.

Communication Skills. Concurrent with these locomotor and cognitive changes are those in the infant's communication skills, both nonverbal and language-based. During Phase II the infant displays increased visual and vocal engagement with others, and much of his or her interaction is of a turn-taking, prelinguistic format, to which

the caregiver or caregivers tend to respond as if it were intentional (Bates, O'Connell, & Shore, 1987; Bruner, 1981). During Phase III, the infant uses communicative signals in a goal-corrected manner, as part of a repertoire of plans for achieving a set goal that often involves regulating the behaviors of others for various purposes: requesting or rejecting actions or objects; attracting or maintaining another's attention; and/or establishing/maintaining joint attention for purposes of sharing an experience (Bruner, 1981). At first through the infant's display and understanding of nonverbal utterances and signals, later through single-word utterances, and still later (at 18–36 months of age) through complex verbal communication, youngster and caregiver(s) are now able indirectly to alter each other's behavior by directly altering each other's set goals (Marvin, 1977).

All these changes have important implications for the Phase III baby's IWMs. At this point the baby has separate working models of caregiver(s) and of self. These consist of images and plans ordered in some form of a hierarchy—or event schemata or scripts (Nelson & Gruendel, 1981; Stern, 1985)—of self and other, based on the newly developed ability to operate internally on the images and likely behaviors that have been chain-linked during Phase II. The content of the infant's IWMs are probably derived from some combination of the stable, chain-linked sequences of interaction that have already been developed in interaction with the caregiver(s) and the newly stabilizing patterns that emerge with the motor, cognitive, and communication skills that develop during Phase III.

Although they are much more sophisticated than in Phase II, even in Phase III the infant's IWMs remain primitive in at least two ways. First, the infant is limited, at least early in this phase, to thinking about caregiver and self only in terms of their behaviors. The infant has yet to comprehend that the attachment figure has unique perceptions and goals, and that these can differ from his or her own. Second, early in this phase the infant is unable to think about behaviors in terms of long sequences. The early Phase III infant's ability to operate in this internal fashion is limited to individual goal–plan hierarchies or event schemata, with each thought activated and terminated by specific stimuli.

The Exploratory System. The fourth important change that takes place during Phase III is especially related to the changes in the infant's locomotor and cognitive changes—namely, the elaboration of his or her exploration behavior system. The development of locomotion and of object permanence, the more sophisticated understanding of means–ends relations, the ability increasingly to organize exploration on the basis of goal-corrected behavior, and emerging imitation and conversational skills (e.g., Piaget, 1952) all enhance the infant's ability to learn about and interact with the physical and social environment, to test and learn the "rules" that govern those interactions, and to categorize those interactions symbolically and linguistically.

The Sociable System. Closely related to the exploration system is the infant's sociable system. Phase III infants are particularly likely to display wariness toward other conspecifics, yet tend at the same time to be attracted to them. Although there appear to be both temperament and relationship differences, these infants are likely to stop exploration when confronted by a strange person, to remain wary (or even fearful) for some moments, and either to remain stationary or to move away from the stranger and toward the attachment feature. After some few moments, if the stranger displays positive affect, is not intrusive, and matches his or her responses to the infant's behavior, the infant is likely to interact sociably, with rapidly decreasing wariness (e.g., Bretherton & Ainsworth, 1974).

The Wary System. The fifth and final major Phase III change to be considered involves the infant's wary behavior system. Wariness toward novel, and especially sudden, nonhuman events has obvious survival value. Less obvious are the nature, developmental course, and role played by wariness toward unfamiliar *humans*. Despite the earlier bias toward responding to human stimuli, during the last quarter of the first year infants increasingly are more wary of unfamiliar adults than they are of unfamiliar nonhuman objects (Bretherton & Ainsworth, 1974). Although there may be individual and reproductive gene pool differences in temperamental reactivity to strangers (e.g., Kagan, 1989), this developmental shift appears to exist whether the infant is raised in a culture in which the norm is single or multiple caregivers (cf. Ainsworth, 1967).

Reciprocal linkages among the older infant's wary, sociable, and attachment behavior systems are more obvious and predictable than they have been earlier. If the wary system is highly activated, the infant tends to retreat to the parent as a haven of safety; if it is not, the infant may continue to stare at a nonintrusive stranger, or may initiate or respond sociably. In many cases, one can see a cycling of conflicting behavior systems, with the infant moving back and forth from parent to stranger as the distance from each tends to activate one behavior system and terminate the other.

Sensitive Periods. That infants became more, rather than less, wary toward unfamiliar humans over the period from 6 months to 18–24 months of age is important for at least two reasons. First, infants *are* vulnerable to danger from other humans, and until they are more able to predict which individuals are dangerous, it is adaptive that their initial reaction be wariness. Second, one of the developmental mechanisms involved in the consolidation of the infant's attachment is the reduction in the range of individuals able to activate and terminate his or her attachment behavior (Bowlby, 1969/1982). The infant comes more and more to approach familiar caregiver(s) and to retreat from unfamiliar individuals of the same species. In its general form, this phenomenon is characteristic of many species, and is common in the study of "sensitive periods" in development (see Bateson, 1976).

There are many examples of sensitive periods in nonhuman and human ontogeny, from the extreme of imprinting in many avian species to that of language development in humans. Bowlby (1969/1982) proposed that the consolidation of infant–caregiver attachment during Phase III is one such period. The reorganization of the infant's increasingly active attachment behavior along goal-corrected lines, combined with heightened wariness of the unfamiliar and the strong emotions associated with the activation of attachment and wary behavioral systems, results in this being a period during which the infant is particularly ready to focus attachment behavior and IWMs of attachment on one or a few familiar figures. Presumably, parallel neurological changes take place as well. It is after these changes have stabilized that disruption of the bond is so likely to lead to the short- and sometimes long-term effects that led Bowlby to the study of this early tie.

Bowlby (1969/1982) suggested that the readiness to become quickly attached remains intact at least through the end of the first year. This does not imply that the specific attachment, a more versus less adaptive *form* of attachment, or the lack of an attachment is completely irreversible after this sensitive period. Nor, it is important to note, does it invoke the construct of "critical periods" (see Bateson, 1976). Although there are few relevant data, the results emerging from studies of infants raised in Eastern European orphanages and adopted into low-risk homes suggest that children *can* form attachments for the first time well after 1 year, but that these attachments are at increased risk of being organized in a significantly less adaptive manner than would usually be expected of children raised in a low-risk home (e.g., Chisholm, Carter, Ames, & Morison, 1995; Goldberg et al., 1996).

Organization among Behavioral Systems. It is during Phase III that the dynamic balance described earlier among the four behavioral systems fully emerges (Ainsworth et al., 1978). For most infants, this balance culminates in organizing essentially all the new developments of this phase into what Ainsworth (1990) has referred to as the "hallmark" of an attachment—the infant's use of the attachment figure as a secure base for exploration. Stable *variations* in this organization are evident in the different insecure strategies of attachment (Ainsworth et al., 1978; Main & Solomon, 1990). In the "avoidant" strategy, the infant tends, when the attachment system is highly activated, to inhibit attachment behavior and (often) to activate the exploration system. In the "resistant" strategy, the infant tends to over-amplify the attachment and wariness systems. In the case of infants classified as having a "disorganized" attachment, the simultaneous and/or sequential activation and termination of behavior systems are especially contradictory and take a form that puts the infant at risk of not being protected (e.g., activation of the attachment system also serves to activate wary behavior toward the caregiver).

Subordinate Attachment Figures and Types of Relationships. It is apparent that throughout human evolution children have been raised in families, which themselves are part of larger groups of varied size and composition. Most children have experienced multiple caregivers, giving them the opportunity to form specific attachments to a number of figures. Even in his early writings, Bowlby (e.g., 1958) proposed that infants tend to become attached to a number of caregivers, and that "for a child of 18 months to have only one attachment figure is quite exceptional" (Bowlby, 1969/1982, p. 304).

Several studies across many cultures have suggested that a minority of infants select more than one attachment figure almost as soon as they begin to show any differential attachment behavior, and that a majority do so by 18 months (e.g., Ainsworth, 1967; Konner, 1976; Marvin, Van Devender, Iwanaga, LeVine, & LeVine, 1977; Schaffer & Emerson, 1964). These and other studies (e.g., Myers, Jarvis, & Creasey, 1987), however, suggest that not all attachment figures are treated by the infant as equivalent. Infants are attached to a range of caregivers; however, that attachment behavior tends (especially when the infant is distressed, hungry, tired, or ill) to be focused on a particular person when both that person and other attachment figures are available. Thus most infants seem to have a network of attachment figures, but the available data suggest that they may tend to choose one figure as the "primary" attachment figure. Importantly, others may be chosen as the primary figures for play or other types of interactions (see van IJzendoorn & Sagi, Chapter 31, this volume).

Development of Attachment during the Toddler and Preschool Years

Most research on social and emotional development during the postinfancy preschool period has focused on issues other than attachment (e.g., autonomy, self-control, independence, and socialization). These issues imply a decline in attachment behavior as the youngster deals with these later "developmental tasks." Although the framework of developmental tasks can be helpful in guiding our research, it can also lead us astray by restricting the focus to single issues. A full understanding requires viewing development across multiple domains. In fact, while the child *is* becoming more autonomous and self-reliant during these preschool years, he or she remains vulnerable to a range of dangers. The child makes increasingly distant forays from the attachment figure while exploring the environment, but is still at an early point in developing the skills needed for self-protection. The close attachment to the caregiver thus remains crucially important to the child's survival and socialization. It is adaptive, rather than "regressive," that attachment behavior remains easily activated.

The general systems model outlined at the beginning of this chapter suggests a focus on the functional relations among various behavior systems in the child, and between the child's organization and that of caregivers and larger social context, such that (1) the child will be protected from danger; (2) he or she will take increased responsibility in self-protection and the integration of behavior with others; and (3) changes across multiple developmental domains will tend to occur simultaneously.

As we move to the study of attachment in the postinfancy years, we must also be careful not to lose the focus on *behavior* as the child's representational and communicative abilities become increasingly noticeable. Because infants' mental models of attachment cannot possibly be symbolic (i.e., language-based), it must be assumed that those cognitive structures that relate to attachment *behavior* in infancy constitute the mental model (Bretherton, 1993). There is a natural shift in research on attachment past infancy to move more and more to the level of cognitive–emotional representation. The trap is to move to the cognitive level, to the relative exclusion of behavior. This would be a terrible error. Bowlby's whole theory—or the cognitive-behavioral part of it—is based on the important linkage between IWMs and behavior. The point is that older children do not move from the level of behavior to the level of internal representation; they become able to process and manipulate plans and goals at that internal level, and increasingly to control behavior with that internal processing. We must remember that the function of an IWM is to organize behavior in more flexible ways.

Changes in Attachment Behavior during the Toddler/Preschool Years

Although most of our knowledge about the ontogeny of attachment behavior is restricted to the first 12–15 months of life, a few naturalistic studies (e.g., Blurton-Jones, 1972; Konner, 1976) and a number of laboratory-based studies (e.g., Main & Cassidy, 1988; Marvin, 1977; Marvin & Greenberg, 1982) provide a general outline of the normative course of attachment behavior over the preschool and early school years. In reviewing the literature, Bowlby (1969/1982) suggested that during the second and most of the third year of life, attachment behavior is shown neither at less intensity nor at less frequency than at the first birthday. In fact, use of attachment figures as a secure base is a critical component of the child's rapidly expanding physical and social world, and attachment behavior therefore remains a major part of his or her behavioral organization.

Overall, 2-year-olds tend to maintain as much

(or more) proximity to their mothers as do 1-year-olds. At the same time, they also make more extensive excursions away in order to explore with their more elaborate cognitive and motor abilities. Several studies (e.g., Schaffer & Emerson, 1964) have found that a toddler tends actively to monitor not only the mother's movements, but also her attention; when she is not attending to him or her, the child often executes attachment behavior with the set goal of regaining her attention. This adaptive behavior pattern is unappreciated in Western cultures, in which it is commonly seen as regressive or controlling "attention seeking," and as such is frustrating to parents.

Before the third birthday, a child is much less adept at maintaining proximity to the attachment figure when the figure is moving. The perception of the caregiver's moving off is typically a condition that terminates the toddler's exploratory behavior and activates attachment behavior. At this younger age, the child can follow the caregiver around the familiar home, but finds it difficult to follow if he or she is moving steadily off. In this situation, one or both members of the dyad initiate physical contact, and the toddler is carried. After the third birthday, with much improved locomotor skills, the child is much less likely to be carried under relaxed circumstances. In fact, in his study of the Zhuntwa hunter–gatherers, Konner (1976) found that in day-to-day living, children in that culture maintain very close physical ties with their mothers until sometime between 3 and 4 years of age; after this, ties to the multiage peer group become increasingly important.

When undergoing a separation from their mothers that is not of their own initiative, 2-year-olds tend to be as distressed as 1-year-olds, although they are more able to rely on calling and active search behaviors rather than crying. Many 3- and 4-year-olds also become mildly upset by such brief separations, but they are less so than 2-year-olds, and they are more willing than younger children to be left for brief periods in the company of friendly adults. By the third birthday, it appears that it is being left *alone* that is especially upsetting and likely to elicit strong attachment behavior. If briefly left alone, or if mildly distressed by being left with a friendly adult, most 3- and 4-year-olds are able to wait for the attachment figure's return before executing attachment behavior (Marvin, 1977).

When the caregiver returns after a brief separation in a laboratory setting, 2-year-olds tend to seek proximity and contact in much the same way as 1-year-olds, albeit with much more locomotor efficiency. They also tend to require a short period of physical contact with the caregiver before being able to move off again to explore, and display the same secure, avoidant, resistant/ambivalent, and disorganized strategies in a form so similar to 1-year-olds that the same attachment classification procedure (Ainsworth et al., 1978) can be used, with only minor changes and extrapolation.

By the third birthday things have changed. At least partially because they are less distressed by brief separations, most children 3 years and older seem to require less physical contact with the attachment figure on reunion before returning to exploration. In one study, however, most 3-year-olds did seek brief proximity to their mothers before returning to exploration, in spite of the fact that they were less distressed by the separation than 2-year-olds were (Marvin, 1977). Four-year-olds, especially boys, were less likely to seek physical proximity or contact on reunion than the 1- to 3-year-olds.

Whereas there is clearly a decrease in physical proximity and contact across the preschool period, it is not the case that the older child is any less attached to the caregiver(s). In addition to the obvious fact that older children continue to retreat to their attachment figures when distressed or frightened, at least two lines of research suggest that the *organization* of the attachment system changes significantly between the ages of 3 and 5 years. First, Marvin (1977) and Marvin and Greenberg (1982) found that 4-year-olds, but not 3-year-olds, tended not to be distressed by brief separations if they and their mothers had negotiated or agreed upon a shared plan regarding the separation and reunion prior to the mothers' departure; the 3-year-olds tended to accept or protest the impending departure, but did not negotiate a shared plan. Second, Cassidy et al. (1992) and Main and Cassidy (1988) found physical proximity and contact to be less important in distinguishing among strategies of attachment in preschool and early-school-age children, relative to infants and toddlers. These older children increasingly organized their intimate interactions with their attachment figures on the basis of physical orientation, eye contact, nonverbal expressions, and affect, as well as conversations about personal matters such as the separation and reunion, feelings, and shared activities and plans.

These two lines of research suggest the importance of Bowlby's (1969/1982) proposed final phase in the development of attachment—the phase of the "goal-corrected partnership." They are also congruent with earlier research suggesting that sometime around age 4, children are much less dependent on physical proximity and contact with their attachment figures to maintain a sense of security, and are increasingly comfortable spending appreciable periods of time in the company of nonfamilial peers and adults (Blurton-Jones, 1972; Konner, 1976). In what follows, we briefly review literature on other developmental domains relevant to the changes in attachment behavior outlined above, and then review the theoretical and empirical work on the goal-corrected partnership.

Developmental Changes in Relations among Behavior Systems

Ainsworth et al. (1978) showed how, in 1-year-olds, the attachment, exploratory, wary, and sociable systems function in the dynamic equilibrium described earlier. Observation of young children's behavior when introduced to a friendly adult stranger presents an excellent opportunity to study this dynamic balance, and has yielded some evidence that this organization changes over the preschool years in a way consistent with a youngster's gradually increased responsibility for protecting himself or herself through increasingly sophisticated behavioral organization.

Greenberg and Marvin (1982) studied young children's initial reactions to a friendly stranger. The most common response among 3- and 4-year-olds was to (apparently) ignore the stranger and continue exploring without activation of either the wariness or attachment behavior systems. The next most common response was the *simultaneous* activation of the wary and sociable systems (usually in the form of coy expressions), and coincidental activation of the attachment system. No 2-year-olds displayed this more complex pattern. Most children of all three ages eventually played sociably with the stranger. Whereas a few of the younger children remained fearful of the stranger throughout the situation, none of the older children did so. Finally, all 2-year-olds (but none of the 3- or 4-year-olds) who displayed wariness toward the stranger while the mother was gone also displayed attachment behavior. Greenberg and Marvin (1982) suggested that this decreased developmental coupling of the wary and attachment behavior systems, and the increased developmental coupling of the wary and sociable systems, may have important implications for children's increasing ability to cope with strangers on their own. The careful approach implied by the coincidental activation of the wary and sociable systems, whether in the form of coy expressions or shy conversation, may provide the basis for strategies of social interaction that can fulfill the same protective function earlier fulfilled by the close physical bond between the child and his or her attachment figure(s).

Changes in Locomotor and Self-Care Skills

Humans exhibit a developmental organization during the preschool years that suggests the crucial importance of a continuing protective attachment, while at the same time providing the young child with the independence necessary to learn the skills that will be required during the following phase. The emergence of milk teeth is complete between 2 and 3 years of age, and by 3 years children are quite independent in feeding themselves. Although Western cultures are now clearly different, in less industrialized cultures breast feeding tapers off between 3 and 4 years of age. By age 3, the child's locomotor skills have developed to the point where he or she can assume much of the responsibility for gaining and maintaining proximity to the attachment figure under most conditions, as well as engage in vigorous play with other children and practice many of the social skills he or she will use in a more stable fashion during the juvenile (school-age) period. By the beginning of the juvenile period, the child is capable of most of the motor skills of older children, although strength, endurance, coordination, and so forth continue to improve.

Changes in Communication Skills

Consistent with studies of nonhuman primates, it is during the preschool period that children develop most of the communication skills that will later be required for stable integration into their social groups, independent of the close physical ties to their attachment figures. By 30 months, children increasingly communicate about past and future events and about emotional states, and connected narrative discourse emerges as children begin to relate logical sequences of events across many utterances (e.g., Bretherton, 1993; Dunn, 1994). Dunn found that during the second and third years children were increasingly able to recognize, understand, and converse about the feelings and behaviors of other family members; they comforted, teased, argued, joked, and blamed. She concludes that by 3 years of age—

much younger than previously thought—children understand surprisingly complex rules for social interaction, interpret others' feelings and goals, and use such rules to manipulate others' internal states. It now seems clear that by age 4, most children are becoming competent at one of our species' most sophisticated communication skills—that is, thinking and conversing about the feelings, goals, and plans of others with whom they are interacting (see Lewis & Mitchell, 1994). As Bowlby (1969/1982) and Marvin (1977) have suggested, this skill should have important implications for the organization of attachment interactions.

Although there has been little recent research on the ontogeny of nonverbal expressions in preschool children, some of the early work in human ethology (Blurton-Jones, 1972; Hinde, 1976) suggests that many of the expressions used to regulate interactions during childhood and adolescence develop, and are employed with increasing effectiveness, during the preschool years. Furthermore, studies of coy expressions (Marvin, 1997) and of posed expressions of happiness, surprise, anger, fear, sadness, and disgust (Lewis, Sullivan, & Vasen, 1987) again suggest that the period between the third and fourth birthdays is especially important in the development elaboration and understanding of a range of complex expressions used to regulate interactions.

Changes in Information-Processing Skills and IWMs

The work of Bretherton (1993), Cassidy and Marvin (1992), Dunn (1994), Marvin and Greenberg (1982), Nelson and Gruendel (1981), Slough and Greenberg (1990), and Stern (1985), among others, suggests that during the second through sixth years of life, children are elaborating more and more sophisticated and accurate (in the sense of nonegocentric) IWMs of both their own and others' behavior and internal events. At the same time, they are developing surprisingly sophisticated IWMs of implicit and explicit rules for social behavior and interaction. The reader is referred to the studies listed above and to other chapters in this volume for information about the *content* of, and individual differences in, these IWMs; in this section we focus on developmental changes in their underlying *form*.

This work was not available at the time Bowlby (1969/1982) first developed his model and Marvin (1977) expanded it. Bowlby's model of information processing during the preschool years relied predominantly on Piaget's (e.g., 1952) theory of the preoperational stage, and the role played by the child's emerging ability to make accurate inferences about others' goals. Although not contradictory to Piaget's theory, Bowlby's model is actually more consistent with contemporary work on cognition and with script and event representation theories (see Bretherton & Munholland, Chapter 5, this volume; Nelson & Gruendel, 1981).

Drawing on Bowlby's general model of the organization and ontogeny of behavioral systems, Marvin (1977) proposed that the developmental changes in IWMs during the preschool years should demonstrate a formal parallel to the changes Bowlby had earlier identified with respect to behavioral organization and development in general. Specifically, the early Phase III IWM has developed to the point where the toddler is able to represent individual goal-corrected image–plan hierarchies. At that point, the internal "experiments" the child conducts take place as image sequences, in which images serve as activating and terminating conditions for other images. These schemas or action representations can also be activated or terminated by conditions or events in the child's environment. As Phase III progresses, the toddler establishes a growing number of increasingly complex, internal, "chain-linked" action images (or "event representations"); consistent with more recent work (see Bretherton, 1993), these links may actually take the form of a network rather than a linear chain. It is these structures that the preschool child is so curious and energetic in building, as to be constantly asking "Why?" in an attempt to establish more links in the network. It is also in the context of conversations between the youngster and caregivers that so many of these links are established (Bretherton, 1993; Dunn, 1994).

Marvin (1977) proposed that one important component of this elaboration is the child's eventual ability to inhibit the execution of a plan in order to formulate a more complex IWM of the situation, devise a more complex plan for achieving a given set goal, or postpone execution of some step in a plan until an anticipated and appropriate link in the chain exists. With the concurrent elaboration of conversational skills, this ability to inhibit ongoing thought and behavior sets the stage for the child to "insert" one of the caregiver's plans or goals into his or her own action plan. Thus the child and caregiver are able to interact under a shared goal plan hierarchy, or a partnership (Bowlby, 1969/1982).

There is, however, an additional parallel (in Piagetian terms, a "vertical decalage") between the operation of the Phase II infant's behavior and that of the older child in this partnership. At first, the partnership between child and attachment figure is a predictable outcome of their interaction, and is not (yet) goal-corrected on the child's part. This youngster cannot alter the goals or plans of self or other *in order* to achieve a shared goal or plan. That is, the youngster cannot internally *operate on* this emerging network of event representations; he or she can only *operate behaviorally in terms of* them. In order for these internal events themselves to operate in a goal-corrected manner, they need the input (increased "variety," in the terms of Ashby, 1956) of another person who already has this ability.

Later in this phase (sometime between 3½ and 5 years of age), the child's information-processing skills undergo a further hierarchical reorganization (Marvin, 1977), in line with Piaget's theory of the shift to the intuitive period, followed soon by concrete operations. This reorganization is essentially a "second-order" abstraction, through which the child is now able internally to operate in a goal-corrected manner on already existing network of event representations. No longer limited to sequential processing through a chain-linked network of thoughts–images–plans, this older preschooler can now comprehend two or more of these images as component parts of a yet higher-order image–goal–plan. This is consistent with what Piaget (1952) termed "operational reversibility." One type of this higher-order image or schema is a representation of the coordination of the child's own plans with those of another with whom he or she is interacting. Whereas the younger preschool child is able to think of and converse about the goals and plans of self and others, he or she is unable to operate on them simultaneously. Although the child will often refer to others' internal events, and will often do so "correctly," Marvin (1977) suggested that this limitation should often result in the child's confusing his or her own perspective with that of the other.

Once the child's IWMs have achieved this later hierarchical reorganization, however, the child should be able internally to operate on his or her own perspective and representation of the caregiver's perspective simultaneously; this enables the child to keep them distinct, to recognize when they are shared or in conflict, and to organize a plan to construct a *shared* perspective. If this shared perspective becomes a new set goal in the child's relationship with the caregiver, then the child should (1) become disequilibrated or distressed when that set goal of a shared set of plans is unattainable; and (2) execute plans to establish that shared perspective, usually by attempting to change the caregiver's goals.

There remains some controversy regarding the age by which a young child is able to make such complex inferences about others' internal events and their relations to his or her own (see Lewis & Mitchell, 1994). There is ample evidence that between the second and third birthdays children come to realize that others have their own feelings, goals, and plans, and that their IWMs are significantly influenced by that realization. There is also evidence that by the fourth birthday most children are able accurately to distinguish between their own and others' perspectives, and to maintain both perspectives in awareness simultaneously while assessing whether or not they match (Marvin, Greenberg, & Mossler, 1976). By this same age, most children are able to reason in a nonegocentric manner about the causal relationship between others' goals/plans and the others' behavior (Greenberg, Marvin, & Mossler, 1977). These are all component skills that allow the child and caregiver *both* to take responsibility, when their goals or plans conflict, in negotiating in a goal-corrected way toward a shared set of plans.

Phase IV: Implications of the Partnership for the Organization of Attachment Behavior during the Preschool Years

Although this partnership is certainly a general-purpose skill used in interactions with family members, other adults, and peers, it is likely that it will first be applied in emotionally powerful interactions such as attachment–caregiving interactions. Marvin (1977) and Marvin and Greenberg (1982) studied its application to this type of interaction, and suggested two important organizational changes. The first is related to the young preschooler's ability to inhibit attachment behavior and to insert the caregiver's plans into the child's own plan for proximity—what might be called the "emergent partnership." The second is related to the older preschooler's ability simultaneously to operate internally on the goals and plans of self and other, to understand objectively (i.e., nonegocentrically) the causal relations between the caregiver's goals/plans and behavior, and to engage in goal-corrected negotiations with the caregiver regarding a shared

plan for proximity—the goal-corrected partnership.

With regard to the first, Bowlby (1969/1982) proposed that a toddler's attachment plans vary in the extent to which they are designed to influence the behavior of the attachment figure. He suggested that the earliest goal-corrected plans for changing the caregiver's behavior are primitive (e.g., pushing the caregiver in certain directions, knocking a book of his or her lap, throwing a tantrum). These early attempts are based either on changing the caregiver's behavior directly through physical means or indirectly though crying and anger. During this same period, parents rely largely on techniques such as distracting the toddler to influence his or her behavior.

However, the changes associated with the early form of the partnership already outlined offer the dyad a new opportunity. As the dyad's conversational skills become elaborated and as the child becomes more able to inhibit his or her ongoing behavior, it should become increasingly the case that child and mother are able to change each other's behavior indirectly by inserting one of each other's goals or plans into the goal or plan structure of the other through linguistic communication. Although the child cannot yet negotiate a shared plan with the caregiver in a goal-corrected manner, the child *can* attempt to change the caregiver's goal or plan, inhibit ongoing behavior, insert one of the caregiver's goals into his or her own plan for action, and thus function in an interaction that has the "predictable outcome" of shared goals.

Marvin (1977) provided an initial test for this hypothesis by administering two analogous procedures to a sample of 2-, 3-, and 4-year-old children: one relevant to interaction in a nonattachment context (a waiting task), and the other in an attachment–caregiving context (the strange situation). The results of both procedures suggest that by 3 years of age a child is usually able to inhibit ongoing, goal-corrected behavior across at least two types of interactions, to insert one of the mother's communicated goals into his or her own plan, and to wait until the circumstances are appropriate for both mother and child before executing the plan. These findings are consistent with Bowlby's (1969/1982) suggestion that children are more able to feel secure in the presence of alternative (even unfamiliar) caregivers by the third birthday, and that the frequency and intensity of attachment behavior are likely to diminish because of developmental changes in the processes that control its activation and termination. The results are also consistent with the conclusion that the 3-year-old's attachment set goal continues to be represented in physical–spatial–temporal terms, and that separations that are not directly under his or her own control continue to disturb or disequilibrate that set goal.

The results also suggest a further change in the organization of attachment behavior sometime around the fourth birthday. As implied earlier, the hierarchical reorganization of the older preschooler's IWMs/information-processing skills that enables the child to operate in a nonegocentric fashion *simultaneously* on the perspectives of self and others, and to construct shared plans with the caregiver in a goal-corrected manner, should have important implications for the organization of attachment behavior. Marvin (1977) suggested that at least five component skills are involved: (1) the ability to recognize that the attachment figure possesses internal events (including thoughts, goals, plans, feelings, etc.); (2) the ability to distinguish between the caregiver's point of view and the child's own, especially when they differ; (3) the ability to infer, from logic and/or experience, what factors control the caregiver's goals and plans; (4) the ability to assess the degree of coordination, or match, between their respective points of view; and 95) the ability to influence the caregiver's goals and plans in a goal-corrected manner. On the basis of much research over the past 20 years (see Bretherton, 1993; Dunn, 1994; Greenberg et al., 1977), it seems possible that by 3 years of age and certainly by 4, children possess the first two component skills. In a series of studies, Marvin and his colleagues (e.g., Greenberg et al., 1977; Marvin, 1977; Marvin & Greenberg, 1982; Marvin et al., 1976; Stewart & Marvin, 1984) studied these five components and how they are associated with the organization of attachment behavior in 2- to 6-year-old children. The results of these studies suggest that by their fourth birthdays, most children raised in low-risk settings have all five skills.

Marvin and Greenberg (1982) examined the behavior patterns of young children during leave-taking, separation, and reunion events. The purpose was to see whether those children who demonstrated the communication and perspective-taking components required for a goal-corrected partnership in fact behaved during the strange situation in a manner consistent with such developmental reorganization. Simply stated, the model suggests that the set goal for these children should no longer be mere physical prox-

imity or contact; rather, it should be a *shared plan for that proximity.* Using specific behavioral criteria based on this model, Marvin and Greenberg (1982) found that most of the 3-year-olds conformed to the separation and reunion pattern consistent with the emergent partnership (i.e., the set goal was still structured in terms of physical proximity and contact), whereas most of the 4-year-olds conformed to the pattern consistent with the goal-corrected partnership. The expected association between level of partnership and ability to reason objectively about the mother's perspective and behavior also emerged. Stewart and Marvin (1984) found essentially the same within-child association between accurate perspective-taking components and separation–reunion behavior patterns that reflected a goal-corrected partnership.

These studies of developmental changes in attachment during the preschool years thus suggest, consistent with Bowlby's (1969/1982) theory, that from 1 until about 3 years of age the organization of the youngster's attachment to the caregiver remains relatively unchanged. Toward the third birthday, significant elaboration of the child's IWMs is exemplified by a more complex network of event schemata, and by an increased ability to inhibit ongoing behavior in a way that allows the child increasingly to integrate his or her goals, plans, and behavior with those of the attachment figure. By this point the child's attachment behavior has become organized in terms of an emergent partnership, and the amount and intensity of attachment behavior become somewhat attenuated. However, the set goal in the attachment–caregiving component of the relationship with the caregiver continues to be structured in terms of physical proximity.

By the fourth birthday, with the newly developed ability internally to operate simultaneously on both his or her own perspective and that of the caregiver, the child is now able to function within a relationship that is no longer so dependent on physical proximity and contact. The child's IWMs of caregiver and self have developed to the point where he or she can conceive of, and maintain in a goal-corrected way, a relationship that is based on shared goals, plans, and feelings. To the extent that child and caregiver are able to maintain this goal-corrected partnership, the child's set goal with respect to attachment–caregiving interactions should shift from some specifiable degree of physical proximity and contact to some specifiable degree of availability in case of need (Bowlby, personal communication, 1987, cited in Ainsworth, 1990). To the same extent, attachment behavior should be further attenuated.

This is not meant to imply that children 4 years or older do not want, need, or enjoy physical proximity and contact with their attachment figures. Under conditions of distress, illness, and fear, children—even much older children—continue to retreat to their attachment figures as a haven of safety. As suggested by the attachment classification systems developed by Cassidy and Marvin (1992) and Main and Cassidy (1988), preschool and young school-age children also continue to maintain and enjoy this close tie through a range of intimate behaviors. What is implied by the model is that the older preschooler has come to organize attachment behavior in a new way—one that enables the child to realize that he or she and an attachment figure have a continuing relationship, whether or not they are in close proximity. This new organization is one in which the child is increasingly responsible for maintaining whatever protective proximity is necessary. In conjunction with the other recently developed locomotor, communication, and information-processing skills, this organization allows the child entering the juvenile phase of development to maintain a close tie to the attachment figure(s) while increasingly moving off and spending more time with a peer group, teachers, and other conspecifics.

Changes in Attachment Behavior beyond the Preschool Years

Bowlby (1969/1982) suggested that the goal-corrected partnership is probably the last phase in the ontogeny of attachment. By this he seems to have meant that there are no further "stage" changes in this behavioral system. The attachment behavioral system, however, remains important throughout the lifespan, and it does continue to undergo significant changes. These probably include further elaborations at the same "level," as well as changes in the relations between the attachment and other behavioral systems (the higher-order control structures), activating and terminating conditions, and IWMs. Certainly there are also changes in specific individuals who serve as attachment figures. One clear implication is that attachment becomes increasingly difficult to measure as it becomes more sophisticated, more abstract, and less dependent on proximity and contact, and as the behavioral systems become elaborated into more

and more complex systems (Bowlby, 1969/ 1982).

During middle childhood, or the juvenile period in primate terminology, children continue to be vulnerable to a wide range of dangers, and continue to use their attachment figures as secure bases from which to explore. Increasingly, however, they use other adults and groups of specific peers in the same manner. With their much more sophisticated communication skills and IWMs, they become able to assume primary responsibility for their own protection through their integration into the larger social structure for longer periods of time and under conditions of greater physical separation from their parents.

The child–parent relationship, however, remains a close one, and attachment–caregiving interactions remain organized according to an increasingly sophisticated goal-corrected partnership. The attachment behavioral system is no less important than earlier, in that school-age children still do not have the wisdom or knowledge to make decisions completely on their own regarding their activities, their supervision, or their protection while away from their parents. Not only is it important for children to know where their parents are and to have a secure sense of the parents' accessibility, but the parents themselves must know where the child is and who is responsible for the child's protection. For this system to function well, an effective goal-corrected partnership is necessary.

Bowlby anticipated this complex state of affairs when he proposed that *availability* of the attachment figure, rather than physical proximity, becomes the set goal of the attachment system in older children and adults. This, he said, "turns on cognitive processes: (a) belief that lines of communication with the attachment figure are open, (b) that physical accessibility is possible, and (c) that the attachment figure will respond if called upon for help" (Bowlby, personal communication, 1987, cited in Ainsworth, 1990). The work of Marvin (1977) and Marvin and Greenberg (1982) suggests that this shift begins to take place during the late preschool years. Certainly it continues to develop and elaborate through the remainder of childhood, and enables children to maintain their attachment to their parents while being increasingly separated from them.

This goal-corrected partnership needs much research. Very little is known except for the general construct, its early development, some implications regarding its relations with self-concept and academic performance during middle childhood (Moss, St-Laurent & Parent, in press), and its importance for the relationship between adolescents and their parents (e.g., Allen & Land, Chapter 15, this volume; Kobak, 1994). In this context it will be important to remember that the goal-corrected partnership is, in Bowlby's terms, a general-purpose skill—one that is used in much wider contexts than attachment–caregiving interactions, despite the suggestion that attachment interactions may be the first type in which it is used. Standardized procedures for studying attachment during the juvenile years are needed. These procedures should include observations of interactions between children and attachment figures in situations designed to mildly activate attachment–caregiving interactions, as well as interview and projective techniques designed to access children's IWMs regarding this part of the relationship. It will also be important to include procedures for gathering information about children's attachments to nonparental figures, including both adults and other children.

Observations and shared experiences regarding relationships during the school-age period suggest that most children develop other close, helping relationships with a range of other children and adults. Older siblings, specific teachers, adult members of the child's extended family, older neighbors, coaches, and the like all become very important people in the lives of school-age children and adolescents. Are these relationships affectional bonds? And are they attachment bonds, or other types of bonds? Given the specificity and strong emotional component of many of these relationships, some certainly quality as bonds, despite the fact that many of them are relatively short-lived (Ainsworth, 1990). Many of them, however, fall under the category of "peer affectional bonds," whose similarities to and differences from attachment bonds need much research. Others (e.g., relationships with some teachers and older neighbors) can be helping and/or protective relationships without constituting actual bonds, as defined earlier. It is likely that some of these relationships actually reflect coordinations of the attachment behavioral system with other behavioral systems, and will not fully be understood outside that context. Although we already know something about the relations between individual differences in early attachment–caregiving bonds and the quality of other, later bonds (see Berlin & Cassidy, Chapter 30, this volume), there has been almost no research on the normative developmental course involved.

Child–parent attachment interactions organized in terms of a goal-corrected partnership also continue through adolescence, as these older children continue to use their parents as a secure base for expanding their increasing autonomy (Allen & Land, Chapter 15, this volume). As throughout life, attachment behaviors are especially evident when an adolescent is distressed, ill, afraid, or reunited with an attachment figure after a long absence (Ainsworth, 1990; Bowlby, 1979). The degree, however, to which movements by adolescents away from parental proximity and control are interspersed with adaptive, temporary returns to that safe haven is greatly underestimated in the developmental literature. The developmental course of these cycles, the complex combinations of attachment behavior with patterns from other behavioral systems, and the parental caregiving behaviors that terminate or continually activate those cycles constitute much of the core of adolescent and family therapy (e.g., Haley, 1977), and will be some of the most important topics for the study of attachment during adolescence.

During adolescence and young adulthood, another developmental change takes place that is precipitated by hormonal changes. During these years the adolescent or young adult begins to search for a permanent, goal-corrected partnership with an agemate, usually of the opposite sex. The biological function of this relationship is to produce offspring and raise them to reproductive age. This reproductive partnership, or adult pair bond (see Hazan & Zeifman, Chapter 16, this volume), does not imply the cessation of attachments to parents. In fact, knowledge of most cultures, as well as recent shifts in Western culture toward more adult offspring's living with their own parents in two- and three-generation homes, suggest that attachment–caregiving relationships between adult offspring and parents often actively continue while the offspring are forming their own "nuclear" family. As Ainsworth (1990) suggests, what it does imply is that these earlier attachments no longer penetrate as many aspects of an adult child's life as they did before.

For understandable reasons, there is a tendency in lifespan developmental, social, and clinical psychology to base research on the assumption that the adult pair bond is a homologue to, or at least a direct outgrowth of, the earlier child–parent attachment–caregiving bond. In the field of attachment research specifically, Hazan and Shaver (1994) argue that there is a correspondence between adult pair bonds and individuals' earlier attachment styles: The history of interactions with one's primary attachment figures is hypothesized to produce a trait-like "style" for involvement in close relationships.

Bowlby (1956), like psychoanalysts before him, noted the important parallels between child–parent and adult pair bonds: "Indeed, this profound attachment to a particular person is both as strong as, and often as irrational as, falling in love, and the very similarity of these two processes suggest strongly that they may have something in common" (p. 63). He argued strongly, however, for shifting the emphasis from taking for granted the similarities to taking for granted the *differences* between the two behavioral systems. Attachment–caregiving relationships and adult pair bond relationships need to be distinguished from each other because the two systems are activated and terminated by different conditions, because they are directed toward different objects, and because they have different sensitive phases in their development (Bowlby, 1969/1982). At the same time, like so many adult behavior patterns and relationships, they do appear to share some components.

Bowlby (1969/1982) and Ainsworth (e.g., 1990) have proposed that at least three basic behavioral systems are involved in sexual pair bonds: the reproductive, attachment, and caregiving systems. We suspect that the sociability behavior system (or some component reflecting close friendship) is an equally important component in many pair bonds. In most pair bonds, each partner displays each of these components toward the other, sometimes simultaneously and at other times in a complementary manner. There may also be individual and cultural differences in the overall stable balance among these components. As an example specifically related to attachment research, in some couples the attachment and caregiving components may predictably be *symmetrical* and *reciprocal* (i.e., the partners share/alternate equally in taking each role). In others, there may be a relatively stable and *complementary* organization (cf. Hinde, 1979), with one partner usually seeking protection and care from the other, who is viewed as stronger and wiser. As Ainsworth (1990) suggests, the latter relationship may not be ideally secure, but it may be nonetheless enduring.

This complex bond does not develop directly out of the individual's earlier attachment behavioral system. If the underlying principles of Bowlby's theory of development presented earlier in this chapter are correct, it develops instead through a complex systemic process involving the coordination and organization of multiple behavioral systems, with changes in activating and terminating conditions, into a more complex, functional whole. We are convinced that unless these principles of development are applied, the study of adult pair bonds will remain as naive as the psychoanalytic and social learning theories of the infant–parent bond in opposition to which Bowlby initially developed his theory. In order to be successful, a theory of adult pair bonds will have to include attachment and caregiving components—but also, and just as importantly, sexual and friendship components. It will also require much descriptive research on the entire developmental pathway from the early attachment–caregiving bond, through peer affectional bonds, to the adult pair bond itself. It will require explicit recognition that characteristics of later-developing components along this pathway may exacerbate or attenuate the effects of earlier components. For example, a young child who has a very insecure goal-corrected attachment partnership with his or her parent may develop an intimate and smoothly functioning peer bond—a bond that may constitute a branch along the developmental pathway and provide increased likelihood of a secure adult pair bond. To understand this complex development fully, we need to know more than the fact that the secure peer bond is a predictor of a secure adult pair bond; we need as well to know *how* the secure peer bond component is structurally and developmentally *organized* within the larger pair bond.

Finally, Ainsworth (1990) proposes that attachment behavior remains especially important throughout the period of aging. It is usually considered malfunctional for the parent and young child to reverse roles, such that the child is the one providing care, support, and security. However, in the case of an aging or ill parent of an adult offspring, this role reversal may be both appropriate and functional. As the aging or illness begins to make the parent less able to protect himself or herself, the parent tends to seek an attachment–caregiving relationship with a younger, stronger adult. Traditionally this new attachment figure is the adult offspring, with the aging parent now functioning as the less autonomous member of the partnership. The changes over this period—including possible "uncoupling" of some of the systems that have become progressively coupled earlier in development; individual differences in attachment patterns among the aged; and the conflict the aged must experience between wanting to be protected and still wanting control over their own lives—will all be important research questions reflecting Bowlby's belief that attachment behavior functions "from the cradle to the grave."

CONCLUSION

Attachment theory began with Bowlby's (e.g., 1958) attempt to understand the psychopathological effects of maternal deprivation by studying the normative course of the ontogeny of this earliest relationship. Bowlby's hope was that if we better understood this normative course, we would be in an improved position to understand the effects of its disruption. We are convinced that Bowlby's attempt to integrate the study of individual differences with that of normative development is as important today as it was 40 years ago.

Whether the issue is the consolidation of the infant's attachment late in the first year of life (e.g., Ainsworth, 1967), identification of patterns of caregiving associated with secure versus insecure attachments during the preschool period (e.g., Britner, Marvin, & Pianta, 1997; Stevenson-Hinde & Shouldice, 1995), increased numbers of children in foster care (Rutter & O'Connor, Chapter 36, this volume), children's relationships with peers (e.g., Berlin & Cassidy, Chapter 30, this volume; Cassidy, Kirsh, Scolton, & Parke, 1996), or adult intimate relationships in this time of high divorce rates (Feeney, Chapter 17, this volume), a full understanding of the isolated issue will not be possible without placing the study in the context of the particular organization of the individual's attachment behavioral system at the particular period in development being studied. In fact, the most powerful design would be to *integrate* normative and differential approaches through the use of developmental-pathway models (see Bowlby, 1982; Waddington, 1957). These models should reflect the underlying theme of this chapter: that distinct pathways are taken by different strategies of attachment and intimate relationships in coincidently functioning to protect the individual and providing the opportunity to be as self-reliant as possible, at each point in development.

NOTE

1. In order to avoid confusion between the organization of observable behaviors, and the cognitive or emotional organization that governs the behaviors, we adopt Greenberg and Marvin's (1982) use of the terms "behavior system" to refer to the organization of observable behaviors, and "behavioral system" to refer to the entire system, consisting of both behaviors *and* their corresponding cognitive or emotional components.

REFERENCES

Ainsworth, M. D. S. (1967). *Infancy in Uganda: Infant care and the growth of love.* Baltimore: Johns Hopkins University Press.

Ainsworth, M. D. S. (1990). Some considerations regarding theory and assessment relevant to attachments beyond infancy. In M. T. Greenberg, D. Cicchetti, & E. M. Cummings (Eds.), *Attachment in the preschool years: Theory, research, and intervention* (pp. 463–488). Chicago: University of Chicago Press.

Ainsworth, M. D. S., Blehar, M. C., Waters, E., & Wall, S. (1978). *Patterns of attachment: A psychological study of the strange situation.* Hillsdale, NJ: Erlbaum.

Ashby, W. R. (1952). *Design for a brain.* New York: Wiley.

Ashby, W. R. (1956). *An introduction to cybernetics.* New York: Wiley.

Bandura, A. (1978). Social learning of aggression. *Journal of Communication, 28,* 12–29.

Bates, E., O'Connell, B., & Shore, C. (1987). Language and communication in infancy. In J. D. Osofsky (Ed.), *Handbook of infant development* (2nd ed., pp. 149–203). New York: Wiley.

Bateson, P. P. G. (1976). Rules and reciprocity in behavioral development. In P. P. G. Bateson & R. A. Hinde (Eds.), *Growing points in ethology* (pp. 401–421). Cambridge, England: Cambridge University Press.

Baumrind, D. (1980). New directions in socialization research. *American Psychologist, 35,* 639–652.

Bell, S. M. V. (1970). The development of the concept of the object as related to infant–mother attachment. *Child Development, 40,* 291–311.

Blurton-Jones, N. (1972). *Ethological studies of child behavior.* New York: Cambridge University Press.

Bowlby, J. (1956). The growth of the independent child. *Royal Society of Health Journal, 76,* 587–591.

Bowlby, J. (1958). The nature of the child's tie to his mother. *International Journal of Psycho-Analysis, 39,* 350–373.

Bowlby, J. (1969/1982). *Attachment and loss: Vol. 1. Attachment.* New York: Basic Books.

Bowlby, J. (1973). *Attachment and loss: Vol. 2. Separation.* New York: Basic Books.

Bowlby, J. (1979). *The making and breaking of affectional bonds.* London: Tavistock.

Bowlby, J. (1980). *Attachment and loss: Vol. 3. Loss.* New York: Basic Books.

Bretherton, I. (1993). From dialogue to internal working models: The co-construction of self in relationships. In C. A. Nelson (Ed.), *Minnesota Symposia on Child Psychology: Vol. 26. Memory and affect in development* (pp. 237–263). Hillsdale, NJ: Erlbaum.

Bretherton, I., & Ainsworth, M. D. S. (1974). Responses of 1-year-olds to a stranger in a Strange Situation. In M. Lewis & L. A. Rosenblum (Eds.), *The origins of fear* (pp. 131–164). New York: Wiley.

Britner, P. A., Marvin, R. S., & Pianta, R. C. (1997). *Maternal caregiving behavior and child attachment in the preschool Strange Situation.* Manuscript in preparation, University of Connecticut.

Bruner, J. (1981). The social context of language acquisition. *Language and Communication, 1,* 155–178.

Burlingham, D., & Freud, A. (1944). *Young children in wartime.* London: Allen & Unwin.

Cassidy, J., & Berlin, L. (1994). The insecure/ambivalent pattern of attachment: Theory and research. *Child Development, 65,* 971–991.

Cassidy, J., Kirsh, S., Scolton, K. L., & Parke, R. D. (1996). Attachment and representations of peers. *Developmental Psychology, 32,* 892–904.

Cassidy, J., & Marvin, R. S., with the MacArthur Working Group. (1992). *Attachment organization in preschool children: Procedures and coding manual.* Unpublished manuscript, University of Virginia.

Chisholm, K. M., Carter, M. C., Ames, E. W., & Morison, S. J. (1995). Attachment security and indiscriminately friendly behavior in children adopted from Romanian orphanages. *Development and Psychopathology, 3,* 397–411.

Cicchetti, D., Cummings, E. M., Greenberg, M. T., & Marvin, R. S. (1990). An organizational perspective on attachment beyond infancy. In M. T. Greenberg, D. Cicchetti, & E. M. Cummings (Eds.), *Attachment in the preschool years: Theory, research, and intervention* (pp. 3–49). Chicago: University of Chicago Press.

Dunn, J. (1994). Changing minds and changing relationships. In C. Lewis & P. Mitchell (Eds.), *Children's early understanding of mind: Origins and development* (pp. 297–310). Hillsdale, NJ: Erlbaum.

Erikson, E. H. (1950). *Childhood and society.* New York: Norton.

Fonagy, P., Steele, H., & Steele, M. (1991). Maternal representations of attachment during pregnancy predict the organization of infant–mother attachment at one year of age. *Child Development, 62,* 891–905.

Freedman, D. G., & Gorman, J. (1993). Attachment and the transmission of culture: An evolutionary perspective. *Journal of Social and Evolutionary Systems, 16,* 297–329.

Freud, A. (1965). *Normality and pathology in childhood: Assessments of development.* New York: International Universities Press.

George, C., & Solomon, J. (1996). Representations of relationships: Links between caregiving and attachment. *Infant Mental Health Journal, 17,* 198–216.

Goldberg, S., Marvin, R., & Sabbagh, V. (1996). *Child–parent attachment and indiscriminately friendly behavior toward strangers in Romanian orphans adopted into Canadian families.* Paper presented at the biennial meeting of the International Society for Infant Studies, Providence, RI.

Greenberg, M. T., & Marvin, R. S. (1982). Reactions of preschool children to an adult stranger: A behavioral systems approach. *Child Development, 53,* 481–490.

Greenberg, M. T., Marvin, R. S., & Mossler, D. G. (1977). The development of conditional reasoning skills. *Developmental Psychology, 13,* 527–528.

Haley, J. (1977). *Problem solving therapy.* San Francisco: Jossey-Bass.

Harlow, H. F., & Harlow, M. K. (1965). The affectional systems. In A. M. Schrier, H. F. Harlow, & F. Stollnitz (Eds.), *Behavior of nonhuman primates* (Vol. 2, pp. 287–334). New York: Academic Press.

Hazan, C., & Shaver, P. R. (1994). Deeper into attachment theory: Authors' response. *Psychological Inquiry, 5*(1), 68–79.

Heinicke, C., & Westheimer, I. (1966). *Brief separations.* New York: International Universities Press.

Hinde, R. A. (1976). On describing relationships. *Journal of Child Psychology and Psychiatry, 17,* 1–19.

Kagan, J. (1989). *Unstable ideas: Temperament, cognition, and self.* Cambridge, MA: Harvard University Press.

Kobak, R. (1994). Adult attachment: A personality or relationship construct? *Psychological Inquiry, 5*(1), 42–44.

Konner, M. (1976). Maternal care, infant behavior and development among the !Kung. In R. Lee & I. DeVore (Eds.), *Kalahari hunter gatherers: Studies of the !Kung San and their neighbors* (pp. 377–394). Cambridge, MA: Harvard University Press.

Lewis, C., & Mitchell, P. (Eds.). (1994). *Children's early understanding of the mind: Origins and development.* Hillsdale, NJ: Erlbaum.

Lewis, M., Sullivan, M. W., & Vasen, A. (1987). Making faces: Age and emotion differences in the posing of emotional expressions. *Developmental Psychology, 23,* 690–697.

Mahler, M., Pine, F., & Bergman, A. (1975). *The psychological birth of the human infant.* New York: Basic Books.

Main, M., & Cassidy, J. (1988). Categories of response to reunion with the parent at age six: Predictable from infant attachment classifications and stable over a one-month period. *Developmental Psychology, 24,* 415–426.

Main, M., & Goldwyn, R. (in press). Adult attachment scoring and classification system. In M. Main (Ed.), *A typology of human attachment organization assessed in discourse, drawings, and interviews.* New York: Cambridge University Press.

Main, M., Kaplan, N., & Cassidy, J. (1985). Security in infancy, childhood, and adulthood: A move to the level of representation. In I. Bretherton & E. Waters (Eds.), *Growing points of attachment theory and research. Monographs of the Society for Research in Child Development, 50*(1–2, Serial No. 209), 66–104.

Main, M., & Solomon, J. (1990). Procedures for identifying infants as disorganized/disoriented during the Ainsworth Strange Situation. In M. T. Greenberg, D. Cicchetti, & E. M. Cummings (Eds.), *Attachment in the preschool years: Theory, research, and intervention* (pp. 134–146). Chicago: University of Chicago Press.

Marvin, R. S. (1977). An ethological–cognitive model for the attenuation of mother–child attachment behavior. In T. M. Alloway, L. Krames, & P. Pliner (Eds.), *Advances in the study of communication and affect: Vol. 3. Attachment behavior* (pp. 25–60). New York: Plenum Press.

Marvin, R. S. (1997). Ethological and general systems perspectives on child–parent attachment during the toddler and preschool years. In N. Segal, G. Weisfeld, & C. Weisfeld (Eds.), *Genetic, ethological, and evolutionary perspectives on human development* (pp. 189–216). Washington, DC: American Psychological Association.

Marvin, R. S., & Britner, P. A. (1996). *Classification system for parental caregiving patterns in the preschool Strange Situation.* Unpublished manuscript, University of Virginia.

Marvin, R. S., & Greenberg, M. T. (1982). Preschoolers' changing conceptions of their mothers: A social-cognitive study of mother–child attachment. In D. Forbes & M. T. Greenberg (Eds.), *New directions for child development: No. 18. Children's planning strategies* (pp. 47–60). San Francisco: Jossey-Bass.

Marvin, R. S., Greenberg, M. T., & Mossler, D. G. (1976). The early development of conceptual perspective taking:

Distinguishing among multiple perspectives. *Child Development, 47,* 511–514.

Marvin, R. S., Van Devender, T. L., Iwanaga, M., LeVine, S., & LeVine, R. A. (1977). Infant–caregiver attachment among the Hausa of Nigeria. In H. M. McGurk (Ed.), *Ecological factors in human development* (pp. 247–260). Amsterdam: North-Holland.

McGraw, M. B. (1943). *The neuromuscular maturation of the human infant.* New York: Columbia University Press.

Moss, E., St-Laurent, D., & Parent, S. (in press). Disorganized attachment and developmental risks at school age. In J. Solomon & C. George (Eds.), *Attachment disorganization.* New York: Guilford Press.

Myers, B. J., Jarvis, P. A., & Creasey, G. L. (1987). Infants' behavior with their mothers and grandmothers. *Infant Behavior and Development, 10,* 245–259.

Nelson, K., & Gruendel, J. (1981). Generalized event representations: Basic building blocks of cognitive development. In M. E. Lamb & A. Brown (Eds.), *Advances in developmental psychology* (Vol. 1, pp. 131–158). Hillsdale, NJ: Erlbaum.

Piaget, J. (1952). *The origins of intelligence in children.* New York: International Universities Press.

Robertson, J. (1953). *A two-year-old goes to hospital* [Film]. London: Tavistock Child Development Research Unit.

Schaffer, H. R., & Emerson, P. E. (1964). The development of social attachments in infancy. *Monographs of the Society for Research in Child Development, 29*(3, Serial No. 94).

Slough, N. M., & Greenberg, M. T. (1990). Five-year-olds' representations of separation from parents: Responses for self and a hypothetical child. In I. Bretherton & M. Watson (Eds.), *New directions for child development: No. 48. Children's perspectives on the family* (pp. 67–84). San Francisco: Jossey-Bass.

Sroufe, L. A., & Waters, E. (1977). Attachment as an organizational construct. *Child Development, 48,* 1184–1199.

Stern, D. (1985). *The interpersonal world of the infant.* New York: Basic Books.

Stevenson-Hinde, J., & Shouldice, A. (1995). Maternal interactions and self-reports related to attachment classifications at 4.5 years. *Child Development, 66,* 583–596.

Stewart, R. B., & Marvin, R. S. (1984). Sibling relations: The role of conceptual perspective taking in the ontogeny of sibling caregiving. *Child Development, 55,* 1322–1332.

Suomi, S. J. (1995). Influence of attachment theory on ethological studies of biobehavioral development in non-human primates. In S. Goldberg, R. Muir, & J. Kerr (Eds.), *Attachment theory: Social, developmental, and clinical perspectives* (pp. 185–201). Hillsdale, NJ: Analytic Press.

Thelen, E., & Ulrich, B. D. (1991). Hidden skills: A dynamic systems analysis of treadmill stepping during the first year of life. *Monographs of the Society for Research in Child Development, 56*(1, Serial No. 223).

Waddington, C. H. (1957). *The strategy of the genes.* London: Allen & Unwin.

Wolff, P. H. (1969). The natural history of crying and other vocalizations in early infancy. In B. M. Foss (Ed.), *Determinants of infant behavior* (Vol. 4, pp. 81–109). New York: Barnes & Noble.

4

The Nature of Individual Differences in Infant–Caregiver Attachment

❖

NANCY S. WEINFIELD
L. ALAN SROUFE
BYRON EGELAND
ELIZABETH A. CARLSON

Developing an attachment relationship with a caregiver in infancy is a normative phenomenon. Almost every infant will develop an affective tie with a caregiver, and will endeavor to use that caregiver as a source of comfort and reassurance in the face of challenges or threats from the environment. The nature of the affective tie and the effectiveness with which the caregiver can be used as a source of comfort in the face of danger, however, differ across infant–caregiver dyads. These variations are individual differences in the quality of attachment relationships.

This chapter describes the nature of individual differences in infant–caregiver attachment as John Bowlby and Mary Ainsworth conceptualized it in their theory of attachment. It reviews how individual differences are described and assessed in infancy, as well as the meaning of attachment classification as an assessment of relationship history. This chapter also discusses theoretical predictions regarding the meaning of individual differences in early attachment relationships for subsequent relationships. Bowlby's theoretical perspective on continuity is discussed, and empirical support for these theoretical claims is briefly reviewed.

INDIVIDUAL DIFFERENCES IN ATTACHMENT: DEVELOPMENT AND DEFINITIONS

An initial distinction between the *presence* of an attachment relationship and the *quality* of an attachment relationship is important. According to Bowlby, a human infant will form an attachment to a caregiver as long as someone is there to interact with the infant and serve as an attachment figure. Forming attachments is strongly built into the human repertoire through evolution. Children will be unattached only if there is no stable interactive presence, such as is the case in certain kinds of institutional rearing. For all others, even those who are mistreated, attachment relationships are formed with caregivers. Individual differences in these attachment relationships are dependent on and reflective of differences in the history of care.

Individual differences in attachment relationships do not arise suddenly, nor are they carried solely in the traits of the infant or the caregiver (Ainsworth, Blehar, Waters, & Wall, 1978; Bowlby, 1969/1982; Sroufe & Waters, 1977). The patterns of interaction are built out of a history of bids and responses within the dyad, and these patterns of interaction, rather than individual behaviors, reveal the underlying character of the relationship.

Through repeated interactions with the same adults over time, infants begin to recognize their caregivers and to anticipate the behavior of primary caregivers. Bowlby and Ainsworth were the first to elaborate on these early relationships in terms of both survival behavior and psychological processes. They described the infant as being biologically predisposed to use the caregiver, usually the mother, as a "haven of safety" and as a "secure base" while exploring the environment (Ainsworth, 1967; Ainsworth et al., 1978; Bowlby, 1969/1982). So when the infant feels threatened, he or she will turn to the caregiver for protection and comfort. In fact, Bowlby and Ainsworth described a delicate balance in the infant between exploration and seeking proximity to the caregiver when exploration proves threatening. Individual differences are most easily seen in this attachment–exploration balance. From this theoretical perspective, assessments of attachment security in infancy must be related to such secure-base behavior.

When seeking comfort or reassurance, infants direct behaviors toward their caregivers such as approaching, crying, seeking contact, and seeking to maintain that contact. These behaviors are called "attachment behaviors" (Ainsworth et al., 1978; Bowlby, 1969/1982). Attachment behaviors do not yield sufficient information, however, if one studies only the number of behaviors expressed. All infants display attachment behaviors at some point, and the number of behaviors may vary with the degree of threat the infant perceives in the environment. In a dangerous environment, when protection is needed, it will be maladaptive for an infant to refrain from expressing attachment behaviors. In an environment that poses little danger and warrants exploration, it may be maladaptive for an infant to forgo exploration in favor of seeking out the caregiver. The study of attachment behaviors becomes most meaningful when one focuses on individual differences in the timing and effectiveness of their expression. Thus the issue at hand in studying individual differences in attachment relationships is not the quantity of attachment behaviors expressed, but rather the organization of attachment-related behavior in the relationship—the quality of the attachment relationship (Ainsworth, 1972; Sroufe & Waters, 1977).

Individual differences in quality of attachment

relationships have been broadly divided into two categories: "secure" attachment relationships and "anxious" or "insecure" attachment relationships (Ainsworth, 1972; Ainsworth et al., 1978; Bowlby, 1973). The term "secure" or the term "anxious" does not describe simply the manifest behaviors of the infant within the attachment relationship. Rather, the terms describe the infant's apparent perception of the availability of the caregiver if a need for comfort or protection should arise, and the organization of the infant's responses to the caregiver in light of those perceptions of availability.

Security of attachment does not mean that the infant never feels fear or apprehension (Bowlby, 1973). Fear and anxiety are normal human reactions. All infants will occasionally feel unsettled or fearful of something in the environment, and such reactions are adaptive because they prompt proximity to the protective caregiver. Security in the relationship with an attachment figure indicates that an infant is able to rely on that caregiver as an available source of comfort and protection if the need arises. Infants with secure attachment relationships may direct few attachment behaviors (such as crying or clinging) toward their caregivers when there are no threats in the environment. When threat-based feelings of apprehension arise, however, infants in secure relationships are able to direct attachment behaviors to their caregivers and take comfort in the reassurance offered by their caregivers. Secure relationships promote infants' exploration of the world and expand their mastery of the environment, because experience tells such infants that if the exploration proves unsettling, they can rely on their caregivers to be there and alleviate their fears. Infants with secure attachment relationships are confident in the sensitive and responsive availability of their caregivers, and consequently these infants are confident in their own interactions with the world.

This confidence is not instilled by the experience of infants who have anxious attachment relationships with their caregivers. Infants with anxious attachment relationships have not experienced consistent availability of and comfort from their caregivers when the environment has proven threatening. Bids for attention may have been met with indifference, with rebuffs, or with notable inconsistency (Ainsworth et al., 1978; Bowlby, 1973). The result of such histories is that these infants are anxious about the availability of their caregivers, fearing that the caregivers will be unresponsive or ineffectively responsive when needed. They may also be angry with their caregivers for this lack of responsiveness. Anger seems to be a normative reaction to inaccessibility of caregivers, similar to that which occurs in prolonged separation (Robertson & Robertson, 1971). Bowlby (1973) speculated that angry reactions may have evolved because they punish caregivers for unresponsiveness, and may be intended to discourage caregivers from further unresponsiveness.

A history of unresponsiveness or erratic responsiveness results in infants' being unable to direct attachment behaviors at caregivers when appropriate. When there is no apparent danger in the environment, some infants with anxious attachment relationships may still direct many attachment behaviors to their caregivers, reflecting a constant low-level anxiety about the availability of the caregivers. When there is a perceived threat from the environment, and anxiety is high, some infants may not be able to direct appropriate attachment behaviors at their caregivers, or may not be easily comforted by caregivers who have been unreliable in the past. Because anxiously attached infants are not free to explore the environment without worry, they cannot achieve the same confidence in themselves and mastery of their environments that securely attached infants can.

Anxious attachments are nonoptimal organizations of attachment behaviors because they compromise exploration in some circumstances. At the same time, patterns of anxious attachment may be viewed as adaptations, in that they are suitable responses to the unresponsiveness of the caregivers. Main and Hesse (1990), for example, argue that establishing a low threshold for threat can be described as "maximizing" expressions of attachment even in low-threat situations. This may assure that inconsistent caregivers will be available if genuine threat should occur. Alternatively, some infants can be described as "minimizing" expressions of attachment, even in conditions of mild threat. This may forestall alienating caregivers who are already rejecting, and it may leave open the possibility of responsiveness if a more serious threat should arise.

Within the theoretical tradition of Bowlby and Ainsworth, all infants are viewed as adapting their attachment behavioral systems to the caregiving environment at the same time as the environment adapts to them. In a proximal sense, both secure and anxious attachments can be considered adaptive: They promote proximity to caregivers, and consequently survival past the vulnerable period of infancy and to the age of reproductive maturity. In purely evolutionary terms, secure and anxious attachments are both distally adaptive as well, in that neither pattern should compromise reproductive success (Sroufe, 1988). In nonevolutionary terms, however, there are ways in which a history of anxious attachment may compromise an individual's subsequent development.

THEORETICAL PREDICTIONS REGARDING INDIVIDUAL DIFFERENCES IN ATTACHMENT

Bowlby (1969/1982, 1973) proposed two major hypotheses regarding individual differences in attachment. The first centered on antecedents of attachment relationships of varying quality. Bowlby defined security of attachment in terms of preferential desire for contact with the caregiver under conditions of threat, and secure-base behavior more generally. He viewed both as manifestations of a child's confidence in a caregiver's responsiveness. Through a history of responsive care, infants will evolve expectations (or, in Bowlby's terms, "internal working models") of their caregivers' likely responses to signs of distress or other signals of the desire for contact. The specific prediction, then, is that caregiver responsiveness early in infancy is related to individual differences in attachment security later in infancy. In the most simple terms, Bowlby postulated that what infants expect is what has happened before. Not all aspects of parental care are related to attachment security, and caregiver responsiveness is not related to all aspects of infant behavior. For example, infants may vary in terms of activity level, preferred modes of signaling, and various aspects of behavioral style, none of which should have a significant impact on attachment security.

Bowlby's second hypothesis concerned the likely consequences of individual differences in attachment security for the child's development, particularly personality development (Bowlby, 1973). Bowlby argued that because attachment relationships are internalized or represented, these early experiences and subsequent expectations get taken forward to serve later behavioral and emotional adaptation, even in totally new contexts and with different people. In particular, internal working models are a foundation not only for expectations concerning the self, but also for later relationships with caregivers and noncaregivers alike. Responsiveness by caregivers (and the ensuing confidence in that responsiveness) is more than a foundation for the developing parent–child relationship. The model of parent as responsive is inevitably associated with a complementary model of the self as effective, since the child is predictably effective at eliciting a parental response. By generalization, this pattern of responsiveness also leads to the idea that relationships may be a context in which needs are met. Thus there are implications for later efficacy, self-esteem, and involved social relationships.

This is not meant to imply that these early relationships alone are destiny. In Bowlby's (1973) view, adaptation always depends both on the prior history of adaptation *and* on current circumstances, with established patterns influencing selection, interpretation, and reactions to the environment, and with current experience capable of transforming adaptation and subsequent expectations, while not erasing the influence of history. Bowlby adapted Waddington's (1957) pathway model to argue both that change is always possible, and that change is at the same time constrained by prior adaptation.

These issues are elaborated in the sections to follow. Then we conclude with a discussion of current issues in the arena of individual differences in attachment, including when attachment-based differences are not expected.

DESCRIPTIONS AND ANTECEDENTS OF INDIVIDUAL DIFFERENCES IN ATTACHMENT SECURITY

Research on Bowlby's first hypothesis—namely, that individual differences in attachment arise from differential experiences and consequently differential expectations regarding the availability of caregivers—was pioneered by Ainsworth, who was the first to provide a formal description of individual differences in human infants' attachment security. Inspired by Bowlby's theory and her own ethological observations of caregiving practices and infant behavior in Uganda (Ainsworth, 1967), Ainsworth began by making hours of detailed observations of exploratory behavior, crying, and other attachment-related behaviors in the home for a small sample of infants. She also developed carefully crafted, behaviorally anchored rating scales for caregiver qualities: the Sensitivity to Signals, Cooperation–Interfer-

ence, Acceptance–Rejection, and Availability–Unavailability scales. Thus, prior to developing her procedure for assessing attachment security in the laboratory at the end of the first year, Ainsworth established anchors in attachment behavior in the home, as well as in assessments of caregiver sensitivity. This methodical pursuit of information to be used for validation was an essential first step in the development of her measure of attachment security. This step was particularly impressive, in light of the fact that few researchers devote the time and resources necessary to validate laboratory measures against the naturalistic occurrence of the behaviors they are intended to capture.

It is not possible to observe directly the conscious and unconscious processes that guide the infant's responses within the attachment relationship. And as mentioned previously, observing the number of attachment behaviors expressed in a given situation is not sufficient, because infants with anxious attachment relationships may not be making attachment-related overtures to their caregivers in an adaptive fashion. The key to assessing attachment rests in determining how an infant organizes attachment behaviors to balance the need for protection and comfort with the desire to explore the environment.

The strange situation (Ainsworth et al., 1978; Ainsworth & Wittig, 1969) was the method Ainsworth developed for assessing the infant–caregiver attachment relationship, and it has become the standard by which measures at later ages are judged. The strange situation is so named because it is intended to be a mildly to moderately stressful experience for an infant, akin to an experience in a doctor's office waiting room. It introduces several strange and therefore stressful elements to an infant—a laboratory context that is unfamiliar, an unfamiliar adult who interacts with the child, and two brief separations from the mother. The premise of the situation is that the multiple increasing stressors will activate the infant's attachment behavioral system, and that individual differences in the child's expectations about the availability of the caregiver will thus be revealed. The situation also reveals the infant's ability to balance exploration of a new environment with a need for reassurance from the caregiver (see Solomon & George, Chapter 14, this volume, for a detailed discussion of the strange situation).

Based on the pattern of interactive behavior across the session and especially the two reunions, each relationship is classified as "secure," "avoidant," or "resistant" (Ainsworth et al., 1978). An additional classification, "disorganized/disoriented," is now also used because some infants exhibit unusual behaviors that prevent them from being classified easily as displaying a single organization of attachment behavior, or that reflect striking episodes of disorientation (Main & Solomon, 1990). Such infants, like avoidant and resistant infants, are considered anxiously attached.

An infant classified as secure with his or her caregiver in the strange situation is able to use the caregiver as a secure base for exploration in the novel room. The infant may check back with the caregiver, but usually engages in exploring the toys. Upon separation the infant may be overtly distressed, and play may become impoverished. A secure infant may be friendly with the stranger, and may even be somewhat comforted by the overtures of the stranger during separation, but there is a clear preference for comfort by the caregiver. Upon reunion with the caregiver, a distressed secure infant will seek proximity or contact with the caregiver, will maintain contact as long as it is needed, and will be readily comforted by the proximity or contact. Eventually, most secure infants will return to play. Even when not distressed, a secure infant is quite responsive to the caregiver's return, greeting with a smile or vocalization and initiating interaction.

An infant classified as avoidant with his or her caregiver will usually engage with the toys in the presence of the caregiver. The infant is unlikely to show affective sharing (e.g., smiling or showing toys to the caregiver) before the first separation, although the infant may engage the caregiver for instrumental assistance (Waters, Wippman, & Sroufe, 1979). Upon separation the infant is unlikely to be distressed, although some distress when left alone is possible. The infant with an avoidant relationship tends to treat the stranger in much the same way as he or she does the caregiver, and in some cases the infant is actually more responsive with the stranger. Upon reunion with the caregiver, an avoidant infant shows signs of ignoring, looking or turning away, or moving past the caregiver rather than approaching. If picked up, an avoidant infant will make no effort to maintain the contact.

Infants classified as resistant with caregivers in the strange situation are conspicuously unable to use the caregivers as a secure base for exploration of the novel setting. These infants may seek proximity and contact with the caregivers even before separation occurs, and may be quite wary of the situation and the stranger. Upon separation infants classified as resistant are likely to be quite distressed, and are not easily calmed by the stranger. Upon reunion they are likely to want proximity or contact with their caregivers, but not to be calmed by the contact. Some resistant infants may display unusual passivity, continuing to cry but failing to seek contact actively. In most cases, however, the hallmark of this classification is seeking contact, then resisting contact angrily once it is achieved. Thus there is an obvious ambivalence in many of these relationships.

An infant who is classified as disorganized/disoriented in the strange situation (in addition to an alternate, best-fitting classification of secure, avoidant, or resistant) exhibits conflicted or disoriented behaviors that indicate an inability to maintain one coherent attachment strategy in the face of distress (Main & Solomon, 1990). Thus, an infant classified as disorganized/disoriented with the caregiver in the strange situation shows such contradictory or conflicted behaviors as behavioral stilling, stereotypies, or direct apprehension with regard to the parent.

Ainsworth et al. (1978) reported extensively on the home behaviors of their participants over the first year of the infants' lives leading up to the strange situation. Although the full sample size used for the development of the strange situation coding procedures was 106 dyads, the more intensive study of home behavior was undertaken only for one subsample of 23 dyads. In general, a small sample size reduces the likelihood of finding significant between-group differences. The fact that Ainsworth and her colleagues found group differences despite the small sample size attests to the strength of these differences. They found that infants who would later be classified as anxiously attached (both avoidant and resistant) with their mothers in the strange situation were more overtly angry and noncompliant at home and cried more at home than infants who would later be classified as secure. The mothers of infants who would later be classified as anxious with them were less sensitive in interactions, more interfering with the children's behavior, and less accessible to the children's bids than mothers of infants who would later be classified as secure. In addition, mothers of infants who would later be classified as avoidant were particularly striking in that they expressed an aversion to physical contact when their infants sought it, and expressed little emotion during interactions with them.

More recently, Waters and Deane (1985) introduced an observation-based Attachment *Q*-Sort that uses extended observations of the home behavior of children as indicators of attachment. This measure was designed for use either by the mother or by a trained observer, and the final result is not a separation into attachment classifications, but rather a continuous score for security. Items in the *Q*-set of the Attachment *Q*-Sort were chosen specifically to represent a series of home behaviors that should be relevant to attachment and that should discriminate between different organizations of attachment behavior. These behaviors include predominant mood, proximity and contact seeking, reactions to frightening stimuli, crying, communication skills and efficacy, and many other behaviors. An observer or the child's mother spends several hours observing the child's behavior at home. The reporter then sorts the *Q*-set cards to describe the child's behavior at home. This sort is compared to a criterion sort (developed through the input of many experts in the field of attachment) to determine security, resulting in a score along a security dimension. Vaughn and Waters (1990) found that infants who were secure with their mothers in the strange situation had significantly higher security scores on the Attachment *Q*-Sort when this was completed by observers, confirming the link between home behavior and strange situation classification.

Numerous others have replicated the core findings of a relation between caregiver insensitivity and later anxious attachment (Bates, Maslin, & Frankel, 1985; Grossmann, Grossmann, Spangler, Suess, & Unzer, 1985; Isabella, 1993; Kiser, Bates, Maslin, & Bayles, 1986; National Institute of Child Health and Human Development [NICHD] Early Child Care Research Network, 1997). In our own research, Egeland and Farber (1984) found that mothers of infants who would later be classified as secure were more sensitive and expressive during a feeding situation than mothers of avoidant or resistant infants. Mothers of avoidant infants were insensitive to their infants' timing cues and seemed to dislike close physical contact with their infants.

The magnitude of the relation between caregiver sensitivity and later attachment security is often not large, especially when compared to the findings in Ainsworth et al.'s (1978) original study, and there have been occasional nonreplications (e.g., Seifer, Schiller, Sameroff, Resnick, & Riordan, 1996). Some of the problems in replicating these findings may be found in the difficulty of devising a good measure of caregiver sensitivity, as well as in the different numbers of hours of home observation that form the basis for the different sensitivity measures. Despite the existence of some nonreplications, a meta-analysis based on 66 studies of varying quality did find a significant relation between sensitivity and attachment (DeWolff & van IJzendoorn, 1997). In addition, the recent multisite NICHD study of day care ($n = 1,153$), although finding little impact of day care on attachment, supported the significance of caregiver sensitivity in predicting individual differences in attachment (NICHD Early Child Care Research Network, 1997).

The finding that infant home behavior during the first year of life was related to later strange situation classification led to the suggestion that attachment classification could be a simple manifestation of temperamental characteristics of the infant, and not a product of the relationship (see Vaughn & Bost, Chapter 10, this volume). Direct comparisons of temperament and attachment in research, however, have suggested that there is not in fact a direct link between temperament and security of attachment (Belsky & Rovine, 1987; Crockenberg, 1981; Egeland & Farber, 1984; Gunnar, Mangelsdorf, Larson, & Hertsgaard, 1989; Seifer et al., 1996; Vaughn, Lefever, Seifer, & Barglow, 1989). Other research has demonstrated that what can be predicted by temperament are specific behaviors during the strange situation, particularly distress during separation from, but not during reunion with, the mother (Gunnar et al., 1989; Vaughn & Bost, Chapter 10, this volume; Vaughn et al., 1989). These findings bolster the supposition that the relationship between the mother and infant is not determined directly by infant temperament.

Other researchers have sought to explain the relation between temperament and attachment by looking at the interaction of maternal and infant characteristics. Although Crockenberg (1981) found no direct relation between infant temperament and attachment classification, she did find a significant interaction between maternal social support and infant temperament in predicting attachment classification. Those mothers with irritable infants (as assessed shortly after birth) and poor social support were more likely to have anxiously attached infants. When social support was high, infant irritability had no impact on attachment quality. Mangelsdorf, Gunnar, Kestenbaum, Lang, and Andreas (1990) looked at infant temperament and maternal personality in relation to attachment. Like previous researchers, they found no main effects of temperament or personality when predicting attachment; however, they did find a significant interaction. Infants who were highly prone to distress and had mothers who were rigid and traditional were more likely to be anxiously attached. In our own research project, Susman-Stillman, Kalkoske, Egeland, and Waldman (1996) found that maternal sensitivity during the first year of life predicted attachment security, that infant temperamental characteristics predicted type of insecurity, and that maternal sensitivity mediated the link between infant irritability and attachment security.

Thus, although some of the behaviors seen in the strange situation may be related to temperament, neither the patterning of the infant–caregiver relationship nor the confidence of the infant in the caregiver is determined by infant temperament (see Vaughn & Bost, Chapter 10, this volume, for a more extensive discussion of attachment and temperament).

PREDICTIVE MEANING OF INDIVIDUAL DIFFERENCES IN INFANT ATTACHMENT

Bowlby's second hypothesis concerns the developmental significance of individual differences in early attachment relationships. What are meaningful variations in infant–caregiver attachment? What features of development do they affect? And what are the processes by which this effect occurs? Bowlby and Ainsworth articulated their ideas regarding individual differences over the course of three decades. The theory and research described in this section draw from these precise, well-reasoned, and sophisticated ideas.

Bowlby described two types of variation in attachment: presence versus absence of an attachment relationship, and individual differences in organization of secure-base behavior across infant–caregiver dyads. Although absence of attachment is likely to affect survival, Bowlby did not predict that individual differences in attachment security have an influence on survival or reproductive success. It is sometimes argued (e.g., Belsky, Chapter 7, this volume) that the existence of the avoidant and resistant patterns in human infants means that these patterns must have evolved to ensure reproductive success in some circumstances. By definition, of course, humans have evolved to have these patterns in

the behavioral repertoire. It is not logically essential, however, that these patterns have specific reproductive advantage; not all behaviors characteristic of a species do. Consider, for example, distress responses in the face of parental death. When no conspecifics are available, distress reactions that alert predators and cannot elicit protection from a deceased caregiver are not helpful. But distress signals in response to separation from a living caregiver *are* functional, and nature did not build-in a more discriminative system (perhaps because infants whose caregivers die are so unlikely to survive). It is interesting, then, to note that the resistant and avoidant attachment patterns are quite reminiscent of the protest–despair–detachment sequences seen in the face of loss (Heinicke & Westheimer, 1966; Robertson & Robertson, 1971). These attachment patterns, seen with caregivers who are physically present, may be contextual distortions of patterns available to all infants. It is extremely unlikely that they represent separate streams of evolution.

Individual differences in attachment security, because of their impact on emotional regulation and exploration, were viewed as important for both personality development and psychopathology. Whereas evolutionary theory is sufficient for explaining the consequences of failures to attach, understanding the developmental implications of individual differences in attachment behavioral organization for those infants who do become attached required the wedding of evolutionary theory, psychoanalytic theory, and general developmental theory. Bowlby argued, as Freud had previously, that early attachment experiences are of special importance because of their implications for mastery, emotional regulation, and interpersonal closeness. Rejecting the notion of drive reduction, Bowlby expanded on Freud's original focus on the role of actual experience. Bowlby elaborated on the idea of an internal world of mental processes as central to the ongoing influence of early history (Sroufe, 1986). Human expectations, according to Bowlby, are based upon the quality and patterning of early care. From a history of responsive care and smooth dyadic emotional regulation come a sense of efficacy, a capacity for serviceable self-regulation, and positive expectations regarding interpersonal relationships. Within this developmental process, the individual is viewed as active—adapting, coping, and shaping his or her own experiences.

There are at least four possible explanations

for why early attachment relationships influence later development. These explanations are not mutually exclusive, and it is likely that each plays a part in the continuing influence of attachment. First, it is possible that the experiences within the early attachment relationship influence the developing brain, resulting in lasting influences at a neuronal level (Schore, 1994). This possibility, though compelling, is not a focus of the present discussion (see Cicchetti & Tucker, 1994). Second, as suggested by Isabella (1993), Cassidy (1994), and Sroufe (1979, 1996), the early attachment relationship may serve as a foundation for learning affect regulation. The caregiver's responses to the infant's distress are an external source of emotion regulation before the infant learns to self-regulate. Early attachment relationships, then, may affect a child both through the mother's actions and through the patterns of regulation internalized from the relationship. Individual differences in attachment may thus be carried forward in the form of differences in affect regulation. A third possible avenue for attachment to influence subsequent development is through behavioral regulation and behavioral synchrony. Through observing and interacting with an attachment figure, an infant learns what it is like to behave in a relationship (Elicker, Englund, & Sroufe, 1992; Gianino & Tronick, 1988; Pastor, 1981). Secure children develop abilities such as self-control and behavioral reciprocity, which result in more skilled interactions than those of anxious children. These interactional skills can then be applied to new settings and new relationships, resulting in continued differences that are strengthened across development. The fourth way in which individual differences in attachment influence later development is through representation. According to Bowlby (1969/1982), from the early attachment relationship the child begins to represent what to expect from the world and from other people, as well as how he or she can expect to be treated by others. These beliefs and expectations, or "internal working models," begin in the relationship with the caregiver as the infant begins to anticipate the behavior of the caregiver in response to the infant's signals. An infant who is treated in a consistently sensitive manner grows to see the world as good and responsive, and the self as deserving such consideration. An infant who is responded to harshly, erratically, or not at all grows to see the world as unpredictable and insensitive, and the self as not deserving better

treatment. These internal working models are then carried forward to new relationships and new experiences, guiding the child's expectations and behavior.

Bowlby proposed a very particular view of individual differences over time, based on an adaptation of Waddington's (1957) "developmental pathways" (analogous to branching tracks in a train yard; see Sroufe, 1997). In this view, early differences in attachment do not directly *cause* later differences in functioning; rather, they initiate pathways that are probabilistically related to certain later outcomes. Any outcome is always the joint product of earlier history *and* current circumstances. Thus changes in pattern of adaptation always remain possible. Prior adaptation, however, constrains subsequent development—both in the sense that the longer a pathway has been followed, the more difficult it is to achieve substantial change in direction, and in the sense that not all patterns of subsequent adaptation are equally likely. Not only may circumstances remain the same (thus supporting the original pattern of adaptation), but individuals interpret, select, and influence the people and circumstances surrounding them (Scarr & McCartney, 1983; Sroufe, Egeland, & Kreutzer, 1990). In Bowlby's terms (1973, 1980), the environment is engaged within the confines of "working models" of self, other, and relationships that have been previously formulated.

There are specific predictions regarding individual differences in early attachment quality and later outcomes. Particular patterns are expected to have particular correlates, in terms of both personality and psychopathology. Moreover, not all developmental outcomes, whether of good or poor quality, are viewed as related to attachment history. As we discuss later, many outcomes are viewed as independent of the attachment system.

Bowlby did not conceive of the internal working model as a model for all things, but rather as a model of expectations and beliefs about oneself, other people, and relationships. Consequently, attachment should be expected to exert its influence on a child's later adaptation primarily in the context of beliefs about the self and relationships, rather than indiscriminately predicting all things, both good and bad. The affective regulation and behavioral reciprocity learned in this early relationship should also be most influential in the realm of subsequent relationship and interpersonal issues.

Even within the parent–child relationship, not

all interactions are driven by the attachment–exploration balance. Minimally stressful free-play sessions, for example, may appear quite similar for secure and anxious dyads (Ainsworth, 1990). Other elements of parent–child relationships, and other elements of children's lives overall, predict individual differences in adaptation as well. It would be naive and incorrect to suggest that infant attachment is solely and directly responsible for adaptation during childhood and adolescence. Attachment does contribute, however, to explaining individual differences in the course of adaptation during childhood, particularly when combined with other assessments of later or concurrent functioning. The idea that early attachment experiences maintain an influence and work together with subsequent experiences to predict development is faithful to Bowlby's (1973, 1980) idea that adaptation arises from a combination of early experience, subsequent experience, and current circumstances.

Theory dictates that the influence of infant attachment relationships should be particularly apparent in some specific domains of adjustment and developmental challenges. These domains include dependency, self-reliance, and efficacy; anxiety, anger, and empathy; and interpersonal competence (Ainsworth, 1972; Ainsworth & Bell, 1974; Bowlby, 1969/1982, 1973, 1988; Sroufe, 1988; Sroufe & Fleeson, 1986, 1988). These issues should be specifically related to attachment because they are intricately connected to the affect regulation, behavioral reciprocity, and expectations and beliefs about self and other that arise from early attachment relationships. Theoretical predictions and empirical findings follow not only from individual differences in secure versus anxious attachment, but also in some cases from more specific individual differences between those with a history of avoidant attachment and those with a history of resistant attachment (and, in some cases, those with a history of disorganized/disoriented attachment).

In the following section, we review empirical predictions from individual differences in infant attachment to theoretically relevant dimensions of behavior in childhood and adolescence. The empirical findings are drawn from the findings of the Minnesota Parent–Child Project, from a Minnesota longitudinal study of middle-class families, and from other longitudinal studies in which attachment with the primary caregiver was assessed with the strange situation during infancy.

EMPIRICAL STUDIES OF INFANT ATTACHMENT AND LATER ADAPTATION

Dependency, Self-Reliance, and Efficacy

Infants whose caregivers are sensitive and responsive to cues learn that they can readily get their needs met and that they have an effect on the world. Such infants grow to believe that they can influence the world around them successfully. Infants whose caregivers are unresponsive or erratically responsive to cues learn that they are not able to influence the world to meet their needs. These infants do not acquire the confidence to function autonomously (Ainsworth & Bell, 1974; Sroufe, Fox, & Pancake, 1983). Such a prediction was a cornerstone of Bowlby's theory, as described in a chapter entitled "The Growth of Self-Reliance" in the second volume of his classic trilogy (Bowlby, 1973).

When the attachment construct was first introduced, it was necessary for researchers to differentiate between attachment and dependency (Ainsworth, 1969, 1972; Bowlby, 1969/1982; Sroufe et al., 1983). Because attachment behavior and signs of dependency are similar (e.g., crying, clinging, seeking proximity), attachment quality was misunderstood to be a measure of dependency (Gewirtz, 1972). Some secure infants were mistakenly thought to be dependent, whereas avoidant infants were thought to be precociously independent. In Bowlby's view, however, it is not possible for an infant to be either too dependent or truly independent. Rather, infants may be effectively or ineffectively dependent.

The key to the relation between infant attachment, dependency, and self-reliance has been articulated by Sroufe et al. (1983), who explained that infants who are effectively dependent will become effectively independent. Using sensitive caregivers effectively to meet needs will lead infants to believe, as children, that they can influence the world to meet their needs and achieve their goals. This confidence allows the children to function autonomously and with a belief that they will be successful in their efforts. Thus the ongoing influence of attachment is brought forward through affect regulation, behavioral reciprocity, and representation. Several studies have examined the relation between attachment and dependency, and between attachment and environmental mastery.

In the Minnesota Parent–Child Project, dependency has been studied in preschool, middle childhood, and adolescence. Sroufe et al. (1983) and Sroufe (1983) studied dependent behavior in preschool. "Dependency" was defined in terms of seeking attention and proximity to the teacher, extreme reliance on the teacher for help, and seeking teacher attention at the expense of peer relations, as well as other indices. Data were obtained through multiple methods, including observer data and teacher rankings and Q-sorts. Teachers and observers were all unaware of the children's attachment histories, and all indicated that children with anxious histories were more dependent on teachers than those with secure histories. Those with resistant or avoidant histories had more interactions with teachers, sat next to them more often during circle time, and were judged to be more dependent overall. Children with secure histories did seek teacher attention, but they tended to seek attention in positive ways, and not at the expense of peer relations. Dependency was later studied at age 10 in a summer camp context by Urban, Carlson, Egeland, and Sroufe (1991), who assessed dependency through camp counselor ratings and observer data on contact sought with adults. As in the preschool context, they found that children with anxious histories, both resistant and avoidant, were rated as more dependent. Children with secure histories sought less contact with adults at the camp overall.

Differences in dependency continued to be manifest at age 15, the latest age we have examined to date (Sroufe, Carlson, & Shulman, 1993). Both those adolescents with histories of resistant attachment *and* those with histories of avoidant attachment continued to show more dependency on adults than those with secure histories. This finding held even when variance attributable to contemporary parenting measures was taken into account.

Confidence, belief that one can succeed, and tolerance of frustration in goal seeking have also been studied in relation to attachment history. In our research, this took the form of studying "ego resilience," or a child's ability to respond flexibly to the changing requirements of a situation, particularly in the face of frustration. Sroufe (1983) reported that children with secure histories were rated as more ego-resilient than children with anxious attachment histories by their preschool teachers (all of whom were unaware of the children's attachment histories). Most striking was the fact that there was no overlap on ego resilience between the secure and avoidant groups.

These dimensions of personal efficacy were also explored in another longitudinal Minnesota study, a study of middle-class families. At the age of 2 years, children and their mothers were seen in a tool use situation. Matas, Arend, and Sroufe (1978) found that children with secure histories appeared more competent in the tool use tasks than those with anxious histories, showing more enthusiasm, compliance with maternal directives, and persistence. When these children were in preschool, Arend, Gove, and Sroufe (1979) found the same relation between attachment and ego resilience that would later be replicated in the Parent–Child Project: Children with secure histories were judged to be more ego-resilient than their anxious counterparts in a teacher Q-sort.

Other studies have explored these efficacy constructs as well. Frankel and Bates (1990), in a replication of Matas et al. (1978), found that toddlers with secure histories were more persistent in a tool use task than children with anxious histories. In an Israeli kibbutz study of attachment between young children and their *metaplot* (the primary caregivers in a kibbutz children's house), Oppenheim, Sagi, and Lamb (1988) found that children who had secure histories with their *metaplot* were described (by their *metaplot*, in Q-sorts) as more goal-directed and achievement-oriented than children with anxious/resistant histories. In a German study of interaction with a stranger, Lütkenhaus, Grossmann, and Grossmann (1985) looked at 3-year-old children's responses to playing a competitive game with an unfamiliar experimenter. When the children were made aware of the possibility that they were failing, those with secure histories increased their efforts, whereas those with anxious histories decreased their efforts. This finding was interpreted as indicating that the children with secure histories believed they had more control over their environments and could succeed by using their skills if they tried.

Overall, these findings on dependency, self-reliance, and efficacy suggest that early attachment history does contribute to a child's growing effectiveness in the world. Children with secure histories seem to believe that, as was true in infancy, they can get their needs met through their own efforts and bids. In contrast, children with anxious histories seem to believe that, as in their early attachment relationships, their efforts are often ineffective, and they must rely extensively on others who may or may not meet their needs.

Anxiety, Anger, and Empathy

Chronic unavailability of and rejection by the caregiver, which are characteristic of anxious attachment, take their toll on an infant over the course of development. Unlike a secure infant, who can count on the responsiveness of the caregiver, an anxiously attached infant must deal with the constant possibility of needing an unavailable caregiver, as well as dealing with the accumulating frustration and dysregulation inherent in being treated insensitively (Bowlby, 1973).

According to Bowlby (1973) and Stayton and Ainsworth (1973), anxiously attached infants must be constantly concerned about the whereabouts of their caregivers, because the caregivers cannot be relied upon to be accessible in times of need. Because of the potential unavailability of the caregivers, these infants live with the constant fear of being left vulnerable and alone. This fear of separation or abandonment continues beyond infancy, because the fear of being alone when comfort or protection is needed continues throughout childhood and adulthood (Bowlby, 1973). Thus the anxiety associated with this fear of separation lasts beyond infancy as well. Such anxiety should be particularly characteristic of individuals with resistant attachment history, because these relationships are characterized by an unpredictable, erratic responsiveness that can prove particularly anxiety-provoking and can give rise to a coping strategy centered on chronic vigilance (Bowlby, 1973; Cassidy & Berlin, 1994).

Another response to unavailable, rejecting caregiving is anger. Some anger is a natural response to the fear engendered by a separation from an attachment figure, because it serves to express displeasure over the separation and to prevent it from recurring (Bowlby, 1973). Chronic anger as a response to chronic unavailability, however, can be highly maladaptive. Such anger may manifest itself through angry or aggressive behavior toward the caregiver. When the expectation of being hurt, disappointed, and afraid is carried forward to new relationships, the anxious infant becomes an angry, aggressive child. Avoidant infants, who are chronically rejected, and disorganized/disoriented infants, who are conflicted in the face of frightened or frightening caregivers, are the most likely to show these angry, aggressive responses later (Ainsworth et al., 1978; Bowlby, 1973, 1980; Lyons-Ruth, Alpern, & Repacholi, 1993; Renken, Egeland, Marvinney, Mangelsdorf, & Sroufe, 1989).

Empathy is in many ways the complement or counterpoint to aggression. Whereas aggression often reflects an alienation from others, empathy reflects an amplified connectedness, and whereas aggression reflects a breakdown or warping of dyadic regulation, empathy reflects heightened affective coordination. In fact, in many ways aggression is dependent upon a lack of empathy or emotional identification with others.

Attachment theory makes a strong prediction with regard to the development of empathic capacity. Given that not only roles but basic properties of relating are learned within the attachment relationship (Sroufe & Fleeson, 1986), the responsiveness that underlies security is also predicted to give rise to empathy. Earlier we have argued, following Bowlby, that consistently providing for infants' needs does not condemn them to perpetual dependency, but in fact serves as the springboard for self-reliance because it instills a sense of efficacy concerning the environment. Similarly, being consistently nurtured and responded to empathically leads not to a spoiled, self-indulged child, but rather to an empathic child. All children learn about the patterning of relating and dyadic emotion regulation through experience. Those whose caregivers are responsive to their tender needs learn that when one person is needy, the other responds; when one person is emotionally overaroused, the other provides comfort or reassurance. All that these children require are the cognitive advances necessary to play the more mature role. Recapitulating understood patterns of dyadic interaction and regulation is a natural human tendency. For some, particularly those with secure attachment histories, this gives rise to the capacity for empathy. Empirical studies on anxiety, anger, and empathy and their relation to infant attachment are reviewed below.

Both in laboratory assessments and in school settings, those with histories of resistant attachment have been found to be less forceful and confident, more hesitant in the face of novelty, and generally more anxious than those with either secure histories or avoidant histories. For example, using Banta's (1970) curiosity box situation at age 4½, Nezworski (1983) found the resistant group to be more hesitant about engaging this novel object than either the avoidant or the secure group. Likewise, from problem behavior checklist data provided by elementary school teachers, children with resistant histories were identified as more passive and withdrawn than children with secure or avoidant histories

(Renken et al., 1989). Further data on anxiety are reported in the section on psychopathology.

Anger, and particularly aggression, as related to attachment history have been examined in several samples. In our research, angry and aggressive behavior was assessed in preschool and in elementary school. During preschool, teacher Q-sorts and detailed behavioral coding by observers indicated that more negative affect, anger, and aggression were expressed by children with anxious attachment histories than by those with secure histories. Q-sort data from elementary school teachers yielded the same results. Teachers and observers were always unaware of the children's histories (for more details, see Sroufe, 1983; Sroufe, Schork, Motti, Lawroski, & LaFreniere, 1984).

Another analysis revealed differences between those with avoidant and resistant histories. Troy and Sroufe (1987) observed children in the preschool setting who were assigned to play pairs by attachment history. Analysis of the interactions between the children in each pair revealed a systematic relation between victimization and attachment. Children with avoidant histories were significantly more likely than other children to victimize their play partners. Children with secure histories were never victimizers, nor were they ever victims, whereas children with resistant histories were likely to be victims if they were paired with children with avoidant histories. In a study examining peer interaction in preschool in relation to attachment history in a German sample, Suess, Grossmann, and Sroufe (1992) also found that children with avoidant attachment histories exhibited more hostility and scapegoating of other children than did children with secure histories.

In the middle-class Minnesota sample mentioned previously, differences as a function of attachment history were found on expressions of anger and aggression toward mothers at 2 years of age (Matas et al., 1978). Matas and her colleagues found that children with anxious histories were more likely than children with secure histories to display aggressive behavior toward their mothers during a tool use task. These findings were replicated by Frankel and Bates (1990), using the same procedure in an independent sample. Interestingly, no difference in aggression was found between the groups with avoidant and resistant histories when the aggression was directed at mothers rather than peers.

Empathy has also been studied in relation to attachment history. In our research, empathic behavior was assessed in two ways. First, ratings were composited from preschool teacher Q-sort descriptions on items pertaining to empathy (e.g., "shows concern for others," "is empathic"). Teachers were unaware of the early attachment histories of the children. The ratings significantly distinguished those with secure and anxious histories, often at the item level (see also Waters et al., 1979). In the written descriptions teachers provided of individual children, those described as "empathic" in each case had secure histories, whereas those described as "mean" were always those with avoidant histories. Second, empathic behavior was assessed from videotapes of preschool interaction (Kestenbaum, Farber, & Sroufe, 1989; Sroufe, 1983). Tapes made of freeplay interactions were examined for instances in which a child in the frame was distressed, and then any children in the vicinity of the distressed child were rated for empathic responses. Results indicated that children with secure histories were more empathic than children with avoidant histories. Children with resistant histories did not differ significantly from either of the other attachment groups on these measures, although they did seem to have trouble maintaining a boundary between someone else's distress and their own; that is, they became distressed in response to witnessing distress in another. This is consistent with the idea that differences in attachment will be reflected in differences in affect regulation.

Overall, attachment history does seem to contribute to the prediction of anxiety, anger, and empathy during childhood. Children with resistant attachment histories seem to be more likely than children with other histories to have problems with anxiety, perhaps in response to the constant vigilance they have developed in their early attachment relationships. Children with avoidant or disorganized/disoriented histories are most likely to show hostile, aggressive behavior, both with parents and with peers, perhaps as a response to chronic rejection and insensitivity from their caregivers. In contrast, children with secure histories seem to have acquired a foundation for empathy from their early relationships; they take to new relationships the ability to be sensitive to another's emotional cues, as well as a pattern of dyadic affect regulation in which the one who is not distressed helps to regulate the other.

Social Competence

Social competence is clearly an important task of development. According to Waters and Sroufe

(1983), competence in general is defined by two capacities: (1) being able to make use of the environment, and (2) being able to make use of personal resources in order to achieve a good developmental outcome. Navigating the world of social relationships is especially important.

One way in which attachment relationships influence later social competence is by providing a foundation for a child's expectations about and approach to other relationships (Sroufe & Fleeson, 1986, 1988). Secure infants, as they develop, bring forward with them expectations that social partners will be responsive to them and that they are worthy of such positive responses. Anxious infants, as they develop, bring forward expectations that they will be treated inconsistently or rejected outright by social partners, and that they are not worthy of better treatment (Bowlby, 1969/1982).

Another way in which the attachment relationship influences social competence is through teaching the infant about behavioral synchrony and communication (Ainsworth & Bell, 1974; Sroufe, Egeland, & Carlson, in press). The sensitive, responsive behavior of the caregiver in a secure dyad teaches the secure infant that communication is contingent upon each partner's cues and responses. The insensitive, uncoordinated interactions of an anxious dyad teach the anxious infant that communication is not a responsive interaction, but a series of poorly coordinated bids and responses. All infants carry with them the expectations of how they should respond to social partners, and how social partners are likely to respond to them.

The data on social competence illustrate particularly well the continuity between early attachment differences and later functioning, despite changes in settings and constructs assessed. Early studies in our laboratory revealed differences in orientation toward peers as early as the toddler period (Pastor, 1981). With entry to preschool, however, the adaptive challenge expands. Children must not only engage in more extensive give-and-take with particular partners, but they must also begin to function with some proficiency in a group. When teacher ratings were focused on such capacities, children with secure histories were found to be dramatically more competent (Sroufe, 1983).

Greater complexity is confronted in middle childhood. A child not only must interact with others, but must sustain personal relationships over time (i.e., forge loyal friendships), must find a place in the more organized peer group, and

must coordinate friendships with group functioning. Again, global ratings by school teachers have confirmed the greater interpersonal competence of those with secure histories. More detailed study of 47 children revealed differences with regard to each of the age-related competence issues. Those with secure histories, compared to those with anxious histories, more often formed friendships at a summer camp (and more often with those who also had been secure), as revealed by reciprocated sociometric choices, counselor nominations, and direct observations of frequency of interaction (Elicker et al., 1992). Those with secure histories were also more accepted by the group and adhered more to group norms, such as those regarding maintenance of gender boundaries, than those with anxious histories (Sroufe, Bennett, Englund, Urban, & Shulman, 1993). Finally, those with secure histories were better able to coordinate these tasks than those with anxious histories, as witnessed by the ease of incorporating others into their activities while still maintaining a reciprocated focus with their partners (Shulman, Elicker, & Sroufe, 1994).

In adolescence, those with secure histories were effective in the above-described ways; they were also rated by camp counselors as more competent in general, and more effective in the mixed-gender crowd in particular (Sroufe, Bennett, et al., 1993; Weinfield, Ogawa, & Sroufe, 1997). In addition, ratings in group problem-solving situations revealed greater leadership abilities of those with secure histories, who were also significantly more often elected spokespersons for their groups (Englund, Levy, & Hyson, 1997). In an interview study of the total sample, the friendships of girls with secure histories were judged to be more intimate (Ostoja, 1996). Differences for boys were not significant, perhaps due to the interview format with this lower-socioeconomic-status sample. Also, again at age 16 years, competence rankings by high school teachers using the total sample favored those with secure histories (Sroufe et al., in press).

In these studies, it was also the case that social competence assessments at each age were predicted by earlier assessments of competence and also were predictive of competence at later ages. Attachment history, along with earlier social competence, did predict later social competence better than attachment alone, as developmental theory derived from Bowlby would predict. But it was also the case that attachment history accounted for additional variance in the later outcomes, even after earlier social competence was taken into account (Sroufe et al., in press). We return to this point later. Overall, the social competence data from our study and those of others (see Thompson, Chapter 13, this volume) are strongly supportive of Bowlby's theory.

INFANT ATTACHMENT AND PSYCHOPATHOLOGY

In the conceptualization presented here, adapted from Bowlby, individual differences in infant attachment quality are not in themselves viewed as pathological or nonpathological. In the pathways perspective, the hypothesis is that patterns of anxious attachment represent initiations of pathways that, if pursued, will increase the likelihood of pathological conditions. Thus, although anxious attachment is considered a risk factor for pathology, not all, or even most, anxiously attached infants will develop psychopathology. Psychopathology, like social competence, is a developmental construction involving a myriad of influences interacting over time (Sroufe, 1997). Similarly, secure attachment is not a guarantee of mental health, but rather is viewed as a protective factor. Research has demonstrated that children with secure histories are more resistant to stress (Pianta, Egeland, & Sroufe, 1990) and more likely to rebound toward adequate functioning following a period of troubled behavior (Sroufe et al., 1990). Thus resilience, too, is viewed as a developmental construction within this framework. Children who are resilient in the face of stress, or recover following struggle, have been found either to have early supportive care or increased support during the time of recovery; resilience is a process rather than a trait (Egeland, Carlson, & Sroufe, 1993). Secure attachment appears to be part of this process. There is minimal evidence that some children simply are inherently resilient (Sroufe, 1997).

There are numerous reasons why anxious attachment histories may put children at risk for psychopathology. The anxiety and low frustration tolerance of some individuals with resistant histories, and the alienation, lack of empathy, and hostile anger of those with avoidant histories, may make the former vulnerable to anxiety disorders and the latter vulnerable to conduct problems and certain personality disorders. Both may be vulnerable to depression, but for different reasons (passivity and helplessness on the one hand,

alienation and aloneness on the other). Both struggle with social relationships, which may exacerbate developmental problems (e.g., through mistreatment by others or through association with deviant peer groups) and may limit social support, thus reducing an important buffer for stress. Those with histories of disorganized attachment, characterized by a failure to maintain a coherent attachment strategy and postures resembling trance-like states (Main & Hesse, 1990), may be at risk for diverse forms of pathology and in particular, dissociation (Main & Morgan, 1996).

At present, there are limited data with regard to these issues. Still, the data from our research are promising. From individual interviews with the Schedule for Affective Disorders and Schizophrenia for Adolescents (administered at age $17\frac{1}{2}$), we first created an overall index of psychopathology based on the number and severity of disorders manifested. The combination of avoidant and disorganized attachment histories across our 12- to 18-month assessments accounted for more than 16% of the variance in this outcome—a highly significant result, and particularly impressive over this length of time and given the difficulties of measuring these constructs. It was also the case, consistent with the developmental-construction view, that later assessments (including other aspects of parenting) added to the predictability of pathology, ultimately accounting for more than 30% of the variance. Attachment history remained significant after other variables were accounted for, and early measures based on competing hypotheses, such as infant temperament, did not predict outcome significantly (Carlson, 1998).

To turn to more specific predictions, a history of resistant attachment was found to be related specifically and uniquely to anxiety disorders (Warren, Huston, Egeland, & Sroufe, 1997). Resistant attachment history did not predict externalizing disorders, and other forms of anxious attachment did not predict anxiety disorders. Some measures of infant "neurological status" (e.g., "slow to habituate" on the Brazelton Neonatal Behavioral Assessment Scale) also predicted anxiety disorders, although not as powerfully as resistant attachment, and resistant attachment remained significant after differences on the Brazelton measure were taken into account.

Predicting anxiety-related symptoms in an independent sample was also one focus of a study by Lewis, Feiring, McGuffog, and Jaskir (1984).

In a longitudinal study extending from infancy to age 6, they examined the connection between infants' attachment history and later maternal reports of the children's psychopathological symptoms. They found that boys with resistant histories were more likely than boys with secure histories to have somatic complaints at age 6, and that boys with anxious histories (both avoidant and resistant) were more likely than boys with secure histories to be socially withdrawn.

As part of our research (Renken et al., 1989), conduct problems in elementary school were assessed through ratings on the Child Behavior Checklist (Achenbach, 1978) by the children's teachers in first through third grades. Results indicated that boys with avoidant attachment histories were rated as more aggressive by teachers than boys with secure or resistant histories.

Finally, disorganized attachment was significantly related to dissociative symptoms, based on the Child Behavior Checklist at age 16 and the Putnam Dissociative Experience Scales at age 19. Dissociation was, of course, also predicted by a history of maltreatment and trauma (Carlson, 1998; Ogawa, Sroufe, Weinfield, Carlson, & Egeland, 1997), but the relation between disorganized attachment and dissociation remained after childhood trauma was partialed out (Ogawa, Egeland, & Carlson, 1998).

A DEVELOPMENTAL PERSPECTIVE ON INDIVIDUAL DIFFERENCES IN ATTACHMENT: BEHAVIOR AS THE JOINT PRODUCT OF PRIOR ADAPTATION AND CURRENT CIRCUMSTANCES

Bowlby's theory led to a particular model of individual differences in development, the developmental-pathways model (Sroufe, 1997). In this model, individual differences in infant attachment are viewed neither as linear traits inexorably manifested over time, nor as infinitely elastic and easily altered by each new experience. Rather, individual differences are viewed in terms of distinctive developmental trajectories that, though requiring support for their maintenance and remaining open to modification, nonetheless embody a "homeorhetic" tendency; that is, a direction once set it itself an influence on developmental course. In other words, following a particular developmental pathway constrains the probable degree and nature of change,

resulting in change that is lawful rather than unpredictable.

Stability of the surrounding environment is certainly a partial explanation for the stability of individual differences. There is, however, a transaction between individual history and environment. One reason why change away from maladaptive behavioral patterns is difficult is that the environment itself is influenced by the individual; it does not simply wash over the person as an independent force. Individuals select, elicit, and interpret particular reactions from the environment that are consonant with their experience-based history of adaptation (Sroufe, 1983). Patterns of maladaption *are* maladaptive in part because they lead to environmental experiences that perpetuate them. Take, for example, the case of avoidant attachment. If such children encounter responsive peers and teachers, countering the rejection they have experienced previously, in time one would expect changes in their working models of self and relationships. Such environmental inputs become less likely, however, because children with these histories are more likely to isolate themselves (Sroufe, 1983), to interpret the ambiguous or even supportive efforts of others as hostile (Suess et al., 1992), and to be rejected by both peers and teachers. In our research, for example, the children with avoidant histories were the only children in the nursery school who made teachers angry, perhaps because of their cool defiance or aggression toward vulnerable children (Sroufe & Fleeson, 1988; Troy & Sroufe, 1987). It is because children have a role in creating their own later experiences that describing individual history and stability of the environment as completely separate influences is unduly simplistic.

The patterns of adaptation reflected in early attachment patterns are, of course, subject to change. The pathways model implies two things about change: (1) The earlier a change is seen in circumstances (the shorter the time a pathway has been pursued), the more readily change may be accomplished; and (2) the more sustained the forces of change, the more permanent the change will be. Attachment classification itself has been shown to change between 12 and 18 months with changes in caregiver life stress (Egeland & Farber, 1984; Vaughn, Egeland, Sroufe, & Waters, 1979). Beyond infancy, the later functioning of children who were securely (or anxiously) attached as infants is sometimes worse (or better) than would have been predicted from attachment alone. Such change is lawful, with the most potent factors identified thus far being changes in caregiver life stress, social support, and depression (Erickson, Sroufe, & Egeland, 1985; Pianta et al., 1990).

Current patterns of care and other environmental circumstances are clearly related to current adaptation, but this does not erase the influence of prior history. Early attachment history has been shown to add to the prediction of functioning even after the influence of contemporary experiences has been taken into account. For example, in our research we have shown that the peer competence and psychopathology measures obtained in adolescence are well predicted by assessments of family functioning at age 13 years. Nonetheless, early history of care and adaptation still adds predictive power (Englund et al., 1997). Even in the face of changes in adaptation, early experience still contributes to prediction of later behavior (Sroufe et al., 1990).

ON FINDING AND NOT FINDING DEMONSTRABLY MEANINGFUL PREDICTIONS FROM ATTACHMENT

Researchers do not always find the degree of stability and predictability with regard to individual differences in attachment that we have reported here (primarily from our own research). Our findings with regard to attachment are often modest as well. There is some inconsistency in the literature (see Thompson, Chapter 13, this volume), with some findings being small or nonsignificant, and others being quite powerful. There are many possible reasons for these varied results.

One issue that warrants consideration is measurement. Constructs such as secure and anxious attachment and subsequent behavioral outcomes are extraordinarily difficult to assess. Salient features of socioemotional development are often difficult to capture in research. In studying such issues, investigators face not only the complexity of the constructs themselves, but also their changing manifestations across development.

Adequacy of measurement is a basic requirement for research of any type. With regard to early attachment, the only laboratory measure that is currently validated against secure-base behavior at home is Ainsworth's strange situation coding scheme, as used for infants between 12 and 20 months old. Beyond 20 months of age, the existing observational paradigm and coding scheme need to be modified or changed entirely to ac-

count for developmental changes in the child and relationship (Ainsworth et al., 1978; Marvin, 1972). Other laboratory procedures for assessing early attachment, though perhaps promising, have yet to be validated against home behavior (see Solomon & George, Chapter 14, this volume). Thus research using laboratory measures other than the strange situation to assess attachment relationships may be introducing as-yet-unidentified measurement error into analyses.

Single assessments of particular constructs can also introduce some unanticipated measurement error into analyses. In our own research, we dealt with this issue by using multiple measurements at different times, as well as multiple reporters. We assessed attachment security twice, at 12 and 18 months, and often pooled these assessments for a more robust indicator of attachment. In order to reduce measurement error further, at both ages each case was coded independently by two raters who conferred about disagreements. All raters were highly experienced and had established reliability with Ainsworth (there are now standard reliability cases for this purpose). We also pooled outcome assessments to establish more robust variables. Although we found that individual differences in attachment did relate to teacher appraisals of social competence or behavior problems for our total sample of 175 participants, relations based on the report of one teacher for each participant (from the more than 100 different schools attended by our participants) were significant but very small. Combining the reports of multiple teachers across years increased effect sizes. Pooling the reports of four independent counselors in our summer camps served a similar purpose, yielding dramatically more impressive findings.

Reports of null results often lead to questions regarding the psychometric properties of the measures used. If measurement issues can be ruled out, null results or counterintuitive results can be informative. A useful example comes from the work of the Grossmanns concerning the unusually high rate of avoidant attachment in their original Bielefeldt sample (Grossmann et al., 1985). Avoidant attachment in this sample was demonstrated to be related to caregiver sensitivity at 6 months and to other external correlates of avoidant attachment that had been established in previous samples, thus reducing the likelihood that the results could be attributed to measurement error. Further assessments showed this high rate of avoidant attachment to be a cohort effect, reflecting difficult societal circumstances at the time that may have influenced caregiving environments. This seemingly counterintuitive high rate of avoidant attachment in fact represented a coherent and informative consequence of a characteristic of the sample. Such research holds an important place in the study of attachment, because it allows us to understand more about the processes that influence individual differences.

Beyond these measurement concerns, conceptual problems are often at issue. Not only are many aspects of early care outside of the attachment domain (e.g., the socialization of impulse control; Sroufe, 1997), but variations in quality of care, even broadly conceived, are not responsible for all aspects of development and behavior. For example, one early inconsistency in the literature concerned details of the relation between attachment security and the age of mirror self-recognition (Cicchetti, 1986; Lewis, Brooks-Gunn, & Jaskir, 1985). In our own research, we found no relation between attachment security and self-recognition (Sroufe, 1988). Such inconsistencies should not diminish the value of Bowlby and Ainsworth's elaboration of attachment theory, however, because nothing in the theory would lead to a strong prediction regarding a variable that is so heavily influenced by cognitive maturation. To the extent that such relations are found in research, they are most likely indirect, and are not validations of attachment theory per se. We have recently reported an impressive link between infant attachment and math achievement at age 16 years (Teo, Carlson, Mathieu, Egeland, & Sroufe, 1996). Surely this relation did not come about because attachment security has a direct influence on the brain's ability to process math problems. More likely, math achievement requires regular attendance at school and perhaps specific support at home. Those adolescents with secure histories, both because their parents remain more involved and for a variety of other reasons, attend school more regularly. Relations between attachment history and reading achievement in high school are less strong, probably because reading proficiency is established early. Although this finding is interesting, it cannot be taken as a confirmation of attachment theory.

Attachment theory is concerned with social behavior and emerging expectations of self, others, and relationships. The strong theoretical predictions relate to feelings of self-worth, expectations regarding others, and capacities for close relationships. One could argue that these areas of

personality and interpersonal functioning may influence diverse aspects of life, but the core predictions of the theory are clear.

Even within the domain of psychopathology, it is not reasonable to expect individual differences in attachment to be equally predictive of all problems. In our research, we deliberately singled out anxiety problems, conduct problems, and dissociation as prototypic resistant, avoidant, and disorganized outcomes, respectively. Anxiety and alienation (along with impoverished empathic capacity) are clear derivatives of the patterns of care associated with resistance and avoidance, respectively, and the disorganization and disorientation inherent in the failure to maintain an attachment orientation should have consequences for self-integration. Other kinds of problems should not be expected to be closely related to attachment history. For example, we have demonstrated that attention-deficit/hyperactivity disorder is more consistently related to other aspects of parenting than to attachment history; it is predictably related to early patterns of overstimulation and parent–child boundary violations (Carlson, Jacobvitz, & Sroufe, 1995). A full understanding of development and developmental problems requires much more than a knowledge of attachment history.

A final reason for varying results among studies might be the particular samples studied. Participants in the Minnesota Parent–Child Project were at risk because of poverty. At-risk samples tend to have higher rates of maladaptation in general and psychopathology in particular; indeed, this was our rationale for studying this population. Certainly the increased range of outcomes might have strengthened the relation between anxious attachment and pathology, particularly as compared to smaller middle-class samples with a more restricted range of outcomes. Middle-class samples have some advantages in that they include more stable attachments and much stronger relations with certain outcomes, in part because of more stable life circumstances. Waters, Merrick, Treboux, Crowell, and Albersheim (1998) found dramatic continuity between infant attachment classification and Adult Attachment Interview classification in a young adult middle-class sample. In our sample, a nonsignificant relation was found between infant attachment classification and Adult Attachment Interview classification at age 19 (Weinfield, Sroufe, & Egeland, 1998). We believe that the difference in the samples is at the heart of the difference in findings. In both samples, negative attachment-related life experiences were associated with instability of attachment classifications. The middle-class sample allows us to see that attachment can be stable over a long period of time; the higher rate of discontinuity (and the higher rate of negative life events) in our sample, however, allows for a more in-depth examination of types of experiences related to stability and change. Both middle-class samples and samples that are more at risk for developmental difficulties are needed in continuing research.

CONCLUSION

In general, the meaning of individual differences in attachment security, as conceptualized by Bowlby and Ainsworth, has been well substantiated by research. At times, of course, well-conceptualized studies by rigorous researchers have failed to obtain predictive relations. Development is extraordinarily complex, and longitudinal research is very difficult to carry out. Despite these challenges, well-conceived studies have repeatedly confirmed core propositions of this individual-differences theory.

In this chapter we have described Bowlby's ideas about attachment security with regard to the normative function of attachment relationships, antecedents and qualities of individual differences in attachment, and consequences of individual differences in attachment for personality development. Bowlby viewed attachment as tied to evolutionary theory. He did not view individual differences in attachment quality as linked directly to eventual reproductive success, although they may well be tied to qualities of adult love and qualities of later parenting behavior. Bowlby focused on attachment because of its evolutionary value in the survival of the human infant, and because of its central role in subsequent human adaptation and development. The normative stages of attachment formation he proposed (see Marvin & Britner, Chapter 3, this volume) inspired Ainsworth's assessment procedure. The similarity of resistance and avoidance to the patterns of protest, anger, and detachment that are normal responses in the face of loss of a caregiver led Ainsworth to focus on these behaviors in ongoing infant–caregiver relationships. The advent of the strange situation procedure has spawned 20 years of research on the meaning and consequences of individual differences in infant attachment for development.

The nature of modern society (thankfully) should not allow for further examination of the place of the attachment behavioral system in the survival of human infants to reproductive maturity. Nor will it allow for systematic examination of suppositions that avoidant and resistant patterns represent separate, evolved strategies because of their reproductive advantages in certain past environments (see Belsky, Chapter 7, this volume). Bowlby's theories about the implications of individual differences in attachment for personality development, however, remain not only testable but also critically important to our understanding of the role of early experience in socioemotional development. These ideas have guided much research, as the contents of this volume demonstrate, and will no doubt continue to contribute to our understanding of development.

ACKNOWLEDGMENT

Work on this chapter was supported in part by a grant from the National Institute of Mental Health (No. MH40864-08).

REFERENCES

Achenbach, T. (1978). The Child Behavior Profile: I. Boys aged 6–11. *Journal of Consulting and Clinical Psychology, 46,* 478–488.
Ainsworth, M. D. S. (1967). *Infancy in Uganda.* Baltimore: Johns Hopkins University Press.
Ainsworth, M. D. S. (1969). Object relations, dependency, and attachment: A theoretical review of the infant–mother relationship. *Child Development, 40,* 969–1025.
Ainsworth, M. D. S. (1972). Attachment and dependency: A comparison. In J. L. Gewirtz (Ed.), *Attachment and dependency* (pp. 97–137). Washington, DC: V. H. Winston.
Ainsworth, M. D. S. (1990). Epilogue: Some considerations regarding theory and assessment relevant to attachments beyond infancy. In M. T. Greenberg, D. Cicchetti, & E. M. Cummings (Eds.), *Attachment in the preschool years* (pp. 463–488). Chicago: University of Chicago Press.
Ainsworth, M. D. S., & Bell, S. M. (1974). Mother–infant interaction and the development of competence. In K. Connolly & J. Bruner (Eds.), *The growth of competence* (pp. 97–118). New York: Academic Press.
Ainsworth, M. D. S., Blehar, M., Waters, E., & Wall, S. (1978). *Patterns of attachment: A psychological study of the strange situation.* Hillsdale, NJ: Erlbaum.
Ainsworth, M. D. S., & Wittig, B. A. (1969). Attachment and exploratory behavior in one-year-olds in a Strange Situation. In B. M. Foss (Ed.), *Determinants of infant behaviour* (Vol. 4, pp. 111–136). London: Methuen.
Arend, R., Gove, F., & Sroufe, L. A. (1979). Continuity of individual adaptation from infancy to kindergarten: A predictive study of ego-resiliency and curiosity in preschoolers. *Child Development, 50,* 950–959.
Banta, T. J. (1970). Tests for the evaluation of early child-

hood education: The Cincinnati Autonomy Test Battery (CATB). In J. Hellmuth (Ed.), *Cognitive studies* (pp. 424–490). New York: Brunner/Mazel.

Bates, J., Maslin, C., & Frankel, K. (1985). Attachment security, mother–child interactions, and temperament as predictors of behavior problem ratings at age three years. In I. Bretherton & E. Waters (Eds.), Growing points in attachment theory and research. *Monographs of the Society for Research in Child Development, 50*(1–2, Serial No. 209), 167–193.

Belsky, J., & Rovine, M. (1987). Temperament and attachment security in the Strange Situation: An empirical rapprochement. *Child Development, 58,* 787–795.

Bowlby, J. (1969/1982). *Attachment and loss: Vol. 1. Attachment.* New York: Basic Books.

Bowlby, J. (1973). *Attachment and loss: Vol. 2. Separation.* New York: Basic Books.

Bowlby, J. (1980). *Attachment and loss: Vol. 3. Loss.* New York: Basic Books.

Bowlby, J. (1988). Developmental psychiatry comes of age. *American Journal of Psychiatry, 145,* 1–10.

Carlson, E., Jacobvitz, D., & Sroufe, L. A. (1995). A developmental investigation of inattentiveness and hyperactivity. *Child Development, 66,* 37–54.

Carlson, E. (1998). A prospective longitudinal study of attachment disorganization/disorientation. *Child Development, 69,* 1107–1128.

Cassidy, J. (1994). Emotion regulation: Influences of attachment relationships. In N. Fox (Ed.), The development of emotion regulation. *Monographs of the Society for Research in Child Development, 59*(2–3, Serial No. 240), 228–249.

Cassidy, J., & Berlin, L. (1994). The insecure/ambivalent pattern of attachment: Theory and research. *Child Development, 65,* 971–981.

Cicchetti, D. (1986, April). *Organization of the self-system in atypical populations.* Paper presented at the biennial meeting of the International Conference on Infant Studies, Los Angeles.

Cicchetti, D., & Tucker, D. (1994). Development and self-regulatory structures of the mind. *Development and Psychopathology, 4,* 533–549.

Crockenberg, S. (1981). Infant irritability, mother responsiveness, and social support influences on the security of infant–mother attachment. *Child Development, 52,* 857–865.

DeWolff, M., & van IJzendoorn, M. (1997). Sensitivity and attachment: A meta-analysis on parental antecedents of infant attachment. *Child Development, 68,* 571–591.

Egeland, B., Carlson, E., & Sroufe, L. A. (1993). Resilience as process. *Development and Psychopathology, 5,* 517–528.

Egeland, B., & Farber, E. (1984). Infant–mother attachment: Factors related to its development and changes over time. *Child Development, 55,* 753–771.

Elicker, J., Englund, M., & Sroufe, L. A. (1992). Predicting peer competence and peer relationships in childhood from early parent–child relationships. In R. Parke & G. Ladd (Eds.), *Family–peer relationships: Modes of linkage* (pp. 77–106). Hillsdale, NJ: Erlbaum.

Englund, M., Levy, A., & Hyson, D. (1997, April). *Development of adolescent social competence: A prospective longitudinal study of family and peer contributions.* Poster session presented at the biennial meeting of the Society for Research in Child Development, Washington, DC.

Erickson, M. F., Sroufe, L. A., & Egeland, B. (1985). The relationship of quality of attachment and behavior problems in preschool in a high risk sample. In I. Bretherton & E. Waters (Eds.), Growing points in attachment theory and research. *Monographs of the Society for Research in Child Development, 50*(1–2, Serial No. 209), 147–186.

Frankel, K. F., & Bates, J. E. (1990). Mother–toddler problem solving: Antecedents in attachment, home behavior, and temperament. *Child Development, 61,* 810–819.

Gewirtz, J. L. (1972). Attachment, dependence, and a distinction in terms of stimulus control. In J. L. Gewirtz (Ed.), *Attachment and dependency* (pp. 179–215). Washington, DC: V. H. Winston.

Gianino, A., & Tronick, E. Z. (1988). The mutual regulation model: The infant's self and interactive regulation coping and defensive capacities. In T. Field, P. McCabe, & N. Schneiderman (Eds.), *Stress and coping* (pp. 47–68). Hillsdale, NJ: Erlbaum.

Grossmann, K., Grossmann, K. E., Spangler, G., Suess, G., & Unzer, L. (1985). Maternal sensitivity and newborn orienting responses as related to quality of attachment in northern Germany. In I. Bretherton & E. Waters (Eds.), Growing points of attachment theory and research. *Monographs of the Society for Research in Child Development, 50*(1–2, Serial No. 209), 233–256.

Gunnar, M., Mangelsdorf, S., Larson, M., & Hertsgaard, L. (1989). Attachment, temperament, and adrenocortical activity in infancy: A study of psychoendocrine regulation. *Developmental Psychology, 25,* 355–363.

Heinicke, C., & Westheimer, I. (1966). *Brief separations.* New York: International Universities Press.

Isabella, R. (1993). Origins of attachment: Maternal interactive behavior across the first year. *Child Development, 64,* 605–621.

Kestenbaum, R., Farber, E., & Sroufe, L. A. (1989). Individual differences in empathy among preschoolers: Relation to attachment history. In N. Eisenberg (Ed.), *New directions for child development: No. 44. Empathy and related emotional responses* (pp. 51–64). San Francisco: Jossey-Bass.

Kiser, L., Bates, J., Maslin, C., & Bayles, K. (1986). Mother–infant play at six months as a predictor of attachment security at thirteen months. *Journal of the American Academy of Child Psychiatry, 25,* 68–75.

Lewis, M., Brooks-Gunn, J., & Jaskir, J. (1985). Individual differences in visual self-recognition as a function of mother–infant attachment relationship. *Developmental Psychology, 21,* 1181–1183.

Lewis, M., Feiring, C., McGuffog, C., & Jaskir, J. (1984). Predicting psychopathology in six-year-olds from early social relations. *Child Development, 55,* 123–136.

Lütkenhaus, P., Grossmann, K. E., & Grossmann, K. (1985). Infant–mother attachment at twelve months and style of interaction with a stranger at the age of three years. *Child Development, 56,* 1538–1542.

Lyons-Ruth, K., Alpern, L., & Repacholi, B. (1993). Disorganized infant attachment classification and maternal psychosocial problems as predictors of hostile–aggressive behavior in the preschool classroom. *Child Development, 64,* 572–585.

Main, M., & Hesse, E. (1990). Parents' unresolved traumatic experiences are related to infant disorganized attachment status: Is frightened and/or frightening parental behavior the linking mechanism? In M. T. Greenberg, D. Cicchetti, & E. M. Cummings (Eds.), *Attachment in the preschool years* (pp. 161–182). Chicago: University of Chicago Press.

Main, M., & Morgan, H. (1996). Disorganization and disorientation in infant strange situation behavior: Phenotypic resemblance to dissociative states. In L. Michelson & W. Ray (Eds.), *Handbook of dissociation: Theoretical, empirical, and clinical perspectives* (pp. 107–138). New York: Plenum Press.

Main, M., & Solomon, J. (1990). Procedures for identifying infants as disorganized/disoriented during the Ainsworth Strange Situation. In M. T. Greenberg, D. Cicchetti, & E. M. Cummings (Eds.), *Attachment in the preschool years* (pp. 121–160). Chicago: University of Chicago Press.

Mangelsdorf, S., Gunnar, M., Kestenbaum, R., Lang, S., & Andreas, D. (1990). Infancy proneness-to-distress temperament, maternal personality, and mother–infant attachment: Associations and goodness of fit. *Child Development, 61,* 820–831.

Marvin, R. S. (1972). *Attachment and cooperative behavior in two-, three-, and four-year-olds.* Unpublished doctoral dissertation, University of Chicago.

Matas, L., Arend, R., & Sroufe, L. A. (1978). Continuity of adaptation in the second year: The relationship between quality of attachment and later competence. *Child Development, 49,* 547–556.

National Institute of Child Health and Human Development (NICHD) Early Child Care Research Network. (1997). The effects of infant child care on mother–infant attachment security. *Child Development, 68,* 860–879.

Nezworski, T. (1983). *Continuity in adaptation into the fourth year: Individual differences in curiosity and exploratory behavior of preschool children.* Unpublished doctoral dissertation, University of Minnesota.

Ogawa, J. R., Egeland, B., & Carlson, E. A. (1998). [The relation between disorganized attachment, childhood trauma, and psychopathological dissociation.] Unpublished raw data.

Ogawa, J. R., Sroufe, L. A., Weinfield, N. S., Carlson, E., & Egeland, B. (1997). Development and the fragmented self: A longitudinal study of dissociative symptomatology in a nonclinical sample. *Development and Psychopathology, 9,* 855–879.

Oppenheim, D., Sagi, A., & Lamb, M. (1988). Infant–adult attachments on the kibbutz and their relation to socioemotional development four years later. *Developmental Psychology, 24,* 427–433.

Ostoja, E. (1996). *Developmental antecedents of friendship competence in adolescence: The roles of early adaptational history and middle childhood peer competence.* Unpublished doctoral dissertation, University of Minnesota.

Pastor, D. (1981). The quality of mother–infant attachment and its relationship to toddlers' initial sociability with peers. *Developmental Psychology, 17,* 326–335.

Pianta, R., Egeland, B., & Sroufe, L. A. (1990). Maternal stress in children's development: Predictions of school outcomes and identification of protective factors. In J. E. Rolf, A. Masten, D. Cicchetti, K. Neuchterlen, & S. Weintraub (Eds.), *Risk and protective factors in the development of psychopathology* (pp. 215–235). New York: Cambridge University Press.

Renken, B., Egeland, B., Marvinney, D., Mangelsdorf, S., & Sroufe, L. A. (1989). Early childhood antecedents of aggression and passive withdrawal in early elementary school. *Journal of Personality, 57,* 257–281.

Robertson, J., & Robertson, J. (1971). Young children in brief separation: A fresh look. *Psychoanalytic Study of the Child, 26,* 264–315.

Scarr, S., & McCartney, K. (1983). How people make their own environments: A theory of genotype → environment effects. *Child Development, 54,* 424–435.

Schore, A. (1994). *Affect regulation and the origin of the self: The neurobiology of emotional development.* Hillsdale, NJ: Erlbaum.

Seifer, R., Schiller, M., Sameroff, A., Resnick, S., & Riordan, K. (1996). Attachment, maternal sensitivity, and infant temperament during the first year of life. *Developmental Psychology, 32,* 12–25.

Schulman, S., Elicker, J., & Sroufe, L. A. (1994). Stages of friendship growth in preadolescence as related to attachment history. *Journal of Social and Personal Relationships, 11,* 341–361.

Sroufe, L. A. (1979). The coherence of individual development. *American Psychologist, 34,* 834–841.

Sroufe, L. A. (1983). Infant–caregiver attachment and patterns of adaptation in preschool: The roots of maladaptation and competence. In M. Perlmutter (Ed.), *The Minnesota Symposia on Child Psychology: Vol. 16. Development and policy concerning children with special needs* (pp. 41–83). Hillsdale, NJ: Erlbaum.

Sroufe, L. A. (1986). Bowlby's contribution to psychoanalytic theory and developmental psychopathology. *Journal of Child Psychology and Psychiatry, 27,* 841–849.

Sroufe, L. A. (1988). The role of infant–caregiver attachment in development. In J. Belsky & T. Nezworski (Eds.), *Clinical implications of attachment* (pp. 18–38). Hillsdale, NJ: Erlbaum.

Sroufe, L. A. (1996). *Emotional development: The organization of emotional life in the early years.* New York: Cambridge University Press.

Sroufe, L. A. (1997). Psychopathology as outcome of development. *Development and Psychopathology, 9,* 251–268.

Sroufe, L. A., Bennett, C., Englund, M., Urban, J., & Shulman, S. (1993). The significance of gender boundaries in preadolescence: Contemporary correlates and antecedents of boundary violation and maintenance. *Child Development, 64,* 455–466.

Sroufe, L. A., Carlson, E., & Shulman, S. (1993). Individuals in relationships: Development from infancy through adolescence. In D. C. Funder, R. Parke, C. Tomlinson-Keesey, & K. Widaman (Eds.), *Studying lives through time: Approaches to personality and development* (pp. 315–342). Washington, DC: American Psychological Association.

Sroufe, L. A., Egeland, B., & Carlson, E. A. (in press). One social world. In W. A. Collins & B. Laursen (Eds.), *The Minnesota Symposium on Child Psychology: Vol. 30. Relationships as developmental context.* Mahwah, NJ: Erlbaum.

Sroufe, L. A., Egeland, B., & Kreutzer, T. (1990). The fate of early experience following developmental change: Longitudinal approaches to individual adaptation in childhood. *Child Development, 61,* 1363–1373.

Sroufe, L. A., & Fleeson, J. (1986). Attachment and the construction of relationships. In W. Hartup & Z. Rubin (Eds.), *Relationships and development* (pp. 239–252). Hillsdale, NJ: Erlbaum.

Sroufe, L. A., & Fleeson, J. (1988). The coherence of individual relationships. In R. A. Hinde & J. Stevenson-Hinde (Eds.), *Relationships within families: Mutual influences* (pp. 27–47). Oxford: Oxford University Press.

Sroufe, L. A., Fox, N., & Pancake, V. (1983). Attachment and dependency in developmental perspective. *Child Development, 54,* 1615–1627.

Sroufe, L. A., Schork, E., Motti, E., Lawroski, N., & LaFreniere, P. (1984). The role of affect in social competence. In C. Izard, J. Kagan, & R. Zajonc (Eds.), *Emotions, cognition and behavior* (pp. 289–319). New York: Cambridge University Press.

Sroufe, L. A., & Waters, E. (1977). Attachment as an organizational construct. *Child Development, 48,* 1184–1199.

Stayton, D., & Ainsworth, M. D. S. (1973). Individual differences in infant responses to brief, everyday separations as related to other infant and maternal behaviors. *Developmental Psychology, 9,* 226–235.

Suess, G. J., Grossmann, K. E., & Sroufe, L. A. (1992). Effects of infant attachment to mother and father on quality of adaptation in preschool: From dyadic to individual organisation of self. *International Journal of Behavioral Development, 15,* 43–65.

Susman-Stillman, A., Kalkoske, M., Egeland, B., & Waldman, I. (1996). Infant temperament and maternal sensitivity as predictors of attachment security. *Infant Behavior and Development, 19,* 33–47.

Teo, A., Carlson, E., Mathieu, P., Egeland, B., & Sroufe, L. A. (1996). A prospective longitudinal study of psychosocial predictors of achievement. *Journal of School Psychology, 34,* 285–306.

Troy, M., & Sroufe, L. A. (1987). Victimization among preschoolers: The role of attachment relationship theory. *Journal of the American Academy of Child and Adolescent Psychiatry, 26,* 166–172.

Urban, J., Carlson, E., Egeland, B., & Sroufe, L. A. (1991). Patterns of individual adaptation across childhood. *Development and Psychopathology, 3,* 445–460.

Vaughn, B. E., Egeland, B., Sroufe, L. A., & Waters, E. (1979). Individual differences in infant–mother attachment at twelve and eighteen months: Stability and change in families under stress. *Child Development, 50,* 971–975.

Vaughn, B. E., Lefever, G. B., Seifer, R., & Barglow, P. (1989). Attachment behavior, attachment security, and temperament during infancy. *Child Development, 60,* 728–737.

Vaughn, B. E., & Waters, E. (1990). Attachment behavior at home and in the laboratory: *Q*-sort observations and Strange Situation classifications of one-year-olds. *Child Development, 61,* 1965–1973.

Waddington, C. (1957). *The strategy of the genes.* London: Allen & Unwin.

Warren, S. L., Huston, L., Egeland, B., & Sroufe, L. A. (1997). Child and adolescent anxiety disorders and early attachment. *Journal of the American Academy of Child and Adolescent Psychiatry, 36,* 637–644.

Waters, E., & Deane, K. (1985). Defining and assessing individual differences in attachment relationships: Q-methodology and the organization of behavior in infancy and early childhood. In I. Bretherton & E. Waters (Eds.), Growing points of attachment theory and research. *Monographs of the Society for Research in Child Development, 50*(1–2, Serial No. 209), 41–65.

Waters, E., Merrick, S., Treboux, D., Crowell, J., & Albersheim, L. (1998). *Attachment security in infancy and early adulthood: A 20-year longitudinal study.* Manuscript submitted for publication.

Waters, E., & Sroufe, L. A. (1983). Social competence as a developmental construct. *Developmental Review, 3,* 79–97.

Waters, E., Wippman, J., & Sroufe, L. A. (1979). Attachment, positive affect, and competence in the peer group: Two studies in construct validation. *Child Development, 50,* 821–829.

Weinfield, N. S., Sroufe, L. A., & Egeland, B. (1998). *Attachment from infancy to early adulthood in a high-risk sample: Continuity, discontinuity and their correlates.* Manuscript submitted for publication.

Weinfield, N. S., Ogawa, J. R., & Sroufe, L. A. (1997). Early attachment as a pathway to adolescent peer competence. *Journal of Research on Adolescence, 7,* 241–265.

5

Internal Working Models in Attachment Relationships

A Construct Revisited

❖

INGE BRETHERTON
KRISTINE A. MUNHOLLAND

Attachment theory underscores the central role of relationships in human development from the cradle to the grave (Bowlby, 1969/1982, 1973, 1980). Beginning in infancy and continuing throughout the life course, an individual's mental health is seen as intimately tied to relationships with attachment figures who afford emotional support and protection:

> For not only young children, it is now clear, but human beings of all ages are found to be at their happiest and to be able to deploy their talents to best advantage when they are confident that, standing behind them, there are one or more trusted persons who will come to their aid should difficulties arise. The person trusted provides a secure base from which his [or her] companion can operate. (Bowlby, 1973, p. 359)

Human attachment relationships, according to Bowlby (1979), are regulated by a behavioral–motivational system that develops in infancy and that is shared with other primates. This system monitors the physical proximity and psychological availability of a "stronger and wiser" attachment figure, and activates/regulates attachment behavior directed toward that figure. As long as an attached individual feels at ease, the attachment figure functions as a secure base of operations whose supportive presence fosters explo-

ration, play, or other social behaviors. When the attached individual feels afraid, however, exploratory goals are overridden by the impetus to seek refuge with and reassurance from the attachment figure, especially if the attached individual is an infant or young child. An individual's attachment to one or a few specific figures therefore becomes most visible under conditions of perceived threat. By seeking an attachment figure's protection, immature offspring are believed to increase the likelihood of their survival and reproductive success.

How well attachment can fulfill its function of physical and psychological protection, however, turns on the mutually responsive quality of interactions between an attached individual and his or her attachment figure(s). Beyond infancy, attachment relations come to be additionally governed by internal (or mental) working models that young individuals construct from the experienced interaction patterns with their principal attachment figures. These internal working models are conceived as "operable" models of self and attachment partner, based on their joint relationship history. They serve to regulate, interpret, and predict both the attachment figure's and the self's attachment-related behavior, thoughts, and feelings. If appropriately revised in line with developmental and environmental changes, internal working models enable reflection and communication about past and future attachment situations and relationships, thus facilitating the creation of joint plans for proximity regulation and the resolution of relationship conflicts. Moreover, an individual who can count on an attachment figure's responsiveness, support, and protection is free to give full attention to other concerns, such as exploration and/or companionable interaction.

In this chapter, we reexamine ideas about the formation, development, function, and intergenerational transmission of internal working models of self and attachment figures. We begin with a brief historical exposition linking attachment theory and psychoanalysis, followed by a summary of Bowlby's ideas on the topic as laid out in his seminal trilogy, *Attachment and Loss* (Bowlby, 1969/1982, 1973, 1980). Next we consider some possible elaborations and extensions of the concept of the working model, and present a selective review of the burgeoning empirical literature on attachment at the representational level. We end with suggestions for future research.

BOWLBY AND THE PSYCHOANALYTIC INNER WORLD

That Bowlby emphasized the function of representation in the conduct of interpersonal relationships is not surprising. As a member of the British Psycho-Analytic Society, he was familiar with Freud's thinking about the inner or representational world, as well as with Klein's (1932), Fairbairn's (1952), and Winnicott's (1958) ideas about internalized relationships. Indeed, Freud's (1940/1963) definition of the inner world in *An Outline of Psychoanalysis* uncannily prefigures Bowlby's notion about the function of "internal working models":

> The yield brought to light by scientific work from our primary sense perceptions will consist of an insight into connections and dependent relations which are present in the external world, which can somehow be reliably *reproduced or reflected in the internal world of our thought and a knowledge of which enables us to 'understand' something in the external world, to foresee it and possibly to alter it.* (p. 53; emphasis added)

Freud also spoke quite explicitly about the function of the inner world in guiding an individual's behavior:

> [The ego's] constructive task consists in interpolating between the demand made by an instinct and the action that satisfies it, *the activity of thought which, after taking its bearing in the present and assessing earlier experiences, endeavours by means of experimental actions to calculate the consequences of the course of action proposed.* In this way the ego comes to a decision on whether the attempt to obtain satisfaction is to be carried out or postponed, or whether it may not be necessary for the demand by the instinct to be completely suppressed altogether as being dangerous. (p. 56; emphasis added)

When Freud wrote these comments, mainstream psychologists had lost interest in the role mental representations play in the conduct of everyday life. Instead they investigated more limited and decontextualized processes, such as how individuals remember word lists and form concepts. Some completely eschewed the examination of mental processes.

Little had changed 15 years after the posthumous publication of Freud's *Outline*, when Bowlby began to recast Freudian ideas about personality and relationship development in terms of post-Freudian evolutionary biology, ethology, control systems theory, and emerging findings from developmental and information-processing research. Mainstream psychology was still dominated by behaviorist ideas and provided few conceptual tools for thinking about the organization and function of the "inner world." A major inspiration came from the writings of a neurobiologist (Young, 1964) who had adopted ideas proposed by Kenneth Craik, a brilliant young pioneer in what would later be called "artificial intelligence." Taking an evolutionary perspective, Craik (1943) proposed that organisms capable of forming complex "internal working models" of their environment considerably improve their chances of survival, because the ability to construct and use mental models to evaluate the potential consequences of alternative courses of action makes for much more flexible and adaptive behavior. Note that Craik's definition of internal working models bears a striking resemblance to Freud's notions about the inner world:

> By a model we thus mean any physical or chemical system which has a similar relation-structure to that of the process it imitates. By 'relation-structure' I do not mean some obscure nonphysical entity which attends the model, but the fact that it is a physical working model which works in the same way as the process it parallels. . . . If the organism carries a 'small-scale model' of external reality and

of its own possible actions within its head, it is able to try out various alternatives, conclude which is the best of them, react to future situations before they arise, utilize the knowledge of past events in dealing with the present and future, and in every way to react in a much fuller, safer and more competent manner to the emergencies which face it. (Craik, 1943, p. 61)

Thus a crucial aspect of internal working models is their relation-structure (i.e., the spatiotemporal causal relations among the events, actions, objects, goals, and concepts represented). To be serviceable, Craik argued, working models need not capture every conceivable aspect of reality, but do need to conserve the relation-structure of those aspects that make it possible to evaluate the probable outcome of alternative behaviors. Internal working models, then, were conceived as a range of simple to complex analogues of important aspects of the world, represented and operable internally.

Bowlby favored Craik's metaphor of "internal working model" over related terms with more static connotations, such as "image" or "map," because both "working" and "model" suggested representations upon which an individual can mentally operate in order to generate predictions. He also claimed that to be of use in novel situations, working models had to be capable of extension to cover potential, not just experienced, realities (Bowlby, 1969/1982).

What is often overlooked is that Bowlby's conception of the working model is a very general one. It applies to *all* representations and is not restricted to working models of self and other in attachment relationships. It is, however, with respect to these particular self–other representations that Bowlby most extensively elaborated his ideas about the building, use, and revision of mental models.

The Development of Working Models of Self and Attachment Figure

Because internal working models are believed to reflect experienced interaction patterns between an attached individual and his or her attachment figure(s), the developing working models of self and of the attachment figure(s) are *ipso facto* complementary:

In the working model of the world that anyone builds a key feature is his notion of who his attachment figures are, where they may be found, and

how they may be expected to respond. Similarly, in the working model of the self that anyone builds a key feature is his notion of how acceptable or unacceptable he himself is in the eyes of his attachment figures. On the structure of these complementary models are based that person's forecasts of how accessible and responsive his attachment figures are likely to be should he turn to them for support. And, in terms of the theory now advanced, it is on the structure of those models that depends, also, whether he feels confident that his attachment figures are in general readily available or whether he is more or less afraid that they will not be available— occasionally, frequently or most of the time. (Bowlby, 1973, p. 203)

A working model of self as valued and competent, according to this view, is constructed in the context of a working model of parents as emotionally available, but also as supportive of exploratory activities. Conversely, a working model of self as devalued and incompetent is the counterpart of a working model of parents as rejecting or ignoring of attachment behavior and/or interfering with exploration. Thus the developing complementary models of self and parents, taken together, represent both sides of the relationship (see also Sroufe & Fleeson, 1986).

Developmental Change in Working Models as a Requirement for Continued Security

The term "secure," in the context of attachment theory, describes an individual's confidence that a protective, supportive figure will be accessible and available, whether the individual is an infant, child, or adult. This usage should not, however, erroneously be taken to imply lack of developmental change in the complexity of working models. Indeed, the opposite is the case: Bowlby repeatedly warned of the pathogenic potential of working models that are *not* updated.

Bowlby maintained that a child's continuing security and age-appropriate self-reliance will be imperiled if the child's and the parents' complementary working models are not adapted in step with the child's developing physical, social, and cognitive competencies. In situations in which an infant still requires protection, a toddler may be able to manage "all by myself." Conversely, whereas a toddler may not fear the dark, a preschooler may need reassurance about imagined danger, such as monsters under the bed.

Because Craik's writings were not concerned with the emergence and increasing sophistication of a child's working models, Bowlby had to cast the net for developmental ideas elsewhere. He found what he was looking for in Piaget (1951, 1952, 1954), whose writings on the sensorimotor period had just become available in English. Akin to Piaget's ideas that infants' understandings of objects result from actions on manipulable objects, Bowlby saw infants' sensorimotor understandings of relationships as developing in the context of repeated interactions with caregiving figures. Such embryonic forms of self–other representation, Bowlby argued, enable even very young infants to recognize the patterning of transactions, and hence to anticipate what the caregiver is likely to do next. As infants' developing recall memory allows them to understand that objects (including parents) continue to exist when out of sight, working models slowly become more deliberately "operable." Infants can now begin to use working models to make and evaluate simple attachment plans, such as where to search for an attachment figure. They can also communicate some of their attachment needs through language, and make simple predictions concerning whether and how the figure may respond to comfort seeking:

> Starting, we may suppose, towards the end of his first year, and probably especially actively during his second and third when he acquires the powerful and extraordinary gift of language, a child is busy constructing working models of how the physical world may be expected to behave, how his mother and other significant persons may be expected to behave, how he himself may be expected to behave, and how each interacts with the other. Within the framework of these working models he evaluates his situation and makes his plans. And within the framework of the working models of his mother and himself he evaluates special aspects of his situation and makes his attachment plans. (Bowlby, 1969/1982, p. 354)

As they enter the preschool years, children with supportive attachment figures become increasingly able to rely on working models to feel secure even when the figures are not physically present. At the same time, they begin to understand that their attachment figures' goals and motives can differ from their own. Together with the growing mastery of verbal communication, these emerging abilities usher in a period of dramatic change, resulting in what Bowlby called a "goal-corrected partnership." Illustrating this change from a child's perspective, Bowlby (1969/1982) invited his readers to consider the

relative sophistication underlying the behavior of a schoolboy who heard of his mother's plan for a trip to visit relatives, and who then searched her out in a neighbor's house to talk her into taking him along. To generate a strategy for retaining access to his mother, the boy had to take note of his mother's goals, not just his own (i.e., he did not ask her to stay home with him). Compare this with the much simpler situation at an earlier time when, as a 1-year-old, the same boy simply toddled after his mother or cried as she was leaving the room.

Bowlby's notions about the goal-corrected partnership are supported by recent research showing that children's understanding of others' desires, intentions, and emotions develops much earlier than was once thought (e.g., Bretherton & Beeghly, 1982; for an extensive review of this burgeoning literature, see Wellman, 1990).

Resistance to Change in Working Models

Despite the developmental requirements for adaptive updating, internal working models as conceived by Bowlby are not in a state of minute-to-minute flux. Some resistance to change is built in via the process of assimilation (borrowed from Piaget). That is, representations of prior transactions bias what individuals expect, and, within limits, regulate the perception of upcoming experiences with attachment figures. Therefore an attachment figure's occasional lapses in sensitivity are not likely to undermine a child's confidence in the figure's emotional availability. Relatedly, ways of acting and thinking that were at one time under deliberate control tend to become less conscious or inaccessible to consciousness as they become habitual and automatic. Automatic processing is more efficient because it makes fewer demands on attention, but the resulting efficiency comes at the price of some loss in flexibility. Finally, the fact that two individuals' working models and expectations are involved in attachment interactions also engenders some stability. When one partner's interactive behavior changes, the other's expectations are violated. In response, the first may at least initially resist or misinterpret a partner's unexpected interactive behaviors, be they positive or negative. These normal stabilizing processes usually give way, however, once a child (or adult) becomes conscious that the old model no longer works.

Change in the Affective Quality of Working Models

As noted, working models can remain affectively stable (i.e., can reflect secure or insecure attachment relations) as they become developmentally more complex. A securely attached infant, however, does not always become a secure child. Affective change in working models can be triggered, for example, when a previously empathic and supportive parent becomes highly stressed or deeply depressed owing to events such as sudden unemployment, chronic illness, or loss of previously available social support. If such a parent then repeatedly threatens to abandon the child or to commit suicide, or becomes extremely unresponsive, the child's confidence in him or her as a secure base may be shaken, leading the child to reconstruct his or her working model of parent and self (Bowlby, 1973). Conversely, when life circumstances improve, or effective support from others becomes available, a parent may become able to respond more sensitively to his or her child's attachment needs, leading the child to construct revised working models of self as valued and of parents as caring. However, defensive aspects of working-model organization in insecure attachment relations, discussed next, may render such reconstructions more difficult.

Working-Model Organization in Light of Defensive Processes

Bowlby's psychoanalytic background is most evident in his discussion of the role defensive processes play in the building of working models. Convinced that Freudian notions about the role of defense and the operation of defense mechanisms were valuable but needed rethinking, Bowlby turned to research on human information processing and memory (see Dixon, 1971; Erdelyi, 1985; Norman, 1976). A central claim of the information-processing literature is that humans selectively exclude available but irrelevant information, in order to focus their limited processing capacities more effectively on what is most salient to the task at hand. Defensive exclusion, Bowlby argued, may rely on similar processes, but with the goal of warding off perceptions, feelings, and thoughts that would otherwise cause unbearable anxiety and psychological suffering.

Although defensive exclusion serves adaptive self-protective functions in the short run, Bowlby warned that it may subsequently interfere with the adequate updating of working models. If defensive exclusion prevents the uptake and incorporation into working models of relevant available information, the attachment system may not be appropriately alerted, leading in turn to its misregulation or deactivation (attenuation or exaggeration of attachment behaviors, feelings, and thoughts).

Note that defensive processes as understood by Bowlby are not necessarily unconscious, but run the gamut from involuntary repression to deliberate suppression or avoidance of perceptions, behaviors, and thoughts. In addition, the degree to which exclusion is successful may vary. Research on procedural ("I know how . . ."), semantic ("I know that . . ."), and episodic ("I remember when . . .") memory systems (e.g., Tulving, 1972) led Bowlby (1980) to speculate that defensive exclusion may be facilitated by the segregation of contradictory information in different memory systems. Patients in treatment, he noted, often give very glowing general descriptions of their parents' admirable qualities (semantic memory), which are contradicted by subsequent more detailed memories of how their parents actually behaved (episodic memory). If information in the two systems is segregated, detection of conflict among representations may be rendered more difficult, Bowlby speculated.

Bowlby saw young children as especially prone to defensive exclusion because of the frequency and intensity with which attachment behavior is activated during the early years. Two situations, he believed, are especially likely to give rise to defensive exclusion: (1) when a child's attachment behavior is intensely aroused, but is not assuaged and is perhaps even punished or ridiculed by a parent; and (2) when a child has come to know something about the parent that the parent does not "wish him to know about and would punish him for accepting as true" (Bowlby, 1980, p. 73). To relieve anxiety, Bowlby proposed, such a child is likely to defensively exclude relevant memories from awareness, retaining conscious access only to what he or she has been told (for example, about sexual abuse or one parent's suicide).

As a consequence of defensive exclusion, Bowlby postulated, a child may come to operate with two incompatible sets of working models of self and of attachment figure: a consciously accessible set, based on false information; and a consciously inaccessible or only intermittently accessible set, reflecting the child's experience/ interpretation of the situation at the time. Sometimes, however, a child may defensively exclude only the identity of the person (e.g., an attachment figure) toward whom he or she harbors hostile feelings, diverting these feelings to another, less salient person. Likewise, some children defensively redirect toward themselves the anger they initially felt toward an attachment figure, producing defensive self-blame. Bowlby noted that a common diversionary behavior in cases of bereavement is compulsive caregiving, based on an intense, often obsessive concern with the welfare of another individual or individuals, who may find the attention irksome rather than helpful. By engaging in this type of caregiving behavior, individuals are believed to divert attention from their own attachment needs.

Bowlby deliberately abstained from use of traditional psychoanalytic labels for defense mechanisms, such as "projection," "projective identification," "denial," or "displacement." Not only do these labels have overlapping meanings, he argued, but their use may prevent a therapist from adequately exploring the personal reality underlying an individual's framework of meanings:

> The more details one comes to know about the events in a child's life, and about what he has been told, what he has overheard and what he has observed but is not supposed to know, the more clearly can his ideas about the world and what may happen in the future be seen as perfectly reasonable constructions. (Bowlby, 1979, p. 23)

Along similar lines, Bowlby and Parkes (1970) recommended that terms such as "magical thinking" and "fantasy" are to be used with extreme caution. They strongly urged that terms such as "disbelief that X has occurred," "belief that Y may still be possible," or "making plans to achieve Z" be used instead.

As this brief review demonstrates, Bowlby made defensive exclusion and diversion of attention responsible for a host of phenomena. Some of these seem to require processes beyond mere exclusion of information from awareness—a point to which we return later.

Communication and Intergenerational Transmission

In Bowlby's view, nonverbal and verbal communication patterns are the processes through which internal working models of secure and insecure attachment relations are generated and maintained, and through which they are in turn transmitted to the next generation. Through the manner in which a parent habitually responds to an infant, he or she also communicates that the infant is or is not worth responding to. In his discussions of verbal communication, Bowlby— like other psychoanalysts (e.g., Stern, 1985) —dwelled most extensively on the role played by deliberate parental *miscommunications* in disorganizing or confusing children's internal working models. However, he also (albeit more briefly) acknowledged parents' facilitating role in helping their children construct and revise working models through dialogue. Parents who have experienced transactions with responsive, accepting attachment figures in childhood, he argued, are better able to respond to their own children's distress with empathy and emotional support. As a result, their children are likely not only to feel understood, valued, and competent, but to be in a better position to construct functional working models of self and caregiver:

> Thus the family experience of those who grow up anxious and fearful is found to be characterized not only by uncertainty about parental support but often also by covert yet strongly distorting parental pressures: pressure on the child, for example, to act as caregiver for a parent; *or to adopt, and thereby to confirm, a parent's false models—of self, of child and of their relationship.* Similarly the family experience of those who grow up to become relatively stable and self-reliant is characterized not only by unfailing parental support when called upon but also by a steady yet timely encouragement toward increasing autonomy, and *by the frank communication by parents of working models—of themselves, of child and of others—that are not only tolerably valid but are open to be questioned and revised. . . .* the inheritance of mental health and mental ill health through the medium of family microculture . . . may well be far more important, than is their inheritance through the medium of genes. (Bowlby, 1973, pp. 322–323; emphasis added)

In addition to elucidating the intergenerational transmission of working models through communication patterns, these statements are noteworthy because they extend the parental role of secure base to the psychological realm. That is, Bowlby apparently suggested that parents serve as secure bases for their children's exploration of the inner world by engaging in verbal dialogue *about* working models.

PERSPECTIVES FROM OTHER COGNITIVE AND SOCIAL-PSYCHOLOGICAL THEORIES

Bowlby systematically sought validation and support for his ideas and hunches from outside the psychoanalytic domain. Before the "cognitive revolution" took hold in psychology, he adopted Craik's (1943) enormously powerful concept of representation as model building and model use. He then wedded this idea to Piaget's theory of cognitive development and to findings from the emerging field of information processing to show how internal working models, conjointly with the attachment system, are vitally involved in the regulation of attachment relationships. In this section, we present selected ideas from other theoretical approaches that can shed further light on the concept of internal working models.

In discussing representation as the creation and use of internal working models, Bowlby claimed that "to understand human behavior it is difficult to do without such a hypothesis" (1969/1982, p. 81). However, a number of researchers (e.g., Dunn, 1993) have criticized the concept as being too vague, too general, and not able to generate directly testable hypotheses. Their criticism may derive from two misunderstandings: (1) that representation conceived as the construction and operation of internal models is specific to attachment, and (2) that ascribing complementary working models of self and other in relationships to an infant or toddler is not consonant with what we know about the development of social-cognitive capacities.

The usefulness of the working-models approach to representation, along the lines proposed by Craik (1943), was more recently reiterated by a cognitive psychologist (Johnson-Laird, 1983) and two philosophers (McGinn, 1989; Metzinger, 1993). Like Bowlby, these theoreticians take the term "working model" or "mental model" to mean that salient aspects of the causal network of relations humans perceive in the course of interacting with the physical and social world must somehow be reproduced internally in order to create subsequent mental simulations. In other words, representations at the most basic level are deemed to be in certain respects analogues of what they represent, retaining the dynamic relational properties of what they model, so that they can be activated (operated) to make predictions by running the model in "mental time." Mental representations, then, are useful representations to the extent that they capture important causal/relational properties of the environment and the self well enough to allow an individual to operate successfully in that environment. Even a simple model of self and attachment figure can be adequate for certain purposes ("If I hold up my arms, Mommy will usually pick me up," "If I point to a cookie, Mommy will usually give it to me").

Representational Theories Consonant with the Working-Model Approach

Useful notions regarding the function, structure, and development of working models derive from the literature on scripts (Schank & Abelson, 1977) and event schemas (Nelson, 1986), but also from classic symbolic interactionism as propounded by Mead (1934) and ideas put forth by Lewin (1933) and Heider (1958) that led to the creation of attribution theory. Some of these ideas predate and others postdate Bowlby's formulation of attachment theory.

Although Bowlby assumed that humans possess a representational system *capable* of operating as an internal working model of the world and the self within it, few notions about how such a system may be organized and work as a functioning whole were available to him. In the late 1970s and early 1980s, a number of theorists began to propose hypothetical entities termed "scripts" or "event schemas" that seemed to have some of the required properties. For example, Schank and Abelson (1977) contended that in the course of repeated similar experiences, individuals generate sequentially ordered "scripts" (in which agents act toward recipients in specific locations to attain particular goals). Scripts are automatically "instantiated" or called up whenever a current experience resembles the script, enabling the individual to predict more or less successfully what is likely to happen next. Building on Bartlett's (1932) long-neglected schema theory of memory, Nelson (1986) proposed similar sequentially organized skeletal structures called "event schemas" that represent who does what to whom, when, where, why, and how. Like Schank and Abelson, Nelson argued that event schemas may be the building blocks from which children construct their basic representational system. More abstract concepts such as "the mother role" or what mothers generally do (comforting, feeding, disciplining) may then be derived from event schemas by further processing.

Having concluded that the notion of scripts was insufficiently flexible to supply the needed variety of representational building blocks, Schank (1982) postulated that events stored in short-term memory may be broken down into and stored in long-term memory as smaller (but still schematized) units, which can then be recombined and/or sequenced and summarized in various ways. He envisaged many different types of complex summary scripts and simple mini-scripts/schemas (e.g., action sequences, roles, affective themes, causal relations) that may be cross-indexed in a variety of systematic, yet-to-be understood ways to form an organized system capable of generating novel representations.

An advantage of conceptualizing the building of mental models along these lines is that it allows us to think more concisely about the intuitively obvious fact that facets of experiences can be separately recalled; recalled in terms of different levels of generality; and retrieved/reactivated and joined together in different ways to create mental models representing hypothetical, feared or hoped-for, probable or improbable, or just playful interactions of interpersonal relationships. In the type of system envisaged by Schank, a unique experience—say, an attachment experience with one's father—may be remembered as a very experience-near schema of being comforted in a way unique to this relationship (e.g., being picked up while distressed, held on his lap, leaning against his chest, being talked to with specific comforting words, then feeling soothed). That same experience may also serve as input to a summary script, verbally expressed as "When I feel sad, Dad will comfort me." The general comforting schema in turn may be embedded in a summary supportiveness schema, "Dad is always there for me when I need him," representing overall trust in the father's availability. Schema networks representing differing aspects of specific attachment relationships (i.e., internal working models of self with father in many situations besides comforting) will then constitute the working model of the father, and in turn may become inputs to a working model of the father role in general. Such schemas/models may also govern what the child expects in relationships with others, such as teachers and close friends (see Berlin & Cassidy, Chapter 30, this volume; Weinfield, Sroufe, Egeland, & Carlson, Chapter 4, this volume), and may perhaps even contribute to an individual's internal working model of human nature in general and the world as a more or less trustworthy or malignant place. In accord with this view, Catlin and Epstein (1992) found that favorable relationships with parents in childhood predicted a belief in a meaningful and predictable/controllable world.

Mead and the Social Construction of Attachment Reality

Central to Bowlby's conception of representation is the social origin of internal working models. This aspect of attachment theory is interestingly paralleled by George Herbert Mead's (1934) and other symbolic interactionists' notions about the social self, though Bowlby was apparently not familiar with their work. Mead (1910, 1913, 1934) proposed that young children learn about themselves from the responses of important others (usually parents) to their social acts. According to this line of thinking, children learn to understand themselves through the responses others make to their social bids. If an infant's gesture of holding up the arms to be picked up is habitually ignored by a parent, this particular way of signaling will, in Mead's view, lose meaning for the infant.

However, attachment theory claims more. Because evolutionary processes are believed to have prepared infants to *expect* caring parental responsiveness to attachment signals, parental ignoring of an infant's attachment signals does not render the infant's communication meaningless, but rather conveys rejection, expressed verbally as "Your signals do not count." Eventually such parental responses, if pervasive and consistent, are incorporated into an internal working model of self that can be stated verbally as "My needs are not important" (Bretherton, 1990). Seen in this way, meanings derived from attachment interactions hold tremendous emotional significance for the child's developing working models of self in relation to attachment figures.

Also relevant to the concept of working models are Mead's speculations about the social origins of thought (i.e., operations on working models). Thought, for Mead, consists of inner conversations with imagined others or oneself. For young children, he suggested, these inner conversations should be viewed as "dramatic," literally involving reenactments of conversations between the child and a parent. "Later, the inner stage changes into the forum and workshop of thought. The features and intonations of the dramatis personae fade out and the emphasis falls upon inner speech, though thought can always return to the personal mode" (Mead, 1910, p. 377).

These speculative ideas shed light on Bowlby's notion that supportive parents serve as psychological secure bases for their children by engaging in verbal dialogue. As Bowlby noted, parents who openly share their reflections about working models with their children help children in turn to construct and adequately revise their own internal working models. Mead's ideas suggest that young children's thinking about attachment interactions may in some instances consist of holding inner conversations derived from actual conversations with parents (such as repeating reassurances to themselves that the monster under the bed is only a shadow).

Interestingly, the important role of parent–child conversations in the construction of social reality and the social self has so far been studied primarily outside the attachment domain (Goodman, Quas, Batterman-Faunce, Riddlesberger, & Kuhn, 1994; Miller, Hoogstra, Mintz, Fung, & Williams, 1993; Nelson, 1993; for a more detailed discussion, see Bretherton, 1993). These studies reveal links between parents' style of discussing past events and children's own emerging capacity to talk about their experiences. They also suggest that children's misunderstandings, including misunderstandings of parental explanations, may interfere as much with the construction of adequate working models as do the parental falsifications that Bowlby believed to be primary in the instigation of defensive processes in children (e.g., Goodman et al., 1994; Steward, 1993). Fortunately, in a secure relationship characterized by open communication, such misunderstandings are more likely to be discovered and corrected.

Lewin and Heider: The Representation of Meaning

Our earlier quotes from Bowlby's work reveal quite clearly that he did not intend the concept of working models to be construed in terms of dispassionate mappings of an objective reality. For Bowlby, emotional and motivational goals and appraisals are an integral part of representation—a way of thinking that has much in common with the theorizing and research of social psychologists Kurt Lewin (1933) and Fritz Heider (1958). Little concerned with the hegemony of behaviorism at the time, these two theorists wrote extensively about the making of personal and interpersonal meaning, although their work

was not widely known outside social psychology.

For Lewin (1933) and Heider (1958), action and interaction are the basis for meaning making and hence for representation. The environment, Lewin believed, is construed in terms of personal meanings—that is, in terms of the actions it is seen to invite, repel, permit, or prohibit, given an individual's current goals and his or her behavioral repertoire. For example, for an infant who is just learning to crawl, a staircase represents an insuperable barrier to rejoining the mother who has disappeared upstairs. For a toddler, the same staircase is a surmountable challenge, and for a preschooler, it is a taken-for-granted way to reach the mother. Related ideas have reemerged in James and Eleanor Gibson's concept of "affordance" (see Gibson, 1982).

The relevance of Lewin's ideas to attachment theory is illustrated by a thought-provoking statement, tucked away in an almost forgotten article that substantially antedates Bowlby's writings. There Lewin explained that a young child's perception of an environment as safe or not safe depends in part on the presence or absence of the mother, because her presence engenders a feeling of protectedness:

In such cases the presence or absence of the mother changes the total structure of the psychological environment very essentially, especially the child's feeling of security or insecurity. As a consequence of the close psychological relationship between the mother and the child's own person, the real abilities of the mother, her effectiveness as against the things and persons of the environment, *have for the child the functional significance of an extension of his own security and power against the environment.* A departure of the mother thus means to the child a weakening of his strength against the environment. (Lewin, 1933, pp. 620–621; emphasis added)

Heider (1958) extended Lewin's (1933) concept of the person in his or her psychological environment or life space to the interpersonal context. He noted that when people react to other persons, they do not usually perceive the others' actions as movement patterns that have to be laboriously interpreted. Rather, people understand others' behaviors (i.e., they construct working models) in terms of how the others make them feel, and what they believe the others to be intending, thinking, perceiving, and feeling. Adults generally make such inferences with extreme rapidity, relying on the redundant information available in the total situation. This includes not only the other persons' emotional expressions and the situational context, but also knowledge of past interactions (drawing on working models). What distinguishes children's from adults' internal working models, we suggest, is the complexity of the attribution making and meaning making involved.

Whether a parent attributes a child's crying to fatigue (temporary factors), the "terrible twos" (developmental stage), or stubbornness/malice (unchangeable personality trait) makes a substantial difference in the way the parent is likely to respond. A mother who sees her infant's fussy behavior as intended to bother her is likely to react with impatience or rejection, while another who ascribes the fussiness to temporary distress or stress that she can alleviate is more likely to respond with comforting. Similarly, the child who interprets a parent's lack of responsiveness as intentional rejection is likely to evaluate the parent and the self more adversely than a child who is cognitively advanced enough to realize that the parent's prolonged nonresponsiveness may have been caused by the parent's lengthy illness. Indeed, although they do not explicitly draw on attribution theory, George and Solomon (1996 and Chapter 28, this volume) have shown that parents' interpretation of children's behavior predicts their actual caregiving behavior.

Working-Model Change and Defensive Processes

The theoretical notions just reviewed also suggest new ways of thinking about defensive information processing in relation to working-model change. Revised script theory as proposed by Schank (1982) implies that profound change in a working model requires revisions in many related schemas at many levels and in many interrelated domains. Thus, for a schema representing somewhat general qualities of a relationship (e.g., "My mother supports me when I am afraid") to be revised, many less general schemas underlying it must also be changed or reinterpreted. However, when a parent's action calls a very general attachment schema (e.g., "My mother is there for me when I need her") into serious question, great anxiety is likely to ensue. As a result, a child may engage not just in defensive exclusion, but in defensive *misattribution*. Instead of accepting an extremely abusive event as overwhelming evidence that the current working model is substantially invalid, the child may try to reinterpret the event defensively (e.g.,

"My mother loves me" and "My mother hits me" may lead to the defensive misattribution "My mother hits me because she loves me"). Since information in everyday life (as opposed to the experimental situations generally used in attribution research) is usually incomplete and interpretable in multiple ways, defensive inclusion or defensive manipulation of specific types of information in generating attachment attributions may be as important in the construction of working models as defensive exclusion.

Heider did not make these links with defensive processes or defensive reality management, even though he postulated that attributions are influenced by an individual's value system and wishes, such that "one's idea of the environment or of one's relation to the environment is kept inviolate or even supported" (Heider, 1958, p. 121). However, if one takes seriously Bowlby's suggestion that defensive processes run the gamut from conscious suppression to unconscious repression, some of the phenomena Bowlby described make more sense in terms of defensive misattributions than merely in terms of defensive exclusion and diversion. Moreover, the label "defensive" may be a misnomer for optimistic attributions based on hope. As Bandura (1982) noted, positive self-efficacy beliefs that are not strictly realistic, but are *slight* overestimations of likely success or mastery, can exert positive influences on coping and self-regulation by influencing how an individual responds to initial difficulties. Attribution theory thus highlights the function of representation (internal working models) as a reality-regulating and reality-creating, not just a reality-reflecting system.

Summary

In summary, we argue here that internal working models of self and attachment figure are part and parcel of a multiply connected schema network whose organized complexity we do not at present fully understand, but in which related information is represented as schemas at different levels of generality. In line with symbolic interactionism, we also argue that attachment-relevant conversations, not only attachment interactions, are involved in the construction of our working models of self with attachment figure. Therefore, operations on working models may at times seem to take the form of inner conversations or interactions with others. Furthermore, we argue that working models have regulatory (defensive, but also positive self-enhancing) functions through which individuals create individual and socially shared realities or meanings.

Working models, we suggest, are subjective, in that they necessarily represent reality from the perspective of a particular individual with his or her specific history of meaning or attribution making (see Metzinger, 1993). Because meaning making is acquired within relationships, however, working models are likely to be at least partially shared with relationship partners and with society at large.

As yet there has been little *developmental* research on attachment attributions, although attribution theory has been used in socialization research (e.g., Dix, Ruble, & Zambarano, 1989). Given the plethora of recent findings about children's theory of mind (Wellman, 1990), the study of mutual attributions and misattributions ought to be a fruitful new approach to studying the goal-corrected attachment partnership—examining parent–child interactions in terms of the "interplay of working models." Interestingly, it is in the field of social psychology that some of the ideas presented in this section have become very influential and have guided attachment theory's application to couple relationships (e.g., Baldwin, 1992; Collins, 1995; Collins & Read, 1990; Shaver, Collins, & Clark, 1996; Shaver & Hazan, 1993). These studies are discussed in the next section, as part of our review of empirical work on attachment at the representational level.

INTERNAL WORKING MODELS IN ATTACHMENT RESEARCH

When empirical studies are grounded in a particular theory, they often claim to test hypotheses based on the tenets of that theory. This cannot strictly be said of attachment research. Rather, attachment theory and attachment research have coevolved and continue to do so. Ainsworth's Baltimore study of infant attachment (summarized in Ainsworth, Blehar, Waters, & Wall, 1978) was inspired by some of Bowlby's seminal writings (e.g., Bowlby, 1958), but he in turn incorporated prepublication findings from Ainsworth's pioneering work on maternal sensitivity into the first volume of his trilogy (Bowlby, 1969/1982). Likewise, Main, Kaplan, and Cassidy's (1985) groundbreaking longitudinal study, which claimed to raise attachment research "to the level of representation," was not initially motivated by an attempt to test Bowlby's notions about working models, but was inspired by extensions of Ainsworth's thinking about patterns of infant attachment. This work was nevertheless acknowledged by Bowlby (1988) as highly relevant to his formulations about internal working models.

A Developmental View of Security

A child's level of perspective taking and attribution making does not *determine* security, although secure attachment may foster the capacity to reflect on relationship issues, where security is defined as the capacity to engage directly, flexibly, creatively, and actively in the solution of interpersonal and intrapsychic attachment problems as they arise.

In infancy and early childhood, this requires the continuing support of a responsive and trustworthy parent (for a more extensive discussion, see George & Solomon, Chapter 28, this volume), but we hypothesize that a secure older child, adolescent, or adult may be better able to weather adverse events even when the attachment figure is temporarily less responsive or not available. For example, a secure older child may be able to better cope with parental irritability caused by illness or job loss because he or she does not attribute the parent's behavior to intentional parental rejection.

Attachment and Communication in Infancy

Ainsworth et al.'s (1978) painstaking naturalistic observations of mothers and infants at home revealed that mothers who were able to respond appropriately (in line with the principles of attachment theory) and promptly to their infants' social signals at home during the first 3 months of life had more harmonious relationships with them during the last quarter of the first year. In turn, these infants seemed to trust in their mothers' availability for protection and comfort. They frequently communicated with the mothers by means other than crying, cooperated with maternal requests, and were eager to explore the physical world. In a laboratory procedure known as the strange situation (for details, see Solomon & George, Chapter 14, this volume), infants of sensitively responsive mothers tended to make a full approach after a brief maternal absence, calmed in response to being held if they had become distressed, and returned to play relatively quickly. Their relationships with their mothers were classified as "secure."

A substantial minority of mothers in the Ainsworth et al. (1978) longitudinal study not only were relatively unresponsive when their infants cried at home, but rarely engaged in affectionate holding and tended to limit close bodily contact to routine care situations. Later in the first year, these mothers often rejected their infants' bids for physical closeness. Their infants cried more and showed more unprovoked aggressive behavior toward the mothers at home. In the strange situation, these infants displayed little or no attachment behavior during reunions. Instead, they snubbed the mother by turning away as she reentered the room and/or ignored her when she tried to engage her child in social interaction. These infants were classified as "avoidant." Ainsworth et al. regarded avoidance as a defensive (self-protective) adaptation to expected maternal rejection in stressful situations. Interestingly, some of these infants were quite anxious about brief separations from the mothers at home.

A small minority of mothers in the Ainsworth et al. (1978) longitudinal study responded with inconsistent sensitivity to infant signals at home during the first 3 months. Although they were sometimes quite responsive, these mothers frequently ignored or rejected their infants' social bids, but without rejecting or curtailing close bodily contact. In the strange situation, these infants were more clingy, cried intensely during the very brief period while their mothers were absent, and wanted to be picked up when they returned. However, they failed to gain the expected solace from physical contact: Instead of comfortably "sinking in" while being held, they squirmed and sometimes kicked. One subgroup seemed very angry, while another was more passive. Generally, these infants did not return to play. They were classified as "ambivalent" or "resistant."

That the patterns of infant–mother interaction during strange situation reunions represent an underlying organization or behavioral strategy vis-à-vis the attachment relationship with the mother is thus supported by the correlations of strange situation behavior with the home observation data. As many other chapters in this volume document, the validity of this claim is supported by a host of other studies, examining sequelae of attachment patterns assessed in the strange situation in infancy (see, e.g., Thompson, Chapter 13, this volume; Berlin & Cassidy, Chapter 30, this volume). Importantly, Main and her colleagues (Main, 1995; Main et al., 1985) discovered a strong link between these infant *behavioral* attachment strategies and parental *representational* strategies. Their findings were based on analyses of parental narratives based on lengthy, open-ended interviews about parental attachment experiences in the family of origin.

Moving to the Level of Representation and Intergenerational Transmission

Previous theorizing (e.g., Bowlby, 1973, 1980) and research (e.g., Belsky, 1984) had focused on the transmission of maladaptive parenting patterns, especially with respect to the so-called "cycle of abuse." Findings obtained with the Adult Attachment Interview (AAI; George, Kaplan, & Main, 1985) brought incisive new insights to this discussion. Main et al. (1985) were able to demonstrate that parents do not necessarily repeat the parenting they remember. In their study, it was *not* the reported *content* of attachment experiences in childhood, but the overall *organization* of the parents' narratives about these experiences (and by inference the organization of their internal working models), that predicted infant–parent attachment in the next generation.

A majority of parents in Main et al.'s (1985; see also Main, 1995) longitudinal study were able to provide coherent, emotionally open, and vivid accounts of childhood attachments during the AAI—a style of responding termed "secure/ autonomous" or "free to evaluate." Most of the parents falling into this group reported reasonably secure childhoods, but a minority described quite adverse attachment experiences in their families of origin. A parent's coherent AAI predicted secure infant strange situation classifications with that parent, regardless of whether remembered family-of-origin attachments were secure or insecure. Mothers whose AAIs were classified as secure/autonomous, then, had infants who were confident of obtaining comfort from their mothers when they needed it.

By contrast, a sizable minority of parents— termed "dismissing"—had a propensity to ward off interview questions with "I don't know" statements, to make generalizations that were unsupported or contradicted by detailed memories, and to discount or derogate the influence of attachment experiences on their development. Infants of these parents received avoidant classifications in the strange situation. Thus a parent's deflection of attention from or avoidance of attachment topics during the AAI paralleled the infant's behavioral avoidance of proximity to and interaction with that parent in the strange situation.

A smaller minority of parents—termed "preoccupied"—produced many conflictual/angry attachment memories during the AAI, interspersed with some positive ones. They often lost track of the interview questions and appeared to avoid deeper reflection on their childhood memories. In the strange situation, their infants tended to be classified as ambivalent. The infants' highly aroused attachment behavior, accompanied by overt anger, was matched at the representational level by their parent's lengthy attachment discussions, infused with unresolved anger.

A fourth group of parents produced interviews that were classified as "unresolved" (Main & Solomon, 1990). During the AAI, these parents had repeated representational lapses that disrupted the narrative flow during discussions of a parent's death or other traumatic events. Infants of these parents were classified as "disorganized" in the strange situation—a classification created by Main and Solomon (1990) to describe infants with puzzling behaviors (such as disoriented movements, dazed expressions, brief gestures of fearfulness, prolonged stilling, and stereotypies) that repeatedly and unaccountably intrude into the more familiar reunion patterns (for further details, see Solomon & George, Chapter 14, and Lyons-Ruth & Jacobvitz, Chapter 23, this volume). Main and Hesse (1990) attribute this disorganization to intruding perceptions of the parent as frightening or frightened (see Hesse, Chapter 19, this volume). Hence lapses in coherent processing characterize disorganized infants at the behavioral level and unresolved parents at the representational level.

Fonagy, Steele, Moran, Steele, and Higgitt (1993; see also Fonagy, Steele, & Steele, 1991) attribute the concordances between secure/autonomous AAI classifications and secure strange situation classifications to parents' capacity for self-reflectiveness, defined as understanding self and other in mentalizing terms (e.g., motivated by wishes, beliefs, regrets, values, and purposes). A highly self-reflective parent, Fonagy and colleagues maintain, is better able to see a situation from his or her infant's perspective, to empathize with the infant's emotions, and hence to respond to the infant's attachment signals with caring behavior that successfully meets the infant's needs for comforting. Insecure parents, by contrast, appear inadvertently to teach infants the very defensive strategies they themselves employ. For example, a mother who

laughingly disowned attachment feelings during the AAI strenuously tried to get her crying infant to laugh after a strange situation separation, rather than first trying to assuage the infant's distress.

To validate the concordances between AAI and strange situation classifications obtained by Main's group (Main, 1995; Main et al., 1985), van IJzendoorn (1995) submitted replication studies comprising 18 samples (over 800 dyads) from the United States, Great Britain, Israel, and the Netherlands to a meta-analysis. He found significant AAI–strange situation correlations for each of the three major classifications (i.e., secure/autonomous, dismissing, and preoccupied AAI classifications tended to be associative with secure, avoidant, and ambivalent strange situation classifications, respectively). Effect sizes were quite large and not dependent on whether the AAI was administered to a parent before or after the birth of the child. Of particular methodological importance was the finding that effect sizes were larger when coders had more extensive training in performing AAI classifications. Effect sizes were also smaller for father–child than for mother–child dyads, and for samples using separation–reunion procedures designed for preschoolers as opposed to the infant strange situation.

Attachment and Communication in Toddlers and Preschoolers

As expectable from attachment theory, strange situation classifications predict the quality of observed parent–child communication patterns beyond infancy (e.g., Beeghly & Cicchetti, 1994; Matas, Arend, & Sroufe, 1978; Radke-Yarrow, Cummings, Kuczynski, & Chapman, 1985). Interestingly, communication patterns between mothers and toddlers or preschoolers (e.g., Crowell & Feldman, 1988; Haft & Slade, 1989) also predict parental AAI classifications and children's attachment representations. In studies assessing the latter, children between 3 and 6 years of age are invited to respond to attachment-relevant family pictures or to enact and narrate attachment-relevant scenarios with small family figures and props (for a more detailed discussion, see Solomon & George, Chapter 14, this volume).

The first such study, conducted by Main et al. (1985), employed a revised version of the Separation Anxiety Test (SAT), adapted from Klagsbrun and Bowlby (1976). Each child interviewee was presented with a standard set of drawings showing parent–child separation situations ranging in severity from saying good night to parents' going on a 2-week trip. The child was then asked what the depicted boy or girl was feeling and what he or she was going to do. Six-year-olds' constructive and relevant responses were moderately correlated with secure attachment classifications both concurrently and in infancy. Revised versions of the SAT, used in subsequent studies with preschoolers (Shouldice & Stevenson-Hinde, 1992; Slough & Greenberg, 1990) corroborated Main et al.'s (1985) results. Cho (1994) additionally reported that children with secure SAT evaluations were judged by their mothers to be more positively responsive and less detached/distancing.

Building on Main et al.'s (1985) findings and ideas, Bretherton and Ridgeway devised an Attachment Story Completion Task (ASCT) that combined narrative and enactive techniques to assist younger children, for whom a purely verbal task was expected to be too difficult (see the Appendix to Bretherton, Ridgeway, & Cassidy, 1990). Again, coherently resolved, emotionally open story completions were moderately correlated with concurrent and earlier secure attachment classifications. They were also correlated with a maternal insight/sensitivity scale applied to interviews that explored a mother's thoughts and feelings about her relationship with her child (Bretherton, Biringen, Ridgeway, Maslin, & Sherman, 1989). Irrelevant, avoidant, or bizarre child responses (e.g., after the members of a separated family are reunited, their house burns down) were correlated with insecure attachment classifications both concurrently and in infancy. Analogous findings were reported by Cassidy (1988), who created a similar story completion procedure. Finally, Verschueren, Marcoen, and Schoefs (1996) reported intercorrelations among 5-year-olds' responses to the SAT, shortened versions of the ASCT, and Cassidy's (1988) story set, demonstrating that these measures assess a common underlying construct. That enactive–narrative techniques are useful beyond the preschool period was shown by Granot and Mayseless (1996), who found that ASCT portrayals of the child protagonist's attitude vis-à-vis threatening situations, and the coherence of narrative structure, were correlated with socially competent behavior by Israeli school children.

Thus a growing body of findings supports the view that a preschooler's ability to communicate openly and coherently about attachment topics with a friendly, nonjudgmental interviewer indexes a secure child–mother attachment relationship. Internal working models of self as valued and parents as supportive and caring, it is believed, allow the child to address anxiety-provoking situations (including story situations) constructively. Hence, as Oppenheim, Emde, and Warren (1997) point out, story resolutions need not be literal reenactments of experience to reveal security–insecurity. Children often include themes that represent hopes (e.g., the reunion of divorced families) and fears (e.g., child abandonment or parental death), along with analogues of actual experiences (Bretherton, Page, & Golby, 1997). Secure children's ability to explore their inner world freely, we suggest, is what explains their ability to tell coherent attachment stories (see also Solomon, George, & DeJong, 1995).

Adolescent Attachment and Working Models

In a chapter entitled "The Growth of Self-Reliance," Bowlby (1973) provided evidence for the continued importance of child–parent attachment during the period from preadolescence to early adulthood, claiming that "an unthinking confidence in the unfailing accessibility and support of attachment figures is the bedrock on which stable and self-reliant personalities are built" (p. 322). That is, unlike other theorists (e.g., A. Freud, 1958), Bowlby did not regard adolescent rebellion as a requirement for healthy individuation. Only recently have a majority of researchers in adolescent development come to share Bowlby's view that close relations with parents foster the growth of adolescent self-reliance and individuation (e.g., Grotevant & Cooper, 1986; Steinberg, 1990).

Although parents are eventually replaced by intimate partners as *principal* attachment figures, recent findings by Freeman (1997) show that in secure dyads, this does not generally occur during the high school years. Using an adolescent version of the SAT developed by Reznick (1993), Freeman evaluated and classified students' responses to separation pictures on the basis of rating scales closely modeled after AAI classifications devised by Main and Goldwyn (1994): emotional openness, coherence, dismissing/devaluing, self-blame, resistance/withholding, preoccupied anger, displacement of feelings, and anxiety. In addition, students were asked to nominate their principal attachment figures. Of those with secure SAT classifications, 80% nominated a parent (usually the mother) as the principal attachment figure, in preference to peers (including boyfriends and girlfriends), nonparental adults, and the self. Of those classified as dismissing, almost one-third named *themselves* as their primary support person. However, this did not imply feelings of mastery and confidence, as exemplified by the response of a dismissing adolescent who commented: "I think I rely on myself, yeah. I've always been somewhat apathetic. Like I said, I learn to live with things as they come 'cuz mostly you can't change" (pp. 80–81). The remainder of the dismissing students selected a friend or sibling (only 1 in 26 chose a parent), but many indicated that these relationships were not particularly close: "Like, I said, I really don't have time to sit and talk to them about it" (p. 81). Students with preoccupied SATs, on the other hand, chose siblings and best friends (two-thirds) and parents (one-third) as their primary support figures, with only 2 of 28 choosing themselves. The preoccupied students described being overly dependent on one source of support, but tended to passively expect the attachment figure to "pick up the pieces for you and take care of you" (p. 4). Even in young adulthood, a majority of individuals still nominated their parents as attachment figures (Fraley & Davis, 1997), although by then more were transferring their primary attachment to intimate partners.

Not only do secure adolescents regard a parent (usually the mother) as their primary attachment figure; they are also better able to communicate with this parent about attachment-related issues. Kobak, Cole, Ferenz-Gillies, Fleming, and Gamble (1993) found that adolescents assessed as secure-autonomous on the basis of their AAI transcripts were able to discuss a potentially stressful and contentious attachment-related topic with their mothers more constructively than those classified as insecure. When they disagreed with their mothers, these adolescents showed little dysfunctional anger, concentrating on problem solving rather than avoiding engagement or extensively dwelling on relationship problems. Insecure adolescents, by contrast, tended to interpret their mothers' contributions to the discussion as attacks on them or to use the discussion as an opportunity to attack their mothers.

Finally, in one of the few longitudinal studies tracking children and their families from birth to adolescence, Zimmermann and Grossmann (1996) found complex correlations between strange situation classifications in infancy and maternal as well as adolescent AAI classifica-

tions. The children's strange situation classifications with mother predicted the mothers' AAI classifications (the AAI was administered to mothers when the children were 6 years old). Maternal AAIs in turn predicted adolescent AAIs at age 16, but only after families with risk factors such as parental divorce, separation, and/or life-threatening illnesses were eliminated from the sample. These risk factors were associated with insecure AAI classifications, particularly preoccupation. On the other hand, an infant's strange situation patterns with mother or father did not predict adolescent AAIs, but at age 10, children who had been secure with their mothers in infancy reported seeking out attachment figures when sad, anxious, or angry. By contrast, 10-year-olds classified as avoidant in infancy reported using avoidant strategies when stressed or distressed. Also, 10-year-olds who later received dismissing AAI evaluations as adolescents perceived their mothers as less available and avoided everyday problems in school. Zimmermann and Grossmann's study thus illustrates that working-model changes are apparently set in train by stressful life events during the postinfancy years.

Attachment and Adult Pair Bonds

The assumption that committed adult couple relationships can be regarded as attachments underlay Bowlby's (1980) comparisons of widows' mourning with young children's responses to loss of a parent. However, the study of ongoing marital and couple relationships from an attachment perspective began much more recently.

There are, of course, important differences between parent–child and couple attachments: In addition to the bond-maintaining role of sexuality, couple relationships are reciprocal rather than asymmetrical (see Weiss, 1982; West & Sheldon-Keller, 1994). Whereas in child–parent relationships it is considered optimal for one person (the parent) to give and for another person (the child) to receive protection and care, in an adult love relationship such one-sidedness would be regarded as problematic. In addition, members of a couple enter their relationship with a lengthy history of attachments to parents and others behind them, in contrast to an infant, who is "inducted" into attachment patterns by parents.

Adults' internal working models of attachment to partners have been studied in two very different ways. One approach, taken by Owens et al. (1995), was to use a Current Relationship Interview (CRI) modeled on the AAI. Given that AAI classifications are believed to index an ability to reflect on attachment issues with emotional openness and coherence, significant concordances between individuals' style of responding to the AAI and the CRI were expected and obtained. However, the within-couple CRI concordances (discussing the couple relationship) were greater than the same couples' AAI concordances. In a few cases, both partners were able to discuss their couple relationship coherently, even though their AAI responses were classified as insecure and therefore not coherent. These findings suggest that the AAI and CRI do not assess a trait-like ability to talk about all attachment relationships in a particular manner. Instead, they suggest that openness or defensiveness/incoherence in communicating about attachment relationships is somewhat more relationship-specific than some earlier findings led us to believe.

A different approach to the study of internal working models in partner relationships was developed by Hazan and Shaver (1987) within the field of social psychology. Hazan and Shaver created three brief paragraphs describing adult analogues of Ainsworth et al.'s (1978) secure, avoidant, and ambivalent strange situation attachment patterns, into which they asked adults to classify themselves. In line with the reciprocity of adult attachments, however, the statements included direct and implied references to a partner as both providing and eliciting support and care. Adults subscribing to the secure style agreed that they found it relatively easy to get close to others, were comfortable with depending on others and having others depend on them, and were not often worried about being abandoned. Adults identifying with the avoidant style, by contrast, assented to being somewhat uncomfortable with closeness to others, found it difficult to trust others completely or to allow themselves to depend on them, and got nervous when love partners wanted to get too close. Individuals who chose the ambivalent style agreed that others were reluctant to get as close to them as they would like; worried that their partners did not really love them or would not want to stay with them; and wanted to get very close to their partners, although they knew that this sometimes scared people away.

In a subsequent study, Bartholomew and Horowitz (1991) identified two subgroups of avoidant individuals, whom they labeled "fearful" and "dismissing." Those in the fearful group wanted close relationships, but felt uncomfortable with closeness because, fearing rejection, they found it difficult to trust others completely, or to let themselves depend on them. Those in the dismissing group said that they were comfortable without close relationships, needed to feel independent and self-sufficient, and preferred neither to depend on others nor to have others depend on them. When study participants were provided with descriptions of fearful and dismissing avoidance, significantly more females identified themselves as fearful, whereas significantly more males self-identified as dismissing. These gender effects were not apparent before the two types of avoidance were differentiated.

Although Hazan and Shaver's (1987) adult self-classification procedure is theoretically linked to individual differences in infant attachment quality described by Ainsworth et al. (1978), the underlying approach differs radically from that taken by the AAI and related assessments, which are evaluated in terms of the overall coherence and organization of responses. Developmental attachment researchers in the AAI tradition have shied away from content analyses of answers to direct questions because of the confusions, contradictions, and idealizations they detected in responses to the AAI (e.g., Kobak & Sceery, 1988). Underlying the use of the self-classification procedure, by contrast, is the assumption that defensive processes will not seriously bias an individual's ability to identify with a specific attachment style. Supporting this assumption is the finding that a substantial proportion of individuals select one of the insecure styles, even though they do not necessarily regard these styles as preferable or optimal. For example, when individuals were asked with which kind of partner they would feel best, most selected the secure style for the ideal partner (Carnelley & Pietromonaco, 1991). In addition, the many theoretically expected correlates of the self-classifications strongly suggest that the AAI and the attachment style measures are tapping into similar underlying constructs, though further studies are needed. A useful beginning in this direction has been offered by Bartholomew and Shaver (1998).

Among the multitude of theoretically interesting findings that have resulted from the Hazan and Shaver (1987) self-classification procedure and related self-ratings (see Crowell, Fraley, & Shaver, Chapter 20, this volume), we review only a few that are particularly striking. Simpson, Rholes, and Nelligan (1992) assessed the attachment styles of dating men and women, and then observed each couple's caregiving and care-seeking behavior after the female partner was given a stress induction in the absence of the male partner. After the couples were reunited, secure women who had become anxious as a result of the induction tended to seek and accept reassurance from their male partners, whereas avoidant women did not. Likewise, secure men provided more reassurance and support to anxious partners, whereas avoidant men were less inclined to do so. In another study, individuals with differing attachment styles exhibited divergent attributional biases vis-à-vis imagined behavior by a partner (Collins, 1995). In response to vignettes describing unresponsive partner behavior, secure individuals expressed more confidence about the future of the hypothetical relationship and were less likely to view the imagined behavior as intentionally rejecting than were individuals with preoccupied or dismissing styles (note that Collins used AAI terminology to label attachment styles). Preoccupied and dismissing individuals, by contrast, feared that the event described in the vignette would put the relationship in jeopardy, and interpreted the hypothetical partner's behavior as unresponsive, untrustworthy, and purposefully rejecting. Finally, Mikulincer and Nachshon (1991) were able to show that secure individuals tend to adopt a more open communication style, thus corroborating findings that related AAI classifications to the quality of dyadic communication. When observed with partners, both secure and ambivalent individuals engaged in self-disclosure and were attracted to self-disclosing partners more than avoidant individuals. Ambivalent individuals, however, differed from secure ones by showing significantly less "disclosure flexibility and topical reciprocity" (p. 321).

Brennan, Clark, and Shaver (1998) recently reviewed studies using the self-classification approach, including rating scales based on the categorical statements. They identified two bipolar dimensions—security–anxiety and closeness–avoidance—that, in their view, best capture the gist of the self-categorizations. Interestingly, these dimensions resemble those underlying the infant strange situation classifications (Ainsworth et al., 1978).

Summary

It is now time to take stock and evaluate what the empirical studies of attachment at the representational level have taught us about internal working models. In general, the findings fit with Bowlby's claim that well-organized and revisable internal working models of attachment relationships go with open and coherent communication between parents and children from infancy to adolescence. From AAI patterns based on the organization of responses to structured open-ended questions about attachment-related memories, we can infer that defensive processes indeed interfere with the organization of working models. Individuals who are able to access and reflect on attachment-related memories with emotional openness and coherence, and who present a relevant, believable, consistent, and vivid account of parent–child attachment relations in their families of origin, tend to be effective attachment figures for their own infants and children. Importantly, patterns analogous to the AAI can be detected in these parents' accounts of caregiving (see George & Solomon, Chapter 28, this volume).

Given, however, that not all adults with coherent AAIs remember a secure childhood, a strict three-generation transmission model is not tenable. *What appears to count, in terms of transmitting patterns of relating from parents to children, is a parent's ability to product a coherently organized account of his or her own childhood attachment experiences as currently remembered and interpreted.* This extremely important finding sheds new light on both continuities and discontinuities in the intergenerational transmission of attachment patterns. It also corroborates what therapists and analysts since Freud have claimed as the desired outcome of successful therapy—namely, that the ability to tell a coherent life story is in some way linked to mental health (Marcus, 1984).

FUTURE DIRECTIONS

Like all important research, the rapidly growing body of findings about individual differences in the organization of attachment representations not only provides useful insights, but raises a myriad of new questions. We conclude this chapter by suggesting that attachment researchers focus on five areas concerned with the development, integration, and operation of working models: (1) developmental changes in child–parent attachment relationships as a function of the growing child's attribution-making and perspective-taking capacities; (2) the development/integration of the self in families where an infant's or child's attachment classifications with the two parents are nonconcordant; (3) the mutual negotiation/construction of attachment relationships in adulthood, especially when partners have different AAI classifications or attachment styles; (4) the development of attachment biographies, representing the vicissitudes of attachment relationships over time, especially for individuals who report insecure childhoods but present coherent accounts of these experiences; and (5) perhaps most importantly, the regulatory role of representation in attachment relationships. Our recommendations draw on ideas from the research on event memory, attribution theory, and symbolic interactionism discussed earlier in this chapter.

Developmental Changes in Child–Parent Attachment Relationships as Reflections of and as Reflected in Working Models

Attachment researchers have focused their efforts primarily on the development of measures that reliably identify attachment patterns, their continuity–discontinuity, and their intergenerational transmission. There is a dearth of research focusing on the implications of developmental changes in a child's working models for the actual functioning of attachment relationships from infancy to adolescence. Marvin and Greenberg (1982) did try to elucidate Bowlby's concept of the goal-corrected partnership during the preschool period; their work, however, did not lead to an upsurge of studies emphasizing the developmental changes in the everyday transaction as opposed to the security of attachment relationships (for a theoretical discussion, see Bretherton, 1991; Case, 1995).

Secure attachments in infancy foster a developing self-reflective capacity, which enhances an individual's ability to take another person's perspective and to process interpersonal feedback (e.g., Fonagy et al., 1993; Kobak & Sceery, 1988; Main, 1991). On the basis of this claim, it would make sense to investigate whether secure individuals develop more differentiated and resilient attachment relationships with others as they grow up. At the same time, the development of a greater capacity to make complex attributions may also lead to new ways of experiencing insecurity (see Noam, 1992, 1996). The systematic study of developmental changes in the experience and conduct of secure and insecure attachment relationships, we propose, may be especially enhanced by taking the meaning-

making approach to representation discussed earlier in this chapter.

Selves in Different Relationships

Despite modest concordances between an infant's strange situation classification with mother and father, as revealed by Fox, Kimmerly, and Schaefer's (1991) meta-analysis, a non-negligible number of infants and children are classified as secure with one parent and insecure with the other. Bowlby did not consider the case of a child's nonconcordant (conflicting) attachment experiences to two parents in the same family, focusing instead on defensive processes that ensue when a child constructs two conflicting (nonintegrated) working models of self and the same attachment figure. Empirical studies probing nonconcordant attachments to parents have so far been exclusively correlational, and can therefore do no more than document outcomes of infants' attachment to fathers and to mothers. In many of these investigations, a child's attachment classification with the mother is more predictive of later functioning (e.g., van IJzendoorn & Bakermans-Kranenburg, 1996); in others, however, children who have two secure attachment relationships fare better than those with two insecure attachments, with children who have nonconcordant attachments (secure with one parent, insecure with the other) falling in between. By recourse to the AAI and related measures and to other in-depth interviews, we may be able to gain insight into whether and how children, adolescents, and adults develop an integrated working model of self in the context of discordant attachments to their two parents (or other primary caregiving figures).

The Negotiation of Couple Attachment Relationships

As a result of the concordances between an infant's strange situation classification with a particular parent and the same parent's AAI classification, the AAI is sometimes regarded as a relationship measure. Yet, despite its power to predict infant–parent attachment, the AAI is neither a measure of a parent's attachment quality in the family of origin nor a measure of the parent's relationship to the infant/child. Nor does the AAI assess couple relationships. As previously noted, individuals classified as secure with the AAI are only slightly more likely than expected by chance to choose a secure partner (van IJzendoorn, 1995). Similarly, adult partners assessed with the Hazan and Shaver (1987) measure and related measures are not likely to seek partners with the same attachment style, ambivalent–ambivalent and avoidant–avoidant pairings being especially rare (Shaver & Hazan, 1993). Rather than providing insight into an individuated internal working model, co-constructed with a particular partner in a specific relationship, both the AAI and the Hazan–Shaver measures appear to access a more general working model or metamodel of how to enter into and behave in attachment relationships—or, as Main terms it, a state of mind vis-à-vis attachment relations (for a related discussion, see Crittenden, 1989).

Hence, despite extensive use of the AAI and especially of the Hazan–Shaver and similar measures in couple research, we are still fairly ignorant about how partners with differing attachment styles/AAI classifications go about the co-construction or joint negotiation of their attachment *relationship.* Owens et al. (1995) found concordances between two partners' AAI classifications to be lower than analogous concordances obtained with the CRI. However, partners' CRI concordances were not perfect. It will be important to discover whether the secure partner in a nonconcordant relationship tends to be security-promoting, eliciting more trust from and fostering a more open communication with an insecure partner than would have been expected if both partners were insecure. It is especially important to find out whether a relationship with a secure partner may eventually enable an insecure partner to revise his or her general working model of attachment relations, or whether any working-model change is limited to the particular relationship. It is also possible that an insecure individual may undermine a secure partner's style/strategy over time, perhaps even indirectly influencing how that partner relates to his or her child. So far we have learned that one parent's AAI classification does not predict an infant's strange situation classification with the other parent (Fonagy et al., 1993), but this study concerned only short-term outcomes. We need research tracking change in couple relationships over several years.

A Biographical Perspective

In addition to developing more complex working models based on more sophisticated perspective-taking and attribution-making abilities, individuals beyond infancy construct narratives about the course of their attachment relationships over time (Noam, 1988). So far the biographical aspect is almost absent from theorizing about internal working models, although the AAI could be interpreted from this point of view. Noam's (1996) distinction of "schemata" (high levels of perspective taking, self-reflectiveness, and meta-representational awareness) and "themata" (biographical life themes) may be useful for the analysis of attachment accounts. Unlike many cognitive theorists and some attachment theorists, Noam does not write themata off as "uninteresting content" in preference to more interesting organizational structure, such as integration or coherence, which is the focus of AAI classifications. Rather, he points out, it is through their life histories and hence their themata that individuals attain a unique identity. A themata-based approach to the study of attachment histories might explore how individuals represent the meaning of their attachment and caregiving experiences across the life course, allowing us to understand more clearly how earlier selves and patterns of relating are either incorporated into later selves/relationships or partially or wholly repudiated.

Representation as a Regulatory System

Finally, we urge that defensive processes in attachment relationships be studied as only one aspect of the much more general, regulatory function of representation. The internal modeling of self and other in relationship, we argue, regulates an individual's relationship adaptation through interpretive/attributional processes that are at the same time reality-reflecting and reality-creating—not only for the individual himself or herself, but for relationship partners as well. Insecure relationships, it appears, encourage self-deceptive and other-deceptive regulatory processes that are restrictive and maladaptive in the long run, as they undermine an individual's capacity to attend to and process attachment-relevant information. On the other hand, secure, supportive relationships encourage the creation of realities that are optimizing and enhancing for both self and other (see Bandura's [1982] research on self-efficacy). A trusting attitude is likely to elicit reciprocal trust, whereas a distrustful stance predisposes an individual to interpret others' neutral and even positive behaviors as ill-intentioned, in turn eliciting negative behavior from them (e.g., Cassidy, Kirsh, Scolton, & Parke, 1996; Dodge, Bates, & Pettit, 1990;

Suess, Grossmann, & Sroufe, 1992). In both cases, meaning making and attribution making at the same time reflect and create relational realities. Instead of putting primary emphasis only on the negative, defensive side of the meaning-regulating and meaning-creating function of representation, it is equally important to a acquire a deeper understanding of its positive side.

In conclusion, we advocate a more process-oriented approach to the study of working models as they are constructed, developed, and revised through participation in attachment relationships. The working-model approach to the study of representational processes in attachment relationships, we maintain, is a useful and fruitful one whose potential has by no means been exhausted.

ACKNOWLEDGMENTS

During the writing of this chapter, Inge Bretherton received support from the Vilas Trust. Helpful comments from Carol George are gratefully acknowledged.

REFERENCES

Ainsworth, M. D. S., Blehar, M. C., Waters, E., & Wall, S. (1978). *Patterns of attachment: A psychological study of the strange situation.* Hillsdale, NJ: Erlbaum.

Baldwin, M. W. (1992). Relational schemas and the processing of social information. *Psychological Bulletin, 112,* 461–484.

Bandura, A. (1982). Self-efficacy mechanism in human agency. *American Psychologist, 37,* 122–147.

Bartholomew, K., & Horowitz, L. M. (1991). Attachment styles among young adults: A test of a four-category model. *Journal of Personality and Social Psychology, 61,* 226–244.

Bartholomew, K., & Shaver, P. R. (1998). Methods of assessing adult attachment: Do they converge? In J. A. Simpson & W. S. Rholes (Eds.), *Attachment theory and close relationships* (pp. 25–45). New York: Guilford Press.

Bartlett, F. C. (1932). *Remembering.* Cambridge, England: Cambridge University Press.

Beeghly, M., & Cicchetti, D. (1994). Child maltreatment, attachment, and the self-system: Emergence of an internal state lexicon in toddlers at high social risk. *Development and Psychopathology, 6,* 5–30.

Belsky, J. (1984). The determinants of parenting: A process model. *Child Development, 55,* 83–96.

Bowlby, J. (1958). The child's tie to his mother. *International Journal of Psycho-Analysis, 39,* 350–373.

Bowlby, J. (1969/1982). *Attachment and loss: Vol. 1. Attachment.* New York: Basic Books.

Bowlby, J. (1973). *Attachment and loss: Vol. 2. Separation.* New York: Basic Books.

Bowlby, J. (1979). *The making and breaking of affectional bonds.* London: Tavistock.

Bowlby, J. (1980). *Attachment and loss: Vol. 3. Loss: Sadness and depression.* New York: Basic Books.

Bowlby, J. (1988). *A secure base.* New York: Basic Books.

Bowlby, J., & Parkes, C. M. (1970). Separation and loss within the family. In E. J. Anthony & C. Koupernik (Eds.), *The child in his family* (pp. 197–216). New York: Wiley.

Brennan, K. A., Clark, C. L., & Shaver, P. R. (1998). Self-report measurement of adult attachment: An integrative overview. In J. A. Simpson & W. S. Rholes (Eds.), *Attachment theory and close relationships* (pp. 46–76). New York: Guilford Press.

Bretherton, I. (1990). Open communication and internal working models: Their role in the development of attachment relationships. In R. A. Thompson (Ed.), *Nebraska Symposium on Motivation: Vol. 36. Socioemotional development* (pp. 59–113). Lincoln: University of Nebraska Press.

Bretherton, I. (1991). Pouring new wine into old bottles: The social self as internal working model. In M. Gunnar & L. A. Sroufe (Eds.), *Minnesota Symposia on Child Psychology: Vol. 23. Self processes in development* (pp. 1–41). Hillsdale, NJ: Erlbaum.

Bretherton, I. (1993). From dialogue to representation: The intergenerational construction of self in relationships. In C. A. Nelson (Ed.), *Minnesota Symposia on Child Psychology: Vol. 26. Memory and affect in development* (pp. 237–263). Hillsdale, NJ: Erlbaum.

Bretherton, I., & Beeghly, M. (1982). Talking about internal states: The acquisition of an explicit theory of mind. *Developmental Psychology, 18,* 906–921.

Bretherton, I., Biringen, Z., Ridgeway, D., Maslin, C., & Sherman, M. (1989). Attachment: The parental perspective. *Infant Mental Health Journal, 10,* 203–221.

Bretherton, I., Page, T., & Golby, B. (1997, April). *Narratives about attachment and authority by preschoolers in postdivorce families.* Papers presented at the biennial meeting of the Society for Research in Child Development, Washington, DC.

Bretherton, I., Ridgeway, D., & Cassidy, J. (1990). Assessing internal working models of the attachment relationship: An Attachment Story Completion Task for 3-year-olds. In D. Cicchetti, M. Greenberg, & E. M. Cummings (Eds.), *Attachment during the preschool years: Theory, research, and intervention* (pp. 272–308). Chicago: University of Chicago Press.

Carnelley, K. B., & Pietromonaco, P. R. (1991). *Thinking about a romantic relationship: Attachment style and gender influence emotional reactions and perceptions.* Paper presented at the third annual meeting of the American Psychological Society, Washington, DC.

Case, R. (1995). The role of psychological defenses in the representation and regulation of close personal relationships across the lifespan. In K. Fischer & G. Noam (Eds.), *Development and vulnerability in close relationships* (pp. 59–88). Hillsdale, NJ: Erlbaum.

Cassidy, J. (1988). Child–mother attachment and the self in six-year-olds. *Child Development, 59,* 121–134.

Cassidy, J., Kirsh, S. J., Scolton, K. L., & Parke, R. D. (1996). Attachment and representations of peers. *Developmental Psychology, 32,* 892–904.

Catlin, G., & Epstein, S. (1992). Unforgettable experiences: The relation of basic beliefs to extreme life events and childhood relationships with parents. *Social Cognition, 10,* 189–209.

Cho, E. (1994). *Mothers' authoritative and authoritarian parenting: Attitudes related to preschoolers' attachment representations and teacher-rated social competence.* Unpublished doctoral dissertation, University of Wisconsin–Madison.

Collins, N. L. (1995). Working models of attachment: Implications for explanation, emotion, and behavior. *Journal of Personality and Social Psychology, 71,* 810–832.

Collins, N. L., & Read, S. J. (1990). Adult attachment, working models, and relationship quality in dating couples. *Journal of Personality and Social Psychology, 58,* 644–663.

Craik, K. (1943). *The nature of explanation.* Cambridge, England: Cambridge University Press.

Crittenden, P. (1989). Internal representational models of attachment relationships. *Infant Mental Health Journal, 11,* 259–277.

Crowell, J. A., & Feldman, S. S. (1988). Mothers' internal working models of relationships and children's behavioral and developmental status: A study of mother–infant interaction. *Child Development, 59,* 1273–1285.

Dix, T., Ruble, D., & Zambarano, R. J. (1989). Mothers' implicit theory of discipline: Child effects, parent effects, and the attribution process. *Child Development, 60,* 1373–1391.

Dixon, N. F. (1971). *Subliminal perception: The nature of a controversy.* London: McGraw-Hill.

Dodge, K., Bates, J. E., & Pettit, G. S. (1990). Mechanisms in the cycle of violence. *Science, 250,* 1678–1683.

Dunn, J. (1993). *Young children's close relationships: Beyond attachment.* Newbury Park, CA: Sage.

Erdelyi, H. M. (1985). *Psychoanalysis: Freud's cognitive psychology.* San Francisco: W. H. Freeman.

Fairbairn, W. R. D. (1952). *An object-relations theory of the personality.* New York: Basic Books.

Fonagy, P., Steele, M., Moran, G., Steele, H., & Higgitt, M. D. (1993). Measuring the ghost in the nursery: An empirical study of the relation between parents' mental representation of childhood experiences and their infants' security of attachment. *Journal of the American Psychoanalytic Association, 41,* 957–989.

Fonagy, P., Steele, H., & Steele, M. (1991). Intergenerational patterns of attachment: Maternal representations during pregnancy and subsequent infant–mother attachments. *Child Development, 62,* 891–905.

Fox, N., Kimmerly, N. L., & Schaefer, W. D. (1991). Attachment to mother/attachment to father: A meta-analysis. *Child Development, 62,* 210–225.

Fraley, R. C., & Davis, K. (1997). Attachment formation and transfer in young adults' close friendships and romantic relationships. *Personal Relationships, 4,* 131–144.

Freeman, H. (1997). *Who do you turn to?: Individual differences in late adolescent perceptions of parents and peers as attachment figures.* Unpublished doctoral dissertation, University of Wisconsin–Madison.

Freud, A. (1958). Adolescence. *Psychoanalytic Study of the Child, 13,* 255–278.

Freud, S. (1963). *An outline of psychoanalysis* (J. Strachey, Trans.). New York: Norton. (Original work published 1940)

George, C., Kaplan, N., & Main, M. (1985). *Adult Attachment Interview* (2nd ed.). Unpublished manuscript, University of California at Berkeley.

George, C., & Solomon, J. (1996). Representational models of relationships: Links between caregiving and attachment. *Infant Mental Health Journal, 17,* 198–216.

Gibson, E. J. (1982). The concept of affordances in development: The renascence of functionalism. In W. A. Collins (Ed.), *Minnesota Symposia on Child Psychology: Vol. 15.*

The concept of development (pp. 55–81). Hillsdale, NJ: Erlbaum.

Goodman, G. S., Quas, J. A., Batterman-Faunce, J. M., Riddlesberger, M. M., & Kuhn, J. (1994). Predictors of accurate and inaccurate memories of traumatic events experienced in childhood. *Consciousness and Cognition, 3,* 269–294.

Granot, D., & Mayseless, O. (1996, August). *The relationships between attachment patterns and adaptive functioning in the school environment amongst children in middle childhood.* Poster session presented at the biennial meeting of the Society for the Study of Behavioral Development, Québec City, Québec, Canada.

Grotevant, H. D., & Cooper, C. R. (1986). Individuation in family relationships. *Human Development, 29,* 82–100.

Haft, W., & Slade, A. (1989). Affect attunement and maternal attachment: A pilot study. *Infant Mental Health Journal, 10,* 157–172.

Hazan, C., & Shaver, P. R. (1987). Romantic love conceptualized as an attachment process. *Journal of Personality and Social Psychology, 52,* 511–524.

Heider, F. (1958). *The psychology of interpersonal relations.* New York: Wiley.

Johnson-Laird, P. N. (1983). *Mental models.* Cambridge, MA: Harvard University Press.

Klagsbrun, M., & Bowlby, J. (1976). Responses to separation from parents: A clinical test for young children. *British Journal of Projective Psychology, 21,* 7–21.

Klein, M. (1932). *The psycho-analysis of children.* London: Hogarth Press.

Kobak, R. R., Cole, H. E., Ferenz-Gillies, R., Fleming, W. S., & Gamble, W. (1993). Attachment and emotion regulation during mother–teen problem solving: A control theory analysis. *Child Development, 64,* 231–245.

Kobak, R. R., & Sceery, A. (1988). Attachment in late adolescence: Working models, affect regulation, and perceptions of self and others. *Child Development, 59,* 135–146.

Lewin, K. (1933). Environmental forces. In C. Murchison (Ed.), *A handbook of child psychology* (2nd ed., pp. 590–625). Worcester, MA: Clark University Press.

Main, M. (1995). Recent studies in attachment. In S. Goldberg, R. Muir, & J. Kerr (Eds.), *Attachment theory: Social, developmental, and clinical perspectives* (pp. 407–474). Hillsdale, NJ: Analytic Press.

Main, M., & Goldwyn, R. (1994). *Adult Attachment Interview scoring and classification manual.* Unpublished manuscript, University of California at Berkeley.

Main, M., & Hesse, E. (1990). The insecure disorganized/disoriented attachment pattern in infancy: Precursors and sequelae. In M. Greenberg, D. Cicchetti, & E. M. Cummings (Eds.), *Attachment during the preschool years: Theory, research, and intervention* (pp. 161–182). Chicago: University of Chicago Press.

Main, M., Kaplan, K., & Cassidy, J. (1985). Security in infancy, childhood and adulthood: A move to the level of representation. In I. Bretherton & E. Waters (Eds.), *Growing points of attachment theory and research. Monographs of the Society for Research in Child Development, 50*(1–2, Serial No. 209), 66–104.

Main, M., & Solomon, J. (1990). Procedures for identifying infants as disorganized/disoriented during the Ainsworth Strange Situation. In M. T. Greenberg, D. Cicchetti, & E. M. Cummings (Eds.), *Attachment in the preschool years: Theory, research, and intervention* (pp. 121–160). Chicago: University of Chicago Press.

Marcus, S. (1984). Freud and Dora: Story, history and case history. In S. Marcus (Ed.), *Freud and the culture of psy-*

choanalysis (pp. 42–86). Winchester, MA: Allen & Unwin.

Marvin, R. S., & Greenberg, M. T. (1982). Preschoolers' changing conceptions of their mothers: A social-cognitive study of mother–child attachment. In D. Forbes & M. T. Greenberg (Eds.), *New directions for child development: No. 18. Children's planning strategies* (pp. 47–60). San Francisco: Jossey-Bass.

Matas, L., Arend, R. A., & Sroufe, L. A. (1978). Continuity and adaptation in the second year: The relationship between quality of attachment and later competence. *Child Development, 49,* 547–556.

McGinn, C. (1989). *Mental content.* New York: Blackwell.

Mead, G. H. (1910). Social consciousness and the consciousness of meaning. *Psychological Bulletin, 7,* 397–405.

Mead, G. H. (1913). The social self. *Journal of Philosophy, Psychology and Scientific Methods, 10,* 374–380.

Mead, G. H. (1934). *Mind, self, and society.* Chicago: University of Chicago Press.

Metzinger, T. (1993). *Subjekt und Selbstmodell: Die Perspektivität phänomenalen Bewusstseins vor dem Hintergrunt einer naturalistischen Theories mentaler Repräsentation.* Paderborn, Germany: Schönigh.

Mikulincer, M., & Nachshon, O. (1991). Attachment styles and patterns of self-disclosure. *Journal of Personality and Social Psychology, 61,* 321–331.

Miller, P. J., Hoogstra, L., Mintz, J., Fung, H., & Williams, K. (1993). Troubles in the garden and how they get resolved: The history of a story in one child's life. In C. A. Nelson (Ed.), *Minnesota Symposia on Child Psychology: Vol. 26. Memory and affect in development.* Hillsdale, NJ: Erlbaum.

Nelson, K. (1986). *Event knowledge: Structure and function in development.* Hillsdale, NJ: Erlbaum.

Nelson, K. (1993). Events, narratives, memory: What develops? In C. A. Nelson (Ed.), *Minnesota Symposia on Child Psychology: Vol. 26. Memory and affect in development* (pp. 1–24). Hillsdale, NJ: Erlbaum.

Noam, G. G. (1988). The self, adult development, and the theory of biography and transformation. In D. K. Lapsley & F. C. Power (Eds.), *Self, ego, and identity: Integrative approaches* (pp. 3–29). New York: Springer.

Noam, G. G. (1992). Development as the aim of clinical intervention. *Development and Psychopathology, 4,* 679–696.

Noam, G. G. (1996). High-risk youth: Transforming our understanding of human development. *Human Development, 39,* 1–17.

Norman, D. A. (1976). *Memory and attention: Introduction to human information processing* (2nd ed.). New York: Wiley.

Oppenheim, D., Emde, R. N., & Warren, S. (1997). Emotion regulation in mother–child narrative co-construction: Associations with children's narratives and adaptation. *Developmental Psychology, 33,* 284–294.

Owens, G., Crowell, J. A. Pan, H., Treboux, D., O'Connor, E., & Waters, E. (1995). The prototype hypothesis and the origins of attachment working models: Adult relationships with parents and romantic partners. In E. Waters, B. E. Vaughn, G. Posada, & K. Kondo-Ikemura (Eds.), Caregiving, cultural, and cognitive perspectives on secure-base behavior and working models: New growing points of attachment theory and research. *Monographs of the Society for Research in Child Development, 60*(2–3, Serial No. 244), 216–233.

Piaget, J. (1951). *Play, dreams and imitation in childhood.* New York: Norton.

Piaget, J. (1952). *The origins of intelligence in children.* New York: Norton.

Piaget, J. (1954). *The child's construction of reality.* New York: Basic Books.

Radke-Yarrow, M., Cummings, E. M., Kuczynski, L., & Chapman, M. (1985). Patterns of attachment in two- and three-year-olds in normal families and families with parental depression. *Child Development, 56,* 884–893.

Reznick, G. (1993). *Measuring attachment in early adolescence: A manual for the administration, coding and interpretation of the Separation Anxiety Test for 11 to 14 year olds.* Unpublished manuscript, Westat, Inc., Rockville, MD.

Schank, R. C. (1982). *Dynamic memory: A theory of reminding and learning in computers and people.* Cambridge, England: Cambridge University Press.

Schank, R. C., & Abelson, R. P. (1977). *Scripts, plans, goals and understanding.* Hillsdale, NJ: Erlbaum.

Shaver, P. R., Collins, N., & Clark, C. L. (1996). Attachment styles and internal working models of self and relationship partners. In G. J. O. Fletcher & J. Fitness (Eds.), *Knowledge structures in close relationships: A social psychological approach* (pp. 25–61). Mahwah, NJ: Erlbaum.

Shaver, P., & Hazan, C. (1993). Adult romantic attachment: Theory and evidence. In D. Perlman & W. Jones (Eds.), *Advances in personal relationships* (Vol. 4, pp. 29–70). London: Jessica Kingsley.

Shouldice, A., & Stevenson-Hinde, J. (1992). Coping with security distress: The Separation Anxiety Test and attachment classification at 4.5 years. *Journal of Child Psychology and Psychiatry, 33,* 331–348.

Simpson, J. A., Rholes, W. S., & Nelligan, J. S. (1992). Support-seeking and support-giving within couple members in an anxiety-provoking situation: The role of attachment styles. *Journal of Personality and Social Psychology, 62,* 434–446.

Slough, N., & Greenberg, M. (1990). Five-year-olds' representations of separation from parents: Responses for self and a hypothetical child. In I. Bretherton & M. Watson (Eds.), *New directions for child development: No. 48. Children's perspectives on the family* (pp. 67–84). San Francisco: Jossey-Bass.

Solomon, J., George, C., & DeJong, A. (1995). Children classified as controlling at age six: Evidence of disorganized representational strategies and aggression at home and school. *Development and Psychopathology, 7,* 447–464.

Sroufe, L. A., & Fleeson, J. (1986). Attachment and the construction of relationships. In W. Hartrup & Z. Rubin (Eds.), *Relationships and development* (pp. 51–71). Hillsdale, NJ: Erlbaum.

Steinberg, L. (1990). Autonomy, conflict and harmony in the family relationship. In S. S. Feldman & G. R. Elliott (Eds.), *At the threshold: The developing adolescent* (pp. 255–276). Cambridge, MA: Harvard University Press.

Stern, D. N. (1985). *The interpersonal world of the infant.* New York: Basic Books.

Steward, M. S. (1993). Medical procedures: A context for studying memory and emotion. In C. A. Nelson (Ed.), *Minnesota Symposia on Child Psychology: Vol. 26. Memory and affect in development* (pp. 171–225). Hillsdale, NJ: Erlbaum.

Suess, G. J., Grossmann, K. E., & Sroufe, L. A. (1992). Effects of infant attachment to mother and father on quality of adaptation in preschool: From dyadic to individual organization of self. *International Journal of Behavioral Development, 15,* 43–65.

Tulving, E. (1972). Episodic and semantic memory. In E.

Tulving & W. Donaldson (Eds.), *Organization of memory* (pp. 381–403). New York: Academic Press.

van IJzendoorn, M. H. (1995). Adult attachment representations, parental responsiveness, and infant attachment: A meta-analysis on the predictive validity of the Adult Attachment Interview. *Psychological Bulletin, 117,* 387–403.

van IJzendoorn, M. H., & Bakermans-Kranenburg, M. J. (1996). Attachment representations in mothers, fathers, adolescents, and clinical groups: A meta-analytic search for normative data. *Journal of Consulting and Clinical Psychology, 64,* 8–27.

Verschueren, K., Marcoen, A., & Schoefs, V. (1996). The internal working model of the self, attachment and competence in 5-year-olds. *Child Development, 67,* 2493–2511.

Weiss, R. S. (1982). Attachment in adult life. In C. M. Parkes & J. Stevenson-Hinde (1992), *The place of attachment in human behavior* (pp. 171–184). New York: Basic Books.

Wellman, H. M. (1990). *The child's theory of mind.* Cambridge, MA: MIT Press.

West, M., & Sheldon-Keller, A. (1994). *Patterns of relating: An adult attachment perspective.* New York: Guilford Press.

Winnicott, D. W. (1958). *Collected papers: Through pediatrics to psychoanalysis.* New York: Basic Books.

Young, J. Z. (1964). *A model for the brain.* London: Oxford University Press.

Zimmermann, P., & Grossmann, K. (1996, August). *Transgenerational aspects of stability in attachment quality between parents and their adolescent children.* Paper presented at the biennial meeting of the International Society for the Study of Behavioral Development, Québec City, Québec, Canada.

II
BIOLOGICAL PERSPECTIVES

❖

6

Attachment Theory in Modern Evolutionary Perspective

❖

JEFFRY A. SIMPSON

It has often been assumed that animals were in the first place rendered social, and that they feel as a consequence uncomfortable when separated from each other, and comfortable whilst together; but it is a more probable view that these sensations were first developed, in order that those animals which would profit by living in society, should be induced to live together, . . . for with those animals which were benefited by living in close association, the individuals which took the greatest pleasure in society would best escape various dangers; whilst those that cared least for their comrades and lived solitary would perish in greater numbers.

—DARWIN (1871/1981, Vol. 1, p. 80)

In some respects, as this quotation suggests, Charles Darwin may have been the first attachment theorist. Although he focused on "society" (instead of significant persons in an individual's life) and "comrades" (instead of attachment figures), Darwin was the first person to appreciate the degree to which human social nature may have been the product of strong, directional selection pressures. John Bowlby, who not only admired Darwin's theoretical vision but served as one of his principal biographers (see Bowlby, 1991), spent much of his remarkable career treading an intellectual path that Darwin had established. Melding ideas from Darwin's theory of evolution by natural selection, object relations theory, control systems theory, evolutionary biology, and the fields of ethology and cognitive psychology, Bowlby (1969/1982, 1973, 1980) developed a grand theory of personality development across the lifespan—attachment theory. One reason why attachment theory is so unique, generative, and prominent in contemporary social and behavioral sciences is because of its deep, foundational ties to principles of evolution. Indeed, as we shall see, attachment theory *is* an evolutionary theory.

Bowlby's interest in the cognitive, emotional, and behavioral ties that bind humans to one another began with an astute observation. Across all human cultures and even several primate species, young and vulnerable infants tend to display a specific sequence of reactions following separation from their stronger, older, and often wiser caregivers. Immediately after separation, infants often protest vehemently, crying, screaming, and throwing temper tantrums as they search for their caregivers. Bowlby reasoned that strong protest during the early phases of caregiver absence is a good initial strategy to promote survival, particularly in species with developmentally immature and highly dependent infants. Intense protests often bring caregivers back to their infants, who, during evolutionary history, should have been vulnerable to injury or predation if left unattended even for brief periods of time.

If loud and persistent protests fail to retrieve their caregivers, infants soon enter a second stage—despair, during which their motor activity slows down and they fall silent. From an evolutionary standpoint, Bowlby realized that despondency is a logical second strategy to promote survival. Excessive movement for long periods of time may result in accident or injury, and loud protests coupled with movement are likely to draw predators. Thus, if protests fail to retrieve caregivers, the next best survival strategy is to avoid actions that may increase the long-term risks of self-inflicted harm or predation.

Bowlby noted that after a period of despair, infants who are not reunited with their caregivers enter a third and final stage—detachment. During this phase, an infant slowly begins to resume normal activity in the absence of a caregiver, often behaving in a highly independent and self-reliant manner. Bowlby (1969/1982) hypothesized that the function of detachment is to clear the way for new affectional bonds with other potential caregivers. According to this view, emotional ties with former caregivers must be partially if not fully relinquished before new bonds can be formed. From the vantage point of evolution, detachment allows infants to cast off old ties and begin the process of forming new ones with caregivers who are willing to provide the resources infants need for survival. Bowlby's insight about the possible evolutionary function of detachment re-mains one of his greatest theoretical achievements.

Bowlby believed that the cognitive, emotional, and behavioral reactions that characterize each stage reflect the operation of an innate attachment system. The reason why the attachment system evolved and remains so deeply ingrained in human nature is that it provided a good solution to one of the greatest adaptive problems our ancestors faced: how to increase the chances of survival through the most vulnerable years of development. Guided by Darwin, Bowlby believed that the attachment system was genetically "wired" into our species through intense directional selection during evolutionary history.

There were, of course, some limitations to Bowlby's early understanding and application of evolutionary thinking. Perhaps the most glaring shortcoming was his exclusive focus on the differential *survival* of individuals, rather than on their differential *reproduction* (and especially the differential replication of their genes). To enhance reproductive fitness, individuals must not only survive to reproductive age; once there, they must successfully mate and raise children, who in turn must mate and raise their own children, and so on. Survival to adulthood means nothing in the currency of evolutionary fitness without successful reproduction and parenting. Contrary to common folklore, evolution is not about the "survival of the fittest." Rather, it focuses on differential reproduction of one's genetic material—that is, being able to maximize the representation of one's genes in future generations. Of course, survival is a mandatory prerequisite to successful reproduction, and Bowlby was wise to build the foundation of attachment theory on this component of reproductive fitness.

Perhaps the biggest impediment to Bowlby's understanding of evolution, however, was the stagnant state of evolutionary thinking when he started to formulate attachment theory. The foundation of attachment theory was firmly in place well before several important "middle-level" theories of evolution—theories addressing the major adaptive problems that humans probably confronted during different life stages throughout evolutionary history—were introduced in the mid-1960s and early 1970s. As a result, Bowlby was not privy to much of what we now know as the "modern" evolutionary perspective when he started to erect the major tenets of attachment theory. Until recently, relatively few of these modern evolutionary theories have been linked to attachment theory and research. One objective of this chapter is to facilitate this process.

Other chapters in this volume provide excellent summaries of research on attachment at various points in the lifespan. The main goal of the present chapter is to place attachment theory in a modern (or neo-Darwinian) evolutionary perspective. As we shall see, the modern evolutionary perspective consists of an array of theories, principles, and assumptions, all of which share a premise: that much of the human mind and human social behavior reflect adaptations to major obstacles to inclusive fitness that humans recurrently faced in evolutionary history.

The chapter has five major sections. The first section reviews recent theoretical developments that have transformed Darwin's original theory of natural selection into the modern evolutionary perspective. Where attachment theory fits within the hierarchy of evolutionary principles and middle-level theories is discussed. The second section describes the major adaptive problems that our ancestors had to overcome, along with the probable nature of the social environment(s) they inhabited during the last 100,000 years. Reviewing anthropological evidence from hunter–gatherer tribes, I identify the most stable features of our social "environment of evolutionary adaptedness" (EEA; Bowlby, 1969/1982).

The third section focuses on how the two major components of attachment theory—the normative component and the individual-difference component—fit within an evolutionary view of human behavior. The discussion of normative attachment begins with a review of infant–mother bonding in the first days of life, followed by the species-typical course through which attachment bonds develop over the lifespan. Different patterns or styles of attachment are viewed as adaptive, ecologically contingent behavioral strategies that exist because they facilitate the basic functions that the attachment system evolved to serve, given different rearing environments. The fourth section indicates how Trivers' (1974) theory of parent–offspring conflict sheds new light on several attachment-related phenomena, including how and why parents and children negotiate issues of weaning, parental investment, and the child's eventual independence from his or her parents. Guided by principles from life history theory (Stearns, 1992; Williams, 1966), the final major section reviews recent evolutionary models that suggest how and why different attachment patterns in childhood may affect the trajectory of social and personality development, culminating in different reproductive strategies in adulthood.

THE PLACE OF ATTACHMENT THEORY IN MODERN EVOLUTIONARY THINKING

Although it remains one of the great intellectual accomplishments in the history of science, Darwin's original theory of evolution was incomplete and imprecise, especially in view of recent theoretical advances that have shaped the modern evolutionary perspective. Darwin's thinking was constrained by several factors. First, his theory predated our understanding of genes and patterns of inheritance. Gregor Mendel's pioneering research on heritable traits in plants, although first published in 1866, was neither understood nor appreciated until after the turn of the century. Second, because Darwin did not focus on genes as the principal units on which natural selection operates, he was not able to solve the enigma of why some organisms engage in self-sacrificial or nonreproductive behavior. It was not until the ap-

pearance of William Hamilton's seminal 1964 paper titled "The Genetical Evolution of Social Behaviour" that the groundbreaking concept of inclusive fitness finally solved this perplexing riddle. Third, Darwin had only a dim understanding of how sexual recombination and genetic mutations provide the variation from which better adaptations and new species are selected. Finally, Darwin did not fully appreciate the extent to which specific adaptations are associated with both benefits and costs. Darwin was inclined to focus more on the benefits bestowed by certain adaptations, and to gloss over the costs. Modern evolutionary theorists now use cost–benefit analyses to understand the nature of adaptations (see Cronin, 1991). Perhaps the clearest sign of Darwin's brilliance was his ability to sketch the broad outlines of how natural selection operates without the benefits of this later knowledge.

The Rise of Modern Evolutionary Theories

Surprisingly few theoretical advances were made for more than a century after Darwin published his second landmark book, *The Descent of Man*, in 1871. At the dawn of the 1960s, one historian lamented: "With respect to the origin of man's distinctively human attributes, Darwin would be disappointed to find matters little advanced beyond his own speculations in *The Descent of Man*" (Greene, 1961/1963, p. 114). This state of affairs began to change rapidly in 1964. With the development of the concept of inclusive fitness, Hamilton (1964) ushered in the theory of kin selection. By focusing on the gene instead of the individual organism as the primary unit upon which selection pressures operate, Hamilton was able to solve perhaps the biggest paradox that Darwin never unraveled: Namely, in the evolutionary struggle for reproductive fitness, why do some organisms forgo reproduction in order to assist the reproductive efforts of their close kin?

Hamilton solved this riddle by realizing that an individual's total (inclusive) fitness should depend on his or her own reproductive output plus the total reproductive output of kin, who share a portion of the individual's genes. If genes are the units on which selection operates, and if individuals can facilitate the reproductive output of their biological relatives, then occasions may arise when it will pay to sacrifice one's own reproductive output to help facilitate the reproduction of close relatives. Unlike Darwin, Hamilton was able to calculate the degree to which pairs of individuals are likely to share novel genes. Given the way sexual recombination works, parents on average share half of their genes with their children; full siblings share half of their genes with one another; grandparents share one-quarter of their genes with their grandchildren; aunts and uncles share one-quarter of their genes with their nieces and nephews; and first cousins share one-eighth of their genes.

With this knowledge in hand, Hamilton was able to show that self-sacrificial behavior should have been selected in situations where the costs of engaging in an act were less than the benefits to be gained times the degree to which individuals were biologically related (i.e., altruistic behavior should have been seen when $C < Br$, where C = costs, B = benefits, and r = the degree of relatedness). Under these assumptions, for example, one's inclusive fitness would have been increased if one sacrificed oneself (and thus future personal reproductive potential) to save the lives of three brothers or sisters (each of whom carried half one's genes). Sacrificing oneself in order to save only one sibling would have lowered inclusive fitness, because only 50% of one's genes would have had a chance to be propagated in the future gene pool. Saving two siblings would have amounted to an even trade, since the two surviving siblings would, on average, have carried 100% of one's genes. But saving three siblings might have allowed 150% of one's genes to make it to the next generation. Hamilton's intellectual breakthrough marked the beginning of the modern evolutionary perspective. Indeed, inclusive-fitness theory is the general, overarching theory of natural selection from which nearly all middle-level evolutionary theories are derived.

In the decade that followed Hamilton's work, several highly influential theories appeared, each of which addressed specific adaptive problems that humans confronted and had to "solve" in our ancestral past. Although Hamilton's research was not cited by Bowlby (1969/1982), Bowlby's first major statement on attachment was one of the first middle-level evolutionary theories. In developing attachment theory, Bowlby was trying to understand and explain how our ancestors successfully "solved" the first barrier to inclusive fitness—how to survive through the perils of infancy.

A flood of theoretical advances ensued in the 1970s, most of which were launched by Robert Trivers. In 1971, Trivers introduced the theory of reciprocal altruism, which is an attempt to account for why organisms with inherently "selfish" genes should at times be inclined to behave in a cooperative manner with non-kin. Trivers outlined specific conditions under which selective reciprocal altruism should enhance an individual's inclusive fitness. Using computer simulations, Axelrod (1984) has demonstrated how a quid pro quo strategy toward helping others (i.e., a "tit-for-tat" strategy) could evolve and become stable amid a host of competing strategies.

A year later, Trivers (1972) unveiled the theory of parental investment and sexual selection. This broad middle-level theory proposes that different amounts of parental investment in children govern sexual selection, accounting for why males and females in many species tend to differ in certain physical attributes (e.g., relative body size) and behavioral characteristics (e.g., propensity toward aggression). According to Trivers, in species where one sex typically invests more time, effort, resources, and energy in producing and raising offspring (usually women, in the case of human beings), the other sex (usually men) should compete among themselves to mate with the higher-investing sex. The intense intrasexual competition that results should have produced some of the modal physical, behavioral, and emotional differences between men and women.

In 1974, Trivers introduced the theory of parent–offspring conflict. This theory attempts to explain why parents and their children—pairs of individuals who share half their genes and should be strongly dependent on each other to pass them on to future generations—tend to have relationships filled with strife and turmoil. Because the theory of parent–offspring conflict has a number of fascinating and important implications for how patterns of attachment between children and their caregivers can be understood, the theory is discussed in more detail later in this chapter.

More recently, life history theory has emerged as a major perspective in evolutionary thinking (see Clutton-Brock, 1991; Lessells, 1991; Stearns, 1976, 1992; Williams, 1966). To leave descendants, individuals must solve problems of survival, growth, development, and reproduction across the lifespan. Depending on life circumstances, the time, effort, and energy that an individual expends can be allotted to somatic effort (i.e., investing in growth and development of the body to facilitate survival en route to eventual reproduction) and reproductive effort (i.e., funneling effort toward progeny). Reproductive effort has two components: mating effort (i.e., locating, courting, and retaining a suitable mate) and parenting effort (i.e., gestating, giving birth, and engaging in postnatal child care). Life history theory deals with how individuals optimally allocate somatic versus reproductive effort, given current life circumstances.

Attachment Theory in the Hierarchy of Evolutionary Theories

To comprehend the place of attachment theory within a modern evolutionary perspective, one must understand what the major middle-level evolutionary theories are and how they relate to one another. Figure 6.1, adapted from Buss (1995), shows the hierarchical structure of evolutionary theories that treat the individual (i.e., novel genes) as the unit upon which natural selection operates. Inclusive-fitness theory, which incorporates Darwin's concept of fitness due to one's own reproduction and Hamilton's concept of fitness due to the reproduction of one's biological relatives, is the superordinate, general theory of evolution from which nearly all middle-level theories are derived. The middle-level theories, each of which addresses special adaptive problems that humans faced during evolutionary history, lie one level below inclusive-fitness theory. Each middle-level theory in turn contains a small number of basic principles that reside at the next level down. Most evolutionary hypotheses and predictions are derived from these basic principles.[1]

Sexual-selection theory, for example, comprises two major principles concerning mate selec-

tion. It suggests that the search for mates should be driven by the degree to which (1) prospective mates are likely to be good investors in and providers for future offspring, and (2) prospective mates have desirable attributes (e.g., physical attractiveness or other mate-attracting features) that could be passed on to offspring. Specific predictions and hypotheses come from each of these principles. Similarly, attachment theory comprises two major theoretical principles or components. The normative component of attachment theory makes predictions about relatively universal, stable patterns of behavior in response to situations in which individuals feel ill, fatigued, or distressed. The individual-difference component offers predictions about the ontogenic origins of different patterns or styles of attachment, including why each pattern is likely to be "adaptive" in specific environments. Life history theory is likewise partitioned into two basic components: the investment of time, energy, and resources in somatic effort versus reproductive effort.

Although middle-level theories were formulated to deal with different problems of adaptation, many of them have overlapping implications for social behavior. The theory of kin selection, for example, specifies when conflict should arise between parents and their children; the theory of parent–offspring conflict indicates when reciprocal altruism ought to occur between different sets of parents; and the theory of reciprocal altruism has implications for when men and women should try to achieve status and ascend social hi-

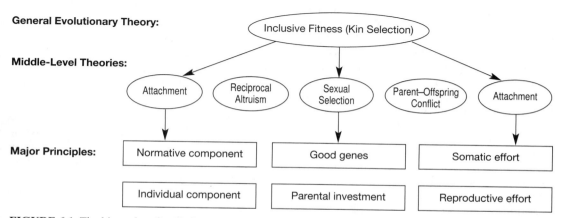

FIGURE 6.1. The hierarchy of evolutionary theories. Only a subset of the major middle-level evolutionary theories—the ones most relevant to attachment theory—are depicted here. For illustrative purposes, the major principles underlying only three of the five theories are shown.

erarchies in local groups. In some instances, middle-level theories generate slightly different hypotheses and predictions about a given outcome or social behavior. This highlights an important point that is often misunderstood: For some phenomena, there is no single evolutionary prediction, particularly if competing middle-level theories are involved (see Buss, 1995). Although inclusive-fitness theory contains the general, overarching principles from which most middle-level theories draw their basic assumptions and premises, there are as many middle-level evolutionary theories as there are major adaptive problems that humans had to solve throughout evolutionary history. In a subsequent section, I review the major barriers that individuals had to surmount in order to enhance their inclusive fitness.

Levels of Explanation

The conditions that give rise to a specific behavior can be investigated at different levels of conceptual analysis. In particular, questions of the form "Why does organism A engage in behavior X?" can be studied at three distinct levels (Sherman, 1988; Tinbergen, 1963). Questions of ultimate causation, which are the central focus of most evolutionary theories, are intended to explicate the phylogenetic origins and evolutionary history of a particular behavior or set of coadapted behaviors. Why, for instance, do most infants in every known culture pass through the same three stages—protest, despair, and detachment—following separation from their primary caregivers? How might this seemingly innate, universal sequence of emotional and behavioral reactions increase an infant's chances of survival, and ultimately his or her inclusive fitness? The normative component of attachment theory addresses these ultimate-causation questions.

Questions of ontogeny focus on how a behavior (or a set of behaviors) develops and changes across the lifespan. Ontogenetic questions fall into two general classes (Tooby & Cosmides, 1990). Some ontogenetic questions address how and why early environmental experiences shunt individuals toward different developmental trajectories, resulting in the enactment of different behavioral strategies. For example, if an infant's needs for protection and security are not met by the primary caregiver, how does the infant adjust his or her emotional and behavioral reactions to make the best of a nonoptimal situation, thereby achieving some level of protection and felt secu-

rity? The individual-difference component of attachment theory, which has been most eloquently articulated by Ainsworth and her associates, addresses these kinds of ontogenetic questions. Other ontogenetic questions focus on how and why specific developmental experiences produce different "thresholds of activation" for certain behaviors. What kinds of early social experiences, for instance, lead certain people (e.g., those classified as ambivalently attached) to have attachment systems that are easily triggered and chronically activated?

Finally, questions of proximate causation address how and why factors in an individual's immediate environment activate, maintain, and regulate a given behavior. These questions, which tend to be the focus of laboratory research, are often asked by social and personality psychologists. What kinds of situations or events tend to trigger the attachment system in children and adults? Once a person's attachment style is formed, what sorts of personal experiences lead him or her to change it?

No specific behavior can be fully understood unless it is addressed at all three levels of explanation. Few contemporary theories—including some middle-level evolutionary theories—make clear predictions about important facets of human social behavior at each level. Attachment theory attempts to explain (1) the evolutionary basis for the formation and maintenance of human bonds, (2) the ontogenic pathways through which different attachment styles are forged, and (3) the proximal factors that control and regulate attachment styles and activation of the attachment system. This is one of attachment theory's most remarkable and appealing features.

THE ENVIRONMENT OF EVOLUTIONARY ADAPTEDNESS, MAJOR LIFE TASKS, AND THE ADAPTED MIND

The Social EEA

To gain a deeper understanding of the context in which the attachment system evolved and the problems it was designed to "solve," one must consider the physical and social environments that humans probably inhabited throughout most of evolutionary history. Although attachment theorists have speculated to some extent about what the EEA might have been like (particularly the physical EEA; see Bowlby, 1969/1982,

1973), considerably less attention has been focused on features of the social EEA. Regrettably, we do not know many details about the environments in which our ancestors lived. What we do know is that, given their diverse patterns of migration, humans inhabited a wide variety of geographical and climatic environments—ranging from arid and barren deserts to lush tropical jungles. Thus there was no single EEA, particularly no monolithic physical environment. Nevertheless, the social environments in which humans evolved, while by no means identical across tribes, may have shared some stable features.

For most of human evolutionary history, people have been hunters and gatherers (see Kelly, 1995). Anthropological observations of contemporary hunter–gatherer tribes, such as the !Kung San of the Kalahari Desert in Africa, the Inuit (Eskimos) of the Arctic, the Ache of Paraguay, and the Aborigines of Australia, therefore, provide us with perhaps the best view of what ancient tribal life might have been like. For thousands of generations, our ancestors probably lived in small cooperative groups (Eibl-Eibesfeldt, 1989). Most people in a tribe were biologically related to one another, and strangers were encountered rather infrequently, probably during periods of intertribal trading or war (see Wright, 1994). Although people occasionally migrated in and out of their natal groups, most people probably remained with the same tribe throughout their lives.

Most men and women formed long-term pair bonds (Eibl-Eibesfeldt, 1989), although serial monogamy may have been common. On average, children were born approximately 4 years apart and were raised with considerable help from the extended family and perhaps the entire group (Wright, 1994); few children were raised solely by their biological parents. Younger children probably spent considerable time being socialized by older children (Eibl-Eibesfeldt, 1989). Both men and women were involved in securing food, with men doing more of the hunting and women doing more of the gathering (Konner, 1982). Although some of these inferences are more speculative than others, the human mind probably evolved to deal with problems that arose in social environments containing most of these features.[2] Brewer and Caporael (1990) have proposed that participation in the daily functioning of small cooperative groups may have been a principal "survival strategy" of early humans.

Psychological Mechanisms and Major Life Tasks

The modern evolutionary perspective represents an attempt to identify and understand how the human mind was designed by natural selection to "solve" the major adaptive problems humans faced in evolutionary history (see Tooby & Cosmides, 1990; Williams, 1966). Buss (1995) has suggested that the human mind contains numerous domain-specific psychological mechanisms, each of which evolved to address one or more adaptive problems. Psychological mechanisms have three defining properties. First, psychological mechanisms exist because they solved a specific problem that impeded survival or reproduction in evolutionary history. Second, they are activated by specific stimuli or information that cue the individual about which adaptive problem needs to be addressed. Third, once activated, psychological mechanisms affect behavior via "decision rules," many of which are unconscious and operate in an automatic fashion. These decision rules can regulate physiological arousal, act as stimuli that trigger other psychological mechanisms, or produce overt behavior. Psychological mechanisms are believed to be evolved solutions to adaptive problems if they show evidence of "special design" (Williams, 1966)—that is, if they provide a precise, specialized, efficient, economical, and reliable solution to a specific adaptive problem (Tooby & Cosmides, 1992).

Some psychological mechanisms presumably evolved in response to stable features of social EEAs, such as the recurrent structures, rules, roles, and perils associated with living in small groups. Though small cooperative groups should have facilitated the inclusive fitness of most group members by providing greater protection from predators and better access to mates and food (Trivers, 1971), group living should have posed some unique adaptive problems. To minimize the adverse effects of "cheaters," for example, humans have apparently developed a keen ability to detect people who do not reciprocate equitably in groups over time (Cosmides, 1989).

Most psychological mechanisms, however, probably evolved to address one of three major barriers to inclusive fitness: problems associated with survival to reproductive age, problems associated with mating and reproduction, and problems associated with raising offspring (or biological relatives) to reproductive age (Bowlby, 1980; Clutton-Brock, 1991). Several psychological mechanisms may have evolved primarily to promote survival, either in infancy per se or throughout the lifespan. Beginning almost precisely at the age when infants become mobile (and therefore can venture away from their primary caregivers), they become sensitive to separations from these caregivers (Ainsworth, Blehar, Waters, & Wall, 1978). By the age of 3 or 4, children have developed strong and distinct fears of snakes, heights, open spaces, and darkness (Marks, 1987), all of which posed considerable danger to humans—particularly young children—during evolutionary history. From an evolutionary perspective, selection pressures should have generated sex differences only when males and females confronted different adaptive problems (Buss, 1995). Because situations posing threats to survival should have been similar for the sexes, males and females should have developed and utilized similar evolved mechanisms to deal with threats to survival. One of the most striking features of research on attachment is the paucity of systematic sex differences (Hazan & Shaver, 1994), particularly in children (see Belsky & Cassidy, 1994, for a review).

Men and women should have faced slightly different adaptive problems with regard to mating and reproduction (see Buss & Schmitt, 1993; Symons, 1979; Trivers, 1972). Their different roles in reproduction should have created different kinds of problems, generating evolved psychological mechanisms that either were different for the sexes or were calibrated for different activation thresholds. However, men and women should have confronted many of the same adaptive problems associated with raising children to adulthood. One of the most pressing problems should have been assuring that one's parental investment was being funneled into carriers of one's genes. Indeed, humans appear to possess subtle psychological mechanisms that result in the preferential allocation of resources to biological children or the imposition of costs to nonbiological children. Among preschool children, child abuse is 40 times greater in stepfamilies than in families with two genetic parents (Daly & Wilson, 1987). Although caregivers seem prepared to bond easily and strongly with their biological offspring almost from birth (Eibl-Eibesfeldt, 1989), certain conditions can mitigate bonding, resulting in discriminative parental solicitude (Daly & Wilson, 1988). According to Daly (1989), bonding between parents and young children tends to be hampered when (1) one or both parents are not biological relatives; (2) the father's paternity is uncertain;

(3) a child is deformed or appears weak; and (4) poverty, lack of food, or too many children in the family reduce the chances of long-term survival. In traditional societies, these are the conditions in which infanticide by parents occurs (Daly & Wilson, 1988; Dickemann, 1975; Minturn & Stashak, 1982).

NORMATIVE AND INDIVIDUAL-DIFFERENCE COMPONENTS OF ATTACHMENT

Attachment theory has two components: (1) a normative component, which explains modal, species-typical patterns and stages of attachment bonds in humans; and (2) an individual-difference component, which accounts for deviations from the modal patterns and stages. This bifurcation—explaining the species-typical patterns of attachment behavior and individual differences that diverge from these patterns—is a hallmark of modern evolutionary models (Wright, 1994). Bowlby and Ainsworth, in fact, were among the first evolutionary theorists to appreciate the importance of trying to account not only for normative behavior, but for systematic individual differences as well. In this section, I review research indicating how each major component fits within evolutionary/ethological models of human behavior.

Normative Features of Attachment

Compared to the young of most species, human infants are born in an underdeveloped and premature state (Eibl-Eibesfeldt, 1989). Yet almost from the moment of birth, human infants are prepared to bond with their caregivers. Due to the release of hormones at birth, newborns are very alert during the first few hours of life—particularly at 20–30 minutes postpartum, when they first have an opportunity to bond (Archavsky, 1952). Newborns' initial attempts at nursing stimulate the release of oxytocin in their mothers, which accelerates emotional bonding and stimulates further nursing. This period of active alertness may have evolved to promote initial bonding between infants and their caregivers (Lagercrantz & Slotkin, 1986).

Newborns who are 16 hours old preferentially respond to the sound of human language with coordinated, rhythmic body movements (Condon & Sander, 1974). Newborns just 2 days old can discriminate their mothers' faces and odors from those of strangers (Field, Cohen, Garcia, & Greenberg, 1984). At 3 days, they show a clear preference for human voices, especially the voices of their mothers (DeCasper & Fifer, 1980; Mills & Melhuish, 1974). Six-day-old newborns prefer the smell of their mothers' clothes over that of strangers' clothes (MacFarlane, 1975, 1977; Russell, 1976). At 3–5 weeks, infants spend considerable time looking at the contours of human faces, focusing mainly on the eyes (Eibl-Eibesfeldt, 1989). Between 9 and 11 weeks, the eyes of others—especially those of a caregiver—draw most of their visual attention. Beginning at 3 and 4 months, infants start to initiate social contact with their mothers. Mothers who breast-feed during this period tend to be more sensitive to the needs of their children (Eibl-Eibesfeldt, 1989), probably because of hormones released during breast feeding. At 3–4 months, infants also start to avoid eye contact when interactions with their parents are unpleasant. Indeed, one indicator of disturbed parent–child relations at this age is the pattern and quality of reciprocal eye contact (Eibl-Eibesfeldt, 1989).

Many postpartum reactions of mothers operate in synchrony with those of their newborns, acting to facilitate the initial formation of infant–caregiver bonds. Immediately after delivery, mothers experience a release of hormones that tend to make them feel euphoric and receptive to emotional bonding (Eibl-Eibesfeldt, 1989). After one brief contact with their infants, mothers can easily distinguish their own newborns from other newborns at a mere 6 hours postpartum (Russell et al., 1983). Mothers with young infants are better at differentiating among cries signaling pain, hunger, and frustration than are pregnant women or mothers with older children (Sagi, 1981). Without instructions, mothers in all cultures interact at a distance of about 30 centimeters from their young infants—an optimal distance given infants' developing vision (Eibl-Eibesfeldt, 1989). Mothers make great efforts to establish eye contact with their infants (Klaus & Kennell, 1976). When infants reciprocate eye contact, mothers become livelier, speak with greater voice inflections, and approach the infants more closely (Grossmann, 1978, cited in Eibl-Eibesfeldt, 1989). Eye contact and smiling by infants are tremendously rewarding to new mothers, who tend to interpret such cues as signs of affection (Eibl-Eibesfeldt, 1989). When interacting with their infants, mothers typically exaggerate their facial expressions, change them

more slowly, and maintain visual contact for longer periods of time (Eibl-Eibesfeldt, 1989), all of which are well suited to infants' developing visual systems. When talking to their infants, mothers slow their speech, accentuate certain syllables, and often talk one octave above normal speech (Anderson & Jaffe, 1972; Grieser & Kuhl, 1988). This pattern of speech, known as "motherese", is preferred by infants who are 4 months old (Fernald, 1985). This form of speech may be an adaptation to infants' developing auditory skills.

Although no single period of development is critical for the formation of attachment bonds, some empirical evidence suggests that extensive contact between infants and caregivers immediately after birth may promote emotional bonding. Klaus and Kennell (1976) found that mothers who nursed their infants twice in the first 3 hours after birth and then spent more than 15 hours with them during the next 3 days (compared to mothers who had minimal postpartum contact) displayed greater emotional attraction to their infants 1 month later. Moreover, home observations 2 years later revealed that mothers with more postpartum contact spoke with their children in a more animated manner, asked more questions, used more adjectives, and issued fewer commands. Mothers who were not allowed to spend time with their newborns after birth were more likely to mistreat their children, and their children were more likely to be diagnosed as failing to thrive in early childhood (see also O'Connor, Vietze, Hopkins, & Altemeier, 1977). Mothers with extensive postpartum contact tend to exhibit more parenting competence than mothers with less contact (Sostek, Scanlon, & Abramson, 1982). Three months after birth, mothers with more early contact make more visual contacts with their infants and display more affection toward them, whereas mothers with less early contact are more likely to engage in instrumental child care activities (e.g., cleaning the infants; DeChateau & Wiberg, 1977). The positive effects of early maternal contact, however, are often confined to the first weeks of life (Myers, 1984a, 1984b; Schaller, Carlsson, & Larsson, 1979), and they may be much weaker than some have claimed (see Herbert, Sluckin, & Sluckin, 1982; Lamb & Hwang, 1982). Indeed, given the paramount importance of strong infant–caregiver bonds, evolutionary pressures should have permitted the formation of strong bonds at multiple stages of development beyond early infancy.

According to Bowlby (1980), attachment behaviors include any actions that increase proximity between children and their attachment figures. Young children engage in three classes of behaviors to establish or maintain proximity to their caregivers (Belsky & Cassidy, 1994). Signaling behaviors (e.g., vocalizing, smiling) regularly draw caregivers toward children, usually for positive interactions. Aversive behaviors (e.g., crying, screaming) bring caregivers to children, typically to terminate such actions. Active behaviors (e.g., approaching, following) function to move children toward caregivers. Although different phenotypically, these classes of behavior serve the same biological function: to keep vulnerable infants in close physical proximity to their caregivers, thereby increasing their chances of survival. Because death prior to reproduction should have been the first major barrier to inclusive fitness, Bowlby claimed that strong directional selection should have shaped the attachment system in humans, setting the stage for their highly social nature.

Attachment propensities develop through four phases in humans (Bowlby, 1982). In the first phase, which takes place between birth and 2–3 months, infants respond to a wide variety of social stimuli and people, not showing particularly strong preferences for a single attachment figure. Although Bowlby may have overestimated the degree to which young infants are open to contact comfort from multiple caregivers (see above), he probably was correct in believing that infants are malleable concerning with whom they can bond during the first 2–3 months of life. During the second phase, which extends from 2–3 months to about 7 months, infants show greater discrimination in social responsiveness. They begin to distinguish caregivers and family members from strangers; they show a clear preference for certain persons; and their attachment behaviors are elicited and quelled by specific attachment figures.

In the third phase, which lasts from 7 months to approximately 3 years, children begin to play a more active role in seeking proximity and initiating social contact. They also develop "internal working models" (i.e., psychological mechanisms formed from experiences with attachment figures) of the self and significant others (Bowlby, 1973). During this phase, all three primary functions of attachment can be seen in a child's behavior: proximity maintenance (staying near to, and resisting separations from, the attachment figure), safe haven (turning to the attachment figure for comfort and support), and secure base (using the attachment figure as a base from which to engage in nonattachment behaviors, such as play and exploration). If children in this phase encounter prolonged separations from their attachment figures, they will experience the three stages of response to separation: protest, despair, and detachment. The fourth phase, which begins at about age 3, marks the beginning of behaviors signifying the development of a "goal-corrected partnership." That is, with the advent of language, children start to see the world from the perspective of their interaction partners. This allows children to incorporate the goals, plans, and desires of their interaction partners into their decision making, resulting in the negotiation of joint plans and activities.

As children pass through the toddler years, the desire for physical proximity is slowly replaced by a desire to achieve and maintain psychological proximity (i.e., felt security; Sroufe & Waters, 1977). Early in adolescence, the overt behavioral manifestations of attachment bonds with parents begin to subside (Hinde, 1976). Hazan and Shaver (1994) have proposed that the three major functions of attachment—proximity maintenance, safe haven, and secure base—are gradually transferred in a sequential fashion from parents to peers and romantic partners as adolescents enter adulthood.

The attachment system is one of several biologically based behavioral systems that develop in early childhood. Although Bowlby (1973) mentioned several systems, he devoted most attention to two with close ties to the attachment system: fear and exploration. The primary biological function of the fear system is to motivate children to stay clear of, or extricate themselves from, potentially dangerous situations. According to Bowlby, natural clues to danger include loud noises, sudden movements, darkness, looming objects, or being alone, all of which should have been harbingers of danger in the EEA. Although some frightening events should reliably trigger the attachment system (e.g., looming objects), others can be handled without having to turn to attachment figures (e.g., fleeing from poisonous snakes). In general, however, the presence of an attachment figure should dampen activation of the fear system.

The exploratory behavioral system ostensibly evolved to ensure that young children learn about their environment and develop skills important for later stages of development (e.g., securing food, fending off attacks, establishing and maintaining social contacts). Most children use their attachment figures as a comforting base from which to explore the environment (Ainsworth, 1963), typically striking a balance between attachment and exploration (Ainsworth, Bell, & Stayton, 1971). When the attachment system is quiescent, play and exploration increase; when the system is activated, play and exploration quickly abate (Ainsworth & Wittig, 1969; Rheingold, 1969).

Individual Differences in Attachment

Though infants are biologically predisposed to form strong attachment bonds with their caregivers, the types of bonds they form should depend on the nature of the environments in which they are raised. According to evolutionary theorists (e.g., Tooby & Cosmides, 1992), psychological mechanisms should be triggered by specific environmental cues, resulting in the enactment of ecologically contingent strategies that evolved to solve specific adaptive problems posed by certain kinds of environments. Infants, of course, do not have the cognitive ability to appraise the "quality" of local environmental conditions (e.g., whether the local environment is safe, plentiful, and rich in resources vs. threatening, harsh, and impoverished). However, they *do* have the ability to discern whether their caregivers are providing them with the level of sensitivity, responsiveness, and attention dictated by their biological needs. This information, in turn, may provide reliable clues about the nature and quality of current— and perhaps future—environmental conditions. If caregivers in evolutionary history were able to devote the time, effort, and energy necessary to be sensitive, responsive, and attentive to the needs of their infants, the local environment was probably safe and rich in resources; if caregivers were insensitive, nonresponsive, and spent less time with their infants, these behaviors should have conveyed that the local environment was more difficult and less hospitable.

From an evolutionary standpoint, Ainsworth's strange situation is well suited to detect different patterns of attachment because it presents infants with two common "cues to danger" in the EEA: being left alone and being left with a stranger. In examining reunions between mothers and their 12- to 18-month-old infants, Ainsworth et al. (1978) documented three basic patterns of attachment: "secure," "ambivalent," and "avoidant."[3] Upon reunion, securely attached children use their caregivers to regulate and attenuate

their distress, often resuming other activities (e.g., exploration) quickly after calming down. In contrast, avoidantly attached children retract from their caregivers upon reunion, opting to control and dissipate their negative affect in an independent, self-reliant manner. Ambivalently attached children make inconsistent and conflicted attempts to derive comfort and support from their caregivers, often intermixing clinginess with overt anger.

Each attachment pattern reflects a different ecologically contingent strategy designed to solve adaptive problems posed by different rearing environments. Mothers of securely attached infants are available and responsive to the needs and signals of their infants (Ainsworth et al., 1978; Grossmann, Grossmann, Spangler, Suess, & Unzner, 1985). They are highly attuned to signs that their infants are distressed (Crockenberg, 1981); provide moderate and appropriate levels of stimulation (Belsky, Rovine, & Taylor, 1984); are synchronous in interactions with their infants (Isabella & Belsky, 1990; Isabella, Belsky, & von Eye, 1989); and behave in a warm, involved, and contingently responsive manner (Bates, Maslin, & Frankel, 1985). Largely because their caregivers are sensitive and responsive, securely attached children need not worry about the availability and responsiveness of their caregivers. This frees them to attend to and focus on issues other than attachment.

Ambivalent children, on the other hand, have caregivers who behave in an inconsistent manner (Ainsworth et al., 1978), perhaps due to deficient parenting skills. Caregivers of ambivalent infants tend to respond erratically to the needs and signals of their infants, often appearing to be underinvolved as parents (Belsky et al., 1984; Isabella et al., 1989; Lewis & Feiring, 1989; Smith & Pederson, 1988). Among children who are maltreated, ambivalent children are more likely to have been the victims of parental neglect (Youngblade & Belsky, 1989). The vehement protests and demanding nature of ambivalent children may therefore reflect an ecologically contingent strategy designed to obtain, retain, and improve the amount of attention and quality of responsiveness from habitually inattentive caregivers (Cassidy & Berlin, 1994; Main & Solomon, 1986). In other words, the constellation of behaviors characteristic of ambivalent children may have evolved to redress deficiencies in caregiving by young, naive, overburdened, and/or underinvolved parents. For children with such parents, this behavioral strategy should have permitted greater proximity to the caregivers, solicited better care, and increased the children's chances of survival.

Avoidant children have caregivers who are consistently cold and rejecting (Ainsworth et al., 1978). Mothers of avoidant children are less responsive to their infants' distress (Crockenberg, 1981), use overly stimulating styles of interaction (Belsky et al., 1984), and have a disdain for close body contact (Ainsworth et al., 1978). Among maltreated children, avoidant individuals are more likely to have suffered physical or emotional abuse from their parents (Youngblade & Belsky, 1989). The evolutionary origins of avoidance may be more complex and multifaceted than the origins of ambivalence. Bowlby (1980) suggested that avoidance allowed infants to disregard cues that might have activated the attachment system. If such cues had been fully processed, avoidant infants might have recognized the inaccessibility and rejecting demeanor of their caregivers. Although this explanation is tenable, it does not address how avoidance might have enhanced survival in children.

At least two viable evolutionary explanations for avoidance in childhood have been offered. Main (1981) has proposed that the distant, self-reliant behavior characteristic of avoidant infants may have allowed them to maintain reasonably close proximity to belligerent or overwhelmed caregivers without driving them away. That is, avoidance may have evolved to redress deficiencies in caregiving provided by highly distressed, hostile, or unmotivated parents. This behavioral strategy should have increased survival among infants in evolutionary history who, if they had placed too many demands on their parents, might have been abandoned. Alternatively, earlier reproduction may have facilitated inclusive fitness in some circumstances, especially in harsh environments with scarce resources (Trivers, 1985). If maternal rejection served as an early cue about the severity of future environments, avoidant tendencies would have allowed infants to explore their environments earlier and more extensively, perhaps facilitating the development of self-sufficient skills necessary for survival and early reproduction in arduous environments.

Bowlby (1969/1982) and Ainsworth (1979) originally believed that the secure pattern of attachment was "nature's prototype." Security may have been the most common pattern of attachment in evolutionary history. However, as we have seen, selection pressures should *not* have generated a single prototype. As Hinde (1982, pp. 71–72) points out:

> There is no best mothering (or attachment) style, for different styles are better in different circumstances, and natural selection would act to favor individuals with a range of potential styles from which they select appropriately . . . mothers and babies will be programmed (by evolution) not simply to form one sort of relationship but a range of possible relationships according to circumstances . . . optimal mothering (and attachment) behavior will differ according to the sex of the infant, its ordinal position in the family, the mother's social status, caregiving contributions from other family members, the state of physical resources, and so on . . . a mother–child relationship which produces successful adults in one situation may not do so in another.

Nonetheless, security may be the primary or default strategy of the attachment system *if* environmental conditions are suitable (Main, 1990). In line with this view, secure patterns of attachment tend to be more stable than insecure patterns over time (Egeland & Farber, 1984). Moreover, it may be easier for individuals to shift from insecure to secure attachment patterns than vice versa (see Belsky & Cassidy, 1994).

Given the complicated neural foundation of the attachment system, the basic functions of the system ought to remain the same over the lifespan (Konner, 1982). As children move into adolescence, cumulative experiences in relationships are continually assimilated into internal working models. These models reflect the degree to which individuals (1) believe they are worthy of love/affection and (2) view significant others as loving/affectionate (Bartholomew & Horowitz, 1991; Collins & Read, 1994). Unlike the attachment system in childhood, however, the system in adulthood becomes integrated with the mating and caregiving behavioral systems (see Shaver, Hazan, & Bradshaw, 1988; Zeifman & Hazan, 1997). As discussed in a later section, individual differences in attachment during adolescence and adulthood may reflect different reproductive strategies designed by evolution to enhance reproductive fitness in certain environments.

ATTACHMENT THEORY AND PARENT–OFFSPRING CONFLICT THEORY

One middle-level evolutionary theory with considerable relevance to attachment theory is Trivers' (1974) theory of parent–offspring conflict. This theory, which is a direct extension of Hamilton's (1964) theory of kin selection, was the first to recognize that children (who share only 50% of their genes with parents and full siblings) should desire greater investment than their parents have been selected to provide. Consequently, parents and offspring should possess slightly divergent reproductive interests, resulting in periods of conflict that climax during the final stages of weaning.

Parent–Offspring Conflict Theory and Parental Investment

Parental investment includes any actions performed by a parent for an offspring that increase the offspring's chances of survival while reducing the parent's ability to invest in other offspring, either existing children or future ones (Trivers, 1972). The level of investment is a function of the costs and benefits associated with a given parental act or behavior. "Costs" are defined as units of forgone reproductive success by any other current or future offspring, and "benefits" are defined as units of reproductive success of the current offspring (Trivers, 1974). In humans, acts of investment include the devotion of time, effort, energy, and resources to children through such activities as feeding, protecting, sheltering, and teaching. The amount of investment children seek and parents are willing to provide should be based on how both parties view the costs and benefits of different forms of parental investment. Hamilton has shown that altruistic behaviors (i.e., acts that lower one individual's future reproductive success while raising the recipient's reproductive success) should have evolved if beneficiaries were likely to be biological relatives carrying the same altruistic genes. When $1 < r (B/C)$ (where r = the degree of relatedness [.5 between parents and their offspring], B = benefits of an altruistic act, and C = costs of the act), altruism should have increased inclusive fitness, and therefore should have been selected for.

When infants are young and highly dependent on their parents for care and resources, the costs of investment to parents are relatively low and the benefits to infants are quite high, from the reproductive vantage point of both parents and infants. During the early stages of child rearing, therefore, the reproductive interests of parents and their offspring coincide. However, as infants grow, consume more resources, and become more self-sufficient, the reproductive interests of

parents and offspring should begin to diverge. From the parents' perspective, the costs of investment continue to rise over time, while the benefits the infants derive from additional investment gradually level off. During this phase, directing investment toward new offspring may enhance parents' reproductive success more than continuing to invest heavily in increasingly autonomous, self-sufficient current children. During evolutionary history, this was the point at which weaning typically occurred.

Because children share only half of their genes with their parents and full siblings, two of an infant's siblings must survive and reproduce successfully if the infant's genes are to be fully propagated in future generations. As a result, infants should devalue the costs of investment incurred by their parents by 50%, expecting twice as many benefits as their parents have been selected to offer. Children and parents should therefore experience conflict until, from the perspective of the parents, the cost of parental investment is more than twice the benefit to the infants (or, from the perspective of the children, the cost of parental investment exceeds self-benefit). When this point is reached, an infant's inclusive fitness will be lowered if he or she demands further investment. Thus conflict subsides as the infant accepts the diversion of parental investment to other siblings.

Trivers (1974) conjectured that the intensity and duration of parent–offspring conflict should depend on factors that affect the cost–benefit ratio over time. Several interesting and novel predictions can be derived from the theory. For instance, conflict should be heightened when half-siblings exist in families. Because half-siblings share only 25% of their genes, four half-siblings must survive and reproduce if the genes of an infant are to be fully propagated. In blended families, therefore, offspring should demand approximately four times as much investment as their parents are willing to give, resulting in particularly long and intense periods of parent–offspring conflict. Conflict should also be pronounced in families with very young mothers. Because younger mothers have more reproductive years ahead of them (and therefore more and possibly better future reproductive opportunities) than older mothers who are approaching menopause, younger mothers should be less tolerant of enduring the demands of high-cost infants.

Similar to virtually all evolutionary theories developed before 1974, attachment theory does not fully recognize and account for the slightly different reproductive interests of infants and their caregivers. Indeed, many attachment theorists implicitly assume that the biological interests of parents and their children are isomorphic, and that (barring significant abnormalities) each child should be of equal "reproductive value" to its parents. Both of these assumptions are dubious. The reproductive value of a child should depend on several conditions (Daly & Wilson, 1981; Trivers, 1974), including attributes of (1) the infant (e.g., his or her health, normality); (2) the mother (e.g., her health, age, ability to invest in the infant); (3) the father (e.g., the certainty of his paternity, his resources, his willingness to invest in the infant); (4) the nuclear family (e.g., the number of existing children, their birth spacing); and (5) the local environment (e.g., the extent to which resources are available to minimize the costs and maximize the benefits of parental investment). When the costs of investing in a given child are disproportionately high relative to the benefits, parents should display discriminative parental solicitude (i.e., preferential investment in certain children; see Daly & Wilson, 1981). In certain circumstances, attachment insecurity may arise from these conditions that reduce parental investment. Lower investment should be revealed by inadequate or poor caregiving behaviors, including parental inattentiveness, neglect, rejection, abuse, and even infanticide in extreme cases.[4]

Cross-cultural research indicates that parental investment is lower in families with at least one stepparent; when fathers question their paternity; when infants are ill, weak, or deformed; during periods of famine; when families are poor or lack social support; when mothers are very young; when families have too many children; and when birth spacing is too short (for reviews, see Daly & Wilson, 1984, 1988; Dickemann, 1975; Minturn & Stashak, 1982). The incidence of parental neglect, abuse, and sometimes infanticide jumps to alarmingly high levels when certain conditions are present. For example, when the prevalence of stepfamilies is adjusted for, the probability of child abuse is up to 100 times greater in households containing at least one stepparent than in households with two biological parents (Daly & Wilson, 1985). Stepparents—especially stepfathers—are many times more likely to kill their biologically unrelated stepchildren than are biological parents (Daly & Wilson, 1988). If they maltreat their children, biological parents tend to neglect their offspring,

usually for reasons stemming from poverty (Daly & Wilson, 1981). Even when financial resources and marital status are held constant, younger mothers are more likely to kill their infants than are older mothers (Daly & Wilson, 1988), and older mothers are less likely to abuse or harm their infants (Daly & Wilson, 1985).

From an evolutionary perspective, each of the precipitating conditions listed above should have incrementally deleterious effects on the quality and quantity of mother–infant interactions, setting the stage for the development of insecure attachment. For children with congenital handicaps (e.g., blindness, mental retardation, severe emotional disturbances) or for mothers who feel overburdened (due to youth, depression, lack of paternal investment, or inadequate social support), neonatal emotional bonding may be disrupted by limited mother–infant postpartum contact or the inability of mothers and infants to communicate in ways known to facilitate early bonding (Daly & Wilson, 1981). Mothers deprived of postpartum interaction sometimes report feeling emotionally detached from their infants (Kennell, Trause, & Klaus, 1975). Indeed, infants who are separated from their mothers in the first 2 days of life are more likely to be abused as toddlers (Klaus & Kennell, 1976; Lynch, 1975; O'Connor et al., 1977), and both disabled children and overburdened mothers are more likely to experience early separations (Irvin, Kennell, & Klaus, 1976; Sugarman, 1977). If precipitating conditions persist over time, parents should continue to engage in insensitive caregiving, with more precipitating conditions resulting in greater insensitivity. Biological parents, who usually neglect their children if they maltreat them, should be more likely to have ambivalent infants, since neglect usually leads to ambivalence (Youngblade & Belsky, 1989). Stepparents, who typically abuse stepchildren if they maltreat them, should be more likely to have avoidant infants, given that abuse is a precursor of avoidance (Youngblade & Belsky, 1989).

Parental Investment and Attachment

Little is known about whether the conditions hypothesized to reduce parental investment actually generate insecure attachment in infants and young children. However, certain contextual factors have been linked to different attachment patterns. Parents with better psychological health and well-being provide their infants with higher-quality care (Belsky, 1984; Gelfand & Teti,

1990), and their infants are more securely attached to them (Belsky & Isabella, 1988; Benn, 1986; Ricks, 1985). Clinically depressed mothers, who engage in more intrusive/hostile and detached/unresponsive styles of caregiving (Gelfand & Teti, 1990), are more likely to raise insecurely attached infants (Gaensbauer, Harmon, Cytryn, & McKnew, 1984; Radke-Yarrow, 1991).

Spouses involved in happier and more supportive marriages when their children are infants and toddlers also display better and more sensitive parenting skills (Cox, Owen, & Lewis, 1989; Crnic, Greenberg, Ragozin, Robinson, & Basham, 1983; Goldberg & Easterbrooks, 1984), and in turn tend to have securely attached infants (Goldberg & Easterbrooks, 1984; Howes & Markman, 1989). Spouses who display the lowest levels of support have infants with the most severe form of insecurity—the disorganized/disoriented attachment pattern (Spieker, 1988; Spieker & Booth, 1988). Recently, Isabella (1994) has developed a process model of the intervening links between marital quality and infant attachment. Higher levels of marital quality (assessed prenatally) predict greater maternal role satisfaction at 4 months postpartum. Greater maternal sensitivity (assessed by observations of mother–infant interaction at 9 months postpartum) in turn predicts greater attachment security (assessed in the strange situation at 12 months postpartum).

External social support also has a positive impact on both parenting behavior and attachment security in infants and young children. Mothers who have more support from the community interact with their 4-month-old infants more positively (Crnic et al., 1983), whereas mothers with less external support are less sensitive when interacting with their premature 6-month-olds (Zarling, Hirsch, & Landry, 1988). Poor mothers who are given material resources are more likely to hold, touch, kiss, and vocalize with their 3-month-old infants (Feiring, Fox, Jaskir, & Lewis, 1987). Indeed, in samples of high-risk infants, the total amount of social support mothers receive correlates positively with the subsequent attachment security of their infants (Crnic, Greenberg, & Slough, 1986). This effect appears to be mediated by the quality of daily care provided by the mothers (Crittenden, 1985). Although some studies have found no straightforward association between social support and attachment security (e.g., Crockenberg, 1981), recent experimental studies have documented

this link (see Jacobson & Frye, 1991; Lieberman, Weston, & Pawl, 1991; Lyons-Ruth, Connell, & Grunebaum, 1990).

The theory of parent–offspring conflict offers keen insights about conditions that should reduce parental investment in a given child. Attachment theorists have not taken full advantage of these insights. Although the degree of caregiver sensitivity appears to be the proximal cause of secure versus insecure attachments in most infants and young children, attachment theorists must consider the full range of contextual factors that, from the perspective of ultimate causation, should affect caregiver sensitivity. Not all offspring were equal in terms of their reproductive value to parents during evolutionary history. Humans should have evolved psychological mechanisms capable of ascertaining the degree to which infants were valuable from a reproductive standpoint. Those deemed more valuable should have received greater parental investment; those deemed less valuable should have received less investment. The level of parental investment should have been conveyed through the quality and sensitivity of parental care, which in turn should have directly affected the formation of secure versus insecure attachment patterns.

EVOLUTIONARY MODELS OF SOCIAL DEVELOPMENT ACROSS THE LIFESPAN

Attachment theory is a theory of social and personality development across the lifespan (Bowlby, 1979). Nonetheless, research on attachment has traditionally focused on certain barriers to inclusive fitness (e.g., problems associated with infant survival and adult parenting) to the relative exclusion of other barriers (e.g., problems related to mating). Despite the fact that some theorists (e.g., Main, 1981) have conjectured that different patterns of attachment in children might represent different evolutionary strategies for enhancing inclusive fitness in certain environments, only recently have different patterns of attachment witnessed in children been theoretically linked to the development of different romantic attachment styles and mating orientations in adults.

Life history theory, one of the major middle-level evolutionary theories, has been the driving force behind this movement. According to this theory (see Stearns, 1992), humans should have evolved to employ differing, ecologically contingent behavioral "strategies" to solve problems related to survival, growth, and reproduction across the lifespan. Dictated by the nature of the local environment, "optimal" solutions to problems at earlier stages of development (e.g., enhancing one's survival, given a specific pattern of attachment with one's caregiver) should affect later stages of development (e.g., patterns of mating and parenting).[5] During development, individuals should invest different amounts of time, energy, and resources at different rates of expenditure into somatic effort (growth and development of the body) versus reproductive effort (which encompasses both mating effort and parenting effort), depending on prevailing environmental conditions.

The Belsky, Steinberg, and Draper Model

Inspired by life history theory and prior research on father absence during childhood and the emergence of deviant behaviors in adolescence (see Draper & Harpending, 1982), Belsky, Steinberg, and Draper (1991) have developed a comprehensive evolution-based lifespan model of human social development. They contend that the principal evolutionary function of early social experience is to provide children with diagnostic information about the kinds of social and physical environments they are most likely to encounter during their lifetime. This information should permit individuals to facultatively adopt an appropriate reproductive strategy—one that should increase inclusive fitness—in future environments. Hinde (1986), for example, has suggested that if maternal rejection is induced by harsh environments in which competition for limited resources is intense, offspring who are aggressive and noncooperative may have higher reproductive fitness as adults than offspring without these attributes. Conversely, offspring raised in less hostile environments with more abundant resources should increase their fitness by developing a cooperative and communal orientation toward others in adulthood.

The Belsky et al. (1991) model, which is depicted in Figure 6.2, contains five stages. Belsky et al. claim that (1) early contextual factors in the family of origin (e.g., the amount of stress, spousal harmony, and financial resources) affect (2) early child-rearing experiences (e.g., the level of sensitive, supportive, and responsive caregiving). These experiences then affect (3) psychological and behavioral development (e.g., patterns of attachment, the nature of working models), which influences (4) somatic development (how quickly sexual maturation is reached) and ultimately (5) the adoption of particular reproductive strategies.

The model describes two developmental trajectories culminating in two reproductive strategies in adulthood. One strategy involves a short-term, opportunistic orientation toward mating and parenting, in which sexual intercourse with multiple partners occurs earlier in life, pair bonds are short-term and relatively unstable, and parental investment is lower. This orientation is geared toward increasing the *quantity* of offspring. The second strategy involves a long-term, investing orientation, in which sexual intercourse occurs later in life with fewer partners, pair bonds are long-term and more stable, and parental investment is greater. This orientation focuses on maximizing the *quality* of offspring. These two strategies are phenotypically similar to r versus K strategies of reproduction, which have been used to classify the reproductive tactics of different species (MacArthur, 1962). The r strategy is characterized by early and rapid reproduction, numerous offspring, and minimal parental investment, whereas the K strategy has the opposite features. The Belsky et al. model is based on cumulative conditional probability. That is, the phenotypic outcome of a later stage of development has a higher probability when a larger number of outcomes from earlier, antecedent stages exist for a given individual.

To date, most evidence supporting this model comes from cross-sectional research on the links between pairs of stages. Research has shown that higher stress in families is associated with more insensitive, harsh, rejecting, inconsistent, and/or unpredictable parenting behavior. Specifically, economic hardship (Burgess & Draper, 1989; McLoyd, 1990), occupational stress (Bronfenbrenner & Crouter, 1982), marital discord (Belsky, 1981; Emery, 1988), and psychological distress (McLoyd, 1990) are all precursors of dysfunctional parenting styles. In contrast, greater social support and more economic resources appear to facilitate warmer and more sensitive rearing practices (Lempers, Clark-Lempers, & Simons, 1989), perhaps because less taxed parents are more patient with (or tolerant of) their young children (Belsky, 1984).

As reviewed earlier, the link between parental sensitivity and the psychological/behavioral development of children is also well established. During the first year of life, insensitive and unresponsive caregiving forecasts the development of insecure attachment (Ainsworth et al., 1978; Grossmann et al., 1985). Insecurity is associated with a myriad of behavior problems. As 2-year-olds, insecurely attached children are less tolerant of frustration (Matas, Arend, & Sroufe, 1978). Insecurely attached preschoolers are more likely to be socially withdrawn (Waters, Wippman, & Sroufe, 1979), are less likely to display sympathy for peers who are upset (Waters et al., 1979), are less willing to interact with friendly adults (Lütkenhaus, Grossmann, & Grossman, 1985), and are liked less by their classmates (LaFreniere & Sroufe, 1985). During elementary school, insecure children exhibit more severe behavior problems, especially aggression and disobedience (Erickson, Sroufe, & Egeland, 1985; Lewis, Feiring, McGuffog, & Jaskir, 1984). According to the Belsky et al. (1991) model, these behaviors are governed by insecure working models, which begin to prepare a child for negative, noncommunal relationships in adulthood.

The most novel and controversial connection in the model is that between psychological/behavioral development and somatic development. Belsky et al. (1991) propose that children who are exposed to high levels of stress, who develop insecure attachments, and who have behavior disorders should reach puberty (and therefore reproductive capacity) earlier than children without these attributes. According to life history theory (Chisholm, 1993; Promislow & Harvey, 1990), environments in which resources are scarce and relationship ties are tenuous should lead people to channel more effort toward rapid physical development, earlier mating, and multiple, short-term relationships. Delayed maturation and reproduction in such arduous environments may cost individuals dearly, since they are more likely to die before reproducing. In contrast, environments in which resources are plentiful and relationship ties are more reciprocal and enduring should shunt people toward slower physical development, later mating, and long-term pair bonds structured around greater parental investment. In such environments, reproductive fitness should be enhanced by deferring reproduction until prospective parents have acquired the skills and resources needed to maximize the quality of each offspring.

Empirical evidence for the link between psychological/behavioral development and somatic development is currently limited and indirect. Girls who report more acrimonious relationships with their parents (especially their mothers) tend to mature more quickly over a 12-month period, relative to girls who start the year at the same stage of puberty but report better relationships with their parents (Steinberg, 1988). For girls, father absence and greater family conflict in early childhood predict earlier menarche, even when body weight is statistically controlled for (Moffitt, Caspi, Belsky, & Silva, 1992; see also Graber, Brooks-Gunn, & Warren, 1995). In addition, girls raised in homes without fathers reach menarche earlier than do girls in homes where fathers are present throughout development (Jones, Leeton, McLeod, & Wood, 1972; Moffit et al., 1992; Surbey, 1990). The impact of father absence on physical maturation, however, may stem from the increased stress associated with divorce and/or being raised in an economically disadvantaged, single-parent family (McLanahan & Booth, 1989; McLoyd, 1990).

The link between pubertal timing and reproductive behavior has received more attention and support. Individuals who mature earlier start having sexual intercourse at a younger age than their more slowly maturing peers (Aro & Taipale, 1987; Smith, Udry, & Morris, 1985), mainly in response to hormonal changes that increase sex drive (Smith et al., 1985; Udry, 1987). Adolescents who are raised by single parents, who are delinquent, or who use drugs also become sexually active at a younger age than do adolescents without these attributes (Jessor, Costa, Jessor, & Donovan, 1983; Newcomer & Udry, 1987). Moreover, family conflict and divorce are associated with increased heterosexual activity. Compared to girls from intact families, girls from divorced families are more sexually assertive (Hetherington, 1972) and date more frequently (Booth, Brinkerhoff, & White, 1984), especially if family conflict remains high following divorce. Individuals with divorced parents marry at a younger age than those from intact families (Carlson, 1979; Mueller & Pope, 1977), making them in turn more susceptible to marital difficulties (Glenn & Supanic, 1984). Indeed, individuals whose parents divorced are more likely to experience divorce in their own marriages (Glenn & Kramer, 1987).

The Belsky et al. (1991) model does not fully establish empirical associations among adult romantic attachment styles, sexual behavior, and parenting behavior. Recent research on adult attachment has begun to fill this void. Brennan and Shaver (1995) have found that avoidantly attached adults tend to have an "unrestricted" sociosexual orientation, whereby they become in-

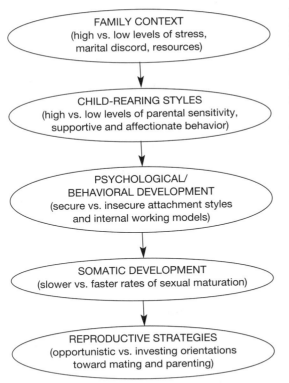

FIGURE 6.2. Developmental stages leading to opportunistic versus investing reproductive strategies. Based on the model of Belsky, Steinberg, and Draper (1991).

volved in multiple, short-term sexual relationships characterized by less closeness and commitment. Securely attached adults, on the other hand, tend to have a "restricted" sociosexual orientation, characterized by involvement in longer-term, closer, and more committed sexual relationships (see Simpson & Gangestad, 1991). This is the most direct evidence to date linking patterns of adult attachment with different mating strategies.

Adult romantic attachment styles also correspond with different expectations about children and parenting, even *before* individuals have children. Rholes, Simpson, Blakely, Lanigan, and Allen (1997) have found that, relative to securely attached individuals, avoidant and ambivalent individuals expect to be easily aggravated by young children, advocate stricter disciplinary practices, expect to convey less warmth to their (future) children, and are less confident about their ability to relate well with their children. Furthermore, avoidant people—but not ambiva-

lent or secure ones—anticipate less satisfaction from caring for young children and express less interest in having them. Once they have children, avoidantly attached mothers are less emotionally supportive of their preschoolers, often adopting a detached, controlling, or instrumental mode of relating to them (Crowell & Feldman, 1988, 1991; Rholes, Simpson, & Blakely, 1995). Mothers with secure orientations are more sensitive to cues displayed by their children and are more supportive of them (see van IJzendoorn, 1995, for a review). Similarly, secure fathers tend to provide warmer, more supportive care (Cohn, Cowan, Cowan, & Pearson, 1992; van Ijzendoorn, Kranenburg, Zwart-Woudstra, van Busschbach, & Lambermon, 1992).

In sum, the Belsky et al. (1991) model proposes that early environmental factors that heighten stress should promote harsh, rejecting, or insensitive styles of parenting, which generate insecure working models and patterns of attachment in young children. These models in turn should accentuate and confirm the tenuous, unpredictable nature of close relationships, leading to an opportunistic interpersonal orientation characterized by internalizing or externalizing behavioral disorders. These cues should accelerate sexual maturation, culminating in a short-term reproductive strategy geared toward early reproduction and less parental investment. Early environments that contain less stress should result in warmer, more contingent, and more sensitive parenting styles, generating secure working models and patterns of attachment in children. Secure models should highlight and reaffirm beliefs that close relationships are communal and partners are trustworthy, producing a reciprocally rewarding interpersonal orientation in which interactions with others are harmonious and mutually beneficial. This should produce slower sexual maturation and a long-term reproductive strategy characterized by later reproduction and greater parental investment. Internal working models are conjectured to play a major role in shunting individuals down these divergent developmental pathways (see Belsky, Chapter 7, this volume; for a recent extension of the model, see Kirkpatrick, 1998).

The Chisholm Model

Chisholm (1993, 1996) has proposed a slightly revised and expanded model of differing reproductive strategies, based heavily on the Belsky et al. (1991) model. Recent work has indicated that local mortality rates may act as the proximal environmental cues that direct people toward different reproductive strategies (Chisholm, 1993). According to bet-hedging theory (Horn & Rubenstein, 1984; Promislow & Harvey, 1990), when mortality rates are high in an area, the optimal reproductive strategy should be an early, short-term one in which current fertility is maximized. When mortality rates are low, the best strategy ought to involve deferred, long-term reproduction in which fewer progeny are given better care. In abundant and safe environments, a delayed/high-investment reproductive strategy should increase the total number of descendants over multiple generations by minimizing the variance of surviving offspring *within* each generation, reducing the likelihood that an entire generation will fail to reproduce (see Chisholm, 1993).

High mortality rates, which should have indexed the difficulty and harshness of local environments in the EEA, may be a principal evolutionary source of deficient caregiving. According to Chisholm, parental indifference or insensitivity may be used by children as a diagnostic cue of local mortality rates, leading them to develop avoidant working models and attachment behaviors better suited to facilitating fitness in difficult environments containing less cooperative people. Low mortality rates, which should have signaled more hospitable environments in the EEA, may be a primary evolutionary source of good, attentive caregiving. Sensitive parenting should have communicated to children that premature death was less likely, resulting in secure working models and attachment behaviors that enhanced fitness in benign environments containing more cooperative people.

In the EEA, there were probably two salient parent-based threats to the survival and growth of children: parents' inability to invest in offspring and/or parents' unwillingness to do so. Chisholm (1996) suggests that children and adolescents should have psychological mechanisms to detect and respond to these different sources of threat. Young infants are in fact very skilled observers of their parents' moods and motivations (Cohn & Tronick, 1983). According to Chisholm's model, secure attachment is in part a facultative adaptation to parents' ability *and* willingness to provide high investment. Avoidant attachment is an adaptation to parents' unwillingness to invest (regardless of their ability), whereas ambivalent attachment is an adaptation to parents' inability to invest (most likely be-

cause of limited resources). The model proposes that warm, sensitive caregiving should have been a reliable indicator of parents' ability and willingness to invest. Cold, rejecting caregiving, on the other hand, should have indicated parents' unwillingness to invest, whereas inconsistent, unpredictable caregiving should have conveyed parents' inability to invest given inadequate or unpredictable resources.

Expanding on the Belsky et al. (1991) model, Chisholm (1996) specifies how all three attachment patterns should be related to the course of development and the emergence of different reproductive strategies. During childhood, secure individuals should maximize long-term learning in order to enhance their developmental quality. In terms of ultimate causation, this might explain why securely attached children tend to grow faster than insecure children in high-risk samples (Valenzuela, 1990) and why secure children evince more advanced cognitive-perceptual and socioemotional skills earlier in development (Belsky & Cassidy, 1994; Sroufe, 1988). When parents are able and willing to invest and local environments are nonthreatening, more effort can be allocated to long-term developmental quality, and therefore to future (long-term) reproductive potential. Thus secure adults should seek long-term mates, be able and willing parents, invest heavily in their children, and provide unconditionally sensitive and responsive child care, all in the service of facilitating the phenotypic quality of their children.

Because avoidantly attached children must deal with rejecting (and potentially dangerous) parents who force them to become independent and self-reliant at an early age, avoidant children must devote more effort to short-term survival. When parents are unwilling to invest and local environments are threatening, less effort and fewer resources can be directed to physical growth. Consequently, effort should be shifted to current, short-term reproduction, accelerating sexual maturation. As a result, avoidant adults should have short-term relationships, be less willing to invest in their children, devote more time and energy to mating effort, and be more rejecting of their children, all in an attempt to increase the quantity of offspring.

Chisholm's (1996) life history predictions for ambivalent individuals constitute a distinct departure from the Belsky et al. (1991) model. He contends that ambivalent children should channel greater effort toward early sexual maturity while striving to extract greater investment from their impoverished or underinvolved caregivers. According to life history theory, when parents are unable to invest because of difficult local environments, children should engage in tactics designed to obtain as many resources as possible, funneling most of them to earlier sexual reproduction. From the perspective of ultimate causation, this might explain why ambivalent children are so irritable, demanding, and/or preoccupied about gaining and maintaining attention from their caregivers (see Belsky & Cassidy, 1994; Kunce & Shaver, 1994). It also might explain why adults with ambivalent romantic attachment styles experience early and extreme sexual attraction to others (Hazan & Shaver, 1987). According to Chisholm's model, ambivalent adults should engage in short-term mating, be willing yet less able to invest in their children, devote considerable time and energy to parenting effort, and behave inconsistently toward their children. Belsky (Chapter 7, this volume) proposes that ambivalence may reflect an evolved "helper-at-the-nest" reproductive strategy, in which parenting effort is directed toward kin.

Although provocative, the Belsky et al. (1991) and Chisholm (1993, 1996) models of social development have some shortcomings. First, neither model considers the complete, complex array of factors that, from an evolutionary standpoint, should influence the adoption of specific reproductive strategies. Mate selection should be contingent on a multitude of factors—ranging from a potential mate's genetic quality, to his or her ability to accrue and share resources, to his or her capacity to impart knowledge and information to offspring. These factors are not fully incorporated into current lifespan models. Second, current models are not sufficiently sensitive to the different roles that men and women assume in the process of reproduction (Hinde, 1991). The fact that women make substantially greater initial investments in offspring than men do should differentially affect how men and women make reproductive decisions, and consequently the mating strategies they ultimately adopt (Alexander & Noonan, 1979; Hinde, 1984; Trivers, 1972). Sex-differentiating factors are not adequately addressed in current lifespan models. Third, no empirical evidence has shown that stress experienced *early* in life directly affects the timing of puberty in either men or women. Since this is the most novel and perhaps critical hypothesis underlying both the Belsky et al. and the Chisholm models, direct evidence showing that early stress actually accelerates puberty is vital to evaluating these models. Fourth, because stress is related to many variables in a curvilinear fashion (see Berlyne, 1960), many different models forecasting the effects of stress on social behavior can be confirmed, depending on where individuals lie on the stress continuum. Current lifespan models must specify more clearly the precise level of stress that research participants have experienced. Despite these drawbacks, the Belsky et al. and Chisholm models represent new, potentially important advances in our understanding of attachment across the lifespan.

CONCLUSIONS

Attachment theory is, at a fundamental level, an evolutionary theory of human social behavior "from the cradle to the grave" (Bowlby, 1979, p. 129). Although the theory's initial ties to evolution focused on how the normative and individual-difference components of attachment should have promoted infant survival, recent work has begun to highlight how attachment patterns across the lifespan—including adult romantic attachment styles—may have evolved to increase reproductive fitness within certain environments. These recent theoretical advances are important because they suggest that patterns of attachment in adulthood may not be inconsequential evolutionary "artifacts" of the attachment system in children. According to life history theory, the attachment system in young children evolved to facilitate survival and development through the most vulnerable periods of early childhood. In adulthood, the attachment system serves the evolutionary function of increasing inclusive fitness through the adoption of environmentally contingent reproductive strategies.

In the future, attachment scholars need to ground more of their thinking about human social behavior in the context of modern, middle-level evolutionary theories. We must continue to tread the intellectual path first established by Darwin and extended by Bowlby and other contemporary evolutionary theorists. Various middle-level theories—especially parent–offspring conflict theory, the theory of parental investment and sexual selection, and life history theory—have a great deal to offer scholars interested in attachment phenomena. Indeed, significant advances in attachment theory and research will rest on the successful and complete integration of attachment theory into a modern evolutionary perspective.

ACKNOWLEDGMENT

Work on this chapter was partially supported by National Institute of Mental Health Grant No. MH49599.

NOTES

1. A few other middle-level evolutionary theories have been developed (e.g., host–parasite coevolution theory: Hamilton & Zuk, 1982; Tooby, 1982). They are not depicted in Figure 6.1.

2. Attachment theorists have commented little about the social environments in which our ancestors may have evolved. This is unfortunate, because modern societies—especially affluent and socially stratified Western cultures—differ in numerous ways from the environments in which the attachment system probably evolved. Today, many people live in relative social or emotional isolation amid dozens (sometimes hundreds) of strangers. Many people live far from their biological relatives, whom they see infrequently. Few people live their entire lives in the same town, let alone the same neighborhood. Most children are raised primarily by their biological parents, with help from babysitters, friends, or day care workers—most of whom are not biological relatives. And until recently, the division of labor outside the home has been drastically skewed, with men engaged in more work-related activities outside the home than women. Thus, in many respects, humans no longer live in the social environments for which they were adapted. These disparities between ancestral and modern environments may have implications for both the ease with which the attachment system is activated in modern humans and the base rates of different attachment styles.

3. Main and Solomon (1990) have identified a fourth attachment pattern in children labeled "disorganized/disoriented." These children do not exhibit a clear, coherent strategy for managing negative affect, often mixing avoidant and ambivalent behaviors. This pattern, which has the lowest base rate, is witnessed when primary caregivers are highly abusive, depressed, or emotionally disturbed (Crittenden, 1988; Main & Hesse, 1990; see Lyons-Ruth & Jacobvitz, Chapter 23, this volume, for a review).

4. These precipitating conditions should interact in interesting ways. For example, males in most polygynous species have a much wider range of reproductive success than females (Trivers, 1985). In our ancestral past, virtually all fertile females reproduced and had approximately the same number of children, whereas some males had large numbers of children and others did not reproduce. Trivers and Willard (1973) have proposed that when environmental resources are limited, daughters should receive greater parental investment than sons. Most daughters will bear children even if environmental conditions are harsh, whereas sons who cannot amass resources and display evidence of their fitness should be less likely to attract mates. When environmental conditions are more plentiful, however, sons should receive greater investment than daughters, because the most reproductively successful males should be able to propagate their parents' genes more extensively than daughters. This line of reasoning suggests that when environmental conditions are harsh, the pattern of parental investment may lead to more daughters than sons being securely attached, whereas the reverse should be true when environmental conditions are more favorable.

5. The term "strategy" refers to a collection of coevolved anatomical, physiological, psychological, and behavioral traits designed by natural selection to enhance inclusive fitness. Use of the term does *not* necessarily imply foresight, conscious awareness, or premeditation prior to engaging in a set of behaviors. Moreover, the term "optimal" does *not* imply that natural selection is geared to produce a single perfect phenotype. Optimal strategies are sets of coevolved traits that are best suited to increasing inclusive fitness in specific environments.

REFERENCES

Ainsworth, M. D. (1963). The development of infant–mother interaction among the Ganda. In B. Foss (Ed.), *Determinants of infant behavior* (Vol. 2, pp. 114–138). New York: Wiley.

Ainsworth, M. D. (1979). Infant–mother attachment. *American Psychologist, 34*, 932–937.

Ainsworth, M. D., Bell, S. M., & Stayton, D. J. (1971). Individual differences in strange situation behavior of one-year-olds. In H. R. Schaffer (Ed.), *The origins of human social relations* (pp. 17–52). New York: Academic Press.

Ainsworth, M. D. S., Blehar, M. C., Waters, E., & Wall, S. (1978). *Patterns of attachment: A psychological study of the strange situation.* Hillsdale, NJ: Erlbaum.

Ainsworth, M. D., & Wittig, B. A. (1969). Attachment and exploratory behaviour of one-year-olds in a strange situation. In B. Foss (Ed.), *Determinants of infant behaviour* (Vol. 4, pp. 129–173). London: Methuen.

Alexander, R. D., & Noonan, K. M. (1979). Concealment of ovulation, parental care, and human social evolution. In N. A. Chagnon & W. W. Irons (Eds.), *Evolutionary biology and human social behavior* (pp. 436–453). North Scituate, MA: Duxbury.

Anderson, S. W., & Jaffe, J. (1972). *The definition, detection and timing of vocalic syllables in speech signals* (Scientific Report No. 12). New York: Department of Communication Sciences, New York State Psychiatric Institute.

Archavsky, I. A. (1952). Immediate breast-feeding of newborn infants in the prophylaxis of the so-called physiological loss of weight. *Vopr. Pediat., 20*, 45–53.

Aro, H., & Taipale, V. (1987). The impact of timing of puberty on psychosomatic symptoms among fourteen- to-sixteen-year-old Finnish girls. *Child Development, 58,* 261–268.

Axelrod, R. (1984). *The evolution of cooperation.* New York: Basic Books.

Bartholomew, K., & Horowitz, L. M. (1991). Attachment styles among young adults: A test of a four-category model. *Journal of Personality and Social Psychology, 61,* 226–244.

Bates, J. E., Maslin, C. A., & Frankel, K. A. (1985). Attachment security, mother–child interaction, and temperament as predictors of behavior-problem ratings at age three years. In I. Bretherton & E. Waters (Eds.), Growing points in attachment theory and research. *Monographs of the Society for Research in Child Development, 50*(1–2, Serial No. 209), 167–193.

Belsky, J. (1981). Early human experience: A family perspective. *Developmental Psychology, 17,* 3–23.

Belsky, J. (1984). The determinants of parenting: A process model. *Child Development, 55,* 83–96.

Belsky, J., & Cassidy, J. (1994). Attachment: Theory and evidence. In M. Rutter & D. Hay (Eds.), *Development through life: A handbook for clinicians* (pp. 373–402). Oxford: Blackwell.

Belsky, J., & Isabella, R. (1988). Maternal, infant, and social-contextual determinants of attachment security. In J. Belsky & T. Nezworski (Eds.), *Clinical implications of attachment* (pp. 41–94). Hillsdale, NJ: Erlbaum.

Belsky, J., Rovine, M., & Taylor, D. G. (1984). The Pennsylvania Infant and Family Development Project: III. The origins of individual differences in infant–mother attachment: Maternal and infant contributions. *Child Development, 55,* 718–728.

Belsky, J., Steinberg, L., & Draper, P. (1991). Childhood experience, interpersonal development, and reproductive strategy: An evolutionary theory of socialization. *Child Development, 62,* 647–670.

Benn, R. K. (1986). Factors promoting secure attachment relationships between employed mothers and their sons. *Child Development, 57,* 1224–1231.

Berlyne, D. E. (1960). *Conflict, arousal, and curiosity.* New York: McGraw-Hill.

Booth, A., Brinkerhoff, D., & White, C. (1984). The impact of parental divorce on courtship. *Journal of Marriage and the Family, 46,* 85–94.

Bowlby, J. (1969/1982). *Attachment and loss: Vol. 1. Attachment.* New York: Basic Books.

Bowlby, J. (1973). *Attachment and loss: Vol. 2. Separation: Anxiety and anger.* New York: Basic Books.

Bowlby, J. (1979). *The making and breaking of affectional bonds.* London: Tavistock.

Bowlby, J. (1980). *Attachment and loss: Vol. 3. Loss.* New York: Basic Books.

Bowlby, J. (1991). *Charles Darwin: A new life.* New York: Norton.

Brennan, K. A., & Shaver, P. R. (1995). Dimensions of adult attachment, affect regulation, and romantic relationship functioning. *Personality and Social Psychology Bulletin, 21,* 267–283.

Brewer, M. B., & Caporael, L. R. (1990). Selfish genes versus selfish people: Sociobiology as origin myth. *Motivation and Emotion, 14,* 237–243.

Bronfenbrenner, U., & Crouter, A. (1982). Work and family through time and space. In S. Kamerman & C. Hayes (Eds.), *Families that work* (pp. 39–83). Washington, DC: National Academy Press.

Burgess, R., & Draper, P. (1989). The explanation of family violence: The role of biological behavioral and cultural selection. In L. Ohlin & M. Tonry (Eds.), *Family violence* (pp. 59–116). Chicago: University of Chicago Press.

Buss, D. M. (1995). Evolutionary psychology: A new paradigm for psychological science. *Psychological Inquiry, 6,* 1–30.

Buss, D. M., & Schmitt, D. P. (1993). Sexual strategies theory: A contextual evolutionary analysis of human mating. *Psychological Review, 100,* 204–232.

Carlson, E. (1979). Family background, school, and early marriage. *Journal of Marriage and the Family, 41,* 341–353.

Cassidy, J., & Berlin, L. J. (1994). The insecure/ambivalent pattern of attachment: Theory and research. *Child Development, 65,* 971–991.

Chisholm, J. S. (1993). Death, hope, and sex: Life-history theory and the development of reproductive strategies. *Current Anthropology, 34,* 1–24.

Chisholm, J. S. (1996). The evolutionary ecology of attachment organization. *Human Nature, 7,* 1–38.

Clutton-Brock, T. (1991). *The evolution of parental care.* Princeton, NJ: Princeton University Press.

Cohn, D., Cowan, P., Cowan, C., & Pearson, J. (1992). Mothers' and fathers' working models of childhood attachment relationships, parenting style, and child behavior. *Development and Psychopathology, 4,* 417–431.

Cohn, J., & Tronick, E. (1983). Three-month-old infants' reactions to simulated depression. *Child Development, 54,* 185–193.

Collins, N. L., & Read, S. J. (1994). Cognitive representations of attachment: The structure and function of working models. In K. Bartholomew & D. Perlman (Eds.), *Attachment processes in adulthood* (pp. 53–90). London: Jessica Kingsley.

Condon, W. S., & Sander, L. W. (1974). Neonate movement is synchronized with adult speech: Interactional participation and language acquisition. *Science, 183,* 99–101.

Cosmides, L. (1989). The logic of social exchange: Has natural selection shaped how humans reason? *Cognition, 31,* 187–276.

Cox, M. J., Owen, M. T., & Lewis, J. M. (1989). Marriage, adult adjustment, and early parenting. *Child Development, 60,* 1015–1024.

Crittenden, P. M. (1985). Social networks, quality of child rearing, and child development. *Child Development, 56,* 1299–1313.

Crittenden, P. M. (1988). Relationships at risk. In J. Belsky & T. Nezworski (Eds.), *Clinical implications of attachment* (pp. 136–174). Hillsdale, NJ: Erlbaum.

Crnic, K. A., Greenberg, M. T., Ragozin, A. S., Robinson, N. M., & Basham, R. B. (1983). Effects of stress and social support on mothers and premature and full-term infants. *Child Development, 54,* 209–217.

Crnic, K. A., Greenberg, M. T., & Slough, N. M. (1986). Early stress and social support influences on mothers' and high-risk infants' functioning in late infancy. *Infant Mental Health Journal, 7,* 19–33.

Crockenberg, S. B. (1981). Infant irritability, mother responsiveness, and social support influences on the security of infant–mother attachment. *Child Development, 52,* 857–869.

Cronin, H. (1991). *The ant and the peacock.* Cambridge, England: Cambridge University Press.

Crowell, J., & Feldman, S. (1988). Mothers' internal models of relationships and children's behavioral and developmental status: A study of mother–child interaction. *Child Development, 59,* 1273–1285.

Crowell, J., & Feldman, S. (1991). Mothers' working models

of attachment relationships and mother and child behavior during separation and reunion. *Developmental Psychology, 27*, 597–605.

Daly, M. (1989). Parent–offspring conflict and violence in evolutionary perspective. In R. W. Bell & N. J. Bell (Eds.), *Sociobiology and the social sciences* (pp. 25–43). Lubbock: Texas Tech University Press.

Daly, M., & Wilson, M. I. (1981). Abuse and neglect of children in evolutionary perspective. In R. D. Alexander & D. W. Tinkle (Eds.), *Natural selection and social behavior: Recent research and new theory* (pp. 405–416). Oxford: Blackwell.

Daly, M., & Wilson, M. (1984). A sociobiological analysis of human infanticide. In G. Hausfater & S. B. Hrdy (Eds.), *Infanticide* (pp. 487–502). New York: Aldine de Gruyter.

Daly, M., & Wilson, M. (1985). Child abuse and other risks of not living with both parents. *Ethology and Sociobiology, 6*, 197–210.

Daly, M., & Wilson, M. (1987). Children as homicide victims. In R. J. Gelles & J. B. Lancaster (Eds.), *Child abuse and neglect: Biosocial dimensions* (pp. 201–214). New York: Aldine de Gruyter.

Daly, M., & Wilson, M. (1988). *Homicide.* New York: Aldine de Gruyter.

Darwin, C. (1981). *The descent of man, and selection in relation to sex* (2 vols.). Princeton, NJ: Princeton University Press. (Original work published 1871)

DeCasper, A. H., & Fifer, W. P. (1980). Of human bonding: Newborns prefer their mother's voice. *Science, 208*, 1174–1176.

DeChateau, P., & Wiberg, B. (1977). Long-term effect on mother–infant behaviour of extra contact during the first hour postpartum: II. Follow-up at three months. *Acta Paediatrica Scandinavica, 67*, 169–175.

Dickemann, M. (1975). Demographic consequences of infanticide in man. *Annual Review of Ecology and Systematics, 7*, 107–137.

Draper, P., & Harpending, H. (1982). Father absence and reproductive strategy: An evolutionary perspective. *Journal of Anthropological Research, 38*, 255–273.

Egeland, B., & Farber, E. A. (1984). Infant–mother attachment: Factors related to its development and changes over time. *Child Development, 55*, 753–771.

Eibl-Eibesfeldt, I. (1989). *Human ethology.* New York: Aldine de Gruyter.

Emery, R. (1988). *Marriage, divorce, and children's adjustment.* Beverly Hills, CA: Sage.

Erickson, M. F., Sroufe, L. A., & Egeland, B. (1985). The relationship between quality of attachment and behavior problems in preschool in a high risk sample. In I. Bretherton & E. Waters (Eds.), Growing points of attachment theory and research. *Monographs of the Society for Research in Child Development, 50*(1–2, Serial No. 209), 147–193.

Feiring, C., Fox, N. A., Jaskir, J., & Lewis, M. (1987). The relation between social support, infant risk status and mother–infant interaction. *Developmental Psychology, 23*, 400–405.

Fernald, A. (1985). Four-month-old infants prefer to listen to motherese. *Infant Behavior and Development, 8*, 181–195.

Field, T. M., Cohen, D., Garcia, R., & Greenberg, R. (1984). Mother–stranger face discrimination by the newborn. *Infant Behavior and Development, 7*, 19–25.

Gaensbauer, T. J., Harmon, R. J., Cytryn, L., & McKnew, D. H. (1984). Social and affective development in infants with a manic–depressive parent. *American Journal of Psychiatry, 141*, 223–229.

Gelfand, D., & Teti, D. (1990). The effects of maternal depression on children. *Clinical Psychology Review, 10*, 329–353.

Glenn, N., & Kramer, K. (1987). The marriages and divorces of the children of divorce. *Journal of Marriage and the Family, 49*, 811–825.

Glenn, N., & Supanic, M. (1984). The social and demographic correlates of divorce and separation in the United States: An update and reconsideration. *Journal of Marriage and the Family, 46*, 563–576.

Goldberg, W. A., & Easterbrooks, M. A. (1984). The role of marital quality in toddler development. *Developmental Psychology, 20*, 504–514.

Graber, J., Brooks-Gunn, J., & Warren, M. (1995). The antecedents of menarcheal age. *Child Development, 66*, 346–359.

Greene, J. C. (1963). *Darwin and the modern world view.* New York: New American Library. (Original work published 1961)

Grieser, D. L., & Kuhl, P. K. (1988). Maternal speech to infants in a tonal language: Support for universal prosodic features in motherese. *Developmental Psychology, 24*, 14–20.

Grossmann, K., Grossmann, K. E., Spangler, G., Suess, G., & Unzner, L. (1985). Maternal sensitivity and newborns' orientation responses as related to quality of attachment in northern Germany. In I. Bretherton & E. Waters (Eds.), Growing points in attachment theory and research. *Monographs of the Society for Research in Child Development, 50*(1–2, Serial No. 209), 233–257.

Hamilton, W. D. (1964). The genetical evolution of social behaviour. *Journal of Theoretical Biology, 7*, 1–52.

Hamilton, W. D., & Zuk, M. (1982). Heritable true fitness and bright birds: A role for parasites? *Science, 218*, 384–387.

Hazan, C., & Shaver, P. R. (1987). Romantic love conceptualized as an attachment process. *Journal of Personality and Social Psychology, 52*, 511–524.

Hazan, C., & Shaver, P. R. (1994). Attachment as an organizational framework for research on close relationships. *Psychological Inquiry, 5*, 1–22.

Herbert, M., Sluckin, W., & Sluckin, A. (1982). Mother-to-infant bonding? *Journal of Child Psychology and Psychiatry, 23*, 205–221.

Hetherington, E. M. (1972). Effects of paternal absence on personality development in adolescent daughters. *Developmental Psychology, 7*, 313–326.

Hinde, R. A. (1976). On describing relationships. *Journal of Child Psychology, 17*, 1–19.

Hinde, R. A. (1982). Attachment: Some conceptual and biological issues. In C. M. Parkes & J. Stevenson-Hinde (Eds.), *The place of attachment in human behavior* (pp. 60–76). New York: Basic Books.

Hinde, R. A. (1984). Why do the sexes behave differently in close relationships? *Journal of Social and Personal Relationships, 1*, 471–501.

Hinde, R. A. (1986). Some implications of evolutionary theory and comparative data for the study of human prosocial and aggressive behavior. In D. Olweus, J. Block, & M. Radke-Yarrow (Eds.), *Development of antisocial and prosocial behavior* (pp. 13–32). Orlando, FL: Academic Press.

Hinde, R. A. (1991). When is an evolutionary approach useful? *Child Development, 62*, 671–675.

Horn, H., & Rubenstein, D. (1984). Behavioural adaptations and life history. In J. Krebs & N. Davies (Eds.), *Behav-*

ioural ecology: An evolutionary approach (2nd ed.). Oxford: Blackwell.

Howes, P., & Markman, H. J. (1989). Marital quality and child functioning: A longitudinal investigation. *Child Development, 60,* 1044–1051.

Irvin, N. A., Kennell, J. H., & Klaus, M. H. (1976). Caring for parents of an infant with a congenital malformation. In M. H. Klaus & J. H. Kennell (Eds.), *Maternal–infant bonding* (pp. 167–208). St. Louis, MO: C. V. Mosby.

Isabella, R. (1994). Origins of maternal role satisfaction and its influences upon maternal interactive behavior and infant–mother attachment. *Infant Behavior and Development, 17,* 381–387.

Isabella, R., & Belsky, J. (1990). Interactional synchrony and the origins of infant–mother attachment: A replication study. *Child Development, 62,* 373–384.

Isabella, R., Belsky, J., & von Eye, A. (1989). Origins of infant–mother attachment: An examination of interactional synchrony during the infant's first year. *Developmental Psychology, 25,* 12–21.

Jacobson, S. W., & Frye, K. F. (1991). Effect of maternal social support on attachment: Experimental evidence. *Child Development, 62,* 572–582.

Jessor, R., Costa, F., Jessor, L., & Donovan, J. (1983). Time of first intercourse: A prospective study. *Journal of Personality and Social Psychology, 44,* 608–626.

Jones, B., Leeton, J., McLeod, I., & Wood, C. (1972). Factors influencing the age of menarche in a lower socio-economic group in Melbourne. *Medical Journal of Australia, 21,* 533–535.

Kelly, R. L. (1995). *The foraging spectrum: Diversity in hunter–gatherer lifeways.* Washington, DC: Smithsonian Institution Press.

Kennell, J. H., Trause, M. A., & Klaus, M. H. (1975). Evidence for a sensitive period in the human mother. In T. Brazelton, E. Tronick, L. Adamson, H. Als, & S. Wise (Eds.), *Parent–infant interaction* (pp. 87–101). New York: Elsevier/Excerpta Media/North Holland.

Kirkpatrick, L. A. (1998). Evolution, pair-bonding, and reproductive strategies: A reconceptualization of adult attachment. In J. A. Simpson & W. S. Rholes (Eds.), *Attachment theory and close relationships* (pp. 353–393). New York: Guilford Press.

Klaus, M., & Kennell, J. (1976). Parent-to-infant attachment. In D. Hull (Ed.), *Recent advances in pediatrics* (pp. 129–152). New York: Churchill Livingstone.

Konner, M. (1982). *The tangled wing: Biological constraints on the human spirit.* New York: Holt, Rinehart, & Winston.

Kunce, L. J., & Shaver, P. R. (1994). An attachment-theoretical approach to caregiving in romantic relationships. In K. Bartholomew & D. Perlman (Eds.), *Attachment processes in adulthood* (pp. 205–237). London: Jessica Kingsley.

LaFreniere, P. J., & Sroufe, L. A. (1985). Profiles of peer competence in the preschool: Interrelations between measures, influence of social ecology, and relation to attachment history. *Developmental Psychology, 21,* 56–69.

Lagercrantz, H., & Slotkin, T. A. (1986). The stress of being born. *Scientific American, 254,* 92–102.

Lamb, M. E., & Hwang, C. P. (1982). Maternal attachment and mother–neonate bonding. In M. E. Lamb & A. L. Brown (Eds.), *Advances in developmental psychology* (Vol. 2, pp. 1–39): Hillsdale, NJ: Erlbaum.

Lempers, J., Clark-Lempers, D., & Simons, R. (1989). Economic hardship, parenting, and distress in adolescence. *Child Development, 60,* 25–49.

Lessells, C. (1991). The evolution of life histories. In J.

Krebs & N. Davies (Eds.), *Behavioural ecology: An evolutionary approach* (3rd ed.). Oxford: Blackwell.

Lewis, M., & Feiring, C. (1989). Infant, mother, and mother–infant interaction behavior and subsequent attachment. *Child Development, 60,* 831–837.

Lewis, M., Feiring, C., McGuffog, C., & Jaskir, J. (1984). Predicting psychopathology in six-year-olds from early social relations. *Child Development, 55,* 123–136.

Lieberman, A. F., Weston, D. R., & Pawl, J. H. (1991). Preventive intervention and outcome with anxiously attached dyads. *Child Development, 62,* 199–209.

Lütkenhaus, P., Grossmann, K. E., & Grossmann, K. (1985). Infant–mother attachment at twelve months and style of interaction with a stranger at the age of three years. *Child Development, 56,* 1538–1542.

Lynch, M. A. (1975). Ill-health and child abuse. *Lancet, ii,* 317–319.

Lyons-Ruth, K., Connell, D. B., & Grunebaum, H. U. (1990). Infants at social risk: Maternal depression and family support services as mediators of infant development and security of attachment. *Child Development, 61,* 85–98.

MacArthur, R. H. (1962). Some generalized theorems of natural selection. *Proceedings of the National Academy of Sciences USA, 48,* 1893–1897.

MacFarlane, J. A. (1975). *The psychology of childbirth.* Cambridge, MA: Harvard University Press.

MacFarlane, J. A. (1977). Olfaction in the development of social preferences in the human neonate. In *The human neonate in parent–infant interaction* (Ciba Foundation Symposium No. 33, pp. 103–117).

Main, M. (1981). Avoidance in the service of attachment: A working paper. In K. Immelmann, G. Barlow, M. Main, & L. Petrinovich (Eds.), *Behavioral development: The Bielefeld Interdisciplinary Project* (pp. 651–693). New York: Cambridge University Press.

Main, M. (1990). Cross-cultural studies of attachment organization: Recent studies, changing methodologies, and the concept of conditional strategies. *Human Development, 33,* 48–61.

Main, M., & Hesse, E. (1990). Parents' unresolved traumatic experiences are related to infant disorganized status: Is frightened and/or frightening parental behavior the linking mechanism? In M. T. Greenberg, D. Cicchetti, & E. M. Cummings (Eds.), *Attachment in the preschool years: Theory, research, and intervention* (pp. 161–184). Chicago: University of Chicago Press.

Main, M., & Solomon, J. (1986). Discovery of an insecure–disorganized/disoriented attachment pattern: Procedures, findings, and implications for the classification of behavior. In T. B. Brazelton & M. Yogman (Eds.), *Affective development in infancy* (pp. 95–124). Norwood, NJ: Ablex.

Main, M., & Solomon, J. (1990). Procedures for identifying disorganized/disoriented infants in the Ainsworth Strange Situation. In M. T. Greenberg, D. Cicchetti, & E. M. Cummings (Eds.), *Attachment in the preschool years: Theory, research, and intervention* (pp. 121–160). Chicago: University of Chicago Press.

Marks, I. M. (1987). *Fears, phobias, and rituals.* New York: Oxford University Press.

Matas, L., Arend, R., & Sroufe, L. A. (1978). Continuity in adaptation in the second year: The relationship between quality of attachment and later competence. *Child Development, 49,* 547–556.

McLanahan, S., & Booth, K. (1989). Mother-only families: Problems, prospects, and politics. *Journal of Marriage and the Family, 51,* 557–580.

McLoyd, V. (1990). The declining fortunes of black children: Psychological distress, parenting, and socioemotional development in the context of economic hardship. *Child Development, 61*, 311–346.

Mills, M., & Melhuish, E. (1974). Recognition of mother's voice in early infancy. *Nature, 252*, 123–124.

Minturn, L., & Stashak, J. (1982). Infanticide as a terminal abortion procedure. *Behavior Science Research, 17*, 70–90.

Moffitt, T. E., Caspi, A., Belsky, J., & Silva, P. A. (1992). Childhood experience and the onset of menarche: A test of a sociobiological model. *Child Development, 63*, 47–58.

Mueller, C., & Pope, H. (1977). Marital instability: A study of its transmission between generations. *Journal of Marriage and the Family, 39*, 83–93.

Myers, B. J. (1984a). Mother–infant bonding: The status of this critical-period hypothesis. *Developmental Review, 4*, 240–274.

Myers, B. J. (1984b). Mother–infant bonding: Rejoinder to Kennell and Klaus. *Developmental Review, 4*, 283–288.

Newcomer, S., & Udry, J. (1987). Parental marital status effects on adolescent sexual behavior. *Journal of Marriage and the Family, 49*, 235–240.

O'Connor, S. M., Vietze, P. M., Hopkins, J. B., & Altemeier, W. A. (1977). Postpartum extended maternal–infant contact: Subsequent mothering and child health. *Pediatric Research, 11*, 380.

Promislow, D., & Harvey, P. (1990). Living fast and dying young: A comparative analysis of life-history variation among mammals. *Journal of the Zoological Society of London, 220*, 417–437.

Radke-Yarrow, M. (1991). Attachment patterns in children of depressed mothers. In C. M. Parkes, J. Stevenson-Hinde, & P. Maras (Eds.), *Attachment across the life cycle* (pp. 115–126). London: Tavistock/Routledge.

Rheingold, H. L. (1969). The effect of a strange environment on the behavior of infants. In B. Foss (Ed.), *Determinants of infant behavior* (Vol. 4, pp. 137–166). London: Methuen.

Rholes, W. S., Simpson, J. A., & Blakely, B. S. (1995). Adult attachment styles and mothers' relationships with their young children. *Personal Relationships, 2*, 35–54.

Rholes, W. S., Simpson, J. A., Blakely, B. S., Lanigan, L., & Allen, E. A. (1997). Adult attachment styles, the desire to have children, and working models of parenthood. *Journal of Personality, 65*, 357–385.

Ricks, M. H. (1985). The social transmission of parental behavior: Attachment across generations. In I. Bretherton & E. Waters (Eds.), Growing points in attachment theory and research. *Monographs of the Society for Research in Child Development, 50* (1–2, Serial No. 209), 211–227.

Russell, M. J. (1976). Human olfactory communication. *Nature, 260*, 520–522.

Sagi, A. (1981). Mothers' and non-mothers' identification of infant cries. *Infant Behavior and Development, 4*, 37–40.

Schaller, J., Carlsson, S. G., & Larsson, K. (1979). Effects of extended post-partum mother–child contact on the mother's behavior during nursing. *Infant Behavior and Development, 2*, 319–324.

Shaver, P. R., Hazan, C., & Bradshaw, D. (1988). Love as attachment: The integration of three behavioral systems. In R. J. Sternberg & M. L. Barnes (Eds.), *The psychology of love* (pp. 68–99). New Haven, CT: Yale University Press.

Sherman, P. W. (1988). The levels of analysis. *Animal Behavior, 36*, 616–619.

Simpson, J. A., & Gangestad, S. W. (1991). Individual differences in sociosexuality: Evidence for convergent and discriminant validity. *Journal of Personality and Social Psychology, 60*, 870–883.

Smith, E., Udry, J., & Morris, N. (1985). Pubertal development and friends: A biosocial explanation of adolescent sexual behavior. *Journal of Health and Social Behavior, 26*, 183–192.

Smith, P. B., & Pederson, D. R. (1988). Maternal sensitivity and patterns of infant–mother attachment. *Child Development, 59*, 1097–1101.

Sostek, A. M., Scanlon, J. W., & Abramson, D. C. (1982). Postpartum contact and maternal confidence and anxiety: A confirmation of short-term effects. *Infant Behavior and Development, 5*, 323–329.

Spieker, S. J. (1988). Patterns of very insecure attachment in samples of high-risk infants and toddlers. *Topics in Early Childhood Special Education, 6*, 37–53.

Spieker, S. J., & Booth, C. (1988). Maternal antecedents of attachment quality. In J. Belsky & T. Nezworski (Eds.), *Clinical implications of attachment* (pp. 95–135). Hillsdale, NJ: Erlbaum.

Sroufe, L. A. (1988). The role of infant–caregiver attachment in development. In J. Belsky & T. Nezworski (Eds.), *Clinical implications of attachment* (pp. 18–38). Hillsdale, NJ: Erlbaum.

Sroufe, L. A., & Waters, E. (1977). Attachment as an organizational construct. *Child Development, 48*, 1184–1199.

Stearns, S. (1976). Life-history tactics: A review of the ideas. *Quarterly Review of Biology, 51*, 3–47.

Stearns, S. (1992). *The evolution of life histories*. New York: Oxford University Press.

Steinberg, L. (1988). Reciprocal relation between parent–child distance and pubertal maturation. *Developmental Psychology, 24*, 122–128.

Sugarman, M. (1977). Perinatal influences of maternal–infant attachment. *American Journal of Orthopsychiatry, 47*, 407–421.

Surbey, M. (1990). Family composition, stress, and human menarche. In F. Bercovitch & T. Zeigler (Eds.), *The socioendocrinology of primate reproduction* (pp. 71–97). New York: Alan R. Liss.

Symons, D. (1979). *The evolution of human sexuality*. New York: Oxford University Press.

Tinbergen, N. (1963). On the aims and methods of ethology. *Zeitschrift für Tierpsychologie, 20*, 410–433.

Tooby, J. (1982). Pathogens, polymorphism, and the evolution of sex. *Journal of Theoretical Biology, 97*, 557–576.

Tooby, J., & Cosmides, L. (1990). On the universality of human nature and the uniqueness of the individual: The role of genetics and adaptation. *Journal of Personality, 58*, 17–68.

Tooby, J., & Cosmides, L. (1992). Psychological foundations of culture. In J. Barkow, L. Cosmides, & J. Tooby (Eds.), *The adapted mind* (pp. 19–136). New York: Oxford University Press.

Trivers, R. L. (1971). The evolution of reciprocal altruism. *Quarterly Review of Biology, 46*, 35–57.

Trivers, R. L. (1972). Parental investment and sexual selection. In B. Campbell (Ed.), *Sexual selection and the descent of man, 1871–1971* (pp. 136–179). Chicago: Aldine-Atherton.

Trivers, R. L. (1974). Parent–offspring conflict. *American Zoologist, 14*, 249–264.

Trivers, R. L. (1985). *Social evolution*. Menlo Park, CA: Benjamin/Cummings.

Trivers, R. L., & Willard, D. E. (1973). Natural selection of parental ability to vary the sex ratio of offspring. *Science, 179*, 90–92.

Udry, J. (1987). Hormonal and social determinants of adolescent sexual initiation. In J. Bancroft (Ed.), *Adolescence and puberty* (pp. 147–163). New York: Oxford University Press.

Valenzuela, M. (1990). Attachment in chronically underweight young children. *Child Development, 61*, 1984–1996.

van IJzendoorn, M. (1995). Adult attachment representations, parental responsiveness, and infant attachment: A meta-analysis on the predictive validity of the Adult Attachment Interview. *Psychological Bulletin, 117*, 387–403.

van IJzendoorn, M., Kranenburg, M., Zwart-Woudstra, H., van Busschbach, A., & Lambermon, M. (1992). Parental attachment and children's socio-emotional development: Some findings on the validity of the Adult Attachment Interview in the Netherlands. *International Journal of Behavioral Development, 14*, 375–394.

Waters, E., Wippman, J., & Sroufe, L. A. (1979). Attachment, positive affect, and competence in the peer group: Two studies in construct validation. *Child Development, 50*, 821–829.

Williams, G. (1966). *Adaptation and natural selection.* Princeton, NJ: Princeton University Press.

Wright, R. (1994). *The moral animal.* New York: Vintage.

Youngblade, L. M., & Belsky, J. (1989). Child maltreatment, infant–parent attachment security, and dysfunctional peer relationships in toddlerhood. *Topics in Early Childhood Special Education, 9*, 1–15.

Zarling, C. L., Hirsch, B. J., & Landry, S. (1988). Maternal social networks and mother–infant interactions in full-term and very low birthweight, pre-term infants. *Child Development, 59*, 178–185.

Zeifman, D., & Hazan, C. (1997). Attachment: The bond in pair-bonds. In J. A. Simpson & D. T. Kenrick (Eds.), *Evolutionary social psychology* (pp. 237–263). Mahwah, NJ: Erlbaum.

7

Modern Evolutionary Theory and Patterns of Attachment

❖

JAY BELSKY

It is not uncommon to read in child and human development textbooks (Bee, 1995; Cole & Cole, 1989; Harris & Liebert, 1992; Hetherington & Parke, 1993; Sigelman & Shaffer, 1995; Turner & Helms, 1995) and in scholarly publications that attachment behavior evolved because it protected infants from predators, and in so doing promoted the survival of the species. From the perspective of modern evolutionary biology, it is clear that such arguments, as far as they go, are insufficient to account for the evolution of attachment behavior (or any other, for that matter), for two reasons (see Simpson, Chapter 6, this volume). First, evolution works at the levels of the gene and the individual, not the species; second, evolution is about differential reproduction, not just survival.

Genetic replication is the goal of (all) life, and thus the ultimate target of natural selection. That is, simple survival is not selected for. Only if survival fosters the *reproduction of the surviving individual's genes* (via his or her own survival and/or that of kin, including descendants), rather than those of the species, does natural selection operate on a behavior or behavior system—perhaps like attachment—that fosters survival. In fact, the goals of reproductive success and survival are often in conflict; when such conflict occurs, the genes and behavior that enhance reproductive success are selected for, not the genes and behavior that promote survival. This can be seen clearly in many species, including birds and monkeys, in which individual organisms that make loud calls to warn others of the presence of predators reduce their own survival prospects by drawing the predators' attention to themselves.

Why should any individual engage in such potentially self-destructive behavior? That is, why has behavior that is so clearly a threat to individual survival evolved? The answer to this question is founded on the fact that those most likely to benefit from the warning call are relatives of the caller and thus possess some of the very same genes as the caller does (i.e., inclusive fitness). Because the benefactors of the warning call have the potential to collectively replicate the caller's genes (through their own reproduction), more than would be the case were no call given, calling behavior that ends up enhancing the reproductive fitness of the caller while simultaneously reducing the caller's probability of survival evolves.

What this analysis should make clear is that attachment behavior would not have evolved if it had only functioned to protect the child and thereby to promote survival, because survival per se is clearly not the goal of natural selection. Thus, unless survival enhanced the reproductive prospects and especially the reproductive fitness of ancestral human infants, there would have been insufficient evolutionary pressure for attachment behavior to evolve. To the extent, then, that evolution had anything to do with human attachment—as Bowlby believed it did, and as the theory he promulgated presumes—it is because the protection and survival it promoted fostered successful reproduction of those individuals whose inclination it was to maintain proximity to, and/or seek contact with, their caregivers.

It is not surprising that many still presume that attachment behavior evolved because it promoted survival of the species, rather than because it promoted the eventual reproductive success of those individual infants who developed a propensity to remain in proximity to their caregivers. After all, in Bowlby's (1969/1982) original formulation of the theory in 1969, he used this argument (among others) to account for attachment behavior (and also to discount secondary-drive theory): "The ultimate outcome for which all structures of a living organism are adapted is neither more nor less than species survival" (p. 54). Yet, as a lifelong learner, Bowlby (1969/1982, pp. 55–56) came to recognize, acknowledge, and correct his "survival of the species" analysis in the second edition of the first volume of his trilogy in 1982, in order to emphasize individual reproduction:

> Darwin's phrase "the welfare of each species" suggests that it is the whole species that is adapted. . . . Others . . . have suggested that the unit of adaptation is the interbreeding population (as was proposed in the first edition of this book).
> All these ideas are discredited now, however. . . .
> The basic concept of the genetical theory of natural selection is that the unit central to the whole process is the individual gene. . . . What this means in practice is that through the process of differential breeding success, individuals that are carrying certain genes increase in numbers whilst individuals that are carrying others diminish . . . the ultimate outcome to be attained is always survival of the genes an individual is carrying.

Despite this explicit updating of the evolutionary theorizing that served as one of several cornerstones of Bowlby's (1969/1982) attachment theory, the fact remains that many old-fashioned ideas about evolution continue to permeate thinking about attachment. In many ways these understandings, either explicitly promulgated by Bowlby or inferred by many of his intellectual descendants, turn out to be mistaken when viewed from the perspective of contemporary evolutionary theory (e.g., Chisholm, 1996; Hinde, 1982; Lamb, Thompson, Charnov, & Estes, 1985). I hope to show in this chapter, which integrates contemporary attachment theory and research with modern evolutionary theory (Hamilton, 1964; Trivers, 1972, 1974), that these "errors" in evolutionary theorizing and reasoning

about attachment do not reflect fatal flaws in the theory, as has been implied at times (Lamb, Thompson, Gardner, & Charnov, 1984); rather, they provide opportunities for enhancing the depth and scope of the theory (Belsky, Steinberg, & Draper, 1991; Chisholm, 1996; Hinde & Stevenson-Hinde, 1990; Main, 1990). In contrast to Lamb and colleagues (1984, 1985), who I believe missed an opportunity to reinterpret Bowlby and contemporary attachment theory in light of modern evolutionary thinking when they accurately criticized some of the evolutionary bases of attachment theory over a decade ago, I argue that "variations in attachment security that Bowlby's theory so clearly anticipated evolved to serve reproductive fitness goals in an ecologically sensitive manner" (Belsky et al., 1991, p. 63). Indeed, it is my specific purpose to move beyond just distinguishing secure from insecure attachments, as my colleagues and I did (Belsky et al., 1991) in our evolutionary analysis of socialization. I argue here that understanding of the three originally identified patterns of attachment—"secure," "avoidant," and "resistant" (B, A, and C, respectively)—can be enhanced by considering each of them from the perspective of modern evolutionary biology.

Toward this end, I begin by analyzing some of what must be regarded as antiquated evolutionary assumptions that were either built into Bowlby's original theorizing or filtered into the subsequent development, articulation, and/or interpretation of the theory by its many adherents. Next I discuss a particular segment of contemporary evolutionary theory, referred to as "life history theory," which provides a new lens for viewing patterns of attachment from an evolutionary perspective. This sets the stage for the application of this evolutionary perspective to current understanding of the three original patterns of attachment and their theorized sequelae in adulthood. To be noted is that virtually all of the evidence to be reviewed here concerning attachment and mating was not available for consideration when we (Belsky et al., 1991) published our evolutionary theory of socialization. Before drawing some general conclusions, I briefly address two persistent theoretical challenges that confront attachment theory: those pertaining to (1) heritability and temperament and (2) multiple internal working models of attachment figures. To be noted is that "disorganized" (D) attachments barely figure at all in this chapter, because it remains unclear to me whether such patterns can be conceptualized in terms of reproductive strategy. Moreover, there are few data linking the D classification in adulthood to mating, and even fewer linking it to parenting behavior.

ATTACHMENT THEORY AND MODERN EVOLUTIONARY THEORY

It is not only with respect to issues of reproduction versus survival and individuals versus species that there remains some confusion about evolution and attachment. As Chisholm (1996, p. 14) has succinctly noted, current evolutionary, anthropological, and archeological thinking holds "that the EEA [environment of evolutionary adaptedness] was neither as uniform nor as benign as Bowlby seems to have imagined (e.g., Edgarton, 1992; Foley, 1992)." Although it was certainly likely that in some ecological niches resources were abundant and maternal care was notably sensitively responsive, as it appears to be in select hunter–gatherer societies today, it is more than likely that in others (or at least at certain times), resources were scarce or of poor quality; probably in consequence, care was as much insensitive as sensitive, if not notably insensitive. Evidence for such less-than-ideal caregiving in the face of harsh and demanding contextual conditions can be found in research by developmental psychologists studying poverty in the contemporary United States (for a review, see McLoyd, 1990), by anthropologists studying child rearing in the Third World (e.g., Scheper-Hughes, 1992), and by primatologists studying the effect of foraging conditions on maternal solicitude (e.g., Rosenblum & Paully, 1984).

To presume, then, as have so many students of attachment theory, that the EEA was a relatively benign environment that promoted sensitive responsiveness and thereby attachment security seems to be a case of equating *one* condition of ancestral human experience with *the* experience of our early hominid ancestors. That natural variation in ancestral rearing conditions might have had consequences for the evolution of attachment behavior is certainly suggested by experimental evidence indicating that secure-base-like behavior among infant monkeys varies as a function of the foraging conditions to which their mothers are exposed. When food is abundant and easy to find, infant offspring frequently separate from their mothers to explore a novel environment, but when the mothers' access to food is more unpredictable and/or difficult, the offspring

look decidedly less secure (Andrews & Rosenblum, 1991, 1994).

Once it is acknowledged that there were many different EEAs, and it is accepted that attachment behavior probably evolved in response to varying selection pressures over the course of human history, it becomes increasingly difficult if not untenable to embrace the notion that one pattern of attachment (i.e., proximity-seeking and contact-maintaining security) was or is "species-typical"—or, even if it were, that such a pattern is "normal" or functioned as the "target" of selection (Chisholm, 1996; Hinde & Stevenson-Hinde, 1990). As Lamb et al. (1985) noted more than a decade ago, "the modern biological view of adaptation . . . leads . . . to question[ing] the belief that there is a single, normative, pattern of parental behavior forming the sole adaptive niche for human infants and that infantile behavior must also accord with a single adaptive behavioral template" (p. 52). Under the diverse conditions in which hominids evolved, it seems more reasonable to presume that no pattern of attachment was primary and others secondary, but rather that what evolved was a repertoire of attachment behaviors that could be flexibly organized into different patterns contingent on ecological and caregiving conditions (Belsky et al., 1991; Chisholm, 1996; Hinde, 1982). That is, in the same way that natural selection shaped the body to store fat under some ecological conditions but not others, so it shaped patterns of attachment. If a particular set of rearing conditions was encountered over a period of time, then one enduring organization of attachment behavior developed; if a different set of conditions was encountered repeatedly, then a different attachment pattern emerged. In other words, what evolved was not merely attachment behaviors, but the ability to organize those behaviors into a pattern that fit the rearing conditions and in so doing promoted reproductive fitness (not just survival).

Although it may be the case in contemporary Western society that one pattern, which has come to be known as "secure," predominates (as it still may in some aboriginal societies), this should not be taken to mean that in any particular EEA this was the species-typical or normative pattern. Indeed, it seems reasonable to speculate that the organizations of attachment behavior typically observed in the strange situation (A, B, and C) reflect only those that current living conditions foster, rather than the full range of possibilities that could emerge from the evolved repertoire of attachment behavior.

Perhaps the best evidence in favor of such an argument is to be found in Main and Solomon's (1986) "discovery" of so-called "disorganized" attachments, especially within high-risk populations (e.g., maltreating parents). It seems likely that had such high-risk rearing conditions not been studied, the D pattern (or patterns) would not have convincingly emerged from research on low-risk populations. Now consider the probability of discovering disorganized attachment if cultural development had advanced to the point where poverty, child maltreatment, maternal depression, and other apparently D-envoking social ecologies were exceedingly rare or even nonexistent by the time research on attachment was initiated. However fanciful this thought experiment may be, it should alert us to the fact that social-ecological conditions that once existed but no longer do (or have not yet been identified or studied) may have fostered (or foster) attachment patterns that would not fit the contemporary A, B, C, or even D classifications. Thus, within the repertoire of human attachment organization, we may currently be observing only a subset of those patterns that might have once been observable over the course of human evolutionary history. It remains possible, of course, that what is observed today reflects the full range of attachment patterns that exist within the human repertoire. Since behavior does not fossilize, there is no way to resolve this theoretically important issue. Nevertheless, because of the possibility that other patterns may have existed (or may still be identified), and because, as I shall argue, patterns of attachment reflect evolved responses to environmental conditions, there remains no compelling reason to presume that any pattern is more primary, more natural, or more species-typical than any other.

In fact, I suspect that the fundamental reason why security has come to be seen by many students of attachment theory (if not by its originator) as the ancestral psychological experience of the infant is that from the very inception of attachment theory, evolutionary theory and mental health theory became intertwined in a way that violated the former while reifying the latter. In light of the facts that Bowlby was a psychiatrist, and that psychologists rather than biologists have played such a central role in developing and promulgating the theory, this is not surprising. For example, Sroufe's (1979) attachment-based theory of developmental tasks, just like Erikson's (1950) theory of psychosocial development and Maslow's (1976) theory of self actualization,

epitomizes a view of mental health that can be traced back to the romantic philosophy of Rousseau, if not before. Central to this view is the evolutionarily untenable notion that human beings' natural state is one of grace—to trust others and care for them, giving as much as receiving, if not more so. Only when barriers to this natural state exist will the caring, stress-resilient course of human development be sidetracked, leading to mistrust/insecurity, to dependency (rather than autonomy), and eventually to problematic relations with others and poor mental health.

From the standpoint of modern evolutionary theory, this mental health view of development, which has so much in common with contemporary thinking about attachment, romanticizes and thus mischaracterizes both the human condition and the nature of evolved life on our planet. This seems especially so in current discussions of attachment theory (and parent–child relations more generally), because there is virtually no acknowledgment that it is not always in a parent's best interest to provide sensitive care (Daly & Wilson, 1980; Hrdy, 1995; Simpson, Chapter 6, this volume; Trivers, 1972, 1974). Thus, even though current theory acknowledges that just as infants evolved to seek contact, comfort, and protection from the caregiver, mothers evolved a reciprocal tendency to provide care, students of attachment theory still fail to highlight what is now recognized as a central evolutionary truth about parent–child relations: the inherent conflict of interest between parent and child, which itself derives from the fact that parent and child share only 50% (not 100%) of their genes (Simpson, Chapter 6, this volume; Trivers, 1972, 1974). Thus, as every parent knows, what a child wants is not always what a parent wants. But more fundamental, and more unappreciated by developmentalists, is the idea that what is in the biological best interest of the parent is not always in the biological best interest of the child (and vice versa). Thus, in just the same way and for just the same reasons that the capacity to provide security-promoting sensitive and responsive care may have evolved, so too may have the capacity to provide insensitive care (i.e., discriminative parental solicitude; Daly & Wilson, 1980).

If a parent's reproductive fitness in the EEA was enhanced by attending to a mate, a potential mate, another child, or the means of economic production, rather than to a child bidding for care and attention, then natural selection would have been as likely to design into the human caregiver the (discriminating) capacity to provide insensitive care as sensitive care. From the perspective of modern evolutionary theory, then—with its emphasis on reproductive fitness rather than survival or mental health—there is no reason to presume that sensitive responsiveness is any more species-typical, normative, or characteristic of ancestral humans than insensitivity. Once again, it is important to acknowledge that because behavior does not fossilize and because evolutionary pressures could have selected for insensitive as well as sensitive care, it cannot be presumed that the natural state of motherhood is to be sensitively responsive. Nor, though, should we presume that sensitivity did not itself have reproductive-fitness payoffs, at least in certain environments.

Furthermore, it seems problematic to argue that insecure attachments "are *mal*adaptations" because "these patterns *compromise* the capacity for dealing with subsequent developmental issues, especially those surrounding intimate social relationships and parenting" (Sroufe, 1988, p. 25, emphasis added) when, as I shall argue, it may make just as much sense to regard these as *evolved* responses to contextual demands (i.e., mothering practices) that *enable* the individual to reproduce "successfully" (or at least once did so in some EEAs). Even though it is now widely accepted that insecure attachment patterns are strategic responses to certain styles of maternal behavior (Sroufe, 1988), as most clearly articulated in Main's (1990) "conditional-strategy" analysis, it remains the case (as the preceding quotation indicates) that these strategies are regarded as "secondary" and as "compromises" that are less optimal in some basic developmental sense. Simply put, from an evolutionary perspective, they are not. They are just as natural and species-typical as their opposite. Although they may not yield developmental outcomes that a mental health perspective values or that our society wants to promote, contemporary (or even enduring) cultural values should not be confused with biological desiderata (Hinde & Stevenson-Hinde, 1990).

In summary, security and insecurity may be equally natural and species-typical conditions, in which case it makes little evolutionary sense to regard one pattern of attachment fostered by sensitivity as primary and others fostered by insensitivity as secondary. To the extent that attachment behavior evolved—and, along with it, the capacity to organize attachment behavior into a variety of patterns—secure and insecure patterns evolved for the very same reason: to promote reproductive fitness. That one pattern was or is more frequent than others, then, does not make it more primary or better, only more frequent. Moreover, we have no way of knowing whether patterns that are more frequent today were always more frequent, or whether patterns of attachment that have been identified to date reflect the full range of patterns that exist within the human behavioral repertoire or just those that current ecological conditions evoke. Finally, even though we may today value developmental sequelae associated with one pattern of attachment more than we do those associated with another, we should not presume that evolution was guided by issues of mental health or happiness. As already noted, when it makes biological sense not to survive, organisms often behave in ways that foster their demise. Thus, we should expect that when it makes biological sense—or at least once did (in an EEA)—for parents to treat their offspring poorly, and for children to disregard the feelings of others and selfishly pursue their own desires, evolution would have surely found a way to get those behavioral jobs done.

LIFE HISTORY THEORY

Readers of this chapter, like most developmentally oriented thinkers, take for granted the life cycle and life history of *Homo sapiens*. But beyond appreciating that the early helplessness of the human newborn is a direct result of its "premature" (relative to that of other mammals) expulsion from the womb in order to accommodate what will become an especially large head, and that the infant's resultant helplessness favored the evolution of attachment behavior and the remarkable learning capacity of our species, students of human development tend not to recognize the relatively distinctive nature of the life history of our species.

Variation in the organization and timing of species-characteristic life courses is the subject, within evolutionary biology, of life history theory. And what evolution-oriented life history researchers and theorists have come to recognize, and what I regard as centrally important to understanding the place of attachment in the human condition, is that life histories themselves are adaptations that have evolved through natural selection (Charnov, 1993; Stearns, 1993). That is, species that bear infants more capable than our own, mature faster, bear more offspring per pregnancy, or parent their offspring less intensively than humans do so because their ensemble of life course traits fits the ecological niches in which they have evolved. That is, the species-specific set of life history features (e.g., rate of growth, time to sexual maturity, litter size, degree of parental investment) promotes the reproductive fitness of the individual members of the species. Thus, in the same way that natural selection has favored the white fur of a fox living on the Alaskan tundra, natural selection has fostered the rapid development and short life course of some species and the slower development and longer life course of others.

Within-Species Variation

Not unreasonably, the reader may wonder at this juncture what all of this has to do with human attachment. Life history theory becomes pertinent when we recognize that not only do life histories vary *across* species; they also can vary *within* species (Gross, 1996)—and can do so for reproductively strategic reasons. That is, life history variation within a species has evolved because it enhances reproductive fitness. A species may evince two (or more) distinctive life histories that vary in any number of characteristics, including size at birth (or maturity), age at reproduction, mating tactics, litter size, and parental investment, because different "versions" of the species are adapted to different ecological niches. What works—that is, what promotes reproductive fitness—in one niche simply does not do as well as in another. "Ecological niche" may itself be defined in any number of ways, including, as I show below, the number of other variants of the species. Ultimately, I argue that it may prove useful to think about patterns of attachment in terms of within-species life history variation.

Divergent varieties of the same species are known as "morphs," and the bluegill sunfish provides an excellent example of variation in growth and mating strategy (Wilson, 1994). One life history pattern within this species is characterized by large size among males at maturity, which enables males to defend their nests; these male bluegills are known as "parentals." Males that mature at a smaller body size are known initially as "sneakers," because they use their small size to sneak into territory controlled by larger males and deposit their own sperm at the moment a parental male mates with a female. Interestingly, "sneakers" continue to develop so that they eventually resemble females. Now known as "mim-

ics," they continue to parasitize the nests of "parentals" by fertilizing female eggs intended for a "parental." The central point here is not simply that male bluegill sunfish come in different varieties with respect to growth, development, and mating, but that behavioral differences at the heart of this variation appear to have evolved in order to promote reproductive fitness. Because the smaller variety of the fish is less successful at defending a territory and attracting mates, it has evolved an alternative tactic for replicating its genes (sneaking).

"Polymorphism" is the term used by evolutionary scientists to describe such systematic variation in life histories and reproductive strategies within a species. I regard this concept as especially pertinent to this chapter, which is concerned not with species-typical attachment behavior (the primary evolutionary concern of Bowlby), but with individual differences in patterns of attachment. Polymorphisms, whether morphological or behavioral, may evolve and be maintained within a population because the environment is heterogeneous, with different morphs adapted to different habitats (as I shall argue, and others have suggested, is the case for varying attachment patterns) (Cook, 1991). In such cases, the relative frequency of the different morphs should to some extent reflect the relative frequency of the different microhabitats in the environment (Cook, 1991). Applied to individual differences in attachment, this account suggests that approximately two-thirds to three-quarters of most samples of infants are classified as secure because this percentage of caregiving environments is predominantly sensitively responsive (i.e., security-promoting) in nature.

A second account of polymorphism emphasizes its "frequency-dependent" origins. That is, a particular morph is only advantageous if it is shown by no more than a certain proportion of the population. If the morph becomes too common, its advantages are reduced, and the proportion of individuals of that particular morph declines. But when a morph becomes less common, its characteristics become more advantageous, and the proportion possessing it increases. As a result, the polymorphism stabilizes when possessors of different characteristics on average all achieve roughly the same reproductive success (Baker & Bellis, 1995). This is considered a "balanced polymorphism," and the possibility seems worth considering that one reason why distributions of attachment classifications seem more rather than less similar across cultures (van

IJzendoorn & Krooneberg, 1988) is that they represent balanced polymorphisms.

Environmental Influences

Divergent morphs, adapted as they are to different environments, may reflect distinctive genotypes (Wilson, 1994). In light of Ricciuti's (1992) behavior-genetic study of twins showing that patterns of infant–mother attachment (A, B, C; security–insecurity) are not heritable (though emotionality in the strange situation is: A1–B2 vs. B3–C2), it seems reasonable to conclude—at least for the time being and consistent with traditional attachment theory—that if varying patterns of attachment do represent distinct morphs, as I argue, they do not arise from distinctive genotypes. Ricciuti's data take on special importance in light of the fact that in some species, divergent life histories are environmentally induced in ways that make evolutionary sense. That is, organisms sometimes modify their life histories in reaction to environmental experience, so as promote reproductive fitness. Such variation is often discussed in terms of "reproductive strategy" and, when subject to environmental influence, is conceptualized as "facultative." *Central to the modern evolutionary perspective on attachment advanced in this chapter is the proposition that patterns of attachment represent facultative responses (to caregiving environments) that evolved in the service of reproductive goals.*

Fish provide excellent and dramatic examples of facultative—that is, environmentally induced—variation in reproductive strategy (Gross, 1996). Consider, for example, reef-living cleaner fish, which have permanent territories in which males control a harem of females and in which individual organisms actually change sex when the reproductive advantage gained by doing so is substantial. In this species, when the dominant male dies, the dominant female (in the female dominance hierarchy), who is invariably the largest female, takes over the male's territory and within 1 hour of the male's death behaves as a male toward the other females. About 2 weeks later, the now-male female (or once-female male) is producing sperm (Charnov, 1982). Why has this remarkable developmental response to environmental experience evolved? Certainly not to make fish mentally healthy, or even to promote survival. The payoff is reproduction. By becoming a male, the former dominant female increases the number of progeny she (now he) can produce.

Somewhat similar social control of sex change in the service of reproductive goals has been observed among a very common and much-studied planktivorous reef fish species that lives in the Red Sea, off the Sinai Peninsula, and in the Philippines (Charnov, 1982). This fish lives in groups consisting of mostly immatures and females, with group sizes averaging about 30, but sometimes as large as 370. Females, it has been discovered, change to males when the proportion of males reaches a critically low level, because at that point the reproductive advantages of being male exceed those of being female. In fact, when investigators systematically removed from 1 to 9 males from each of 26 different groups, they were replaced on an almost 1:1 basis by females who became males.

Needless to say, the species described illustrate rather amazing changes in life history organization as a function of environmental, and especially social, circumstances. Reef-living fish, however, only illustrate how a relatively *contemporaneous* environmental factor (presence vs. absence of dominant males) can alter features of life history. More pertinent to the forthcoming argument that patterns of attachment are central components of facultative reproductive strategies in humans is evidence that *developmentally antecedent* experiences can influence life history (Gross, 1996). Consider in this regard the case of a ground-nesting bee that can develop either into a fighter phenotype that is flightless, has large mandibles, and mates within the nest, or into a distinctly smaller-headed phenotype with wings that mates outside the nest. What determines which developmental course an individual organism will follow? The answer is maternal provisioning. When mothers provide more nutrients during the larval stage of the bee's life cycle, growth is greater, and this leads to the development of a fighter morph following metamorphosis; in contrast, poorer provisioning by mothers during the larval stage results in the development of the alternative morph. Male coho salmon are somewhat similarly influenced, but not by maternal provisioning. Those that mature precociously as a result of greater availability and adequacy of nutrients, yet remain small and cryptic, are known as "jacks" and sneak onto the spawning grounds to reproduce without ever swimming out to sea. In contrast, those that grow more slowly and mature when older and larger ("hooknoses") swim out to sea as juveniles and return to their home pools as adults to fight for spawning opportunities (Gross, 1991). In the case of both the bee and the salmon, then, experience (i.e., nutrition) shapes development (i.e., growth and behavior) in a way that fosters reproductive success rather than happiness or survival. For both, alternative life history tactics are genotypically possible, but experience determines which developmental trajectory characterizes an individual's life course.

What about Humans?

However fascinating these examples of environmentally induced alternative life history tactics, there is reason to wonder whether anything similar occurs within humans or their close relatives, primates. In fact, extensive evidence indicates that life history characteristics are subject to environmental influence in the case of primates, once again in the service of reproductive goals. Pubertal maturation and sexual development in particular are affected by troop membership in Old World monkeys (e.g., macaques and baboons) and orangutans. Among stumptail macaques raised in captivity, for example, the adolescent growth spurt is delayed among males living in the group unless the dominant male is removed. Shortly after the dominant male is taken out, the next-highest-ranking male of sufficient biological maturity begins sexual development. Interestingly, similar processes have been observed with females in the case of monogamous New World monkeys, such as tamarins and marmosets. Here reproduction by female adolescents is inhibited by the presence of the mother. The established effects are the suppression of ovulation among pubertal female marmosets living in the presence of their mothers, the slowing of sexual maturation among female cotton-top tamarins living in their natal groups, and the suppression of fertility among female cotton-top tamarins living in the presence of their mothers (Snowdon, Ziegler, & Widowski, 1993). Similar social influences on pubertal onset in other mammals show similar patterns of effects (for a review, see Steinberg, 1989). In all cases, the biologic seems to be that inhibition of fertility reduces conflict with more dominant conspecifics, which would pose problems for any offspring— or for the animal seeking to produce offspring. When reproduction is deferred until the dominant male or female is no longer in a position to dominate the potential mother or father, the well-being and reproductive fitness of the potential parent are enhanced more than would be the case if that parent were to mature and produce progeny who would be at serious risk of not surviving to reproductive age.

It may not only be the life histories of species other than our own that have evolved to be responsive to environmental experience in the service of reproductive goals. Some years ago, we (Belsky et al., 1991), drawing on the principles of modern evolutionary theory, advanced a theory of socialization based upon a life history framework; a central premise of this theory was that early human experience influences not only psychological and behavioral functioning (including attachment security), but physical development and reproductive behavior as well. In contrast to the aforementioned work on primates, which highlights *contemporaneous* influences upon development (e.g., the suppressive effect of the presence of a dominant male on the sexual development of a subordinate male at about the time when the juvenile might be expected to mature physically), our theory emphasized the effect of *developmentally antecedent* experiences on subsequent psychological, physical, and behavioral development. More specifically, we theorized that under conditions of stress and resource unpredictability, human caregivers treat offspring in less sensitive, responsive, and supportive ways than would otherwise be the case, and that such caregiving responses to these ecological conditions evolved to promote in the offspring opportunistic interpersonal orientations, earlier timing of puberty and reproduction, and limited parental investment. Although much in our theory was consistent with other perspectives on human development (including traditional attachment theory), as well as with data linking patterns of early care with later psychological and interpersonal functioning (including patterns of mating and parenting), our life-history-based prediction that timing of puberty should also be affected by early experience was what made the theory unique. Noteworthy, though, was the fact that our theorizing was consistent with formal models in the field of behavioral ecology, which indicate that when the future is uncertain, short-term benefits (i.e., more offspring born early and cared for poorly) have more value than long-term benefits (i.e., fewer offspring born later and cared for more intensively) (Chisholm, 1995; Clark, 1991; Krebs & Kacelnik, 1991; Rogers, 1994).

Our theoretical proposition (Belsky et al., 1991) concerning the relation between earlier experience and pubertal timing was based upon the premise that humans evolved to adjust their life histories in response to environmental experiences in the service of reproductive goals. By maturing earlier, individuals whose experiences had unconsciously informed them (1) that resources (including, if not most especially, parental care and attention) were scarce and/or unpredictable, (2) that others could not be trusted, and (3) that relationships were not enduring would have been in a position to pursue a quantity-versus-quality reproductive strategy. That is, by pursuing short-term, opportunistic relationships rather than enduring, mutually beneficial ones, such individuals would have maximized matings and presumably conceptions (at least in a particular EEA), but not parental investment. By engaging in behavior that would have resulted (at least in the EEA) in bearing more offspring and taking less care of them, individuals would have enhanced their reproductive fitness more than if they had pursued a reproductive strategy oriented toward quality (of mating and parenting). In essence, early maturation evolved to be part of a life history pattern that enhanced reproductive fitness, given the ecological conditions under which the organism developed. Maccoby (1991) argued that developmental processes would not have evolved to operate in the way we theorized, particularly in the case of females. However, it seems noteworthy that studies stimulated by the Belsky et al. (1991) theory, and especially our prediction regarding early experience and pubertal timing, have documented the hypothesized association between indicators of stressful rearing experience (including father absence, conflicted parent–child relations, and depression) and earlier age of puberty, at least in the case of females (e.g., Graber, Brooks-Gunn, & Warren, 1995; Moffitt, Caspi, Belsky, & Silva, 1992).

What these several illustrations of organisms' responses to environmental experience are intended to demonstrate is that environmentally induced modifications in life history traits occur and appear reproductively strategic. That is, an organism's response to environmental input appears not to be random, but rather to promote the reproductive fitness of the organism. In other words, the effect of nurture (i.e., environment) is in the service of nature (i.e., biology). This formulation not only provides a means of resolving aspects of the nature–nurture debate, which pits these two broad sources of influence against each other, but should foster thinking about environmental influences in terms of biological functions. This should prove especially beneficial in

the case of phenomena that are considered to pertain to issues of mating and parenting, as it is generally recognized that the more a phenomenon concerns reproduction—as mating and parenting certainly do—the more subject it has been to selection pressures. Of course, there is much about human attachment that is relevant to mating (a potential sequela of attachment) and parenting (both an antecedent and a sequela of attachment); it is for this reason that the preceding discussion of modern evolutionary theory, including life history theory, is relevant to thinking about attachment. In the remainder of this chapter, I argue that evolution is relevant to human attachment because patterns of attachment served as vehicles for "translating" information about prevailing ecological conditions into a fitness-enhancing reproductive strategy.

Before doing so, however, I must make this clear: It would be a mistake to presume that the evolutionary interpretation of patterns of attachment to be advanced requires for confirmation evidence that reproductive fitness is currently associated with different patterns of attachment. Even though it may be, evolutionary psychologists have highlighted the fact that what evolution selected were (among other things) many psychological processes that served to foster reproductive fitness in the EEAs. Because the modern world is so different from the EEAs, the ancestral-fitness consequences of evolved psychological mechanisms such as attachment may no longer be realized. Nevertheless, the psychological processes that evolved in the service of them remain operative (Buss, 1995; Cosmides & Tooby, 1987).

PATTERNS OF ATTACHMENT AS (COMPONENTS OF) REPRODUCTIVE STRATEGIES

Even though all the necessary longitudinal studies are not yet available, much in contemporary attachment theory and research leads to the expectation that individuals with varying attachment patterns in infancy and childhood will develop differently over time. The general assumption has been not only that individuals with secure attachment histories will cope with stress more successfully than those with insecure histories, but also that the former will be more motivated to establish, and skilled in maintaining, close interpersonal relationships than the latter. In consequence, secure attachment history may well foster more harmonious and stable pair bonds (i.e., marriages) in adulthood, and certainly more sensitive and security-promoting parenting once children are born (Belsky & Cassidy, 1994). To be noted, of course, is that contemporary attachment theory also acknowledges—most explicitly in research using the Adult Attachment Interview (AAI)—that experiences promoting insecurity will not inevitably promote unstable and unsatisfying close relationships and insensitive parenting in adulthood. After all, individuals who have "worked through" and gained perspective on their adverse and insecurity-promoting childhood experiences, and are classified as "earned secure" on the AAI, are expected (and have been found) to parent sensitively and foster security in their own progeny (Pearson, Cohn, Cowan, & Cowan, 1994).

The very fact that attachment theory postulates probabilistic relations between attachment security–insecurity in infancy and early childhood and interpersonal functioning in adulthood—including patterns of mating and parenting—raises the prospect that the attachment system evolved as a reproductive-fitness-maximizing behavioral system. In fact, consistent with the arguments we originally advanced (Belsky et al., 1991), I develop the proposition in the remainder of this chapter that patterns of attachment represent nascent facultative reproductive strategies that evolved to promote reproductive fitness in particular ecological niches. Regardless of whether that ultimate goal of evolution is still achieved in contemporary Western culture, I argue that the various psychologies reflected and sustained by individual differences in attachment were fostered by natural selection.

Relation to Main's Conditional-Strategy View

The functional and evolutionary analysis that I advance regarding why young children develop varying patterns of attachment, apparently in response to variations in caregiving experience, is fundamentally different from (though not opposed to) functional analyses that have been offered by other students of attachment theory, even evolution-oriented ones. For the most part, variation in attachment behavior in infancy and early childhood has been discussed in terms of its immediate consequences and survival value, but certainly not with regard to reproductive-fitness consequences. Thus, Main (1981, 1991) argued that avoidant attachment developed as a

"conditional" behavioral strategy in response to the caregiver's unwillingness or inability to accept and sensitively respond to the child's "primary" behavioral strategy of seeking proximity and contact when the attachment system is activated (see also Cassidy & Kobak, 1988). More recently, Cassidy and Berlin (1994) argued that in contrast to the rejected infant's proclivity to minimize the expression of attachment needs and thus to develop an avoidant pattern of attachment as a means of protecting itself from the caregiver's rejecting behavior, the infant who experiences inconsistently responsive care develops a strategy of maximizing or exaggerating expressions of attachment needs in hopes of evoking more support and care from the caregiver. Furthermore, in both cases these conditional strategies function to promote survival. Note how in both of these attempts to illuminate theoretically the nature of insecure attachment patterns, emphasis is placed upon the immediate needs and survival of the infant, but no discussion or analysis of the reproductive goals is offered. As a result, although these psychological analyses are adequate from the standpoint of proximate explanations of why a behavior or behavior pattern develops, they provide only the most limited insight into why such patterns of response to proximate environmental conditions might have evolved in the first place. This is because, as argued earlier, survival is an insufficient biological goal when it comes to an evolutionary analysis.

Limits and Assumptions

In attempt to recast patterns of attachment in a modern evolutionary framework emphasizing reproduction, not just survival, I summarize below the hypothesized evolutionary function of secure attachment and then proceed to consider avoidant and resistant attachments. Throughout the analysis to follow, evidence pertaining to relations between attachment on the one hand and mating and parenting on the other is examined, in order to situate this functional analysis in a life history framework. It must be noted at the outset that the forthcoming analysis is more heuristic than definitive, and this is so for a variety of reasons. To begin with, basically all the attachment-based data pertaining to functioning in intimate relationships in adulthood (i.e., mating) are derived from cross-sectional or relatively short-term longitudinal investigations carried out by social psychologists relying upon brief questionnaires to measure attachment styles in romantic relationships. Thus, unless otherwise indicated in the forthcoming analysis, all attachment findings related to mating, dating, and romantic-relationship functioning in adulthood are based upon self-reports of attachment style in romantic relationships. Because no longitudinal evidence yet exists indicating that these romantic-relationship-oriented measurements are themselves systematically related to infants', toddlers', or even older children's attachment classifications, it should not be presumed that the data to be cited demonstrate that early attachment predicts reproductive behavior in adulthood, even though results from the available studies are discussed in such terms (for heuristic reasons). Moreover, given the fact that it remains uncertain whether attachment styles founded upon these self-reports are systematically related to classifications derived from the AAI, which assesses current state of mind regarding rearing experience in childhood there are further grounds for not drawing definite conclusions from the analysis to follow.

It needs to be pointed out as well that the discussion of empirically chronicled linkages between individual differences in attachment and mating/parenting behavior in the context of a life history analysis of the evolutionary basis of variation in attachment is predicated on two basic assumptions. The first is that attachment patterns are relatively stable from the opening years of life through adolescence and young adulthood. Given recent evidence that attachment classifications as currently measured using the strange situation are not stable across a 6-month period in the second year of life (Belsky, Campbell, Cohn, & Moore, 1996), this would seem a rather precarious assumption. For the purpose of the arguments presented in this chapter, however, I regard it as a mistake to equate an empirical measurement (i.e., strange situation classification) with the theoretical construct it is designed to assess (i.e., internal working model), given the fallibility of current approaches to measuring attachment security (and many other developmental constructs). To be noted, nevertheless, is that despite evidence showing that attachment classifications are not as stable across short developmental periods as some have assumed, there is repeated indication that early classifications at some ages are in fact predictive of internal working models in middle childhood (Main & Cassidy, 1988), as well as in late adolescence and young adulthood (as measured using the AAI) (Hamilton, 1994; Waters, Merrick, Albersheim,

& Treboux, 1995; Zimmermann, 1994; but see Grossmann, Grossmann, & Zimmermann, Chapter 33, this volume, for evidence to the contrary). Clearly, more work is called for before any definitive conclusions are drawn regarding relations between early and later attachment. Therefore, although the empirical evidence linking attachment patterns measured in adulthood (using a variety of different methodologies; for a review, see Crowell & Treboux, 1995) and mating and parenting in adulthood discussed *as if* attachment patterns are more rather than less stable, it must be made explicit that this too is a working assumption rather than an established fact.

A second assumption that needs to be made explicit with regard to my discussion of (theorized) relations between early attachment and later mating and parenting concerns the relative stability of environmental conditions across the first two decades or so of the human lifespan in the EEAs. Because it is being argued that patterns of attachment developing early in life represent facultative responses to caregiving conditions in the service of reproductive goals (i.e., central components of reproductive strategies), it is assumed that in the EEAs ecological conditions were relatively stable across the first two decades or so of human lifespans. Only if there was reasonable stability would it have been adaptive for organisms to develop during their juvenile years reproductive orientations that would not have been expressed fully until adulthood. If ecological conditions during childhood and during the young adult years were basically unrelated, then it would surely have proved maladaptive in an evolutionary sense for the reproductive strategy that an organism was going to follow when sexually mature to be initiated on the basis of experiences during childhood. Because there is no way of knowing exactly how stable environmental conditions were across the first two decades of the human lifespan in the EEAs, we are left to assume relative environmental stability.

Some will argue, not unreasonably—and often on the basis of the contemporary world—that a presumption of relative stability of ecological conditions is problematic, and that it would have made much more biological sense for a reproductive "program" to have evolved that remained as open as possible until the age of maturation and even afterward. I would caution that it may be problematic to presume that rates of environmental change we witness in the modern world are in the least bit informative about life in the EEAs. Moreover, currently unrecognized biological constraints on biological and psychological development may have required organisms to commit themselves to alternative reproductive strategies at some point in the life cycle, which would have precluded the possibility of a totally open and ever-reprogrammable reproductive program. Thus, a presumption of *relative* (though certainly not absolute) stability in ecological conditions from childhood to young adulthood seems reasonable and thus a viable basis for interpreting patterns of attachment established during the first 5–7 years of life—not just in the first year—as components of facultatively developed reproductive strategies.

Secure Attachment and Mating/Parenting

When we (Belsky et al., 1991) first advanced our argument that the capacity for divergent patterns of attachment evolved as a central component of facultatively induced reproductive strategies, we theorized that these divergent life trajectories promoted (at least in some EEAs) the reproductive fitness of both parents and children. More specifically, caregivers providing sensitive care were responding to ecological conditions (in their own past, as well as in their child-rearing present) that indicated (or at least were perceived as indicating) that resources were reasonably available and would remain so for the foreseeable future. As a result, parents' often unconscious goal was to provide their children with early experiences that would induce in the progeny the sense (1) that the world was more benign, if not benevolent, than hostile, and (2) that others could be trusted because (3) relationships were enduring and rewarding. Such awareness would itself have promoted an orientation toward and capacity for close, enduring relationships (including pair bonds) that were mutually rewarding to the individuals involved, as well as the desire and ability to invest heavily in parental care. Although such a reproductive strategy emphasizing parenting over mating would have delayed mating and reduced the number of offspring conceived, it would have simultaneously increased the individuals' likelihood of survival to reproductive age and their capacity to promote the survival and eventual reproduction of their own progeny. In consequence, a quality-oriented (rather than quantity-oriented) strategy of mating and parenting, fostered as it would have been (at least in some EEAs) by sensitive, responsive care in infancy and early childhood, would have promoted the reproductive fitness of both grandparents (who initially cared for the parents in a sensitive manner) and parents (who developed a secure attachment in response to sensitive, responsive care during childhood). Although no evidence exists pertaining to actual reproductive fitness, research consistent with this evolutionary analysis comes (1) from investigations of the functioning in close heterosexual relationships of individuals classified as secure on the AAI, or evincing higher levels of security on questionnaires developed by social psychologists to appraise attachment in close relationships; and (2) from studies of the parenting of mothers classified as "autonomous" (i.e., secure) on the AAI.

Mating

With respect to mating and functioning in close relationships, observational studies of couple interaction during problem-solving and self-disclosure tasks indicate that secure men engage in more positive and supportive interactions with their spouses than do insecure men (Cohn, Cowan, Cowan, & Pearson, 1992b; Ewing & Pratt, 1995; Kobak & Hazan, 1992). In fact, when Simpson, Rholes, and Nelligan (1992) placed the female members of college dating couples in a stressful situation, women categorized as secure in their romantic relationships sought more emotional support and accepted more physical contact from their male partners than did insecure women, perhaps because secure men—who, as other work shows, are disproportionately likely to be the partners of secure women (van IJzendoorn & Bakermans-Kranenburg, 1996)—provided more emotional support than did insecure men, made more reassuring comments, and displayed greater concern for their partners' well-being. In light of these behavioral findings, it should be of little surprise that in their study of married couples, Cohn et al. (1992b) observed that conflict and negative affect were most frequent in couples in which both partners were insecure. Relatedly, Senchak and Leonard (1992) reported in their study of more than 300 newlywed couples that those in which both partners were secure engaged in the least negative interaction.

Evidence that lower levels of conflict, as well as more competent strategies for managing conflict, are found in secure individuals' relationships also comes from nonobservational studies. O'Connor et al. (1995) found, for example, that secure women experienced less conflict with their husbands on topics related to time spent together and household division of labor—two common conflict areas—than did insecure women. Owens (1993) also reported that secure women experienced less discord with their partners. Perhaps more noteworthy, though, is Pistole's (1989) discovery that secure individuals were more likely than insecure individuals to engage in mutually focused—as opposed to self- or other-focused—strategies for managing conflict in romantic relationships. Not only does such a conflict management style suggest why conflict may be less frequent in the case of secure individuals, but these data also underscore the notion that security sets the stage for the development of mutually rewarding relationships.

Certainly consistent with this analysis are data indicating that secure individuals evince higher levels of satisfaction when dating (Simpson, 1990) and when married (Kobak & Hazan, 1992; Owens, 1993). Moreover, greater commitment to the relationship and stronger feelings of love for the partner have also been found to characterize the heterosexual experiences of secure individuals (Owens, 1993). Indeed, Hazan and Shaver (1987) reported in the very first study of attachment security and romantic relationships that secure individuals characterized their most significant love relationships as more positive, trusting, and supportive than insecure individuals described their relationships.

It is likely that the features of relationship feelings and functioning of secure individuals summarized to this point account for why such persons have also been found to have longer-lasting love relationships (Hazan & Shaver, 1987). In perhaps the most impressive work to date, Kirkpatrick and Davis (1994) followed a sample of over 300 dating couples studied for 3 years and observed that secure males and females were most likely to have stable and satisfying relationships. And in another longitudinal investigation, this one of a diverse sample of respondents to a newspaper survey, Kirkpatrick and Hazan (1994) found that those who were secure 4 years earlier were most likely to have married at the time of the follow-up.

Parenting

The modern evolutionary perspective on secure attachment being advanced in this chapter anticipates not only that a history of security will foster the development of mutually rewarding and stable pair bonds, but that it will do so in the service of promoting high-investment parenting. For purposes of this analysis, and consistent with research stimulated by traditional attachment theory, "high-investment parenting" is defined as parenting that is sensitively responsive to the individualized needs of a child, and that thereby fosters the development of security in the child. Evidence that security is associated with high-investment parenting comes from two sources. The first shows that mothers and fathers classified as autonomous/secure on the AAI are disproportionately likely to have offspring who are themselves classified as secure when observed in the strange situation with their mothers (for a meta-analysis, see van IJzendoorn, 1995), even when the AAI is administered prior to a child's birth (Fonagy, Steele, & Steele, 1991; Ward & Carlson, 1995). The second and related source of relevant information are investigations showing that mothers classified as autonomous/secure on the AAI provide more sensitively responsive care to their children than mothers classified as insecure (e.g., Crowell & Feldman, 1988, 1991; Grossmann, Fremer-Bombik, Rudolph, & Grossmann; Haft & Slade, 1989). In fact, a meta-analysis of 10 investigations revealed that the relation between secure attachment in adulthood and responsive caregiving is sufficiently robust that it would take 155 studies with null results to generate an insignificant statistical relation (van IJzendoorn, 1995). Notable as well is that two investigations that have examined fathering show the same expected relation between security in adulthood and the provision of warm, supportive care (Cohn, Cowan, Cowan, & Pearson, 1992a; van IJzendoorn, Kranenburg, Zwart-Woudstra, van Busschbach, & Lambermon, 1992).

In summary, and consistent with the evolutionary perspective under consideration, there are grounds for tentatively concluding that secure attachment in childhood may be a central part of a developing, facultative reproductive strategy designed to promote a quality-versus-quantity orientation toward reproduction. By promoting the establishment and maintenance of mutually rewarding and enduring pair bonds, as well as sensitively responsive and security-inducing parenting, security in childhood is theorized to provide a means of translating contextually significant information about the availability and predictability of resources—including parental care and attention—into a developmental strategy for promoting reproductive fitness. Whether reproductive fitness is actually enhanced in the modern world is less central to this analysis than the argument that natural selection fostered psychological and developmental processes that afforded such consequences in some EEAs and that remain operative today.

Avoidant Attachment and Mating/Parenting

Although we (Belsky et al., 1991) detailed an alternative reproductive strategy associated with insecure attachment as part of our evolutionary theory of socialization, we failed to distinguish between the resistant and avoidant forms of insecure attachment. In retrospect, it is clear that the analysis offered had more to do with the latter than with the former pattern of attachment. Arguing that limited and unpredictable resources would have led parents to provide insensitive and rejecting care as a means of fostering in their progeny a view (1) that the world was an uncaring place, (2) that others could therefore not be trusted, and thus (3) that relationships were not likely to be mutually rewarding or enduring, we contended (Belsky et al., 1991) that humans evolved to react to such early experiences in such ways because it promoted the reproductive fitness of parents and children. A child so "programmed" by experiences fostering an avoidant attachment pattern would have pursued disproportionately self-serving, opportunistic interpersonal relations (rather than mutually rewarding ones), and as a result would have experienced unstable pair bonds, multiple matings, and the conceptions of many children who would receive limited parental investment.

Under these adverse environmental conditions, the quantity-versus-quality strategy of mating and parenting associated with avoidant attachment would have enhanced the reproductive fitness of grandparents and parents alike. Because of the limited and unpredictable nature of resources to support parenting and child functioning, the prospect of a precarious future made it more likely that some offspring would not survive and/or reproduce. Thus a reproductive strategy that emphasized mating (and procreation) over parenting would have been most likely to promote reproductive fitness: Since the risks to progeny's eventual reproductive success were great and uncontrollable, the way to ensure that some would survive to reproduce would involve the production of many offspring, even if they were not going to be well cared for. Arguing along the same lines, Chisholm (1996, p. 12; emphasis in original) has noted that

when the flow of resources is chronically low or unpredictable—which is when we might otherwise expect parental investment to be *most* critical for offspring reproductive value—it may in fact be (or have been) biologically (i.e., evolutionary) adaptive to *reduce* parental investment, to allocate resources not to parenting (or even, beyond some threshold, to the parents' own health or longevity), but to *offspring production* instead (Borgerhoff Mulder, 1992; Harpending, Draper, & Pennington, 1990; Kaplan, 1994; Pennington & Harpending, 1988).

Although no research on the sequelae and correlates of attachment (in childhood or adulthood) has been stimulated by such a life history perspective, data that have been gathered on mating and parenting are rather consistent with such theorizing.

Mating

With regard to mating and close relationships, Brennan and Shaver (1995) reported that individuals classified as avoidant in terms of self-reported romantic attachments were most unrestricted in their sexual behavior (Simpson & Gangestad, 1991); that is, they were most willing and ready to engage in sex in the absence of strong feelings of love or an enduring relationship. Moreover, Hazan, Zeifman, and Middleton (1994) found that such individuals were most likely to report involvement in one-night stands and sex outside established relationships, and that they preferred purely sexual contact (e.g., oral and anal sex) to more emotionally intimate sexual contact (e.g., kissing, cuddling). Relatedly, Miller and Fishkin (1997) found that insecure men desired a greater number of partners over the next 30 years of their lives. And Kirkpatrick and Hazan (1994) observed that over a 4-year period, avoidant individuals were most likely to be dating more than one person. All these data seem rather consistent with Simpson's (1990) evidence that among dating college students, those who scored high on avoidance in romantic relationships scored lowest on commitment and trust and had partners who also reported low levels of commitment and trust. This may explain, in part, why Feeney and Noller (1992) found in their study of college students that those who were avoidant in romantic relationships were most likely to have experienced a relationship breakup.

The instability of close relationships in the case of these avoidant individuals was probably stimulated as well by the ways in which avoidant individuals behave when someone in the relationship is anxious. Simpson et al. (1992) found that when the women in college dating couples were stressed, avoidant men withdrew support from their anxious partners, and avoidant women decreased support seeking. The fact that avoidant individuals report engaging in the most coercive and least affectionately supportive behavior in close relationships also helps account for limitations in their close relationships (Kunce & Shaver, 1994). Perhaps such callousness derives from the beliefs of such individuals that romantic relationships are fictional and that true love is rare (Hazan & Shaver, 1987; see also Feeney & Noller, 1990). In any event, the kind of relationship functioning just described as characteristic of avoidant individuals is consistent with the notion that such persons engage in opportunistic and self-serving rather than mutually rewarding relationships. Such relationships can be expected to be short-term in nature, and although they may foster early and frequent conceptions (or at least would have done so in some EEAs), it is unlikely that they will support high levels of parental investment.

Parenting

As it turns out, evidence pertaining to the parenting of avoidant—or, in adult attachment terms, "dismissing"—individuals suggests that however frequent their matings may be, the quality of the care they provide their progeny is limited. The aforementioned meta-analysis by van IJzendoorn (1995) demonstrates that mothers classified as dismissing on the AAI provide consistently less sensitively responsive care than do mothers of secure infants, perhaps because they have been found in work using social-psychological measures of adult attachment (i.e., self-reports) to be less desirous of having children than more secure individuals (Rholes, Simpson, Blakely, Lanigan, & Allen, 1997). Particularly notable with regard to actual parenting are two studies by Crowell and Feldman (1988, 1991) indicating that during a series of interactional tasks, dismissing mothers were less emotionally supportive and helpful with their preschoolers, and tended to be cold, remote, and controlling—a pattern that seemed consistent with mothers' self-descriptions of being pushed to become independent as children. Just prior to a separation from their 2- to 4-year-olds, dismissing mothers evinced the least anxiety of all mothers, perhaps accounting for their

particularly speedy departures. Upon reunion, these same mothers were least responsive and affectionate with their children. Probably because of comparably insensitive care in their own infancy (see Belsky & Cassidy, 1994, for a review), mothers classified as dismissing on the AAI were found in van IJzendoorn's (1995) meta-analysis to be disproportionately likely to have children classified as avoidant in the strange situation. Although van IJzendoorn's (1995) analysis also showed that quality of parenting (i.e., sensitive responsiveness) did not entirely mediate the relation between adult and infant attachment, his findings are consistent with the notion that adult attachment influences parenting, and thereby attachment security in the child.

As in the case of data pertaining to mating, again we see evidence consistent with the reproductive-strategy perspective being advanced in this chapter. Avoidant or dismissing attachment appears to be related not only to more "problematic" heterosexual relations in adulthood, but to limited parental investment as well. Although classical attachment theory offers an account of how and perhaps even why such patterns of functioning in adulthood are associated with this pattern of attachment, it cannot explain the evolutionary foundations of these developmental linkages. The present reformulated perspective on attachment, which underscores the *reproductive* significance of mating/parenting and conceptualizes avoidance as a central feature of an opportunistic and facultative reproductive strategy, accomplishes just that.

Resistant Attachment and Mating/Parenting

Having outlined the evolutionary logic behind the development of secure and avoidant attachment patterns, and having summarized some evidence consistent with them, I now turn to the third and final pattern to be considered in this modern evolutionary perspective on attachment—namely, resistant attachment. Central to this pattern, as Cassidy and Berlin (1994) recently observed, is the tendency to exaggerate one's need for care and attention (see also Main & Solomon, 1986). Through extensive whining, clinging, and seeking proximity to (what might be regarded as) an excessive extent, the infant or young child is considered to be pursuing a conditional strategy to obtain more and better-quality care than he or she has inconsistently received.

Even though Cassidy and Berlin (1994) insightfully note that the immediate, proximate function of behavior associated with resistant attachment is to recruit more care and attention from an inconsistently responsive caregiver, and they highlight the benefit of such behavior with regard to survival (and thereby reproduction; Chisholm, 1996), the biological "payoff" of such helpless dependency on the part of the child *for the parent* who fosters the development of resistant attachment remains unclear.

In light of the inherent conflict of interest between parent and child (Trivers, 1974), this is a theoretically noteworthy lacuna. Just because a behavior (or, in this case, a behavior pattern) benefits the child, this is not necessarily sufficient for the capacity for such a behavior (or behavior pattern) to evolve—especially if the behavior (pattern) in question is influenced by the parent or is costly to the parent, as whining dependency would seem to be. It is usually only where there is some biological "payoff" for the parent as well as for the child that we should expect a parentally influenced and costly pattern of child functioning to evolve. Once again, I suggest that consideration of the behavioral development of nonhuman species may provide insight into the evolutionary history of attachment.

Many animals, ranging from eusocial insects (e.g., wasps, bees, ants) to birds (e.g., acorn woodpeckers) and a few mammals (e.g., naked mole rats), produce offspring that are physically or behaviorally sterile (Baker & Bellis, 1995). Rather than leaving the parental home range to reproduce, they remain and help parents raise their siblings. In the case of some avian species, direct reproduction may not be altogether abandoned, but rather deferred until a time when reproductive prospects have improved (Emlen, Wrege, & Demong, 1995). Until that point, efforts to support the reproduction of kin by provisioning or protecting younger siblings, half-siblings, and cousins afford a means of indirect reproduction (i.e., inclusive fitness). Such seemingly nonreproductive behavior has even been observed among humans. Clark (1996), upon analyzing the reproductive consequences of human migration in 19th-century Sweden, has shown that women who stayed in their native villages had a higher likelihood of remaining childless, whereas those who stayed and bore children had, on average, more offspring than those who migrated from their home range. The possibility has been raised that the childless women who remained at home may have assumed the role of

sterile helpers to their parents and siblings—a process of lineage reproduction that has been observed in other societies, such as the Kipsigis (Borgerhoff Mulder, 1992).

In the most speculative comments to be made in this reinterpretation of the evolutionary basis of attachment in humans, especially patterns of attachment, I propose that the capacity for developing resistant attachments evolved as a means of fostering indirectly reproductive "helper-at-the-nest" behavior. That is, by inducing helpless dependency in a child, inconsistently responsive parenting evolved to promote a reproductive strategy designed to facilitate the direct reproductive success of kin (especially parents), and thereby the indirect reproductive success of the resistant individual.

Mating

Although data on the functioning of resistant—or, in adult attachment terms, "preoccupied"—individuals in close relationships provides limited evidence that could be interpreted as consistent with this view (for a review, see Shaver & Hazan, 1993), one finding stands out as particularly noteworthy. Kunce and Shaver (1994) found that resistant women reported the highest levels of "compulsive caregiving." That is, these individuals were most likely to endorse items such as "I can't seem to stop from 'mothering' my partner too much." Perhaps this proclivity merely reflects what transpires when a psychological orientation that evolved to ensure the care of younger siblings or other relatives is deployed in a mating relationship. What had originally been fostered in some EEAs to enable a child to become a caregiver while still young simply continues in the contemporary world to function in adulthood in relation to one's spouse.

Parenting

That a resistant attachment style originally fostered in infancy and early childhood continues to function in adulthood is also suggested by evidence linking the preoccupied attachment style in adulthood—presumed to derive largely from childhood experience—with the way in which mothers care for their children. Several investigations suggest that preoccupied mothers "behave in ways that interfere with their child's autonomy or exploration" (Cassidy & Berlin, 1994, p. 981) and thereby promote dependency, perhaps in the service of inducing "helper-at-the-nest" behavior in their own offspring. Certainly consistent with this view are findings indicating (1) that preoccupied mothers appea especially oriented and responsive toward expressions of fear in their babies, but are disinclined to attune to or validate their infants' expressions of initiative and exuberance during play (Haft & Slade, 1989); (2) that preoccupied mothers of toddlers tend to have difficulty separating from their toddlers, and separate in ways that can be expected to foster child anxiety while discouraging independence (Crowell & Feldman, 1988, 1991); and (3) that preoccupied mothers of adolescents about to depart from home to attend college are inclined to express anxiety and convey doubts about their children's ability to function autonomously (Kobak, Ferenz-Gilles, Everhart, & Seabrook, 1994). In addition to fostering anxiety and undermining the autonomous functioning of offspring, all such behavior would seem to create a psychological environment that would keep a child physically near a parent and perhaps especially susceptible to the parent's manipulations. Just such features would seem essential for promoting "helper-at-the-nest" behavior.

To the extent that this clearly speculative analysis is correct, one might expect to find resistant attachment in some ecological niches more often than in others. Perhaps, for example, firstborns and especially female firstborns are more likely to receive C classifications. But this may only prove to be the case under rearing conditions in which maternal caregiving is excessively taxed, perhaps because surrogate adult caregivers are unavailable. What these few suggestions should make clear is that particular attachment patterns may emerge under particular ecological conditions, and that these may vary over time within a family.

ENDURING THEORETICAL CONUNDRUMS

Before I draw some general conclusions, it seems appropriate to comment upon two enduring conundrums that confront attachment theory: one having to do with the role of temperament, and the other with the sequelae of multiple internal working models (derived from multiple attachment relationships). When an evolutionary perspective is applied to temperament, it raises the possibility that infants and children may vary, for heritable reasons, in their susceptibility to en-

vironmental influence (Belsky, 1997). Thus it seems plausible to entertain the prospect that for inborn, constitutional/temperamental reasons, some infants may be very strongly predisposed to develop secure, avoidant, or resistant attachments almost regardless of the quality of care they experience, and thereby to enact reproductive strategies consistent with such inborn individual differences. Other infants (perhaps most), in contrast, are likely to be much more environmentally reactive, so that through processes of emotion regulation and development fostered by caregiving experience, they develop whatever patterns of attachment and follow whatever reproductive strategies are consistent with their rearing experience.

Such variation in environmental reactivity, if it exists, may provide parents with means of "hedging their bets" in the game of life. Because non-malleable progeny are likely to fit (sometimes across generations) the ecological niche in which they find themselves, such fixed types should episodically flourish and thus remain in the gene pool. And because the more malleable types are able to fit more niches, they should achieve reproductive success sufficiently often to preserve this facultative developmental strategy in the gene pool as well. What such an analysis suggests, of course, is that the arguments advanced in the preceding sections, which imply that all children are equally reactive to caregiving experience (in the service of reproductive goals), may be overstated; thus the developmental processes outlined having to do with caregiving influence may apply to some individuals more than to others.

In the case of multiple working models, the evolutionary arguments advanced herein may run into serious conceptual trouble unless one of two alternative perspectives is adopted (for a related discussion, see Shaver, Collins, & Clark, 1996). The first and perhaps traditional perspective—that children develop a hierarchy of working models, and that the primary one exerts the most influence—seems consistent with the perspective promulgated throughout this chapter. Instead, though, it may be the case that alternative models provide the developing individual with multiple reproductive templates that can later be enacted, depending upon the mating and parenting (i.e., reproductive) circumstances he or she subsequently encounters. Thus patterns of attachment that do not develop early in life may simply not be available for use as reproductive strategies. Of course, the two views just mentioned are not mutually exclusive. A hierarchy may exist, with the primary model serving as the default option and the secondary model coming "on-line" only when the primary fails. Needless to say, the ideas just advanced are clearly not sufficient, given the state of empirical work, to resolve the issues pertaining to temperament and multiple internal working models—issues that continue to challenge all attachment theorists.

CONCLUSION

The evolutionary interpretation of patterns of attachment advanced in this chapter is not intended to deny or dismiss the central contributions of what can be regarded as classical attachment theory and the amazingly rich program of theory development and research it has spawned. This should be most evident in my extensive reliance upon findings generated by research derived from this paradigm, whether based upon data using the strange situation, the AAI, or self-report measures of romantic-relationship styles. Clearly, however, the core proposition of this chapter—that patterns of attachment represent central features of facultatively induced reproductive strategies—will be new to many. Some will find it difficult to reconcile a non-value-laden, evolutionary perspective on attachment (which regards all three patterns discussed as equally adaptive in terms of promoting reproductive fitness in the ecological niches that gave rise to them) with the more traditional, mental-health-oriented perspective (which views security as the pattern that is inherently "best," rather than "best" in current society or from a mental health perspective, and insecurity as some kind of psychological maladaptation if not pathology). But Main's (1990) "conditional-strategy" perspective already laid the foundation for the former view by highlighting the functional nature of different patterns of attachment, as did Lamb et al. (1984, 1985) and Hinde (1982; Hinde & Stevenson-Hinde, 1990) in their evolutionary critiques of attachment theory. Where the current perspective goes beyond the conditional-strategy framework, and beyond the biological issues raised by Lamb et al. and by Hinde, is in placing what has to this point been an essentially psychological analysis of attachment patterns into a modern evolutionary framework. And what is central to such a framework is a focus upon reproductive fitness, rather than upon adaptation to the immediate caregiving en-

vironment and survival. This leads, as I have shown, to an emphasis upon mating and parenting—core features of life history strategies that play a central role in an organism's effort to reproduce itself.

Ultimately, the perspective advanced here is more similar to than different from the traditional view. Both regard rearing experience as central to the development of individual differences in attachment patterns, and both regard early experiences as shaping developmental trajectories in ways that influence not only short-term psychological functioning, but longer-term relationship functioning as well. What is different is that the modern evolutionary perspective places reproductive fitness at the core of attempts to understand individual differences in attachment. As a result, issues of mental health and psychological well-being are deemphasized, and the issue of reproducing one's genes moves to center stage.

In fact, the central argument advanced in the last half of this chapter is that we see divergent patterns of attachment today precisely because these patterns, and the entire attachment system out of which they develop, evolved in order to promote reproductive fitness in the EEAs. It is only through understanding the central importance of genetic replication that we can understand not only why there is an attachment system, but why the human organism may develop in such a way that juvenile patterns of attachment become systematically related to mating and parenting in adulthood. Classical attachment theory emphasized the survival function of the attachment behavior system and attempted to account (via its emphasis on mothering) for how an infant becomes secure (or insecure), and (via its emphasis on the internal working model) for how attachment early in life comes to shape later development (including mating and parenting). However, it never adequately addressed two fundamental questions: (1) Why should human development have evolved in such a manner that attachment security is shaped by mothering experience (rather than by temperament and genetics)? (2) Why should early attachment be at all related to later social and emotional development (rather than be totally unrelated to it)? In this chapter, I have sought to provide answers to these core theoretical questions by arguing that patterns of attachment evolved in the human behavioral repertoire as means of promoting reproductive fitness in Bowlby's EEAs.

ACKNOWLEDGMENTS

Work on this chapter was supported by grants from the National Institute of Mental Health (No. MH44604) and the Scaife Family Foundation.

REFERENCES

Andrews, M., & Rosenblum, L. (1991). Attachment in monkey infants raised in variable- and low-demand environments. *Child Development, 62*, 686–693.

Andrews, M., & Rosenblum, L. (1994). The development of affiliative and agonistic social patterns in differentially reared monkeys. *Child Development, 65*, 1398–1404.

Baker, R., & Bellis, M. (1995). *Human sperm competition.* New York: Chapman & Hall.

Bee, H. (1995). *The growing child.* New York: Harper-Collins.

Belsky, J. (1997). Variation in susceptibility to environmental influence: An evolutionary argument. *Psychological Inquiry, 8*, 82–186.

Belsky, J., & Cassidy, J. (1994). Attachment: Theory and evidence. In M. Rutter & D. Hay (Eds.), *Development through life: A handbook for clinicians* (pp. 373–402). Oxford: Blackwell.

Belsky, J., Campbell, S., Cohn, J., & Moore, G. (1996). Instability of attachment security. *Developmental Psychology, 32*, 905–914.

Belsky, J., Steinberg, L., & Draper, P. (1991). Childhood experience, interpersonal development and reproductive strategy: An evolutionary theory of socialization. *Child Development, 62*, 647–670.

Borgerhoff Mulder, M. (1992). Reproductive decisions. In E. A. Smith & B. Winterholder (Eds.), *Evolutionary ecology and human behavior* (pp. 129–147). New York: Aldine de Gruyter.

Bowlby, J. (1969/1982). *Attachment and loss: Vol. 1. Attachment.* Harmondsworth, England: Penguin Books.

Brennan, K. A., & Shaver, P. R. (1995). Dimensions of adult attachment, affect regulation, and romantic relationship functioning. *Personality and Social Psychology Bulletin, 21*, 267–283.

Buss, D. (1995). Evolutionary psychology: A new paradigm for psychological science. *Psychological Inquiry, 6*, 1–3.

Cassidy, J., & Berlin, L. (1994). The insecure/ambivalent pattern of attachment: Theory and research. *Child Development, 65*, 971–991.

Cassidy, J., & Kobak, R. (1988). Avoidance and its relation to other defensive processes. In J. Belsky & T. Nezworski (Eds.), *Clinical implications of attachment* (pp. 300–326). Hillsdale, NJ: Erlbaum.

Charnov, E. (1982). *The theory of sex allocation.* Princeton, NJ: Princeton University Press.

Charnov, E. (1993). *Life history invariants.* New York: Oxford University Press.

Chisholm, J. (1995). Life history theory and life style choice: Implications for Darwinian medicine. *Perspectives in Human Biology, 1*, 19–28.

Chisholm, J. (1996). The evolutionary ecology of attachment organization. *Human Nature, 7*, 1–38.

Clark, C. (1991). Modeling behavioral adaptations. *Behavioral and Brain Sciences, 14*, 85–117.

Clark, C. (1996). Reproductive consequences of human dispersal in 19th century Sweden. *Behavioral Ecology, 41*, 17–31.

Cohn, D., Cowan, P., Cowan, C., & Pearson, J. (1992a). Mothers' and fathers' working models of childhood attachment relationships, parenting style, and child behavior. *Development and Psychopathology, 4*, 417–431.

Cohn, D., Cowan, P., Cowan, C., & Pearson, J. (1992b). Working models of childhood attachment and couples relationships. *Journal of Family Issues, 13*, 432–449.

Cole, M., & Cole, S. (1989). *The development of children.* New York: Freeman.

Cook, L. (1991). *Genetic and ecological diversity: The sport of nature.* London: Chapman & Hall.

Cosmides, L., & Tooby, J. (1987). From evolution to behavior: Evolutionary psychology as the missing link. In J. Dupre (Ed.), *The latest and the best: Essays on evolution and optimality* (pp. 277–306). Cambridge, MA: MIT Press.

Crowell, J., & Feldman, S. (1988). Mothers' internal models of relationships and children's behavioral and developmental status: A study of mother–child interaction. *Child Development, 59*, 1273–1285.

Crowell, J., & Feldman, S. (1991). Mothers' working models of attachment relationships and mother and child behavior during separation and reunion. *Developmental Psychology, 27*, 597–605.

Crowell, J., & Treboux, D. (1995). A review of adult attachment measures: Implications for theory and research. *Social Development, 4*, 294–327.

Daly, M., & Wilson, M. (1980). Discriminative parental solicitude: A biological perspective. *Journal of Marriage and the Family, 42*, 277–288.

Edgarton, R. (1992). *Sick societies: Challenging the myth of primitive harmony.* New York: Free Press.

Emlen, S., Wrege, P., & Demong, N. (1995). Making decisions in the family: An evolutionary perspective. *American Scientist, 83*, 148–158.

Erikson, E. (1950). *Childhood and society.* New York: Norton.

Ewing, K., & Pratt, M. (1995, March). *The role of adult romantic attachment in marital communication and parenting stress.* Poster presented at the biennial meeting of the Society for Research in Child Development, Indianapolis, IN.

Feeney, J., & Noller, P. (1990). Attachment style as a predictor of adult romantic relationships. *Journal of Personality and Social Psychology, 58*, 281–291.

Feeney, J., & Noller, P. (1992). Attachment style and romantic love: Relationship dissolution. *Australian Journal of Psychology, 44*, 69–74.

Foley, R. (1992). Evolutionary ecology and fossil hominids. In E. Smith & B. Winterholder (Eds.), *Evolutionary ecology and human behavior* (pp. 29–64). New York: Aldine de Gruyter.

Fonagy, P., Steele, H., & Steele, M. (1991). Maternal representations of attachment during pregnancy predict the organization of infant–mother attachment at one year of age. *Child Development, 62*, 891–905.

Graber, J., Brooks-Gunn, J., & Warren, M. (1995). The antecedents of menarcheal age. *Child Development, 66*, 346–359.

Gross, M. R. (1991). Salmon breeding behavior and life history evolution in changing environments. *Ecology, 72*, 1180–1186.

Gross, M. R. (1996). Alternative reproductive strategies and tactics: Diversity within sexes. *Trends in Ecology and Evolution, 11*, 92–109.

Grossmann, K., Fremer-Bombik, E., Rudolph, J., & Grossmann, K. E. (1988). Maternal attachment representation as related to patterns of infant–mother attachment and maternal care during the first year. In R. Hinde & J. Stevenson-Hinde (Eds.), *Relationships within families* (pp. 241–262). Oxford: Clarendon Press.

Haft, W., & Slade, A. (1989). Affect attunement and maternal attachment: A pilot study. *Infant Mental Health Journal, 10*, 157–172.

Hamilton, C. E. (1994). *Continuity and discontinuity of attachment from infancy through adolescence.* Unpublished doctoral dissertation, University of California at Los Angeles.

Hamilton, W. (1964). The genetical theory of social behaviour. *Journal of Theoretical Biology, 7*, 1–52.

Harpending, H., Draper, P., & Pennington, R. (1990). Cultural evolution, parental care, and mortality. In A. Swedland & G. Armelagos (Eds.), *Disease in populations in transition* (pp. 83–107). New York: Bergin & Garvey.

Harris, J., & Liebert, R. (1992). *Infant and child.* Englewood Cliffs, NJ: Prentice-Hall.

Hazan, C., & Shaver, P. (1987). Romantic love conceptualized as an attachment process. *Journal of Personality and Social Psychology, 52*, 511–524.

Hazan, C., Zeifman, D., & Middleton, K. (1984, July). *Attachment and sexuality.* Paper presented at the 7th International Conference on Personal Relationships, Groningen, The Netherlands.

Hetherington, E., & Parke, P. (1993). *Child psychology* (4th ed.). New York: McGraw-Hill.

Hinde, R. (1982). Attachment: Some conceptual and biological issues. In C. M. Parkers & J. Stevenson-Hinde (Eds.), *The place of attachment in human behavior* (pp. 14–37). New York: Basic Books.

Hinde, R., & Stevenson-Hinde, J. (1990). Attachment: Biological, cultural and individual desiderata. *Human Development, 33*, 62–72.

Hrdy, S. (1995). Natural-born mothers. *Natural History, 104*, 30–42.

Kaplan, H. (1994). Evolutionary and wealth flows theories of fertility: Empirical test and new models. *Population and Development Review, 20*, 753–791.

Kirkpatrick, L. A., & Davis, K. (1994). Attachment style, gender and relationship stability: A longitudinal analysis. *Journal of Personality and Social Psychology, 66*, 502–512.

Kirkpatrick, L., & Hazan, C. (1994). Attachment styles and close relationships: A four year prospective study. *Personal Relationships, 1*, 123–142.

Kobak, R., Ferenz-Gillies, R., Everhart, E., & Seabrook, L. (1994). Maternal attachment strategies and emotion regulation with adolescent offspring. *Journal of Research on Adolescence, 4*, 553–566.

Kobak, R., & Hazan, C. (1992). *Parents and spouses: Attachment strategies and marital functioning.* Unpublished manuscript, University of Delaware.

Krebs, J., & Kacelnik, A. (1991). Decision making. In J. Krebs & N. Davies (Eds.), *Behavioural ecology: An evolutionary approach* (3rd ed., pp. 119–139). Oxford: Blackwell.

Kunce, L., & Shaver, P. (1994). An attachment-theoretical approach to caregiving in romantic relationships. In K. Bartholomew & D. Perlman (Eds.), *Attachment processes in adulthood* (pp. 205–237). London: Jessica Kingsley.

Lamb, M., Thompson, R., Charnov, E., & Estes, D. (1985). *Infant–mother attachment.* Hillsdale, NJ: Erlbaum.

Lamb, M., Thompson, R., Gardner, W., & Charnov, E. (1984). Security of infantile attachment as assessed in the "Strange Situation": Its study and biological interpretation. *Behavioral and Brain Sciences, 7*, 127–171.

Maccoby, E. (1991). Different reproductive strategies in males and females. *Child Development, 62*, 676–681.

Main, M. (1981). Avoidance in the service of proximity: A working paper. In K. Immelmann, G. Barlow, L. Petrinovitch, & M. Main (Eds.), *Behavioral development: The Bielefeld Interdisciplinary Project* (pp. 651–693). New York: Cambridge University Press.

Main, M. (1990). Cross-cultural strategies of attachment and attachment organization: Recent studies, changing methodologies, and the concept of conditional strategies. *Human Development, 33*, 48–61.

Main, M. (1991). Metacognitive knowledge, metacognitive monitoring and singular (coherent) versus multiple (incoherent) models of attachment: Findings and directions for future research. In C. M. Parkes, J. Stevenson-Hinde, & P. Marris (Eds.), *Attachment across the life cycle* (pp. 127–159). New York: Routledge.

Main, M., & Cassidy, J. (1988). Categories of response with the parent at age six: Predicted from infant attachment classification. *Developmental Psychology, 24*, 415–426.

Main, M., & Solomon, J. (1986). Discovery of a new, insecure–disorganized/disoriented attachment pattern. In T. B. Brazelton & M. Yogman (Eds.), *Affective development in infancy* (pp. 95–124). Norwood, NJ: Ablex.

Maslow, A. (1976). *Farther reaches of human nature.* New York: Viking.

McLoyd, V. (1990). The declining fortunes of black children: Psychological distress, parenting, and socioemotional development in the context of economic hardship. *Child Development, 61*, 311–346.

Miller, L., & Fishkin, S. (1997). On the dynamics of human bonding and reproductive success. In J. Simpson & D. Kenrick (Eds.), *Evolutionary social psychology* (pp. 86–101). Mahwah, NJ: Erlbaum.

Moffitt, T., Caspi, A., Belsky, J., & Silva, P. (1992). Childhood experience and the onset of menarche: A test of a sociobiological model. *Child Development, 63*, 47–58.

O'Connor, E., Pan, H., Treboux, D., Waters, E., Crowell, J., Teti, D., & Posada, G. (1995). *Women's adult attachment security and quality of marriage.* Unpublished manuscript, State University of New York at Stony Brook.

Owens, G. (1993). *An interview-based approach to the study of adult romantic relationships.* Unpublished manuscript, State University of New York at Stony Brook.

Pearson, J., Cohn, D., Cowan, P. A., & Cowan, C. (1994). Earned- and continuous-security in adult attachment: Relation to depressive symptomology and parenting style. *Development and Psychopathology, 6*, 359–373.

Pennington, R., & Harpending, H. (1988). Fitness and fertility among the Kalahari !Kung. *American Journal of Physical Anthropology, 7*, 303–319.

Pistole, M. (1989). Attachment in adult romantic relationships: Styles of conflict resolution and relationship satisfaction. *Journal of Social and Personal Relationships, 6*, 505–510.

Rholes, W., Simpson, J., Blakely, B. S., Lanigan, L., & Allen, E. (1997). Adult attachment styles, the desire to have children, and working models of parenthood. *Journal of Personality, 65*, 357–367.

Ricciuti, A. (1992). *Child–mother attachment: A twin study.* Unpublished doctoral dissertation, University of Virginia.

Rogers, A. (1994). Evolution of time preference by natural selection. *American Economics Review, 84,* 460–481.

Rosenblum, L., & Paully, G. (1984). The effects of varying environmental demands on maternal and infant behavior. *Child Development, 55,* 305–314.

Scheper-Hughes, N. (1992). *Death without weeping: The violence of everyday life in Brazil.* Berkeley: University of California Press.

Senchak, M., & Leonard, K. (1992). Attachment style and marital adjustment among newlywed couples. *Journal of Social and Personal Relationships, 9,* 51–64.

Shaver, P., Collins, N., & Clark, C. (1996). Attachment styles and internal working models of self and relationship partners. In G. Fletcher & J. Fitness (Eds.), *Knowledge structures in close relationships* (pp. 25–62). Mahwah, NJ: Erlbaum.

Shaver, P., & Hazan, C. (1993). Adult romantic attachment: Theory and evidence. In D. Perlman & W. Jones (Eds.), *Advances in personal relationships* (Vol. 4, pp. 29–70). London: Jessica Kingsley.

Sigelman, C., & Shaffer, D. (1995). *Life-span human development* (2nd ed.). Pacific Grove, CA: Brooks/Cole.

Simpson, J. (1990). Influences of attachment styles on romantic relationships. *Journal of Personality and Social Psychology, 59,* 971–980.

Simpson, J., & Gangestad, S. (1991). Individual differences in sociosexuality: Evidence for convergent and discriminant validity. *Journal of Personality and Social Psychology, 60,* 870–883.

Simpson, J., Rholes, W., & Nelligan, J. (1992). Support seeking and support giving within couples in an anxiety-provoking situation: The role of attachment styles. *Journal of Personality and Social Psychology, 62,* 434–446.

Snowdon, C., Ziegler, T., & Widowski, T. (1993). Further hormonal suppression of eldest daughter cotton tamarin following birth of infants. *American Journal of Primatology, 31,* 11–21.

Sroufe, L. A. (1979). The coherence of individual development. *American Psychologist, 34,* 834–841.

Sroufe, L. A. (1988). The role of infant–caregiver attachment in development. In J. Belsky & T. Nezworski (Eds.), *Clinical implications of attachment* (pp. 18–38). Hillsdale, NJ: Erlbaum.

Stearns, S. (1993). The role of development in the evolution of life histories. In J. Bonner (Ed.), *Evolution and development.* New York: Springer-Verlag.

Steinberg, L. (1989). Reciprocal relation between parent–child distance and pubertal maturation. *Development Psychology, 24,* 122–128.

Trivers, R. (1972). Parental investment and sexual selection. In B. Campbell (Ed.), *Sexual selection and the descent of man, 1871–1971* (pp. 136–179). Chicago: Aldine-Atherton.

Trivers, R. (1974). Parent–offspring conflict. *American Zoologist, 24,* 249–264.

Turner, J., & Helms, D. (1995). *Lifespan development* (5th ed.) New York: Harcourt, Brace.

van IJzendoorn, M. (1995). Adult attachment representations, parental responsiveness, and infant attachment: A meta-analysis on the predictive validity of the Adult Attachment Interview. *Psychological Bulletin, 117,* 387–403.

van IJzendoorn, M., & Bakermans-Kranenburg, M. (1996). Attachment representations in mothers, fathers, adolescents, and clinical groups: A meta-analytic search for normative data. *Journal of Clinical and Consulting Psychology, 64,* 8–21.

van IJzendoorn, M., Kranenburg, M., Zwart-Woudstra, H., van Busschbach, A., & Lambermon, M. (1992). Parental attachment and children's socio-emotional development: Some findings on the validity of the Adult Attachment Interview in the Netherlands. *International Journal of Behavioral Development, 14,* 375–394.

Ward, M. J., & Carlson, E. (1995). Associations among adult attachment representations, maternal sensitivity, and infant–mother attachment in a sample of adolescent mothers. *Child Development, 66,* 69–79.

Waters, E., Merrick, S., Albersheim, L., & Treboux, D. (1995, March). *Attachment security from infancy to early adulthood: A 20-year longitudinal study.* Paper presented at the biennial meeting of the Society for Research in Child Development, Indianapolis, IN.

Wilson, D. (1994). Adoptive genetic variation and human evolutionary psychology. *Ethology and Sociobiology, 15,* 219–235.

Zimmermann, P. (1994). *Bindung im Jugendalter: Entwicklung und Umgang mit aktuellen Andorderungen* [Attachment in adolescence: Development and interaction with present circumstances]. Unpublished doctoral dissertation, University of Regensburg, Regensburg, Germany.

8

Psychobiological Origins of Infant Attachment and Separation Responses

❖

H. JONATHAN POLAN
MYRON A. HOFER

John Bowlby's great achievement was to place filial attachment firmly within the small group of behavioral systems that have been most essential for the survival of humans and many other species of mammals during evolution. By showing how attachment may be regarded as a motivational system in its own right, on a par with sex and appetite, he cut through a long-standing debate on the origin of the child's tie with the mother. But in so doing he left open the early developmental processes leading to the formation of attachment. Although Bowlby hypothesized that in slowly developing (altricial) mammals such as rats, dogs, and primates, processes analogous to "imprinting" (as in rapidly developing birds and sheep) occurred, the actual processes involved in acquisition of the intense and specific behaviors that keep such infants close to their mothers remained unknown. Because Bowlby (1973) and other, more recent theorists explain the infant's complex responses to separation in terms of this attachment behavior, our understanding of separation also rests on an uncertain foundation. Research on attachment, at least in humans, has moved on to the developmental role and generational transmission of qualitatively different patterns of attendant behavior (Main, 1996), as if the basic nature of and the processes underlying attachment and separation were settled.

Since the essential phenomena of infant attachment—maternally directed proximity seeking and the response to maternal separation—

occur in most mammals studied thus far, they appear to be strongly conserved in evolution; that is, the basic underlying mechanisms (from genes to neurobehavioral systems) are likely to be similar in all mammals. And studies in the last two decades have strongly supported this inference. Reviews have appeared that summarize research on attachment across a number of mammalian species (Kraemer, 1992; Leon, 1992), so we are not taking that approach here. Instead, we think that more can be gained from an in-depth analysis and interpretation of recent research on a single species. In the last two decades, we have learned more about the psychobiological processes underlying the parent–infant relationship in the rat than in any other species. The multiple analytic experiments on which this knowledge is based require a rapidly developing, inexpensive, easily accessible, laboratory-adapted animal and are thus not suited to primate species, especially humans. Naturally, studies on rats cannot settle questions about human development. But they can suggest new ways to interpret human behavior, new ideas about what to look for, and new hypotheses about underlying biological processes. Above all, they can give us a comparative perspective and suggest how attachment in humans evolved.

In this chapter we review what is known about the biological and psychological processes underlying the development of behavioral responses characteristic of attachment in the young rat.

We show that "attachment," like "appetite," is a unitary descriptive term for a group of behaviors that have been found to depend on component processes working in parallel, as well as in sequence. Much of the work described in this chapter was done by researchers who did not think of themselves as studying attachment. Indeed, when these kinds of studies began more than 20 years ago, few scientists thought that newborn rat pups were capable of more than simple reflexive behaviors. Thus investigators studied the development of the separate systems mediating orienting behavior, suckling, vocalization, and other behaviors of rat pups in the context of infant–mother interactions. Out of these studies have emerged new views of the development of maternally directed proximity seeking and maternal separation responses in this species, which differ in a number of ways from currently accepted views and may have implications for our understanding of human attachment.

Volume 1 of Bowlby's trilogy (Bowlby, 1969/1982) emphasized that the foundation of a filial attachment system is the ability to recognize and seek proximity to a specific individual parent. In the past two decades, the broad outlines of some of the processes by which altricial mammals recognize, acquire preferences for, and seek proximity with their mothers have been revealed. In the next section we focus on four areas that are fundamental to understanding the development of maternally directed proximity seeking in the infant rat. First, it has been learned that the development of preferences for highly specific olfactory features of the mother begins soon after birth, and that the infant rat's behavioral responses show rapid modification through learning. Thus specificity (i.e., recognition and preference by the infant for its mother as distinct from other familiar objects) is not a late manifestation of a mature attachment system, dependent on extensive postnatal experience. Furthermore, the motivational component of proximity seeking (the intensification of this behavior after periods of separation) is also present very early, rather than requiring extensive experience with the brief separations and contingent maternal responses of an evolving relationship. Second, several different sensory systems are involved in eliciting and maintaining a complex repertoire of approach behaviors and in quieting a separated pup; there is no single system (e.g., the tactile properties of the mother's soft and yielding surface) that is the only significant basis for the formation of attachment. Third, the oral stimulation of sucking and

the provision of milk play powerful roles in forging the rat pup's tie to its mother, in contrast to the minimization of such "secondary reinforcement" in most formulations of human filial attachment. These different sensory and motivational systems develop in parallel but independently of each other. This contrasts with the idea of a developmental progression, in which control of attachment behavior shifts in a sequence from one cue to the next, under the control of a single motivational system. Fourth, maternal recognition and preference responses have prenatal origins.

Accompanying this new view of how the infant's tie to the mother first develops has been an equally important change in our concept of how separation from the mother can produce behavioral and physiological changes in the infant. The response to separation is generally taken as the most dramatic feature of infantile attachment. Yet our studies in rat pups have revealed another, different way in which the response to separation can be understood. Central to this new understanding of the separation response has been the discovery that certain components of the mother–infant interaction *regulate* the infant's behavioral and physiological systems. That is, the mother rat maintains the level and pattern of her pup's behavior and physiology by her interactions with it. Different components of the interaction (e.g., warmth, nutrients, olfactory or tactile stimulation) regulate different behavioral and/or physiological systems, independently of each other. The loss of all these component "hidden" regulators together in maternal separation is what results in the pattern of changes known as the "protest" and "despair" phases of the separation response. Thus the relationship between attachment and the response to separation can be understood in an entirely new way. The fact that the infant and mother stay close and interact intensely with each other creates the setting in which "hidden" regulators can develop. But the response to separation can be understood independently of the infant's tie to its mother.

Finally, cognitive processes involved in maternal recognition and separation responses are highlighted to illustrate the emergence of a simple maternal representation, or "working model." We propose that the infant rat's maternal representation provides a paradigm system for investigating the developmental cognitive neuroscience of mammalian working models.

Bowlby (1969/1982) began Volume 1 of his great trilogy with a chapter entitled "Observations to Be Explained." This chapter contains a new set of such observations, and our attempts to explain them have led us to question some of the central tenets of attachment theory: whether attachment is a unitary motivational system "in its own right," whether the responses of infants to maternal separation are evidence for the system's existence, and whether the evolutionary purpose of attachment is defense against predators. By keeping these questions in mind, readers will be able to decide for themselves how their own conceptual models of attachment might be modified.

DEVELOPMENT OF MATERNALLY DIRECTED PREFERENCE AND PROXIMITY SEEKING

Development and Mechanisms of Olfactory Preference

Exclusive, or preferential, orienting and proximity seeking by an offspring directed toward the mother are the defining behaviors of a filial attachment system. To perform them, the offspring must be able to recognize the mother and to discriminate between maternal and nonmaternal stimuli. Although a rat pup is unable to see or hear until at least 11 days of age, the pup's sense of smell, on the way to becoming far more sensitive and discriminating than a human's, is quite competent at birth. Analytic studies designed to rule out the influence of all other sensory modalities have determined that olfaction plays a key role in the rat pup's maternally directed orienting and proximity seeking. Immediately after birth, a newborn already has an orienting response (lateral head movement) that is extremely specifically directed toward the odor of its own mother's amniotic fluid in preference to that of another dam (Hepper, 1987). By postnatal day 10, a pup approaches the odor of its mother in preference to that of a nonlactating female (Nyakas & Endroczi, 1970). This early specific olfactory response is bolstered in the third week by approaching an odor emitted by lactating females in the caecotrophe portion of their anal excreta (Leon, 1974). During the same period of development, pups also begin to recognize and approach other familiar odors, such as that of their home nest shavings, which they approach in preference to fresh shavings (Gregory & Pfaff, 1971; Johanson, Turkewitz, & Hamburgh, 1980) and to shavings from the nest of a nonlactating

female (Gregory & Pfaff, 1971). However, the studies just cited left unclear whether rat pups simply discriminate familiar from unfamiliar odors, or whether they can discriminate *among the familiar odors* in their environment—specifically, between those of their mothers and their home shavings. Such an ability would be evidence of *filial* attraction, rather than a less specific orienting toward *any* familiar cues, and its onset would mark an important developmental milestone for an infant. Therefore, we tested 1- to 10-day-old pups on fine mesh over a two-choice test chamber, comparing proximity seeking toward their mothers with proximity seeking toward the home nest.

We found that pups as young as 4–5 days crawled closer to their mothers' odor than to that of their home nest shavings, and that they performed certain other behaviors, such as probing with their snouts into the test platform, more when responding to their mothers' odor (Polan, Kajunski, & Hofer, 1995). Furthermore, pups increased both maternal preference and differential responding to their mothers' scent after overnight isolation, demonstrating early development of a motivational component. We also found that if we supplied as little as 0.5°C of additional warmth over the maternal side of the test chamber, then even 2-day-old pups would express a preference for maternal odor (Polan & Hofer, 1998), whereas 1-day-old pups in our test paradigm did not yet show a preference for this odor over that of equally familiar home nest shavings. These results suggest that preference for the maternal odor over that of home shavings may be acquired between 1 and 2 days of age, and that the earliest distinction between mother and home shavings may require the convergence in time and space of both olfactory and thermal cues.

Although it had long been suspected that infant rats *learn* their olfactory preferences, we found some rather surprising reinforcers of that learning. During the first 9 postnatal days of a rat pup's life, in classical conditioning experiments using novel odors as the conditioned stimulus, we documented the effectiveness of several reinforcers that neither satisfy an obvious physiological need state, the way milk and warmth do, nor are themselves attractive (Sullivan, Hofer, & Brake, 1986). Examples of these reinforcers include tail pinching, vigorous repetitive stroking with a soft brush (Sullivan & Hall, 1988), and mild foot shock (Camp & Rudy, 1988). Each of these artificial reinforcers is thought to imitate something that the mother does to the pups in the normal course of returning to the nest and initiating a nursing bout. When she returns to the nest she often steps on the pups, then picks them up with her teeth one by one, carries them, and then begins to lick them with rapid vigorous strokes of her tongue before replacing them in the litter pile. Thus, tail pinching may mimic the sensation of being stepped on, and stroking may mimic the sensation of being licked; perhaps mild shock mimics the sensation of teeth gripping the skin. What these and the other primary reinforcers in neonates (even milk ingestion) have in common is that they are vigorously behaviorally arousing to pups. These classical conditioning experiments (reviewed in Sullivan & Hall, 1988; Sullivan & Wilson, 1994; and Wilson & Sullivan, 1994) have thus shown that a wide variety of stimuli that seem to mimic specific maternal behaviors toward the pups, and that all vigorously activate pups, also support the learning of a preference to a novel odor with which they are paired. It is now known that norepinephrine plays a key role in mediating these events. Thus it is theorized that in infant rats, during a sensitive period extending through the first week and a half of life, associative preference learning depends on an activated norepinephrinergic state induced by the reinforcer.

What advantage might there be in newborn rats' predisposition to learn approach responses to a wide range of unconditioned stimuli, some of which might seem noxious to us at worst and not very maternal at best, but which nevertheless get the pups' attention and activate them physiologically? We believe that this ability was selected in evolution precisely because it enables pups to learn from the widest range of maternal interactions and cues. Thus they begin to learn about the mother from the moment she reenters the nest and activates them by her movements. They are not limited to the cues that accompany the rewarming of the litter pile after she settles over it, or to just the sensations of milk letdown. Because the mother activates her young pups repeatedly—up to 20 times a day at each return to the nest—we can see how by stepping on, retrieving, licking, crouching over, and providing milk to them, she powerfully conditions an attraction in them to her own odor and tactile cues (fur texture, etc.). These findings, in essence, substantiate Bowlby's (1969/1982) positing of an imprinting-like basis for the formation of mammalian attachment. We can see that this process of approach behavior conditioning by a broad range of activating stimuli during the 9-day sensitive period, and its continuance beyond 9 days for cues originally conditioned during the sensitive period (Sullivan, 1996), is the *functional equivalent* of imprinting in an altricial mammalian species.

Implications for Human Attachment

Many of these reinforcers are counterintuitive for human investigators, yet the licking, pickup, and stepping on by the mother rat may be the equivalent of the holding, rocking, and cooing by a human mother. We hypothesize that evolution has, appropriately enough, equipped neonates of each mammalian species with central nervous system responses to the species-typical maternal repertoire that supports learning to approach her physical features. Moreover, the discovery of activating reinforcers in rat pups has opened up a new avenue of investigation into the earliest processes of human filial learning. Sullivan et al. (1991) presented newborn human infants with a novel odor while they lay in a bassinet isolated from their mothers; if the odor was paired with rubbing the infants' torsos to mimic maternal care, the next day the infants activated and turned their head toward the same odor. This experiment and others like it suggest that learning an olfactory cue for orientation, reinforced by association with an activating tactile cue, is a basic process in mammalian newborns that has been conserved across evolution. These phenomena also suggest a new view of the paradox that abused children are no less strongly attached to their mothers than those that are well treated. The prevailing view holds that the filial attraction to the mother, once established, inevitably directs approach toward the mother *despite* the mother's herself being the source of the threat. However, this explanation begs the question of how an attraction to such a mother becomes established. We are raising the possibility that the attachment may have been formed in part *because of* the abusive behavior. That is, due to the unique biology of the infant, abusive treatment may, by its activating properties, reinforce approach and even preference for the caregiver. This may itself seem paradoxical; however, in the unpredictable and dangerous environments in which all mammals (including humans) evolved, it may have been adaptive for maternal behavioral reinforcers of infant proximity seeking to include a much wider range of behaviors than are appropriate to modern life.

Complex Multisensory Repertoire of Maternally Directed Orienting and Proximity-Seeking Behaviors

The study of olfactory preference—measuring lateralized orienting in response to laterally presented odors—has, by its very elegance and simplicity, yielded important new insights into the psychobiological basis of filial attachment. Nevertheless, rat pups do not live in such a simple world of two physical dimensions and one sensory modality. New studies in our laboratory have revealed an unexpected complexity to the repertoire of pups' maternally directed proximity-seeking behaviors, and to the range of maternal sensory cues that guide these behaviors.

A rat pup is born into a "sandwich" world, consisting of the substrate of its nest materials beneath it and the canopy of its mother's ventrum presented as she hovers above. In this environment, the newborn pup must (1) burrow underneath the canopy of the mother's ventrum after she assumes her crouch over the litter and (2) orient and maintain itself in relation to her ventrum, so that (3) contact with the ventral surface will permit heat transfer, protection, nipple grasp, and access to ongoing maternal cues that regulate the pup's endocrinological, physiological, and behavioral processes. In this sandwich world, the mother's body is both the source of stimuli to which the pup is responding *and* the superstructure upon which the pup organizes its responses. In naturalistic observations of nest behavior, we identified a surprisingly organized repertoire of maternally directed proximity-seeking and orienting behaviors not previously systematically described: wedging and wriggling under the mother's body, turning upside down under her ventrum, ventroflexing while upside down, and barking audibly (Polan, Soo-Hoo, & Hofer, 1997).

Based on these naturalistic observations, we hypothesized that this impressive repertoire is guided, at least in part, by *tactile* cues from the mother's ventrum. Using a test chamber that simulated the sandwich world and permitted the experimenter to vary the stimulus properties of the overhead surface or "roof" (which simulated the mother's ventrum), we analyzed the behaviors' environmental controls (Polan & Hofer, in press). Each pup was placed prone onto the test platform. The roof, supported by the corral walls, was lowered over the pup until it made light contact with the dorsal surfaces of the pup's head, snout, and torso.

In the first experiment, testing whether tactile cues guide the behaviors, we used a fine-wire-mesh roof acting as a "bare-minimum" simulation of the maternal ventrum, providing a slightly elastic surface with a curved ventrum-like contour overhead, but lacking dam-like features in other sensory modalities. Pups from 1 to 9 days old became aroused, traveled, wedged themselves into the declining slope, wriggled, turned upside down, and audibly barked under it. Once upside down, supported by the floor under their back, some pups traveled across the mesh. We inferred that tactile stimulation by an overhead wire mesh roof evokes specific behaviors, which appear identical in form to those we observed in the nest, and by which pups orient toward and seek proximity with the maternal ventrum.

Our initial presumption was that these behaviors are simple reflexes elicited by nonspecific tactile stimulation of a pup's dorsum. However, it was conceivable that the behaviors might be graded responses to increasingly specific mother-like cues. The next experiment tested whether adding more mother-like cues to the wire roof, in order to increase the specificity of the simulation of the awake dam's ventrum, would increase the frequencies of the maternally directed behavior repertoire. Pups from 2 to 3 days old were tested under either the wire mesh, the mesh lined with soft absorbent cotton, the mesh covered with a dam's fur pelt, or a pup's own anesthetized dam's ventrum suspended from the same height as the other roofs through a cutout form. Each roof condition added one or more mother-like features to the overhead surface: Cotton added softness and thermal insulation; the pelt, whose natural odor was removed by the tanning process, added the specific texture of the dam's fur; and the anesthetized dam's ventrum, the nipples of which were covered by small spots of tape, added the mother's natural odor and heat source. An open condition with no roof served as a control.

We found, to our surprise, that this stepwise stimulus increase led to a stepwise increase in response. Thus, early maternally directed proximity-seeking behaviors are graded responses to maternal features, not simple reflexes to nonspecific tactile stimulation.

Having found that multiple modalities of maternal cues elicited a graded response, suggesting a more sophisticated response system than expected, we next asked whether that system might be responsive to changes in a pup's motivational state. Operationally, we asked whether a period of acute deprivation is necessary for the expression of the maternally directed orienting and proximity-seeking behaviors. Therefore we compared the behaviors of pups that had received acute overnight deprivation with the behavior of nondeprived pups. We found that maternal deprivation was not *necessary* to the performance of the behaviors; however, it did significantly *enhance* responding to the cotton roof and the anesthetized ventrum, but not to the open condition. These findings suggest that the motivational component of the system specifically modulates maternally directed orienting behaviors, but not those elicited by isolation on the platform.

Finally, we asked how early in development the entire repertoire of behaviors is present and when the behaviors come under the sensory guidance of maternal features. We tested newborn pups that were deprived just before and just after their very first nursing bout. We found that after the first nursing experience, the behaviors were already subject to sensory guidance by maternal features, whereas prior to any nursing, pups performed the behaviors vigorously but independently of the type of stimulus encountered. Thus the first experience of nursing organizes an important transition in the control of these orienting behaviors, from reflex-like action patterns to responsiveness to specific maternal features.

Implications for Human Attachment

So far, we have outlined the development of a highly specific maternally directed orienting and proximity-seeking(i.e., filial attachment) system. In both rats and humans, compound features in several sensory modalities come to elicit attachment behavior, but one highly developed sense in each species provides tremendous discriminative power—vision in humans and olfaction in rats. Each of these dominant senses provides the sensory acuity necessary to distinguish between an infant's own mother and another mother. Just as a human infant discerns the mother's identity by her facial features, so the infant rat discriminates, and prefers, its own dam from another dam of the same colony fed a different diet (Leon, 1974).

Extreme maternal specificity—indeed, the capacity for exclusivity—is a hallmark of human infant attachment. Interestingly, although rat pups are also capable of discrimination and preference for their own dams as individuals in their approach behavior, they are far less specific in their comfort response (i.e., the quieting of their isolation vocalizations). Any dam, and even littermates, will have this effect on them. This asymmetry of specificity for approach and com-

fort in the infant rat may have survival advantages in the burrow environment of interconnecting passages and dens, inhabited by closely related members of a colony. Even human infants show a marked capacity to adapt the specificity of their comfort responses to more communal caregiving. For example, human infants in day care will accept comforting from a larger set of adults than did the children reared strictly within a nuclear family who were first described by Bowlby and his colleague, Robertson (Robertson, 1953).

Contribution of Suckling to Attachment

What is it about the first experience of nursing that may organize this complex repertoire of behaviors into specifically *maternally directed* behaviors? In this section we present evidence that nipple grasp, sucking, and orogustatory stimulation by milk contribute to the development of filial attachment. With the experimental work by Harlow (Harlow, 1961; Harlow & Zimmerman, 1959) and Scott (1963), showing so clearly that food reward was not *necessary* for the formation of strong attachments in two highly social mammals (rhesus monkeys and beagle dogs), thinkers in the field reacted strongly against the view held for so long that attachment in mammals depended upon the "oral gratification" or "reinforcing properties" of mother's milk. Bowlby (1969/ 1982), in his masterful synthesis, and current attachment theorists (e.g., Bretherton, 1985; Kraemer, 1992), have not given suckling or maternal milk delivery any clear role in the formation of the human infant's tie to the mother.

Harlow's paradigm, by its radical partitioning of suckling from other experience, fails to address how suckling experience may influence the formation of attachment under normal circumstances, when the infant interacts with a mother who possesses the full complement of maternal sensory qualities and serves as both an object of social comfort and a source of milk. Shortly after the initial publication of Harlow's major findings (Harlow & Zimmerman, 1959), Igel and Calvin (1960) reported results of a similar experiment with dogs. They confirmed Harlow's basic result that milk reinforcement did not result in a strong attachment to a wire surrogate, whereas a non-milk-providing cloth surrogate elicited a substantial attachment. But they also tested the impact of adding milk reinforcement to each type of surrogate and found that puppies reared with a "lactating" cloth surrogate spent significantly more nonfeeding time with it than puppies with a "nonlactating" cloth surrogate spent with theirs, whereas a "lactating" wire surrogate was no more attractive than a "nonlactating" one. These data imply that suckling a mother surrogate does strengthen attachment if, and only if, that surrogate possesses other sufficiently potent proximity-promoting qualities.

Much research using the rat model over the past two decades likewise suggests that suckling, far from being irrelevant to the development of attachment, serves as an important organizer of attachment. The early orienting behaviors discussed in the preceding section result in close physical contact with the maternal body surface in ventrum-to-ventrum orientation. Once this proximity is achieved, a pup searches for and orally grasps a nipple. Although in all mammals the most obvious function of the infant's oral grasp of the maternal nipple is to prepare the infant to extract milk, in cached (hidden in nests) altricial infants such as rat pups, it also serves to latch an infant to the mother's body; this assures the maintenance of close contact, just as does clinging by primate infants and following by precocial infants such as ungulates. The mothers of some marsupial (Hunsaker, 1977) and rodent species (King, 1963) actually employ their infants' secure hold on their nipples as a means of transporting the young out of harm's way.

Indeed, in rat pups the performance and control of nipple attachment are independent of nutritional status: Until 10 days of age, the time it takes a pup to grasp a nipple when placed near one is the same for a recently fed pup as for a deprived pup (Hall, Cramer, & Blass, 1977). In contrast, once a pup is attached to a nipple, sucking frequency (Brake & Hofer, 1980) and rate of milk intake (Cramer & Blass, 1983) are a function of nutritional state, indicating that nutritional status regulates consummatory oral behavior, but not the oral grasp. Furthermore, milk letdown is not necessary to sustain the pup's oral grip and lip seal around the nipple. Normally, pups attached to the nipples of a lactating dam receive milk ejections about five times an hour (Wakerly & Drewett, 1975); yet pups presented with an anesthetized dam, which gives no milk, remain nipple-attached and engage in "dry suckling" for at least 3 hours (Brake & Hofer, 1980; Hall et al., 1977)—the longest interval tested. Finally, although pups separated from their dams and artificially reared by tube feedings from the third through fifth day after birth lose the ability to attach themselves to nipples, milk delivery

through a nipple is not necessary to reinstate it. All that are required are nipple search and attachment "practice" sessions with a nonlactating anesthetized dam during the period of artificial rearing (Stoloff, Kenny, Blass, & Hall, 1980).

These facts demonstrate the independence of nipple attachment from milk ingestion in neonatal rats and are consistent with the idea that nipple attachment subserves a proximity maintenance (or filial attachment) function, as well as providing nutrients. This view is further supported by the finding that the act of dry suckling is itself a powerful reinforcer of approach learning in young rat pups. Kenny and Blass (1977) found that as early as 7 days (the youngest age tested), pups learn to negotiate a maze to suckle a nonlactating nipple. In our laboratory, Brake (1981) showed that 11- to 14-day-olds acquired a preference in a two-choice test paradigm for a novel odor presented during a 1-hour period of dry suckling. Thus we can begin to discern nipple attachment's likely role in the development of the rat pup's overall filial attachment system. The act of orally grasping a nipple assures continued infant–mother proximity; during its continuation, the act of suckling itself, independent of milk ingestion, reinforces further proximity seeking in response to increasingly specific maternal cues.

Orogustatory stimulation by milk is an additional reward. Brake (1981) found that when milk accompanies the act of suckling, learning is reinforced even more effectively. Johanson and Hall (1979) found that milk itself, delivered into the mouths of 1-day-old pups by an implanted cannula (thus bypassing the act of suckling), also supports instrumental and olfactory preference learning.

Interestingly, Blass's group has begun to dissect the central neurochemical bases of the tactile reward system of nipple grasp from the gustatory reward system of milk. The evidence confirms the independence of these two systems: The reward provided by milk's flavor is mediated by opioid receptors (Blass & Fitzgerald, 1988), whereas the rewarding properties of sucking are mediated by nonopioid systems (Blass, Fillion, Weller, & Brunson, 1990). These results, together with those reviewed in previous sections of this chapter, lead us to hypothesize that maternally directed proximity seeking, nipple attachment, sucking, and milk ingestion are parallel motivational systems, which are organized by the performance of the first nursing bout and forge an integrated filial attachment system very quickly after birth.

Implications for Human Attachment

This view puts into perspective the roles of suckling and milk reward in the formation of attachment. Suckling and all of its associated activities include a cluster of reinforcers, just one of which is the traditional primary reinforcer of milk. Thus, in a strict sense, the secondary-drive theory of attachment—which postulated that attachment owes its origination *solely* to association of the mother with milk reward—is false, as Harlow declared. But in a deeper sense, all the interactions with the mother that normally lead to suckling, acting in concert with milk reward, provide the momentum that drives the formation of the infant's attachment.

Blass has begun to apply the rat model to human research on the orogustatory effects of suckling. He has found that, as with the rat pup, orogustatory stimulation in the human newborn has potent rewarding properties and is separable into two components: a tactile component, related to nipple grasp and suck, and an orogustatory component, related to the presence of milk in the mouth (Blass & Ciaramitaro, 1994; Smith, Fillion, & Blass, 1990). Just as in the rat, both stimuli calm a crying infant, and whereas milk's comforting effect lasts well beyond its delivery into the mouth, the effect of non-nutritive sucking coincides with the presence of the pacifier. These remarkable behavioral parallels raise the intriguing possibility that they involve the same central neural mechanisms in both species; studies of human infants born to mothers maintained on methadone provide indirect evidence to support this (Blass & Ciaramitaro, 1994).

Prenatal Origins of Attachment and Pre- and Postnatal Continuities

It makes good teleological sense that orienting and approach behaviors directed toward the mother and needed right after birth may have their origins in behavioral capabilities of the fetus, and that behaviors with which the newborn comes equipped may serve as building blocks from which a filial attachment system can be constructed. It makes even more sense when one considers that the prenatal and immediate postnatal environments are both supplied by the mother's body. Despite the obvious differences between being inside and being outside the uterus, one might expect certain sensory continuities (e.g., thermal, chemosensory, and rhythmic) to help construct an experiential and behavioral

bridge between these two phases of life. There is good evidence to support this view.

The best-established evidence for such prenatal "building blocks" concerns nipple attachment and responsiveness to milk. Smotherman, Robinson, and their colleagues found that the late-term rat fetus possesses organized appetitive responses to features of its mother that have never been encountered and will not be encountered until after birth—namely, her nipples and her milk. While each rat dam was anesthetized by spinal blockade and immersed in a thermoneutral saline bath, the investigators carefully removed fetal rat subjects from the uterus and amniotic membranes while maintaining intact umbilical connections to the placenta, and observed the behavioral responses to various stimuli. Remarkably, an artificial nipple made of soft vinyl presented to rat fetuses elicited an oral grasping response from day 19 through term (Robinson et al., 1992). On gestational day 21, fetuses mouthed, licked, and orally grasped the artificial nipple while treadling with their forelimbs—behaviors that strongly resemble the postnatal repertoire of a neonate in relation to its mother's ventrum.

Since fetal rats can taste and smell, Smotherman and Robinson (1992) fit test fetuses with an intraoral cannula that delivered pulses of stimulus fluids. They found that milk, unlike other liquid stimuli, consistently evoked mouthing activity during the 15 seconds after presentation, and that prior exposure to an artificial nipple increased this mouthing. Moreover, they discovered that 70% of day 20 or 21 fetuses had the so-called "stretch response" (limb extension and trunk dorsiflexion) to pulses of intraoral milk on the first exposure, which had been thought to occur only in neonatal infants after they had attached themselves to nipples and received milk ejections. Both the fetal nipple grasp and the stretch responses strongly suggest that a rat fetus enters its extrauterine world with an assortment of "made-to-order" proximity-maintaining and appetitive stimulus–response predispositions directed toward the essential features of its first postnatal encounter with the mother.

Furthermore, milk has comforting properties, even to a fetus (Robinson, Arnold, Spear, & Smotherman, 1993). Late-term fetuses display an organized "face-wiping" response (moving the forepaws along the side of the head in a rostral direction), which is elicited by the intraoral presentation of novel chemical stimuli other than milk, and by tactile stimulation of the vibrissal pads. Just as the stretch response is seen as a prototypical acceptance response, the face-wiping is seen as an exemplar of aversion. Oral milk blunts the face-wiping response to later snout tactile stimulation in fetal rats. This "comfort" response of milk has been found to be mediated by the endogenous opioid system, which is functional in the fetus.

There is even some evidence for prenatal precursors of the maternally directed proximity-seeking behaviors described earlier. Smotherman and Robinson (1986) observed the ontogeny of spontaneous fetal behaviors in three microenvironments: inside the translucent walls of the uterus; within the transparent intact amniotic sac; and outside the amnion, supported in a thermoneutral isotonic saline bath. In addition to mouth, head, and limb movements, the investigators noted behaviors that they called "curling" and "stretching." Curls and stretches accounted for some 14% of all fetal activity from gestational days 16 through 21; judging by the authors' descriptions, they closely resembled the wriggling, rolling, and flexing actions performed by our neonates under the experimental roof. Especially intriguing was the finding that curls and stretches were significantly more frequent in the less restrictive microenvironments (the amnion and the bath) than inside the uterus itself, suggesting to us the possibility that fetuses may develop the capacity for these behaviors prenatally, but that the confines of the uterine walls may inhibit their expression while the fetuses await their arrival into a more accommodating surround. The externalized amniotic sac, a saline bath, and the postnatal nest covered by the soft, yielding canopy of the mother's ventrum could all be such surrounds.

We have just reviewed compelling evidence for "hard-wired" prenatal behavioral dispositions toward the nipple and milk. Yet in utero learning also shapes the first filial behaviors. In rats, olfactory cues in the vicinity of the nipples direct infants to those specific areas on the maternal body surface (Hofer, Shair, & Singh, 1976). In the first attachment to the nipple in the infant rat, the odor of amniotic fluid bridges the prenatal and the postnatal phases of the infant's early life. During parturition, rat mothers deposit amniotic fluid on their nipple lines; this acts as a necessary local stimulus to elicit nipple grasping, a lip seal, and the intraoral negative pressure that holds the pups firmly to the mothers. Without the olfactory and taste stimulation of amniotic fluid, a new-born rat does not appear to recognize the nipple as such. It fails to attach, and nursing cannot be initiated. As mentioned earlier, an infant rat in the first hours after birth can discriminate and will turn preferentially toward the scent of its own mother's amniotic fluid rather than the amniotic fluid of another mother (Hepper, 1987). Thus even in the immediate postnatal period, we can already identify a set of native behaviors by which the infant maintains proximity to the mother, as well as an acquired capacity to discriminate and cling to its *own* mother.

Knowing that rat pups will not grasp washed nipples (Hofer et al., 1976), but that amniotic fluid applied to washed nipples reinstates the grasp response (Teicher & Blass, 1977), Pedersen and Blass (1982) hypothesized that the amniotic fluid odor cue is learned *in utero*. Reasoning that it might be possible to "teach" fetuses an artificial cue by mimicking key events of late gestation and early postnatal life, they injected citral (the compound that gives lemon its characteristic odor) into the amniotic sac of each fetus on day 20 of gestation. At term, 2 days later, the rats were delivered by cesarean section and then exposed for 1 hour to a nest saturated with citral while they were stroked with a soft brush, mimicking the mother's postpartum licking as a reinforcer. Pups were then tested for their ability to attach to nipples of a recently parturient dam. When held with their snouts in contact with the nipples of the anesthetized test dam, the citral-exposed pups grasped the nipples only if citral-soaked shavings were placed around the nipples to scent the immediate area. These pups even grasped nipples that had been thoroughly washed with organic solvents to remove all natural scents that might direct or elicit nipple grasping, as long as citral was provided. A second experiment showed that citral was effective in directing pups' first nipple attachment only if they received exposure to it both *in utero* and immediately postnatally, along with stroking.

These results are evidence that rat fetuses enter the world equipped with the "knowledge" of what cue should guide their first filial act, nipple attachment, having learned it in the womb. Through prenatal exposure, a fetus acquires a highly specific olfactory–gustatory cue that enables it as a newborn to find its own mother's teat, and that initiates a series of oral behaviors generating the prolonged physical attachment to the teat that is necessary for suckling.

Implications for Human Attachment

Research with human infants has proceeded along similar lines with strikingly parallel results. Varendi, Porter, and Winberg (1996) have essentially replicated the findings of Teicher and Blass (1977) in human newborns, demonstrating that amniotic fluid placed on the areola guides a newborn to the breast and is preferred to an untreated breast. Although this result is not proof of prenatal learning, it certainly points to it as a strong possibility. The best evidence for prenatal learning of preferences for maternal features comes from research by Fifer's group (Moon, Bever, & Fifer, 1992) using audition, which is functional in human fetuses. They found that newborn infants preferred to hear their own mothers' voices over that of a strange adult female. Moreover, 72-hour-old newborns preferred to hear an "intrauterine version" of their mothers' voices, created by low-pass filtering of a recording of the mothers' speech, rather than the nonfiltered recording (Moon & Fifer, 1990); this finding suggests that early preferences for human mothers are learned *in utero*. Pursuing this hypothesis, Fifer and Moon (1994) have begun to describe the physiological state changes (including heart rate slowing) of 36- to 40-week fetuses on hearing their own mothers speaking, providing direct evidence that attention and information processing are engaged by this stimulus.

RESPONSES TO SEPARATION

Up to this point, we have explored new views of the processes by which approach and proximity-seeking behaviors develop in infant rats. But behavioral systems that maintain an infant in close proximity to the mother and that promote physical attachment to the nipple, do not fulfill our criteria for a fully developed attachment system. Another essential component is a particular set of responses to maternal separation. In fact, Bowlby's attachment theory was developed in order to explain the separation responses that became all too evident during the societal devastations of World War II (Bowlby, 1969/1982). On the basis of subsequent systematic studies by Robertson, Heinecke, and others, Bowlby proposed that when an attachment system is sufficiently developed, the infant comes to respond to separation from the mother as a signal of danger. The affect of security, established during the pre-

vious close interactions with the mother, is now replaced by the affect of fear and the behaviors and physiological changes that express this state. Separation anxiety, Bowlby reasoned, is activated when attachment behaviors are elicited but fail to result in the infant's reaching the appropriate terminating stimuli for this instinctual system. Proximal behaviors of approach give way to more distal attachment behaviors of searching and vocalization. These rise to a frantic intensity that expresses the affects elicited by nontermination of the instinctual behaviors and by the signal event of separation. Thus the explanation of the separation response afforded by attachment theory depends not only upon the development of an attachment system, but also upon the presence of an organism capable of perceiving the danger signal of separation and of responding affectively to it. The behavioral and physiological changes induced by separation are viewed as parts of an integrated psychophysiological response, as is commonly understood to occur in emotional responses to stress.

Hidden Regulators: From Attachment to Loss

Our experiments have provided a different explanation for the early responses of infants to separation—one based upon loss, rather than upon a response to a signal of danger inherent in the event of separation, or a response to disruption of an affective bond. The loss involves some of the very interactions we have been describing, involving rat pups' tactile, olfactory, thermal, and oral sensory pathways. We came to this conclusion as the result of a series of experiments aimed at ruling out different possible signals (summarized in Hofer, 1995). We found that a pup was not responding to a single cue, but instead that different systems in the pup were responding to different aspects of the mother's absence. Those elements of the interaction with the dam whose loss we had considered as possible signals eliciting the separation response turned out to produce their effect through loss of an unexpected regulatory control they exerted over the infant's developing neural systems *prior* to separation. When these elements were withdrawn simultaneously by maternal separation, the infant's systems gradually responded to loss of this ongoing regulation. We found that the direction of the separation response in a given behavioral or physiological system was determined by the direction of the regulatory effect of the mother–infant interaction prior to separation. For example, if the regulatory effect of interacting with the dam had been to increase sympathetic autonomic cardiac drive, the response to separation was found to be a decrease in sympathetic tone and thus a fall in cardiac rate.

A pup's response to separation thus appeared in a new light, as an assemblage of individual components reflecting the withdrawal or *loss* of a number of different regulatory processes that had been hidden within the pup's relationship with its dam. By experimentally providing or withholding different elements of the interaction, we were able to produce pups that showed some of the responses to separation without others. And these interactions were found to exert graded regulatory effects on infant systems, rather than all-or-none signal effects. For example, by providing different amounts of heat to separated pups (so as to alter their body temperature within the naturally occurring range), we were able to produce pups with behavioral reactivity levels ranging from depressed to hyperactive, but always with low heart rates. And by providing nutrients by stomach to separated pups, we could produce pups with heart rates ranging from slightly above normal (500 per minute) to well below normal (250 per minute), but always with the same behavioral reactivity levels.

This degree of experimental control over behavioral reactivity and cardiac rate as responses to separation gave us confidence that we had learned something fundamental about the processes involved. By analyzing the mother–infant interaction into its component events, isolating these events, inventing ways to reproduce each of them separately, and providing them individually to pups after maternal separation, we had developed a method that could specify which element of the loss was responsible for a given component of the response. Release from these regulatory controls within the mother–infant relationship provided us with a way of understanding the response to separation that did not depend upon recognition of a danger signal or disruption of an inferred affective "bond."

Temporal Factors in the Separation Response: Rapid Regulation of Affective State

Different components of the mother–infant interaction exert their regulatory control by different pathways and over different time frames. In addition, the infant systems that are regulated have different rates of response to loss of the particular regulatory interaction (Hofer, 1995). Thus, after abrupt separation, the fall in cardiac rate and the rise in behavioral reactivity take 8 hours to become clearly evident and do not peak until 18–20 hours. The fall in growth hormone and in the brain enzyme ornithine decarboxylase, however, are clearly evident 20 minutes after separation, and the vocalization response usually peaks in the first few minutes unless a pup remains asleep at the time of separation.

With the accumulation of evidence in the infant rat, there does not appear to be any fundamental difference in eliciting mechanisms between the rapid ("protest") and slowly developing ("despair") phases of the response to separation, as was once thought (Hofer, 1983). The infant rats' immediate calling response to separation can be continuously varied in rate according to the intensity of a given regulator (e.g., warmth or odor) that is present in the isolation chamber, or according to the number of modalities (e.g., texture, contour, warmth, odor) provided in an artificial surrogate. Thus, a pup's calling rate can be down-regulated in a graded fashion by natural and artificial stimuli that possess some of the mother's traits, and the pup can be completely "comforted" by an artificial surrogate that provides enough of these stimuli (Hofer, 1996). Thus, calling can be continuously inhibited by interaction with the dam over many hours, as can the pup's general activity level (Hofer, 1975), although each behavior has different regulators operating over different pathways.

Another regulator of infant calling involves an entirely different pathway. As discussed above, milk and other nutrients powerfully reduce infant calling rates, due to their stimulation of intraoral sensory receptors—an effect mediated by both endogenous opioids and cholecystokinin (Blass & Fitzgerald, 1988; Blass & Shide, 1993). This links the attachment behaviors organized around suckling to the quieting of vocalization in the comfort response, further tying oral/ingestive behavior into the experiences responsible for development of the attachment system.

The role of affect in these responses is beginning to become evident. The rate of calling that a young rat shows in response to separation has been found to reflect a balance among at least four major brain neuromodulator systems (reviewed in Hofer, 1996). The striking fact about this neural control system is its similarity to our current understanding of the neural basis for anxiety in humans. The same drugs that are effective in reducing anxiety (e.g., benzodiazepines) selectively decrease calling rates in rat pups, and synthetic compounds that produce severe anxiety in human volunteers selectively raise pups' calling rates. These findings suggest that the brain states of the young rat that is suddenly separated and then reunited with its mother are similar to the affective states of anxiety and comfort/security that we consider to accompany those states in humans. And in this system we have a relatively simple model of maternal regulation of infant emotions.

Regulatory Interactions and Attachment Theory

How does this system of component regulators differ from the regulatory system of Bowlby's attachment theory? First of all, a great deal more is regulated than an infant's proximity and affective state. Without the experiments we have done, one could not know that the infant's autonomic, endocrine, thermal, and digestive systems are involved, as well as those controlling behavior. Second, the many processes of mutual regulation between mother and infant are also more varied in their pathways and modes of action than the goal-corrected proximity maintenance system that Bowlby proposed. In Bowlby's system, the mother simply provides the terminating stimuli for the proximity-seeking behaviors. Thirdly, Bowlby inferred from the behaviors he observed that "intense affects arise during the formation, maintenance, disruption and renewal of the attachment relationship" (Bowlby, 1980, p. 40). These affective states in turn determine any physiological changes induced by separation or reunion, according to his view. We now have a different way of accounting for separation-induced changes, both in physiology and in affective states.

Finally, Bowlby (1969/1982) proposed that an "internal working model" of the attachment relationship is gradually built up out of the child's interactions—a mental representation of the self and the mother, upon which the child's approach to future social interactions is based. Such a development, he believed, allows the infant to form expectations of the likely consequences of his or her behavior toward the mother. Ainsworth, Blehar, Waters, and Wall (1978) demonstrated that, depending on the quality of the relationship previously experienced, infants exhibited qualitatively different patterns of behavior toward their

mothers and toward strangers in standardized tests. The behavioral and physiological regulatory systems we have described cannot in themselves account for such events. Instead, they appear to belong to an earlier stage in development, out of which such mental representations are built. Possible processes by which early regulators may play a role in the formation of later mental representations have been discussed elsewhere (Hofer, 1995). But even in the rat we can see how these may develop.

Developing Complexity in the Vocal Response to Separation

A recent finding suggests that older rat pups, like human infants, develop expectancies as a result of the quality of their recent interactions with their mother and alter their attachment behavior accordingly. We discovered that if a 2-week-old pup experienced a brief (1- to 3-minute) period of contact with its dam just prior to isolation, even if she was entirely passive (anesthetized), it would subsequently call at two to three times its usual rate. This effect, which we call "potentiation," was enhanced if the dam was awake and active rather than passive (Hofer, Brunelli, Masmela, & Shair, 1996). This potentiated isolation–calling response was specific to the mother; it did not follow brief periods of contact with littermates, the home cage nest, or a second novel test box. Unlike the initial vocal response to separation that develops on the second postnatal day, potentiation did not develop until pups were more than a week old. The later effect of the maternal contact was found to depend on both its quality and its duration. If the period of contact was 30 minutes or longer and the dam remained passive (anesthetized), a pup no longer showed an enhanced response when separated from her. But if the dam actively interacted with the pup, the pup continued to show an enhanced response even after 30 minutes.

The sequence of events in these experiments bears some similarity to the common experience of a human mother who returns briefly to the day care center after dropping her toddler off in the morning, only to find a much more severe response to her leaving this second time. These experiments add a new dimension to the separation response of the young rat, in which the pup is not simply responding to the presence or absence of maternal stimuli in its immediate environment, but instead is responding to certain patterns of interaction with its mother prior to isolation. We are currently attempting to discover the crucial signal or regulating interaction that is responsible for this potentiation of the infant's separation response. Whether or not these experiments are telling us that a rat pup builds up an internal working model based on certain expectancies created during interactions with its dam prior to separation is not yet clear (see below). There may be other explanations, but this response does appear to represent an increasing complexity in the pup's response to separation that develops only after several days of experience with the regulatory interactions of the early mother–infant relationship.

TOWARD A PSYCHOBIOLOGY OF MATERNAL REPRESENTATION

Investigators and theorists of human infant attachment are increasingly interested in the "maternal representation" (i.e., the memories, or templates, that encode the infant's experiences of the mother). Just as with the concept of attachment itself, debate about maternal representation is focused largely on its psychological nature and psychosocial role, while we still have little understanding of its biological substrates. However, a comparison of the maternal representations of the infant human and rat reveals parallels at basic levels of structure and content, making the rat a potentially valuable model system with which to investigate the developmental neuroscience of the maternal representation.

Bowlby's concept of the representation as a "working model" connotes an internal construct with enduring core features and considerable plasticity, revised in accord with changing functional capacities of the offspring in relation to the mother, as well as with changes in the mother herself. One fundamental function of the representation's core features is maternal recognition—the ability to respond differentially or selectively to the mother. Picture an 8-month-old infant in day care who studies every mother who arrives to pick up her baby. Each woman captures the infant's attention, but as soon as a woman proves not to be his or her mother, the infant either loses interest in her or continues to study her with a kind of neutral interest. In sharp contrast, when the infant's mother appears, she is recognized and met with a burst of joyous greeting. The infant has compared each mother with an internal visual–auditory template, or representation of his or her *own* mother; she, and only

she, matches this representation, triggering the excited response and behavior of reunion.

Recognition involves different cognitive operations in different contexts. During the more distal task of proximity–seeking, recognition requires the learning of cues that act as signals or predictors of the mother's presence, whereas proximal, intimate interactions engage an increasingly complex representation. To illustrate these distal and proximal aspects of maternal recognition and their implications for the resulting representations in human infants, picture the same child's having been in day care for several weeks. Now the infant reacts excitedly to the sound of the mother's footsteps; the sound alone elicits eager anticipation as he or she orients toward the door to greet the mother, having learned that a distal cue (the sound of footsteps) predicts her presence. On the other hand, when that same infant as a toddler is enfolded into the mother's embrace, he or she may react with puzzlement, even dismay, if an important detail of the maternal gestalt is altered—perhaps by a new, more pungent perfume or a hug less vigorous than usual.

Our studies of the infant rat reveal analogous examples of the construction of the maternal representation's core features and the functioning of these features in recognition tasks. The following are two examples of such processes. In the first example, preference and approach behavior, which require a maternal odor *and* a thermal gradient at age 2 days, come to be elicited by the olfactory cue alone by 4–5 days of age. Evidently the more distal (olfactory) cue comes to signal the original olfactory–thermal combination and mobilizes an initial response. The thermal cue is not "forgotten," nor has it become irrelevant; when added to the olfactory cue, it still causes older pups to respond more fully than to the odor alone. Rosenblatt (1983) postulated this kind of learning as a paradigm of how altricial mammals acquire a maternal representation: A physiologically relevant stimulus (warmth) by association imparts *incentive* value to an otherwise neutral stimulus (maternal odor).

In our second example, association results in the construction of a tightly specified compound representation of the dam's nipple. During the first 24 hours after birth, either the olfactory sense *or* the trigeminal tactile system (snout and whiskers) is capable of guiding successful nipple attachment. After 3–4 days of nursing, however, the loss of either system results in a total failure of suckling (Hofer, Fisher, & Shair, 1981), and the pups die. If the pheromone that replaces amniotic fluid as the olfactory cue for nipple attachment (Hofer et al., 1976) is washed from the maternal ventrum, the pups with substantial nursing experience fail to become attracted to that area or aroused when near it, and fail to show the normal pattern of rapid lateral head swings and vertical probing of the maternal ventrum that would bring them into tactile contact with the teat. If a pup's snout and vibrissal (whisker) pad and upper lip are anesthetized, the arousal and the probing are left intact, but the pup's lower lip and tongue pass over the protruding teat without the pup's opening its mouth and grasping it. In both cases, even if the teat is manually placed in the pup's mouth (which is also intact sensorially), it will not grasp it, attach, or suck. Apparently the specific odor of the dam's ventrum and the tactile properties of the teat, sensed by the vibrissae and snout, have together become integrated with the intraoral sensation of the teat into a tightly specified multisensory stimulus complex in the first few days after birth. Without any one of these key features, the teat is not recognized as such, and no attachment to it takes place. The focusing and the detail necessary for this response suggest that the pup has constructed a highly specified representation of the ventrum and teat to which the behavioral responses of nipple attachment are linked. Parallels between these phenomena and those of human infants and children suggest that similar basic processes may be at work.

A remaining mystery is whether (and, if so, how) these core features are assembled into a coherent, whole maternal representation, rather than just a set of function-specific parts. Stern (1985, pp. 111–116), an influential current theorist who draws from both cognitive psychology and the object relations tradition of psychoanalysis, hypothesizes that a realistic working model is integrated from representations of the mother in specific interactions that have been generalized, or "RIGs." He and other object relations theorists explain certain types of adult psychopathology (e.g., borderline personality disorder) as the failure of this integration.

What are these early processes of representational integration? Clues may come from a body of work showing how infant rats weld classically conditioned cues into wholes by *breaking* certain rules of adult learning. Spear and his colleagues (e.g., Mellon, Kraemer, & Spear, 1991; Molina, Hoffman, Serwatka, & Spear, 1991; Spear, Kraemer, Molina, & Smoller, 1988; Spear & McKinzie, 1994) have shown that stronger cues in one sensory modality presented to infant and preweanling rats are likely to potentiate (to add conditioned strength to) weaker cues in another modality with which they are paired, whereas in adult animals stronger cues are likely to overshadow (to subtract conditioned strength from) weaker ones. Furthermore, in infant rats but not in adults, different stimuli associated with the same reinforcer tend to be treated as equivalent (e.g., reinforcement of one increases the conditioned strength of the other)—a process Spear's group calls "unitization." In plain language, young animals tend to be "lumpers" of conditioned stimuli, whereas adults tend to be "splitters." We hypothesize that stimulus lumping provides young altricial mammals with a learning strategy they need for efficient processing of cues from their first environment, their mother. Maternal stimuli with the greatest associative potency take hold first and provide the informational scaffolding onto which others are laid, sparing pups from having to learn to associate every maternal stimulus with every other one. In essence, an infant assumes, correctly, that the mother it smells is the same as the mother it feels, and thus represents her as a whole object. As the young animal acquires independent locomotion and feeding, and cues of nonmaternal origin become more frequent and salient in its environment, ontogenetically timed splitting (overshadowing) becomes the dominant and appropriate strategy to differentiate the maternal representation from nonmaternal objects and to distinguish among various nonmaternal objects. Thus potentiation, unitization, and overshadowing may be fundamental principles that first establish coherence among the complex array of conditioned memory traces of maternal origin, and then differentiate that complex representation from the nonmaternal surround. These phenomena, and the reinforcing of approach responses to the wide array of activating maternal behaviors (discussed earlier), demonstrate that infant rats possess an impressive repertoire of ontogenetically adaptive learning strategies that may help explain how a coherent maternal representation is quickly constructed. These considerations provide new testable hypotheses for the study of the development of the maternal representation in human infants.

Much recent discussion of maternal representation has centered on "metacognition" (Main, 1991), the higher-order appraisal and reorganization of memories, which in turn alter the individual's expectancies in relation to his or her attachment figures. Good evidence now indicates that these higher-order processes are as important in determining the ultimate form, function, and affective impact of the maternal representation (Main, 1991) as its raw content. Although many of these uniquely human processes begin in early childhood, perhaps coincident with language, nonverbal groundwork for them may be laid by 12 months of age. During separation, infants show certain patterns of adaptive and/or defensive attachment behavior, using attentional shifts (Main, 1995) apparently based on altered expectancies in their interactions with their mothers. For example, as is well known, infants whose mothers have consistently rejected their cues at home dramatically ignore their mothers under the stress of the Ainsworth strange situation; these infants are thus classified as "avoidant" (Ainsworth et al., 1978). Consider another example from about the same point in development. Stern (1985, pp. 149–151) showed mothers videotapes of themselves playing with their 8-month-old infants and pointed out their "affect attunements," or spontaneous nonverbal responses to their children's expressed emotions. Each mother was then asked to refrain from attuning during the next play session; instead, she was instructed to maintain a neutral face, voice, and posture when her baby expressed itself affectively. Videotapes of the experimentally altered interaction captured each infant's puzzlement, and even distress, the moment after the mother would have attuned. Evidently the infant's representation of its intimate affective dialogue with the mother had come to regulate its affective states; the sudden cessation of a maternal response violated an expectancy.

As the last example illustrates, compelling evidence for the operation of an expectancy is the sudden disruption of behavior that occurs when the infant is surprised by a situation of nonreward or negative contrast (see, e.g., Tolman, 1932). Thus expectancy is revealed not simply by the gradual decrement of a conditioned response that transpires during extinction when the reinforcer is withheld. Rather, it is evidenced by an immediate active disturbance of behavior, or the performance of new behaviors that suggest "frustration" (Amsel, 1992), after a single instance of a reduced or absent reinforcement. Such responses suggest that a specific rewarding event was anticipated.

We regard the maternal potentiation of the rat pup's isolation calling, discussed earlier, as an example of the operation of a simple expectancy in the maternal representation. Recall that if pups experienced a brief return of their mothers after an initial separation, their calling rate during the subsequent separation increased severalfold. The developmental onset of potentiation several days after the appearance of primary separation calling is consistent with a learned response. What has been learned may be that reunion with the mother is followed by the multiple potent rewards embedded in the interaction with her. Interruption of that interaction, with its consequent failure to obtain those rewards, is a violation of the infant's expectancy; this is expressed by the resumption of isolation calling at dramatically higher than usual rates. This frustration behavior may serve the adaptive function of communicating distress to the mother while her likelihood of responding is high.

In applying the term "representation" to rat pups, we are not suggesting that infant rodents internally reorganize memories of interactions to create novel configurations, as do children. Rather, we are pointing out that the affective valence of a pup's maternal representation is sensitively tuned to its recent experience, resulting in a remarkable flexibility of response patterning and communication. At present we can only point out the *analogies* between aspects of rat pups' and human infants' working models. Whether these analogies derive from *homologies* of underlying brain mechanisms is an essential topic for further research.

In this discussion of maternal representation, we acknowledge, and at the same time defer resolution of, the question of *mental* representations. We do not infer from animal research the existence of mind, consciousness, or conscious awareness, thoughts, intentions, or desires. As Blumberg and Wasserman (1995) have argued, inferring a complex mental life from complex and adaptable behavior systems is a conceptual Scylla and Charybdis. Nor do we assume that maternal representations in young mammals are merely "mechanical and mindless processes"— Blumberg and Wasserman's phrase for the sign-tracking behaviors of pigeons. We take the position of comparative cognition, which rejects the assumption that all human cognitive processes are unique and, following Darwin's assertion that cognitive processes evolved (Darwin, 1871/1981), entertains the testable hypothesis that "there is some continuity of evolved cognitive processes across species" (Rilling & Neiworth, 1986, p. 19). The question of cognitive continuity across mammalian species during early development has not been the subject of a thorough research program; comparative studies of the construction of maternal representations could provide a paradigm for investigating this question.

SUMMARY, IMPLICATIONS, AND PERSPECTIVE

In this chapter we have described a number of component behavioral systems that together act to bring the infant into close proximity to the mother, continue to keep the infant close, act to reunite the separated infant with the mother, and cause a complex patterned response to prolonged maternal separation. These several components tell us that an "enduring social bond" (to use Bowlby's term) has been formed, but we can now understand the bond in terms of separate processes that can be delineated as they work independently, serially, or in parallel to produce the familiar behavioral signs of "attachment." The discovery of these component processes allows us to begin to understand what makes up the "glue" that holds the infant to the mother. The discovery of regulatory interactions within the mother–infant relationship allows us to escape the circularity of the traditional attachment model, in which the response to separation is attributed to disruption of a social bond, the existence of which is inferred from the presence of that same separation response. Some of the individual processes described allow us to understand how the infant comes to identify and orient toward the mother by different means at different stages in development. Beginning before birth and continuing in the newborn period, novel processes of associative learning have been discovered that allow us for the first time to understand the mysterious "imprinting-like processes" that Bowlby envisioned as the functional equivalent of imprinting in infant altricial mammals. And, finally, we can begin to see how one of the consequences of these early learning processes, acting within repeated regulatory interactions, is to provide a novel source of experiences for the formation of the representation of the infant–mother relationship.

What are the implications of this recent experimental work for Bowlby's attachment theory? We believe that these laboratory studies have revealed an extensive layer of biological and behavioral processes underlying the control system and mental-representational constructs of attachment theory. Experimental analyses of the early proximity maintenance behaviors that Bowlby referred to as "component instinctual processes" have shown that these behaviors are much more flexible and complex than previously thought, and that later they continue to play important roles in other functions within the relationship, rather than becoming focused entirely on maintaining the "set goals" of an attachment system. Thus the developing behaviors that are viewed in attachment theory as reflecting the progressive unfolding of a unitary hierarchical attachment system have come to be seen as components of a larger developing organization—the mother–infant relationship as a whole.

With this enlarged view, some processes have been discovered to play an important role in the development of proximity maintenance between infant and mother that were not previously considered to be important (e.g., prenatal learning, milk provision). And events that were thought to be central to attachment have been found to be produced by other, independent mechanisms (e.g., separation responses). More broadly, our understanding of the evolutionary survival value of remaining close to the mother has been expanded to include the many pathways available for regulation of the infant's physiological and behavioral systems by its interactions with the caregiver. The relationship thus provides an opportunity for the mother to shape both the developing physiology and the behavior of her offspring, through her patterned interactions with the infant. Behavioral adaptations to environmental change occurring in the life of the mother can thus lead to biological changes in the offspring—a novel evolutionary mechanism.

Conceptually, the results of our research have moved us from using a hierarchical goal-corrected control system as our model, to using a self-organizing regulatory system composed of mother and infant as a unit. In this way of thinking about close relationships, a great deal more is regulated than the proximity of the infant to the mother, as described above. The behaviors and responses that Bowlby sought to explain are now viewed as part of a larger whole, shaped and even determined by processes that Bowlby did not envision, and in turn influencing and making possible features of the whole that fall outside of Bowlby's attachment system. A major advantage of viewing the mother–infant interaction as the unit of understanding is that the regulatory effects of the infant on the mother are included, and their role in the formations of her internal working model can be readily understood. The bidirectional flow of signals and other forms of regulatory exchange are not included in the control system of attachment theory, although these play an important role in proximity maintenance as well as in the formation of internal working models of the relationship.

The discovery of regulatory processes hidden within the observable parent–infant interactions, which occur in a rhythmic pattern during the early lives of mammals, provides a very different way to explain the dramatic observations that led Bowlby to formulate his theory of attachment: the responses of children to separation. The word "loss" has long been used in connection with grief and the response to separation. But what is lost and how this loss comes about can now be specified. The role of attachment behavior can now be seen in a new light: It provides the "glue" that holds mother and infant together and allows the whole mutual regulatory system to be formed and maintained.

In the foregoing, we have emphasized the ways in which recent research has led us to question some of the central tenets of John Bowlby's theory. Yet as long ago as 1958, Bowlby called for a "far-reaching programme of experimentation . . . with ethological concepts and methods . . . into the social responses in the preverbal period of infancy" (p. 365). We believe that Bowlby would delight in the ways that this "programme" has contributed thus far to the growth of our understanding of the mother–infant relationship, which he did so much to advance.

In the spirit of Bowlby (who, as noted earlier, began the first volume of his trilogy with a chapter entitled "Observations to Be Explained"), we offer further questions to be investigated, some of which are already the subject of study in a number of laboratories:

• What is the precise relation between the development of proximity seeking and separation or loss responses? Is the achievement of one necessary for the emergence of the other? If so, what mechanisms link them?
• Can individual differences in separation and reunion responses be modeled in the laboratory by programmed differences in the early mother–infant interaction? If so, what biobehavioral mechanisms underlie this plasticity?
• Do individual differences in separation responses arise from genetically based substrates?

A selective breeding study in our laboratory is now investigating this possibility.
• How might a psychophysiologically integrated fear response to separation as a danger signal develop from the primitive separation "anxiety" that results from the disruption of maternal regulation?
• How do maternal regulators arise? Are there prenatal antecedents? Why do they persist when pups are fully mobile and capable of free living? What are the implications of these systems for development throughout the lifespan?
• What is the neural basis of infant rats' ontogenetic learning adaptations?
• What is the relation of later differentiated affects to early primitive affective states, such as norepinephrine-mediated activation, opioid-mediated suckling reward, and benzodiazepine-receptor-mediated separation and comfort responses?
• What is the relation between filial preferences and other social attachments through the life cycle, such as mate selection ("sexual imprinting") and parental behavior? Do characteristics of early experience and/or biological substrates influence the quality (security) of attachment in infancy *and* adulthood?

What brain structures underlie these early attachment and separation response systems?

Clinical research on human infant attachment is coming of age. Attachment has already acquired status as a causal agent; its disturbances are often hypothesized to contribute to social and psychological pathologies of childhood (Main, 1996). At this juncture, it is critical for basic researchers to provide clinical researchers and clinicians with clarity concerning the biobehavioral origins of attachment. We have advanced a point of view indicating that the concept of attachment in infant rats has also come of age. We have presented evidence that the infant rat develops a surprisingly complex attachment relationship to its mother—one that has operationally defined behavioral, motivational, neurochemical, and representational aspects. We believe that as investigation into the development of attachment in the infant rat proceeds, this model will begin to inform new hypotheses concerning the biobehavioral bases of normal human infant attachment, as well as of disorders of human infancy (e.g., anaclitic depression, failure to thrive, separation anxiety, autism, etc.) that may involve primary or secondary disturbances of filial attachment.

REFERENCES

Ainsworth, M. D. S., Blehar, M. C., Waters, E., & Wall, S. (1978). *Patterns of attachment: A psychological study of the strange situation.* Hillsdale, NJ: Erlbaum.

Amsel, A. (1992). *Frustration theory: An analysis of dispositional learning and memory.* New York: Cambridge University Press.

Blass, E. M., & Ciaramitaro, V. (1994). Oral determinants of state, affect, and action in newborn humans. *Monographs of the Society for Research in Child Development, 59* (1, Serial No. 239), 1–96.

Blass, E. M., Fillion, T. J., Weller, A., & Brunson, L. (1990). Separation of opioid from nonopioid mediation of affect in neonatal rats: Nonopioid mechanisms mediate maternal contact influences. *Behavioral Neuroscience, 104,* 625–636.

Blass, E. M., & Fitzgerald, E. (1988). Milk-induced analgesia and comforting in 10-day-old rats: Opioid mediation. *Pharmacology, Biochemistry and Behavior, 29,* 9–13.

Blass, E. M., & Shide, D. J. (1993). Endogenous cholecystokinin reduces vocalization in isolated 10-day-old rats. *Behavioral Neuroscience, 107,* 488–492.

Blumberg, M. S., & Wasserman, E. A. (1995). Animal mind and the argument from design. *American Psychologist, 50,* 133–144.

Bowlby, J. (1958). The nature of the child's tie to his mother. *International Journal of Psycho-Analysis, 39,* 350–371.

Bowlby, J. (1969/1982). *Attachment and loss: Vol. 1. Attachment.* New York: Basic Books.

Bowlby, J. (1973). *Attachment and loss: Volume 2. Separation.* New York: Basic Books.

Bowlby, J. (1980). *Attachment and loss: Volume 3. Loss.* New York: Basic Books.

Brake, S. (1981). Suckling infant rats learn a preference for a novel olfactory stimulus paired with milk delivery. *Science, 211,* 506–508.

Brake, S. C., & Hofer, M. A. (1980). Maternal separation and "dry" suckling influences nonnutritive sucking responses in neonatal rat pups. *Physiology and Behavior, 24,* 185–189.

Bretherton, I. (1985). Attachment theory: Retrospect and prospect. In I. Bretherton & E. Waters (Eds.), *Growing points of attachment theory and research. Monographs of the Society for Research in Child Development, 50*(1–2, Serial No. 209), 3–35.

Camp, L. L., & Rudy, J. W. (1988). Changes in the categorization of appetitive and aversive events during postnatal development of the rat. *Developmental Psychobiology, 21,* 25–42.

Cramer, C. P., & Blass, E. M. (1983). Mechanisms of control of milk intake in suckling rats. *American Journal of Physiology, 245 (Regulatory Integrative Comparative Physiology, 14),* R154–R159.

Darwin, C. (1981). *The descent of man, and selection in relation to sex* (2 vols.). Princeton, NJ: Princeton University Press. (Original work published 1871)

Fifer, W. P., & Moon, C. (1995). The effects of fetal experience with sound. In J. P. Lecanuet, N. A. Krasnegor, W. P. Fifer, & W. P. Smotherman (Eds.), *Fetal development: A psychobiological perspective* (pp. 351–366). Hillsdale, NJ: Erlbaum.

Gregory, E. H., & Pfaff, D. W. (1971). Development of olfactory guided behavior in infant rats. *Physiology and Behavior, 6,* 573–576.

Hall, W. G., Cramer, C. P., & Blass, E. M. (1977). Ontogeny of suckling in rats: Transitions toward adult ingestion. *Journal of Comparative and Physiological Psychology, 91,* 1141–1155.

Harlow, H. F. (1961). The development of affectional patterns in infant monkeys. In B. M. Foss (Ed.), *Determinants of infant behaviour* (Vol. 1., pp. 75–88). London: Methuen.

Harlow, H. F., & Zimmerman, R. R. (1959). Affectional responses in the infant monkey. *Science, 130,* 421–431.

Hepper, P. G. (1987). The amniotic fluid: An important priming role in kin recognition. *Animal Behaviour, 35,* 1343–1346.

Hofer, M. A. (1975). Studies on how early maternal separation produces behavioral change in young rats. *Psychosomatic Medicine, 37,* 245–264.

Hofer, M. A. (1983). On the relationship between attachment and separation processes in infancy. In R. Plutchik & H. Kellerman (Eds.), *Emotion: Theory, research, and experience* (Vol. 2, pp. 199–216). New York: Academic Press.

Hofer, M. A. (1995). Hidden regulators: Implications for a new understanding of attachment, separation, and loss. In S. Goldberg, R. Muir, & J. Kerr (Eds.), *Attachment theory: Social, developmental, and clinical perspectives* (pp. 203–230). Hillsdale, NJ: Analytic Press.

Hofer, M. A. (1996). Multiple regulators of ultrasonic vocalization in the infant rat. *Psychoneuroendocrinology, 21,* 203–217.

Hofer, M. A., Brunelli, S. A., Masmela, J., & Shair, H. N. (1996). Maternal interactions prior to separation potentiate isolation-induced calling in rat pups. *Behavioral Neuroscience, 110,* 1158–1167.

Hofer, M.A., Fisher, A., & Shair, H. (1981). Effects of infraorbital nerve section on survival, growth, and suckling behaviors of developing rats. *Journal of Comparative and Physiological Psychology, 95,* 123–133.

Hofer, M. A., Shair, H., & Singh, P. (1976). Evidence that maternal ventral skin substances promote suckling in infant rats. *Physiology and Behavior, 17,* 131–136.

Hunsaker, D. (1977). Behavior of new world marsupials. In D. Hunsaker (Ed.), *The biology of marsupials* (pp. 279–347). New York: Academic Press.

Igel, G. J., & Calvin, A. D. (1960). The development of affectional responses in infant dogs. *Journal of Comparative Physiology and Psychology, 53,* 302–305.

Johanson, I. B., & Hall, W. G. (1979). Appetitive learning in 1-day-old rat pups. *Science, 205,* 419–421.

Johanson, I. B., Turkewitz, G., & Hamburgh, M. (1980). Development of home orientation in hypothyroid and hyperthyroid rat pups. *Developmental Psychobiology, 13,* 331–342.

Kenny, J. T., & Blass, E. M. (1977). Suckling as an incentive to instrumental learning in preweanling rats. *Science, 196,* 898–899.

King, J. A. (1963). Maternal behavior in Peromyscus. In H. L. Rheingold (Ed.), *Maternal behavior in mammals* (pp. 58–93). New York: Wiley.

Kraemer, G. (1992). A psychobiological theory of attachment. *Behavioral and Brain Sciences, 15,* 493–541.

Leon, M. (1974). Maternal pheromone. *Physiology and Behavior, 13,* 441–453.

Leon, M. (1992). The neurobiology of filial learning. *Annual Review of Psychology, 43,* 377–398.

Main, M. (1991). Metacognitive knowledge, metacognitive monitoring, and singular (coherent) vs. multiple (incoherent) models of attachment: Findings and directions for future research. In C. M. Parkes, J. Stevenson-Hinde, & P. Marris (Eds.), *Attachment across the life cycle* (pp. 127–159). London: Tavistock/Routledge.

Main, M. (1995). Recent studies in attachment: Overview, with selected implications for clinical work. In S. Goldberg, R. Muir, & J. Kerr (Eds.), *Attachment theory: Social, developmental, and clinical perspectives* (pp. 407–474). Hillsdale, NJ: Analytic Press.

Main, M. (1996). Introduction to the special section on attachment and psychopathology: 2. Overview of the field of attachment. *Journal of Consulting and Clinical Psychology, 64,* 237–243.

Mellon, R. C., Kraemer, P. J., & Spear, N. E. (1991). Development of intersensory function: Age-related differences in stimulus selection of multimodal compounds in rats as revealed by Pavlovian conditioning. *Journal of Experimental Psychology: Animal Behavior Processes, 17,* 448–464.

Molina, J. C., Hoffman, H., Serwatka, J., & Spear, N. E. (1991). Establishing intermodal equivalence in preweanling and adult rats. *Journal of Experimental Psychology: Animal Behavior Processes, 17,* 433–447.

Moon, C., & Fifer, W. P. (1990). Syllables as signals for 2-day-old infants. *Infant Behavior and Development, 13,* 377–390.

Moon, C., Bever, T. G., & Fifer, W. P. (1992). Canonical and non-canonical syllable discrimination by two-day-old infants. *Journal of Child Language, 19,* 1–17.

Nyakas, C., & Endroczi, E. (1970). Olfaction guided approaching behaviour of infantile rats to the mother in maze box. *Acta Physiologica Academiae Scientiarum Hungaricae, 38,* 59–65.

Pedersen, P. E., & Blass, E. M. (1982). Prenatal and postnatal determinants of the first suckling episode in albino rats. *Developmental Psychobiology, 15,* 349–355.

Polan, H. J., & Hofer, M. A. (1998). Olfactory preference for mother over home next shavings by newborn rats. *Developmental Psychobiology, 33,* 5–20.

Polan, H. J., & Hofer, M. A. (in press). Maternally-directed orienting behaviors of newborn rats. *Developmental Psychobiology.*

Polan, H. J., Kajunski, E., & Hofer, M. A. (1995). Rat pups discriminate their mothers from nest shavings by olfaction. *Developmental Psychobiology, 29,* 293. (Abstract)

Polan, H. J., & Hofer, M. A. (1997). Differential orienting responses in neonatal rats: Origins of attachment? *Developmental Psychobiology, 30,* 237. (Abstract)

Rilling, M. E., & Neiworth, J. J. (1986). Comparative cognition: A general processes approach. In D. F. Kendricks, M. E. Rilling, & M. R. Denny (Eds.), *Theories of animal memory* (pp. 19–33). Hillsdale, NJ: Erlbaum.

Robertson, J. (1953). Some responses of young children to loss of maternal care. *Nursing Times, 49,* 382–386.

Robinson, S. R., Arnold, H. M., Spear, N. E., & Smotherman, W. P. (1993). Experience with milk and an artificial nipple promotes conditioned opioid activity in the rat fetus. *Developmental Psychobiology, 26,* 375–387.

Robinson, S. R., Hoeltzel, T. C., Cooke, K. M., Umphress, S. M., Smotherman, W. P., & Murrish, D. E. (1992). Oral capture and grasping of an artificial nipple by rat fetuses. *Developmental Psychobiology, 25,* 543–555.

Rosenblatt, J. S. (1983). Olfaction mediates developmental transition in the altricial newborn of selected species of mammals. *Developmental Psychobiology, 16,* 347–375.

Scott, J. P. (1963). Process of primary socialization in canine and human infants. *Monographs of the Society for Research in Child Development, 28*(1, Serial No. 85), 1–47.

Smith, B. A., Fillion, T. J., & Blass, E.M. (1990). Orally-mediated sources of calming in one to three day-old human infants. *Developmental Psychology, 26,* 731–737.

Smotherman, W. P., & Robinson, S. R. (1986). Environmental determinants of behaviour in the rat fetus. *Animal Behaviour, 34,* 1859–1873.

Smotherman, W. P., & Robinson, S. R. (1992). Prenatal experience with milk: Fetal behavior and endogenous opioid systems. *Neuroscience and Biobehavioral Reviews, 16,* 351–364.

Spear, N. E., Kraemer, P. J., Molina, J. C., & Smoller, D. E. (1988). Developmental change in learning and memory: Infantile disposition for unitization. In J. Delacour & J. C. S. Levy (Eds.), *Systems with learning and memory abilities* (pp. 27–52). Amsterdam: Elsevier.

Spear, N. E., & McKinzie, D. L. (1994). Intersensory integration in the infant rat. In D. J. Lefkowicz & R. Lickliter (Eds.), *The development of intersensory perception* (pp. 133–161). Hillsdale, NJ: Erlbaum.

Stern, D. (1985). *The interpersonal world of the infant.* New York: Basic Books.

Stoloff, M. L., Kenny, J. T., Blass, E. M., & Hall, W. G. (1980). The role of experience in suckling maintenance in albino rats. *Journal of Comparative and Physiological Psychology, 94,* 847–856.

Sullivan, R. M. (1996, November). *Neural correlates of neonatal olfactory learning.* Paper presented at the meeting of the International Society for Developmental Psychobiology, Washington, DC.

Sullivan, R. M., & Hall, W. G. (1988). Reinforcers in infancy: Classical conditioning using stroking or intra-oral infusions of milk as UCS. *Developmental Psychobiology, 21,* 215–223.

Sullivan, R. M., Hofer, M. A., & Brake, S. (1986). Olfactory-guided orientation in neonatal rats is enhanced by a conditioned change in behavioral state. *Developmental Psychobiology, 19,* 615–623.

Sullivan, R. M., Taborsky-Barbar, S., Mendoza, R., Itino, A., Leon, M., Cotman, C. W., Payne, T. F., & Lott, I. (1991). Olfactory classical conditioning in neonates. *Pediatrics, 87,* 511–518.

Sullivan, R. M., & Wilson, D. A. (1994). The locus coeruleus, norepinephrine, and memory in newborns. *Brain Research Bulletin, 35,* 467–472.

Teicher, M. H., & Blass, E. M. (1977). First suckling response of the newborn albino rat: The roles of olfaction and amniotic fluid. *Science, 198,* 635–636.

Tolman, E. C. (1932). *Purposive behavior in animals and men.* New York: Century.

Varendi, H., Porter, R. H., & Winberg, J. (1996). Attractiveness of amniotic fluid odor: Evidence of prenatal olfactory learning? *Acta Pediatrica, 85,* 1223–1227.

Wakerly, J. B., & Drewett, R. F. (1975). Pattern of suckling in the infant rat during spontaneous milk-ejection. *Physiology and Behavior, 15,* 277–281.

Wilson, D. A., & Sullivan, R. M. (1994). Neurobiology of associative learning in the neonate: Early olfactory learning. *Behavioral and Neural Biology, 61,* 1–18.

9

Attachment in Rhesus Monkeys

❖

STEPHEN J. SUOMI

Attachment is not an exclusively human phenomenon. Although the theory that John Bowlby conceived and developed during the 1950s and 1960s reflected his clinical observations of infants and young children (even in the face of his psychoanalytic training), it also had a strong basis in his knowledge of (and near-constant interest in) ethological studies of developmental phenomena in animals, especially nonhuman primates. Indeed, it can be argued that Bowlby (1969/1982) tailored several essential features of his attachment theory specifically to account for clear-cut commonalities in the strong behavioral and emotional ties that infants inevitably develop with their mothers—not only across all of humanity, but also among our closest evolutionary relatives.

At about the time that Bowlby published, with James Robertson, his seminal studies of infant separation via hospitalization (Robertson & Bowlby, 1952), he became aware of the classic ethological studies of filial imprinting in precocial birds. During this period, he developed a close friendship with Robert Hinde, a world-class ethologist at Cambridge University, who was in the process of shifting his own basic research interests from song-learning in birds to mother–infant interactions in rhesus monkeys. Hinde soon had rhesus monkey mothers raising babies in small captive social groups (e.g., Hinde, Rowell, & Spencer-Booth, 1964), and Bowlby came to recognize patterns of behavior

shown by the infant monkeys toward their mothers—but not toward other adult females in the group—that strikingly resembled recurrent response patterns of human infants and young children he had observed over years of clinical practice. These common patterns provided Bowlby with powerful evidence supporting his assumption that attachment has its basis in biology.

Indeed, virtually all of the basic features of human infant behavior that Bowlby's attachment theory specifically ascribed to our evolutionary history could be observed in the normative mother-directed behaviors of rhesus monkey infants described by Hinde and other primate researchers. For Bowlby (1958, 1969/1982), the fact that rhesus monkey infants and human babies share unique physical features, behavioral propensities, and emotional labilities linked to highly specific circumstances was consistent with the view that they also share significant parts of their respective evolutionary histories. He argued that these features, present in newborns of each species but often largely absent (or at least mostly hidden) in older individuals, represent successful adaptations to selective pressures over millions of years. To Bowlby, those characteristics common to human and monkey infants reflect evolutionary success stories and should be viewed as beneficial, if not essential, for survival of both the individual infant and the species.

What are those common characteristics—and

what is their relevance for attachment theorizing? This chapter begins by describing how attachment relationships between rhesus monkey infants and their mothers are normally established and maintained throughout development. Next, those features that are unique to rhesus monkey infant–mother attachment relationships are examined, as is conflict within these relationships. Attachment relationships in rhesus monkeys and other primates are subject to influence from a variety of sources, and some of these influences are reviewed next. Some long-term biobehavioral consequences of different early attachment experiences are then examined in detail. Finally, the implications for attachment theory of recent findings regarding cross-generational transmission of specific attachment patterns in rhesus monkey families are discussed.

NORMATIVE PATTERNS OF INFANT–MOTHER ATTACHMENT IN RHESUS MONKEYS

The first detailed longitudinal studies of species-normative attachment relationships in rhesus monkeys were carried out over 30 years ago (e.g., Hansen, 1966; Harlow, Harlow, & Hansen, 1963; Hinde & Spencer-Booth, 1967). These seminal investigations provided descriptions of infant behavioral development and emerging social relationships that not only appear remarkably accurate even in today's light, but also have been repeatedly shown to generalize to other rhesus monkey infants growing up in a range of naturalistic settings, as well as to infants of other Old World monkey and ape species (see Higley & Suomi, 1986, for one of many comprehensive reviews). Virtually all infants in these species spend their initial days, weeks, and (for infant apes) months of life in near-continuous physical contact with their biological mothers, typically clinging to the mothers' ventral surface for most of their waking (and all of their sleeping) hours each day. Rhesus monkey neonates clearly and consistently display four of the five "component instinctual responses" that Bowlby (1958) listed as universal human attachment behaviors in his initial monograph on attachment: sucking, clinging, crying, and following (the fifth, smiling, is universally seen in chimpanzee but not monkey infants). All of these response patterns reflect efforts on the part of the infant to obtain and maintain physical contact with or proximity to its mother.

Rhesus monkey mothers, in turn, provide their newborns with essential nourishment; physical and psychological warmth (e.g., Harlow, 1958); and protection from the elements, potential predators, and even other members of the social group, including pesky older siblings. During this time a strong and enduring social bond inevitably develops between mother and infant—a bond that is unique in terms of its exclusivity, constituent behavioral features, and ultimate duration. The attachment bond that a rhesus monkey infant inevitably develops with its mother is like no other social relationship it will experience in its lifetime, except (in reciprocal form) for a female when she grows up to have infants of her own. Furthermore, for a male infant this bond will last at least until puberty, while for a female it will be maintained as long as mother and daughter are both alive (Suomi, 1995).

In their second month of life, most rhesus monkey infants start using their mothers as a "secure base" from which to begin exploring their immediate physical and social environment. At this age monkey infants are inherently curious (Harlow, 1953), and most attempt to leave their mothers' side for brief periods as soon as they become physically able. Mothers typically monitor these attempts quite closely, and they often physically restrain their infants' efforts—or retrieve them if they have wandered beyond arm's length—at the slightest sign of potential danger. Numerous studies (e.g., Hinde & White, 1974) have demonstrated that at this stage of infant development the mother is primarily responsible for maintaining mutual contact and/or proximity. With the emergence of social fear in the infant's emotional repertoire between 2 and 3 months of age (functionally and developmentally equivalent to human infant 9-month "stranger anxiety"; cf. Sackett, 1966; Suomi & Harlow, 1976), this pattern reverses; thereafter, the infant is primarily responsible for maintaining proximity and actual physical contact with its mother.

Once any rhesus monkey infant has become securely attached to its mother, it can then use her as an established base from which to make exploratory ventures toward stimuli that have caught its curiosity. The infant soon learns that if it becomes frightened or is otherwise threatened by the stimuli it has sought out, it can always run back to its mother, who can provide immediate safety and comfort via mutual ventral contact even if she has not already actively intervened on its behalf. Several studies have documented that initiation of ventral contact with the mother promotes rapid decreases in hypothalamic–pituitary–adrenal (HPA) activity (as indexed by lowered plasma cortisol concentrations) and in sympathetic nervous system arousal (as indexed by reductions in heart rate), along with other physiological changes commonly associated with soothing (e.g., Gunnar, Gonzalez, Goodlin, & Levine, 1981; Mendoza, Smotherman, Miner, Kaplan, & Levine, 1978; Reite, Short, Seiler, & Pauley, 1981).

As they grow older, most monkey infants voluntarily spend increasing amounts of time at increasing distances from their mothers, apparently confident that they can return to the mothers' protective care without interruption or delay should circumstances warrant it. Their mothers' presence as a secure base clearly promotes exploration of their ever-expanding physical and social world (Dienske & Metz, 1977; Harlow et al., 1963; Simpson, 1979). On the other hand, when rhesus monkey infants develop less than optimal attachment relationships with their mothers, their exploratory behavior is inevitably compromised (e.g., Arling & Harlow, 1967; Suomi, 1995); this is consistent with Bowlby's observations regarding human attachment relationships (e.g., Bowlby, 1969/1982, 1988), as will be discussed later.

At about 3 months of age, monkey infants begin to develop distinctive social relationships with other members of their social group. Increasingly, these come to involve other infants of like age and comparable physical, cognitive, and socioemotional capabilities. Following weaning (usually in the fourth and fifth months) and essentially until puberty (during the third or fourth year), play with peers represents the predominant social activity for young monkeys (Ruppenthal, Harlow, Eisele, Harlow, & Suomi, 1974). During this time the play interactions become increasingly gender-specific and sex-segregated (i.e., males tend to play more with males, and females with females; e.g., Harlow & Lauersdorf, 1974). Peer play also becomes more and more behaviorally and socially complex, and by the third year the play bouts typically involve patterns of behavior that appear to simulate the full range of adult social activity (e.g., Suomi & Harlow, 1975). By the time they reach puberty, most rhesus monkey juveniles have had ample opportunity to develop, practice, and perfect behavioral routines that will be crucial for functioning as a normal adult, especially those patterns involved

in reproduction and in dominance/aggressive interactions (Suomi, 1979a). Virtually all of them have also maintained close ties with their mothers (e.g., Berman, 1982).

The onset of puberty is associated with major life transitions for both male and female rhesus monkeys. Adolescence is associated not only with major hormonal alterations, pronounced growth spurts, and other obvious physical changes, but also with major social changes for both sexes (Suomi, Rasmussen, & Higley, 1992). Males experience the most dramatic and serious social disruptions: They sever all social ties not only with their mothers and other kin, but also with all others in their natal social troop. Virtually all of these adolescent males soon join all-male "gangs," and after several months most of them then attempt to enter a different established troop—typically one composed entirely of individuals of all ages and both genders, and largely unfamiliar to the adolescent males (Berard, 1989). Field data show that the process of natal group emigration represents an exceedingly dangerous transition for adolescent males. The mortality rate for these males from the time they leave their natal group until they become successfully integrated into another full-fledged group can be as high as 50%, depending on local circumstances (e.g., Dittus, 1979). Recent field studies have also identified and characterized substantial interindividual variability in both the timing of male emigration and the basic strategies followed in attempting to join other established social groups (Mehlman et al., 1995; Suomi et al., 1992).

Adolescent females, by contrast, never leave their maternal family or natal social group (Lindburg, 1971). Puberty for them is instead associated with increases in social activities directed toward maternal kin, typically at the expense of interactions with unrelated peers. Family interactions are heightened even more when these young females begin to have offspring of their own. Indeed, the birth of a new infant (especially to a new mother) often has the effect of "invigorating" the matriline—drawing its members closer both physically and socially, and, conversely, providing a buffer from external threats and stressors for mother and infant alike. Rhesus monkey females continue to be involved in family social affairs for the rest of their lives, even after they cease having infants of their own. Thus their experiences with specific attachment relationships tend to be lifelong (Suomi, 1998).

UNIQUE ASPECTS OF RHESUS MONKEY INFANT–MOTHER ATTACHMENT RELATIONSHIPS

Is infant–mother attachment different from any or all other social relationships a young rhesus monkey (or, for that matter, a human infant) will establish during its lifetime? Some aspects of the attachment relationship are clearly exclusive to the mother–infant dyad, because only the mother, and nobody else, provides an infant not only with all that passes through the placenta, but also with a prenatal environment uniquely attuned to her own circadian and other biological rhythms. In addition, there is increasing evidence of predictable fetal reactions that can be traced to specific activities (including vocalizations) of the mother, perhaps providing the basis for exclusive multimodal proto-communication between mother and fetus (e.g., Busnell & Granier-Deferre, 1981; DeCasper & Fifer, 1980; Fifer, 1987; Schneider, 1992). Such types of prenatal stimulation are, of course, routinely (and exclusively) provided by pregnant females of virtually all mammalian species, except perhaps for the egg-laying monotremes.

Some of these aspects of maternal support and stimulation are basically continued into an infant's initial postnatal months, including obviously the mother's status as the primary (if not sole) source of its nutrition. Mothers also keep sharing their own specific antibodies with their infants postnatally via the nursing process. Moreover, the essentially continuous contact or proximity between a mother and newborn provides the infant with extended exposure to its mother's odor, taste (of milk, at least), relative warmth, sound, and sight, representing a range and intensity of social stimulation seldom if ever provided by any other family or group members. In addition, rhesus monkey mothers continue to communicate their internal circadian and other biological rhythms to their offspring via extended ventral–ventral contact, and there is some evidence that their offspring typically develop synchronous parallel rhythms during their initial weeks of life (cf. Boyce, Champoux, Suomi, & Gunnar, 1995). As before, these maternally specific postnatal aspects of infant support and stimulation are not limited to the higher primates, but instead are characteristic of mothers of virtually all mammalian species (including the monotremes), at least up to the time of weaning (e.g., Hofer, 1995). But other aspects of a rhesus monkey mother's relationship with her infant are not shared by other mammalian mothers, not even by mothers of some other primate species.

What are these unique features of a rhesus monkey (and human) mother's relationship with her infant? It turns out that they are the very characteristics that Bowlby made the defining features of infant–mother attachment: (1) the mother's ability to reduce fear in her infant via direct social contact and other soothing behavior, and (2) the mother's capacity to provide a secure base to support her infant's exploration of the environment. Numerous longitudinal studies of rhesus monkey social ontogeny, carried out in both laboratory and field environments, have consistently found that mothers have a virtual monopoly on these capabilities—or at least the opportunity to express them with their infants (e.g., Berman, 1982; Harlow & Harlow, 1965). Thus, rhesus monkey infants rarely if ever use other group members (even close relatives) as secure bases, or even as reliable sources of ventral contact (Suomi, 1979b). Moreover, on those occasions when they "mistakenly" seek the company of someone other than their mothers, they are unlikely to experience decreases in physiological arousal comparable to those resulting from contact with their mothers; often, they experience increases in arousal instead.

The attachment relationship a rhesus monkey infant establishes with its mother differs in other fundamental ways from all other social relationships it will ever develop during its lifetime. Although numerous laboratory and field studies have shown that a rhesus monkey routinely develops a host of distinctive relationships with different siblings, peers, and adults of both sexes throughout development, each is strikingly different from the initial attachment to the mother in terms of primacy, constituent behaviors, reciprocity, and course of developmental change (Suomi, 1979b). Given these findings, perhaps Bowlby was not entirely correct when he argued that the infant's attachment to the mother provides the prototype for all subsequent social relationships (Bowlby, 1969/1982). On the other hand, Bowlby was absolutely correct (at least for rhesus monkeys) when he argued that the nature of the specific attachment relationship an infant develops with the mother can profoundly affect both concurrent and future relationships the infant may develop with others in its social sphere, as will be discussed in detail later.

A different issue regarding unique aspects of rhesus monkey attachment concerns not whether infant–mother attachment differs from other social relationships with conspecifics, but rather whether attachment as originally defined by Bowlby generalizes to other species, including other primates. As outlined above, Bowlby clearly believed that basic features of attachment phenomena are essentially homologous in rhesus monkey infants and human babies—but are these characteristic features of attachment seen in other mammalian species as well? It all depends on how one defines "attachment," or such terms as "partner preference" and "imprinting."

Without question, infant preference for the mother (and vice versa) represents an exceedingly widespread phenomenon across most mammalian and avian species, as well as in numerous other taxa (Wilson, 1975). One specific (and, for Bowlby, a particularly relevant) form of partner preference involves "imprinting." According to Lorenz's (1937) classical definition, imprinting is restricted to those partner preferences that are (1) acquired during a critical (or "sensitive") period (or "phase"), (2) irreversible, (3) generally species-specific, and (4) typically established prior to any behavioral manifestation of the preference. According to this definition, imprinting-like phenomena can be observed in numerous insect, fish, avian, and mammalian species, including most if not all primates (Immelmann & Suomi, 1981).

On the other hand, it can be argued that infant–mother attachment as originally defined by Bowlby (1958, 1969/1982) represents a special case of imprinting that may itself be limited largely to Old World monkeys, apes, and humans (Suomi, 1995). To be sure, infants of all the other primate species (i.e., prosimians and New World monkeys) are initially at least as dependent on their mothers for survival, and spend at least as much time in physical contact with them, as rhesus monkey (and human) infants (Higley & Suomi, 1986). In these other primate species, however, the predominant form of mother–infant physical contact is usually different (dorsal–ventral vs. ventral–ventral); the frequency and diversity of mother–infant interactions are generally reduced; the patterns of developmental change differ dramatically; and, most importantly, the basic (indeed defining) features of attachment are largely absent.

Consider the case of capuchin monkeys (*Cebus apella*), a highly successful New World species whose natural habitat covers much of South America, including both Amazonian and Andean regions. These primates are remarkable in many respects, not the least of which is an amazing capability for manufacturing and using tools to manipulate their physical environment (Darwin, 1794; Visalberghi, 1990). In this respect they are clearly superior to rhesus monkeys—and, for that matter, all other primates except chimpanzees and humans. On the other hand, capuchin mother–infant relationships seem somewhat primitive by rhesus monkey standards.

A capuchin monkey spends virtually all of the first 3 months of life clinging to its mother's back, moving ventrally only during nursing bouts (Welker, Becker, Hohman, & Schafer-Witt, 1987). During this time there is very little visual, vocal, or grooming interaction between mother and infant, in marked contrast to a rhesus monkey infant, who by 3 months of age is already participating in extensive one-on-one interactions involving a wealth of visual, auditory, olfactory, tactile, and vestibular stimulation, and who typically has been using its mother as a secure base for exploration for over 2 months. When capuchin monkeys finally get off their mothers' backs in their fourth month, they seem surprisingly independent and can spend long periods away from the mothers without getting upset. If frightened, they are almost as likely to seek protective contact from other group members as from their mothers (Byrne & Suomi, 1995). At this age and thereafter, capuchin monkey youngsters spend only about one third as much time grooming their mothers as rhesus monkeys do, and their other activities with the mothers are not markedly different from their activities with siblings, peers, or unrelated adults (Byrne & Suomi, 1995; Welker, Becker, & Schafer-Witt, 1990), in sharp contrast to rhesus monkey of comparable age. All in all, capuchin monkey infants seem far less attached to their biological mothers in terms of the prominence of the relationship, the relative uniqueness of constituent behaviors, and the nature and degree of secure-base-mediated exploration. One wonders how Bowlby's attachment theory might have looked if Hinde had been studying capuchin rather than rhesus monkeys!

Comparative studies of infant–mother relationships in other New World monkey and prosimian species have found that in most cases the relationships more closely resemble those of capuchin monkeys than those of rhesus monkeys (e.g., Fragaszy, Baer, & Adams-Curtis, 1991); in a few species (e.g., some marmosets and tamarins), the mother is not even an infant's primary caregiver (Higley & Suomi, 1986). To be sure, infants in all these primate species appear to be "imprinted" on their mothers, according to Lorenz's (1937) definition. However, attachment involves considerably more developmental complexity and reciprocity, especially with respect to secure-base phenomena, than do classical notions of imprinting. Indeed, it can be argued that, strictly speaking, attachment represents a special, *restricted case* of imprinting. Moreover, because infant–mother attachment is most apparent in humans and their closest phylogenetic kin, it also may well represent a relatively recent evolutionary adaptation among primates (Suomi, 1995).

CONFLICT IN RHESUS MONKEY INFANT–MOTHER RELATIONSHIPS

The relationships that rhesus monkeys develop with their mothers over time involve many behavioral patterns that go beyond attachment phenomena per se (Hinde, 1976). Indeed, a rhesus monkey female is extensively involved in a wide variety of interactions with her mother virtually every day that both are alive (and a male is thus involved every day until adolescence). However, this does not mean that all of these interactions are uniformly positive and pleasant. To the contrary, conflicts between mothers and offspring are frequent and often predictable, if not inevitable, occurrences in everyday rhesus monkey social life.

Sociobiologists have long argued that although mothers and infants share many genes and (therefore) many long-term goals, their short-term interests are not always mutual, and hence periodic conflict is inevitable (Trivers, 1974). Regardless of the validity of this view, an obvious instance of parent–offspring conflict occurs for virtually every rhesus monkey infant at around 20 weeks of age, when its mother begins to wean it from her own milk to solid food. Whether this process begins because the mother "wants" her infant to cease nursing (so she can stop lactating, begin cycling, and be able to produce another offspring, as the sociobiologists propose); because she "knows" that she cannot continue to produce enough milk to sustain her infant's rapidly growing energy requirements; or because her infant's erupting teeth make nursing increasingly uncomfortable is certainly open to question. What *is* clear is that weaning is almost always associated with significant changes in the basic nature of the infant's relationship with its mother, and those changes are seldom placid (e.g., Hinde & White, 1974).

Mothers, for their part, make increasingly frequent efforts to deny their infants access to their nipples, albeit with considerable variation in the precise form, timing, and intensity of their weaning behavior, ranging from the exquisitely subtle to what borders on abuse. Infants, on the other hand, dramatically increase their efforts to obtain and maintain physical contact with their mothers, even when nipple contact is not attainable. As with mothers, there is substantial variation in the nature, intensity, and persistence of the infants' efforts to prevent or at least delay the weaning process (Berman, Rasmussen, & Suomi, 1993). In virtually all cases, an infant's newfound preoccupation with maintaining maternal contact clearly inhibits its exploratory behavior, and noticeably alters and diminishes its interactions with peers (and often other kin) as well. Indeed, it usually takes a month or more (if at all) before those interaction patterns return to some semblance of normality (Hinde & White, 1974; Ruppenthal et al., 1974). Weaning therefore appears to undermine basic attachment security for the infant, perhaps permanently in some cases.

Postweaning "normality" for a young rhesus monkey seldom lasts for more than a few additional weeks before a second form of conflict with its mother typically arises. Most mothers return to reproductive receptivity at about the time their infants are 6–7 months old, at which point they begin actively soliciting selected adult males for the next 2 or 3 months (rhesus monkeys are seasonal breeders in nature). Throughout this period they may enter into consort relationships with several different males, typically lasting 1–3 days each. During this time a female and her chosen partner usually leave the main body of the monkey troop for most (if not all) of the time they are together, often seeking relative seclusion to avoid harassment or other interruptions from other troop members (Manson & Perry, 1993). At the same time, the offspring from the previous year's consort tends to be ignored, actively avoided, or even physically rejected by both the mother and her current mate (Berman, Rasmussen, & Suomi, 1994).

Not surprisingly, most rhesus monkey yearlings become quite upset in the face of such functional maternal separations; indeed, a few actually develop dramatic behavioral and physiological symptoms that parallel Bowlby's (1960, 1973) descriptions of separation-induced depression in human infants and young children (Suomi, 1995). Most of their cohorts likewise exhibit an initial period of intense protest following loss of access to their mothers, but soon begin directing their attention elsewhere. Interestingly, female offspring "left behind" by their mothers during consorts tend to seek out other family members during their mothers' absence, whereas young males are more likely to increase interactions with peers while their mothers are away (Berman et al., 1994). These gender differences in the prototypical response to maternal separation at 6–7 months of age thus appear to presage the much more dramatic gender differences in life course that emerge during adolescence and continue throughout adulthood.

It would seem that a rhesus monkey mother would always have the upper hand in conflicts with her offspring during both weaning and breeding periods, given her great size and strength advantage over even the most persistent 5- to 7-month-old infant. A number of research findings, however, suggest that infants bring resources of their own into these conflicts. For example, Simpson, Simpson, Hooley, and Zunz (1981) reported that infants who remained in physical contact with their mothers more and explored less during the preweaning months were more likely to delay the onset of weaning by several weeks, and in some cases even to preempt their mothers' cycling during the normal breeding season; this pattern was especially clear for male infants. More recently, Berman et al. (1993) found that infants who achieved the most frequent nipple contacts with their mothers during the breeding season had mothers who were least likely to conceive, even if they entered into relationships with multiple consorts during that period. The end result in both cases was that these infants could, by their own actions, "postpone" their mothers' next pregnancy for another year, thus gaining additional opportunities for unfettered access to her not shared by agemates whose mothers had become pregnant during the same period. In the process, such an infant was also able to postpone by at least a year the appearance of a new source of conflict—that of "rivalry" with the mother's next infant.

The birth of a new sibling has major consequences for a yearling rhesus monkey. From that moment on, the yearling's relationship with the mother is altered dramatically, especially with respect to attachment-related activities. No longer is a yearling the primary focus of its mother's attention. Instead, many of its attempts to use her as a source of security and comfort are often ignored or rebuffed, especially when its newborn sibling is nursing or merely clinging to the mother's ventrum (Suomi, 1982). Moreover, whenever the yearling tries to push its younger sibling off the mother, to obstruct its access to her, or to disrupt its activity when it moves away from her, the mother's most likely response is to physically punish the yearling quickly, without warning, and often with considerable severity. In contrast, the mother seldom if ever punishes the younger sibling when it interrupts the yearling's attempts to interact with her or otherwise disrupts the yearling's activities (Berman, 1992).

Thus the arrival of a younger sibling inevitably alters the yearling's attachment relationship with its mother. This relationship generally continues to wane (i.e., proximity seeking and secure-base exploratory behavior both diminish) throughout the rest of the childhood years, especially after the birth of each succeeding sibling. For males, the waning process continues into puberty, eventually culminating with their natal troop emigration, which effectively terminates any remnant of their relationship with their mothers. Although attachment-related activities likewise decline throughout childhood for females, the daughters tend to increase other forms of affiliative interaction with their mothers (e.g., mutual grooming bouts), most notably after they start having offspring of their own. Coincidentally, episodes involving obvious conflict with their mothers become increasingly frequent for both male and female offspring as they approach puberty; thereafter, any semblance of attachment-like behavior directed toward mothers is infrequent at best among daughters and, of course, impossible for sons once they have left their natal troop (Suomi, 1998).

FACTORS INFLUENCING ATTACHMENT RELATIONSHIPS IN RHESUS MONKEYS

Although Bowlby (1969/1982) believed that attachment has a strong biological basis and represents the product of evolutionary processes, he also observed that there is substantial variation among mother–infant dyads in fundamental aspects of their attachment relationships, and he recognized the potential developmental significance of such variation. Indeed, he lived to see his research associate Mary Ainsworth's strange situation assessment paradigm become almost reified in its identification and characterization of different "types" (viz., A, B, C, and [more recently] D) and even "subtypes" (e.g., A1, A2, B3,

or B4) of human infant–mother attachment relationships (e.g., Goldberg, 1995). Perhaps not surprisingly, there appears to be comparable variation in the attachment relationships formed by
different rhesus monkey mother–infant dyads.
Indeed, there exist compelling parallels in rhesus
monkey attachment relationships to each of the
major human attachment types, and at least ar-
guable similarities for most of the classical subtypes (e.g., Higley & Suomi, 1989). Moreover,
an increasing body of research has identified numerous factors that clearly can influence the nature and ultimate developmental trajectory of
these different attachment relationships. Some of
these influences derive from characteristics of
the infant, some from characteristics of the
mother, and still others to factors external to the
mother–infant dyad.

Rhesus monkey infants are born with distinctive physical and physiognomic features, relatively mature sensory systems with preestab-
lished preferences and biases, and behavioral
propensities that serve to promote essential contact with their mothers. These include not only
the above-mentioned "component instinctual responses" identified by Bowlby (1958), but also
the full range of items on the Brazelton Neonatal
Assessment Scale (Brazelton, 1973), as adapted
for monkeys with surprisingly minimal modification (e.g., Schneider & Suomi, 1992). To the
extent that any of these species-normative features, preferences, or propensities might be compromised in individual monkeys as a result of genetic defects, fetal insults, and/or perinatal
complications, one might expect some degree of
disruption in their emerging relationships with
their mothers. Indeed, the literature generally
bears this out, although there are compelling
anecdotal reports of mothers (and others in the
social group) who make compensatory adjustments in long-term support of offspring who are
clearly developmentally disabled (e.g., Fedigan
& Fedigan, 1977). On the other hand, cases of severe infant developmental disability in which the
affected individual survives beyond infancy are
relatively rare in the wild. A more common
source of infant variance in rhesus monkey attachment relationships comes from differences
among infant monkeys in their temperamental
characteristics and the physiological processes
that underlie their behavioral expression.

Researchers studying rhesus and other monkey species in both laboratory and field settings
have long recognized developmentally stable individual differences along certain temperamental
dimensions. Perhaps the most thoroughly studied
area of monkey temperamental research to date
has focused on individual differences in prototypical biobehavioral response to environmental
novelty and/or challenge. Several sets of investigators have identified a subgroup of "high-reactive" monkeys, constituting perhaps 15–20% of
both wild and captive populations studied to
date, who consistently respond to such mildly
stressful situations with obvious behavioral expressions of fear and anxiety, as well as significant (and often prolonged) cortisol elevations,
unusually high and stable heart rates, and dramatic increases in central nervous system metabolism of the neurotransmitter norepinepherine
(e.g., Capitanio, Rasmussen, Snyder, Laudenslager, & Reite, 1986; Clarke & Boinski, 1995;
Suomi, 1981, 1983, 1991; Suomi, Kraemer,
Baysinger, & Delizio, 1981).

High-reactive monkeys can be readily identified in their first few weeks of life. Most begin
leaving their mothers later, and explore their
physical and social environments less, than the
other monkeys in their birth cohort. High-reactive infants also tend to be shy and withdrawn in
their initial encounters with peers. Laboratory
studies have shown that they exhibit higher and
more stable heart rates and greater cortisol output in such interactions than do their less reactive
agemates (Suomi, 1991). These distinctive behavioral and physiological features appear early
in infancy, they show remarkable interindividual
stability throughout development, and there is increasing evidence that they are highly heritable
(cf. Higley et al., 1993).

One consequence of such biobehavioral tendencies is that high-reactive infants tend to spend
more time with their mothers and less time with
peers during their initial weeks and months of
life. Their attachment relationships with their
mothers tend disproportionately to be "C"-like
(ambivalent), especially in the face of such challenges as brief separations from their mothers.
High-reactive young monkeys are also far more
likely to exhibit depressive-like reactions to
functional maternal separations during the breeding season, as described above, than the rest of
their birth cohort (cf. Berman et al., 1994; Suomi, 1995). On the other hand, a high-reactive infant may ultimately be more "successful" than
others in its peer group in postponing its mother's next pregnancy and, eventually, a new sibling
rival for her attention (Berman et al., 1993;
Simpson et al., 1981; Suomi, 1998). These and
other findings provide impressive evidence that

temperamental reactivity on the part of the infant can influence, if not alter substantially, fundamental aspects of its relationship with its mother throughout development.

Rhesus monkey infants in a second subgroup, constituting approximately 5–10% of populations studied to date, consistently exhibit response styles that are perhaps best described as highly impulsive in nature, especially in social settings (where such behavior often leads to aggressive exchanges). This temperamental pattern is most readily apparent in peer play interactions. Impulsive males in particular seem unable to moderate their behavioral responses to rough-and-tumble play initiations from peers, instead escalating initially benign play bouts into full-blown, tissue-damaging aggressive exchanges, disproportionately at their own expense (Higley, Suomi, & Linnoila, 1996). Prospective longitudinal studies have shown that individuals who develop such response patterns typically exhibit poor state control and significant deficits in visual orienting capabilities during their first month of life (Champoux, Suomi, & Schneider, 1994). They also tend to exhibit chronically low rates of brain metabolism of serotonin, a prominent inhibitory neurotransmitter implicated in ubiquitous aspects of metabolic, regulatory, and emotional functioning (cf. Coccaro & Murphy, 1990). In particular, impulsive monkeys consistently have lower cerebrospinal fluid (CSF) concentrations of the primary central serotonin metabolite, 5-hydroxyindoleacetic acid (5-HIAA), than their peers throughout development (e.g., Champoux, Higley, & Suomi, 1997; Higley & Suomi, 1996; Higley, King, et al., 1996; Mehlman et al., 1994). As is the case for high reactivity, these behavioral and neurochemical characteristics of impulsive aggressivion are remarkably stable throughout development, and they also appear to be highly heritable (cf. Higley et al., 1993; Higley & Suomi, 1996).

Highly impulsive rhesus monkeys typically develop difficult attachment relationships with their mothers. They seem to be unusually fussy in their initial weeks (reflecting their generally poor state control; cf. Champoux et al., 1994), and their conflicts with their mother intensify substantially during and shortly after the time of weaning (Suomi, in press). In Ainsworth's strange situation terminology, these infants tend to form "A"-like (avoidant) and "D"-like (disorganized) attachment relationships. As they grow older, highly impulsive youngsters usually continue to exhibit difficulties in their social interactions with their mothers, with peers, and with others in their social group, and these social problems generally carry over into adolescence and adulthood (cf. Higley & Suomi, 1996; Suomi, in press).

Thus, certain infant temperamental characteristics seem to have a strong influence on the nature and long-term course of mother–infant attachment relationships in rhesus monkeys. Numerous other studies have shown that differences among monkey mothers in their characteristic maternal "style" can also affect the type of attachment relationships they develop with their offspring. Although a comprehensive review of the relevant literature is beyond the scope of this chapter, it is worth noting that most primate females tend to be remarkably consistent in the specific manner in which they rear their infants, at least after their initial pregnancy (cf. Higley & Suomi, 1986; Suomi, 1987). It is also worth noting that some of the differences one can observe among monkey mothers in their respective maternal styles can be related to specific temperamental characteristics they displayed as infants, as well as the nature of the attachment relationship they formed with their own mothers (e.g., Champoux, Byrne, Delizio, & Suomi, 1992; Suomi, 1995, in press; Suomi & Ripp, 1983), as will be discussed later.

Factors other than infant temperament or maternal "style" per se can also influence emerging infant–mother attachment relationships in monkeys. For example, numerous studies carried out over the past 30 years have demonstrated that most rhesus monkey mothers, no matter what their characteristic maternal style might be, are usually highly sensitive to those aspects of their immediate physical and social environment that pose a potential threat to their infants' well-being, and they appear to adjust their maternal behavior accordingly (Berman, Rasmussen, & Suomi, 1997). Both laboratory and field studies have consistently shown that low-ranking mothers typically are much more restrictive of their infants' exploratory efforts than are high-ranking mothers, whose maternal style tends to be more "laissez-faire." The standard interpretation of these findings has been that low-ranking mothers risk reprisal from others if they try to intervene whenever their infants are threatened, so they minimize such risk by restricting their infants' exploration. High-ranking mothers usually have no such problem and hence can afford to let their infants explore as they please (cf. Suomi, 1998).

Other studies have found that mothers generally become more restrictive and increase their levels of infant monitoring when their immediate social environment becomes less stable, such as when major changes in dominance hierarchies take place or when a new male tries to join the social group. Changes in various aspects of the physical environment, such as the food supply's becoming less predictable, have also been associated with increases in maternal restriction of early infant exploration (e.g., Andrews & Rosenblum, 1991). For those infants whose opportunities to explore are chronically limited during their first few months of life, their ability to develop species-normative relationships with others in their social group (especially peers) can be compromised, often with long-term consequences for both the infants and the troop (cf. Suomi, 1998).

EFFECTS OF DIFFERENTIAL ATTACHMENT RELATIONSHIPS ON LONG-TERM DEVELOPMENTAL TRAJECTORIES FOR RHESUS MONKEYS

Although considerable evidence from both field and laboratory studies has shown that individual differences among rhesus monkeys in certain temperamental characteristics tend to be quite stable from infancy to adulthood and are at least in part heritable, this does not mean that these behavioral and physiological features are necessarily fixed at birth or are immune to subsequent environmental influence. On the contrary, an increasing body of evidence from laboratory studies demonstrates that prototypical biobehavioral response patterns can be modified substantially by certain early experiences. In this respect, individual differences among monkeys in their early attachment relationships are especially relevant.

One set of studies has focused on rhesus monkey infants raised with peers instead of their biological mothers. Those infants were permanently separated from their biological mothers at birth; hand-reared in a neonatal nursery for their first month of life; housed with same-age, like-reared peers for the rest of their first 6 months; and then moved into larger social groups containing both peer-reared and mother-reared agemates. During their initial months, these infants readily developed strong social attachment bonds to each other, much as mother-reared infants develop attachments to their own mothers (Harlow, 1969). However, because peers are not nearly as effec-

tive as typical monkey mothers in reducing fear in the face of novelty, or in providing a "secure base" for exploration, the attachment relationships that these peer-reared infants developed were almost always "anxious" in nature (Suomi, 1995). As a result, while peer-reared monkeys showed completely normal physical and motor development, their early exploratory behavior was somewhat limited. They seemed reluctant to approach novel objects, and they tended to be shy in initial encounters with unfamiliar peers (Suomi, in press).

Even when peer-reared youngsters interacted with their same-age cagemates in familiar settings, their emerging social play repertoires were usually retarded in both frequency and complexity. One possible explanation for their relatively poor play performance is that their cagemates had to serve both as attachment figures and playmates—a dual role that neither mothers nor mother-reared peers have to fulfill. Another is that they faced difficulties in developing sophisticated play repertoires with basically incompetent play partners. Perhaps as a result of either or both these factors, peer-reared youngsters typically dropped to the bottom of their respective dominance hierarchies when they were grouped with mother-reared monkeys their own age (Higley, King, et al., 1996).

Several prospective longitudinal studies have found that peer-reared monkeys consistently exhibit more extreme behavioral, adrenocortical, and noradrenergic reactions to social separations than do their mother-reared cohorts, even after they have been living in the same social groups for extended periods (Higley & Suomi, 1989). Such differences in prototypical biobehavioral reactions to separation persist from infancy to adolescence, if not beyond. Interestingly, the general nature of the separation reactions of peer-reared monkeys seems to mirror that of "naturally occurring" high-reactive mother-reared subjects. In this sense, early rearing by peers appears to have the effect of making rhesus monkey infants generally more high-reactive than they might have been if reared by their biological mothers (Suomi, 1997).

Early rearing with peers has another long-term developmental consequence for rhesus monkeys: It tends to make them more impulsive, especially if they are males. Like the previously described impulsive monkeys growing up in the wild, peer-reared males initially exhibit aggressive tendencies in the context of juvenile play; as they approach puberty, the frequency and severity of their aggressive episodes typically exceed those of mother-reared group members of similar age. Peer-reared females tend to groom (and be groomed by) others in their social group less frequently and for shorter durations than their mother-reared counterparts, and, as noted above, they usually stay at the bottom of their respective dominance hierarchies. These differences between peer-reared and mother-reared agemates in aggression, grooming, and dominance remain relatively robust throughout the preadolescent and adolescent years (Higley, Suomi, & Linnoila, 1996). Peer-reared monkeys also consistently show lower CSF concentrations of 5-HIAA than their mother-reared counterparts. These group differences in 5-HIAA concentrations appear well before 6 months of age, and they remain stable at least throughout adolescence and into early adulthood (Higley & Suomi, 1996). Thus peer-reared monkeys as a group resemble the impulsive subgroup of wild-living (and mother-reared) monkeys, not only behaviorally but also in terms of decreased serotonergic functioning (Suomi, 1997).

Other laboratory studies utilizing peer-reared monkeys have disclosed additional differences from their mother-reared counterparts—differences that are not readily apparent in free-ranging populations of rhesus monkeys. For example, peer-reared adolescent and adult males require larger doses of the anesthetic ketamine to reach a comparable state of sedation. They also exhibit significantly higher rates of whole-brain glucose metabolism under mild isoflurane anesthesia, as determined by positron emission tomography (PET) imaging, than mother-reared controls (Doudet et al., 1995). Finally, peer-reared adolescent monkeys consistently consume larger amounts of alcohol under comparable *ad libitum* conditions than their mother-reared agemates (Higley, Hasert, Suomi, & Linnoila, 1991). Recent follow-up studies have demonstrated that the peer-reared subjects quickly develop a greater tolerance for alcohol; this can be predicted by their central nervous system serotonin turnover rates (Higley et al., in press), which in turn appear to be associated with differential serotonin transporter availability (Heinz et al., 1998).

This association between serotonin turnover rate and serotonin transporter availability has led to a collaboration with Lesch and his colleagues, who have recently identified and characterized the serotonin transporter gene (5-HTT) —a candidate gene for impaired serotonergic function,

in that it mediates serotonin neurotransmission and is a target both for antidepressant compounds such as Prozac and for certain drugs of abuse (Lesch et al., 1996). They have shown that length variation of the 5-HTT gene-linked polymorphic region (5-HTT-LPR) results in allelic variation in 5-HTT expression, such that the "short" allele of the 5-HTT-LPR confers low transcriptional efficiency to the 5-HTT gene promoter (relative to the "long" allele), suggesting that the low 5-HTT expression may result in decreased serotonergic function (Heils et al., 1998). Although this genetic polymorphism was first detected in humans, it also appears in rhesus monkeys; in fact, it is found uniquely among simian primates and humans (Lesch et al., 1997).

We have recently been able to apply polymerase-chain-reaction-based genotype analysis to most of the rhesus monkeys in our laboratory at the National Institutes of Health, in order to determine the relative frequencies of the "short" and "long" alleles of the 5-HTT gene. Some of these genotyped monkeys were peer-reared, while others were reared by their biological mothers since birth. We found that the relative frequency of subjects possessing the "short" 5-HTT allele did not differ significantly between the two rearing groups; this was not overly surprising, given that these monkeys had been more or less randomly preassigned to their respective rearing conditions at birth. Because we had collected CSF samples from these monkeys during their second and fourth years of life under comparable experimental conditions (and while they were all living in comparable social groups), it was possible to determine whether their 5-HIAA concentrations differed as a function of their 5-HTT polymorphic status, as might be expected from the extant literature. Interestingly, we did find such a predictive relationship, with individuals possessing the "short" allele having significantly lower 5-HIAA concentrations—*but only among peer-reared subjects.* For mother-reared subjects, 5-HIAA concentrations were essentially identical for monkeys with either allele (Bennett et al., 1998).

Thus there appears to be a significant genotype–environment *interaction* in the brain metabolism of serotonin, wherein the ultimate effect of a polymorphism in a specific gene for a given individual is, in fact, highly dependent on the specific early attachment experience of that individual. We are currently carrying out additional analyses involving other behavioral and physiological measures that have already been collected on those mother- and peer-reared monkeys whose 5-HTT polymorphic status has been individually specified. For example, we are now trying to determine whether rearing-condition differences in the incidence of impulsive aggressiveness per se can be traced to potentially different consequences of possessing the "short" allele as a function of peer vs. mother rearing, as appears to be the case for rearing-condition differences in 5-HIAA concentrations.

An additional risk that peer-reared females carry into adulthood concerns their maternal behavior. Peer-reared mothers are significantly more likely to exhibit neglectful and/or abusive treatment of their first born offspring than are their mother-reared counterparts, although their risk for inadequate maternal care is not nearly as great as is the case for females reared in social isolation; moreover, their care of subsequent offspring tends to improve dramatically (Ruppenthal, Arling, Harlow, Sackett, & Suomi, 1976). Nevertheless, most multiparous mothers who experienced early peer rearing continue to exhibit non-normative developmental changes in ventral contact with their offspring throughout the whole of their reproductive years (Champoux et al., 1992).

To summarize, early rearing by peers seems to make rhesus monkey infants both more highly reactive and more impulsive. Moreover, their resulting developmental trajectories not only resemble those of naturally occurring subgroups of rhesus monkeys growing up in the wild, but also persist in that vein long after their period of exclusive exposure to peers has been completed and they have been living in more species-typical social groups. Indeed, some effects of early peer rearing may well be passed on to the next generation via aberrant patterns of maternal care, as appears to be the case for both high-reactive and impulsive mothers rearing infants in their natural habitat (Suomi & Levine, 1998). As noted by Bowlby and other attachment theorists for the human case, the effects of inadequate early social attachments may be both lifelong and cross-generational in nature.

What about the opposite situation? That is, are there any consequences, either short- or long-term, of *enhanced* early social attachment relationships for rhesus monkeys? We attempted to address this question by rearing rhesus monkey neonates selectively bred for differences in temperamental reactivity with foster mothers who differed in their characteristic maternal "style," as determined by their patterns of care of previous offspring. In this work, specific members of a captive breeding colony were selectively bred to produce offspring who, on the basis of their genetic pedigree, were either unusually high-reactive or within the normal range of reactivity. These selectively bred infants were then cross-fostered to unrelated multiparous females preselected to be either unusually nurturant with respect to attachment-related behavior or within the normal range of maternal care of previous offspring. The selectively bred infants were then reared by their respective foster mothers for their first 6 months of life, after which they were moved to larger social groups containing other cross-fostered agemates, as well as those reared by their biological mothers (Suomi, 1987).

During the period of cross-fostering, control infants (i.e., those whose pedigrees suggested normative patterns of reactivity) exhibited essentially normal patterns of biobehavioral development, independent of the relative nurturance of their foster mother. In contrast, dramatic differences emerged among genetically high-reactive infants as a function of their type of foster mother: Whereas high-reactive infants cross-fostered to control females exhibited expected deficits in early exploration and exaggerated responses to minor environmental perturbations, high-reactive infants cross-fostered to nurturant females actually appeared to be behaviorally precocious. They left their mothers earlier, explored their environment more, and displayed less behavioral disturbance during weaning than not only the high-reactive infants cross-fostered to control mothers, but even the control infants reared by either type of foster mother. Their attachment relationships with their nurturant foster mothers thus appeared to be unusually secure (Suomi, 1987).

When these monkeys were permanently separated from their foster mothers and moved into larger social groups at 6 months of age, additional temperament–rearing interaction effects appeared, marked by optimal outcomes for those high-reactive youngsters who had been reared by nurturant foster mothers. These individuals became especially adept at recruiting and retaining other group members as allies during agonistic encounters; perhaps as a consequence, most rose to and maintained top positions in their group's dominance hierarchy. In contrast, high-reactive youngsters who had been foster-reared by control females tended to drop to and remain at the bottom of the same hierarchies (Suomi, 1991).

Finally, some of the cross-fostered females

from this study have since become mothers themselves, and their maternal behavior toward their firstborn offspring has been assessed. It appears that these young mothers have adopted the general maternal style of their foster mothers, independent of both their own original reactivity profile and the type of maternal style shown by their biological mothers. Thus the apparent benefits accrued by high-reactive females raised by nurturant foster mothers can seemingly be transmitted to the next generation of offspring, even though the mode of transmission is nongenetic in nature (Suomi & Levine, 1998). Clearly, high reactivity need not always be associated with adverse outcomes. Instead, following certain early experiences high-reactive infants appear to have relatively normal (if not actually optimal) long-term developmental trajectories, which in turn can be amenable to cross-generational transmission. Whether the same possibilities exist for genetically impulsive rhesus monkey infants is the focus of ongoing research.

These and other findings from studies with monkeys demonstrate that differential early social experiences can have major long-term influences on an individual's behavioral and physiological propensities, over and above any heritable predispositions. The nature of early attachment experiences appears to be especially relevant: Whereas insecure early attachments tend to make monkeys more reactive and impulsive, unusually secure early attachments seem to have essentially the opposite effect, at least for some individuals. In either case, the type of attachment relationship a rhesus monkey infant establishes with its mother (or mother substitute) can markedly affect its biobehavioral developmental trajectory, even long after its interactions with her have ceased (as is always the case for a male living in the wild).

CROSS-GENERATIONAL CONSEQUENCES OF EARLY ATTACHMENT RELATIONSHIPS: IMPLICATIONS FOR HUMAN ATTACHMENT THEORY

Among the most intriguing aspects of the long-term consequences of different early attachment experiences is the apparent transfer of specific features of maternal behavior across successive generations. Several studies of rhesus monkeys and other Old World monkey species have demonstrated strong continuities between the type of attachment relationship a female infant develops with her mother and the type of attachment relationship she develops with her own infant(s) when she becomes a mother herself. In particular, the pattern of ventral contact a female infant has with her mother (or mother substitute) during her initial months of life is a powerful predictor of the pattern of ventral contact she will have with her own infants during their first 6 months of life (Champoux et al., 1992; Fairbanks, 1989). This predictive cross-generational relationship is as strong in females who were foster-reared from birth by unrelated multiparous females as it is for females reared by their biological mothers, strongly suggesting that cross-generational transmission of at least one fundamental component of mother–infant attachment —patterning of mutual ventral contact—necessarily involves nongenetic mechanisms (Suomi & Levine, 1998). What those nongenetic mechanisms might be, and through what developmental processes they might act, are questions at the heart of ongoing investigations.

Contemporary attachment theorists considering the long-term consequences of differential early attachment relationships in humans have also been examining possible cross-generational continuities in attachment styles. Some authors have posited the likely existence of strong cross-generational continuities, such that mothers who experienced secure attachments when they were infants might tend to develop secure attachments with their own infants, while those who experienced avoidant or ambivalent attachments with their own mothers might tend to promote avoidant or ambivalent attachments as mothers themselves (e.g., Berlin & Cassidy, Chapter 30, this volume; Main, 1995). Moreover, current attachment theorists attribute these postulated infancy-to-parenthood continuities in attachment type to "internal working models" initially based on early memories and periodically transformed by more recent experiences. Most of the empirical findings that have led to these hypotheses have come from comprehensive interviews of adults (e.g., the Adult Attachment Interview) retrospectively probing memories of events and experiences. On the other hand, the most powerful empirical support for apparently parallel long-term continuities in attachment behavior from the nonhuman primate literature comes from prospective longitudinal observations and physiological recordings, both in controlled experimental settings and in naturalistic habitats, as reviewed above.

One insight that the nonhuman primate data

bring to discussions about long-term consequences of early experiences is that strong developmental continuities can unfold *in the absence of language or complex imagery*. It is difficult to argue that rhesus monkeys, for example, possess sufficient cognitive capabilities to develop "internal working models" requiring considerable self-reflection, given that they are probably not capable of "self-awareness" or "self-recognition" (e.g., Gallup, 1977; Povinelli, Parks, & Novak, 1992). What cognitive, emotional, and mnemonic processes might underlie these continuities— and do they have parallels in human nonverbal mental processes?

Alternatively, one might argue that working models are exclusively human constructions built upon a basic foundation that is essentially biological in nature and universal among the more advanced primate species. According to this view, cognitive constructions per se may not be necessary for long-term developmental or cross-generational continuities in attachment phenomena to transpire; that is, such continuities are essentially "programmed" to occur in the absence of major environmental disruption, and are in fact the product of strictly biological processes that reflect the natural evolutionary history of advanced primate species, human and nonhuman alike. If this is the case, then working models (or other comparable cognitive processes) might represent a "luxury" for humans that might enable individuals to cognitively "reinforce" the postulated underlying biological foundation, in which case the predicted developmental continuity might actually be strengthened.

On the other hand, the existence of a working model that has the potential to be *altered* by specific experiences (and/or insights) in late childhood, adolescence, or adulthood, might provide a basis for "breaking" an otherwise likely continuity between one's early attachment experiences and subsequent performance as a parent. These important issues deserve not only further theoretical consideration, but empirical investigation as well. As Bowlby (1988) himself said, "All of us, from cradle to the grave, are happiest when life is organized as a series of excursions, long or short, from the secure base provided by our attachment figure(s)" (p. 62). Research with nonhuman primates has clearly provided compelling evidence in support of a strong biological foundation for attachment phenomena. Indeed, such a foundation may well serve as a "secure base" for future research excursions in the realm of attachment phenomena.

REFERENCES

Andrews, M. W., & Rosenblum, L. A. (1991). Security of attachment in infants raised in variable- or low-demand environments. *Child Development, 62,* 686–693.

Arling, G. L., & Harlow, H. F. (1967). Effects of social deprivation on maternal behavior of rhesus monkeys. *Journal of Comparative and Physiological Psychology, 64,* 371–377.

Bennett, A. J., Lesch, K. P., Heils, A., Long, J., Lorenz, J., Shoaf, S. E., Suomi, S. J., Linnoila, M., & Higley, J. D. (1998). *Serotonin transporter gene variation, strain, and early rearing environment affect CSF 5–HIAA concentrations in rhesus monkeys (Macaca mulatta).* Manuscript submitted for publication.

Berard, J. (1989). Male life histories. *Puerto Rican Health Sciences Journal, 8,* 47–58.

Berman, C. M. (1982). The ontogeny of social relationships with group companions among free-ranging rhesus monkeys: I. Social networks and differentiation. *Animal Behavior, 30,* 149–162.

Berman, C. M. (1992). Immature siblings and mother–infant relationships among free-ranging rhesus monkeys on Cayo Santiago. *Animal Behavior, 44,* 247–258.

Berman, C. M., Rasmussen, K. L. R., & Suomi, S. J. (1993). Reproductive consequences of maternal care patterns during estrus among free-ranging rhesus monkeys. *Behavioral Ecology and Sociobiology, 32,* 391–399.

Berman, C. M., Rasmussen, K. L. R., & Suomi, S. J. (1994). Responses of free-ranging rhesus monkeys to a natural form of maternal separation: I. Parallels with mother–infant separation in captivity. *Child Development, 65,* 1028–1041.

Berman, C. M., Rasmussen, K. L. R., & Suomi, S. J. (1997). Group size, infant development, and social networks: A natural experiment with free-ranging rhesus monkeys. *Animal Behavior, 53,* 405–421.

Bowlby, J. (1958). The nature of the child's tie to his mother. *International Journal of Psycho-Analysis, 39,* 1–24.

Bowlby, J. (1960). Separation anxiety. *International Journal of Psycho-Analysis, 51,* 1–25.

Bowlby, J. (1969/1982). *Attachment and loss: Vol. 1.* New York: Basic Books.

Bowlby, J. (1973). *Attachment and loss: Vol. 2. Separation.* New York: Basic Books.

Bowlby, J. (1988). *A secure base.* New York: Basic Books.

Boyce, T. W., Champoux, M., Suomi, S. J., & Gunnar, M R. (1995). Salivary cortisol in nursery-reared rhesus monkeys: Interindividual stability, reactions to peer interactions, and altered circadian rhythmicity. *Developmental Psychobiology, 28,* 257–267.

Brazelton, T. B. (1973). *Clinics in developmental medicine: No. 50. Neonatal Behavioral Assessment Scale.* London: Heinemann.

Busnell, M.-C., & Granier-Deferre, C. (1983). And what of fetal audition? In A. Oliverio & M. Zappella (Eds.), *The behavior of human infants* (pp. 93–126). New York: Plenum Press.

Byrne, G. D., & Suomi, S. J. (1995). Activity patterns, social interaction, and exploratory behavior in *Cebus apella* infants from birth to 1 year of age. *American Journal of Primatology, 35,* 255–270.

Capitanio, J. P., Rasmussen, K. L. R., Snyder, D. S., Laudenslager, M. L., & Reite, M. (1986). Long-term follow-up of previously separated pigtail macaques: Group and individual differences in response to unfamiliar situations. *Journal of Child Psychology and Psychiatry, 27,* 531–538.

Champoux, M., Byrne, E., Delizio, R. D., & Suomi, S. J. (1992). Motherless mothers revisited: Rhesus maternal behavior and rearing history. *Primates, 33,* 251–255.

Champoux, M., Higley, J. D., & Suomi, S. J. (1997). Behavioral and physiological characteristics of Indian and Chinese–Indian hybrid rhesus macaque infants. *Developmental Psychobiology, 31,* 49–63.

Champoux, M., Suomi, S. J., & Schneider, M. L. (1994). Temperamental differences between captive Indian and Chinese–Indian hybrid rhesus macaque infants. *Laboratory Animal Science, 44,* 351–357.

Clarke, A. S., & Boinski, S. (1995). Temperament in nonhuman primates. *American Journal of Primatology, 37,* 103–125.

Coccaro, E. F., & Murphy, D. L. (1990). *Serotonin in major psychiatric disorders.* Washington, DC: American Psychiatric Press.

Darwin, E. (1794). *Zoonomia, or the laws of organic life.* London: Johnson.

DeCasper, A. J., & Fifer, W. P. (1980). Of human bonding: Newborns prefer their mothers' voices. *Science, 208,* 1174–1176.

Dienske, H., & Metz, J. A. J. (1977). Mother–infant body contact in macaques: A time interval analysis. *Biology of Behaviour, 2,* 3–21.

Dittus, W. P. J. (1979). The evolution of behaviours regulating density and age-specific sex ratios in a primate population. *Behaviour, 69,* 265–302.

Doudet, D., Hommer, D., Higley, J. D., Andreason, P. J., Moneman, R., Suomi, S. J., & Linnoila, M. (1995). Cerebral glucose metabolism, CSF 5–HIAA, and aggressive behavior in rhesus monkeys. *American Journal of Psychiatry, 152,* 1782–1787.

Fairbanks, L. A. (1989). Early experience and cross-generational continuity of mother-infant contact in vervet monkeys. *Developmental Psychobiology, 22,* 669–681.

Fedigan, L. M., & Fedigan, L. (1977). The social development of a handicapped infant in a free-living troop of Japanese monkeys. In S. Chevalier-Skolnikoff & F. E. Poirier (Eds.), *Primate bio-social development: Biological, social, and ecological determinants* (pp. 205–222). New York: Garland Press.

Fifer, W. P. (1987). Neonatal preference for mother's voice. In N. A. Krasnagor, E. M. Blass, M. A. Hofer, & W. P. Smotherman (Eds.), *Perinatal development: A psychobiological perspective* (pp. 39–60). New York: Academic Press.

Fragaszy, D. M., Baer, J., & Adams-Curtis, L. (1991). Behavioral development and maternal care in tufted capuchins (*Cebus apella*) and squirrel monkeys (*Saimiri sciureus*) from birth through seven months. *Developmental Psychobiology, 24,* 375–393.

Gallup, G. G. (1977). Self-recognition in primates: A comparative approach to the bidirectional properties of consciousness. *American Psychologist, 32,* 329–338.

Goldberg, S. (1995). Introduction. In S. Goldberg, R. Muir, & J. Kerr (Eds.), *Attachment theory: Social, developmental, and clinical perspectives* (pp. 1–15). Hillsdale, NJ: Analytic Press.

Gunnar, M. R., Gonzalez, C. A., Goodlin, B. L., & Levine, S. (1981). Behavioral and pituitary–adrenal responses during a prolonged separation period in rhesus monkeys. *Psychoneuroendocrinology, 6,* 65–75.

Hansen, E. W. (1966). The development of maternal and infant behaviour in the rhesus monkey. *Behaviour, 27,* 109–149.

Harlow, H. F. (1953). Mice, monkeys, men, and motives. *Psychological Review, 60,* 23–35.

Harlow, H. F. (1958). The nature of love. *American Psychologist, 13,* 673–685.

Harlow, H. F. (1969). Age-mate or peer affectional system. In D. S. Lehrman, R. A. Hinde, & E. Shaw (Eds.), *Advances in the study of behavior* (Vol. 2, pp. 333–383). New York: Academic Press.

Harlow, H. F., & Harlow, M. K. (1965). The affectional systems. In A. M Schrier, H. F. Harlow, & F. Stollnitz (Eds.), *Behavior of nonhuman primates* (Vol. 2, pp. 287–334). New York: Academic Press.

Harlow, H. F., Harlow, M. K., & Hansen, E. W. (1963). The maternal affectional system of rhesus monkeys. In H. L. Rheingold (Ed.), *Maternal behavior in mammals* (pp. 254–281). New York: Wiley.

Harlow, H. F., & Lauersdorf, H. E. (1974). Sex differences in passions and play. *Perspectives in Biology and Medicine, 17,* 348–360.

Heils, A., Teufel, A., Petri, S., Stober, G., Riederer, P., Bengel, B., & Lesch, K. P. (1996). Allelic variation of human serotonin transporter gene expression. *Journal of Neurochemistry, 6,* 2621–2624.

Heinz, A., Higley, J. D., Gorey, J. G., Saunders, R. C., Jones, D. W., Hommer, D., Zajicek, K., Suomi, S. J., Weinberger, D. R., & Linnoila, M. (1998). *In vivo* association between alcohol intoxication, aggression, and serotonin transporter availability in nonhuman primates. *American Journal of Psychiatry, 155,* 1023–1028.

Higley, J. D., Hasert, M. L., Suomi, S. J., & Linnoila, M. (1991). A new nonhuman primate model of alcohol abuse: Effects of early experience, personality, and stress on alcohol consumption. *Proceedings of the National Academy of Sciences USA, 88,* 7261–7265.

Higley, J. D., Hommer, D., Lucas, K., Shoaf, S., Suomi, S. J., & Linnoila, M. (in press). CNS serotonin metabolism rate predicts innate tolerance, high alcohol consumption, and aggression during intoxication in rhesus monkeys. *Archives of General Psychiatry.*

Higley, J. D., King, S. T., Hasert, M. F., Champoux, M., Suomi, S. J., & Linnoila, M. (1996). Stability of individual differences in serotonin function and its relationship to severe aggression and competent social behavior in rhesus macaque females. *Neuropsychopharmacology, 14,* 67–76.

Higley, J. D., & Suomi, S. J. (1986). Parental behaviour in primates. In W. Sluckin & M. Herbert (Eds.), *Parental behaviour in mammals* (pp. 152–207). Oxford: Blackwell.

Higley, J. D., & Suomi, S. J. (1989). Temperamental reactivity in nonhuman primates. In G. A. Kohnstamm, J. E. Bates, & M. K. Rothbard (Eds.), *Handbook of temperament in children* (pp. 153–167). New York: Wiley.

Higley, J. D., & Suomi, S. J. (1996). Reactivity and social competence affect individual differences in reaction to severe stress in children: Investigations using nonhuman primates. In C. R. Pfeffer (Ed.), *Intense stress and mental disturbance in children* (pp. 3–58). Washington, DC: American Psychiatric Press.

Higley, J. D., Suomi, S. J., & Linnoila, M. (1996). A nonhuman primate model of Type II alcoholism?: Part 2. Diminished social competence and excessive aggression correlates with low CSF 5-HIAA concentrations. *Alcoholism: Clinical and Experimental Research, 20,* 643–650.

Higley, J. D., Thompson, W. T., Champoux, M., Goldman, D., Hasert, M. F., Kraemer, G. W., Scanlan, J. M., Suomi, S. J., & Linnoila, M. (1993). Paternal and maternal genetic and environmental contributions to CSF monoamine metabolites in rhesus monkeys (*Macaca mulatta*). *Archives of General Psychiatry, 50,* 615–623.

Hinde, R. A. (1976). On describing relationships. *Journal of Child Psychology and Psychiatry, 17,* 1–19.

Hinde, R. A., Rowell, T. E., & Spencer-Booth, Y. (1964). Behavior of socially living monkeys in their first six months. *Proceedings of the Zoological Society of London, 143,* 609–649.

Hinde, R. A., & Spencer-Booth, Y. (1967). The behaviour of socially living rhesus monkeys in their first two and a half years. *Animal Behaviour, 15,* 169–176.

Hinde, R. A., & White, L. E. (1974). Dynamics of a relationship: Rhesus mother–infant ventro–ventro contact. *Journal of Comparative and Physiological Psychology, 86,* 8–23.

Hofer, M. A. (1995). Hidden regulators: Implications for a new understanding of attachment, separation, and loss. In S. Goldberg, R. Muir, & J. Kerr (Eds.), *Attachment theory: Social, developmental, and clinical perspectives* (pp. 203–230). Hillsdale, NJ: Analytic Press.

Immelmann, K., & Suomi, S. J. (1981). Sensitive phases in development. In K. Immelmann, G. W. Barlow, L. Petrinovich, & M. Main (Eds.), *Behavioral development: The Bielefeld Project* (pp. 395–431). New York: Cambridge University Press.

Lesch, K. P., Bengel, D., Heils, A., Sabol, S. Z., Greenberg, B. D., Petri, S., Benjamin, J., Muller, C. R., Hamer, D. H., & Murphy, D. L. (1996). Association of anxiety-related traits with a polymorphism in the serotonin transporter gene regulatory region. *Science, 274,* 1527–1531.

Lesch, L. P., Meyer, J., Glatz, K., Flugge, G., Hinney, A., Hebebrand, J., Klauck, S. M., Poustka, A., Poustka, F., Bengel, D., Mossner, R., Riederer, P., & Heils, A. (1997). The 5–HT transporter gene-linked polymorphic region (5-HTTLPR) in evolutionary perspective: Alternative biallelic variation in rhesus monkeys. *Journal of Neural Transmission, 104,* 1259–1266.

Lorenz, K. (1937). Der Kumpan in der Umwelt des Vogels. *Journal für Ornithologie, 83,* 137–213, 289–413.

Lindburg, D. G. (1971). The rhesus monkey in north India: An ecological and behavioral study. In L. A. Rosenblum (Ed.), *Primate behavior: Developments in field and laboratory research* (Vol. 2, pp. 1–106). New York: Academic Press.

Main, M. (1995). Recent studies in attachment: Overview, with selected implications for clinical work. In S. Goldberg, R. Muir, & J. Kerr (Eds.), *Attachment theory: Social, developmental, and clinical perspectives* (pp. 407–474). Hillsdale, NJ: Analytic Press.

Manson, J. H., & Perry, S. E. (1993). Inbreeding avoidance in rhesus macaques: Whose choice? *American Journal of Physical Anthropology, 90,* 335–344.

Mehlman, P. T., Higley, J. D., Faucher, I., Lilly, A. A., Taub, D. M., Vickers, J., Suomi, S. J., & Linnoila, M. (1994). Low cerebrospinal fluid 5–hydroxyindoleacetic acid concentrations are correlated with severe aggression and reduced impulse control in free-ranging nonhuman primates (*Macaca mulatta*). *American Journal of Psychiatry, 151,* 1485–1491.

Mehlman, P. T., Higley, J. D., Faucher, I., Lilly, A. A., Taub, D. M., Vickers, J. M., Suomi, S. J., & Linnoila, M. (1995). CSF 5–HIAA concentrations are correlated with sociality and the timing of emigration in free-ranging primates. *American Journal of Psychiatry, 152,* 907–913.

Mendoza, S. P., Smotherman, W. P., Miner, M., Kaplan, J., & Levine, S. (1978). Pituitary–adrenal response to separa-

tion in mother and infant squirrel monkeys. *Developmental Psychobiology, 11,* 169–175.

Povinelli, D. J., Parks, K. A., & Novak, M. A. (1992). Role reversal by rhesus monkeys, but no evidence of empathy. *Animal Behavior, 44,* 269–281.

Reite, M., Short, R., Seiler, C., & Pauley, J. D. (1981). Attachment, loss, and depression. *Journal of Child Psychology and Psychiatry, 22,* 141–169.

Robertson, J., & Bowlby, J. (1952). Responses of young children to separation from their mothers. *Cours du Centre International de l'Enfance, 2,* 131–142.

Ruppenthal, G. C., Arling, G. L., Harlow, H. F., Sackett, G. P., & Suomi, S. J. (1976). A 10–year perspective on motherless mother monkey mothering behavior. *Journal of Abnormal Psychology, 88,* 341–349.

Ruppenthal, G. C., Harlow, M. K., Eisele, C. D., Harlow, H. F., & Suomi, S. J. (1974). Development of peer interactions of monkeys reared in a nuclear family environment. *Child Development, 45,* 670–682.

Sackett, G. P. (1966). Monkeys reared in isolation with pictures as visual input: Evidence for an innate releasing mechanism. *Science, 154,* 1468–1472.

Schneider, M. L. (1992). Delayed object permanence in prenatally stressed rhesus monkey infants. *Occupational Therapy Journal of Research, 12,* 96–110.

Schneider, M. L., & Suomi, S. J. (1992). Neurobehavioral assessment in rhesus monkey neonates (*Macaca mulatta*): Developmental changes, behavioral stability, and early experience. *Infant Behavior and Development, 15,* 155–177.

Simpson, M. J. A. (1979). Daytime rest and activity in socially living rhesus monkey infants. *Animal Behaviour, 27,* 602–612.

Simpson, M. J. A., Simpson, A. E., Hooley, J., & Zunz, M. (1981). Infant-related influences on birth intervals in rhesus monkeys. *Nature, 290,* 49–51.

Suomi, S. J. (1979a). Peers, play, and primary prevention in primates. In M. Kent & J. Rolf (Eds.), *Primary prevention in psychopathology: Vol. 3. Social competence in children* (pp. 127–149). Hanover, NH: University Press of New England.

Suomi, S. J. (1979b). Differential development of various social relationships by rhesus monkey infants. In M. Lewis & L. A. Rosenblum (Eds.), *The child and its family: Vol. 2. Genesis of behavior* (pp. 219–244). New York: Plenum Press.

Suomi, S. J. (1981). Genetic, maternal, and environmental influences on social development in rhesus monkeys. In A. B. Chiarelli & R. S. Corruccini (Eds.), *Primate behavior and sociobiology: Selected papers (Part B) of the VIII Congress of the International Primatological Society, 1980* (pp. 81–87). New York: Springer-Verlag.

Suomi, S. J. (1982). Sibling relationships in nonhuman primates. In M. E. Lamb & B. Sutton-Smith (Eds.), *Sibling relationships: Their development and significance* (pp. 284–309). Hillsdale, NJ: Erlbaum.

Suomi, S. J. (1983). Social development in rhesus monkeys: Considerations of individual differences. In A. Oliverio & M. Zappella (Eds.), *The behavior of human infants* (pp. 71–92). New York: Plenum.

Suomi, S. J. (1987). Genetic and maternal contributions to individual differences in rhesus monkey biobehavioral development. In N. A. Krasnagor, E. M. Blass, M. A. Hofer, & W. P. Smotherman (Eds.), *Perinatal development: A psychobiological perspective* (pp. 397–420). New York: Academic Press.

Suomi, S. J. (1991). Up-tight and laid-back monkeys: Individual differences in the response to social challenges. In S. Brauth, W. Hall, & R. Dooling (Eds.), *Plasticity of development* (pp. 27–56). Cambridge, MA: MIT Press.

Suomi, S. J. (1995). Influence of Bowlby's attachment theory on research on nonhuman primate biobehavioral development. In S. Goldberg, R. Muir, & J. Kerr (Eds.), *Attachment theory: Social, developmental, and clinical perspectives* (pp. 185–201). Hillsdale, NJ: Analytic Press.

Suomi, S. J. (1997). Early determinants of behaviour: Evidence from primate studies. *British Medical Bulletin, 53,* 170–184.

Suomi, S. J. (1998). Conflict and cohesion in rhesus monkey family life. In M. Cox & J. Brooks-Gunn (Eds.), *Conflict and cohesion in families* (pp. 283–296). Mahwah, NJ: Erlbaum.

Suomi, S. J. (in press). Developmental trajectories, early experiences, and community consequences: Lessons from studies with rhesus monkeys. In D. Keating & C. Hertzman (Eds.), *Developmental health: The wealth of nations in the information age.* New York: Guilford Press.

Suomi, S. J., & Harlow, H. F. (1975). The role and reason of peer friendships. In M. Lewis & L. A. Rosenblum (Eds.), *Friendships and peer relations* (pp. 310–334). New York: Basic Books.

Suomi, S. J., & Harlow, H. F. (1976). The facts and functions of fear. In M. Zuckerman & C. D. Spielberger (Eds.), *Emotions and anxiety: New concepts, methods, and applications* (pp. 3–34). Hillsdale, NJ: Erlbaum.

Suomi, S. J., Kraemer, G. W., Baysinger, C. M., & Delizio, R. D. (1981). Inherited and experiential factors associated with individual differences in anxious behavior displayed by rhesus monkeys. In D. G. Klein & J. Rabkin (Eds.), *Anxiety: New research and changing concepts* (pp. 179–200). New York: Raven Press.

Suomi, S. J., & Levine, S. (1998). Psychobiology of intergenerational effects of trauma: Evidence from animal studies. In Y. Danieli (Ed.), *International handbook of multigenerational legacies of trauma* (pp. 623–637). New York: Plenum Press.

Suomi, S. J., Rasmussen, K. L. R., & Higley, J. D. (1992). Primate models of behavioral and physiological change in adolescence. In E. R. McAnarney, R. E. Kriepe, D. P. Orr, & G. D. Comerci (Eds.), *Textbook of adolescent medicine* (pp. 135–139). Philadelphia: Saunders.

Suomi, S. J., & Ripp, C. (1983). A history of motherless mother monkey mothering at the University of Wisconsin Primate Laboratory. In M. Reite & N Caine (Eds.), *Child abuse: The nonhuman primate data* (pp. 49–77). New York: Alan R. Liss.

Trivers, R. L. (1974). Parent–offspring conflicts. *American Zoologist, 14,* 249–264.

Visalberghi, E. (1990). Tool-use in *Cebus. Folia Primatologica, 54,* 146–154.

Welker, C., Becker, P., Hohman, H., & Schafer-Witt, C. (1987). Social relations in groups of the black-capped capuchin *Cebus apella* in captivity: Interactions of group-born infants during their first 6 months of life. *Folia Primatologica, 49,* 33–47.

Welker, C., Becker, P., & Schafer-Witt, C. (1990). Social relations in groups of the black-capped capuchin (*Cebus apella*) in captivity: Interactions of group-born infants during their second half-year of life. *Folia Primatologica, 54,* 16–33.

Wilson, E. O. (1975). *Sociobiology.* New York: Cambridge University Press.

10

Attachment and Temperament

Redundant, Independent, or Interacting Influences on Interpersonal Adaptation and Personality Development?

❖

BRIAN E. VAUGHN
KELLY K. BOST

For nearly two decades, a vigorous research effort has been directed at documenting and explaining relations between attachment and temperament in infancy, childhood, and adulthood (for reviews, see Goldsmith & Alansky, 1987; Goldsmith & Harman, 1994; Seifer & Schiller, 1995). Although the data generated from this effort reveal the overlap across behavioral domains relevant to constructs arising from attachment theory and from theories of temperament, interpretations of this overlap vary (largely as a function of the theoretical preferences of investigators reporting on these relations). The purpose of this chapter is to review the literature relating attachment and temperament constructs in light of the theoretical claims arising from attachment theory and from theories of temperament. The chapter is divided into three major sections. First, we present brief treatments of the conceptual and empirical domains embraced and claims advanced by attachment theory and by the major individual-difference theories of temperament. Second, we document the history of communication between temperament and attachment theorists at both conceptual and empirical levels. This section includes a detailed review of literature organized both in terms of the conceptual territory in dispute and in terms of the approach to assessing temperament employed by investigators. In the final section of the chapter, the conclu-

sions justified by empirical findings are summarized and critically evaluated in the context of the claims about social adaptation and personality development proffered from attachment theory and from the major theories of temperament.

PRÉCIS OF ATTACHMENT AND TEMPERAMENT THEORIES

The Bowlby–Ainsworth theory of attachment explains how and why infant–parent bonds are assembled over the first years of life, and how interpersonal experiences in the context of attachment relationships set developmental trajectories with regard to the assembly of subsequent interpersonal relationships, especially love relationships. Although implications for personality development and functioning are implicit in attachment theory, attachment relationships are explicitly social, and the primary emphases of the theory are on the construction, maintenance, and subjective meaning of attachment bonds. In contrast, most temperament theories have been proposed as explanations of endogenously organized individual differences in styles of action or in the actions themselves (see Strelau, 1983, for a treatment of temperament that does not emphasize individual differences as the core phenomena to be explained). Temperament dimensions are often connected explicitly to personality functioning, and in certain theories give rise to personality traits (see Buss & Plomin, 1984). For most temperament theorists, temperamental attributes carry implications for social functioning, but interpersonal exchanges and relationships are not explicit components of temperament (see Goldsmith et al., 1987).

The Bowlby–Ainsworth Theory of Attachment

Bowlby (1969/1982) acknowledged four broad intellectual influences on his thinking about the nature of the child's tie to the mother: psychoanalytic theory, especially its object relations variants; ethology and animal behavior; general systems theory; and cognitive psychology. To this mix of influences, Ainsworth added security theory as it was described by Blatz and elaborated in her own thinking and research (see Ainsworth & Marvin, 1995) before she joined in the attachment enterprise with Bowlby.

From psychoanalytic theory, Bowlby borrowed insights concerning the nature of the early child–caregiver bond (e.g., the infant–caregiver relationship is a true love relationship, and therefore the dissolution of the child–caregiver bond through prolonged separations results in a full-fledged grief experience for the child; the early child–caregiver bond serves as a model for subsequent intimate relationships; psychological adjustment can be fruitfully viewed as the capacity to work, love, and play well). To the extent that the early love relationship constructed in the context of caregiver–infant interactions constitutes the foundation for learning to "love well," the child–caregiver attachment can be construed as a primary cornerstone for inter- and intrapersonal adjustment across a lifetime. Ethology supplied Bowlby with the motivational tools and empirical data he needed to explain the child's tendency to seek and maintain proximity to caregivers, once the psychoanalytic motivational model was discarded. He used the ethological concept of a "behavioral system," organized to maintain proximity to the caregiver, as the mechanism governing attachment behavior. Bowlby explained the presence of this behavioral system in terms of evolution by natural selection. Locating the motivation for proximity seeking and contact maintenance in evolutionary "deep time" rather than in ontogenetic time allowed Bowlby to decouple attachment behavior from other motivational systems (e.g., hunger, warmth) that both psychoanalysts and behaviorists had used to explain the child's tie to the caregiver. Control systems theory provided him with key features of the behavioral system, including "set goal," "goal correction," and "feedback."

Finally, Bowlby was careful to coordinate the developmental schedule for the emerging attachment relationship with Piaget's periods of sensorimotor and preoperational intelligence. He shared the Genevan bias that the child actively participates in her or his own development, and he saw this as a defining distinction between attachment theory and other theoretical explanations of the child–caregiver bond. However, Piaget was not the primary cognitive-psychological influence on attachment theory. Bowlby based his concept of "internal working models" (e.g., Bowlby, 1973, 1980) on the ideas of Craik (1943), who had suggested that people construct mental models for all kinds of physical and social phenomena as heuristics for explanation of the operation and functioning of those phenomena (see also Johnson-Laird, 1983). Bowlby found the concept attractive because it suggested both a process and a structure for preserving the child's attachment relationship in the absence of overt attachment behavior and in the absence of the caregiver altogether.

Normative Claims

From this eclectic mix of influences, Bowlby formulated attachment theory. In essence, the child's tie to the caregiver is assumed to constitute a special sort of relationship (i.e., a love relationship) that arises from the operation of a behavioral system designed over the course of human evolution to promote proximity and contact with the primary caregiver in the service of survival. As the system is activated in both normal and emergency situations (i.e., when the infant is stressed by internal or by external inputs) and as the set goal is attained (i.e., contact or proximity is achieved and maintained) on many occasions, the pattern of individual interactions becomes organized as a recognizable and unique relationship characterizing the child–caregiver dyad (see Hinde, 1987, and Hinde & Stevenson-Hinde, 1987, for discussions of connections between interactions and relationships). This relationship is assembled or co-constructed with the caregiver over time in a regular, expectable sequence that parallels (but is not derivative of) the growth of sensorimotor intelligence during the first years of life. Further activity of the behavioral system in the context of the attachment relationship provides input for the assembly of an internal working model of the relationship, and of collateral models of the attachment figure and the self. Because these models take their initial forms from interactions and emotions experienced prior to the onset of verbal representation, Bowlby (1980) argued that core aspects of internal working models may be difficult to bring into conscious awareness. These assumptions constitute the normative, species-specific claims for attachment theory (see also, Waters, Kondo-Ikemura, Posada, & Richters, 1991).

Individual Differences

A fifth influence on Bowlby's thinking about attachment arose from his association with Mary Ainsworth. Ainsworth's work focused on the construct of "security" (i.e., a feeling of safety and comfort arising from the satisfaction of basic physical and psychological needs, and from knowledge that future satisfaction of needs is not at risk). She met Bowlby in the early 1950s (see Ainsworth & Marvin, 1995) and recognized immediately that the attachment relationship should serve as the primary source of security for a young child. That this relationship is indeed a source of security can be inferred from the organization of the child's behavior with reference to the caregiver. As Ainsworth observed, the child uses the caregiver as a base for exploring the surrounding environment in both familiar and unfamiliar settings. Furthermore, when the child is distressed, threatened, or simply bored, proximity and contact with the caregiver generally return the "system" to its prior state, allowing the child to continue exploration. Ainsworth refers to the balance of attachment and exploratory behavior organized around a specific caregiver as the "secure-base" and "haven-of-safety" phenomena. These organized patterns of behavior, when coherent over time and context, constitute diagnostic criteria for the existence of an attachment relationship between child and caregiver.

In its primary formulation, attachment theory is a normative account of how and why child–caregiver bonds emerge and are maintained. It is, however, both explicit and implicit in the theory that attachments have important individual-difference implications in the domains of personality and interpersonal adaptation. Security theory provided a venue for exploring those implications. Fieldwork convinced Ainsworth (e.g., Ainsworth, 1967; Ainsworth, Blehar, Waters, & Wall, 1978) that differences in the patterns of interaction characterizing different child–mother pairs are indicative of differences in the effectiveness of the attachment relationship as a source of security. Although these differences were apparent in home observations (e.g., Ainsworth et al., 1978; Vaughn & Waters, 1990; Waters & Deane, 1985; Waters et al., 1991), they were more clearly differentiated in her strange situation (SS) procedure. In most samples, from 50% to 70% of cases are assigned to the "secure" (Group B) classification, whereas the remaining cases are assigned to one of three "insecure" (Groups A, C, D) classifications.

Ainsworth argued that qualitative differences in the organization of attachment-relevant behavior seen in the SS arise as a consequence of the histories of interactions characterizing various child–mother pairs. In her own data (e.g., Ainsworth, 1967; Ainsworth et al., 1978), differences in the patterning of infant–mother interactions were evident from the first 3 months of life. Other researchers (e.g., Egeland & Farber, 1984; Grossmann, Grossmann, Spangler, Suess, & Unzner, 1985; Pederson & Moran, 1995) have also distinguished securely from insecurely attached infants on the basis of home observations summarized in terms of "maternal sensitivity." Caregivers who are sensitively responsive to their children's communicative signals tend to have securely attached children.

Individual-Difference Claims

Attachment theory assumes that individual differences in the organization of secure-base behavior and associated differences in affective expression arise as a consequence of quantitative and qualitative differences in the patterns of interactions over the first years of life. Differences with respect to interactive contexts support the construction of qualitatively distinct internal working models of the attachment relationship, the caregiver, the self, and the general social world. Differences in working models and in experienced attachment relationships influence personality development and psychosocial adjustment by virtue of their influences on expectations about the self and about the self in relation to others (Waters, Vaughn, Posada, & Kondo-Ikemura, 1995).

Temperament Theories

Whereas attachment theory's roots and major claims are relatively easy to specify, finding the core concepts and enumerating the major claims of temperament theories are quite complicated. This is because theorists from at least five different (and somewhat independent) perspectives have suggested possible dimensions of temperament (see Goldsmith et al., 1987). The perspectives differ in terms of their characterization of the domain of temperament, the relation of temperament dimensions to biological substrates (e.g., genes, physiological processes, accidents of birth), and the intersection between temperament and development. For the purposes of this chapter, we have grouped the perspectives into four broad categories: behavioral style theory, emergent personality theory, emotion/physiological regulation theories, and social construction theory. We recognize that this grouping is ad hoc, insofar as all perspectives imply some form of biologically based, endogenously organized traits that appear early in life and tend to show at least moderate ordering consistency for samples of individuals across time. We also recognize that some approaches do not fall neatly into a single category, and that many of the empirical efforts aimed at connecting temperament dimensions with attachment constructs have employed methods derived from more than one perspective. Nevertheless, this scheme helps us to organize the assumptions and claims of temperament theories, especially with reference to domains of action and behavioral style that overlap the domains of action, affect, and cognition claimed by attachment theory.

Behavioral-Style Theory

The notion that "temperament" refers to the style in which behaviors are exhibited, rather than to the content of behavior or its motivational underpinnings, is associated with Thomas and Chess (e.g., Thomas & Chess, 1977; Thomas, Chess, & Birch, 1968; Thomas, Chess, Birch, Hertzig, & Korn, 1963). The treatment of temperament as behavioral style is grounded in interpretations going back to ancient Greek philosophers and retains its appeal in the popular press of today. Thomas and Chess (in Goldsmith et al., 1987) assert that temperament is a property of persons that is not derivative of any other attribute or motivational source, and that the expression of temperament is dynamically tuned to the constraints imposed by external stimuli, opportunities, expectations, and demands. They further argue that temperament should be assessed in social contexts, in part because the constraints of specific social contexts will lead to variations in the expression of the underlying temperamental attribute. From their perspective, temperamental attributes codetermine properties of the environment, although neither the processes through which codetermination is exercised nor the other codeterminants are specified. Ordering consistency is expected across time, but this approach to temperament is sufficiently elastic as to accommodate marked changes in the rank orderings of individuals on temperament dimensions, because the dimensions are malleable under certain (not specified) constraints imposed by the social environment. Finally, Thomas and Chess see no necessary connection between "personality" (broadly construed) and temperament.

Thomas and Chess suggest that temperament should be assessed in the context of deep and comprehensive interviews with knowledgeable informants. For infants and young children, this usually means parents or other primary caregivers. In most research contexts, the interview format is not practical, so questionnaires have been constructed to capture the nine temperament dimensions proposed (i.e., activity level, adaptability, approach vs. withdrawal, distractibility, intensity of affect expression, quality of mood, rhythmicity of biological functions, persistence/attention span, and sensory threshold). Multivariate analyses of scale scores derived from either of the two formats indicate that the nine dimensions are not orthogonal and can be reduced efficiently to three or four dimensions (see Seifer, Sameroff, Barrett, & Krafchuk, 1994). The "adaptability," "approach," "intensity," and "mood" scales are often grouped together to yield a dimension called "temperamental difficulty."

Carey and associates (e.g., Carey & McDevitt, 1978; Fullard, McDevitt, & Carey, 1984) designed a set of questionnaires that are widely used in temperament research across the periods of infancy and childhood. Temperament scores from the Carey protocols have yielded modest to moderate estimates of reliability and validity. Temporal stability of temperament scores from the Carey protocols ranges from low to moderate over periods of time ranging from 3 to 24 months. Agreement across knowledgeable raters (e.g., mothers and fathers) tends to be modest for most of the behavioral-style scales (e.g., Martin, 1988; Martin & Halverson, 1991). Moderate associations between behavioral-style dimensions and laboratory assessments of temperament have been reported (e.g., Matheny, Riese, & Wilson, 1985).

The behavioral-style theory of temperament was proposed to explain why infants and children differ with respect to how they behave in everyday life. These differences are believed to reflect variations in constitutionally grounded temperamental attributes. Thomas and Chess (in Goldsmith et al., 1987) claim that these attributes are present and can be assessed from early infancy, that they are at least moderately stable from infancy to childhood, and that they codetermine the responses of social partners to the child. Although the characteristic profile of temperament may change as a consequence of instruction in a specific and constraining social environment, most intraindividual variations in the expression of temperament do not reflect lability in the underlying temperamental attribute (see Thomas & Chess in Goldsmith et al., 1987, p. 509). Thus, although change per se with respect to the salience of a temperamental attribute may be observed and can be explained in a specific case, the behavioral-style perspective does not specify a normative developmental trajectory for temperament.

Emergent-Personality Theory

Buss and Plomin (1975, 1984) characterize temperament as basic personality primitives that are genetically grounded and highly heritable, can be detected early in life, and demonstrate relatively high rank-order stability across developmental periods. Buss and Plomin (1984) identify three traits that meet these criteria: emotionality, activity, and sociability. They reject as candidates for temperament traits individual-difference dimensions (e.g., rhythmicity of vegetative activities) that decline in salience for personality beyond infancy. Also excluded from the domain of temperament are behavioral and psychological individual-difference attributes (e.g., maturation rate, mental ability) that do not have obvious relations with personality. Finally, personality traits that arise primarily from social experience (e.g., shame) are not considered to be temperament traits. From this perspective, temperament is indistinguishable from personality during infancy. However, with increasing age these personality primitives become differentiated; for example, primordial distress, the indicator of emotionality during infancy, is assumed to split into fear and anger after the first year (see Buss & Plomin in Goldsmith et al., 1987, p. 518). Furthermore, Buss and Plomin indicate that normative changes in the level of expression of temperament traits are expectable (e.g., the expression of emotionality declines past infancy in response to pressures from the social environment and in response to maturation of the central nervous system and associated regulatory mechanisms).

Because the defining feature of the emergent-personality perspective is its grounding in the genetic substrate, Buss and Plomin have devoted considerable energy to the construction of assessment instruments that provide reliable and coherent estimates of their three temperament traits. Data collected with their instruments have shown the three dimensions to be differentiated, even though modest correlations among them are frequently reported. Data from adoption studies indicate that these traits are moderately heritable and stable across developmental periods (e.g., DeFries, Plomin, & Fulker, 1994; Plomin & DeFries, 1985). Other researchers, using a similar temperament taxonomy but with different instruments (e.g., Susman-Stillman, Kalkoske, Egeland, & Waldman, 1996), have reported moderate (negative) correlations between sociability and emotionality. Nevertheless, these traits seem to satisfy the criteria stated by Buss and Plomin for inclusion in the temperament domain. The three dimensions are also included in recent considerations of temperament as an early indicator of the "Big Five" personality traits (see chapters in Halverson, Kohnstamm, & Martin, 1994).

Although the behavior-genetic approach used by DeFries et al. (1994) and by Plomin and DeFries (1985) would seem ideally suited to testing hypotheses about the heritability of attachment behaviors and classifications, there have been very few attempts to do so. A PsycLIT search identified only a single published study bearing on this issue. In a study of adult twins, Livesley, Jang, Jackson, and Vernon (1993) reported that adult behaviors associated with early attachment problems had low heritability. Results from a more directly relevant study based on data from the Louisville Twin Study (Finkel, Wille, & Matheny, 1997) suggest that monozygotic twins show greater concordance for attachment classifications than do dizygotic twins. Although this study used a nonstandard method for assessing attachment security, the authors did attempt to evaluate congruence of classifications between their procedure and the Ainsworth SS with reasonable success (78% classified similarly) in an independent sample of twins.

These results reported by Finkel et al. (1997) seem promising, but they must be interpreted in light of results from other studies of siblings. Two studies of attachment in nontwin siblings reported cross-sibling concordance rates of 64% and 61% for attachment security (i.e., Teti, Nakagawa, Das, & Wirth, in press; Ward, Vaughn, & Robb, 1988), which is at the level reported by Finkel et al. for monozygotic twins. Perhaps even more compelling are results reported by Sagi et al. (1995), who found that unrelated children cared for in the same family-based kibbutz had concordance rates between 68% and 70% when observed in the SS with a given *metapelet* (i.e., caregiver). These studies suggest that the degree of concordance across dizygotic twins reported by Finkel et al. (1997) is much *lower* than should be expected, and that their concordance for monozygotic twins is at about the level that could be expected for any pair of siblings seen with the same parent. Until these issues can be addressed in a single, large-*n* study, behavior-genetic interpretations of attachment security and attachment behavior seem premature.

Theories of Emotional/Physiological Regulation

Two theoretical approaches (i.e., those of Goldsmith and Campos and of Rothbart and Derryberry) and two related empirical positions (temperamental "proneness to distress" [e.g., Gunnar and associates] and "proneness to behavioral inhibition" [Kagan and associates; Fox and associates]) are reviewed here.

Goldsmith and Campos (e.g., Goldsmith in Goldsmith et al., 1987; Goldsmith & Campos, 1986, 1990) have proposed a theory of temperament that is grounded in the functionalist perspective on emotions and emotional development articulated by Campos and associates (e.g., Campos, Campos, & Barrett, 1989; Campos, Mumme, Kermoian, & Campos, 1994; Goldsmith & Campos, 1990). This perspective on emotional development differs in several ways from traditional approaches to understanding the development of emotion and emotional expression (e.g., Izard & Malatesta, 1987). The functionalist perspective assumes that primary emotions (e.g., joy/pleasure, anger, fear) regulate internal psychological processes, regulate so-

cial/interpersonal activity, are specifiable in terms of unique and measurable behavioral patterns, and require no instruction from the social environment for their expression (Goldsmith in Goldsmith et al., 1987). In this theoretical framework, temperament is defined as individual differences in the tendencies to experience and express the primary emotions. Relations between temperament and personality are relatively straightforward, insofar as traits such as "aggressiveness" are expected to be affected by individual differences in the experience and expression of the primary emotion "anger" (see Goldsmith in Goldsmith et al., 1987, p. 511). This theory allows for other influences on the assembly of personality traits, but assumes a strong relation between individual differences on these traits and individual differences on temperament dimensions. Goldsmith also includes motor activity in the list of temperament-relevant attributes, because activity level may reflect emotional arousal that is not differentiated with respect to the primary emotions.

Although this perspective shares behavioral content with the behavioral-style and emergent-personality theories, Goldsmith and Campos distinguish their position from these others by including motivational components and by relaxing the heritability requirement. Goldsmith (in Goldsmith et al., 1987) notes that many emotional expressions imply motivational states; he also notes that species-specific traits are strongly canalized but are not heritable in the behavioral-genetic sense. For Goldsmith and Campos, primary emotions and their innate communication system have the same status as the attachment behavioral system in the Bowlby–Ainsworth theory of attachment: They are biological primitives or "givens" that support goals of individual and inclusive fitness, and that provide a foundation for the construction of individual differences in patterns of behavior over the life course.

Developmentally, each primary emotion retains its set goal, but the means through which that goal is maintained, both in expressive and in receptive aspects, may change as a child becomes more socially and cognitively sophisticated. One change concerns the integration of expression and internal state. For most primary emotions, integration should be complete by the end of the first year of life. This suggests that stability with respect to rank orderings of individuals is not likely to be attained from early infancy. It further implies that although there may be coordinations between temperament and ongoing exchanges in the physical and social environments throughout infancy, these coordinations should not be expected to forecast other such coordinations over more than a very short period of time until the temperament dimension itself becomes "integrated." Since the inputs into temperament integrations will almost certainly come both from within and from outside the infant, it should be important to identify the social experiences that aid in the achievement and consolidation of such integrations. Goldsmith, Bradshaw, and Rieser-Danner (1986) considered potential influences of temperament, construed in this manner, on attachment.

The Rothbart and Derryberry temperament theory (e.g., Rothbart & Derryberry, 1981) incorporates the behavioral phenomena discussed by Goldsmith and Campos (although Rothbart and Derryberry do not necessarily endorse the functionalist approach), but it does not limit the domain of temperament to emotional experience and expression. Rothbart (1989a, 1989b, 1989c, 1991) has indicated that the scope of this theory extends to physiological and cognitive mechanisms underlying reactivity and regulation more generally. She has defined temperament as constitutionally based individual differences in reactivity and self-regulation, with constitutional referring to the person's relatively enduring biological makeup, influenced over time by heredity, maturation, and experience (Rothbart, 1989a). "Reactivity" refers to arousal in motor, affective, autonomic, or endocrinological domains, whereas "self-regulation" refers to processes that modulate the local level of reactivity in response to endogenous and exogenous parameters. Although the reactivity and self-regulation constructs are distinct, they are not conceived of as orthogonal at the level of measurement. That is to say, a single observed behavior can be motivated by both reactive and self-regulative processes. According to this theory, temperament-relevant behavior may be observed in emotional, attentional, and motor activities. Thus the domain of temperament covers much that might otherwise be considered in studies of cognitive development (e.g., Ruff & Rothbart, 1996) and interpersonal/social development (Rothbart, 1989c).

Rothbart (e.g., 1989c, 1991) suggests that temperament undergoes normative developmental change in conjunction with the maturational timetable governing shifts in the organization of physiological and cognitive processes, which in turn underlie reactivity and self-regulation. Although different component processes may follow asynchronous maturational timetables, normative changes tend to manifest themselves as punctuations rather than as continuous, gradual changes. Furthermore, because the underlying maturational timetables are not necessarily synchronized, some temperamental attributes may show normative and/or individual rank-order changes, while other attributes remain static (Rothbart in Goldsmith et al., 1987, p. 516). Finally, certain temperamental attributes are emergent rather than being specified in the earliest months of life. For example, Rothbart (1989c) discusses the development of "behavioral inhibition," which is not clearly defined until the second half of the first year and is dependent on achievements in motor and cognitive domains. As a result of the asynchronies of maturation for underlying mechanisms, and as a consequence of the phenomenon of emergence, an individual's temperamental profile is expected to undergo reorganization and transformation during the early years of life, and individual differences may be less stable over the period of infancy than in the periods from toddlerhood onward. Nevertheless, Rothbart (1989c) reports that most temperamental traits show significant, albeit modest, degrees of rank-order stability even during infancy.

The Rothbart–Derryberry theory is distinguished from Goldsmith and Campos's approach in terms of the breadth of content within the domain of "temperament." Rothbart distinguishes her approach from the emergent-personality approach in terms of both breadth and specificity. For example, whereas Buss and Plomin assert that negative emotionality/distress is the primary heritable temperamental attribute (e.g., Buss & Plomin in Goldsmith et al., 1987), Rothbart (1989a) includes both positive and negative emotionality as independent temperamental dimensions. Rothbart and Derryberry are also more explicit than other theorists in connecting temperament to physiological and cognitive domains. Their theory bears a structural similarity to attachment theory, insofar as the normative components undergo development according to species-specific maturational timetables and insofar as the consolidation of individual differences is not expected until the underlying components have been established.

In addition to standing as an independent conceptual framework for describing and explaining normative and individual-difference aspects of temperament, the Rothbart–Derryberry theory serves as the springboard for two important (and related) approaches to temperament that have been explicitly directed at explaining the behavioral phenomena addressed by the Bowlby–Ainsworth attachment theory: namely, "proneness to distress" and "behavioral inhibition." The construct of behavioral inhibition was popularized by Kagan and associates (e.g., Garcia-Coll, Kagan, & Reznick, 1984; Kagan, Reznick, & Snidman, 1988). They argued that being at the extremes of the behavioral-inhibition dimension (either "inhibited" or "bold") is associated with a characteristic pattern of autonomic nervous system and neuroendocrine responses (e.g., Fox, 1989; Kagan, Reznick, & Snidman, 1987), which broadly reflects central nervous system functioning and is stable from the late toddler period forward. Kagan and associates (e.g., Kagan, Resnick, & Snidman, 1989) differ from other theorists in that their construal of temperament does not *require* continuous dimensions. Rather, the salience of the behavioral-inhibition construct is appreciated primarily at the extremes (the top or bottom 10–15% of cases in convenience samples) and is expected to show continuity only for the extreme cases. Kagan implies (e.g., Kagan, 1984) that individual differences with regard to behavioral inhibition can explain the behaviors characteristic of children assigned to different classification categories according to Ainsworth's criteria for the SS.

Fox and associates (e.g., Calkins & Fox, 1992, 1994; Calkins, Fox, & Marshall, 1996; Fox, 1989, 1994) have reported findings consistent with Kagan's notion that individual differences along the behavioral-inhibition dimension have antecedents in both autonomic and central nervous system functioning. Their general findings are, however, more consistent with a "continuous-dimension" interpretation than with a "discrete-type" interpretation. Like Rothbart and Derryberry, Fox and associates argue that behavioral inhibition arises as an individual-difference dimension later in development than does reactivity. Calkins (1994) also suggests that socialization influences interact with endogenously organized trajectories of reactivity to produce inhibited or bold types in early childhood.

Gunnar and associates have been more concerned with Rothbart and Derryberry's construct of negative reactivity (usually operationalized as "proneness to distress" in Gunnar's research) and its concomitant relations with the functioning of the hypothalamic–pituitary–adrenocortical (HPA) system (e.g., Gunnar, 1990, 1994; Stansbury & Gunnar, 1994). Gunnar's data suggest that individual differences in HPA functioning can be assessed reliably very early in life, and that these differences have expectable correlates in behavioral outcomes assessed some months later (e.g., Gunnar, Porter, Wolf, & Rigatuso, 1995). Her findings tend to support the notion from Rothbart and Derryberry's theory concerning the primacy of reactivity and regulation as sources of temperament-relevant behaviors.

Gunnar's model of relations among psychoneuroendocrine systems, central nervous system functioning, temperament, and social interactions and relationships is dynamic, complex, and not comprehensively described here. Her interpretations of the data differ from those offered by Kagan and Fox in that Gunnar does not posit a necessarily causal relation between HPA indicators and temperament. Rather, these systems may interact and be mutually regulating (e.g., Gunnar, Larson, Hertsgaard, Harris, & Broderson, 1992). Indeed, Gunnar's data suggest that the quality of parent–child attachments moderates relations between negative emotional reactivity (temperament) and behavioral outcome (e.g., Gunnar, Mangelsdorf, Larson, & Hertsgaard, 1989; Mangelsdorf, Gunnar, Kestenbaum, Lang, & Andreas, 1990).

Temperament as Social Construction

Bates (e.g., Bates, 1980; Bates & Bayles, 1984; Bates, Freeland, & Lounsbury, 1979) has proposed an approach to conceptualizing temperament in terms of observable behaviors, but without making a strong interpretation regarding the underlying sources of individual differences along the several temperamental dimensions. The most salient temperamental attribute from this perspective is "difficultness," a construct first introduced by behavioral-style theorists (e.g., Thomas & Chess, 1977; Thomas et al., 1963). Bates's (1980) difficultness construct differs from the behavioral-style construct in that individual differences arise as much from the observer's (usually a parent's) perception that the behavior of the child is difficult for that observer as they may from some endogenously organized attribute of the child. Bates and Bayles (1984) documented diverse subjective and objective correlates of difficultness in children across the infancy period, using measures designed within this perspective. Although the problem of observer subjectivity with regard to ratings of temperament-relevant behavior has been noted repeatedly (e.g., Sameroff, Seifer, & Elias, 1982; Vaughn, Bradley, Joffe, Seifer, & Barglow, 1987), Bates was the first major temperament theorist to face the issue directly. When the subjective biases of observers are admitted into the mix of parameters contributing to characterizations of temperament, questions that are typically glossed over or avoided in the temperament literature can be explored (e.g., Bates, 1980). For example, Bates's approach affords the possibility of considering low correlations between temperament ratings provided by equally knowledgeable raters (mothers and fathers) as a legitimate phenomenon worthy of scientific interest, rather than as an embarrassing skeleton to be directed into a closet after some mention of the significance of values in the .2 to .3 range.

The behavioral territory claimed by Bates's theory resembles that of behavioral-style theory and the theories of emotional expression/regulation. Unlike other temperament theories, however, Bates's construal of temperament comes close to a social co-construction. In this aspect, Bates's temperament dimensions are similar to attachment relationships. That is, both temperamental difficultness and attachments require the contributions of interacting partners, and both temperament and attachments are seen as instrumental in setting a trajectory for later positive or negative adaptations in intra- and interpersonal realms of activity (see Bates, 1989a; Bates, Maslin, & Frankel, 1985; Erickson, Egeland, & Sroufe, 1985).

Common Themes
across Temperament Theories

At the level of observable behavior, the theories of temperament broadly agree. The characteristic level of expression and/or experience of negative (and perhaps positive) affect, and the tendency to express this affect as a reaction to perturbations in the environment, are central to the meanings of temperamental difficultness, emotionality, and reactivity (see Bates, 1989b; Goldsmith, Rieser-Danner, & Briggs, 1991). Temperament is also (usually) characterized in terms of the degree of psychomotor arousal/activity and the capacity for its regulation. The theorists agree that individual differences along temperament dimensions carry implications for frequencies and qualities of exchanges between a child and the physical and social objects in the child's environment, and that these exchanges may modify the characteristic expression of temperament. They

also agree that individual differences along temperament dimensions should be detectable from early infancy. Furthermore, all theoretical positions reviewed suggest connections between temperament and personality, even though the specifics of these connections vary from theory to theory.

Theorists are not in complete agreement regarding the nature of temperamental dimensions (e.g., behavioral styles, emergent personality, emotional experience, physiological reactivity/regulation, social perception), and there is no consensus with respect to the specific biological substrates that give rise to individual differences along dimensions of temperament. Nor is there consensus on the optimal technique(s) for measuring individual differences in temperament, even though parent reports are the method of convenience. Finally, although most temperament theories allow for changes in the behavioral indicators of temperament as a function of growth and experience, there is no broad consensus concerning either normative or individual developmental trajectories. Thus questions regarding the temporal stability of individual differences are answered somewhat differently from theory to theory.

CONCEPTUAL AND EMPIRICAL CONNECTIONS BETWEEN ATTACHMENT AND TEMPERAMENT

Potential and Realized Points of Conceptual Contact

On the surface, it seems that biological temperament constructs should converge with the normative understandings of attachment (Bowlby, 1969/1982), because both Bowlby's explanation for the presence of the attachment behavioral system and temperament constructs depend to a greater or lesser extent on genetic transmission. Surprisingly, there has been little interest among temperament researchers in the normative development of attachment behavior or attachment system functioning. For example, Bowlby's notion that a species-specific, neurally based behavioral system governs proximity and contact maintenance between children and adult caregivers retains its uniqueness and specificity under any of the temperament theories. Likewise, the notion that the child–caregiver relationship, from its earliest expression, is best characterized as a love relationship (and that loss in a love relationship is the source of grief reactions) has no alternative (or even parallel) characterization in the temperament theories. All major theories of social relationships mark the period from about 10 to about 20 months of age as "special" in terms of the qualities of relationships observable in child–caregiver interactions (e.g., Bowlby, 1969/1982; Kaye, 1982; Sander, 1964; Stern, 1985). The establishment of such a relationship is normative for the human species and may be a necessary foundation for assembling the skills required to establish and maintain intimate, loving relationships in later developmental periods (e.g., Owens et al., 1995; Sroufe & Fleeson, 1986). Again, this normative aspect of attachment theory is uncontested by theories of temperament.

Bowlby's assumption that this love relationship is assembled in the context of interactions over the first few years of life and parallels the construction of intelligence (in the senses of both Piaget and Vygotsky) during the first few years of life is not contradicted by any of the temperament theories. All relationships are emergent from interaction and from patterns of interaction over time (see Hinde, 1979; Hinde & Stevenson-Hinde, 1987). Attachment relationships are no different. Although temperament theories may include corollaries about the content or quality of specific interactions and relationships, there is no disagreement that construction of the child–caregiver relationship requires a history of interaction. In this respect, the theories of temperament and attachment theory are congruent.

Whereas the biologically grounded aspects of attachment theory have not been considered, much less contested, in temperament research, individual differences in quality (or security) that characterize specific attachment relationships have been studied extensively from the perspective of temperament (for reviews and commentary, see Goldsmith & Alansky, 1987; Goldsmith & Harman, 1994; Kagan, 1984; Seifer & Schiller, 1995). Interest in attachment behavior and attachment quality by temperament theorists and researchers is motivated by the recognition that many of the affect-laden terms used by attachment researchers in descriptions of interactions between children and their caregivers (e.g., "pleasure," "joy," "positive expectations," and "enthusiasm" vs. "distress," "anger," "fear," and "lethargy") bear close resemblance to aspects of the phenotypic indicators of the primary difficultness/emotionality/reactivity/distress-prone-ness dimension of temperament (see Vaughn et al., 1992). Because both attachment theory and the temperament theories are explicit in making connections between their content domains and personality/self-concept development (e.g., Bowlby, 1980, 1988; chapters in Halverson et al., 1994), the interpretation of individual variability relevant to this primary temperament dimension has been considered nontrivial by temperament theorists. Baldly stated, the "temperament" interpretation has been that the attachment security construct is redundant as a predictor of behavioral variability and personality dimensions, after the contributions of endogenously organized traits are considered. Resistance to interaction and avoidance of interaction/contact (which are considered by attachment theorists to reflect an interaction history) are interpretable as manifestations of individual differences along dimensions or across categories of temperament (e.g., Kagan, 1984).

As noted earlier in this chapter, Ainsworth's theoretical propositions and data (and her opinions; see Ainsworth & Marvin, 1995) imply that individual differences in the patterning of attachment behavior (i.e., secure-base and haven-of-safety phenomena) arise as a consequence of variations in child–caregiver interaction (which are in turn thought to arise as consequences of variability in caregivers' capacity for interpreting and responding to their infants' communicative signals) and not as a consequence of endogenously organized properties of children. If early-appearing temperament were found to be directly implicated in differences in the patterning of attachment behavior, and if those same temperamental attributes were also found to affect the aspects of children's behavior assumed to arise as a consequence of attachment security, and if such effects were shown to be independent of the effects of child–parent interaction quality and parental sensitivity to children's communicative signals, then Ainsworth's understandings of these patterns of behavior as indicative of differences along a dimension of attachment security would be called into question.

On the other hand, Seifer and associates (e.g., Seifer & Schiller, 1995; Seifer, Schiller, Sameroff, Resnick, & Riordan, 1996) note that both temperament and attachment security interpretations may be sustained if it is demonstrated that both sensitivity and temperamental attributes contribute to the quality of the child–mother interactions that lead to individual differences in the patterning of secure-base and haven-of-safety behavior observed in both "emergency" (e.g., the SS) and "ordinary" (e.g., home observation) contexts. Below, we review the empirical findings relevant to these questions.

Empirical Contact

A search of the PsycINFO journal index using the key words "attachment" and "temperament" identified 112 published papers from 1981 to 1996 in which both sets of constructs were assessed. Examination of the abstracts indicated that 54 of these papers evaluated relations between concept domains for normally developing infants and young children. Papers excluded from our review were concerned with older children (age >7–8 years), used constructs from the attachment and temperament domains as independent predictors of some third domain (e.g., problem behaviors), or used samples from atypical populations (e.g., developmentally disabled children, parents with diagnosed mental illness). A summary of the results from these published papers is presented in Table 10.1. Sections of Table 10.1 are organized by the temperament approach adopted by the investigator(s); however, we caution that this organizational contrivance is not entirely adequate, because assessment strategies spanning two or more of the approaches outlined above were included in several studies (e.g., Seifer et al., 1996), and some authors (e.g., Belsky, Fish, & Isabella, 1991; Susman-Stillman et al., 1996) reported on data collected with instrument(s) from one approach from the perspective of another approach. When results relevant to different approaches were included in a single study, we have listed the article in more than one section of Table 10.1. Columns in Table 10.1 indicate whether the analyses were concerned with relations between temperament construct(s) and attachment security (coded as a continuous dimension), patterns of attachment behavior (i.e., SS classifications), attachment behaviors (e.g., proximity seeking, crying, secure-base behavior), and/or maternal sensitivity.

Attachment and Temperament as Behavioral Style

Relations between behavioral-style measures of temperament and attachment security (and/or interactive antecedents to security) were reported for 14 different samples (reported in 12 separate articles and chapters). In 10 samples, the SS classifications and/or behaviors during reunion

served as indicators of attachment. In seven samples (Seifer et al., 1996, collected both Q-sort and SS data), the Waters Attachment Q-Sort (AQS) security score was the indicator of attachment. Sample sizes ranged from 23 to 166; age at initial assessment for temperament ranged from 6 to 12 months, and from 12 to 42 months for attachment assessments. The samples were heterogeneous for indicators of socioeconomic status, although most participants were middle-class and of European American ethnic status. In all samples save one (i.e., Stevenson-Hinde & Shouldice, reported in Vaughn et al., 1992), mothers served as the informants for temperament. In the Seifer et al. (1996) report, observed behavior indicators of behavioral style were obtained in addition to maternal reports.

Results suggest that behavioral-style measures of temperament show modest associations with attachment security measures, but this generalization is qualified by the specific measure of attachment used. Significant between-group differences were reported in only 2 of the 10 samples using SS classifications as the indicators of attachment security. Of these two, one (i.e., Kemp, 1987) reported as significant a discriminant function with a probability of $p < .07$. Kemp distinguished the avoidant (Group A) cases from both secure (Group B) and resistant (Group C) cases. Avoidant cases were described by their mothers as temperamentally "easier" than were cases classified otherwise. In the second of these studies, Rieser-Danner, Roggman, and Langlois (1987) reported the results of a multiple-regression analysis that cannot be interpreted in terms of security of attachment, because they split the secure cases into two groups on the basis of emotionality criteria rather than on the basis of attachment security. Rieser-Danner et al. (1987) also included a single resistant (Group C) infant in their regression analysis. The only legitimate conclusion that can be drawn from their analysis is that B3 infants are perceived by their mothers as temperamentally more difficult than are other secure (i.e., Subgroups B1, B2) and avoidant (Group A) infants. Although such an interpretation may be consistent with the hypothesis that temperament is associated with the manner in which security or insecurity is constructed, it is not consistent with the hypothesis that temperament is a foundation parameter determining security versus insecurity (see also Belsky & Rovine, 1987, for a related discussion).

In three samples, the insecure cases (i.e., Groups A and C) were combined and contrasted

TABLE 10.1. Empirical Associations between Attachment and Temperament

Temperament perspective	Attachment measure	Temperament measure	Security	B vs. A and/or C and/or D	A vs. C	SS behavior	Maternal sensitivity–responsivity
Temperament as behavioral style							
Bohlin, Hagekull, Germer, Anderson, & Lindberg (1989)	Separation–reunion[a]	BBQ[2]	N/A	N/A	N/A	−	+
Egeland & Farber (1984)	SS[a, b]	ITQ[1, 3]	N/A	−	−	N/A	N/A
Frodi, Bridges, & Shonk (1989)	SS[a]	ITQ-R[2]	N/A	+	−	N/A	N/A
Kemp (1987)	SS[a]	ITQ[3]	N/A	+	+	−	N/A
Mangelsdorf, Gunnar, Kestenbaum, Lang, & Andreas (1990)*	SS[a]	LTA[3]	N/A	−	−	−	+
Rieser-Danner, Roggman, & Langlois (1987)	SS[a]	ITQ[3]	N/A	+	+	N/A	N/A
Seifer, Schiller, Sameroff, Resnick, & Riordan (1996)*	SS[a] AQS(O)	ITQ-R[3]	N/A +	− N/A	− N/A	N/A N/A	− −
Stevenson-Hinde & Shouldice (1992)	AQS(M)[d]	BSQ[5]	+	N/A	N/A	N/A	N/A
Trudel (reported in Vaughn et al., 1992)	AQS(M)[b]	TTS, modified[4]	+	N/A	N/A	N/A	N/A
Vaughn, Lefever, Seifer, & Barglow (1989)	SS[a]	ITQ-R[3]	N/A	−	−	+	N/A
Hron-Stewart (reported in Vaughn et al., 1992)	AQS(O)[c]	TTS[4]	−	N/A	N/A	N/A	N/A
Joffe (reported in Vaughn et al., 1992)	AQS(O)[a]	ITQ-R[3]	−	N/A	N/A	N/A	N/A
Wachs & Desai (1993)	AQS(M)[c]	TTS[4]	+	N/A	N/A	N/A	+
Weber, Levitt, & Clark (1986)	SS[a]	DOTS[3]	N/A	−	−	+	NA
Temperament as emerging personality							
Belsky, Fish, & Isabella (1991)	SS[a]	ICQ + observations[2, 3]	N/A	−	N/A	N/A	−
Bretherton, Biringen, Ridgeway, Maslin, & Sherman (1989)	PI[b] AQS(M)[c, d]	CCTI[4, 5]	N/A	N/A	N/A	N/A	+
Crockenberg (1981)	SS[a]	NBAS[1]	N/A	−	−	−	+
Crockenberg & McCluskey (1986)	SS[a]	NBAS[1]	N/A	N/A	N/A	+	+
Lewis & Feiring (1989)	Other separation–reunion[a]	Observed sociability[2]	N/A	+	+	+	N/A

(continued)

TABLE 10.1 *(continued)*

Temperament perspective	Attachment measure	Temperament measure	Security	B vs. A and/or C and/or D	A vs. C	SS behavior	Maternal sensitivity–responsivity
Seifer et al. (1996)*	SS[a]	EAS[3]	N/A	–	–	N/A	–
	AQS(O)		+	N/A	N/A	N/A	–
Susman-Stillman, Kalkoske, Egeland, & Waldman (1996)	SS[a]	Observation[1] ITQ[2,3]	N/A	–	+	N/A	+
van den Boom (1989)	SS[a]	NBAS[1] ICQ[3]	N/A	+	N/A	N/A	+
van den Boom (1994)	SS[a]	NBAS[1]	N/A	+	+	N/A	+
Waters, Vaughn, & Egeland (1980)	SS[a]	NBAS[1]	N/A	+	+	N/A	N/A

Temperament as biologically founded substrates:
Physiological regulation, reactivity, proneness to distress, and behavioral inhibition

Balleyguier (1991)	SS[a]	Neonatal irritability[1]	N/A	+	–	N/A	+
Bradshaw, Goldsmith, & Campos (1987)	SS[a]	IBQ[3]	N/A	–	–	+	N/A
Braungart & Stifter (1991)	SS[a]	Reactivity[3]	N/A	+	–	+	N/A
		Regulation[3]		+	–	+	N/A
Calkins & Fox (1992)	SS[a]	Neonatal reactivity[1] 5-month reactivity[2]	N/A	+	–	+	N/A
		IBQ[2]	N/A	+	–	N/A	N/A
		TBAQ[3,4]	N/A	–	–	N/A	N/A
Denham & Moser (1994)	PI	IBQ[3]	N/A	N/A	N/A	N/A	+
Del Carmen, Pedersen, Huffman, & Bryan (1993)	SS[a]	BRP[2]	N/A	–	–	N/A	N/A
Gunnar, Mangelsdorf, Larson, & Hertsgaard (1989)	SS[a]	LTA[3]	N/A	–	–	+	N/A
Hertsgaard, Gunnar, Erikson, & Nachmias (1995)	SS[b]	Cortisol levels[4]	N/A	–	–	N/A	N/A
Izard, Haynes, Chisholm, & Baak (1991)	SS[a]	IBQ[3] Emotional expressiveness[2,3]	+	N/A	N/A	N/A	N/A
Kanaya (1986)	Other separation–reunion[a]						
Kochanska (1995)	AQS(M)[c,d]	Observed fearfulness[5]	+	N/A	N/A	N/A	N/A

(continued)

TABLE 10.1 (continued)

Temperament perspective	Attachment measure	Temperament measure	Security	B vs. A and/or C and/or D	A vs. C	SS behavior	Maternal sensitivity–responsivity
		CBQ composite[5]					
Kotsaftis (reported in Vaughn et al., 1992)	AQS(M)[d]	CBQ[5]	+	N/A	N/A	N/A	N/A
Mangelsdorf et al. (1990)*	SS[a]	LTA[3]	N/A	–	–	–	+
Miyake & Chen (1984)	SS[a]	Irritability/ proneness to distress[1, 2]	N/A	+	N/A	N/A	N/A
Miyake, Chen, & Campos (1985)	SS[a]	Irritability/ proneness to distress[1, 2]	N/A	+	N/A	N/A	N/A
Nachmias, Gunnar, Mangelsdorf, Parritz, & Buss (1996)	SS[b]	TBAQ[4] Inhibition[3]	N/A N/A	– –	– –	N/A N/A	N/A N/A
Seifer, et al. (1996)	SS[a] AQS(O)	IBQ[3]	N/A +	– N/A	– N/A	N/A N/A	+
Thompson, Connell, & Bridges (1988)	SS[a, b]	Temperamental fear[3, 4]	N/A	N/A	N/A	+	N/A
Thompson & Lamb (1984)	SS[a]	Observed emotional responsiveness[3, 4]	N/A	+	+	+	N/A
Temperament as social construction							
Bates, Maslin, & Frankel (1985)	SS[a]	ICQ[2, 3]	N/A	–	–	+	N/A
Belsky & Rovine (1987)	SS[a]	NBAS[1] ICQ[2]	N/A N/A	+ –	+ –	N/A N/A	N/A N/A
Seifer et al. (1996)*	SS[a] AQS(O)	ICQ[3]	N/A +	– N/A	– N/A	– N/A	–
Volling & Belsky (1992)	SS (Father)[a]	ICQ (Mother)[2]	N/A	+	N/A	N/A	N/A

Note. More articles are represented in Table 10.1 than are cited in the text. +, effect tested and significant; –, effect tested and not significant; N/A, effect not tested.

*Multiple category placements.

Attachment measures: AQS-M (Attachment *Q*-Sort—Mother); AQS-O (Attachment *Q*-Sort—Observers); PI (parent interview); SS (Strange Situation); other separation–reunion. [a]Attachment assessed between 11 and 15 months; [b]attachment assessed between 16 and 20 months; [c]attachment assessed between 21 and 36 months; [d]attachment assessed after 36 months.

Temperament measures: BBQ (Baby Behavior Questionnaire); BRP (Behavioral Responsiveness Paradigm); BSQ (Behavioral Style Questionnaire); CBQ (Children's Behavior Questionnaire); CCTI (Colorado Child Temperament Inventory); DOTS (Dimensions of Temperament Survey); EAS (Emotionality, Activity, Sociability); IBQ (Infant Behavior Questionnaire); ICQ (Infant Characteristics Questionnaire); ITQ (Infant Temperament Questionnaire); ITQ-R (Infant Temperament Questionnaire—Revised); LTA (Louisville Temperament Assessment); NBAS (Neonatal Behavioral Assessment Scale); TBAQ (Toddler Behavior Assessment Questionnaire); TTS (Toddler Temperament Scale). [1]Temperament assessment during neonatal period; [2]temperament assessment in first half of first year; [3]temperament assessment between 6 and 15 months; [4]temperament assessment between 16 and 24 months; [5]temperament assessment between 25 and 42 months; [6]temperament assessment after 42 months.

with the secure (Group B) cases (i.e., Frodi, Bridges, & Shonk, 1989; Kemp, 1987; Mangelsdorf et al., 1990). This comparison was not significant in the Kemp or Mangelsdorf et al. analyses, but significant differences were reported by Frodi et al. (1989). Using an extreme-groups comparison ("difficult" vs. "easy"), Frodi et al. reported that 100% of their temperamentally "easy" infants ($n = 9$) were classified as secure, whereas only 60% of their temperamentally "difficult" infants (4 out of 7) were classified as secure. More interestingly, the three "difficult" infants classified as insecure were from the avoidant group. Thus, the Kemp (1987) and Frodi et al. (1989) studies both reported finding the avoidant group to be distinguishable from the secure cases, but whether these babies were temperamentally less difficult (Kemp) or more difficult (Frodi et al.) remains an open question. Clearly, such inconsistencies across studies present a conundrum to theorists attempting to interpret attachment behavior in terms of temperamental difficultness.

In 3 of the 14 samples, results of correlation analyses relating behavioral-style dimensions of temperament to reunion behaviors in the SS were reported. Bohlin, Hagekull, Germer, Anderson, and Lindberg (1989) found no direct relations between temperament and measures of avoidance and resistance in reunion episodes of an adapted SS procedure. This study must be interpreted cautiously, because the adaptation of the SS consisted of conducting the separation–reunion sequences in the child's own home and no reliability or validity data for the resulting classifications are reported. Likewise, Vaughn, Lefever, Seifer, and Barglow (1989) failed to find any significant correlations between a measure of temperamental "difficulty" and the five criterial behaviors from reunion episodes of the SS. Weber, Levitt, and Clark (1986) reported finding 2 of 15 correlations between individual temperament dimension scores and reunion behavior significant, and they reported a significant correlation between a summary "difficulty" score and resistance in the reunion episodes of the SS.

Only Seifer et al. (1996) considered relations between maternal sensitivity and temperament scores. The maternal reports of child behavioral style were consistently unrelated to observers' ratings of sensitivity at both 6 and 9 months of age. However, independent observers' ratings of mood and approach (based on child behavior) were related to observer ratings of sensitivity at both 6 and 9 months. At 9 months, observer assessments of the "intensity" temperament dimension were also significantly correlated with observer assessments of maternal sensitivity.

Taken together, the results of studies in which SS classifications and/or behavioral criteria are used to assess attachment security suggest that security is not strongly related to behavioral-style indices of temperament. Even the studies suggesting such relations are inconsistent, with one suggesting that prototypical secure cases (B3) are more difficult than other infants (Rieser-Danner et al., 1987); another suggesting that temperamentally difficult infants are likely to be classified as avoidant in the SS (Frodi et al., 1989); another suggesting that avoidant infants are temperamentally easier than are other cases (Kemp, 1987); and yet another suggesting that resistant infants may be more temperamentally difficult (Weber et al., 1986). Correlations between behavioral-style indices of temperament and behavioral criteria are also consistent with this interpretation. Temperament as behavioral style bears little relation to attachment behavior. Seifer et al.'s (1996) findings regarding temperament and maternal sensitivity are particularly intriguing, insofar as they suggest that sensitive mothers have infants who appear less temperamentally difficult to observers, but not to the mothers themselves.

To turn to studies in which the AQS was used to index attachment security, behavioral-style indicators of temperamental difficulty proved to be significantly correlated with attachment security in five of the seven samples. Correlational data suggested that cases rated by the parents as more temperamentally "difficult" had lower attachment security scores. The range of correlation values was wide (r's from $-.04$ to $-.54$), and these values were more likely to reach significance when mothers completed both the temperament ratings and the AQS. Although the results from these studies are not entirely consistent (i.e., significant correlations were not obtained in two samples reported by Vaughn et al. [1992], and Seifer et al.'s [1996] sample yielded significant associations between AQS attachment security assessed at 12 months and behavioral style measured at 6 and 12 months, but not at 9 months), they do suggest that behavior observed at home will not be parsed easily into "temperament-relevant" and "attachment-relevant" categories. This problem is likely to be especially apparent when dimensions such as positive and negative mood are assessed, because both attachment and temperament theories contain postulates and propose hypotheses concerning mood and its vicissitudes (e.g., secure infants are supposed to display positive mood when interacting with their attachment figures). In addition, mood and other aspects of affect expression in the context of interaction with the mother play an important role in the definition of attachment security with the AQS. Given this context, it is surprising that correlations between the AQS security score and the behavioral-style scores are so modest.

Whereas these findings stand in contrast to those from studies using the SS (reviewed above), it is important to note that the shared variance across the AQS and behavioral-style measures is not large (range from 0.2% to 29% common variance) in these studies. Clearly, the construction and maintenance of a secure-base relationship entails more than a child's possession of an appropriate profile of stylistic attributes (and conversely, parental ratings of temperament as behavioral style are influenced by a broader range of child behaviors, interactional episodes and contexts, and other extrarelationship factors than are necessary and sufficient for the assembly of an attachment relationship). Nevertheless, there is common ground between the behavioral-style approach to temperament and the attachment security construct. We return to questions concerning the nature of this common ground and suggestions for adjusting theoretical propositions to accommodate it in the final section of this chapter (see also Vaughn et al., 1992).

Attachment and Temperament as Emergent Personality

Our literature search revealed two reports in which the Buss and Plomin measures were used to index temperament (i.e., Bretherton, Biringen, Ridgeway, Maslin, & Sherman, 1989; Seifer et al., 1996). In addition, irritability/distress during the neonatal period has been studied by several investigators in a manner consistent with Buss and Plomin's perspective, and these studies are reviewed here also. Studies in which early distress/irritability is interpreted in terms of Kagan's concepts of proneness to distress and behavioral inhibition are reviewed in a subsequent section.

Seifer et al. (1996) included the Emotionality scale from the Buss and Plomin (1984) version of the Emotionality, Activity, Sociability (EAS)

instrument at their 6-, 9-, and 12-month assessments. The Emotionality score was not related to SS classification for any of the three time periods. The 9- and 12-month scores did, however, correlate significantly with the AQS security score at 12 months. The 6-month Emotionality score was not significantly related to AQS security. Seifer and associates also examined relations between emotionality and maternal sensitivity. No significant associations were obtained (zero of four tests were significant). In contrast, Bretherton et al. (1989) reported a significant, negative association ($r = -.57, p < .001$) between maternal ratings of infant emotionality at 18 months of age and maternal sensitivity (scored from an interview with each mother) approximately 7 months later (i.e., when each child was 25 months of age). These investigators also reported positive and significant associations between temperamental dimensions labeled "sociability" and "attention span" (scored from an adaptation of the EAS) and their measure of maternal sensitivity.

A number of studies relating irritability during early infancy to later attachment status have been reported in a manner consistent with Buss and Plomin's perspective on temperament as early personality. Waters, Vaughn, and Egeland (1980) used a broad-band composite score formed from the items of the Neonatal Behavioral Assessment Scale (NBAS; Brazelton, 1973) as an indicator of early psychophysiological integrity, and found a relation between scores on this indicator and later attachment status. Specifically, infants identified on postnatal day 7 as less well integrated were more likely than other infants to be classified as resistant (Group C) in the SS. Many of the items included in the composite were indicative of irritability and general fussiness. It is important to note that this relation was not reproduced when NBAS data from postnatal day 10 were used. Nevertheless, the results of their study suggest that temperament-like attributes characterizing an infant very early in life may contribute to a pattern of interactions between the child and caregiver that is a precursor to a specific pattern of insecurity. This idea has been echoed more recently by Cassidy and Berlin (1994), who suggested that Group C infants are more biologically vulnerable than are Group A or Group B babies. When early vulnerability is combined with weak exploratory competence, these children often appear immature in the SS.

Studies by Crockenberg and by Egeland and associates (e.g., Crockenberg, 1981; Crockenberg & McCluskey, 1986; Susman-Stillman et al., 1996) have explored additional implications of infant irritability for attachment security and for attachment behavior assessed in the SS. Crockenberg (1981) did not find a direct relation between neonatal irritability (again using the NBAS to index irritability) and security of attachment (B vs. A + C cases). But she discovered an interaction between neonatal irritability and social support for mothers, such that irritability *was* significantly associated with insecurity when mothers lacked sufficient external social support, but not when social support was relatively high. In a subsequent report, Crockenberg and McCluskey (1986) analyzed additional data from the original (i.e., Crockenberg, 1981) sample and found that neonatal irritability was positively related to maternal responsiveness to crying at 3 months of age ($r = .29$, $p < .05$), but negatively related ($r = -.17$, n.s.) to their measure of maternal sensitivity at 12 months. The difference between these two correlations was significant. Crockenberg's findings are consistent with the speculation offered by Waters et al. (1980) to the effect that more irritable newborns potentiate interactive trajectories leading to different attachment outcomes from those for less irritable babies.

Susman-Stillman et al. (1996) conducted additional analyses for the sample originally described by Waters et al. (1980) and by Egeland and Farber (1984). Susman-Stillman et al.'s irritability measure was composed of items from a behavioral-style questionnaire completed by mothers at 3 and 6 months postpartum (but not using the original dimensions), and from observational assessments made by members of the neonatal nursing staff while the infants were in postdelivery rooms. Infant irritability did not predict security of attachment (assessed using SS classifications) directly in analyses of either 3- or 6-month data. However, a moderating relation between irritability and maternal sensitivity was found for the 3-month data. At 3 months of age, sensitivity predicted later attachment security *only* for the low-irritability infants. This effect was not reproduced in analyses of the 6-month data. Analyses within the insecure group (i.e., avoidant and resistant cases) suggested a role for irritability in the assembly of resistant attachment relationships, but this trend was only marginally significant ($p < .15$, in the predicted direction). An additional temperament-relevant variable ("sociability") distinguished avoidant from resistant cases: Group A (avoidant) infants

had been more temperamentally sociable as 3-month-olds than had been Group C (resistant) infants. Further analyses suggested that the Group A infants shared temperamental attributes (i.e., sociability) with secure infants from Subgroups B1 and B2, whereas the Group C infants shared attributes with the secure infants from Subgroups B3 and B4 (i.e., irritability). Although Susman-Stillman et al.'s findings do not precisely replicate either the Waters et al. (1980) results or Crockenberg's (1981) data, the results of the three studies are consistent with speculation that emotionality/distress (operationalized in terms of a young infant's tendency to be fussy across a range of stimulus conditions) is associated with the kind of fussiness in the SS that leads to a classification as resistant.

This interpretation is challenged by van den Boom's (1989, 1994) findings in two separate samples of infants from the Netherlands. She followed two groups of highly irritable infants (as determined by scores on NBAS items), who were recruited from a low-socioeconomic-status population, from birth to 12 months of age; she found that the majority were classified as insecure in the SS. The majority of these insecure cases were classified as avoidant (26 of 39 cases in her nonintervention groups, 1994 sample). Thus her data suggest that highly irritable newborns are likely to assemble avoidant relationships with their caregivers, rather than resistant ones (as suggested by Waters et al., 1980, and Susman-Stillman et al., 1996). Lewis and Feiring (1989) reached a similar conclusion regarding the Group A infants, but with respect to the sociability dimension. That is to say, in Lewis and Feiring's study, avoidant infants in modified SS assessments were *less social* during the first year of life than were nonavoidant infants.

van den Boom (1994) also conducted an intervention with half of her second sample that was intended to improve the sensitivity of the mothers to infant communicative signals. For the intervention group (highly irritable as newborns), the proportion of securely attached cases was significantly greater than for the nonintervention control group. Indeed, the percentage of secure cases in the treatment group approached that reported for low-income samples unselected for differences in temperamental attributes (i.e., 62% secure, 38% insecure in the treatment group). This result is consistent with the conclusion reached by Susman-Stillman et al. (1996) to the effect that influences of irritability on subsequent attachment are subordinate to influences of maternal sensitivity. Of course, it is also possible that increases in maternal sensitivity contingent on the intervention acted to reduce the level of infant irritability, which in turn promoted interactions conducive to the assembly of secure attachments.

The final study reviewed in this section was reported by Belsky et al. (1991). They operationalized negative emotionality in terms of observations of fussiness during parent–child interactions and the Fussy/Difficult scale from the Infant Characteristics Questionnaire (ICQ; Bates, Freeland, & Lounsbury, 1979), which mothers completed at 3 and 9 months postpartum. They operationalized positive emotionality in terms of observed behavior and individual items from the ICQ that concerned smiling and other forms of positive affect. Although they did not find direct relations between security of attachment (assessed in the SS) and negative emotionality, Belsky et al. (1991) reported that children high with respect to negative emotionality *and* low with respect to positive emotionality tended to be classified as insecure. No analyses by insecure classification category were reported.

Overall, the results of studies relating temperament from the Buss and Plomin (1975, 1984) perspective to attachment security are inconclusive. On the one hand, all reports suggest some overlap between these conceptual domains; on the other, most of the significant associations reported could not be replicated in other studies. For example, Waters et al. (1980) and Susman-Stillman et al. (1996) suggest that irritable infants are more likely than other infants to be later classified as resistant in the SS, whereas van den Boom (1989, 1994) suggests that such infants are more likely to be classified as avoidant. Likewise, Bretherton et al. (1989) reported substantial relations between negative emotionality and maternal sensitivity, whereas Seifer et al. (1996) failed to find a significant relation between measures of the same constructs. Clearly, some problems with interpretation of these results arise from different operationalizations of emotionality (which may have markedly variable psychometric properties), from differences in the timing of assessments, and perhaps from other threats to validity across studies. Nevertheless, the fact that such large differences can arise from premises that were so similar in their initial formulation (e.g., temperamental emotionality/irritability predicts patterns of interaction that lead to the assembly of insecure attachments) suggests that both the temperament-as-early-emotion theory and the interactions antecedent to the assembly of attachments need additional conceptual and/or empirical specification before these two construct domains can be meaningfully juxtaposed.

Attachment and Temperament as Emotional/Physiological Regulation and Reactivity

The Goldsmith–Rothbart Approach. Analyses relating assessments of emotional and psychophysiological regulation (in the spirit of Goldsmith's and Rothbart's approaches to temperament) to assessments of attachment security and/or attachment behavior were reported for seven samples of infants and young children. In an additional sample, maternal ratings of infant temperament (using Rothbart's Infant Behavior Questionnaire [IBQ]) were related to self-reports of feeling attached to the child. Additional studies adopting Kagan's empirical perspective on proneness to distress/behavioral inhibition are reviewed in the next subsection.

Seifer et al. (1996) tested relations between IBQ characterizations of temperament and SS classifications. The test was not significant. Significant associations between IBQ scores and the AQS attachment security score were reported in three studies (i.e., Kochanska, 1995 [reported there in footnote 4, p. 607]; Kotsaftis [in Vaughn et al., 1992]; Seifer et al., 1996). Kochanska and Kotsaftis used composite scores for "negative reactivity," and Seifer et al. used the single Distress to Limits scale. Seifer et al. also reported that Distress to Limits scores were associated with their measures of maternal sensitivity at 6 (but not 9) months. In a similar study, Bradshaw, Goldsmith, and Campos (1987) reported that a composite of positive versus negative affect from the IBQ was positively and significantly correlated with avoidance scored in the SS. The same composite showed a negative relation (not significant) with resistance scored in the SS. Although not directly relevant to infants' attachment security, findings reported by Denham and Moser (1994) are consistent with the results reported above. Denham and Moser found that mothers who described their infants as being more temperamentally difficult (based on scores from the IBQ) also reported feeling less attached to their infants at both 6 weeks of age and 9 months of age.

Three other studies examined relations between individual differences in the regulation of affect and SS classifications. Del Carmen, Pedersen, Huffman, and Bryan (1993) assessed temperamental attributes when infants in their sample were 3 months old, using a procedure developed by Garcia-Coll et al. (1988). Four temperament dimensions were scored (negativity, positivity, soothability, and sociability). Attachment was assessed at 12–13 months of age. A discriminant function analysis failed to distinguish the secure from the insecure cases. However, a follow-up analysis indicated that insecure cases had *lower* scores on the negativity scale than did the secure cases. Of 11 insecure cases in this sample, 10 had been classified as avoidant, so this relation is consistent with the findings reported by Bradshaw et al. (1987) to the effect that avoidance in the SS is related to low negative affect (but see van den Boom, 1994).

Relations between negative reactivity and emotional responsiveness in the SS were examined in two studies. Thompson and Lamb (1984) reported reliable episode-by-episode differences for variables representing "peak intensity" and "range" of emotional expressiveness in the SS. In general, infants classified as B1 or B2 tended to have lower scores for facial and vocal aspects of peak intensity of emotion than did infants classified as B3, B4, or C. These infants also tended to recover from distress more rapidly than did the B3, B4, and C cases. Trends for infants classified as avoidant paralleled those for the B1 and B2 cases, but were not as consistently different from the B3, B4, and C cases. For their emotion measures, cases classified as avoidant did not differ from cases classified as B1 or B2, and cases classified as resistant did not differ from those classified as B3 or B4 (with the exception that recovery scores for resistant infants were higher, indicating longer recovery time, in the first reunion episode of the SS). Thompson and Lamb concluded that individual differences in the tendencies to experience emotion in the SS are not determinants of security of attachment, but may influence the form in which security or insecurity was manifest.

Braungart and Stifter (1991) extended the Thompson and Lamb (1984) analyses to behaviors used by infants in the SS to regulate their distress in separation and reunion episodes. Again, B1 and B2 infants differed from B3 and B4 infants in terms of their use of self-regulatory strategies during separation and reunion. Avoidant infants also differed from B3 and B4 infants in terms of their use of specific self-regulatory strategies. Interestingly, avoidant infants were rated similarly to B3 and B4 infants with respect to negative emotion in separation. Braungart and Stifter concluded that there may be important differences between secure and insecure infants with respect to the strategies and tactics they use to regulate effects of emotional arousal. Unfortunately, Braungart and Stifter's data do not afford the opportunity to evaluate the determinants of these regulatory tactics, because they were assessed in the context of the SS itself. It would be most interesting to consider whether attachment security (or antecedent interaction history) is a cause or consequence of these differences in regulatory strategies (see Cassidy, 1994; Field, 1994; and Hofer, 1994, for extended discussions of such possibilities for human and nonhuman animals).

The Kagan–Fox Approach. Unlike most of the other approaches reviewed here, Kagan's interest in temperament and its possible relation to attachment security has tended to be narrowly focused on a single dimension (reactivity or proneness to distress at the unfamiliar during infancy, which is a precursor to behavioral/emotional inhibition during childhood) (e.g., Kagan, 1984, 1994a, 1994b; Kagan & Snidman, 1991). Like Rothbart (e.g., Rothbart, 1988), Kagan argues that individual differences with respect to reactivity–inhibition are intimately tied to autonomic and central nervous system structures. However, in contrast to Rothbart and to most other researchers in the area, Kagan's research characterizes temperament in terms of discrete types (e.g., low-reactivity vs. high-reactivity, inhibited vs. uninhibited), rather than on continuous dimensions of temperament (see Kagan, 1994a; Kagan, Reznick, & Gibbons, 1989). Consequently, research from Kagan's laboratory tends to emphasize extreme-group comparisons and frequently excludes from analyses those cases in the midrange who are neither strongly high-reactivity (inhibited) nor strongly low-reactivity (uninhibited). Although Kagan has speculated repeatedly on temperamental explanations of SS classifications as a function of inhibited versus uninhibited types (e.g., Kagan, 1982, 1984), we found no research from his group testing this speculation. Other research teams (e.g., Fox and associates, Gunnar and associates, Miyake and associates) have not adopted the extreme-group designs preferred by Kagan, and it may be that the research we now review would not be considered an adequate test of his speculations.

Miyake and associates (e.g., Miyake & Chen, 1984; Miyake, Chen, & Campos, 1985; Usi & Miyake, 1984) summarized research completed in Japan relevant to relations between irritability/proneness to distress and SS classifications. They concluded that infant irritability/proneness to distress from the neonatal period forward was associated with being classified as resistant (Group C) in the SS. Although Miyake et al. did not collect psychophysiological data that might connect their findings with the speculations offered by Kagan, their findings were interpreted as being consistent with Kagan's hypotheses.

Fox and associates (e.g., Calkins & Fox, 1992) examined the development of reactivity and inhibition in relation to attachment for children assessed longitudinally over the first 2 years of life. Temperament was assessed via Rothbart's IBQ at 5 and 14 months of age. No measure of temperamental reactivity/proneness to distress made during the first year of life showed a significant relation to the A-B-C classifications made from 14-month SS assessments. However, one secure–insecure contrast proved significant: Insecure cases (i.e., the combined A and C groups) were more likely than secure infants to have fussed and cried at the removal of a pacifier as newborns. This variable from the neonatal period also had a modest but significant association with crying at reunion in the SS. The 5-month IBQ Activity Level score also distinguished avoidant from secure cases (avoidant cases were more active). Perhaps most interestingly, 14-month attachment classifications were associated with assessments of inhibition at 24 months. Resistant infants tended to be more inhibited at age 2 than were infants classified as avoidant. Thus, although reactivity/proneness to distress did not strongly predict attachment classifications, resistance in the SS did forecast later tendencies to inhibition.

Gunnar and associates have conducted the most programmatic series of studies relevant to Kagan's hypotheses concerning attachment security and temperament (e.g., Gunnar et al., 1989; Hertsgaard, Gunnar, Erickson, & Nachmias, 1995; Mangelsdorf et al., 1990; Nachmias, Gunnar, Mangelsdorf, Parritz, & Buss, 1996). Using a variety of questionnaire (e.g., Mangelsdorf et al., 1990), neuroendocrine (e.g., Gunnar et al., 1989; Hertsgaard et al., 1995; Nachmias et al., 1996), and behavioral (e.g., Mangelsdorf et al., 1990; Nachmias et al., 1996) assessments, Gunnar and associates have tested relations between indicators of proneness to distress and attach-ment security. In virtually all of the analyses reported, they failed to find a significant association between this dimension of temperament and traditional attachment classifications from the SS. This has been true even when tests for extreme inhibited–uninhibited groups have been conducted (e.g., Nachmias et al., 1996, p. 516). However, in one study a strong association between levels of salivary cortisol (a neuroendocrine indicator for stress) and classification as disorganized/disoriented in the SS (see Main & Solomon, 1986, 1990) was found. Although this finding does not bear directly on Kagan's hypotheses concerning attachment classifications, it does suggest that attachment security has implications for understanding individual differences in reactions to stressful events (see Hertsgaard et al., 1995, for additional discussion).

Overall, the sophisticated empirical data from the laboratories of both Fox and Gunnar provide scant support for the notion that individual differences in reactivity or proneness to distress during early infancy bear a meaningful relation to the quality of attachment assessed in the SS. At the same time, their research does suggest that the temperamental-reactivity or proneness-to-distress dimension itself shows moderate stability across infancy and may be meaningfully related to later individual differences along the dimension of inhibition. Furthermore, Calkins and Fox (1992) suggest the possibility that both reactivity and attachment security predict later status as inhibited or uninhibited. Finally, results reported by Nachmias et al. (1996) suggest that behavioral inhibition interacts with attachment security in regard to levels of salivary cortisol. That is, cortisol values were higher after two different stressful procedures (one was the SS) for highly inhibited and insecure cases than for highly inhibited and secure cases. Thus security may moderate the effects of high inhibition when an infant is faced with challenging and potentially stressful tasks or events.

Attachment and Perceived Temperament

In contrast to the other approaches to temperament, only a handful of studies were found that used as the indicator of temperament Bates et al.'s (1979) ICQ. Bates et al. (1985) examined relations between ICQ scales at 6, 13, and 24 months of age and a security scale derived from a weighting algorithm applied to insecure; B1, B2, and B4; and finally B3 cases. No relations between temperament and attachment security were reported for the 6- or 24-month analyses. At 13 months of age, less secure cases tended to be less socially responsive. Frankel and Bates (1990) reported that both attachment and temperament showed associations with child behavior in a problem-solving task at age 2, but the two predictor domains were (apparently) nonoverlapping. Belsky and Rovine (1987) found no significant relations between ICQ scores at 3 months and the A-B-C classifications; however, Belsky (reported in Vaughn et al., 1992) did find an association between a summary score for infant difficulty from the ICQ and the AQS security score. Seifer et al. (1996) reported trends ($p < .10$) for the ICQ Difficult/ Fussy dimension and SS classifications for temperament data collected at 9 and 12 months of age (but not for their 6-month data). They also reported a significant correlation between the ICQ Difficult/Fussy dimension score and the AQS security score at 12 months (but not in their 6- or 9-month data). Volling and Belsky (1992) found that maternal perceptions of infant temperamental difficulty assessed at 3 months of age (but not at 9 months) distinguished infants later classified as secure versus insecure with the infants' *fathers*. Infants subsequently classified as secure were perceived to be *more* difficult at 3 months than were infants subsequently classified as insecure.

Following Thompson's (e.g., Frodi & Thompson, 1985; Thompson & Lamb, 1984) suggestion that infants be grouped according to the level of distress displayed in the SS, Belsky and Rovine (1987) regrouped the avoidant cases with B1 and B2 cases and compared them against a regrouping of the resistant cases with B3 and B4 cases. Analyses of a "difficultness composite" proved significant, with the A1 through B2 cases being less difficult than the B3 through C cases. Although infants classified as A through B2 fuss and cry less and may be less emotionally intense (see; Frodi & Thompson, 1985; Thompson & Lamb, 1984) than infants in the B3 through C group, subsequent attempts to replicate the Belsky and Rovine (1987) findings have largely failed. Using the same and different assessment protocols, Gunnar et al. (1989), Mangelsdorf et al. (1990), Seifer et al. (1996), and Vaughn et al. (1989) found no relations between these SS groups and temperament. Indeed, Seifer et al. reported a significant effect in exactly the opposite direction: In their data, the A through B2 cases were significantly more difficult than were the B3 through C cases. When these findings are

combined with van den Boom's data (e.g., van den Boom, 1989) indicating that irritable newborns are more likely to be later classified in the SS as avoidant than as secure or resistant, it seems fair to conclude that temperamental difficulty, however defined, is not necessarily a significant determinant of the kind of fussiness and irritability that leads to differences in attachment classification in the SS.

CONCLUSIONS AND CRITICAL COMMENTARY

Explicit in the title of this chapter are questions concerning the nature of the overlap between the domains of attachment and temperament, especially as they relate and co-relate to emerging personality during infancy and early childhood. Such questions do not pertain to the normative aspects of the Bowlby–Ainsworth theory dealing with the assembly of a relationship between infant and caregiver over the first years of life. Rather, they focus on qualitative differences in the meaning and effectiveness of that relationship (i.e., security of attachment) and possible relations of security to dimensions of temperament. Our review of connections between attachment and temperament should answer one of these questions definitively. Namely, *attachment security cannot be considered as redundant with temperament in the explanation of personality and/or in explanations of qualities of interpersonal action*. This appears to be the case across the full range of temperament construals reviewed above. The data suggest also that there is more to temperament than can be explained by individual differences in parent–child relationships. We now consider whether and how these two domains should be considered as independent or interactive contributors to personality and interpersonal development.

Regarding the independence of the two construct domains, the data reviewed in Table 10.1 suggest that answers will depend on how both attachment security and temperament are construed. When differences between secure (Group B) and insecure (Groups A, C, D) infants are examined, temperament dimensions derived from the four major approaches are typically orthogonal to attachment security. That is, parent reports of temperamental difficulty, negative reactivity, emotionality, and so forth generally do not distinguish securely attached infants from insecurely attached infants. However, when temperament is construed in terms of irritability assessed at very early ages (e.g., the neonatal period), differences between secure and insecure infants have been reported (e.g., Crockenberg, 1981; Susman-Stillman et al., 1996; van den Boom, 1994; Waters et al., 1980). The results from these studies are qualified by interactions with low levels of social and/or economic resources; nevertheless, the fact that irritability during early infancy increases the risk for insecurity later in the first year suggests that endogenously organized (or disorganized) attributes of infants may potentiate inadequate caregiving practices when caregivers themselves are also stressed. In this regard, van den Boom's (1994) report of improved attachment quality when mothers received appropriate training and support indicates that temperament need not imply attachment destiny, even in at-risk groups.

Although the secure–insecure distinction is not especially coordinated with dimensions of temperament, we recognize that the most strongly contested question has been that of the potential association(s) between temperament dimensions reflecting difficultness, emotionality, negative reactivity, and so on, and irritability/distress as exhibited in the SS. Such irritability/distress often distinguishes the avoidant cases (and the B1 + B2 subgroups) from the resistant cases (and the B3 + B4 subgroups) and is frequently correlated with parent reports about infant temperament (e.g., Vaughn et al., 1989). This fact has prompted some researchers (e.g., Kagan, 1984) to speculate that the differences between avoidant and resistant cases are primarily differences of temperament rather than of interaction histories.

If it were the case that resistant infants in the SS were invariably (or even typically) reactive/inhibited and avoidant infants were not prone to distress/inhibition, Kagan's speculations would have to be taken seriously. Indeed, research reported by Belsky and Rovine (1987), Miyake et al. (1985), and Thompson and Lamb (1984) has been interpreted in this manner. However, these findings must be considered in light of data reported by Seifer et al. (1996) and by van den Boom (1994) to the effect that negative reactivity/proneness to distress during early infancy is associated with avoidance and with avoidant classifications in the SS, rather than with resistant classifications. These opposing sets of findings suggest (at the least) that additional conceptual work on temperament is required before strong claims of a direct influence of tempera-

ment on behavior in and attachment classifications from the SS can be entertained.

Whereas temperament dimensions appear to explain little about attachment security assessed in the SS, these same dimensions frequently do correlate significantly with attachment security assessed in terms of secure-base behavior in ordinary situations and settings when the AQS is used to index secure-base behavior. The correlations are small to moderate (r's from .04 to .57) across the range of ages from 12 to 47 months, and with assessment instruments from all of the major approaches to temperament (Seifer et al., 1996; Vaughn et al., 1992). Infants and young children characterized as being more difficult, prone to distress, reactive, and so on are less likely to use their caregivers as a secure base and haven of safety than are less temperamentally difficult children. Since temperament assessments are often completed prior to the time that a secure-base relationship (attachment) has been assembled (e.g., Belsky [reported in Vaughn et al., 1992]; Seifer et al., 1996), it is necessarily true that temperament is antecedent to being attached. It is not, however, necessarily true that temperament is causally antecedent to individual differences in attachment quality.

There are at least three ways to interpret the temporal relation between temperament and attachment security. A strong interpretation explains individual differences with respect to attachment security in terms of preexisting temperamental differences present from the earliest weeks of life. This interpretation is not consistent with the modest associations between temperament assessed early in the first year (6 months of age and earlier) and AQS security scores at 12 to 18 months of age (see Seifer et al., 1996; Vaughn et al., 1992). Although the magnitudes of association between assessments of temperament and attachment security tend to increase with increasing child age, in no study has the correlation between measures suggested that these constructs share as much as 50% of variance. The extant data do not support a strong temperament interpretation of individual differences in attachment security. Rather, they have been interpreted by Vaughn et al. (1992) as indications of common content across the assessment instruments, perhaps especially with respect to indicators of general mood.

A second, less strong interpretation of the temperament–attachment association is that an infant whose temperament is perceived as difficult, reactive, prone to distress, and so forth may elicit different and less optimal caregiving than infants with other temperamental attributes may. Temperamental differences should thus act indirectly on security by potentiating less optimal tactics and interactions from the caregiving environment. Put simply, it may be challenging for the "average" parent to be sensitive to the communicative signals of a temperamentally difficult baby. Only Seifer et al. (1996) have provided an explicit test of this hypothesis. For observer assessments of temperament, significant associations were found between infant mood and approach at 6 and 9 months of age and observer-coded indicators of the quality and appropriateness of maternal behavior (i.e., sensitivity). But maternal perceptions of infant temperament did not yield similar correlations with sensitivity. Although observers found mothers of (observed) difficult infants to be less sensitive, mothers' own perceptions of their infants as difficult did not predict observer ratings of their sensitivity. Furthermore, for this sample, the relation between temperament and attachment security was not mediated by interaction quality (i.e., maternal sensitivity).

Results reported by Crockenberg (1981), Susman-Stillman et al. (1996), and van den Boom (1994), showing that irritable infants in low-resource environments tend to become insecure, suggest the plausibility of a moderated three-stage pathway—from temperament to interaction/sensitivity to attachment security. It may be that when a parent's economic, social, and/or psychological resources are strained, an irritable or otherwise difficult infant elicits less than optimal caregiving, which in turn potentiates the assembly of an insecure attachment. In such a scenario, difficult temperament may be interpreted either as an additional stressor for the parent or as an independent factor leading to suboptimal interactions and (indirectly or directly) to insecure attachment. These alternative hypotheses should be tested across a range of socioeconomic status categories to determine whether either one (or both) can be supported.

A third interpretation of the temperament–attachment relation is that individual differences in both domains arise in the context of infant–caregiver interactions. On this interpretation, neither domain is causally related to the other, and both are causally connected to interaction histories. This formulation does not require either temperament or the attachment relationship to arise entirely as a consequence of personality or interactional attributes of the caregiver;

rather, it requires the *relation* between security and temperament to reflect interaction histories. This interpretation is consistent with findings that temperament reports from different informants (e.g., mothers, fathers, teachers, research assistants) are only moderately related (e.g., Bates & Bayles, 1984; Field & Greenberg, 1982; Jones & Parks, 1983; Martin & Halverson, 1991; Seifer et al., 1994) and with the fact that infant–caregiver attachments show only modest congruence for the same infant with two caregivers (Fox, Kimmerly, & Schafer, 1991; Sagi et al., 1995). Given this interpretation, we would expect that reports of temperament and attachment will be more strongly related when both are filtered through the eyes (and experience) of a single caregiver. Existing data support this hypothesis (e.g., Bates & Bayles, 1988; Belsky's and Kotsaftis's samples in Vaughn et al., 1992; Wachs & Desai, 1993), although equally strong associations can arise when mothers rate temperament and observers describe children's secure-base behavior (Seifer et al., 1996).

The interpretation that both attachment security and temperament depend (in part) on qualities of infant–parent interaction receives support in reports from Belsky's (e.g., Belsky et al., 1991) and Seifer's (e.g., Seifer et al., 1998) laboratories. Both groups reported on normative and non-normative changes in temperament during the first year. Most interesting to us are non-normative changes to increasing difficultness. In Seifer et al.'s sample, when infants moved from being less negative/difficult to being more negative/difficult over the first few months, they were likely to be characterized as insecurely attached at 12 months. In Belsky et al.'s sample, infants who changed from high to low *positive* emotionality between 3 and 9 months of age were more likely to be classified as insecure. Although normative changes in temperament have been documented before (e.g., Guerin & Gottfried, 1994; Hooker, Nesselroade, Nesselroade, & Lerner, 1987), these studies are the first to examine the implications of idiographic changes in temperament for interpersonal relationships. Their findings justify increasing empirical and conceptual efforts to understand the processes and circumstances leading to diverse patterns of change in the expression of temperament. When these are better understood, questions regarding relations between attachment and temperament will be formulated more precisely and may yield more penetrating insights.

At the beginning of this chapter, we noted that

both attachment and temperament theories have been proposed to explain interpersonal functioning and personality growth during childhood. However, the connections among (1) secure-base behavior, working models, and so on; (2) emotionality, reactivity, mood, and so on; and (3) relevant dimensions of personality have rarely been made explicit. Thus it is not obvious that these conceptual domains are competing as explanations for the same personality or interactive/relationship phenomena. It seems clear, however, that the existing data do not support any strong conclusion, save that attachment and temperament domains are related (to a modest degree) but clearly not isomorphic. We suggest that the nature and implications of relations between domains remain to be worked out (see also Stevenson-Hinde, 1991). It seems likely that both will influence the formation and expression of personality and self-concepts as these are assembled during early childhood. Future research should evaluate potential interactions between individual differences with respect to attachment security and individual differences along temperament dimensions.

ACKNOWLEDGMENTS

Preparation of this chapter was supported in part by Grant No. 95-14563 from the National Science Foundation. We would like to thank Ronald Seifer, who read and critiqued an earlier version of this chapter. His comments helped us improve the organization and quality of the chapter. The responsibility for any remaining mistakes, misinterpretations, or lack of clarity is our own.

REFERENCES

Ainsworth, M. D. S. (1967). *Infancy in Uganda: Infant care and the growth of love.* Baltimore: Johns Hopkins University Press.

Ainsworth, M. D. S., Blehar, M. C., Waters, E., & Wall, S. (1978). *Patterns of attachment: A psychological study of the strange situation.* Hillsdale, NJ: Erlbaum.

Ainsworth, M. D. S., & Marvin, R. S. (1995). On the shaping of attachment theory and research: An interview with Mary D. S. Ainsworth (Fall, 1994). In E. Waters, B. E. Vaughn, G. Posada, & K. Kondo-Ikemura (Eds.), Caregiving, cultural, and cognitive perspectives on secure-base behavior and working models: New growing points of attachment theory and research. *Monographs of the Society for Research in Child Development, 60* (2–3, Serial No. 244), 3–21.

Balleyguier, G. (1991). The development of attachment ac-

cording to the temperament of the newborn. *Psychiatrie de l'Enfant, 34,* 641–657.

Bates, J. E. (1980). The concept of difficult temperament. *Merrill–Palmer Quarterly, 26,* 299–319.

Bates, J. E. (1989a). Concepts and measures of temperament. In G. A. Kohnstamm, J. E. Bates, & M. K. Rothbart (Eds.), *Temperament in childhood* (pp. 3–26). New York: Wiley.

Bates, J. E. (1989b). Applications of temperament concepts. In G. A. Kohnstamm, J. E. Bates, & M. K. Rothbart (Eds.), *Temperament in childhood* (pp. 321–355). New York: Wiley.

Bates, J. E., & Bayles, K. (1984). Objective and subjective components in mothers' perceptions of their children from age 6 months to 3 years. *Merrill–Palmer Quarterly, 30,* 111–130.

Bates, J. E., & Bayles, K. (1988). The role of attachment in the development of behavior problems. In J. Belsky & T. Nezworski (Eds.), *Clinical implications of attachment* (pp. 253–299). Hillsdale, NJ: Erlbaum.

Bates, J. E., Freeland, C. A. B., & Lounsbury, M. L. (1979). Measurement of infant difficultness. *Child Development, 50,* 794–803.

Bates, J. E., Maslin, C., & Frankel, K. (1985). Attachment security, mother–child interaction, and temperament as predictors of behavior problem ratings at age three years. In I. Bretherton & E. Waters (Eds.), Growing points of attachment theory and research. *Monographs of the Society for Research in Child Development, 50*(1–2, Serial No. 209), 167–193.

Belsky, J., Fish, M., & Isabella, R. (1991). Continuity and discontinuity in infant negative and positive emotionality: Family antecedents and attachment consequences. *Developmental Psychology, 27,* 421–431.

Belsky, J., & Rovine, M. (1987). Temperament and attachment security in the Strange Situation: An empirical rapprochement. *Child Development, 58,* 787–795.

Bohlin, G., Hagekull, B., Germer, M., Anderson, K., & Lindberg, L. (1989). Avoidant and resistant reunion behaviors as predicted by maternal interactive behavior and infant temperament. *Infant Behavior and Development, 12,* 105–117.

Bowlby, J. (1969/1982). *Attachment and loss: Vol. 1. Attachment.* New York: Basic Books.

Bowlby, J. (1973). *Attachment and loss: Vol. 2. Separation: Anxiety and anger.* New York: Basic Books.

Bowlby, J. (1980). *Attachment and loss: Vol. 3. Loss: Sadness and depression.* New York: Basic Books.

Bowlby, J. (1988). *A secure base: Clinical applications of attachment theory.* London: Tavistock.

Bradshaw, D., Goldsmith, H., & Campos, J. (1987). Attachment, temperament, and social referencing: Interrelationships among three domains of infant affective behavior. *Infant Behavior and Development, 10,* 223–231.

Braungart, J., & Stifter, C. (1991). Regulation of negative reactivity during the Strange Situation: Temperament and attachment in 12-month-old infants. *Infant Behavior and Development, 14,* 349–364.

Brazelton, T. B. (1973). *Neonatal Behavioral Assessment Scale.* Philadelphia: Lippincott/Spastics International.

Bretherton, I., Biringen, Z., Ridgeway, D., Maslin, C., & Sherman, M. (1989). Attachment: The parental perspective. *Infant Mental Health Journal, 10,* 203–221.

Buss, A. H., & Plomin, R. (1975). *A temperament theory of personality.* New York: Wiley-Interscience.

Buss, A. H., & Plomin, R. (1984). *Temperament: Early developing personality traits.* Hillsdale, NJ: Erlbaum.

Calkins, S. D. (1994). Origins and outcomes of individual differences in emotion regulation. In N. A. Fox (Ed.), The development of emotion regulation: Biological and behavioral considerations. *Monographs of the Society for Research in Child Development*, 59(2–3, Serial No. 240), 53–72.

Calkins, S. D., & Fox, N. (1992). The relations among infant temperament, security of attachment, and behavioral inhibition at twenty-four months. *Child Development*, 63, 1456–1472.

Calkins, S. D., & Fox, N. A. (1994). Individual differences in the biological aspects of temperament. In J. Bates & T. Wachs (Eds.), *Temperament: Individual differences at the interface of biology and behavior* (pp. 199–217). Washington, DC: American Psychological Association.

Calkins, S. D., Fox, N. A., & Marshall, T. R. (1996). Behavioral and physiological correlates of inhibition in infancy. *Child Development*, 67, 523–540.

Campos, J. J., Campos, R. G., & Barrett, K. C. (1989). Emergent themes in the study of emotional development and emotion regulation. *Developmental Psychology*, 25, 294–402.

Campos, J. J., Mumme, D. L., Kermoian, R., & Campos, R. G. (1994). A functionalist perspective on the nature of emotion. In N. A. Fox (Ed.), The development of emotion regulation: Biological and behavioral considerations. *Monographs of the Society for Research in Child Development*, 59 (2–3, Serial No. 240), 284–303.

Carey, W. B., & McDevitt, S. C. (1978). Revision of the Infant Temperament Questionnaire. *Pediatrics*, 61, 735–739.

Cassidy, J. (1994). Emotion regulation: Influences of attachment relationships. In N. A. Fox (Ed.), The development of emotion regulation: Biological and behavioral considerations. *Monographs of the Society for Research in Child Development*, 59(2–3, Serial No. 240), 228–249.

Cassidy, J., & Berlin, L. J. (1994). The insecure/ambivalent pattern of attachment: Theory and research. *Child Development*, 65, 971–981.

Craik, K. (1943). *The nature of explanation.* Cambridge, England: Cambridge University Press.

Crockenberg, S. B. (1981). Infant irritability, mother responsiveness, and social support influences on the security of infant–mother attachment. *Child Development*, 52, 857–865.

Crockenberg, S., & McCluskey, K. (1986). Change in maternal behavior during the baby's first year of life. *Child Development*, 57, 746–753.

DeFries, J. C., Plomin, R., & Fulker, D. W. (1994). *Nature and nurture during middle childhood.* Cambridge, MA: Blackwell.

Denham, S., & Moser, M. (1994). Mothers' attachment to infants: Relations with infant temperament, stress, and responsive maternal behavior. *Early Child Development and Care*, 98, 1–6.

Del Carmen, R., Pedersen, F. A., Huffman, L. C., & Bryan, Y. E. (1993). Dyadic distress management predicts subsequent security of attachment. *Infant Behavior and Development*, 16, 131–147.

Egeland, B., & Farber, E. (1984). Infant–mother attachment: Factors related to its development and changes over time. *Child Development*, 55, 753–771.

Erickson, M., Egeland, B., & Sroufe, L. A. (1985). The relationship between quality of attachment and behavior problems in a high risk sample. In I. Bretherton & E. Waters (Eds.), Growing points in attachment theory and research. *Monographs of the Society for Research in Child Development*, 50(Nos. 1–2, Serial No. 209), 147–186.

Field, T. (1994). The effects of mother's physical and emotional unavailability on emotion regulation. In N. A. Fox (Ed.), The development of emotion regulation: Biological and behavioral considerations. *Monographs of the Society for Research in Child Development*, 59(2–3, Serial No. 240), 208–277.

Field, T., & Greenberg, R. (1982). Temperament ratings by parents and teachers of infants, toddlers, and preschool children. *Child Development*, 53, 160–163.

Finkel, D., Wille, D., & Matheny, A. P., Jr. (1997). *Preliminary results from a twin study of infant–caregiver attachment.* Manuscript.

Fox, N. A. (1989). Psychophysiological correlates of emotional reactivity during the first year of life. *Developmental Psychology*, 25, 364–372.

Fox, N. A. (1994). Dynamic cerebral processes underlying emotion regulation. In N. A. Fox (Ed.), The development of emotion regulation: Biological and behavioral considerations. *Monographs of the Society for Research in Child Development*, 59(2–3, Serial No. 240), 152–166.

Fox, N., Kimmerly, N. L., & Schafer, W. D. (1991). Attachment to mother/attachment to father: A meta-analysis. *Child Development*, 62, 210–225.

Frankel, K., & Bates, J. (1990). Mother–toddler problem solving: Antecedents in attachment, home behavior, and temperament. *Child Development*, 61, 810–819.

Frodi, A., Bridges, L., & Shonk, S. (1989). Maternal correlates of infant temperament ratings and of infant–mother attachment: A longitudinal study. *Infant Mental Health Journal*, 10, 273–289.

Frodi, A., & Thompson, R. A. (1985). Infants' affective responses in the Strange Situation: Effects of prematurity and quality of attachment. *Child Development*, 56, 1280–1290.

Fullard, W., McDevitt, S. C., & Carey, W. B. (1984). Assessing temperament in one- to three-year-old children. *Journal of Pediatric Psychology*, 9, 205–217.

Garcia-Coll, C. T., Emmons, L., Vohr, B. R., Ward, A. M., Brann, B. S., Shaul, P. W., Mayfield, S. R., & Oh, W. (1988). Behavioral responsiveness in preterm infants with intraventricular hemorrhage. *Pediatrics*, 81, 412–418.

Garcia-Coll, C., Kagan, J., & Reznick, J. S. (1984). Behavioral inhibition in young children. *Child Development*, 55, 1005–1019.

Goldsmith, H. H., & Alansky, J. A. (1987). Maternal and infant temperamental predictors of attachment: A meta-analytic review. *Journal of Consulting and Clinical Psychology*, 55, 805–816.

Goldsmith, H. H., Bradshaw, D. L., & Rieser-Danner, L. A. (1986). Temperament as a potential developmental influence on attachment. In J. V. Lerner & R. M. Lerner (Eds.), *New directions for child development: No. 31.* (pp. 5–34). San Francisco: Jossey-Bass.

Goldsmith, H. H., Buss, A. H., Plomin, R., Rothbart, M. K., Thomas, A., Chess, S., Hinde, R. A., & McCall, R. R. (1987). Roundtable: What is temperament? Four approaches. *Child Development*, 58, 505–529.

Goldsmith, H. H., & Campos, J. J. (1986). Fundamental issues in the study of early temperament: The Denver Twin Temperament Study. In M. Lamb, A. Brown, & B. Rogoff (Eds.), *Advances in developmental psychology* (Vol. 4, pp. 7–37). Hillsdale, NJ: Erlbaum.

Goldsmith, H. H., & Campos, J. J. (1990). The structure of temperamental fear and pleasure in infants. *Child Development*, 61, 1944–1964.

Goldsmith, H. H., & Harman, C. (1994). Temperament and

attachment: Individuals and relationships. *Current Directions in Psychological Science, 3*, 53–57.

Goldsmith, H. H., Rieser-Danner, L. A., & Briggs, S. (1991). Evaluating convergent and discriminant validity of temperament questionnaires for preschoolers, toddlers, and infants. *Developmental Psychology, 27*, 566–579.

Grossmann, K., Grossmann, K. E., Spangler, G., Suess, G., & Unzner, L. (1985). Maternal sensitivity and newborns' orientation responses as related to quality of attachment in northern Germany. In I. Bretherton & E. Waters, (Eds.), Growing points of attachment theory and research. *Monographs of the Society for Research in Child Development, 50*(1–2, Serial No. 209), 233–256.

Guerin, D. W., & Gottfried, A. W. (1994). Developmental stability and change in parent reports of temperament: A ten-year longitudinal investigation from infancy through preadolescence. *Merrill–Palmer Quarterly, 40*, 334–355.

Gunnar, M. R. (1990). The psychobiology of infant temperament. In J. Colombo & J. Fagen (Eds.), *Individual differences in infancy: Reliability, stability, prediction* (pp. 387–409). Hillsdale, NJ: Erlbaum.

Gunnar, M. R. (1994). Psychoneuroendocrine studies of temperament and stress in early childhood: Expanding current models. In J. E. Bates & T. D. Wachs (Eds.) *Temperament: Individual differences at the interface of biology and behavior* (pp. 175–198). Washington, DC: American Psychological Association.

Gunnar, M., Larson, M., Hertsgaard, L., Harris, M., & Broderson, L. (1992). The stressfulness of separation among 9-month-old infants: Effects of social context variables and infant temperament. *Child Development, 63*, 290–303.

Gunnar, M., Mangelsdorf, S., Larson, M., & Hertsgaard, L. (1989). Attachment, temperament, and adrenocortical activity in infancy: A study of psychoendocrine regulation. *Developmental Psychology, 25*, 355–363.

Gunnar, M. R., Porter, F. L., Wolf, C. M., & Rigatuso, J. (1995). Neonatal stress reactivity: Predictions to later emotional temperament. *Child Development, 66*, 1–13.

Halverson, C. F., Jr., Kohnstamm, G. A., & Martin, R. P. (Eds.). (1994). *The developing structure of temperament and personality from infancy to adulthood*. Hillsdale, NJ, Erlbaum.

Hertsgaard, L., Gunnar, M., Erickson, M. F., & Nachmias, M. (1995). Adrenocortical responses to the strange situation in infants with disorganized/disoriented attachment relationships. *Child Development, 66*, 1100–1106.

Hinde, R. A. (1979). *Towards understanding relationships*. New York: Academic Press.

Hinde, R. A. (1987). *Individuals, relationships and culture: Links between ethology and the social sciences*. New York: Cambridge University Press.

Hinde, R. A., & Stevenson-Hinde, J. (1987). Interpersonal relationships and child development. *Developmental Review, 7*, 1–21.

Hofer, M. A. (1994). Hidden regulators in attachment, separation, and loss. In N. A. Fox (Ed.), The development of emotion regulation: Biological and behavioral considerations. *Monographs of the Society for Research in Child Development, 59*(2–3, Serial No. 240), 192–207.

Hooker, K., Nesselroade, D. W., Nesselroade, J. R., & Lerner, R. M. (1987). The structure of intraindividual temperament in the context of mother–child dyads: *P*-technique factor analyses of short-term change. *Developmental Psychology, 23*, 332–346.

Izard, C. E., Haynes, O. M., Chisholm, G., & Baak, K.

(1991). Emotional determinants of infant–mother attachment. *Child Development, 62*, 906–917.

Izard, C. E., & Malatesta, C. (1987). Perspectives on emotional development: I. Differential emotions: Theory of early emotional development. In J. D. Osofsky (Ed.), *Handbook of infant development* (2nd ed. pp. 355–379). New York: Wiley.

Johnson-Laird, P. N. (1983). *Mental models: Towards a cognitive science of language, inference, and consciousness*. Cambridge, MA: Harvard University Press.

Jones, C., & Parks, P. (1983). Mother-, father-, and examiner-reported temperament across the first year of life. *Research in Nursing and Health, 6*, 183–189.

Kagan, J. (1982). *Psychological research on the human infant: An evaluative summary*. New York: W. T. Grant Foundation.

Kagan, J. (1984). *The nature of the child*. New York: Basic Books.

Kagan, J. (1994a). On the nature of emotion. In N. A. Fox (Ed.), The development of emotion regulation: Biological and behavioral considerations. *Monographs of the Society for Research in Child Development, 59*(2–3, Serial No. 240), 7–24.

Kagan, J. (1994b). *Galen's prophecy: Temperament in human nature*. New York: Basic Books.

Kagan, J., Reznick, J. S., & Gibbons, J. (1989). Inhibited and uninhibited types of children. *Child Development, 60*, 838–845.

Kagan, J., Reznick, J. S., & Snidman, N. (1987). The physiology and psychology of behavioral inhibition in children. *Child Development, 58*, 1459–1473.

Kagan, J., Reznick, J. S., & Snidman, N. (1988). Biological bases of childhood shyness. *Science, 240*, 167–171.

Kagan, J. J., Reznick, S., & Snidman, N. (1989). Issues in the study of temperament. In G. A. Kohnstamm, J. E. Bates, & M. K. Rothbart (Eds.), *Temperament in childhood* (pp. 133–144). New York: Wiley.

Kagan, J., & Snidman, N. (1991). Infant predictors of inhibited and uninhibited profiles. *Psychological Science, 2*, 40–44.

Kanaya, Y. (1986). Are maternal emotions associated with infant temperament and attachment? *Annual Report of the Research and Clinical Center for Child Development, 9*, 51–58.

Kaye, K. (1982). *The mental and social life of babies: How parents create persons*. Chicago: University of Chicago Press.

Kemp, V. (1987). Mothers' perceptions of children's temperament and mother–child attachment. *Scholarly Inquiry for Nursing Practice, 1*, 51–68.

Kochanska, G. (1995). Children's temperament, mothers' discipline, and security of attachment: Multiple pathways to emerging internalization. *Child Development, 66*, 597–615.

Lewis, M., & Feiring, C. (1989). Infant, mother, and mother–infant interaction behavior and subsequent attachment. *Child Development, 60*, 831–837.

Livesley, W. J., Jang, K. L., Jackson, D. N., & Vernon, P. A. (1993). Genetic and environmental contributions to dimensions of personality disorder. *American Journal of Psychiatry, 150*, 1826–1831.

Main, M., & Solomon, J. (1986). Discovery of an insecure-disorganized/disoriented attachment pattern. In T. B. Brazelton & M. W. Yogman (Eds.), *Affective development in infancy* (pp. 95–124). Norwood, NJ: Ablex.

Main, M., & Solomon, J. (1990). Procedures for identifying infants as disorganized/disoriented during the Ainsworth strange situation. In M. T. Greenberg, D. Cicchetti, & E. M. Cummings (Eds.), *Attachment in the preschool years: Theory, research, and intervention* (pp. 121–160). Chicago: University of Chicago Press.

Mangelsdorf, S., Gunnar, M., Kestenbaum, R., Lang, S., & Andreas, D. (1990). Infant proneness-to-distress, temperament, maternal personality, and mother–infant attachment. *Child Development, 61*, 820–831.

Martin, R. P. (1988). *The Temperament Assessment Battery for Children: Manual.* Brandon, VT: Clinical Psychology Press.

Martin, R. P., & Halverson, C. F., Jr. (1991). Mother–father agreement in temperamental ratings: A preliminary investigation. In J. Strelau & A. Angleitner (Eds.), *Explorations in temperament: International perspectives on theory and measurement* (pp. 235–248). London: Plenum Press.

Matheny, A. P., Riese, M. L., & Wilson, R. S. (1985). Rudiments of infant temperament: Newborn to 9 months. *Developmental Psychology, 21*, 486–494.

Miyake, K., & Chen, S. (1984). Relation of temperamental disposition to classification of attachment: A progress report. *Annual Report of the Research and Clinical Center for Child Development, 7*, 17–25.

Miyake, K., Chen, S., & Campos, J. (1985). Infant temperament, mother's mode of interaction, and attachment in Japan: An interim report. In I. Bretherton & E. Waters (Eds.), Growing points of attachment theory and research. *Monographs of the Society for Research in Child Development, 50*(1–2, Serial No. 209), 276–297.

Nachmias, M., Gunnar, M. R., Mangelsdorf, S., Parritz, R. H., & Buss, K. (1996). Behavioral inhibition and stress reactivity: The moderating role of attachment security. *Child Development, 67*, 508–522.

Owens, G., Crowell, J. A., Pan, H., Treboux, D., O'Connor, E., & Waters, E. (1995). The prototype hypothesis and the origins of attachment working models: Adult relationships with parents and romantic partners. In E. Waters, B. E. Vaughn, G. Posada, & K. Kondo-Ikemura (Eds.), Caregiving, cultural, and cognitive perspectives on secure-base behavior and working models: New growing points of attachment theory and research. *Monographs of the Society for Research in Child Development, 60*(2–3, Serial No. 244), 216–233.

Pederson, D. R., & Moran, G. (1995). A categorical description of infant–mother relationships in the home and its relation to Q-sort measures of infant–mother interaction. In E. Waters, B. E. Vaughn, G. Posada, & K. Kondo-Ikemura (Eds.), Caregiving, cultural, and cognitive perspectives on secure-base behavior and working models: New growing points of attachment theory and research. *Monographs of the Society for Research in Child Development, 60*(2–3, Serial No. 244), 111–132.

Plomin, R., & DeFries, J. C. (1985). *Origins of individual differences in infancy: The Colorado Adoption Project.* New York: Academic Press.

Rieser-Danner, L. A., Roggman, L., & Langlois, J. H. (1987). Infant attractiveness and perceived temperament in the prediction of attachment classifications. *Infant Mental Health Journal, 8*, 144–155.

Rothbart, M. K. (1988). Temperament and the development of the inhibited approach. *Child Development, 59*, 1241–1250.

Rothbart, M. K. (1989a). Temperament in childhood: A framework. In G. A. Kohnstamm, J. E. Bates, & M. K. Rothbart (Eds.), *Temperament in childhood* (pp. 59–73). New York: Wiley.

Rothbart, M. K. (1989b). Biological processes in temperament. In G. A. Kohnstamm, J. E. Bates, & M. K. Rothbart (Eds.), *Temperament in childhood* (pp. 77–110). New York: Wiley.

Rothbart, M. K. (1989c). Temperament and development. In G. A. Kohnstamm, J. E. Bates, & M. K. Rothbart (Eds.), *Temperament in childhood* (pp. 187–247). New York: Wiley.

Rothbart, M. K. (1991). Temperament: A developmental framework. In J. Strelau & A. Angleitner (Eds.), *Explorations in temperament: International perspectives on theory and measurement* (pp. 235–260). London: Plenum Press.

Rothbart, M. K., & Ahadi, S. A. (1994). Temperament and the development of personality. *Journal of Abnormal Psychology, 103*, 55–66.

Rothbart, M. K., & Derryberry, D. (1981). Development of individual differences in temperament. In M. E. Lamb & A. L. Brown (Eds.), *Advances in developmental psychology* (Vol. 1, pp. 37–86). Hillsdale, NJ: Erlbaum.

Ruff, H. A., & Rothbart, M. K. (1996). *Attention in early development: Themes and variations.* New York: Oxford University Press.

Sagi, A., van IJzendoorn, M. H., Aviezer, O., Donnell, F., Koren-Karie, N., Joels, & Harel, Y. (1995). Attachments in multiple-caregiver and multiple-infant environment: The case of the Israeli kibbutzim. In E. Waters, B. E. Vaughn, G. Posada, & K. Kondo-Ikemura (Eds.), Caregiving, cultural, and cognitive perspectives on secure-base behavior and working models: New growing points of attachment theory and research. *Monographs of the Society for Research in Child Development, 60*(Nos. 2–3, Serial No. 244), 71–91.

Sameroff, A. J., Seifer, R., & Elias, P. K. (1982). Sociocultural variability in infant temperament ratings. *Child Development, 53*, 164–171.

Sander, L. W. (1964). Adaptive relationships in early mother–child interaction. *Journal of the American Academy of Child Psychiatry, 3*, 231–264.

Seifer, R., Sameroff, A. J., Barrett, L. C., & Krafchuk, E. (1994). Infant temperament measured by multiple observations and mother report. *Child Development, 65*, 1478–1490.

Seifer, R., & Schiller, M. (1995). The role of parenting sensitivity, infant temperament, and dyadic interaction in attachment theory and assessment. In E. Waters, B. E. Vaughn, G. Posada, & K. Kondo-Ikemura (Eds.), New growing points of attachment theory and research. *Monographs of the Society for Research in Child Development, 60*(2–3, Serial No. 244), 146–174.

Seifer, R., Schiller, M., Sameroff, A., Hayden, L., Dickstein, S., Wheeler, E., Hermann, M., & St. Martin, A. (1998). *Individual patterns of change and longitudinal characteristics of infant temperament: Description and association with relationship development.* Manuscript submitted for publication.

Seifer, R., Schiller, M., Sameroff, A., Resnick, S., & Riordan, K. (1996). Attachment, maternal sensitivity, and infant temperament during the first year of life. *Developmental Psychology, 32*, 12–25.

Sroufe, L. A. (1985). Attachment classification from the perspective of infant–caregiver relationships and infant temperament. *Child Development, 56*, 1–14.

Sroufe, L. A., & Fleeson, J. (1986). Attachment and the construction of relationships. In W. Hartup & Z. Rubin (Eds.), *Relationships and development* (pp. 51–71). Hillsdale, NJ: Erlbaum.

Stansbury, K., & Gunnar, M. R. (1994). Adrenocortical activity and emotion regulation. In N. A. Fox (Ed.), The development of emotion regulation: Biological and behavioral considerations. *Monographs of the Society for Research in Child Development, 59*(2–3, Serial No. 240), 108–134.

Stern, D. N. (1985). *The interpersonal world of the infant: A view from psychoanalysis and developmental psychology.* New York: Basic Books.

Stevenson-Hinde, J. (1991). Temperament and attachment: An eclectic approach. In P. Bateson (Ed.), *The development and integration of behaviour: Essays in honor of Robert Hinde* (pp. 315–329). Cambridge, England: Cambridge University Press.

Stevenson-Hinde, J., & Shouldice, A. (1995). Maternal interactions and self-reports related to attachment classifications at 4.5 years. *Child Development, 66,* 583–596.

Strelau, J. (1983). *Temperament, personality, affectivity.* New York: Academic Press.

Susman-Stillman, A., Kalkoske, M., Egeland, B., & Waldman, I. (1996). Infant temperament and maternal sensitivity as predictors of attachment security. *Infant Behavior and Development, 19,* 33–47.

Teti, D. M., Nakagawa, M., Das, R., & Wirth, O. (in press). Concordance and non-concordance of child–mother attachment among infant–sibling pairs: An examination of mother–child interaction. In E. Waters, B. E. Vaughn, G. Posada, & D. M Teti (Eds.), *Patterns of secure base behavior: Q-sort perspectives on attachment and caregiving in infancy and childhood.* Mahwah, NJ: Erlbaum.

Thomas, A., & Chess, S. (1977). *Temperament and development.* New York: Brunner/Mazel.

Thomas, A., Chess, S., & Birch, H. G. (1968). *Temperament and behavior disorders in children.* New York: New York University Press.

Thomas, A., Chess, S., Birch, H. G., Hertzig, M. E., & Korn, S. (1963). *Behavioral individuality in early childhood.* New York: New York University Press.

Thompson, R., Connell, J., & Bridges, L. (1988). Temperament, emotion, and social interactive behavior in the Strange Situation: A component process analysis of attachment system functioning. *Child Development, 59,* 1102–1110.

Thompson, R. A., & Lamb, M. (1984). Assessing qualitative dimensions of emotional responsiveness in infants: Separation reactions in the Strange Situation. *Infant Behavior and Development, 7,* 423–445.

Usi, H., & Miyake, K. (1984). Infant temperament: Its relationship with attachment classification and longitudinal data analysis: A progress report. *Annual Report of the Research and Clinical Center for Child Development, 7,* 37–48.

van den Boom, D. C. (1989). Neonatal irritability and the development of attachment. In G. Kohnstamm, J. Bates, & M. Rothbart (Eds.), *Temperament in childhood* (pp. 299–318). New York: Wiley.

van den Boom, D. (1994). The influence of temperament and mothering on attachment and exploration: An experimental manipulation of sensitive responsiveness among lower-class mothers with irritable infants. *Child Development, 65,* 1457–1477.

Vaughn, B. E., Bradley, C. B., Joffe, L. S., Seifer, R., & Barglow, P. (1987). Maternal characteristics measured prenatally predict ratings of temperamental "difficulty" on the Carey Infant Temperament Questionnaire. *Developmental Psychology, 23,* 160–170.

Vaughn, B. E., Lefever, G., Seifer, R., & Barglow, P. (1989). Attachment behavior, attachment security, and temperament during infancy. *Child Development, 60,* 728–737.

Vaughn, B. E., Stevenson-Hinde, J., Waters, E., Kotsaftis, A., Lefever, G. B., Shouldice, A., Trudel, M., & Belsky, J. (1992). Attachment security and temperament in infancy and early childhood: Some conceptual clarifications. *Developmental Psychology, 28,* 463–473.

Vaughn, B. E., & Waters, E. (1990). Attachment behavior at home and in the laboratory: Q-sort observations and strange situation classifications of one-year-olds. *Child Development, 61,* 1965–1973.

Volling, B., & Belsky, J. (1992). Infant, father, and marital antecedents of infant–father attachment security in dual-earner and single-earner families. *International Journal of Behavioral Development, 15,* 83–100.

Wachs, T., & Desai, S. (1993). Parent reports of toddler temperament and attachment: Their relation to each other and to the social microenvironment. *Infant Behavior and Development, 16,* 391–396.

Ward, M. J., Vaughn, B. E., & Robb, M. (1988). Attachment and adaptation in siblings: The role of the mother in cross-sibling consistency. *Child Development, 59,* 643–651.

Waters, E., & Deane, K. (1985). Defining and assessing individual differences in attachment relationships: Q-methodology and the organization of behavior in infancy and early childhood. In I. Bretherton & E. Waters (Eds.), Growing points of attachment theory and research. *Monographs of the Society for Research in Child Development, 50*(1–2, Serial No. 209).

Waters, E., Kondo-Ikemura, K., Posada, G., & Richters, J. E. (1991). Learning to love: Mechanisms and milestones. In M. R. Gunnar & L. A. Sroufe (Eds.), *Minnesota Symposia on Child Psychology: Vol. 23. Self processes in development* (pp. 178–225). Hillsdale, NJ: Erlbaum.

Waters, E., Vaughn, B. E., & Egeland, B. (1980). Individual differences in infant–mother attachment relationships at age one: Antecedents in neonatal behavior in an economically disadvantaged sample. *Child Development, 51,* 208–216.

Waters, E., Vaughn, B. E., Posada, G., & Kondo-Ikemura, K. (Eds.). (1995). Caregiving, cultural, and cognitive perspectives on secure-base behavior and working models: New growing points of attachment theory and research. *Monographs of the Society for Research in Child Development, 60*(2–3, Serial No. 244).

Weber, R., Levitt, M., & Clark, C. (1986). Individual variation in attachment security and Strange Situation behavior: The role of maternal and infant temperament. *Child Development, 57,* 56–65.

11

Psychophysiological Measures in the Study of Attachment

❖

NATHAN A. FOX
JUDITH A. CARD

"Psychophysiology" is the study of how physiological processes intersect with and influence psychologically relevant behavior. Psychophysiological research includes the measurement of physiological systems as correlates of observed behavioral responses, as well as the manner in which individual differences in the level of a physiological response predispose subjects to certain types of behavior. Developmental psychologists have measured multiple physiological responses and have inferred certain psychological processes from these measurements. This is particularly true of research on the preverbal human infant: Researchers have measured physiology in an attempt to understand the competencies of the young infant, and have inferred the presence or absence of specific affective states on the basis of these physiological responses. These studies are usually based upon certain assumptions about the role of physiological systems in the generation of behavioral responses. Such assumptions are the product of a long history of research in psychophysiology with adults and older children. Before tackling the psychophysiological literature on attachment, we provide a brief overview of the use of psychophysiological methods in psychology.

PSYCHOPHYSIOLOGICAL METHODS IN PSYCHOLOGY

Heart rate (HR) has the longest history as a psychophysiological measure of preverbal infants' cognitive and affective responses. As a result of the work of Lacey and Lacey (1958), researchers investigated HR responses of infants to a variety of stimuli (e.g., Lewis, 1975; Lewis, Kagan, Campbell, & Kalafat, 1966). Lacey and Lacey reported that adult subjects displayed HR acceleration during periods of cognitive processing (e.g., mental arithmetic) when it was necessary to reject external distractions. Subjects displayed HR deceleration during periods of quiet attention to stimuli presented to them. The Laceys argued that these directional changes in HR facilitate cognitive processing. HR acceleration prevents attention to external events and provides an individual with the opportunity to concentrate on "internal thinking," whereas HR deceleration allows the individual to focus and attend to external events.

Graham and Clifton (1966) took this model and adapted it to the study of cognitive processing in the human infant. They argued that one can assess an infant's psychological response to a

226

stimulus via measurement of the infant's HR. HR acceleration was viewed by Graham and Clifton as a defensive response, in which external stimuli are blocked out and the infant can organize itself metabolically to fight or flee from external threat. HR deceleration, in response to stimulus presentation, was thought to reflect both the orienting response (OR) and subsequent infant attention. In Graham and Clifton's view, repeated stimulus presentation should produce habituation of HR deceleration (though not necessarily habituation of the OR). Presentation of novel stimuli should reelicit the OR and HR deceleration. Thus, they argued, HR responses can be used to index such processes as attention and learning in the preverbal infant.

Developmental researchers such as Kagan (Lewis et al., 1966) and Lewis (1975) attempted to assess attention to auditory and visual stimuli as well as habituation responses in infants, using HR change as the dependent measure. These studies met with qualified success: Researchers were able to demonstrate that under certain conditions, infants could exhibit HR deceleration to the presentation of a novel stimulus, and that with repeated presentation they would exhibit habituation of that response. There was, however, a great deal of intersubject variability in infant HR responses.

Not all psychophysiologists viewed directional changes in HR as reflecting psychological processes such as attention. Obrist, Webber, Sutterer, and Howard (1970) argued that HR decelerations or accelerations in response to stimulus presentation reflect, in the main, changes in metabolic demand, rather than the direct influence of cognitive or psychological state. Obrist et al. called attention to the fact that body metabolism, primarily muscular, has a major influence on the autonomic nervous system (ANS), particularly on HR. They argued that changes in HR are products of these demands, and that the OR and attention or defensive responses are enhanced by these metabolic and autonomic changes.

In addition to being used as a measure of attention, HR and other measures of the ANS have been used to assess subjects' degree of general arousal (Schachter & Singer, 1962). A number of researchers suggested that a subject's emotional state can be indexed by measurement of ANS activity (Duffy, 1957, 1962). Increases in ANS measures were thought to reflect increased emotional arousal. Lacey (1967), however, argued that there is no general physiological reaction

that can be called "arousal." Instead, he suggested that individual measures of autonomic activity each reflect independent processes. Lacey called this model "response stereotypy," by which he meant that different measures of ANS activity will not necessarily respond in the same direction (either up or down), but will change as a function of the processes they reflect. As evidence for this model, Lacey reported low intercorrelations among ANS measures in subjects who were placed in situations designed to elicit affective arousal. Lacey argued that it is imperative to examine the underlying physiological mechanisms involved in the production of each specific ANS change. Porges et al. (1980) challenged Lacey's "response stereotypy" model. They suggested that the lack of intercorrelation among ANS measures is a function of measurement problems and does not reflect the lack of integration across physiological and psychological processes; rather, they argued, ANS arousal can be characterized by the changing relations among ANS variables.

A number of researchers have highlighted the importance of individual differences in determining the direction of HR response. Wilder (1967) and Benjamin (1963) were among the first to suggest that initial level of HR may be a determining factor in the direction and magnitude of HR phasic responses. This principle, known as the "law of initial values," was to add an important qualifier for studies examining HR change. According to this principle, resting or initial HR level will determine the degree to which subjects can display HR acceleration or deceleration. Subjects with fast HRs, for example, should not display the same degree of acceleration as those with slower HRs. As a solution, researchers employed change scores or analysis of covariance to account for initial HR differences.

This brief overview of the literature involved in the interpretation of HR responses is presented as a prologue to the next section of this chapter. In this section, we introduce some of the issues surrounding the use of psychophysiological measures in the study of behavior. Most of the issues briefly touched upon above are relevant not only to HR but to any psychophysiological measure. These issues include the multidetermined nature of a response; the psychological inferences that are made regarding a response; the problem of artifactual inflation of the measured response; and the consequences of individual differences in initial level of the response.

Following a consideration of measurement issues, we review studies that have included measures of psychophysiological responses of infants during Ainsworth's strange situation (Ainsworth & Wittig, 1969). These studies concentrate on the measurement of HR or cortisol activity in infants undergoing assessment in the strange situation. We then consider studies in which infant psychophysiological responses were assessed as correlates of behavior in the strange situation. Such studies focus on individual differences in reactivity that may be related to attachment classification or infant behavior in the strange situation. Following this section, we review studies of caregiver sensitivity and responsivity that included psychophysiological measures, and we end with a section on recent studies that have used psychophysiological responses to inform research on the Adult Attachment Interview (AAI). Throughout these reviews, we hope to provide the reader with both the problems and the benefits of using psychophysiological measures to study different aspects of attachment behavior.

MEASUREMENT CONSIDERATIONS

Multidetermined Nature of the Response

HR can be measured by anyone who can feel a pulse and count. Yet for all its simplicity of measurement, HR is complexly determined; there are both neural and extraneural influences on it. Extraneural influences include hormonal effects that are the result of sympathetic activity, or metabolic effects that may be a function of somatic activity ranging from digestion to muscle movement. There are mechanical influences on HR; changes in respiratory activity affect HR via the stretch receptors (Porges & Byrne, 1992). There are also intrinsic influences on HR; the heart beats at a particular rate as a function of electrical discharge via pacemaker cells at the sinoatrial node. HR responds to changes in other systems, such as fluctuations in blood pressure. Most neural influence on the heart is via the vagus or 10th cranial nerve (Katona & Jih, 1985). The vagus nerve, which originates in the brain stem, has complex interconnections with neural centers regulating respiration and is linked with both afferent and efferent connections to the midbrain and cortical regions of the brain (Porges, 1995). Thus, HR (and HR change) may

be the result of multiple physiological factors, only some of which may directly affect psychological state.

Most psychophysiological measures share with HR the same problems with regard to their multidetermined nature. There is a good deal of ambiguity, for example, regarding the source of electrical signals recorded off the scalp (Nuwer, 1997). Electrical activity recorded off the scalp is affected by the thickness of the dura, by skull bone, and by the spread of electrical activity across the cortex. Whereas methods exist for estimating the source of specific brain electrical responses (e.g., evoked responses), these methods are complex and often impractical (Scherg & von Cramon, 1985). In the absence of concomitant neuroimaging techniques, measures of the electroencephalogram (EEG) from specific scalp locations remain at best indirect estimates of neural activity.

Changes in cortisol level are also multidetermined. Cortisol is a hormone secreted by the actions of the hypothalamic–pituitary–adrenocortical (HPA) axis. It is the hormone of energy and hence is released as a result of many aspects of an organism's interaction with the environment, including response to novelty, appetitive behavior, sexual response, and response to injury or illness, as well as response to psychological stressors (Gunnar, 1994). The secretion of cortisol within the HPA system has its own circadian rhythm, and the adrenocortical system is slow to respond, so that it may take 25 to 30 minutes before a change in cortisol levels can be detected.

The multidetermined nature of psychophysiological responses requires, at the very least, careful methodological consideration. The measurement of HR has involved recording of somatic activity to rule out these influences on rate. Attempts have also been made to extract from the HR signal the portion of variance that can be exclusively related to neural influence (e.g., Porges & Bohrer, 1991). Researchers using EEG or evoked responses must be careful in the placement of electrodes on the scalp. The topographic location for electrode placement changes with age. Studies that utilize magnetic resonance imaging (MRI) and EEG simultaneously confirm the accuracy of electrode placement (Lagerlund et al., 1993). Studies of cortisol response should take into account time of day for sample collection, because of changes due to circadian rhythms. These precautions and concerns are critical in allowing inferences about psychophysiological responses to be made.

Inferences Regarding Psychological Processes

Although it is now more than 30 years since Lacey (1959) published his critique of Darrow's (1929) and Lindsley's (1939) arousal theory, researchers continue to attribute increases in HR to increases in general arousal (e.g., Frodi, Lamb, Leavitt, Donovan, Neff, & Sherry, 1978; Spangler & Grossmann, 1993). Similar inferences have been made for EEG power as the dependent measure (Gale & Edwards, 1986). Lacey argued against a notion of uniform arousal, in part because he found that ANS measures did not rise together in a similar manner during periods of so-called "arousal." Lacey's stand presaged the position of researchers who also argued against the notion of general emotional arousal (Ekman, Levenson, & Friesen, 1983; Izard, Huebner, Risser, & Dougherty, 1980). Instead, researchers such as Ekman felt that situations designed to arouse emotion in subjects elicit a series of discrete emotions, each of which has its unique set of central and ANS correlates. Ekman et al. (1983) demonstrated that subjects who posed discrete facial expressions of emotion displayed changes in ANS measures specific to those emotions. In that study, for example, ANS measures differentiated between the emotions of fear and anger. It is not clear, however, whether such differences in autonomic activity will hold for spontaneous expressions of emotions.

Successful mapping of physiology to behavior allows the investigator to draw inferences about the role of underlying physiology in psychological processes. The success of mapping HR deceleration to attentional processes, for example, is a result of careful experimental design in which stimulus presentation is synchronized to the ongoing measurement of physiology (HR). In a series of studies, Richards (1985, 1987) was able to describe the various components of the HR response, during different phases of attention, by linking observable changes in behavioral attention to specific changes in the pattern of HR during those attentional phases.

Fox and Davidson (1988) examined the pattern of infant EEG activity during the expression of different discrete emotions. Infant EEG was recorded during stimulus situations designed to elicit particular discrete emotions (joy, sadness, distress). Each infant was videotaped continuously, and the videotaped records were synchronized with the continuous EEG record. Segments of videotape during which an infant displayed a particular discrete facial expression were identified, and the EEG was extracted for those precise times. In this way, inferences about the pattern of the EEG during the expression of these discrete emotions could be made.

Three procedural elements are critical in making psychological inferences about physiological changes. First, behavior and physiology should be simultaneously recorded and synchronized, in order to allow for the coding and extraction of synchronous portions of behavior and physiology (Fox & Davidson, 1986b). Second, because most physiological responses have fast response times, multiple trials or epochs should be recorded, to allow for averaging across epochs so that a stable estimate can be obtained (Rushton, Brainerd, & Pressley, 1983). Third, behavior should be considered the anchor, so that inferences about psychological state are based on the convergence of both measurement systems rather than on the physiological response alone.

Artifactual Inflation of the Measured Response

In the late 1970s and 1980s, a number of studies were conducted in which infant HR was measured during the approach of the mother and an unfamiliar adult. Researchers conducting these studies found large phasic increases in HR during the approach of an unfamiliar adult, particularly if the mother was not in the room (Campos, Emde, Gaensbauer, & Sorce, 1973). The HR acceleration was interpreted as the infant's defensive response to the approaching unfamiliar adult or to the mother's departure. An infant, however, was not affectively neutral or passively sitting by as the unfamiliar adult approached (particularly when the mother was not in the room). Rather, the infant was likely to express negative affect, including crying and motoric behavior, indicating withdrawal from the situation. Such behavioral responses would cause large phasic accelerative responses in HR. If HR acceleration reflects increased metabolic demands that accompany behavioral change, how should this HR change be interpreted? Does the HR acceleration reflect a "true" psychological state or simply the consequences of increased muscle movement? In order to answer this question, we must make the distinction between movement influences on the electrical signal and movement-mediated physiological responses. HR is routinely recorded during exercise. Increases in HR reflect true demands on the heart that are not the result of artifact. This increased HR may or may not reflect a psychological state elicited during exercise. If we assume accurate determination of HR, when HR accelerates because of movement the HR acceleration is real and reflects a true metabolic shift.

Measurement of the EEG (and, indeed, all physiological measures) is highly sensitive to such factors as gross motor movement, eye movement activity, limb movement, and state change. For example, infants may show increased slow-wave activity during the course of a study reflecting state change. If the EEG is recorded properly, then the state change as reflected in the EEG may be informative (e.g., testing an infant during naptime). The increased slow-wave activity, however, may also be evidence of poor experimental design. Relatedly, Gunnar and colleagues (Larson, Gunnar, & Hertsgaard, 1991) reported that some infants napped en route to the lab, and that this behavior affected their subsequent cortisol responses to various laboratory manipulations. Such inadvertent manipulations may make data difficult to interpret.

Individual Differences in Initial Level of Response

The "law of initial values" states that the initial baseline level of a physiological system will affect the degree to which that system responds to stimulus presentation. For example, subjects with high levels of basal cortisol may respond differently to a stressor than those with more normative levels. The notion is that there is a ceiling level above which the system usually does not operate. It is important, therefore, that individual differences in baseline level be incorporated into any analysis of phasic responses. The usual approaches include computing change scores between baseline and phasic responses, or using analysis of covariance with baseline level as the covariate.

The issue of baseline level is complicated when researchers are assessing infants and young children. Since these subjects cannot be instructed to sit quietly for a baseline recording, researchers have attempted to devise methods for recording psychophysiological responses during which infants are not responding to strong stimulus challenge. The key is to record "baseline" during a noninvasive condition that may be replicated across subjects. It is often necessary to record behavior during such "baseline" recordings, to ensure that all subjects are in the same state.

Baseline differences may also speak to the underlying physiological mechanisms that affect magnitude of response. Porges, Stamps, and Walter (1974) noted that some infants did not display HR deceleration in response to the presentation of a visual stimulus. These infants exhibited fast HRs. Upon further investigation, Porges et al. found that this same group also displayed low HR variability. When subjects were grouped into those displaying high resting HR variability and those with low resting HR variability, those with high resting variability were more likely to show the decelerative pattern. In his subsequent work, Porges (1991, 1996; Porges, Doussard-Roosevelt, Portales, & Suess, 1994) has argued that initial baseline differences in HR are due to vagal control of the heart, and that the differences in the degree of this control predict HR responsivity.

The recording and analysis of psychophysiological responses require an understanding of the underlying physiology and of behavior–physiology interactions. Psychophysiological research involves a set of methodological problems and technological procedures for recording and analysis of responses. Once these technical aspects are mastered, however, the knowledge obtained linking physiology and behavior may be great. In particular, when researchers are working with preverbal infants, psychophysiological responses may provide important information regarding subjects' psychological responses to a variety of situations. Ultimately, though, psychophysiological study should strive for understanding the manner in which physiological changes affect behavior and behavior affects physiology. Such work provides the greatest insight into psychological behaviors.

PSYCHOPHYSIOLOGICAL MEASUREMENT OF INFANTS WITHIN THE STRANGE SITUATION

Heart Rate

The strange situation (Ainsworth & Wittig, 1969) was designed to assess the quality of an infant's attachment to the primary caregiver. The strange situation presents the infant with a series of conditions beginning with the infant and caregiver together in an unfamiliar playroom, followed by the introduction of an unfamiliar adult, separation from the caregiver, and the infant's being left alone in the playroom. There are two conditions of reunion between caregiver and infant; principally on the basis of the infant's behavior during these reunion episodes, the infant is classified as being "securely" or "insecurely" attached to that caregiver. There are four subtypes of secure infants, ranging from those who show little proximity seeking during reunion to those who seek a good deal of contact and comfort. Infants may cry and become distressed in response to separation from their caregivers, though such distress is not a prerequisite behavior for a secure attachment. There are three insecure classifications: "avoidant," "resistant," and "disorganized." Avoidant infants ignore their caregivers' return and may actively avoid proximity and contact; resistant infants display proximity- and contact-seeking behaviors, while at the same time displaying resistance to caregiver attempts to soothe distress; and disorganized infants are likely to display contradictory emotions, to appear confused and apprehensive, to make incomplete or undirected movements, and to show depressed affect and possibly behavioral stilling. Unlike the disorganized infants, the secure, avoidant, and resistant infants are viewed as having a coherent strategy for coping with the separation, although the secure infants are viewed as having a more adaptive strategy to stressful situations.

Within the confines of the strange situation paradigm, infants may locomote where they please in the unfamiliar playroom. Some infants run to the door after their caregivers leave. Some infants move close to their caregivers when the unfamiliar adult enters, whereas other infants play and explore around the room. The high mobility within the confines of the experimental setting places limitations on the ability of researchers to measure ongoing physiological activity during this procedure. Nevertheless, there have been a number of attempts to assess psychophysiological reactions during the strange situation.

One of the first attempts to record HR during the strange situation was described by Sroufe and Waters (1977). They described individual case studies of infant HR response during preseparation, separation, and reunion episodes. Infant HR was recorded via telemetry: Each infant wore a small transmitter that sent an FM radio signal containing the electrocardiogram (EKG) to a receiver—a procedure that allowed the infant complete mobility within the playroom. The authors were primarily interested in the HR responses of

insecure infants. Avoidant infants, who usually appear undisturbed by the separation, seem to exhibit "displacement behavior" during reunion, in which they continue to play with toys in a rigid or uninspired way. Sroufe and Waters hypothesized that these infants, although showing no overt behavioral distress at reunion, are in fact upset and should therefore show elevations in HR during reunion, in contrast to the decelerative HR responses shown by most infants during object play prior to separation. Similarly, Sroufe and Waters were interested in the HR patterns of resistant infants, who appear highly distressed during separation and have difficulty being soothed by their caregivers during reunion. Resistant infants, they thought, should continue to show elevated HRs during the reunion episodes, reflecting their inability to regulate their heightened arousal.

Sroufe and Waters (1977) reported that secure, avoidant, and resistant infants all showed increased HRs upon separation, which remained elevated during reunion. Secure infants' HRs recovered on average after less than 1 minute of contact with their mothers. After the secure infants were put down, they showed HR deceleration when they returned to play and attended to objects. Resistant infants, in contrast, requested to be put down before their HRs recovered to the preseparation level; then, after being put down with their HRs still elevated, they reached up to be held again. Avoidant infants showed an increase in HR from the beginning of separation until long into the reunion session, even though they outwardly appeared to be unaffected by the separation. These case studies demonstrated that HR could be recorded from infants in the strange situation and that changes in HR were helpful in interpreting the behavior of different types of infants.

Donovan and Leavitt (1985a) also examined HR response in infants during the strange situation. These researchers, using telemetry, recorded EKG synchronized to the ongoing sequence of behavioral episodes of the strange situation. Thirty-seven infants were tested, and 29 of these had usable EKG data. Of the 29 infants, 22 were classified as securely attached, 4 as avoidant, and 3 as resistant. Because of the low number of infants in the insecure categories, most of the statistical analyses were computed only on the subcategories (B1 through B4) of the secure infants. The data suggested that in response to the entrance and approach of the unfamiliar adult, secure infants displayed HR deceleration, relative to a preentrance baseline. In addition, in response to impending separation (when their mothers said goodbye), secure infants displayed acceleratory trends in their HR. Although no statistical comparisons were completed, Donovan and Leavitt presented the mean HR data for the combined avoidant and resistant infants during these same situations. These insecure infants did not appear to display HR deceleration to either stranger entrance or approach; they did, however, display HR acceleration to the impending separation. Donovan and Leavitt interpreted the deceleratory responses of secure infants as indexing attention and orienting to the stranger, whereas they viewed the acceleratory responses to impending separation as a defensive response. Unfortunately, the small number of insecure infants, and the need to combine avoidant and resistant infants, precluded any assessment of the hypotheses proposed by Sroufe and Waters (1977) regarding the utility of HR in distinguishing the behaviors of avoidant and resistant infants.

In this same study, Donovan and Leavitt (1985a) also examined the HR changes of the mothers and their infants. The HR data for the 22 securely attached infants and their mothers paralleled each other, whereas the HR data for the combined insecurely attached infants and their mothers did not. Securely attached infants and their mothers both displayed HR decreases as the stranger entered the room and approached the infant. Donovan and Leavitt suggested that this concordance between the secure infants and their mothers reflects a mother's involvement in her infant's behavior. Specifically, by responding to an infant's gaze and/or events surrounding her infant, a mother displays a sensitivity that contributes to the development of a secure attachment. The mothers of insecurely attached infants failed to show consistency to the stranger's entrance and approach. The authors suggested that this inconsistency reflects less involvement on the part of a mother in the infant's behavior.

A later attempt to examine HR responses of infants during the strange situation provided little support for differentiating between avoidant and secure attachment classifications. Spangler and Grossmann (1993) observed 41 infants in the strange situation, recording EKG via telemetry during the paradigm. Although no description was provided of how behavior and physiology were synchronized, the authors reported usable HR data for 18 secure, 6 avoidant, and 6 disorganized infants. The analyses revealed no group differences in infant HR change during any of

the reunion episodes. The one episode in which significant group differences in HR change appeared was Episode 6, when the infant was alone in the room. In this episode, disorganized infants displayed greater HR acceleration than did the other two groups (avoidant and secure). Interestingly, the secure and disorganized infants displayed similar levels of negative vocalizations during this episode, whereas only the disorganized infants displayed the elevated HR pattern. Spangler and Grossmann suggested that disorganized infants may be intensely alarmed by the strange situation separation, to the point that activation of their attachment behavior cannot be systematically controlled.

Spangler and Grossmann (1993) also examined the HRs of attachment-classified infants during object manipulation and play with their mothers. They found that the avoidant infants did not display HR acceleration when looking at their mothers, whereas the secure and disorganized infants did. The avoidant infants did, however, display acceleration while looking at objects or during object manipulation, whereas the disorganized and secure infants displayed HR deceleration. It appears that these behavior–EKG links were aggregates of data from across the different episodes of the strange situation, thus clouding the interpretation of these differences. Similarly, it is unclear why secure and disorganized infants displayed similar HR patterns while the HR patterns of avoidant infants differed, particularly during visual regard of their mothers. Spangler and Grossmann state that "the heightened heart rate when looking to the mother indicates that visual contact with mother was initiated specifically during episodes of physiological arousal" (p. 1447). In the absence of a precise linkage between measures of visual regard and specification of when these behaviors were coded, such an explanation seems post hoc at best.

In a more recent study, Bono and Stifter (1995) examined the relations between measures of HR and HR variability assessed immediately before and after the strange situation as a function of infant attachment classification at 18 months of age. The authors reported that infants categorized as resistant displayed faster HRs and less heart period variability than secure infants after the strange situation. These differences, however, may be due to the extreme degree of upset displayed by resistant infants and their inability to be soothed during reunion. To the extent that resistant infants display behavioral problems in regulating their affect in the strange situation and immediately thereafter, autonomic activity will mimic those patterns of dysregulation. At the moment, it is not possible to say whether the elevated HR is an artifact or an example of a converging indicator of the infants' distress.

Cortisol

A number of studies have measured cortisol in infants who have undergone testing in the strange situation. Cortisol response takes place over a much longer time course than other physiological systems. Thus measurement of cortisol in saliva or plasma 15 to 30 minutes after completion of the strange situation may accurately reflect an infant's HPA response during the experimental paradigm.

Gunnar, Mangelsdorf, Larson, and Hertsgaard (1989) observed 66 infants in the strange situation at 13 months of age. Saliva was obtained from these infants, first at home prior to coming to the lab, then immediately before the strange situation and immediately after the strange situation; salivary cortisol was measured from these three sets of samples. Of the 66 infants, 37 were classified as secure, 10 as avoidant, 16 as resistant, and 3 as disorganized. There were no differences among attachment groups in either cortisol level or the degree of cortisol change. In a follow-up, Gunnar, Colton, and Stansbury (1992) examined differences in salivary cortisol between 47 securely attached infants and 24 insecurely attached infants. Again, saliva was collected immediately prior to and immediately after the strange situation. Again, no differences in salivary cortisol reactivity among infants classified as avoidant, resistant, and secure were found.

Spangler and Grossmann (1993), on the other hand, reported finding differences in salivary cortisol reactivity between their infant attachment groups. In their study of 41 infants, saliva was collected immediately prior to the strange situation and then 15 and 30 minutes afterwards. They found significant cortisol increases in infants categorized as disorganized compared to secure infants 15 minutes after the strange situation, and significant secure–insecure differences 30 minutes after the strange situation. Spangler and Grossmann argued that these data support a cortisol–coping hypothesis, with secure infants better able to cope with the stress of separation in the strange situation than insecure infants. Span-

gler and Grossmann also commented on the differences between their findings and those of the two studies conducted by Gunnar's group (Gunnar et al., 1989, 1992). They stated that these differences could have resulted from variation in the length of time after the session before saliva was collected. In the Gunnar et al. studies, saliva was collected 5 to 10 minutes after the session; in the Spangler and Grossmann study, it was collected at 15 and then again at 30 minutes after the strange situation. Given the slow response time of cortisol, the Gunnar et al. data may not have reflected the full effect of the strange situation upon the insecure infants.

In a subsequent study, Hertsgaard, Gunnar, Erickson, and Nachmias (1995) examined 38 infants from a high-risk population. Unlike other studies, this one did not control for time of day at which saliva was obtained, nor was there any pretest cortisol measurement. Of the 34 subjects with usable data, 17 were classified as secure, 5 as avoidant, 1 as resistant, and 11 as disorganized. Results of the analyses revealed, first, that the infants with disorganized classifications had elevated cortisol levels compared to all of the other infants combined. Further inspection of the data revealed that the main difference in level was between the avoidant and disorganized infants. That is, avoidant infants displayed the lowest cortisol values, and disorganized infants displayed the highest. The authors argued that these data support the notion that infants categorized as disorganized may have greater vulnerability to stressful situations. It is, of course, also interesting that the infants classified as avoidant did not show elevated cortisol levels. If in fact avoidant infants are physiologically stressed during the strange situation, one would expect their cortisol levels to be higher than those of secure infants. It is also important to note that the initial level of cortisol was not assessed; therefore, it is unclear whether the cortisol levels represent different responses to the strange situation stress or initial differences between groups in levels of cortisol.

More recently, Nachmias, Gunnar, Mangelsdorf, Parritz, and Buss (1996) examined 73 children at 18 months of age in the strange situation. There were 13 children classified as avoidant, 12 classified as resistant, and 48 classified as secure. Salivary samples were collected immediately prior to the strange situation and 45 minutes after the onset of the testing session. The children had also been observed on a previous occasion responding to presentation of several novel events for assessment of behavioral inhibition. "Behavioral inhibition" was defined as the tendency to restrain or restrict one's approach to new people, places, events, and/or objects (Kagan & Snidman, 1991). Although the authors did not find a relation between inhibition and security of attachment, they did find that children with higher behavioral inhibition had higher postsession cortisol levels if they were also insecure. Secure inhibited children did not exhibit significant cortisol reactivity—nor, for that matter, did insecure infants who were low in inhibition. Thus the degree of cortisol reactivity to the strange situation in insecure children was heightened among those with higher behavioral inhibition. These results nicely illustrate Gunnar's stress model, in which the security of attachment is viewed as a buffer against stress; in this model, infants who are securely attached should exhibit a reduced stress response. In fact, inhibited infants who were securely attached did show lower cortisol responses.

In sum, the results of studies conducted to examine the physiological correlates of attachment classification during the strange situation have been mixed. Few studies have measured HR responses of infants in the strange situation, despite the technical feasibility of doing so. Those studies that have measured HR responses in the strange situation contain small numbers of subjects in different attachment categories, so that interpretation of the HR data is problematic. Greater success has been found in studies utilizing cortisol in the strange situation. The results indicate that infants who appear stressed during the strange situation are more likely to exhibit increases in cortisol levels.

MEASUREMENT OF INDIVIDUAL DIFFERENCES IN INFANT PSYCHOPHYSIOLOGICAL RESPONSE AS RELATED TO BEHAVIOR IN THE STRANGE SITUATION

Heart Rate

Although attachment theorists believe that an infant's temperament is orthogonal to the quality of the attachment the child has with the primary caregiver (Sroufe, 1985), there have been attempts to reconcile temperament and attachment positions (see Vaughn & Bost, Chapter 10, this volume). Belsky and Rovine (1987), for example, argued that temperament may play a role in the manner in which behaviors are expressed within the strange situation, regardless of attachment classification. That is, temperamentally reactive and fearful infants may be more likely to cry during separation and may have more difficulty in being soothed during reunion. Belsky and Rovine suggested that instead of comparing secure (B), avoidant (A), and resistant groups, one should compare A1-through-B2 infants with B3-through-C2 infants (the former group is relatively avoidant, whereas the latter group is relatively resistant). Organizing attachment classifications in this manner may assist in conceptualizing the influence of temperament on behavior in the strange situation. One might expect infants in the A1-through-B2 range not to react as intensively to separation as infants in the B3-through-C2 range.

Several researchers interested in the psychophysiological correlates of temperament have examined the physiological correlates of reactivity and regulation in infants (e.g., Fox, 1989; Stifter & Fox, 1990). Some of these workers have attempted to relate their findings to subsequent attachment behavior or status (Izard et al., 1991). For example, Porges et al. (1994) conceptualized their measure of vagal tone as reflecting the degree to which infants will be reactive and able to self-regulate. Infants with high vagal tone are thought to display more mature autonomic regulation and thus may exhibit both greater reactivity and superior self-regulatory strategies. Izard et al. (1991) examined the relation between vagal tone measured at 3, 4½, 6, and 9 months and attachment status at 13 months of age in 54 infants. Forty infants were classified as securely attached, 8 as avoidant, and 6 as resistant. Measures of vagal tone, HR, and HR variance were collected at each age assessed during the first year of life. A continuous measure of security was utilized as the dependent measure, and vagal tone scores were computed for each of the different assessment points on that score. Izard et al. reported that measures of vagal tone at the earliest months significantly predicted attachment insecurity at 13 months. Specifically, infants with high vagal tone at 3 months and high HR variance at 4½ months were more likely to be classified as insecure at 13 months, though there were no differences between avoidant and resistant infants. Izard et al.'s findings seem contrary to Porges's (1991) prediction regarding the role of vagal tone in emotion regulation. Porges argues that high vagal tone should reflect more mature autonomic regulation and greater regulatory capacity. It is unclear why these autonomic measures at this young age differed in the direction that they did, nor is it clear why there was a lack of differentiation at each of the other ages assessed.

Fox and colleagues conducted a series of studies aimed at examining relations among individual differences in emotion expression and emotion regulation and measures of autonomic activity (Fox, 1989; Fox & Gelles, 1984; Stifter & Fox, 1990). Fox and Gelles (1984) found that 3-month-old infants who displayed high HR variability and low HR were more likely to express positive emotions in response to maternal bids than were infants with high HR and low HR variability. "HR variability" was defined in this study as the mean of the successive differences in HR over the recording epoch. HR variability (particularly of the mean successive differences) is highly correlated with measures of respiratory sinus arrhythmia such as vagal tone. The authors reasoned that high HR variability, like vagal tone, should reflect an infant's ability to display an organized behavioral response. This was confirmed when they found that infants with high HR variability displayed more positive interactive behavior. In subsequent studies, Fox (e.g., Fox, 1985) found that infants with high vagal tone were more reactive as young infants and also more likely to display positive social behaviors as toddlers. In contrast to Izard et al.'s (1991) findings, but consistent with Porges's prediction, these data suggest that high vagal tone is associated with more organized social responsivity. Porges has argued that the level of vagal tone reflects the degree to which the organism will exhibit an organized response to stimulus challenge. The manner of response of the ANS is reflected in organized overt behavior. Thus infants with high vagal tone should display less dysregulated and more organized behavioral responses to novelty and challenge; infants with low vagal tone should display less organized behavioral responses to stimulation.

Fox (1985) related individual differences in HR variability to attachment status within a high-risk (premature) infant sample. In a sample of 60 infants, Fox reported relations among measures of HR variability at 3 months of age and attachment status at 12 months of age. Of the 60 infants in the sample, 43 were classified at 12 months of age as secure, 16 as avoidant, and only 1 as resistant. Although there were no differences between attachment classification groups (avoidant vs. secure) on any of the autonomic measures, individual differences in behavior in the strange situation were related to 3-month HR variability. Specifically, infants who cried during the strange situation at 12 months had higher HR variability at 3 months. In addition, infants with high HR variability at 3 months displayed greater regulation at reunion during the strange situation; that is, they resumed playing in a shorter period of time. Fox argued that high HR variability, like vagal tone, reflects better physiological organization, such that children with high variability are more reactive but are also better able to self-regulate than infants with low variability.

Brain Electrical Activity

Brain electrical activity (EEG) is measured by recording the voltage off the scalp, which is supposedly generated from the cortex itself. The measure of brain activity is usually expressed in electrical units and reflects the amplitude of the signal at a particular frequency or frequency band. The square of the amplitude is known as "power." Berger (1929, 1932a, 1932b) was the first to postulate that power and activation are inversely related. He did so on the basis of the following observation: When subjects rested with their eyes closed, EEG power, particularly in the alpha frequency (8–13 Hz), was high in amplitude. When subjects were instructed to open their eyes and attend to an external stimulus, the amplitude of the alpha waves decreased. Berger (and later Lindsley & Wicke, 1974) argued that during attention and cognition, multiple centers in the brain actively process external information, leading to desynchronization of alpha waves and a decrease in alpha amplitude. When subjects are resting, alpha waves are more synchronous, and hence the amplitude of the EEG is higher. Thus, when the EEG signal displays high-amplitude waves, the assumption is made that there is less "brain" activation than when the EEG signal displays reduced-amplitude waves.

The asymmetry index, used in laterality studies, reflects the difference in EEG power between homologous regions (identical scalp locations from the left and right hemispheres). This index is either expressed as a ratio score (Right − Left/Right + Left) or a difference score between the natural log values of the left right hemispheres (LnR − LnL). For example, if there are 10 units of power measured from the left frontal scalp lead and 6 units of power measured from the right frontal scalp lead, the asymmetry index will be $(6 - 10)/(16)$, or $-.25$. Similarly, if there are 6 units of power measured from the left frontal scalp lead and 10 units from the right frontal scalp lead, the asymmetry index will be $(10 - 6/16)$, or $+.25$. The sign (positive or negative) of the index indicates whether the asymmetry reflects greater relative left or right activation. In the case where the asymmetry score is $-.25$ (less power, and hence more activation, measured from the right hemisphere [6 units] than from the left hemisphere [10 units]), it indicates right frontal asymmetry. In the case where the asymmetry score is $+.25$, the score reflects left frontal asymmetry for similar reasons. Right frontal asymmetry indicates relatively greater activation in the right hemisphere, whereas left frontal asymmetry indicates relatively greater activation in the left hemisphere.

Various data from a number of different sources have implicated the anterior regions of the left and right cerebral hemispheres as being involved in the expression and/or experience of different emotions (Davidson & Fox, 1982; Fox, 1991; Fox & Davidson, 1984). In an initial study, Davidson and Fox (1982) found that 10-month-old infants viewing a video tape of an actress portraying either positive affect (smiling and laughter) or negative affect (sad expression and crying) exhibited asymmetric activation in frontal scalp leads, depending upon the valence of the video stimulus. While viewing the positive segment, infants exhibited left frontal EEG asymmetry (relatively greater activation in the left frontal region). Follow-up studies found this asymmetry in frontal EEG activity to be present also in infants' response to sweet and sour tastes (Fox & Davidson, 1986a), as well as the approach of the infants' mothers or a stranger (Fox & Davidson, 1988). Infants exhibited left frontal EEG asymmetry during the expression of positive affects and right frontal EEG asymmetry during the expression of negative affects (Fox & Davidson, 1984). Fox and Davidson (1984) argued that the functional significance of frontal asymmetry with regard to emotion may be conceptualized in terms of the motivational systems of approach and withdrawal. The right frontal region may be specialized for behaviors associated with withdrawal, while the left may be specialized for behaviors associated with approach. Subsequently, Fox (1991, 1994) speculated that activity in the frontal region may also be involved in the regulation of approach or withdrawal behaviors. He based this position in part

upon the literature on the behavioral effects of unilateral frontal brain damage. Patients with either left or right frontal lesions often report an inability to control or regulate the expression of negative or positive affects; these same patients can, if requested, produce facial expressions of either positive or negative affect. Their deficit thus appears to be in the control of emotion expression, rather than in the ability to produce the expressions themselves. Fox argued, then, that both left and right frontal activation may be associated with the ability to modulate approach or withdrawal behaviors. Left frontal activation may be associated with the ability to control approach behavior and the expression of positive affect. A decrement in left frontal activation may be associated with the absence of the expression of positive affect. Right frontal activation may be associated with the ability to control withdrawal behaviors and the expression of negative affect. A decrement in right frontal activation may be associated with the absence of the expression of negative affect. There is some evidence for this model.

Henriques and Davidson (1990) found that depressed individuals (even those who had previously been depressed and were currently in remission) exhibited right frontal EEG asymmetry. Inspection of the EEG power values revealed that the asymmetry in these individuals was a function of less activity in the left frontal region. The authors argued that some depression may be characterized by an absence of positive affect rather than the presence of extreme negative affect. On the other hand, Davidson and Fox (1988) found that infants with right frontal EEG asymmetry were more likely to cry at maternal separation than were those displaying left frontal EEG asymmetry. Fox, Bell, and Jones (1992) replicated this finding and reported that the locus of effect was in the right hemisphere: Infants most likely to cry were those displaying less power in the right frontal region (e.g., right frontal asymmetry). In addition, Calkins, Fox, and Marshall (1996) found that inhibited infants displayed right frontal EEG asymmetry, which was a function of right frontal activation. Finally, Schmidt, Shahinfar, and Fox (1996) reported that toddlers selected for externalizing behaviors exhibited left frontal EEG asymmetry, which was a function of high right frontal power (less right activation). They speculated that this pattern may reflect a decreased ability to experience punishment among aggressive children.

Both Davidson (1993a, 1993b) and Fox (1994) have argued that the pattern of resting or tonic frontal EEG activation may be thought of as reflecting a predisposition toward the expression and experience of affects associated with approach or withdrawal. For example, infants exhibiting tonic right frontal EEG asymmetry (as a function of right frontal activation) may be more likely to display distress at separation and to have difficulty in regulating that distress. Infants displaying left frontal EEG asymmetry (as a function of left frontal activation) may be more likely to express positive affect and perhaps to be better regulated in their behavioral responses.

Although there are no data directly assessing EEG differences in the prediction of attachment classification, there is indirect evidence of a relation between dispositional patterns of frontal EEG asymmetry and attachment classification. In a series of studies, Fox and colleagues (Calkins & Fox, 1992; Calkins et al., 1996; Fox, Calkins, & Bell, 1994) examined the pattern of EEG asymmetry in temperamentally inhibited infants. These infants displayed a pattern of right frontal EEG asymmetry as early as 9 months of age. Indeed, infants displaying stable right frontal EEG asymmetry across the first 2 years of life were more likely to display reticence and social withdrawal at age 4 than were infants whose pattern was unstable or who showed a stable pattern of left frontal EEG asymmetry over that period of time (Fox et al., 1994). In a parallel study, Calkins and Fox (1992) reported that inhibited infants were more likely to be categorized as resistant than were uninhibited infants. Fifty infants were seen at both 14 and 24 months of age. At 14 months of age, the infants were videotaped in the strange situation, and later 34 were classified as secure, 7 as avoidant, and 9 as resistant. At 24 months of age, these same infants were seen in the laboratory and assessed for behavioral inhibition. The pattern of cross-age findings revealed that at 24 months avoidant infants were likely to be assessed as uninhibited, resistant infants were likely to be assessed as highly inhibited, and secure infants were likely to display behaviors around the mean. The temperamentally inhibited infants displayed right frontal EEG asymmetry, suggesting an underlying predisposition toward withdrawal. Inhibited infants displaying right frontal EEG asymmetry were most likely to be categorized as resistant in their attachment, due to their disposition to express negative affect in response to mild stress and their inability to modulate that affective response.

Similar findings have been reported in a study examining the influence of maternal depression with both clinical and nonclinical populations on attachment security (Dawson, Klinger, Panagiotides, Spieker, & Frey, 1992). These workers reported that secure infants of symptomatic mothers displayed reduced left frontal EEG activity in response to a positive-affect elicitor, compared to securely attached infants of nonsymptomatic mothers. They argue that the infants of symptomatic mothers may have more difficulty expressing positive affect, as indexed by the reduced left frontal EEG activity. The small number of subjects and lack of comparison to insecure infants, however, do not allow for generalization of the role of the EEG as indicative of affect expression in attachment.

The cognitive functions that are mediated by the frontal cortex may also assist in modulating emotional responses. For example, researchers have long investigated the role of the frontal lobes in certain aspects of attention (Rothbart & Posner, 1985). In particular, the frontal lobes have been implicated in subjects' abilities to switch set and to inhibit a prepotent motor response (Goldman-Rakic, 1987). In addition, certain areas of the frontal region have been implicated in aspects of planful behavior, including attentional flexibility (Welsh, Pennington, & Groisser, 1991). Rothbart and Posner (1985) have suggested that these aspects of attention are critical elements in the regulation of affective responses. For example, a child's ability to refocus attention from one stimulus to another may assist him or her in regulating distress. Harman and Fox (1997) found that infants who were able to refocus attention were less likely to remain distressed than were those unable to shift attention.

Although the influence of individual differences in temperament on attachment security remains a point of discussion and dissension among researchers, there appears to be evidence for psychophysiological markers of certain infant dispositions. In particular, proneness to distress and negative affect seem to have distinct physiological markers. These dispositions most certainly have some influence upon behavior in the strange situation and perhaps on attachment classification. More importantly, the manner in which caregiving styles interact with such dispositions to produce attachment classification and social competencies should be a productive avenue of research.

PSYCHOPHYSIOLOGICAL RESPONSES OF CAREGIVERS AND ATTACHMENT

The development of the attachment relationship is thought to be based on the manner in which the caregiver responds to the infant's signals. Ainsworth and her colleagues have argued that the degree to which a mother is sensitive and responsive to an infant's signals will contribute to the quality of the infant's attachment to the mother. A mother who is insensitive and ignoring of the infant's needs contributes to the development of an avoidant attachment; a mother who is inconsistent in her responses contributes to the development of a resistant attachment; and a mother who is sensitive and responsive to the infant contributes to the development of a secure attachment (Ainsworth, 1973). It is for this reason that a good deal of research has examined the parameters of sensitivity and responsivity in maternal behavior during the first year of life, and its association with the subsequent quality of attachment (Ainsworth, 1973; Ainsworth, Bell, & Stayton, 1971; Ainsworth, Blehar, Waters, & Wall, 1978; Bell & Ainsworth, 1972; Belsky & Isabella, 1987; Egeland & Farber, 1984).

Among studies assessing these parameters and subsequent quality of attachment are those that have utilized psychophysiological measures to examine maternal sensitivity to infant signals, as well as the underlying aspects of sensitive caregiving behavior (e.g., Donovan & Leavitt, 1985a, 1985b, 1989; Frodi, Lamb, Leavitt, & Donovan, 1978). For example, in a study assessing the behavioral sensitivity of mothers to their infants during a feeding session, Donovan and Leavitt (1978) showed that physiological reactivity (the degree of a mother's HR deceleration) to an infant's signals predicted the mother's behavioral sensitivity when feeding the infant. HR deceleration was interpreted as reflecting maternal attention. The authors suggested that mothers showing the HR deceleration pattern were more attentive to their infants' needs than mothers who did not show this pattern of HR deceleration.

Researchers have argued that the quality of maternal responsiveness is in part influenced by the infant's behavior. In order to examine this, researchers have presented adult participants with audiotapes or videotapes of different types of cries of familiar and unfamiliar infants, and measured the autonomic responses to these cries. Frodi, Lamb, Leavitt, and Donovan (1978) presented 48 mother–father pairs with a 6-minute videotape showing either a smiling infant or a crying infant. The infant in the videotape was randomly labeled prior to presentation as either "normal," "difficult," or "premature." Blood pressure and skin conductance were recorded while the participant watched the tape. Results revealed little autonomic change in response to the smiling infant, but significant increases in blood pressure (interpreted as reflecting an "aversive state" or a "disposition to aggress") and skin conductance (interpreted as an index of autonomic arousal to "aggress") in response to the crying infant, with the highest increases in parents who were told that the infant was premature. The authors speculated that perception of an infant's difficultness may lead some individuals to respond aversively to that infant's signals. In a follow-up study, these same authors (Frodi, Lamb, Leavitt, Donovan, Neff, & Sherry, 1978) examined 64 parents who were presented with a videotape of either a full-term or a premature infant and heard, paired with it, either a full-term or a premature infant's cry. HR and skin conductance were measured and found to be significantly elevated when subjects heard the cry of a premature infant, particularly when this cry was paired with the video of the premature infant. The increases in HR and skin conductance were interpreted within a general model of arousal as reflecting aversiveness. The authors speculated that "high-risk" infants may emit cries that are more aversive and thus more likely to reduce caregivers' responsiveness.

Several other studies have employed variants of the paradigm described above to examine factors that might influence parental response to infant cries (these data are reviewed extensively in Donovan & Leavitt, 1985b). For example, Boukydis and Burgess (1982) examined the effects of parity on a parent's response to infant crying, finding that primiparous parents showed higher levels of skin potential response. Wiesenfeld, Malatesta, and DeLoach (1981) reported that both mothers and fathers responded with HR deceleration to unfamiliar infant cries, although mothers were better able than fathers to discriminate between their own infants' cries and those of an unfamiliar infant.

In most of these studies, HR deceleration has been interpreted as reflecting attention to the stimulus, whereas HR acceleration has been considered evidence of an aversive or defensive response. Such correspondence may not always be evident, however. For example, Wiesenfeld and

Klorman (1978) found that mothers responded with HR acceleration to videotapes of their own infants' smiles. Similarly, Donovan, Leavitt, and Balling (1978) found an initial HR acceleration in mothers in response to their smiling 3-month-old infants. The acceleration of HR found in such studies does not easily fit a model of linking acceleration and defensive response. Nevertheless, the finding of HR deceleration across studies in response to "normal" infant cries does seem to reflect an early component of the attention system and may play a role in directing maternal responses to a distressed infant.

In a series of innovative studies, Donovan and Leavitt studied factors that may elicit an attentional response in mothers of young infants (Donovan & Leavitt, 1989; Donovan, Leavitt, & Walsh, 1990, 1997). They examined the degree to which mothers felt they had control over the termination of an infant's cry. Their task, a modification of the illusion-of-control paradigm (Alloy & Abramson, 1979), consisted of having each mother make one of two responses, with the goal of terminating an infant's cry, after which the mother was asked to estimate her perceived control over the event. On each of 42 trials, a red light was followed by cry onset. Subjects had the option of either pressing or not pressing a button. Responses were followed by a fixed schedule of cry termination in half the trials and cry continuation in the other half. On trial 41, the cry stimulus was omitted. After the trials, mothers of 5-month-old infants were asked to rate the degree to which they felt they had control over cry termination during the task.

HR was monitored continuously during the task, and change scores were computed between prestimulus HR level and levels during (1) the 10-second interval prior to onset of the cry, (2) the initial 5 seconds of the cry, (3) the 20-second interval during omission of the cry on trial 41, and (4) the 10-second period on trial 42. Mothers were grouped into those who reported either a high illusion of control, a midlevel illusion of control, or a low illusion of control during the task. Mothers in the high-illusion group displayed an augmented HR acceleration in anticipation of the impending cry, which habituated rapidly and remained low during the middle of the task, and displayed increasing acceleration toward the final trials. Mothers in the high-illusion group did not show the same pattern of deceleration to the omitted cry that mothers in the middle- and low-illusion groups did. Thus maternal HR reflected attentional processes in a

mother's response to her perception of control over an infant's cries. Mothers with a high illusion of control displayed more aversive responses, coped less well over time (as reflected in their pattern over trials), and were not as attentive to the omitted cry. Donovan and Leavitt (1989) claimed that this pattern of HR findings reflects a degree of insensitivity to infant signals.

In this same study, Donovan and Leavitt assessed the mothers and infants in the strange situation when the infants were 15 months of age. Infants were classified as either secure or insecure, and comparisons were made with the 5-month sensitivity ratings. Four insecurely attached infants had mothers in the low- or middle-illusion groups, and three had mothers in the high-illusion group. These small group sizes precluded any direct test of the relations between illusion group and attachment security. Donovan and Leavitt also reported that mothers of insecurely attached infants were more depressed at 5 (but not at 16) months than mothers of securely attached infants. And mothers of insecurely attached infants exhibited cardiac acceleration to the impending cry.

In two follow-up studies, Donovan and Leavitt (Donovan et al., 1990, 1997) further refined their model of illusion of control in relation to sensitive caregiving. Donovan et al. (1990) presented mothers of 5-month-olds with the illusion-of-control task. A week later, the mothers participated in a learned-helplessness paradigm, in which they were presented with an infant cry and told to try to terminate it by pressing a button. For all mothers, pushing the button had no effect on the cry. Mothers were then given a second task consisting of a shuttle box with a movable handle. Again, they were asked to attempt to terminate the cry by moving the handle. HR was recorded throughout the session.

As in the earlier study, mothers were categorized as high, middle, or low on illusion of control. In addition, mothers completed a temperament questionnaire designed to assess their own infants' behavior; based on their responses, their infants were categorized as either "easy" or "difficult." The HR data revealed an interaction between illusion group and infant temperament. Mothers in the high-illusion group who rated their infants as difficult responded with cardiac acceleration in the learned-helplessness task. Only mothers in the middle-illusion group displayed significant cardiac deceleration to the impending cry as they completed the task. Donovan et al. (1990) argued that mothers who had a high illusion of control were less attentive and more "defensive" in response to infant signals than were mothers in the other two groups.

In a recent study, Donovan et al. (1997) assessed mothers of 4- to 6-month-olds in their lab twice—once with the illusion-of-control task, and a second time with a signal detection task in which they were asked to differentiate infant cries that varied in frequency. HR was monitored throughout the illusion-of-control task. Mothers were divided into three groups based on sensitivity scores collected during the signal detection task. Analysis of the HR data revealed that only the most sensitive mothers exhibited a smooth pattern of habituation over trials in HR; mothers in the latter two groups failed to habituate across trials. Thus greater sensitivity of mothers to infant cries was associated with habituation of the HR response during the illusion-of-control task. In addition, mothers' perception of their ability to control terminating an infant cry was related to their sensitivity to discriminate between different infant cry patterns.

The Donovan and Leavitt work has systematically addressed factors that may be associated with maternal sensitivity to infant cries, and possibly to a secure pattern of attachment. They reported across studies that maternal sensitivity was related to the degree to which mothers realistically estimated the control they had over terminating an infant's cry, as well as the degree to which they were susceptible to learned helplessness. The picture emerging from this body of work is one in which particular maternal personality characteristics contribute to a mother's lack of sensitivity toward her infant's signals. This apparent insensitivity is further supported by the absence of clear deceleratory HR patterns in the data. The links among this apparent insensitivity, maternal personality characteristics, and associated HR response have not yet been fully explored, however. In only one study (Donovan & Leavitt, 1989) did these investigators follow up the mothers and children to age 15 months and assess them in the strange situation. As with many studies of this type, the number of insecure children who had mothers in the high-illusion group was too small to permit any definite conclusions to be drawn. Nevertheless, the work represents the best available attempt to integrate physiological indices of attention with cognitive and personality attributes of caregiving, in order to clarify the factors involved in maternal sensitivity.

PSYCHOPHYSIOLOGY AND THE ADULT ATTACHMENT INTERVIEW

Recent conceptual advances in the study of attachment have led to the development of an instrument for assessing an adult's current state of mind regarding attachment to his or her parents. Researchers administering the AAI (George, Kaplan, & Main, 1984) ask subjects to describe experiences they may have had as children interacting with their parents. Particular emphasis is placed on themes of separation and loss. Subjects are asked to generate memories regarding their parents' caregiving and to characterize the relationships they had with their parents. Interviews are recorded on audiotape and then scored from verbatim transcripts. Important elements in the scoring are a subject's coherence and nature of discourse. That is, an interview is scored for the degree to which there is consistency across responses and the extent to which a coherent story is generated. On the basis of these scores, subjects are classified into one of four attachment groups: "secure/autonomous," "dismissing," "preoccupied," or "unresolved" (see Hesse, Chapter 19, and Crowell, Fraley, & Shaver, Chapter 20, this volume).

There are at least two possible positions that attachment theorists may take with regard to the importance of early experience for adult state of mind as rendered by the AAI (Fox, 1995). One may argue that early experience is critical for the formation of working models, and thus for the states of mind that are reflected by the AAI data. In this case, what actually happened in infancy is critical, whether the person remembers it accurately or not. Hence one would expect researchers to search for continuity across infancy to adulthood—even though an adult may not remember the events of the past. If there were a way to elicit or identify accurate childhood memories via psychophysiological methods, this should be interesting to attachment researchers. A second position may be that early experience is not critical for the formation of adult states of mind regarding attachment. AAI data are the product of a long history over time with many transformations, and perhaps current psychological state is more important in understanding current state of mind about attachments than is prior early experience. In this case, the veracity of early memories about childhood may not be an important issue.

Attachment theory seems closer to the second than to the first position outlined above. Main,

Kaplan, and Cassidy (1985) have argued that the AAI assesses the current state of mind about attachment relationships, and hence that the interviewer need not be concerned about the veracity of the memories. Attachment theorists have also written about the intergenerational transmission of attachment and are interested in the manner in which security is communicated across generations (e.g., Bakersman-Kranenburg & van IJzendoorn, 1993; van IJzendoorn, 1992). Implicit in the subjects' accounts is a concern for the continuity within the attachment-based cognitions formed early in life. It is, of course, possible that continuity of working models exists (subjects classified as secure in infancy are classified as autonomous as adults), but the memories that subjects describe are current interpretations of their own childhoods rather than accurate representations of the occurrences. Reports of childhood experiences may in fact be reconstructions of past experiences. While details of the memory may be filled in over time, there may be an affective core to the memory that reflects security or insecurity. To the extent that attachment researchers are interested in this affective core, there may be methods for examining these early memories in older children and adults.

There is currently great interest within the field of cognitive neuroscience in studying the neural correlates of episodic memory. Episodic memory is one of two "types" of memory that constitute the explicit (or conscious) memory system. According to Tulving (1983), who first made the distinction, episodic memory "is concerned with unique, concrete personal experiences dated in the rememberer's past" (p. 1). Although Tulving explicitly required conscious recollection of events in the past as a hallmark of episodic memory, several researchers have been interested in whether individuals have access to certain types of episodic memories, particularly autobiographical memories from childhood (Damasio, 1990; Fink et al., 1996; Fletcher et al., 1995). Researchers in this area are interested in examining the quality of the information that may be stored over time in the brain, and in the possibility that under certain conditions, this information may be successfully retrieved.

There is neuropsychological evidence implicating certain regions of the cerebral cortex as being crucially involved in the recollection of autobiographical material. Early reports (Milner, 1966) centered on the temporal lobes (specifically, the hippocampal formation), whereas more recent studies have also implicated the frontal lobes as being involved in the recollection of autobiographical material (see Squire et al., 1992, for a review). Although most of this work has been completed with adults, there is some research on the recall of autobiographical information from children. Some researchers (e.g., Newcombe & Fox, 1994) found that subjects had poor conscious recall of autobiographical information, while others (Fivush, 1995) found that recall for particular discrete occurrences (e.g., a trip to Sea World) seems to last for many years, although the details that are remembered seem to change. In addition, there is some indication that early memories are not accessible to conscious recall (Newcombe & Fox, 1994). For example, Newcombe and Fox (1994) presented 22 children aged 8 to 10 with pictures of 3-year-olds, some of whom had attended preschool with the subjects 5 to 7 years earlier. The skin conductance of each child was measured in response to the child's viewing of each picture. Newcombe and Fox reported that although children could not consciously identify the children in the pictures or even reliably state that they were familiar, the pictures of children with whom they had attended preschool elicited reliable skin conductance responses. Newcombe and Fox argued that these data suggest that certain early memories are stored but inaccessible to conscious recall.

The implication from this study is that early childhood memories may remain with an individual even after conscious recall has disappeared. In addition, these memories may hold an affective charge that can influence subsequent behavior (e.g., Zajonc, 1980). It is possible that childhood memories regarding interactions with parents (particularly about events such as separation or loss), though inaccessible to conscious recall, continue to be stored and maintain an affective charge. Recent work on adult autobiographical memory supports this possibility. Fink et al. (1996) performed a study utilizing positron emission tomography (PET), which allows imaging of metabolism in different areas of the brain. Two weeks prior to being studied with the PET procedure, subjects provided an experimenter with autobiographical memories. Within the PET procedure, subjects heard, in a counterbalanced fashion, descriptions of events that either corresponded to their own personal memories or were not related to their past. While being scanned, subjects were asked to imagine each event. Results revealed that when subjects heard and imagined their own personal events, there was greater right-brain activation, including (though not singular to) the right prefrontal area. When subjects heard and imagined events not related to their past, cerebral activity increased symmetrically, particularly in both temporal areas. The data suggest that autobiographical memories are stored and seem to have a strong affective component.

Fink et al.'s (1996) findings are interesting, in light of research by both Fox and Davidson (Davidson & Fox, 1982; Fox, 1991; Fox & Davidson, 1984) implicating the left and right prefrontal cortices in the experience and expression of different emotions. In the study described above, Fink et al. did not control for the valence of the autobiographical material that was presented to the subjects. Examples such as "He tore off his shirt to demonstrate his scars to the nurse" suggest that at least some of the material may have had a negative valence. When subjects were asked to imagine the scene, they may have been experiencing dysphoric affect, thus implicating activity of the right prefrontal area. Autobiographical material carries with it an important affect content, which is stored and organized in distinct ways within the brain. Neuroimaging techniques such as PET or functional MRI (fMRI) may be useful in examining the neural correlates of presumed childhood memories, particularly memories about attachment experiences.

SUMMARY

The use of psychophysiological measures involves complex technologies and has its own set of methodological issues. If such approaches are to be informative, they should be used in studies asking questions that cannot easily be answered without the addition of psychophysiological data. One example is the question of reactivity of avoidant infants. For quite some time, attachment researchers have been interested in whether infants who are classified as avoidant undergo stress during the strange situation. Research utilizing HR or cortisol has attempted to answer this question, albeit with limited success. Psychophysiological approaches have been more successful in describing individual differences in infant disposition, including reactivity to stress. Using measures of cortisol response or EEG asymmetry, studies have identified physiological markers of infant temperament that influence infant behavior toward caregivers and behavior in the strange situation. The use of these measures

has also aided our understanding of the manner in which attachment may act as a buffer or moderator of initial physiological disposition. Future studies should examine whether these initial physiological dispositions change as a function of such moderators. Such work holds great promise for understanding the interplay of biology and environment as they shape personality.

REFERENCES

Ainsworth, M. D. S. (1973). The development of infant–mother attachment. In B. M. Caldwell & H. N. Ricciuti (Eds.), *Review of child development research* (Vol. 3, pp. 1–94). Chicago: University of Chicago Press.

Ainsworth, M. D. S., Bell, S. M. V., & Stayton, D. J. (1971). Individual differences in strange-situation behavior of one year olds. In H. R. Schaffer (Ed.), *The origins of human social relations* (pp. 17–58). New York: Academic Press.

Ainsworth, M. D. S., Blehar, M. C., Waters, E., & Wall, S. (1978). *Patterns of attachment*. Hillsdale, NJ: Erlbaum.

Ainsworth, M. D. S., & Wittig, B. A. (1969). Attachment and exploratory behaviour of one-year-olds in a strange situation. In B. M. Foss (Ed.), *Determinants of infant behaviour* (Vol. 4, pp. 113–136). London: Methuen.

Alloy, L. B., & Abramson, L. Y. (1979). Judgment of contingency in depressed and nondepressed students: Sadder but wiser? *Journal of Experimental Psychology: General, 108*, 441–487.

Bakersman-Kranenburg, M. J., & van IJzendoorn, M. H. (1993). A psychometric study of the Adult Attachment Interview: Reliability and discriminate validity. *Developmental Psychology, 29*, 870–879.

Bell, S. M., & Ainsworth, M. D. S. (1972). Infant crying and maternal responsiveness. *Child Development, 43*, 1171–1190.

Belsky, J., & Isabella, R. (1987). Maternal, infant, and social-contextual determinants of attachment security: A process analysis. In J. Belsky & T. Nezworski (Eds.), *Clinical implications of attachment* (pp. 40–94). Hillsdale, NJ: Erlbaum.

Belsky, J., & Rovine, M. (1987). Temperament and attachment security in the strange situation: An empirical rapprochement. *Child Development, 58*, 787–795.

Benjamin, L. S. (1963). Statistical treatment of the law of initial values (LIV) in autonomic research: A review and recommendation. *Psychosomatic Medicine, 25*, 556–566.

Berger, H. (1929). Uber das Elektrenkephalogramm des Menschen: I. *Archiv für Psychiatrie und Nervenkrankheiten, 87*, 527–570.

Berger, H. (1932a). Uber das Elektrenkephalogramm des Menschen: IV. *Archiv für Psychiatrie und Nervenkrankheiten, 97*, 6–26.

Berger, H. (1932b). Uber das Elektrenkephalogramm des Menschen: V. *Archiv für Psychiatrie und Nervenkrankheiten, 98*, 231–254.

Bono, M., & Stifter, C. A. (1995, April). Changes in infant cardiac activity elicited by the Strange Situation and its relation to attachment status. In C. A. Brownell (Chair), *Early development of self-regulation in the context of the mother–child relationship*. Symposium conducted at the biennial meeting of the Society for Research in Child Development, Indianapolis, IN.

Boukydis, C. F. Z., & Burgess, R. (1982). Adult physiological response to infant cries: Effects of temperament, parental status, and gender. *Child Development, 53,* 704–713.

Calkins, S. D., & Fox, N. A. (1992). The relations among infant temperament, security of attachment, and behavioral inhibition at twenty-four months. *Child Development, 63,* 1456–1472.

Calkins, S. D., Fox, N. A., & Marshall, T. R. (1996). Behavioral and physiological antecedents of inhibition in infancy. *Child Development, 67,* 523–540.

Campos, J., Emde, R. N., Gaensbauer, T., & Sorce, J. (1973, March). *Cardiac and behavioral responses of human infants to strangers: Effects of mother's absence and of experimental sequence.* Paper presented at the biennial meeting of the Society for Research in Child Development, Philadelphia.

Damasio, A. R. (1990). Category-related recognition defects as a clue to neural substrates of knowledge. *Trends in Neuroscience, 13,* 95–98.

Darrow, C. W. (1929). Electrical and circulatory responses to brief sensory and ideational stimuli. *Journal of Experimental Psychology, 12,* 267–300.

Davidson, R. J. (1993a). The neuropsychology of emotion and affective style. In M. Lewis & J. M. Haviland (Eds.), *Handbook of emotions* (pp. 143–154). New York: Guilford Press.

Davidson, R. J. (1993b). Childhood temperament and cerebral asymmetry: A neurobiological substrate of behavioral inhibition. In K. H. Rubin & J. B. Asendorf (Eds.), *Social withdrawal, inhibition, and shyness in childhood* (pp. 31–48). Hillsdale, NJ: Erlbaum.

Davidson, R. J., & Fox, N. A. (1982). Asymmetrical brain activity discriminates between positive and negative affective stimuli in human infants. *Science, 218,* 1235–1237.

Davidson, R. J., & Fox, N. A. (1988). Frontal brain asymmetry predicts infants' response to maternal separation. *Journal of Abnormal Psychology, 98,* 127–131.

Dawson, G., Klinger, L. G., Panagiotides, H., Spieker, S., & Frey, K. (1992). Infants of mothers with depressive symptoms: Electroencephalographic and behavioral findings related to attachment status. *Development and Psychopathology, 4,* 67–80.

Donovan, W. L., & Leavitt, L. A. (1978). Early cognitive development and its relation to maternal physiologic responsiveness. *Child Development, 49,* 1251–1254.

Donovan, W. L., & Leavitt, L. A. (1985a). Physiological assessment of mother–infant attachment. *Journal of the American Academy of Child Psychiatry, 24,* 65–70.

Donovan, W. L., & Leavitt, L. A. (1985b). Physiology and behavior: Parents' response to the infant cry. In B. Lester & C. F. Z. Boukydis (Eds.), *Infant crying: Theoretical and research perspectives* (pp. 241–261). New York: Plenum Press.

Donovan, W. L., & Leavitt, L. A. (1989). Maternal self-efficacy and infant attachment: Integrating physiology, perceptions, and behavior. *Child Development, 60,* 460–472.

Donovan, W. L., Leavitt, L. A., & Balling, J. D. (1978). Maternal physiological response to infant signals. *Psychophysiology, 15,* 68–74.

Donovan, W. L., Leavitt, L. A., & Walsh, R. O. (1990). Maternal self-efficacy: Illusory control and its effect on susceptibility to learned helplessness. *Child Development, 61,* 1637–1647.

Donovan, W. L., Leavitt, L. A., & Walsh, R. O. (1997). Cognitive set and coping strategy affect mothers' sensitivity to infant cries: A signal detection approach. *Child Development, 5,* 760–772.

Duffy, E. (1957). The psychological significance of the concept of "arousal" and "activation." *Psychological Review, 64,* 265–275.

Duffy, E. (1962). *Activation and behavior.* New York: Wiley.

Egeland, B., & Farber, E. A. (1984). Infant–toddler attachment: Factors related to its development and changes over time. *Child Development, 55,* 753–771.

Ekman, P., Levenson, R. W., & Friesen, W. V. (1983). Autonomic nervous system activity distinguishes between emotions. *Science, 221,* 1208–1211.

Fink, G. R., Markowitsch, H. J., Reinkemeier, M., Bruckbauer, T., Kessler, J., & Heiss, W. D. (1996). Cerebral representation of one's own past: Neural networks involved in autobiographical memory. *Journal of Neuroscience, 16,* 13, 4275–4282.

Fivush, R. (1995). Language, narrative, and autobiography. *Consciousness and Cognition: An International Journal, 4,* 100–103.

Fletcher, P. C., Frith, C. D., Grasby, P. M., Shallice, T., Frackowiak, R. S. J., & Dolan, R. J. (1995). Brain systems for encoding and retrieval of auditory-verbal memory: An *in vivo* study in humans. *Brain, 118,* 401–416.

Fox, N. A. (1985). Behavioral and autonomic antecedents of attachment in high-risk infants. In M. Reite & T. Field (Eds.), *The psychobiology of attachment and separation* (pp. 389–414). Orlando, FL: Academic Press.

Fox, N. A. (1989). Psychophysiological correlates of emotional reactivity during the first year of life. *Developmental Psychology, 25,* 364–372.

Fox, N. A. (1991). If it's not left, it's right: Electroencephalogram asymmetry and the development of emotion. *American Psychologist, 46,* 863–872.

Fox, N. A. (1994). Dynamic cerebral processes underlying emotion regulation. In N. A. Fox (Ed.), The development of emotion regulation: Biological and behavioral considerations. *Monographs of the Society for Research in Child Development, 59* (2–3, Serial No. 240), 152–166.

Fox, N. A. (1995). Of the way we were: Adult memories about attachment experiences and their role in determining infant–parent relationships: A commentary on van IJzendoorn (1995). *Psychological Bulletin, 117,* 404–410.

Fox, N. A., Bell, M. A., & Jones, N. A. (1992). Individual differences in response to stress and cerebral asymmetry. *Developmental Neuropsychology, 8,* 161–184.

Fox, N. A., Calkins, S. D., & Bell, M. A. (1994). Neural plasticity and development in the first year of life: Evidence from cognitive and socio-emotional domains of research. *Development and Psychopathology, 6,* 677–696.

Fox, N. A., & Davidson, R. J. (1984). Hemispheric substrates of affect: A development model. In N. A. Fox & R. J. Davidson (Eds.), *The psychobiology of affective development* (pp. 353–382). Hillsdale, NJ: Erlbaum.

Fox, N. A., & Davidson, R. J. (1986a). Taste-elicited changes in facial signs of emotion and the asymmetry of brain electrical activity in human newborns. *Neuropsychologia, 24,* 417–422.

Fox, N. A., & Davidson, R. J. (1986b). Psychophysiological measures of emotion: New directions in developmental research. In C. E. Izard & P. Read (Eds.), *Measuring emotions in infants and children* (Vol. 2, pp. 13–47). New York: Cambridge University Press.

Fox, N. A., & Davidson, R. J. (1988). Patterns of brain electrical activity during the expression of discrete emotions in ten-month-old infants. *Developmental Psychology, 24,* 230–236.

Fox, N. A., & Gelles, M. (1984). Face-to-face interaction in term and preterm infants. *Infant Mental Health Journal, 5,* 192–205.

Frodi, A., Lamb, M. E., Leavitt, L., & Donovan, W. (1978). Fathers' and mothers' responses to infant smiles and cries. *Infant Behavior and Development, 1,* 187–198.

Frodi, A., Lamb, M. E., Leavitt, L., Donovan, W., Neff, C., & Sherry, D. (1978). Fathers' and mothers' responses to the appearance and cries of premature and normal infants. *Developmental Psychology, 14,* 490–498.

Gale, A., & Edwards, J. A. (1986). Individual differences. In M. Coles, E. Donchin, & S. W. Porges (Eds.), *Psychophysiology: Systems, processes, and applications* (pp. 431–507). New York: Guilford Press.

George, C., Kaplan, N., & Main, M. (1984). *The Attachment Interview for Adults.* Unpublished manuscript, University of California at Berkeley.

Goldman-Rakic, P. S. (1987). Development of cortical circuitry and cognitive function. *Child Development, 58,* 601–622.

Graham, F. K., & Clifton, R. K. (1966). Heart-rate change as a component of the orienting response. *Psychological Bulletin, 65,* 305–320.

Gunnar, M. R. (1994). Human developmental psychoneuroendocrinology: A review of research on neuroendocrine responses to challenge and threat in infancy and childhood. In M. E. Lamb, L. A. Brown, & B. Rogoff (Eds.), *Advances in developmental psychology* (Vol. 4, pp. 51–103). Hillsdale, NJ: Erlbaum.

Gunnar, M. R., Colton, M., & Stansbury, K. (1992, May). *Studies of emotional behavior, temperament, and adrenocortical activity in human infants.* Paper presented at the 8th International Conference on Infant Studies, Miami, FL.

Gunnar, M. R., Mangelsdorf, S., Larson, M., & Hertsgaard, L. (1989). Attachment, temperament, and adrenocortical activity in infancy: A study of psychoendocrine regulation. *Developmental Psychology, 25,* 355–363.

Harman, C., & Fox, N. A. (1997). Frontal and attentional mechanisms regulating distress experience and expression during infancy. In N. A. Krasnegor, G. R. Lyon, & P. S. Goldman-Rakic (Eds.), *Development of the prefrontal cortex: Evolution, neurobiology, and behavior* (pp. 191–208). Baltimore: Paul H. Brookes.

Henriques, J. B., & Davidson, R. J. (1990). Regional brain electrical asymmetries discriminate between previously depressed and healthy control subjects. *Journal of Abnormal Psychology, 99,* 22–31.

Hertsgaard, L., Gunnar, M., Erickson, M. F., & Nachmias, M. (1995). Adrenocortical responses to the Strange Situation in infants with disorganized/disoriented attachment relationships. *Child Development, 66,* 1100–1106.

Izard, C. E., Huebner, R. R., Risser, D., & Dougherty, L. (1980). The young infant's ability to produce discrete emotion expressions. *Developmental Psychology, 16,* 132–140.

Izard, C. E., Porges, S. W., Simons, R. F., Haynes, O. M., Hyde, C., Parisi, M., & Cohen, B. (1991). Infant cardiac activity: Developmental changes and relations with attachment. *Developmental Psychology, 27,* 432–439.

Kagan, J., & Snidman, N. (1991). Infant predictors of inhibited and uninhibited profiles. *Psychological Science, 2,* 40–44.

Katona, P. G., & Jih, F. (1985). Respiratory sinus arrhythmia:

A noninvasive measure of parasympathetic cardiac control. *Journal of Applied Physiology, 39,* 801–805.

Lacey, J. I. (1959). Psychophysiological approaches to the evaluation of psychotherapeutic process and outcome. In E. A. Rubinstein & M. B. Parloff (Eds.), *Research in psychotherapy* (pp. 161–196). Washington, DC: American Psychological Association.

Lacey, J. I. (1967). Somatic response patterning and stress: Some revisions of activation theory. In M. H. Appley & R. Trumbull (Eds.), *Psychological stress: Issues in research* (pp. 14–27). New York: Appleton-Century-Crofts.

Lacey, J. I., & Lacey, B. C. (1958). The relationship of resting autonomic activity to motor impulsivity. *Research Publications of the Association for Research in Nervous and Mental Disease, 36,* 144–209.

Lagerlund, T. D., Sharbrough, F. W., Rack, C. R., Erickson, B., Strelow, D. C., Cicora, K. M., & Busacker, N. E. (1993). Determination of 10–20 system electrode locations using magnetic resonance image scanning with markers. *Electroencephalography and Clinical Neurophysiology, 86,* 1–209.

Larson, M. C., Gunnar, M. R., & Hertsgaard, L. (1991). The effects of morning naps, car trips, and maternal separation on adrenocortical activity in human infants. *Child Development, 62,* 362–372.

Lewis, M. (1975). The cardiac response during infancy. In R. F. Thompson & M. M. Patterson (Eds.), *Methods in physiological psychology: Vol. 1-C. Recording of bioelectric activity* (pp. 201–229). New York: Academic Press.

Lewis, M., Kagan, J., Campbell, H., & Kalafat, J. (1966). The cardiac response as a correlate of attention in infants. *Child Development, 37,* 63–71.

Lindsley, D. B., & Wicke, J. D. (1974). The EEG: Autonomous electrical activity in man and animals. In R. Thompson & M. N. Patterson (Eds.), *Bioelectrical recording techniques* (pp. 3–83). New York: Academic Press.

Lindsley, D. B. (1939). A longitudinal study of the occipital alpha rhythm in normal children: Frequency and amplitude standards. *Journal of Genetic Psychology, 55,* 197–213.

Main, M., Kaplan, N., & Cassidy, J. (1985). Security in infancy, childhood, and adulthood: A move to the level of representation. In I. Bretherton & E. Waters (Eds.), *Growing points of attachment theory and research. Monographs of the Society for Research in Child Development, 50* (1–2, Serial No. 209), 66–104.

Milner, B. (1966). Amnesia following operation on the temporal lobes. In C. W. M. Whitty & O. L. Zangwill (Eds.), *Amnesia* (pp. 109–133). London: Butterworth.

Nachmias, M., Gunnar, M., Mangelsdorf, S., Parritz, R., & Buss, K. (1996). Behavioral inhibition and stress reactivity: The moderating role of attachment security. *Child Development, 67,* 508–522.

Newcombe, N., & Fox, N. A. (1994). Infantile amnesia: Through a glass darkly. *Child Development, 65,* 31–40.

Nuwer, N. (1997). Assessment of digital EEG, quantitative EEG, and EEG brain mapping: Report of the American Academy of Neurology and the American Clinical Neurophysiological Society. *Neurology, 49,* 277–292.

Obrist, P. A., Webber, R. A., Sutterer, J. R., & Howard, J. L. (1970). Cardiac deceleration and reaction time: An evaluation of two hypotheses. *Psychophysiology, 6,* 695–706.

Porges, S. W. (1991). Vagal tone: An autonomic mediator of affect. In J. A. Garber & K. A. Dodge (Eds.), *The development of affect regulation and dysregulation* (pp. 111–128). New York: Cambridge University Press.

Porges, S. W. (1995). Orienting in a defensive world: Mammalian modifications of our evolutionary heritage. A polyvagal theory (Presidential Address, 1994). *Psychophysiology, 32,* 301–318.

Porges, S. W. (1996). Physiological regulation in high-risk infants: A model for assessment and potential intervention. *Development and Psychopathology, 8,* 43–58.

Porges, S. W., & Bohrer, R. E. (1991). The analysis of periodic processes in psychophysiological research. In J. T. Cacioppo & L. G. Tassinary (Eds.), *Principles of psychophysiology: Physical, social, and inferential elements* (pp. 708–753). New York: Cambridge University Press.

Porges, S. W., Bohrer, R. E., Cheung, M. N., Drasgow, F., McCabe, P. M., & Keren, G. (1980). New time-series statistic for detecting rhythmic co-occurrence in the frequency domain: The weighted coherence and its application to psychophysiological research. *Psychological Bulletin, 88,* 580–587.

Porges, S. W., & Byrne, E. A. (1992). Research methods for measurement of heart rate and respiration. *Biological Psychology, 34,* 93–130.

Porges, S. W., Doussard-Roosevelt, J. A., Portales, A. L., & Suess, P. E. (1994). Cardiac vagal tone: Stability and relation to difficultness in infants and 3-year-olds. *Developmental Psychology, 27,* 289–300.

Porges, S. W., Stamps, L. E., & Walter, G. F. (1974). Heart-rate variability and newborn heart-rate responses to illumination changes. *Developmental Psychology, 10,* 507–513.

Richards, J. E. (1985). Respiratory sinus arrhythmia predicts heart rate and visual responses during visual attention in 14- and 20-week old infants. *Psychophysiology, 22,* 101–109.

Richards, J. E. (1987). Infant visual sustained attention and respiratory sinus arrythmia. *Child Development, 58,* 488–496.

Rothbart, M. K., & Posner, M. I. (1985). Temperament and the development of self-regulation. In L. C. Hartlage & C. F. Telzrow (Eds.), *Neuropsychology of individual differences: A developmental perspective* (pp. 93–123). New York: Plenum Press.

Rushton, J. P., Brainerd, C. J., & Pressley, M. (1983). Behavioral development and construct validity: The principle of aggregation. *Psychological Bulletin, 94,* 18–38.

Schachter, S., & Singer, J. E. (1962). Cognitive, social, and psychological determinants of emotion. *Psychological Review, 69,* 379–399.

Scherg, M., & von Cramon, D. (1985). Two bilateral sources of the late AEP as identified by a spatio-temporal dipole model. *Electroencephalography and Clinical Neurophysiology, 62,* 32–44.

Schmidt, L. A., Shahinfar, A., & Fox, N. A. (1996). Frontal EEG correlates of dysregulated social behavior in children. *Psychophysiology, 33,* S8. (Abstract)

Spangler, G., & Grossmann, K. E. (1993). Biobehavioral organization in securely and insecurely attached infants. *Child Development, 64,* 1439–1450.

Squire, L. R., Ojemann, J. G., Miezin, F. M., Petersen, S. E., Videen, T. O., & Raichle, M. E. (1992). Activation of the hippocampus in normal infants: A functional anatomical study of memory. *Proceedings of the National Academy of Sciences USA, 89,* 1837–1841.

Sroufe, L. A. (1985). Attachment classification from the perspective of infant–caregiver relationships and infant temperament. *Child Development, 56,* 1–14.

Sroufe, L. A., & Waters, E. (1977). Heart rate as a convergent measure in clinical and developmental research. *Merrill–Palmer Quarterly, 23,* 3–27.

Stifter, C. A., & Fox, N. A. (1990). Infant reactivity: Physiological correlates of newborn and 5-month temperament. *Developmental Psychology, 26,* 582–588.

Tulving, E. (1983). *Elements of episodic memory.* Oxford: Oxford University Press.

van IJzendoorn, M. H. (1992). Intergenerational transmission of parenting: A review of studies in nonclinical populations. *Developmental Review, 12,* 76–99.

Welsh, M. C., Pennington, B. F., & Groisser, D. B. (1991). A normative-developmental study of executive function: A window on prefrontal function in children. *Developmental Neuropsychology, 7,* 131–149.

Wiesenfeld, A. R., & Klorman, R. (1978). The mother's psychophysiological reactions to contrasting expressions by her own and unfamiliar infant. *Developmental Psychology, 14,* 294–304.

Wiesenfeld, A. R., Malatesta, C. Z., & DeLoach, L. L. (1981). Differential parental response to familiar and unfamiliar infant distress signals. *Infant Behavior and Development, 4,* 281–295.

Wilder, J. (1967). *Stimulus and response: The law of initial value.* Bristol, UK: J. Wright.

Zajonc, R. B. (1980). Feeling and thinking: Preferences need no inferences. *American Psychologist, 35,* 151–175.

III

ATTACHMENT IN INFANCY
AND CHILDHOOD

❖

12

Interactional and Contextual Determinants of Attachment Security

❖

JAY BELSKY

Why do some infants develop secure attachments to their primary caregivers, whereas others establish insecure relationships? That is the central question to be addressed in this chapter. In certain respects, one might regard such a question as more North American than British. This is because even though John Bowlby, a British psychiatrist, was concerned with the consequences of variation in the quality of early attachment, it was his Canadian colleague, psychologist Mary Ainsworth, who brought the topic of the origins of individual differences in infant–parent attachment security to center stage. Whereas Bowlby's (1944, 1958) original thinking on the roots of security–insecurity was organized around the development of disorders (e.g., juvenile delinquency) and led to a focus on major separations from parents early in life, Ainsworth (1973) was the first to devote considerable empirical and theoretical energies to consideration of the determinants of secure and insecure infant–mother attachments in the normal, nonclinical population.

At the core of Ainsworth's extension of Bowlby's theory of attachment was the contention that a sensitive, responsive caregiver is of fundamental importance to the development of a secure as opposed to an insecure attachment bond during the opening years of life. According to Ainsworth, a caregiver capable of providing security-inducing, sensitive, responsive care understands the child's individual attributes, accepts the child's behavioral proclivities, and is thus capable of orchestrating harmonious interactions between self and infant (especially those involving the soothing of distress) on a relatively consistent

basis. In elaborating on and thereby further developing Bowlby's theory, Ainsworth never stated the belief that the development of the relationship between infant and mother is determined entirely by the mother. Nevertheless, Ainsworth was convinced that the developing relationship between child and adult is not shaped equally by the two individuals involved. Recognizing the greater maturity and power of the mother, Ainsworth attributed disproportionate influence to her rather than to the child.

Nonetheless, the notion of maternal sensitivity championed by Ainsworth in her efforts to account for individual differences in attachment security was defined in terms of what the child brings to the relationship and, more specifically, how the child behaves at a particular time. By definition, then, care that is sensitive and theorized to promote security in the child does not take exactly the same form for all children. Nor does it take the same form across all situations in the case of a particular child. This was why Ainsworth (1973) adopted the methodology of rating maternal behavior after extensive observation, rather than microcoding interactions on a moment-by-moment basis. To evaluate sensitivity accurately, she believed, it is best to observe a mother with her infant across a variety of situations and circumstances. Only in so doing can an observer learn, for example, whether a mother's practice of permitting a mildly fussy infant to fall asleep on his or her own does or does not reflect a more general pattern of unresponsiveness. If such seemingly insensitive care is observed again when the infant awakes, then the label "insensitive" may be far more appropriate than if the same mother proves highly responsive to her rested and hungry (rather than tired) infant.

The first part of this chapter contains a summary of research on the effects of mothering and mother–infant interaction on attachment security—the issues raised most directly by Ainsworth. Related evidence pertaining to the effects of the quality of fathering and of nonparental caregivers' care on attachment to fathers and to nonparental caregivers, respectively, is also considered. Attention is devoted to the origins of security in these nonmaternal infant–adult relationships, because they too underscore the role of sensitive care in promoting attachment security.

In the second part of the chapter, the broader social context of attachment is considered. At about the same time that interest in the interactional origins of attachment security was growing in the field of developmental psychology, Bronfenbrenner (1979) advanced an ecological perspective, which drew attention to the broader context of human development beyond the confines of the mother–child relationship. Even though some (including Bronfenbrenner) regarded his framework as a challenge to a developmental psychology that seemed to be excessively concerned with the mother–child relationship, those who were already intrigued by Ainsworth's ideas saw Bronfenbrenner's ecological framework as a means for expanding the attachment research agenda. This was because it drew attention to issues that were not explicitly emphasized in attachment theory, but that seemed latent in the theory.

Whereas caregiver sensitivity is regarded within attachment theory as the principal determinant of whether an infant develops a secure or insecure relationship with the caregiver, from an ecological perspective the psychological attributes of the mother, her relations with her partner, and the degree to which she has access to other social agents who provide instrumental and emotional support should also be associated with the security of the infant–mother relationship. This is because these factors are theorized to affect the quality of care that a mother (or other caregiver) provides (for reviews, see Belsky, 1984, 1990). Thus, whereas attachment theory is essentially a theory of the microprocesses of development, emphasizing the daily interactional exchanges between parent and child and the developing internal working model of the child, the ecological/social-contextual perspectiv draws attention to the contextual factors and processes

likely to influence these microdevelopmental processes. In essence, then, the ecological perspective turns what is an independent variable in attachment theory—patterns of mother–infant interaction—into a dependent variable, something itself to be explained. This ecological or contextual view of attachment theory and research in no way violates the premises of the theory or research traditions it has spawned; rather, it enriches them while preserving their strengths.

THE QUALITY OF MATERNAL AND NONMATERNAL CARE

Not long after Ainsworth (1973) first advanced her ideas regarding the role of maternal sensitivity in fostering the development of a secure attachment relationship, she published results from her small but intensively investigated Baltimore sample of 26 middle-class mother–child dyads, which proved consistent with her theorizing (Ainsworth, Blehar, Waters, & Wall, 1978). Thereafter, what might be regarded as a "cottage industry" developed within the field of developmental psychology, seeking to replicate—or refute—her findings. Child temperament was the major focus of those seeking to disconfirm Ainsworth's theory and evidence, and it is thus difficult to consider the role of maternal sensitivity and the quality of maternal care more generally without devoting at least some attention to what might be regarded as a competing theoretical perspective.

The Role of Temperament

According to various temperament theorists, the source of security and insecurity lies not in the caregiver's ministrations, but in the constitutional attributes of the child. Some, like the child psychiatrist Stella Chess, regarded the Ainsworth–Bowlby view as little more than refurbished psychoanalysis, which attributes far too much influence to parents and "blames" them for difficulties inherent in the child (Chess & Thomas, 1982).

Two basic views regarding the role temperament plays in the development and assessment of individual differences in infant–mother attachment relationships merit discussion here. One, embraced principally by students of attachment theory, is that temperament does not directly influence the quality of attachment that develops between infant and mother, because even a difficult infant, given the "right" care, can become secure—there being multiple pathways to security (Sroufe, 1985). Thus no main effect of temperament on attachment security is expected.

The second school of thought regarding the temperament–attachment association contends that an infant's temperament (particularly his or her susceptibility to distress) directly affects the development of the attachment relationship via its impact upon mother–infant interaction, *and* is the principal determinant of behavior used to evaluate attachment security in the strange situation (Chess & Thomas, 1982; Kagan, 1982). The claim has been advanced, moreover, that infants classified as securely attached are simply less upset by separation in the strange situation, whereas those infants classified as insecurely attached are simply more distressed—despite the fact that both secure *and* insecure infants display the same kinds of discrete behaviors (i.e., crying) in the strange situation. A meta-analysis of some 18 studies, performed over a decade ago, nonetheless provides some support for the assertion that insecurity is a direct function of an infant's proneness to distress (Goldsmith & Alansky, 1987). Resistant behavior in the strange situation (e.g., kicking legs, pushing away upon reunion) was found to be reliably, though weakly, associated with proneness to distress.

Notably, however, the most extensive investigation done to date on the topic of temperament/ irritability and attachment security challenges these meta-analytic findings. In a sample of economically at-risk families in the Netherlands, van den Boom (1990, 1994) longitudinally followed 100 infants who scored very high on irritability on two separate neonatal examinations. Contrary to the Goldsmith and Alansky (1987) findings, more than three of every four distress-prone infants whose mothers received no intervention services ($n = 50$) and who were classified as insecure were categorized as avoidant, not as resistant. As van den Boom (1990) noted, these data directly challenge the assumption of Chess and Thomas (1982) and Kagan (1982), who have contended that variation in security of attachment is a product of temperamental differences among babies. After all, how does a temperament-based theory of attachment account for the fact that infants who were highly irritable as newborns express limited negative affect in the strange situation?

In addition to these Dutch findings and the more extensive evidentiary base considered by Vaughn and Bost (Chapter 10, this volume),

which collectively discount the effect of temperament on attachment security, one further consideration should be raised in any discussion of attachment and temperament. Throughout much of the temperament–attachment debate over the past 15 years, temperament has been treated more or less as a fixed trait. Yet there is not only evidence that temperament can and does change (Rothbart & Bates, 1997), but that features of families, including the quality of care that parents provide, contribute to changes in temperament (for evidence and a review, see Belsky, Fish, & Isabella, 1991). The most important implication of this latter fact is that even when data linking temperament, especially measured late in the first year (or thereafter), covary with attachment security, it cannot be presumed—as it so often is—that such a finding reflects an effect of temperament on attachment rather than an effect of parental care. This is because the very same features of care that (as will be seen) predict attachment security have been implicated in the few available studies of change in temperament.

Maternal Care

A critical review of the data available well over a decade ago led Lamb, Thompson, Gardner, Charnov, and Estes (1984) to conclude that the evidence pertaining to Ainsworth's (1973) proposition that the quality of mothering is the primary determinant of the child's attachment security was not particularly strong. Despite the fact that these scholars' analysis of Ainsworth et al.'s (1978) study was insufficiently appreciative of the contributions of her seminal research, their final conclusion was difficult to fault. Not only was Ainsworth's sample particularly small ($n = 26$) and far from representative, but a good deal of the other evidence available at the time Lamb et al. (1984) produced their review could be interpreted as either consistent or inconsistent with Ainsworth's ideas regarding the role of maternal sensitivity in promoting security (for a more detailed analysis, see Belsky & Isabella, 1988). Nevertheless, as Clarke-Stewart (1988, p. 51) astutely noted with regard to the evidence in question, we are "doomed to frustration [when it comes to drawing conclusions regarding the effect of maternal behavior on the development of attachment security] . . . if we demand complete consistency across different studies and different measures." We should not expect exact duplication among our results, she further observed, concluding that "the problem is probably with the measure (of sensitivity), not with the hypothesis about maternal sensitivity."

When one looks at the data now, it is even more apparent that Clarke-Stewart (1988)—just like many attachment theorists and researchers before her—was correct about maternal sensitivity. Even though the evidence is still not perfectly uniform (Murray, Fiori-Cowley, Hooper, & Cooper, 1996; Schneider-Rosen & Rothbaum, 1993; Seifer, Schiller, Sameroff, Resnick, & Riordan, 1996), there can be little doubt that with more and better data, the contribution of caregiving behavior is clear. Consistent with Ainsworth's (1973) original theorizing, ratings of maternal sensitivity in the first year are linked to security in the strange situation in samples of middle-class U.S. (Ainsworth et al., 1978; Cox, Owen, Henderson, & Margand, 1992; Fish & Stifter, 1995 [girls only]; Isabella, 1993; Teti, Gelfand, Messinger, & Isabella, 1995), Canadian (Pederson & Moran, 1996), and German (Grossmann, Grossmann, Spangler, Suess, & Unzner, 1985) families, as well as economically disadvantaged, often single-parent ones (Egeland & Farber, 1984; Krupka, Moran, & Pederson, 1996; Susman-Stillman, Kalkoske, Egeland, & Waldman, 1996). Furthermore, security is associated with prompt responsiveness to distress (Crockenberg, 1981; Del Carmen, Pedersen, Huffman, & Bryan, 1993), with moderate, appropriate stimulation (Belsky, Rovine, & Taylor, 1984; Feldstein, Crown, Beebe, & Jaffe, 1995), and with interactional synchrony (Isabella & Belsky, 1991; Isabella, Belsky, & von Eye, 1989; Leyendecker, Lamb, & Scholmerich, 1997), as well as with warmth, involvement, and responsiveness (Bates, Maslin, & Frankel, 1985; Leyendecker, Lamb, Fracasso, Scholmerich, & Carson, 1997; National Institute of Child Health and Human Development [NICHD] Early Child Care Network, 1997; O'Connor, Sigman, & Kasasi, 1992). In contrast, avoidant attachments are related to intrusive, excessively stimulating, controlling interactional styles, and resistant attachments are related to an unresponsive, underinvolved approach to caregiving (Belsky et al., 1984; Isabella et al., 1989; Lewis & Fiering, 1989; Malatesta, Grigoryev, Lamb, Albin, & Culver, 1986; Smith & Pederson, 1988; Vondra, Shaw, & Kevinides, 1995). In addition to such associations from studies using the strange situation procedure, similar contemporaneous and time-lagged relations have emerged in North American research relying

upon Waters and Deane's (1985) Attachment Q-Sort measure (1996; Moran, Pederson, Pettit, & Krupka, 1992; Pederson et al., 1990; Seifer et al., 1996; Scholmerich, Fracasso, Lamb, & Broberg, 1995) and in related research conducted in Japan (Vereijken, Riksen-Walraven, & Kondo-Ikemura, 1997). Thus, consistent with attachment theory and Clarke-Stewart's (1988, p. 51) decade-old analysis of the available evidence, "there does seem to be a significant degree of predictability from parents' behavior to infants' attachment classifications."

This is not to say that the strength of the discerned association is large. As Goldsmith and Alansky (1987) observed in their meta-analysis of 15 studies carried out between 1978 and 1987, "the effect [of maternal interactive behavior on attachment security] that has enjoyed the confidence of most attachment researchers is not as strong as was once believed" (p. 811). Recently, DeWolff and van IJzendoorn (1997) reexamined relations between parenting and attachment security from a meta-analytic perspective. Drawing upon data from 66 investigations involving some 4,176 infant–mother dyads, they discerned an overall effect size of .17 between measures of mothering and of mother–child interaction and attachment security. For this analysis, they included studies employing a quite diverse array of measures of maternal care, including ones focused upon maternal sensitivity, contiguity of maternal response, physical contact, and cooperation. When meta-analysis was restricted to only the subset of 30 investigations that measured sensitivity ($n = 1,666$), the effect size was somewhat larger (.22). And when the 16 studies ($n = 837$) that relied on Ainsworth's original sensitivity rating scales were considered, the effect size was larger still (.24). Nevertheless, effect sizes across investigations that relied upon different operationalizations of mothering and mother–infant interaction were more similar than different. Moreover, the magnitude of the discerned effects was not affected (i.e., moderated) by the length of observations of mother–child interaction, or by whether security was assessed using the strange situation or the Attachment Q-Sort. Worth noting as well is that DeWolff and van IJzendoorn (1997) did not include the findings of the original Ainsworth et al. (1978) study in their meta-analyses, because its results—like the more recent (null) ones of Seifer et al. (1996) (which were included)—were regarded as outliers relative to the entire corpus of findings.

Even though the effect size of .16 that Goldsmith and Alansky (1987) generated between sensitivity and attachment was remarkably similar to the overall combined effect size across all study outcomes that DeWolff and van IJzendoorn (1997) generated (.17), and not too different from the somewhat larger figure derived from research using Ainsworth's sensitivity ratings (.24), these two sets of meta-analysts appraised their results quite differently. Whereas Goldsmith and Alansky characterized the effect size as "weak," DeWolff and van IJzendoorn point out that even weak correlations—and the aforementioned effect size statistics were in the form of correlations—"may nevertheless indicate powerful causal mechanisms" (p. 585).

Whether one regards the magnitude of the effect of maternal care (and especially of sensitivity rated with Ainsworth's original rating scales) as weak or moderate, two points merit consideration. First, as I have argued elsewhere (Belsky, 1997), the DeWolff and van IJzendoorn (1997) results demonstrate, as did the original Goldsmith and Alansky (1987) analysis, that Ainsworth's core theoretical proposition linking maternal sensitivity with attachment security has been empirically confirmed. But as DeWolff and van IJzendoorn (1997) themselves note, it should be clear that even though their results point to the important role of maternal behavior and especially sensitivity in the development of attachment security, they just as plainly document the fact that the quality of a mother's care does not play an exclusive role in determining whether a child develops a secure or insecure attachment.

The modesty of the meta-analytically derived correlation between maternal behavior and attachment security, coupled with the logical possibility that this reliably discerned association may be a product of the effect of infant characteristics (especially temperament) on maternal interactive style, provides a basis for questioning the causal role of maternal care in fostering security or insecurity. Fortunately, van den Boom's (1990) investigation of 100 irritable Dutch infants from economically at-risk families puts the issue to rest, especially the argument that insecurity reflects negative emotionality or difficult temperament. In her study design, van den Boom included an experimental manipulation to heighten maternal sensitivity and evaluated its effects on attachment security. Three home visits designed to foster mothers' "contingent, consistent, and appropriate responses to both positive and nega-

tive infant signals" were administered to 50 mothers randomly assigned to an experimental group. The home visitor/intervenor "aimed to enhance mothers' observational skills . . . [and] assisted mothers to adjust their behaviors to their infant's [*sic*] unique cries" (p. 208). Control group mothers were simply observed in interaction with their babies. Importantly, the two groups of mothers were equivalent in terms of maternal behavior prior to the implementation of the intervention.

Impressively, not only did postintervention observations reveal that maternal sensitivity was greater in the experimental group, but results of strange situation evaluations 4 months after the termination of the intervention were strongly consistent with predictions derived from attachment theory: Whereas a full 68% (34 of 50) of the infants in the control group were classified as insecure, this was true of only 28% (14 of 50) of the experimental subjects! No doubt these findings resulted from the fact that "experimental mothers respond[ed] to the whole range of infant signals [during postintervention home observation], while control mothers mainly focus[ed] on very negative infant signals" (van den Boom, 1990, p. 236). More specifically, in the insecurity-producing control group,

mildly negative infant behaviors like fussing are ignored for most of the time or are responded to ineffectively. Positively toned attachment behaviors, on the contrary, are ignored for the most part. And infant exploration is either ignored or interfered with.

The program mothers' infants' negative actions boost maternal positive actions. Maternal anger is not observed. . . . Positive social infant behaviors are also responded to in a positive fashion. And program mothers are attentive to the infant's [*sic*] exploration, but they do not interfere in the process. (van den Boom, 1990, p. 236)

These findings chronicling a causal—not just correlational—impact of the quality of maternal care on attachment security are, in the main, in accord with those emanating from other experimental investigations. In a meta-analysis of intervention studies, van IJzendoorn, Juffer, and Duyvestyn (1995) showed that interventions are effective in enhancing maternal sensitivity, and in particular that short-term interventions (like van den Boom's) can, in so doing, increase the probability of an infant's developing a secure attachment to the mother. Indeed, the combined effect size for the effectiveness of the attachment interventions was impressive (d = .48). These re-sults extend those from correlational studies in documenting a truly causal effect of maternal care on attachment security.

Nonmaternal Care

Although attachment theory is often cast as a theory of the infant–*mother* relationship, most attachment theorists and researchers consider at-tachment to be involved in emotionally close child–*adult* relationships more generally. Indeed, Bowlby made it clear that in writing about moth-ers he was assuming that mothers are usually the primary caregivers. If, as is now widely recog-nized, infants and young children can establish relationships with more than a single individu-al (neither Bowlby nor Ainsworth argued other-wise), a theoretically important question is whether the interactional processes highlighted as important to the development of secure rela-tionships with mothers also operate in other cas-es. The few available studies of fathers and of nonparental caregivers indicate that this is indeed the case.

Infant–Father Attachment

In fact, even though the majority of investiga-tions examining the relation between quality of parental care and infant–father attachment secu-rity individually failed to document a significant effect of fathering on attachment security (Bel-sky, 1983; Caldera, Huston, & O'Brien, 1995; Easterbrooks & Goldberg, 1984; Grossmann & Grossmann, 1992; Schneider-Rosen & Roth-baum, 1993; Volling & Belsky, 1992), a different picture emerged when the results of these studies and two others showing a significant relation (Cox et al., 1992; Goossens & van IJzendoorn, 1990) were combined and subjected to meta-analysis. When data from all eight investigations were considered together, a significant ($p <$ .001), even if small (.13), effect size emerged (n = 546) (van IJzendoorn & DeWolff, 1997). And as the authors of this meta-analysis have pointed out, this small effect size represented the lower boundary of the association between paternal sensitivity and infant–father attachment. This was because nonsignificant findings, which were insufficiently specified in the original research reports, had to be replaced with zero correlations (or probability values of .50) when they might actually have been higher. Nevertheless, and no-tably, the association between paternal sensitivity

and infant–father attachment was statistically—and significantly—weaker than the association between maternal sensitivity and infant–mother attachment.

Infant–Caregiver Attachment

I now turn to evidence pertaining to nonparental caregivers. Even though no meta-analysis of this limited data base has yet been undertaken, a brief summary of relevant studies proves instructive. Work in the United States by Howes, Rodning, Galluzzo, and Myers (1988) using the Attach-ment Q-Sort reveals that 12- to 24-month-olds are more likely to score low on security of at-tachment to a nonparental caregiver if the care-giver frequently ignores them and if the caregiver cares for many children. These results have been replicated and extended in a series of subsequent reports by Howes (see Howes, Chapter 29, this volume, for a summary). Howes and Hamilton (1992) and Howes, Phillips, and Whitebook (1992) related attachment security with caregiver to behavior of the caregiver toward the child and found that sensitivity, involvement, and appropri-ate caregiving significantly predicted Attach-ment Q-Sort security. These results were further confirmed in a large sample by Howes and Smith (1995), in which classifications of child–caregiv-er relations as secure and insecure based upon Attachment Q-Sort scores (i.e., top two-thirds and bottom third of the distribution, respectively) were related to caregiver involvement. Additional evidence from the Netherlands indicates that in-fants classified in the strange situation as secure-ly attached to their caregivers have caregivers who provide more sensitive care (Goossens & van IJzendoorn, 1990). In sum, interactional processes similar to those delineated in studies of mothering appear relevant to the development of secure relationships with others with whom a child is expected to develop a close, affectional bond.

Conclusions

When considered in its entirety, the evidence summarized in this section pertaining to mother-ing, fathering, and the care provided by some other consistent caregiver provides support for Ainsworth's (1973) extension of Bowlby's theory of attachment. Individual differences in attach-ment security, whether measured with the labora-tory-based strange situation or the home-based Attachment Q-Sort procedure, are systematically related to the quality of the care that an infant or toddler experiences with a particular caregiver. What makes the evidence particularly convincing is that it is both correlational and experimental in nature; it is longitudinal as well as cross-sectional; and it applies to fathers and child care providers as well as to mothers. Even though infant temperamental characteristics may contribute to the quality of interaction between caregiver and child, the evidence that such attributes are the primary determinants of attachment security is especially limited.

PSYCHOLOGICAL AND SOCIAL-CONTEXTUAL DETERMINANTS

Having considered the interactional determinants of attachment security, I turn now to the role of more "distal" factors implicated by an ecological perspective and likely to affect the quality of care that mothers—and other caregivers—provide. First to be considered are personality and psychological attributes of mothers. The influence of maternal state of mind regarding attachment is not considered in this section or in this chapter, because Hesse (Chapter 19, this volume) addresses this topic. After considering maternal personality and psychological well-being, I turn to the broader context of child–parent attachment relationships, and thus to social-contextual sources of stress and support—specifically, the marital/partner relationship and social support from nonspousal associates.

Parental Psychological Resources/Personality

Because the provision of security-inducing sensitive care requires the accurate reading of, and timely and empathic responding to, a child's affective and behavioral cues, there are theoretical grounds for expecting a caregiver's psychological attributes to be related to the security of attachment that a child develops. Moreover, much theory and research not based on the writings of Bowlby and Ainsworth indicates that both mothers' and fathers' psychological health and well-being affect the quality of care that parents provide (for reviews, see Belsky, 1984; Belsky & Vondra, 1989; Gelfand & Teti, 1990). Evidence involving both normal and clinical samples and pertaining to the relation between parental personality/psychological well-being and infant–parent attachment security reveals, in the main,

that psychologically healthier parents are more likely than less psychologically healthy parents to have infants who are securely attached to them.

Normal Samples

Cross-sectional studies (Benn, 1986; Ricks, 1985) and longitudinal ones (in which personality is measured prior to attachment security) indicate that in nondisturbed populations, secure attachment relationships are more likely to develop when mothers are psychologically healthy. For example, one large-sample project ($n = 160$) found that mothers of secure infants scored higher on a series of personality subscales measuring nurturance, understanding, autonomy, inquisitiveness, and dependence, and lower on a subscale assessing aggressiveness, than did mothers of insecure infants (Maslin & Bates, 1983). More recently, Del Carmen et al. (1993) reported that mothers who scored higher on prenatal anxiety were more likely to have insecure 1-year-olds than those scoring lower on anxiety; and O'Connor (1997) found that mothers of secure infants were likely to describe themselves as self-confident, independent, cheerful, adaptable, and affectionate. It is notable that such findings are not restricted to economically advantaged families, but also emerge in research on high-risk, low-socioeconomic-status households (Jacobson & Frye, 1991). For example, studying a sample of 100 African American infants growing up in high-rise public housing noted for high levels of violence and crime, Sims, Hans, and Cox (1996) observed that mothers of insecure infants had significantly more psychological symptoms (e.g., feeling irritable, worthless) than mothers of secure infants. Teti, Sakin, Kucera, Corns, and Das Eiden (1996) discerned the same relation when studying toddlers and preschoolers whose middle-class mothers were about to have, and had recently delivered, a second child. Finally, in the largest study to date (involving more than 1,100 infants), maternal personality was assessed when infants were 1 month of age; it was found that mothers of infants classified as secure at 15 months of age scored higher on a composite index of psychological adjustment (agreeableness + extraversion – neuroticism – depression) than mothers of insecure infants (NICHD Early Child Care Network, 1997).

Relations between psychological functioning and attachment security also emerge in the case of fathers. Caldera (in press) reported that men who were higher in self-esteem had 14- and 18-month-olds who scored as more secure on the Attachment *Q*-Sort (completed by fathers); similar results were found in the case of mothers. Moreover, fathers who felt more in control of their own destinies (i.e., internal locus of control) when their infants were 6 months of age had toddlers who were more secure when studied at home 2½ years later by trained observers using the Attachment *Q*-Sort (Caldera et al., 1995).

Not all relevant investigations, however, provide evidence of statistically significant associations between parental personality and attachment security (Barnett, Blignault, Holmes, Payne, & Parker, 1987; Belsky, Rosenberger, & Crnic, 1995; Levitt, Weber, & Clark, 1986; Zeanah et al., 1993). Perhaps more noteworthy, though, is the fact that no evidence indicates that parents of secure infants are *less* psychologically healthy than other parents. Evidence from clinical samples reveals a similar pattern of results.

Clinical Samples

Depression in its various manifestations—unipolar and bipolar—is the clinical disorder most often studied in relation to attachment security. On the basis of evidence linking both unresponsive/detached and intrusive/rejecting mothering with maternal depression (for a review, see Gelfand & Teti, 1990), there are strong grounds for expecting children of depressed mothers to be at heightened risk of insecure attachment. Perusal of the available evidence reveals seemingly inconsistent findings, however. Whereas some research has failed to discern the expected significant association between maternal psychological disorder and elevated rates of insecurity (Frankel, Maslin-Cole, & Harmon, 1991; Lyons-Ruth, Zoll, Connell, & Grunebaum, 1986 [12 month data]; Sameroff, Seifer, & Zax, 1982), other investigations have documented such a linkage (Campbell, Cohn, Meyers, Ross, & Flanagan, 1993; D'Angelo, 1986; Das Eiden & Leonard, 1996; DeMulder & Radke-Yarrow, 1991; Gaensbauer, Harmon, Cytryn, & McKnew, 1984; Lyons-Ruth, 1988 [18-month data]; Murray et al., 1996; Radke-Yarrow, 1991; Radke-Yarrow, Cummings, Kuczynski, & Chapman, 1985; Spieker & Booth, 1988; Teti et al., 1995).

The age at which attachment security is measured may account for why the relation between depression and insecurity achieves conventional levels of significance in some samples but not in others, as 7 of the 11 investigations chronicling

the expected depression–insecurity relation assessed attachment security at or after age 15 months (DeMulder & Radke-Yarrow, 1991; Gaensbauer et al., 1984; Lyons-Ruth, 1988; Murray et al., 1996; Radke-Yarrow, 1991; Radke-Yarrow et al., 1985; Teti et al., 1995). Such results suggest that amount of exposure to a depressed caregiver may account for some of the apparent inconsistency in the literature—a conclusion supported by evidence from two longitudinal investigations, which failed to discern a significant effect of depression when security was assessed at 12 months, but did document such an effect 6 months later (Gaensbauer et al., 1984; Lyons-Ruth, 1988).

These findings raise the prospect that the extent to which a child experiences care by a depressed mother may be the critical factor, thereby pointing to the importance of severity and chronicity of depression as important determinants of insecure attachment. Notably, five different studies directly draw attention to the issues of severity and chronicity in the case of depression and attachment security (Campbell et al., 1993; Lyons-Ruth et al., 1986; Radke-Yarrow, 1991; Radke-Yarrow et al., 1985; Teti et al., 1995). For example, Radke-Yarrow (1991; Radke-Yarrow et al., 1985) found that children whose mothers were more severely disturbed, suffering from bipolar depression, were more likely to be classified as insecure than were children whose mothers received a unipolar diagnosis. Moreover, children classified as disorganized in their attachment—the most insecure of all insecure attachments (see Lyons-Ruth & Jacobvitz, Chapter 23, this volume)—had the most severely depressed mothers. Further evidence that degree of exposure to a depressed (or severely disordered) mother is what matters most comes from evidence that infants of depressed mothers were less likely to be insecure when cared for during their first year in a nonmaternal care arrangement while their mothers worked outside the home than when cared for primarily by their (depressed) homemaker mothers (Cohn, Campbell, & Ross, 1991).

In sum, the relation between depression and insecurity is likely to be moderated by (i.e., dependent upon) exposure to a depressed mother, and more specifically to experiencing care on a day-to-day basis that is adversely affected by maternal depression. This analysis is consistent with the mediational thinking that underlies this entire chapter. It stipulates that even though maternal psychological well-being, as well as the marital/partner relationship and social support, may directly affect attachment insecurity (through some unspecified process), most of the effect of such distal factors will be determined by their impact on the quality of care that a mother actually provides. Perhaps the best evidence of such a mediational process involving maternal psychological well-being comes from a study of nondisordered women, which serves as a useful conclusion to this section. Benn (1986) found that when a composite index of psychological well-being—labeled "emotional integration" and drawn from clinical interview ratings of competence, emotional responsivity, warmth, and acceptance of motherhood—was statistically controlled for, a previously discerned and significant association between maternal sensitivity and attachment security was substantially attenuated. Such results are clearly in accord with the mediational view, which links distal factors with attachment security via more proximal processes of parenting.

The Marital/Partner Relationship

An abundance of evidence indicates that supportive spousal relationships during the infancy and toddler years are correlated with the very kinds of parenting theorized (and found) to predict attachment security (for narrative reviews of relevant literature, see Belsky, 1984, 1990; for a meta-analysis, see Erel & Burman, 1995). In fact, such findings emerge when observed parental behavior serves as the dependent variable in studies where the focus is on middle-class parents rearing healthy children in the United States (Cox, Owen, Lewis, & Henderson, 1989; Dickie, 1987; Goldberg & Easterbrooks, 1984; Jouriles, Pfiffner, & O'Leary, 1988; Oates & Heinicke, 1985), Japan (Durrett, Richards, Otaki, Pennebaker, & Nyquist, 1986), Israel (Levy-Schiff & Israelashvili, 1988), and Germany (Engfer, 1988; Meyer, 1988); where the focus is upon middle-class parents caring for premature infants (Crnic, Greenberg, Ragozin, Robinson, & Basham, 1983); and where the focus is on impoverished inner-city mothers rearing premature infants (Feiring, Fox, Jaskir, & Lewis, 1987).

Given such data linking marital quality with many of the aspects of parenting found to be predictive of attachment security (DeWolff & van IJzendoorn, 1997), there are strong grounds to expect a relation between marital functioning and infant–parent attachment security. The fact that a mediational perspective leads to such a prediction does not preclude the possibility that

marital quality may come to be related to attachment security via direct rather than via parenting-mediated processes. Not only does Davies and Cummings's (1994) emotional-security hypothesis lead to such a prediction, but Owen and Cox's (1997) failure to find evidence of a parent-mediated linkage is consistent with it. Especially in the case of overt marital conflict, it is not difficult to imagine how exposure to such aversive interaction between mother and father could foster insecurity directly.

In any event, available evidence is consistent with both mediational and direct-effect theorizing. That is, children growing up in families with better-functioning marriages are more likely to develop secure attachments than those growing up in households where spouses are less happy in their marriages. Such results emerge from cross-sectional studies carried out in the United States (Crnic, Greenberg, & Slough, 1986; Goldberg & Easterbrooks, 1984; Howes & Markman, 1989; Jacobson & Frye, 1991) and in Japan (Durrett, Otaki, & Richards, 1984). Moreover, in their aforementioned investigation of poor African American mothers and infants, Sims et al. (1996) found that when fathers were physically violent with mothers, infants were more likely to be insecurely attached to their mothers.

More important than these results from cross-sectional studies are those from several longitudinal ones. In one such investigation, Howes and Markman (1989) found that wives who prenatally reported higher levels of marital satisfaction and lower levels of spousal conflict had children who scored higher on the Attachment Q-Sort measure 1 to 3 years later. Tracking similar middle-class families across a somewhat shorter time period, Lewis, Owen, and Cox (1988) reported that 1-year-old daughters (but not sons) were more likely to be securely attached to their mothers when marriages were more harmonious during pregnancy. More recently, Teti et al. (1996) showed that greater marital harmony before a second child was born predicted greater security (via the Attachment Q-Sort) on the part of the firstborn, both in the last trimester of the mother's pregnancy and up to 2 months following the birth of the younger sibling. Relatedly, Owen and Cox (1997) reported that more marital conflict—observed both prenatally and at 3 months postpartum—predicted less secure infant–father attachments and greater disorganization in infant–mother relationships (assessed at 12 months), even after each parent's psychological maturity was controlled for. Such findings would seem consistent with others (Belsky & Isabella, 1988) indicating that marital quality declined more precipitously across the transition to parenthood in the case of infants subsequently classified as insecurely attached to their mothers in the strange situation than it did in the case of infants subsequently classified as secure. Also noteworthy is Spieker's (1988; Spieker & Booth, 1988) research on high-risk mother–infant dyads, which indicated that the lowest levels of spousal support measured prenatally and at 3 months postpartum characterized the marriages in families in which infants developed the most insecure form of attachments to their mothers (i.e., disorganized attachments).

Despite the seeming persuasiveness of the cross-sectional and longitudinal data, it would be a mistake to selectively cite only the aforementioned research and leave the impression that all studies of marriage and attachment present such positive and statistically significant results. Not only is it the case that a number of investigations have discerned no significant association between some index of marital quality and infant–parent attachment security (Belsky, 1996; Belsky et al., 1995; Das Eiden & Leonard, 1996; Levitt et al., 1986; Teti, Nakagawa, Das, & Wirth, 1991; Zeanah et al., 1993), but one study actually produced results directly contrary to those presented above. In this research, which involved an unusual sample of upper-middle-class Japanese mothers temporarily living in the United States as a result of their husbands' employment, higher levels of marital quality were associated with lower Attachment Q-Sort security scores (Nakagawa, Teti, & Lamb, 1992). Although this contrary result is difficult to reconcile with the remainder of the evidence, the null findings just reported present less severe obstacles to interpretation.

In fact, two recent studies draw attention to the possibility that null findings may reflect the limits of inquiring into direct effects only, rather than the absence of a relation between marital quality and attachment security. In one important piece of work, Isabella (1994) found that even though no direct relation between marital quality (measured prenatally) and attachment security (measured when infants were 1 year of age) could be discerned, an indirect pathway of influence did appear to exist: Higher levels of marital quality predicted greater maternal role satisfaction at 4 months postpartum, which itself predicted greater maternal sensitivity 5 months later, and thereby attachment security.

Whereas the work of Isabella (1994) underscores an indirect—and typically unstudied—process by which marital quality may affect the infant–mother attachment bond, work by Das Eiden, Teti, and Corns (1993) draws attention to the need to study marital quality in context. Although Das Eiden et al. found that higher levels of marital quality were related to higher levels of Attachment Q-Sort security, further analyses revealed that this relation was restricted to families in which mothers were classified as insecure on the Adult Attachment Interview. What is fascinating about these data is not only that they are consistent with other research showing that a mother with a risky developmental history is less likely to mother poorly if she has a supportive marriage (see Belsky & Pensky, 1988, for a review); they also suggest that for a full understanding of the marital relationship's impact on the development of secure or insecure attachment bonds, additional information about the family is useful.

This theme of multiple determinants is one to which I return in the concluding section of this chapter. For now, it suffices to point out that acceptance of null findings may be premature when only direct effects are examined. Developmental influences do not operate only directly. There is a need to take into consideration both mediational processes (e.g., via role satisfaction and mothering) and moderational ones (e.g., interactions with maternal state of mind) in considering linkages between marriage and attachment.

Nonspousal Social Support

It is not just marital/partner relations that are systematically related to what transpires between parents and their children. Consistent with the theorizing of Cochran and Brassard (1979) and Cochran and Niego (1995), numerous investigations now provide evidence that the amount and nature of contact with and support from significant others affect the way parents (especially mothers) interact with their infants (for a meta-analysis, see Andersen & Telleen, 1992). For example, middle-class European American mothers with more prenatal social support are more sensitive when interacting with their 3-month-olds (Goldstein, Diener, & Mangelsdorf, 1996); low-income African American mothers with larger social networks tend to be more responsive in interaction with their infants (Burchinal, Follmer, & Bryand, 1996); and poor Hispanic women who receive more material resources from friends and relatives engage in more proximal (touching, kissing, holding) and distal (vocalizing, looking) interaction with their 3-month-old premature infants (Feiring et al., 1987). Given the mediational view that is central to this chapter, such findings lead to the expectation that nonspousal social support should be positively associated with attachment security.

Ten studies pertaining to the relation between nonspousal social support and infant–mother attachment security have been reported, and seven of these have failed to yield the expected association (Belsky et al., 1995; Belsky & Isabella, 1988; Crnic et al., 1986; Levitt et al., 1986; Spieker, 1988; Spieker & Booth, 1988; Zeanah et al., 1993). Notably, the three studies supporting the hypothesis that more social support should significantly predict attachment security focused on samples at risk for insensitive maternal care or insecure attachment. Thus Crockenberg (1981) found that the absence of social support predicted insecure attachment, but only in the case of highly irritable infants. Crnic et al. (1986) reported that an index of total community support was positively correlated with attachment security in a sample of premature infants. And Crittenden (1985) showed that in a group of infants with abusive or neglectful mothers, low social support predicted insecurity. Perhaps more interesting and theoretically significant, however, is that this effect of social support in the Crittenden investigation disappeared once quality of maternal care (i.e., abuse or neglect) was controlled for, consistent with the mediational arguments advanced throughout this chapter.

Once again, Isabella's (1994) research cautions against concluding that attachment security is not affected by social support, even when direct effects of social support do not emerge as expected. He found, as he did with marital quality, that high social support significantly predicted high maternal role satisfaction, and thereby quality of maternal care and attachment security. Thus, even though the contribution of social support to attachment security was neither overwhelming nor direct, a process of influence postulated by Isabella (1994)—and consistent with the mediational-process argument developed throughout this chapter—was confirmed. Given the conflicting results across correlational studies, as well as the fact that mediational processes may be a more appropriate venue for understanding the effects of social support on attachment security, it is inappropriate to embrace the null hypothesis of no relation between social support and infant–mother attachment.

INTEGRATION AND GENERAL CONCLUSIONS

Evidence considered in the first part of this chapter has documented the role played by the quality of maternal and nonmaternal care in fostering secure and insecure attachments to mothers and fathers/nonparental caregivers, respectively. Importantly, the evidence pertaining to infant–mother attachment security has been experimental (and thereby causal) as well as correlational in nature. Nevertheless, the effects of mothering have by no means been large, except perhaps in the van den Boom (1994) research. The modest effect sizes, even in studies in which sensitivity was rated using Ainsworth's scales, raise the prospect that infants may differ in their susceptibility to rearing influence (Belsky, 1997). Thus security–insecurity may be more a heritably determined feature in the case of some children and a rearing-determined one (in accordance with attachment theory) in the case of others. If this were found to be so, it might explain why the effect sizes for mothering appear so modest, as a small effect may emerge when children who are and are not affected by the quality of care they receive are combined in a single analysis. Intriguingly, van den Boom's (1994) dramatic experimental results, along with Crockenberg's (1981) correlational ones, raise the possibility that more fussy and irritable infants may be the ones most susceptible to rearing influences—in the case of attachment security, as well as other developmental outcomes (Belsky, 1997).

In the second half of this chapter, determinants of attachment suggested by an ecological perspective have been examined. Central to the discussion of psychological and contextual factors is the assumption that so-called "distal" influences—whether they are less distant, like personality, or more distant, like social support—exert their impact by influencing more proximal processes of parent–child interaction. Although ample evidence provides grounds for concluding that all the factors considered play a role in shaping the development of a secure or insecure attachment bond, inconsistency in the evidence has been repeatedly and purposefully highlighted. Up to this point, however, these factors have themselves not been placed "in context." By organizing the second part of the chapter around various factors, even while emphasizing mediational processes of influence, I may have risked leaving the impression that these sources of influence on the parent–child relationship—and thus on the child's attachment to his or her parent—operate in isolation. Nothing could be farther from the truth.

My own theorizing and that of others draw attention to the need to consider stresses and supports simultaneously (Belsky, 1984; Belsky & Isabella, 1988), or, in the terms of developmental psychopathology, risk and protective factors (Cicchetti, 1983; Sroufe & Rutter, 1984). Central to both of these theoretical orientations is the postulate that risks can be balanced by strengths, and moreover that the risks of problematic developmental outcomes (including attachment insecurity) are more likely to be realized as risk factors accumulate and are not balanced by supports or compensatory factors. Consider in this regard Das Eiden and Leonard's (1996) findings that heavy paternal alcohol consumption amplified the effect of maternal depression on attachment security: Even though higher depression scores were related to greater likelihood of insecure attachment, this was especially the case when fathers were heavy alcohol users.

My colleagues and I have obtained related results in a series of studies concerning the effect of the accumulation of risks on attachment security. Perhaps most notable are our most recent results, showing that even though not a single one of the factors considered in this chapter individually distinguished secure and insecure attachments (to mothers or to fathers), a decidedly different story emerged when indices of personality, marital quality, social support, infant temperament, occupational stressors, and socioeconomic status were simultaneously considered. When a composite of risk scores on these factors was created, a clear and significant relation with attachment emerged, replicating earlier findings (Belsky & Isabella, 1988). Specifically, the more indications there were that a family and a specific infant–parent relationship were "at risk" due to lower levels of parental psychological adjustment, poorer marital quality, more negative and less positive infant temperament, less social support, more work–family stress, and lower socioeconomic status, the more likely it was that the infant–mother or infant–father relationship would be insecure (Belsky, 1996; Belsky et al., 1995).

These results underscore the final point to be made in this chapter: To understand how psychological and social contexts influence the development of the child–parent attachment relationship, multiple factors must be considered simultaneously. Having a mother who is depressed is likely to have a dramatically different effect if a marriage is also conflicted and an infant is temperamentally difficult than if a spouse is supportive and an infant is easy to care for. Thus not only do processes of mediation need to be central to our understanding of the origins of individual differences in attachment (distal factors → parent–child interaction → attachment security), but so too do moderational ones, as the impact of one source of influence is highly likely to be contingent on another. As Bronfenbrenner (1979, p. 38) so astutely noted, in the ecology of human development—and thus with respect to the etiology of secure and insecure infant–parent attachment bonds—"the principal main effects are likely to be interactions."

REFERENCES

Ainsworth, M. D. (1973). The development of infant–mother attachment. In B. M. Caldwell & H. N. Ricciuti (Eds.), *Review of child development research* (Vol. 3, pp. 1–94). Chicago: University of Chicago Press.

Ainsworth, M. D., Blehar, M. C., Waters, E. & Wall, S. (1978). *Patterns of attachment: A psychological study of the strange situation.* Hillsdale, NJ: Erlbaum.

Andersen, P., & Telleen, S. (1992). The relationship between social support and maternal behavior and attitudes: A meta-analytic review. *American Journal of Community Psychology, 20*, 753–774.

Barnett, B., Blignault, I., Holmes, S., Payne, A., & Parker, G. (1987). Quality of attachment in a sample of 1-year-old Australian children. *Journal of the American Academy of Child and Adolescent Psychiatry, 26*, 303–307.

Bates, J. E., Maslin, C. A., & Frankel, K. A. (1985). Attachment security, mother–child interaction, and temperament as predictors of behavior-problem ratings at age three years. In I. Bretherton & E. Waters (Eds.), Growing points of attachment theory and research. *Monographs of the Society for Research in Child Development, 50*(1–2, Serial No. 209), 167–193.

Belsky, J. (1983). *Father–infant interaction and security of attachment: No relationship.* Unpublished manuscript, Pennsylvania State University.

Belsky, J. (1984). The determinants of parenting: A process model. *Child Development, 55*, 83–96.

Belsky, J. (1990). Parental and nonparental care and children's socioemotional development: A decade in review. *Journal of Marriage and the Family, 52*, 885–903.

Belsky, J. (1996). Parent, infant, and social-contextual determinants of attachment security. *Developmental Psychology, 32*, 905–914.

Belsky, J. (1997). Theory testing, effect-size evaluation, and differential susceptibility to rearing influence: The case of mothering and attachment. *Child Development, 68*, 598–601.

Belsky, J., Fish, M., & Isabella, R. (1991). Continuity and discontinuity in infant negative and positive emotionality:

Family antecedent and attachment consequences. *Developmental Psychology, 27,* 421–431.

Belsky, J., & Isabella, R. (1988). Maternal, infant, and social-contextual determinants of attachment security. In J. Belsky & T. Nezworski (Eds.), *Clinical implications of attachment* (pp. 41–94). Hillsdale, NJ: Erlbaum.

Belsky, J., & Pensky, E. (1988). Developmental history, personality and family relationships: Toward an emergent family system. In R. Hinde & J. Stevenson-Hinde (Eds.), *Relationships within families: Mutual influences* (pp. 193–217). Oxford: Clarendon Press.

Belsky, J., Rosenberger, K., & Crnic, K. (1995). Maternal personality, marital quality, social support and infant temperament: Their significance for infant–mother attachment in human families. In C. Pryce, R. Martin, & D. Skuse (Eds.), *Motherhood in human and nonhuman primates* (pp. 115–124). Basel: Karger.

Belsky, J., Rovine, M., & Taylor, D. G. (1984). The Pennsylvania Infant and Family Development Project: III. The origins of individual differences in infant–mother attachment: Maternal and infant contributions. *Child Development, 55,* 718–728.

Belsky, J., & Vondra, J. (1989). Lessons from child abuse: The determinants of parenting. In D. Cicchetti & V. Carlson (Eds.), *Current research and theoretical advances in child maltreatment* (pp. 153–202). Cambridge, England: Cambridge University Press.

Benn, R. K. (1986). Factors promoting secure attachment relationships between employed mothers and their sons. *Child Development, 57,* 1224–1231.

Bowlby, J. (1944). Forty-four juvenile thieves: Their characters and home life. *International Journal of Psycho-Analysis, 25,* 19–52.

Bowlby, J. (1958). The nature of the child's tie to his mother. *International Journal of Psycho-Analysis, 39,* 350–373.

Bronfenbrenner, U. (1979). *The ecology of human development.* Cambridge, MA: Harvard University Press.

Burchinal, M., Follmer, A., & Bryand, D. (1996). The relations of maternal social support and family structure with maternal responsiveness and child outcomes among African American families. *Developmental Psychology, 6,* 1073–1083.

Caldera, Y. M. (in press). Paternal involvement and infant–father attachment: A Q-set study. In B. Vaughn & E. Waters (Eds.), *Patterns of secure base behavior: Q-sort perspectives on attachment and caregiving.* Mahwah, NJ: Erlbaum.

Caldera, Y. M., Huston, A., & O'Brien, M. (1995, April). *Antecedents of father–infant attachment: A longitudinal study.* Paper presented at the biennial meeting of the Society for Research in Child Development, Indianapolis, IN.

Campbell, S. B., Cohn, J. F., Meyers, T. A., Ross, S., & Flanagan, C. (1993, April). Chronicity of maternal depression and mother–infant interaction. In D. Teti (Chair), *Depressed mothers and their children: Individual differences in mother–child outcome.* Symposium conducted at the biennial meeting of the Society for Research in Child Development, New Orleans, LA.

Chess, S., & Thomas, A. (1982). Infant bonding: Mystique and reality. *American Journal of Orthopsychiatry, 5,* 213–222.

Cicchetti, D. (1983). The emergence of developmental psychopathology. *Child Development, 55,* 1–7.

Clarke-Stewart, K. A. (1988). Parents' effects on children's development: A decade of progress? *Journal of Applied Developmental Psychology, 9,* 41–84.

Cochran, M., & Brassard, J. (1979). Child development and personal social networks. *Child Development, 50,* 601–616.

Cochran, M., & Niego, S. (1995). Parenting and social networks. In M. Bornstein (Ed.), *Handbook of parenting* (Vol. 3, pp. 393–418). Mahwah, NJ: Erlbaum.

Cohn, J., Campbell, S., & Ross, S. (1991). Infant response in the still face paradigm at 6 months predicts avoidant and secure attachment at 12 months. *Developmental Psychopathology, 3,* 367–376.

Cox, M., Owen, M. T., Henderson, V. K., & Margand, N. A. (1992). Prediction of infant–father and infant–mother attachment. *Developmental Psychology, 28,* 474–483.

Cox, M., Owen, M. T., Lewis, J., & Henderson, V. K. (1989). Marriage, adult adjustment, and early parenting. *Child Development, 60,* 1015–1024.

Crittenden, P. M. (1985). Social networks, quality of child rearing, and child development. *Child Development, 56,* 1299–1313.

Crnic, K. A., Greenberg, M. T., Ragozin, A. S., Robinson, N. M., & Basham, R. B. (1983). Effects of stress and social support on mothers and premature and full-term infants. *Child Development, 54,* 209–217.

Crnic, K. A., Greenberg, M. T., & Slough, N. M. (1986). Early stress and social support influences on mothers' and high-risk infants' functioning in late infancy. *Infant Mental Health Journal, 7,* 19–33.

Crockenberg, S. B. (1981). Infant irritability, mother responsiveness, and social support influences on the security of infant–mother attachment. *Child Development, 52,* 857–869.

D'Angelo, E. J. (1986). Security of attachment in infants with schizophrenic, depressed, and unaffected mothers. *Journal of Genetic Psychology, 147,* 421–422.

Das Eiden, R., & Leonard, K. (1996). Paternal alcohol use and the mother–infant relationship. *Development and Psychopathology, 8,* 307–323.

Das Eiden, R., Teti, D., & Corns, K. (1993, April). *Maternal working models of attachment, marital adjustment, and the parent–child relationship.* Paper presented at the biennial meeting of the Society for Research in Child Development, New Orleans, LA.

Davies, P., & Cummings, E. (1994). Marital conflict and child adjustment: An emotional security hypothesis. *Psychological Bulletin, 116,* 387–411.

Del Carmen, R., Pedersen, F., Huffman, L., & Bryan, Y. (1993). Dyadic distress management predicts security of attachment. *Infant Behavior and Development, 16,* 131–147.

DeMulder, E. K., & Radke-Yarrow, M. (1991). Attachment with affectively ill and well mothers: Current behavioral correlates. *Developmental Psychopathology, 3,* 227–242.

DeWolff, M., & van Ijzendoorn, M. (1997). Sensitivity and attachment: A meta-analysis on parental antecedents of infant attachment. *Child Development, 68,* 571–591.

Dickie, J. (1987). Interrelationships within the mother–father–infant triad. In P. W. Berman & F. A. Pederson (Eds.), *Men's transitions to parenthood: Longitudinal studies of early family experience* (pp. 113–144). Hillsdale, NJ: Erlbaum.

Durrett, M. E., Otaki, M., & Richards, P. (1984). Attachment and the mother's perception of support from the father. *International Journal of Behavioral Development, 7,* 167–176.

Durrett, M. E., Richards, P., Otaki, M., Pennebaker, J. W., & Nyquist, L. (1986). Mother's involvement with her infant and her perception of spousal support, Japan and America. *Journal of Marriage and the Family, 48,* 187–194.

Easterbrooks, M. A., & Goldberg, W. A. (1984). Toddler development in the family: Impact of father involvement and parenting characteristics. *Child Development, 55,* 744–752.

Egeland, B., & Farber, E. A. (1984). Infant–mother attachment: Factors related to its development and changes over time. *Child Development, 55,* 753–771.

Engfer, A. (1988). The interrelatedness of marriage and the mother–child relationship. In R. Hinde & J. Stevenson-Hinde (Eds.), *Relationships within families: Mutual influences* (pp. 104–118). Oxford: Clarendon Press.

Erel, O., & Burman, B. (1995). Interrelatedness of marital relations and parent–child relations. *Psychological Bulletin, 118,* 108–132.

Feiring, C., Fox, N. A., Jaskir, J., & Lewis, M. (1987). The relation between social support, infant risk status, and mother–infant interaction. *Developmental Psychology, 23,* 400–405.

Feldstein, S., Crown, C., Beebe, B., & Jaffe, J. (1995, April). *Temporal coordination and the prediction of mother–infant attachment.* Paper presented at the biennial meeting of the Society for Research in Child Development, Indianapolis, IN.

Fish, M., & Stifter, C. (1995). Patterns of mother–infant interaction and attachment. *Infant Behavior and Development, 18,* 435–446.

Frankel, K., Maslin-Cole, C., & Harmon, R. (1991, April). *Depressed mothers of preschoolers.* Paper presented at the biennial meeting of the Society for Research in Child Development, Seattle, WA.

Gaensbauer, T. J., Harmon, R. J., Cytryn, L., & McKnew, D. H. (1984). Social and affective development in infants with a manic–depressive parent. *American Journal of Psychiatry, 141,* 223–229.

Gelfand, D., & Teti, D. (1990). The effects of maternal depression on children. *Clinical Psychology Review, 10,* 329–353.

Goldberg, W. A., & Easterbrooks, M. A. (1984). The role of marital quality in toddler development. *Developmental Psychology, 20,* 504–514.

Goldsmith, H. H., & Alansky, J. A. (1987). Maternal and infant temperamental predictors of attachment: A meta-analytic review. *Journal of Consulting and Clinical Psychology, 55,* 805–816.

Goldstein, L., Diener, M., & Mangelsdorf, S. (1996). Maternal characteristics and social support across the transition to motherhood: Associations with maternal behavior. *Journal of Family Psychology, 10,* 60–71.

Goossens, F., & van IJzendoorn, M. (1990). Quality of infants' attachment to professional caregivers. *Child Development, 61,* 832–837.

Grossmann, K., & Grossmann, K. E. (1992). Newborn behavior, the quality of early parenting, and later toddler–parent relationships in a group of German infants. In J. K. Nugent, B. M. Lester, & T. B. Brazelton (Eds.), *The cultural context of infancy* (Vol. 2, pp. 3–38). Norwood, NJ: Ablex.

Grossmann, K., Grossmann, K. E., Spangler, G., Suess, G., & Unzner, L. (1985). Maternal sensitivity and newborns' orientation responses as related to quality of attachment in northern Germany. In I. Bretherton & E. Waters (Eds.), Growing points of attachment theory and research. *Monographs of the Society for Research in Child Development, 50*(1–2, Serial No. 209), 233–257.

Howes, C., & Hamilton, C. E. (1992). Children's relationships with caregivers: Mothers and child care teachers. *Child Development, 63,* 859–866.

Howes, C., & Markman, H. J. (1989). Marital quality and child functioning: A longitudinal investigation. *Child Development, 60,* 1044–1051.

Howes, C., Phillips, D. A., & Whitebook, M. (1992). Thresholds of quality: Social development in center based child care. *Child Development, 63,* 449–460.

Howes, C., Rodning, C., Galluzzo, D. C., & Myers, L. (1988). Attachment and child care: Relationships with mother and caregiver. *Early Childhood Research Quarterly, 3,* 403–416.

Howes, C., & Smith, E. W. (1995). Children and their child care caregivers: Profiles of relationships. *Social Development, 4,* 44–61.

Isabella, R. A. (1993). Origins of attachment: Maternal interactive behavior across the first year. *Child Development, 64,* 605–621.

Isabella, R. A. (1994). Origins of maternal role satisfaction and its influences upon maternal interactive behavior and infant–mother attachment. *Infant Behavior and Development, 17,* 381–388.

Isabella, R., & Belsky, J. (1991). Interactional synchrony and the origins of infant–mother attachment: A replication study. *Child Development, 62,* 373–384.

Isabella, R., Belsky, J., & von Eye, A. (1989). Origins of infant–mother attachment: An examination of interactional synchrony during the infant's first year. *Developmental Psychology, 25,* 12–21.

Jacobson, S. W., & Frye, K. F. (1991). Effect of maternal social support on attachment: Experimental evidence. *Child Development, 62,* 572–582.

Jouriles, E., Pfiffner, L., & O'Leary, S. (1988). Marital conflict, parenting, and toddler conduct problems. *Journal of Abnormal Child Psychology, 16,* 197–206.

Kagan, J. (1982). *Psychological research on the human infant: An evaluative summary.* New York: W. T. Grant Foundation.

Krupka, A., Moran, G., & Pederson, D. (1996, April). *The quality of mother–infant interactions in families at risk for maladaptive behavior: A window on the process of attachment.* Paper presented at the biennial meeting of the International Conference on Infant Studies, Providence, RI.

Lamb, M. E., Thompson, R. A., Gardner, W. P., Charnov, E. L., & Estes, D. (1984). Security of infantile attachment as assessed in the "strange situation": Its study and biological interpretation. *Behavioral and Brain Sciences, 7,* 127–172.

Levitt, M., Weber, R., & Clark, M. (1986). Social network relationships as sources of maternal support and well-being. *Developmental Psychology, 22,* 310–316.

Levy-Schiff, I., & Israelashvili, I. (1988). Antecedents of fathering: Some further exploration. *Developmental Psychology, 24,* 434–440.

Lewis, M., & Feiring, C. (1989). Infant, mother, and mother–infant interaction behavior and subsequent attachment. *Child Development, 60,* 831–837.

Lewis, M., Owen, M. T., & Cox, M. J. (1988). The transition to parenthood: III. Incorporation of the child into the family. *Family Process, 27,* 411–421.

Leyendecker, B., Lamb, M., Fracasso, M., Scholmerich, A., & Larson, C. (1997). Playful interaction and the antecedents of attachment. *Merrill–Palmer Quarterly, 43,* 24–47.

Leyendecker, B., Lamb, M., & Scholmerich, A. (1997). Studying mother–infant interaction: Effects of context and length of observation in two cultural groups. *Infant Behavior and Development, 20,* 325–339.

Lyons-Ruth, K. (1988, April). *Maternal depression and in-*

fant disturbance. Paper presented at the biennial meeting of the International Conference on Infant Studies, Washington, DC.

Lyons-Ruth, K., Zoll, D., Connell, D., & Grunebaum, H. (1986). The depressed mother and her one-year-old infant: Environmental context, mother–infant interaction and attachment. In E. Tronick & T. Field (Eds.), *Maternal depression and infant disturbance* (pp. 61–82). San Francisco: Jossey-Bass.

Malatesta, C. Z., Grigoryev, P., Lamb, C., Albin, M., & Culver, C. (1986). Emotion socialization and expressive development in preterm and full-term infants. *Child Development, 57,* 316–330.

Maslin, C. A., & Bates, J. E. (1983). *Precursors of anxious and secure attachments: A multivariate model at age 6 months*. Paper presented at the biennial meeting of the Society for Research in Child Development, Detroit, MI.

Meyer, H. J. (1988). Marital and mother–child relationships: Developmental history, parent personality and child difficulties. In R. A. Hinde & J. Stevenson-Hinde (Eds.), *Relationships within families: Mutual influences* (pp. 119–142). Oxford: Clarendon Press.

Moran, G., Pederson, D., Pettit, P., & Krupka, A. (1992). Maternal sensitivity and infant–mother attachment in a developmentally delayed sample. *Infant Behavior and Development, 15,* 427–442.

Murray, L., Fiori-Cowley, A., Hooper, R., & Cooper, P. (1996). The impact of postnatal depression and associated adversity on early mother–infant interactions and later infant outcome. *Child Development, 67,* 2512–2526.

Nakagawa, M., Teti, D. M., & Lamb, M. E. (1992). An ecological study of child–mother attachments among Japanese sojourners in the United States. *Developmental Psychology, 28,* 584–592.

National Institute of Child Health and Human Development (NICHD) Early Child Care Network. (1997). The effects of infant child care on infant–mother attachment security: Results of the NICHD Study of Early Child Care. *Child Development, 68,* 860–879.

Oates, D. S., & Heinicke, C. (1985). Prebirth prediction of the quality of the mother–infant interaction: The first year of life. *Journal of Family Issues, 6,* 523–542.

O'Connor, M. (1997, March). *Maternal personality characteristics on the MMPI and infant attachment*. Paper presented at the biennial meeting of the Society for Research in Child Development, Washington, DC.

O'Connor, M., Sigman, M., & Kasasi, C. (1992). Attachment behavior of infants exposed prenatally to alcohol. *Developmental Psychopathology, 4,* 243–256.

Owen, M., & Cox, M. (1997). Marital conflict and the development of infant–parent attachment relationships. *Journal of Family Psychology, 11,* 152–164.

Pederson, D., & Moran, G. (1996). Expressions of the attachment relationship outside of the Strange Situation. *Child Development, 67,* 915–927.

Pederson, D., Moran, G., Sitko, C., Campbell, K., Ghesqure, K., & Acton, H. (1990). Maternal sensitivity and the security of infant–mother attachment. *Child Development, 61,* 1974–1983.

Radke-Yarrow, M. (1991). Attachment patterns in children of depressed mothers. In C. M. Parkes, J. Stevenson-Hinde, & P. Marris (Eds.), *Attachment across the life cycle* (pp. 115–126). London: Tavistock/Routledge.

Radke-Yarrow, M., Cummings, E. M., Kuczynski, L., & Chapman, M. (1985). Patterns of attachment in two- and three-year-olds in normal families and families with parental depression. *Child Development, 56,* 884–893.

Ricks, M. H. (1985). The social transmission of parental behavior: Attachment across generations. In I. Bretherton & E. Waters (Eds.), Growing points of attachment theory and research. *Monographs of the Society for Research in Child Development, 50*(1–2, Serial No. 209), 211–227.

Rothbart, M., & Bates, J. (1997). Temperament. In W. Damon (Series Ed.) & N. Eisenberg (Vol. Ed.), *Handbook of child psychology: Vol. 3. Social, emotional, and personality development* (5th ed., pp. 308–418). New York: Wiley.

Sameroff, A. J., Seifer, R., & Zax, M. (1982). Early development of children at risk for emotional disorder. *Monographs of the Society for Research in Child Development, 47.*

Schneider-Rosen, K., & Rothbaum, F. (1993). Quality of parental caregiving and security of attachment. *Developmental Psychology, 29,* 358–367.

Scholmerich, A., Fracasso, M., Lamb, M., & Broberg, A. (1995). Interactional harmony at 7 and 10 months of age predicts security of attachment as measured by Q-sort ratings. *Social Development, 34,* 62–74.

Seifer, R., Schiller, M., Sameroff, A., Resnick, S., & Riordan, K. (1996). Attachment, maternal sensitivity, and infant temperament during the first year of life. *Developmental Psychology, 32,* 12–25.

Sims, B., Hans, S., & Cox, S. (1996, April). *Raising children in high-risk environments: Mothers' experience of stress and distress related to attachment security*. Poster presented at the biennial meeting of the International Conference on Infant Studies, Providence, RI.

Smith, P. B., & Pederson, D. R. (1988). Maternal sensitivity and patterns of infant–mother attachment. *Child Development, 59,* 1097–1101.

Spieker, S. J. (1988). Patterns of very insecure attachment in samples of high-risk infants and toddlers. *Topics in Early Childhood Special Education, 6,* 37–53.

Spieker, S. J., & Booth, C. (1988). Maternal antecedents of attachment quality. In J. Belsky & T. Nezworski (Eds.), *Clinical implications of attachment* (pp. 95–135). Hillsdale, NJ: Erlbaum.

Sroufe, L. A. (1985). Attachment classification from the perspective of infant–caregiver relationships and infant temperament. *Child Development, 56,* 1–14.

Sroufe, L. A., & Rutter, M. (1984). The domain of developmental psychopathology. *Child Development, 55,* 17–29.

Susman-Stillman, A., Kalkoske, M., Egeland, B., & Waldman, I. (1996). Infant temperament and maternal sensitivity as predictors of attachment security. *Infant Behavior and Development, 19,* 33–47.

Teti, D., Gelfand, D., Messinger, D., & Isabella, R. (1995). Maternal depression and the quality of early attachment. *Developmental Psychology, 31,* 364–376.

Teti, D., Nakagawa, M., Das, R., & Wirth, O. (1991). Security of attachment between preschoolers and their mothers: Relations among social interaction, parenting stress, and mothers' sorts of the Attachment Q-Set. *Developmental Psychology, 27,* 440–447.

Teti, D., Sakin, J., Kucera, E., Corns, K., & Das Eiden, R. (1996). And baby makes four. *Child Development, 67,* 579–596.

van den Boom, D. (1990). Preventive intervention and the quality of mother–infant interaction and infant exploration in irritable infants. In W. Koops et al. (Eds.), *Developmental psychology behind the dikes* (pp. 249–270). Amsterdam: Eburon.

van den Boom, D. (1994). The influence of temperament and mothering on attachment and exploration. *Child Development, 65,* 1457–1477.

van IJzendoorn, M., & DeWolff, M. (1997). In search of the absent father: Meta-analysis of infant–father attachment. *Child Development, 68*, 604–609.

van IJzendoorn, M., Juffer, F., & Duyvesteyn, M. (1995). Breaking the intergenerational cycle of insecure attachment: A review of the effects of attachment-based interventions on maternal sensitivity and infant security. *Journal of Child Psychology and Psychiatry, 36*, 225–248.

Vereijken, C., Riksen-Walraven, J., & Kondo-Ikemura, K. (1997). Maternal sensitivity and infant attachment security in Japan: A longitudinal study. *International Journal of Behavioral Development, 21,* 35–49.

Volling, B. L., & Belsky, J. (1992). Infant, father, and marital antecedents of infant–father attachment security in dual-earner and single-earner families. *International Journal of Behavioral Development, 15*, 83–100.

Vondra, J., Shaw, D., & Kevinides, M. (1995). Predicting infant attachment classification from multiple, contemporaneous measures of maternal care. *Infant Behavior and Development, 18,* 415–425.

Waters, E., & Deane, K. E. (1985). Defining and assessing individual differences in attachment relationships: *Q*-methodology and the organization of behavior in infancy and early childhood. In I. Bretherton & E. Waters (Eds.), Growing points of attachment theory and research. *Monographs of the Society for Research in Child Development, 50*(1–2, Serial No. 209), 41–65.

Zeanah, C., Benoit, D., Barton, M., Regan, C., Hirshberg, L., & Lipsett, L. (1993). Representations of attachment in mothers and their one-year-old infants. *Journal of the American Academy of Child and Adolescent Psychiatry, 32*, 278–286.

13

Early Attachment and Later Development

❖

ROSS A. THOMPSON

Throughout much of human history, philosophers have speculated about how the child foreshadows the adult that is to be. During the past century of psychological theorizing, scientific answers to this classic question have been sought in studies of the long-term sequelae of early differences in intelligence or temperament. At the same time, psychoanalytic theorists have argued that early relational influences also have enduring consequences for psychological growth. This view was crystallized in Freud's (1940/1963, p. 45) famous dictum that the infant–mother relationship is "unique, without parallel, established unalterably for a whole lifetime as the first and strongest love-object and as the prototype of all later love-relations." Drawing on this psychoanalytic heritage, Bowlby (1969/1982, 1973) enlisted formulations from evolutionary biology, developmental psychology, and control systems theory to argue that a warm and continuous relationship with a caregiver promotes psychological health and well-being throughout life in a manner that accords with the adaptive requirements of the human species. In collaboration with Ainsworth (1967, 1973), he proposed that differences in the security of infant–mother attachment may have significant long-term implications for later intimate relationships, self-understanding, and even psychopathology.

It is unsurprising that with the development and validation of the strange situation procedure for measuring variations in early attachment security, Bowlby's provocative theoretical formulations would be tested in a series of short-term longitudinal studies. Beginning in the late 1970s, researchers observed infants in the strange situation and in later follow-up assessments to determine whether a secure or insecure attachment foreshadowed later psychological functioning. It is perhaps more surprising to survey the scope and breadth of research on the consequences of early attachment in the two decades that followed. Individual differences in attachment in infancy have been studied in relation to a dizzying variety of later outcomes, including parent–child interaction; relations with peers, friends, and siblings; behavior with unfamiliar adults; competence in preschool and kindergarten; exploration and play; intelligence and language ability; ego resilience and ego control; frustration tolerance; curiosity; self-recognition; social cognition; behavioral problems and other indicators of incipient psychopathology; and many other variables. Longitudinal follow-up studies have spanned periods of several months to decades, and have included observations; self-reports; reports from parents, teachers, and peers; standardized tests; and a variety of other assessments. Guided by a general expectation that a secure attachment predicts better later functioning, researchers have proposed a broad variety of specific formulations to account for hypothesized relations between attachment security and later sociopersonality attributes.

This intensive research inquiry has been fruitful, yielding a number of substantive conclusions concerning the importance of a secure attachment for psychological growth—together with a variety of questions remaining to be answered, and new ways of conceptualizing the associations between attachment in infancy and later behavior. The goal of this chapter is to survey this empirical landscape, identifying what is known and what remains to be explored, and outlining new directions for future theory and research. The latter is important because of the manner in which attachment research permits the exploration of some of the most compelling general questions of developmental theory. With respect to questions concerning the consequences of early relational influences, for example, studies summarized in this chapter suggest that relationships are multi-influential, that outcomes are multidetermined, and that continuity is complex and multifaceted. Such conclusions are relevant to understanding developmental influences beyond the confines of attachment theory.

This chapter begins with a discussion of the theoretical reasons why attachment security may be expected to predict later psychosocial functioning. Subsequently, reasons why prediction may *not* be anticipated, or why "it depends," are considered as a counterpoint to these theoretical views, and to sharpen expectations of the conditions in which attachment is likely to have the strongest association with later sociopersonality characteristics. The empirical literature is reviewed next, and the chapter concludes with a summary of this research and considerations for future inquiry.

In a chapter covering this broad terrain, two caveats should be noted. The first concerns assessment (see Solomon & George, Chapter 14, this volume). Attachment in infancy is operationalized solely in the strange situation procedure, a 21-minute behavioral observation conducted in a laboratory playroom involving the mother and a stranger (Ainsworth, Blehar, Waters, & Wall, 1978). By contrast, several assessments of childhood attachment have been validated—the most prominent being the Attachment *Q*-Sort (AQS), a 90-item observer report instrument (Waters & Deane, 1985). Although alternative age-appropriate assessments of attachment security are an advantage to researchers, they can be problematic to reviewers of research because each measure offers a some-

what different portrayal of the security of attachment, consistent with the changing capacities of the developing child. The AQS differs from the strange situation, for example, because it employs multiple assessment contexts, incorporates a broader range of behavioral criteria, operationalizes security in multifaceted ways, and uses different rating procedures and different informants. Although AQS security scores and strange situation classifications converge, it is perhaps unsurprising that AQS security scores have somewhat different correlates (such as with infant temperament) than do attachment classifications (see Thompson, 1998). Because they offer somewhat different portrayals of attachment security, therefore, the limited existing literature using the AQS and other well-validated later-age assessments is distinguished from the strange situation literature in this chapter's review of research on the sequelae of attachment.

Second, it is also important to distinguish research concerning the concurrent correlates of attachment security from studies of its predictive relations. A secure attachment can have a network of contemporaneous associations that are different from its connections to future behavior. One reason is that predictive relations may be altered as new developmental challenges or subsequent events (e.g., changing family circumstances) that also affect predicted outcomes intervene. Contemporaneous associations between attachment and other psychosocial variables are not influenced by these changes, and may be strengthened by common influences (e.g., sensitive care) at a single period of time. For this reason, this review emphasizes the predictive relations between attachment and later psychological outcomes, although contemporaneous associations are noted where pertinent.

SOURCES OF DEVELOPMENTAL CONTINUITY

The enduring appeal of attachment theory is based in part on its theoretical breadth and integration. Bowlby's explanations for the importance of a warm, continuing early caregiving relationship to psychological well-being were based on considerations related to the biological heritage of the human species, relational dynamics, and developing understanding of self and others. Consequently, attachment theory offers several reasons for expecting that security will foreshadow later psychosocial growth.

Internal Working Models

Central to these predictive formulations is Bowlby's (1980, 1988) concept of an "internal working model" of self and relationships, based on object relations theory. He proposed that early experiences of sensitive or insensitive care contribute to the growth of broader representations concerning a caregiver's accessibility and responsiveness, as well as to beliefs about one's deservingness of such care. Such expectations not only enable immediate forecasts of the sensitivity of the caregiver's responsiveness, but also guide future relational choices and expectations, self-appraisal, and behavior toward others. Specifically, Bowlby believed that individuals with secure working models of relationships seek and begin to expect supportive, satisfying encounters with old and new partners, and the decision rules for relating to others that are implicit in their relational models cause them to behave in a positive, open manner that elicits such support. By contrast, individuals with insecure working models may, because of the distrust or uncertainty engendered by their relational expectations, anticipate less support from others and may actually deter the kind of supportive care from which they would benefit. In fact, when their partners respond negatively to their distrust or hostility, it confirms their expectations concerning the unreliability of others' acceptance, and their views of themselves as unworthy of such care. Sroufe (1979, 1990, 1996; Sroufe & Fleeson, 1986, 1988), Bretherton (1991, 1993), Crittenden (1990, 1994), Thompson (1998), and Main (1991; Main, Kaplan, & Cassidy, 1985) have each offered contemporary extensions of Bowlby's theory of working models.

Consistent with contemporary formulations of schema theory (e.g., Baldwin, 1992), therefore, Bowlby portrayed working models as largely unconscious interpretive filters through which relationships and other social experiences are construed and self-understanding is constructed. They provide implicit decision rules for relating to others that may, for better or worse, help to confirm and maintain intuitive expectations about others and oneself. These internal representations are self-perpetuating, both because of confirmation biases inherent in their functioning and because they cause young children to elicit complementary responses from partners that are consistent with their relational expectations (in a manner analogous to the way a young child's temperamental style, whether easy or difficult, shapes how others perceive and react to the child). It is easy to see, therefore, how the development of internal working models of self and relationships may be a source of continuity between early attachment and later psychosocial functioning.

To be sure, internal working models are developing representations. More precisely, working models are based on a network of developing representations that emerge successively but interactively with age (Thompson, 1998). At least four interrelated representational systems are encompassed within the conscious and unconscious features of working models: (1) fundamental social expectations of the attributes of caregivers and other partners, created during the first year and subsequently elaborated; (2) event representations, by which general and specific memories of attachment-related experiences are conceived and retained in long-term memory, beginning during the third year (Hudson, 1993; Nelson, 1989); (3) autobiographical memories, by which specific events are conceptually connected because of their relation to a continuing personal narrative and developing self-understanding, beginning in the fourth year (Nelson, 1993; Welch-Ross, 1995); and (4) understandings of other people and their psychological characteristics (such as their thoughts, motives, and intentions), by which the behavior of attachment partners and the nature of relationships is understood, beginning in the third and fourth years (this is sometimes studied under the rubric of "theory of mind"; see Wellman, 1990). In each conceptual domain, representations (of events, self, others, and relationships) develop and mature as a consequence of the child's direct experiences with others, evolving conceptual skills, and indirect representations of experiences derived from shared discourse with others, especially caregivers (see Thompson, 1998, and Bretherton, 1991, 1993, for further details).

Understanding the developmental processes entailed in the growth, elaboration, and consolidation of multifaceted working models is important for grasping their role in the continuity between early attachment and later psychosocial behavior. This is true for several reasons. First, insofar as the earliest representations of the caregiving relationship—which contribute to a secure or insecure attachment in infancy—consist largely of simple social expectations for the caregiver's characteristics, they probably do not provide the conceptual foundation for the more sophisticated and complex representations of self and relationships to emerge in later years. Conceptions of one's worthiness of love can be anticipated only dimly, at best, in the earliest proto-working models in infancy. This early simplicity of representational processes may in fact contribute to the plasticity of working models until the consolidation of these belief systems with the integrative, metarepresentational capabilities of adolescence (Bowlby, 1973). Thus understanding the processes mediating the transition from the simple social expectations of infancy to the more complex representational systems of later ages, and their relevance to continuity or change in a child's security-relevant behavior, is central to grasping how attachment security in infancy foreshadows later functioning.

Second, because working models are being continuously revised and updated throughout development, their impact on a child's psychosocial functioning at any particular age may depend on the security of the representations that are developing at that particular time. Thus a secure attachment at age 6 may, for instance, be of greater significance for emergent self-image than a secure attachment in infancy or early childhood, insofar as the self-representational facets of working models are becoming expanded and refined at this time in particular. To be sure, a history of security is better than a history of insecurity as self-image is progressively constructed throughout childhood, but it is likely that *contemporary* working models are most influential during the significant advances in self-understanding and other aspects of social representation in childhood. In short, different facets of working models (e.g., social expectations, autobiographical memory) have not only different developmental timetables but perhaps also different periods of critical influence.

Finally, because young children's earliest representations of personal experiences, self, and relationships are shaped in the context of shared discourse with others (Fivush, 1994; Nelson, 1993; Oppenheim & Waters, 1985), caregivers assume an important role in guiding the nature of children's early working models. Through their own interpretations of significant events in children's lives, caregivers can influence how children construe the experiences they encounter and their personal meaning, as well as shaping early constructions of emotion, morality, and self that emerge from such conversations. Moreover, as children gradually develop the conceptual skills necessary to represent personal experience in more sophisticated ways, they are likely to appropriate the viewpoints and interpretations that have been provided earlier in discourse with caregivers. In this respect, therefore, attachment figures doubly influence working models: Both through the quality of care they provide and through the interpretations of events they offer in the context of shared conversations with children, secure or insecure representations of relational experience are engendered and maintained in young children.

Taken together, these considerations underscore that the attributes of fully developed working models do not characterize the simpler, developing representational systems of young children. Consequently, it is important to consider working models in a developmental context (as Bowlby did) in order to understand them as a source of developmental continuity. Doing so not only enables attachment theorists to consider the developmental impact of working models more closely in accord with a child's developing conscious and unconscious representations of experience, but also encourages the consideration of various influences that may mediate between early forms of working models and later psychosocial functioning. In many respects, this defines an important research agenda for future work on the representational features of attachment relationships and their importance to developmental continuity.

Ontogenetic Adaptations

Following Bowlby (1969/1982), attachment theorists have long regarded attachment as one of several species-typical behavioral systems that have evolved to promote infant survival. Specifically, attachment motivates infants to seek the protective proximity of adults, especially when offspring are distressed, alarmed, or in danger. Contemporary behavioral ecologists have also underscored the sensitivity of offspring to the variations that may exist in parental care and their meaning not only for a child's immediate survival, but also for long-term reproductive success (e.g., Clutton-Brock, 1991; see Simpson, Chapter 6, and Belsky, Chapter 7, this volume). In one view, Chisholm (1996) has argued that the secure, avoidant, and resistant attachment classifications can be regarded as "facultative adaptations" (i.e., environmentally contingent adjustments) to alternative patterns of parental investment in offspring (see Hinde, 1982, and Lamb, Thompson, Gardner, & Charnov, 1985, for similar views). In this formulation, the sensitively responsive parental care leading to a secure attachment reflects the adult's ability and willingness to provide for the child. By contrast, alternative patterns of attachment insecurity derive from parental behavior that reflects either an inability to invest resources in offspring or an unwillingness to do so. According to Chisholm, the behavioral characteristics of securely and insecurely attached children are adaptive responses to perceptions of these variations in parental solicitude, revealed in the confident play and exploration of secure children (which in other ways enhance the children's reproductive success) or in either the clingy, dependent behavior or the independent activity that may be necessary to obtain needed resources in other ways.

Chisholm proposes that these behavioral patterns may have long-term sequelae owing to the alternative survival and reproductive strategies they inaugurate, since variations in early parental solicitude probably reflect broader characteristics of environmental provision or deprivation in the ecological contexts of human evolution. A similar view has been advanced by Belsky, Steinberg, and Draper (1991), who have argued that infant attachment patterns may be related, through similar adaptive strategies, to the subsequent timing of sexual maturity, preferences in pair bonding, and mature reproductive strategy. In each case, attachment patterns in infancy are conceived of as "ontogenetic adaptations," which are significant early in life but also become incorporated into behavioral patterns that are adaptive throughout life.

The view of attachment security as an ontogenetic adaptation provides another viewpoint for understanding the associations between infant attachment and later psychosocial functioning. To the extent that clear theoretical predictions concerning the later consequences of early facultative adaptations for reproductive strategy can be derived from current thinking in behavioral ecology and evolutionary biology, the short- and long-term sequelae of secure and insecure patterns of attachment can be examined more incisively. However, considerably more theoretical work is necessary before these hypotheses can be formulated and tested, because many mediating influences between early attachment and later adaptations are essential to identify (especially for modeling the behavior of organisms as psychologically complex as humans) but currently remain underspecified. As a consequence, at times the tests of these adaptive formulations have revealed greater complexity than predicted

(e.g., Moffitt, Caspi, Belsky, & Silva, 1992). Thus the view of attachment patterns as ontogenetic adaptations remains heuristically powerful but requires greater theoretical development.

Emergent Personality and Social Skills

Another explanation for developmental continuity, consistent with the foregoing, is that attachment in infancy shapes emergent personality processes that, as they mature and become consolidated in succeeding years, exert a continuing influence on psychosocial functioning. A secure or insecure attachment in infancy can shape many aspects of developing personality, including sociability, emotional predispositions, curiosity, self-esteem, independence, cooperation, and trust. The importance of attachment is not only in its multifaceted potential influences on emergent personality, but also in its effects on personality organization, because diverse features of personality are likely to be influenced in concert by attachment security.

This potential role of attachment in personality development is thoughtfully conceptualized in the "organizational perspective," which portrays personality growth in terms of a succession of age-salient developmental challenges around which critical issues of personality development are focused (Cicchetti, 1990; Sroufe, 1979, 1990, 1996). During the first year, of course, the growth of a secure attachment relationship is central; in successive years, relevant developmental issues include the growth of an autonomous self, the acquisition of effective peer relations, and successful adaptation to school. Within this neo-Eriksonian perspective, the successful mastery of earlier developmental challenges is believed to provide a stronger psychological foundation for surmounting subsequent challenges, largely because of the supportive features of personality growth (such as ego development) that have occurred as a result. It is not entirely clear, however, how broadly attachment is believed to influence success in subsequent developmental challenges, or by which specific developmental processes it is influential. Conceivably, within this formulation, attachment security can have either a portentous influence in later personality functioning or a significantly narrower one; without greater specification of the processes by which attachment affects later adaptation, it is difficult to clarify its organizational role.

A somewhat narrower perspective on developmental continuity, which is nevertheless consistent with the organizational perspective, focuses on the acquisition and maintenance of social skills and (more broadly) social predispositions as a consequence of early attachment (e.g., Thompson & Lamb, 1983). Because infancy is a period of rapidly developing sociability in which differences between securely and insecurely attached infants are very apparent, the legacy of early attachment relationships includes the enhanced, flexible, and positive (or restricted, inflexible, and/or maladaptive) social skills that are acquired in this first relationship. As these skills and predispositions are generalized to other circumstances and other social partners, they are likely to elicit complementary responses from partners that tend to reinforce and maintain these characteristics. Moreover, as children increasingly select the partners and settings that they find congenial, these social characteristics become still further consolidated through the self-selection of social demands and opportunities. Through either the broader organization of personality or narrower shaping of emergent social skills (or both), therefore, attachment may provide a foundation for later sociopersonality functioning.

Taken together, there are multiple, overlapping reasons to expect attachment in infancy to foreshadow later psychosocial functioning, based on intrapsychic functioning, behavioral individuality, and even species heritage. Considered in concert, they provide a range of hypotheses concerning the sequelae of attachment that can be tested empirically.

REASONS FOR DEVELOPMENTAL DISCONTINUITY OR "IT DEPENDS"

Although the formulations of attachment theory predicting consistency between early attachment patterns and later psychological functioning are indeed powerful, there are also a number of reasons, from both within and outside attachment theory, to argue that there may be very limited continuity between early attachment and later behavior. Portrayed most strongly, these perspectives argue that researchers should expect essentially little or no relation between infant attachment and later functioning. In most cases, however, these explanations indicate that whether continuity will be found depends on a number of mediators or other considerations.

Juvenile Adaptations

One argument from evolutionary biology is that attachment patterns in infancy may be facultative adaptations to alternative patterns of parental investment but, like many early adaptive behaviors, constitute "juvenile adaptations" with no necessary long-term behavioral importance. Many behaviors aid individuals through their immaturity but either disappear or have little value afterwards; such behaviors include early reflexes, crying, cooing and other preverbal behavior, and prelocomotor activity. In each case, they enable the developing organism to reach maturity, but individual differences in these capabilities have no necessary enduring significance. If attachment patterns are conceived of as juvenile adaptations, they will be regarded as facultative adaptations to early patterns of parental investment that enable young offspring to reach a level of functional maturity, but are not necessarily relevant to long-term reproductive success. If offspring survive early childhood and reach reproductive maturity, in other words, the particular attachment pattern that has enabled them to do so is irrelevant to their later psychosocial functioning. From this perspective, therefore, there is little reason why infant attachment patterns alone should foreshadow long-term psychological or behavioral functioning.

Consistency and Change in Parent–Child Relationships

A secure attachment in infancy is the beginning of what Maccoby (1983, 1984) has called a "mutual interpersonal orientation of positive reciprocity" between parent and child. This is a relationship characterized by mutual cooperation, in which a child is intrinsically and eagerly receptive to the caregiver's socialization incentives because of the general harmony of their interactions. In this mutually responsive relationship, the parent is sensitive to the child's interest, and the child in turn is committed to the relationship with the parent. To the extent that the reciprocally cooperative orientation inaugurated by a secure parent–infant attachment endures, therefore, it is likely to promote many positive features of psychosocial growth by heightening the child's receptivity to many other socialization influences concerned with achieving competence, behavioral compliance, or other developmental goals (see Waters, Kondo-Ikemura, Posada, & Richters, 1991). For example, Kochanska (1995) has found that a secure attachment predicts later conscience development for certain toddlers, and speculates that the creation and maintenance of a mutually responsive orientation between parent and offspring account for this association (see also Kochanska & Thompson, 1997).

From this perspective, therefore, a secure attachment in infancy sets the stage for subsequent psychosocial achievements if the sensitive, supportive care initially contributing to attachment security is maintained (conversely, insensitive parenting contributes to insecure attachment, and to less optimal later functioning if it also endures over time). If, however, the harmony of the secure parent–child relationship changes and their mutually cooperative orientation is disrupted or lost, there may be no apparent sequelae of an initially secure attachment. The mediational role of continuing parent–offspring comity is particularly important in understanding the sequelae of infant attachment because of the frequency with which the security of attachment can change in the early years of life, owing to life transitions, family crises, and other normative and non-normative events (see Thompson, 1998, for a review of this research). It is important also because of the relatively simple social expectations that constitute the representational basis for a secure attachment in infancy. In some respects, the continuing harmony of the parent–child relationship may constitute the bridge between a secure attachment in infancy and more sophisticated later working models of the reliability of parental care, and of one's deservingness of love, if the harmony of that relationship is maintained over childhood.

The harmony of parent–child relationships may change over time, however. Change can occur as the result of normative developmental transitions, which include emergent capabilities of the child that impose new demands on parents and require that they acquire added skills as mentors, teachers, mediators, and disciplinarians. Parents also experience life changes, such as marital or work changes or the birth of additional children, that can alter their sensitive responsiveness to offspring. Consequently, parents who have found it easy to respond sensitively to a dependent baby may have greater difficulty with an autonomy-seeking toddler, partly because the qualities of parental care that engender security in an infant are different from those that maintain confidence in a toddler or preschooler, and partly because parents' lives change also. Because of the ways normative developmental changes in the lives of offspring and parents can alter their

relationship, it is perhaps unsurprising that conventional measures of parenting show limited stability over time and across situations (Holden & O'Dell, in press).

The dynamic changes in parent–child relationships that can occur over time are illustrated in a study by Teti, Sakin, Kucera, Corns, and Das Eisen (1996), who used the AQS to study attachment security in toddlers following the birth of a new sibling. They found that security in firstborn preschoolers decreased following the new birth, and that the children whose security scores dropped most dramatically had mothers with significantly higher scores on depression and anxiety. Social support to a mother from her partner also mediated the impact of a new birth on a preschooler's attachment, suggesting that the extent to which the interactional harmony of mother and child was altered by this event was influenced by her capacities to cope with the new birth. In more extreme circumstances, marital conflict between parents can significantly challenge young children's attachment security by altering parent–offspring relationships and the confidence the children derive from them, as suggested by the "emotional security hypothesis" of Cummings and Davies (1994; Davies & Cummings, 1994). Whether initially secure (or insecure) parent–child relationships remain that way over time depends, therefore, on the frequency and extent of family events that can disrupt early relational quality (see Waters, Merrick, Albersheim, & Treboux, 1995, and Zimmermann, Fremmer-Bombik, Spangler, & Grossmann, 1997, for illustrative longitudinal data).

When parent–child relationships change over time, it is unlikely that the security of parent–infant attachment will significantly predict later psychosocial functioning in children. This is illustrated in several recent longitudinal studies. Youngblade and Belsky (1992; see also Youngblade, Park, & Belsky, 1993) found that the security of attachment with mother (at 12 months) and with father (at 13 months) poorly predicted how an offspring interacted with a same-sex close friend at age 5. However, measures of the harmony of mother–child and father–child interaction at age 3 were significantly related to later peer interaction. Youngblade and her colleagues noted that the poor predictive power of infant attachment security was explained in part by the very weak relation between early attachment and parent–child harmony at age 3. In the absence of continuity in parent–child relationships, in other words, attachment did not predict later peer interaction. Other researchers have reported similar results. Erickson, Sroufe, and Egeland (1985; see also Egeland, Kalkoske, Gottesman, & Erickson, 1990) noted that when infant attachment security failed to predict behavior problems at ages 4½ to 5, it was often due to intervening changes in the quality of the parent–child relationship (see also Sroufe, Egeland, & Kreutzer, 1990).

When these findings are considered together, it is likely that one answer to the question of whether the security of attachment in infancy predicts later psychosocial functioning is that "it depends" on the subsequent quality of the parent–child relationship. To the extent that the mutually responsive orientation that initially led to attachment security is maintained, it is likely to foster the growth of independent competence, curiosity, self-esteem, and other positive subsequent achievements through a young child's heightened receptiveness to the caregiver's socialization influences and through the continuing support provided by responsive caregiving. If normative developmental changes or significant life transitions modify or disrupt this interpersonal orientation, however, there may be little apparent predictive relation between early attachment and later psychosocial characteristics. Instead, there may be a waning of the influence of early attachment as parent–child relationships become more complex and assume new qualities over time (Lamb, 1987; Lamb et al., 1985).

Multidetermined and Differentiated Outcomes

Another manner in which the prediction of the sequelae of infant attachment is mediated concerns the outcomes under consideration. In short, outcomes are diverse and multidetermined, making their relation to early attachment security complex and contingent.

As earlier noted, a broad variety of outcomes has been studied in relation to attachment security, ranging from variables measuring social competence to cognitive functioning to self-understanding to linguistic skill. But clearly attachment is not expected to foreshadow *every* important subsequent accomplishment in a child's life. On what basis, therefore, should researchers predict strong relations between attachment and subsequent behavior, and by contrast expect weaker or negligible relations with other behavioral domains? In what circumstances does attachment have a causal relation to later psychosocial characteristics, and in what circumstances is it associated noncausally with later functioning?

Attachment theorists have offered various perspectives on these questions, but generally have differentiated narrow versus broad portrayals of the sequelae of attachment (see, e.g., Belsky & Cassidy, 1994). In a narrow view, for example, a secure attachment should also foreshadow the child's later trust and confidence in the parent, and perhaps in other close partners. These outcomes have in common the challenges of relational intimacy with which attachment security is most directly concerned, and for which the strongest predictive relation to attachment may be expected. In a somewhat broader view, a secure attachment should also predict the child's sociability, understanding of others, and orientation toward others—that is, a wider network of relational dispositions applied to familiar and unfamiliar partners. Attachment security may be related to this broader range of outcomes, but more weakly and perhaps mediated by other influences. In a much broader view (such as the neo-Eriksonian organizational perspective), attachment security should foreshadow cognitive competence, exploratory skill, emotion regulation, communication style, and other outcomes through its general effects on the child's self-confidence, initiative, ego functioning, and other broader personality processes. This network of predictive relations extends attachment influences most broadly to features of emergent personality organization, and predictions are most speculative.

Other theorists have parsed the range of outcome domains somewhat differently. Bowlby (1969/1982) for example, believed that even in infancy, attachment is only one of several dimensions of the parent–child relationship. Parents are significant attachment figures, but they are important to young offspring also as play partners, in feeding, and in other activities that are guided by other behavioral systems. Based on this view, attachment security in infancy should be most directly associated with outcomes that are relevant to the maintenance of relational security in fearful or stressful contexts; thus a secure attachment should predict differences in dependency and self-reliance, emotion regulation, and interpersonal competence (see Weinfield, Sroufe, Egeland, & Carlson, Chapter 4, this volume). Other attachment theorists, emphasizing the representational features of attachment processes, have primarily explored the relations between attachment security and later self-concept, conceptions of friendship, and other features of social cognition. From this perspective, the central sequelae of attachment concern the transmission of beliefs, values, and understanding (e.g., Bretherton, Golby, & Cho, 1997).

Thus in regard to the relations between attachment and later behavior, the outcome domain is an important consideration, although attachment theorists differ about the outcomes most directly pertinent to attachment processes. Further clarification of the specific scope of the sequelae of infant attachment is perhaps the most important theoretical issue for attachment researchers, for several reasons. As noted by several commentators (e.g., Belsky & Cassidy, 1994; Sroufe, 1988), clarity in theoretical hypotheses of the sequelae of attachment in infancy ensures that issues of the discriminant validity of attachment patterns also receive attention. It may be as important to attachment theory to determine what a secure attachment does *not* predict, and why, as it is to understand its network of predictable consequences. Furthermore, attention to issues of discriminant validity also helps to ensure that attachment theory is not tested against predictive formulations that it should not and perhaps cannot embrace. In other words, in clarifying the scope of behavioral outcomes that are reasonably predicted by a secure infant attachment, theorists help to ensure that attachment theory is not tested against inappropriate or unwarranted extensions of the theory. Moreover, when clear expectations concerning the domain(s) of the expectable sequelae of attachment are formulated, unexpected relations between attachment and other outcome variables can be reexamined more incisively. If, for example, attachment security has an apparent but unanticipated relation to later sociolinguistic competence, this may be due to their joint relation to a common antecedent influence (such as parental sensitivity in early conversations about emotional themes) rather than to a direct link between the two. This reflects a noncausal longitudinal association between attachment and later behavior, not a causal relation, and this reformulation can then be more carefully examined in subsequent research.

Even when attachment security has a strong hypothesized causal association with a predicted outcome, it may not be readily apparent because outcomes are multidetermined. Although an insecure attachment in infancy and early childhood may contribute to behavior problems in preschool, for example, many other factors in a child's experience and social ecology may contribute to the same outcome. This makes longitudinal follow-up studies with single categorical predictors (such as attachment security) inherently low in predictive power. Indeed, in longer-term follow-up studies the initial effects of a secure or insecure attachment on later behavior may be superseded by other, more contemporary influences, contributing to a waning of its predictive power. Not surprisingly, therefore, some researchers have found that outcome prediction is boosted by the inclusion of other variables (such as early day care experience), some of which may interact with the influence of a secure or insecure attachment in predicting psychosocial outcomes (Egeland & Hiester, 1995; Vaughn, Deane, & Waters, 1985).

The multidetermination of behavioral outcomes predicted by attachment is especially provocative when multiple attachment relationships are considered in relation to each other. Clearly infants and young children develop emotionally salient attachments to multiple partners, which include mothers and fathers but also older relatives and day care teachers (see Howes, Chapter 29; Berlin & Cassidy, Chapter 30; and van IJzendoorn & Sagi, Chapter 31, this volume). In general, research on the impact of multiple attachments on later psychosocial outcomes has applied a hierarchy-of-relationships approach, in which the relative effects of secure attachments to mothers and fathers are compared. This research has generally concluded that maternal attachments have stronger predictive power for later psychosocial functioning than do paternal attachments, although secure attachment to *both* parents is optimal (Belsky, Garduque, & Hrncir, 1984; Easterbrooks & Goldberg, 1990; Main et al., 1985; Main & Weston, 1981; Suess, Grossmann, & Sroufe, 1992; see van IJzendoorn, Sagi, & Lambermon, 1992, for a review). But examining a hierarchy of attachment influences may be asking the wrong question, because different caregivers develop qualitatively different kinds of relationships, often in different circumstances or interactional contexts, with the children in their care. Instead, it may be more reasonable to expect that attachment relationships with different caregivers predict qualitatively different aspects of a child's behavioral functioning, depending on the salient interactional contexts characterizing their relationship.

This is provocatively illustrated in a study of Israeli children who were raised on traditional kibbutzim (Oppenheim, Sagi, & Lamb, 1988). Having assessed the security of the attachments of these children to their mothers, fathers, and *metaplot* (i.e., communal caregivers) in infancy, these researchers studied the same children again at ages 4½ to 5 on various measures of socio-emotional and personality functioning. Some-what surprisingly, there were no significant dif-ferences on these measures when children were compared who had been securely or insecurely attached to their mothers or their fathers in infan-cy. However, when children were compared on the basis of their earlier attachments to the *meta-plot,* a network of predicted relations was con-firmed that was consistent with theoretical expectations. These researchers concluded that because of the communal conditions of care they had experienced in infancy, the infant–*metaplot* attachments had been more salient to the growth of the particular socioemotional outcomes they studied (which were assessed, incidentally, in the child care setting). In a similar vein, Howes and her colleagues have found that peer interaction and play were predicted in preschoolers by the security of attachment to their day care teachers, but not to their mothers (Howes, Hamilton, & Matheson, 1994; Howes, Matheson, & Hamilton, 1994).

These considerations, taken as a whole, indi-cate that the theoretical relation between attach-ment in infancy and later psychological functioning is neither clear, simple, nor straightforward. Although some facets of attachment theory sug-gest a general association between attachment and later behavior, a more thoughtful assessment of attachment theory suggests that attachment se-curity is likely to have stronger (rather than weaker), causal (rather than noncausal), and di-rect (rather than mediated) relations with certain outcome domains (especially those concerned with relational intimacy) as compared with oth-ers. Empirically, moreover, the effects of attach-ment on hypothesized outcomes may be contin-gent on a variety of other influences, including other attachment relationships. These reflections suggest that new research strategies are needed to elucidate the complex associations between at-tachment and later sociopersonality characteris-tics—strategies that extend beyond simple an-tecedent–consequent longitudinal designs and include multiple assessments of attachment secu-rity, as well as of potential mediating influences over the period of study. At the same time, greater theoretical clarification of the outcome domains relevant to early attachment, and of the possible relationship specificity of early attach-ment relationship sequelae, is also needed.

EMPIRICAL PERSPECTIVES

Two decades of inquiry into the sequelae of early attachments yield this confident conclusion: Sometimes attachment in infancy predicts later psychosocial functioning, and sometimes it does not. Consistent with the theoretical formulations outlined earlier, the prediction of later outcomes is contingent on the outcome domain, on the time span between attachment and later behavior, on stability and change in caregiving influences, on the partner(s) included in the follow-up as-sessment, and on other factors. The following re-view is organized by different outcome domains, with special attention to mediating influences on developmental continuity, and to hypotheses for further study (see also Colin, 1996, and Thomp-son, 1998).

Parent–Child Relationship

The narrowest and strongest predictive relation between infant attachment and later psychologi-cal growth should concern the parent–child rela-tionship: A secure attachment in infancy may be expected to provide the basis for more positive subsequent parent–offspring interaction. This ex-pectation is confirmed in short-term follow-up assessments during the second year of life, when securely attached children show greater enthusi-asm, compliance, and positive affect (and less frustration and aggression) during shared tasks with their mothers (Frankel & Bates, 1990; Matas, Arend, & Sroufe, 1978; see also Bates, Maslin, & Frankel, 1985), as well as affective sharing (Waters, Wippman, & Sroufe, 1979, Study 1) and compliance during free play with their mothers (Londerville & Main, 1981; see also Main, 1983, and Main, Tomasini, & Tolan, 1979). Securely attached infants tend to main-tain more harmonious relations with parents in the second year.

It is likely that both infants and mothers con-tribute to their continuing relational harmony. This is indicated by the assessments of concur-rent maternal behavior in each study cited above (except Waters et al., 1979, which did not assess maternal behavior), showing that the mothers of securely attached children also acted consistently more supportively, sensitively, and helpfully to-ward their offspring in follow-up assessments than did the mothers of insecurely attached tod-dlers. Thus the more positive behavior of chil-dren could have resulted from the more positive initiatives of their caregivers. This is reflected also in a study by Slade (1987) examining the relations between attachment and the symbolic play of toddlers. As predicted, securely attached infants later showed longer and more complex episodes of symbolic play in the second year than did insecurely attached infants. Not surprisingly, their mothers also acted more supportively during the follow-up play assessments. However, group differences were most apparent in experimental contexts in which the mothers were allowed to contribute the most to the children's play activity: In these circumstances, securely attached toddlers showed significantly more advanced play than their insecurely attached counterparts. Slade's conclusion that "secure dyads 'work' better" together is consistent with the conclusions of research concerning the maintenance of parent–child harmony into the second year (p. 83).

However, the beneficial effects of attachment security in infancy for later parent–child harmony may wane over time. Researchers have not found enduring associations between a secure attachment in infancy and parent–child interaction at ages 2½ (in Japan; Takahashi, 1990), 3 (Youngblade & Belsky, 1992), and 5 (in the Netherlands; van IJzendoorn, van der Veer, & van Vliet-Visser, 1987). Grossmann and Grossmann (1991) found that follow-up assessments of parent–child and family interaction at ages 6 and 10 yielded a very mixed pattern of associations with infant attachment in a study in Germany. On the other hand, two research groups have used a 1-hour separation and reunion procedure to assess attachment security in 6-year-olds, and each has reported that more than 80% of their samples obtained the same attachment classifications with mothers in infancy and at age 6 (Main & Cassidy, 1988; Wartner, Grossmann, Fremmer-Bombik, & Suess, 1994).

The inconsistency in the results of these studies concerning long-term continuity in parent–child relationships mirrors the inconsistent findings of other studies concerning the stability of attachment classifications over time (see Thompson, 1998). Taken together, they suggest both considerable flexibility in the interactive harmony of parent–child relationships in the early years, and the possibility of consistency in these relationships under certain conditions (most likely involving stability in family circumstances and the capacity of family members to adjust to changing life demands when they occur; see Waters et al., 1995; Zimmerman et al., 1997; for a review, see Thompson, 1998). Consequently, although attachment security in infancy may reliably inaugurate short-term continuity in the harmony of parent–child relations, the evidence concerning long-term consistency is mixed, with continuity probably depending on important mediating conditions in the ecology of family life.

Other Close Relationships

A somewhat broader view of the sequelae of attachment security in infancy is that a secure attachment enables young children to enter more successfully into other intimate relationships at later ages. This is consistent both with Bowlby's formulations and with Freud's famous dictum concerning the mother–infant relationship. But the research evidence tends to be inconclusive. Teti and Ablard (1989) found that siblings who were each securely attached to their parents displayed more harmonious interaction than did insecurely attached dyads (see also Volling & Belsky, 1992). Parents, however, assume an obvious role in creating and maintaining sibling harmony, so it is unclear whether this reflects the effects of each child's attachment or the continuing influence of sensitive (or insensitive) parenting.

Children also develop close relationships with teachers and counselors. In an extensive longitudinal study of socioeconomically disadvantaged families in Minneapolis (see Weinfield et al., Chapter 4, this volume), preschoolers with secure attachment histories were less dependent on their teachers than were insecurely attached children (Sroufe, 1983; Sroufe, Fox, & Pancake, 1983). The same children were, at age 10, also found to be less dependent on their counselors at a summer camp than were children with insecure histories (Urban, Carlson, Egeland, & Sroufe, 1991).

There has been extensive inquiry into whether a secure attachment foreshadows more successful peer relationships and friendships in later years. There is evidence that securely attached infants socialize more competently and are more popular with well-acquainted peers as preschoolers (LaFreniere & Sroufe, 1985; Sroufe, 1983; Troy & Sroufe, 1987; Vandell, Owen, Wilson, & Henderson, 1988; Waters et al., 1979, Study 2). However, similar to the mixed research results concerning parent–child relationships, longer-term follow-up studies reveal weak or unexpected associations between attachment security and peer interactions at age 4 (Howes, Hamilton, & Matheson, 1994; Howes, Matheson, & Hamilton, 1994), interactions with close friends at age 5

(Youngblade & Belsky, 1992; Youngblade et al., 1993), self-reported loneliness at ages 5–7 (Berlin, Cassidy, & Belsky, 1995), and self-reported friendships at age 9 (Lewis & Feiring, 1989). On the other hand, both Elicker, Englund, and Sroufe (1992) and Grossmann and Grossmann (1991) have reported greater social competence and stronger friendships among 10-year-olds with secure attachment histories (see also Shulman, Elicker, & Sroufe, 1994; Sroufe, Carlson, & Shulman, 1993; Suess et al., 1992). In the Minneapolis project, children with secure attachment histories continued to exhibit greater peer competence through middle adolescence (see Weinfield et al., Chapter 4, this volume).

The design of these studies unfortunately does not permit an examination of reasons for these inconsistent findings: They could derive from the influence of intervening events on later friendships, changes (or continuity) in parent–child relationships, social-ecological stress or support, or other factors. It appears, however, that the benefits of a secure attachment in infancy for subsequent close relationships are apparent in short-term assessments, but less certain for longer-term follow-ups. The infant–mother relationship may constitute a prototype for later close relations at least for a few years, if not for a whole lifetime.

The short-term benefits of attachment security for close relationships are not limited to infancy. Wartner et al. (1994) used an attachment assessment involving an hour-long separation from the mother in the laboratory (based on Main & Cassidy, 1988), and found that securely attached 6-year-olds were more competent in their play and conflict resolution in preschool than were insecurely attached children. Using the same attachment assessment, Cohn (1990) found in a short-term follow-up that securely attached boys were better liked by teachers and peers than were insecurely attached boys (there were no effects for girls). Turner (1991) also noted sex differences in a contemporaneous study of attachment (using a similar separation–reunion procedure) and peer interaction in 4-year-olds, with insecurely attached boys exhibiting greater aggressive, assertive, controlling, and attention-seeking behavior than their securely attached counterparts, and insecurely attached girls showing greater compliance than insecurely attached boys. In the only research on predictive validity using the AQS, Kerns (1994) reported that friendship pairs composed of securely attached preschoolers (assessed via maternal reports at age 4) were, at age

5, more positive and well coordinated in their interactions than were pairs of insecurely attached children (see also Park & Waters, 1989, and Kerns, 1996). Kerns, Klepac, and Cole (1996) have also used a self-report Security Scale to assess grade school children's perceptions of security in their relationships with their mothers, and found in contemporaneous assessments that secure children were more accepted by peers, had more reciprocated friendships, and were less lonely than children who rated their relationships with their mothers as less secure. Although there are drawbacks to self-report measures of attachment security, this research provides a useful example of much-needed research on the correlates of attachment with older children.

Encounters with Unfamiliar Partners

A further extension of the possible network of the sequelae of attachment security in infancy concerns a child's initial encounters with unfamiliar partners, whether adults or peers. If a secure or insecure attachment instills expectations concerning the behavioral propensities of a caregiver, these expectations may be extended to unfamiliar partners and bias the child's first encounters with them (Thompson & Lamb, 1983). After all, if young children do not know what to expect from someone unfamiliar, it is not unreasonable for them to generalize the expectations they have derived from familiar caregivers.

There is evidence from contemporaneous assessments of attachment and stranger sociability that infants do indeed behave toward adult strangers in a manner that resembles their parent–directed behavior in the strange situation (Easterbrooks & Lamb, 1979; Lamb, Hwang, Frodi, & Frodi, 1982 [with fathers, not mothers]; Main & Weston, 1981; Thompson & Lamb, 1983; but see Sagi, Lamb, & Gardner, 1986). In predictive studies, securely attached infants have also been found to be more sociable with unfamiliar adults during the second or third year, although the evidence is not uniform (Londerville & Main, 1981; Lütkenhaus, Grossmann, & Grossmann, 1985; Main, 1983; Plunkett, Klein, & Meisels, 1988; but see Frodi, 1983, and Thompson & Lamb, 1983, for failures to find this association). A colleague and I (Thompson & Lamb, 1983) found that attachment was associated with stranger sociability contemporaneously but not predictively, because, we argued, of the high rates of change in attachment between earlier and later assessments. Thus infants may behave toward adult strangers in a way that draws on the social skills and predispositions currently fostered in their attachments to familiar caregivers, with prediction to later sociability dependent on the consistency of attachment over time.

The evidence concerning the advantages of securely attached infants in their initial encounters with unfamiliar peers is less consistent (Booth, Rose-Krasnor, & Rubin, 1991; Jacobson & Wille, 1986; Pastor, 1981; Takahashi, 1990; Vandell et al., 1988). This may derive from the fact that peers are less competent social partners, challenging the skills of even the most gregarious young child, and perhaps undermining the potential benefits that may derive from a secure attachment relationship to the mother.

It is important to note that because of the wariness that initial encounters with unfamiliar people can create, mothers were present during each of the stranger and peer sociability assessments of these studies. Because of this research design, the effects of a secure or insecure attachment on peer or adult sociability were confounded with the immediate support provided by the attachment figure; indeed, in each study in which concurrent maternal behavior was evaluated, the mothers of securely attached children were found to be more supportive and child-centered with their offspring than were the mothers of insecurely attached children. It is thus difficult to conclude confidently, without further research, that the security of attachment better equips infants in their initial encounters with unfamiliar people, independently of the immediate assistance of a sensitive, helpful caregiver.

Personality

The broadest range of hypothesized sequelae of a secure attachment in infancy consists of personality characteristics that are believed to derive from the trust and confidence engendered by the attachment relationship. Whether viewed in terms of formulations of the organizational perspective, Bowlby's theory of internal working models of self and relationships, or even ontogenetic adaptations, early attachment is believed to shape emergent personality processes that will be revealed in follow-up assessments. Within this general formulation, however, a wide variety of specific predictions concerning the personality sequelae of attachment security has been posed, and most of these predictions have been tested in only one study. For example, the Minneapolis longitudinal study of disadvantaged families found that infants with secure attachment histories were observed as preschoolers to be more empathic and were rated by their teachers as higher on self-esteem, emotional health, agency, compliance, and positive affect (Kestenbaum, Farber, & Sroufe, 1989; Sroufe, 1983; Sroufe et al., 1983; Sroufe & Egeland, 1991; Sroufe, Schork, Motti, Lawroski, & LaFreniere, 1984). In summer camp at age 10, secure children from this study were rated by counselors as higher in emotional health/self-esteem and self-confidence (Elicker et al., 1992), and in the most recent findings, measures of psychopathology in late adolescence were modestly but significantly predicted by infant attachment (see Weinfield et al., Chapter 4, this volume). However, Feiring and Lewis (1996) failed to find an association between infant attachment (using a modified strange situation) and adolescent psychopathology, and no other research has been designed to replicate the impressive findings of the Minneapolis research. Consequently, this review focuses on two personality variables that have been most often studied in follow-up research.

The two personality variables that have been of greatest interest to attachment researchers are ego resiliency and behavioral problems in the preschool years, and each has yielded a fairly perplexing array of research results. Arend, Gove, and Sroufe (1979) reported, for example, that securely attached toddlers received significantly higher scores on Q-sort and behavioral measures of ego resiliency in a follow-up assessment at age 5½. Sroufe (1983) reported a similar difference for the preschool follow-up assessment of a subsample of children from the Minneapolis study, as did Grossmann and Grossmann (1991) for their German sample at age 5. However, the association between attachment and ego resilience has not been replicated by other researchers (Easterbrooks & Goldberg, 1990; Howes, Hamilton, & Matheson, 1994; Howes, Matheson, & Hamilton, 1994; Oppenheim et al., 1988; van IJzendoorn et al., 1987, 1992).

Extending the formulations of attachment theory to clinical concerns, some attachment theorists have hypothesized that infants with insecure attachments should be more prone to the development of behavior problems in later years. However, several studies using behavioral inventories and observations in follow-up assessments throughout the preschool years have failed to discern a straightforward association between attachment and later problematic behavior (Bates & Bayles, 1988; Bates et al., 1985; Erickson et al., 1985; Fagot & Kavanagh, 1990; Lewis, Feiring, McGuffog, & Jaskir, 1984; Lyons-Ruth, Alpern, & Repacholi, 1993). In some studies (e.g., Erickson et al., 1985; Lewis et al., 1984; Lyons-Ruth et al., 1993), the association between attachment and later behavior problems was mediated by intervening experiences for a child, such as those involving environmental stress, difficulty in the parent–child relationship, or other factors. In other research, predictable sex differences in the association between attachment and later problematic behavior were apparent (Renken, Egeland, Marvinney, Mangelsdorf, & Sroufe, 1989). As a consequence, the authors of one report in this literature cautioned against drawing clinical implications from early attachment classifications (Fagot & Kavanagh, 1990).

In general, therefore, it is hard to find reliable, consistent personality sequelae of a secure or insecure attachment in infancy, largely because so few hypothesized correlates have been replicated in more than one sample. But even when multiple investigators have examined predicted personality sequelae, studies have yielded inconsistent results, perhaps because these personality characteristics are multiply influenced throughout development. As earlier noted, many factors are likely to affect the growth of characteristics in a young child, including those that contribute to the development of behavior problems or ego resiliency in the preschool years. This makes studies that rely on any single predictor (such as attachment security) inherently weak in predictive power, especially when the predictor is a categorical variable and when outcome variables are often measured in diverse ways. Since a secure attachment in infancy is also likely to interact, both contemporaneously and subsequently, with other factors that influence personality development (such as relationships formed with day care or elementary school teachers, peer relationships, or social support provided by a grandparent or other partner), the prediction of complex personality sequelae is likely to require multivariate longitudinal analyses. Some of the research reviewed in this chapter exemplifies such an approach to studying the sequelae of early attachment, but much more is needed.

Representations of Self, Others, and Relationships

Inspired by contemporary interest in the social-representational features of attachment relationships, researchers have recently devoted consid-

erable attention to how a secure or insecure attachment history influences a child's developing conceptions of self, other people, and relational processes. Such an effort is important for several reasons. First, it enables theoretical linkages between attachment and other developing capabilities of the young child, including the growth of theory of mind, event representation, autobiographical memory, conscience, self-concept, and emotional understanding (see Kochanska & Thompson, 1997; Oppenheim & Waters, 1995; Thompson, 1998). Attachment researchers can draw on considerable empirical work on these topics in their efforts to understand the role of attachment security in their development. Second, research on the social-representational features of attachment relationships may clarify the empirical picture of the sequelae of attachment outlined above, especially if these representations are found to mediate the behavioral outcomes of a secure or insecure attachment. For example, if individual differences in friendship conceptions are associated with attachment security, this may help to clarify the inconsistent empirical relations between infant attachment and friendship formation in later years; it may also lead to more incisive future empirical strategies. Third, systematic empirical work on the representational dimensions of attachment can help to clarify the meaning and developmental significance of Bowlby's concept of working models, which has been criticized for undue vagueness and generality in its use by attachment researchers (Hinde, 1988; Rutter, 1995). At present, however, a rather limited range of social-representational correlates of attachment security has been examined. The following review is thus a promissory note for potential advances to come.

How is attachment security associated with developing self-concept? In a study of contemporaneous associations with a measure of attachment in 6-year-olds (based on Main & Cassidy, 1988), Cassidy (1988) found that securely attached children described themselves in generally positive terms but were capable of admitting that they were imperfect. By contrast, insecurely attached children either revealed a more negative self-image or resisted admitting flaws (see also Verschueren, Marcoen, & Schoefs, 1996). Further study of the associations between attachment security and children's emerging self-image is needed, especially because of its relevance to Bowlby's views of the importance of attachment processes to developing working models of self. Cassidy's research is also noteworthy for assessing attachment and self-image contemporaneously at an age when the latter is becoming differentiated in young children and increasingly important to them; it thus offers a good model for further study.

Another recent investigation explored the relations between attachment in infancy and later information processing of emotional issues. Belsky, Spritz, and Crnic (1996) predicted that children with secure attachment histories would be less distractible during positive than during negative events, and would thus remember positive events more accurately than negative events. They expected that the reverse would be true for insecurely attached children. In a study in which 3-year-olds' delayed recognition memory for positive and negative events during a previously viewed puppet show was assessed, these expectations were confirmed. Children deemed securely attached in infancy remembered positive events more accurately than negative events, although there were no differences on attentional measures. The findings of this study are potentially important—and thus deserve follow-up study—because of their broader relevance to Bowlby's concern for the differential retention in memory of personal events, based on working models derived from attachment security.

Because of these findings, we (Laible & Thompson, 1998) explored further the contemporaneous associations between attachment security and emotional understanding in preschoolers. We expected that owing to the more open communication shared with their caregivers, securely attached children would be more advanced in emotion identification and role-taking tasks than would insecure children. But we also studied preschoolers' differential understanding of positive and negative emotions. We found that children deemed to be securely attached (based on the AQS) obtained higher scores on two assessments of emotional understanding, but that this was due primarily to secure children's greater competence in understanding negative emotion. The security of attachment fostered, we reasoned, greater understanding (rather than avoidance) of negative emotions and their consequences.

In three studies, Cassidy, Kirsh, Scolton, and Parke (1996) examined the relations between attachment and children's representations of peer relationships. Infant attachment classifications were not strongly predictive of preschoolers' responses to story questions concerning negative peer events with ambiguous intent, contrary to the expectations that securely attached children would be more likely to attribute benign motives to the story characters and insecure children to infer hostile intent. However, in contemporaneous assessments of attachment (using Main & Cassidy's [1988] procedure) and the same story questions, securely attached kindergartners and first-graders responded as predicted, and these representations of peer relationships were found to mediate individual differences in peer sociometric status. The latter finding is particularly important, because this is the first study to confirm expected associations among attachment, social representations, and social behavior in young children.

Taken together, these studies indicate that there is considerable value to exploring the representational features of attachment further, using age-appropriate measures of attachment and social representation. In addition to the benefits of doing so that are outlined above, such research explores catalysts to individual differences in representations of self, others, and relationships in the postinfancy years, when such conceptions truly flourish. In addition, it is noteworthy that some of the strongest associations between attachment and social representation have thus far emerged in contemporaneous assessments. Such an assessment strategy could well be emulated by future investigators examining other variables—such as emotion self-regulation (see Cassidy, 1994, and Thompson, 1994) and exploratory competence (see Cassidy & Berlin, 1994)—that emerge developmentally in the postinfancy years.

Other Sequelae

In general, there have been few associations between attachment classifications and contemporaneous or subsequent measures of intelligence (e.g., Egeland & Farber, 1984; Elicker et al., 1992; Jacobson & Wille, 1986; Pastor, 1981; Slade, 1987; Waters et al., 1979; but see Main, 1983, and Londerville & Main, 1981, for differences in developmental quotient in one sample). This is an instance of discriminant validity confirmed by the empirical literature, because, as Sroufe (1983) has noted, infants should be capable of benefiting from a secure attachment relationship independently of variations in intellectual functioning within the normal range.

Securely attached infants have been found to be more sophisticated in aspects of their play behavior, particularly symbolic play (Londerville

& Main, 1981; Main, 1983; Matas et al., 1978; Slade, 1987; but see Jacobson & Wille, 1986). However, these differences have been observed in the context of maternal involvement, in which differences in the support provided by the mothers of securely and insecurely attached children have also been noted. Thus it is difficult to conclude unequivocally that the security of attachment is associated with play competence independently of immediate maternal support (although see Belsky et al., 1984, for group differences in elicited play outside of immediate maternal support).

Schneider-Rosen and Cicchetti (1984) reported that securely attached toddlers were more advanced in visual self-recognition than insecurely attached toddlers, in contemporaneous assessments with a sample that included children who had been maltreated. However, this association was not replicated in a predictive study by Lewis, Brooks-Gunn, and Jaskir (1985), who studied attachment at 12 months and visual self-recognition several months later (see also Pipp, Easterbrooks, & Harmon, 1992).

THE LESSONS OF EARLY RELATIONSHIPS

The belief that the child foreshadows the adult that is to be is so deeply rooted in Western philosophy and North American psychology that recent voices questioning the formative significance of infancy (e.g., Fogel, 1993; Lewis, 1997; Scarr, 1992) are disconcerting. Yet these discordant voices force a reconsideration of the reasons for expecting continuity of individual differences from infancy to later life; the conditions fostering such continuity (and, conversely, discontinuity and change in individual characteristics); and the broader relation between rapid developmental change and consistency of individual attributes in the early years. Attachment research is often guided by a general expectation that a secure attachment in infancy predicts good psychosocial outcomes in later years. But as noted above, considerably greater theoretical precision is essential to guide future research into the outcomes of attachment security; such precision will ensure that attachment theory is not evaluated against predictive expectations that it cannot endorse, as well as permit more incisive interpretation of research results. This level of theoretical precision does not currently exist, with the result that the many findings surveyed in this chapter

reflect the variety of "minitheories" of attachment and its outcomes that have proliferated during the past 25 years under the broad heuristic umbrella of Bowlby's provocative but general formulations (Belsky & Cassidy, 1994).

What can we conclude from this network of empirical results? At the outset, it is apparent that the strength of the relation between infant security and later sociopersonality functioning is modest (Belsky & Cassidy, 1994; Lamb et al., 1985). To be sure, problems of measurement error that are inherent in research on early psychosocial development, together with the fact that nonsignificant trends in research data are often in the predicted direction, suggest that the empirical landscape may underestimate the extent to which the predictions of attachment theory hold true in early development. Moreover, one of the most thoughtfully designed, intensive longitudinal studies in Minneapolis concerned with the outcomes of attachment security has yielded impressively strong findings for the predictive validity of early attachment (see Weinfield et al., Chapter 4, this volume). However, even when the outcome domains that are most directly pertinent to attachment formulations are considered, current research yields few reliable, long-term consequences of attachment security in infancy that would justify the classic theoretical portrayals of mother–infant attachment as a prototype of later love relationships, or the current formulations of attachment as a foundation for later adaptation.

Instead, the outcomes of attachment security appear to be more contingent and provisional than earlier expected. The most reliable outcome of a secure attachment in infancy is a more harmonious parent–child relationship in the immediate years to come. This relationship benefits from the greater cooperation and responsiveness of both securely attached children and their mothers, and is thus in this sense a dyadic outcome. Such a relationship, if it is maintained, heightens the young child's receptiveness to the caregiver's socialization incentives in many aspects of early sociopersonality development, including conscience, emotion self-regulation, and behavioral competence and self-control. A secure attachment in infancy also provides short-term advantages for the creation and maintenance of other close relationships (such as friendships), although it is unclear whether this is due to social expectations, social skills, maternal support, or other correlates of a secure attachment.

These conclusions are consistent with the view

that attachment security instills competence with the challenges of relational intimacy, especially in the parent–child relationship, although these benefits are not necessarily long-lasting. Research examining the longer-term consequences of attachment for close relationships yield a strikingly mixed picture, suggesting that intervening events (including changes in attachment security, family circumstances, social stress, and/or the growth of normative developmental capabilities) can alter the expected outcomes of attachment in infancy. Both consistency and change in psychosocial sequelae are consistent with Bowlby's (1969/1982) portrayal of the plasticity of attachment processes in early childhood prior to the consolidation of internal representations of attachment in later years. But these conclusions suggest that the strongest correlates of early attachment will be found in contemporaneous or short-term longitudinal studies focused on competence in close relationships, and that further study of the processes underlying change in early attachments and their sequelae is warranted (see Belsky, Campbell, Cohn, & Moore, 1996, for an example).

By contrast, there is less support for the view that early attachment shapes emergent personality processes or broader adaptive strategies. No reliable personality correlates of attachment security have been discerned, and the provocative findings of the Minneapolis project remain to be replicated. This may be unsurprising, both for theoretical and for empirical reasons. The variety of influences on early sociopersonality growth, and the multidetermination of complex characteristics such as ego resiliency together suggest that attachment security may have rather limited predictive power for broad personality attributes. Moreover, relational influences on early personality development include multiple attachments—attachments experienced not only at home (with fathers as well as mothers), but also elsewhere (e.g., at day care)—contributing to a more complex predictive equation. There is considerable value in understanding the origins of differences in ego functioning and behavioral problems in young children, but greater reflection on the role of attachment processes in their emergence is needed.

Attachment researchers have recently devoted considerable attention to the representational features of attachment security, and these also present considerable conceptual and empirical challenges. Although the "move to the level of representation" (Main et al., 1985) in attachment

thinking has been heuristically powerful for researchers, basic questions must still be addressed concerning developmental changes in internal working models, relational influences on event representation, and empirical methods for studying early social representation, to ensure that "working models" do not become a catchall explanation within attachment research (Hinde, 1988; Rutter, 1985). Although nascent representations of relational partners are apparent in infancy, it may not be until childhood that these representations assume sufficient scope and sophistication to provide the basis for more sustained beliefs concerning self, others, and relationships. In the meantime, continuing harmony in the parent–child relationship may provide a bridge between the simple social expectations of the infant and the more fully developed representations of the older preschooler. For this reason, and because social representations are themselves developing processes, a secure attachment may have a stronger *contemporaneous* than a *predictive* relation to emergent self-understanding, friendship conceptions, and emotional understanding in childhood, and the limited empirical evidence seems to support this view. Future researchers should explore these developing social representations in relation to the other cognitive accomplishments of early childhood, much as Bowlby originally sought to do in formulating attachment theory.

As a whole, therefore, the empirical landscape is both challenging and hopeful for attachment theory. Although research findings undermine straightforward expectations that a secure attachment in infancy foreshadows diverse long-term benefits for children, such predictions may not have been theoretically warranted anyway. Instead, the research underscores the need for the following: greater clarity in theoretical predictions of the outcome domains most pertinent to attachment security, attention to diverse mediating influences, consideration of whether contemporaneous rather than long-term predictive associations should be expected, and reflection on the developing conceptual capabilities of the young child. These constitute a formidable empirical as well as conceptual challenge for the future.

One additional challenge awaits attachment researchers. As Bowlby (1969/1982) noted, attachment is only one of several dimensions of the parent–child relationship. Even in infancy, parents are important in feeding, in play, and in other ways that complement but extend beyond the attachment relationship they share with off-spring. Their influence extends far beyond the security they provide in difficult or stressful contexts. Although attachment theorists have reasonably had little to say about the relations between attachment security in the early years and other features of the parent–child relationship that are emerging at the same time, there may be value in integrating attachment formulations into a broader view of parent–offspring relations in infancy and beyond.

There are in fact many lessons to be learned within early relationships (Thompson, 1996). Several are encompassed within attachment theory. Early relational experience with caregivers provides provisional lessons that answer the question "What do others do when I am upset?" These lessons instill a sense of security, or insecure uncertainty, when young children are distressed, fearful, or anxious. Similarly, the lessons yielded by provisional answers to the question "What happens when I venture to explore?" are central to the attachment–exploration balance that derives from the caregiver's functioning as a secure base. Other lessons of early relationships are less directly tied to attachment concerns. Parents may figure prominently in how young children begin to answer the question "What can I accomplish?" as the children seek to comprehend the extent of personal agency and efficacy. But a parent is influential less as a secure base and more as a mentor (in a Vygotskian sense) in shared experience. In this respect, the attachment relationship is less central to this lesson than are other dimensions of the parent–child relationship, even though this lesson is also relevant to self-image, dependency, exploratory competence, and other sequelae of attachment.

Another lesson of early relationships is "What must I do to maintain good relations with others?" This reflects the emergence, late in the first year, of reciprocal obligations in the parent–child relationship. As noted by Campos, Kermoian, and Zumbahlen (1992) and Biringen, Emde, Campos, and Appelbaum (1995), the growth of self-produced locomotion late in the first year changes the parent–child relationship. Young offspring become more assertive and goal-oriented, and parents more actively monitor their children's activity; they increasingly use prohibitions and sanctions to protect and control their offspring, and they expect compliance. Positive affectional exchanges increase between a parent and child (reflecting the growth of attachment), but so also do clashes of will (Campos et al.,

1992). At the same time that attachment security is taking shape, therefore, parent–child interaction is also being forged by the negotiation of behavioral expectations and shared experiences affording potential conflict. There is every reason to believe that the latter are important to psychological development: As Vygotskian theory predicts, considerable growth in social understanding and self-awareness results from the conflict of expectation and intention between younger and older social partners.

The psychosocial characteristics that have been studied as the outcome of attachment security are probably affected, therefore, by other emerging features of the parent–child relationship that are focused not on warmth and harmony, but on issues of personal agency and conflict and its resolution. Recognizing that early relationships are multi-influential, an important challenge for future attachment researchers is to consider the place of attachment within the broader context of the developing parent–child relationship.

ACKNOWLEDGMENTS

I am grateful for many helpful comments on an earlier version of this chapter from Jay Belsky, Jude Cassidy, Phil Shaver, and Brian Vaughn.

REFERENCES

Ainsworth, M. D. S. (1967). *Infancy in Uganda: Infant care and the growth of love.* Baltimore: Johns Hopkins University Press.

Ainsworth, M. D. S. (1973). The development of infant–mother attachment. In B. Caldwell & H. Ricciuti (Eds.), *Review of child development research* (Vol. 3, pp. 1–94). Chicago: University of Chicago Press.

Ainsworth, M. D. S., Blehar, M. C., Waters, E., & Wall, S. (1978). *Patterns of attachment.* Hillsdale, NJ: Erlbaum.

Arend, R., Gove, F. L., & Sroufe, L. A. (1979). Continuity of individual adaptation from infancy to kindergarten: A predictive study of ego-resiliency and curiosity in preschoolers. *Child Development, 50,* 950–959.

Baldwin, M. W. (1992). Relational schemas and the processing of social information. *Psychological Bulletin, 112,* 461–484.

Bates, J. E., & Bayles, K. (1988). Attachment and the development of behavior problems. In J. Belsky & T. Nezworski (Eds.), *Clinical implications of attachment* (pp. 253–299). Hillsdale, NJ: Erlbaum.

Bates, J. E., Maslin, C. A., & Frankel, K. A. (1985). Attachment security, mother–child interaction, and temperament as predictors of behavior-problem ratings at age three years. In I. Bretherton & E. Waters (Eds.), Growing points of attachment theory and research. *Monographs of the So-*

ciety for Research in Child Development, 50(1–2, Serial No. 209), 167–193.

Belsky, J., Campbell, S. B., Cohn, J. F., & Moore, G. (1996). Instability of infant–parent attachment security. *Developmental Psychology, 32,* 921–924.

Belsky, J., & Cassidy, J. (1994). Attachment: Theory and evidence. In M. Rutter & D. Hay (Eds.), *Development through life* (pp. 373–402). Oxford: Blackwell.

Belsky, J., Garduque, L., & Hrncir, E. (1984). Assessing performance, competence, and executive capacity in infant play: Relations to home environment and security of attachment. *Developmental Psychology, 20,* 406–417.

Belsky, J., Spritz, B., & Crnic, K. (1996). Infant attachment security and affective–cognitive information processing at age 3. *Psychological Science, 7,* 111–114.

Belsky, J., Steinberg, L., & Draper, P. (1991). Childhood experience, interpersonal development, and reproductive strategy: An evolutionary theory of socialization. *Child Development, 62,* 647–670.

Berlin, L. J., Cassidy, J., & Belsky, J. (1995). Loneliness in young children and infant–mother attachment: A longitudinal study. *Merrill–Palmer Quarterly, 41,* 91–103.

Biringen, Z., Emde, R. N., Campos, J. J., & Appelbaum, M. I. (1995). Affective reorganization in the infant, the mother, and the dyad: The role of upright locomotion and its timing. *Child Development, 66,* 499–514.

Booth, C. L., Rose-Krasnor, L., & Rubin, K. H. (1991). Relating preschoolers' social competence and their mothers' parenting behaviors to early attachment security and high-risk status. *Journal of Social and Personal Relationships, 8,* 363–382.

Bowlby, J. (1969/1982). *Attachment and loss: Vol. 1. Attachment.* New York: Basic Books.

Bowlby, J. (1973). *Attachment and loss: Vol. 2. Separation: Anxiety and anger.* New York: Basic Books.

Bowlby, J. (1980). *Attachment and loss: Vol. 3. Loss: Sadness and depression.* New York: Basic Books.

Bowlby, J. (1988). *A secure base: Parent–child attachment and healthy human development.* New York: Basic Books.

Bretherton, I. (1991). Pouring new wine into old bottles: The social self as internal working model. In M. R. Gunnar & L. A. Sroufe (Eds.), *Minnesota Symposia on Child Psychology: Vol. 23. Self processes in development* (pp. 1–41). Hillsdale, NJ: Erlbaum.

Bretherton, I. (1993). From dialogue to internal working models: The co-construction of self in relationships. In C. A. Nelson (Ed.), *Minnesota Symposia on Child Psychology: Vol. 26. Memory and affect in development* (pp. 237–263). Hillsdale, NJ: Erlbaum.

Bretherton, I., Golby, B., & Cho, E. (1997). Attachment and the transmission of values. In J. Grusec & L. Kuczynski (Eds.), *Parenting and children's internalization of values: A handbook of contemporary theory* (pp. 103–134). New York: Wiley.

Campos, J. J., Kermoian, R., & Zumbahlen, M. R. (1992). Socioemotional transformations in the family system following infant crawling onset. In N. Eisenberg & R. A. Fabes (Eds.), *Emotion and its regulation in early development* (pp. 25–40). San Francisco: Jossey-Bass.

Cassidy, J. (1988). Child–mother attachment and the self in six-year-olds. *Child Development, 59,* 121–134.

Cassidy, J. (1994). Emotion regulation: Influences of attachment relationships. In N. A. Fox (Ed.), The development of emotion regulation: Biological and behavioral considerations. *Monographs of the Society for Research in Child Development, 59*(2–3, Serial No. 240), 228–249.

Cassidy, J., & Berlin, L. J. (1994). The insecure/ambivalent pattern of attachment: Theory and research. *Child Development, 65,* 971–991.

Cassidy, J., Kirsh, S. J., Scolton, K. L., & Parke, R. D. (1996). Attachment and representations of peer relationships. *Developmental Psychology, 32,* 892–904.

Chisholm, J. S. (1996). The evolutionary ecology of attachment organization. *Human Nature, 1,* 1–37.

Cicchetti, D. (1990). The organization and coherence of socioemotional, cognitive, and representational development: Illustrations through a developmental psychopathology perspective on Down syndrome and child maltreatment. In R. A. Thompson (Ed.), *Nebraska Symposium on Motivation: Vol 36. Socioemotional development* (pp. 259–366). Lincoln: University of Nebraska Press.

Clutton-Brock, T. J. (1991). *The evolution of parental care.* Princeton, NJ: Princeton University Press.

Cohn, D. A. (1990). Child–mother attachment of 6-year-olds and social competence at school. *Child Development, 61,* 152–162.

Colin, V. L. (1996). *Human attachment.* New York: McGraw-Hill.

Crittenden, P. M. (1990). Internal representational models of attachment relationships. *Infant Mental Health Journal, 11,* 259–277.

Crittenden, P. M. (1994). Peering into the black box: An exploratory treatise on the development of self in young children. In D. Cicchetti & S. L. Toth (Eds.), *Rochester Symposium on Developmental Psychopathology: Vol. 5. Disorders and dysfunctions of the self* (pp. 79–148). Rochester, NY: University of Rochester Press.

Cummings, E. M., & Davies, P. T. (1994). *Children and marital conflict.* New York: Guilford Press.

Davies, P. T., & Cummings, E. M. (1994). Marital conflict and child adjustment: An emotional security hypothesis. *Psychological Bulletin, 116,* 387–411.

Easterbrooks, M. A., & Goldberg, W. A. (1990). Security of toddler–parent attachment: Relation to children's socio-personality functioning during kindergarten. In M. T. Greenberg, D. Cicchetti, & E. M. Cummings (Eds.), *Attachment in the preschool years* (pp. 221–244). Chicago: University of Chicago Press.

Easterbrooks, M. A., & Lamb, M. E. (1979). The relationship between quality of infant–mother attachment and infant competence in initial encounters with peers. *Child Development, 50,* 380–387.

Egeland, B., & Farber, E. A. (1984). Infant–mother attachment: Factors related to its development and changes over time. *Child Development, 55,* 753–771.

Egeland, B., & Hiester, M. (1995). The long-term consequences of infant day-care and mother–infant attachment. *Child Development, 66,* 474–485.

Egeland, B., Kalkoske, M., Gottesman, N., & Erickson, M. F. (1990). Preschool behavior problems: Stability and factors accounting for change. *Journal of Child Psychology and Psychiatry, 31,* 891–909.

Elicker, J., Englund, M., & Sroufe, L. A. (1992). Predicting peer competence and peer relationships in childhood from early parent–child relationships. In R. D. Parke & G. W. Ladd (Eds.), *Family–peer relationships: Modes of linkage* (pp. 77–106). Hillsdale, NJ: Erlbaum.

Erickson, M. F., Sroufe, L. A., & Egeland, B. (1985). The relationship between quality of attachment and behavior problems in preschool in a high-risk sample. In I. Bretherton & E. Waters (Eds.), Growing points of attachment theory and research. *Monographs of the Society for Research in Child Development, 50*(1–2, Serial No. 209), 147–166.

Fagot, B. I., & Kavanagh, K. (1990). The prediction of anti-social behavior from avoidant attachment classifications. *Child Development, 61,* 864–873.

Feiring, C., & Lewis, M. (1996). Finality in the eye of the beholder: Multiple sources, multiple time points, multiple paths. *Development and Psychopathology, 8,* 721–733.

Fivush, R. (1994). Constructing narrative, emotion, and self in parent–child conversations about the past. In U. Neisser & R. Fivush (Eds.), *The remembering self: Construction and accuracy in the self-narrative* (pp. 136–157). Cambridge, England: Cambridge University Press.

Fogel, A. (1993). *Developing through relationships.* Chicago: University of Chicago Press.

Frankel, K. A., & Bates, J. E. (1990). Mother–toddler problem solving: Antecedents in attachment, home behavior, and temperament. *Child Development, 61,* 810–819.

Frodi, A. (1983). Attachment behavior and sociability with strangers in premature and full-term infants. *Infant Mental Health Journal, 4,* 13–22.

Freud, S. (1963). *An outline of psychoanalysis* (J. Strachey, Trans.). New York: Norton. (Original work published 1940)

Grossmann, K. E., & Grossmann, K. (1991). Attachment quality as an organizer of emotional and behavioral responses in a longitudinal perspective. In C. M. Parkes, J. Stevenson-Hinde, & P. Marris (Eds.), *Attachment across the life cycle* (pp. 93–114). London: Routledge.

Hinde, R. A. (1982). Attachment: Some conceptual and biological issues. In J. Stevenson-Hinde & C. M. Parkes (Eds.), *The place of attachment in human behavior* (pp. 60–76). New York: Basic Books.

Hinde, R. A. (1988). Continuities and discontinuities: Conceptual issues and methodological considerations. In M. Rutter (Ed.), *Studies of psychosocial risk: The power of longitudinal data* (pp. 367–383). Cambridge, England: Cambridge University Press.

Holden, G. W., & O'Dell, P. C. (in press). Just how stable is parental behavior?: Meta-analysis and reformulation. *Psychological Bulletin.*

Howes, C., Hamilton, C. E., & Matheson, C. C. (1994). Children's relationships with peers: Differential associations with aspects of the teacher–child relationship. *Child Development, 65,* 253–263.

Howes, C., Matheson, C. C., & Hamilton, C. E. (1994). Maternal, teacher, and child care history correlates of children's relationships with peers. *Child Development, 65,* 264–273.

Hudson, J. A. (1993). Understanding events: The development of script knowledge. In M. Bennett (Ed.), *The child as psychologist: An introduction to the development of social cognition* (pp. 142–167). New York: Harvester Wheatsheaf.

Jacobson, J. L., & Wille, D. E. (1986). The influence of attachment pattern on developmental changes in peer interaction from the toddler to the preschool period. *Child Development, 57,* 338–347.

Kerns, K. A. (1994). A longitudinal examination of links between mother–child attachment and children's friendships in early childhood. *Journal of Social and Personal Relationships, 11,* 379–381.

Kerns, K. A. (1996). Individual differences in friendship quality: Links to child–mother attachment. In W. M. Bukowski, A. F. Newcomb, & W. W. Hartup (Eds.), *The company they keep: Friendship in childhood and adolescence* (pp. 137–157). Cambridge, England: Cambridge University Press.

Kerns, K. A., Klepac, L., & Cole, A. (1996). Peer relationships and preadolescents' perceptions of security in the child–mother relationship. *Developmental Psychology, 32,* 457–466.

Kestenbaum, R., Farber, E. A., & Sroufe, L. A. (1989). Individual differences in empathy among preschoolers: Relation to attachment history. In N. Eisenberg (Ed.), *Empathy and related emotional responses* (pp. 51–64). San Francisco: Jossey-Bass.

Kochanska, G. (1995). Children's temperament, mothers' discipline, and security of attachment: Multiple pathways to emerging internalization. *Child Development, 66,* 597–615.

Kochanska, G., & Thompson, R. A. (1997). Precursors of moral transmission. In J. E. Grusec & L. Kuczynski (Eds.), *Parenting and children's internalization of values: A handbook of contemporary theory* (pp. 53–77). New York: Wiley.

LaFreniere, P. J., & Sroufe, L. A. (1985). Profiles of peer competence in the preschool: Interrelations between measures, influence of social ecology, and relation to attachment history. *Developmental Psychology, 21,* 56–69.

Laible, D. J., & Thompson, R. A. (1998). Attachment and emotional understanding in preschool children. *Developmental Psychology, 34,* 1038–1045.

Lamb, M. E. (1987). Predictive implications of individual differences in attachment. *Journal of Consulting and Clinical Psychology, 55,* 817–824.

Lamb, M. E., Hwang, C. P., Frodi, A., & Frodi, M. (1982). Security of mother– and father–infant attachment and its relation to sociability with strangers in traditional and non-traditional Swedish families. *Infant Behavior and Development, 5,* 355–367.

Lamb, M. E., Thompson, R. A., Gardner, W., & Charnov, E. L. (1985). *Infant–mother attachment: The origins and developmental significance of individual differences in Strange Situation behavior.* Hillsdale, NJ: Erlbaum.

Lewis, M. (1997). *Altering fate: Why the past does not predict the future.* New York: Guilford Press.

Lewis, M., Brooks-Gunn, J., & Jaskir, J. (1985). Individual differences in visual self-recognition as a function of the mother–infant attachment relationship. *Developmental Psychology, 21,* 1181–1187.

Lewis, M., & Feiring, C. (1989). Early predictors of childhood friendship. In T. J. Berndt & G. W. Ladd (Eds.), *Peer relationships in child development* (pp. 246–273). New York: Wiley.

Lewis, M., Feiring, C., McGuffog, C., & Jaskir, J. (1984). Predicting psychopathology in six-year-olds from early social relations. *Child Development, 55,* 123–136.

Londerville, S., & Main, M. (1981). Security of attachment, compliance, and maternal training methods in the second year of life. *Developmental Psychology, 17,* 289–299.

Lütkenhaus, P., Grossmann, K. E., & Grossmann, K. (1985). Infant–mother attachment at twelve months and style of interaction with a stranger at the age of three years. *Child Development, 56,* 1538–1542.

Lyons-Ruth, K., Alpern, L., & Repacholi, B. (1993). Disorganized infant attachment classification and maternal psychosocial problems as predictors of hostile–aggressive behavior in the preschool classroom. *Child Development, 64,* 572–585.

Maccoby, E. E. (1983). Let's not overattribute to the attribution process: Comments on social cognition and behavior. In E. T. Higgins, D. N. Ruble, & W. W. Hartup (Eds.), *Social cognition and social development* (pp. 356–370). Cambridge, England: Cambridge University Press.

Maccoby, E. E. (1984). Socialization and developmental change. *Child Development, 55,* 317–328.

Main, M. (1983). Exploration, play, and cognitive functioning related to infant–mother attachment. *Infant Behavior and Development, 6,* 167–174.

Main, M. (1991). Metacognitive knowledge, metacognitive monitoring, and singular (coherent) versus multiple (incoherent) models of attachment: Findings and directions for future research. In C. M. Parkes, J. Stevenson-Hinde, & P. Marris (Eds.), *Attachment across the life cycle* (pp. 127–159). London: Routledge.

Main, M., & Cassidy, J. (1988). Categories of response to reunion with the parent at age 6: Predictable from infant attachment classifications and stable over a 1-month period. *Developmental Psychology, 24,* 415–426.

Main, M., Kaplan, N., & Cassidy, J. (1985). Security in infancy, childhood, and adulthood: A move to the level of representation. In I. Bretherton & E. Waters (Eds.), *Growing points of attachment theory and research. Monographs of the Society for Research in Child Development, 50*(1–2, Serial no. 209), 66–104.

Main, M., Tomasini, L., & Tolan, W. (1979). Differences among mothers of infants judged to differ in security. *Developmental Psychology, 15,* 472–473.

Main, M. B., & Weston, D. R. (1981). The quality of the toddler's relationship to mother and to father: Related to conflict behavior and the readiness to establish new relationships. *Child Development, 52,* 932–940.

Matas, L., Arend, R. A., & Sroufe, L. A. (1978). Continuity of adaptation in the second year: The relationship between quality of attachment and later competence. *Child Development, 49,* 547–556.

Moffitt, T. E., Caspi, A., Belsky, J., & Silva, P. A. (1992). Childhood experience and the onset of menarche: A test of the sociobiological model. *Child Development, 63,* 47–58.

Nelson, K. (Ed.). (1989). *Narratives from the crib.* Cambridge, MA: Harvard University Press.

Nelson, K. (1993). The psychological and social origins of autobiographical memory. *Psychological Science, 4,* 7–14.

Oppenheim, D., Sagi, A., & Lamb, M. E. (1988). Infant–adult attachments on the kibbutz and their relation to socioemotional development 4 years later. *Developmental Psychology, 24,* 427–433.

Oppenheim, D., & Waters, H. A. (1995). Narrative processes and attachment representations: Issues of development and assessment. In E. Waters, B. E. Vaughn, G. Posada, & K. Kondo-Ikemura (Eds.), Caregiving, cultural, and cognitive perspectives on secure-base behavior and working models: New growing points of attachment theory and research. *Monographs of the Society for Research in Child Development, 60*(2–3, Serial No. 244), 197–215.

Park, K. A., & Waters, E. (1989). Security of attachment and preschool friendships. *Child Development, 60,* 1076–1081.

Pastor, D. L. (1981). The quality of mother–infant attachment and its relationship to toddlers' initial sociability with peers. *Developmental Psychology, 17,* 326–335.

Pipp, S., Easterbrooks, M. A., & Harmon, R. J. (1992). The relation between attachment and knowledge of self and mother in one- to three-year-old infants. *Child Development, 63,* 738–750.

Plunkett, J. W., Klein, T., & Meisels, S. J. (1988). The relationship of preterm infant–mother attachment to stranger sociability at 3 years. *Infant Behavior and Development, 11,* 83–96.

Renken, B., Egeland, B., Marvinney, D., Mangelsdorf, S., & Sroufe, L. A. (1989). Early childhood antecedents of aggression and passive-withdrawal in early elementary school. *Journal of Personality, 57,* 257–281.

Rutter, M. (1995). Clinical implications of attachment concepts: Retrospect and prospect. *Journal of Child Psychology and Psychiatry, 36,* 549–571.

Sagi, A., Lamb, M. E., & Gardner, W. (1986). Relations between Strange Situation behavior and stranger sociability among infants on Israeli kibbutzim. *Infant Behavior and Development, 9,* 271–282.

Scarr, S. (1992). Developmental theories for the 1990s: Development and individual differences. *Child Development, 63,* 1–19.

Schneider-Rosen, K., & Cicchetti, D. (1984). The relationship between affect and cognition in maltreated infants: Quality of attachment and the development of visual self-recognition. *Child Development, 55,* 648–658.

Shulman, S., Elicker, J., & Sroufe, L. A. (1994). Stages of friendship growth in preadolescence as related to attachment history. *Journal of Social and Personal Relationships, 11,* 341–361.

Slade, A. (1987). Quality of attachment and early symbolic play. *Developmental Psychology, 23,* 78–85.

Sroufe, L. A. (1979). The coherence of individual development: Early care, attachment, and subsequent developmental issues. *American Psychologist, 34,* 834–841.

Sroufe, L. A. (1983). Infant–caregiver attachment and patterns of adaptation in preschool: The roots of maladaptation and competence. In M. Perlmutter (Ed.), *Minnesota Symposia on Child Psychology: Vol. 16. Development and policy concerning children with special needs* (pp. 41–83). Hillsdale, NJ: Erlbaum.

Sroufe, L. A. (1988). The role of infant–caregiver attachment in development. In J. Belsky & T. Nezworski (Eds.), *Clinical implications of attachment* (pp. 18–38). Hillsdale, NJ: Erlbaum.

Sroufe, L. A. (1990). An organizational perspective on the self. In D. Cicchetti & M. Beeghly (Eds.), *The self in transition: Infancy to childhood* (pp. 281–307). Chicago: University of Chicago Press.

Sroufe, L. A. (1996). *Emotional development.* Cambridge, England: Cambridge University Press.

Sroufe, L. A., Carlson, E., & Shulman, S. (1993). Individuals in relationships: Development from infancy through adolescence. In D. C. Funder, R. D. Parke, C. Tomlinson-Keasey, & K. Widaman (Eds.), *Studying lives through time: Personality and development* (pp. 315–342). Washington, DC: American Psychological Association.

Sroufe, L. A., & Egeland, B. (1991). Illustrations of person–environment interaction from a longitudinal study. In T. D. Wachs & R. Plomin (Eds.), *Conceptualization and measurement of organism–environment interaction* (pp. 68–84). Washington, DC: American Psychological Association.

Sroufe, L. A., Egeland, B., & Kreutzer, T. (1990). The fate of early experience following developmental change: Longitudinal approaches to individual adaptation in childhood. *Child Development, 61,* 1363–1373.

Sroufe, L. A., & Fleeson, J. (1986). Attachment and the construction of relationships. In W. W. Hartup & Z. Rubin (Eds.), *Relationships and development* (pp. 51–71). Hillsdale, NJ: Erlbaum.

Sroufe, L. A., & Fleeson, J. (1988). The coherence of family relationships. In R. A. Hinde & J. Stevenson-Hinde (Eds.), *Relationships within families* (pp. 27–47). Oxford: Clarendon Press.

Sroufe, L. A., Fox, N. E., & Pancake, V. R. (1983). Attachment and dependency in developmental perspective. *Child Development, 54,* 1615–1627.

Sroufe, L. A., Schork, E., Motti, E., Lawroski, N., & LaFreniere, P. (1984). The role of affect in emerging social competence. In C. Izard, J. Kagan, & R. Zajonc (Eds.), *Emotion, cognition, and behavior* (pp. 289–319). New York: Cambridge University Press.

Suess, G. J., Grossmann, K. E., & Sroufe, L. A. (1992). Effects of infant attachment to mother and father on quality of adaptation in preschool: From dyadic to individual organization of self. *International Journal of Behavioral Development, 15,* 43–65.

Takahashi, K. (1990). Are the key assumptions of the "Strange Situation" procedure universal?: A view from Japanese research. *Human Development, 33,* 23–30.

Teti, D. M., & Ablard, K. E. (1989). Security of attachment and infant–sibling relationships: A laboratory study. *Child Development, 60,* 1519–1528.

Teti, D. M., Sakin, J., Kucera, E., Corns, K. M., & Das Eisen, R. (1996). And baby makes four: Predictors of attachment security among preschool-aged firstborns during the transition to siblinghood. *Child Development, 67,* 579–596.

Thompson, R. A. (1994). Emotion regulation: A theme in search of definition. In N. A. Fox (Ed.), The development of emotion regulation: Biological and behavioral considerations. *Monographs of the Society for Research in Child Development, 59*(2–3, Serial No. 240), 25–52.

Thompson, R. A. (1996, October). *The lessons of early relationships.* Kendon Smith Lecture, University of North Carolina–Greensboro.

Thompson, R. A. (1998). Early sociopersonality development. In W. Damon (Series Ed.) & N. Eisenberg (Vol. Ed.), *Handbook of child psychology: Vol. 3. Social, emotional, and personality development* (5th ed., pp. 25–104), New York: Wiley.

Thompson, R. A., & Lamb, M. E. (1983). Security of attachment and stranger sociability in infancy. *Developmental Psychology, 19,* 184–191.

Troy, M., & Sroufe, L. A. (1987). Victimization among preschoolers: Role of attachment relationship history. *Journal of the American Academy of Child and Adolescent Psychiatry, 26,* 166–172.

Turner, P. J. (1991). Relations between attachment, gender, and behavior with peers in preschool. *Child Development, 62,* 1475–1488.

Urban, J., Carlson, E., Egeland, B., & Sroufe, L. A. (1991). Patterns of individual adaptation across childhood. *Development and Psychopathology, 3,* 445–460.

Vandell, D. L., Owen, M. T., Wilson, K. S., & Henderson, V. K. (1988). Social development in infant twins: Peer and mother–child relationships. *Child Development, 59,* 168–177.

van IJzendoorn, M. H., Sagi, A., & Lambermon, M. W. E. (1992). The multiple caretaker paradox: Data from Holland and Israel. In R. C. Pianta (Ed.), *New directions for child development: No. 57. Beyond the parent: The role of other adults in children's lives* (pp. 5–24). San Francisco: Jossey-Bass.

van IJzendoorn, M. H., van der Veer, R., & van Vliet-Visser, S. (1987). Attachment three years later: Relationships between quality of mother–infant attachment and emotional/cognitive development in kindergarten. In L. W. C. Tavecchio & M. H. van IJzendoorn (Eds.), *Attachment*

in social networks (pp. 185–224). Amsterdam: Elsevier.

Vaughn, B. E., Deane, K. E., & Waters, E. (1985). The impact of out-of-home care on child–mother attachment quality: Another look at some enduring questions. In I. Bretherton & E. Waters (Eds.), Growing points of attachment theory and research. *Monographs of the Society for Research in Child Development, 50*(1–2, Serial No. 209), 110–135.

Verschueren, K., Marcoen, A., & Schoefs, V. (1996). The internal working model of the self, attachment, and competence in five-year-olds. *Child Development, 67,* 2493–2511.

Volling, B. L., & Belsky, J. (1992). The contribution of mother–child and father–child relationships to the quality of sibling interaction: A longitudinal study. *Child Development, 63,* 1209–1222.

Wartner, U. G., Grossmann, K., Fremmer-Bombik, E., & Suess, G. (1994). Attachment patterns at age six in south Germany: Predictability from infancy and implications for preschool behavior. *Child Development, 65,* 1014–1027.

Waters, E., & Deane, K. E. (1985). Defining and assessing individual differences in attachment relationships: Q-methodology and the organization of behavior in infancy and early childhood. In I. Bretherton & E. Waters (Eds.), Growing points of attachment theory and research. *Monographs of the Society for Research in Child Development, 50*(1–2, Serial No. 209), 41–65.

Waters, E., Kondo-Ikemura, K., Posada, G., & Richters, J. E. (1991). Learning to love: Mechanisms and milestones. In M. R. Gunnar & L. A. Sroufe (Eds.), *Minnesota Symposia on Child Psychology: Vol. 23. Self processes and development* (pp. 217–255). Hillsdale, NJ: Erlbaum.

Waters, E., Merrick, S. K., Albersheim, L., & Treboux, D. (1995, April). From the Strange Situation to the Adult Attachment Interview: A 20-year longitudinal study of attachment security in infancy and early adulthood. In J. A. Crowell & E. Waters (Chairs), *Is the parent–child relationship a prototype of later love relationships?: Studies of attachment and working models of attachment.* Symposium conducted at the biennial meeting of the Society for Research in Child Development, Indianapolis, IN.

Waters, E., Wippman, J., & Sroufe, L. A. (1979). Attachment, positive affect, and competence in the peer group: Two studies in construct validation. *Child Development, 50,* 821–829.

Welch-Ross, M. K. (1995). An integrative model of the development of autobiographical memory. *Developmental Review, 15,* 338–365.

Wellman, H. M. (1990). *The child's theory of mind.* Cambridge, MA: MIT Press.

Youngblade, L. M., & Belsky, J. (1992). Parent–child antecedents of 5-year-olds' close friendships: A longitudinal analysis. *Developmental Psychology, 28,* 700–713.

Youngblade, L. M., Park, K. A., & Belsky, J. (1993). Measurement of young children's close friendship: A comparison of two independent assessment systems and their associations with attachment security. *International Journal of Behavioral Development, 16,* 563–587.

Zimmermann, P., Fremmer-Bombik, E., Spangler, G., & Grossmann, K. E. (1997). Attachment in adolescence: A longitudinal perspective. In W. Koops, J. B. Hoeksma, & D. C. van den Boom (Eds.), *Development of interaction and attachment: Traditional and non-traditional approaches* (pp. 281–292). Amsterdam: North-Holland.

14

The Measurement of Attachment Security in Infancy and Childhood

❖

JUDITH SOLOMON
CAROL GEORGE

In this chapter we examine the methods of assessing attachment security in infancy and early childhood, at both the level of behavior and the level of representation. Our first goal is to provide the reader with an overview and summary of available measures, including new or lesser-known measures, along with information about their psychometric properties and the ways in which they have been used in research. Our second goal is to evaluate the current state of measurement in the field of attachment. How well do the available instruments and protocols actually reflect the construct of attachment security? How useful are these measures for testing core predictions in attachment theory?

This chapter can be used in several ways. Some readers, especially those new to research in this area, can use this chapter as a source of information to help select measures appropriate to their research. For readers who are familiar with childhood attachment assessment and well grounded in attachment theory, this may be their first opportunity to examine all of the measures together. This kind of overview is important for understanding the development of the field and providing a sense of new directions and opportunities for theory and research.

THE DOMAIN OF ATTACHMENT SECURITY

"Attachment security" is defined by Ainsworth, Blehar, Waters, and Wall (1978) as the state of being secure or untroubled about the availability of the attachment figure. As a construct, security can never be directly observed, but must be inferred from that which is observable. Furthermore, a construct is "evidenced in a variety of forms of behavior and not perfectly so in any one of them" (Nunnally, 1978, p. 84). How, then, do we determine whether a particular measure of attachment security is a "good" or valid measure of this construct?[1]

In practice, psychologists typically follow a three-step process. First, they operationalize the construct, either intuitively or with respect to theory or prior research. Second, they establish the basic reliability of the measure, asking themselves, "Can it be replicated over time [short-term stability of scores or categories], and, to the extent that the measure is tester-derived and thus requires some judgment, can scores, codes, and so forth, be agreed upon?" Finally, they evaluate how well the measure predicts (in the broadest sense) other theoretically important variables

287

(convergent validity) or is uncorrelated with the-oretically unrelated variables (discriminant valid-ity) (Campbell & Fiske, 1959).

Although this approach is well accepted, Nun-nally (1978) has pointed out that it is based upon an inherent circularity in logic. We predict a rela-tion between constructs, we "find" it using mea-sures of the constructs at hand, and we thereby infer that our measures are valid. Optimally, con-struct validation requires three somewhat differ-ent steps (Cronbach & Meehl, 1955; Nunnally, 1978): (1) The domain of relevant indices or variables ("observables") must be specified, indi-cating which variables are indicative of security and which are not; (2) the intercorrelations among multiple concurrent measures of the con-struct must be ascertained; and (3) each measure must be cross-validated with respect to a network of other theoretically important constructs that have been similarly validated. Rather than being sequential, these three steps constitute a reflec-tive process, in which knowledge gained from one step transforms our understanding of the oth-ers.

For attachment researchers, the domain of "observables," at least for infancy and toddler-hood (12 to 20 months), is currently drawn from Bowlby's (1969/1982, 1973, 1980) ethological attachment theory. "Attachment behaviors" are those that increase proximity to or maintain con-tact with a particular attachment figure. They are understood to be organized with respect to an in-ternal system of control (the attachment system) that has the adaptive function of protection and the set goal of physical proximity or felt security (Sroufe, 1979). A critical feature of this model, with important implications for measurement, must be emphasized: The type of attachment be-havior observed depends upon the degree to which the attachment system is activated. When a young child is alarmed, he or she can be ex-pected to signal clearly for proximity to and con-tact with the attachment figure (crying, ap-proaching, reaching, clinging). Once these are achieved, and in the absence of further distur-bance, the child can be expected to accept some distance from the attachment figure and return to exploration. Attachment behavior under condi-tions of low activation, often referred to as "se-cure-base behavior," can be difficult to distin-guish from friendly, affiliative behavior and can be very much influenced by features of the exter-nal environment (e.g., how far away the child can wander, how visible the mother is) (Carr, Dabbs, & Carr, 1975; Rheingold & Eckerman, 1970).

Ainsworth et al. (1978) have argued that this basic pattern (a shift from exploration to attach-ment behaviors and back) will appear disturbed or distorted to the extent that the infant perceives the attachment figure to be inaccessible or unre-sponsive. Thus, Ainsworth's classic measure of attachments in infancy (the strange situation), and the more recent Waters and Deane Attach-ment Q-Sort measure (AQS; Waters, 1987, 1995; Waters & Deane, 1985), which are described more fully later, focus on deviations from this basic pattern as a measure of insecurity in in-fant–parent attachment.

Attachment theory is less specific regarding appropriate measures of security in the third and fourth years of life and beyond. The attachment system is believed to function throughout this pe-riod, and indeed throughout the lifespan, but with diminishing sensitivity. Fewer situations are per-ceived as threatening, and knowledge of the par-ent's accessibility (rather than actual proximity or contact) is increasingly effective in terminat-ing attachment behavior. In addition, the broader and more flexible behavioral repertoire of the older child, as well as the child's capacity to com-prehend cognitively and therefore to anticipate and coordinate with the parent's behavior, can make it more difficult for scientific observers to perceive the underlying organization of attach-ment behavior. At the same time, the achieve-ment of language and symbolic operations dur-ing this period begins to make it feasible to assess attachment security at the representational level.

CORE THEORETICAL PREDICTIONS

Whether one is following Nunnally's model of optimal construct validation or the commonly ac-cepted but more approximate procedures of most investigators, the predictive (retrodictive, concur-rent, predictive) validity of a measure is a funda-mental concern. There are probably as many the-oretically interesting relations among constructs in the field of attachment as there are researchers to propose them. Attachment theory as articulat-ed by Bowlby and Ainsworth, however, provides certain key predictions regarding the relation be-tween security and other variables that are core to the theory itself. The validity of any particular measure of security should be assessed at a mini-mum with respect to these. Acknowledging that there may be some dispute in the boundary areas, we propose the following core predictions:

1. *Attachment security should be positively related to the caregiver's accessibility and responsiveness to the child.* This prediction is implicit in the definition of security itself—that is, the state of being untroubled (confident) that the attachment figure will be available and will permit proximity and contact to the extent needed. An important corollary to this prediction is that attachment security with one caregiver should be independent of security with the other, insofar as the sensitivity of the two caregivers can be shown to differ. This follows from the definition of attachment security as a reflection of a particular relationship (Ainsworth et al., 1978; Hinde, 1982) and not (entirely) a property of the child (i.e., not a function of temperament or some other quality).

2. *Attachment security in a particular caregiver–child relationship should tend to remain stable over time.* Although Bowlby (1973, 1980) was well aware of destabilizing influences on infant–caregiver attachment (e.g., repeated separation, life stress) and avoided adherence to a doctrine of critical periods, he proposed that the quality of attachment should tend to remain increasingly stable and resistant to change as a function of mutual adaptation in interaction patterns and in each party's expectations about the other and the relationship. Sroufe and Waters (1977) emphasized the organizational quality of attachment; that is, although particular attachment behaviors may show little stability (due to the situation or the child's development), the underlying quality or organization of the relationship should be expected to remain stable.

3. *Attachment security should predict other important aspects of development.* Related to the notion of continuity, but distinct from it, is the general hypothesis argued by Bowlby (1973) and elaborated both theoretically and empirically by Sroufe (1979) that attachment security should predict other key aspects of development. Bowlby emphasized the effects of insecurity arising from separation and loss on the development of psychopathology. In contrast, Sroufe articulated the more normative construct of "coherence" in development; that is, successes or failures in one developmental task (such as attachment in infancy) should predispose the child (and the caregiver–child dyad) to success or failure in subsequent developmental tasks (e.g., autonomy, social competence). Sroufe's notion, though perhaps less central to attachment theory proper, parallels in many respects Erikson's (1950) classic formulation of developmental stages and has captured the attention of many researchers. It is important to note that it implies prediction to constructs other than attachment security, either concurrently or from one developmental period to another. In contrast, continuity implies prediction from an attachment security measure at one time to the same or a different measure of attachment security at another. Demonstration of *coherence* across time does not necessarily establish *continuity* in the attachment relationship.

4. *Attachment security can be assessed using similar or parallel measures cross-culturally and across attachment figures.* In the first two volumes of his *Attachment and Loss* trilogy, Bowlby (1969/1982, 1973, 1980) painstakingly built a case for the species-specific and therefore universal nature of attachment behavior in the young child. To the degree that a measure is based upon ethological attachment theory, it should function similarly across cultures; that is, it should be as effective in describing the range of attachment relationships found in one culture (society, ethnic group, social class) as it is in any other. In addition, it should be expected to be correlated in similar ways to measures of other theoretically important constructs, particularly to caregiver behavior. By virtue of the same reasoning, the effectiveness of security measures and the pattern of correlations to caregiver behavior should be similar for all attachment figures (e.g., mother, father, other caregivers).

ORGANIZATION OF THIS CHAPTER

For the period of infancy through early childhood (ages 12 to approximately 72 months), measures of attachment security are based on observation of behavior of one type or another. These measures can be further divided according to whether they focus on the organization of attachment behavior directed toward the caregiver or on the child's linguistic or play behavior (representational measures of attachment). Although the field of attachment has its theoretical origins in Bowlby's ethological theory of attachment, its empirical origins and the foundation of almost all subsequent efforts at assessment lie in the classification approach to attachment relationships pioneered by Ainsworth et al. (1978). This system of multidimensional categories of relationship, assessed on the basis of the infant's behavior in a laboratory separation and reunion context, has been both intuitively and theoretically compelling. The majority of measures for the period beyond early toddlerhood have been designed deliberately to capture these same or similar qualitative differences in child–caregiver attachment at both the behavioral and representational levels. A second strand of development is represented by Waters's (1995) AQS method, which is designed to permit observers (either trained observers or caregivers) to describe infant or child attachment behavior in the home. We begin by describing Ainsworth's classification system and a recent modification of it (specifically, the inclusion of the disorganized/disoriented category). This is followed by a description and discussion of classification systems for reunion behavior and mental representation of preschool and kindergarten-age children, and then by information on the AQS approach. Each section includes a brief discussion of unresolved issues in the construct validation of the measure(s) in question. We conclude with a general discussion of measurement in the field.[2]

ATTACHMENT CLASSIFICATION IN INFANCY: THE STRANGE SITUATION

Attachment classification is based on the behavior of the young toddler (12 to 20 months of age) in the strange situation. This is a laboratory procedure that was designed to capture the balance of attachment and exploratory behavior under conditions of increasing though moderate stress (Ainsworth et al., 1978). Full directions for running the session and for classification are presented in Ainsworth et al. (1978). An outline of the episodes that make up the strange situation is shown in Table 14.1. Ainsworth's system provides instructions for classifying the infant's attachment relationship into one of three main groups: a "secure" group (B) and two "insecure" groups, "avoidant" (A) and "resistant" or "ambivalent" (C). Table 14.2 provides a brief description of classification criteria. Instructions are also available for designating eight subgroups, but the subgroups are rarely examined separately (due to limited sample sizes) and are not considered further here. Classification is based on the infant's behavior toward the caregiver during the two reunion episodes, viewed in the context of behavior in the preceding and intervening episodes and in response to the caregiver's current behavior. The infant's behavior during reunions can also be rated with respect to four scales of infant–caregiver interactive behavior

that are used in the process of classification: proximity seeking, contact seeking, avoidance, and resistance to contact and interaction.

About 15% of attachments in normative samples and much higher percentages in high-risk samples are difficult to classify using the original A-B-C criteria (see Main & Solomon, 1986, 1990, for a complete discussion). Main and Solomon described the range of behaviors found in such unclassifiable infants, and developed guidelines for classification of most of these insecure infants into a fourth classification group termed "disorganized/disoriented" (D). Infants classified into Group D show a diverse set of behaviors that are characterized by a lack of observable goal, purpose, or explanation in the immediate situation, and, at a higher level of explanation, suggest that the child lacks a coherent attachment strategy with respect to the parent. (Further information about this category can be found in Lyons-Ruth & Jacobvitz, Chapter 23, this volume.)

Validation of the Measure

Beginning with Ainsworth's seminal work, validation of the infant classification system has been an ongoing priority. Many chapters in this volume summarize this progress, and the reader is referred to pertinent chapters throughout this section. In what follows, we briefly summarize the literature with respect to the construct validity criteria established earlier.

Reliability

Intercoder Agreement. The Ainsworth system and the other classification measures that we describe elsewhere in this chapter require extensive training. Some systems require certification or proof that the researcher can meet a minimum reliability standard. This is a departure from measures commonly used in psychology, and some further explanation may be helpful. Unlike event coding, which involves tallies of relevant, precisely defined acts, the classification process requires matching a particular case to a multidimensional, categorical template or prototype. Manuals for classification are composed mainly of written descriptions of these templates. These written descriptions cannot capture, however, the range and nuance of behavior and context that determine placement in a particular group. Only in training, where a student can see many cases

TABLE 14.1. Episodes of the Strange Situation

Episode	Duration	Description
1	1 minute	*Parent, infant*: Dyad introduced to room.
2	3 minutes	*Parent, infant*: Infant settles in, explores. Parent assists only if necessary.
3	3 minutes	*Parent, infant, stranger*: Introduction of a stranger. Stranger plays with infant during final minute.
4	3 minutes	*Infant, stranger*: Parent leaves infant with stranger. *First separation.*
5	3 minutes	*Parent, infant*: Parent returns. Stranger leaves quietly. *First reunion.*
6	3 minutes	*Infant*: Parent leaves infant alone in room. *Second separation.*
7	3 minutes	*Infant, stranger*: Stranger enters room and stays with infant, interacting as necessary.
8	3 minutes	*Parent, infant*: Parent returns. Stranger leaves quietly. *Second reunion.*

of a particular type, can the student develop the expertise that will permit evaluation of new cases in terms of their fit to a particular attachment category.

Within-laboratory agreement for trained coders tends to be very high, ranging from 100% in the original Ainsworth and Bell study (Ainsworth et al., 1978) to 85–95% for researchers who were trained by Ainsworth or her students (e.g., Main & Weston, 1981; Waters, 1979). In the one published study that examined the important question of interlaboratory agreement on A-B-C classification, five expert coders and Ainsworth independently coded all or a subset of 37 cases (videotapes), several of which were chosen because of the classification difficulties

TABLE 14.2. Strange Situation Classification Groups

Group	Brief description
Secure (B) (Ainsworth et al., 1978)	Uses mother as secure base for exploration. Separation: Signs of missing parent, especially during the second separation. Reunion: Actively greets parent with smile, vocalization, or gesture. If upset, signals or seeks contact with parent. Once comforted, returns to exploration.
Avoidant (A) (Ainsworth et al., 1978)	Explores readily, little display of affect or secure-base behavior. Separation: Responds minimally, little visible distress when left alone. Reunion: Looks away from, actively avoids parent; often focuses on toys. If picked up, may stiffen, lean away. Seeks distance from parent, often interested instead in toys.
Ambivalent or resistant (C) (Ainsworth et al., 1978)	Visibly distressed upon entering room, often fretful or passive; fails to engage in exploration. Separation: Unsettled, distressed. Reunion: May alternate bids for contact with signs of angry rejection, tantrums; or may appear passive or too upset to signal, make contact. Fails to find comfort in parent.
Disorganized/disoriented (D) (Main & Solomon, 1990)	Behavior appears to lack observable goal, intention, or explanation—for example, contradictory sequences or simultaneous behavioral displays; incomplete, interrupted movement; stereotypies; freezing/stilling; direct indications of fear/apprehension of parent; confusion, disorientation. Most characteristic is lack of a coherent attachment strategy, despite the fact that the baby may reveal the underlying patterns of organized attachment (A, B, C).

Note. Descriptions in Groups A, B, and C are based on Ainsworth et al. (1978). Descriptions in Group D are based on Main and Solomon (1990).

that they presented (Carlson & Sroufe, 1993). Agreement percentages ranged from 50% to 100%, with the highest agreement (86%) found between Ainsworth and others. The fact that not all coders were trained to identify the disorganized/disoriented group may have influenced average reliability. The overall level of agreement is reassuring, especially considering the difficulty of the cases. The wide range of intercoder agreement, however, leaves room to question what level would have been achieved with a more diverse and less experienced group of coders. In studies that made use of coders trained to identify the disorganized/disoriented group, across- and within-laboratory agreement ranged from 80% to 88% (Carlson, in press; Carlson, Cicchetti, Barnett, & Braunwald, 1989; Lyons-Ruth, Repacholi, McLeod, & Silva, 1991).[3]

Short-Term Stability. Issues surrounding the short- and long-term stability of classifications are discussed thoroughly by Grossmann, Grossmann, and Zimmerman (Chapter 33, this volume). We note briefly here that classification stability is generally high (from 50% to 96%) when laboratory assessments are spaced 2 to 6 months apart or longer. The highest stability levels are generally found in middle-class samples, and the lowest in disadvantaged ones (Connell, 1976, cited in Waters, 1982; Lyons-Ruth et al., 1991; Main & Weston, 1981; Vondra, Hommerding, & Shaw, 1996; Waters, 1979; see Belsky, Campbell, Cohn, & Moore, 1996, and Thompson, Lamb, & Estes, 1981, for lower reliability estimates in middle-class samples). Stability of the D attachment classification over the course of the second year of life may be lower than that of the standard A-B-C classifications (Lyons-Ruth et al., 1991: 86%; Main & Weston, 1981: 50%; Vondra et al., 1996: 68%). Lyons-Ruth et al. and Vondra et al. reported an increase in numbers of disorganized/disoriented infants between 12 and 18 months. In a meta-analysis of nine samples ($n = 840$), however, in which the time-lag between assessments ranged from 2 to 60 months, van IJzendoorn, Schuengel, and Bakersman-Kranenberg (in press) estimate stability of the D classification to be strong ($r = .34$). Repeated assessments of the strange situation over the very short term (i.e., 2 to 4 weeks) result in much lower stability, presumably reflecting sensitization of infants to the separation procedure (Ainsworth et al., 1978). Thus, where research designs require repeated testing, researchers should avoid close spacing of assessments.

Relation to Other Measures of Security

One of the most compelling aspects of Ainsworth's original work was in the exceptional effort she and her colleagues made to validate the classification groups with respect to infant behavior toward the mother in the home. Home observation data for the original sample of 23 babies was based on detailed narrative records of monthly visits over the course of the first year of life. Drawing on this work, Ainsworth was able to develop a rich and complex portrait of each relationship. (See Weinfield, Sroufe, Egeland, & Carlson, Chapter 4, this volume.) Well-known findings from the study link classification in the strange situation to a set of variables reflecting the frequency and quality of infant attachment behavior in the home. Attachment classifications have also been assessed against home-based measures of attachment security—both a category system developed by Ainsworth and the AQS, which yields a summary security score reflecting the quality of an infant's secure-base behavior in the home. Broadly speaking, the results using all three approaches have been consistent: Secure versus insecure laboratory attachment classifications were related to different patterns of infant behavior in the home in ways predicted by theory. The two main insecure groups (A and C), however, were generally less well discriminated from each other in the home (Ainsworth et al., 1978; Vaughn & Waters, 1990). In addition, several studies using the AQS method have failed to find any relation between AQS security scores and attachment classification. (See the later section on the AQS.)

Prediction to Core Variables

Mother–Child Interaction. Ainsworth's original home observations established key differences among mothers of secure, avoidant, and ambivalent infants with respect to four highly intercorrelated variables: sensitivity (defined as prompt and appropriate responsiveness to the infant's signals), acceptance (vs. rejection), cooperation, and psychological accessibility. Mothers of secure infants were high on all four dimensions; mothers of avoidant infants provided the infants with little positive experience with physical proximity and were rejecting; and mothers of ambivalent infants were inconsistent or unresponsive to infant distress and other signals. These findings have been replicated in several studies in both naturalistic and structured situations, although the strength of the associations has been weaker in the replications. In a recent meta-analysis, DeWolff and van IJzendoorn (1997) concluded that parental sensitivity, although clearly important, does not appear to be the exclusive factor in the development of secure attachment. Given the centrality of the sensitivity construct in contemporary attachment theory, this is a radical notion. It should be noted that failure to replicate Ainsworth's original findings may reflect various kinds of measurement error—for example, reliance on more limited sampling of mother–child interaction (e.g., Pederson & Moran, 1995) and shifts in the operational definition of sensitivity away from Ainsworth's original emphasis on appraisal of signals and appropriate responding toward an emphasis on warmth, acceptance, and support (Seifer & Schiller, 1995).

The identification of the disorganized/disoriented category may be another influence on the strength of the association found between sensitivity and attachment security. Children classified into this group usually receive an alternate classification corresponding to the Ainsworth category they most nearly resemble. Perhaps the alternate classification corresponds to the general level of maternal sensitivity, whereas disorganization of the attachment strategy reflects other types of experience with the mother (Main & Hesse, 1990; Solomon & George, 1996, in press). In some cases, attachment disorganization may also arise from neurological vulnerabilities in the children (Spangler, Fremmer-Bombik, & Grossmann, 1996), although van IJzendoorn et al. (in press) found no association between temperament and D classification in their meta-analysis. There has been very little actual observation of patterns of mother–infant interaction related to the D classification. Reports from other investigators using Main and Solomon's criteria, however, strongly suggest a link between attachment disorganization and dysfunctional mother–infant interaction, including maltreatment (Carlson et al., 1989; Lyons-Ruth & Block, 1996; Lyons-Ruth et al., 1991; O'Connor, Sigman, & Brill, 1987; Schuengel, van IJzendoorn, & Bakersmans-Kranenburg, in press).

Individual studies have shown no relation between attachment security to mothers and to fathers (e.g., Belsky & Rovine, 1987; Main & Weston, 1981), supporting the basic premise that classifications reflect particular relationships and not, for example, an infant's temperament. However, meta-analysis has revealed a small but significant concordance in an infant's classification to both parents (Fox, Kimmerly, & Schafer, 1991; van IJzendoorn & De Wolff, 1997). This concordance may reflect the effect of negative emotionality (i.e., temperament) on the manifest expression of distress in the strange situation (Goldsmith & Alansky, 1987), as well as mutual influences and temperamental similarities between parents. The independence of attachment classifications to mothers and to other caregivers has also been found in several different contexts (see Howes, Chapter 29, this volume). Although a child's temperament may influence the development of regulatory strategies in the parent–child relationship and present a challenge to the parent's capacity to be sensitive, current evidence does not suggest that attachment classifications can be simply reduced to temperamental differences among children (Fogel & Thelen, 1987; Goldsmith & Harman, 1994; Seifer & Schiller, 1995). (See also Vaughn & Bost, Chapter 10, this volume.)

Continuity. Long-term stability or continuity of classification conducted between the ages of 12 to 18 months and 60 months has been reported to be very high (82%) in two studies that have made use of Main and Cassidy's classification system for kindergarten-age children (Main & Cassidy, 1988; Wartner, Grossmann, Fremmer-Bombik, & Suess, 1994) but considerably lower when attachment is assessed in preschoolers (Cassidy, Berlin, & Belsky, 1990). Substantial (72–77%) continuity of secure versus insecure classifications from the ages of 18 months to 20 years (attachment classifications derived from the Adult Attachment Interview [AAI]; George, Kaplan, & Main, 1984, 1985, 1996) has been reported (Hamilton, in press; Waters, Treboux, Crowell, Merrick, & Albersheim, in press). Stability has been found to be lower in other samples, however (Grossmann, Grossmann, & Zimmerman, Chapter 33, this volume; Thompson, Chapter 13, this volume). In the Waters et al. (1995) study, stability within the insecure group was lower than in the secure group, and changes in classification were linked to experiences of loss, abuse, or major illness over the course of development. Consistent with this view, Weinfield, Sroufe, and Egeland (in press) report little stability in secure versus insecure classifications in a high-risk poverty sample. Thus it appears that long-term continuity should not be expected in samples that have undergone major changes in family functioning or status and/or when the family is under chronic stress.

Coherence. Beginning with Sroufe's (1979) early articulation of the coherence of development across developmental tasks, he and other researchers have established links between infant patterns of attachment and autonomy, peer relationships, social competence, and cognitive and socioemotional functioning (see Thompson, Chapter 13, this volume). In contrast to Bowlby's predictions, however, A-B-C classifications tend not to be strongly related to later measures of maladaptation—that is, to clinical indices (Carlson, 1998; Lyons-Ruth, 1996; Lyons-Ruth, Alpern, & Repacholi, 1993; Ogawa, Sroufe, Weinfield, Carlson, & Egeland, 1997). In a study of high-risk infants, the investigators reported that 71% of the sample in preschool and 83% of 7-year-olds who showed above-normal levels of hostility in the classroom had been classified as disorganized/disoriented in infancy (Lyons-Ruth, 1996; Lyons-Ruth et al., 1993). In addition, ratings of disorganization in the strange situation in infancy have been found to predict psychopathology in late adolescence (Carlson, 1998; Ogawa et al., 1997).

Cross-Cultural Predictions and Predictions to Other Caregivers. Studies of infants from cultures beyond North America in the strange situation have mainly been limited to Western Europe, but researchers have also examined infants and their mothers in Israel, Japan, and two sites in Africa (Kermoian & Leiderman, 1986; Miyake, Chen, & Campos, 1985; Sagi et al., 1985; Takahashi, 1986; True, 1994; see van IJzendoorn & Sagi, Chapter 31, this volume). Although secure classifications appear to be normative cross-culturally (Sagi, 1990), cultural differences have emerged in the proportions of attachment types, and debate continues regarding the cross-cultural interpretation of strange situation classifications (e.g., Levine & Miller, 1990). Corresponding observations of maternal behavior in the home (e.g., Grossmann, Grossmann, Spangler, Suess, & Unger, 1985) suggest that differences in the distributions of classifications may reflect systematic cultural differences in maternal behavior. They may also reflect differences in the frequency with which infants in different cultures and subcultures experience even brief separations from their mothers (Jackson, 1993; Miyake et al., 1985; Takahashi, 1986).

Investigators have reported no difficulty in classifying infant–father attachment relationships from the strange situation. In several but not all studies, the modal classification category is secure (Easterbrooks & Goldberg, 1984; Main & Weston, 1981; Schneider-Rosen & Rothbaum, 1993; but see Cox, Owen, Henderson, & Margand, 1992, and Grossmann, 1997). Nevertheless, at least in conventional two-parent families, infants seem to prefer their mothers as a haven of safety when they are distressed (Lamb, 1976). In the last two decades, influenced in part by prevailing social politics, developmental psychologists have attempted to demonstrate that mothers and fathers are interchangeable as caregivers. Measures of paternal sensitivity to infant signals in various contexts (paralleling Ainsworth's scales for maternal behavior) have not been found to predict secure infant–father attachment, however. Measures of reciprocity during play and a father's sensitive support of a child's exploration have emerged as the strongest predictors of secure classifications, suggesting that fathers promote their infants' security in different ways than do mothers (Cox et al., 1992; Grossmann, 1997; van IJzendoorn & DeWolff, in press). Belsky (1996) reported that in comparison to infant–mother attachments, infant–father attachments were more closely related to marital satisfaction and to both paternal and infant temperament. These data highlight the fact that the early infant–father relationship is subject in many respects to the mother–father relationship, which influences whether the father chooses and/or is permitted to enter the "circle" of the infant–mother bond (Solomon & George, 1996). The manner in which these complex family relationships come to influence the security of the infant's attachment to the father remains unknown.

Discussion

There can be little doubt that attachment classification by highly trained judges captures fundamental and far-reaching qualities of the infant–mother relationship. The reliability, stability, and predictive validity of Ainsworth's classification measure are well established in U.S. and Western European populations. However, important questions still remain about the psychometric properties and meaning of the measure for infant–father relationships, relationships with other caregivers, and attachment relationships in non-Western societies.

One of the most significant contributions of the method stems from its recognition of attachment relationship patterns or types, which has permitted researchers to describe and explicate individual differences in early relationships in a parsimonious and predictively very powerful way (see Weinfield et al., Chapter 4, this volume). Ainsworth's observational and coding skills remain unsurpassed. Indeed in a recent set of meta-analyses, van IJzendoorn noted that the magnitudes of the associations between theoretically important variables reported by Ainsworth have yet to be matched by other researchers (DeWolff & van IJzendoorn, in press; van IJzendoorn, Vereijken, & Riksen-Walreven, in press). It should not be forgotten, however, that the A-B-C groups were based on the study of a middle-class sample of only 23 mothers and infants, observed three decades ago. As researchers have investigated larger samples and high-risk groups, inconsistencies and gaps as well as new research opportunities have emerged. For example, Belsky et al. (1996) recently reported less than 50% short-term stability of A-B-C classifications. The sample for this study was considerably larger than that studied in early stability samples (Connell, 1976, cited in Waters, 1982; Main & Weston, 1981; Waters, 1979). Mothers' work patterns and the degree of father's involvement in the lives of very young children have also changed considerably since the early work was undertaken. A replication of Belsky et al.'s finding would raise important new questions and force us to revisit assumptions about attachment stability.

The disorganized/disoriented group would not have been identified had researchers not attempted to replicate early findings in larger and atypical populations, and had they not been open to unexpected variations in strange situation behavior (Main & Solomon, 1990). Although more information is required regarding the demarcation, etiology, and sequelae of the D category, findings from several studies strongly suggest that the explanatory power of Ainsworth's methodology is increased when this category is included in the study. As researchers focus on additional and larger groups of various risk samples, stable subgroups within this very heterogeneous category may yet be identified (Solomon & George, in press; Teti, in press).

We would also like to note an important methodological implication of Ainsworth's reliance on a categorical approach to qualitative differences in attachment. This approach reflected her background in clinical assessment, as well as her conviction that the patterns of behavioral constellations, rather than individual differences in particular behaviors, distinguish types of attach-

ment (Ainsworth & Marvin, 1995). Statistically less sensitive than dimensional measures, categorical systems require larger samples to establish reliable group differences. Many researchers who make use of Ainsworth's classification system (or other systems derived from it) are forced to reduce variability to a simple secure–insecure dimension because of inadequate sample size, usually in the insecure groups. As a result, these studies are unable to provide complete validation of the three- and four-group classification systems. When the literature is based on small samples, researchers are also at risk of deriving false conclusions from inconsistencies in results that arise simply from sampling error.[4]

Infant classification procedures have become so closely identified with the construct of security that it is difficult for either new or established attachment researchers to conceive that different or additional measures may be necessary or feasible. In part, this state of affairs reflects the simple brilliance of the strange situation procedure: It is hard to imagine another situation that can as reliably and ethically activate attachment behavior in the second year of life. The procedure makes use of a "natural cue to danger" (Bowlby, 1973), separation from the attachment figure, to activate the attachment system. The use of distinct episodes allows the coder to observe the infant's immediate response to particular events and the coherence of behavior across episodes. Furthermore, the situation appears to provide the "right" amount of stress. Too little stress does not activate the attachment system adequately, judging by the results of home observations (e.g., Ainsworth et al., 1978; Vaughn & Waters, 1990), and therefore may not allow critical distinctions among insecure groups to be revealed. Very high stress, such as that provided by repeating the procedure twice in 2 weeks, appears to result in a breakdown of defensive strategies, again obscuring important differences among groups. Finally, given that the primary threat to the child in the strange situation is a (transitory) threat to the relationship, the inferential leap from an observed pattern of attachment behavior to the infant's confidence regarding the psychological responsiveness of the caregiver seems to be a relatively modest one.

Whatever its appeal, from a technical standpoint the validity of the security construct as measured by the strange situation requires its cross-validation with one or more other measures of security. Since the validation of the single alternative measure of security in early toddlerhood, the AQS, is still at an early (though promising) stage, it is fair to conclude that construct validation for attachment classifications has yet to be established definitively. We hope that this rather unsettling realization will inspire researchers to participate in the validation of the AQS measure, as well as to devise other alternative measurement approaches.

CLASSIFICATION OF ATTACHMENT RELATIONSHIPS IN THE PRESCHOOL AND KINDERGARTEN PERIOD

Investigators have followed two approaches to developing classification systems for children's attachment behavior beyond infancy. The dominant approach is based on an assumption of continuity between infancy and older ages, with allowances for developmental changes in the actual behaviors indicative of one or another type of relationship. Beginning with the challenges of interpreting the strange situation behavior of children older than 18 months, Marvin (1977) and later Schneider-Rosen (1990) developed general guidelines to identify the traditional Ainsworth classification groups among toddlers. These researchers modified assessment criteria developmentally; for example, the timing and quality of distance interaction (including talking) was used as an index of security, instead of the proximity seeking and contact maintenance of the very young child. Marvin also emphasized the importance of considering additional aspects of parent–child interaction, such as the quality of parent–child negotiations around departures and reunions, as an index of the quality of the goal-corrected partnership that begins to emerge in the older toddler (Bowlby, 1969/1982, 1973, 1980).

The first major effort along these lines was that of Main and Cassidy (1988), who attempted to apply the continuity framework to developing a set of classification criteria for 6-year-olds. This system was developed using children whose infant attachment classifications were known. This effort was followed by the work of Cassidy, Marvin, and the MacArthur Working Group on Attachment, who attempted to adjust the kindergarten system downward to develop a classification system for the preschool-age child (2½ to 4½ years old). Both systems can therefore be said to be founded on *a priori* notions of developmental transformation in the early years of

life, as informed by careful and extensive observations of children in the various age ranges.

The second approach, called by Crittenden (1992a, 1992b, 1994) the "dynamic-maturational approach," emphasizes dynamic changes in the quality of attachment that arise from the interaction between maturation and current experience. Based on the concept of developmental pathways, this approach emphasizes more strongly than the continuity approach the possibilities for changes in quality of the attachment relationship over time. In addition, greater emphasis is placed in this system on inferences regarding the function of the child's behavior toward the parent. Crittenden originally participated in the MacArthur Working Group, so that there are strong similarities between her system and the Cassidy–Marvin system, as well as subtle but nonetheless significant differences. In both systems, attachment groups are distinguished by identifying the communicative or defensive goals that underlie attachment patterns. In both, the avoidant pattern is viewed as a defensive behavioral strategy organized around the goal of decreasing the probability of emotional involvement or confrontation. In Crittenden's Preschool Assessment of Attachment (PAA), however, this defensive strategy includes both cool or neutral avoidance of the parent (as in the Main–Cassidy and Cassidy–Marvin systems) and behavior that might be seen as somewhat role-reversed (i.e. placating, guiding, or acting solicitously toward the parent). The latter, according to Crittenden, is linked to cool neutrality by the fact that in both strategies, the child takes the major initiative in regulating proximity and communication with the parent.

Both approaches to preschool attachment use the strange situation procedure, especially the two separations and reunions of the original. Some investigators have introduced variations to accommodate the older age of the children, such as longer separations (Moss, Parent, Gosselin, Rousseau, & St-Laurent, 1996; Stevenson-Hinde & Shouldice, 1995). Other variations include changing the role and/or gender of the stranger (DeMulder & Radke-Yarrow, 1991; Stevenson-Hinde & Shouldice, 1990), changing the instructions to the caregiver (Cassidy & Marvin, 1987, 1990, 1991, 1992), and blending the strange situation with other laboratory tasks and procedures (DeMulder & Radke-Yarrow, 1991; Stevenson-Hinde & Shouldice, 1995). There has been no systematic determination of whether these variations materially affect the reunion behavior of the children. Although the Main and Cassidy system for 6-year-olds was developed earlier, we present information about the Cassidy–Marvin and Crittenden systems first because they apply to chronologically younger children.

The Cassidy–Marvin System and the Work of the MacArthur Group

The Cassidy–Marvin system (Cassidy & Marvin, 1987, 1990, 1991, 1992) for preschool-age children provides guidelines for a "secure" group (B) and four "insecure" groups as follows:

"avoidant" (A), "ambivalent" (C), "controlling/disorganized" (D), and "insecure/other" (IO). Each classification group includes a set of subgroups, including types that expand upon the infant subgroups. A brief description of classification criteria is shown in Table 14.3, and we summarize information on reliability and validity below.

Reliability

Intercoder Agreement. The majority of researchers using the Cassidy–Marvin system par-

TABLE 14.3 Early Childhood Laboratory Separation–Reunion Classification Systems: Major Classification Groups

Group	Cassidy–Marvin	PAA	Main–Cassidy
B	*Secure:* Uses parent as secure base for exploration. Reunion behavior is smooth, open, warm, positive.	*Secure/balanced:* Relaxed, intimate, direct expression of feelings, desires. Able to negotiate conflict or disagreement.	*Secure:* Reunion behavior is confident, relaxed, open. Positive, reciprocal interaction or conversation.
A	*Avoidant:* Detached, neutral nonchalance, but does not avoid interaction altogether. Avoids physical or psychological intimacy.	*Defended:* Acts to reduce emotional involvement or confrontation. Focuses on play and exploration at expense of interaction.	*Avoidant:* Maintains affective neutrality; subtly minimizes and limits opportunities for interaction.
C	*Ambivalent:* Protests separation strongly. Reunion characterized by strong proximity-seeking, babyish, coy behavior.	*Coercive:* Maximizes psychological involvement with parent; exaggerates problems and conflict. Is coercive, for example, threatening (resistant, punitive) and/or disarming (innocent, coy)	*Ambivalent:* Heightened intimacy and dependency on parent. Reunion characterized by ambivalence, subtle hostility, exaggerated cute or babyish behavior.
D	*Controlling/disorganized:* Characterized by controlling behavior (punitive, caregiving) or behaviors associated with infant disorganization.		*Controlling:* Signs of role reversal: punitive (rejecting, humiliating) or caregiving (cheering, reassuring, falsely positive).
A/C		*Defended/coercive:* Child shows both defended and coercive behaviors, appearing together or in alternation.	
AD		*Anxious depressed:* Sad/depressed; stares, extreme distress/panic.	
IO or U	*Insecure/other:* Mixtures of insecure indices that do not fit into any of the other groups.	*Insecure/other:* Mixture of insecure indices; acts incoherently in relation to parent.	*Unclassifiable:* Mixture of insecure indices that do not fit into any of the other groups.

Note. Cassidy–Marvin, Main–Cassidy: Organized groups = A, B, C. PAA: Organized groups = A, B, C, A/C.

ticipated in the MacArthur Working Group on Attachment (a collection of attachment researchers who collaborated to create the system), report establishing reliability with this group, and/or brought in a classification judge who established reliability on the system. The MacArthur Group requires a minimum of 75% agreement for certification. The range of training reliability scores reported in published studies includes percentages a bit lower: 75–92% (Achermann, Dinneen, & Stevenson-Hinde, 1991; Bretherton, Ridgeway, & Cassidy, 1990; Cassidy et al., 1990; Cicchetti & Barnett, 1991; Crittenden & Claussen, 1994; Easterbrooks, Davidson, & Chazan, 1993; Greenberg, Speltz, DeKlyen, & Endriga, 1991; Marvin & Pianta, 1996; Moss et al., 1996; Shouldice & Stevenson-Hinde, 1992; Speltz, Greenberg, & DeKlyen, 1990; Stevenson-Hinde & Shouldice, 1995; Turner, 1991).

Short-Term Stability. There are no published studies of short-term stability.

Relation to Other Measures
of Attachment Security

Some convergence between Cassidy–Marvin classifications and concurrent representational measures of attachment security has been demonstrated, especially for the secure–insecure dichotomy. It must be emphasized, however, that the representational measures are also new and that their validity has not been independently and thoroughly established. (See the section on representational measures, below.) Classification as secure versus insecure with the Cassidy–Marvin system significantly predicted classification as secure versus insecure with Bretherton's doll-play attachment representation measure (Bretherton et al., 1990) and was significantly related to scales designed to capture qualities of secure attachment representation in the Separation Anxiety Test (SAT; Shouldice & Stevenson-Hinde, 1992). In neither study were investigators able to discriminate among the insecure reunion classifications with the representational measures. It is unclear whether this reflects a shortcoming in one or both types of security measures. Posada, Waters, Marvin, and Cassidy (in press) report no relation between concurrent AQS assessment and Cassidy–Marvin classifications.

Prediction to Core Variables

Mother–Child Interaction. There are a limited number of studies demonstrating the validity

of Cassidy–Marvin classifications with respect to core theoretical predictions. Detailed descriptive work on mother–child relationships in the home, particularly with a focus on maternal behavior in situations in which the attachment system is presumed to be activated, has not yet been carried out. Based on brief observations in the home and laboratory, however, Stevenson-Hinde and her colleagues found some predicted differences between the secure and insecure groups in measures of mothers' sensitivity, socialization, and positive involvement with their children. Differences between the secure and the various insecure groups were revealed in one type of situation or the other, depending upon the group (Acherman et al., 1991; Stevenson-Hinde & Shouldice, 1990, 1995). Moss, Rousseau, Parent, St-Laurent, and Saintonge (1998) found overall smoother and more positive interaction during a brief free play between mothers and secure 5- to 6-year-olds, in comparison to dyads in which the children were judged insecure. In both samples, dyads with children judged controlling were characterized by the poorest mother–child coordination. Crittenden and Claussen (1994) found no relation between Cassidy–Marvin classifications and ratings of maternal sensitivity in a brief play situation, but did find a difference between mothers of secure and insecure children in maternal involvement and positive affect during laboratory cleanup. Studies in non-normative samples provide indirect evidence to suggest that classification reflects differences in maternal behavior. Maltreated children were more likely to be classified as insecure, especially D (controlling/disorganized) or IO (insecure/other) (Cicchetti & Barnett, 1991). Manassis, Bradley, Goldberg, Hood, and Swinson (1994) found that only 25% of children were secure in a sample of preschoolers with anxiety-disordered mothers; 65% of the children were rated as D or IO. Children whose mothers were rated as unresolved with respect to the children's diagnosis of a chronic, debilitating disorder were also more likely to be classified as insecure (Marvin & Pianta, 1996). Finally, Marcovitch et al. (1997) found that the distribution of attachment classifications among Romanian adoptees differed significantly from that of a normal comparison sample, with D the most common classification. (See Note 1.)

Continuity. There is only one report addressing continuity of classification. Cassidy et al. (1990) reported 66% stability of A-B-C classification groups from infancy to age 3 for a sample of 53 children. Stability was found mainly in the secure group, whereas children judged as avoidant and resistant in infancy with the strange situation were more likely at age 3 to be judged as secure with the Cassidy–Marvin system. This estimate of continuity is somewhat lower than that obtained over longer periods of time (see the discussion of the Main–Cassidy system, below) and could suggest that the Cassidy–Marvin system overestimates the numbers of secure relationships in the preschool years.

Coherence. A few studies report differences between secure and insecure children in other developmental domains. Secure children appear to be more cooperative with their mothers in brief laboratory tasks (Acherman et al., 1990; Cassidy et al., 1990), are less likely to show behavioral problems in the clinical range (Moss et al., in press), and are less likely to be diagnosed with conduct disorders in clinical populations (Greenberg et al., 1991; Speltz et al., 1990). In the one study focusing on peer relationships, secure children were found to be less gender-stereotyped in behavior than insecure children (Turner, 1991).

Cross-Cultural Studies and Other Relationships. The Cassidy–Marvin system has been used to study attachment in the United States and England. There is no published information on preschooler attachment in countries or cultures other than these, on the father–child relationship, or on relationships with other caregivers.

The Preschool Assessment of Attachment

Crittenden's PAA (Crittenden, 1992b, 1994) provides guidelines for six major classification groups as follows: "secure" (B), "defended" (A), "coercive" (C), "defended/coercive" (A/C), "anxious depressed" (AD), and "insecure/other" (IO). Each classification group includes a set of subgroups, including typologies that expand upon the infant classifications by integrating a maturational/developmental perspective on preschooler behavior into the system. Classification criteria are shown in Table 14.3. Despite the apparent overlap with the Cassidy–Marvin system in group designations, it should be noted that the PAA depends upon an expanded set of criteria, including inferred regulation of internal feeling states, parent–child negotiation, the responsiveness of the attachment figure, and the observer's affective response to interaction. Published papers using the PAA are based on children ranging in age from 21 months to 65 months.

Reliability

Intercoder Agreement. Investigators report high intercoder agreement with Crittenden (80–90%) and within laboratories (82–87%) (Crittenden & Claussen, 1994; Fagot & Pears, 1996; Teti, Gelfand, Messenger, & Isabella, 1995). No cross-laboratory reliability figures are available.

Short-Term Reliability. There are no studies of short-term reliability.

Relation to Other Attachment Measures

There is no information regarding the association of PAA classifications with measures of child attachment in the home. Crittenden and her colleagues, however, used both the Cassidy–Marvin system and the PAA to classify two samples of preschoolers—one a maltreatment group, the other a heterogeneous community sample that included some maltreated children (Crittenden & Claussen, 1994). Agreement on main classification group (with PAA Groups A/C, AD, and IO treated as equivalent to Cassidy–Marvin Group D) between the two systems was poor (38% and 39%). These figures, however, partially reflect the fact that Crittendon "forced" the very high proportion of Cassidy–Marvin IO classifications into the otherwise best-fitting A, B, or C group. Within the Cassidy–Marvin system, these cases would have been combined with the D group. Agreement between the two systems on a secure–insecure split was 82% in the maltreatment sample, but only 64% in the community sample. Agreement for insecure classifications was considerably better than for secure classifications in both samples. This result exemplifies the serious lack of consensus about what constitutes secure behavior in the preschool years, and the corresponding lack of fundamental descriptive data on parents and children at this age.

Prediction to Core Variables

Mother–Child Interaction. The PAA involves an explicit departure from the Ainsworth system and its descendants, and predictions regarding maternal behavior differ slightly as well (Crittenden, 1992a). Secure attachment is predicted to be related to sensitive, stable mothering; the defended pattern is believed to reflect a predictable negative parental response to a child's display of negative affect; and the coercive pattern is believed to reflect unpredictability (whether this is unpredictability in response to a child's positive and/or negative affect or in general living circumstances is not specified). These predictions have been partially tested in brief, semistructured home and laboratory observations. Mothers of secure children received highest ratings for sensitivity, low controllingness, positive involvement, and positive affect. Mothers of defended children showed little involvement in cleanup in the laboratory, but otherwise the groups of insecure children's mothers were not differentiated (Crittenden & Claussen, 1994). In a study of normative, middle-class children, Fagot and Pears (1996) found that children who moved from either security or avoidance at 18 months to coerciveness at 30 months had mothers who differed from their stable counterparts, but not in ways that clearly indicated unpredictability of the mothers' behavior toward the children. Finally, indirect evidence of differences in maternal behavior is suggested by links among PAA patterns, maltreatment history, and maternal depression. Crittenden and Claussen (1994) found secure attachments to be modal among nonmaltreated infants; the mixed A/C pattern was significantly associated with maltreatment. Teti et al. (1995) found that the AD and IO patterns were, as would be expected, particularly common in a sample of preschoolers whose mothers were depressed.

Continuity. The PAA explicitly predicts discontinuity—a shift from a defended pattern of attachment to a coercive one—in some proportion of children as a reflection of unpredictability in maternal behavior and maturational changes in children from infancy to preschool age. In the study referred to above by Fagot and Pears (1996), a normative sample of mother–toddler dyads was assessed when the children were 18 and 30 months and 7 years of age. They found shifts from A to C and the reverse in the preschool period, with an overall increase in C classifications from 10% to 36% of the sample. Disorganized/disoriented attachment classifications were not made at 18 months; since it is likely that this group overlaps with both A and C in the PAA system, it is difficult to evaluate the actual discontinuity in attachment relationships.

Coherence. Specific relations between PAA patterns and maladaptive development, both at home and with peers, have been predicted. In line with predictions, Crittenden and Claussen (1994) found maternal ratings of social withdrawal to be associated with the defended pattern, but was unable to show that A and C children differed from one another as predicted with respect to conduct disorder, anxiety, and attentional difficulties. Fagot and Pears found that the coercive pattern predicted teacher reports of poor peer relationships at age 7.

Cross-Cultural Studies and other Relationships. The PAA has been used in studies of normative and high-risk samples in the United States. There are no published studies of the PAA as a measure of security in other relationships (e.g., father–child, other caregiver–child).

The Main–Cassidy Attachment Classification for Kindergarten-Age Children

The Main and Cassidy (1988) attachment classification system for kindergarten-age children was developed on a sample of 33 children whose infant attachment classifications in the strange situation (A, B, and D) were known and who had experienced no major change in caretaking relationships. The system was further tested and extended on a new sample of 50 children that afforded enough C children to establish classification guidelines for this group. Classification is based on a child's behavior during the first 3 or 5 minutes of reunion with the parent following a one-hour separation, rather than on the episodes and timing of the strange situation. Guidelines are provided for five major classification groups: "secure" (B), "avoidant" (A), "ambivalent" (C), "controlling" (D), and "unclassified" (U). Criteria for subgroup classifications are also provided. Rating scales for security and avoidance have also been developed. The major criteria for classification are shown in Table 14.3.

Reliability

Intercoder Agreement. In the majority of studies, intercoder reliability between Main or Cassidy and other investigators ranges from 70% to 82% (Cassidy, 1988; Cohn, 1990; Main & Cassidy, 1988; Wartner et al., 1994). Intercoder agreement on the security and avoidance rating scales is in the same range. However, in one study completed before the system was finalized, agreement between expert coders was 52%, with the majority of disagreements involving the controlling (D) category (Solomon, George, & Silverman, in press).

Short-Term Stability. Stability of classification over a 1-month period in Main and Cassidy's sample of 50 was 62%. Instability was largely due to change involving the controlling group. Given that (as noted below) long-term continuity of classification is much higher, it is likely, as with infant classifications, that instability in part reflects sensitization to the test situation.

Relation to Other Measures of Security

Main–Cassidy classifications have been shown to be strongly related to classifications based on two different procedures for classifying children's representation of attachments. We (Solomon, George, & De Jong, 1995) reported 79% agreement (kappa = .74) between Main–Cassidy classifications and classifications based on children's responses in a structured doll-play situation. Agreement between the systems was very high for children in the secure, ambivalent, and controlling groups, but lower for those in the avoidant group. A high level of agreement between Main–Cassidy classifications and classifications of children's responses to pictures of attachment-related events has also been reported (Jacobsen, Edelstein, & Hofmann, 1994; Jacobsen & Hofmann, in press). Slough and Greenberg (1990) found that ratings of child security, as assessed from children's responses to the SAT (Hansburg, 1972; Klagsbrun & Bowlby, 1976), were positively related to Main–Cassidy security ratings during reunion. (For a full description of these studies, see the section on representational measures, below.)

Prediction to Core Variables

Mother–Child Interaction. We (Solomon et al., in press) found significant correlations between ratings based on Main–Cassidy classifications of security, avoidance, and ambivalence and observer sorts of maternal behavior in the home (Maternal Caretaking *Q*-Sort). Security was related to age-appropriate maternal involvement and support; avoidance to rejection and affective distance; and ambivalence to indulgent and in-

fantalizing behavior. Mothers of children rated high in controlling behavior were distinguished solely by high scores on the *Q*-sort item "Treats child like a playmate or companion."

Continuity. In their original development study, Main and Cassidy (1988) reported a match of 82% (kappa = .76) between 12-month and 6-year A-B-C-D classifications with mothers and 62% stability (kappa = .28) in classifications with fathers. Wartner et al. (1994) reported an 82% match in classifications with mothers (kappa = .72) over the same period in their independent German sample.

Coherence. Cohn (1990) and Wartner et al. (1994) have investigated the links between classifications at age 6 and social competence and peer acceptance in school. In both studies, the securely attached children were judged to be more socially competent and accepted than the insecurely attached children, although the studies differed as to which insecure group showed the greatest deficit (C or A, respectively). Paralleling these findings at the representational level of assessment, Cassidy (1988), found that secure children had more positive representations of peers' feelings, as assessed from social problem-solving vignettes, than did insecure children. We (Solomon et al, 1995) found that middle-class controlling and unclassifiable kindergarten children showed the highest levels of behavioral problems (especially hostility) at home and school, but that the secure, avoidant, and ambivalent groups did not differ significantly on these measures. Secure versus insecure Main–Cassidy classifications have also been found to be related to representational measures of self-esteem and attachment, with secure children judged to be more open about themselves and about feelings of vulnerability than insecure children (Cassidy, 1988; Slough & Greenberg, 1990).

Cross-Cultural Studies. The Main–Cassidy system has been used in the United States, Iceland, and Germany.

Discussion

Given the range of options for attachment classification in early childhood, readers may find themselves perplexed as to which system is most appropriate for their own research. At present, there are two classification systems available for the preschool period—the Cassidy–Marvin system and the PAA. To complicate matters further, a few investigators (Easterbrooks et al., 1993; Moss et al., 1996, 1998) have recently extended the use of the Cassidy–Marvin system to classification of attachment in kindergartners, the age range of the Main–Cassidy system.

The greater ambiguity at present surrounds the measures for the preschool range proper (i.e., 21 to 48 months). The Cassidy–Marvin and PAA systems overlap in several areas, but they differ just enough to make comparisons difficult. Both systems rely on inferences regarding a child's attachment strategy with respect to a parent, but on somewhat different bases. A key conceptual difference concerns what constitutes a disorganized attachment strategy. In the Cassidy–Marvin system, behavior that either is clearly disorganized or is aimed at controlling the parent can result in placement into the D category. The link between these morphologically different behaviors is supported by continuity in these categories between infancy and age 6 (Main & Cassidy, 1988) and by the finding that children who were classified as controlling at age 6, on the basis of reunion with their parents were judged to be disorganized at the level of representation on the basis of a doll-play measure (Solomon et al., 1995). In contrast, the PAA defines as organized any strategy that is coherent and whose goal in the immediate situation is apparent. Thus it places greater emphasis on a parent's behavior and a child's response in the moment, and it requires a more abstract level of inference.

Although the overlap between Cassidy–Marvin and PAA classifications for identical cases is limited, both systems appear to capture at least some of the variance in preschool mother–child relationships. Secure classifications in both systems are related to global measures of positive/smooth interaction between a mother and child (Cassidy et al., 1990; Crittenden & Claussen, 1994; Fagot & Pears, 1996; Moss et al., in press; Stevenson-Hinde & Shouldice, 1995). Particular categories in both systems (Cassidy–Marvin: D, IO; PAA: A/C, AD, IO) seem to be closely associated with clinical antecedents (i.e., maltreatment, maternal depression, conduct disorders). Beyond these broad distinctions, however, the relative value, utility, or validity of one system over another cannot be determined at present.

A possible limitation to both preschool measures is their reliance on the brief separation and reunion episodes of the strange situation. Theoretically, the quality of attachment behavior will depend on the degree to which the attachment system is activated, and it is not clear that 2-, 3-, and 4-year old children will find a 3-minute separation sufficiently arousing. On the other hand, very long separations may also mask group differences by overstressing the attachment system (Slough & Greenberg, 1990). Research should begin to establish the optimal separation time for this age.

A long separation is part of the Main–Cassidy procedure for classifying attachment relationships at age 6. This may partly explain the comparative success researchers have had with this measure in finding unique and theoretically expected differences for each of the major classification groups at the older age. Maturational differences between kindergarten and preschool children may also result in differential validity of classification at the two ages. For example, in both the Main–Cassidy and Cassidy–Marvin systems, the quality (especially the elaboration and coherence) of verbal communication is a distinguishing characteristic of a securely attached child. In the preschool years, however, verbal skills are generally more limited and are still quite unevenly distributed. The classifier is forced therefore to rely on subtler (less reliable) behavioral indices. This greater variability in the behavior of preschoolers is reflected in the Cassidy–Marvin manual, which is both more inclusive and less precise in spelling out criteria for categorization than is the Main–Cassidy manual for older children.

This leads us to consider which system to use with children ages 5 to 7. If the kindergarten-age child is indeed "easier" to classify than the preschool-age child, researchers trained in the Cassidy–Marvin system should have little trouble using the Main–Cassidy system. Two groups of researchers have used the former to generate classifications for kindergarten-age children (Easterbrooks et al., 1993; Moss et al., 1996), with each group having established reliability on a small subsample with a coder trained in both systems.[5] This procedure may indicate that the Cassidy–Marvin system is identical to the Main–Cassidy system when used with older children, or it may reflect the skillfulness of one or both sets of researchers; however, it is not sufficient for establishing the validity of the Cassidy–Marvin system for children in the transition to the middle childhood period (cf. Moss et al., 1998). At present, therefore, investigators working with 5- to 7-year-olds would be well advised to rely on the Main–Cassidy system.

ATTACHMENT SECURITY MEASURES BASED ON SYMBOLIC REPRESENTATION

It is generally believed that infants and toddlers encode knowledge, including knowledge about their relationships with attachment figures, in terms of enactive or sensorimotor representation. Early in the preschool years, children begin to use symbolic forms of mental representation and to organize knowledge conceptually (Bretherton, 1985). These conceptual structures and processes can be observed in contexts in which a child is asked to develop scripts for actions and events. As a result of this developmental achievement, the child is ripe for assessments that tap internal working models of attachment. Internal representational models of relationships are believed to arise from actual experiences in a relationship. They have been conceptualized as consisting of both specific content, including affect, and information-processing rules that integrate and determine perception and memory (Bowlby, 1969/1982; Bretherton, 1985; Main, Kaplan, & Cassidy, 1985). Because of their link to experience, individual differences in these models can be expected to parallel individual differences in a child's actual behavior with an attachment figure; that is, they should be systematically related to measures of attachment security based on reunion and/secure-base behavior in early childhood and thereafter.

The measures that have been developed are of two kinds—those based on children's responses to pictured situations, and those based on children's doll-play narratives and enactment of attachment-related scenarios. Some researchers have attempted to develop classification schemes to parallel the Ainsworth system. Other researchers have developed scales to reflect aspects of attachment security or related constructs, but have not attempted to understand patterning of responses in such a way as to derive classifications.

Picture Response Procedures

Three interrelated measures have been developed to assess internal representations of attachment on the basis of children's responses to projective pictures or stories. Two measures (Kaplan, 1995; Slough & Greenberg, 1990) incorporate the procedures of the SAT, a picture response protocol that was first developed by Hansburg (1972) for adolescents and later modified for children ages 4–7 by Klagsbrun and Bowlby (1976). The pro-

cedure consists of a set of six photographs depicting attachment-related scenes ranging from mild (a parent says goodnight to a child in bed) to stressful (a child watches a parent leave). Each picture is introduced by an adult, and the child is asked to describe how the child in the picture feels and what that child will do.

Kaplan (1987) developed a classification system for children's responses to the pictures that differentiates attachment groups on the basis of children's emotional openness and ability to envision constructive solutions to feelings engendered by separation. The system was developed on a small sample of middle-class 6-year-olds whose attachment classifications with their mothers at 12 months were known. Children classified as "resourceful" (B) were able to discuss coping with separation in constructive ways. There was no evidence that they denied feelings of vulnerability, and no evidence that they became disorganized or disoriented. Children were classified as "inactive" (A) when they offered responses indicating feelings of vulnerability or distress at separation. but were at a loss to suggest ways in which the child in each picture might cope. Children classified as "ambivalent" (C) typically demonstrated a contradictory mixture of responses; for example, a child might seem angry toward the parent, but would shift to wanting to please the parent. Children were classified as "fearful" (D) on the basis of several types of responses: inexplicable fear, lack of constructive strategies for coping with separation, or disorganized or disoriented thought processes. Although Kaplan's classification system has been very influential in the design of other representational measures, information regarding its reliability and validity when used with the SAT pictures is limited to Kaplan's original study. She reached 76% reliability with a second trained judge on her sample of 38 children. Correspondence between SAT responses and infant strange situation classifications was 68% for the four groups (kappa = .55) (see Grossmann & Grossmann, 1991, for data relating to a small modification of Kaplan's procedures).

Jacobsen and her colleagues (Jacobsen et al., 1994; Jacobsen & Hofmann, in press) adapted Kaplan's classification system for use with a series of pictures depicting a long separation from parents (Chandler, 1973). These investigators were unusually thorough in establishing the validity of the measure. As in Kaplan's study, Jacobsen et al.'s Icelandic children were 7 years old when assessed. Judges were trained by Kaplan and established excellent within-laboratory agreement (kappa = .80–87). Short-term stability 1 year later was substantial (kappa = .78). Representational classifications agreed closely with concurrent classifications based upon reunion behavior (Main & Cassidy, 1988): Agreement on secure versus insecure classifications was 89%, and for the three groups (B, A, D) it was 80%. Representational classifications also showed significant correspondence to strange situation classifications completed when the children were 18 months of age (82% agreement on main groups). Finally, secure versus insecure representational classification (especially the D pattern) successfully predicted the following theoretically related variables for children between the ages of 7 and 15, even when differences in IQ were controlled for: performance on cognitive-developmental tasks, self-esteem, teacher-reported attention and participation in class, insecurity about self, and grade point average. Classification was unrelated to emotion recognition for the Chandler pictures and to teacher-rated extraversion and disruptive behavior.

A limited amount of information is available about a third representational measure of attachment security, designed by Slough and Greenberg (1990). These investigators used the SAT pictures and developed four scales, apparently adapted from Kaplan's early classification criteria (Main et al., 1985), to rate attachment security. The attachment scales (acknowledgment of separation-related affect in stressful separations; statements of well-being in mild separations) were positively related to security ratings (Main & Cassidy, 1988) of 5-year-olds upon reunion with their mothers following a 3-minute separation, and negatively related to ratings of avoidance. Representation ratings were unrelated, however, to reunion behavior following a second, longer (90-minute) separation. Since the Main–Cassidy ratings were based on nonstandard separation–reunion procedures, the validity of the findings is open to question. No information is available regarding intercoder reliability or test–retest stability of the Slough and Greenberg measure.

Doll Play

A second approach to developing representation-based attachment security measures is founded on observation of children's doll play centering on attachment-relevant themes. Bretherton and her colleagues developed a doll-play procedure

to assess attachment security in 3-year-olds; this procedure involves of a set of five stories (child spills juice, child hurts her knee, child "discovers" a monster in the bedroom, parents depart, and parents return). An adult introduces each story with a story stem that describes what has happened, and a child is asked to describe and enact what happens next. Bretherton developed a classification system that identifies the four main attachment groups (A, B, C, D). Detailed transcripts are made of children's verbal behavior and enactment of each story and classifications are based on children's predominant responses to the stories. Separate criteria for each story were established on *a priori* grounds or based on Kaplan's (SAT) findings. Secure (B) children demonstrate coping behavior in relation to the attachment theme. For example, upon separation from parents, a secure child spontaneously (without prompting from the administrator) plays with the grandmother doll. Avoidant (A) children appear to avoid responding; for example, they request another story or say "I don't know." No consistent patterns have been identified for ambivalent (C) children. Children are classified as disorganized (D) if they give odd or disorganized responses—for example, throwing the child doll on the floor.

No intercoder or test–retest reliability figures are available. However, Bretherton et al. examined the concordance between secure and insecure doll-play classifications and corresponding classifications of children with the Cassidy–Marvin preschool system. A secure–insecure match was found for 75% of the 28 children. There was no match, however, for type of insecurity across the two measures. Doll-play classifications were converted to security scores and were found to be highly correlated with AQS security scores at 25 months and marginally correlated with (concurrent) AQS security scores at 37 months. Representation security scores showed significant, moderate relations to marital satisfaction, family adaptation and cohesiveness, child temperament (sociability, shyness), and language and cognition as assessed by the Bayley Scales of Infant Development. This broad network of correlations raises some question regarding the discriminant validity of the system.

We have developed a second approach to classification based on doll-play responses (George & Solomon, 1994; Solomon et al., 1995). This system focuses on the Bretherton et al. separation–reunion stories taken as a unit and was developed for kindergarten-age children. We also introduced some changes to the Bretherton et al. procedures to facilitate symbolic play and enhance involvement.

The system identifies four attachment groups (classifications are based on complete transcripts of the children's verbal and behavioral responses): "confident" (B), "casual" (A), "busy" (C), and "frightened" (D). The basic criteria for the groups were developed on a pilot sample whose concurrent attachment classifications were known. Classification involves a consideration of both story content and structure. The stories of children in the pilot sample who were classified as confident (B) depicted themes of danger and rescue by competent adults. Symbolic play was constructive, and stories were integrated into coherent narratives. The stories of children classified as casual (A) depicted ordinary events portrayed in a schematic or stereotyped fashion. Explicit concerns about separation issues were minimized or absent, and family members were unavailable at reunion. The stories of children classified as busy (C) emphasized affectively positive themes of caregiving or having fun during the parents' absence. Reunions were delayed or interrupted, and narratives were highly digressive. The stories of children classified as frightened (D) were either chaotic and destructive or inhibited and constricted.

Intercoder reliability was 71% for the entire sample and 95% for disorganized (D) versus organized (A-B-C) classifications. The concordance between representation classifications and attachment classifications based on reunion behavior (Main & Cassidy, 1988) was 79% (kappa = .74). There are no stability studies and no published studies examining the relation between the representational classifications and other theoretically relevant variables for this system.

Other Representational Measures

Several investigators have presented preliminary findings on other promising security measures based on symbolic representation. For example, Kaplan and Main (1986) developed a preliminary classification system for use with kindergarten-age children's drawings of their families. Some investigators, including Kaplan, have reported concordance between this system (or slight modifications of it) and reunion behavior classifications (Fury, Carlson, & Sroufe, 1997; Main et al., 1985; Pianta, Longmaid, & Ferguson, in press); however, this finding has not been replicated in all studies (see Main, 1995) and

thus may be seen as an interesting correlate of, but not a measure of, attachment (Main, personal communication, 1998). Cassidy (1988) developed a classification system based on children's doll-play responses to tap representations of the self in relation to the attachment figure. Classification based on doll play was significantly related to classification based on laboratory reunion (Main–Cassidy system); however, discrepancies between the systems were also substantial, so that the usefulness of this system as a measure of attachment representation is unclear. Other investigators have used variations of the picture or story stem procedures described above, along with rating systems or their own classification criteria, often derived from Kaplan's or Bretherton et al.'s security classification systems. Investigators typically report modest though significant relations between representational measures and other attachment measures or theoretically relevant variables (Oppenheim & Waters, 1995; Shouldice & Stevenson-Hinde, 1992).

Discussion

The development of attachment security measures based on children's symbolic behavior is a relatively new endeavor, and it is clear that there is much work to be done. Although these measures are at an early stage of development, their potential is twofold. First, the variety of children's symbolic behavior permits the development and comparison of different measures, which is necessary to establish construct validity. This has been an elusive goal for measures based on interaction. We encourage researchers to undertake the systematic cross-validation of these measures, especially with respect to the four core hypotheses we have outlined earlier in this chapter.

Second, investigators who have used representational materials in work with young children find them to be a rich source of information and a fruitful base for hypothesis generation. At their best, representational data reveal both the content and the structure of young children's thought, or, in Main's (1995) terms, "state of mind" regarding attachment. They may make it possible to explore psychologically important regulatory processes in young children, such as fantasy and defense, and to trace the links between children's and adults' construction of representational models. For this promise to be realized, investigators should take care to establish the congruence of new measures with interaction-based measures of attachment security. This continues to be necessary because a high level of abstraction is inherent in the construct of an attachment representation, and children's cognitive and language development can influence the quality of their responses to representational stimuli.

One of the most encouraging signs from work with representational measures to date is the degree of overlap between systems in the classification criteria for the various attachment groups. These criteria have direct analogues to qualitative differences in parent–infant and parent–child interaction, as well as to representational processes already identified in adults. For example, the behavior of the secure infant and kindergartner is characterized by open and direct communication of affect and by active, persistent, and unambivalent expression of attachment behavior. Criteria for security in Kaplan's SAT classification system also include direct acknowledgment of affect (sadness, longing, anger) and a clear sense that reassurance or relief is forthcoming. In our own doll-play classification system, secure children symbolically depict separation anxiety as well as confidence in the favorable resolution to these fears and concerns. Furthermore, the cognitive complexity and narrative structure of their play clearly parallel the coherence and integration of thought characteristic of the attachment representations of secure adults (Main, 1995).

We briefly note two areas that need special attention as measures continue to be refined. First, we encourage investigators to develop measures directly from the representational material produced by a particular procedure, instead of relying in *a priori* considerations alone or "borrowing" criteria from one measure and applying them to another. For example, it appears that in response to SAT stimuli, avoidant children will often say "I don't know." We find that this response is not characteristic of avoidant children when responding to doll-play scenarios; when repeated or mixed with other "response-avoidant" tactics, it is instead characteristic of some disorganized/controlling children. Transfer of Kaplan's picture-based criteria to doll-play materials may be one reason why, for example, Bretherton et al.'s doll-play classification system has failed to distinguish among insecure classification groups.

Researchers should also consider the degree to which representational procedures activate the attachment system. Our experience in comparing the responses of children ages 3 through 7 to the Bretherton et al. procedure (George & Solomon, 1996a), suggests that different stories result in better discrimination between classification groups at different ages. In the stories of 3-year-olds, we see clearer distinctions in response to the "monster in the bedroom" story than to any of the other stories, including the separation–reunion scenario. In older children, we see clearer distinctions among the classification groups in response to the "hurt knee" and "separation–reunion" story stems, and less distinctiveness in response to the "monster" story. These differences may reflect an interaction between the attachment system and cognitive development. For the young preoperational child—who is unable to distinguish between reality and fantasy, and whose perceptions of the world are driven by appearances (Flavell, 1986)—imaginary monsters are real and scary. This story may more readily activate the attachment system and the corresponding internal working model of attachment than other stimuli. For the concrete operational child (ages 5 to 7)—who is able to distinguish between fantasy and reality, is not driven by appearances, and is in a new "practicing" phase with respect to autonomy—the "hurt knee" and "separation–reunion" stories may be sufficiently evocative to activate the attachment system. Indeed, by the time children reach age 7 or so, the thought of an overnight separation from the parents is no longer very disturbing; children's stories then become more matter-of-fact. When these materials are used toward the end of the age range, therefore, it may be necessary to modify the scenario to evoke clear individual differences in attachment representations.

THE ATTACHMENT *Q*-SORT: INFANCY THROUGH 5 YEARS

In contrast to systems of classifying child behavior and representation, the AQS assesses the quality of a child's secure-base behavior in the home. The system was developed by Waters to provide a practical alternative to the Ainsworth home observation narratives. Within the AQS system, "secure-base behavior" is defined as the smooth organization of and appropriate balance between proximity seeking and exploration (Posada, Gao, et al., 1995). The *Q*-set for the AQS consists of 90 items designed to tap a range of dimensions believed to reflect either the secure-base phenomenon itself or behavior associated with it in children ages 1 to 5. These items are sorted into one of nine piles, according to whether the item is considered characteristic or uncharacteristic of a child's behavior. Sorts can be completed by trained observers or by parents. Waters (1995) recommends that sorts by observers should be based on two to three visits for a total of 2–6 hours of observation in the home, with additional observations if observers fail to agree.

The AQS permits the salience of a behavior in the child's repertoire to be distinguished from the frequency with which the behavior occurs. In addition, it helps to prevent observer biases and lends itself to an array of qualitative and quantitative analyses. AQS data can be analyzed in terms of individual items or summary scales, or they permit a comparison of the child's Q-sort profile to a criterion sort. Waters (1995) has developed criterion sorts for the construct of attachment security and for several other constructs (social desirability, dependence, sociability) by collecting and averaging the sorts of experts in the field. The child's security score is the correlation coefficient between the observer's sort and the criterion sort, and it represents the child's placement on a linear continuum with respect to security. Although some researchers have used different criterion sorts for the second and fourth years of life, E. Waters (personal communication, 1997) now recommends the use of a single criterion across this age range (12 to 60 months). Validated sorts for the A, C, or D insecure attachment groups defined by the strange situation are not available, although some researchers have developed classifications on *a priori* grounds for particular purposes (e.g., Howes & Hamilton, 1992; Pederson & Moran, 1995).

Validation of the Measure

Reliability

Intercoder Agreement. In comparison to classification systems, reliability on the AQS does not require extensive training or certification of reliability. Studies report interobserver reliability (correlations between sorts) ranging from .72 to .95. The correlation between mothers' and trained observers' sorts tends to be moderate in small to moderate-size samples (approximately 35 to 60 subjects), but improves considerably as a function of training and supervision of mothers

and the degree to which observers are trained and have opportunity to see a sufficient range of child behavior (Teti & McGourty, 1996). We return to this issue at the conclusion of this section.

Short-Term Stability. Short-term stability of parent-generated AQS security scores varies considerably across studies (.04 to .75) (Bretherton et al., 1990; Teti, Sakin, Kucera, Corns, & Das Eiden, 1996; van Dam & van IJzendoorn, 1988). Observer sorts of children's separations and reunions at day care at 6-month intervals from 18 to 42 months (Howes & Hamilton, 1992) were at the low end of this range ($r = .04–.39$), and no stability was shown for observer sorts in a Japanese sample (Vereijken & Kondo-Ikemura, in press).

Relation to Other Measures of Attachment

AQS security scores have been found to differentiate 12- to 18-month-old infants classified as secure or insecure in the strange situation in several but not all published studies (Belsky & Rovine, 1990; Bosso, Corter, & Abramovitch, in press; Bretherton et al., 1990; Mangelsdorf et al. 1996; Sagi et al., 1995; van Dam & van IJzendoorn, 1988; Vaughn & Waters, 1990). The strength of the relation tends to be moderate, with average security scores for the secure group of about .50, and average security scores for the insecure groups of about .25. Paralleling Ainsworth's original finding, distinctive differences between children classified as A or C in the strange situation do not emerge clearly in the AQS data. In the preschool period, the relation between the AQS and other security measures is less certain. As noted earlier, Posada et al. (in press) failed to find a relationship between preschool reunion-based classifications and observer AQS scores. Bretherton et al. (1990) reported a strong correlation between maternal sorts completed at age 25 months and Bretherton's representational measure of attachment, but the relation between measures was considerably weaker when concurrent 37-month maternal sorts were used.

Prediction to Core Variables

Mother–Child Interaction. For the infancy period, scores or ratings of maternal sensitivity and competence based on brief home visits have been found in several studies to correlate moderately with observer and/or maternal AQS scores

(Pederson et al., 1990; Pederson & Moran, 1995; Schölmerich, Fracasso, Lamb, & Broberg, 1995; Teti, Nakagawa, Das, &Wirth, 1991; van Dam & van IJzendoorn, 1988). In the preschool period, Silverman (see Solomon et al., in press) found relations between AQS security scores and maternal Q-sort items reflecting maternal enjoyment, psychological availability, and authoritative control. More indirectly, researchers have found significant differences in AQS security of preschoolers whose mothers were classified as secure or insecure with the AAI (Posada, Waters, Crowell, & Lay, 1995).

In contrast to what has been found for strange situation classifications, Vaughn and Bost (Chapter 10, this volume) note that assessments of temperament, especially negative reactivity, show moderate correlations with AQS security. In a theoretically related set of findings, several studies report moderate concordance between mothers' and fathers' AQS security scores (Belsky & Rovine, 1990; Del Carmen, Pedersen, Huffman, & Bryan, in press; Howes & Markman, 1989; LaFreniere, Provost, & Dubeau, 1992). These findings suggest some limitation in the discriminant validity of AQS security, although the shared variance is not great.

Continuity. Belsky and Rovine (1990) reported low to moderate long-term stability between ages 1 and 3 (mothers: $r = .23$; fathers: $r = .53$; social desirability partialed out).

Coherence. AQS security in the infancy and preschool periods has been found to be related to higher-quality and more positive interaction with peers and siblings, and to lower levels of behavior problems (Bosso et al., in press; LaFreniere et al., 1992; Del Carmen et al., in press; Park & Waters, 1989; Teti & Ablard, 1990; cf. Belsky & Rovine, 1990). A variety of parental and marital variables (e.g., marital quality, social support, parenting stress) have also been shown to be related to AQS security (Howes & Markman, 1989; Nakagawa, Teti, & Lamb, 1992; Teti et al., 1991).

Cross-Cultural Studies. In a major study on the cross-cultural validity of the AQS, researchers determined that mothers and experts can discriminate attachment security from the constructs of dependency and social desirability in a range of countries (China, Japan, Israel, Columbia, Germany, Norway, United States) (Posada, Gao, et al., 1995). Although the structure of the data is broadly similar cross-culturally, the

correlations of maternal sorts across cultures tend to be low (ranges = .15–.32) (see also Strayer, Verissimo, Vaughn, & Howes, 1995; Vaughn, Strayer, Jacques, Trudel, & Seifer, 1991). This suggests that ecological factors may have a powerful effect on the patterning of young children's secure-base behavior in the home.

Discussion

The great promise of the AQS lies in its emphasis on naturalistic observation in ecologically valid contexts. For the infancy period, there is correspondence with security or insecurity in the strange situation and with maternal sensitivity, suggesting that the AQS taps some of the variance associated with the construct of attachment security. Even for infants, however, the strength of relationship among these variables is moderate or low; there is also no direct evidence that classifications and AQS security are congruent in the preschool period (in part because there are so few studies). Because of their paradoxical finding that the strength of association between AQS security and attachment classification is weaker than that between AQS scores and maternal sensitivity, van IJzendoorn et al. (in press) raise the unsettling suggestion that these measures do not tap the same underlying construct. It is not to be expected—indeed, it may not even be desirable—for any two measures of a construct to be perfectly correlated. Nonetheless, it may be helpful to explore the sources of nonconvergence in order to better estimate and understand the underlying construct of security.

A besetting question for this method is whether mothers or trained observers are the more appropriate sources of secure-base data. There is empirical evidence of bias or measurement error in parental sorts. For example, Belsky and Rovine (1990) found that only when social desirability was partialed out of mothers' AQS descriptions could a relation to strange situation classifications be demonstrated. In comparison to observer sorts, maternal sorts are more likely to be correlated with temperament measures, suggesting that mothers' sorts are biased by their perceptions of their children's temperaments (van IJzendoorn et al., in press). Investigators have also demonstrated systematic (although apparently contradictory) differences between mother and observer sorts corresponding to children's strange situation classifications (Stevenson-Hinde & Shouldice, 1990) or to maternal sensitivity (Vereijken & Kondo-Ikemura, in press). It is likely that these sorting biases reflect the same maternal information-processing biases that are believed to be causal factors in the development of the different types of attachment relationships (Cassidy & Kobak, 1988; George & Solomon, 1996b; Main, 1995).

Observers may be susceptible to different sorts of bias or error. The results of meta-analysis show that mothers' and observers' sorts predict strange situation classifications about equally well (or poorly) (van IJzendoorn et al., in press). Yet the association between maternal sensitivity and AQS security is considerably higher when observers sort than when mothers do. In contrast to the strange situation, a mother's behavior is not constrained in the home, and it is quite likely that the observer's impression of one partner influences his or her impression of the other. In Deane's original Q-sort study (Waters & Deane, 1985), and in Teti and McGourty's (1996) more recent effort, maternal and observer agreement was moderate to very strong (.50–.80) when observers had sufficient opportunity to see relevant child behavior. If an observer's perceptions as he or she learns more about a child become more like a mother's, which is the more accurate observer?

In our view, the lack of congruence between the AQS and strange situation classifications is rooted in the different contexts of the home and of the laboratory separation and reunion. In the placid and relatively safe environment of the middle-class home, there is little to activate the attachment system. Consequently, a certain amount of what is observed in the home is quite likely to be a function of child temperament (including sociability), the immediate physical and social environment, the family milieu (e.g., marital harmony), and more transitory influences (e.g., the health, mood, and current activities of the participants). That is, the AQS as generally employed will necessarily be imprecise with respect to a child's generalized expectations regarding maternal availability and responsiveness, which are what are believed to be assessed in the strange situation. The context of observation can be expected to be increasingly important past infancy, since situations that strongly activate attachment are very rarely observed in the home as children mature (Solomon et al., in press). Observations of mothers and children under more stressful or threatening conditions (e.g., busy parks, stores, doctors' offices, airports) might increase the convergence of AQS scores with reunion-based classifications and allow the quality

of the attachment relationship to be disentangled from other influences in the home.

The effect of context on measures of attachment security may be even more complex. Ainsworth et al. (1978) noted that discrepancies between patterns of secure-base behavior in the home and attachment classifications could often be explained by recent changes in maternal sensitivity. Thus home observations may be rather accurate as to the current state of a mother–child relationship, but the child's expectations regarding the mother's responsiveness may lag behind.[6] A final possibility is that the strange situation classification reflects a child's experience of the mother as responsive (or not) when the child is under stress, but not his or her experience of the mother under conditions of low stress. This certainly would be consistent with the nature of more mature relationships. We are unlikely to hold it against those we depend on if they snub us mildly in everyday life, as long as they are truly there for us when we feel we *really* need them. The inverse should also be true: We may dismiss, discount, or at least hesitate to put faith in the sensitive responsiveness of others if we still cannot forgive them for the times they failed or disappointed us.

Finally, questions may be asked about the validity of the expert (criterion) sorts themselves. AQS researchers have emphasized that the organization of secure-base relevant behaviors (i.e., the child's profile relative to the expert Q-sort of the security construct) is the best measure of security (Posada, Gao, et al., 1995). Experts may agree, and yet the criterion sort may still require some revision.[7] The validity of the criterion sort for 3-year-olds is especially problematic: At this time, there simply is not a sufficient descriptive base from which to derive a sound criterion. A general concern is that expert sorts may confound core attachment phenomena with other behaviors, which are correlated with attachment patterns under some circumstances but not others. For example, in some cultures the infant is very rarely out of proximity with the mother; distance communication (including affective sharing between mother and baby) is rare, as is the provision of toys or maternal involvement in cognitive stimulation (Ainsworth, 1967; Brazelton, 1977; Goldberg, 1977; Levine & Miller, 1990; M. True, personal communication, 1996). Within the infant criterion sort, however, some items reflecting these kinds of interactions are given great weight (i.e., have relatively extreme placement in the sort). The only way to determine whether the current weighting of items is appropriate is to test and refine criterion sorts against strange situation classifications cross-culturally and with respect to extensive naturalistic observations.

SUMMARY AND CONCLUSIONS

Our overview of attachment security measures reveals a robust field in a period of active expansion and experimentation. In the last decade, several new measures have emerged as researchers have attempted to validate the original Ainsworth classification measure and to test and extend attachment theory past the second year of life. Many researchers have given attention to the basic requirements of construct validation as we have outlined them here. At the same time, it must be acknowledged that few have been entirely systematic or thorough in this regard. Not surprisingly, as the strange situation was developed nearly 30 years ago, the most complete information is available for it. Researchers who use other measures should be aware of the substantial gaps that remain in their validation.

In our view, the greatest uncertainty surrounds assessment of attachment security in the early preschool years (approximately 21 to 48 months). As discussed earlier, this period of development presents special challenges. The attachment system is not as easily activated in the preschool-age child as in the infant, and the behavioral repertoire exhibited by children in this age group is broader. In contrast to those of older children, the linguistic and representational capacities of preschoolers are still primitive and vary greatly between children and across situations. Thus both brief observational measures and representational measures appear to be less robust and less sensitive than might be expected. There is a tremendous need for long-term, naturalistic studies of attachment relationships in this theoretically critical age range.

The study of attachment security had its beginnings in Ainsworth's careful, ethologically influenced observations. These early studies, despite their reliance on small, homogeneous samples, provided a relatively sturdy base for a paradigm shift in the study of social and emotional development. Ainsworth's approach moved the field away from a trait-like view of infant dependency to one in which patterns of attachment were understood to reflect qualitative differences in the organization of the attachment and exploratory behavioral systems (Ainsworth, 1969). Similarly, Ainsworth's focus on maternal sensitivity definitively moved the field away from behaviorist and psychoanalytic approaches to the development of infant–parent bonds, and toward an emphasis on the contingent, reciprocal nature of mother–child interaction. Unfortunately, the explanatory appeal of the Ainsworth research paradigm and its predictive successes have engendered certain theoretical and methodological confusions or errors. We would like to comment on two of them here.

An error at the conceptual or theoretical level is a common, implicit assumption in the literature that secure child–mother attachment will in all contexts predict maternal sensitivity, positive affect on the part of the child, and harmonious interaction. In other words, attachment has come to stand for the whole of the multifaceted child–parent relationship (Hinde, 1982). One result of this thinking is that most researchers have given inadequate thought to the contexts in which they have observed parents and children. In contrast, we have emphasized throughout this chapter that attachment behavior is elicited by, and is best observed in, situations that are stressful, threatening, or fear-inducing for the child or that evoke those states in the child's memory. Assessments of the child–mother relationship in other contexts (e.g., play, problem solving) may yield measures that are correlated with attachment security measured under stressful circumstances, but are not equivalent to it. We have gone on to hypothesize that attachment security and insecurity are based primarily upon the infant's experiences with the caregiver in those moments in which the infant's attachment system is activated.

The other problem to which we draw attention is a methodological one that arises from the accelerated pace of research in attachment over the last decade. This acceleration seems to have been accompanied by a kind of frontier mentality regarding the development and use of new measures, at least by some investigators. In some ways this movement can be likened to a gold rush, and the prospect of discovering empirical "gold" may sometimes blind researchers to important validation issues. We especially caution researchers with regard to the following procedures, which have appeared in both published papers and conference presentations: (1) using measures developed for one age range (e.g., 24–48 months) in studies of earlier or later ages without prior, independent validation of the measure for the new period; (2) incorporating one or more procedures, measures, or coding systems into a new measure, and claiming validation for the new measure on the basis of data collected for the original procedures; (3) developing a coding or classification system for a new measure based only on *a priori,* theoretical considerations or only on findings with a theoretically similar measure, without refining these on the basis of empirical findings; (4) referring solely to the opinion of an "expert" by way of establishing reliability or validity for a new measure; and (5) asserting a new measure to be valid based on similarities in the distribution of classifications that emerge in the new system, compared to the distribution of classifications found with other measures or at other ages.

These procedures can be seen as creative shortcuts to the very real problems of measure development in the field. They are attractive because attachment research tends to require considerable training by experts, as well as lengthy, time-consuming, repeated, and hence expensive observations of subjects. Pressure within academia to publish quickly, ever more limited funding, and journal preferences all work against deliberation and caution in developing and validating new measures. It is a rare researcher who wishes to dedicate his or her career to validating existing measures. This enterprise is basic to the scientific endeavor, however, and should be taken as a collective responsibility within the field as a whole.

NOTES

1. It must be emphasized that the construct of security is meaningful only for a relationship in which a child has already developed an attachment to a particular caregiver. In situations in which this is in doubt, such as in studies involving transitions to foster care, the interpretation of any measure of security is problematic.

2. Because of space constraints, we rely for this review mainly on the published literature. This may have the unintended consequence of exaggerating rather than minimizing the appearance of a relation between any two variables, but it ensures that the studies have undergone peer review.

3. In evaluating the magnitude of intercoder stability or continuity figures, one should note that when classification groups are disproportionately represented in the sample, high overall concordance may mask poor concordance for one or several of the (less common) groups. This is a particular problem in attachment research, because secure classifications usually account for at least 50% of cases in normative samples. Indeed, several investigators have noted that high stability in classification is actually disproportionately due to stability (continuity) in the secure group, but not in the insecure groups (Belsky, Campbell, Cohn, & Moore, 1996; Solomon & George, 1996; van IJzendoorn, Juffer, & Duyvesteyn, 1995; Waters, Treboux, Crowell, Merrick, & Albersheim, 1995). It is recommended that researchers report kappa statistics, which are adjusted for the relative frequencies of categories, along with raw reliability/stability figures. A large discrepancy between the raw (unweighted) concordance statistic and kappa indicates that agreement, stability, and so on are unevenly distributed in the sample.

4. The interactive scales, along with measures of other aspects of infant behavior in the strange situation, have been used to derive two discriminant functions (broadly representing avoidance and resistance in the strange situation) (Richters, Waters, & Vaughn, 1988). These can be used to produce "classifications" with high correspondence to classification by trained judges. Only a few researchers have made use of this empirical approach to classification (see Ainsworth et al., 1978; Belsky et al., 1996). Individual differences in scores on these two functions could theoretically be used to provide more sensitive, dimensional data in attachment studies. The discriminant functions do not tap aspects of behavior relevant to attachment disorganization, however, and are therefore not appropriate for studies in which attachment disorganization is a focus of interest.

5. Easterbrooks et al. (1993) used the Main and Cassidy manual, but were trained on the Cassidy–Marvin system; Moss et al. (1996) relied entirely on the Cassidy–Marvin system.

6. A similar possibility is suggested by a review of the effects of clinical interventions on attachment classification (van IJzendoorn et al., 1995). Several studies reviewed by these investigators reported improvements in maternal sensitivity to a child without a concomitant move by the child to a secure classification.

7. According to data provided by Posada, Gao, et al. (1995), the expert sort seems to describe best the 3-year-old child of mature graduate student parents in Norway. Modal security scores in this sample were the highest of any of those studied.

REFERENCES

Achermann, J., Dinneen, E., & Stevenson-Hinde, J. (1991). Cleaning up at 2.5 years. *British Journal of Developmental Psychology, 9,* 365–376.

Ainsworth, M. D. S. (1967). *Infancy in Uganda: Infant care and the growth of love.* Baltimore: Johns Hopkins University Press.

Ainsworth, M. D. S. (1969). Object relations, dependency, and attachment: A theoretical review of the infant–mother relationship. *Child Development, 40,* 969–1025.

Ainsworth, M. D. S., Blehar, M. C., Waters, E., & Wall, S.

(1978). *Patterns of attachment: A psychological study of the strange situation.* Hillsdale, NJ: Erlbaum.

Ainsworth, M. D. S., & Marvin, R. S. (1995). On the shaping of attachment theory and research: An interview with Mary D. S. Ainsworth. In E. Waters, B. E. Vaughn, G. Posada, & K. Kondo-Ikemura (Eds.), Caregiving, cultural, and cognitive perspectives on secure-base behavior and working models. *Monographs of the Society for Research in Child Development, 60*(2–3, Serial No. 244), 3–12.

Ainsworth, M. D. S., & Wittig, B. A. (1969). Attachment and exploratory behaviour of one-year olds in a strange situation. In B. M. Foss (Ed.), *Determinants of infant behaviour* (Vol. 4, pp. 113–136). London: Methuen.

Belsky, J. (1996). Parent, infant, and social-contextual antecedents of attachment security. *Developmental Psychology, 32*, 905–913.

Belsky, J., Campbell, S., Cohn, J., & Moore, G. (1996). Instability of attachment security. *Developmental Psychology, 32*, 921–924.

Belsky, J., & Rovine, M. (1987). Temperament and attachment security in the Strange Situation: An empirical rapprochement. *Child Development, 58*, 787–795.

Belsky, J., & Rovine, M. (1990). *Q*-sort security and first-year non-maternal care. In K. McCartney (Ed.), *New directions in child development: No. 49. The social ecology of daycare* (pp. 7–22). San Francisco: Jossey-Bass.

Bosso, O. R., Corter, C. M., & Abramovitch, R. (in press). Attachment security in three-year-old first born children: Relations to Strange Situation classifications and to behavior toward a younger sibling. In E. Waters, B. Vaughn, & D. Teti (Eds.), *Patterns of secure base behavior: Q-sort perspectives on attachment and caregiving.* Mahwah, NJ: Erlbaum.

Bowlby, J. (1969/1982). *Attachment and loss: Vol. 1. Attachment.* New York: Basic Books.

Bowlby, J. (1973). *Attachment and loss: Vol 2. Separation.* New York: Basic Books.

Bowlby, J. (1980). *Attachment and loss: Vol 3. Loss.* New York: Basic Books.

Brazelton, T. B. (1977). Implications of infant development among the Mayan Indians of Mexico. In P. H. Leiderman, A. Tulkin, & A. Rosenfield (Eds.), *Culture and infancy* (pp. 151–187). New York: Academic Press.

Bretherton, I. (1985). Attachment theory: Retrospect and prospect. In I. Bretherton & E. Waters (Eds.), Growing points of attachment theory and research. *Monographs of the Society for Research in Child Development, 50*(1–2, Serial No. 209), 3–35.

Bretherton, I., Ridgeway, D., & Cassidy, J. (1990). Assessing internal working models of the attachment relationship: An attachment story completion task for 3-year-olds. In M. T. Greenbergh, D. Cicchetti, & E. M. Cummings (Eds.), *Attachment in the preschool years* (pp. 273–308). Chicago: University of Chicago Press.

Campbell, D., & Fiske, D. (1959). Convergent and discriminant validation by the multitrait multimethod matrix. *Psychological Bulletin, 56*, 81–105.

Carlson, E. A. (1998). A prospective longitudinal study of disorganized/disoriented attachment. *Child Development, 69*, 1107–1128.

Carlson, E. A., & Sroufe, L. A. (1993, Spring). Reliability in attachment classification. *Society for Research in Child Development Newsletter*, p. 12.

Carlson, V., Cicchetti, D., Barnett, D., & Braunwald, K. (1989). Finding order in disorganization. In D. Cicchetti & V. Carlson (Eds.), *Child maltreatment: Theory and re-search on the causes and consequences of child abuse and neglect* (pp. 494–528). New York: Cambridge University Press.

Carr, S. J., Dabbs, J. M., & Carr, T. S. (1975). Mother–infant attachment: The importance of the mother's visual field. *Child Development, 46*, 331–338.

Cassidy, J. (1988). Child–mother attachment and the self in six-year olds. *Child Development, 59*, 121–134.

Cassidy, J., Berlin, L., & Belsky, J. (1990, April). *Attachment organization at age 3: Antecedent and concurrent correlates.* Paper presented at the biennial meeting of the International Conference on Infant Studies, Montreal.

Cassidy, J., & Kobak, R. R. (1988). Avoidance and its relation to other defensive processes. In J. Belsky & T. Nezworski (Eds.), *Clinical implications of attachment* (pp. 300–323). Hillsdale, NJ: Erlbaum.

Cassidy, J., & Marvin, R. S. (1987). *Attachment organization in preschool children: Coding guidelines.* Unpublished manuscript, MacArthur Working Group on Attachment, Seattle, WA.

Cassidy, J., & Marvin, R. S. (1990). *Attachment organization in preschool children: Coding guidelines* (2nd ed.). Unpublished manuscript, MacArthur Working Group on Attachment, Seattle, WA.

Cassidy, J., & Marvin, R. S. (1991). *Attachment organization in preschool children: Coding guidelines* (3rd ed.). Unpublished manuscript, MacArthur Working Group on Attachment, Seattle, WA.

Cassidy, J., & Marvin, R. S. (1992). *Attachment organization in preschool children: Coding guidelines* (4th ed.). Unpublished manuscript, MacArthur Working Group on Attachment, Seattle, WA.

Chandler, M. J. (1973). Egocentrism and antisocial behavior: The assessment and training of social perspective-taking skills. *Developmental Psychology, 9*, 326–332.

Cicchetti, D., & Barnett, D. (1991). Attachment organization in maltreated preschoolers. *Development and Psychopathology, 3*, 397–411.

Cohn, D. A. (1990). Child–mother attachment of six-year-olds and social competence at school. *Child Development, 61*, 152–162.

Cox, M. J., Owen, M. T., Henderson, V. K., & Margand, N. A. (1992). Prediction of infant–father and infant–mother attachment. *Developmental Psychology, 28*, 474–483.

Crittenden, P. M. (1992a). The quality of attachment in the preschool years. *Development and Psychopathology, 4*, 209–241.

Crittenden, P. M. (1992b). *Preschool Assessment of Attachment.* Unpublished manuscript, Family Relations Institute, Miami, FL.

Crittenden, P. M. (1994). *Preschool Assessment of Attachment* (2nd ed.). Unpublished manuscript, Family Relations Institute, Miami, FL.

Crittenden, P. M., & Claussen, A. H. (1994). *Validation of two procedures for assessing quality of attachment in the preschool years.* Paper presented at the biennial meeting of the International Conference on Infant Studies, Paris.

Cronbach, L. J., & Meehl, P. E. (1955). Construct validity in psychological tests. *Psychological Bulletin, 52*, 281–302.

Del Carmen, R., Pederson, F., Huffman, L. C., & Bryan, Y. E. (in press). Maternal and paternal constructions of three-year-olds' secure base behavior: Concurrent and antecedent relationships. In E. Waters, B. Vaughn, & D. Teti (Eds.), *Patterns of secure base behavior: Q-sort perspectives on attachment and caregiving.* Mahwah, NJ: Erlbaum.

DeMulder, E. K., & Radke-Yarrow, M. (1991). Attachment

with affectively ill and well mothers: Concurrent behavioral correlates. *Development and Psychopathology, 3*, 227–242.

DeWolff, M. S., & van IJzendoorn, M. H. (1997). Sensitivity and attachment: A meta-analysis on parental antecedents of infant attachment. *Child Development, 68*, 571–591.

Easterbrooks, M. A., Davidson, C. E., & Chazan, R. (1993). Psychosocial risk, attachment, and behavior problems among school-aged children. *Development and Psychopathology, 5*, 389–402.

Easterbrooks, M. A., & Goldberg, W. A. (1984). Toddler development in the family: Impact of father involvement and parenting characteristics. *Child Development, 55*, 1273–1285.

Erikson, E. H. (1950). *Childhood and society*. New York: Norton.

Fagot, B. I., & Pears, K. S. (1996). Changes in attachment during the third year: Consequences and predictions. *Development and Psychopathology, 8*, 325–344.

Flavell, J. H. (1986). The development of children's knowledge about the appearance–reality distinction. *American Psychologist, 41*, 418–424.

Fogel, A., & Thelen, E. (1987). Development of early expressive and communicative action: Reinterpreting the evidence from a dynamic systems perspective. *Developmental Psychology, 23*, 747–761.

Fox, N. A., Kimmerly, N. L., & Schafer, W. D. (1981). Attachment to mother/attachment to father: A meta-analysis. *Child Development, 62*, 210–225.

Fury, G. S., Carlson, E. A., & Sroufe, L. A. (1997). Children's representations of attachment in family drawings. *Child Development, 68*, 1154–1164.

George, C., Kaplan, N., & Main, M. (1984). *Adult Attachment Interview*. Unpublished manuscript, University of California at Berkeley.

George, C., Kaplan, N., & Main, M. (1985). *Adult Attachment Interview* (2nd ed.). Unpublished manuscript, University of California at Berkeley.

George, C., Kaplan, N., & Main, M. (1996). *Adult Attachment Interview* (3rd ed.). Unpublished manuscript, University of California at Berkeley.

George, C., & Solomon, J. (1994). *Six-year attachment doll play procedures and classification system*. Unpublished manuscript, Mills College, Oakland, CA.

George, C., & Solomon, J. (1996a, August). *Assessing internal working models of attachment through doll play*. Paper presented at the biennial meeting of the International Society for the Study of Behavioral Development, Québec City, Québec, Canada.

George, C., & Solomon, J. (1996b). Representational models of relationships: Links between caregiving and attachment. *Infant Mental Health Journal, 17*, 198–216.

Goldberg, S. (1977). Infant development and mother-infant interaction in urban Zambia. In P. H. Leiderman, A. Tulkin, & A. Rosenfield (Eds.), *Culture and infancy* (pp. 211–243). New York: Academic Press.

Goldsmith, H. H., & Alansky, J. (1987). Maternal and infant temperamental predictors of attachment: A meta-analytic review. *Journal of Consulting and Clinical Psychology, 55*, 805–816.

Goldsmith, H. H., & Harman, C. (1994). Temperament and attachment: Individuals and relationships. *Current Directions in Psychological Science, 3*, 53–57.

Greenberg, M. T., Speltz, M. L., DeKlyen, M., & Endriga, M. (1991). Attachment security in preschoolers with and without externalizing behavior problems: A replication. *Development and Psychopathology, 3*, 413–430.

Grossmann, K. E., & Grossmann, K. (1991). Attachment quality as an organizer of emotional and behavioral responses in a longitudinal perspective. In C. M. Parkes, J. Stevenson-Hinde, & P. Marris (Eds.), *Attachment across the life cycle* (pp. 93–114). Tavistock, UK: Routledge.

Grossmann, K. (1997, April). *Infant–father attachment relationship: Sensitive challenges during play with toddler is the pivotal feature*. Poster presented at the biennial meeting of the Society for Research in Child Development, Washington, DC.

Grossmann, K., Grossmann, K. E., Spangler, G., Suess, G., & Unzer, L. (1985). Maternal sensitivity and newborns' orientation responses as related to quality of attachment in northern Germany. In I. Bretherton & E. Waters (Eds.), Growing points of attachment theory and research. *Monographs of the Society for Research in Child Development, 50*(1–2, Serial No. 209), 233–256.

Hamilton, C. E. (in press). Continuity and discontinuity of attachment from infancy through adolescence. *Child Development*.

Hansburg, H. G. (1972). *Adolescent separation anxiety: Vol. 1. A method for the study of adolescent separation problems*. Springfield, IL: Charles C. Thomas.

Hinde, R. A. (1982). Attachment: Some conceptual and biological issues. In C. M. Parkes & J. Stevenson-Hinde (Eds.), *The place of attachment in human behavior* (pp. 60–70). New York: Basic Books.

Howes, C., & Hamilton, C. E. (1992). Children's relationships with child-care teachers: Stability and concordance with parental attachments. *Child Development, 63*, 867–878.

Howes, C., & Markman, H. J. (1989). Marital quality and child functioning: A longitudinal investigation. *Child Development, 60*, 1044–1051.

Jackson, J. I. (1993). Multiple caregiving among African-Americans and infant attachment: The need for an emic approach. *Human Development, 36*, 87–102.

Jacobsen, T., Edelstein, W., & Hofmann, V. (1994). A longitudinal study of the relation between representations of attachment in childhood and cognitive functioning in childhood and adolescence. *Developmental Psychology, 30*, 112–124.

Jacobsen, T., & Hofmann, V. (in press). Children's attachment representations: Longitudinal relations to school behavior and academic competency in middle childhood and adolescence. *Developmental Psychology*.

Kaplan, N. (1987). *Individual differences in six-year-olds' thoughts about separation: Predicted from attachment to mother at one year of age*. Unpublished doctoral dissertation, University of California at Berkeley.

Kaplan, N., & Main, M. (1986). *A system for the analysis of children's family drawings in terms of attachment*. Unpublished manuscript, Department of Psychology, University of California at Berkeley.

Klagsbrun, M., & Bowlby, J. (1976). Responses to separation from parents: A clinical test for young children. *British Journal of Projective Psychology, 21*, 7–21.

Kermoian, R., & Leiderman, P. H. (1986). Infant attachment to mother and child caretaker in an East African community. *International Journal of Behavioral Development, 9*, 455–469.

Lamb, M. E. (1976). Effects of stress and cohort on mother- and father-infant interaction. *Developmental Psychology, 12*, 435–443.

LaFreniere, P. J., Provost, M. A., & Dubeau, D. (1992). From an insecure base: Parent–child relations and internalizing behavior in the pre-school. *Early Development and Parenting, 1,* 137–148.

Levine, R. A., & Miller, P. M. (1990) Commentary. *Human Development, 33,* 73–80.

Lyons-Ruth, K. (1996). Attachment relationships among children with aggressive behavior problems: The role of disorganized early attachment problems. *Journal of Consulting and Clinical Psychology, 64,* 64–73.

Lyons-Ruth, K., Alpern, L., & Repacholi, B. (1993). Disorganized infant attachment classification and maternal psychosomatic problems as predictors of hostile–aggressive behavior in the preschool classroom. *Child Development, 64,* 572–585.

Lyons-Ruth, K., & Block, D. (1996). The disturbed caregiving system: Relationships among childhood trauma, maternal caregiving, and infant affect and attachment. *Infant Mental Health Journal, 17,* 257–275.

Lyons-Ruth, K., Repacholi, B., McLeod, S., & Silva, E. (1991). Disorganized attachment behavior in infancy: Short-term stability, maternal and infant correlates, and risk-related subtypes. *Development and Psychopathology, 3,* 377–396.

Main, M. (1995). Recent studies in attachment: Overview, with selected implications for clinical work. In S. Goldberg, R. Muir, & J. Kerr (Eds.), *Attachment theory: Social, development, and clinical implications* (pp. 407–474). Hillsdale, NJ: Analytic Press.

Main, M., & Cassidy, J. (1988). Categories of response to reunion with the parent at age 6: Predictable from infant attachment classifications and stable over a 1-month period. *Developmental Psychology, 24,* 1–12.

Main, M., & Hesse, E. (1990). Parents' unresolved traumatic experiences are related to infant disorganized attachment status: Is frightened or frightening parental behavior the linking mechanism? In M. T. Greenberg, D. Cicchetti, & E. M. Cummings, (Eds.), *Attachment in the preschool years* (pp. 161–184). Chicago: University of Chicago Press.

Main, M., Kaplan, N., & Cassidy, J. (1985). Security in infancy, childhood and adulthood: A move to the level of representation. In I. Bretherton & E. Waters (Eds.), *Growing points of attachment theory and research. Monographs of the Society for Research in Child Development, 50*(1–2, Serial No. 209), 66–104.

Main, M., & Solomon, J. (1986). Discovery of a new, insecure–disorganized/disoriented attachment pattern. In T. B. Brazelton & M. Yogman (Eds.), *Affective development in infancy* (pp. 95–124). Norwood, NJ: Ablex.

Main, M., & Solomon, J. (1990). Procedures for identifying infants as disorganized/disoriented during the Ainsworth strange situation. In M. T. Greenberg, D. Cicchetti, & E. M. Cummings (Eds.), *Attachment in the preschool years* (pp. 121–160). Chicago: University of Chicago Press.

Main, M., & Weston, D. R. (1981). The quality of the toddler's relationship to mother and father: Related to conflict behavior and readiness to establish new relationships. *Child Development, 52,* 932–940.

Manassis, K., Bradley, S., Goldberg, S., Hood, J., & Swinson, R. P. (1994). Attachment in mothers with anxiety disorders and their children. *Journal of the American Academy of Child and Adolescent Psychiatry, 33,* 1106–1113.

Mangelsdorf, S. C., Plunkett, J. W., Dedrick, C. F., Berlin, M., Meisels, S. J., McHale, J. L., & Dichtellmiller, M. (1996). Attachment security in very low birth weight babies. *Developmental Psychology, 32,* 914–920.

Marcovitch, S., Goldberg, S., Gold, A., Washington, J., Wasson, C., Krekewich, K., & Handley-Derry, M. (1997). Determinants of behavioral problems in Romanian children adopted in Ontario. *International Journal of Behavioral Development, 20,* 17–31.

Marvin, R. S. (1977). An ethological–cognitive model of the attenuation of mother–child attachment behavior. In T. Alloway, L. Krames, & P. Pilner (Eds.), *Advances in the study of communication and affect: Vol. 3. Attachment behavior* (pp. 25–60). New York: Plenum Press.

Marvin, R. S., & Pianta, R. C. (1996). Mothers' reactions to their child's diagnosis: Relations with security of attachment. *Journal of Clinical Child Psychology, 25,* 436–445.

Miyake, K., Chen, S., & Campos, J. J. (1985). Infant temperament, mother's mode of interaction, and attachment in Japan: An interim report. In I. Bretherton & E. Waters (Eds.), Growing points of attachment theory and research. *Monographs of the Society for Research in Child Development, 50*(1–2, Serial No. 209), 276–297.

Moss, E., Parent, S., Gosselin, C., Rousseau, D., & St-Laurent, D. (1996). Attachment and teacher-reported behavior problems during the preschool and early school-age period. *Development and Psychopathology, 8,* 511–525.

Moss, E., Rousseau, D., Parent, S., St-Laurent, D., & Saintonge, J. (1998). Attachment at school-age: Maternal reported stress, mother–child interaction, and behavior problems. *Child Development, 69,* 1390–1405.

Nakagawa, M., Teit, D. M., & Lamb, M. E. (1992). An ecological study of child–mother attachments among Japanese sojourners in the United States. *Developmental Psychology, 28,* 584–592.

Nunnally, J. C. (1978). *Psychometric theory.* New York: McGraw-Hill.

O'Connor, M., Sigman, M., & Brill, N. (1987). Disorganization of attachment in relation to maternal alcohol consumption. *Journal of Consulting and Clinical Psychology.*

Ogawa, J. R., Sroufe, L. A., Weinfield, N. S., Carlson, E., & Egeland, B. (1997). Development and the fragmented self: Longitudinal study of dissociative symptomatology in a nonclinical sample. *Developmental Psychopathology, 9,* 855–879.

Oppenheim, D., & Waters, H. S. (1995). Narrative processes and attachment representations: Issues of development and assessment. In E. Waters, B. E. Vaughn, G. Posada, & K. Kondo-Ikemura (Eds.), Caregiving, cultural, and cognitive perspectives on secure-base behavior and working models. *Monographs of the Society for Research in Child Development, 60*(2–3, Serial No. 244), 197–233.

Park, K. A., & Waters, E. (1989). Security of attachment and preschool friendships. *Child Development, 60,* 1076–1081.

Pederson, D. R., & Moran, G. (1995). A categorical description of infant–mother relationships in the home and its relation to Q-sort measures of infant–mother interaction. In E. Waters, B. E. Vaughn, G. Posada, & K. Kondo-Ikemura (Eds.), Caregiving, cultural, and cognitive perspectives on secure-base behavior and working models. *Monographs of the Society for Research in Child Development, 60*(2–3, Serial No. 244), 111–132.

Pederson, D. R., Moran, G., Sitko, C., Campbell, K., Ghesquire, K., & Acton, H. (1990). Maternal sensitivity and the security of infant–mother attachment: A Q-sort study. *Child Development, 61,* 1974–1983.

Pianta, R. C., Longmaid, K., & Ferguson, J. E. (in press). Attachment-based classifications of children's family drawings: Psychometric properties and relations with children's adjustment in kindergarten. *Journal of Clinical Child Psychology.*

Posada, G., Gao, Y., Wu, F., Posada, R., Tascon, M.,

Schöelmerich, A., Sagi, A., Kondo-Ikemura, K., Haaland, W., & Synnevaag, B. (1995). The secure-base phenomenon across cultures: Children's behavior, mothers' preferences, and experts' concepts. In E. Waters, B. E. Vaughn, G. Posada, & K. Kondo-Ikemura (Eds.), Caregiving, cultural, and cognitive perspectives on secure-base behavior and working models. *Monographs of the Society for Research in Child Development, 60*(2–3, Serial No. 244), 27–48.

Posada, G., Waters, E., Crowell, J., & Lay, K. (1995). Is it easier to use a secure mother as a secure base: Attachment Q-Set correlates of the Adult Attachment Interview. In E. Waters, B. E. Vaughn, G. Posada, & K. Kondo-Ikemura (Eds.), Caregiving, cultural, and cognitive perspectives on secure-base behavior and working models. *Monographs of the Society for Research in Child Development, 60*(2–3, Serial No. 244), 133–144.

Posada, G., Waters, E., Marvin, R., & Cassidy, J. (in press). Three-year-olds' ability to use the mother as a secure base: A comparison of the MacArthur strange situation classifications with naturalistic observations using the attachment Q-set. In E. Waters, B. Vaughn, G. Posada, & D. Teti (Eds.), *Patterns of secure base behavior: Q-sort perspectives on attachment and caregiving in infancy and childhood.* Mahwah, NJ: Erlbaum.

Rheingold, H. L., & Eckerman, C. O. (1970). The infant separates himself from his mother. *Science, 168,* 78–83.

Richters, J., Waters, E., & Vaughn, B. (1988). Empirical classification of infant–mother relationships from interactive behavior and crying during reunion. *Child Development, 59,* 512–522.

Sagi, A. (1990). Attachment theory and research from a cross-cultural perspective. *Human Development, 33,* 10–22.

Sagi, A., Lamb, M. E., Lewkowicz, K. S., Shoham, R., Dvir, R., & Estes, D. (1985). Security of infant–mother, –father, and –*metapelet* attachments among kibbutz-reared Israeli children. In I. Bretherton & E. Waters (Eds.), Growing points of attachment theory and research. *Monographs of the Society for Research in child development, 50*(1–2, Serial No. 209), 257–275.

Sagi, A., van IJzendoorn, M., Aviezer, O., Donnell, F., Koren-Karie, N., Joels, T., & Harel, Y. (1995). Attachments in a multiple-caregiver and multiple-infant environment: The case of the Israeli kibbutzim. In E. Waters, B. E. Vaughn, G. Posada, & K. Kondo-Ikemura (Ed.), Caregiving, cultural, and cognitive perspectives on secure-base behavior and working models. *Monographs of the Society for Research in Child Development, 60*(2–3, Serial No. 244), 71–91.

Scheungel, C., van IJzendoorn, M. H., & Bakermans-Kranenburg, M. J. (in press). Frightening maternal behavior linking unresolved loss and disorganized infant attachment. *Journal Consulting and Clinical Psychology.*

Schneider-Rosen, K. (1990). The developmental reorganization of attachment relationships: Guidelines for classification beyond infancy. In M. T. Greenberg, D. Cicchetti, & E. M. Cummings (Eds.), *Attachment in the preschool years* (pp. 185–220). Chicago: University of Chicago Press.

Schneider-Rosen, K., & Rothbaum, R. (1993). Quality of parental caregiving and security of attachment. *Developmental Psychology, 29,* 358–367.

Scholmerich, A., Fracasso, M. P., Lamb, M. E., & Broberg, A. G. (1995). Interactional harmony at 7 and 10 months of age predicts security of attachment as measured by Q-sort ratings. *Social Development, 4,* 62–74.

Seifer, R., & Schiller, M. (1995). The role of parenting sensitivity, infant temperament, and dyadic interaction in attachment theory and assessment. In E. Waters, B. E. Vaughn, G. Posada, & K. Kondo-Ikemura (Eds.), Caregiving, cultural, and cognitive perspectives on secure-base behavior and working models. *Monographs of the Society for Research in Child Development, 60*(2–3, Serial No. 244), 146–174.

Shouldice, A., & Stevenson-Hinde, J. (1992). Coping with security distress: The Separation Anxiety Test and attachment classification at 4.5 years. *Journal of Child Psychology and Psychiatry, 33,* 331–348.

Slough, N. M., & Greenberg, M. T. (1990). Five-year olds' representations of separation from parents: Responses from the perspective of self and other. In I. Bretherton & M. W. Watson (Eds.), *New directions for child development: No. 48. Children's perspectives on the family* (pp. 67–84). San Francisco: Jossey-Bass.

Solomon, J., & George, C., (1996, April). *The effects on attachment of overnight visitation in divorced and separated families.* Paper presented at the biennial meeting of the International Conference on Infant Studies, Providence, RI.

Solomon, J., & George, C. (in press). The place of disorganization in attachment theory: Linking classic observations with contemporary findings. In J. Solomon & C. George (Eds.), *Attachment disorganization.* New York: Guilford Press.

Solomon, J., George, C., & De Jong, A. (1995). Children classified as controlling at age six: Evidence of disorganized representational strategies and aggression at home and at school. *Development and Psychopathology, 7,* 447–463.

Solomon, J., George, C., & Silverman, N. (in press). Maternal caretaking Q-sort: Describing age-related changes in mother–child interaction. In E. Waters, B. Vaughn, & D. Teti (Eds.), *Patterns of secure base behavior: Q-sort perspectives on attachment and caregiving.* Mahwah, NJ: Erlbaum.

Speltz, M., Greenberg, M. T., & DeKlyen, M. (1990). Attachment in preschoolers with disruptive behavior: A comparison of clinic-referred and non-problem children. *Development and Psychopathology, 2,* 31–46.

Spangler, G., Fremmer-Bombik, E., & Grossmann, K. (1996). Social and individual determinants of attachment security and disorganization during the first year. *Infant Mental Health Journal, 17,* 127–139.

Sroufe, L. A. (1979). The coherence of individual development. *American Psychologist, 34,* 834–841.

Sroufe, L. A. & Waters, E. (1977). Attachment as an organizational construct. *Child Development, 48,* 1184–1199.

Stevenson-Hinde, J., & Shouldice, A. (1990). Fear and attachment in 2.5-year olds. *British Journal of Developmental Psychology, 8,* 319–333.

Stevenson-Hinde, J., & Shouldice, A. (1995). Maternal interactions and self-reports related to attachment classifications at 4.5 years. *Child Development, 66,* 583–596.

Strayer, F. F., Verissimo, M., Vaughn, B. E., & Howes, C. (1995). A quantitative approach to the description and classification of primary social relationships. In E. Waters, B. E. Vaughn, G. Posada, & K. Kondo-Ikemura (Eds.), Caregiving, cultural, and cognitive perspectives on secure-base behavior and working models. *Monographs of the Society for Research in Child Development, 60*(2–3, Serial No. 244), 49–70.

Takahashi, K. (1986). Examining the strange situation procedure with Japanese mothers and 12-month-old infants. *Developmental Psychology, 22,* 265–270.

Teti, D. H. (in press). Conceptualizations of disorganization in the preschool years: An integration. In J. Solomon & C. George (Eds.), *Attachment disorganization.* New York: Guilford Press.

Teti, D. M., & Ablard, K. E. (1990). Security of attachment and infant–sibling relationships: A laboratory study. *Child Development, 60,* 1519–1528.

Teti, D. M., Gelfand, D. M., Messinger, D. S., & Isabella, R. (1995). Maternal depression and the quality of early attachment: An examination of infants, preschoolers, and their mothers. *Developmental Psychology, 31,* 364–376.

Teti, D. M., & McGourty, S. (1996). Using mothers versus trained observers in assessing children's secure base behavior: Theoretical and methodological considerations. *Child Development, 67,* 597–605.

Teti, D. M., Nakagawa, M., Das, R., & Wirth, O. (1991). Security of attachment between preschoolers and their mothers: Relations among social interaction, parenting stress, and mothers' sorts. *Developmental Psychology, 27,* 440–447.

Teti, D. M., Sakin, J. W., Kucera, E., Corns, K. M. & Das Eiden, R. (1996). And baby makes four: Predictors of attachment security among preschool-age firstborns during the transition to siblinghood. *Child Development, 67,* 579–596.

Thompson, R. A., Lamb, M. E., & Estes, D. (1981). Stability of infant–mother attachment and its relationship to changing life circumstances in an unselected middle-class sample. *Child Development, 53,* 144–148.

True, M. (1994). *Mother–infant attachment and communication among the Dogon of Mali (West Africa).* Unpublished doctoral dissertation, University of California at Berkeley.

Turner, P. (1991). Relations between attachment, gender, and behavior with peers in preschool. *Child Development, 62,* 1475–1488.

van Dam, M., & van IJzendoorn, M. H. (1988). Measuring attachment security: Concurrent and predictive validity of the parental Attachment Q-set. *Journal of Genetic Psychology, 149,* 447–457.

van IJzendoorn, M. H. & DeWolff, M. S. (1997). In search of the absent father: Meta-analysis of infant–father attachment. A rejoinder to our discussants. *Child Development, 68,* 604–609.

van IJzendoorn, M. H., Juffer, F., & Duyvesteyn, M. G. C. (1995). Breaking the intergenerational cycle of insecure attachment: A review of the effects of attachment-based interventions on maternal sensitivity and infant security. *Journal of Child Psychology and Psychiatry, 36,* 225–248.

van IJzendoorn, M. H., Schuengel, C., & Bakersman-Kranenburg, M. J. (in press). Disorganized attachment in early childhood: Meta-analysis of presursors, concomitants, and sequelae. *Development and Psychopathology.*

van IJzendoorn, M. H., Vereijken, C. M. J. L., & Riksen-Walraven, M. J. M. A. (in press). Is the Attachment Q-Sort a valid measure of attachment security in young children? In E. Waters, B. Vaughn, & D. Teti (Eds.), *Patterns of secure base behavior: Q-sort perspectives on attachment and caregiving.* Mahwah, NJ: Erlbaum.

Vaughn, B. E., Strayer, F. F., Jacques, M., Trudel, M., & Seifer, R. (1991). Maternal descriptions of two- and three-year-old children: A comparison of Attachment Q-Sorts in two socio-cultural communities. *International Journal of Behavioural Development, 14,* 279–291.

Vaughn, B. E., & Waters, E. (1990). Attachment behavior at home and in the laboratory: Q-sort observations and Strange Situation classifications of one-year olds. *Child Development, 61,* 1865–1973.

Vereijken, C. M. J. L., & Kondo-Ikemura, K. (in press). Attachment security and maternal sensitivity in Japan: Mother and observer Attachment Q-Sorts related to maternal behaviors. In E. Waters, B. Vaughn, & D. Teti (Eds.), *Patterns of secure base behavior: Q-sort perspectives on attachment and caregiving.* Mahwah, NJ: Erlbaum.

Vondra, J. I., Hommerding, K. D., & Shaw, D. S. (1996). *Stability and change in infant attachment in a low income sample.* Unpublished manuscript.

Wartner, U. G., Grossmann, K., Fremmer-Bombik, E., & Suess, G. (1994). Attachment patterns at age six in south Germany: Predictability from infancy and implications for preschool behavior. *Child Development, 65,* 1010–1023.

Waters, E. (1979). The reliability and stability of individual differences in infant–mother attachment. *Child Development, 49,* 483–494.

Waters, E. (1982). The stability of individual differences in infant attachment: Comments on the Thompson, Lamb, & Estes contribution. *Child Development, 54,* 516–520.

Waters, E. (1987). *Attachment Behavior Q-Set* (Revision 3.0). Unpublished manuscript, State University of New York at Stony Brook.

Waters, E. (1995). The Attachment Q-Set. In E. Waters, B. E. Vaughn, G. Posada, & K. Kondo-Ikemura (Eds.), Caregiving, cultural, and cognitive perspectives on secure-base behavior and working models. *Monographs of the Society for Research in Child Development, 60*(2–3, Serial No. 244), 247–254.

Waters, E., & Deane, K. E. (1985). Defining and assessing individual differences in attachment relationships: Q-methodology and the organization of behavior in infancy and early childhood. In I. Bretherton & E. Waters (Eds.), Growing points of attachment theory and research. *Monographs of the Society for Research in Child Development, 50*(1–2, Serial No. 209), 41–65.

Waters, E., Merrick, S. K., Treboux, D., Crowell, J., & Albersheim, L. (in press). Attachment security from infancy to early adulthood: A 20-year longitudinal study. *Child Development.*

Weinfield, N., Sroufe, L. A., Egeland, B. (in press). Attachment from infancy to early adulthood in a high-risk sample: Continuity, discontinuity, and their correlates. *Child Development.*

IV

ATTACHMENT
IN ADOLESCENCE
AND ADULTHOOD

15

Attachment in Adolescence

❖

JOSEPH P. ALLEN
DEBORAH LAND

Adolescent attachment behavior appears at first glance to depart sharply from patterns of attachment behavior seen at earlier ages. Adolescents often appear to be engaged in an active, purposeful flight *away* from attachment relationships with parents and other parental attachment figures. Attachment bonds to parents are treated by many adolescents more like ties that restrain than like ties that anchor and secure, and a key task of adolescence is to develop autonomy so as no longer to need to rely (as much) on parents' support when making one's way through the world (Allen, Hauser, Bell, & O'Connor, 1994; Collins, 1990; Grotevant & Cooper, 1985; Hill & Holmbeck, 1986; Moore, 1987; Steinberg, 1990). Yet research is increasingly showing that adolescent autonomy is most easily established not at the expense of attachment relationships with parents, but against a backdrop of secure relationships that are likely to endure well beyond adolescence (Allen, Hauser, Bell, & O'Connor, 1994; Allen, Hauser, Eickholt, Bell, & O'Connor, 1994; Fraley & Davis, 1997). Rather than being antithetical to the developmental challenge facing adolescents, the attachment system appears to play an integral role in helping adolescents meet this challenge. This is but one example of the variety of ways in which adolescent behavior toward attachment figures may seem conflicted, confused, and contradictory *unless it is viewed in the context of the developmental changes of adolescence.* This chapter begins with a brief consideration of a number of these changes, and then uses this developmental perspective to consider both the ways that individual differences in attachment organizations are manifested in adoles-

cence and the ways that adolescence fits into theories explaining continuities in attachment processes across the lifespan. Ultimately, the challenges posed to attachment theory by adolescent behavior are seen as useful in clarifying and refining our understanding of the workings of the attachment system across the lifespan.

NORMATIVE DEVELOPMENT OF THE ATTACHMENT SYSTEM IN ADOLESCENCE

From an attachment perspective, adolescence is a transitional period. At the onset of this period, the adolescent is beginning to make tremendous efforts to become less dependent on caregiving from primary attachment figures. Little more than half a decade later, in late adolescence, the possibility of becoming an attachment figure to one's own offspring has fully emerged (Ward & Carlson, 1995). Yet adolescence is not simply the span that bridges these two periods of intense involvement with attachment experiences. Rather, it is a period of profound *transformations* in specific emotional, cognitive, and behavioral systems, as the adolescent evolves from being a receiver of care from parents to being a potential caregiver.

Cognitive and Emotional Transformations in Adolescent Attachment Behavior

A fundamental change from infancy to adulthood is the emergence of a single overarching attachment organization, which predicts future behavior with offspring and with marital partners, from the multiple distinct patterns of attachment behavior that infants display with different caregivers (Cox, Owen, Henderson, & Margand, 1992; Fox, Kimmerly, & Schafer, 1991; O'Connor, Pan, Waters, & Posada, 1995; Steele, Steele, & Fonagy, 1996; van IJzendoorn, 1992, 1995; Waters, Merrick, Albersheim, & Treboux, 1995). This is not to say that the adolescent no longer recognizes distinctions between qualities of specific relationships with the mother, with the father, and with others; indeed, these distinctions may be clarified and sharpened during this period. Rather, it is to say that something else is also emerging—an integrated strategy for approaching attachment relationships that is highly predictive of future behavior in new attachment (and caregiving) relationships (Main & Goldwyn, in press; Steele et al., 1996; Waters et al., 1995). This in turn implies a degree of generalization and abstraction that permits the emergence of a generalized stance toward attachment from the multiple models held of different attachment relationships in infancy and childhood.

Although this development could in theory occur anywhere from middle childhood to adolescence, it appears most likely to occur during adolescence for several reasons. Adolescence brings with it the capacity for formal operational thinking, including logical and abstract reasoning abilities (Keating, 1990); this lets the individual begin to construct, from experiences with multiple caregivers, a more overarching stance toward attachment experiences (Main, Kaplan, & Cassidy, 1985; Ricks, 1985). Adolescence is also characterized by dramatic increases in differentiation of self and other (Bowlby, 1973). Such differentiation allows for a more consistent view of the self as existing apart from interactions with caregivers, in contrast to the action/script-oriented view of the self in relationships that is believed to predominate in infancy and early childhood (Ricks, 1985). This in turn may allow adolescents to view themselves as distinct from their caregivers to a far greater extent than previously. Views of oneself in attachment relationships can thus become more internally based and less centered around a particular relationship.

The advent of formal operational thinking also allows an adolescent to give extended consideration to abstract and counterfactual possibilities, which in turn allow the adolescent to compare relationships with different attachment figures both to one another and to hypothetical ideals.

For example, a child may represent multiple divergent attachment experiences without considering how they relate to one another, holding views such as "My mother always helps me feel better" and "My father ignores me when I'm upset." The adolescent, in contrast, can entertain more integrative propositions, such as "I can get help when I need it from some people, but not from everyone, so I have to be careful in deciding which people to get close to." The potential to consider attachment relationships in the abstract brings with it the ability to recognize that parents may be deficient in some ways in meeting attachment needs (Kobak & Cole, 1994). This recognition that parents can (and perhaps should) behave differently also implies that other relationships may meet attachment needs better than current relationships with parents may. Although this process can leave an adolescent prone to becoming angrily preoccupied with or derogatorily dismissive of the "deficient" parent(s), ideally it will lead to greater openness, objectivity, and flexibility in reevaluating past attachment relationships—characteristics that mark the presence of secure attachment organization in adolescence and young adulthood (Kobak & Duemmler, 1994; Main & Goldwyn, in press).

Transformations in the Parental Relationship

The adolescent's developing cognitive capacities do not merely affect the ability to ponder the concept of attachment in a vacuum. Rather, they (along with the myriad other physical and social changes of adolescence) are also likely to produce dramatic changes in day-to-day interactions with parents. One result of growth in the adolescent's cognitive capacities is increased sophistication in managing the "goal-corrected partnership" with each parent, in which behavior is determined not only by the adolescent's current needs and desires, but also by recognition of the need to manage certain "set goals" for the partnership (Bowlby, 1973; Kobak & Duemmler, 1984). For example, an adolescent who wants to stay out past an agreed-on curfew considers not only the desire to stay out late, but also the overarching set goal of maintaining trust and warmth in relation to parents. Goal-corrected systems in secure dyads allow such adjustments to be made flexibly as needed. A secure adolescent who has never broken curfew before may expect only minimal disruption to the relationship from a first transgression and give it a try, whereas a secure adolescent who has just had a serious breach in parental trust (e.g., an arrest for minor vandalism) may be more attentive to reestablishing this trust and maintaining a positive relationship with parents. Although elements of the goal-corrected partnership are evident far earlier in development (Bowlby, 1973), this partnership reaches new levels of complexity and coordination as a result of adolescents' enhanced perspective-taking ability and capacity to consider attachment relationships from both their own and their parents' points of view.

The increasingly goal-corrected nature of the parent–adolescent relationship provides an important context for considering one of the most important and intriguing changes of adolescence: the decreased reliance on parents as attachment figures. A critical distinction here is that this change appears primarily to reflect the adolescent's becoming less *dependent* on parents in a number of ways, rather than the relationship's becoming unimportant as a whole (Buhrmester, 1992; Buhrmester & Furman, 1987; Larson, Richards, Moneta, Holmbeck, & Duckett, 1996; Wilks, 1986). The development of the ability to function with greater social, cognitive, and emotional autonomy vis-à-vis parents is now recognized as a critical developmental task of adolescence (Collins, 1990; Hill & Holmbeck, 1986). As noted at the outset of this chapter, however, such autonomy does not ideally develop in isolation, but in the context of a close, enduring *relationship* with parents (Allen, Hauser, Bell, & O'Connor, 1994; Collins, 1990).

Research on adolescent autonomy and relatedness is beginning to link these developmental processes to an individual's attachment organization both before and after adolescence (Allen & Hauser, 1996; Becker-Stoll & Fremmer-Bombik, 1997). A recent study showed that infant security was more clearly predictive of observed qualities of autonomy and relatedness in adolescent–parent interactions than it was of interview-based assessments of adolescent security (Becker-Stoll & Fremmer-Bombik, 1997). This suggests that successful balancing of efforts to attain autonomy and maintain a sense of relatedness in adolescent–parent interactions related to disagreements may even potentially be considered a stage-specific manifestation of attachment security in adolescence (Allen, Kuperminc, & Moore, 1997). From this perspective, the seemingly contradictory process of learning *not* to get one's attachment needs met by a primary attachment figure is actually quite in keeping with what we know about attachment at earlier points in the lifespan. In several respects, this process appears only slightly different from attachment processes in infancy, in which the infant seeks to explore the environment and will move away from parents if necessary to do so *except* when stressed (Ainsworth, 1989). In early to midadolescence, most young people will still turn to parents under conditions of extreme stress (Steinberg, 1990), and parents are still often used as attachment figures even in young adulthood (Fraley & Davis, 1997). Adolescents may be on the edge of tears far less often than infants, but when they are this distressed, their likelihood of turning to parents for help still increases dramatically. Thus, to some extent, the differences between adolescents' attachment behaviors and those of infants and younger children are clearly not as large as they at first appear.

In other ways, however, adolescent behavior toward attachment figures does seem to represent a clear break with prior patterns of attachment behavior. Very little behavior at earlier stages of development matches the intensity of an adolescent's efforts to overcome the need to depend on parents (Steinberg, 1990), which may lead the adolescent at times *actively to avoid* relying on parents when stressed. If one asks a teenager in front of friends and under moderate stress, "Do you want to go get help from your mom?", the answer nearly always comes back as a strong (perhaps overly so) "NO!" This is not to say that this type of behavior does not occur earlier in the lifespan as well, but it clearly occurs with much more striking force and regularity in the adolescent years. This behavior differs from what we see in infancy, where the infant explores the environment except when stressed; the adolescent may at times avoid a parent, *particularly* when stressed.

Bowlby's (1973) view of competing behavioral systems, and his emphasis on the balance of the attachment and exploratory systems, can still accommodate these observations if we now view adolescence as a point in the lifespan where it is most important for the exploratory system to be highly activated and fully developed. Adolescent autonomy-seeking behavior can be viewed as part of the exploratory system, which may at times not just have opposing goals to the attachment system, but may actually have as a goal the minimization of the power of the attachment system with respect to parents. That is, the adolescent seeks to explore living (to some extent) without being emotionally dependent on his or her parents. In adolescence, the exploratory system may well take on greater primacy, particularly with respect to attachments to parents (though not peers), as adolescents' developing capacities make them increasingly less dependent on their parents. Without such exploration, accomplishing the major tasks of social development in adolescence and young adulthood, such as establishing long-term romantic relationships and productive careers, may well be difficult if not impossible. This is not different in principle from the competing influence of the exploratory and attachment systems on infant behavior, although the press for autonomy in adolescence may be more relentless and more directly in competition with the attachment system than it is during infancy (Allen, Kuperminc, & Moore, 1997; Steinberg, 1990). To some extent, an adolescent's cognitive capacities come to the rescue in managing these conflicting systems by allowing the adolescent to recall that the parents remain available as attachment figures when truly needed, even as the adolescent attempts to develop a relationship with the parents in which seeking of comfort is largely avoided for long periods of time. In this sense, the analogy to exploratory and secure-base behavior in infancy remains apt: Adolescents can explore (emotionally) the possibility of living independently from parents, in part because they know that they can turn to parents in cases of real need. This notion receives support from research suggesting that the presence of adolescent autonomy-seeking behavior tends to be highly correlated with evidence of an underlying positive relationship with parents (Allen, Hauser, Bell, & O'Connor, 1994).

As this autonomy-seeking process unfolds, it also appears likely to further adolescents' capacities to reevaluate the nature of the attachment relationship with parents. For with increased independence from parents as attachment figures may also come a certain degree of freedom from the need to monitor and assure parents' availability to meet attachment needs (Kobak & Cole, 1994). Main and Goldwyn (in press) refer to this cognitive and emotional freedom as "epistemic space," and suggest that it allows individuals to evaluate their parents as attachment figures more objectively. This epistemic space is likely to be as important to the emerging capacity to think more autonomously about attachment relationships as are the developing cognitive capacities discussed earlier. For even with fully developed cognitive capacities, it is likely to be very difficult to attain

the critical distance needed to begin objectively evaluating the qualities of an attachment relationship on which one feels totally dependent. In such a dependent relationship, strongly negative feelings about and evaluations of an attachment figure may well be too threatening to acknowledge openly, given that the expression of these feelings may engender negative feelings and behaviors in return. As independence increases, so too will the emotional distance necessary to put developing cognitive capacities to work in reevaluating the nature of the attachment relationship with parents. Uncomfortable as this critical distance and objective evaluation may be to parents, it seems likely to be fundamental to an adolescent's capacity to develop an accurate, thoughtful response to attachment experiences. This in turn may be crucial to resolving attachment difficulties in relationships with parents in ways that allow some adolescents to form more secure relationships with others, such as peers, in the future.

Transformations in Peer Relationships

By midadolescence, interactions with peers have begun to take on many of the functions that they will serve for the remainder of the lifespan—providing important sources of intimacy, feedback about social behavior, social influence and information, and ultimately attachment relationships and lifelong partnerships (Ainsworth, 1989; Fuligni & Eccles, 1993; Gavin & Furman, 1989, 1996; Hartup, 1992). The development of peer relationships in adolescence is characterized by the gradual emergence of the capacity for adult-like intimacy and supportiveness (Hartup, 1992; Jones & Dembo, 1989; Tesch, 1983). Although these new components of relationships are seen in embryonic form in childhood peer relationships, they appear most clearly in an individual's developmental history in attachment relationships with *parents* (Gavin & Furman, 1989, 1996; Kahen, Katz, & Gottman, 1994). This suggests that the nature of developing peer attachment relationships may derive as much or more from prior attachment relationships with parents as from prior relationships with peers. Childhood peer relationships, although an essential aspect of normal social development (Hartup, 1983), are viewed as unlikely to serve much of an attachment function under most conditions (Ainsworth, 1989).

Ainsworth (1989) delineates four characteristics that distinguish attachment relationships from other social relationships, and that help clarify the ways in which peer relationships do and do not serve attachment functions in adolescence. These characteristics include (1) proximity seeking; (2) secure-base behavior (freer exploration in the presence of an attachment figure); (3) safe-haven behavior (retreat to the attachment figure when facing a perceived threat); and (4) separation protest when separations are involuntary. Ainsworth's delineation makes quite clear the ways in which childhood playmates differ from attachment figures. It also makes clear the extent to which these distinctions become increasingly fuzzy when one is considering adolescent peer relationships. By late adolescence, long-term relationships can be formed in which peers (as romantic partners or as very close friends) indeed serve as attachment figures in all senses of the term (Buhrmester, 1992). What prompts this growth in the attachment qualities of peer relationships? One source is obviously the same set of cognitive, developmental, and social changes described earlier, which improves the capacity of both an adolescent and his or her peers to serve as attachment figures to one another (Youniss & Haynie, 1992). In particular, the growing push for autonomy from parents may create healthy pressure to begin to use peers as attachment figures, so that attachment needs can be met while establishing autonomy in the relationship with parents (Steinberg, 1990).

From this perspective, adolescence is not a period in which attachment needs and behaviors are relinquished; rather, it is one in which they are gradually transferred to peers. This transfer also involves a *transformation* from hierarchical attachment relationships (in which one primarily receives care from a caregiver) to peer attachment relationships (in which one both receives and offers care and support). Adolescents' seemingly inappropriate dependence on peers, particularly in early adolescence, may be viewed as the awkward first step toward learning to use peers as attachment figures. In this respect, phenomena such as heightened susceptibility to peer pressure are quite understandable: To the extent that peers begin replacing multiple parental functions, adolescents may reflexively tend to "obey" peer directives just as they have previously done with parental directives, and may experience an almost reflexive desire to please peers just as they have previously done with parents. The transition to use of peers as attachment figures is thus clumsy at first, and may even be dysfunctional in some ways at certain times, but it is only

the necessity for adolescents to struggle with this process that encourages their capacities for adult-like attachment relationships to develop fully.

One of the endpoints of developing peer relationships in adolescence is the development of romantic relationships that may eventually become lifelong attachment relationships (Ainsworth, 1989). Romantic relationships do not solely result from developing interests in forming attachments with peers, of course; they also reflect the operation of a sexual/reproductive system that is likely to be every bit as biologically rooted and critical to species survival as the attachment system (Ainsworth, 1989; Hazan & Shaver, 1987; Shaver, Hazan, & Bradshaw, 1988; see Simpson, Chapter 6, this volume). The sexual and attachment systems both push toward the establishment of new peer relationships characterized by sufficient intensity, shared interests, and strong affect to begin to take over some of the many functions of prior parent–child relationships. The sexual component of these relationships may also help advance the attachment component by providing consistent motivation for interaction; experience with intense, intimate affect; and a history of shared unique experience. It also seems likely that prior attachment experiences and current patterns of approach to attachment thoughts and feelings will in turn shape the nature of these developing romantic relationships (Hazan & Shaver, 1994).

INDIVIDUAL DIFFERENCES IN ADOLESCENT ATTACHMENT STRATEGIES

With some notion of the transformations in attachment cognitions, feelings, and behavior that occur during adolescence, it is now possible to consider what we know about individual differences in attachment in adolescence. Before considering the differences between secure and insecure adolescents, we must first recognize the question of just what "security" and "insecurity" actually mean for the adolescent who has developed (1) a characteristic *strategy* for dealing with attachment-related thoughts, feelings, and memories; (2) *specific memories* and representations of interactions with attachment figures; and (3) *ongoing relationships* with his or her attachment figures. Recent research suggesting high concordance rates between the attachment organization of individual adults and their parents (Benoit &

Parker, 1994) raises the possibility that it may even make sense to speak of secure or insecure dyads under some conditions. This chapter focuses primarily on adolescents' characteristic strategies for dealing with attachment thoughts and memories—in part because they represent the only research with demonstrated empirical connections to the infant attachment literature, and in part because they appear to offer the best empirical basis for predicting future behavior in attachment relationships. Although a number of different and promising tools have been developed to assess attachment models, strategies, and organization in adolescence and adulthood, this chapter primarily reviews findings based on assessments made with the Adult Attachment Interview (AAI; George, Kaplan, & Main, 1996; Main & Goldwyn, in press).[1]

Families

Although attachment processes appear to follow certain normative developmental pathways for all adolescents, for families of adolescents with secure attachment strategies, these paths appear fairly straight, smooth, and easily traversed; for families with insecure adolescents, they may be filled with twists, detours, dead ends, and difficulties. These differences are manifested in a much smoother process of balancing autonomy and attachment needs in families with secure adolescents, perhaps because these adolescents have more confidence that their relationships will remain intact and functional in spite of disagreements. For example, in the task of learning to resolve differences of opinion between parents and adolescents, teens with secure attachment strategies tend to engage in productive, problem-solving discussions that balance autonomy strivings with efforts to preserve the current relationship with parents (Allen & Hauser, 1996; Becker-Stoll & Fremmer-Bombik, 1997; Kobak, Cole, Ferenz-Gillies, Fleming, & Gamble, 1993). These discussions may be heated or intense at times, but nevertheless maintain a focus on solving the disagreement at hand. In contrast, insecure teen–parent dyads are more likely to be characterized by avoidance of problem solving and lower levels of adolescent confidence in interactions, and by higher levels of disengagement, dysfunctional anger, and use of pressuring tactics that tend to undermine autonomy (Becker-Stoll & Fremmer-Bombik, 1997; Kobak et al., 1993). Disagreements that secure dyads try to resolve directly lead insecure dyads either to withdraw or to become hostile and pressuring. As noted earlier, these patterns of difficulty in handling issues of autonomy and relatedness are predictable from attachment insecurity seen both in infancy and at age 6 (Becker-Stoll & Fremmer-Bombik, 1997).

One explanation for both the avoidance and the dysfunctional anger and pressuring behavior of insecure dyads is that these behaviors are understandable responses if the dyads are interpreting adolescents' efforts to establish autonomy in disagreements as presenting a real threat to the dyadic relationship. A second explanation is that insecure adolescents (and parents) may be overwhelmed by the affect brought on by the disagreement (Kobak & Cole, 1994). Although all parents and teens occasionally become upset during disagreements, insecure teens and their parents may be more likely to have a history of difficulties in getting their upset feelings assuaged in attachment relationships. This may leave them more vulnerable to having angry, hurt feelings spin out of control, and may lead both parties in a disagreement to move rapidly from reasoned discussions to a "fight-or-flight" stance. A third explanation is that an insecure adolescent is easily frustrated because he or she does not expect to be heard or understood by a parent whose insecurity makes it hard to tune in accurately to the adolescent's perspectives and feelings. These three explanations are not mutually exclusive, as a relationship history that leads to adolescent insecurity would also appear likely to lead to difficulties in handling any unpleasant feelings that arise in the relationship.

The interaction patterns of families of insecure adolescents may be problematic at any point in development, but they are particularly problematic in adolescence, when autonomy strivings (and the developmental forces that drive them) almost certainly require some sensitive renegotiation of the relationship with parents (Allen, Kuperminc, & Moore, 1997; Youniss, 1980). This is a task for which the family of an insecure adolescent may be particularly ill suited. The moodiness, changing relationships, tension, and growing emotional and behavioral independence from parents that characterize adolescent development may all conspire to create a chronic state of activation of the attachment system, thus increasing the impact of an insecure parental relationship on the adolescent. Ironically, this occurs at the same time that the adolescent is trying to begin to reduce the centrality of the parental relationship in his or her life.

Evidence is now accumulating to suggest that distinctions among specific types of insecure attachments in families with adolescents may be understood in terms of adolescents' balancing of efforts to attain autonomy while maintaining positive relationships in interactions. Becker-Stoll and Fremmer-Bombik (1997) note that dismissing adolescents show the least autonomy and relatedness in interactions with parents of all attachment groups observed; this suggests that dismissing individual's characteristic withdrawal from engagement with attachment figures may particularly hinder the task of renegotiating the nature of parent–adolescent relationships. Reimer, Overton, Steidl, Rosenstein, and Horowitz (1996) also note that families of dismissing adolescents tend to be less responsive to their adolescents than do families of preoccupied adolescents. Allen and Hauser (1996) report that one indicator of preoccupation with attachment in young adulthood—use of passive thought processes, reflecting mental entanglement between self and caregivers—was predicted by adolescents' overpersonalized behaviors toward fathers in arguments 10 years earlier and by adolescents' lack of simple withdrawal from/avoidance of arguments. Avoidance of problem solving and of renegotiating relationships thus appears linked to less overall security and more specifically to dismissing attachment organizations, but also to less likelihood of being insecurely preoccupied with attachment relationships. Insecure preoccupation, in contrast, appears to be best predicted from heightened and unproductive overengagement with parents in arguments that ultimately undermine an adolescent's autonomy.

Psychosocial Functioning

A number of recent studies suggest the existence of substantial links between the adolescent's attachment organization and psychosocial functioning. Two insecure attachment strategies, the preoccupied and dismissing strategies, have been implicated in problems of psychosocial functioning, although the two are associated with somewhat different patterns of problems. Adolescents' use of preoccupied strategies has been most closely linked to internalizing problems, particularly to adolescents' self-reports of depression (Allen, Moore, Kuperminc, & Bell, 1998; Kobak, Sudler, & Gamble, 1991). Adolescent depression has been related to *maternal* attachment insecurity (Homann, 1997), and these relations

hold even after maternal strategies of affect regulation and maternal depression are accounted for. Adam, Sheldon-Keller, and West (1996) also report that suicidality in adolescence is related to a combination of a preoccupied and an unresolved attachment status. Together, these findings suggest a strong connection between adolescent depression and attachment insecurity (in both adolescents and their mothers), with a particular relation of depression to adolescent preoccupied attachment organization.

Externalizing problem behaviors (e.g., aggression and delinquency) have also been related to insecurity, although the attachment system appears to interact with other aspects of the adolescent relationship in producing these relationships (Allen et al., 1998). For example, maternal control of adolescent behavior—long a recognized inverse correlate of adolescent deviance (Patterson, DeBaryshe, & Ramsey, 1989)—has been found to provide a buffer against deviant behavior, but only for adolescents with either secure or preoccupied attachment strategies. It thus appears that maternal control may be effective as a buffer against deviance only when adolescents are open to thinking about the maternal relationship (in either a secure or a preoccupied fashion). This finding suggests an important extension of existing theories about the importance of maternal control in adolescence, and also provides an example of the importance of beginning to integrate attachment research into existing theories of adolescent social development.

The type of insecurity to which externalizing behaviors are linked in adolescence is less clear. When examining psychiatrically hospitalized adolescents, almost all of whom were insecure, Rosenstein and Horowitz (1996) reported that preoccupied attachment strategies were associated with internalizing symptoms, whereas dismissing strategies were associated with externalizing symptoms. Preoccupied adolescents were more likely to be depressed, whereas dismissing adolescents were more likely to be substance abusing and conduct disordered. Allen et al. (1998) found that preoccupation was related to adolescent deviance, even after levels of security were accounted for, but only in the presence of additional demographic risk factors (e.g., male gender and low income). Thus, for male adolescents and for adolescents from poor families, preoccupation was associated with externalizing behavior even after accounting for levels of security. Allen and Kuperminc (1995), in contrast, found evidence that preoccupation was directly related to externalizing behaviors when these were assessed via adolescents' self-reports.

In attempting to reconcile these findings, it is important to note that adolescent problem behaviors and symptoms may serve not only as expressions of distress or of psychopathology, but also as attempts to change the nature of interactions within a parent–adolescent dyad. Externalizing problem behaviors may even serve as attachment behaviors themselves, in that they may call for help and intervention by the parent on behalf of the adolescent (Allen et al., 1998; Kobak et al., 1993). An adolescent who has adopted preoccupied strategies for dealing with attachment-related concerns and whose attachment system is chronically hyperactivated may actually use problematic behavior as one of many extreme and ambivalent means of seeking a response from a caregiver (Cassidy & Berlin, 1994). Much as the resistant infant may call for help from a caregiver while angrily resisting the caregiver's efforts, the preoccupied adolescent may well use hostile, self-destructive, and infuriating behaviors (e.g., getting arrested for shoplifting while carrying plenty of spare cash) as a way both to engage parental attention and to express anger and resistance. This may be particularly likely to occur in adolescence, where growing perspective-taking abilities allow the adolescent to envision in advance how parents will respond to given behaviors (Kobak et al., 1993). This process may help explain why preoccupation is linked not just to internalizing symptoms (as has been frequently reported at other points in the lifespan; Cassidy & Berlin, 1994; Pianta, Egeland, & Adam, 1996; Rubin & Lollis, 1988), but also to some adolescent reports of externalizing behaviors. Even though externalizing behaviors are often associated with dismissing or avoidant attachment strategies both earlier and later in the lifespan (Allen & Hauser, 1996; Renken, Egeland, Marvinney, Mangelsdorf, & Sroufe, 1989; Rothbaum, Schneider, Pott, & Beatty, 1995), in adolescence externalizing problems may also serve a preoccupied function.

Moreover, both preoccupied and dismissing attachment strategies may lead to the development of problem behaviors by influencing the ways that adolescents process negative affect. Rosenstein and Horowitz (1996) note that the intense focus on parents that is characteristic of preoccupied strategies may lead to failure to learn to self-regulate negative affect, as well as to failure to develop the exploratory competence necessary to learn regulatory skills from other sources. This is offered as an explanation for the depression associated with adolescent preoccupation. It may also help explain externalizing behaviors, given that these behaviors are closely linked to deficits in social competence that may result from failure to explore and develop relationships apart from parents (Allen, Aber, & Leadbeater, 1990; Dodge, 1993; Leadbeater, Hellner, Allen, & Aber, 1989; Patterson et al., 1989).

Kobak and Cole (1994) suggest that different attachment strategies may predict different clusters of psychological symptoms because the strategies reflect different approaches to dealing with distress-related cues. Adolescents using dismissing strategies may take on symptoms that distract themselves and others from these cues, whereas preoccupied individuals take on symptoms that focus on distress-related cues and leave the attachment system in a more highly activated state. Kobak and Cole support this explanation with findings that eating-disordered individuals in a college population were disproportionately likely to use dismissing strategies (with the attention given to eating behaviors distracting the individuals from feelings of internal emotional distress), and that depressed individuals tended to use more preoccupied strategies. This is also in accord with the findings of Nolen-Hoeksema and colleagues that depressed individuals tend to adopt ruminative strategies for coping with negative life events and accompanying negative affect—strategies that heighten and maintain their attention to distressing internal cues (Nolen-Hoeksema & Girgus, 1994; Nolen-Hoeksema, Parker, & Larson, 1994).

Peers

There are several reasons to expect close links between an adolescent's attachment organization and qualities of ongoing peer relationships. A secure attachment organization, which is characterized in adolescence and adulthood by coherence in talking (and presumably thinking) about attachment-related experiences and affect, should permit similar experiences and affect in peer relationships to be processed more accurately and coherently as well. In contrast, the defensive exclusion of information about attachment that is characteristic of insecure organizations may lead to distorted communications and negative expectations about others, both of which have been linked to problems in social functioning at various points in the lifespan (Cassidy, Kirsh,

Scolton, & Parke, 1996; Dodge, 1993; Slough & Greenberg, 1990). Similarly, discomfort with attachment-related affect and experiences may also lead adolescents with dismissing attachment strategies to push away peers, particularly those who could become close friends (Kobak & Sceery, 1988). This last hypothesis is consistent with the finding that for college students, hostility and lack of social skills as rated by close friends are linked to students' insecure attachment organizations (Kobak & Sceery, 1988). A related mechanism by which attachment organization may be linked to peer relationships is that insecure attachment organization co-occurs with (and serves to mark) problematic ongoing difficulties with parents, which make it difficult to move freely beyond the relationships with parents to establish successful new relationships with peers (Gavin & Furman, 1996).

Several studies have found links between attachment security and peer relationships in adolescence. Zimmermann, Scheuerer-Englisch, and Grossmann (1996) found that security was linked to overall friendship quality among a sample of 16-year-olds. Similarly, Allen et al. (1998) found that in a sample of academically at-risk adolescents, social acceptance by peers was positively related to adolescent attachment security. Even after the current quality of the maternal relationship was accounted for in this study, security remained a significant predictor of peer social acceptance, suggesting that attachment organization in adolescence functioned as more than just a marker of the quality of the ongoing maternal relationship. Similar research with samples of high-functioning late adolescents in college has also found consistent relationships of security to higher-quality peer relationships (Kobak & Sceery, 1988; Treboux, Crowell, Owens, & Pan, 1994). These findings are consistent with the notion that qualities of the models of attachment held by adolescents with respect to primary attachment relationships may generalize to influence behaviors with peers, or that the emotional capacities necessary to produce secure discourse in the AAI are also useful in peer relationships (Allen et al., 1998; Cassidy et al., 1996). (For more extensive discussion of the correspondence between attachment and peer relationships, see Berlin & Cassidy, Chapter 30, and Thompson, Chapter 13, this volume).

One of the most important new facets of peer interactions to develop in adolescence is that of romantic and sexual relationships (Cullari & Mikus, 1990; Treboux & Busch-Rossnagel,

1990; Wright, Peterson, & Barnes, 1990). Here the evidence about relations to attachment organization is mixed. O'Beirne and Allen (1996) reported that adolescent security was not linked to whether a sample of at-risk 16-year-olds had begun having intercourse yet, but among those adolescents who had begun, security was linked to having first intercourse at a later as opposed to an earlier age. This suggests that insecurity may be linked to a very early age of first intercourse, but not to the occurrence of first intercourse around or after age 16. Moore (1997) reported that among sexually active adolescents, security was associated with having fewer sexual partners and with greater use of contraception. Moore also found slight evidence that after security was accounted for, use of dismissing attachment strategies was predictive of earlier age of initiation into sexual intercourse. Januszewski, Turner, Guerin, and Flack (1996) reported in a study of 21-year-olds that secure females displayed a trend toward being more likely to require some emotional commitment from partners before engaging in sex, and were also likely to have somewhat less permissive attitudes toward sexuality. These findings are consistent with the hypotheses put forward by Belsky (Chapter 7, this volume) that for evolutionary reasons, secure attachment organizations are likely to be associated with a "quality-versus-quantity" approach to sexual relationships, whereas dismissing attachment organizations are more likely to be associated with a "quantity-versus-quality" approach. Alternatively, these findings can just as easily be interpreted as similar to the findings about broader peer relationships discussed above, in which insecurity is simply linked to behavior with romantic partners that is less functional in nature (i.e., it increases the risk of sexually transmitted diseases and unwanted pregnancies) and more likely to be considered an externalizing problem behavior (Donovan & Jessor, 1985).

CONTINUITY IN THE MEANING AND STATUS OF ATTACHMENT FROM INFANCY THROUGH ADOLESCENCE

We have been considering many of the features of adolescent attachment strategies, while thus far avoiding a much more fundamental question: Just what *is* attachment in adolescence? Our working empirical answer to this question—that attachment strategies are reflected in a type of discourse about memories of experience and affect in early attachment relationships, as assessed in the AAI—is fundamentally unsatisfying for several reasons that apply as much to attachment theory in general as to adolescent attachment. First, we want to know how adolescent attachment organization is related to attachment at other points in the lifespan—particularly infancy, where our knowledge base and theories are most fully developed. Second, our current ad hoc definition provides little theoretical basis for understanding how or why such a longitudinal relationship should exist. Finally, we want to know just what the attachment system has become in adolescence. If the attachment behavioral system is no longer essential to physical survival, then just what is its role and function?

One approach to addressing these questions is to empirically assess continuities in attachment across the lifespan: Is adolescent attachment simply the stage-specific manifestation of the same attachment processes that are observed in infancy? As we are now moving into the third decade since the development of the strange situation, studies are beginning to emerge that have tracked individuals from infancy into adolescence. Thus far, the results of these studies are mixed. Waters et al. (1995) reported that late adolescent (i.e., age 21) security in the AAI was concordant with infant strange situation security at a rate of 70% (kappa = .40). When individuals who had undergone major life events that are known potentially to alter attachment classification (e.g., death of a parent) were excluded, the concordance rate rose to 78% (kappa = .52). For those individuals with significant major life events, the concordance rate was only 44% and was nonsignificant. Main (1997) found a high degree of concordance between infant strange situation classifications and AAI classifications obtained at age 19. Hamilton (1994, 1995) also reported findings of slight continuity from infancy to adolescence. Other research has found no significant associations between infant strange situation behavior with either mothers or fathers and adolescent attachment classifications (Weinfield, 1996; Zimmermann, Fremmer-Bombik, Spangler, & Grossmann, 1995).

Waters et al.'s (1995) findings may be most important for explaining these discrepant results, because they highlight the ways in which long-term continuities are mediated by intervening social-environmental factors. It is almost certainly important that an adolescent who has been fol-lowed since infancy and who retains the same attachment classification over time is probably also living with parents who have retained some degree of stability in their approach to their relationship with the adolescent (Thompson, Chapter 13, this volume; van IJzendoorn, 1996). This view receives further support and elaboration from recent findings that the degree of concordance between maternal and adolescent attachment organization is much higher for adolescents living with both biological parents than for adolescents living in other family structures (Allen, Land, Liebman, Bell, & Jodl, 1997), although it generally appears somewhat modest overall (Zimmermann et al., 1995). In addition, mother–adolescent attachment concordance appears to be greater for older than for younger adolescents, suggesting that perhaps the stresses created by the changes of early adolescence may at least temporarily disrupt either adolescents' underlying attachment organization or the capacity to assess it (Allen, Land, et al., 1997). Somewhat in contrast, however, Rosenstein and Horowitz (1996) have reported a concordance of over 80% in maternal and adolescent attachment strategies among psychiatrically disturbed adolescents, suggesting robustness in mother–adolescent attachment concordance under some extreme conditions. Together, these findings suggest that adolescent attachment organization (and its relation to prior infant and current maternal attachment organization) may be significantly influenced both by developmental changes and by challenges in the current environment.

Of particular interest in this regard are findings from the Regensburg longitudinal study (Becker-Stoll & Fremmer-Bombik, 1997) that infant attachment classifications predicted adolescent displays of autonomy and relatedness with parents, which have been found in other studies to predict attachment organization in young adulthood (Allen & Hauser, 1996). These predictions to family interaction behaviors were found even though there was *no* direct prediction of adolescent attachment classification from infant attachment status. These findings are in some ways similar to findings that serious psychiatric disturbance in adolescence is also predictive of attachment insecurity a decade later in young adulthood (Allen, Hauser, & Borman-Spurrell, 1996). These findings suggest that perhaps during adolescence, there are underlying structural continuities with attachment at earlier and later stages of development that are more clearly manifested in specific, discrete interactions with parents and in levels of psychosocial functioning than in overall attachment organization as it is currently conceptualized. Another possibility is that the strength of the adolescent's efforts to establish autonomy at certain points in adolescence makes it more difficult to *assess* actual underlying attachment organization via interviews. This latter interpretation is consistent with findings of greater reticence on the part of adolescents (as compared to adults) when participating in attachment interviews (Ward & Carlson, 1995), although it is somewhat undercut by the numerous findings discussed above suggesting the validity of the AAI in adolescence.

Evidence about continuities from adolescent attachment organization to the attachment organization of the offspring of adolescents (i.e., forward into the next generation) is not extensive, but is remarkably consistent with evidence about such continuities with adult parents and their offspring. Ward and Carlson (1995) reported concordances between the three-category attachment status of adolescent mothers, assessed with the AAI, and their offspring, assessed with the strange situation, of 78% (kappa = .54). Thus, predictions from the attachment organization of parents to the attachments of their infant offspring do not appear to differ depending on whether the parents are adolescents or adults.

Taken together, these findings suggest substantial continuities between attachment organization in adolescence and at other points in the lifespan. Adolescent attachment strategies display very strong concordances with attachments of adolescents' infant offspring, moderately strong concordances with parents' attachment organization, and some evidence of weaker long-term continuities from infant attachment organization. Results from several of these studies (e.g., Allen, Land, et al., 1997; Waters et al., 1995) also suggest the presence of sources of lawful discontinuity in attachment in adolescence as a result of disruptions from both developmental and demographic factors. In some ways, these findings are reassuring in suggesting that the assessment of adolescent attachment on which we have relied does indeed tap the same construct that appears at other points in the lifespan. Yet in other ways these findings raise profound questions about just what "attachment strategies" mean in adolescence (and, by extension, in adulthood as well).

These findings raise the possibility that observed continuities between infant strange situation behavior and later adolescent attachment strategies reflect primarily continuities in *parenting received,* rather than continuities that result from an *internal,* stable working model of the self in attachment relationships (Thompson, Chapter 13, this volume; van IJzendoorn, 1996). van IJzendoorn questions whether in fact any *internal* stability in attachment actually does exist from infancy to adolescence, and notes evidence that observed continuities over this time frame may primarily reflect stability in parents' attachment strategies. It is not unreasonable to assume that attachment as assessed in infants and young children is mainly an epiphenomenon, marking an adaptive response to a relatively stable pattern for handling affect on the part of the *parents.* Infant attachment organization may predict many future outcomes (including the nature of attachment strategies and autonomy behaviors used in adolescence) simply because it marks an important, stable aspect of parenting likely to persist over time, but in this case the essential elements of the attachment may reside more within the parents than within the infants.

A critical empirical question for the field thus becomes the following: When does attachment organization become a property of the individual and not just a reflection of qualities of major ongoing attachment relationships? To answer this question, we will need to observe individuals whose caregivers change substantially in caregiving behavior (e.g., becoming more secure following psychotherapy, or becoming insecure and unresolved following a major loss). The key issue is identification of the point in the lifespan at which an individual's attachment organization begins to remain stable, even following changes in the care received from the primary caregiver. This process may well occur gradually over a period of years, such that adolescent attachment organization in part reflects an enduring internal state and in part reflects a response set developed to adapt to the current behaviors of the adolescent's major attachment figures. It is also possible that attachment organization *never* fully exists without being to some extent dependent on the nature of specific existing attachment relationships. Main's pioneering work on the failure to resolve the loss of attachment figures, even in adulthood, suggests that at least some aspects of the attachment system remain subject to social and environmental influences throughout the lifespan (Main & Hesse, 1990; Main & Solomon, 1986).

To the extent that an adolescent's attachment organization reflects a response to the ongoing relationship with a caregiver, we need to develop a theory for the transmission of attachment organization from parent to offspring that is broad enough to encompass this process as it occurs not just in infancy, but also in adolescence. Although one could make a case that adolescent attachment organization is attuned to caregiver behavior because it serves many of the same survival functions as in infancy, this rationale is necessarily weaker in adolescence: Adolescents simply do not need their parents' support for survival in the same way that infants do. We believe that a far better case can be made that parent-to-adolescent transmission of attachment organization results from the function of the attachment system in supporting the adolescent's developing capacities for emotion regulation. This in turn may well have provided an evolutionary advantage, in terms of future likelihood of reproduction, by increasing the adolescent's social skills or by tuning the adolescent's strategies to his or her social environment (Belsky, Chapter 7, this volume).

EMOTION-REGULATING FUNCTIONS OF ADOLESCENT ATTACHMENT ORGANIZATION

Parents frequently deal with their adolescents' states of emotional upheaval (Larson et al., 1994), and although an adolescent's actual survival is rarely threatened, emotional dysregulation frequently appears in the form of emotional "crises" in which the adolescent feels he or she simply cannot go on or cope with a situation judged to be intolerable. A central function of the adolescent's attachment relationship with parents may be to provide an emotional secure base from which the adolescent can explore the wide range of emotional states that arise when he or she is learning to live as a relatively autonomous adult. Developing the capacity to regulate affect without distortions, even in regard to highly charged issues (e.g., "Where and with whom will I live next year?"), may well enhance the ability to form and sustain future relationships and ultimately to nurture one's own offspring. From this perspective, the last major caregiving task of parents becomes supporting their adolescent's capacity to cope with the affect engendered in learning to live independently of parental caregiving.

It is fairly easy to see ways in which adolescents' discourse in the AAI may come to match

parental emotion-regulating strategies. One of the most prominent features of the classification system used to code the AAI is its implicit assessment of the degree of coherence, clarity, and organization brought to bear in discussing highly affectively charged situations (Cassidy, 1994; Main & Goldwyn, in press). The dismissing adolescent or adult is characterized by a tendency to avoid discussion or consideration of a range of strong affects, such as fear, anger, disappointment, hurt, and loneliness; he or she may thus idealize past relationships, minimize the importance of past difficulties, or present the self as relatively invulnerable. One can readily imagine that a dismissing parent may treat his or her adolescent's difficulties with such feelings in a similar fashion, and that the adolescent may thus learn that handling his or her own feelings of distress in this fashion is the most adaptive available strategy, given the parent's inability to respond in a supportive way. Similar patterns can easily be envisioned with respect to use of preoccupied attachment strategies: An adolescent may learn, for example, that becoming deeply involved in anger regarding close relationships is the least painful, most self-protective way to cope with a parent who consistently utilizes this approach when dealing with the adolescent.

A focus on the emotion-regulating functions of attachment organization may help clarify one of the thornier issues in the assessment of attachment organization beginning in adolescence: In contrast to the emphasis in infant attachment theory on the content of the infant's internal working models of the self in relation to attachment figures, the actual classification of adolescent (and adult) interviews relies virtually not at all on assessment of the *content* of these internal working models. Rather, the content is duly noted, but the critical distinctions with respect to overall assessments of security/autonomy in adolescent and adult attachment revolve around the ways in which the adolescent or adult *processes* emotion-charged memories of attachment experiences. What is noteworthy, for example, about the dismissing adolescent's recounting of past experiences with parents is not necessarily the specific content of what is recalled. Such recountings may range from glowing but vague descriptions of parenting received to detailed, negative descriptions that lack any indication of the emotional impact they had on the interviewee. What is consistent, however, is that all discourse steers the individual away from in-depth consideration of possible negative feelings (i.e., loss, missing, regret) surrounding attachment figures. Although this pattern of emotion regulation is first easily assessed in adolescence via the AAI, infant strange situation behavior can be similarly interpreted in terms of the infant's regulation of affect aroused by attachment needs. Avoidance of parents on reunion may reflect efforts to minimize the affectively arousing nature of such reunions, as well as the affect experienced during the separation. Similarly, ambivalence or resistance may well reflect an overwhelmed, arousal-enhancing style of coping with strong affect. In infancy, patterns of emotion regulation with a caregiver tend to correlate with characteristics of the infant's internal working model of self in relationship to that caregiver (Cassidy, 1994; Thompson, Flood, & Lundquist, 1995), and there may be relatively little distinction between the two with respect to attachment organization. In adolescence, the processes used for handling strong emotion may well diverge from the content of any given internal model, and the individual's coherence, openness, and flexibility in describing affectively charged attachment memories are used to distinguish secure from insecure adolescent (and adult) attachment organization (Main & Goldwyn, in press).

A focus on emotion-regulating aspects of adolescent attachment organization also offers a clear prediction about the timing and conditions under which attachment organization will become a stable internal property of the developing individual, rather than a reflection of the current relationship with a primary caregiver. If attachment organization reflects primarily a strategy for handling intense affect, then it is likely to come to reside within the individual, to the extent that the individual has developed independent capacities for handling such affect without reliance on his or her primary caregiver. As long as the caregiver must be relied on extensively in regulating affect, then it is adaptive for the strategy used by the adolescent in affect regulation to match that of his or her caregiver. It makes little sense to try to ignore attachment-related cues, for example, when one is interacting with a primary caregiver who is preoccupied with attachment. It is only when one no longer relies as heavily on a caregiver to regulate affect that one can develop an independent, potentially divergent approach to affect regulation. This prediction in turn brings us back to adolescence as the stage in life when this transformation appears most likely to occur, given the extent to which adolescence is characterized by the developing

capacity to regulate affect and behavior independently of reliance on a primary caregiver (Kobak & Cole, 1994).

Understanding when attachment strategies take on a degree of internal stability is critical to understanding when these strategies are truly "passed on" from generation to generation. Prior to this stabilization, continuity between parent and offspring attachments may exist, but it may merely reflect offspring reaction to current interactions with the parent. In essence, such continuity is little more than a mirroring of parenting behavior. After this internalization process occurs, in contrast, an attachment strategy has truly been transmitted to the next generation and will display continuity into the future. Knowing when this transition takes place is essential to thinking about when and how to intervene to alter attachment strategies in individuals (should one focus on parents, on an adolescent, or on both, for example?). It is also essential to understanding just what attachment means in adolescence.

CONCLUSIONS

In some ways we know a great deal about attachment in adolescence, yet in other respects we know disconcertingly little. As at other stages of development, attachment strategies of adolescents are related to numerous aspects of psychosocial functioning. These strategies are also lawfully related to parents' attachment strategies, to the attachment strategies of the infant offspring of adolescent parents, and (to a lesser extent) to the prior attachment strategies of adolescents observed as far back as infancy. Yet attempts to assess attachment in adolescence inevitably must confront the questions of what attachment becomes and what function it serves during this stage of the lifespan. These questions are critical to understanding attachment in adolescence, but they also have important implications for our efforts to define attachment across the lifespan in a way that both conforms to our knowledge regarding infancy and yet is flexible enough to account for the changes in the nature of the attachment system in adolescence and beyond.

ACKNOWLEDGMENTS

This chapter was completed with the assistance of grants from the Spencer Foundation and National Academy of Education, the National Institute of Mental Health, and the W. T. Grant Foundation to Joseph P. Allen.

NOTES

1. The AAI focuses primarily on state of mind with respect to attachment [to parents] as assessed through coded discourse. It places primary emphasis on the coherence of discourse about childhood relationships with parents. This chapter focuses on research utilizing this measure, because thus far it is the only measure that has demonstrated an empirical connection to the attachment construct as assessed in infancy (as evidenced by small continuities that have sometimes been observed from attachment organization in infancy to that in adulthood assessed with the AAI, and much more robust predictions from the AAI to the capacity to establish a secure attachment relationship with one's infant offspring).

There are also studies of adolescent attachment based on several different self-report instruments. For example, the Inventory of Parent and Peer Attachment (Armsden & Greenberg, 1987) has been used in several studies (e.g., Papini & Roggman, 1992; Papini, Roggman, & Anderson, 1991: Paterson, Pryor, & Field, 1995; Schultheiss & Blustein, 1994a, 1994b) with subjects as young as 12 years of age to assess perceived quality (i.e., security) of relationships with mothers, fathers, and peers. Self-report measures of romantic attachment (e.g., Bartholomew & Horowitz, 1991; Hazan & Shaver, 1987, 1990) have been used in scores of studies involving 18- and 19-year-old college students (see Feeney, Chapter 17, this volume, for a review of literature on romantic attachment). Recently this kind of measure was used in a large representative-sample study of black and white adolescents (Cooper, Shaver, & Collins, 1998). The associations and differences between the AAI and self-report attachment measures are discussed in Chapter 20 of the present volume by Crowell, Fraley, and Shaver.

REFERENCES

Adam, K. S., Sheldon-Keller, A. E., & West, M. (1996). Attachment organization and history of suicidal behavior in clinical adolescents. *Journal of Consulting and Clinical Psychology, 64,* 264–272.

Ainsworth, M. D. S. (1989). Attachments beyond infancy. *American Psychologist, 44,* 709–716.

Allen, J. P., Aber, J. L., & Leadbeater, B. J. (1990). Adolescent problem behaviors: The influence of attachment and autonomy. *Psychiatric Clinics of North America, 13,* 455–467.

Allen, J. P., & Hauser, S. T. (1996). Autonomy and relatedness in adolescent–family interactions as predictors of young adults' states of mind regarding attachment. *Development and Psychopathology, 8,* 793–809.

Allen, J. P., Hauser, S. T., & Borman-Spurrell, E. (1996). Attachment insecurity and related sequelae of severe adolescent psychopathology: An eleven-year follow-up study. *Journal of Consulting and Clinical Psychology, 64,* 254–263.

Allen, J. P., Hauser, S. T., Bell, K. L., & O'Connor, T. G. (1994). Longitudinal assessment of autonomy and relatedness in adolescent–family interactions as predictors of adolescent ego development and self-esteem. *Child Development, 65,* 179–194.

Allen, J. P., Hauser, S. T., Eickholt, C., Bell, K. L., & O'Connor, T. G. (1994). Autonomy and relatedness in family interactions as predictors of expressions of negative adolescent affect. *Journal of Research on Adolescence, 4,* 535–552.

Allen, J. P., & Kuperminc, G. P. (1995, March–April). *Adolescent attachment, social competence, and problematic behavior.* Paper presented at the biennial meeting of the Society for Research in Child Development, Indianapolis, IN.

Allen, J. P., Kuperminc, G. P., & Moore, C. M. (1997). Developmental approaches to understanding adolescent deviance. In S. S. Luthar, J. A. Burack, D. Cicchetti, & J. Weisz (Eds.), *Developmental psychopathology: Perspectives on risk and disorder* (pp. 548–567). Cambridge, England: Cambridge University Press.

Allen, J. P., Land, D. J., Liebman, S. E., Bell, K., & Jodl, K. M. (1997, April). *Maternal attachment organization as a predictor of mother–adolescent interactions and adolescent attachment organization.* Paper presented at the biennial meeting of the Society for Research in Child Development, Washington, DC.

Allen, J. P., Moore, C. M., Kuperminc, G. P., & Bell, K. L. (1998). Attachment and adolescent psychosocial functioning. *Child Development, 69,* 1406–1419.

Armsden, G. C., & Greenberg, M. T. (1987). The Inventory of Parent and Peer Attachment: Individual differences and their relationship to psychological well-being in adolescence. *Journal of Youth and Adolescence, 16,* 427–454.

Bartholomew, K., & Horowitz, L. M., (1991). Attachment styles among young adults: A test of a four-category model. *Journal of Personality and Social Psychology, 61,* 226–244.

Becker-Stoll, F., & Fremmer-Bombik, E. (1997, April). *Adolescent–mother interaction and attachment: A longitudinal study.* Paper presented at the biennial meeting of the Society for Research in Child Development, Washington, DC.

Benoit, D., & Parker, K. C. H. (1994). Stability and transmission of attachment across three generations. *Child Development, 65,* 1444–1456.

Bowlby, J. (1973). *Attachment and loss: Vol. 2. Separation: Anxiety and anger.* New York: Basic Books

Buhrmester, D. (1992). The developmental courses of sibling and peer relationships. In F. Bou & J. Dunn (Eds.), *Children's sibling relationships* (pp. 192–240). Hillsdale, NJ: Erlbaum.

Buhrmester, D., & Furman, W. (1987). The development of companionship and intimacy. *Child Development, 58,* 1101–1113.

Cassidy, J. (1994). Emotion regulation: Influences of attachment relationships. In N. A. Fox (Ed.), The development of emotion regulation: Biological and biobehavioral considerations. *Monographs of the Society for Research in Child Development, 59*(2–3, Serial No. 240), 228–249.

Cassidy, J., & Berlin, L. J. (1994). The insecure/ambivalent pattern of attachment: Theory and research. *Child Development, 65,* 971–991.

Cassidy, J., Kirsh, S., Scolton, K., & Parke, R. D. (1996). Attachment and representations of peer relationships. *Developmental Psychology, 32,* 892–904.

Collins, W. A. (1990). Parent–child relationships in the transition to adolescence: Continuity and change in interaction, affect, and cognition. In R. Montemayor, G. R. Adams, & T. P. Gullotta (Eds.) *Advances in adolescent development: Vol. 2. From childhood to adolescence: A transitional period?* (pp. 85–106). Newbury Park, CA: Sage.

Cooper, M. L., Shaver, P. R., & Collins, N. L. (1998). Attachment styles, emotion regulation, and adjustment in adolescence. *Journal of Personality and Social Psychology, 74,* 1380–1397.

Cox, M. J., Owen, M. T., Henderson, V. K., & Margand, N. A. (1992). Prediction of infant–father and infant–mother attachment. *Developmental Psychology, 28,* 474–483.

Cullari, S., & Mikus, R. (1990). Correlates of adolescent sexual behavior. *Psychological Reports, 66,* 1179–1184.

Dodge, K. A. (1993). Social-cognitive mechanisms in the development of conduct disorder and depression. *Annual Review of Psychology, 44,* 559–584.

Donovan, J. E., & Jessor, R. (1985). Structure of problem behavior in adolescence and young adulthood. *Journal of Consulting and Clinical Psychology, 53,* 890–904.

Fraley, R. C., & Davis, K. E. (1997). Attachment formation and transfer in young adults' close friendships and romantic relationships. *Personal Relationships, 4,* 131–144.

Fox, N. A., Kimmerly, N. L., & Schafer, W. D. (1991). Attachment to mother/attachment to father: A meta-analysis. *Child Development, 62,* 210–225.

Fuligni, A. J., & Eccles, J. S. (1993). Perceived parent–child relationships and early adolescents' orientation toward peers. *Developmental Psychology, 29,* 622–632.

Gavin, L. A., & Furman, W. (1989). Age differences in adolescents' perceptions of their peer groups. *Developmental Psychology, 25,* 827–834.

Gavin, L. A., & Furman, W. (1996). Adolescent girls' relationships with mothers and best friends. *Child Development, 67,* 375–386.

George, C., Kaplan, N., & Main, M. (1996). *Adult Attachment Interview* (3rd ed.). Unpublished manuscript, University of California at Berkeley.

Grotevant, H. D., & Cooper, C. R. (1985). Patterns of interaction in family relationships and the development of identity exploration in adolescence. *Child Development, 56,* 415–428.

Hamilton, C. E. (1994). *Continuity and discontinuity of attachment from infancy through adolescence.* Unpublished doctoral dissertation. University of California at Los Angeles.

Hamilton, C. E. (1995, March–April). *Continuity and discontinuity of attachment from infancy through adolescence.* Paper presented at the biennial meeting of the Society for Research in Child Development, Indianapolis, IN.

Hartup, W. W. (1983). Peer relations. In P. H. Mussen (Series Ed.) & E. M. Hetherington (Vol. Ed.), *Handbook of child psychology: Vol. 4. Socialization, personality, and social development* (4th ed., pp. 301–349). New York: Wiley.

Hartup, W. W. (1992). Friendships and their developmental significance. In H. McGurk (Ed.), *Childhood social development: Contemporary perspectives* (pp. 175–205). Hillsdale, NJ: Erlbaum.

Hazan, C., & Shaver, P. R. (1987). Romantic love conceptualized as an attachment process. *Journal of Personality and Social Psychology, 52,* 511–524.

Hazan, C., & Shaver, P. R. (1990). Love and work: An attachment-theoretical perspective. *Journal of Personality and Social Psychology, 59,* 270–280.

Hazan, C., & Shaver, P. R. (1994). Attachment as an organizational framework for research on close relationships. *Psychological Inquiry, 5,* 1–22.

Hill, J. P., & Holmbeck, G. N. (1986). Attachment and autonomy during adolescence. *Annals of Child Development, 3,* 145–189.

Homann, E. (1997, April). *Attachment and affect regulation in depressed mothers and their adolescent daughters.* Paper presented at the biennial meeting of the Society for Research in Child Development, Washington, DC.

Januszewski, B., Turner, R., Guerin, L., & Flack, A. (1996, March). *Working models of attachment, sociosexual orientation, and sexual problems.* Paper presented at the biennial meeting of the Society for Research on Adolescence, Boston.

Jones, G. P., & Dembo, M. H. (1989). Age and sex role differences in intimate friendships during childhood and adolescence. *Merrill–Palmer Quarterly, 35,* 445–462.

Kahen, V., Katz, L. F., & Gottman, J. M. (1994). Linkages between parent–child interaction and conversations of friends. *Social Development, 3,* 238–254.

Keating, D. (1990). Adolescent thinking. In S. S. Feldman & G. Elliott (Eds.), *At the threshold: The developing adolescent* (pp. 54–90). Cambridge, MA: Harvard University Press.

Kobak, R., & Cole, C. (1994). Attachment and metamonitoring: Implications for adolescent autonomy and psychopathology. In D. Cicchetti (Ed.), *Rochester Symposium on Development and Psychopathology: Vol. 5. Disorders of the self* (pp. 267–297). Rochester, NY: University of Rochester Press.

Kobak, R. R., Cole, H. E., Ferenz-Gillies, R., Fleming, W. S., & Gamble, W. (1993). Attachment and emotion regulation during mother–teen problem solving: A control theory analysis. *Child Development, 64,* 231–245.

Kobak, R., & Duemmler, S. (1994). Attachment and conversation: Toward a discourse analysis of adolescent and adult security. In K. Bartholomew & D. Perlman (Eds.), *Advances in personal relationships: Volume 5. Attachment processes in adulthood* (pp. 121–149). London: Jessica Kingsley.

Kobak, R. R., & Sceery, A. (1988). Attachment in late adolescence: Working models, affect regulation, and representations of self and others. *Child Development, 59,* 135–146.

Kobak, R. R., Sudler, N., & Gamble, W. (1991). Attachment and depressive symptoms during adolescence: A developmental pathways analysis. *Development and Psychopathology, 3,* 461–474.

Larson, R. W., Richards, M. H., Moneta, G., Holmbeck, G., & Duckett, E. (1996). Changes in adolescents' daily interactions with their families from ages 10 to 18: Disengagement and transformation. *Developmental Psychology, 32,* 744–754.

Leadbeater, B. J., Hellner, I., Allen, J. P., & Aber, J. L. (1989). The assessment of interpersonal negotiation strategies in multi-problem youth. *Developmental Psychology, 25,* 465–472.

Main, M. (1997, December). *Attachment: Theory, research, application.* Paper presented at the meeting of the American Psychoanalytic Society, New York.

Main, M., & Goldwyn, R. (in press). Adult attachment rating and classification systems. In M. Main (Ed.), *A typology of human attachment organization assessed in discourse, drawings and interviews.* New York: Cambridge University Press.

Main, M., & Hesse, E. (1990). Parents' unresolved traumatic experiences are related to infant disorganized attachment status: Is frightened and/or frightening parental behavior the linking mechanism? In M. T. Greenberg, D. Cicchetti, & E. M. Cummings (Eds.), *Attachment in the preschool years* (pp. 161–184). Chicago: University of Chicago Press.

Main, M., Kaplan, N., & Cassidy, J. (1985). Security in infancy, childhood, and adulthood: A move to the level of representation. In I. Bretherton & E. Waters (Eds.) Growing points of attachment theory and research. *Monographs of the Society for Research in Child Development, 50*(1–2, Serial No. 9), 66–104.

Main, M., & Solomon, J. (1986). Discovery of a new, insecure–disorganized/disoriented attachment pattern. In T. B. Brazelton & M. Yogman (Eds.), *Affective development in infancy* (pp. 95–124). Norwood, NJ: Ablex.

Moore, C. W. (1997). *Models of attachment, relationships with parents, and sexual behavior in at-risk adolescents.* Unpublished doctoral dissertation, University of Virginia.

Moore, D. (1987). Parent–adolescent separation: The construction of adulthood by late adolescents. *Developmental Psychology, 23,* 298–307.

Nolen-Hoeksema, S., & Girgus, J. S. (1994). The emergence of gender differences in depression during adolescence. *Psychological Bulletin, 115,* 424–443.

Nolen-Hoeksema, S., Parker, L. E., & Larson, J. (1994). Ruminative coping with depressed mood following loss. *Journal of Personality and Social Psychology, 67,* 92–104.

O'Beirne, H. A., & Allen, J. P. (1996, March). *Adolescent sexual behavior: Individual, peer, and family correlates.* Paper presented at the biennial meeting of the Society for Research on Adolescence, Boston.

O'Connor, E. M., Pan, H., Waters, E., & Posada, G. (1995, March–April). *Attachment classification, romantic jealousy, and aggression in couples.* Paper presented at the biennial meeting of the Society for Research in Child Development, Indianapolis, IN.

Papini, D. R., & Roggman, L. A. (1992). Adolescent perceived attachment to parents in relation to competence, depression, and anxiety: A longitudinal study. *Journal of Early Adolescence, 12,* 420–440.

Papini, D. R., Roggman, L. A., & Anderson, J. (1991). Early-adolescent perceptions of attachment to mother and father: A test of emotional-distancing and buffering hypotheses. *Journal of Early Adolescence, 11,* 258–275.

Paterson, J., Pryor, J., & Field, J. (1995). Adolescent attachment to parents and friends in relation to aspects of self-esteem. *Journal of Youth and Adolescence, 24,* 365–376.

Patterson, G. R., DeBaryshe, B. D., & Ramsey, E. (1989). A developmental perspective on antisocial behavior. *American Psychologist, 44,* 329–335.

Pianta, R. C., Egeland, B., & Adam, E. K. (1996). Adult attachment classification and self-reported psychiatric symptomatology as assessed by the Minnesota Multiphasic Personality Inventory—2. *Journal of Consulting and Clinical Psychology, 64,* 273–281.

Reimer, M. S., Overton, W. F., Steidl, J. H., Rosenstein, D. S., & Horowitz, H. (1996). Familial responsiveness and behavioral control: Influences on adolescent psychopathology, attachment, and cognition. *Journal of Research on Adolescence, 6,* 87–112.

Renken, B., Egeland, B., Marvinney, D., Mangelsdorf, S., & Sroufe, L. A. (1989). Early childhood antecedents of aggression and passive-withdrawal in early elementary school. *Journal of Personality, 57,* 257–281.

Ricks, M. H. (1985). Social transmission of parental behavior: Attachment across generations. In I. Bretherton & E. Waters (Eds.), Growing points of attachment theory and research. *Monographs of the Society for Research in Child Development, 50*(1–2, Serial No. 9), 211–227.

Rosenstein, D. S., & Horowitz, H. A. (1996). Adolescent attachment and psychopathology. *Journal of Consulting and Clinical Psychology, 64,* 244–253.

Rothbaum, F., Schneider, K., Pott, M., & Beatty, M. (1995). Early parent–child relationships and later problem behavior: A longitudinal study. *Merrill–Palmer Quarterly, 41,* 133–151.

Rubin, K. H., & Lollis, S. P. (1988). Origins and consequences of social withdrawal. In J. Belsky & T. Nezworski (Eds.), *Clinical implications of attachment* (pp. 219–252). Hillsdale, NJ: Erlbaum.

Schultheiss, D. E. P., & Blustein, D. L. (1994a). Role of adolescent–parent relationships in college student development and adjustment. *Journal of Counseling Psychology, 41,* 248–255.

Schultheiss, D. E. P., & Blustein, D. L. (1994b). Contributions of family relationship factors to the identity formation process. *Journal of Counseling and Development, 73,* 579–599.

Shaver, P., Hazan, C., & Bradshaw, D. (1988). Love as attachment: The integration of three behavioral systems. In R. J. Sternberg & M. Barnes (Eds.), *The psychology of love* (pp. 68–99). New Haven, CT: Yale University Press.

Slough, N. M., & Greenberg, M. T. (1990). Five-year-olds' representations of separation from parents: Responses from the perspective of self and other. In I. Bretherton & M. W. Watson (Eds.), *New directions for child development: No. 48. Children's perspectives on the family* (pp. 67–84). San Francisco: Jossey-Bass.

Steele, H., Steele, M., & Fonagy, P. (1996). Associations among attachment classifications of mothers, fathers, and their infants. *Child Development, 67,* 541–555.

Steinberg, L. (1990). Interdependence in the family: Autonomy, conflict, and harmony in the parent-adolescent relationship. In S. Feldman & G. Elliott (Eds.), *At the threshold: The developing adolescent* (pp. 255–276). Cambridge, MA: Harvard University Press.

Tesch, S. A. (1983). Review of friendship development across the lifespan. *Human Development, 26,* 266–276.

Thompson, R. A, Flood, M. F., & Lundquist, L. (1995). Emotional regulation: Its relations to attachment and developmental psychopathology. In D. Cicchetti & S. L. Toth (Eds.), *Rochester Symposium on Developmental Psychopathology: Vol. 6. Emotion, cognition, and representation* (pp. 261–299). Rochester, NY: University of Rochester Press.

Treboux, D., & Busch-Rossnagel, N. A. (1990). Social network influences on adolescent sexual attitudes and behaviors. *Journal of Adolescent Research, 5,* 175–189.

Treboux, D., Crowell, J. A., Owens, G., & Pan, H. (1994, February). *Attachment behaviors and working models: Relation to best friendships and romantic relationships.* Paper presented at the biennial meeting of the Society for Research in Adolescence, San Diego, CA.

van IJzendoorn, M. H. (1992). Intergenerational transmission of parenting: A review of studies in nonclinical populations. *Developmental Review, 12,* 76–99.

van IJzendoorn, M. H. (1995). Adult attachment representations, parental responsiveness, and infant attachment: A meta-analysis on the predictive validity of the Adult Attachment Interview. *Psychological Bulletin, 117,* 387–403.

van IJzendoorn, M. H. (1996). Commentary. *Human Development, 39,* 224–231.

Ward, M. J., & Carlson, E. A. (1995). Associations among adult attachment representations, maternal sensitivity, and infant–mother attachment in a sample of adolescent mothers. *Child Development, 66,* 69–79.

Waters, E., Merrick, S. K., Albersheim, L., & Treboux, D. (1995, March–April). *Attachment security from infancy to early adulthood: A 20-year longitudinal study.* Paper presented at the biennial meeting of the Society for Research in Child Development, Indianapolis, IN.

Weinfield, N. S. (1996). *Attachment and the representation of relationships from infancy to adulthood: Continuity, discontinuity, and their correlates.* Unpublished doctoral dissertation, University of Minnesota.

Wilks, J. (1986). The relative importance of parents and friends in adolescent decision making. *Journal of Youth and Adolescence, 15,* 323–334.

Wright, D. A., Peterson, L. R., & Barnes, H. L. (1990). The relation of parental employment and contextual variables with sexual permissiveness and gender role attitudes of rural early adolescents. *Journal of Early Adolescence, 10,* 383–398.

Youniss, J. (1980). *Parents and peers in social development.* Chicago: University of Chicago Press.

Youniss, J., & Haynie, D. L. (1992). Friendship in adolescence. *Journal of Developmental and Behavioral Pediatrics, 13,* 59–66.

Zimmermann, P., Fremmer-Bombik, E., Spangler, G., & Grossmann, K. E. (1995, March–April). *Attachment in adolescence: A longitudinal perspective.* Paper presented at the biennial meeting of the Society for Research in Child Development, Indianapolis, IN.

Zimmermann, P., Scheuerer-Englisch, H., & Grossmann, K. E. (1996, May). *Social relationships in adolescence: Continuity and transformations.* Paper presented at the biennial meeting of the European Association for Research on Adolescence, Liege, Belgium.

16

Pair Bonds as Attachments

Evaluating the Evidence

❖

CINDY HAZAN
DEBRA ZEIFMAN

Anyone familiar with John Bowlby's writings can readily understand the common (mis)perception that attachment theory applies exclusively to relationships between infants and their caregivers. Although he made repeated reference to attachment as a lifespan phenomenon, the principal focus of his theorizing was "the nature of the child's tie to his mother" (Bowlby, 1958). His oft-cited claim that attachment is an integral part of human behavior from "the cradle to the grave" (Bowlby, 1979) was more a hypothesis than a thoroughly documented, empirically established fact.

The absence of a comprehensive theory of attachment beyond childhood may have delayed the initiation of research forays into the area, but it did not preclude them. In the last decade alone, investigations of adult attachment have proliferated at a rate comparable to that of infant attachment studies during the years immediately following the publication of Ainsworth's (1967) original findings. Adult attachment research has proceeded largely on the faith that Bowlby was right about two things: that patterns of attachment established in early life are relatively stable across development, and that pair-bond relationships are the prototypical adult instantiation of attachment.

The present chapter does not address continuity in attachment patterns between infancy and adulthood. Instead, our focus is the second assumption—that romantic relationships qualify as attachment bonds and thus constitute the appropriate context in which to investigate adult attachment phenomena. Although these assumptions may appear to be inextricably interrelated, they actually represent independent issues, at least from an empirical standpoint. Consider the possible outcomes of stability studies: a finding of relative continuity in patterns of attachment from infancy to adulthood, or, alternatively, no systematic connections between infants' strange situation classifications and their subsequent adult attachment categorization. Neither outcome would provide a definitive answer to the question of whether the attachment system is active in adult life or implicated in pair bonds. Continuity of individual differences is not the same as continuity of function; these are separate issues requiring distinct types of evidence. Thus the validity of our arguments concerning the second assumption is not dependent on the results of empirical investigations relating to the first.

The importance of the question—whether romantic bonds are attachments in the technical sense—can hardly be overestimated. The entire field of adult attachment research has been constructed on the premise that they are. If it were to turn out that Bowlby was mistaken, either about the lifespan significance of attachment or about the preeminence of romantic partners as attachment figures in adult life, it could potentially undermine the whole body of findings. Therefore, it is crucial to the adult attachment enterprise that this foundational assumption be examined and evaluated in light of the evidence.

One reason for questioning the assumption that romantic relationships are genuine attachments concerns the presumed function of attachment bonds. In theory, the attachment behavioral system evolved in response to selection pressures in the "environment of evolutionary adaptedness" (EEA) that made it advantageous for infants to maintain proximity to protectors (Bowlby, 1958, 1969/1982). Thus the hypothesized ultimate function of attachment is *protection.* Few would argue with the adaptiveness of a system that in situations of real or perceived danger led vulnerable young to seek protection from their more mature and competent guardians, or with the necessity of such a system for human infant survival.

What is considerably less apparent is how attachment might contribute to *adult* survival. It cannot simply be assumed that adult attachment—if it exists—serves the same function as infant attachment. The burden of providing empirical evidence for this and related assumptions rests squarely with adult attachment researchers. A solid foundation is essential to support the already large and rapidly expanding body of findings.

Is there compelling evidence that the attachment system is operative in adult romantic relationships? If so, does it serve the same function as in infancy? Do pair-bond partners replace parents in their roles as primary attachment figures, as Bowlby hypothesized? And, if so, by what processes does the transition occur? These are some of the questions addressed in this chapter. In our own research, we started with the last ones—whether attachments are transferred from parents to partners, and how. We therefore begin with a brief summary of these results. This is followed by a review of the literature, including some of our own work, as it relates to the question of whether pair bonds are attachments in the technical sense. Throughout the chapter and in the third major section especially, we address issues related to the function and evolutionary significance of attachment bonds in adulthood. Finally, we outline a model of the processes by which attachment bonds are formed between romantic partners.

FROM PARENTAL ATTACHMENT TO PAIR BONDS

How Attachment Is Defined

Bowlby took care to define the specific type of socioemotional bond to which his theory applied, and to distinguish it from other kinds of social ties. Attachment bonds have four defining features: "proximity maintenance," "separation distress," "safe haven," and "secure base." These are readily observable in the overt behavior of an infant in relation to a primary caregiver (usually the mother). She serves as a base of security from which the infant engages in interactions with the social and physical world. The infant continuously monitors her proximity and availability. If the infant senses danger or feels anxious for any reason, he or she will retreat to the mother as a source of comfort and haven of safety. Because separations from her signal potential danger, the infant will object to and be distressed by them. But as long as the mother is perceived to be sufficiently near and responsive, the infant will be motivated to explore and learn about his or her environment.

Theoretically, this dynamic balance between attachment and exploration is an integral part of behavior during all phases of development. Nevertheless, changes as a function of maturation are expected. One predictable change concerns the time and distance from the attachment figure that can be comfortably tolerated. A typical 12-month-old will exhibit greater distress (and more disrupted exploration) as the result of even brief separations from a caregiver than will the average 36-month-old. By late childhood or early adolescence, longer separations are usually negotiated without undue upset, and separation distress is rare except in the case of unexpected and/or extended caregiver unavailability.

Perhaps the preeminent change in attachment relationships concerns their mutuality. The asymmetrical (complementary) attachments of early life—in which infants seek and derive security from caregivers but do not provide security in return—are hypothesized to be replaced by more symmetrical (reciprocal) attachments. According to Bowlby, the pair bond—in which sexual partners *mutually* derive and provide security—is the prototype of attachment in adulthood. Thus, in the course of normative development, the sexual mating, caregiving (parenting), and attachment systems become integrated (Hazan

& Shaver, 1994; Shaver, Hazan, & Bradshaw, 1988).

The Ontogeny of Infant Attachment

Given the opportunity, all normal human infants become attached to their primary caregivers, typically within the first 8 months of life. Attachment formation proceeds through a series of phases, beginning in the first weeks of life and ending sometime toward the end of the second year with the establishment of a "goal-corrected partnership" (Bowlby, 1969/1982). The process begins with close physical proximity, which is initially maintained by intentional actions of the caregiver and reflexive behavior on the part of the infant (e.g., crying, sucking, clinging). In time, the infant learns to associate the caregiver with comfort and alleviation of distress (safe haven). Typically around 8 months of age, and concurrent with the onset of self-produced locomotion and stranger wariness, the infant begins to protest separations and to use the caregiver as a base of security for exploration. Separation distress is the accepted indicator that an attachment bond is fully formed. Note that these components, which together define attachment, do not emerge simultaneously but in sequence.

Although multiple attachments are the norm, attachment figures are not treated equivalently. An infant shows clear discrimination and consistent preferences for the primary caregiver (Colin, 1985, 1987; Cummings, 1980). Even if several caregivers are regularly available, an infant reliably seeks and maintains proximity to one, especially when distressed (Ainsworth, 1967, 1982). The infant also exhibits more intense protest upon being separated from the primary attachment figure as compared to others (Schaffer & Emerson, 1965), and in unfamiliar settings is most reassured by this figure's presence (Ricciuti, 1974; Shill, Solyom, & Biven, 1984). The primary attachment figure is not simply one among a coterie of possible protectors, but the individual with whom the infant has a privileged relationship. Bowlby (1958, 1969/1982) referred to this tendency to form one special attachment as "monotropy," and he considered it a crucial aspect of the survival-enhancing function of attachment.

Over the course of development, changes are to be expected in the composition and structure of individuals' attachment hierarchies. New people may be added and/or others dropped. According to Bowlby, parental figures tend to be permanent members of the attachment hierarchy, but eventually assume a position secondary in importance to the pair-bond partner. Exactly when and how this change from complementary (parental) to reciprocal (peer) attachment comes about was not specified within attachment theory. We explored these questions of timing and process in two related studies. (For more details, see Hazan & Zeifman, 1994.)

Study 1: Attachment Behavior in Childhood and Adolescence

Background and Objectives

Peer relationships during childhood and adolescence are usually characterized as "affiliative"— that is, as functionally distinct from parental attachments and presumably regulated by a different behavioral system. Although there is obvious overlap in the behaviors that typify these two types of social bonds (e.g., friendly approaches, sharing), affiliative relationships primarily provide stimulation and increase arousal, in contrast to the arousal-moderating and security-enhancing provisions of attachment bonds. Yet a review of the research suggests that *some* components of attachment may be present in peer relationships fairly early in development.

By age 3, children are capable of sustaining complex social interactions with agemates (Gottman, 1983; Rubin, 1980). Not only do they possess the necessary skills for engaging their peers, but they show a growing interest in doing so. The preference for spending time with peers relative to parents increases steadily. Thus, one aspect of attachment—proximity seeking— seems to be present in and typical of peer relationships by childhood, although such relationships would not quality as attachments in the full sense of the term.

By middle childhood, youngsters are capable of developing more intimate relationships with their peers (Buhrmester & Furman, 1986, 1987; Buhrmester & Prager, 1995; Furman & Buhrmester, 1985; Hartup, 1983; Lewis, 1982) and increasingly turn to them for comfort. There is evidence that by late adolescence, peers come to be preferred over parents as sources of emotional support (Steinberg & Silverberg, 1986). The confiding and support-seeking aspects of peer relationships appear to be functionally similar to the parent-directed safe-haven behavior of infancy and early childhood.

In sum, there may be normative developmental changes in the *target* of different attachment behaviors, such that some get redirected toward peers during childhood and adolescence. On the basis of these kinds of findings, we reasoned that a key to understanding the transfer of attachment from parents to peers might lie in an analysis of attachment at the component level.

Method

We developed an interview measure of the four components of attachment and administered it (individually) to a diverse cross-section of over 100 children and adolescents ranging in age from 6 to 17. In constructing the interview items, we operated on the assumption that the components would be functionally and psychologically equivalent to their behavioral manifestations in infancy. For each, we asked several related questions: questions pertaining to proximity maintenance (e.g., "Whom do you like to spend time with, be near to?"); safe haven ("Whom do you turn to when you're upset, feeling down?"); separation distress ("Whom do you hate to be away from, miss most during separations?"); and secure base ("Whom do you feel you can always count on, know would do almost anything for you?"). Subjects were asked to respond to each of the questions by naming the single most preferred person in each situation.

Because we were primarily interested in the distinction between parental figures and peers, responses were grouped into these two categories. The "parents" category included mothers, fathers, stepparents, and grandparents; "peers" included friends, boyfriends, and girlfriends. Together, the two categories covered 91% of the responses. The consistency of responses to items within each component was generally high, but consistency across components was not. That is, participants tended to name the same person for all items measuring one component, but often named different people in response to items measuring other components. This can be taken as evidence of the internal consistency of the components, as well as their distinctiveness. Several age-related changes in the target of attachment behaviors were observed.

Results and Discussion

Nearly all children and adolescents in the sample were peer-oriented in terms of proximity seeking. That is, they preferred to spend their time in the company of peers rather than parents. In regard to the safe-haven component, there was an apparent shift between the ages of 8 and 14, with peers coming to be preferred over parents as sources of comfort and emotional support. For the majority, parents continued to serve as bases of security and as the primary sources of separation distress. Only among the oldest adolescents (the 15- to 17-year-old group) did we find what could be considered full-blown attachments to peers—that is, peer relationships containing all four components. Of this minority who considered a peer to be their primary attachment figure, the overwhelming majority (83%) named a boyfriend or girlfriend—that is, a *romantic* partner. Our findings are consistent with those of other studies that have documented developmental changes in the constellation of social relationships during the transition from childhood to adolescence (Blyth, Hill, & Theil, 1982; Furman & Wehner, 1994).

Study 2: Attachment Behavior in Adulthood

Background and Objectives

Research on the formation and development of romantic relationships suggests that whether attachment features are present—and, if so, which ones—may depend on how long a couple has been together. For example, romantic couples typically experience on especially strong desire for physical proximity and contact in the initial stages of a relationship (Berscheid, 1985), whereas the provision of mutual support and care becomes more important in later stages (Reedy, Birren, & Schaie, 1981; Sternberg, 1986). Similarly, reactions to separations seem to vary according to relationship length and stage (Weiss, 1988). Thus, in adult–adult relationships as well as infant–caregiver relationships, the presence or absence of attachment components may depend on the stage of relationship development.

Method

We administered essentially the same interview used in our child/adolescent study to an equally diverse sample of over 100 adults ranging in age from 18 to 82, but this time we grouped subjects by stage of relationship development, rather than by age. Three relationship status groups were identified: "not in a romantic relationship," "in a romantic relationship for less than 2 years," and "in a romantic relationship for 2 or more years." It is important to note that these cutoffs were empirically derived. Other cutoffs were examined, but the data indicated that relationships of less than 2 years' duration were qualitatively different from those of longer duration, at least in the components we measured.

The data also suggested response categories that differed in two ways from those used in the previous study. First, siblings were named more often than they had been by younger subjects. (This was especially true for our oldest participants, many of whose parents were no longer living.) Second, peers were subdivided into the two most common response categories: friends and romantic partners. When we averaged across components, 85% of all responses were covered by the following three categories: "parent/adult sibling," "friend," and "romantic partner."

Results and Discussion

The adults were clearly peer-oriented in both proximity-seeking and safe-haven behaviors. Nearly all of our adult respondents reported a preference for spending time with and seeking emotional support from their friends and/or partners rather than their parents or siblings. But findings for the other two components varied as a function of relationship status. Subjects involved in romantic relationships of at least 2 years' duration overwhelmingly named partners in response to the items covering separation distress and secure base (compared to approximately one-third of those in the under-2-years group, and none in the less-than-1-year subgroup of this group). Those in shorter-term romantic relationships and those without partners tended to name a parent as the individual whose absence was most distressing and whose presence served as a base of security.

Conclusions

In the introduction, we have posed the question of whether romantic relationships (i.e., pair bonds) are true attachments. Evidence that they are would support Bowlby's claims that the attachment system is active throughout the lifespan and that sexual partners assume the role of attachment figures in adult life. Moreover, such evidence would provide empirical justification for the common practice of using romantic relationships as the context for investigating adult attachment phenomena. We reasoned that a logical starting point for addressing this question was to discover first whether romantic relationships meet the definitional criteria of attachment. In addition, it was necessary to demonstrate that romantic partners assume preeminent status in the attachment hierarchy by replacing parental figures as the predominant source of emotional security.

The results of these two studies (and a replication of the second by Fraley & Davis, 1997) are consistent with and thus provide preliminary support for Bowlby's hypothesis. Full-blown attachments, among adolescent as well as adult subjects, were observed almost exclusively in two kinds of social relationships—with parents or with romantic partners. By this standard, pair bonds quality as bona fide attachments. Furthermore, and just as Bowlby predicted, pair-bond partners did assume the status of primary attachment figures (by being preferred over parents).

The findings may also reveal something about the basic processes by which primary attachments are transferred from parents to peers. The establishment of a goal-corrected partnership in early childhood facilitates social exploration. As such, the endpoint in the development of complementary attachments to parents serves as the starting point for reciprocal attachments to peers. Increased time spent in the company of peers fosters mutual confiding, comforting, and a reliance on peers as havens of safety, thereby paving the way for attachment formation. However, it is important to note that most of our adolescent and adult subjects were not attached—in the technical sense—to their friends. Peer relationships meeting the definitional criteria of attachment were almost exclusively of the romantic variety.

Apparently sex plays a central role in peer attachment. Sexual maturation may serve as a catalyst for redirecting social attention and activity toward mating, as is the case in many other species (Hinde, 1983). Furthermore, sexual exchanges create a social context that is conducive to attachment formation. (We return to this issue below.)

THE NATURE OF THE BOND IN PAIR BONDS

So far, evidence has been presented that pair-bond relationships are characterized by the same features as infant–caregiver attachments and develop according to the same process, at least in terms of the sequence in which various components come into play. These findings alone provide support for the assertion that the same behavioral system is involved in pair bonds and in infant–caregiver relationships. But the similarities do not end there, nor should they. If the attachment system is operative in pair bonds, its effects would be expected to be far more pervasive, and to be conspicuous in other aspects of relationship functioning. In fact, the congruences are far-reaching. They include the nature of physical contact that typifies and distinguishes attachment bonds; the factors that influence the selection of attachment figures; reactions to attachment disruption and loss; and the role of attachment in biological and psychological fitness. We discuss each of these in turn.

Physical Contact

Freud was among the first to write about the striking similarities in the physical intimacy that typifies lovers and mother–infant pairs. Like caregivers and their infants, adult sexual partners (at least initially) spend much time engaged in mutual gazing, cuddling, nuzzling, suckling, and kissing, in the context of prolonged face-to-face, skin-to-skin, belly-to-belly contact and the touching of body parts otherwise considered "private." What we find interesting and particularly compelling is that in virtually every culture, these most intimate of human interpersonal exchanges are limited to parent–infant and pair-bond relationships (Eibl-Eibesfeldt, 1975). Although some forms of intimate contact may occur in isolation within other types of social relationships (e.g., kissing among friends), their collective occurrence is typically more restricted.

The universal existence of prohibitions against physical intimacy outside recognized pair bonds (at least for females) has generally been attributed to the fact that copulations outside such bonds reduce confidence in paternity. Such restrictions may also reflect an implicit understanding that close physical contact with another can lead to a subsidiary emotional bond that will jeopardize a primary one. In subcultures where extrarelationship sexual contact is permitted, efforts to avoid emotional involvement are common. For example, prostitutes commonly refuse to engage in kissing, nuzzling, and other forms of intimate face-to-face contact with their clients (Nass & Fisher, 1988). Members of gay male couples who consensually engage in extrarelationship sexual activity usually reserve kissing

and cuddling for their primary partners (Blumstein & Schwartz, 1983). And ground rules among so-called "swinging" heterosexual couples often forbid regular or frequent sexual contact with the same person (O'Neill & O'Neill, 1972). Such practices may serve the ultimate function of maintaining paternity confidence (e.g., heightened arousal could foster more effective sperm competition; see Baker & Bellis, 1995) while preventing the proximate mechanism of repeated physical intimacy leading to bonding. If an emotional bond is not desired in the context of a physically intimate relationship, special steps must be taken to protect against its formation.

There is some evidence that the chemical basis for the effects of close physical contact may be the same for lovers and for mother–infant pairs. Oxytocin, a substance released during suckling/nursing interactions and thought to induce infant attachment and maternal caregiving, is also released at sexual climax and has been implicated in the cuddling that often follows sexual intercourse (i.e., "afterplay"; Carter, 1992). Cuddling, or contact as was demonstrated by Harlow, is crucial for the establishment of emotional bonds.

In sum, pair bonds and infant–caregiver relationships show conspicuous similarities in the nature of physical contact, and these differentiate them from other classes of social relationships. The consequence of repeated interactions of this uniquely intimate sort is the development of a specific and distinctive type of bond—namely, an attachment. It follows that the attachment system is active in both.

Selection Criteria

If pair-bond relationships involve the attachment system, one would expect at least some overlap between infants and adult romantic partners in the criteria on which selections are based. But the attributes that make one a good mother or father are not necessarily the same qualities that make one appealing as a sexual partner. There is the additional complication of well-documented sex differences in mate selection criteria, which are attributed to differences in parental investment that are present and influential even before conception (Trivers, 1972).

Differential parental investment theory holds that sexual encounters will have potentially different consequences for males and females. Males have an abundant supply of small sperm cells, which are produced at a rate of approximately 500 million per day (Zimmerman, Maude, & Moldawar, 1965), whereas females have a far more limited supply of large egg cells, which are produced at a rate of about one per month during a much shorter period of life. Added to this are the female burdens of gestation and lactation, requiring years of investment. For males, whose contribution to offspring can be as limited as a few sperm, the most effective strategy may be to take advantage of all opportunities for sex with fertile partners. The female, for whom every sexual encounter is potentially quite costly, may be expected to be far choosier in accepting or encouraging copulations. Once her egg is fertilized, she has to forgo other reproductive opportunities for a relatively long time. Her most effective strategy may thus be to limit her sexual encounters to males who possess and appear willing to share valuable resources with her and the offspring she will have to nurture.

In a survey of 37 cultures, Buss (1989) found that sex differences in mate selection criteria are consistent with male–female differences in parental investment. For example, males generally assign greater importance than females to the physical appearance of potential mates, preferring partners who look youthful and healthy—both of which are reasonably good indices of fertility (Buss, 1989; Symons, 1979). In contrast, females typically care more than males about the social status and earning power of potential partners; this is a sensible mate selection strategy for ensuring that offspring are well provided for.

Although these differences in mate selection criteria are reliably found, sex differences are negligible when it comes to evaluating potential partners for a long- versus a short-term relationship (Kenrick, Groth, Trost, & Sadalla, 1993). Given that we humans tend to reproduce in the context of long-term relationships, short-term strategies may be less relevant to understanding mating in our species. Moreover, although sex differences in the relative importance of such traits as physical appearance and social status are reliable, less attention is given to the fact that *neither* trait is assigned highest priority by *either* sex. For both men and women, the most highly valued qualities in a potential mate are "kind/understanding" and "intelligent" (Buss, 1989). In choosing among potential reproductive partners, males *and* females prefer those who are responsive and competent, and these traits matter more to them than wealth or beauty.

It follows from the norm of assortative mating that men and women tend to choose partners who are similar to themselves on numerous dimensions, including socioeconomic status and physical attractiveness (Berscheid, 1985; Berscheid & Reis, 1997; Hinsz, 1989; Rubin, 1973). This may reflect the more general tendency to prefer what is familiar. In the case of mating, preexisting similarities draw potential partners into the same activities and social circles, thereby increasing familiarity, and similarity can create a false sense of familiarity. The word "familiar" comes from the Latin *familia,* which connotes family or household. Others who are similar can seem like family members and may be especially appealing partners for kin relationships.

We find it noteworthy that the factors found to exert the greatest influence on the selection of pair-bond partners are so similar to those used by infants in "choosing" among potential attachment figures. In the case of infants, "preference" is given to individuals who are kind, responsive, competent, and familiar—especially in the context of distress alleviation. The one who most consistently and most competently reduces the discomfort caused by hunger, soiled diapers, fatigue, illness, and strange environments (i.e., the *primary* caregiver) is the one to whom an infant is most likely to become attached (Bowlby, 1958, 1969/1982). Such considerations make perfect sense in the choice of attachment figures during infancy. But why should adults be sensitive to cues of familiarity, responsiveness, or competence in potential reproductive partners? More importantly, why should they care more about these qualities than about cues of fertility or resources?

It is because pair-bond relationships are relatively enduring that attachment-relevant criteria are taken into account when mates are selected. Further evidence that mating decisions are not reducible to sex differences in parental investment comes from studies of facial attractiveness. In a series of detailed analyses involving facialmetric methods and cross-cultural samples, Cunningham, Druen, and Barbee (1997) have sought to identify the features that make potential sexual partners most appealing. Although the findings vary somewhat (and systematically) as a function of gender, the combination of features judged to be most attractive is much the same for men and women. Sexual appeal—whether the individual being evaluated is male or female—is significantly enhanced by the co-occurrence of three types of facial features: expressive, neotenous, and sexual-maturational. Expressive features (e.g., size of smile area) serve as cues of warmth and sensitivity. Neotenous features (e.g., large eyes) signal vulnerability and need for nurturance. Facial features associated with sexual maturation (e.g., prominent cheekbones) function as cues of reproductive capability.

We have noted earlier that prototypical pair bonds are hypothesized to involve the integration of three social-behavioral systems: sexual mating, caregiving (parenting), and attachment. Cunningham et al.'s (1997) findings lend support to this conceptualization of pair bonds. Why should females find neotenous features (which signal vulnerability) appealing in a male if their primary concern is to choose a mate who will provide protection and resources? Why should males be drawn to expressive (attachment-affording) qualities in a female if their objective is to select a mate who is young and fertile? And why, as Buss found, should both males and females give highest priority to qualities indicating a mate's suitability for satisfying attachment needs? Bowlby anticipated the answer: Pair bonds are regulated by multiple behavioral systems, each of which influences mate selection, and one of which is attachment. Clearly it is important to choose a mate who is fertile, but studies have shown that well over 90% of all postpubescent young people are (Symons, 1979). Attachment is relevant to mating because we humans need to select reproductive partners who will be good parents and good companions.

Reactions to Separation and Loss

Additional evidence that attachment is an integral part of pair-bond relationships comes from the literature on bereavement, as well as from studies of routine marital separation. The original inspiration for attachment theory came from Bowlby's observations of infants and children separated from their primary caregivers. He found it remarkable that the separations were so distressing, given that the children's nutritional and hygienic needs were being met quite adequately by surrogates. Even more striking was the similarity across children in how they responded. Bowlby identified what appeared to be a universal pattern of reactions, which he labeled the "protest–despair–detachment" sequence. The initial reaction is characterized by agitation, hyperactivity, crying, resistance to others' offers of comfort, and extreme anxiety, often to the point of panic. Eventually this active protest subsides, only to be replaced by a period of lethargy, inac-

tivity, despair, and disrupted sleeping and eating behavior. In time, a degree of emotional detachment from the lost attachment figure facilitates the resumption of normal, preseparation activities and functioning.

If the attachment system is operative in pair bonds, adult reactions to the loss of a partner should be similar. In fact, they are. Several studies have documented essentially the same sequence in adults grieving for the loss of a spouse: initial anxiety and panic, followed by lethargy and depression, and eventually by recovery through emotional detachment (Hazan & Shaver, 1992; Parkes & Weiss, 1983; Weiss, 1975) or emotional reorganization (Fraley & Shaver, Chapter 32, this volume). This sequence of reactions is not limited to situations of permanent loss. Even brief, routine separations are enough to trigger the same pattern of responses in marital partners (Vormbrock, 1993).

It makes good adaptive sense to react with anxiety and protest to even the temporary "loss" of an individual who serves as a primary source of emotional and/or physical security. The fact that this reaction is the norm among adults separated from their long-term partners, and is *not* the normal reaction to the loss of other kinds of social ties, is yet another indication that the attachment system is active in pair bonds.

Physical and Psychological Health Effects

The notion that attachment is a very real biological need, at least in early life, was established in studies of infants reared in orphanages and other institutional settings (Robertson, 1953; Spitz, 1946). Although adults are clearly less dependent on social bonds for basic survival, there is ample evidence that they incur health benefits from having such bonds, and suffer health decrements as a consequence of the absence or loss of these bonds. Relationship disruption (especially divorce) makes one more susceptible to a wide range of physical and psychological ills, including disease, impaired immune functioning, accidents, substance abuse, suicide, and various other forms of psychopathology (e.g., Bloom, Asher, & White, 1978; Goodwin, Hurt, Key, & Sarrett, 1987; Lynch, 1977; Uchino, Cacioppo, & Kiecolt-Glaser, 1996).

Obviously, the detrimental health effects of disrupted adult relationships cannot in and of themselves serve as conclusive evidence that such bonds are true attachments. Many different unexpected and undesirable events have been shown to induce high levels of stress (Holmes & Rahe, 1967), which in turn can undermine both physical and psychological well-being. But several additional findings bolster the present assertions.

First, among the most common stressors, attachment-related losses cause the most subjective distress. Death of a spouse is the leading stressful event on the Social Readjustment Rating Scale, followed by divorce and marital separation (Holmes & Rahe, 1967). Second, a number of investigations have helped to highlight the distinctiveness of attachment relationships. For instance, Weiss (1973) found that loneliness takes at least two distinct forms, depending on whether social deprivation is due to the absence of an intimate companion (which he labeled "emotional loneliness") or a lack of friends ("social loneliness"). This distinction was supported by the results of a national survey, which found the two types to be associated with different antecedents and symptoms (Rubenstein & Shaver, 1982). Consistent with Weiss's theory, the loss or absence of a pair-bond relationship was found to be associated with emotional loneliness and feelings of "desperation" and anxiety. In contrast, a lack of friendship predicted social loneliness, which was experienced as "restless boredom." Additional corroboration comes from a recent study by Stroebe, Stroebe, Abakoumkin, and Schut (1996), who found that social support in the form of friendship did not help alleviate the distress of losing a spouse. And Vormbrock's (1993) review of the literature on war- and job-related routine marital separations led to a similar conclusion: The social provisions of pair bonds are sufficiently distinctive that other social relationships—even close friendships or kin ties—cannot compensate for their loss. Interestingly, Vormbrock did find that renewing relationships with parental *attachment* figures was helpful in moderating the anxiety caused by spousal absence.

If attachment bonds have exceptional effects on physical and psychological functioning, such effects should be absent not only in other types of relationships, but even in the kinds of relationships that typically develop into attachments but that have yet to achieve that status. This appears to be the case. Early maternal deprivation is associated with long-term developmental consequences *only* if it occurs after an attachment bond between infant and mother has been established (Bowlby, 1958). Separations prior to 8 months of age do not increase the probability of

poor developmental outcomes. Earlier in this chapter, we have reported our finding that most romantic relationships qualified as attachments only after they had endured for at least 2 years. Weiss (1988) found that widows and widowers married for less than 2 years did not show the same sequence of reactions (protest–despair–detachment/reorganization) as those grieving for the loss of longer-term bonds.

In sum, the results of a number of studies indicate that bonds between adult partners and infant–caregiver pairs are similarly and uniquely powerful in their impact on physical and psychological well-being. Other kinds of interpersonal relationships offer valuable social provisions, but emotional security does not appear to be one of them; otherwise disruptions would give rise to anxiety, which they do not. If separation distress is the marker of attachment, then bonds between long-term adult partners clearly qualify.

THE FUNCTION OF ATTACHMENT IN ADULT LIFE

Evolutionary thinking figured prominently in Bowlby's theory. The attachment system, he argued, is a species-typical characteristic that evolved to serve a protective, survival-enhancing function. In the EEA, an infant who identified, became attached to, and then stayed close to a protector had significantly better chances of living to reproductive age than an infant who failed to develop such bonds. His hypotheses concerning the function of attachment and its evolutionary origins pose a challenge for adult attachment research and theory.

Some evolutionary theorists (e.g., Kirkpatrick, 1998) have rejected the notion that the attachment system is integral to pair bonds by reasoning as follows: Reflexively seeking proximity in the face of danger would have been adaptive for infants but maladaptive for adults. Specifically, a propensity to seek protection from a mate, rather than aiding in the fight against some external threat, would have been more likely to jeopardize adult survival. Moreover, the fact that human females are generally smaller and weaker than their male counterparts makes it particularly doubtful that men could have gained a survival advantage by turning to their female partners for refuge in the face of danger. Therefore, attachment cannot serve the same protective function in adulthood that it does in infancy. Furthermore, given the unlikelihood that an entire system will be retained yet undergo a qualitative change in its function, pair bonds cannot involve the attachment system. The flaws in this line of reasoning include a limited conceptualization of protection, misplaced emphasis on survival rather than on reproductive success, and a failure to acknowledge normative developmental change in the system and related behaviors.

One major shortcoming of this argument is its limited conceptualization of the protective function of attachment. Although the risk of predation in the EEA was undoubtedly reduced for infants who became attached to their caregivers, the benefits of the bond would have extended far beyond this specific type of protection. Then and now, attachments also help ensure that infants receive adequate routine care in the form of food, warmth, shelter, guidance, and monitoring—all of which enhance survival. Clearly the protective function of attachment is not limited to brawn, even in infancy.

By relying on a narrow definition of protection, the argument also fails to take into account normative developmental change in the behavioral manifestations of attachment. Very young and vulnerable infants do indeed rely entirely on their caregivers for protection and sustenance. But increases in maturity and competence are associated with corresponding decreases in the most primitive forms of attachment behavior, such as reflexive proximity seeking. Although older children and adolescents continue to depend on parents for many aspects of care, they do not typically run to them for physical cover at the slightest hint of danger. Their developing capacities for self-protection and self-reliance, however, do not mean that they no longer benefit from having someone who is deeply committed to and invested in their welfare looking out for them, and reliably available to help if needed.

To expect attachment to be manifested in exactly the same behaviors in infancy and adulthood is to ignore ontogenic reality; to require pair-bond relationships to be typified by infantile behavior in order to qualify as true attachments is misguided. The mere fact that behavior during disparate phases of development is not identical is insufficient proof that such behavior subserves different functions (Tinbergen, 1963). Feeding behavior, for example, also changes dramatically from infancy to adulthood, yet the basic function is the same.

In the preceding sections, we have reviewed a diverse set of empirical findings that together provide strong support for Bowlby's claims that the attachment system is active in adult life and integral to pair bonds. Relationships with long-term partners qualify as attachments in the technical sense by containing all four defining components. This fact makes them similar to infant–caregiver bonds and distinct from other kinds of social ties, even close relationships with friends and kin. The processes by which pair bonds and infant–caregiver relationships develop appear to be quite similar. The nature of physical contact that typifies these two types of relationships also serves to distinguish them from other classes of social bonds. In addition, there is considerable overlap in the criteria used to select attachment figures in infancy and mates in adulthood. A similar sequence of reactions characterizes the responses of infants separated from primary caregivers and adults separated from long-term partners—a sequence not observed in reaction to other types of social loss. And the mental and physical health effects of infant attachments and pair-bond relationships appear to be uniquely and similarly profound and pervasive. In the absence of a compelling alternative explanation of these multiple and varied similarities, the postulation that they are due to the active involvement of the same behavioral system is not only the most parsimonious explanation of the facts; in our view, it is the only logical conclusion to be drawn from them.

But what about the question of function? To seriously evaluate the possibility that attachment serves the same protective function in adulthood as in infancy requires that "protection" be defined in a manner that encompasses its full meaning and acknowledges normative developmental change. An answer to the function question, however, calls for more than simply establishing that pair-bond partners provide each other with protection. It must be established that such protection would have afforded adaptive advantage by translating reliably into enhanced survival and reproductive success in the EEA. Hence a key to understanding the function of attachment in adulthood lies in an examination of the circumstances in which pair bonding evolved.

The Evolution of Pair Bonds

If human reproductive success required nothing more than conception, reproductive partners could part ways as soon as a viable pregnancy was achieved. In actuality, however, the vast majority of human males and females opt to remain with the same partner for a more extended period of time (Eibl-Eibesfeldt, 1989; Mellen, 1981). This trend is thought to have followed a birthing crisis in which an infant's large head, housing a more fully developed brain, could not easily pass through the birth canal of our bipedal female ancestors (Trevathan, 1987). Infants who were born prematurely, with less developed brains and smaller heads, were more likely to survive (as were their mothers). Immaturity at birth also offered the advantage of a longer period of learning during a time of heightened neural plasticity. This would have been a distinct advantage in a species with such complex social organization as our own. However, with the benefits of premature birth came new risks and challenges. The effort required to care adequately for such dependent offspring during such a protracted period of immaturity, along with the major tasks of socialization and training, made paternal investment an advantage if not a necessity. Exceptionally helpless and vulnerable offspring would have had rather poor chances of surviving to reproductive age or developing the necessary skills for their own eventual mating and parenting roles without an adequately strong force to keep fathers around and involved.

Many unique features of human sexuality appear to have evolved for the purpose of fostering and maintaining an enduring bond between reproductive partners. The most striking change in our reproductive physiology, in comparison to that of other mammalian species, is the loss or absence of outward signs of estrus in the female. Most mammals mate only during the short estrus periods of the female, but human sexual desire and activity are not so restricted. Women can be sexually receptive during any phase of their reproductive cycle, despite the fact that conception is possible only during a small fraction of it. This physiological adaptation enables the couple to maintain a continuous tie on the basis of sexual reward (Eibl-Eibesfeldt, 1975). Hidden ovulation may also serve to diminish the benefits of straying. Males of many diverse species guard their mates during periods of sexual receptivity so as to ensure paternity. When a female's fertile period has ended, a male can safely move on to another receptive partner. However, if ovulation is hidden, making it impossible for the male to determine just when fertilization will be possible, his optimal strategy may shift toward guarding and remaining with the same sexual partner for longer periods of time (Alcock, 1989).

Genital differences between us and our closest primate relatives also suggest the important role of sex in maintaining the integrity of the human pair bond. For example, the average length of the erect human penis is 13 cm, compared with approximately 3 cm for the gorilla (which is a much larger animal in terms of overall body size). Although penis size alone is not an accurate predictor of monogamous versus polygamous mating patterns among primates, the exceptional length of the erect human penis, in marked contrast to that of all the great apes, made possible a wide variety of copulatory positions, including more intimate face-to-face, mutually ventral (i.e., bond-promoting) positions. In addition, by increasing the probability of female orgasm, it may have served to heighten the female's readiness for engaging in sexual activity, thereby strengthening the bond with her mate (Short, 1979).

The physiological changes associated with sexual climax may also stimulate bond formation between partners. As noted previously, orgasms trigger a release of oxytocin in both males and females (Carter, 1992), resulting in a state of calm and contentment. It also stimulates a desire for continued close physical contact and cuddling, again increasing the chances that a bond will develop.

When the adaptive problem of immature offspring and the corresponding need for paternal investment arose in the course of human evolution, our species—by virtue of its altricial nature—already had available a well-designed, specialized, flexible, but reliable mechanism for ensuring that two individuals would be highly motivated to stay together and vigorously resist being separated. The mechanism was attachment. In light of the generally conservative tendencies of evolution and natural selection, it is highly probable that this preexisting mechanism would have been exploited for the purpose of keeping reproductive partners together. Pair bonds are primarily reproductive relationships, but sex serves more than a reproductive function in our species. The unique features of human reproductive physiology and anatomy help to ensure that partners will engage in the kinds of intimate exchanges known to stimulate attachment formation.

Reproductive Advantages of Pair Bonds

In our species, reproductive success requires negotiation of at least three adaptive challenges:

surviving to reproductive age, mating, and providing adequate care to offspring so that they too will survive to reproduce. We have just argued that the relative immaturity of human newborns created a situation in the EEA in which survival depended not only on their forming a strong bond to a protector, but also on the joint investment of their parents. This necessitated a mechanism that would hold reproductive partners together for an extended period of time. We have proposed that the attachment system, which had evolved to ensure an enduring bond between infants and caregivers, was exploited for this additional purpose. But the advantages of pair bonding extend beyond its role in offspring survival: Benefits include enhanced survival and reproductive fitness for *mates,* as well as their offspring.

There is mounting evidence that offspring mating strategies may depend critically on the pair-bond status of parents, especially mothers. Adolescents from father-absent homes show precocious sexual interest, relatively early sexual maturation, more negative attitudes toward potential mates, and less interest in long-term relationships than do their counterparts reared in father-present homes (Belsky, Chapter 7, this volume; Draper & Belsky, 1990; Draper & Harpending, 1982; Surbey, 1990). In other words, if parents choose not to remain together, their children are more likely to adopt approaches to mating that emphasize quantity over quality. Parental divorce has also been found to affect offspring mating behavior. Female children of divorce tend to fear closeness and have difficulty establishing committed relationships, whereas the effects for males are evidenced in a lack of achievement orientation (Wallerstein, 1994) and lower socioeconomic status (Lillard & Gerner, in press). Thus the failure of reproductive partners to maintain long-term bonds may have a negative effect on the mating appeal and success of their offspring.

Whether opportunistic, short-term mating strategies are inferior to stable, long-term approaches is the source of much current debate (e.g., Belsky, Chapter 7, this volume; Buss, 1997; Chisholm, 1996). Most research and theorizing on short- versus long-term mating presume that they represent mutually exclusive strategies. That is, individuals choose to engage in copulation with multiple partners or to opt instead for a monogamous relationship. In reality, both males and females can establish enduring pair bonds and still pursue short-term mating opportunities outside these bonds. According to life

history theory (Stearns, 1992), organisms possess a finite amount of resources that must be allocated across various evolutionary challenges, including survival, growth, mating, and parental investment. Local circumstances determine the balance of time and energy an individual devotes to each. From this perspective, it may be most sensible for adolescents from unstable families to adopt a strategy of mating early and often. Thus, both long- and short-term strategies can be viewed as reasonable and comparably adaptive responses to different ecologies.

Although it is clearly advantageous for humans to be capable of facultative mating adaptations that take account of varying ecological conditions (Buss & Schmitt, 1993; Daly & Wilson, 1988), the correlates of short- and long-term mating strategies are not supportive of the view that they are different but essentially equal (see Belsky, Chapter 7, this volume, for an alternative viewpoint). The ability to adjust behavior to nonoptimal circumstances is obviously important, but such adjustments are unlikely to produce optimal results. Take feeding behavior, for example. Survival depends on the regular intake of food, and if humans are hungry enough, they will consume garbage to stay alive. But refuse is unlikely to have the same nutritional value as a well-rounded meal, nor is it expected to support physical development equally well. Likewise, quick and frequent copulation coupled with an avoidance of parental investment may be the best available strategy in some circumstances, but it hardly qualifies as generally optimal. For instance, infant mortality rates are higher among children without an investing father (Hill & Hurtado, 1995). It has also been found that women suffering from infertility of unknown biological cause tend to have an avoidant attachment style (Justo, Maia, Ferreira-Diniz, Santos, & Moreira, 1997). In the currency of evolution, a superior strategy is one that ensures survival and enhances reproductive success. It is a matter of empirical fact that pair-bonds not only contribute to the survival of offspring, but also leave them better equipped to attract and retain mates of their own, which in turn would be expected to improve the reproductive fitness of their own offspring.

In addition to the multiple direct and indirect benefits that accrue to the progeny of stable pair bonds, there are also advantages for the mates themselves. There is at least one indication that long-term bonds between partners directly enhance the partners' own reproductive success. It is well documented that women ovulate more regularly if they are in a stable sexual relationship (e.g., Cutler, Garcia, Huggins, & Preti, 1985; Veith, Buck, Getzlaf, Van Dalfsen, & Slade, 1983). They also tend to continue ovulating into their middle years and to reach menopause significantly later if sexual activity is consistent. Earlier, we have cited evidence that partners in long-term relationships enjoy more robust physical and mental health. Clearly, the more fit an individual is, the better able he or she is to function in all the various roles adults are required to fill—including those of mate, parent, and grandparent. A healthy member of any social group is more valued and more valuable (and, we might add, more capable of protecting self as well as loved ones). A stable bond with a trusted and reliable companion also promotes the kind of exploration and productive engagement in activity on which family welfare depends (Hazan & Shaver, 1990). As for the protective aspects of this kind of companionship, adults too need someone to look out for them and keep track of them—someone to initiate a search if they fail to show up at the expected time, to care for them when they are sick, dress their wounds, help defend them against external threats, reassure them, and keep them warm at night.

What is the function of attachment in adult life? On the basis of the evidence, we would argue that the attachment system serves essentially the same purpose in adulthood as it does in infancy. It cements an enduring emotional bond between individuals that translates today, as it did in the EEA, into differential survival and reproductive success.

A MODEL OF ADULT ATTACHMENT FORMATION

In arguing that attachment is an integral part of adult pair bonds, we have hinted at the processes by which a sexual partner comes to replace parents in the hierarchy of attachment relationships. In this final major section of the chapter, we offer a more detailed account of these processes. Although we have incorporated many diverse empirical findings to support our perspective, the model we propose is largely theoretical. Firm conclusions about how two adults make the transformation from relative indifference to profound psychological and physiological interdependence must therefore await the results of more direct tests.

Before we present the model, a few caveats are

in order. In contrast to the preponderance of attachment research, which emphasizes individual differences, our model stresses normative processes. There is good reason to expect that the processes will vary somewhat as a function of the working models that individual couple members bring to a relationship, but there is not space for a discussion of all these various possibilities. Also, in our effort to build a persuasive case that pair bonds are true attachments, we have necessarily stressed the similarities between pair bonds and infant–caregiver relationships over their differences. The differences are both numerous and profound, but three strike us as particularly important.

First, the reciprocal nature of prototypical adult attachments means dual roles for the partners. Each mate uses the other as an attachment figure and source of security; each also serves as an attachment figure and provider of security to the other. This implicates not only the attachment system, but the caregiving (parenting) system as well. And because pair-bond members are sexual partners, the sexual mating system is also involved. Therefore, adult attachments are qualitatively different from infant attachments by virtue of their mutuality and sexual nature.

Second, we have referred earlier to the crucial role of physical contact in fostering attachment formation. The motivation for proximity seeking is another major source of difference between infants and adults. When an infant approaches or signals the caregiver for contact, distress alleviation is often the goal. Babies are, after all, helpless to meet their own physical needs. Although adult partners also turn to each other for comfort, sexual attraction is a major impetus for contact, especially in the initial phases of relationship development.

Third, a consideration of the evolutionary roots of pair-bond attachment highlights yet another fundamental difference between lovers and parent–child pairs. Beyond the reality that infants cannot survive without protection and care, in most instances they are also biologically related to their caregivers. The issue of genetic relatedness is an important one. Although the expected fitness of mates is correlated (due to their shared genetic interests), it is generally assumed that this correlation can be reversed rather easily, as in the case of sexual infidelity, whereas the genetic interests of relatives are forever linked (Daly & Wilson, 1996). This presumes that mates are not genetically related. In fact, with the exception of first-degree relatives, a high degree of inbreeding has been the norm in our species (Thornhill, 1991). In a survey of 370 cultures, fully 26% prescribed or strongly preferred marriage between cousins (Broude, 1994). Moreover, the low incidence of interracial marriage and the prevalence of look-alike partners (Hinsz, 1989) indicate that individuals tend to select mates from their own genetic pool. Although mates will not typically be first-degree relatives, they are still more likely to be "related" than two randomly selected individuals.

It is also worth noting that attachment is not synonymous with sexual fidelity. Results of genetic analyses provide objective evidence that even so-called "monogamous" species engage in copulations outside pair bonds (Carter et al., 1997; Mendoza & Mason, 1997). Our goal is not to argue that because pair bonds are regulated by the attachment system, they are therefore indissoluble or even as durable as parent–offspring bonds. The current high rate of divorce, particularly in Western cultures, is but one indication that relationships between mates are more fragile. Nevertheless, a close examination of the data reveals that the majority of marriages that end in divorce do so within the first few years—perhaps before an attachment has been established—and that breakups are significantly less common among couples who have at least one child (Fisher, 1992). Once partners have become attached and/or commingled their genes, their relationship is more likely to endure.

How do adults become attached to each other? Bowlby identified four phases in the development of infant–caregiver attachments. We propose a parallel four-phase process model to integrate and explain the phenomenology of pair-bond development. We have adopted Bowlby's labels for each of the phases and supplemented them with their hypothesized romantic-relationship equivalents. (See Zeifman & Hazan, 1997, for a more detailed explication of the model.)

Preattachment: Attraction and Flirting

Specific attachments in infancy take months to develop and are typically not evident until the second half of the first year of life. However, the propensities that facilitate their formation are present almost from birth. In infancy, the preattachment phase is characterized by a readiness for and inherent interest in social interaction. Very young babies are rather indiscriminate in their social signaling and generally welcome approaches from virtually anyone who appears friendly. Their vocalizations and body language make it clear that they find such exchanges stimulating and exciting. The eventual development of an exclusive bond begins with openness to the types of social interaction that support its formation.

This combination of preparedness for social engagement and relatively promiscuous signaling of interest is at the heart of adult flirting. The telling behaviors are universally recognizable: smiling, making eye contact, talking animatedly (with heightened pitch, inflection, and volume), and exaggerated gestures and facial expressions. Eibl-Eibesfeldt (1989) called this unique and distinctive pattern of behavior the "proceptive program."

Is there any reason to believe that adult flirtation involves the attachment system? It seems more likely that the excitement and arousal associated with flirtatious exchanges are due to the activation of the sexual mating system, rather than to attachment per se. We acknowledge the predominantly sexual nature of adult flirtation, but we also find it telling that flirting individuals are responsive to attachment-relevant cues. When flirtations are initiated with more than immediate sexual gratification as the goal, and more specifically with the hope or possibility of a more lasting association, attachment-relevant cues such as warmth, responsiveness, and reciprocal liking are particularly important (Aron, Dutton, Aron, & Iverson, 1989; Backman & Secord, 1959; Clark, Shaver, & Abrahams, in press; Curtis & Miller, 1986). That is, the "attachment-worthiness" of potential partners is a consideration in and has an effect on the sexual attraction itself.

In order for an attachment bond to develop between two individuals, they first have to be drawn together. The motivations for social proximity seeking no doubt vary as a function of many individual characteristics, including age. Sexual attraction helps to ensure that adults will seek and maintain close proximity to individuals to whom they may become attached.

Attachment in the Making: Falling in Love

Sometime between 2 and 3 months of age, the indiscriminate signaling of an infant becomes more selective. The infant begins to direct social signals preferentially toward the individual who has played a primary role in his or her care, especially in distress alleviation. The vocal and physical interactions of a caregiver–infant dyad during this phase take on the appearance of synchrony and attunement. Prolonged mutual gazing, nuzzling, and cuddling also reflect the increasingly intimate nature of the relationship.

Similar behaviors are typical of a new couple. As adults make the transition from attraction to falling in love, their interactions become smoother and more intimate. Still, the predominant psychological and physical states that accompany infatuation are ones of heightened arousal. Sleeplessness, reduced food intake, and (paradoxically) unbounded energy are common features of in-love experiences (Tennov, 1979). Nevertheless, there is a noticeable increase in behaviors that have a more calming than arousing effect. For example, reassuring, "parental" forms of physical contact, such as hand holding or placing an arm around the other's shoulder, are typical among new lovers and can be contrasted with the less intimate and more arousing touches that typify flirtations or purely sexual encounters. Also, as noted earlier, sexual climax triggers a release of oxytocin (Carter, 1992), effecting a sense of subjective well-being in the arms of the partner.

This trend toward increasingly comforting exchanges is not limited to physical contact. Changes in voice quality can also be noted, including soothing whispers and "baby talk." Whereas self-disclosures in the preattachment stage are usually limited to positive or neutral facts, adults begin to share more personal information as they fall in love, including stories of painful experiences and fears (Altman & Taylor, 1973). Revelations of this type may constitute a test of commitment and future reliability, as well as a bid for acceptance and care. As the members of a couple start to serve as mutual sources of emotional support, their relationship takes on an additional component of attachment—namely, safe haven.

Clear-Cut Attachment: Loving

At what point does a relationship partner become an attachment figure? The answer may lie in the predictable changes that occur as partners make the transition from being in love to loving each other. For example, the frequency of sexual activity declines (Fisher, 1992; Traupmann & Hatfield, 1981), while the importance of emotional supportiveness and nurturance increases (Kotler, 1985; Reedy et al., 1981). As couple members become increasingly familiar with each other, simply being together is no longer as arousal-

inducing, and arousal is insufficient to maintain their satisfaction with the relationship. This constitutes a major change in the way partners relate to each other and may signal a qualitative change in the nature of the bond between them.

Leibowitz (1983) has proposed an explanation for the arousing-to-comforting transformation that occurs in developing romantic relationships. He hypothesizes that the arousal that accompanies infatuation is mediated by phenylethylamine, which is similar in its effects to amphetamines. Eventual habituation to phenylethylamine is thought to stimulate the production and release of endorphins, which induce a contrasting state of calm and contentment. It is worth noting that in diverse species, opioid administration ameliorates the disorganizing effects of separation, whereas opioid blockage exacerbates them (Panksepp, Siviy, & Normansell, 1985). In addition to alleviating anxiety, opioids are powerful conditioning agents. Through classical conditioning, stimuli paired with opioid drugs rapidly become associated with their calming effects and are strongly preferred. Moreover, such preferences are extremely difficult to extinguish.

Opioid conditioning is the expected result of repeated anxiety- and/or tension-alleviating interactions. Exchanges of this kind are a common feature of both infant–caregiver relationships and adult romantic relationships. When a parent comforts a crying infant, the parent becomes associated (in the infant's mind and brain) with the alleviation of distress. Similarly, through repeated comforting exchanges, including the release of tension brought about by sexual climax, a lover comes to be associated with stress reduction and calming. Relationships that develop into attachment bonds appear to be those in which heightened physiological arousal is repeatedly attenuated by the same person and in a context of close bodily contact. As such, attachment may involve the conditioning of an individual's opioid system to the stimulus of a specific other.

The transition from an arousal-enhancing to an arousal-moderating effect of the partner's presence signals clear-cut (adult) attachment. The "flip side" of each partner's ability to calm the other reflects the presence of another attachment component—separation distress.

Goal-Corrected Partnership: The Postromance Phase (or Life as Usual)

An important change takes place sometime between the second and third years of life in the way infants (now toddlers) relate to their primary caregivers. The frequency of attachment behavior decreases, and the need for close physical contact is somewhat attenuated. Children exhibit increased interest in exploration, especially social contact with peers. The reliability of the caregiver is well established, and the resulting confidence and security provide support for nonattachment activities. Attention is shifted from the attachment figure to the external world.

A parallel transformation occurs in the development of relationships between adult pairs. Physical contact, mutual gazing, sexual exchanges, and other bond-promoting behaviors decline in frequency. The mental energy consumed by preoccupation with the partner and the relationship is freed up to be redirected toward other real-world obligations and interests (e.g., friendships and work obligations), which are often neglected by individuals in the throes of romantic passion. At this point, the bond between partners is not as readily apparent in their overt interactions, but beneath the surface lies a profound emotional interdependence (Berscheid, 1983).

Hofer (1984; see also Polan & Hofer, Chapter 8, this volume) has proposed that this deeper interdependence involves the coregulation of physiological systems. In essence, each partner has come to serve as one of the external cues or stimuli that provide regulatory input to internal systems (just as light–dark cycles influence sleep). Hofer refers to this physiological interdependence as "entrainment." The removal of the cues provided by the partner help to explain the disorganization—both psychological and physiological—that follows the loss of a long-term partner. The emotional security inherent in such close bonds makes the distress of even brief separations understandable.

This psychological and physiological tether, once established, may not be obvious in the day-to-day, routine interactions between members of a pair bond. Nor is the deep emotional connection between parents and their offspring as older children or adolescents easily observed under normal circumstances. But having an individual who can be trusted and depended on for long-term accessibility and assistance makes it easier for humans of all ages to go about the daily business of exploring and learning about the environment, and making whatever contribution to it they are capable of. A goal-corrected partnership—in childhood as well as adulthood—serves as a base of security from which to operate in the world.

CONCLUSIONS

Our primary goal in this chapter has been to evaluate the claim that attachment is integral to pair bonds. The evidence we have reviewed indicates that such bonds are similar in many respects to the one interpersonal tie that most researchers agree does involve the attachment system—infant–caregiver bonds. Furthermore, the similarities extend far beyond the superficial to include fundamental features, functions, dynamics, and processes. From this extensive evidence, we conclude that attachment is indeed integral to pair bonds.

Critics of this viewpoint (e.g., Kirkpatrick, 1998) acknowledge the many resemblances between infant–caregiver and romantic relationships, but reject such evidence as circumstantial. Research and theory in the social sciences are built almost entirely on a foundation of circumstantial evidence. Few if any of our most interesting and cherished constructs can be directly observed or measured, and attachment is no different. Even in infancy, the evidence is circumstantial. Proximity maintenance and separation distress, as well as safe-haven and secure-base behaviors, are the data from which the existence and regulatory role of the attachment behavioral system are *inferred*. Evidence that the attachment system is operative in pair bonds is by necessity indirect, but is no less solid. Given the consistency and strength with which extant findings support Bowlby's pair-bond attachment hypothesis, it would make sense to reject it only if there were an alternative that could provide a more parsimonious explanation of the facts.

As for the functions of attachment in adult life, we have argued that they are essentially the same as in infancy. The attachment system helps to ensure the development of an enduring bond that enhances survival and reproductive fitness in direct as well as indirect ways. Pair bonds are not simply mutually beneficial alliances based on the principles of reciprocal altruism. Instead, they involve a profound psychological and physiological interdependence, such that the absence or loss of one partner can be literally life-threatening for the other.

Bowlby's original hypotheses concerning pair-bond attachment were based on little more than his formidable powers of observation and deep insights into human affectional behavior. In the time since their formulation, a substantial body of empirical data on relationships has been amassed—one that, on the whole, supports his initial speculations (see Feeney, Chapter 17, this volume). The evidence indicates that attachment needs persist from the cradle to the grave. And, just as Bowlby surmised, in adulthood such needs are satisfied by pair bonds.

ACKNOWLEDGMENTS

We would like to thank Rick Canfield, Jude Cassidy, Phillip Shaver, and Joanna Scheib for providing critical and valuable feedback on earlier drafts. Work on this chapter was supported by a National Science Foundation grant (No. SBR-9320364) to Cindy Hazan.

REFERENCES

Ainsworth, M. D. S. (1967). *Infancy in Uganda: Infant care and the growth of attachment.* Baltimore: Johns Hopkins University Press.

Ainsworth, M. D. S. (1982). Attachment: Retrospect and prospect. In C. M. Parkes & J. Stevenson-Hinde (Eds.), *The place of attachment in human behavior* (pp. 3–30). New York: Basic Books.

Alcock, J. (1989). *Animal behavior: An evolutionary approach.* Boston: Sinauer.

Altman, I., & Taylor, D. A. (1973). *Social penetration: The development of interpersonal relationships.* New York: Holt, Rinehart & Winston.

Aron, A., Dutton, D. G., Aron, E. N., & Iverson, A. (1989). Experiences of falling in love. *Journal of Social and Personal Relationships, 6,* 243–257.

Backman, C. W., & Secord, P. F. (1959). The effect of perceived liking on interpersonal attraction. *Human Relations, 12,* 379–384.

Baker, R. R., & Bellis, M. A. (1995). *Human sperm competition: Copulation, masturbation, and infidelity.* London: Chapman & Hall.

Berscheid, E. (1983). Emotion. In H. H. Kelley, E. Berscheid, A. Christenson, J. H. Harvey, T. L. Huston, G. Levinger, E. McClintock, L. A. Peplau, & D. R. Peterson (Eds.), *Close relationships* (pp. 110–168). New York: Freeman.

Berscheid, E. (1985). Interpersonal attraction. In G. Lindzey & E. Aronson (Eds.), *Handbook of social psychology* (3rd ed., pp. 413–484). New York: Random House.

Berscheid, E., & Reis, H. T. (1998). Attraction and close relationships. In S. Fiske, D. Gilbert, & G. Lindzey (Eds.), *Handbook of social psychology* (4th ed., pp. 193–281). New York: McGraw-Hill.

Bloom, B. L., Asher, S. J., & White, S. W. (1978). Marital disruption as a stressor: A review and analysis. *Psychological Bulletin, 85,* 867–894.

Blumstein, P., & Schwartz, P. (1983). *American couples: Money, work and sex.* New York: Pocket Books.

Blyth, D. A., Hill, J. P., & Theil, K. S. (1982). Early adoles-

cents' significant others: Grade and gender differences in perceived relationships with familiar and non-familiar adults and young people. *Journal of Youth and Adolescence, 11,* 425–449.

Bowlby, J. (1958). The nature of the child's tie to his mother. *International Journal of Psycho-Analysis, 39,* 350–373.

Bowlby, J. (1969/1982). *Attachment and loss: Vol. 1. Attachment.* New York: Basic Books.

Bowlby, J. (1980). *Attachment and loss: Vol. 3. Loss: Sadness and depression.* New York: Basic Books.

Broude, G. (1994). *Marriage, family, and relationships: A cross-cultural encyclopedia.* Santa Barbara, CA: ABC-Clio.

Buhrmester, D., & Furman, W. (1986). The changing functions of friends in childhood. In V. J. Derlega & B. A. Winstead (Eds.), *Friendship and social interaction* (pp. 41–62). New York: Springer-Verlag.

Buhrmester, D., & Furman, W. (1987). The development of companionship and intimacy. *Child Development, 58,* 1101–1113.

Buhrmester, D., & Prager, K. (1995). Patterns and functions of self-disclosure during childhood and adolescence. In K. J. Rotenberg (Ed.), *Disclosure processes in children and adolescents* (pp. 10–56). New York: Cambridge University Press.

Buss, D. M. (1989). Sex differences in human mate preferences: Evolutionary hypotheses tested in 37 cultures. *Behavioral and Brain Sciences, 12,* 1–49.

Buss, D. M. (1997). The emergence of evolutionary social psychology. In J. A. Simpson & D. T. Kenrick (Eds.), *Evolutionary social psychology* (pp. 387–400). Mahwah, NJ: Erlbaum.

Buss, D. M., & Schmitt, D. P. (1993). Sexual strategies theory: An evolutionary perspective on human mating. *Psychological Review, 100,* 204–232.

Carter, C. S. (1992). Oxytocin and sexual behavior. *Neuroscience and Biobehavioral Reviews, 16,* 131–144.

Carter, C. S., DeVries, A. C., Taymans, S. E., Roberts, R. L., Williams, J. R., & Getz, L. L. (1997). Peptides, steroids, and pair bonding. *Annals of the New York Academy of Sciences, 807,* 260–272.

Chisholm, J. S. (1996). The evolutionary ecology of attachment organization. *Human Nature, 7,* 1–38.

Clark, C. L., Shaver, P. R., & Abrahams, M. F. (in press). Strategic behaviors in romantic relationship initiation. *Personality and Social Psychology Bulletin.*

Colin, V. (1985). *Hierarchies and patterns of infants' attachments to parents and day caregivers: An exploration.* Unpublished doctoral dissertation, University of Virginia.

Colin, V. (1987). *Infant's preferences between parents before and after moderate stress activates behavior.* Paper presented at the biennial meeting of the Society for Research in Child Development, Baltimore.

Cummings, E. M. (1980). Caregiver stability and attachment in infant day care. *Developmental Psychology, 16,* 31–37.

Cunningham, M. R., Druen, P. B., & Barbee, A. P. (1997). Angels, mentors, and friends: Tradeoffs among evolutionary, social, and individual variables in physical appearance. In J. A. Simpson & D. T. Kenrick (Eds.), *Evolutionary social psychology* (pp. 109–140). Mahwah, NJ: Erlbaum.

Curtis, R. C., & Miller, K. (1986). Believing another likes or dislikes you: Behaviors making the beliefs come true. *Journal of Personality and Social Psychology, 51,* 284–290.

Cutler, W. B., Garcia, C. R., Huggins, G. R., & Preti, G. (1986). Sexual behavior and steroid levels among gynecologically mature premenopausal women. *Fertility and Sterility, 45,* 496–502.

Daly, M., & Wilson, M. (1988). *Homicide.* New York: Aldine de Gruyter.

Daly, M., & Wilson, M. (1996). Evolutionary psychology and marital conflict. In D. M. Buss & N. M. Malamuth (Eds.), *Sex, power, conflict: Evolutionary and feminist perspectives* (pp. 9–28). New York: Oxford University Press.

Draper, P., & Belsky, J. (1990). Personality development in evolutionary perspective. *Journal of Personality, 58,* 141–161.

Draper, P., & Harpending, H. (1988). A sociobiological perspective on the development of human reproductive strategies. In K. MacDonald (Ed.), *Sociobiological perspectives on human development* (pp. 340–372). New York: Springer-Verlag.

Eibl-Eibesfeldt, I. (1975). *Ethology: The biology of behavior.* New York: Holt, Rinehart & Winston.

Eibl-Eibesfeldt, I. (1989). *Human ethology.* New York: Aldine de Gruyter.

Fisher, H. E. (1992). *Anatomy of love.* New York: Norton.

Fraley, R. C., & Davis, K. E. (1997). Attachment formation and transfer in young adults' close friendships and romantic relationships. *Personal Relationships, 4,* 131–144.

Furman, W., & Buhrmester, D. (1985). Children's perceptions of the personal relationships in their social networks. *Developmental Psychology, 21,* 1016–1024.

Furman, W. W., & Wehner, E. A. (1994). Romantic views: Toward a theory of adolescent romantic relationships. In R. Montemayor, G. R. Adams, & T. P. Gullotta (Eds.), *Personal relationships during adolescence* (pp. 168–195). Thousand Oaks, CA: Sage.

Goodwin, J. S., Hurt, W. C., Key, C. R., & Sarrett, J. M. (1987). The effect of marital status on stage, treatment and survival of cancer patients. *Journal of the American Medical Association, 258,* 3125–3130.

Gottman, J. M. (1983). How children become friends. *Monographs of the Society for Research in Child Development, 48*(3, Serial No. 201).

Hartup, W. (1983). Peer relations. In P. H. Mussen (Series Ed.) & E. M. Hetherington (Vol. Ed.), *Handbook of child psychology: Vol. 4. Socialization, personality, and social development* (4th ed., pp. 301–349). New York: Wiley.

Hazan, C., & Shaver, P. R. (1990). Love and work: An attachment theoretical perspective. *Journal of Personality and Social Psychology, 59,* 270–280.

Hazan, C., & Shaver, P. R. (1992). Broken attachments. In T. L. Orbuch (Ed.), *Close relationship loss: Theoretical approaches* (pp. 90–108). Hillsdale, NJ: Erlbaum.

Hazan, C., & Shaver, P. R. (1994). Attachment as an organizational framework for research on close relationships. *Psychological Inquiry, 5,* 1–22.

Hazan, C., & Zeifman, D. (1994). Sex and the psychological tether. In K. Bartholomew & D. Perlman (Eds.), *Advances in personal relationships: Vol. 5. Attachment processes in adulthood* (pp. 151–177). London: Jessica Kingsley.

Hill, K., & Hurtado, M. (1995). *Demographic/life history of Ache foragers.* New York: Aldine de Gruyter.

Hinde, R. A. (1983). The human species. In R. A. Hinde (Ed.), *Primate social relationships* (pp. 334–349). Oxford: Blackwell.

Hinsz, V. B. (1989). Facial resemblance in engaged and married couples. *Journal of Social and Personal Relationships, 6,* 223–229.

Hofer, M. A. (1984). Relationships as regulators: A psy-

chobiologic perspective on bereavement. *Psychosomatic Medicine, 46,* 183–197.

Holmes, T. H., & Rahe, R. H. (1967). The Social Readjustment Rating Scale. *Journal of Psychosomatic Research, 11,* 213–218.

Justo, J. M. R. M., Maia, C. B., Ferreira-Diniz, F., Santos, C. L., & Moreira, J. M. (1997, June). *Adult attachment style among women with infertility of unknown biological cause.* Paper presented at the International Network on Personal Relationships Conference, Miami University, Oxford, OH.

Kenrick, D. T., Groth, G. E., Trost, M. R., & Sadalla, E. K. (1993). Integrating evolutionary and social exchange perspectives on relationships: Effects of gender, self-appraisal, and involvement level on mate selection criteria. *Journal of Personality and Social Psychology, 64,* 951–969.

Kirkpatrick, L. A. (1998). Evolution, pair-bonding, and reproductive strategies: A reconceptualization of adult attachment. In J. A. Simpson & W. S. Rholes (Eds.), *Attachment theory and close relationships* (pp. 353–393). New York: Guilford Press.

Kotler, T. (1985). Security and autonomy within marriage. *Human Relations, 38,* 299–321.

Leibowitz, M. (1983). *The chemistry of love.* New York: Berkeley Books.

Lewis, M. (1982). Social development in infancy and early childhood. In J. B. Osofsky (Ed.), *Handbook of infant development* (2nd ed., pp. 419–493). New York: Wiley.

Lillard, D., & Gerner, J. (in press). Getting to the Ivy League: How family composition affects college choice. *Journal of Higher Education.*

Lynch, J. J. (1977). *The broken heart: The medical consequences of loneliness.* New York: Basic Books.

Mellen, S. L. W. (1981). *The evolution of love.* San Francisco: Freeman.

Mendoza, S. P., & Mason, W. A. (1997). Attachment relationships in New World primates. *Annals of the New York Academy of Sciences, 807,* 203–209.

Nass, G. D., & Fisher, M. P. (1988). *Sexuality today.* Boston: Jones & Bartlett.

O'Neill, N., & O'Neill, G. (1972). *Open marriage: A new lifestyle for couples.* New York: M. Evans.

Panksepp, J., Siviy, S. M., & Normansell, L. A. (1985). Brain opioids and social emotions. In M. Reite & T. Field (Eds.), *The psychobiology of attachment and separation* (pp. 3–50). London: Academic Press.

Parkes, C. M., & Weiss, R. S. (1983). *Recovery from bereavement.* New York: Basic Books.

Reedy, M. N., Birren, J. E., & Schaie, K. W. (1981). Age and sex differences in satisfying love relationships across the adult life span. *Human Development, 24,* 52–66.

Ricciuti, H. N. (1974). Fear and the development of social attachments in the first year of life. In M. Lewis & L. Rosenblum (Eds.), *Origins of fear* (pp. 73–106). New York: Wiley.

Robertson, J. (1953). Some responses of young children to the loss of maternal care. *Nursing Times, 49,* 382–386.

Rubenstein, C., & Shaver, P. R. (1982). *In search of intimacy.* New York: Delacorte.

Rubin, Z. (1973). *Liking and loving.* New York: Holt, Rinehart & Winston.

Rubin, Z. (1980). *Children's friendships.* Cambridge, MA: Harvard University Press.

Schaffer, H. R., & Emerson, P. E. (1964). The development of social attachments in infancy. *Monographs of the Soci-*

ety for Research in Child Development, 29(3, Serial No. 94).

Shaver, P. R., Hazan, C., & Bradshaw, D. (1988). Love as attachment: The integration of three behavioral systems. In R. J. Sternberg & M. L. Barnes (Eds.), *The psychology of love* (pp. 68–99). New Haven, CT: Yale University Press.

Shill, M. A., Solyom, P., & Biven, C. (1984). Parent preference in the attachment-exploration balance in infancy: An experimental psychoanalytic approach. *Child Psychiatry and Human Development, 15,* 34–48.

Short, R. V. (1979). Sexual selection and its component parts: Somatic and genital selection as illustrated in man and the great apes. *Advances in the Study of Behavior, 9,* 131–155.

Spitz, R. A. (1946). Anaclitic depression. *Psychoanalytic Study of the Child, 2,* 313–342.

Stearns, S. (1992). *The evolution of life histories.* New York: Oxford University Press.

Steinberg, L., & Silverberg, S. B. (1986). The vicissitudes of autonomy in early adolescence. *Child Development, 57,* 841–851.

Sternberg, R. J. (1986). A triangular theory of love. *Psychological Review, 93,* 119–135.

Stroebe, W., Stroebe, M., Abakoumkin, G., & Schut, H. (1996). The role of loneliness and social support in adjustment to loss: A test of attachment versus stress theory. *Journal of Personality and Social Psychology, 70,* 1241–1249.

Surbey, M. (1990). Family composition, stress, and human menarche. In F. Bercovitch & T. Zeigler (Eds.), *The socioendocrinology of primate reproduction* (pp. 71–97). New York: Alan R. Liss.

Symons, D. (1979). *The evolution of human sexuality.* New York: Oxford University Press.

Tennov, D. (1979). *Love and limerence: The experience of being in love.* New York: Stein & Day.

Thornhill, N. W. (1991). An evolutionary analysis of rules regulating human inbreeding and marriage. *Behavioral and Brain Sciences, 14,* 247–281.

Tinbergen, N. (1963). On aims and methods of ethology. *Zeitschrift für Tierpsychologie, 20,* 410–433.

Traupmann, J., & Hatfield, E. (1981). Love: Its effects on mental and physical health. In J. March, S. Kiesler, R. Fogel, E. Hatfield, & E. Shana (Eds.), *Aging: Stability and change in the family* (pp. 253–274). New York: Academic Press.

Trevathan, W. (1987). *Human birth.* New York: Aldine de Gruyter.

Trivers, R. L. (1972). Parental investment and sexual selection. In B. Campbell (Ed.), *Sexual selection and the descent of man, 1871–1971* (pp. 136–179). Chicago: Aldine.

Uchino, B. N., Cacioppo, J. T., & Kiecolt-Glaser, J. K. (1996). The relationship between social support and physiological processes: A review with emphasis on underlying mechanisms and implications for health. *Psychological Bulletin, 119,* 488–531.

Veith, J. L., Buck, M., Getzlaf, S., Van Dalfsen, P., & Slade, S. (1983). Exposure to men influences the occurrence of ovulation in women. *Physiology and Behavior, 31,* 313–315.

Vormbrock, J. K. (1993). Attachment theory as applied to war-time and job-related marital separation. *Psychological Bulletin, 114,* 122–144.

Wallerstein, J. S. (1994). Children after divorce: Wounds that don't heal. In L. Fenson & J. Fenson (Eds.), *Human development, 94/95* (pp. 160–165). Guilford, CT: Dushkin.

Weiss, R. S. (1973). *Loneliness: The experience of emotional and social isolation.* Cambridge, MA: MIT Press.

Weiss, R. S. (1975). *Marital separation.* New York: Basic Books.

Weiss, R. S. (1988). Loss and recovery. *Journal of Social Issues, 44,* 37–52.

Zeifman, D., & Hazan, C. (1997). A process model of adult attachment formation. In S. Duck (Eds.), *Handbook of personal relationships* (2nd ed., pp. 179–195). Chichester, England: Wiley.

Zimmerman, S. J., Maude, M. B., & Moldawar, M. (1965). Frequent ejaculation and total sperm count, motility and forms in humans. *Fertility and Sterility, 16,* 342–345.

17

Adult Romantic Attachment and Couple Relationships

❖

JUDITH A. FEENEY

"My partner is extremely affectionate, which suits me down to the ground. I've always, always craved affection all my life, mainly through parental—*bad* parental relationships. So, I don't know, but I put it down to that. And she's the only person I've ever gone out with that's actually given me the affection I've wanted."

It is not unusual for people, in describing the quality of their romantic relationships, to emphasize the impact of early experiences with caregivers; such an emphasis is reflected in this brief quotation from a research participant. Other descriptions of romantic relationships explore in more detail the continuity between early and later social relations, focusing in particular on the legacy of negative experiences with caregivers. Consider the following comment, made by a participant in a study of long-term dating relationships:

"It took E. a long time to want to get close to me, because I think her mother has destroyed her trust in people and the way people express emotions. Her mother just flits in and out of moods, and she's always put E. down. So I think E. had lost the ability to get close to people. She is often really quiet and upset, and has trouble talking about her problems. She listens, but she doesn't like to reciprocate with any discussion of her troubles. She's starting to overcome this, but only in the last

couple of months, because I've raised it as a very damaging issue in our relationship. I feel separated from her because of her silence—it makes me feel like I can't make her happy. Also, E.'s never had any attention from her father. He hasn't taken an interest in what she does, and I think she feels that he hasn't had any input in her emotional development."

Comments such as these are consistent with Bowlby's (1969/1982, 1973, 1980) theory of attachment, which recognizes the enormous importance of the bonds formed between children and their caregivers. They also support Bowlby's claim that attachment behavior plays a vital role throughout the life cycle. This chapter focuses on the proposition that romantic love can be conceptualized as an attachment process, which is influenced in part by earlier experiences with caregivers. My aims are to present the original theoretical and empirical work on which this proposition is based, to outline the considerable advances that have since been made in this research area, and to explore the unresolved issues and likely future directions.

THE FIRST STUDIES OF ROMANTIC LOVE AS ATTACHMENT

Although Bowlby's attachment theory dealt primarily with the bonds formed between infants and their caregivers, theoretical work dating from the early 1980s has argued for the relevance of attachment principles to adults' close relationships. These arguments have centered on an analysis of the functions of attachment bonds. Specifically, infant attachment bonds involve "proximity maintenance" and "separation protest" (seeking proximity to the attachment figure, and resisting separation), "secure base" (using the attachment figure as a base from which to explore the environment), and "safe haven" (turning to the attachment figure for comfort in times of threat). According to Weiss (1982, 1986, 1991), these features of infant–caregiver bonds apply to most marital and committed nonmarital romantic relationships. That is, the person derives comfort and security from the partner, wants to be with the partner (especially in times of stress), and protests when the partner threatens to become unavailable. Similarly, Ainsworth (1989) has pointed to sexual pair bonds as a prime example of adult attachments.

Other key concepts of attachment theory suggest a link between the *quality* of infant and adult attachment relationships. Bowlby proposed that during the years of "immaturity" (infancy to adolescence), individuals gradually build up expectations of attachment figures, based on experiences with these individuals. Expectations about the availability and responsiveness of attachment figures are incorporated into "working models" of these figures, which guide perceptions and behavior in later relationships.

Despite claims of continuity between childhood and adult relationships, the attachment perspective on adults' romantic relationships did not become an active area of research interest until Hazan and Shaver reported their seminal studies of romantic love (Hazan & Shaver, 1987; Shaver & Hazan, 1988; Shaver, Hazan, & Bradshaw, 1988). In these papers, Hazan and Shaver argued that romantic love can be conceptualized as an attachment process. That is, relationships between spouses and between unmarried but committed lovers are affectional bonds that involve complex socioemotional processes. They further argued that variations in early social experience produce relatively lasting differences in relationship styles, and that the three major attachment styles described in the infant literature ("secure," "avoidant," and "ambivalent") are manifested in romantic love.

In support of these arguments, Hazan and Shaver presented theoretical analyses of love and attachment, integrated with new empirical data. Their theoretical analyses (Shaver & Hazan, 1988) addressed several issues, including the concept of love as the integration of behavioral systems, and comparison of the attachment perspective with previous theories of love. These issues are briefly discussed later in this chapter.

The empirical studies (Hazan & Shaver, 1987) assessed the link between attachment style and aspects of childhood and adult relationships. Hazan and Shaver developed a forced-choice, self-report measure of adult attachment, which consisted of three paragraphs written to capture the main features typifying the three attachment styles. Subjects were asked to choose the paragraph most descriptive of their feelings in close relationships. This measure was used with a large sample of respondents to a "Love Quiz" printed in a local newspaper, and with an undergraduate sample. Subjects completed questionnaires assessing general attitudes to close relationships, together with experiences specific to their "most important romance." Results showed that the frequencies of the three styles were similar to those observed among infants: Just over half the adults described themselves as secure; of the remainder, slightly more classified themselves as avoidant than as ambivalent. Consistent with predictions based on attachment theory, the three attachment groups differed in their reports of early family relationships, working models of attachment, and love experiences.

In reporting their results, Hazan and Shaver (1987) noted the limitations of their initial studies. Because of constraints on data collection, the measures were brief and simple. Moreover, subjects described their experience of a single romantic relationship; hence the focus was on relationship qualities that differentiated the three attachment groups. Although this focus might seem to imply a trait approach, the authors recognized that relationship qualities are influenced also by "factors unique to particular partners and circumstances" (Hazan & Shaver, 1987, p. 521). This important point is taken up again later in this chapter.

EARLY STUDIES OF ADULT ROMANTIC ATTACHMENT: REPLICATIONS AND EXTENSIONS

Despite the limitations of their initial research, Hazan and Shaver succeeded in providing both a *normative* account of romantic love (i.e., an account of the typical processes of romantic attachment) and an understanding of *individual differ-*

ences in adult relationship styles. Providing a bridge between infant attachment theory and theories of romantic love, their work generated intense interest among relationship researchers. As a result, their initial papers were soon followed by studies reporting replications and extensions of their findings. Most of these early studies made some attempt to address the limitations noted by Hazan and Shaver, but focused primarily on other issues: on conceptualizing love and attachment, on linking theories of attachment style and affect regulation, and on establishing the salience of attachment issues to subjects in romantic relationships. (Early studies focusing on adult attachment style as a predictor of relationship quality are presented in a later section of this chapter.)

Conceptualizing Love and Attachment

The first two studies discussed here focus on the conceptualization of love and attachment. Shaver and Hazan (1988) proposed that previous theories of love (theories of "love styles," of "anxious" love, and of the components of love) can be integrated within the attachment perspective. To test this proposition, Levy and Davis (1988) assessed the links between attachment style and measures of the love styles described by Lee (1973, 1988) and the components of love discussed by Sternberg (1986).

The love styles described by Lee are "eros" (passionate love), "ludus" (game-playing love), "storge" (friendship love), "mania" (possessive, dependent love), "pragma" (logical, "shopping-list" love), and "agape" (selfless love). Shaver and Hazan (1988) argued that this typology can be reduced to the three major attachment styles. Secure attachment should correspond to a combination of eros and agape; avoidant attachment should correspond to ludus; and ambivalent attachment should correspond to mania (Shaver & Hazan did not see storge and pragma as forms of romantic love). Levy and Davis's (1988) results, based on ratings of each attachment and love style, largely supported this formulation: Secure attachment was related positively to eros and agape, and negatively to ludus; avoidant attachment was related positively to ludus, and negatively to eros; and ambivalent attachment was related positively to mania. These relations, however, were modest in size.

In terms of Sternberg's (1986) model of love, the three components (intimacy, passion, commitment) were all related positively to secure attachment, and negatively to avoidant and ambivalent attachment. These results supported the link between secure attachment and better relationship functioning, but failed to establish a unique set of correlates for each insecure style. Other measures employed by Levy and Davis did, however, distinguish between forms of insecure attachment; in particular, ambivalence was associated with a more dominating style of response to conflict.

The second study considered here (Feeney & Noller, 1990) was designed to replicate Hazan and Shaver's (1987) work, and to assess their proposed integration of theories of love. Using a large undergraduate sample, Noller and I reported attachment group differences on measures of family history and working models, which largely supported the earlier work. A new and noteworthy finding was that avoidant subjects were more likely than others to report having experienced a lengthy separation from their mothers during childhood (a finding consistent with attachment theory).

Like Levy and Davis (1988), we (Feeney & Noller, 1990) were interested in relating the attachment perspective to previous theories of love (Table 17.1 summarizes the findings of these two studies.) In particular, we argued that the link between "anxious love" and ambivalent attachment warranted attention. Shaver and Hazan (1988) described theories of anxious love as unidimensional, but did not test whether measures of anxious love were unidimensional, or how they related to attachment style. Using factor analysis, we assessed the structure of a broad range of measures: self-esteem, loving, love styles, and anxious love ("limerence," "love addiction"). This procedure resulted in 16 scales. Of particular interest was the fact that measures of anxious love were multidimensional. The limerence measure, for example, tapped four aspects of anxious love: obsessive preoccupation, self-conscious anxiety in dealing with partners, emotional dependence, and idealization of partners.

Four higher-order factors emerged from the 16 scales: "neurotic love" (high scores on preoccupation, dependence, and idealization), "self-confidence" (high scores on self-esteem and lack of self-conscious anxiety), "avoidance of intimacy" (high scores on ludus and low scores on loving, eros, and agape), and "circumspect love" (high scores on friendship and pragma). All four scales strongly differentiated the attachment groups. Secure subjects were high on self-confidence, low on neurotic love, and low on avoidance of in-

TABLE 17.1. Measures of Love Associated with the Three Major Attachment Styles

Measure	Secure	Avoidant	Ambivalent
Love styles	Eros (passionate love), agape (selfless love)	Ludus (game-playing love)	Mania (possessive love)
Components of love	High on intimacy, passion, and commitment	Low on intimacy, passion, and commitment	Low on intimacy, passion, and commitment
Higher-order factors	High on self-confidence (high on self-esteem and lack of self-conscious anxiety with partners); low on avoidance of intimacy; low on neurotic love	High on avoidance of intimacy (high on ludus and low on eros, agape, and loving); low on self-confidence; low on neurotic love	High on neurotic love (high on preoccupation, dependence, and idealization); low on circumspect love (friendship, pragma); low on self-confidence; low on avoidance of intimacy

timacy. Both insecure groups lacked self-confidence, but whereas avoidant subjects reported avoidance of intimacy, ambivalent subjects were high on neurotic love and low on circumspect love. These results support Shaver and Hazan's (1988) theoretical analysis, but with qualifications. In particular, although Shaver and Hazan equated anxious love with ambivalent attachment, it seems that at least one aspect of anxious love (self-conscious anxiety in dealing with partners) characterizes both avoidant and ambivalent persons.

Affect Regulation with Peers and Romantic Partners

A second focus of early studies of adult attachment was on affect regulation—that is, on ways of dealing with negative emotion. Differences in attachment style are thought to reflect experiences of regulating distress with caregivers. Through these experiences, an individual learns strategies for organizing emotional experience and handling negative feelings, and these strategies come to be applied to other distressing situations. Secure individuals, having experienced responsive caregiving, are expected to handle negative feelings in a relatively constructive manner by acknowledging distress and turning to others for support. Avoidant individuals are likely to restrict acknowledging and expressing negative feelings, having learned self-reliance as a way of reducing conflict with rejecting or insensitive caregivers. Ambivalent individuals are expected to show heightened awareness and expression of negative feelings, learned as a way of maintaining contact with inconsistent caregivers.

Kobak and Sceery (1988) examined attachment patterns, representations of self and others, and affect regulation in a student sample. On the basis of interviews that asked about subjects' relationships with their parents, subjects were classified as "secure," "dismissing of attachment" (cf. avoidant), or "preoccupied" (cf. ambivalent). Representations of self and others were measured via self-report scales (e.g., social competence, distress), and affect regulation (e.g., hostility, anxiety) was measured via peer Q-sort ratings. As expected, both self-reports and peer Q-sort ratings showed that secure subjects were well adjusted and handled their negative feelings in constructive ways. Although dismissing subjects were rated as hostile by peers, they reported levels of social competence and distress similar to those of secure subjects, suggesting a failure to acknowledge negative feelings. For preoccupied subjects, self-reports and peer ratings indicated high levels of distress and anxiety, supporting the claim that ambivalent individuals show both heightened awareness and heightened expression of negative feelings.

The link between attachment style and the regulation of negative affect *within* romantic relationships was explored by Simpson (1990), in one of the first attachment studies to recruit both partners in ongoing (dating) relationships. Simpson was interested in the link between attachment style and reports of emotional experience, both in terms of the emotional quality of the relationship itself, and in terms of responses to relationship breakup. The emotional quality of current relationships was assessed by asking subjects how often they experienced each of 28 different emotions that varied in valence (positive vs. negative) and intensity (mild vs. intense). Secure subjects reported more frequent positive emotions and less frequent negative emotions (both mild and intense) than did avoidant and ambivalent subjects. This result may reflect two interrelated effects: Secure individuals may form relationships of higher quality, and they may also perceive and interpret relationship events in a more positive way (Simpson, 1990).

Responses to relationship breakup were assessed at 6-month follow-up by asking dating partners who were no longer together about the extent of emotional distress following their breakups. Consistent with attachment theory, avoidant attachment was associated with less distress, although this effect was obtained only for men. This result is partially supported by other research linking attachment style with emotional responses to relationship breakup. We (Feeney & Noller, 1992) found that avoidant attachment was related negatively to upset and positively to relief, whereas ambivalent attachment was related positively to surprise and upset and negatively to relief (secure attachment was unrelated to reports of emotional response).

Salience of Attachment Issues to Perceptions of Romantic Relationships

The studies reported so far pointed to meaningful relations among styles of adult romantic attachment, love experiences, and reports of negative emotions. However, these studies tended to rely on closed-ended, self-report measures. Even Kobak and Sceery (1988), who supplemented such measures with peer reports and interviews, used relatively structured instruments. Because structured measures may lead to response sets such as experimenter demand and social desirability, we (Feeney & Noller, 1991) argued that early studies of adult attachment had not established the *salience* of attachment issues to subjects' evaluations of their relationships. That is, attachment issues may not be very important to individuals, except when they are introduced by measurement procedures.

To address this problem, we asked subjects who were currently in dating relationships to provide open-ended verbal descriptions of their relationships. Subjects were asked to speak for 5 minutes, telling "what kind of person your partner is, and how you get along together." The descriptions were audiotaped and transcribed for content analysis. Two weeks later, subjects completed Hazan and Shaver's (1987) measure of attachment style.

The salience of attachment issues was assessed by examining whether subjects spontaneously referred to issues that are central to working models of attachment: openness, closeness, dependence, commitment, and affection. Each of these issues was spontaneously mentioned by at least 25% of subjects, with 89% of the sample referring to at least one of the five issues. The salience of attachment issues was further supported by the finding that in terms of word counts, one-fifth of the content of transcripts was devoted on average to discussing these issues.

We (Feeney & Noller, 1991) also examined the link between attachment style (using the three-group measure) and open-ended reports of relationships. Attachment groups differed markedly in the content of their reports, as illustrated by the sample extracts in Table 17.2. Secure subjects emphasized partners' mutual support, but advocated "balance" in terms of the extent to which partners depended on each other. Both secure and avoidant subjects described their relationships as based on friendship; unlike secure subjects, however, those who saw themselves as avoidant preferred clear limits to closeness, dependence, commitment, and displays of affection. Ambivalent subjects, in contrast, preferred unqualified closeness, commitment, and affection, and tended to idealize their partners. These results fit neatly with attachment theory, and with studies using structured measures of relationship experiences.

ADVANCES IN CONCEPTUALIZATION AND MEASUREMENT

Understanding the more recent studies of adult romantic attachment and relationship experiences requires us to consider briefly the advances in conceptualization and measurement on which they are based. In terms of measurement, Hazan and Shaver's (1987) forced-choice item had clear limitations (as they themselves noted). Reliance on a single item raised concerns about reliability of measurement. These concerns were exacerbated by the forced-choice format, which required subjects to choose from complex alternatives, and which seemed to imply that attachment styles were mutually exclusive. Given these problems, researchers soon sought more refined

TABLE 17.2. Extracts from Open-Ended Reports of Romantic Relationships, Supplied by Subjects from the Three Attachment Groups

Secure: "We're really good friends, and we sort of knew each other for a long time before we started going out—and we like the same sort of things. Another thing which I like a lot is that he gets on well with all my close friends. We can always talk things over. Like if we're having any fights, we usually resolve them by talking it over—he's a very reasonable person. I can just be my own person, so it's good, because it's not a possessive relationship. I think that we trust each other a lot."

Avoidant: "My partner is my best friend, and that's the way I think of him. He's as special to me as any of my other friends. His expectations in life don't include marriage, or any long-term commitment to any female, which is fine with me, because that's not what my expectations are as well. I find that he doesn't want to be overly intimate, and he doesn't expect too much commitment—which is good. . . . Sometimes it's a worry that a person can be that close to you, and be in such control of your life."

Ambivalent: "So I went in there . . . and he was sitting on the bench, and I took one look, and I actually melted. He was the best-looking thing I'd ever seen, and that was the first thing that struck me about him. So we went out and we had lunch in the park . . . so we just sort of sat there—and in silence—but it wasn't awkward . . . like, you know, when you meet strangers and you can't think of anything to say, it's usually awkward. It wasn't like that. We just sat there, and it was incredible—like we'd known each other for a real long time, and we'd only met for about 10 seconds, so that was—straightaway my first feelings for him started coming out."

measures. Before these refinements are discussed, however, three comments on measurement should be made.

First, despite the calls for more refined instruments, the three-group measure has remained popular. This popularity presumably reflects its ease of administration, its conceptual link with infant attachment theory, and the general appeal of simple typologies.

Second, consistent links between the three-group measure and relationship variables support its reliability and validity. Thus, the question is not whether this measure produces meaningful results, but rather how it might be improved psychometrically.

Finally, it is important to note that Hazan and Shaver were not the first researchers to measure adult attachment. The Adult Attachment Interview (AAI; George, Kaplan, & Main, 1985) taps memories of childhood relationships with parents, as well as the subject's evaluations of the effects of these experiences on his or her adult personality. Interview transcripts can be used to identify three attachment patterns (cf. Kobak & Sceery, 1988): "secure" (marked by the valuing of attachment experiences, and by ease and objectivity in discussing attachment episodes), "dismissing" (marked by the devaluing of attachment relationships, and by difficulty in recalling specific attachment experiences), and "preoccupied" (marked by confused or incoherent accounts of attachment relationships). The validity of this measure is supported by links between

parents' attachment classification as assessed by the AAI, and their children's attachment classification as assessed earlier by observers (Main & Goldwyn, 1985). AAI classifications have also been related to marital quality (Cohn, Silver, Cowan, Cowan, & Pearson, 1992), as noted later in this chapter. Most of the measures discussed in the following sections differ from the AAI in two important respects: They focus on romantic attachment (as opposed to current state of mind with respect to childhood attachment), and they require less in-depth training to administer and score.

From Forced-Choice to Multiple-Item Measures

The first variation of Hazan and Shaver's (1987) measure involved a minor revision: the three descriptions were presented intact, but instead of being forced to choose between them, subjects used rating scales to indicate the applicability of each one (Levy & Davis, 1988). This measurement approach recognizes that not all subjects choosing a particular attachment style (e.g., secure) will find the associated description equally applicable; some will be more "secure" than others. It also allows researchers to consider patterns of scores across attachment styles. Subjects who see themselves as secure, for example, will differ in their degree of avoidance and ambivalence, and these differences may have implications for individual and relationship outcomes.

Even this version, however, assumes that the various themes within each attachment description form a consistent whole. To test this assumption, researchers next developed measures in which each description was broken into a number of statements to be rated by subjects. This approach permits factor-analytic investigation of the structure of attachment measures. Item content has varied slightly from study to study, however (researchers have broken the descriptions down in different ways, and some have omitted or added items). For this reason, consensus concerning the underlying structure has been rather slow to emerge. Nevertheless, several studies point to two major dimensions, tapping "comfort with closeness" and "anxiety over relationships" (Feeney, Noller, & Callan, 1994; Simpson, Rholes, & Nelligan, 1992; Strahan, 1991). Comfort with closeness, a bipolar dimension, contrasts elements of the original secure and avoidant descriptions (e.g., "I find it relatively easy to get close to others" vs. "I am nervous when anyone gets too close"). Anxiety over relationships deals with themes central to ambivalent attachment, such as concerns about love, worries about abandonment, and the need for extreme closeness (e.g., "I often worry that my partner doesn't really love me," "I find that others are reluctant to get as close as I would like"). More broadly based pools of items, designed to cover the basic themes of attachment theory, have yielded similar dimensions (Brennan, Clark, & Shaver, 1998; Feeney, Noller, & Hanrahan, 1994).

A Four-Group Model of Adult Attachment

At the same time as the three-group measure was being refined, a four-group model of adult attachment was proposed, based on Bowlby's claim that attachment patterns reflect working models of self and others (Bartholomew, 1990; Bartholomew & Horowitz, 1991). Bartholomew argued that models of self can be dichotomized as positive (the self is seen as worthy of love and attention) or negative (the self is seen as unworthy). Similarly, models of others can be positive (others are seen as available and caring) or negative (others are seen as unreliable or rejecting). Working models of self and others jointly define four attachment styles, including two avoidant styles, "dismissing" and "fearful" (see Figure 17.1). Dismissing individuals emphasize achievement and self-reliance, maintaining a sense of self-worth at the expense of intimacy. Fearful individuals desire intimacy but distrust others; they avoid close involvements, which may lead to loss or rejection.

Self-report prototypes of the four attachment

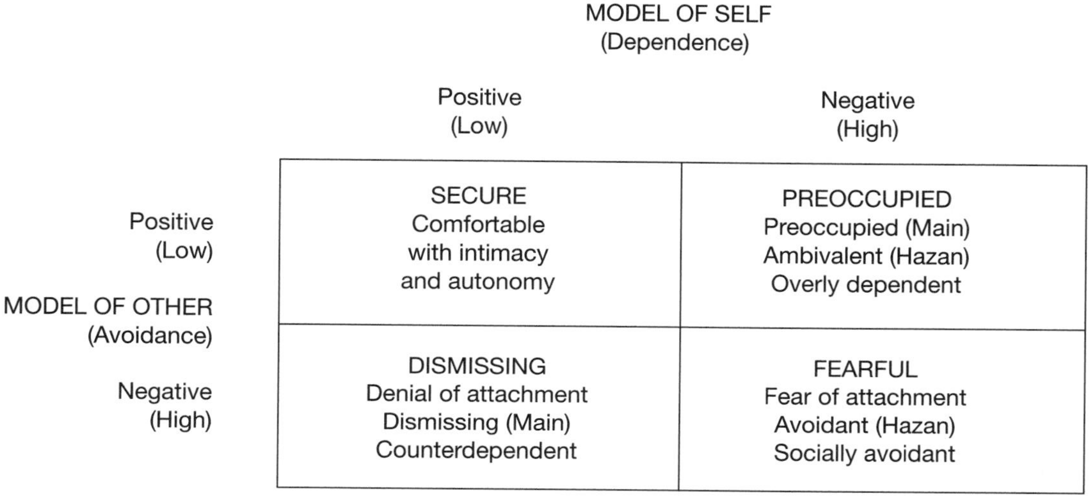

	MODEL OF SELF (Dependence)	
	Positive (Low)	Negative (High)
MODEL OF OTHER (Avoidance) Positive (Low)	SECURE Comfortable with intimacy and autonomy	PREOCCUPIED Preoccupied (Main) Ambivalent (Hazan) Overly dependent
Negative (High)	DISMISSING Denial of attachment Dismissing (Main) Counterdependent	FEARFUL Fear of attachment Avoidant (Hazan) Socially avoidant

FIGURE 17.1. The four adult attachment styles defined by Bartholomew in terms of working models of self and others. From Bartholomew (1990). Copyright 1990 by Sage Publications, Inc. Reprinted by permission.

styles have been developed (similar in form to Hazan and Shaver's three descriptions), together with interview schedules yielding ratings on the four prototypes (Bartholomew & Horowitz, 1991). Considerable convergence has been established between Bartholomew's interview and self-report measures, and between classifications from Bartholomew's interview schedule and those based on the AAI (Bartholomew & Shaver, 1998). The four-group and three-group categorical measures also show meaningful relations with each other (Brennan, Shaver, & Tobey, 1991). As expected, subjects who choose the secure category of one measure are also likely to choose the secure category of the other, and those choosing Bartholomew's preoccupied category are likely to describe themselves as ambivalent in terms of Hazan and Shaver's measure. Bartholomew's fearful group is drawn largely from Hazan and Shaver's avoidant group (this result is not surprising, given that Hazan and Shaver's description of avoidance emphasizes discomfort with closeness), but the dismissing group is drawn from both secure and avoidant groups.

The four-group model is validated by empirical support for two distinct types of avoidance. The interpersonal problems of fearful individuals involve social insecurity and lack of assertiveness, whereas those of dismissing individuals involve excessive coldness (Bartholomew & Horowitz, 1991). Furthermore, we (Feeney, Noller, & Hanrahan, 1994) found that the five attachment scales of our measure defined four attachment groups that were generally similar to those proposed by Bartholomew. Compared with dismissing individuals, fearful individuals reported less confidence in self and others, as well as more discomfort with closeness, need for approval, and preoccupation with relationships. Similarly, Brennan et al. (1998) reported four attachment groups consistent with Bartholomew's typology, based on a cluster analysis using the higher-order factors of avoidance and anxiety. Finally, the two avoidant groups have been found to differ markedly in their responses to affect-laden situations (Feeney, 1995; Fraley, Davis, & Shaver, 1998).

Given these findings, researchers have increasingly adopted the four-group model of adult attachment. This model is consistent with infant research suggesting the importance of a fourth attachment group showing characteristics of both avoidance and ambivalence (Crittenden, 1985); in particular, fearful adults tend to endorse both avoidant and ambivalent attachment prototypes (Brennan et al., 1991). The four groups of Bartholomew's model are also closely tied to the two major attachment dimensions discussed earlier. The dismissing and fearful groups report less comfort with closeness than the secure and preoccupied groups; this result suggests that comfort with closeness is related to working models of others (Feeney, 1995; Feeney, Noller, & Hanrahan, 1994). Preoccupied and fearful groups report greater anxiety over relationships than secure and dismissing groups; thus anxiety over relationships is related to working models of self (Feeney, 1995; Feeney, Noller, & Hanrahan, 1994). (See Crowell, Fraley, & Shaver, Chapter 20, this volume, for a more detailed discussion of adult attachment measures.)

STABILITY OF ADULT ATTACHMENT AND WORKING MODELS

Although studies have shown reasonable stability of attachment patterns across the early childhood years, the extent of stability is still an issue both for developmental researchers and for investigators of adult attachment. This issue is tied to other contentious issues, particularly the "trait versus relationships" debate, discussed later.

The stability of adult romantic attachment has been assessed over intervals ranging from 1 week to 4 years. With forced-choice (three- or four-group) measures, a change in attachment type across assessments is shown by approximately one in four subjects (Baldwin & Fehr, 1995; Kirkpatrick & Hazan, 1994). This figure varies little with the time lag between assessments. Ratings of attachment prototypes are moderately stable, as are multiple-item scales (Collins & Read, 1990; Feeney, Noller, & Callan, 1994); when the limited reliability of scales is considered, their stability is quite high (Scharfe & Bartholomew, 1994). Interview measures (whether forced-choice measures or ratings) tend to be more stable than self-reports or peer reports (Scharfe & Bartholomew, 1994).

The fact that more refined measures are more stable suggests that some of the instability in adult romantic attachment reflects unreliability of measurement. However, some instability undoubtedly reflects actual change in attachment organization over time. This finding is not contrary to attachment theory, which asserts that significant relationship experiences and other major life events may alter attachment organization and associated working models (see also the following sections). In a study of young couples, for example, involvement in satisfying relationships at one point in time was associated with increased security at a later time (Hammond & Fletcher, 1991). Furthermore, in a 4-year prospective study, relationship breakups were associated with change from secure to insecure attachment, and avoidant subjects who formed new relationships were less likely to remain avoidant than those who did not (Kirkpatrick & Hazan, 1994).

To understand the sources of stability and instability in adult romantic attachment, we need to consider the concept of working models in some detail. Bowlby proposed working models as the mechanism by which childhood attachment experiences affect a person throughout life. (See Bretherton & Munholland, Chapter 5, this volume, for an extensive discussion of internal working models.) Early studies of adult attachment relied on simple measures of working models; these included new self-report items designed to assess attitudes to self and to others (Hazan & Shaver, 1987), as well as existing self-report scales (Collins & Read, 1990). Neither of these methods fits closely with other work on childhood and adulthood attachment bonds, which has tended to emphasize the processes involved in mental representation of events, along with the role of defensive exclusion (e.g., Bretherton, 1987, 1991). Recent research into working models of adult attachment has become more sophisticated, however. The following sections deal with two concepts central to this research: first, that working models guide experience in intimate relationships; and second, that working models are in turn influenced by relationship experiences.

Influence of Working Models on Relationship Experiences

The increasing sophistication of theory and research in this area can be seen in Collins and Read's (1994) work on the structure and function of working models. With regard to the structure of working models, these researchers have argued that individuals develop a hierarchy of models. A set of generalized models lies at the top of the hierarchy, with models for particular classes of relationships (e.g., family members, peers) at an intermediate level, and models for particular relationships (e.g., father, spouse) at the lowest level. Models higher in the hierarchy

apply to a wider range of others but are less predictive for any specific situation.

Collins and Read (1994) have further suggested that working models include four interrelated components: memories of attachment-related experiences; beliefs, attitudes, and expectations of self and others in relation to attachment; attachment-related goals and needs; and strategies and plans for achieving these goals. All four components vary across the major attachment groups, as summarized in Table 17.3 (the three-group model is used here, because much of the research is based on this model). For example, secure individuals tend to remember their parents as warm and affectionate, avoidant individuals to remember their mothers as cold and rejecting, and ambivalent individuals to remember their fathers as unfair (Feeney & Noller, 1990; Hazan & Shaver, 1987; Rothbard & Shaver, 1994). These findings from retrospective reports fit with predictions from attachment theory, although we cannot be sure to what extent the memories are affected by current views of the world.

In terms of the functions of working models, Collins and Read (1994) claimed that these models shape individuals' cognitive, emotional, and behavioral responses to others. Working models affect cognitive responses by directing people to pay attention to certain aspects of the stimuli that confront them (particularly goal-related stimuli), by creating biases in memory encoding and retrieval, and by affecting explanation processes. For example, secure adults show faster recognition of positive-outcome words set in an interpersonal context, whereas avoidant adults show faster recognition of negative-outcome words (Baldwin, Fehr, Keedian, Seidel, & Thomson, 1993). Furthermore, explanations of relationship events by secure subjects reflect their stronger perceptions of security and greater confidence in their partners' availability (Collins, 1996).

With regard to emotional response patterns, working models are thought to affect both primary and secondary appraisals. "Primary appraisal" refers to the immediate emotional reaction to a given situation. In "secondary appraisal," cognitive processing may either maintain, amplify, or lessen the initial emotional response, depending on how the individual interprets the experience. For example, someone who is initially elated at receiving a phone call from an attractive acquaintance may maintain that elation by thinking of the recent conversation, may amplify it by imagining a rosy future with the person, or may

TABLE 17.3. Attachment Group Differences in Working Models

Secure	Avoidant	Ambivalent
Memories		
Parents warm and affectionate	Mothers cold and rejecting	Fathers unfair
Attachment-related beliefs, attitudes		
Few self-doubts; high in self-worth	Suspicious of human motives	Others complex and difficult to understand
Generally liked by others	Others not trustworthy or dependable	People have little control over own lives
Others generally well-intentioned and good-hearted	Doubt honesty and integrity of parents and others	
Others generally trustworthy, dependable, and altruistic	Lack confidence in social situations	
Interpersonally oriented	Not interpersonally oriented	
Attachment-related goals and needs		
Desire intimate relationships	Need to maintain distance	Desire extreme intimacy
Seek balance of closeness and autonomy in relationships	Limit intimacy to satisfy needs for autonomy	Seek lower levels of autonomy
	Place greater weight on goals such as achievement	Fear rejection
Plans and strategies		
Acknowledge distress	Manage distress by cutting off anger	Heightened displays of distress and anger
Modulate negative affect in constructive way	Minimize distress-related emotional displays; withhold intimate disclosure	Solicitous and compliant to gain acceptance

lessen it by assuming that the caller will never phone again.

Working models affect behavioral responses through the activation of stored plans and strategies, and through the construction of new plans and strategies (Collins & Read, 1994). An example of a stored strategy that is likely to have developed in childhood is an individual's "running home to Mother" whenever conflict with the spouse arises. In the absence of an available existing strategy, new strategies may be devised for current situations. Hence working models may affect decisions about whether to discuss a conflictual issue openly with one's spouse or to avoid it.

Influence of Relationship Experiences on Working Models

Several factors promote the stability of working models. First, individuals tend to select environ-

ments that fit their beliefs about self and others. For instance, there is evidence (Kirkpatrick & Davis, 1994; see later discussion) that relationships involving an ambivalent female and an avoidant male are quite stable (although not very happy). The clingy, anxious female presumably confirms the avoidant male's belief that it is unwise to let others get too close, and the avoidant male confirms the ambivalent female's belief that others are less concerned about love relationships than she is. Second, working models may be self-perpetuating. For example, someone who believes that others cannot be trusted may approach them defensively, increasing the likelihood of further rejection. Third, the information-processing biases discussed earlier lead people to perceive social events in ways that support existing models (Collins & Read, 1994).

Despite these forces promoting stability, change in working models does occur, particularly when significant events in the social environment disconfirm existing expectations. For example, becoming involved in a stable, satisfying relationship may lead to change for those whose models of self and others have led to skepticism about the possibility of having such a relationship. The high percentage of secure subjects generally found in samples of stable couples supports this effect (Feeney, Noller, & Callan, 1994; Senchak & Leonard, 1992), as does the following comment made by a research participant (Feeney, 1998; this study is described more fully later):

"I had a real problem trusting anyone at the start of any relationship. A couple of things happened to me when I was young,which I had some emotional difficulties getting over. At the start of our relationship, if P. had been separated from me, I would have been constantly thinking: 'What was he doing?'; 'Was he with another girl?'; 'Was he cheating on me?'; all that would have been running through my head. Over a 3-year period of going out, you look at it in a different light; you learn to trust him."

Similarly, a secure person who is involved in a particularly negative relationship may become insecure as a result of that experience, as indicated by a comment from another participant in the same study.

"Before I started seeing T., I was in another long relationship with another fellow. That lasted for about a year, and things then were just totally different from things now. It was good up until about 10 months, and then the last couple of months were really bad. I was always really confident about myself and secure about myself, but he made me feel in 2 months—just seemed to ruin everything I'd ever felt good about myself, and I felt bad about everything I did, and he made me feel bad. And so I've got this constant thing in the back of my head that maybe that might happen again."

Of course, the impact of such negative experiences is likely to depend on how long they last, as well as on the extent to which they are seen as emotionally significant. Working models may also change as individuals arrive at new understandings of their past experiences, particularly those that are attachment-related.

ROMANTIC ATTACHMENT STYLE, WORKING MODELS, AND RELATIONSHIP QUALITY

In studies described in an earlier section, Levy and Davis (1988) and Simpson (1990) also explored the link between attachment style and the quality of dating relationships. Both of these studies linked secure attachment with high levels of trust, commitment, satisfaction, and interdependence. By contrast, avoidant and ambivalent attachment were negatively related to trust and satisfaction, and avoidant attachment was also related to low levels of interdependence and commitment. These results are consistent with attachment theory.

Another important study of dating relationships (Collins & Read, 1990) used a measure of attachment style that included scales assessing comfort with closeness and anxiety over relationship issues. Some findings were robust across gender. For example, men and women who were comfortable with closeness reported being able to get other people to open up and talk about personal information, and men and women who were anxious about relationships reported distrusting their partners. Other results concerning the implications of attachment dimensions for relationship quality were gender-specific. For females, anxiety over relationships was a strong correlate of relationship quality, being linked with jealousy and with low levels of communication, closeness, partner responsiveness, and satisfaction. For males, comfort with closeness was the crucial attachment dimension, being linked with most indices of relationship quality. These gender differences may reflect sex-role stereotypes, whereby women are socialized to value emotional closeness and men are socialized to value self-reliance. Given that a relationship is rated negatively when the woman is anxious about relationship issues and when the man is uncomfortable with intimacy, it seems that extreme conformity to sex-role stereotypes may be detrimental to relationship quality.

In a 3-year study of dating couples, Kirkpatrick and Davis (1994) reported results that paralleled those of Collins and Read (1990): Ambivalent women rated their relationships negatively, as did avoidant men. The relationships of ambivalent women and of avoidant men were quite stable over time, however, despite the negative ratings of relationship quality. Why might this be? Ambivalent women may strive particularly hard to maintain their relationships (note that women tend to act as the emotional caretakers of close relationships); furthermore, they are frequently paired with avoidant men, for whom their dependent behavior may confirm working models (Belsky & Cassidy, 1994). Similarly, the relationships of avoidant men may be stable because they tend to involve secure or ambivalent partners. Avoidant men may also engage in such behaviors as conflict avoidance, which may contribute to long-term stability, although not to concurrent happiness. As Kirkpatrick and Davis (1994) noted, the differing implications of attachment style for current happiness and for long-term stability caution against simplistic statements about "good" or "bad" attachment styles.

Studies of marriage have also linked attachment style with relationship quality, including independent observers' ratings of spouses' behavior. Kobak and Hazan (1991) investigated the role of working models of attachment in marital functioning. Spouses completed measures of dyadic satisfaction and working models, and also engaged in two interaction tasks: (1) a problem-solving interaction, and (2) a confiding task in which they shared a loss or disappointment unrelated to the marriage. Problem-solving discussions were rated for rejection and support/validation, and confiding interactions were rated for speakers' disclosure and listeners' acceptance of distress. Spouses with secure working models reported higher dyadic satisfaction than those with insecure models. Secure husbands were less rejecting and more supportive during problem solving, and secure wives were less likely to be rejected by husbands on the same task. Accuracy of working models (the level of one's agreement with the spouse about one's own working models) was also related to dyadic satisfaction, and to observers' ratings of communication in the problem-solving and confiding tasks.

Another study of attachment and marriage defined attachment type at the level of the couple, based on spouses' responses to the three-group attachment measure (Senchak & Leonard, 1992). Three "couple types" were defined: "secure" (in which both spouses chose the secure description), "insecure" (in which both spouses chose insecure descriptions), and "mixed" (in which one spouse chose the secure description and the other described himself or herself as insecure). Secure couples showed better marital adjustment than both mixed and insecure couples, in terms of reports of marital intimacy, partners' relationship functioning, and partners' withdrawal and

verbal aggression in response to conflict. The finding that mixed couples (those with one insecure spouse) showed similar marital adjustment to insecure couples suggests that in a mixed couple, the attitudes and behavior of the insecure spouse may have an overriding influence on the quality of the marriage. Because the couple was adopted as the unit of analysis, however, the actual role of each partner within the couple is unclear. Furthermore, because all measures were self-report, the association between attachment style and marital adjustment may have been inflated by common-method variance.

Marital quality has also been linked to attachment classification (secure vs. insecure) on the AAI (Cohn et al., 1992). These researchers found that attachment classification was unrelated to self-reported marital satisfaction, but was related to observers' ratings of couple interactions. Specifically, couples with secure husbands engaged in less conflict and in more positive behaviors. This observed link between AAI classifications and observers' ratings cannot be attributed to common-method variance (unlike the findings of Senchak & Leonard, 1992). Also in contrast to the work of Senchak and Leonard, mixed couples in Cohn et al.'s study (those with one secure and one insecure spouse) were rated by observers as similar to secure couples, and as functioning better than insecure couples. Hence it remains unclear whether, as Cohn et al. suggest, a secure partner can buffer the negative effects of insecure attachment on relationship quality.

Attachment and Relationship Quality: The Role of Communication

Several findings from the studies of dating and marriage reported above point to attachment style differences in communication patterns. The relevance of attachment to communication patterns is further supported by the claim that for infants and children, communication is the main avenue through which goal conflicts are negotiated and attachment relationships are maintained (Bretherton, 1990; Kobak & Duemmler, 1994).

A number of researchers have explicitly addressed the relation between attachment style and communication in adults' close relationships, and some have supplemented self-report questionnaires with behavioral observation and structured diary records. Pistole (1989) investigated the implications of attachment style for reports of conflict resolution in a sample of students involved in love relationships. She found that secure individuals were more likely to use an integrating (or problem-solving) strategy than those who were insecure, and that they also used more compromising than ambivalent individuals in particular. Ambivalent participants were more likely to oblige their partners than were avoidant participants. These findings support the tendency for secure individuals to use constructive strategies in dealing with conflict—that is, strategies that reflect their concern both for protecting their own interests and for enhancing the quality of their relationships.

Patterns of self-disclosure (another key aspect of communication) have been linked with attachment style, in studies using both self-report and behavioral methods (Keelan, Dion, & Dion, 1998; Mikulincer & Nachshon, 1991). In general, secure and ambivalent individuals reported more self-disclosure than avoidant individuals. Secure individuals showed the most reciprocity, in terms of discussing the particular topics raised by their partners. They also showed the most flexibility, in terms of the range of self-disclosure reported across various social situations, and the ability to differentiate between partners and strangers as potential targets of disclosure.

In a comprehensive study of the links among attachment, communication, and relationship satisfaction, we (Feeney, Noller, & Callan, 1994) assessed married couples across the first 2 years of marriage. We measured two attachment dimensions (comfort with closeness, anxiety over relationships) and three aspects of communication: the quality of day-to-day interactions (assessed via diary reports), self-reported conflict style, and nonverbal accuracy (assessed via a standard content paradigm involving ambiguous messages that could be positive, neutral, or negative, depending on the nonverbal behavior). In day-to-day interactions, husbands' comfort with closeness was related to their ratings of involvement, recognition, disclosure, and satisfaction; wives' anxiety over relationships was related to their ratings of domination, conflict, low involvement and dissatisfaction. With regard to conflict style, the key attachment variable was anxiety over relationships. Both husbands and wives who were high on this scale reported their conflicts as coercive, distressing, and lacking in mutual negotiation, suggesting that anxiety over relationship issues is related to destructive patterns of marital conflict. Husbands high in anxiety were low in nonverbal accuracy for all three message types, and wives high in comfort were more accurate for neutral and negative messages.

Analyses over time showed that attachment scales predicted later relationship variables. Specifically, comfort with closeness predicted later nonverbal accuracy for wives; anxiety over relationships predicted later negative conflict patterns for wives, and lower nonverbal accuracy and relationship satisfaction for husbands. However, the quality of marital interaction (as defined by measures of communication and satisfaction) also predicted later attachment security for husbands. This finding supports the idea that working models of attachment may be revised on the basis of experience within intimate relationships. Given that attachment style is linked with both communication and relationship satisfaction, we (Feeney, Noller, & Callan, 1994) suggested that the link between attachment style and satisfaction may stem in part from the ways in which the different attachment groups communicate. That is, the link between attachment and satisfaction may be mediated by communication patterns. However, our data did not support this hypothesis. Rather, the findings suggested that in these early marriages, attachment and communication had independent effects on satisfaction.

In a study of conflict patterns, attachment, and marital satisfaction across the marital life cycle (Feeney, 1994), security of attachment was associated with marital satisfaction, although mutual negotiation of conflict was the single most important predictor of satisfaction for both husbands and wives. In contrast to the study just described (Feeney, Noller, & Callan, 1994), the link between secure attachment and marital satisfaction was mediated by communication patterns for wives. In other words, the higher satisfaction reported by secure wives appeared to reflect their more constructive ways of communicating during conflict episodes. For husbands, conflict style only partially mediated the link between secure attachment and marital satisfaction, and anxiety over relationships explained variance in marital satisfaction over and above that related to communication patterns.

Although the studies of dating and marital relationships discussed so far highlight the importance of attachment style, the diverse ways of measuring this construct make convergent results less readily apparent. Table 17.4 summarizes the major findings linking subjects' own attachment style to relationship quality. I now turn to the issue of how relationship quality is linked with the attachment style of subjects' partners.

TABLE 17.4. Key Aspects of Relationship Quality Associated with Subjects' Own Attachment Style

Comfort with closeness (cf. secure vs. avoidant attachment)	Anxiety over relationships (cf. ambivalent attachment)
Trust	Lack of trust
Relationship satisfaction (M)	Relationship dissatisfaction (F)
Commitment	Jealousy
Closeness/interdependence	High levels of conflict (F)
Supportiveness	Coercion, domination, and distress in response to dyadic conflict
Self-disclosure, including flexibility and reciprocity of disclosure	Lack of compromise in dyadic problem solving
Involvement and satisfaction in daily interactions with partner (M)	Low involvement and satisfaction in daily interactions with partner (F)

Note. (M) indicates that these associations have been reported primarily for males; (F) indicates that these associations have been reported primarily for females.

Relationship Quality: Effects of Partners' Attachment Style

Most of the studies of ongoing relationships reported above employed both members of couples, allowing researchers to assess whether perceptions of relationship quality were related to partners' attachment style, as well as to subjects' own attachment style. (As noted earlier, Hazan and Shaver recognized that relationship quality is likely to be influenced by factors unique to particular partners.) Collins and Read (1990) found that relationship evaluations were related to partners' attachment style, in ways that parallelled the effects of subjects' own attachment style: Men's comfort with closeness was related strongly to their partners' relationship evaluations, whereas women's anxiety over abandonment was related strongly (and negatively) to their partners' evaluations. Subjects' own and partners' effects were roughly comparable in size.

Other studies of dating couples have partially supported these results. Consistent with Collins and Read's findings, Simpson (1990) reported a robust negative effect of women's ambivalence on partners' relationship evaluations. In contrast to that study, however, effects were generally less consistent for partners' attachment than for subjects' own attachment. Similarly, in the study by Kirkpatrick and Davis (1994), the most robust effect of partner attachment was the tendency for men paired with ambivalent women to rate their relationships negatively.

Studies of married couples have also reported reliable partner effects, using a range of methodologies (questionnaires, behavioral observation, and diary records). Kobak and Hazan (1991) found that wives of less secure husbands were more rejecting and less supportive than other wives, and that husbands of secure wives listened more effectively during problem solving. Similarly, we (Feeney, Noller, & Callan, 1994) found that communication patterns and marital satisfaction were related to both subjects' own and partners' attachment dimensions (comfort with closeness, anxiety over relationships), although the links were somewhat stronger for subjects' own attachment. (As noted earlier, the relative importance of comfort and anxiety depended on gender and on the relationship variable being considered.) For couples sampled across the life cycle, spouses' marital satisfaction has been related both to subjects' own and to partners' levels of comfort and anxiety, as assessed by simple correlations (Feeney, 1994). When the independent contribution of each attachment dimension was assessed via regression analysis, the strongest partner effect was the negative relation between wives' anxiety and husbands' satisfaction; this finding supports the substantial literature on attachment and dating relationships.

To summarize, the literature attests to the effects of both subjects' own and partners' attachment style on relationship quality; better relationship quality is reported both by subjects who are securely attached, and by those whose partners are securely attached. These findings raise a further question: Namely, do attachment styles of subjects and partners *interact* to predict relationship quality? That is, does the effect of a partner's attachment style depend on a subject's own attachment style? Studies addressing this issue are further examples of the increasing sophistication of research into adult attachment.

First, an experiment was conducted in which subjects were given a written profile of a hypothetical relationship partner (Pietromonaco & Carnelley, 1994). They were asked to imagine themselves in a relationship with that partner, and to evaluate the partner and the relationship along several dimensions. Subjects' attachment style was assessed with the three-group measure. The hypothetical partner's attachment style was manipulated by varying the content of the profile to reflect either secure, avoidant, or preoccupied behavior, thus allowing the researchers to see how subjects responded to different kinds of partners. As with studies of real couples, relationship evaluations were related to attachment styles of both self and partner, as indicated by reliable main effects. Some measures also showed interactive effects of subjects' own and the hypothetical partner's attachment style. For example, secure subjects reported less positive feelings about relationships with either type of insecure partner; by contrast, insecure subjects (especially avoidant subjects) responded less fa-

vorably to an avoidant partner than to a preoccupied partner.

Second, a recent study of real married couples assessed interactive effects of subjects' own and partners' attachment styles (Feeney, 1994). Couples sampled across the marital life cycle completed measures of attachment (comfort with closeness, anxiety over relationships) and marital satisfaction. For the full sample, satisfaction was related to both subjects' own and partners' attachment dimensions (main effects). Interaction effects were restricted to couples married for 10 years or less. For these couples, wives' anxiety and husbands' comfort jointly affected satisfaction. Specifically, wives' anxiety was linked with husbands' and wives' dissatisfaction only for couples in which the husbands were low in comfort (see Figures 17.2a and 17.2b). By contrast, husbands' anxiety was linked with lower satisfaction for both partners, regardless of wives' comfort (a main effect). It seems that in a more recent marriage, the anxious husband's dependent behavior is destructive, perhaps because it violates the male gender-role stereotype. The anxious wife's dependent behavior (which seems to confirm the female stereotype) may have less harmful effects except when she has a husband

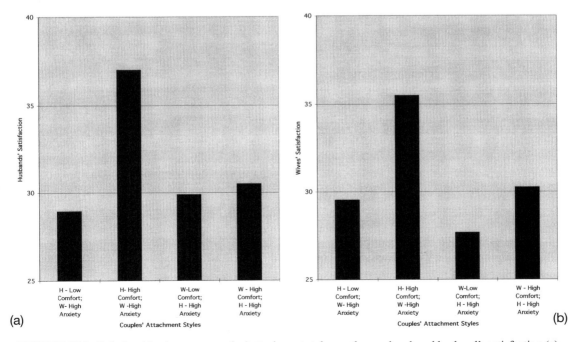

(a)

(b)

FIGURE 17.2. Relationships between couples' attachment styles on the one hand, and husband's satisfaction (a) and wives' satisfaction (b) on the other. H, Husband; W, wife.

who, being uncomfortable with intimacy, fails to provide the support and reassurance she craves. (Recall, however, that many studies of dating couples have found anxiety over relationships to be more problematic in women than in men.)

Relationship Quality: Integrating Attachment, Caregiving, and Sexuality

A comprehensive approach to the study of attachment and relationship quality is provided by Shaver et al. (1988), who have argued that sexuality and caregiving are independent behavioral systems that are integrated with the attachment system in prototypical romantic love. In other words, romantic love involves the three components of attachment, caregiving, and sexuality, with the relative importance of these components following a predictable pattern over time (Hazan & Shaver, 1994). Because the attachment system appears very early in the course of an individual's development, and because it plays a vital role in the formation of working models, the attachment system influences the expression of caregiving and sexuality. Hence the attachment system is viewed as pivotal to the establishment and maintenance of romantic relationships.

What support exists for these propositions? Empirical studies clearly support the separate importance of each of the proposed components of romantic love. We have already discussed the strong link between attachment style and relationship quality. The importance of caregiving in intimate bonds is supported by the finding that marital satisfaction is predicted more strongly by an index of caregiving and care receiving than by measures of personality, health, or material circumstances (Kotler, 1985). Similarly, sexual satisfaction is an acknowledged predictor of relationship quality and stability (Sprecher & McKinney, 1993). Support is also emerging for links between attachment style and each of the other proposed components of love (caregiving and sexuality), as discussed below. Although there appears to be no published empirical work integrating all three components of romantic bonds, such integrative work offers the promise of a comprehensive theory of romantic love.

Attachment and Caregiving

In a study of dating and married couples, Carnelley, Pietromonaco, and Jaffe (1996) assessed the link between attachment style and caregiving, and the implications of these variables for rela-

tionship satisfaction. Attachment style was defined by measures of fearful avoidance and preoccupation, and caregiving was defined in terms of a composite measure of "beneficial care." Subjects' own attachment security was linked with the provision of more beneficial care to romantic partners. Moreover, subjects' own attachment security, partners' attachment security, and partners' provision of beneficial care all contributed to relationship satisfaction.

Additional support for the link between attachment and caregiving comes from the work of Kunce and Shaver (1994). These researchers developed self-report items to assess the quality of caregiving in intimate dyads, based on the infant–caregiver literature. Factor analysis of these items revealed four scales: proximity (vs. distance), sensitivity (vs. insensitivity), cooperation (vs. control), and compulsive caregiving. In a student sample, these scales differentiated attachment groups as defined by a four-group measure. As expected, secure subjects reported high proximity and sensitivity, while dismissing subjects reported low proximity and sensitivity; both these groups reported a lack of compulsive caregiving. Consistent with their need for the approval of others, preoccupied and fearful subjects reported high compulsive caregiving but low sensitivity (Kunce & Shaver, 1994).

Finally, a study using Kunce and Shaver's caregiving measure in a sample of married couples (Feeney, 1996) showed that secure attachment was associated with beneficial caregiving to the spouse. Specifically, high comfort with closeness and low anxiety over relationships were related both to a lack of compulsive care and to more responsive care (a composite of the scales assessing proximity, sensitivity and cooperation). In addition, marital satisfaction was higher for securely attached spouses and for those whose partners reported more responsive caregiving. For husbands, however, the link between partners' caregiving and their own satisfaction was restricted to those in shorter-term marriages and to those high in anxiety over relationships.

Attachment and Sexuality

Support is also emerging for the link between attachment style and sexual attitudes and behaviors. We (Feeney, Noller, & Patty, 1993) found that avoidant individuals had more accepting attitudes toward casual sex than members of other attachment groups did. Similarly, Brennan and

Shaver (1995) found that avoidant individuals were more likely than secure individuals to engage in "one-night stands" and to endorse the idea that sex without love is pleasurable. In a 6-week diary study, however, we (Feeney et al., 1993) found that female avoidant and male ambivalent subjects were the least likely to report engaging in sexual intercourse. This finding suggests that gender and attachment style interact in their effects on sexual behavior. Furthermore, the low level of intercourse reported by female avoidant subjects is surprising, given avoidant individuals' greater acceptance of casual sex; this highlights the need to assess the effects of attachment style on both sexual attitudes and sexual behaviors.

To date, Hazan, Zeifman, and Middleton (1994) have reported the most comprehensive study of the link between attachment and the expression of sexuality. This study employed a sample of 100 adults, who completed measures of attachment style and of the frequency and enjoyment of various sexual behaviors. Three distinct sexual styles were identified, consistent with the three major attachment styles. Secure individuals were less likely to be involved in one-night stands or to have sex outside of the primary relationship, and more likely to be involved in mutually initiated sex and to enjoy physical contact. Avoidant individuals tended to report activities indicative of low psychological intimacy (one-night stands, extrarelationship sex, sex without love), as well as less enjoyment of physical contact. Ambivalent females reported involvement in exhibitionism, voyeurism, and domination/bondage, whereas ambivalent males appeared to be more sexually reticent. For both sexes, ambivalent attachment was associated with enjoyment of holding and caressing, but not of more clearly sexual behaviors.

Attachment Style and Couple Relationships under Stress

What can attachment theory tell us about relationship partners' responses to stress? In infancy, the attachment system organizes the balance between an infant's proximity-seeking and exploratory behavior. When the attachment figure is nearby and the environment is familiar, the infant is likely to engage in exploratory activity. By contrast, when the infant is in a strange or threatening situation, attachment behavior is likely to be evident. Three types of conditions activate infant attachment behavior: conditions in the environment, such as alarming events; conditions within the attachment relationship, such as the caregiver's absence or discouraging of proximity; and conditions of the child, such as hunger and sickness (Bowlby, 1969/1982).

Although some of these specific conditions (e.g., hunger) may elicit attachment behavior only in the helpless infant, the broad typology is relevant to adult behavior. Hence three types of situations are likely to activate attachment behavior in adults: stressful conditions in the social or physical environment; conditions that appear to threaten the future of the attachment relationship; and conditions of the individual, such as ill health. The research discussed below focuses on environmental conditions and conditions threatening close relationships; these two conditions have been studied in the context of couples' attachment relationships and, as we shall see, are relevant to the conceptualization of adult attachment.

Stressful Environmental Conditions

Most of the early research on adult attachment linked attachment style with global evaluations of relationship quality. Such research implies that attachment style influences behavior across a range of settings. This assumption is not contrary to attachment theory; indeed, the robust links identified by these studies point to pervasive differences between attachment groups. Nevertheless, because attachment behavior is likely to be activated under stressful conditions, individual differences in attachment behavior should be most pronounced under these conditions (Simpson & Rholes, 1994; Simpson et al., 1992).

On the basis of this argument, Simpson et al. (1992) investigated the effect of an environmental stressor on attachment behavior in couples. Dating couples took part in a laboratory study in which the female member of each couple was told that she would shortly be exposed to a stressful set of experimental procedures. Couples were unobtrusively videotaped during the alleged "waiting" time, in order to assess the extent to which females turned to their partners for support (support seeking) and the extent to which their partners provided support (support giving). Attachment style was defined in terms of two self-report scales: secure versus avoidant (cf. comfort with closeness) and anxious versus nonanxious (cf. anxiety over relationships). Independent coders rated females' support seeking and males' support giving, as well as females' anxiety in response to the experimental situation.

The key finding to emerge from this study was that support seeking and support giving were jointly influenced by attachment (secure vs. avoidant) and by females' anxiety in response to the stressful situation. For more securely attached women, high levels of observer-rated anxiety were associated with high levels of support seeking; for more avoidant women, high levels of anxiety were associated with physical and emotional withdrawal from partners. Similarly, for more securely attached men, high levels of partner anxiety were associated with high levels of support giving; for more avoidant men, high partner anxiety was associated with low levels of support. These results highlight the need to define the context of interactions when describing the characteristics of particular attachment styles. It is inappropriate, for example, to describe avoidant individuals as cold and distant, if such descriptors apply only to behavior under stressful conditions (Simpson et al., 1992).

Attachment style differences in responses to environmental stress have also been studied in the context of missile attacks occurring in Israel during the Persian Gulf War (Mikulincer, Florian, & Weller, 1993). Secure, avoidant, and ambivalent groups differed in their emotional reactions to the attacks: Both avoidant and ambivalent individuals reported high levels of hostility and psychosomatic symptoms, with the latter group also reporting high levels of anxiety and depression. Attachment groups also differed in the strategies used to cope with the stress. Secure individuals were the most likely to seek support from others; avoidant individuals tended to distance themselves from the threat (by trying to "forget the whole thing"); ambivalent individuals focused on their emotional responses (by wishing they felt differently and criticizing themselves). These results support the proposition that secure attachment is linked with constructive responses to stress, and they highlight the contrasting features of the two major insecure groups.

Conditions Threatening the Attachment Relationship

Researchers have also begun to study how individuals with different attachment styles respond to conditions that they view as threatening their attachment relationships. These conditions include absence or discouraging of proximity on the part of the partner, and relationship conflict.

Cafferty, Medway, O'Hearn, and Chappell (1994) studied reunion dynamics among U.S. couples in which the male spouse was deployed overseas during the Gulf War. Four months after reunion, the men and their wives completed self-report questionnaires assessing attachment style, marital satisfaction, conflict, and affect during reunion. For both deployed men and their wives, secure attachment was associated with higher marital satisfaction and with less postreunion conflict. Preoccupied subjects showed particularly low levels of satisfaction and particularly high levels of conflict. Links between attachment style and affect during reunion were confined to men, for whom secure attachment was related to reports of more positive and less negative affect. The stronger results for affect among the deployed men may reflect the more stressful nature of their separation experience.

A recent study of dating couples related attachment style to responses to separation from partners, and to situations involving partners' discouraging of proximity (Feeney, 1998). This study involved two parts. In the first part, members of the couples independently provided open-ended reports of their experiences of being physically separated from their current partners. Content analyses indicated that secure attachment was associated with less insecurity in response to separation, with more constructive coping strategies, and with the perception that the separation experience had actually strengthened a couple's relationship.

In the second part of the study, couples participated in three conflict-centered interactions. One of these interactions involved conflict over a specific issue (use of leisure time); the other two were designed to elicit attachment-related anxiety by having one partner rebuff the other's attempts to maintain closeness (the role of the distant, discouraging partner was adopted by the male in one interaction, and by the female in the other). Prior to these interactions, participants ("insiders") rated their expectations of their partners' behavior and motives; after each interaction, they rated their own discomfort and own satisfaction with the interaction. From videotapes of the interactions, independent coders ("outsiders") rated participants' affect, nonverbal behavior, and conversation patterns.

In terms of insider ratings, secure attachment was related to positive expectations of partners' behavior and motives, and to less discomfort and greater satisfaction, for both issue-based and relationship-based conflict. In terms of outsider ratings, secure attachment was unrelated to responses to the issue-based conflict, but was linked with less negative affect, less avoidant nonverbal behavior, and more constructive conversation patterns in response to partners' distancing. These results neatly integrate two separate findings reported by previous researchers: Attachment style exerts pervasive effects on *global perceptions* of relationship functioning; at the same time, attachment style differences in *observable behavior* are strongest under conditions that seem to threaten an individual or an attachment relationship.

A recent laboratory study of attachment and relationship conflict in dating couples (Simpson, Rholes, & Phillips, 1996) also employed both insider and outsider data. In this study, more ambivalent men and women reported feeling more distress and hostility during problem-centered discussion. Trained raters (outsiders) rated ambivalent men and women as exhibiting greater anxiety, and avoidant men as engaging in lower-quality interactions. These effects were more pronounced for couple members who were asked to discuss major problems than for those who were asked to discuss minor problems. This result supports the finding (Feeney, 1998) that attachment differences are stronger under conditions that seem to threaten the relationship. Ambivalent men and women who discussed major problems also reported more negative perceptions of the partner/relationship after the discussion than before, and these changes were not mediated by the quality of the discussion. The latter result suggests that these negative perceptions may reflect negative expectations embodied in working models, supporting the assertion that attachment style exerts pervasive effects on perceptions of relationship functioning (Feeney, 1998).

Attachment Style and Relationship Quality: Further Conceptual Issues

The studies discussed above are important conceptually, because they clarify the extent to which attachment style differences emerge in response to stressful situations. A more general conceptual issue is raised by the link between attachment style and relationship quality, evidenced in the studies discussed throughout this chapter. That is, there are at least two ways of conceptualizing attachment style, both of which are consistent with the observed link with relationship quality. On one hand, adult attachment style can be conceptualized as an enduring, trait-like characteristic of an individual that influences functioning in close relationships. On the other hand, it can be conceptualized as reflecting recent relationship experiences—that is, experiences specific to particular relationships.

This question of "traits versus relationships" is addressed by studies of the stability of attachment, described earlier. These studies offer some support for both perspectives. Longitudinal data point to moderately high stability, especially for the more refined measures; indeed, some data suggest that attachment styles are more stable than is relationship status (Kirkpatrick & Hazan, 1994). On the other hand, the link between relationship events and change in attachment style points to the important role of recent relationship experiences in perceptions of attachment security.

It is important to note here that although attachment measures seem to tap relatively enduring individual differences, and although they are linked with personality (Bartholomew & Horowitz, 1991; Collins & Read, 1990; Shaver & Brennan, 1992), attachment style is not redundant with basic dimensions of personality. Relations between measures of attachment style and personality tend to be modest in size. Furthermore, relationship outcomes such as satisfaction and commitment are better predicted by attachment measures than by general personality measures (Shaver & Brennan, 1992).

Most importantly, the "traits versus relationships" question does not involve two mutually exclusive perspectives. Rather, individual characteristics and relationship events are bound up together. By choosing particular partners, individuals are likely to find themselves in situations that confirm their expectations of relationships (Kirkpatrick & Davis, 1994; Kirkpatrick & Hazan, 1994). Supporting the notion that relationship partners are chosen to confirm preexisting expectations, systematic patterns of partner "matching" have been identified by studies of dating and married couples. Secure individuals tend to be paired with secure partners (Collins & Read, 1990; Feeney, 1994; Senchak & Leonard, 1992); involvement with a secure and responsive partner is likely to confirm positive working models of attachment. There is also evidence that an avoidant individual tends to be paired with an ambivalent individual—a pattern likely to confirm each partner's expectations (Kirkpatrick & Davis, 1994).

Of course, patterns of partner matching are not easy to interpret. It is possible that secure individuals are attracted to secure partners, and hence that this "pairing" effect is evident at the earliest stages of relationships. Alternatively, being in an ongoing relationship with a secure individual may help the partner to revise existing negative models of attachment; in this case, the tendency for secure individuals to be paired with other secure individuals may be evident only in established relationships. Researchers have also studied individuals' responses to hypothetical relationship partners of different attachment types (Frazier, Byer, Fischer, Wright, & DeBord, 1996; Pietromonaco & Carnelley, 1994). These studies have produced conflicting findings concerning patterns of partner matching, however, and have limited ecological validity. These issues can be resolved only by longitudinal studies that track participants' attachment styles over the full course of relationship development.

SUMMARY AND FUTURE DIRECTIONS

The proposition that adults' close relationships can be understood in terms of attachment principles has generated immense interest, and as of late 1998, almost 400 authors had cited Hazan and Shaver's (1987) groundbreaking studies. The attachment perspective has important strengths, as Shaver and Hazan (1988) and others (e.g., Clark & Reis, 1988) have noted. Attachment theory addresses a wide range of relationship issues, including anxiety, loneliness, and grief; it enables healthy and unhealthy forms of love to be explained in terms of the same principles; and it is developmental in focus (the concept of working models can account for the continuity of early patterns of relating, as well as for the possibility of change).

Attachment theory seems to be especially useful in addressing certain key issues in the study of close relationships, such as conflict. This theory helps us to understand both the sources of relationship conflict and individual differences in handling conflict. Research suggests that the "anxiety over relationships" dimension of attachment is of particular importance here. Individuals high on this dimension report more relationship conflict, suggesting that much of this conflict is driven by basic insecurities over issues of love, loss, and abandonment. Those who are anxious about their relationships also engage in

coercive and distrusting ways of dealing with conflict, which are likely to bring about the very outcomes they fear most.

The studies discussed in this chapter point to considerable advances within adult attachment research. Methodological developments include the move from categorical to continuous measures, which provide fuller description of attachment patterns, and the development of the four-group model, which is grounded in Bowlby's concept of working models of self and others. Researchers are also increasingly recognizing that different measures of adult attachment are not interchangeable. As noted earlier, the AAI taps "current state of mind with regard to attachment," whereas most other measures assess, in part, the quality of current romantic relationships.

Although many of the romantic attachment studies conducted to date involve correlations among self-report measures, several studies have connected these measures with behavioral ratings (Feeney, Noller, & Callan, 1994; Kobak & Hazan, 1991; Mikulincer & Nachshon, 1991; Simpson et al., 1992), interview and diary-based reports (Feeney & Noller, 1991; Feeney, Noller, & Callan, 1994; Pietromonaco & Barrett, 1997; Tidwell, Reis, & Shaver, 1996), measures of cognitive processing of relational information (Baldwin et al., 1993), relationship outcomes predicted over time (Feeney & Noller, 1992; Shaver & Brennan, 1992), and corroborative reports by friends (Bartholomew & Horowitz, 1991) and partners (Kobak & Hazan, 1991). Furthermore, recent studies have supported specific theory-based predictions concerning the relative strength of association between adult attachment measures and particular behaviors: for example, behavior during discussion of relationship-centered issues versus concrete issues (Feeney, 1998), and behavior during discussion of major versus minor relationship problems (Simpson et al., 1996). These studies are sufficient in number and diversity to indicate that measures of adult romantic attachment do not simply tap a generalized tendency to perceive or report events more or less favorably.

Despite these advances, important questions remain. Controversial questions raised in this chapter include (1) how stable attachment style is, and (2) whether attachment patterns are properties of individuals or of relationships. Resolution of these questions requires longitudinal studies that follow couples over the course of long-term relationships, and, just as importantly, studies that track those individuals who move from relationship to relationship. We are also a long way from understanding the link between children's experiences with their caregivers and the expectations that the children develop of romantic relationships as they mature. It has been argued that whereas the matching between parent and child attachment styles is guided by identification, the matching between romantic partners may reflect self-verification processes (i.e., the tendency to prefer those who confirm expectations of the self in relation to others; see Pietromonaco & Carnelley, 1994). Although this explanation is plausible, it is not clear how or when self-verification processes become relevant to partner matching.

Among the more recent directions in adult attachment research, some stand out as particularly promising. These include longitudinal studies of attachment across several generations, using interview and observational methods (Jacobvitz & Burton, 1994), and studies of the cognitive processes associated with working models (Baldwin et al., 1993; Mikulincer, 1995). Initiatives such as these are likely to broaden the contribution made by the attachment perspective on close relationships.

REFERENCES

Ainsworth, M. D. S. (1989). Attachments beyond infancy. *American Psychologist, 44,* 709–716.

Baldwin, M. W., & Fehr, B. (1995). On the instability of attachment style ratings. *Personal Relationships, 2,* 247–261.

Baldwin, M. W., Fehr, B., Keedian, E., Seidel, M., & Thomson, D. W. (1993). An exploration of the relational schemata underlying attachment styles: Self-report and lexical decision approaches. *Personality and Social Psychology Bulletin, 19,* 746–754.

Bartholomew, K. (1990). Avoidance of intimacy: An attachment perspective. *Journal of Social and Personal Relationships, 7,* 147–178.

Bartholomew, K., & Horowitz, L. M. (1991). Attachment styles among young adults: A test of a four-category model. *Journal of Personality and Social Psychology, 61,* 226–244.

Bartholomew, K., & Shaver, P. R. (1998). Methods of assessing adult attachment: Do they converge? In J. A. Simpson & W. S. Rholes (Eds.), *Attachment theory and close relationships* (pp. 25–45). New York: Guilford Press.

Belsky, J., & Cassidy, J. (1994). Attachment and close relationships: An individual-difference perspective. *Psychological Inquiry, 5,* 27–30.

Bowlby, J. (1969/1982). *Attachment and loss: Vol. 1. Attachment.* New York: Basic Books.

Bowlby, J. (1973). *Attachment and loss: Vol. 2. Separation: Anxiety and anger.* New York: Basic Books.

Bowlby, J. (1980). *Attachment and loss: Vol. 3. Loss.* New York: Basic Books.

Brennan, K. A., Clark, C. L., & Shaver, P. R. (1998). Self-report measurement of adult attachment: An integrative overview. In J. A. Simpson & W. S. Rholes (Eds.), *Attachment theory and close relationships* (pp. 46–76). New York: Guilford Press.

Brennan, K. A., & Shaver, P. R. (1995). Dimensions of adult attachment, affect regulation, and romantic relationship functioning. *Personality and Social Psychology Bulletin, 21,* 267–283.

Brennan, K. A., Shaver, P. R., & Tobey, A. E. (1991). Attachment styles, gender, and parental problem drinking. *Journal of Social and Personal Relationships, 8,* 451–466.

Bretherton, I. (1987). New perspectives on attachment relations: Security, communication, and internal working models. In J. D. Osofsky (Ed.), *Handbook of infant development* (2nd ed., pp. 1061–1100). New York: Wiley.

Bretherton, I. (1990). Open communication and internal working models: Their role in the development of attachment relationships. In R. A. Thompson (Ed.), *Nebraska Symposium on Motivation: Vol. 36. Socioemotional development* (pp. 59–113). Lincoln: University of Nebraska Press.

Bretherton, I. (1991). Pouring new wine into old bottles: The social self as internal working model. In M. R. Gunnar & L. A. Sroufe (Eds.), *Minnesota Symposia on Child Psychology: Vol. 23. Self processes in development* (pp. 1–41). Hillsdale, NJ: Erlbaum.

Cafferty, T. P., Davis, K. E., Medway, F. J., O'Hearn, R. E., & Chappell, K. D. (1994). Reunion dynamics among couples separated during Operation Desert Storm: An attachment theory analysis. In K. Bartholomew & D. Perlman (Eds.), *Advances in personal relationships: Vol. 5. Attachment processes in adulthood* (pp. 309–330). London: Jessica Kingsley.

Carnelley, K. B., Pietromonaco, P. R., & Jaffe, K. (1996). Attachment, caregiving, and relationship functioning in couples: Effects of self and partner. *Personal Relationships, 3,* 257–277.

Clark, M. S., & Reis, H. T. (1988). Interpersonal processes in close relationships. *Annual Review of Psychology, 39,* 609–672.

Cohn, D. A., Silver, D. H., Cowan, C. P., Cowan, P. A., & Pearson, J. (1992). Working models of childhood attachment and couple relationships. *Journal of Family Issues, 13,* 432–449.

Collins, N. L. (1996). Working models of attachment: Implications for explanation, emotion, and behavior. *Journal of Personality and Social Psychology, 71,* 810–832.

Collins, N. L., & Read, S. J. (1990). Adult attachment, working models, and relationship quality in dating couples. *Journal of Personality and Social Psychology, 58,* 644–663.

Collins, N. L., & Read, S. J. (1994). Cognitive representations of attachment: The structure and function of working models. In K. Bartholomew & D. Perlman (Eds.), *Advances in personal relationships: Vol. 5. Attachment processes in adulthood* (pp. 53–90). London: Jessica Kingsley.

Crittenden, P. (1985). Social networks, quality of child-rearing, and child development. *Child Development, 56,* 1299–1313.

Feeney, J. A. (1994). Attachment style, communication patterns, and satisfaction across the life cycle of marriage. *Personal Relationships, 1,* 333–348.

Feeney, J. A. (1995). Adult attachment and emotional control. *Personal Relationships, 2,* 143–159.

Feeney, J. A. (1996). Attachment, caregiving, and marital satisfaction. *Personal Relationships, 3,* 401–416.

Feeney, J. A. (1998). Adult attachment and relationship-centered anxiety: Responses to physical and emotional distancing. In J. A. Simpson & W. S. Rholes (Eds.), *Attachment theory and close relationships* (pp. 189–218). New York: Guilford Press.

Feeney, J. A., & Noller, P. (1990). Attachment style as a predictor of adult romantic relationships. *Journal of Personality and Social Psychology, 58,* 281–291.

Feeney, J. A., & Noller, P. (1991). Attachment style and verbal descriptions of romantic partners. *Journal of Social and Personal Relationships, 8,* 187–215.

Feeney, J. A., & Noller, P. (1992). Attachment style and romantic love: Relationship dissolution. *Australian Journal of Psychology, 44,* 69–74.

Feeney, J. A., Noller, P., & Callan, V. J. (1994). Attachment style, communication and satisfaction in the early years of marriage. In K. Bartholomew & D. Perlman (Eds.), *Advances in personal relationships: Vol. 5. Attachment processes in adulthood* (pp. 269–308). London: Jessica Kingsley.

Feeney, J. A., Noller, P., & Hanrahan, M. (1994). Assessing adult attachment: Developments in the conceptualization of security and insecurity. In M. B. Sperling & W. H. Berman (Eds.), *Attachment in adults: Clinical and developmental perspectives* (pp. 128–152). New York: Guilford Press.

Feeney, J. A., Noller, P., & Patty, J. (1993). Adolescents' interactions with the opposite sex: Influence of attachment style and gender. *Journal of Adolescence, 16,* 169–186.

Fraley, R. C., Davis, K. E., & Shaver, P. R. (1998). Dismissing-avoidance and the defensive organization of emotion, cognition, and behavior. In J. A. Simpson & W. S. Rholes (Eds.), *Attachment theory and close relationships* (pp. 249–279). New York: Guilford Press.

Frazier, P. A., Byer, A. L., Fischer, A. R., Wright, D. M., & DeBord, K. A. (1996). Adult attachment style and partner choice: Correlational and experimental findings. *Personal Relationships, 3,* 117–136.

George, C., Kaplan, N., & Main, M. (1985). *Adult Attachment Interview* (2nd ed.). Unpublished manuscript, University of California at Berkeley.

Hammond, J. R., & Fletcher, G. J. O. (1991). Attachment styles and relationship satisfaction in the development of close relationships. *New Zealand Journal of Psychology, 20,* 56–62.

Hazan, C., & Shaver, P. R. (1987). Romantic love conceptualized as an attachment process. *Journal of Personality and Social Psychology, 52,* 511–524.

Hazan, C., & Shaver, P. R. (1994). Attachment as an organizational framework for research on close relationships. *Psychological Inquiry, 5,* 1–22.

Hazan, C., Zeifman, D., & Middleton, K. (1994, July). *Adult romantic attachment, affection, and sex.* Paper presented at the 7th International Conference on Personal Relationships, Groningen, The Netherlands.

Jacobvitz, D. B., & Burton, H. (1994, July). *Attachment processes in mother–child relationships across generations.* Paper presented at the 7th International Conference on Personal Relationships, Groningen, The Netherlands.

Keelan, J. P. R., Dion, K. K., & Dion, K. L. (1998). Attachment style and relationship satisfaction: Test of a self-disclosure explanation. *Canadian Journal of Behavioural Science, 30,* 24–35.

Kirkpatrick, L. A., & Davis, K. E. (1994). Attachment style, gender, and relationship stability: A longitudinal analysis.

Journal of Personality and Social Psychology, 66, 502–512.

Kirkpatrick, L. E., & Hazan, C. (1994). Attachment styles and close relationships: A four-year prospective study. *Personal Relationships, 1,* 123–142.

Kobak, R. R., & Duemmler, S. (1994). Attachment and conversation: Toward a discourse analysis of adolescent and adult security. In K. Bartholomew & D. Perlman (Eds.), *Advances in personal relationships: Vol. 5. Attachment processes in adulthood* (pp. 121–149). London: Jessica Kingsley.

Kobak, R. R., & Hazan, C. (1991). Attachment in marriage: Effects of security and accuracy of working models. *Journal of Personality and Social Psychology, 60,* 861–869.

Kobak, R. R., & Sceery, A. (1988). Attachment in late adolescence: Working models, affect regulation, and representations of self and others. *Child Development, 59,* 135–146.

Kotler, T. (1985). Security and autonomy within marriage. *Human Relations, 38,* 299–321.

Kunce, L. J., & Shaver, P. R. (1994). An attachment-theoretical approach to caregiving in romantic relationships. In K. Bartholomew & D. Perlman (Eds.), *Advances in personal relationships: Vol. 5. Attachment processes in adulthood* (pp. 205–237). London: Jessica Kingsley.

Lee, J. A. (1973). *The colors of love: An exploration of the ways of loving.* Toronto: New Press.

Lee, J. A. (1988). Love-styles. In R. J. Sternberg & M. Barnes (Eds.), *The psychology of love* (pp. 38–67). New Haven, CT: Yale University Press.

Levy, M. B., & Davis, K. E. (1988). Lovestyles and attachment styles compared: Their relations to each other and to various relationship characteristics. *Journal of Social and Personal Relationships, 5,* 439–471.

Main, M., & Goldwyn, R. (1985). *Adult Attachment Classification System.* Unpublished manuscript, University of California at Berkeley.

Mikulincer, M. (1995). Attachment style and the mental representation of the self. *Journal of Personality and Social Psychology, 69,* 1203–1215.

Mikulincer, M., Florian, V., & Weller, A. (1993). Attachment styles, coping strategies, and posttraumatic psychological distress: The impact of the Gulf War in Israel. *Journal of Personality and Social Psychology, 64,* 817–826.

Mikulincer, M., & Nachshon, O. (1991). Attachment styles and patterns of self-disclosure. *Journal of Personality and Social Psychology, 61,* 321–331.

Pietromonaco, P. R., & Barrett, L. F. (1997). Working models of attachment and daily social interactions. *Journal of Personality and Social Psychology, 73,* 1409–1423.

Pietromonaco, P. R., & Carnelley, K. B. (1994). Gender and working models of attachment: Consequences for perceptions of self and romantic relationships. *Personal Relationships, 1,* 63–82.

Pistole, M. C. (1989). Attachment in adult romantic relationships: Style of conflict resolution and relationship satisfaction. *Journal of Social and Personal Relationships, 6,* 505–510.

Rothbard, J. C., & Shaver, P. R. (1994). Continuity of attachment across the life span. In M. B. Sperling & W. H. Berman (Eds.), *Attachment in adults: Clinical and developmental perspectives* (pp. 31–71). New York: Guilford Press.

Scharfe, E., & Bartholomew, K. (1994). Reliability and stability of adult attachment patterns. *Personal Relationships, 1,* 23–43.

Senchak, M., & Leonard, K. E. (1992). Attachment styles and marital adjustment among newlywed couples. *Journal of Social and Personal Relationships, 9,* 51–64.

Shaver, P. R., & Brennan, K. A. (1992). Attachment styles and the "Big Five" personality traits: Their connections with each other and with romantic relationship outcomes. *Personality and Social Psychology Bulletin, 18,* 536–545.

Shaver, P. R., & Hazan, C. (1988). A biased overview of the study of love. *Journal of Social and Personal Relationships, 5,* 473–501.

Shaver, P. R., Hazan, C., & Bradshaw, D. (1988). Love as attachment: The integration of three behavioral systems. In R. J. Sternberg & M. Barnes (Eds.), *The psychology of love* (pp. 68–99). New Haven, CT: Yale University Press.

Simpson, J. A. (1990). Influence of attachment styles on romantic relationships. *Journal of Personality and Social Psychology, 59,* 971–980.

Simpson, J. A., & Rholes, W. S. (1994). Stress and secure base relationships in adulthood. In K. Bartholomew & D. Perlman (Eds.), *Advances in personal relationships: Vol. 5. Attachment processes in adulthood* (pp. 181–204). London: Jessica Kingsley.

Simpson, J. A., Rholes, W. S., & Nelligan, J. S. (1992). Support seeking and support giving within couples in an anxiety-provoking situation: The role of attachment styles. *Journal of Personality and Social Psychology, 62,* 434–446.

Simpson, J. A., Rholes, W. S., & Phillips, D. (1996). Conflict in close relationships: An attachment perspective. *Journal of Personality and Social Psychology, 71,* 899–914.

Sprecher, S., & McKinney, K. (1993). *Sexuality.* Newbury Park, CA: Sage.

Sternberg, R. J. (1986). A triangular theory of love. *Psychological Review, 93,* 119–135.

Strahan, B. J. (1991). Attachment theory and family functioning: Expectations and congruencies. *Australian Journal of Marriage and Family, 12,* 12–26.

Tidwell, M. O., Reis, H. T., & Shaver, P. R. (1996). Attachment, attractiveness, and social interaction: A diary study. *Journal of Personality and Social Psychology, 71,* 729–745.

Weiss, R. S. (1982). Attachment in adult life. In C. M. Parkes & J. Stevenson-Hinde (Eds.), *The place of attachment in human behavior* (pp. 171–184). New York: Basic Books.

Weiss, R. S. (1986). Continuities and transformations in social relationships from childhood to adulthood. In W. W. Hartup & Z. Rubin (Eds.), *Relationships and development* (pp. 95–110). Hillsdale, NJ: Erlbaum.

Weiss, R. S. (1991). The attachment bond in childhood and adulthood. In C. M. Parkes, J. Stevenson-Hinde, & P. Marris (Eds.), *Attachment across the life cycle* (pp. 66–76). London: Tavistock/Routledge.

18

Same-Sex Romantic Attachment

❖

JONATHAN J. MOHR

Without warning
as a whirlwind
swoops on an oak
love shakes my heart
—Sappho

Same-sex romantic relationships appear to have existed in most cultures throughout recorded history, regardless of prevailing attitudes toward homosexuality and bisexuality (Boswell, 1994; Greenberg, 1988). Despite popular opinions that same-sex couples are less stable, satisfied, and committed than their heterosexual counterparts (Herek, 1991b; Peplau, 1991), the emerging empirical literature on lesbian and gay male relationships provides strong evidence that this is not the case. Indeed, research to date has indicated that the similarities between opposite-sex and same-sex relationships far outweigh the differences (Kurdek, 1995; Peplau, 1993).

The study of same-sex couples has evolved over the past two decades from an early emphasis on atheoretical, descriptive research to a more recent focus on the application of theories that were originally developed to explain opposite-sex relationship functioning (Kurdek, 1995). A steadily growing body of research has shown that current frameworks for understanding intimate relationship functioning, such as those offered by the interdependence, contextual, and problem-solving models, may be profitably applied to the study of both same-sex and opposite-sex couples (Kurdek, 1991a, 1997).

This chapter provides a basis for applying Bowlby's theory of attachment to same-sex love relationships. Although attachment researchers initially focused on the infant–caregiver bond, the past decade has witnessed a tremendous growth in the number of studies using attachment theory as a framework for investigating adult romantic relationships (see Feeney, Chapter 17, this volume). This research has shown not only that romantic love may be profitably conceptualized as part of an attachment-related process, but that many aspects of relationship functioning can be reliably predicted by differences in the ways individuals internally represent their attachment relationships (i.e., differences in their working models of attachment). For example, studies have shown that positive working models of self and other are related to a wide variety of adaptive relationship behaviors, including effective conflict resolution (Pistole, 1989; Simpson, Rholes, & Phillips, 1996), support seeking and giving (Kunce & Shaver, 1994; Simpson, Rholes, & Nelligan, 1992), positive communication (Feeney, Noller, & Callan, 1994), and joint problem solving (Kobak & Hazan, 1991).

The vast majority of work on adult romantic attachment has focused on opposite-sex relationships. Only a small handful of papers have acknowledged the potential relevance of attachment theory to lesbian, gay male, and bisexual

(LGB) people (e.g., Ainsworth, 1985; Feeney & Raphael, 1992), and even fewer have included empirical investigations focusing on this population (e.g., Mohr & Fassinger, 1998). Conducting research with opposite-sex couples may be less challenging (e.g., may require less effort in recruiting participants) and less controversial (i.e., more societally acceptable) than research with same-sex couples; however, the inclusion of same-sex partnerships in attachment research may lead to a broader understanding of adult attachment processes. For example, the study of same-sex attachments may help to illuminate ways in which gender and attachment interact in the dynamics of relationship functioning. Furthermore, relationship difficulties associated with the pervasive societal intolerance for same-sex partnerships (Brown, 1995; Hancock, 1995) may provide an opportunity to understand the role of attachment in how couples manage chronic stress and stigma. Finally, strong arguments have been made concerning the ethical importance of including LGB individuals in mainstream psychological research (Herek, Kimmel, Amaro, & Melton, 1991).

This chapter first explores the evolutionary basis for same-sex attraction and provides an argument for the relevance of the attachment system for LGB adults. The current empirical literature on same-sex couples is then reviewed, with an emphasis on results suggestive of attachment-related processes. Finally, Bowlby's work on fear and loss is used to illustrate ways in which the study of same-sex couples may provide fertile ground for the exploration of questions about the points of intersection between contextual and intrapersonal forces.

EVOLUTION AND SAME-SEX ATTACHMENT

Perhaps one of the cleverest challenges to confront evolutionary theory is homosexuality. Homosexuality seems to be a tailor-made rebuttal of the great evolutionary credo—survival of the fittest. How do we explain what is often a lifelong preference for nonreproductive sex?

—McKnight (1997, p. x)

At the core of Bowlby's theory is the idea that the human propensity for establishing affectional bonds is adaptive from an evolutionary perspective (Bowlby, 1969/1982; Simpson, Chapter 6, this volume). The infant–caregiver bond, the ro-

mantic partnership, and the close friendship all ultimately serve to enhance reproductive success. It is perhaps easiest to intuitively understand the adaptive value of the infant–caregiver bond. In the environment of early humans, the chances of survival were greatest for those infants who were predisposed to engage in behaviors that ensured proximity to their caregivers, so that the caregivers would be in a good position to protect them from natural threats (e.g., attack from predators, drowning). The attachment system has evolved to be activated most strongly in the situations that are potentially most threatening to an infant's well-being, such as lack of proximity to caregivers, presence of strangers, strange surroundings, and weakened infant state. Bowlby (1969/1982) offered evidence of this phenomenon in humans, nonhuman primates, and other animals (e.g., lambs and deer). From an evolutionary perspective, the survival of the infant is in the best interests of both the infant and his or her parents, because they all have a stake in passing along their genes. This explains the proposed survival advantage that has been accorded to parents with a readily activated caregiving system. Parents with a predisposition to maintain proximity to their infants and to respond readily to their infants' attachment behaviors are thought to have been more likely to have children who would survive into adulthood and pass along the parents' genes.

To a great extent, our reproductive advantage as humans is a function of lifespan. The longer we live, the more chances we have to reproduce and raise our children into their healthy adulthood, and to provide care for our children's children. The longer we live, the more opportunities we have to offer help to our kin and thus to support another venue for the survival of our genetic code. From this viewpoint, attachment relationships in adulthood may serve the same adaptive function that they do in infancy. West and Sheldon-Keller (1994) argued that the "function of attachment, the provision of safety and security, remains constant throughout the life span, although the mechanisms of achieving this function change and develop with maturation" (p. 22). Thus, from an attachment perspective, romantic attachments provide adults with reliable relationships upon which they can depend for protection, care, and support during times of greatest need (e.g., sickness, economic hardship, violent attack). The establishment of stable romantic attachments may then increase the likelihood of surviving into old age and enjoying the reproductive advantage that this affords. Further-more, the reciprocal attachments that character-ize adult romantic relationships may serve to dis-courage dissolution and thus provide a more secure environment for children (see Simpson, Chapter 6, this volume).

The existence of same-sex romantic relation-ships has long posed a vexing problem for evolu-tionary theorists. As one writer has put it, "Ho-mosexuals were with us through antiquity and, if recent history is any guide, are a robust minority within society. So why hasn't male homosexuali-ty died out as a less reproductive strain of hu-manity?" (McKnight, 1997, p. 1). Some of the earliest uses of evolutionary theory to address same-sex attractions appeared in the medical lit-erature of the late 19th century (Gibson, 1997). At that time, a common explanation for mental disorders was degeneration theory, which pro-posed that weakness of the nervous system caused individuals to be especially vulnerable to the primitive impulses constituting our evolu-tionary legacy. Individuals unable to resist the "beast within" were thought to fall several notch-es on the evolutionary ladder. Homosexuality was almost always viewed as a form of degenera-tion in which the original "bi-sexuality of the an-cestors of the race, shown in the rudimentary fe-male organs of the male, could not fail to occasion functional, if not organic, reversions when mental or physical manifestations were in-terfered with by disease or congenital defect" (Kiernan, 1888, quoted in Gibson, 1997, p. 115). Although such reversions were viewed in quite negative terms (and, as demonstrated below, were often linked with masturbation), some doctors recognized the existence of genuine romantic at-tachments between members of the same sex:

> [Sexual perversions are] frequently produced on the neurotic soil of the male and female masturbator. The female masturbator of this type usually be-comes excessively prudish, despises and hates the opposite sex, and frequently forms a furious attach-ment for another woman, to whom she unselfishly devotes herself. (Kiernan, 1888, quoted in Gibson, 1997, p. 116)

It is likely that this form of "furious" attach-ment was no more intense than those exhibited in 19th century heterosexual love relationships. By focusing on same-sex love as a form of deviant sexuality, doctors were unable to recognize that such love was much more than a pitiable and loathsome expression of primitive sexual in-stincts. Although the outdated language of this

example may make its absurdity evident, one does not need to look far to find similar exam-ples from our own time. For example, it is not uncommon for same-sex couples today to be ac-cused of flaunting their sexuality when exhibit-ing normal attachment or courting behavior, such as holding hands in public (Herek, 1991a).

Bowlby also discussed homosexuality from an evolutionary perspective, but his thinking was markedly different from that of the degeneration theorists. Whereas 19th century doctors viewed same-sex attraction as a lapse into brutish and uncivilized instinctive behavior, Bowlby ap-peared to think of homosexuality as the product of an efficient but functionally ineffective behav-ioral apparatus. In the first volume of his trilogy, he observed that the sexual behavioral system in same-sex dyads works perfectly well, in that the predictable outcome of orgasm is routinely achieved (Bowlby, 1969/1982). The puzzle, ac-cording to Bowlby, is in why the sexual system would ever be organized in a way that runs ex-plicitly counter to intuitive notions of reproduc-tive fitness. "What makes it [same-sex attraction] functionally ineffective is that for some reason the system has developed in such a way that its predictable outcome is unrelated to function" (pp. 130–131). He illustrated this notion of mis-guided behavior by comparing homosexual sex to an antiaircraft gun that works perfectly, except that it consistently destroys friendly planes rather than enemy ones. This analogy may lack appeal for individuals in same-sex relationships, but it serves to convey Bowlby's idea that the sexual behavioral system of homosexuals is not serving its functional goal of reproduction.

Although Bowlby clearly saw homosexual de-sire as evidence of a functional mistake in the evolutionary sense, his limited discussion of the topic at no time denied that legitimate, psycho-logically healthy same-sex romantic attachments exist. Indeed, his writings about homosexual be-havior in a variety of animals primarily reveal his curiosity about the degree to which the sexual behavioral system is environmentally labile. He did not explicitly discuss same-sex couples, but it is likely that he would view their relationships as subject to the same psychological principles as opposite-sex romantic attachment relationships. Bowlby maintained that the attachment behav-ioral system is active from "the cradle to the grave" (1988, p. 82), and he never gave any indi-cation that he believed this to be true only for in-dividuals in opposite-sex couples. Ainsworth, Bowlby's collaborative partner, noted that same-sex romantic attachments are likely to function in the same manner as opposite-sex attachments (Ainsworth, 1985). She stated that one of the main differences between these two types of romantic attachment is that only one of them (i.e., opposite-sex attachment) is societally sanctioned. This observation points to the importance of context in the development of attachment bonds—a topic discussed later in this chapter.

Bowlby's (1969/1982) discussion of homosexuality was based upon his initial understanding of evolutionary theory, which was not informed by the currently accepted notion that evolutionary success is focused on the survival of the gene (Dawkins, 1976; Kirkpatrick, 1998). As noted below, evolutionary theorists have described possible scenarios wherein homosexuality contributes to reproductive fitness even when lesbians and gay men do not have children themselves.

Within the past several decades, a number of interesting and controversial propositions have been made regarding the evolutionary basis of homosexuality (McKnight, 1997), and these have been met with strident opposition and critique (Dickemann, 1995; McKnight, 1997; Weinrich, 1995). If homosexuality is indeed "one of the cleverest challenges to confront evolutionary theory" (McKnight, 1997, p. 1), then it is not surprising that attempts to explain it in terms of reproductive fitness have created such controversy. Bowlby himself noted that the "task of determining precisely what the function of a certain piece of instinctive behavior is may be considerable" (Bowlby, 1969/1982, p. 133). A complete discussion of recent evolutionary theories of homosexuality is beyond the scope of this chapter, but a few of the most notable theories are mentioned here.

Evolutionary theorists, faced with the problem of explaining the continued appearance of same-sex attraction throughout history, have assumed that there is a genetic component to homosexuality and bisexuality. Although many specific theories have been advanced to address this problem, a number of them come down to the proposition that "gay genes" offer a direct reproductive advantage to women and men who engage in heterosexual relations. Hutchinson (1959) was one the first theorists to offer a scientifically grounded discussion of this possibility (McKnight, 1997). He applied then-current ideas about the adaptive value of the sickle-cell mutation prevalent in some African and Asian populations to evolutionary explanations of homosexuality. The

sickle-cell mutation was found to increase resistance to malaria. Although homozygous sickle-cell children (i.e., children with two sickle-cell genes) exhibited strong resistance to malaria, they would often die of severe anemia before reaching puberty. Heterozygous children (i.e., children with one sickle-cell gene and one "normal" gene) would gain a measure of protection from malaria, but would not develop the lethal anemia. These children thus had an advantage over both the children with two sickle-cell genes and those with two "normal" genes; such an advantage is called "heterozygous superior fitness."

The argument regarding homosexuality runs along similar lines, although little consensus exists regarding the ways in which a "gay gene" may contribute to evolutionary success. Theories regarding the reproductive advantages afforded by gay genetic material include the ideas that the genes are linked to (1) greater male sex drive; (2) greater female sex drive (i.e., the so-called "overloving effect"; Hamer & Copeland, 1994); and (3) traits such as charm, empathy, and intelligence that are attractive to females (McKnight, 1997). Another popular theory is that male homosexuality is somehow linked to a genetic predisposition for kin-selective altruism, although most variants of this theory do not appear to stand up to rigorous inspection (McKnight, 1997). According to one version of the kin-selective hypothesis, males with the gay gene instinctively feel at a reproductive disadvantage and decide to divert their energies into supporting the reproductive fitness of close family members (Dickemann, 1995; Salais & Fischer, 1995; Wilson, 1975). Some scientists have suggested that homosexuality is the by-product of a hypervariable mutation in the X chromosome that serves as part of a larger process of ensuring species variability (Hamer & Copeland, 1994). Observational studies of nonhuman primates have shown that sexual interactions between members of the same sex are as enduring as those between members of the opposite sexes (Pavelka, 1995). Evolutionary explanations of this phenomenon include arguments that same-sex attractions may serve to reduce tension, form coalitions, reduce mating competition, and control the population.

Despite uncertainty regarding the reproductive advantages associated with the hypothesized "gay gene," many evolutionary theorists agree on the mechanisms that maintain this material in the gene pool (McKnight, 1997). A form of natural selection called "balance selection" is thought to favor a heterozygous genetic blend, in which men and women possess some homosexual genetic material, but not so much that they will favor homosexual relationships. Balance selection acts to harmonize the forces of "diversifying selection," which works to create great variation in the genetic code related to sexual orientation, and "directional selection," which works to flush out genes of lesser overall adaptive value (i.e., homosexual genes). The existence of a continuum of sexual preference among humans is considered to be evidence of diversifying selection, whereas the greater number of heterosexual partnerships compared to same-sex partnerships is taken as evidence of directional selection (McKnight, 1997). According to this general approach, evolution performs a balancing act in which so-called "gay genes" are actively maintained in the gene pool, while minimizing the extent to which individuals engage in exclusively same-sex sexual behavior. It is interesting to note that some theorists contend that negative attitudes toward homosexuals are an expression of directional natural selection in the social-evolutionary sphere (Gallup, 1993).

Most evolutionary theories of same-sex attraction tend to focus on the sexual behavioral system and do not explicitly address the formation of same-sex romantic attachments. What is clear from studies of love, satisfaction, and commitment, however, is that adult same-sex romantic attachments exist (Kurdek, 1995; Peplau, 1993).[1] Although such attachments may be the by-products of functional mistakes in the evolutionary sense (Bowlby, 1969/1982), no evidence exists to suggest that same-sex romantic attachments function in inherently different ways than their opposite-sex counterparts do (Mohr & Fassinger, 1997). Regardless of the true evolutionary significance of same-sex attractions, it is apparent that LGB individuals have made important contributions to their families, to their communities, and to society. The attachment system offers these individuals the capacity to enjoy greater safety and security through intimate bonds, and thus to increase their chances of surviving into old age and making contributions to others' lives over time. Also, given the great variability in sexual behavior among LGB-identified individuals, as well as recent developments in artificial insemination and family structures, significant numbers of LGB people have children (Patterson, 1995). Thus same-sex romantic attachments may also increase individuals' ability to provide for their children, as appears to be the case for opposite-sex romantic attachments (Weiss, 1982).

Charles Darwin may not have guessed how long same-sex attractions would remain a mystery when he wrote, "We do not even in the least know the final cause of sexuality: The whole subject is hidden in darkness" (Darwin, quoted in Rosario, 1997, p. 9). Although the evolutionary significance of sexual orientation is still "hidden in darkness," there appears to be no reason to assume that same-sex romantic attachments operate according to a set of different principles (e.g., set goals, functions) than those operating in heterosexual attachments. The remainder of this chapter, then, applies current knowledge regarding heterosexual romantic attachment to male and female same-sex couples.

ATTACHMENT AND SAME-SEX RELATIONSHIP QUALITY

We have been together 40 years and in these 40 years we were waiting for this.
      —Danish citizen Eigel Axgil, 67
      (as quoted by Rule, 1989, p. A8),
      who married Axel Axgil, 74, in
      1989. (They were the first
      officially registered same-sex
      couple in modern history.)

Perhaps the most remarkable feature of the modern same-sex romantic partnership is its resilience in the face of widespread societal condemnation. Recent battles over the legalization of same-sex marriage in the United States have made it eminently clear that same-sex couples are still faced with pervasive stigma, discrimination, and challenges to their legitimacy (Eskridge, 1996). In spite of this hostile climate, many LGB individuals manage to forge long-term intimate relationships (Kurdek, 1995) and to enjoy the sense of security afforded by growing older with a person who is invested in one's well-being over time (Friend, 1991).

The study of romantic relationships from an attachment perspective was stimulated by the seminal work of Hazan and Shaver (1987; Shaver & Hazan, 1988), who demonstrated that the patterns of attachment found in studies of infant behavior could be profitably applied to investigations of adult love experiences. They explored individual differences in romantic attachment by translating the infant typology developed by Ainsworth, Blehar, Waters, and Wall (1978) into terms meaningful for adult relationships. Consistent with the literature on infant attachment, Hazan and Shaver defined three styles of attachment: one secure and two insecure. "Secure" romantic attachment was characterized by comfort with closeness and interdependence with one's partner, as well as by low levels of fear of being abandoned by one's partner. "Avoidance" was predominantly characterized by discomfort with closeness and interdependence, whereas "anxious-ambivalence" was defined by high levels of abandonment anxiety, desire to merge with one's partner, and chronic frustration with a lack of closeness. In this chapter the terms "avoidance" and "discomfort with closeness" are used interchangeably, as are the terms "anxious-ambivalence," "anxiety over relationships," and "abandonment anxiety."

Individuals who rely upon avoidant strategies are thought to minimize their attachment needs due to expectations of rebuff or rejection by romantic partners, especially in times of stress. Anxious-ambivalent strategies are conceptualized as a hyperactivation of the attachment system, in which one's expression of and vulnerability to distress are exaggerated in order to gain the attention of partners who are believed to be inconsistently available (Simpson & Rholes, 1994). A sizable body of research indicates the relevance of these attachment patterns and strategies in predicting indices of relationship quality such as satisfaction and commitment (e.g., Collins & Read, 1990; Hazan & Shaver, 1987; Kirkpatrick & Davis, 1994), as well as secure-base behavior in stressful situations (e.g., Crowell, Gao, Treboux, & Owens, 1997; Simpson et al., 1992, 1996).

As mentioned earlier, little empirical work on same-sex couples has been done from a perspective that is explicitly grounded in attachment theory. A careful reading of past research on same-sex couples, however, finds support for hypotheses that are in line with an attachment perspective. For example, Kurdek and Schmitt (1986) found that individuals in male and female same-sex couples and in opposite-sex couples reported similar levels of dyadic attachment (i.e., valuing dyadic interaction). Dyadic attachment predicted relationship satisfaction, love for partner, and liking of partner for all three types of couples. From the perspective of attachment theory, valuing dyadic attachment indicates an absence of the avoidant tendency to deny needs for closeness. Thus Kurdek and Schmitt's finding suggests that avoidance is inversely associated with reports of relationship quality, which

matches results found in research on opposite-sex couples (e.g., Collins & Read, 1990). Relationship satisfaction and commitment in same-sex couples have been linked to a number of other variables indicative of positive working models of attachment, including capacity for interdependence (Schreurs & Buunk, 1996), few dysfunctional relationship beliefs (Kurdek, 1991a), expressiveness (Kurdek, 1991a), neuroticism (Kurdek, 1997), and verbal and emotional intimacy (Deenen, Gijs, & van Naerssen, 1994).

Studies of conflict in same-sex couples provide further indirect evidence for the role of attachment in relationship quality. For example, Kurdek (1991a) found that members of same-sex couples who used withdrawal as a conflict resolution strategy also tended to be less verbally expressive and to report fewer investments in the relationship. One explanation of this finding is that such individuals draw heavily upon avoidant attachment strategies. Avoidance has been linked to withdrawal in stressful situations (Simpson et al., 1992), as well as to reports of low relationship investment (Pistole, Clark, & Tubbs, 1995). Kurdek (1991a) also found that individuals who frequently complied with their same-sex partners' demands in conflictual situations tended to have negative relationship beliefs and to report high costs to remaining in the relationship. This pattern of compliance and negative beliefs has been shown to be connected to an ambivalent style of attachment organization in members of opposite-sex couples. For example, Pistole (1989) found that ambivalent participants were more likely than avoidant participants to oblige their partners in conflictual situations. Pistole et al. (1995) found that ambivalent adults were more likely to report high relationship costs than were their secure and avoidant counterparts. Although these results from same-sex couple research do not directly test hypotheses based in attachment theory, they provide evidence that same-sex couples exhibit patterns of behavior that are highly suggestive of the adult attachment strategies found in research on opposite-sex couples.

A more direct test of the relations between attachment security and same-sex couple functioning is found in a recent study of female and male same-sex couples (Mohr & Fassinger, 1997). Our preliminary results suggest that attachment security may play a role in basic relationship processes for female and male same-sex couples that is similar to its role for opposite-sex couples. We used a measure of attachment style that included scales measuring anxiety over relationship issues and discomfort with closeness. Both of these dimensions of attachment were associated with a range of relationship variables for female and male same-sex couples, including lower levels of satisfaction and faith in one's partner, and higher levels of communication apprehension and aversive interaction. These results are congruent with those consistently found in studies of opposite-sex couples (e.g., Collins & Read, 1990; Feeney et al., 1994; Levy & Davis, 1988; Simpson, 1990).

In our study (Mohr & Fassinger, 1997), data were gathered from both members of couples, which made it possible to examine the degree to which participants' relationship evaluations were related to their partners' attachment styles. Effects of partners' attachment styles on participants' relationship evaluations have been found in a number of studies of opposite-sex couples (e.g., Collins & Read, 1990; Kirkpatrick & Davis, 1994; Kobak & Hazan, 1991; Simpson, 1990). We found that individuals scoring high on anxiety over relationships were likely to have same-sex partners who scored low on relationship trust and who perceived a high number of serious conflict areas. Avoidantly attached participants tended to have partners who reported infrequent discussion in the relationship. Generally these partner effects were less strong than those related to participants' own attachment ratings, but this was not always the case. For example, relationship satisfaction for men was negatively correlated with their partners' self-reported levels of anxiety over relationships and discomfort with closeness, and these correlations with satisfaction were stronger than those derived from participants' own levels of such anxiety and discomfort.

Several investigations focusing on attachment and relationship satisfaction in opposite-sex couples have uncovered ways in which gender and attachment interact in predicting satisfaction (Feeney, Chapter 17, this volume). Probably the most robust result is that participants' and partners' ratings of relationship quality are best predicted by females' levels of abandonment anxiety and males' levels of avoidance and discomfort with closeness (Collins & Read, 1990; Feeney, 1994; Kirkpatrick & Davis, 1994). It has been hypothesized that these effects may be due to processes related to gender-role socialization. Evidence of these gender-based effects has been found in research on gender and conflict structure in married couples. For example, one study indicated that relationship satisfaction is inversely related to the degree to which marital couples engage in a "wife demands, husband withdraws" style of conflict (Heavey, Layne, & Christensen, 1993). This dynamic is strongly suggestive of a female ambivalent and male avoidant pairing, and couples with this combination of attachment styles are precisely those that have been found to give the lowest ratings of relationship satisfaction (Feeney, 1994; Kirkpatrick & Davis, 1994).

Do these gender-related dynamics emerge in same-sex couples? Preliminary results from our study do not indicate gender effects with regard to attachment (Mohr & Fassinger, 1997). Discomfort with closeness and relationship anxiety predicted a number of indices of relationship quality for both female and male same-sex couples. Perhaps the most striking difference between women and men has already been mentioned: Attachment insecurity predicted partners' relationship satisfaction for men, but not for women. Overall, however, few gender differences were found. This may be related to findings suggesting that no significant differences exist between female and male same-sex couples in approaches to problem solving and conflict resolution (Falbo & Peplau, 1980; Kurdek, 1991a; Metz, Rosser, & Strapko, 1994), and that same-sex couples typically do not draw upon traditional gender roles as a model for long-term relationships (Peplau, 1991).

This apparent lack of gender effects for same-sex couples may be due in part to focusing on hypotheses derived from research with opposite-sex couples. To a great extent, LGB people lack role models and societal norms for intimate relationships, thus it makes sense that findings based on traditional marital roles may not apply to same-sex relationship functioning. One area in which attachment-related gender differences may be expected in same-sex couples is sexual exclusivity. Male same-sex couples have been found to be more likely than any other type of couple to engage in sexual activities outside of the couple relationship (Kurdek, 1995; Peplau, 1991), and no significant differences in relationship satisfaction have been found among male couples based on sexual exclusivity. This suggests that the attachment system and the sexual system may be capable of functioning relatively independently of each other for many gay and bisexual men, whereas this does not appear to be the case for individuals in female same-sex couples or in opposite-sex couples (Kurdek, 1995). Thus, although attachment security has been linked to sexual exclusivity in a primarily heterosexual sample (Hazan, Zeifman, & Middleton, 1994), this connection may not be as strong for men in same-sex relationships. This hypothesis is especially interesting in light of recent theory regarding the evolved functions of jealousy in heterosexual relationships. If, as has been suggested, sexual jealousy serves the evolutionary function of increasing men's paternity certainty (Buss, Larsen, Westen, & Semmelroth, 1992), then this form of jealousy may be less likely to be stimulated in relationships in which paternity certainty is not an issue (e.g., male same-sex relationships).

Finally, studies of opposite-sex couples have suggested that people may tend to seek relationships with partners who confirm their attachment-related beliefs. For example, individuals with anxious-ambivalent styles of attachment tend to be involved with avoidantly attached partners, who give some reality-based weight to their belief that they want more closeness than their partners do (Collins & Read, 1990; Kirkpatrick & Davis, 1994). Preliminary evidence from the study discussed above suggests that this may also be true for same-sex couples (Mohr & Fassinger, 1997). Women and men who were highly anxious over relationships tended to have partners who also reported higher than average levels of such anxiety, as well as higher levels of discomfort with closeness. Participants uncomfortable with closeness tended to be partnered with individuals who reported high levels of relationship anxiety. Thus highly anxious participants were likely to be with anxious or avoidant partners, whereas highly avoidant participants (i.e., those uncomfortable with closeness) were likely to be with anxious but not avoidant partners. The partner-matching effects were stronger for the female couples than the male couples, but they were significant for both types of couples. These results are in line with the experimental findings of Pietromonaco and Carnelley (1994). Participants were given a written profile of a hypothetical romantic partner, and they were asked to imagine themselves in a relationship with that person. The profiles were designed to reflect secure, avoidant, and anxious-ambivalent attachment styles. Participants with avoidant styles of attachment offered the most negative evaluations of a hypothetical partner who exhibited avoidant behavior.

Overall, these findings tentatively suggest that the links found between attachment and relationship quality for opposite-sex couples hold for same-sex couples as well. Individuals in same-sex couples who are able to establish closeness with their partners and have trust in their partners' availability tend to be more satisfied with their relationships and report more positive communication patterns. The gender effects typically encountered in attachment research with opposite-sex couples did not arise in one study of same-sex couples. Although this result may be due in part to the relative lack of reliance on traditional gender roles in same-sex relationship functioning, it may also be due to the lack of longitudinal data. Kirkpatrick and Davis (1994) found that certain pairings of attachment styles in opposite-sex couples tended to be longer-lived, regardless of reports of relationship satisfaction. This points to the potential interest of conducting longitudinal studies of same-sex couples. Also, differences between male and female same-sex couples with regard to sexual exclusivity may prove to be an area worthy of investigation from an attachment-theoretical perspective.

FEAR, SAFETY, AND SAME-SEX RELATIONSHIPS

> Throughout the assault, he talked about how he was acting for God; that what he was doing to me was God's revenge on me because I was a "queer" and getting rid of me would save children and put an end to the movement in Indiana. . . . I still do not have unrestricted freedom; my significant other and I live with constant fear that it will happen again.
> —SARRIS (1992, p. 202)

LGB individuals have achieved substantial political and social gains in the past several decades, but institutional intolerance for and personal antagonism toward the expression of same-sex desire remain realities throughout most of the world today (Herek, 1991a). What are the consequences of these adverse social conditions for relationship functioning in same-sex couples? This question remains largely unanswered, although a few studies have indicated that the climate of intolerance does indeed affect same-sex couples. For example, research findings have suggested that same-sex relationship quality is inversely related to parental disapproval of individuals' sexual orientation (Murphy, 1989; Smith & Brown, 1997) and to chronic nondisclosure of sexual orientation (Berger, 1990). Clinical writings have suggested that both external manifestations of antigay prejudice (e.g., violence, discrimination) and the internalization of negative views of same-sex attraction (e.g., internalized homophobia, chronic sexual orientation confusion) can lead to diminished satisfaction and greater conflict in same-sex couples (Brown, 1995; Hancock, 1995), especially when partners differ with regard to their levels of internalized homophobia and comfort with being "out of the closet" (Brown, 1995; Patterson & Schwartz, 1994).

Understanding the context of LGB individuals' lives is a prerequisite to articulating the unique ways in which attachment variables may play roles in determining same-sex-romantic relationship functioning. The process of developing as a lesbian, a gay male, or a bisexual person often involves confusion, anxiety, and internal conflict. Many adolescents facing their same-sex attractions hide this aspect of their lives and thereby experience a profound sense of emotional isolation (Savin-Williams, 1995). Those who choose to express their sexual orientation openly are often subjected to intense ridicule, rejection, and threat. One major study of LGB youth found that 80% of the participants had experienced verbal insults related to their sexual orientation, 44% had experienced property damage, 33% had had objects thrown at them, 30% had been chased or followed, 22% had been sexually assaulted, 17% had been physically assaulted, and 13% had been spat upon (Hershberger & D'Augelli, 1995). The strongest predictor of self-acceptance for these youth was family support regarding sexual orientation. In addition, family support was found to serve as a buffer against the deleterious effects of victimization, particularly in regard to more threatening acts of violence. Similar results regarding the prevalence of antigay violence have been found in a number of national surveys of LGB adults (Berrill, 1992). The accumulated findings of studies such as these provide a sobering view of the difficult circumstances faced by many LGB individuals.

Given these suboptimal conditions, LGB individuals must learn to identify potential sources of threat and to manage the fear, shame, and anger associated with pervasive antigay stigma and hostility (de Monteflores, 1993; Fassinger, 1991; Troiden, 1993). The process of learning to identify sources of possible danger is an important component of the fear behavioral system. Bowlby (1973) wrote extensively about humans' predisposition to react in a self-protective fashion to certain natural or innately recognized clues to danger (e.g., darkness, sudden noise, alone-

ness), as well as to cultural clues to danger that are learned by observation or personal experience. According to Bowlby, fear reactions are activated both by threatening stimuli (e.g., the approach of a hostile peer) and by inaccessibility of attachment figures (including perceived threats to the accessibility of attachment figures). An individual's total fear reaction at a given time is thought to be an additive function of all of the fear stimuli present in the situation. Bowlby identified three behavioral outcomes of fear reactions: immobility (i.e., freezing), increased distance from the feared situation (i.e., fleeing), and increased proximity to one's attachment figure (i.e., seeking). Individuals who are able to use their attachment figures as a secure base for exploration are believed to be less susceptible to fear stimuli than those with insecure attachments.

How might the attachment and fear systems come into play in the process of LGB identity development? If LGB identity development is conceptualized as an exploratory process, as we have suggested (Mohr & Fassinger, 1998), then "attachment insecurity may increase susceptibility to fear with regard to the tasks of identity development . . . [and thus] curtail the exploration that is often critical in forging a positive gay identity" (p. 9). We found support for this hypothesis in a study of LGB adults. Participants who exhibited a pattern of high attachment avoidance and anxiety were more likely than other participants to fear judgment from others based on sexual orientation, and less likely than other participants to disclose their sexual orientation to work colleagues and heterosexual friends, to identify with and seek involvement in the LGB community, or to interact with heterosexual people. Furthermore, this pattern of attachment insecurity was associated with the internalization of antigay values, especially in male participants. Although the data from this study did not provide a means of exploring causal relations between the attachment and LGB identity variables, the results suggested that attachment insecurity was associated with a heightened fear response to behaviors that are thought to reflect acceptance and openness regarding one's sexual orientation. This fear response may involve actively "fleeing" the challenging tasks of LGB identity development, as well as "freezing" one's identity formation process.

The developmental tasks faced by LGB individuals may present what, from an attachment perspective, are considered "double-bind situations." For example, the process of "coming out" (i.e., disclosing one's sexual orientation) to one's parents may involve risking rejection from the very figures to whom one turns in times of distress. Parents of securely attached LGB children may be more likely than parents of insecurely attached children to respond sensitively to their children throughout the coming-out process. We have found indirect evidence of this, based upon retrospective reports (Mohr & Fassinger, 1998). Also, Holtzen, Kenny, and Mahalik (1995) found that lesbians and gay men who disclosed their sexual orientation to parents reported higher levels of parental attachment security than those who did not disclose. Parents with antigay values may, however, reject their children regardless of the attachment security of the children. An interesting implication of this possibility is that the coming-out process may alter LGB individuals' working models of attachment with regard to their parents. The change in working models need not be only negative: LGB children may actually come to view their parents as more responsive and reliable as a result of a positive coming-out experience.

Same-sex romantic couples are not immune from such double-bind situations. Consider, for example, the case in which one or both partners in a same-sex couple have internalized societal antigay values and attitudes (i.e., have high internalized homophobia). These people are in the position of desiring romantic attachment relationships that go against their own value systems. Those who develop romantic relationships with same-sex partners may experience a push–pull dynamic, in which they simultaneously desire same-sex intimacy while wishing for distance from partners whose sex embodies the very opposite of what they view as acceptable. We (Mohr & Fassinger, 1998) found that attachment insecurity, especially avoidance, was associated with higher levels of internalized homophobia in gay and bisexual men. One interpretation of this association is that internalized homophobia may discourage the formation of same-sex bonds in which intimate closeness and trust can be tolerated. The irony of such a state of affairs is that the inability to use a partner as a secure base for exploration of a gay identity may prevent an individual from gaining the experiences necessary to decrease levels of internalized homophobia.

Attachment and internalized homophobia may be intertwined in other ways in determining same-sex relationship quality. As mentioned earlier, same-sex couples may experience difficul-

ties when partners are dissimilar with regard to variables related to gay identity (Brown, 1995; Patterson & Schwartz, 1994). For example, partners may differ radically in the degree to which they wish to conceal the nature of their relationship in public (i.e., to "pass" as heterosexual), and these differences can lead to difficulties that may seem intractable. These differences may derive from environmental factors (e.g., differences in tolerance of homosexuality in partners' respective workplace environments). As noted earlier, however, various indicators of gay identity difficulties (including lack of "outness" and fear of judgment from others) have been found to be associated with insecure attachment (Mohr & Fassinger, 1998). Thus, a couple with great disparities between the partners in levels of outness and internalized homophobia is likely to have at least one insecurely attached partner. Given that attachment insecurity has been linked to negative communication and conflict patterns in a number of studies (Feeney, Chapter 17, this volume), it may be that such a couple is doubly challenged: The partners must negotiate an inherently formidable difference in the relationship while working with attachment-related communication difficulties.

Acute stressors, such as the experience of antigay violence or threats of violence, may also serve to activate the attachment behavioral system. Indeed, the attachment system is believed to have evolved to ensure individuals' safety at times of greatest threat (Bowlby, 1973). Individual differences in attachment representations are expected to lead to differences in responses to threat (Mikulincer & Florian, 1998; Simpson & Rholes, 1994). No attachment research has been conducted on threats specific to same-sex couples, such as antigay violence, but findings from other studies can be used to generate hypotheses regarding reactions to such threats. Research on responses to acute stress suggests that avoidant victims of antigay violence may be expected to minimize both the impact of such an event and the need for support, whereas ambivalent victims may be expected to focus on their distress, blame themselves, and experience an intense need for soothing from their attachment figures (Mikulincer, Florian, & Weller, 1993; Simpson et al., 1992). Secure victims, however, may be expected to seek direct support for their distress (i.e., to use their partners as a safe haven) and to experience less symptomatology than their insecure counterparts. These different attachment-related strategies for coping may directly affect relationship functioning, or they may affect relationship functioning indirectly through the degree to which they maintain levels of symptomatology resulting from the traumatic stressor. For example, increased use of avoidant behaviors after an incident of antigay violence may affect relationship quality directly through greater avoidance of intimacy and interdependence, and indirectly by maintaining depression levels, which in turn affect couple functioning.

Finally, the relative invisibility of committed same-sex couples may make LGB individuals more vulnerable to negative societal messages regarding prospects for long-term relationships (Brown, 1995). For example, individuals may internalize the message that same-sex partnerships are primarily defined by sex, and thus are under continual jeopardy of dissolution due to sexual temptations outside of the relationship or to sexual boredom. Individuals may also believe that same-sex relationships are less legitimate than their opposite-sex counterparts because of the relative lack of public, legal, and (often) familial recognition of such relationships (Ainsworth, 1985; Brown, 1995). For LGB people with high levels of attachment anxiety, these beliefs may pose serious threats to their sense of security and lead to chronic activation of the attachment behavioral system. Avoidantly attached people, on the other hand, may respond to such beliefs by maintaining even greater distance than usual from attachment figures. Brown (1995) has speculated that individuals who have internalized these types of societal messages may be vulnerable to romantic jealousy because they typically view same-sex partnerships as inherently less stable than their opposite-sex counterparts. Given evidence that insecurely attached individuals are more susceptible to romantic jealousy (Collins & Read, 1990) and to maladaptive responses to jealousy (Sharpsteen & Kirkpatrick, 1997), it is clear that the forces of societal heterosexism and attachment may be intertwined in complex ways.

This section has featured examples of attachment-related issues that are unique to same-sex couples through their association with the pervasive invisibility and hostility faced by LGB individuals. These examples may have given the impression that societal heterosexism, internalized homophobia, and romantic attachment insecurity weave a web so pervasive and formidable that no same-sex couple can escape a miserable fate. As noted earlier, however, same-sex couples appear to be as satisfied and well adjusted as opposite-sex couples (Kurdek, 1995). Brown (1995) observed that all same-sex couples must face heterosexism and internalized homophobia, even couples that have long and happy histories: "I . . . know firsthand the challenges that an oppressive reality can throw in the faces of the most happy and well-functioning couples, even when both partners are skillful communicators with a strong commitment to the functioning and health of the relationship" (p. 276). Perhaps, as Simpson and Rholes (1994) have suggested, successfully facing adversity may actually strengthen such a couple's functioning. Learning with one's same-sex partner to negotiate the challenges posed by heterosexism and internalized homophobia may provide a basis for reworking and improving working models of attachment.

LOSS IN SAME-SEX RELATIONSHIPS

> Several weeks later I was cleaning the garage and found one of his old shirts tossed in a corner. It still smelled like him—that light orange odor. I also found our old beach ball, but I could not let the air out—his breath was in it.
> —McCreary (1991, p. 144)

Bowlby was deeply concerned with the psychological repercussions of losing one's attachment figure—a fact that is not surprising, given the central role he accorded to achieving a sense of security and safety through attachment bonds. The final volume of his *Attachment and Loss* trilogy, *Loss: Sadness and Depression,* is devoted to the study of loss and mourning. Bowlby (1980) attempted to explain the process of bereavement from an ethological perspective, and thus to normalize the intense affective, cognitive, and behavioral shifts that commonly accompany loss. He suggested that reactions to loss can be viewed as part of a broader category of separation from one's attachment figure. From an attachment perspective, the specific sequence of numbing, protest, despair, and reorganization found in infants following a prolonged separation is evidence of an innate behavioral system that has evolved to maximize proximity to caregivers (Bowlby, 1980); this cycle has been amply documented among infants, children, and heterosexual adults (Bowlby, 1980; Fraley & Shaver, Chapter 32, this volume).

Working models of attachment are viewed as moderators of the bereavement process. Preoccupation with attachment relationships (i.e., the ambivalent attachment pattern), for example, has been linked to chronic mourning in adults (Bowlby, 1980). A preoccupied individual who has lost a romantic partner through either death or relationship dissolution is likely to experience an extended period of yearning for the missing partner, characterized by high levels of anxiety and depression, as well as by unusual difficulty in resuming normal daily routines (Fraley & Shaver, Chapter 32, this volume). Conversely, an avoidant individual is likely to have minimal grief reactions to loss. Although Bowlby believed the suppression of grief to be associated with problems adjusting to loss, debate still continues as to the degree to which this is the case (Fraley & Shaver, Chapter 32, this volume).

The attachment literature on loss and bereavement has not yet included reference to same-sex couples, but results from empirical studies of relationship dissolution can be interpreted from an attachment perspective. For example, one study of adjustment to romantic-relationship dissolution indicated that male and female same-sex couples did not differ from opposite-sex couples with regard to reasons for separation or levels of separation distress (Kurdek, 1997). The finding of no difference in distress levels among types of couples suggests that the attachment system may operate similarly for same-sex and opposite-sex couples in the context of relationship dissolution. Kurdek (1997) also found that predissolution levels of neuroticism (which is an indicator of attachment anxiety; Shaver & Brennan, 1992) predicted postdissolution levels of separation distress. This result is consistent with the notion, discussed above, that preoccupied patterns of attachment are associated with especially difficult recovery from loss and prolonged separation. In an earlier study of relationship dissolution, Kurdek (1991b) found that participants who reported experiencing few postdissolution adjustment difficulties placed a low value on dyadic attachment and reported low levels of psychological distress. Given that avoidance is associated with devaluing attachment needs and underreporting symptomatology (Dozier & Lee, 1995), this result may be interpreted as suggesting that avoidant LGB individuals tend to report low levels of adjustment problems after ending a romantic relationship. Similar findings have emerged in research with individuals in opposite-sex relationships. For example, Simpson (1990) found that avoidant men reported especially low levels of emotional distress 6 months after ending a romantic relationship.

The AIDS epidemic has forced many gay male couples to confront issues of death and bereavement prematurely. The literature that has emerged from this epidemic provides ample evidence of loss and grieving in the context of same-sex romantic love. Folkman, Chesney, Collette, Boccellari, and Cooke (1996) conducted one of the most intensive studies of AIDS-related bereavement to date. This study examined preloss predictors of the course of postloss depression in 110 gay men whose partners died of AIDS-related complications. Each man was assessed bimonthly for a 10-month period, starting 3 months before the partner's death. The findings support many of Bowlby's assertions regarding loss, and they raise interesting issues that may contribute to the refinement of theory regarding bereavement. Mean scores on a measure of depression throughout the 10 months exceeded the cutoff score for risk of major depression. The levels and persistence of depression found in this study were comparable to those found in bereaved partners of heterosexual married couples, suggesting that few differences exist in the degree to which bereaved partners in same- and opposite-sex couples experience despair.

Folkman et al. (1996) constructed a predictive model of postloss depression that included variables representing a variety of domains: demographic, mental health, physical health, stress, resources, and coping. The only significantly predictive demographic variable was length of relationship. Interestingly, caregiver burden did not predict the course of postloss depression, but the ability to view caregiving in positive terms was predictive: Men who felt that caregiving contributed positively to their romantic relationship were likely to recover more rapidly from postloss depression than other participants. The data did not describe the patterns of caregiving observed in these men, but this result is consistent with the notion that individuals who are compulsive caregivers or ambivalent with regard to the caregiving role may be especially vulnerable to chronic mourning (Bowlby, 1980).

Level of preloss daily hassles was one of the strongest predictors of nonrecovery from postloss depression. A possible interpretation of this result is based on recent work on the role of neuroticism in exposure and reaction to daily stressors. For example, Bolger and his colleagues (Bolger & Schilling, 1991; Bolger & Zuckerman, 1995) found that high-neuroticism participants experienced more daily conflicts and hassles than their low-neuroticism counterparts, and that they were more likely to react to these every-day stressors with anger and depression. As mentioned earlier, neuroticism is considered to be an indicator of high levels of attachment anxiety. These findings, put together, offer a basis for a plausible attachment-related interpretation of the daily-hassles finding in the bereavement study: Men who reported high levels of preloss daily hassles may have tended to have ambivalent patterns of attachment. If this were the case, then it would not be surprising that these men had a difficult bereavement process, given the association of anxious attachment with chronic mourning (Fraley & Shaver, Chapter 32, this volume). Another interpretation of the research findings, however, is that level of preloss daily hassles may reflect a more chaotic lifestyle that would make recovery from postloss depression difficult for any person, regardless of attachment style.

One important finding of the Folkman et al. (1996) study is that participants who reported high levels of preloss depression were more likely to have a rapid recovery from postloss depression than those who reported low levels of preloss depression. The authors interpreted this result as an example of the process referred to by Klinger (1987) as "disengagement from incentives." Interview data indicated that the caregivers were largely preoccupied with the ongoing losses associated with their partners' illness. Depressive mood in response to these losses may indicate a process wherein individuals were beginning to disengage from their partners in preparation for the impending death. Hoffman (1996) has noted that this type of depression may also reflect anticipatory grief. This process of beginning bereavement prior to the loss of a partner may be viewed as an early phase of what Bowlby (1980) referred to as the stage of "reorganization." Bowlby, in fact, initially called this stage that of "detachment" (Fraley & Shaver, Chapter 32, this volume). According to Bowlby (1980), healthy recovery from loss requires an acknowledgment that the deceased is no longer available, combined with the ability to maintain a continuing secure bond with the deceased. Thus, beginning to disengage from one's partner before the partner's death may facilitate the process of reorganizing one's life and working models of the partner after the loss. Evidence of continuing bonds with deceased partners is found in such important symbols as the AIDS quilt, a memorial to those who have died of AIDS-related causes in the United States (Shelby, 1994). The quilt consists of thousands of panels created by the be-reaved in memory of loved ones. This memorial provides bereaved individuals an opportunity to create a relatively enduring, public symbol of their continuing bond with their partners (as well as their continuing bond with other close friends who have also died of AIDS-related causes). The quilt may also offer the bereaved a reassuring symbol of continuing social support and solidarity in the midst of a climate that is often hostile with regard to AIDS-related issues (Hoffman, 1996).

Another important finding in the Folkman et al. (1996) study is that levels of depression in bereaved partners who were HIV+ did not decrease over the 7-month period following the loss. Similar results were found in another longitudinal study, wherein participants who were both bereaved and HIV+ reported the highest levels of distress in a large urban sample of gay men (Martin & Dean, 1993). From an attachment perspective, HIV+ caregivers may feel the need to serve as strong, reliable figures for their partners while simultaneously experiencing attachment distress related to their own illness and to the unavailability of their partners as caregivers for them. Thus HIV+ caregivers may feel compelled to suppress their own attachment distress, which may subsequently lead to difficulties in processing the impending loss. Shelby (1994), reporting a clinical study of the impact of AIDS on male romantic relationships, found that the mourning process is often especially complex and prolonged for a surviving partner who is HIV+. He noted that such an individual may exhibit a "continued idealization of the deceased partner and an identification with his illness and death" (p. 63), which may lead to increased isolation and depressive mood. According to Shelby, the HIV+ bereaved may become preoccupied with the virus as a "powerful and deadly tie to the deceased partner that cannot be loosed" (p. 63). Such possibilities hint at the complex transformations that representations of self and other may undergo in response to life-threatening illness.

Although little has been written from an attachment perspective on loss in same-sex couples, the research reviewed in this section suggests that responses to loss in same-sex couples are largely consistent with Bowlby's theory. This section has featured examples from the literature on relationship dissolution and AIDS-related bereavement. Loss may also play an important role in LGB identity development. Crespi (1995), for example, writes about the role of mourning in developing a positive lesbian identity. In a society that values heterosexuality more than homosexuality, LGB individuals must face potential losses of status, respectability, physical safety, and relationships with family and friends. Loss of positive regard and support from one's parents may be especially difficult to process and could conceivably affect romantic-relationship functioning (Murphy, 1989; Smith & Brown, 1997). Future investigations of these dynamics may be enriched by including information about the quality of parental attachment prior to disclosure of one's sexual orientation.

SUMMARY AND CONCLUSIONS

The purpose of this chapter has been to begin to articulate ways in which attachment theory may both contribute to and profit from the study of same-sex romantic relationships. Much remains to be learned about the evolutionary underpinnings of both adult attachment and homosexuality, but the steadily growing body of research on same-sex couples strongly suggests that dynamics of romantic attachment are operative for LGB individuals. The preliminary findings discussed in this chapter indicate that many parallels exist with regard to the role of attachment in same-sex and opposite-sex relationship quality (Mohr & Fassinger, 1997). Attachment-related processes may also play unique roles in same-sex couple functioning through their relations with heterosexism and internalized homophobia. Thus the study of same-sex couples promises to illuminate points of intersection between attachment processes and stigma, stress, and societal oppression in romantic-relationship functioning.

The lack of longitudinal work in this area, however, leaves many questions unanswered regarding these points of intersection. For example, recent research has indicated that attachment is related to variables associated with the LGB identity formation process (Mohr & Fassinger, 1998), but it is unclear whether attachment insecurity leads to difficulties in the identity process, whether identity difficulties lead to changes in working models of attachment, or whether a third variable influences both attachment and identity. It is equally unclear what implications this may have for the formation, maintenance, and dissolution of same-sex couples. Furthermore, gender differences may contribute to the complexity of this picture. For example, research has indicated that lesbians and gay men often first begin same-

sex sexual involvements via different routes: Lesbians are more likely to meet partners through friendship networks, and gay men are more likely to meet partners through sexual encounters (Garnets & Kimmel, 1993). Such potential differences in the contexts of romantic-relationship formation for lesbians and gay men suggest the possibility that the role and salience of working models of attachment in the early stages of LGB identity formation are moderated by gender.

The examples offered in this chapter constitute a first step in identifying some possibilities for future study, but the list is hardly exhaustive. For example, longitudinal research on relationships between lesbian ex-lovers (a little-studied, but much-discussed phenomenon; see Becker, 1988) may contribute to the growing literature on jealousy and attachment (e.g., Sharpsteen & Kirkpatrick, 1997). Another potentially interesting line of investigation may be to study the ability of LGB communities to promote secure romantic attachments through their role as a safe haven for LGB individuals and same-sex couples. These examples, along with those discussed earlier, indicate that the study of same-sex couple functioning provides a rich forum for exploring the complex interplay of forces at the individual, dyadic, and societal levels—an interplay that potentially involves the attachment, fear, sex, and exploratoration behavioral systems. Exploration of this uncharted territory will both enhance attachment theory and provide much-needed data on same-sex romantic relationships.

ACKNOWLEDGMENTS

I would like to thank Jude Cassidy, Henry Hogue, Phil Shaver, and Susan Woodhouse for their helpful comments on an earlier draft of this chapter.

NOTE

1. It may be more accurate to say that same-sex romantic attachments exist to the extent that *any* adult romantic attachments exist. Developments in evolutionary theory have led some theorists (e.g., Kirkpatrick, 1998) to question the assumption held among many attachment researchers that the attachment behavioral system is salient in opposite-sex romantic relationships. These arguments are worth extending to same-sex romantic relationships and integrating with current perspectives on evolution and homosexuality

(McKnight, 1997). The ideas presented in this chapter, however, assume the salience of the attachment system in romantic couples (see Hazan & Zeifman, Chapter 16, this volume).

REFERENCES

Ainsworth, M. D. S. (1985). Attachments across the lifespan. *Bulletin of the New York Academy of Medicine, 61,* 792–812.

Ainsworth, M. D. S., Blehar, M. C., Waters, E., & Wall, S. (1978). *Patterns of attachment: A psychological study of the strange situation.* Hillsdale, NJ: Erlbaum.

Becker, C. S. (1988). *Unbroken ties: Lesbian ex-lovers.* Boston: Alyson.

Berger, R. M. (1990). Passing: Impact of the quality of same-sex couple relationships. *Social Work, 35,* 328–332.

Berrill, K. T. (1992). Anti-gay violence and victimization in the United States: An overview. In G. M. Herek & K. T. Berrill (Eds.), *Hate crimes: Confronting violence against lesbians and gay men* (pp. 19–45). Newbury Park, CA: Sage.

Bolger, N., & Schilling, E. A. (1991). Personality and the problems of everyday life: The role of neuroticism in exposure and reactivity to daily stressors. *Journal of Personality, 59,* 355–386.

Bolger, N., & Zuckerman, A. (1995). A framework for studying personality in the stress process. *Journal of Personality and Social Psychology, 69,* 890–902.

Boswell, J. (1994). *Same-sex unions in premodern Europe.* New York: Villard Books.

Bowlby, J. (1969/1982). *Attachment and loss: Vol. 1. Attachment.* New York: Basic Books.

Bowlby, J. (1973). *Attachment and loss: Vol. 2. Separation: Anxiety and anger.* New York: Basic Books.

Bowlby, J. (1980). *Attachment and loss: Vol. 3. Loss: Sadness and depression.* New York: Basic Books.

Bowlby, J. (1988). *A secure base: Parent–child attachment and healthy human development.* New York: Basic Books.

Brown, L. S. (1995). Therapy with same-sex couples: An introduction. In N. S. Jacobson & A. S. Gurman (Eds.), *Clinical handbook of couple therapy* (pp. 274–294). New York: Guilford Press.

Buss, D. M., Larsen, R. J., Westen, D., & Semmelroth, J. (1992). Sex differences in jealousy: Evolution, physiology, and psychology. *Psychological Science, 3,* 251–255.

Collins, N. L., & Read, S. J. (1990). Adult attachment, working models, and relationship quality in dating couples. *Journal of Personality and Social Psychology, 58,* 644–663.

Crespi, L. (1995). Some thoughts on the role of mourning in the development of a positive lesbian identity. In T. Domenici & R. C. Lesser (Eds.), *Disorienting sexuality: Psychoanalytic reappraisals of sexual identities* (pp. 19–32). New York: Routledge.

Crowell, J., Gao, Y., Treboux, D., & Owens, G. (1997). Current relationship representations: Relation to secure base behavior in marital interactions. In J. Crowell & E. Waters (Chairs), *The secure base phenomenon in adult attachment relationships: Exploration of the core of the attachment system.* Symposium conducted at the biennial meeting of the Society for Research on Child Development, Washington, DC.

Dawkins, R. (1976). *The selfish gene.* New York: Oxford University Press.

Deenen, A. A., Gijs, L., & van Naerssen, A. X. (1994). Intimacy and sexuality in gay male couples. *Archives of Sexual Behavior, 23,* 421–431.

de Monteflores, C. (1993). Notes on the management of difference. In L. D. Garnets & D. C. Kimmel (Eds.), *Psychological perspectives on lesbian and gay male experiences* (pp. 218–247). New York: Columbia University Press.

Dickemann, M. (1995). Wilson's panchreston: The inclusive fitness hypothesis of sociobiology re-examined. *Journal of Homosexuality, 28,* 147–183.

Dozier, M., & Lee, S. W. (1995). Discrepancies between self- and other-report of psychiatric symptomatology: Effects of dismissing attachment strategies. *Development and Psychopathology, 7,* 217–226.

Eskridge, W. N. (1996). *The case for same-sex marriage: From civil liberty to civilized commitment.* New York: Free Press.

Falbo, T., & Peplau, L. A. (1980). Power strategies in intimate relationships. *Journal of Personality and Social Psychology, 38,* 618–628.

Fassinger, R. E. (1991). The hidden minority: Issues and challenges in working with lesbian women and gay men. *The Counseling Psychologist, 19,* 157–176.

Feeney, J. A. (1994). Attachment style, communication patterns, and satisfaction across the life cycle of marriage. *Personal Relationships, 1,* 333–348.

Feeney, J. A., Noller, P., & Callan, V. J. (1994). Attachment style, communication and satisfaction in the early years of marriage. In K. Bartholomew & D. Perlman (Eds.), *Advances in personal relationships: Vol. 5. Attachment processes in adulthood* (pp. 269–308). London: Jessica Kingsley.

Feeney, J. A., & Raphael, B. (1992). Adult attachments and sexuality: Implications for understanding risk behaviors for HIV infection. *Australian and New Zealand Journal of Psychiatry, 26,* 399–407.

Folkman, S., Chesney, M., Collette, L, Boccellari, A., & Cooke, M. (1996). Postbereavement depressive mood and its prebereavement predictors in HIV+ and HIV– gay men. *Journal of Personality and Social Psychology, 70,* 336–348.

Friend, R. A. (1991). Older lesbian and gay people: A theory of successful aging. *Journal of Homosexuality, 20,* 99–118.

Gallup, G. G. (1993). Have attitudes toward homosexuals been shaped by natural selection? *Ethology and Sociobiology, 16,* 53–70.

Garnets, L. D., & Kimmel, D. C. (1993). Lesbian and gay male dimensions in the psychological study of human diversity. In L. D. Garnets & D. C. Kimmel (Eds.), *Psychological perspectives on lesbian and gay male experiences* (pp. 1–51). New York: Columbia University Press.

Gibson, M. (1997). Clitoral corruption: Body metaphors and American doctors' constructions of female homosexuality. In V. A. Rosario (Ed.), *Science and homosexualities* (pp. 108–132). New York: Routledge.

Greenberg, D. F. (1988). *The construction of homosexuality.* Chicago: University of Chicago Press.

Hamer, D. H., & Copeland, P. (1994). *The science of desire: The search for the gay gene and the biology of behavior.* New York: Simon & Schuster.

Hancock, K. A. (1995). Psychotherapy with lesbians and gay men. In A. R. D'Augelli & C. J. Patterson (Eds.), *Lesbian, gay, and bisexual identities over the lifespan: Psychologi-*

cal perspectives (pp. 398–432). New York: Oxford University Press.

Hazan, C., & Shaver, P. (1987). Romantic love conceptualized as an attachment process. *Journal of Personality and Social Psychology, 52,* 511–524.

Hazan, C., Zeifman, D., & Middleton, K. (1994, July). *Adult romantic attachment, affection, and sex.* Paper presented at the 7th International Conference on Personal Relationships, Groningen, The Netherlands.

Heavey, C. L., Layne, C., & Christensen, A. (1993). Gender and conflict structure in marital interaction: A replication and extension. *Journal of Consulting and Clinical Psychology, 64,* 16–27.

Herek, G. M. (1991a). Stigma, prejudice, and violence against lesbians and gay men. In J. C. Gonsiorek & J. D. Weinrich (Eds.), *Homosexuality: Research implications for public policy* (pp. 60–80). Newbury Park, CA: Sage.

Herek, G. M. (1991b). Myths about sexual orientation: A lawyer's guide to social science research. *Law and Sexuality, 1,* 133–172.

Herek, G. M., Kimmel, D. C., Amaro, H., & Melton, G. B. (1991). Avoiding heterosexist bias in psychological research. *American Psychologist, 46,* 957–963.

Hershberger, S. L., & D'Augelli, A. R. (1995). The impact of victimization on the mental health and suicidality of lesbian, gay, and bisexual youths. *Developmental Psychology, 31,* 65–74.

Hoffman, M. A. (1996). *Counseling clients with HIV disease: Assessment, intervention, and prevention.* New York: Guilford Press.

Holtzen, D. W., Kenny, M. E., & Mahalik, J. R. (1995). Contributions of parental attachment to gay or lesbian disclosure to parents and dysfunctional cognitive processes. *Journal of Counseling Psychology, 42,* 350–355.

Hutchinson, G. E. (1959). A speculative consideration of certain possible forms of sexual selection in man. *American Naturalist, 93,* 81–91.

Kirkpatrick, L. A. (1998). Evolution, pair-bonding, and reproductive strategies: A reconceptualization of adult attachment. In J. A. Simpson & W. S. Rholes (Eds.), *Attachment theory and close relationships* (pp. 353–393). New York: Guilford Press.

Kirkpatrick, L. A., & Davis, K. E. (1994). Attachment style, gender, and relationship stability: A longitudinal analysis. *Journal of Personality and Social Psychology, 66,* 502–512.

Klinger, E. (1987). Current concerns and disengagement from incentives. In F. Halisch & J. Kuhl (Eds.), *Motivation, intention, and volition* (pp. 337–347). Berlin: Springer-Verlag.

Kobak, R. R., & Hazan, C. (1991). Attachment in marriage: Effects of security and accuracy of working models. *Journal of Personality and Social Psychology, 60,* 861–869.

Kunce, L. J., & Shaver, P. R. (1994). An attachment-theoretical approach to caregiving in romantic relationships. In K. Bartholomew & D. Perlman (Eds.), *Advances in personal relationships: Vol. 5. Attachment processes in adulthood* (pp. 205–237). London: Jessica Kingsley.

Kurdek, L. A. (1991a). Correlates of relationship satisfaction in cohabiting gay and lesbian couples: An integration of contextual, investment, and problem-solving models. *Journal of Personality and Social Psychology, 61,* 910–922.

Kurdek, L. A. (1991b). The dissolution of gay and lesbian couples. *Journal of Social and Personal Relationships, 8,* 265–278.

Kurdek, L. A. (1995). Lesbian and gay couples. In A. R.

D'Augelli & C. J. Patterson (Eds.), *Lesbian, gay, and bisexual identities over the lifespan: Psychological perspectives* (pp. 243–261). New York: Oxford University Press.

Kurdek, L. A. (1997). Relation between neuroticism and dimensions of relationship commitment: Evidence from gay, lesbian, and heterosexual couples. *Journal of Family Psychology, 11,* 109–124.

Kurdek, L. A., & Schmitt, J. P. (1986). Relationship quality of partners in heterosexual married, heterosexual cohabiting, and gay and lesbian relationships. *Journal of Personality and Social Psychology, 51,* 711–720.

Levy, M. B., & Davis, K. E. (1988). Lovestyles and attachment styles compared: Their relations to each other and to various relationship characteristics. *Journal of Social and Personal Relationships, 5,* 439–471.

Martin, J. L., & Dean, L. (1991). Effects of AIDS-related bereavement and HIV-related illness on psychological distress among gay men: A 7-year longitudinal study, 1985–1991. *Journal of Personality and Social Psychology, 61,* 94–103.

McCreary, K. (1991). Remembrance. In E. Hemphill (Ed.), *Brother to brother: New writings by black gay men* (p. 144). Boston: Alyson.

McKnight, J. (1997). *Straight science?: Homosexuality, evolution, adaptation.* London: Routledge.

Metz, M. E., Rosser, B. R. S., & Strapko, N. (1994). Differences in conflict-resolution styles among heterosexual, gay, and lesbian couples. *Journal of Sex Research, 31,* 293–308.

Mikulincer, M., & Florian, V. (1998). The relationship between adult attachment styles and emotional and cognitive reactions to stressful events. In J. A. Simpson & W. S. Rholes (Eds.), *Attachment theory and close relationships* (pp. 143–165). New York: Guilford Press.

Mikulincer, M., Florian, V., & Weller, A. (1993). Attachment styles, coping strategies, and posttraumatic psychological distress: The impact of the Gulf War in Israel. *Journal of Personality and Social Psychology, 64,* 817–826.

Mohr, J. J., & Fassinger, R. E. (1997, August). Attachment, sexual identity and relationship functioning in same-sex couples. In K. M. O'Brien (Chair), *The role of attachment in psychological and vocational well-being.* Symposium conducted at the annual meeting of the American Psychological Association, Chicago.

Mohr, J. J., & Fassinger, R. E. (1998). *Individual differences in lesbian/gay identity: An attachment perspective.* Manuscript submitted for publication.

Murphy, B. C. (1989). Lesbian couples and their parents: The effects of perceived parental attitudes on the couple. *Journal of Counseling and Development, 68,* 46–51.

Patterson, C. (1995). Lesbian mothers, gay fathers, and their children. In A. R. D'Augelli & C. J. Patterson (Eds.), *Lesbian, gay, and bisexual identities over the lifespan: Psychological perspectives* (pp. 262–290). New York: Oxford University Press.

Patterson, D. G., & Schwartz, P. (1994). The social construction of conflict in intimate same-sex couples. In D. D. Cahn (Ed.), *Conflict in personal relationships* (pp. 3–26). Hillsdale, NJ: Erlbaum.

Pavelka, M. S. (1995). Sexual nature: What can we learn from a cross-species perspective? In P. R. Abramson & S. D. Pinkerton (Eds.), *Sexual nature, sexual culture* (pp. 17–36). Chicago: University of Chicago Press.

Peplau, L. A. (1991). Lesbian and gay relationships. In J. C. Gonsiorek & J. D. Weinrich (Eds.), *Homosexuality: Re-*

search implications for public policy (pp. 177–196). Newbury Park, CA: Sage.

Peplau, L. A. (1993). Lesbian and gay relationships. In L. D. Garnets & D. C. Kimmel (Eds.), *Psychological perspectives on lesbian and gay male experiences* (pp. 395–419). New York: Columbia University Press.

Pietromonaco, P. R., & Carnelley, K. B. (1994). Gender and working models of attachment: Consequences for perceptions of self and romantic relationships. *Personal Relationships, 1,* 63–82.

Pistole, M. C. (1989). Attachment in adult romantic relationships: Style of conflict resolution and relationship satisfaction. *Journal of Social and Personal Relationships, 6,* 505–510.

Pistole, M. C., Clark, E. M., & Tubbs, A. L. (1995). Love relationships: Attachment style and the investment model. *Journal of Mental Health Counseling, 17,* 199–209.

Rosario, V. A. (1997). Homosexual bio-histories: Genetic nostalgias and the quest for paternity. In V. A. Rosario (Ed.), *Science and homosexualities* (pp. 1–26). New York: Routledge.

Rule, S. (1989, October 2). Rights for gay couples in Denmark. *The New York Times,* p. A8.

Salais, D., & Fischer, R. B. (1995). Sexual preference and altruism. *Journal of Homosexuality, 28,* 185–196.

Sarris, K. (1992). Survivor's story. In G. M. Herek & K. T. Berrill (Eds.), *Hate crimes: Confronting violence against lesbians and gay men* (pp. 201–203). Newbury Park, CA: Sage.

Savin-Williams, R. C. (1995). Lesbian, gay male, and bisexual adolescents. In A. R. D'Augelli & C. J. Patterson (Eds.), *Lesbian, gay, and bisexual identities over the lifespan: Psychological perspectives* (pp. 165–189). New York: Oxford University Press.

Schreurs, K. M. G., & Buunk, B. P. (1996). Closeness, autonomy, equity, and relationship satisfaction in lesbian couples. *Psychology of Women Quarterly, 20,* 577–592.

Sharpsteen, D. J., & Kirkpatrick, L. A. (1997). Romantic jealousy and adult romantic attachment. *Journal of Personality and Social Psychology, 72,* 627–640.

Shaver, P. R., & Brennan, K. A. (1992). Attachment styles and the "Big Five" personality traits: Their connections with each other and with romantic relationship outcomes.

Personality and Social Psychology Bulletin, 18, 536–545.

Shaver, P. R., & Hazan, C. (1988). A biased overview of the study of love. *Journal of Social and Personal Relationships, 5,* 473–501.

Shelby, R. D. (1994). Mourning within a culture of mourning. In S. A. Cadwell, R. A. Burnham, Jr., & M. Forstein (Eds.), *Therapists on the front line: Psychotherapy with gay men in the age of AIDS* (pp. 53–79). Washington, DC: American Psychiatric Press.

Simpson, J. A. (1990). Influence of attachment styles on romantic relationships. *Journal of Personality and Social Psychology, 59,* 971–980.

Simpson, J. A., & Rholes, W. S. (1994). Stress and secure base relationships in adulthood. In K. Bartholomew & D. Perlman (Eds.), *Advances in personal relationships: Vol. 5. Attachment processes in adulthood* (pp. 181–204). London: Jessica Kingsley.

Simpson, J. A., Rholes, W. S., & Nelligan, J. S. (1992). Support seeking and support giving within couples in an anxiety-provoking situation: The role of attachment styles. *Journal of Personality and Social Psychology, 62,* 434–446.

Simpson, J. A., Rholes, W. S., & Phillips, D. (1996). Conflict in close relationships: An attachment perspective. *Journal of Personality and Social Psychology, 71,* 899–914.

Smith, R. B., & Brown, R. A. (1997). The impact of social support on gay male couples. *Journal of Homosexuality, 33,* 39–61.

Troiden, R. R. (1993). The formation of homosexual identities. In L. D. Garnets & D. C. Kimmel (Eds.), *Psychological perspectives on lesbian and gay male experiences* (pp. 191–217). New York: Columbia University Press.

Weinrich, J. D. (1995). Biological research on sexual orientation: A critique of the critics. *Journal of Homosexuality, 28,* 197–213.

Weiss, R. S. (1982). Attachment in adult life. In C. M. Parkes & J. Stevenson-Hinde (Eds.), *The place of attachment in human behavior* (pp. 171–184). New York: Basic Books.

West, M. L., & Sheldon-Keller, A. E. (1994). *Patterns of relating: An adult attachment perspective.* New York: Guilford Press.

Wilson, E. O. (1975). *Sociobiology: The new synthesis.* Cambridge, MA: Harvard University Press.

19

The Adult Attachment Interview
Historical and Current Perspectives

❖

ERIK HESSE

In 1985, the publication of a monograph entitled "Growing Points of Attachment Theory and Research" (Bretherton & Waters, 1985) marked a major turning point for the direction of the field. Here, Main, Kaplan, and Cassidy (1985) reported that an interview-based method of classifying a parent's state of mind with respect to attachment was strongly associated with the infant's behavior toward that parent during Ainsworth's strange situation procedure conducted 5 years previously (Ainsworth, Blehar, Waters, & Wall, 1978). At the same time, infant attachment classification with the mother was found predictive of verbatim transcripts of children's responses to Kaplan's version of the Separation Anxiety Test at age 6 (see also Kaplan, 1987), and both mother–child and father–child discourse patterns were found sharply predicted by strange situation behavior towards the same parent in infancy (see also Strage & Main, 1985, and Main, 1995). Taken together, the above discoveries led these authors to appropriately subtitle this publication "A Move to the Level of Representation" in attachment research.

Until that time, research in attachment had focused almost exclusively upon nonverbal behavior as observed in or found to be correlated with the Ainsworth strange situation. This structured laboratory separation and reunion procedure yields three traditional categories of infant attachment with respect to a particular parent (secure, avoidant, and resistant or ambivalent; a fourth category, disorganized/disoriented, has subsequently been added). Studies of nonverbal behavior as related to these categories centered primarily upon (1) home observations of mother–infant interactions (see Belsky, Chapter 12, this volume) and (2) follow-up investigations examining corresponding differences in preschool and kindergarten behavior. In this latter context, children judged secure with their mothers during infancy were repeatedly found to enjoy more favorable outcomes (see Weinfield, Sroufe, Egeland, & Carlson, Chapter 4, this volume). It was not until the advent of the Adult Attachment Interview (AAI; George, Kaplan, & Main, 1984, 1985, 1996), however, that representational processes as the likely mediator of differences in parental caregiving behavior were fully comprehended and made accessible to investigation.

The AAI protocol was developed in the early 1980s, as was an accompanying system for scoring and classification (Main & Goldwyn, 1984a, 1998a). Main and Goldwyn's initial analysis showed that several continuous rating scales appearing to reflect a parent's current state of mind with respect to his or her own attachment experiences were substantially related to aspects of the infant's behavior toward that parent in the strange situation 5 years previously. For example, scores for an infant's avoidance of the mother during the reunion episodes of the strange situation were correlated with her insistence upon lack of memory for childhood within the AAI, and with her idealization of her own mother. Finally, a strong relation was uncovered between the four categories of parental AAI response (secure/autonomous, dismissing, preoccupied, and unresolved/disorganized, described below) and the infant's strange situation response to the parent (secure, avoidant, resistant or ambivalent, and disorganized/disoriented; see Main, 1985, 1995, 1996; Main et al., 1985; Main & Goldwyn, 1998; Main & Hesse, 1990; Main & Solomon, 1990).

Since these initial publications first reporting a marked correspondence between the parent's AAI classification and the infant's strange situation response, the relation between Adult Attachment Interview and infant strange situation categories has been replicated in over 18 samples. In addition, the instrument has been extensively tested for its psychometric properties; secure-autonomous parents have repeatedly been found to be more sensitive than others to infant signals; and remarkably few subjects in clinical populations have been found secure/autonomous. Finally, when the system of interview analysis described here has been used (as opposed to alternative approaches; see below), in three out of four low-risk samples, an infant's secure versus insecure strange situation response to the mother has predicted the coherence of that individual's life narrative 16 to 20 years later.

This chapter begins with an overview of the AAI protocol and a summary of the adult attachment categories. Here the specific relations between parental AAI and infant strange situation responses are noted. Next the development of the AAI and of the scoring and classification system are considered from a historical perspective, culminating in a discussion of the greater emphasis now placed upon the analysis of the discourse properties of the interview. These properties were later found to be consonant with the principles of cooperative, rational discourse described by the linguistic philosopher P. Grice (1975, 1989). Third, AAI training institutes and their effects are mentioned briefly. Fourth, a review of present and emerging empirical findings is provided. Finally, several common queries and sources of confusion regarding the AAI and its analysis are addressed.

THE ADULT ATTACHMENT INTERVIEW: PROTOCOL AND OVERVIEW OF THE CATEGORIES

Protocol

The AAI is a semistructured, hour-long protocol consisting of 18 questions (see excerpts in Table 19.1). The entire interview exchange is transcribed verbatim (i.e., the full conversational interaction between the interviewer and the subject), although any cues to intonation, prosody, or nonverbal behavior are omitted. The interview begins with a call for a general description of relationships to parents in childhood, followed by a request for five adjectives that would best represent the relationship with each parent. After the adjectives are provided (first for the mother), the speaker is probed for specific episodic memories that would illustrate or support why each descriptor was chosen. This process is then repeated for the father, and for any other significant attachment figure (e.g., a stepfather or nanny). The protocol goes on to ask what the speaker did when emotionally upset, physically hurt, or ill, and how the parents responded. The subject is asked about salient separations, possible experiences of rejection, threats regarding discipline, and any experiences of abuse. The speaker is then queried regarding the effects of these experiences on his or her adult personality; whether any experiences constituted a significant setback to development; and why the parents are believed to have behaved as they did.

An especially important feature of the AAI protocol is the section addressing experiences of loss of significant persons through death. Each report of such an experience is systematically probed regarding reactions to the event, changes in feelings over time, and effects upon adult personality. Finally, the speaker is asked about the nature of the current relationship with parents, and any speaker who is now a parent himself or herself is asked how experiences of being parented may have affected responses to his or her own child.

Summary of the AAI Categories

Hesse (1996) has suggested that the central task presented to the subject by this interview is that of (1) producing and reflecting upon memories related to attachment while *simultaneously* (2) maintaining coherent (in Grices's conceptualiza-

TABLE 19.1. Brief Précis of the Adult Attachment Interview Protocol Excerpted from George, Kaplan, and Main (1996)

1. To begin with, could you just help me to get a little bit oriented to your family—for example, who was in your immediate family, and where you lived?
2. Now I'd like you to try to describe your relationship with your parents as a young child, starting as far back as you can remember.
3–4. Could you give me five adjectives or phrases to describe your relationship with your mother/father during childhood? I'll write them down, and when we have all five I'll ask you to tell me what memories or experiences led you to choose each one.
5. To which parent did you feel closer, and why?
6. When you were upset as a child, what did you do, and what would happen? Could you give me some specific incidents when you were upset emotionally? Physically hurt? Ill?
7. Could you describe your first separation from your parents?
8. Did you ever feel rejected as a child? What did you do, and do you think your parents realized they were rejecting you?
9. Were your parents ever threatening toward you—for discipline, or jokingly?
10. How do you think your overall early experiences have affected your adult personality? Are there any aspects you consider a setback to your development?
11. Why do you think your parents behaved as they did during your childhood?
12. Were there other adults who were close to you—like parents—as a child?
13. Did you experience the loss of a parent or other close loved one as a child, or in adulthood?
14. Were there many changes in your relationship with parents between childhood and adulthood?
15. What is your relationship with your parents like for you currently?

Note. The AAI cannot be conducted on the basis of this brief, modified précis of the protocol, which omits several questions as well as the critical follow-up probes. The full protocol, together with extensive directions for administration, can be obtained by writing to Professor Mary Main, Department of Psychology, University of California at Berkeley, Berkeley, CA 94720. Adapted from George, Kaplan, and Main (1996). Copyright 1996 by the authors. Adapted by permission.

tion, consistent/collaborative) discourse with the interviewer. This is not as easy an undertaking as it might appear, and George et al. (1984, 1985, 1996) have remarked upon the potential of the protocol to "surprise the unconscious." The interview moves at a relatively rapid pace, requiring the speaker to reflect upon and answer a multitude of complex questions regarding life history. Ample opportunities are thereby provided for speakers to contradict themselves, to find themselves unable to answer questions clearly, and/or to be stimulated into excessively lengthy or digressive discussions of particular topics. To maintain a consistent and collaborative narrative, a speaker must remember (and potentially reflect upon) what he or she has said, in order to integrate the overall presentation as it unfurls.

In the current system of AAI analysis (see below for a historical overview), speakers are judged "secure/autonomous" when they produce an acceptably coherent and collaborative narrative, whether experiences are reported as having been favorable or unfavorable. In essence, these speakers appear to answer questions with sufficient (but not excessive) elaboration, and then return the conversational turn to the interviewer. This, again, can be achieved whatever the nature

of the experiences being described, and thus, for example, an individual providing a coherent narrative that includes descriptions of physical or sexual abuse by parents will, following this rule system, be judged secure/autonomous. The children of coherent speakers are consistently classified as secure.

Interviews are classified as "dismissing" when discourse appears aimed at minimizing the discussion of attachment-related experiences. Typically, these transcripts violate coherence in that they are internally inconsistent, while responses are often excessively terse (e.g., "I don't remember"). Descriptions of parents are most often favorable to highly favorable. Unlike secure individuals utilizing similar descriptors, however, those classified as dismissing fail to provide supportive evidence for these globally positive representations, and not infrequently contradict them. For example, it is not uncommon for dismissing speakers to respond to later interview queries in ways clearly at odds with the positive impression presented at the outset (e.g., describing instances of being afraid to go to a parent when badly hurt). Speakers falling in this category have repeatedly been found to have children classified as avoidant.

Individuals classified as "preoccupied," while not necessarily internally inconsistent, produce narratives that nonetheless violate the principle of collaboration (described below). Thus the interview questions appear to stimulate memories, but the speaker is often unable to maintain a focus or to contain his or her responses to a given question. In many cases, therefore, the memories aroused, rather than the intent of the question itself, appear to draw the subject's attention and guide the subject's speech (Hesse, 1996). Among some preoccupied speakers, this is evidenced in lengthy, angry discussions of childhood interactions with the parent(s), which may inappropriately move into the present tense and/or into discussions of the present relationship. Preoccupied speakers may also digress to remote topics, use vague language, and on occasion oscillate regarding their view of a parent several times within the same sentence. Infants of these speakers are typically judged resistant/ambivalent.

The above provides a summary of what Main (1995) has termed the three central or "organized" AAI categories. These categories, again, parallel and predict the three original infant strange situation response patterns delineated by Ainsworth et al. (1978). Although both dismissing and preoccupied narratives have been described as incoherent, they are each nonetheless considered organized because a singular strategy or approach to the discourse task is manifested. More specifically, dismissing speakers attend chiefly to providing a positive impression of childhood experiences while avoiding discussing particular events. Preoccupied speakers, in contrast, maximize attention to attachment-related experiences and their effects at the expense of retaining appropriate conversational collaboration.

Two additional AAI categories involve either local disorganization surrounding discussions of potentially traumatic events, or failure to maintain an organized discourse strategy across the interview as a whole. The first, termed "unresolved/disorganized" is assigned when substantial lapses in the monitoring of reasoning or discourse occur during discussions of potentially traumatic events (e.g., significant loss experiences or abuse; see below). Unresolved attachment has repeatedly been found to be predictive of disorganized/disoriented infant strange situation behavior, a category added to Ainsworth's original three-part classification system by Main and Solomon (1986, 1990). An overview of the first four adult attachment categories as seen in relation to infant strange situation behavior is

provided in Table 19.2. This table incorporates several references to Grice's maxims, discussed at length below.

Finally, the recently delineated "cannot classify" category (Hesse, 1996) is assigned when the interview manifests a combination of contradictory and incompatible linguistic patternings. This category is too new to have been subjected to psychometric examination, and has not yet been found to be related to any specific infant strange situation response (other than disorganized, see Ammaniti & Speranza, 1994). The cannot classify category has, however, been found to be associated with adults' histories of psychiatric disorder, marital and criminal violence, and sexual abuse.

To this point, the global linguistic features of the five AAI categories have been briefly summarized, and four of these categories have been noted to be predictive of particular infant strange situation response patterns. What is most striking about this association is that it suggests that the form in which an individual presents his or her life narrative (regardless of its content) predicts caregiving behavior in highly specific and systematic ways. Thus the combination of internal consistency and collaboration in a speaker's discourse regarding attachment predicts that speaker's capacity to impart security to an infant. The specificity of these linkages between language and nonverbal behavior is unprecedented.

THE DEVELOPMENT OF THE ADULT ATTACHMENT INTERVIEW: A BRIEF HISTORY

Evolution of the Protocol

The AAI and its accompanying scoring and classification system evolved in the context of a 6-year follow-up study of mothers, fathers, and their children who had been seen in the strange situation when the children were 12 (mothers) and 18 (fathers) months of age. Data collection began in January 1982, with families participating in several procedures: free play (Main et al., 1985), sandbox play (Weston & Richardson, 1985), and parent–child reunions (Main et al., 1985; Main & Cassidy, 1988). Early pilot-testing of the interview protocol was conducted by Carol George and Nancy Kaplan. George's doctoral dissertation (George, 1984) focused on videotaping family responses to watching excerpts from a documentary about a 2-year-old undergoing fos-

TABLE 19.2. AAI Classifications and Corresponding Patterns of Infant Strange Situation Behavior

Adult state of mind with respect to attachment	Infant strange situation behavior
Secure/autonomous (F)	Secure (B)
Coherent, collaborative discourse. Valuing of attachment, but seems objective regarding any particular event/relationship. Description and evaluation of attachment-related experiences is consistent, whether experiences are favorable or unfavorable. Discourse does not notably violate any of Grice's maxims.	Explores room and toys with interest in preseparation episodes. Shows signs of missing parent during separation, often crying by the second separation. Obvious preference for parent over stranger. Greets parent actively, usually initiating physical contact. Usually some contact maintaining by second reunion, but then settles and returns to play.
Dismissing (Ds)	Avoidant (A)
Not coherent. Dismissing of attachment-related experiences and relationships. Normalizing ("excellent, very normal mother"), with generalized representations of history unsupported or actively contradicted by episodes recounted, thus violating Grice's maxim of quality. Transcripts also tend to be excessively brief, violating the maxim of quantity.	Fails to cry on separation from parent. Actively avoids and ignores parent on reunion (i.e., by moving away, turning away, or leaning out of arms when picked up). Little or no proximity or contact-seeking, no distress, and no anger. Response to parent appears unemotional. Focuses on toys or environment throughout procedure.
Preoccupied (E)	Resistant or ambivalent (C)
Not coherent. Preoccupied with or by past attachment relationships/experiences, speaker appears angry, passive, or fearful. Sentences often long, grammatically entangled, or filled with vague usages ("dadadada," "and that"), thus violating Grice's maxims of manner and relevance. Transcripts often excessively long, violating the maxim of quantity.	May be wary or distressed even prior to separation, with little exploration. Preoccupied with parent throughout procedure; may seem angry or passive. Fails to settle and take comfort in parent on reunion, and usually continues to focus on parent and cry. Fails to return to exploration after reunion.
Unresolved/disorganized (U)	Disorganized/disoriented (D)
During discussions of loss or abuse, individual shows striking lapse in the monitoring of reasoning or discourse. For example, individual may briefly indicate a belief that a dead person is still alive in the physical sense, or that this person was killed by a childhood thought. Individual may lapse into prolonged silence or eulogistic speech. The speaker will ordinarily otherwise fit Ds, E, or F categories.	The infant displays disorganized and/or disoriented behaviors in the parent's presence, suggesting a temporary collapse of behavioral strategy. For example, the infant may freeze with a trance-like expression, hands in air; may rise at parent's entrance, then fall prone and huddled on the floor; or may cling while crying hard and leaning away with gaze averted. Infant will ordinarily otherwise fit A, B, or C categories.

Note. Descriptions of the adult attachment classification system are summarized from Main, Kaplan, and Cassidy (1985) and from Main and Goldwyn (1984a, 1998a). Descriptions of infant A, B, and C categories are summarized from Ainsworth, Blehar, Waters, and Wall (1978), and the description of the infant D category is summarized from Main and Solomon (1990). Data from Main (1996).

ter care placement ("Thomas"; see Robertson & Robertson, 1967–1972); Kaplan's master's thesis investigated 6-year-olds' responses to an adaptation of Hansburg's Separation Anxiety Test using pictured parent–child separations (Kaplan, 1984). Nancy Kaplan and a visiting London anthropology student, Ruth Goldwyn, served as AAI interviewers, and by the summer of 1982 Main and Goldwyn had begun to devise a scoring and classification system for interview analysis.

Recognition of the Match between Responses to Protocol Inquiries and the Quality of the Infant's Attachment to the Speaker

The Adult Attachment Interview evolved, then, somewhat serendipitously out of a diverse group of research aims. At the time of its original development, however, the ways in which it would actually be employed in research were somewhat unclear. During a review of the early protocols,

Main became intrigued by a particular narrative that, for reasons not yet fully specifiable, appeared to contain discourse of a kind that would be produced by a parent whose baby would be classified B4 in the strange situation. B4 is a subclassification of security in which emotional expressions of distress and desire for contact after separation are exaggerated, as compared to prototypically secure (B3) infants. Although Main had not yet operationalized the reasons leading to the initial conclusion that the particular speaker under study would have had a child showing a B4 response to him 5 years earlier, this in fact turned out to be the case.

How was it that when this transcript was read, the speaker was predicted to be the parent of a B4 infant? Although there are no definitive answers to this question, several possible explanations arise. The first is that perhaps the reader imagined how this speaker would, as a parent, stimulate and shape an infant response which—although essentially secure—nonetheless required exaggeration of affect in order to maintain the speaker's attention. In contrast, like a B4 infant, the speaker could have conveyed the impression of attempting in a mildly exaggerated way to draw the listener's attention and perhaps even to evoke a caring or sympathetic response. A third possibility is, of course, that both factors were contributory.

The discovery of this correspondence was so intriguing that additional transcripts were read, and the strange situation response of the infant was often correctly predicted. This preliminary outcome led Main and Goldwyn to attempt to develop a formal rule system for capturing the processes involved in making these distinctions. The approach taken to this task began with the random selection of a series of 44 "development" transcripts, which were then categorized, with feedback regarding the strange situation status of each speaker's infant being obtained after each narrative was analyzed. When an appropriate match was found, the "rules" that had been generated to classify the transcript were retained and at times elaborated (see Main & Cassidy, 1988, for a description of a similar development procedure). As this process moved forward, and further matches and mismatches appeared, the existing rules were confirmed, disconfirmed, and refined (Main, 1993, 1995). Gradually, a preliminary system for classifying transcripts into one of three categories predictive of Ainsworth's original infant strange situation response patterns was de-

veloped. Later, rules for identifying transcripts predictive of Main and Solomon's (1986, 1990) fourth strange situation category were generated.

Formalizing the Relation between Parental AAI and Infant Strange Situation Response

After the 44 transcripts in the development sample were discarded, the rule system was tested "blind" on the remaining 66 transcripts. Here no feedback respecting individual cases was provided, and no further adjustments were made to the system. This original rule system was largely composed of a set of general descriptors of the overarching characteristics that made each of the three categories unique. These descriptors have remained active and critical components in the classification process to the present time.

The AAI categories were introduced above via an emphasis upon the discourse process itself—that is, the production of a coherent or incoherent life narrative emerging out of an interaction between two speakers. Although the original category descriptors are now always considered within this larger conversational context, the reader should also be familiar with their more content-oriented parameters. These can be summarized as follows (Main & Goldwyn, 1998a, pp. 148–177).

Secure/Autonomous: Freely Valuing and Yet Objective (F)

Transcripts are placed in the secure/autonomous category when the speaker appears to value attachment relationships and regard attachment-related experiences as influential, but seems relatively independent and objective (autonomous) regarding any particular experience or relationship, and free to explore thoughts and feelings during the course of the interview. If one or both parents are described as loving, there is sufficient evidence to support this description. If, in contrast, the parents are portrayed negatively, these descriptions appear reflective, thoughtful, and often implicitly forgiving. Discussions tend to include "an avowal of a need to depend on others . . . setting parents in relevant contexts when criticizing them, or showing a sense of proportion and balance through humor" (Main & Goldwyn, 1998a, p. 160). Finally, these speakers often evidence a capacity for metacognitive monitoring of their memories and language (Main, 1991), described as "an ability to examine the evidence afresh, even while the interview is in progress" (Main & Goldwyn, 1998a, p. 161).

Some speakers manifesting the above-described characteristics will seem to have had highly unfavorable attachment-related experiences, in which case they are often referred to as "earned secure." This designation is based on the notion that the nature of their experiences as presented would ordinarily create a pathway to an insecure state of mind, suggesting that "earned secure" individuals have gained access to a trajectory that would not have been anticipated. "Earned secure" status has been of interest to many investigators, especially in view of the fact that as parents these individuals have to date been found no less sensitive and responsive to their children than those with apparently more favorable early attachment-related experiences (Pearson, Cohn, Cowan, & Cowan, 1994), even when parenting under stressful conditions (Phelps, Belsky, & Crnic, 1998). Later, however, some of the complexities involved in assessing "earned secure" attachment status are discussed.

Dismissing of Attachment: Dismissing, Devaluing, or "Cut Off" from Attachment Relationships and Experiences (Ds)

The dismissing category is assigned to transcripts in which the speaker's state of mind seems to indicate an attempt to limit the influence of attachment relationships in thought, in feeling, or in daily life. There is an implicit claim to strength, normality, and/or independence, and parents are often presented in positive to highly positive terms that are either unsupported or contradicted. In addition, potential negative effects of parenting or other untoward experiences are denied or minimized, or (rarely) attachment figures or attachment-related phenomena are derogated. What dismissing adults appear to have in common is an organization of thought that permits attachment to remain relatively deactivated (Main, 1995).

Preoccupied: Preoccupied with or by Early Attachments or Attachment-Related Experiences (E)

Interviews are placed in the preoccupied category when the transcript suggests an excessive, confused, and unobjective preoccupation with

particular attachment relationships or experiences. Discussions of these experiences often appear neither fruitful, objective, nor incisive. Descriptions of early relationships may seem vague and uncritical, or else angry, conflicted, and unconvincingly analytical. Finally, some (rare in low-risk samples) seem fearfully preoccupied with and overwhelmed by traumatic experiences, the discussion of which interrupts portions of the interview focused on other topics.

Correspondence of the First Three Categories with Strange Situation Classifications

In Main and Goldwyn's first formal investigation, the three organized infant strange situation classifications (secure, avoidant, and resistant/ambivalent) were compared with the three existing organized AAI classifications (secure/autonomous, dismissing, and preoccupied), and a significant correspondence was uncovered for both the mother–infant and father–infant subsamples (Main, 1985; Main & Goldwyn, 1998b). The three-way match for the 32 mothers and infants seen in the strange situation 5 years previously was 75% (37% expected by chance, kappa = .61, $p < .001$), while the three-way match for the 35 fathers and infants was 69% (46% expected by chance, kappa = .41, $p < .005$). In addition, a highly significant correspondence appeared regarding subcategories (46% match across the eight corresponding infant and adult subcategories, with 17% match expected by chance).

Hence, what had begun with a single transcript suspected of belonging to the parent of a B4 infant, but yet to be operationalized with respect to the characteristics leading to this conclusion, had now been developed into a global system encompassing all the categories and subcategories corresponding to those originally delineated for the strange situation (Ainsworth et al., 1978). The system, then, had been sufficiently refined within the development sample to allow the replication of this original prediction in a larger sample subjected to "blind," formal analysis.

AAI Scale Scores for Inferred Early Experiences and Current State of Mind

In addition to the classification descriptors, a preliminary set of continuous (9-point) scales regarding (1) inferred early experiences with each parent and (2) the speaker's current state of mind with respect to attachment had been developed. Strikingly, AAI scale scores were found to be correlated with continuous scores for particular infant strange situation behavior patterns, so that, for example, across this sample of 32 mothers scores for idealization of the speaker's mother (r = .47) and father (r = .43), and her insistence on lack of memory for childhood (r = .41) were found to be associated with infant scores for avoidance of the mother 5 years previously, while the mother's preoccupied anger in speaking of her own mother (r = .56) was correlated with her infant's earlier angry resistance (Main & Goldwyn, 1984b, 1998b). Similar patterns of correlations emerged among the 35 fathers seen in this sample, so that, for example, the infant's avoidance of the father in the strange situation 5 years earlier was associated with father's insistence upon lack of memory for childhood (r = .47), his idealization of his own mother (r = .53), and interestingly, most strongly of all, with his idealization of his own father (r = .64).

Several new scales have since been developed, and Table 19.3 provides an overview of selected continuous scoring systems (Main & Goldwyn, 1998a). Based on five AAI samples (364 subjects, including a large subgroup of Bay Area subjects collected by Main, Hesse, and van IJzendoorn), Fyffe and Waters (1997) have recently demonstrated the close fit between the continuous scale scores assigned to interview transcripts and interview classifications. Thus, two multiple discriminant functions (secure vs. insecure, and dismissing vs. preoccupied) have been derived, which (1) permit researchers to test for expectable relations between scale scores and classifications in new samples and (2) allow secure, preoccupied, and dismissing states of mind to be approached from a continuous, as well as a categorical, perspective. The continuous scales are also each of import in themselves and are

coming into increasing use in emerging studies. For reasons of space, however, this review of AAI studies must necessarily focus upon categorical findings.

Unresolved/Disorganized with Respect to Potentially Traumatic Experiences (U)

The next discovery regarding the AAI (Main & Hesse, 1990) was that marked lapses in the metacognitive monitoring of reasoning or discourse during the discussion of loss experiences (see below) were related to disorganized infant behavior as defined by Main and Solomon (1990). More specifically, in a subsample of 53 mothers and infants drawn from the Main and Goldwyn study, it was reported that in "blind" analyses only 16% (3 of 19) of mothers showing no significant lapses had disorganized infants, while 91% (11 of 12) with marked discourse/reasoning lapses (unresolved mothers) had infants who had been judged disorganized with them in the strange situation 5 years previously. Thus there was now an AAI category corresponding to and predictive of each of the four strange situation categories in use at that time.

Elaborations and Reconceptualizations in the AAI Scoring and Classification System

Since its inception, the AAI scoring and classification system has undergone a number of changes, the most significant being a refinement of the continuous scales. This made it possible to quantify distinctions in narrative form in ways that took the discourse process itself (i.e., the conversational interaction between interviewer and subject) more fully into consideration. This advance led in turn to the realization that the approach being utilized in fact fit well with the

---

TABLE 19.3. "State-of-Mind" Scales Used in the AAI, Related to the Three Major Categories

Scales associated with the secure/autonomous adult attachment category

Coherence of transcript. For the highest rating, the speaker exhibits a "steady and developing flow of ideas regarding attachment." The person may be reflective and slow to speak, with some pauses and hesitations, or speak quickly with a rapid flow of ideas; overall, however, the speaker seems at ease with the topic, and his or her thinking has a quality of freshness. Although verbatim transcripts never look like written narratives, there are few significant violations of Grice's maxims of quantity, quality, relation, and manner. The reader has the impression that on the whole this text provides a "singular" as opposed to a "multiple" model of the speaker's experiences and their effects (see Main, 1991).

(continued)

TABLE 19.3. *(continued)*

Metacognitive monitoring. For the highest rating, evidence of active monitoring of thinking and recall is evident in several places within the interview. Thus the speaker may comment on logical or factual contradictions in the account of his or her history, possible erroneous biases, and/or the fallibility of personal memory. Underlying metacognitive monitoring (Forguson & Gopnik, 1988) is active recognition of an appearance–reality distinction (the speaker acknowledges that experiences may not have been as they are being presented); representational diversity (e.g., a sibling may not share the same view of the parents); and representational change (e.g., the speaker remarks that what is said today might not have been said yesterday).

Scales associated with the dismissing adult attachment category

Idealization of the speaker's primary attachment figure(s). This scale assesses the discrepancy between the overall view of the parent taken from the subject's speech at the abstract or semantic level, and the reader's inferences regarding the probable behavior of the parent. Since the reader has no knowledge of the speaker's actual history, any discrepancies come from within the transcript itself. For the highest rating, there is an extreme lack of unity between the reader's estimate of the speaker's probable experience with the primary attachment figure(s) and the speaker's positive to highly positive generalized or "semantic" description. Despite inferred experiences of, for example, extreme rejection or even abuse, the portrait of the parent is consistently positive, and gratuitous praise of the parents may be offered (e.g., references to "wonderful" or "excellent" parents).

Insistence on lack of memory for childhood. This scale assesses the speaker's insistence upon her inability to recall her childhood, especially as this insistence is used to block further queries or discourse. The scale focuses upon the subject's direct references to lack of memory ("I don't remember"). High ratings are given to speakers whose first response to numerous interview queries is "I don't remember," especially when this reply is repeated or remains firmly unelaborated. Low scores are assigned when speakers begin a response with a reference to lack of memory, but then actively and successfully appear to recapture access to the experience they have been asked to describe.

Active, derogating dismissal of attachment-related experiences and/or relationships. This scale deals with the cool, contemptuous dismissal of attachment relationships or experiences and their import, giving the impression that attention to attachment-related experiences (e.g., a friend's loss of a parent) or relationships (those with close family members) is foolish, laughable, or not worth the time. High ratings are assigned when a speaker makes no effort to soften or disguise his or her dislike of the individual or of the topic, so that—in keeping with the apparent intent of casting the individual (or topic) aside ("My mother? A nobody. No relationship. Next question?")—the sentences used are often brief and the topic is quickly dropped. Moderately low scores are given for "gallows" humor: "Oh hell, I didn't mind another separation, I guess that one was #13." (Note: Speakers receiving high scores on this scale are assigned to a relatively rare adult attachment subcategory, Ds2, in which attachment figures are derogated rather than idealized.)

Scales associated with the preoccupied adult attachment category

Involved/involving anger expressed toward the primary attachment figure(s). Accurate ratings on this scale depend upon close attention to the form of the discourse in which anger towards a particular attachment figure is implied or expressed. Direct descriptions of angry episodes involving past behavior ("I got so angry I picked up the soup bowl and threw it at her") or direct descriptions of current feelings of anger ("I'll try to discuss my current relationship with my mother, but I should let you know I'm really angry at her right now") do not receive a rating on the scale. High ratings are assigned to speech that includes, for example, run-on, grammatically entangled sentences describing situations involving the offending parent; subtle efforts to enlist interviewer agreement; unlicensed, extensive discussion of surprisingly small recent parental offenses; extensive use of psychological jargon (e.g., "My mother had a lot of material around that issue"); angrily addressing the parent as though the parent were present; and, in an angry context, slipping into unmarked quotations from the parent.

Passivity or vagueness in discourse. High scores are assigned when, throughout the transcript, the speaker seems unable to find words, seize on a meaning, or focus upon a topic. The speaker may, for example, repeatedly use vague expressions or even nonsense words; add a vague ending to an already completed sentence ("I sat on his lap, and that"); wander to irrelevant topics; or slip into pronoun confusion between the self and the parent. In addition, as though absorbed into early childhood states or memories, the subject may inadvertently (not through quotation) speak as a very young child ("I runned very fast") or describe experiences as they are described to a young child ("My mother washed my little feet"). Vague discourse should not be confused with restarts, hesitations, or dysfluency.

work of the linguistic philosopher Grice (1975, 1989) regarding the principles of cooperative discourse.

Incorporating Discourse Properties as Conceptualized by Grice into the Interview Analysis

From the beginning, scores for overall coherence of AAI transcript were found to be a strong correlate of infant security of attachment (e.g., r [31] = .48 for mothers, r [34] = .53 for fathers; Main, 1985; Main & Goldwyn, 1998). *Webster's Dictionary* (1959, p. 520) states that the term "coherence" is derived from the Latin, meaning approximately "a sticking together or uniting of parts." Elaborating upon this definition, Main and Goldwyn (1998a) have stated that "coherence" may be identified as "a connection or congruity arising from some common principle or relationship; consistency; [or] connectedness of thought, such that the parts of the discourse are clearly related, form a logical whole, or are suitable or suited and adapted to context" (p. 44). From this point of view, coherence involves more than simply internal consistency. This is made clear in the statement "form a logical whole, *or are suitable to . . . and adapted to context*" (emphasis added). In other words, even if an individual speaks in a manner that is plausible and internally consistent, thereby adhering to the first aspect of the criterion, he or she may still discuss a topic at excessive length or make obscure analogies, thus failing to shape speech in a manner suitable to the discourse exchange. Thus conversational cooperation, as well as internal consistency, was an important component in Main and Goldwyn's original conceptualization of coherence (Main, in press).

Grice's principles of cooperative, rational discourse thus appeared to relate to the scoring and classification system already constructed for the AAI. Grice (1975, 1989) identified rational or coherent discourse as following an overriding "Cooperative Principle," which normally[1] requires adherence to four maxims and can be summarized as follows:

Quality—be truthful, and have evidence for what you say.
Quantity—be succinct, and yet complete.
Relation—be relevant to the topic at hand.
Manner—be clear and orderly.

To participate most effectively in the interview, then, the speaker must respond to each question as relevant, and then relinquish his or her conversational turn. Discourse is judged coherent when a subject appears able to access and evaluate memories while *simultaneously* remaining plausible (consistent, or implicitly truthful) and collaborative (Hesse, 1996). In presentations of this kind, the discussion and evaluation of attachment-related experiences are reasonably consistent, clear, relevant, and succinct, leading to relatively high AAI coherence scores and placement in the secure/autonomous category.

As discussed earlier, in dismissing interviews typically one or both parents are described in positive terms that are unsupported or contradicted. Intriguingly, in the Main and Goldwyn scoring system, these speakers had already been identified via high scores for idealization of the parent(s), which pointed to a violation of Grice's maxim of quality ("have evidence for what you say"). Many dismissing speakers had also been described as excessively succinct, violating quantity by cutting short the conversational exchange by using such statements as "I don't remember." These speech habits had been quantified as insistence on lack of memory.

Preoccupied speakers tend primarily to violate Grice's maxims of relevance, quantity, and manner, which can be termed the maxims of collaboration. With respect to relevance, some preoccupied speakers wander from topic to topic or move away from the context of the query (e.g., discussing current relations with parents when asked about childhood experiences), while others became embroiled in excessively lengthy descriptions of past or current problems with parents. Violations of manner also typify certain preoccupied speakers, as seen in vague speech ("sort of, sort of—and that"), excessive use of psychological jargon ("my mother had a lot of material around that issue"), and use of nonsense words ("dididididi"). Phenomena conforming to these violations and pointing to the preoccupied classification had already been quantified in continuous scales identifying passivity or vagueness of discourse (manner) and involved/involving anger (relevance, quantity, and manner).

Development of the Unresolved/Disorganized Attachment Category

Main and Goldwyn had noted as early as 1984 that the parents of disorganized/disoriented infants often spoke in unusual ways regarding loss experiences. At that time, however, the specific linguistic features that led to considering such individuals as tentatively "unresolved" were not well operationalized. Unresolved or "disordered" mourning had most commonly been understood as falling into two general categories: (1) "chronic mourning," a continuing strong grief reaction that does not abate over an extended period of time (but see Fraley & Shaver, Chapter 32, this volume); or (2) "failed mourning," in which expectable grief is substantially minimized or does not occur (see Bowlby, 1980). As the analysis of discussions of loss experiences within the AAI development sample proceeded, however, it became evident that the linguistic indicators of "unresolved" attachment status in adults that predicted disorganized attachment in infants did not appear as explicit manifestations of chronic or failed mourning.

Over time, it would become increasingly clear that what the parents of disorganized infants had in common were various indications of what was ultimately termed "lapses in metacognitive monitoring" during discussions of potentially traumatic experiences (Hesse & Main, in press). More specifically, the AAI transcripts of these individuals were distinguished by the appearance of (ordinarily) brief slips in the apparent monitoring of thinking or the discourse context during the discussion of loss or (later) other potentially traumatic events. These discourse/reasoning lapses appear suggestive of temporary alterations in consciousness or working memory, and are believed to represent either interference from normally dissociated memory or belief systems, or unusual absorptions involving memories triggered by the discussion of traumatic events (Hesse & Main, 1999; Hesse & van IJzendoorn, 1998; Hesse & van IJzendoorn, in press).

Lapses in the monitoring of *reasoning* are manifested in statements suggesting that the speaker is temporarily expressing ideas that violate our usual understanding of physical causality or time–space relations. Marked examples of reasoning lapses are seen when speakers make statements indicating that a deceased person is believed simultaneously dead and not-dead in the physical sense—for example, "It was almost better when she died, because then *she could get on with being dead* and I could get on with raising my family" (Main & Goldwyn, 1998a, p. 118; emphasis added). This statement implies a belief, operative at least in that moment, that the deceased remains alive in the physical sense (albeit perhaps in a parallel world). Statements of this kind may thus indicate the existence of incompatible belief and memory systems, which, nor-

mally dissociated, have intruded into consciousness simultaneously as a result of queries regarding the nature of the experience and its effects.

Lapses in the monitoring of discourse, in contrast, sometimes suggest that the topic has triggered a "state shift" indicative of considerable absorption, frequently appearing to involve entrance into peculiar, compartmentalized states of mind (Hesse, 1996; Hesse & van IJzendoorn, in press). Thus, for example, an abrupt alteration or shift in speech register inappropriate to the discourse context occurs when a subject moves from his or her ordinary conversational style into a eulogistic or funereal manner of speaking, or provides excessive attention to detail.

Both state shifts and the sudden appearance of incompatible ideas suggest momentary but qualitative changes in consciousness.[2] Discourse/reasoning lapses of the kinds just described often occur in a high-functioning individual and are normally not representative of the speaker's overall conversational style. For this reason, among others, transcripts assigned to the unresolved/disorganized (hereafter, unresolved) category are given a best-fitting alternate classification (e.g., U/Ds or unresolved/dismissing).

Emergence of the Cannot Classify Adult Attachment Category

As mentioned earlier, a fifth interview category, "cannot classify," emerged as expert judges began noting a small percentage of transcripts that failed to meet criteria for placement in one of the three central or organized attachment categories. This was first observed in transcripts where, for example, an unsupported positive description of one of the parents led to a relatively high idealization score, while in direct contradiction to the expected global patterning, this same parent was later discussed in an angrily preoccupied manner. Thus the idealization score called for placement in the dismissing category, while other portions of the transcript called for preoccupied category placement. Main and Hesse (see Hesse, 1996) therefore concluded that these transcripts were unclassifiable and should be placed in a separate group.

TRAINING INSTITUTES AND THEIR EFFECTS

Since its inception, the AAI has been used in many different countries and research contexts, with new studies emerging on a continuous basis. The methodology is complex, however, and achieving competence at scoring and classifying transcripts requires a significant investment of time.

The first formal 2-week AAI training institute, which included 12 attendees, was held at the University of Virginia in 1985, with Mary Ainsworth acting as host and participant. A second institute was organized by John Bowlby and John Byng-Hall at the Tavistock Clinic in 1987, and in 1988 two additional institutes were held at the University of Virginia. Having established reliability across 100 transcripts, Mary Ainsworth served as cotrainer for the first of these institutes with Mary Main. At this time, the 2-week training emphasized a "top-down" or global-features approach to mastering a recognition of the differing categories.

In 1989, the first institute made up of nonnative English speakers was organized by Massimo Ammaniti and Nino Dazzi at the University of Rome. This institute was taught by Mary Main and Erik Hesse, and it was concluded that because of potential complications created by working from English texts, participants would undertake the analysis of only one case (as opposed to two or three cases) per day. The surprising result of this "experiment" was that trainees appeared to gain a grasp of the system more quickly, and to apply it with greater accuracy. Future institutes therefore followed this format, and in 1991 a further important change was implemented, in that greater emphasis was given to a "bottom-up" or scale-oriented approach to the transcripts and their classification.

From 1989 to 1997, only Mary Main and Erik Hesse served as qualified trainers in the AAI. In 1997, a 2-week "training to train" institute was organized at Berkeley, certifying four new trainers (Nino Dazzi, Deborah Jacobvitz, David Pederson, and June Sroufe) to teach the scoring and classification system. As in the case of the 2-week strange situation training institutes held at Minnesota (see A. Sroufe, 1990), all AAI institutes are now followed by a 30-case reliability check.

EMPIRICAL FINDINGS AND EMERGING DIRECTIONS

Empirical work regarding the AAI can be roughly divided into six topical or conceptual areas. The first is the series of studies replicating the capacity of the AAI to predict an infant's strange situation response to the speaker. It has also been critical to test the psychometric properties of the instrument; to examine relations to parental behavior, particularly parental sensitivity to infant signals; to investigate clinical populations; and to compare strange situation assessments in infancy and the *same* individuals' later responses to the AAI. At present, the AAI is also being used to address many new research topics, including, for example, attachment in couples and the applicability of the instrument to latency-age children.

Predicting Infant Strange Situation Response from Parental Adult Attachment Interviews

Despite the impressive nature of the initial findings regarding the prediction of infant strange situation response from parental attachment interviews, replication remained a first necessity. Using a Charlottesville sample with interviews coded by Mary Ainsworth 2 to 6 months following the strange situation ($n = 45$), Ainsworth and Eichberg (1991)—"blind" to infant strange situation status—replicated the relation between the three organized AAI categories and infant strange situation behavior (80% correspondence; for reasons of space limitation, statistics are no longer given for early individual studies of AAI–strange situation correspondence, but see van IJzendoorn, 1995, below).

Ainsworth (personal communication, 1988) also replicated the adult to infant sub-classification match reported by Main and Goldwyn (1998b), finding 45% correspondence (18% expected by chance). Additionally, as in the Main and Hesse (1990) report, unresolved attachment status strongly predicted disorganized strange situation response (89% correspondence). As regards unresolved adult attachment status, Ainsworth and Eichberg demonstrated that loss in and of itself (even early loss of a parent) did not predict infant disorganization. Instead, infant disorganization was related specifically to lapses in discourse or reasoning surrounding the discussion of loss.

Another critical issue regarding Adult Attachment Interview–strange situation correspondence was the possible influence of the offspring upon the parent's state of mind. To rule out this potential confound, it was necessary to administer the interview prior to the birth of the subject's first child. The pioneering work in this area was conducted by Fonagy, Steele, and Steele (1991).

Here 96 London mothers were interviewed *before* childbirth, and strange situation assessments at 12 months were conducted by judges unaware of the mothers' AAI status. The overall two-way (secure–insecure) match between mothers' prenatal interviews and children's security of attachment was 75%, and the three-way match was 66%.

Several additional prebirth studies have now been conducted, with similarly impressive results. Using an Australian sample of 44 dyads that included the unresolved category, Radojevic (1994) was the first to replicate the Bay Area findings relating fathers' AAI status to "blind" assessments of their infants' strange situation behavior. The secure–insecure match between fathers' prebirth interviews and infants' response to the father at 15 months was 77%, and 60% of unresolved fathers had disorganized infants. Prebirth AAIs in the London study uncovered similar secure–insecure correspondence between fathers' interviews and infant strange situation response (71%; Steele, Steele, & Fonagy, 1996).

Benoit and Parker (1994) are to date the only investigators to complete a three-generation study, examining the match between AAIs conducted with mothers and their adult daughters. A striking three-way correspondence of 75%—directly comparable to the mother–infant matches reported in previous studies—was found between mothers (grandmothers) and their adult daughters, with secure grandmothers tending overwhelmingly to have secure adult daughters. In addition, the daughters' AAI status was assessed prior to their infants' birth, yielding an 81% three-way and 77% four-way AAI–strange situation correspondence. A simple parent-to-child transmission model was found to account for the results, and grandmothers' adult attachment categories were significantly related to those of their grandchildren.

Ward and Carlson (1995) were the first to examine the correspondence between AAI and strange situation response in a high-risk sample of unmarried inner-city adolescent mothers and infants. Seventy-four mothers were administered the AAI prior to the birth of each mother's first child, and their infants were seen in the strange situation at 15 months. Independent, "blind" codings replicated the three-way (78%) and four-way (68%) mother–infant associations reported for middle-class samples.

In 1995, van IJzendoorn provided a meta-analytic overview of the parent–infant matches in the 14 studies then available (18 samples, 854 dyads). This analysis was based on investigations conducted in six countries, and included two reports comparing the AAI to Waters's (secure–insecure) Attachment Q-Sorts of child behavior observed in the home (Eiden, Teti, & Corns, 1995; Posada, Waters, Crowell, & Lay, 1995). For the secure–insecure split, the combined correspondence across samples was 75%. The combined effect size (d) was 1.06 (equal to a Fisher's Z of 0.51), $r = .49$ (biserial $r = .59$), and maternal attachments tended to be related somewhat more strongly to children's attachment ($d = 1.14$, $r = .50$) than did paternal attachments ($d = 0.80$, $r = 0.37$). Cohen (1988) notes that an effect size of 0.50 should be considered moderate, while one of 0.80 should be considered strong, and van IJzendoorn calculated that it would take 1,087 studies with null results to diminish the combined one-tailed p level to insignificance (Rosenthal, 1991).

For the three organized categories, the correspondence across studies was 70% (kappa = .46). The combined effect size for the match between the adult dismissing and the infant avoidant categories was 1.02, and for the match between the adult preoccupied and infant ambivalent categories it was 0.93.

Nine studies had been conducted utilizing a four-way analysis (548 dyads), and the overall four-category correspondence was 63% (kappa = .42). Given that unresolved attachment status is most often assigned on the basis of only a few sentences, while disorganized infant attachment status is normally established via only a few seconds of behavior (Main & Solomon, 1990), it was striking indeed that the unresolved adult category was specifically predictive of the disorganized infant category (combined $d = 0.65$, $r = .31$). Amount of training was strongly associated with differences in effect sizes relating unresolved adult attachment status to infant disorganized attachment: More training was associated with much larger effects.

Finally, van IJzendoorn's (1995) meta-analysis showed that the parent–infant correspondence for the five prebirth samples (389 dyads) was equivalent to that seen in the remaining studies. This further emphasized the likelihood that individual differences in infants' contribution to interactions with the parents could not account for the relation between the interview and strange situation behavior.

Since 1995, studies of AAI–strange situation correspondence have continued. Sagi et al. (1997) uncovered "contextual constraints" on intergenerational transmission in Israeli kibbutzim, depending upon whether infants slept in communal groups (40% mother–infant match) or had home-based sleeping arrangements (76% match). In studies involving 20 Italian, 28 German, and 60 Canadian dyads, notable mother–infant correspondences were reported by Ammaniti, Speranza, and Candelori (1996, 85% secure–insecure match), by Gloger-Tibbelt and Gomille (1999, 82% match), and by Pederson, Gleason, Moran, and Bento (1998, 80% match), respectively.

In addition, two recent investigations have compared Main and Cassidy's (1988) attachment classification system for 6-year-old children to concurrent AAIs conducted with mothers. In a "blind" study of 32 middle-class 6-year-olds and their mothers, George and Solomon (1996) uncovered a four-way match of 82% (kappa = .74, p < .0001) between mothers' AAI status and their 6-year-olds' attachment. Similarly, Ammaniti et al. (1996) reported a 95% secure–insecure match between mothers' AAIs and 6-year-olds' attachment. In the Pederson et al. (1998) study, a 60% three-way match (kappa = .30, p < .01) was found between mothers' AAIs and infants' attachment as assessed via Pederson and Moran's (1996) home attachment classification system.

Three final points should be made in this discussion. First, the correspondence between the AAI and Main and Cassidy's (1988) classification system for 6-year-olds, Waters's (1995) home Attachment Q-Sort, and Pederson and Moran's (1996) home attachment classifications shows that parental attachment representations as they relate to infant attachment security are not the consequence of "method bias" (i.e., are not tied to one particular way of assessing the offspring's attachment). As an illustration, discourse/reasoning lapses during the discussion of potentially traumatic events can alternately be seen as instances of (linguistic) "disorganization and disorientation," which, as the reader is aware, has repeatedly been found to be associated with disorganized/disoriented strange situation behavior. At 6, however, children disorganized as infants no longer show disorganized behavior upon reunion, but are instead punitive or caregiving (termed "D-controlling"). At this age, therefore, the relations between the unresolved category and D-controlling behavior (87% correspondence; George & Solomon, 1996) cannot rely upon "mirroring." Thus, a parent's "state of mind" and a child's attachment remain systematically related, despite differing methods of assessing the child's attachment and despite developmental transformations.

Second, van IJzendoorn's (1995) meta-analysis has shown that within the insecure AAI categories, the dismissing, preoccupied, and unresolved classifications are each specifically predictive of the corresponding infant attachment classifications. This means (van IJzendoorn, 1995, p. 396) that the predictive validity of the instrument is not restricted to the global secure–insecure attachment distinction, but meets one of the most important validity requirements in being able to distinguish among the three insecure categories as well.

Finally, a test's reliability establishes an upper limit on its validity, and van IJzendoorn (1995) suggested that with further standardization of training, the effect sizes reported in his meta-analysis might be found to have underestimated the "true" degree of correspondence between adult and infant classifications. Later, van IJzendoorn and Bakermans-Kranenburg (1997) estimated inter-judge agreement at 80%, while an informal survey of available publications undertaken by the present writer yields an average inter-judge agreement of 82% across studies for both the three-way and four-way analyses (mean kappa = .71 for both as well). It should be noted, however, that these figures may underestimate the ability of investigators to obtain valid results. Some investigators have used two or more coders for all cases, and used consensual agreement (or submission to a third judge) on disagreed cases; others used fully trained judges for published data, but provide interrater reliability estimates using a judge who has not completed training in the instrument.

Psychometric Properties of the Adult Attachment Interview

van IJzendoorn and Bakermans-Kranenburg (1996) reported that in a combined (meta-analytic) sample of 584 nonclinical mothers, 24% were classified as dismissing, 58% as secure/autonomous, and 18% as preoccupied. With the unresolved category included, a four-way analysis of the available 487 nonclinical mothers showed the following distribution: 16% dismissing, 55% secure/autonomous, 9% preoccupied, and 19% unresolved. The combined distribution of nonclinical fathers was highly similar. Interestingly, a meta-analysis of five studies that included both wives and husbands (226 couples) showed a three-way correspondence comparable to a correlation of $r = .28$, accounted for by the fact that secure men and women married each other at greater than chance levels. In the four-way analysis ($n = 152$), the secure–insecure association was not found; however, unresolved individuals appeared to have married more often than expected by chance.

AAI distributions in adolescent samples did not differ significantly from distributions in the nonclinical adult samples. However, combined samples with very low-socioeconomic-status backgrounds ($n = 995$) did differ significantly from nonclinical mother samples, with the unresolved and dismissing categories being overrepresented, and the secure/autonomous category correspondingly underrepresented. The AAI was found to be unrelated to social desirability (Bakermans-Kranenburg & van IJzendoorn, 1993; Crowell et al., 1996; Sagi et al., 1994), and showed only a modest association with social adjustment (Crowell et al., 1996). Although the AAI was only weakly related to content-based retrospective parenting style measures and appeared to be independent of general personality measures (van IJzendoorn, 1995), more recently persons classified as preoccupied have been found to report more symptoms on the Minnesota Multiphasic Personality Inventory than others, whereas dismissing individuals report fewer (Pianta, Egeland, & Adam, 1996).

The AAI has been subjected to a series of rigorous psychometric tests of its stability and discriminant validity (van IJzendoorn, 1995). Stability studies typically employ different interviewers across the time period in question, with coders unaware of one another's classifications. With interviews conducted 2 months apart ($n = 83$), Bakermans-Kranenburg and van IJzendoorn (1993) found 78% stability (kappa = .63) across the three organized attachment categories (the unresolved category was less stable), while an Israeli study of 59 college students conducted 3 months apart yielded 90% test–retest stability (kappa = .79; Sagi et al., 1994). The mean inter-judge agreement for this latter study was 95%. Both studies reported that category placement could not be attributed to the influence of a particular interviewer.

Stability has also been tested across an 18-month period in New York (86% three-category stability, kappa = .73; Crowell et al., 1996), and across a 4-year period in Rome (95% secure–insecure correspondence, 70% three-category correspondence, Ammaniti et al., 1996). In their study of Canadian mothers, Benoit and Parker

(1994) found 90% three-category stability between a prebirth interview and interviews conducted at 11 months of infant age ($n = 84$). The outcome of this last investigation is particularly important since the major life transition occasioned by the birth of a first child might have been expected to change a mother's "state of mind with respect to attachment."

Because of the weight given to "coherence" scores when AAI transcripts are being assigned to secure versus insecure attachment status, it has been critical to establish that in five out of six studies conducted to date, secure versus insecure adult attachment status has been found to be unrelated to intelligence, including assessments specific to verbal fluency (Crowell, Fraley, & Shaver, Chapter 20, this volume; van IJzendoorn, 1995). Moreover, because insistence on lack of memory for childhood is associated with the dismissing category, it has been necessary to assess general abilities involving memory. Thus, if persons assigned to the dismissing category suffer from overall difficulties with childhood memories, their insistence on lack of recall for early relationships and interactions might not pertain to state of mind specific to attachment history. This question was first examined by Bakermans-Kranenburg and van IJzendoorn (1993), who found the AAI categories to be independent of nonattachment-related memory. An Israeli study (Sagi et al., 1994) used an even broader range of memory tests. Here, the accuracy of memories for childhood events was ingeniously tested, and subjects were also examined for "immediate" memory skills in a test of (non-attachment-related) paired associates. No differences were found across the categories.

One of the most critical questions pertaining to the discriminant validity of the AAI stems from its reliance upon individual differences in discourse characteristics. If these characteristics were found to generalize to non-attachment-related topics, the inability of the parents of insecure infants to produce coherent and collaborative AAI narratives could not readily be attributed to an (insecure) state of mind arising specifically from a request for a review and evaluation of their attachment history. This question was addressed by Crowell, Waters, and their colleagues, using an "Employment Experience Interview," which followed the form of the AAI protocol, but focused upon technical aspects of the speaker's work history (Crowell et al., 1996). Although transcripts of the Employment Experience Interview could be reliably classified as secure/autonomous, dismissing, or preoccupied, these classifications were orthogonal to the secure/autonomous, dismissing, and preoccupied classifications assigned to the same 53 mothers within the AAI. Thus it appears that the attachment-related content of the AAI protocol does in fact have a direct influence upon the linguistic form manifested in the interview transcript.

The AAI as Predictive of Caregiving

Ainsworth's original studies of infant–mother interaction uncovered a strong relation between a mother's "sensitivity and responsiveness to infant signals and communications" and infant security as indicated by strange situation behavior (Ainsworth et al., 1978; see also Belsky, Chapter 12, this volume). Therefore, almost as soon as the match between parental and infant attachment classification was uncovered, reports relating secure/autonomous adult attachment to sensitive, or otherwise positive, behavior toward an infant or preschooler began to emerge (e.g., Crowell & Feldman, 1988, 1991). van IJzendoorn (1995) provided a meta-analytic overview of 10 studies ($n = 389$) comparing secure vs. insecure parental attachment representations to observations of parents' sensitivity, warmth, structure, and supportiveness as seen in interactions with their infants or preschoolers. The combined effect size across these investigations was 0.72, equivalent to $r = .34$. Intriguingly, whereas the match between the AAI and the infant's strange situation behavior was somewhat lower (but still strong, $d = .80$) for fathers as compared to mothers, the predictability of caregiving responsiveness from the AAI was greater for fathers than for mothers.

Although only a small proportion of studies had applied Ainsworth's sensitivity scales to observations of parent–infant interaction, one aim of van IJzendoorn's analysis was of course to test the hypothesis that parental sensitivity acted as the mediator between the AAI and infant strange situation response. To act as a mediator sufficient to account for the strong ($r = .49$, biserial $r = .59$) relation between the AAI and strange situation behavior, however, parental sensitivity would have to be (1) highly related to parental state of mind, and (2) highly related to infant security of attachment. With this in mind, and utilizing a selection of the most adequate studies from Goldsmith and Alansky's (1987) estimate ($r = .32$) of the relation between maternal sensitivity and infant security of attachment as assessed in the strange situation, van IJzendoorn demonstrated that there was a marked "transmission gap" in our understanding of the nature of the interactions accounting for the relation between the AAI and the strange situation. Indeed, van IJzendoorn's calculations showed that the largest part of the influence of adult mental representation on infant security of attachment was as yet unspecified (i.e., could not be accounted for by parental sensitivity and responsiveness as currently assessed).

A later investigation undertaken to improve upon anomalies in some of the studies included in van IJzendoorn's meta-analysis ultimately served to confirm the existence of van IJzendoorn's "transmission gap." In this study of 60 Canadian infant–mother dyads, not only was the AAI strongly related to infant strange situation response, but maternal sensitivity was found to be strongly related to infant security ($r = .60$; Pederson et al., 1998). However, the relation between a mother's attachment status and sensitivity to her infant was modest, and the direct path between parental autonomy and infant security accounted for approximately five times the variance accounted for by the mediated path (maternal sensitivity).

Both van IJzendoorn (1995) and Pederson et al. (1998) have noted that difficulties in assessing parental sensitivity may account in part for the transmission gap, since neither training institutes nor reliability checks are available to those utilizing this observational approach. van IJzendoorn has further suggested that genetic transmission, and emotional interactions more subtle than are (or can be) captured in the usual assessments of maternal sensitivity (such as the indices of "affect attunement" found to be related to AAIs in a pilot study by Haft & Slade, 1989), could also contribute to the existing association between parental and infant attachment. To these suggestions, Pederson and his colleagues have added the possible contribution of a parent's ability to make accurate attributions regarding the nature of an infant's mental processes (Fonagy, Steele, Steele, Moran, & Higgitt, 1991; Main, 1991), and the socialization and regulation of infant emotions (Cassidy, 1994). In this latter context, it is noteworthy, for example, that dismissing mothers have been found to be more likely than others to have a negative response to a videotape of a crying infant (Zeanah et al., 1993). Moreover, in a first report from a larger study focused on narrowing the "transmission gap" via the investigation of parental responsiveness to video-tapes of infants in varying emotional states, Goldberg, Blokland, Cayetano, and Benoit (1998) are finding that dismissing mothers seem least interested in and responsive to infant affect; preoccupied mothers inappropriately responsive; and secure–autonomous mothers the most likely to be empathetic, being the only mothers to mirror negative infant expressions with negative expressions of their own. Finally—in keeping with Bowlby's original (1969/1982) emphasis upon the close relations between the attachment and the fear ("escape") systems, and Main's recent emphasis upon the role of fear in individual differences in the organization (or disorganization) of attachment relationships (Hesse & Main, 1999; Main, 1995)—secure–autonomous mothers were also found superior in their ability to recognize fearful infant facial expressions, while dismissing mothers were least likely to recognize them and most likely to identify fear as "interest."

It is evident that van IJzendoorn's identification of the "transmission gap" will provide the basis for much future observational (and perhaps also experimental) research. Among other possibilities mentioned by van IJzendoorn and by Pederson et al., one in particular warrants special examination. This is the likelihood that the parent's early influence may sufficiently launch the infant on a path toward a particular state of attachment organization (or disorganization), so that, in a kind of feedforward model, the infant comes to participate in the formation of its own attachment, simultaneously shaping—and in some cases altering—the degree and type of parental responsiveness that can thereafter be observed. If so, then earlier observations of parental behavior may be found to be more strongly related to parental AAIs than later ones. Interestingly, observations of maternal sensitivity made earlier in the first year of life have been found to be more strongly related to 12-month infant strange situation response than observations made later (Grossmann, Grossmann, Spangler, Suess, & Unzer, 1985; Isabella, 1993; see also Sroufe, Egeland, & Kreutzer, 1990).

The upshot of this argument is that once enough time has elapsed, children's behavior may already have been sufficiently shaped by parental (un)responsiveness that observers have, for example, little opportunity to witness the parents' responsiveness to (no longer evident) expressions of distress (Pederson et al., 1998). In keeping with this hypothesis, Beckwith, Cohen, and Hamilton (in press) have reported that mater-

nal sensitivity at 1 month was a stronger predictor of security as assessed in AAIs administered at age 18 than was sensitivity assessed at 8 or 24 months, while maternal sensitivity at 12 years showed no relation to adolescent AAI status.

An investigation that may ultimately aid in throwing further light on this question is currently being undertaken by Dozier and her colleagues at Delaware (Stovall & Dozier, 1998), who have completed a single-subject analysis of newly evolving attachment relationships in 10 foster mother–infant dyads. Here, infants placed with secure–autonomous foster mothers before 12 months of age were independently found secure both in the strange situation and according to diary entry data recorded by the mother. However, children placed with secure–autonomous foster mothers after 12 months were insecure both in the strange situation and as recorded in the mother's diary.

Comparing Adult Attachment Classifications in Clinical and Nonclinical Populations

As discussed earlier, the central categories of the AAI were developed and refined with respect to a 1-year-old's (secure vs. insecure) response to the speaker in a stressful situation. No examination of interview responses within clinical samples had been undertaken, however, and it is therefore surprising that—without adjustment—this system would ultimately be shown to discriminate between clinical and nonclinical populations (van IJzendoorn & Bakermans-Kranenburg, 1996). Indeed, the effect size discriminating clinical from nonclinical populations ($d = 1.03$) was found to be almost identical to that discriminating the parents of secure infants from the parents of insecure infants ($d = 1.06$). Ultimately, in a four-way analysis, only 8% of members of clinical samples were judged secure.

Attachment Status in the Mothers of Clinically Distressed Children

In the first study of mothers of clinically distressed infants, Benoit, Zeanah, and Barton (1989) reported that only 1 of 23 mothers of 7- to 8-month-old infants hospitalized for failure to thrive was judged secure/autonomous, whereas distributions in their comparison group of mothers of infants hospitalized for chronic and acute physical illnesses did not diverge from those of other samples. In another study, among 20 mothers of severely sleep-disordered infants, not one was identified as secure/autonomous (Benoit, Zeanah, Boucher, & Minde, 1992).

Using a three-way analysis, Crowell and Feldman (1988) found that 17 out of 20 mothers of children with behavior problems (85%) were insecure, while all 20 mothers of children suffering jointly from developmental delay and clinical problems (100%) were insecure. Later, mothers of children with conduct and disruptive/aggressive disorders were found to be almost exclusively insecure, although, importantly, only 6 out of 10 mothers of children suffering from attention-deficit/hyperactivity disorder uncomplicated by conduct and aggressive/disruptive disorders were insecure (Crowell & Feldman, 1991). Similar outcomes are emerging for adolescents; thus, for example, Rosenstein and Horowitz (1996) reported that among 27 mothers of psychiatrically hospitalized adolescents only 2 were secure.

Moreover, in four-way analyses, conduct disorder is being found to be related to unresolved maternal attachment. For example, DeKlyen (1996) found 19 out of 25 mothers of conduct-disordered children insecure; 11 of these were unresolved or cannot classify (for comparable results, see also Constantino, 1996; Greenberg, Speltz, DeKlyen, & Endriga, 1991; Speltz, Greenberg, & DeKlyen, 1990).

Attachment Status in Clinically Distressed Adolescents and Adults

Many studies of clinically distressed adolescents and adults have now been conducted or are in progress. Although most of these investigations focus on fairly large samples, some have examined carefully matched individuals who differ only in terms of diagnoses.

A study of the latter kind (24 closely comparable female subjects, 12 borderline and 12 dysthymic, none comorbid) was conducted at the Tavistock Clinic, using a coder who was unaware of either subjects' diagnoses or the aims of the investigation (Patrick, Hobson, Howard, Castle, & Maughan, 1994). Borderline patients were selected for having met at least seven out of the eight *Diagnostic and Statistical Manual of Mental Disorders,* third edition, revised (DSM-III-R) criteria. All of the twelve borderline patients— but only 4 dysthymic patients—were classified as preoccupied (Fisher's exact test, two-tailed, $p = .001$). Moreover, 10 of the 12 borderline patients were classified into one particular (very

rare) AAI subcategory, E3, meaning that descriptions of frightening events repeatedly and inappropriately interrupted responses to queries regarding other topics. The overall rates of experiences of trauma and loss as defined by Main and Goldwyn did not differ between groups, but all 9 of the borderline subjects reporting loss or trauma were classified as primarily unresolved (e.g., U/E3) as compared to only 2 of the 10 dysthymic patients reporting loss or trauma (Fisher's exact test, two-tailed, $p = .0007$).

Fonagy et al. (1996) undertook a large-scale study of 82 clinically distressed young adults at a national center for the inpatient treatment of severe personality disorders in London, comparing interviews to those of 85 well-matched controls. The transcripts were screened for references to hospital treatment, and were analyzed using both the continuous scoring systems and the four major classifications.

Only 9 of the 82 psychiatric patients, but 50 of the 85 control patients, were judged secure/autonomous with the four-category system ($\chi^2 = 78.4, p < .001$). In addition, many of the AAI experience and state-of-mind scales, as well as Fonagy's "reflective-self" scale (Fonagy, Steele, Steele, Moran, & Higgitt, 1991; see below), sharply differentiated the psychiatric patients from the controls. The category most strongly differentiating the groups was unresolved (76% inpatients vs. 7% controls), and—as in an earlier study of anxiety-disordered subjects conducted by Manassis, Bradley, Goldberg, and Hood (1994; 14 of 18 or 78% unresolved)—anxiety-disordered subjects were found especially likely to be unresolved (38 of 44 or 86%). Among the subclassifications, fearful preoccupation with traumatic events (E3) was found to be unexpectedly common in the psychiatric group (28% vs. 1%). Replicating earlier outcomes (Patrick et al., 1994), 47% of the borderline patients were classified E3[3].

Adam, Sheldon-Keller, and West (1996) examined attachment status and suicidality in 133 adolescents (mean age = 15½ years) from Canadian inpatient and outpatient treatment centers. Fifty-three of the 69 adolescents placed in the suicidal group had made suicide attempts, and 13 had severe suicidal ideation. Transcripts were coded by judges unaware of case status.

In this study, history of exposure to attachment-related trauma had similar prevalence in each group (86% suicidal, 78% comparison). However, among those adolescents who were exposed to trauma, the unresolved classification had a significantly higher prevalence for the suicidal group (73% vs. 44%). Preoccupied attachment was also associated with suicidality, and strikingly, 77% of subjects who were both unresolved and preoccupied (U/E) were found in the suicidal group. It was concluded (1) that cognitive disorganization surrounding traumatic events as assessed within the AAI may mediate the relation between earlier traumatic experience and adolescent suicidal behavior found in previous studies; and (2) that preoccupied individuals may be especially vulnerable to disorganization.

In a highly informative and different kind of investigation (Allen, Hauser, & Borman-Spurrell, 1996), the interview was administered to 66 young adults (mean age = 26) who had been psychiatrically hospitalized 11 years previously, and to a matched (nonhospitalized, $n = 76$) control sample. Both groups came from upper-middle-class families, and individuals suffering from psychosis or organic impairment were excluded from the hospitalized sample. Interviews were "blinded" for any evidence of previous hospitalization.

Surprisingly, the proportion of secure/autonomous transcripts among individuals hospitalized 11 years previously (7.6%) was no higher than that found in studies examining individuals experiencing current distress. Moreover, the interview transcripts of 25.8% of the hospitalized group were judged cannot classify, as compared to 6.6% of the comparison group. Speakers who had been hospitalized were far less coherent than controls, were more likely to express contempt or derogation for attachment-related experiences and attachment figures, and received higher scores for unresolved responses to abuse experiences. The latter two scales were also found to be related to criminal behavior, and derogation was related to hard drug use. Notably, Rosenstein and Horowitz (1996)—who found only 1 of 60 psychiatrically hospitalized adolescents to be secure/autonomous—also found substance abuse to be related to the dismissing category. Among males, these authors found conduct disorders highly predictive of the dismissing attachment category (14/15 cases).

In other recent studies involving adolescents, Ivarsson, Broberg, and Gillberg (1998) found 11 of 15 participants seen in Swedish outpatient clinics for depressive disorders dismissing, and only one secure. In Rome, 36 patients suffering from eating disorders (mean age, 17 years) were administered the AAI. Few were secure, and interestingly, anorexia was associated with the dismissing category, while bulimic subjects tended to be preoccupied (Candelori & Ciocca, 1998).

Descriptive Case Studies

Recently, "blind" case studies have examined clinical distress in relation to the AAI. Focusing on a troubled adolescent mother placed in the rare AAI subcategory termed "derogating of attachment" (Ds2) on the basis of speech characteristics observed in the AAI, Zeanah, Finley-Belgrad, and Benoit (1997) found that (a) the subject's mother had threatened to kill her, and (b) had herself experienced similar threats from the subject's grandmother. Sharply in keeping with her speech characteristics, the young mother's treatment of her own children was observed to be initially cruel, teasing, and derogating.

As the reader will recall, speakers are assigned to the cannot classify category when contradictory discourse strategies appear within the AAI. With this in mind, it is of particular interest that a mother judged cannot classify by Hughes and MacGauley (1997) exhibited marked neglect and carelessness to a degree inviting of external injury, while making alternating sudden trips to the hospital occasioned by fear of germs. Another mother described as cannot classify by Minde and Hesse (1996) demanded (successfully) to have her child removed by Caesarean section 1 month early, then insisted on staying with the infant in intensive care for periods that far exceeded usual hospital practices. Like the other mother described above, she later alternated periods of overinvolvement with periods of neglect. In keeping with the hypothesis that discourse usage in the AAI should be predictive of caregiving, then, these two case studies of "unclassifiable" discourse were found to reflect "unclassifiable" behavior towards the offspring.

AAI Status and Psychopathology in a Nonclinical Sample

In the clinical studies discussed above, individuals diagnosed with varying disorders have been examined for their accompanying adult attachment classifications. Recently, Lee, Polan, and Ward (1998) completed an investigation of a *nonclinical* New York sample of 60 adult women, who were seen in the Adult Attachment Interview as well as in the diagnostic setting. Using the "organized" (secure–autonomous, dismissing, and preoccupied) attachment categories in the analysis, a majority of women with insecure attachment classifications were diagnosed with psychopathology. Further, the authors tested how DSM III-R Axis I and Axis II psychopathology (none, Axis I or I and II combined, Axis II only) might be related to the three organized classifications. A significant association was found between psychopathology and AAI status, such that placement in the dismissing category was associated with Axis I (or Axis I and Axis II, comorbid) while placement in the preoccupied category was associated with Axis II placement. Finally, when the unresolved category was utilized, unresolved subjects whose alternative placement was secure–autonomous (unresolved/secure) were found significantly less likely to be diagnosed with psychopathology than subjects with unresolved/insecure classifications, although unresolved/secure–autonomous subjects did experience some difficulties with daily functioning (e.g., marital discord, physical symptoms).

Longitudinal Studies of Attachment Status

Despite the fact that the AAI focuses on an individual's presentation and evaluation of attachment-related experiences, until recently it has chiefly been known for its implied ability to predict caregiving behavior via the infant's strange situation response. This is, of course, not informative regarding the potential of the instrument either to identify the probable nature of the speaker's early attachment relationships, or to assist in systematically tracing pathways involving change.

Recently, however, five studies have compared infant attachment as assessed nonverbally in the strange situation to discourse regarding attachment-related experiences in AAIs conducted with the same individuals 15 to 21 years later. In all of these investigations, judges coding the interview have been unaware of infant attachment classification.

Waters, Merrick, Treboux, Crowell, and Albersheim (in press) conducted AAIs with 50 lower- to middle-class young adults (aged 20 to 22) seen in the Ainsworth strange situation at 12 months. In a first, three-way analysis ($n = 50$), 64% of subjects were placed in the adult attachment category corresponding to their original strange situation response (kappa = .40), while for 72% of subjects (kappa = .44), secure versus insecure infant strange situation behavior was predictive of coherent vs. incoherent interview

texts. Attachment status was, however, significantly less stable for young adults who had experienced loss of a parent, parental divorce, life-threatening illness in a parent or self, parental psychiatric disorder, or physical or sexual abuse prior to age 18. Among the 32 subjects who did *not* report such events, the three-way correspondence was 72% (kappa = .46), while the two-way correspondence was 78% (kappa = .52).

Hamilton (in press) examined the predictability of AAI responses in a sample of 30 adolescents (aged 17 to 19) who had been raised in unconventional lifestyles (e.g., communal living groups).[4] In a three-way analysis, 63% of subjects were placed in adult attachment categories corresponding to their strange situation response to their mothers during infancy, while the two-way (secure vs. insecure) correspondence was 77% (kappa = .49). Negative life events were associated with maintenance of an insecure attachment pattern.

Two of the five studies using the Main and Goldwyn system did not find continuity between strange situation and AAI response. One investigation involved a low-risk sample of German 16-year-olds (Zimmermann, Grossmann, & Fremmer-Bombik, 1998; information regarding this study is limited, since these outcomes were discovered as this chapter was going to press). The second investigation included many subjects experiencing substantial intervening trauma. In this latter study, Weinfield, Sroufe, and Egeland (in press) conducted interviews with 57 adolescents (aged 18 to 19) drawn from an at-risk poverty sample. Although only 39% of participants had been judged insecure with their mothers in infancy, 68% were judged insecure in adolescence (60% dismissing). In addition, while 78% of adolescents insecure with their mothers in infancy were incoherent and noncollaborative (insecure) in the AAI, 65% who had been secure as infants were also incoherent and noncollaborative in adolescence. Hence, no association between strange situation behavior and AAI response was uncovered, although child maltreatment, maternal depression, and assessments of family functioning provided some evidence for lawful discontinuity. In keeping with Bowlby's earliest writings (Bowlby, 1969/1982, 1973, 1980; Robertson & Bowlby, 1952), then, the findings from the Minnesota study are incompatible with a "critical period" hypothesis respecting attachment.

The disorganized infant attachment category was not utilized in the above-described studies.

Forty-five subjects from the Bay Area longitudinal sample have, however, now been administered the AAI at age 19 (Main & Hesse, 1998), and about 90% of interviews have been analyzed. With the disorganized category included, strong predictability of secure versus insecure AAI response from infants' strange situation response to their mothers is being uncovered. A majority of subjects secure with their mothers in infancy have been found to be coherent and collaborative (secure/autonomous) in discussing their attachment-related experiences during adolescence. In contrast, only a small minority of subjects avoidant or resistant with their mothers during infancy have been judged secure/autonomous. Finally, among the 12 adolescents given a disorganized category placement in infancy, not one has been judged secure/autonomous.

A fifth longitudinal investigation of adolescents in a low-risk sample (Lewis, 1997) used Kobak's AAI *Q*-Sort (described below), and, as in the German study (Zimmermann et al., 1998), reported that *Q*-Sorted attachment status in adolescence could not be predicted from infant "strange situation" behavior. Ainsworth's two-separation procedure was not utilized, however, and instead, attachment was assessed on the basis of a single separation and reunion. Thus these results are difficult to interpret.

Three further studies bearing upon issues of long-term predictability of attachment status should be noted briefly here. As discussed earlier, an investigation of 81 Canadian (grand)mothers and their adult daughters (Benoit & Parker, 1994) found 75% three-way correspondence in attachment status (kappa = .51). In addition, Rosenstein and Horowitz (1996) uncovered an 81% three-way correspondence (kappa = .62) between 27 mothers and their psychiatrically hospitalized adolescents. It is yet be determined, however, whether the impressive correspondence reported in these two studies reflect long-term stability in the offspring's attachment, continuing or concurrent interactions between mother and offspring, similarity of circumstances, or some combination of these factors.

In a study bearing more directly upon long-term predictability, Beckwith et al. (in press) saw 86 premature infants in naturalistic home observations (1, 8, and 24 months), followed up with ("blind") AAI codings (secure/autonomous, dismissing, or preoccupied) at 18 years of age. Simple event coding had been used to assess maternal sensitivity across 15-second intervals, so that at 1 month, for example, the "sensitivity" score had summed maternal positive attentiveness, talk to the infant, holding, contingency to infant distress, and mutual gaze. The mothers of the 35 dismissing 18-years-olds (i.e., those who normalized or presented an idealized portrait of their parents, often while insisting on lack of memory for childhood) were found to have consistently received the lowest sensitivity scores.

New Directions

The AAI is currently being extended to new populations and areas of inquiry. Due to space considerations, only a few of these investigations can be summarized here.

Extension to Younger Samples

As noted earlier, Ward and Carlson (1995) reported "blind" matches between adolescent mothers' prebirth AAIs (mean age, 16 years) and infant strange situation response identical to those found for adult mothers and their children. Similarly, "blinded" clinical studies of adolescent populations have obtained expectable relations between diagnostic groups (e.g., Adam et al., 1996, above: mean age of subjects, 15 years).

Currently, the applicability of the AAI to even younger ages is being tested. Using a version of the interview that included age-appropriate adjustments (Ammaniti, Candelori, Dazzi, DeCoro, Muscetta, et al., 1990), 31 children were seen at 10 and again at 14 years of age (Ammaniti, van IJzendoorn, Speranza, & Tambelli, 1998). Two coders worked with each interview (mean interjudge agreement, 82%, kappa = .64) and arrived at a consensual judgment, with coders unaware of the child's attachment status at separate ages. The four-way classification distributions did not differ from AAI distributions in comparable but older samples. Moreover, Fyffe and Waters's (1997) beta-weights for deriving the three organized classifications from discriminant functions based upon "state of mind" scale scores in adults and older adolescents living in the United States were applied to the state of mind scores assigned to this Rome sample, and 90% of the 10-year attachment classifications (kappa = .80) and 81% of the 14-year classifications were correctly predicted (kappa = .68). Strikingly, considerable stability of attachment was observed between 10 and 14 years of age for both the two-way (75%, kappa = .48) and the four-way analyses (71%, kappa = .48).

At the Tavistock Clinic, even younger sexually abused (vs. control) children and young adolescents are also being interviewed, with the preliminary results of "blind" coding indicating the expected differences (see Trowell, 1997). Finally, at Trinity College, Dublin, mothers and daughters seen in the strange situation are both participating in the AAI when the girls have reached 11 years (M. Gaffney, personal communication, 1998).

Attachment in Deaf Populations

The AAI is now being used with deaf (signing) populations, and several faculty members at Gallaudet University (Patrick Brice, Irene Leigh, and Kathryn Meadow-Orlans) are conducting projects that will assess, for example, (1) ways in which varying aspects of interview response of import to AAI discourse (e.g., "lapses in metacognitive monitoring") may be revealed in American Sign Language (ASL), and (2) the relation between signed AAI response and infant strange situation behavior. At the University of Western Ontario, Chovaz McKinnon (1998) has administered the AAI to 50 deaf adults skilled in ASL who, raised in an era in which parents were discouraged from learning sign language, had also been sent away to residential schools at age 5. Unexpectedly, despite the limitations imposed upon communication with parents and early long-term separations, a majority of these deaf adults were found to be secure/autonomous. Moreover, despite the absence of either hearing or signed communication with parents, continuous secure deaf adults satisfactorily supported positive descriptions of early parenting.

Adult Attachment Related to Violence

The AAI has been and continues to be used to investigate both violent offenders and victims of offense. Sullivan-Hanson (1990), for example, reported that virtually no subjects seen in shelters for battered women were secure/autonomous, and that many fit to the "fearfully preoccupied" (E3) subclassification. Stalker and Davies (1995) found that only 5 out of 40 sexually abused women were secure/autonomous. Twenty-four were unresolved, and over one-third (whether or not unresolved) met the criteria for cannot classify. Three of the five secure women had no DSM Axis II personality disorder, while the remaining subjects were likely to have multiple diagnoses.

Levinson and Fonagy (1998) found evidence for an association between insecure adult attachment and criminality, particularly with respect to crimes against persons as opposed to less violent crimes. Holtzworth-Munroe, Stuart, and Hutchinson (1997) conducted a "blind" study comparing nonviolent, maritally nondistressed men (n = 15); nonviolent, maritally distressed men (n = 15); and violent, maritally distressed men (n = 30). A secure state of mind was virtually absent among men exhibiting violence toward their wives (26 of 30 insecure), and many were judged cannot classify (11 of 30). Among personality-disordered violent criminal offenders, van IJzendoorn et al. (1997) reported that only 2 out of 40 subjects (5%) were classified secure/autonomous, with 53% unresolved and/or cannot classify. In keeping with their display of mixed discourse strategies, subjects in the cannot classify group had more personality disorders. Intriguingly, as in the Stalker and Davies (1995) study, the secure/autonomous subjects in the Dutch study exhibited the fewest disorders.

Political Extremism and Authoritarianism

In keeping with an interest in the origins of authoritarianism, Hopf (1993; Hopf & Hopf, 1997) hypothesized that German right-wing extremist youth (e.g., those expressing tolerance for violence, deflecting criticism away from Germany for Nazi crimes, and disparaging outgroups) would most likely be classified dismissing. As anticipated, among 30 right-wing subjects, 23 of 30 (77%) were judged dismissing, and none were secure/autonomous. In contrast, 10 of 19 (53%) non-right-wing subjects were secure.

Corroborating this outcome, in a "blind" study of a large sample of college students (Hesse & van IJzendoorn, 1998b; see also van IJzendoorn, 1997) found that the dismissing participants obtained significantly higher scores on an authoritarianism scale. Hopf had expected as well that dismissing states of mind would be linked to aggression towards peers, and indeed Kobak and Sceery (1988) have reported that dismissing college students are considered hostile (and anxious) by their peers.

Attachment, Couple Interactions, and Family Systems

An emerging area of special interest is the connection between attachment status and family systems. Byng-Hall (1995), for example, has stressed the import of early loss upon marital distress, and Bakermans-Kranenburg and van IJzendoorn (1997) reported that women classified as unresolved were the most likely to have experienced previous breakups in romantic relationships. Allen and Hauser (1996) found that several aspects of AAI status at age 25 could be predicted from (two-parent) family interactions at age 14. Moreover, among families with 13-year-olds in the Minnesota poverty sample, "family balance" scores devised by June Fleeson Sroufe (Fleeson, 1988) predicted secure versus insecure AAI status at age 19 (Weinfield et al., in press). In addition, Crowell, Waters, and their colleagues have examined "secure base" behavior in couples engaged in a standard marital interaction task. Here, secure/autonomous individuals were found to be more able both to turn to their partners as a secure base and to act as a secure base for their partners (see Crowell et al., Chapter 20, this volume).

The Cowans and their colleagues (e.g., Cowan, Cohn, Cowan, & Pearson, 1996) have investigated both parenting and couple interactions as a function of joint as well as individual attachment status. For example, child–parent relationships were particularly compromised when both parents were insecure (Cohn, Cowan, Cowan, & Pearson, 1992). For insecure women married to secure men, however, this risk was minimized, with a secure father apparently acting as a "buffer" against less competent parenting. Similar results were obtained when couple interactions were examined (Cohn, Silver, Cowan, Cowan, et al., 1992).

In an AAI analysis of the first 40 romantic couples within a larger sample of romantic adolescent couples, G. Creasey (personal communication, 1999; see also Creasey, Boston, Tingley, Craft, & Kurtz, 1999) has uncovered "buffering" effects of having a secure partner previously obtained by the Cowans. Thus, in 20-minute conflict interactions, couples in which both or only one partner was secure exhibited similar mean numbers of negative behaviors (64 and 73). However, more than twice as many negative behaviors (147) were observed in couples in which both partners were insecure with respect to their own attachment histories. Using three-way analyses ($n = 80$), secure/autonomous individuals were markedly the most positive and the least negative in conflict situations, while individuals preoccupied with their own attachment histories were the most negative, and the least positive. In addition, in keeping with the results of a study of infant–mother interaction conducted at Leiden (discussed below), unresolved subjects whose secondary or alternative attachment category was secure/autonomous (unresolved–secure) showed almost three times as many positive behaviors during conflict interactions as did unresolved–insecure subjects. Unresolved–secure subjects also showed fewer negative behaviors than unresolved–insecure subjects.

Unresolved Attachment Status as Predictive of Frightened/Frightening Behavior toward the Offspring

Until recently, most studies investigating caregiving behavior as related to adult attachment status have focused upon overall differences in "sensitive responsiveness" in secure versus insecure parents. However, more fine-grained approaches may be profitable, as seen in the case studies described above.

A new area of investigation involves the relationship among unresolved parental attachment status, frightened/frightening parental behavior, and disorganized infant attachment. Main and Hesse (Hesse & Main, 1999, in press; Main & Hesse, 1990) have hypothesized that the discourse/reasoning lapses occurring during discussions of traumatic events that mark unresolved attachment may often stem from alterations in normal consciousness occasioned by the intrusion of partially dissociated, frightening ideas or memories. Since the interview queries appear sufficient to produce these disturbances in consciousness, it is not unreasonable to presume that frightened, frightening, and occasionally dissociated behavior may occur during interactions with the infant. Behavior of this kind is expected to place the infant in a paradox, in which it can neither flee from nor approach the attachment figure, and hence has been expected on theoretical grounds to produce disorganized behavior in the strange situation (Main & Hesse, 1990). Frightened/frightening maternal behavior has currently been found predictive of disorganized strange situation attachment status in several different countries and settings. These include a study of Dutch mothers observed in the home (Schuengel, Bakermans-Kranenburg, & van IJzendoorn, 1999); Boston mothers observed in the strange situation (Lyons-Ruth, Bronfman, & Parsons, in press); Bay Area mothers video-taped in free play with their infants (K. Abrams, personal communication, 1998); and villagers of the Dogan ethnic group observed in natural (both open and hut) settings in Mali, West Africa (True, Pasani, Ryan, & Oumar, 1998). Because frightened/frightening parental behavior appears, then, to be a substantial predictor of disorganized infant attachment status—which has in turn been repeatedly found predictive of vulnerability to psychopathology (see Lyons-Ruth & Jacobvitz, Chapter 23, this volume)—it is particularly important to determine its associations with lapses in reasoning or discourse (i.e., unresolved attachment) as observed in the parent.

Two large-scale, "blind" studies have investigated the association between unresolved attachment and frightened/frightening behavior, using a coding system developed by Main and Hesse (1992, 1998b). Schuengel et al. (1999) observed 85 mothers and their 10- to 11-month-olds in 2 two-hour home visits, administering the AAI 2 months later. Mothers found to be unresolved/insecure (e.g., U/Ds or U/E) did indeed exhibit frightened/frightening behavior in their infants' presence. However, unresolved mothers whose alternative attachment category was secure/autonomous (U/F) did *not* exhibit frightened/frightening behavior. This suggested that an underlying secure/autonomous attachment organization might act as a buffer between unresolved aspects of a mother's mental state and her behavior toward her infant. This intriguing suggestion finds partial support in recent studies by Lee et al. (1998) and by Creasey (1999) mentioned earlier.

In a sample of 113 mother–infant dyads, Jacobvitz, Hazen, and Riggs (1997; see also Lyons-Ruth & Jacobvitz, Chapter 23, this volume) compared *prebirth* AAI assessments to interactions with firstborn infants observed at 8 months of infant age. In this study, as opposed to the Leiden study, mothers were required to interact with their infants in potentially stressful contexts, such as feeding and changing. As predicted, mothers classified as unresolved prior to their infants' birth were markedly more frightened, frightening, and dissociated than other mothers, and (in contrast to the Dutch study) these results held whether the unresolved mother's underlying or "alternative" AAI classification was secure or insecure. However, in keeping with the "buffering" effects suggested by the Dutch study, unresolved/secure mothers tended to be somewhat less frightening than unresolved/insecure mothers.

Adult Attachment Status
and Responsiveness to Therapy

Although the AAI has repeatedly been found to discriminate between clinical and nonclinical populations, it has only recently been used to assess the outcomes of therapeutic interventions (see Cortina, in press; Main, 1993, 1995, 1996; and Slade, Chapter 25, this volume, for discussions of both the practical and philosophical implications of this use of the AAI). Here too, case studies are proving instructive. For example, a coding system focusing upon "dismissing" and "preoccupied" violations of Grice's maxims developed by Dazzi, DeCoro, Ortu, and Speranza (in press) was applied to an adolescent patient's AAI transcript, and later to therapeutic sessions (the coder was unaware of session order). Coherence violations were found to decrease as the sessions progressed (Muscetta, Dazzi, De Coro, Ortu, & Speranza, in press; see also Diamond et al., in press, for a description of insecure-to-secure AAI category changes in two borderline patients).

Fonagy and his colleagues were among the first to study responsiveness to therapy. In a preliminary report from a larger project (Fonagy et al., 1995), change in interview status was studied in 35 nonpsychotic inpatients following 1 year of intensive psychodynamic psychotherapy. All 35 patients were classified as insecure upon intake, but 14 (40%) were judged secure upon discharge.

In addition, Fonagy examined changes in overall functioning (on the DSM's Global Assessment of Functioning Scale) between admission and discharge as related to AAI classification, as well as a set of other potential predictors (below). Intriguingly (and as discussed at some length within the report), across the 82 subjects, the proportion of individuals who improved was higher in the dismissing group (93%) than in the preoccupied (41%) and secure/autonomous (3 of 9 subjects or 33%) groups, with effect sizes of 1.84, 1.09, and 0.51 respectively. Not one of the other potential predictors, including the Symptom Checklist–90, the Beck Depression Inventory, the Eysenck Personality Questionnaire, the Spielberger State–Trait Anxiety Inventory, or DSM Axis I and Axis II diagnoses, was predictive of responsiveness to therapy.

Routh, Hill, Steele, Elliott, and Dewey (1995) reported on inferred responsiveness to a "parent management training" course for 37 parents of children suffering from conduct disorder. As in the studies of the parents of conduct disordered children mentioned earlier, a marked proportion of parents (43%) fell into the unresolved category. As compared to the children of other mothers, the children of the 16 unresolved mothers showed strikingly little change across the course of treatment.

Korfmacher, Adam, Ogawa, and Egeland (1997) described responsiveness to a year of home visits and group therapy (conducted across alternate weeks by the same facilitator) among 55 first-time mothers living in poverty. Facilitators kept case notes and responded to questionnaires over the course of treatment, and the AAI was administered only following the intervention. The unresolved mothers displayed the greatest difficulties, as evidenced in low levels of participation and commitment, and negative interactions with facilitators and in groups; additionally, mothers unresolved for past trauma were also notable for having a "crisis orientation" response to intervention. Dismissing mothers, in contrast, were described as having an "emotionally shallow" involvement with the program, emphasizing simple companionship and engaging in supportive therapy less than other mothers. None of these mothers accepted crisis work—a finding consonant with the dismissing tendency to emphasize strength and normality. The secure/autonomous mothers showed high levels of emotional commitment to the interventions and were distinguished for participation in problem-solving treatment (in which a mother accepts practical advice from the facilitator) and supportive therapy (in which a mother shares her deeper feelings with the facilitator and the group). (For other evidence of differential responsiveness to interventions, see Bakermans-Kranenburg, Juffer, and van IJzendoorn, 1998, as well as Tyrell, Dozier, Teague, & Fallot, 1998).

ADDITIONAL APPROACHES TO SCORING AND CLASSIFYING THE ADULT ATTACHMENT INTERVIEW

As noted earlier, over the 17 years since its inception, Main and Goldwyn have substantially refined the AAI classification and scoring system. In addition, three groups of investigators

thoroughly familiar with the system have developed alternative approaches to the analysis of AAI transcripts.

The earliest of these—and still the only one serving to predict infant strange situation behavior in "blind" tests—was developed by Fremmer-Bombik in Germany (see Grossmann, Fremmer-Bombik, Rudolph, & Grossmann, 1988). This system followed Main and Goldwyn's in attempting to determine whether or not the speaker was "valuing (or devaluing) of attachment." Each sentence in the interview was coded into approximately 20 available categories, and an algorithm was developed that assigned varying weights to categories, ultimately deriving four parameters (e.g., parents' supportive acts, formal linguistic characteristics regarding Main's coherency analyses, and number of reflections regarding the parents' behavior) that permitted each transcript to be classified as either secure or insecure. When two German longitudinal samples were combined, the two-way concordance of AAI and infant attachment for 82 mother–infant pairs was 78% (kappa = .56, $p < .001$). For the 67 father–infant pairs the two-way concordance was 64% (kappa = .29, $p < .05$; Zimmermann et al., 1998).

Taking a different point of entry, Kobak (1993) developed a 100-item Q-Sort for the analysis of the interview, with most items derived from the Main and Goldwyn system identifying the three organized attachment categories (Kobak, Cole, Ferenz-Gillies, Fleming, & Gamble, 1993, p. 235). Like Fyffe and Waters's (1997) discriminant analysis of the continuous scores in the Main and Goldwyn system, this method yields two dimensions (secure vs. anxious and dismissing vs. preoccupied). A criterion or "ideal" prototype sort is used to identify the three organized adult categories, and two persons independently read and sort each transcript. Kobak (personal communication, October 1998) recommends that at least one sorter should be trained in the Main and Goldwyn system. A third (and occasionally a fourth) rater is added when criterion levels of agreement are not met.

A first, blind application of the system to adolescent interview transcripts indicated an overlap of 79% (Kobak et al., 1993). Further applications of the Q-Sort system to transcripts independently coded using the Main and Goldwyn system show overlap ranging from 61% (Borman-Spurrell,

Allen, Hauser, Carter, & Cole-Detke, 1998; 71% agreement omitting unresolved and cannot classify subjects) to 74% (Allen, Moore, Kuperminc, & Bell, in press).

The Q-Sort system has yielded many impressive results, including studies of adolescent–parent interactions (e.g., Kobak et al., 1993), clinical process (e.g., Dozier, Cue, & Barnett, 1994), and psychiatrically distressed populations (Borman-Spurrell et al., 1998; Cole-Detke & Kobak, 1996). In addition, it was used in a groundbreaking investigation by Dozier and Kobak (1992), which first connected adult attachment to psychophysiology. Here it was reported that, as predicted, subjects using a dismissing strategy showed a rise in skin conductance when responding to queries regarding rejection and separation. (In this context, it should be noted as well that [the Main and Goldwyn system, Adam, 1998] found security associated with healthier physiological stress system functioning—for example, greater security predicted a stronger basal cortisol cycle with higher morning values and a steeper downward drop across the day.)

The Q-Sort system contrasts with the Main and Goldwyn system in that the unresolved and cannot classify categories are not identified; moreover, as in Fremmer-Bombik's system, the individual's parenting experiences, as well as current state of mind, enter partially into the final dimensional score. This means that "earned secure" status may be somewhat less likely to be identified with prototype scores, and can only be assessed by using item-level analyses. The Q-Sort may therefore be especially useful for the study of adolescents, but less applicable to older and clinical samples, where a higher proportion of unresolved, cannot classify, and "earned secure" subjects may be expected. The Q-Sort has not been tested against an infant's strange situation response to the speaker.

The most recent addition to AAI analysis has been a scale for "reflective self function" developed by Fonagy and his colleagues (Fonagy, Steele, Steele, Moran, & Higgitt, 1991; see also Fonagy, Steele, Steele, Higgitt, et al., 1994). This scale takes its origins in psychology's emerging interest in theory of mind, and attempts to score AAI transcripts for the speaker's recognition of the existence and nature of mental processes taking place in both the self and others (especially, of course, the parents). The scale bears some resemblance to Fremmer-Bombik's original system of interview analysis, which emphasized reflections upon and explanations of the parent's behavior or influence. It is also based in part on Main's scale for meta-cognitive monitoring of errors in the speaker's own present or past thinking (Main, 1991, see Table 3), but ultimately places greatest emphasis on the recognition of thoughts, intentions, wishes, and a general awareness of mental states in others.

Like coherence of transcript (e.g., Allen et al., 1996; Fonagy et al., 1996), reflective self has to date served well to discriminate clinical from nonclinical populations, with individuals suffering from (1) borderline disorders (Fonagy et al., 1996) and (2) depressive disorders (Ivarsson et al., 1998), as well as those in criminal populations (Levinson & Fonagy, 1998) being markedly low on reflective self function. Fonagy et al.'s interpretation of the failure of reflective self function to appear in individuals with borderline diagnoses rests on inhibition in the development of recognition of intentionality in others due to their early experiences of extreme abuse (Fonagy et al., 1996). Similarly, criminal acts against others may be more readily undertaken by individuals failing to recognize the existence of mind in those who are being harmed (Levinson & Fonagy, 1998).

A first study of reflective-self function scored by individuals who had already undertaken both the AAI and strange situation scoring for the same sample showed impressive relations to both parental and infant security (Fonagy et al., 1991). "Blind" studies relating reflective self to either adult or infant attachment status have yet to emerge, however, so that, like the relation between security of attachment and Main's metacognitive monitoring scale, the relation between security of attachment and Fonagy's reflective self-function remains to be estimated. Main and Fonagy (1998) are presently developing a brief "theory-of-mind" interview to follow the final queries of the AAI. This interview should increase the opportunity of uncovering existing relations among attachment, metacognitive monitoring, and reflective self. Like other new approaches to the analysis of the AAI described here, reflective self function has still to be subjected to psychometric tests.

COMMON CONFUSIONS AND QUERIES REGARDING THE ADULT ATTACHMENT INTERVIEW

Over time, it has become apparent that there are a number of questions and confusions regarding the AAI which are manifested with sufficient regularity as to warrant closer consideration. The most common confusions center primarily upon (1) what the AAI actually assesses, and (2) the role that temperament may play in the production of AAI response. There are additionally a wide variety of recurring questions ranging from the practicalities of assessment of the AAI directly from videotape to the influence of emotion upon the discourse process.

Secure versus Insecure Attachment Status: What Is being Assessed?

One of the most common misconceptions regarding the AAI is that it assesses whether or not adults are "securely attached" to a second person (e.g., Eagle, 1997). Although close adult relationships undoubtedly involve attachment (Hazan & Shaver, 1994), the (secure vs. insecure) organization of one person's attachment to another specific person is not what the AAI assesses. The AAI appears instead to provide a means of assessing an individual's overall "state of mind with respect to attachment," together with specific states of mind that arise during the discussion of particular topics (as seen in the continuous scales).

The above confusion has perhaps arisen out of the widespread recognition that assessment of attachment in infants and children always involves the quality of their attachment to a particular caregiver (Ainsworth et al., 1978; Main & Cassidy, 1988). In these cases, we recognize that the infant or child is not secure or insecure in itself, but rather is securely or insecurely attached to one parent, and may be securely or insecurely attached to the other. This way of thinking, which rightly underscores the inability of an infant or young child to be "secure–autonomous," may have inadvertently become generalized to the AAI.

Adults assessed via the AAI are not considered securely versus insecurely attached, but rather as being in a secure versus insecure *state of mind with respect to attachment,* in part because the interview does not focus upon another single person, but rather asks for descriptions and evaluations of relations to several significant individuals. Thus a first problem with referring to secure versus insecure attachment in an adult as derived from the AAI is this: Secure versus insecure with respect to whom? A related problem is that ordinarily a singular classification is derived from the interview, despite the fact that the protocol covers many early and current relationships, which may vary in terms of security.

Note further that a coherent (secure–autonomous) speaker may in fact be discussing adverse early relationships to both parents, neither of whom could currently serve as sources of security. Moreover, whether or not in principle the parents would be able to provide security, in many cases—especially with older adults—the parents are no longer alive.

Why Is the Adult Attachment Interview Analyzed Exclusively from Verbatim Speech Transcripts?

A frequently raised question is why AAI analysis is restricted to verbatim speech transcripts, and does not take advantage of as many modalities of communication as are potentially available during the interview process. For example, if cues to emotional expressions, physical movement, eye contact, et alia were added to the interview transcription, or were derived directly from visual material, might this additional information both speed classification and increase its accuracy? Or, why not use the classification system as it is and simply analyze the AAI directly from videotape?

The first question bears on the intrinsic meaning of the methodology, and the second involves issues of practicality and practicability. Since the AAI has been primarily utilized as a predictive measure, a natural inclination is to seek ways of furthering its predictive strength. As an example, let us assume that avoidance of eye contact with the interviewer is associated with dismissing attachment status. Let us further assume that frequency counts of eye contact increase predictability of caregiving, clinical status, or the nature of the speaker's early attachment to the parent from (transcript-identified) dismissing attachment status. From the standpoint of prediction, this would of course be a valuable advance. However, the classification and scoring system is not just about prediction; it is specifically about how much and what can be predicted from the analysis of *discourse* regarding attachment-related experiences. Therefore, if we are to use the instrument to achieve a better understanding of the relations between language and attachment, additions to or modifications in the present system intended to increase its predictability logically should be confined to uncovering new parameters of language. Both the unresolved category and the recently emerging cannot classify category—each of which has increased our power to predict infant attachment status and/or clinical status—are examples of the productivity of this approach.

We should also consider the fact that there is an upper limit to predictability, which, utilizing the (linguistically based) system as it stands, is already rapidly being approached. If nonverbal cues were to be added to the linguistic system currently utilized, the rate of increase in predictability would likely be small; moreover (see below) there would be considerable danger of actually reducing accuracy of prediction. In view of all of these factors, it seems clear that any nonlinguistic correlates of the AAI can and should be investigated separately from the existing system.

We can now consider the practical issues involved in a visual versus a transcribed analysis of the interview utilizing the traditional methodology. Although this writer's attempts at analyses of the AAI from videotapes have been limited, the process appears to be far more cumbersome than that involving printed text. First, it immediately becomes necessary, ironically, to take written notes on what the subject is saying in order to make comparisons with various aspects of future portions of the discussion. Second, it is much more difficult to cross-check different sections of the interview. For example, if it is stated that a cousin died when the subject was 5 years old, somewhere around the beginning of the tape, and then stated again 45 minutes later that the cousin died when the subject was 10, either the judge would have to have noted the age at which the death was said to have occurred at the outset of the tape, or the tape would have to be rewound to the beginning in an attempt to find the initial relevant sentence (or this "spoken" index of unresolved attachment might well be missed altogether). As another example, idealization scores are derived from careful study of the subject's descriptions of parents—not only as given at the beginning of the procedure, but elsewhere during the interview as well. These generalized descriptions, taken from varying points in the text, are compared to discussions of "actual events." In working with a printed text, cross-checking of this kind is fast and simple. If a videotape is used, in contrast, the judge is not only again confronted with the necessity of taking notes, but also is subjected to the cumbersome and time-consuming task of repeatedly rewinding and forwarding the video, at some considerable risk of error.

Another problem with classificatory (and scoring) analysis taken from videotapes is that, in the absence of a separate system for identifying adult attachment status solely from visual cues, much potential "noise" is introduced into the existing process. The judge has a visual impression of the subject—whether the subject is nervous or well dressed, for example, and how much eye contact the subject makes with the interviewer. Moreover, in some cases judges will have "gut" positive or negative reactions to individuals' visual and behavioral characteristics, which may have no systematic relation to the form of their discourse or attachment status. It should be underscored that this "noise" may in many cases potentially be turned into lawful correlates of the AAI (see above), but as they bear upon the text analysis itself visual and behavioral cues are likely to interfere with the judges' objectivity and hence become a detriment to the classification and scoring process.

Adult Attachment and Self-Report Inventories

Self-report measures regarding adult attachment have been developed by a variety of researchers with differing aims. Some—for example, Main, Hesse, and van IJzendoorn, as well as Lichtenstein and Cassidy (see Crowell et al., Chapter 20, this volume) have attempted to design self-report instruments that would predict adult attachment status as assessed by the AAI. The primary aim of these endeavors has been to make the assessment of "state of mind with respect to attachment" more readily accessible to other investigators.

As regards the long-term (and still ongoing) project in which the present writer participated, a first study of a college student sample ($n = 50$) utilized self-identified subject-to-parent attachment classifications devised by the authors and presented in brief paragraphs. No relation was found between AAI status and a subject's self-identified attachment classification (secure/autonomous, dismissing, preoccupied). In point of fact, not only were insecure subjects likely to term themselves secure, but secure subjects were likely to consider themselves insecure. Later, a set of Likert scales containing both "direct" and "indirect" items were developed. These scales were stable and psychometrically sound, but to date have reached satisfactory levels of association with AAI categories in only one sample.

Similarly, no relation to infants' security of attachment to their mothers appeared in Hamilton's

(1995) investigation of 200 adolescents' self-reported feelings of security with their mothers as assessed by Armsden and Greenberg's Inventory of Peer and Parent Attachment (IPPA; see Crowell et al., Chapter 20, this volume). In contrast, strange situation behavior to the mother *did* predict responses to the AAI (Hamilton, in press, $n = 30$). Self-reported IPPA security with mothers during adolescence additionally failed to predict the adolescents' AAI (Hamilton, 1995). Crowell, Treboux, and Waters (in press) have also recently found self-reported quality of attachment with parents to be unrelated ($r = .11$) to the AAI.

Other investigators have developed self-report measures of romantic "attachment styles." These focus upon romantic or partner relationships, using either self-classifications as, for example, secure, dismissing or preoccupied, or else brief multi-item inventories (see Crowell et al., Chapter 20, this volume). These measures are producing intriguing and coherent results in many areas, including observed couple interactions (e.g., Simpson, Rholes, & Nelligan, 1992; Simpson, Rholes, & Phillips, 1996), psychophysiology (e.g., Fraley, & Shaver, 1997), cognitive organization and biases (e.g., Mikulincer & Orbach, 1995), and projective tests related to affect regulation (e.g., Mikulincer, Florian, & Tolmacz, 1990). In addition, using an interview concerning couple relationships modeled after the AAI, Crowell and her colleagues found a 69% correspondence between secure versus insecure status on this interview and secure versus insecure status assessed in a self-report inventory ($n = 36$, kappa = .38; see Crowell et al., Chapter 20, this volume).

Considered together, these findings suggest that, as opposed to state of mind with respect to early attachment relations and experiences—which has yet to be satisfactorily identified through self-report—individuals may have more "conscious" access to their current approach to relating to romantic partners (M. Main, personal communication, 1998).

Crowell (Crowell et al., Chapter 20, this volume, Table 20.1) has reviewed three studies indicating absence of relationship between self-reports of romantic attachment styles and attachment organization as assessed by the AAI ($r = -.12$, $r = .04$, and $r = .21$). In addition to the three studies reviewed by Crowell et al., absence of relation between romantic self-report inventories and AAI status (as coded by the present writer, $n = 60$), was also reported by Holtzworth-Munroe

et al. (1997). Here, Griffin and Bartholomew's Relationship Styles Questionnaire (RSQ, 1994; see also Bartholomew & Horowitz, 1991), which yields categorical placement (secure, dismissing, preoccupied, or fearful) based on the predominant score on continuous scales, was compared directly to AAI classification. Only 45% of men classified as secure/autonomous on the AAI were similarly classified as secure on the RSQ, and only 24% of men classified as secure on the RSQ were classified as secure/autonomous on the AAI. In addition, rather than a participant's being classified on the basis of his highest subscale score, his scores on all four RSQ scales were considered. However, the multivariate analysis of variance comparing RSQ subscale scores of men given different AAI classifications was nonsignificant, indicating that men given different classifications on the AAI did not differ on their overall pattern of RSQ scores.

Thus it is not surprising that, to the knowledge of this writer, romantic or partner self-report inventories have not as yet been found to be related either to the quality of an infant's attachment to the subject, or to the subject's strange situation response in infancy. Indeed, such results would be surprising, given the absence of relation between romantic or partner attachment self-report inventories and the AAI.

The Adult Attachment Interview, Memory, and Experience

We know from introspection as well as from direct observations and experiments (e.g., Bartlett, 1932; Loftus, 1994) that the ways in which events and experiences are recalled are highly subject to distortions and inaccuracies. This fact raises a variety of important questions and touches on the issue of whether real events are significantly causal in the organization of our subjective states. The AAI circumvents this issue, however, because no claim is made that the contents of any given interview represent an accurate reconstruction of experience—or, more specifically, that coherence of interview response and accuracy in recounting of early experience are related. How construction of narrative and actual experience may be related is, of course, an important question, but this topic can only be investigated via interviews that have been preceded by extensive observations of subjects across the period covered by the AAI protocol (approximately 4 to 14 years of age).

As noted earlier, in studies using low-risk longitudinal samples, secure versus insecure attachment status in infancy has predicted secure versus insecure AAI responses in the same individual. Unfortunately, these studies cannot address the issue of accuracy of recall, for the reasons mentioned directly above. Moreover, and somewhat ironically, the outcomes of these studies may in fact lead to some renewed confusion regarding the nature of assessment involving the AAI. Thus, because an individual's likelihood of having had favorable versus unfavorable experiences with the mother during the first year of life has now been found to be associated with security versus insecurity in late adolescence, the AAI may incorrectly be assumed to be assessing the subject's memories for "real" events. Again, what is actually being assessed is the form in which an individual's life history is presented and discussed. Thus, for example, whether or not a secure/autonomous individual's memories are accurate, their narrative is identified by its coherence.

Conversely, this point can be illustrated by considering the association between an insecure-avoidant strange situation response to the mother in infancy and a dismissing state of mind with respect to attachment reported in three low-risk samples (Hamilton, in press; Main & Hesse, 1998a; Waters et al., in press). It will be recalled that an individual classified as dismissing typically presents a favorable description of attachment-related experiences, which is insufficiently supported. If the taxonomic methodology of Main and Goldwyn's system of discourse analysis relied upon a speaker's general descriptions of his or her experiences, those speakers who had been classified as avoidant as infants would almost always be classified as secure/autonomous in the AAI. Were this the case, the existing relations between AAI and strange situation response would never have been found. It is, again, precisely because the AAI emphasizes the coherence (form) versus the content of the individual's presentation that these matches to infancy are being uncovered.

What Role Might Emotion Play in Responses to the Adult Attachment Interview?

Although the analysis of the AAI rests upon verbatim speech transcripts rather than, for example, facial expression, vocal tone, or psychophysiological indices of emotion (see above), it is nonetheless assumed that emotion plays a central role in shaping discourse respecting attachment. To begin with, a close reading of the organized category descriptors reveals much direct reference to emotional states as they are made manifest through the speaker's language. For example, the secure/autonomous category is described as being associated with forgiveness, compassion, humor, and references to missing and needing other persons. The dismissing category is associated with a notable absence of expressions of emotional vulnerability, and the marker of one dismissing subcategory is contempt. Finally, two of the three preoccupied subcategories are associated with expressions of anger and of fear, respectively.

Individuals classified as dismissing and preoccupied are identified, at least in part, then, via linguistic indications of negative emotional states arising during discussions involving attachment. Thus, it is ordinarily inferred that (whether attachment experiences are described positively or negatively) these speakers have most often had attachment-related difficulties. As discussed above, however, secure/autonomous individuals can also report unfavorable (as well as favorable) early attachment histories.

A central factor leading to these varying outcomes no doubt involves differences in both the quality of and the capacity to regulate and integrate emotion. Thus, for speakers having had apparently favorable experiences, emotional responses accompanying the interview process are unlikely to be unpleasant, making the discourse task a relatively straightforward one. For secure/autonomous individuals discussing adverse early experiences, however, the production of a coherent narrative may involve the capacity to "contain" reactions to uncomfortable or stressful feelings—a proposition that could be tested through simultaneous recording of psychophysiological reactions and/or emotional expression. Individuals falling into the dismissing and preoccupied attachment categories, in contrast, seem unable to respond fluidly to the interview process, perhaps because of potential discomfort stimulated by attachment-related topics, with some (dismissing) appearing to attempt to "avoid" the topic, and others (preoccupied) becoming overwhelmed.

With respect to unresolved attachment status, relations to early attachment on the part of the speaker are as yet unknown. However, the role of emotion has been clearly specified at the theoretical level, as it has been hypothesized that in the majority of cases fear underlies those processes leading to discourse/reasoning lapses during the discussion of potentially traumatic experiences (Hesse & Main, 1999; in press; Main & Hesse, 1990).

Can Temperament Account for the Phenomena Observed in the Strange Situation and the Adult Attachment Interview?

Because there is room for some misunderstanding regarding the role that temperament may play in phenomena surrounding both the AAI and its relation to the strange situation (Fox, 1995), a discussion of these topics is warranted.

Temperament, Strange Situation Behavior, and the AAI

Within the field of attachment as a whole, there is to date little evidence for stable hereditary factors in shaping strange situation classifications in infancy. First, if hereditary and stable characteristics are what are reflected in strange situation behavior, then the secure, avoidant, or resistant infant should behave similarly with each parent. Strange situation responses are, however, largely independent, with many infants judged secure with one parent and insecure with the other (van IJzendoorn & DeWolff, 1997; see also an earlier meta-analysis conducted by Fox, Kimmerly, & Schafer, 1991). Second, infants who are insecure with their mothers at 12 months are significantly likely to become secure by 18 months if there are favorable changes in the mothers' life circumstances (see Sroufe, 1985). Third, if—rather than supposing that security, avoidance, and resistance were specific and stable infant characteristics—it were more generally presumed that mothers are responding (i.e., sensitively versus insensitively) to "easy" versus "difficult" infant temperament, then handicapped, sick, and otherwise "difficult" infants should not be found equally as likely as infants in low-risk samples to be judged secure, as in fact they have been (see van IJzendoorn, Goldberg, Kranenburg, & Frenkel, 1992).

Finally, if infant temperament is shaping infant–parent interaction in ways pertinent to offspring attachment status, then it should be more difficult to predict strange situation behavior from the AAI before than after birth. This is because in an AAI conducted prior to the birth of the first child, the parent's state of mind cannot be influenced by the individual behavioral char-

acteristics of the infant. As noted earlier, however, van IJzendoorn's (1995) meta-analysis showed that an infants' strange situation response to the mother and to the father are predicted equally well whether the AAI is administered prior to or succeeding birth.

It is indeed the case, however, that to this point dyads involved in AAI–strange situation studies have been biologically related. Main (1996) has therefore suggested that a new set of studies should be conducted in which the interview is administered to parents prior to adoption, and compared, as in studies of biological dyads, to infants' strange situation behavior at 12 months of age. If the usual concordance failed to appear across a set of several such studies, compelling evidence for genetic input would be established. A first investigation of this kind is being undertaken (van Londen, Juffer, & van IJzendoorn, 1998).

What Relative Roles Might Heritable and Environmental Factors Play in Adult Attachment Status?

The discussion above addresses attachment classifications observed in infancy as related to the AAI. However, we may also ask whether or not an adult's state of mind with respect to attachment is the product of heritable factors. A preliminary investigation using a questionnaire designed to assess temperamental dimensions of emotionality, activity, and sociability (Buss & Plomin, 1984) in a Dutch sample of 83 mothers administered the AAI yielded no significant relations (DeHass, Bakermans-Kranenburg, & van IJzendoorn, 1994). Main (1996), however, takes the position that while genetic input appears to play at most a minor role in security of attachment to the parents during the first year of life, genetically influenced factors may have an as yet unspecified influence upon state of mind with respect to attachment in adulthood, particularly with regard to "earned security." Thus, for example, it has been suggested that variations in genetically biased levels of metacognitive skills may play a significant role in making some, but not other, individuals more resilient in the face of a difficult childhood (Main, 1991, 1996).

It is indeed an intriguing question how certain individuals whose early experiences appear to have been highly difficult produce coherent and collaborative AAI narratives, and have secure infants, without undertaking psychotherapy or having had any other obvious form of potentially helpful intervention. Positive early experiences with friends, an influential teacher, or (later) a relationship with a supportive partner could of course contribute to these outcomes.

In addition, we must leave open the possibility that because the AAI does not necessarily provide valid information about an individual's actual experiences, we do not know whether those who appear to be "earned secure" have in fact had substantially positive early experiences that are now, ironically, coherently misrepresented. Furthermore, it is conceivable that some individuals considered "earned secure" on the basis of their coherent recounting of a harsh childhood may have been secure with at least one parent for the first year or two of life—a fact that is, of course, unlikely to be readily consciously accessed. In this instance, favorable preverbal experiences could somehow be aiding the speaker in a coherent reconstruction of the experiences that are remembered, despite the fact that those experiences were indeed unfavorable. These and other important questions regarding the role of "forgotten" early experiences (as opposed to heritable genetic factors) in making some individuals more likely than others to be placed in an "earned secure" category can only be addressed via longitudinal studies.

SUMMARY AND CONCLUSIONS

The Adult Attachment Interview (George et al., 1984, 1985, 1996) is a semistructured protocol focusing upon an individual's description and evaluation of salient early attachment experiences and the effects of these experiences on current personality and functioning. The interview is analyzed via an accompanying scoring and classification system (Main & Goldwyn, 1984a, 1998a) that includes a set of general category descriptors for identifying five differing (secure, dismissing, preoccupied, unresolved, and cannot classify) "states of mind with respect to attachment," as well as continuous scales for scoring the text with respect to both the speaker's current state of mind and his or her inferred childhood experiences.

The analysis of the interview originally focused primarily upon content-oriented aspects of the global category descriptors (e.g., "valuing of attachment and yet seemingly objective," "dismissing or devaluing of attachment," "preoccupied by past attachment experiences") and utilized only a few continuous scales (e.g.,

"coherence of transcript," "idealization of parents," "insistence on lack of recall"). Over time, interview analysis came to include new scales pertaining more specifically to the discourse process (e.g., "vague discourse usages"), and hence began to more explicitly incorporate the ways in which specific aspects of the conversational exchange related to the secure versus insecure adult attachment categories. It was later discovered that this advance in text analysis fit well with the work of the linguistic philosopher Grice (1975, 1989) as it pertained to the ideal of cooperative, rational discourse.

At present, interview analysis takes into consideration each of the factors above, and thus scale scores and general category descriptors are now viewed within the larger context of the overall discourse exchange. Perhaps the most critical implication of this approach to the analysis of language is that *the parents of insecure infants appear unable to discuss their own attachment-related experiences without significantly violating Grice's conversational maxims.* Thus notable failure in the maintenance of coherence and/or collaboration during these discussions has repeatedly been shown to predict insecure infant attachment.

Since the original studies that demonstrated the power of the interview to predict the strange situation response of a speakers' infant, clinical and developmental researchers have applied the AAI to an increasingly wide variety of domains. Coherent, collaborative (secure/autonomous) interview responses have been found to be associated with sensitive, responsive caregiving, and the psychometric properties of the instrument have been rigorously tested. Furthermore, AAI studies have been extended to clinical populations, and very few clinically distressed individuals (or parents of clinically distressed children and adolescents) have been found to be secure/autonomous. Longitudinal studies are now emerging demonstrating that an infant's strange situation behavior toward the mother (in the absence of highly stressful intervening life events) predicts secure versus insecure interview responses in the same individual during adolescence and young adulthood. The AAI has been or is now being utilized in a variety of other areas, including studies of criminal populations, political extremism, couple interactions, and readiness for and responsiveness to clinical interventions.

In addition to providing a history and overview of AAI research, this chapter has addressed a number of frequent questions and sources of confusion surrounding the interview and its assessment. The first involves a common misunderstanding regarding what the AAI does in fact assess. The AAI does not assess an adult's secure versus insecure attachment to any other specific person, but rather evaluates an individual's overall state of mind with respect to attachment—a state no doubt influenced by a wide variety of past and current relationships. The assessment of the AAI via nonverbal behavior has been considered, as has classification derived directly from videotapes; it has been suggested (1) that nonverbal behavior should be considered separately from rather than in conjunction with the Main and Goldwyn system, and (2) that using this current, language-based system to classify directly from videotapes is likely to prove both cumbersome and less accurate. In addition, the assessment of attachment through self-report inventories has been discussed. Here differing approaches have been delineated, and it has been noted that attempts to capture adult state of mind with respect to attachment using self-reports have yet to be proven successful. In contrast, self-reports of romantic and couple attachment relationships—while not related to the AAI—are producing intriguing and coherent outcomes.

With respect to "emotion," because the AAI is scored and classified from verbatim speech transcripts, descriptions of its analysis may initially appear remote from the affective components involved in the discourse exchange. Emotion (as indicated in conjunction with both theoretical considerations and category descriptors) is nonetheless believed to play a central role in production of the varying forms of AAI narrative. As regards temperament, the influence of hereditary versus environmental factors upon individual differences in AAI response remains unclear, particularly with respect to individuals classified as "earned secure." Finally, regarding issues of memory and experience bearing on coherence versus incoherence within the AAI, no claim is made that the contents of any speaker's presentation represent an accurate reconstruction of his or her life history. How construction of narrative and actual experience may be related is of central import, but this topic has yet to be investigated.

Levy, Blatt, and Shaver (1998) have termed the match between AAI and infant strange situation behavior "astonishing," and it is remarkable indeed that this relation has now been reported by so many investigators. From the point of view of this writer, what is perhaps most fascinating about the analysis of the AAI is that it suggests that language can provide an "empirical window" into aspects of cognition and emotion that systematically mediate caregiving behavior. Main (1991, 1995, 1996, in press) has suggested that individual differences in cognition and the expression and/or regulation of emotion as manifested in the AAI may reflect differences in capacities for flexibility of attentional processes pertaining to attachment. This line of reasoning can be clarified by considering that accessing and reflecting upon attachment-related experiences, while simultaneously monitoring the discourse context within the interview, must require relatively high capabilities for flexibility of attention (Hesse, 1996). Because maintaining flexibility of attention while discussing attachment-related experiences appears to be a central component in the production of a coherent/collaborative text, this capacity may well be a necessary prerequisite to sensitive and responsive caregiving.

This proposition is brought into relief when the three central insecure categories of adult attachment are considered. A speaker classified as dismissing—via failing to integrate descriptions of experience, as seen, for example, in insistence on lack of memory—appears to restrict attention to the level of semantic representations. This restriction leads to incoherence in narrative, and, relatedly, predicts an avoidant infant strange situation response. Speakers classified as preoccupied appear to exaggerate attention to the interview queries, focusing upon particular (episodic) aspects of their history at the expense of monitoring the discourse context. Thus flexibility of attention is compromised here as well, and these speakers—excessively focused upon their own histories—have infants who, during the strange situation, are excessively focused upon them. Finally, among unresolved speakers, disorganization in discourse and reasoning appears to indicate disruptions in attentional processes, whether otherwise flexible or inflexible. Here it has been suggested that a (temporary) collapse in attention is occasioned by the arousal of unintegrated fear (Hesse & Main, 1999, in press; Main & Hesse, 1990). Strikingly, the infants of these speakers manifest disruptions (disorganization/disorientation) in attention and behavior during the strange situation.

Within the AAI, the organization of language

pertaining to attachment thus appears to be a manifestation of the "dynamics" of cognition and emotion as mediated by attention. Individual differences in attentional flexibility regarding attachment may therefore influence patterns of caregiving, which in turn may shape responses in the offspring that influence the organization of its own developing attentional propensities.

The importance of this point can initially be difficult to comprehend. It is not the simple exposition of the notion that the way one person speaks and acts will influence another to follow suit. Recall that Crowell et al. (1996) demonstrated that the form of discourse used by a given speaker in the AAI is orthogonal to that speaker's discussion of work-related experiences. Thus the form of language appearing within the AAI is most likely a manifestation of highly specific aspects of mental processes that represent the speaker's potential capacities for caregiving, perhaps including subtle aspects of emotional attunement (Haft & Slade, 1989), emotion regulation (Cassidy, 1994; Kobak, Chapter 2, this volume), and the ability to accurately conceptualize the infant's wishes and intentions (see Ainsworth et al., 1978; Fonagy et al., 1991, 1996; Main, 1991). The discovery that differing forms of discourse regarding attachment appear to be predictive of differences in this potential has no doubt permanently altered the way language will be considered within the context of clinical and developmental research.

ACKNOWLEDGMENTS

I am grateful to the Irving Brooks Harris Foundation of Chicago and to Kohler-Stiftung of Munich for their support of varying aspects of this project.

NOTES

1. In fact, interview analysis takes into account that, as Mura (1983) has pointed out, speakers can "license" violations of Grice's maxims. For example, "If you really want to hear about that one, let me ask you about your dinner plans" licences a violation of quantity; "I'm sorry, but I need to back up and digress" licenses a violation of relevance.

2. Rarely, speakers are placed in the unresolved category for reports of extreme behavioral reactions to loss or other traumatic experiences.

3. These findings emerged when Gunderson's classification criteria for borderline status were used.

4. The strange situation classification distributions

of these nonconventional dyads did not, however, differ from those of conventional low-risk samples.

REFERENCES

Adam, E. K. (1998). *Emotional and physiological stress in mothers of toddlers: An adult attachment model.* Unpublished doctoral dissertation, University of Minnesota.

Adam, K. S., Sheldon-Keller, A. E., & West, M. (1996). Attachment organization and history of suicidal behavior in adolescents. *Journal of Consulting and Clinical Psychology, 64,* 264–292.

Ainsworth, M. D. S., Blehar, M. C., Waters, E., & Wall, S. (1978). *Patterns of attachment: A psychological study of the Strange Situation.* Hillsdale, NJ: Erlbaum.

Ainsworth, M. D. S., & Eichberg, C. G. (1991). Effects on infant–mother attachment of mother's unresolved loss of an attachment figure or other traumatic experience. In C. M. Parkes, J. Stevenson-Hinde, & P. Marris (Eds.), *Attachment across the life cycle* (pp. 160–183). London: Routledge.

Allen, J. P., & Hauser, S. T. (1996). Autonomy and relatedness in adolescent–family interactions as predictors of young adults' states of mind regarding attachment. *Development and Psychopathology, 8,* 793–809.

Allen, J. P., Hauser, S. T., & Borman-Spurrell, E. (1996). Attachment theory as a framework for understanding sequelae of severe adolescent psychopathology: An eleven-year follow-up study. *Journal of Consulting and Clinical Psychology, 64,* 254–263.

Allen, J. P., Moore, C., Kuperminc, G., & Bell, K. (in press). Attachment and adolescent psycho-social functioning. *Child Development.*

Ammaniti, M., & Speranza, A. M. (1994, June). *Maternal representations and disorganized patterns of attachment in children.* Poster presented at the International Conference on Infant Studies, Paris.

Ammaniti, M., Speranza, A. M., & Candelori, C. (1996). Stability of attachment in children and intergenerational transmission of attachment. *Psichiatria dell'Infanzia e dell'Adolscenza, 63,* 313–332.

Ammaniti, M., Candelori, C., Dazzi, N., DeCoro, A., Muscetta, S., Ortu, F., Pola, M., Speranza, A. M., Tambelli, R., & Zampino, F. (1990). *I. A. L.: Intervista sull'attacamento nella latenza (A. I. C. A. Attachment Interview for Childhood and Adolescence).* Unpublished protocol, University of Rome "La Sapienza."

Ammaniti, M., van IJzendoorn, M. H., Speranza, A. M., & Tambelli, R. (1998). *Internal working models of attachment during late childhood and early adolescence: An exploration of stability and change.* Manuscript submitted for publication.

Bakermans-Kranenburg, M. J., & van IJzendoorn, M. H. (1993). A psychometric study of the Adult Attachment Interview: Reliability and discriminant validity. *Developmental Psychology, 29,* 870–879.

Bakermans-Kranenburg, M. J., & van IJzendoorn, M. H. (1997). Adult attachment and the break-up of romantic relationships. *Journal of Divorce and Remarriage, 27,* 121–139.

Bakermans-Kranenburg, M. J., Juffer, F., & van IJzendoorn, M. H. (1998). Intervention with video feedback and attachment discussions: Does type of maternal insecurity make a difference? *Infant Mental Health Journal, 19,* 202–219.

Bartholomew, K., & Horowitz, L. M. (1991). Attachment styles among young adults: A test of a four-category model. *Journal of Personality and Social Psychology, 61,* 226–244.

Bartlett, F. C. (1932). *Remembering: A study in experimental and social psychology.* Cambridge, England: Cambridge University Press.

Beckwith, L., Cohen, S. E., & Hamilton, C. E. (in press). Maternal sensitivity during infancy and subsequent life-events relate to attachment representation at early adulthood. *Developmental Psychology.*

Benoit, D., & Parker, K. (1994). Stability and transmission of attachment across three generations. *Child Development, 65,* 1444–1456.

Benoit, D., Zeanah, C. H., & Barton, M. L. (1989). Maternal attachment disturbances in failure to thrive. *Infant Mental Health Journal, 10,* 185–202.

Benoit, D., Zeanah, C. H., Boucher, C., & Minde, K. K. (1992). Sleep disorders in early childhood: Association with insecure maternal attachment. *Journal of the American Academy of Child and Adolescent Psychiatry, 31,* 86–93.

Borman-Spurrell, E., Allen, J., Hauser, S., Carter, A., & Cole-Detke, H. (1998). *Assessing adult attachment: A comparison of interview-based and self-report methods.* Manuscript submitted for publication.

Bowlby, J. (1969/1982). *Attachment and loss: Vol. 1. Attachment.* London: Hogarth Press.

Bowlby, J. (1973). *Attachment and Loss: Vol 2. Separation.* New York: Basic Books.

Bowlby, J. (1980). *Attachment and Loss: Vol. 3. Loss.* New York: Basic Books.

Bretherton, I., & Waters, E. (Eds.). (1985). Growing points of attachment theory and research. *Monographs of the Society for Research in Child Development, 50*(1–2, Serial No. 209).

Buss, A. H., & Plomin, R. (1984). *Temperament: Early developing personality traits.* Hillsdale, NJ: Erlbaum.

Byng-Hall, J. (1995). Creating a secure family base: Some implications of attachment theory for family systems. *Family Process, 34,* 45–58.

Candelori, C., & Ciocca, A. (1998). Attachment and eating disorders. In P. Bria, A. Ciocca & S. DeRisio (Eds.), *Psychotherapeutic issues in eating disorders: Models, methods, and results* (pp. 139–154). Rome: Societia Editrice Universo.

Cassidy, J. (1994). Emotion regulation: Influences of attachment relationships. In N. A. Fox (Ed.), The development of emotion regulation. *Monographs of the Society for Research in Child Development, 59*(2–3, Serial No. 240), 53–72.

Chovaz McKinnon, C. J. (1998). *Relationship representations of deaf adults.* Unpublished doctoral dissertation, University of Western Ontario, London, Ontario, Canada.

Cohen, J. (1988). *Statistical power analysis for the behavioral sciences.* Hillsdale, NJ: Erlbaum.

Cohn, D. A., Cowan, P. A., Cowan, C. P., & Pearson, J. (1992). Mothers' and fathers' working models of childhood attachment relationships, parenting styles, and child behavior. *Development and Psychopathology, 4,* 417–431.

Cohn, D. A., Silver, D. H., Cowan, C. P., Cowan, P. A., et al. (1992). Working models of childhood attachment and couple relationships. *Journal of Family Issues, 13,* 432–449.

Cole-Detke, H., & Kobak, R. (1996). Attachment processes in eating disorder and depression. *Journal of Consulting and Clinical Psychology, 64,* 282–290.

Constantino, J. (1996). Intergenerational aspects of the development of aggression: A preliminary report. *Journal of Developmental and Behavioral Pediatrics, 17,* 176–182.

Cortina, M. (in press). Causality, adaptation, and meaning: A perspective from attachment theory and research. *Psychoanalytic Dialogues.*

Cowan, P. A., Cohn, D. A., Cowan, C. P., & Pearson, J. L. (1996). Parents' attachment histories and children's externalizing and internalizing behaviors: Exploring family systems models of linkage. *Journal of Consulting and Clinical Psychology, 64,* 53–63.

Creasey, G., Boston, A., Tingley, L., Craft, A., & Kurtz, S. (1999, April). *Working models of attachment as predictors of observed conflict management behavior with adolescent romantic couples.* Paper to be presented at the biennial meeting of the Society for Research in Child Development, Albuquerque, NM.

Crowell, J. A., & Feldman, S. S. (1988). Mothers' internal models of relationships and children's behavioral and developmental status: A study of mother–child interaction. *Child Development, 59,* 1273–1285.

Crowell, J. A., & Feldman, S. S. (1991). Mothers' working models of attachment relationships and mother and child behavior during separation and reunion. *Developmental Psychology, 27,* 597–605.

Crowell, J. A., Treboux, D., & Waters, E. (in press). The Adult Attachment Interview and the Relationship Questionnaire: Relations to reports of mothers and partners. *Personal Relationships.*

Crowell, J. A., Waters, E., Treboux, D., O'Connor, E., Colon-Downs, C., Feider, O., Golby, B., & Posada, G. (1996). Discriminant validity of the Adult Attachment Interview. *Child Development, 67,* 2584–2599.

Dazzi, N., DeCoro, A., Ortu, F., & Speranza, A. M. (in press). L'intervista sull' attaccamento in preadolescenza: un' analisi delia dimensione della coerenza. *Psicologia Clinica dello Svilupp.*

DeHass, M., Bakermans-Kranenburg, M., & van IJzendoorn, M. H. (1994). The Adult Attachment Interview and questionnaires for attachment style, temperament, and memories of parental behavior. *Journal of Genetic Psychology, 155,* 471–486.

DeKlyen, M. (1996). Disruptive behavior disorder and intergenerational attachment patterns: A comparison of normal and clinic-referred preschoolers and their mothers. *Journal of Consulting and Clinical Psychology, 64,* 357–365.

DeWolff, M. S., & van IJzendoorn, M. H. (1997). Sensitivity and attachment: A meta-analysis on parental antecedents of infant attachment. *Child Development, 68,* 571–591.

Diamond, D., Clarkin, J., LeVine, H., Levy, K., Foelsch, P., & Yoemans, F. (in press). Borderline conditions and attachment: A preliminary report. *Psychoanalytic Inquiry.*

Dozier, M., Cue, K. L., & Barnett, L. (1994). Clinicians as caregivers: Role of attachment organization in treatment. *Journal of Consulting and Clinical Psychology, 62,* 793–800.

Dozier, M., & Kobak, R. R. (1992). Psychophysiology in attachment interviews: Converging evidence for deactivating strategies. *Child Development, 63,* 1473–1480.

Eagle, M. (1997). Attachment and psychoanalysis. *British Journal of Medical Psychology, 70,* 217–229.

Eiden, R. D., Teti, D. M., & Corns, K. M. (1995). Maternal working models of attachment, marital adjustment, and the parent–child relationship. *Child Development, 66,* 1504–1518.

Fleeson, J. (1988). *Assessment of parent–adolescent relation-*

ships: Implications for adolescent development. Unpublished doctoral dissertation, University of Minnesota.

Fonagy, P., Leigh, T., Steele, M., Steele, H., Kennedy, G., Mattoon, M., Target, M., & Gerber, A. (1996). The relation of attachment status, psychiatric classification, and response to psychotherapy. *Journal of Consulting and Clinical Psychology, 64,* 22–31.

Fonagy, P., Steele, H., & Steele, M. (1991). Maternal representations of attachment during pregnancy predict the organization of infant–mother attachment at one year of age. *Child Development, 62,* 891–905.

Fonagy, P., Steele, M., Steele, H., Moran, G., & Higgitt, A. C. (1991). The capacity for understanding mental states: The reflective self in parent and child and its significance for security of attachment. *Infant Mental Health Journal, 12,* 201–218.

Fonagy, P., Steele, M., Steele, H., Higgitt, A., et al. (1994). The Emmanuel Miller Memorial Lecture 1992: The theory and practice of resilience. Emmanuel Miller Lecture at the First Congress of the Association of Child Psychiatry & Allied Disciplines (1992). *Journal of Child Psychology and Psychiatry and Allied Disciplines, 35,* 231–257.

Fonagy, P., Steele, M., Steele, H., Leigh, T., Kennedy, R., Mattoon, G., & Target, M. (1995). Attachment, the reflective self, and borderline states: The predictive specificity of the Adult Attachment Interview and pathological emotional development. In S. Goldberg, R. Muir, & J. Kerr (Eds.), *Attachment theory: Social, developmental, and clinical perspectives* (pp. 233–278). Hillsdale, NJ: Analytic Press.

Fonagy, P., Target, M., Steele, M., Steele, H., & others. (1997). Morality, disruptive behavior, borderline personality disorder, crime, and their relationship to security of attachment. In L. Atkinson & K. J. Zucker (Eds.), *Attachment and psychopathology* (pp. 233–274). New York: Guilford Press.

Forguson, L., & Gopnik, A. (1988). The ontogeny of common sense. In J. W. Astington, P. L. Harris, & D. R. Olson (Eds.), *Developing theories of mind* (pp. 226–243). New York: Cambridge University Press.

Fox, N. A. (1995). Of the way we were: Adult memories about attachment experiences and their role in determining infant–parent relationships: A commentary on van IJzendoorn. *Psychological Bulletin, 117,* 404–410.

Fox, N. A., Kimmerly, N. L., & Schafer, W. D. (1991). Attachment to mother/attachment to father: A meta-analysis. *Child Development, 62,* 210–225.

Fraley, R. C., & Shaver, P. R. (1997). Adult attachment and the suppression of unwanted thoughts. *Journal of Personality and Social Psychology, 73,* 1080–1091.

Fyffe, C. E., & Waters, E. (1997, April). *Empirical classification of adult attachment status: Predicting group membership.* Paper presented at the biennial meeting of the Society for Research in Child Development, Washington, DC.

George, C. (1984). *Individual differences in affective sensitivity: A study of five-year-olds and their parents.* Unpublished doctoral dissertation, University of California at Berkeley.

George, C., Kaplan, N., & Main, M. (1984). *Adult Attachment Interview Protocol.* Unpublished manuscript, University of California at Berkeley.

George, C., Kaplan, N., & Main, M. (1985). *Adult Attachment Interview Protocol* (2nd ed.). Unpublished manuscript, University of California at Berkeley.

George, C., Kaplan, N., & Main, M. (1996). *Adult Attachment Interview Protocol* (3rd ed.). Unpublished manuscript, University of California at Berkeley.

George, C., & Solomon, J. (1996). Representational models of relationships: Links between caregiving and attachment. *Infant Mental Health Journal, 17,* 198–216.

Goldberg, S., Blokland, K., Cayetano, P., & Benoit, D. (1998, May). *Across the transmission gap: Adult attachment and response to infant emotions.* Paper presented at the Waterloo Conference on Child Development, University of Waterloo, Waterloo, Ontario.

Goldsmith, H. H., & Alansky, J. A. (1987). Maternal and infant temperamental predictors of attachment: A meta-analytic review. *Journal of Consulting and Clinical Psychology, 55,* 805–816.

Gomille, B., & Gloger-Tibbelt, G. (1999). Transgenerationale Vermittlung von Bindung. Zusammenhänge zwischen den mentalen Bindungsmodellen von müttern, den Bindungsmustern ihrer Kleinkinder sowie Erlebens- und Verhaltensweisen der Mütter beim Ubergang zur Elternschaft. *Praxis der Kinderpsychologie und Kinderpsychiatrie.*

Greenberg, M. T., Speltz, M. L., DeKlyen, M., & Endriga, M. C. (1991). Attachment security in preschoolers with and without externalizing behavior problems: A replication. *Development and Psychopathology, 3,* 413–430.

Grice, P. (1975). Logic and conversation. In P. Cole & J. L. Moran (Eds.), *Syntax and semantics: Vol. 3. Speech acts* (pp. 41–58). New York, Academic Press.

Grice, P. (1989). *Studies in the way of words.* Cambridge, MA: Harvard University Press.

Griffin, D. W., & Bartholomew, K. (1994). The metaphysics of measurement: The case of adult attachment. In K. Bartholomew & D. Perlman (Eds.), *Advances in personal relationships: Vol. 5. Attachment processes in adulthood* (pp. 17–52). London: Jessica Kingsley.

Grossmann, K., Fremmer-Bombik, E., Rudolph, J., & Grossmann, K. (1988). Maternal attachment representations as related to patterns of infant–mother attachment and maternal care during the first year. In R. A. Hinde & J. Stevenson-Hinde (Eds.), *Relationships within families: Mutual influences* (pp. 241–260). Oxford: Clarendon Press.

Grossmann, K., Grossmann, K. E., Spangler, G., Suess, G., & Unzner, L. (1985). Maternal sensitivity and newborns' orientation responses as related to quality of attachment in northern Germany. In I. Bretherton & E. Waters (Eds.), Growing points of attachment theory and research. *Monographs of the Society for Research in Child Development, 50*(1–2, Serial No. 209), 233–256.

Gunderson, J. G., Kolb, J. E., & Austin, V. (1981). The diagnostic interview for borderline patients. *American Journal of Psychiatry, 138,* 896–903.

Haft, W. L., & Slade, A. (1989). Affect attunement and maternal attachment: A pilot study. *Infant Mental Health Journal, 10,* 157–172.

Hamilton, C. E. (1995, March). *Continuity and discontinuity of attachment from infancy through adolescence.* Paper presented at the biennial meeting of the Society for Research in Child Development, Indianapolis.

Hamilton, C. E. (in press). Continuity and discontinuity of attachment from infancy through adolescence. *Child Development.*

Hazan, C., & Shaver, P. R. (1994). Attachment as an organizational framework for research on close relationships. *Psychological Inquiry, 5,* 1–22.

Hesse, E. (1996). Discourse, memory, and the Adult Attachment Interview: A note with emphasis on the emerging cannot classify category. *Infant Mental Health Journal, 17*, 4–11.

Hesse, E., & Main, M. (1999). Frightened behavior in traumatizing but non-maltreating parents: Previously unexamined risk factor for offspring. In D. Diamond & S. J. Blatt (Eds.), Psychoanalytic theory and attachment research I: Theoretical considerations. *Psychoanalytic Inquiry, 19.*

Hesse, E., & Main, M. (in press). Disorganization in infant and adult attachment: Descriptions, correlates, and implications for developmental psychopathology. *Journal of the American Psychoanalytic Association.*

Hesse, E., & van IJzendoorn, M. H. (1998a). Parental loss of close family members and propensities towards absorption in offspring. *Developmental Science, 1*, 299–305.

Hesse, E., & van IJzendoorn, M. H. (1998b). *Attachment and politics.* Unpublished manuscript, Leiden University.

Hesse, E., & van IJzendoorn, M. H. (in press). Propensities towards absorption are related to lapses in the monitoring of reasoning or discourse during the Adult Attachment Interview: A preliminary investigation. *Attachment and Human Development.*

Holtzworth-Munroe, A., Stuart, G. L., & Hutchinson, G. (1997). Violent versus nonviolent husbands: Differences in attachment patterns, dependency, and jealousy. *Journal of Family Psychology, 11*, 314–331.

Hopf, C. (1993). Rechtsextremismus und Beziehungserfahrungen. *Zeitschrist fur Soziologie, 22*, 449–463.

Hopf, C., & Hopf, W. (1997). *Familie, Personlichkeit, Politik: Eine Einfuhrung in die politische Sozialisation* [Family, personality, politics: An introduction to political socialization]. Munich: Juventa.

Hughes, P., & MacGauley, G. (1997). Mother–infant interaction during the first year with a child who shows disorganization of attachment. *British Journal of Psychotherapy, 14*, 147–158.

Isabella, R. (1993). Origins of attachment: Maternal interactive behavior across the first year. *Child Development, 64*, 605–624.

Ivarsson, T., Broberg, A. G., & Gillberg, C. (1998). *Depressive disorders in adolescence: An exploratory study of attachment characteristics and reflective functioning.* Manuscript submitted for publication.

Jacobvitz, D. B., Hazen, N. L., & Riggs, S. (1997, April). *Disorganized mental processes in mothers, frightened/frightening behavior in caregivers, and disoriented, disorganized behavior in infancy.* Paper presented at the biennial meeting of the Society for Research in Child Development, Washington, DC.

Kaplan, N. (1984). *Internal representations of separation experiences in six-year-olds: Related to actual experiences of separation.* Unpublished master's thesis, University of California at Berkeley.

Kaplan, N. (1987). *Individual differences in six-year-old's thoughts about separation: Predicted from attachment to mother at age one.* Unpublished doctoral dissertation, University of California at Berkeley.

Kobak, R. R. (1993). *The Attachment Q-Sort.* Unpublished manuscript, University of Delaware.

Kobak, R. R., Cole, H. E., Ferenz-Gillies, R., Fleming, W. S., & Gamble, W. (1993). Attachment and emotion regulation during mother–teen problem solving: A control theory analysis. *Child Development, 64*, 231–245.

Kobak, R. R., & Sceery, A. (1988). Attachment in late adolescence: Working models, affect regulation, and representations of self and others. *Child Development, 59*, 135–146.

Korfmacher, J., Adam, E., Ogawa, J., & Egeland, B. (1997). Adult attachment: Implications for the therapeutic process in a home intervention. *Applied Developmental Science, 1*, 43–52.

Lee, S. S., Polan, H. J., & Ward, M. J. (1998). *Internal working models of attachment and psychopathology in a nonclinical sample of adult women.* Manuscript submitted for publication.

Levy, K. N., Blatt, S. J., & Shaver, P. R. (1998). Attachment styles and parental representations. *Journal of Personality and Social Psychology, 74*, 407–419.

Levinson, A., & Fonagy, P. (1998). *Criminality and attachment: The relationship between interpersonal awareness and offending in a prison population.* Manuscript submitted for publication.

Lewis, M. (1997). *Altering fate: Why the past does not predict the future.* New York: Guilford Press.

Loftus, E. F. (1994). The repressed memory controversy. *American Psychologist, 49*, 443–445.

Lyons-Ruth, K., Bronfman, E., & Parsons, E. (in press). Maternal disrupted affective communication, maternal frightened or frightening behavior, and disorganized infant attachment strategies. In J. Vondra & D. Barnett (Eds.), Atypical patterns of infant attachment: Theory, research, and current directions. *Monographs of the Society for Research in Child Development.*

Main, M. (Chair). (1985, April). *Attachment: A move to the level of representation.* Symposium conducted at the meeting of the Society for Research in Child Development, Toronto.

Main, M. (1991). Metacognitive knowledge, metacognitive monitoring, and singular (coherent) vs. multiple (incoherent) models of attachment: Findings and directions for future research. In C. M. Parkes, J. Stevenson-Hinde, & P. Marris (Eds.), *Attachment across the life cycle* (pp. 127–159). London: Routledge.

Main, M. (1993). Discourse, prediction, and recent studies in attachment: Implications for psychoanalysis. *Journal of the American Psychoanalytic Association, 41*(Suppl.), 209–244.

Main, M. (1995). Attachment: Overview, with implications for clinical work. In S. Goldberg, R. Muir & J. Kerr (Eds.), *Attachment theory: Social, developmental, and clinical perspectives* (pp. 407–474). Hillsdale, NJ: Analytic Press.

Main, M. (1996). Introduction to the special section on attachment and psychopathology: II, Overview of the field of attachment. *Journal of Consulting and Clinical Psychology, 64*, 237–243.

Main, M. (in press). The Adult Attachment Interview: Fear, attention, safety, and discourse processes. *Journal of the American Psychoanalytic Association.*

Main, M., & Cassidy, J. (1988). Categories of response to reunion with the parent at age six: Predicted from infant attachment classifications and stable over a one-month period. *Developmental Psychology, 24*, 415–426.

Main, M., & Fonagy, P. (1998). *Theory of mind: An interview protocol.* Manuscript in preparation.

Main, M., & Goldwyn, R. (1984a). *Adult attachment scoring and classification system.* Unpublished manuscript, University of California at Berkeley.

Main, M., & Goldwyn, R. (1984b). Predicting rejection of her infant from mother's representation of her own experience: Implications for the abused–abusing intergenerational cycle. *International Journal of Child Abuse and Neglect, 8*, 203–217.

Main, M., & Goldwyn, R. (1998a). *Adult attachment scoring and classification system.* Unpublished manuscript, University of California at Berkeley.

Main, M., & Goldwyn, R. (1998b). *Interview-based adult attachment classifications: Related to infant–mother and infant–father attachment.* Unpublished manuscript, University of California at Berkeley.

Main, M., & Hesse, E. (1990). Parents' unresolved traumatic experiences are related to infant disorganized attachment status: Is frightened and/or frightening parental behavior the linking mechanism? In M. T. Greenberg, D. Cicchetti & E. M. Cummings (Eds.), *Attachment in the preschool years: Theory, research, and intervention* (pp. 161–182). Chicago: University of Chicago Press.

Main, M., & Hesse, E. (1992). *Coding system for identifying frightened, frightening, dissociated, and disorganized parental behavior.* Unpublished manuscript, University of California at Berkeley.

Main, M., & Hesse, E. (1998a). *Predicting Adult Attachment Interview response in late adolescence from infant Strange Situation behavior with mother and father.* Manuscript in preparation, University of California at Berkeley.

Main, M., & Hesse, E. (1998b) *Coding system for identifying frightened, frightening, dissociated, and disorganized parental behavior* (6th ed.). Unpublished manuscript, University of California at Berkeley.

Main, M., Kaplan, N., & Cassidy, J. (1985). Security in infancy, childhood, and adulthood: A move to the level of representation. In I. Bretherton & E. Waters (Eds.), Growing points of attachment theory and research. *Monographs of the Society for Research in Child Development, 50*(1–2, Serial No. 209), 66–104.

Main, M., & Solomon, J. (1990). Procedures for identifying infants as disorganized/disoriented during the Ainsworth strange situation. In M. T. Greenberg, D. Cicchetti, & E. M. Cummings (Eds.), *Attachment in the preschool years: Theory, research, and intervention* (pp. 121–160). Chicago: University of Chicago Press.

Manassis, K., Bradley, S., Goldberg, S., Hood, J., & Swinson, R. P. (1994). Attachment in mothers with anxiety disorders and their children. *Journal of the American Academy of Child & Adolescent Psychiatry, 33,* 1106–1113.

Mikulincer, M., Florian, V., & Tolmacz, R. (1990). Attachment styles and fear of personal death: A case study of affect regulation. *Journal of Personality and Social Psychology, 58,* 273–280.

Mikulincer, M., & Orbach, I. (1995). Attachment styles and repressive defensiveness: The accessbility and architecture of affective memories. *Journal of Personality and Social Psychology, 68,* 917–925.

Minde, K., & Hesse, E. (1996). The role of the Adult Attachment Interview in parent–infant psychotherapy: A case presentation. *Infant Mental Health Journal, 17,* 115–126.

Mura, S. S. (1983). Licensing violations: Legitimate violations of Grice's conversational principle. In R. T. Craig & K. Tracy (Eds.), *Conversational coherence: Form, structure, and strategy.* Beverly Hills, CA: Sage.

Muscetta, S., Dazzi, N., DeCoro, A., Ortu, F., & Speranza, A. M. (in press). States of mind with respect to attachment and change in a psychotherapeutic relationship: A study of the coherence of transcript in short-term psychotherapy with an adolescent. *Psychoanalytic Inquiry.*

Patrick, M., Hobson, R. P., Castle, D., Howard, R., & Maughan, B. (1994). Personality disorder and the mental representation of early social experience. *Development and Psychopathology, 6,* 375–388.

Pearson, J. L., Cohn, D. A., Cowan, P. A., & Cowan, C. P.

(1994). Earned- and continuous-security in adult attachment: Relation to depressive symptomatology and parenting style. *Development and Psychopathology, 6,* 359–373.

Pederson, D. R., Gleason, K. E., Moran, G., & Bento, S. (1998). Maternal attachment representations, maternal sensitivity, and the infant–mother attachment relationship. *Developmental Psychology, 34,* 925–933.

Pederson, D. R., & Moran, G. (1996). Expressions of the attachment relationship outside of the strange situation. *Child Development, 67,* 915–927.

Phelps, J. L., Belsky, J., & Crnic, K. (1998). Earned security, daily stress, and parenting: A comparison of five alternative models. *Development and Psychopathology, 10,* 21–38.

Pianta, R. C., Egeland, B., & Adam, E. K. (1996). Adult attachment classification and self-reported psychiatric symptomatology as assessed by the Minnesota Multiphasic Personality Inventory—2. *Journal of Consulting and Clinical Psychology, 64,* 273–281.

Posada, G. , Waters, E., Crowell, J., & Lay, K. L. (1995). Is it easier to use a secure mother as a secure base?: Attachment Q-Sort correlates of the Berkeley Adult Attachment Interview. In E. Waters, B. Vaughn, G. Posada, & K. Kondo-Ikemura, (Eds.). Caregiving, cultural, and cognitive perspectives on secure-base phenomena and working models: New growing points of attachment theory and research. *Monographs of the Society for Research in Child Development, 60*(2–3, Serial No. 244), 133–145.

Radojevic, M. (1994). Mental representations of attachment among prospective Australian fathers. *Australian and New Zealand Journal of Psychiatry, 28,* 505–511.

Robertson, J., & Bowlby, J. (1952). Responses of young children to separation from their mothers. *Cours du Centre Internationale de l'Enfance, 2,* 131–142.

Robertson, J., & Robertson, J. (1967–1972). *Young children in brief separations* [Film series]. London: Tavistock Institute of Human Relations.

Rosenthal, R. (1991). *Meta-analytic procedures for social research* (rev. ed.). Newbury Park, CA: Sage.

Rosenstein, D., & Horowitz, H. A. (1996). Adolescent attachment and psychopathology. *Journal of Consulting and Clinical Psychology, 64,* 244–253.

Routh, C. P., Hill, J. W., Steele, H., Elliott, C. E., & Dewey, E. W. (1995). Maternal attachment status, psychosocial stressors, and problem behavior: Follow-up after parent training courses for conduct disorder. *Journal of Child Psychology and Psychiatry, 36,* 1179–1198.

Sagi, A., van IJzendoorn, M. H., Scharf, M. H., Joels, T., Koren-Karie, N., Mayseless, O., & Aviezer, O. (1997). Ecological constraints for intergenerational transmission of attachment. *International Journal of Behavioral Development, 20,* 287–299.

Sagi, A., van IJzendoorn, M. H., Scharf, M. H., Koren-Karie, N., Joels, T., & Mayseless, O. (1994). Stability and discriminant validity of the Adult Attachment Interview: A psychometric study in young Israeli adults. *Developmental Psychology, 30,* 771–777.

Schuengel, C., Bakermans-Kranenburg, M. J., & van IJzendoorn, M. H. (1999). Frightening maternal behavior linking unresolved loss and disorganized infant attachment. *Journal of Consulting and Clinical Psychology, 67*(1).

Simpson, J. A., Rholes, W. S., & Nelligan, J. S. (1992). Support-seeking and support-giving within couple members in an anxiety-provoking situation: The role of attachment styles. *Journal of Personality and Social Psychology, 62,* 434–446.

Simpson, J. A., Rholes, W. S., & Phillips, D. (1996). Conflict in close relationships: An attachment perspective. *Journal of Personality and Social Psychology, 71,* 899–914.

Speltz, M. L., Greenberg, M. T., & DeKlyen, M. (1990). Attachment in preschoolers with disruptive behavior: A comparison of clinic-referred and nonproblem children. *Development and Psychopathology, 2,* 31–46.

Sroufe, L. A. (1985). Attachment classification from the perspective of infant–caregiver relationships and infant temperament. *Child Development, 56,* 1–14.

Sroufe, L. A. (1990, Autumn). The role of training in attachment assessment. *Newsletter of the Society for Research in Child Development.*

Sroufe, L. A., Egeland, B., & Kreutzer, T. (1990). The fate of early experience following developmental change: Longitudinal approaches to individual adaptation in childhood. *Child Development, 61,* 1363–1373.

Stalker, C. A., & Davies, F. (1995). Attachment organization and adaptation in sexually abused women. *Canadian Journal of Psychiatry, 40,* 234–240.

Steele, H., Steele, M., & Fonagy, P. (1996). Associations among attachment classifications of mothers, fathers, and infants: Evidence for a relationship-specific perspective. *Child Development, 2,* 541–555.

Stovall, K. C., & Dozier, M. (1998). *The evolution of attachment in new relationships: Single subject analyses of ten foster infants.* Manuscript submitted for publication.

Strage, A., & Main, M. (1985, April). *Parent–child discourse patterns at six years predicted from the organization of infant attachment relationships.* Paper presented at the biennial meeting of the Society for Research in Child Development, Toronto.

Sullivan-Hanson, J. (1990). *The early attachment and current affectional bonds of battered women: Implications for the impact of spouse abuse on children.* Unpublished doctoral dissertation, University of Virginia.

Trowell, J. (1997). *Attachment in children: Development from a study with sexually abused girls* (Association for Child Psychology and Psychiatry Occasional Papers, No. 14). London: Association for Child Psychology and Psychiatry.

True, M., Pasani, L., Ryan, R., & Oumar, F. (1998). *Maternal behaviors related to disorganized infant attachment in West Africa.* Paper presented at the annual meeting of the Western Psychological Association, Albuquerque.

Tyrell, C., Dozier, M., Teague, G. B., & Fallot, R. D. (1998). *Effective treatment for persons with serious psychiatric disorders: The importance of attachment states of mind.* Manuscript submitted for publication.

van IJzendoorn, M. H. (1995). Adult attachment representations, parental responsiveness, and infant attachment: A meta-analysis on the predictive validity of the Adult Attachment Interview. *Psychological Bulletin, 117,* 387–403.

van IJzendoorn, M. H. (1997). Attachment, emergent morality, and aggression: Toward a developmental socioemotional model of antisocial behavior. *International Journal of Behavioral Development, 21,* 703–727.

van IJzendoorn, M., & Bakermans-Kranenburg, M. (1996). Attachment representations in mothers, fathers, adolescents and clinical groups: A meta-analytic search for normative data. *Journal of Consulting and Clinical Psychology, 64,* 8–21.

van IJzendoorn, M. H., & DeWolff, M. S. (1997). In search of the absent father—meta-analysis of infant–father attachment: A rejoinder to our discussants. *Child Development, 68,* 604–609.

van IJzendoorn, M. H., Feldbrugge, J. T. T. M., Derks, F. C. H., deRuiter, C., Verhagen, et al. (1997). Attachment representations of personality-disordered criminal offenders. *American Journal of Orthopsychiatry, 67,* 449–459.

van IJzendoorn, M. H., & Bakermans-Kranenburg, M. J. (1997). Intergenerational transmission of attachment: A move to the contextual level. In L. Atkinson & K. J. Zucker (Eds.), *Attachment and psychopathology* (pp. 135–170). New York: Guilford Press.

van IJzendoorn, M. H., Goldberg, S., Kroonenberg, P. M., & Frenkel, O. J. (1992). The relative effects of maternal and child problems on the quality of attachment: A meta-analysis of attachment in clinical samples. *Child Development, 63,* 840–858.

van Londen, M., Juffer, F., & van IJzendoorn, M. H. (1998). *Predicting infant attachment organization from prebirth Adult Attachment Interviews in first-time adoptive mothers.* Manuscript in preparation, Leiden University.

Ward, M. J., & Carlson, E. A. (1995). The predictive validity of the Adult Attachment Interview for adolescent mothers. *Child Development, 66,* 69–79.

Waters, E., Merrick, S. K., Treboux, D., Crowell, J., & Albersheim, L. (in press). Attachment security from infancy to early adulthood: A 20–year longitudinal study. *Child Development.*

Waters, E. (1995). The Attachment Q-set, Version 3.0. In E. Waters, B. Vaughn, G. Posada, & K. Kondo-Ikemura (Eds.), Caregiving, cultural, and cognitive perspectives on secure-base phenomena and working models: New growing points of attachment theory and research. *Monographs of the Society for Research in Child Development, 60*(2–3, Serial No. 244), 133–145.

Webster's new international dictionary of the English language. (1959). W. A. Neilson (Ed.). (2nd ed., unabridged). Springfield, MA: Merriam.

Weinfield, N., Sroufe, L. A., & Egeland, B. (in press). Attachment from infancy to early adulthood in a high risk sample: Continuity, discontinuity, and their correlates. *Child Development.*

Weston, D., & Richardson, E. (1985, April). *Children's world views: Working models and the quality of attachment.* Poster presented at the biennial meeting of the Society for Research in Child Development, Toronto.

Zeanah, C. H., Benoit, D., Barton, M., Regan, C., Hirshberg, L. M., & Lipsitt, L. P. (1993). Representations of attachment in mothers and their one-year-old infants. *Journal of the American Academy of Child and Adolescent Psychiatry, 32,* 278–286.

Zeanah, C. H., Finley-Belgrad, E., & Benoit, D. (1997). Intergenerational transmission of relationship psychopathology: A mother–infant case study. In L. Atkinson & K. J. Zucker (Eds.), *Attachment and psychopathology* (pp. 292–318). New York: Guilford Press.

Zimmermann, P., Grossmann, K. E., & Fremmer-Bombik, E. (1998). *Attachment in infancy and adolescence: Continuity of attachment or continuity of transmission of attachment?* Manuscript submitted for publication.

20

Measurement of Individual Differences in Adolescent and Adult Attachment

❖

JUDITH A. CROWELL
R. CHRIS FRALEY
PHILLIP R. SHAVER

Attachment theory is a lifespan developmental theory. According to Bowlby (1969/1982), human attachments play a "vital role . . . from the cradle to the grave" (p. 208). Ainsworth (1989) devoted her American Psychological Association Distinguished Scientific Contribution Award address to "attachments beyond infancy," and included discussions of adolescents' and adults' continuing relationships with parents, their relationships with especially close friends, and the role of attachment in heterosexual and homosexual "pair bonds." Although Bowlby and Ainsworth clearly identified the importance of the attachment system across the lifespan, they provided relatively few guidelines concerning its specific function and expression in later life.

Early research on attachment followed Bowlby's and Ainsworth's primary focus on young children and explored the developmental roots of the attachment system, examining infants' attachment to their parents, especially their mothers. (These studies are reviewed in many of the other chapters in this volume.) Beginnin in the mid-1980s, the groundwork was laid for examining the attachment system in older children and adults, and several new lines of research emerged. Following an interest in attachment representations, George, Kaplan, and Main

(1984) created the Adult Attachment Interview (AAI) "to assess the security of the adult's overall working model of attachment, that is, the security of the self in relation to attachment in its generality rather than in relation to any particular present or past relationship" (1985, p. 78). As explained below, the AAI assesses adults' representations of attachment based on their discussion of childhood relationships with their parents, and of those experiences' effects on their development as adults and as parents. At about the time the AAI was being developed, Pottharst and Kessler (as described in Pottharst, 1990b) created an Attachment History Questionnaire (AHQ) to assess adults' memories of attachment-related experiences in childhood (e.g., separation from parents, loss of parents, quality of relationships with attachment figures). In a separate research effort, Armsden and Greenberg (1987) developed the Inventory of Parent and Peer Attachment (IPPA), which assesses the security, or perceived quality, of adolescents' current relationships with parents and peers. Similarly, West and Sheldon-Keller (1994; West, Sheldon, & Reiffer, 1987) developed the Reciprocal Attachment Questionnaire for Adults to assess security with respect to a primary attachment figure (parent, peer, or partner) in adulthood. Also at about this time, Hazan and Shaver (1987; Shaver, Hazan, & Bradshaw, 1988) began to consider the applicability of attachment theory in general, and of Ainsworth's infant classification scheme in particular, to the study of feelings and behavior in adolescent and adult romantic relationships.

Given the independence of these several groups of investigators, and their different domains of interest and varied professional backgrounds, the lines of research they initiated have developed in different ways. Each kind of work has inspired variations and offshoots, so that today there are many different measures of adolescent and adult attachment—and a great deal of confusion about what they measure, what they are supposed to measure, and how they are related (if at all) to each other. In the present chapter we attempt to organize and review this rapidly growing, very complex measurement literature and to provide guidelines for researchers undertaking research on adolescent or adult attachment. In particular, we show that the different kinds of measures cannot sensibly be substituted for one another in empirical studies.

The chapter begins with a brief discussion of attachment theory, especially the elements that are key to understanding the attachment system in adults, and hence to assessing it. The AAI and related measures are discussed in the next section. The third section deals with the AHQ, the IPPA, and the Reciprocal Attachment Questionnaire. These three measures are considered in a single section because they all use a self-report methodology and because none is meant to capture the attachment patterns delineated by Ainsworth, Blehar, Waters, and Wall (1978) in their work with the strange situation (SS). The fourth major section deals with some of the measures of romantic attachment that grew out of Hazan and Shaver's (1987) attempt to apply Ainsworth's discoveries to the study of romantic relationships. The final section is an attempt to summarize the overlaps and distinctions among measures developed in different lines of research on adolescent and adult attachment, and to provide guidelines for future research.

ADULT ATTACHMENT: THEORETICAL ISSUES

The title of this chapter identifies two ideas from attachment theory that are critical to measurement. The first is that the attachment system is normative—that is, relevant to the development of all people, and active and important in adult life. The second is that there are individual differences in the expression of attachment behavior in the context of attachment relationships.

Adult Attachment

Although some of Bowlby's original inspiration for attachment theory came from his work as a clinician, he primarily drew from research in ethology, observations of animal behavior, and cognitive psychology when developing the theory. He described the attachment behavioral system as an evolutionarily adaptive motivational–behavioral control system. The attachment system has the goal of promoting safety in infancy and childhood through the child's relationship with an attachment figure or caregiver (Bowlby, 1969/1982). Attachment behavior is activated in times of danger, stress, and novelty, and has the outcome of gaining and maintaining proximity and contact with an attachment figure. Hence, the behavioral manifestations are context-specific (evident in times of danger or anxiety), although the attachment system is considered active at all times, continuously monitoring the environment and the availability of attachment figures (Ainsworth et al., 1978; Bretherton, 1985). The child can confidently explore the environment with the active support of a caregiver, secure in the knowledge that this attachment figure is there if any need should arise. Ainsworth et al. (1978) termed this interaction between child and caregiver the "secure base phenomenon," a phenomenon central to attachment theory.

Bowlby (1969/1982) hypothesized that the attachment relationship in infancy is similar in nature to later love relationships, and he drew few distinctions among those close relationships, be they parent to child, partner to partner, or adult child to older parent. Mary Ainsworth (1991) highlighted the function of the attachment behavioral system in adult relationships, emphasizing the secure-base phenomenon as the critical element. She stated that a secure attachment relationship is one that facilitates functioning and competence outside of the relationship: There is "a seeking to obtain an experience of security and comfort in the relationship with the partner. If and when such security and comfort are available, the individual is able to move off from the secure base provided by the partner, with the confidence to engage in other activities" (1991, p. 38). Attachment relationships are distinguished from other adult relationships as those that provide feelings of security and belonging, and without which there is loneliness and restlessness. This function is distinct from aspects of relationships that provide guidance or companionship; sexual gratification; or opportunities to feel needed or to share common interests or experiences, feelings of competence, or alliance and assistance (Ainsworth, 1985; Weiss, 1974). The behavioral elements of attachment in adult life are similar to those observed in infancy, and an adult shows a desire for proximity to the attachment figure when stressed, increased comfort in the presence of the attachment figure, and anxiety when the attachment figure is inaccessible (Shaver et al., 1988; Weiss, 1991). Grief is felt at the loss of an attachment figure (Bowlby, 1980; Fraley & Shaver, Chapter 32, this volume).

A major difference between adult–adult attachment and child–parent attachment is that the attachment behavioral system in adults is reciprocal; in other words, adult partners are not assigned to or set in the role of "attachment figure/caregiver" or "attached individual/care receiver." Both attachment and caregiving behavior are observable in adults, and partners shift between the two roles (Ainsworth, 1991; Kunce & Shaver, 1994; Shaver et al., 1988). The potential for flexible reciprocity adds complexity to the measurement of adult attachment.

Individual Differences and Mental Representations or Working Models

The study of attachment in adults has focused largely on individual differences in the organization of attachment behavior and in expectations regarding attachment relationships, rather than on normative, developmental aspects of the attachment system. The idea of individual differences emerged from the work of Ainsworth et al. (1978), who broadly characterized the patterns of attachment as "secure" and "anxious" or "insecure" (see also Bretherton, 1985). In addition to the security–insecurity distinction, Ainsworth et al. (1978) drew a second distinction between "avoidance and conflict relevant to close bodily contact" (p. 298)—that is, the avoidance and resistance behaviors that distinguish two of the major insecure patterns. It is important to note that individual differences in attachment security do not represent differences in strength or quantity of attachment; "the most conspicuous dimension that has emerged so far is not strength of attachment but security vs. anxiety in the attachment relationship. This does not imply substitution of

degree of security for degree of strength" (Ainsworth et al., 1978, p. 298).

Differences among attachment patterns in infancy are thought to develop primarily from different experiences in interaction with an attachment figure, rather than being heavily influenced by child temperament or other child characteristics (Ainsworth et al., 1978; Vaughn & Bost, Chapter 10, this volume). The secure pattern characterizes the infant who seeks and receives protection, reassurance, and comfort when stressed. Confident exploration is optimized because of the support and availability of the caregiver. The child comes to feel secure with the attachment figure; hence the behavioral system connects with feelings and the expression of emotion at least in the context of attachment-related experiences. The major insecure patterns ("avoidant," "ambivalent") develop when attachment behavior is met by rejection, inconsistency, or even threat from the attachment figure, leaving the infant "anxious" about the caregiver's responsiveness should problems arise. To reduce this anxiety, the infant's behavior comes to fit or complement the attachment figure's behavior; in other words, it is strategic and adaptive within the context of that relationship (Main, 1981, 1990). However, the need to attend to the caregiver in this anxious, strategic way, which compromises exploratory behavior, is considered maladaptive outside of that particular relationship.

Current theory and research on adult attachment draw heavily on Bowlby's concept of attachment representations or working models. Importing ideas from cognitive psychology, Bowlby (1973, 1980) hypothesized that individuals develop attachment representations of the functioning and significance of close relationships. These representations, or models, consist of a person's beliefs and expectations about how attachment relationships operate and what he or she gains from them. As noted above, individual differences emerge in the expression of attachment behavior in the context of attachment relationships. Patterns of attachment develop in the course of behavioral interactions between an infant/child and parents (Bowlby, 1980) and reflect expectations about the child's own behavior and a parent's likely behavior in various situations. Cognitive–affective structures develop that mirror the behavioral patterns. They are called "working" models or representations because they are the basis for action in attachment-related situations and because in principle they are open to revision as a function of significant attachment-related experiences. The models are relatively stable and can operate automatically without the need for conscious appraisal; they guide behavior in relationships with parents and influence expectations, strategies, and behavior in later relationships (Bretherton, 1985). Bowlby's incorporation of mental representations into attachment theory allows for a lifespan perspective on the attachment behavioral system, providing a way of understanding developmental change in the expression of attachment and its ongoing influence on development and behavior in relationships.

An individual's model of attachment involves stable postulates about the roles of both parent and child in the relationship, because individual differences in attachment stem from a particular caregiving environment. In other words, working models are models of attachment relationships (Bretherton, 1985). Bowlby (1973) wrote:

> In the working model of the world that anyone builds, a key feature is his notion of who his attachment figures are, where they may be found, and how they may be expected to respond. Similarly, in the working model of the self that anyone builds a key feature is his notion of how acceptable or unacceptable he himself is in the eyes of his attachment figures. . . . Confidence that an attachment figure is . . . likely to be responsive can be seen to turn on two variables: (a) whether or not the attachment figure is judged to be the sort of person who in general responds to calls for support and protection; (b) whether or not the self is judged to be the sort of person towards whom . . . the attachment figure is likely to respond in a helpful way. Logically these variables are independent. In practice, they are apt to be confounded. As a result, the model of the attachment figure and the model of the self are likely to develop so as to be complementary and mutually confirming. (pp. 203–204)

Bowlby (1973, 1980) also wrote about the dilemma presented by the situation in which a child is presented with a negative view of the self and other, and/or with incompatible data about his or her experiences—that is, when the "child's first-hand experience" of the attachment figure is in opposition to what the parent tells the child about the meaning of the parental behavior. Because information relevant to characterizing an attachment relationship comes from multiple sources (Bowlby, 1973), conflicting information challenges the development of a coherent representation. Bowlby (1973) and Main (1981, 1990, 1991), among others, have written about the strategies required to maintain cognitive organi-

zation in the face of stress and conflicting information. These secondary strategies (Main, 1990) (as opposed to the primary strategy of approach, contact seeking, and contact maintenance when the attachment system is activated) are defensive maneuvers that require "manipulating the level of output usually called for by the [attachment] system—[and, in addition, manipulating cognitive processes to maintain] a given attachment organization" (p. 48). Such strategies develop because there are inconsistencies, incompatibilities, and a lack of internal connectedness in the elements of the attachment representation (Bowlby, 1973; Main, 1990, 1991). Strategies may include avoidance of the attachment figure in stressful situations (Main, 1981), oscillation between the two viewpoints (i.e., "child good, parent bad," "child bad, parent good"), acceptance of the parent's view while denying one's own experience (Bowlby, 1973).

A central developmental hypothesis in attachment theory is that early parent–child relationships are prototypes of later love relationships— a Freudian insight preserved and modified by Bowlby (Waters, Kondo-Ikemura, Posada, & Richters, 1991). Bowlby did not claim that there is a critical period in infancy that has implications across the lifespan (the most extreme interpretation of the prototype hypothesis), but rather that there is a strong tendency toward continuity in parent–child interactions, which then feed back into the attachment behavioral system. That is, in addition to having effects on individual personality characteristics, child–parent relationships should be related to subsequent patterns of family organization and should play a role in intergenerational transmission of family attachment patterns. Much of adult attachment research has been based on the assumption that there are parallel individual differences between infant and adult patterns of attachment and attachment representation (e.g., see Hazan & Shaver, 1987; Main, Kaplan, & Cassidy, 1985). However, ideas about the origins of these attachment patterns in adults and disagreement about the structure of the attachment system are in part responsible for some of the confusion in the adult attachment field.

Bowlby (1969/1982) also discussed the concept of change in attachment patterns, an issue relevant to adult patterns of attachment. In childhood, if an attachment pattern changes, there should be a corresponding change in the quality of parent–child interactions (Bowlby, 1969/1982). Bowlby also hypothesized that change in attachment patterns can occur in later life through the influence of new attachment relationships and the development of formal operational thought. This combination of events should allow the individual to reflect on and reinterpret the meaning of past and present experiences (Bowlby, 1973, 1980). It is also possible that a new relationship can lead to the co-construction of a new attachment representation, which takes into account both partners' attachment representations as well as other elements of the relationship (Oppenheim & Waters, 1995; Owens et al., 1995). This may or may not lead to full representational change in the individual's original model of attachment. In general, it can be said that researchers have attributed the development of adult attachment patterns to three broad sources, although the relative importance and influence of the three sources is debated and is a critical research issue (for examples, see Fraley, 1998; Owens et al., 1995; Waters et al., 1991). The three sources are (1) parent–child attachment relationships; (2) peer and romantic relationship experiences, including the experience of the parents' marriage; and (3) the current adult attachment relationship.

In summary, two central aspects of attachment theory are key to understanding attachment in adulthood and to evaluating existing measures of adult attachment: The attachment system is active in adults, and there are individual differences in adult attachment behavior that have their foundations in attachment experiences and are embodied in attachment representations.

NARRATIVE MEASURES OF ATTACHMENT REPRESENTATIONS

The use of narrative to assess attachment is based on the idea that "mental processes vary as distinctively as do behavioral processes" (Main et al., 1985, p. 78), and that behavioral and representational processes are reflected in language. The scoring of the narrative measures described in this section is based on the concept of attachment security—that is, the ability of an individual to use an attachment figure as a secure base from which to explore and a safe haven in times of distress or danger (secure), versus the inability to do so (insecure). The assessments ultimately derive their validity from observations of attachment behavior in natural settings. Each measure was designed to have the same basic structure—that is, to include an assessment of the continu-um from secure to insecure, and secondarily, to assess differences among insecure strategies.

Adult Attachment Interview

In what Main et al. (1985) called "a move to the level of representation" (in contrast to the previous focus on behavior in the assessment of parent–child attachment relationships), Main and her coworkers developed a semistructured interview for adults about childhood attachment experiences and the meaning currently assigned by an individual to past attachment-related experiences (George et al., 1984, 1985, 1996). The development of the AAI and its scoring were based on several key ideas about attachment. These include the ideas that working models operate at least partially outside of conscious awareness; that they are based on attachment-relevant experiences; that infants begin to develop models that guide behavior in attachment relationships in the first year of life; that representations provide guidelines for behavior and affective appraisal of experience; that formal operational thought allows the individual to observe and assess a given relationship system, and hence that the model of the relationship can be altered without an actual change in experiences in the relationship; and that the models are not templates, but are processes that serve to "obtain or to limit access to information" (Main et al., 1985, p. 77). In addition, the scoring system is linked to Bowlby's and Main's ideas about secondary strategies, defensive processes, and incompatible models described earlier.

An adult is interviewed about his or her general view of the relationship with parents; ordinary experiences with parents in which the attachment system is presumed to be activated (upset, injury, illness, separation); experiences of loss; and finally the meaning that the adult attributes to these experiences in terms of the parents' behavior and the development of the interviewee's adult personality and behavior as a parent (if applicable). The resulting narrative is transcribed and examined for material directly expressed by the individual, and also for unintended qualities of discourse, such as incoherence and inconsistency. Scoring is based on (1) the coder's assessment of the individual's childhood experiences with parents; (2) the language used by the individual in the interview; and (3) most importantly, the individual's ability to give an integrated, believable account of experiences and their meaning. The speaker's language and discourse style are considered reflections of the "current state of mind with respect to attachment" (Main & Goldwyn, 1994; Main et al., 1985; Hesse, Chapter 19, this volume).

Main and Goldwyn's Scoring System

The AAI scoring system was developed by examining 44 parental interviews for which the SS classifications of the interviewees' infants were already known, and identifying qualities of content and discourse that distinguished them. Hence the AAI was expressly developed to capture the issues tapped by the SS, especially an individual's ability to use an attachment figure as a secure base. The system has been refined and somewhat expanded over the past 15 years (Main & Goldwyn, 1994), but has not yet been published. Extensive training is required to administer and score the interview.

Scoring is done from a transcript, using scales that characterize the individual's childhood experiences with each parent *in the opinion of the coder.* There are two sets of scales: parental behavior and state of mind scales. That is, the parental behavior is rated from the specific memories and descriptions given of parental behavior, and not from the general assessment or summary of the parenting given by the individual. The parental behavior scales, rated separately for mother and father, are as follows: loving, rejecting, neglecting, involving, and pressuring. The state of mind scales assess discourse style and particular forms of coherence and incoherence: idealization, insistence on lack of recall, active anger, derogation, fear of loss, metacognitive monitoring, and passivity of speech. Using the ratings of the specific forms of incoherence and the overall coherence of the transcript, the coder also assigns scores for coherence of transcript and coherence of mind. The concept of "coherence" is based on Grice's maxims (1975) regarding discourse: High coherence means that the narrative adheres to Grice's maxims of *quality* (it is believable, without contradictions or illogical conclusions), *quantity* (enough, but not too much, information is given to permit the coder to understand the narrative), *relevance* (the individual answers the questions asked), and *manner* (the individual uses fresh, clear language rather than jargon, canned speech, or nonsense words).

Patterns of scale scores are used to assign an adult to one of three major classifications: a secure category ("autonomous") or one of two insecure categories ("dismissing" or "preoccupied"), with the coherence scales being used to make the secure–insecure distinction. The three categories parallel the three infant attachment patterns identified by Ainsworth et al. (1978), and the discourse style used in the interviews reflects the behavioral elements in infant attachment patterns.

Individuals classified as autonomous in the AAI maintain a balanced view of early relationships, value attachment relationships, and view attachment-related experiences as influential in their development. In parallel to the direct approach of the secure infant, the autonomous adult's approach to the interview is open, direct, and cooperative, regardless of how difficult the material is to discuss. The interview itself contains coherent, believable reports of behavior by parents; simply put, the adult's summarizing descriptions of the parenting he or she received match the specific memories given of parental behavior. Because security is inferred from coherence, any kind of childhood experience may be associated with being classified as autonomous, although in many cases parental behavior is summarized as loving, and there are clear and specific memories given of loving behavior by the parents.

The two insecure classifications are associated with incoherent accounts, meaning that interviewees' assessment of experience is not matched by their actual descriptions of parental behavior. There is little to no support provided for a parent's serving as a secure base; and discourse, whether dismissing or preoccupied, mirrors the lack of exploration and inflexibility of insecure infants. The classifications reflect the strategies used to manage the anxiety of having a parent who failed in this regard. Corresponding to the behavior of avoidant infants in the SS, adults classified as dismissing are uncomfortable with the topic of the interview, deny the impact of early attachment relationships on their personality development, have difficulty recalling specific events, and often idealize experiences. This classification is associated with descriptions of rejection in the coder's opinion (pushing a child away in attachment-activating situations), in the context of an adult's giving an overarching assessment of having loving parents. Just as ambivalent infants are resistant in the SS, adults classified as preoccupied display confusion or oscillation about past experiences, and descriptions of relationships with parents are marked by active anger or passivity. The preoccupied classification is associated with memories of nonloving but involving, even role-reversing parenting, in which a child needed to be alert to parental needs in preference to his or her own.

Individuals may be classified as "unresolved," in addition to being assigned one of the three major classifications. Unresolved adults report attachment-related traumas of loss and/or abuse, and manifest confusion and disorganization in the discussion of that topic. The unresolved classification is given precedence over the major classification in categorizing the individual, and is considered an insecure classification. A "cannot classify" designation is assigned when scale scores reflect elements rarely seen together in an interview (e.g., high idealization of one parent and high active anger toward the other) (Hesse, 1996). Such interviews are often markedly incoherent and thus are considered to reflect a high degree of insecurity. Fremmer-Bombik and colleagues devised an algorithm for classifying people with the AAI, which is discussed by Hesse (Chapter 19, this volume).

Q-Sort Scoring System

The Adult Attachment Q-Sort is an alternative method of scoring the AAI and was derived from the original scoring system (Kobak, 1993; Kobak, Cole, Ferenz-Gillies, Fleming, & Gamble, 1993). Its underlying structure parallels that of the SS and the Main and Goldwyn scoring systems, but it emphasizes the relation between affect regulation and attachment representations by examining the use of secure versus insecure emotional strategies and minimizing ("deactivating") versus maximizing ("hyperactivating") emotional strategies. The interview is scored from a transcript according to a forced distribution of descriptors, and yields scores for two conceptual dimensions: security–anxiety and deactivation–hyperactivation. Security is inferred from or defined as coherence and cooperation within the interview, and often (although not necessarily) memories of supportive attachment figures in the coder's opinion. Deactivation corresponds to dismissing strategies, whereas hyperactivation corresponds to the excessive detail and active anger seen in the transcripts of many preoccupied subjects. The strategies of deactivating and hyperactivating lie at opposite ends of a single dimension, which is assumed to be orthogonal to the secure–anxious (insecure) dimension. An individual's transcript is rated by two or more coders, using 100 Q-sort items and instructions that impose a forced normal distribution along a 9-point continuum (Kobak et al., 1993). The individual's sorts can then be correlated with expert-based prototypic sorts for the two major dimensions. The dimensional scores can be used to classify the adult into the categories of the Main and Goldwyn system. When this is done, approximately 80% of individuals receive the same classification with the Q-sort system as with the original system (kappa = .65); there is more overlap on the deactivation–hyperactivation dimension than on the secure–insecure dimension (Kobak et al., 1993).

Reflective Self-Concept Scoring

A third method of coding the AAI has been developed; this method departs conceptually from Main and Goldwyn's original classification system and from the system developed by Kobak and colleagues. Fonagy, Steele, Steele, Moran, and Higgitt (1991) use a scoring system that captures the "reflective self"—that is, the adult's quality of understanding his or her own and another's intentions and motivations. In a study of 200 parents, the self-reflection function derived from AAI transcripts related highly to coherence, yet was a stronger predictor of infant security than was coherence. The authors note that it is unclear whether the AAI is the best source of data with which to examine the self-reflection function.

Distribution of Classifications

In a meta-analysis, the distribution of AAI classifications in nonclinical samples of women, men, and adolescents was 58% autonomous (secure), 24% dismissing, and 18% preoccupied (Bakermans-Kranenburg & van IJzendoorn, 1993). About 19% of individuals also received an unresolved classification in association with a major classification. Within these normative samples, about 11% of people classified as autonomous, 26% of the dismissing group, and 40% of the preoccupied group were also classified as unresolved; and of people classified as unresolved, 38% had a major classification of autonomous, 24% of dismissing, and 38% of preoccupied. The base rate of insecurity in clinical and at-risk samples was much higher: 8% autonomous, 26% dismissing, 25% preoccupied, and 40% unresolved (Bakermans-Kranenburg & van IJzendoorn, 1993).

Stability and Discriminant Validity

High stability of attachment classifications (78–90% for three classification groups across periods ranging from 2 weeks to 18 months) has been observed in a number of studies using the original AAI scoring system (e.g., kappa = .73, 86%, over 18 months; Crowell, Waters, Treboux, & O'Connor, 1995). (See also Bakermans-Kranenburg & van IJzendoorn, 1993; Benoit & Parker, 1994; Crowell & Treboux, 1995; Sagi et al., 1994.) There are no gender differences in distribution of classifications when the original scoring system is used (van IJzendoorn & Bakersmans-Kranenburg, 1996), but with the Q-sort method of scoring, it appears that men may be more likely to be classified as dismissing (Borman-Spurrell, Allen, Hauser, Carter, & Cole-Detke, 1998).

Because the capacity to speak coherently about attachment may conceivably be based on non-attachment-related cognitive abilities such as intelligence or memory, the discriminant validity of the original AAI scoring system has been investigated. Security as assessed with the AAI is not usually associated with intelligence, and is not associated with memory, social desirability, or discourse style on an unrelated topic (Bakermans-Kranenburg & van IJzendoorn, 1993; Crowell et al., 1996; Sagi et al., 1994). There is a small relation between AAI experience scores as rated by the coder and self-reports of how one was parented (de Haas, Bakermans-Kranenburg, & van IJzendoorn, 1994).

Scale Scores

Discriminant analysis has enabled AAI security to be represented as a continuous variable (Fyffe & Waters, 1997). Two linear combinations of coding scales (such as mother loving and coherence of transcript) were obtained from two separate discriminant analyses of data from 364 adults in five study samples. One function distinguished between the autonomous (secure) category and all insecure categories (89% correct prediction), and the other distinguished the dismissing category from the preoccupied category (96% prediction). The two functions correlated .49 with each other, because in these samples preoccupied people were scored as less coherent than dismissing people. Neither scoring system for the AAI suggests that level of incoherence is a distinguishing feature between the two insecure groups; nor would this be predicted on a theoretical basis or from the work of Ainsworth and colleagues. The coder rating of "coherence of transcript" correlated .96 with the security function, indicating that the secure–insecure judgment made by coders was virtually identical with the coherence judgment. Although this finding seems to suggest that researchers can get a good assessment of AAI security simply by reliably coding coherence of transcript, this is difficult to do because the other scales are used in establishing and checking the coherence rating.

Research with the AAI

The AAI had its origins in investigations of the child–parent attachment relationship, and most of the studies based on the AAI have used it for this purpose. There is a consistent link among AAI classifications, parenting behavior, and child attachment status (van IJzendoorn, 1995). A few studies have used the AAI to examine attachment between adult romantic partners. It is important to bear in mind that the AAI does not directly assess secure-base behavior in adults, although the validity of the measure arises from its conceptual and empirical association with the secure-base phenomenon.

Studies of Adults as Individuals

Prospective Longitudinal Studies. To examine the idea that early attachment patterns correspond to attachment patterns in adult life, several studies have assessed the relation between infant attachment security and AAI classifications in late adolescence and young adulthood. Two studies have found a 70–75% correspondence of AAI and SS security–insecurity in late adolescents and young adults who participated as infants in studies of attachment (e.g., kappa = .44, Waters, Merrick, Treboux, Crowell, & Albersheim, 1998; see also Hamilton, 1998). As predicted by Bowlby's ideas about change in attachment representations in childhood, lack of correspondence between infant and adult classifications was related to life stresses that significantly altered the caregiving environment, including death of a parent, life-threatening illness in subject or parent, and divorce.

Two studies have failed to find correspondence between infant SS classifications and later AAI scores. A study of a high-risk sample (Weinfield, Sroufe, & Egeland, 1998) did not find correspondence between infant SS and adolescent AAI classifications, again consistent with the lack of attachment stability in circumstances of high life stress and change (Vaughn, Egeland, Sroufe, & Waters, 1979). There was no correspondence between AAI classifications scored with Kobak's Q-sort in a German sample of mid-adolescents and their SS classifications during infancy (Zimmermann, Fremmer-Bombik, Spangler, & Grossmann, 1997). In a meta-analysis of all studies examining the stability of attachment, Fraley (1998) found that the continuity between security as assessed in the SS in infancy and the AAI in young adulthood ranges from $r = -.10$ to $r = .50$. Precise explanations of cross-study differences in observed continuity remain to be tested and replicated, but it seems likely that the effort to explain stability and instability will be successful. In other words, discontinuity will turn out to be "principled" rather than mysterious or haphazard.

The Dismissing Strategy. Adults classified as dismissing use strategies that minimize, dismiss, devalue, or deny the impact of negative attachment experiences. When asked during the AAI about separations, rejection, effects of childhood on current personality, why their parents behaved as they did, and changes in the relationship with parents since childhood, college students who used dismissing strategies showed an increase in skin conductance (Dozier & Kobak, 1992). In other words, despite their efforts to minimize negative aspects of childhood and the importance of early relationships, they nevertheless showed signs of physiological distress and arousal when challenged with these topics. Such strategies have been related to the fact that adults classified as dismissing underreport distress, psychological symptoms, or problems in interpersonal relationships, compared with the reports of others who know them well (Dozier & Lee, 1995; Kobak & Sceery, 1988). The strategy of avoidance or dismissal has led to difficulties in the development of self-report assessments that discriminate the AAI dismissing group from the AAI autonomous group (Crowell, Treboux, & Waters, in press).

Self-Esteem, Loneliness, Adjustment, and Psychopathology. In studies examining the construct of self-esteem, when college students and low-socioeconomic-status mothers with ill children were classified as autonomous (secure) on the AAI, they rated themselves as higher in self-esteem (Benoit, Zeanah, & Barton, 1989; Tre-

boux, Crowell, & Colon-Downs, 1992). In the study of college students (Treboux et al., 1992), those classified as secure were more likely to report themselves as likable and lovable than insecure students, but they did not differ on subscales of the Multidimensional Self-Esteem Inventory (O'Brien & Epstein, 1983), such as moral approval, personal power, competence, and body appearance. In several samples of young adults, however, no relation between classification and global assessment of self-esteem was found (Borman-Spurrell et al., 1998; Waters & Crowell, 1994; Zeanah et al., 1993). Secure college students in another study were rated by peers as more ego-resilient, less anxious, and less hostile than insecure students (Kobak & Sceery, 1988). In the insecure group, the dismissing subjects were rated by peers as hostile and anxious; the preoccupied group was rated as most anxious. Reporting feelings about relationships late in the first year, secure students reported less loneliness, and higher levels of social support than dismissing students. However, dismissing students did not differ from secure students on the self-report measures of distress or perceived social competence (Kobak & Sceery, 1988). In contrast, the students classified as preoccupied did not report more loneliness or less social support, but they did perceive themselves as less socially competent than the secure students, and they reported more anxiety and distress.

A moderate relation was found between security and ratings of social adjustment (Crowell et al., in press). Clinical populations have a much higher proportion of insecure classifications than the general population, but few specific relations between AAI classification and psychopathology have emerged (van IJzendoorn & Bakermans-Kranenburg, 1996; van IJzendoorn et al., 1998). In one study, depressive symptoms were related to ratings of negative past and present relationships with parents, but were unrelated to coherence in the AAI (Pearson, Cohn, Cowan, & Cowan, 1994). This suggests that awareness of difficulties in one's past (i.e., the capacity to self-report problems) may be related to depressive symptoms, regardless of AAI attachment status.

The unresolved group has been overrepresented in clinical samples, and this has led to suggestions that it is more pathological than other insecure classifications (van IJzendoorn & Bakermans-Kranenburg, 1996). To explore this question, the relation of the unresolved classification to psychosocial functioning was examined within demographically matched former clinical and nonclinical samples (Colon-Downs, Crowell, Allen, Hauser, & Waters, 1997). Individuals in either sample classified as unresolved were not more disturbed in severity of reported symptoms or other assessments of psychosocial functioning than other insecure individuals. Unresolved for abuse and unresolved for loss proved not to be equivalent categories, insofar as the former classification was associated with clinical status and the latter was not. In general, the unresolved status did not yield more information regarding general psychosocial functioning than that provided by the knowledge that the individual had experienced trauma.

Studies of the Parent–Child Relationship

Attachment Classifications across Generations. A number of investigators have found high correspondence between parental attachment classifications and infant SS classifications when the parents are the caregiver (kappa = .46 for three classifications; kappa = .44 for four classifications) (Fonagy, Steele, & Steele, 1991; Sagi et al., 1992; Steele, Steele, & Fonagy, 1996; van IJzendoorn, 1992; see meta-analysis by van IJzendoorn, 1995). Mother–infant correspondence has been greater than father–infant correspondence (Main et al., 1985; Steele et al., 1996; van IJzendoorn, 1992). A three-generation study revealed concordance between grandmothers' and mothers' AAI classifications, and attachment correspondence between grandmothers and infants was mediated by mothers' classifications (Benoit & Parker, 1994). In a study using parental AAI classifications and preschoolers' attachment status assessed with home observations, children of secure mothers were more secure than children of insecure mothers (Posada, Waters, Crowell, & Lay, 1995).

Parent–Child Studies: Infancy. Mothers classified as autonomous on the AAI are observed to be more responsive, sensitive, and attuned to their infants in the first year of life (Grossmann, Fremmer-Bombik, Rudolph, & Grossmann, 1988; Haft & Slade, 1989; Ward & Carlson, 1995). A study using a videotaped scenario of a crying child to assess mothers' perceptions of infants' emotions and behavior found that women classified as dismissing viewed the child as more spoiled, negative, and insecure than did autonomous women (Zeanah et al., 1993).

Parent–Child Studies: Preschool. Parental security of attachment is associated with parents' providing help, support, and structure during observed tasks (Cohn, Cowan, Cowan, & Pearson, 1992; Crowell & Feldman, 1988; Das Eiden, Teti, & Corns, 1995), and marital functioning and attachment status of partners have moderating effects (Cohn, Cowan, et al., 1992; Das Eiden et al., 1995). Autonomous mothers prepared their preschoolers most effectively for separation and were most responsive to their children before and after separation (Crowell & Feldman, 1991). Mothers classified as preoccupied had the most difficulty with separation and prepared their children the least well; dismissing mothers left their children abruptly.

Parent–Child Studies: School Age. In a clinical sample of children studied in semistructured interaction with their mothers, secure mothers were warmer, more supportive, and smoother in transitioning between activities than insecure mothers (Crowell, O'Connor, Wollmers, Sprafkin, & Rao, 1991). In the insecure group, mothers classified as dismissing were more abrupt in transitioning between tasks than preoccupied mothers. Ratings of behavior and affective symptoms by parents, teachers, and children themselves find that children of insecure parents, especially those classified as dismissing, have the highest ratings of problem behavior and child distress (Cowan, Cohn, Cowan, & Pearson, 1996; Crowell et al., 1991).

Parent–Child Studies: Adolescence. Autonomy and relatedness in family interactions of parents and their 14-year-olds predicted the adolescents' AAI coherence at age 24–25 years (Allen & Hauser, 1991). Adolescents later classified as unresolved were more hostile toward their mothers in interactions than adolescents subsequently classified as secure. Both preoccupied and unresolved classifications were related to blurring of interpersonal boundaries and to restricting of autonomy in adolescents' interactions with mothers. The ego development of the same adolescents, and of their fathers, also predicted security of attachment in young adult life (Hauser, 1992).

In another study, secure mothers described their teenage daughters as more ego-resilient than did insecure mothers, but the groups did not differ in descriptions of sons (Kobak et al., 1993). During discussions of future plans, mothers with preoccupied/hyperactivating strategies were most anxious and their teenagers had trouble focusing on the topic. (See Allen & Land, Chapter 15, this volume, for a more complete review.)

Studies of Romantic Relationships

Couples: Concordance of Attachment Status. A meta-analysis of AAI attachment classifications of 226 couples showed modest concordance (50–60%, equivalent to a kappa of .20, for three major classifications) between partners for attachment status, and this was accounted for by the secure–secure pairings (van IJzendoorn & Bakersmans-Kranenburg, 1996). Not surprisingly, this finding suggests that factors other than attachment security are active in partner selection and maintenance.

Couples: Marital Satisfaction and Reports of the Relationship. Little relation between the broad construct of marital satisfaction and AAI classification has been found, but feelings of intimacy are related (Benoit et al., 1989; Cohn, Silver, Cowan, Cowan, & Pearson, 1992; Crowell, Treboux, Owens, & Pan, 1995; Gao, Treboux, Owens, Pan, & Crowell, 1995; O'Connor, Pan, Waters, & Posada, 1995; Zeanah et al., 1993). Associations between attachment security and the use of physical aggression in couples' relationships are consistently obtained (Crittenden, Partridge, & Claussen, 1991; Gao et al., 1995; A. Holtzworth-Munroe, personal communication, 1993; O'Connor et al., 1995; Sullivan-Hanson, 1990).

Couples' Interactions. In two studies, men classified as secure were in better-functioning marriages and had more positive interactions in structured task situations (Cohn, Silver, et al., 1992; Kobak & Hazan, 1992). In addition, "insecure–insecure" couples showed more conflict and negative affect than "secure–secure" couples. The "insecure–secure" couples did not differ in interactions from "secure–secure" couples (Cohn et al., 1992). In a study examining secure-base behavior in the interactions of engaged couples, AAI security was related to the quality of secure-base support and secure-base use of both men and women observed in a standard marital interaction task (Gao, Crowell, Treboux, & Waters, 1997). In other words, individuals classified as autonomous (secure) with the AAI are better able to use a secure base and act as a secure base for their partners.

Self-Reports of Peer/Romantic Attachment. As can be seen later in Table 20.1, the average correlation between the AAI and self-report measures of peer/romantic attachment is about .15. This matter is discussed further in subsequent sections of this chapter.

Current Relationship Interview

The Current Relationship Interview (CRI; Crowell & Owens, 1996) is one of several interviews that have been developed to assess adult attachment within close relationships (e.g., Bartholomew & Horowitz, 1991; Carlson, Onishi, & Gjerde, 1997; Cowan & Cowan, 1991). The CRI was developed as a way to examine the prototype hypothesis—the hypothesis that adult close relationships are similar in organization to infant–parent attachment relationships. More specifically, it explores the process by which a new attachment relationship may be integrated into an already existing representation of attachment, or by which a new representation develops. As a narrative assessment, it is intended to examine the influence of the partner's attachment behavior and ideas on the individual's representation of attachment and his or her own attachment behavior.

The CRI investigates the representation of attachment within the adult partnership. The interview asks the adult for descriptions of the relationship and for instances of the use of and giving of secure-base support in the relationship. The interview is scored from a transcript and the subject is classified into one of three major groups, according to the profile of scores on a variety of rating scales. Rating scales are used to characterize (1) the participant's behavior and thinking about attachment-related issues (e.g., valuing of intimacy and independence); (2) the partner's behavior; and (3) the subject's discourse style (e.g., anger, derogation, idealization, passivity of speech, fear of loss, and overall coherence).

The CRI and its scoring system parallel the AAI in structure. The secure–insecure dimension is based on coherent reports of being able to use the partner as a secure base and to act as a secure base, or the coherently expressed desire to do so. Individuals who cannot coherently discuss secure-base use and support in the interview are divided between those who avoid discussion of these behaviors or dismiss their significance, and those who appear to heighten or control the attachment elements of the relationship. CRI scoring is based on state of mind regarding attachment, as well as the individual's specifically reported attachment behaviors of secure-base support and use. These factors are given primacy in the determination of attachment security, rather than the individual's reported feelings about the relationship or the behaviors of the partner. Thus, whereas most individuals who are classified as secure with the CRI have good relationships with their partners, this is not a requirement for such a classification. Rather, they must value attachment and coherently describe their relationships with respect to the secure base elements. Similarly, a number of individuals classified as insecure with the CRI are satisfied with their current relationships. They are classified as insecure because they are incoherent in describing the secure-base phenomenon within the relationship.

The secure[CRI] interview is characterized by coherence; that is, the subject convincingly describes his or her own and the partner's secure-base behavior, or can coherently discuss negative partner behavior. The subject expresses the idea that an adult relationship provides support for the individuals involved and for their joint development. Attachment elements of the relationship are valued, such as the desire for intimacy and shared support, whether or not the relationship is actually providing these elements. The dismissing[CRI] classification is given when there is little evidence that the individual views attachment, support, and comfort within the relationship as important, even if the partner is convincingly described as loving. The discourse is incoherent, in that the relationship may be idealized or "normalized." A need for autonomy and separateness within the relationship may be emphasized, and there may be a focus on concrete or material aspects of the relationship (e.g., buying a house, going on vacations, and having fun). The preoccupied[CRI] classification is given when the subject expresses strong dependence on anxious involvement with the partner, or attempts to control the partner. The individual may be dissatisfied or anxious about the partner's ability to fulfill his or her needs, and may express ambivalence or confusion about the relationship, the partner, and/or the self, regardless of the nature of the partner's actual behavior. An unresolved[CRI] classification is given, along with one of the three major classifications, if a previous romantic relationship is currently exerting a disruptive or disorganizing influence on the individual's language or reasoning.

Distribution and Concordance of Classification in Couples

Distribution of CRI classifications in a sample of 124 engaged adults (62 couples) was 46% secure, 38% dismissing, 14% preoccupied, and 2% unresolved (Crowell & Waters, 1997a). Distribution of the couple classifications was as follows: both secure, 33%; secure man–insecure woman, 7%; insecure man–secure woman, 30%; both insecure, 30%. Concordance between partners for CRI classifications was 63% premaritally (kappa = .29) and 65% after 15 months of marriage (kappa = .30).

Stability and Discriminant Validity

Security on the CRI is unrelated to intelligence, education, gender, duration of relationship, or the endorsement of symptoms of depression (Owens, 1993; Treboux, 1997). Unlike the AAI, the CRI draws upon a current relationship, subject to life events and the partner's behaviors. Hence the CRI classifications are expected to be less stable than those of the AAI, especially in the early phases of relationship development. In a study of young adults assessed in the transition to marriage, 66% of the men (kappa = .28) and 74% of the women (kappa = .49) had the same classification across an 18-month interval (Crowell & Waters, 1997a). Overall, 50% of the couples (kappa = .31) had the same status across 18 months. The most stable group was that in which both partners were classified as insecure.

Research with the CRI

Reports of Relationships and Marital Satisfaction

In studies comparing young adults in nondistressed relationships, those classified as secure[CRI] reported greater satisfaction in the relationship, greater commitment and feelings of love overall, and fewer problems in the relationship than insecure[CRI] individuals (Crowell & Waters, 1997a; Owens, 1993; Treboux, 1997). When couples were assessed, those in which partners were both classified as insecure reported higher levels of verbal and physical aggression before marriage, and lower levels of intimacy and satisfaction, than other pairings. The CRI was not related to reported feelings of passion or to jealousy in men.

Behavioral Observations

The relation between spouses' observed secure-base use and secure-base support and CRI status, both premaritally and 18 months later, was examined in one study (Crowell & Waters, 1997b). CRI security was positively related to both secure-base use and secure-base support for both men and women.

Correspondence with the AAI

In a sample of 124 young adults who were about to marry, the correspondence between the AAI and the CRI (the three-category classification system was used for each interview) was 55% for men (kappa = .19) and 62% for women (kappa = .27) (Crowell & Waters, 1997a). After 18 months of marriage, the correspondence was 62% for men (kappa = .21) and 71% for women (kappa = .43). The correlation of the security scores from the AAI and CRI was .51 (Gao, Waters, Crowell, & Treboux, 1998).

When the predictive abilities of the AAI and CRI with respect to reports about the marital relationship were examined, the premarital CRI predicted feelings of commitment, intimacy, and self and partner verbal and physical aggression 18 months later (Crowell, Treboux, Owens, & Pan, 1995). The relation between the AAI and marital variables was mediated by CRI security. However, the AAI also directly predicted feelings of intimacy, threats to abandon the partner, the partner's threats to abandon the subject, and partner's physical aggression.

When the relations of AAI and CRI to secure-base behaviors were examined, the common components of AAI and CRI security significantly predicted secure-base behaviors (Gao et al., 1998). The unique contribution of the CRI predicted secure-base behaviors in women but not men. The unique contribution of the AAI predicted secure-base behaviors in men but not women.

Self-Reports of Attachment

In a study of 36 young adults who were given the CRI and the Experiences in Close Relationships scale (ECR; Brennan, Clark, & Shaver, 1998), there was 69% correspondence between secure and insecure classifications (kappa = .38). Together, the avoidance and anxiety scales of the ECR explained 29% of the variance in CRI security status (about the same as that explained by

the AAI), with the avoidance scale being the sole contributor (Treboux, 1997). Security on the CRI was moderately related to marital satisfaction, discord, intimacy, and dedication. Security on the ECR was highly related to marital satisfaction and discord, and moderately related to passion, intimacy, dedication, and the endorsement of depressive symptoms.

Summary

In summary, attempts to measure adult attachment with narratives have produced many interesting findings. The measures draw upon the links between attachment and cognition identified by Bowlby. The AAI in particular draws the core of its validity from its association with observations of attachment behavior on the part of infants (especially in the home) and with behavior in adult romantic/marital relationships, and it appears to be relatively specific to the attachment behavioral system. In other words, it is not highly related to broad-based assessments of social competence or to reports of feelings in or about relationships.

Because narrative assessments are expensive and difficult to administer and score, a number of researchers (including Benoit, Lichtenstein and Cassidy, and Main, Hesse, and van IJzendoorn) have tried to develop self-report assessments that capture the same information as the AAI. Other measures of adult attachment under development include projective tests (see West & Sheldon-Keller, 1994, for preliminary information) and the observations of secure-base behavior noted above developed by Crowell and Waters. So far, none of these new instruments has been published or widely used.

SELF-REPORT MEASURES OF ATTACHMENT HISTORY, SECURITY OF ATTACHMENT TO PARENTS AND PEERS, AND DIMENSIONS OF RECIPROCAL ATTACHMENTS

As mentioned in our introduction, the measures reviewed in this section are heterogeneous in focus and method, but all are self-report measures of adolescent and adult attachment that were not based on attempts to capture the attachment patterns identified by Ainsworth et al. (1978). None of the measures included in the present section has generated as much research as either the AAI and its offshoots or the Hazan and Shaver measure of romantic attachment style and its off-shoots (see below), but they raise interesting questions and provide valuable leads for further research.

Attachment History Questionnaire

The AHQ, copyrighted by Pottharst and Kessler in 1982, is described by Pottharst (1990b). The questionnaire contains sections on demographic variables, family history (including losses, divorce, etc.), patterns of family interactions, parental discipline techniques, and friends and support systems. Most of the items were based on Bowlby's writings. Fifty-one items are answered on 7-point response scales, in addition to which there are several open-ended questions, checklists, and so forth. A principal-components analysis, followed by varimax rotation, was computed on the 51 scaled items, and four factors were obtained: "secure attachment base" (e.g., trusted parents, amount of love from mother), "parental discipline" (e.g., not allowed to see friends, parents took things away), "threats of separation" (e.g., parents threatened to leave, parents threatened to call police), and "peer affectional support" (e.g., dependability of friends, having been supported by friends). In many studies the subscales are combined to yield a single security score with an alpha coefficient of .91.

A book edited by Pottharst (1990a), *Explorations in Adult Attachment,* describes several studies using the measure. These studies reveal that AHQ insecurity, on one or more AHQ subscales, is related to dysfunctional or pathological outcomes (e.g., being the mother in a family in which father and daughter have an incestuous relationship, abusing one's children, becoming a prostitute, and having severe psychological problems following loss of a spouse). In general, Pottharst and his colleagues have focused on the extreme circumstances that originally captured Bowlby's interest and led to his thinking about attachment as a normative process with potential for clinically significant deviations.

Inventory of Parent and Peer Attachment

Armsden and Greenberg (1987) developed the IPPA to assess adolescents' perceptions of their relationships with parents and close friends (not romantic partners). The authors argue that in adolescents, "the 'internal working model' of attachment figures may be tapped by assessing (1)

the positive affective/cognitive experience of trust in the accessibility and responsiveness of attachment figures, and (2) the negative affective/cognitive experiences of anger and/or hopelessness resulting from unresponsive or inconsistently responsive attachment figures" (p. 431). Accordingly, the IPPA assesses three broad constructs as they apply to mothers, fathers, and peers: "degree of mutual trust" (e.g., "My mother respects my feelings"), "quality of communication" (e.g., "I like to get my mother's point of view on things I'm concerned about"), and "degree of anger and alienation" (e.g., "My mother expects too much from me"). The dimensions are highly correlated within each relationship type and are therefore commonly aggregated to yield a composite index of security versus insecurity with respect to parents or peers. Security with respect to parents and security with respect to peers are correlated only about .30, indicating that adolescents relate differently within different kinds of close relationships, although the qualities assessed in different relationship domains may share common roots (Armsden & Greenberg, 1987).

Reliability estimates of the IPPA subscales are high. Three-week test–retest estimates and Cronbach's alphas are approximately .90. The IPPA has been used extensively to assess security in adolescents and has been related to a number of theoretically relevant outcome variables. For example, adolescents who report security with parents also report less conflict between their parents (Armsden, 1986). Secure peer and parental ratings are positively correlated with self-esteem and life satisfaction (Armsden & Greenberg, 1987), the use of problem-solving coping strategies (Armsden, 1986), low levels of loneliness (Armsden, 1986), less symptomatology and distress (Bradford & Lyddon, 1993; Kenny & Perez, 1996), and enhanced identity formation (Schultheiss & Blustein, 1994). Larose and Boivin (1997) found that security was related to anxiety and loneliness, but this relation was partially mediated by levels of social support. Holtzen, Kenny, and Mahalik (1995) found that among a sample of young homosexual adults, those who were secure with their parents were more likely to have disclosed their sexual orientation to their parents. Interestingly, in a sample of 10- to 16-year-old psychiatric patients, adolescents with clinical depression reported more insecure relationships with parents, but those who had recovered from depression did not (Armsden, McCauley, Greenberg, Burke, & Mitchell, 1990).

Security is unrelated or only weakly related to socioeconomic status and parental education levels (Armsden, 1986).

As mentioned, the IPPA was not designed to differentiate among the attachment patterns delineated by Ainsworth and her colleagues: "It is not clear what the development[al] manifestations of 'avoidant' or 'ambivalent' would be in adolescence, or if other conceptualizations of insecure attachment would be more appropriate" (Armsden & Greenberg, 1987, p. 447). Recent analyses by Brennan et al. (1998) indicate that the IPPA subscales of trust and communication primarily load on one of two dimensions common to self-report measures of romantic/peer attachment, anxiety (about being abandoned or unloved). The IPPA alienation subscale loads relatively highly on both anxiety and the second common dimension, avoidance. (These structural issues are discussed in more detail in the next major section of this chapter.)

Reciprocal and Avoidant Attachment Questionnaires for Adults

West and Sheldon-Keller (West & Sheldon, 1988; West et al., 1987; West & Sheldon-Keller, 1992, 1994) have developed two multi-item self-report instruments for measuring individual differences in adult attachment: the Reciprocal Attachment Questionnaire for Adults and the Avoidant Attachment Questionnaire for Adults. Based on Bowlby's (1980) clinical observations concerning loss and its impact on attachment behavior and functioning in children and adults, West and Sheldon-Keller's Reciprocal Attachment Questionnaire operationalizes various components of the attachment system in adults—proximity seeking (e.g., "I feel lost if I'm upset and my attachment figure is not around"), separation protest (e.g., "I feel abandoned when my attachment figure is away for a few days"), feared loss (e.g., "I'm afraid that I will lose my attachment figure's love"), availability (e.g., "I am confident that my attachment figure will try to understand my feelings"), and use of the attachment figure (e.g., "I talk things over with my attachment figure"). It also operationalizes general patterns of attachment—angry withdrawal (e.g., "I get frustrated when my attachment figure is not around as much as I would like"), compulsive caregiving (e.g., "I put my attachment figure's needs before my own"), compulsive self-reliance (e.g., "I feel it is best not to rely on my

attachment figure"), and compulsive care seeking (e.g., "I would be helpless without my attachment figure").

A unique feature of the instruments developed by West and Sheldon-Keller is that each participant is instructed to answer the questions with respect to an individual he or she considers to be a primary attachment figure. Thus the instruments do not assess attachment with respect to romantic relationships, friendship relationships, or parental relationships in particular. Instead, they assess the quality of attachment to whoever is identified as an individual's most important attachment figure. West and Sheldon-Keller created a separate questionnaire, the Avoidant Attachment Questionnaire, for adults who claim not to have a primary attachment figure. This instrument contains four subscales: "maintains distance in relationships" (e.g., "I'm afraid of getting close to others"), "high priority on self-sufficiency" (e.g., "My strength comes only from myself"), "attachment relationship is a treat to security" (e.g., "Needing someone would make me feel weak"), and "desire for close affectional bonds" (e.g., "I long for someone to share my feelings with").

The subscales of the Reciprocal Attachment Questionnaire have fairly high internal consistency and test–retest reliability over 4 months (approximately .75). Factor analyses of the items indicate that a two-factor solution provides a relatively good fit to the inter-item correlations (West & Sheldon-Keller, 1994). Among the component subscales of the Reciprocal Attachment Questionnaire, availability, feared loss, and proximity seeking load highly on one factor, and use of the attachment figure and separation protest load highly on a second factor. Analyses of the general attachment patterns from the Reciprocal Attachment Questionnaire indicate that compulsive self-reliance and angry withdrawal load highly on one factor, and compulsive caregiving and compulsive care seeking load highly on a second factor. A similar two-dimensional structure appears to underlie the Avoidant Attachment Questionnaire. As Brennan et al. (1998) have shown, and as we discuss in the next section, the two-factor structure is conceptually similar to the one uncovered in analyses of most self-report measures of adult attachment. One factor broadly represents concerns about availability and responsiveness of the attachment figure, and the other broadly represents proximity-seeking strategies and the use of the attachment figure as a secure base.

SELF-REPORT (AND RELATED INTERVIEW) MEASURES OF ROMANTIC ATTACHMENT

The study of romantic attachment began in the late 1970s and early 1980s, in an attempt to understand the nature and etiology of adult loneliness and the various ways that people experience love. It had been noticed that many lonely adults report troubled childhood relationships with parents and either distant or overly enmeshed romantic relationships, suggesting that attachment history may play a role in the experience of adult loneliness (Rubenstein & Shaver, 1982; Shaver & Hazan, 1987; Weiss, 1973). Also, social psychologists and anthropologists had observed that there is considerable variability in the way people approach love relationships (ranging from intense preoccupation to active avoidance), and they were developing individual-difference taxonomies to capture this variability; examples of these include Lee's "love styles" (Hendrick, 1986; Lee, 1973, 1988) and Sternberg's "components of love" (Sternberg, 1986). Despite these rich descriptions, there was no compelling theoretical framework within which to organize or explain the observed individual differences (Hazan & Shaver, 1994).

In an attempt to address this issue, Hazan and Shaver (1987) published a paper in which they conceptualized romantic love (or "pair bonding," to use the term common in contemporary evolutionary psychology) as an attachment process, involving the interplay among attachment, caregiving, and sexual/reproductive behavioral systems. Hazan and Shaver noted that many of the emotional and behavioral dynamics characteristic of infant–mother relationships also characterize adult romantic relationships. For example, both kinds of relationships involve periods of ventral–ventral contact, "baby talk," and cooing. More importantly, in each case an individual feels safest and most secure when the other is nearby, accessible, and responsive. Under such circumstances, the partner may be used as a "secure base" from which to explore the environment. When an individual is feeling distressed, sick, or threatened, the partner is used as a "safe haven"—a source of safety, comfort, and protection (see Shaver et al., 1988, for further discussion of these parallels).

Hazan and Shaver (1987; Shaver & Hazan, 1988) argued that the various approaches to love and the experience of loneliness described by so-cial psychologists reflect individual differences in the organization of the attachment system during adulthood. Specifically, they argued that the major patterns of attachment organization described by Ainsworth (secure, ambivalent, and avoidant) were conceptually similar to the "love styles" observed among adults. Although Bowlby and Ainsworth had discussed the role of attachment in adult romantic relationships, no one had actually attempted to assess, in the adult pair-bonding context, the kinds of individual differences among infants noted by Ainsworth et al. (1978).

Attachment Style Questionnaires

When Hazan and Shaver (1987) began their work on romantic attachment, they adopted Ainsworth's threefold typology as a framework for organizing individual differences in the ways adults think, feel, and behave in romantic relationships. In their initial studies, Hazan and Shaver (1987, 1990) developed brief multisentence descriptions of each of the three proposed attachment types—avoidant, secure, and ambivalent:

"I am somewhat uncomfortable being close to others; I find it difficult to trust them completely, difficult to allow myself to depend on them. I am nervous when anyone gets too close, and often, others want me to be more intimate than I feel comfortable being" (avoidant).

"I find it relatively easy to get close to others and am comfortable depending on them and having them depend on me. I don't worry about being abandoned or about someone getting too close to me" (secure).

"I find that others are reluctant to get as close as I would like. I often worry that my partner doesn't really love me or won't want to stay with me. I want to get very close to my partner, and this sometimes scares people away" (ambivalent).

These descriptions were based on a speculative extrapolation of the three infant patterns summarized in the final chapter of Ainsworth et al. (1978). Respondents are asked to think back across their history of romantic relationships and say which of the three descriptions best captures the way they *generally* experience and act in romantic relationships. The descriptions refer to a person's characteristic desires, feelings, and behaviors, and to comments made by relationship partners—*not to discourse coherence or defenses*. In other words, the manifest content of the measure is quite different from the discourse focus of the AAI and CRI, discussed earlier in this chapter. In their initial studies, Hazan and Shaver (1987) found that people's self-reported romantic attachment patterns related to a number of theoretically relevant variables, including beliefs about love and relationships (working models of romantic relationships) and recollections of early experiences with parents.

Many researchers adopted Hazan and Shaver's categorical, forced-choice measure because of its brevity, face validity, and ease of administration. Nonetheless, a few investigators quickly recognized some of the measure's limitations (e.g., Collins & Read, 1990; Levy & Davis, 1988; Simpson, 1990). For example, the categorical measurement model assumes that variation among people within a particular category is unimportant or does not exist, and that individuals do not vary in the extent to which they can be characterized by each pattern. In addition, as Baldwin and Fehr (1995) pointed out, the test–retest stability of the categorical measure was only 70% (equivalent to a Pearson r of approximately .40) and did not decrease as a function of the magnitude of the test–retest interval. This suggests that the instability was due to measurement error resulting from classification artifacts, not to "true" change in attachment security (Fraley & Waller, 1998; Scharfe & Bartholomew, 1994; but see Baldwin & Fehr, 1995).

To address these issues, many attachment researchers began to use continuous rating scales. For example, Levy and Davis (1988) asked participants to rate how well each attachment pattern described their general approach to relationships. Test–retest reliability estimates for ratings of the three alternatives tend to be about .60 over time frames ranging from 1 to 8 weeks (Baldwin & Fehr, 1995; Feeney & Noller, 1996). Subsequently, Collins and Read (1990) and Simpson (1990) decomposed the three multisentence descriptions to form separate items that could be individually rated on Likert-type response scales. On average, these relatively brief multi-item scales have alpha and test–retest (over periods ranging from 1 week to 2 years) reliability estimates of .70 (Carpenter & Kirkpatrick, 1996; Collins & Read, 1990; Fuller & Fincham, 1995; Scharfe & Bartholomew, 1994; Simpson, Rholes, & Nelligan, 1992; Simpson, Rholes, & Phillips, 1996).

In recent years, a number of researchers have proposed new measures of adult romantic attachment patterns (e.g., Brennan & Shaver, 1995; Carver, 1997; Feeney, Noller, & Hanrahan, 1994; Griffin & Bartholomew, 1994a; see Brennan et al., 1998, for a comprehensive list and review of 14 measures). In the midst of these efforts, Bartholomew (1990; Bartholomew & Horowitz, 1991; Griffin & Bartholomew, 1994b) has been influential in proposing a more elaborate conceptualization of what most investigators have come to call "attachment orientations," "attachment patterns," or "attachment styles." The various attempts to create multi-item scales revealed that there are two major dimensions underlying self-report measures: anxiety (about abandonment or insufficient love) and avoidance (of intimacy and emotional expression).

These two dimensions are conceptualized by Brennan et al. (1998) as corresponding to the two dimensions underlying Ainsworth's infant typology (see Fig. 10 of Ainsworth et al., 1978). In a discriminant analysis involving 105 infants who had been categorized and scored by coders on Ainsworth's infant behavior scales (e.g., crying, contact maintenance, exploratory behavior, resistance, avoidance), two linear combinations of coding scales were created that discriminated well among the three infant categories. One function distinguished ambivalent (angry, tearful) from secure and avoidant infants, thereby reflecting variability in ambivalent attachment. The other distinguished avoidant from secure and ambivalent infants, thereby reflecting avoidance. Conceptually, these two dimensions are viewed as 45-degree rotations of Kobak's secure–insecure and deactivation–hyperactivation dimensions discussed earlier in this chapter. (See Brennan et al., 1998, and Shaver & Clark, 1994, for detailed discussions of this point.)

Bartholomew (1990) provided an interpretation of these dimensions in terms of what Bowlby called working models of self and attachment figures. (Recall the quotation from Bowlby on p. 437 of this chapter.) Bartholomew argued that the two dimensions underlying measures of adult attachment can be conceptualized as "model of self" (positive vs. negative) and "model of others" (positive vs. negative). She also pointed out that combinations of the two dimensions can be viewed as yielding four, rather than three, major attachment patterns. She borrowed names for the four patterns from a mixture of the Ainsworth, Hazan/Shaver, and Main et al. (1985) typologies, calling the positive–positive group "secure," the negative–positive group "preoccupied," the positive–negative group "dismissing," and the negative–negative group "fearful." In line with the quotation from Bowlby, in most populations studied to date there are more secure and fearful than preoccupied and dismissing individuals, suggesting that most people harbor affectively congruent models of self and others (both positive or both negative). The conceptual dimensions themselves, however, and the measures designed to tap them, are distinct (in Bowlby's terms, "logically independent").

Following Hazan and Shaver's lead, Bartholomew and Horowitz (1991) developed the Relationship Questionnaire (RQ), a short instrument containing multi-sentence descriptions of each of the four theoretical types:

"It is easy for me to become emotionally close to others. I am comfortable depending on them and having them depend on me. I don't worry about being alone or having others not accept me" (secure).
"I am uncomfortable getting close to others. I want emotionally close relationships, but I find it difficult to trust others completely, or to depend on them. I worry that I will be hurt if I allow myself to become too close to others" (fearful).
"I want to be completely emotionally intimate with others, but I often find that others are reluctant to get as close as I would like. I am uncomfortable being without close relationships, but I sometimes worry that others don't value me as much as I value them" (preoccupied).
"I am comfortable without close emotional relationships. It is very important to me to feel independent and self-sufficient, and I prefer not to depend on others or have others depend on me" (dismissing).

Notice that the wording of three of the four type descriptions (secure, preoccupied, and fearful) is very similar to the wording of the three Hazan and Shaver descriptions (secure, ambivalent, and avoidant). However, the compulsive self-reliance and independence depicted in Bartholomew's dismissing description are not represented in the original Hazan and Shaver taxonomy.

As with Hazan and Shaver's instrument, respondents choose the RQ description that best characterizes them and rate each description according to how well it describes them. In general, the reliability estimates of the RQ classifications (kappas about .35) and ratings (*r*'s of about .50)

are comparable to those of the original Hazan and Shaver three-category instrument (Scharfe & Bartholomew, 1994). More recently, Griffin and Bartholomew (1994a) developed the Relationship Styles Questionnaire (RSQ), a 30-item inventory that contains content from both the Hazan and Shaver descriptions and the RQ descriptions. The RSQ can be scaled to create a score for each person on each of the four attachment patterns. That is, each individual can be assigned secure, fearful, preoccupied, and dismissing scores. Also, the RSQ can be used to score people on the two dimensions (model of self and model of other) that underlie these patterns. Due to its multi-item nature, the RSQ exhibits somewhat higher reliability estimates than the RQ (*r*'s of about .65 for the brief scales assessing each of the four attachment patterns; Fraley & Shaver, 1997).

In the most recent attempt to refine multi-item romantic attachment scales, Brennan et al. (1998) factor-analyzed the nonredundant items from all extant self-report attachment measures. They found that two major factors (anxiety and avoidance) underlie these measures and can be represented well by two 18-item scales (combined in the ECR, mentioned earlier), each having an alpha coefficient greater than .90. As mentioned in the discussion of the CRI, the two subscales of the ECR capture the gist of the Armsden and Greenberg IPPA and the West and Sheldon-Keller Reciprocal and Avoidant Attachment Scales for Adults; this suggests that all self-report attachment scales, whether conceived originally in terms of Bowlby's specific constructs (e.g., West & Sheldon-Keller, 1994) or Ainsworth's (e.g., Hazan & Shaver, 1987), load substantially on the same two major factors. These factors can be thought of in terms of either their affective–behavioral names, "anxiety" and "avoidance," or their cognitive/representational (working-model-related) names, "model of self" and "model of other."

Current Issues in the Measurement of Adult Attachment with Self-Reports

Despite conceptual and methodological advances in the study of romantic attachment, a number of important controversies and problems remain. The first concerns whether adult attachment patterns are best conceptualized and measured as types or dimensions (Fraley & Waller, 1998; Griffin & Bartholomew, 1994b). Recent taxometric work indicates that the adult attachment patterns assessed with self-report measures are best accounted for by a latent dimensional model (Fraley & Waller, 1998). Fraley and Waller (1998) review many of the problems that can arise when categorical models are used to assess dimensional phenomena, and they recommend that researchers adopt dimensional measurement models to study adult attachment. Interestingly, this argument suggests that many published findings from research on romantic attachment might have been stronger if researchers had used dimensional rather than categorical assessment procedures (see Brennan et al., 1998, for examples).

A second issue concerns how best to conceptualize the two dimensions that underlie adult attachment. Specifically, it is unclear whether measurement should be focused on assessing variation in the content of working models or variation in the functional operation of the attachment system. Within Bartholomew's framework, individual differences in attachment are conceptualized as being due to differences in the beliefs people hold about themselves and others. Accordingly, many researchers have attempted to specify the actual beliefs that people with different attachment orientations hold (e.g., Baldwin, Fehr, Keedian, Seidel, & Thomson, 1993; Collins, 1996; Klohnen & John, 1998). When Hazan and Shaver originally applied attachment theory to adults, however, they conceptualized individual differences as emerging from variations in the functional organization of the attachment system involving affect regulation and behavior regulation processes, only some of which are characterized as "cognitive" (Shaver et al., 1988; Shaver & Hazan, 1988).

According to Hazan and Shaver's perspective, individual differences in attachment patterns are attributable to two different components of the attachment system. One component involves anxious monitoring of the psychological proximity of the attachment figure (i.e., being especially vigilant to attachment-related cues about availability and responsiveness). When either the attachment figure is perceived as being available and responsive (the "secure" stance) or the attachment figure's availability is not viewed as critical to personal safety (the "dismissing" stance), an individual feels able to function effectively in the environment (or to "explore"). This component is closely related to individual differences on the anxiety dimension. The second component is responsible for regulation of attachment behavior with respect to attachment-related concerns. For example, to regulate attachment-related anxiety, people can either seek contact with an attachment figure (i.e., use the figure as a safe haven) or withdraw and attempt to handle the threat alone. This component is largely responsible for individual differences on the avoidance dimension.

Viewed in these terms, further specification of the concerns, appraisals, and emotional processes that underlie adult romantic attachment experiences and behavior need not necessarily be limited to positive and negative beliefs about self and other. Thus, although researchers from both the "internal working models" and the "behavioral systems" perspectives currently assess individual differences in terms of the same empirical dimensions (model of self/anxiety and model of other/avoidance), there are differences in the way these dimensions are conceptualized—and, accordingly, differences in the way measurement instruments are being revised and refined within each framework.

Finally, there is debate concerning whether attachment patterns are best assessed with self-report or interview methodologies, and whether the two kinds of methods converge on the same phenomena (Bartholomew & Shaver, 1998; Carlson et al., 1997; Crowell & Treboux, 1995; Crowell et al., in press). We return to this issue in the final section of the chapter, because it is responsible for considerable tension between the AAI and self-report romantic traditions within the field of contemporary attachment research. In the meantime, however, it is worth noting that Bartholomew (Bartholomew & Horowitz, 1991; Griffin & Bartholomew, 1994a, 1994b) and other attachment researchers (Carlson et al., 1997) have developed semistructured interview techniques for assessing adult romantic attachment. These methods are all influenced by the AAI and its scoring system, but some (most notably Bartholomew's) are scored in terms of the two dimensions discussed in the present section, anxiety and avoidance, whereas the AAI and CRI are not. It is important to note that individual differences, when assessed with Bartholomew's interview technique, tend to correspond reasonably well with patterns assessed by self-report instruments (Bartholomew & Horowitz, 1991; Bartholomew & Shaver, 1998; Griffin & Bartholomew, 1994b).

The Nomological Network and Construct Validity

As explained earlier, the AAI coding system was initially developed empirically to maximize the prediction of an adult parent's *infant's* classification in the SS. In this sense, there was an obvious "gold standard" for the AAI's validity—the categories of the SS, which are based on naturalistic observations of infants' secure-base behavior. In contrast, the self-report instruments of the Hazan and Shaver tradition were not designed to predict any single criterion. Instead, their validity and the value of the research tradition from which they derive rest on their ability to empirically reproduce the network of covariates postulated by the theory (Cronbach & Meehl, 1955). In this section we discuss the construct validity of measures of adult romantic attachment, focusing on relationship processes, the dismissing strategy in particular, and general adjustment and psychopathology (for more detailed reviews, see Bartholomew & Perlman, 1994; Feeney, Chapter 17, this volume; Feeney & Noller, 1996; Reis & Patrick, 1996; Shaver & Clark, 1994; Shaver & Hazan, 1993; Simpson & Rholes, 1998; Sperling & Berman, 1994). We begin with a brief rationale for the use of self-report instruments in the assessment of attachment security in adults.

The Rationale for Assessing Adult Attachment with Self-Report Methods

A number of authors have questioned the validity of assessing adult attachment with self-report instruments (Carlson et al., 1997; Crowell & Treboux, 1995), noting the difficulty of assessing unconscious or automatic processes with measures that tap people's conscious reports. There are, however, at least three reasons why self-report instruments are appropriate for investigating individual differences in adult attachment. First, according to Bowlby, attachment plays an important role in people's emotional lives (Volumes 2 and 3 of the *Attachment and Loss* trilogy deal primarily with anxiety, anger, sadness, grief, and depression). Adults are able to provide valuable information about their emotional experiences and behavior. Second, most adults have sufficient experience in close relationships to recount how they behave in such relationships and the kinds of things their partners have said to them about their behavior. Third, conscious and unconscious processes typically operate in the same direction to achieve a goal (Jacoby, Toth, Lindsay, & Debner, 1992). Bowlby himself (e.g., Bowlby, 1980) talked about both conscious and unconscious forms of defense.

In some cases, however, the conscious beliefs people hold are inaccurate reflections of the underlying organization of their attachment system.

Some people defensively report that they are not anxious when actually they are; others may simply lack insight into their true motives and behavior. Nonetheless, even in these cases it is possible to use attachment theory to derive the kinds of conscious beliefs that defensive people may hold about themselves. For example, an avoidant person should believe that he or she is "independent" and "self-sufficient," does not "worry about abandonment," and does not "need close relationships." Holding such beliefs is an important part of defensively excluding attachment-related thoughts and emotions. It is a separate question whether people endorsing such statements in a questionnaire actually do or do not need close relationships to the same extent as other kinds of people, or whether they can function well without others.

Although self-reports are frequently used to assess individual differences in attachment security, they are rarely used alone to investigate the dynamics of attachment and defense. In other words, placing a person in the two-dimensional attachment style space is not, by itself, the same as determining *why* the person is located in a particular region of the space. (Similarly, coding someone as having poor recall in the AAI for attachment-related events in childhood does not automatically reveal the *reasons* for poor recall.) To probe these deeper issues, researchers typically employ behavioral observations (Fraley & Shaver, 1998), psychophysiological assessments (Carpenter & Kirkpatrick, 1996; Feeney & Kirkpatrick, 1996, Fraley & Shaver, 1997), peer reports (Banai, Weller, & Mikulincer, 1998; Bartholomew & Horowitz, 1991; Gjerde, Block, & Onishi, 1998), projective tests (Mikulincer, Florian, & Tolmacz, 1990; Woike, Osier, & Candella, 1996), diary techniques (Pietromonaco & Feldman Barrett, 1997; Tidwell, Reis, & Shaver, 1996), and experimental cognitive research methodologies (Baldwin et al., 1993; Fraley & Shaver, 1997, 1999; Mikulincer, 1995, 1998; Mikulincer & Orbach, 1995). With such a diverse array of methods, the complex meanings of scores on self-report attachment measures have gradually been revealed, and the results fit coherently with attachment theory (see Shaver & Clark, 1994, for a review).

Relationship Processes

According to attachment theory, individual differences in the organization of the attachment system emerge from caregiving interactions with attachment figures (Ainsworth et al. 1978; Bowlby, 1973) and subsequently have numerous influences on relationship dynamics, potentially ranging from partner selection to mechanisms of relationship maintenance and dissolution.

Partner Selection. Cross-cultural studies suggest that the secure pattern of attachment in infancy is universally considered the most desirable pattern by mothers (see van IJzendoorn & Sagi, Chapter 31, this volume). For obvious reasons, there is no similar study asking infants whether they would prefer a security-inducing caregiver or attachment figure. Adults seeking long-term relationships identify responsive caregiving qualities, such as attentiveness, warmth, and sensitivity, as most "attractive" in potential dating partners (Baldwin, Keelan, Fehr, Enns, & Koh-Rangarajoo, 1996; Chappell & Davis, 1998; Frazier, Byer, Fischer, Wright, & DeBord, 1996; Miller & Fishkin, 1997; Pietromonaco & Carnelley, 1994; Zeifman & Hazan, 1997). Despite the attractiveness of secure qualities, however, not everyone is paired with a secure partner. Some evidence suggests that people end up in relationships with partners who confirm their existing beliefs about attachment relationships (Brennan & Shaver, 1995; Collins & Read, 1990; Frazier et al., 1997; but see Kirkpatrick & Davis, 1994).

Implications for Secure-Base and Safe-Haven Behavior. Overall, secure adults tend to be more satisfied in their relationships than insecure adults. Their relationships are characterized by greater longevity, trust, commitment, and interdependence (Feeney, Noller, & Callan, 1994; Keelan, Dion, & Dion, 1994; Kirkpatrick & Davis, 1994; Kirkpatrick & Hazan, 1994; Senchak & Leonard, 1992; Simpson, 1990), and they are more likely to use romantic partners as a secure base from which to explore the world (Fraley & Davis, 1997). A large proportion of research on adult attachment has been devoted to uncovering the behavioral and psychological mechanisms that promote security and secure-base behavior in adults. There have been two major discoveries thus far. First, and in accordance with attachment theory, secure adults are more likely than insecure adults to seek support from their partners when distressed. Furthermore, they are more likely to provide support to their distressed partners. Second, the attributions that insecure individuals make concerning their part-

ners' behavior during and following relational conflicts exacerbate, rather than alleviate, their insecurities.

Concerning the first dynamic, Simpson et al. (1992) found in a laboratory study that secure women who were overtly distressed were more likely than insecure women to seek emotional support from their partners. Also, secure men were more likely than insecure men to provide support to their distressed partners. In a naturalistic observational study, Fraley and Shaver (1998) found that secure women who were separating from their partners in an airport were more likely than insecure women to express their anxiety, seek comfort from their partners, and provide comfort for their partners (attending to them, holding their hands, etc.). In contrast, avoidant women were more likely to pull away or withdraw from their partners. Collins and Feeney (in press) found that secure individuals were more likely to offer care and support to their partners during a laboratory discussion of a stressful event. Similar findings have been obtained in studies of self-reported behavioral strategies during stressful situations. For example, Pistole (1989) found that secure adults were more likely than insecure adults to use conflict resolution strategies involving compromise and integration. Gaines et al. (1997) found that secure individuals tended not to use defensive and destructive strategies for dealing with conflictual situations. Prospective studies corroborate these observations (e.g., Scharfe & Bartholomew, 1995).

These findings suggest that part of the reason why some individuals feel more secure in their relationships is that they openly express their worries and receive reassurance and support. Furthermore, the data suggest that some people feel insecure in their relationships because they cannot turn to their partners for comfort and support. Existing research has not been able to tease apart the precise causal structure of these processes. It may be that having a responsive partner influences the way an individual comes to think and behave in a relationship. In addition, perhaps individuals who enter relationships with secure expectations are more likely to seek support from others and to elicit responsive behavior from them. In general, the evidence suggests that the causal relations are bidirectional (Fuller & Fincham, 1995). In support of the first interpretation, Simpson et al. (1996) observed partners who were instructed to discuss and resolve a major issue in their relationship. They found that anxious adults were most likely to view their partners in a negative light after a major conflict. These adults felt more anger and hostility toward their partners than less anxious individuals, and viewed their relationship as involving less love, commitment, and mutual respect. In contrast, secure individuals viewed their partners in a more positive light after discussing a conflictual topic (see Fuller & Fincham, 1995, for related findings). Thus conflictual relationship events, despite their negative valence, may provide an opportunity for secure individuals to build their trust in each other. In contrast, such conflicts appear to magnify insecure partners' insecurities and doubts.

Recent work also suggests that beliefs and expectations people hold prior to entering a relationship affect secure-base behavior and relationship development. Collins (1996) conducted an experiment in which participants were instructed to read hypothetical relationship scenarios depicting a partner behaving in ambiguous ways that could be construed in a negative light (e.g., losing track of the partner during a party). She found that anxious participants inferred hostile and rejecting intentions, whereas secure participants inferred more positive intentions. Similarly, Mikulincer (1998) found that insecure adults were more likely to attribute hypothetical trust-violating events (but not trust-validating events) to their partners' intentions. Over time, such attributional processes appear to diminish the degree of trust that both partners extend toward each other (Fuller & Fincham, 1995). For example, Keelan et al. (1994) found that insecure adults experienced decreases in trust and relationship satisfaction over a 4-month period.

Changes in Attachment over Time. Cross-sectional and longitudinal studies indicate that the longer partners have been together, the less anxious they become about attachment-related issues such as separation or abandonment (Fraley & Shaver, 1998; Klohnen & Bera, 1998; Mickelson, Kessler, & Shaver, 1997). In other words, scores on the anxiety dimension generally decrease over time. Cross-sectional evidence also suggests that partners become more similar to each other in security over time (Fraley & Shaver, 1998). This observation suggests that attachment security is affected by reciprocal influence processes as a relationship develops (Fuller & Fincham, 1995).

The Dismissing Strategy

According to attachment theory, people differ in the kinds of strategies they adopt to regulate the distress associated with nonoptimal caregiving. Following a separation and reunion, for example, some insecure children approach, but with ambivalence and resistance, whereas others withdraw, apparently minimizing attachment-related feelings and behavior (Main & Weston, 1982). These different strategies have been referred to as "hyperactivating" or "maximizing" strategies and "deactivating" or "minimizing" strategies, respectively (Cassidy & Kobak, 1988; Fraley, Davis, & Shaver, 1998; Main, 1990).

Recent research on romantic attachment has attempted to illuminate some of the defense mechanisms underlying these behavioral strategies. In an experimental task in which adults were instructed to discuss losing their partners, Fraley and Shaver (1997) found that dismissing individuals were just as physiologically distressed (as assessed by skin conductance measures) as other individuals. When instructed to suppress their thoughts and feelings, however, dismissing individuals were able to do so effectively. That is, they could deactivate their physiological arousal to some degree and minimize the attention they paid to attachment-related thoughts. (Interestingly, preoccupied adults experienced an *increase* in arousal, relative to control conditions, when trying to suppress attachment-related anxiety.) Fraley and Shaver (1997) argued that such deactivation is possible because avoidant individuals (1) have less complex networks of attachment-related representations, (2) can effectively redirect their attention away from anxiety-provoking stimuli, and (3) can keep their interpersonal world structured so as to minimize attachment-related experiences.

In support of these propositions, Mikulincer and Orbach (1995) found that when asked to recall emotional childhood memories, avoidant adults recalled memories that were characterized by emotional discreteness. That is, when asked to recall a sad memory, avoidant individuals recalled memories that contained only elements of sadness and not elements of anger and anxiety, which tend to be present in the sad memories of secure and especially of preoccupied individuals. In recent work, Fraley and Shaver (1999) have replicated this finding in a study assessing latency to retrieve attachment-related memories specific to romantic experiences. These authors found that avoidant individuals took longer to retrieve episodic memories of occasions when they felt anxious or loved in their current relationships. In contrast, they took no longer than others to retrieve memories unrelated to attachment issues (e.g., occasions when they felt tired or hungry). Research has also shown that dismissing individuals are less likely to engage in attachment behaviors with their partners (Fraley & Davis, 1997; Fraley & Shaver, Chapter 32, this volume) and are less likely to engage in behaviors thought to promote affectional bonding, such as eye-to-eye contact, kissing, and open communication about feelings (Fraley et al., 1998). In summary, individuals organize their interpersonal behavior in a way that minimizes attachment-related issues. This defensive strategy is reflected in the ways they regulate their attention, behavior, and emotions (Fraley et al., 1998).

General Adjustment and Psychopathology

In general, individuals who are secure with respect to attachment have high self-esteem (Bartholomew & Horowitz, 1991; Brennan & Bosson, 1998; Brennan & Morris, 1997; Collins & Read, 1990; Feeney & Noller, 1990; Shaver et al., 1996) and are considered well adjusted, nurturing, and warm by their peers (Bartholomew & Horowitz, 1991; Gjerde et al., 1998). As found in studies using the AAI (reviewed earlier in this chapter), *kind* of self-esteem is also meaningfully related to attachment organization. For example, although autonomous and dismissing adults typically report high levels of self-esteem, Brennan and Morris (1997) found that secure adults were more likely to derive their self-esteem from internalized positive regard from others, whereas dismissing adults were more likely to derive their self-esteem from various abilities and competencies.

Not surprisingly, adults with a variety of clinical disorders are more likely to report themselves as insecure. Depressed adults are more likely to report themselves as insecure, especially preoccupied and fearful (Carnelley, Pietromonaco, & Jaffe, 1994; Hammen et al., 1995). Furthermore, individuals with eating disorders, such as bulimia nervosa and anorexia nervosa, are more likely to report themselves as insecure (Brennan & Shaver, 1995; Burge et al., 1997). College students who felt their parents had drinking problems were more likely to rate themselves as insecure (Brennan, Shaver, & Tobey, 1991) and were reportedly more likely to "drink to cope" themselves (Brennan & Shaver, 1995). Brennan and Shaver (1998) recently examined the structure of self-report measures of 13 personality disorders (e.g., schizoid, paranoid, avoidant, obsessive–compulsive) and discovered that two of the three dimensions underlying these scales are the now-familiar dimensions underlying adult romantic attachment patterns.

Woike et al. (1996) examined the association between self-reported attachment and the use of violent imagery in the Thematic Apperception Test. These authors found that anxious individuals were the most likely to use violent imagery, and suggest that such imagery may stem from frustration with romantic partners who thwart attachment needs. Consistent with this line of reasoning, Dutton, Saunders, Starzomski, and Bartholomew (1994) found a high incidence of fearful and preoccupied men (i.e., the two groups highest on the anxiety dimension) within a sample that had been referred for treatment for wife assault. Similarly, Bookwala and Zdaniuk (1998) found that preoccupied and fearful adults were the most likely to be involved in reciprocally aggressive romantic relationships. The anger that accompanies insecure attachment among adults appears to have ramifications for the way people treat their children as well. Moncher (1996) found that parents who abused their children were more likely to rate themselves as insecure than secure.

Discriminant Validity

Part of the validity of measures of romantic attachment stems from their empirical associations with a variety of theoretically important variables and phenomena, including relationship dynamics, intrapsychic processes, and psychopathology. Indeed, Bowlby (e.g., 1980, 1988) believed that the way an individual comes to organize his or her behavior with respect to attachment-related goals will be reflected in many aspects of his or her life. Nonetheless, the validity of self-report attachment measures would be called into question if they overlapped too much with measures of constructs viewed as theoretically distant from attachment organization (Shaver & Brennan, 1992). Several constructs have been proposed as alternatives to attachment style in explaining what self-report measures of adult attachment actually measure. First, some writers have expressed concern over the possibility that self-report measures of adult attachment are simply assessing relationship satisfaction (Bartholomew, 1994). Although security *is* correlated with relationship satisfaction, the average magnitude of the correlation is only about .30 (e.g., Senchak & Leonard, 1992; Simpson, 1990). Secure people tend to be in relationships in which they are happy and satisfied, but the correlation is not high enough to suggest that self-report measures of attachment and measures of satisfaction assess the same construct. Another reason for believing that self-report measures of attachment security do not simply assess relationship satisfaction is that they show relations with other theoretically meaningful variables among individuals who are *not* currently involved in relationships.

Another factor related to close-relationship phenomena is physical attractiveness (Hatfield & Sprecher, 1986). However, Tidwell et al. (1996) found no association between physical attractiveness (rated from photographs) and adult attachment style, suggesting that existing findings regarding attachment security are not confounded by physical attractiveness.

During the last decade, a number of personality theorists have rallied around the five-factor model of personality (see John, 1990, for a review). Research in this area suggests that personality variability can be captured reasonably well by a five-dimensional model consisting of neuroticism, extraversion, openness to experience, agreeableness, and conscientiousness (see Block, 1995, and Pervin, 1994, for critiques of this model). Thus, questions arise as to how the attachment dimensions fit into this structure and whether they are redundant with one or more of the five factors. Shaver and Brennan (1992) and Carver (1997) examined associations between the five traits and the attachment dimensions and found that the anxiety dimension is correlated approximately .30 with neuroticism, and that security is correlated approximately .30 with agreeableness and extraversion. Thus the attachment dimensions, although correlating with some of the major personality variables focused on by trait theorists, are not simply redundant with those variables. Moreover, Shaver and Brennan (1992) examined the relative ability of the attachment dimensions and the five traits to predict relationship outcomes over time. In general, the attachment dimensions were better predictors of relationship variables, such as relationship length, satisfaction, and commitment, than were the five-factor model's variables.

Self-report measures of adult attachment have also been found to be uncorrelated with verbal intelligence (Treboux, 1997), and to correlate less than .20 with measures of social desirability response set (Fraley et al., 1998; Kunce & Shaver, 1994; Mikulincer & Orbach, 1995).

DISCUSSION

From a topic area that virtually did not exist in 1980, the study of adult attachment has grown to become one of the most visible areas in developmental, social, personality, and clinical psychology. Between 1987 and 1997, some 800 articles and chapters dealing with adult attachment were published. In general, the findings obtained by adult attachment researchers have been interesting, consistent, and compatible with Bowlby's and Ainsworth's theories. Nevertheless, among the interesting and challenging concerns in the study of adult attachment is that of measurement. One problem is how the various measures of adult attachment relate to one another, and another is what measures researchers should use to investigate "adult attachment."

A number of studies have included more than one measure of some aspect of adult attachment, including measures that tap different relational domains (e.g., parents, peers, or romantic partners) and embody different methods (e.g., coded interviews, self-report questionnaires). Table 20.1 presents a preliminary summary of such studies. The table indicates that when we collapse data across methods, the association between adult attachment within the parental and peer (romantic partners or nonparental attachment figures) domains is roughly equivalent to a correlation of .23. The estimate is, of course, higher when similar methods are used to assess attachment in both domains ($r = .31$) and lower when each attachment domain is measured with a different kind of technique (interview vs. self-reports, $r = .15$). In the former case, the higher estimate presumably benefits in part from common method variance (e.g., focusing on an individual's coherence of discourse in interviews about two kinds of relationships). In fact, the average correlation for studies employing the same kind of method, with data collapsed across domains, is .57, whereas the average correlation for studies employing different methods is .27.

Although not definitive, this set of studies suggests that adult attachment within the parental domain is related to that within the peer domain, but not strongly so—an observation that has important implications for understanding the

TABLE 20.1. Relations between Various Measures of Adult Attachment, as a Function of Method and Domain

Same domain (both assessments referred to parents, or both to romantic partners)		Different domains (e.g., parents and romantic partners)	
Source	r	Source	r
Methods were the same (both interviews or both self-reports)			
AAI (test–retest)	.73	Armsden & Greenberg (1987) (parents and peers)	.28
CRI (test–retest)	.38		
Multi-item self-report romantic attachment scales (averages of test–retest and internal consistency)	.80	Baldwin et al. (1996) (parents and romantic partners)	.14
IPPA (averages of test–retest and internal consistency)	.90	Bartholomew & Shaver (1998) (parents and peers/partners)	.42
Reciprocal Attachment Questionnaire for Adults (averages of test–retest and internal consistency)	.75	Collins & Read (1990) (parents and romantic partners)	.28
		Crowell et al. (in press) (parents and romantic partners)	.26
		Fraley & Shaver (1999) (parents and romantic partners)	.29
		Gao et al. (1998) (parents and romantic partners)	.51
		Owens et al. (1995) (parents and romantic partners)	.30
Average = .75		Average = .31	
Methods were different (interview and self-report)			
Bartholomew & Shaver (1998) (romantic partner)	.34	Bartholomew & Shaver (1998) (parent interview and partner self-report)	.20
Carlson et al. (1997) (romantic partner)	.49	Borman-Spurrell et al. (1998) (AAI and partner self-report)	.04
Crowell et al. (in press) (AAI and self-report of parents)	.11	Borman-Spurrell et al. (1998) (Kobak/AAI and partner self-report)	.26
Treboux (1997) (romantic partner)	.54	Crowell et al. (in press) (AAI and partner self-report)	.21
Bartholomew & Shaver (1998) (different interview coding systems)	.44	Shaver et al. (1998) (AAI coding scales and partner self-report)	.30
		Steele et al. (1998) (AAI and partner self-report)	−.12
Average = .39		Average = .15	

Note. The upper left quadrant (same method to assess attachment security in the same domain) contains rough estimates of the reliabilities of each measure discussed in this chapter. Averages within each quadrant are based on Fisher's r-to-z and z-to-r transformations.

attachment system in adulthood, and for measuring adult attachment. If we assume that there is an attachment behavioral system in adults, then it appears that this system can be organized or calibrated differently for different relationships or for different kinds of relationships. That this is possible has been known from early in the history of attachment research on infants, when it became evident that a particular infant could exhibit different attachment patterns when tested independently with mother and father (Main & Weston, 1981), despite some overlap (Fox, Kimmerly, & Schafer, 1991). Nonetheless, it has often been assumed that the various measures of adult attachment, despite differences in the kinds of attachment relationships on which they focus, can be readily substituted for one another. This assumption is clearly false.

Researchers need to adopt assessment techniques that are specific to the kind of relationship under study. For example, if a researcher is interested in studying romantic attachment dynamics, he or she should use one of the multi-item self-report techniques (e.g., the ECR) or one of the romantic interview techniques (Bartholomew's peer/partner interview, Crowell and Owen's CRI, or Carlson et al.'s interview). Investigators interested in assessing the common variance underlying adolescents' and adults' various attachment orientations will have to assess attachment variation across multiple domains (e.g., parents, close friends, romantic partners), preferably using a variety of methods (e.g., self-reports, interviews) and latent structural modeling techniques (see Griffin & Bartholomew, 1994b).

As we have explained throughout this chapter, each measure was developed for a particular purpose. Therefore, in determining which one or more instruments to use for a particular study, a researcher should consider the theoretical assumptions underlying each instrument. The AAI classifies an adult based on his or her current "state of mind with respect to attachment," as inferred from narrative measures of experiences with parents during childhood. Its focus on discourse is based on the assumption that the ability to describe secure-base experiences reflects either the nature of those experiences or, in the case of those who have "earned security," to understand them in a coherent and believable way. It is a rich and well-validated measure, especially for the study of current representations of early attachment relationships. Its utility in the investigation of attachment between adults (e.g., romantic partners) is still under investigation, but it shows promise. Nevertheless, the AAI is expensive and difficult to learn to score.

The AHQ, the IPPA, and the Reciprocal Attachment Questionnaire for Adults were developed to assess attachment history, relationship behaviors, and feelings of security in relationships with parents and peers, but they were not designed to tap the attachment patterns observed in infants and children by Ainsworth et al. (1978). In contrast, the self-report romantic attachment measures were designed to assess patterns such as those described by Ainsworth and her colleagues, under the assumption that these patterns reflect natural variation in the organization of the attachment system at any age. The self-report measures assume that people can accurately describe some of their thoughts, feelings, and behaviors in romantic attachment relationships. Such measures are not ideal for investigating mechanisms and strategies per se, but they have been used in conjunction with other techniques (such as psychophysiological, behavioral, and cognitive procedures) to uncover important aspects of intrapsychic processes and behavior in close relationships.

In summary, before adopting a measure to assess adult attachment, researchers should consider (1) the assumptions underlying each technique and each technique's connection with attachment theory, and (2) the relationship domain to be investigated (e.g., parents, close friends, romantic partners). In light of the substantial differences among adult attachment measures, we urge caution in how researchers present their findings and in how they generalize across measures with respect to attachment theory. Furthermore, we encourage researchers to continue investigating the many measurement issues inherent in the study of adult attachment. There is still much work to be done in understanding the relations among the various instruments and the best ways to assess normative development and individual differences in adult attachment organization. We hope that the present overview will provide a useful foundation for further exploration of the complex measurement landscape of adult attachment.

REFERENCES

Ainsworth, M. D. S. (1985). Attachments across the life span. *Bulletin of the New York Academy of Medicine, 61*(9), 792–811.

Ainsworth, M. D. S. (1989). Attachments beyond infancy. *American Psychologist, 44,* 709–716.

Ainsworth, M. D. S. (1991). Attachments and other affectional bonds across the life cycle. In C. M. Parkes, J. Stevenson-Hinde, & P. Marris (Eds.), *Attachment across the life cycle* (pp. 33–51). London: Routledge.

Ainsworth, M. D. S., Blehar, M., Waters, E., & Wall, S. (1978). *Patterns of attachment: A psychological study of the strange situation.* Hillsdale, NJ: Erlbaum.

Allen, J. P., & Hauser, S. T. (1991, April). *Prediction of young adult attachment representations, psychological distress, social competence, and hard drug use from family interactions in adolescence.* Paper presented at the biennial meeting of the Society for Research in Child Development, Seattle, WA.

Armsden, G. (1986). *Attachment to parents and peers in late adolescence: Relationships to affective status, self-esteem, and coping with loss, threat, and challenges.* Unpublished doctoral dissertation, University of Washington.

Armsden, G. C., & Greenberg, M. T. (1987). The Inventory of Parent and Peer Attachment: Relationships to well-being in adolescence. *Journal of Youth and Adolescence, 16,* 427–454.

Armsden, G. C., McCauley, E., Greenberg, M. T., Burke, P., & Mitchell, J. (1990). Parent and peer attachment in early adolescent depression. *Journal of Youth and Adolescence, 12,* 373–386.

Bakermans-Kranenburg, M., & van IJzendoorn, M. (1993). A psychometric study of the Adult Attachment Interview: Reliability and discriminant validity. *Developmental Psychology, 29,* 870–879.

Baldwin, M. W., & Fehr, B. (1995). On the instability of attachment style ratings. *Personal Relationships, 2,* 247–261.

Baldwin, M. W., Fehr, B., Keedian, E., Seidel, M., & Thomson, D. W. (1993). An exploration of the relational schemata underlying attachment styles: Self report and lexical decision approaches. *Personality and Social Psychology Bulletin, 19,* 746–754.

Baldwin, M. W., Keelan, J. P. R., Fehr, B., Enns, V., & Koh-Rangarajoo, E. (1996). Social-cognitive conceptualization of attachment working models: Availability and accessibility effects. *Journal of Personality and Social Psychology, 71,* 94–109.

Banai, E., Weller, A., & Mikulincer, M. (1998). Interjudge agreement in evaluation of adult attachment style: The impact of acquaintanceship. *British Journal of Social Psychology, 37,* 95–109.

Bartholomew, K. (1990). Avoidance of intimacy: An attachment perspective. *Journal of Social and Personal Relationships, 7,* 147–178.

Bartholomew, K. (1994). Assessment of individual differences in adult attachment. *Psychological Inquiry, 5,* 23–27.

Bartholomew, K., & Horowitz, L. (1991). Attachment styles among young adults: A test of a four category model. *Journal of Personality and Social Psychology, 61,* 226–244.

Bartholomew, K., & Perlman, D. (Eds.). (1994). *Advances in personal relationships: Vol. 5. Attachment processes in adulthood.* London: Jessica Kingsley.

Bartholomew, K., & Shaver, P. R. (1998). Methods of assessing adult attachment: Do they converge? In J. A. Simpson & W. S. Rholes (Eds.), *Attachment theory and close relationships* (pp. 25–45). New York: Guilford Press.

Benoit, D., & Parker, K. (1994). Stability and transmission of attachment across three generations. *Child Development, 65,* 1444–1456.

Benoit, D., Zeanah, C., & Barton, M. (1989). Maternal attachment disturbances in failure to thrive. *Infant Mental Health Journal, 10,* 185–202.

Block, J. (1995). A contrarian view of the five-factor approach to personality description. *Psychological Bulletin, 117,* 187–215.

Bookwala, J., & Zdaniuk, B. (1998). Adult attachment styles and aggressive behavior within dating relationships. *Journal of Social and Personal Relationships, 15,* 175–190.

Borman-Spurrell, E., Allen, J., Hauser, S., Carter, A., & Cole-Detke, H. (1998). *Assessing adult attachment: A comparison of interview-based and self-report methods.* Manuscript submitted for publication.

Bowlby, J. (1969/1982). *Attachment and loss: Vol. 1. Attachment.* New York: Basic Books.

Bowlby, J. (1973). *Attachment and loss: Vol. 2. Separation: Anxiety and anger.* New York: Basic Books.

Bowlby, J. (1980). *Attachment and loss: Vol. 3. Loss: Sadness and depression.* New York: Basic Books.

Bowlby, J. (1988). *A secure base.* New York: Basic Books.

Bradford, E., & Lyddon, W. J. (1993). Current parental attachment: Its relation to perceived psychological distress and relationship satisfaction in college students. *Journal of College Student Development, 34,* 256–260.

Brennan, K. A., & Bosson, J. K. (1998). Attachment-style differences in attitudes toward and reactions to feedback from romantic partners: An exploration of the relational bases of self-esteem. *Personality and Social Psychology Bulletin, 24,* 699–714.

Brennan, K. A., Clark, C. L., & Shaver, P. R. (1998). Self-report measurement of adult attachment: An integrative overview. In J. A. Simpson & W. S. Rholes (Eds.), *Attachment theory and close relationships* (pp. 46–76). New York: Guilford Press.

Brennan, K. A., & Morris, K. A. (1997). Attachment styles, self-esteem, and patterns of seeking feedback from romantic partners. *Personality and Social Psychology Bulletin, 23,* 23–31.

Brennan, K. A., & Shaver, P. R. (1995). Dimensions of adult attachment, affect regulation, and romantic relationship functioning. *Personality and Social Psychology Bulletin, 21,* 267–283.

Brennan, K. A., & Shaver, P. R. (1998). Attachment styles and personality disorders: Their connections to each other and to parental divorce, parental death, and perceptions of parental caregiving. *Journal of Personality, 66,* 835–878.

Brennan, K. A., Shaver, P. R., & Tobey, A. E. (1991). Attachment styles, gender, and parental problem drinking. *Journal of Social and Personal Relationships, 8,* 451–466.

Bretherton, I. (1985). Attachment theory: Retrospect and prospect. In I. Bretherton & E. Waters (Eds.), Growing points of attachment theory and research. *Monographs of the Society for Research in Child Development, 50*(1–2, Serial No. 209), 3–35.

Burge, D., Hammen, C., Davila, J., Daley, S. E., Paley, B., Lindberg, N., Herzberg, D., & Rudolph, K. D. (1997). The relationship between attachment cognitions and psychological adjustment in late adolescent women. *Development and Psychopathology, 9,* 151–167.

Carlson, K., Onishi, M., & Gjerde, P. (1997, August). *Assessment of romantic attachment: Comparison of self-report and interview methodologies.* Paper presented at the annual meeting of the American Psychological Association, Chicago.

Carnelley, K. B., Pietromonaco, P. R., & Jaffe, K. (1994). Depression, working models of others, and relationship functioning. *Journal of Personality and Social Psychology, 66,* 127–140.

Carpenter, E. M., & Kirkpatrick, L. A. (1996). Attachment style and presence of a romantic partner as moderators of psychophysiological responses to a stressful laboratory situation. *Personal Relationships, 3,* 351–367.

Carver, C. S. (1997). Adult attachment and personality: Converging evidence and a new measure. *Personality and Social Psychology Bulletin, 23,* 865–883.

Cassidy, J., & Kobak, R. R. (1988). Avoidance and its relation to other defensive processes. In J. Belsky & T. Nezworski (Eds.), *Clinical implications of attachment* (pp. 300–323). Hillsdale, NJ: Erlbaum.

Chappell, K. D., & Davis, K. E. (1998). Attachment, partner choice, and perceptions of romantic partners: An experimental test of the attachment-security hypothesis. *Personal Relationships, 5,* 327–342.

Cohn, D., Cowan, P., Cowan, C., & Pearson, J. (1992). Mothers' and fathers' working models of childhood attachment relationships, parenting style, and child behavior. *Development and Psychopathology, 4,* 417–431.

Cohn, D., Silver, D., Cowan, P., Cowan, C., & Pearson, J.

(1992). Working models of childhood attachment and couples relationships. *Journal of Family Issues, 13,* 432–449.

Collins, N. L. (1996). Working models of attachment: Implications for explanation, emotion, and behavior. *Journal of Personality and Social Psychology, 71,* 810–832.

Collins, N. L., & Feeney, B. C. (in press). A safe haven: An attachment theory perspective on support-seeking and caregiving in adult romantic relationships. *Journal of Personality and Social Psychology.*

Collins, N. L., & Read, S. J. (1990). Adult attachment, working models, and relationship quality in dating couples. *Journal of Personality and Social Psychology, 58,* 644–663.

Colon-Downs, C., Crowell, J. A., Allen, J. P., Hauser, S. T., & Waters, E. (1997, April). *Investigating the unresolved adult attachment classification: A pattern of attachment or an index of general psychosocial functioning.* Paper presented at the biennial meeting of the Society for Research in Child Development, Washington, DC.

Cowan, C., & Cowan, P. (1991). *Couples' Attachment Interview.* Unpublished manuscript, University of California at Berkeley.

Cowan, P., Cohn, D., Cowan, C., & Pearson, J. (1996). Parents' attachment histories and children's externalizing and internalizing behavior: Exploring family systems models of linkage. *Journal of Consulting and Clinical Psychology, 64,* 53–63.

Crittenden, P., Partridge, M., & Claussen, A. (1991). Family patterns of relationships in normative and dysfunctional families. *Development and Psychopathology, 3,* 491–512.

Cronbach, L. J., & Meehl, P. M. (1955). Construct validity in psychological tests. *Psychological Bulletin, 52,* 281–302.

Crowell, J. A., & Feldman, S. S. (1988). Mothers' internal models of relationships and children's behavioral and developmental status: A study of mother–child interaction. *Child Development, 59,* 1273–1285.

Crowell, J. A., & Feldman, S. S. (1991). Mothers' working models of attachment relationships and mother and child behavior during separation and reunion. *Developmental Psychology, 27,* 597–605.

Crowell, J. A., O'Connor, E., Wollmers, G., Sprafkin, J., & Rao, U. (1991). Mothers' conceptualizations of parent–child relationships: Relation to mother-child interaction and child behavior problems. *Development and Psychopathology, 3,* 431–444.

Crowell, J. A., & Owens, G. (1996). *Current Relationship Interview and scoring system.* Unpublished manuscript, State University of New York at Stony Brook.

Crowell, J. A., & Treboux, D. (1995). A review of adult attachment measures: Implications for theory and research. *Social Development, 4,* 294–327.

Crowell, J. A., Treboux, D., Owens, G., & Pan, H. (1995, March). *Is it true the longer you're together the more you think alike?: Examining two hypotheses of attachment theory.* Paper presented at the biennial meeting of the Society for Research in Child Development, Indianapolis, IN.

Crowell, J. A., Treboux, D., & Waters, E. (in press). The Adult Attachment Interview and the Relationship Questionnaire: Relations to reports of mothers and partners. *Personal Relationships.*

Crowell, J. A., & Waters, E. (1997a, April). *Couples' attachment representations: Stability and relation to marital behavior.* Poster presented at the biennial meeting of the So-

ciety for Research in Child Development, Washington, DC.

Crowell, J. A., & Waters, E. (1997b, April). *The secure base phenomenon in adult attachment relationships: Exploration of the core of the attachment system.* Poster presented at the biennial meeting of the Society for Research in Child Development, Washington, DC.

Crowell, J. A., Waters, E., Treboux, D., & O'Connor, E. (1995, March). *Stability of attachment representations and experiences of life events in newly married couples.* Poster presented at the biennial meeting of the Society for Research in Child Development, Indianapolis, IN.

Crowell, J. A., Waters, E., Treboux, D., O'Connor, E., Colon-Downs, C., Feider, O., Golby, B., & Posada, G. (1996). Discriminant validity of the Adult Attachment Interview. *Child Development, 67,* 2584–2599.

Das Eiden, R., Teti, D., & Corns, K. (1995). Maternal working models of attachment, marital adjustment, and the parent–child relationship. *Child Development, 66,* 1504–1518.

Dozier, M., & Kobak, R. R. (1992). Psychophysiology in attachment interviews: Converging evidence for deactivating strategies. *Child Development, 63,* 1473–1480.

Dozier, M. & Lee, S. W. (1995). Discrepancies between self- and other-report of psychiatric symptomatology: Effects of dismissing attachment strategies. *Development and Psychopathology, 7,* 217–226.

de Haas, M., Bakermans-Kranenburg, M., & van IJzendoorn, M. (1994). The Adult Attachment Interview and questionnaires for attachment style, temperament, and memories of parental behavior. *Journal of Genetic Psychology, 155,* 471–486.

Dutton, D. G., Saunders, K., Starzomski, A., & Bartholomew, K. (1994). Intimacy–anger and insecure attachment as precursors of abuse in intimate relationships. *Journal of Applied Social Psychology, 24,* 1367–1386.

Feeney, B. C., & Kirkpatrick, L. A. (1996). Effects of adult attachment and presence of romantic partners on physiological responses to stress. *Journal of Personality and Social Psychology, 70,* 255–270.

Feeney, J. A., & Noller, P. (1990). Attachment style as a predictor of adult romantic relationships. *Journal of Personality and Social Psychology, 58,* 281–291.

Feeney, J. A., & Noller, P. (1996). *Adult attachment.* Thousand Oaks, CA: Sage.

Feeney, J. A., Noller, P., & Callan, V. J. (1994). Attachment style, communication, and satisfaction in the early years of marriage. In K. Bartholomew & D. Perlman (Eds.), *Advances in personal relationships: Vol. 5. Attachment processes in adulthood* (pp. 269–308). London: Jessica Kingsley.

Feeney, J. A., Noller, P., & Hanrahan, M. (1994). Assessing adult attachment: Developments in the conceptualization of security and insecurity. In M. B. Sperling & W. H. Berman (Eds.), *Attachment in adults: Clinical and developmental perspectives* (pp. 128–152). New York: Guilford Press.

Fonagy, P., Steele, H., & Steele, M. (1991). Maternal representations of attachment during pregnancy predict the organization of infant–mother attachment. *Child Development, 62,* 891–905.

Fonagy, P., Steele, M., Steele, H., Moran, G. S., & Higgitt, A. C. (1991). The capacity for understanding mental states: The reflective self in parent and child and its significance for security of attachment. *Infant Mental Health Journal, 12,* 201–218.

Fox, N. A., Kimmerly, N. L., & Schafer, W. D. (1991). Attachment to mother/attachment to father: A meta-analysis. *Child Development, 62,* 210–225.

Fraley, R. C. (1998). *Attachment continuity from infancy to adulthood: Meta-analysis and dynamic modeling of developmental mechanisms.* Manuscript submitted for publication.

Fraley, R. C., & Davis, K. E. (1997). Attachment formation and transfer in young adults' close friendships and romantic relationships. *Personal Relationships, 4,* 131–144.

Fraley, R. C., Davis, K. E., & Shaver, P. R. (1998). Dismissing-avoidance and the defensive organization of emotion, cognition, and behavior. In J. A. Simpson & W. S. Rholes (Eds.), *Attachment theory and close relationships* (pp. 249–279). New York: Guilford Press.

Fraley, R. C., & Shaver, P. R. (1997). Adult attachment and the suppression of unwanted thoughts. *Journal of Personality and Social Psychology, 73,* 1080–1091.

Fraley, R. C., & Shaver, P. R. (1998). Airport separations: A naturalistic study of adult attachment dynamics in separating couples. *Journal of Personality and Social Psychology, 75,* 1198–1212.

Fraley, R. C., & Shaver, P. R. (1999). *Defensive memory and attentional strategies in adult attachment.* Manuscript in preparation, University of California at Davis.

Fraley, R. C., & Waller, N. G. (1998). Adult attachment patterns: A test of the typological model. In J. A. Simpson & W. S. Rholes (Eds.), *Attachment theory and close relationships* (pp. 77–114). New York: Guilford Press.

Frazier, P. A, Byer, A. L., Fischer, A. R., Wright, D. M., & DeBord, K. A. (1996). Adult attachment style and partner choice: Correlational and experimental findings. *Personal Relationships, 3,* 117–136.

Fuller, T. L., & Fincham, F. D. (1995). Attachment style in married couples: Relation to current marital functioning, stability over time, and method of assessment. *Personal Relationships, 2,* 17–34.

Fyffe, C., & Waters, E. (1997, April). *Empirical classification of adult attachment status: Predicting group membership.* Poster presented at the biennial meeting of the Society for Research in Child Development, Washington, DC.

Gaines, S. O., Reis, H. T., Summers, S., Rusbult, C. E., Cox, C. L., Wexler, M. O., Marelich, W. D., & Kurland, G. J. (1997). Impact of attachment style on reactions to accommodative dilemmas in close relationships. *Personal Relationships, 4,* 93–113.

Gao, Y., Crowell, J., Treboux, D., & Waters, E. (1997, April). *Is it easier for a secure person to use and to serve as a secure base?* Poster presented at the biennial meeting of the Society for Research in Child Development, Washington, DC.

Gao, Y., Crowell, J., Waters, E., & Treboux, D. (1998, June). *Attachment working models and secure base behavior.* Paper presented at the biennial meeting of the International Society for the Study of Relationships, Saratoga Springs, NY.

Gao, Y., Treboux, D., Owens, G., Pan, H., & Crowell, J. (1995, April). *Working models of adult relationships: Foundation in childhood, fine tuning in marriage.* Poster presented at the biennial meeting of the Society for Research in Child Development, Indianapolis, IN.

George, C., Kaplan, N., & Main, M. (1984). *Adult Attachment Interview.* Unpublished manuscript, University of California at Berkeley.

Gjerde, P. F., Block, J., & Onishi, M. (1998). *Personality implications of romantic attachment styles in young adults: A multi-method study.* Manuscript submitted for publication.

Grice, P. (1975). Logic and conversation. In P. Cole & J. L. Moran (Eds.), *Syntax and semantics III: Speech acts* (pp. 41–58). New York: Academic Press.

Griffin, D. W., & Bartholomew, K. (1994a). The metaphysics of measurement: The case of adult attachment. In K. Bartholomew & D. Perlman (Eds.), *Advances in personal relationships: Vol. 5. Attachment processes in adulthood* (pp. 17–52). London: Jessica Kingsley.

Griffin, D. W., & Bartholomew, K. (1994b). Models of the self and other: Fundamental dimensions underlying measures of adult attachment. *Journal of Personality and Social Psychology, 67,* 430–445.

Grossmann, K., Fremmer-Bombik, E., Rudolph, J., & Grossmann, K. (1988). Maternal attachment representations as related to patterns of infant–mother attachment and maternal care during the first year. In R. A. Hinde & J. Stevenson-Hinde (Eds.), *Relationships within families: Mutual influences* (pp. 241–260). Oxford: Clarendon Press.

Haft, W., & Slade, A. (1989). Affect attunement and maternal attachment: A pilot study. *Infant Mental Health Journal, 10,* 157–172.

Hamilton, C. E. (1998). *Continuity and discontinuity of attachment from infancy through adolescence.* Manuscript submitted for publication.

Hammen, C. L., Burge, D., Daley, S. E., Davila, J., Paley, B., & Rudolph, K. D. (1995). Interpersonal attachment cognitions and prediction of symptomatic responses to interpersonal stress. *Journal of Abnormal Psychology, 104,* 436–443.

Hatfield, E., & Sprecher, S. (1986). *Mirror, mirror . . . : The importance of looks in everyday life.* Albany: State University of New York Press.

Hauser, S. (1992). *Adolescent attachment and parental ego development antecedents of young adult attachment representations: Longitudinal studies.* Paper presented at the biennial meeting of the Society for Research in Adolescence, Washington, DC.

Hazan, C., & Shaver, P. R. (1987). Romantic love conceptualized as an attachment process. *Journal of Personality and Social Psychology, 52,* 511–524.

Hazan, C., & Shaver, P. R. (1990). Love and work: An attachment theoretical perspective. *Journal of Personality and Social Psychology, 59,* 270–280.

Hazan, C., & Shaver, P. R. (1994). Attachment as an organizational framework for research on close relationships. *Psychological Inquiry, 5,* 1–22.

Hendrick, C., & Hendrick, S. S. (1986). A theory and method of love. *Journal of Personality and Social Psychology, 50,* 392–402.

Hesse, E. (1996). Discourse, memory and the Adult Attachment Interview: A note with emphasis on the emerging cannot classify category. *Infant Mental Health Journal, 17,* 4–11.

Holtzen, D. W., Kenny, M. E., & Mahalik, J. R. (1995). Contributions of parental attachment to gay or lesbian disclosure to parents and dysfunctional cognitive processes. *Journal of Counseling Psychology, 42,* 350–355.

Jacoby, L. L., Toth, J. P., Lindsay, D. S., & Debner, J. A., (1992). Lectures for a layperson: Methods for revealing unconscious processes. In R. F. Bornstein & T. S. Pittman (Eds.), *Perception without awareness* (pp. 81–120). New York: Guilford Press.

John, O. P. (1990). The "Big Five" factor taxonomy: Dimensions of personality in the natural language and in questionnaires. In L. A. Pervin (Ed.), *Handbook of personality: Theory and research* (pp. 67–100). New York: Guilford Press.

Keelan, J. P. R., Dion, K. L., & Dion, K. K. (1994). Attachment style and heterosexual relationships among young adults: A short-term panel study. *Journal of Social and Personal Relationships, 11,* 201–214.

Kenny, M. E., & Perez, V. (1996). Attachment and psychological well-being among racially and ethnically diverse first-year college students. *Journal of College Student Development, 37,* 527–535.

Kirkpatrick, L. A., & Davis, K. E. (1994). Attachment style, gender, and relationship stability: A longitudinal analysis. *Journal of Personality and Social Psychology, 66,* 502–512.

Kirkpatrick, L. A., & Hazan, C. (1994). Attachment styles and close relationships: A four-year prospective study. *Personal Relationships, 1,* 123–142.

Klohnen, E. C., & Bera, S. (1998). Behavioral and experiential patterns of avoidantly and securely attached women across adulthood: A 31-year longitudinal study. *Journal of Personality and Social Psychology, 74,* 211–223.

Klohnen, E. C., & John, O. P. (1998). Working models of attachment: A theory-based prototype approach. In J. A. Simpson & W. S. Rholes (Eds.), *Attachment theory and close relationships* (pp. 115–140). New York: Guilford Press.

Kobak, R. R. (1993). *The Attachment Interview Q-Set.* Unpublished manuscript, University of Delaware.

Kobak, R. R., Cole, H., Ferenz-Gillies, R., Fleming, W., & Gamble, W. (1993). Attachment and emotional regulation during mother-teen problem solving: A control theory analysis. *Child Development, 64,* 231–245.

Kobak, R. R., & Hazan, C. (1992). *Parents and spouses: Attachment strategies and marital functioning.* Unpublished manuscript, University of Delaware/Cornell University.

Kobak, R. R., & Sceery, A. (1988). Attachment in late adolescence: Working models, affect regulation, and representations of self and others. *Child Development, 59,* 135–146.

Kunce, L. J., & Shaver, P. R. (1994). An attachment-theoretical approach to caregiving in romantic relationships. In K. Bartholomew & D. Perlman (Eds.), *Advances in personal relationships: Vol. 5. Attachment processes in adulthood* (pp. 205–237). London: Jessica Kingsley.

Larose, S., & Boivin, M. (1997). Structural relations among attachment working models of parents, general and specific support expectations, and personal adjustment in late adolescence. *Journal of Social and Personal Relationships, 14,* 579–601.

Lee, J. A. (1973). *The colors of love: An exploration of the ways of loving.* Toronto: New Press.

Lee, J. A. (1988). Love-styles. In R. J. Sternberg & M. Barnes (Eds.), *The psychology of love* (pp. 38–67). New Haven, CT: Yale University Press.

Levy, M. B., & Davis, K. E. (1988). Lovestyles and attachment styles compared: Their relations to each other and to various relationship characteristics. *Journal of Social and Personal Relationships, 5,* 439–471.

Main, M. (1981). Avoidance in the service of attachment: A working paper. In K. Immelman, G. Barlow, M. Main, & L. Petrinovitch (Eds.), *Behavioral development: The Bielefeld interdisciplinary project* (pp. 651–693). New York: Cambridge University Press.

Main, M. (1990). Cross-cultural studies of attachment organization: Recent studies, changing methodologies, and the concept of conditional strategies. *Human Development, 33,* 48–61.

Main, M. (1991). Metacognitive knowledge, metacognitive monitoring, and singular (coherent) versus multiple (incoherent) models of attachment: Findings and directions for future research. In C. M. Parkes, J. Stevenson-Hinde, & P. Marris (Eds.), *Attachment across the life cycle* (pp. 127–159). London: Routledge.

Main, M. (1995). Recent studies in attachment: Overview, with selected implications for clinical work. In S. Goldberg, R. Muir, & J. Kerr (Eds.), *Attachment theory: Social, developmental, and clinical perspectives* (pp. 407–474). Hillsdale, NJ: Analytic Press.

Main, M., & Goldwyn, R. (1994). *Adult attachment rating and classification system: Manual in draft* (Version 6.0). Unpublished manuscript, University of California at Berkeley.

Main, M., Kaplan, N., & Cassidy, J. (1985). Security of infancy, childhood, and adulthood: A move to the level of representation. In I. Bretherton & E. Waters (Eds.), Growing points of attachment theory and research. *Monographs of the Society for Research in Child Development, 50*(1–2, Serial No. 209), 66–106.

Main, M., & Weston, D. R. (1981). The quality of the toddler's relationship to mother and to father: Related to conflict behavior and the readiness to establish new relationships. *Child Development, 52,* 932–940.

Mickelson, K. D., Kessler, R. C., & Shaver, P. R. (1997). Adult attachment in a nationally representative sample. *Journal of Personality and Social Psychology, 73,* 1092–1106.

Mikulincer, M. (1995). Attachment style and the mental representation of the self. *Journal of Personality and Social Psychology, 69,* 1203–1215.

Mikulincer, M. (1998). Attachment working models and the sense of trust: An exploration of interaction goals and affect regulation. *Journal of Personality and Social Psychology, 74,* 1209–1224.

Mikulincer, M., Florian, V., & Tolmacz, R. (1990). Attachment styles and fear of personal death: A case study of affect regulation. *Journal of Personality and Social Psychology, 58,* 273–280.

Mikulincer, M., & Orbach, I. (1995). Attachment styles and repressive defensiveness: The accessibility and architecture of affective memories. *Journal of Personality and Social Psychology, 68,* 917–925.

Miller, L. C., & Fishkin, S. A. (1997). On the dynamics of human bonding and reproductive success: Seeking windows on the adapted-for human–environmental interface. In J. A. Simpson & D. T. Kenrick (Eds.), *Evolutionary social psychology* (pp. 197–235). Mahwah, NJ: Erlbaum.

Moncher, F. J. (1996). The relationship of maternal adult attachment style and risk of physical child abuse. *Journal of Interpersonal Violence, 11,* 335–350.

O'Brien, E., & Epstein, S. (1983). *The Multidimensional Self-Esteem Inventory.* Unpublished manuscript, University of Massachusetts.

O'Connor, E., Pan, H., Waters, E., & Posada, G. (1995, March). *Attachment classification, romantic jealousy, and aggression in couples.* Poster presented at the biennial meeting of the Society for Research in Child Development, Indianapolis, IN.

Oppenheim, D., & Waters, E. (1995). Narrative processes and attachment representations: Issues of development and assessment. In E. Waters, B. Vaughn, G. Posada, & K. Kondo-Ikemura (Eds.), Caregiving, cultural, and cognitive perspectives on secure-base behavior and working models: New growing points of attachment theory and research. *Monographs of the Society for Research in Child Development, 60*(2–3, Serial No. 244), 197–215).

Owens, G. (1993). *An interview-based approach to the study of adult romantic relationships.* Unpublished manuscript, State University of New York at Stony Brook.

Owens, G., Crowell, J., Pan, H., Treboux, D., O'Connor, E., & Waters, E. (1995). The prototype hypothesis and the origins of attachment working models: Adult relationships with parents and romantic partners. In E. Waters, B. Vaughn, G. Posada, & K. Kondo-Ikemura (Eds.), Caregiving, cultural, and cognitive perspectives on secure-base behavior and working models: New growing points of attachment theory and research. *Monographs of the Society for Research in Child Development, 60*(2–3, Serial No. 244), 216–233).

Pearson, J., Cohn, D., Cowan, P., & Cowan, C. P. (1994). Earned- and continuous-security in adult attachment: Relation to depressive symptomatology and parenting style. *Development and Psychopathology, 6,* 359–373.

Pearson, J., Cowan, P., Cowan, C., & Cohn, D. (1993). Adult attachment and adult child–older parent relationships. *American Journal of Orthopsychiatry, 63,* 606–613.

Pervin, L. A. (1994). A critical analysis of current trait theory. *Psychological Inquiry, 5,* 103–113.

Pietromonaco, P. R., & Carnelley, K. B. (1994). Gender and working models of attachment: Consequences for perceptions of self and romantic relationships. *Personal Relationships, 1,* 63–82.

Pietromonaco, P. R., & Feldman Barrett, L. (1997). Working models of attachment and daily social interactions. *Journal of Personality and Social Psychology, 73,* 1409–1423.

Pistole, M. C. (1989). Attachment in adult romantic relationships: Style of conflict resolution and relationship satisfaction. *Journal of Social and Personal Relationships, 6,* 505–510.

Posada, G., Waters, E., Crowell, J., & Lay, K. (1995). Is it easier to use a secure mother as a secure base?: Attachment Q-sort correlates of the Adult Attachment Interview. In E. Waters, B. Vaughn, G. Posada, & K. Kondo-Ikemura (Eds.), Caregiving, cultural, and cognitive perspectives on secure-base behavior and working models: New growing points of attachment theory and research. *Monographs of the Society for Research in Child Development, 60*(2–3, Serial No. 244), 133–145).

Pottharst, K. (Ed.). (1990a). *Explorations in adult attachment.* New York: Peter Lang.

Pottharst, K. (1990b). The search for methods and measures. In K. Pottharst (Ed.), *Explorations in adult attachment* (pp. 9–37). New York: Peter Lang.

Reis, H. T., & Patrick, B. C. (1996). Attachment and intimacy: Component processes. In E. T. Higgins & A. W. Kruglanski (Eds.), *Social psychology: Handbook of basic principles* (pp. 523–563). New York: Guilford Press.

Rubenstein, C., & Shaver, P. R. (1982). *In search of intimacy.* New York: Delacorte.

Sagi, A., Aviezer, O., Joels, T., Korne-Karje, N., Mayseless, O., Scharf, M., & van IJzendoorn, M. (1992, July). *The correspondence of mother's attachment with infant–mother attachment relationship in traditional and non-traditional kibbutzim.* Paper presented at the 25th International Congress of Psychology, Brussels.

Sagi, A., van IJzendoorn, M., Scharf, M., Korne-Karje, N., Joels, T., & Mayseless, O. (1994). Stability and discriminant validity of the Adult Attachment Interview: A psychometric study in young Israeli adults. *Developmental Psychology, 30,* 771–777.

Scharfe, E., & Bartholomew, K. (1994). Reliability and stability of adult attachment patterns. *Personal Relationships, 9,* 51–64.

Scharfe, E., & Bartholomew, K. (1995). Accommodation and

attachment representations in young couples. *Journal of Social and Personal Relationships, 12,* 389–401.

Schultheiss, D. E. P., & Blustein, D. L. (1994). Contributions of family relationship factors to the identity formation process. *Journal of Counseling and Development, 73,* 159–166.

Senchak, M., & Leonard, K. E. (1992). Attachment styles and marital adjustment among newlywed couples. *Journal of Social and Personal Relationships, 9,* 51–64.

Shaver, P. R., Belsky, J., & Brennan, K. A. (1998). *Comparing measures of adult attachment: An examination of interview and self-report methods.* Manuscript submitted for publication.

Shaver, P. R., & Brennan, K. A. (1992). Attachment styles and the "Big Five" personality traits: Their connections with each other and with romantic relationship outcomes. *Personality and Social Psychology Bulletin, 18,* 536–545.

Shaver, P. R., & Clark, C. L. (1994). The psychodynamics of adult romantic attachment. In J. M. Masling & R. F. Bornstein (Eds.), *Empirical perspectives on object relations theory* (pp. 105–156). Washington, DC: American Psychological Association.

Shaver, P. R., & Hazan, C. (1987). Being lonely, falling in love: Perspectives from attachment theory. *Journal of Social Behavior and Personality, 2,* 105–124.

Shaver, P. R., & Hazan, C. (1988). A biased overview of the study of love. *Journal of Social and Personal Relationships, 5,* 473–501.

Shaver, P. R., & Hazan, C. (1993). Adult romantic attachment: Theory and evidence. In D. Perlman & W. Jones (Eds.), *Advances in personal relationships* (Vol. 4, pp. 29–70). London: Jessica Kingsley.

Shaver, P. R., Hazan, C., & Bradshaw, D. (1988). Love as attachment: The integration of three behavioral systems. In R. J. Sternberg & M. L. Barnes (Eds.), *The psychology of love* (pp. 68–99). New Haven, CT: Yale University Press.

Shaver, P. R., Papalia, D., Clark, C. L., Koski, L. R., Tidwell, M., & Nalbone, D. (1996). Androgyny and attachment security: Two related models of optimal development. *Personality and Social Psychology Bulletin, 22,* 582–597.

Simpson, J. A. (1990). The influence of attachment styles on romantic relationships. *Journal of Personality and Social Psychology, 59,* 971–980.

Simpson, J. A., & Rholes, W. S. (Eds.). (1998). *Attachment theory and close relationships.* New York: Guilford Press.

Simpson, J. A., Rholes, W. S., & Nelligan, J. S. (1992). Support-seeking and support-giving within couple members in an anxiety-provoking situation: The role of attachment styles. *Journal of Personality and Social Psychology, 62,* 434–446.

Simpson, J. A., Rholes, W. S., & Phillips, D. (1996). Conflict in close relationships: An attachment perspective. *Journal of Personality and Social Psychology, 71,* 899–914.

Sperling, M. B., & Berman, W. H. (Eds.). (1994). *Attachment in adults: Clinical and developmental perspectives.* New York: Guilford Press.

Steele, H., Steele, M., & Fonagy, P. (1996). Associations among attachment classifications of mothers, fathers, and their infants. *Child Development, 67,* 541–555.

Steele, J., Waters, E., Crowell, J., & Treboux, D. (1998, June). *Self-report measures of attachment: Secure bonds to other attachment measures and attachment theory?* Paper presented at the biennial meeting of the International Society for the Study of Personal Relationships, Saratoga Springs, NY.

Sternberg, R. J. (1986). A triangular theory of love. *Psychological Review, 93,* 119–135.

Sullivan-Hanson, J. (1990). *The early attachment and current affectional bonds of battered women: Implications for the impact of spouse abuse on children.* Unpublished doctoral dissertation, University of Virginia.

Tidwell, M. O., Reis, H. T., & Shaver, P. R. (1996). Attachment, attractiveness, and social interaction: A diary study. *Journal of Personality and Social Psychology, 71,* 729–745.

Treboux, D. (1997, April). *Are self-reports reliable measures of secure base behavior?* Poster presented at the biennial meeting of the Society for Research in Child Development, Washington, DC.

Treboux, D., Crowell, J., & Colon-Downs, C. (1992, March). *Self-concept and identity in late adolescence: Relation to working models of attachment.* Paper presented at the biennial meeting of the Society for Research in Adolescence, Washington, DC.

van IJzendoorn, M. H. (1992). Intergenerational transmission of parenting: A review of studies in non-clinical populations. *Developmental Review, 12,* 76–99.

van IJzendoorn, M. H. (1995). Adult attachment representations, parental responsiveness, and infant attachment: A meta-analysis on the predictive validity of the Adult Attachment Interview. *Psychological Bulletin, 117,* 387–403.

van IJzendoorn, M. H., & Bakersmans-Kranenburg, M. (1996). Attachment representations in mothers, fathers, adolescents and clinical groups: A meta-analytic search for normative data. *Journal of Clinical and Consulting Psychology, 64,* 8–21.

van IJzendoorn, M., Feldbrugge, J., Derks, F., de Ruiter, C., Verhagen, M., Philipse, M., van der Stark, C., & Riksen-Walraven, M. (1998). *Attachment, personality disorders, and staff–patient interactions in mentally disturbed criminal offenders.* Manuscript submitted for publication.

Vaughn, B., Egeland, B., Sroufe, L. A., & Waters, E. (1979). Individual differences in infant–mother attachment at twelve and eighteen months: Stability and change in families under stress. *Child Development, 50,* 971–975.

Ward, M. J., & Carlson, E. A. (1995). Associations among adult attachment representations, maternal sensitivity, and infant–mother attachment in a sample of adolescent mothers. *Child Development, 66,* 69–79.

Waters, E., & Crowell, J. (1994) [Self-esteem and attachment classification]. Unpublished raw data, State University of New York at Stony Brook.

Waters, E., Merrick, S., Treboux, D., Crowell, J., & Albersheim, L. (1998) *Attachment security from infancy to early adulthood: A 20-year longitudinal study.* Manuscript submitted for publication.

Waters, E., Kondo-Ikemura, K., Posada, G., & Richters, J. (1991). Learning to love: Mechanisms and milestones. In M. Gunnar & L. A. Sroufe (Eds.), *Self processes and development* (pp. 217–255). Hillsdale, NJ: Erlbaum.

Weinfield, N., Sroufe, L. A., & Egeland, B. (1998). *Attachment from infancy to early adulthood in a high risk sample: Continuity, discontinuity, and their correlates.* Manuscript submitted for publication.

Weiss, R. (1973). *Loneliness: The experience of emotional and social isolation.* Cambridge, MA: MIT Press.

Weiss, R. (1974). The provisions of social relationships. In Z. Rubin (Ed.), *Doing unto others* (pp. 17–26). Englewood Cliffs, NJ: Prentice-Hall.

Weiss, R. (1991). Attachment in adult life. In C. M. Parkes, J. Stevenson-Hinde, & P. Marris (Eds.), *Attachment across the life cycle* (pp. 171–184). London: Routledge.

West, M., & Sheldon, A. E. (1988). The classification of pathological attachment patterns in adults. *Journal of Personality Disorders, 2,* 153–160.

West, M., Sheldon, A. E. R., & Reiffer, L. (1987). An approach to the delineation of adult attachment: Scale development and reliability. *Journal of Nervous and Mental Disease, 175,* 738–741.

West, M. L., & Sheldon-Keller, A. E. (1992). The assessment of dimensions relevant to adult reciprocal attachment. *Canadian Journal of Psychiatry, 37,* 600–606.

West, M. L., & Sheldon-Keller, A. E. (1994). *Patterns of relating: An adult attachment perspective.* New York: Guilford Press.

Woike, B. A., Osier, T. J., & Candella, K. (1996). Attachment styles and violent imagery in thematic stories about relationships. *Personality and Social Psychology Bulletin, 22,* 1030–1034.

Zeanah, C., Benoit, D., Barton, M., Regan, C., Hirshberg, L., & Lipsett, L. (1993). Representations of attachment in mothers and their one-year-old infants. *Journal of the American Academy of Child and Adolescent Psychiatry, 32,* 278–286.

Zeifman, D., & Hazan, C. (1997). Attachment: The bond in pair-bonds. In J. A. Simpson & D. T. Kenrick (Eds.), *Evolutionary social psychology* (pp. 237–263). Mahwah, NJ: Erlbaum.

Zimmermann, P., Fremmer-Bombik, E., Spangler, G., & Grossmann, K. E. (1997). Attachment in adolescence: A longitudinal perspective. In W. Koops, J. B. Hoeksma, & D. C. van den Boom (Eds.), *Development of interaction and attachment: Traditional and non-traditional approaches* (pp. 281–292). Amsterdam: North-Holland.

V

CLINICAL APPLICATIONS OF ATTACHMENT THEORY AND RESEARCH

❖

21

Attachment and Psychopathology in Childhood

❖

MARK T. GREENBERG

This chapter reviews what is currently known about the relations between attachment and psychopathology in childhood. Given the existence of excellent recent reviews on this topic by others (Carlson & Sroufe, 1995; Cicchetti, Toth, & Lynch, 1995; Lyons-Ruth, Zeanah, & Benoit, 1996; Rutter, 1997), this review focuses on the more common externalizing and internalizing disorders of childhood and does not cover developmental disabilities. The chapter begins with general comments on the role of attachment in the development of psychopathology. It then addresses two fundamental questions. First, how has the study of attachment contributed to the understanding of childhood disorders? The answer includes a review of how attachment has been linked to childhood difficulties, a discussion of modes of transmission and differential pathways of influence, and the presentation of a heuristic model for understanding the role of attachment relations. The second question is this: How can the field of childhood psychopathology enrich the further study of attachment? The chapter closes with suggestions for future research.

The nature of the parent–child relationship during infancy and toddlerhood is believed to be one of the central causal factors in the child's personality (Bowlby, 1969/1982; Bronfenbrenner, 1979; Erikson, 1963; Freud, 1965; Greenspan, 1981). Numerous empirical findings indicate that the development of a secure attachment with caregiver(s) in the first 2 years of life is related to higher sociability with other adults and children, higher compliance with parents, and more effective emotional regulation (Ainsworth, Blehar, Waters, & Wall, 1978; Bretherton, 1985; Richters & Waters, 1991). Moreover, insecure attachment prior to age 2 has been related to lower sociability, poorer peer relations, symptoms of anger, and poorer behavioral self-control during the preschool years and beyond (Carlson & Sroufe, 1995; see Thompson, Chapter 13, this volume).

The idea that social relationships both affect and are affected by developing psychopathology in childhood is fundamental to most modern theories of development. Furthermore, object relations theorists (Mahler, Pine, & Bergman, 1975; Winnicott, 1965) and ego psychologists (Freud, 1965) have hypothesized that a child's earliest and closest relationships have the greatest impact on the development of mental health and illness. Yet it was not until John Bowlby (1969/1982, 1973) focused the fields of child development and child psychiatry on the study of infant and child attachment relationships that researchers truly began to study the associations between the child's closest relationships and the development of various forms of behavioral disorder. In spite of Bowlby's original focus, attachment research focused almost entirely during its early stages on infant development in normal settings (Bretherton, 1992; Main, 1996). Although scattered projects in the 1970s and 1980s began to study at-risk populations of children or adults with disorders (Belsky & Nezworski, 1988), researchers have only quite recently fully turned their attention to fulfilling Bowlby's legacy of utilizing attachment theory in the service of understanding and treating disorders in which relationship factors are a putative cause (Cicchetti et al., 1995).

With the initial studies of attachment and psychopathology during the last decade, attachment theory is beginning to make a major contribution beyond infancy and beyond the confines of its own advocates. This is an exciting development, because attachment theory can provide a critical developmental frame for understanding how early and continued close relationships affect the cognitive–affective structures that children use to construct their expectancies, views of the world, and coping strategies. As indicated in other chapters in this volume (see Dozier, Stovall, & Albus, Chapter 22; Kobak, Chapter 2; Lyons-Ruth & Jacobvitz, Chapter 23; and Weinfield, Sroufe, Egeland, & Carlson, Chapter 4), the management of anxiety, anger, and sadness through the healthy use of secure-base figures and mature defenses is likely to be an important protective factor against various forms of psychopathology across the lifespan (Carlson & Sroufe, 1995; Fonagy et al., 1995; Main, 1996).

THE ROLE OF ATTACHMENT IN UNDERSTANDING DEVELOPMENTAL PSYCHOPATHOLOGY

There are two general ways by which attachment theory and research may inform the study of psychopathology. First, in some cases, atypical attachment patterns in the first years of life may themselves be considered early disorders or incipient forms of psychopathology (Lieberman & Zeanah, 1995). In these cases, it is believed that early relationships—probably in concert with other risk factors in a child's ecology—have led to patterns of relating and associated behaviors that can be considered diagnostic of incipient disorder and are in need of treatment. The second broad way in which attachment may contribute to later disorder is by either increasing risk or buffering the effects of other risk factors (i.e., operating as a protective factor). Each of these two aspects of attachment is considered here.

Early Attachment Disorders

The Historical Context

For many years, clinicians in the fields of child psychiatry, pediatrics, and social work have seen children with significant impairments in their behavior, cognitions, and affect that were believed to result from deprivations or disruptions in relations with significant caregivers. These impairments usually derived from one of the following conditions: the absence of a significant attachment relationship (usually due to institutional rearing), significant distortions in the quality of care, or traumatic disruptions or losses of attachments in childhood. These concerns were part of the Zeitgeist that led Bowlby and others (Goldfarb, 1955; Spitz, 1946) to begin to investigate the effects of "maternal deprivation" just after World War II (Bowlby, 1953). As discussed by both Rutter (1981) and Bowlby, it is critical to distinguish among deprivation that results from not developing a close attachment during the infancy and toddler period; distortions in care that are the result of insensitivity, unresponsiveness, and often physical neglect and abuse within an attachment relationship; and, finally, the effects of loss of a relationship that has been established. In spite of the known consequences of the first two conditions for maladaptation, diagnostic systems did not recognize that disorder might result from disturbed or absent attachment relations until the third edition of the *Diagnostic and Statistical Manual of Mental Disorders* (DSM-III) appeared in 1980. When it was first recognized and termed "reactive attachment disorder," it was characterized as a disorder marked by pervasive disturbance across relationships; it needed to occur before 8 months of age; and it had associated symptoms related to "failure to thrive" that had little or no association with attachment relations (Richters & Volkmar, 1994; Zeanah, 1996). Revisions in DSM-III-R, as well as the ninth revision of the *International Classification of Diseases* (ICD-9), altered both the age of onset (to 5 years of age or younger) and dropped criteria related to failure to thrive. Beginning with these revised systems (and continuing with DSM-IV and ICD-10), these diagnostic systems distinguish two types of reactive attachment disorder: "inhibited" and "disinhibited" (see Zeanah, 1996, for further description). The inhibited subtype is marked by hypervigilance and fear that is manifested by withdrawal and ambivalence. The disinhibited subtype is distinguished by indiscriminate friendliness and the absence of a selective attachment to a discriminated figure who is sought for comfort. In DSM-IV there is a further requirement of the documentation of pathogenic care by the caregiver.

Problems in Current Nosology

Although these nosological revisions have indicated some progress in understanding the pathogenesis that can result in the early years from distortions in attachment, they suffer from a number of difficulties (Lyons-Ruth et al., 1996; Zeanah, 1996). First, the criteria are still focused on aberrant behavior in general, rather than on the attachment relationship and its specific consequences. This is unfortunate, because a child may experience an attachment disorder with the primary caregiver that causes considerable dysfunction, but may react in positive ways to other adults or peers (Lieberman & Zeanah, 1995). Second, attachment disorders have been narrowly defined as due to severe deprivation and maltreatment; however, it is possible for attachment disorder to develop in a stable and unhealthy relationship that is not characterized by severe maltreatment (Rutter, 1997). Third, as attachment disorders are by their very nature relational disorders, they do not fit comfortably into nosological systems that characterize the disorder as person-centered. A significant advance has been made in the diagnostic manual of Zero to Three (1994), which includes both a specific axis of parent–child relationship disorders and a global assessment scale of parent–child relationships. Types of relationship disorders include "overinvolved," "underinvolved," "abusive," "angry/hostile," "anxious/tense," and "mixed." However, the manual also retains the traditional notion of reactive attachment disorder and is thus not fully informed by recent research on attachment (Lieberman & Zeanah, 1995).

Insecure Attachment versus Early Attachment Disorder

Recent theory and research have led to important innovations in the formulation of systems for describing attachment disorders in the early years. A central issue is how to distinguish insecure attachments, as studied in the Strange Situation or similar laboratory separation and reunion sequences, from attachment disorders. Although it is likely that children with attachment disorders will show insecure attachments in such situations, very few children with insecure attach-

ments are considered to have an attachment disorder. Zeanah, Mammen, and Lieberman (1993) have distinguished insecurity from disorder by the degree to which the emotions and behaviors that a child shows in his or her attachment relationship indicate profound disturbances in the child's feeling of safety and lead to risk for persistent distress or disability (Wakefield, 1992). Furthermore, it has long been noted that focusing solely on separation and reunion behavior provides too narrow a measure of the relationship (Bowlby, 1988; Rutter, 1981). Returning to the basis of attachment theory, Lieberman and Pawl (1988, 1990) refocused this discussion by considering attachment disorders to be rooted in distortions in behavior (Cicchetti, Cummings, Greenberg, & Marvin, 1990). Using this foundation, Zeanah et al. (1993) have proposed a list of behavioral features that should be considered in assessing the nature of the attachment relationship in naturalistic settings.

An Alternative Taxonomy of Attachment Disorders

On the basis of both attachment theory and current research, Lieberman and Zeanah (1995) have provided an alternative taxonomy of attachment disorders in the early years. This taxonomy distinguishes among conditions of "nonattachment," "disordered attachment," and "disruption of attachments." Disorders of nonattachment follow closely the diagnostic systems of DSM-IV and ICD-10 in describing infants who do not exhibit a preferred attachment (e.g., Bowlby's description of a discriminated figure) and have reached the cognitive level of 10 to 12 months. This latter criterion is not part of the other diagnostic systems, but aids in distinguishing attachment disorder from cognitive disorders and pervasive developmental disorders (Zeanah, 1996). There are two subtypes, "withdrawn/inhibited" and "indiscriminately social."

Disordered attachments are distinguished by their distortions in secure-base behavior and follow from the richly described case studies of Lieberman and her colleagues (Lieberman & Pawl, 1988, 1990; Lieberman & Zeanah, 1995). Three forms of disordered attachment have been distinguished. These include subtypes characterized by extreme inhibition (clinging and little exploration); reckless self-endangerment (failure to use the secure base in times of risk); and role reversal, wherein the child shows excessive concern and worry regarding the attachment figure.

The third type of attachment disorder involves patterns of grief reaction of children under age 3 subsequent to the loss of an attachment figure. These are based on the clinical observations of the Robertsons (Robertson & Robertson, 1989) and Bowlby, and are based on the premise that loss of the primary attachment figure in infancy is inherently pathogenic. Lieberman and Zeanah (1995) do not make clear whether, or how, normal grief reactions may be distinguished from those that are pathological at this age, as Bowlby (1980) did with respect to older children and adults.

These major advances in the development of new systems of nosology that are specific to attachment relationships bring the study of attachment back to its clinical origins and begin to make the findings of attachment research available to clinicians working with children who experience trauma and loss. However, there is a need both for further validation of the diagnostic reliability of these conditions and for examination of the developmental trajectory of children who show these early extreme attachment difficulties. There is also a great need for parallel work in the field of early and middle childhood.

Although the development of diagnostic categories based on attachment-related phenomena has the potential to lead to great advances in understanding early disorder and its genesis, diagnostic models are unlikely to capture the more general role that attachment plays in the genesis of maladaptation.

Attachment as a Risk or Protective Factor for Later Disorder

The second general way in which attachment may contribute to later disorder is either to increase risk or to buffer the effects of other risk factors (i.e., to operate as a protective factor). Given the potential contribution of attachment theory and research, the enthusiasm to utilize attachment theory can lead to overinterpretation of findings and a fruitless search for the "Holy Grail" of psychopathology. Some investigators, employing simplistic models, have considered the test of the contribution of attachment research to be whether there are long-term main effects of infant attachment on later psychopathology. However, like any contributory risk or protective factor, attachment is likely to show its greatest influence in the context of other risk factors that are part of the child and family ecology (Greenberg, Speltz, & De-

Klyen, 1993). A short digression into key tenets of risk factor models in developmental psychopathology will provide a frame for considering the role of attachment relations.

Risk Factors in Developmental Psychopathology

Research on risk factors for childhood disorder has led to seven general conclusions. First, development is complex, and it is unlikely that there is a single cause for most disorders; even in the case of disorders in which a biochemical or genetic mechanism has been discovered, the expression of the disorder is influenced by other biological or environmental events. Thus, it is doubtful that attachment insecurity alone will lead to a disorder (Sroufe, 1983, 1990), although it may increase its likelihood. However, this statement should be qualified in cases in which severe and continued maltreatment (especially physical abuse) accompany this insecurity. A corollary of this principle is that it is unlikely that most childhood disorders can be eliminated by merely treating causes that are purported to lie in the child alone (Rutter, 1982). Thus, even when a powerful biological cause is implicated (e.g., autism), the parent–child relationship in general and attachment relations in particular may be a focus for treatment.

A second tenet of developmental psychopathology is the notion of multiple pathways both to and from disorder (Cicchetti & Rogosh, 1997). That is, different combinations of risk factors may lead to the same disorder (i.e., "equifinality"). In the most common childhood mental disorders, no single cause may be either necessary or sufficient (Greenberg et al., 1993), and the effect of a risk factor will depend on its timing and relation to other risk factors ("multifinality").

Third, risk factors occur not only at the level of the individual or family, but at other levels in ecological models (Kellam, 1990). For example, risk at the level of the peer group (e.g., peer networks, deviance) and the neighborhood (e.g., its density, dangerousness, resources) may significantly affect risk for disorder. Furthermore, the nature of connections between the family and other social institutions, as well as regulatory features and legislation, may have effects at the macro level (Bronfenbrenner, 1979; Weissberg & Greenberg, 1997).

Fourth, there appears to be a nonlinear relationship (often quadratic or exponential) between

risk factors and outcomes. Although one or two risk factors may show little prediction to poor outcomes, there appears to be a rapidly increasing rate of disorder with additional risk factors (Rutter, 1979; Sameroff, Seifer, Barocas, Zax, & Greenspan, 1987). It is currently unclear whether certain risk factors or certain combinations of risk factors matter more than others. To examine this issue requires person-oriented analyses that assess the predictive value of different risk factors. In the domain of juvenile delinquency, Loeber and Dishion (1983) have demonstrated how the use of odds ratios for different risk factors may assist in making these determinations. Recent findings (Greenberg, Speltz, DeKlyen, & Jones, 1998; Lyons-Ruth, Alpern, & Repacholi, 1993; Shaw, Owens, Vondra, Keenan, & Winslow, 1997) provide examples of initial attempts to examine this question in regard to attachment security.

Fifth, many developmental risk factors are not disorder-specific, but instead are related to a variety of maladaptive outcomes. Thus the combination of poverty, family violence, and parental psychopathology has been associated with a variety of childhood disorders. Risk factors predict multiple outcomes, and there is often great overlap between problem behaviors. For example, attachment has been considered a risk factor for both internalizing and externalizing disorders. In contrast to most other common-cause risk factors, specific forms of insecurity may be linked to specific forms of disorder (Carlson & Sroufe, 1995).

A sixth guiding principle is that certain risk factors may have differential action or influence in different developmental periods. For example, secure attachment may be more important in early development, whereas cognitive ability and motivation may be more important in middle childhood, and parental norms regarding behavior may be most critical during adolescence. There is a need for basic research to elucidate the differential timing of risk factors. For example, attachment theory predicts that children who are securely attached in the first few years of life and later experience traumatic circumstances should be at less risk for disorder than those who are insecurely attached in their early years. However, it is unclear how long (i.e., up to what age) a child needs a secure relationship in order to receive this protection. In contrast, if a child develops an insecure and harmful early attachment, it is not known at what age rehabilitation of that relationship, or change to a new "secure" caregiver, may

counter the effects of early insecurity on later maladaptation.

Finally, risk factors may vary in influence with host factors such as gender and ethnicity, and with environmental factors such as family atmosphere. Moreover, a factor that presumably confers risk for one disorder (e.g., conduct disorder) may reduce the risk for other disorders. For example, avoidant attachment is considered a risk factor, but it may decrease the risk of suicide (Adam, Sheldon-Keller, & West, 1995).

Protective Factors

In contrast to risk factors, protective factors are those that reduce the risk of maladaptive outcomes under conditions of risk. Although much less is known about protective factors and their operation (Kazdin, 1990; Luthar, 1993; Rutter, 1985), at least three broad types of protective factors have been identified. These include characteristics of the individual (e.g., temperamental qualities and intelligence; Luthar & Zigler, 1992), the quality of the child's relationships, and broader ecological factors such as high-quality schools, safe neighborhoods, and regulatory activities (e.g., laws or regulations that protect and/or support children and families). Within the domain of the quality of the child's social relations, the importance of secure attachment to parents (Carlson & Sroufe, 1995) and of healthy relationships with peers (Parker, Rubin, Price, & DeRosier, 1995) has been demonstrated.

There is considerable controversy regarding the designation of specific factors as serving either a risk or a protective function (Luthar, 1993; Rutter, 1987; Stouthamer-Loeber et al., 1993: Zimmerman & Arunkumar, 1994). In some studies a factor (e.g., social class, attachment security, peer group status) may be conceptualized as a risk factor, and in others it may be treated as a protective factor. This may depend on which end of the spectrum is being studied, the nature of the sample population, and the theoretical bent of the investigator. For example, attachment insecurity may be conceptualized as a risk factor that contributes significantly to disorder (Sroufe, 1983). However, under conditions of great risk, a secure attachment may be conceptualized as conferring protection from maladaptation (Morisset, Barnard, Greenberg, Booth, & Speiker, 1990).

Prospective longitudinal designs are critical to understanding how protective factors operate and how they interact with risk. Such well-planned basic studies can identify (1) which risk factors are predictive of different developmental stages of a problem, (2) how risk and protective factors are dynamically related in different developmental periods, and (3) what factors are most likely to protect or buffer persons with multiple risk factors from negative outcomes. Coie et al. (1993) suggest that protective factors may work in one or more of the following four ways: The presence of a protective factor may directly decrease dysfunction; the protective factor may interact with the risk factor to buffer its effect; the protective factor may disrupt the mediational chain by which risk leads to disorder; or it may prevent the initial occurrence of the risk factor.

Empirical Support for the Role of Infant Attachment in Later Maladaptation

In the past decade, numerous studies have examined the effects of infant and toddler attachment on later development. Within this large body of work, more and more projects have begun to assess outcomes related to behavioral risk and/or psychopathology. As most studies have followed children only through the early school years, and have focused primarily on the outcome of externalizing behavior problems, less is known about incipient forms of internalizing disorders or their more complete forms. These studies are reviewed here in four groups: those examining middle-class and relatively advantaged samples; those examining families at high social risk; those examining families with infants at high medical risk; and those examining families with caregivers who have psychiatric diagnoses or other risk factors.

Low-Risk Samples

Numerous studies of low-risk populations have now addressed the question of whether insecure attachment in the first 2 years is related to higher rates of disruptive behavior problems in the 4- to 7-year age range. Subject samples in these studies are drawn in a nonrandom manner from the population (i.e., easily obtainable volunteers from the community), are primarily middle-class, show a relatively low percentage of insecure children (30% or less), and are likely to evidence low rates of significant problems at follow-up in childhood. Furthermore, given their relatively small sample size and low base rate of psychopathology, these studies have little power to detect significant relationships. In four illustrative studies (Bates, Maslin, & Frankel, 1985;

Bates, Bayles, Bennett, Ridge, & Brown, 1991; Fagot & Kavanaugh, 1990; Goldberg, Lojkasek, Minde, & Corter, 1990; Lewis, Feiring, McGuffog, & Jaskir, 1984), no significant main effects were found between insecure attachment and later externalizing problems. Moreover, there was little investigation of mediator or moderator effects, with one exception: Lewis et al. (1984) reported a gender × attachment interaction, with 40% of insecure boys as compared to 6% of secure boys scoring above the 90th percentile on the Child Behavior Checklist (CBCL) Total Problem Score. Follow-up of this sample at age 13 revealed no long-term main effect of infant attachment status, and no interaction between attachment and stress exposure on teacher or mother ratings of psychopathology (Feiring & Lewis, 1997).

These findings, as well as more general notions regarding the simplicity of single-cause models, indicate that longitudinal main-effects models will be of little interest in middle-class convenience samples and will probably provide little of value of understanding the potential linkages between attachment and externalizing psychopathology. Such studies neither prove nor disprove the effects of attachment, unless one expects strong main effects. Thus low-risk samples may be inadequate for addressing this question (Fagot & Kavanaugh, 1990). Larger population-based studies with adequate sampling (National Institute of Child Health and Human Development [NICHD] Early Child Care Research Network, 1994) should soon begin to provide data generalizable to a larger segment of society. A second and more adequate strategy is indicated by studies that examine the effects of attachment transactionally in populations that share risk factors in other domains (difficult temperament or organic process within the child, poor parental management strategies, family adversity, and parent psychopathology) and have a high base rate of psychopathology.

Families at High Social Risk

Several investigators have studied high-social-risk populations (Lyons-Ruth, Connell, Zoll, & Stahl, 1987; Rodning, Beckwith, & Howard, 1991; Shaw & Vondra, 1995; Spieker & Booth, 1988). Researchers in two studies have examined high-risk populations into middle childhood or later, and these studies are reviewed here in some detail (Egeland & Sroufe, 1981; Lyons-Ruth et al., 1993). Only the Minnesota Parent–Child Project (Egeland & Sroufe, 1981; Erickson, Sroufe, & Egeland, 1985; Sroufe, 1983) has followed a sample through childhood and into adolescence and has assessed aspects of psychopathology (see Weinfield et al., Chapter 4, this volume). In this project, a high-social-risk sample consisting of infants of primarily young, single mothers was followed from birth (long-term sample size of 174). The investigators assessed attachment at both 12 and 18 months and categorized children as "secure" (B), "avoidant" (A), or "ambivalent" (C), as a result of consistent patterns across both time periods. This methodology is likely to create more accurate sampling of stable patterns of attachment, and to avoid inaccuracy due to both error variance and short-term fluctuations in family stressors with significant effects on attachment security (Vaughn, Egeland, Sroufe, & Waters, 1979). However, at different ages of follow-up, different measures (combined across time vs. only 12 months) were utilized as the predictors. Follow-up assessments in the preschool years (Erickson et al., 1985; Sroufe, 1983; Troy & Sroufe, 1987), in the early elementary school years (Renken, Egeland, Marvinney, Mangelsdorf, & Sroufe, 1989; Sroufe, 1990; Sroufe, Egeland, & Kreutzer, 1990), and in the preadolescent period (Urban, Carlson, Egeland, & Sroufe, 1991) consistently revealed that children in high-social-risk environments who showed early insecure relations were significantly more likely to show poor peer relations, moodiness, and symptoms of depression and aggression than children who showed early security.

For externalizing outcomes, predictions from attachment and early parent–child relations were much stronger for boys than for girls (which might be expected, given the expected high base rate of externalizing in males). Although main effects in the high-risk environment were found, transactional processes were identified in the preschool years that might increase the risk of disruptive behavior problems for secure infants as well as decrease the risk of such problems in insecure children. Compared to the secure group without behavior problems, the secure infants with later behavior problems had mothers who were less supportive and encouraging at both 24 and 42 months; at the later assessment the mothers were less effective teachers, providing little support, unclear expectations, and inconsistent limits. Furthermore, at 30 months these homes had fewer play materials and less maternal involvement. These mothers also reported more confusion and disorganized mood states than did

mothers of secure infants who did not later show behavior problems. Compared to insecurely attached infants with later behavior problems, those without such problems had mothers who were warmer, more supportive, and more appropriate at limit setting at 42 months. The children were also more positive in their affect and more compliant and affectionate with their mothers at 42 months. The home environment of insecure infants without later problems contained more appropriate play materials and were characterized by higher maternal involvement.

At ages 10–11, 47 of the 174 children were carefully observed at a 4-week summer day camp (Urban et al., 1991). Children who had been rated as secure as infants were less dependent, more ego-resilient, more socially competent, and more likely to interact effectively with camp counselors; in most instances, however, avoidant and ambivalent children were not distinguishable. Ambivalent children were particularly dependent in their relations with counselors. An examination of the development of friendship patterns indicated that secure children were more likely to form a friendship (as assessed by both observer and peer sociometric reports), and that security affected friendship choice and formation, with secure–secure friendships occurring more frequently than expected (Elicker, Englund, & Sroufe, 1992). In these more recent reports, transactional patterns had not yet been explored.

Two recent follow-ups of the Minnesota sample (Ogawa, Sroufe, Weinfield, Carlson, & Egeland, 1997; Warren, Huston, Egeland, & Sroufe, 1997) have examined the relation between infant attachment and psychopathology in adolescence. Warren et al. (in press) examined predictors of anxiety disorders in 172 individuals (and thus much larger samples than the Elicker et al. and Urban et al. reports in later childhood and early adolescence) who received a psychiatric interview at age 17. Fifteen percent of the sample had a current diagnosis or lifetime history of an anxiety disorder. The results supported the hypothesized relations between ambivalent infant attachment and later anxiety disorders (Cassidy, 1995): 28% of ambivalent infants had such disorders, as compared to 16% of avoidant and 12% of secure infants. After infant temperament and maternal ratings of anxiety in infancy were accounted for, ambivalent attachment accounted for a significant but modest percentage (4%) of the variance in predicting anxiety disorders. However, secure infants did not show a lower rate of overall disorders (including diagnoses other than anxiety disorders) than did ambivalent infants. Compared to both secure infants (39%) and ambivalent infants (40%), those who were avoidant showed the highest overall rate of disorders (70%). As this report focused only on the anxiety disorders and did not examine the roles of moderators or mediators of infant attachment, it is only an initial report of this long-term follow-up.

Ogawa et al. (1997) examined the relationship of developmental factors and the experience of trauma to symptoms of dissociation in adolescence (age 17) and young adulthood (age 19). In addition to examining the role of attachment classifications (secure, avoidant, ambivalent) at ages 12 and 18 months, the strange situation data were scored on Main's Disorganized/Disoriented Scale (Main & Solomon, 1990). Findings indicated that infant attachment was a significant factor in predicting dissociation at both time periods. In adolescence, both avoidant classification and higher ratings of disorganization contributed to the differentiation of clinical levels of dissociation vs. normality. In young adulthood, infancy ratings of disorganization played a substantial role in prediction of later dissociation. These findings are supportive of the theoretical model of Liotti (1995) linking early disorganization and trauma to later dissociative disorders.

Thus the quality of early attachment was related in a predictable manner to preschool measures of behavior problems, as well as to adolescent measures of anxiety and dissociation, and this association was in some cases mediated by later aspects of the parent–child relationship and family circumstances. The findings of this study clearly support a transactional/multipathway model by demonstrating that information about early security of attachment and later parent–child and family relationships may be necessary to predict later behavior problems accurately (Erickson et al., 1985; Sroufe et al., 1990). The fact that the Minnesota findings show more and stronger effects of infant attachment than studies of low-risk samples have done may indicate that secure attachment operates as a protective factor in high-risk environments (Morisset et al., 1990; Rutter, 1987), or that insecure attachment combined with family adversity is one potent pathway to later disruptive behavior problems (Lyons-Ruth, Zoll, Connell, & Grunebaum, 1989). It should be noted that with the exception of the Ogawa et al. (1997) report (which utilized the Disorganized/Disoriented Scale) this project did not include assessment of the more recent "disorganized/disoriented" (D) classification in infancy, which may have reduced its power of prediction. The disorganized/disoriented pattern is exhibited at high rates in samples in which there is parent psychopathology, child abuse, or very high social risk (Cicchetti & Barnett, 1991; Crittenden, 1988; Lyons-Ruth et al., 1987; O'Connor, Sigman, & Brill, 1987; Spieker & Booth, 1988).

Two recent longitudinal investigations of attachment in high-social-risk populations have also indicated its predictive power (Lyons-Ruth et al., 1989; Shaw & Vondra, 1995). Lyons-Ruth and colleagues have followed a sample of high-social-risk families in Cambridge, Massachusetts, in which many caregivers were depressed. Follow-up of 80% (n = 64) of the sample in the preschool period utilized teachers as independent raters of anxiety, hostility, and hyperactivity. Preschoolers who were rated as hostile with peers and adults were significantly more likely to have been insecure as infants, especially disorganized/disoriented, and to have caregivers with chronic depressive symptoms; 71% of the hostile preschoolers had been classified as disorganized at age 18 months, while only 12% of hostile children had been classified as secure. If a child was classified as disorganized and had a mother with psychosocial problems, there was a 55% rate of hostile behavior in kindergarten, as compared to a 5% rate for low-income children without either risk factor. Lyons-Ruth, Easterbrooks, Davidson Cibelli, and Bronfman (1995) reported that the combination of low infant intelligence and insecure attachment was highly predictive of teacher-rated externalizing problems at age 7; however, neither factor alone was predictive. Fifty percent of the disorganized/low-intelligence group showed externalizing problems, as compared to 5% of the sample with neither risk factor. In the same sample, internalizing symptoms were predicted by avoidant (not disorganized) attachment at 8 months, but only maternal depression predicted internalizing scores at clinical levels. In a recent follow-up of this Cambridge sample, Easterbrooks, Davidson, and Chazan (1993) reported that children who were coded as insecure at age 7 (with the Main & Cassidy [1985] coding system) showed significantly higher internalizing and externalizing problems by both parent and teacher report, and this connection was maintained after accounting for family risk.

Shaw and Vondra (1995), studying a high-social-risk sample in Pittsburgh, found that infant attachment insecurity modestly predicted preschool behavior problems at age 3. In a more recent analysis of this sample predicting to parental ratings of behavior problems on the CBCL at age 5, Shaw et al. (1997) found that insecure infant attachment at 12 months was uniquely predictive (i.e., it predicted outcome after all other risk factors were accounted for). Whereas 60% of disorganized children showed clinically elevated levels of aggression, 31% of avoidant, 28% of ambivalent, and only 17% of secure infants did so. Most importantly, the combination of disorganized attachment and parental rating of difficult temperament at age 2 were potent predictors; children with *both* risk factors were in the 99th percentile for aggression, whereas children with only disorganized attachment or only difficult temperament were in the normal range. Logistic regression analysis showed that insecure attachment (odds ratio = 3.4) and maternal personality (odds ratio = 8.4) contributed uniquely in predicting clinical-level difficulties at age 5.

In both the Shaw et al. and Lyons-Ruth et al. studies, the insecure pattern that was most closely related to later problems was the newly developed insecure attachment category of disorganized/disoriented or D (see Hesse, Chapter 19, and Lyons-Ruth & Jacobvitz, Chapter 23, this volume; Main & Hesse, 1990). Disorganized attachment may be a general vulnerability factor for later problems in adaptation, given that in the Cambridge sample, 50% of 7-year-olds classified as disorganized were rated as showing poor general adaptation to school (Lyons-Ruth et al., 1995). Nevertheless, it should be made quite clear that an insecure attachment is not itself a measure of psychopathology. In some cases an insecure attachment may set a trajectory that, along with other risk factors, increases the risk for either externalizing or internalizing psychopathology.

Infants at Medical Risk

Most research on infants with medical risk has focused on those who are born preterm. Several projects with a diverse set of preterm infants have led to the conclusion that preterm birth itself does not lead to higher rates of insecurity (Crnic, Greenberg, & Slough, 1986; Easterbrooks, 1989; Frodi & Thompson, 1985; Goldberg, 1988). Nonetheless, the combination of preterm status and a high-stress, low-resource family environment (Wille, 1991), or accompanying serious medical conditions (Plunkett,

Meisels, Steifel, & Pasik, 1986), may lead to higher rates of insecurity in this population.

Goldberg, Gotowiec, and Simmons (1995) examined infant attachment in children without health problems, those with cystic fibrosis, and those with congenital heart defects. Two findings are of interest. First, both medically diagnosed groups showed lower rates of secure attachment at 12 to 18 months than did the healthy group; this was mostly accounted for by higher rates of disorganized attachments in both of the medically diagnosed groups. Second, infants who were avoidant showed higher ratings on both internalizing and externalizing scores at age 4 (mother and father ratings combined) than did secure children. Neither ambivalent nor disorganized children showed higher rates of problems than did secure infants.

Marvin and Pianta (1996) reported findings on two medically ill groups: 1- to 4-year-olds with either cerebral palsy (CP) or epilepsy. There was a slightly increased risk for insecure attachment in the CP group and a very significant increased risk for insecurity in the epilepsy group; the latter had a high rate of disorganized and insecure/other classifications, which was presumed to be partially a function of neurological impairment (R. S. Marvin, personal communication, July 1997). Findings from an innovative, brief interview of parental representations of response to diagnosis (the Response to Diagnosis Interview, or RDI) indicated significant linkages in the CP group between the RDI and toddler attachment security (Marvin & Pianta, 1996) and between the RDI and the Adult Attachment Interview (AAI) (Morog, 1996). Parents who were resolved regarding the diagnosis were more likely to be scored as autonomous on the AAI and were more likely to have children who were securely attached. However, no such linkages (either between the RDI and AAI or between RDI and child attachment) were found in the epilepsy sample (Marvin & Pianta, 1996; Morog, 1996). Furthermore, there was a higher rate of lack of resolution on the RDI in the epilepsy group, and this may reflect the continuing crisis of having a child with an unpredictable course of seizures, as compared to the stable development of children with CP.

Speltz, Endriga, Fisher, and Mason (1997) examined attachment at 12 months of age, comparing infants with craniofacial disorders and matched controls. They reported that children with both cleft lip and palate had high rates of security (80% secure) that were comparable to their matched controls' rates (72% secure). However, those children with only cleft palate showed somewhat lower rates of security (54% secure). As infants with the combination of cleft lip and palate are more facially disfigured, these findings indicate that the children's facial malformation itself had little effect on the formation of secure attachment.

In summary, with the exception of epilepsy, it appears that child-associated physical and/or medical risk conditions are not associated with a significant elevation of risk for insecure attachment. These findings provide continued support for the conclusions of the meta-analysis of van IJzendoorn, Goldberg, Kroonenberg, and Frenkel (1992), which found that maternal problems, family problems, and child maltreatment were more likely to increase risk than were infant risk conditions.

Caregivers with Psychiatric Diagnoses or Other Risk Factors

Of related interest are studies of risk due to parent psychopathology. Radke-Yarrow and colleagues examined the attachment patterns of children between the ages of 15 and 52 months, whose mostly middle-class mothers had either bipolar depression, major unipolar depression, mild depression, or no affective disorder (DeMulder & Radke-Yarrow, 1991; Radke-Yarrow, Cummings, Kuczynski, & Chapman, 1985). In two different reports using somewhat different systems of coding separation and reunion patterns (a developmentally adapted version of Ainsworth's original coding system vs. the MacArthur Preschool Attachment Assessment System [PAAS]; Cassidy & Marvin, with the MacArthur Working Group on Attachment, 1992), similar findings were reported. In both analyses, children in the maternal bipolar group showed high rates of insecurity (approximately 70%), and the majority of these insecure classifications were disorganized/disoriented. The rates of child insecurity in the normal and mildly depressed groups did not differ, whereas that in the unipolar group was somewhat elevated. These findings on unipolar depression are comparable to those of Cohn, Campbell, and Ross (1991), who also studied a volunteer middle-class sample.

Manassis, Bradley, Goldberg, Hood, and Swinson (1994) reported the first study of children of mothers with diagnosed anxiety disorders. This is a particularly important group, giv-

en the key role of anxiety in attachment theory (Bowlby, 1973; Bretherton, 1992; Cassidy, 1995). Studying 20 children ages 22 to 51 months old, the authors utilized the PAAS coding system (Cassidy et al., 1992). Eighty percent of the children of anxious mothers were coded as insecure, with a high percentage of children rated as controlling/disorganized or as insecure/other. Two children in the sample met criteria for childhood anxiety disorders, and both were classified as avoidant. There were four secure children, and none met criteria for an anxiety disorder. These secure children were distinguished from the remainder of the sample by the significantly lower life stress and higher reported parenting competence of their anxious mothers. The authors also utilized a temperamental measure of inhibition, which they hypothesized would be the active factor predicting both attachment insecurity and childhood anxiety. However, they found no relation between behavioral inhibition and either attachment security or childhood anxiety disorder in this sample.

In addition to the effects of maternal psychiatric diagnosis, other, nondiagnostic familial risk factors have been repeatedly related to insecure attachment. These include the amount of life stress and family adversity experienced during a child's infancy (Egeland & Sroufe, 1981; Spieker & Booth, 1988; Vaughn et al., 1979), maternal alcoholism and drug abuse (O'Connor et al., 1987; Rodning et al., 1991), and marital satisfaction and parental social support satisfaction (Crnic et al., 1986; Crockenberg, 1981). However, as Belsky, Rosenberger, and Crnic (1995) illustrate, individual family risk variables often do not show main effects on infant security, and there is a need for risk factor research to examine multiple determinants in *a priori* models that investigate moderator and mediator effects. For example, Das Eiden, Teti, and Corns (1995) showed that marital satisfaction did not directly predict infant Attachment *Q*-Sort scores, but instead operated as a protective factor in moderating the effects of insecure maternal adult attachment status.

Concurrent Relations between Attachment and Psychopathology during Early Childhood

Recently classification systems have been developed for assessing the quality of attachment through the use of laboratory separations and reunions in children between the ages of 3 and 6 years (Cassidy et al., 1992; Crittenden, 1992; Main & Cassidy, 1985; see Solomon & George, Chapter 14, this volume, for a review). These assessments allow the examination of contemporaneous relations between attachment and psychopathology, as well as between attachment and other dimensions of functioning. However, as they are contemporaneous measurements, they leave unresolved the question of direction of causality. I first review studies on the concurrent relations between attachment and adaptive functioning in samples of children with clinical diagnoses and of late adoptees. Finally, I review findings from nonclinical populations.

Oppositional Defiant Disorder

Three studies have examined attachment security in clinic-referred samples of children who met criteria for oppositional defiant disorder (ODD) and comparison children matched on age, social class, and family composition (DeKlyen, Speltz, & Greenberg, 1996; Greenberg, Speltz, DeKlyen, & Endriga, 1991; Speltz, Greenberg, & DeKlyen, 1990). In the first two studies, approximately 80% of the clinic children demonstrated insecure attachments, as compared to 30% of the comparison children. Although the clinic children showed all styles of insecurity (avoidant, ambivalent, controlling), they showed a disproportionately higher rate of the controlling classification. This classification is characterized by a child's attempt to actively direct control of the interaction with the parent upon reunion; many of the children who showed this pattern were either punitive and hostile or rejecting of their mothers. Main and Cassidy (1988) have hypothesized that this controlling pattern is a developmental transformation of the recently described infant disorganized/disoriented (D) pattern shown at high rates in social risk samples.

Three other findings from these clinical samples bear discussion. First, the fact that 15–20% of the clinic-referred sample showed secure attachments indicates that attachment is not merely assessing ODD and that attachment may be a component of only some pathways leading to ODD. Campbell (1990) has similarly noted that in some families in which there are high rates of aggression and hyperactivity, the mother–child relationship appears warm and trusting. Second, in the first study (Speltz et al., 1990), the relation between attachment status and clinic status was found only among boys (there were few girls, and thus there was little power to test the effect

among girls). The replication study (Greenberg et al., 1991) included only boys. Third, the finding of high concurrent concordance between an independent assessment of maternal attachment and child attachment in the clinic group (DeKlyen, 1996) increases the likelihood that these children's attachments in infancy were also insecure and that attachment processes may influence the development of disruptive problems. Utilizing a third cohort of 80 clinically referred boys and 80 carefully matched controls, DeKlyen et al. (1996) again found that children with early ODD had higher rates of insecurity. In this sample, however, only 55% of clinic children were coded as insecure. In the same cohort, attachment to fathers showed a similar pattern with greater rates of insecurity in the clinic sample (55%) as compared to the comparison sample (85%) (DeKlyen, Speltz, & Greenberg, 1998).

Other findings on the relations between the AAI (George, Kaplan, & Main, 1984) and behavior problems in early childhood (Crowell & Feldman, 1988; Dozier et al., Chapter 22, this volume) support a link between parental representations of attachment and childhood externalizing problems. DeKlyen (1996) has proposed that parental attachment status may have implications for mode or style of child and family treatment. Routh, Hill, Steele, Elliot, and Dewey (1995) presented clinical findings indicating that parents with autonomous (secure) adult attachment classifications had children who showed greater clinical improvement.

Gender Identity Disorder

Birkenfeld-Adams (1996, cited in Goldberg, 1997) used the PAAS to assess preschool attachment classification in a group of boys with gender identity disorder, and compared them to a nonspecific clinic sample with behavioral difficulties and to a comparison sample. Both clinic samples showed lower rates of security and could be differentiated by type of insecurity. Boys with gender identity disorder were more likely to show ambivalent attachments, whereas the nonspecific clinic sample showed higher rates of avoidant and controlling/disorganized classifications.

The Effects of Institutional Rearing and Late Adoption

As maternal loss and deprivation have been central to attachment theory since its inception

(Bowlby, 1953, 1969/1982), it is surprising that there is a dearth of studies on children who have suffered traumatic loss of attachment figures or who have been adopted after infancy. Marcovitch et al. (1997) reported findings on attachment security during the preschool years, using the PAAS in a sample of Romanian children adopted by Canadian families. They contrasted two groups: children who had spent significant time in a deprived institutional rearing setting prior to adoption, and those who were adopted in the first months of life. In both groups, there was a significantly higher rate of insecurity than in a normally home-reared Canadian sample. What was remarkable was that although there were quite high rates of both ambivalent and controlling/disorganized attachments in both adoptee groups, not one adoptee was classified as avoidant. The authors suggest that avoidance would be a particularly maladaptive strategy for an adoptee. Likewise, it would be unlikely for parents who are highly motivated to adopt to show parenting patterns related to avoidance (e.g., rejection) during the relationship formation stage. This also fits with Bowlby's original observations of high proximity seeking in institutionalized children. The authors comment on the need for a classification system that is more sensitive to the types of behaviors shown by formerly institutionalized children (e.g., indiscriminate relating to adults).

In a second study of Romanian adoptees in Canada, Chisholm, Carter, Ames, and Morison (1995) examined attachment security with a short form of the Attachment Q-Sort (Waters & Deane, 1985). The study contrasted three groups of preschool children: those in depriving Romanian orphanages for at least the first 8 months of life, those adopted before 4 months of age, and a home-reared Canadian sample. The early institutionalized (late-adopted) group showed significantly more parent report items indicating insecurity. The authors concluded that the early-depriving institutional setting affected these children's ability to develop a secure attachment. Paralleling the findings of Marcovitch et al. (1997), the early-institutionalized children also showed significantly greater indiscriminate friendliness to adults. This may be related to the observations of Bowlby (1953), Goldfarb (1955), and Tizard and Hodges (1978) that children in or after long-term institutionalization show a pattern of indiscriminately friendly behavior to unfamiliar adults. Although some investigators have conceptualized indiscriminate socializing with adults as a sign of nonattachment (Lieber-man & Pawl, 1988), this did not appear to be the case in this sample: Parent-reported security scores were unrelated to indiscriminate friendliness. Two limitations in this report are notable: It used a nonvalidated short form of a parent report attachment measure, and face-to-face interviews were used for the early-institutionalized group, whereas phone interviews were used for the other two samples. The findings of this investigation confirm those of Singer, Brodzinsky, Ramsay, Steer, and Waters (1985) that infants adopted in the first months show the same rates of security as those reared by their biological parents.

Nonclinical Samples

Other studies from nonclinical populations have also related attachment in childhood to psychopathology. In a middle-class sample of 6-year-olds, children given the controlling classification had higher rates of parent- and teacher-rated aggression (Solomon, George, & De Jong, 1995). No elevated rate of problems was found for either concurrently avoidant or ambivalent children. Further evidence supporting the hypothesis of a concurrent relation between the controlling classification and teacher-rated maladaptation was found in a study of normative French Canadian children ages 5 to 7 (Moss, Parent, Gosselin, Rousseau, & St.-Laurent, 1996). They reported that children with controlling classifications were more likely to show some form of teacher-reported problem behavior over a 2-year period. Ambivalent children showed higher rates of externalizing problems than did any other attachment group, and none of the groups was distinguishable on internalizing problems. Fagot and Pears (1996) examined how attachment security at age 3 related to teacher ratings of behavioral and peer problems at age 7. This study was distinctive in using the Crittenden (1992) model for scoring attachment at age 3. Follow-up findings indicated that children who were labeled "coercive" at age 3 showed greater rates of behavioral problems and peer problems at age 7, compared to children labeled "secure" or "defended."

Two recent studies have examined the concurrent relations between attachment and peer relations. Cohn (1990), studying a sample of 6-year-olds, found that boys with insecure attachments to their mothers were perceived as more aggressive by peers and were reported by their teachers to show greater behavior problems. No such associations were found for girls. Turner (1991), studying a sample of English 4-year-olds, reported that boys with concurrent insecurity with their mothers showed more aggression, disruption, and attention seeking in preschool than did secure boys. Insecure girls showed more dependent and less assertive and controlling behavior than did secure girls, but no differences were found in aggression or disruption.

Developmental Models of Pathways from Early Attachment to Later Disorder

There are a number of issues involved in the use of developmental models that link earlier patterns of attachment to later disorder. These include, first, the possibility of specific linkages between *types* of insecurity and later outcomes and disorders. Second, in order for developmental models to be useful and testable, there is a need to specify processes through which early attachment may influence the course of development. Third, there is a need for clearer conceptualization of the role of attachment insecurity in complex models of risk. These issues are reviewed below.

Are There Specific Links between Attachment Patterns and Later Disorders?

Beginning with Bowlby (1973), several theorists have proposed models of the differing developmental pathways that may ensue from variations in early attachment patterns. Sroufe (1983), for instance, has proposed that both avoidant and ambivalent infants may develop externalizing behavior problems, but that the meaning of their behavior and the specific manifestations may differ in predictable ways (although current diagnostic criteria may fail to differentiate them). An avoidant child may develop a hostile, aggressive, antisocial pattern in response to experience with a rejecting and emotionally unavailable caregiver. The underlying anger, which is not directed to its source, may be manifested through lying, bullying others, and blaming and being insensitive to others. The ambivalent child, on the other hand, may be easily overstimulated, showing impulsivity, restlessness, short attention span, and low frustration tolerance. Both children may be aggressive, but for different reasons.

Rubin, Hymel, Mills, and Rose-Krasnor (1991) suggest that avoidant children are more likely than ambivalent children to become disruptive preschoolers. In a model that includes child temperament, socioecological factors, and parental social setting and attitudes, as well as attachment effects, they delineate a pathway in which an anxious, unresponsive, rejecting mother responds to an avoidant infant in an authoritarian, hostile manner, sometimes resulting in aggressive child behavior. In contrast, they predict that unresponsive parenting with an ambivalent infant is more likely to lead to internalizing problems.

A review of findings regarding the specificity of linkages between avoidant attachment and later externalizing problems, and between ambivalent attachment and internalizing disorders, is inconclusive. The strongest links have been found in the Minnesota Parent–Child Project, in which findings at two different time periods showed differentiation. First, teacher ratings in middle childhood showed that infant avoidance was linked to later aggressiveness, and ambivalence was linked to passive withdrawal; however, relations were significant only for boys (Renken et al., 1989). Second, at age 17, infant ambivalent attachment was linked specifically to anxiety disorders (Warren et al., 1997). At other ages (e.g., later preschool years and early adolescence), clear differentiation was not detected. Furthermore, findings by Moss et al. (1996) and Goldberg (1997) do not support these differential pathways.

Although models linking avoidant versus ambivalent attachment to later maladaptation have utility, their utility may be limited because they do not address the newly developed insecure attachment category of disorganized/disoriented (Main & Hesse, 1990). As noted earlier, the disorganized pattern is shown at high rates in samples in which there is parent psychopathology, child abuse, or very high social risk (Carlson, Cicchetti, Barnett, & Braunwald, 1989; Crittenden, 1988; Lyons-Ruth et al., 1987; O'Connor et al., 1987; Spieker & Booth, 1988). Given these high rates of D classifications in children who are at risk for psychopathology, this pattern requires further exploration if early attachment is to be linked with later psychopathology (Ogawa et al., 1997). Lyons-Ruth (1996) has reviewed the current literature on the relations between the D classification and aggression, as well as its potential roots in intergenerational risk factors experienced by caregivers. Unfortunately, in comparison to other infancy classifications, there are not sufficient data regarding the home environment in which the D pattern develops. Main and Hesse (1990) postulate that the traumatized mother of the disorganized infant is unpredictably frightening to her child, and that disorganization is a response to this fear and inconsistency. Given the high rate of the disorganized pattern in infants who are at high biological risk, either perinatally (from alcohol or drug abuse, smoking, and/or nutrition deficiencies), postnatally (from child abuse), or both, there is a need for further investigation of potential neurological and neuropsychological correlates of this pattern. (See also George & Solomon, Chapter 28, and Lyons-Ruth & Jacobvitz, Chapter 23, this volume.)

From the findings to date, it appears that attachment insecurity may be an important but nonspecific risk factor that increases risk for a number of forms of psychopathology. There are not yet sufficient longitudinal data from infancy to permit researchers to ascertain whether specific pathways exist between types of insecure attachment and differing forms of psychopathology. This is a promising area for further research. It is also clear that insecure attachment is not itself a measure of psychopathology, but may set a trajectory that, along with other risk factors, may increase the risk for either externalizing or internalizing psychopathology (Rutter, 1985). Further study of the role of attachment as both a mediator and a moderator in developmental psychopathology is warranted.

Models of Continuity and the Process of Developmental Transformation: The Contributions of Early Attachment Relations

In order to consider the possibility that a child's attachment may be a cause (not just a predictor or a correlate) of later behavioral maladaptation, theoretically based process models must be posited (Greenberg & Speltz, 1988; Sroufe & Fleeson, 1986; Waters, Kondo-Ikemura, Posada, & Richters, 1991). Four complementary processes, other than continuity of care (Thompson, Chapter 13, this volume), have been delineated that may link early attachment to later maladaptation: cognitive–affective structures; the neurophysiology of emotion regulation; observed behaviors; and functional, motivational processes.

The first process involves the development of representations of relationships (Main, Kaplan, & Cassidy, 1985). Attachment theory posits that the particular organization of infant attachment behavior is maintained at both the behavioral and representational levels. Thus sensitive and responsive parenting during infancy not only leads to differences in observable attachment patterns

directed toward caregivers, but also leads the child to develop a cognitive–affective schema or "working model" of both self and others. The working model includes the child's expectations regarding intimacy and care from others, and is believed to selectively affect perception, cognition, and motivation (Bretherton, 1985; Bretherton & Munholland, Chapter 5, this volume; Sroufe & Fleeson, 1986). As the toddler's representational skills and understanding of affective states become increasingly complex, these models undergo further specification and differentiation. Main et al. (1985) define the internal working model "as a set of conscious and/or unconscious rules for the organization of information relevant to attachment, and for obtaining and limiting access to that information, i.e., to information regarding attachment related experiences, feelings, ideations" (pp. 66–69). Thus individual differences in attachment behavior patterns are viewed as manifestations of individual differences in the child's internal working models of specific relationships.

At present there is little understanding of how resistant the child's working models are to revision, given change in the quality of his or her relationships or traumatic experiences, or whether there are any specific ages/stages during childhood in which such models may become extremely resistant to revision. With age, these models are believed to become increasingly resistant to change. As working models stabilize, they serve as a conservative force that resists change by biasing perception of the actions and desires of others (Bowlby, 1973).

Because there are reciprocal linkages between the working models of the self and of attachment figures, it is believed that secure attachments will also lead to generalized perceptions of competence and self-esteem. Furthermore, when a secure and trusting bond forms between parent and child, the parent reciprocally develops a favorable working model of the child—one that includes attributions of responsiveness, warmth, and trust, and thus sets the stage for reciprocal and cooperative interactions (George & Solomon, Chapter 28, this volume; Richters & Waters, 1991). Thus one mechanism through which insecure attachment may play a causal role in later maladaptation is the crystallization of working models characterized by anger, mistrust, anxiety, and fear (Main, 1995). This model fits well with recent work on attributional biases in children with both internalizing and externalizing difficulties. For example, Dodge (1991) has hypothesized that insecure attachments may lead to hostile working models containing attributional biases in which hypervigilance and unresolved child anger lead to reactive aggression. Support for this proposition was provided by Cassidy, Kirsh, Scolton, and Parke (1996) in a study of kindergarten and first-grade children. In response to hypothetical peer dilemmas, they reported that children with higher security scores (security was assessed with the Main & Cassidy [1985] procedure) showed more positive representations of why events happened, how the hypothetical child would feel, and what would happen next. Thus the study provides evidence that attachment security may be linked to representational models of the self in peer relations.

A second possible process by which attachment may affect later disorder is this: It may bring about changes in emotion regulation that have effects on neural organization. Although these ideas are quite speculative at this point, a number of theorists have elaborated ways in which patterns of emotion regulation established in early childhood may substantially alter both the fear-conditioning processes in the amygdala (LeDoux, 1995) and the development of connections between the limbic system and the prefrontal cortex (Schore, 1996). There may also be linkages among affective communication, attachment processes, and neural organization (Bretherton, 1995; Greenberg & Snell, 1997; Grossmann, 1995). Because both attachment and prefrontal processing have been linked to both depression (Dawson, Hessl, & Frey, 1994) and externalizing disorders (Goleman, 1995), further investigation of this potential pathway is warranted.

A third process by which early attachment may be linked to some forms of later maladaptation is at the level of observable behavior. We (Greenberg et al., 1993) have hypothesized that some of the behaviors labeled "disruptive" in young children may also be viewed as evidence of attachment strategies with considerable power to regulate caregiving patterns, especially when other and more adaptive strategies have been ineffective or unavailable to the children. Thus disruptive behaviors such as whining, noncompliance, and other negative forms of attention seeking may in some cases serve the function of regulating parent or teacher proximity to, and monitoring of, a child under conditions of past or present nonoptimal care and/or insecurity. Although these attachment strategies have some short-term adaptive significance (e.g., caregiver physical or "verbal" proximity is often reduced

by child negativity), they are likely to serve as a "setting" condition for the development of maladaptive family processes.

In a similar manner, one might consider Main and Hesse's (1990) hypothesis that because of the absence of a coherent and predictable pattern of responding, the disorganized (D) infant begins to take control of the management of aspects of the parent–child relationship during the preschool years. This pattern of role reversal in the preschooler, although helping to maintain connection to the parent, evidences some of the features that index such a child's behavioral difficulties (e.g., bossiness, domination). Finally, the ambivalent pattern, highlighted by immature behaviors that often mix anger and dependency, may also illustrate how behaviors that serve the attachment system (need to maintain proximity and attention of caregivers) may themselves be symptoms or precursors of a variety of later maladaptations (Cassidy, 1995; Cassidy & Berlin, 1994). At the broader family level, Marvin and Stewart (1990) discuss how such patterns of child behavior may both serve the attachment needs of the child and fit larger family patterns of maladaptation that have been identified by family theorists.

A fourth process by which attachment may contribute to maladaptation relates to its motivational properties during social intercourse. Attachment may promote a generalized positive or resistant social orientation in the child, providing differential levels of readiness for socialization (Richters & Waters, 1991). Children with warm, contingent relations in early life are more likely to comply with parent controls and directives during toddlerhood and the preschool years (Maccoby & Martin, 1983; Sroufe & Fleeson, 1986). Thus attachment processes may provide the "motivational cornerstone" in explaining how a prosocial orientation develops and how identification processes proceed in early and middle childhood (Waters et al., 1991). As such, attachment may mediate aspects of motivation that deter children from deviance and create the positive bonding (discussed in social control theories) that protects children from delinquency and social and personal destructiveness (Hawkins, Arthur, & Catalano, 1995).

The Role of Attachment in Risk Factor Models

At times, attachment theory and research have been misunderstood as stating that early attachment relations are necessarily stable and inexorably lead to either healthy or pathological outcomes. This misunderstanding may be in part the result of the developmental processes in subdisciplines of psychology. As attachment research has now been clearly established and attachment researchers have begun to work in closer collaboration with researchers and theorists from different traditions (e.g., temperament, neuropsychology, family processes), the role of attachment in psychopathology is becoming more clearly delineated.

As the preceding review indicates, attachment processes have shown both predictive and concurrent associations with maladaptation in childhood and early adolescence. With few exceptions, however, it is unlikely that insecure attachment is either a necessary or a sufficient cause of later disorder, and in some cases it may in fact be an effect of the disorder itself (Cicchetti et al., 1995). We (Greenberg et al., 1993) have proposed a risk factor model for conceptualizing the early-starter pattern of disruptive behavior problems, which incorporates attachment as a critical dimension. The four general risk domains include child characteristics (temperament, biological vulnerability, neurocognitive function); quality of early attachment relations; parental management/socialization strategies; and family ecology (e.g., family life stress and trauma, family instrumental resources, intra- and extrafamilial social support). It is likely that this risk factor model has generality, and that these same general classes of risk factors are also likely to contribute to the development of early internalizing disorders (anxiety disorders, childhood depression, somatization, and dissociative states). However, as Rubin et al. (1991) and others (Manassis & Bradley, 1994; Shaw & Bell, 1993) have hypothesized, it is likely that different aspects or dimensions of these general risk factors may predict different disorders. For example, temperament may be considered a general risk factor for disorder; reactive versions may be related to externalizing problems, whereas inhibited and withdrawn types create risk for internalizing difficulties. Furthermore, these differing temperamental qualities may interact differentially in moderating other risk factors. Similarly, in the domain of parent management, parental punitiveness and underinvolvement may create risk for externalizing problems (Patterson, DeBaryshe, & Ramsey, 1989). In contrast, parental overcontrol and the absence of autonomy promotion may predict internalizing difficulties (Allen, Hauser, & Bor-

man-Spurell, 1996; Kobak, Sudler, & Gamble, 1991). Few data, however, indicate that any of the four domains of risk factors *alone* directly causes later problems. That is, taken alone, an atypical temperament, or family chaos/poor home environment, or an insecure attachment, or poor parental management is unlikely to "cause" disorder.

Figure 21.1 is a graphic model of these risk factors. The purpose of this model is not to illustrate the actual degree of overlap between risk factors (this will vary among individuals and is also unknown in most populations), but only to illustrate that in a particular case a child may have none of the four risk factors, only one, or more than one overlapping factor. The circle for each of the four risk factors denotes high risk status on the factor (e.g., insecure attachment, high family risk, atypical temperament, ineffective parenting). Thus, any child/family ecology may show none (in which case the child would not be represented in Figure 21.1 at all), one, or more of these factors. The cross-hatched area represents types of cases in which the probability of a significant psychopathology during childhood rises significantly above the base rate.

Because the model involves four major risk factors, a two-dimensional drawing cannot adequately represent all possible interactions (e.g., behavior problems may occur in the presence of only family stressors and poor discipline—an interaction that would be visible in a three-dimensional model). The model considers the assessment of risk in each domain as being both qualitative (cutoff scores for risk classification can be derived) and quantitative (levels of severity within each risk factor may be meaningful and could be portrayed on a fourth dimension). Although a diagram is by nature static, the relations among these four factors and maladaptation are expected to be transactional; significant variations may occur in risk status across time, especially in family adversity as a result of nonnormative traumas. Furthermore, it is likely that some domains are of more importance to certain disorders. For example, ineffective parenting may be found to contribute more to externalizing than to internalizing disorders (Patterson et al., 1989), whereas child trauma may be more related via attachment processes to dissociative disorder (Liotti, 1995; Ogawa et al., 1997). Figure 21.1 does not indicate proximal versus distal influences or the possible pathways by which the influence of each factor may be mediated. Indeed, these pathways will be quite different depending

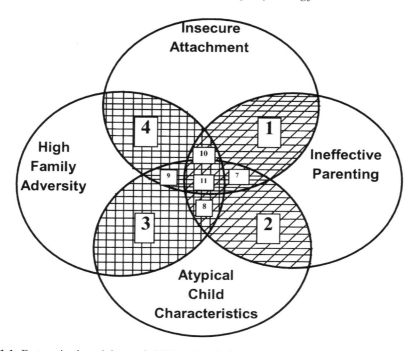

FIGURE 21.1. Factors in the etiology of childhood maladaptation. Areas 1 through 4, two-factor intersection (visible); Area 5 (high family adversity and parent management), two-factor intersection (invisible); Area 6 (insecure attachment and child characteristics), two-factor intersection (invisible); Areas 7 through 10, three-factor intersections; Area 11, four-factor intersections.

upon the number and type of risk factors involved, their developmental timing, and their sequence. Furthermore, one should consider other domains with further development. It is necessary to add peer relations at about the time of school entry (Parker et al., 1995), and by middle childhood the domain of neighborhood ecology is likely to be a risk factor for some forms of disorder.

The role that the sex of the child plays in potentiating risk is as yet unclear. Current findings indicate that attachment is often moderated by sex: Insecure attachment is more often linked to the development of identifiable (usually externalizing) problems in early and middle childhood in boys. These findings fit well with the generally greater vulnerability of boys to high-risk environments as well as to poverty (Duncan, Brooks-Gunn, & Klebanov, 1994; Zaslow & Hayes, 1986). It is not clear whether this greater vulnerability is due to the higher base rate of such problems in boys in middle childhood, and further findings on both boys and girls in the adolescent period will be necessary to clarify this issue.

It appears evident that with the intersection of two, three, or four risk factors in a child's ecology, there is an increasing probability of later problems. Numerous studies reviewed above have demonstrated this empirically (e.g., Erickson et al., 1985; Lyons-Ruth et al., 1995; Shaw et al., 1997). We (Greenberg, DeKlyen, Speltz, & Endriga, 1997) have examined this four-factor model in order to predict the classification of oppositional, clinic-referred preschoolers compared to normally behaving children. Using logistic regression, we found that child characteristics, parental management strategies (harsh punishment), and concurrent attachment security all provided unique information in differentiating the two groups; the fourth factor of family ecology did not provide additional unique information for the sample. In addition, results indicated that it was extremely unlikely that a child with risk in less than two domains would receive a diagnosis, whereas clinic children were 34 times as likely to have risk in all four domains.

It should be considered that different combinations of risk factors (e.g., insecure attachment and family adversity vs. difficult temperament and poor parent management) may lead to differing disorders (i.e., differences in the symptoms or natural course) requiring different treatments (Speltz, 1990). Campbell (1991) presents a cluster analysis in which three different types of families were identified by distinct sets of risk factors.

Given the large number of possible combinations between factors identified in Figure 21.1, a few exemplar patterns may be identified. The first pattern is one in which all risk factors are present: Early insecure attachment, family stress, and difficult temperament interact with poor parent management in the preschool years (Rubin et al., 1991). However, depending on the type/form of insecurity and the nature of the atypical temperament, different forms of disorder may eventuate. A second important pattern highlights the child's characteristics. In this scenario, a child's high activity level and temperamental difficulty may combine with either lax or very harsh management strategies during the preschool years, leading to a vicious cycle of parent irritability and child defiance. In this case, only child characteristics and their interaction with parent management may be of etiological significance, and infant attachment security may not play a putative role.

A third pattern may indicate the role of factors occurring only during the preschool period, with little risk being evident in infancy. In one possible scenario, family disruption (divorce or parent death) or other family trauma may disrupt parenting practices. Again, insecure attachment may not have occurred during infancy and thus may not be of etiological significance or increase risk. However, the premorbid quality of attachment may alter the significance of the traumatic event. Given this patterning of risk factors, in some cases secure early attachment may serve to protect the child from negative outcomes in spite of family disruption, breakdown of parental management, and so forth. We (Greenberg et al., 1991), as well as Campbell (1990), have presented clinical case studies of children with externalizing problems in which it appeared that parent–child attachment was concurrently secure. In some of these cases, it appeared that symptoms were primarily related to recent psychosocial stressors, uncomplicated by a history of difficult temperament, poor parent–child interaction, or parental psychopathology. In other cases, both biological vulnerability and family history of trauma and disorder were apparent. Similarly, Manassis et al. (1994) have reported a small percentage of children of anxious mothers who were secure, and

have shown security to be at least in part affected by the family ecology.

The development and refinement of risk factor models will require longitudinal prospective studies of normal and high-risk children in which these (and possibly other risk factors) are gathered across developmental periods. Although epidemiologically based large samples are critical to this task, longitudinal case studies and studies of samples selected with strong theoretical rationales can also provide important contributions.

THE ROLE OF DEVELOPMENTAL PSYCHOPATHOLOGY IN UNDERSTANDING ATTACHMENT

The Measurement Roadblock

The Preschool Years and Late Adolescence/Adulthood

Attachment theory derives in part from a long tradition of utilizing clinical case studies as a means of deriving theories regarding developmental pathways to disorders. One of the unique aspects of the theory is that it bridges basic theory and research in developmental, evolutionary, and cognitive psychology (Bowlby, 1969/1982, 1973, 1980). Unfortunately, in its transition from the child clinic to its normative study in infancy, it has often been reified in a way that has reduced attachment research to validated research paradigms by which aspects of attachment have been carefully assessed (primarily the strange situation). This was surely not the intention of Ainsworth or others (Ainsworth & Marvin, 1995), and it has led to limitations in measurement in both normal and clinical populations. There are two issues to be explored regarding both theory and measurement. The first is that of alternative measures and their development. The second is the question of how returning to the clinic might facilitate this development.

As detailed by others (Ainsworth, 1989; Cicchetti et al., 1995; Greenberg, Cicchetti, & Cummings, 1990; Main & Cassidy, 1988; Crowell, Fraley, & Shaver, Chapter 20, this volume; Solomon & George, Chapter 14, this volume), there have been dramatic advances in the measurement of attachment in both early childhood and later adolescence and adulthood. As discussed earlier in this chapter, the use of separation and reunion situations has led to significant findings, as have Q-sort assessments. Furthermore, the use of the AAI (George et al., 1984) in late adolescence and adulthood has quickly been appropriated by psychopathologists, and this instrument is providing important information regarding the contribution of representations of close relationships to adult psychopathologies (see Dozier et al., Chapter 22, this volume).

Middle Childhood

Considerably less progress has been made in the development of measures for use with children between age 5 and midadolescence. Three types of measures have been developed. The first type includes behavioral measures of reunion behavior (Main & Cassidy, 1985); to date, however, these have not been utilized after age 7 (Easterbrooks et al., 1993). The second type consists of representational measures of attachment, and these have primarily been used with 3- to 6-year-olds (Bretherton, Ridgeway, & Cassidy, 1990; Cassidy, 1988; Main et al., 1985; Oppenheim, Nir, Warren & Emde, 1997; Oppenheim & Waters, 1995; Slough & Greenberg, 1990). A number of studies have shown these measures to be concurrently related to measures of reunion behavior in community samples (Cassidy, 1988; Shouldice & Stevenson-Hinde, 1992; Slough & Greenberg, 1997). To date, there has been little application of these measures to children with early disorders. We (Greenberg et al., 1997), however, found that the attachment narratives appeared to underrate insecurity in a clinic-referred sample and to overrate insecurity somewhat in the controls.

For children above age 6, a number of self-report measures have been utilized; however, without other validated measures of attachment to relate them to, their validity is uncertain (Cook, Greenberg, & Kusche, 1995; Kerns, Klepac, & Cole, 1996; Lynch & Cicchetti, 1991). Several significant difficulties impede further measure development in this age range. The first is that there is an assumption that observational paradigms will not reveal individual differences at this period of life. Second, at these ages children may be less able or willing to reveal their representations of relationships in an interview similar to the AAI. Although the development of measures that may be sensitive for the normative populations in middle childhood is sorely needed, investigation of children with a variety of disorders in which attachment is believed either to play a direct role or to potentiate risk may pro-

vide important advances. Furthermore, there is a great clinical need to develop measures of attachment that can be utilized to provide assessment benchmarks in many clinical situations involving children (e.g., decisions regarding removal from the home, the effects of foster care, adaptation to late adoption, etc.) (Pilowsky & Kates, 1995). It is likely, in spite of the above-stated assumption, that observational measures may ultimately prove useful in middle childhood, but this will require a fine-grained analysis and possibly more age-appropriate stressors.

Evolving Standardized Measurement Models from the Clinical Setting

Studying clinical samples in middle childhood in which patterns of insecurity are more marked may be a useful strategy in beginning to identify such patterns. Such a strategy would also deal with a further concern raised about both child and adult measures of attachment; that is, because they have been derived from normative samples, they may not capture important aspects of attachment relationships in clinical populations (Adam et al., 1995; Crittenden, 1995; Goldberg, 1997; Levine & Tuber, 1993). Given both these concerns, it is remarkable that there has been little study of childhood difficulties that are believed to relate to attachment. I briefly discuss three common conditions in childhood that may yield important insights: aggressive, depressive, and anxiety disorders (also see Alexander, 1992, regarding early sexual abuse, and Liotti, 1995, regarding early attachment and dissociative disorders).

Childhood Aggression and Conduct Problems

Conduct problems in early childhood have received considerable attention from attachment researchers. Reasons for this interest include their early appearance (and thus the application of existing attachment measures), as well as the fact that both theory and research have shown attachment to be a significant risk factor for such problems (Greenberg et al., 1993). Findings at present (reviewed earlier) lead to the conclusion that both avoidant and controlling/disorganized children (as well as children classified as "coercive," according to Crittenden's [1992] classification system) may be at greatest risk for conduct problems. Recently a number of alternative theories have been proposed to explain how attachment may be related to conduct problems.

Solomon et al. (1995) hypothesize that the absence of a coherent strategy, rather than security versus insecurity, is linked to maladaptation. This hypothesis does not fit well with three separate cohorts of aggressive children reported earlier, in which high rates of aggression were related to avoidance. Furthermore, findings from the Minnesota Parent–Child Project also indicated that early avoidance is related to later aggression.

Research on the links between attachment relations and later adolescent delinquency and adult criminality (as well as antisocial personality disorder) are needed. Fonagy et al. (1997) present a model that links early attachment to later attachment and criminality. They hypothesize that internal working models of specific attachment figures are globalized during the adolescent years into more generalized relations, often discussed as attachment or bonding to social institutions (Hawkins et al., 1995; Hirschi, 1969). That is, parent–child attachment bonds are reconfigured as bonds to social institutions (e.g., schools and businesses) and the adults who represent them (e.g., teachers and employers). Children who show a lack of bonding to institutions, as well as deviant peer relations, are at significantly greater risk for substance use and criminal careers (Brook, Whiteman, & Finch, 1993: Le Blanc, 1994). Fonagy et al. hypothesize that secure early and continued attachments facilitate greater awareness of the mental states of others, and that this "mentalizing" both inhibits malevolent acts and facilitates further relationship building during childhood. Thus insecure attachment is linked to criminality via the absence of developmentally appropriate consideration of the needs and feelings of others, as well as via deficient bonding to social institutions. Fonagy et al. further hypothesize that children with avoidant attachments may be most likely to follow this pathway. Although few data support these propositions, they raise a number of research questions. First, what is the relationship between "mentalizing" or "theory of mind" and attachment relations in older children? Second, if this relationship is specific to conduct problems, might such relations be absent in depression or other disorders? Third, what is the developmental process by which specific working models become generalized, and when they are discrepant, which model may affect the adolescent transition (Bretherton, 1985)? Finally, if the theory is supported, what will counterexamples (i.e., children with insecure internal working models who do bond to social institutions) tell us about the process?

Childhood Depression

Although there has been considerable theorizing about the role attachment may play in the pathogenesis of depression (Cicchetti & Cummings, 1990; Kobak et al., 1991), there has as yet been no investigation of attachment behavior or representational models in children with dysthymia or major depression. Although adolescent samples have shown the expected relations between attachment and depression (Dozier et al., Chapter 22, this volume), and children of depressive parents show higher rates of insecurity, study of children with depression is clearly a next step in the research agenda. As with conduct problems, both clinicians and researchers should consider the fact that in some cases attachment relations will either have no relation to the disorder or may be an effect of the disorders. Only careful case histories of attachment patterns, as well as contemporaneous assessments, will illuminate these pathways.

Childhood Anxiety Disorders

Given that anxiety can be considered the fundamental condition underlying insecure attachment (Bowlby, 1973), it is both surprising and curious that there has been so little attention paid to anxiety disorders and their relation to attachment (Cassidy, 1995). I found no published studies of attachment in any childhood population with anxiety disorders. This lack of research is most surprising in the area of separation anxiety disorder (SAD). Although there has been considerable theorizing by clinicians and developmental psychopathologists about the role of parent–child relations in SAD (Klein, 1994; Mannasis & Bradley, 1994; Thurber, 1996), little is known about either the behavioral or representational patterns of children with SAD and how these may be related to age of onset of SAD, parent–child behavior, or recent family or child trauma. Furthermore, it is not clear what patterns of parent–child communication (e.g., parental communication that focuses on the symptoms and their concern, reinforcement of dependent and anxious behavior in the attachment relationship, maternal distress) may lead to different manifestations or courses of the disorder.

Because the symptoms of SAD may be normal responses in early childhood, it is only when these symptoms are both excessive and developmentally inappropriate that SAD can be diagnosed. The anxiety must occur specifically in response to anticipated separation from home or an attachment figure and must persist for at least 4 weeks to meet DSM-IV diagnostic criteria. Community studies indicate that it occurs in approximately 3.5% of early adolescents (Anderson, Williams, McGee, & Silva, 1987; Bowen, Offord, & Boyle, 1990), but little is known about its prevalence in younger children. It is often accompanied by somatic complaints, as well as more global symptoms of anxiety (Francis, Last, & Strauss, 1987), and it is marked by age-related symptoms: greater crying and attempts to resist separation in younger children, verbalization of fear and somatization in middle childhood, and greater muscle rigidity in adolescents (Ollendick & Francis, 1988).

In a study comparing mothers of children diagnosed with SAD versus phobias, mothers of SAD were much more likely to report their own anxiety-based school refusal than were mothers of phobic children or controls (Last & Strauss, 1990). Furthermore, SAD can be reliably distinguished from both specific school phobia (Bernstein, Svingen, & Garfinkel, 1990) and DSM-III-R overanxious disorder (Morreau & Follett, 1993), and it is associated with gender identity disorder (Zucker, Bradley, & Sullivan, 1996). SAD is also believed to be a risk factor for a variety of adult psychiatric disorders, including depression, agoraphobia, and panic disorder. Recently Shear (1996) has provided a potential model of the role of attachment in the development of both agoraphobia and panic. Although family systems models (Kearney & Silverman, 1995), behavioral models, and psychopharmacological models have been utilized in the treatment of SAD (Klein, 1994), attachment theory has had little impact on either case conceptualization or treatment processes. This is remarkable, given the attention paid to the topic by Bowlby himself, and longitudinal studies of children with SAD are clearly a next step. Marvin (1992) has noted relations between SAD-like symptoms, experience of loss, and psychogenic pain, and he has elaborated a treatment model that incorporates both attachment and family systems theory.

FAMILY SYSTEMS, ATTACHMENT, AND PSYCHOPATHOLOGY

As the study of attachment in childhood has developed, there has been increasing interest in its study in systems larger than the dyad. This has been especially important in clinical settings, given the important role of family systems models in the treatment of childhood disorders. There have been several illuminating formulations of the relation between attachment theory and family systems theory (Byng-Hall, 1995; Byng-Hall & Stevenson-Hinde, 1991; Jacobvitz, Morgan, Kretchmar, & Morgan, 1991; Marvin & Stewart, 1990). Empirical research has indicated the indirect role father behavior plays in affecting infant–mother attachment (Das Eiden & Leonard, 1996), the role of father attachment in child adjustment (Cowan, Cohn, Cowan, & Pearson, 1996; DeKlyen et al., 1998), and the role of intergenerational patterns (Benoit & Parker, 1994; Spieker & Bensley, 1994). Furthermore, the role of attachment processes in psychopathology is complicated, and family systems considerations will be essential to understanding the role of attachment processes (Radke-Yarrow et al., 1995). The development of diagnostic models of attachment processes at the level of the family system is a considerable challenge. The emergent properties at this level of analysis may be important in explaining how unexpected patterns of attachment between children and their individual parents are linked to the development of psychopathology.

SUMMARY

The study of attachment and its relation to developmental pathways of normality and psychopathology has made significant advances in the past decade. Research with both normal and clinical populations has led to this improved knowledge base. Advances have also been made both in attachment theory regarding the processes of transmission, and in developmental psychopathology regarding the various ways that attachment processes may affect divergent pathways for different forms of maladaptation. Greater attention to the validation of attachment indices in early and middle childhood is necessary if researchers are to fully investigate the transactional relations between attachment and both risk and psychopathology. Longitudinal studies of representative normative populations, high-risk populations, and samples in which there are specific forms of maladaptation are needed to provide a fuller picture of the role of attachment in risk for psychopathology in childhood.

REFERENCES

Adam, K. S., Sheldon Keller, A. E., & West, M. (1995). Attachment organization and vulnerability to loss, separation, and abuse in disturbed adolescents. In S. Goldberg, R. Muir, & J. Kerr (Eds.), *Attachment theory: Social, developmental, and clinical perspectives* (pp. 309–341). Hillsdale, NJ: Analytic Press.

Ainsworth, M. D. S. (1989). Attachments beyond infancy. *American Psychologist, 44,* 709–716.

Ainsworth, M. D. S., Blehar, M. C., Waters, E., & Wall, S. (1978). *Patterns of attachment.* Hillsdale, NJ: Erlbaum.

Ainsworth, M. D. S., & Marvin, R. S. (1995). On the shaping of attachment theory and research: An interview with Mary D. S. Ainsworth (Fall 1994). In E. Waters, B. E. Vaughn, G. Posada, & K. Kondo-Ikemura (Eds.), Caregiving, cultural, and cognitive perspectives on secure-base behavior and working models: New growing points of attachment theory and research. *Monographs of the Society for Research in Child Development, 60*(2–3, Serial No. 244), 3–21.

Alexander, P. C. (1992). Application of attachment theory to the study of sexual abuse. *Journal of Consulting and Clinical Psychology, 60,* 185–195.

Allen, J. P., Hauser, S. T., & Borman-Spurell, E. (1996). Attachment theory as a framework for understanding sequelae of severe adolescent psychopathology: An 11-year follow-up study. *Journal of Consulting and Clinical Psychology, 64,* 254–263.

Anderson, J. C., Williams, S., McGee, R. A., & Silva, P. (1987). DSM-III disorders in preadolescent children: Prevalence in a large sample form a general population. *Archives of General Psychiatry, 44,* 69–76.

Bates, J. E., Maslin, C. A., & Frankel, K. A. (1985). Attachment security, mother–child interaction, and temperament as predictors of behavior problem ratings at age three years. In I. Bretherton & E. Waters (Eds.), Growing points of attachment theory and research. *Monographs of the Society for Research in Child Development, 50*(1–2, Serial No. 209), 167–193.

Bates, J. E., Bayles, K., Bennett, D. S., Ridge, B., & Brown, M. M. (1991). Origins of externalizing behavior problems at eight years of age. In D. J. Pepler & K. H. Rubin (Eds.), *The development and treatment of childhood aggression* (pp. 93–120). Hillsdale, NJ: Erlbaum.

Belsky, J., & Nezworski, T. (Eds.). (1988). *Clinical implications of attachment.* Hillsdale, NJ: Erlbaum.

Belsky, J., Rosenberger, K., & Crnic, K. (1995). The origins of attachment security: Classical and contextual determinants. In S. Goldberg, R. Muir, & J. Kerr (Eds.), *Attachment theory: Social, developmental, and clinical perspectives* (pp. 153–183). Hillsdale, NJ: Analytic Press.

Benoit, D., & Parker, K. C. H. (1994). Stability and transmission of attachment across three generations. *Child Development, 65,* 1444–1456.

Bernstein, G. A., Svingen, P. H., & Garfinkel, B. D. (1990). School phobia: Patterns of family functioning. *Journal of*

the American Academy of Child and Adolescent Psychiatry, 29, 24–30.

Bowen, R. C., Offord, D. R., & Boyle, M. H. (1990). The prevalence of overanxious disorder and separation anxiety disorder: Results for the Ontario Child Health Study. *Journal of the American Academy of Child and Adolescent Psychiatry, 29,* 753–758.

Bowlby, J. (1953). *Child care and the growth of love.* Harmondsworth, England: Penguin.

Bowlby, J. (1969/1982). *Attachment and loss: Vol. 1. Attachment* (2nd ed.). New York: Basic Books.

Bowlby, J. (1973). *Attachment and loss: Vol. 2. Separation.* New York: Basic Books.

Bowlby, J. (1980). *Attachment and loss: Vol. 3. Loss.* New York: Basic Books.

Bowlby, J. (1988). *A secure base.* New York: Basic Books.

Bretherton, I. (1985). Attachment theory: Retrospect and prospect. In I. Bretherton & E. Waters (Eds.), Growing points in attachment theory and research. *Monographs of the Society for Research in Child Development, 50*(1–2, Serial No. 209), 3–35.

Bretherton, I. (1992). The origins of attachment theory: John Bowlby and Mary Ainsworth. *Developmental Psychology, 28,* 759–775.

Bretherton, I. (1995). Attachment theory and developmental psychopathology. In D. Cicchetti & S. L. Toth (Eds.), *Rochester Symposium on Developmental Psychopathology: Vol. 6. Emotion, cognition, and representation* (pp. 231–260). Rochester, NY: University of Rochester Press.

Bretherton, I., Ridgeway, D., & Cassidy, J. (1990). Assessing internal working models of the attachment relationship. In M. T. Greenberg, D. Cicchetti, & E. M. Cummings (Eds.), *Attachment in the preschool years: Theory, research, and intervention* (pp. 273–308). Chicago: University of Chicago Press.

Bronfenbrenner, U. (1979). *The ecology of human development.* Cambridge, MA: Harvard University Press.

Brook, J. S., Whiteman, M., & Finch, S. (1993). Role of mutual attachment in drug use: A longitudinal study. *Journal of the American Academy of Child and Adolescent Psychiatry, 32,* 982–989.

Byng-Hall, J. (1995). *Rewriting family scripts.* New York: Guilford Press.

Byng-Hall, J., & Stevenson-Hinde, J. (1991). Attachment relationships within a family system. *Infant Mental Health Journal, 12,* 187–200.

Campbell, S. B. (1990). *Behavior problems in preschool children: Clinical and developmental issues.* New York: Guilford Press.

Campbell, S. B. (1991). Longitudinal studies of active and aggressive preschoolers: Individual differences in early behavior and outcome. In D. Cicchetti & S. L. Toth (Eds.), *Rochester Symposium on Developmental Psychopathology: Vol. 2. Internalizing and externalizing expressions of dysfunction* (pp. 57–90). Hillsdale, NJ: Erlbaum.

Carlson, E. A., & Sroufe, L. A. (1995). Contributions of attachment theory to developmental psychopathology. In D. Cicchetti & D. J. Cohen (Eds.), *Developmental psychopathology* (Vol. 1, pp. 581–617). New York: Wiley.

Carlson, V., Cicchetti, D., Barnett, D., & Braunwald, K. (1989). Disorganized/disoriented attachment relationships in maltreated infants. *Developmental Psychology, 25,* 525–531.

Cassidy, J. (1988). Child–mother attachment and the self in six-year-olds. *Child Development, 59,* 121–134.

Cassidy, J. (1995). Attachment and generalized anxiety disorder. In D. Cicchetti & S. L. Toth (Eds.), *Rochester Symposium on Developmental Psychopathology: Vol. 6. Emotion, cognition, and representation* (pp. 343–370). Rochester, NY: University of Rochester Press.

Cassidy, J., & Berlin, L. J. (1994). The insecure/ambivalent pattern of attachment: Theory and research. *Child Development, 65,* 971–981.

Cassidy, J., Kirsh, S. J., Scolton, K., & Parke, R. D. (1996). Attachment and representation of peer relationships. *Developmental Psychology, 32,* 892–904.

Cassidy, J., & Marvin, R. S., with the MacArthur Working Group on Attachment. (1992). *Attachment organization in three and four year olds: Procedures and coding manual.* Unpublished manuscript, University of Virginia.

Chisholm, K. M., Carter, M. C., Ames, E. W., & Morison, S. J. (1995). Attachment security and indiscriminately friendly behavior in children adopted from Romanian orphanages. *Development and Psychopathology, 7,* 283–294.

Cicchetti, D., & Barnett, D. (1991). Attachment organization in maltreated preschoolers. *Development and Psychopathology, 3,* 397–411.

Cicchetti, D., & Cummings, E. M. (1990). Towards a transactional model of relations between attachment and depression. In M. T. Greenberg, D. Cicchetti, & E. M. Cummings (Eds.), *Attachment in the preschool years: Theory, research, and intervention* (pp. 339–374). Chicago: University of Chicago Press.

Cicchetti, D., Cummings, E. M., Greenberg, M. T., & Marvin, R. S. (1990). An organizational perspective on attachment beyond infancy. In M. T.. Greenberg, D. Cicchetti, & E. M. Cummings (Eds.), *Attachment in the preschool years: Theory, research, and intervention* (pp. 3–49). Chicago: University of Chicago Press.

Cicchetti, D., & Rogosh, F. A. (1997). Equifinality and multifinality in developmental psychopathology. *Development and Psychopathology, 8,* 597–600.

Cicchetti, D., Toth, S. L., & Lynch, M. (1995). Bowlby's dream comes full circle: The application of attachment theory to risk and psychopathology. In T. H. Ollendick & R. J. Prinz (Eds.), *Advances in clinical child psychology* (Vol. 17, pp. 1–75). New York: Plenum Press.

Cohn, D. A. (1990). Child–mother attachment of six-year-olds and social competence at school, *Child Development, 61,* 152–162.

Cohn, J. F., Campbell, S. B., & Ross, S. (1991). Infant response in the still-face paradigm at 6 months predicts avoidant and secure attachment at 12 months. *Development and Psychopathology, 3,* 367–376.

Coie, J. D., Watt, N. F., West, S. G., Hawkins, J. D., Asarnow, J. R., Markman, H. J., Ramey, S. L., Shure, M. B., & Long, B. (1993). The science of prevention: A conceptual framework and some directions for a national research program. *American Psychologist, 48,* 1013–1022.

Cook, E. T., Greenberg, M. T., & Kusche, C. A. (1995, March). *People in my life: Attachment relationships in middle childhood.* Paper presented at the biennial meeting of the Society for Research in Child Development, Indianapolis, IN.

Cowan, P. A., Cohn, D. A., Cowan, C. P., & Pearson, J. L. (1996). Parents' attachment histories and children's externalizing and internalizing behaviors: Exploring family systems models of linkages. *Journal of Consulting and Clinical Psychology, 64,* 53–63.

Crittenden, P. M. (1988). Relationships at risk. In J. Belsky & T. Nezworski (Eds.), *Clinical implications of attachment* (pp. 136–176). Hillsdale, NJ: Erlbaum.

Crittenden, P. M. (1992). Quality of attachment in the preschool years. *Development and Psychopathology, 4,* 209–241.

Crittenden, P. M. (1995). Attachment and psychopathology. In S. Goldberg, R. Muir, & J. Kerr (Eds.), *Attachment theory: Social, developmental, and clinical perspectives* (pp. 367–406). Hillsdale, NJ: Analytic Press.

Crnic, K. A., Greenberg, M. T., & Slough, N. M. (1986). Early stress and social support influence on mothers' and high-risk infants' functioning in late infancy. *Infant Mental Health Journal, 7,* 19–33.

Crockenberg, S. (1981). Infant irritability, mother responsiveness, and social influences on the security of infant–mother attachment. *Child Development, 52,* 857–865.

Crowell, J. A., & Feldman, S. S. (1988). Mothers' internal models of relationships and children's behavioral and developmental status: A study of mother–child interaction. *Child Development, 59,* 1273–1285.

Das Eiden, R., Teti, D. M., & Corns, K. M. (1995). Maternal working model of attachment, marital adjustment, and the parent–child relationship. *Child Development, 66,* 1504–1518.

Das Eiden, R., & Leonard, K. E. (1996). Paternal alcohol use and the mother–infant relationship. *Development and Psychopathology, 8,* 307–324.

Dawson, G., Hessl, D., & Frey, K. (1994). Social influences of early developing biological and behavioral systems related to risk for affective disorder. *Development and Psychopathology, 6,* 759–779.

DeKlyen, M. (1996). Disruptive behavior disorders and intergenerational attachment patterns: A comparison of normal and clinic-referred preschoolers and their mothers. *Journal of Consulting and Clinical Psychology, 64,* 357–365.

DeKlyen, M., Speltz, M. L., & Greenberg, M. T. (1996, January). *Predicting early starting behavior disorders: A clinic sample of preschool oppositional defiant boys.* Paper presented at the International Society for Research in Child and Adolescent Psychopathology, Santa Monica, CA.

DeKlyen, M., Speltz, M. L., & Greenberg, M. T. (1998). Fathers and early starting conduct problems: Positive and negative parenting, father–son attachment, and the marital context. *Clinical Child and Family Psychology Review, 1,* 3–21.

DeMulder, E. K., & Radke-Yarrow, M. (1991) Attachment with affectively ill and well mothers: Concurrent behavioral correlates. *Development and Psychopathology, 3,* 227–242.

Dodge, K. A. (1991). The structure and function of reactive and proactive aggression. In D. J. Pepler & K. H. Rubin (Eds.), *The development and treatment of childhood aggression* (pp. 201–218). Hillsdale, NJ: Erlbaum.

Duncan, G. J., Brooks-Gunn, J., & Klebanov, P. K. (1994). Economic deprivation and early childhood development. *Child Development, 65,* 296–318.

Easterbrooks, M. A. (1989). Quality of attachment to mother and father: Effects of perinatal risk status. *Child Development, 60,* 825–830.

Easterbrooks, M. A., Davidson, C. E., & Chazan, R. (1993). Psychosocial risk, attachment, and behavior problems among school-aged children. *Development and Psychopathology, 5,* 389–402.

Egeland, B., & Sroufe, L. A. (1981). Developmental sequelae of maltreatment in infancy. *New directions for child development: No. 11.* (pp. 77–92). San Francisco: Jossey-Bass.

Elicker, J., Englund, M., & Sroufe, L. A. (1992). Predicting peer competence and peer relations in childhood from early parent–child relationships. In R. Parke & G. Ladd (Eds.), *Family–peer relationships: Models of linkage* (pp. 77–106). Hillsdale, NJ: Erlbaum.

Erickson, M. F., Sroufe, L. A., & Egeland, B. (1985). The relationship between quality of attachment and behavior problems in preschool in a high-risk sample. In I. Bretherton & E. Waters (Eds.), Growing points of attachment theory and research. *Monographs of the Society for Research in Child Development, 50*(1–2, Serial No. 209), 147–156.

Erikson, E. H. (1963). *Childhood and society* (2nd ed.). New York: Norton.

Fagot, B. I., & Kavanaugh, K. (1990). The prediction of antisocial behavior from avoidant attachment classifications. *Child Development, 61*, 864–873.

Fagot, B. I., & Pears, K. C. (1996). Changes in attachment during the third year: Consequences and predictions. *Development and Psychopathology, 8*, 325–344.

Feiring, C., & Lewis, M. (1997). Finality in the eye of the beholder: Multiple sources, time points, multiple paths. *Development and Psychopathology, 8*, 721–733.

Fonagy, P., Target, M., Steele, M., Steele, H. Leigh, T., Levinson, A., & Kennedy, R. (1997). Crime and attachment: Morality, disruptive behavior, borderline personality, crime, and their relationships to security of attachment. In L. Atkinson & K. J. Zucker (Eds.), *Attachment and psychopathology* (pp. 223–274). New York: Guilford Press.

Fonagy, P., Steele, M., Steele, H., Leigh, T., Kennedy, R., Mattoon, G., & Target, M. (1995). Attachment, the reflective self, and borderline states. In S. Goldberg, R. Muir, & J. Kerr (Eds.), *Attachment theory: Social, developmental, and clinical perspectives* (pp. 233–278). Hillsdale, NJ: Analytic Press.

Francis, G., Last, C. G., & Strauss, C. C. (1987). Expression of separation anxiety disorder: The roles of age and gender. *Child Psychiatry and Human Development, 18*, 82–89.

Freud, A. (1965). *The writings of Anna Freud: Vol. 6. Normality and pathology in childhood: Assessments of development.* New York: International Universities Press.

Frodi, A., & Thompson, R. (1985). Infants' affective responses in the Strange Situation: Effects of prematurity and quality of attachment. *Child Development, 56*, 1280–1290.

George, C., Kaplan, N., & Main, M. (1984). *Adult Attachment Interview.* Unpublished manuscript, University of California at Berkeley.

Goldberg, S. (1988). Risk factors in infant–mother attachment. *Canadian Journal of Psychology, 42*, 173–188.

Goldberg, S. (1997). Attachment and childhood behavior problems in normal, at-risk, and clinical samples. In L. Atkinson & K. J. Zucker (Eds.), *Attachment and psychopathology* (pp. 171–195). New York: Guilford Press.

Goldberg, S., Gotowiec, A., & Simmons, R. J. (1995). Infant–mother attachment and behavior problems in healthy and chronically ill preschoolers. *Development and Psychopathology, 7*, 267–282.

Goldberg, S., Lojkasek, M., Minde, K., & Corter, C. (1990). Predictions of behavior problems in children born prematurely. *Development and Psychopathology, 1*, 15–30.

Goldfarb, W. (1955). Emotional and intellectual consequences of psychological deprivation in infancy: A reevaluation. In P. Hoch & D. Zubin (Eds.), *Psychopathology in childhood* (pp. 105–119). New York: Grune & Stratton.

Goleman, D. (1995). *Emotional intelligence.* New York: Bantam.

Greenberg, M. T., Cicchetti, D., & Cummings, E. M. (Eds.). (1990). *Attachment in the preschool years: Theory, research, and intervention.* Chicago: University of Chicago Press.

Greenberg, M. T., DeKlyen, M., Speltz, M. L., & Endriga, M. C. (1997). The role of attachment processes in externalizing psychopathology in young children. In L. Atkinson & K. J. Zucker (Eds.), *Attachment and psychopathology* (pp. 196–222). New York: Guilford Press.

Greenberg, M. T., & Snell, J. (1997). The neurological basis of emotional development. In P. Salovey (Ed.), *Emotional development and emotional literacy* (pp. 93–119). New York: Basic Books.

Greenberg, M. T., & Speltz, M. L. (1988). Contributions of attachment theory to the understanding of conduct problems during the preschool years. In J. Belsky & T. Nezworski (Eds.), *Clinical implications of attachment* (pp. 177–218). Hillsdale, NJ: Erlbaum.

Greenberg, M. T., Speltz, M. L., & DeKlyen, M. (1993). The role of attachment in the early development of disruptive behavior problems. *Development and Psychopathology, 5*, 191–213.

Greenberg, M. T., Speltz, M. L., DeKlyen, M., & Endriga, M. C. (1991). Attachment security in preschoolers with and without externalizing problems: A replication. *Developmental and Psychopathology, 3*, 413–430.

Greenberg, M. T., Speltz, M. L., DeKlyen, M., & Jones, K. (1998). *The differential role of risk factors in predicting clinic referral for early conduct problems.* Unpublished manuscript, University of Washington.

Greenspan, S. I. (1981). *Psychopathology and adaptation in infancy and early childhood: Principles of clinical diagnosis and preventive intervention.* New York: International Universities Press.

Grossmann, K. E. (1995). The evolution and history of attachment research and theory. In S. Goldberg, R. Muir, & J. Kerr (Eds.), *Attachment theory: Social, developmental, and clinical perspectives* (pp. 85–121). Hillsdale, NJ: Analytic Press.

Hawkins, J. D., Arthur, M. W., & Catalano, R. F. (1995). Preventing substance abuse. In M. Tonry & D. Farrington (Eds.), *Crime and justice: A review of research, Vol. 19. Building a safer society: Strategic approaches to crime prevention* (pp. 343–427). Chicago: University of Chicago Press.

Hirschi, T. (1969). *Causes of delinquency.* Berkeley: University of California Press.

Jacobvitz, D. B., Morgan, E., Kretchmar, M. D., & Morgan, Y. (1991). The transmission of mother–child boundary disturbances across three generations. *Development and Psychopathology, 3*, 513–527.

Kazdin, A. E. (1990, June). *Prevention of conduct disorder.* Paper presented at the National Conference on Prevention Research, National Institute of Mental Health, Bethesda, MD.

Kearney, C. A., & Silverman, W. K. (1995). Family environment of youngsters with school refusal behavior: A synopsis with implications for treatment and assessment. *American Journal of Family Therapy, 23*, 59–72.

Kellam, S. G. (1990). Developmental epidemiological framework for family research on depression and aggression. In G. R. Patterson (Ed.), *Depression and aggression in family interaction* (pp. 11–48). Hillsdale, NJ: Erlbaum.

Kerns, K. A., Klepac, L., & Cole, A. K. (1996). Peer relationships and preadolescents' perceptions of security in the child–mother relationship. *Developmental Psychology, 32*, 457–466.

Klein, R. G. (1994). Anxiety disorders. In M. Rutter, E. Taylor, & L. Hersov (Eds.), *Child and adolescent psychiatry.* (pp. 242–261). Oxford: Blackwell.

Kobak, R. R., Sudler, N., & Gamble, W. (1991). Attachment and depressive symptoms during adolescence: A developmental pathways analysis. *Development and Psychopathology, 3*, 461–474.

Last, C. G., & Strauss, C. C. (1990). School refusal in anxiety-disordered children and adolescents. *Journal of the American Academy of Child and Adolescent Psychiatry, 29*, 31–35.

Le Blanc, M. (1994). Family, school, delinquency and criminality: The predictive power of an elaborated social control theory for males. *Criminal Behavior and Mental Health, 4*, 101–117.

LeDoux, J. E. (1995). Emotion: Clues from the brain. *Annual Review of Psychology, 46*, 209–235.

Levine, L. V., & Tuber, S. B. (1993). Measures of mental representation: Clinical and theoretical considerations. *Bulletin of the Menninger Clinic, 57*, 69–87.

Lewis, M., Feiring, C., McGuffog, C., & Jaskir, J. (1984). Predicting psychopathology in six-year-olds from early social relations. *Child Development, 55*, 123–136.

Lieberman, A. F., & Pawl, J. H. (1988). Clinical applications of attachment theory. In J. Belsky & T. Nezworski (Eds.), *Clinical implications of attachment* (pp. 327–347). Hillsdale, NJ: Erlbaum.

Lieberman, A. F., & Pawl, J. H. (1990). Disorders of attachment and secure base behavior in the second year of life: Conceptual issues and clinical intervention. In M. T. Greenberg, D. Cicchetti, & E. M. Cummings (Eds.), *Attachment in the preschool years: Theory, research, and intervention* (pp. 375–398). Chicago: University of Chicago Press.

Lieberman, A. F., & Zeanah, C. H. (1995). Disorders of attachment in infancy. *Child and Adolescent Psychiatric Clinics of North America, 4*, 571–687.

Liotti, G. (1995). Disorganized/disoriented attachment in the psychotherapy of dissociative disorders. In S. Goldberg, R. Muir, & J. Kerr (Eds.), *Attachment theory: Social, developmental, and clinical perspectives* (pp. 343–366). Hillsdale, NJ: Analytic Press.

Loeber, R., & Dishion, T. (1983). Early predictors of male delinquency: A review. *Psychological Bulletin, 93*, 68–99.

Luthar, S. S. (1993). Annotation: Methodological and conceptual issues in research on childhood resilience. *Journal of Child Psychology and Psychiatry, 34*, 441–453.

Luthar, S. S., & Zigler, E. (1992). Intelligence and social competence among high-risk adolescents. *Development and Psychopathology, 4*, 287–299.

Lynch, M., & Cicchetti, D. (1991). Patterns of relatedness in maltreated and nonmaltreated children: Connections among multiple representational models. *Development and Psychopathology, 3*, 207–226.

Lyons-Ruth, K. (1996). Attachment relationships among children with aggressive behavior problems: The role of disorganized early attachment patterns. *Journal of Consulting and Clinical Psychology, 64*, 64–73.

Lyons-Ruth, K., Alpern, L., & Repacholi, B. (1993). Disorganized infant attachment classification and maternal psychological problems as predictors of hostile–aggressive behavior in the preschool classroom. *Child Development, 64*, 572–585.

Lyons-Ruth, K., Connell, D., Zoll, D., & Stahl, J. (1987). Infants at social risk: Relationships among infant maltreatment, maternal behavior, and infant attachment behavior. *Developmental Psychology, 23*, 223–232.

Lyons-Ruth, K., Easterbrooks, M. A., Davidson Cibelli, C. E., & Bronfman, E. (1995, April). *Predicting school-age externalizing symptoms from infancy: Contributions of disorganized attachment strategies and mild mental lag.* Paper presented at the biennial meeting of the Society for Research in Child Development, Indianapolis, IN.

Lyons-Ruth, K., Zeanah, C., & Benoit, D. (1996). Disorders and risk for disorders during infancy and toddlerhood . In E. J. Mash & R. Barkley (Eds.), *Child psychopathology* (pp. 457–491). New York: Guilford Press.

Lyons-Ruth, K., Zoll, D., Connell, D., & Grunebaum, H. U. (1989). Family deviance and family disruption in childhood: Associations with maternal behavior and infant maltreatment during the first years of life. *Development and Psychopathology, 1*, 219–236.

Maccoby, E. E., & Martin, J. A. (1983). Socialization in the context of the family: Parent–child interaction. In P. H. Mussen (Series Ed.) & E. M. Hetherington (Vol. Ed.), *Handbook of child psychology: Vol. 4. Socialization, personality, and social development* (4th ed., pp. 1–101) New York: Wiley

Mahler, M. S., Pine, F., & Bergman, A. (1975). *The psychological birth of the human infant.* New York: Basic Books.

Main, M. (1995). Recent studies in attachment: Overview, with selected implications for clinical work. In S. Goldberg, R. Muir, & J. Kerr (Eds.), *Attachment theory: Social, developmental, and clinical perspectives* (pp. 407–474). Hillsdale, NJ: Analytic Press.

Main, M. (1996). Introduction to the special section on attachment and psychopathology: 2. Overview of the field of attachment. *Journal of Consulting and Clinical Psychology, 64*, 237–243.

Main, M., & Cassidy, J. (1985). *Assessments of child–parent attachment at six years of age.* Unpublished manuscript.

Main, M., & Cassidy, J. (1988). Categories of response to reunion with the parent at age six: Predictable from infant attachment classifications and stable over a one-month period. *Developmental Psychology, 24*, 415–426.

Main, M., & Hesse, E. (1990). Parents' unresolved traumatic experiences are related to infant disorganized attachment status: Is frightened and/or frightening parental behavior the linking mechanism. In M. T. Greenberg, D. Cicchetti, & E. M. Cummings (Eds.), *Attachment in the preschool years: Theory, research, and intervention* (pp. 161–184). Chicago: University of Chicago Press.

Main, M., Kaplan, N., & Cassidy, J. (1985). Security in infancy, childhood, and adulthood: A move to the level of representation. In I. Bretherton & E. Waters (Eds.), Growing points of attachment theory and research. *Monographs of the Society for Research in Child Development, 50*(1–2, Serial No. 209), 66–104.

Main, M., & Solomon, J. (1990). Procedures for identifying infants as disorganized/disoriented during the Ainsworth Strange Situation. In M. T. Greenberg, D. Cicchetti, & M. Cummings (Eds.), *Attachment in the preschool years: Theory, research, and intervention* (pp. 121–160). Chicago: University of Chicago Press.

Manassis, K., & Bradley, S. (1994). The development of childhood anxiety disorders: Toward an integrated model. *Journal of Applied Developmental Psychology, 15*, 345–366.

Manassis, K., Bradley, S., Goldberg, S., Hood, J., & Swinson, R. P. (1994). Attachment in mothers with anxiety disorder and their children. *Journal of the American Academy of Child and Adolescent Psychiatry, 33,* 1106–1113.

Marcovitch, S., Goldberg, S., Gold, A., Washington, J., Wasson, C., Krekewich, K., & Handley-Derry, M. (1977). Determinants of behavioral problems in Romanian children adopted in Ontario. *International Journal of Behavioral Development, 20,* 17–31.

Marvin, R. S. (1992). Attachment and family systems-based intervention in developmental psychopathology. *Development and Psychopathology, 4,* 697–711.

Marvin, R. S., & Pianta, R. C. (1996). Mothers' reaction to their child's diagnosis: Relations with security of attachment. *Journal of Clinical Child Psychology, 25,* 436–445.

Marvin, R. S., & Stewart, R. B. (1990). A family systems framework for the study of attachment. In M. T. Greenberg, D. Cicchetti, & E. M. Cummings (Eds.), *Attachment in the preschool years: Theory, research, and intervention* (pp. 51–86). Chicago: University of Chicago Press.

Morisset, C. T., Barnard, K. E., Greenberg, M. T., Booth, C. L., & Spieker, S. J. (1990). Environmental influences on early language development: The context of social risk. *Development and Psychopathology, 2,* 127–149.

Morog, M. C. (1996). *Trauma and its relation to working models of relationships: Attachment and loss in mothers of children with disabilities.* Unpublished doctoral dissertation, University of Virginia.

Morreau, D., & Follett, C. (1993). Panic disorder in children and adolescents. *Child and Adolescent Psychiatric Clinics of North America, 2,* 581–602.

Moss, E., Parent, S., Gosselin, C., Rousseau, D., & St-Laurent, D. (1996). Attachment and teacher-reported behavior problems during the preschool and early school-age period. *Development and Psychopathology, 8,* 511–526.

National Institute of Child Health and Human Development (NICHD) Early Child Care Research Network. (1994). Child care and child development. The NICHD Study of Early Child Care. In S. Friedman & C. Haywood (Eds.), *Developmental follow-up: Concepts, domains, and methods* (pp. 337–396). New York: Academic Press.

O'Connor, M. J., Sigman, M., & Brill, N. (1987). Disorganization of attachment in relation to maternal alcohol consumption. *Journal of Consulting and Clinical Psychology, 55,* 831–836.

Ogawa, J. R., Sroufe, L. A., Weinfield, N. S., Carlson, E. A., & Egeland, B. (1997). Development and the fragmented self: Longitudinal study of dissociative symtomatology in a nonclinical sample. *Development and Psychopathology, 9,* 855–879.

Ollendick, T. H., & Francis, G. (1988). Behavioral assessment and treatment of childhood phobias. *Behavior Modification, 12,* 165–204.

Oppenheim, D., Nir, A., Warren, S., & Emde, R. N. (1997). Emotion regulation in mother–child narrative co-construction: Association with children's narratives and adaptation. *Developmental Psychology, 33,* 284–294.

Oppenheim, D., & Waters, H. S. (1995). Narrative processes and attachment representations: Issues of development and assessment. In E. Waters, B. E. Vaughn, G. Posada, & K. Kondo-Ikemura (Eds.), Caregiving, cultural, and cognitive perspectives on secure-base behavior and working models: New growing points of attachment theory and research. *Monographs of the Society for Research in Child Development, 60*(2–3, Serial No. 244), 197–215.

Parker, J. G., Rubin, K. H., Price, J. M., & DeRosier, M . E. (1995). Peer relations, child development, and adjustment: A developmental psychopathology perspective. In

D. Cicchetti & D. J. Cohen (Eds.), *Developmental psychopathology* (Vol. 2, pp. 96–161). New York: Wiley.

Patterson, G. R., DeBaryshe, B. D., & Ramsey, E. (1989). A developmental perspective on antisocial behavior. *American Psychologist, 44,* 329–335.

Pilowsky, D. J., & Kates, W. G. (1995). Foster children in acute crisis: Assessing critical aspects of attachment. *Journal of the American Academy of Child and Adolescent Psychiatry, 35,* 1095–1097.

Plunkett, J. W., Meisels, S. J., Steifel, G. S., & Pasik, P. L. (1986). Patterns of attachment among preterm infants of varying biological risk. *Journal of the American Academy of Child Psychiatry, 25,* 794–800.

Radke-Yarrow, M., Cummings, E. M., Kuczynski, L., & Chapman, M. (1985). Patterns of attachment in two- and three-year-olds in normal families and families with parental depression. *Child Development, 56,* 884–893.

Radke-Yarrow, M., McCann, K., DeMulder, E., Belmont, B., Martinez, P., & Richardson, D. T. (1995). Attachment in the context of high-risk conditions. *Development and Psychopathology, 7,* 247–266.

Renken, B., Egeland, B., Marvinney, D., Mangelsdorf, S., & Sroufe, L. A. (1989). Early childhood antecedents of aggression and passive-withdrawal in early elementary school. *Journal of Personality, 57,* 257–281.

Richters, J. E., & Waters, E. (1991). Attachment and socialization: The positive side of social influence. In M. Lewis & S. Feinman (Eds.), *Social influences and socialization in infancy* (pp. 185–213). New York: Plenum Press.

Richters, M. M., & Volkmar, F. R. (1994). Reactive attachment disorder of infancy or early childhood. *Journal of the American Academy of Child and Adolescent Psychiatry, 33,* 328–332.

Robertson, J., & Robertson, J. (1989). *Separations and the very young.* London: Free Association Books.

Rodning, C., Beckwith, L., & Howard, J. (1991). Quality of attachment and home environments in children prenatally exposed to PCP and cocaine. *Development and Psychopathology, 3,* 351–366.

Routh, C. P., Hill, J. H., Steele, H., Elliot, C. E., & Dewey, M. E. (1995). Maternal attachment status, psychosocial stressors, and problem behavior: Follow-up after parent training courses for conduct disorder. *Journal of Child Psychology and Psychiatry, 36,* 1179–1198.

Rubin, K. H., Hymel, S., Mills, S. L., & Rose-Krasnor, L. (1991). Conceptualizing different developmental pathways to and from social isolation in childhood. In D. Cicchetti & S. L. Toth (Eds.), *Rochester Symposium on Developmental Psychopathology: Vol. 2. Internalizing and externalizing expressions of dysfunction* (pp. 91–122). Hillsdale, NJ: Erlbaum.

Rutter, M. (1979). Protective factors in children's responses to stress and disadvantage. In M. W. Kent & J. Rolf (Eds.), *Primary prevention of psychopathology: Vol. 3. Social competence in children* (pp. 49–74). Hanover, NH: University Press of New England.

Rutter, M. (1981). *Maternal deprivation reassessed* (2nd ed.). Harmondsworth, England: Penguin.

Rutter, M. (1982). Prevention of children's psychosocial disorders: Myth and substance. *Pediatrics, 70,* 883–894.

Rutter, M. (1985). Resilience in the face of adversity: Protective factors and resistance to psychiatric disorder. *British Journal of Psychiatry, 147,* 598–611.

Rutter, M. (1987). Psychosocial resilience and protective mechanisms. *American Journal of Orthopsychiatry, 57,* 316–331.

Rutter, M. (1997). Clinical implications of attachment concepts: Retrospect and prospect. In L. Atkinson & K. J. Zucker (Eds.), *Attachment and psychopathology* (pp. 17–46). New York: Guilford Press.

Sameroff, A. J., Seifer, R., Barocas, R., Zax, M., & Greenspan, S. (1987). Intelligence quotient scores of 4-year-old children: Social-environmental risk factors. *Pediatrics, 79*, 343–350.

Schore, A. N. (1996). The experience-dependent maturation of a regulatory system in the orbital prefrontal cortex and the origin of developmental psychopathology. *Development and Psychopathology, 8*, 59–87.

Shaw, D. S., & Bell, R. Q. (1993). Developmental theories of parental contributions to antisocial behavior. *Journal of Abnormal Child Psychology, 21*, 493–518.

Shaw, D. S., Owens, E. B., Vondra, J. I., Keenan, K., & Winslow, E. B. (1997). Early risk factors and pathways in the development of early disruptive behavior problems. *Development and Psychopathology, 8*, 679–700.

Shaw, D. S., & Vondra, J. I. (1995). Infant attachment security and maternal predictors of early behavior problems: A longitudinal study of low-income families. *Journal of Abnormal Child Psychology, 23*, 335–357.

Shear, K. M. (1996). Factors in the etiology and pathogenesis of panic disorder: Revisiting the attachment-separation paradigm. *American Journal of Psychiatry, 153*, 125–136.

Shouldice, A. E., & Stevenson-Hinde, J. (1992). Coping with security distress: The Separation Anxiety Test and attachment classifications at 4.5 years. *Journal of Child Psychology and Psychiatry, 33*, 331–348.

Singer, L. M., Brodzinsky, D. M., Ramsay, D., Steer, M., & Waters, E. (1985). Mother–infant attachment in adoptive families. *Child Development, 56*, 1543–1551.

Slough, N. M., & Greenberg, M. T. (1990). Five-year-olds' representations of separation from parents: Responses from the perspective of self and other. In I. Bretherton & M. W. Watson (Eds.), *New directions for child development: No. 48. Children's perspectives on the family* (pp. 67–84). San Francisco: Jossey-Bass.

Slough, N. M., & Greenberg, M. T. (1997, April). *Assessment of attachment in five-year-olds: Validation of a revised version of the Separation Anxiety Test*. Paper presented at the biennial meeting of the Society for Research in Child Development, Washington, DC.

Solomon, J., George, C., & De Jong, A. (1995). Children classified as controlling at age 6: Evidence of disorganized representational strategies and aggression at home and at school. *Development and Psychopathology, 7*, 447–463.

Speltz, M. L. (1990). The treatment of preschool conduct problems: An integration of behavioral and attachment concepts. In M. T. Greenberg, D. Cicchetti, & E. M. Cummings (Eds.), *Attachment in the preschool years: Theory, research, and intervention* (pp. 399–426). Chicago: University of Chicago Press.

Speltz, M. L., Endriga, M. C., Fisher, P. A., & Mason, C. A. (1997). Early predictors of attachment in infants with cleft lip and/or palate. *Child Development, 68*, 12–25.

Speltz, M. L., Greenberg, M. T., & DeKlyen, M. (1990). Attachment in preschoolers with disruptive behavior: A comparison of clinic-referred and nonproblem children. *Development and Psychopathology, 2*, 31–46.

Spieker, S. J., & Bensley, L. (1994). Roles of living arrangement and grandmother social support in adolescent mothering and infant attachment. *Developmental Psychology, 30*, 102–111.

Spieker, S. J., & Booth, C. L. (1988). Maternal antecedents of attachment quality. In J. Belsky & T. Nezworski (Eds.),

Clinical implications of attachment (pp. 95–135). Hillsdale, NJ: Erlbaum.

Spitz, R. (1946). Anaclitic depression: An inquiry into the genesis of psychiatric conditions in early childhood—II. *Psychoanalytic Study of the Child, 2*, 313–342.

Sroufe, L. A. (1983). Infant–caregiver attachment and patterns of adaptation in preschool: The roots of maladaptation and competence. In M. Perlmutter (Ed.), *Minnesota Symposia on Child Psychology: Vol. 16. Development and policy concerning children with special needs* (pp. 41–83). Hillsdale, NJ: Erlbaum.

Sroufe, L. A. (1990). Pathways to adaptation and maladaptation: Psychopathology as developmental deviation. In D. Cicchetti (Ed.), *Rochester Symposium on Developmental Psychopathology: Vol. 1. The emergence of a discipline* (pp. 13–40). Hillsdale, NJ: Erlbaum.

Sroufe, L. A., & Fleeson, J. (1986). Attachment and the construction of relationships. In W. W. Hartup & Z. Rubin (Eds.), *The nature of relationships* (pp. 51–71). Hillsdale, NJ: Erlbaum.

Sroufe, L. A., Egeland, B., & Kreutzer, T. (1990). The fate of early experience following developmental change: Longitudinal approaches to individual adaptation in childhood. *Child Development, 61*, 1363–1373.

Stouthamer-Loeber, M., Loeber, R., Farrington, D. P., Zhang, Q., Van Kammen, W. & Maguin, E. (1993). The double edge of protective and risk factors for delinquency: Interrelations and developmental patterns. *Development and Psychopathology, 5*, 683–701.

Thurber, C. A. (1996). Separation anxiety disorder and the collapse of anxiety disorders of childhood and adolescence. *Anxiety Disorders Practice Journal, 2*, 115–135.

Tizard, B., & Hodges, J. (1978). The effect of early institutional rearing on the development of eight-year-old children. *Journal of Child Psychology and Psychiatry, 19*, 99–118.

Troy, M., & Sroufe, L. A. (1987). Victimization among preschoolers: The role of attachment relationship history. *Journal of the American Academy of Child and Adolescent Psychiatry, 26*, 166–172.

Turner, P. (1991). Relations between attachment, gender, and behavior with peers in the preschool. *Child Development, 62*, 1475–1488.

Urban, J., Carlson, E., Egeland, B., & Sroufe, L. A. (1991). Patterns of individual adaptation across childhood. *Development and Psychopathology, 3*, 445–460.

van IJzendoorn, M. H., Goldberg, S., Kroonenberg, P. M., & Frenkel, O. J. (1992). The relative effects of maternal and child problems on the quality of attachment: A meta-analysis of attachment in clinical samples. *Child Development, 63*, 840–858.

Vaughn, B., Egeland, B., Sroufe, L. A., & Waters, E. (1979). Individual differences in infant–mother attachment at 12 and 18 months: Stability and change in families under stress. *Child Development, 50*, 971–975.

Wakefield, J. C. (1992). The concept of mental disorder. *American Psychologist, 47*, 373–388.

Warren, S. L., Huston, L., Egeland, B., & Sroufe, L. A. (1997). Child and adolescent anxiety disorders and early attachment. *Journal of the American Academy of Child and Adolescent Psychiatry, 36*, 637–644.

Waters, E., & Deane, K. E. (1985). Defining and assessing individual differences in attachment relationships: Q-sort methodology and the organization of behavior in infancy and early childhood. In I. Bretherton & E. Waters (Eds.), Growing points of attachment theory and research. *Mono-*

graphs of the Society for Research in Child Development, *50*(1–2, Serial No. 209), 41–65.

Waters, E., Kondo-Ikemura, K., Posada, G., & Richters, J. E. (1991). Learning to love: Mechanisms and milestones. In M. Gunnar & L. A. Sroufe (Eds.), *Minnesota Symposia on Child Psychology: Vol. 23. Self processes in development* (pp. 217–255). Hillsdale, NJ: Erlbaum.

Weissberg, R., & Greenberg, M. T. (1997). Community and school prevention. In I. Siegel & A. Renninger (Eds.), *Handbook of child psychology: Vol. 4. Child psychology in practice* (5th ed., pp. 877–954). New York: Wiley.

Wille, D. E. (1991). Relation of preterm birth with the quality of infant-mother attachment at age one. *Infant Behavior and Development, 14,* 227–240.

Winnicott, D. W. (1965). *The maturational processes and the facilitating environment.* New York: International University Press.

Zaslow, M. S., & Hayes, C. D. (1986). Sex differences in children's responses to psychosocial stress: Toward a cross-context analysis. In M. Lamb, A. Brown, & B. Ro-goff (Eds.), *Advances in developmental psychology* (Vol. 4, pp. 298–337). Hillsdale, NJ: Erlbaum.

Zeanah, C. H. (1996). Beyond insecurity: A reconceptualization of attachment disorders in infancy. *Journal of Consulting and Clinical Psychology, 64,* 42–52.

Zeanah, C. H., Mammen, O., & Lieberman, A. (1993). Disorders of attachment. In C. H. Zeanah (Ed.), *Handbook of infant mental health* (pp. 322–349). New York: Guilford Press.

Zero to Three, Task Force on Diagnostic Classification in Infancy. (1994). *Diagnostic classification of mental health and developmental disorders of infancy and early childhood.* Arlington, VA: Zero to Three.

Zimmerman, M. A., & Arunkumar, R. (1994). Resiliency research: Implications for schools and social policy. *Social Policy Report, 8*(4), 1–20.

Zucker, K. J., Bradley, S. J., & Sullivan, C.B.L. (1996). Traits of separation anxiety in boys with gender identity disorder. *Journal of the American Academy of Child and Adolescent Psychiatry, 35,* 791–798.

22

Attachment and Psychopathology in Adulthood

❖

MARY DOZIER
K. CHASE STOVALL
KATHLEEN E. ALBUS

Bowlby (1969/1982, 1973, 1980) proposed a model of development with clearly articulated implications for psychopathology. According to this model, an infant's development of an attachment to the caregiver is a key developmental task that influences not only the child's representations of self and other, but also strategies for processing attachment-related thoughts and feelings. Attachment-related events, such as loss and abuse, lead to modifications in these internal representations and affect a child's strategies for processing thoughts and feelings. Bowlby (1973, 1980) suggested that when children develop negative representations of self or others, or when they adopt strategies for processing attachment-related thoughts and feelings that compromise realistic appraisals, they become more vulnerable to psychopathology. In this chapter we consider how the quality of the infant's attachment to his or her caregiver, subsequent attachment-related experiences, and concurrently assessed states of mind with regard to attachment (Main & Goldwyn, in press) may be related to risk for psychopathology or to psychological resilience in adulthood.

ATTACHMENTS TO CAREGIVERS

Infants develop expectations about their caregivers' availability through interactions with primary caregivers. According to Bowlby (1969/1982), these expectations then serve as the basis for infants' working models of the self and of the other. When experiences lead to a "confident expectation" (Winnicott, 1971) that caregivers will be lovingly responsive, infants develop a model of the self as loved and valued, and a model of the other as loving (Bretherton, 1985). This confidence allows infants to develop secure strategies for seeking out their caregivers when distressed or in need, with the expectation that needs will be met. When infants instead have experiences that lead them to expect caregivers to be rejecting or undependable, they develop a model of the self as unloved or rejected, and a model of the other as unloving or rejecting. These children do not expect that caregivers will be available when needed, and they develop alternative, insecure strategies for coping with their distress.

Insecure strategies vary primarily along the dimension of attempts to minimize or maximize the expression of attachment needs. When children use minimizing strategies, they defensively turn attention away from their distress and from issues of caregiver availability. They therefore have limited access to their own feelings and develop an unrealistic portrayal of parents' availability. When children use maximizing strategies, they defensively turn their attention to their own

497

distress and to issues of caregiver availability. Because they are so "enmeshed" (Main & Goldwyn, in press) in issues of caregiver availability, they are unable to appraise accurately whether threats exist and whether caregivers are available. Either of these strategies may leave children at greater risk for psychopathology. Minimizing strategies may predispose a child to externalizing disorders because attention is turned away from the self, without the resolution of negative representations. Maximizing strategies may predispose a child to internalizing disorders because attention is riveted on caregiver availability, and negative representations remain painfully alive.

Carlson and Sroufe (1995; Sroufe, 1997) have emphasized the importance of the organizational function of the attachment system in integrating affective, motivational, and behavioral components of experience. As representational capacities change, so too do the processes of thinking about attachment figures and experiences (Carlson & Sroufe, 1995). Various factors make continuity in development likely, including continuity in quality of care and the limitations of previous levels of adaptation (Sroufe, 1996). Nonetheless, changes in environmental quality can result in changes in developmental trajectories. According to Sroufe (1997), discontinuity, as well as continuity, is lawful. Bowlby (1973) considered issues such as loss of caregivers, traumatic experiences, and the continuing level of caregiver availability as critical to continuity and discontinuity. For example, experiences of loss or abuse may leave a child vulnerable and without emotionally available attachment figures. The child may then revise earlier models of trusting caregivers. The family context, however, appears central to the likelihood and the nature of traumatic events such as abuse, and may be integral to the child's ability to cope with loss. For example, ongoing abuse may be unlikely to occur if the child has a competent and emotionally available caregiver (Alexander, 1992).

OVERVIEW OF THE CHAPTER

If we were to limit our discussion in this chapter to evidence linking attachment behavioral strategies in infancy with adult psychopathology, this would be a very brief chapter indeed. The evidence specifically linking infants' attachment behavioral strategies to psychopathology in adulthood is limited to two studies reporting data from the Minnesota Parent–Child Project's longi-

tudinal sample (Carlson, 1998; Warren, Huston, Egeland, & Sroufe, 1997). In this chapter, therefore, we cast our net more broadly, looking at relationships between attachment-relevant events in childhood (e.g., trauma and separation from parents) and later psychopathology. In addition, we examine the association between concurrently assessed attachment states of mind and psychopathology.

We limit our consideration of attachment states of mind to Main and Goldwyn's (in press) formulation and operationalization. Although the constructs of "attachment styles" (Hazan & Shaver, 1987, 1994) and "attachment states of mind" share a conceptual framework, there are key differences that lead to different operationalizations (see Bartholomew & Shaver, 1998; Crowell, Fraley, & Shaver, Chapter 20, this volume). Main and Goldwyn's system assesses state of mind with regard to attachment as a function of discourse coherence and defensive strategy. By contrast, attachment style assesses the individual's self-reported style of forming adolescent and adult attachments. As expected, given the different operationalizations of the variables, they are not strongly related to each other (Bartholomew & Shaver, 1998; Crowell et al., Chapter 20, this volume; Waters, Merrick, Albersheim, & Treboux, 1995). Because we are interested in differences in processing attachment-related thoughts and feelings, we deal only with findings linking attachment states of mind with psychopathology in this chapter.[1]

We progress through the major psychopathological disorders, considering first the Axis I disorders, or clinical syndromes. We start with affective disorders, followed by anxiety disorders. Each of these groups of disorders is heterogeneous with regard to heritability and symptomatology; therefore, it would be surprising if clear findings emerged with regard to attachment-related issues without further specification of parameters. We move from there to a discussion of dissociative disorders. Although dissociative phenomena have been discussed throughout the 20th century, the recognition of dissociative disorders as a bona fide diagnostic category is recent and remains controversial. Nonetheless, the evidence linking attachment in infancy and attachment-related traumas to later dissociative symptoms, and the evidence linking concurrent states of mind with dissociative symptoms, converge to make a compelling picture. We consider eating disorders next; these disorders are often comorbid with personality disorders and affective disorders. Finally, we end the discussion of Axis I disorders with schizophrenia, a disorder that is highly heritable.

From here we move to a consideration of two of the most prevalent Axis II, or personality, disorders: borderline personality disorder and antisocial personality disorder. We include these two disorders because they are prevalent and largely distinct from other Axis I disorders. (As we discuss later, rates of borderline personality disorder and depression comorbidity are high, but the disorders themselves are distinguishable.) Genetic involvement in personality disorders is variable, with relatively high heritability for antisocial personality disorder and low heritability for borderline personality disorder. The concept of borderline personality disorder emerged from the perspective of problematic early relationships with caregivers.

For each disorder or group of disorders considered, we begin with a general description of the disorder(s), prevalence and comorbidity rates, and evidence regarding genetic involvement. We then discuss attachment theory's contributions to an understanding of the disorder(s). From there we move to a consideration of the empirical evidence linking attachment phenomena to the disorder(s).

AFFECTIVE DISORDERS

Unipolar and bipolar affective disorders are very different with respect to symptomatology, genetic involvement, course, level of associated dysfunction, and the probable role of attachment in the etiology and course of the disorders. The basic distinction between unipolar and bipolar affective disorders is that unipolar affective disorders are characterized only by a depressed mood, whereas bipolar disorders are also characterized by elevated (manic or hypomanic) mood.

When unipolar affective disorder is severe and disabling, and represents a change from a previous level of functioning, major depressive disorder is present. When unipolar affective disorder is milder but more chronic (of at least 2 years' duration), dysthymic disorder is present. On the basis of a large epidemiological study (Kessler et al., 1994), 5–10% of the population were estimated to have major depressive disorder within a 1-year period, and 2–5% to have dysthymic disorder. The heritability of unipolar disorders may be linearly related to severity, with severe unipolar disorders more heritable than less severe

ones, and moderately severe disorders intermediate in heritability (Moldin, Reich, & Rice, 1991; Nigg & Goldsmith, 1994). In a large Danish sample, the concordance among monozygotic twins was 43%, as contrasted with 20% for dizygotic twins (Bertelsen, Harvald, & Hauge, 1977).

The primary category of bipolar affective disorders (bipolar I) is characterized by the presence of manic episodes and possibly (but not necessarily) depressive episodes. Although bipolar disorders can be quite debilitating when untreated, treatment with lithium allows many with bipolar disorders to function well, with relatively little dysfunction. The prevalence of bipolar disorders is substantially lower than the prevalence of unipolar disorders, estimated at 0.5% of the population in a given year (Kessler et al., 1994). Bipolar disorders are highly heritable, with the concordance among monozygotic twins estimated to be as high as 70–86%, as contrasted with 25% concordance or lower for dizygotic twins (e.g., McGuffin & Katz, 1986). Although there are several theories with regard to the involvement of specific genes in bipolar disorders, the findings are as yet inconclusive (Nurnberger & Gershon, 1992). Because very little work on the involvement of family factors in bipolar disorders has been reported in the literature, most of our comments concern unipolar disorders.

The heterogeneity among the unipolar affective disorders is important to consider in relation to attachment. First, major depression and dysthymia differ with regard to heritability; it is therefore reasonable to expect that they may differ with regard to the importance of attachment-related issues as well. Second, even within diagnostic categories, severity seems an important dimension to consider (Brown & Harris, 1993). Third, within diagnostic categories, the differential reliance on internalizing versus externalizing coping strategies is important, and central to states of mind with regard to attachment. Some persons with unipolar affective disorders show predominantly internalizing symptoms, with self-blame and self-deprecation primary. Others show a preponderance of externalizing symptoms, with interpersonal hostility primary. As argued by Cole-Detke and Kobak (1996), preoccupied states of mind, which involve a preoccupation with one's own thoughts and feelings, seem consistent with internalizing symptoms. On the other hand, dismissing states of mind, which involve a turning away from one's own distress, seem consistent with externalizing symptoms. Findings of differential treatment responsiveness between persons with depression who use internalizing versus externalizing coping strategies suggest the importance of the distinction we are making (Barber & Muenz, 1996; Beutler et al., 1991). Unfortunately, distinctions between internalizing and externalizing symptoms are not frequently made within a diagnosis of depression, and this dimension has not been considered in research relating states of mind to depression.

Attachment and Affective Disorder: Theoretical Links

Bowlby (1980) suggested that three major types of circumstances are most likely to be associated with the later development of depression. First, when a child's parent dies, and the child experiences little control over ensuing circumstances, he or she is likely to develop a sense of hopelessness and despair in reaction to traumatic events. Second, when a child is unable, despite many attempts, to form stable and secure relationships with caregivers, he or she develops a model of the self as a failure. Any subsequent loss or disappointment is then likely to be perceived as reflecting that the child is a failure. Third, when a parent gives a child the message that he or she is incompetent or unlovable, the child develops complementary models of the self as unlovable and of the other as unloving (Bretherton, 1985). Thus the child and later the adult will expect hostility and rejection from others when in need. Cummings and Cicchetti (1990) have suggested that these experiences of having a psychologically unavailable parent are similar to the experience of actually losing a caregiver, in that the child experiences frequent or even chronic losses of the parent.

Interestingly, Bowlby's formulation is compatible with Seligman's learned-helplessness theory of depression (Seligman, Abramson, Semmel, & von Baeyer, 1979), as Bowlby (1980) himself noted. Seligman proposed that hopelessness, and hence depression, develops when noxious events occur that are experienced as uncontrollable. Each of the sets of circumstances specified by Bowlby involves a sense of uncontrollability on the part of the child. In the second and third sets of circumstances, the child feels a sense of uncontrollability as the result of the parent's disappointing responses to the child. In circumstances involving parental death, the child feels lack of control over the loss of the caregiver and over subsequent caregiving experiences.

Children's Attachment-Related Experiences and Later Depression

The circumstances Bowlby proposed as central to the development of depression have received strong empirical support. Several longitudinal investigations provide converging evidence that the death of a parent in early childhood puts a child at risk for later depression (e.g., Harris, Brown, & Bifulco, 1990). Harris et al. found that when a child's mother died before the child was 11 years old, the child was at increased risk for later depression. Indeed, of those women whose mothers died before they were 11 years old, 42% were later diagnosed with depression, contrasted with 14% of those whose mothers died after they were 11. Furthermore, loss by death was associated with more severe forms of depression, which were accompanied by vegetative signs such as psychomotor retardation. Loss by separation was associated with less severe, but angrier, forms of depression. Bowlby (1980) explained this distinction by suggesting that the death of a child's mother may well lead to a sense of total despair, whereas separation from the mother may lead to a belief that events are reversible (i.e., that there is still hope).

Just as important as the loss itself are the child's subsequent caregiving experiences. Harris, Brown, and Bifulco (1986) found that inadequate care following the loss doubled the risk of depression in adulthood, particularly in cases of separation rather than death. Inadequate care often consisted of neglect, indifference, and low levels of parental control. Cummings and Cicchetti (1990) suggested that the impact of a loss also depends on the quality of the child's internal working models prior to the loss and on the quality of the original relationship.

Retrospective recall of parental support and rejection by persons with depression provides some support for Bowlby's hypothesized relation between parental emotional availability and depression. In several studies (e.g., Raskin, Boothe, Reatig, Schulterbrandt, & Odel, 1971), persons with depression described their parents as having been more unsupportive and rejecting than did persons without diagnosed psychiatric disorders. In Fonagy et al.'s (1996) study, ratings of "probable experience" of parenting were made by coders on the basis of interview data. Parents of persons with depression were rated as unloving and as moderately rejecting; this did not differentiate the depressed persons from others with psychiatric diagnosis, but it did differentiate them from persons without psychiatric diagnoses.

Attachment States of Mind and Unipolar Depression

Main and Goldwyn (in press) proposed that different attachment states of mind are associated with different patterns of processing attachment-related thoughts, feelings, and memories. The classification system they developed involves discourse analysis of transcribed responses to the Adult Attachment Interview (AAI; George, Kaplan, & Main, 1985). Responses are coded primarily with regard to "state of mind" with regard to attachment experiences, and secondarily with regard to "probable experiences" with parents. (See Hesse, Chapter 19, and Crowell et al., Chapter 20, this volume.) "Autonomous" transcripts are characterized by coherence; the speaker's representation of attachment experiences is straightforward, clear, and consistent with evidence presented. "Dismissing" transcripts are characterized most especially by lack of recall, idealization of one or both parents, or (more infrequently) derogation of attachment experiences. "Preoccupied" transcripts are characterized by current angry involvement with attachment figures, or by passive speech, such as rambling discourse (Main & Goldwyn, in press). These classifications make up the three-category system. A fourth category, "unresolved with regard to loss or trauma," is used for transcripts in which the speaker experiences lapses in reasoning or lapses in monitoring discourse regarding a loss or trauma. When an unresolved classification is given, a secondary classification (of autonomous, preoccupied, or dismissing) is also made. Reports of research using the AAI often specify whether the four-group coding scheme (including unresolved) or the three-group coding scheme (forcing unresolved subjects into the best-fitting secondary classification) is used.

The findings regarding the association between states of mind and affective disorders have been somewhat inconsistent, with some studies finding depression associated with preoccupied states of mind (Cole-Detke & Kobak, 1996; Fonagy et al., 1996; Rosenstein & Horowitz, 1996), but some finding depression associated more closely with dismissing states of mind (Patrick, Hobson, Castle, Howard, & Maughan, 1994). We suggest that there may be systematic differences on the internalizing–externalizing dimension in the groups labeled as "depressed" in these stud-

ies, and that these may account for the discrepancies in findings.

First, Rosenstein and Horowitz (1996) examined the states of mind of adolescents who had been admitted to a psychiatric hospital. Adolescents were classified as having affective disorders if they met diagnostic criteria for major depressive disorder, dysthymia, or schizoaffective disorder, and if they did not meet criteria for conduct disorder. Adolescents were classified as having conduct disorder if they met criteria for conduct disorder or oppositional defiant disorder but not criteria for depression. Adolescents were classified in a third group (comorbid affective disorder and conduct disorder) if they met criteria for both disorders. Thus, the "pure" affective disorder group excluded persons who showed externalizing symptoms of conduct disorder, but did not exclude those who were comorbid for a more internalizing disorder. Those in the "pure" affective disorder group were classified as having preoccupied states of mind significantly more often than those in the comorbid or the conduct disorder group. More specifically, 69% of the affective disorder group were classified as preoccupied, whereas 25% of the comorbid group and 14% of the conduct disorder group were classified as preoccupied. (See Table 22.1.)

Cole-Detke and Kobak (1996) examined the states of mind of women who reported depressive symptoms, eating disorder symptoms, both types of symptoms, or neither. The distribution of women who reported only depressed symptoms was relatively even across the three categories of attachment. Although depressed women were classified as preoccupied more often than were women with eating disorders, the majority fell into categories other than preoccupied. Again, the criteria for the depressed group excluded at least some with comorbid externalizing, but not internalizing, symptoms.

On the other hand, Patrick et al. (1994) limited their depressed group to women inpatients without any borderline personality disorder symptomatology, thus excluding some with internalizing symptomatology. Patrick et al. assessed the states of mind of 24 female inpatients who had diagnoses of either dysthymia or borderline personality disorder. Women were included in the dysthymic group only if they met none of the criteria for borderline personality disorder. The distribution of states of mind was significantly different for the two groups. This was a function of a clear pattern's emerging for the women in the borderline group (where 100% were classified as pre-

TABLE 22.1. Diagnostic Groups and AAI Classifications

	Three-way classifications			Four-way classifications			
	F	E	Ds	F	E	Ds	U
Axis I							
Affective disorders							
Unipolar							
Cole-Detke & Kobak (1996) (dep. symp.)	4	6	4				
Rosenstein & Horowitz (1996) (mixed)	0	22	10	0	19	8	6
Tyrrell & Dozier (1997) (MDD)	5	1	0	3	1	0	2
Patrick et al., 1994 (dysthymia)	2	4	6				
Bipolar							
Tyrrell & Dozier (1997)	0	0	7	0	0	3	4
Mixed affective							
Fonagy et al. (1996)	18	41	13	9	6	5	52
Schizoaffective							
Tyrrell & Dozier (1997)	1	1	6	1	0	5	2
Anxiety disorders							
Fonagy et al. (1996)	7	29	8	2	1	3	38
Eating disorders							
Cole-Detke & Kobak (1996)	3	1	8				
Fonagy et al. (1996)	1	9	4	0	0	1	13
Substance abuse							
Fonagy et al. (1996)	6	23	8	4	3	2	28
Schizophrenia							
Tyrrell & Dozier (1997)	3	0	24	1	0	16	12
Comorbid groups							
Eating disorders and depression							
Cole-Detke & Kobak (1996)	4	10	5				
Conduct disorders and depression							
Rosenstein & Horowitz (1996)	0	3	9	0	1	6	5
Axis II							
Borderline personality disorder							
Fonagy et al. (1996)	3	27	6	2	1	1	32
Patrick et al. (1994)	0	12	0				
Antisocial personality disorder							
Rosenstein & Horowitz (1996) (CD)	0	1	6	0	1	6	0
Fonagy et al. (1996)	8	9	5	3	1	1	17

Note. F, autonomous; E, preoccupied; Ds, dismissing; U, unresolved; dep. symp., depressive symptoms; mixed, mixed unipolar affective disorder diagnoses; MDD, major depressive disorder; CD, conduct disorder.

occupied) rather than for the women in the dysthymic group (where 50% were classified as dismissing).

Several points are worth making with regard to these findings. First, the distribution of state-of-mind classifications among persons with depressive symptoms in two of the studies (Cole-Detke & Kobak, 1996; Patrick et al., 1994) was quite similar, but the findings have been cited in the literature as if they suggest opposite conclusions.

Second, the exclusion criteria in each of these three studies created depressed groups that were systematically different from one another. For example, Rosenstein and Horowitz (1996) excluded persons from the affective disorder group who were comorbid for antisocial disorders. This comorbid group was classified primarily as dismissing. Although the remaining group was more diagnostically "pure," the exclusion process systematically excluded persons likely to have dismissing classifications, and not those likely to have preoccupied classifications. The exclusion criteria used by Patrick et al. are likely to have had the opposite effect, because those who met any criteria for borderline personality disorder were excluded. On a related issue, it is likely in each of these studies that the apparently diagnostically "pure" affective disorder group included a number of persons who had other relevant diagnoses. For example, in the Rosenstein and Horowitz study, 75% of the affective disorder group had Axis II (personality disorder) diagnoses, and most persons with personality disorders were classified as having preoccupied states of mind with regard to attachment. We suggest, therefore, that these several studies yield very important data relating states of mind to eating disorders, conduct disorders, and borderline personality disorder. Conclusions regarding states of mind and depression, however, are more complicated.

Given that the experience of loss is hypothesized as a significant vulnerability factor for depression, it follows that persons with unipolar affective disorder may be likely to be unresolved with regard to loss. In the several studies that have examined unresolved status among persons with depression, the results have also been inconsistent. In Fonagy et al.'s (1996) large sample of inpatients, 72% of persons with depression were classified as unresolved, as contrasted with 18% in Rosenstein and Horowitz's (1996) adolescent inpatient sample and 16% of Patrick et al.'s (1994) outpatient sample. The low percentage in Patrick et al.'s sample could be attributable to their excluding women who had lost both parents to death or separation before the age of 16—a subgroup that was likely to have a large proportion classifiable as unresolved with regard to loss.

Fonagy et al. (1996) found that different subtypes of depression were differentially related to states of mind. Compared with other affective disorders, major depression in the Fonagy et al. study was more often associated with autonomous states of mind. In Tyrrell and Dozier's (1997) study of persons with serious psychopathological disorders, five of six persons with major depression were classified as autonomous when the three-category system was used, and half were classified as autonomous when the four-category system was used. Fonagy et al. suggested that these findings could be attributable to the episodic nature of major depression. Major depression may not interfere with the maintenance of coherent states of mind as pervasively as chronic dysthymia does. An alternative is that major depression is more heritable than dysthymia; thus less in the way of unfavorable caregiving may be necessary for the disorder to emerge.

The primary criterion for autonomous states of mind is coherence. It is possible to have coherent states of mind even if life experiences have been difficult and caregivers have been generally unavailable. Persons who seem to have developed autonomous states of mind despite difficult life circumstances are termed "earned autonomous" (Main & Goldwyn, in press), as contrasted with persons who have had basically loving parents throughout their lives, who are termed "continuous autonomous." Pearson, Cohn, Cowan, and Cowan (1994) studied differences in reported depression, tapped with the Center for Epidemiologic Studies Depression Scale (Radloff, 1977), among women with these two types of autonomous classifications. Women in the earned autonomous group reported significantly more depression than women in the continuous autonomous group. These results suggest that difficult life experiences may predispose individuals to depression, even if an autonomous state of mind is developed.

The data relating state of mind and bipolar disorders are limited. Fonagy et al. (1996) found that persons with bipolar disorders were significantly more likely to be classified as dismissing than were persons with other affective disorders. Tyrrell and Dozier (1997) found that all seven persons with bipolar disorders were classified as dismissing when Main and Goldwyn's (in press) three-category system was used, and that four of those seven were classified as unresolved when the four-category system was used.

These various findings point to the importance of diagnostic issues when one is considering linkages between attachment states of mind and affective disorders. The first critical distinction to be made is between unipolar and bipolar affective disorders. These types of disorders are quite different in a number of ways. The preliminary findings emerging suggest that these disorders can also be distinguished by the states of mind with which they are associated. Second, several distinctions among the unipolar affective disorders appear important. Compared with dysthymia, major depression is less frequently associated with loss, and more frequently associated with autonomous states of mind. Within the categories of major depressive disorder and dysthymia, we suggest that differences in the extent to which disorders are self-blaming (internalizing) versus other-blaming (externalizing) are important in terms of states of mind. A related issue is comorbidity. Although a diagnosis of unipolar affective disorder may not provide evidence of the extent to which symptoms are internalizing or externalizing, other comorbid diagnoses, such as borderline personality disorder, eating disorders, and particular anxiety disorders may provide such evidence. Several studies have highlighted how important it is to consider comorbid diagnoses in analyses.

ANXIETY DISORDERS

Like affective disorders, anxiety disorders are quite heterogeneous. Most of these disorders are characterized by a combination of fear and avoidance, with the balance differing for different disorders. We suggest that when fear predominates, the disorder involves primarily internalizing symptoms, whereas when avoidance predominates, the disorder involves primarily externalizing symptoms. As discussed previously, strategies that maximize the expression of attachment needs are expected to be associated with more internalizing disorders, and strategies that minimize the expression of attachment needs are expected to be associated with more externalizing disorders. The disorder in which fear most clearly predominates is generalized anxiety disorder. Persons who have this disorder experience chronic anxiety regarding at least several life circumstances. Panic disorder is also characterized primarily by fear. Yet, given that agoraphobia accompanies panic disorder more often than not in clinic samples (American Psychiatric Association, 1994), avoidance is also often associated with panic disorder. Phobic disorders (including specific phobia, social phobia, and agoraphobia) are characterized by fear when the individual does not successfully avoid the feared stimulus, but avoidance often predominates. Similarly, in obsessive–compulsive disorder, fear is experienced to the extent that self-prescribed compulsive behaviors are not engaged in.

The prevalence of anxiety disorders among the general population is estimated at about 15% in a given year, with lifetime prevalence rates of about 30% (Kessler et al., 1994). Specific phobias and panic disorder with agoraphobia are the most common anxiety disorders, and generalized anxiety disorder is the least common. Moreover, comorbidity with other diagnoses is common; in particular, anxiety disorders and depressive disorders often co-occur (Kendler, Heath, Martin, & Eaves, 1987). The estimates of heritability of anxiety disorders vary enormously from study to study, in part because of variability within the disorders. Different anxiety disorders appear more heritable than others, with minimal genetic involvement for generalized anxiety disorder (Cassidy, 1995; Torgerson, 1988), for example, and significant genetic involvement for obsessive–compulsive disorder (Torgerson, 1988). Even within specific anxiety disorder diagnoses (e.g., animal phobia vs. situational phobia as types of specific phobias; Kendler, Neale, Kessler, Heath, & Eaves, 1992), the genetic component varies.

Attachment and Anxiety Disorders: Theoretical Links

Bowlby (1973) proposed that all forms of anxiety disorders (with the exception of specific animal phobias) are best accounted for by anxiety regarding the availability of the attachment figure. Several types of family environments were specified as most likely by Bowlby, all of which involve parental control through overprotection or rejection. Included among these are family environments in which a child worries about a parent's survival in the child's absence (because of parental fighting or suicide attempts), environments in which the child worries about being rejected or abandoned (because of threats from parents), environments in which the child feels the need to remain home as a companion to the parent, and environments in which a parent has difficulty letting the child go because of overwhelming feelings that harm will come to the child.

Infant Attachment and Later Anxiety Disorders

Warren et al. (1997) examined the association between attachment in infancy and anxiety disorders, diagnosed when children were 17½ with the Schedule for Affective Disorders and Schizophrenia for School-Age Children, Modified Present State/Epidemiologic version (K-SADS-MPE; Orvaschel, Puig-Antich, Chambers, Tabrizi, & Johnson, 1982). Infants with resistant attachments were significantly more likely than infants with secure or avoidant attachments to be diagnosed with anxiety disorders as adolescents. Warren et al. also assessed whether this relation between resistant attachment and anxiety disorders was attributable to temperamental differences, as determined via neonatal nurse ratings of reactivity (Terreira, 1960) as well as the Neonatal Behavioral Assessment Scale (Brazelton, 1973). Even when differences in temperament were controlled for, resistant attachments emerged as significant predictors of later anxiety disorders.

Children's Attachment-Related Experiences and Later Anxiety Disorders

Consistent with Bowlby's position, problematic family environments have been linked with anxiety disorders. Faravelli, Webb, Ambonetti, Fonnesu, and Sessarego (1985) found that persons with agoraphobia had experienced early separation from their mothers or parental divorce significantly more often than a control group with no psychiatric disorder. Brown and Harris (1993) found that persons with panic disorder had frequently experienced early loss of a caregiver or extremely inadequate caregiving, compared with persons who had no psychiatric diagnosis.

Cassidy (1995) found that persons with generalized anxiety disorder reported more rejection by their parents and role reversal than persons who did not endorse symptoms of generalized anxiety. Similarly, Chambless, Gillis, Tran, and Steketee (1996) found that most persons with anxiety disorders described their parents as unloving and controlling. Specific anxiety disorder diagnosis (obsessive–compulsive disorder vs. panic disorder with agoraphobia) did not differentially predict parental care (Chambless et al., 1995). The underlying personality cluster, as assessed by the Structured Clinical Interview for DSM-III-R (Spitzer, Williams, & Gibbon, 1987), was related to reported care, however: Persons who engaged in more avoidant behavior reported that their mothers had been neglectful, whereas persons who engaged in dependent or passive–aggressive behavior reported that their mothers had been overprotective.

Attachment States of Mind and Anxiety Disorders

There has been little published work investigating the association between states of mind and anxiety disorders. Of adolescents who were clinically elevated on the anxiety scale of the Millon Multiaxial Personality Inventory (Millon, 1983), 65% had preoccupied states of mind and 35% had dismissing states of mind (Rosenstein & Horowitz, 1996). Similarly, Fonagy et al. (1996) found that most persons with anxiety disorders were classified as preoccupied in the three-category system, which did not differentiate them from other clinical groups. What did differentiate them was that they were disproportionately unresolved with regard to loss or trauma, relative to other clinical groups. Cassidy (1995) found that, contrasted with persons without symptoms of generalized anxiety disorder, persons with generalized anxiety disorder reported greater anger and vulnerability on the Inventory of Adult Attachment (Lichtenstein & Cassidy, 1991). Feelings of anger and vulnerability are consistent with preoccupied states of mind.

We reiterate the importance of considering specific diagnoses within the anxiety disorders. Although it has not yet been investigated, we speculate that differences in internalizing versus externalizing symptomatology will be more relevant to attachment states of mind than the more general label of "anxiety disorder."

DISSOCIATIVE DISORDERS

Dissociative disorders, as the same suggests, are characterized by a dissociation of parts of the self that are usually integrated. Minor dissociative states are commonplace—for example, becoming so absorbed in a conversation while driving as to be unaware of the passing landscape. The dissociative disorders specified in the *Diagnostic and Statistical Manual of Mental Disorders*, fourth edition (DSM-IV; American Psychiatric Association, 1994) involve dissociation of one's identity (dissociative identity disorder and dissociative fugue), memory (dissociative amnesia), and consciousness (depersonalization disorder). Transient experiences of depersonalization are seen in about 40% of hospitalized patients (American Psychiatric Association, 1994) and appear to be experienced at some point by many nonpatients. The more serious dissociative disorders have been diagnosed relatively rarely until recently, with a sharp recent rise in rates diagnosed. Waller and Ross (1997) found no evidence for genetic influences in a dissociative taxon.

Attachment and Dissociation: Theoretical Links

Dissociation involves turning away, presumably not volitionally, from some aspect of the environment. Dissociation clearly has an adaptive function, in that it allows a person not to become overwhelmed in the face of trauma. Indeed, Perry, Pollard, Blakley, Baker, and Vigilante (1995) have argued that dissociation and arousal have different behavioral and physiological courses. When a person experiences a threat, an immediate response is alarm, which is associated with hyperarousal of the sympathetic nervous system. If threat continues for a long time, however, and/or if the person is largely helpless, the continued high arousal becomes difficult to sustain. Rather, the person may enter a dissociative state, which is both behaviorally and physiologically different from the state of high arousal. Here the behavioral reaction is freezing accompanied by a trance-like state.

Perry et al. (1995) have argued further that evolution has predisposed infants and children to experience dissociative states readily in the face of threat. According to these authors, survival was most likely for children who did not fight or flee in the face of danger, but rather experienced dissociative states. Perry et al. argue that the cost of experiencing dissociative states frequently as a child, however, is a sensitized and compromised neural network. This is especially true because children are undergoing critical periods for the organization of brain systems. Once sensitization has occurred, less is required to evoke dissociative states subsequently. Thus a child who repeatedly enters dissociative states will more readily enter such states under conditions of mild stress.

When a traumatic event (e.g., a natural disaster, loss, or even abuse at the hands of another adult) is experienced, but the caregiver can provide sensitive care and a sense of protection, the child is not in a position of experiencing "fright without solution" (Main & Hesse, 1990). In these cases, the child can continue to rely on the caregiver for protection. If, however, the caregiver cannot protect the child under conditions that the child experiences as threatening, or if the parent is actually the source of the threat, the child may experience the threat as overwhelming and enter a dissociative state (Main & Morgan, 1996). Kluft (1985) has proposed a model of the development of dissociative disorders, in which a susceptible child in a susceptible period (ages 4–6, when imagination is very active) is abused without protection from a caregiver, and thus learns to create alternate identities as a defense.

One predictor of the "susceptible child" may be a disorganized/disoriented attachment in infancy (Carlson, 1996). Evidence of dissociation can be seen among some babies during the strange situation (see Lyons-Ruth & Jacobvitz, Chapter 23, this volume; Main & Morgan, 1996). For most children, the strange situation is distressing, but an organized attachment system orchestrates behaviors with the caregiver. Some babies experience a breakdown of attachment strategies. Abused babies, as well as the babies of caregivers who are themselves unresolved with regard to trauma or loss, are likely to show this breakdown in strategies (Carlson, Cicchetti, Barnett, & Braunwald, 1989; Main & Morgan, 1996). Main and Hesse (1990) have proposed that frightened or frightening parental behavior is what leaves these children "frightened without solution." According to Main and Hesse (1990) and Liotti (1996), early experiences with a frightened or frightening caregiver cause a child to develop multiple, incompatible models of the self and the other. In interactions with the caregiver, the child experiences rapid shifts in which the caregiver is at first frightened, then no longer frightened, then caring for the child. With each shift, a different model of self (perpetrator of fright, rescuer, loved child) and of the caregiver (victim, rescued victim, competent caregiver) is operative. These multiple models of the self and other cannot be integrated by young children and are retained as multiple models (Liotti, 1996; Main & Hesse, 1990). These children have an unsolvable dilemma when distressed: They are neither able to go to their caregivers for nurturance, nor able to turn away and distract themselves. Because they experience this continued threat without resolution, they are at risk for entering a minor dissociative state during the strange situation and under other threatening conditions. Liotti (1992) has pointed out that these behaviors are most phenotypically similar to dissociative states in adulthood, thus suggesting a possible connection between early trance-like states and later dissociative disorders. Given Perry et al.'s (1995) suggestion that the experience of dissociative states in childhood leads to a sensitized neurobiology that predisposes individuals to experiencing later dissociative states, disorganized attachment in infancy and childhood experiences of abuse without caregiver protection may predispose individuals to dissociative states in adulthood (Carlson, 1996).

Infant Attachment and Dissociation in Adulthood

Carlson (1998) examined the relationship between disorganized attachment in infancy and dissociative symptoms during childhood and adolescence in the Minnesota longitudinal sample. Babies in this study had originally been classified with Ainsworth's three-category system (Ainsworth, Blehar, Waters, & Wall, 1978), because the fourth category of disorganized/disoriented attachment had not yet been conceptualized or operationalized (Main & Solomon, 1986). Carlson recoded these babies for disorganized/disoriented behavior; she found that 35% of the babies could be classified as disorganized/disoriented at 12 months, and that 43% could be thus classified at 18 months. To provide a teacher assessment of dissociative symptoms, Carlson selected items from the Teacher Report Form of the Child Behavior Checklist (Achenbach & Edelbrock, 1986) that were consistent with a diagnosis of dissociative disorder. Infant disorganization was associated with higher teacher ratings of dissociative symptoms both in elementary school and in high school. Furthermore, disorganized/disoriented behavior in the strange situation predicted the self-report of more dissociative symptomatology on the Dissociative Experiences Scale (Carlson & Putnam, 1993) at age 19. Thus two sets of raters converged in pointing to symptoms of dissociation for adolescents who were assessed as disorganized/disoriented in infancy, and the relations persisted over time. One might wonder whether some gross neurological deficit contributed to the ratings of dissociation in both infancy and adolescence. No associations emerged between disorganized/disoriented attachment and any of the variables assessing endogenous vulnerability, such as prenatal difficulties, difficulties during childbirth, and maternal drug and alcohol use (Carlson, 1998).

Children's Attachment-Related Experiences and Later Dissociative Disorders

As noted earlier, Main and Hesse (1990) have proposed that disorganized or disoriented behavior in the strange situation results from the caregiver's behaving in a frightened or frightening manner toward the child. This caregiver, who is herself often unresolved with regard to attachment, is unable to protect the child adequately from later threats, or may even perpetrate threats. Thus it seems that a child who is disorganized in infancy may be at increased risk for later abuse because of the caregiver's qualities. Children who have formed disorganized attachments to caregivers in infancy, and are later repeatedly abused, may be particularly susceptible to later dissociative disorders (Liotti, 1996). Two findings provide preliminary support for this hypothesis. First, E. A. Carlson (personal communication, August 1996) found that the three adolescents in the Minnesota sample who had dissociative disorders (rather than only dissociative symptoms) each had had disorganized/disoriented attachments to caregivers as infants. Second, the incidence of abuse among persons with dissociative disorders is extremely high, with figures reported as high as 97% in some studies (Putnam, 1991).

Main and Hesse (1990) have proposed an intergenerational model of the transmission of dissociative symptoms. They suggest that unresolved loss and trauma are the underlying causes of parents' behaving in frightening or frightened ways with their children. Losses require some time to resolve, according to Main and Goldwyn (in press). Very recent losses are not considered in the scoring of unresolved status in the Main and Goldwyn system, because lack of resolution in such cases is normative. Even recent losses can have disorganizing effects on parental behavior, however. Therefore, it follows that a parent's experiencing the death of someone close may make disorganized attachment and even later dissociative states in a child more likely. Indeed, Liotti (1996) found that 62% of adults diagnosed with dissociative disorders had mothers who had lost a close relative within 2 years of their birth.

Attachment States of Mind and Dissociative Disorders

Attachment states of mind are classified as unresolved with regard to loss or trauma when some notable lapse of reasoning or monitoring of discourse is evident in the AAI. Thus, like the classification of disorganized/disoriented attachment in the strange situation, the classification of unresolved status is based on behavior that is similar to dissociative phenomena. For example, when a person becomes lost in recounting episodes of abuse or loss, appearing frightened in the retelling, he or she may be experiencing a dissociative-like state. When a person gives details at one point in the discourse regarding loss or trauma that contradict other details, he or she may be once again experiencing a dissociative-like state. Thus it seems likely that unresolved status may be associated with dissociative disorders and symptoms. To our knowledge, however, persons with dissociative disorders have not yet been included as participants in a study assessing attachment states of mind.

EATING DISORDERS

Eating disorders include anorexia nervosa and bulimia nervosa. Anorexia nervosa is characterized by maintaining a body weight that is dangerously low, accompanied by distorted body image and fears of becoming fat. Bulimia nervosa is characterized by binge eating accompanied by behaviors intended to compensate for the bingeing, such as purging and taking laxatives. Typically these disorders emerge in adolescence, particularly at stressful times such as college entry. The vast majority (90%) of those diagnosed with eating disorders are women (American Psychiatric Association, 1994). About 1% of young women meet the criteria for anorexia nervosa, and about 1–3% meet the criteria for bulimia nervosa (American Psychiatric Association, 1994), although a much larger percentage show some bulimic or anorexic symptoms (e.g., Hart & Ollendick, 1985). Many women with eating disorders are also depressed, with rates of reported comorbidity as high as 75% (Mitchell & Pyle, 1985).

Attachment and Eating Disorders: Theoretical Links

Bowlby (1973) suggested that a child feels inadequate and out of control if given the message that he or she will have difficulty functioning independently or that he or she is unlovable. As discussed previously, children who receive such messages may feel their own anxiety exquisitely, developing generalized anxiety disorder or agoraphobia, for example. If these children have developed an avoidant strategy of turning their attention away from their own distress, however, they may be more likely to develop externalizing symptoms. Cole-Detke and Kobak (1996) have suggested that a young woman who develops an eating disorder may be attempting to control her world through her eating behavior by directing her attention away from her own feelings of distress.

Children's Attachment-Related Experiences and Later Eating Disorders

Much of the evidence linking early attachment-related experiences to eating disorders relies on retrospective accounts of parenting availability. The findings that emerge are complicated. First, women with anorexia nervosa typically describe both their parents negatively. Palmer, Oppenheimer, and Marshall (1988) found that women with eating disorders reported generally lower-quality parental care than others without eating disorders. Second, fathers are often described as emotionally unavailable and rejecting (Cole-Detke & Kobak, 1996; Rhodes & Kroger, 1992). Third, mothers are described as domineering, overprotective, and perfectionistic (Minuchin, Rosman, & Baker, 1980). Finally, parents appear to act in ways that thwart efforts at independence. Kenny and Hart (1992) found that women with eating disorders described their parents as generally unsupportive of their independence.

An observational study conducted by Humphrey (1989) provides converging evidence for this pattern of family interaction. In interactional analyses, parents were found to communicate double messages, suggesting support for daughters while simultaneously undermining their confidence. The effects of these interactions can be seen in the daughters' feelings of inadequacy. For example, Armstrong and Roth (1989) found that women with eating disorders responded to imagined minor separations from loved ones in extreme ways. Thus a picture generally emerges of an overcontrolling, perfectionistic mother who communicates lack of support for her daughter's autonomy striving; an emotionally rejecting father; and a daughter who feels rejected, controlled, and inadequate. Although sexual abuse has been suggested as a causal factor for eating disorders, the preponderance of evidence suggests that such abuse is not strongly related to the development of either anorexia nervosa or bulimia nervosa (e.g., Pope, Mangweth, Negrao, Hudson, & Cordas, 1994; Welch & Fairburn, 1994).

Attachment States of Mind and Eating Disorders

Two studies (Cole-Detke & Kobak, 1996; Fonagy et al., 1996) have examined the association between states of mind and eating disorders, and obtained somewhat contradictory results. As reviewed previously, Cole-Detke and Kobak used the self-report of a sample of college women for the assessment of eating disorders. The methodology yielded information about the three major categories of states of mind (preoccupied, dismissing, and autonomous), but not about the fourth category (unresolved with respect to loss or abuse). The breakdown of states of mind differed significantly for women reporting eating disorders, depression, a combination of the two, or neither. Women who reported eating disorders only were most frequently classified as dismissing. Women who reported a combination of eating disorders and depression were most frequently classified as preoccupied (similar to women who reported only depression).

In the investigation by Fonagy et al. (1996), 64% of persons with eating disorders were classified as having preoccupied states of mind. With the four-category system, all but 1 of the 14 persons with eating disorders were classified as unresolved with regard to a loss or trauma. Persons with eating disorders did not differ significantly from persons with other psychiatric disorders in the breakdown of state-of-mind classifications. In the Cole-Detke and Kobak (1996) study, over half (61%) of the women reporting eating disorders also reported depression, and were thus not included in the "pure" eating disorder group. If a similar proportion of persons in Fonagy et al.'s study was comorbid for depression, the majority of the remaining "pure" eating disorder group might have been classified as dismissing, thus matching Cole-Detke and Kobak's results.

Consistent with the patterns of family interaction described above, Cole-Detke and Kobak (1996) have argued that women with eating disorders are attempting to control their worlds through their eating behavior and that the type of control exerted is externally oriented. This type of control is chosen because women with eating disorders do not have the ability to examine their own psychological states, and cope instead by diverting distress to a focus on their own bodies. Cole-Detke and Kobak have proposed, therefore, that eating disorders allow the diversion of attention away from attachment-related concerns, and toward the more external and more "attainable" goal of body change.

SCHIZOPHRENIA

The schizophrenias are the group of disorders associated with the greatest dysfunction of any of the Axis I disorders. These disorders are characterized most especially by psychosis (i.e., loss of touch with reality), as manifested often in delusions or hallucinations. The schizophrenias appear to have high heritability. For example, although the prevalence among the general population is about 1%, the concordance for monozygotic twins is usually estimated at about 50%, as opposed to 15% for dizygotic twins (Gottesman, 1991). Even in adoption studies, when the influence of the environmental effects associated with biological parents are minimized, the influence of biological parents appears more predictive of the development of schizophrenia than the influence of adoptive parents (Gottesman, 1991). The mechanism for the transmission has not been clearly specified as a single-gene or single-chromosome locus. Many researchers are now exploring what seems the more likely explanation that multiple genes are involved, and that the involvement of specific genes will be variable across the schizophrenias (Gottesman, 1991).

Children's Attachment-Related Experiences and Later Schizophrenia

Several family environment variables have been suggested as causal in the etiology of schizophrenia, including double-binding communication (Bateson, Jackson, Haley, & Weakland, 1956), pseudomutuality (Wynne, 1970), communication deviance, and expressed emotion (Goldstein, 1985). With the exception of communication deviance and expressed emotion, none of these theories has received substantial empirical support. The evidence linking communication deviance and expressed emotion to the development of schizophrenia is limited to a single study (Goldstein, 1985). Communication deviance is characterized by "disordered communication" among family members (Goldstein, 1990, p. 410), including, for example, messages that have double meanings. High levels of expressed emotion are characterized by familial overinvolvement and/or criticality. Communication deviance and expressed emotion assessed in the families of adolescents with mild to moderate clinical disturbances predicted schizophrenia and schizophrenia-spectrum disorders (schizoid, schizotypal, and paranoid personality disorders) 15 years later (Goldstein, 1985). Even though these results suggest that parental behavior is important in the onset of schizophrenia, it is also possible that the parents' behaviors reflected sensitivity to different premorbid behaviors of their children who later developed schizophrenia. For example, Walker, Grimes, Davis, and Smith (1993) found that in home videotapes taken years before the onset of schizophrenia, the children who later developed schizophrenia could be reliably differentiated from their siblings who did not develop schizophrenia.

The evidence regarding familial influences on the *recurrence* of schizophrenia is more compelling, and findings have been replicated in a number of studies (e.g., Brown, Birley, & Wing, 1972; Leff & Vaughn, 1985). Indeed, persons in high-expressed-emotion families relapse at about four times the rate of persons in low-expressed-emotion families. Even in studies where expressed emotion is manipulated through family intervention, high expressed emotion is related strongly to relapse (Goldstein, 1985).

Attachment States of Mind and Schizophrenia

Dozier and her colleagues have examined states of mind in several samples of persons with schizophrenia (Dozier, Cue, & Barnett, 1994; Tyrrell & Dozier, 1997). Only the most recent investigation (Tyrrell & Dozier, 1997) used the Main and Goldwyn (in press) classification system, however. In this most recent study, nearly all (89%) persons with schizophrenia were classified as dismissing of attachment when the three-category system was used. When the four-category system was used, 44% were classified as unresolved.

We argue, however, that these results tell us little about factors predisposing to schizophrenia. First, we suggest that findings of higher rates of unresolved status among persons with schizophrenia should be interpreted with caution. Indeed, schizophrenia, which is characterized most especially by thought disorder, involves "lapses in monitoring of reasoning and discourse" (Main & Goldwyn, in press)—the characteristics that define unresolved status. Thus persons with thought disorder may appear unresolved with regard to loss or abuse because of their thought disorder. Second, we suggest that the failure to find many autonomous transcripts among persons with schizophrenia is to be expected, in that the incoherence associated with thought disorder is inconsistent with a coherent transcript. Although we urge caution in thinking of states of mind as preceding psychopathology when measured concurrently, we suggest that differences in states of mind are important in how relationships are approached and how treatment is used (see Slade, Chapter 25, this volume).

BORDERLINE PERSONALITY DISORDER

Persons with borderline personality disorder have a notably unstable sense of self (American Psychiatric Association, 1994). Similarly, representations of others are undeveloped and unstable, such that others are idealized at times and devalued at other times. A central issue is the fear of abandonment by an idealized other. Because the unstable sense of self is dependent on validation from the idealized other, the threat of abandonment is experienced as potentially devastating. This instability of internal representations is often associated with emotional volatility. In particular, strong feelings of anger and dysphoria can be readily precipitated by subtle suggestions of rejection. Thus a number of factors contribute to create conditions in which interpersonal relationships are likely to be intense and tumultuous. Such factors also point to probable attachment-relevant influences on the etiology of borderline personality disorder.

Although the prevalence of borderline personality disorders is only about 1% of the general population, the prevalence among persons receiving treatment is much greater—about 15% among outpatients, and about 50% among outpatients diagnosed with personality disorders (Widiger, 1993). Thus persons with borderline personality disorder are relatively more likely than others to seek out treatment; this finding is not surprising, given that "crying out for help" is characteristic of the disorder.

There has been less research on genetic involvement in borderline personality disorder than in most other disorders considered. Nigg and Goldsmith (1994) concluded on the basis of a number of family studies that the incidence of borderline personality disorder among first-degree relatives of someone with a borderline diagnosis is about 11%. Studies investigating concordance among twins have not found evidence for genetic transmission (Torgerson & Psychol, 1984). The diagnostic label "borderline" was originally intended to refer to the border between neurotic and psychotic, and this suggests a possible link between borderline and psychotic disorders (i.e., schizophrenia). There is little evidence for a genetic link between borderline and schizophrenic disorders, however (Nigg & Goldsmith,

1994). Borderline and affective disorders are often comorbid, though, with rates of comorbidity as high as 50% in clinic samples (Alnaes & Torgerson, 1988).

Attachment and Borderline Personality Disorder: Theoretical Links

Main and Hesse (1990) have suggested that the experience of trauma without the support of a caregiver predisposes individuals to the development of either borderline or dissociative pathology. As described previously, Main and Hesse have proposed that the child cannot integrate the various qualities of a caregiver into single models of self and other when the caregiver behaves in a frightened or frightening way; thus unintegrated models are maintained. This formulation is consistent with Gunderson, Kerr, and Englund's (1980) characterization of borderline pathology, in which attentional and behavioral processes are described as unintegrated.

Borderline pathology is generally associated with the exaggeration of symptomatology and of negative affect, as well as a "preoccupation" with concerns about current and previous relationship difficulties. The readiness to report distress is consistent with the maximizing of the expression of attachment needs, seen in babies with resistant attachment and in adults who are preoccupied with regard to attachment. Working models of caregivers as incompetent or inconsistently available, and of the self as inconsistently valued, seem as central to a diagnosis of borderline personality disorder as to a classification of preoccupied attachment.

Children's Attachment-Related Experiences and Later Borderline Personality Disorder

The evidence for problematic conditions within the family in the development of borderline personality disorder is compelling. Indeed, the family histories of persons with borderline personality disorder are fairly indistinguishable from those of persons with dissociative disorders. Most especially, as in dissociative disorders, early abuse is often seen in the histories of persons diagnosed with borderline personality disorder. For example, Herman, Perry, and van der Kolk (1989) found that 81% of persons with borderline personality disorder reported physical or sexual abuse, or were witnesses to such abuse when they were children. For 57% of these chil-

dren, the trauma occurred before the age of 7. Similarly, Ogata et al. (1990) found that 71% of women with borderline personality disorder were sexually abused, contrasted with only 22% of women with affective disorders. The only notable exception to these very high rates is Brown and Anderson's (1991) finding that 29% of inpatients with borderline personality disorder reported that they had been abused as children. Sanders and Giolas (1991) found evidence of higher rates of documented abuse histories in the hospital records of borderline patients than in the histories of other patients. Thus these results do not appear to reflect a reporting bias only.

Persons with borderline personality disorder report very high rates of prolonged separations from caregivers during their childhoods (Zanarini, Gunderson, Marino, Schwartz, & Frankenburg, 1989), most especially from their mothers (Soloff & Millward, 1983). They also report emotional neglect when their caregivers were physically present (Patrick et al., 1994; Zanarini et al., 1989).

Attachment States of Mind and Borderline Personality Disorder

Using Main and Goldwyn's (in press) three-category system, Fonagy et al. (1996) found that 75% of persons with borderline personality disorder had preoccupied states of mind, and that half of those with preoccupied states of mind fell into a rarely used subgroup, fearfully preoccupied with regard to traumatic events. Similarly, in Patrick et al.'s (1994) study, all women with borderline personality disorder were classified as preoccupied, and 10 of the 12 were classified as preoccupied with regard to loss or trauma. This subgroup of preoccupied state of mind (E3) often co-occurs with unresolved status. Not surprisingly, then, 89% and 75% of persons with borderline personality disorder were classified as unresolved in the Fonagy et al. and Patrick et al. studies, respectively. Thus the combination of maximizing strategies and the experience of unresolved abuse appears central to borderline personality disorder.

ANTISOCIAL PERSONALITY DISORDER

Antisocial personality disorder, as described in the DSM-IV (American Psychiatric Association, 1994), is characterized by a consistent disregard for the rights and feelings of others and for the basic laws of society. Characteristics of antisocial personality disorder include deceitfulness, impulsivity, irresponsibility, irritability, and lack of remorse. The links between childhood or adolescent conduct disorder and later adult antisocial personality disorder have been noted in numerous studies (e.g., McCord, 1979; Robins, 1966). Indeed, one of the criteria for antisocial personality disorder is the presence of earlier conduct disorder.

The evidence for the heritability of antisocial personality disorder is strong (Nigg & Goldsmith, 1994), and heritability appears moderate to high. First-degree relatives of males with antisocial personality disorder are five times more likely to have the disorder than the general population, whereas first-degree relatives of females are 10 times more likely to have the disorder (Baker, Mack, Moffitt, & Mednick, 1989). On the basis of the Epidemiologic Catchment Area study, Robins and Regier (1991) estimated a lifetime prevalence of about 7% for males and 1% for females. The lower incidence among women, and the increased likelihood of the disorder among first-degree relatives for women, combine to suggest that the genetic influence is greater for women than for men with the disorder (Nigg & Goldsmith, 1994).

Attachment and Antisocial Personality Disorder: Theoretical Links

Bowlby (1973) proposed that, when children experience separations from parents, and when parents threaten abandonment, children feel intense anger. Ordinary but stressful separations are often met with anger, which is functional in communicating to the parents the children's feelings about the separation. When prolonged separations are combined with frightening threats, however, Bowlby suggested that children are likely to feel a dysfunctional level of anger toward parents, often involving intense hate. Initially the anger may be directed toward the parents. Because that may prove dangerous in maintaining the relationship with the parents, however, the anger is often repressed and directed toward other targets (Bowlby, 1973; Stott, 1950).

Children's Attachment-Related Experiences and Later Antisocial Personality Disorder

Prolonged separations from primary caregivers (as the result of divorce or separation rather than death), fathers' antisocial or deviant behavior, and mothers' unaffectionate, neglectful care are several of the conditions associated with antisocial personality disorder (McCord, 1979; Robins, 1966). Robins (1966) found that parental desertion, divorce, or separation was associated with the diagnosis of antisocial personality disorder. Zanarini et al. (1989) found that 89% of persons with antisocial personality disorder had experienced prolonged separations from a caregiver at some point during their childhood. Given that loss by death was not associated with later antisocial personality disorder, however, it does not seem to be simply the absence of a caregiver that is important (Robins, 1966). McCord (1979) found that antisocial personality disorder was a likely outcome only when mothers were also unaffectionate and did not provide adequate supervision, and when fathers were deviant. Many persons with antisocial personality disorder report that they experienced physical abuse, or at least harsh discipline, during childhood (e.g., Zanarini et al., 1989).

Attachment States of Mind and Antisocial Personality Disorder

Most of the empirical evidence suggests that antisocial personality disorder (or conduct disorder in adolescents) is associated with unresolved and dismissing states of mind (Allen, Hauser, & Borman-Spurrell, 1996; Rosenstein & Horowitz, 1996). Allen et al. assessed states of mind among adolescents who were psychiatric inpatients and a control group of high school students. Criminality and use of "hard drugs" were then assessed approximately 10 years later. The most impressive finding was that ratings from the adolescents' attachment interviews predicted criminality 10 years later, even after previous psychiatric hospitalization was accounted for. In particular, derogation of attachment and lack of resolution of trauma predicted criminal behavior. "Derogation of attachment" is a rarely occurring subtype of dismissing attachment in which the person derogates attachment figures or attachment experiences. Among this sample of psychiatric inpatients in the Allen et al. study, 15% of the interviews were unclassifiable ("cannot classify") because they met criteria for multiple, incompatible categories. This group of persons with unclassifiable interviews reported the most criminal behavior, followed by persons classified as dismissing and unresolved. Post hoc analyses revealed that the unclassifiable group showed higher levels of criminal behavior than the secure and preoccupied groups, and that the dismissing group showed significantly higher levels than the secure group.

Rosenstein and Horowitz (1996) found that among adolescents with conduct disorder only, six of seven were classified as dismissing, and none was classified as unresolved. In the group of adolescents comorbid for conduct disorder and affective disorder, half of the adolescents were classified as dismissing, and nearly half were classified as unresolved with regard to loss or trauma. Fonagy et al. (1996) obtained very different results for a combined group made up of persons with antisocial and paranoid personality disorders, however. When the three-category system was used, more were classified as preoccupied and as autonomous than as dismissing. When the four-category system was used, most were classified as unresolved.

SUMMARY AND CONCLUSIONS

Attachment in Infancy

At this point, the only clear connections between infant attachment and adult psychopathology that can be made are between disorganized attachment and dissociative symptoms in adolescence (Carlson, 1998) and between resistant attachment and anxiety disorders in adolescence (Warren et al., 1997). These associations are compelling for a number of reasons. First, the "phenotypic similarity" of the phenomena is striking when one considers the association between disorganized attachment and dissociative symptoms (Liotti, 1996; Main & Morgan, 1996) and between resistant attachment and anxiety (Cassidy, 1995). Second, the caregiving experiences predictive of disorganized and resistant attachment are similar to the caregiving experiences predictive of dissociative symptoms and anxiety symptoms, respectively. More specifically, the occurrence of attachment-related trauma, especially abuse, is known to be associated both with disorganized attachment (Carlson et al., 1989) and with dissociative disorders (e.g., Putnam, 1991). This association between abuse and later dissociation may be accounted for partially by the development of a sensitized neurobiology when a child experiences frightening events from which escape is not possible. Similarly, unavailable or inconsistently available caregiving appears predictive of both resistant attachment and

symptoms of anxiety (Cassidy, 1995). Carlson (1998) has suggested that the child who frequently becomes hyperaroused (rather than disorganized) when threatened with an unavailable caregiver develops a sensitized neurobiology that predisposes him or her to later anxiety. Finally, the categories of adult attachment that parallel infant disorganized and resistant attachment are characterized by behaviors consistent with the predicted symptomatology. Adults who are unresolved with regard to loss or trauma are characterized by a "lapse in reasoning or in the monitoring of discourse" when discussing loss or trauma (Main & Goldwyn, in press). Similarly, the discourse of adults who are preoccupied with regard to attachment is affected by anxiety that may be either more diffuse (e.g., similar to the anxiety associated with generalized anxiety disorder) (Cassidy, 1995) or more focused (e.g., similar to the anxiety associated with a phobic disorder). Thus the categories of adult attachment that parallel infant disorganized and resistant attachment are themselves characterized by some level of dissociation and anxiety, respectively.

Attachment-Related Circumstances

Loss

Loss predicts multiple disorders, including depression, anxiety, and antisocial personality disorder. To some degree, the type of loss experienced appears to affect the development of psychopathology differentially. Depression is associated generally with the early loss of the mother. Major depression in particular, or depression involving vegetative signs, has been found to be related to permanent loss of a caregiver, whereas depression characterized by anger and other externalizing symptoms has been found to be related to separation (Brown & Harris, 1993). Anxiety appears to be associated more closely with threats of loss and instability than with permanent loss (Monroe & Simons, 1991). Antisocial personality disorder is associated with loss through desertion, separation, and divorce (McCord, 1979).

For affective and anxiety disorders, the circumstances prior to and subsequent to the loss appear to be as important in determining risk or resilience as the loss itself. With regard to vulnerability to depression and anxiety, experiences with the mother prior to the loss and with other caregivers subsequent to the loss affect the child's resilience or vulnerability (Brown & Harris, 1993). A nurturing relationship with the mother, and nurturing, continuous relationships with the father or other caregivers, seem to protect the child from the effects of the loss. An emotionally unavailable mother and/or neglectful care subsequent to the loss can leave the child desperately vulnerable, and thus at risk for later depression and anxiety (Harris et al., 1986). Bowlby (1980) suggested that children who have had rejecting caregivers may then experience a subsequent loss as overwhelming.

Caregiving experiences prior and subsequent to loss appear central to the development of antisocial personality disorder as well. Paternal deviance and inadequate maternal caregiving are correlates of divorce and desertion. The results of several studies (McCord, 1979; Robins, 1966) suggest that these caregiving conditions themselves, rather than loss, are what predict antisocial personality disorder.

Abuse

Reports of abuse are consistently high among persons with borderline personality disorder, dissociative disorder, and antisocial personality disorder. When children have caregivers who do them harm, they experience unresolvable conflicts, because the very persons who should be providing protection from threat are themselves threatening. Thus Liotti (1996) has proposed that multiple models of caregivers develop for several reasons. First, the actual behavior of a caregiver often vacillates quickly from hurtful to loving, in ways that cannot be accommodated by a single model of the caregiver (Liotti, 1996; Main & Morgan, 1996). When parents' behavior remains menacing, children often "fix parents up" (Harris, 1995, p. 57) so that they can derive some security from them, however illusory that security might be. The act of "fixing them up" involves a distortion too great to be accommodated within a single model of such a parent.

Alexander (1992) has argued that abuse is often symptomatic of the system of caregiving within the family. The nature and duration of the abuse are not random, therefore, but systematically related to the family's functioning (Alexander, 1992). Furthermore, the system of caregiving may be as important to later adjustment as the abuse itself, if not more so. For instance, dismissing parents may be likely to minimize the evidence or effects of abuse, according to Alexander, thus allowing the abuse to continue

over time. Preoccupied parents may get their own needs met by role-reversing children, such that they fail to take a competent position in protecting children. Parents with unresolved states of mind who abuse their children may be acting out their models of their own caregivers that they internalized as children (Sroufe, 1988), whereas their unresolved partners may be too disoriented to protect children (Alexander, 1992). Thus extended abuse often occurs in a context of disordered caregiving. When abuse occurs in a caregiving context in which caregivers are competent and emotionally available, however, the caregivers are likely to intervene quickly, providing support and protection so that children can successfully resolve the effects of the trauma.

Quality of Caregiving

Reports of inadequate caregiving of one type or another are associated with all forms of psychopathology. Considering combinations of rejection and/or neglect with overprotection or inadequate control allows some specificity in the prediction of specific disorders. Affective and anxiety disorders tend to be associated most frequently with parental rejection combined with loss. Antisocial personality disorders are most frequently associated with parental rejection, harsh discipline, and inadequate control. Eating disorders are associated with maternal rejection and overprotection combined with paternal neglect, and borderline personality disorder is associated most consistently with parental neglect.

Attachment States of Mind

There are relatively few findings regarding the distribution of attachment states of mind among persons with psychiatric disorders. The findings that do exist are consistent in some respects, as described below, but are inconsistent in others. We suggest that there may be several important reasons for the discrepancies. First, the classification system has been evolving in recent years, and few coders have yet been certified as reliable. To our knowledge, of the AAI studies cited here, only Allen et al. (1996) used a certified coder (Erik Hesse) for all interviews. Thus, it is possible that although laboratories achieved reliability among coders, the classifications may not always correspond well with the Main and Goldwyn (in press) system. Even though we suggest the possibility of "lab effects," we hasten to add that such effects will be reduced in the years ahead as raters across laboratories are certified as reliable, as recommended by Main and Goldwyn (in press). A second possible reason for discrepancies in findings is that diagnostic groups are defined differently in different studies. We suggest that diagnostic groupings be created that are as specific as possible, with researchers systematically assessing the effects of other comorbid diagnoses and symptomatology. Furthermore, we urge attention to heterogeneity within disorders. In particular, we expect that differences related to the internalization–externalization dimension that cuts across some disorders may be quite important to consider in relation to states of mind.

Nonetheless, several consistent findings have emerged. One finding that has emerged consistently is that psychiatric disorders are nearly always associated with nonautonomous states of mind. Furthermore, unresolved status is the most overrepresented state of mind among persons with psychiatric disorders. What these findings mean in terms of the causal connection between attachment state of mind and psychiatric disorders is unclear. Only in the Allen et al. (1996) longitudinal study were states of mind assessed significantly earlier in time than psychopathology data were collected. Allen et al. provided evidence that ratings of derogation and ratings of lack of resolution of abuse can predict problematic behaviors (in particular, criminal behavior and hard-drug use) in a high-risk sample. Some of the longitudinal studies now being conducted with high-risk samples will address the association between states of mind and the emergence of different psychiatric disorders more comprehensively.

We suggest that the classification of unresolved status may be more meaningful for some psychiatric disorders than for others. For disorders where disorganization is not a key feature, we expect that unresolved classifications are more likely to indicate lack of resolution of loss or trauma. For disorders where disorganization is a key feature, we expect that unresolved status may not indicate whether the person interviewed is actually unresolved with regard to a loss or trauma. In particular, persons with schizophrenia and bipolar affective disorders are at times highly disorganized in speech. Therefore, disorganization when discussing loss or trauma is consistent with this general presentation, rather than suggesting anything more specific about their states of mind.

Dismissing states of mind seem to reflect at-tempts to minimize attachment needs, whereas preoccupied states of mind reflect the maximizing of attachment needs (Cassidy, 1994; Main, 1990). Therefore dismissing states of mind should be associated with disorders that involve turning attention away from one's own feelings, such as antisocial personality disorder, eating disorder, substance abuse and dependence, hostile forms of depression, and externalizing forms of anxiety disorders. Preoccupied states of mind should be associated with disorders that involve absorption in one's own feelings, such as internalizing forms of depression and anxiety, as well as borderline personality disorder. The evidence available thus far is mixed with regard to these connections. As discussed previously, the findings of Rosenstein and Horowitz (1996), Cole-Detke and Kobak (1996), and Patrick et al. (1994) can be interpreted as consistent in suggesting that some externalizing disorders (i.e., eating disorders and conduct disorders) are associated with dismissing states of mind, and that an internalizing disorder (i.e., borderline personality disorder) is associated with preoccupied states of mind. We suggest that both depression and anxiety are more heterogeneous disorders, subsuming those who are more self-focused (i.e., internalizing) and those who are less self-focused (i.e., externalizing).

The Metaphor of the Branching Railway Lines

Bowlby (1973) described "branching railway lines" as a metaphor for the development of psychopathology and psychological health. Infants with emotionally available caregivers begin their development moving out from the "metropolis" in different directions from those with emotionally unavailable caregivers. Future experiences with caregivers, and experiences of loss and abuse, have differential effects on these children because they are on different branching pathways (Sroufe, 1997). No circumstances, including the quality of early caregiving or the experiences of loss or abuse, fully constrain development. Nonetheless, certain pathways become more or less likely, because there evolves within a child an organized system for coping with his or her experiences (Sroufe, 1996). The research we have examined in this chapter provides tentative support for this model. In the next decade, a number of longitudinal investigations will be completed that follow children from infancy to adulthood, thus allowing fuller tests of this model of "psychopathology as an outcome of development" (Sroufe, 1997, p. 251).

NOTE

1. Relations between self-report romantic attachment and various forms of psychopathology are discussed in Brennan and Shaver (1995, 1998); Cooper, Shaver, and Collins (1998); Mickelson, Kessler, and Shaver (1998); and Shaver and Clark (1994).

REFERENCES

Achenbach, T., & Edelbrock, C. (1986). *Manual for the Teacher's Report Form and Teacher Version of the Child Behavior Profile.* Burlington: University of Vermont, Department of Psychiatry.

Ainsworth, M., Blehar, M., Waters, E., & Wall, S. (1978). *Patterns of attachment: A psychological study of the Strange Situation.* Hillsdale, NJ: Erlbaum.

Alexander, P. C. (1992). Application of attachment theory to the study of sexual abuse. *Journal of Consulting and Clinical Psychology, 60,* 185–195.

Allen, J. P., Hauser, S. T., & Borman-Spurrell, E. (1996). Attachment theory as a framework for understanding sequelae of severe adolescent psychopathology: An 11-year follow-up study. *Journal of Consulting and Clinical Psychology, 64,* 254–263.

Alnaes, R., & Torgerson, S. (1988). The relationship between DSM-III symptom disorders (Axis I) and personality disorders (Axis II) in an outpatient population. *Acta Psychiatrica Scandinavica, 78,* 485–492.

American Psychiatric Association. (1994). *Diagnostic and statistical manual of mental disorders* (4th ed.). Washington, DC: Author.

Armstrong, J. G., & Roth, D. M. (1989). Attachment and separation difficulties in eating disorders: A preliminary investigation. *International Journal of Eating Disorders, 8,* 141–155.

Baker, L. A., Mack, W., Moffitt, T. E., & Mednick, S. (1989). Sex differences in property crime in a Danish adoption cohort. *Behavior Genetics, 19,* 355–370.

Barber, J. P., & Muenz, L. R. (1996). The role of avoidance and obsessiveness in matching patients to cognitive and interpersonal psychotherapy: Empirical findings from the Treatment for Depression Collaborative Research Program. *Journal of Consulting and Clinical Psychology, 64,* 951–958.

Bartholomew, K., & Shaver, P. R. (1998). Measures of attachment: Do they converge? In J. A. Simpson & W. S. Rholes (Eds.), *Attachment theory and close relationships* (pp. 25–45). New York: Guilford Press.

Bateson, G., Jackson, D., Haley, J., & Weakland, J. (1956). Toward a theory of schizophrenia. *Behavioral Science, 1,* 251–264.

Bertelsen, A., Harvald, B., & Hauge, M. (1977). A Danish twin study of manic depressive disorders. *British Journal of Psychiatry, 130,* 330–351.

Beutler, L. E., Engle, D., Mohr, D., Daldrup, R. J., Bergan, J., Meredith, K., & Merry, W. (1991). Predictors of differential response to cognitive, experiential, and self-directed

psychotherapeutic procedures. *Journal of Consulting and Clinical Psychology, 59,* 333–340.

Bowlby, J. (1969/1982). *Attachment and loss: Vol. 1. Attachment.* New York: Basic Books.

Bowlby, J. (1973). *Attachment and loss: Vol. 2. Separation.* New York: Basic Books.

Bowlby, J. (1980). *Attachment and loss: Vol. 3. Loss.* New York: Basic Books.

Brazelton, T. B. (1973). *Neonatal Behavioral Assessment Scale.* Philadelphia: Lippincott.

Brennan, K. A., & Shaver, P. R. (1995). Dimensions of adult attachment, affect regulation, and romantic functioning. *Personality and Social Psychology Bulletin, 21,* 267–283.

Brennan, K. A., & Shaver, P. R. (1998). Attachment styles and personality disorders: Their connections to each other and to parental divorce, parental death, and perceptions of parental caregiving. *Journal of Personality, 66,* 835–878.

Bretherton, I. (1985). Attachment theory. Retrospect and prospect. In I. Bretherton & E. Waters (Eds.), Growing points of attachment theory and research. *Monographs of the Society for Research in Child Development, 50*(1–2, Serial No. 209), 3–35.

Brown, G. R., & Anderson, B. (1991). Psychiatric morbidity in adult inpatients with childhood histories of sexual and physical abuse. *American Journal of Psychiatry, 148,* 55–61.

Brown, G. W., Birley, J. L. T., & Wing, J. K. (1972). Influence of family life on the course of schizophrenic disorders: A replication. *British Journal of Psychiatry, 121,* 241–258.

Brown, G. W., & Harris, T. O. (1993). Aetiology of anxiety and depressive disorders in an inner city population: 1. Early adversity. *Psychological Medicine, 23,* 143–154.

Carlson, E. A. (1998). *A prospective longitudinal study of disorganized/disoriented attachment. Child Development, 69,* 1107–1128.

Carlson, E. A., & Sroufe, L. A. (1995). Contributions of attachment theory to developmental psychopathology. In D. Cicchetti & D. J. Cohen (Eds.), *Developmental psychopathology: Vol. 1. Theory and methods* (pp. 581–617). New York: Wiley.

Carlson, E. B., & Putnam, F. W. (1993). An update on the Dissociative Experiences Scale. *Dissociation, 7,* 16–27.

Carlson, V., Cicchetti, D., Barnett, D., & Braunwald, K. (1989). Disorganized/disoriented attachment relationships in maltreated infants. *Developmental Psychology, 25,* 525–531.

Cassidy, J. (1994). Emotion regulation: Influences of attachment relations. In N. A. Fox (Ed.), The development of emotion regulation: Biological and behavioral considerations. *Monographs of the Society for Research in Child Development, 59*(2–3, Serial No. 240), 228–249.

Cassidy, J. (1995). Attachment and generalized anxiety disorder. In D. Cicchetti & S. Toth (Eds.), *Rochester Symposium on Developmental Psychopathology: Vol. 6. Emotion, cognition, and representation* (pp. 343–370). Rochester, NY: University of Rochester Press.

Chambless, D. L., Gillis, M. M., Tran, G. Q., & Steketee, G. S. (1996). Parental bonding reports of clients with obsessive compulsive disorder and agoraphobia. *Clinical Psychology and Psychotherapy, 3,* 77–85.

Cole-Detke, H., & Kobak, R. (1996). Attachment processes in eating disorder and depression. *Journal of Consulting and Clinical Psychology, 64*(2), 282–290.

Cooper, M. L., Shaver, P. R., & Collins, N. L. (1998). Attachment styles, emotion regulation, and adjustment in adolescence. *Journal of Personality and Social Psychology, 74,* 1380–1397.

Cummings, E. M., & Cicchetti, D. (1990). Toward a transactional model of relations between attachment and depression. In M. T. Greenberg, D. Cicchetti, & E. M. Cummings (Eds.), *Attachment in the preschool years* (pp. 339–372). Chicago: University of Chicago Press.

Dozier, M., Cue, K., & Barnett, L. (1994). Clinicians as caregivers: Role of attachment organization in treatment. *Journal of Consulting and Clinical Psychology, 62,* 793–800.

Faravelli, C., Webb, T., Ambonetti, A., Fonnesu, F., & Sessarego, A. (1985). Prevalence of traumatic early life events in 31 agoraphobic patients with panic attacks. *American Journal of Psychiatry, 142,* 1493–1494.

Fonagy, P., Leigh, T., Steele, M., Steele, H., Kennedy, R., Mattoon, G., Target, M., & Gerber, A. (1996). The relation of attachment status, psychiatric classification, and response to psychotherapy. *Journal of Consulting and Clinical Psychology, 64,* 22–31.

George, C., Kaplan, N., & Main, M. (1985). *Adult Attachment Interview* (2nd ed.). Unpublished manuscript, University of California at Berkeley.

Goldstein, M. J. (1985). Family factors that antedate the onset of schizophrenia and related disorders: The results of a fifteen year prospective study. *Acta Psychiatrica Scandinavica, 71,* 7–18.

Goldstein, M. (1990). Family relations as risk factors for the onset and course of schizophrenia. In J. Rolf, A. S. Masten, D. Cicchetti, K. H. Nuechterlein, & S. Weintraub (Eds.), *Risk and protective factors in the development of psychopathology* (pp. 408–423). New York: Cambridge University Press.

Gottesman, I. I. (1991). *Schizophrenia genesis.* New York: Freeman.

Gunderson, J. G., Kerr, J., & Englund, D. W. (1980). The families of borderlines: A comparative study. *Archives of General Psychiatry, 37,* 27–33.

Harris, M. (1995). *The loss that is forever.* New York: Dutton.

Harris, T. O., Brown, G. W., & Bifulco, A. (1986). Loss of parent in childhood and adult psychiatric disorder: The Walthamstow Study. 1. The role of lack of adequate parental care. *Psychological Medicine, 16,* 641–659.

Harris, T. O., Brown, G. W., & Bifulco, A. T. (1990). Depression and situational helplessness/mastery in a sample selected to study childhood parental loss. *Journal of Affective Disorders, 20,* 27–41.

Hart, K. J., & Ollendick, T. H. (1985). Prevalence of bulimia in working and university women. *American Journal of Psychiatry, 142,* 851–854.

Hazan, C., & Shaver, P. (1987). Romantic love conceptualized as an attachment process. *Journal of Personality and Social Psychology, 52,* 511–524.

Hazan, C., & Shaver, P. (1994). Attachment as an organizational framework for research on close relationships. *Psychological Inquiry, 5,* 1–22.

Herman, J. L., Perry, J. C., & van der Kolk, B. A. (1989). Childhood trauma in borderline personality disorder. *American Journal of Psychiatry, 146,* 490–495.

Humphrey, L. L. (1989). Observed family interactions among subtypes of eating disorders using Structural Analysis of Social Behavior. *Journal of Consulting and Clinical Psychology, 57,* 206–214.

Kendler, K. S., Heath, A. C., Martin, N. G., & Eaves, L. J. (1987). Symptoms of anxiety and symptoms of depression. *Archives of General Psychiatry, 44,* 451–457.

Kendler, K. S., Neale, M. C., Kessler, R. C., Heath, A. C., & Eaves, L. J. (1992). Generalized anxiety disorder in women. *Archives of General Psychiatry, 49,* 267–272.

Kenny, M. E., & Hart, K. (1992). Relationship between parental attachment and eating disorders in an inpatient and a college sample. *Journal of Counseling Psychology, 39,* 521–526.

Kessler, R. C., McGonagle, K. A., Zhao, S., Nelson, C. B., Hughes, M., Eshleman, S., Wittchen, H. U., & Kendler, K. S. (1994). Lifetime and 12-month prevalence of DSM-III-R psychiatric disorders in the United States. *Archives of General Psychiatry, 51,* 8–19.

Kluft, R. P. (1985). *Childhood antecedents of multiple personality.* Washington, D.C.: American Psychiatric Press.

Leff, J., & Vaughn, C. (1985). *Expressed emotion in families.* New York: Guilford Press.

Lichtenstein, J., & Cassidy, J. (1991). *The Inventory of Adult Attachment: Validation of a new measure.* Paper presented at the biennial meeting of the Society for Research in Child Development, Seattle, WA.

Liotti, G. (1992). Disorganized/disoriented attachment in the etiology of the dissociative disorders. *Dissociation, 4,* 196–204.

Liotti, G. (1996). *Understanding the dissociative processes: The contribution of attachment theory.* Manuscript submitted for publication.

Main, M. (1990). Cross-cultural studies of attachment organization: Recent studies, changing methodologies, and the concept of conditional strategies. *Human Development, 33,* 48–61.

Main, M., & Goldwyn, R. (in press). Adult attachment rating and classification system. In M. Main (Ed.), *A topology of human attachment organization assessed in discourse, drawings, and interviews.* New York: Cambridge University Press.

Main, M., & Hesse, E. (1990). Parents' unresolved traumatic experiences are related to infant disorganized attachment status: Is frightened and/or frightening parental behavior the linking mechanism? In M. T. Greenberg, D. Cicchetti, & E. M. Cummings (Eds.), *Attachment in the preschool years* (pp. 161–182). Chicago: University of Chicago Press.

Main, M., & Morgan, H. (1996). Disorganization and disorientation in infant Strange Situation behavior. In L. K. Michelson & W. J. Ray (Eds.), *Handbook of dissociation: Theoretical, empirical, and clinical perspectives* (pp. 107–138). New York: Plenum Press.

Main, M., & Solomon, J. (1986). Discovery of a new, insecure–disorganized/disoriented attachment pattern. In T. B. Brazelton & M. Yogman (Eds.), *Affective development in infancy* (pp. 95–124). Norwood, NJ: Ablex.

McCord, J. (1979). Some child-rearing antecedents of criminal behavior in adult men. *Journal of Personality and Social Psychology, 37,* 1477–1486.

McGuffin, P., & Katz, R. (1986). Nature, nurture, and affective disorder. In J. F. W. Deakin (Ed.), *The biology of depression* (pp. 26–52). London: Royal College of Psychiatrists/Gaskell Press.

Mickelson, K. D., Kessler, R. C., & Shaver, P. R. (1997). Adult attachment in a nationally representative sample.

Journal of Personality and Social Psychology, 73, 1092–1106.

Millon, T. (1983). *The Millon Clinical Multiaxial Inventory manual* (3rd ed.). Minneapolis, MN: National Computer Systems.

Minuchin, S., Rosman, B. L., & Baker, L. (1980). *Psychosomatic families: Anorexia nervosa in context.* Cambridge, MA: Harvard University Press.

Mitchell, J. E., & Pyle, R. L. (1985). Characteristics of bulimia. In J. E. Mitchell (Ed.), *Anorexia nervosa and bulimia: Diagnosis and treatment* (pp. 29–47). Minneapolis: University of Minnesota Press.

Moldin, S. O., Reich, T., & Rice, J. P. (1991). Current perspectives on the genetics of unipolar depression. *Behavior Genetics, 21,* 211–242.

Monroe, S. M., & Simons, A. D. (1991). Diathesis–stress theories in the context of life stress research: Implications for the depressive disorders. *Psychological Bulletin, 110,* 406–425.

Nigg, J. T., & Goldsmith, H. H. (1994). Genetics of personality disorders: Perspectives from personality and psychopathology research. *Psychological Bulletin, 115,* 346–380.

Nurnberger, J. I., & Gershon, E. S. (1992). Genetics. In E. S. Paykel (Ed.), *Handbook of affective disorders* (2nd ed., pp. 131–148). New York: Guilford Press.

Ogata, S. N., Silk, K. R., Goodrich, S., Lohr, N. E., Westen, D., & Hill, E. M. (1990). Childhood sexual and physical abuse in adult patients with borderline personality disorder. *American Journal of Psychiatry, 147,* 1008–1013.

Palmer, R. L., Oppenheimer, R., & Marshall, P. D. (1988). Eating disordered patients remember their parents: A study using the Parental Bonding Instrument. *International Journal of Eating Disorders, 7,* 101–106.

Patrick, M., Hobson, R. P., Castle, D., Howard, R., & Maughan, B. (1994). Personality disorder and the mental representation of early social experience. *Development and Psychopathology, 6,* 375–388.

Pearson, J. A., Cohn, D. A., Cowan, P. A., & Cowan, C. P. (1994). Earned- and continuous-security in adult attachment: Relation to depressive symptomatology and parenting style. *Development and Psychopathology, 6,* 359–373.

Perry, B. D., Pollard, R. A., Blakley, T. L., Baker, W. L., & Vigilante, D. (1995). Childhood trauma, the neurobiology of adaptation, and "use dependent" development of the brain: How "states" become "traits." *Infant Mental Health Journal, 16,* 271–291.

Pope, H. G., Mangweth, B., Negrao, A. B., Hudson, J. I., & Cordas, T. A. (1994). Childhood sexual abuse and bulimia nervosa: A comparison of American, Austrian, and Brazilian women. *American Journal of Psychiatry, 151,* 732–737.

Putnam, F. W. (1991). Recent research on multiple personality disorder. *Psychiatric Clinics of North America, 14,* 489–502.

Radloff, L. S. (1977). The CES-D scale: A self-report depression scale for research in the general population. *Applied Psychological Measurement, 1,* 385–401.

Raskin, A., Boothe, H. H., Reatig, N. A., Schulterbrandt, J. G., & Odel, D. (1971). Factor analyses of normal and depressed patients' memories of parental behavior. *Psychological Reports, 29,* 871–879.

Rhodes, B., & Kroger, J. (1992). Parental bonding and separation–individuation difficulties among late adolescent

eating disordered women. *Child Psychiatry and Human Development, 22,* 249–263.

Robins, E., & Regier, D. A. (1991). *Psychiatric disorders in America.* New York: Free Press.

Robins, L. (1966). *Deviant children grown up.* Baltimore: Williams & Wilkins.

Rosenstein, D. S., & Horowitz, H. A. (1996). Adolescent attachment and psychopathology. *Journal of Consulting and Clinical Psychology, 64*(2), 244–253.

Sanders, B., & Giolas, M. H. (1991). Dissociation and childhood trauma in psychologically disturbed adolescents. *American Journal of Psychiatry, 148,* 50–54.

Seligman, M. E. P., Abramson, L. Y., Semmel, A., & von Baeyer, C. (1979). Depressive attributional style. *Journal of Abnormal Psychology, 88,* 242–247.

Shaver, P. R., & Clark, C. L. (1994). The psychodynamics of adult romantic attachment. In J. M. Masling & R. F. Bornstein (Eds.), *Empirical perspectives on object relations theories* (pp. 105–156). Washington, DC: American Psychological Association.

Soloff, H. P., & Millward, J. W. (1983). Developmental histories of borderline patients. *Comprehensive Psychiatry, 24,* 574–588.

Spitzer, R. L., Williams, J. B., & Gibbon, M. (1987). *Instruction manual for the Structured Clinical Interview for DSM-III-R (SCID).* New York: Biometrics Research Department, New York State Psychiatric Institute.

Sroufe, L. A. (1988). The role of infant–caregiver attachment in development. In J. Belsky & T. Nezworski (Eds.), *Clinical implications of attachment* (pp. 18–38). Hillsdale, NJ: Erlbaum.

Sroufe, L. A. (1996). *Emotional development.* New York: Cambridge University Press.

Sroufe, L. A. (1997). Psychopathology as development. *Development and Psychopathology, 9,* 251–268.

Stott, D. H. (1950). *Delinquency and human nature.* Dunfermline, Scotland: Carnegie UK Trust.

Terreira, A. (1960). The pregnant woman's attitude and its reflection on the newborn. *American Journal of Orthopsychiatry, 30,* 553–561.

Torgerson, S. (1988). Genetics. In C. Last & M. Hersen (Eds.), *Handbook of anxiety disorders* (pp. 159–170). New York: Pergamon Press.

Torgerson, S., & Psychol, C. (1984). Genetic and nosological aspects of schizotypal and borderline personality disorders. *Archives of General Psychiatry, 37,* 546–554.

Tyrrell, C., & Dozier, M. (1997). *The role of attachment in therapeutic process and outcome for adults with serious psychiatric disorders.* Paper presented at the biennial meeting of Society for Research in Child Development, Washington, DC.

Walker, E. F., Grimes, K. E., Davis, D. M., & Smith, A. J. (1993). Childhood precursors of schizophrenia: Facial expressions of emotion. *American Journal of Psychiatry, 150,* 1654–1660.

Waller, N. G., & Ross, C. (1997). The prevalence and biometric structure of pathological dissociation in the general population: Taxonomic and behavior genetic findings. *Journal of Abnormal Psychology, 106,* 499–510.

Warren, S. L., Huston, L., Egeland, B., & Sroufe, L. A. (1997). Child and adolescent anxiety disorders and early attachment. *Journal of the American Academy of Child and Adolescent Psychiatry, 36,* 637–644.

Waters, E., Merrick, S. K., Albersheim, L., & Treboux, D. (1995, April). From the Strange Situation to the Adult Attachment Interview: A 20-year longitudinal study of attachment security in infancy and early childhood. In J. A. Crowell & E. Waters (Chairs), *Is the parent–child relationship a prototype of later love relationships?: Studies of attachment and working models of attachment*. Symposium conducted at the meeting of the Society for Research in Child Development, Indianapolis, IN.

Welch, S. L., & Fairburn, C. G. (1994). Sexual abuse and bulimia nervosa: Three integrated case control comparisons. *American Journal of Psychiatry, 15*, 402–407.

Widiger, T. A. (1993). The DSM-III-R categorical personali-

ty diagnoses: A critique and an alternative. *Psychological Inquiry, 4*, 75–90.

Winnicott, D. W. (1971). *Therapeutic consultations in child psychiatry*. New York: Basic Books.

Wynne, L. C. (1970). Communication disorders and the quest for relatedness in families of schizophrenics. *American Journal of Psychoanalysis, 30*, 100–114.

Zanarini, M. C., Gunderson, J. G., Marino, M. F., Schwartz, E. O., & Frankenberg, F. R. (1989). Childhood experiences of borderline patients. *Comprehensive Psychiatry, 30*, 18–25.

23

Attachment Disorganization

Unresolved Loss, Relational Violence, and Lapses in Behavioral and Attentional Strategies

❖

KARLEN LYONS-RUTH
DEBORAH JACOBVITZ

The conceptual cornerstone of our understanding of disorganized attachment behaviors in infancy was laid when Main and Solomon (1986) chose the term "disorganized/disoriented" to describe the diverse array of previously unrecognized fearful, odd, disorganized, or overtly conflicted behaviors exhibited during Ainsworth's strange situation procedure. As described by Main and Solomon (1986, 1990), infants are to be considered "disorganized/disoriented" when, for example, they appear apprehensive, cry and fall huddled to the floor, or put their hands to their mouths with hunched shoulders in response to their parents' return following a brief separation. Other disorganized infants display conflicting behavioral movements, such as turning in circles while simultaneously approaching their parents. Still others appear disoriented, freezing all movements while exhibiting a trance-like expression. Main and Hesse (1990, 1992; see also Hesse & Main, in press-a, in press-b) have proposed that a parent who enters altered states of consciousness during discussions of loss and trauma—states such as trance-like or dissociative states—is more likely to engage in inexplicably frightening and/or frightened behavior with a child. The caregiver, who at once becomes the source of comfort and the source of alarm, arouses contradictory responses in the infant—that is, the infant experiences inherently contradictory tenden-

cies to both flee from and approach the caregiver, resulting in an experience of "fright without solution" (Main, 1995). Under this condition, a collapse of behavioral strategies necessarily occurs and the infant is likely to display mistimed, interrupted, and/or incomplete movements and expressions, as well as the behaviors described directly above.

Main and colleagues' descriptions of disorganized/disoriented behavioral patterns in infancy (e.g., Main, 1973; Main & Solomon, 1986, 1990; Main & Weston, 1981) have led to an explosion of more than 80 empirical and theoretical publications on the developmental origins, correlates, and outcomes of attachment disorganization (see van IJzendoorn, Schuengel, & Bakermans-Kranenburg, in press). This chapter begins with a review of the literature on attachment disorganization in infancy, including its definition, prevalence, and associated correlates in infant behavior. The second major section, "Family Correlates of Disorganized Attachment Behavior," summarizes studies of family risk factors, parental states of mind regarding attachment assessed with the Adult Attachment Interview (AAI; George, Kaplan, & Main, 1984, 1985, 1996; Main & Goldwyn, 1998; Main, Kaplan, & Cassidy, 1985), and frightened or frightening parental behavior toward an infant. In the third major section of the chapter, data describing the

520

longitudinal reorganization of disorganized infant behavior into controlling forms of attachment behavior are reviewed, along with evidence linking both disorganized and controlling forms of attachment behavior with disruptive behavior disorders and dissociative symptoms. The fourth section of the chapter reviews recent data and theoretical models linking disorganized/controlling forms of attachment with adult violence, trauma, and child maltreatment. The later development of aggression and violence is only one of a number of developmental pathways related to early attachment disorganization, but it has received the most consistent research attention and is important because of the serious social consequences of such behavior. It should be emphasized, however, that this is a pathway followed by a minority of infants or adults in the disorganized group. The final major section of the chapter, "An Integrative Conceptual Framework: Loss, Trauma, and the Relational Diathesis," outlines a theoretical framework capable of encompassing the diverse presentations of disorganized/controlling attachment behavior across the lifespan. It also offers a proposed model to account for some of the variations in behavior and adaptation within the disorganized spectrum at any given age.

DISORGANIZED ATTACHMENT BEHAVIOR IN INFANCY: DEFINITION, PREVALENCE, AND ASSOCIATED INFANT CHARACTERISTICS

Definition of Disorganized/Disoriented Behavior

Understanding the central role of fear in attachment theory, including the infant's response to situations that arouse anxiety, is critical to understanding attachment disorganization (Hesse & Main, in press-a, in press-b; Main, 1995; Main & Hesse, 1990). Bowlby's (1969) initial formulation of attachment theory emphasized the organization of a diverse set of behaviors around the set goal of maintaining physical proximity or contact as a basis for describing how a child's tie to the mother functions at the level of observable behavior. During the first year of life, the infant's attachment to the caregiver is expressed through an increasingly sophisticated behavioral system that functions at an evolutionary level to protect the infant from harm and at a psychological level

to reduce infant distress and arousal and maintain a sense of security (Bowlby, 1969). Although the infant continually monitors the physical location of attachment figure(s), signs of danger or potential danger to the infant (such as strangeness, hunger, fatigue, illness, injury, or cues to anything frightening) result in higher levels of activation of the infant's attachment behavioral system. When the attachment system is strongly aroused, physical interaction with the caregiver (e.g., touching, clinging, cuddling) may be necessary to terminate the infant's attachment behavior. When the environment is benign and the mother is present or her whereabouts are well known, the child typically ceases to exhibit attachment behavior and instead explores the environment (Bowlby, 1969).

Separation from an attachment figure in unfamiliar circumstances, although not necessarily truly dangerous, produces physiological arousal in virtually all infants. This arousal is assumed to be a preadapted mechanism to protect the infant from harm, because separation from an adult caregiver exposes the infant to an increased risk of danger (Bowlby, 1969). What appear to vary across infants are their responses to their caregivers in the face of the arousal produced by separation in an unfamiliar environment. Ainsworth, Blehar, Waters, and Wall (1978) discovered three patterns of behavior displayed by infants when they are distressed following an unwanted separation from their caregivers in the strange situation. Some infants, termed "avoidant," show minimal displays of affect. For example, they direct attention toward objects and away from their caregivers; they turn away or look away rather than seek contact and comfort (Ainsworth et al., 1978). Other infants, termed "resistant" (and alternatively termed "ambivalent" by Ainsworth as well as others), mingle proximity and contact-seeking with angry behavior. For example, a resistant infant may raise his or her arms, signaling to be held, but then arch away and resist contact as the caregiver tries to pick him or her up. Resistant children seem unable to be comforted and calmed by their caregivers, and rather than returning to exploration following reunion, they often continue to cry and otherwise exhibit distress as the reunion episode ends. Finally, "secure" infants seek proximity and contact with little or no avoidance or angry resistance toward their caregivers. The contact and comfort they receive are effective in calming them, allowing them to return to play. These three attachment categories have been identified in families from a range of socioeconomic backgrounds in the United States and in various cultures around the world. (For comprehensive reviews, see Thompson, Chapter 13; van IJzendoorn & Sagi, Chapter 31; and Weinfield, Sroufe, Egeland, & Carlson, Chapter 4, this volume.)

For many years, researchers noted that some infants did not fit the three established attachment patterns (Crittenden, 1985; Lyons-Ruth, Connell, Zoll, & Stahl, 1987; Main & Weston, 1981; Radke-Yarrow, Cummings, Kuczynski, & Chapman, 1985). It was unclear what should be done with children who did not fit the standard categories. Researchers simply put these children aside or forced them into the best-fitting attachment category. The description of the disorganized/disoriented attachment category was grounded in a recognition that many infants in the strange situation were difficult or impossible to classify, as well as in the direct observation of conflict behaviors in infants and toddlers (Main, 1973; Main & Solomon, 1986, 1990).

Based on ethologists' descriptions of "conflict behaviors" observed in nonhuman primates (i.e., behaviors believed to result from the simultaneous activation of incompatible systems; see Hinde, 1970), Main (1979; see also Main, 1973) developed a scale for assessing "disorganized/disordered" behaviors in human infants. This scale was used to code infant behavior in a procedure in which each of a group of 1-year-old infants was exposed to an initially silent, unmoving, masked "clown" in the parent's presence (Main & Weston, 1981). One week later, each infant participated in Ainsworth's strange situation procedure with the same parent. Thirteen percent of the infants were judged "unclassifiable" with Ainsworth's three-category attachment classification system, and disorganized behavior in the "clown session" was most pronounced among these infants (Main & Weston, 1981).

To gain a better understanding of why some infants were unclassifiable, Main and Solomon (1986, 1990) reexamined over 200 anomalous strange situation videotapes. They concluded that most of the children seemed to lack any coherent, organized strategy for dealing with the stress of separation. Main and Solomon (1986, 1990) provide several striking illustrations throughout their texts. For example, one unclassifiable infant cried loudly while attempting to gain her mother's lap, then suddenly fell silent and stopped moving for several seconds. Others were observed approaching the parent with head averted; rocking on hands and knees following an abortive approach; moving away from the parent to the wall when apparently frightened by the stranger; screaming for the parent by the door upon separation, then moving silently away at reunion; raising hand to mouth in an apprehensive gesture immediately upon reunion; and, while in an apparently good mood, slowly swiping at the parent's face with a trancelike expression. What these infants had in common was the display of one or several disorganized behaviors—that is, contradictory movements and expressions corresponding to an inferred contradiction in intentions or plans (approaching a parent with head averted), or behaviors that involved apprehension either directly (fearful facial expressions, oblique approaches) or indirectly (disoriented behaviors, including dazed and trance-like expressions; freezing of all movement at a parent's entrance).

Main and Solomon (1986, 1990) called this new category "disorganized/disoriented." They proposed that infants be considered disorganized/disoriented when, in the presence of the caregiver in the strange situation, they display behaviors falling into one or more of the following seven thematic headings:

1. Sequential display of contradictory behavior patterns, such as very strong attachment behavior suddenly followed by avoidance, freezing, or dazed behavior.
2. Simultaneous display of contradictory behaviors, such as strong avoidance with strong contact seeking, distress, or anger.
3. Undirected, misdirected, incomplete, and interrupted movements and expressions—for example, extensive expressions of distress accompanied by movement away from, rather than toward, the mother.
4. Stereotypies, asymmetrical movements, mistimed movements, and anomalous postures, such as stumbling for no apparent reason and only when the parent is present.
5. Freezing, stilling, and slowed "underwater" movements and expressions.
6. Direct indices of apprehension regarding the parent, such as hunched shoulders or fearful facial expressions.
7. Direct indices of disorganization and disorientation, such as disoriented wandering, confused or dazed expressions, or multiple rapid changes in affect.

Disorganization in infancy was slow to be identified, because the behaviors are fleeting and often out of context. For example, disorganized behavior is seen when a child who appears to be in a good mood suddenly strikes at the mother, or when a child stops with a dazed expression for 20 seconds during an approach to the mother. Such behaviors are clearly unusual from the perspective of a well-trained observer. Those who are new to the system, however, may not take notice of such behaviors, since they happen quickly and by definition lack coherence; they do not make sense to the observer. However, high interrater reliability on the classification of infant behavioral patterns as disorganized/disoriented has been established in a variety of studies (Lyons-Ruth, Connell, Grunebaum, & Botein, 1990; Main & Solomon, 1990; Owen & Cox, 1997), while across all studies conducted to date reliability (80%) is acceptable (van IJzendoorn, Schuengel, & Bakermans-Kranenburg, in press).

Crittenden (1992) offers a somewhat different conceptualization of children originally considered "unclassifiable." Similar to Main and her colleagues, she proposes that some of these children show a mixture of avoidant and resistant strategies. Crittenden (1992), however, assigns them to a "defended/coercive" category and suggests that many of them should be viewed as displaying an organized attachment pattern, because they are strategically adapting their behavior to the constraints present in the caregiving relationship.

Theoretical Model

Main and Hesse (1990; see also Hesse & Main, in press-a, in press-b) have hypothesized that disorganized infant attachment behavior arises from the infant's experiencing the attachment figure herself as frightening. Infants are likely to find their attachment figures frightening under several conditions. Some attachment figures engage in directly frightening behavior, ranging from creeping up from behind an infant and sliding both hands around the infant's neck and throat to incidents of physical or sexual abuse. Other attachment figures, however, appear frightened of their own infants. Hesse and Main (in press-b; Main & Hesse, 1995) describe frightened parental behaviors as including entrance into dissociative or trance-like states (e.g., freezing of all movement with a "dead" stare, unblinking), seeking safety and comfort from an infant (e.g., showing deferential behavior), and viewing an infant as a source of alarm (e.g., one parent backed away from her infant while stammering in an unusual and frightened voice, "D-don't fol-low me, d-don't"). Main and Hesse (1990; see also Hesse & Main, in press-b) propose that frightened parental behavior occurs spontaneously and is triggered internally, stemming from parents' thoughts or from events or objects in the environment associated with their own traumatic and/or frightening experiences. According to these authors (Hesse & Main, in press-b; Main & Hesse, 1990), the apparent inexplicability of such frightened parental behavior will inevitably be alarming to an infant.

A frightened or frightening attachment figure presents an inherent conflict for an infant. Fear of the parent activates the attachment system, and the infant feels compelled to seek proximity; however, proximity-seeking increases the infant's fear, and he or she then contradicts the approach. The attachment figure is "at once the source of and the solution to its alarm" (Main & Hesse, 1990, p. 163). This paradox results in a collapse of the infant's behavioral and attentional strategies. Unable to maintain a single coherent strategy, the infant shows disorganized and/or disoriented attachment behavior. Although Hesse and Main (in press-a, in press-b) have specified that disorganized attachment behavior may stem from experiences other than frightened or frightening caregiving, the central conflict thought to distinguish disorganized infants from other insecurely attached infants is that they cannot find a solution to the paradox of fearing the figures whom they must approach for comfort in times of stress. Infants frequently frightened by the primary caregiver are believed, then, to be exposed repeatedly to experiences of "fright without solution" (Main, 1995).

Prevalence and Stability of Disorganized Attachment Patterns

A meta-analysis conducted by van IJzendoorn, Schuengel, and Bakermans-Kranenburg (in press) indicated that the percentage of infants classified as disorganized was 14% in middle-class, nonclinical groups in North America ($n = 1,882$) and 24% in low-socioeconomic-status (low-SES) samples ($n = 493$). Results of studies investigating the stability over time of disorganized attachment behaviors have been mixed. The stability of the disorganized pattern in the maltreatment study conducted by Barnett, Ganiban, and Cicchetti (in press) was 67% from 12 to 18 months and 81% from 18 to 24 months, compared to stabilities of secure attachments of 75% and 69%, respectively. Vondra, Hommerding, and Shaw (in press) also reported a stability rate of 67% in disorganized classifications from 12 to 18 months of age in a low-income sample. These stability rates are much higher than Cicchetti and Barnett (1991) reported among 30- to 48-month-old maltreated preschoolers. Barnett et al. (in press) attribute the change in apparent stability across the two studies to Cicchetti and Barnett's (1991) use of scoring criteria for the preschool period based on the system of Cassidy, Marvin, and the MacArthur Working Group on Attachment (1991)—a coding system that has not been used and refined in relation to high-risk samples as extensively as the infant scoring system for disorganization.

Lyons-Ruth, Repacholi, McLeod, and Silva (1991) reported a much lower stability rate from 12 to 18 months, primarily because of a substantial increase in the number of disorganized attachments from 12 to 18 months of age. Vondra et al. (in press) and Beckwith and Rodning (1991) also reported increases in disorganized attachment behavior from 12 to 18 months in low-income samples, and Barnett et al. (in press) reported a significant increase in vocal distress among disorganized infants from 12 to 18 months (but not from 12 to 24 months). Thus some shifts in infant presentation of disorganized behavior are likely to be occurring during this period, and these deserve further description. Vondra et al. (1997) also found that disruptive family events were related to change to a disorganized classification from 12 to 18 months of age. A meta-analysis of nine samples, including a total of 515 participants from lower- and higher-SES backgrounds, indicated significant stability of disorganized attachments across time periods ranging from 1 to 60 months ($r = .36$, van IJzendoorn, Schuengel, & Bakermans-Kranenburg, in press).

Temperament and Disorganized Attachment Behavior

Given the behavioral maladaptation evident in many disorganized attachment behaviors, one important question is whether a difficult temperament, or individual differences in emotional reactivity or behavioral disorganization, may underlie or precede the disorganized attachment classification. However, recent studies have shown that infants are unlikely to be classified as disorganized with more than one caregiver (Main & Solomon, 1990; Steele, Steele, & Fonagy, 1996; van IJzendoorn, Schuengel, & Bakermans-Kranenburg, in press). For example, Main and

Solomon (1990) reported that 31 of 34 infants classified as disorganized with one parent were not classified as disorganized with the other parent. These findings suggest that attachment disorganization emerges within a particular relationship; they do not support the notion of attachment disorganization as an individual trait or inborn characteristic of the infant. Based on a meta-analysis of 12 samples including 1,877 participants, van IJzendoorn, Schuengel, and Bakermans-Kranenburg (in press) reported a nonsignificant association between disorganized attachment behavior in infancy and constitutional and temperamental variables ($r = .003$). In the eight studies ($n = 1,639$) that examined the association between difficult temperament in particular and disorganized attachment classification, the effect size ($r = .02$) was small and not significant.

Other types of evidence also indicate that individual differences in emotional reactivity, infant difficultness, or general behavioral disorganization are unlikely to account for disorganized attachment behavior. Following up V. Carlson, Cicchetti, Barnett, and Braunwald's (1989) sample of maltreated and nonmaltreated 1-year-olds, Barnett et al. (in press) explored directly whether 18- and 24-month-olds classified as disorganized at 1 year were more emotionally reactive—that is, exhibited higher levels of separation distress—than nondisorganized infants. Emotionality was assessed by rating distress vocalizations at 15-second intervals to create a measure combining peak distress level and duration of distress. There were no significant relations between disorganized attachment classification and emotionality ratings at 12, 18, or 24 months. In addition, emotionality at 12 or 18 months did not predict disorganization at a subsequent assessment. Since high negative emotional reactivity is a core component of the construct of difficult temperament, this evidence also weighs against a view of disorganized infants as having a generally difficult temperament. In another longitudinal study following 157 infants from birth to 18 months, E. Carlson (1998) found that ratings of attachment disorganization in the strange situation at 12 and 18 months were not related to maternal history of serious medical or psychological problems, medical complications during pregnancy or delivery, infant anomalies, Brazelton Neonatal Behavioral Assessment Scale (NBAS) scores when the infants were 7 and 10 days old, or infant temperament ratings at 3 months. Finally, Vondra et al. (in press) found no relation between maternal ratings of difficultness or observers' ratings of fussy behavior at 12 or 18 months and infant disorganized classifications at 12 or 18 months.

However, in one study, disorganized attachment patterns in infancy were predicted by newborn behavioral organization. In a middle-income sample of 88 mother–infant pairs, Spangler, Fremmer-Bombik, and Grossmann (1996) found that infants displaying disorganized attachment patterns exhibited lower orientation on the Brazelton NBAS. Newborns' behavioral dimensions, however, did not predict the three organized attachment patterns. Since findings that have related scores on the NBAS to both organized and disorganized attachment patterns have not replicated, caution is needed in interpreting this finding (E. Carlson, 1998; Crockenberg, 1981; Grossmann, Grossmann, Spangler, Suess, & Unzner, 1985; Spangler et al., 1996).

Cortisol Secretion and Disorganized Attachment Behaviors

Several studies have investigated the extent to which attachment security helps children cope with stress. In animal models, cortisol secretion is correlated with an animal's inability to mobilize an effective strategy to cope with a stressor. To date, three studies have examined the association between infants' attachment behavior and their stress levels as indexed by salivary cortisol levels. In two of the three studies, infants with disorganized attachment classifications showed significantly higher cortisol levels than those of secure infants in response to brief separations (Hertsgaard, Gunnar, Erickson, & Nachmias, 1995; Spangler & Grossmann, 1993). Significant differences in the level of salivary cortisol were not evident prior to participation in the strange situation but did appear 30 minutes after the strange situation (Spangler & Grossmann, 1993). These findings are consistent with Main and Solomon's (1986) view that disorganized infant behaviors reflect the lack of an effective strategy for coping with stress; this lack results in higher and more enduring levels of stress hormones after the strange situation.

Cognitive Correlates of Disorganized Infant Attachment Behaviors

Few studies have explored the cognitive correlates of infant disorganized attachment behavior. However, Bowlby's (1969) formulation of the complementary relations between attachment and exploration posits that continued activation of the attachment system will inhibit exploration of the environment. Therefore, some relations between attachment and cognitive development may be expected. Studying low-income mothers and their controls, Lyons-Ruth, Repacholi, et al. (1991) found that infant disorganized attachment classification was related to infant mental development scores, even after maternal verbal IQ estimates, maternal involvement at home, and maternal hostile/intrusive behavior at home were controlled for. They also found that infant disorganization was related to a pattern of mild "mental lag," in which mental scores on the Bayley Scales of Infant Development lagged behind Bayley motor scores by one half of a standard deviation or more. Although only 33% of disorganized infants and 8% of nondisorganized infants displayed this pattern, this subgroup of disorganized infants contributed disproportionately to the group of children who were highly externalizing by age 7 (Lyons-Ruth, Easterbrooks, & Cibelli, 1997). Whether such cognitive effects will also be observed in middle-income settings, or whether these effects represent an interaction between infant disorganization and other aspects of the low-income environment, still needs to be explored. A later section of this chapter discusses cognitive effects in middle childhood.

FAMILY CORRELATES OF DISORGANIZED ATTACHMENT BEHAVIOR

Disorganized Attachment Behavior and Family Risk Factors

The incidence of disorganized attachment classifications in infancy has ranged from 13% to 82%, depending on the presence and types of family risk factors. Serious family risk factors, including child maltreatment, parental major depressive disorder, parental bipolar disorder, and parental alcohol intake have been associated with significant increases in the incidence of disorganized attachment patterns in infancy.

In both middle- and low-income samples, maltreatment by parents has been associated with disorganization in infancy. In a study of physically abused toddlers from middle-income backgrounds, George and Main (1979) initially described abused toddlers' behaviors with their peers and caregivers in a day care center. These behaviors were similar to indices of disorganized/disoriented infant behavior in the strange situation; for example, the toddlers showed proximity seeking accompanied by head aversion, detours, and oblique approaches. V. Carlson et al. (1989) found that 82% of the maltreated infants in their low-income sample were classified as disorganized, compared to 18% of those in the low-income control group. Lyons-Ruth et al. (1990) found that 55% of maltreated infants who had received extensive home-visiting services were classifiable as disorganized.

Several studies have examined the relationship between maternal depression and attachment disorganization, because depression in mothers has been shown to be associated with both irritable and inconsistent caregiving. The results of such studies have been mixed. Several studies have found an association between maternal depression or bipolar disorder and attachment disorganization in infants. Teti, Gelfand, Messinger, and Isabella (1995), studying middle-income depressed mothers in treatment, found that 40% of the infants (aged 16–21 months) of depressed mothers were classified as disorganized, compared to 10% in the nondepressed group. In addition, using Crittenden's Preschool Assessment of Attachment (PAA), they found that 29% of older children of depressed mothers (aged 21–26 months) were also classified in the PAA "anxious depressed," "defended/coercive," and "insecure/other" groups compared to 9% of controls. (Crittenden views these groups as comparable to the disorganized attachment classification.) It is notable that the depressed mothers in this study were all receiving psychotherapeutic treatment, including medication when indicated, and that two-thirds had also received 1 year of additional parenting services prior to these attachment assessments.

In another study of middle-income families, DeMulder and Radke-Yarrow (1991) reported that 50% of the infants and preschoolers of mothers suffering from bipolar disorder were classified as disorganized, compared to 25% of children of unipolar depressed mothers, and 18% of the children of controls. In addition, mothers of disorganized/controlling children were the most negative in their affect tone, displaying a high level of downcast affect, high levels of more than one kind of negative affect, and low levels of tenderness and affection. Finally, in an intervention study of depressed mothers on welfare and their controls, Lyons-Ruth et al. (1990) reported that 62% of the infants of chronically depressed low-income mothers were classified as disorganized if the families received no intervention services. Maternal depressive symptoms in this sample were serious enough to warrant referral to a home-visiting service and were stable over a 3½-year period (Alpern & Lyons-Ruth, 1991).

A meta-analysis of 16 studies ($n = 1,053$) examining the relationship between maternal depressive symptoms and infant disorganization in a wide variety of samples, however, showed only a marginally significant relationship ($r = .06$, $p < .06$; van IJzendoorn, Schuengel, & Bakermans-Kranenburg, in press). Only 3 of the 16 studies reported that infant disorganization was more common among depressed mothers than among nondepressed mothers. In a large National Institute of Child Health and Human Development (NICHD) study on day care, involving 1,131 families, no significant relationship was found between attachment disorganization in infants and the psychological adjustment of their mothers, as assessed by the Center for Epidemiologic Studies Depression Scale and the Neuroticism, Extraversion, and Openness Personality Inventory (NICHD Early Child Care Research Network, 1997). It appears that more chronic and severe maternal depression resulting in significant clinical impairment is necessary before associations with infant disorganization become apparent.

Only one study has examined the relationship between maternal alcohol intake and attachment disorganization in infants. O'Connor, Sigman, and Brill (1987) found that infants of middle-income mothers who had consumed moderate to heavy amounts of alcohol prior to pregnancy were more likely to be classified as disorganized than a comparison group of infants whose mothers were either abstinent or light drinkers. Replication of this finding is needed for confirmation.

Prevalence of Subgroups within the Disorganized Attachment Category by Family Risk Factors

The coding directions for assigning a disorganized classification include instructions also to assign a secondary best-fitting organized attachment classification—either secure, avoidant, or ambivalent—to each infant. In the disorganized/secure subgroup, the infant seeks contact with the caregiver without marked avoidance or ambivalence and is soothed by his or her presence but shows other unusual signs of hesitation, confusion, apprehension, dysphoria, or conflict in relation to the caregiver. Disorganized/avoidant and disorganized/ambivalent infants often display unexpected combinations of distress, contact seeking, avoidance, resistance, or other apprehensive or conflict behaviors. In 20 studies across 25 samples (*n* = 1,219), van IJzendoorn, Schuengel, and Bakermans-Kranenburg (in press) reported that, in 34% of the cases, disorganized attachment was accompanied by a secondary classification of avoidance (disorganized/avoidant infants); in 14% of the cases, it was accompanied by a secondary secure classification (disorganized/secure infants); and in 46% of the cases, disorganization was accompanied by an ambivalent classification (disorganized/ambivalent infants).

Although on most measures reviewed in this chapter disorganized infants have shown similar profiles regardless of the best-fitting secondary classification, a few studies have found differences based on the secondary classification. For example, the incidence of disorganized/secure infants was found to be highest in low-risk, middle-SES samples, as shown in Table 23.1 (Lyons-Ruth, Repacholi, et al., 1991). Compared with behavior shown by the disorganized/secure group, disorganized forms of avoidant or ambivalent infant behavior have been associated with low SES, with more severe maternal psychosocial problems (e.g., chronic maternal depression), and with a history of documented child maltreatment (Lyons-Ruth, Repacholi, et al., 1991).

In addition, mothers of disorganized/insecure infants were shown in one study to be more intrusive and negative with their infants at home than mothers of disorganized/secure infants. In contrast, mothers of disorganized/secure infants displayed more withdrawal from the infant (Lyons-Ruth, Repacholi, et al., 1991; see also the sections below on frightened/frightening caregiving). Further work is needed to explore potential subgroups in the disorganized category and to assess whether such subgroups constitute distinct precursors to the caregiving and punitive subgroups that emerge within the disorganized spectrum during the preschool period (see the section on longitudinal studies below).

Disorganized Attachment Behavior and Parental Unresolved States of Mind on the AAI

Exploring the parental mental representations, or internal working models of attachment relationships, that are associated with infants' displays of particular attachment patterns has deepened our understanding of the intergenerational transmission of attachment. According to attachment theory, as patterns of interaction and affective re-

TABLE 23.1. Subtypes of Disorganized Attachment Behavior Reported in Previous Studies by Risk Status of Sample

	Age of infant (in months)	*n*	Risk status	*n* (D)	% D/secure
Low risk					
Main & Solomon (1990)	12–18	268	Middle-class	34	61.7
Ainsworth & Eichberg (1991)	12–18	45	Middle-class	15	53.3
Moderate risk					
O'Connor, Sigman, & Brill (1987)	12	46	Middle-class (12 prenatal heavy drinkers)	16	50.0
High risk:					
Lyons-Ruth, Connell, Grunebaum, & Botein (1990)	18	70	Low-income/ at-risk	33	30.3
Carlson, Cicchetti, Barnett, & Braunwald (1989)	11–16	43	Low-income/ maltreated	22	27.3
Spieker & Booth (1988)	13	60	Low-income/ at-risk	17	5.9[a]

Note: Comparing distribution of D/secure and D/insecure subclassifications within the disorganized category by low, moderate, or high risk, χ^2 (2, *n* = 120) = 9.77, *p* < .01 (Spieker & Booth, 1988, omitted due to different reporting procedures). From Lyons-Ruth, Repacholi, McLeod, and Silva (1991). Copyright 1991 by Cambridge University Press. Reprinted by permission.

[a]20 uncertain B (secure) eliminated from sample.

sponse are repeated in close relationships over time, children build expectations about future interactions with parents and others that guide their interpretations and behaviors in new situations. As these expectations, which are largely unconscious, become elaborated and organized they are termed "internal working models of attachment relationships." These working models of self and others tend to perpetuate themselves in the absence of specific influences for change and become incorporated as stable interpersonal tendencies which endure over time and guide later parental behavior (Bowlby, 1973; Bretherton, this volume).

Main, Kaplan, and Cassidy (1985) have demonstrated that when parents' representations of their childhood attachment relationships are explored in an open-ended interview format, four broad classifications of the adult's state of mind regarding attachment can be reliably assigned (George, Kaplan, & Main, 1984, 1985, 1996; Main & Goldwyn, 1998). These four classifications, labeled "autonomous," "dismissing," "preoccupied," and "unresolved," predict the four infant attachment classifications: "secure," "avoidant," "resistant" (or "ambivalent") and "disorganized." Adults classified as secure "value attachment relationships and regard attachment experiences as influential, but they are relatively independent and objective regarding any particular experience or relationship" (Main & Goldwyn, 1998, p. 159). Secure adults are aware of the nature of their experiences with their parents during childhood and have considered the effects of these experiences on them. Adults considered secure appear free to explore their thoughts and feelings during the course of the interview. Adults classified as dismissing devalue, minimize, or dismiss the importance of attachment relationships and experiences. They may dismiss possible imperfections in their parents in the face of contradictory evidence or they may contemptuously derogate attachment figures or attachment-related experiences. Finally, adults classified as preoccupied appear "confused, unobjective and preoccupied with past relationships within the family and/or past experiences" (Main & Goldwyn, 1998, p. 168). Preoccupied adults may appear "passive and vague, fearful and overwhelmed, and/or angry, conflicted, and unconvincingly analytical" (Main & Goldwyn, 1998, p. 168) during discussions of early family relationship experiences. Recent studies have demonstrated that an adult's internal working model of attachment, assessed prior to the birth

of the first child, predicts the security of the infant–parent attachment relationship at 1 year (van IJzendoorn, 1995; see Crowell, Fraley, & Shaver, Chapter 20, and Hesse, Chapter 19, this volume, for discussions of the AAI).

The unresolved classification is assigned to adults who show signs of disorientation and disorganization during discussions of potentially traumatic events (i.e., loss by death, physical abuse, or sexual abuse). As detailed by Main and Goldwyn (1998), one such index is a lapse in the monitoring of discourse, whereby the speaker enters a state of mind in which he or she no longer appears appropriately conscious of the interview situation and has in fact "lost awareness of the discourse context." Main and Morgan (1996) provide striking examples: "Some adults fall silent in the middle of a sentence discussing loss or trauma, and then complete the sentence 20 seconds or more later, as if no time had passed. Others may never complete the sentence, as 'he died, and his face [52-second pause]. I guess I was just finishing high school'" (p. 125). Indications of losing the discourse context include a sudden shift to an odd or poetic phrasing in discussing loss or trauma. For example, "She was young, she was lovely, she was dearly beloved by all who knew her and who witnessed her as she was torn from the ground at its moment of splendor" (Main & Goldwyn, 1998, p. 123).

Other indices of unresolved loss or trauma involve lapses in the monitoring of reasoning. Lapses in the monitoring of reasoning are usually brief and should not be confused with "irrational" thinking in the transcript as a whole. These lapses can take several forms, including indications of a belief that a lost person is simultaneously dead and alive (in a physical rather than a religious sense). For example, one speaker said, "It's probably better that he is dead, because now he can get on with being dead and I can get on with raising a family" (Main & Goldwyn, 1998, p. 118). Such lapses may also include disbelief that the person is dead (e.g., discussing a parent in the present tense even though the parent died 20 years earlier). Like disorganized infants, parents classified as unresolved are also given a best-fitting alternate classification that identifies the pattern most closely corresponding to the overall organization of the interview (e.g., unresolved/autonomous).

Early loss of a parent through death has been associated with infant disorganization. Main and Hesse (1990) reported that 15% of the adults in their sample had lost a parent through death before having completed high school; 56% of these parents had infants classified as disorganized. Put another way, only 8% of the parents of avoidant, resistant, or secure babies had experienced such loss, whereas 39% of the parents of disorganized babies had done so. Lyons-Ruth, Repacholi, et al. (1991) reported a similar association between parental death and infant disorganization. Early loss of an attachment figure in itself, however, does not inevitably lead to infant disorganization (Ainsworth & Eichberg, 1991). Rather, the lack of resolution of the loss, as revealed in parents' lapses in the monitoring of reasoning and discourse during discussions of loss on the AAI, is what forecasts attachment disorganization in their infants. A meta-analysis of nine studies ($n = 548$) revealed an effect size of .65 ($r = .31$) for the relation between child disorganization and parental unresolved status (van IJzendoorn, 1995). The effect sizes across studies varied very strongly in relation to the amount of training coders had received in the system for coding disorganized attachment, with more training being associated with stronger effect sizes.

Unresolved Parental States of Mind and Frightened/Frightening Caregiving

One of the critical questions needing further study is why unresolved loss or trauma on the part of parents is related to their infants' display of disorganized attachment behavior. To what extent are lapses in the monitoring of discourse and reasoning in discussions of loss and trauma related to the quality of care parents provide their children, and how do these caregiving behaviors contribute to disorganized infant attachment behaviors? Lapses in the monitoring of reasoning and discourse are notable because they involve a sudden shift or alteration in the quality of discourse. Hesse (1996) suggests that these lapses involve "frightening and/or overwhelming experiences that may momentarily be controlling or altering discourse" (p. 8). Hesse and Main (in press-a, in press-b) suggest that such a parent is still overwhelmed either by a past experience of maltreatment, which is inherently frightening, or by "incompletely remembered loss experiences." When the still-traumatized parent responds to memories or ideas surrounding loss or trauma, Main and Hesse (1990) propose that the parent will engage in frightened and frightening behavior with the infant. More recently, Jacobvitz, Hazen, and Riggs (1997), Schuengel, van IJzendoorn, Bakermans-Kranenburg, and Blom (in

press), and Lyons-Ruth, Bronfman, and Parsons (in press) tested aspects of Main and Hesse's (1990) hypothesis regarding the role of frightened or frightening parental behavior as the mediator of the effect of unresolved parental states of mind on infant disorganization. Results of the three studies converged in somewhat unexpected ways.

Using Main and Hesse's (1995) coding system for identifying frightened or frightening behaviors, Jacobvitz et al. (1997) found very strong associations between a *prenatal* assessment of maternal unresolved loss on the AAI and a mother's display of frightened or frightening behaviors toward her firstborn infant at 8 months in a sample of 113 middle-income families. Frightening maternal behaviors included unusual vocal patterns, such as simultaneously voicing and devoicing intonations; baring teeth; invasions into vulnerable areas of the infant's personal space, such as hands suddenly, silently sliding from behind across the infant's throat; sudden looming into the infant's face; and movements or postures that seemed to be part of a pursuit/hunt sequence (Main & Hesse, 1992b, 1995; see also Main & Hesse, 1990). One mother in the study conducted by Jacobvitz and her colleagues (1997; see also Thalhuber, Jacobvitz, & Hazen, 1998) appeared to enter a trance-like state, sitting immobilized in an uncomfortable position (with her hand in the air) and blankly staring into space for 50 consecutive seconds. She entered into what appeared to be an altered state on several occasions for a total of 5 minutes during a 20-minute feeding session. This mother was classified as unresolved on the AAI. Indications that a mother was afraid of her baby included instances in which the mother handled the baby as if the baby were an inanimate object and in which the mother moved her hand away suddenly as if fearful of being hurt (see Hesse & Main, in press-b).

As predicted, then, mothers classified prenatally as unresolved differed significantly from mothers not classified as unresolved on the 9-point frightened/frightening scale. However, mothers classified as unresolved did not differ significantly from other mothers on any other negative parenting interaction patterns observed in the mothers' homes, including maternal insensitivity, interference, or rejection (Jacobvitz et al., 1997). This difference between unresolved mothers and other mothers occurred regardless of whether the unresolved mothers were given a secondary secure or insecure adult classification (Jacobvitz, 1998). Not all mothers classified as unresolved, however, engaged in frightened or frightening behaviors toward their infants. Compared to unresolved mothers who were also assigned a secondary insecure classification, unresolved mothers who were also assigned a secondary secure (i.e., autonomous) classification showed a marginally significant trend in the direction of engaging in fewer frightened or frightening behaviors toward their infants.

In a sample of 85 mother–child dyads, Schuengel et al. (in press) found a relation between maternal unresolved loss on the AAI when an infant was 12 months old and maternal display of frightened or frightening behaviors toward the infant at 10 or 11 months using the Main and Hesse (1992b) coding system, but this finding occurred only among the subgroup of mothers classified as unresolved/insecure on the AAI (analogous to the disorganized/insecure infant subgroup). Like Jacobvitz et al. (1997), Schuengel et al. (in press) found that mothers classified as unresolved/insecure displayed significantly more frightened or frightening behaviors than mothers classified as unresolved/secure. However, in a more puzzling finding that goes counter to the findings reported by Jacobvitz (1998), Schuengel et al. (in press) found that mothers classified as secure displayed significantly *more* frightened or frightening behaviors than did mothers classified unresolved/secure. This finding, if replicated, suggests some overall behavioral inhibition on the part of mothers classified as unresolved/secure, since the secure but not unresolved mothers displayed more frightened or frightening behaviors than did this unresolved subgroup. One explanation for the discrepant findings across the two studies is that Jacobvitz and her colleagues created a more stressful situation for mother and child than did Schuengel et al. (in press). In the Jacobvitz et al. (1997) study, mothers were instructed to feed their babies, play with them, and change their babies' clothes. Not only were parents forced to interact with their children, but most of the 8-month-olds resisted having their clothes changed. Schuengel et al. (in press), in contrast, did not structure the home observations. Stressful conditions may trigger thoughts associated with earlier losses or trauma, resulting in the display of frightened and/or frightening caregiving behavior.

To understand further why some mothers classified unresolved did or did not display frightened or frightening behaviors toward their infants, Jacobvitz and her colleagues explored factors associated with the loss experience. Bowlby (1980) has suggested that the closer the relationship of the person lost, the more difficult the resolution process, particularly if the death occurred during childhood. Ainsworth and Eichberg (1991) did not find this to be the case; they found no significant association between either a mother's age when the loss occurred or her relationship to the deceased (e.g., attachment figure vs. someone else) and unresolved states of mind on the AAI. Replicating Ainsworth and Eichberg's study with a larger sample ($n = 113$), Jacobvitz (1998) also found that the mother's age when the loss occurred was unrelated to the mother's resolution of loss but did find that mothers who were unresolved were more likely to have lost a parent than to have lost a less important figure. Moreover, both the mother's age when the loss occurred and the mother's relationship to the deceased discriminated between unresolved mothers who engaged in frightened or frightening behavior toward their infants and those who did not (Jacobvitz et al., 1997). Ninety-one percent of unresolved mothers who either lost an attachment figure or were younger than 17 when the unresolved loss occurred engaged in frightened or frightening behaviors toward their infants. In contrast, only 20% of the unresolved mothers who were 17 or older when the loss occurred and did not lose an attachment figure displayed frightened or frightening behavior (Jacobvitz et al., 1997). Therefore, degree of kinship and timing of the loss may be important in predicting whether the mother's unresolved state of mind impinges on her caregiving behavior.

Frightened/Frightening Caregiving and Disorganized Attachment Behavior in Infancy

Schuengel, van IJzendoorn, Bakermans-Kranenburg, and Blom (1997, in press) and Lyons-Ruth, Bronfman, and Parsons (in press) tested Main and Hesse's hypothesis that maternal frightened and/or frightening behavior would be related to the infant's attachment disorganization. In the study by Schuengel et al. (in press), maternal frightened or frightening behavior marginally predicted infant disorganized attachment classification ($p < .05$, one-tailed). However, the subscale for maternal dissociated behavior more strongly predicted infant disorganized behavior, as did a broader set of maternal "disorganized" behaviors that included the frightened or frightening behavior codes (Schuengel et al., 1997). Schuengel et al. (1997, in press) did not examine maternal frightened or frightening behaviors separately for the two subgroups of disorganized infants, as they did for the two subgroups of unresolved mothers. It is notable that maternal self-reported scores on the Dissociative Experiences Scale (DES) did not predict infant disorganization nor did the closeness of kin of a mother's experienced loss. Lyons-Ruth and Block (1996) also failed to find a relation between maternal scores on the DES and infant disorganization.

Similar to Schuengel et al. (1997), Lyons-Ruth, Bronfman, and Parsons (in press) found that a broader set of maternal behaviors that included the frightened or frightening behavior codes (Main & Hesse, 1992b) significantly predicted an infant's rating for disorganized behavior and marginally predicted an infant's disorganized attachment classification. Lyons-Ruth and colleagues expanded on Main and Hesse's construct of frightened or frightening behavior to include two other broad aspects of maternal behavior hypothesized to be theoretically related to infant fear and disorganization of attachment strategies. These included extreme parental misattunement to the specific content of an infant's attachment-related communications and the display of competing caregiving strategies that both elicited and rejected infant attachment affects and behaviors. This broader set of behaviors, termed "disrupted affective communication between mother and infant," included codes for affective communication errors, role confusion, negative/intrusive behaviors, disorientation, and withdrawal. Maternal behavior was coded in the strange situation at 18 months among 65 mother–infant dyads. When the frightened or frightening behavior codes were analyzed separately, they significantly predicted infant disorganized behavior. However, with all frightened or frightening behaviors excluded, the level of disrupted maternal affective communication also significantly predicted infant disorganization.

However, when the two subgroups of disorganized infants were examined separately on the frequency of maternal frightened or frightening behavior and on the frequency of disrupted communication more generally, only the mothers of disorganized/insecure infants differed significantly from mothers of infants with organized patterns of attachment. This finding echoed Schuengel et al.'s (in press) identification of elevated frightened or frightening behavior only among mothers in the unresolved/insecure subgroup. Mothers of infants in the disorganized/insecure subgroup showed elevated rates of frightening behavior, affective communication

errors, hostile/intrusive behavior, and role confusion, compared to mothers of organized infants.

However, mothers of disorganized/secure infants were distinguished from mothers of organized infants when the *patterning* of maternal frightened or frightening behavior and disrupted communication was taken into account. Mothers of disorganized/secure infants exhibited a fearful, inhibited pattern of behavior. This pattern was characterized by subtle frightened behavior in the absence of high levels of frightening, dissociated, and role-reversed maternal behavior. In addition, mothers of disorganized/secure infants exhibited a pattern of withdrawn, but not hostile, interaction on the disrupted communication codes (Lyons-Ruth, Bronfman, & Atwood, in press).

A study of 20 village-living mother–infant dyads in the Dogon ethnic group of Mali, an African country, provides preliminary cross-cultural support for a relationship between frightened or frightening maternal behavior and attachment disorganization (True, Pasani, Ryan, & Oumar, 1998). Although none of the mothers scored above the midpoint on the frightened or frightening behavior scale, infants whose mothers scored above 1 on the frightened or frightening behavior scale were more often classified as disorganized in the strange situation than infants whose mothers showed no frightened or frightening indices.

Taken together, these studies suggest that maternal frightened or frightening behaviors are related both to infant disorganized attachment status and to parental unresolved states of mind. However, the most broadly based applications of the coding inventories for fear-related maternal behaviors were the most successful in predicting disorganized infant behavior. In addition, it appears that the overall patterning of parental behaviors within the disorganized spectrum may take quite different forms. Because of these potential differences in the profiles of maternal behavior within the disorganized classification, future researchers may need to plan their data analyses carefully to capture both the fearful, inhibited subgroup and the more pervasively frightening subgroup.

Other Studies of the Caregiving Behavior of Disorganized Infants

Several prospective longitudinal studies following disorganized infants over time have demonstrated that their mothers may show a particularly impaired ability to engage in well-attuned affective communications with their young children. Hann, Castino, Jarosinski, and Britton (1991) examined mother–infant interactions at 20 months among 67 low-income adolescent mothers and their infants (the infant's attachment strategies had been assessed at 13 months). In this sample of low-income adolescent mothers, 60% of the infants were classified as disorganized with a secondary insecure classification. They found that negotiation of conflict was significantly impaired among mothers of disorganized/insecure infants. The secure 20-month-olds and their mothers in this study were the most likely to make social initiations, initiate nonaggressive conflict behavior, and follow nonaggressive conflict with further nonaggressive conflict. The small number of toddlers with insecure but organized attachment strategies demonstrated intermediate levels of initiative and intermediate frequencies of nonaggressive conflict initiations. In contrast, compared to the other toddlers, those previously classified as disorganized/insecure more often initiated aggressive conflict with their mothers and refused their mothers' social initiatives, and were the least likely to initiate social exchanges with their mothers. Moreover, aggressive conflicts initiated by the children in the disorganized/insecure group were less likely to be resolved than those initiated by their mothers. In addition, compared to the other mothers, mothers of disorganized infants (regardless of their secondary classification) were less affectionate. They initiated more interactions but complied less frequently with their children's initiatives. This study indicates that mother–toddler exchanges in dyads from the disorganized/insecure group were more often conflicted and asynchronous.

Other longitudinal studies have reported similar results. Main et al. (1985), studying a middle-income sample, initially reported that mothers of disorganized infants and mothers of avoidant infants exhibited low fluency and balance in discourse with these same children at age 6 (see Strage & Main, 1985). Similarly, Easterbrooks, Lyons-Ruth, Biesecker, and Carper (1996), in a low-income sample, showed that mothers of 18-month-old infants classified as disorganized were rated lower in emotional availability when they were observed with their children at 7 years of age. Similar results were reported by Moss, Parent, Gosselin, Rousseau, and St-Laurent (1996) in their study of a middle-income sample. Mothers of children classified as controlling at

ages 5 to 7 displayed the least reciprocal and least balanced communication, compared to mothers of children in other attachment categories.

Spieker and Booth (1988), studying low-income mothers and infants, conducted a number of analyses of measures taken both prenatally and at 6 weeks and 3 months postpartum. Mothers of disorganized infants did not differ from mothers of secure infants on 23 interview measures of social support, emotional symptoms, or satisfaction with available resources. However, mothers of both disorganized and avoidant infants were rated lower than mothers of secure infants on total teaching skills and on positive parent–infant mutuality.

Ratings of maternal insensitivity, as assessed using Ainsworth's sensitivity–insensitivity scale, have not been associated with attachment disorganization in infancy. In a meta-analysis of 12 studies, van IJzendoorn, Schuengel, and Bakermans-Kranenburg (in press) reported no significant relationship between disorganized attachment in infants and ratings of parental insensitivity. The sensitivity–insensitivity scale, which is a global rating of maternal caregiving, does not appear to be differentiated and specific enough regarding the affective communications involved in fear-related behavior to predict infant disorganization.

LONGITUDINAL REORGANIZATION OF DISORGANIZED FORMS OF ATTACHMENT BEHAVIOR INTO CONTROLLING FORMS OF ATTACHMENT BEHAVIOR

Two prospective longitudinal studies have demonstrated a shift from disorganized behavior during infancy to controlling behavior with mothers (of either a punitive or a caregiving type) at 6 years of age (Main & Cassidy, 1988; Wartner, Grossmann, Fremmer-Bombik, & Suess, 1994). In a study of 33 families in Berkeley, California, Main and Cassidy (1988) developed an assessment of parent–child attachment at age 6. Children's behavioral and verbal response patterns to a reunion with a parent after an hour-long separation were classified into four categories that corresponded to the four infant attachment classifications, including "secure," "avoidant," "ambivalent," and "controlling." Children are classified as "controlling" if they "seem to actively attempt to control or direct the parent's attention and behavior and assume a role which is usually considered more appropriate for a parent with reference to a child" (Main & Cassidy, 1988, p. 418). Eighty-four percent of the infants classified as disorganized at 1 year were also classified as displaying controlling behavior toward the parent when they were 6 years old (Main & Cassidy, 1988). Combining data from two studies (Main & Cassidy, 1988; Wartner et al., 1994), van IJzendoorn, Schuengel, and Bakermans-Kranenburg (in press) reported a strong association ($r = .55$) between attachment disorganization in infancy and later controlling attachment behavior. Interestingly, after correcting for coding error, van IJzendoorn and his colleagues found that continuity from attachment disorganization in infancy to controlling behavior during the preschool years was much stronger than short-term stability either in disorganized attachment behavior in infancy or in controlling behavior in preschool children (Main & Cassidy, 1988). The array of studies exploring correlates

of disorganized attachment behavior at later ages is reviewed below and summarized in Table 23.2.

Controlling Attachment Behavior and Parental Internal Models

Like disorganized behavior in infancy, controlling/disorganized behavior in preschool children has been related to mothers' mental representations of attachment. Several researchers have reported an association between controlling/disorganized behavior in children and unresolved loss or trauma (as assessed on the AAI) in their mothers (George & Solomon, 1996; Greenberg, Speltz, DeKlyen, & Endriga, 1991). George and Solomon (1996) have further extended our understanding of the mental representations of caregiving among mothers whose children were classified as controlling (see also George & Solomon, Chapter 28, this volume). In semistructured interviews about mothers' relationships to their 6-year-olds, George and Solomon

TABLE 23.2. Longitudinal Outcomes of Disorganization in Infancy and Correlates of Controlling Behavior in Preschool and Elementary School

Authors	Children's ages	Assessment instruments	Outcomes and correlates of disorganization
Carlson (1998)	18, 24, and 42 months; 4½–5 years; grades 1, 2, 3, 6; 17½ years	Strange situation, Main and Solomon coding; birth complications; Neonatal Behavioral Assessment Scale; Carey Infant Temperament Questionnaire; observations of mother–child interactions; preschool behavior problem index; teachers' completion of Child Behavior Checklist and emotional health rank; Schedule of Affective Disorders and Schizophrenia for School-Age Children (K-SADS)	Less confident with mothers (24 months); avoidance of mothers (42 months); dissociation and internalizing behavior (grades 1, 2, 3, and 6), lower emotional health rank (Grades 1, 2, 3, and 6); overall behavior problems, internalizing problems, & dissociative symptoms (17½ years); and higher ratings of psychopathology in general and dissociation specifically on the K-SADS (17½ years)
Cohn (1990)	6 years	Main and Cassidy system; peer behavior nominations; teacher and peer liking ratings; teacher completion of Classroom Adjustment Rating Scales and Health Resources Inventory	No significant results for girls or boys, but disorganized unclassifiable infants were not included

(continued)

TABLE 23.2. *(continued)*

Authors	Children's ages	Assessment instruments	Outcomes and correlates of disorganization
DeMulder & Radke-Yarrow (1991)	Preschool	Main and Cassidy system	Mothers of controlling preschoolers displayed the most negative affective tone
Greenberg, Speltz, DeKlyen, & Endriga (1991)	Preschool	Main and Cassidy system; DSM-III-R criteria	Diagnosis of oppositional defiant disorder
Hann, Castino, Jarosinski, & Britton (1991)	13 and 20 months	Strange situation, Main and Solomon coding; observations of mother–infant interactions	Fewest social initiatives and more refusals of mothers' initiatives; initiation of conflict by aggressive behavior
Hubbs-Tait, Osofsky, Hann, & Culp (1994)	13 and 54 months	Strange situation, Main and Solomon coding; Child Behavior Checklist and Child Behavior Checklist Social Scale completed by mothers	Externalizing behavior problems; no relationship between attachment and maternal reports of children's social skills and friendship
Jacobsen et al. (1994)	7, 9, 12, 15, and 17 years	Piagetian cognitive tasks; Chandler's perspective-taking task, Kaplan's coding; behavioral ratings of self-confidence by interviewers	Lower self-confidence, difficulties with deductive reasoning, including poor performance on syllogistic reasoning task
Jacobvitz & Hazen (in press)	18, 20, 24, 30, 36, 42, and 54 months	Strange situation, Main and Solomon coding; observations of mother–child and father–child interactions, of family dinners, of interactions with two different peers, and of peer interactions in preschool classrooms	Controlling behavior toward mothers, either caregiving or punitive; fearful/disorganized responses; emotional disconnection; and aggression toward peers
Kaplan (1987)	1 and 6 years	Strange situation, Main and Solomon coding; Kaplan's Separation Anxiety Test	Fearful/disorganized (e.g., catastrophic fantasies) or silent responses
Lyons-Ruth, Alpern, & Repacholi (1993)	18 months; 5 years	Strange situation, Main and Solomon coding; home observations of mother–infant interactions; Bayley Scales of Infant Development; teachers' completion of Preschool Behavior Questionnaire	Hostile/aggressive behavior toward peers at age 5
Lyons-Ruth, Easterbrooks, & Cibelli (1997)	18 months; 7 years	Strange situation, Main and Solomon coding; home observations of mother–infant interactions; Bayley Scales of Infant	Externalizing behavior problems at age 7; mild mental lag combined with disorganization at 18 months was a risk factor for externalizing problems

(continued)

TABLE 23.2. *(continued)*

Authors	Children's ages	Assessment instruments	Outcomes and correlates of disorganization
		Development; teachers' completion of Child Behavior Checklist	
Main & Cassidy (1988)	1 and 6 years	Strange situation, Main and Solomon coding; Main & Cassidy system	Controlling (role-reversing) behavior toward parent, either punitive or caregiving
Moss, Parent, Gosselin, Rousseau, & St-Laurent (1996)	3–5 years; 1–7 years	Main and Cassidy system; questionnaires completed by parents and teachers, including the Preschool Socio-Affective Profile and Child Behavior Checklist	Lower social competence in preschool; behavior problems shown over time, with no clear pattern of internalizing or externalizing problems
Moss, Rousseau, Parent, St-Laurent, & Saintong (1998)	5–7 years; 9–11 years	Main and Cassidy system; questionnaires completed by teachers, including the Preschool Socio-Affective Profile and Child Behavior Checklist	Externalizing and internalizing behavior problems in boys and girls; lower mathematics scores and lower academic self-esteem at age 8 than secure or resistant children
Ogawa, Sroufe, Weinfeld, Carlson, & Egeland (1997)	12, 18, 24, 42, 54, and 61 months; grades 1, 2, 3, 6; 16, 17½, and 19 years	Strange situation, Main and Solomon coding; Child Behavior Checklist completed by mothers and teachers; life stress measures; assessments of physical abuse, neglect, and witnessing trauma; Putnam's Child Dissociative Checklist; K-SADS; Dissociative Experiences Scale	Dissociation at 16 to 17½ years and 19 years; higher dissociation scores at age 19 for young adults classified as disorganized in infancy who also faced trauma (vs. 19-year-olds who were not classified as disorganized or were classified as disorganized but did not experience trauma)
Shaw, Owens, Vondra, Keenan, & Winslow (1996)	6–9, 18 months; 1, 2, 3, and 5 years	Strange situation, Main and Solomon coding; mothers' completion of Infant Characteristics Questionnaire, Child Behavior Checklist, Personality Research Form, Marital Adjustment Test, Child-Rearing Disagreements Scale, and Parenting Daily Hassles	Disorganization at 1 year combined with parent ratings of difficultness at age 2 predicted aggression at age 5
Speltz, Greenberg, & DeKlyen (1990)	5–7 years	Main and Cassidy system; DSM-III-R criteria	Aggression and externalizing behaviors toward peers
Solomon, George, & de Jong (1995)	6 years	Main and Cassidy system; children's response to stories about a hurt knee, a monster in the bedroom,	Depiction of self and caregiver as frightening (e.g., themes of catastrophe and helplessness), or

(continued)

TABLE 23.2. *(continued)*

Authors	Children's ages	Assessment instruments	Outcomes and correlates of disorganization
		and parent–child separation and reunion	complete inhibition
Teti, Gelfand, Messinger, & Isabella (1995)	16–21 months; 21–26 months	Strange situation, Main and Solomon coding; Crittenden's Preschool Assessment of Attachment	Maternal depression was associated with anxious depressed, defended/coercive, and insecure/other preschool classifications
Wartner, Grossmann, Fremmer-Bombik, & Suess (1994)	1, 5, and 6 years	Strange situation, Main and Solomon coding; Main and Cassidy system; observations of preschool play groups; social perceptions task (cartoons depicting themes of aggression)	Infant disorganization was associated with controlling behavior at age 6; social incompetence in play groups (5 years) was associated with controlling behavior at age 6

(1996) found that a helpless parental stance was related significantly to controlling attachment behavior on the part of a child. In some cases, this helpless stance involved failing to provide reassurance and protection to the child, while in other cases the helpless stance included fear either of the child or of the mother's own loss of control in some way. In still other cases, the mother described feeling that the child was in control of the relationship, either because of the child's precocious positive capabilities or because of the child's unmanageability. Moreover, in George and Solomon's (1996) middle-income sample, 62% of parents with unresolved loss or trauma described their relationships with their children in helpless terms. Helpless stances have not yet been related to disorganized attachment behavior in infancy, however.

Disorganized/Controlling Attachment Patterns and Children's Internal Representations of Attachment Figures

As described earlier, an infant's display of disorganized attachment behaviors is thought to occur because the infant is faced with an unresolvable paradox. When fear is aroused, the infant experiences unresolvable conflict with respect to seeking comfort from a frightened or a frightening caregiver who is also the only haven of safety. Several studies examining children's depictions of self and caregiver show that many children classified as disorganized in infancy still display "fright without solution" at age 6 (Main, 1995).

Kaplan (1987) administered her Separation Anxiety Test to children in the Berkeley sample to assess children's responses to drawings of parent–child separations. The responses of children classified as disorganized at 1 year were fearful and disorganized. Some children appeared afraid and yet unable to do anything about it, while others remained silent throughout the task. Still others engaged in catastrophic fantasies, indicating that the attachment figure would be hurt or killed.

In another study of a middle-income sample of 69 kindergartners, children were asked to respond to a set of doll play stories about attachment-related themes (Solomon, George, & de Jong, 1995). The doll play of controlling children was characterized by themes of catastrophe and helplessness, including nightmares and violent fantasies, or by complete inhibition of play. Compared to the other children in the study, those classified as controlling more often depicted themselves as helpless and their caregivers as frightening. Although this helpless stance in kindergartners has not been linked empirically with attachment disorganization in infancy, such helplessness is compatible theoretically with a collapse of behavioral strategies resulting in an inhibition of attachment behavior. Jacobsen et al. (1992) also found an association between children's controlling behavior with the caregiver and fearful and disorganized responses to a series of cartoon illustrations depicting a parent–child separation and coded with Kaplan's system (see Kaplan, 1987).

Disorganized/Controlling Attachment Patterns and Cognitive Correlates

Several studies have demonstrated associations between disorganized/controlling attachment patterns and the quality of children's cognitive functioning. In a 10-year longitudinal study assessing 85 Icelandic children at ages 7, 9, 12, 15, and 17, Jacobsen, Edelstein, and Hofmann (1994) examined the relationship between attachment security assessed at age 7 and later cognitive functioning. Both disorganized/controlling children and other insecure children differed from secure children on Piagetian tasks assessing concrete and formal operational reasoning from 7 to 15 years of age. These cognitive differences by attachment group disappeared when self-confidence was controlled. However, on the subset of formal operational measures that assessed syllogistic reasoning, disorganized/controlling children differed significantly from other secure and insecure children from ages 9 to 17, and these differences remained when self-confidence, IQ, and attention problems were included in the analyses. Disorganized/controlling children were particularly likely to give contradictory responses on these tasks compared to other attachment groups, and attachment group differences increased with age, with disorganized/controlling adolescents as a group never reaching formal operational level. However, these results need replication due to the small number of disorganized/controlling children in the analyses of syllogistic reasoning ($n = 6$). The syllogistic reasoning tasks involved answering hypothetical questions posed by an experimenter rather than the direct experimentation involved in the other Piagetian tasks with objects. Jacobsen et al. (1994) suggest that disorganized children may perform poorly because they are particularly vulnerable to disregulated thought processes generated by their anxieties regarding the reactions of others. In another longitudinal study following 35 children in Germany over 5 years, Jacobsen, Huss, Fendrich, Kruesi, and Ziegenhain (1997) examined the relationship between attachment and self-regulatory abilities related to cognitive functioning. Compared to the other children, those classified as disorganized/controlling had the most difficulty waiting on a standard delay-of-gratification task.

All of these difficulties with cognitive functioning suggest that disorganized children may be at risk for academic problems. Moss, Rousseau, Parent, St-Laurent, and Saintong (1998) found that children classified as disorganized at age 5–7 had lower mathematics scores and lower academic self-esteem at age 8 than did children classified as secure or resistant. Moreover, such results were obtained even after the children's IQs were controlled for. As in the findings reported by Jacobsen et al. (1994), the relationship between disorganized/controlling attachment and mathematics performance disappeared after children's self-confidence with schoolwork was controlled for.

Disorganized/Controlling Attachment Patterns and the Development of Peer Relationships

Most studies of the relationship between attachment disorganization and peer interaction have relied on behavior checklists completed by mothers and/or teachers, as shown in Table 23.2. Only a few studies have obtained ratings of friendship quality from the peers themselves or from trained observers (Cohn, 1990; Jacobvitz & Hazen, in press; Wartner et al, 1994). In one cross-sectional study of 40 children, trained observers rated 6-year-olds classified as disorganized/controlling as more incompetent in play quality and conflict resolution than secure children, but the ratings of disorganized/controlling children's friendship quality did not differ from those given to avoidant children (Wartner et al., 1994). Furthermore, compared with secure children, disorganized/controlling children were rated as more incompetent overall in three or more (but not in two or fewer) of the areas assessed. In another cross-sectional study, in which ratings of peer liking, sociometric status, and peer nominations were obtained from the children themselves, disorganized/controlling children did not differ from the other attachment groups (Cohn, 1990). However, contrary to other investigators, nine children who were disorganized/unclassifiable were eliminated from the study, creating a small and possibly unrepresentative group of children in the disorganized/controlling category.

Few studies have examined the development of peer relationships among children classified as disorganized in infancy. As part of a larger longitudinal study conducted by Hazen, Jacobvitz, and Hazen (in press) followed 66 infants over 3 years who had been classified as secure, avoidant, resistant, or disorganized at 18 months. Mother–child, father–child, and peer interactions were videotaped when the children were 20, 26, 32, 44, and 56 months old. At each age, mother–child and father–child interactions were videotaped in play, cleanup, and problem-solving situations. In addition, at all five ages, each child was videotaped in the day care classroom and in dyadic play and cleanup with two different peers identified by the child's teacher as "friends," or children with whom the child interacted most.

Preschoolers classified as secure, avoidant, or resistant in infancy behaved in similar ways with the two different peers. However, based on case study data, children classified as disorganized at 18 months were observed to act quite differently with one peer as compared to another at both the 44- and 56-month assessments. For example, one child spent much of his interaction with one peer trying to annoy him, shining a flashlight in his eyes, using a puppet to try to grab his nose, and periodically shoving toy animals in his face. With the other peer, however, the same child did not interact at all and progressively withdrew. By the end of the session, he was lying face down and burying his head under a large pillow.

Jacobvitz and Hazen (in press) have proposed that disorganized children may be more likely than other children to carry unintegrated models of the same caregiver into their interactions with peers, such that they draw on different models with different peers. Moreover, only after a disorganized child develops a way to interact with the caregiver (e.g., using controlling behavior) may the child be able to develop a consistent behavioral style, even though often not an optimal one, for interacting with peers. In the Jacobvitz and Hazen study, children who took longer to establish more consistent ways of interacting with their caregivers also took longer to sustain peer interactions, even aggressive or passive interchanges.

Disorganized/Controlling Attachment Patterns and the Development of Behavior Problems

Recent studies demonstrate an association between attachment disorganization and the development of peer aggression or externalizing behaviors. Early studies of low-income samples that used only the three traditional attachment classifications reported that avoidant attachment behavior in infancy predicted aggressive behavior toward peers in preschool (Troy & Sroufe, 1987) and elementary school (Renken, Egeland, Marvinney, Mangelsdorf, & Sroufe, 1989). Studies of middle-income samples did not replicate those findings (Bates, Maslin, & Frankel, 1985; Fagot & Kavanaugh, 1990; Goldberg, Perotta, Minde, & Corter, 1986; Lewis, Feiring, McGuf-

fog, & Jaskir, 1984). In a subsequent study of a low-income sample that included the disorganized classification, Lyons-Ruth, Alpern, and Repacholi (1993) found that avoidant behavior was often displayed in combination with disorganized behavior in low-income samples and the disorganized component predicted later aggression, whether or not the disorganization included avoidant behaviors. Several more recent longitudinal studies distinguishing between avoidant and disorganized/controlling attachments have replicated this association (Goldberg, Gotowiec, & Simmons, 1995; Hubbs-Tait, Osofsky, Hann, & Culp, 1994; Lyons-Ruth et al., 1997; Shaw, Owens, Vondra, Keenan, & Winslow, 1996; see also van IJzendoorn et al., in press).

Cross-sectional studies have also found an association between children's disorganized/controlling behavior with mother and aggression or externalizing behaviors. In two studies of clinic-referred preschoolers with oppositional behavior and their normal controls, oppositional preschoolers were more often classified as controlling toward their mothers (Greenberg et al., 1991; Speltz, Greenberg, & DeKlyen, 1990). In a cross-sectional sample of low-risk preschoolers, controlling children were rated higher by parents and teachers on both internalizing and externalizing behavior (Solomon et al., 1995). Finally, in another cross-sectional study of low-risk 5- to 7-year-olds, children classified as controlling scored lower on maternal ratings of social competence and higher on a checklist of childhood behavior problems also completed by mothers (Moss et al., 1996). At a 2-year follow-up, teachers rated 7- to 9-year-olds previously classified as controlling higher on internalizing and externalizing behaviors (Moss et al., 1998).

However, in one prospective longitudinal study, avoidant or resistant attachments at age 1 also predicted aggression in preschool when other risk factors were present at age 2 (Shaw et al., 1996). In another longitudinal study following low-income children from birth to adolescence, infants classified as disorganized scored higher on teacher ratings of dissociative behavior and internalizing behavior in first, second, third, and sixth grades, and on both internalizing behavior and overall psychopathology in adolescence (E. Carlson, 1998).

Cohn (1990) also assessed teacher-rated behavior problems in a cross-sectional study using all four attachment categories. She found that ambivalent boys were rated as displaying the most behavior problems. However, contrary to most other investigators, she discarded the data from 8 boys judged to be disorganized/unclassifiable, leaving only 4 boys in the disorganized/controlling group. Wartner et al. (1994) also coded all four attachment groupings at age 6 and coded problem behaviors based on half-day observations of children's play groups. Problem behaviors included a low threshold for distress, tics, social isolation, hostility, and temper outbursts. No differences were found among the attachment groupings in such a brief observation.

Other recent studies of both low- and middle-income samples have reported a relation between an avoidant attachment pattern and internalizing rather than externalizing problems (Goldberg et al., 1995; Hubbs-Tait et al., 1994; Lyons-Ruth et al., 1997; Moss et al., 1996). One study that distinguished between children cross-classified as disorganized and avoidant from those classified as avoidant found only elevated internalizing problems among avoidant children, and elevated externalizing *and* internalizing problems among children classified as both disorganized and avoidant (Lyons-Ruth et al., 1997).

On the basis of these data, we might expect disorganized attachment relationships in infancy to predict social-relational disorders of childhood characterized by aggressive control tactics and by mixed externalizing and internalizing symptoms. However, Lyons-Ruth et al. (1997) found that only 25% of disorganized infants in a high-risk sample were rated specifically as highly externalizing at age 7, whereas 50% were rated over the clinical cutoff score for generally maladaptive behavior at age 7. Similarly, following children prospectively from 18 to 54 months of age, Jacobvitz and Hazen (in press) found that some preschoolers classified as disorganized/disoriented in infancy later displayed hostile/aggressive behaviors toward peers. However, other children appeared disconnected—for example, moving backward when peers approached, cautiously sidestepping along the wall when approaching peers, or burying their heads under pillows in the corner of the room during a peer interaction task. These findings suggest that the forms of later maladaptation associated with early disorganization may not be entirely captured by conventional checklists for internalizing and externalizing symptoms. Instead, more subtle and more organizationally oriented assessments may be needed of the odd, intrusive, controlling, or incompetent social behaviors that may be correlates of disorganized/controlling attachment patterns.

Attachment Disorganization and Altered States of Consciousness in Young Adulthood

Main and Hesse (1990, 1992a; see also Hesse & Main, in press-a) have proposed that parents who are unresolved with respect to loss or trauma may be vulnerable to entering altered states of consciousness, such as trance-like states. Support for this hypothesis comes from a study of 140 low-risk subjects who were administered the AAI and the Tellegen Absorption Scale (TAS), which includes items such as "I sometimes 'step outside' my usual self and experience an entirely different state of mind," and "At times I feel the presence of someone who is not physically there" (Hesse & van IJzendoorn, in press-a). Unresolved subjects showed significantly elevated scores on the TAS when compared with subjects classified into the remaining adult attachment categories (autonomous, dismissing, preoccupied, and cannot classify). See also Muscetta, Dazzi, De Coro, Ortu, and Speranza (in press) for a discussion of the relationship between unresolved attachment status and dissociative symptoms.

Main and Hesse (1990) have proposed that parents who temporarily enter altered states of consciousness will be more likely to engage in inexplicably frightened and/or frightening behavior with their children. Frightened and/or frightening parental behavior is theorized to arouse contradictory responses in an infant, who simultaneously experiences tendencies to approach and to flee from the caregiver, resulting in attachment disorganization in the child. Because hypnotic states can be induced by using "confusion techniques" (e.g., very rapidly urging a subject to engage in contradictory movements that cannot be carried out simultaneously), Liotti (1992; see also Liotti, in press-a, in press-b) has proposed that disorganization and disorientation in infancy will increase a child's vulnerability to altered states or dissociative disorders (e.g., fugues, trance states, dissociative identity disorder, experiences of depersonalization and derealization, and ideas of possession).

Empirical support for Liotti's hypothesis comes from a prospective longitudinal study following 129 children from birth to age 17½ (E. Carlson, 1998). Infants classified as disorganized at 12 and 18 months of age (vs. the other infants) more often displayed symptoms of dissociation in elementary school and high school, as reported by teachers on the Teacher Report Form of the Child Behavior Checklist, and by the adolescents themselves on the Schedule of Affective Disorders and Schizophrenia for School-Age Children (K-SADS). Moreover, attachment disorganization in infancy showed a significant association with scores on the Dissociative Experience Scale at age 17½ ($r = .36$; Carlson, 1998).

Indirect evidence for Liotti's hypothesis comes from studies examining the relationship between dissociative disorders in adults and their parents' experiences of important losses near the time of their own births. Liotti, Intreccialagli, and Cecere (1991) reasoned that if a parent's unresolved response to loss predicts attachment disorganization in the infant, then loss near the birth of an infant should increase the likelihood of a disorganized attachment to the mother. Attachment disorganization, in turn, should increase a person's propensity to enter an altered state of consciousness. Liotti et al. (1991) asked 46 patients diagnosed as suffering from dissociative disorders and 119 patients with other psychiatric diagnoses whether their mothers had suffered a loss through death of a parent, sibling, spouse or another child during the 2 years before or after their births. Approximately 62% of the dissociative patients and only 13% of the controls were the offspring of mothers who had lost an important person near the time of the patient's birth.

Hesse and van IJzendoorn (in press-b) reported similar results in a study of two low-risk samples (n's = 138 and 308). Young adults were asked whether their own parents had lost another child or another loved one within 2 years preceding or following their births. Reports of loss of a child or another loved one within two years of their births were related to elevated levels of absorption in an altered state of reality, as assessed on Tellegen's Absorption Scale.

Not all infants classified as disorganized show dissociative symptoms later in life. Based on the prevailing view of dissociation as a defense against trauma (see Putnam, 1997), Liotti (1992, in press-a) has further proposed that infants classified as disorganized will be particularly vulnerable to dissociative disorders if traumatic circumstances continue or appear in later life. Empirical support for this idea comes from a longitudinal study following 168 children from birth to age 19. Ogawa, Sroufe, Weinfield, Carlson, and Egeland (1997) compared scores on the DES for three groups: (1) young adults classified as disorganized during infancy who had not faced trauma (defined as near-catastrophic events [including death of a family member] at any age, life-threatening illnesses before 54 months of age, or at least a month's separation of mother and child before age 54 months; $n = 10$); (2) young adults classified as disorganized during infancy who had faced such trauma ($n = 35$); and (3) other young adults not previously classified as disorganized ($n = 83$). This group was not divided by trauma history. A significant elevation in DES scores was found only among 19-year-olds classified as disorganized during infancy who had experienced trauma, providing further support for Liotti's theory. It is also notable that 78% of those classified as disorganized during infancy had experienced later trauma. This high rate suggests that caregiving environments associated with infant disorganization also place the infant at risk for further exposure to trauma or loss.

DISORGANIZED/CONTROLLING ATTACHMENTS AND RELATIONSHIP VIOLENCE, TRAUMA, AND MALTREATMENT

Prospective Cohorts and Deviant Groups: Complementary Research Strategies in the Study of Attachment

Given the emerging web of relations linking unresolved trauma, dissociation, and maladaptive social behavior to disorganized forms of attachment in infancy and childhood, investigators are beginning to consider the implications of these data for delineating the pathways to adult relational violence and maltreatment. The body of work just reviewed, tracing pathways prospectively from prebirth parental states of mind to attachment status in infancy to outcomes in childhood and adolescence, exemplifies one critical strategy for testing tenets of attachment theory. This approach asks how many disorganized infants have maladaptive outcomes. However, the most seriously traumatized children, such as those in violent or criminal families or those subjected to multiple foster placements, will be underrepresented in most longitudinal studies.

Identifying children who are disorganized in infancy and then studying the various outcomes of such early patterns over time needs to be complemented by a second research strategy—a follow-back strategy. This strategy involves asking how many children or adults with the most deviant relational pathologies have disorganized/controlling attachment histories. Attachment theory makes strong predictions that the subset of children and adults with seriously pathological relational behavior should have histories of disorganized attachment patterns in infancy or childhood, as well as further exacerbating factors. Identifying the forms of relational pathology consistent with these predictions, as well as the forms of later pathology *not* related to attachment history, requires supplementing normative and prospective samples with samples already displaying serious deviance. The public policy importance of attachment theory and research will derive in part from the degree to which the most serious later relational disorders are captured within the larger groups who are classified as disorganized/controlling in early life. Therefore, relations among attachment, violence, and maltreatment will continue to be pivotal in testing tenets of attachment theory and in stimulating new ideas.

Adequate exploration of the relations between disorganized forms of attachment and disordered forms of adult or child relational behavior will necessarily continue to involve a recursive process of observation and instrument development. For example, the identification and description of disorganized forms of infant attachment behavior emerged partially from theoretically incongruous findings. Namely, in studies of maltreated infants using the initial three-category attachment classification system, sizable proportions of maltreated infants were classified as secure (Crittenden, 1985; Lyons-Ruth et al., 1987). Those incongruous findings became part of a recursive process. First, methods of assessing attachment in low-risk populations were extended to studying high-risk populations. Then assessment instruments were revised to include the atypical adaptations encountered in high-risk environments and reapplied in high-risk studies, with a much better fit to the data (e.g., Crittenden, 1985; Lyons-Ruth et al., 1987, 1990; Main & Solomon, 1986, 1990). This process began with research on attachment in infancy and has not progressed to the same point in the study of age groups beyond infancy. Over the next decade, more differentiated subgroupings and coding procedures are likely to emerge in assessments of older children, adolescents, and adults as a critical mass of research develops on high-risk populations in these age groups. The continual development of well-validated attachment assessment instruments for the study of attachment organization in groups at very high risk for attachment disorganization is one current frontier of attachment research (see also Dozier, Stovall, & Albus, Chapter 22, and Hesse, Chapter 19, this volume).

An Attachment Perspective on Relationship Violence

Attachment theory has a fundamental contribution to make in placing serious relational disorders, such as violent or maltreating behavior, into a broader conceptual context—a context that includes concepts of internal working models, mental segregation, and controlling relational behavior. An attachment perspective on violence and abuse needs to integrate four basic aspects of attachment theory: (1) the presence of an attachment behavioral control system; (2) the role of anger in that control system; (3) the operation of both intersubjective and intrapsychic mechanisms in channeling the experience and expression of attachment-related affects, as well as the fear, anger, and unregulated physiological arousal resulting from frustration of attachment goals; and (4) the intergenerational transmission of relational patterns. These basic postulates of an attachment model are reviewed in detail in other chapters of the present volume.

Of particular relevance to the study of violence, Bowlby (1973) has pointed out that anger is a natural response to frustration and serves as an important communicative signal to the attachment partner that something is awry. If the attachment relationship is in jeopardy or the attachment figure is unresponsive, anger is one way of increasing the intensity of the communication to the attachment figure. Thus anger may occur in the service of the attachment relationship. To the extent that the increased emotional signaling works well enough to elicit the partner's ongoing participation in protection and arousal regulation, the attachment relationship will maintain a consistent and predictable, albeit possibly insecure, organization.

Should the child's increased anger and distress fail to elicit an adequate parental response to the child's fearful arousal, however, increasingly frantic and futile anger and distress may mount, and strategic behavioral organization may break down or take increasingly deviant forms as the communication fails to achieve its goal. Bowlby (1980) described these processes as part of the "protest" and "despair" phases of the child's response to loss of the caregiver in the absence of an adequate substitute. When an infant is confronted not with a loss but with a fearful infant–caregiver relationship, attempts to organize a consistent strategy appear to disintegrate into the conflict behaviors represented in disorganized attachment behavior. Such conflict behaviors may appear in the form of anger or distress and alternate with fear and avoidance, or may appear in disguised forms (e.g., inexplicable, aim-inhibited action sequences). Therefore, in the absence of adequate caregiving regulation of fearful arousal, various intersubjective, intrapsychic, and physiological compensatory mechanisms are set in motion, resulting in maladaptive, contradictory, or controlling behavioral and mental organizations. Violence in intimate relationships can be one outcome of such a deviation in the organization of attachment relationships, and one in which great intensity of positive longing, anger, and fear may be combined with a lack of felt security, lapses in attention, dysfluent communication, and unregulated arousal.

The relations between attachment and adult maltreatment, physical aggression, or violence need to be explored from at least two perspectives—that of the recipient of aggression or maltreatment, and that of the aggressor or perpetrator of maltreatment. We first consider the effects of maltreatment on children from an attachment perspective and then consider the still fragmentary evidence concerning working models of attachment among adults who are either recipients or perpetrators of maltreatment, violence, or abuse.

Child Maltreatment and Attachment

Child Outcomes and Family Correlates of Child Maltreatment

A large literature deals with aspects of the adaptation of maltreated children outside the context of attachment research (see reviews by Cicchetti, Lynch, Schonk, & Todd-Manly, 1992; Wolfe, 1985). A complete review of this literature goes beyond the scope of the present chapter. The literature is briefly summarized here, however, in order to examine how an attachment perspective deepens and extends our understanding of the developmental pathways associated with child and adult aggression.

Not surprisingly, the literature on child abuse and neglect has established that many negative developmental outcomes are associated with maltreatment. Peer relations are disturbed, with maltreated children exhibiting more withdrawal from and avoidance of their peers. Physically abused children, in particular, display more aggression toward other children (George & Main, 1979; Mueller & Silverman, 1989). Maltreated children also display unusual or aggressive behavior in response to the distress of peers (Main & George, 1985) and have more depressive symptoms (Kazdin, Moser, Colbus, & Bell, 1985).

The school functioning of maltreated children is also compromised, compared to that of controls. Sexually abused children are a noted exception to this pattern, however, as elaborated further below (Eckenrode, Laird, & Doris, 1993). There are suggestions that representational models of self and other are more negatively toned and less coherent among maltreated children (Lynch & Cicchetti, 1991; Schneider-Rosen & Cicchetti, 1991). In relation to the family environment, maltreated children experience distortions in ongoing parent–child interaction, in addition to specific incidents of abuse (Crittenden, 1981; Lyons-Ruth, Connell, & Zoll, 1989). As noted earlier, Carlson et al. (1989) found that 82% of maltreated infants displayed disorganized patterns of attachment to their caregivers, compared to only 17% of socioeconomically similar controls. Lyons-Ruth et al. (1990) obtained figures of 55% among maltreated infants and 34% among low-income controls in a context where all maltreating families had received clinical home-visiting services. Thus there is ample evidence that maltreated children experience more negative family relationships and exhibit poorer developmental outcomes on multiple dimensions, as well as having early disorganized attachment relationships. As parents themselves, maltreated children are at elevated risk for maltreating their own children (Egeland, Jacobvitz, & Papatola, 1987; Kaufman & Zigler, 1987).

Children's Physiological Adaptations to Maltreating Environments

In addition to the earlier-reviewed elevated cortisol responses to stress among disorganized infants, evidence is accruing that the most extremely impaired early attachment relationships are associated with even more pervasive changes in the organization and functioning of the hypothalamic–pituitary–adrenal (HPA) axis. M. Carlson et al. (1995) found that normal diurnal variation in cortisol secretion was altered among Romanian orphans, with peak values occurring in late morning or early afternoon, rather than at rising. M. Carlson and Earls (1997) also found that degree of cortisol elevation among Romanian orphans was related to decrements in infant developmental scores on the Bayley Scales. Boyce, Champoux, Suomi, and Gunnar (1996) found similar alterations in diurnal cycles of cortisol secretion among rhesus monkeys raised in social isolation.

Blunted cortisol responses to stress may be another outcome of particularly deviant early attachment experiences. Kraemer and Clarke (1996) reported that compared to mother-reared monkeys, rhesus monkeys randomly assigned to a peer-rearing condition showed subsequent blunting of physiological responses to stress, while still showing behavioral signs of disturbance (see also Clarke, 1993). Similarly, Hart, Gunnar, and Cicchetti (1995) found that school-age children who were maltreated were less likely to show cortisol elevations after conflicts with peers than were nonmaltreated children. Hart et al. (1995) speculated that when a child is exposed to chronic stress in abusive family contexts, the HPA axis may down-regulate to avoid chronic hyperactivation. The low cortisol levels observed among Vietnam veterans exposed to combat provide convergent support among human subjects for the hypothesis that unbuffered stress leads to down-regulation of the HPA axis (Boscarino, 1996; Yehuda, Southwick, Giller, Ma, & Mason, 1990).

These more extreme alterations in functioning of the HPA axis have not yet been studied in relation to disorganized/controlling attachment patterns per se. More work is now needed exploring the interrelations among very deviant early attachment experiences, disorganized attachment behaviors, cognitive development, and chronically elevated or blunted physiological responses to stress.

Disorganized/Disoriented Attachment Patterns and the Maltreated Child

The attachment literature has made several important contributions to the conceptualization and further development of the literature on maltreatment. The first contribution has been an attachment organizational perspective on the understanding of these multiple negative correlates. The postulate that early infant–caregiver relational patterns are represented and carried forward as prototypes for how to interact with others in close relationships shifts the conceptual framework from a narrower focus on abuse incidents per se to a more organizational view of the integrated behavioral, affective, physiological, and representational patterns that are being transmitted from parent to child (Crittenden & Ainsworth, 1989).

A more recent and specific contribution of attachment research is the finding that the *disorganization* of the attachment relationship, rather than simply its *insecurity*, may be a central mechanism in the emergence of many of the disturbances associated with maltreatment. Therefore, we predict that maltreatment should also be associated with the developmental sequelae of disorganized attachment patterns—sequelae that also appear in nonmaltreated groups, including disorganized/controlling attachment patterns, verbal deficits, aggressive and other maladaptive behavior problems, altered physiological responses to stress, and contradictory and unintegrated mental representations of relationships. The literature on developmental outcomes among maltreated children just reviewed is consistent with these predictions, although the predictions have not yet been thoroughly tested using attachment assessments per se.

Once the mental and behavioral components of disorganized attachment patterns are considered, the question emerges of whether children or adults who have been recipients of sexual or physical maltreatment will display patterns of behavior *not* shared with other children with disorganized attachment histories. There are indications in the literature that the type of abuse does affect the way social behavior and symptomatology are organized later in childhood or adulthood. For example, in several studies, hospitalized sexually abused girls were more likely to present dissociative and posttraumatic symptoms, whereas physically abused hospitalized adolescents were more likely to present depressive symptoms and conduct symptoms (Deblinger, McLeer, Atkins, Ralphe, & Foa, 1989; McLeer, Callaghan, Henry, & Wallen, 1994; Pelcovitz et al., 1994). Consistent with this picture, physically abused school children were more likely to perform poorly academically, to be sent to the principal more often, and to be suspended from school more often, while sexually abused girls exhibited none of these school problems (Eckenrode et al., 1993). In adulthood, mothers who had been physically abused in childhood were more likely to be intrusive and covertly hostile in interactions with their infants, while mothers who had been sexually abused but not physically abused were more likely to be withdrawn and uninvolved with their infants but were not more likely to be hostile (Lyons-Ruth & Block, 1996). Overall, it appears that sexually abused women are less likely than physically abused women to act aggressively toward others, more likely to conform to social expectations, and more likely to use dissociative defenses to maintain areas of appropriate social functioning.

Lyons-Ruth and Block (1996) have speculated that the different stances of physically abused and sexually abused mothers toward their infants are related to the abused women's differential overt identification with the aggressor or the victim position in the earlier abusive relationship. Identification with a sexual aggressor may be psychologically unlikely for women, whereas identification with a physically abusive parent may be more psychologically and behaviorally feasible. Consistent with an attachment framework, however, difficulties in intimate relationships, unintegrated mental representations, negative self-concepts, and problems with affect regulation are expected to be core features of a disorganized attachment relationship. These features should be common to identification with either the aggressor or the victim position in an abusive relationship. The abuse literature confirms that both groups of maltreated adolescents display these core features.

In summary, qualitative differences between children or adults who have suffered physical or sexual abuse and children or adults whose disorganized attachment relationships stem from other kinds of traumatic attachment-related experiences have yet to be demonstrated. Although differences between these groups may be anticipated, these distinctions have not yet been made and remain at the frontier of current work.

States of Mind Regarding Attachment among Violent, Maltreating, or Maltreated Adults

Unresolved States of Mind among Maltreating or Maltreated Adults

From an attachment perspective, there is a strong presumption that a maltreating caregiver is a frightened or frightening caregiver whose current mental state is characterized by a lack of resolution of loss or trauma, resulting in contradictory and unintegrated mental contents. However, empirical data addressing this prediction are rare. Few studies have examined maltreating adults' own internal models of attachment. Some data are available relating these adults' own histories of trauma or abuse to attachment-related outcomes in adulthood. Lyons-Ruth and colleagues have demonstrated a link between the severity of trauma or abuse in a mother's own childhood and her child's display of disorganized rather than organized forms of insecure behavior, as well as her own display of withdrawn or hostile behavior toward the child (Lyons-Ruth & Block, 1996; Lyons-Ruth, Zoll, Connell, & Grunebaum, 1989). Several other studies have related re-

sponses on the AAI to an adult's earlier history of trauma. These studies have implicated both unresolved (U) states of mind and rarer states of mind, such as "preoccupied/overwhelmed by trauma" (E3) and "cannot classify" (CC), as sequelae of maltreatment. These two rarer AAI subgroups are described briefly before we present the empirical findings.

Both the preoccupied/overwhelmed by trauma (E3) and cannot classify (CC) AAI subgroups occur rarely in low-risk samples but are seen with increasing frequency among clinical populations (see Hesse, this volume). Neither AAI subgroup has a corresponding infant attachment subgroup, and neither subgroup has been validated against infant data. As described by Main and Goldwyn (1998), both of these AAI subgroups may also be given a primary classification of unresolved with respect to loss or trauma if they also meet the coding criteria for lack of resolution.

The preoccupied/overwhelmed by trauma (E3) subgroup is one of three subtypes of a preoccupied state of mind identified in the Main and Goldwyn (1998) AAI coding manual. This adult subtype has no corresponding infant resistant subtype as its expected intergenerational counterpart, as do the other two preoccupied subtypes. Because of its rarity, this subtype also receives a relatively brief description in the coding manual and has no corresponding detailed coding scale for identifying and rating overwhelmed manifestations in the transcript, as do the other two preoccupied subtypes. Interviews are classified as preoccupied/overwhelmed by trauma if material related to traumatic experiences repeatedly intrudes into the interview context. Adults whose interviews are classified as E3 are often grouped with adults in the other two preoccupied subgroups for purposes of data analysis, and, theoretically, their infants are expected to display resistant attachment patterns rather than disorganized attachment patterns.

Adult interviews are placed in the cannot classify (CC) category when the discourse manifests a collapse of strategy at a global level rather than only during discussions of loss or trauma (Hesse, 1996; Minde & Hesse, 1996). This global breakdown in strategy is characterized by the display of two contrasting states of mind over the course of the interview that should be incompatible (dismissing and preoccupied), or by a general inability to implement an organized stance (as seen in transcripts with low coherence scores, as well as low scores for both dismissing and preoccupied strategies).

Patrick, Hobson, Castle, Howard, and Maughan (1994) found that 9 of 12 clinic patients exhibiting borderline personality disorder were classified as both preoccupied/overwhelmed by trauma (E3) and unresolved with respect to childhood trauma. The remaining three patients with borderline personality disorder were classified preoccupied/overwhelmed by trauma only. In contrast, clinic patients with dysthymic disorder were significantly less likely to show these unresolved/overwhelmed characteristics on interview, despite a similarly high rate of childhood trauma. Comparable results, including the high rates of childhood trauma among psychiatric patients compared to controls, were reported by Fonagy et al. (1996). Neither of these studies coded the cannot classify category. Stalker and Davies (1995), studying 40 women in psychiatric treatment who were sexually abused in childhood, also found that 7 of 8 abused women with borderline personality organization (88%) were classified as unresolved on the AAI, and that 5 of these 7 (71%) were also classified in the preoccupied group (the authors did not provide a breakdown of the frequencies of the three subtypes in the preoccupied group). Among all sexually abused women, 60% were classified as unresolved, and 88% of those were also classified in the preoccupied group. Stalker and Davies also reported that 37.5% of both resolved and unresolved women also met criteria for the cannot classify category, although this category was not considered in their data analyses.

Thus childhood trauma that eventuates in adult borderline personality disorder is clearly associated with a concomitant unresolved and overwhelmed state of mind with respect to attachment. Sexual abuse survivors in psychiatric treatment are also likely to show these characteristics, whether or not they also exhibit borderline personality disorder, but psychiatric patients with dysthymic disorder are not, even in the context of a history of trauma. These data support the prediction from attachment theory that adults with severe problems in maintaining close relationships—a characteristic associated with borderline personality disorder—will exhibit unresolved states of mind with respect to attachment. However, the data also indicate that indices of lack of resolution of trauma by themselves are not sufficient to capture these states of mind. These studies have been conducted among clinical samples rather than general-population samples, however, so they represent the more impaired end of the spectrum of trauma-exposed adults. General-population samples are needed to fully explore the distribution of attachment-related states of mind among adults exposed to childhood trauma.

Disorganized Attachment Patterns and Violence between Intimate Partners

We have noted above the overlap in correlates of disorganized attachment patterns and correlates of childhood abuse. West and George (1998) have pointed to a similar overlap in the correlates associated with disorganized attachment relationships and those associated with marital violence. They have proposed that violence in intimate relationships is rooted in disorganized attachment relationships and have outlined a model of marital relational violence based on the literature on disorganized/controlling attachment patterns. West and George (1998) have further pointed out that marital violence is associated with a constellation of adult characteristics that are also related to disorganized/unresolved attachment relationships. This constellation includes a history of trauma or abuse, borderline personality organization, intense abandonment anxiety, controlling behavior toward the partner, and unintegrated or dissociated mental contents associated with trauma.

There are still relatively few data directly exploring the attachment behaviors or states of mind of those who display marital violence, however. Owen and Cox (1997) found that elevated rates of marital conflict observed between marital partners in a laboratory assessment were associated with elevated rates of disorganized attachment classifications on the part of their infants. However, Shaw et al. (1996) did not replicate this finding. Steiner, Zeanah, Stuber, Ash, and Angell (1994) found that mothers who reported higher levels of partner violence were more likely to have infants with disorganized attachments. In the study by Lyons-Ruth and Block (1996), infants of mothers who were not abused but had witnessed violence between others in childhood were as likely to display a disorganized attachment strategy as were infants whose mothers had directly experienced physical or sexual abuse. Bearman and Ogawa (1993) reported, in particular, that mothers who displayed indicators of lack of resolution in relation to violence witnessed in childhood were more likely to have infants classified as disorganized.

The few existing studies of marital violence and AAI responses suggest that in addition to unresolved states of mind, rarer adult states of mind such as preoccupied/overwhelmed by trauma (E3) and cannot classify (CC) appear with increased frequency among both perpetrators and victims of violent behavior. Holtzworth-Monroe, Stuart, and Hutchinson (1997) found that male batterers were significantly more often classified cannot classify on the AAI than were nonbatterers, and Sullivan-Hanson (1990), studying battered women, found that women in shelters had a high prevalence of E3 classifications on the AAI (the unresolved classification was not coded in that study).

Two other studies have examined states of mind with respect to attachment among mentally disturbed criminal offenders. Levinson and Fonagy (1998) collected AAIs from 22 mentally disturbed criminal offenders. Both offenders and nonclinical controls were less likely than psychiatric controls to be classified as unresolved (36% and 0% vs. 82%). Eighty-two percent of offenders, but only 36% of psychiatric controls and 4% of normals, had been abused in childhood, and current anger toward attachment figures was described as "intense" among offenders. Both offenders and psychiatric controls were more likely to be classified preoccupied than nonclinical controls (45% and 64% vs. 14%). Levinson and Fonagy did not report whether most of the people classified as preoccupied were in the E3 (overwhelmed by trauma) subgroup. Because the group of criminal offenders would be strongly predicted to show unresolved states of mind with respect to attachment, based on their histories of abuse, current anger, and violent behavior toward others, these findings run counter to theory.

Although Levinson and Fonagy found that offenders were less likely to display unresolved states of mind than psychiatric controls, a study by van IJzendoorn, Feldbrugge, et al. (in press) of 40 mentally disturbed criminal offenders did not replicate that finding—a difference that may be accounted for by the latter authors' inclusion of cannot classify codes with unresolved codes in reporting the data. van IJzendoorn, Feldbrugge, et al. (in press) found that autonomous AAI classifications were almost absent (5%) among offenders, while the combined unresolved/cannot classify groups constituted 53% of the sample. This distribution is a significant departure from the distribution of AAI classifications reported in low-risk middle-income samples, where about 14% are classified as unresolved (van IJzendoorn, Schuengel, & Bakermans-Kranenburg, in press). However, criminal offenders were *not* more likely than other *clinical* groups to display unresolved or cannot classify states of mind. van IJzendoorn and coworkers did not present the frequencies for unresolved and cannot classify subgroups separately, however, nor did they report how many unresolved subjects received a subclassification of E3 or CC.

The data as a whole suggest that violence-prone and disturbed men may be particularly likely to display the more globally contradictory states of mind associated with the cannot classify category, while abused and distressed women may be more likely to display both unresolved and overwhelmed (E3) states of mind with respect to attachment. As discussed in more depth in the next section of this chapter, however, we would not expect this division to be a rigid one. Rather, we would expect the abused–abuser internal working model of attachment to include representations of both positions in this dyadic relational pattern, with the potential for either overwhelmed or contradictory states of mind to be expressed, depending on context, temperament, gender role, and other factors.

Data are particularly needed tying these rarer groups (including the CC and E3 classifications) to infant and child attachment data, since the parental risk factors associated with these groups overlap with the risk factors for infant disorganization. On the basis of their sample of sexually abused women, Stalker and Davies (1995) suggested that the AAI categories need continued expansion "to avoid placing individuals with relatively mild information-processing distortions in the same category as those with serious distortions. Delineation of the subgroups of the category currently labeled cannot classify (CC) may be the means by which such expansion can be achieved" (p. 238). We would also add the E3 subgroup to the group of AAI categories for which more infant data and coding description are needed. This emerging evidence of the prevalence of E3 and CC states of mind among violent or abused adults suggests that there may be a wider spectrum of parental states of mind that would be expected to predict infant disorganization beyond the unresolved group alone. Further research on the childhood antecedents and intergenerational outcomes associated with these adult states of mind will be crucial to understanding the interface between attachment relationships and psychopathology. Further exploration of the attachment-related correlates both of childhood abuse and of adult violence and psychiatric disorder constitutes an active area of current attachment research, and new findings are likely to emerge (see Dozier et al., Chapter 22, and Hesse, Chapter 19, this volume).

AN INTEGRATIVE CONCEPTUAL FRAMEWORK: LOSS, TRAUMA, AND THE RELATIONAL DIATHESIS

The literature reviewed in this chapter on disorganized/controlling attachment patterns, unresolved loss or trauma, and frightened or frightening caregiving behavior raises a number of issues. A recurring theme regarding the disorganized attachment category across the lifespan is a theme of contradictory and unintegrated behavioral strategies and mental contents. Contradictions are observed within such an individual's behavioral strategies and mental contents and contradictions are also observed at the level of the composition of the disorganized group, which includes such sharply contrasting subgroups as punitive versus caregiving and frightened versus frightening. Here we point to three of the most pressing questions raised by this literature and elaborate a framework to account for such apparent discontinuities.

One question that merits more attention in the literature is why some experiences of loss, parental death, or trauma become resolved and others do not. A second related question that has not been addressed is how processes of intergenerational transmission of disorganized forms of attachment work. In the model to date, caregivers are viewed as developing an unresolved state of mind in relation to a specific experience of loss or trauma—an experience usually occurring later than the first few years of life and often much later. In contrast, infants are viewed as developing a disorganized attachment strategy through exposure to their caregivers' unintegrated fear. This leads to the conundrum that if a disorganized infant grows up without further loss or trauma, then he or she will not be codable as unresolved on the AAI. Do we assume, then, that all disorganized infants grow out of disorganized forms of attachment behavior unless further unresolved loss or trauma occurs? Or is a caregiver's frightened or frightening behavior sufficient in itself to lead to intergenerational transmission of disorganized attachment behavior? A third question posed by the current data is how to explain the apparently very different behavioral and mental organizations that emerge out of a common fear-based dynamic. Why are some parents frightened and some frightening, some disorganized infants approaching and some avoiding, and some controlling children battling with their parents while others are caregiving toward their parents?

Lyons-Ruth, Bronfman, and Atwood (in press) have pointed out that placing the process of fear and its modulation into a relational context points to a way out of these impasses. If attachment disorganization or lack of resolution is a function both of the intensity of fear-producing experience and of the adequacy of the attachment relationship to help resolve the fearful affect, then potential answers emerge. At one end of the spectrum, particularly abrupt or shocking trauma, or trauma that also impairs the caregiver, may be sufficient in itself to disorganize the attachment strategy of a child or adult who has had otherwise adequate attachment relationships. At the other end of the spectrum, even the normative distress-producing experiences of infancy may remain unbuffered and lead to disorganized attachment responses in the presence of a frightened or frightening caregiver who experiences unresolved fear in relation to the infant's attachment behaviors. If the early attachment relationship remains disorganized/controlling throughout childhood, further loss or trauma may not be necessary for intergenerational transmission of disorganization to occur.

In this relational-diathesis model, organized dismissing or preoccupied attachment relationships should provide sufficient protection and caretaking in response to uncomplicated experiences of loss to allow integrated mental functioning. Only if the loss or traumatic experience falls well outside the norm should we expect to see the kinds of behavioral and mental lapses associated with disorganization. Similarly, only if the degree of communication and protection available from the attachment figure falls outside the spectrum associated with organized attachment strategies should we expect to see disorganized attachment responses even in the absence of loss or trauma. This implies that there should be an additive or interactive effect between the presence and characteristics of the trauma and the quality of the childhood attachment relationship in producing disorganized/controlling/unresolved states. This stress–relational-diathesis model is consistent with the primate literature demonstrating that peer-nurtured monkeys that have experienced early maternal deprivation (the relational diathesis) display adequate social behavior until stressed, at which time the early relational diathesis becomes manifest again in atypical social behaviors. By itself, however, the stress is not sufficient to produce atypical behaviors in peers that have not been maternally deprived (Suomi, 1991).

The concept of a relational diathesis, or vulnerability to disorganization in the face of trauma, is foreshadowed in Bowlby's (1980) discussion of the conditions affecting the course of mourning. He states that "adults whose mourning takes a pathological course are likely before their bereavement to have been prone to make affectional relationships of certain special, albeit contrasting, kinds" (p. 202). He lists the three classes of affectional relationships as those "suffused with overt or covert ambivalence," those in which "there is a strong disposition to engage in compulsive caregiving," and those in which "there are strenuous attempts to claim emotional self-sufficiency and independence of all affectional ties" (p. 202). A similar point was made by Freud (1917/1957), who described persons prone to pathological mourning as those who have experienced marked but consciously unacceptable ambivalence toward the lost person. In short, the more insecure the underlying attachment, the more difficult the mental resolution of a loss becomes.

Ainsworth and Eichberg (1991) provided empirical grounding for this concept in their finding that mothers who were classified as unresolved in relation to past loss or trauma were more likely to receive secondary classifications of preoccupied or dismissing rather than autonomous on the AAI (for meta-analytic data, see van IJzendoorn, Schuengel, & Bakermans-Kranenburg, in press). Although in all the above-cited literature the relevant processes were placed in the adult personalities or states of mind of the bereaved, it is in keeping with Bowlby's broader theory to derive these states of mind in part from patterns of caregiving experienced in childhood.

In conceptualizing the childhood relational processes most likely to interfere with the resolution of loss or trauma, however, we should distinguish between those caregiving behaviors that allow the maintenance of organized but insecure attachment patterns, such as the preoccupied or dismissing classifications, and those caregiving behaviors more likely to be associated with disorganized or controlling patterns of child attachment. At present, from a parent's AAI data alone, a distinction cannot be made between the parent's carrying forward the experience of a disorganized or controlling attachment relationship from childhood and the parent's further experience of a loss or trauma that fails to be resolved. Longitudinal data from infancy or childhood will be needed to assess separately how the prevalence and severity of childhood trauma and the extent of insecurity in early attachment relationships contribute to the intergenerational transmission of disorganization. We predict, however, that trauma will both occur more frequently and be more difficult to resolve in the context of an already disorganized caregiving system, suggesting both direct and indirect effects of early disorganized caregiving on later adult outcomes. The data of Ogawa et al. (1997) provide some support for these predictions in relation to adult dissociative symptoms, as noted earlier.

Finally, the sharply contrasting behavioral styles that make up the disorganized category, such as punitive or caregiving control in childhood, can be viewed as stemming from the nature of the relational diathesis itself. If a caregiver has not experienced comfort and soothing in relation to his or her own early fear-evoking experiences, the infant's pain and fear will evoke unresolved fearful affects in the caregiver, including memories of his or her own helplessness as a child in obtaining comfort. To prevent reexperiencing his or her own unresolved fearful affects, the caregiver must restrict attention and responsiveness to the infant's fear and distress. As a result, the caregiver's fluid responsiveness to the infant's attachment-related cues will inevitably be restricted (Fraiberg, Adelson, & Shapiro, 1975; Main, 1995, 1996; Main et al., 1985; Strage & Main, 1985). The more pervasive these restrictions, the more the caregiver's mental states take precedence over the infant's attachment-related communications and initiatives. To the extent that the caregiver's unresolved fearful experiences are attended to at the expense of attention to the child's current states, the interaction between the two partners will become less balanced and less mutually regulated to meet the needs of both partners.

Such unbalanced relational processes provide a conceptually powerful construct that can order many additional aspects of the findings regarding disorganized attachment patterns. Both Bowlby (1980) and his forebears in psychoanalytic scholarship emphasized that mental representations of relationships are inherently dyadic (see also Sroufe & Fleeson, 1986). What is represented is not only the individual's way of participating in the relationship—for example, as the coercively controlled child—but the entire dyadic relational pattern of controlled child and controlling parent. The more the parent must respond to his or her own need to regulate fearful arousal rather than to the child's states, the more skewed these relational polarities become, and the more discontinuous and self-contradictory are the internalized models that accommodate both relational possibilities (e.g., "I should accept external control and take no initiative" vs. "I should control the other by overriding the other person's initiative").

In a relational model, the unintegrated dualities that recur in the disorganized group both at the individual level (unintegrated mental contents) and at the level of the disorganized group as a whole (frightened or frightening behavior, coercive or caregiving behavior, chaotic or inhibited play) can be understood as partially rooted in a disorganized child's history of participation in such unbalanced relationships. Inherent in a model of unbalanced relationships is an asymmetry of power in which one partner's (attachment-related) goals or initiatives are elaborated at the expense of the other's. By definition, then, one partner is more helpless in the relationship and the other more controlling, whether the control is exerted through active aggression or through the more covert mechanisms of withdrawal, guilt induction, or self-preoccupation (see Fraiberg et al., 1975, and Zahn-Waxler & Kochanska, 1990, for examples). Thus, a helpless versus hostile/controlling dyadic dichotomy in relationship roles should be especially evident among individuals in disorganized attachment relationships, and this may partially account for the bifurcation into punitive or caregiving stances that occurs among disorganized infants during the preschool period. Because such internal models include both contradictory relationship roles, however, an individual with such a model may mentally or behaviorally activate either role sequentially or simultaneously, depending on contextual and temperamental factors; this may lead to highly contradictory behavioral or mental sequences.

Lyons-Ruth and Atwood (1998) present preliminary evidence that these helpless or hostile/controlling stances can be identified in the AAI, independently of indices of unresolved states of mind. These authors have speculated that these two AAI patterns are associated with the overwhelmed by trauma (E3) and cannot classify (CC) subgroups that often seem to cluster with the unresolved classification. In this formulation, the E3 and CC subgroups represent overall states of mind that correspond to an unbalanced helpless versus hostile/controlling internal working model, which may manifest itself in either helpless or hostile interpersonal stances (or both in alternation) and should be tied to childhood experiences of participation in very unbalanced or controlling relationships. A fuller exposition of this model is available in Lyons-Ruth, Bronfman, and Atwood (in press).

Lyons-Ruth and Atwood (1998) have developed initial conventions for coding hostile/controlling or helpless states of mind on the AAI, and Hesse (1996; Minde & Hesse, 1996) has described the more interview-wide characteristics that constitute the CC designation. More needs to be done to conceptualize and code the extremes of relational imbalance in childhood, both as revealed by the AAI and as observed in parent–child transactions, to better differentiate hostile/controlling or helpless states of mind from the less extreme parental rejection or overinvolvement consistent with the child's maintenance of an organized attachment strategy.

CONCLUSIONS

In summary, Main and colleagues' (Main et al., 1985; Main & Solomon, 1986, 1990) discovery of a disorganized attachment pattern in infancy has opened up new ground in understanding the interface between development and psychopathology. Theoretically, Main and coworkers (Hesse & Main, in press; Main & Hesse, 1990; Main & Morgan, 1996) have pointed to "fear without solution" as the core dilemma facing infants who display inexplicable and conflicting attachment behaviors. These authors have proposed that frightened or frightening maternal behaviors, such as trance-like or dissociative states, sudden unusual vocal patterns, or sudden looming into the infant's face, are related to the mother's earlier unresolved trauma. When cues in the current environment activate these unintegrated trauma-related representations, fear-related maternal behaviors occur out of context and are therefore inexplicable to the infant. Such inexplicable behaviors are likely to alarm the infant. Since infants rely on their attachment figures to protect them from harm should dangers arise, fear stemming from their own caregivers places infants in an unresolvable paradox. Such an attachment figure is "at once the source of and the solution to [an infant's] alarm" (Main & Hesse, 1990, p. 163). At the same time that the infant experiences a tendency to approach the caregiver for comfort, the infant experiences a competing tendency to flee.

Competing and irreconcilable tendencies to move toward and away from the caregiver, who is both the source of alarm and the haven of safety, intensifies the infant's fear, resulting in a collapse of behavioral and attentional strategies.

Contradictory behavioral tendencies inhibit the infant from employing the strategies used by other infants who are alarmed—namely, seeking comfort and support from the caregiver (i.e., evidence of security), shifting attention away from the caregiver (i.e., avoidance), or oscillating between seeking and resisting comfort (i.e., ambivalent or resistant behavior). As elaborated earlier, attachment disorganization in infancy forecasts controlling behavior with caregivers, aggressive and fearful peer relationships, and internalizing and externalizing problems in preschool, kindergarten, and elementary school, as well as dissociative symptoms and elevated psychopathology during adolescence.

The parent's fearful affect, which is thought to underlie frightened and frightening caregiving behavior, is related theoretically to the parent's lack of resolution of fear-arousing experiences of loss or trauma. "Lack of resolution" refers here to the failure to integrate fully the reality of the loss or traumatic experience and to rework mental representations of attachment experiences. To the extent that multiple, conflicting, and unintegrated models of past traumatic experiences are maintained in segregated areas of consciousness, a caregiver is likely to display conflicting and unintegrated behaviors with his or her own child. As a result, affects or behaviors related to earlier trauma may be reactivated unpredictably in parent–child interactions in ways that are not monitored by an overarching, integrated, and coherent parental state of mind. These basic theoretical postulates are gaining substantial support from recent empirical studies. In turn, new questions are emerging that have to do with exploring the limiting conditions of these propositions, and with determining how processes related to disorganization of attachment strategies interface with the three organized classifications on the one hand and with clearly defined psychopathology on the other. In this direction lie some of the future developments of attachment theory and research.

REFERENCES

Ainsworth, M. D. S., Blehar, M., Waters, E., & Wall, S. (1978). *Patterns of attachment.* Hillsdale, NJ: Erlbaum.

Ainsworth, M. D. S., & Eichberg, C. G. (1991). Effects on infant–mother attachment of mother's unresolved loss of an attachment figure or other traumatic experience. In C. M. Parkes, J. Stevenson-Hinde, & P. Marris (Eds.), *Attachment across the life cycle* (pp. 161–183). London: Routledge.

Alpern, L., & Lyons-Ruth, K. (1993). Preschool children at social risk: Chronicity and timing of maternal depressive symptoms and child behavior problems at school and at home. *Development and Psychopathology, 5,* 371–387.

Barnett, D., Ganiban, J., & Cicchetti, D. (in press). Maltreatment, emotional reactivity, and the development of Type D attachments from 12 to 24 months of age. In J. Vondra & D. Barnett (Eds.), Atypical patterns of infant attachment: Theory, research, and current directions. *Monographs of the Society for Research in Child Development.*

Bates, J. E., Maslin, C. A., & Frankel, K. A. (1985). Attachment security, mother–child interaction, and temperament as predictors of behavior problem ratings at age three years. In I. Bretherton & E. Waters (Eds.), Growing points of attachment theory and research. *Monographs of the Society for Research in Child Development, 50*(1–2, Serial No. 209), 167–193.

Beckwith, L., & Rodning, C. (1991, April). Stability and correlates of attachment classifications from 13 to 36 months in a sample of preterm infants. In R. S. Marvin & J. Cassidy (Chairs), *Attachment during the preschool years: Examination of a new measure.* Symposium conducted at the biennial meeting of the Society for Research in Child Development, Seattle, WA.

Berman, D., & Ogawa, J. R. (1993, April). *Seeing is believing: Observed trauma as an alternate route to unresolved status in the Adult Attachment Interview.* Poster presented at the biennial meeting of the Society for Research in Child Development, New Orleans, LA.

Boscarino, J. (1996). Post-traumatic stress disorder, exposure to combat, and lower plasma cortisol among Vietnam veterans: Findings and clinical implications. *Journal of Consulting and Clinical Psychology, 64,* 191–201.

Bowlby, J. (1969). *Attachment and loss: Vol. 1. Attachment.* New York: Basic Books.

Bowlby, J. (1973). *Attachment and loss: Vol. 2. Separation: Anxiety and anger.* New York; Basic Books.

Bowlby, J. (1980). *Attachment and loss: Vol. 3. Loss.* New York: Basic Books.

Boyce, T. W., Champoux, M., Suomi, S. J., & Gunnar, M. R. (1995). Salivary cortisol in nursery-reared rhesus monkeys: Reactivity to peer interactions and altered Circadian activity. *Developmental Psychobiology, 28,* 12.

Carlson, E. A. (1998). A prospective longitudinal study of disorganized/disoriented attachment. *Child Development, 69,* 1970–1979.

Carlson, V., Cicchetti, D., Barnett, D., & Braunwald, K. (1989). Disorganized/disoriented attachment relationships in maltreated infants. *Developmental Psychology, 25,* 525–531.

Carlson, M., Dragomir, C., Earls, F., Farrell, M., Macovei, O., Nystrom, P., & Sparling, J. (1995). Effects of social deprivation on cortisol regulation in institutionalized Romanian infants. *Society for Neurosciences Abstracts, 218,* 12.

Carlson, M., & Earls, F. (1997). Psychological and neuroendocrinological sequelae of early social deprivation in institutionalized children in Romania. *Annals of the New York Academy of Sciences, 807,* 419–428.

Cassidy, J., Marvin, R. S., & The MacArthur Working Group on Attachment. (1991). *Attachment organization in preschool children: Coding guidelines* (3rd ed.). Unpublished manuscript.

Cicchetti, D., & Barnett, D. (1991). Attachment organization in maltreated preschoolers. *Development and Psychopathology, 3,* 397–411.

Cicchetti, D., Lynch, M., Schonk, S., & Todd-Manly, J. (1992). An organizational perspective on peer relations in maltreated children. In R. D. Parke & G. M. Ladd (Eds.), *Family–peer relationships: Modes of linkage* (pp. 345–383). Hillsdale, NJ: Erlbaum.

Clarke, A. S. (1993). Social rearing effects on HPA axis activity over early development and in response to stress in young rhesus monkeys. *Developmental Psychobiology, 26,* 433–447.

Cohn, D. (1990). Child–mother attachment in six-year-olds and social competence in school. *Child Development, 61,* 152–162.

Crittenden, P. M. (1981) Abusing, neglecting, problematic, and adequate dyads: Differentiating by patterns of interaction. *Merrill-Palmer Quarterly, 27,* 201–208.

Crittenden, P. M. (1985). Maltreated infants: Vulnerability and resilience. *Journal of Child Psychology and Psychiatry, 26,* 85–96.

Crittenden, P. M. (1992). Quality of attachment in the preschool years. *Development and Psychopathology, 4,* 209–241.

Crittenden, P. M., & Ainsworth, M. D. S. (1989). Child maltreatment and attachment theory. In D. Cicchetti & V. Carlson (Eds.), *Child maltreatment: Theory and research on the causes and consequences of child abuse and neglect* (pp. 432–463). New York: Cambridge University Press.

Crockenberg, S. (1981). Infant irritability, mother responsiveness, and social support influences on the security of infant attachment. *Child Development, 52,* 857–865.

Deblinger, E., McLeer, S., Atkins, M., Ralphe, D., & Foa, E. (1989). Post-traumatic stress in sexually abused, physically abused, and nonabused children. *Child Abuse and Neglect, 13,* 403–408.

DeMulder, E. K., & Radke-Yarrow, M. (1991). Attachment with affectively ill and well mothers: Concurrent behavioral correlates. *Development and Psychopathology, 3,* 227–242.

Easterbrooks, A. M., Lyons-Ruth, K., Biesecker, G., & Carper, A. (1996). Infancy predictors of emotional availability in middle childhood: The role of attachment and maternal depression. In J. Robinson (Chair), *Emotional availability in mother–child dyads: Predictors across development and risk status.* Symposium conducted at the International Conference on Infant Studies, Providence, RI.

Eckenrode, J., Laird, M., & Doris, J. (1993). School performance and disciplinary problems among abused and neglected children. *Developmental Psychology, 29,* 53–62.

Egeland, B., Jacobvitz, D., & Papatola, K. (1987). Intergenerational continuity of parental abuse. In J. Lancaster & R. Gelles (Eds.), *Biosocial aspects of child abuse* (pp. 255–278). San Francisco: Jossey-Bass.

Fagot, B. I., & Kavanagh, K. (1990). The prediction of antisocial behavior from avoidant attachment classifications. *Child Development, 61,* 864–873.

Fonagy, P., Leigh, T., Steele, M., Steele, H., Kennedy, G., Mattoon, M., Target, M., & Gerber, A. (1996). The relation of attachment status, psychiatric classification, and response to psychotherapy. *Journal of Consulting and Clinical Psychology, 64,* 22–31.

Fraiberg, S., Adelson, E., & Shapiro, V. (1975). Ghosts in the nursery. *Journal of the American Academy of Child Psychiatry, 14,* 387–421.

Freud, S. (1957). Mourning and melancholia. In J. Strachey (Ed. and Trans.), *The standard edition of the complete psychological works of Sigmund Freud* (Vol. 14, pp. 237–260). London: Hogarth Press. (Original work published 1917)

George, C., Kaplan, N., & Main, M. (1984) *Adult Attachment Interview* (1st ed.). Unpublished manuscript, University of California at Berkeley.

George, C., Kaplan, N., & Main, M. (1985). *Adult Attachment Interview* (2nd ed.). Unpublished manuscript, University of California at Berkeley.

George, C., Kaplan, N., & Main, M. (1996). *Adult Attachment Interview* (3rd ed.). Unpublished manuscript, University of California at Berkeley.

George, C., & Main, M. (1979). Social interaction of young abused children: Approach, avoidance, and aggression. *Child Development, 50,* 306–318.

George, C., & Solomon, J. (1996). Representational models of relationships: Links between caregiving and attachment. *Infant Mental Health Journal, 17,* 198–216.

Goldberg, S., Gotowiec, A., & Simmons, R. J. (1995). Infant–mother attachment and behavior problems in healthy and chronically ill preschoolers. *Development and Psychopathology, 7,* 267–282.

Goldberg, S., Perotta, M., Minde, K., & Corter, C. (1986). Maternal behavior and attachment in low birthweight twins and singletons. *Child Development, 57,* 34–46.

Greenberg, M. T., Speltz, M. L., DeKlyen, M., & Endriga, M. C. (1991). Attachment security in preschoolers with and without externalizing behavior problems: A replication. *Development and Psychopathology, 3,* 413–430.

Grossmann, K., Grossmann, K. E., Spangler, G., Suess, G., & Unzner, L. (1985). Maternal sensitivity and newborn's orientation responses as related to quality of attachment in northern Germany. In I. Bretherton & E. Waters (Eds.), *Growing points of attachment theory and research. Monographs of the Society for Research in Child Development, 50*(1–2 Serial No. 209), 233–256.

Hann, D. M., Castino, R. J., Jarosinski, J., & Britton, H. (1991, April). Relating mother–toddler negotiation patterns to infant attachment and maternal depression with an adolescent mother sample. In J. Osofsky & L. Hubbs-Tait (Chairs), *Consequences of adolescent parenting: Predicting behavior problems in toddlers and preschoolers.* Symposium conducted at the biennial meeting of the Society for Research in Child Development, Seattle, WA.

Hart, J., Gunnar, M., & Cicchetti, D. (1995) Salivary cortisol in maltreated children: Evidence of relations between neuroendocrine activity and social competence. *Development and Psychopathology, 7,* 11–12.

Hertsgaard, L., Gunnar, M., Erickson, M. F., & Nachmias, M. (1995). Adrenocortical response to the strange situation in infants with disorganized/disoriented attachment relationships. *Child Development, 66,* 1100–1106.

Hesse, E. (1996). Discourse, memory, and the Adult Attachment Interview: A note with emphasis on the emerging cannot classify category. *Infant Mental Health Journal, 17,* 4–11.

Hesse, E., & Main, M. (in press-a). Frightened behavior in traumatized but non-maltreating parents: Previously unexamined risk factor for offspring. *Psychoanalytic Inquiry.*

Hesse, E., & Main, M. (in press-b). Disorganization in infant and adult attachment: Description, correlates, and implications for developmental psychopathology. *Journal of the American Psychanalytic Association.*

Hesse, E., & van IJzendoorn, M. (in press-a). Propensities towards absorption are related to lapses in the monitoring of reasoning or discourse during the Adult Attachment Interview: A preliminary investigation. *Attachment and Human Development.*

Hesse, E., & van IJzendoorn, M. (in press-b). Parental loss of close family members and propensities toward absorption in offspring. *Developmental Science.*

Hinde, R. A. (1970). *Animal behavior: A synthesis of ethology and comparative psychology* (2nd ed.). New York: McGraw-Hill.

Holtzworth-Munroe, A., Stuart, G. L., & Hutchinson, G. (1997). Violent vs. nonviolent husbands: Differences in attachment patterns, dependency, and jealousy. *Journal of Family Psychology, 11,* 314–331.

Hubbs-Tait, L., Osofsky, J., Hann, D., & Culp, A. (1994). Predicting behavior problems and social competence in children of adolescent mothers. *Family Relations, 43,* 439–446.

Jacobsen, T., Edelstein, W., & Hofmann, V. (1994). A longitudinal study of the relation between representations of attachment in childhood and cognitive functioning in childhood and adolescence. *Developmental Psychology, 30,* 112–124.

Jacobsen, T., Huss, M., Fendrich, M., Kruesi, M. J. P., & Ziegenhain, U. (1997). Children's ability to delay gratification: Longitudinal relations to mother-child attachment. *Journal of Genetic Psychology, 158,* 411–426.

Jacobsen, T., Ziegenhain, U., Muller, B., Rottmann, U., Hofmann, V., & Edelstein, W. (1992, September). *Predicting stability of mother–child attachment patterns in day-care children from infancy to age 6.* Poster presented at the Fifth World Congress of Infant Psychiatry and Allied Disciplines, Chicago.

Jacobvitz, D. (1998, March). *Frightening caregiving: Links with mothers' loss and trauma.* Paper presented at the biennial meeting of the Southwestern Society for Research in Human Development, Galveston, TX.

Jacobvitz, D., & Hazen, N. (in press). Developmental pathways from infant disorganization to childhood peer relationships. In J. Solomon & C. George (Eds.), *Attachment disorganization.* New York: Guilford Press.

Jacobvitz, D., Hazen, N., & Riggs, S. (1997, April). Disorganized mental processes in mothers, frightening/frightened caregiving, and disoriented/disorganized behavior in infancy. In D. Jacobvitz (Chair), *Caregiving correlates and longitudinal outcomes of disorganized attachments in infants.* Symposium conducted at the biennial meeting of the Society for Research in Child Development, Washington, DC.

Kaplan, N. (1987). *Individual differences in 6–year-olds' thoughts about separation: Predicted from attachment to mother at age 1.* Unpublished doctoral dissertation, University of California at Berkeley.

Kaufman, J., & Zigler, E. (1987). Do abused children become abusive parents? *American Journal of Orthopsychiatry, 57,* 186–192.

Kazdin, A. E., Moser, J., Colbus, D., & Bell, R. (1985). Depressive symptoms among physically abused and psychiatrically disturbed children. *Journal of Abnormal Psychology, 94,* 298–307.

Kraemer, G. W., & Clarke, A. S. (1996). Social attachment, brain function, and aggression. *Annals of the New York Academy of Sciences, 794,* 121–135.

Levinson, A., & Fonagy, P. (1998). *Criminality and attachment: The relationship between interpersonal awareness and offending in a prison population.* Manuscript submitted for publication.

Lewis, M., Feiring, C., McGuffog, C., & Jaskir, J. (1984). Predicting psychopathology in six-year-olds from early social relations. *Child Development, 55,* 123–136.

Liotti, G. (1992). Disorganized/disoriented attachment in the etiology of the dissociative disorders. *Dissociation, 4,* 196–204.

Liotti, G. (in press-a). Understanding the dissociative processes: The contribution of attachment theory. *Psychoanalytic Inquiry.*

Liotti, G. (in press-b). Disorganization of attachment as a model for understanding dissociative psychopathology. In J. Solomon & C. George (Eds.), *Attachment disorganization.* New York: Guilford Press.

Liotti, G., Intreccialagli, B., & Cecere, F. (1991). Esperienza di lutto nella madre e facilitazione dello sviluppo di disturbi dissociativi nella prole: Unio studio caso–controllo.

[Unresolved mourning in mothers and development of dissociative disorders in children: A case–control study]. *Rivista di Psichiatria, 26,* 283–291.

Lynch, M., & Cicchetti, D. (1991). Patterns of relatedness in maltreated and nonmaltreated children: Connections among multiple representational models. *Development and Psychopathology, 3,* 207–226.

Lyons-Ruth, K., Alpern, L., & Repacholi, B. (1993). Disorganized infant attachment classification and maternal psychosocial problems as predictors of hostile–aggressive behavior in the preschool classroom. *Child Development, 64,* 572–585.

Lyons-Ruth, K., & Atwood, G. (1998) *Elaborating the concept of unresolved mental states: A relational diathesis model of hostile–helpless states of mind.* Unpublished manuscript.

Lyons-Ruth, K., Bronfman, E., & Atwood, G. (in press). A relational diathesis model of hostile–helpless states of mind: Expressions in mother–infant interaction. In J. Solomon & C. George (Eds.), *Attachment disorganization.* New York: Guilford Press.

Lyons-Ruth, K., & Block, D. (1996). The disturbed caregiving system: Relations among childhood trauma, maternal caregiving, and infant affect and attachment. *Infant Mental Health Journal, 17,* 257–275.

Lyons-Ruth, K., Bronfman, E., & Parsons, E. (in press). Maternal disrupted affective communication, maternal frightened or frightening behavior, and disorganized infant attachment strategies. In J. Vondra & D. Barnett (Eds.), *Atypical patterns of infant attachment: Theory, research, and current directions. Monographs of the Society for Research in Child Development.*

Lyons-Ruth, K., Connell, D., & Zoll, D. (1989). Patterns of maternal behavior among infants at risk for abuse: Relations with infant attachment behavior and infant development at 12 months of age. In D. Cicchetti & V. Carlson (Eds.), *Child maltreatment: Theory and research on the causes and consequences of child abuse and neglect* (pp. 464–494). New York: Cambridge University Press.

Lyons-Ruth, K., Connell, D., Grunebaum, H., & Botein, S. (1990). Infants at social risk: Maternal depression and family support services as mediators of infant development and security of attachment. *Child Development, 61,* 85–98.

Lyons-Ruth, K., Connell, D., Zoll, D., & Stahl, J. (1987). Infants at social risk: Relations among infant maltreatment, maternal behavior, and infant attachment behavior. *Developmental Psychology, 23,* 223–232.

Lyons-Ruth, K., Easterbrooks, A., & Cibelli, C. (1997). Infant attachment strategies, infant mental lag, and maternal depressive symptoms: Predictors of internalizing and externalizing problems at age 7. *Developmental Psychology, 33,* 681–692.

Lyons-Ruth, K., Repacholi, B., McLeod, S., & Silva, E. (1991). Disorganized attachment behavior in infancy: Short-term stability, maternal and infant correlates, and risk-related subtypes. *Development and Psychopathology, 3,* 377–396.

Lyons-Ruth, K., Zoll, D., Connell, D., & Grunebaum, H. (1989). Family deviance and family disruption in childhood: Associations with maternal behavior and infant maltreatment during the first two years of life. *Development and Psychopathology, 1,* 219–236.

Main, M. (1973). *Exploration, play, and cognitive functioning as related to child–mother attachment.* Unpublished doctoral dissertation, Johns Hopkins University.

Main, M. (1979). *Scale for disordered/disoriented infant be-*

havior in response to the Main and Weston clown sessions. Unpublished manuscript, University of California at Berkeley.

Main, M. (1995). Recent studies in attachment: Overview, with selected implications for clinical work. In S. Goldberg, R. Muir, & J. Kerr (Eds.), *Attachment theory: Social, developmental, and clinical perspectives* (pp. 407–474). Analytic Press: Hillsdale, NJ.

Main, M. (1996). Introduction to the special section on attachment and psychopathology: 2. Overview of the field of attachment. *Journal of Consulting and Clinical Psychology, 64,* 237–243.

Main, M., & Cassidy, J. (1988). Categories of response to reunion with the parent at age 6: Predicted from infant attachment classifications and stable over a 1–month period. *Developmental Psychology, 24,* 415–426.

Main, M., & George, C. (1985). Response of abused and disadvantaged toddlers to distress in agemates: A study in the day care setting. *Developmental Psychology, 21,* 407–412.

Main, M., & Goldwyn, R. (1998). *Adult attachment scoring and classification system.* Version 6.3. Unpublished manuscript, University of California at Berkeley.

Main, M., & Hesse, E. (1990). Parents' unresolved traumatic experiences are related to infant disorganized attachment status: Is frightened and/or frightening parental behavior the linking mechanism? In M. T. Greenberg, D. Cicchetti, & E. M. Cummings (Eds.), *Attachment in the preschool years: Theory, research, and intervention* (pp. 161–182). Chicago: University of Chicago Press.

Main, M., & Hesse, E. (1992a). Disorganized/disoriented infant behavior in the strange situation, lapses in the monitoring of reasoning and discourse during the parent's Adult Attachment Interview, and dissociative states. In M. Ammaniti & D. Stern (Eds.), *Attachment and psycho-analysis* (pp. 80–140). Rome: Guis, Laterza & Figl.

Main, M., & Hesse, E. (1992b). *Frightening, frightened, dissociated, or disorganized behavior on the part of a parent: A coding system for parent–infant interactions* (4th ed.). Unpublished manuscript, University of California at Berkeley.

Main, M., & Hesse, E. (1995). *Frightening, frightened, dissociated, or disorganized behavior on the part of the parent: A coding system for parent–infant interactions* (5th ed.). Unpublished manuscript. University of California at Berkeley.

Main, M., Kaplan, N., & Cassidy, J. (1985). Security in infancy, childhood, and adulthood: A move to the level of representation. In I. Bretherton & E. Waters (Eds.), *Growing points of attachment theory and research. Monographs of the Society for Research in Child Development, 50*(1–2, Serial No. 209), 66–104.

Main, M., & Morgan, H. (1996). Disorganization and disorientation in infant strange situation behavior: Phenotypic resemblance to dissociative states? In L. K. Michelson & W. J. Ray (Eds.), *Handbook of dissociation: Theoretical, empirical, and clinical perspectives* (pp. 107–138). New York: Plenum Press.

Main, M., & Solomon, J. (1986). Discovery of a new, insecure-disorganized/disoriented attachment pattern. In T. B. Brazelton & M.W. Yogman (Eds.), *Affective development in infancy* (pp. 95–124). Norwood, NJ: Ablex.

Main, M., & Solomon, J. (1990). Procedures for identifying infants as disorganized/disoriented during the Ainsworth strange situation. In M. T. Greenberg, D. Cicchetti, & E. M. Cummings (Eds.), *Attachment in the preschool years:*

Theory, research, and intervention (pp. 121–160). Chicago: University of Chicago Press.

Main, M., & Weston, D. R. (1981). The quality of the toddler's relationship to mother and to father: Related to conflict behavior and the readiness to establish new relationships. *Child Development, 52,* 932–940.

McLeer, S., Callaghan, M., Henry, D., & Wallen, J. (1994). Psychiatric disorders in sexually abused children. *Journal of the American Academy of Child and Adolescent Psychiatry, 33,* 313–319.

Minde, K., & Hesse, E. (1996). The role of the Adult Attachment Interview in parent–infant psychotherapy: A case presentation. *Infant Mental Health Journal, 17,* 115–126.

Moss, E., Parent, S., Gosselin, C., Rousseau, D., & St-Laurent, D. (1996). Attachment and teacher-reported behavior problems during the preschool and early school-age period. *Development and Psychopathology, 8,* 511–525.

Moss, E., Rousseau, D., Parent, S., St-Laurent, D., & Saintong, J. (1998). Correlates of attachment at school age: Maternal reported stress, mother-child interaction, and behavior problems. *Child Development, 69,* 1390–1405.

Mueller, E., & Silverman, N. (1989). Peer relations in maltreated children. In D. Cicchetti & V. Carlson (Eds.), *Child maltreatment: Theory and research on the causes and consequences of child abuse and neglect* (pp. 529–578). New York: Cambridge University Press.

Muscetta, S., Dazzi, N., De Coro, A., Ortu, F., & Speranza, A. M. (in press). States of mind with respect to attachment and change in a psychotherapeutic relationship: A study of the coherence of transcript in short-term psychotherapy with an adolescent. *Psychoanalytic Inquiry.*

National Institute of Child Health and Human Development (NICHD) Early Child Care Research Network. (1997). The effects of infant child care on infant–mother attachment security: Results of the NICHD study of early child care. *Child Development, 68,* 860–879.

O'Connor, M. J., Sigman, M., & Brill, N. (1987). Disorganization of attachment in relation to maternal alcohol consumption. *Journal of Consulting and Clinical Psychology, 55,* 831–836.

Ogawa, J. R., Sroufe, L. A., Weinfield, N. S., Carlson, E. A., & Egeland, B. (1997). Development and the fragmented self: Longitudinal study of dissociative symptomatology in a nonclinical sample. *Development and Psychopathology, 9,* 855–879.

Owen, M. T., & Cox, M. J. (1997). Marital conflict and the development of infant–parent attachment relationships. *Journal of Family Psychology, 11,* 152–164.

Patrick, M., Hobson, R. P., Castle, P., Howard, R., & Maughan, B. (1994). Personality disorder and mental representation of early social experience. *Development and Psychopathology, 6,* 375–388.

Pelcovitz, D., Kaplan, S., Goldenberg, B., Mandel, F., Lehane, J., & Guarrera, J. (1994). Post-traumatic stress disorder in physically abused adolescents. *Journal of the American Academy of Child and Adolescent Psychiatry, 33,* 305–312.

Putnam, F. W. (1997). *Dissociation in children and adolescents: A developmental perspective.* New York: Guilford Press.

Radke-Yarrow, M., Cummings, E. M., Kuczynski, L., & Chapman, M. (1985). Patterns of attachment in two- and three-year-olds in normal families and families with parental depression. *Child Development, 56,* 884–893.

Renken, B., Egeland, B., Marvinney, D., Mangelsdorf, S., & Sroufe, L. A. (1989). Early childhood antecedents of aggression and passive-withdrawal in early elementary school. *Journal of Personality, 5,* 257–281.

Schneider-Rosen, K., & Cicchetti, D. (1991). Early self-knowledge and emotional development: Visual self-recognition and affective reactions to mirror self-image in maltreated and nonmaltreated toddlers. *Developmental Psychology, 27,* 481–488.

Schuengel, C., van IJzendoorn, M., Bakermans-Kranenburg, M., & Blom, M. (1997, April). Frightening, frightened and/or dissociated behavior, unresolved loss, and infant disorganization. In D. Jacobvitz (Chair), *Caregiving correlates and longitudinal outcomes of disorganized attachments in infants.* Symposium conducted at the biennial meeting of the Society for Research in Child Development, Washington, DC.

Schuengel, C., van IJzendoorn, M., Bakermans-Kranenburg, M., & Blom, M. (in press). Frightening, frightened and/or dissociated behavior, unresolved loss, and infant disorganization. *Journal of Consulting and Clinical Psychology.*

Shaw, D. S., Owens, E. B., Vondra, J. I., Keenan, K., & Winslow, E. B. (1996). Early risk factors and pathways in the development of early disruptive behavior problems. *Development and Psychopathology, 8,* 679–699.

Solomon, J., George, C., & de Jong, A. (1995). Children classified as controlling at age six: Evidence of disorganized representational strategies and aggression at home and at school. *Development and Psychopathology, 7,* 447–463.

Spangler, G., Fremmer-Bombik, E., & Grossmann, K. (1996). Social and individual determinants of infant attachment security and disorganization. *Development and Psychopathology, 17,* 127–139.

Spangler, G., & Grossmann, K. E. (1993). Biobehavioral organization in securely and insecurely attached infants. *Child Development, 64,* 1439–1450.

Speltz, M. L., Greenberg, M. T., & DeKlyen, M. (1990). Attachment in preschoolers with disruptive behavior: A comparison of clinic-referred and nonproblem children. *Development and Psychopathology, 2,* 31–46.

Spieker, S. J., & Booth, C. (1988). Maternal antecedents of attachment quality. In J. Belsky & T. Nezworski (Eds.), *Clinical implications of attachment* (pp. 300–323). Hillsdale, NJ: Erlbaum.

Sroufe, L. A., & Fleeson, J. (1986). Attachment and the construction of relationships. In W. Hartup & Z. Rubin (Eds.), *Relationships and development* (pp. 51–72). Hillsdale, NJ: Erlbaum.

Stalker, C., & Davies, F. (1995). Attachment organization and adaptation in sexually abused women. *Canadian Journal of Psychiatry, 40,* 234–240.

Steele, H., Steele, M., & Fonagy, P. (1996). Associations among attachment classifications of mothers, fathers, and their infants. *Child Development, 67,* 541–555.

Steiner, H., Zeanah, C. H., Stuber, M., Ash, P., & Angell, R. (1994). The hidden faces of trauma: An update on child psychiatric traumatology. *Scientific Proceedings of the Annual Meeting of the American Academy of Child and Adolescent Psychiatry, 31.*

Strage, A., & Main, M. (1985, April). Attachment and parent–child discourse patterns. In M. Main (Chair), *Attachment: A move to the level of representation.* Paper presented at the biennial meeting of the Society for Research in Child Development, Toronto.

Sullivan-Hanson, J. M. (1990). *The early attachment and current affectional bonds of battered women: Implications for the impact of spouse abuse on children.* Unpublished doctoral dissertation, University of Virginia.

Suomi, S. (1991). Early stress and adult emotional reactivity in rhesus monkeys. In *The childhood environment and adult disease.* (Ciba Foundation Symposium 156, pp. 171–188). Chichester, England: Wiley.

Teti, D. M., Gelfand, D. M., Messinger, D. S., & Isabella, R. (1995). Maternal depression and the quality of early attachment: An examination of infants, preschoolers, and their mothers. *Developmental Psychology, 34,* 361–376.

Thalhuber, K., Jacobvitz, D., & Hazen, N. L. (1998, March). *Effects of mothers' past traumatic experiences on mother–infant interactions.* Paper presented at the biennial meeting of the Southwestern Society for Research in Human Development, Galveston, TX.

Troy, M., & Sroufe, L. A. (1987). Victimization among preschoolers: Role of attachment relationship history. *Journal of the American Academy of Child and Adolescent Psychiatry, 26,* 166–172.

True, M., Pasani, L., Ryan, R., & Oumar, F. (1998). *Maternal behaviors related to disorganized infant attachment in West Africa.* Paper presented at the annual meeting of the Western Psychological Association, Albuquerque, NM.

van IJzendoorn, M. H. (1995). Adult attachment representations, parental responsiveness, and infant attachment: A meta-analysis on the predictive validity of the Adult Attachment Interview. *Psychological Bulletin, 117,* 387–403.

van IJzendoorn, M., Feldbrugge, J., Derks, F., de Ruiter, C., Verhagen, M., Philipse, M., van der Staak, C., & Riksen-Walraven, J. (in press). Attachment representations of personality disordered criminal offenders. *American Journal of Orthopsychiatry.*

van IJzendoorn, M. H., Schuengel, C., & Bakermans-Kranenburg, M.J. (in press). Disorganized attachment in early childhood: Meta-analysis of precursors, concomitants, and sequelae. *Development and Psychopathology.*

Vondra, J., Hommerding, K. D., & Shaw, D. S. (in press). Stability and change in infant attachment in a low-income sample. In J. Vondra & D. Barnett (Eds.), Atypical patterns of infant attachment: Theory, research, and current directions. *Monographs of the Society for Research in Child Development.*

Wartner, U. G., Grossmann, K., Fremmer-Bombik, E., & Suess, G. (1994). Attachment patterns at age six in south Germany: Predictability from infancy and implications for preschool behavior. *Child Development, 65,* 1014–1027.

West, M., & George, C. (1998). *Abuse and violence in intimate adult relationships: New perspectives from attachment theory.* Unpublished manuscript.

Wolfe, D. A. (1985). Child abusive parents: An empirical review and analysis. *Psychological Bulletin, 97,* 461–482.

Yehuda, R., Southwick, S. M., Nussbaum, G., Wahlby, V., Giller, E. L., & Mason, J. W. (1990). Low urinary cortisol excretion in patients with post-traumtic stress disorder. *Journal of Nervous and Mental Disease, 178,* 366–369.

Zahn-Waxler, C., & Kochanska, G. (1990). The origins of guilt. In R. Thompson (Ed.), *Nebraska Symposium on Motivation: Vol. 36. Socioemotional development* (pp. 183–258). Lincoln: University of Nebraska Press.

24

Contributions of Attachment Theory to Infant–Parent Psychotherapy and Other Interventions with Infants and Young Children

❖

ALICIA F. LIEBERMAN
CHARLES H. ZEANAH

The goal of this chapter is to examine how attachment theory and research have influenced clinical practice, with a particular focus on infant–parent psychotherapy and other preventive interventions that promote infant mental health by addressing early disturbances in parent–child relationships. Only programs and approaches with clearly articulated clinical and preventive goals are described. The chapter is divided into four major sections. The first section describes the shared psychoanalytic origins of attachment theory and infant–parent psychotherapy, provides an overview of infant–parent psychotherapy and its relation to attachment theory and psychoanalysis, and explores attachment theory's evolving contributions to clinical practice. The second section illustrates the integration of attachment theory and infant–parent psychotherapy into several clinical programs for infants and toddlers. The third section describes other programs and approaches influenced by attachment theory. The final section reviews the few studies evaluating the efficacy of attachment-focused interventions. Some brief concluding remarks highlight the importance of a trust-

ing working alliance, empathy, and sensitive responsiveness to emotional signals as the hallmarks of clinical approaches based on attachment theory.

ATTACHMENT THEORY AND INFANT–PARENT PSYCHOTHERAPY: SHARED ORIGINS

There is an inherent affinity between attachment theory and infant–parent psychotherapy because of their common emphasis on the importance of the mother–child relationship in the first 3 years of life as the bedrock for healthy emotional development. Both attachment theory (Bowlby, 1969/1982) and infant–parent psychotherapy (Fraiberg, Adelson, & Shapiro, 1975) emerged in the 1970s as seminal influences on the then-emerging field of infant mental health. Although representing different conceptual frameworks, Bowlby and Fraiberg were both psychoanalysts, and their work bears the unmistakable imprint of the object relations approach to psychoanalytic theory that was the prevailing clinical *Zeitgeist*.

Yet the striking similarities and mutual influences between the approaches have only recently begun to be formally recognized (Lieberman, 1991).

Infant–Parent Psychotherapy: Overview

Infant–parent psychotherapy was developed as an effort to treat disturbances in the infant–parent relationship in the first 3 years of life (Fraiberg, 1980). The basic premise of this approach is that such disturbances are the manifestations in the present of unresolved conflicts that one or both of a baby's parents have with important figures from their own childhood. The current baby is not perceived by the parents as a baby in his or her own right. Rather, in Fraiberg's (1980) highly eloquent words, the baby has become

> the representative of figures within the parental past, or a representative of an aspect of the parental self that is repudiated or negated. In some cases the baby himself seems engulfed in the parental neurosis and is showing the early signs of emotional disturbance. In treatment, we examine with the parents the past and the present in order to free them and their baby from old "ghosts" that have invaded the nursery, and then we must make meaningful links between the past and the present through interpretations that will lead to insight. At the same time . . . we maintain the focus on the baby through the provision of developmental information and discussion. We move back and forth, between present and past, parent and baby, but we always return to the baby. (p. 61)

The Baby's Presence in the Sessions

The presence of the baby during the therapeutic sessions is a central ingredient of this approach to psychotherapy. This was a revolutionary innovation when Fraiberg introduced it, and it has become the sine qua non of most therapeutic approaches to the treatment of infants and toddlers. The widespread acceptance of this often demanding therapeutic format stems from a recognition that parental reporting is no substitute for direct observation of the baby and of the parent–baby interaction. The therapist's observational skill allows him or her to identify themes, detect defensive distortions, capture emotional nuances, and monitor infant development in ways that would not be possible even with the most sincere efforts at parental self-disclosure and description of the infant. Similarly, the baby's presence allows for an emotional immediacy to therapeutic intervention that could not be replicated if the parents were recollecting a particular scene.

The Present as a Bridge to the Past

Fraiberg's metaphor of "ghosts in the nursery" (Fraiberg et al., 1975) has galvanized theoreticians and clinicians alike, because it evokes the powerful and enduring hold that a sad and frightening childhood can have on adult experience. In individual psychotherapy, it is found again and again that clients can overcome crippling psychological symptoms and self-defeating patterns of living when they are able to reconnect emotionally and come to grips with the pain, fear, anger, and helplessness evoked by childhood circumstances and key childhood events. Similarly, one of the most extraordinary experiences afforded to the infant–parent psychotherapist is witnessing the amazing transformation in feelings and behavior toward a baby that can occur when a parent is able to trace ambivalence, anger, and rejection of the baby to early childhood experiences. The parallel transformation of the baby from a fussy, muted, withdrawn, and angry creature to a lively, thriving, and engaged human being is the most rewarding aspect of this work.

Yet it is also true that retrieving the past is not invariably the key to healing in the present, even when it is a key to clinical understanding. This is particularly the case when a parent does not rely on language as the primary form of self-expression, when he or she is not psychologically minded, or when the parent's psychological functioning is too fragile or constricted to tolerate delving into painful early memories. Moreover, a parent with severe characterological difficulties may be quite able to relive past experiences with great emotional intensity and to be fully aware of the repetition of the past in his or her present feelings toward the baby, and yet may neither find emotional relief in these insights nor develop more positive ways of relating to the child. In such a case, verbal interpretations of the links between the past and the present do not hold the key to improvement, and the most effective interventions are not spoken but rather enacted through the therapist's empathic attitude and behavior toward the parent and the baby (Lieberman & Pawl, 1993; Pawl & Lieberman, 1997).

Another obstacle to the therapeutic value of finding links between the past and the present is that many distressed and ambivalent parents choose not to speak about their childhoods even when they have been in treatment for a long time; they view therapeutic efforts to discuss their past as tactless and intrusive. They prefer to focus instead on the difficulties they experience in present relationships with important figures in their lives—a spouse, a boss, a partner, a friend, a sibling, a parent, and even the infant–parent psychotherapist. This may well be a sign that such a parent's defenses against anxiety are unconsciously experienced as too fragile, and that the parent is afraid of not being able to withstand the onslaught of recovered affect without emotional collapse. In these circumstances, therapeutic progress can take place not by cajoling the parent to bring up the walled-off past, but by focusing instead on the feeling states involving salient current relationships and by exploring how these feeling states may also be present in relation to the baby (see Silverman, Lieberman, & Pekarsky, 1997, for a clinical example).

In all cases, hypothesized links between a parent's past and his or her present feelings toward the baby are entertained by the therapist even when not explicitly discussed, and these hypotheses may provide the basis for clinical interventions. Whether such links become concrete foci for insight-oriented interpretations depends on clinical need, as well as on the parent's interest in pursuing such connections and the parent's emotional capacity to withstand the pain of revisiting the past without significant or lasting emotional deterioration.

Even when the recovery of lost affective connections with the past opens new psychological perspectives and brings new emotional freedom, the emerging insights often need to go hand in hand with conscious, determined, and sometimes very courageous efforts to change behavior in order to achieve lasting positive change in parenting styles. For this reason, versatility and flexibility are hallmarks of infant–parent psychotherapy. In addition to insight-oriented interventions, Fraiberg (1980) described three other therapeutic modalities that are employed in infant–parent psychotherapy: brief crisis intervention, developmental guidance, and supportive treatment. The specific therapeutic modality that predominates in the treatment may vary according to the specific circumstances, both across families and with a particular family in the course of treatment.

In current practice with families facing a multiplicity of socioeconomic as well as emotional stresses, the different therapeutic modalities are often used either simultaneously within a session or in rapid succession from one session to another (Lieberman & Pawl, 1993; Pawl & Lieberman, 1997). A successful crisis intervention may resolve an acute problem and generate enough trust in the therapist to allow treatment to become deeper and more insight-oriented. Conversely, a well-timed interpretation may assuage a parent's resistance to the point that he or she may accept developmental information that had previously been angrily rejected. Emotional support is always a component of infant–parent psychotherapy, whether by itself or in conjunction with psychodynamic interpretations, because the therapist's empathic understanding is considered an essential ingredient in giving parents the courage to explore themselves and to try out new ways of behaving with their babies.

Across therapeutic modalities, concrete assistance with problems of living (in the forms, for example, of providing a ride to the pediatrician, making phone calls to the housing authorities to advocate for better housing, or interceding with public agencies to secure necessary services) can help to create and maintain a valuable therapeutic alliance when a parent is having difficulty in these areas due to cognitive or emotional problems, depression, or lack of knowledge. The therapeutic legitimacy and importance given to concrete actions advocating for the family are reflections of Selma Fraiberg's genius in integrating her dual vocation and training as social worker and psychoanalyst.

The Baby and the Therapist as Transference Objects

Fraiberg's (1980) original concept of the baby rather than the therapist as the object of the parent's transference continues to have much clinical usefulness. Infant–parent psychotherapists do not see themselves as the center of the therapeutic process, in the sense that they do not deliberately cultivate or interpret parental emotional reactions toward themselves. The focus of therapeutic attention is a parent's feelings and behaviors toward the baby, not toward the therapist.

In spite of this transferential focus on the baby, parental transference to the therapist is ubiquitous. Just as a troubled parent perceives the baby through the lens of early emotional experiences, it is only natural that the perception of the therapist as a powerful figure in the parent's life should be influenced by a similar lens as well. (In attachment theory terms, we would say that the working models of attachment and caregiving that affect a parent's behavior toward the baby also inform the parent's perception of the therapist. This point is elaborated in the next section.) Sometimes the therapist is idealized by a needy and grateful parent as the wise, generous, and knowledgeable provider of help and support. When this happens, the therapist uses the parent's positive emotional investment as a vehicle toward change, while perhaps giving the parent lighthearted permission to detect and complain about the therapist's mistakes whenever these come to the parent's attention.

Perhaps more often, a parent may perceive the therapist as a deceptively benign person who might become critical and punitive at any time, and who has the legal power to alert the child protection authorities about situations that might lead to the child's removal from the home and placement in foster care. When this covert negative transference prevails, the first task of the infant–parent therapist is to address the parent's anger, mistrust, and fear with tact and understanding, in the knowledge that the negative transference is likely to be an indication of painful experiences of abuse and powerlessness in the parent's childhood, in his or her immediate past, and/or perhaps also in current circumstances.

In these situations, the therapist's positive regard, attentiveness to the parent's needs, and empathic responsiveness are considered to be primary mutative factors in infant–parent psychotherapy. Through their relationship to the therapist, parents learn, often for the first time, ways of relating that are characterized by mutuality and caring rather than by anger and fear (Lieberman & Pawl, 1993). Because of its power to change negative expectations and create a new and more trusting experience of how to be with another, this aspect of the therapeutic relationship can be regarded as a corrective attachment experience (Lieberman, 1991). Through such a corrective experience, an ambivalent and angry parent can begin to experience and practice more protective and nurturing ways of relating to the baby.

Contributions of Attachment Theory to Infant–Parent Psychotherapy

Readers familiar with attachment theory will recognize the implicit influence of this viewpoint in the description of infant–parent psychotherapy outlined above. This influence is made more ex-

plicit in recent writings on infant–parent psychotherapy (e.g., Lieberman, 1991, 1996, 1997). In particular, clinical practice has been profoundly influenced by the concept of internal working models of the self and of attachment (Bowlby, 1980; Main, 1991). When viewed from this perspective, the intergenerational transmission of conflict from one generation to the next can be understood in different (yet complementary) terms from the explanatory mechanisms posited by Fraiberg (1980). The "ghosts in the nursery" model posits that unresolved parental conflicts are reenacted in relation to the baby—in other words, that unconscious impulses are displaced or projected from their original objects to the current transference object represented by the infant. In the framework of internal working models, this reference to psychoanalytic drive theory need not be invoked. We would say instead that internalized early experiences provide a structural framework that serves to sort out, select, and encode current emotional events. For example, the concept of "corrective emotional experience" (Lieberman, 1991), described in the section above, refers to the changes in the working model of the self in relation to attachment that can occur when the therapist provides the opportunity for sustained exploration of attachment-related emotional events in the context of empathic support and permission to experience and express a range of positive and negative affects. This respect for the mutative power of the therapist–parent relationship per se would not be tenable in a model that emphasizes insight-related psychological change as stemming from a redirection of negative affects from current targets to early recipients of them.

The contribution of attachment theory to infant–parent psychotherapy is explicitly elaborated in recent writings, but this influence was also quite apparent when infant–parent psychotherapy was in the process of first being developed, as illustrated in the examples below:

1. Fraiberg (1977) chose the term "attachment" to refer to the clinically relevant aspects of the mother–child relationship, including the expressions "lost and broken attachments" and "disorders of attachment."

2. Real-life events such as separation, loss, abuse, deprivation, and maltreatment were recognized as crucial pathogenic factors in a child's development (Fraiberg, 1977, 1980) and were major foci of therapeutic attention.

3. Observable behaviors in both parent and

child were used in infant–parent psychotherapy as indicators of underlying psychological processes, and these behaviors were used at the onset and the conclusion of infant–parent psychotherapy to evaluate the effectiveness of treatment (Fraiberg, Lieberman, Pekarsky, & Pawl, 1981).

4. Much emphasis was placed on the importance of enhancing maternal empathy and responsiveness to the baby's signals as the primary vehicle for fostering the child's mental health (Fraiberg et al., 1981).

5. There was a specific focus on infant attachment behavior and defenses against anxiety (Fraiberg, 1982), including avoidance, which was first identified as a defensive response by Ainsworth, Blehar, Waters, and Wall (1978).

Remarkably, in light of this unmistakable borrowing of attachment theory's terminology and methods, Fraiberg cited neither Bowlby nor Ainsworth as major influences in her writings, although she thought highly of their work (S. Fraiberg, personal communications, 1976, 1979, 1980). This absence of explicit reference to the impact of attachment theory on the genesis of infant–parent psychotherapy constitutes an interesting historical footnote in the chronicle of the infant mental health field. As a psychoanalyst, Fraiberg believed firmly in the usefulness of the economic and dynamic principles of psychoanalysis—the very viewpoints so decisively discarded in Bowlby's work (see the next section for an elaboration of this point). For example, addressing the relation among love, sexuality, and aggression, Fraiberg (1977) wrote that "it matters a great deal whether we include drives in our theory or not" (p. 36); she went on to use standard psychoanalytic drive terminology in discussing what she called "the origins of human bonds," which she understood, in classical psychoanalytic fashion, to be the by-products of the conflicting discharge aims of aggression and sexuality. Yet unexpectedly, in the midst of a fairly conventional psychoanalytic account of libidinal and drive matters, she stated:

All of this means that in the process of redirection and the ritualization of aggression in the service of love, a new pattern emerges which acquires *full status as an instinct* and a high degree of autonomy from the aggressive and sexual instincts from which it derived. *Not only are the patterns of love part of an autonomous instinct group, but they have a motive force equal to or greater than that of aggression under a wide range of conditions.* (p. 44; emphasis added)

These sentences could be mistaken for ones written by Bowlby if it were not for the earlier emphasis on drives. It is clear that with the ostensible purpose of discussing Konrad Lorenz's (1967) views on aggression, Fraiberg was indirectly incorporating into her thinking Bowlby's (1969/1982) groundbreaking application of ethological thinking to human behavior, without citing him or referring to him. Rather than openly incorporating the contributions of attachment theory into her writings, she chose instead to translate into classical psychoanalytic drive theory Bowlby's (1969/1982) claim that the attachment behavioral system constitutes an autonomous instinct.

Fraiberg's failure to acknowledge Bowlby's influence is a pointed example of the prolonged ostracism of attachment theory in the psychoanalytic world. In the following section, we discuss the different factors that coalesced into this state of affairs.

Attachment Theory, Psychoanalysis, and Clinical Practice

Attachment theory is the theory of socioemotional development best supported by empirical research (see Belsky & Cassidy, 1994, for a review). Still, it has been remarkably slow in influencing clinical practice with children and adults, although this situation is fortunately changing (Fonagy, 1991; Holmes, 1993; Slade, Chapter 25, this volume).

There are several interrelated reasons for the persistent reluctance of clinicians to incorporate attachment theory into their understanding of clinical issues. One major factor is that for many years after its appearance, attachment theory was rebuked by Bowlby's fellow psychoanalysts as a radical departure from the core of their discipline (see Grosskurth, 1986, and Karen, 1994, for excellent reviews). The reception was so uniformly frosty and even hostile that it led Bowlby (1988) to complain that "a problem encountered by every analyst who has proposed new theoretical ideas is the criticism that the new theory is 'not psychoanalysis'" (p. 58). The preeminence of psychoanalysis at the time as the leading influence in clinical training and practice meant that attachment theory remained consistently marginalized within these areas. In addition to these external circumstances, several issues related to the development of attachment theory contributed to its slowness in being adopted by clinicians.

One intrinsic drawback to its clinical application was that attachment theory is not a total personality theory because it does not include a systematic exploration of other motivational systems (e.g., sexuality, dominance, and aggression) and their interrelation with the attachment system (Lichtenberg, 1989; Lieberman, 1996; Seligman, 1991; Slade & Aber, 1992). For clinicians facing the multiplicity of conflicts and motivations reported by their clients, the unwavering focus on security and protection often seemed overly constricted and constricting. In order to become aware of the clinical usefulness of attachment theory, clinicians needed to be shown how to apply it in their everyday practice. Yet this focus on direct clinical application was for a long time not available within attachment theory.

At least at the outset of his career, Bowlby himself seemed less interested in influencing clinical practice than in redressing what he viewed as the unscientific aspects of psychoanalysis and in promoting changes in the cultural mores about child rearing. This dual emphasis on scientific legitimacy and on much-needed social reform regarding attitudes and policies toward children is probably related at least in part to Bowlby's modest self-appraisal as a clinician. In a disarmingly candid interview with Jeremy Holmes (1993), he is quoted as saying: "I am not strong on intuition. . . . I often shudder to think how inept I have been as a therapist and how I have ignored or misunderstood material a patient has presented. Clearly, the best therapy is done by a therapist who is naturally intuitive and also guided by the appropriate theory" (p. 32). Bowlby's personal preferences as well as his intellectual honesty naturally steered him in the direction where he believed he could contribute the most: providing clinicians with "the appropriate theory" to guide their work.

This was necessarily a slow approach to influencing clinical practice, because people tend to read writers in their own field of endeavor. The many publications stemming from attachment theory focused on theory and developmental research rather than on clinical practice, and seemed off limits to most clinicians in their focus and terminology (e.g., Ainsworth et al., 1978; Bowlby, 1969/1982, 1973, 1980). The first book exploring the clinical applications of attachment theory had a developmental researcher as its senior editor (Belsky & Nezworski, 1988). Bowlby himself wrote only sparsely on clinical practice, and then quite late in his career (Bowlby, 1988). Mary Ainsworth, although a gifted clinician, did

not do so at all. The dearth of clinical writings from the seminal figures in attachment theory, combined with the hostility with which leading psychoanalysts regarded this approach, led to the widespread assumption that attachment theory had academic rather than clinical relevance.

It is useful to review briefly the connections between attachment theory and psychoanalysis because of the enduring influence of the psychoanalytic origins of attachment theory, and because of Bowlby's own consistent view of his theory as "the attachment version of psychoanalysis" (J. Bowlby, personal communication, 1989).

Bowlby's continued allegiance to the psychoanalytic perspective can be explained by his recognition of the explanatory power of three basic viewpoints that form part of the metapsychology of psychoanalysis. These are the "genetic" viewpoint, which seeks the origins of a psychological phenomenon by investigating antecedent experiences; the "structural" viewpoint, which makes propositions regarding the building blocks or components of the psyche; and the "adaptive" viewpoint, which concerns itself with the ways in which psychological functioning represents an accommodation to the specific conditions and demands of an individual's environment (Rapaport & Gil, 1959). All three of these principles were clearly at work in the original formulation of attachment theory (Bowlby, 1969/1982), as well as in more recent developments in attachment theory and research.

On the other hand, Bowlby explicitly discarded two other basic psychoanalytic principles: the "economic" viewpoint, which proposes the existence of a psychic energy (named "libido") that is distinct from physical energy; and the "dynamic" viewpoint, which proposes the existence of psychological forces (called "instinctual drives"—i.e., sex and aggression) that strive for expression through discharge. Bowlby replaced these notions with a more modern biological approach to the understanding of instinct and a cybernetic model of affective life. Such a radical theoretical innovation had a paradoxical effect. Although ensuring the scientific legitimacy of attachment theory as a framework open to empirical investigation, these radical innovations also led to the rejection of attachment theory by psychoanalysts, who regarded Bowlby's innovations as mechanistic, bland, and out of touch with the basic conflicts of the human psyche (Grosskurth, 1986; Holmes, 1993).

Not content with discarding some of the basic principles of psychoanalysis, Bowlby (1969/ 1982) also introduced four bold propositions that could not easily be assimilated into the psychoanalytic practice of the time. First, he proposed that certain aspects of human psychological functioning and behavior should be understood from an ethological perspective, with survival and fitness as the explanatory mechanisms for the biological functions of certain behavioral systems. Second, within this context, he introduced the concept of attachment as an autonomous motivational system on a par with hunger and sexuality in its importance for survival. This also placed primary emphasis on the importance of real-life events, as opposed to the person's fantasies or subjective perception of such events, for understanding the development of psychopathology in children and for tracing back the origins of psychopathology in adults (Bowlby, 1969/1982, 1973, 1980). Among such pathogenic real-life events are separation from parents, loss, and maltreatment (Bowlby, 1969/ 1982, 1973, 1980). Finally, Bowlby advocated applying the ethological tradition of behavioral observation to the understanding of psychological processes in humans, rather than relying primarily on verbalization, as was the psychoanalytic tradition.

These conceptual innovations have important clinical implications. They lead the psychotherapist to understand the patient or client not only as an individual but also as a representative of the human species, endowed with species-specific behavioral propensities that may have their origin in biological imperatives and may not be amenable to change as a result of cultural practices. Attachment theory also turns the clinician's attention to the importance of real-life events in shaping development and in coloring current functioning, emphasizing that actual events have more parsimonious explanatory power for understanding psychopathology than the drive-related fears and fantasies postulated by classical psychoanalysis. In keeping with contemporary developmental research, attachment theory considers infants to be closely tied to immediate experiences and (at least for most of the first 18 months of life) cognitively incapable of the kinds of fantasies attributed to them by some psychoanalytic theorists (Cassidy, 1990; Slade & Aber, 1992; Stern, 1985).

The premises of attachment theory also place a great deal of importance on the observation of

behavior as an indicator of a person's emotional responses, as opposed to relying mostly on verbal reports, fantasies, wishes, or dreams. Yet the pioneering spirit of these innovations put attachment theory in a "no man's land" from a clinical point of view. For clinicians influenced by a behaviorist approach, attachment theory seemed too close to its psychoanalytic origins; for psychoanalysts, it was too iconoclastic. As a result, attachment theory did not find a ready audience for a clinical exploration of its implications.

The current rapprochement between psychoanalysis and attachment theory was set in motion by three simultaneous developments. One was the increasingly sophisticated elaboration within attachment theory of a focus on internal representation and working models of the self in relation to attachment (e.g., Bretherton, 1984; Cassidy, 1988; Main, 1991; Main & Cassidy, 1988; Main, Kaplan, & Cassidy, 1989; Zeanah & Barton, 1989; Zeanah & Benoit, 1995). Another and converging trend was the growing openness of psychoanalysis to the importance of real-life events in influencing the course of personality formation (e.g., Wallerstein, 1973), as well as to approaches emphasizing intersubjectivity and a narrative account of the patient's experience (e. g., Emde, 1988, 1994; Fonagy, 1991; Lichtenberg, 1989; Stern, 1985, 1995). Finally, the emergence of clinicians trained both in developmental research and in psychodynamic theory and practice is creating useful bridges between the two disciplines (e.g., Emde, 1988; Lieberman, 1991, 1996; Lyons-Ruth, 1991; Osofsky, 1993; Slade, Chapter 25, this volume; Slade & Aber, 1992; Zeanah & Barton, 1989). These simultaneous and mutually influential developments have led to a new appreciation of the value of attachment theory for clinical practice.

Nevertheless, the systematic application of attachment theory to clinical issues is still in a rudimentary stage of development. As recently as 1992, Erickson, Korfmacher, and Egeland (1992) reported that a computer search of peer-reviewed journals uncovered only "an eclectic assortment of attachment-related therapy articles," but no comprehensive conceptualization of the clinical applications of attachment theory (p. 498). They also pointed out that "most practitioners who make use of attachment theory in their clinical work seem to apply it in idiosyncratic ways" (p. 499). These authors singled out infant–parent psychotherapy (Fraiberg et al., 1975) as the most notable exception to this state of affairs.

THE APPLICATION OF ATTACHMENT THEORY AND INFANT–PARENT PSYCHOTHERAPY IN INFANCY AND EARLY CHILDHOOD MENTAL HEALTH PROGRAMS

Several mental health programs oriented to infants, toddlers, preschoolers, and their families have integrated attachment theory and infant–parent psychotherapy in varying degrees into their clinical approaches. This section provides a review of some of these programs.

The Infant–Parent Program: The Ann Arbor/San Francisco Model

The Infant–Parent Program (IPP) is an iteration of the original Child Development Project at the University of Michigan, Ann Arbor (Fraiberg, 1980), which was a demonstration program designed to develop and test infant–parent psychotherapy as a treatment of choice for relationship disorders of infancy. Established in 1979 at the San Francisco General Hospital by Fraiberg and colleagues, the IPP is partially funded by community mental health and other city funds with the goal of offering infant–parent psychotherapy to families of infants in the 0–3 age range who experience or are at risk for abuse, neglect, and relationship disorders (Lieberman & Pawl, 1993; Pawl & Lieberman, 1997). The families seen at the program are among the most impoverished and disenfranchised in the city, reflecting the characteristics of the population traditionally served by the San Francisco General Hospital, which is a teaching hospital of the University of California at San Francisco. More often than not, the family circumstances include poverty, lack of education, joblessness, homelessness, inadequate housing, mental illness, substance abuse, community and domestic violence, or other risk factors. Approximately 30% of the referrals originate in child protective services, with another 15% stemming from juvenile court or family court. The remaining sources of referral include public health nurses, pediatricians, psychiatrists, and community agencies serving high-risk families and their children.

The theoretical and clinical underpinnings of the program are essentially identical to those outlined in the section "Infant–Parent Psychotherapy: Overview." However, the original emphasis on the links between parents' early childhood experiences and their current feelings, perceptions, attitudes, and behaviors toward their babies (Fraiberg, 1980), though still a core component of the program, has been complemented by an increased appreciation for individual differences in babies and for the very real and immediate contribution that the parents' stressful current circumstances make to maladaptive patterns of caregiving. The hopelessness and suspiciousness often generated by these parents' difficult life conditions demand a painstaking attunement to their immediate subjective experience of the therapist and of the therapeutic process. As a result, much attention is given to the parents' own definition of their problems, their concepts of what they need, their expectations of treatment, and their response to the therapist's interventions. The quality of the parent–therapist relationship is often considered the primary mutative factor under these conditions (Pawl & Lieberman, 1997).

The children's emotional and behavioral difficulties are the foci of sustained therapeutic attention in the context of the parents' perception of these problems. The children's symptom picture includes failure to thrive, depression, separation anxiety, multiple and seemingly inexplicable fears, severe and prolonged tantrums, distractibility, impulsiveness, lack of age-appropriate impulse control, and uncontrolled anger.

An important subset of the clinical population treated at the IPP consists of infants and toddlers diagnosed with reactive attachment disorder as described in the *Diagnostic and Statistical Manual of Mental Disorders*, fourth edition (DSM-IV) and in the Zero to Three diagnostic classification. These children have not been able to form a sustained, focused relationship because of loss of the original attachment figure, followed by institutional care or multiple changes in foster care placement. They show the symptom picture typical of this condition, including withdrawal, irritability, lack of responsiveness to human contact, and lethargy, or their reverse—namely, indiscriminate sociability and shallowness in human relations. Many of these children also show prolonged and seemingly intractable tantrums and unpredictable bouts of aggression.

Regardless of the immediate presenting problem, IPP intervention invariably begins with an extended assessment process that lasts approximately 6 weeks and is geared to building a reliable working alliance with each child's parent(s) or caregiver(s), as well as to gathering comprehensive information about the child, the family, and their circumstances. Except in exceptional circumstances, the assessment is carried out by the same clinician who will conduct the treatment if infant–parent psychotherapy is considered the treatment of choice at the end of the assessment. This is done in order to maximize the continuity of human connection between parent and intervenor, and to avoid a repetition of the history of separation, loss, and short-lived relationships with intimate others as well as with service providers that is the rule in this population. The intervenors are master's-level and pre- and postdoctoral therapists representing a variety of disciplines, including social work, psychology, psychiatry, pediatrics, and nursing. Whenever clinically appropriate, a developmental neuropsychology evaluation involving at least three sessions is conducted in order to obtain a systematic picture of the child's cognitive, sensorimotor, and emotional functioning, and to provide feedback to the parents. Great care is taken to determine the timing of this evaluation and to integrate it with the ongoing clinical assessment and treatment of the child and the family (Lieberman, Van Horn, Grandison, & Pekarsky, 1997).

The sessions involve the parent(s) and the child and take place either in the home or in the office playroom, as clinically indicated or as preferred by the parents. Whenever possible, at least one home visit is conducted during the assessment process in order to obtain a more accurate understanding of the family's living conditions. The format of joint parent–child sessions is dictated by the ongoing need to learn as much as possible about the child's and parents' functioning and the quality of their relationship; however, variations in this basic format are possible, depending on family composition, the child's age, and other factors. For example, individual sessions with one or both parents or meetings with the couple are sometimes called for when private time for the adults is needed in order to discuss emotionally charged issues that affect the child's welfare but are not appropriate to discuss in the child's presence.

Both the assessment and the treatment sessions are unstructured, with the themes largely determined by each parent's free associations and by the unfolding interactions between the parents and the child. The intervenor observes how the parents and the child relate to each other and how each of them responds to the emotions that emerge during the sessions. Child observations are used to determine the child's level and quality of functioning in the sensorimotor, social, and emotional domains, and these observations are used to supplement and enrich the formal developmental neuropsychology evaluation. Questions, probings, joint play, developmental guidance, expressions of emotional support, and insight-oriented interpretations are used as clinically indicated to help the parents modify their rigid, constricted, and distorted perceptions of the child and to construct a more developmentally appropriate, empathic, and nuanced behavioral repertoire in their interactions with the child. These interventions have the goal of helping the child become more securely reliant on the parents.

In every aspect of treatment, the therapist is aware of the pervasiveness of a parallel process between what transpires between the parents and the therapist and what transpires between the parents and the child. In keeping with this awareness, the therapist is careful at all times to be empathically responsive to the emotional needs of both the parents and the child, and not to force the disclosure or expression of negative feelings or psychological conflicts in either the parents or the child.

Many of the recent writings involving the work of the IPP emphasize the compatibility of infant–parent psychotherapy with assessment procedures and therapeutic techniques influenced by attachment theory. In particular, a randomized treatment outcome study of the effectiveness of infant–parent psychotherapy, conducted with a Latino subsample, utilized the strange situation procedure and other assessment instruments derived from attachment theory research to assess the intervention and control groups before and after treatment (Lieberman, Weston, & Pawl, 1991). This study demonstrated significant differences between the intervention and control groups in maternal empathy, dyadic goal-corrected partnership, and children's avoidance, resistance, and anger toward their mothers, with the scores in all of these measures significantly favoring the treatment group. The results support the theoretical and clinical compatibility of concepts central to both attachment theory and infant–parent psychotherapy, and point the way toward a fruitful collaboration of research and clinical intervention within an integrated paradigm.

The Child Trauma Research Project: A San Francisco Innovation

The Child Trauma Research Project (CTRP) is a treatment outcome research program that utilizes age-modified infant–parent psychotherapy in order to assess and treat children in the first 5 years of life who have been traumatized by domestic violence—specifically, by the experience of witnessing their mothers being battered and/or raped by partners. This program seeks to integrate the assessment and intervention strategies of attachment theory and infant–parent psychotherapy into a researchable model of child–mother psychotherapy that addresses the disruption in attachment pattern resulting from violence-related trauma to both a mother and a child (Lieberman et al., 1997). The goal of the program is to investigate the effectiveness of dyadic psychotherapy in helping to address and alleviate the traumatic effects of violence on the child–mother relationship. The clinical objectives are to enable the mother to enter into and to appreciate the child's inner world; to help the child and the mother to jointly construct a narrative of their experiences, including the impact of violence; and to offer mother and child a safe space that allows them to enact their conflicts in order to find more adaptive ways of resolving them. In order to reduce the chances of retraumatization in the course of treatment, only families where the mothers no longer have active relationships with the perpetrators are included. Exclusionary criteria involve homelessness and maternal psychosis, mental retardation, and substance abuse, in order to increase sample homogeneity and reduce the need for multiple treatment approaches.

The treatment outcome research component of the CTRP informs the assessment process, dictating the need for standardized instruments and assessment procedures. At the same time, the fundamental clinical principles of infant mental health assessment are integral parts of the assessment. These principles involve the importance of a collaborative relationship between the mother and the therapist; the assessment of the child's functioning in the context of his or her primary relationships; the need to assess the child in familiar settings, including the home and the child care setting; and the need for an assessment period lasting several weeks, in order to gain a detailed understanding of the prevailing emotional themes, range of functioning in both the child and the mother, degree of variation in the quality of the attachment relationship, and the influence of situational factors as compared to stable family circumstances and chronic stressors. With these principles firmly in place, the use of standardized instruments for the mother and for the child does not detract from the working alliance that must be established during the assessment process. The instruments include measures of depression, anxiety, and posttraumatic stress disorder to assess the mother's condition; other measures to assess the mother's perceptions of her child; and a final set of measures to ascertain the child's cognitive functioning and dimensions of attachment.

The clinical premise underlying the intervention is directly derived from an integration of attachment theory and psychoanalytic insights into children's inner lives. The assumption is that watching the mother being battered by a partner is traumatizing because it shatters the child's confidence in the mother as a source of protection, and because it makes real the very young child's age-appropriate fantasies about the destructiveness of feelings of anger and aggression. As a result, the child can no longer rely on the mother as a secure base because, from the child's perspective, she was damaged and unable to help when the child most needed her. The child's predicament can be expressed in the following questions: "If Mommy can't protect herself, how can she protect me? If something happens to Mommy, what will become of me? Who will take care of me?"

When the perpetrator is also the father of the child and he is out of the home, the child's longings for the loving aspects of the father get mixed up with the fear of the destructive parts of the father and the fear of being like him. We hear many 3- and 4-year-olds, both boys and girls, say to their mothers: "I will kill you. I will beat you up. I will call Daddy and ask him to kill you because you are bad." In making these statements, a child is asking: "Am I dangerous like Daddy? Will you, Mommy, let me do to you the things that Daddy did to you? What will happen to you if I am like Daddy? Will I hurt you and kill you? And will you make me go away the way you made Daddy go away?"

All these questions are far from rhetorical; they have a powerful existential immediacy. They are real because the events to which they refer actually happened and can happen again at any time. The simultaneous framing of the clinical challenges in terms of attachment theory and in terms of the fantasies engendered by real-life events allow for forms of intervention in which the actual interactions between mother and child are addressed, contained, and redirected in ways that restore a feeling of security and protection for both mother and child.

An evaluation of the effectiveness of this program is currently underway.

Steps Towards Effective, Enjoyable Parenting: The Minnesota Program

Steps Towards Effective, Enjoyable Parenting (STEEP) emerged as a community-oriented application of research findings from the Minnesota Parent–Child Project (Erickson et al., 1992). A program involving multiple services, STEEP has the underlying goal of influencing a mother's internal working model of attachment by focusing on her feelings, attitudes, and representations of the mother–child relationship. The original program focused on first-time mothers, although subsequent community applications have expanded to mothers with more than one child as well. The initial focus on primiparous women was prompted by the desire to develop a proactive preventive approach that could be implemented before a mother felt she had failed at being a parent. The participants are selected on the basis of being at risk for parenting problems due to stressful life circumstances, poverty, youth, lack of education, and social isolation.

The STEEP program begins with home visits that start to take place during the second trimester of pregnancy. These visits focus on helping a mother to prepare for the birth of her baby, both by anticipating the baby's needs and by discussing the mother's feelings and expectations about parenthood. These home visits take place every other week and continue until the babies' first birthdays. In order to build cohesiveness and continuity, the same intervenor conducts the group sessions and the individual home visits.

STEEP relies on both insight and the therapeutic relationship as ways of affecting the mother's internal working model of attachment. Within each of these two approaches to intervention, the intervenor uses specific principles that include the identification and explicit affirmation of strengths in the mother and the child; the mother's empowerment as someone who is competent and worthy of respect; clear communications that describe patterns of interaction and attempt to alter working models; and verbal articulation of the patterns of interaction between the mother and the intervenor, with the purpose of establishing parallels between these patterns and the mother's history. The simultaneous use of individual and group sessions, which is a unique feature of this approach, allows mothers the freedom to explore different facets of their experience in the intimacy of the individual relationship with the intervenor or in the group setting, as they choose. At the same time, the continuity provided by having the same intervenor in both settings allows the intervenor to gain a better understanding of each mother and facilitates a deepening of the mother's trust in relationships.

Preliminary results of this intervention found no significant effects of the intervention on attachment status, perhaps because of a remarkably high proportion of securely attached infants in the control group, but the intervention has been adapted by various community agencies for use with high-risk dyads (Erickson et al., 1992).

Attachment Theory and a Transactional Approach to Intervention: The Rochester Program

Cicchetti and Toth (1987, 1995) apply a transactional risk model to intervention with infants and parents who demonstrate a variety of risk factors, including maltreatment and maternal depression. Working at the Mount Hope Family Center in Rochester, New York, a center for the prevention of child maltreatment, they take an integrative approach toward research and the provision of services. Their transactional risk model makes use of a clear identification of vulnerability factors and buffering factors that serve a protective function in a child's development. In this model, the achievement of a secure attachment is identified as the central stage-salient developmental issue between 6 and 12 months of age, and it interacts with the development of an autonomous sense of self in the toddler period. Psychopathology in the child is understood within this model to be the result of interplay among maladaptive processes involving parental, environmental, and child-related factors. Intervention is geared to setting in place support mechanisms that bolster the protective factors, as well as to tailoring intervention to the specific risk factors identified in each child and family. The services involve a multidisciplinary approach that includes social workers, special educators, speech therapists, psychologists, and psychiatrists, depending on the risk factors and specific interventions identified.

Infant–parent psychotherapy is among the services provided when indicated. The versatility of this program and its capacity to meet a variety of family needs are enhanced by the availability of a home-based component for families unable to attend the center, as well as a therapeutic preschool and concrete services (e.g., transportation, babysitting, and liaison with agencies providing food, clothing, and shelter). The multidisciplinary approach allows for a "division of labor" within the program that preserves the energies of the intervenors and prevents burnout in the taxing work with multirisk families. To date, no formal evaluation of this program has been conducted.

A Relationship-Based Intervention for Maltreated Infants and Toddlers: The New Orleans Program

Another clinical approach developed from attachment theory that illustrates how infant–parent psychotherapy is integrated within a comprehensive intervention program is an intervention program for maltreated infants and toddlers in foster care (Larrieu & Zeanah, in press; Zeanah et al., 1997). By definition, infants and toddlers treated in this program have experienced disrupted and disordered attachment relationships, either prior to or during foster care or both. All of the infants and toddlers (newborn to 48 months) living within a defined geographic area who have been maltreated, removed from their families of origin, and placed in foster care are referred to this program. Once the courts have determined that abuse or neglect has occurred, and that the maltreatment is of sufficient severity to warrant foster care, the infants and all of their important caregivers are referred for evaluation by a multidisciplinary team of infant mental health professionals.

Infants and toddlers less than 4 years old are not only the children most vulnerable to physical injury from abuse and neglect; they are also the most vulnerable to psychological injury from the disruption of attachment relationships that foster care necessarily entails. There is an urgency about resolving the questions regarding who their primary attachment figures are to be and about ensuring that these caregivers are sufficiently physically and psychologically available to the infants to facilitate their development. The question posed to the intervention team is this: "What is necessary to reunite this infant or toddler with this parent, so that the infant will be safe (at least) and thrive (if possible)?"

The primary purpose of the program is to reduce the amount of time that an infant spends in foster care by identifying what the family needs, providing it, and determining whether the family responds within a reasonable period of time. If a family is successful in reaching minimal standards of safety, the infant is returned to the family's care, and ongoing support is provided. If the parents are not successful in responding to treatment and recognize that they are not likely to be able to provide the infant with necessary care, they may surrender their rights to the child. If the family is not successful in responding to treatment and unwilling to surrender parental rights, then the state attempts to terminate these rights by proving the parents unfit.

The evaluation of infants and families begins with a series of home visits to foster and biological families. These visits are designed to build rapport, to explain the program, to attempt to identify strengths and problems in caregivers, and to begin to establish common goals. Following one or more home visits, caregivers attend the clinic for purposes of being assessed both with and without their infants in various standardized procedures. Chiefly, these procedures are designed to examine each caregiver's interactions with and internal representations of each infant.

The focus of the assessment is on neither the infant nor the caregiver, but always on the infant in the context of his or her important caregiving relationships. For this reason, comparing an infant in one caregiving relationship to the same infant in another caregiving relationship allows the clinicians to begin to understand specific strengths and weaknesses in particular relationships, as well as infant characteristics that are cross-contextual.

Having assessed the infant and all involved caregivers, and having developed recommendations for treatment, the primary clinician sends a copy of the findings to child protective services and to the juvenile court judge. The judge then orders a treatment plan for the family of origin. Typically, the treatment plan includes infant–parent psychotherapy for any identified relationship conflicts, and other treatments designed to address problems within the infant, the caregiver, and/or the unique fit between the two that are interfering with a healthy attachment relationship. These other treatments may include interaction guidance (McDonough, 1993; see later description in this chapter), mother–infant groups, medication, substance abuse counseling and Twelve-Step programs, couple therapy, family therapy, and/or individual therapy. Evaluation of the effectiveness of this intervention is underway.

Attachment theory and research inform this assessment and intervention program in a number of ways:

1. The program operates with a fundamental underlying assumption, drawn from Bowlby (1969/1982), that attachment is biologically hard-wired into the human infant and that only extremes of intrinsic (e.g., severe mental retardation) or extrinsic (e.g., serious neglect or multiple placements) circumstances will interfere with infants' becoming attached to their primary caregivers. The absence of attachment in an infant or toddler who has a mental age of at least 10 months suggests that reasons for the absence must be identified quickly, and that establishment of a meaningful attachment relationship is a first clinical priority.

2. Following from this fundamental assumption is a related one that primary caregivers are biologically drawn to infants, who engender powerful affiliative and protective feelings in their caregivers. An extensive literature describing features of what Bowlby described as the attachment/caregiving system in adults has delineated the powerful effects that infants have on adults (e.g., Berlin & Cassidy, Chapter 30, this volume; Solomon & George, 1996; George & Solomon, Chapter 28, this volume). When caregivers are not drawn to their own infants with powerful affiliative and protective urges, whatever factors seem to be compromising this powerful biological disposition become important foci of treatment.

3. These two fundamental assumptions lead immediately to a third assumption—namely, that identifying and removing obstacles to a healthy infant–caregiver attachment relationship will lead to substantial improvements in that relationship. Obstacles may arise from within the infant, the caregiver, or the caregiving context, or (more typically) from some combination of all of these (Zeanah et al., 1997). The clinical task is to move beyond broad indices of risk and to make inferences about which particular factors are most importantly involved in the relationship disturbance.

For this reason, careful attention is paid to individual differences among infants, in terms of both the clinician's perceptions of an infant and different caregivers' perceptions of the infant. Assessing an infant in all of his or her important contexts enhances appreciation for the infant's contribution to these relationships (Lieberman, 1991). Furthermore, the caregivers' relationship histories, social supports and current stressors, and mental health are all assessed as potential sources of strength upon which to build or as problem areas that need to be ameliorated. Obstacles to a healthy infant–caregiver relationship that seem most amenable to intervention will be higher clinical priorities. Therefore, the assessment must move beyond a phenomenological description of problem areas and toward an understanding of the reasons why a particular attachment relationship is disturbed. This in turn helps in designing the most appropriate interventions to address the underlying reasons for attachment disturbances.

4. Attachment relationship patterns are intergenerationally transmitted, as outlined by Bowlby (1969/1982, 1973, 1980) and as documented by considerable research (Main et al., 1985; van IJzendoorn, 1995, 1997). Furthermore, caregivers' perspectives on their own attachment histories give important direction to the specific kind of intervention that is developed. The inclusion in this treatment program of attention to caregivers' own attachment histories, as well as to here-and-now interactions with their infants, places the treatment more clearly in an intergenerational context.

5. Infant–parent psychotherapy is often used in this intervention program as a way to focus treatment efforts on the infant–caregiver relationship disturbances as derived from intergenerational patterns. In the face of multiple competing problem areas for a caregiver, this has the effect of focusing the intervention so that other areas are addressed only to the extent that they significantly and negatively influence the caregiver's capacity to relate to the infant.

6. One of the clearest findings from developmental research is that attachment is a relationship characteristic, and that an infant may have qualitatively different attachment relationships with different caregivers, based upon the infant's actual experiences with those caregivers (van IJzendoorn & DeWolff, 1977). This finding provides a rationale for careful assessment of each of the infant's important caregiving relationship, which often leads clinicians to discover dramatic differences in different infant–caregiver relationships for the same infant (Zeanah et al., 1997). Clearly, treatment for relationship disturbances must be individualized.

ATTACHMENT THEORY AND OTHER PARENT–INFANT INTERVENTIONS

Attachment also has provided the impetus for the development of other approaches to parent–infant intervention beyond infant–parent psychotherapy. Simultaneously and reciprocally, the influence of infant–parent psychotherapy is apparent in the specific clinical modalities and interventions adopted by many of these programs and approaches. The shared clinical origins of attachment theory and infant–parent psychotherapy are so inextricably linked that the explanatory mechanisms postulated in intervention are often matters of theoretical preference.

Attachment and Cognitive-Behavioral Parent Training Approaches: The Seattle Approach

The relationship between attachment in infancy and toddlerhood and later externalizing symptomatology and disruptive behavior disorders has been the subject of considerable research in recent years (e.g., Goldberg, 1997; Greenberg, DeKlyen, Speltz, & Endriga, 1997; Greenberg, Speltz, DeKlyen, 1993; Shaw, Keenan, & Vondra, 1994). Although the emotional quality of the parent–child relationship had been implicated as an important risk factor for behavior disorders for a number of years, the coherence of attachment theory and the ease of measuring its important constructs significantly advanced the study of the early childhood antecedents of later externalizing symptomatology. Furthermore, attachment theory and research have influenced preventive intervention efforts aimed at reducing externalizing symptomatology and disruptive behavior disorders. One programmatic example of efforts to integrate the insights of attachment theory and research into parent training programs derived from learning theory has been described by Speltz and colleagues (Greenberg & Speltz, 1988; Speltz, 1990).

The rationale for this intervention program is that many of the symptoms and signs of disruptive behavior disorders may be viewed from the framework of attachment as breakdowns in the efforts at joint communication, negotiation, and planning that are central to the goal-corrected partnership. Indeed, a reasonable degree of toddler cooperation is the hallmark of the successful goal-corrected partnership, and a lack of such cooperation is the hallmark of disruptive behav-ior. Noting that most parent training programs designed to intervene with symptomatic toddlers have not included attention to the negotiating skills of the parent–child dyad, Speltz (1990) proposes that traditional programs can be enhanced by greater attention to the developmentally salient issue of toddler–parent verbal communication.

The Seattle intervention begins with a two- to three-session evaluation designed to obtain detailed descriptions of the child's presenting problem, the child's developmental status, the attachment history of the parent–child relationship, the parent's own attachment history, and observation of interaction between parent and child. The interactions include episodes of child-directed and parent-directed play, as well as two separations and reunions. The assessment is designed to address a number of questions that are used in the intervention itself, including the developmental capability of the child to communicate his or her needs, the emotional capability of the parent to respond to the child's communications, the child's primary strategies for regulating the caregiver's behavior, the quality of the child's attachment to the parent during the first 2 years of life, the extent of parent relationship conflicts beyond problems with the child, the ability of the parent and child to negotiate conflicting goals, and the extent to which family relationship conflicts affect the parent–child dyad. A feedback session with the parent follows the assessment and is designed to provide an understanding of the problem and to propose an intervention.

The intervention itself comprises 10–16 sessions divided into four phases. The first phase (1–2 sessions) is designed to educate each parent about the developmental issues relevant to the child's problems. In this phase, the child's behavior is reinterpreted from the standpoint of the child's need for increased control and autonomy, and unrealistic parental expectations for child behavior are tempered. In the second phase (3–5 sessions), the parent is observed during play sessions with the child and coached to allow the child to direct the play. The dual focus of this phase of the intervention is on allowing the child to experience a reasonable sense of control in the relationship and on continuing to focus on parental attributions and beliefs about the child's behavior. The third phase of the intervention (2–3 sessions) focuses on limit setting and a least-restraint principle for approaching it. Each parent learns how to distinguish behaviors that require a response from those that can be ignored, how to gain child compliance and praise success, and how to set limits directly for non-compliant or aggressive behavior. The final phase (4–6 sessions) focuses directly on parent–child communication and negotiation. Efforts are directed at enabling the parent to structure the process of negotiation and to assist the child by "filling in" verbally during a time when the child's verbal capacities are new and limited.

This approach to assessment and intervention is informed by attachment theory and research in a number of ways:

1. Coherence of discourse between child and caregiver has emerged as a central construct in attachment in the preschool years. This approach clearly makes enhancing coherence of discourse a major focus of treatment.

2. Beyond enhanced communication, the approach also attempts to enhance both the parent's and the child's problem-solving skills, especially regarding the conflicting goals and agendas that characterize the goal-corrected partnership.

3. In keeping with the emphasis in attachment theory on the child's sense of self in relation to the attachment figure, this approach attempts to enhance the child's sense of self-efficacy ("What I feel and say matters to someone quite important to me") and sense of the parent as responsive ("He or she understands my point of view").

4. Attachment theory has always been concerned with the child's ability to self-regulate emotions and behaviors. The child's ability to recognize and label his or her own emotional states ("I feel sad") is enhanced by this approach, which in turn promotes development of healthier emotional and behavioral self-regulation.

No formal evaluation of the efficacy of this approach has been published.

Attachment and Interaction Guidance: The Ann Arbor Approach

Some approaches to early intervention are less explicitly derived from attachment theory, although they share with it basic components of the conceptual framework. One example of such an approach is "interaction guidance," a form of brief psychotherapy for caregivers and infants described by McDonough (1993). The approach was designed specifically for families who have proven hard to reach through more traditional methods, although it has wide applicability and

has been used in clinical settings with both disadvantaged and middle-class families (Cramer et al., 1990; McDonough, 1993). This form of treatment may be used with an infant–caregiver dyad, a caregiver and several children, or even an entire family.

Interaction guidance begins with an initial visit with the family. Usually this visit occurs at the family's home, although it may also occur at a human services agency, a hospital, or some other site, depending upon the referral source and the family's situation and preferences. One or more home visits are conducted in order to help the therapist understand the family's situation and to hear the story of the caregiver's relationship with the infant. In addition, the therapist outlines the content and process of interaction guidance and offers to work with the family. Much effort is made to have the family members become active partners in treatment, and a major goal of these early sessions is developing a therapeutic alliance with the family. The nonspecific factors typical to most clinical approaches are important, but they are enhanced through focusing explicitly on the family's strengths and competence, through encouraging the caregiver to participate actively in the development of goals for the treatment, and through inviting the caregiver to critique the ongoing process of treatment and to suggest any changes that seem necessary.

Formal treatment sessions are clinic-based, and usually they are held in a specially equipped playroom. Videotaping capabilities are essential, as jointly observing infant–caregiver interactions is at the core of this approach. Generally 8–12 sessions are conducted over 3 to 9 months, with more frequent sessions initially.

Each session follows a typical format, and the predictability of the session itself is considered a component of the treatment (McDonough, 1993). First, the therapist asks the family about any important events or issues that have arisen since the previous session. Following this, the therapist invites the caregiver to play with the young child as they "usually play at home" for about 5 or 6 minutes. As a rule, the therapist remains with the family during this time, as an observer rather than as a participant. The play period is videotaped; following its completion, the therapist and caregiver watch the "movie" they have made.

Initially, during this review time, the therapist solicits comments from the caregiver about what he or she observes on the tape. Caregivers are encouraged to comment on any aspect of themselves, their children, or anything else that catches their eye. Associations to perceptions of their infants or feelings about themselves as parents are common during this part of the session. Following this period of eliciting comments from the caregiver, the therapist reviews the tape again, this time carefully highlighting strengths in the interaction, such as positive parental behaviors or instances of sensitive reading of the infant's cues. The therapist generally ignores negative or conflicted interactions unless the caregiver brings them into the discussion. If this happens, the therapist seeks to explore the caregiver's feelings, both at the time of the interaction and in the here-and-now moment of looking back retrospectively at the behavior ("How did you feel when you said that to Chris?" "How do you feel now watching it?"). The purpose of viewing the videotape is to create an observing ego in the caregiver within the supportive, holding environment of the therapy, in order to facilitate exploration and understanding.

Following the viewing of the tape, the caregiver and infant resume play, and the therapist and caregiver resume their dialogue about what occurred in the tape sequence or about other concerns. The session concludes with a discussion about treatment progress or its lack, and with a reiteration or renegotiation of previously established goals. The therapist then asks the family members whether they would like to schedule another appointment, again emphasizing their active role in the treatment process.

In general, the focus of treatment is on the immediate interactions of caregiver and infant. Many other concerns may come up for discussion in treatment, and if generated by the family, they are considered important. Nevertheless, the therapist makes no special efforts to explore previous relationships, including the caregiver's childhood relationship experiences. Nondidactic developmental guidance may be offered, but generally only after the caregiver has made an implicit or explicit request for assistance with a particular problem. The infant's perspective is a common focus, and the therapist may speak for the baby playfully in order to convey this perspective to the caregiver. Caregiver transference reactions to the infant are more likely than reactions to the therapist to be a focus of exploration.

Although atheoretical in its origins, interaction guidance has several features linking it conceptually to attachment theory. These include the following:

1. A central premise both of attachment theory and of interaction guidance is that a special relationship between a caregiver and a therapist can ameliorate a disturbed caregiver–infant relationship. That is, the caregiver can use the relationship with the therapist to explore new ways of being with the infant.

2. The link between the caregiver representation and the caregiver's behavior, which has been demonstrated so convincingly by attachment research (reviewed by van IJzendoorn, 1995), is assumed by the interaction guidance therapist as he or she moves back and forth among the caregiver's subjective experience of the infant, the interaction between the infant and the caregiver, and the infant's putative internal experience.

3. Both attachment theory and interaction guidance place special emphasis on the individual's emotional experience in relationships. Bowlby (1980) asserted that representational models guide people's interpretation and evaluation of social relationships and their emotional reactions to others. Furthermore, according to Bowlby, changing the assumptions of these models or creating different models altogether constitutes the essence of the psychotherapeutic process. Similarly, McDonough (1993) has suggested that interaction guidance allows caregivers to develop new feelings about their infants and about themselves as caregivers through exploring alternative beliefs and behaviors in the context of a therapeutic relationship that is a source of security and strength for each caregiver.

In a preliminary study in Switzerland, interaction guidance was found to be as effective as brief psychoanalytic psychotherapy in improving mothers' interactions with their infants, perceptions of their infants, and symptomatology in a middle-class, clinic-referred sample.

EVALUATING PREVENTIVE INTERVENTIONS FOR DISTURBANCES OF ATTACHMENT

A number of investigations have attempted to address the efficacy of preventive interventions designed to improve clinical disturbances of attachment. Stern-Bruschweiler and Stern (1989) and Stern (1995) have provided a compelling theoretical model for understanding these approaches. Their model proposes that the infant–parent relationship be conceptualized as an open system with four components: (1) the infant's and (2) the parent's interactive behaviors, which constitute the external components of the relationship; and (3) the infant's and (4) the parent's representations, which constitute the internal components of the relationship. Various infant–parent psychotherapies and interventions are conceptualized as addressing one of these four components of the relationship. Because the relationship is an open system, however, therapeutic effects directed toward one component of the system are expected to have effects on the other components as well. Studies on the effects of attachment have addressed each of these components, although no single study has yet addressed all of them.

There have been eight studies of low-socioeconomic-status (low-SES) samples of mothers, in which strange situation classifications at 12 to 14 months were the outcomes. Four of these studies involved supportive interventions, and one involved insight-oriented psychotherapy applied to high-risk mothers. All of the studies were designed to change the mothers' interactions with their infants and the infants' attachment classifications. Each of these studies examined maternal sensitivity and responsiveness as one outcome and infant attachment as another outcome. Two of the interventions had no demonstrable effect on maternal sensitivity but significantly increased the proportion of secure infant attachment (Jacobsen & Frye, 1991; Lyons-Ruth, Connell, Grunebaum, & Botein, 1990), whereas the other three interventions significantly improved maternal sensitivity but failed to increase rates of secure infant attachment (Barnard et al., 1988; Beckwith, 1988; Egeland & Erickson, 1993). In an Australian sample that included mothers from a wider range of SES backgrounds, a supportive intervention over the first year significantly reduced maternal anxiety in the intervention group but had no effect on infant attachment (Barnett, Blignault, Holmes, Payne, & Parker, 1987).

Brief interventions conducted in The Netherlands, which involved teaching mothers to be more sensitive, have also produced mixed results. Two studies found improvements in both maternal sensitivity and infant attachment (Juffer, 1993; van den Boom, 1991), and one found improvements in neither (Meij, 1991).

Only one investigation has attempted to change infant attachment between the second and third years. Lieberman et al. (1991) applied infant–parent psychotherapy to high-risk, low-SES, unacculturated Mexican and Central American immigrant mothers and their infants in the San Francisco area. The treatment was provided for 1 year in the home when infants were aged 12 to 24 months. The therapy helped mothers (1) to identify, express, and come to terms with painful feelings about adverse experiences in their own childhood relationships, and (2) to link these early experiences to current feelings, perceptions, and attitudes toward their babies, as well as to actual maladaptive child-rearing practices. The results showed increased maternal empathy, dyadic capacity to resolve conflicts constructively (goal-connected partnership), and decreased child avoidance, resistance, and anger involving mothers as the outcomes of intervention.

In an effort to evaluate the effect size of these interventions and to attempt to resolve apparent inconsistencies in these findings, van IJzendoorn, Juffer, and Duyvesteyn (1995) conducted a meta-analysis. They found a medium effect size for intervention on maternal sensitivity, and a modest effect size for intervention on infant attachment. The overall pattern of these results seems not to support the Stern-Bruschweiler and Stern (1989) model; however, it is far from clear that this model has been tested adequately by studies conducted to date. Widely varying sample characteristics, inconsistencies in the interventions themselves, variability in the degree to which they were designed to address different outcomes, and incomplete assessments of the essential components of the relationship make lumping them together for meta-analytic purposes a poor approximation of the proposed model. For example, no single investigation to date has simultaneously assessed maternal representations, maternal sensitivity, and infant representations (i.e., strange situation classifications) before and after intervention. As we look to the future, more comprehensive measures in theoretically driven interventions will be necessary to clarify previous discrepant findings in this area.

CONCLUSIONS

Attachment theory has made substantial contributions to clinical practice with young children and their families—both directly, through programs that have translated its premises into intervention practices, and indirectly, by influencing the ongoing evolution of psychoanalytically oriented infant–parent psychotherapy. Although there are substantial differences among these programs, they all share the overarching principle that sensitive and age-appropriate responsiveness to a child's signals needs to characterize both a parent's and a therapist's stance, in order to promote the child's mental health and socioemotional and cognitive development. The need for the unstinting clinical application of this principle is nowhere more apparent than in the treatment of children suffering from reactive attachment disorder and other disturbances resulting in aggressive, defiant, and disruptive behaviors that tend to evoke a punitive response in adults. Pseudotheoretical and pseudoclinical postulates are sometimes offered as rationalizations when a therapist finds himself or herself engaging in behaviors that provoke pain, fear, emotional outbursts, or affective withdrawal in a child. In these circumstances, it is essential to keep in mind that stress-producing interventions, even when well-intentioned and carefully thought-out, reinforce and perpetuate the aggressive and victimizing relationship patterns that have shaped children with disorders of attachment. In this sense, the deliberate or accidental inflicting of pain or encouragement of anger as part of the therapeutic intervention runs counter to Bowlby's (1988) concept of the therapist as a secure base for the exploration of feeling, and detracts from the value of clinical intervention as an opportunity for corrective attachment experiences (Lieberman, 1991). When tempted to react punitively to trying therapeutic situations, therapists working within the attachment theory tradition need to remind themselves that interventions relying on emotional pressure or developmentally inappropriate efforts at behavior modification represent lapses of therapeutic empathy that endanger the value of the therapeutic enterprise, as well as children's mental health. Such a lapse can and should be corrected by an authentic dialogue in which a therapist acknowledges his or her empathic lapse with the child and with the parent, and explicitly attempts to reestablish a working relationship characterized by the hallmarks of attachment theory—reciprocity, emotional contingency, and mutual trust.

REFERENCES

Ainsworth, M. D. S., Blehar, M.C., Waters, E., & Wall, S. (1978). *Patterns of attachment*. Hillsdale, NJ: Erlbaum.

Barnard, K., Magyary, D., Sumner, G., Booth, C. L., Mitchell, S. K., & Spieker, S. (1988). Prevention of parenting alterations for women with low social support. *Psychiatry, 51*, 248–253.

Barnett, B., Blignault, I., Holmes, S., Payne, A., & Parker, G.

(1987). Quality of attachment in a sample of 1-year-old Australian children. *Journal of the American Academy of Child and Adolescent Psychiatry, 26*, 303–307.

Beckwith, L. (1988). Intervention with disadvantaged parents of sick preterm infants. *Psychiatry, 51*, 242–247.

Belsky, J., & Cassidy, J., (1994). Attachment: Theory and evidence. In M. Rutter & D. F. Hay (Eds.), *Development through life: A handbook for clinicians* (pp. 373–402). Oxford: Blackwell.

Belsky, J., & Nezworski, T. (Eds.). (1988). *Clinical implications of attachment*. Hillsdale, NJ: Erlbaum.

Bowlby, J. (1969/1982). *Attachment and loss: Vol. 1. Attachment*. New York: Basic Books.

Bowlby, J. (1973). *Attachment and loss: Vol. 2. Separation*. New York: Basic Books.

Bowlby, J. (1980). *Attachment and loss: Vol. 3. Loss*. New York: Basic Books.

Bowlby, J. (1988). *A secure base*. New York: Basic Books.

Bretherton, I. (1984). Representing the social world in symbolic play: Reality and fantasy. In I. Bretherton (Ed.), *Symbolic play: The development of social understanding* (pp. 1–41). New York: Academic Press.

Cassidy, J. (1988). Child–mother attachment and the self in 6-year-olds. *Child Development, 59*, 121–134.

Cicchetti, D., & Toth, S. L. (1987). The application of a transactional risk model to intervention with multi-risk maltreating families. *Zero to Three: Bulletin of the National Center for Clinical Infant Programs, 7*, 1–8.

Cicchetti, D., & Toth, S. L. (1995). Child maltreatment and attachment organization: Implications for intervention. In S. Goldberg, R. Muir, & J. Kerr (Eds.), *Attachment theory: Social, developmental, and clinical perspectives*. Hillsdale, NJ: Analytic Press.

Cramer, B., Robert-Tissot, C., Stern, D. N., Serpa-Rusconi, S., De Muralt, M., Besson, G., Palacio-Espasa, F., Bachmann, J.-P., Knauer, D., Berney, C., & D'Arcis, U. (1990). Outcome evaluation of brief mother–infant psychotherapy. *Infant Mental Health Journal, 11*, 278–300.

Egeland, B., & Erickson, M. F. (1993). Attachment theory and findings: Implications for prevention and intervention. In S. Kramer & H. Parens (Eds.), *Prevention in mental health: Now, tomorrow, ever?* (pp. 21–50). Northvale, NJ: Aronson.

Emde, R. (1988). Development terminable and interminable: 1. Innate and motivational factors from infancy. *International Journal of Psycho-Analysis, 69*, 23–42.

Erickson, M. F., Korfmacher, J., & Egeland, B. (1992). Attachments past and present: Implications for the therapeutic intervention with mother–infant dyads. *Development and Psychopathology, 4*, 495–507.

Fonagy, P. (1991). Thinking about thinking: Some clinical and theoretical considerations in the treatment of a borderline patient. *International Journal of Psycho-Analysis, 72*, 639–656.

Fraiberg, S. (1977). *Every child's birthright: In defense of mothering*. New York: Basic Books.

Fraiberg, S. (1980). *Clinical studies in infant mental health: The first year of life*. New York: Basic Books.

Fraiberg, S. (1982). Pathological defenses in infancy. *Psychoanalytic Quarterly, 51*, 612–635.

Fraiberg, S., Adelson, E., & Shapiro, V. (1975). Ghosts in the nursery: A psychoanalytic approach to impaired infant–mother relationships. *Journal of the American Academy of Child Psychiatry, 14*, 1387–1422.

Fraiberg, S., Lieberman, A., Pekarsky, J., & Pawl, J. (1981). Treatment and outcome in an infant psychiatry program. *Journal of Preventive Psychiatry, 1*, 89–111.

Goldberg, S. (1997). Attachment and childhood behavior problems in normal, at-risk, and clinical samples. In L. Atkinson & K. J. Zucker (Eds.), *Attachment and psychopathology* (pp. 171–195). New York: Guilford Press.

Greenberg, M. T., DeKlyen, M., Speltz, M., & Endriga, M. C. (1997). The role of attachment processes in externalizing psychopathology in young children. In L. Atkinson & K. J. Zucker (Eds.), *Attachment and psychopathology* (pp. 196–222). New York: Guilford Press.

Greenberg, M. T., & Speltz, M. (1988). Contributions of attachment theory to the understanding of conduct problems during the preschool years. In J. Belsky & T. Nezworski (Eds.), *Clinical implications of attachment* (pp. 177–218). Hillsdale, NJ: Erlbaum.

Greenberg, M. T., Speltz, M., & DeKlyen, M. (1993). The role of attachment in the early development of disruptive behavior problems. *Development and Psychopathology, 5,* 191–213.

Grosskurth, P. (1986). *Melanie Klein: Her world and her work.* Cambridge, MA: Harvard University Press.

Holmes, J. (1993). *John Bowlby and attachment theory.* London: Routledge.

Jacobson, S. W., & Frye, K. F. (1991). Effect of maternal social support on attachment: Experimental evidence. *Child Development, 62,* 572–582.

Juffer, F. (1993). *Verbonden door adoptie: Een experimenteel onderzoek bij gezinnen met een adoptiebaby [Attached through adoption: An experimental study in families with adopted infants].* Amersfoort, The Netherlands: Academische Uitgeverij.

Karen, R. (1994). *Becoming attached.* New York: Warner Books.

Larrieu, J., & Zeanah, C. H. (1998). An intensive intervention for infants and toddlers in foster care. *Child and Adolescent Psychiatric Clinics of North America, 7,* 357–391.

Lichtenberg, J. D. (1989). *Psychoanalysis and motivation.* Hillsdale, NJ: Analytic Press.

Lieberman, A. F. (1991). Attachment theory and infant–parent psychotherapy: Some conceptual, clinical and research issues. In D. Cicchetti & S. Toth (Eds.), *Rochester Symposium on Developmental Psychopathology: Vol. 3. Models and integrations* (pp. 261–288). Hillsdale, NJ: Erlbaum.

Lieberman, A. F. (1996). Aggression and sexuality in relation to toddler attachment: Implications for the caregiving system. *Infant Mental Health Journal, 17,* 276–292.

Lieberman, A. F. (1997). Toddlers' internalization of maternal attributions as a factor in quality of attachment. In L. Atkinson & K. Zucker (Eds.), *Attachment and psychopathology* (pp. 277–291). New York: Guilford Press.

Lieberman, A. F., Van Horn, P., Grandison, C. M., & Pekarsky, J. H. (1997). Mental health assessment of infants, toddlers, and preschoolers in a service program and a treatment outcome research program. *Infant Mental Health Journal, 18,* 158–170.

Lieberman, A. F., & Pawl, J. (1993). Infant–parent psychotherapy. In C. H. Zeanah (Ed.), *Handbook of infant mental health* (pp. 427–442). New York: Guilford Press.

Lieberman, A. F., Weston, D., & Pawl, J. (1991). Preventive intervention and outcome with anxiously attached dyads. *Child Development, 62,* 199–209.

Lorenz, K. (1967). *On aggression.* New York: Harcourt, Brace & World.

Lyons-Ruth, K. (1991). Rapprochement or approchement: Mahler's theory reconsidered from the vantage point of recent research on early attachment relationships. *Psychoanalytic Psychology, 8,* 1–23.

Lyons-Ruth, K., Connell, D., Grunebaum, H., & Botein, S. (1990). Infants at social risk: Maternal depression and family support services as mediators of infant development and security of attachment. *Child Development, 61,* 85–98.

Main, M. (1991). Metacognitive knowledge, metacognitive monitoring, and singular (coherent) vs. multiple (incoherent) models of attachment: Findings and direction for future research. In C. M. Parkes, J. Stevenson-Hinde, & P. Marris (Eds.), *Attachment across the life cycle* (pp. 127–159). London: Routledge.

Main, M., Kaplan, N., & Cassidy, J. (1985). Security in infancy, childhood, and adulthood: A move to the level of representation. In I. Bretherton & E. Waters (Eds.), *Growing points in attachment theory and research. Monographs of the Society for Child Development, 50*(1–2, Serial No. 209), 66–104.

McDonough, S. (1993). Interaction guidance. In C. H. Zeanah (Ed.), *Handbook of infant mental health* (pp. 414–426). New York: Guilford Press.

Meij, J. (1991). *Sociale ondersteuning, gehechtheidskwaliteit en vroegkinderlijke competentie-ontwikkeling.* (Social support, quality of attachment, and early development of competence.) Unpublished doctoral dissertation, University of Nijmegen, The Netherlands.

Osofsky, J. (1993). Applied psychoanalysis: How research with infants and adolescents at high psychosocial risk informs psychoanalysis. *Journal of the American Psychoanalytic Association, 41*(Suppl.), 193–208.

Pawl, J., & Lieberman, A. F. (1997). Infant–parent psychotherapy. In J. Noshpitz (Ed.), *Handbook of child and adolescent psychiatry* (Vol. 1, pp. 339–351). New York: Basic Books.

Rapaport, D., & Gil, M. M. (1959). The points of view and assumptions of metapsychology. *International Journal of Psycho-Analysis, 40,* 153–162.

Seligman, S. (1991). Conceptual and methodological issues in the study of internal representation: A commentary. *Infant Mental Health Journal, 12,* 126–129.

Shaw, D. S., Keenan, K., & Vondra, J. I. (1994). Developmental precursors of externalizing behavior: Ages 1 to 3. *Developmental Psychology, 30,* 355–364.

Silverman, R., Lieberman, A. F., & Pekarsky, J. H. (1997). Anxiety disorder. In A. F. Lieberman, S. Wieder, & E. Fenichel (Eds.), *Casebook of the Zero To Three diagnostic classification of mental health and developmental disorders of infancy and early childhood* (pp. 47–59). Arlington, VA: Zero to Three.

Slade, A., & Aber, J. L. (1992). Attachments, drives, and development: Conflicts and convergences in theory. In J. Barron, M. Eagle, & D. Wolintzky (Eds.), *Interface of psychoanalysis and psychology* (pp. 154–185). Washington, DC: American Psychological Association.

Solomon, J., & George, C. (1996). Defining the caregiving system: Toward a theory of caregiving. *Infant Mental Health Journal, 17,* 183–197.

Speltz, M. (1990). The treatment of preschool conduct problems: An integration of behavioral and attachment concepts. In M. T. Greenberg, D. Cicchetti, & M. Cummings (Eds.), *Attachment in the preschool years: Theory, research, and intervention* (pp. 399–426). Chicago: University of Chicago Press.

Stern, D. N. (1985). *The interpersonal world of the infant.* New York: Basic Books.

Stern, D. N. (1995). *The motherhood constellation: A unified* view of parent–infant psychotherapy. New York: Basic Books.

Stern-Bruschweiler, N., & Stern, D. N. (1989). A model for conceptualizing the role of the mother's representational world in various mother–infant therapies. *Infant Mental Health Journal, 10,* 142–156.

van den Boom, D. C. (1991). *Neonatal irritability and the development of attachment: Observation and intervention.* Unpublished doctoral dissertation, University of Leiden, The Netherlands.

van IJzendoorn, M. H. (1995). Adult attachment representations, parental responsiveness, and infant attachment: A meta-analysis on the predictive validity of the Adult Attachment Interview. *Psychological Bulletin, 117,* 387–403.

van IJzendoorn, M. H. (1997). Intergenerational transmission of attachment: A move to the contextual level. In L. Atkinson & K. J. Zucker (Eds.), *Attachment and psychopathology* (pp. 135–170). New York: Guilford Press.

van IJzendoorn, M. H., & DeWolff, M. S. (1997). In search of the absent father: Meta-analysis of infant–father attachment. *Child Development, 68,* 604–609.

van IJzendoorn, M. H., Juffer, F., & Duyvesteyn, M. G. C. (1995). Breaking the intergenerational cycle of insecure attachment: A review of the effects of attachment-based interventions on maternal sensitivity and infant security. *Journal of Child Psychology and Psychiatry, 36,* 225–248.

Wallerstein, R. (1973). Psychoanalytic perspectives on the problem of reality. *Journal of the American Psychoanalytic Association, 21,* 5–33.

Zeanah, C. H., & Barton, M. L. (1989). Introduction: Internal representations and parent–infant relationships. *Infant Mental Health Journal, 10,* 135–141.

Zeanah, C. H., & Benoit, D. (1995). Clinical applications of a parent perception interview. *Child Psychiatric Clinics of North America, 4,* 539–554.

Zeanah, C. H., Boris, N. W., Heller, S. S., Hinshaw-Fuselier, S., Larrieu, J., Lewis, M., Palomino, R., Rovaris, M., & Valliere, J. (1997). Relationship assessment in infant mental health. *Infant Mental Health Journal, 18,* 182–197.

25

Attachment Theory and Research

Implications for the Theory and Practice of Individual Psychotherapy with Adults

❖

ARIETTA SLADE

ATTACHMENT THEORY AND PSYCHOANALYSIS: THE BREACH AND THE RAPPROCHEMENT

Attachment theory began with John Bowlby's (1969/1982, 1973, 1980) elegant and parsimonious descriptions of his ideas about the nature and function of human attachments. These formulations inspired the interest of his colleague Mary Ainsworth (Ainsworth, Blehar, Waters, & Wall, 1978), whose pioneering research was to provide empirical validation of many of Bowlby's basic principles and establish a foundation for the thousands of research investigations that evolved from her original research findings (see Belsky & Cassidy, 1994; Bretherton, 1995; Karen, 1998). However, despite the fact that Bowlby was a psychiatrist and psychoanalyst who spent the bulk of his time working as a therapist and analyst, and whose theory evolved directly from his clinical work with delinquent children, the relation between attachment theory and individual psychotherapy has received relatively little attention from clinicians *or* attachment researchers until recently. In fact, Bowlby himself noted:

It is a little unexpected that, whereas attachment theory was formulated by a clinician for use in the diagnosis and treatment of emotionally disturbed patients and families, its usage hitherto has been mainly to promote research in developmental psychology. Whilst I welcome the findings of this research as enormously extending our understanding of personality development and psychopathology, and thus as of the greatest clinical relevance, it has not the less been disappointing that clinicians have been so slow to test the theory's uses. (1988, pp. ix–x)

Bowlby was right: Attachment theory has had a dramatic impact on developmental psychology; until recent years, however, it had little palpable impact on clinical theory and practice.

The reasons underlying the fact that Bowlby's work was marginalized, derided, or simply ignored by psychoanalysts, psychiatrists, and clinical psychologists for over 30 years are complex, but of course have much to do with the core elements of attachment theory. Today, given the past two decades' remarkable advances in infancy research (Beebe & Lachmann, 1988; Beebe & Stern, 1977; Mahler, Pine, & Bergman, 1975; Stern, 1985; Tronick, 1989), and the evolution of psychoanalysis into a relational and interpersonal theory (Aron, 1995; Mitchell, 1988), Bowlby's ideas no longer seem revolutionary and indeed have much in common with current developmental and psychoanalytic theory. In the 1940s and 1950s, however, his ideas were seen as radical and heretical. (See Cassidy, Chapter 1, this volume, for a review of Bowlby's theory.)

Bowlby's considerable theoretical opus emphasized several key notions: (1) A child is born with a predisposition to become attached to his or her caregivers; (2) the child will organize his or her behavior and thinking in order to maintain these attachment relationships, which are key to his or her psychological and physical survival; (3) the child will often maintain such relationships at great cost to his or her own functioning; and (4) the distortions in feeling and thinking that stem from early disturbances in attachment occur most often in response to the parents' inability to meet the child's needs for comfort, security, and emotional reassurance. Environmental failure—be it in the overt trauma of abandonment or loss, of abuse, or the more covert trauma of parental neglect, rejection, and emotional unavailability—often leads to the distortions in thinking and feeling that are at the root of much psychopathology, and that typically underlie the need for psychiatric intervention.

These ideas, and specifically Bowlby's rejection of drive theory, were to lead to his dramatic breach with the psychoanalytic establishment. Despite the fact that he has been described by Storr (1992) as one of the "three or four finest psychiatrists of the twentieth century," Bowlby's theory and its tremendous ramifications for clinical work were for decades "virtually airbrushed out of the psychoanalytic record—rather like some dissident in Stalinist times" (Holmes, 1995, p. 20). Grotstein (1990) has called Bowlby's extrusion "one of the most dreadful, shameful and regrettable chapters in the history of psychoanalysis" (p. 62). Space limitations preclude a fuller discussion of the theoretical, historical, and political reasons underlying the breach; however, these have been fully described by Fonagy (Chapter 26, this volume), Holmes (1993b, 1995), Karen (1998), and van Dijken (1996). In any case, the principal effects of the events of this period were straightforward: From the standpoint of psychoanalysis, psychiatry, and clinical psychology, Bowlby all but ceased to exist for at least three decades. It was not until nearly 40 years after he published his first clinical and theoretical papers, and over a decade after he published the first volume of his attachment trilogy (Bowlby, 1969), that clinicians began to consider some of the ways attachment theory might be applicable to clinical work.

It is easy to assign all the blame for Bowlby's extrusion and subsequent exclusion from the clinical literature upon the psychoanalytic establishment; however, it is important to note that Bowlby himself played a significant role in the standoff that was to have such unfortunate consequences for the field as well as for Bowlby personally. Bowlby was incensed and indignant at his psychoanalytic colleagues' unwillingness to consider the effects of real experience. In an interview in 1991 (Hunter, 1991), he noted that although he and the reigning psychoanalytic giants of the day—Donald Winnicott and Anna Freud—saw the essentials of healthy development in much the same light, they could not agree upon theory. Speaking of Anna Freud, he noted: "It was rather strange because in all matters practical—home, young, small children, we were in complete agreement, and all the work on separation she valued very highly. But when we came to talking theory, she had no use for my ideas at all" (Hunter, 1991, p. 170).

As the split widened, Bowlby increasingly took a position that discounted the role of internal experience—fantasies, urges, and impulses—in shaping psychological life. The rigidity of his position was probably influenced by the tenor of what became a bitter and political dispute. Whatever the cause, Bowlby maintained that psychological life is determined by the response of the environment to the child's earliest feelings and needs. He rejected the notion that an aspect of the individual's response to the world emerges *sui generis*; as a consequence, his position left little room for the distorting effects of wish and impulse on the development of an inner life, or for the notion that an individual's own idiosyncratic wishes and personal desires may interfere with the capacity to become attached. The result was a relatively underdeveloped view of the nature of subjective experience.

The failure of clinical psychiatry, psychology, and psychoanalysis to embrace Bowlby's ideas must also be seen as a function of the relative limitations of his clinical writings. Bowlby saw himself as a scientist who especially valued the domains of hypothesis and proof. And while he recognized and valued the "artistic" dimensions of psychoanalysis, he wrote little about the specific application of his theory to clinical process, and some of what he did write seems—relative to the richness and complexity of his developmental and theoretical writings—less evolved and dimensional. For instance, Bowlby appears in some of his writings (e.g., Bowlby, 1988) to imply that once patients are faced with the irrationality of their internal working models, or learn that the "reality" of such models is no longer applicable, they will abandon lifelong beliefs and expectations. As much as he speaks to the difficulty of such work, his clinical publications for the most part give relatively short shrift to the examination of such complexities. Bowlby (1988) himself remarked that he was a much better scientist and theoretician than he was a therapist, and there can be little doubt that his overarching views of the role and function of attachment in the development of personality and psychopathology have had a far greater impact than his clinical writings.

At present, there is a small but steadily growing literature on the relation between attachment theory and clinical process, spurred largely by developments in the assessment of adult attachment (Main, Kaplan, & Cassidy, 1985). For the most part, the current literature has focused on three separate domains: (1) the relation between attachment theory and psychoanalysis (Diamond & Blatt, 1994; Eagle, 1995, 1997; Fonagy, Chapter 26, this volume; Fonagy et al., 1995; Fonagy & Target, 1998; Marrone, 1984; Osofsky, 1995; Silverman, 1991; Slade, 1996; Slade & Aber, 1992; Zelnick & Buchholz, 1990), (2) the relevance of attachment theory to the treatment of infants and their parents (Lieberman, 1992; Lieberman & Pawl, 1993; Lieberman & Zeanah, Chapter 24, this volume; Minde & Hesse, 1996; Zeanah, Mammen, & Lieberman, 1993); and (3) the application of attachment research to the theory and practice of psychotherapy (Biringen, 1994; Byng-Hall, 1991; Gunderson, 1996; Hamilton, 1987; Holmes, 1993a, 1993b, 1995, 1996; Mackie, 1981; Rutter, 1995; Sable, 1983, 1989, 1992, 1994; Sperling & Lyons, 1994; Sheldon & West, 1989; West & Keller, 1994; West, Sheldon, & Reiffer, 1989). A number of self and relational psychoanalysts have also included Bowlby in their revisions of psychoanalytic metapsychology (Lichtenberg, 1989; Mitchell, 1988), although it must be noted that these authors consider Bowlby's theory to be largely consistent with the basic principles of the British object relations school, which in certain subtle ways it is not. The issue of the relation between object relations theory and attachment theory is addressed by Fonagy in Chapter 26 of this volume. Various writers have addressed the relation between attachment disruption and the development of specific clinical syndromes; for instance, Coates and Wolfe (1997) have linked childhood gender identity disorder to attachment derailment in the first 2 years of life, and have suggested specific treatment strategies in relation to derailed attachment between mother and child.

The implications of attachment theory and research for the theory and practice of individual, psychoanalytically oriented adult psychotherapy constitute the focus for this chapter.[1] I wish to make explicit that I am not making a case for a specific "type" of therapy—specifically, "attachment therapy" (Biringen, 1994). Instead, I suggest, in keeping with many colleagues (Fonagy et al., 1995; Fonagy & Target, 1996; Holmes, 1993b, 1995, 1996; Pine, 1990; Silverman, 1991; Target & Fonagy, 1996), that an understanding of the nature and dynamics of attachment *informs* rather than *defines* intervention and clinical thinking. Attachment theory offers a broad and far-reaching view of human functioning that has the potential to change the way clinicians think about and respond to their patients, and the way they understand the dynamics of the therapeutic relationship. At the same time, an understanding of attachment organization does not define all aspects of human experience. Nor does it substitute for other, equally important, and equally valid kinds of clinical understanding.

In discussing how attention to attachment processes affects clinical thinking, it is useful to distinguish between the implications of attachment *theory* for psychotherapy, and the implications of attachment *research* and specifically attachment *classification* for psychotherapy. Given the interrelation between attachment theory and research, this distinction may seem problematic; however, for the sake of clarity, it is useful to separate them. To date, most of the literature in this area has addressed the implications of attachment theory for clinical work. Bowlby (1988) himself devoted a number of publications to this subject, and a number of primarily British or European authors—many of whom either worked with or were indirectly influenced by Bowlby and his work at the Tavistock Clinic in London—followed suit (Byng-Hall, 1991; Hamilton, 1987; Heard & Lake, 1986; Holmes, 1993a, 1993b, 1995, 1996, in press; Liotti, 1993, 1995; Mackie, 1981; Marrone, 1984). These writings make it evident that Bowlby's unique view of the role of early relationships in the development of the mind, along with his theory of the infant's inborn motivation to establish and maintain attachment relationships, has the potential to shift the therapist's understanding of various dimensions of the therapeutic situation. Relational theorists have described a similar (but in some critical respects distinct) paradigm shift stemming from developments within object relations theory and infant research (Mitchell, 1988).

What have received considerably less attention in the literature, and therefore serve as the focus of this chapter, are the implications of recent developments in attachment research and classification for the clinical process. Although clinical psychiatry, psychoanalysis, and psychology remained relatively closed to Bowlby's ideas for decades (and to a large extent still remain so), these same ideas have been widely embraced by a number of developmental and academic psychologists, largely as a function of the pioneering efforts of Mary Ainsworth. Her development of a system for the classification of attachment was to make Bowlby's fundamental hypotheses open to empirical investigation, and was to move attachment theory out of the domain of psychoanalysis and into the domain of developmental study. As a consequence, attachment theory was to develop along a completely different trajectory than it might have if it had remained essentially a clinical theory about early development. Today, the notion that attachment quality can be classified is at the heart of attachment research; especially relevant to this chapter are recent developments in the classification of adult attachment, much of which has been pioneered by Mary Main and her colleagues (Main et al., 1985).

In this chapter, I address the implications of adult attachment research for clinical listening and clinical process. I then consider the implications of attachment classification for the process and aims of psychotherapy. I begin with a brief history of attachment classification and related research, and then turn to a discussion of each of the issues mentioned above. Questions of the relation between diagnosis, severity of psychopathology, and attachment classification are addressed in other chapters if this volume (Dozier, Stovall, & Albus, Chapter 22; Greenberg, Chapter 21).

A BRIEF HISTORY OF ATTACHMENT CLASSIFICATION AND RELATED RESEARCH

Bowlby believed that parental behavior leads to the development of established and predictable modes of response in the infant, and to the development of *patterns* of attachment. These behavioral patterns are the first manifestations of what will become "internal working models" or representations of attachment, and that will guide the individual's feelings, thoughts, and expectations in later relationships (see Bretherton, 1985,

1987; Bretherton & Munholland, Chapter 5, this volume; Main et al., 1985). Bowlby was powerfully influenced by cognitive psychology, and particularly by the information-processing model of neural and cognitive functioning. Just as cognitive psychologists defined representational models in terms of access to particular kinds of information and data, Bowlby suggested that different patterns of attachment reflect differences in an individual's degree of access to certain kinds of thoughts, feelings, and memories. Certain types of insecure models permit only limited access to attachment-related thoughts, feelings, and memories, whereas others provide exaggerated or distorted access to attachment-relevant information. Thus, Bowlby suggested, cognitive as well as emotional access to attachment-relevant information emerges as a function of the history of the mother–child relationship; in essence, the structure and functioning of the child's mind are determined by the types of feelings that are recognized and allowed expression within the dyad. These ideas were to be developed first by Mary Ainsworth and later by Mary Main. Their work gave rise to an extraordinarily rich and complex body of developmental research, and was to change the course of attachment research and indeed developmental theory in profound ways.

Mary Ainsworth and the Study of Mother–Infant Attachment

Mary Ainsworth was, without question, the individual single-handedly responsible for the dramatic impact attachment theory was to have upon developmental and academic psychology. Her research paved the way for what is now a vast collection of empirical studies of the antecedents and sequelae of children's attachment to their caregivers (for reviews, see Belsky & Cassidy, 1994; Cassidy, Chapter 1, this volume; Karen, 1998). Most relevant to this chapter is Ainsworth et al.'s (1978) discovery that variations in the quality of maternal responsiveness and sensitivity during the first year of life lead to demonstrable differences in infants' patterns of seeking comfort from their mothers. These empirical findings confirmed Bowlby's central hypothesis: that patterns of seeking care and nurture and of expressing affect emerge *as a function* of the mother's response to them. A child learns, from an early age, which responses will elicit care from the mother and which will not. Those that elicit or assure at least limited security become preferred and safe ways of interacting with those who care for the child.

Central to Ainsworth's thinking was the notion that the quality of maternal responsiveness is directly tied to patterns of infantile behavior, particularly comfort seeking and contact maintenance. On the basis of her observations of infantile patterns of separation and reunion in the laboratory separation procedure known as the strange situation, Ainsworth was able to distinguish three primary attachment classifications: "secure," "avoidant," and "resistant." These patterns were linked to mothers' success or failure in responding to and meeting infant needs. Infants whose mothers had responded to them in a sensitive fashion during the first year of life were likely to seek the mothers' comfort following separation; these children were classified as secure. Mothers who were rejecting or inconsistent in their responsiveness during the first year were likely to have children who either avoided their mothers or could not be comforted or contained by them upon reunion; these infants were classified as avoidant or resistant, respectively. In later research, Main and Solomon (1986, 1990) described a third insecure category, the "disorganized/disoriented" category. This pattern of attachment, in which infants showed evidence of disorganization and dissociation upon reunion, was also linked to maternal behavior—specifically, disorganization and dissociation in the discussion of early trauma and loss (Main & Hesse, 1990). For Ainsworth, then, and for a subsequent generation of attachment researchers, infantile behavior in relationships is predictably and lawfully related to maternal behavior during the first year of life. That is, *patterns* of behavior in attachment-relevant situations emerge as a direct function of the mother–infant relationship.

Mary Main and the Study of Adult Attachment

Mary Main's studies of adult attachment have proven to be as significant within attachment research as those of Bowlby and Ainsworth; these contributions have also been instrumental in bringing the study of attachment to the attention of psychoanalysts and psychotherapists. In the remainder of this chapter, I consider the relevance of research on adult attachment to the therapeutic process. Main and her colleagues (George, Kaplan, & Main, 1985; Main et al., 1985) set out to examine the relations between a parent's early relationship experiences and his or her infant's attachment status: How might patterns in the parent's early attachment experiences be linked to patterns in their infant's behavior? Along with colleagues Carol George and Nancy Kaplan, Main developed a deceptively simple semistructured interview known as the Adult Attachment Interview (AAI), in which adults are asked to describe childhood attachment relationships, as well as experiences of loss, rejection, and separation (George et al., 1985). From her analysis of AAI transcripts (Main & Goldwyn, 1984, 1998), Main discovered patterns of representation that were analogous to infantile patterns of behavior in the strange situation. These patterns were manifested not in adults' descriptions of the *events* of their lives, but in the way such events were remembered and organized. Indeed, Main found that adults who had had especially difficult childhoods were not necessarily insecure; what distinguished them from their insecure counterparts was the quality of their representations of attachment.

Main and her colleagues originally described three patterns of adult attachment: the "autonomous," "dismissing," and "preoccupied" patterns of attachment. Autonomous adults, like secure infants (who express distress and need in clear and communicative ways), had ready and coherent access to a range of positive and negative feelings about their early attachment experiences. Their representations of early attachment experiences were coherent and flexible. Insecure adults, by contrast, described such experiences in incoherent, contradictory ways. Dismissing adults idealized early relationship experiences and described painful events in a detached, often contradictory way, whereas preoccupied adults seemed overwhelmed and flooded by the affect associated with early attachment experiences. Dismissing adults, like avoidant infants, minimized and overregulated affects that would disrupt their functioning, whereas preoccupied adults, like resistant children, were unable to contain and regulate memories and affects associated with early attachment. Some time after the publication of her original findings, Main suggested that subjects whose interviews revealed disorganization and other indices of disordered thinking in the discussion of mourning or trauma could be classified as "unresolved/disorganized with respect to mourning or trauma" (Main & Hesse, 1990); these subjects manifested the effects of trauma in cognitive or affective disorientation and confusion, dissociation, lapses in consciousness, and the like. Recently a fifth classification, "cannot classify," has been described (Hesse, 1996). This category is used when "no single state of mind with respect to attachment is prominent" (Main & Goldwyn, 1998); typically, this classification is used when the subject fluctuates between dismissing and preoccupied states of mind, although it can also be used when the subject fails to rely upon any "single strategy for organizing information relevant to attachment; that is, there appears to be a breakdown of strategy at a global level" (Minde & Hesse, 1996, p. 119). (Both infant and adult classifications are described more fully in Belsky & Cassidy, 1994; Main, 1995b; and Slade & Aber, 1992. See also Crowell, Fraley, & Shaver, Chapter 20, Hesse, Chapter 19, and Solomon & George, Chapter 14, this volume.)

Main and her colleagues found that parents who were autonomous in their representation of attachment had children who were secure in the strange situation (Main et al., 1985). Those who were dismissing of attachment had avoidant children, and those who were preoccupied had resistant children. Parents who were unresolved/disorganized in relation to loss and trauma had children who were disorganized in relation to attachment. These relationships were especially strong for mothers. Meta-analyses of the 14 studies replicating these findings have confirmed the strength of the association between infant and adult security (van IJzendoorn, 1995; van IJzendoorn & Bakermans-Kranenburg, 1996), although complex and important issues of discordance and discontinuity have yet to be resolved (Slade et al., 1995; Zeanah, Benoit, et al., 1993).

Metacognitive Monitoring, Reflective Functioning, and Affect Regulation: Theoretical Contributions of Main, Fonagy, and Others

Main's description of specific categories for the classification of adult attachment was to change the course of attachment research. At the same time, it was to give rise to a theoretical revolution in the understanding of representational processes—specifically narrative coherence, metacognitive monitoring, and reflective functioning. Although these constructs are intimately tied to the notion of attachment security, Main's groundbreaking work on representation led to a number of theoretical and clinical inquiries separate from her original work on the classification of adult

attachment. These developments have been particularly relevant to the clinical enterprise.

For Main, the capacity to represent past experiences in a *coherent* and *collaborative* fashion is certainly the most significant and compelling aspect of adult security, and is clearly the most predictive of infant security. A coherent interview is one that seems both believable and "true" to the listener; in a coherent interview, the events and affects intrinsic to early relationships are conveyed without distortion, contradiction, or derailment of discourse. The subject collaborates with the interviewer, clarifying his or her meanings, and working to make sure he or she is understood. Such a subject is thinking as the interview proceeds, and is aware of thinking with and communicating to another; thus coherence and collaboration are inherently intertwined and interrelated. Life events and early relationships are examined afresh as the subject strives to make sense of his or her experience for the listener; pain and discomfort are managed with insight and humor. Main (1990, 1991, 1995a) views this critical aspect of narrative process as a manifestation of what she refers to as "metacognitive monitoring"—the adult's capacity to "step back and consider his or her own cognitive processes as objects of thought or reflection" (1991, p. 135). Coherence reflects an active, "constructivist" process at work; the subject is reevaluating the story while telling it. Descriptions are given in the first person, in narratives that are succinct, believable, and clear, even when traumatic memories and experiences are described.

Main suggests that coherence and the capacity to collaborate with the listener are the sequelae of the adult's having formed a single, internally consistent working model of attachment; such a model allows for the integration of all attachment-relevant information and memories. All aspects of experience are allowed access to consciousness, without distortion or contradiction. Multiple models of attachment are formed when the acknowledgment of disturbing feelings or memories threatens the self or current relationships; distortion and incoherence are the cognitive and linguistic manifestations of multiple contradictory models. For Main, coherence is also a critical element in the intergenerational transmission of attachment: The mother who is able to openly acknowledge, access, and evaluate her own attachment experiences will be able to respond to her child's attachment needs in a sensitive and nurturing way.

Peter Fonagy and his colleagues (Fonagy, Steele, Moran, Steele, & Higgitt, 1991; Fonagy et al., 1995; Fonagy, Steele, Steele, & Target, 1997; Fonagy & Target, 1996; Target & Fonagy, 1996) have extended Main's work on metacognitive monitoring in ways that are particularly relevant to understanding both the action of therapy and the dynamics of the therapeutic relationship. Fonagy and his colleagues suggest that coherence and other manifestations of metacognitive monitoring signal the capacity to *reflect* upon internal affective experience in a complex and dynamic fashion. The "reflective function refers to the psychological processes underlying the capacity to mentalize . . . mentalizing refers to the capacity to perceive and understand oneself and others' behavior in terms of mental states, i.e., reflection" (Fonagy et al., 1997, p. 5). The reflective function is what allows the individual to make sense of his or her own and others' psychological experience, to enter into another's experience, to "read" another's mind. The development of the reflective function allows the child to make others' behavior meaningful and predictable, and permits him or her to respond adaptively in a range of interpersonal situations. It permits a more developed, complex, and affective representation of the self, inner experience, and intimate relationships. Above all, it may provide protection against the damaging effects of abuse and trauma (Fonagy et al., 1995).

The mother's capacity to understand her child's mental states, and her "readiness to contemplate these in a coherent manner" (Fonagy et al., 1995, p. 255), are what create the context for a secure attachment relationship. The mother who is able to reflect upon her own as well as her infant's inner experience forms a representation of her infant as intentional—that is, as "mentalizing, desiring, believing." The image of the intentional infant is internalized by the child, and "constitutes the core of [his or her] mentalizing self" (Fonagy et al., 1995, p. 257). Because it gives the child a sense of his or her inner life and affective experience, the mother's capacity to enter her child's mind and give reality to the child's internal experience is probably a vital aspect of empathic and sensitive mothering. The experience of the self as real, known, and intentional is central to the experience of security.

A vital aspect of security (and a direct outgrowth of the reflective capacity) is the ability to regulate and thus fully experience a range of affects, specifically distress and pleasure (Slade, in

press). With understanding comes the capacity to regulate and contain mental states. Presumably this capacity too has its roots in the mother–child relationship. The mother who is able to reflect upon and thus modulate and integrate her own affective experience will not be dysregulated by her infant or toddler's aggression or other negative affects, because the vagaries of emotion are familiar to her. And because she is sensitive to the meaning of emotion, she will respond to her infant's signals as if they are patterned, sequential, bounded, and meaningful. Infant signals are perceived by the mother as coherent, organized communications that—like all interpersonal dialogue—have a function and a message. The mother's capacity to give voice to her own experiences, to describe them meaningfully and coherently, allows her to understand the meaningfulness of her infant's affective communications and to represent them within the context of their ongoing dialogue. Thus they become known, familiar, and communicable to the child.

There are various ways to consider the clinical relevance of this body of work. In the following sections, I first consider the relevance of such general constructs as coherence, metacognitive monitoring, and reflective functioning for the clinical process. I then consider how notions of attachment classification may inform and guide the clinician's thinking regarding clinical formulation, the aims of psychotherapy, and the dynamics of processes of transference and countertransference.

THE RELEVANCE OF COHERENCE, REFLECTIVE FUNCTIONING, AND METACOGNITIVE MONITORING FOR CLINICAL LISTENING

Main's work on metacognitive monitoring and Fonagy's subsequent work on reflective functioning were to change the course of attachment theory in dramatic ways. At the same time, this work was to add to the extant literature on clinical process in both direct and indirect ways. Main's initial emphasis in her work on narrative was on the particular significance and meaning of narrative coherence. Rather than attend specifically to the content of an individual's story, Main focuses upon the structure of the story. For Main, the critical issue is not what kind of story the person tells, but where, when, and how this story breaks down. How is the story told, and what can the subject (or patient) allow himself or herself to know, feel, and remember in telling the story, particularly as such knowing occurs in the presence of and in collaboration with the interviewer? Main suggests that experiences that cannot be known or spoken about are at the root of incoherence in discourse. Incoherence is manifested in a number of ways—in breaks and disruptions in the story, inconsistencies, contradictions, lapses, irrelevancies, and shifts in person. These are linguistic efforts to manage what cannot be integrated or regulated in experience or memory. Fonagy has elaborated this work by focusing specifically on what he terms the capacity to "mentalize" affective experience—to reflect upon and contemplate the complexity and diversity of one's internal, mental states.

In many ways, this attention to narrative process operationalizes what has always been intrinsic to good clinical listening: listening for changes in voice; for contradictions, lapses, irrelevancies, and breakdowns in meaning; and for the subtle, ongoing disruptions and fluctuations in the structure and organization of discourse. Indeed, these ways of listening for moments when experience cannot be contemplated or mentalized offer the therapist a view of how the patient defends himself or herself against the intrusion of unacceptable feelings or memories into conscious thought. They offer a means to understanding how an individual lives in the world and in relation to others, what the individual can tolerate feeling, and what he or she needs to make others feel in order to feel personally safe. It tells the therapist what can be known, what can be felt, what can be spoken, and what cannot be contained.

Attending to what can and cannot be told, and to how it is told, also helps the therapist to imagine patients' early experience in powerful and direct ways. It helps him or her to imagine the dynamic patterns that evolved in early childhood, to understand early empathic breaks with caregivers, and to identify islands of dissociated, unintegrated affective experience. It makes it possible to think much more closely about how early interactive experiences may be affecting responses to emotional upheaval and conflict, and may be affecting the way a patient thinks or does not think about emotion. It allows the therapist to understand the *function* of particular patterns of thought and feeling, as they protect the patient from intolerable experiences, and as they are designed to elicit ways of thinking and behaving in

others (in both real and transferential aspects of such relationships). In essence, this way of hearing language and understanding the organization of thought implies that experiences of seeking comfort and care constitute nodal, organizing events in the development of the mind.

In my own clinical work, for instance, if a patient disavows an emotional experience in the course of an hour, I may wonder whether this was an emotion the patient's mother could imagine and embrace, or whether she subtly abandoned the patient when he or she expressed it. Or when a patient continually conveys a sense of chaos and helplessness, I may wonder whether this is the patient's way of communicating a need for structure and containment. What was the nature of emotional exchanges between the child and each parent, and at what cost to the child (now an adult) was regulation achieved? Were the mother's ministrations organizing and containing? Were they disorganizing and fragmenting? Or did they subtly encourage the child to disappear? How do the organizational qualities of the patient's narrative convey his or her needs and expectations in relationship to primary caregivers? What does it tell me about what the patient believes can be responded to and heard in his or her story? When does language convey a sense of agency and personal ownership, and when does it convey a sense of being lost and helpless in the face of affective upheaval?

One of the primary aspects of coherence, in Main's view, is the capacity to integrate semantic generalizations and episodic memories; in other words, the adult is able to provide specific memories as evidence supporting the general descriptions of his or her primary relationships. Certainly clinicians are well aware of the fact that the organization of memory is central to their work, and many therapists work directly with early memories and fantasies. However, what Main's work suggests is that it may sometimes be useful to ask for specific memories, and to ask patients to describe their early interactions and relationships in some detail. A patient's remembering (or imagining) what it was like to be with his or her mother and father offers the therapist a means of listening for covert abandonments, as well as the more overt disruptions of early loss, abandonment, separation, and trauma. Although these constructions may have little relation to what "actually" happened, they are nevertheless meaningful stories, and they will become more coherent, organized, and vital over the course of treatment.

ATTACHMENT CLASSIFICATION AND CLINICAL FORMULATION

Main's approach to language is not only aimed at discerning islands of coherence and incoherence; it is also aimed at uncovering *patterns* of representation—specifically the dismissing, preoccupied, and unresolved/disorganized patterns of attachment. What relevance do these constructs have for the clinical enterprise? Certainly the notion of insecurity has clinical utility. Many of the patients seen in psychotherapy today would be classified as insecure, by virtue of the nonautonomous or insecure nature of their internal working models of attachment; in other words, they would be classified (to a greater, lesser, or overlapping extent) as dismissing, preoccupied, or unresolved/disorganized in relation to attachment. In a review of research examining the links between attachment processes and adult psychopathology, Dozier et al. (Chapter 22, this volume) note that "psychiatric disorders are nearly always associated with nonautonomous states of mind." (p. 515). This is not to say that insecurity is synonymous with psychopathology (Cassidy, 1997; Cicchetti, 1989; Sroufe, 1989). Many complex factors lead to psychopathology; nevertheless, insecurity may be considered a significant, but not determining, risk factor. Furthermore, it is not necessarily the case that all patients seeking psychotherapy are insecure, nor does the designation of insecurity describe the breadth or complexity of any clinical picture. However, thinking about a patient's attachment classification is useful in much the same way that thinking about a patient's diagnosis is—that is, as a guide to understanding and making sense of the patient's experience.

But what of the categories themselves? Is attachment classification useful clinically? Thinking about attachment in terms of patterns overlaps in certain ways with more traditional ways of thinking about diagnosis; and, like diagnosis, it has both advantages and disadvantages in the clinical situation. I discuss some of these issues below. I begin with a description of the attachment classification system from a clinical perspective.

Attachment classification offers a distinct way of thinking about psychological structure along what is essentially a continuum of affect regulation and structure. At one end of the continuum is the avoidant/dismissing category, where free expression of (particularly negative) affect is minimal, and the structures for regulating, con-

taining, and suppressing affect are rigid and highly organized. Affects, memories, and cognitions relevant to attachment are overregulated. Attachment researchers have suggested that such affect regulation strategies serve to "deactivate" (Kobak & Sceery, 1988; Main, 1990) or "minimize" (Cassidy, 1994) affects that would disrupt attachment relationships. Although the dismissing classification does not in and of itself reflect psychopathology, certain individuals who fall into this category might also be described as obsessional, schizoid, or narcissistic.

At the other end of the continuum is the resistant/preoccupied category. The polar opposite of the avoidant/dismissing category, the resistant/preoccupied category is characterized by the relative absence of structures for regulating affect. Feelings, memories, and cognitions relevant to attachment are underregulated. Here structures do not suppress affect; rather, affect routinely dissolves or overwhelms structures, rendering them useless or only transiently organizing. These strategies are understood as "hyperactivating" or "heightening" affective cues to caregivers, thus assuring continuing comfort and care (Cassidy, 1994; Cassidy & Berlin, 1994; Main & Solomon, 1986). Some (although again not all) individuals falling into this category might well be described diagnostically as hysterical or borderline in their personality organization.

The secure/autonomous category falls at the midpoint of this continuum. Here structure and affect exist in a balance. Affects, including a range of negative affects, can be represented and acknowledged in a flexible and coherent way. Affective experience is neither constricted nor overwhelming, indicating the presence of well-functioning capacities for affect regulation and modulation. This balance is reflected in the coherence and "truth" of narrative, and in the flexibility and cohesiveness of representational structures. Although these individuals may certainly demonstrate neurotic pathology, such as anxiety or depression, they are unlikely to receive diagnoses indicative of more severe character disturbance.

The fourth attachment category, unresolved/disorganized, cannot easily be placed along this continuum. It is in some sense an extreme form of the resistant/preoccupied category, in that it is typified by incoherence and disorganization not unlike that seen in the resistant/preoccupied category. Further confirmation of the similarity between these two categories is provided by the fact that clinical researchers find that individuals with borderline personality disorder are most often classified as either resistant/preoccupied or disorganized/unresolved, or both (Adam, Sheldon-Keller, & West, 1995; Ainsworth & Eichberg, 1991; Allen, Hauser, & Borman-Spurrell, 1996; Fonagy et al., 1995). This category, along with the resistant/preoccupied category, has also been linked to childhood trauma or loss (Adam et al., 1995; Allen et al., 1996; Fonagy et al., 1995) and to dissociative disorders (Liotti, 1993, 1995). The fifth category, cannot classify, similarly cannot be easily placed along this continuum, for it often contains elements of both types of insecure organizations; and, like the unresolved/disorganized classification, it has been linked with indices of psychopathology (Hesse, 1996 and Chapter 19, this volume).

From the perspective of psychoanalytic theory, there are two major problems with the notion of attachment classification: It is adevelopmental and mutually exclusive. I begin with the issue of development. In one way, the notion of attachment classification is indeed adevelopmental; that is, the notion of attachment type is not explicitly wedded to developmental success or failure. Psychoanalysts of course assume that lower levels of functioning and failures in differentiation are associated with more primitive defenses and modes of regulating affect, whereas higher levels of functioning and success in the realms of differentiation and autonomy are associated with higher-level defenses and modes of regulating affect (Freud, 1965). Attachment theorists suggest instead that the dynamics of a secure relationship predispose a child toward more differentiated, coherent, and flexible functioning (Diamond & Blatt, 1994). Thus early patterns of defense, as manifested in the secure, avoidant, and resistant patterns, emerge not as a function of developmental progression, but as a function of the child's orientation to affect as it arises in his or her earliest relationships.

Although these ways of thinking about structural differences do not specifically include consideration of the different tasks inherent in stages of development, they map easily onto psychoanalytic developmental theory. For instance, an avoidant child's move through separation and individuation (Mahler et al., 1975) will necessarily be different from a resistant child's experience of autonomy and exploration. Similarly, an avoidant child's ways of managing the complexities of Oedipal love will differ greatly from those of a resistant child. Each of the "affectively charged moments" (Pine, 1985) that define infancy,

childhood, and adulthood will be navigated in a way consistent with attachment organization.

In other words, although attachment theory is not a stage theory, there is certainly reason to think that attachment quality significantly affects a child's capacity to move through and resolve developmental challenges throughout the lifespan. Notions of type, however, are less easily reconciled with psychoanalytic theory. In fact, notions of classification and type have provided the biggest impediment to psychoanalytic clinicians' acceptance of attachment research.

Some attachment researchers have avoided the problem of type by suggesting that attachment be considered in terms of two overlapping dimensions: the secure–insecure dimension and the dismissing–preoccupied dimension (Kobak & Sceery, 1988; Shaver & Clark, 1994; Shaver & Hazan 1993). In these schemas, an individual's classification is considered in terms of its overall security (i.e., coherence and organization) and its dominant defensive style (dismissing or preoccupied). Both Main's notion of coherence/collaboration and Fonagy's notion of reflective functioning avoid the problem of type altogether, by conceptualizing these variables along a single, unitary dimension. Nevertheless, most attachment researchers conceive of attachment in terms of categories that are more or less mutually exclusive; the individual in question either falls into one category or another. An individual is classified as having a single, primary attachment classification, although there are some instances in which individuals receive dual or mixed classifications (Hesse, 1996), suggesting a more complex view of this aspect of attachment theory.

Although the notion of distinct categories of attachment, or of "styles" of affect regulation, has recently received some support from the domain of neurobiology (Schore, 1994),[2] the assumptions underlying the assignment of attachment type remain unacceptable to many clinicians. Just as they are leery of the problems inherent in the notion of diagnostic categories and labels, they are wary if not outright rejecting of attachment classification, and skeptical as to its clinical relevance. Given the history of psychoanalysis as the study of the complex and developing nature of the human mind, it is obvious why the notion of attachment "types" raises hackles among psychoanalytic clinicians. It simply does not make sense to think of patients in terms of a single, mutually exclusive attachment classifications that presumably remain stable within the clinical situation. It is too often the case that patients fluctuate among modes of defense, particularly when they have been in treatment for some time and their defenses necessarily become more fluid.

Nevertheless, thinking about structure and representation in this way does indeed provide clinicians with a way to listen to and think about clinical material in working with adults. Using attachment classifications as metaphors or guides in clinical listening (Blatt, 1995; Lichtenberg, 1989), rather than as singular, mutually exclusive types, offers an important means of understanding how patients live in relationships, how they organize their inner experiences and inner lives, how they manage the developmental thrusts of separation and individuation, and how they modulate desire and aggression. Most important, understanding the *function* of the regulatory strategies associated with specific attachment classifications allows therapists to understand the dynamic properties of patients' representational models—how the patients' ways of thinking and behaving in relationships are meant to evoke particular kinds of responses and relationships. In the same way that diagnosis serves as a guide (but not a recipe) in the treatment situation, notions of attachment organization provide a therapist with metaphors for thinking about early patterns of affect regulation and defense, and of imagining and speaking to a patient's experience.

In essence, attachment categories tell a story. They tell a story about how emotion has been regulated, what experiences have been allowed into consciousness, and to what degree an individual has been able to make meaning of his or her primary relationships. For Main and many other attachment theorists, these categories represent a way of being in the world that is set in place at an early age, as a function of early experience. Thus, these "modes of experience" or (in Main's terms) "states of mind" necessarily determine an individual's experience of development and its vicissitudes, of change, and of basic relatedness. It is also important to note, however (M. Main, personal communication, April 18, 1998), that inherent in each of the insecure categories are aspects and components of the other insecure categories. Thus, although individuals learn a specific, conscious strategy that dictates attachment behavior, there is another, *unconscious* representation that exists out of awareness but that may well be accessible in the clinical situation.

From this perspective, listening for the ways attachment themes and organization are both consciously and unconsciously expressed changes how therapists observe their patients and make sense of their stories; it also changes the way they respond to patient narratives, and to the particular aspects of these narratives that emerge as a function of attachment organization. Thus the nature of a therapist's efforts to transform and enter into a patient's narrative will be profoundly shaped by the individual's attachment security. How therapists talk to patients and what they endeavor to do in their talking and in their listening will vary as a function of the patients' predominant (at a given point in treatment) attachment organization.

In a recent paper, Jeremy Holmes (1998) suggests that the work of therapy involves both "story-making and story breaking," helping the patient at once to tell a coherent story and to allow this story to be told in a different, and perhaps more healing light. Holmes states: "Implicit in my argument so far is the view that psychological health (closely linked to secure attachment) depends on a dialectic between story-making and story breaking, between the capacity to form narrative, and to disperse it in light of new experience." By definition, insecure representational models either preclude story making (knitting together the events of one's life in a coherent way) or story breaking (examining the events of one's life anew in the light of new insight). Holmes (in press) defines "three prototypical pathologies of narrative capacity: clinging to rigid stories (the dismissing pattern); being overwhelmed by unstoried experience (the preoccupied pattern); or being unable to find a narrative strong enough to contain traumatic pain (the unresolved pattern)." These "pathologies of narrative capacity" have profound and distinct effects upon the clinical process.

Let me consider the clinical implications of each of the two primary insecure patterns in turn. In work with patients who seem primarily dismissing in their attachment organization, therapy revolves around finding ways of allowing affects into experience and into consciousness—that is, of allowing for "story breaking." These are individuals who constrict rather than contain their emotional experience, and who are strangers to feelings, motivations, or inner life. With such patients, the import of psychological experience, intimacy (Holmes, 1996), and attachment is minimized and diminished, or at the very least seems far out of reach. Often when it is suggested to such patients that they may be feeling sad, longing, or angry, or that they might have felt that way as children, their response is usually some variant of "Well, I must have, or maybe I do, but I really don't feel it right now," or "I guess so, I suppose so." They often speak in the second person: "Well, you know, when you're dealing with your child, you can feel angry and frustrated." Thus denial and avoidance appear in the form of the discourse markers described by Main as indicative of a patient's detachment.

From a therapeutic perspective, then, the therapist who recognizes a dismissing attachment organization in a patient must turn her attention to finding ways into the patient's affective experience and memory. Such avenues are often blocked by what Holmes (1998) refers to as "nodal memories," or rigid, inflexible versions of the patient's story that must be "reworked . . . unpacked . . . and then reassembled, taking on a new perspective." As the patient comes to tell his or her story in treatment, this singular view of life's events must be recast in light of new information. There are often multiple roadblocks to joining the patient in his or her pain and confusion, because the adherence to rigid stories precludes the patient's experiencing aspects of his or her life that have been long denied and forgotten.

By contrast, treatment with individuals whose attachment organization can be described as preoccupied revolves around the slow creation of structures for the modulation of affect. These patients (particularly those in Main's E2 and E3 categories; see Main & Goldwyn, 1998) often seem overwhelmed and indeed tormented by feelings, and much of treatment revolves around containing and organizing such feelings. In Holmes's (1998) terms, work with many preoccupied adults involves the therapist's finding a way "of capturing the confusion and vagaries of overwhelming feelings." Thus, whereas the absence of affect typifies individuals who are dismissing of attachment, the relative absence of structures to contain an abundance of emotion is typical of many preoccupied individuals. Indeed, the major challenge of working with these patients is to find ways to help them manage and contain affect; often the development of real, internalized structures seems virtually impossible. They often seem to derive very little from therapeutic attempts to organize their experience. Structures seem to evaporate readily and are replaced with raw affect. Their general understanding of relationships seems superficial and hackneyed, and not at all deeply related to internal consolidation (Main, 1995b). Therapeutic in-

sights, instead of paving the way toward the development of real structure, take on a hollow, unintegrated feel. Within the session, these patients are so "driven" by feeling that they jump from one issue to the next, without any sense of a focus or inner purpose. Fonagy et al. (1996) have noted that these patients are especially difficult to treat, and have the least success in outcome studies.

Work with patients who are unresolved/disorganized with respect to mourning or trauma poses a different set of issues, primarily because much of the affect underlying the lack of resolution has been dissociated and profoundly distorted. Here there is often a slow and painstaking recreation of what might have happened; this process often involves working from the barest of clues, and at the same time engenders terror and further dissociation in the patient (Liotti, 1993, 1995).

ATTACHMENT ORGANIZATION AND THE THERAPEUTIC RELATIONSHIP

Therapeutic work takes place within a therapeutic relationship. As all important relationships are affected to a greater or lesser extent by the dynamics of attachment processes, so will the therapeutic relationship be affected by these same dynamics. On the one hand, attachment organization and attachment history will have a profound effect upon the patient's feelings about as well as conscious and unconscious expectations of the therapist. And attachment dynamics will also influence the therapist's feelings about and responses to the patient, although these effects are more subtle and (ideally) more acknowledged.

From an attachment perspective, the model of a successful or helpful treatment involves a patient's capacity to make use of therapy and of a therapist in a "secure" way—namely, to be able to reflect upon his or her life story together with the therapist, and then to bring that shared understanding and meaning into everyday life in a way that is transforming and healing. In other words, treatment provides the patient a means to contemplate and indeed reexperience his or her life story within a safe and healing context, with an emotionally available and sensitive other who "marks" (Gergely & Watson, 1996), and thus gives new meaning and shape to, life events and the patient's sense of self and relationships. But the degree to which a patient is able to involve himself or herself in treatment, to join with the therapist in the task of mutual understanding, is very much a function of the patient's attachment security. Even when the therapist provides a "secure base," serving as an emotionally available, responsive, and empathic "companion" to the patient (Bowlby, 1988), patients whose attachment organization is insecure are likely to respond to the therapist in ways that are consistent with their lifelong patterns of defense, affect regulation, and security operations.

Reliance upon a therapist need not necessarily be seen as a manifestation of transference. Indeed, turning to a therapist for help and guidance at a time of emotional distress and turmoil derives from a "universal human need to feel protected and comforted" when alarmed or frightened (M. Cortina, personal communication, January 4, 1997). Thus the impulse to seek therapy may well derive from a healthy sense that one can be helped by someone "stronger and wiser" (Bowlby, 1988; Farber, Lippert, & Nevas, 1995), and from a view of others as capable of providing care and comfort. However, for individuals with insecure attachment histories, such normal human processes often become distorted and transformed by what are rightly called "transferential expectations" that the therapist will not understand, will not be available, or will in some way violate the patient's sense of (albeit shaky) safety and security. And, as might be expected, the "shape" of such responses to treatment will emerge as a function the individual's attachment organization.

Individuals with a dismissing organization will typically find the treatment process emotionally challenging and difficult. These individuals often seem cool and somewhat remote, and tend to dismiss the importance of relationships as well as feelings. They often describe difficulty in maintaining relationships. Difficulties in these relationships are minimized, even though it may be evident from the patients' life circumstances that their distance has caused them a great deal of pain. "There may be a smooth, seemingly friendly exterior that appears self-assured and less afraid than others might be. But the apparent good adaptation is superficial and underneath 'the springs of love are frozen and independence is hollow' (Bowlby, 1960)" (Sable, 1983, p. 378). Psychotherapy poses explicit challenges to such patients' defensive strategies. Mary Dozier and her colleagues have carried out a series of studies investigating the impact of attachment organiza-

tion on the treatment process. With respect to dismissing adults, Dozier and her colleagues (Dozier, 1990; Dozier, Lomax, & Tyrrell, 1996) have noted that such individuals often seem quite resistant to treatment. Dozier (1990) reports that within the context of therapy, they deny their need for help so as to protect themselves from the possibility that the caregiver will be unavailable. Often they are rejecting of treatment, rarely asking for help and pulling back from help that is offered. In other work, Dozier et al. (1996) report that when individuals with dismissing attachment organizations *do* confront emotional issues, they often try to divert the clinician's attention. They may become somewhat disorganized in discussing emotional issues.

Dozier's findings are entirely consistent with my own experience as a therapist. I too have found such individuals to be rejecting of help, unmoved by my references to their hurt or fear, and likely to experience my efforts to imagine their feelings as intrusive or overly emotional. They rarely acknowledge the effects or distress of separation; appointments may be missed, rescheduled, or forgotten with apparent equanimity. They are able to acknowledge their dependency upon me in only the most oblique ways. It is only after a reasonable length of time that such patients are able to acknowledge feelings of loss, sadness, need, and rejection, and often such revelations are followed by periods of sealing over and denial. Emotional outbursts are often brief, intense, and contained, and efforts at minimization quickly become apparent.

Adults who are preoccupied in relation to attachment pose very different challenges to the treatment process and to the formation and maintenance of a treatment alliance. The inability to collaborate with and thus take in the therapist's words and support is what makes therapy with such individuals so difficult. Preoccupied adults are thought to heighten or maximize their expression of attachment needs and feelings, in order to ensure their caregivers' care and availability (Cassidy, 1994; Main & Solomon, 1986). Indeed, these individuals "present themselves (in treatment) as needy and dependent, and demand much of their attachment figures" (Dozier, 1990, p. 57). They are far more likely to call therapists between sessions, to demand extra appointments, to become extremely dependent upon their therapists, and to demand advice and support. In other words, these patients are far more likely than dismissing individuals to challenge the parameters of psychotherapy and endeavor to turn the treatment situation into a relationship more reminiscent of a parent–child relationship. On the one hand, such ways of being in relationship to the therapist are not transference manifestations in the classical sense, but manifestations of the patients' primary mode of relatedness. Need and distress presumably function to keep the therapist involved. What is transferential, however, is the experience of the therapist as insufficiently helpful and available; this may well result in a great deal of hostility toward the therapist as the rage and chaos of primary relationships is elicited in the transference. Gunderson (1996) notes that these patients cannot tolerate being alone; thus, specific technical interventions are required to manage both resulting transference and countertransference manifestations.

ATTACHMENT ORGANIZATION AND COUNTERTRANSFERENCE

I have described some of the ways dismissing and preoccupied individuals may respond to the treatment process. But what of the feelings these individuals evoke in the therapist? Clearly, given that attachment patterns function to evoke feelings in others, they will function to evoke feelings in the therapist (see also Sroufe & Fleeson, 1988). Insecure adults—namely, those who have suffered some early assault on their capacity to develop relationships—bring their insecure representational models into the therapeutic relationship in vivid and immediate ways, and these form the basis for a range of countertransferential reactions in the therapist. Deadlocked in their rigid representations, dismissing patients lock the therapist out as they themselves were locked out by their attachment figures. Faced with the impermeability of such a patient's narratives, the therapist experiences himself or herself as caught in the same barren landscape as the patient; however, the therapist experiences what the patient cannot—the hopelessness of change and of attaining intimacy. And the therapist is left feeling much as the patient once felt as a child: angry, unacknowledged, silly, and inept.

As Dozier (1990) has pointed out, these patients often do succeed in driving clinicians away, and thus lose the help they need. Countertransference reactions can be quite intense, and therapists treating such patients often feel intrusive, melodramatic, helpless, ridiculous, and excluded. Such patients can be very rejecting and

hurtful; it is natural to withdraw in response to these kinds of rejections. Often, a therapist's unconscious response to such rejections manifests itself in "forgetting" to bring things to a patient's attention and failing to address critical transference issues. These are vivid examples of how the therapist unwittingly colludes with the patient's inability to grapple with the exigencies of his or her emotional life. A different and somewhat more sadistic variation of possible countertransference reactions to such a patient is the attempt to force them to acknowledge disturbing feelings. This reaction, like withdrawal, stems from the frustration of being utterly shut out, as well as from the projection of the patient's unmetabolized feelings (especially rage) onto the therapist.

The emotional "feel" of working with a preoccupied patient is of course quite different from that of working with a dismissing one. Patients who are primarily preoccupied with respect to attachment are trying very hard to get the therapist to lessen their sense of confusion and take care of them, and yet collaboration with the therapist is all but impossible for these patients. And the therapist feels much the way the patients once did as a child: swamped, angry, helpless, confused, and dysregulated. As a consequence, countertransference reactions to such patients can be quite powerful—feelings of being devoured and overwhelmed, as well as annoyed and confused. And, in natural response to becoming mired in such feelings, a therapist will often try to organize and structure a preoccupied patient; in effect, the therapist may start trying too hard to (in Holmes's terms) "make" stories for the patient. These efforts are sometimes not helpful and may in fact increase the patient's feeling of chaos and confusion. Progress in work with patients who are primarily preoccupied in relation to attachment is hard-won. It seems to follow not from words or interpretation, but from the therapist's long-term emotional availability and tolerance for fragmentation and chaos. Such flexibility and emotional availability provide the structure that is most likely to lead to internal consolidation and genuine structural change.

Dozier (1990) and Fonagy et al. (1996) have noted that these individuals are not necessarily more compliant in treatment, nor are they more likely to be helped by treatment. In fact, in the only large-scale outcome study of attachment classification and therapy outcome, Fonagy et al. (1996) reported that dismissing adults were far more likely to improve in psychotherapy than preoccupied individuals. Interestingly, Horowitz, Rosenberg, and Bartholomew (1996) reported that dismissing adults do not do well in brief psychotherapy; in line with Fonagy et al.'s findings, as well as the clinical writings of Liotti (1993, 1995), they suggested instead that "long-term dynamic psychotherapy, cognitive therapy, or pharmacotherapy may be more appropriate" (p. 558). For preoccupied patients, however, the capacity to *reflect* upon emotions in self and others rather than *respond* to them is notably absent. This is undoubtedly a factor in the finding that such individuals seem not to do well in psychotherapy (see also Korfmacher, Adam, Ogawa & Egeland, 1997, for a discussion of therapeutic process and outcome in a home visitation intervention).

Thus far, I have addressed the question of therapist response from the vantage point of the patient's attachment classification. But what aspects of therapist response, and specifically of negative countertransferential responses, evolve from the therapist's own history and attachment classification? Bowlby (1988) viewed the therapist's emotional availability as central to healing in psychotherapy, because only when the therapist behaves in a sensitive, empathic (i.e., secure) way is the patient able to separate childhood projections from his or her real experience in psychotherapy. In fact, Bowlby implied that for some patients therapeutic neutrality may well trigger experiences of rejection, neglect, and abandonment, whereas for others the therapist's overinvolvement and intrusiveness may well trigger fears of engulfment or enhance dependency. But to what extent is a therapist's sensitivity and emotional availability contingent upon his or her own attachment history and attachment classification?

Therapy concerns itself over and over again with loss, separation, and reunion—both in its consideration of such events in patients' lives, and in the constant separations and reunions that are intrinsic to the therapeutic process. And just as losses, separations, and reunions have meaning for patients, so do they have meaning for therapists. Similarly, just as being *cared for* may be quite evocative for patients, so may the experience of *caring* be evocative for therapists. Many therapists have suffered early loss and abandonment; naturally, they will vary in the degree to which they have reconciled and come to terms with these experiences. And, regardless of the degree to which a therapist has come to terms

with his or her own early experience, different patients will engage the therapist's attachment dramas in different ways.

From an attachment perspective, the readiness to care for patients is as normal in therapists as it is normal for patients to turn to them for care. Indeed, it may be seen as a corollary to the parental "caregiving system" (Bowlby, 1980; Solomon & George, 1996; see George & Solomon, Chapter 28, this volume). "Care" within the therapeutic context can be defined in myriad ways (providing a secure base, reflecting upon and entering into the patient's experience, etc.); in any case, it implies an emotional connection that flows from therapist to patient as well as from patient to therapist. In a secure therapist, these feelings create an atmosphere of safety and connection. The therapist's feelings of connection to the patient, as well as his or her capacity to care for the patient, may well contribute to the therapist's capacity for empathy and to the resulting therapeutic success, and may well be understood in light of attachment processes. But in an insecure therapist, the predilection to care is as vulnerable to distortion as it is in the insecure patient; these are the perils of countertransference.

In one study, Dozier, Cue, and Barnett (1994) offered fascinating support for the notion that the attachment organization of the therapist may influence treatment outcome. Dozier and her colleagues reported that secure therapists were more able than insecure therapists to hear and respond to the dependency needs of their dismissing patients, and were thus less vulnerable to intense countertransference reactions toward these individuals. The overt demands and explicit dependency needs of patients who are preoccupied in relation to attachment may also be better managed by secure therapists. Insecure therapists are often most likely to become entangled with such patients, responding to their obvious needs rather than their underlying needs. By contrast, secure therapists are more likely to respond to less direct and subtle manifestations of need and dependency. These findings add an interesting dimension to considering the emerging attachment of patient to therapist. A therapist's own security, manifested in the capacity to remain open to his or her experience as well as to the patient's, is likely to be most predictive of a healthy and successful psychotherapy. Obviously, these findings raise a number of issues in the training and supervision of therapists (Main, 1995b).

CLOSING NOTES

I have outlined various implications of attachment theory and research for the theory and practice of individual psychotherapy—for clinicians' thinking about the therapeutic relationship, development, defense, and clinical process. The understanding of defense, affect regulation, motivation, and the dynamics of relationships that is provided by latter-day attachment theory does not replace other ways of understanding developmental and relational processes. Optimally, it should add to therapists' ways of listening to and understanding clinical material, and will be helpful with some patients and not others. As Pine (1990) has noted in introducing his view that a "multiplicity of variables" are central to human function, "The complexity of the human animal is sufficiently great such that we gain in our understanding by having multiple perspectives on it" (p. 4). Attachment and attachment processes constitute only one (admittedly very important) aspect of human functioning, and although attachment processes define an aspect of human experience, they do not *define* an individual in all his or her complexity. Nevertheless, an understanding of the processes so richly described by Bowlby, Ainsworth, and Main, along with a broad array of attachment theorists and researchers, can shed much light on the clinical enterprise and can serve as a valuable adjunct to good clinical work.

Today clinicians are under increasing pressure to administer short, cost-effective, problem-centered treatments. From the vantage point of attachment theory (as well as psychoanalytic theory more generally), the brief psychotherapies are unlikely to result in the "reworking" of representational models, or in changing the quality of attachment representations. They are also unlikely to allow for the development of healthy and curative attachment processes between patient and therapist. Given that issues surrounding the "making and breaking of affectional bonds" (Bowlby, 1979) are so often at the center of therapeutic inquiry, we cannot ignore the fact that it takes time and a relationship to change lifelong patterns of attachment. Attachment-related issues also raise a number of questions about training: How can we sensitize upcoming generations of therapists to the vicissitudes of attachment? And, more importantly, how can we increase the likelihood that therapist trainees have examined the vagaries of their own histories? We now know that this is critical to good clinical work.

These are but a few of the matters raised by the research and theory reviewed here. Let us hope that further understanding by clinicians of the complex and rich literature on attachment will shed even more light on how the dynamics and organization of attachment affect clinical outcome and clinical process, and will pave the way toward development of even more effective ways of listening to patients and helping them to change their lives.

ACKNOWLEDGMENTS

This chapter is based in part on a paper delivered to Section 5 of Division 39 of the American Psychological Association, January 27, 1996. I would like to thank the editors for their careful and comprehensive reading of earlier versions of this chapter; their comments were enormously helpful and made for a more coherent and accurate final version. I would also like to thank the many colleagues who read and commented on early drafts for helping me sharpen my thinking, and for their support and encouragement—particularly Sheldon Bach, Susan Coates, Mauricio Cortina, Peter Fonagy, Jeremy Holmes, Alicia Lieberman, Mary Main, Justine McCabe, Jill Scharff, and David Scharff.

NOTES

1. "Psychotherapy" is a term used to describe a wide range of therapeutic approaches that vary in duration, in intensity, and in their aims and goals, and that can be administered to families, couples, groups, and individual children or adults. A discussion of the complexity of and overlap among different forms of psychotherapy is beyond the scope of this chapter. Here I limit myself to a consideration of what is variously called "psychoanalytically oriented psychotherapy," "insight-oriented psychotherapy," and "dynamic psychotherapy." All of these terms refer to the idea that there exists a dynamic relation between early childhood experience and current adaptation; the aim of treatment in this form of psychotherapy is to illuminate the emotional and structural links between past and present experience. Bowlby himself was a psychoanalytic psychotherapist; thus an emphasis on the representation of early childhood experience is intrinsic to both attachment theory and psychoanalytic psychotherapy.

2. In view of the recent developments in understanding the link between neurobiology and attachment, it should be noted that the differences inherent in working with dismissing and preoccupied patients

may involve differential involvement of left- and right-brain functioning (P. Thomas, personal communication, June 24, 1997). If therapy leads to the transformation of neurobiological structures, the nature and type of transformation sought by the therapist may well differ as a function of attachment category. Main and Hesse (M. Main, personal communication, May 27, 1998) have been using a self-report inventory to examine these phenomena, with interesting preliminary results. Notably, they have found that certain states of mind in relation to attachment are differentially related to left- and right-brain functioning.

REFERENCES

Adam, K. S., Sheldon Keller, A. E., & West, S. (1995). Attachment organization and vulnerability to loss, separation, and abuse in disturbed adolescents. In S. Goldberg, R. Muir, & J. Kerr (Eds.), *Attachment theory: Social, developmental, and clinical perspectives* (pp. 309–343). Hillsdale, NJ: Analytic Press.

Ainsworth, M. D. S., Blehar, M. C., Waters, E., & Wall, S. (1978). *Patterns of attachment: A psychological study of the strange situation.* Hillsdale, NJ: Erlbaum.

Ainsworth, M. D. S., & Eichberg, C. (1991). Effects on infant–mother attachment of mother's unresolved loss of an attachment figure, or other traumatic experience. In C. Parkes, J. Stevenson-Hinde, & P. Marris, (Eds.), *Attachment across the life cycle* (pp. 199–216). London: Routledge.

Allen, J. P., Hauser, S. T., & Borman-Spurrell, E. (1996). Attachment theory as a framework for understanding sequelae of severe adolescent psychopathology: An eleven year follow-up study. *Journal of Consulting and Clinical Psychology, 61,* 254–263.

Aron, L. (1995). *A meeting of minds: Mutuality in psychoanalysis.* Hillsdale, NJ: Analytic Press.

Beebe, B., & Lachmann, F. M. (1988). Mother–infant mutual influence and precursors of psychic structure. In A. Goldberg (Ed.), *Frontiers in self-psychology* (Vol. 3, pp. 3–26). Hillsdale, NJ: Analytic Press.

Beebe, B., & Stern, D. N. (1977). Engagement–disengagement and early object experiences. In N. Freedman & S. Grand (Eds.), *Communicative structures and psychic structures* (pp. 35–55). New York: Plenum Press.

Belsky, J., & Cassidy, J. (1994). Attachment: Theory and evidence. In M. Rutter & D. Hay (Eds.), *Development through life* (pp. 373–402). Oxford: Blackwell.

Biringen, Z. (1994). Attachment theory and research: Application to clinical practice. *American Journal of Orthopsychiatry, 64,* 404–420.

Blatt, S. (1995). Representational structures in psychopathology. In D. Cicchetti & S. L. Toth (Eds.), *Rochester Symposium on Developmental Psychopathology: Vol. 6. Emotion, cognition, and representation* (pp. 1–33). Rochester, NY: University of Rochester Press.

Bowlby, J. (1960). Grief and mourning in infancy and early childhood. *Psychoanalytic Study of the Child, 15,* 19–52.

Bowlby, J. (1969/1982). *Attachment and loss: Vol. 1. Attachment.* New York: Basic Books.

Bowlby, J. (1973). *Attachment and loss: Vol. 2. Separation.* New York: Basic Books.

Bowlby, J. (1979). *The making and breaking of affectional bonds.* London: Tavistock.

Bowlby, J. (1980). *Attachment and loss: Vol. 3. Loss.* New York: Basic Books.

Bowlby, J. (1988). *A secure base: Parent–child attachment and healthy human development.* New York: Basic Books.

Bretherton, I. (1985). Attachment theory: Retrospect and prospect. In I. Bretherton & E. Waters (Eds.), Growing points of attachment theory and research. *Monographs of the Society for Research in Child Development, 50*(1–2, Serial No. 209), 3–39.

Bretherton, I. (1987). New perspectives on attachment relations: Security, communication, and internal working models. In J. Osofsky (Ed.), *Handbook of infant development* (2nd ed., pp. 1061–1100). New York: Wiley.

Bretherton, I. (1995). The origins of attachment theory: John Bowlby and Mary Ainsworth. In S. Goldberg, J. Kerr, & R. Muir (Eds.), *Attachment theory: Social, developmental, and clinical perspectives* (pp. 45–84). Hillsdale, NJ: Analytic Press.

Byng-Hall, J. (1991). The application of attachment theory to understanding and treatment in family therapy. In C. Parkes, J. Stevenson-Hinde, & P. Marris (Eds.), *Attachment across the life cycle* (pp. 199–216). London: Routledge.

Cassidy, J. (1994). Emotion regulation: Influences of attachment relationships. In N. A. Fox (Ed.), The development of emotion regulation: Biological and behavioral foundations. *Monographs of the Society for Research in Child Development, 59*(2–3, Serial No. 240), 228–250.

Cassidy, J. (1997). Attachment theory. In J. Noshpitz (Ed.), *Handbook of child and adolescent psychiatry: Vol. 1. Infants and preschoolers: Development and syndromes* (pp. 236–250). New York: Wiley.

Cassidy, J., & Berlin, L. J. (1994). The insecure/ambivalent pattern of attachment: Theory and research. *Child Development, 65,* 971–992.

Cicchetti, D. (1989). Developmental psychopathology: Past, present, and future. In D. Cicchetti (Ed.), *Rochester Symposium on Developmental Psychopathology: Vol. 1. The emergence of a discipline* (pp. 1–12). Hillsdale, NJ: Erlbaum.

Coates, S., & Wolfe, S. (1997). Gender identity disorders of childhood. In J. Noshpitz (Ed.), *Handbook of child and adolescent psychiatry* (pp. 452–473). New York: Wiley.

Diamond, D., & Blatt, S. (1994). Internal working models and the representational world in attachment and psychoanalytic theories. In M. Sperling & W. Berman (Eds.), *Attachment in adults: Clinical and developmental perspectives* (pp. 72–98). New York: Guilford Press.

Dozier, M. (1990). Attachment organization and treatment use for adults with serious psychopathological disorders. *Development and Psychopathology, 2,* 47–60.

Dozier, M., Cue, K., & Barnett, L. (1994). Clinicians as caregivers: Role of attachment organization in treatment. *Journal of Consulting and Clinical Psychology, 62,* 793–800.

Dozier, M., Lomax, L., & Tyrrell, C. (1996). *Psychotherapy's challenge for adults using deactivating attachment strategies.* Unpublished manuscript, University of Delaware.

Eagle, M. (1995). The developmental perspectives of attachment and psychoanalytic theory. In S. Goldberg, R. Muir, & J. Kerr (Eds.), *Attachment theory: Social, developmental, and clinical perspectives* (pp. 123–153). Hillsdale, NJ: Analytic Press.

Eagle, M. (1997). Attachment and psychoanalysis. *British Journal of Medical Psychology, 70,* 217–229.

Farber, B. A., Lippert, R. A., & Nevas, D. B. (1995). The therapist as attachment figure. *Psychotherapy, 32,* 204–212.

Fonagy, P., Leigh, T., Steele, M., Steele, H., Kennedy, R., Mattoon, G., Target, M., & Gerber, A. (1996). The relation of attachment status, psychiatric classification and response to psychotherapy. *Journal of Consulting and Clinical Psychology, 64,* 22–31.

Fonagy, P., Steele, M., Moran, G., Steele, H., & Higgitt, A. C. (1991). The capacity for understanding mental states: The reflective self in parent and child and its significance for security of attachment. *Infant Mental Health Journal, 13,* 200–216.

Fonagy, P., Steele, M., Steele, H., Leigh, T., Kennedy, R., Mattoon, G., & Target, M. (1995). Attachment, the reflective self, and borderline states: The predictive specificity of the Adult Attachment Interview and pathological emotional development. In S. Goldberg, R. Muir, & J. Kerr (Eds.), *Attachment theory: Social, developmental, and clinical perspectives* (pp. 233–279). Hillsdale, NJ: Analytic Press.

Fonagy, P., Steele, M., Steele, H., & Target, M. (1997). *Reflective functioning manual.* Unpublished manuscript, University College, London.

Fonagy, P., & Target, M. (1996). Playing with reality: I. Theory of mind and the normal development of psychic reality. *International Journal of Psychoanalysis, 77,* 217–233.

Fonagy, P., & Target, M. (1998). Mentalization and the changing aims of child psychoanalysis. *Psychoanalytic Dialogues, 8,* 87–114.

Freud, A. (1965). *Normality and pathology in childhood.* New York: Norton.

Gergely, G., & Watson, J. (1996). The social biofeedback theory of parental affect-mirroring: The development of emotional self-awareness and self-control in infancy. *International Journal of Psychoanalysis, 77,* 1181–1212.

George, C., Kaplan, N., & Main, M. (1985). *Adult Attachment Interview* (2nd ed.). Unpublished manuscript, University of California at Berkeley.

Grotstein, J. (1990). Introduction. In M. Little (Ed.), *Psychotic anxieties and containment.* Northvale, NJ: Aronson.

Gunderson, J. (1996). The borderline patient's intolerance of aloneness: Insecure attachments and therapist availability. *American Journal of Psychiatry, 153,* 752–758.

Hamilton, V. (1987). Some problems in the clinical application of attachment theory. *Psychoanalytic Psychotherapy, 3,* 67–83.

Heard, D., & Lake, B. (1986). The attachment dynamic in adult life. *British Journal of Psychiatry, 149,* 430–438.

Hesse, E. (1996). Discourse, memory, and the Adult Attachment Interview: A note with emphasis on the emerging cannot classify category. *Infant Mental Health Journal, 17,* 4–11.

Holmes, J. (1993a). Attachment theory: A biological basis for psychotherapy. *British Journal of Psychiatry, 163,* 430–438.

Holmes, J. (1993b). *John Bowlby and attachment theory.* London: Routledge.

Holmes, J. (1995). Something there is that doesn't love a wall: John Bowlby, attachment theory, and psychoanalysis. In S. Goldberg, R. Muir, & J. Kerr (Eds.), *Attachment theory: Social, developmental, and clinical perspectives* (pp. 19–45). Hillsdale, NJ: Analytic Press.

Holmes, J. (1996). *Attachment, intimacy, and autonomy.* New York: Aronson.

Holmes, J. (1998). Defensive and creative uses of narrative in psychotherapy: An attachment perspective. In G. Roberts & J. Holmes (Eds.), *Narrative in psychotherapy and psychiatry* (pp. 49–68). Oxford: Oxford University Press.

Horowitz, L. M., Rosenberg, S. E., & Bartholomew, K. (1996). Interpersonal problems, attachment styles, and outcome in brief dynamic psychotherapy. *Journal of Consulting and Clinical Psychology, 61,* 549–560.

Hunter, V. (1991). John Bowlby: An interview. *Psychoanalytic Review, 78,* 159–175.

Karen, R. (1998). *Becoming attached: First relationships and how they impact our capacity to love.* New York: Oxford University Press.

Kobak, R. R., & Sceery, A. (1988). Attachment in later adolescence: Working models, affect regulation, and representations of self and others. *Child Development, 59,* 135–146.

Korfmacher, J., Adam, A., Ogawa, J., & Egeland, B. (1997). Adult attachment: Implications for the therapeutic process in a home visitation intervention. *Applied Developmental Science, 1,* 43–52.

Lichtenberg, J. (1989). *Psychoanalysis and motivation.* Hillsdale, NJ: Analytic Press.

Lieberman, A. F. (1992). Infant–parent psychotherapy with toddlers. *Development and Psychopathology, 4,* 559–574.

Lieberman, A. F., & Pawl, J. H. (1993). Infant–parent psychotherapy. In C. H. Zeanah (Ed.), *Handbook of infant mental health* (pp. 427–441). New York: Guilford Press.

Liotti, G. (1993). Disorganized attachment and dissociative experiences: An illustration of the developmental–ethological approach to cognitive therapy. In H. Rosen & K. T. Kuehlwein (Eds.), *Cognitive therapy in action* (pp. 213–239). San Francisco: Jossey-Bass.

Liotti, G. (1995) Disorganized/disoriented attachment in the psychotherapy of the dissociative disorders. In S. Goldberg, R. Muir, & J. Kerr (Eds.), *Attachment theory: Social, developmental, and clinical perspectives* (pp. 343–367). Hillsdale, NJ: Analytic Press.

Mackie, A. J. (1981). Attachment theory: Its relevance to the therapeutic alliance. *British Journal of Medical Psychology, 54,* 203–212.

Mahler, M., Pine, F., & Bergman, A. (1975). *The psychological birth of the human infant.* New York: Basic Books.

Main, M. (1990). Cross-cultural studies of attachment organization: Recent studies, changing methodologies, and the concept of conditional strategies. *Human Development, 33,* 48–61.

Main, M. (1991). Metacognitive knowledge, metacognitive monitoring, and singular (coherent) vs. multiple (incoherent) model of attachment: Findings and directions for future research. In C. Parkes, J. Stevenson-Hinde, & P. Marris (Eds.), *Attachment across the life cycle* (pp. 127–160). London: Routledge.

Main, M. (1995a). Discourse, prediction, and studies in attachment: Implications for psychoanalysis. In T. Shapiro & R. N. Emde (Eds.), *Research in psychoanalysis: Process, development, outcome* (pp. 209–245). Madison, CT: International Universities Press.

Main, M. (1995b). Recent studies in attachment: Overview, with selected implications for clinical work. In S. Goldberg, R. Muir, & J. Kerr (Eds.), *Attachment theory: Social, developmental, and clinical perspectives* (pp. 407–475). Hillsdale, NJ: Analytic Press.

Main, M., & Goldwyn, R. (1984). *Adult attachment scoring and classification systems.* Unpublished manuscript, University of California at Berkeley.

Main, M., & Goldwyn, R. (1998). *Adult attachment scoring*

and classification systems (2nd ed.). Unpublished manuscript, University of California at Berkeley.

Main, M., & Hesse, E. (1990). Lack of mourning in adulthood and its relationship to infant disorganization: Some speculations regarding causal mechanisms. In M. T. Greenberg, D. Cicchetti, & E. M. Cummings (Eds.), *Attachment in the preschool years: Theory, research, and intervention* (pp. 161–182). Chicago: University of Chicago Press.

Main, M., Kaplan, N., & Cassidy, J. (1985). Security in infancy, childhood, and adulthood: A move to the level of representation. In I. Bretherton & E. Waters (Eds.), Growing points of attachment theory and research. *Monographs of the Society for Research in Child Development, 50*(1–2, Serial No. 209), 66–107.

Main, M., & Solomon, J. (1986). Discovery of a new, insecure–disorganized/disoriented attachment pattern. In T. B. Brazelton & M. Yogman (Eds.), *Affective development in infancy* (pp. 95–124). Norwood, NJ: Ablex.

Main, M., & Solomon, J. (1990). Procedures for identifying infants as disorganized/disoriented during the Ainsworth Strange Situation. In M. T. Greenberg, D. Cicchetti, & E. M. Cummings (Eds.), *Attachment in the preschool years: Theory, research, and intervention* (pp. 95–124). Chicago: University of Chicago Press.

Marrone, M. (1984). Aspects of transference in group analysis. *Group Analysis, 17*, 179–190.

Minde, K., & Hesse, E. (1996). The role of the Adult Attachment Interview in parent–infant psychotherapy: A case presentation. *Infant Mental Health Journal, 17*, 115–126.

Mitchell, S. (1988). *Relational concepts in psychoanalysis: An integration.* Cambridge, MA: Harvard University Press.

Osofsky, J. D. (1995). Perspectives on attachment and psychoanalysis. *Psychoanalytic Psychology, 12*, 347–363.

Pine, F. (1985). *Developmental theory and clinical process.* New Haven, CT: Yale University Press.

Pine, F. (1990). *Drive, ego, object, and self.* New York: Basic Books.

Rutter, M. (1995). Clinical implications of attachment concepts: Retrospect and prospect. *Journal of Child Psychology and Psychiatry, 36*, 549–557.

Sable, P. (1983). Overcoming fears of attachment in an adult with a detached personality. *Psychotherapy, 20*, 376–382.

Sable, P. (1989). Attachment, anxiety, and the loss of a husband. *American Journal of Orthopsychiatry, 59*, 550–556.

Sable, P. (1992). Attachment theory: Application to clinical practice with adults. *Clinical Social Work Journal, 20*, 271–283.

Sable, P. (1994). Attachment, working models, and real experiences. *Journal of Social Work Practice, 8*, 25–33.

Schore, A. (1994). *Affect regulation and the origin of the self.* Hillsdale, NJ: Erlbaum.

Shaver, P., & Clark, C. L. (1994). The psychodynamics of adult romantic attachment. In J. M. Masling & R. F. Bornstein (Eds.), *Empirical perspectives on object relations theory* (pp. 105–156). Washington, DC: American Psychological Association.

Shaver, P., & Hazan, C. (1993). Adult romantic attachment: Theory and evidence. In D. Perlman & W. H. Jones (Eds.), *Advances in personal relationships* (Vol. 44, pp. 29–70). London: Jessica Kingsley.

Sheldon, A. E. R., & West, S. (1989). The functional discrimination of affiliation and attachment: Theory and empirical demonstration. *British Journal of Psychiatry, 155*, 18–23.

Silverman, D. (1991). Attachment patterns and Freudian theory: An integrative proposal. *Psychoanalytic Psychology, 8*, 169–193.

Slade, A. (1996). A view from attachment theory and research. *Journal of Clinical Psychoanalysis, 5*, 112–123.

Slade, A. (in press). Representation, symbolization, and affect regulation in the concomitant treatment of a mother and child: Attachment theory and child psychotherapy. *Psychoanalytic Inquiry.*

Slade, A., & Aber, J. L. (1992). Attachments, drives, and development: Conflicts and convergences in theory. In J. Barron, M. Eagle, & D. Wolitzky (Eds.), *Interface of psychoanalysis and psychology* (pp. 154–186). Washington, DC: American Psychological Association.

Slade, A., Dermer, M., Gerber, J., Gibson, L., Graf, F., Siegel, N., & Tobias, K. (1995, March). *Prenatal representation, dyadic interaction, and quality of attachment.* Paper presented at the biennial meeting of the Society for Research in Child Development, Indianapolis, IN.

Solomon, J., & George, C. (1996). Defining the caregiving system: Toward a theory of caregiving. *Infant Mental Health Journal, 17*, 183–198.

Sperling, M., & Lyons, L. S. (1994). Representations of attachment and psychotherapeutic change. In M. Sperling & W. Berman (Eds.), *Attachment in adults: Clinical and developmental perspectives* (pp. 331–349). New York: Guilford Press.

Sroufe, L. A. (1989). Relationships, self, and individual adaptation. In A. J. Sameroff & R. N. Emde (Eds.), *Relationship disturbances in early childhood: A developmental approach* (pp. 70–94). New York: Basic Books.

Sroufe, L. A., & Fleeson, J. (1988). The coherence of family relationships. In R. A. Hinde & J. Stevenson-Hinde (Eds.), *Relationships within families: Mutual influences* (pp. 27–47). Oxford: Oxford University Press.

Stern, D. N. (1985). *The interpersonal world of the infant.* New York: Basic Books.

Storr, A. (1992). John Bowlby. *Munks Roll.* London: Royal College of Physicians.

Target, M., & Fonagy, P. (1996). Playing with reality: II. The development of psychic reality from a theoretical perspective. *International Journal of Psycho-Analysis, 77*, 459–479.

Tronick, E. (1989). Emotions and emotional communication in infants. *American Psychologist, 44*, 112–119.

van Dijken, S. (1996). *The first half of John Bowlby's life: A search for the roots of attachment theory.* Unpublished doctoral dissertation, University of Leiden, The Netherlands.

van IJzendoorn, M. H. (1995). Adult attachment representations, parental responsiveness, and infant attachment: A meta-analysis on the predictive validity of the Adult Attachment Interview. *Psychological Bulletin, 117*, 387–403.

van IJzendoorn, M. H., & Bakermans-Kranenburg, M. J. (1996). Attachment representations in mothers, fathers, adolescents, and clinical groups: A meta-analytic search for normative data. *Journal of Consulting and Clinical Psychology, 64*, 8–21.

West, M., & Sheldon, A. (1994). Psychotherapy strategies for insecure attachment in personality disorders. In M. Sperling & W. Berman (Eds.), *Attachment in adults: Clinical and developmental perspectives* (pp. 313–331). New York: Guilford Press.

West, M., Sheldon, A., & Reiffer, L. (1989). Attachment theory and brief psychotherapy: Applying current research to clinical interventions. *Canadian Journal of Psychiatry, 34*, 369–374.

Zeanah, C., Benoit, D., Barton, M., Regan, C., Hirshberg, L., & Lipsitt, L. P. (1993). Representations of attachment in mothers and their one-year-old infants. *Journal of the American Academy of Child and Adolescent Psychiatry, 32*, 278–286.

Zeanah, C., Mammen, O., & Lieberman, A. F. (1993). Disorders of attachment. In C. H. Zeanah (Ed.), *Handbook of infant mental health* (pp. 322–349). New York: Guilford Press.

Zelnick, L., & Buchholz, E. S. (1990). The concept of mental representations in the light of recent infant research. *Psychoanalytic Psychology, 1*, 29–58.

26

Psychoanalytic Theory from the Viewpoint of Attachment Theory and Research

❖

PETER FONAGY

There is bad blood between psychoanalysis and attachment theory. As with many family feuds, it is hard to identify where the problem began. In the early 1960s a number of major psychoanalytic figures turned on John Bowlby, following the publication of his article in the *Psychoanalytic Study of the Child* (Bowlby, 1960). Attachment theory was criticized as mechanistic, nondynamic, and explicated according to thorough misunderstandings of psychoanalytic theory (e.g., A. Freud, 1960/1969). Opposition to his views provided one small area of common ground for the followers of Anna Freud and Melanie Klein (Grosskurth, 1986), and for the next few decades Bowlby was a relatively isolated figure in psychoanalysis.

The critiques, which were compounded at fairly regular intervals by major figures such as Engel (1971) and Hanley (1978), have raised a variety of issues but can be boiled down to relatively few simple disagreements. Bowlby has been seen as having renounced drives, unconscious processes, and complex internalized motivational and conflict-resolving systems. He has further been seen as having discarded the richness of the array of human emotions—affects experienced by the ego and involving socialization, as well as sources of pleasure rooted in the infant's physical body. Attachment theory has been seen as ignoring biological vulnerabilities other than those rooted in the caregiver's behavior, and as reduc-

ing etiological considerations to a single variable: that of physical separation. Bowlby has been accused of failing to consider the impact of the developmental state of the ego on the child's ability to make attachments and react to loss. He has also been accused of ignoring negative attachment related to fear of the mother and to trauma other than physical separation. He has been viewed as a reductionist in his emphasis on evolutionary considerations at the expense of full recognition of complex symbolic functioning. As recently as 1992, Lilleskov wrote: "Bowlby's disregard of drive theory may have made observations of behavior easier but has reduced the explanatory power of these observations" (p. 128).

Rather than engaging these historic figures of psychoanalysis in debate, and taking issue with the crassness of their critiques and the profound misapprehension of attachment theory these have often implied, we should look briefly at Bowlby's presentation of psychoanalysis. This, I am sad to say, was at times unworthy of his genius. In Chapter 22 of the second volume of his *Attachment and Loss* trilogy (Bowlby, 1973), titled "Pathways for the Growth of Personality," Bowlby compared two alternative theoretical models to two types of railway systems. He described the psychoanalytic model of personality development as a single-track rail along which stops can occur. In this model, adult pathological states are the results of fixations at, or regressions to, early phases of normal development. The other model, which Bowlby derived from the biologist C. H. Waddington (1966), consists of several alternative developmental pathways—a single main route branching out into a number of distinct tracks. Although Bowlby's point was clear, it was also disingenuous. He was very familiar with the work of Anna Freud, Erik Erikson, and others, all of whom posited similar "multitrack" developmental networks. Bowlby was thus guilty of combating a psychoanalytic straw figure. Similarly, in his 1958 paper, Bowlby was at pains to demonstrate that psychoanalysts had been trying in vain to free themselves from what he called "secondary-drive theory." The primary drive, being based on oral and other physical needs, creates a secondary drive for bonding. By contrast, he placed social bonds in the position of a primary biological given. Again, Anna Freud and Burlingham (1944) had already recognized the child's instinctual need to be attached to the mother. Even earlier, the Hungarian psychoanalyst Imre Hermann (1923) had proposed a primary instinct to "cling" to the caregiver, based on primate observations not dissimilar to Bowlby's use of Harlow's work.

Bowlby maintained this blinkered attitude to the end. In his epilogue to the collection of papers edited by Parkes and Stevenson-Hinde (Bowlby, 1980b), he restated his disappointment with psychoanalysis: "Psychoanalysis gave weight to the internal workings of the human mind and recognized the special status of intimate human relationships, but its metapsychology, already obsolescent, was a handicap, while its fixation on a single, retrospective research method gave no means of resolving differences of opinion" (p. 310). Bowlby here appeared to rule out the relevance of psychoanalytic observation on *a priori* grounds without wishing to explore the ideas in detail. In the same section, he commented that different investigative methods have intrinsic strengths and vulnerabilities and can be fruitfully used in combination: "the strength of one may make good at least some of the weaknesses of the other" (p. 312). But by this time psychoanalysis had disappeared from his epistemic horizon.

Thus, just as psychoanalysts have consistently and somewhat tendentiously misread attachment theory and found it wanting in richness and explanatory power, so Bowlby consistently focused on the weakest facets of the psychoanalytic corpus, almost as if he wished to forestall a mutually corrective interrelationship. There have been ex-

ceptions to this trend. Bretherton (1987) presented a thoughtful comparative review of attachment theory, separation–individuation theory, and the theory of infant–mother relatedness proposed by Stern. There are some other excellent examples of integrative attempts, including those of Eagle (1995, 1997) and Holmes (1993, 1997).

In this chapter a similar integrative attempt is undertaken, with the aim of demonstrating that the relationship between attachment theory and psychoanalysis is more complex than adherents of either community have generally recognized. Indeed, there are many points of contact—some obvious, others more subtle, and yet others perhaps tenuous. There are also points of significant divergence. As psychoanalytic theory is not at this time a coherent set of propositions, there appears to be no shortcut to exploring areas of overlap by looking individually at selected major schools of psychoanalytic thought in relation to attachment theory. The present review starts with Sigmund Freud and ends with the work of Daniel Stern. Much that is relevant has to be omitted because of constraints of space and the even more significant limitations imposed by my own ignorance.

FREUD'S MODELS

It is misleading to attempt to trace commonalities and differences between Freud's thinking and current attachment theory. Freud's theory does not represent a homogeneous corpus (Sandler, Holder, Dare, & Dreher, 1997). Traditionally, his contribution is divided into four phases. The first is the prepsychoanalytic phase, covering a series of papers mostly on neurological topics; second is the affect–trauma phase, during which Freud put forward the view that the etiology of neurosis rests in the actual events of childhood development; third is the topographical phase, in which Freud emphasized fantasy driven by biological drive states; the fourth phase includes the dual-instinct theory and the structural model of the mind. Each of these phases has distinct points of correspondence with and divergence from attachment theory, and a skillful Freud scholar could readily construct a picture in which the originator of psychoanalysis is seen as either a friend or a foe of attachment theory.

Points of Contact

Freudian psychoanalysis and attachment theory both concern themselves with unconscious processes. However, whereas the exclusion of specific meanings from consciousness is the cornerstone of Freud's system, for Bowlby and later attachment theorists it is only one aspect of mental functioning. Freud, like Bowlby, started his voyage of discovery with concern about the psychological consequences of significant early deprivation (Bowlby, 1973; Freud & Breuer, 1893/1954). But whereas Bowlby went on to elaborate the psychological, social, and biological underpinnings of this association, Freud turned away from his "seduction hypothesis" in favor of his second model, emphasizing the psychosexual theory of development. Uninformed reviewers of Bowlby may take exception to the therapeutic realism of his approach, in which cathartic recollections of traumatic events appear once again to be occupying pride of place (Bowlby, 1977). The critical difference between the naive realism of Freud's early theories and Bowlby's epistemology lies in Bowlby's attention to the representation of experience (Bowlby, 1980a). This refutes any suggestion that Bowlby's theory represents a return to the naive realist reductionism of the affect–trauma model. Freud's move from the affect–trauma model to the topographical model did signal a shift from realist reductionism and extreme environmentalism toward idealism, in which the phenomena described were chiefly seen as products of the mind bearing no actual relationship to reality. To Bowlby, this shift was unpalatable (Bowlby, 1981), and the divergence between the topographical model and attachment theory is far greater than that between Freud's earlier and later ideas.

The social environment again found a preeminent place within the fourth phase of Freud's development (Freud, 1923/1961). At this stage Freud recognized that anxiety is a biologically determined epiphenomenal experience linked to the perception of both external and internal dangers (Freud, 1926/1959). The prototypical danger situation is one of loss. The loss of the object (the mother) was considered by Freud as a threat of comparable order to the fear of loss of a body part or of self-regard. Freud's structural model provided a useful background to attachment theory in other ways. Freud (1923/1961) hypothesized that conflicts within the human mind are organized around three themes corresponding to three psychic agencies (id, ego, and superego). Freud's conflict themes concerning wish and reality and internal and external reality remained essential building blocks for Bowlby and other

attachment theorists. In particular, the ego's capacity to create defenses that organize characterological and symptomatic constructions as part of the developmental process became a cornerstone of Bowlby's trilogy, particularly the last volume (Bowlby, 1980a). Here he considered in detail mechanisms of perceptual and cognitive distortions necessary for the functioning of internal working models (IWMs).

Bowlby himself reviewed Freud's contributions on the child's attachment to the mother (e.g., Bowlby, 1958); he noted the ways in which his thinking was congruent with Freud's, as well as points of difference. To summarize briefly:

1. He pointed out that Freud's awareness of the importance of attachment to the mother developed late and was reported only in his paper on "Female Sexuality" (Freud, 1931/1961).
2. Bowlby noted Freud's (1920/1955) observation that abandonment and isolation distress infants at 18 months of age.
3. Bowlby also acknowledged that in Freud's understanding, anxiety is rooted in fear of the loss of the mother, although this is seen as a fear of ungratified instincts (Freud, 1926/1959).
4. Freud (1940/1964) acknowledged that the child's relation to the mother is unique and laid down unalterably at an early stage to become the prototype for all later love relations. Freud also acknowledged that there is more to this love relationship than food, and that the experience of being cared for relates directly to self-esteem (narcissistic cathexis).
5. Bowlby pointed out, however, that Freud emphasized phylogenetic foundations of this relationship in preference to the quality of mothering received by the infant. Thus Freud's theory seems ultimately to hold no place for a primal need to be attached to another person.

Points of Divergence

When we examine Freud's corpus as a whole, it becomes evident that points of divergence substantially outnumber points of correspondence. The following is an abbreviated list of areas where attachment theory has diverged from Freudian ideas:

1. Freud was quite narrow in terms of the cultural and social context he envisioned for development; his focus was undoubtedly on cultural absolutes that precluded awareness of the cultural diversity even within his own society.

2. Freud's concern with the Oedipal period in the third and fourth years of life reduced his interest in early childhood experience. His views of infancy were abstract, fictional, and not based on direct observation.

3. Related to this, and notwithstanding his awareness of the impact of extreme environments, Freud had relatively little to say concerning the developmental significance of real behavior with the real parents, real relationships, and other environmental determinants.

4. Freud was unclear about the synthesizing role of the self. More specifically, in Freud's theory the ego performs the functions of both an organizing agency (a grouping of psychological mechanisms) and an integrative phenomenal representation, the coherence of which has to be preserved.

5. Freud (1920/1955) accounted for the reemergence in adulthood of childhood patterns of relating in terms of the repetition compulsion, ultimately the death instinct. This is inconsistent with the cognitive formulation of attachment theory, which emphasizes the accumulation of relationship experience.

6. Finally, Freud's view of development was somewhat mechanistic and linear rather than systemic. Although the move from an affect–trauma model to a topographical model gave an additional role to the child in shaping his or her destiny, this was restricted to fantasy and conceived of in terms of distortions of reality.

On balance, it would be wrong to consider attachment theory as closely related to Freudian theory. There are some points of contact, and Bowlby never denied his intellectual heritage, but his development of Freudian psychoanalysis left far more of the theory behind than it carried forward. But Freud is not the be-all and end-all of psychoanalytic theory. In order to explore points of contact and divergence between psychoanalytic and attachment theories, we have to consider major developments of Freud's theory over the past century.

STRUCTURAL APPROACHES

The North American Structural Approach

Freud's (1923/1961) introduction to the tripartite (or structural) model did not mark the end of the emphasis placed on instincts in his topographical

frame of reference. His sequence of stages of libidinal development remained the cornerstone of his theory until the introduction of ego psychology by Heinz Hartmann (Hartmann, Kris, & Loewenstein, 1946), first in Vienna and then in New York. Hartmann's ideas spread quickly in the postwar psychiatric community of North America. Ego psychology, as it came to be known, detailed the ways in which the ego, oriented toward internal and external adaptations, comes to form a coherently functioning organization that is more complex than the sum of its parts (Hartmann, 1952/1964). Within this framework the ego has a developmental line, with fixation points to which, under pressure, an individual may return (Arlow & Brenner, 1964). Although regressions in the ego are generally considered pathological, Kris (1952) emphasized that they may serve adaptive functions in, for example, artistic or creative sensitivity. Modern structural theorists (see, e.g., Boesky, 1989) retain the notion of the tripartite model but dispense with problematic notions such as psychic energy. They retain the central premise of the ubiquitous nature of intrapsychic conflict (see Brenner, 1982).

Structural theory dominated North American psychoanalysis throughout the development of attachment theory, and attachment theory was treated with considerable hostility by ego psychologists (see below). This might suggest that there are few points of contact between the two theories. This, however, is not the case. I turn first to issues that would have warranted closer collaboration between ego psychologists and attachment theorists, and later explore some possible reasons why such integration proved impossible.

Points of Contact

There are several major figures within the tradition of ego psychology whose contribution to the attachment field (explicit or implicit) should be given serious consideration.

René Spitz (1959) identified how "psychic organizers" such as smiling are linked to underlying advances in the formation of mental structures and herald dramatic shifts in an infant's interpersonal interaction. He ascribed primary importance to the role of the mother and the mother–infant interaction in a theory of developmental stages, and highlighted the role of affect in the development of self-regulation. Spitz saw the mother's emotional expression as at first serving a soothing or containing function, which facilitates the restoration of homeostasis and emotional equilibrium. Later, the infant uses the mother's emotional response as a signaling device to indicate safety. Later still, the affective response is internalized and used as part of the child's own emotional reaction, signaling safety or danger (Emde, 1980). Thus Spitz's views are closely connected to the emphasis placed by modern attachment theorists on emotion regulation as a key developmental function of the attachment system (e.g., Sroufe, 1990).

Edith Jacobson (1964) advanced our understanding of constructs closely linked to attachment theory. Her contributions were critical, although this is rarely acknowledged, in introducing the conceptualization of "images" or representations of self and other as key determinants of mental functioning. She advanced the idea that the infant acquires self and object representations with good (loving) or bad (aggressive) valences, depending on experiences of gratification or frustration with the caretaker. She introduced the term "representation" to stress that this concept refers to the experiential impact of internal and external worlds, and that representations are subject to distortion and modification, regardless of physical reality. Her ideas are clearly closely linked to Bowlby's notion of the IWM and in some ways are more complex and sophisticated. Jacobson substantially altered the climate of psychoanalytic thinking. Her contributions ultimately made way for the attachment theory's frame of reference, although this took several decades. She anticipated many key constructs, particularly that of the representational world.

Erik Erikson (1950, 1959) was the first to expand the problematic erotogenic-zone model of Freud in his surprisingly subtle concept of "organ modes." In 1950 he wrote: "In addition to the overwhelming need for food, a baby is, or soon becomes receptive in many other respects. As he is willing and able to suck on appropriate objects and to swallow whatever appropriate fluids they emit, he is soon also willing and able to 'take in' with his eyes whatever enters his visual field. His tactile senses, too, seem to 'take in' what feels good" (p. 57). In this way he made a critical distinction between drive expression and mode of functioning, which opened up new vistas for the psychoanalytic understanding of human behavior.

The drive expression model binds understanding of social interaction to the gratification of biological needs. The notion of "mode of functioning," on the other hand, frees us to think about characteristic manners of obtaining gratification or relating to objects at particular developmental stages. As Erikson saw it, basic trust is the mode of functioning of the oral stage. He viewed the mouth as the focus of a general approach to life —the incorporative approach. Erikson stressed that through these processes, interpersonal patterns are established that center on the social modality of taking and holding onto objects, both physical and psychic. Erikson defined "basic trust" as a capacity "to receive and accept what is given" (1950, p. 58).

Erikson became interested in the give and take between infant and caregiver in the sharing and dosing of stimuli at about the same time John Bowlby did. Like Bowlby, Erikson saw development as a continuous process, starting within the first few minutes of postnatal experience and extending throughout life, taking different forms at different times. Erikson also shared Bowlby's pioneering lifespan perspective, and his outlook on how "cultures, in various ways, underline and mutualize the child's larger social potentiality" as these gradually become available (Erikson, 1950, p. 86). Erikson's (1950) brilliant insight, far ahead of his time, was in identifying that such microexperiences will eventually become aggregated, leading to "the firm establishment of enduring patterns for the balance of basic trust over basic mistrust . . . [the] amount of trust derived from earliest infantile experience does not seem to depend on absolute quantities of food or demonstrations of love, but rather on the *quality* of the maternal relationship" (1959, p. 63; emphasis in original).

Several similarities between current attachment theory and Erikson's views emerge: (1) the notion of the accumulation of lower-order episodic experiences in higher-order neural structures; (2) broken attachment to the primary caregiver as the opposite pole of whatever is the basis for the continuation of the child's "healthy personality"; (3) the idea that the quality of the maternal relationship determines the sense of trust that mothers create in their children and that then persists throughout life; (4) Erikson's anticipation of the growing interest among attachment theorists in cross-generational cycles of advantage and disadvantage; and (5) the notion of coherence of mental representations as the key to how a trustful or secure pattern of relationships may be transferred across generations.[1] Moreover, (6) Erikson described the transactional nature of these interactions. For example, he wrote that "it is as true to say that babies control and bring up their families as it is to say the converse. A family can bring up a baby only by being brought up by him" (1959, p. 55).

The parameters of care that have been shown to predict infant security could have been drawn from *Childhood and Society*. Maternal sensitivity, Ainsworth's key construct, has been mentioned above. In a footnote, Erikson described the importance of moderate stimulation, which he defined as "a certain ratio between the positive and the negative, which if the balance is towards the positive, will help him to meet later crises with a better chance of unimpaired development" (1950, p. 61, n.). Erikson saw nonintrusiveness of the parent (Malatesta, Grigoryev, Lamb, Albin, & Culver, 1986) as the mother's not trying to control the interaction too much. Interactional synchrony (Isabella & Belsky, 1991) is equivalent to Erikson's description of "reciprocity or mutual regulation" (1950, p. 58).

There are two distinct traditions in the literature on the determinants of attachment, and both can be found in the work of Erikson. Whereas Erikson invariably stressed the importance of individual or interactional factors such as the ones considered above, he was also quick to point out that cultural factors (contextual or ecological factors, in attachment terminology) are also critical. Indeed, cultural differences (as well as similarities) in attachment have been clear from the start (see van IJzendoorn & Sagi, Chapter 31, this volume, and van IJzendoorn, Goldberg, Kroonenberg, & Frenkel, 1992). Erikson also emphasized that the immediate social context of the mother may be critical, and indeed support from the partner (Goldberg & Easterbrooks, 1984) and others in the mother's social environment (Crnic, Greenberg, Ragozin, Robinson, & Basham, 1983) has been shown to be important.[2] This underscores Erikson's point concerning the value of studying environmental influences in the context of the culturally conditioned expectations of the caregivers.

Points of Divergence

So how is it that despite the contributions of Spitz, Jacobson, Erikson, and others, attachment theory did not and could never have emerged from the ego-psychological frame of reference? First of all, the *pseudo*biological character of the ego-psychological model is fundamentally incompatible with the attachment model, which seeks to identify genuine phenomena in biology

in order to achieve concrete reference points for its conceptual framework. Building attachment theory on the structural frame of reference would have required double standards: one taking a metaphorical approach to biological processes, the other treating biological knowledge as providing absolute constraints on theorization. The implausibility of the biological framework for the structural model has been broadly recognized since the 1970s (see, e.g., Klein, 1976).

A related incompatibility rests in the primacy of sexuality in psychoanalytic explanations of psychopathology. Hanley (1978), for example, has asserted that "it is inconceivable for any behavioral system not to come under the influence of the libidinal instinct" (p. 367). Thus early attachment must, by definition in the ego-psychological perspective, be formed as part of psychosexual development in the oral phase. Within classical structural theory, sexuality, although the outcome of earlier developmental phases, is also assumed to undergo qualitative changes during the fourth and fifth years of life, with radical implications for later development and neurotic psychopathology. The primacy of sexuality in explanations of psychopathology has been regarded as a misconception by many psychoanalysts (e.g., Klein, 1980).

A further issue concerns the relative emphasis given to the individual ego in contrast to interpersonal relations. Although Erikson stressed the importance of social agents for the facilitation of psychological development and for the ongoing articulation of the individual ego, his emphasis was not on the social relationship, but rather on the antecedents and consequences of the attainment of self-identity. Like other psychoanalytic developmental theorists (e.g., Mahler, Spitz, Anna Freud, and others), Erikson placed separation–individuation ahead of social involvement. For example, he wrote that "true engagement with the other is the result and test of firm self-delineation" (Erikson, 1968, p. 167). The importance of attachment, as we have seen, is not omitted from Erikson's model but is deemphasized, perhaps as a consequence of his somewhat unidimensional schematization of developmental progression, and his emphasis on self-identity as the emergence of the self as separate and autonomous. The focus of ego psychology is on the individual rather than on the relationship. Identity consolidation is the central goal. Attachment plays a secondary role; it either facilitates identity development or is its by-product. Attachment is relegated to the status of an intermediary link in the process of development toward individuation, which, in its turn, is the precondition of a mature relationship.

Modifications of the Structural Model

There are three major modifications of the structural model, all associated with figures involved in work with children, which have points of contact with attachment theory. The three theorists are (1) Freud's daughter, an originator of child psychoanalysis, Anna Freud; (2) an American analyst, a pioneer of infant observation, Margaret Mahler; and (3) a British colleague of Anna Freud's at Hampstead, Joseph Sandler, who contributed enormously to refining the most commonly used concepts of psychoanalysis.

Anna Freud's Work: Points of Contact and Divergence

Anna Freud was one of the first psychoanalysts to adopt a coherent developmental perspective on psychopathology. Her model (A. Freud, 1965) is both cumulative and epigenetic, with each developmental phase being constructed on the basis of the previous one. She argued that psychological disorder can be most effectively studied in its developmental evolution. She based her theory on the metaphor of developmental lines (A. Freud, 1963), which is similar to Waddington's (1966) metaphor as used by Bowlby. Anna Freud asserted that it is the profile or patterns among these lines of development that best captures the nature of the risk faced by the individual child. The lines, which she described in terms of their respective beginnings and endpoints, include the line from dependency to self-reliance to adult object relations, the line from irresponsibility to responsibility in body management, the line from egocentrism to social partnership, and so forth. Unevenness of development was considered a risk factor, and treatment was seen as incorporating a developmental component (developmental help) to restore the child to the path of normal development (Kennedy & Moran, 1991).

Anna Freud (1963) postulated continuities as the cornerstone of her developmental and epigenetic points of view—continuities in which one layer of psychological attainment leads stepwise to the next. One faulty step leaves a weakness in the structure. This is essentially the same as Bowlby's conceptualization of the growth of personality (Bowlby, 1973, Ch. 22). In practice, Anna Freud's notion of developmental assistance

leads to a powerful, relationship-oriented therapy (Kennedy & Yorke, 1980). Assistance focuses on learning to regulate affect, tolerate social proximity, and understand the psychological aspects of relating to another (Bleiberg, Fonagy, & Target, 1997).

Anna Freud's (1936/1946) early work on ego defenses suggests an alternative frame of reference to the association of patterns of attachment and adult outcomes. Attachment patterns can be seen as mechanisms of defense, mustered by the child to cope with the idiosyncratic styles of interaction of his caregivers (Fonagy, Steele, Steele, & Higgitt, 1992). Patterns of attachment are habitual ways of relating, developed by the ego to minimize anxiety and maximize adaptation. Avoidant attachment, for example, may be rooted in the infant's behavioral strategy of avoidance, evocatively described by Selma Fraiberg (1982). The resistant pattern of attachment, rooted in the resistant, fighting response of the infant (aimed at reducing anxiety by replacing a passive strategy with an active one), may further adaptation by maximizing the chances of eliciting the caregiver's attention. The disorganized pattern can be reformulated as an indication of the relative immaturity of the ego and its inability to muster coherent strategies of response.

This reformulation may be of more than semantic significance. Anna Freud's framework, for example, offers an interesting model of the relationship between attachment classification and psychological disturbance, with the latter only becoming a manifest problem once the mechanisms of defense have proved inadequate to the task of protecting the child from anxiety. Pathology can be seen as the malfunctioning of attachment strategies, rooted in conflict between mutually exclusive strategies, their maladaptive evolution, and their incoherent internal organization. They are neither cause nor consequence, yet they are important as pieces within the complex puzzle of early disruptive behavior. The link between attachment strategies encoded in IWMs and psychopathology may be found in the interrelationship of IWMs.

Notwithstanding these important points of contact, Anna Freud was deeply unsympathetic to the work of attachment theorists. Despite her own observations to the contrary, in her theoretical writings she based the child's early relationship to the mother on sexual instinctual needs. Although she was well aware of unevenness in ego development, she rarely saw this as caused by relationship disturbance. She commonly neglected the influence of the external environment in favor of the vicissitudes of instincts. Even in discussing observations of attachment behavior, she added the theoretical coda (for which she had no observational evidence) that "by means of the constantly repeated experience of satisfaction of the first body needs, the libidinal interest of the child is lured away from exclusive concentration on the happenings in his own body and directed toward those persons in the outside world (the mother or mother substitute) who are responsible for providing satisfaction" (A. Freud & Burlingham, 1944, p. 291).

There is a peculiar disharmony within Anna Freud's work. Her observations were astute, accurate, and innovative. For example, she observed and reported on the significance of attachment relationships in her observational work in the Hampstead War Nurseries (A. Freud, 1941–1945/1974). However, her theory was greatly limited by her conservative use of the drives of the structural model. She was unwilling or unable to abandon what she perceived as the most scientific aspects of her father's contributions.

Margaret Mahler's Work: Points of Contact and Divergence

Mahler's focus was on tracing the growth of the separate self from the unity of "I" and "not-I." "Separation" refers to the child's emergence from a symbiotic fusion with the mother, whereas "individuation" consists of those achievements marking the child's assumption of his or her own individual characteristics (Mahler, Pine, & Bergman, 1975, p. 4). Mahler's model assumes that the child develops from "normal autism" through a symbiotic period to the four sequentially unfolding subphases of the separation–individuation process (Mahler & Furer, 1968). The separation–individuation process is thought to begin at 4 to 5 months of age. In the hatching subphase, the infant begins to differentiate himself or herself from the mother (Mahler et al., 1975). The second subphase, practicing, is discussed further below. The rapprochement subphase is dated from 15–18 to 24 months; there is an awareness of separateness, separation anxiety, and an increased need to be with the mother (Mahler et al., 1975, p. 77). The fourth subphase is the consolidation of individuality and the beginning of emotional object constancy (Mahler et al., 1975, p. 109), which begins in the third

year of life. Mahler's contribution was significant, since it enabled clinicians treating adults to make more accurate reconstructions of the preverbal period, thereby making patients more accessible to psychoanalytic clinical interventions.

Mahler's work is well known to and often cited by attachment theorists, and thus it is not reviewed here in depth. Carlson and Sroufe (1995), in their comprehensive, state-of-the-art chapter, have referred to the practicing subphase (9–17 months) of the separation–individuation process and the infant's tendency to return for "emotional refueling" as clearly analogous to Bowlby's "secure-base" phenomenon. Similarly, Mahler's proposed link between a history of well-regulated relationships with the caregiver and the smooth transition toward more autonomous functioning by the age of 2 is common ground between the two frames of reference (Burland, 1986). Mahler makes clear that it is only with attributes selectively evoked by the mother that the baby establishes a symbiotic dual unity, which is on the way to self–object differentiation and reciprocal object relations (Mahler et al., 1975). These ideas speak to the recently emerging research on the role of the mother's representations of her infant in mediating the relationship between her general state of mind in relation to attachments and her behavior with the specific infant (Slade, Belsky, Aber, & Phelps, in press).

Followers of Mahler have been helpful in elaborating the specific tasks of parenting in the second year of life, which take the field beyond the generic endorsement of sensitivity to be found in the classical attachment literature (Ainsworth, Blehar, Waters, & Wall, 1978). Settlage (1977), for example, identified eight developmental tasks of the rapprochement subphase, including (1) gradual deflation of the sense of omnipotence of the symbiotic unity; (2) compensation for the loss of omnipotence through an increased sense of autonomy; and (3) firming up of the core sense of self. Thus the mother of the infant in the second year must combine emotional availability with a gentle push toward independence. An excessive push toward independence, or its opposite, undermines the child's potential to invest the environment with sufficient interest, and the child's pleasure and confidence in his or her own functioning might be impaired. The caregiver's role in gradually dissolving the manifestations of the attachment bond (e.g., the decreasing need for physical proximity, etc.) is not fully considered by attachment theorists.

The rapprochement subphase is seen by

"Mahlerians" as the critical period of character formation. Its crucial conflict between separateness and closeness, autonomy and dependency, is repeated throughout development—particularly in periods that accompany loss, illness, drug-induced states, and the like (Kramer & Akhtar, 1988). The attachment system seems under particular stress in this subphase, and behaviors associated with anxious attachment are frequently observable in most children. The mother's failure empathetically to support the child during the rapprochement subphase, when the child's ambivalence between autonomy and fusion is at its height, will lead to the collapse of the child's omnipotence, and the enhancement of the self from within (through autonomous activities) will be in jeopardy. Such individuals will therefore have no clear image of themselves or their objects; may wish to avoid or control them; may search for symbiosis with a perfect object; and may have difficulty tolerating ambivalence, criticisms, or setbacks, which challenge their view of the other. Although Bowlby (1973, Ch. 18, particularly p. 265) did not explicitly favor the concept of symbiosis, he seemed to refer to what Mahlerians call "bad symbiosis" when he discussed the inversion of the normal parent–child relationship in reference to phobias in childhood.

There are divergences between Mahler's approach and attachment theory. These are in part epistemological. For example, Mahler was content to define the symbiotic phase largely without reference to behavioral descriptions. According to Mahler, during the first half of the first year, the infant is in a state of primary narcissism; psychic functioning is dominated by the pleasure principle, and the structuralization of the mind into id and ego, self and other, inner and outer has not yet taken place. Evidence from infant research casts considerable doubt on this formulation (Bahrick & Watson, 1985). Gergely (1992) and Stern (1994) both argue that the key feature of these early capacities is the infant's sensitivity to abstract, amodal properties and cross-modal invariances rather than to modality-specific, physical features. Thus the infant seems not to be a concrete experiencer of the physical world, as Mahler assumed, but rather to be biologically prepared for the establishment of early social relationships, as Bowlby suggested.

As we have seen, Mahler emphasized the process of separation–individuation—the gradual distancing of the child from the mother, the transition from dependency to independent functioning. In fact, Mahler extended this to the en-

tire life cycle, which she regarded as constituting a more or less successful process of distancing "from the introjection of the lost symbiotic mother" (Mahler, 1972, p. 130). The establishment of relationships is not a developmental goal in its own right. In Mahler's framework, it is the disengagement from attachment, which is considered the hallmark of progress and the enrichment of the self. Thus, although Mahler considered emotional availability of the caregiver to be essential, she viewed this as a precondition of the separation–individuation process.

There is a further point of divergence. Mahler showed consistent concern with the infant's experience of body boundaries, awareness of body parts, and the development of the body self (Mahler & McDevitt, 1980, p. 403). The critical aspect of the mother–infant relationship in the practicing subphase is the establishment of an experience of contingency in relation to self-initiated physical acts. The mother's support in engendering such an experience of control may be critical to the physical integration of the "I." Mahler thus also saw the development of the representation of the body as a function of the infant–caregiver relationship. Clinical experience with severe personality pathology can strikingly illustrate the ambivalent and chaotic representations some individuals manifest of their own bodies (e.g., self-mutilation, self-starvation). In conduct-disordered and delinquent boys, the disruption of attachment (Bowlby, 1973) is often coupled with a limited capacity to experience ownership over their own bodily actions, which permits interpersonal violence (Fonagy, Target, Steele, & Steele, 1997). In general, Mahler's model is far more enlightening about the nature of aggression than Bowlby's framework is. Parens (1979) pointed out that aggression begins to emerge in the second subphase of separation–individuation, in the service of both separation and individuation. This stance marks a clear departure from Freud's nativist views, as well as perhaps providing a helpful growth point for attachment theory (Fonagy et al., 1997).

Joseph Sandler's Work: Points of Contact and Divergence

Sandler's contributions are qualitatively different from those of Anna Freud and Margaret Mahler. His contribution has been conceptual and systemic rather than content-oriented (Fonagy & Cooper, in press). Like Mahler and Anna Freud, Sandler developed a new theory based on the structural model, which also encompassed the relational framework of British and modern North American analysts (see below). His major contribution has been the restatement of structural theory in representational terms and in the light of observations of child analytic process at the Hampstead Clinic (Sandler & Sandler, 1978). In essence, Sandler has reformulated the structural model of instincts into a model of wishes represented by and acting upon mental representations of role relationships. Sandler has been one of the key figures in the "quiet revolution" that psychoanalysis has undergone during the last 30 years.

Sandler's general approach is fully consistent with the psychological model of attachment theory, in that he attempts to describe how complex representations of self and objects are shaped by everyday affectively laden experiences, fantasies, and memories of the individual alone and in interaction with others. He puts the "shape" metaphor to good use. Identification is the modification of the self-representation to resemble the shape of the object representation. Projection adds unwanted parts of the self-representation to the representation of the other. He attributes a central role to these representations in the causation of behavior (Sandler, 1993). Sandler is more concerned about how representations may be distorted by internal states than by external events, but his formulation can deal with both sets of experiences equally well.

For example, Sandler (see Sandler & Sandler, 1998) has elaborated a model of the two-person interaction in which the direct influence of one on the other is accounted for by the evocation of particular roles in the mind of the other person who is being influenced. The behavior or role of the influencing person is crucial in eliciting a complementary response from the participant. Sandler suggests that in this way infantile and childhood patterns of relationships may be actualized or enacted in adult relationships; he even suggests that all relationships are guided by individuals' needs to explore the "role responsiveness" of the other. Sandler and Sandler (1978) see mother–infant interactions as the context for the earliest formulations of self-representations and object representations, and believe that these interactions provide the basic unit of self-representation. Critically, most psychoanalytic workers since Sandler who have adopted the developmental framework would assume that the cognitive–affective structures of self and other representation regulate children's behavior with their caregivers, and in due course behavior in all significant relationships, including eventually their relationships with their own children. Thus there is little substantive difference between Sandler's formulation and the notion of IWMs.

Sandler's ego-psychological model of the representational world and the suggestions of developmentalists concerning IWMs of attachment relationships may differ in terms of the respective role given to fantasy and drives, but even here they agree in many fundamentals. The framework proposed by Sandler (1985) places an inborn wish to maintain safety at the center of the infant's motivational field, in a manner analogous to Bowlby's (1969) emphasis on the innate propensity for attachment. Sandler's safety concept has reoriented the psychoanalytic theory of motivation. The unique emphasis on instinctual gratification is replaced by the pursuit of a prototypical sense of safety as a unifying goal. It is probable that Sandler and Bowlby were describing analogous ideas. Sandler's description of the "background of safety" may be the phenomenological counterpart of attachment theorists' "secure-base" concept or Sroufe and Waters's (1977) notion of "felt security." The difference between the two approaches may be attributed to their respective points of origin. Bowlby's concern was with the external, whereas Sandler's is with subjective experience.

The strength of Sandler's formulation rests in the clear framework it offers to clinicians. It has coherent implications for the transference–countertransference relationship, which most psychoanalytic clinicians use to guide their work. The motivational system is simplified as well as linked to attachment and other theories. Safety is the experience of the ego not threatened by drive states, moral pressures, the environment, or its own disintegration. Safety as a phenomenal experience arises from the infant–mother relationship (the infant's feeling protected, held at the breast), but then acquires autonomy and comes to organize intrapsychic as well as interpersonal life. The abused child seeks contact with the abusing caregiver because, paradoxically, the predictable, familiar, but adverse experience (which includes a clear representation of the child's role) generates a greater sense of safety than an unfamiliar, nonabusive one (for which the child has no role relationship representations). In psychoanalysis, the past is explored because of the light that it sheds on the developmental origin of representations of role relationships. Outdated, maladaptive schematas are worked through and newer, more adaptive relational models are worked towards. Thus Sandler's model of a structural change is consistent with attachment theory. It is not structures of drives and defenses that are transformed, but rather affectively toned self–other configurations. Sandler's model can be seen as an elaboration of attachment theory from an intrapsychic standpoint.

THE KLEINIAN MODEL

The gap between attachment theory and psychoanalysis has narrowed considerably with the rise of object relations theories in psychoanalysis, one of which was Melanie Klein's (1932/1975). There are several key concepts in the Kleinian model. She saw mental structures as arising out of a variety of internal objects (phantasies about people in the infant's life), which change in character in unconscious phantasy as the child develops from infancy. The infant's phantasies are modified by actual experiences of interaction with the environment. In her work with children, Klein was impressed that the children she analyzed had extremely ruthless sadistic phantasies about which they characteristically felt very guilty and anxious (Spillius, 1994). Klein (1935/1975) assumed that the infant's self is, from the beginning, constantly threatened by destruction from within by the aggressive drive—Freud's death instinct (Freud, 1920/1955).

In the Kleinian model, the human psyche has two basic positions: the paranoid–schizoid (P-S) and the depressive (Klein, 1935/1975). In the P-S position, the relationship to the object (the caregiver) is to a part object, split into a persecutory and idealized relationship, and the ego (the self) is similarly split. In the depressive position, the relation is to an integrated parental image. The individual recognizes his or her destructive wishes toward the object. This brings with it a certain characteristic sadness (hence the term "the depressive position"), but, correspondingly, the ego is more integrated. In the P-S position, the person moves between states of exaggerated perception of goodness (idealization of both self and other) and similarly extreme persecutory perceptions of both self and other as bad. In the early depressive position, primitive envy represents a particularly malignant form of innate aggression (Klein, 1957/1975). This is because unlike other forms of destructiveness, which are turned against *bad* objects already seen as persecutory, envy is hatred directed at the *good* object and arouses a premature expression of depressive anxiety about damage to the good object.

Points of Contact

It is not widely recognized that Bowlby was deeply influenced by Kleinian thought. His training and experience in the British Psychoanalytic Society were predominantly Kleinian. His focus on the first year of life as a crucial determinant of later developmental outcome is of course highly compatible with the Kleinian approach. Many of his ideas (or at least the way he expressed them) were, however, clear reactions against the Kleinian influence prevailing at the time. In a 1981 interview (Holland, 1990), Bowlby described Klein as "inspirational, the antithesis of what I try to be" (p. 135). He considered her to be "totally unaware of the scientific method." Thus Bowlby completely rejected his Kleinian heritage. Nevertheless, there is something to be gained from reexamining Kleinian and neo-Kleinian ideas in relation to attachment theory.

First, one may consider whether there might be a significant overlap between the dichotomies of the P-S and depressive positions and of security and insecurity in infant–mother attachment. According to Klein, the two positions alternate, but in particular individuals one may predominate over the other, suggesting that the depressive position may be associated with attachment security while the P-S position shares characteristics with attachment insecurity.

1. A key marker of the P-S position is "splitting"—the attribution of all goodness and love to an idealized object, and all pain, distress, and badness to a persecutory one (Klein, 1932/1975). Splitting, brilliantly operationalized as semantic–episodic memory discrepancy, is an important marker of insecurity (particularly the dismissing category) in Main and Goldwyn's system for coding Adult Attachment Interview (AAI) narratives (Main & Goldwyn, 1995). Good is experienced as rapidly turning into bad; the bad gets worse and the good becomes increasingly idealized.

2. By contrast, the depressive position is thought to be marked by the infant's capacity to see the mother as a whole person, the cause of both good and bad experiences (Klein, 1935/1975). The operationalization of security in an attachment history narrative seems to pull for a balance between love and hate—the recognition

and acceptance of imperfection in the caregiver.

3. Kleinian theory holds that the psychic pain associated with the integration of the split (good and bad) part objects may be so great that the infant may resort to massive (manic) denial, obsessional reparation, or contempt. Once more, the AAI coding scheme is specifically keyed to identify narratives marked by derogation (contempt), incapacity to recall (denial), or idealization (manic reparation) as insecure.

4. Segal (1957) linked the capacity for symbolization and sublimation to depressive reparation. AAI coding is strongly oriented toward the analysis of speech and discourse, with individuals who manifest secure states of mind in relation to attachment showing substantially greater competence in this domain.

5. Spillius (1992) has suggested that the depressive position may be initiated by the child's attribution of an "intentional stance" (perception of him or her as thinking and feeling) to the caregiver. Elsewhere, my colleagues and I have suggested that "mentalizing" (or "reflective capacity")—the ability coherently to describe the actions of one's caregivers and one's own actions in mental state terms—may be crucial in the assessment of attachment security in the AAI (Fonagy, Steele, Moran, Steele, & Higgitt, 1991).

Kleinian commentary on infant mental states overlaps with the classification of adult attachment narratives. It might be argued that as Klein's observations were of older children and adults, she was describing the *sequelae* of insecure infantile attachment based on the narratives of these patients. Her description of the P-S position may well be considered by attachment theorists as a relatively apt portrayal of an insecure adult state of mind with respect to attachment. Indeed, it would be a great deal more difficult to attempt to identify P-S features in the behavior of insecure infants in the strange situation. Perhaps Bowlby's dissatisfaction with the Kleinian perspective was rooted in part in the attempted "adultomorphization" of the fictional and metaphorical infants of early Kleinian theory. The Kleinian perspective highlights an approach to attachment security as a mode of mental functioning that can involve rapid cycling between "secure" and "insecure" modes. The frequency of such cycles is the stable personal attribute, not the class or category that best fits the individual at any time point.

A second point of contact is the notion of projective identification. Klein (1957/1975) portrayed projective identification as an unconscious infantile phantasy by which an infant is able to relocate persecutory experiences by separating (splitting) them from the self-representation and making them part of the image of a particular object. It is assumed that disowned unconscious feelings of rage or shame are firmly believed by the child to exist within the mother. By acting in subtle but influential ways, the child may achieve a confirming reaction of criticism or even persecution. A phantasy of magical control over an object may be achieved in this way. Thus projective identification is not a truly internal process; it involves the object, who may experience it as manipulation, seduction, or a myriad of other forms of psychic influence. Spillius (1994) has suggested the use of the term "evocatory projective identification" to designate instances in which the recipient of projective identification is put under pressure to have the feelings appropriate to the projector's phantasy.

The relationship of projective identification and attachment is undoubtedly complex. Here I would like to draw attention to only one interesting feature. The disorganized attachment pattern in infancy (Main & Solomon, 1990) manifests itself as controlling behavior in the preschool years (Cassidy, Marvin, & The MacArthur Working Group on Attachment, 1989) and the early school years (Main & Cassidy, 1988). Such children appear to take control of the relationship, sometimes treating their parents in an apparently condescending or humiliating manner. Although explanations for such behavioral discontinuity may be offered in terms other than those of projective identification, the background of such children makes an account in terms of pathological projective identification more likely. Disorganized attachment organization has been shown to be associated with parental experience of unresolved trauma (Main & Hesse, 1990), infant histories of maltreatment (Carlson, Cicchetti, Barnett, & Braunwald, 1989), maternal depression (Radke-Yarrow, Cummings, Kuczynski, & Chapman, 1985), and prenatal parental drug and alcohol abuse (O'Connor, Sigman, & Brill, 1987; Rodning, Beckwith, & Howard, 1991). It is likely that children exposed to such deprivation are repeatedly confronted with intolerable levels of confusing and hostile caregiving, and are forced to internalize aspects of their caregivers that they are incapable of integrating. Their self-structure is thus formed around a fragmented and flawed image, which they are forced to externalize in order to retain any measure of coherence. The process of projective identification fits the behavioral description of these children as attempting to experience themselves as coherent selves and to force these alien, unassimilable parts of themselves into another. They maintain the illusion that these parts are now outside through subtle manipulative control of the other's behavior (Fonagy & Target, 1997).

A further point of contact concerns the distinction between the dismissing and preoccupied patterns of adult attachment and Rosenfeld's Kleinian developmental model of narcissism. Rosenfeld (1971/1988) described narcissistic states as characterized by omnipotent object relations and defenses that deny the identity and separateness of the object. He distinguished between "thin-skinned" and "thick-skinned" narcissism, and his description closely matches the preoccupied and dismissing AAI categories, respectively (Main & Goldwyn, 1995). In the case of "thick-skinned" narcissism, Rosenfeld assumed that with the assistance of projective identificatory processes, the individual deposits his or her own perceived inadequacies in others, whom he or she can then dismiss, denigrate, and devalue. In the case of "thin-skinned" narcissism, Rosenfeld assumed that the patient's dependency causes him or her to feel intolerable vulnerability to the other, which the patient attempts to ward off through continuous, unprovoked angry attacks on those whose dependability appears to mock his or her own feelings of helplessness and defectiveness. This description fits the angry/resentful subcategory of the preoccupied classification. The former description points to the dismissing classification, where the individual denies the value of the caregivers, or his or her need of them.

This analogy may be of relevance beyond the level of description. A number of clinicians note the interchangeability of the "thin-skinned" and "thick-skinned" patterns (e.g., Bateman, 1996). This should alert attachment theorists to the possibility of a lack of stability in this aspect of the classification in particular individuals who score at extreme levels. Alternatively, Rosenfeld's and similar psychoanalytic concepts may be helpful in the elaboration of the "cannot classify" category of the AAI (Main & Goldwyn, in press), where a mixture of narrative styles precludes the unambiguous assignment of either a dismissing or a preoccupied classification.

Points of Divergence

One of Bowlby's central objections to Kleinian psychoanalytic theory was to its neglect of actual experience and the assumption that the child's anxieties arise predominantly from constitutional tendencies (Klein, 1936/1964). The criticism is less apt in the case of post-Kleinian psychoanalysts, who have been quite successful at integrating environmental accounts with her ideas (e.g., Rosenfeld, 1965). The child's capacity to cope with the pain and anxiety of the depressive position, seeing himself or herself as destructive and envious, is also attributed to external as well as constitutional factors.

Notwithstanding this increased respect for the external environment, at present there is not room in attachment theory for a concept such as the death instinct. Kleinian ideas continue to pivot around the innate destructiveness of the human infant. In truth, the concept may not be as critical to Kleinian theory as it is often supposed to be (see Parens, 1979). Envy may be triggered by frustration or inconsistent mothering or the child's inadequate capacity to appreciate time and space. However, aggression may not be inevitably linked to deprivation. The child may resent the inevitable limitations of maternal care, find it hard to tolerate the mother's control, and prefer to destroy it rather than experience frustration (envy). Attachment theory could explore in greater depth the constitutional variability among infants, some of whom may indeed be genetically predisposed to violent responses (e.g., Reiss et al., 1995) that could interfere with the establishment of secure attachment, regardless of their caregivers' sensitivity.

Finally, the concept of "positions" to describe a dimension at least analogous to the security–insecurity dimension highlights the nondeterministic nature of the developmental processes that may underlie quality of attachment. Attachment researchers have produced impressive data demonstrating the stability of individual differences predicted by infant–caregiver classification. This can be readily understood in terms of underlying differences in basic mechanisms such as emotion regulation, which are likely to provide continuity for patterns of behavior. An alternative explanation, of course, may be couched in terms of the continuity of environmental characteristics (Lamb, 1987). Kleinian theory highlights yet another possibility. Kleinian psychoanalysts consider the term "position" as implying a particular constellation of object relationships, phantasies, anxieties, and defenses to which an individual is likely to return throughout life. Specific environments may trigger a P-S or a depressive reaction, an insecure or a secure relationship pattern. The infant can develop secure or insecure relationships with different caregivers (Steele, Steele, & Fonagy, 1996). Consequently, we have to assume the concurrent presence of several, perhaps both secure and insecure, IWMs in the child's mind. Which one becomes dominant for the adult may depend on the importance of the specific caregiver in the child's life. Thus the notion of alterations of IWMs, in much the same way that Kleinians envisioned the oscillation of positions, is at least a theoretical possibility.

Inspiring though Kleinian ideas may be to some, there is no getting away from the "fuzziness" of Kleinian descriptions. On the one hand, the Kleinian emphasis on "phantasy" as the building block of mental structure transcends the gap between the experiential and nonexperiential aspects of mental functioning and moves mental structuralization to the experiential realm. This has the advantage of providing experience-nearness and ridding the theory of much reified pseudoscientific terminology. On the other hand, this creates an unbridgeable gulf between it and the attachment theory approach, which is committed to pursuing questions about the nature of the mechanisms underpinning mental functions.

THE INDEPENDENT SCHOOL OF BRITISH PSYCHOANALYSIS

Unlike the other psychoanalytic orientations, the British school should not be considered a unified approach. Fairbairn (1954) was perhaps the key theoretician. Winnicott (1958a, 1971), Balint (1959), and Kahn (1978/1983) may be considered some of the key contributors. These workers did not subscribe to a single coherent framework; hence, their usual collective description as "the Independents" is probably highly appropriate (see Rayner, 1991).

The Independents abandoned the structural model and developed a "self–object" theory in which parts of the self are in dynamic interaction with each other and with complementary internal and external objects. Self and affect become crucial agents of motivation, and for Fairbairn (1954), there is no emotion without the self and no self without emotion. Winnicott (1958a) postulated an inherent desire to develop a sense of self—a desire that can be hidden or falsified.

Fairbairn (1954) asserted that the basic striving is not for pleasure but for a relationship. Pleasure and anxiety reduction follow the attainment of a desired relationship between self and other. There was a further important shift away from unconscious contents and repression and toward the notion of incompatible ideas. Fairbairn suggested that the loss of optimal intimacy will give rise to "splitting" in the ego, and that these conflicting multiple self-object systems are the developmental roots of psychopathology.

Winnicott (1965e) contributed most constructively toward providing a developmental description of the origins of the self in the infant–caregiver relationship. He saw the child as evolving from a unity of mother and infant. Three functions of this unity facilitate healthy development: (1) holding, leading to integration of sensorimotor elements; (2) handling, facilitating personalization (autonomy); and (3) object relating, resulting in the establishment of a human relationship (Winnicott, 1962/1965b). The mother's primary maternal preoccupation of heightened sensitivity to her own self, her body, and the baby offers the infant the illusion that the mother responds accurately to his or her gesture because she is the infant's own creation (i.e., a part of him or her).

In contrast to Winnicott, who assumed no idyllic phase in early childhood, Balint (1965) proposed that a desire to be loved is a primary form of love. Balint conceived of this as a lack of differentiatedness felt toward early objects who do not frustrate the infant. A disruption of this state leads to a basic fault, a profound misordering of which the individual is conscious throughout life.

Points of Contact

Attachment theory has its psychoanalytic roots in the work of British analysts from the Independent school. What is described as "attachment" in Bowlby's (1969/1982) terms is "primary love" in Balint's (1965) terms, "object seeking" in Fairbairn's (1952), "ego relatedness" in Winnicott's (1965e), and "personal relations" in Guntrip's (1961). This is explicit in Bowlby's acknowledgments of these analysts, even though he felt that he had moved beyond them by establishing a firm biological and evolutionary basis for object relations theory. Points of contact between attachment theory and the object relations theories of Fairbairn and Winnicott have been extensively and imaginatively reviewed by Sroufe (1986),

Eagle (1995), and Holmes (1993), among others. Here I focus only on certain specific issues less well covered in these reviews.

Bowlby was influenced by Balint's (1952) concept of primary object relations, but he used it chiefly to add weight to his emphasis on non-oral components of the early need for the object. Balint (1959) identified two characteristic defenses in the child's management of anxiety: One is to love and even to be intensely dependent upon the newly emerging objects (the "oc-nophilic attitude"); the other is to dislike attachments to others, but to love the spaces between them (the "philobatic attitude"). Instead of investing in objects, the philobat is thought to invest in his or her own ego skills. Balint's description is perhaps the clearest statement of the match between analytic accounts of narcissism and a dismissing attachment pattern. The philo-batic attitude is a metaphoric statement of an avoidant, dismissing pattern, while the description of its counterpart fits the resistant, preoccupied one.

A first point of contact is between attachment theory and Winnicott's ideas about sensitive caregiving. For Winnicott, the mother has to be "good enough," but her failure is expectable and is in fact the major motivator of growth. This is consistent with the observation of attachment researchers that moderate degrees of maternal involvement are preferable to highly contingent responses (Malatesta, Culver, Tesman, & Shepard, 1989). Moderate levels of acceptance (Murphy & Moriarty, 1976) and maternal involvement (Belsky, Rovine, & Taylor, 1984) are more beneficial to growth than perfect matching. But Winnicott also stressed that the baby must not be challenged too soon or too intensely about the mother's "realness" (her independence as a person). This would force the infant to negotiate the "me and the not-me" distinction before acquiring sufficient experiences of being omnipotent to form the ego nuclei, which will in time become integrated in the real experience of the "I" (the true self). Insensitive parenting may have more powerful effects where the child's ego needs are not met. Where the child's knowing, as opposed to willing, is impinged upon or confused, this may lead to disintegration, disorientation, withdrawal, and a sense of annihilation—a fragmentation of the line of continuity of being. Measurement of sensitivity could be sharpened if Winnicott's distinction between willing and knowing were to be subjected to separate measurement.

The holding environment provides the setting for the fusion of aggression and love, which prepares the way for the toleration of ambivalence and the emergence of concern, as well as the acceptance of responsibility (Winnicott, 1963a/ 1965e). An analogous idea concerning the role of the mother's contribution to the development of the infant's sense of self through the understanding and processing of the infant's negative emotional states was suggested by Wilfred Bion from a Kleinian perspective in his concept of the mother's "containing function" (Bion, 1962). Relatedness is born of the experience of being allowed to be alone in the presence of somebody else (Winnicott, 1971). For the infant to be able to be alone, a sense of safety must be associated with experiencing the inner world. For the infant to learn about and represent the experience of distress, it must be met by a combination of external feedback (e.g., the mother's face and tone) that "explains" to the infant what he or she is feeling (Gergely & Watson, 1996) and a simultaneous communication of having coped with the distress (Fonagy et al., 1995). The secure mother (or other caregiver) may be thought to soothe by combining a resonant response with an affect display incompatible with that of the child. If secure attachment is the outcome of a sense of safety associated with experiencing the inner world, insecure attachment may be the consequence of the mother's manifest defensive behavior in this regard. A dismissing mother may altogether fail to mirror the child's distress because of the painful experiences this evokes for her, or because she lacks the capacity to create a coherent image of the child's mental state. By contrast, the preoccupied mother may represent the infant's internal experience with excessive clarity, or the response may be complicated by the mother's ambivalent preoccupation with her own experience at the expense of communicating coping, and the child's opportunity to "experience" his or her inner world safely is lost.

Winnicott further pointed to the importance of the infant's opportunity to generate spontaneous creative gestures. Winnicott considered sucking the thumb or smiling after a good feeding to be creative gestures, because they are within the infant's control. Sensitive caregiving must therefore actively lend coherence to the physical body of the infant by acknowledging the goal-orientedness of his or her physical being.[3] If handled satisfactorily, the infant looks at the mother's face rather than her breast. When the infant overcomes his or her preoccupation with physical needs, his or her concerns with mind and meaning can develop.

The natural evolution of the self occurs when individuals who look after the child do not unnecessarily impinge on the infant by substituting their own impulses while curtailing or redirecting the infant's creative gestures. The caregivers need to maintain or restore their own sense of well-being before they can act as tension regulators for the infant. This is Winnicott's perspective on the transcultural transmission of attachment security (van IJzendoorn, 1995).

A second major facet of Winnicott's (1963d/1965e) theory relevant to attachment theory concerns environmental failure and the infant's reaction to it. On the one hand, internal and external impingements and the lack of a holding environment can lead to aggression and antisocial behavior. This is characterized by the use of physical action as self-expression, a lack of concern for the other, and a definition of the self in opposition to the environment. On the other hand, external impingement and the substitution of the gestures of the other for the gestures of the self engenders a "false self" (Winnicott, 1960a/1965e), which appears real, performs and complies, and may be true in highly selected aspects or based on wholesale identification with the object. In either case, notwithstanding the superficially convincing nature of such a presentation, the self put forward by such individuals is fragile, vulnerable, and phenomenologically empty.

From the point of view of attachment theory, the two categories of environmental failure may be seen as alternative coping strategies to deal with insensitive caretaking (impingement). Insensitive caregiving limits the child's developing capacity to envision mental states in self and other (Fonagy & Target, 1997). The developmental failure is different, however. The aggressive, antisocial pattern may be linked to the defensive inhibition of mentalizing capacity, leading to highly abnormal patterns of social interaction (Fonagy, 1991). A false self appears not to be inconsistent with mentalization. My colleagues and I would maintain that this kind of mentalization, as Winnicott suggested, is not genuine. Such individuals have been able to come to an understanding of intentionality in their caregivers, but have achieved this at the expense of self-understanding. They defensively separate mentalization from the actual state of the self. As a consequence, their mentalization may appear "hyperactive"—an intense but ultimately fruitless pursuit of psychological understanding.

Even when accurate, the products of such efforts feel shallow and empty and do not influence behavior.

Points of Divergence

The attachment theory account of the repetition of early patterns of behavior in later life is primarily cognitive, explained in terms of the influence of the IWM. The object relations account of the persistence of early structures is more dynamic. Fairbairn (1952) proposed that there is a "devotion" or "obstinate attachment" to certain early perceptions of the object (p. 117). To adopt new modes of relating might involve a betrayal of the early relationship, which is impeded by attendant guilt (Eagle, 1997) and the terror of an empty, objectless world where no relationship is available. Thus, in Fairbairn's view, repetition is motivated by the avoidance of guilt and avoidance of the terror of emptiness.

Winnicott's theory, like attachment theory, makes the self the focus of the psychology of the mind: Representations of self and objects are seen as intertwined and reciprocally influencing agents; relationships are construed as organized to safeguard self-structures; and so forth. However, in relation to the holding environment, Winnicott (1962b/1965e) assumed that this interpretation of the notion of sensitive caretaking shields the infant from unbearable mental experience—unthinkable, primitive, or archaic anxiety in the vulnerable process of moving from an unintegrated to an integrated state. Such extravagant speculations about the internal state of the infant are not consistent with attachment theory. It is also important to note that for Winnicott, who was strongly influenced by Klein and Bion, the infant's predisposition has a highly significant role in determining the nature of the mother–infant relationship. Thus maternal care is not the only determinant of the holding environment. The balance within the baby himself or herself—the initial balance with which the infant starts life—contributes to the likely success of maternal care. Perhaps there is a greater role for temperament in Winnicott's theory than in Bowlby's. Winnicott (1960a) was more deeply rooted in instinct theory than is generally realized. The "good enough" mother does not simply give meaning to behavior, but permits the child's spontaneous expression of a need or impulse. Mothers who are not good enough communicate that such impulses are dangerous. Thus Winnicott, unlike Bowlby, did not consider relationships to be independent from instincts. Furthermore, Winnicott's focus was on the mother as the "root" of all the child's potential difficulties. In attachment theory, many other sources of "impingements" from the external environment are contemplated. The descriptions of infancy by the British Independent analysts all suffer from "mother-centrism," which can easily give rise to mother blaming.

NORTH AMERICAN OBJECT RELATIONS THEORISTS AND ATTACHMENT THEORY

British object relations theory has influenced North American psychoanalysis over the last 30 years. In some cases (such as the Kleinian influence on Kernberg), this has been openly acknowledged. In others (such as Winnicott's influence on Kohut), it has been left for the reader to discover. Here I consider only three of the major North American object relations theorists from the point of view of attachment theory: Heinz Kohut, Otto Kernberg, and Daniel Stern.

Heinz Kohut

Whatever one might think of the adequacy of his theories, there can be no doubt that Kohut revolutionized North American psychoanalysis. He broke the iron grip of ego psychology by forcing psychoanalysts to think in less mechanistic terms—in terms of selfhood rather than psychological function, in terms of "selfobjects" rather than the drive gratification provided by the object.

Kohut (1971, 1977; Kohut & Wolf, 1978) made the innovative suggestion that the development of narcissism (originally self-love or self-esteem) has its own developmental path, and that caregiving individuals (objects) serve special functions along this line of development as selfobjects. A selfobject functions to evoke the experience of selfhood. Empathic responses from the selfobject facilitate the unfolding of the infantile grandiosity and encourage feelings of omnipotence, which enable the building of an idealized image of the parent with whom the child wishes to merge. "Transmuting internalization of the mirroring function" leads gradually to a consolidation of the nuclear self (Kohut & Wolf, 1978, pp. 414–416). The idealization of the selfobject leads to the development of ideals. At the opposite pole of this "bipolar self" is a representation

of natural talents gained through the mirroring function. Selfobjects continue to be needed throughout life, to some degree, to sustain self-cohesion (Kohut, 1984). They are experienced as part of oneself, serving to maintain the self's organization, while objects can become targets of desires once the self-concept is sufficiently demarcated.

Points of Contact

Kohut's self psychology relies on the notion of attachment as a central motivation of the self for the establishment and maintenance of self-cohesiveness (Shane, Shane, & Gales, 1997). Consistent with the suggestion of Bowlby, Kohut replaced the dual drives of classical analysis with a relational construct. Like Winnicott, Kohut linked self-development to mirroring or maternal sensitivity. Like attachment theorists, he reversed the relationship of drives and self-structure, regarding the self as superordinate and drive conflicts as indications of "an enfeebled self" (Kohut, 1977). For example, he characterized the Oedipus complex as the child's reaction to the parent's failure to enjoy and participate empathically in the child's growth. Unempathic parents are likely to react to their Oedipal child with counterhostility or counterseduction. Such reactions may stimulate destructive aggression and isolated sexual fixation. Kohut identified castration anxiety and penis envy, as Bowlby might have been inclined to do, as imposed from outside rather than being the consequence of a constitutional predisposition to Oedipal experiences.

Kohut specified some aspects of the IWM associated with insensitive caregiving. When parents fail to provide for the child's narcissistic needs, the representation of the self as omnipotent and the representation of the caregiver as perfect become "hardened" and will not be integrated into later structures. They continue to exist within the individual's representational world and cause disturbances of interpersonal relationships, as well as dysfunctional self-representations. For example, the grandiose self may pose a threat to the self-organization.

Kohut's view of narcissism (Kohut & Wolf, 1978), the most influential of his propositions, is closely linked to attachment constructs. He suggested that primary infantile narcissism is impinged upon by disappointment in the caregivers, which is then fended off by the "normal" grandiose self. The grandiose self can be gradually neutralized by age-specific mirroring responses of the caregivers, but if a parent is unempathic or insensitive, the idealized but faulty parental image will be internalized in place of the representation of the child's own capacities. In attachment theory terms, the child's IWM will be a dual one—one component containing a set of omnipotent expectations, based on the child's view of the parent's capacities mixed with infantile omnipotence; the other component portraying total helplessness and enfeeblement, the expectations of an infant facing an unempathic caregiver. Kohut (1972) showed how injured narcissism may call forth rage to protect the self, together with fantasies of grandiosity, in order to cover a sense of infantile vulnerability.

Points of Divergence

Unlike attachment theorists, Kohut viewed cohesion of the self as the primary motivation guiding human behavior rather than as a biologically predefined relationship pattern. He separated anxiety about object loss from anxiety about disintegration of the self. At the root of anxiety for Kohut is the self's experience of a defect, a lack of cohesiveness and lack of continuity in the sense of self. This subtle but important shift of emphasis relegates the importance of the attachment figure to second place. Related to this is Kohut's apparent lack of interest in aspects of functioning other than the individual's relation to his or her own grandiosity and exhibitionism—a lack of consideration for the capacity for intimacy, mutuality, and reciprocity in interpersonal relations.

The concept of self as used by Kohut is in fact somewhat alien to the attachment theory approach. Using the concept as a superordinate structure with a mental apparatus runs into the same problems of mechanistic thinking and reification that, as has been noted, hindered ego psychology (Stolorow, Brandchaft, & Atwood, 1987). Although Kohut presented the self in representational terms, he ascribed to it motivational properties and tendencies, such as goals, plans, and self-esteem motivation (Kohut, 1971). Thus the self comes to denote almost all of personality and thereby becomes a superfluous term.

It is difficult to identify within attachment theory a concept analogous to grandiosity or omnipotence as naturally occurring in infant development. The notion of infantile omnipotence is certainly challenged by findings indicating that on the majority of occasions the infant is not able to elicit synchronous (mirroring) behavior from the mother (Gianino & Tronick, 1988). Although infants undoubtedly enjoy experiences of mastery (DeCasper & Carstens, 1981), there is no evidence that this leads to a sense of omnipotence. It seems far more likely that we are encountering again a central limitation of psychoanalytic thinking. This is the description of infant behavior in terms of adultomorphic constructs—the very problem Bowlby's entire theoretical work aimed to address.

Otto Kernberg

Kernberg is the most frequently cited living psychoanalyst. His preeminent position is an indication of the remarkable coherence he has achieved in creating a structural object relations theory (Kernberg, 1976). In Kernberg's theory, affects serve as the primary motivational system (Kernberg, 1982). He proposes that psychic structure is made up of combinations of (1) self-representations, (2) object representations, and (3) an affect state linking them (which also defines a relationship). Representations are of the self and object linked by a dominant affect state. He accepts the existence of drives in the mature child and adult, but sees these as the products rather than the motivators of development. He treats them as hypothetical constructs that come to be organized from congruent affect states around the theme of sexuality and aggression if a normal developmental path has been followed. Drives manifest themselves in mental representations as emotional experience. The major psychic structures (id, ego, and superego) are also hypothetical constructs that refer to groupings of self–object relationships under the influence of specific emotional states. Self–object relations are internalized relationship experiences colored by the prevailing affective states. For example, the superego may be harsh because the affect state prevailing at the time was one of anger and criticism.

Points of Contact

There are fewer key points of contact between Kernberg and Bowlby and other attachment theorists than one might expect, given their common respect for the empiricist tradition. Kernberg's (1984) model of neurotic pathology uses a version of the IWM concept. Individuals with high levels of personality organization are considered to be able to integrate positive and negative representations of self and others. These evolved through childhood phases in which good and bad representations of self and others were combined across affective valences, and representations containing both loving and hostile elements were formed. Kernberg regards these representations as influential in governing future object relationships. Even relatively well-integrated representations contain units that reflect a defensive or impulsive aspect of conflict. Anxiety, characteristic of neurotic pathology, is likely to arise when representations of self and objects are highly charged affectively but are poorly differentiated. For example, the self may be represented as weak and vulnerable, and the object as ruthless and domineering. The prevalent affective tone may be violent and hostile. When this configuration is activated in a social situation, the individual may become highly anxious. The main difference from an IWM formulation is that Kernberg assumes that the manifest IWM may be a defense against an underlying painful internal representation of relationships in which the original source of hostility was the self.

Even more severe disturbances of IWM functioning may be found in borderline personality organizations (Kernberg, 1987). Here the self–object–affect triads are thought to be dramatically lacking in integration. The consequences are profound splitting, impulsivity, lack of empathy, and unmodulated expression of sexuality and aggression. The underlying cause relates closely to Kleinian formulations of primitive object representations. The units of psychic structure are based not on genuine internalizations of self–other relationships, but rather on so-called "part-object" representations originating in states of mind (P-S positions) in which the representation of the entire person was beyond the capacity of the individual. Instead of the more readily comprehensible, relatively realistic relationship patterns of neurotic personalities, Kernberg identifies highly unrealistic, sharply idealized, or persecutory representations of self and objects. These part representations can never be traced back into the past because they never actually existed in this form. They represent a specific, small fragment of an actual person, experienced at a moment characterized by overwhelming and diffuse affect (positive or negative, depending on the affective valance of the part-object representation). Of course, disorganized attachment, with accompanying inadequate affect regulation, is bound to increase the likelihood of forming such part-object representations.

Because object relations are poorly integrated, the reversals and enactments of representations of the self and others are likely to be extremely frequent and rapid. Relationships with such individuals will be correspondingly confusing and even chaotic. There is evidence from AAI studies of borderline patients of exactly such confusing internal representations of attachment (Fonagy et al., 1996; Patrick, Hobson, Castle, Howard, & Maughan, 1994). Thus Kernberg's formulation of borderline pathology, translated into attachment theory language, might be that it is the activation of poorly structured, highly distorted unstable IWMs with loose assignments of object and subject. Kernberg's criteria for borderline personality disorder include a diffuse sense of identity, which may be the consequence of a disintegrated system of models of relationship representations.

Points of Divergence

Kernberg (unlike attachment theorists and other object relations theorists) does not privilege early experience. In fact, there is little in attachment theory that might preclude giving weight to later experience; the focus on infancy may be a carryover from the ethological concept of critical periods, or even a historical artifact of the relatively slow progress in developing preschool and middle-childhood attachment measures (Goldberg, 1995). Kernberg's determination to maintain dialogue with the North American psychoanalytic community obliges him to retain the notions of drives and psychic agencies. These have no place in an attachment theory framework. It should be noted that in contrast to other psychoanalytic writers, for Kernberg these are hypothetical constructs, not biological givens. They are the products of development and integration.

Kernberg (1976) has directly criticized Bowlby for not taking account of "the internal world" and for neglecting "instinct as intra-psychic developments and internalized object relations as major structural organizers of psychic reality" (p. 121). This is undoubtedly an unwarranted criticism, particularly in the light of Bowlby's emphasis on such constructs as the IWM (see, e.g., Ch. 17 of Bowlby, 1969/1982). It would be more accurate to say that Bowlby's conceptualization of the internal world is different from Kernberg's. It is interesting that Kernberg makes no reference in this section to Bowlby's later book (Bowlby, 1973). He is also silent about Bowlby's restatement of the psychoanalytic concept of the internal world in terms of "environmental and organismic models" (Bowlby, 1969/ 1982, p. 82).

More substantive discrepancies exist. For example, in Kernberg's model (Kernberg, 1977), the root cause of borderline states is the intensity of destructive and aggressive impulses, coupled with a relative weakness of the ego structures available to handle them. He sees this as presenting a constant threat to the good introject, thus forcing the individual to use "primitive" defenses (splitting) in an attempt to separate contradictory images of self and other. As we have seen, the notion of an aggressive predisposition in the infant is not currently part of attachment theory. A more standard formulation might be one proposed by Shaw, Owens, Vondra, Keenan, and Winslow (1996). Here infant temperament and negative parental reaction are seen as leading to avoidant attachment, which in its turn may bring about maternal withdrawal, further aggressive attention seeking, impulsive and unsystematic disciplinary practices, oppositional behavior, and ultimately aggression. The assumption of high levels of innate aggression is clearly reductionist, and it simply short-circuits the more sophisticated transactional developmental model.

Daniel Stern

Daniel Stern occupies a unique place in psychoanalysis (Stern, 1985). He has been able to bridge the gulf between developmentalists and psychoanalysts in a highly successful and productive way. His primary concern is with the development of self structure. He distinguishes four stages of early formation of the self: (1) The sense of emergent self (0–2 months) involves the process of the self's coming into being and forming initial connections; (2) the sense of core self and the domain of core relatedness (2–6 months) are based on the single organizing subjective perspective and a coherent physical self; (3) the sense of subjective self and the domain of intersubjective relatedness (7–15 months) emerge with the discovery of subjective mental states beyond physical events; and (4) the sense of verbal self forms after 15 months.

Points of Contact

Stern (1985, 1994) distinguishes three types of relationships of self-with-other: self–other complementing, state sharing, and state transforming. Although these relationships can be characterized by the degree of attachment or separateness they imply, it is their contribution to the structuralization of the self through the schematization of experience that interests Stern. He takes the concept of relationship beyond the meaning ascribed to it by the separation theories, which view the self–other relationship as a means toward the development of a sense of the self as separate, as well as beyond the meaning ascribed to the relationship by attachment theories, which consider the relationship a goal.

Stern's most important point of contact with attachment theory is probably in the elaboration of the IWM (Stern, 1994). In particular, he has elaborated the concept of the representational world. His starting point is the "emerging moment," which is the subjective integration of all aspects of lived experience. The "moment" takes its input from emotions, behaviors, sensations, and all other aspects of the internal and external world from schematic representations of various types (e.g., event representations, semantic representations or conceptual schemas, perceptual schemas, and sensorimotor representations). He adds to these two further modes of representations: "feeling shapes" and "proto-narrative envelopes." These schemas form a network, which he terms "the schema of a-way-of-being-with."

The "schema of a-way-of-being-with" is conceptualized by Stern (1998) from the assumed subjective perspective of the infant in interaction with the caregiver. The infant organizes his or her experience around a motive and a goal. The goals are not only biological, but include object relatedness (cf. Fairbairn), affect states (cf. Kernberg), states of self-esteem (cf. Kohut), and safety (cf. Sandler), as well as the gratification of physical needs, whether hunger, thirst, sexuality, or aggression (cf. Freud's structural model). The representation includes a proto-plot with an agent, an action, an instrumentality, and a context—all essential elements in the understanding of human behavior (see Bruner, 1990). Stern's theory elaborates Winnicott's (1971). Attunement satisfies the infant's need for omnipotence, while the caregiver's capacity to accept protest without retaliation or anxiety satisfies the child's needs to have confidence in the caregiver as resilient to the infant's attacks.

The schemas of ways-of-being-with come closest to providing a neuropsychologically valid model of the representation of interpersonal experience. Certain features of the model are critical in this regard: (1) These schemas are emergent properties of the nervous system and the mind; (2) they make use of multiple, simultaneous representations of the lived experience; (3) they are based on prototypes, and are less affected by single experiences and naturally aggregating common patterns of lived experience; (4) the model allows room for modification from inside as well as outside, and internally generated activation (fantasy) may strengthen or alter and potentially distort objective experience; and (5) in adopting Edelman's (1987) concept of neural Darwinism, Stern opens an important avenue for further work on the fate of representations that lose out in the process of neural natural selection.

Stern's model is helpful to attachment theory, because it casts new light on the notion of IWMs and brings it into closer contact with mental-model theory (Johnson-Laird, 1990). Mental-model theory assumes that to understand is to construct mental models from knowledge and from perceptual or verbal evidence. To formulate a conclusion is to describe what is represented in the models. To test validity is to search for alternative models that refute the putative conclusion. IWMs, like all mental models (including Stern's schema of a-way-of-being-with), may or may not be accessible to consciousness. What matters for Bowlby's and Stern's proposed mechanisms are the structures created, which are isomorphic with the structures of the states of affairs to which they pertain (whether perceived or conceived), and which are thus able to represent. Stern's theory assumes that mental operations are invariant. In the maturation of thought, development is not the evolution of new mental operations—as has been assumed, for example, by Piaget—but the derivation of new concepts and models of the world (Johnson-Laird, 1990). Mental models of the kind envisaged by Stern, and implicitly also by Bowlby, offer a form of data structure that plays a central role in the computational architecture of the mind.

Points of Divergence

Stern's framework has much to offer attachment theory, particularly in terms of the careful integration of infant observation studies with concepts concerning interpersonal development. Nevertheless, it lacks two critical dimensions essential to attachment theory. First, it lacks a genuine longitudinal observational perspective. A great strength of attachment theory is its almost unique empirical handle on longitudinal and cross-generational predictions. Although Stern's observations are well operationalized in terms of mother–infant interaction and infant develop-

ment, they lack operationalization in the context of adult behavior, and therefore longitudinal studies based on Stern's framework have rarely been attempted. Second, while Stern probably appropriately claims that "schemas of ways-of-being-with" are the building blocks of IWMs (Stern, 1998), close links between the two systems have not yet been demonstrated. There is important pioneering work by Beatrice Beebe and her group (Beebe, Lachmann, & Jaffe, 1997), but the bulk of the empirical work remains to be performed.

EVALUATION AND SUMMARY

Limitations of Current Psychoanalytic Models

Given the current spate of critiques of psychoanalytic ideas (e.g., Crews, 1995; Webster, 1995), it seems hardly necessary to list once again the limitations of psychoanalytic theoretical constructs. Nevertheless, as these considerations affect the generalizability of the conclusions below, a brief overview appears justified. First of all, most psychoanalytic conjectures have not been tested empirically. In the absence of data, psychoanalysts use indirect evidence, such as unsystematic clinical observations or appeal to authority; they therefore risk confirmatory bias, overelaboration of theory, and failure to identify good theories among multiple alternative explanations. Second, psychoanalytic models tend to assume uniformity regarding the relationship between the pattern of abnormality and developmental course, and to lump diverse aspects of phenomena under single headings such as "object relations" (which subsumes empathy, the ability to sustain relationships, representations of self and objects, etc.). Furthermore, psychoanalytic accounts display little sophistication about the nature of environmental factors.[4] They are also weak in incorporating the wider social context in which development occurs. Finally, psychoanalytic models all too frequently confidently assert a one-to-one correspondence between specific developmental phases and particular forms of psychopathology, generally with an overemphasis on early experience.

Some Attractive Features of Psychoanalytic Models

If psychoanalytic theory had no attractive features, it would be hard to justify a continuing interest in such an epistemically weak discipline. Some specific implications for attachment theory are considered below. Here I mention four relatively strong general features that recommend the approach. First, there is a great deal of generativity within the field; psychoanalytic ideas have inspired important lines of empirical investigation (e.g., learned helplessness, schema theory, and, arguably, attachment theory). Second, psychoanalytic theories offer attractive unifying explanations of diverse overt behaviors by postulating a single underlying covert anomaly. For example, why are narcissistic individuals often forgetful of names, prejudiced, inconsiderate of others' time, and unable to remain in love? Psychoanalytic accounts, whether self-psychological or based on other object relations views, attempt to find a single explanation for such diverse phenomena. Third, the psychoanalytic approach sees development as a series of compromise formations. For example, both nonconscious and conscious self-representations are helpfully viewed as the product of competing environmental pressures and intrapsychic processes with a function to regulate positive and negative affect. Finally, because psychoanalytic theorization is rooted in clinical practice, the person of the therapist provides a valuable device for creating understanding of thoughts, feelings, and behavior that lie beyond the normal range of conscious experience and common-sense psychology (Wollheim, 1995). It is possible that the understanding they offer is more complex and psychologically deeper than other so-called "omnibus" theories of human behavior (cognitive-behavioral, humanistic, systemic), even if psychoanalysis is therapeutically no more effective than these other approaches.

Summary of Common Ground between Psychoanalytic and Attachment Theories

This section summarizes the points of contact between attachment theory and various psychoanalytic traditions. Naturally this is not intended to be an exhaustive listing, but it is hoped that the substantial number of common assumptions between the two frameworks puts to rest the prevailing view of incompatibility between the two frames of reference.

The Phenomenon of Attachment

To begin with, a number of analysts have described phenomena very similar to attachment, while naturally using different terms to describe these. Erikson used the concept of "basic trust"; Anna Freud described attachment phenomena but did not incorporate them into her theory; Sandler describes the "secure base" but calls it the "background of safety"; and so on. In addition, many psychoanalysts now accept that the infant–caregiver relationship is based not on physical need, but rather on the need for a relationship. Current formulations differ, with some analysts postulating a specific relationship instinct (e.g., Modell), others a genetic predisposition (e.g., Balint, Winnicott), and yet others a need secondary to a primal need for psychic organization (e.g., Fairbairn, Kernberg). Still others assume that relationships arise as defenses against the vicissitudes of the child's internal world (e.g., Erikson, Klein).

Determinants of Attachment Security

Both approaches share the view that *personality* may be best studied in relation to the *social environment*. This view is dominant in the writings of almost all psychoanalytic theorists, particularly Anna Freud and Erikson. There is also substantial agreement on the formative nature of the first years of life, particularly the mother–infant relationship. This view was propounded by Spitz; reaffirmed by Erikson, Mahler, and Sandler; and, from a separate perspective, endorsed by Klein and Winnicott. Moreover, maternal sensitivity is seen by both traditions as the key to determining quality of relationship regulation between infant and mother. Within certain perspectives (e.g., Erikson's), sensitivity is conceptualized as the mother's behavior, whereas object relations theorists tend to highlight the infant's experience of being contained, which entails substantial problems of operationalization. Furthermore, both traditions have come to the conclusion that the ideal level of sensitivity from the point of view of infant development is not perfect, but rather moderate in responsivity and intensity to the infant's state. Both Erikson and Winnicott were strongly of this opinion. Finally, the transactional nature of mother–infant interaction was recognized by Erikson, Mahler, and others.

Sequelae of Attachment Status

First, there is a common assumption that a well-regulated early relationship with the caregiver leads to a good outcome, particularly in terms of the development of an autonomous and robust sense of self. This is basic to the formulations of Erikson, Mahler, the modern Kleinians, Winnicott, Modell, Kohut, and others. There is also common ground in seeing dysynchrony of mother–infant interaction as problematic because it risks a distortion of the child's core self. More specifically, if the child is not perceived and responded to accurately, the caregiver's defense will be internalized in place of the self (e.g., Jacobson, Winnicott; see also Crittenden, 1994). In addition, both attachment theory and psychoanalytic theory assume that mediation from experience during infancy to later behavior is assured by the internalization of certain psychological functions, such as emotion regulation from the primary caregiver (e.g., Spitz, Winnicott). A related claim concerns the impact of a harmonious mother–infant relationship on the optimal development of the child's symbolic function (e.g., Winnicott; see similar claims by Bretherton, Bates, Benigni, Camaioni, & Volterra, 1979, and Main, 1991). Lastly, Bowlby and attachment theorists are not alone in making assumptions concerning the cross-generational transmission of relationship patterns (e.g., Erikson, Masterson, Rinsley).

Adult Attachment

There is common ground between the two theories in seeing narratives as providing particularly useful access to relationship representations (Stern), and in seeing security as being linked to coherent experience of the caregiver (Erikson). A speculative link has also been made between adult insecurity and security, and the P-S and depressive positions of the Kleinian model, respectively. Such a link could imply that insecurity (rather than security) is the "basic position," and that the persistence of splitting is a consequence of suboptimal intimacy (Fairbairn). Moreover, a number of clinicians have described patterns of behavior and interpersonal relationship representations that are similar to classifications of adult attachment (e.g., Rosenfeld on "thick-skinned" and "thin-skinned" narcissism; Balint on ocnophilic and philobatic styles of relating).

Sexuality and Aggression

First, there is partial commonality in how aggressive behavior is understood. Many analysts have agreed with attachment theorists that aggression is the "breakdown product" of disappointment and frustration, particularly of dependency and

attachment needs (e.g., Balint, Winnicott, Kohut). Similarly, problems of sexuality and aggression have not been seen by all psychoanalysts as primary determinants of behavior, but rather as consequent on the impoverished regulatory structures, which in their turn are related to inadequate mother–infant relationships. For example, within self psychology, classically crucial developmental problems (such as the Oedipus complex, castration anxiety, and penis envy) are all assumed to be imposed from outside by unempathic, insensitive parenting.

The Representational System

Most analysts (e.g., Jacobson, Sandler, Stern) have concurred with attachment theory in considering mental representation of relationships as key determinants of interpersonal behavior. The correspondence is even closer with those theorists who have postulated representational structures in which roles are encoded for both subject and object (e.g., Sandler, Kernberg, Stern). Many of these psychoanalytic representational accounts emphasize, in common with attachment theory, that mental representations of relationships account for the continuity of the effect of early experience across the lifespan (e.g., Emde, Kernberg). In addition, some analysts have recognized that microexperiences of infant–mother interaction become aggregated into enduring structures that subserve stable patterns of behavior (e.g., Erikson, Stern). There is also the common assumption among some psychoanalysts and attachment theorists that the representational world influences behavior via nonconscious procedures based on the distinction between implicit and declarative memory (e.g., Stern, and my own group). Finally, the frameworks have in common the important assumption that perception and experience are distorted by expectations, both conscious and unconscious, encoded in the representational system. (This is a fundamental tenet of Freudian psychology, much of which is concerned with describing the internal mechanisms that are responsible for the discrepancy between actual and psychic reality.)

Potential "Points of Growth" of Attachment Theory, Based on Theoretical Insights from Psychoanalysis

In this review I have identified a number of areas in attachment theory that could be elaborated in the context of psychoanalytic ideas. I list these briefly in summary form.

With important exceptions (e.g., Bretherton, 1991), attachment theory pays relatively little attention to distortions of the child's perception of the external world. Comparable caregiver behavior may be experienced and encoded differently by different infants, greatly complicating the relationship of actual experience and its representation (Eagle, 1997). Such distortions can arise as a consequence of internal states (fantasies, affects, cognitions) and may lead to an inaccurate representation of the parental figure. IWMs may be distorted by conflict, and there may be conflict between IWMs. There is likely to be a hierarchy of internal representations of relationships. Some representations may have greater access to consciousness than others. IWMs may sometimes evolve with development; alternatively, the evolution of some IWMs may stop. They may then become marked by the mode and level of functioning (interpersonal awareness, self–other differentiation, etc.) prevalent at the time of their construction. Psychoanalysis, as we have seen, has struggled with these issues since its inception, and its discoveries should not be ignored.

In general, notwithstanding the developmental richness of attachment theory as a tradition, there has been relatively little work on discontinuities of attachment. Few have attempted to account for discontinuities (rather than continuities) in children's behavior in attachment theory terms. Instances where experience appears to have little effect on a child's social development (e.g., resilience) are little studied. Some psychoanalytic workers (Erikson, Anna Freud) have touched on these ideas, and their notion of lifespan development is closely related to and could in certain instances inform attachment theory. Sensitive caregiving probably remains a formative influence beyond infancy. Kohut's work on narcissism and on the caregiver's failure to help the child perceive his or her "real" limitations is but one example.

As we have seen, a number of analysts have been concerned with notions of caregiver sensitivity, using somewhat different terms (Bion, "containing"; Winnicott, "holding"; etc.). Some of the distinctions proposed may be helpful (e.g., Winnicott's distinction between sensitivity to what the child knows and what the child wants; Gergely's description of mirroring as a process that organizes affective states; the communication of a resonating yet coping attitude in mirroring; etc.). A refined notion of sensitivity may help us to understand better the cross-generational transmission of attachment.

Objections to attachment theory from psychoanalysts usually focus on the allegedly simplistic categorical system offered. This is a misunderstanding, because Bowlby's theory was anything but simplistic. Yet workers in the field often appear to conflate the operationalization of the theory in terms of attachment categories with attachment theory itself. Such conflation gives rise to the reification of attachment categories as if these were theoretical entities rather than observed clusters of behavior. This may bring an artificial closure to what "attachment" means, and a potentially fruitful integration of psychoanalytic discoveries with attachment theory ideas may be lost. For example, we have seen that insecurity may be construed as a habitual mode of defense (Anna Freud) or as a representational organization strongly influenced by P-S modes of functioning (Klein). The psychoanalytic ideas reviewed in this chapter suggest for the most part that attachment security is best considered as a dimensional rather than as a categorical construct. Insecurity of attachment is a psychological position that may be activated more or less readily in all of us.

A further recurrent theme in this review has been the connection between the concept of attachment and the child's awareness of the other as a psychological entity. Psychoanalysts view healthy development as intrinsically linked to the child's acquiring a capacity to perceive the caregiver as a separate but complete human individual—a psychological entity with an intentional stance, motivated by wishes, beliefs, and feelings. Associated with the perception of the other as a coherent being is a perception of the self as a mental rather than a physical entity. Following the ideas of Winnicott and others, we may see the coherently perceived mirroring other as the core of the self-representation of the infant. Attachment in this context is a sense of comfort and security in the safe exploration not just of the external world, but perhaps even more importantly, the internal one. This may explain the dialectic that we repeatedly encounter in theoretical writings between autonomy and intimacy: Does intimacy grow out of autonomy or autonomy out of intimacy? The coherent mentalizing self, itself the product of primary intersubjectivity (where the other is not yet the other but the generator of representations of internal states), may enable both separateness and dependency.

A number of useful ideas emerge from exploring common points between the two kinds of theories concerning severe personality disorder. For example, borderline personality disorder may be a dysfunction of IWMs in which representations of self and objects oscillate rapidly (Kernberg) and representations of others are grossly distorted, with relationship representations frequently lacking human social quality (my colleagues and I). Rapid alterations between IWMs, as well as the absence of coherence within them, may be associated with an inhibition of a metacognitive or a reflective capacity that normally serves the function of self-organization. The abandonment of reflection may be seen as constitutional or as an extreme defensive response of individuals confronted with social situations (e.g., child abuse) in which they find the contemplation of mental states in self and other overwhelming. They "voluntarily" abandon this crucial psychological capacity, with sometimes disastrous consequences.

Psychoanalysis has classically prioritized instincts and bodily processes rather than relationships in the creation of psychic organization. Attachment theory has less to say about the bodily self. Building on Winnicott's ideas, we can see that early attachment is linked to the child's growing sense of ownership of the body. Various disorders of conduct, particularly violence and self-harm, may be associated with the looseness of the link between a sense of psychological and physical self. The attachment relationship may be critical in establishing such integration. A similar approach may be taken to the issue of sexuality. Although it is evident that the two systems (attachment and sexual relationships) can exist independently (Holmes, 1993), there are also evident links between mature sexual relationships and a secure state of mind with regard to attachment (Eagle, 1997).

Finally, the therapeutic application of attachment theory may be enriched by psychoanalytic ideas. Attachment status is clearly linked to psychotherapy process, although this branch of research is still in its infancy (Holmes, 1997; Slade, Chapter 25, this volume). The closeness of object relations and attachment theory formulations is evident in the links between secure attachment (basic trust) and therapeutic alliance, IWMs and concepts such as role responsiveness (accounting for transference and countertransference phenomena), disorganization of attachment and the clinical observation of projective identification, the notion of coherence and the overlapping notion of narrativization of one's history,

and so on. The generic goals of psychoanalytic psychotherapy may be readily stated in attachment theory terms: Intimacy and autonomy are its basic goals, rooted in the opposition of attachment and exploration (Holmes, 1997). Clinical observations of patterns of relationship or relationship styles between therapist and patient could enrich studies of attachment, because the psychotherapeutic relationship can readily be conceptualized as an attachment relationship (Bowlby, 1988). Equally, attachment classification of psychoanalytic patients could be helpful in the evaluation of the psychoanalytic process, and in attempts at predicting individual differences in responses to therapy. Preoccupied, entangled personality-disordered patients respond less well to inpatient psychotherapy than dismissing ones do (Fonagy et al., 1996). We may speculate that whereas avoidant, dismissive individuals defensively exclude attachment cues, and this tendency is modified in therapy, entangled, preoccupied persons need help in giving up a fantasy of recovering what they experience as a lost relationship (even if that relationship only ever existed as a fantasy) (Eagle, 1997, p. 227). The relinquishing of infantile fantasies is seen by a number of psychoanalysts as an essential element of successful treatment (e.g., Fairbairn, 1952). The nature of therapeutic strategies, and the transferential feelings engendered, are likely to be determined by the nature of the primary attachment ties (Mallinckrodt, Gantt, & Coble, 1995).

Conclusion

Attachment theory and psychoanalytic theory have common roots but have evolved in epistemologically distinct ways. Ironically, psychoanalysis, like Bowlby's graphic description of the growth of personality, evolves along multiple and sometimes intersecting tracks, whereas attachment theory, with a more mature scientific method, evolves linearly, with new discoveries building on past achievements. The distinct epistemologies may blind us to the obvious fact that both "rail systems" attempt to cover the same terrain—that of a developmental approach to psychological disorder. Common ground exceeds points of divergence. When psychoanalytic theory is considered as a whole, many important aspects of attachment theory may be argued to have been observed on the couch as well as in the laboratory. There are some areas where attachment theory has not yet had the opportunity to venture.

Both psychoanalytic theory and clinical work might be greatly enriched if these relatively unexplored areas were to become the focus of future attachment research.

ACKNOWLEDGMENT

I would like to express my admiration and gratitude to Phil Shaver for his extensive help and guidance in the preparation of this chapter. His good-humored suggestions and forbearance went a considerable way beyond what an author has a right to expect from an editor.

NOTES

1. He considered basic trust to be transmitted across generations by "the experience of the caretaking person as a *coherent* being, who reciprocates one's physical and emotional needs in expectable ways and therefore deserves to be endowed with trust, and whose face is recognized as it recognizes" (Erikson, 1964, p. 117).

2. In the London Parent–Child Project, my colleagues and I found that the difference between support anticipated by the mother and actually obtained from the father, rather than absolute levels of support, turned out to be the most potent predictor (Fonagy, Steele, Steele, Higgitt, & Target, 1994).

3. Daniel Stern (1985) has explored these ideas most fully in his elaboration of the development of self-agency in the 4- to 6-month-old, where both proprioceptive feedback and the experience of forming plans are seen as contributing to the continuity of the sense of self.

4. For example, moving away from Melanie Klein's constitutional explanation of pathology, Winnicott asserted that "babies are not men—i.e., they are neither paranoid nor depressive (1948/1958b, p. 159). The only alternative account available to him rooted psychopathology in the mother. Yet transactional processes predominate in the generation of risk (Rutter, 1994).

REFERENCES

Ainsworth, M. D. S., Blehar, M. C., Waters, E., & Wall, S. (1978). *Patterns of attachment: A psychological study of the strange situation.* Hillsdale, NJ: Erlbaum.

Arlow, J. A., & Brenner, C. (1964). *Psychoanalytic concepts and the structural theory.* New York: International Universities Press.

Bahrick, L. R., & Watson, J. S. (1986). Detection of intermodal proprioceptive-visual contingency as a potential basis of self-perception in infancy. *Developmental Psychology, 21,* 963–973.

Balint, M. (1952). On love and hate. *International Journal of Psycho-Analysis, 33,* 355–362.

Balint, M. (1959). *Thrills and regressions.* London: Hogarth Press.

Balint, M. (1965). *Primary love and psycho-analytic technique.* London: Tavistock.

Bateman, A. (1996, July). *The concept of enactment and "thick-skinned" and "thin-skinned" narcissism.* Paper presented at the European Conference of English-Speaking Psychoanalysts, London.

Beebe, B., Lachmann, F., & Jaffe, J. (1997). Mother–infant interaction structures and presymbolic self and object representations. *Psychoanalytic Dialogues, 7,* 113–182.

Belsky, J., Rovine, M., & Taylor, D. G. (1984). The Pennsylvania Infant and Family Development Project: III. The origins of individual differences in infant–mother attachment: Maternal and infant contributions. *Child Development, 55,* 718–728.

Bion, W. R. (1962). *Learning from experience.* London: Heinemann.

Bleiberg, E., Fonagy, P., & Target, M. (1997). Child psychoanalysis: Critical overview and a proposed reconsideration. *Psychiatric Clinics of North America, 6,* 1–38.

Boesky, D. (1989). A discussion of evidential criteria for therapeutic change. In A. Rothstein (Ed.), *How does treatment help?: Models of therapeutic action of psychoanalytic therapy* (pp. 171–180). Madison, CT: International Universities Press.

Bowlby, J. (1958). The nature of the child's tie to his mother. *International Journal of Psycho-Analysis, 39,* 350–373.

Bowlby, J. (1960). Grief and mourning in infancy and early childhood. *Psychoanalytic Study of the Child, 15,* 3–39.

Bowlby, J. (1969/1982). *Attachment and loss: Vol. 1. Attachment.* London: Hogarth Press and the Institute of Psycho-Analysis.

Bowlby, J. (1973). *Attachment and loss: Vol. 2. Separation: Anxiety and anger.* London: Hogarth Press and the Institute of Psycho-Analysis.

Bowlby, J. (1977). The making and breaking of affectional bonds: II. Some principles of psychotherapy. *British Journal of Psychiatry, 130,* 421–431.

Bowlby, J. (1980a). *Attachment and loss: Vol. 3. Loss: Sadness and depression.* London: Hogarth Press and the Institute of Psycho-Analysis.

Bowlby, J. (1980b). Epilogue. In C. M. Parkes & J. Stevenson-Hinde (Eds.), *The place of attachment in human behavior* (pp. 301–312). New York: Basic Books.

Bowlby, J. (1981). Psychoanalysis as natural science. *International Review of Psycho-Analysis, 8,* 243–255.

Bowlby, J. (1988). *A secure base: Clinical applications of attachment theory.* London: Routledge.

Brenner, C. (1982). *The mind in conflict.* New York: International Universities Press.

Bretherton, I. (1987). New perspectives on attachment relationships: Security, communication, and internal working models. In J. D. Osofsky (Ed.), *Handbook of infant development* (2nd ed., pp. 1061–1100). New York: Wiley.

Bretherton, I. (1991). Pouring new wine into old bottles: The social self as internal working model. In M. R. Gunnar & L. A. Sroufe (Eds.), *Minnesota Symposia on Child Psychology: Vol. 23. Self processes and development* (pp. 1–41). Hillsdale, NJ: Erlbaum.

Bretherton, I., Bates, E., Benigni, L., Camaioni, L., & Volterra, V. (1979). Relationships between cognition, communication, and quality of attachment. In E. Bates, L. Benigni, I. Bretherton, L. Camaioni, & V. Volterra (Eds.), *The emergence of symbols.* New York: Academic Press.

Bruner, J. (1990). *Acts of meaning.* Cambridge, MA: Harvard University Press.

Burland, J. A. (1986). The vicissitudes of maternal deprivation. In R. F. Lax, S. Bach, & J. A. Burland (Eds.), *Self and object constancy: Clinical and theoretical perspectives* (pp. 324–347). New York: Guilford Press.

Carlson, E., & Sroufe, L. A. (1995). Contribution of attachment theory to developmental psychopathology. In D. Cicchetti & D. J. Cohen (Eds.), *Developmental psychopathology: Vol. 1. Theory and methods* (pp. 581–617). New York: Wiley.

Carlson, V., Cicchetti, D., Barnett, D., & Braunwald, K. (1989). Disorganized/disoriented attachment relationships in maltreated infants. *Developmental Psychology, 25,* 525–531.

Cassidy, J., Marvin, R. S., & The MacArthur Working Group on Attachment. (1989). *Attachment organization in three and four year olds: Coding guidelines.* Unpublished scoring manual, University of Illinois.

Crews, F. (1995). *The memory wars: Freud's legacy in dispute.* London: Granta Books.

Crittenden, P. M. (1994). Peering into the black box: An exploratory treatise on the development of self in young children. In D. Cicchetti & S. L. Toth (Eds.), *Rochester Symposium on Developmental Psychopathology: Vol. 5. Disorders and dysfunctions of the self* (pp. 79–148). Rochester, NY: University of Rochester Press.

Crnic, K. A., Greenberg, M. T., Ragozin, A. S., Robinson, N. M., & Basham, R. B. (1983). Effects of stress and social support on mothers and premature and full-term infants. *Child Development, 54,* 209–217.

DeCasper, A. J., & Carstens, A. A. (1981). Contingencies of stimulation: Effects on learning and emotion in neonates. *Infant Behavior and Development, 4,* 19–35.

Eagle, M. (1995). The developmental perspectives of attachment and psychoanalytic theory. In S. Goldberg, R. Muir, & J. Kerr (Eds.), *Attachment theory: Social, developmental, and clinical perspectives* (pp. 123–150). Hillsdale, NJ: Analytic Press.

Eagle, M. (1997). Attachment and psychoanalysis. *British Journal of Medical Psychology, 70,* 217–229.

Edelman, G. M. (1987). *Neural Darwinism.* New York: Basic Books.

Emde, R. N. (1980). A developmental orientation in psychoanalysis: Ways of thinking about new knowledge and further research. *Psychoanalysis and Contemporary Thought, 3,* 213–235.

Engel, G. L. (1971). Attachment behaviour, object relations, and the dynamic point of view: A critical review of Bowlby's *Attachment and loss. International Journal of Psychoanalysis, 52,* 183–196.

Erikson, E. H. (1950). *Childhood and society.* New York: Norton.

Erikson, E. H. (1959). *Identity and the life cycle.* New York: International Universities Press.

Erikson, E. H. (1968). *Identity: Youth and crisis.* New York: Norton.

Fairbairn, W. R. D. (1952). *An object-relations theory of the personality.* New York: Basic Books.

Fairbairn, W. R. D. (1954). Observations on the nature of hysterical states. *British Journal of Medical Psychology, 29,* 112–127.

Fonagy, P. (1991). Thinking about thinking: Some clinical and theoretical considerations in the treatment of a borderline patient. *International Journal of Psycho-Analysis, 72,* 1–18.

Fonagy, P., & Cooper, A. (in press). Joseph Sandler's contributions to psychoanalysis. In P. Fonagy, A. Cooper, & R. Wallerstein (Eds.), *Psychoanalysis on the move.* London: Routledge.

Fonagy, P., Leigh, T., Steele, M., Steele, H., Kennedy, R., Mattoon, G., Target, M., & Gerber, A. (1996). The relation of attachment status, psychiatric classification, and response to psychotherapy. *Journal of Consulting and Clinical Psychology, 64,* 22–31.

Fonagy, P., & Moran, G. S. (1994). Psychoanalytic formulation and treatment of chronic metabolic disturbance in insulin dependent diabetes mellitus. In A. Erskine & D. Judd (Eds.), *The imaginative body: Psychodynamic psychotherapy in health care.* London: Whurr Publications.

Fonagy, P., Steele, H., Moran, G. S., Steele, M., & Higgitt, A. (1991). The capacity for understanding mental states: The reflective self in parent and child and its significance for security of attachment. *Infant Mental Health Journal, 13,* 200–217.

Fonagy, P., Steele, M., Moran, G. S., Steele, H., & Higgitt, A. (1992). The integration of psychoanalytic theory and work on attachment: The issue of intergenerational psychic processes. In D. Stern & M. Ammaniti (Eds.), *Attaccamento e psiconalis* (pp. 19–30). Bari, Italy: Laterza.

Fonagy, P., Steele, M., Steele, H., Higgitt, A., & Target, M. (1994). The Emmanuel Miller lecture 1992: The theory and practice of resilience. *Journal of Child Psychology and Psychiatry, 35,* 231–257.

Fonagy, P., Steele, M., Steele, H., Leigh, T., Kennedy, R., Mattoon, G., & Target, M. (1995). Attachment, the reflective self, and borderline states: The predictive specificity of the Adult Attachment Interview and pathological emotional development. In S. Goldberg, R. Muir, & J. Kerr (Eds.), *Attachment theory: Social, developmental, and clinical perspectives* (pp. 233–278). Hillsdale, NJ: Analytic Press.

Fonagy, P., & Target, M. (1997). Attachment and reflective function: Their role in self-organization. *Development and Psychopathology, 9,* 679–700.

Fonagy, P., Target, M., Steele, M., & Steele, H. (1997). The development of violence and crime as it relates to security of attachment. In J. D. Osofsky (Ed.), *Children in a violent society* (pp. 150–177). New York: Guilford Press.

Fraiberg, S. (1982). Pathological defenses in infancy. *Psychoanalytic Quarterly, 51,* 612–635.

Freud, A. (1946). *The ego and the mechanisms of defence* (C. Baines, Trans.). New York: International Universities Press. (Original work published 1936)

Freud, A. (1954). The widening scope of indications for psychoanalysis: Discussion. *Journal of the American Psychoanalytical Association, 2,* 607–620.

Freud, A. (1963). The concept of developmental lines. *Psychoanalytic Study of the Child, 18,* 245–265.

Freud, A. (1965). *Normality and pathology in childhood.* Harmondsworth, England: Penguin Books.

Freud, A. (1969). Discussion of Dr. Bowlby's paper ("Grief and mourning in infancy and early childhood"). In *The Writings of Anna Freud* (pp. 167–186). New York: International Universities Press. (Original work published 1960)

Freud, A. (1974). Reports on the Hampstead Nurseries. In *The writings of Anna Freud.* New York: International Universities Press. (Original work published 1941–1945).

Freud, S., & Breuer, J. (1893/1954). On the psychical mechanism of hysterical phenomena: Preliminary communication. In J. Strachey (Ed.), *The standard edition of the complete psychological works of Sigmund Freud* (Vol. 2, pp. 3–17). London: Hogarth Press.

Freud, A., & Burlingham, D. (1944). *Infants without families.* New York: International Universities Press.

Freud, S. (1955). Beyond the pleasure principle. In J. Strachey (Ed. and Trans.), *The standard edition of the complete psychological works of Sigmund Freud* (Vol. 18, pp. 1–64). London: Hogarth Press. (Original work published 1920)

Freud, S. (1959). Inhibitions, symptoms, and anxiety. In J. Strachey (Ed. & Trans.), *The standard edition of the complete psychological works of Sigmund Freud* (Vol. 20, pp. 77–172). London: Hogarth Press. (Original work published 1926)

Freud, S. (1961). The ego and the id. In J. Strachey (Ed. & Trans.), *The standard edition of the complete psychological works of Sigmund Freud* (Vol. 19, pp. 1–59). London: Hogarth Press. (Original work published 1923)

Freud, S. (1961). Female sexuality. In J. Strachey (Ed. & Trans.), *The standard edition of the complete psychological works of Sigmund Freud* (Vol. 21, pp. 221–246). London: Hogarth Press. (Original work published 1931)

Freud, S. (1964). An outline of psycho-analysis. In J. Strachey (Ed. & Trans.), *The standard edition of the complete psychological works of Sigmund Freud* (Vol. 23, pp. 139–208). London: Hogarth Press. (Original work published 1940)

Gergely, G. (1992). Developmental reconstructions: Infancy from the point of view of psychoanalysis and developmental psychology. *Psychoanalysis and Contemporary Thought, 14,* 3–55.

Gergely, G., & Watson, J. (1996). The social biofeedback model of parental affect-mirroring. *International Journal of Psycho-Analysis, 77,* 1181–1212.

Gianino, A. F., & Tronick, E. Z. (1988). The mutual regulation model: The infant's self and interactive regulation and coping and defensive capacities. In T. M. Field, P. M. McCabe, & N. Schneiderman (Eds.), *Stress and coping across development* (pp. 47–68). Hillsdale, NJ: Erlbaum.

Goldberg, S. (1995). Introduction. In S. Goldberg, R. Muir, & J. Kerr (Eds.), *Attachment theory: Social, developmental, and clinical perspectives* (pp. 1–15). Hillsdale, NJ: Analytic Press.

Goldberg, W. A., & Easterbrooks, M. A. (1984). The role of marital quality in toddler development. *Developmental Psychology, 20,* 504–514.

Goldberg, S., Muir, R., & Kerr, J. (Eds.). (1995). *Attachment theory: Social, developmental, and clinical perspectives.* Hillsdale, NJ: Analytic Press.

Grosskurth, P. (1986). *Melanie Klein: Her world and her work.* New York: Knopf.

Guntrip, H. (1961). *Personality structure and human interaction.* New York: International Universities Press.

Hanley, C. (1978). A critical consideration of Bowlby's ethological theory of anxiety. *Psychoanalytic Quarterly, 47,* 364–380.

Hartmann, H. (1964). The mutual influences in the development of ego and id. In *Essays on ego psychology* (pp. 155–182). New York: International Universities Press. (Original work published 1952)

Hartmann, H., Kris, E., & Loewenstein, R. (1946). Comments on the formation of psychic structure. *Psychoanalytic Study of the Child, 2,* 11–38.

Hermann, I. (1923). Zur Psychologie der Chimpanzen. *Internazional Zeitschrift für Psychoanalyse, 9,* 80–87.

Holland, R. (1990). Scientificity and psychoanalysis: Insights from the controversial discussions. *International Review of Psychoanalysis, 17,* 133–158.

Holmes, J. (1993). *John Bowlby and attachment theory.* London: Routledge.

Holmes, J. (1997). Attachment, autonomy, intimacy: Some clinical implications of attachment theory. *British Journal of Medical Psychology, 70,* 231–248.

Isabella, R., & Belsky, J. (1991). Interactional synchrony and the origins of infant–mother attachment: A replication study. *Child Development, 62,* 373–384.

Jacobson, E. (1964). *The self and the object world.* New York: International Universities Press.

Johnson-Laird, P. N. (1990). The development of reasoning ability. In G. Butterworth & P. Bryant (Eds.), *Causes of development: Interdisciplinary perspectives* (pp. 85–110). Hillsdale, NJ.: Erlbaum.

Kahn, M. (1983). Secret and potential space. In *Hidden selves.* London: Hogarth. (Original work published in 1978)

Kennedy, H., & Moran, G. (1991). Reflections on the aims of child psychoanalysis. *Psychoanalytic Study of the Child, 46,* 181–198.

Kennedy, H., & Yorke, C. (1980). Childhood neurosis v. developmental deviations: Two clinical case histories. *Dialogue: A Journal of Psychoanalytic Perspectives, 4,* 20–33.

Kernberg, O. F. (1976). *Object relations theory and clinical psychoanalysis.* New York: Aronson.

Kernberg, O. F. (1977). The structural diagnosis of borderline personality organization. In P. Hartocollis (Ed.), *Borderline personality disorders: The concept, the syndrome, the patient* (pp. 87–121). New York: International Universities Press.

Kernberg, O. F. (1982). Self, ego, affects, and drives. *Journal of the American Psychoanalytic Association, 30,* 893–917.

Kernberg, O. F. (1984). *Severe personality disorders: Psychotherapeutic strategies.* New Haven, CT: Yale University Press.

Kernberg, O. F. (1987). Borderline personality disorder: A psychodynamic approach. *Journal of Personality Disorders, 1,* 344–346.

Klein, G. S. (1976). Freud's two theories of sexuality. *Psychological Issues, 36,* 14–70.

Klein, M. (1964). The psychotherapy of the psychoses. In *Contributions to psychoanalysis, 1921–1945.* New York: McGraw-Hill. (Original work published 1936)

Klein, M. (1975). The psycho-analysis of children. In *The writings of Melanie Klein.* London: Hogarth Press. (Original work published 1932)

Klein, M. (1975). A contribution to the psychogenesis of manic–depressive states. In *The writings of Melanie Klein* (pp. 236–289). London: Hogarth Press. (Original work published 1935)

Klein, M. (1975). Envy and gratitude. In *The writings of Melanie Klein* (Vol. 3, pp. 176–235). London: Hogarth Press. (Original work published 1957)

Klein, M. (1980). On Mahler's autistic and symbiotic phases: An exposition and evolution. *Psychoanalysis and Contemporary Thought, 4,* 69–105.

Kohut, H. (1971). *The analysis of the self.* New York: International Universities Press.

Kohut, H. (1972). Thoughts on narcissism and narcissistic rage. *Psychoanalytic Study of the Child, 27,* 360–400.

Kohut, H. (1977). *The restoration of the self.* New York: International Universities Press.

Kohut, H. (1984). *How does analysis cure?* Chicago: University of Chicago Press.

Kohut, H., & Wolf, E. S. (1978). The disorders of the self and their treatment: An outline. *International Journal of Psycho-Analysis, 59,* 413–425.

Kramer, S., & Akhtar, S. (1988). The developmental context of internalized preoedipal object relations: Clinical applications of Mahler's theory of symbiosis and separation–individuation. *Psychoanalytic Quarterly, 57,* 547–576.

Kris, E. (1952). *Psychoanalytic explorations in art.* New York: International Universities Press.

Lamb, M. (1987). Predictive implications of individual differences in attachment. *Journal of Consulting and Clinical Psychology, 55,* 817–824.

Lilleskov, R. (1992). [Review of *Attachment in the preschool years: Theory, research, and intervention*]. *International Review of Psycho-Analysis, 19,* 126–130.

Mahler, M. S. (1972). On the first three subphases of the separation–individuation process. *International Journal of Psycho-Analysis, 53,* 333–338.

Mahler, M. S., & Furer, M. (1968). *On human symbiosis and the vicissitudes of individuation: Vol. 1. Infantile psychosis.* New York: International Universities Press.

Mahler, M. S., & McDevitt, J. F. (1980). The separation–individuation process and identity formation. In S. I. Greenspan & G. H. Pollock (Eds.), *The course of life: Psychoanalytic contributions toward understanding personality development: Vol. 1. Infancy and early childhood* (DHHS Publication No. ADM 80-786, pp. 395–406). Washington, DC: U.S. Government Printing Office.

Mahler, M. S., Pine, F., & Bergman, A. (1975). *The psychological birth of the human infant: Symbiosis and individuation.* New York: Basic Books.

Main, M. (1991). Metacognitive knowledge, metacognitive monitoring, and singular (coherent) vs. multiple (incoherent) model of attachment: Findings and directions for future research. In C. M. Parkes, J. Stevenson-Hinde, & P. Marris (Eds.), *Attachment across the life cycle* (pp. 127–159). London: Tavistock/Routledge.

Main, M., & Cassidy, J. (1988). Categories of response to reunion with the parent at age 6: Predictable from infant attachment classifications and stable over a 1-month period. *Developmental Psychology, 24,* 415–426.

Main, M., & Goldwyn, R. (in preparation). Adult attachment classification system. In M. Main (Ed.), *Behavior and the development of representational models of attachment: Five methods of assessment.* New York: Cambridge University Press.

Main, M., & Goldwyn, R. (in press). Adult attachment rating and classification systems. In M. Main (Ed.), *A typology of human attachment organization assessed in discourse, drawings, and interviews.* New York: Cambridge University Press.

Main, M., & Hesse, E. (1990). Parents' unresolved traumatic experiences are related to infant disorganized attachment status: Is frightened and/or frightening parental behavior the linking mechanism? In M. Greenberg, D. Cicchetti, & E. M. Cummings (Eds.), *Attachment in the preschool years: Theory, research, and intervention* (pp. 161–182). Chicago: University of Chicago Press.

Main, M., & Solomon, J. (1990). Procedures for identifying infants as disorganized/disoriented during the Ainsworth strange situation. In M. Greenberg, D. Cicchetti, & E. M. Cummings (Eds.), *Attachment during the preschool years: Theory, research, and intervention* (pp. 121–160). Chicago: University of Chicago Press.

Malatesta, C. Z., Culver, C., Tesman, J. R., & Shepard, B. (1989). The development of emotion expression during the first two years of life. *Monographs of the Society for Research in Child Development, 54,* 1–104.

Malatesta, C. Z., Grigoryev, P., Lamb, C., Albin, M., & Culver, C. (1986). Emotional socialization and expressive development in pre-term and full-term infants. *Child Development, 57,* 316–330.

Mallinckrodt, B., Gantt, D., & Coble, H. (1995). Attachment patterns in the psychotherapy relationship: Development of a Client Attachment to the Therapist Scale. *Journal of Counseling Psychology, 42,* 307–317.

Murphy, L. B., & Moriarty, A. E. (1976). *Vulnerability, coping, and growth: From infancy to adolescence.* New Haven, CT: Yale University Press.

O'Conner, M. J., Sigman, M., & Brill, N. (1987). Disorganization of attachment in relation to maternal alcohol consumption. *Journal of Consulting and Clinical Psychology, 55,* 831–836.

Parens, H. (1979). *The development of aggression in early childhood.* New York: Aronson.

Patrick, M., Hobson, R. P., Castle, D., Howard, R., & Maughan, B. (1994). Personality disorder and the mental representation of early social experience. *Developmental Psychopathology, 6,* 375–388.

Radke-Yarrow, M., Cummings, E. M., Kuczynski, L., & Chapman, M. (1985). Patterns of attachment in two- and three-year-olds in normal families and families with parental depression. *Child Development, 56,* 884–893.

Rayner, E. (1991). *The independent mind in British psychoanalysis.* London: Free Association Books.

Reiss, D., Hetherington, E. M., Plomin, R., Howe, G. W., Simmens, S. J., Henderson, S. H., O'Connor, T. J., Bussell, D., Anderson, E. R., & Law, T. (1995). Genetic questions for environmental studies: Differential parenting and psychopathology in adolescence. *Archives of General Psychiatry, 52,* 925–936.

Rodning, C., Beckwith, L., & Howard, J. (1991). Quality of attachment and home environment in children prenatally exposed to PCP and cocaine. *Development and Psychopathology, 3,* 351–366.

Rosenfeld, H. (1965). *Psychotic states: A psychoanalytic approach.* New York: International Universities Press.

Rosenfeld, H. (1988). Contribution to the psychopathology of psychotic states: The importance of projective identification in the ego structure and object relations of the psychotic patient. In E. B. Spillius (Ed.), *Melanie Klein today* (pp. 117–137). London: Routledge. (Original work published 1971)

Rutter, M. (1994). Beyond longitudinal data: Causes, consequences, changes, and continuity. *Journal of Consulting and Clinical Psychology, 62,* 928–940.

Sandler, J. (1985). Towards a reconsideration of the psychoanalytic theory of motivation. *Bulletin of the Anna Freud Centre, 8,* 223–243.

Sandler, J. (1993). Communication from patient to analyst: Not everything is projective identification. *British Psycho-Analytical Society Bulletin, 29,* 8–16.

Sandler, J., Holder, A., Dare, C., & Dreher, A. U. (1997). *Freud's models of the mind: An introduction.* London: Karnac Books.

Sandler, J., & Sandler, A.-M. (1978). On the development of object relationships and affects. *International Journal of Psycho-Analysis, 59,* 285–296.

Sandler, J., & Sandler, A.-M. (1998). *Object relations theory and role responsiveness.* London: Karnac Books.

Segal, H. (1957). Notes on symbol formation. *International Journal of Psycho-Analysis, 38,* 391–397.

Settlage, C. F. (1977). The psychoanalytic understanding of narcissistic and borderline personality disorders: Advances in developmental theory. *Journal of the American Psychoanalytic Association, 25,* 805–833.

Shane, M., Shane, E., & Gales, M. (1997). *Intimate attachments: Toward a new self psychology.* New York: Guilford Press.

Shaw, D. S., Owens, E. B., Vondra, J. I., Keenan, K., & Winslow, E. B. (1996). Early risk factors and pathways in the development of early disruptive behavior problems. *Development and Psychopathology, 8,* 679–699.

Slade, A., Belsky, J., Aber, L., & Phelps, J. L. (in press). Maternal representations of their toddlers: Links to adult attachment and observed mothering. *Developmental Psychology.*

Spillius, E. B. (1992, June). *Discussion of "Aggression and the Psychological Self" (shortened version of present paper), given at scientific meeting "Psychoanalytic Ideas and Developmental Observation" in honour of George S. Moran.* Paper presented at the University College, London.

Spillius, E. B. (1994). Developments in Kleinian thought: Overview and personal view. *Psychoanalytic Inquiry, 14,* 324–364.

Spitz, R. A. (1959). *A genetic field theory of ego formation: Its implications for pathology.* New York: International Universities Press.

Sroufe, L. A. (1986). Bowlby's contribution to psychoanalytic theory and developmental psychopathology. *Journal of Child Psychology and Psychiatry, 27,* 841–849.

Sroufe, L. A. (1990). An organizational perspective on the self. In D. Cicchetti & M. Beeghly (Eds.), *The self in transition: Infancy to childhood* (pp. 281–307). Chicago: University of Chicago Press.

Steele, H., Steele, M., & Fonagy, P. (1996). Associations among attachment classifications of mothers, fathers, and their infants: Evidence for a relationship-specific perspective. *Child Development, 67,* 541–555.

Stern, D. N. (1985). *The interpersonal world of the infant: A view from psychoanalysis and developmental psychology.* New York: Basic Books.

Stern, D. N. (1994). One way to build a clinically relevant baby. *Infant Mental Health Journal, 15,* 36–54.

Stern, D. N. (1998). The process of therapeutic change involving implicit knowledge: Some implications of developmental observations for adult psychotherapy. *Infant Mental Health Journal.*

Stolorow, R., Brandchaft, B., & Atwood, G. (1987). *Psycho-analytic treatment: An intersubjective approach.* Hillsdale, NJ: Analytic Press.

van IJzendoorn, M. H. (1995). Adult attachment representations, parental responsiveness, and infant attachment: A meta-analysis on the predictive validity of the Adult Attachment Interview. *Psychological Bulletin, 117,* 387–403.

van IJzendoorn, M. H., Goldberg, S., Kroonenberg, P. M., & Frenkel, O. J. (1992). The relative effects of maternal and child problems on the quality of attachment: A meta-analysis of attachment in clinical samples. *Child Development, 59,* 147–156.

Waddington, C. H. (1966). *Principles of development and differentiation.* New York: Macmillan.

Webster, R. (1995). *Why Freud was wrong: Sin, science and psycho-analysis.* London: Harper Collins.

Winnicott, D. W. (1958a). *Collected papers: Through paediatrics to psycho-analysis.* London: Tavistock.

Winnicott, D. W. (1958b). Paediatrics and psychiatry. In *Collected papers: Through paediatrics to psycho-analysis* (pp. 157–173). London: Tavistock. (Original work published 1948)

Winnicott, D. W. (1965a). Ego distortion in terms of true and false self. In *The maturational processes and the facilitating environment* (pp. 140–152). London: Hogarth Press. (Original work published 1960)

Winnicott, D. W. (1965b). Ego integration in child development. In *The maturational processes and the facilitating environment* (pp. 56–63). London: Hogarth Press. (Original work published 1962)

Winnicott, D. W. (1965c). Communicating and not communicating leading to a study of certain opposites. In *The maturational processes and the facilitating environment* (pp. 179–192). London: Hogarth Press. (Original work published 1963a)

Winnicott, D. W. (1965d). Psychotherapy of character disorders. In *The maturational processes and the facilitating environment* (pp. 203–216). London: Hogarth Press. (Original work published 1963b)

Winnicott, D. W. (1965e). *The maturational processes and the facilitating environment.* London: Hogarth Press.

Winnicott, D. W. (1971). *Playing and reality.* London: Tavistock.

Wollheim, R. (1995). *The mind and its depths.* Cambridge, MA: Harvard University Press.

27

Family and Couple Therapy

Toward Greater Security

❖

JOHN BYNG-HALL

John Bowlby wrote one of the first family thera-py papers (Bowlby, 1949). It vividly conveys his excitement on discovering the power of family therapy to produce change. At that time he con-templated developing this as a way of doing psy-chotherapy. He was a scientist as well as a clini-cian, however, and felt that the family was too complex to research, so he decided to study the dyadic aspects of attachment as a first step (J. Bowlby, personal communication, 1982). He never doubted, however, that family research would eventually be undertaken, and he became a steadfast supporter of family therapy (Byng-Hall, 1991b). The exciting challenge of studying whole-family attachment patterns is now upon us.

For nearly 40 years, Bowlby ran seminars in which clinicians of various approaches and re-searchers from different fields brought their thoughts together. It was a remarkably fruitful approach. I was a member of these seminars for 12 years. Bowlby would listen with respect to therapists, despite their apparently woolly ideas, because they were confronting important issues; at the same time, researchers gained the respect of the clinicians as they elucidated issues rele-vant to therapeutic work. Bowlby was brilliant in the use of both research and therapeutic perspec-tives in case consultations. He would elucidate the attachment elements to tell a coherent story, and then help the clinician relate this to the whole clinical picture. I hope that this chapter will continue this rich tradition of cross-fertiliza-tion by adding family and marital therapists' clinical perspectives to the debate, and by indi-cating what aspects of attachment research have been useful and what will be valuable to know more about. Family and marital therapists need—and already use—concepts that encom-pass a wider context than the dyad, to include tri-ads and whole families. Some of these concepts may be useful to attachment researchers.

Unfortunately, family therapists have for vari-ous reasons become interested in attachment the-ory only relatively recently (Byng-Hall, 1991b). One reason for the delay has been attachment theory's focus on the dyad and not the whole family. Not surprisingly, then, there are few em-pirical studies of family or couple therapy using an attachment paradigm. Equally, there is limited clinical family therapy literature that uses attach-ment as its central theory. There are, however, an increasing number of publications whose authors refer to attachment research to inform part of their practice; this is appropriate, because attach-ment is only one aspect of family relationships.

The main aim of this chapter is to explore how the family can either increase or undermine the sense of security of its members, and how this knowledge can provide family and couple thera-pists with suitable goals for their work. The chapter starts by considering attachment patterns in families and couples, and links concepts from different bodies of attachment research to family systems concepts. A table summarizes these links and also shows how relevant terms used in attachment research are related to each other. Various conceptual frameworks that can be used for understanding families are considered, initially from the perspective of overall patterns; systems theory and the concept of distance regulation are explored. Then the chapter focuses on the "inner" family, looking at shared internal working models, object relations theory, and the individual's capacity to understand family interaction. After this, the implications of attachment theory for family and couple therapy are discussed—first with respect to the overall aims of the therapist, and second when applied to particular situations. The last major section of the chapter suggests avenues for future exploration.

ATTACHMENT IN THE FAMILY AND COUPLE SYSTEM: CONCEPTUAL ISSUES

Ways of Studying Family Attachment Patterns

What units are most fruitful to study when one is exploring the family system? Emde (1988) offers a heuristic proposition that family therapy mostly works on the effect of relationships on relationships. Berlin and Cassidy (Chapter 30, this volume) discuss the current state of knowledge about relations between relationships; they conclude that there is good evidence that early attachments influence later relationships. Those who have early secure dyadic affectional bonds are later more likely to have harmonious and supportive relationships with their siblings, friends, and romantic partners, and their own children. Those who have "earned" security— that is, those who appear to have had unsupportive childhoods, yet have become secure as adults—show that the influence of early attachments on later relationships can be modified. It has been shown that subsequent attachment experiences (e.g., marriage and psychotherapy) can be key sources of such changes. Berlin and Cassidy's review also concludes that infant–parent relationships can be influenced by other relationships, such as the parents' relationships with their own parents, the parents' marriage, therapeutic relationships, and more general social support. This suggests that therapy—including family therapy during an insecure childhood, or couple therapy later—may have preventative roles to play.

Emde (1991) has explored the level of com-

plexity in the influence of dyadic relationships on one another. For instance, a triad has only three dyadic relationships influencing one another, whereas in a family of four there are 15, and in a family of eight there are 378! This suggests that studying the triad is a good way to build on the dyadic research. Emde (1991) discusses why triads are considered particularly meaningful in therapy, and suggests that this may be because so many feelings are evoked by a person's being either left out of or included in dyads. For example, children have fears and wishes about exclusion from or inclusion in the parents' relationship, as well as parent–sibling relationships. Bowen (1978), a pioneer family systems therapist, considered the triad rather than the dyad to be the basic building block of relationships. He described how problems in one relationship can be rerouted through another relationship; for example, parental tension may be lessened by directing conflict toward a child. Donley (1993) extends this thinking to attachment patterns.

Another approach to exploring attachments in families is to study aspects of family relationships that are shared. Family therapists consider that shared family beliefs and shared family rules about behavior, which are encoded in repeated patterns of interaction, are important in determining how the family functions. Marvin and Stewart (1990) have proposed the term "shared working model," and I (Byng-Hall, 1995a) have used the concept of "family script," which is composed of the family's shared expectations of how family roles are to be performed in various contexts (including that of attachment/caregiving).

From a wider perspective, it has proved possible to research factors ranging from those within the individual to those outside the family that are linked together in the model of a family system. Cowan, Powell, and Cowan (1997) describe six different mutually influencing domains of the family system that are relevant to the dyadic relationship involved in parenting. These are factors related to the individual; past and present relationships with the previous generation; quality of the parents' relationship; quality of sibling relationships; relationships between nuclear family and the outside world; and each parent–child relationship. Cowan et al. then discuss studies showing each domain's links with the parenting relationship, which in turn influences the family. The authors go on to draw lessons for parenting interventions. Cowan, Cohn, Cowan, and Pearson (1996) have used a similar multidomain model, as well as path-analytic statistics, to explore how parents' attachment histories are linked to children's externalizing and internalizing behaviors. This thorough approach to the investigation of links between aspects of family life, and domains of the family system in which attachments are included, promises to be very fruitful.

Security in the Family: The Concept of a Secure Family Base

Some of the ways that the family system is organized can influence both the current felt security of its members and the capacity for attachment relationships to provide security. The clinical concept of a "secure family base" has been proposed (Byng-Hall, 1995b) in order to suggest features of the family system that may contribute to greater security in the family. The secure family base has been defined as "a family that provides a reliable and readily available network of attachment relationships, and appropriate caregivers, from which all members of the family are able to feel sufficiently secure to explore their potential" (Byng-Hall, 1997b, p. 27). This clinical concept has not yet been researched, and implies an ideal to work toward on a continuum of secure–insecure. The concept involves a shared family responsibility; it assures everyone that any member who is in need of help will be cared for, even when certain members are unavailable (either temporarily or permanently). For small children, a secure family base means an expectation of reliable handover and handback within the family network or with suitable outside caregivers.

The capacity for collaboration among caregivers becomes the crucial attribute that joins attachment relationships into a functioning network. Cobb (1996) studied collaboration in 62 triads consisting of two parents with a young adolescent. This study showed that the capacity to collaborate in problem solving within these triads correlates positively with those in which the adolescent has secure attachments with both parents; the capacity to collaborate also correlated positively with the capacity for exploration within these triads, suggesting that a safe base was being provided. In triads in which the adolescent had preoccupied attachments to both parents the family was able to collaborate, but they were not able to explore, which suggests that collaboration is not sufficient on its own to provide

a secure base. Avoidant attachments did not support either collaboration or exploration. Collaboration in caregiving requires the capacity to keep in mind not only children (or ill and old members of the family) but also other caregivers, and to maintain a supportive and trusting attitude to other appropriate attachment relationships. This facilitates the mutual support, planning, and delegation that are required for handing over care in ways that a child can trust.

A secure family base requires a shared awareness that attachment relationships need to be protected and not undermined. A central family rule is that care is always given priority when it is needed, even when there are other very pressing family preoccupations. This enables family members to have conflicts and to express anger (a functional part of family life), safe in the knowledge that care remains ensured. The shared working model of a secure family base is one of family members' supporting one another in their care for family members, whatever happens. The concept of a secure family base is useful, as it focuses the therapist's attention on factors that either support or undermine the security of the family base. Factors that undermine security can include loss or threatened loss of an attachment figure; competition for care, or a parent's being "captured" by one member of the family to the exclusion of others; turning to inappropriate caregivers, such as a parent's turning to a child; expectations of losses similar to those encountered in previous generations, which lead to inappropriate precautions in current parenting; abuse within the family; and conflicts that disrupt caregiving, mainly involving power battles or distance conflicts (Byng-Hall, 1995a, 1997b).

If family members are experienced as having a right to family care from extended family members, this can increase the size of the available network. The boundaries of family membership and the number of people to whom members have privileged access, especially in a crisis, vary across families and cultures. Children slowly develop a model of "our family," and may get to know about boundaries either directly or through family stories. Collaboration in caregiving in the extended family, especially between female members, may also have been selected during evolution as a way of passing on one's genes—by making sure that the children of relatives, as well as one's own, survive to reproductive age (Stevenson-Hinde & Shouldice, 1995).

The research needed to validate the concept of the secure family base includes studying working models of collaboration during caregiving, beliefs about family membership, and rules about priority of care. Triadic questions about parents' supporting each other to look after children, or ill and needy members of any age, may also be fruitful. Studying attitudes and approaches to other family members' relationships is crucial. Grandparents who cherish and enjoy their children's relationships with their own children, without attempting to take over, can also provide a good model to explore.

Attachment in Couples: Two Approaches

The parents' attachment relationship has been studied from two different directions. Social psychologists have used self-report techniques to explore adult romantic attachments, whereas developmental researchers have used adults' description of their childhood experiences of attachments. These two bodies of work and the relations between them are fully discussed by Crowell, Fraley, and Shaver (Chapter 20, this volume). An outline of each approach is given here, focusing on some, but not all, of the instruments involved. The outline starts with a description of the relation between the Adult Attachment Interview (AAI; George, Kaplan, & Main, 1984, 1985 ,1996; Main & Goldwyn, 1985, 1996) and the strange situation (SS), because it is necessary to understand the dyadic patterns found in child–parent attachments before translating the patterns to the couple relationship.

The AAI is an interview with an adult about his or her childhood attachment relationships. Adjectives are requested that describe each parent, and then the interviewee is asked to describe an episode to illustrate each adjective. This procedure picks up any discrepancies between semantic memory (based on what the adult was told as a child) and episodic memory (based on what the adult experienced). Questions are also asked about what happened to the adult when he or she was ill or upset as a child, and about how his or her personality was influenced by childhood relationships. This reveals the adult's current state of mind about attachments. It is not meant to be a measure of what actually happened in childhood.

Ratings are made of the interview transcript, and one of four main classifications is assigned:

1. *Autonomous/free (F)*. If the individual is able to tell a coherent story about childhood experiences that indicates his or her awareness of the significance of attachments for children, he or she is classified as F. Such adults, as parents, have been shown to be more likely than insecure adults to have children who are securely attached to them. They are available and responsive when needed, which allows their children to feel secure enough to explore. One of the other three classifications is assigned when a person's interview is relatively incoherent.

2. *Dismissing (D)*. This kind of adult dismisses the importance of attachments and is likely to have a child who has an avoidant attachment. The child is rejected if he or she makes demands when upset, and so avoids the parent when distressed. This maintains the attachment, but at a cost in emotional distance and coolness.

3. *Preoccupied/entangled (E)*. The adult who is preoccupied with unresolved attachment issues from the past, and who tells long, rambling stories, is likely to have a child with an ambivalent attachment. Because the parent is only intermittently emotionally available, the child demands to be noticed. The child may also reverse roles and provide the distressed parent with care, thus becoming indispensable and trying thereby to assure the continuing presence of the attachment figure. These strategies are likely to maintain constant contact, thus preserving the attachment.

4. *Unresolved (U)*. This kind of individual may tell a coherent story for much of the time, but becomes incoherent when asked about an important dead attachment figure or abuse from an attachment figure. Such incoherence is considered to indicate unresolved loss or trauma. An unresolved adult is likely to have a child with a disorganized attachment—a child who does not have a clear strategy for maintaining the attachment and seems caught in an approach–avoidance conflict with the parent.

Fisher and Crandell (1997) describe the various possible pairings of AAI classifications of each partner (excluding unresolved). Pairings may consist either of partners in the same category (autonomous [F-F], dismissing [D-D], or preoccupied [E-E]) or of partners in different categories (autonomous and insecure [F-D or F-E] or dismissing and preoccupied [D-E]. Fisher and Crandell have noted that the last pairing (D-E) is common in couples seeking help. As space does not allow for descriptions of all the pairings, the D-E attachment pairing (similar to the avoidant–ambivalent pairing found in research on adult romantic attachment) provides the focus for discussion throughout the rest of the chapter, to illustrate how various concepts relate to couple attachments. This expository strategy has the advantage of being both clinically relevant and descriptive of two major forms of insecure attachment. Fisher and Crandell describe the D-E pairing as producing a highly conflictual relationship in which the preoccupied partner is expressing most of the discontent, while the dismissing partner sees the only problem with the relationship as the other's discontent. The preoccupied partner feels chronically deprived and abandoned, while the dismissing partner is disdainful of his or her dependency needs. As the preoccupied partner escalates the appeal to have dependency needs met, this escalates the dismissing partner's defensive response of distancing, which leads to subsequent pursuer–distancer escalations (see below).

Radojevic (1996) has gone through the same exercise, except that she has added the unresolved category. She discusses the need to do grieving work or posttraumatic work in these couples, in addition to the normal tasks of couple therapy.

Feeney (Chapter 17, this volume) discusses research on romantic attachment styles. Hazan and Shaver (1987) initially used a self-classification procedure in which a person was asked to choose the most self-descriptive of three descriptions of feeling and behavior in relationships. The three descriptions were based on the SS categories (Ainsworth, Blehar, Waters, & Wall, 1978) of "secure," "ambivalent," and "avoidant." Because a forced choice of one of the descriptions was required, a three-group model of romantic attachment was involved. Further refinement of this model followed, addressing some of the problems of using a forced-choice measure (e.g., Brennan, Clark, & Shaver, 1998). The three descriptions were broken down into a number of agree–disagree statements. Factor analysis of these statements pointed to two major dimensions: "comfort with closeness" and "anxiety over relationships." Comfort with closeness is a bipolar dimension with secure at one pole and avoidant at the other; anxiety over relationships deals with themes central to ambivalent attachments. Bartholomew and Horowitz (1991) added a fourth category to the two-dimensional model by dividing avoidant attachment into "fearful" and "dismissing" types. They also argued that the anxiety dimension can be viewed as a reflection of positive versus negative models of self, and

the avoidance dimension as a reflection of positive versus negative models of others. Avoidants with high self-esteem are categorized as dismissing; they emphasize achievement and self-reliance, maintaining a sense of self-worth at the expense of intimacy. In contrast, avoidants with low self-esteem are categorized as fearful; they desire intimacy but distrust others, avoiding close involvements that may lead to loss or rejection. This distinction fits with my clinical experience and helps to explain the difference between these two contrasting manifestations of avoidance, which call for very different therapeutic approaches. The three-group and the four-group models show meaningful relations to each other, but the four-group model is validated by empirical support for the two distinct types of avoidance.

The AAI and Bartholomew's interview schedule show some convergence (Bartholomew & Shaver, 1998), but it is clear that important differences exist. The relations between the two measures and the corresponding research literatures are discussed by Crowell et al. (Chapter 20, this volume). As a clinician, I find the AAI research particularly useful in understanding strategies used in insecure relationships that carry a parent–child component, even if these are manifested in a couple. It is also invaluable in understanding clients' narratives (Slade, Chapter 25, this volume). The adult romantic research is particularly helpful in understanding issues associated with attitudes toward intimate relationships (the new element in romantic attachments), especially the difference between dismissing and fearful avoidance in couple members. Table 27.1 shows how the various categories are linked and from which research domain they come.

Links between Family Therapy Concepts and Attachment Research

Lyman Wynne (1984), a leading family therapist, described the development of relational systems. He portrayed attachment/caregiving as the first stage in the epigenesis of relational systems, followed by communication, then joint problem solving, and finally mutuality. Bowlby (personal communication, 1984) agreed that these functions are closely linked, but pointed out that the four processes are overlapping rather than following each other in an epigenetic sequence. Despite this conceptual problem, the article has been important in drawing family therapists' attention to attachment and has influenced prac-

TABLE 27.1. Security of Attachments: Individuals, Couples, and Families

Domain of attachments	Attachment patterns			
Child				
SS classification	Secure (B)	Avoidant (A)	Ambivalent or resistant (C)	Disorganized/ disoriented (D, or A + C)
Child's pattern with parent	Autonomous; explores readily	Avoids closeness; attachment behavior deactivated	Demanding and/or angry; attachment behavior overactivated	Disorganized; becomes controlling or excessively caregiving when older
Parent				
AAI classification	Autonomous/free (F)	Dismissing (D)	Preoccupied/ entangled (E)	Unresolved (U) in regard to loss or trauma
Adult romantic attachment style	Secure	Avoidant (dismissing or fearful)	Ambivalent or preoccupied	
Narrative	Coherent	Incoherent; dismisses importance of attachment	Incoherent; preoccupied with past	Incoherent in discussing losses or traumas
Parental style	Sensitively responsive	Rejecting	Intermittently available	Maltreatment (by some); "frightened or frightening"
Couple and family relationships				
Distance	Free to go to and from when appropriate	Distant	Overly close; intrusive	Approach–avoidance conflict (some)
Family transactional style	Adaptable	Disengaged	Enmeshed	Sometimes disoriented
Shared strategy	Maintenance of contact with other	Avoidance of emotional or physical closeness	Mutual monitoring; blurred boundaries; role reversal	No common strategy; perhaps dissociation

tice, notably that of Doane and Diamond (1994, and see below).

The circumplex model of family functioning (Olson, Sprenkle, & Russell, 1979) was developed by taking 50 concepts commonly used by family and marital therapists and placing them in three main categories: "cohesion," "adaptability," and "communication." The items are used in a self-report questionnaire, and many are related to features of attachment. Much research has been devoted to this model. Unfortunately, it is difficult to see how the results relate to attachment, because the concepts used are so global. However, it may be valuable for an attachment researcher to see whether attachment elements can be extracted from the existing data based on this model.

Marvin and Stewart (1990) have noted that Salvador Minuchin's (1974) classification of family organization, which has been widely used by family therapists, is very similar to the way in which Ainsworth et al. (1978) classified the security of children's attachments. Minuchin's "adaptive" families are like secure attachments; "enmeshed" families are similar to ambivalent attachments; and "disengaged" families are like avoidant attachments. Stevenson-Hinde (1990) illustrated this similarity with the use of a table matching Minuchin's categories of family functioning to AAI classification, SS classification, and the child's interaction style with the parent. Moreover, she included a "chaotic" family also described by Minuchin, matching it tentatively with the disorganized SS classification. Table

27.1 includes adult romantic attachment categories. Links are illustrated by matching each factor to the type of attachment relationship with which it is associated. A more detailed exploration of concepts useful in understanding attachment and security within the family follows.

Systems Theory as a Framework for Thinking about Attachments

Marvin and Stewart (1990) have argued that attachment theory and family systems theory can be related to each other, to the advantage of both. Family therapists use systems theory to help them understand how members of a family mutually influence one another and create a whole that is more than the sum of its parts. General systems theory was proposed by Bertalanffy (1968) in order to explore the interrelationships among all elements of whatever kind. He argued against isolating elements as a way of trying to study them; instead, each has to be understood within its own context. Patricia Minuchin (1985), a psychologist with a family systems orientation, believes that attachment theory, despite its narrow focus, is one of the more suitable developmental theories to be integrated into systems theory. This is because it explores bidirectional relationships in which each participant provides the context for the other's behavior. Minuchin states: "If the individual is part of an organized family system, he or she is never truly independent and can only be understood in context" (1985, p. 290). Stevenson-Hinde (1990) has described the place of attachment within the family system and has provided an overview of the characteristics of systems theory.

Bowlby (personal communication, 1982) was interested in general systems theory at an early point in its history and selected control systems theory, one aspect of cybernetics, as the area of systems theory most relevant to attachment (Bowlby, 1982). Circular causality is one of the central ideas used to explain mutual influence. Instead of a simple linear causality in which a particular cause produces a specific effect, circular causality consists of "a series of cause and effect sequences that eventually leads back to a first cause, and either confirms or changes that cause" (Simon, Steirlin, & Wynne, 1985, p. 37). The effects of any action thus circle back—either directly from the other person within the dyad, or via other people—to affect how the original actor behaves next time around in the cycle of interaction. Interactive cycles, which include both ac-

tions and verbal components, act as information feedback loops. These either discourage any deviation from the norm (negative feedback) and so maintain the stability of the pattern, or they encourage and strengthen a new form of behavior (positive feedback), which encourages change and disruption of the previous pattern of interaction. Bowlby (1969/1982) proposed the concept of "goal-corrected behavior," in which feedback loops come into action if the interaction is deviating from the pathway to the goal. The goals of attachment/caregiving (proximity and protection) involve two people, and shared goal-corrected behavior is required if parent and child are to collaborate in gaining and maintaining proximity.

Certain situations create "mutual positive" feedback loops within dyadic relationships, which make them potentially unstable and frequently lead to triangulation of other people in order to stabilize the relationships (Hoffman, 1971). In the S family (encountered in my clinical practice), the father, Mr. S, had an avoidant style of attachment to his wife and when under stress would withdraw from Mrs. S, who had an ambivalent style of attachment and when under stress would cling to Mr. S. (This family is also used later to illustrate other concepts related to avoidant–ambivalent couple attachments.) Mr. S's withdrawal would then act as positive feedback to his wife's clinging, thereby increasing her clinging, which in turn acted as positive feedback to his withdrawal. Thus there was an escalating crisis in the relationship, of the type known as "pursuer–distancer" (see the discussion of distance regulation, below). Their son would then be brought into the cycle of interaction, because his attachment behavior became activated. When he ran to his mother, she encouraged it, because her own attachment behavior was still activated and she wanted to be with someone. At this moment, the goal of gaining proximity was shared by mother and son. When the son's attachment system was assuaged, however, hers was not. So when he tried to go off to play, she would stop him, thus giving his exploratory behavior negative feedback. The original shared goal-corrected behavior of the mother and son's getting together now included the mother's goal of gaining caregiving from her son through a reversal of roles. She could no longer respond to his cues indicating his readiness to explore. Over time mother and son became inseparable, and he would not go to school. These kinds of unstable parental relationships can potentially involve anyone available; mothers-in-law are favorites, and therapists are also common. Cycles of interaction often involve an entire family or extended family.

Patricia Minuchin (1985, p. 290) has said that "the irreducible unit is the cycle of interaction. Change must be directed towards that cycle." Family therapists include as many as possible of those who get involved in the cycle of interaction, in order to change the cycle. In the case of the S family, seeing the son on his own or seeing dyads only would not have altered the cycle so quickly, although work with the parents on their relationship was required for a long-term solution. Family therapists see the linear concept of pathology or illness as an unhelpful explanation for emotional distress, because it locates the whole problem in one person and leaves the other family members to continue unwittingly making their contributions to the distress. This can scapegoat the individual and prevent any real change.

Marvin and Stewart (1990) provide an extensive discussion of systems theory as it relates to family attachments and to their maladaptations. They discuss systems concepts that are useful in understanding how the family's stability and change is managed. These include relations between whole systems and their subsystems, maintenance of invariant relationships, self-regulation, and self-organization. A colleague and I (Byng-Hall & Stevenson-Hinde, 1991) have described a way of exploring videotapes of family therapy sessions that can identify various influences, including the family interactions that maintain a relationship pattern. Radojevic (1996) has used the systems concepts of "first-order" and "second-order" change. First-order change involves parts changing but not the whole structure; second-order change involves a change in the underlying rules that alters the whole structure. Family therapy aims at achieving second-order, lasting change by altering the family's working models.

Distance Regulation in the Family System

According to Bowlby (1988, p. 123), "The attachment control system maintains a person's relation to his attachment figure between certain limits of distance and accessibility." In a family context, each person's distance and accessibility are being regulated in an attempt to accommodate all family members' needs to achieve some

security. Family therapists are usually witnesses to situations in which this is not achieved, at least for some members. Increasing closeness in one relationship may merely increase the distance to an insecure level in another, and vice versa. Family therapists usually do not have data about their clients' attachment status. Therapists can, however, observe signs of felt insecurity in each family member, note his or her attachment strategies, see how these are responded to, and note whether this then affects the distance from others (who may, especially if feeling left out, attempt to counter such changes). The way a family regulates distance can provide the focus for interventions aimed at changing the pattern.

"Too Close–Too Far" Couple and Family Systems

Elsewhere (Byng-Hall, 1980, 1997a; Byng-Hall & Campbell, 1981), I have proposed the concept of a "too close–too far" family system. In these families, certain relationships are experienced by one member of the relationship as being too close (either intrusive or entrapping), thus evoking distancing behavior, while another member feels the same relationships to be too far away to be secure, thus activating attachment behavior. This can happen at times in many different family relationships, such as the one between a parent and an adolescent or the one between the parents. Pistole (1994), who uses adult romantic attachment concepts, has explored the struggles that emerge when the distance between members of a couple cannot be negotiated to suit both partners. She points out that "so long as the partner is perceived as physically or symbolically close and accessible enough, the attachment system is calm" (p. 148). If a tolerable range of distance is exceeded, one partner's separation anxiety is triggered, and this can set off a distance struggle in the form of pursuit–distance cycles (recall the S couple discussed earlier) if the anxiety is not responded to by the other partner. This can happen in any couple, even those with secure attachment styles, in response to changing situations, typically when one partner is seeking closeness and the other is not emotionally able to respond at that time. The cycles can usually be resolved by a renegotiation of the distance or by a "kiss and make up" scenario. Pistole describes how a couple combination of avoidant and ambivalent attachment styles (Bartholomew & Horowitz, 1991; Hazan & Shaver, 1987) can contribute to a pursuit–distance cycle's becoming a major and continuing feature of the relationship. The ambivalent partner focuses unduly on the attachment information within the relationship, especially any that might be indicative of the partner's lack of accessibility, while the avoidant partner restricts attention to the environment. Such partners are then likely to misconstrue each other's style as evidence of intention and react accordingly, setting up a pursuit–distance cycle.

Triangulation of Others as Distance Regulators

Following pursuer–distancer escalations between parents, one parent is likely to turn to a child, as in the S family. A child's mixed feelings about the parents' marriage—on the one hand, wanting one parent to himself or herself; on the other, wanting the parents to be together—means that the child will try to divide the parents when they get too close and unite them when they seem too far apart. This gives the child the role of distance regulator to the parents' marriage and stops the dangerous escalations (Byng-Hall, 1980). A variation on this pattern is a child who "captures" a parent and excludes all others, including the other parent; capturing is maintained if it resolves the parent's distance conflict (Byng-Hall & Stevenson-Hinde, 1991). Siblings may also act as a team, one acting to bring the parents together while the other divides them. Often this leads to conflict between the siblings. A steadier distance can be maintained between the parents in these ways.

Illnesses and Emotional Problems That Become Distance Regulators

Another clinically common phenomenon can arise when a family member (say, a child) becomes ill or develops an emotional problem, which may itself be the result of the stress due to being a distance regulator (Byng-Hall, 1980, 1995a). The illness or problem may then help to stabilize the too close–too far parental system by bringing the parents together to look after the child. This shared nonintimate caregiving (or disciplinary) role does not threaten the relationship by making it too close; it also provides a reason for not separating. In other words, the illness or problem resolves the parents' too close–too far conflict, and thus becomes the distance regulator of the parents' relationship. Another pattern is that of the distancing parent who does not engage in collaborative caregiving, becomes isolat-

ed, and eventually leaves. Both these situations can make it more difficult for the child to get better (Byng-Hall, 1997a).

Research on Family Distance

Bell, Erikson, Cornwell, and Bell (1991) explored closeness–distance in 79 normal families, using the Family Paper Sculpture to gain the family members' consensus as to their distance. This procedure showed that families in which relationships were experienced as very close or very distant at one point in time might experience their relationships as extreme in the opposite direction at another point. The authors postulated that the experiences of extreme closeness and extreme distance may be different manifestations of the same underlying process. Global coding of taped family interactions showed that the families exhibiting extremes had more conflict, less ability to resolve differences, and less warmth and support among family members. This would suggest that the too close–too far family configuration in more troubled families would justify further investigation. In order to explore the too close–too far system further, it would be necessary to include studies in which the distancing and clinging in dyads were also measured, preferably in the context of taped family interactions.

Shared, and Contradictory, Working Models

Working models "direct not only behavior but also attention, memory and cognition, insofar as these relate directly or indirectly to attachment" (Main, Kaplan, & Cassidy, 1985, p. 67; see Bretherton & Munholland, Chapter 5, this volume, for a discussion of working models). Thus the ways in which working models guide responses to feedback loops involve many modalities. Marvin and Stewart (1990) have proposed the concept of "shared working models," which allow for family members to anticipate one another's likely plans and actions. This facilitates collaboration and the creation of shared goal-corrected aims. The more accurately each member can assess another's working model, the better they are able to collaborate. Models can be extended to self, the other, and others; in other words, there are models of how the other person relates to third parties. The final step in creating a systemic internal working model consists of how others, working together, relate back to the self. The care seeker's model deals with "how Mother and Father (or the family) help each other to look after me." The caregiver's model deals with "how we together look after him or her." At a higher level of abstraction, all members of the family have a shared model of "how we look after each other when it is necessary." The model at a lower level of abstraction can relate to contributions from specific family members (e.g., a model that helps to explain each person's attachment strategy).

Bowlby (1973) suggested that children may develop working models that are contradictory or incompatible for the same significant situation, which can create insecurity and narrative incoherence (Main, 1991). The contradiction may be between two versions of the same situation in one person; for instance, an episodic memory can contradict a semantic memory if what the child saw happening contradicts what the child was told was happening. This contradiction may also be a manifestation of a family ethos of keeping secrets. Moreover, different people may hold models of what to do in a particular situation that are incompatible with each other. In this case, each person may interpret the other's actions in terms of his or her own model, which is likely to be wrong and lead to inappropriate action (Pistole, 1994). A good example of this misconstruing can be found in the internal working models of avoidant and ambivalent adults in families like the S family. The problem arises because their strategies for the same thing—how to maintain insecure attachments—are diametrically opposite to each other in the direction that they take. Mr. S's strategy was to withdraw while Mrs. S's was to cling when the relationship was threatened. Mrs. S interpreted her husband's withdrawal as showing that he was intending to leave; he, dismissing the importance of attachment, saw her clinging as a sign that she intended to control and entrap him, rather than that she needed his help. What was interesting in terms of cybernetics was that Mr. S actually intended his withdrawal to be negative feedback to stop his wife's clinging, while she intended her clinging to be negative feedback to his withdrawal. Instead, both actions were taken as positive feedback. If therapy is done with all members of such a family present, the emerging new models can be shared to a greater extent; where they continue to differ, the members can become aware of their differences, which they can then take into account instead of misconstruing other people's intentions.

Attachments, Object Relations Theory, and Mutual Projections

Heard (1978) and Fonagy (Chapter 26, this volume) describe how attachment theory can be understood within object relations theory. Fisher and Crandell (1997) discuss how research findings with the AAI and SS can be related to object relations theory as it is practiced in the Tavistock Marital Studies Institute. They explore the concepts of "projection" and "defense" as used in object relations theory. Some couple and family therapists use the concept of "mutual projections," in which each partner becomes the repository of the other's disowned selves. Another way of thinking about this is that mutual projections solve the problem of incompatible internal working models of attachment held by each partner. Instead of each person's holding both contradictory models of the self uncomfortably within consciousness, the working model that is least acceptable, together with the emotions and actions it encourages, is attributed to someone else and is attacked there. Distressing attachment-related emotions are defensively excluded by the dismissing individual and attributed to the preoccupied partner, who readily expresses distressed feelings. The tendency of the preoccupied individual to reject or angrily push away the partner, at the same time as clinging, is ever present within his or her ambivalence. However, the rejecting aspect can be attributed to the dismissing partner, while his or her own angry pushing away is perceived as merely an expression of justifiable rage at the partner's failure to meet his or her needs. This is a neat solution to the discomfort of owning ambivalent feelings. In the dismissing–preoccupied couple, both partners' defenses are supported by the process of mutual projection. Indeed, this process may have contributed to the partners' choosing each other in the first place. Family and marital therapists attempt to help people "own" their feelings, which allows them to be more sensitive to others' actual feelings, instead of just perceiving their own disowned feelings in others and attacking them there.

The Capacity to Observe Group Process

One object relations concept discussed by Fisher and Crandell (1997) is that of "triangular space" (Britton, 1989), which gives an individual the possibility of experiencing being a participant in a relationship while being observed by a third person, as well as being an observer of a relationship between two other people. "This provides us with a capacity for seeing ourselves in interaction with others and for entertaining another point of view whilst retaining our own, for reflecting on ourselves whilst being ourselves" (Britton, 1989, p. 87). This capacity has some similarities to the concept of the "reflective self." A Reflective Self Function scale can be applied to AAI data to predict the security of the attachment that an interviewee's child has to the interviewee; this suggests that the capacity to reflect is important for secure attachments (Fonagy, Steele, Steele, Moran, & Higgitt, 1991). This capacity to be an observer to the process in which one is a participant can also be valuable in group situations. In families, this can be called "interactional awareness"—the capacity to be aware of how what is unfolding in family scenarios may be affecting all those involved. The aware individual also has some notion of his or her own input and of why all the others respond as they do (Byng-Hall, 1995a, p. 39). Shared capacity for interactional awareness allows for collaboration in protecting family members from potentially disturbing aspects of what is happening, and thus supports the security of the family base.

IMPLICATIONS OF ATTACHMENT THEORY FOR FAMILY THERAPY PRACTICE

Overall Aims of the Therapist

Family therapists usually work with relationships *in vivo*. Advantages of this approach include the following:

1. What is learned in the session is shared and so can be taken away and worked on at home, unlike individual therapy, in which the family member returns after the session to an unchanged set of pressures from the family system.
2. New cycles of interaction can be created within the sessions, and the family can use these at home right away.
3. Work can be done on both interactions and the meaning of those interactions; this bridges the gap between episodic and semantic memory, and so is more likely to provide a coherent view of attachments.

Family therapists usually see the whole family together, but they will also see subsystems at times—say, the parents together, a group of siblings, or individual members. This is done, however, as part of a coordinated attempt to change the whole family system.

Bowlby (1988) discussed the role of the therapist in individual psychotherapy. He outlined five tasks for the therapist to perform: (1) providing a secure therapeutic base, (2) exploring relationships with significant others, (3) exploring the relationship with the therapist, (4) reviewing how current ways of relating may be due to past experiences, and (5) recognizing that these images from the past may or may not be appropriate for the future. These tasks are used here as a frame for thinking about the tasks of family therapy (the fourth and fifth tasks are combined below).

Providing a Secure Therapeutic Base

A family therapist can provide a temporary secure base for the whole family during therapy (Byng-Hall, 1995a; Heard, 1982; Marvin, 1992). The overall aim is to use this therapeutic secure base to help the family members to explore ways of improving the security of the family base. This helps them to explore and solve their own problems during and following therapy. The following steps, informed by attachment theory, help to provide a secure therapeutic base.

Availability of the Therapist. In one family therapy model guided by attachment theory (Byng-Hall, 1995a), the therapist makes himself or herself available as quickly as possible, and then maintains contact for an adequate period of time. The family can be telephoned in order to establish the beginnings of a relationship. In the first session, the therapist engages warmly with each member of the family; this ensures that each feels that the therapist is emotionally available to him or her, while modeling how everyone else is also offered that possibility, and none is left out. The family is initially seen weekly to establish an attachment. Once this is achieved, the frequency is tapered off to fortnightly or monthly sessions, and then to sessions every 3–6 months. After discharge, the therapist makes it clear that he or she is still available. In this way families are usually seen between 6 and 16 times, but these are spread over 1 to 3 years. Thus the family is offered what amounts to a brief intervention in terms of therapy time, but a much longer-term secure base. Many family therapists see families every 3–4 weeks, which, although reducing the intensity of therapeutic attachment, nevertheless emphasizes that a family has to provide its own secure family base.

Roles of the Therapist as an Attachment Figure. To be experienced as a potential secure base, the therapist has to show the capacity to fulfill two important functions of an attachment figure: to be alert to potential dangers, and to facilitate exploration (Byng-Hall, 1995a, p. 123). A sense of security emerges from knowing that the therapist is able to address the family's most worrying situations in a helpful way, so an attempt is made to reach core anxieties and conflicts in the first session. The discussion of feared issues may also help to activate the family's attachment to the therapist. When the family is feeling more secure, the therapist helps the family to explore how, when, and why these conflicts arise, and to improvise alternative ways of relating.

Working with Current Significant Relationships

Reframing the Meaning of Attachment Strategies: A Competence-Based Approach. Feeling understood is crucial to family members' establishing secure attachments to the therapist. Attachment theory can offer explanations that are clear to both therapist and family, and that make sense out of what may be otherwise perplexing. For instance, a child who is angry, demanding, and controlling is often seen as intentionally bad, but the child can be seen in a completely different light if described as insecure and trying to make sure he or she is in the parents' minds when he or she feels unloved and unlovable. Equally telling is a discussion about how this sets up a vicious circle as the parents become exasperated and make the child even more insecure, and so on. Here is a cycle of interaction that the family can understand and attempt to rectify. Family therapists use the term "reframing" when a particular behavior that has been seen in one way is given a fresh meaning. Reframing is "a therapeutic strategy that effects an alteration in a client's or family's internal model of the world" (Simon et al., 1985, p. 286). Marvin (1992) points out that attachment theory portrays strategies within insecure attachments as adaptations that are appropriate to that situation and are thus competent ways of coping. Even though these strategies can become problematic if adopted again later in life, they nevertheless remain attempts to be competent. Family therapists have increasingly found that validating families' attempts at competence,

known as "positive labeling," is more productive than identifying faults, especially in front of other family members who may then blame the individual. Once the family members feel validated by knowing that the therapist has appreciated how much they have already struggled to sort things out, they can turn to trying to understand why it has not worked and start to explore fresh ways of handling the problem.

Creating a More Coherent Narrative Style in the Family. Family stories and narrative styles have been categorized along lines similar to AAI classifications: "coherent," "incoherent/dismissive," "incoherent/preoccupied," "contradictory" (about too close–too far situations), and "unresolved mourning" (Byng-Hall, 1997a, 1999). Therapeutic techniques to achieve greater coherence are described in detail elsewhere (Byng-Hall, 1995a, 1997a, 1999). One approach is for the therapist to become the narrator to the process as it unfolds in the session, which models how the family members can tell their own story about their own process. Another technique reported in one case was to help parents with a "contradictory" story about (and models of) attachments (one parent was avoidant, the other ambivalent). The story enabled them to see that despite their opposing strategies, both of their attachment styles were actually aimed at maintaining their marriage. In this way a story was told about a clash between ways of trying to achieve the same thing, rather than a story about mutual opposition (Byng-Hall, 1997a). Techniques for telling more coherent stories about illness and loss can be used to help families with serious illnesses (Byng-Hall, 1997a). Pianta, Marvin, Brittner, and Borowitz (1996) explored the narratives of parents of chronically sick children when they were asked to discuss their response to hearing the children's diagnoses.

Resolving Distance Conflicts. Family therapists know that changing the distance within one relationship can merely switch the distance problem elsewhere; this is only first-order change. For instance, creating greater space in an overly close mother–child relationship may merely lead to a sibling's taking over the same role, unless whatever it is that leaves the mother needing a close relationship with a child is changed. Addressing the whole pattern is important, and no one should be left out. Some of the shifts in distance can be made in the session, others outside. The family can be encouraged to do certain things between sessions. The father in the S family taught his son to swim; the mother and her mother took the daughter to a puppet theatre; and the parents went to a restaurant. Space can also be used in the session. Structural family therapists (e.g., Minuchin, 1974) move chairs around so that the intensity of engagement can be increased in one relationship while distancing others. For instance, the mother and father can be put facing each other, excluding the children, and then given the task of resolving a disagreement. In addition, experiential techniques can be used to evoke intense emotion to mobilize greater closeness (Doane & Diamond, 1994; Johnson, 1996).

Conflict over Authority and Power Battles. Parental power battles and children who are disputing authority usually make everyone in the family feel insecure, and exploration is therefore inhibited. Structural family therapy techniques (Minuchin, 1974) can help to restore parental authority and set boundaries that keep children from being drawn into their parents' arguments. One important sign that this has happened is that children can play while parents argue. They can do this when they sense that their parents are now trying to sort themselves out, so the parents will not need to draw the children into their battles. Elsewhere (Byng-Hall, 1995a), I have explored the mutual influences between attachment/caregiving systems and authority systems. Some strategies within relationships, such as role reversal, can play a part in both systems. For instance, a child who has a role-reversed attachment can more readily be recruited into parental power battles as an ally of one parent against the other. This infringes the family hierarchy and is called a "cross-generational coalition." The choice of which parent the child is for or against may depend on what type of role reversal is involved. One clinical hypothesis is that if the role reversal is caretaking in style, the child may become the ally of the parent. If it is punitive or controlling in form, the child may be recruited in alliance against the parent (Byng-Hall, 1997b). From the perspective of the family influence on role reversal, it may be that a caring ethos encourages a caretaking form, whereas a battling family encourages a punitive form.

A secure family base allows family members to engage in conflicts, safe in the knowledge that care will not be threatened. As resolving conflict is a necessary aspect of authority, a secure family base supports functional authority systems. In turn, functional authority facilitates caregiving,

especially when parents are setting limits (e.g., sending children to bed). Conversely, insecure family bases help to disrupt authority, and dysfunctional authority disrupts security. Family therapists have to work on both authority and attachments because of mutual influence between the two domains. When authority issues predominate in a family, however, power conflicts have to be worked on first before the family can feel secure enough to explore attachment issues.

When violence occurs in couples, their attachments warrant particular care and attention in therapy. Goldner, Penn, Sheinberg, and Walker (1990) have discussed the therapeutic implications of couples' staying together because of their attachments, despite continuing violence. For a discussion of attachment and relationship violence, see De Zulueta (1993) and Lyons-Ruth and Jacobvitz (Chapter 23, this volume).

Couple and Sexual Therapy. Fisher and Crandell (1997) have used the AAI as a base for theorizing about couple therapy; their work has been discussed above. Elsewhere (Byng-Hall, 1985), I have discussed couple therapy using the concepts of distance regulation and resolution of distance conflict, also discussed above. Johnson (1996) uses the four-group model of romantic attachments (Bartholomew & Horowitz, 1991) in emotionally focused marital therapy (EFMT), in which emotional responses are seen as the primary signaling system of attachment. Distressed partners are helped to reprocess their emotional responses so that they can interact in new ways (Johnson, 1996). Johnson quotes Gottman's (1991) finding that critical attack and nonresponsive withdrawal are particularly corrosive to marital relationships. Central are ideas from childhood separations that lead to anger as part of the bereavement process. Johnson (1997) believes that much of the anger expressed in couples has similar origins: "If one partner's cruelty is really a frantic protest against the loss of attachment, the other's withdrawal expresses the equally primordial urge to protect oneself when one's partner looks like a predator" (p. 40). The approach–avoidance conflict is used to explain some of the dynamics observed. For instance, Johnson quotes material clearly taken from a disorganized/disoriented reunion in the SS—"One insecure girl ran towards her mother and then turned her back and walked backward for the last few feet" (p. 39)—which is given as an example of how some spouses may behave. The identification of patterns of insecure interactions is used to alert the therapist to the fact that an individual may be feeling insecure rather than destructive.

EFMT takes 8–20 sessions and consists of nine steps. Of particular interest to attachment theorists are Step 4, in which the problem is reframed in terms of underlying emotions and attachment needs, and the last two steps (8 and 9), which are devoted to establishing a secure base to explore problems. Seven studies show favorable treatment outcomes with different populations (Johnson, 1996). EFMT is most successful in couples where the partners wish to restructure their relationship in terms of a closer bond but have become alienated by negative interaction cycles, often of a blame–withdrawal nature. Johnson and Talitman (1997) showed that couples containing male partners who were reluctant to turn to their spouses for contact and support were most likely to benefit from EFMT. This is an important finding, because such couples are frequently encountered in clinical settings.

Roberts (1992) links the nonverbal responses of attachment behavior to sexual behavior. He suggests a therapeutic model for sexual therapy that uses exploration of the couple's childhood attachments and the early experiences of their romantic love, and then reinforces new ways of interacting with homework assignments and rituals.

Extended Families, Substitute Caregivers, and Schools. Bowlby (1988) emphasized the importance of grandmothers. Family therapists commonly work with grandparents and other relatives who are currently involved in care for families (Byng-Hall, 1982; Crose, 1994; Shields, King, & Wynne, 1995). This can be achieved either by bringing grandparents in for sessions or by planning trips for family members to visit relatives between sessions to explore different ways of relating (Bowen, 1978). It can be important to explore the nonfamily care network, because it is common to find dysfunctional caregiving by child minders, au pairs, or nannies going unnoticed or unreported. Schools are also major caregivers. Work can be done to facilitate collaboration between the school system and the family system (Dowling & Osborne, 1994; Howes, Chapter 29, this volume).

Exploring the Relationship to the Therapist

The therapist is likely to feel powerfully drawn into family roles in the family script; this is the equivalent of transference and countertransference in individual therapy (Byng-Hall, 1995a). An insecure family is likely to recruit the therapist into one of the unsatisfactory caregiving roles typical of the family. Becoming aware of the process gives clues as to what is going on and helps the therapist to avoid merely becoming part of the family system. Some family therapists share their own experience with the family members about how they are drawn into the family transactions and how this feels. This helps family members to understand how they make each other feel. In distance struggles (Byng-Hall, 1995a; Pistole, 1994), the therapist is likely to be triangulated into distance-regulating roles in too close–too far conflicts, in much the same way that family members are. The therapist, however, has to find ways of managing that role differently—of handing responsibility back to the parents, so that they can negotiate their own relationship and no longer need to triangulate other distance regulators. Family therapists may also use a one-way mirror and an observing team to help them maintain a therapeutic stance. The relationship between the family and the observing group then becomes important, and the group can communicate its thoughts in various ways to the family. Sometimes the family is invited to observe the group reflecting on what they saw going on in the session. This is interesting in terms of Britton's (1989) concept of triangular space: It provides an experience of first being observed, then having some feedback from the observers, and then observing others relate. In some ways, the observing group can represent a well-intentioned extended family. Some families say that they become quite "attached" to the team members, whom they often meet in the first session.

*Comparing Past and Present:
Understanding Developmental Pathways*

Family therapists vary in the extent to which they work with family history. Many hold that it is more important to change what is going on in the present. Others use "genograms" (family trees) to explore transgenerational family patterns; this can be a powerful tool for exploring unresolved losses and separations (Walsh & McGoldrick, 1991). The affect aroused in describing past bereavements within the family can provide powerful motivation for the members to come together to comfort one another. The overall aim is to help family members to support one another in the grieving process and to enable them to complete unresolved mourning (Byng-Hall, 1991a). The family tree may reveal when current family members have been used as replacements for dead members in order to avoid mourning—for example, when a child is conceived immediately after a death (Byng-Hall, 1995a). When members of the family use an adjective to describe a relative, they can be asked to illustrate it with an episode, in a way similar to the AAI. Exploring the connections between stories of what happened in past generations and what is happening now in the session can help the therapist and the family members to elucidate what comes from the past, and then to assess whether or not behaving in old ways is helpful now. Asking what happened in the lives of each parent when they were at the age that their child developed a problem may reveal the transgenerational component of current difficulties in attachments (e.g., an earlier unmourned family loss). During therapy each parent can come to understand the origins of his or her own and the partner's parenting and caregiving patterns, and children can make sense of how their parents behave. In this way, empathy with each other's current attachment experiences can be deepened.

Families and Couples in Particular Situations

Illness and Attachment

Marvin (1992) conducted a classic research study on family therapy in cases of pediatric psychogenic pain, using an attachment- and family-systems-based approach to developmental psychopathology. He devised a brief intervention for this type of pain, which is usually difficult to treat. The study can be used as a paradigm for designing an intervention. Marvin conceptualizes attachment-related developmental disorders as stemming from adaptive strategies used earlier in life and suitable to the context at that time, but reemployed later in inappropriate circumstances. These strategies provide temporary solutions to family crises, especially those centering around transitions (e.g., anxiety about an adolescent's leaving home). The symptom is thus conceptualized as competence-based and not as pathology; the problem, however, creates a deviation in the developmental pathway. Interventions are aimed at returning the developmental pathway to that which is age-appropriate for the child.

Marvin (1992) studied a group of 19 adolescents. He viewed the development of psychogenic pain in these adolescents in the following way. In most of the families, one or both parents were preoccupied with threatened or real loss, and so were not so attentive to the adolescent. Attachment/caregiving was then activated by what was usually a minor illness, which got better. After 1 or 2 days, however, the pain returned at a much more severe level, which was hypothesized to have arisen out of a state of self-hypnosis. The prolonged pain provided the adolescent with relief from responsibilities. The parents lost executive power through lack of knowledge about the illness or its cure, and the child became more controlling. The time each parent spent on the adolescent increased, while time with each other decreased. The adolescent was being looked after like a younger, more demanding child—a situation that interfered with the parents' marital interaction.

The intervention designed by Marvin involves five steps over 4 days. The first step involves giving the family members an overall frame of understanding. They are told that pain is valuable to protect injured parts, but that in this case the mechanism for switching it off has not worked for some reason. It is now unnecessary though very real pain; it is not psychological pain. In the second step, the therapist hypnotizes the child, using a dimmer switch as a metaphor. Symptoms are greatly reduced by the end of the second day, and parents are enthusiastic. Marvin considers this improvement to be important in the early establishment of the therapist as a safe base, and key to the success of a brief intervention. Hypnosis is continued twice a day, and the child is taught self-hypnosis. In the third step, the family patterns are returned to normal; the therapist explains that it is appropriate to expect normal behavior, as this pain is unnecessary. Family routines are explored in detail. The fourth step involves plans to elevate the child to an appropriate developmental level. Age-appropriate responsibilities are returned to the adolescent, as well as appropriate privileges. In the final step, the parents are told that the most necessary part of the intervention is for them to go out together once a week. They are not to tell the children what they are doing, and not to talk about the children when they are out. This disentangles the marriage from the parenting. These interventions are designed to reverse the pattern set up by the symptom. In Marvin's (1992) study, all of the patients were symptom-free at discharge; at a 6-month follow-up, 17 of the 19 adolescents were symptom-free. One of Marvin's working hypotheses to explain this high success rate is that the program is in large part competence-based rather than pathology-based.

Severely Disturbed Hospitalized Patients

The Yale Psychiatric Institute studied severely disturbed and hospitalized young adults suffering from schizophrenia, affective disorders, or borderline personality disorder (Doane & Diamond, 1994). The program was based on Wynne's (1984) epigenetic model of the development of relational systems, in which attachment is seen as the first step. Family therapy was one of the regular parts of the treatment regimen offered. Diamond (1986a) developed a measure of attachment based on the Five Minute Speech Sample (FMSS), in which an individual (on his or her own) is asked to speak spontaneously for 5 minutes about a particular relative. He or she describes what sort of person the relative is or was, and how they get or got along together. Each parent is asked to speak in this way about each of his or her own parents (the patient's grandparents), and also about the patient; the patient speaks about each parent. An intergenerational picture is thus built up (Diamond & Doane, 1994). In the Yale research, this approach generated categories that the investigators described as roughly corresponding to SS categories and their counterpart AAI categories. Each relationship described was categorized as: (1) "positive secure," similar to secure or autonomous attachment; (2) "negative," similar to avoidant or dismissing attachment; or (3) "ambivalent," similar to ambivalent or preoccupied attachment. These categories were based on freely expressed opinions; in the AAI, by contrast, the unconscious is "surprised" by the structuring of the interview, and coding is based on overall coherence of the description. This difference meant that the negative attachment classification was made without an interviewer being able to pick up any of the idealization or denial that would have been revealed by a contrast between semantic and episodic memory. A study comparing the AAI and the FMSS would help to clarify the relation between the two classifications, and would add validity to the instrument. In Diamond and Doane's study, the FMSS was validated by the Parental Bonding Instrument (Parker, Tuppling, & Braun, 1979). It was also correlated with a 2-hour-long Intergenerational Family Attachment, Bonding, and Separation–Individuation Instrument (Diamond, 1986b), based on a therapeutic interview.

The Yale project may not have measured exactly the same phenomena as the classical attachment research paradigms. The references to "positive," "negative," "disturbed," "strong," and "weak" attachments and to "disconnected" families suggest either that a rather different view of attachments prevailed, or that the population under study had additional severe psychological problems and perhaps different manifestations of attachment. Many may have had disorganized/disoriented attachments as children, or unresolved mourning issues, which were not accounted for in Doane and Diamond's classification system. It is interesting that this research, based on coded narratives, was being developed at a similar time as Main and her associates were developing the AAI, and that similarities were revealed. This project's findings are interesting and clinically impressive. Unfortunately, space limitations preclude a discussion of the specialized interventions used with this very disturbed group.

Foster and Adoptive Families

Levy and Orlans (1995) use an intensive 2-week-long therapy for foster and adoptive families in which severely damaged, attachment-disordered children have been placed, and in which the placement is subsequently threatened. Each child is resident with a therapeutic foster family during the period of treatment. Notably, a one-way mirror is used, so that the long-term foster or adoptive parents can observe the therapy when they are not directly involved. This procedure helps to break up dysfunctional family interactions while still allowing the parents to stay involved, and it uses the therapists as models for how to handle the children. The intervention is designed to "open the door" for conventional treatment to be effective afterwards.

Divorce: Implications for Therapy

Argles (1983) has identified types of separation threats, warnings, and symptoms encountered in family therapy that can be signs of anxious attachment, and has discussed the therapeutic implications. Malon (1986) has described couple therapy in which there are real or implied threats of divorce, and has equated these with anxious attachment. Intense pursuit–avoidance patterns are described, and the desperation tactics of the couple are considered to represent an attempt to renegotiate the love bond. Therapeutic strategies are described. Thweatt (1980) has used attachment theory to inform a rapid crisis intervention and time-limited treatment. Todorski (1995) has used Ahrons and Rogers's (1981) classification system to categorize the relationship of postdivorce couples, and has related these to AAI categories. She links "perfect pals" and "cooperative colleagues" to the autonomous category, "angry associates" to the preoccupied category, "fiery foes" to the unresolved category, and "dissolved duos" to the dismissing category. These associations are clinical, however, not research-based.

Old Age

Crose (1994) states that clinical experience often reveals patterns of attachment in older families similar to those found earlier in life. She describes techniques for working with individuals of each attachment style to help them cope. She claims that intensive family therapy can be productive in completing unfinished business before it is too late and parents die with regrets, leaving adult children to live with unresolved guilt. Shields et al. (1995) have described a family life review, which uses the tendency to reminisce to good advantage. Parents can tell the stories of their courtship and marriage; pregnancies, births, and miscarriages; and the early lives of their children. This helps the generations to develop a more realistic view of each other and to set appropriate boundaries between them.

RESEARCH STRATEGIES: SOME PROMISING IDEAS FOR THE FUTURE

Family therapists observe how attachment patterns appear to vary over time, both within relationships and between different contexts. Aspects of different attachment styles may emerge in the same person in response to various family members and to changes in the situation. A parent, for instance, can appear to have a different attachment with each of his or her children. However, people are not chameleon-like; each person has a major style that is relatively stable over time. For family therapists, the subcategory coding of each major attachment category may fit this picture and help to explain how one person's attachments can differ. Will subcategories of each individual's attachment status turn out to play a major role in research on family patterns? The mutual effects of all dyadic relationships in families of three or four members may start to elucidate family at-

tachment patterns. Studying two children in a family may throw light on the question of whether siblings can have different attachments to the same parent, and may give us more information about sibling attachment styles. (See Berlin & Cassidy, Chapter 30, this volume.)

Research that moves beyond the dyad to the family can take several directions: developing the triadic research, extending the understanding of working models to encompass families, observing whole-family interaction and family therapy sessions, and exploring couple and family narrative styles. In the meantime, therapists await with interest the further elucidation of disorganized (SS)/unresolved (AAI) attachment, because many clinical families are likely to have some family members with this form of attachment.

Triadic Research

Stewart (1977) observed mothers, fathers, and babies in a modified SS. Fathers played a different role from mothers: They were more solitary but would come in to support their infants at points of potential stress, such as when the mothers were leaving the room. Marvin and Stewart (1984) examined triads of mothers, infants, and older siblings. Preschool-age older siblings played a comforting role similar to that Stewart found for fathers, although older siblings who were toddlers were unable to do so. It is possible to devise a modification of the SS including both parents with one child, in which each parent has a reunion with the infant and also both parents come back into the room together (see below). This may be revealing of the family pattern.

Triadic questions can be asked in questionnaires or interviews similar to the AAI. These can include questions about the parents' relationship with each other, especially about how they support or undermine each other's parenting of their troubled child.

Family Group Procedures

Clinicians have long adapted the SS techniques to yield clues about the quality of whole-family attachments. In a family separation procedure that has been used for clinic families (Byng-Hall, 1995a), both parents leave together and return through the door side by side at the same moment. This reveals how siblings comfort each other when left alone together by their parents and which parent each sibling turns to on reunion. The procedure also provides some indication as to what each child's attachment to each parent may be like, and how parents collaborate in handling the situation. In a single-case study (Byng-Hall, 1995a; Cotgrove, 1993), each of two siblings (ages 1 and 3), whose attachment status with each parent was known, was studied in this way. The attachment pattern observed in the procedure was very similar to the configuration adopted by the family members when they first came into the consulting room in the first session. This finding lends some support to clinicians' observations that the first 5 minutes in the "strange" therapy situation can evoke attachment behavior and give clues to family attachment patterns.

Narrative Investigation: Reports in Progress

Fisher and Crandell (1997) have described an instrument currently being employed to study their ideas about family attachments (discussed above). It is called the Couple Attachment Joint Interview, in which couples are interviewed jointly and are asked about attachment issues within their relationship (e.g., how they respond to illness, loss, and separations, and whether or not they can depend on each other). They are then asked to describe episodes that illustrate these ideas. The interview is similar to the AAI in form but resembles the SS in its setting, as it is the couple's interaction that is being assessed. For instance, do the partners demonstrate a capacity to see and consider each other's position in each other's presence?

Hill (1992) described a process in which whole families were interviewed with a view to exploring family attachment narratives. The family members were asked for adjectives to describe family relationships and were asked to illustrate these with descriptions. This interview is currently being developed further.

Family Therapy Research

Outcome research in which attachment measures are taken before and following family and marital therapy is feasible. There are many interesting questions to be answered. For instance, which form of therapy alters internal working models or attachment status most effectively—individual psychotherapy, mother–infant therapy, or family therapy? What effect does each approach have, and on which symptoms? Akister (1998), in a research update of attachment theory and systemic practice, recommends prospective studies to assess the effectiveness of interventions.

Process research is more difficult. I spent several years developing seven instruments for coding videotapes of each family therapy session in random order. Instruments included ones for each attachment style and for interventions focused on these styles. So far, interesting results have been obtained with these instruments in single-case studies. For instance, one family (already described in Byng-Hall & Stevenson-Hinde, 1991), demonstrated a too close–too far system in which when one partner was clinging, the other was distancing. There were peaks of synchronized pursuing–distancing and periods of quiescence with no distance struggle. Therapy started with no distance struggle and remained so while the child was triangulated in a cross-generational coalition. Once the cross-generational coalition stopped, there was a peak of pursuing–distancing; this suggests that triangulation of the child may have protected the parents from pursuing–distancing escalations. This peak receded following interventions aimed at the distance conflict (Byng-Hall & Roberts, 1996). Adequate interrater reliability has not yet been achieved, although the rater of the case above may have been sufficiently consistent in her random-order ratings of family sessions to indicate changes of baselines. The changes demonstrated were consistent with clinical assessment of the case and were clinically helpful. So many variables are encountered during ongoing family therapy, such as the number and ages of family members, that it is very difficult to code behaviors similarly across families.

CONCLUSIONS

Bowlby's 50-year-old dream of family attachment research remains an exciting challenge, although a substantial start has been made. Family research is difficult but potentially very rewarding. Such research may be one of the most interesting developments in the early years of the next millennium. Will researchers take up the challenge in a thorough way? It may happen only when researchers start routinely to consider how what they propose to do relates to the family context, or whether any aspect of the research can illuminate family or triadic issues, even if the research is not primarily focused on the family. An example of this may be adding questions about how the individual experienced his or her parents' (or relevant caretakers') collaboration with each other over their parenting, when studying internal working models of attachment, and to feel that the study is incomplete if this is not considered. From a family therapist's perspective, it appears as if attachment researchers have a professional working model of the dyad, not of the family. With no disrespect meant, a reappraisal and extension of the model may take some time, especially as the dyadic model has proved to be so successful.

This chapter has highlighted some of the major issues raised by family and couple therapy, and informed researchers of what therapists will find helpful to know more about. I have made some suggestions about research strategies, but researchers themselves are more likely to devise the best methodology. I have also attempted to illustrate some of the salient features of family and couple therapy—inevitably expressing some woolly ideas, as happened in Bowlby's productive seminars, in the hope that this will evoke creative responses from researchers. In the meantime, it is clear that the most immediately feasible research is outcome research done by therapists, so the most pointed challenge goes out to my therapist colleagues.

ACKNOWLEDGMENTS

Help with this chapter was generously given by Carolyn Cowan, Philip Cowan, Juliet Hopkins, Bob Marvin, and Joan Stevenson-Hinde.

REFERENCES

Ahrons, C. R., & Rogers, R. H. (1981). *Divorced families.* New York: Norton.

Ainsworth, M. D. S., Blehar, M. C., Waters, E., & Wall, S. (1978). *Patterns of attachment: A psychological study of the strange situation.* Hillsdale, NJ: Erlbaum.

Akister, J. (1998). Attachment theory and systemic practice: Research update. *Journal of Family Therapy, 10,* 353–366.

Argles, P. (1983). Identifying separation threats in family therapy. *Journal of Marital and Family Therapy, 9,* 209–211.

Bartholomew, K., & Horowitz, L. M. (1991). Attachment styles among young adults: A test of a four-category model. *Journal of Personality and Social Psychology, 61,* 226–244.

Bartholomew, K., & Shaver, P. R. (1998). Methods of assessing adult attachment: Do they converge? In J. A. Simpson & W. S. Rholes (Eds.), *Attachment theory and close relationships* (pp. 25–45). New York: Guilford Press.

Bell, L. G., Erikson, L., Cornwell, C., & Bell, D. C. (1991). Experienced closeness and distance among family members. *Contemporary Family Therapy, 13,* 231–245.

Bertalanffy, L. von. (1968). *General systems theory.* New York: Braziller.

Bowen, M. (1978). *Family therapy in clinical practice.* New York: Aronson.

Bowlby, J. (1949). The study and reduction of group tensions in the family. *Human Relations, 2,* 123–128.

Bowlby, J. (1969/1982). *Attachment and loss: Vol 1. Attachment* (2nd ed.). London: Hogarth Press.

Bowlby, J. (1973). *Attachment and loss: Vol. 2. Separation: Anxiety and anger.* London: Hogarth Press.

Bowlby, J. (1988). *A secure base: Clinical applications of attachment theory.* London: Routledge.

Britton, R. (1989). The missing link: Parental sexuality in the Oedipus complex. In J. Steiner (Ed.), *The Oedipus complex today: Clinical implications* (pp. 83–101) London: Karnac Books.

Brennan, K. A., Clark, C. L., & Shaver, P. R. (1998). Self-report measurement of adult attachment: An integrative overview. In J. A. Simpson & W. S. Rholes (Eds.), *Attachment theory and close relationships* (pp. 46–76). New York: Guilford Press.

Byng-Hall, J. (1980). The symptom bearer as marital distance regulator: Clinical implications. *Family Process, 19,* 355–365.

Byng-Hall, J. (1982). Grandparents, other relatives, friends, and pets. In A. Bentovim, A. Cooklin, & G. Gorrel Barnes (Eds.), *Family therapy: Complementary frameworks of theory and practice* (Vol. 2, pp. 361–370). London: Academic Press.

Byng-Hall, J. (1985). Resolving distance conflicts. In A. Gurman (Ed.), *Casebook of marital therapy* (pp. 1–19). New York: Guilford Press.

Byng-Hall, J. (1991a). Family scripts and loss. In F. Walsh & M. McGoldrick (Eds.), *Living beyond loss: Death in the family* (pp. 130–143). New York: Norton.

Byng-Hall, J. (1991b). An appreciation of John Bowlby: His significance for family therapy. *Journal of Family Therapy, 13,* 5–16.

Byng-Hall, J. (1995a). *Rewriting family scripts: Improvisation and systems change.* New York: Guilford Press.

Byng-Hall, J. (1995b). Creating a secure family base: Some implications of attachment theory for family therapy. *Family Process, 34,* 45–58.

Byng-Hall, J. (1997a). Toward a coherent story in illness and loss. In R. Papodopoulos & J. Byng-Hall (Eds.), *Multiple voices: Narratives in systemic family psychotherapy* (pp. 103–124). London: Duckworth.

Byng-Hall, J. (1997b). The secure family base. In *Bonding and attachment* (ACPP Occasional Papers, No.14) (pp. 27–30). London: Association for Child Psychology and Psychiatry.

Byng-Hall, J. (1999). Creating a coherent story in family therapy. In G. Roberts & J. Holmes (Eds.), *Narrative approaches in psychiatry and psychotherapy.* Oxford: Oxford University Press.

Byng-Hall, J., & Campbell, D. C. (1981). Resolving conflicts in distance regulation: An integrative approach. *Journal of Marital and Family Therapy, 7,* 321–330.

Byng-Hall, J., & Roberts, A. (1996). *Single-case study of family therapy: Use of videotape coding.* Paper presented at the Annual Residential Conference, Child and Adolescent Section of the Royal College of Psychiatrists, St. Helier, Jersey, United Kingdom.

Byng-Hall, J., & Stevenson-Hinde, J. (1991). Attachment relationships within a family system. *Infant Mental Health Journal, 12,* 187–200.

Cobb, C. L. H. (1996). Adolescent–parent attachments and family problem-solving. *Family Process, 35,* 57–82.

Cotgrove, A. J. (1993). *Attachment theory and the family: A single case study to pilot measures of attachment and change in family therapy.* Unpublished master's thesis, Tavistock Clinic, London.

Cowan, P. A., Cohn, D. A., Cowan, C. P., & Pearson, J. L. (1996). Parents' attachment histories and children's externalizing and internalizing behaviors: Exploring family systems models of linkage. *Journal of Consulting and Clinical Psychology, 64,* 53–63.

Cowan, P. A., Powell, D., & Cowan, C. P. (1997) Parenting interventions: A family systems perspective. In I. E. Sigel & K. A. Renninger (Eds.), *Handbook of child psychology: Vol. 4. Child psychology in practice* (5th ed.). New York: Wiley.

Crose, R. (1994). Family bonding and attachment patterns in late life. *Family Therapy, 21,* 17–21.

De Zulueta, F. (1993). *From pain to violence: The traumatic roots of destructiveness.* London: Whurr.

Diamond, D. (1986a). *Attachment and separation–individuation.* Unpublished manuscript, Yale University.

Diamond, D. (1986b). *Intergenerational family attachment, bonding, and separation–individuation interview schedule.* Unpublished manuscript, Yale University.

Diamond, D., & Doane, J. A. (1994). Disturbed attachment and negative affective style: An intergenerational style. *British Journal of Psychiatry, 164,* 770–781.

Doane, J. A., & Diamond, D. (1994). *Affect and attachment in the family: A family-based treatment of major psychiatric disorder.* New York: Basic Books.

Donley, G. D. (1993). Attachment and the emotional unit. *Family Process, 32,* 3–20.

Dowling, E., & Osborne, E. (1994). *The family and school: A joint systems approach to problems with children* (2nd ed.). London: Routledge.

Emde, R. N. (1988). The effects of relationships on relationships: A developmental approach to clinical intervention. In R. A. Hinde & J. Stevenson-Hinde (Eds.), *Relationships within families* (pp. 354–364). Oxford: Oxford University Press.

Emde, R. N. (1991). The wonder of our complex enterprise: Steps enabled by attachment and the effect of relationships on relationships. *Infant Mental Health Journal, 12,* 164–173.

Fisher, J. V., & Crandell, L. E. (1997). Complex attachment: Patterns of relating in the couple. *Sexual and Marital Therapy, 12,* 211–224.

Fonagy, P., Steele, M., Steele, H., Moran, G. S., & Higgitt, A. C. (1991). The capacity for understanding mental states: The reflective self in parent and child and its significance for security of attachment. *Infant Mental Health Journal, 12,* 201–218.

George, C., Kaplan, N., & Main, M. (1984). *Adult Attachment Interview.* Unpublished manuscript, University of California at Berkeley.

George, C., Kaplan, N., & Main, M. (1985). *Adult Attachment Interview* (2nd ed.). Unpublished manuscript, University of California at Berkeley.

George, C., Kaplan, N., & Main, M. (1996). *Adult Attachment Interview* (3rd ed.). Unpublished manuscript, University of California at Berkeley.

Goldner, V., Penn, P., Sheinberg, M., & Walker, G. (1990). Love and violence: Gender paradoxes in volatile attachments. *Family Process, 29,* 343–364.

Gottman, J. M. (1991). Predicting the longitudinal course of marriages. *Journal of Marital and Family Therapy, 17,* 3–7.

Hazan, C., & Shaver, P. (1987). Romantic love conceptualized as an attachment process. *Journal of Personality and Social Psychology, 52,* 511–524.

Heard, D. (1978). From object relations to attachment theory. *British Journal of Medical Psychology, 51,* 67–76.

Heard, D. (1982). Family systems and the attachment dynamic. *Journal of Family Therapy, 4,* 99–116.

Hill, J. (1992). *The family attachment interview: An exploration.* Paper presented at the conference of the Liverpool Psychotherapy Society. Liverpool, England, United Kingdom.

Hoffman, L. (1971). Deviation-amplifying processes in natural groups. In J. Haley (Ed.), *Changing families: A family therapy reader* (pp. 285–311). New York: Grune & Stratton.

Johnson, S. M. (1996). *The practice of emotionally focused marital therapy.* New York: Brunner/Mazel.

Johnson, S. M. (1997). The biology of love: What therapists need to know about attachment. *Family Therapy Networker, 21,* 36–41.

Johnson, S. M., & Talitman, E. (1997). Predictors of success in emotionally focused marital therapy. *Journal of Marital and Family Therapy, 23,* 135–152.

Levy, T. M., & Orlans, M. (1995). Intensive short-term therapy with attachment-disordered children. In L. Vande-Creek, S. Knapp, & T. L. Jackson (Eds.), *Innovations in clinical practice: A sourcebook* (Vol.14, pp. 227–251). Sarasota, FL: Professional Resource Press.

Main, M. (1991). Metacognitive knowledge, metacognitive monitoring, and singular (incoherent) vs. multiple (incoherent) model of attachment: Findings and directions for future research. In C. M. Parkes, J. Stevenson-Hinde, & P. Marris (Eds.), *Attachment across the life cycle* (pp. 127–160). London: Tavistock/Routledge.

Main, M., & Goldwyn, R. (1985). *Adult attachment scoring and classification system.* Unpublished manuscript, University of California at Berkeley.

Main, M., & Goldwyn, R. (1996). *Adult attachment scoring and classification system* (2nd ed.). Unpublished manuscript, University of California at Berkeley.

Main, M., Kaplan, N., & Cassidy, J. (1985). Security in infancy, childhood, and adulthood: A move to the level of representation. In I. Bretherton & E. Waters (Eds.), *Growing points of attachment theory and research. Monographs of the Society for Research in Child Development, 50*(1–2, Serial No. 209), 66–104.

Malon, D. W. (1986). Dealing with anxious attachment when divorce impends: A re-courting strategy. *Family Therapy, 13,* 227–238.

Marvin, R. S. (1992). Attachment- and family systems-based intervention in developmental psychopathology. *Development and Psychopathology, 4,* 697–711.

Marvin, R. S., & Stewart, R. B. (1984). Sibling relations: The role of conceptual perspective-taking in the ontogeny of sibling caregiving. *Child Development, 55,* 1322–1332.

Marvin, R. S., & Stewart, R. B. (1990). A family systems framework for the study of attachment. In M. T. Greenberg, D. Cicchetti, & E. M. Cummings (Eds.), *Attachment in the preschool years: Theory, research, and intervention* (pp. 51–86). Chicago: University of Chicago Press.

Minuchin, P. (1985). Families and individual development: Provocations from the field of family therapy. *Child Development, 56,* 289–302.

Minuchin, S. (1974). *Families and family therapy.* Cambridge, MA: Harvard University Press.

Olson, D. H., Sprenkle, D. H., & Russell, C. S. (1979). Circumplex model of marital and family systems. *Family Process, 18,* 29–45.

Parker, G., Tuppling, H., & Braun, L. B. (1979). A parental bonding instrument. *British Journal of Medical Psychology, 52,* 1–10.

Pianta, R. C., Marvin, R. S., Brittner, P. A., & Borowitz, K. C. (1996) Mothers' resolution of their children's diagnosis: Organized patterns of caregiving representations. *Infant Mental Health Journal, 17,* 239–256.

Pistole, M. C. (1994). Adult attachment styles: Some thoughts on closeness–distance struggles. *Family Process, 33,* 147–160.

Radojevic, M. (1996). Adult attachment: Some considerations for family therapy. *Australian and New Zealand Journal of Family Therapy, 17,* 33–41.

Roberts, T. W. (1992). Sexual attraction and romantic love: Forgotten variables in marital therapy. *Journal of Marital and Family Therapy, 18,* 357–364.

Shields, C. G., King, D. A., & Wynne, L. C. (1995). Interventions with later life families. In R. H. Mikesell, D. D. Lusterman, & S. H. McDaniel (Eds.), *Handbook of family psychology and systems theory* (pp. 144–158). Washington, DC: American Psychological Association.

Simon, F. B., Steirlin, H., & Wynne, L. C. (1985). *The language of family therapy: A systemic vocabulary and source book.* New York: Family Process.

Stevenson-Hinde, J. (1990). Attachment within family systems: An overview. *Infant Mental Health Journal, 11,* 218–227.

Stevenson-Hinde, J., & Shouldice, A. (1995). 4.5 to 7 years: Fearful behavior, fears, and worries. *Journal of Child Psychology and Psychiatry, 36,* 1027–1038.

Stewart, R. (1977). *Parent–child interaction in a quasi-naturalistic situation.* Unpublished master's thesis, Pennsylvania State University.

Todorski, J. (1995). Attachment and divorce: A therapeutic view. *Journal of Divorce and Remarriage, 22,* 189–204.

Thweatt, R. W. (1980). Divorce: Crisis intervention guided by attachment theory. *American Journal of Psychotherapy, 34,* 240–245.

Walsh, F., & McGoldrick, M. (Eds.). (1991). *Living beyond loss: Death in the family.* New York: Norton.

Wynne, L. C. (1984). The epigenesis of relational systems: A model for understanding family development. *Family Process, 23,* 297–318.

VI
EMERGING TOPICS
AND PERSPECTIVES

❖

28

Attachment and Caregiving

The Caregiving Behavioral System

❖

CAROL GEORGE
JUDITH SOLOMON

An 8-month-old infant clambers on . . . a fallen tree while its mother sits about 7 feet below. The infant slips and hangs by two hands. [His mother] looks up, stands on two legs, and barely reaches the foot of her infant. She pulls it to her chest but it wriggles free, repeats the climb only to slip at the same place again, to be rescued once more by its mother.
—SCHALLER (1963, p. 263, describing gorillas)

Gremlin's concern for Gimble went way beyond merely responding to his appeals for help: like a good mother she would anticipate trouble. . . . Once, as she was carrying him along a trail, she saw a small snake ahead. Carefully she pushed Gimble off her back and kept him behind her as she shook branches at the snake until it glided away.
—GOODALL (1990, p. 169, describing chimpanzees)

One day Effie was observed contentedly feeding about twenty feet behind the group, while Poppy, some six feet behind her mother, was solo playing and swinging in a Seneco tree . . . suddenly Effie twirled around and stared at Poppy. . . . Poppy had fallen and was hanging by her neck in a narrow fork of the tree. The infant could only feebly kick her legs and flail her arms as the stranglehold began cutting off her oxygen. Instantly Effie ran to her baby. With considerable effort she tugged at Poppy, trying to release her from a potentially fatal position. Effie was wearing a horrified expression of fear similar to that of a human parent whose child is in mortal danger. . . . At last Effie succeeded in releasing her infant from the tree's stranglehold. Immediately upon regaining her breath, Poppy began to whimper, then attached herself to Effie's nipple for four minutes before her mother carried her off, in a protective ventral position, toward the group, which were unaware of the drama that had unfolded behind them.
—FOSSEY (1983, p. 88, describing gorillas)

Bowlby's attachment theory has inspired a dramatic shift in the way we understand the development of the early infant–caregiver relationship and of relationships across the lifespan. In particular, his reframing of relationships in terms of the ethological concept of "behavioral systems" has added new meaning to our understanding of relationship development and function. The term "attachment" has become a shorthand phrase for an enduring relationship encompassing classes of observable behavior that, according to ethological theory, are regulated by the attachment system. The attachment system is one of many behavioral systems that have evolved to promote survival and reproductive success (Hinde, 1982a). The goal of attachment behavior is to seek protection by maintaining proximity to the attachment figure or parent in response to real or perceived stress or danger (Bowlby, 1969/1982). Although the actual behavior may vary according to context and age, the goal of that behavior remains the same across the lifespan. The empirical evidence supporting the role of the attachment relationship in the child's development is impressive. Almost three decades of research have shown that this relationship is an important contributing factor to the individual's ability to accomplish age-appropriate socioemotional and cognitive tasks in childhood and adulthood (see, e.g., Jacobsen, Edelstein, & Hofmann, 1994; Sroufe, 1988; Thompson, Chapter 13, this volume; Weinfield, Sroufe, Egeland, & Carlson, Chapter 4, this volume; Weiss, 1991). Research has shown that marked aberrations in the organization of this relationship are associated with problems in behavior and mental health in children (Solomon & George, in press-a; Lyons-Ruth & Jacobvitz, Chapter 23, this volume) and adults (Adam, 1994; Adam, Sheldon-Keller, & West, 1995; Fonagy et al., 1995; Manassis, Bradley, Goldberg, Hood, & Swinson, 1994; Pianta, Egeland, & Adam, 1996).

According to attachment theory, the most important factor guiding this pivotal relationship is the child's experience with caregivers. All infants who receive some form of basic regular care appear to select attachment figures, suggesting that simple propinquity of an attachment figure is sufficient for the development of attachment (Bowlby, 1969/1982). The quality of care determines the qualitative organization of the relationship through its effect on the child's confidence in the availability of the caregiver (i.e., security—Ainsworth, Blehar, Waters, & Wall, 1978; DeWolff & van IJzendoorn, 1997; Weinfeld et al., Chapter 4, this volume). What are the origins of the attachment figure's sensitivity? What indeed causes parents to provide care for their infants—care that sometimes requires costly personal sacrifices on the part of the parents?

Bowlby (1969/1982, 1988) proposed that the behavior of the attachment figure is organized by a caregiving behavioral system. Until recently there has been neither interest in caregiving as an organized behavioral system, nor consideration of how of the caregiving system contributes to the development of the child–parent relationship. It is likely that this lack of interest is the product of several interacting factors. First, because they were aligned with child-centered disciplines (psychoanalysis, developmental psychology, pe-

diatrics, social work), Bowlby and subsequent attachment researchers focused predominantly on the needs and development of the child. The parent has been considered an adjunct to the child's development. We do not mean to suggest here that the parent has been viewed as unimportant. Indeed, this is not the case; the literature on parenting in developmental psychology, for example, is comprehensive and covers a wide range of topics and concerns (Bornstein, 1995). What is lacking from these disciplines, however, is a view that integrates parental goals with child outcomes. Second, the concept of behavioral systems, which was extrapolated from biology and is foreign to developmental psychology and psychoanalysis, has been overshadowed by the dominant explanatory constructs of these disciplines. Developmental psychology has emphasized discrete behavior or behavior patterns (following learning theory) and, more recently, parental attitudes and attributions (following cognitive and social cognitive theory). Evolutionary theory has only just reemerged as an area of interest in psychology and has never had a place in traditional or contemporary psychoanalysis. Third, the historical focus of developmental psychology has been almost exclusively on the development of children through adolescence. Even today the empirical study of adult development, with the exception of some aspects of personality and cognitive development, is the purview of lifespan developmental psychology—a branch of psychology that adheres to different theoretical models and generally does not address issues regarding continuity or coherence from childhood to adulthood.

With the development of the Adult Attachment Interview (AAI; George, Kaplan, & Main, 1984, 1985, 1996), a semistructured clinical-style interview asking adults to describe their childhood attachment experiences, the field has seen a burst of research linking parents' mental representations of attachment to child attachment and developmental outcome (Hesse, Chapter 19, and Crowell, Fraley, & Shaver, Chapter 20, this volume; van IJzendoorn, 1995). The AAI has also provided a model of assessment for a small group of pioneering researchers interested in parents' mental representations of their children. Following the semistructured format of the AAI, these researchers have developed interviews asking parents to describe their perceptions and subjective experiences of their children, interactions with their children, and their relationship with their children (Aber, Slade, Cohen, & Meyer,

1989; Bretherton, Biringen, Ridgeway, Maslin, & Sherman, 1989; Cox, Owen, Henderson, & Margand, 1992; Cramer et al., 1990; Pianta & Marvin, 1992; Zeanah & Barton, 1989). Parental representations are typically analyzed in terms of rating scales drawn from (1) the AAI (e.g., coherence, lack of resolution—Main & Goldwyn, 1985, 1991, 1994); (2) Ainsworth's original maternal interaction scales (e.g., sensitivity, acceptance), and (3) other scales derived from attachment theory or research (e.g., intensity of involvement, joy, anger). Although their approaches differ somewhat, these researchers have been successful in describing individual differences in parental attributions and perceptions of children as related to the children's attachment (Benoit, Parker, & Zeanah, in press; Bretherton et al., 1989; Marvin & Pianta, 1996; Zeanah, Benoit, Hirschberg, Barton, & Regan, 1994), the children's behavior (Aber, Belsky, Slade, & Crnic, 1997; Benoit, Zeanah, Parker, Nicholson, & Coolbear, 1997; Slade, Belsky, Aber, & Phelps, 1997; Slade & Cohen, 1996), and the mothers' adult attachment classifications (Benoit et al., 1997; Slade et al., 1997; Slade & Cohen, 1996) These approaches have provided important insight into child attachment, parental perceptions and attitudes, and developmental risk. They do not, however, take an organized behavioral-systems approach to understanding caregiving behavior.

Recently we have begun to outline an approach to the study of caregiving, based on the postulate that caregiving behavior is organized within a behavioral system that is independent from, but linked developmentally and behaviorally to, attachment (George & Solomon, 1996; Solomon & George, 1996). In this chapter we expand upon this perspective and present a behavioral-systems framework for conceptualizing and studying caregiving. Like our colleagues, we have based our approach on our research on mental representations of caregiving. One unique contribution of our approach is noting the importance for the parent of making the shift away from the perspective of *being protected* (the goal of the child) to the perspective of *providing protection* (the goal of the parent). In our view, consideration of this shift is fundamental to understanding the meaning of, and motivation underlying, critical aspects of parental behavior; cultural differences in providing care; the development of the infant's attachment; and the mechanisms of intergenerational transmission. We propose that understanding this shift will also

contribute to intervention with parents of children "at risk." The chapter begins with a review of the defining characteristics of behavioral systems and an examination of variations in patterns of care from a functionalist or evolutionary perspective. We then describe a behavioral-systems-based model outlining major influences on the etiology of the caregiving system. We follow with a summary of our own research and describe the ways in which our studies of mothers' mental representations of caregiving have informed us about the caregiving system. We end with a discussion of what the behavioral-systems approach to caregiving adds to our understanding of parent–child interaction, and of how this perspective may be used to enhance relationship-based intervention.

DEFINING THE CAREGIVING BEHAVIORAL SYSTEM

A Behavioral-Systems Model of Caregiving

Bowlby grounded attachment theory in ethology. In this section we examine behavioral systems, one of the key components of the ethological approach. According to ethologists, much of the behavioral repertoire in humans and other species is organized by behavioral systems. Briefly, behavioral systems are defined by the following basic principles (Bowlby, 1969/1982; Hinde, 1982a): They (1) comprise behavior that is coordinated to achieve a specific goal and adaptive function; (2) are activated and terminated by endogenous and environmental cues; (3) are "goal-corrected" (i.e., are regulated by goals that extend over long periods of time, with the behaviors needed to achieve those goals being adjusted flexibly, in a nonrandom fashion, to a wide range of environments and to the development of the individual); (4) are guided at the biological level by a feedback system that monitors internal cues (central nervous system activity, hormones) and environmental cues leading to the system's activation or termination; (5) are related to and interact with other behavioral systems; (6) involve developmental integration of sequences of behavior that become functional over time as the product of organism–environment interaction; and (7) are believed to be organized and integrated by specific cognitive control systems (in the case of humans, mental representations). We begin our discussion of caregiving by examining the first four of these principles. The remaining principles are discussed in later sections.

We assume (as did Bowlby) that the caregiving system is reciprocal to, and evolved in parallel with, the attachment system. The way in which the infant's behavioral systems (e.g., attachment, exploration, affiliation) interact with one another was outlined thoroughly in Bowlby's and Ainsworth's original work and has become a standard feature of attachment theory and research (Cassidy, Chapter 1, this volume). The ways in which the infant's behavioral systems interact with those of the caregiver, and the ways in which the caregiver's behavioral systems interact among one another, are as yet largely unexplored.

The first step in defining the caregiving system is to delineate its adaptive function and behavioral goal. Following Bowlby, we propose that the adaptive function of the caregiving system, like that of attachment, is protection of the young and, ultimately, of one's reproductive fitness (see also Belsky, Chapter 7, this volume; Simpson, Chapter 6, this volume). Following ethological theory, and paralleling Bowlby's (1969/1982) discussion of attachment, we believe that the behavioral goal of the caregiving system is to provide protection for the child. Central to Bowlby's theory was his identification of factors involved in the activation, termination, and regulation of the child's attachment system. Internal or external cues or stimuli associated with situations that the child perceives as frightening, dangerous, or stressful should activate the attachment system. It follows that with regard to the caregiving system, internal or external cues associated with situations that the *parent* perceives as frightening, dangerous, or stressful for the child should activate the caregiving system. These situations include, but are not limited to, separation, child endangerment, and the child's verbal and nonverbal signals of discomfort and distress. Once the system is activated, the caregiver can call upon a repertoire of behaviors. The goal of these behaviors—including retrieval, maintaining proximity, carrying, following, signaling the child to follow, calling, looking, and in humans, smiling—is to ensure protection of the child.[1] The child's attachment system is deactivated by proximity and/or physical or psychological contact with the attachment figure when he or she responds to the child's attachment needs in a satisfactory manner. Again following Bowlby's template for attachment, the parent's caregiving system should be deactivated by physical or psychological proximity and signs that the child is comforted, contented, or satisfied. Just as Bowlby proposed attachment to be associated with and regulated by strong feelings, including joy and anger in response to whether or not the caregiver is within proximity, caregiving is also associated with and regulated by strong emotions. Mothers express intense feelings of pleasure and satisfaction when they are able to provide protection for their children; they experience heightened anger, sadness, anxiety, and despair when they are separated from their children or when their ability to protect the children is threatened or blocked.

Behavioral systems are goal-corrected—a feature that potentially allows for maximum behavioral flexibility. This suggests that the specific type and range of caregiving behavior will vary, depending upon context, age, and experiences of parent or child. We also presume, as with the attachment system, that this goal-corrected quality is regulated in part by neurological systems in the brain. The actual mechanisms related to providing care and the ways in which physiological substrates are influenced by learning and experience need further investigation. There have been studies, however, that examine physiological responses in the young to attachment-activating situations. Rats, monkeys, apes, and human infants respond to separation with an increase in stress-related hormones (e.g., cortisol) and other physiological indicators of heightened stress (e.g., heart rate acceleration) (Hertsgaard, Gunnar, Erickson, & Nachmias, 1995; Hofer, 1995; Sroufe & Waters, 1977; Suomi, 1995, and Chapter 9, this volume). Examination of the attachment figure's hormonal and physiological responses to caregiving situations would contribute to our understanding of the biological basis of caregiving.

Once the caregiving system is activated, the caregiver must "decide" whether and how to behave. The caregiver's behavior depends upon his or her conscious and unconscious evaluation of competing sources of information. One source of information is the caregiver's evaluation of the child's signals. Another source of information is his or her own perception of danger or threat. In the role of caregiver, the parent must always be vigilant, scanning regularly for cues from these sources. From the caregiver's perspective, he or she must then organize the various perceptions and select a response. Sensitive mothering has been given a central place in the etiology of secure attachment. "Sensitive mothers" have been defined as those who perceive and evaluate their children's cues appropriately, and who respond quickly and contingently (Ainsworth et al., 1978). The concept of sensitivity emphasizes caregiving behavior from a child's perspective. Examining caregiving from a parent's perspective, we note that the parent has access to more information than the child, including a wealth of information drawn from his or her evaluation of the context and personal past experience (as a child and/or as a parent). In addition, especially among humans, a parent is cognitively more mature than a child and thus potentially capable of evaluating caregiving situations from multiple perspectives and in a more sophisticated manner. Of course, in some situations sophisticated cognitive involvement is not a necessary condition for caregiving behavior; that is, some behavior appears to be nearly automatic (e.g., blocking a child from stepping in front of a moving vehicle). As the child gets older, however, caregiving becomes more difficult. Consider, for example, situations in which the parent's caregiving system is activated but the child's attachment system is not. As parents who have "survived" their children's adolescence know, a parent's desire to protect his or her child is often in conflict with the child's desire for the parent to relinquish demonstrative protective behavior (frequently interpreted by the adolescent as parental control or intrusion). This conflict between parents' and children's behavioral systems is a major source of the arguments between teens and their parents. In North American culture at least, it often behooves a parent to consider as many perspectives on the situation as possible (i.e., multiple perspective taking and metacognitive capabilities are involved) before deciding how or whether to takes steps to protect his or her child. In sum, providing care is extremely complex, and ultimately the information and affect that contribute to a parent's response have more to do with the internal organization of his or her caregiving system than with the child's cues or behavior. The child's cues activate the system. What happens next is influenced strongly by the parent's caregiving system.

The Caregiving System: Interaction and Competition among Behavioral Systems

According to ethological theory, behavior is the product of the *interaction* among behavioral systems (Hinde, 1982a). We propose, therefore, that another important step in defining the caregiving system is to examine the interaction between the parent's caregiving system and other behavioral systems that may compete with providing care for any particular child (Bowlby, 1969/1982; Solomon & George, 1996; Stevenson-Hinde, 1994). This is true at the ultimate (functional) as well as at the proximate (psychological and physiological) level of analysis. Trivers (1974) pointed out that from a functionalist's standpoint, although parent and child have overlapping interests, they also have inherent and inevitable conflicts. This point is fundamental to evolutionary analyses of successful adaptation (i.e., reproductive fitness) and is a point that has been lost in recent discussions of attachment and parental care (Belsky, Chapter 7, this volume; Belsky, Steinberg, & Draper, 1991; Solomon & George, 1996). At the ultimate level, parent–child conflict is an especially important component of discussions of caregiving, because becoming a parent (having a baby or raising a child) is the defining condition of the parent's fitness (unless, as in some other species, the individual decides to become an "auntie," accomplishing reproductive success through a less direct pathway). Furthermore, a child acts to protect his or her own survival and reproductive success, but a parent's fitness depends on the fitness of all his or her children. At the proximate level, conflict among behavioral systems is also an inherent part of caregiving. Parents' adult roles are both biologically and socially defined. When we consider parents' roles in terms of other behavioral systems, a parent may be some or all of the following: a caregiver for other children, a friend (affiliative system), a sexual partner (sexual system), a worker (exploratory system), and a child to his or her own parents (attachment system). We have noted elsewhere that just as an infant or child must seek a dynamic balance between attachment and other behavioral systems (e.g., exploration, affiliation), a parent must strike a balance between his or her need to protect and care for the child and the need to pursue other goals (Solomon & George, 1996). As a consequence, the optimal caregiving strategy requires the parent to be flexible in relation to all his or her goals. In relation to the ultimate or functional level of causality, parental behavior is constrained or determined by environmental factors, such as distribution of resources and environmental hazards (Kaplan, 1996). At the proximate level, the parent is constrained by cultural and individual factors. Elsewhere we have detailed the ecological, developmental, and cultural constraints that may influence caregiving strategies (Solomon & George, 1996).

Flexible care (i.e., a high level of involvement through toddlerhood, followed by less direct supervision as the child matures) appears to characterize all humans. This flexibility is founded upon the mother's ability to attend to and balance cues both from the child (including developmental cues) and from the environment (including cultural press) in order to determine when protection is and is not needed (Ainsworth et al., 1978; Belsky & Isabella, 1988; Isabella, 1993; Solomon, George, & Silverman, in press). Flexibility appears to contribute to selective advantage under difficult environmental conditions (Kermoian & Liederman, 1986). Under other conditions, it may be more appropriate or more advantageous to the parent to develop alternative or compromise strategies that are manipulations of a primary strategy in a particular behavioral system (Hinde, 1982b; Hinde & Stevenson-Hinde, 1991). With regard to the attachment system, Main (1990) has argued that security is the primary attachment strategy, and that avoidant and ambivalent attachment are conditional patterns that allow the child to maintain proximity to the mother. Following this thinking, we have proposed that mothers of avoidant and ambivalent children develop alternative strategies of care, and that cultures with high levels of avoidant and ambivalent children promote alternative caregiving strategies (e.g., Grossmann & Grossmann, 1990; Miyake, Chen, & Campos, 1985; Sagi, 1990). Under conditions in which it is desirable from the mother's perspective for the infant to become precociously independent, providing care "from a distance" may be more advantageous. Under conditions in which it is desirable for the child to delay maturity, care that encourages physical and psychological closeness may be more advantageous (for a full discussion, see George & Solomon, 1996; Solomon & George, 1996; Solomon, George, & De Jong, 1995; for an alternative view, see Belsky, Chapter 7, this volume). In either case, conditional caregiving strategies afford the child some degree of proximity to the mother, yet also leave the child somewhat more vulnerable than children whose mothers engage in flexible care. Distant care limits the mother's ability or desire to attend to her child and limits her accessibility; keeping the child close decreases the mother's need to attend to cues from both the child and the environment, because she assumes that her child is safe simply by virtue of the child's physical proximity to her. On the basis of the conditional-strategies argument, we have proposed elsewhere that flexible care is the caregiving pattern associated with attachment security; similarly, we have argued that distant and close care are patterns associated with avoidance and ambivalence, respectively (Solomon & George, 1996).

The success of flexible, distant, or close caregiving patterns can be evaluated in terms of the relative costs and benefits to parent and child. A functional analysis of these patterns from the viewpoint of adult reproductive success is made difficult by the range of culture-specific factors determining reproductive behavior (e.g., social scripts pertaining to sexual behavior, birth control, and parenting). If we are correct in assuming, however, that the goal of caregiving is protection of the young, then a very broad range of caregiving strategies may be considered to be "good enough," to the extent that the mother's behavior *under conditions of risk or threat to the child* is organized around protection. We argue later that from this perspective, mothers of infants classified as avoidant and resistant as well as secure may be considered "good enough." In contrast to these mothers, we argue, the mothers of infants classified as disorganized may properly be labeled "disabled" as caregivers, because they intermittently or persistently abdicate their protective role. We acknowledge that our definition of "good enough" departs somewhat from what was originally intended by the term "good enough" (Winnicott, 1958), as well as from the common judgment about mothers of insecure children within the field of attachment, where maternal sensitivity is the yardstick by which caregiving is judged. We believe that our view is supported indirectly, however, by accumulating evidence that disorganized attachment, in contrast to the organized secure, avoidant, and ambivalent patterns, is associated with pathological risk (Carlson, 1997; Fagot & Kavanagh, 1990; Lyons-Ruth, 1996; Lyons-Ruth & Block, 1996; Moss, Parent, Gosselin, Rousseau, & St-Laurent, 1996; Moss, Rousseau, Parent, St-Laurent, & Saintonge, 1998; Solomon, George, & De Jong, 1995; Solomon & George, in press-b, in press-c—for parallel findings in adults, see, e.g., Adam et al., 1995; Fonagy et al., 1995; Liotti, in press; West & George, 1998).

In sum, our functional view, in combination with the findings of attachment studies that include recent research focusing on attachment disorganization, suggests the following: (1) Distant and close caregiving patterns may be somewhat out of balance, as compared with the flexible care that supports attachment security; however, (2) in the absence of other risk factors to the mother, the child, or the relationship, it is likely that these caregiving patterns contribute to the mother's and the child's fitness. One hallmark of our work is the suggestion that the field may benefit from considering these caregiving patterns (and the patterns of attachment associated with them) as "good enough." This view moves away from the position of early research and theory. We return to the issue of "good enough" care later in this chapter.

A Note about Caregiving in Mothers versus Fathers

It is likely that interaction and competition among behavioral systems are somewhat different, depending on the gender of the parent. Attachment research has focused on mothers; although there is a smattering of research on fathers' behavior in relation to child attachment, no attention has been devoted to defining the caregiving system in relation to other behavioral systems for human fathers. Our emphasis in the remainder of this chapter, therefore, is on mothers. Before leaving the subject of fathers, however, we note that the function of the caregiving system is protection, and we have no doubt that fathers protect their young. It is likely, however, that the behaviors organized by the caregiving system and the contexts that activate the system differ for mothers and fathers. That maternal caregiving both in humans and in nonhuman species involves direct forms of care and protection has been well documented. Descriptions of protection of the young by fathers in nonhuman primates are qualitatively different from those for mothers. Bowlby (1969/1982) noted that in some instances a male may attack or threaten the infant when danger approaches, sending the infant fleeing to its mother. In gorillas, males provide protection more generally for the group as a whole (including the juveniles), signaling danger by chest beating or hooting (Schaller, 1963). Researchers have demonstrated that human fathers are perfectly capable of sensitive care, but that, like nonhuman primate fathers, they remain less involved than mothers with their infants (Lamb, 1997). In attachment research, behaviors associated with sensitivity as defined for mothers have not successfully predicted infants' attachment security in the strange situation for fathers. Rather, security seems to be associated with paternal

play and problem-solving interactions (Belsky, 1993; Easterbrooks & Goldberg, 1984; Grossmann, 1997; Schneider-Rosen & Rothbaum, 1993). From a behavioral-systems view, these kinds of father behavior may be expressions of the affiliation or exploration behavioral systems rather than the caregiving system. In sum, the field is beginning to explicate the nature of father–infant interaction, but the nature of the attachment and caregiving systems in the father–child relationship remains somewhat of a mystery.

ONTOGENY OF MATERNAL CAREGIVING

Intergenerational Transmission?

As a reflection of the psychoanalytic roots of attachment theory, and in the absence of a broad biological and developmental view of caregiving, attachment theorists and researchers have emphasized caregiving as the developmental endpoint of early attachment experiences (Bowlby, 1969/1982; Bretherton, 1985; Sroufe & Fleeson, 1986). We have described this view as the "assimilation model" of caregiving (Solomon & George, 1996). According to cognitive-developmental theory, "assimilation" is the process by which new experiences and information are integrated into existing schemes; attachment theorists have suggested that under normal circumstances, a mother integrates her experiences with her child into her mental schemes of attachment.

The assimilation model has been endorsed by a growing number of attachment theorists (Bretherton, 1985; Fonagy et al., 1995; Main, 1995; Main, Kaplan, & Cassidy, 1985; van IJzendoorn, 1995). This model has long been accepted as the mechanism of intergenerational continuity in psychoanalysis (Fonagy, 1994, and Chapter 26, this volume). At first glance, the assimilation model appears to be supported empirically. Most researchers studying this phenomenon have reported a strong correspondence between mothers' representations of attachment and the quality of their infants' attachments to them (Ainsworth & Eichberg, 1991; Benoit & Parker, 1994; Benoit et al., in press; Bus & van IJzendoorn, 1992; Crowell & Feldman, 1988; Fonagy, Steele, & Steele, 1991; George & Solomon, 1996; Grossmann, Fremmer-Bombik, Rudolph, & Grossmann, 1988; Haft & Slade, 1989; Main et al., 1985; Slade et al., 1995; van IJzendoorn,

1995; Ward, Botyanski, Plunket, & Carlson, 1991; Zeanah, Hirshberg, Danis, Brennan, & Miller, 1995). Concordances have been seen as the product of direct transmission of mothers' representation of childhood attachment. According to the assimilation model, the mechanism for transmission across generations is maternal sensitivity. That is, based on her mental representations of attachment, a mother responds to her infant's signals and thus contributes to the building blocks for her baby's attachment. Indeed, from a recent meta-analysis of the extensive number of studies investigating some aspect of maternal sensitivity, DeWolff and van IJzendoorn (1997) concluded that maternal sensitivity does indeed contribute to attachment security.

On the surface there appears to be strong evidence for the assimilation model, and without a doubt, the mother's representation of attachment contributes greatly to her interaction with her child. As we have discussed previously (Solomon & George, 1996), more careful examination of the data shows, however, that concordance between mother and child attachment is found predominantly for mothers judged secure. Concordance is lowest for mothers of insecure children, particularly when mothers are unresolved about early loss. In addition, looking more carefully at the evidence supporting maternal sensitivity as the mechanism of transmission, DeWolff and van IJzendoorn noted that the correlations between sensitivity and attachment security are moderate at best. They concluded, "Sensitivity has lost its privileged position as the only important causal factor. A multidimensional approach of parenting antecedents should replace the search for the unique contribution of sensitivity" (p. 583). Their statement echoes the voices of a small number of attachment researchers who have called for a contextual understanding of attachment, in particular examining characteristics of the mother, the family system, and the environment (e.g., Belsky & Isabella, 1988; Cowan, Cohn, Cowan, & Pearson, 1996; Grossmann & Grossmann, 1990; Jackson, 1993; Miyake et al., 1985; Solomon & George, 1996).

Development of Maternal Behavior

The next step, then, in defining the caregiving system is to describe a contextual framework for caregiving. There have been contributions to such a framework from a variety of disciplines. Following Bronfenbrenner's (1979) ecological systems theory, Belsky and his colleagues have proposed a model of the "determinants of parenting" (Belsky, 1984, and Chapter 12, this volume; Belsky & Isabella, 1988; Belsky, Rosenberger, & Crnic, 1995), which emphasizes proximal contextual influences on attachment relating to the parent (e.g., personality), the child (e.g., temperament), and the context (e.g., the parent's marriage). Fleming and Corter (Corter & Fleming, 1995; Fleming, Corter, & Steiner, 1995) have described the similarities and differences associated with birth for rat and human mothers (see also Polan & Hofer, Chapter 8, this volume). They discuss proximal factors that influence maternal behavior, including sensory (e.g., tactile stimulation of the young), biological (e.g., adrenal and ovarian hormones), and experiential (i.e., value of the mother's experience with the young) influences. Similarly, Keverne (1995), emphasizing the remarkable similarity across species of hormonal priming associated with pregnancy and birth, has examined species differences in the neurological systems influenced by hormones and experience that maintain maternal behavior. Pryce (1995) has developed the only comprehensive model of mothering, including a discussion of the developmental pathways that may lead to the development of "good" and "bad" mothering (based on Cicchetti & Rizley's [1981] discussion of the sequelae of child abuse). Pryce stresses the importance of interacting developmental influences: species and genotype, the mother's neurobiological development, developmental history (including sensitive periods), and culture. In addition to the transaction among these childhood factors, he suggests that maternal behavior is also guided by such adult influences as hormonal changes, caregiving environment (e.g., social support, stress), characteristics of the infant, and "maternal motivation" (defined as the mother's motivation to provide care, based on the reward value of the baby).

Although the goals and caregiving dimensions described in these models differ, the general premise on which these models are based overlaps with the view presented here. Central to our argument is that the development of the caregiving system, and therefore of caregiving behavior, is the product of a complex transaction among an array of biological and experiential factors. Following attachment theory, and similar to the position advanced by Pryce, we propose that the caregiving system has important roots in childhood as well as adult influences. Belsky, Fleming, and Corter, as well as Kerverne, have confined their models to examining influences on the female once she has become a mother. And although Belsky and Pryce both suggest that their models add to the understanding of the development of the child's attachment behavioral system, they differ from the view presented here in that these models do not examine mothering from the perspective of a separate caregiving behavioral system. Furthermore, although Pryce offers a comprehensive look at influences on caregiving, his discussion is not linked specifically to attachment research.

As the reader will recall, one basic tenet of a behavioral-systems model concerns the development and integration of behavior over time. In the remainder of this section, we outline ontogenetic factors beyond the mother's own attachment experience that we consider important to the development of the caregiving system. Some of these developmental influences have been considered briefly by other researchers as they are related to the development of maternal behavior (e.g., Fraiberg, 1980; Sroufe & Fleeson, 1986), but not in terms of their relation to the caregiving system. Our discussion here is an extension of our earlier work (George & Solomon, 1989, 1996; Solomon & George, 1996) and is influenced by the models of caregiving we have described above. We consider the following discussion as work in progress and do not intend it to be a definitive statement on caregiving. Our primary goal is to stimulate future thinking about the development of the caregiving system.

Factors Important to the Development of the Caregiving System

Childhood Influences

All behavioral systems begin with immature forms of behavior that are integrated to become fully organized or "mature." Behavioral systems contribute to the individual's fitness, but they do not develop at the same rate or at the same time during the life course. Behavioral systems essential for the survival of the young (e.g., the attachment and feeding systems) mature quickly. Behavioral systems important to later stages of development (e.g., the caregiving and sexual systems) mature more slowly. Immature, isolated, and incomplete forms of behavior associated with a behavioral system can be observed before the system has reached maturity (see, e.g., Bowl-

by's [1969/1982] description of the phases of attachment; see also Marvin & Britner, Chapter 3, this volume). Behavior resulting from immature systems also differs qualitatively from behavior resulting from mature systems. The stimuli activating immature behavioral systems are more varied than those that activate mature behavioral systems. Upon maturity, the individual discriminates stimuli better, and the system becomes organized, integrated, and goal-corrected (Bowlby, 1969/1982).

The caregiving system appears to be first expressed by isolated, immature, nonfunctional forms of care and affection—elements of which are observable at early ages in primates, including humans. For example, "play-mothering" is common among juveniles in primate species, especially females (Pryce, 1995). Throughout childhood and adolescence, human children typically express the desire to provide care and the behavior associated with providing care when they are near babies, animals (especially baby animals), or playing with dolls. There are important differences, however, between play-mothering and mature caregiving. One difference is that in play-mothering the behavior is fragmented and behavioral sequences are incomplete (i.e., a child does not follow through in providing complete or satisfactory care). Another crucial difference is that the child's attention is easily distracted away from the infant (Pryce, 1995), which means that the child may place a baby in jeopardy.

Behavioral biologists emphasize that maternal behavior in a juvenile is probably cued not only by the presence of an infant, but also by the child's own experiences of maternal care (Pryce, 1995). Play-mothering does not occur, for example, in rhesus macaques who are isolated from their own mothers during the first year of life. Furthermore, when these monkeys become mothers themselves, they fail to show normal preferences for their own infants over infants of other females (Pryce, 1995). Sroufe and Fleeson (1986) and Bretherton (1985) have suggested that a child develops a sense of caregiving (specifically, mental representations of providing care) through his or her experiences with the mother.

Although there is no research on caregiving behavior during middle childhood (roughly ages 5–11), we expect that under child-rearing conditions in which a child does not assume *primary* responsibility for providing care and protection for siblings or their parents, the caregiving system matures gradually. In many cultures, siblings take on major responsibility for care of siblings; in these contexts, mothers typically tutor and guide their older children in caring for younger ones. The degree to which this experience contributes to the early maturity of a child's caregiving system (i.e., to making it fully organized and integrated) is an empirical question.

Adolescence

We propose that the caregiving system begins a transformation toward maturity during adolescence (Solomon & George, 1996). This view fits with the developmental perspective that adolescence is the period during which many child characteristics (e.g., physical, mental, psychological) mature into adult forms. Fullard and Reiling (1976) found that when given a choice between pictures of adults and infants, children between the ages of 7 and 12 preferred adults. A shift to adult-like preferences for pictures of infants was observed for girls aged 12 to 14 and boys aged 14 to 16. These shifts in preferences coincide with the average ages at which girls and boys become capable of reproduction. It is likely that the adolescent transformation of the caregiving system is partly based on the biological changes associated with puberty. Kerverne (1995) has noted that evolutionary biologists define parental care in terms of the biological capabilities of gamete production and placental development (i.e., the development associated with puberty). When one takes the evolutionary view, then, the transition to parenting emerges at a younger age for most females (with the exception of young teens) than when one defines parental care from the psychological perspective (pregnancy and postnatal care). In girls, changes in the hypothalamus, pituitary, and ovaries result in menarche and are associated with dramatic changes in primary and secondary sexual characteristics, including ovulation and the production of adrenocorticotropic hormone (ACTH). As we describe in more detail below, given the influence of hormones on mammalian and primate mothering, we speculate that these changes may initiate the transition toward maturity of the caregiving system during adolescence. This transition is also influenced by experience. Stressful childhood experience, for example, may provoke the early onset of menarche (Moffitt, Caspi, Belsky, & Silva, 1992). With regard to actual mothering, in cultures like our own that discourage adolescent sexual behavior and pregnancy, the influence of cultural mores and taboos may override a girl's biological predisposition for a baby. It is our experience, however, that despite cultural pressures against adolescents' having babies, many older adolescent girls (e.g., ages 17–19) suddenly reveal remarkable interest and thoughtfulness regarding mothering that extend beyond the intellectual knowledge of reproduction. During these later adolescent years, girls are often consumed by questions about whether or not they will be good mothers, how a mother comes to love a baby, and what it is like to be responsible for an infant.

Transition to Parenthood

The caregiving system probably undergoes its greatest development during the transition to parenthood (pregnancy, birth, and the months following birth). Developmentalists conceptualize transition as a "crisis" or "bio-social-behavioral shift" that results from the transaction among unique biological, psychological, and social factors (Cole & Cole, 1996; Lee, 1995). Our model of caregiving emphasizes a similar kind of qualitative shift during this period. At the biological level, this period for mothers is accompanied by intense hormonal and neurological changes that especially influence the hypothalamus and the limbic system (Pryce, 1995). For example, in nonhuman mammals (e.g., rats), ovarian steroids (e.g., oxytocin, progesterone, and estradiol) produced during this period have been shown to influence maternal behavior directed toward infants. In humans, maternal behavior may be more closely related initially to adrenal hormones (e.g., ACTH—related to attention of sensory systems) than to ovarian steroids (Fleming et al., 1995). Fleming et al. have proposed that hormones may have an important (though not exclusive) role in producing sensory acuity, emotional calm, and closeness with infants in human mothers, similar to the role that has been demonstrated in animal mothers. Finally, researchers have noted an enormous upsurge in thoughts, doubts, and worries about the self as a parent, the spouse, and the past in this period; some have suggested that this upwelling of anxiety is essential for a reorganization of the self (Ammaniti, 1994; Benedek, 1959; Bibring, Dwyer, Huntington, & Valenstein, 1961; Brazelton, 1981; Cowan, 1991; Deutscher, 1971; Lee, 1995; Liefer, 1980).

The caregiving system has been shown to be influenced by the experience of childbirth itself, including the hormonal milieu and stimuli emanating from the young (Bahr, 1995; Fleming et al., 1995). Among rats and goats, for example, mothers need contact with their young immediately following birth in order to accept their babies (Klaus, Kennell, & Klaus, 1995). Factors surrounding birth were once thought to be critical to mothering in human mothers as well, although the strong interpretation of these effects has now been tempered (Klaus et al., 1995). Providing human mothers with bonding experiences (i.e., the opportunity for extended closeness and physical contact with their infants immediately following birth) has been found to enhance touching, kissing, talking to the babies, and nursing, especially for mothers at risk (e.g., those experiencing economic risk, high stress, or unplanned or unwanted pregnancies). A mother's bonding experiences have not been found to be related to a child's attachment security later in infancy (Rode, Chang, Fisch, & Sroufe, 1981). Manning-Orenstein (1997), however, found that a mother's birthing experience was significantly related to her representations of self as a caregiver. In this study, mothers who were assisted by a *doula* (a woman who assists the mother with labor and the delivery process) showed a significantly greater representational shift between the last trimester of pregnancy and the first trimester following birth toward caregiving security (associated with child attachment security), and away from rejection and helplessness (associated with child avoidant and disorganized attachment), than mothers who were assisted by a Lamaze coach. (We discuss the relation between caregiving security vs. helplessness and child attachment in a later section.) Manning-Orenstein argued that the *doula,* as compared with the Lamaze coach, served as a "secure base" for a mother during this transition period and raised the mother's confidence in herself as a mother.

In our view, the degree to which childbirth and other influences associated with the transition to parenthood influence the caregiving system is a question that needs further investigation. The experiences that a mother brings to her baby's birth, her representation of herself as a caregiver, her interpretation of the birth experience, and her experience of the birth itself (e.g., miscarriage—Slade et al., 1995; premature birth—Steele & Steele, 1994; foster care—Dozier & Stovall, 1997; birthing technique—Manning-Orenstein, 1997) may be synergistic factors that together could influence (positively or negatively) the caregiving system for at least a subset of mothers.

The Baby

Other factors that may influence the development of the caregiving system are associated with the baby itself (Bell, 1968; Crockenberg, 1986; Fraiberg, 1980; Sameroff, 1993). The baby has enormous power to evoke caregiving behavior. Lorenz (1943) suggested that the physical features of "babyness," a combination of the prominent features of an infant (e.g., rounded, oversized head; large eyes), evoke caregiving behavior in adults. In addition to physical attractiveness, Suomi (1995) noted that neonatal behavioral, perceptual, and social biases, including distinctive emotional expressions, make human infants and their closest primate relatives (Old World monkeys and apes) attractive to any caregiver. In humans, adults, particularly women, prefer pictures of infants over pictures of adults (Fullard & Reiling, 1976). Physical abnormalities in a baby can elicit maternal rejection and neglect. Babies perceived by their mothers as unattractive receive less attention than attractive babies do (Langlois, Ritter, Casey, & Sawin, 1995). Infants with physical malformations are often rejected and, in other species or in other cultures or historical periods in humans, killed or abandoned (Langlois, 1988). Infant cues and proximity have been shown to influence patterning of behavior and the mother's motivation to respond in rats and humans. In rats, the pups' odor (chemosensory cues) appears to be an attractant for the mother. The stimulation of touching the pups produces retrieval behavior and lactation. Human mothers recognize and prefer their own babies' cries and odors, and their babies' vocalizations elicit affectionate behavior and instrumental caretaking (Fleming et al., 1995). Anisfeld, Casper, Nozyce, and Cunningham (1990) found that physical contact with an infant through using a soft baby carrier, as compared with an infant seat, was associated with increased sensitivity in early infancy and attachment security at 1 year.

It is likely that the influence of the baby on the caregiving system is part of a feedback loop; in other words, it is transactional, rather than linear and unidirectional. The activation of the caregiving system, and the resulting caregiving behavior elicited by the baby, appear to be influenced heavily by other factors associated with the mother, including (as discussed earlier) her own representations of attachment. The mother's perception of her infant and their relationship appears to be a more important factor than any single quality in the baby (Egeland & Farber, 1984; Pianta, Marvin, Britner, & Borowitz, 1996), and we believe that her perception of the infant is influenced by her caregiving system. Temperament (the infant's emotional reactivity, degree of psychomotor arousal, and capacity for regulation) does not appear to have a direct influence on whether or not a baby will develop a secure attachment to the mother (Belsky & Rovine, 1987; Vaughn & Bost, Chapter 10, this volume), although some researchers have found irritability or neurological difficulties in ambivalent infants (Cassidy & Berlin, 1994; Vaughn & Bost, Chapter 10, this volume) and disorganized infants (Spangler, Fremmer-Bombik, & Grossmann, 1996; Spangler & Grossmann, in press).

The notion of the importance of this feedback loop for the mother–infant relationship is supported by the results of some intervention studies. Suomi (1995) reported that when temperamentally reactive or behaviorally inhibited rhesus monkey infants were reared by highly nurturing foster mothers, these infants developed "secure" relationships; when infants with similar reactive temperaments were raised by punitive foster mothers, they developed "insecure" relationships. The attachment that developed between foster mothers and temperamentally uninhibited infants, on the other hand, seemed to be little affected by the type of foster mother. The results of this research suggest that the mother–infant transaction is especially important for fragile infants. In humans, the transaction between mother and infant behavior has been examined in the context of clinical interventions aimed at changing a mother's behavior. Intervention that teaches a mother to be more sensitive to her baby has had some short-term success (see van IJzendoorn, Juffer, & Duyvesteyn, 1995, for a review). van den Boom (1994) found in a low-socioeconomic-status sample that enhancing maternal sensitivity and responsiveness in mothers with irritable babies increased security of attachment at 12 months, compared with that of irritable infants whose mothers received no intervention. Intervention studies concentrating on changing a mother's mental representation of attachment have been less successful. This form of intervention may require more time; that is, it may have a "sleeper effect" (van IJzendoorn et al., 1995). It appears that strategies that emphasize immediate changes in a mother's perceptions

and behavior may be the most effective ways to begin intervention. We return to this issue specifically with regard to the caregiving system at the end of this chapter.

Social-Contextual Factors Related to Providing Care

Social-contextual variables, such as the extent of a mother's satisfaction with her social support network, her marriage, or her economic circumstances, can either support or compete with her ability to focus on providing care for her child. These factors have been found by some researchers to be related to the quality of the parent–child relationship (Anisfeld et al., 1990; Belsky, Gilstrap, & Rovine, 1984; Belsky et al., 1995; Cowan, Cowan, Heming, & Miller, 1991; Diamond, Heinicke, & Mintz, 1996; Kerig, Cowan, & Cowan, 1993).

In our view, it is likely that the mother's partnership with the baby's father or another coparent may especially influence her ability to provide care (see also Gable, Belsky, & Crnic, 1992). From a behavioral-systems perspective, the parent's partner can either enhance or compete directly with the ability or desire to be a caregiver. Marital satisfaction, in and of itself, has not been found to be a strong predictor of child attachment with the mother (Belsky et al., 1995). Other aspects of the marriage, however, may influence child attachment and maternal caregiving. In our research, we have been particularly interested in parental conflict and communication patterns. We found in a recent study of infants of divorce that a mother's reports of high parent conflict and low communication with the baby's father was related to the baby's attachment insecurity with the mother, especially attachment disorganization (Solomon & George, in press-b). Our analyses of mothers' caregiving interviews (this interview asks a mother to describe her experiences with the child and her view of herself as a caregiver; George & Solomon, 1989, 1996) showed that relationship conflict was sometimes the product of the fathers' inability or unwillingness to participate in a caregiving partnership. In some of the more severe cases in our sample, the fathers actually blocked the mothers from providing care and protection for the babies.

The importance of the marital context to a mother's capacity to parent has also been demonstrated in the Cowans' studies of the family system. These investigators examined the links between a mother's and a father's adult attachment representations, marital quality, and a child's development. Overall, their studies showed that quality of marital interaction and the father's AAI classification were related to the child's adjustment to school. They found that both secure and insecure women functioned better as wives and mothers when they were married to secure men (Cohn, Silver, Cowan, Cowan, & Pearson, 1992; Cowan et al., 1996). In other words, a secure husband appeared to buffer a mother, regardless of her own attachment status, from personal distress, marital dissatisfaction, and poor interactions with her child (lack of warmth and controlling parenting style). Our caregiving-system-based interpretation of these findings is that the secure partner provides a "secure base" for the mother. It is likely that the secure partner participates in a caregiving partnership by not placing other conflicting demands on the mother or drawing her attention away from the child, by allowing her to take care of other competing needs, and by participating to some degree in caring directly for the child. Finally, it is also likely that the secure partner is the mother's "haven of safety"—that is, the one to whom she turns when her own attachment system is aroused (see also Berman, Marcus, & Berman, 1994).

Representational Models of Caregiving

According to ethological theory, behavioral systems are regulated in the mind by working cognitive models that evaluate, emotionally appraise, and organize the organism's real-life experience (Bowlby, 1969/1982). These models are updated and reworked to achieve internal consistency, and are available for use in novel situations or as the basis of future plans. Since Main et al.'s (1985) expansion of the concept of mental representation over a decade ago, the definition and nuances of representational models of attachment are well known and do not require elaboration here (see Bretherton & Munholland, Chapter 5, this volume).

If the caregiving system is a behavioral system in its own right, then it should be guided by a set of representational schemes related to providing care. In our work, we have sought to define the representational schemes of the caregiving system as assessed via a semistructured caregiving interview (George & Solomon, 1989, 1996). Briefly, we found that mothers of secure children were best characterized as flexible in their mental representations of caregiving. Mothers of se-

cure children were positive and realistic about potential threats to child security as they responded to questions that asked them to describe themselves as parents, their children, and their relationship with the children. They evaluated caregiving in relation to the situation, their children's personalities and developmental needs, their child-rearing goals, and their own needs. Their responses to questions were forthright and did not appear to reflect any predominant form of defensive processing.

Mothers of avoidant and ambivalent children appeared to have developed conditional representational models of caregiving. Mothers of avoidant children described strategies of protecting the children from a distance (a conditional strategy we have described earlier from a functionalist perspective), guided at the representational level by mild rejection. They evaluated themselves and their children as unwilling and unworthy individuals, and emphasized the negative aspects of their interactions. The most discriminating feature that set mothers of avoidant children apart from mothers of children in other attachment groups was the quality of their defensive processes in response to our interview. Mental representations of rejecting mothers were characterized by cognitive *deactivation*. The mothers dismissed or devalued their children's attachment needs, thus deactivating their caregiving system; they never, however, abandoned their role in providing care and protection. In contrast to mothers of avoidant children, mothers of ambivalent children were characterized by their behavioral and representational uncertainty. They described strategies to keep their children close (a conditional strategy we have also described earlier from a functionalist perspective), promoted dependency, and appeared insensitive to child cues. In terms of defensive processes, the mental representations of uncertain mothers were characterized by cognitive *disconnection*, as revealed by their inability to integrate positive and negative, good and bad, desirable and undesirable. This mental position appeared to leave them confused, and as a product of their uncertainty, their caregiving appeared to be heightened but somewhat ineffective.

Now that we have described the mental representations of caregiving associated with flexible, rejecting, and uncertain mothering, we return to examine our proposition that these three caregiving groups are associated with "good enough" protection and care. The reader will recall that within a behavioral-systems framework, maternal behavior is the product not only of activation and termination of the mother's caregiving system, but also of the mother's integration of her own and the child's competing behavioral systems. At the representational level, we found that the hallmark of caregiving associated with attachment security (flexible care) was a mother's commitment to finding a way to integrate and balance her own behavioral systems (i.e., her multiple roles and own attachment needs) with those of her child (George & Solomon, 1989, 1996). Mothers stated that often this balancing act was very difficult to achieve, and many mothers of secure children in our samples reported situations that made them unhappy or distressed (i.e., security was not a synonym for happiness). In particular, mothers in the infant divorce sample described tremendous stress associated with conflicting goals and great difficulty reaching a satisfactory resolution. What stood out in their interviews, however, was that this conflict was resolved through finding some acceptable balance.

What was apparent in the interviews of rejecting and uncertain mothers was the degree to which they were successful at the representational level in establishing approximations of behavioral-system integration, although their emphases when evaluating contextual cues and their own and the children's behavior appeared to be somewhat out of balance. Rejecting mothers were, under some circumstances, unwilling to integrate fully cues that would activate their caregiving system and require immediate provisions of care. For example, one mother put several "distancing" caregiving strategies into place, including providing swimming lessons and putting the child's older sibling in charge rather than staying in proximity when the child was in the pool. These mothers emphasized themselves and their own needs and desires over those of their children. They described investing more time and energy in their perceived *role* as caregivers than in responding to their children's actual attachment cues. For example, rejecting mothers often reported that mothering was the most important "job" that they could ever have; yet they would interpret their children's hurt or distress as attempts at manipulation (note, however, that they were not oblivious to the children's cues). They also stressed the importance of activities and goals associated with other behavioral systems (e.g., relationships with romantic partners) over their caregiving system. Uncertain mothers tended to overemphasize caregiving and to overinterpret their children's attachment cues. They emphasized their children over themselves, sacrificing the goals of other behavioral systems to caregiving and the children's attachment. These mothers, for example, were so concerned with their availability to their children that they deliberately scheduled their employment hours or errands to occur when the children were in school or asleep. Although their caregiving appeared out of balance, mothers in both the rejecting and uncertain groups, as compared with the mothers we describe in the next section, emphasized providing some degree of care and protection for their children.

The Disabled Caregiving System: Abdication of Care, Helplessness, and Disorganized Attachment

In contrast to mothers of children with organized attachment, we found *abdicated caregiving* to characterize mothers of disorganized and controlling children (George & Solomon, 1996; Solomon & George, 1996). These mothers evaluated themselves as helpless to protect their children (and often themselves) from threats and danger; their discussion of caregiving and their children brought out strong themes of inadequacy, helplessness, and losing control. The majority of mothers in this group described how they lacked effective and appropriate resources to handle caregiving situations. In some instances, this was due to their perception of themselves as totally ineffective or unable to find or utilize resources. In other instances, they described attempts to provide care that they felt were blocked by other individuals or by the circumstances at hand (e.g., court-imposed visitation with a father a mother does not trust; Solomon, George, & Wallerstein, 1995). These mothers also described themselves as helpless to provide assurance for their frightened children. As a result, at the behavioral-systems level, these mothers were markedly out of balance (i.e., dysequilibrated); at the representational level, these mothers portrayed themselves as being out of control or desperately struggling to remain in control of themselves, the children, or the circumstances.

For most mothers, descriptions of their children generally paralleled descriptions of themselves. The children were described as being out of control (e.g., wild, acting like "maniacs," strong-willed, defiant, or hysterical), and the mothers themselves as helpless to combat or organize the children's behavior. Some mothers, however, viewed their children as completely different from themselves—as precocious and amazingly in control of the situation or of others. In particular, these children were described as especially sensitive (e.g., skilled caregivers, adultified) or as possessing extraordinary gifts or qualities. We viewed these mothers as abdicating care because, as a result of the children's caregiving, role reversal, or special gifts, the mothers interpreted their own caregiving as relatively unimportant or ineffective. In addition, it was clear that for some of these mothers their concerns for themselves overshadowed caring for the children; and often, oblivious to the needs of the children, these mothers appeared relieved that the children were so advanced that they could care for themselves. Finally, for some mothers, caregiving and control were not in the forefront of their thinking because of their "special" understanding or relationship with their children. These mothers described the children and themselves as psychologically merged ("I am one with this child"); thus their reported behavior and thoughts about providing care for the children were based on evaluations of themselves. In short, all of these mental representations reflected a caregiving system that had been disabled by a mother's helplessness (Solomon & George, 1996).

In contrast to the interviews of mothers of avoidant and ambivalent children, the interviews of mothers of disorganized children failed to reveal any predominant defensive processing strategies. Rather, these mothers described their own extreme behavioral reactions or feelings of impotence or constriction, and their inability to select, evaluate, or modify their own behavior or that of their children. Evaluations of themselves or their children as helpless were often associated with strong emotions and affective dysregulation, and these mothers evaluated themselves as unable to control affect.[2]

We propose that abdication disables the caregiving system, and that the result is a disorganized and dysfunctional form of providing care (Solomon & George, 1996).[3] Under some circumstances, it may be in a mother's best interest to abdicate care. Under extreme conditions, a mother may abandon or kill her infant (Clutton-Brock, 1991; Miller, 1987; Scheper-Hughes, 1987); however, these forms of physical abdication are relatively rare, may interfere with the mother's reproductive fitness (exceptions include cases when a mother finds a better mate), and in our own culture are considered pathological. Of particular interest to us is a subset of mothers who do not dispose of their infants but who nevertheless abdicate their caregiving system, thus leaving their infants or children without adequate care or protection. For such a mother, when her caregiving system is disabled, her attachment and caregiving systems are disequilibrated. This means that these reciprocal behavioral systems fail to inform each other, and the caregiving system fails to mediate between the mother's own attachment system and the child's. As a result, the mother experiences caregiving and her relationship with the child in terms of profound helplessness and fear. This picture of relationship disorganization is supported not only by our caregiving data, but also by representational studies of attachment in children and adults. Disorganized children depict themselves and their attachment figures as helpless, threatening, or out of control (Bretherton, Ridgeway, & Cassidy, 1990; Kaplan, 1995; Solomon, George, & De Jong, 1995); unresolved adults portray themselves and others as isolated, threatened, unprotected, and unable to contain or prevent danger (George, West, & Pettem, in press).

In sum, evidence from representational studies of caregiving and attachment suggests that these mothers are afraid, although the mothers need not be constantly preoccupied with or consciously aware of their fear. Main and Hesse (1990) have suggested that a mother's fear, specifically as expressed by frightened or frightening behavior toward the infant, is what causes attachment disorganization. Recent studies have begun to find some empirical support for this hypothesis (see Lyons-Ruth & Jacobvitz, Chapter 23, this volume). We have proposed, however, that for a full understanding of attachment disorganization, mother–child interaction must also be examined from the perspective of the caregiving system (Solomon & George, in press-a). Based on this perspective, two guiding caregiving-related questions emerge: What is the mother afraid of? And what is it about the mother's caregiving behavior that frightens the child?

We suggest that the mother is afraid of her own profound helplessness—a helplessness that may be the product of overlapping fears. She may be afraid for the safety and protection of herself and/or her child. She may also fear losing control of her emotions and her behavior, and/or of circumstances or people (self, child, or others) that threaten her fragile resources. Determining the immediate causes of the mother's fear (i.e., the situational cues that elicit the mother's fear in the moment) is more difficult; these causes are likely to be very idiosyncratic and related to her own childhood and/or current experience. Unresolved childhood loss and trauma have been linked to attachment disorganization (Ainsworth & Eichberg, 1991; Main & Hesse, 1990; Manassis et al., 1994). This link has not been supported empirically, however, in a recent study of disorganized attachment in middle childhood; in contrast to the findings of previous studies, the majority of disorganized children in this study did not have mothers with unresolved loss or trauma (George & Solomon, 1998). More research is needed, therefore, to determine whether lack of resolution is linked explicitly to a mother's fears and helplessness, and to explore other mechanisms by which the attachment relationship may become disorganized. In addition to childhood trauma, we propose that the mother's caregiving system may be immobilized because she is afraid of the challenges raised by a particular child or circumstances (Pianta et al., 1996; Solomon & George, in press-a, in press-b, in press-c). Fear is known to be associated with increased stress and arousal, as well as with hypervigilance (Perry, Pollard, Blakley, Baker, & Vigilante, 1995). We believe that in order to isolate the particular features of interaction that lead to attachment disorganization, it is necessary to observe a mother and child under stressful circumstances—specifically, situations that threaten the mother's ability to manage (regulate) either her child's negative affect or behavior or her own. Our data suggest that mothers of disorganized children can sometimes provide organized protective care (Solomon et al., in press), and that under some circumstances they evaluate themselves as effective. Observations of mother–child interaction under low-stress conditions have failed to differentiate between organized and disorganized groups (Scheungel, van IJzendoorn, Bakersman-Kranenburg, & Blom, in press; Solomon et al., in press; Stevenson-Hinde & Shouldice, 1995), as compared with observations of mother–child interaction under more stressful circumstances (Jacobvitz, Hazen, & Riggs, 1997; Stevenson-Hinde & Shouldice, 1995). Links between stress and helplessness (and therefore disorganization) have also been found in studies directly measuring parental stress. Parents who reported high levels of helplessness (as assessed by a measure derived from our helplessness rating scale) also reported attributions of severe daily stress (Magana, 1997) and marked posttraumatic stress symptoms (Coulson, 1995). Thus a moth-

er's fear must be understood in the context of those stressful events or cues that dysregulate her and leave her feeling vulnerable, unprotected, and helpless.

In order to explain what in the mother's behavior frightens the child, let us examine the chain of events that we propose is likely to prevail during mother–child interaction in disorganized dyads. Hypervigilant and lacking robust, organized defenses, the mother is susceptible to being overwhelmed by helplessness and fear as the result of cues from the baby, from the environment, or perhaps from within (e.g., being flooded by affect). This state of panic or helplessness is disabling to caregiving, because it renders the mother herself closed (impermeable) to the child's attachment cues. Thus the mother is not able to care for or respond to the child's needs or distress for some period of time. Importantly, from a caregiving-system perspective, we stress that *what frightens the child is the mother's simultaneous abdication of care and impermeability to the child's cues or bids for care.* As Main and Hesse (1990) have suggested, in her frightened state, the mother may also exhibit fear behavior. Following Perry et al. (1995), we suggest that the mother's fear may be expressed through one or more of the following classes of fear behavior: freezing, flight, and frightened facial expressions or movements. These behaviors may frighten the child in and of themselves, or the child may be frightened by the mother's extreme unresponsiveness. In either case the child's attachment system is activated, and a parallel chain of events is then set in motion. The child becomes hypervigilant, and potentially frightened and disorganized, depending on his or her evaluation of the mother's availability. The child's evaluation of the mother and resulting behavioral (and relationship) disorganization reflect his or her individual history of interaction with the mother and developmental status. Behavioral constriction, hypercompliance, flight, freezing, defiance, dissociation, disorientation, numbing, and aggression are all possible reactions (see Perry et al., 1995). Note that some of these fear behaviors have been described to characterize children judged to be disorganized in the laboratory or thought to be disorganized due to experiences with their parents (e.g., George & Main, 1979; Main & Cassidy, 1988; Main & George, 1985; Main & Solomon, 1990). As a result of fear and the mother's impermeability, the child's attachment system becomes "closed" (Bowlby, 1980), and the child's desire and ability to seek protection and care from the mother (even if she should try to provide care) are blocked. Mother and child are left simultaneously vulnerable, mutually impermeable, helpless, and afraid, leading to a dialectic cycle of failed protection. We propose that it is under conditions of failed protection—that is, abdication of the caregiving system—that the mother fails to provide "good enough" care for the child.

CONCLUSIONS
AND IMPLICATIONS

We believe that by focusing on the attachment system alone, the field has missed important insights into the child–parent relationship that emerge only when the perspective of the caregiving system is added. Indeed, this chapter has been dedicated to describing those insights. Attachment researchers, and more broadly developmental psychologists and psychoanalysts, have historically approached the mother as a "variable." Maternal behavior has been carved into an almost infinite list of qualities and behaviors. Attachment theorists have described mothers, for example, as sensitive, rejecting, accepting, intrusive, or frightened. In this chapter we have argued that in order to understand caregiving, theorists need to move from the level of considering the mother as a "variable" to seeking to understand the mother as an individual in her own right. Mothers as individuals represent a complex interplay of developmental factors and challenges, including, as we emphasize in this chapter, an integration of competing behavioral systems.

What is added to our understanding of maternal caregiving and attachment by looking at the mother and her behavior through the lens of the caregiving behavioral system? We propose that this lens has important implications for understanding the development of caregiving behavior throughout the lifespan, and we have made specific suggestions for future research throughout this chapter. We now consider a major clinical implication of this view of the caregiving system.

The caregiving system provides clinicians with a powerful tool—a tool that frames a mother's behavior and perceptions of her child in terms of *protection*. The mother's desire and ability to provide protection are the central organizing features of the child's attachment. Behavioral interventions usually focus on changing the mother's "bad" behavior. Furthermore, as we

have discussed earlier, attachment theory (and therefore intervention) has assumed that maternal sensitivity is the strongest determinant of attachment security. Captivated by this concept, the field has focused on getting mothers to be more sensitive to their children in a variety of interactive settings (e.g., play, problem solving, or feeding), and has strayed away from the type of sensitive interaction that is fundamental to attachment—sensitivity to a child's needs for protection. Even mothers with very traumatic and disturbed attachment histories are strongly motivated to protect their children (Fraiberg, 1980). In our experience, mothers with serious intellectual, behavioral, or adjustment problems, who may not be able to benefit immediately from insight-oriented therapy or some forms of didactic parent education, have been able to understand what it means to provide or fail to provide protection for their children. Attachment theorists are beginning to suggest that there may be other ways to influence mother–child attachment. We propose that one powerful influence that has been overlooked is intervention organized around the framework of the caregiving system—that is, a mother's evaluation of herself as effective in providing protection for her child.

NOTES

1. A good question is raised here as to whether other maternal caregiving behaviors, also central to the baby's survival, may be considered "parts" of this system (e.g., nursing, cleaning, behavioral thermoregulation, "affectionate" behavior, grooming/licking/washing). Whether or not these behaviors are included, it is clear that a much wider variety of maternal behaviors can and must be brought to bear (organized) to serve the goal of protection, especially when an infant is immature and immobile.

2. One might expect the interviews of these mothers to resemble the AAI discourse patterns of lack of resolution, since the unresolved adult attachment group appears to be the adult form of child disorganization (George, West, & Pettem, in press), and lack of resolution is seen as one of the major caregiving contributions to disorganized attachment (Main & Hesse, 1990). The hallmark of lack of resolution is an individual's inability to monitor discourse or reasoning. Interestingly, these monitoring-related features of thought were not found when mothers of disorganized/controlling children described their caregiving, despite the fact that many of them were classified as unresolved with respect to loss on the AAI (George & Solomon, 1996). We see this as evidence in further support of our view that a mother's thinking about her caregiving

and her attachment experiences are regulated by separate representational models for the attachment and caregiving behavioral systems.

3. Dysfunction as associated with attachment disorganization has only been defined to date in terms of developmental or mental health risk. Dysfunction from a functionalist view (i.e., in the environment of evolutionary adaptedness) would take into consideration caregiving that undermines a mother's adaptive fitness.

REFERENCES

Aber, J. L., Belsky, J., Slade, A., & Crnic, K. (in press). Maternal representations of the relationship with their toddlers: Links to attachment and observed mothering. *Developmental Psychology.*

Aber, J. L., Slade, A., Cohen, L., & Meyer, J. (1989, April). *Parental representations of their toddlers: Their relationship to parental history and sensitivity and toddler security.* Paper presented at the biennial meeting of the Society for Research in Child Development, Baltimore, MD.

Adam, K. S. (1994). Suicidal behavior and attachment: A developmental model. In M. B. Sperling & W. H. Berman (Eds.), *Attachment in adults* (pp. 175–198). New York: Guilford Press.

Adam, K. S., Sheldon-Keller, A., & West, M. (1995). Attachment organization and vulnerability to loss, separation, and abuse in disturbed adolescents. In S. Goldberg, R. Muir, & J. Kerr (Eds.), *Attachment theory: Social, developmental, and clinical perspectives* (pp. 309–342). Hillsdale, NJ: Analytic Press.

Ainsworth, M. D. S., Blehar, M. C., Waters, E., & Wall, S. (1978). *Patterns of attachment: A psychological study of the strange situation.* Hillsdale, NJ: Erlbaum.

Ainsworth, M. D. S., & Eichberg, C. (1991). Effects on infant–mother attachment of mother's unresolved loss of an attachment figure, or other traumatic experience. In C. M. Parkes, J. Stevenson-Hinde, & P. Marris (Eds.), *Attachment across the life cycle* (pp. 160–186). London: Routledge.

Ammaniti, M. (1994). Maternal representations during pregnancy and early infant–mother interaction. In M. Ammaniti & D. S. Stern (Eds.), *Psychoanalysis and development: Representations and narratives* (pp. 79–96). New York: New York University Press.

Anisfeld, E., Casper, V., Nozyce, M., & Cunningham, N. (1990). Does infant carrying promote attachment?: An experimental study of the effects of increased physical contact on the development of attachment. *Child Development, 61,* 1617–1627.

Bahr, N. I. (1995). Environment factors and hormones: Their significance for maternal behavior in captive gorillas. In C. R. Pryce, R. D. Martin, & D. Skuse (Eds.), *Motherhood in human and nonhuman primates* (pp. 94–105). Basel: Karger.

Bell, R. (1968). A reinterpretation of the direction of effects in studies of socialization. *Psychological Review, 75,* 81–95.

Belsky, J. (1993). Promoting father involvement: An analysis and critique. *Journal of Family Psychology, 7,* 287–292.

Belsky, J. (1984). The determinants of parenting: A process model. *Child Development, 55,* 83–96.

Belsky, J., Gilstrap, B., & Rovine, M. (1984). The Pennsylvania Infant and Family Development Project: I. Stability and change in mother–infant and father–infant interaction in a family setting at one, three, and nine months. *Child Development, 55,* 692–705.

Belsky, J., & Isabella, R. (1988). Maternal, infant, and social contextual determinants of attachment security. In J. Belsky & T. Nezworski (Eds), *Clinical implications of attachment* (pp. 41–94). Hillsdale, NJ: Erlbaum.

Belsky, J., Rosenberger, K., & Crnic, K. (1995). The origins of attachment security: "Classical" and contextual determinants. In S. Goldberg, R. Muir, & J. Kerr (Eds.), *Attachment theory: Social, developmental, and clinical perspectives* (pp. 153–183). Hillsdale, NJ: Analytic Press.

Belsky, J., & Rovine, M. (1990). Patterns of marital change across the transition to parenthood: Pregnancy to three years postpartum. *Journal of Marriage and the Family, 52,* 5–19.

Belsky, J., Steinberg, L., & Draper, P. (1991). Childhood experience, interpersonal development, and reproductive strategy: An evolutionary theory of socialization. *Child Development, 62,* 647–770.

Benedek, T. (1959). Parenthood as a developmental phase: A contribution to the libido theory. *Journal of the American Psychoanalytic Association, 7,* 389–417.

Benoit, D., & Parker, K. (1994). Stability and transmission of attachment across three generations. *Child Development, 65,* 1444–1456.

Benoit, D., Parker, K. C. H., & Zeanah, C. H. (in press). Mothers' internal representations of their infants during pregnancy: Stability over time and association with infants' attachment classifications at 12 months. *Journal of Child Psychology and Psychiatry.*

Benoit, D., Zeanah, C. H., Parker, K. C. H., Nicholson, E., & Coolbear, J. (1997). "Working model of the child interview": Infant clinical status related to maternal perceptions. *Infant Mental Health Journal, 18,* 107–121.

Berman, W. H., Marcus, L., & Berman, E. R. (1994). Attachment in marital relations. In M. B. Sperling & W. H. Berman (Eds.), *Attachment in adults* (pp. 204–231). New York: Guilford Press.

Bibring, G., Dwyer, T., Huntington, D., & Valenstein, A. (1961). A study of the psychological processes in pregnancy and of the earliest mother–child relationship. *Psychoanalytic Study of the Child, 16,* 9–24.

Bornstein, M. (Ed.). (1995). *Handbook of parenting* (4 vols.). Hillsdale, NJ: Erlbaum.

Bowlby, J. (1969/1982). *Attachment and loss: Vol. 1. Attachment.* New York: Basic Books.

Bowlby, J. (1980). *Attachment and loss: Vol. 3. Loss.* New York: Basic Books.

Bowlby, J. (1988). *A secure base.* New York: Basic Books.

Brazelton, T. B. (1981). *On becoming a family.* New York: Delacorte Press/Lawrence.

Bretherton, I. (1985). Attachment theory: Retrospect and prospect. In I. Bretherton & E. Waters (Eds.), Growing points of attachment theory and research. *Monographs of the Society for Research in Child Development, 50*(1–2, Serial No. 209), 3–35.

Bretherton, I., Biringen, Z., Ridgeway, D., Maslin, D., & Sherman, M. (1989). Attachment: The parental perspective. *Infant Mental Health Journal, 10,* 203–221.

Bretherton, I., Ridgeway, D., & Cassidy, J. (1990). Assessing internal working models of attachment relationships: An attachment story completion task for 3-year-olds. In M. T. Greenberg, D. Cicchetti, & E. M. Cummings (Eds.), *Attachment in the preschool years* (pp. 273–308). Chicago: University of Chicago Press.

Bronfenbrenner, U. (1979). Ecology of the family as a context for human development: Research perspectives. *Developmental Psychology, 22,* 723–742.

Bus, A. G., & van IJzendoorn, M. H. (1992). Patterns of attachment in frequently and infrequently reading mother–child dyads. *Journal of Genetic Psychology, 153,* 395–403.

Carlson, E. (1997, April). *A prospective longitudinal study of consequences of attachment disorganization/disorientation.* Paper presented at the biennial meeting of the Society for Research in Child Development, Washington, DC.

Cassidy, J., & Berlin, L. J. (1994). The insecure/ambivalent pattern of attachment theory and research. *Child Development, 65,* 971–991.

Cicchetti, D., & Rizley, R. (1981). Developmental perspectives on the etiology, intergenerational transmission, and sequelae of child maltreatment. *New Directions in Child Development, 11,* 31–55.

Clutton-Brock, T. H. (1991). *The evolution of parent care.* Princeton, NJ: Princeton University Press.

Cohn, D. A., Silver, D. H., Cowan, C. P., Cowan, P. A., & Pearson, J. (1992). Working models of childhood attachment and couple relationships. *Journal of Family Issues, 13,* 432–449.

Cole, M., & Cole, S. R. (1996). *The development of children.* New York: Freeman.

Corter, C., & Fleming, A. S. (1995). Psychobiology of maternal behavior in humans: Sensory, experiential, and hormonal factors. In M. Bornstein (Ed.), *Handbook of parenting* (Vol. 2, pp. 59–85). Hillsdale, NJ: Erlbaum.

Coulson, W. (1995). *Disruptive caregiving strategies in mothers with symptoms of posttraumatic stress.* Unpublished undergraduate thesis, Mills College, Oakland, CA.

Cowan, C. P., Cowan, P. A., Heming, G., & Miller, N. B. (1991). Becoming a family: Marriage, parenting, and child development. In P. A. Cowan & E. M. Hetherington (Eds.), *Family transitions* (Vol. 2, pp. 79–109). Hillsdale, NJ: Erlbaum.

Cowan, P. A. (1991). Individual and family life transitions: A proposal for a new definition. In P. A. Cowan & E. M. Hetherington (Eds.), *Family transitions* (Vol. 2, pp. 3–30). Hillsdale, NJ: Erlbaum.

Cowan, P. A., Cohn, D. A., Cowan, C. P., & Pearson, J. L. (1996). Parents' attachment histories and children's externalizing and internalizing behavior: Exploring family systems models of linkage. *Journal of Consulting and Clinical Psychology, 64,* 53–63.

Cox, M., Owen, M. T., Henderson, V. K., & Margand, N. A. (1992). Prediction of infant–father and infant–mother attachment. *Developmental Psychology, 28,* 474–483.

Cramer, B., Robert-Tissot, C., Stern, D., Serpa-Rusconi, S., De Muralt, M., Besson, G., Palacio-Espasa, F., Bachmann, J.-P., Knauer, D., Berney, C., & D'Arcis, U. (1990). Outcome evaluation in brief mother–infant psychotherapy: A preliminary report. *Infant Mental Health Journal, 11,* 278–300.

Crockenberg, S. B. (1986). Are temperamental differences in babies associated with predictable differences in caregiving? In J. V. Lerner & R. M. Lerner (Eds.), *Temperament and social interaction in infants and children* (pp. 53–75). San Francisco: Jossey-Bass.

Crowell, J. A., & Feldman, S. S. (1988). Mothers' internal models of relationships and children's behavioral and developmental status: A study of mother–child interaction. *Child Development, 59,* 1273–1285.

Deutscher, M. (1971). First pregnancy and family formation.

In D. Milmen & G. Goldman (Eds.), *Psychoanalytic contributions to community psychology* (pp. 233–255). Springfield, IL: Charles C Thomas.

de Wolff, M. S., & van IJzendoorn, M. H. (1997). Sensitivity and attachment: A meta-analysis on parental antecedents of infant attachment. *Child Development, 68,* 571–591.

Diamond, D., Heinicke, C., & Mintz, J. (1996). Separation–individuation as a family transactional process in the transition to parenthood. *Infant Mental Health Journal, 17,* 24–42.

Dozier, M., & Stovall, K. C. (1997, April). *Coping with disruption in early caregiving: Factors affecting attachment strategies among foster infants.* Paper presented at the biennial meeting for the Society for Research in Child Development, Washington, DC.

Easterbrooks, M. A., & Goldberg, W. A. (1984). Toddler development in the family: Impact of father involvement and parenting characteristics. *Child Development, 55,* 740–752.

Egeland, B., & Farber, I. A. (1984). Infant–mother attachment: Factors related to its development and changes over time. *Child Development, 55,* 753–771.

Fagot, B. I., & Kavanagh, K. (1990). The prediction of antisocial behavior from avoidant attachment classifications. *Child Development, 61,* 864–873.

Fleming, A. S., Corter, C., & Steiner, M. (1995). Sensory and hormonal control of maternal behavior in rat and human mothers. In C. R. Pryce, R. D. Martin, & D. Skuse (Eds.), *Motherhood in human and nonhuman primates* (pp. 106–114). Basel: Karger.

Fonagy, P. (1994). Mental representations from an intergenerational cognitive science perspective. *Infant Mental Health Journal, 15,* 37–68.

Fonagy, P., Steele, H., & Steele, M. (1991). Maternal representations of attachment during pregnancy predict organization of infant–mother attachment at one year of age. *Child Development, 62,* 891–905.

Fonagy, P., Steele, M., Steele, H., Leigh, T., Kennedy, R., Mattoon, G., & Target, M. (1995). Attachment, the reflective self, and borderline states: The predictive specificity of the Adult Attachment Interview and pathological emotional development. In S. Goldberg, R. Muir, & J. Kerr (Eds.), *Attachment theory: Social, developmental, and clinical perspectives* (pp. 233–278). Hillsdale, NJ: Analytic Press.

Fossey, D. (1983). *Gorillas in the mist.* Boston: Houghton Mifflin.

Fraiberg, S. (1980). *Clinical studies in infant mental health: The first year of life.* New York: Basic Books.

Fullard, W., & Reiling, A. M. (1976). An investigation of Lorenz's babyness. *Child Development, 47,* 1191–1193.

Gable, S., Belsky, J., & Crnic, K. (1992). Marriage, parenting, and child development: Progress and prospects. *Journal of Family Psychology, 5,* 276–294.

George, C., Kaplan, N., & Main, M. (1984). *Adult Attachment Interview.* Unpublished manuscript, University of California at Berkeley.

George, C., Kaplan, N., & Main, M. (1985). *Adult Attachment Interview* (2nd ed.). Unpublished manuscript, University of California at Berkeley.

George, C., Kaplan, N., & Main, M. (1996). *Adult Attachment Interview* (3rd ed.). Unpublished manuscript, University of California at Berkeley.

George, C., & Main, M. (1979). Social interactions of young abused children: Approach, avoidance, and aggression. *Child Development, 50,* 306–318.

George, C., & Solomon, J. (1989). Internal working models

of caregiving and security of attachment at age six. *Infant Mental Health Journal, 10,* 222–237.

George, C., & Solomon, J. (1996). Representational models of relationships: Links between caregiving and attachment. *Infant Mental Health Journal, 17,* 198–216.

George, C., & Solomon, J. (1998, July). *Attachment disorganization at age six: Differences in doll play between punitive and caregiving children.* Paper presented at the meeting of the International Society for the Study of Behavioural Development, Bern, Switzerland.

George, C., West, M., & Pettem, O. (in press). The Adult Attachment Projective: Mental representations of disorganized attachment in adults: In J. Solomon & C. George (Eds.), *Attachment disorganization.* New York: Guilford Press.

Goodall, J. (1990). *Through a window: My thirty years with the chimpanzees of Gombe.* Boston: Houghton Mifflin.

Grossmann, K. (1997, April). *Infant–father attachment relationship: A play situation, not the strange situation, is the pivot situation.* Paper presented at the biennial meeting of the Society for Research in Child Development, Washington. DC.

Grossmann, K., Fremmer-Bombik, E., Rudolph, J., & Grossmann, K. E. (1988). Maternal representations as related to patterns of infant–mother attachment and maternal care during the first year. In R. A. Hinde & J. Stevenson-Hinde (Eds.), *Relationships within families* (pp. 241–260). Oxford: Oxford University Press.

Grossmann, K. E., & Grossmann, K. (1990). The wider concept of attachment in cross-cultural research. *Human Development, 33,* 31–47.

Haft, W., & Slade, A. (1989). Affect attunement and maternal attachment: A pilot study. *Infant Mental Health Journal, 10,* 157–172.

Hertsgaard, L., Gunnar, M., Erickson, M. F., & Nachmias, M. (1995). Adrenocortical responses to the strange situation in infants with disorganized/disoriented attachment relationships. *Child Development, 66,* 1100–1106.

Hinde, R. A. (1982a). *Ethology.* New York: Oxford University Press.

Hinde, R. A. (1982b). Attachment: Some conceptual and biological issues. In C. M. Parkes & J. Stevenson-Hinde (Eds.), *The place of attachment in human behavior* (pp. 60–78). London: Tavistock.

Hinde, R. A., & Stevenson-Hinde, J. (1991). Perspectives on attachment. In C. M. Parkes, J. Stevenson-Hinde, & P. Marris (Eds.), *Attachment across the life cycle* (pp. 52–65). London: Routledge.

Hofer, M. A. (1995). Hidden regulators: Implications for a new understanding of attachment, separation, and loss. In In S. Goldberg, R. Muir, & J. Kerr (Eds.), *Attachment theory: Social, developmental, and clinical perspectives* (pp. 203–230). Hillsdale, NJ: Analytic Press.

Isabella, R. A. (1993). Origins of attachment: Maternal interactive behavior across the first year. *Child Development, 64,* 605–621.

Jackson, J. (1993). Multiple caregiving among African Americans and infant attachment: The need for an emic approach. *Human Development, 36,* 87–102.

Jacobsen, T., Edelstein, W., & Hofmann, V. (1994). A longitudinal study of the relation between representations of attachment in childhood and cognitive functioning in childhood and adolescence. *Developmental Psychology, 30,* 112–124.

Jacobvitz, D., Hazen, N. L., & Riggs, S. (1997, April). *Disorganized mental processes in mothers, frightening/frightened caregiving, and disoriented, disorganized behavior*

in infancy. Paper presented at the biennial meeting of the Society for the Research for Child Development, Washington, DC.

Kaplan, H. (1996). A theory of fertility and parental investment in traditional and modern societies. *Yearbook of Physical Anthropology, 39,* 91–136.

Kaplan, N. (1995). *Patterns of response to imagined separation in six-year-olds judged secure, avoidant, ambivalent and disorganized with mother in infancy: Resourceful, inactive, ambivalent, and fearful.* Unpublished manuscript, University of California at Berkeley.

Kerig, P. K., Cowan, P. A., & Cowan, C. P. (1993). Marital quality and gender differences in parent–child interaction. *Developmental Psychology, 29,* 931–939.

Kermoian, R., & Liederman, P. H. (1986). Infant attachment to mother and child caretaker in an East African community. *International Journal of Behavioral Development, 9,* 455–469.

Keverne, E. B. (1995). Neurochemical changes accompanying the reproductive process: Their significance for maternal care in primates and in other mammals. In C. R. Pryce, R. D. Martin, & D. Skuse (Eds.), *Motherhood in human and nonhuman primates* (pp. 69–77). Basel: Karger.

Klaus, M. H., Kennell, J. H., & Klaus, P. H. (1995). *Bonding.* Reading, MA: Addison-Wesley.

Lamb, M. E. (1997). The development of father–infant relationships. In M. E. Lamb (Ed.), *The role of the father in child development* (pp. 261–285). New York: Wiley.

Langlois, J. (1988). The role of physical attractiveness in the observation of adult–child interactions: Eye of the beholder or behavioral reality? *Developmental Psychology, 24,* 254–263.

Langlois, J. H., Ritter, J. M., Casey, R. J., & Sawin, D. B. (1995). Infant attractiveness predicts maternal behaviors and attitudes. *Developmental Psychology, 31,* 464–472.

Lee, R. E. (1995). Women look at their experience of pregnancy. *Infant Mental Health Journal, 16,* 192–205.

Liefer, M. (1980). *Psychological effects of motherhood.* New York: Praeger.

Liotti, G. (in press). Disorganization of attachment as a model for understanding dissociative psychopathology. In J. Solomon & C. George (Eds.), *Attachment disorganization.* New York: Guilford Press.

Lorenz, K. (1943). Die angeboren formen moglichend Erfahrun. *Zeitschrift für Tierpsychologie, 5,* 233–409.

Lyons-Ruth, K. (1996). Attachment relationships among children with aggressive behavior problems: The role of disorganized early attachment strategies. *Journal of Consulting and Clinical Psychology, 64,* 64–73.

Lyons-Ruth, K., & Block, D. (1996). The disturbed caregiving system: Relations among childhood trauma, maternal caregiving, and infant affect and attachment. *Infant Mental Health Journal, 17,* 257–275.

Magaña, L. (1997). *Unresolved trauma and environmental stress in relation to the caregiving behavioral system: Disorganization of caregiving strategies.* Unpublished undergraduate thesis, Mills College, Oakland, CA.

Main, M. (1990). Cross-cultural studies of attachment organization: Recent studies, changing methodologies, and the concept of conditional strategies. *Human Development, 33,* 48–61.

Main, M. (1995). Recent studies in attachment: Overview, with selected implications for clinical work. In S. Goldberg, R. Muir, & J. Kerr (Eds.), *Attachment theory: Social, developmental, and clinical perspectives* (pp. 407–474). Hillsdale, NJ: Analytic Press.

Main, M., & Cassidy, J. (1988). Categories of response to reunion with the parent at age 6: Predictable from infant attachment classifications and stable over a 1-month period. *Developmental Psychology, 24,* 415–426.

Main, M., & George, C. (1985). Response of abused and disadvantaged toddlers to distress in agemates: A study in the daycare setting. *Developmental Psychology, 21,* 407–412.

Main, M., Kaplan, N., & Cassidy, J. (1985). Security in infancy, childhood, and adulthood: A move to the level of representation. In I. Bretherton & E. Waters (Eds.), Growing points of attachment theory and research. *Monographs of the Society for Research in Child Development, 50*(1–2, Serial No. 209), 66–104.

Main, M., & Goldwyn, R. (1985). *Adult attachment scoring and classification systems.* Unpublished manuscript, University of California at Berkeley.

Main, M., & Goldwyn, R. (1991). *Adult attachment scoring and classification systems* (2nd ed.). Unpublished manuscript, University of California at Berkeley.

Main, M., & Goldwyn, R. (1994). *Adult attachment scoring and classification systems* (3rd ed.). Unpublished manuscript, University of California at Berkeley.

Main, M., & Hesse, E. (1990). Parents' unresolved traumatic experiences are related to infant disorganized attachment status: Is frightened and/or frightening parental behavior the linking mechanism? In M. T. Greenberg, D. Cicchetti, & E. M. Cummings (Eds.), *Attachment in the preschool years* (pp. 161–182). Chicago: University of Chicago Press.

Main, M., & Solomon, J. (1990). Procedures for identifying infants as disorganized/disoriented during the Ainsworth strange situation. In M. T. Greenberg, D. Cicchetti, & E. M. Cummings (Eds.), *Attachment in the preschool years* (pp. 121–160). Chicago: University of Chicago Press.

Manassis, K., Bradley, S., Goldberg, S., Hood, J., & Swinson, R. P. (1994). Attachment in mothers with anxiety disorders and their children. *Journal of the American Academy of Child and Adolescent Psychiatry, 33,* 1106–1113.

Manning-Orenstein, G. (1997). *Birth intervention: Comparing the influence of doula assistance at birth vs. Lamaze birth preparation on first-time mothers' working models of caregiving.* Unpublished doctoral dissertation, Saybrook Institute, San Francisco, CA.

Marvin, R. S., & Pianta, R. C. (1996). Mothers' reaction to their child's diagnosis: Relations with security of attachment. *Journal of Clinical Child Psychology, 25,* 436–445.

Miller, B. D. (1987). Female infanticide and child neglect in rural North India. In N. Scheper-Hughes (Ed.), *Child survival: Anthropological perspectives on the treatment and maltreatment of children* (pp. 164–181). Boston: Reidel.

Miyake, K., Chen, S. J., & Campos, J. J. (1985). Infant temperament, mother's mode of interaction, and attachment in Japan: An interim report. In I. Bretherton & E. Waters (Eds.), Growing points of attachment theory and research. *Monographs of the Society for Research in Child Development, 50*(1–2, Serial No. 209), 276–297.

Moffitt, T. E., Caspi, A., Belsky, J., & Silva, P. A. (1992). Childhood experience and the onset of menarche: A test of a sociobiological model. *Child Development, 63,* 47–58.

Moss, E., Parent, S., Gosselin, C., Rousseau, D., & St-Laurent, D. (1996). Attachment and teacher-reported behavior problems during the preschool and early school-age period. *Development and Psychopathology, 8,* 511–525.

Moss, E., Rousseau, D., Parent, S., St-Laurent, D., & Saintonge, J. (1998). Correlates of attachment at school-age: Maternal reported stress, mother–child and behavior problems. *Child Development, 69,* 1390–1405.

Perry, B. D., Pollard, R. A., Blakley, T. L., Baker, W. L., & Vigilante, D. (1995). Childhood trauma, the neurobiology of adaptation, and "use dependent" development of the brain: How "states" become "traits." *Infant Mental Health Journal, 16,* 271–289.

Pianta, R. C., Egeland, B., & Adam, E. M. (1996). Adult attachment classification and self-reported psychiatric symptomatology as assessed by the Minnesota Multiphasic Personality Inventory. *Journal of Consulting and Clinical Psychology, 64,* 273–281.

Pianta, R. C., & Marvin, R. S. (1992). *The Reaction to Diagnosis Interview.* Unpublished manuscript, University of Virginia.

Pianta, R. C., Marvin, R., Britner, P., & Borowitz, K. (1996). Mothers' resolution of their children's diagnoses: Organized patterns of caregiving representations. *Infant Mental Health Journal, 17,* 239–256.

Pryce, C. R. (1995). Determinants of motherhood in human and nonhuman primates: A biosocial model. In C. R. Pryce, R. D. Martin, & D. Skuse (Eds.), *Motherhood in human and nonhuman primates* (pp. 1–15). Basel: Karger.

Rode, S. E., Chang, P., Fisch, R. O., & Sroufe, L. A. (1981). Attachment patterns in infants separated at birth. *Developmental Psychology, 17,* 188–191.

Sagi, A. (1990). Attachment theory and research from a cross-cultural perspective. *Human Development, 33,* 10–22.

Sameroff, A. J. (1993). Models of development and developmental risk. In C. H. Zeanah (Ed.), *Handbook of infant mental health* (pp. 3–14). New York: Guilford Press.

Schaller, G. B. (1963). *The mountain gorilla: Ecology and behavior.* Chicago: University of Chicago Press.

Scheper-Hughes, N. (1987). Culture, scarcity, and maternal thinking: Mother love and child death in Northeast Brazil. In N. Scheper-Hughes (Ed.), *Child survival: Anthropological perspectives on treatment and maltreatment of children* (pp. 291–317). Boston: Reidel.

Schneider-Rosen, K. S., & Rothbaum, F. (1993). Quality of parental caregiving and security of attachment. *Developmental Psychology, 29,* 358–367.

Schuengel, C., van IJzendoorn, M. H., Bakermans-Kranenburg, M. J., & Blom, M. (in press). Frightening, frightened, and/or dissociated behavior, unresolved loss, and infant disorganization. In J. Solomon & C. George (Eds.), *Attachment disorganization.* New York: Guilford Press.

Slade, A., Belsky, J., Aber, J. L., & Phelps, J. L. (in press). Maternal representations of their toddlers: Links to adult attachment and observed mothering. *Developmental Psychology.*

Slade, A., & Cohen, L. J. (1996). The process of parenting and the remembrance of things past. *Infant Mental Health Journal, 17,* 217–238.

Slade, A., Dermer, M., Gerber, J., Gibson, L., Graf, F., Siegal, N., & Tobias, K. (1995, March). *Prenatal representation, dyadic interaction, and the quality of attachment.* Paper presented at the biennial meeting of the Society for Research in Child Development, Indianapolis, IN.

Solomon, J., & George, C. (1996a). Defining the caregiving system: Toward a theory of caregiving. *Infant Mental Health Journal, 17,* 183–197.

Solomon, J., & George, C. (in press-a). The place of disorganization in attachment theory: Linking classic observations with contemporary findings. In J. Solomon & C. George (Eds.), *Attachment disorganization.* New York: Guilford Press.

Solomon, J., & George, C. (in press-b). The development of attachment in separated and divorced families: Effects of overnight visitation, parent, and couple variables. *Attachment and Human Development.*

Solomon, J., & George, C. (in press-c). The caregiving behavioral system in mothers of infants: A comparison of divorcing and married mothers. *Attachment and Human Development.*

Solomon, J., George, C., & De Jong, A. (1995). Children classified as controlling at age six: Evidence of disorganized representational strategies and aggression at home and school. *Development and Psychopathology, 7,* 447–464.

Solomon, J., George, C., & Silverman, N. (in press). Maternal caregiving *Q*-sort: Describing age-related changes in mother–infant interaction. In E. Waters, B. Vaughn, & D. Teti (Eds.), *Patterns of attachment behavior: Q-sort perspectives in secure base behavior and caregiving in infancy and childhood.* Mahwah, NJ: Erlbaum.

Spangler, G., Fremmer-Bombik, E., & Grossmann, K. (1996). Social and individual determinants of infant attachment security and disorganization. *Infant Mental Health Journal, 17,* 127–139.

Spangler, G., & Grossmann, K. (in press). Individual and physiological correlates of attachment disorganization in infancy. In J. Solomon & C. George (Eds.), *Attachment disorganization.* New York: Guilford Press.

Sroufe, L. A. (1988). The role of infant–caregiver attachment in development. In J. Belsky & T. Nezworski (Eds.), *Clinical implications of attachment* (pp. 18–38). Hillsdale, NJ: Erlbaum.

Sroufe, L. A., & Fleeson, J. (1986). Attachment and the construction of relationships. In W. Hartup & Z. Rubin (Eds.), *The nature and development of relationships* (pp. 51–71). Hillsdale, NJ: Earlbaum.

Sroufe, L. A., & Waters, E. (1977). Heart rate as a convergent measure in clinical and developmental research. *Merrill–Palmer Quarterly, 23,* 3–27.

Steele, H., & Steele, M. (1994). Intergenerational patterns of attachment. In *Advances in personal relationships* (Vol. 5, pp. 93–120). London: Jessica Kingsley.

Stevenson-Hinde, J. (1994). An ethological perspective. *Psychological Inquiry, 5,* 62–65.

Stevenson-Hinde, J., & Shouldice, A. (1995). Maternal interactions and self-reports related to attachment classifications at 4.5 years. *Child Development, 66,* 583–596.

Suomi, S. J. (1995). Attachment theory and nonhuman primates. In S. Goldberg, R. Muir, & J. Kerr (Eds.), *Attachment theory: Social, developmental, and clinical perspectives* (pp. 185–201). Hillsdale, NJ: Analytic Press.

Trivers, R. L. (1974). Parent–offspring conflict. *American Zoologist, 11,* 249–264.

van den Boom, D. C. (1994). The influence of temperament and mothering on attachment and exploration: An experimental manipulation of sensitive responsiveness among lower-class mothers with irritable infants. *Child Development, 65,* 1457–1477.

van IJzendoorn, M. H. (1995). Adult attachment representations, parental responsiveness, and infant attachment: A meta-analysis on the predictive validity of the Adult Attachment Interview. *Psychological Bulletin, 117,* 387–403.

van IJzendoorn, M. H., Juffer, F., & Duyvesteyn, M. G. C. (1995). Breaking the intergenerational cycle of insecure attachment: A review of the effects of attachment-based interventions on maternal sensitivity and infant security. *Journal of Child Psychology and Psychiatry, 36,* 225–248.

Ward, M. J., Botyanski, N., Plunket, S., & Carlson, E. (1991, April). *The concurrent and predictive validity of the Adult Attachment Interview for adolescent mothers.* Paper presented at the biennial meeting of the Society for Research in Child Development, Seattle, WA.

Weiss, R. S. (1991). The attachment bond in childhood and adulthood. In C. M. Parkes, P. Marris, & J. Stevenson-Hinde (Eds.), *Attachment across the life cycle* (pp. 66–76). London: Routledge.

West, M., & George, C. (1998). *Violence in intimate relationships: An attachment theory perspective.* Manuscript submitted for publication.

Winnicott, D. W. (1958). *Collected papers.* London: Tavistock.

Zeanah, C. H., & Barton, M. L. (1989). Internal representations and parent–infant relationships. *Infant Mental Health Journal, 10,* 135–141.

Zeanah, C. H., Benoit, D., Hirschberg, L., Barton, M. L., & Regan, C. (1994). Mothers' representations of their infants are concordant with infant attachment classification. *Developmental Issues in Psychiatry and Psychology, 1,* 1–14.

Zeanah, C. H., Hirshberg, L., Danis, B. A., Brennan, M., & Miller, D. (1995, March). *On the specificity of the Adult Attachment Interview in a high risk sample.* Paper presented at the biennial meeting of the Society for Research in Child Development, Indianapolis, IN.

29

Attachment Relationships in the Context of Multiple Caregivers

❖

CAROLLEE HOWES

In his early writings, Bowlby (1969/1982) proposed that a child develops a hierarchy of attachment relationships—first to the mother as the primary caregiver and then to others, specifically the father. In 1967, Ainsworth wrote that "nearly all the babies in this sample who became attached to their mothers during the period spanned by our observations became attached also to some other familiar figure—father, grandmother, or other adult in the household, or to an older sibling" (p. 315). The Ainsworth sample was composed of Ganda infants in East Africa. Ainsworth's next major work was the Baltimore study of child–mother attachment (Ainsworth, Blehar, Waters, & Wall, 1978). Although this work was concerned with patterns of infant–mother attachment relationships, Ainsworth still acknowledged the possibility of other attachment figures: "The mother figure is, however, the principal caregiver, whether the natural mother or someone else plays that role" (Ainsworth et al., 1978, p. 5).

Although, as these quotations show, recognition of alternative attachment figures has been part of attachment theory since its development, attachment research has largely been conducted on the child–mother attachment relationship. Thus, we know considerably less about attachments to other familiar figures. In the United States, however, families outside the dominant culture (particularly people of color, immigrant families, and families living in or close to poverty) have historically used a variety of child-rearing configurations involving networks of caregiving adults rather than a single caregiver (Jackson, 1993). In order to understand children's development in these families, it may be useful to consider a network of attachment relationships, rather than to focus only on the child–mother relationship. As the roles of women and men in family life have changed, and as the two-income family has become an economic necessity in many cases, most children even in dominant U.S. culture are now regularly cared for by more than one adult. Furthermore, new work driven by a developmental perspective on attachment, by a move toward a concern with attachment representations as well as secure-base behaviors, and by increasing understanding of the importance of teacher–child relationships in school-age children has expanded the definition of attachment figures beyond adults who attend to children's physical needs. Therefore, we must study attachments with multiple caregivers.

The inclusion of multiple caregivers in the study of attachment relationships adds new dimensions to a number of theoretical issues within the field of attachment research. These issues are used in this chapter to organize the growing empirical literature on attachment relationships in the context of multiple caregivers. Once a child is considered to have more than one attachment relationship, we must identify which adults in the child's social network are attachment figures. Central to attachment theory is a set of propositions about how attachments are formed and about the influence of attachment relationships on subsequent development. Because alternative attachment relationships are formed in different contexts than maternal attachments, and often in different developmental periods (i.e., subsequent to maternal attachments), examining antecedents of alternative attachment relationships can inform and expand theory. Similarly, examining the predictive power of alternative attachment for children's development can expand our understanding of relationships in development. Including multiple caregivers in our theories of attachment requires that we reexamine our understanding of the organization of internal working models. Finally, the issue of multiple caregivers is closely tied to questions of whether child care is related to attachment.

WHO IS AN ATTACHMENT FIGURE?

There is little disagreement that in most Western families, the child's biological mother is an attachment figure. Bowlby's (1969/1982) original formulation of attachment assumed that the child's mother is the primary attachment figure. Currently, in most families, the mother is responsible for either the actual caregiving of the children or the management and delegation of that caregiving.

Three underlying questions are important in identifying alternative attachment figures:

1. Are certain kinds or categories of caregivers (e.g., grandparents or child care providers) considered attachment figures for all children, or do attachment figures for a given child need to be determined by individual circumstances? If a necessary criterion for an alternative attachment figure is emotional presence over time, then certain categories of adults—for example, mothers and fathers in two-parent families—appear to be categorical choices. On the other hand, identifying a set of alternative attachment figures for individual children leads to complex and fundamental questions about the nature of an attachment relationship. For example, mothers and fathers may be categorically considered attachment figures, but should an individual father be considered an attachment figure if and only if he participates in caregiving tasks?

2. Do the criteria for the identification of attachment figures change over development? That is, does an attachment figure need to participate in caregiving activities to be considered when a child is an infant, but not when the child reaches school age? Is it sufficient then for the attachment figure to be emotionally central to the child's daily life? For example, a father who does not participate in caregiving tasks may be influential in the organization of family social and emotional interactions and of everyday activities. Identification of alternative attachment figures across developmental stages leads us to consider how attachment behaviors change with development.

3. How consistent over time does the alternative attachment figure need to be? Child care providers are often identified as alternative attachment figures, but a particular person in the role of child care provider is rarely present for more than a year or two. However, children regularly have a child care provider as a caregiver for 10 years of their lives. Can we examine continuity in children's relationships with a series of people who fill the role of child care provider, or should we only consider alternative attachment figures to be persons who remain present in a child's life for a number of years?

Criteria for Identification of Attachment Figures

Two different research groups have proposed criteria for the identification of attachment figures beyond the mother. van IJzendoorn, Sagi, and Lambermon (1992) have suggested five criteria, and my colleagues and I (Howes, Hamilton, & Althusen, in press) have suggested three. The two sets of criteria differ on a number of dimensions. I begin with broad descriptions, comparing the two sets, and then move to a detailed discussion of each.

The van IJzendoorn et al. (1992) criteria involve assessing attachment security, its antecedents, and its consequences. The Howes et al. (in press) criteria are independent of attachment security. The van IJzendoorn et al. criteria may be best used to identify classes or categories of attachment figures, whereas the Howes et al. criteria also may be used to differentiate between individuals within a category. The van IJzendoorn et al. criteria may be most useful when one is considering infants and toddlers, whereas the Howes et al. criteria can be used throughout several developmental periods. The van IJzendoorn et al. criteria can be implemented using well-established attachment measures, while the Howes et al. criteria may require both an assessment of a child's social network and multiple informants' perspectives on each caregiver's emotional investment in the child.

The Van IJzendoorn et al. Criteria

After reviewing the existing empirical literature, van IJzendoorn et al. (1992) concluded that child care providers and *metaplot* (caregivers on Israeli kibbutzim) categorically meet their criteria for being alternative attachment figures.

> (a) Infant–caregiver samples do not show an overrepresentation of avoidant classification; (b) Infant–caregiver samples do not show an overrepresentation of unclassifiable cases; (c) Infant–caregiver classifications are independent of infant–parent classifications; (d) Caregiver sensitivity is related to the infant–caregiver strange situation classifications; and (e) Infant–caregiver classifications predict later socio-emotional functioning. (van IJzendoorn et al., 1992, p. 9)

Following the publication of the van IJzendoorn analysis, a colleague and I (Howes & Smith, 1995a) published an analysis of child care provider–child attachment relationships (n = 1,379). Children in the sample were cared for in relatives' homes, other private homes, or child care centers. Child care quality varied from poor to good, but not excellent. We generated subscale scores from the Attachment Q-Sort (Waters, 1990), and used these scores in a cluster analysis to group the children into attachment behavior profiles consistent with security categories derived from the Ainsworth strange situation (Ainsworth et al., 1978). All children could be clustered, and thus van IJzendoorn et al.'s second criterion (no overrepresentation of unclassifiable cases) was met. Children in the secure cluster were also more positively involved with their caregivers than children in other clusters, thereby meeting the fourth criterion (a relation between caregiver sensitivity and attachment security) of van IJzendoorn et al. As will be explored later in this chapter, there is growing empirical evidence for van IJzendoorn et al.'s third and fifth criteria (independence of parental attachments and prediction of later functioning).

However, 50% of the children in the Howes and Smith (1995a) sample were classified as avoidant. In addition, more children aged 3 years and over were classified as avoidant than as difficult (resistant) or secure. And more boys than girls were classified as avoidant. These results are particularly noteworthy in light of van IJzen-

doorn et al.'s (1992) first criterion (no overrepresentation of avoidance).

Further examination of the Howes and Smith avoidant group suggests that approximately one-third of the children who were placed in the avoidant cluster because of high scores on an "avoiding the caregiver" subscale had high security scores. These children in the avoidant cluster with high security scores often sought comfort from and were engaged in positive negotiations and interactions with their caregivers. Therefore, these children appear to have been empirically misclassified as insecure. These misclassified children also tended to be preschoolers rather than toddlers. This suggests that an older child in child care may sometimes construct a secure attachment relationship with a caregiver in which the child uses the caregiver to organize his or her social and learning environment, but spends little time in close contact with the caregiver. This profile of behavior suggests a goal-corrected partnership (Bowlby, 1969/1982). For preschoolers, behavior indicative of a goal-corrected partnership is more developmentally appropriate than the contact-seeking behaviors of toddlers. Moreover, the notion of caregivers as organizers, rather than as providers of comfort, may be particularly true of caregivers who are teachers (Pianta & Walch, 1995).

Further support for this idea of caregivers as organizers is provided by a study of children's cognitive activities in child care (Howes & Smith, 1995b). In this study, children with higher security scores with their caregivers were most frequently engaged in competent exploration of the environment and enhanced cognitive activity, even when richness of available activities and teacher facilitation of individual children's play were controlled for. What appeared to be important, therefore, was the children's felt security with their caregivers rather than the extent of involvement with them.

The Howes et al. Criteria

We have proposed the following three criteria for identification of attachment figures other than the mother (Howes et al., in press): (1) provision of physical and emotional care; (2) continuity or consistency in a child's life; and (3) emotional investment in the child. These criteria are principally meant to be applied to adults within individual children's social networks. That is, they are meant to identify specific attachment figures for a particular child, rather than to identify categories of attachment figures. Therefore, for example, fathers generally meet the criteria, but individual children may or may not have fathers who are involved in physical and emotional care, continuously present in their lives, and emotionally invested in their well-being.

Although these criteria and the criteria used by Ainsworth in her early work to identify attachment figures are similar in that they identify particular individuals for particular children, they differ in two dimensions. Ainsworth (1967) did not include physical and emotional care as a criterion; she stated that infants are attached to adults who never provide care (e.g., some fathers in Uganda). Furthermore, when Ainsworth (1967) identified multiple attachment figures, she started with observations of the children. When children directed attachment behaviors to, or organized their attachment system around, adults other than their mothers, those adults were considered attachment figures. Likewise, Schaffer and Emerson's (1967) work in a Scottish village followed children to identify attachment figures. The social context of a village in which all participants in the children's lives could be readily observed may have allowed for this method of identification. The Howes et al. (in press) criteria, instead of beginning with observations of children, identify broad categories of people who may be attachment figures—parents, relatives, child care providers—and attempt through interviews and social network analysis to determine which of these potential caregivers are attachment figures for individual children and should be observed.

Using the Howes et al. (in press) criteria requires social network analysis (Bost, Cielinski, Newell, & Vaughn, 1997). First, the adults with whom a child has had opportunities to construct alternative attachment relationships must be identified. Then for each figure, these questions must be asked: Does this person provide physical and emotional care? Is this person a consistent presence in the child's social network? And is this person emotionally invested in the child?

The mother (or the parent who is primarily responsible for the organization of a child's daily life) is the usual informant in research on children's social networks, although preschool children are increasingly used as informants as well (Bost et al., 1997; Reid, Landesman, Treder, & Jaccoby, 1989). Most mothers can readily provide information on who cares for their children in their absence, and can report on whether caregiving arrangements involving potential alternative attachment figures are consistent and predictable. Therefore, teachers, regular child care providers, and grandparents who spend regular time with their grandchildren are considered to meet the criterion of consistency, because the children can regularly predict or expect them to be there.

The Problem of Consistency over Time: Categories or Individuals?

Continuity or consistency over time is a problematic criterion when researchers are identifying child care providers and teachers as alternative attachment figures. Children rarely have the same person in the role of child care provider or teacher for more than a year or two. Most children in the United States, however, have a series of persons who care for them as child care providers or teachers. Therefore, there is continuity in categories of alternative attachment figures.

There is growing evidence for continuity in relationship quality with the same child care providers and teachers. In two longitudinal samples, when the persons serving as child care providers remained stable, relationship quality was consistent over time. Initially, when the child care providers changed, so did relationship quality (Howes & Hamilton, 1992a). This suggests that children constructed new representations of their relationships with their new providers. When children experienced more than one change in child care providers, there was more consistency in relationship quality (Howes & Hamilton, 1992a). This consistency suggests that children begin to treat child care providers as a category of alternative attachment relationships. Nine-year-old children from one of these longitudinal samples were interviewed about their relationships with their current teachers. Children's attachment security with their first child care providers predicted their perception of their relationships with their current teachers (Howes, Hamilton, & Phillipsen, 1998). Likewise, teacher perception of teacher–child relationship quality was consistent over the transition from child care to kindergarten (Howes & Phillipsen, in press) and from kindergarten to second grade (Pianta, Steinberg, & Rollins, 1995). In both of these longitudinal samples, relationship quality with the child care providers and teachers at each time point was independent of child–mother attachment security and child temperament.

Emotional Investment as a Criterion

Within a social network interview, mothers are far less able to report on the emotional investment of the alternative caregivers than they are to report on their children's caregiving arrangements. Measures of an adult's perception of an adult–child relationship assess the adult's emotional investment in the child (Pianta & Steinberg, 1992; Tinsley & Parke, 1983). Another strategy for assessing emotional investment is derived from research that examines parents' internal models of caregiving (George & Solomon, 1996). In an interview format similar to the Adult Attachment Interview (George, Kaplan, & Main, 1985), parents are asked to describe how they think about and interact with their children in terms of providing protection and care (George & Solomon, 1996). A similar format can be used with alternative attachment figures in relation to children for whom they provide care.

If the ultimate criterion for identifying attachment figures is the children's organization of their attachment behavior (Ainsworth, 1967), asking adults whether they are emotionally invested in the children is problematic. Children become attached to neglecting parents who appear emotionally uninvested, although such parents may fight having their children taken away (Carlson, Cicchetti, Barnett, & Braunwald, 1989). Fortunately, by preschool age, children can be used as informants on their social contact with and the support provided by adults (Bost et al., 1997; Reid et al., 1989). Children's perceptions may also help us to understand the emotional investment of alternative attachment figures. Advances in interview and narrative methods for assessing attachment representations in early and middle childhood (Oppenheim & Waters, 1995) provide another means of identifying children's perceptions of alternative attachment figures. For example, 6-year-old children in one study were able to tell coherent and differentiated stories about their mothers and their child care providers (Matheson, 1992).

In summary, two groups of researchers have provided guidelines for identifying alternative attachment figures. The van IJzendoorn et al. (1992) approach identifies two categories of alternative attachment figures, child care providers

and *metaplot*, on the basis of existing empirical research. The identification of further categories necessitates further research. In contrast, the Howes et al. (in press) approach allows a set of attachment figures to be identified for each child. The first two of the Howes et al. criteria (i.e., caregiving and consistency) can be identified through well-established network analysis. The third criterion (emotional investment) is the most speculative of the criteria, and is in need of measurement development and empirical support before it can be widely adopted.

Categories of Alternative Attachment Figures

For the purposes of this chapter, certain categories of adults frequently available in children's social networks are considered as alternative attachment figures. These categories are fathers, grandparents, child care providers, and teachers. There is a considerable literature on attachment relationships with fathers and child care providers, as well as a growing literature on attachment relationships with teachers; however, there is almost no literature on attachment relationships with grandparents. Nevertheless, grandparents are often mentioned in adult accounts of important supplemental caregiving relationships. The existing empirical literature does suggest that according to either the van IJzendoorn et al. (1992) or the Howes et al. (in press) criteria, persons who fall within these categories of caregivers may be attachment figures.

A second set of caregiver categories is also considered. These categories are not characteristic of typical children. However, they are included because either (as in the case of the *metaplot*) there is a considerable body of empirical research on attachments to these caregivers, or (as in the cases of foster and adoptive parents, shelter and group home caregivers, and therapeutic teachers) there are compelling theoretical reasons to include them. Relationships with foster and adoptive parents and with shelter and group home caregivers are often formed after an initial attachment relationship has been constructed and then lost. Relationships with therapeutic teachers are formed in the context of previous difficulties in relationships with adults. Thus investigation of these relationship categories has the potential to expand our understanding of attachment theory.

PATHWAYS TO THE ESTABLISHMENT OF ALTERNATIVE ATTACHMENT RELATIONSHIPS

Developmental Issues

Beyond the identification of attachment figures, the study of multiple caregivers leads to considerations of pathways to the establishment of attachment relationships. Attachment theory assumes that a mother and infant will begin to construct their relationship from the moment of birth. Children's repertoire of social signals and their capacities for memory, internal representation, and affective cognitions develop at the same time as the child–mother attachment. Children encounter alternative attachment figures at varying points in their development. In contrast to an infant–mother attachment constructed from birth, an attachment relationship between a child and a child care provider may begin when the child is 6 or 8 months old. This alternative attachment relationship is formed within a different developmental context than the infant–mother attachment relationship. An infant–child care provider relationship begun within the first year of the child's life is still formed prior to the developmental period (6–8 months) when attachment representations emerge. Children with early infant child care experiences simultaneously construct internal models of two (or more) attachment relationships. We may expect different pathways to attachment formation when a child and an alternative attachment figure begin their relationship after the child has already established one or more attachment relationships. This sequentially formed attachment relationship is constructed within a different developmental period than the infant–mother attachment, and in the context of an already established relationship history.

Simultaneously Formed Attachment Relationships

The largest body of literature on simultaneously formed attachment relationships pertains to the categories of mothers and fathers. In two-parent families, children simultaneously, and from birth onward, are assumed to construct attachment relationships with their mothers and with their fathers (Easterbrooks & Goldberg, 1987). None of the literature reviewed for this chapter questions the assumption that fathers are attachment figures. The comparison of processes underlying

mother and father attachment formation is complicated, however, because families vary considerably in the organization of caregiving responsibilities, and the organization of caregiving in families appears to change as children develop. Most studies of mother and father attachment to date have not documented family caregiving organization.

A large literature suggests that when fathers take on caregiving activities, there are few differences between child–mother and child–father relationships (Parke & Asher, 1983). An early study by Lamb (1977a) is illustrative, in that when mothers, fathers, and infants were all present for evening observations, infants directed attachment behaviors to both mothers and fathers; although this finding was consistent with those of other studies, child–mother and child–father social interaction patterns were different. In this longitudinal study, children over time (7 to 13 months) came to prefer to engage with either of their parents rather than with an increasingly familiar visitor. By age 2 the children showed no preference for one parent over the other in the nonstressed context of the home (Lamb, 1977b).

More recent literature suggests that within the traditional family, the organization of caregiving may alter the course of attachment formation. Steele, Steele, and Fonagy (1995) examined associations among mothers' and fathers' adult attachment classifications and the attachment classifications of their infants. The pattern of associations suggests that infant–mother interaction may influence father–infant interaction, which in turn influences father–infant attachment. That is, in a traditional family in which the mother is the primary caregiver, the mother may constrain and shape father–infant interaction.

As noted above, there is almost no literature on grandparent–child attachment relationships. There is a small literature on adolescent parents that includes the parents of the adolescents, who are, of course, the grandparents of the infants. Living with and/or receiving support from a grandmother appears to enhance attachment security between an adolescent mother and her child (Spieker & Bensley, 1977). Perhaps, through processes similar to those identified by Steele et al. (1995) for mothers and fathers, a grandmother's representations of attachment appear to influence an adolescent mother's caregiving and attachment relationship with her child (Ward, Carlson, Plunket, & Kessler, 1991). Although life events, including having a baby, appear to be catalysts for positive change in adults' representations of attachment (Ward & Carlson, 1995). Benoit and Parker (1994) report continuity of attachment representations between grandmothers and mothers and between these representations and child–mother attachment security. Further examination of grandparents as alternative attachment figures could lead to an expanded understanding of pathways toward attachment relationships and of the intergenerational transmission of caregiving behaviors.

Sequentially Formed Attachment Relationships

Toddlers or older children who encounter alternative attachment figures already have at least one internal model of an attachment relationship. In sequentially formed attachments, both the developmental context and the relationship history are different from those affecting infant–mother attachment. As an example, consider a toddler–foster parent attachment relationship. A toddler and foster parent begin constructing a relationship when the toddler has more social and cognitive capacities than an infant, and when the toddler has experienced constructing a relationship with another caregiver. Thus, in the study of antecedents of attachment relationships with multiple caregivers, we must determine not only whether these antecedents are the same as in infant–mother attachments, but also what the influences of different developmental and life history contexts are. By studying divergent pathways to the establishment of attachment relationships, we may come to understand the establishment of attachment relationships in general.

New Relationships with Child Care Providers and Teachers

The formation of infant–mother attachment relationships can be observed as children track or follow their mothers, cry to alert the mothers to their distress, or maintain social contact through smiles and vocalizations. Research on the formation of new attachment relationships with child care providers has also examined the role of attachments behaviors in the formation of attachment relationships.

Three studies have explicitly examined the formation of attachment relationships between toddlers and child care providers. Raikes (1993) had center-based providers complete Attachment Q-Sorts for the children in their care. Security scores increased as the children spent more time with the providers, indicating relationship formation. Barnas and Cummings (1997) compared children's attachment behaviors with long-term staff members (3 months or more in the center) and short-term staff members. Children directed more attachment behaviors to the long-term staff, and long-term staffers were more successful in soothing distressed children than short-term staffers. We (Howes & Oldham, in press) observed toddlers daily and then weekly during their first 6 months in child care. The frequency of attachment behavior decreased over the children's first 2 months in child care. However, the initial frequency of attachment behaviors and their rate of decrease over time were unrelated to the children's attachment security by the end of 6 months in child care.

Thus the formation of attachment relationships in child care settings appears to be a similar process to that of infant–mother attachment formation. When children begin child care, they direct attachment behaviors to the caregivers; with time in the setting, children's experiences of interacting with the caregivers become more organized. Children respond differently to providers who are present for longer periods of time and are therefore more predictable. Children develop an attachment organization for particular providers that can be captured with standard measurement tools.

The emerging literature on children's relationships with elementary school teachers (e.g., Pianta & Walsh, 1995) has not yet explicitly examined relationship formation. As discussed earlier, however, there is evidence for consistency. That is, as children make the transition from child care to school (Howes & Phillipsen, 1995) and from kindergarten to second grade (Pianta et al., 1995), their relationships with teachers are consistent in quality. As the definition of school adjustment is expanded to include social and emotional adjustment as well as academic achievement (Ladd, 1989), the study of how children form relationships with their teachers becomes increasingly important.

New Relationships with Alternative Adults for Children with Prior Difficult Relationships

The bulk of the literature on attachment relationship formation with child care providers is based on typical children who have not necessarily had difficulties with prior relationships. A small literature examines relationship formation in atypical children whose prior relationship history is more problematic. These studies suggest that children with prior maladaptive relationships can form secure attachment relationships with new caregivers, and therefore that they construct each relationship based on interactions with a particular adult.

Classic studies of adoptive children indicated that children adopted after the beginnings of attachment relationship formation (6–8 months) have difficulty forming positive, trusting relationships with their adoptive parents (Tizard & Rees, 1975; Yarrow, Goodwin, Manheimer, & Milowe, 1973). Attachment was not directly assessed in these studies, however. Some subsequent studies have more directly examined attachment formation in adoptive children. Singer, Brodzinsky, Ramsay, Steir, and Waters (1985) examined attachment formation in children adopted before or during the developmental period of attachment formation. There were no differences in rates of attachment security between these two groups of adopted infants, or between the adopted infants and a control group of non-adopted infants. Furthermore, for these early-adopted infants, the number of foster placements prior to adoption was unrelated to attachment security. Similarly, a recent study of infants adopted from Romania found no differences in attachments to adoptive mothers between infants who had spent less than 6 months in an orphanage and infants who had spent 6 months or more (Marcovitch et al., 1997). Finally, Dontas, Maratos, Fafoutis, and Karangelis (1985) examined attachment formation in orphans who had spent their early months in an orphanage with multiple caregivers. Each infant (7 to 9 months old) was seen in a modification of the strange situation with his or her favorite orphanage caregiver immediately prior to adoption. Two weeks after adoption, the children were again seen in the strange situation with their adoptive mothers. Infants preferentially directed attachment behaviors to their adoptive mothers. These more recent studies suggest that attachment formation in infants adopted prior to or during the optimal developmental period for this process is similar to attachment formation between infants and their biological mothers.

Adoptive children change attachment figures, but do not necessarily have maladaptive relationships with their first caregivers. In contrast, abused and neglected children are likely to have insecure attachment relationships with their parents (Carlson et al., 1989). We (Howes & Segal, 1993) observed toddlers removed from their homes because of maternal abuse or neglect and placed in high-quality shelter care. After 2 months in shelter care, almost half of the children (47%) had developed secure relationships with caregivers, as assessed with the Attachment Q-Sort. Children who had remained in the shelter longer were more secure than children with shorter stays.

Howes and Ritchie (in press) observed changes in children's attachment organization with teachers in a therapeutic preschool. The out-of-control behavior of these 3- to 4-year-old children had led to their removal from community child care environments and placement in a setting designed to foster a secure relationship through predictable and sensitive caregiving. Children's attachment security was assessed by an independent observer who used the Attachment Q-Sort at 2 months and again at 6 months after the children's entry into the program. Security scores increased over time, suggesting that children were reorganizing their attachments to the teachers following repeated positive interactions.

In summary, the small but growing literature on attachment formation to alternative caregivers suggests that this process is similar to that of infant–mother attachment. Although the developmental context is different for relationships formed when children are toddlers rather than infants, children in both periods construct their attachment relationships on the basis of repeated interactions with caregiving adults. Children with prior relationship difficulties, when moved to settings with sensitive caregivers, appear to be able either to reorganize their attachment representations when they encounter caregivers who respond sensitively or to construct independent relationships based on experiences with the new caregivers.

PATHWAYS TO SECURE ALTERNATIVE ATTACHMENT RELATIONSHIPS

Two other issues underlie or follow the issue of pathways to the establishment of attachments to alternative caregivers: Are the pathways to secure attachments with alternative attachment figures similar to or different from pathways to secure infant–mother attachments? And how do we distinguish between insecure attachment relationships and the absence of an attachment relationship?

Similar or Different Pathways to Attachment Security?

About two-thirds of typical infant–mother pairs will construct secure attachment relationships (e.g., Ainsworth et al., 1978). In the case of an infant with multiple caregivers, it may take much greater caregiver sensitivity to co-construct a secure relationship. If an alternative attachment relationship is constructed simultaneously with the maternal attachment, this adult (e.g., a child care provider) may be less emotionally involved than the mother, or the child may spend considerably less time with the adult (e.g., a grandmother) than with the mother. The construction of a secure attachment relationship when the adult is emotionally detached or regularly present for only a short period of time may require particularly responsive behaviors from the adult.

If the alternative attachment relationship is constructed sequentially with the maternal attachment, as in the case of a toddler–foster parent attachment, the child may approach the new caregiver as if he or she is not to be trusted. Similarly, a child with a history of avoiding child care providers is unlikely to bring behaviors to kindergarten that make forming a secure teacher–child relationship easy. In these situations, constructing a secure alternative attachment relationship will require even greater effort and skill on the part of the adult. For various reasons, therefore, the antecedents of secure alternative attachment relationships may be different from those of secure infant–mother attachment relationships.

Similar Pathways to Attachment Security: Typical Children with Fathers and Child Care Providers

Fathers and some child care providers care for children with no prior attachment history (simultaneous formation); other child care providers care for typical children with secure attachment

histories (sequential formation). The literature for both of these kinds of alternative caregivers suggests that more sensitive caregiving in earlier or current periods is linked to more secure attachment relationships (Anderson, Nagel, Roberts, & Smith, 1981; Cox, Owen, Henderson, & Margand, 1992; Easterbrooks & Goldberg, 1987; Goossen & van IJzendoorn, 1990; Howes & Hamilton, 1992b; Howes & Smith, 1995a). Consistent with our earlier discussion of fathers and caregiving, the accurate prediction of father–child security can be increased if a father's attitudes about the infant, the parent role, and time spent with the infant are known (Cox et al., 1992). Fathers who express more positive feelings about their infants and their role as parents, and who assign a high priority to time spent with the infants, have more secure infants.

Different Pathways to Attachment Security: Children Who Have Had Prior Difficult Life Experiences

To construct a secure attachment relationship with a child who has experienced prior difficult life circumstances, a caregiver may have to behave very sensitively indeed toward the child. Chisholm, Carter, Ames, and Morison (1995) studied attachment security in three groups of toddlers. Two of the groups were composed of Romanian orphans who had experienced extreme neglect in the form of unstable and inattentive caregivers. One group of orphans were adopted before they were 4 months old, the other after they were at least 8 months old. The third group was a comparison group of nonadopted infants. Children in the group of orphans adopted after 8 months of age had lower attachment security scores as assessed by the Attachment *Q*-Sort than children in the other two groups. Only in this late-adopted group was parental commitment to the parent role associated with attachment security.

Ritchie (1995) compared attachment security with home caregivers (biological mothers, foster mothers, adoptive mothers, and grandmothers) in two groups of 4-year-old children prenatally exposed to alcohol and/or other drugs. One group attended community preschool centers; the other group of children had been asked to leave community preschools. This second group was enrolled in a therapeutic preschool. At the time of assessment with the Attachment *Q*-Sort, children in the community preschool group were more likely to have been adopted (75%) and to have lived in homes without substance-abusing caregivers (75%). Children in the therapeutic preschool group were more likely to have experienced multiple changes in caregivers ($M = 4.2$ changes), to have been in foster care (82%), to be living with their biological mothers (73%), and to have received care from a substance-abusing caregiver (82%). Children in the community preschool group had higher attachment security scores with their caregivers at home than children in the therapeutic preschool group. This suggests that children at risk for poor relationships are better able to construct secure relationships when life events are more stable and consistent.

Marcus (1991) conducted one of the few attachment studies of foster children. Unlike the other studies reviewed in this chapter, this study employed a nonstandard measure of attachment: Foster parents reported on children's reunion behaviors, and attachment security scores were derived from this index. Foster care workers rated foster parents' sensitivity toward their children's feelings. Foster parents with higher sensitivity scores had foster children with higher security scores. Children who had spent more time with their foster parents also had higher security scores.

These three studies on attachment relationships between children with prior difficult life experiences and alternative caregivers suggest that in order to construct a secure attachment relationship with such a child, an adult may need to be much more sensitive than is the case in typical child–adult attachment.

Insecure Attachments or the Absence of an Attachment?

Given potential constraints on the construction of secure attachment relationships between children and alternative caregivers, the issue of whether such a relationship is insecure or is not an attachment relationship at all becomes particularly salient. A basic assumption of attachment theory is relevant to this argument: If an adult is providing regular physical and emotional care, then the child forms an attachment relationship with that adult (Bowlby, 1969/1982). The organization of the attachment relationship may be maladaptive, in that the child does not trust the caregiver to keep him or her safe, but it is an adaptation to the particular history of interactions between this adult and this child. According to this assumption, if an adult is identified as an attachment figure, then the child is attached, albeit insecurely. It is unreasonable, therefore, to use security with a caregiver as a criterion for the identification of an alternative attachment figure. It is reasonable to look closely at the organization of the attachment relationship between a child and an alternative attachment figure, and to consider extreme insecurity as one mode of organization.

When children are extremely insecure, particularly if they are avoidant of an attachment figure, they may appear not to be attached. When the attachment figure is an alternative attachment figure, it becomes difficult at times to distinguish between nonattachment and extremely insecure attachment. For example, when the Attachment Q-Sort (Waters, 1990) is used with children and their child care providers under conditions of very poor-quality care, the attachment security scores can range as low as −.57 (possible range −1.0 to 1.0) (Howes et al., in press). If, from a child's point of view, the child care provider is taking care of him or her, then these scores indicate a very low degree of felt security. It is of course difficult to ascertain from infants and toddlers whether the children expect their child care providers to take care of them. However, children are left with child care providers by their mothers, who explicitly or implicitly tell them that the child care providers are in charge of them while the mothers are gone; thus it may be reasonable to assume that children do expect child care providers to take care of them, albeit in some cases very poorly.

The issue of nonattachment is complicated by the psychiatric diagnosis of reactive attachment disorder. This diagnosis is becoming a common one for severely disturbed children under age 3 (Zeanah, 1995). Some children with multiple caregivers (e.g., foster children or abused children placed in shelter care) engage in behaviors concordant with this diagnosis. These children may appear indiscriminately friendly, perhaps clinging to strangers, or may act as if they have never bonded with their attachment figures. It must be noted that the focus of this chapter is on attachment relationships, whereas the diagnosis of reactive attachment disorder is based on a set of behaviors of a child rather than a relationship (Zeanah, 1995). It also is clear that we know relatively little about this issue of disordered attachment.

ORGANIZATION OF INTERNAL MODELS IN THE MULTIPLE-CAREGIVER CONTEXT

The examination of attachment in the context of multiple caregivers necessitates consideration of the organization of multiple attachment relationships within a child's internal working models. According to attachment theory, the child forms internal representations of self and of relationships with others, based on repeated experiences of interaction with an attachment figure (Bowlby, 1969/1982; see Bretherton & Munholland, Chapter 5, this volume). If the child's experiences with the adult provide the child with comfort, protection, and opportunities to explore the environment, the child constructs a positive model of relationships. Bowlby (1958) proposed that children develop separate internal models based on separate experiences, but did not elaborate on how children's internal models are organized when they have divergent experiences with more than one attachment figure.

Hierarchical Organization

Several different possibilities for the organization of internal models of attachment relationships in the multiple-caregiver context have been suggested. Bretherton (1985) posits a hierarchical organization in which a child's representation of the most salient caregiver, most often the mother, is always the most influential. The hierarchical organization also suggests that maternal attachment security influences the security of all subsequent attachment relationships. If attachment representations are organized in a hierarchical fashion, then we should expect to find the strongest predictions of consequences for attachment security to derive from maternal attachment. We should also expect that the organization of attachment relationships of multiple caregivers will be concordant with maternal attachments.

Integrative Organization

An alternative organizational structure, in which children integrate all of their attachment relationships into a single representation, has been suggested. This integrative organization is assumed in the study of attachment networks (van IJzendoorn et al., 1992). This organizational structure predicts that developmental consequences of attachment relationships can best be predicted by considering the quality of all attachment relationships in a child's network. There is no assumption that one attachment relationship will be more salient than another, so all relationships are given equal weight. Two secure attachment relationships are assumed to be more powerful in predicting positive developmental outcomes than one that is secure and one that is insecure; the latter configuration, in turn, is expected to be more powerful in predicting positive outcomes than two insecure relationships. In the assumption of an integrative organization of internal working models, there is no prediction that attachment relationships of multiple caregivers will be concordant in quality. Instead, the quality of each attachment relationship is assumed to be independent of each other relationship. The literature on integrative organization of multiple attachment relationships into the internal model does not include substantial discussions of the process by which a child integrates these multiple representations.

Independent Organization

A third alternative is an organizational model that considers each attachment representation as independent both in quality and in its influence on development. The independent model argues that different attachment relationship representations are differentially influential for different developmental domains. Thus, for example, child–father attachment representations may influence children's negative affect and tension in interpersonal conflict, while child–mother attachment representations more generally influence competence (Suess, Grossmann, & Sroufe, 1992). The independent model can be tested by examining predictive relations between attachment security of various attachment figures and behavior in different developmental domains. This process clearly works best when there is a theory to predict why different attachment figures should be more or less influential in a developmental domain.

Empirical Examination of Organization of Internal Models

In order to find empirical support for the organization of internal models, two bodies of literature must be considered. In one body of literature, researchers have examined the concordance or nonconcordance of children's attachment quality to more than one caregiver. In the second body of literature, researchers have compared the predictability of children's developmental outcomes from their attachment security with different caregivers.

Concordance of Attachment Quality

The largest literature concerning attachment quality concordance consists of studies comparing infant–mother and infant–father attachment security. Fox, Kimmerly, and Schafer (1991) conducted a meta-analysis of 11 studies that examined the concordance of infant–mother and infant–mother attachment security. They concluded that mother and father relationships were modestly concordant; that is, they were not independent. One explanation for this finding, favored by Fox et al. (1991), is that a child's temperament is influential in the quality of attachment. An alternative explanation is that parents are similar in their interactions with children. This explanation is consistent with the literature suggesting that the mother shapes the father–child relationship (Steele et al., 1995), and it supports a hierarchical model of organization.

In contrast, studies of concordance in attachment quality between mother–child and child care provider–child attachment (Goossen & van IJzendoorn, 1990; Howes & Hamilton, 1992) and among mother–, father–, and *metapelet–*child attachment (Sagi et al., 1985) find little evidence for concordance. Mothers and fathers, unlike mothers and child care providers or parents and *metaplot,* share a child-rearing setting. In addition, mothers and fathers may share a value system that leads to consistency in caregiving behaviors. Further support for this idea is provided by a report (Howes & Matheson, 1992) that when child care settings and homes are more similar in child-rearing and belief systems, child–childcare provider and child–mother attachments are more concordant.

In summary, the literature on concordance of attachment relationships provides inconclusive support for the hierarchical model. Adults who share child-rearing values and behaviors are most concordant in their relationships with children. But when the alternative adults are dissimilar, so is the relationship quality.

Prediction of Developmental Outcomes

Studies in which mother– and father–child attachment security are used to predict children's competence have generally found that child–mother attachment security is more influential (Main, Kaplan, & Cassidy, 1985; Suess et al., 1992; Volling & Belsky, 1992). These studies clearly support the hierarchical model, with the mother being the most important attachment figure.

Other studies, however, and some of the findings of the studies just mentioned, are less conclusive. The Main et al. (1985) results were based on assessments of children when they were 6 years old. When these same children were toddlers, father–child attachment security best predicted children's friendliness with a stranger (Main & Weston, 1981). Similar results were found in a Swedish sample (Lamb, Hwang, Frodi, & Frodi, 1982). In the Suess et al. (1992) study, negative affect and tension in interpersonal conflict were best predicted by father–child attachment security. Easterbrooks and Goldberg (1987) found that father–child attachment best predicted problem solving. And whereas in the Volling and Belsky (1992) study father–infant attachment security did not predict sibling interaction at age 6, father–child interaction at age 3 was predictive. This second set of results supports an independent model better than it does a hierarchical model.

When we move beyond fathers as alternative attachment figures and examine the predictability of attachment security with child care providers and *metaplot,* as well as mothers, there is more support for the independent and integrative models than for the hierarchical model. Two studies find that security of attachment to a child care provider (Howes, Matheson, & Hamilton, 1997) or to a *metapelet* (Oppenheim, Sagi, & Lamb, 1998) predicted preschool children's social competence with peers better than child–mother attachment security did. The authors suggest that in each of these child-rearing settings, children's orientation to peers occurs when the primary caregiver is not the mother.

When networks of child care providers, fathers, and mothers (van IJzendoorn et al., 1992) or networks of mothers, child care providers, and teachers (Howes, Rodning, Galluzzo, & Myers, 1988; Howes et al., 1998) are used to predict children's outcomes, there is considerable support for an integrative model. In both Israeli and Dutch samples, networks of attachment relationships predicted children's socioemotional development better than single attachment relationships did. In a U.S. sample of toddlers in their first year in child care, social behavior with peers was best predicted by a combination of maternal and child care provider attachment security (Howes et al., 1988).

Continuity and Change in Internal Models

In infant–mother attachment, earliest representations of the attachment relationship are considered most important (Bowlby, 1969/1982). Early representations are more salient because they are the least accessible to the conscious mind, and because the patterns of interaction based on these representations become well established. Mothers' behavior to children is constrained by their own internal models and by their values and beliefs about child rearing, making change unlikely.

Alternative attachment representations can be discordant, and therefore they have the potential to introduce change in children's internal models. For example, a child may have developed an early secure child–mother attachment; within the context of disputed parental custody at age 5, however, the child may develop an avoidant attachment relationship with a harsh and punitive father, who now cares for him or her half the time. Tapping into older children's representations when we know their history of multiple caregiving may inform our understanding of continuity and change in internal models, as well as of the potential for nonconcordant attachment relationships to compensate for or to buffer each other. Almost no empirical data are available to support or disconfirm these speculations. With advances in our ability to examine representations in older children, and with expansions in our notions of attachment figures to include multiple caregivers throughout childhood, there is great potential for research in this area.

RELATIONS BETWEEN CHILD CARE AND MATERNAL ATTACHMENT

One of the largest increases in multiple caregiving in the United States is attributable to the increasing use of child care by families of every income level. By the mid-1980s, the number of mothers with infants under 1 year of age in the United States who were in the paid labor force had reached 50%. Unlike past generations, when working mothers were primarily poor women or women of color, in the 1980s well-educated, affluent mothers with infants were working. This social change marked far-reaching changes in the economic and social organizations of families (Fein & Fox, 1990). In 1988, Belsky published a controversial paper about the influences of nonmaternal care on infant socioemotional development, and this launched a debate concerning the possibility that nonmaternal care may increase the incidence of insecure mother–child attachment. The debate was carried out in the national press as well as in more scholarly venues. I conclude this chapter by reviewing the theoretical and empirical evidence related to this debate.

At the time of Bowlby's (1969/1982) original formulation of attachment theory, relatively few mothers with very young children worked regularly outside the home. Those mothers who did tended to use child care that was not in the public eye (care by nannies in their homes or by relatives). Thus, although Bowlby did focus on and see as detrimental the more dramatic forms of maternal separation (e.g., hospitalization), regular and predictable separations with familiar caregivers were not discussed. It was left to the interpreters of traditional attachment theory to make theoretical predictions about the influences of child care on infant–mother attachment security.

Belsky (1988) argued that the repeated separations between mother and infant necessitated by nonmaternal care may interfere with the construction of a secure attachment relationship, particularly if child care begins prior to the establishment of the relationship. He presented early data suggesting an association between child care attendance prior to the first birthday and avoidant infant–mother attachment relationships. Belsky suggested two ways in which the experience of child care may interfere with the construction of secure infant–mother attachments: (1) The repeated separations may leave an infant with an underlying mistrust about the availability of the mother; or (2) the experience of working may leave the mother less emotionally available and sensitive to the needs of her infant. Sroufe (1988), in reviewing Belsky's argument, pointed out that one feature of child care is that mothers return. Therefore, children in child care not only experience repeated separations; they also learn that separations are predictable and predictably terminated. He suggested that what is important for secure infant–mother attachments in children experiencing child care is the mothers' ability to remain emotionally available and close to the infants in the context of daily separations.

Clarke-Stewart (1988), again in response to Belsky, suggested that using the strange situation as an assessment tool may influence the proportion of secure versus insecure attachments in children with nonmaternal care experiences. She argued that the procedures of the strange situation are too similar to the experience of child care (i.e., being left with a friendly stranger) to permit comparison of children with and without child care experience. What appears to be avoidance in the strange situation may instead be independence. Furthermore, she suggested that mothers who work may place more value on their own and their infants' independence than mothers who stay at home with their infants.

Finally, Phillips, McCartney, Scarr, and Howes (1987) argued that there is no compelling theoretical reason for child care to interfere with the establishment of secure mother–child attachment. Instead, just as the sensitivity of child–mother interaction at home predicts infant–mother attachment security, the quality of the child care environment should predict the child's experiences in child care. Therefore, children's developmental outcomes should be a product of experiences in both environments.

All of the reviewers of the empirical literature published prior to 1987 agreed that there was an increase in avoidant infant–mother attachments when working mothers were compared to nonworking mothers (Belsky, 1988; Clarke-Stewart, 1988). Beyond disagreements over the theoretical meaning of these findings, there was disagreement about sample composition and assessment procedures, as well as whether the increase in avoidant infant–mother attachments was large enough to be meaningful.

In part as a response to the child care debate, the National Institute of Child Health and Human Development (NICHD) funded a longitudinal 10-site study of 1,357 families with young children, beginning when the children were newborns. In this NICHD sample, there were no differences in infant–mother attachment security (assessed via the strange situation) at 12 months between infants with working and nonworking mothers (NICHD Early Child Care Research Network, in press). Instead, security of infant–mother attachment was related to the mothers' sensitivity and responsiveness. Children were most likely to have insecure infant–mother attachments if they received the least sensitive and responsive care from their mothers and from their child care providers. The findings of the NICHD study indicate "that child care by itself constitutes neither a risk nor a benefit for the development of the infant–mother attachment" (NICHD Early Child Care Research Network, in press). These findings strengthen the argument that attachment relationships are constructed through ongoing interactions between children and their attachment figures.

All of the children in these studies of infant–mother attachment who experienced working mothers also experienced caregiving in the context of multiple caregivers. The theory and empirical research reviewed in this chapter suggest, as did Bowlby and Ainsworth, that children form multiple attachment relationships. It appears that to the extent that these alternative attachments are outside the familiar caregiving system, the quality of these alternative attachment relationships is independent of infant–mother attachments.

SUMMARY AND CONCLUSIONS

Many if not most of the infants in the United States today will have multiple caregivers. The identification of particular alternative attachment figures and of categories of attachment figures requires addressing fundamental issues within attachment theory, including the nature of emotional care, the interaction of development and caregiving, and the consistency or continuity of attachment figures. The construction of attachment relationships between children and their alternative caregivers appears similar to the construction of infant–mother attachment. There is some indication that within two-parent traditional families, maternal representations of attachment influence the development of infant–father attachment, and that within grandmother–mother–child family configurations, grandmothers' representations of attachment may influence infant–mother attachment. When alternative attachments are formed outside the family (i.e., in child care settings), the process of attachment formation appears similar to the processes within families. A growing literature on alternative attachment relationships for children with prior difficult relationships suggests that the process of attachment formation in such cases are similar to those of typical children, but that the construction of secure attachments appears dependent on particularly skilled and sensitive adult behaviors. Much has yet to be learned about the influence and role of alternative attachment relationships in the long-term development of children. Particularly for children with difficult life circumstances, however, it seems possible that alternative attachment figures can provide children with a "safety net" for their future development.

ACKNOWLEDGMENT

Thanks to Sharon Ritchie for her understandings of how attachments with multiple caregivers develop and change, particularly for children who have the most difficulty forming relationships.

REFERENCES

Ainsworth, M. D. S. (1967). *Infancy in Uganda: Infant care and the growth of love.* Baltimore: Johns Hopkins University Press.

Ainsworth, M. D. S., Blehar, M., Waters, E., & Wall, S. (1978). *Patterns of attachment.* Hillsdale, NJ: Erlbaum.

Anderson, C. W., Nagel, P., Roberts, M., & Smith, K. (1981). Attachment in substitute caregivers as a function of center quality and caregiver involvement. *Child Development, 52,* 53–51.

Barnas, M. V., & Cummings, E. M. (1997). Caregiver stability and toddlers' attachment-related behaviors towards caregivers in day care. *Infant Behavior and Development, 17,* 171–177.

Belsky, J. (1988). The "effects" of infant day care reconsidered. *Early Childhood Research Quarterly, 3,* 3–70.

Benoit, D., & Parker, K. C. H. (1994). Stability and transmission of attachment across three generations. *Child Development, 65,* 1444–1456.

Bost, K., Cielinski, K., Newell, W. H., & Vaughn, B. (1997). Social networks of children attending Head Start from the perspective of the child. *Early Childhood Research Quarterly, 9,* 777–752.

Bowlby, J. (1958). The nature of the child's tie to his mother. *International Journal of Psycho-Analysis, 39,* 350–373.

Bowlby, J. (1969/1982). *Attachment and loss: Vol. 1. Attachment.* New York: Basic Books.

Bretherton, I. (1985). Attachment theory: Retrospect and prospect. In I. Bretherton & E. Waters (Eds.), *Growing points of attachment theory and research. Monographs of the Society for Research in Child Development, 50*(1–2, Serial No. 209), 3–35.

Carlson, V., Cicchetti, D., Barnett, D., & Braunwald, K. G. (1989). Disorganized/disoriented attachment relationships in maltreated infants. *Developmental Psychology, 25,* 525–531.

Chisholm, K., Carter, M. C., Ames, E. W., & Morison, S. J. (1995). Attachment security and indiscriminately friendly behavior in children adopted from Romanian orphanages. *Development and Psychopathology, 7,* 283–297.

Clarke-Stewart, K. A. (1988). "The effects of infant day care reconsidered" reconsidered. *Early Childhood Research Quarterly, 3,* 58–97.

Cox, M. J., Owen, M., Henderson, V. K., & Margand, N. A. (1992). Prediction of infant–father and infant–mother attachment. *Developmental Psychology, 28,* 777–783.

Dontas, C., Maratos, O., Fafoutis, M., & Karangelis, A. (1985). Early social development in institutionally reared Greek infants: Attachment and peer interaction. In I. Bretherton & E. Waters (Eds.), Growing points of attachment theory and research. *Monographs of the Society for Research in Child Development, 50*(1–2, Serial No. 209), 135–175.

Easterbrooks, M. A., & Goldberg, W. (1987). Toddler development in the family: Impact of father involvement and parenting characteristics. *Child Development, 55,* 770–752.

Fein, G., & Fox, N. A. (1990). *Infant day care: The current debate.* Norwood, NJ: Ablex.

Fox, N. A., Kimmerly, N. L., & Schafer, W. D. (1991). Attachment to mother/attachment to father: A meta-analysis. *Child Development, 52,* 210–225.

George, C., Kaplan, N., & Main, M. (1985). *Adult Attachment Interview* (2nd ed.). Unpublished manuscript, University of California at Berkeley.

George, C., & Solomon, J. (1996). Representational models of relationship: Links between caregiving and representation. *Infant Mental Health Journal, 17,* 198–216.

Goossen, F. A., & van IJzendoorn, M. H. (1990). Quality of infants' attachment to professional caregivers: Relation to infant–parent attachment and daycare characteristics. *Child Development, 51,* 832–837.

Howes, C., & Hamilton, C. E. (1992a). Children's relationships with child care teachers: Stability and concordance with maternal attachment. *Child Development, 53,* 879–892.

Howes, C., & Hamilton, C. E. (1992b). Children's relationships with caregivers: Mothers and child care teachers. *Child Development, 53,* 859–878.

Howes, C., Hamilton, C. E., & Althusen, V. (in press). Using the Attachment *Q*-Set to describe non-familial attachments. In B. Vaughn & E. Waters (Eds.), *Attachment.* Mahwah, NJ: Erlbaum.

Howes, C., & Matheson, C. C. (1992). Contextual constraints on the concordance of child–mother and teacher–child relationships. In R. C. Pianta (Ed.), *New directions for child development: No. 57. Beyond the parent: The role of other adults in children's lives* (pp. 25–70). San Francisco: Jossey-Bass.

Howes, C., Matheson, C. C., & Hamilton, C. E. (1997). Maternal, teacher and child care history correlates of children's relationships with peers. *Child Development, 55,* 257–273.

Howes, C., & Oldham, E. (in press). Attachment formation in child care: Processes in the formation of attachment relationships with alternative caregivers. In A. Goncu & E. Klein (Eds.), *Children in play, story, and school.* New York: Greenwood.

Howes, C., & Phillipsen, L. C. (in press). The consistency and predictability of teacher–child relationships during the transition to kindergarten. *Journal of School Psychology.*

Howes, C., Hamilton, C. E., & Phillipsen, L. C. (1998). Stability and continuity of child–caregiver relationships. *Child Development, 69,* 418–426.

Howes, C., & Ritchie, S. (1998). Changes in child–teacher relationships in a therapeutic preschool program. *Early Education and Development, 4,* 411–422.

Howes, C., Rodning, C., Galluzzo, D. C., & Myers, L. (1988). Attachment and child care: Relationships with mother and caregiver. *Early Childhood Research Quarterly, 3,* 703–715.

Howes, C., & Segal, J. (1993). Children's relationships with alternative caregivers: The special case of maltreated children removed from their homes. *Journal of Applied Developmental Psychology, 17,* 71–81.

Howes, C., & Smith, E. W. (1995a). Children and their child care caregivers: Profiles of relationships. *Social Development, 7,* 77–51.

Howes, C., & Smith, E. W. (1995b). Relations among child care quality, teacher behavior, children's play activities, emotional security, and cognitive activity in child care. *Early Childhood Research Quarterly, 10,* 381–707.

Jackson, J. F. (1993). Multiple caregiving among African Americans and infant attachment: The need for an emic approach. *Human Development, 35,* 87–102.

Ladd, G. W. (1989). Children's social competence and social supports: Precursors of early school adjustment. In B. H. Schneider, G. Attili, J. Nadel, & R. Weissburg (Eds.), *Social competence in developmental perspective* (pp. 271–291). Amsterdam: Kluwer.

Lamb, M. E. (1977a). Father–infant and mother–infant interaction in the first year of life. *Child Development, 78,* 157–181.

Lamb, M. E. (1977b). The development of infant–mother and father–infant attachments in the second year of life. *Developmental Psychology, 13,* 537–578.

Lamb, M. E., Hwang, C. P., Frodi, A., & Frodi, M. (1982). Security of mother- and father-attachment and its relation to sociability with strangers in nontraditional Swedish families. *Infant Behavior and Development, 5,* 355–357.

Main, M., Kaplan, N., & Cassidy, J. (1985). Security in infancy, childhood, and adulthood: A move to the level of representation. In I. Bretherton & E. Waters (Eds.), *Growing points of attachment theory and research. Monographs of the Society for Research in Child Development, 50*(1–2, Serial No. 209), 66–104.

Main, M., & Weston, D. R. (1981). The quality of toddlers' relationships to mother and to father: Related to conflict and the readiness to establish new relationships. *Child Development, 52,* 932–970.

Marcovitch, S., Goldberg, S., Gold, A., Washington, J., Wasson, C., Krekewich, K., & Handley-Derry, M. (1997). Determinants of behavioral problems in Romanian children adopted in Ontario. *International Journal of Behavioral Development, 20,* 17–31.

Marcus, R. F. (1991) The attachments of children in foster care. *Genetic, Social, and General Psychology Monographs, 117,* 355–397.

Matheson, C. C. (1992). *Children's perceptions of day care teachers: An attachment theory perspective.* Unpublished doctoral dissertation, University of California at Los Angeles.

National Institute of Child Health and Human Development (NICHD) Early Child Care Research Network. (in press). The effects of infant child care on infant–mother attachment. *Child Development.*

Oppenheim, D., & Waters, H. S. (1995). Narrative processes and attachment representations: Issues of development and assessment. In E. Waters, B. Vaughn, G. Posada, & K. Kondo-Ikemura (Eds.), Caregiving, cultural, and cognitive perspectives on secure-base behavior and working models: New growing points of attachment theory and research. *Monographs of the Society for Research in Child Development, 60*(2–3, Serial No. 244), 197–215.

Oppenheim, D., Sagi, A., & Lamb, M. E. (1988). Infant–adult attachments on the kibbutz and their relation to socio-emotional development four years later. *Developmental Psychology, 27,* 727–733.

Parke, R. D., & Asher, S. R. (1983). Social and personality development. *Annual Review of Psychology, 37,* 755–509.

Phillips, D., McCartney, K., Scarr, S., & Howes, C. (1987). Selective review of infant daycare research: A cause for concern. *Zero to Three, 7,* 18–21.

Pianta, R. C., & Steinberg, M. (1992). Teacher–child relationships and adjusting to school. In R. C. Pianta (Ed.), *New directions for child development: No. 57. Beyond the parent: The role of other adults in children's lives* (pp. 51–80). San Francisco: Jossey-Bass.

Pianta, R. C., Steinberg, M., & Rollins, K. B. (1995). The first two years of school: Teacher–child relationships and deflections in children's classroom adjustment. *Development and Psychopathology, 7,* 295–312.

Pianta, R. C., & Walch, D. J. (1995). *High risk children in schools.* New York: Routledge.

Raikes, H. (1993). Relationship duration in infant care: Time with a high ability teacher and infant–teacher attachment. *Early Childhood Research Quarterly, 8,* 309–325.

Reid, M., Landesman, S., Treder, R., & Jaccoby, J. (1989). My family and friends: Six to twelve year old children's perceptions of social support. *Child Development, 50,* 895–910.

Ritchie, S. (1995). *Attachment relationships of substance-exposed children with their caregivers and their teachers.* Unpublished doctoral dissertation, University of California at Los Angeles.

Sagi, A., Lamb, M., Lewkowicz, K., Shoham, R., Dvir, R., & Estes, D. (1985). Security of infant–mother, infant–father, infant–*metapelet* attachments among kibbutz reared Israeli children. In I. Bretherton & E. Waters (Eds.), *Growing points of attachment theory and research. Monographs of the Society for Research in Child Development, 50*(1–2, Serial No. 209), 257–275.

Schaffer, H. R., & Emerson, P. E. (1967). The development of social attachments in infancy. *Monographs of the Society for Research in Child Development, 32*(3, Serial No.).

Singer, L. M., Brodzinsky, D. M., Ramsay, D., Steir, M., & Waters, E. (1985). Infant–mother attachment in adoptive families. *Child Development, 55,* 1573–1551.

Spieker, S. J., & Bensley, L. (1997). Roles of living arrangements and grandmother social support in adolescent mothering and infant attachment. *Developmental Psychology, 30,* 102–111.

Sroufe, L. A. (1988). A developmental perspective on day care. *Early Childhood Research Quarterly, 3,* 51–50.

Steele, H., Steele, M., & Fonagy, P. (1995). Associations among attachment classifications of mothers, fathers, and their infants. *Child Development, 57,* 571–555.

Suess, G. J., Grossmann, K. E., & Sroufe, L. A. (1992). Effects of infant attachment to mother and father on quality of adaptation in preschool: From dyadic to individual organization of self. *International Journal of Behavioral Development, 15,* 73–55.

Tinsley, B., & Parke, R. (1983). Grandparents as support and socializing agents. In M. Lewis (Ed.), *Beyond the dyad* (pp. 25–75). New York: Plenum Press.

Tizard, B., & Rees, J. (1975). The effect of early institutional rearing on the behavior problems and affectional relationships of four-year-old children. *Journal of Child Psychology and Psychiatry, 15,* 51–77.

van IJzendoorn, M. H., Sagi, A., & Lambermon, M. (1992). The multiple caregiver paradox: Data from Holland and Israel. In R. C. Pianta (Ed.), *New directions for child development: No. 57. Beyond the parent: The role of other adults in children's lives* (pp. 5–27). San Francisco: Jossey-Bass.

Volling, B., & Belsky, J. (1992). The contribution of child–mother and father–child relationships to the quality of sibling interaction: A longitudinal study. *Child Development, 53,* 1209–1222.

Ward, M. J., & Carlson, E. A. (1995). Associations among adult attachment representations, maternal sensitivity, and infant–mother attachment in a sample of adolescent mothers. *Child Development, 55,* 59–79.

Ward, M. J., Carlson, E. A., Plunket, S. W., & Kessler, D. B. (1991). *Adolescent infant–mother attachment: Interactions, relationships, and working models.* Unpublished manuscript, Cornell Medical College.

Waters, E. (1990). *The Attachment Q-Set.* Stony Brook: State University of New York.

Yarrow, L. J., Goodwin, M. S., Manheimer, H., & Milowe, I. D. (1973). Infancy experiences and cognitive and personality development at 10 years. In L. J. Stone, H. T. Smith, & L. B. Murphy (Eds.), *The competent infant: Research and commentary* (pp. 1277–1281). New York: Basic Books.

Zeanah, C. (1995). Beyond insecurity: A reconceptualization of attachment disorders of infancy. *Journal of Consulting and Clinical Psychology, 57,* 72–52.

30

Relations among Relationships

Contributions from Attachment
Theory and Research

❖

LISA J. BERLIN
JUDE CASSIDY

Nobody loves me but my mother
and she could be jivin' too.
Now you see why I act funny, Baby
when you do the things you do.
—B. B. KING (1970)

Questions concerning relations among relationships cut to the heart of attachment theory and research. According to Bowlby, "there is a strong causal relationship between an individual's experiences with his parents and his later capacity to make affectional bonds" (1979, p. 135). By "affectional bonds," Bowlby was referring to particularly close ties "in which the partner is important as a unique individual and interchangeable with none other" (Ainsworth, 1989, p. 711). An attachment is a specific type of affectional bond that one person has to another from whom he or she attempts to derive security, such as the bond of an infant to a mother. Bowlby argued that early attachments play a key role in people's subsequent close relationships—in attachment and nonattachment relationships. Bowlby also specified that the mechanisms underlying the "causal" associations between early attachments and subsequent affectional bonds are "internal working models," mental representations that are forged in repeated daily transactions between infant and parent, and that tend to become stable over time.

In this chapter we focus on the contributions of attachment theory and research to understanding relations among relationships. Attachment theory, of course, offers but one of many perspectives on the links among people's close relationships and on the influence of early relationship experiences on later bonds (see, e.g., Duck, 1988; Dunn, 1988a, 1993; Hartup & Rubin, 1986; Hinde & Stevenson-Hinde, 1988; Maccoby, 1992; Weber & Harvey, 1994). Social learning theories, for example, emphasize children's acquisition of social skills via their learning from and modeling of their parents (e.g., Bandura, 1977). What distinguishes attachment theory from this and other theories is the specificity of its predictions about individual differences and its arguments that mental representations (internal working models) underlie the associations between early attachments and subsequent close relationships. In this chapter we address the distinctive tenets of the theory and the research that has tested them.

We begin this chapter with a brief overview of Bowlby's attachment theory, focusing on its claims about relations among relationships. We

688

then consider the attachment theory and research addressing several specific types of relations among relationships: (1) the influence of infant–parent attachments on subsequent bonds (on relationships with siblings, friends, romantic partners, children, peers), (2) the influence of parents' other relationships (parents' relationships with their own parents, with spouses, with providers of social support, with therapists) on infant–parent attachments, and (3) the concordance of attachment patterns across a caregiver's multiple children, and across a child's multiple caregivers. We aim throughout this review to examine the extent to which attachment research, inspired by Ainsworth's pioneering work (e.g., Ainsworth, Blehar, Waters, & Wall, 1978), supports the claims of the theory. We also aim to identify pressing questions and to suggest next steps for attachment theory and research.

A BRIEF OVERVIEW OF ATTACHMENT THEORY AND ITS PREDICTIONS ABOUT RELATIONS AMONG RELATIONSHIPS

According to attachment theory, the infant–parent attachment relationship is an evolutionarily adaptive relationship whose principal function is the protection of the child (Bowlby, 1969/1982). Bowlby (1969/1982) maintained that the "attachment behavioral system" is one of several species-specific "control systems" that have evolved to facilitate protection, survival, and ultimately "reproductive fitness." According to Bowlby (1969/1982, 1973) individuals develop "cognitive maps" or "internal working models" (also called "representational models") to guide each control system (see also Bretherton & Munholland, Chapter 5, this volume). With respect to the attachment behavioral system, Bowlby (1973) asserted that repeated daily transactions between an infant and a parent lead the infant to develop expectations about the parent's caregiving. These expectations in turn are gradually organized into internal working models of the caregiver, the self in relation to this caregiver, and the attachment relationship as a whole. Sensitive caregiving potentiates a secure attachment and the concomitant development of internal working models of the caregiver as trustworthy and helpful and of the self as deserving of the caregiver's sensitive treatment. Conversely, insensitive caregiving leads to an insecure attachment and to working models of the caregiver as

unavailable and untrustworthy and of the self as unworthy of the caregiver's benevolent treatment.

People's working models guide the development of subsequent relationships. This occurs initially by their guiding individual expectations about others' emotional availability: ". . . the kinds of experiences a person has, especially during childhood, greatly affect . . . whether he expects later to find a secure personal base, or not" (Bowlby, 1979, p. 104). Internal working models also guide both treatment *of* and treatment elicited *from* relationships partners. As Sroufe and Fleeson (1988) noted, "Others are selected, responded to, and influenced in ways that are compatible with previous relationship learning" (p. 29). Sroufe and Fleeson (1986, 1988) also stressed that the working model of the attachment relationship as a coherent whole—the model of how a close relationship should *be*—is what is carried forward. Barring major changes in the environment or the individual, the principal qualities of the infant–parent attachment(s) will be replicated in subsequent close relationships: Secure infants will subsequently form supportive, nurturing close relationships, whereas insecure infants will form close relationships in which the giving of care, the receiving of care, or both are incomplete.

A consideration of Main's (1990) concept of "conditional behavioral strategies" yields even more specific predictions about relations among relationships. Main asserted that in addition to their adaptive propensity to form attachments, infants are equipped with biologically based abilities to tailor the output of the attachment behavioral system to particular caregiving contexts. These tailoring abilities, which function to garner as much parental investment and protection as possible, are attachment strategies. Attachment strategies can also be viewed as unconscious plans, guided by internal working models of relationships, which in turn guide cognition and behavior. In sensitive caregiving environments, attachment strategies allow for a relatively direct relation between the activation of the attachment system and its output. In insensitive caregiving environments, the output of the attachment system must be manipulated to fit the particular demands of the caregiver.

Main (1990) proposed that each of the three principal attachment patterns ("secure," "avoidant," and "ambivalent") reflects a particular attachment strategy. Each pattern in turn is proposed to be linked to particular ways of behaving in close relationships. Secure infants are expected to form relationships in which attachment figures are used as a secure base. Avoidant infants are expected to form relationships in which their attachment behaviors are decreased and muted. Ambivalent infants are hypothesized to form subsequent relationships in which their attachment behaviors are increased and heightened (see also Cassidy & Berlin, 1994; Cassidy & Kobak, 1988; Main, 1981, 1990).

Both Bowlby (1969/1982, 1979) and Ainsworth (1989; Ainsworth & Marvin, 1995) have stressed that attachment theory's predictions about relations among relationships apply principally to *close* relationships. These predictions are in fact more relevant to relationships consisting of attachments than relationships which do not consist of attachments, and more relevant to relationships including affectional bonds than relationships which do not include affectional bonds (see also Belsky & Cassidy, 1994, and Sroufe, 1988). Ironically, much of attachment research has not distinguished between children's subsequent affectional and nonaffectional bonds, and/or has focused on connections between attachments and nonaffectional bonds. Accordingly, one of our aims in reviewing the attachment research on relations among relationships is to examine the extent to which there are stronger associations between attachments and affectional bonds than between attachments and nonaffectional bonds (Belsky & Cassidy, 1994).

Attachment theory addresses not only the influence of early attachments on subsequent relationships but also two other types of relations among relationships. The first is the influence of parents' other relationships on the infant–parent attachment. The second concerns concordance of patterns of attachment across (1) a caregiver's multiple children and (2) a child's multiple caregivers. In the remainder of this chapter, we examine all of these relations among relationships.

THE INFLUENCE OF THE INFANT–PARENT ATTACHMENT ON SUBSEQUENT AFFECTIONAL AND NONAFFECTIONAL BONDS

We begin this section by examining connections between early attachments and what we presume to be early affectional relationships—relationships with siblings and with childhood friends. We next consider the associations between early attachments and subsequent affectional relationships with romantic partners and children. We then examine the relations between early attachments and what we presume to be nonaffectional bonds—ties to peers and strangers. We conclude the section with a discussion of linking mechanisms between early attachments and subsequent affectional and nonaffectional bonds. Throughout this section we review investigations of both longitudinal and contemporaneous relations among child–parent attachments and affectional and nonaffectional bonds. Although the longitudinal data speak most directly to Bowlby's claims about early attachments and individuals' subsequent abilities to form bonds, the contemporaneous data are also relevant. We also note that all of the data we review are correlational findings, which do not provide evidence of causation.

The Influence of the Infant–Parent Attachment on Early Affectional Bonds: Relationships with Siblings and Friends

Relationships with Siblings

Presuming that most sibling relationships consist of affectional bonds (see, e.g., Dunn & Kendrick, 1982, for empirical support for this presumption), attachment theory predicts close links between the qualities of early attachments and sibling relationships. To date, there have been two studies on the associations between infant–parent attachment and sibling relationships, both of which support the predictions of attachment theory by illustrating secure infant–mother attachments going hand in hand with more harmonious sibling interactions. In the first of these investigations, in which the authors examined the contemporaneous connections among the quality of infant–mother attachment, (older) sibling–mother attachment, and sibling interaction, child–mother attachment security was related not only to positive treatment *of* but also to positive treatment *from* the sibling (Teti & Ablard, 1989).

A second study of the associations between infant–parent attachment and the sibling relationship yielded similar results (Volling & Belsky, 1992). Infant–mother—but not infant–father—attachment security was associated with sibling interaction observed in the home approximately 5 years later: Children who had been securely attached were significantly less likely to participate in sibling conflicts than children who had been insecurely attached, and this association held above and beyond associations with both contemporaneous and 3-year maternal behaviors;

there were, however, no attachment group differences in siblings' prosocial interactions.

Relationships with Friends

Several inquiries have addressed the association between infant–parent attachment and affectional bonds in early childhood friendships; all provide theoretically predicted evidence of associations between early attachments and subsequent close relationships. Researchers have examined connections between infant–parent attachment and children's friendships in children as young as 2 years of age and as old as 12. One study revealed connections between infant–mother attachment and "social responsiveness" during a play session with a "best playmate," with children classified as secure at 2 years observed to be more responsive at ages 2 and 5 than children who had been insecure (Pierrehumbert, Ianotti, Cummings, & Zahn-Waxler, 1989). Another study used *Q*-Sort methods to examine concurrent links between infant–mother attachment and several aspects of laboratory free play between 4-year-old best friends (Park & Waters, 1989). Best friendships consisting of two "secure" children received higher scores on "positive interaction" than dyads comprised of one secure and one insecure best friend, but there were no attachment differences in "coordinated interaction," "self-disclosure," or "tempo of play." In a 1-year follow-up study with about half of these dyads, the secure–secure dyads again received higher scores than the secure–insecure pairs on "positive interaction"; the secure–secure dyads also scored higher on "coordinated interaction" (Kerns, 1994).

In a similar longitudinal investigation of infant–parent attachment and best friendship at 6 years of age, children who had been classified as secure with their mothers were less likely to engage in "dyad negative" behavior during laboratory play than children who had been classified as insecure. This relation, however, did not emerge for "dyad positive" behavior, which was, surprisingly, *less* evident in children who had been securely attached to their fathers (Youngblade & Belsky, 1992). Additional analyses of these data with Park and Waters's (1989) Dyadic Relationships *Q*-Sort revealed parallel findings for infant–parent attachment as assessed with the strange situation, though not with the Attachment *Q*-Sort (Youngblade, Park, & Belsky, 1993).

In addition to examining infant–parent attachment and children's early friendships, researchers have recently extended the study of early attachments and friendships to middle childhood. In a follow-up of the pioneering Minnesota Parent–Child Project of low-income families, children were assessed over the course of a 1-month summer camp (Elicker, Englund, & Sroufe, 1992; Shulman, Elicker, & Sroufe, 1994). Children classified as secure with their mothers at both 12 and 18 months were more likely to make friends with other children with secure attachment histories. Similarly, in a longitudinal study of north German families, infant–mother (but not infant–father) attachment predicted children's interviewer-rated "competence in establishing close friendships" at age 10, with children who had been securely attached to their mothers rated as more competent than children who had been insecurely attached (Freitag, Belsky, Grossmann, Grossmann, & Scheuerer-Englisch, 1996).

Consistent with these longitudinal findings are findings from two recent cross-sectional inquiries into attachment quality and fifth- and sixth-grade U.S. children's friendships (Kerns, Klepac, & Cole, 1996). In one study, children who reported a "more secure" attachment to their mothers were more likely to be in reciprocated friendships; they were not, however, more likely to report being in more positive or less negative friendships. In the second investigation, children in "secure–secure" dyads were less critical, more responsive, and marginally more balanced about power than children in "secure–insecure" dyads. Children in secure–secure dyads also reported more companionship in friendship than children in secure–insecure dyads, although there were no attachment differences in self-reported intimacy and affection, or in friendship stability.

Children's attachments to their parents may influence not only the quality but also the quantity of children's friendships. It is intriguing to note that across three studies, children who had been securely attached infants were judged to have made more friends in middle childhood than children who had been insecure (Elicker et al., 1992; Grossmann & Grossmann, 1991; Lewis & Feiring, 1989). Especially notable among these investigations is a follow-up of the same north German children discussed earlier—the only inquiry into early attachment and later affectional bonds to provide any hint regarding minimizing–maximizing processes (Grossmann & Grossmann, 1991). Specifically, 10-year-olds who had been judged secure with their mothers could, when discussing their friendships, identify a number of friends by name, whereas the children who had been judged insecure (83% of whom were classified as avoidant) professed to having many friends but could not name any of them. The discrepancy between these avoidant children's general claims and lack of support for their assertions is strikingly reminiscent of the idealizing discourse of some adults classified as "dismissing" (avoidant) in the Adult Attachment Interview (AAI). Such adults also describe their experiences in glowing generalities, yet fail to substantiate their global descriptions with specific examples. In the AAI, this type of idealizing is considered to reflect defensive exclusion of painful memories, which in turn is consistent with minimizing attachment (i.e., not acknowledging the pain in past attachment experiences precludes the need for comfort and nurturance). For the avoidant north German children, the discrepancy between their claims to have many friends and their inability to name them may have reflected defensive exclusion of painful thoughts about a lack of friends.

Relationships with Siblings and Friends: Summary

In sum, the existing studies of the associations between infant–parent attachment and sibling and friend relationships all lend at least some support to attachment theory's predictions about the influence of the infant–parent attachment on the developing child's subsequent close relationships, with secure infant–mother attachments going hand in hand with more harmonious sibling interactions and friendship quality and quantity.

It is notable that the research on early attachment and subsequent affectional bonds that has included assessments of infant–father attachment has generally indicated either no relation between infant–father attachment (Freitag et al., 1996; Volling & Belsky, 1992) or (in one study—Youngblade & Belsky, 1992) a counterintuitive association. These findings highlight the need for attachment researchers to devote more attention to understanding infant–father attachment, especially vis-à-vis its influence on the child's subsequent relationships (see Belsky, 1996, and van IJzendoorn & DeWolff, 1997). It may be that infant–father relationships influence subsequent relationships quite differently than do infant–mother relationships. Other elements of the child–father relationship, such as the father's be-

havior in play, may overshadow or interact with the influences of the infant–father attachment (see, e.g., Parke, 1995).

Finally, in all of these investigations except the Grossmann and Grossmann (1991) north German inquiry (in which most of the insecure children were avoidant), the avoidant and ambivalent attachment groups were combined, thereby preventing the analysis of minimizing and maximizing attachment strategies. Especially in light of the intriguing hint in the Grossmanns' (1991) data of the insecure (predominantly avoidant) children's possible idealizing—and minimizing—self-reports, we suggest the analysis of minimizing and maximizing processes as an important goal for future inquiries into the links between early attachments and children's sibling relationships and friendships.

The Influence of the Infant–Parent Attachment on Later Affectional Bonds: Relationships with Romantic Partners and Children

Bowlby (1979) highlighted marriage and child-rearing relationships as the subsequent relationships in which the influence of early attachments is likely to be strongest. Understanding the influence of early attachments on romantic and child-rearing relationships, however, requires prospective data on infant–parent attachment and the infant's later (adult) romantic relationships and parenting, which to date are not available. Nonetheless, as we will discuss, some hints into the influence of early attachments on these later relationships have begun to emerge.

A large portion of the research into adult attachment processes has relied on the AAI, which is not a measure of early attachment, but rather a measure of the adult's "current state of mind with respect to attachment" (George, Kaplan, & Main, 1985; Main, Kaplan, & Cassidy, 1985; for reviews, see Crowell, Fraley, & Shaver, Chapter 20, this volume, Crowell & Treboux, 1995, and Hesse, Chapter 19, this volume). Although the AAI draws heavily on recollections of early attachment experiences, it is the way in which these experiences are discussed in the interview that most informs both an individual's classification (as "autonomous" [secure], "dismissing" [avoidant], or "preoccupied" [ambivalent]) and his or her scores on continuous scales measuring "probable experiences" with early attachment figures (e.g., loving, pressure to achieve, rejection) and "current state of mind" (e.g., coherent, idealizing, angry). Subsequent experiences—especially attachment relationships with therapists and spouses—may influence individuals' working models and their "current state of mind." It is the adult's current state of mind, in turn, that is expected to influence an individual's behavior in romantic relationships and as a parent (Main & Goldwyn, in press).

Some insight into the influence of the infant–parent attachment on relationships with romantic partners and children has come from analysis of the coder-rated AAI scales for probable early experiences with each parent. Although these scales have yet to be fully validated, studies drawing on the AAI scales can provide intriguing hints about the links between early attachments and subsequent romantic relationships. Some information on the links between early attachments and subsequent romantic relationships has also come from examining adults' self-reported romantic attachment styles. As we will discuss, however, the use of attachment style questionnaires to examine the influence of the early infant–parent attachment on adults' romantic relationships is complicated by some of the same factors that complicate the use of the AAI to examine this issue.

Relationships with Romantic Partners

Some insight into the influence of the infant–parent attachment on subsequent romantic relationships has come from a recent study in which both mothers' and fathers' (coder-rated) early attachment experiences were associated with the quality of their marriages (Cowan, Cohn, Cowan, & Pearson, 1996). Mothers and fathers who were rated as having had loving parents were also observed to interact more positively with each other at home.

Insight into the links between early attachments and subsequent romantic relationships has also come from a body of research stimulated by Hazan and Shaver's (1987) proposal of a tripartite classification scheme of adults' "attachment styles" in romantic relationships (e.g., Hazan & Shaver, 1987, 1994; Shaver & Hazan, 1993; for reviews, see Crowell & Treboux, 1995, and Feeney, Chapter 17, this volume). Adults' self-reported romantic attachment styles as measured with Hazan and Shaver's (or similar) questionnaires have been linked in theoretically predictable ways to their recollections of their early relationships with their parents (Bartholomew & Horowitz, 1991; Collins & Read, 1990; Feeney

& Noller, 1990; Hazan & Shaver, 1987; Simpson, 1990). For example, in one study, secure adults reported having warmer early relationships with their parents than insecure adults reported having (Hazan & Shaver, 1987). In another inquiry, college students' descriptions of their opposite-sex parents were associated with the students' partners' self-reported tendencies in romantic relationships (Collins & Read, 1990).

Limitations inherent to using these questionnaires, however, demand that these findings be interpreted cautiously. Specifically, in light of the fact that attachment strategies are thought to include distortions (minimizing and maximizing tendencies), attachment research questions and self-report measures may be particularly ill matched. Moreover, like the AAI data, these findings do not speak to the extent to which romantic attachment style is derived from early attachments, and/or the extent to which individuals' current romantic partnerships are coloring their recollections of their parents. Most promising among the measures of attachment style may be Bartholomew's peer and family attachment interviews, which, like the AAI, are scored by trained coders (Bartholomew & Horowitz, 1991; Griffin & Bartholomew, 1994; see also Crowell's [1990] Close Relationship Interview).

We raise two additional issues that are especially pertinent to understanding the influence of early attachments on later romantic partnerships. The first concerns the differences between infant–parent attachments and romantic partnerships. Specifically, although Bowlby singled out future romantic relationships as particularly likely to be influenced by early attachments, infant–parent relationships differ from romantic partnerships in ways that may make understanding the relations between these types of relationships especially challenging. In particular, although both infant–parent relationships and most marriages can be considered attachment relationships, the infant–parent relationship is not reciprocal: Whereas the infant is attached to the parent, and seeks the parent as a secure base, the parent is not attached to the infant. Rather, the parent is said to be bonded to the infant, as that infant's caregiver (Ainsworth, 1989). In most romantic partnerships, however, each partner is an attachment figure to the other: Each is the other's caregiver, and each typically seeks the other as a secure base (Shaver, Hazan, & Bradshaw, 1988). These differences in the two types of close relationships must be considered when researchers are thinking about the influence of early attachments on later romantic bonds.

A second important issue concerns the influence of another type of attachment relationship on individuals' romantic partnerships: their own parents' marriages. Hazan and Shaver (1987), in fact, found links between adults' recollections of the quality of their parents' marriages and these adults' self-reported romantic attachment styles. It is likely that individuals' working models of romantic attachments are informed not only by their relationships with their parents but also by their parents' marital relationships, and that both of these types of relationships influence people's romantic partnerships.

Relationships with Children

A number of inquiries have revealed associations between the AAI coder-rated scores for parents' probable early attachment-related experiences and (1) their own parenting behavior and (2) their infants' attachment to them (e.g., Fonagy, Steele, & Steele, 1991; Main & Goldwyn, 1984). In the first of these inquiries, there was a strong correlation between a mother's (AAI coder-rated) experience of rejection by her own mother and her infant's avoidance of her during the strange situation (Main & Goldwyn, 1984). More recently, mothers of secure infants were found to have reported, during pregnancy, having had more loving mothers than mothers of avoidant (but not ambivalent) infants; notably, there were no differences based on these mothers' early experiences with their fathers (Fonagy et al., 1991).

Perhaps the most intriguing information about the influence of parents' early relationships with their parents on the infant–parent attachment has come from examining the connections among parents' early experiences, parents' current state of mind, and infant–parent attachment in cases when early experiences and current state of mind are *discordant,* as has been illustrated by two recent investigations. In the first study, the researchers examined the parenting behavior of two subgroups of adults classified according to the AAI as autonomous (secure): One "continuously secure" subgroup was coded as having supportive early attachments, and one "earned secure" subgroup had unsupportive early attachments (Pearson, Cohn, Cowan, & Cowan, 1994). Although the earned and continuously secure parents had different early attachment experiences, there were no differences in the observed parenting of earned secure versus continuously secure parents. In addition, the earned secure parents were observed to be warmer and to provide more structure to their preschoolers than insecure parents.

Parallel findings have emerged from another investigation of earned and continuous security in which mothers' "positive" parenting of toddlers was observed under varying degrees of daily parenting stress (Phelps, Belsky, & Crnic, 1998). Under conditions of high stress, earned and continuously secure mothers demonstrated equally positive parenting, again demonstrating that early attachments do not necessarily forecast later relationships. In addition, both groups of secure mothers were more positive with their toddlers than were mothers classified as insecure. There were no attachment group differences under conditions of low stress.

Both of these innovative inquiries speak to the limits of the influence of early attachments on subsequent attachment relationships. These data are consistent with Bowlby's arguments that although working models created within early attachments are expected to exert far-reaching effects, changes in working models can occur and can disrupt the influence of early experiences. Moreover, according to the theory, if there is discontinuity between early and later working models of attachment, current relationships can reflect current as well as former models (Bowlby, 1969/1982, 1979, 1988; Main & Goldwyn, in press).

Another question concerns the parameters of changes in working models. For example, in Pearson et al.'s (1994) study, there were significant differences between the earned and continuously secure parents on depressive symptomatology, with earned secure parents reporting more symptoms of depression than continuously secure parents. This finding implies that there may have been lingering psychological effects of the difficult early attachments that these earned secure parents reported. Depressive symptomatology can in turn affect relationships (DeMulder & Radke-Yarrow, 1991; Downey & Coyne, 1990; Teti, Gelfand, Messinger, & Isabella, 1995). Finally, Bowlby (1979) wrote that "the stronger the emotions . . . the more likely are the earlier and less conscious models to become dominant" (p. 142). Thus, in the same way that attachment group differences in parenting behavior have been illuminated under stressful conditions (Phelps et al., 1998), particular situations or particular relationships—especially those evoking strong feelings—may affect the extent to which people rely on current versus former working models (see also Mikulincer, Florian, & Weller, 1993; Simpson, Rholes, & Nelligan, 1992).

Relationships with Romantic Partners and Children: Summary

In sum, although romantic and child-rearing relationships are hypothesized to be especially susceptible to the influences of early attachments, understanding the links between early attachments and later romantic and child-rearing relationships has been hampered by the absence of prospective studies of infant–parent attachment and adult romantic relationships and parenting. Some insights into the influence of early attachments on these later relationships have come from studies drawing on objective ratings and self-reports of adults' recollections of their early relationships. Researchers have also begun to illuminate the limits of the contributions of early attachments to subsequent relationships.

Interestingly, the further examination of discontinuity between early attachment experiences and later attachment relationships appears to hold the most promise for elucidating the workings of internal models of attachment and attachment strategies. Continuing to probe the connections—and lack of connections—among early experiences, current state of mind, and relationships with romantic partners and children should help illuminate the relative contributions of early and later attachment experiences to adults' close relationships. These types of data in turn may have important clinical implications for understanding how and when change is possible, and may illuminate fundamental issues in developmental psychology, such as the notion of "sensitive periods" in a person's life for various developmental phenomena (see, e.g., Gallagher & Ramey, 1987; Gollin, 1981; Wachs & Gruen, 1982).

The Influence of the Infant–Parent Attachment on Nonaffectional Bonds: Relationships with Peers and Interactions with Strangers

Relationships with Peers

Despite Bowlby's emphasis on the influence of early attachments on later *close* relationships, arguably the largest single body of attachment research addresses the connections between child–parent attachment and children's nonaffectional bonds. In response to findings illustrating the importance of early peer relationships for later mental health (see Parker & Asher, 1987, for a review), many researchers have examined the contribution of the infant–parent attachment to children's relationships with their peers. The research on the links between early attachment and children's peer relationships is multifaceted. There exist contemporaneous and longitudinal investigations of toddlers, preschoolers, and school-age children, with data provided by mothers, teachers, independent observers, and peers on children's behavior *toward* others, as well as treatment received and/or elicited *from* others. Although the findings are by no means uniform, they are strikingly consistent in illustrating a relation between secure child–mother attachment and more harmonious interactions with peers, higher regard from peers, and fewer behavior problems in both preschool and elementary school classrooms.

Relations between attachment quality and children's interactions with peers first emerged in a series of studies conducted by Sroufe and his colleagues (see Elicker et al., 1992, and Kerns, 1996, for reviews). One early investigation used a modified version of the strange situation, in which 15-month-old infants were classified as either "secure" or "anxious" (Waters, Wippman, & Sroufe, 1979). Two years later, observers' *Q*-sorts of children's "peer competence" in the preschool classroom consistently favored the children who had been classified as secure. In another preschool inquiry, teachers rated 4- to 5-year-olds who had been classified as secure as higher on ego control and ego resiliency than children who had been classified as insecure (Arend, Gove, & Sroufe, 1979). In still another preschool study, two classrooms of 4- to 5-year-olds whose attachment classifications were stable from 12 to 18 months were observed extensively over at least one semester (LaFreniere & Sroufe, 1985). Teachers rated secure preschoolers as more socially competent than insecure children, and observers scored the secure children higher on measures of social participation and social dominance than ambivalent children and lower on negative affect than avoidant children. Secure children were also better liked by their classmates than insecure children.

Three additional preschool investigations were based on these same children. One demonstrated attachment group differences on a composite measure of empathy (based on teacher reports and independent observations): Secure children received higher empathy scores than avoidant children, although the ambivalent children did not differ from either the secure or the avoidant children (Kestenbaum, Farber, & Sroufe, 1989). In an inquiry into children's bullying when they were paired with same-sex classmates, secure children were less likely than their insecure counterparts to act as bullies; moreover, none of the children who had been classified as secure was bullied (Troy & Sroufe, 1987). Finally, these same secure children were viewed by both teachers and observers as exhibiting fewer behavior problems than their avoidant and/or ambivalent counterparts (Erickson, Sroufe, & Egeland, 1985; see Fagot & Kavanagh, 1990, for both parallel and contradictory findings; see Bates & Bayles, 1988, and Bates, Maslin, & Frankel, 1985, for contradictory findings).

Findings consistent with those of Sroufe and his colleagues have emerged from a longitudinal inquiry conducted in southern Germany (Suess, Grossmann, & Sroufe, 1992), as well as from two other European investigations in which attachment quality and preschool behavior were examined concurrently at ages 4 (Turner, 1991) and 6 (Wartner, Grossmann, Fremmer-Bombik, & Suess, 1994). Parallel evidence has also come from an inquiry into hostile/aggressive behavior in the preschool classroom: In this study, the recently identified "disorganized/disoriented" attachment classification was most strongly linked to preschool hostility and aggression (Lyons-Ruth, Alpern, & Repacholi, 1993). Contradictory findings emerged from a longitudinal investigation including measures of attachment quality at 12 months and 4 years of age, as well as teacher and observer ratings of preschool behavior: No connections emerged between attachment quality and behavior with peers (Howes, Matheson, & Hamilton, 1994).

Several studies have linked attachment and behavior toward peers in school-age children. In two inquiries, both attachment quality and school behavior were examined at age 6 (Cohn, 1990; Solomon, George, & De Jong, 1995). In the first of these investigations, insecure boys were described by their teachers as less personally and socially competent and as having more behavior problems than secure boys. Insecure boys also were viewed by their classmates as more aggressive than secure boys and were less well liked than secure boys; no attachment group differences emerged for girls (Cohn, 1990). In the sec-

ond of these investigations, which focused on attachment problems, disorganized/controlling children were rated by teachers as having more behavior problems than their secure, avoidant, and ambivalent classmates, and in particular as being more hostile than the secure and ambivalent children (Solomon et al., 1995; see Shaw, Owens, Vondra, Keenan, & Winslow, 1996, for convergent longitudinal data). In a similar study of first- through third-graders in which the focus was on teacher-rated behavior problems, attachment group differences based on 18-month (but not 12-month) assessments were discerned for boys only, with insecure boys less likely than boys who had been securely attached to be classified as aggressive or passive/withdrawn (Renken, Egeland, Marvinney, Mangelsdorf, & Sroufe, 1989; see also Lewis, Feiring, McGuffog, & Jaskir, 1984, for similar findings with mother-rated behavior problems). Finally, in the Minnesota summer camp follow-up, 10- and 11-year-old children who had been secure infants were rated by their counselors as more socially competent than children who had been insecure (Elicker et al., 1992; Shulman et al., 1994), even after concurrent indices of socioemotional functioning were controlled (Sroufe, Egeland, & Kreutzer, 1990).

Interactions with Strangers

As we have discussed, attachment theory emphasizes the influence of early attachments on later close relationships. To the extent that children's interactions with strangers are not relationships at all, children's interactions with strangers may not be influenced by early attachments. Children's interactions with strangers may have more roots in the sociable (affiliative) system than in the attachment system (see Cassidy & Berlin, in press).

At the same time, all close relationships (except, arguably, for familial relationships) begin with interactions between strangers. The way in which people approach strangers—what Main and Weston (1981) discussed as "the readiness to establish new relationships"—may reflect their internal working models of themselves, others, and relationships. Moreover, the extent to which sociability (as opposed to internal working models) "drives" interactions with strangers may depend on the potential for forming a relationship with a given stranger. For example, the attachment system may be more influential in an individual's interactions with someone with whom he or she hopes to form a relationship (e.g., an attractive stranger at a cocktail party), whereas the sociable system may be more influential in an individual's interactions with someone with whom he or she is less likely to form a relationship. Considering the relations between attachment quality and interactions with new people should help elucidate these issues.

Investigations of attachment and children's interactions with unfamiliar children and adults have yielded mixed results. Associations between attachment quality and behavior with unfamiliar children have been indicated in three studies (Lieberman, 1977; Pastor, 1981; van den Boom, 1995), but have not been found in two studies (Jacobson & Wille, 1986; Howes et al., 1994). Two investigations have indicated connections between attachment security and sociability with adults (Main & Weston, 1981; Plunkett, Klein, & Meisels, 1988), but three studies have not revealed such links (Frodi, 1983; Lamb, Hwang, Frodi, & Frodi, 1982; Thompson & Lamb, 1983).

Relationships with Peers and Interactions with Strangers: Summary

In sum, the extensive and multifaceted literature on the associations between child–parent attachment and children's peer relationships offers generally consistent evidence of an association between a secure child–mother attachment and more harmonious interactions with peers. As Belsky and Cassidy (1994) have suggested, in comparison to the research on the relations between early attachments and (1) affectional bonds and (2) interactions with (familiar) peers, the less consistent body of studies on early attachment and interactions with strangers can be taken as tentative support for Bowlby's and Ainsworth's emphasis on the greater contribution of infant–parent attachments to *close* relationships.

It is not enough, however, to compare findings of the relations between attachment quality and affectional and nonaffectional bonds across studies. More conclusive evidence of a closer connection between child–parent attachment and affectional bonds than between child–parent attachment and nonaffectional bonds would come from researchers' identifying "attachments," "affectional bonds," and "nonaffectional bonds" (see Ainsworth, 1989).

In addition, we suggest within-study and/or within-person comparisons of the links between early attachments and nonaffectional bonds, affectional bonds, and attachments. The existing research may be clouded by the likelihood that some of the peer interactions investigated were in fact "unidentified" interactions between friends. Moreover, research on children's peer relationships has indicated that peer acceptance and friendship each play unique roles in children's socioemotional functioning (e.g., Parker & Asher, 1993). It may be that a child's behavior in a classroom in which he or she has a friend differs markedly from the same child's behavior in a classroom in which he or she has no friends, and that the influence of the child–parent attachment is different in these different settings. We propose that attachment researchers attend more carefully not only to the distinctions between children's relationships, but also to the interactions among the influences of these various relationships.

Finally, since the time of Bowlby's writings, scholars focusing on "nature" (vs. "nurture") have argued convincingly for the contributions of genes and/or temperament to individual differences in sociability (e.g., Plomin, 1986; Suomi, 1997). It may be that temperament plays a larger role in interactions with strangers, whereas attachment security plays a larger role in the initiation and maintenance of relationships. In particular, future studies of the development of relationships vis-à-vis people's interactions with peers and strangers could benefit from including measures of temperament.

The literature on the connections between early attachments and nonaffectional relationships also offers some food for thought on minimizing and maximizing attachment strategies, especially in regard to the ways in which behaviors in one relationship can serve the "goals" of another. Specifically, given that peers and strangers are not by definition attachment figures, children's interactions with peers and/or unfamiliar others may serve as an arena in which the children minimize or maximize their attachment *to their parents.* For example, at a birthday party, an ambivalent child may withdraw from peers and cling to the mother's skirt to emphasize (nonconsciously) his or her dependence on the mother.

At the same time, children's interactions with peers and unfamiliar others may contain the seeds of close relationships, and these interactions may serve to minimize or maximize a *potential* attachment to the peer (e.g., at a birthday party an ambivalent child may demonstrate maximizing behavior to another child by shadowing or clinging to the child). These two possibilities are not necessarily mutually exclusive; they may depend on such factors as the child's age and the nature of the situation, including the presence or absence of established attachment figures. For example, the ambivalent child's clinging to the mother at the hypothetical birthday party may also serve as a signal to the child's peers, which may elicit caregiving or, alternatively, bullying. Similarly, a child's clinging to the mother every time the child is dropped off for preschool may elicit extra caregiving from the teacher.

With regard to the avoidant pattern, avoidant children might be expected to minimize attachment to both parents and peers by interacting with their classmates and peers in a neutral, cool, and distant manner that in no way draws attention to themselves, their needs, or their vulnerabilities. In fact, however, the most definitive characterization of avoidant children's interactions with peers comes from the studies of attachment and behavior problems, which have portrayed avoidant children as aggressive and hostile. In Troy and Sroufe's (1987) study of bullying among peers, it is notable that all of the children who bullied were avoidant (see also Renken et al., 1989, for consistent findings; see Fagot & Kavanagh, 1990, for both parallel and contradictory findings). It is also important to note that since the identification of the disorganized/disoriented attachment classification, attachment disorganization has been linked more closely than avoidance to children's hostile/aggressive behaviors, although in several studies this disorganization has also included a high degree of avoidance (e.g., Lyons-Ruth et al., 1993; Solomon et al., 1995; see Lyons-Ruth, 1996, and Lyons-Ruth & Jacobvitz, Chapter 23, this volume, for comprehensive reviews and discussions).

Posthoc reflection on the seemingly antithetical connections between avoidance and hostility suggests ways in which aggression and hostility toward peers are consistent with a minimizing strategy. First, aggressive and hostile behaviors are alienating as well as derogating patterns of behavior, both of which are consistent with the minimization of attachment (Main & Goldwyn, in press). Second, the hostility and aggression associated with the avoidant group may reflect a pattern of unsuccessfully attempting to suppress negative emotions: The individual attempts to suppress negative emotions which eventually build up beyond control and erupt in hostile outbursts (see Cassidy, 1994, and Malatesta-Magai, 1991, for reviews of the notion that the minimization of attachment involves suppression of negative affect). These outbursts, however, may only make the avoidant individual all the more concerned about his negative feelings and the importance of controlling them. In an effort to prevent further outbursts, negative emotions are bottled up again, and the cycle continues.

The Influence of the Infant–Parent Attachment on Subsequent Affectional and Nonaffectional Bonds: Linking Mechanisms

As described earlier, Bowlby posited that people's internal working models guide both cognitive and emotional processes—including expectations, attention deployment, interpretation, and memories—which in turn guide behavior. Given the array of evidence on the connections between early attachments and subsequent relationships, both theorists and researchers have begun to focus more on linking mechanisms and, specifically, on representational models (see Bretherton & Munholland, Chapter 5, this volume; Cassidy & Berlin, in press).

There is increasing evidence to support the argument that representations mediate the associations between early attachments and children's other relationships. First, numerous studies have indicated associations between attachment quality and representations of self, others, and attachment in general (e.g., Cassidy, 1988; Main et al., 1985; Slade, Belsky, Aber, & Phelps, in press). Furthermore, one investigation revealed connections between infant–mother attachment and not only children's representations of their peers but also these children's peer relationships (Suess et al., 1992). A follow-up study reported identical findings when attachment was assessed at age 6 (Wartner et al., 1994). Finally, one investigation has simultaneously linked attachment quality, representations, and relationship quality: Cassidy and her colleagues presented evidence that children's peer/friend representations mediate the association between child–mother attachment and the quality of children's friendships (Cassidy, Kirsh, Scolton, & Parke, 1996). Parallel findings have come from a study of one aspect of college students' representations of relationships, termed "rejection sensitivity" (Feldman & Downey,

1994). This study did not include direct assessments of early attachment quality, but rather focused on early (attachment-relevant) experiences of family violence as assessed via self-reported frequency and severity of parental physical maltreatment and parent–parent aggression. The students' "rejection sensitivity" was found to mediate the association between early experiences of family violence and these students' self-reported romantic attachment styles.

Continued research along these lines, especially research that integrates established assessments of representational processes developed within different but parallel research traditions, should prove fascinating (see Baldwin, 1992, for a discussion of the ubiquity of the emphasis on representational processes across different research traditions). Other promising avenues include examining the development and evolution of cognitive "structures" (see Piaget, 1954) and examining the influence of experience on brain functioning and the development of neural pathways (see, e.g., Cicchetti & Tucker, 1994; Siegel, 1999).

In addition to representational processes, it is also important to consider other types of mechanisms linking early attachments and subsequent affectional and nonaffectional bonds. There may be more direct connections between attachments and other bonds. Parents of secure children may provide their children with more opportunities to establish social networks and to make friends. Some evidence for this supposition comes from Lieberman's (1977) investigation of attachment security and peer relationships, in which attachment security was positively related to the extent of children's contacts with peers. Parents of secure children may also teach their children to value relationships and may advise their children in such a way as to help them develop and maintain harmonious friendships. Secure children also may be more likely to receive supportive treatment from their parents and (as discussed earlier) to observe their parents in harmonious interactions with each other and with the parents' own adult peers and friends. Thus secure children may model their parents' relationships.

THE INFLUENCE OF PARENTS' OTHER RELATIONSHIPS ON THE INFANT–PARENT ATTACHMENT

In the same way that the infant–parent attachment is proposed to contribute importantly to other relationships, parents' other relationships are proposed to contribute importantly to their abilities to provide their infants with a secure base, and thus to the infant–parent attachment. Parents' attachments, especially their bonds to their own parents and to each other, are expected to be especially influential. We begin this section with a brief discussion of the influence of parents' relationships with their parents. Then we consider the influences of parents' marital relationships and parents' social support. Finally, we discuss a less commonplace but equally important influence on infant–parent attachment—the influence of parents' psychotherapeutic relationships.

The Influence of Parents' Relationships with Their Parents on the Infant–Parent Attachment

Arguably the single most important set of relationships to influence the infant–parent attachment are parents' relationships with their own parents. As discussed earlier (under the rubric of the influence of early attachments on subsequent child-rearing relationships), however, understanding the influence of parents' early attachments on their own parenting behavior has been limited by the absence of prospective studies. Some insight has come from the studies using the AAI scales to examine the link between parents' early attachment experiences and their own child-rearing behaviors (as discussed earlier— e.g., Fonagy et al., 1991; Phelps et al., 1998).

In addition to examining parents' retrospective accounts of their early relationships with their parents, researchers have also investigated contemporaneous associations between parents' relationships with their parents and the infant–parent attachment. Although none of these studies include data on parents' early attachments to their parents, they do provide some preliminary evidence of contemporaneous relations between supportive mother–grandmother relationships and a greater likelihood of a secure infant–mother attachment (Frodi et al., 1984; Levitt, Weber, & Clark, 1986; Spieker & Bensley, 1994). In light of the theory's emphasis on the influence of parents' early attachments on their own parenting, the lack of conclusive data on this issue highlights the need for further research on the topic.

The Influence of the Marital Relationship on the Infant–Parent Attachment

In his earliest writings, Bowlby discussed marital harmony as key to infant development: "By providing love and companionship [the husband] support[s] the mother emotionally and help[s] her maintain that harmonious contented mood in the atmosphere of which the infant thrives" (1953, p. 13). Bowlby thus argued that marital quality contributes *indirectly* to the infant–parent attachment. Similarly, Belsky has argued that marital quality is one of several "distal" factors (vs. "proximal" processes, such as mother–infant interaction) that acts in concert—interactively and/or additively—to predict infant–parent attachment (Belsky, 1981, 1984, 1996; Belsky & Isabella, 1988; Belsky, Rosenberger, & Crnic, 1995).

The research on the connections between marital quality and attachment quality has yielded generally consistent evidence of a positive association between the two: These associations have been documented in both low- and high-risk samples in cross-sectional inquiries conducted in the United States (Crnic, Greenberg, & Slough, 1986; Goldberg & Easterbrooks, 1984 [with more consistent findings for infant–father than for infant–mother attachment]; Teti, Nakagawa, Das, & Wirth, 1991), in Japan (Durrett, Otaki, & Richards, 1984), and in England (Stevenson-Hinde & Shouldice, 1995). They have also been documented in longitudinal studies, three of which have linked prenatal and/or postnatal marital quality to infant attachment quality (Belsky & Isabella, 1988; Howes & Markman, 1989; Isabella & Belsky, 1985; Jacobson & Frye, 1991; Lewis, Owen, & Cox, 1988 [for daughter–mother but not son–mother attachment quality]; Spieker & Booth, 1988; Teti, Sakin, Kucera, Corns, & Das Eiden, 1996; see Levitt et al., 1986, and Zeanah et al., 1993, for null findings; see Belsky et al., 1995, for a review).

As Belsky et al. (1995) have discussed, especially provocative findings on the associations between marital quality and early attachment come from two inquiries in particular. The first illustrated the indirect effects of marital quality on infant–mother attachment. Specifically, prenatal marital quality predicted mothers' role satisfaction, which in turn forecast both maternal sensitivity and infant–mother attachment (Isabella, 1994). In the second study, the effects of marital quality were moderated by mothers' current

working models: Mothers' self-reported marital quality correlated positively with children's security, but only for mothers classified as insecure according to the AAI (Das Eiden, Teti, & Corns, 1995). It may be that for secure mothers, current state of mind "drives" marital quality, sensitive parenting, and child attachment, whereas for insecure mothers, current state of mind with respect to attachment is more malleable and open to the influence of the current marriage. That is, relationships that contribute to the infant–parent attachment may be differentially influential for different people. Only additional research will clarify these processes. Especially in light of the fact that marital quality is hypothesized to contribute indirectly to infant–mother attachment, multigenerational, multimeasure studies of the direct and indirect effects of adults' past and present relationships with their parents and with their spouses are essential.

Furthermore, greater attention to methodological issues may facilitate future investigations of the associations between marital quality and child–parent attachment. Specifically, most studies to date have relied on self-report assessments of marital quality, which may in turn obscure associations between marital quality and child–parent attachment, especially if the insecure attachment groups are combined. In particular, given the apparent inclinations of dismissing/avoidant individuals to disavow personal troubles (e.g., Berlin, Cassidy, & Belsky, 1995; Kobak & Sceery, 1988; Main & Goldwyn, in press; see also Stevenson-Hinde & Shouldice, 1995), and given the generally concordant attachment patterns between infants and their parents (van IJzendoorn, 1995), one might expect parents of avoidant infants to deny marital difficulties, perhaps even to the point of defensively idealizing their marriages and reporting the most positive marriages of all three attachment groups. If this is the case, examining the insecure groups individually should prove fruitful. Including more observational measures of marital quality should also be helpful.

In addition, assessments of marital quality vary; some are more global, whereas others tap specific aspects of the marital relationship. It may be that the most important aspect of the marital relationship for the infant–parent attachment is the extent to which an infant's attachment figure perceives emotional support from his or her spouse or partner (i.e., the extent to which the partner serves as a secure base). Other aspects of the spousal relationship, such as partners' abilities to work and have fun together, their financial security, and their sexual compatibility, may be less relevant to understanding attachment processes.

The Influence of Parents' Social Support on the Infant–Parent Attachment

In the same way that parents' close relationships are expected to influence parenting and the infant–parent attachment, parents' more general social support has also been hypothesized to enhance parenting and infant security. Just as the theory posits stronger connections between early attachments and subsequent close (vs. nonaffectional) relationships, attachment theory also calls for stronger influences of the parents' close (vs. nonaffectional) relationships on the infant–parent attachment. More studies than not have in fact found *no* direct connections between parents' social support and infant–parent attachment (Belsky, 1996; Belsky et al., 1995; Belsky & Isabella, 1988; Crockenberg, 1981; Isabella, 1994; Levitt et al., 1986; Zeanah et al., 1993; see Belsky et al., 1995, for a review)—findings that can be taken as support for attachment theory's emphasis on close relationships.

As with the associations between marital quality and infant–parent attachment, the links between social support and infant–parent attachment are complex. One pioneering work, for example, revealed associations between social support and infant–mother attachment only in dyads with temperamentally "irritable" infants (Crockenberg, 1981). Similarly, it is notable that the only study to yield evidence of direct connections between infant–mother attachment and social support was an investigation of high-risk premature infants (Crnic et al., 1986). Taken together, these two investigations raise the question of whether the effects of social support on infant–parent attachment may be moderated by infant risk status. The influence of social support on infant–parent attachment has also been shown to be mediated by maternal role satisfaction (Isabella, 1994), and to act in concert with other "distal" factors (e.g., marital satisfaction and work–family relations) to predict infant–father attachment (Belsky, 1996).

In sum, consistent with some of our previous recommendations for future research, we suggest that studies of social support and attachment will be enhanced by more precise distinctions between affectional and nonaffectional bonds. For example, in Crockenberg's (1981) study, mothers' perceptions of support from their husbands were considered part of "social" support, making it impossible to separate marital quality from the quality of nonaffectional social support. We suggest that it is crucial to separate "social" support derived from intimate relationships from more general social support within the context of nonaffectional bonds. In addition, to the extent that assessments of social support are bound to self-report procedures, researchers must take care to use measures that either circumvent or assess individuals' minimizing and maximizing biases.

The Influence of Parents' Psychotherapeutic Relationships on the Infant–Parent Attachment

Bowlby viewed the psychotherapeutic relationship as a potential attachment relationship with the power to modify the influence of early attachments on subsequent affectional and nonaffectional bonds—in other words, to change relations among relationships. According to Bowlby (1988), a principal job of the therapist is, in fact, to serve as an attachment figure: to provide the patient with a secure base from which to explore and to rework his or her representational models of self, others, and relationships.

Several experimental intervention studies have addressed the effects of parents' participation in attachment-directed interventions (Barnard et al., 1988; Booth, Mitchell, Barnard, & Spieker, 1989; Erickson, Korfmacher, & Egeland, 1992; Jacobson & Frye, 1991; Lambermon & van IJzendoorn, 1989; van den Boom, 1994, 1995; see van IJzendoorn, Juffer, & Duyvesteyn, 1995, for a review and meta-analysis; see also Lieberman & Zeanah, Chapter 24, this volume). What is not completely clear from this body of studies, however, is the extent to which the therapeutic *relationship* per se (1) was designed to be the principal agent of change, and (2) functioned as the principal agent of change. Some of the interventions were explicitly focused on relationships, whereas others were more practical (e.g., didactic) interventions. And even when therapy is explicitly didactic, an important therapeutic relationship may develop. For example, although mothers in one study were assigned to two different types of intervention services, "mental health" and "information/resource," home visitors' records indicated that many of the information/resource mothers actually received mental health services which centered on the establishment of a therapeutic relationship (Booth et al., 1989). In this study, it was receiving mental health services that predicted the quality of mother–child interaction.

Some insight into the influence of mothers' psychotherapeutic relationships on the infant–mother attachment has come from two attachment intervention studies. In one intervention designed to provide a "corrective attachment experience," mothers' "level of involvement" in the therapeutic process was found to relate to these mothers' subsequent interactions with their toddlers, to their toddlers' Attachment Q-Sort security scores, and to a dyadic assessment of the "goal-corrected partnership" (Lieberman, Weston, & Pawl, 1991; see also Lieberman & Pawl, 1988).

In another study, in which the effects on infant–mother attachment of mothers' participation in psychodynamically oriented therapeutic sessions were compared to the effects of more practical intervention services (toy demonstrations and linking families to social services), there were no differences in the two intervention groups' effects on infant–mother attachment (Lyons-Ruth, Connell, Grunebaum, & Botein, 1990). This null finding, however, may be explained by qualitative ratings indicating that both groups of mothers reported "strong positive" relationships with their home visitors (Lyons-Ruth, Botein, & Grunebaum, 1984). These investigations underscore the importance of future studies measuring the quality of the psychotherapeutic relationship and its influence on attachments (see also Berlin, O'Neal, & Brooks-Gunn, 1998; Horvath & Symonds, 1991; Korfmacher, 1998; Nezworski, Belsky, & Tolan, 1988).

Another suggestion for future studies of the connections between parents' psychotherapeutic relationships and infant–parent attachment concerns long-term effects. Although van IJzendoorn et al. (1995) have suggested that longer-term interventions are less effective in changing attachments than short-term interventions, we believe that this conclusion may be premature. It may be instead that deeper-reaching therapeutic interventions require extensive time in which to yield effects (i.e., longer time than the existing studies permitted). That interventions can effect important changes in the infant–mother relationship (e.g., in maternal sensitivity), even if the infant–mother attachment does not change, has been illustrated by several inquiries (Barnard et al., 1988; Beckwith, 1988; Erickson et al., 1992; Lieberman et al., 1991). Moreover, qualitative

analyses within some of these investigations have suggested that deeper changes may have been in progress at the time that intervention outcomes were assessed. For example, in Lieberman et al.'s (1991) inquiry, although there were no associations between mothers' participation in psychotherapy and infant–mother attachment per se, after 6 months of therapy it was noted that the intervention infants who had been avoidant were more likely than the avoidant infants in the control group to have changed attachment classifications—a finding that the authors suggest may have indicated a reduction of defensiveness in the intervention group. Moreover, in Lyons-Ruth et al.'s (1990) investigation, in addition to there being significantly fewer infants classified as disorganized/disoriented in the intervention group, the authors noted that the disorganized infants who were in the intervention group were disproportionately likely to be classified as "disorganized/secure"—that is, as showing some underlying elements of security. This finding may have reflected a growing potential for attachment security within these insecurely attached intervention group infants.

The Influence of Parents' Other Relationships on the Infant–Parent Attachment: Summary

In this section we have reviewed the evidence of the influence of parents' other relationships on the infant–parent attachment. Perhaps the most intriguing data come from the attachment intervention studies. Although these data do not illustrate that the therapeutic *relationship* is what influences or changes the infant–parent attachment, they do provide some intriguing hints along these lines. In their suggestion of the power of therapeutic relationships to change (i.e., to *discontinue*) relations among relationships, the attachment intervention studies highlight the importance of understanding discontinuity. Taken together with our earlier discussions of discontinuity in attachment experiences (such as for the AAI "earned secure" subgroup), these inquiries highlight the value of elucidating *discontinuity* for understanding attachment processes and relations among relationships on the whole.

It is also important for researchers to continue to examine the ways in which the influences of parents' early and later attachments interact. The suggestion from Das Eiden et al.'s (1995) work that people may be differentially susceptible to the influences of certain relationships is especially intriguing; it brings up the question of what factors may influence this susceptibility. There may be attachment-related factors (i.e., the working models of insecurely attached people may be more malleable than the working models of securely attached people) or factors that are not related to attachment, such as age, gender, and temperament (see also Belsky, 1997, for further discussion of this issue). Finally, researchers should consider further the mechanisms linking these other relationships to the infant–parent attachment. Supportive spouses and therapists may, as Bowlby (1953) first suggested, increase parents' security and their abilities to serve as a secure base. These relationships may also enhance self-awareness and awareness of others, which in turn may enhance the parents' sensitivity to their infants' attachment signals (see Belsky, 1984). These possibilities are not necessarily mutually exclusive and, again, may differ for different people.

THE CONCORDANCE OF INFANT–CAREGIVER ATTACHMENTS

Although much of attachment theory and research addresses the bond of one infant to one parent, both the theory and the research also speak to caregivers' multiple bonds to different children and to children's multiple attachments (e.g., Ainsworth, 1989; Bowlby, 1969/1982, 1979; Howes, Chapter 29, this volume; van IJzendoorn & Sagi, Chapter 31, this volume). Given that most parents have more than one child and that most children have more than one attachment figure, understanding these multiple bonds is essential to understanding relations among relationships. Moreover, considering the concordance of infant–parent attachments requires addressing a key argument within attachment theory and research: that the principal mechanisms underlying relations among relationships are internal working models. Specifically, if a primary caregiver's working models of attachment do in fact guide her caregiving behaviors, the caregiver's children should show similar infant attachment patterns, barring major changes between pregnancies. At the same time, if an infant's working models of attachment are in fact specific to each early caregiver, if early caregivers have different working models of at-

tachment and different caregiving styles, infants should form different attachments across caregivers. Investigators have addressed both of these sets of propositions.

The Concordance of Infant–Caregiver Attachments across a Caregiver's Multiple Infants

Researchers have examined the attachment quality of caregivers' multiple infants across twins, siblings, and children assigned to Israeli kibbutz caregivers (Goldberg, Perotta, Corter, & Minde, 1986; Sagi et al., 1985, 1995; Szajnberg, Skrinjaric, & Moore, 1989; Teti & Ablard, 1988; Ward, Vaughn, & Robb, 1988). Four diverse inquiries have indicated approximately 60% concordance of child–mother attachment across (1) high- and low-risk twins (Goldberg et al., 1986; Szajnberg et al., 1989); (2) low-income mothers' infants, each seen in a strange situation at 12 months of age (Ward et al., 1988); and (3) middle-class mothers' infants and young children assessed contemporaneously via the strange situation and maternal Attachment Q-Sort, respectively (Teti & Ablard, 1988). Moreover, in two separate kibbutz investigations, individual caregivers or *metaplot* were found to have infants who formed similar attachments to them, although in the second of these studies this effect emerged only for infants who spent nights with their parents and not for infants who slept in group housing (Sagi et al., 1985, 1995). As Sagi et al. (1995) point out, the lack of biological link between the *metaplot* and their infants and among the infants themselves rules out genetic explanations for attachment concordance, which makes these data especially informative. Taken as a whole, this group of studies illustrates concordance of attachment quality of different children to the same caregiver.

It is also important to remember that attachment theory fully allows for discordant attachments across a caregiver's children, especially in the face of significant change in maternal behavior. Bowlby (1979) explicitly stated that "parents do not treat every child alike and may provide excellent conditions for one and very adverse ones for another" (p. 136). In Ward et al.'s (1988) study, discordance of attachment between siblings was related to instability of maternal behavior over time. This finding raises the question of what factors changed these mothers' parenting behaviors and in turn influenced their infants' attachments. Given some evidence of discordance as well as concordance, researchers now need to scrutinize the conditions under which caregivers' children are similarly and dissimilarly attached.

The Concordance of Infant–Caregiver Attachments across an Infant's Multiple Caregivers

There have been several studies of the relations among infants' attachments to multiple caregivers, including mothers, fathers, child care providers, and kibbutz *metaplot* (Belsky & Rovine, 1987; Easterbrooks, 1989; Fox, Kimmerly, & Schafer, 1991; Goossens & van IJzendoorn, 1990; Grossmann, Grossmann, Huber, & Wartner, 1981; Howes & Hamilton, 1992; Main & Weston, 1981; Sagi et al., 1985, 1995; Steele, Steele, & Fonagy, 1996). These studies have yielded mixed findings. Specifically, although several studies have indicated that one infant can form different types of attachments to different caregivers (Belsky & Rovine, 1987; Goossens & van IJzendoorn, 1990; Grossmann et al., 1981; Howes & Hamilton, 1992; Main & Weston, 1981), there is equally (if not more) substantial evidence of associations between an infant's multiple attachments, especially across the infant's parents (Fox et al., 1991; Goossens & van IJzendoorn, 1990; Steele et al., 1996; van IJzendoorn & DeWolff, 1997).

As Fox et al. (1991) discussed in light of their meta-analytic findings of concordance between infant–mother and infant–father attachment, the two most compelling explanations of concordance of attachment across an infant's multiple caregivers center on (1) infant characteristics and (2) caregivers' shared child-rearing values and practices. There are limited data to address both of these arguments.

With respect to infant characteristics, concordance across an infant's multiple caregivers may be explained by the phenomenon of particular infant characteristics' "eliciting" the same type of caregiving and/or attachment strategy from different caregivers. One study addressed this possibility by examining the association between infant risk status (very low birthweight and prematurity) and the concordance of infant–mother and infant–father attachment (Easterbrooks, 1989). There was no association, however, between infant risk status and the extent of the match between infant–mother and infant–father attachment.

With respect to overlap in caregivers' childrea-

ring values and practices, Howes and Matheson (1992) reported stronger associations between child–mother and child–(nonparental) caregiver attachment when mothers' and caregivers' child-rearing values were more similar. In Steele et al.'s (1996) inquiry, however, it was not the case that when parents had similar AAI classifications (classifications that should have overlapped at least partially with their child-rearing values and practices), there was also greater concordance between infant–mother and infant–father attachment.

The evidence of concordance of attachment across an infant's multiple caregivers also raises the question of whether the quality of one attachment influences the quality of the other. According to Bowlby's concept of "monotropy," infants tend to have a principal attachment figure who is sought preferentially (above other attachment figures) as a secure base in times of trouble (Bowlby, 1958, 1969/1982). The attachment to the principal attachment figure may be more likely than other attachments to influence other bonds, including attachments to other caregivers. In Steele et al.'s (1996) study, which revealed concordance of infant–mother and infant–father attachment, one *post hoc,* empirically supported explanation was in fact that infant–mother attachment was influencing infant–father attachment.

Additional support for the notion that the principal attachment may be especially influential comes from the considerable number of inquiries suggesting a greater contribution from the child–mother attachment (usually the principal attachment) than from the child–father attachment to children's subsequent relationships. Furthermore, findings from more than one investigation have suggested that when children have a secure attachment to one attachment figure and an insecure attachment to another, children whose secure attachment is to their mothers are more socially competent than children whose secure attachment is to other caregivers (e.g., Howes, Rodning, Galuzzo, & Myers, 1988; Main & Weston, 1981).

The Concordance of Infant–Caregiver Attachments: Summary

In sum, the research on the concordance of infant–caregiver attachments has yielded evidence of both concordance and discordance, and has highlighted the importance of understanding the circumstances under which (1) a caregiver's children are similarly and dissimilarly attached and (2) an infant forms similar and dissimilar attachments to his or her caregivers. The key features of such circumstances are likely to include caregivers' child-rearing values and practices, caregivers' stress, and children's temperaments, with some temperamental characteristics (e.g., infant "difficultness") likely to be more influential than others. Echoing suggestions made in previous sections of this chapter, we also urge that researchers more carefully identify infants' attachments, affectional bonds, and nonaffectional bonds. Although most infants do become attached to their fathers, and although many may become attached to familiar child care providers, the bonds of infants to their secondary caregivers (be they mothers, fathers, or others) are not automatically attachments. Clarifying the nature of infants' bonds should help clarify the connections among them.

CONCLUSIONS

Our review of attachment theory and research on relations among relationships has revealed considerable support for the claims of attachment theory; it has also illuminated some inconsistencies that require further attention. More specifically, our review illustrates substantial evidence of associations between a secure infant–parent attachment and children's more harmonious and supportive relationships with siblings, friends, and peers, as well as preliminary though intriguing evidence of connections between infant–parent attachment and subsequent romantic and child-rearing relationships. Our review also demonstrates generally theoretically predictable relations between parents' other relationships and the infant–parent attachment. Our review of the work on the concordance of infant–caregiver attachments has revealed less consistent findings.

Taken as a whole, our review indicates some (albeit tentative) evidence of closer connections between attachments and affectional bonds than between attachments and nonaffectional bonds. Specifically, there is more consistent evidence of relations between infant–parent attachment and children's other *relationships* than between infant–parent attachment and their interactions with strangers. Similarly, parents' close relationships seem to contribute both more importantly and more directly to infant–parent attachment than does parents' more general social support.

These apparently differential associations, however, require more rigorous scrutiny. A recurrent theme in our suggestions for future research has in fact centered on the importance of investigators' distinguishing more clearly among people's nonaffectional bonds, affectional bonds, and attachments.

Another recurring theme in our suggestions for next steps concerns the need to understand more about the role of the infant–father attachment in both influencing and being influenced by other relationships. It may be that the infant–father attachment contributes less to other relationships (including other attachments) than does the infant–mother attachment. It may also be, however, that the infant–father attachment simply exerts a different type of influence than does the infant–mother attachment. Furthermore, these influences may differ by the sex of the infant. Chodorow (1978, 1989), for example, has drawn on psychoanalytic theory to argue convincingly that child–mother relationships exert quite different influences on the future relational tendencies of males and females (see also Gilligan, 1982). We suggest further inquiry into (1) attachment *to* males versus females, (2) attachments *of* males versus females, and (3) the interaction between the two (e.g., what are the implications for future relationships of father–son attachment vs. father–daughter attachment?). There is also some recent evidence that the infant–father attachment is influenced *by* the infant–mother attachment (Steele et al., 1996).

A third recurring suggestion for future attachment theory and research concerns the importance of understanding discontinuous and discordant relations among relationships. More specifically, the investigations of adults classified as "earned secure" illustrate that the influence of early attachments on other relationships can be altered. The studies of the influence of parents' other relationships on the infant–parent attachment, moreover, raise the possibility that subsequent attachment experiences (e.g., marriage, psychotherapy) can be a source of such changes. Researchers must illuminate further the points where established working models cease to guide behavior and new working models are forged. These points are also likely to be different for different people at different developmental periods under different circumstances, especially stressful circumstances. We propose that the continued examination of attachment discontinuities and of discordance in infant–parent attachment will be especially valuable in addressing these issues. For example, it would be intriguing to conduct case studies of families in which one or both parents' adult attachment classifications do *not* match the quality of the infant–parent attachment (see Slade et al., 1995, for findings relevant to this question).

In a related vein, Bretherton (1985) noted well over a decade ago that, given evidence of discordance between an infant's attachments to different caregivers, we need more information about the sequelae of discordance (see also Ainsworth, 1990). The following are some of the most critical questions: How are discordant working models of attachment integrated into an adult's "current state of mind"? What are the forces that facilitate and/or prevent such integration? Are people with discordant working models of attachment more susceptible to the influence of other relationships than people with concordant working models? Addressing these questions could help illuminate the parameters of the influence of various attachment relationships.

It is important to note the limits of the influence of attachment relationships, and indeed the limits of the influence of relationships, period. As Rutter (1995) has argued, "There is a need to consider . . . dyadic relationships in terms that go beyond attachment concepts and to consider social systems that extend beyond dyads" (p. 556; see also Cowan, 1997; Thompson, 1997). It is important to remember that attachment theory emphasizes one aspect of one relationship (the extent to which a parent provides his or her child with a secure base). Hinde (1976), for example, has provided a detailed taxonomy of various other important dimensions of relationships, and Dunn (e.g., 1988b) has focused on the connections between child–sibling relationships and other relationships (see also Dunn, 1988a, 1993). It would enrich attachment theory and research to incorporate some of these other approaches. For example, it would be interesting to contrast the contributions of the child–mother attachment and the child–sibling relationship to subsequent close relationships. Finally, it is essential to bear in mind that numerous factors that have nothing to do with relationships (attachment or otherwise) contribute importantly to the qualities of people's relationships. These include characteristics of the individual, such as temperamental reactivity, physical appearance, IQ, and athletic abilities; characteristics of the family, such as socioeconomic status; and characteristics of the environment, such as the safety of neighborhoods and cultural norms regarding relationships.

A final suggestion for understanding the contributions of attachment theory and research to understanding relations among relationships harkens back to the first volume of Bowlby's *Attachment and Loss* trilogy (Bowlby, 1969/1982) and reflects a renewed interest in the intersection of attachment and evolutionary theory (see Belsky, Chapter 7, this volume, and Simpson, Chapter 6, this volume). Specifically, given Bowlby's emphasis on the evolutionary adaptiveness of the infant–mother attachment, we suggest that it is important to question whether and how relations among relationships were evolutionarily adaptive. Belsky, Steinberg, and Draper (1991) have begun to address this question by arguing that connections between the infant–parent attachment and other relationships reflect "reproductive strategies" of mating and parenting that were originally developed to maximize individuals' reproductive fitness. Belsky (Chapter 7, this volume) has argued further that each of the three principal attachment patterns, with its accompanying relational tendencies, reflects a particular reproductive strategy. The questions of whether the existence of associations between early attachments and later relationships was ever or currently is evolutionarily adaptive require empirical attention. We hope that scholars will take up these and other questions raised in this chapter, in order to advance not only attachment theory and research, but also the broader understanding of relations among relationships.

ACKNOWLEDGMENTS

We thank Jay Belsky, Karlen Lyons-Ruth, Phil Shaver, and Ross Thompson for helpful comments on a previous draft of this chapter. Writing of this chapter was supported, in part, by grants to the second author from the National Institute on Mental Health (MH50773) and from the National Institute of Child Health and Development (HD36635).

REFERENCES

Ainsworth, M. D. S. (1989). Attachments beyond infancy. *American Psychologist, 44,* 709–716.
Ainsworth, M. D. S. (1990). Some considerations regarding theory and assessment relevant to attachment beyond in-

fancy. In M. T. Greenberg, D. Cicchetti, & E. Cummings (Eds.), *Attachment in the preschool years* (pp. 463–488). Chicago: University of Chicago Press.

Ainsworth, M. D. S., Blehar, M. C., Waters, E., & Wall, S. (1978). *Patterns of attachment.* Hillsdale, NJ: Erlbaum.

Ainsworth, M. D. S., & Marvin, R. (1995). On the shaping of attachment theory and research: An interview with Mary D. S. Ainsworth (Fall 1994). In E. Waters, B. E. Vaughn, G. Posada, & K. Kondo-Ikemura (Eds.), Caregiving, cultural, and cognitive perspectives on secure-base behavior and working models: New growing points of attachment theory and research. *Monograph of the Society for Research in Child Development, 60*(2–3, Serial No. 244), 3–21.

Arend, R. A., Gove, F. L., & Sroufe, L. A. (1979). Continuity of individual adaptation from infancy to kindergarten: A predictive study of ego-resiliency and curiosity in preschoolers. *Child Development, 50,* 950–959.

Baldwin, M. W. (1992). Relational schemas and the processing of social information. *Psychological Bulletin, 112,* 461–484.

Bandura, A. (1977). *Social learning theory.* Englewood Cliffs, NJ: Prentice-Hall.

Barnard, K. E., Magyary, D., Sumner, G., Booth, C. L., Mitchell, S. K., & Spieker, S. (1988). Prevention of parenting alterations for women with low social support. *Psychiatry, 51,* 248–253.

Bartholomew, K., & Horowitz, L. (1991). Attachment styles among young adults: A test of a four-category model. *Journal of Personality and Social Psychology, 61,* 226–244.

Bates, J., & Bayles, K. (1988). Attachment and the development of behavior problems. In J. Belsky & T. Nezworski (Eds.), *Clinical implications of attachment* (pp. 253–299). Hillsdale, NJ: Erlbaum.

Bates, J., Maslin, C. A., & Frankel, K. A. (1985). Attachment security, mother–child interaction, and temperament as predictors of behavior-problem ratings at age three years. In I. Bretherton & E. Waters (Eds.), Growing points of attachment theory and research. *Monographs of the Society for Research in Child Development, 50*(1–2, Serial No. 209), 167–193.

Beckwith, L. (1988). Intervention with disadvantaged parents of sick, preterm infants. *Psychiatry, 51,* 242–247.

Belsky, J. (1981). Early human experience: A family perspective. *Developmental Psychology, 17,* 3–23.

Belsky, J. (1984). The determinants of parenting: A process model. *Child Development, 55,* 83–96.

Belsky, J. (1996). Parent, infant, and social-contextual antecedents of father–son attachment security. *Child Development, 32,* 905–913.

Belsky, J. (1997). Theory testing, effect-size evaluation and differential susceptibility to rearing influence: The case of mothering and attachment. *Child Development, 64,* 598–600.

Belsky, J., & Cassidy, J. (1994). Attachment: Theory and evidence. In M. Rutter & D. Hay (Eds.), *Development through life* (pp. 373–402). Oxford: Blackwell.

Belsky, J., & Isabella, R. A. (1988). Maternal, infant, and social-contextual determinants of attachment security. In J. Belsky & T. Nezworski (Eds.), *Clinical implications of attachment* (pp. 41–94). Hillsdale, NJ: Erlbaum.

Belsky, J., Rosenberger, K., & Crnic, K. (1995). The origins of attachment security: "Classical" and contextual determinants. In S. Goldberg, R. Muir, & J. Kerr (Eds.), *Attachment theory: Social, developmental, and clinical per-*

spectives (pp. 153–184). Hillsdale, NJ: The Analytic Press.

Belsky, J., & Rovine, M. (1987). Temperament and attachment security in the strange situation: An empirical rapprochement. *Child Development, 58,* 787–795.

Belsky, J., Steinberg, L., & Draper, P. (1991). Childhood experience, interpersonal development, and reproductive strategy: An evolutionary theory of socialization. *Child Development, 62,* 647–670.

Berlin, L. J., Cassidy, J., & Belsky, J. (1995). Loneliness in young children and infant–mother attachment: A longitudinal study. *Merrill–Palmer Quarterly, 41,* 91–103.

Berlin, L. J., O'Neal, C. R., & Brooks-Gunn, J. (1998). What makes early intervention programs work?: The program, its participants, and their interaction. *Zero to Three, 18,* 4–15.

Booth, C. L., Mitchell, S. K., Barnard, K. E., & Spieker, S. (1989). Development of maternal social skills in multiproblem families: Effects on the mother–child relationship. *Developmental Psychology, 25,* 403–412.

Bowlby, J. (1953). *Child care and the growth of love.* Harmondsworth, England: Penguin Books.

Bowlby, J. (1958). The nature of the child's tie to his mother. *International Journal of Psycho-Analysis, 39,* 350–373.

Bowlby, J. (1969/1982). *Attachment and loss: Vol. 1. Attachment.* New York: Basic Books.

Bowlby, J. (1973). *Attachment and loss: Vol. 2. Separation.* New York: Basic Books.

Bowlby, J. (1979). *The making and breaking of affectional bonds.* London: Tavistock.

Bowlby, J. (1988). *A secure base.* New York: Basic Books.

Bretherton, I. (1985). Attachment theory: Retrospect and prospect. In I. Bretherton & E. Waters (Eds.), Growing points of attachment theory and research. *Monographs of the Society for Research in Child Development, 50*(1–2, Serial No. 209), 3–35.

Cassidy, J. (1988). Child–mother attachment and the self in six-year-olds. *Child Development, 59,* 121–134.

Cassidy, J. (1994). Emotion regulation: Influences of attachment relationships. In N. A. Fox (Ed.), Emotion regulation: Biological and behavioral considerations. *Monographs of the Society for Research in Child Development, 59*(2–3, Serial No. 240), 228–249.

Cassidy, J., & Berlin, L. J. (1994). The insecure/ambivalent pattern of attachment: Theory and research. *Child Development, 65,* 971–991.

Cassidy, J., & Berlin, L. J. (in press). Childhood loneliness: Understanding the origins of contributions of attachment theory. In K. J. Rotenberg & S. Hymel (Eds.), *Loneliness in childhood and adolescence.* New York: Cambridge University Press.

Cassidy, J., Kirsh, S., Scolton, K. L., & Parke, R. D. (1996). Attachment and representations of peer relationships. *Developmental Psychology, 32,* 892–904.

Cassidy, J., & Kobak, R. R. (1988). Avoidance and its relation to other defensive processes. In J. Belsky & T. Nezworski (Eds.), *Clinical implications of attachment* (pp. 300–323). Hillsdale, NJ: Erlbaum.

Chodorow, N. (1978). *The reproduction of mothering.* Berkeley: University of California Press.

Chodorow, N. (1989). *Feminism and psychoanalytic theory.* New Haven, CT: Yale University Press.

Cicchetti, D., & Tucker, D. (1994). Development and self-regulatory structures of the mind. *Development and Psychopathology, 6,* 533–549.

Cohn, D. A. (1990). Child–mother attachment of six-year-olds and social competence at school. *Child Development, 61,* 152–162.

Collins, N. L., & Read, S. J. (1990). Adult attachment, working models, and relationship quality in dating couples. *Journal of Personality and Social Psychology, 58,* 644–663.

Cowan, P. A. (1997). Beyond meta-analysis: A plea for a family systems view of attachment. *Child Development, 68,* 601–603.

Cowan, P. A., Cohn, D. A., Cowan, C. P., & Pearson, J. L. (1996). Parents' attachment histories and children's externalizing and internalizing behaviors: Exploring family systems models of linkages. *Journal of Consulting and Clinical Psychology, 64,* 53–63.

Crockenberg, S. (1981). Infant irritability, mother responsiveness, and social support influences on the security of infant–mother attachment. *Child Development, 52,* 857–865.

Crowell, J. A. (1990). *Close Relationship Interview.* Unpublished manuscript.

Crowell, J. A., & Treboux, D. (1995). A review of adult attachment measures: Implications for theory and research. *Social Development, 4,* 294–327.

Crnic, K., Greenberg, M. T., & Slough, N. M. (1986). Early stress and social support influences on mothers' and high-risk infants' functioning in late infancy. *Infant Mental Health Journal, 7,* 19–33.

Das Eiden, R., Teti, D. M., & Corns, K. M. (1995). Maternal working models of attachment, marital adjustment, and the parent–child relationship. *Child Development, 66,* 1504–1518.

DeMulder, E. K., & Radke-Yarrow, M. (1991). Attachment with affectively ill and well mothers: Concurrent behavioral correlates. *Development and Psychopathology, 3,* 227–242.

Downey, G., & Coyne, J. C. (1990). Children of depressed parents: An integrative review. *Psychological Bulletin, 108,* 50–76.

Duck, S. W. (Ed.). (1988). *Handbook of personal relationships.* New York: Wiley.

Dunn, J. (1988a). Relations among relationships. In S. W. Duck (Ed.), *Handbook of personal relationships* (pp. 193–209). New York: Wiley.

Dunn, J. (1988b). Connections between relationships: Implications of research on mothers and siblings. In R. A. Hinde & J. Stevenson-Hinde (Eds.), *Relationships within families: Mutual influences* (pp. 168–180). Oxford: Clarendon Press.

Dunn, J. (1993). *Young children's close relationships: Beyond attachment.* Newbury Park, CA: Sage.

Dunn, J., & Kendrick, C. (1982). *Siblings: Love, envy and understanding.* Cambridge, MA: Harvard University Press.

Durrett, M., Otaki, M., & Richards, P. (1984). Attachment and the mother's perception of support from the father. *International Journal of Behavioral Development, 7,* 167–176.

Easterbrooks, M. A. (1989). Quality of attachment to mother and to father: Effects of perinatal risk status. *Child Development, 60,* 825–830.

Elicker, J., Englund, M., & Sroufe, L. A. (1992). Predicting peer competence and peer relationships in childhood from early parent–child relationships. In R. D. Parke & G. W. Ladd (Eds.), *Family–peer relationships: Modes of linkages* (pp. 77–106). Hillsdale, NJ: Erlbaum.

Erickson, M. F., Korfmacher, J., & Egeland, B. (1992). At-

tachments past and present: Implications for therapeutic intervention with mother–infant dyads. *Development and Psychopathology, 4,* 495–507.

Erickson, M. F., Sroufe, L. A., & Egeland, B. (1985). The relation between quality of attachment and behavior problems in preschool in a high-risk sample. In I. Bretherton & E. Waters (Eds.), Growing points of attachment theory and research. *Monographs of the Society for Research in Child Development, 50*(1–2, Serial No. 209), 147–166.

Fagot, B., & Kavanagh, K. (1990). The prediction of antisocial behavior from avoidant attachment. *Child Development, 61,* 864–873.

Feeney, J. A., & Noller, P. (1990). Attachment style as a predictor of adult romantic relationships. *Journal of Personality and Social Psychology, 58,* 281–291.

Feldman, S., & Downey, G. (1994). Rejection sensitivity as a mediator of the impact of childhood exposure to family violence on adult attachment behavior. *Development and Psychopathology, 6,* 231–247.

Fonagy, P., Steele, H., & Steele, M. (1991). Maternal representations of attachment during pregnancy predict the organization of infant–mother attachment at one year of age. *Child Development, 62,* 891–905.

Fox, N. A., Kimmerly, N. L., & Schafer, W. D. (1991). Attachment to mother/attachment to father: A meta-analysis. *Child Development, 62,* 210–225.

Freitag, M., Belsky, J., Grossmann, K., Grossmann, K. E., & Scheuerer-Englisch, H. (1996). Continuity in parent–child relationships from infancy to middle childhood and relations with friendship competence. *Child Development, 67,* 1437–1454.

Frodi, A. (1983). Attachment behavior and sociability with strangers in premature and fullterm infants. *Infant Mental Health Journal, 4,* 14–22.

Frodi, A., Keller, B., Foye, H., Liptak, G., Bridges, L., Grolnick, W., Berko, J., McAnarney, E., & Lawrence, R. (1984). Determinants of attachment and mastery motivation in infants born to adolescent mothers. *Infant Mental Health Journal, 5,* 15–23.

Gallagher, J. J., & Ramey, C. T. (1987). *The malleability of children.* Baltimore: Paul H. Brookes.

George, C., Kaplan, N., & Main, M. (1985). *Adult Attachment Interview* (2nd ed.). Unpublished manuscript, University of California at Berkeley.

Gilligan, C. (1982). *In a different voice.* Cambridge, MA: Harvard University Press.

Goldberg, S., Perotta, M., & Minde, K. (1986). Maternal behavior and attachment in low-birth-weight twins and singletons. *Child Development, 57,* 34–46.

Goldberg, W. A., & Easterbrooks, M. A. (1984). The role of marital quality in toddler development. *Developmental Psychology, 20,* 504–514.

Gollin, E. S. (Ed.). (1981). *Developmental plasticity: Behavioral and biological aspects of variations in development.* New York: Academic Press.

Goossens, F., & van IJzendoorn, M. H. (1990). Quality of infants' attachments to professional caregivers: Relation to infant–parent attachment and day-care characteristics. *Child Development, 61,* 832–837.

Griffin, D., & Bartholomew, K. (1994). Models of self and other: Fundamental dimensions underlying measures of adult attachment. *Journal of Personality and Social Psychology, 67,* 430–445.

Grossmann, K. E., & Grossmann, K. (1991). Attachment quality as an organizer of emotional and behavioral responses in a longitudinal perspective. In C. M. Parkes, J.

Stevenson-Hinde, & P. Marris (Eds.), *Attachment across the life cycle* (pp. 93–114). London: Routledge.

Grossmann, K. E., Grossmann, K., Huber, F., & Wartner, U. (1981). German children's behavior towards their mothers at 12 months and their fathers at 18 months in Ainsworth's strange situation. *International Journal of Behavioral Development, 4,* 157–181.

Hartup, W., & Rubin, Z. (Eds.). (1986). *Relationships and development.* Hillsdale, NJ: Erlbaum.

Hazan, C., & Shaver, P. (1987). Romantic love conceptualized as an attachment process. *Journal of Personality and Social Psychology, 52,* 511–524.

Hazan, C., & Shaver, P. (1994). Attachment as an organizational framework for research on close relationships. *Psychological Inquiry, 5,* 1–22.

Hinde, R. A. (1976). On describing relationships. *Journal of Child Psychology and Psychiatry, 17,* 1–19.

Hinde, R. A., & Stevenson-Hinde, J. (Eds.). (1988). *Relationships within families: Mutual influences.* Oxford: Clarendon Press.

Horvath, A. O., & Symonds, B. D. (1991). Relation between working alliance and outcome in psychotherapy: A meta-analysis. *Journal of Consulting and Clinical Psychology, 38,* 139–149.

Howes, C., & Hamilton, C. E. (1992). Children's relationships with child care teachers: Stability and concordance with parental attachments. *Child Development, 63,* 867–878.

Howes, C., & Matheson, C. C. (1992). Contextual constraints on the concordance of mother–child and teacher–child relationships. In R. Pianta (Ed.), *New directions in child development: No. 57. Beyond the parent: The role of other adults in children's lives* (pp. 25–40). San Francisco: Jossey-Bass.

Howes, C., Matheson, C. C., & Hamilton, C. E. (1994). Maternal, teacher, and child care history correlates of children's relationships with peers. *Child Development, 65,* 264–273.

Howes, C., Rodning, C., Galluzzo, D. C., & Myers, L. (1988). Attachment and child care: Relationships with mother and caregiver. *Early Childhood Research Quarterly, 3,* 403–416.

Howes, P., & Markman, H. J. (1989). Marital quality and child functioning: A longitudinal investigation. *Child Development, 60,* 1044–1051.

Isabella, R. A. (1994). Origins of maternal role satisfaction and its influences upon maternal interactive behavior and infant–mother attachment. *Infant Behavior and Development, 17,* 381–387.

Isabella, R. A., & Belsky, J. (1985). Marital change during the transition to parenthood and security of infant–parent attachment. *Journal of Family Issues, 6,* 505–522.

Jacobson, J. L., & Frye, K. F. (1991). Effect of maternal social support on attachment: Experimental evidence. *Child Development, 62,* 572–582.

Jacobson, J. L., & Wille, D. E. (1986). The influence of attachment patterns on developmental changes in peer interaction from the toddler to the preschool period. *Child Development, 57,* 338–347.

Kerns, K. A. (1994). A longitudinal examination of links between mother–child attachment and children's friendships in early childhood. *Journal of Social and Personal Relationships, 11,* 379–381.

Kerns, K. A. (1996). Individual differences in friendship quality and their links to child–mother attachment. In W. M. Bukowski, A. F. Newcomb, & W. W. Hartup (Eds.), *The company they keep: Friendship in childhood and ado-*

lescence (pp. 137–157). New York: Cambridge University Press.

Kerns, K. A., Klepac, L., & Cole, A. (1996). Peer relationships and preadolescents' perceptions of security in the child–mother relationship. *Developmental Psychology, 32,* 457–466.

Kestenbaum, R., Farber, E., & Sroufe, L. A. (1989). Individual differences in empathy among preschoolers: Relation to attachment history. In N. Eisenberg (Ed.), *New directions in child development: No. 44. Empathy and related emotional responses* (pp. 51–64). San Francisco: Jossey-Bass.

King, B. B. (1970). Nobody loves me but my mother. On *Indianola Mississippi seeds.* Universal City, CA: MCA Records.

Kobak, R. R., & Sceery, A. (1988). Attachment in late adolescence: Working models, affect regulation, and representations of self and others. *Child Development, 59,* 135–146.

Korfmacher, J. (1998). Examining the service provider in early intervention. *Zero to Three, 18,* 17–22.

LaFreniere, P. J., & Sroufe, L. A. (1985). Profiles of peer competence in the preschool: Interrelations between measures, influence of social ecology, and relation to attachment history. *Developmental Psychology, 21,* 56–69.

Lamb, M., Hwang, C., Frodi, A., & Frodi, M. (1982). Security of mother– and father–infant attachment and its relation to sociability with strangers in traditional and non-traditional families. *Infant Behavior and Development, 5,* 355–367.

Lambermon, M. W. E., & van IJzendoorn, M. H. (1989). Influencing mother–baby interaction through videotaped or written instruction: Evaluation of a parent education program. *Early Childhood Research Quarterly, 4,* 449–459.

Levitt, M. J., Weber, R. A., & Clark, M. C. (1986). Social network relationships as sources of maternal support and well-being. *Developmental Psychology, 22,* 310–316.

Lewis, M., & Feiring, C. (1989). Early predictors of children's friendships. In T. J. Berndt & G. W. Ladd (Eds.), *Peer relationships in child development* (pp. 246–273). New York: Wiley.

Lewis, M., Feiring, C., McGuffog, C., & Jaskir, J. (1984). Predicting pathology in six-year-olds from early social relations. *Child Development, 55,* 123–136.

Lewis, M., Owen, M. T., & Cox, M. (1988). The transition to parenthood: III. Incorporation of the child into the family. *Family Press, 27,* 411–421.

Lieberman, A. F. (1977). Preschoolers' competence with a peer: Relations with attachment and peer experience. *Child Development, 48,* 1277–1287.

Lieberman, A. F., & Pawl, J. H. (1988). Clinical applications of attachment theory. In J. Belsky & T. Nezworski (Eds.), *Clinical implications of attachment* (pp. 327–351). Hillsdale, NJ: Erlbaum.

Lieberman, A. F., Weston, D. R., & Pawl, J. H. (1991). Preventive intervention and outcome with anxiously attached dyads. *Child Development, 62,* 199–209.

Lyons-Ruth, K. (1996). Attachment relationships among children with aggressive behavior problems: The role of disorganized early attachment patterns. *Journal of Consulting and Clinical Psychology, 64,* 64–73.

Lyons-Ruth, K., Alpern, L., & Repacholi, B. (1993). Disorganized infant attachment classification and maternal psychosocial problems as predictors of hostile–aggressive behavior in the preschool classroom. *Child Development, 64,* 572–585.

Lyons-Ruth, K., Botein, S., & Grunebaum, H. (1984). Reaching the hard-to-reach: Serving isolated and depressed mothers with infants in the community. In B. Cohen & J. Musick (Eds.), *New directions for mental health services: No. 24. Interventions with psychiatrically disabled parents and their young children* (pp. 95–122). San Francisco: Jossey-Bass.

Lyons-Ruth, K., Connell, D. B., Grunebaum, H., & Botein, S. (1990). Infants at social risk: Maternal depression and family support services as mediators of infant development and security of attachment. *Child Development, 61,* 85–98.

Maccoby, E. (1992). The role of parents in the socialization of children: An historical overview. *Developmental Psychology, 28,* 1006–1017.

Main, M. (1981). Avoidance in the service of attachment: A working paper. In K. Immelman, G. Barlow, M. Main, & L. Petrinovich (Eds.), *The Bielefeld interdisciplinary project* (pp. 651–693). New York: Cambridge University Press.

Main, M. (1990). Cross-cultural studies of attachment organization: Recent studies, changing methodologies, and the concept of conditional strategies. *Human Development, 33,* 48–61.

Main, M., & Goldwyn, R. (1984). Predicting rejection of her infant from mothers' representations of her own experience: Implications for the abused–abusing intergenerational cycle. *Child Abuse and Neglect, 8,* 203–217.

Main, M., & Goldwyn, R. (in press). Adult attachment rating and classification systems. In M. Main (Ed.), *A typology of human attachment organization assessed in discourse, drawings, and interviews.* New York: Cambridge University Press.

Main, M., Kaplan, N., & Cassidy, J. (1985). Security in infancy, childhood, and adulthood: A move to the level of representation. In I. Bretherton & E. Waters (Eds.), *Growing points of attachment theory and research. Monograph of the Society for Research in Child Development, 50*(1–2, Serial No. 209), 66–104.

Main, M., & Weston, D. (1981). The quality of the toddler's relationship to mother and to father: Related to conflict behavior and the readiness to establish new relationships. *Child Development, 52,* 932–940.

Malatesta-Magai, C. (1991). Emotional socialization: Its role in personality and developmental psychopathology. In D. Cicchetti & S. L. Toth (Eds.), *Rochester Symposium on Developmental Psychopathology: Vol. 3. Internalizing and externalizing expressions of dysfunction* (pp. 203–224). Hillsdale, NJ: Erlbaum.

Mikulincer, M., Florian, V., & Weller, A. (1993). Attachment styles, coping strategies, and post-traumatic psychological distress: The impact of the Gulf War in Israel. *Journal of Social and Personality Psychology, 64,* 817–826.

Nezworski, T., Belsky, J., & Tolan, W. J. (1988). Intervening in insecure infant attachment. In J. Belsky & T. Nezworski (Eds.), *Clinical implications of attachment* (pp. 352–386). Hillsdale, NJ: Erlbaum.

Park, K., & Waters, E. (1989). Security of attachment and preschool friendships. *Child Development, 60,* 1076–1081.

Parke, R. D. (1995). Fathers and families. In M. Bornstein (Ed.), *Handbook of parenting: Vol. 3. Status and social conditions of parenting* (pp. 27–63). Hillsdale, NJ: Erlbaum.

Parker, J., & Asher, S. R. (1987). Peer acceptance and later personal adjustment: Are low-accepted children at risk? *Psychological Bulletin, 102,* 357–389.

Parker, J., & Asher, S. R. (1993). Friendship and loneliness quality in middle childhood: Links with peer group acceptance and loneliness. *Developmental Psychology, 29,* 611–621.

Pastor, D. (1981). The quality of mother–infant attachment and its relationship to toddlers' initial sociability with peers. *Developmental Psychology, 17,* 326–335.

Pearson, J., Cohn, D. A., Cowan, P. A., & Cowan, C. P. (1994). Earned- and continuous-security in adult attachment: Relation to depressive symptomology and parenting style. *Development and Psychopathology, 6,* 359–373.

Phelps, J. L., Belsky., J., & Crnic, K. (1998). Earned-security, daily stress, and parenting: A comparison of five alternative models. *Development and Psychopathology, 10,* 21–38.

Piaget, J. (1954). *The construction of reality in the child.* New York: Basic Books.

Pierrehumbert, B., Iannotti, R. J., Cummings, E. M., & Zahn-Waxler, C. (1989). Social functioning with mother and peers at 2 and 5 years: The influence of attachment. *International Journal of Behavioral Development, 12,* 85–100.

Plomin, R. (1986). *Development, genetics, and psychology.* Hillsdale, NJ: Erlbaum.

Plunkett, J., Klein, T., & Meisels, S. (1988). The relationship of preterm infant–mother attachment to stranger sociability at 3 years. *Infant Behavior and Development, 11,* 83–96.

Renken, B., Egeland, B., Marvinney, D., Mangelsdorf, S., & Sroufe, L. A. (1989). Early childhood antecedents of aggression and passive-withdrawal in early elementary school. *Journal of Personality, 57,* 257–282.

Rutter, M. (1995). Clinical implications of attachment concepts: Retrospect and prospect. *Journal of Child Psychology and Psychiatry, 36,* 549–571.

Sagi, A., Lamb, M. E., Lewkowicz, K. S., Shoham, R., Dvir, R., & Estes, D. (1985). Security of infant–mother, –father, and –metapelet attachments among kibbutz-reared Israeli children. In I. Bretherton & E. Waters (Eds.), *Growing points of attachment theory and research. Monographs of the Society for Research in Child Development, 50*(1–2, Serial No. 209), 257–275.

Sagi, A., van IJzendoorn, M. H., Avizer, O., Donnell, F., Koren-Karie, N., Joels, T., & Harel, Y. (1995). Attachments in a multiple-caregiver and multiple-infant environment: The case of the Israeli kibbutzim. In E. Waters, B. E. Vaughn, G. Posada, & K. Kondo-Ikemura (Eds.), *Caregiving, cultural, and cognitive perspectives on secure-base behavior and working models: New growing points of attachment theory and research. Monographs of the Society for Research in Child Development, 60*(1–2, Serial No. 244), 71–91.

Shaver, P. R., & Hazan, C. (1993). Adult romantic attachment: Theory and evidence. In D. Perlman & W. Jones (Eds.), *Advances in personal relationships* (Vol. 4, pp. 29–70). London: Jessica Kingsley.

Shaver, P. R., Hazan, C., & Bradshaw, D. (1988). Love as attachment: The integration of three behavioral systems. In R. Sternberg & M. L. Barnes (Eds.), *The psychology of love* (pp. 68–99). New Haven, CT: Yale University Press.

Shaw, D., Owens, E. B., Vondra, J., Keenan, K., & Winslow, E. B. (1996). Early risk factors and pathways in the development of early disruptive behavior problems. *Development and Psychopathology, 8,* 679–699.

Shulman, S., Elicker, J., & Sroufe, L. A. (1994). Stages of friendship growth in preadolescence as related to attachment history. *Journal of Social and Personal Relationships, 11,* 341–361.

Siegel, D. (1999). *The developing mind: Toward a neurobiology of interpersonal experience.* New York: Guilford Press.

Simpson, J. A. (1990). Influence of attachment styles on romantic relationships. *Journal of Personality and Social Psychology, 59,* 971–980.

Simpson, J. A., Rholes, W. S., & Nelligan, J. S. (1992). Support seeking and support giving within couples in an anxiety-provoking situation: The role of attachment styles. *Journal of Personality and Social Psychology, 62,* 434–446.

Slade, A., Belsky, J., Aber, J. L., & Phelps, J. L. (in press). Maternal representations of the relationship with their toddlers: Links to adult attachment and observed mothering. *Developmental Psychology.*

Slade, A., Dermer, M., Gerber, J., Gibson, L., Graf, F., Siegel, N., & Tobias, K. (1995). Prenatal representation, dyadic interaction, and quality of attachment. In A. Slade (Chair), *Mothers' representations of relationships assessed prenatally: Predictions to maternal and child development.* Symposium conducted at the biennial meeting of the Society for Research in Child Development, Indianapolis, IN.

Solomon, J., George, C., & De Jong, A. (1995). Children classified as controlling at age six: Evidence of disorganized representational strategies and aggression at home and at school. *Development and Psychopathology, 7,* 447–463.

Spieker, S. J., & Bensley, L. (1994). Roles of living arrangements and grandmother social support in adolescent mothering and infant attachment. *Developmental Psychology, 30,* 102–111.

Spieker, S. J., & Booth, C. L. (1988). Maternal antecedents of attachment quality. In J. Belsky & T. Nezworski (Eds.), *Clinical implications of attachment* (pp. 95–135). Hillsdale, NJ: Erlbaum.

Sroufe, L. A. (1988). The role of infant–caregiver attachment in development. In J. Belsky & T. Nezworski (Eds.), *Clinical implications of attachment* (pp. 18–38). Hillsdale, NJ: Erlbaum.

Sroufe, L. A., Egeland, B., & Kreutzer, T. (1990). The fate of early experience following developmental change: Longitudinal approaches to individual adaptation in childhood. *Child Development, 61,* 1363–1373.

Sroufe, L. A., & Fleeson, J. (1986). Attachment and the construction of relationships. In W. W. Hartup & Z. Rubin (Eds.), *Relationships and development* (pp. 51–71). Hillsdale, NJ: Erlbaum.

Sroufe, L. A., & Fleeson, J. (1988). The coherence of family relationships. In R. A. Hinde & J. Stevenson-Hinde (Eds.), *Relationships within families: Mutual influences* (pp. 27–47). Oxford: Clarendon Press.

Steele, H., Steele, M., & Fonagy, P. (1996). Associations among attachment classifications of mothers, fathers, and their infants. *Child Development, 67,* 541–555.

Stevenson-Hinde, J., & Shouldice, A. (1995). Maternal interactions and self-reports related to attachment classifications at 4.5 years. *Child Development, 66,* 583–596.

Suess, G. J., Grossmann, K. E., & Sroufe, L. A. (1992). Effects of infant attachment to mother and father on quality of adaptation in preschool: From dyadic to individual organization of self. *International Journal of Behavioral Development, 15,* 43–65.

Suomi, S. J. (1997). Early determinants of behavior: Evidence from primate studies. *British Medical Bulletin, 53,* 170–184.

Szajnberg, N. M., Skrinjaric, J., & Moore, A. (1989). Affect attunement, attachment, temperament, and zygosity: A twin study. *Journal of the American Academy of Child and Adolescent Psychiatry, 28,* 249–253.

Teti, D. M., & Ablard, K. (1989). Security of attachment and infant–sibling relationships. *Child Development, 60,* 1519–1528.

Teti, D. M., Gelfand, D. M., Messinger, D. S., & Isabella, R. (1995). Maternal depression and the quality of early attachment: An examination of infants, preschoolers, and their mothers. *Developmental Psychology, 31,* 364–376.

Teti, D. M., Nakagawa, M., Das, R., & Wirth, O. (1991). Security of attachment between preschoolers and their mothers: Relations among social interaction, parenting stress, and mothers' sorts of the Attachment Q-Set. *Developmental Psychology, 27,* 440–447.

Teti, D. M., Sakin, J. W., Kucera, E., Corns, K., & Das Eiden, R. (1996). And baby makes four: Predictors of attachment security among preschool-aged firstborns during the transition to siblinghood. *Child Development, 67,* 579–596.

Thompson, R. A. (1997). Sensitivity and security: New questions to ponder. *Child Development, 68,* 595–597.

Thompson, R. A., & Lamb, M. E. (1983). Security of attachment and stranger sociability in infancy. *Developmental Psychology, 19,* 184–191.

Troy, M., & Sroufe, L. A. (1987). Victimization among preschoolers: The role of attachment relationship history. *Journal of the American Academy of Child and Adolescent Psychiatry, 26,* 166–172.

Turner, P. J. (1991). Relations between attachment, gender, and behavior with peers in preschool. *Child Development, 62,* 1475–1488.

van den Boom, D. (1994). The influence of temperament and mothering on attachment and exploration: An experimental manipulation of sensitive responsiveness among lower-class mothers with irritable infants. *Child Development, 65,* 1457–1477.

van den Boom, D. (1995). Do first-year intervention effects endure?: Follow-up during toddlerhood of a sample of Dutch irritable infants. *Child Development, 66,* 1798–1816.

van IJzendoorn, M. H. (1995). Adult attachment representations, parental responsiveness, and infant attachment: A meta-analysis on the predictive validity of the Adult Attachment Interview. *Psychological Bulletin, 117,* 387–403.

van IJzendoorn, M. H., & deWolff, M. S. (1997). In search of the absent father: Meta-analysis of infant–father attachment. A rejoinder to our discussants. *Child Development, 68,* 604–609.

van IJzendoorn, M. H., Juffer, F., & Duyvesteyn, M. G. C. (1995). Breaking the intergenerational cycle of insecure attachment: A review of the effects of attachment-based interventions on maternal sensitivity and infant security. *Journal of Child Psychology and Psychiatry, 36,* 225–248.

Volling, B., & Belsky, J. (1992). The contribution of mother–child and father–child relationships to the quality of sibling interaction: A longitudinal study. *Child Development, 63,* 1209–1222.

Wachs, T. D., & Gruen, G. E. (1982). *Early experience and human development.* New York: Plenum Press.

Ward, M. J., Vaughn, B. E., & Robb, M. R. (1988). Social-emotional adaptation and infant–mother attachment in siblings: Role of the mother in cross-sibling consistency. *Child Development, 59,* 643–651.

Wartner, U., Grossmann, K., Fremmer-Bombik, E., & Suess, G. (1994). Attachment patterns at age six in south Germany: Predictability from infancy and implications for preschool behavior. *Child Development, 65,* 1014–1027.

Waters, E., Wippman, J., & Sroufe, L. A. (1979). Attachment, positive affect, and competence in the peer group: Two studies in construct validation. *Child Development, 50,* 821–829.

Weber, A., & Harvey, J. (Eds.). (1994). *Perspectives on close relationships.* Needham Heights, MA: Allyn & Bacon.

Youngblade, L. M., & Belsky, J. (1992). Parent–child an- tecedents of 5-year-olds' close friendships: A longitudinal analysis. *Developmental Psychology, 28,* 700–713.

Youngblade, L. M., Park, K., & Belsky, J. (1993). Measurement of young children's close friendships: A comparison of two independent assessment systems and their associations with attachment security. *International Journal of Behavioral Development, 16,* 563–587.

Zeanah, C., Benoit, D., Barton, M., Regan, C., Hirshberg, L. M., & Lipsitt, L. P. (1993). Representations of attachment in mothers and their one-year-old infants. *Journal of the American Academy of Child and Adolescent Psychiatry, 32,* 278–286.

31

Cross-Cultural Patterns
of Attachment

Universal and Contextual Dimensions

❖

MARINUS H. VAN IJZENDOORN
ABRAHAM SAGI

It was in Uganda, a former British protectorate in East Africa, that Mary Ainsworth (1967) began to create the famous tripartite classification system of "avoidant" (A), "secure" (B), and "resistant" or "ambivalent" (C) infant–mother attachment relationships. In her short-term longitudinal field study, carried out in 1954–1955, she found three patterns of attachment behavior in a small sample of 28 infants. The "securely attached group," consisting of 16 children, cried infrequently and seemed especially content when they were with their mothers. Secure children also used their mothers as a safe base from which to explore the environment. The "insecurely attached group," consisting of 7 babies, cried frequently, not only when left alone by their mothers but also in the mothers' presence; they cried to be picked up and then cried when they were put down. These babies wanted continuous physical contact with their mothers, but at the same time seemed ambivalent about their presence. A "nonattached" group consisting of 5 infants responded similarly to their mothers and to other adults. For example, they were not upset about being left alone by their mothers and did not respond to the mothers' return in any specific way. In fact, from Ainsworth's detailed case studies of these 5 nonattached infants, it can be inferred that in the strange situation procedure (Ains-

worth, Blehar, Waters, & Wall, 1978) they would have been classified as avoidant.

Ainsworth's Uganda study raised some important cross-cultural issues, the first being the universality of the infant–mother attachment relationship and the tripartite classification system. The second issue was the universality of the nomological network surrounding the concept of attachment. Ainsworth (1967) clearly initiated her famous Baltimore study to test the replicability of her Uganda results in another, Western culture. In so doing, she was particularly interested in documenting the crucial role of maternal sensitivity as an antecedent of attachment. The third issue raised by the Uganda research was the culture-specific or contextual dimension of attachment development. It is surprising to see that even in the Uganda study, the presence of multiple caretakers did not interfere with the development of a secure attachment (Weisner & Gallimore, 1977). After Bowlby's (1951; see also Robertson & Robertson, 1971) report on the disastrous effects of fragmented institutional care, the Uganda study showed for the first time that the decisive factors for attachment security were not the number of caretakers per se, but the continuity and quality of the mother–infant interaction. Ainsworth (1967) considered her study as the beginning of a cross-cultural search for antecedents and sequelae of attachment security. The question now is this: What results have four decades of cross-cultural attachment research yielded?

Cross-cultural attachment research has been using the "etic" approach more often than the "emic" approach (Jackson, 1993; van IJzendoorn, 1990). Pike (1967) derived the terms "emic" and "etic" from the two different approaches to the study of sound in language: "phonemics" and "phonetics." Phonetics concerns the sound characteristics of language that are supposed to be universal, whereas phonemics concerns the meaningful, and therefore culture-specific, sound properties of a language. In cross-cultural research, the "etic" approach leads to an emphasis on theories and assessments that have been developed in a specific culture (often a Western, industrialized society). These theories and assessments are then applied in other cultures to test whether the phenomena under scrutiny are really cross-culturally valid rather than culture-specific. The "emic" approach focuses on social and behavioral configurations and developmental trajectories that are specific to the culture, and it tries to understand this culture from within its own frame of reference (see also Berry, 1969).

Most cross-cultural attachment research can be characterized as "etic," because in many cases Bowlby's conceptualization of attachment and Ainsworth's operationalization of attachment have been applied to various non-Western cultures. One of the reasons for this "etic" emphasis may be the ethological foundation of attachment theory. Because attachment processes have also been observed in nonhuman primates and in other species, Bowlby (1969/1982) suggested that the formation of an attachment relationship between infants and their protective caregivers is the outcome of evolution; "inclusive fitness" (Trivers, 1974) was deemed to be facilitated by an innate bias to become attached to a conspecific (see Belsky, Chapter 7, and Simpson, Chapter 6, this volume). Therefore, a core element of attachment theory is the idea of the universality of this bias in infants to become attached, regardless of their specific cultural niche.

From this universality thesis, however, it does not follow that the development of attachment is insensitive to culture-specific influences and idiosyncrasies. On the contrary, the evolutionary perspective leaves room for globally adaptive behavioral propensities that are realized in a specific way, depending on the cultural niche in which children have to survive (Hinde & Stevenson-Hinde, 1990, 1991). If a cultural niche requires the suppression of negative emotions, infants may develop an avoidant attachment pattern to meet this cultural demand. In such a culture, the avoidant attachment pattern may well be normative in the sense that it promotes inclusive fitness and general adaptation, and it may be observed in the majority of cases. That is, the universality thesis predicts only that attachment bonds will be established in any known culture, regardless of child-rearing arrangements and family constellations. It does not imply that one of the three principal attachment patterns is universally normative; evolution may not have equipped human beings with rigid behavioral strategies that would have made it difficult to adapt to changing (natural and social) environments (see Belsky, Chapter 7, and Simpson, Chapter 6, this volume). Nevertheless, one may wonder whether the secure attachment pattern is the primary strategy for adapting to a social environment that is basically supportive of the infant, and whether the insecure strategies should be considered as secondary, in that they constitute deviating but adaptive patterns provoked by less supportive contexts (Main, 1990).

In this chapter, we describe and evaluate the cross-cultural attachment studies that have followed Ainsworth's Uganda example. We limit our discussion to cultures other than the Anglo-Saxon and European cultures. The outcomes of attachment studies in the major English-speaking countries and Europe are of course presupposed in the "etic" application of attachment theory and assessments to non-Western cultures, but we refer to other chapters in this volume for reviews (see Belsky, Chapter 12; Thompson, Chapter 13; and Weinfield, Sroufe, Egeland, & Carlson, Chapter 4). In particular, we presuppose the following findings:

1. In Western countries all infants become attached to one or more specific (parental or nonparental) caregivers, except perhaps in the most extreme cases of neurophysiological impairments, such as extreme mental retardation. For the purpose of cross-cultural research, this finding may be translated into the "universality hypothesis."

2. In Western societies the majority of infants are securely attached, although a considerable number of infants (up to 40%) have been found to be insecurely attached (van IJzendoorn &

Kroonenberg, 1988; van IJzendoorn, Sagi, & Lambermon, 1992), and the number of secure infants may vary considerably across samples within a culture (e.g., Grossmann, Grossmann, Huber, & Wartner, 1981). In stressful circumstances, secure infants appear to settle more easily than insecure infants, as shown by several psychophysiological studies (Hertsgaard, Gunnar, Erickson, & Nachmias, 1995; I. Soarez, personal communication, August, 1996; Spangler & Grossmann, 1993; Verweij-Tijsterman, 1996). Secure attachment therefore seems to be normative in both the numerical and the physiological senses; this may be called the "normativity hypothesis."

3. Attachment security is dependent on child-rearing antecedents, particularly sensitive and prompt responses to the infants' attachment signals, although other factors may be relevant as well (DeWolff & van IJzendoorn, 1997; van IJzendoorn & DeWolff, 1997). The causal relation between sensitive child rearing and attachment security has been documented in several experimental intervention studies (van IJzendoorn, Juffer, & Duyvesteyn, 1995). This is the "sensitivity hypothesis."

4. Attachment security leads to differences in children's competence to regulate their negative emotions (absence of aggression, ego control; Cassidy, 1994), to establish satisfactory relationships with peers and teachers (Bretherton, 1991), and to develop cognitive abilities (emergent literacy, meta-cognition; for reviews, see Meins, 1997; van IJzendoorn, Dijkstra, & Bus, 1995). This is the "competence hypothesis."

The universality, normativity, sensitivity, and competence hypotheses constitute the core hypotheses of attachment theory (Ainsworth et al., 1978; Belsky & Cassidy, 1995; Bowlby, 1969/1982; Bretherton, 1985, 1991; Main, 1990; van IJzendoorn, 1990). "Etic" studies on attachment in various cultures may be heuristically fruitful in documenting (1) the universality of attachment in infancy, (2) the culture-specific dimensions and normativity of the three attachment patterns, and (3) the generalizability of the nomological network of attachment-related constructs across cultures (see Main, 1990, and van IJzendoorn, 1990, for preliminary analyses). From this point on, we discuss attachment studies in several non-European, non-Anglo-Saxon societies: various African cultures, the People's Republic of China, Israel, and Japan. The time has come to describe, evaluate, and integrate the growing points and directions in the cross-cultural study of attachment.

INFANT–MOTHER ATTACHMENT IN A NETWORK OF CAREGIVERS: THE AFRICAN CASE

In her Uganda study, Ainsworth (1967, 1977) described the development of attachment in a multiple-caregiver context. Even in a child-rearing environment in which mothers share their caregiving responsibilities with several other adults and older children, infants nevertheless become attached to their mothers and use them as a secure base to explore the world. The Uganda study, however, was rather small and exploratory, and certainly not representative of the various African cultures (Jackson, 1993).

In this section we discuss some other studies of attachment in Africa, conducted in the years following Ainsworth's (1967) research. We place special emphasis on child development in a network of (child and adult) caregivers, in order to test the idea that a multiple-caregiver environment is in no way incompatible with a unique attachment relationship between child and parent. Attachment in a network of multiple caregivers is of crucial importance, because cross-cultural evidence shows that in most societies nonparental caretaking is either the norm or a frequent form (Weisner & Gallimore, 1977). Only a few studies on attachment in Africa have been published as yet, and of course they cannot be considered representative of the vast African continent. Nevertheless, they may provide cumulative evidence for some of the core hypotheses of attachment theory.

The Gusii Study

Child rearing among the Gusii of Kenya is different from child rearing in Western, industrialized countries in at least two ways. First, mothers share their child-rearing tasks and responsibilities with other caregivers to a larger extent than in many other non-Western cultures; in particular, child caregivers such as older siblings take care of the infants during a large part of the day. Second, the division of tasks between mothers and other caregivers is rather strict, in that mothers provide most of the physical care and are responsible for their children's health, whereas the activities of child caregivers are limited to social and playful interactions (Kermoian & Leiderman, 1986). The strict division of caregiving tasks between mothers and other caregivers provided Kermoian and Leiderman with the opportunity to test whether different attachment relationships would develop between an infant and his or her mother and between that infant and another caregiver, as well as whether the influence of a specific attachment relationship would be restricted to a specific area of competence.

Kermoian and Leiderman (1986) included 26 families in their study, with infants between the ages of 8 and 27 months (mean age: 14½ months). Outside each mother's hut, a modified strange situation procedure was implemented, with two separation–reunion episodes for mother, caregiver, and stranger each. The lack of a strange laboratory environment was meant to be compensated for by the extra separations.

Gusii infants are used to being greeted with a handshake by their mothers and caretakers. During the reunions, the Gusii infants anticipated the handshake in the same way as North American or European infants anticipate a hug. The secure Gusii infants would reach out to an adult with one arm, to receive the handshake enthusiastically, whereas the insecure infants would avoid the adult or reach and then pull away after the adult approached. The insecure children's exploratory behavior was also different: They explored the environment visually instead of manipulatively.

Although the Gusii infants used culture-specific attachment behaviors to express their emotions about the separations and reunions, the patterns of attachment were comparable with Western findings. Sixteen of the infants (61%) were classified as securely attached to their mothers at the first assessment, and 14 infants (54%) were classified as securely attached to their nonmaternal caregivers. Kermoian and Leiderman (1986) did not differentiate between the two insecure categories. The percentages of secure infants are almost identical to the findings in a Dutch study on infants' attachment to mothers, fathers, and professional caregivers (Goossens & van IJzendoorn, 1990). The authors concluded that the development of differential or person-specific attachment behaviors for "polymatric" infants is similar to that observed in "monomatric" Western societies (Reed & Leiderman, 1981).

Because the mothers developed their attachment relationship with their infants in the context of physical care, it was expected that attachment security with mothers would be related to the infants' health status. The child caregivers developed their bond with the infants in the context of stimulating social, verbal, and playful interactions, and attachment security with the caregivers was therefore expected to be associated with the infants' cognitive-developmental status. Indeed, the infants who were securely attached to their nonmaternal caregivers had higher scores on the Bayley Scales of Infant Development than the insecurely attached infants. For the infant–mother relationship, there was no association between security and cognitive development. Furthermore, the nutritional or health status of the infants was related to the security of the infant–mother attachment and not to the security of the infant–caregiver attachment. Infants who were securely attached to their mothers had a recent history of higher nutritional status than insecurely attached infants. In this respect, the infant–caregiver bond appeared to be irrelevant. Thus attachment security appeared to have a different impact on the infants' development, depending on the context in which the bond emerged. (In the section below on the Israeli kibbutzim, we report a similar finding.) Kermoian and Leiderman (1986) suggested that the pervasive influence of the infant–mother attachment relationship in Western cultures may be caused by the absence of role differentiation and task division in most Western families.

The Gusii study also provided some evidence in favor of the sensitivity hypothesis. Kermoian and Leiderman (1986) hypothesized that mothers would be more sensitive to the signals of their infants if they were older, because Gusii women gain status with age, and thus older mothers might be more likely to be emotionally balanced themselves. Furthermore, in a larger household the mothers would be able to share their burden of tasks with more people, and therefore would be able to devote more time and energy to their infants. Lastly, the birth of a new baby was expected to decrease a mother's sensitivity to her older infant (Trivers, 1974). As predicted, maternal age and household density were associated with infants' secure attachment to their mothers. Similar correlations were absent in the case of the caregivers. The birth of a new baby increased the risk for insecure attachment. These results support the cross-cultural validity of the sensitivity hypothesis.

The Hausa Study

The Hausa, who populate a large market town in Nigeria, represent a polymatric culture in which the distribution of child care tasks is somewhat less strict than in the Gusii. Because Hausa men (as Muslims) are allowed to marry as many as four wives, and because these wives do not have to work in the fields, polymatric care is provided mainly by adult caregivers instead of child caregivers. An average of four caregivers share with the mothers the tasks of social, verbal, and playful interactions. Mothers also contribute to a substantial part of these activities. The biological mothers, however, take almost complete responsibility for physical care activities, such as feeding and bathing (Marvin, VanDevender, Iwanaga, LeVine, & LeVine, 1977). Agriculture is the main economy in this flat-savannah, orchard-bush part of the country. The Hausa live in small, round, walled compounds with separate huts for each of the wives. In the middle of each compound is an open common cooking and working area, where open fires and freely accessible tools and other utensils constitute a continuous risk for infants.

Marvin et al. (1977) included 18 infants in their descriptive study, which focused on the occurrence of attachment and exploratory behaviors in the natural setting. When not asleep, these Hausa infants were almost always in close physical contact with or in close proximity to one or more adult caregivers. The infants were not allowed to explore the wider environment alone, because of the dangers involved. The high social density of the Hausa compound led to prompt adult or older sibling responses to any infant attachment signals, such as crying. The Hausa caregivers therefore appeared to be indulgent and sensitive, and at the same time restrictive toward their infants, who were not allowed to move around freely. The restriction of locomotion also led to a different use of adult caregivers as a secure base: Hausa infants explored their immediate environment in visual and manipulative ways, but only in close proximity to an attachment figure, and they ceased to explore as soon as the caregiver had left. The Hausa infants studied by Marvin et al. thus differed from Western infants not only in their preference for manipulative exploration, but also in their use of passive or signaling attachment behaviors, instead of more active proximity-seeking or following behaviors. Nevertheless, the Hausa infants clearly appeared to use adult caregivers as safe bases from which to explore, and they differentiated between attachment figures and strangers.

Furthermore, all infants displayed attachment behavior to more than one caregiver, and on the average they appeared to be attached to three or four different figures, including their fathers. Although they were raised in a network of attachment relationships, most Hausa infants were primarily attached to one attachment figure, to whom they addressed their attachment behaviors most frequently. This principal attachment figure was in most cases the person who held the baby most and who otherwise interacted with him or her most frequently (Marvin et al., 1977). The most important attachment figure was not necessarily the biological mother. Unfortunately, Marvin et al. (1977) did not use the Ainsworth tripartite system to classify the infant–caregiver relationships. It is therefore unclear how attachment security was affected by the prompt and sensitive responses to the infants' signals. However, the Hausa study clearly documents the existence of multiple attachments in a multiple-caregiver context, as well as the infants' preference for one of the attachment figures. The Hausa study provides further support for the universality hypothesis, and shows how attachment serves to protect infants from the dangers of their environment. The culture-specific attachment and exploratory behaviors appear to leave room for the universal occurrence of the secure-base phenomenon.

The Dogon Study

In a more recent crosscultural study of 26 mothers and their 1-year-old infants, True (1994), in cooperation with Pisani and Oumar, tested the hypothesis that secure and insecure dyads among the Dogon of Mali (West Africa) would be characterized by different communication patterns in attachment-related circumstances. Traditionally, the Dogon economy is based on subsistence farming of a single crop, millet, which makes the members of the Dogon society vulnerable to malnutrition. The sample included in True's study was derived from a more acculturated and economically diverse town population. With a few exceptions, these infants were living in compounds with their extended families. The fathers usually had children with several wives. During the first year of their lives, the infants were nursed by their biological mothers. Maternal care was supplemented with care from siblings and other family members (True, 1994). In particular with a firstborn male infant, the primary caregiver during the day was the paternal grandmother; however, the mother was available when the child was hungry, and the mother slept at night with the infant. For other infants, the mothers were mainly responsible during the day and night, but they readily shared the child care with female relatives or older children. Infant mortality was high during the first years of life: 25% of the children did not survive the first 5 years. This threatening ecology may have been one of the reasons why these Dogon mothers breast-fed their infants on demand and very frequently, and kept them in close proximity almost all the time. Physical interaction was favored above verbal or visual interaction, and infant distress signals were met with immediate responses. The process of weaning during the end of the second year was gradual, with fathers and older siblings becoming more important (True, 1994).

The Dogon dyads were filmed in the traditional strange situation procedure, and they were also observed twice in the stressful setting of a standardized well-baby examination, the Weigh-In. For the first time in cross-cultural research in Africa, not only were the strange situation data classified into the classic tripartite A-B-C system, but the additional coding system for disorganized/disoriented attachment behaviors (Main & Solomon, 1990; see Lyons-Ruth & Jacobvitz, Chapter 23; George & Solomon, Chapter 28, this volume) was also applied. The Weigh-In setting was used to assess the communication patterns of the infant–mother dyads during a stressful but naturalistic situation. The mutual orientation ("directness") and cooperation between mothers and infants were rated, and scales assessing violations of communication (e.g., infant avoidance of the mother or maternal withdrawal from the infant) were applied. The most extreme score of a dyad on the communication violation scales was used post hoc to calculate a summary rating (True, 1994).

The Dogon study showed a high percentage of disorganized infants (23%), compared to the percentages in normal Western samples (15–20%). The percentage of secure infant–mother dyads was also high (69%), whereas the avoidant classification appeared to be absent, and few resistant infant–mother dyads were found (8%). True (1994) also "forced" the infants into the best-fitting attachment classification of the tripartite coding system, regardless of the disorganized behaviors (see Lyons-Ruth & Jacobvitz, Chapter 23, this volume). The forced attachment classification distribution was as follows: 88% secure, 12% resistant, and 0% avoidant. The study supports the universality hypothesis in showing how the strange situation procedure remains classifi-

able with the A-B-C-D coding system, even in an African culture. Furthermore, True also demonstrated that the majority of her participants were classified as securely attached, which provides some further cross-cultural evidence for the normativity hypothesis.

To explain the lack of avoidant attachments, True (1994) hypothesized that the strange situation procedure in the Dogon society may have been experienced as highly stressful instead of mildly stressful. The stress of two separations from the mother and two encounters with a stranger may have forced the avoidant infants to seek proximity, and may also have increased the number of disorganized infants. The association between attachment security and communication violations, however, only partly supports this argument. True found a negative correlation ($r = -.40$) between attachment and communication: that is, secure infant–mother dyads were less likely to violate the rules of open communication than were the insecure infant–mother dyads. This outcome is in line with findings in Western societies, and therefore supports the validity of the strange situation in the Dogon society. This post hoc outcome was, however, limited to part of the sample—that is, to those participants who did not show strong avoidance in the Weigh-In and therefore were unable to violate communication rules (True, 1994).

The Environment of Evolutionary Adaptedness: The !Kung and Efé Studies

Bowlby (1969/1982) developed his evolutionary theory of attachment on the basis of speculations about child development and child rearing in the original environment in which the human species spent about 99% of its historical time as hunters and gatherers. In this "environment of evolutionary adaptedness," an infant would be protected against predators and other dangers by staying in close proximity to a protective adult. Only a few societies are left that might resemble this original way of living, and still fewer have been studied from the viewpoint of attachment. Konner's (1977) study of the !Kung San or Bushmen of northwestern Botswana, and Morelli and Tronick's (1991) study on the Efé or Pygmies of the Ituri forest in northeastern Zambia, are outstanding examples of attachment research on hunter–gatherer societies. Hunters and gatherers are characterized by their living in small seminomadic groups with a fluid group structure, absence of strict social rules, and flexible subsistence strategies (Konner, 1977).

The general rules of child rearing in the !Kung society are indulgence, stimulation, and nonrestriction (Konner, 1977). The !Kung infants studied by Konner were fed whenever they cried and whenever they reached for the breast. This feeding on demand led to brief but frequent feeds, amounting to several times an hour during the day. At night the infants slept in close proximity to their mothers, and they were also fed on demand—even without the mothers' awakening. The extent of physical contact was large compared to that in Western infant–mother dyads. An infant was carried around in a sling, which left the infant with constant access to the mother's breast and to decorative objects hanging around her neck. The infant was able to look around freely and to experience extensive physical and cognitive stimulation. Konner found that this stimulating environment led to advanced neuromotor development in the !Kung infants.

The 2- and 3-year-old children studied by Konner were involved in multiage peer groups, in which they spent more time than with their mothers, and in which they readily established new bonds. Konner (1977) suggested that the great social density of this child-rearing environment enabled the mothers to be extremely indulgent and sensitive to the infants' signals, and that at the same time this social network facilitated the gradual transition into the peer group, in which the older peers took responsibility for the care and protection of the younger toddlers. The !Kung study thus provides support for the universality as well as the sensitivity hypothesis. In this hunter–gatherer society, the infant–mother bond seems to fulfill a unique function of protection and stimulation, even in the context of a wider social network of caregivers. Furthermore, a basic tenet of attachment theory is confirmed—namely, that sensitive responses to infants' signals foster independence instead of dependence later on in life.

The Efé employ a system of multiple caregivers throughout the first few years of life (Morelli & Tronick, 1991). Beginning at birth, the newborn is allowed to suckle other adult females besides the mother, child rearing remains the responsibility of a larger network of adult caregivers (Tronick, Morelli, & Winn, 1987). Even the physical care is shared with other caregivers, in contrast with the Hausa and the Gusii, where the mothers are mainly responsible for feeding, bathing, and other physical care activi-

ties. Multiple caregiving is not necessarily related to the unavailability of the mother: Other caregivers may nurse an infant even in the presence of the mother. Morelli and Tronick (1991) reported that the percentage of time the infants they studied spent with other individuals increased from 39% at 3 weeks to 60% at 18 weeks. The number of caregivers in the first 18 weeks amounted to 14.2 on average. This extremely dense social network led to prompt responses to any sign of infant distress.

During the second half of the first year, the infants in this study began to show preference for the care of their own mothers, and they were more likely to be carried by their mothers on trips out of the camp and to protest against their leaving. Morelli and Tronick (1991) proposed that Efé cultural beliefs about infants' growing competence to discriminate between mothers and other caregivers may have been a reason for this shift. They also pointed to the 1-year-olds' interference with adults' work activities, which prevented nonmaternal caregivers from taking on caregiving responsibility during work. Another intriguing reason for the emergence of a special infant–mother bond, despite the multiple-caregiver context, may have been the care provided during the night. At night, only the mothers cared for their infants, and sleep was regularly interrupted by episodes of playful interaction exclusively between infants and their mothers (Morelli & Tronick, 1991). From the perspective of attachment theory, the night may be an especially stressful time during which infants in general need a protective caregiver most (see the description of the Israeli communal kibbutzim, below).

ATTACHMENT IN THE ONLY CHILD: THE CHINESE CASE

Research on socioemotional development in general, and on attachment in particular, is almost nonexistent in the People's Republic of China (Wang, 1993; Wu, 1985; Zhu & Lin, 1991). The dearth of studies on socioemotional development in China is distressing, in view of Kagitcibasi's (1996) suggestion that the Chinese culture favors interdependence instead of independence, and that in Chinese child rearing the model of emotional interdependence is dominant (cf. Chen, Rubin, & Li, 1995; Li-Repac, 1982)—emphases comparable to those in Japanese cultural and parental beliefs (see below). This observation concurs with Ho's (1986) conclusion that Chinese parents tend to emphasize emotional harmony and control in social relationships, whereas Western parents are inclined to stress individuality and spontaneity.

Because China represents one-third of the world population (with more than 1,100,000,000 inhabitants), and is unique in its birth restriction policy of one child per family (Kuotai & Jing-Hwa, 1985), we have decided to discuss the relevant attachment studies, despite the fact that so few have been carried out to date. It should be kept in mind that the vast population of China is not homogeneous, although the majority of the Chinese are said to belong to the ethnic group of the Han. For political reasons, the common ethnicity of the Chinese has often been stressed at the cost of ethnic differentiation. China is composed of at least 56 nationalities (Wang, 1993). The first studies on psychological characteristics of different nationalities have shown remarkable similarities (Wang, 1993), but socioemotional research on intranational differences has yet to be conducted.

The Beijing Q-Sort Study

In their cross-cultural study on attachment in China, Gao and Wu (Posada et al., 1995) addressed the following questions: Does the secure-base phenomenon exist in Beijing? Do mothers and experts evaluate secure attachment in ways similar to those of Western mothers and experts? And do mothers and experts agree with each other about the "ideal" typical secure child? The authors used a Chinese version of the Attachment Q-Sort (Vaughn & Waters, 1990) to stimulate mothers and experts to provide descriptions of real and ideal children from the perspective of attachment theory. The sample consisted of 41 mothers living in the city of Beijing; all but one mother had only one child (age range: 13–44 months). Each Chinese mother was asked to sort the 90 behavioral descriptions of her own child and of the "ideal" child in two separate runs. Mothers were asked to sort the descriptions into nine piles, ranging from "not descriptive of the [ideal] child at all" to "very descriptive of the [ideal] child." Only some of the 90 behavioral descriptions pertain to the secure-base phenomenon, and are thus related to attachment instead of dependence or sociability.

If Chinese mothers or experts had not selected the security descriptions as relevant to a real or ideal Chinese child, there would have been some doubt about the universality of the secure-base phenomenon in general, and its applicability in Chinese culture in particular. The patterning of the attachment behaviors in the range of the more or less pertinent descriptors showed, however, that Chinese parents as well as experts found the concept of attachment applicable in their cultural context. Furthermore, the Chinese mothers' descriptions of their own children were not more highly correlated with one another than with descriptions from various Western (Germany, Norway, United States) and non-Western (Colombia, Japan) societies (Posada et al., 1995). The implication is that Chinese mothers do not systematically deviate from mothers living in a variety of other societies in terms of their descriptions of the relevance of the secure-base phenomenon to their own children. The same appeared to be true for the Chinese mothers' descriptions of the ideal child. This outcome concurs with the results of an anthropological study of Chinese families living in Papua New Guinea; this study focused on attachment behaviors and the parental responses, and did find interactive patterns predicted by attachment theory (Wu, 1985).

The experts' opinion about the "optimally secure" child was also highly associated with the mothers' view of the "ideal" child. That is, Chinese mothers perceived the ideal child as a securely attached child, just as the Chinese experts did, and the experts' descriptions of the optimally secure Chinese child were strongly associated with similar descriptions by experts from various Western and non-Western societies. These results clearly support the universality hypothesis of attachment theory. It is important to note that among these Chinese experts and parents, the idea of emotional interdependence did not seem to regulate their views of the ideal child, at least in certain domains.

This finding appears to replicate the unexpected outcome of the Lin and Fu (1990) study of child-rearing attitudes in Chinese, Chinese American, and European American parents of kindergarten-age and elementary-school-age children. In this study, the Chinese and Chinese American parents rated the importance of encouragement of independence higher than their European American counterparts did. Lin and Fu (1990) suggested that valuing interdependence and filial piety within the family is not necessarily incompatible with individual independence in the wider social context, such as school or work. In fact, being successful in school and at work may be a filial obligation to be reached only through personal autonomy. Furthermore, children's age may be an important factor. Whereas Chinese parents are considered to be indulgent and overprotective of younger children, this parenting attitude changes drastically when the children are deemed to be responsible for their own actions. From that point in time (which may be located anywhere between 2 and 6 years) impulse control and harsh discipline begin to dominate (Ho, 1986).

The First Chinese Strange Situation Study

A pioneering study of attachment in China using the strange situation procedure has been conducted by Hu and Meng (1996) of the Psychology Department of Peking University in Beijing. The authors' aim was to describe patterns of attachment in Chinese infants, as well as the association between attachment and temperament. They also focused on associations between the mothers' involvement in the care of their infants and the quality of the infant–mother attachment relationship. The sample consisted of 31 mother–infant dyads (16 of the infants were boys) from intact families with a "middle-class" background. Each infant was an only child, and all but one family lived with the grandparents. Filial piety has remained functional in the Chinese context of housing shortages, especially for the younger generations. In fact, this is the reason why parents and children tend to live with the grandparents instead of the grandparents with their offspring (C.-F. Yang, 1988; K.-S. Yang, 1988).

The distribution of attachment classifications in this Chinese sample was remarkably similar to the global distribution (van IJzendoorn & Kroonenberg, 1988). The percentage of secure infant–mother dyads was 68%; the avoidant classification was assigned in 16% of the cases; and the resistant classification was used in 16% of the cases. In view of the strict birth control policy and the traditional preference for a male child, it is important to note that the distributions of attachment classifications for male and female infants were virtually the same (Hu & Meng, 1996). Paradoxically, the policy of one child per family may enhance the importance of the only child to such a degree that it overrides the traditional sex-specific preferences (the "little emperor" phenomenon described by Stafford, 1995; see also Kuotai & Jing-Hwa, 1985).

Hu and Meng (1996) expressed some doubts about the validity of the avoidant category. They noted that the avoidant infants did not show stranger anxiety, and they commented on the indifference the avoidant infants expressed toward their mothers at reunion. The Chinese mothers' stress on early independence in their infants, as well as their reliance on nonparental caregivers, may have been responsible for this "indifferent attachment." In some cases, grandparents may have served as the primary attachment figures. An alternative interpretation, however, may refer to the subtle avoidant behaviors that are difficult for even well-trained coders to observe in infants. Without more details about this study, it is difficult to evaluate the authors' claim of the invalidity of the avoidant classification. In this respect, the outcome of this study does not seem to fit easily with Kagan, Kearsly, and Zelazo's (1978) finding that Chinese (American) infants tended to be more apprehensive toward strangers and strange situations than European American infants—in other words, that Chinese infants were more inhibited (Hsu, 1985).

Attachment appeared to be associated with mothers' involvement in the care of their infants. Mothers of avoidant and secure infants worked outside the home every day, whereas mothers of resistant babies stayed at home. Furthermore, mothers of avoidant infants were less involved in child care than mothers of secure infants, and the grandparents played an even larger role as substitute caregivers in the former cases. This outcome may be considered an indirect confirmation of the sensitivity hypothesis of attachment theory.

ATTACHMENT IN THE KIBBUTZ: THE ISRAELI CASE

Until fairly recently, collective sleeping arrangements for children away from their parents constituted probably the most distinctive characteristic of Israeli kibbutz practices in collective child raising. Whereas most institutionalized child rearing in Western cultures involves clinical and multiproblem populations, the collective sleeping arrangements in the kibbutzim were designed for healthy, middle-class, well-functioning, intact families. Many cultures practice multiple caregiving; the patterns are in many ways similar to the practice in kibbutzim (Rabin & Beit-Hallahmi, 1982). However, a worldwide sample of 183 societies showed that none of them maintained a system of having infants sleep away from their parents (Barry & Paxton, 1971). Communal sleeping can be conceived as a unique natural experiment in extremely extended nonparental care with normal children (Beit-Hallahmi & Rabin, 1977). Thus, studying attachment in the Israeli kibbutz, especially where collective sleeping arrangements for infants were practiced, has provided a unique opportunity to examine the four major working hypotheses (Aviezer, van IJzendoorn, Sagi, & Schuengel, 1994).

Collective Sleeping Arrangements

The children's house on a kibbutz serves as the place in which children spend most of their time, eat their meals, and are bathed, in much the same way as they might do at home—hence the term "children's house." Because in the past many kibbutzim adhered to communal sleeping arrangements for children during the night, the children's house was physically designed to fulfill all such functions. Therefore, it consisted of a number of bedrooms (each of which was shared by three or four children), a dining area, showers, and a large space for play activities and learning. Children had private corners in their bedrooms where they kept their personal things, and which were decorated according to each child's preference. When collective sleeping was still in effect, family time was in the afternoon and evening, when both parents tried to be available. Children were returned to the children's house for the night by their parents, who put them to bed; a caregiver or a parent then remained with them until the night watchwomen took over. Communal sleeping started a few months after birth (Aviezer et al., 1994).

Attachment and Collective Sleeping Practices

Sagi et al. (1985) were the first to use the strange situation (Ainsworth et al., 1978; Ainsworth & Wittig, 1969) and its classification system to study the attachments of communally sleeping kibbutz infants to their parents and caregivers. They also examined infant–mother attachment in 36 Israeli infants attending city day care facilities. They found that only 59% of kibbutz infants were securely attached to their mothers, as compared with 75% of Israeli day care infants, and with the 65–70% found in most studies worldwide. Among children with insecure attachments in both Israeli samples, ambivalent relationships were overrepresented (see below). Communal sleeping in children's houses—the unique char-

acteristic of a collective upbringing—was postulated by Sagi and his colleagues to be a possible antecedent for the development of insecure attachments, and a second study was designed to investigate this hypothesis.

In a quasi-experimental study, 23 mother–infant dyads from kibbutzim with communal sleeping arrangements, and 25 dyads from kibbutzim where family-based sleeping had been instituted, were observed in the strange situation (Sagi, van IJzendoorn, Aviezer, Donnell, & Mayseless, 1994). The distribution of attachment patterns for communally sleeping infants was confirmed: Only 48% of the infants were securely attached to their mothers. It should be noted, however, that even in the communal sleeping context, all children appeared to be attached to their mothers; this finding supports the universality hypothesis. The attachment distribution for infants in the family-based sleeping arrangements was completely different. Eighty percent of these infants were securely attached to their mothers—a rate similar to that found among urban Israeli infants (Sagi et al., 1985), as well as to that found in other international samples (van IJzendoorn & Kroonenberg, 1988). As to the normativity hypothesis, across studies the majority of the infants living in the collective sleeping arrangement were still securely attached to their mothers. The disorganized classification was, however, not included in this study.

In order to rule out alternative explanations for the effect of communal sleeping arrangements, assessments were also made of the ecology of the children's house during the day, maternal separation anxiety, infants' temperaments, and mother–infant play interactions. The two groups (i.e., family-based and communal sleepers) were found to be comparable on all of these variables. Thus it was concluded that collective sleeping, experienced by infants as a time during which mothers were largely unavailable and inaccessible, was responsible for the greater insecurity found in this group. Inconsistent responsiveness was inherent in the reality of these infants, given that sensitive responding by a mother or caregiver during the day contrasted sharply with the presence of an unfamiliar person at night. Inconsistent responsiveness has been described as an important antecedent of ambivalent attachment (Ainsworth et al., 1978). This confirms the sensitivity hypothesis.

It should be noted that in several Israeli studies (Sagi et al., 1985, 1994, 1997), the ambivalent classification appeared to be overrepresented and the avoidant classification to be underrepresented, compared to the global distribution (van IJzendoorn & Kroonenberg, 1988). In fact, this finding has been replicated consistently across different Israeli child-rearing arrangements and different kinds of caregivers. We offer two speculations concerning the Israeli bias toward ambivalent attachments. First, the ambivalent attachment strategy may be elicited in the context of continual threats to national and personal security more readily than the avoidant strategy may be. Parental preoccupation with these daily stresses may lead to exaggerated overprotectiveness and impaired sensitivity to children's attachment signals. Second, there is growing evidence that emotional reactivity may be more closely associated with ambivalent attachment than with avoidant attachment (Belsky & Rovine, 1987; Vaughn et al., 1992). The overrepresentation of ambivalent attachment and the near-absence of avoidant attachment may therefore also be attributed to a possible predominance of a high degree of emotional reactivity in Israeli society. To our knowledge, sound empirical evidence on temperament in Israel is still absent. As long as studies of temperament in this cultural context have not yet provided a test of this bold conjecture, our interpretation remains speculative. The finding of a substantial number of dismissing adults with an avoidant stance complicates the matter even further (Sagi et al., 1995, 1997).

Networks of Attachment Relationships

The kibbutz context has also made a unique contribution to the evaluation of the competence hypothesis. Oppenheim, Sagi, and Lamb (1990) assessed a broad spectrum of socioemotional skills in most of the subjects in the Sagi et al. (1985) sample when they were 5 years old, in an attempt to understand the sequelae of early relationships. They found that secure attachment to a nonparental caregiver (the *metapelet*) during infancy was the strongest predictor of a child's being empathic, dominant, independent, achievement-oriented, and behaviorally purposive in kindergarten. On the other hand, no significant associations were found between these socioemotional developments and the quality of children's attachment to their parents. These results suggest that the influence of attachment relationships may be viewed as domain-specific (for similar results, see the Gusii study described earlier in this chapter). Because the infants' relations with

caregivers had been formed in the context of the infant house, they were the best predictor of children's socioemotional behavior in similar contexts.

One can expect attachment relationships in a multiple-caregiver environment, however, to interact in such a way that the predictive power of individual relationships is weaker than that of their combination (Howes, Rodning, Galluzzo, & Myers, 1988; Tavecchio & van IJzendoorn, 1987). Thus we proposed a model of testing multiple-caregiver environments based on the kibbutz experience (Sagi & van IJzendoorn, 1996; van IJzendoorn et al., 1992), in which the interrelations between multiple attachments were examined. More specifically, we examined in the group of kibbutz children the predictive power of the "extended" network of infants' attachments to the three types of caregivers (i.e., attachments to mothers, fathers, and *metaplot*), in comparison to the family network (attachments to mothers and fathers) and the infants' attachment to their mothers only. We found that an extended network was the best predictor of later advanced functioning. This outcome may be interpreted as support for the "integration" model, which assumes that in a network consisting of two or more attachment relationships, secure attachments may compensate for insecure attachments in a linear way (van IJzendoorn et al., 1992).

Ecological Constraints on Intergenerational Transmission of Attachment

The kibbutz is the most unusual cultural setting in which the intergenerational transmission of attachment has been studied. "Intergenerational transmission of attachment" refers to the process through which parents' mental representations of their past attachment experiences influence their parenting behavior and the quality of their children's attachment to them (Bowlby, 1969/1982; Fonagy, Steele, & Steele, 1991; Main, Kaplan, & Cassidy, 1985; see Hesse, Chapter 19, this volume). In several studies of Western cultures, a strong association (concordance rate of about 75%) was found between the security of the parents' mental representation of attachment and the security of the child–parent attachment (for a review, see van IJzendoorn, 1995).

In a recent Israeli study, we (Sagi et al., 1997) presented the Adult Attachment Interview (Main & Goldwyn, in press; see Hesse, Chapter 19, this volume) to 20 mothers from kibbutzim maintaining collective sleeping arrangements, and to 25 mothers from home-sleeping kibbutzim (same design and participants as in Sagi et al., 1994). Parent–child concordance in attachment classifications was low for the communally sleeping group (40%), whereas it was rather high for the home-sleeping group (76%). Thus our data appear to be compatible with a model of intergenerational transmission of attachment in which the ecological context plays a facilitative or inhibiting role. Transmission of attachment across generations appears to depend upon the specific child-rearing arrangements, and contextual factors such as communal sleeping may override the influence of parents' attachment representation and their sensitive responsiveness. This finding indicates the limits of a context-free universal model of transmission.

AMAE, DEPENDENCE, AND ATTACHMENT: THE JAPANESE CASE

The Japanese case can be considered a real challenge to the attachment paradigm—in particular, to the universality, the normativity, and the sensitivity hypotheses. From research on attachment in Japan, three issues have been derived. First, researchers studying attachment in Japan have claimed that ambivalent attachment relationships are overrepresented and that avoidant attachments are underrepresented (Miyake, Chen, & Campos, 1985; Takahashi, 1986). Second, the stressful strange situation, including two separations from the attachment figure, is criticized for being an invalid assessment of attachment in Japanese infants, who are used to continuous close proximity to their mothers. Third, the concept of attachment may not be relevant to the Japanese culture, in which the idea of *amae* (Doi, 1973, 1992) seems to play a more prominent and more adequate role in describing family relationships and its societal implications (Emde, 1992). Doi (1989) emphasizes that *amae* covers the same area as attachment, but that the bond with the parent inevitably implies dependence as well—an implication that, according to Doi, is denied in attachment theory (see Ainsworth, 1969). He argues that "*amae* definitely has an advantage over attachment precisely because it implies a psychological dependence . . ." (Doi, 1989, p. 350). Therefore, an important preliminary question is how attachment, *amae,* and dependence are interpreted and evaluated in Japan.

Amae and Attachment

Vereijken (1996) reports on a study addressing exactly this issue. Eight native Japanese behavioral scientists were asked to describe the concepts of *amae,* attachment, and dependence with the help of the Attachment *Q*-Sort procedure (Vaughn & Waters, 1990). The *Q*-Sort cards contain the description of 90 different behaviors and can be regarded as a standard vocabulary pertinent to children's behavior in a wide variety of settings. The experts were asked to describe a child whom they considered prototypical for *amae* by sorting the 90 cards. Relevant behavioral descriptions of *amae* were "fussiness after playing in presence of mother," "demanding and impatient with the mother," and "enjoys having mother hug or cuddle him [or her]." The experts were strongly in agreement on the description of *amae.* They were also asked to provide ideal typical profiles of a dependent child and of a securely attached child. The descriptions of *amae* and dependence appeared to be very similar, whereas the descriptions of attachment security and *amae* were not associated at all (Vereijken, 1996, p. 85). Furthermore, when the descriptions of the ideal child according to Japanese mothers were compared with the expert's definitions of *amae,* attachment, and dependence, only attachment security appeared to be desirable, whereas *amae* and dependence were not associated with the ideal Japanese child in the eyes of mothers.

In another Japanese study of 42 mothers and 18 experts, the similarity of Japanese mothers' description of the ideal child with the experts' profile of the most secure child was striking ($r = .86$; Posada et al., 1995). Thus, in terms of a culture-specific evaluation of the importance of *amae,* we may conclude that even from a Japanese perspective, attachment security seems to be more desirable to mothers than the behavioral characteristics included in *amae.* It should be noted, however, that the domain of 90 behavioral descriptions may have restricted the range of potential definitions and evaluations of the concepts for which the Attachment *Q*-Sort was not originally constructed (i.e., *amae* and dependence). In an observational study of Japanese sojourners in the United States, however, Mizuta, Zahn-Waxler, Cole, and Hiruma (1996) confirmed Vereijken's (1996) conclusion that *amae* and attachment appear to be orthogonal dimensions that can be reliably distinguished. This empirical evidence is in contrast with Johnson's

(1993) speculation that the concept of attachment may be similar to the intrapsychical dimension of *amae*—that is, a desire to be held, fed, bathed, made safe, and emotionally comforted.

Two studies using the strange situation procedure to assess attachment security in Japan have been reported in the international literature. Durrett, Otaki, and Richards (1984) studied a middle-class sample of 39 intact families with their 12-month-old firstborns in Tokyo. Miyake, Takahashi, Nakagawa, and others studied a total of 60 middle-class intact families with their 12-month-old infants in Sapporo, a large city in the northern part of Japan (Miyake et al., 1985; Nakagawa, Lamb, & Miyake, 1992; Takahashi, 1986). An earlier report of a strange situation study by Takahashi (1982) did not focus on attachment classifications but on attachment behaviors, particularly toward the stranger. In both studies, the mothers were the primary caregivers of the infants, and in both cases the large majority of the mothers were full-time homemakers.

The results of these two studies are rather discrepant. The Tokyo study showed a pattern of avoidant, secure, and resistant infant–mother attachments consistent with the global distribution (13% A, 61% B, and 18% C, with 8% unclassifiable cases). The Sapporo study did not include avoidantly attached children, and it showed a distribution of either 68% securely attached and 32% resistantly attached infants (Takahashi, 1986), or 75% securely attached and 21% resistantly attached infants, with 4% unclassifiable cases and 4 damaged videotapes (Nakagawa, Lamb, & Miyake, 1992). The two studies also differed markedly in their conclusions about the validity of the strange situation procedure for use in the Japanese context. It is of course needless to say that Japan cannot be represented adequately by only two attachment studies of modest size.

The Tokyo Study

The Tokyo study investigated the relationship between the security of infant–mother attachment and the mothers' perception of the positive support they received from their husbands. In accordance with previous studies of social support and attachment, Durrett et al. (1984) hypothesized that mothers who felt supported by their husbands would be more sensitive to their infants' needs and attachment signals, and therefore would be better able to foster the secure attachment of their infants.

The mothers of securely attached infants indeed indicated that they felt more supported by their husbands than did the mothers of avoidantly attached infants, but they did not differ in this regard from the mothers of resistantly attached infants. The differences in support were especially large with respect to a husband's pride in his wife's accomplishments, enjoyment in her activities, and sensitivity to her needs (Durrett et al., 1984). The authors concluded "that in Japan as well as in America the adequacy of mothering seems to be influenced by the support perceived by the mother and the family context" (Durrett et al., 1984, p. 174). The sensitivity hypothesis is only partially and indirectly supported, because the assessment of perceived social support was not equivalent to observed maternal sensitivity. Furthermore, on the basis of perceived support, the resistant category could not be discriminated from the secure category. The Tokyo study confirms the universality and normativity hypotheses more definitively because it did not report difficulties in applying the attachment coding system to this population, and because the normative "modal" category was secure.

The Sapporo Study

The Sapporo study provides a more complicated picture, in particular because the various reports do not converge in terms of the basic data or in terms of the number of cases involved. If we leave out the interim reports on part of the sample (Miyake et al., 1985, included only approximately 20 subjects in most of their analyses), we should concentrate on the longitudinal data provided by Nakagawa, Lamb, and Miyake (1992), who focused on maternal sensitivity. But first we should examine the suggestion that the strange situation procedure may be too stressful for Japanese infants, and therefore invalid.

In order to examine whether the stress level induced by the complete strange situation procedure might be a cause of the overrepresentation of resistantly attached infants, Takahashi (1986) decided to classify the infant–mother attachments also on the basis of the first five strange situation episodes, which include only one separation from the mother and no episode in which the child is alone in the strange room. With this modified procedure, she found that 83% of the infants could be classified as securely attached to their mothers, and only 17% as resistantly attached. Again, she did not find infants who qual-

ified for the avoidant category. More importantly, however, Takahashi (1986) also reported that
in the absence of clear instructions about the curtailing of episodes in case of excessive crying behavior, the maximum duration of a crying
episode was set at 2 minutes. This is considerably
longer than in most attachment studies elsewhere, as Takahashi (1986, p. 266) conceded, because normally crying leads to a curtailed
episode after only 20–30 seconds. The absence
of avoidance in the Sapporo study may therefore
be explained by the "more than mild" stress level
induced in the Japanese version of the strange
situation procedure. We are reminded of
Ainsworth et al.'s (1978) report on a short-term
test–retest study of the original procedure, in
which at the second assessment most avoidant
infants appeared to behave in a "secure" way, and
many secure infants showed resistant behavior.

Because the status of the Sapporo attachment
classifications is unclear (Grossmann & Grossmann, 1989), it is difficult to evaluate the Nakagawa, Lamb, and Miyake (1992) report on the
antecedents of attachment security in this sample. In part of the sample (25–29 families), researchers rated videotaped home interactions at 4
and 8 months after birth; they also conducted 8-
month laboratory assessments on scales for maternal accessibility, acceptance, cooperation, and
sensitivity. The authors found no association between attachment security and antecedent maternal interactive behavior at home or in the laboratory. They suggested that the ratings of maternal
behavior may have been less valid, because the
Japanese mothers looked very self-conscious
during the observations, although they were
asked to behave naturally. Mizuta et al. (1996)
have also remarked that the Japanese mothers in
their study were inclined to show strong defer-
ence, compliance, and reserve toward the experimenter as an authority figure.

In sum, the Sapporo study does not seem to
undermine either the universality or the normativity hypothesis; in fact, the absence of avoidant
infants may have been an artifact of the rigid procedure and/or the unique characteristics of this
sample, which were not shared by the Tokyo
sample (van IJzendoorn & Kroonenberg, 1988).
The sensitivity hypothesis is of course not supported by the results of this study, although plausible alternative interpretations of the absence of
an association between maternal sensitivity and
attachment security have been proposed. It may
be added that in a recent meta-analysis of more
than 65 studies, the association between sensitiv-

ity and attachment was found to be $r = .24$
(DeWolff & van IJzendoorn, 1997). A sample of
fewer than 30 cases does not provide sufficient
power to detect this medium effect size.

Takahashi (1990) followed the Sapporo sample for 2½ years after the attachment assessment,
and she focused on the children's compliance to
their mothers' requests, their curiosity, their social competence, and their cognitive development. The assessments during the second year of
life showed that the secure infants complied
more with their mothers' directions and demands; they also showed more curiosity about a
new object and were more competent in relating
to unfamiliar peers than the resistantly attached
infants. During the third year of life, however, the
resistantly attached children no longer differed
from the securely attached children in terms of
social competence and cognitive development.

Takahashi (1990) concluded that the strange
situation procedure does not predict competence
after infancy, and thus appears to lack cross-
cultural validity. However, studies in Western
countries on the long-term sequelae of attachment security after infancy have not always
yielded strong differences between the secure
and insecure groups, either; in most comparisons, the resistant group was too small to be
studied separately from the avoidant group (see
Thompson, Chapter 13, this volume). Furthermore, during the first 5 years of life, changes in
attachment security should be considered to be
the outcome of the interaction between the developing child and the changing environment
(Bowlby, 1969/1982). The follow-up studies presented by Takahashi (1990) did not include assessments of the potentially changing child rearing context (van IJzendoorn, 1996).

The Attachment *Q*-Sort Study

The cross-cultural debate on attachment in Japan
has focused on the validity of the strange situation procedure, and in fact has been based on the
outcomes of only one study, the Sapporo study.
As we have shown earlier, the Tokyo study does
not confirm the results of the Sapporo study. Fortunately, the strange situation procedure is no
longer the only measure to be used in cross-
cultural research. The Attachment *Q*-Sort
(Vaughn & Waters, 1990) is a viable alternative,
particularly in cases where separations between
parents and children may be uncommon (van
IJzendoorn, Vereijken, & Riksen-Walraven, in
press). Vereijken (1996) constructed a Japanese

version of the Attachment *Q*-Sort, and he studied the association between sensitivity and attachment security in a Tokyo sample of 48 intact families with 14-month-old infants. More sensitive mothers had more secure children, and the association between sensitivity and attachment was impressively strong (all correlations—based on independent coders—were .59 or higher). In a follow-up study 10 months later, the association between sensitivity and attachment was replicated (Vereijken, 1996). The Vereijken (1996) study indeed supports the validity of attachment theory—in particular, the universality and the sensitivity hypotheses.

UNIVERSAL AND CONTEXTUAL DIMENSIONS OF ATTACHMENT

In this section we review the findings of cross-cultural attachment research in two ways. First, we discuss the use of the *concept* of attachment security across cultures. Second, we summarize the cross-cultural support for the core *hypotheses* of attachment theory. Of course, the most powerful test of the universality of attachment theory is the cross-cultural confirmation of its nomological network.

The Concept of Attachment

To start with cross-cultural use of the concept of attachment, we focus on the conceptual normativity of attachment security. The Attachment *Q*-Sort (Vaughn & Waters, 1990) provides the opportunity to test whether experts and parents conceptualize attachment security in a similar manner, within as well across societies. Posada et al. (1995) performed exactly this test, in a cross-cultural comparison of expert and mother samples from China, Colombia, Germany, Israel, Japan, and the United States. They correlated the descriptions of the "optimally secure" child as sorted by the experts from the different societies and the descriptions of the "ideal" child in the eyes of the mothers in each culture. Without exception, the correlations were substantial, indicating that across cultures the experts' conceptualization of attachment was very similar to the mothers' ideas about the ideal child (Posada et al., 1995). Similarly, the experts' opinions about a most secure child and the mothers' views of the most ideal child converged strongly across cultures. It seems, therefore, that across cultures experts as well as mothers interpret attachment se-

curity in a similar manner, and they also appear to evaluate it in the same way, although the reasons for their preference of secure instead of insecure attachments may be different (Harwood, Miller, & Irizarry, 1995).

The conceptual similarity of attachment security across diverging cultures does not mean that exactly the same infant attachment behaviors are considered to be indicative of secure or insecure attachment. In some cultures distal attachment behaviors may be stressed somewhat more than proximal behaviors, or vice versa. The secure-base phenomenon, however, is located at the level of behavior patterns or behavioral organization, at which separate behaviors play only a minor role (Waters, 1977). Gusii infants, for example, are accustomed to being greeted with a handshake instead of a hug by their mothers, as noted earlier. After separations the Gusii infants expect the handshake, whereas Western infants look forward to "more intimate" physical contact. The patterning of attachment behaviors demonstrating the secure base remains the same, regardless of the specific behaviors. The secure Gusii infants studied by Kermoian and Leiderman (1986) would reach out to the adult with one arm, to receive the handshake enthusiastically, whereas the insecure infants would avoid the adult or would reach and then pull away as the adult approached. This is a powerful demonstration of the culture-specific behavioral markers of a universal and normative phenomenon.

A Cross-Cultural Test of the Nomological Network

The evidence for the cross-cultural validity of attachment theory is impressive. In Table 31.1, we present the findings of the cross-cultural studies as they pertain to the four core hypotheses of attachment theory: the universality, normativity, sensitivity, and competence hypotheses. The overview is limited to the studies discussed above.

The universality hypothesis appears to be supported most strongly. In every cross-cultural study, similar patterns of attachment behavior have been observed. Some children may have been difficult to rate—for example, because of the stresses of the assessment procedure—but reports of children who did not show attachment behavior in stressful circumstances are absent. Furthermore, the numbers of children who were difficult to rate do not differ across cultures. In the studies discussed here, these children were

TABLE 31.1. Evidence from Africa, China, Israel, and Japan for the Cross-Cultural Validity of Attachment Theory

Society	Hypothesis			
	Universality	Normativity	Sensitivity	Competence
Africa				
Ganda (Ainsworth, 1967)	+	+	+	0
Gusii (Kermoian & Leiderman, 1986)	+	+	+	0
Dogon (True, 1994)	+	+	0	+
Hausa (Marvin et al., 1977)	+	0	0	0
!Kung San (Konner, 1977)	+	0	(+)	0
Efé (Morelli & Tronick, 1991)	+	0	(+)	0
China				
Beijing (Posada et al., 1995)	+	+	0	0
Beijing (Hu & Meng, 1996)	+	+	+	0
Israel				
Communal kibbutzim (Sagi et al., 1985, 1994)	+	+	+	+
Family-based kibbutzim (Sagi et al., 1994)	+	+	+	0
City (Sagi et al., 1985)	+	+	0	0
Japan				
Tokyo (Durrett et al., 1984)	+	+	±	0
Sapporo (Takahashi, 1986)	+	+	–	±
Tokyo (Vereijken, 1996)	+	+	+	0

Note. +, positive evidence; 0, no evidence available; ±, mixed positive and negative evidence; –, negative evidence; (+), indirect positive evidence.

exceptions rather than the rule, and the application of the coding system for disorganized attachment behavior (Main & Solomon, 1990) might have rendered their interactions interpretable. The cross-cultural studies included here support Bowlby's (1969/1982) idea that attachment is indeed a universal phenomenon, and an evolutionary explanation seems to be warranted. Although in many cultures children grow up with a network of attachment figures, the parent or caregiver who takes responsibility for the care of a child during part of the day or the night becomes the favorite target of infant attachment behaviors. Not only the attachment phenomenon itself, but also the different types of attachment, appear to be present in various Western and non-Western cultures. Avoidant, secure, and resistant attachments have been observed in the African, Chinese, and Japanese studies; even in the extremely diverging child-rearing context of the Israeli communal kibbutzim, the differentiation between secure and insecure attachment could be made.

The cross-cultural evidence for the normativity hypothesis is rather strong as well. In all cross-cultural studies included here, the majority of infants were classified as securely attached. In Table 31.2, the attachment classification distributions of the studies discussed above are presented. When these are combined with Attachment Q-Sort findings about the cross-cultural preference among experts as well as mothers for securely attached children, we may be confident that secure attachment is not just a North American invention or a Western ideal, but a rather widespread and preferred phenomenon. As we have described in the introductory section, the category of secure attachments emerged from Ainsworth's Ganda study, not from her Baltimore study (as is often suggested). Scrutinizing Ainsworth's (1967) report on the Ganda sample, we became acutely aware of its importance in establishing the strange situation procedure and its coding system. In fact, the Baltimore study should be considered much more of a replication than a pioneering exploration into uncharted territory (e.g., Lamb, Thompson, Gardner, Charnov, & Estes, 1984).

The sensitivity and competence hypotheses receive less support. A recent meta-analysis of

TABLE 31.2. Distributions of Infant–Mother Attachment Classifications in Africa, China, Israel, and Japan Compared with Western Europe and the United States

Society	n	Avoidant (A)	Secure (B)	Resistant (C)	Other
Africa					
Ganda (Ainsworth, 1967)	28	18%	57%	25%	—
Gusii (Kermoian & Leiderman, 1986)	26	—[a]	61%	—[a]	—
Dogon (True, 1994)	26	0%	69%	8%	23%
China					
Beijing (Hu & Meng, 1996)	31	16%	68%	16%	—
Israel					
Communal kibbutzim (Sagi et al., 1985, 1995)	104	7%	56%	37%	—
Family-based kibbutzim (Sagi et al., 1995)	25	0%	80%	20%	—
City (Sagi et al., 1985)	36	3%	80%	17%	—
Japan					
Tokyo (Durrett et al., 1984)	39	13%	61%	18%	8%
Sapporo (Takahashi, 1986)	60	0%	68%	32%	—
Western Europe					
9 samples combined (van IJzendoorn & Kroonenberg, 1988)	510	28%	66%	6%	—
United States					
21 samples combined (van IJzendoorn et al., 1992)	1,584	21%	67%	12%	—

[a]No differentiation between avoidant and resistant attachments available.

more than 65 studies showed that the association between attachment and sensitivity is important but modest: The combined effect size in a selected set of pertinent studies was equivalent to $r = .24$ (DeWolff & van IJzendoorn, 1997). Cross-cultural studies on attachment are by necessity small, and the lack of statistical power may have been one of the most important causes for the disconfirming results in the Sapporo study (Takahashi, 1990). Nevertheless, in seven studies unequivocal support for the sensitivity hypothesis was found, and in two other studies support may be indirectly derived from the reports (Konner, 1977; Morelli & Tronick, 1991). The most striking disconfirming data have been found in the Sapporo study, but at the same time supporting evidence has been presented in the Tokyo study. That is, whether findings support or disconfirm the sensitivity hypothesis does not depend on culture, but seems to be associated with specific studies or samples. The Sapporo results cannot be used to invalidate the strange situation,

because of the presence of more positive support in other Japanese research (albeit in another city; Vereijken, 1996), unless there are good reasons to suspect that intracultural differences play an important role. In the discussions of the Sapporo findings, this line of reasoning has never been stressed (Miyake et al., 1985; Takahashi, 1990). Although the sensitivity hypothesis does not appear to be refuted in cross-cultural research, more studies on the antecedents of attachment security are needed to settle the issue more definitively.

The competence hypothesis has been tested only sporadically in cross-cultural research; this concurs with the relative lack of Western studies on the association between attachment and (later) competence (Meins, 1997; van IJzendoorn, Dijkstra, & Bus, 1995). In the Gusii study (Kermoian & Leiderman, 1986), the nutritional status of the secure infants was better than that of the insecure infants. This outcome has been replicated by Valenzuela (1990) in her Chilean study of undernourished infants. Although the relation between attachment and health status is truly remarkable, it is still not clear whether attachment security serves only as the cause and nutritional status only as the effect. A more intricate causal pattern cannot be completely excluded on the basis of the correlational evidence that Kermoian and Leiderman (1986) and Valenzuela (1990) have provided. The Dogon study (True, 1994) does not allow for differentiation between cause and effect, either. We should therefore conclude that the cross-cultural support for the competence hypothesis is still insufficient. The concept of attachment networks may be fruitfully applied in further cross-cultural studies of the competence hypothesis.

CONCLUSIONS

Our analysis and integration of cross-cultural attachment research suggest a balance between universal trends and contextual determinants. Attachment theory without contextual components is as difficult to conceive as attachment theory without a universalistic perspective. If across cultures all infants used the same fixed strategies to deal with attachment challenges, it would leave no room for adaptation to dynamic changes of the environment (Hinde & Stevenson-Hinde, 1990), and to the constraints imposed by different developmental niches (see Belsky, Chapter 7, this volume; DeVries, 1984; Harkness & Super, 1992, 1996; LeVine & Miller, 1990; Simpson, Chapter 6, this volume). Without variation, selection of optimal behavioral strategies would become obsolete (Darwin, 1859/1985). The three basic attachment patterns—avoidant, secure, and ambivalent—can be found in every culture in which attachment studies have been conducted thus far. Even in the Israeli research, some avoidant infant–parent relationships have been found, albeit at a much lower than usual rate.

What seem to be universal are the general cultural pressure toward selection of the secure attachment pattern in the majority of children, and the preference for the secure child in parents across cultures. Even in the extremely deviating context of the communal sleeping arrangement, the majority of children develop secure attachments to their parents. The most dramatic demonstration of the adaptive value of attachment security is its role as a protective factor against malnutrition (True, 1994). Dixon, LeVine, and Brazelton (1982) even identified

malnutrition as a symptom of a "disorder of attachment." Furthermore, in many cultural contexts, the secure attachment strategy seems to emerge from the most sensitive parenting. Although the cross-cultural evidence pertaining to the competence hypothesis is still scarce, secure attachment seems to increase the likelihood of better social competence in the future. Thus the universal validity of attachment theory appears to be confirmed in cross-cultural research.

Cross-cultural studies on attachment have made us sensitive to the importance of wider social networks in which children grow and develop (Harkness & Super, 1996; Nsamenang, 1992; Thompson, 1993). We need a radical change from a dyadic perspective to an attachment network approach (Tavecchio & van IJzendoorn, 1987). In Western as well as non-Western cultures, most children communicate with several attachment figures (Lamb, 1977; Main & Weston, 1981), including siblings (Weisner & Gallimore, 1977). Examining the competence hypothesis only on the basis of infant–mother attachment may decrease predictive power substantially. If Kermoian and Leiderman (1986) had included only mothers in their study, they would not have been able to predict cognitive competence on the basis of their attachment assessments. In the Israeli case, infant–mother attachment did not predict aspects of competence as assessed in a kindergarten context, whereas the extended attachment network was found to predict social competence at age 5 more strongly than any single attachment relationship (van IJzendoorn et al., 1992; Sagi & van IJzendoorn, 1996).

Cross-cultural studies on attachment require major investments on the part of the researchers. It is remarkable that so many studies in various parts of the world have been performed. The cross-cultural studies are rather small-scale, in-depth observational studies, often combined with a longitudinal component. The validity of the cross-cultural data can be regarded as high, because in general the researchers have been carefully adapting their assessments to the particular culture. In this respect, cross-cultural attachment research is not only "etic"; it also contains elements of the "emic" approach, and the two approaches appear compatible (Pike, 1967). For example, the use of the naturally occurring Weigh-In procedure for the purpose of assessing communication patterns between parents and infants (True, 1994) is ecologically valid as well as replicable. Nevertheless, the current cross-cultural data base is almost absurdly small, compared to the domain that should be covered. In cultural anthropology, the number of different cultures (past and present) has been estimated at more than 1,200. Systematic anthropological data are available on at least 186 different cultural areas in the Standard Cross-Cultural Sample (Murdock & White, 1969). In this chapter we have covered only a few cultural areas in China, Japan, Israel, and Africa. Data on attachment in India and the Islamic world are still completely lacking. Furthermore, large parts of China and Africa are uncharted territories with respect to the development of attachment. For example, we have been able to present data from only two Chinese studies. Although these studies represent admirable contributions to the attachment literature, they cannot be considered to be representative of a population of more than 1 billion people from at least 56 nationalities.

Of course, cross-cultural attachment research is not meant to produce representative demographic data. Its most important contribution is the test of some core propositions of attachment theory. The central issue is whether attachment theory is just a middle-class Western invention with no relevance at all to other cultures, or whether its universalistic perspective can be confirmed in non-Western child-rearing circumstances. The cross-cultural studies have not (yet) refuted the bold conjectures of attachment theory about the universality and normativity of attachment, and about its antecedents and sequelae. In fact, taken as a whole, the studies are remarkably consistent with the theory. Attachment theory may therefore claim cross-cultural validity.

ACKNOWLEDGMENT

Support for the preparation of this chapter was provided by a fellowship from the Netherlands Institute for Advanced Study in the Humanities and Social Sciences (NIAS) to Marinus H. van IJzendoorn.

REFERENCES

Ainsworth, M. D. S. (1967). *Infancy in Uganda: Infant care and the growth of love.* Baltimore: Johns Hopkins University Press.

Ainsworth, M. D. S. (1969). Object relations, dependency, and attachment: A theoretical review of the infant–mother relationship. *Child Development, 40,* 969–1025.

Ainsworth, M. D. S. (1977). Infant development and mother–infant interaction among Ganda and American families. In P. H. Leiderman, S. R. Tulkin, & A. H. Rosenfeld (Eds.), *Culture and infancy* (pp. 119–150). New York: Academic Press.

Ainsworth, M. D. S., Blehar, M. C., Waters, E., & Wall, S. (1978). *Patterns of attachment.* Hillsdale, NJ: Erlbaum.

Ainsworth, M. D. S., & Wittig, B. A. (1969). Attachment and exploratory behavior of one year olds in a strange situation. In B. M. Foss (Ed.), *Determinants of infant behavior* (Vol. 4, pp. 113–136). London: Methuen.

Aviezer, O., van IJzendoorn, M. H., Sagi, A., & Schuengel, C. (1994). "Children of the dream" revisited: 70 years of collective early child care in Israeli kibbutzim. *Psychological Bulletin, 116,* 99–116.

Barry, H. I., & Paxton, L. M. (1971). Infancy and early childhood: Cross-cultural codes 2. *Ethnology, 10,* 466–508.

Beit-Hallahmi, B., & Rabin, A. (1977). The kibbutz as a social experiment and as a child-rearing laboratory. *American Psychologist, 12,* 57–69.

Belsky, J., & Cassidy, J. (1995). Attachment: Theory and evidence. In M. Rutter, D. Hay, & S. Baron-Cohen (Eds.), *Developmental principles and clinical issues in psychology and psychiatry.* Oxford: Blackwell.

Belsky, J., & Rovine, M. (1987). Temperament and attachment security in the strange situation: An empirical rapprochement. *Child Development, 58,* 787–795.

Berry, J.W. (1969). On cross-cultural comparability. *International Journal of Psychology, 4,* 119–128.

Bowlby, J. (1951). *Maternal care and mental health.* Geneva: World Health Organization.

Bowlby, J. (1969/1982). *Attachment and loss: Vol. 1. Attachment.* New York: Basic Books.

Bretherton, I. (1985). Attachment theory: Retrospect and prospect. In I. Bretherton & E. Waters (Eds.), Growing points of attachment theory and research. *Monographs of the Society for Research in Child Development, 50* (1–2, Serial No. 209), 3–35.

Bretherton, I. (1991). The roots and growing points of attachment theory. In C. M. Parkes, J. Stevenson-Hinde, & P. Marris (Eds.), *Attachment across the life cycle* (pp. 9–32). London: Tavistock/Routledge.

Cassidy, J. (1986). The ability to negotiate the environment: An aspect of infant competence as related to quality of attachment. *Child Development, 57,* 331–337.

Cassidy, J. (1994). Emotion regulation: Influences of attachment relationships. In N. A. Fox (Ed.), The development of emotion regulation: Biological and behavioral considerations. *Monographs of the Society for Research in Child Development, 59*(2–3, Serial No. 240), 228–249.

Chen, X. Y., Rubin, K. H., & Li, B. S. (1995). Social and school adjustment of shy and aggressive children in China. *Development and Psychopathology, 7,* 337–349.

Darwin, C. (1985). *On the origin of species by means of natural selection, or the preservation of favoured races in the struggle for life.* Harmondsworth, England: Penguin. (Original work published 1859)

DeVries, M. W. (1984). Temperament and infant mortality among the Masai of East Africa. *American Journal of Psychiatry, 141,* 1189–1194.

DeWolff, M. S., & van IJzendoorn, M. H. (1997). Sensitivity and attachment: A meta-analysis on parental antecedents of infant- attachment. *Child Development, 68,* 571–591.

Dixon, S. D., LeVine, R. A., & Brazelton, T. B. (1982). Malnutrition: A closer look at the problem in an East African village. *Developmental Medicine and Child Neurology, 24,* 670–685.

Doi, T. (1973). *The anatomy of dependence.* New York: Kodansha.

Doi, T. (1989). The concept of *amae* and its psychoanalytic implications. *International Review of Psychoanalysis, 16,* 349–354.

Doi, T. (1992). On the concept of *amae. Infant Mental Health Journal, 13,* 7–11.

Durrett, M. E., Otaki, M., & Richards, P. (1984). Attachment and the mother's perception of support from the father. *International Journal of Behavioral Development, 7,* 167–176.

Emde, R. N. (1992). *Amae,* intimacy, and the early moral self. *Infant Mental Health Journal, 13,* 34–42.

Fonagy, P., Steele, H., & Steele, M. (1991). Maternal representations of attachment during pregnancy predict the organization of infant–mother attachment at one year of age. *Child Development, 62,* 891–905.

Goossens, F. A., & van IJzendoorn, M. H. (1990). Quality of infants' attachments to professional caregivers: Relation to infant–parent attachment and day-care characteristics. *Child Development, 61,* 832–837.

Grossmann, K. E., & Grossmann, K. (1989). Preliminary observations on Japanese infants' behavior in Ainsworth's strange situation. In *Annual Report of the Research and Clinical Center for Child Development* (pp. 1–12).

Grossmann, K. E., Grossmann, K., Huber, F., & Wartner, U. (1981). German children's behavior towards their mothers at 12 months and their fathers at 18 months in Ainsworth's strange situation. *International Journal of Behavioral Development, 4,* 157–181.

Harkness, S., & Super, C. M. (1992). Shared child care in East Africa: Sociocultural origins and developmental consequences. In M. E. Lamb, K. J. Sternberg, C. P. Hwang, & A. G. Broberg (Eds.), *Child care in context: Cross-cultural perspectives* (pp. 441–459). Hillsdale, NJ: Erlbaum.

Harkness, S., & Super, C. M. (Eds.). (1996). *Parents' cultural belief systems: Their origins, expressions, and consequences.* New York: Guilford Press.

Harwood, R. L., Miller, J. G., & Irizarry, N. L. (1995). *Culture and attachment: Perceptions of the child in context.* New York: Guilford Press.

Hertsgaard, L., Gunnar, M., Erickson, M. F., & Nachmias, M. (1995). Adrenocortical responses to the strange situation in infants with disorganized/disoriented attachment relationships. *Child Development, 66,* 1100–1106.

Hinde, R. A., & Stevenson-Hinde, J. (1990). Attachment: Biological, cultural, and individual desiderata. *Human Development, 33,* 62–72.

Hinde, R. A., & Stevenson-Hinde, J. (1991). Perspectives on attachment. In C. M. Parkes, J. Stevenson-Hinde, & P. Marris (Eds.), *Attachment across the life cycle* (pp. 52–65). London: Routledge/Tavistock.

Ho, D. Y. F. (1986). Chinese patterns of socialization: A critical review. In M. H. Bond (Ed.), *The psychology of the Chinese people* (pp. 1–37). Hong Kong: Oxford University Press.

Howes, C., Rodning, C., Galluzzo, D. C., & Myers, L. (1988). Attachment and child care: Relationships with mother and caregiver. *Early Childhood Research Quarterly, 3,* 403–416.

Hsu, C. C. (1985). Characteristics of temperament in Chinese infants and young children. In W. S. Tseng & D. Y. H. Wu (Eds.), *Chinese culture and mental health* (pp. 135–152). Orlando, FL: Academic Press.

Hu, P., & Meng, Z. (1996). *An examination of infant–mother attachment in China.* Poster presented at the meeting of the International Society for the Study of Behavioral Development, Québec City, Québec, Canada.

Jackson, J. F. (1993). Multiple caregiving among African Americans and infant attachment: The need for an emic approach. *Human Development, 36,* 87–102.

Johnson, F. A. (1993). *Dependency and Japanese socialization: Psychoanalytic and anthropological investigations into* amae. New York: New York University Press.

Kagan, J., Kearsley, R. B., & Zelazo, P. R. (1978). *Infancy: Its place in human development.* Cambridge, MA: Harvard University Press.

Kagitcibasi, C. (1996). *Family and human development across cultures: A view from the other side.* Hillsdale, NJ: Erlbaum.

Kermoian, R., & Leiderman, P. H. (1986). Infant attachment to mother and child caretaker in an East African community. *International Journal of Behavioral Development, 9,* 455–469.

Konner, M. (1977). Infancy among the Kalahari Desert San. In P. H. Leiderman, S. R. Tulkin, & A. Rosenfeld (Eds.), *Culture and infancy: Variations in the human experience* (pp. 287–328). New York: Academic Press.

Kuotai, T., & Jing-Hwa, C. (1985). The one-child-per-family policy: A psychological perspective. In W. S. Tseng & D. Y. H. Wu (Eds.), *Chinese culture and mental health* (pp. 153–166). Orlando, FL: Academic Press.

Lamb, M. E. (1977). The development of mother–infant and father–infant attachments in the second year of life. *Developmental Psychology, 13,* 637–648.

Lamb, M. E., Thompson, R. A., Gardner, W. P., Charnov, E. L., & Estes, D. (1984). Security of infantile attachment as assessed in the "strange situation": Its study and biological interpretation. *Behavioral and Brain Sciences, 7,* 127–171.

LeVine, R. A., & Miller, P. M. (1990). Commentary. *Human Development, 33,* 73–80.

Lin, C. Y. C., & Fu, V. R. (1990). A comparison of child-rearing practices among Chinese, immigrant Chinese, and Caucasian-American parents. *Child Development, 61,* 429–433.

Li-Repac, D. C. (1982). *The impact of acculturation on the child-rearing attitudes and practices of Chinese-American families: Consequences for the attachment process.* Unpublished doctoral dissertation, University of California at Berkeley.

Main, M. (1990). Cross-cultural studies of attachment organization: Recent studies, changing methodologies, and the concept of conditional strategies. *Human Development, 33,* 48–61.

Main, M., & Goldwyn, R. (in press). Interview-based adult attachment classifications: Related to infant–mother and infant–father attachment. *Developmental Psychology.*

Main, M., Kaplan, N., & Cassidy, J. (1985). Security in infancy, childhood, and adulthood: A move to the level of representation. In I. Bretherton & E. Waters (Eds.), Growing points of attachment theory and research. *Monographs of the Society for Research in Child Development, 50* (1–2, Serial No. 209), 66–104.

Main, M., & Solomon, J. (1990). Procedures for identifying infants as disorganized/disoriented during the Ainsworth Strange Situation. In M. T. Greenberg, D. Cicchetti, & E. M. Cummings (Eds.), *Attachment in the preschool years: Theory, research, and intervention* (pp. 121–160). Chicago: University of Chicago Press.

Main, M., & Weston, D. R. (1981). The quality of the toddler's relationship to mother and to father: Related to conflict behavior and the readiness to establish new relationships. *Child Development, 52,* 932–940.

Marvin, R. S., VanDevender, T. L., Iwanaga, M. I., LeVine, S., & LeVine, R. A. (1977). Infant–caregiver attachment among the Hausa of Nigeria. In H. McGurk (Ed.), *Ecological factors in human development* (pp. 247–259). Amsterdam: North-Holland.

Meins, E. (1997). *Security of attachment and the social development of cognition.* Hove, England: Psychology Press.

Miyake, K., Chen, S. J., & Campos, J. J. (1985). Infant temperament, mother's mode of interaction, and attachment in Japan: An interim report. In I. Bretherton & E. Waters (Eds.), Growing points of attachment theory and research. *Monographs of the Society for Research in Child Development, 50*(1–2, Serial No. 209), 276–297.

Mizuta, I., Zahn-Waxler, C., Cole, P. M., & Hiruma, N. (1996). A cross cultural study of preschoolers' attachment: Security and sensitivity in Japanese and U.S. dyads. *International Journal of Behavioral Development, 19,* 141–159.

Morelli, G. A., & Tronick, E. Z. (1991). Efé multiple caretaking and attachment. In J. L. Gewirtz & W. M. Kurtines (Eds.), *Intersections with attachment* (pp. 41–52). Hillsdale, NJ: Erlbaum.

Murdock, G. P., & White, D. R. (1969). Standard cross-cultural sample. *Ethnology, 8,* 329–369.

Nakagawa, M., Lamb, M. E., & Miyake, K. (1992). Antecedents and correlates of the strange situation behavior of Japanese infants. *Journal of Cross-Cultural Psychology, 23,* 300–310.

Nakagawa, M., Teti, D. M., & Lamb, M. E. (1992). An ecological study of child–mother attachments among Japanese sojourners in the United States. *Developmental Psychology, 28,* 584–592.

Nsamenang, A. B. (1992). *Human development in cultural context: A Third World perspective.* Newbury Park, CA: Sage.

Oppenheim, D., Sagi, A., & Lamb, M. E. (1990). Infant–adult attachments on the kibbutz and their relation to socioemotional development four years later. In S. Chess & M. E. Hertzig (Eds.), *Annual progress in child psychiatry and child development, 1989* (pp. 92–106). New York: Brunner/Mazel.

Pike, K. L. (1967). *Language in relation to a unified theory of the structure of human behavior* (rev. ed.). The Hague: Mouton.

Posada, G., Gao, Y., Wu, F., Posado, R., Tascon, M., Schoelmerich, A., Sagi, A., Kondo-Ikemura, K., Haaland, W., & Synnevaag, B. (1995). The secure-base phenomenon across cultures: Children's behavior, mothers' preferences, and experts' concepts. In E. Waters, B. E. Vaughn, G. Posada, & K. Kondo-Ikemura (Eds.), Caregiving, cultural, and cognitive perspectives on secure-base behavior and working models: New growing points of attachment theory and research. *Monographs of the Society for Research in Child Development, 60*(2–3, Serial No. 244), 27–48.

Rabin, A. I., & Beit-Hallahmi, B. (1982). *Twenty years later.* New York: Springer.

Reed, G., & Leiderman, P. H. (1981). Age-related changes in attachment behavior in polymatrically reared infants: The Kenyan Gusii. In T. M. Field, A. M. Sostek, P. Vietze, & P. H. Leiderman (Eds.), *Culture and early interactions* (pp. 215–236). Hillsdale, NJ: Erlbaum.

Robertson, J., & Robertson, J. (1971). Young children in brief separation: A fresh look. *Psychoanalytic Study of the Child, 26,* 264–315.

Sagi, A., Lamb, M. E., Lewkowicz, K. S., Shoham, R., Dvir, R., & Estes, D. (1985). Security of infant–mother, –father, and –metapelet attachments among kibbutz-reared Israeli children. In I. Bretherton & E. Waters (Eds.), Growing points of attachment theory and research. *Monographs of the Society for Research in Child Development, 50*(1–2, Serial No. 209), 257–275.

Sagi, A., & van IJzendoorn, M. H. (1996). Multiple caregiving environments: The kibbutz experience. In S. Harel & J. P. Shonkoff (Eds.), *Early childhood intervention and family support programs: Accomplishments and challenges* (pp. 143–162). Jerusalem: JDC–Brookale Institute.

Sagi, A., van IJzendoorn, M. H., Aviezer, O., Donnell, F., & Mayseless, O. (1994). Sleeping out of home in a kibbutz communal arrangement: It makes a difference for infant–mother attachment. *Child Development, 65,* 992–1004.

Sagi, A., van IJzendoorn, M. H., Scharf, M., Joels, T., Koren-Karie, N., Mayseless, O., & Aviezer, O. (1997). Ecological constraints for intergenerational transmission of attachment. *International Journal of Behavioral Development, 20,* 287–299.

Spangler, G., & Grossmann, K. E. (1993). Biobehavioral organization in securely and insecurely attached infants. *Child Development, 64,* 1439–1450.

Stafford, C. (1995). *The roads of Chinese childhood: Learning and identification in Angang.* Cambridge, England: Cambridge University Press.

Takahashi, K. (1982). Attachment behaviors to a female stranger among Japanese two-year-olds. *Journal of Genetic Psychology, 140,* 299–307.

Takahashi, K. (1986). Examining the strange-situation procedure with Japanese mothers and 12-month-old infants. *Developmental Psychology, 22,* 265–270.

Takahashi, K. (1990). Are the key assumptions of the 'strange situation' procedure universal? A view from Japanese research. *Human Development, 33,* 23–30.

Tavecchio, L. W. C., & van IJzendoorn, M. H. (1987). *Attachment in social networks: Contributions to the Bowlby–Ainsworth attachment theory.* Amsterdam: North-Holland.

Thompson, R. A. (1993). Socioemotional development: Enduring issues and new challenges. *Developmental Review, 13,* 372–402.

Trivers, R. L. (1974). Parent–offspring conflict. *American Zoologist, 14,* 249–264.

Tronick, E. Z., Morelli, G. A., & Winn, S. (1987). Multiple caretaking of Efé (Pygmy) infants. *American Anthropologist, 89,* 96–106.

True, M. M. (1994). *Mother–infant attachment and communication among the Dogon of Mali.* Unpublished doctoral dissertation, University of California at Berkeley.

Valenzuela, M. (1990). Attachment in chronically underweight young children. *Child Development, 61,* 1984–1996.

van IJzendoorn, M. H. (1990). Developments in cross-cultural research on attachment: Some methodological notes. *Human Development, 33,* 3–9.

van IJzendoorn, M. H. (1995). Adult attachment representations, parental responsiveness, and infant attachment: A meta-analysis on the predictive validity of the Adult Attachment Interview. *Psychological Bulletin, 117,* 387–403.

van IJzendoorn, M. H. (1996). Attachment patterns and their

outcomes: Commentary. *Human Development, 39,* 224–231.

van IJzendoorn, M. H., & DeWolff, M. S. (1997). In search of the absent father: Meta-analyses on infant–father attachment. A rejoinder to our discussants. *Child Development, 68,* 604–609.

van IJzendoorn, M. H., Dijkstra, J., & Bus, A.G. (1995). Attachment, intelligence, and language. *Social Development, 4,* 115–128.

van IJzendoorn, M. H., Juffer, F., & Duyvesteyn, M. G. C. (1995). Breaking the intergenerational cycle of insecure attachment: A review of the effects of attachment-based interventions on maternal sensitivity and infant security. *Journal of Child Psychology and Psychiatry, 36,* 225–248.

van IJzendoorn, M. H., & Kroonenberg, P. M. (1988). Cross-cultural patterns of attachment: A meta-analysis of the strange situation. *Child Development, 59,* 147–156.

van IJzendoorn, M. H., Sagi, A., & Lambermon, M. W. E. (1992). The multiple caretaker paradox: Data from Holland and Israel. In R. C. Pianta (Ed.), *New directions for child development: No. 57. Beyond the parent: The role of other adults in children's lives* (pp. 5–24). San Francisco, CA: Jossey-Bass.

van IJzendoorn, M. H., Vereijken, C. M. J. L., & Riksen-Walraven, J. M. A. (in press). Is the Attachment *Q*-Sort a valid measure of attachment security in young children? In B. Vaughn, E. Waters, & D. Posada (Eds.), *Patterns of secure base behavior:* Q-sort perspectives on attachment and caregiving in infancy and childhood. Mahwah, NJ: Erlbaum.

Vaughn, B. E., Stevenson-Hinde, J., Waters, E., Kotsaftis, A., Lefever, G. B., Shouldice, A., Trudel, M., & Belsky, J. (1992). Attachment security and temperament in infancy and early childhood: Some conceptual clarifications. *Developmental Psychology, 28,* 463–473.

Vaughn, B. E., & Waters, E. (1990). Attachment behavior at home and in the laboratory: Q-sort observations and strange situation classifications of one-year-olds. *Child Development, 61,* 1965–1973.

Vereijken, C. M. J. L. (1996). *The mother–infant relationship in Japan: Attachment, dependency, and* amae. Unpublished doctoral dissertation, Catholic University of Nijmegen, The Netherlands.

Verweij-Tijsterman, E. (1996). *Day care and attachment.* Amsterdam, Academisch Proefschrift Vrije Universiteit.

Wang, Z. M. (1993). Psychology in China: A review dedicated to Li Chen. *Annual Review of Psychology, 44,* 87–116.

Waters, E. (1978). The reliability and stability of individual differences in infant–mother attachment. *Child Development, 49,* 483–494.

Weisner, T. S., & Gallimore, R. (1977). My brother's keeper: Child and sibling caretaking. *Current Anthropology, 18,* 169–190.

Yang, C.-F. (1988). Familism and development: An examination of the role of family in contemporary China mainland, Hong Kong, and Taiwan. In D. Sinha & H. S. R. Kao (Eds.), *Social values and development: Asian perspectives* (pp. 93–123). New Delhi: Sage.

Yang, K.-S. (1988). Will societal modernization eventually eliminate cross-cultural psychological differences? In M. H. Bond (Ed.), *The cross-cultural challenge to social psychology* (pp. 67–85). Beverly Hills, CA: Sage.

Zhu, Z., & Lin, C. (1991). Research and application in Chinese child psychology. *Applied Psychology: An International Review, 40,* 15–25.

32

Loss and Bereavement

Attachment Theory and Recent Controversies Concerning "Grief Work" and the Nature of Detachment

❖

R. CHRIS FRALEY
PHILLIP R. SHAVER

For the majority of his adult life, Charles Darwin suffered from a perplexing set of symptoms, including persistent gastric pains and heart palpitations. Modern scholars have suggested that Darwin's ill health resulted from what is known today as "hyperventilation syndrome," a condition that can be triggered by stressful psychological events. Although it is difficult to ascertain the true etiology of Darwin's illness, scholars have identified a range of possibilities—including Darwin's controversial professional life and his tumultuous interpersonal life, which included the loss of his mother when he was 8 years old.

Given the possible connection between Darwin's ill health and the early death of his mother, it is not surprising that John Bowlby took an ardent interest in Darwin's life. In his final book, *Charles Darwin: A New Life,* Bowlby (1990) attributed Darwin's illness to suppressed grief following the death of his mother. Bowlby believed that the suppression of grief inhibits a natural sequence of painful emotional reactions that, unless allowed to run their full course, can lead to psychological and physical ill health.

Although Bowlby's final book was primarily concerned with understanding Darwin's loss in particular, he was deeply concerned with the psychological consequences of loss throughout his career. In his first empirical study (Bowlby,

1946), he argued that the loss of a primary attachment figure was a predisposing factor in juvenile delinquency. Furthermore, in his landmark trilogy about attachment theory, *Attachment and Loss,* loss received prominent billing and was the focus of the entire third volume (Bowlby, 1980).

Although Bowlby's ideas about loss changed and developed over the course of his career, he continued to portray the loss of an attachment figure as a major factor in personality development. He viewed unresolved and suppressed grief as important pathogenic forces, and viewed grief itself as a natural part of the functioning of what he called the "attachment behavioral system," a system "designed" by natural selection to discourage prolonged separation between an individual and his or her primary attachment figure.

Our aims in this chapter are to summarize Bowlby's theoretical contributions to the study of bereavement, and to review recent research and controversies concerning attachment theory and loss.[1] We begin with a broad review of Bowlby's key ideas as expressed in the *Attachment and Loss* trilogy. We discuss Bowlby's ideas on the function and course of mourning, and review theory and research on patterns of "disordered" mourning. Next we discuss recent controversies that question two of Bowlby's important claims: his claim that the suppression of grief has negative consequences (Bonanno, Keltner, Holen, & Horowitz, 1995; M. Stroebe, 1992; M. Stroebe & W. Stroebe, 1991; Wortman & Silver, 1989), and his purported claim that recovery from loss entails arriving at a state of "detachment" (Klass, Silverman, & Nickman, 1996a). In both cases, we conclude that Bowlby was essentially correct, although not privy to recent findings that allow elaboration and further specification of his ideas.

AN ATTACHMENT PERSPECTIVE ON SEPARATION AND BEREAVEMENT

Bowlby's thoughts on loss and grief were developed over a period of several decades, but expressed most completely in his 1980 volume, *Loss*. In this volume, Bowlby addressed a wide range of issues (e.g., whether or not children are capable of grieving). However, two of his goals are of particular interest for the present chapter. First, Bowlby wished to show that seemingly irrational or "immature" reactions to loss, such as disbelief, anger, searching, and sensing the continued presence of the lost attachment figure, are understandable when viewed from an ethological perspective. Second, Bowlby sought to argue that the way an individual responds to loss stems from the way his or her attachment system has become organized over the course of development. Bowlby believed that individuals whose attachment systems are organized in such a way as to chronically anticipate rejection and loss (preoccupied or anxious-ambivalent individuals) or to defensively suppress attachment-related feelings (avoidant or compulsively self-reliant individuals) are likely to suffer from psychological and physical distress following bereavement. In developing these ideas, Bowlby paid particular attention to the function of attachment behavior and to various factors that may shape the organization of an individual's attachment system.

The Function and Course of Mourning in Infancy and Adulthood

One of Bowlby's most important contributions to the literature on bereavement was an ethological perspective on attachment and loss. Bowlby observed that infants of many species require protection and care from older individuals in order to survive. To obtain this protection, infants have evolved physical adaptations (such as large eyes)

and behavioral adaptations (such as crying) that attract the attention of potential caregivers. In addition to these more basic adaptations, however, infants possess a motivational system (the attachment system) designed by natural selection to regulate and maintain proximity between infants and their caregivers. When the attachment figure is judged to be sufficiently close and accessible, the infant experiences what Sroufe and Waters (1977a) called "felt security" and is more likely to explore the environment and engage in playful social interactions. In contrast, when the attachment figure is judged to be inaccessible or absent, the infant experiences anxiety and vigorously attempts to reestablish contact with the absent figure by calling, searching, and clinging. The following passage illustrates the protest of a 16-month-old girl after learning that her father would be leaving her in the nursery for an extended period of time.

> When Dawn sensed that her father was leaving, she again whined "Mm, mm, mm," and as he got up she broke into a loud cry and clutched him around the neck. Father became upset, put her down and tried to console her. Dawn then threw herself in a temper on the floor and screamed for her father. As he was departing through the door, she almost knocked her head on the floor. When the nurse picked her up, she continued to scream but later comforted herself by sucking her finger and some candy. (Heinicke & Westheimer, 1965, pp. 94–95)

According to Bowlby (1969/1982), these "protest" reactions promote the infant's survival because they help to ensure proximity between the infant and the attachment figure. Furthermore, the yearning and anxiety experienced by the child motivate him or her to continue seeking the missing attachment figure until all efforts have been exhausted. When viewed within this light, many of the seemingly perplexing reactions to separation and loss (such as continued searching even when a lost caregiver is objectively irretrievable) appear reasonable and adaptive. Such protest responses would have served an important biological function in evolutionary history. By doing everything possible to prevent the loss of their attachment figures or by successfully recovering missing attachment figures, infants would have substantially increased their chances of survival, and ultimately their reproductive fitness.

During the protest phase of separation and loss, infants generally react vigorously to their situation. However, the intensity of these reactions eventually wanes if the separation is extended, as is obviously the case following a caregiver's death. Anxiety, anger, and denial eventually give way to despair, sadness, and withdrawal. This second phase, "despair," was viewed by Bowlby as a result of the failure of protest to induce the return of the lost attachment figure. A third phase, "detachment," marks an apparent recovery and gradual renewal of interest in other activities and social relationships. The term "detachment" is somewhat misleading, however, because Bowlby and his coworkers provided evidence that reunion with a lost attachment figure can, after a period of reassurance of the person's stable return and continued interest, cause powerful activation of the attachment system (e.g., crying, following, clinging). The apparent "detachment," therefore, is not a neutral wearing away of an attachment bond, but rather a defensive suppression of attachment responses that have failed for a long while to produce the attachment figure.[2]

Although Bowlby was primarily concerned with understanding infant–caregiver attachment, he viewed adult romantic, or pair-bond, relationships within the same theoretical framework he used to explain infant attachment. Bowlby (1969/1982, 1980) and his colleagues (e.g., Parkes & Weiss, 1983; Weiss, 1975) observed that adults who lose or are separated from their romantic attachment figures undergo a series of reactions similar to those observed in infants. As an illustration, consider the following passage, which describes the protest reaction of a woman whose husband died after spending several months in the hospital with leukemia. Although she had anticipated the loss for some time (in fact, her husband was expected to die that evening), she still felt compelled to hold on to him and keep him from leaving.

> I went over to him. I remember my brother-in-law taking me away from him because he said I kept holding on to him and patting his head. I cried my heart out. But I remember my brother-in-law coming to me and taking me away from him. (Quoted in Parkes & Weiss, 1983, p. 78)

When a loss is prolonged or permanent, the protest phase is often accompanied by an enduring preoccupation with the missing person. An adult often experiences an intense yearning for a lost mate and continues, for some time after the loss, to find it surprising or disquieting when aspects of the normal routine are interrupted by the conspicuous absence of the attachment figure.

> The hardest thing for me, I think, is at night. We have a neighbor [who] works the second shift and we hear his pickup truck every night. And my husband would always say something like, 'When's he going to get his brakes fixed?' And every night I'm sitting here when he comes along, and that's when I really think about my husband, because he would always say something. (Quoted in Parkes & Weiss, 1983, p. 87)

Eventually, when the individual realizes that his or her partner will not be returning, some degree of despair and disorganization is likely. For both adults and children, this phase is characterized by sleeping and eating disturbances, social withdrawal, profound loneliness, and intense sorrow. As Weiss (1973) noted, the feelings of loneliness stem specifically from the absence of the attachment figure and cannot be alleviated by the presence of others (see W. Stroebe, Stroebe, Abakoumkin, & Schut, 1996, for recent empirical evidence on this point). Although many bereaved individuals derive some comfort from the presence of close, supportive friends or family members, these support networks do not fill the emotional gap left by the missing attachment figure.

For most bereaved individuals, the phase of despair and disorganization lasts for many months. In the first few months following conjugal bereavement, roughly 30% to 40% of adults can be classified as clinically depressed (Clayton, Halikas, & Maurice, 1972; Futterman, Gallagher, Thompson, Lovett, & Gilewski, 1990). After this time, however, symptoms of grief appear to decrease in a negative exponential manner. Roughly 12 months after bereavement, approximately 18% to 30% of bereaved adults exhibit signs of depression (Bornstein, Clayton, Halikas, Maurice, & Robins, 1973; Clayton et al., 1972; Jacobs, Hansen, Berkman, Kasl, & Ostfeld, 1989). After 24 to 30 months, approximately 18% of adults exhibit signs of depression (Futterman et al., 1990; Lund et al., 1985; Lund, Caserta, Dimond, & Shaffer, 1989)—a figure almost twice the base rate of depression in a nonbereaved population. Importantly, even many years after a loss, healthy individuals continue to dream of, cry over, and yearn for a deceased partner (Klass et al., 1996a). As one bereaved individual expressed it, in an often quoted remark, "You don't get over it; you just get used to it."

In Bowlby's later work on loss in adulthood (Bowlby, 1980), these particular phases of mourning were supplemented by a new initial phase, "numbing," because research and clinical observations indicated that mourners often fail to register the loss of the attachment figure at first, presumably because the event is too painful and perhaps incomprehensible. The following example describes the initial numbing reaction of a woman whose husband died suddenly and unexpectedly. Upon visiting the morgue, she found it difficult to acknowledge that her husband was dead.

> I didn't believe it. I stayed there for twenty minutes. I rubbed him, I rubbed his face, I patted him, I rubbed his head. I called him, but he didn't answer. And I knew if I called him he'd answer me because he's used to my voice. But he didn't answer me. They said he was dead, but his skin was just as warm as mine. (Quoted in Parkes & Weiss, 1983, p. 84)

Also, on the basis of adults' ability to talk about their troubling experiences, and of their attempts to deal cognitively and emotionally with loss, Bowlby changed the name of the final phase from "detachment" to "reorganization." As explained later in this chapter, this change is particularly important because it reflects Bowlby's belief that many mourners do not defensively "detach" from lost attachment figures, but instead rearrange their representations of self and lost figures so that a continuing bond *and* adjustment to real circumstances are both possible.

As might be expected, given Bowlby's ethological perspective on separation and loss, there is considerable evidence that grief responses are characteristic of many species, not just humans. For many animals born without the capacity to care for themselves, the loss of a primary attachment figure evokes intense anxiety and protest, and leads eventually to despair and sorrow (see Bowlby, 1969/1982). For example, in one of the earliest studies on attachment in rhesus macaques, Seay, Hansen, and Harlow (1962) separated 5-month-old rhesus infants from their mothers for a 3-week period. These infants reacted at first with extreme signs of protest and agitation, including screeching and attempts to break the barriers separating them from their mothers. When these attempts failed to bring them closer to their mothers, the rhesus infants became lethargic and withdrawn. (See Plimpton & Rosenblum, 1987, and Reite & Boccia, 1994, for reviews of more recent studies of reactions to loss in nonhuman primates.)

Such dramatic responses are also characteristic of some nonmammalian species that exhibit attachment behavior. Konrad Lorenz (1963), an ethologist whose work had an enormous impact on the development of Bowlby's ideas, provided a remarkable illustration of these emotional reactions in the greylag goose:

> The first response to the disappearance of the partner consists in the anxious attempt to find him again. The goose moves about restlessly by day and night, flying great distances and visiting all places where the partner might be found, uttering all the time the penetrating trisyllabic long-distance call. . . . The searching expeditions are extended farther and farther, and quite often the searcher himself gets lost, or succumbs to an accident. . . . All the objectively observable characteristics of the goose's behaviour on losing its mate are roughly identical with those accompanying human grief. (Lorenz, 1963, pp. 200–201)

Cross-cultural research on humans also attests to the prevalence of these specific emotional and behavioral responses to loss (Rosenblatt, Walsh, & Jackson, 1976). As W. Stroebe and Stroebe (1987) have observed, however, the specific ways in which grief is manifested varies substantially across cultures. Some societies are structured in ways that accentuate, and perhaps romanticize, the anxiety, anger, and yearning experienced after loss. For example, Mathison (1970) described the structured rituals of certain Trobriand Islanders. As part of their mourning ritual, a widow is expected to cry for several days following the loss of her husband. In contrast to these expressive norms, the display of emotion is restricted to a brief period among the Navajo. After this time, a widow is expected to return to her normal everyday activities and not to speak of the loss or the deceased (Miller & Schoenfeld, 1973). Nevertheless, despite the variability in mourning rituals that has been observed by cultural anthropologists, the loss of a loved one appears to elicit profound distress in humans everywhere (Rosenblatt et al., 1976).

In summary, Bowlby's ethological theory of attachment and loss has made an important contribution to our understanding of the phenomenology of grief and the behavioral and emotional reactions exhibited following the loss of an attachment figure.[3] According to Bowlby's theory, the absence of an attachment figure activates an innate motivational system that compels the individual to search for the person and to do everything possible to regain that person's proximity and care. When these efforts fail, the bereaved individual experiences profound sorrow and despair. Eventually, the bereaved individual reorganizes his or her representations of the world in a way that allows him or her to return to normal activities and seek out or renew social relationships. Because some of the theoretical points surrounding this last stage are controversial, we return to them later in the chapter, in the section titled "Continuing Bonds: A Controversy Concerning Detachment and Resolution."

Bowlby's Conceptualization of Disordered Patterns of Mourning

In addition to offering an explanation of normative reactions to loss of an attachment figure, Bowlby also proposed a framework for conceptualizing atypical forms of mourning. His analysis of these disordered forms suggests that they can be arrayed along a single conceptual dimension running from "chronic mourning" to "prolonged absence of conscious grieving" (Bowlby, 1980, p. 138).[4] Chronic mourning is characterized by protracted grief and prolonged difficulty in normal functioning. Individuals who suffer from chronic mourning may find themselves overly preoccupied with thoughts of their missing partners and unable to return to normal functioning for years after the loss. In contrast, an absence of grief is characterized by a conspicuous lack of conscious sorrow, anger, or distress. According to Bowlby, individuals exhibiting an absence of grief may express relatively little distress following the loss, continue in their jobs or activities without any noticeable disruption, and seek little support or solace from friends and family. It was Bowlby's belief that this manner of reacting to loss can lead to difficulties in long-term adjustment if an individual has lost someone to whom he or she is deeply attached.

For the most part, modern clinicians agree with Bowlby's delineation of these opposing patterns of grief (e.g., Middleton, Raphael, Martinek, & Misso, 1993; W. Stroebe & Stroebe, 1987). According to Middleton et al. (1993), most clinicians distinguish between two forms of disordered mourning: "delayed" and "chronic." Similar to Bowlby's description of a prolonged absence of conscious grieving, delayed mourning is characterized by denials of distress and a continuation of normal affairs without substantial disruption. This category of disordered mourning is similar to what Parkes (1965) referred to as "inhibited" mourning and what Deutsch (1937) called "absent" mourning. Chronic mourning, as understood by contemporary clinicians, encompasses what Bowlby likewise called chronic mourning and is characterized by prolonged symptoms of depression and anxiety. Chronic mourning also includes what contemporary psychologists call "unresolved grief" (e.g., Ainsworth & Eichberg, 1991; Lundin, 1984; Main & Hesse, 1990; Zisook & Devaul, 1985), although the precise meaning of this term varies considerably across theorists, as we explain later.

Research on Patterns of Mourning

It is noteworthy that variants of these two major patterns of problematic grief have been identified in multiple ways throughout the history of attachment research. In the literatures on both infant and adult attachment relationships, researchers have focused on individuals who experience intense distress after losing attachment figures, as well as on individuals who apparently experience little distress following loss or separation. Although this research has not exclusively focused on irretrievable cases of loss (e.g., death of a spouse), it provides important insights into the nature of bereavement, because, according to Bowlby (1980), the same psychological mechanisms underlie reactions to both brief and permanent separations.[5]

One of the earliest researchers to focus on differences in reactions to separation from an attachment figure was Mary Ainsworth. As explained by Solomon and George (Chapter 14, this volume), Ainsworth developed the strange situation assessment procedure (Ainsworth, Blehar, Waters, & Wall, 1978) to investigate the interplay of attachment and exploration in a controlled laboratory setting. The procedure is generally used with infant–caregiver dyads and includes two moderately stressful separations between an infant and one of his or her principal attachment figures. The purpose of the procedure is to classify infants' reactions to these brief but somewhat stressful separations and the reunions that follow. As most readers of this chapter know, the three major patterns are "secure," "anxious-ambivalent," and "avoidant." *Of special interest here is the fact that these patterns, like those identified following an irretrievable loss, can be arrayed along a dimension ranging from intense and chronic distress to an absence or avoidance of distress.*

Anxious-ambivalent infants in the strange situation are marked by a tendency to remain focused on their attachment figure (rather than playing wholeheartedly with the attractive toys provided by the experimenter), to cry profusely during the separation episodes, *and to refuse to calm down once their attachment figure returns.* In other words, they exhibit a miniature version of chronic mourning, becoming extremely distressed by separation and then finding it impossible to "resolve" this upset when conditions would seem to warrant resolution. Avoidant infants in the strange situation are marked by a kind of cool nonchalance regarding their attachment figures' whereabouts, and—at least in some cases—an active ignoring of them when they return following a separation. This can be viewed as a miniature and very short-term version of failure to become anxious, angry, or bereft in the face of loss. Secure infants fall somewhere in between the two major insecure groups, often reacting with considerable distress to the separations but also being quick to "resolve" these negative emotions once their attachment figures return.

Research on adults' reactions to separation from or loss of attachment figures also indicates that responses can be arrayed along a conceptual dimension running from absent to chronic distress. As noted above, research by Parkes and his colleagues (Parkes, 1985; Parkes & Weiss, 1983) suggests that some individuals experience chronic anxiety, whereas others chronically deny the psychological impact of the loss on their well-being. In our research on relationship breakups (Fraley, Davis, & Shaver, 1997) and marital separations (Fraley & Shaver, 1998), we have also identified reactions falling along this dimension. Specifically, after separations from romantic partners or spouses, many individuals report experiencing intense anxiety and sorrow. Furthermore, naturalistic observations indicate that these individuals are highly likely to cling to their partners and to resist separation actively (Fraley & Shaver, 1998). On the other hand, some individuals appear less distressed when separated from their partners. They are less likely to protest separation and appear to be relatively unaffected by the absence of their mates.

Chronic Grief and Anxious-Ambivalent Organization of the Attachment System

One of Bowlby's key ideas was that whether an individual exhibits a healthy or problematic pattern of grief following separation depends on the way his or her attachment system has become organized over the course of development. Individuals who experience chronic grief are thought to have organized their attachment behavior around the implicit assumption that attachment figures will not be consistently accessible or trustworthy. As Bowlby argued, these expectations have their roots in an individual's history of attachment-related experiences:

> [A]lthough those who make anxious and ambivalent attachments are likely to have experienced discontinuities in parenting and/or often to have been rejected by their parents, the rejection is more likely to have been intermittent and partial than complete. As a result the children, still hoping for love and care yet deeply anxious lest they be neglected or deserted, increase their demands for attention and affection, refuse to be left alone and protest more or less angrily when they are. (Bowlby, 1980, pp. 218–219)

By persistently searching for the attachment figure and doing everything possible to prevent separation, the anxious-ambivalent individual increases the chance that he or she will be able to retain the attachment figure's attention and care. Thus the individual's mind is organized in a way that keeps him or her persistently "searching" for cues regarding the attachment figure's availability and presence. When the attachment figure's availability is questionable, this hypervigilance manifests itself in clinginess, jealousy, and inability to focus or concentrate on other activities. In the absence of the attachment figure, however, this vigilance manifests itself in persistent searching behavior, yearning, anxiety, and depression. Because the mind has become organized to detect cues of unavailability or unresponsiveness, a real loss continues to prime the attachment system, making extreme anxiety and sorrow almost unavoidable.

Research on both infant and adult attachment supports Bowlby's idea that the organization of attachment behavior and emotion reflects the history and dynamics of the individual's relationships with his or her principal attachment figures. In infancy and early childhood, a relative lack of care and maternal sensitivity is associated with anxious-ambivalence on the part of a child (Anisfeld, Casper, Nozyce, & Cunningham, 1990; Ainsworth et al., 1978; Grossmann, Grossmann, Spangler, Suess, & Unzner, 1985; van den Boom, 1990; van IJzendoorn, 1995). In contrast, children who are provided with a stable environment, and with sensitive and responsive care, appear to organize their attachment behavior and emotions in a way suggesting that they expect others to be available when needed. As noted above, these secure children become fairly distressed when separated from their mothers in the strange situation, but are easily soothed and comforted when the mothers return. This pattern of behavior differs substantially from that of an anxious-ambivalent child, who essentially punishes the mother for leaving and vigorously attempts to prevent her from leaving again.

In the context of adult romantic attachments, the organization of attachment behavior and emotion also tends to reflect the nature of the romantic attachment relationship (Collins & Read, 1990; Hazan & Shaver, 1987; Kirkpatrick & Davis, 1994). In some of our naturalistic studies, we have observed that adults who exhibit the most distress following separation (similar to a pattern of chronic mourning) are the least likely to have stable relationships with their partners (Fraley & Shaver, 1998). That is, their relationships have lasted for only a brief period of time, and/or their representational models, measured with self-report instruments, indicate that they worry about obtaining the stability, security, and care that they desire in close relationships. This ambivalent, or preoccupied, romantic attachment pattern also appears to be linked to chronic mourning after the end of a relationship. We have also found that preoccupied adults are the most likely to experience distress and disturbance following the end of an exclusive relationship (Fraley et al., 1997). Preoccupied adults are more likely than other adults to cry, cling, and yearn for their missing partners for extended periods of time.

Following bereavement, adults characterized as insecure, dependent, anxious, or fearful are often those who suffer from chronic mourning (Parkes & Weiss, 1983; Sanders, 1989; Vachon et al., 1982). Parkes (1985; Parkes & Weiss, 1983) described the "grief-prone personality," a construct modeled after Bowlby's description of anxiously attached individuals and empirically associated with poor outcomes in Parke's studies. These individuals were intensely anxious, yearned deeply for their lost spouses, and had extreme difficulty in adjusting to prior losses.

In recent years, Mary Main and her colleagues (e.g., Main & Hesse, 1990; Main, Kaplan, & Cassidy, 1985) have devoted a considerable amount of effort to understanding adults' representations of their early attachment relationships. Using a clinical assessment procedure, the Adult Attachment Interview (AAI; George, Kaplan, & Main, 1984), designed to assess "current state of mind with respect to attachment" in adults, Main

and her colleagues have identified a group of individuals whom they classify as "unresolved/disorganized" with respect to loss or trauma." Unresolved loss is marked by

> (1) lapses in the metacognitive monitoring of reasoning, such as indications of disbelief that a person is dead, ideas of being causal in the death, indications of confusion between the dead person and self, and other psychologically confused statements; (2) lapses in the metacognitive monitoring of discourse such as prolonged, inappropriate silences, odd associations, unusual attention to detail, poetic or eulogistic phrasing of speech; (3) reports of extreme behavioral responses at the time of the trauma in the absence of convincing evidence that resolution has taken place. (Main & Goldwyn, 1985, 1994, as summarized by Adam, Sheldon-Keller, & West, 1995, p. 318)

The unresolved designation is assigned when a person receives a relatively high rating on an unresolved coding scale, but he or she is also assigned to a best-fitting primary AAI category (dismissing, autonomous/secure, or preoccupied) as well. In every study of which we are aware, there is an association between unresolved mourning and preoccupied attachment. For example, Ainsworth and Eichberg (1991) found that 50% of the mothers in their sample who received an unresolved classification were also given a secondary classification of preoccupied. In contrast, only 18% of the sample who did not experience a loss or who had resolved their loss were classified as preoccupied. In a recent report by Adam et al. (1995), 49% of an adolescent clinic sample was classified with the AAI as unresolved. Of this subsample, 48% were given a secondary classification of preoccupied, compared to 12% of those not classified as unresolved. These findings provide additional evidence that unresolved or chronic mourning is associated with a preoccupied attachment organization.

There is also a body of research *not* rooted in the attachment perspective that links characteristics associated with an anxious-ambivalent attachment organization to chronic mourning and difficulties in recovery. This research indicates that both neuroticism and low self-esteem, indicators of anxious-ambivalence (Shaver & Brennan, 1992), are correlates of chronic mourning in bereaved individuals. For example, Vachon et al. (1982) and M. Stroebe and Stroebe (1993) found that neuroticism was associated with depression in the months following bereavement. Furthermore, Lund et al. (1989) found that low self-esteem was associated with stress and depression two years after bereavement. (For a more complete discussion of research on personality and bereavement, see reviews by Sanders, 1993, and W. Stroebe & Stroebe, 1987)

In summary, there is considerable empirical support for Bowlby's idea that chronic mourning stems from an anxious-ambivalent attachment organization. He believed that lack of responsiveness on the part of attachment figures (in both childhood and adulthood) heightens an individual's vigilance and sensitivity to cues regarding separation, rejection, and loss. As a result, when irretrievable losses occur, anxious-ambivalent or preoccupied, individuals have difficulty resolving these losses because their attachment systems are primed to continue yearning and searching for the missing attachment figures.

The Absence of Grief

Bowlby (1980) believed that relative absence of distress, or apparent "detachment," is a defensive reaction to loss that may eventually break down and give rise to intense feelings of grief and sorrow. He also entertained the possibility that the suppression of grief can have adverse effects on physical health, as illustrated by the example of Charles Darwin. According to Bowlby, the relative absence of grief exhibited by some individuals following loss is a facet of a more general pattern of personality organization, which he called "compulsive self-reliance." He believed that compulsive self-reliance stems from early attachment experiences in which the expression of emotion is discouraged: "Not infrequently, it seems, a person who grows up to assert his independence of affectional ties has [grown up in a family where] affectional bonds are little valued, attachment behavior is regarded as childish and weak and is rebuffed, all expression of feeling is frowned upon and contempt expressed for those who cry" (pp. 224–225). Bowlby believed that over time, such experiences can lead an individual to assert his or her independence and self-sufficiency, even in situations involving permanent losses.

In Chapter 4 of *Loss,* Bowlby (1980) offered a sophisticated account of the defense mechanisms that may regulate an individual's experience of grief and sorrow, and explained why these mechanisms may pose problems for the individual's long-term well-being. He believed that the process of "defensive exclusion"—a deliberate or automatic redirection of attention away from painful thoughts and feelings about the loss—can eventually lead to the development of segregated or dissociated memory systems for the loss experience. Because these memories still exist, albeit in an unintegrated form, they can continue to influence emotion and behavior without the person's understanding how or why.

When people fail to acknowledge the implications of a loss (i.e., when they avoid confronting the loss), Bowlby believed that they are vulnerable to subsequent physical and psychological illness for two reasons. First, if representations of the experience become relatively dissociated from other representations in memory, people have a difficult time sensitizing themselves to events and thoughts surrounding the loss; they tend not to work through the walled-off memories and expectations. Because the dissociated representations are infrequently activated, it is difficult to habituate naturally to the emotions associated with them. When this is the case, it may take only subtle, but personally meaningful, stimuli to reactivate representations of the attachment figure or the loss and to bring about feelings of anxiety and distress. As an example, Bowlby noted that individuals who fail to express grief in the early months of bereavement may break down when an anniversary takes place or when some other reminder of the attachment figure summons to mind fragmented memories and feelings for the deceased. For a nondefensive individual, these events may not elicit heightened distress, because the meaning of the events and their connections to other aspects of the individual's life have been worked through and integrated into current representations of the world. For the defensive person, in contrast, these unintegrated reactions can be frightening or disorienting.

Bowlby also believed that dissociated or segregated memory systems can lead to long-term physical or psychological distress because their partial activation continues to prime the attachment system. For example, mundane events, such as making dinner, can elicit fairly stressful reactions and tax a person's physical resources if these activities were previously organized around the now-deceased attachment figure. A bereaved individual, however, may not recognize the source of these reactions if he or she has not fully acknowledged the loss or come to recognize the loss-related meaning implicit in seemingly mundane activities. Repeated activation of inexplicable and partially suppressed negative emotions may eventually have a negative impact on psychological well-being or physical health.

Unfortunately, little research has explicitly examined the long-term implications of defensive approaches to loss. However, a few studies have been published in recent years on the role of "grief work," and they appear to call Bowlby's assumptions about defenses into question. In the next two sections, we review this research and discuss its implications for attachment theory.

THE ROLE OF "GRIEF WORK" IN THE RECOVERY PROCESS: A CONTROVERSY CONCERNING THE SUPPRESSION OF GRIEF

Bowlby considered acknowledgment of beliefs, expectations, and emotions related to lost attachment figures to be a fundamental part of the recovery process. That is, he believed that a bereaved individual must reorganize working models in a manner that simultaneously and coherently acknowledges the absence of the attachment figure and does not defensively isolate memories or affects related to the loss. This reorganization process is commonly called "grief work" in the bereavement literature. Bowlby's perspective on grief work has been shared by many clinicians, including those inspired by his theory (Parkes & Weiss, 1983) as well as those who preceded him (Freud, 1917/1957; Lindemann, 1944). Most clinicians consider it important to acknowledge or confront a loss explicitly and to "work though" feelings and emotions related to the loss experience (M. Stroebe, 1992). Similarly, many clinicians consider the suppression of memories and feelings related to the loss, or avoidance of reminders of the loss, to be among the major wellsprings of psychopathology.

In recent years, however, several researchers have questioned the importance of grief work in the recovery process (Bonanno, in press; Bonanno, Znoj, Siddique, & Horowitz, 1996; M. Stroebe, 1992; M. Stroebe & Stroebe, 1991; Wortman & Silver, 1989). Specifically, these researchers have pointed out that the suppression of grief may not be as detrimental as was previously assumed. Because this perspective calls one of Bowlby's major theoretical ideas into question, we review its claims in detail and examine the evidence that bears on them.

Early Critiques of the Grief Work Hypothesis

In a highly influential article entitled "The Myths of Coping with Loss," Wortman and Silver (1989) critically analyzed several assumptions held by clinicians regarding the bereavement process. One of these assumptions is that grief work facilitates recovery. Wortman and Silver pointed out correctly that, given the emphasis clinicians place on grief work, surprisingly little research had examined the value or necessity of the process. Furthermore, Wortman and Silver argued that most of the evidence that did exist actually contradicted the grief work hypothesis.

Wortman and Silver (1989) reviewed two programs of research that they believed addressed the role of grief work in the recovery process. The first was that of Parkes and Weiss (1983), two colleagues of Bowlby's who conducted a frequently cited longitudinal study of bereaved adults. Various measures were taken shortly after the loss, 13 months after the loss, and 2–4 years after the loss. Wortman and Silver (1989) focused on one of these measures—"yearning," a coder rating of the extent to which a bereaved individual pined over a missing spouse. Wortman and Silver interpreted this measure as an indicator of grief work. Parkes and Weiss's (1983) results showed that individuals with the highest yearning scores in the initial interview were *more* likely than others to have poor mental and physical health outcomes 13 months after the loss. According to Wortman and Silver, this indicated that the people who were doing the most grief work were the least likely to adjust to the loss.

As further evidence against the grief work hypothesis, Wortman and Silver (1989) cited their own research on parents who had suffered the sudden death of an infant (Silver & Wortman, 1988, and Wortman & Silver, 1987, both cited in Wortman & Silver, 1989). In these studies, grief work was assessed as "active attempts by the parent to make sense of and process the death, including searching for an answer for why the baby had died, thinking of ways the death could have been avoided, and being preoccupied with thoughts about the loss" (Wortman & Silver, 1989, p. 352). Their results indicated that the more parents engaged in such supposed grief work, the more distressed they were 18 months after the loss. Furthermore, they were also more likely to feel bitter about the loss and easily upset by reminders of it.

According to Wortman and Silver (1989), the results of these studies call into question the usefulness of grief work in the recovery process. As M. Stroebe, van den Bout, and Schut (1994) pointed out, however, Wortman and Silver may have inadvertently examined indicators of distress and preoccupation, rather than indicators of grief work per se. Yearning, in the Parkes and Weiss (1983) study, was conceptualized as a "constant pining [that] interferes with other thinking" (p. 46). Yearning, according to this definition, is thus an indicator of depressive rumination and preoccupation, not of reorganization, acknowledgment, and integration. Similarly, in Wortman and Silver's own studies, operationalizations of grief work appear to have been confounded with distress, worry, and preoccupation. In summary, the studies reviewed by Wortman and Silver as evidence against the grief work hypothesis either inadequately or inaccurately captured the phenomenon as it was conceptualized by Bowlby and other clinicians. Wortman and Silver may have confounded early signs of anxious-ambivalent chronic mourning with more secure approaches to reorganization following loss.

More Recent Critiques of the Grief Work Hypothesis

Although Wortman and Silver's (1989) article had an enormous impact on subsequent theorizing about grief work, many researchers have pointed to the limitations of their analysis. As mentioned above, M. Stroebe et al. (1994) observed that the evidence provided by Wortman and Silver failed to distinguish depressive rumination from the process of working through the loss. Nevertheless, as M. Stroebe et al. (1994) acknowledged, Wortman and Silver's discussion made an important contribution to the field because it drew attention to the relative dearth of research explicitly investigating the value of grief work in the recovery process.

What has been learned since the publication of Wortman and Silver's (1989) critique? In a comprehensive review of the grief work hypothesis, M. Stroebe (1992) concluded that the evidence "does not back the strong claims made by theorists and clinicians in favor of the grief work hypothesis. . . . the grief work hypothesis has neither been confirmed nor disconfirmed empirically" (p. 27). Furthermore, in a subsequent review, Bonanno et al. (1995), concluded that "avoiding unpleasant emotions during bereavement is in fact not such a bad thing" (p. 986).

These conclusions have been drawn from research that was explicitly designed to remedy the shortcomings of the research discussed above. It is worthwhile to consider this newer research in more detail and to examine its implications for Bowlby's theory.

M. Stroebe and Stroebe (1991) conducted a longitudinal study of 30 widows and 30 widowers to determine whether the initial suppression of grief leads to poor adjustment in the long run. As a measure of psychological adjustment, these authors assessed depression (with the Beck Depression Inventory) approximately 4–7 months, 14 months, and 24 months after the loss. As a measure of grief work, the authors created a scale ranging from confrontation to avoidance. Items measuring avoidance included "I avoid anything that would be too painful a reminder" and "At the moment any activity is a welcome distraction."

To assess the effectiveness of grief work in reducing depression, the authors examined the association between early measures of grief work and later measures of depression, while controlling for early levels of depression. The results indicated that for widows, the use of avoidant strategies did not lead to higher levels of depression. For widowers, however, the use of avoidant strategies did lead to higher levels of depression. Given this mixed evidence, M. Stroebe and Stroebe (1991) concluded that it would be premature to draw any definitive conclusions about the role of grief work in recovery.

In another important series of studies, Bonanno and his colleagues (Bonanno et al., 1995, in press; Bonanno, Siddique, Keltner, & Horowitz, 1997) investigated the association between defensive processes and adjustment to bereavement. The research team followed a sample of bereaved individuals from the San Francisco Bay Area over a period of approximately 2 years, assessing grief and adjustment with clinical interviews, questionnaires, and objective and subjective health reports at 6 months, 14 months, and 25 months after loss. The main conclusion the team has drawn from this research is that emotional dissociation or detachment during the bereavement process is predictive of a *healthy* pattern of recovery, not of an increase in symptoms and psychological distress at any subsequent point.

Bonanno et al. (1995) assessed defensive processing at 6 months after loss by examining the discrepancy between verbal reports of distress and autonomic indicators of distress (assessed via heart rate). During a brief interview, bereaved participants were asked to discuss the loss while their heart rate was monitored. After the discussion, participants provided ratings of the negative emotions they had experienced during the interview. The discrepancy between the two measures of distress—one physiological and the other verbal—was used as an indicator of emotional dissociation, with emotional dissociation being characterized by higher autonomic scores than would be expected, given an individual's verbal reports of emotion.

In order to examine the association between emotional dissociation and subsequent adjustment, Bonanno and his colleagues examined patterns of grief (rated by a clinical interviewer) and somatic complaints over an 8-month period. Participants were classified as exhibiting a "minimal" pattern of grief if they had relatively low scores at 6 months and 14 months after loss. Participants were classified as exhibiting a "recovered" pattern of grief if they had high scores at 6 months but fairly low scores at 14 months. "Prolonged" grief patterns were exhibited by individuals who had relatively high grief scores at each time point. Individuals were classified as exhibiting "delayed" grief if they had relatively low scores at 6 months but high scores at 14 months.

According to Bowlby's reasoning about absence of conscious grief, individuals with high levels of emotional dissociation should be more likely than other people to exhibit a delayed negative reaction. According to Bonanno et al.'s results, however, emotionally dissociative individuals were more likely to exhibit a minimal pattern of grief throughout the study. They had relatively low clinical ratings of grief at 6 months and 14 months after loss. Furthermore, in a follow-up at 25 months after loss, they were no more likely than less defensive people to have developed health problems or delayed onset of grief (Bonanno et al., in press).

It is important to note that, consistent with the initial autonomic indicators, these dissociative individuals did have higher levels of self-reported somatic complaints at 6 months after the loss. Therefore, despite their relatively low levels of reported distress, they were experiencing some somatic difficulties during the first few months after loss. Interestingly, however, these somatic complaints did not persist. At the 14-month and 25-month follow-ups, dissociative individuals had relatively low levels of complaints (Bonanno et al., 1995, in press). Therefore, it appears that individuals who exhibit a relative absence of grief do not necessarily suffer for it in the long run, although they may have some physical repercussions initially.

In addition to examining verbal–autonomic dissociations, Bonanno and his colleagues (Bonanno et al., 1997) examined several other indicators of defensive processing in the same subject sample. Bonanno et al. (1997) examined the association between the "repressive coping style" or "dispositional repression" (Weinberger, 1990; Weinberger, Schwartz, & Davidson, 1979) and adjustment to loss. Research on dispositional repression has attempted to distinguish between individuals who honestly report low levels of trait-based anxiety ("truly low-anxiety people") and individuals who defensively report low levels of trait-based anxiety ("repressors"). Generally, such research has shown that although repressive individuals report low levels of anxiety, they exhibit more indirect signs of anxiety (e.g., increased heart rate, increased facial temperature) than truly low-anxiety individuals.

In the Bonanno et al. sample, both repressors and truly low-anxiety individuals had relatively low levels of interviewer-rated grief at each time in the study. Furthermore, repressors were no more likely than truly low-anxiety individuals to report higher levels of distress or poor health. These findings seem to indicate that dispositional repression is *not* associated with long-term difficulties in adjusting to loss. Bonanno and his colleagues also examined "dispositional self-deception" (Paulhus, 1988), a construct similar to that of "repressive coping." In accordance with the previous results, self-deceptive individuals had lower levels of interviewer-rated grief at 14 months and 25 months after loss, even when level of grief at 6 months was controlled for.

In summary, the more recent research has included controls for many of the confounds present in earlier research on grief work (e.g., confounding distress with grief work), and yet it continues to suggest that individuals who suppress their grief do not necessarily experience a relapse in grief or have a difficult time recovering from loss. In fact, individuals who suppress their emotions actually appear to recover from loss with relatively few difficulties.

These findings are hard to reconcile with Bowlby's idea that the absence of grief is a predictor of subsequent difficulties in adjustment. As M. Stroebe (1992) has noted, however, whether or not the suppression of grief is detrimental to recovery is likely to depend on important features of an individual's personality, many of which have not been examined in the existing literature. In the following section, we discuss an important dimension of personality highlighted in recent attachment research, the dismissing-avoidant dimension, which may act as an important moderator in the association between defensive suppression and the experience of grief.

THE ORGANIZATION OF DEFENSES AND THE INHIBITION OF ATTACHMENT FORMATION

Although Bowlby clearly thought that the absence of grief is usually a defensive coverup of covert distress, he also noticed that there are exceptions to this pattern. Consider the following quotations from *Loss* (Bowlby, 1980):

> Some of those who proclaim their self-sufficiency are in fact relatively immune to loss. (p. 213)

> Not everyone [characterized by an assertion of independence of affectional ties] develops a highly organized personality, however. In many the hardness and self-reliance are more brittle and it is from amongst these persons, it seems likely, that a substantial proportion of all those who at some time in their life develop a pathological response to loss are recruited. (p. 225)

> Some individuals having this disposition [of compulsive self-reliance] have made such tenuous ties with parents, or a spouse or a child that, when they suffer loss, they are truly little affected by it. (p. 211)

> Individuals disposed strongly to assert their self-sufficiency fall on a continuum ranging from those whose proclaimed self-sufficiency rests on a precarious basis to those in whom it is firmly organized. (p. 211)

> The more frequently a child is rejected or experiences a separation, moreover, and the more anxious and distressed he becomes the more frequent and painful are the rebuffs he is likely to receive and the thicker therefore will grow his protective shell. In some persons, indeed, the shell becomes so thick that affectional relationships are attenuated to a point at which loss ceases almost to have significance. Immune to mourning they may be; but at what a price! (p. 240)

These quotations reveal two trends in Bowlby's thinking, which he apparently never articulated in further detail. They suggest that Bowlby believed that some people who exhibit an absence of grief are truly unperturbed by loss, or at least less perturbed than others, because (1) they

have never established a close, emotional attachment to their partners in the first place; and/or (2) their defenses have become so "thick," or highly organized, that these people are able to shut off their emotions successfully.

Defenses in the Development of Attachment Relationships

Research and theory on infant–mother attachment has generally adhered to the idea that almost all infants become emotionally attached to their primary caregivers (see Cassidy, Chapter 1, this volume). Therefore, following separation or loss, avoidant behavior on the part of infants involves the suppression of *true* feelings of rejection and distress (see Sroufe & Waters, 1977b, for further discussion on this point). In adult romantic relationships, however, we may encounter a kind of defensive process that does not have the opportunity to unfold in the context of infant–mother relationships. Specifically, in adulthood an individual can avoid becoming attached to his or her romantic partner, even in the course of an extended relationship. When the relationship ends, such a person may not experience intense anxiety or sorrow; moreover, few long-term difficulties should be encountered in such a case, because the loss is not deeply traumatic.

Recall that Bowlby believed that part of the recovery process entails rearranging one's representations of the world in a way that integrates the reality of the loss with one's implicit assumptions about the world. People vary, however, in the extent to which their assumptions about the world are organized around their relationship partners. When a person is relatively unattached to his or her partner, the relationship will be less important to his or her sense of well-being and security. The partner or the partnership will not be a valued aspect of the self, and the person's memories and goals will not be extensively organized around the other individual. When such a relationship ends, there should be substantially less than usual for a person to "work through." Hence, the absence of distress, in these cases, may reflect a true absence of grief and not just a coverup of powerful feelings.

According to our research, dismissing-avoidant adults are less likely than others to become emotionally attached to their partners (Fraley & Davis, 1997). These dismissing individuals are conceptually similar to Bowlby's description of compulsively self-reliant individuals; they highly value their independence, and their peers describe them as somewhat cold and aloof (Bartholomew, 1990; Bartholomew & Horowitz, 1991). Furthermore, when their relationships dissolve, these people exhibit relatively little anxiety or sorrow (Fraley et al., 1997).

We believe that dismissing adults, as captured in this research, are what Bowlby had in mind when discussing people who may be relatively immune to loss. To the extent that they are able to inhibit the development of attachment and interdependence in their romantic relationships, there should be relatively little for them to grieve about when their relationships end. The absence of grief in these individuals should therefore reflect a true absence of grief, rather than a defensive suppression of it. Consequently, they should be unlikely to develop subsequent difficulties, although their chronic pattern of nonengagement combined with only partially acknowledged coldness and hostility (Bartholomew & Horowitz, 1991; Kobak & Sceery, 1988) may cause pain to their relationship partners and families. This important "side effect" should be added to what Bowlby had in mind when he exclaimed, "At what a price!" Presumably he was thinking about the dismissing person's shallow emotional life, but it is also important to think about the not-so-shallow distress such a person can cause to others.

Defenses in the Activation of the Attachment System

As indicated by the quotations above, Bowlby acknowledged that some people have relatively little to grieve about following a loss. He was primarily interested, however, in accounting for those who *do* have something to grieve about and, for some reason, fail to do so. For instance, 8-year-old Charles Darwin appeared to feel genuinely and deeply hurt by his mother's death. But certain factors, including his father's persistent criticism and his older sisters' insistence that their mother not be mentioned around the house, forced Darwin to suppress his natural feelings. It was Bowlby's belief that suppression under such circumstances can lead to problems, unless an individual's defenses are so efficiently organized that he or she is able to deactivate the attachment system to a considerable degree. That is, Bowlby believed that people's defenses fall along a continuum ranging from those resting on a "precarious basis" to those that are "firmly organized."

We have recently conducted research that highlights the importance of this distinction. In a

series of laboratory studies involving people in established romantic relationships (Fraley & Shaver, 1997), we had participants deliberately suppress their thoughts and feelings about a vividly imagined breakup with their romantic partners. Meanwhile, we measured the cognitive accessibility of loss-related thoughts (via stream-of-consciousness reports) and autonomic arousal level (via skin conductance). In general, suppressing loss-related thoughts, as opposed to neutral thoughts, did not lead to a substantial increase or decrease in loss-related thoughts and feelings in subsequent phases of the experiment. This finding is consistent with the literature reviewed above that has failed to find a clear link between suppression and subsequent distress. However, for ambivalent or preoccupied adults, suppressing loss-related thoughts led to an *increase* (a rebound) in such thoughts in later phases of the experiment. In contrast, for dismissing adults, suppressing loss-related thoughts led to a *decrease* in these thoughts and feelings later on. It was as if the dismissing defenses, once activated, continued to do their work even when it was no longer called for by experimental instructions.

The findings from these studies suggest that suppression may actually be helpful for dismissing-avoidant adults. Apparently, dismissing adults have their defenses so well organized that they can shut off feelings in the context of loss (see Fraley, Davis, & Shaver, 1998, for a discussion of the possible mechanisms underlying this ability). In contrast, suppression appears to be harmful for preoccupied adults. In these studies, preoccupied adults actually exhibited a rebound or resurgence in attachment-related thoughts and feelings after they tried to suppress them.

In summary, although Bowlby clearly thought there was an association between the suppression of grief and difficulties in adjustment, his discussion of the links suggests rather complex dynamics, many of which have not been captured in recent research on bereavement. We note first that whether the absence of grief is indicative of latent distress depends on how central the lost individual was to the bereaved. To the extent that the missing person served as an attachment figure, suppression may be detrimental for recovery. In other words, Bowlby's ideas suggest that the association between emotional suppression and recovery is moderated by the importance of the relationship to the bereaved individual. To our knowledge, this interaction has not been taken into account in research that has investigated the links between suppression and adjustment.

Second, Bowlby's theory suggests that suppression may work for some individuals but not for others. Specifically, for individuals who have organized their attachment systems over the course of development in such a way that they can deactivate their feelings fairly successfully (as in the case of dismissing adults), adjustment to loss may be relatively unproblematic. However, other individuals, in whom defenses are more precariously organized, may be expected to suffer following attempts to suppress their emotions. In other words, the theory suggests that the association between suppression and recovery will depend on how and how well an individual's defenses are organized. Some of the research we have conducted suggests that this interaction is critical for understanding the link between defenses and adjustment.

CONTINUING BONDS: A CONTROVERSY CONCERNING DETACHMENT AND RESOLUTION

A second challenge to Bowlby's account of loss and grief appears in *Continuing Bonds: New Understandings of Grief* (Klass et al., 1996a). The editors and authors portray Freud and Bowlby as "modernists," in contrast with their own "postmodernism." They say that the modernist emphasis on extreme individualism and mechanistic science led Freud and Bowlby incorrectly to view mourning as a biological, rigidly sequenced process with a fixed "healthy" endpoint—rapid decathexis and detachment, defined by Klass et al. as complete severance of the emotional bond to a lost attachment figure. In this section, we examine the evidence and rationale for this "postmodern" position. We argue that it involves a caricature of Bowlby's views, and yet we embrace some of its valuable insights, which can easily and beneficially be accommodated within attachment theory. As we intend to show, it is unfortunate that the editors and most of the chapter authors of *Continuing Bonds* have found it necessary to define themselves in contrast or opposition to attachment theory, because in several instances it has caused them not only to distort intellectual history but also to misread their own findings.[6]

Bowlby (1980) was to a large extent reacting *against* Freud's (1917/1957) idea, expressed in "Mourning and Melancholia," that the process of grieving involves "hypercathecting" and then "decathecting" the mental representation of a lost "object" of libidinal instinct. In Bowlby's opinion, this conceptualization caused psychoanalytically inclined therapists to hasten the grieving process, and to view many of its healthy manifestations as pathological. According to Bowlby, the mourning reactions that many psychoanalytic clinicians viewed as immature or pathological—prolonged searching, yearning, and sometimes expressing anger or ambivalence toward a lost attachment figure—reflect the natural dynamics of the attachment system, as explained earlier in this chapter. It was part of Bowlby's general approach to attachment phenomena to be sympathetic to a person of any age whose attachment behavioral system has been activated, and he clearly disapproved of characterizing such individuals' reactions as childish, irrational, or inappropriately dependent. Advocating rapid or complete severance of emotional bonds would have been completely contradictory to his theoretical and therapeutic goals.[7]

Evidence for Continuing Bonds

The accumulation of evidence from many contemporary studies of grief has caused the authors of *Continuing Bonds* to question their own clinical training and previous allegiance to what they mistakenly view as attachment theory. As one of them explains (Balk, 1996, p. 312):

In-depth, qualitative research with bereaved parents led Klass (1987–88) to ask serious questions about the accepted view of attachment and bereavement. He reported that bereaved parents in self-help and support groups commonly mentioned ongoing attachments to their dead children (1992–93, 1993). Hogan and DeSantis (1992) discovered that bereaved adolescents typically maintained ongoing attachments to their dead siblings. Silverman, Nickman, and Worden (1992) noted that bereaved children made conscious efforts to sustain connections to their dead parents and incorporated those attachments into their ongoing social environment. Tyson-Rawson (1993) . . . reported that 14 of her 20 [college student] research participants mentioned "an ongoing attachment to [their deceased fathers], indicating a continuing bond . . ." (p. 166). Ten of the 14 students felt comforted with this ongoing attachment [and] felt it as a real presence in their lives. . . . These 10 women "were also more likely to report that they viewed themselves as having reached some resolution of their grief" (p. 171). In addition to these empirical studies, bereaved individuals have emphasized in therapy [that] they do not accept that bereavement resolution requires relinquishing emotional investments in their dead loved ones. As one widow said, "If that is what experts think grief resolution is about, then I want nothing to do with their ideas."

The editors of *Continuing Bonds* summarize this evidence as follows:

> Rather than letting go, [our subjects] seemed to be continuing the relationship. . . . they kept this relationship by dreaming, by talking to the parent, by believing that the parent was watching them, by keeping things that belonged to the parent, by visiting the grave, and by frequently thinking about the dead parent. . . . we realized that *we were observing phenomena that could not be accounted for within the models of grief that most of our colleagues were using*. . . . what we were observing was not a stage of disengagement, *which we were educated to expect,* but rather, we were observing people altering and then continuing their relationship to the lost or dead person. Remaining connected seemed to facilitate both adults' and children's ability to cope with the loss and the accompanying changes in their lives. These "connections" provided solace, comfort and support, and eased the transition from the past to the future. (Klass, Silverman, & Nickman, 1996b, pp. xvii–xviii; emphasis added)

The authors' perspective is repeatedly contrasted with what they claim was Bowlby's position. Consider the following quotations from *Continuing Bonds*:

> Bowlby continued the [Freudian] model that the purpose of grief is to sever the bond with the dead. . . . He defined a distinct and unvarying sequence of behaviors that can be identified in children separated from their mothers [leading to detachment]. . . . Those who follow the Bowlby/Parkes theory continue to define the resolution of grief as severing bonds rather than as establishing a changed bond with the dead person. (Silverman & Klass, 1996, pp. 9–13)

> In Bowlby's view . . . the attempt to restore proximity [to the deceased attachment figure] is inappropriate or nonfunctional. . . . Like psychoanalytic theory, which focuses on the importance of relinquishing ties, Bowlby's work suggests that bonds with the deceased need to be broken for the bereaved to adjust and recover. . . . Those who retain ties are considered maladjusted. This general impression that ties with the deceased need to be severed is referred to in this chapter as the *breaking bonds* hypothesis. (M. Stroebe, Gergen, Gergen, & Stroebe, 1996, p. 33)

> According to the attachment theory of bereavement resolution, ongoing attachment following a death is unhealthy, if not pathological. (Balk, 1996, p. 311)

What Bowlby Actually Said about Continuing Bonds

Do these statements do justice to Bowlby's theory? Their degree of bias is hinted at in another passage in the book, in which two of the editors say:

> In his early papers on this process [grieving], the final stage that Bowlby described was labeled adaptation, a conceptualization that could be consistent with the thesis of this book. But soon adaptation was defined as detachment. He identified a distinct and unvarying sequence of behaviors that can be identified in children separated from their mothers: protest, despair and yearning, and detachment. (Silverman & Klass, 1996, p. 10)

Silverman and Klass do not discuss the fact that Bowlby presented the phases of grief in a heuristic way, not at all as an "unvarying sequence." Furthermore, they choose not to mention that in his writings on permanent losses, Bowlby (1980) used the term "reorganization" rather than "detachment." It is important to note that the term "detachment" was originally coined to describe a *defensive* reaction to the *return* of a missing attachment figure. When infants are separated from their attachment figures, they at first respond with intense anxiety and/or sadness. Eventually they appear to recover and begin exploring their environments with renewed interest; they seem once again interested in other people. However, if the attachment figures return, Bowlby (1969/1982) noted that many children respond with coldness and an absence of attachment behavior, as if they are punishing the attachment figures for abandoning them or are unsure how to organize their conflicting desires to seek comfort and express anger. Bowlby (1969/1982) emphasized that this defensive response is best described as "apparent" detachment, because once the children reaccept their attachment figures' care, they are particularly clingy and hypervigilant concerning the figures' whereabouts.

Within Bowlby's theoretical framework, the term "detachment" is not meant to characterize the recovery process itself. It is unfortunate that the term is occasionally used in this context, because it carries the Freudian implication that the bereaved eventually "detaches" or "decathects" himself or herself from the attachment figure. We suspect that the term "detachment" was retained for so long because most of the attachment literature has been concerned with relatively brief separations, in which the attachment figure eventually returns, rather than with permanent separations. It is perhaps for this reason that Bowlby (1980), when writing about *permanent* losses, used the term "reorganization" instead of "detachment" to describe the final stage of mourning. He clearly did not believe that an individual must "detach" from the partner in order to recover from the loss. (See Bowlby, 1980, pp. 19–21, 93–100.)

What did Bowlby actually say about the recovery process, the length and difficulty of mourning, and the heuristic flexibility of the phase model? The following quotations from Bowlby (1980) clearly indicate that the authors of *Continuing Bonds* distorted his theory in an attempt to formulate a position that "competes" with their own:

> Loss of a loved person is one of the most intensely painful experiences any human being can suffer. To the bereaved nothing but the return of the lost person can bring true comfort. . . . [There is] a bias that runs through so much of the older literature on how human beings respond to loss . . . there is a tendency to under-estimate how intensely distressing and disabling loss usually is and for how long the distress, and often the disablement, commonly lasts. Conversely, there is a tendency to suppose that a normal healthy person can and should get over a bereavement not only fairly rapidly but also completely. (pp. 7–8)

> Admittedly these phases [of numbing, protest, despair, and reorganization] are not clear cut, and any one individual may oscillate for a time back and forth between any two of them. (p. 85)

> So comforting did widows find the sense of a dead husband's presence [which Bowlby described as persisting for a long time "at its original intensity"] that some deliberately evoked it whenever they felt unsure of themselves or depressed. (pp. 96–97)

> Findings in regard both to the high prevalence of a continuing sense of the presence of the dead person and to its compatibility with a favourable outcome give no support to Freud's well-known and already quoted passage: "Mourning has a quite precise psychical task to perform: its function is to detach the survivor's memories and hopes from the dead." (p. 100)

> Indeed, an occasional recurrence of active grieving, especially when some event reminds the bereaved of her loss, is the rule. I emphasize these findings . . . because I believe that clinicians sometimes have unrealistic expectations of the speed and completeness with which someone can be expected to get over a major bereavement. (p. 101)

There is no reason to regard any of these experiences as either unusual or unfavourable, rather the contrary. For example, in regard to the Boston widows Glick, [Weiss, and Parkes] (1974) report: 'Often the widow's progress toward recovery was facilitated by inner conversations with her husband's presence . . . this continued sense of attachment was not incompatible with increasing capacity for independent action' (p. 154). Although Glick [et al. regard] this finding as paradoxical, those familiar with the evidence regarding the relation of secure attachment to the growth of self-reliance . . . will not find it so. On the contrary, *it seems likely that for many widows and widowers it is precisely because they are willing for their feelings of attachment to the dead spouse to persist that their sense of identity is preserved and they become able to reorganize their lives along lines they find meaningful.* (p. 98; emphasis added)

> [A secure] person . . . is likely to possess a representational model of attachment figure(s) as being available, responsive and helpful and a complementary model of himself as at least a potentially lovable and valuable person. . . . On being confronted with the loss of someone close to him such a person will not be spared grief; on the contrary he may grieve deeply. . . . [But] he is likely to be spared those experiences which lead mourning to become unbearable or unproductive or both. . . . Since he will not be afraid of intense and unmet desires for love from the person lost, he will let himself be swept by pangs of grief; and tearful expression of yearning and distress will come naturally. During the months and years that follow he will probably be able to organize life afresh, *fortified perhaps by an abiding sense of the lost person's continuing and benevolent presence.* (pp. 242–243; emphasis added)

The stream of such quotations could go on indefinitely, but the point is made: There is virtually no support in *Loss* for the criticisms of Bowlby leveled repeatedly by the authors of *Continuing Bonds*.

New Insights Regarding Continuing Bonds

Despite their misrepresentation of Bowlby and attachment theory, the authors of *Continuing Bonds* report a number of interesting findings and ideas that we believe help to extend Bowlby's analysis. For example, Silverman and Nickman (1996) found that five kinds of activities helped children maintain healthy mental connections to their deceased parents:

1. The children located the parents in a place (usually heaven) where they could imagine

the parents continuing to observe and take an interest in the children's activities and needs.

2. They experienced the parents' continuing presence.

3. They "reached out" to the deceased parents to maintain interaction with them.

4. The children made special efforts, often augmented by family members, to remember the deceased's characteristics and love for them.

5. Many children kept objects (e.g., clothing, jewelry) that belonged to their lost parents, and contact with these objects seemed to prolong the sense of closeness and of being loved and protected.

Many of the children studied by Silverman and Nickman seemed to realize that their needs and wishes for continued contact with their parents were partly responsible for their views about their parents' continued existence in another realm. A 14-year-old boy said, "I want my father to see me perform. If I said a dead person can't see then I would not be able to have my wish that he see what I am doing. I believe that the dead see, hear, move. Don't ask me how" (quoted in Silverman & Nickman, 1996, p. 77). A 15-year-old girl said, "I think heaven is not a definite place. . . . I know I'm not imagining him . . . it's not as if I actually see him standing there, but I feel him and, like, in my mind I hear his voice" (quoted, p. 78). A majority of the studied children dreamed of their parents and experienced them, during the dream, as alive: "I dreamed he met me on the way home from school and . . . he hugged me" (quoted, p. 79).

Silverman and Nickman note that the children's touching mixture of credulity and self-understanding regarding their own mental constructions is "similar to what Weisman (1972) called 'middle knowledge': a partial awareness of the reality of death that forms the best compromise between an unpleasant truth and a wished-for state of events" (p. 79). Our impression is that this "middle knowledge" is compatible with what AAI researchers call "coherence of mind," the hallmark of security. The children with middle knowledge were able to articulate their thoughts and wishes in a coherent way, even if this resulted in hovering between thinking of death as final (which the vast majority accepted, at least with respect to further earthly existence) and thinking of death as a passage to another realm that allowed continuing observation of and interaction with loved ones (in the loved ones' minds or imaginations).

According to the authors of another chapter of *Continuing Bonds* (Normand, Silverman, & Nickman, 1996), this kind of coherence and balance characterizes many of the relationships that children construct between themselves and their dead parents:

A sign of the mental openness and "coherence" of this [pattern] is that the positive or even idealized memories are sometimes interspersed with more negative ones. For example, a number of children reminisced about the good times they had shared with their deceased parent, but also at times recalled the pain caused by the death. Similarly, in their description of the deceased, children were more likely in the third [follow-up] interview . . . to be willing to include a few "bad points" along with the deceased's "good points" that had been more easily shared with the interviewer. After talk focused on the deceased and the loss, these children could more easily go on to other topics. (Normand et al., 1996, p. 102)

Distortions Encouraged by the Wish to Reject Bowlby's Analysis of Loss

Unfortunately, while providing many interesting examples of the kinds of processes that Bowlby analyzed in terms of searching and reorganizing working models, the authors of *Continuing Bonds* overlook the implications of some of their most important findings. Because they want to criticize what they regard as Bowlby's advocacy of "broken bonds," they uncritically celebrate all continuing bonds. In the process, they ignore data indicating that ambivalent or chronic grieving can be a sign of serious psychological difficulty. Although it is easy to read emotional pain as a sign of return to the romantic mores of an earlier century, it is dangerous not to consider it within the context of a bereaved individual's long-term psychological well-being. As far as we know, there is no evidence that an ambivalent approach to mourning is a positive predictor of psychological adjustment.

Part of the difficulty with the "postmodern" perspective adopted by the authors is that it oversimplifies the concept of dependence. Consider the following passage from Silverman and Klass (1996, p. 16):

We can see the consequences of [modernism's] valuing autonomy in the criteria for what has been called pathological grief. In the dominant model of grief, dependence has often been seen as a condition for "pathological" grief. [For example], Raphael (1983) assumes that dependent personalities are more prone to pathological grief: " . . . it may be suggested that people with personal characteristics that lead them to form dependent, clinging, ambivalent relationships with their spouses are at greater risk of having a poor outcome" (p. 225).

In the first volume of his *Attachment and Loss* trilogy, Bowlby critically analyzed the concept of dependence (see Bowlby, 1969/1982, pp. 228–229). It was his contention that the psychoanalytic perspective, with its emphasis on neuroses and psychopathology, fails to make an important distinction between two kinds of dependence: secure dependence and anxious dependence. In the case of secure dependence, a person is able to function in a free and autonomous manner due to the security afforded by an attachment figure. In the anxious-ambivalent case, however, autonomy and exploration are compromised by an attachment figure's uncertain accessibility.

Our reading of the various chapters in *Continuing Bonds* suggests that like many of the early psychoanalytic writers on dependence, the authors fail to recognize an important distinction between the two forms of dependence. But unlike early psychoanalytic authors, who focused too much on unhealthy or anxious dependence, the authors of *Continuing Bonds* focus too much on what they think is healthy or secure dependence. This causes them to ignore evidence (from their own research, as well as research reviewed earlier in this chapter) indicating that anxiously dependent or ambivalent people are more vulnerable to psychological difficulties than those who are securely attached.

Some of the examples from Rosenblatt's (1996) chapter illustrate the danger of considering all forms of dependence as adaptive. In line with the "postmodern" theme of the volume, he considers virtually any sign of prolonged grief and psychological pain healthy and common, even quotations such as the following—from an adult woman whose father died when she was an infant, decades before Rosenblatt interviewed her:

I . . . went through some stuff where I feel I caused the death, and that was really, really deep stuff, because I, it was, I couldn't verbalize it. It made no sense to me . . . but I think in searching, I had this sort of replacement idea, that once you had a birth you automatically had a death. And I got born so he died, you know. Why me? And, sort of, so it's been a huge issue, just taking the right to be alive. . . .

When I was 24 I was in a car accident, and looking . . . back on it, I'm sure it was a veiled suicidal kind of thing. (Quoted in Rosenblatt, 1996, p. 51)

Although neither of us is an expert AAI coder, this passage seems to qualify for a high score on the "unresolved" AAI rating scale—a rating that has been associated with troubled childhoods, adult dissociative tendencies, and being at risk for inducing a disorganized/disoriented attachment pattern in one's children. (See Hesse, Chapter 19, this volume.)

In another chapter, Silverman and Nickman (1996) note in passing other individual differences that might ring bells with careful readers of the attachment literature. They encountered children who could not answer the question "What advice would you give another child who had lost a parent?"; such children replied, "I don't know" or "I can't think of anything." The authors write: "These were the same children who did not dream about the deceased, and who did not talk to the deceased [in their minds]" (p. 80). This was in sharp contrast with the secure-sounding children (the majority of subjects in the study) who *did* have helpful answers, which reflected their ability to organize their own experiences and think about which of them might be helpful to others.

Normand et al. (1996) discuss four kinds of relationships that bereaved children constructed with their images of dead parents: "Seeing the Parent as a Visiting Ghost," "Holding on to Memories from the Past," "Maintaining an Interactive Relationship," and "Becoming a Living Legacy." The first type, Seeing the Parent as a Visiting Ghost, should prove especially interesting to AAI researchers who notice signs of unresolved loss. The authors say:

In this cluster, children conceived of their deceased parent as a ghost whose presence was frightening, unpredictable, and out of their control. . . . Most notably, [they] located the deceased as being "right beside me," unlike all the other children in the sample who located their deceased parent either in heaven or were uncertain about his/her location. Unlike any of the other children in the sample who reported feeling watched by the deceased, these children were frightened by the idea. At the 1-year interview, 12-year-old Justin explained, "Like, it's just quiet, and I think she's right there behind me and she's gonna . . . Like when I look in the mirror in the morning, like to comb my hair, I always think that she's gonna pop up behind me and scare me." . . . Their dreams of their mother left them feeling fearful as well. . . . Children who experienced their parent as a visiting ghost did not feel sad or glad, only frightened. These children said they "never" cried during the first year after the death. All the other children in the sample said they cried every day or at least several times a week at that time. Neither of these children talked about the deceased, to avoid getting "all upset and everything." . . . [They] visited the graves—with the rest of their families—and found it unpleasant. In addition, they saw no resemblance between themselves and their deceased parents. (pp. 88–89)

Normand et al. find this pattern "difficult to explain," saying that the children appeared "very distraught" and had hardly changed after 2 years. "Despite the small number of indicators [collected in our study], we favor the interpretation that the parent–child relationship prior to the death must account in part for this representation" (p. 109). This conclusion is consistent with the notion that disorganized attachment results from an attachment figure's "frightening" behavior (e.g., Main & Hesse, 1990).

In a separate study of late-adolescent women whose fathers had died, described in a *Continuing Bonds* chapter by Tyson-Rawson (1996), 30% of the women who had some kind of continuing attachment to their father experienced an "intrusive presence" suggestive of insecure attachment. One woman said:

After he died, I was so depressed that I couldn't go to school or sleep or anything. So they put me on an antidepressant for a while. Lately, I've been feeling that way again. I have these dreams, nightmares, and I can't stop thinking about him dying. I think he's mad at me. . . . I don't know why, no, I think I feel this way because I never said good-bye to him. I knew he was dying and all that time I just stayed away, went to someone else's house. (Quoted in Tyson-Rawson, 1996, p. 138)

Anxiety and guilt were commonly reported by such women. As Tyson-Rawson (1996, p. 128) notes, "these women's responses had a desperate, struggling quality . . . [Their sense of intrusive presence was] typically expressed in nightmares, intrusive thoughts, and high levels of anxiety that debilitated the subject in one or more areas of functioning." Consider the following examples from four women (quoted in Tyson-Rawson, 1996, p. 138). Although the time since death was only 4 months for one subject, it was as long as 4 years for another, and their experiences were similar.

I really got crazy after he died. . . . Now I'm quieter, but I have these dreams that he's there and I'm sup-

posed to do something. I feel guilty and I don't know why. I love him so much.

After four years I still can't study, like, I keep getting scared and jumpy, like there's someone outside the door. I can't be alone since he died.

I'm just so nervous all the time. I keep expecting him to show up . . . I know it's only been four months but I don't know if he'll ever go away.

I don't know what's the matter with me. Sometimes I think I'm crazy and other people just can't see it.

According to Tyson-Rawson (1996),

The common factor that united the experience of these four women was a sense of "unfinished business" (McGoldrick, 1991). Each reported thinking that she had not been able to effect closure in the relationship with her father. . . . [Two] had highly conflicted relationships with their fathers, characterized by cutoff from contact and minimal interaction. In comparison to those who welcomed their father's presence in their lives, *those who experienced an Intrusive Presence were unanimous in reporting no sense of having resolved their grief.* (p. 139; emphasis added)

In other words, in line with earlier sections of the present chapter, a tendency toward preoccupied attachment seems to have presaged later difficulty in constructively resolving grief, viewing the lost attachment figure as security-providing within the realm of imagination, and enjoying positive memories of interactions with the deceased while he was alive.

In the end, the distinction between modernism and postmodernism is not very helpful in conceptualizing either attachment theory (which if anything is more postmodern than modern, by the standards provided in *Continuing Bonds*) or the findings obtained by the authors of *Continuing Bonds*. Although the studies reported in *Continuing Bonds* do add interesting detail to some of Bowlby's claims, which he was able to document only sketchily through clinical case studies, the useful details are easy to lose in the welter of misreadings of attachment theory and bereavement research published since 1980. It is amply clear both that bereaved individuals do construct mental representations of their relationships with deceased attachment figures, and that these constructions and the bonds they incorporate can be either security-enhancing or security-threatening. The concept of resolution in contemporary attachment theory does not entail complete severance of affectional bonds or complete excision of mental representations of dead attachment figures. It focuses more on a person's ability to talk comfortably and coherently about the loss than it does about the particular form of representations of the deceased—representations that are naturally influenced both by personal wishes and by cultural and religious belief systems. In our opinion, none of the findings reported in *Continuing Bonds* would have bothered or even surprised Bowlby, although the repeated distortions of his work might have elicited a raised eyebrow.

SUMMARY AND CONCLUSION

From a combination of attachment theory and numerous clinical case studies, Bowlby (1980) developed a theory of loss, grief, and mourning that remains the deepest and most comprehensive available. His theory is recognized as one of the major theories of bereavement (W. Stroebe & Stroebe, 1987) and has generated an enormous amount of research on reactions to loss and individual differences in the way people respond to and adapt to loss. Not surprisingly, Bowlby's theory has also generated criticism and controversy. In the present chapter we have considered two important criticisms of the theory: one saying that the suppression of intense emotions following loss of an attachment figure is not necessarily damaging (i.e., not necessarily a harbinger of future psychological problems), and another saying that Bowlby was wrong to view detachment as the proper outcome of mourning.

Concerning the first point, we have shown that Bowlby himself recognized that some exceptionally self-reliant individuals can weather losses without showing much grief and without suffering later breakdowns or episodes of serious depression. We agree with Bowlby's critics, however, that he probably overestimated the extent to which suppression of grief is harmful. In retrospect, it appears that the suppression of grief is harmful only for individuals who feel strongly impelled to express their feelings (especially individuals with anxious-ambivalent tendencies) and for some reason cannot. This idea may help to illuminate some of Charles Darwin's health problems, which Bowlby believed were partially instigated by the stress incurred by the death of his mother. Young Darwin was deeply affected by this loss, but was also forced to suppress his feelings. Perhaps if Darwin had been less affected by the loss, or had not been forced by his family to suppress his grief, or had previously developed avoidant defenses, he would have been able to

manage the loss with few ill effects. (We are *not* implying that this would have made him a better person; far from it.)

As for the second criticism—namely, that Bowlby was a harsh modernist who advocated clean breaks in one's affectional bonds—we have shown that this is an unfair reading of a long book designed to make clinicians more sympathetic to their clients' grief. Bowlby's theory was in large part a reaction to Freud's claim (made relatively early in his career, before he experienced some of his own devastating losses) that investment in the lost "object" must be withdrawn for successful recovery to take place. Bowlby viewed a continuing bond with a missing figure to be the natural result of the dynamics of the attachment system—a system designed to ensure proximity between an individual and his or her attachment figure, whether that figure is physically available or not. Healthy recovery, from this perspective, entails finding a way to maintain a secure bond with the attachment figure while simultaneously acknowledging that the person is not physically available to provide comfort and care. As noted by the authors of *Continuing Bonds,* this comfort is often derived from prayer or from a sense that the figure is present and serving a protective function. As Bowlby noted, however, when the continued bond is experienced as frightening and disorganizing, or when it interferes substantially with one's ability to adapt to life, then it should be recognized as problematic.

After considering what has been learned in recent years about loss, grief, and mourning, we are left with several questions and issues for future research, which we list briefly in closing. If it is true that a substantial number of people—ones whom we suspect can be classified as dismissing-avoidant—can withstand the loss of a parent or spouse without extensive grieving, it will be useful to know whether this is possible because their defenses are able to suppress emotions that are actually present at some level, as suggested by Bonanno et al.'s (1995) psychophysiological study, or because they avoid becoming highly invested in their "close" relationships in the first place and so actually have less than other bereaved individuals to become emotional about. Research based on the AAI (e.g., Dozier & Kobak, 1992) has been interpreted as showing that dismissing individuals have emotions (concerning early attachment experiences) that they manage to suppress and mask to a large extent. Such research has also suggested that dismissing individuals may be somewhat hard on their relationship partners, whether or not they are harmful to themselves. Kobak and Sceery (1988) reported that the friends of dismissing individuals viewed them as relatively hostile, in contrast with what the dismissing people said about themselves. Using somewhat different measures of the dismissing orientation, Bartholomew and Horowitz (1991) found that both dismissing college students and their friends recognized that they experienced interpersonal problems falling in the cold–dominant quadrant of an interpersonal-problem circumplex. In addition, a host of studies (reviewed by van IJzendoorn, 1995) show a reliable connection between the dismissing orientation in parents and avoidant attachment on the part of their infants, which has been shown to have negative interpersonal sequelae during childhood. Thus it will be worthwhile to learn more about the defenses of avoidant individuals, the effects of these defenses on their own mental and physical health, and the costs of the defensive stance for relationship partners (see Fraley et al., 1998, for a discussion of this issue).

A further goal for future research should be to examine in more detail the kinds of "continuing bonds" constructed by people with different attachment patterns. An underplayed finding in *Continuing Bonds* is that a small proportion of bereaved individuals had frightening or intrusive or conflicted bonds—in their imagined postloss relationships with attachment figures, as in life. Because the authors of *Continuing Bonds* wanted to emphasize the generally healthy and beneficial nature of continuing bonds, they did not seek to examine or explain the unhealthy examples uncovered by their probing interviews.

What stands out across the various issues discussed in this chapter is that the ways in which people cope with loss are essentially the same as the ways in which they handle relationships with living partners. If there is a message for clinical practitioners from the research conducted so far, it is that there is no one way to experience a loss. If there ever were clinicians who tried to get clients to completely sever mental ties with dead attachment figures, surely they would have been risking harm to secure and preoccupied people, who do not naturally sever ties in that way. Those clients would have needed help, if at all, with establishing workable internal representations of themselves and their deceased partners that were compatible with healthy lives. On the other hand, if there were clinicians who attempted to force dismissingly avoidant clients to engage in emotionally dramatic "grief work" when those clients were not so inclined, we must question whether this would have been more helpful than harmful.

These issues indicate a need for better understanding of the reorganization and recovery process. It seems to us that the process of reorganization following loss is similar in many respects to processes of reorganization during major transitions throughout the lifespan. Hazan, Hutt, Sturgeon, and Bricker (1991) have indicated that as people enter adulthood, they do not *detach* from their early attachment figures as new people (e.g., romantic partners) come to assume the role and functions of primary attachment figures. As adults, we find ways to continue bonds with our early attachment figures even if they live on the opposite side of the country, and even if someone else has assumed a larger emotional role in our current lives. This same process of change in the hierarchy of attachment figures appears to characterize the process of reorganization following loss. Through mourning, we find ways to continue our bonds with attachment figures even though they are no longer physically present and someone new may serve as a more "proximate" attachment figure. In both cases, some people reorganize their attachment systems in a way that facilitates this balance, whereas others have more difficulty. A better understanding of attachment reorganization throughout development would contribute to our understanding of recovery following bereavement.

Bowlby was not able to answer every important question about grief and mourning; nevertheless, having reconsidered his work in light of much that came before and has come since, we are humbled by his ability to incorporate so much of the evidence available to him while keeping an eye on a coherent, comprehensive, and deep theory of human attachment. It is safe to assume that his work will still be influential decades from now among researchers and clinicians interested in grief.

ACKNOWLEDGMENTS

We would like to thank the following people for reading early drafts of this chapter and providing us with critical and valuable feedback: George Bonanno, Jude Cassidy, Carol George, Richard Robins, Margaret Stroebe, Caroline Tancredy, and Robert Weiss.

NOTES

1. Although Bowlby's theory is useful in explaining reactions to the loss of many kinds of objects in which a person may be emotionally invested (e.g., a job, homeland, or child), in the present chapter we focus on the loss of a specific class of objects—attachment figures. (See Cassidy, Chapter 1, this volume, for further discussion on the nature of attachment relationships as compared to other kinds of relationships.) Furthermore, although in principle an individual may be attached to several individuals (e.g., siblings, teachers), we confine our discussion primarily to a child's loss of a parent or an adult's loss of a spouse or romantic partner. We do so because most of the research and controversy concerning separation and bereavement have focused on children's loss of parents or on conjugal loss.

2. Although infants and children eventually seem to recover from the loss of primary attachment figures, there is considerable evidence that the loss can have profound effects on psychological development. For example, Bowlby (1980) discussed some now-classic studies by his colleagues Brown and Harris (1978) that demonstrated a link between early loss and adult depression in women (see also Barry, Barry, & Lindermann, 1965; Bendiksen & Fulton, 1975; Birtchnell, 1972). More recent research has continued to document similar associations (Harris & Bifulco, 1991). The data indicate that although a child eventually recovers from a loss, the loss can leave a fairly deep emotional scar. Later in the chapter, we discuss in more detail the nature of detachment and the prolonged effects of loss in adulthood.

3. Due to Bowlby's emphasis on explaining emotional and behavioral reactions to loss, W. Stroebe and Stroebe (1987) classify Bowlby's theory as a "depression model" of grief, as opposed to a "stress model" of grief. According to W. Stroebe and Stroebe (1987), "depression models construe bereavement in terms of loss and focus on the emotional reaction, stress models view bereavement as a stressful life event, that is, as an experience that overtaxes the coping resources of the individual" (p. 77). Given that Bowlby's theory provides an explanation for why loss is a stressor *and* why people experience the emotions that they do, we fail to understand why his theory is classified as belonging to only one of these two fuzzy categories. It is noteworthy that Bowlby's theory has guided several generations of research on infant–mother separation and the stress response in nonhuman primates (see Reite & Boccia, 1994, for a review).

4. Bowlby (1980) also discussed "compulsive caregiving" as a disordered form of mourning. Because of space limitations and the relative lack of research examining this pattern, we do not discuss it in this chapter.

5. As several reviewers of an earlier draft of this chapter pointed out, the experience of loss differs in many ways from the experience of separation. Although we agree that there are some important differences between these two experiences, we believe that there are good reasons to consider the emotional and behavioral reactions to loss and separation as manifestations of the same underlying process. First, as we will discuss, there are remarkable parallels between reactions to loss and reactions to separation. Both experiences elicit profound anxiety and distress, and after some time can result in profound despair and withdrawal. Furthermore, patterns of individual variation in response to the two situations are similar. Some individuals experience a heightened sense of distress and protest intensely, whereas others avoid such reactions. We suspect that the mechanisms mediating attachment-related emotion and behavior are activated in any situation in which the attachment figure is implicitly perceived as unavailable. Although people can consciously recognize the distinction between separation and loss and can regulate their behavior accordingly, it is unlikely that the more basic emotional and behavioral mechanisms can make this distinction with any clarity. In fact, as Bowlby (1969/1982, 1980) noted, part of the frustration of loss stems from the conscious knowledge that the attachment figure is irretrievable, coupled with the motivation to search for, care for, and be cared for by the missing attachment figure.

6. The reason for taking such a close look at this book is that its authors have, individually and in small groups, produced many interesting and influential papers over the past several years. For our purposes, the book serves as a convenient single example.

7. For a related brief critique of an earlier version of the postmodernist position as outlined by M. Stroebe, Gergen, Gergen, and Stroebe (1992), see Peskin (1993).

REFERENCES

Adam, K. S., Sheldon-Keller, A. E., & West, M. (1995). Attachment organization and vulnerability to loss, separation, and abuse in disturbed adolescents. In S. Goldberg, R. Muir, & J. Kerr (Eds.), *Attachment theory: Social, developmental, and clinical perspectives* (pp. 309–341). Hillsdale, NJ: Analytic Press.

Ainsworth, M. D. S., Blehar, M. C., Waters, E., & Wall, S. (1978). *Patterns of attachment.* Hillsdale, NJ: Erlbaum.

Ainsworth, M. D. S., & Eichberg, C. (1991). Effects on infant–mother attachment of mother's unresolved loss of an attachment figure, or other traumatic experience. In C. M. Parkes, J. Stevenson-Hinde, & P. Marris (Eds.), *Attachment across the life cycle* (pp. 160–183). London: Routledge.

Anisfeld, E., Casper, V., Nozyce, M., & Cunningham, N. (1990). Does infant carrying promote attachment?: An experimental study of the effects of increased physical contact on the development of attachment. *Child Development, 61,* 1617–1627.

Balk, D. E. (1996). Attachment and the reactions of bereaved college students: A longitudinal study. In D. Klass, P. R. Silverman, & S. L. Nickman (Eds.), *Continuing bonds: New understandings of grief* (pp. 311–328). Washington, DC: Taylor & Francis.

Barry, H., Jr., Barry, H., III, & Lindemann, E. (1965). Dependency in adult patients following early maternal bereavement. *Journal of Nervous and Mental Disease, 140,* 196–206.

Bartholomew, K. (1990). Avoidance of intimacy: An attachment perspective. *Journal of Social and Personal Relationships, 7,* 147–178.

Bartholomew, K., & Horowitz, L. M. (1991). Attachment styles among young adults: A test of a four-category model. *Journal of Personality and Social Psychology, 61,* 226–244.

Bendiksen, R., & Fulton, R. (1975). Death and the child: An anterospective test of the childhood bereavement and later behavior disorder hypothesis. *Omega, 6,* 45–59.

Birtchnell, J. (1972). Early parent death and psychiatric diagnosis. *Social Psychiatry, 7,* 202–210.

Bonanno, G. A. (in press). The concept of "working through" loss: A critical evaluation of the cultural, historical, and empirical evidence. In A. Maercker & M. Schuetzwohl (Eds.), *Posttraumatic stress disorder: Vulnerability and resilience in the life-span.* Seattle, WA: Hogrefe & Huber.

Bonanno, G. A., Keltner, D., Holen, A., & Horowitz, M. J. (1995). When avoiding unpleasant emotions might not be such a bad thing: Verbal–autonomic response dissociation and midlife conjugal bereavement. *Journal of Personality and Social Psychology, 69,* 975–989.

Bonanno, G. A., Siddique, H. I., Keltner, D., & Horowitz, M. J. (1997). *Correlates and consequences of dispositional repression and self-deception following the loss of a spouse.* Manuscript submitted for publication.

Bonanno, G. A., Znoj, H., Siddique, H. I., & Horowitz, M. J. (in press). Verbal–autonomic dissociation and adaptation to midlife conjugal loss: A follow-up at 25 months. *Cognitive Therapy and Research.*

Bornstein, P. E., Clayton, P. J., Halikas, J. A., Maurice, W. L., & Robins, E. (1973). The depression of widowhood after thirteen months. *British Journal of Psychiatry, 122,* 561–566.

Bowlby, J. (1946). *Forty-four juvenile thieves: Their characters and home-life.* London: Bailliére, Tindall, & Cox.

Bowlby, J. (1969/1982). *Attachment and loss: Vol. 1. Attachment.* New York: Basic Books.

Bowlby, J. (1980). *Attachment and loss: Vol. 3. Loss: Sadness and depression.* New York: Basic Books.

Bowlby, J. (1990). *Charles Darwin: A new life.* New York: Norton.

Brown, G. W., & Harris, T. (1978). *The social origins of depression: A study of psychiatric disorder in women.* London: Tavistock.

Clayton, P. J., Halikas, J. A., & Maurice, W. L. (1972). The depression of widowhood. *British Journal of Psychiatry, 120,* 71–76.

Collins, N. L., & Read, S. J. (1990). Adult attachment, working models, and relationship quality in dating couples. *Journal of Personality and Social Psychology, 58,* 644–663.

Deutsch, H. (1937). Absence of grief. *Psychoanalytic Quarterly, 6,* 12–22.

Dozier, M., & Kobak, R. R. (1992). Psychophysiology in attachment interviews: Converging evidence for deactivating strategies. *Child Development, 63,* 1473–1480.

Fraley, R. C., & Davis, K. E. (1997). Attachment formation and transfer in young adults' close friendships and romantic relationships. *Personal Relationships, 4,* 131–144.

Fraley, R. C., Davis, K. E., & Shaver, P. R. (1998). Dismissing-avoidance and the defensive organization of emotion, cognition, and behavior. In J. A. Simpson & W. S. Rholes (Eds.), *Attachment theory and close relationships* (pp. 249–279). New York: Guilford Press.

Fraley, R. C., Davis, K. E., & Shaver, P. R. (1997). *Attachment behavior and romantic relationship dissolution.* Unpublished manuscript, University of California, Davis.

Fraley, R. C., & Shaver, P. R. (1998). Airport separations: A naturalistic study of adult attachment behavior and dynamics in separating couples. *Journal of Personality and Social Psychology, 75,* 1198–1212.

Fraley, R. C., & Shaver, P. R. (1997). Adult attachment and the suppression of unwanted thoughts. *Journal of Personality and Social Psychology, 73,* 1080–1091.

Freud, S. (1957). Mourning and melancholia. In J. Strachey (Ed. and Trans.), *The standard edition of the complete psychological works of Sigmund Freud* (Vol. 14, pp. 237–260). New York: Basic Books. (Original work published 1917)

Futterman, A., Gallagher, D., Thompson, L. W., Lovett, S., & Gilewski, M. (1990). Retrospective assessment of marital adjustment and depression during the first two years of spousal bereavement. *Psychology and Aging, 5,* 277–283.

George, C., Kaplan, N., & Main, M. (1984). *The Adult Attachment Interview.* Unpublished manuscript, University of California at Berkeley.

Glick, I. O., Weiss, R. S., & Parkes, C. M. (1974). *The first year of bereavement.* New York: Wiley.

Grossmann, K., Grossmann, K. E., Spangler, G., Suess, G., & Unzner, L. (1985). Maternal sensitivity and newborns' orientation responses as related to quality of attachment in northern Germany. In I. Bretherton & E. Waters (Eds.), Growing points of attachment theory and research. *Monographs of the Society for Research in Child Development, 50*(1–2, Serial No. 209), 233–257.

Harris, T., & Bifulco, A. (1991). Loss of parent in childhood, attachment style, and depression in adulthood. In C. M. Parkes, J. Stevenson-Hinde, & P. Marris (Eds.), *Attachment across the life cycle* (pp. 234–267). London: Routledge.

Hazan, C., Hutt, M. J., Sturgeon, J., & Bricker, T. (1991, April). *The process of relinquishing parents as attachment figures.* Paper presented at the biennial meeting of the Society for Research in Child Development, Seattle, WA.

Hazan, C., & Shaver, P. R. (1987). Romantic love conceptualized as an attachment process. *Journal of Personality and Social Psychology, 59,* 511–524.

Heinicke, C. M., & Westheimer, I. J. (1965). *Brief separations.* New York: International Universities Press.

Hogan, N., & DeSantis, L. (1992). Adolescent sibling bereavement: An ongoing attachment. *Qualitative Health Research, 2,* 159–177.

Jacobs, S., Hansen, F., Berkman, L., Kasl, S., & Ostfeld, A. (1989). Depressions of bereavement. *Comprehensive Psychiatry, 30,* 218–224.

Kirkpatrick, L. A., & Davis, K. E. (1994). Attachment style, gender, and relationship stability: A longitudinal analysis. *Journal of Personality and Social Psychology, 66,* 502–512.

Klass, D. (1987–1988). John Bowlby's model of grief and the problem of identification. *Omega, 18,* 13–32.

Klass, D. (1992–1993). The inner representation of the dead child and the worldviews of bereaved parents. *Omega, 26,* 255–272.

Klass, D. (1993). Solace and immortality: Bereaved parents' continuing bonds with their children. *Death Studies, 17,* 343–346.

Klass, D., Silverman, P. R., & Nickman, S. L. (Eds.).

(1996a). *Continuing bonds: New understandings of grief.* Washington, DC: Taylor & Francis.

Klass, D., Silverman, P. R., & Nickman, S. L. (1996b). Preface. In D. Klass, P. R. Silverman, & S. L. Nickman (Eds.), *Continuing bonds: New understandings of grief* (pp. xvii–xxi). Washington, DC: Taylor & Francis.

Kobak, R. R., & Sceery, A. (1988). Attachment in late adolescence: Working models, affect regulation, and representations of self and others. *Child Development, 59,* 135–146.

Lindemann, E. (1944). Symptomatology and management of acute grief. *American Journal of Psychiatry, 101,* 141–149.

Lorenz, K. (1963). *On aggression.* New York: Bantam.

Lund, D. A., Dimond, M. F., Caserta, M. S., Johnson, R. J., Poulton, J. L., & Connelly, J. R. (1985). Identifying elderly with coping difficulties after two years of bereavement. *Omega, 16,* 213–223.

Lund, D. A., Caserta, M. S., Dimond, M. F., & Shaffer, S. K. (1989). Competencies, tasks of daily living, and adjustments to spousal bereavement in later life. In D. A. Lund (Ed.), *Older bereaved spouses: Research with practical applications* (pp. 135–152). Washington, DC: Taylor & Francis.

Lundin, T. (1984). Morbidity following sudden and unexpected bereavement. *British Journal of Psychiatry, 144,* 84–88.

Main, M., & Goldwyn, R. (1985). *Adult attachment scoring and classification system.* Unpublished manuscript, University of California at Berkeley.

Main, M., & Goldwyn, R. (1994). *Adult attachment scoring and classification system* (2nd ed.). Unpublished manuscript, University of California at Berkeley.

Main, M., & Hesse, E. (1990). Parents' unresolved traumatic experiences are related to infant disorganized attachment status: Is frightened and/or frightening parental behavior the linking mechanism? In M. T. Greenberg, D. Cicchetti, & E. M. Cummings (Eds.), *Attachment in the preschool years: Theory, research, and intervention* (pp. 161–182). Chicago: University of Chicago Press.

Main, M., Kaplan, N., & Cassidy, J. (1985). Security in infancy, childhood, and adulthood: A move to the level of representation. In I. Bretherton & E. Waters (Eds.), Growing points of attachment theory and research. *Monographs of the Society for Research in Child Development, 50*(1–2, Serial No. 209), 66–104.

Mathison, J. (1970). A cross-cultural view of widowhood. *Omega, 1,* 201–218.

McGoldrick, M. (1991). The legacy of loss. In F. Walsh & M. McGoldrick (Eds.), *Living beyond loss: Death in the family* (pp. 104–129). New York: Norton.

Middleton, W., Raphael, B., Martinek, N., & Misso, V. (1993). Pathological grief reactions. In M. S. Stroebe, W. Stroebe, & R. O. Hansson (Eds.), *Handbook of bereavement: Theory, research, and intervention* (pp. 44–61). New York: Cambridge University Press.

Miller, S. I., & Schoenfeld, L. (1973). Grief in the Navajo: Psychodynamics and culture. *International Journal of Social Psychiatry, 19,* 187–191.

Normand, C. L., Silverman, P. R., & Nickman, S. L. (1996). Bereaved children's changing relationships with the deceased. In D. Klass, P. R. Silverman, & S. L. Nickman (Eds.), *Continuing bonds: New understandings of grief* (pp. 87–111). Washington, DC: Taylor & Francis.

Parkes, C. M. (1965). Bereavement and mental illness. *British Journal of Medical Psychology, 38,* 388–397.

Parkes, C. M. (1985). Bereavement. *British Journal of Psychiatry, 146,* 11–17.

Parkes, C. M., & Weiss, R. (1983). *Recovery from bereavement.* New York: Basic Books.

Paulhus, D. L. (1988). Self-deception: Where do we stand? In J. S. Lockard & D. L. Paulhus (Eds.), *Self-deception: An adaptive mechanism?* (pp. 251–255). Englewood Cliffs, NJ: Prentice-Hall.

Peskin, H. (1993). Neither broken hearts nor broken bonds. *American Psychologist, 48,* 990–991.

Plimpton, E. H., & Rosenblum, L. A. (1987). Maternal loss in nonhuman primates: Implications for human development. In J. Bloom-Feshbach & S. Bloom-Feshbach (Eds.), *The psychology of separation and loss* (pp. 63–86). San Francisco: Jossey-Bass.

Raphael, B. (1983). *The anatomy of bereavement.* New York: Basic Books.

Reite, M., & Boccia, M. L. (1994). Physiological aspects of adult attachment. In M. B. Sperling & W. H. Berman (Eds.), *Attachment in adults* (pp. 98–127). New York: Guilford Press.

Rosenblatt, P. C. (1996). Grief that does not end. In D. Klass, P. R. Silverman, & S. L. Nickman (Eds.), *Continuing bonds: New understandings of grief* (pp. 45–58). Washington, DC: Taylor & Francis.

Rosenblatt, P. C., Walsh, R. P., & Jackson, D. A. (1976). *Grief and mourning in cross-cultural perspective.* New Haven, CT: Human Relations Area Files.

Sanders, C. M. (1989). *Grief: The mourning after.* New York: Wiley.

Sanders, C. M. (1993). Risk factors in bereavement outcome. In M. S. Stroebe, W. Stroebe, & R. O. Hansson (Eds.), *Handbook of bereavement: Theory, research, and intervention* (pp. 255–267). New York: Cambridge University Press.

Seay, B., Hansen, E., & Harlow, H. F. (1962). Mother–infant separation in monkeys. *Journal of Child Psychology and Psychiatry, 3,* 123–132.

Shaver, P. R., & Brennan, K. A. (1992). Attachment styles and the "Big Five" personality traits: Their connections with each other and with romantic relationship outcomes. *Personality and Social Psychology Bulletin, 18,* 536–545.

Silverman, P. R., & Klass, D. (1996). Introduction: What's the problem? In D. Klass, P. R. Silverman, & S. L. Nickman (Eds.), *Continuing bonds: New understandings of grief* (pp. 3–25). Washington, DC: Taylor & Francis.

Silverman, P. R., & Nickman, S. L. (1996). Children's construction of their dead parents. In D. Klass, P. R. Silverman, & S. L. Nickman (Eds.), *Continuing bonds: New understandings of grief* (pp. 73–86). Washington, DC: Taylor & Francis.

Silverman, P. R., Nickman, S., & Worden, J. W. (1992). Detachment revisited: The child's reconstruction of a dead parent. *American Journal of Orthopsychiatry, 62,* 494–503.

Sroufe, L. A., & Waters, E. (1977a). Attachment as an organizational construct. *Child Development, 48,* 1184–1199.

Sroufe, L. A., & Waters, E. (1977b). Heart rate as a convergent measure in clinical and developmental research. *Merrill–Palmer Quarterly, 23,* 3–27.

Stroebe, M. (1992). Coping with bereavement: A review of the grief work hypothesis. *Omega, 26,* 19–42.

Stroebe, M., Gergen, M., Gergen, K., & Stroebe, W. (1992). Broken hearts or broken bonds?: Love and death in historical perspective. *American Psychologist, 47,* 1205–1212.

Stroebe, M., Gergen, M., Gergen, K., & Stroebe, W. (1996). Broken hearts or broken bonds? In D. Klass, P. R. Silverman, & S. L. Nickman (Eds.), *Continuing bonds: New understandings of grief* (pp. 31–44). Washington, DC: Taylor & Francis.

Stroebe, M., & Stroebe, W. (1991). Does "grief work" work? *Journal of Consulting and Clinical Psychology, 59,* 479–482.

Stroebe, M., & Stroebe, W. (1993). The mortality of bereavement: A review. In M. S. Stroebe, W. Stroebe, & R. O. Hansson (Eds.), *Handbook of bereavement: Theory, research, and intervention* (pp. 175–195). New York: Cambridge University Press.

Stroebe, M., van den Bout, J., & Schut, H. A. W. (1994). Myths and misconceptions about bereavement: The opening of a debate. *Omega, 29,* 187–203.

Stroebe, W., & Stroebe, M. (1987). *Bereavement and health: The psychological and physical consequences of partner loss.* New York: Cambridge University Press.

Stroebe, W., Stroebe, M., Abakoumkin, G., & Schut, H. (1996). The role of loneliness and social support in adjustment to loss: A test of attachment versus stress theory. *Journal of Personality and Social Psychology, 70,* 1241–1249.

Tyson-Rawson, K. (1993). *College women and bereavement: Late adolescence and father death.* Unpublished doctoral dissertation, Kansas State University.

Tyson-Rawson, K. (1996). Relationship and heritage: Manifestations of ongoing attachment following father death. In D. Klass, P. R. Silverman, & S. L. Nickman (Eds.), *Continuing bonds: New understandings of grief* (pp. 125–145). Washington, DC: Taylor & Francis.

Vachon, M. L. S., Sheldon, A. R., Lancee, W. J., Lyall, W. A. L., Rogers, J., & Freeman, S. J. J. (1982). Correlates of enduring stress patterns following bereavement: Social network, life situation and personality. *Psychological Medicine, 12,* 783–788.

van den Boom, D. (1990). Preventive intervention and the quality of mother–infant interaction and infant exploration in irritable infants. In W. Koops, H. J. G. Soppe, J. L. Van der Linden, P. C. M. Molenaar, & J. J. F. Schroots (Eds.), *Developmental psychology behind the dikes: An outline of developmental psychology research in the Netherlands.* Delft, The Netherlands: Uitgeverij Eburon.

van IJzendoorn, M. (1995). Adult attachment representations, parental responsiveness, and infant attachment: A meta-analysis of the predictive validity of the Adult Attachment Interview. *Psychological Bulletin, 117,* 387–403.

Weinberger, D. A. (1990). The construct validity of the repressive coping style. In J. L. Singer (Ed.), *Repression and dissociation: Implications for personality theory, psychopathology, and health* (pp. 337–386). Chicago: University of Chicago Press.

Weinberger, D. A., Schwartz, G. E., & Davidson, R. J. (1979). Low-anxious, high-anxious, and repressive coping styles: Psychometric patterns and behavioral and physiological responses to stress. *Journal of Abnormal Psychology, 88,* 369–380.

Weisman, A. (1972). *On dying and denying: A psychiatric study of terminality.* New York: Behavioral.

Weiss, R. S. (1973). *Loneliness: The experience of social and emotional isolation.* Cambridge, MA: MIT Press.

Weiss, R. S. (1975). *Marital separation.* New York: Basic Books.

Wortman, C. B., & Silver, R. C. (1989). The myths of coping with loss. *Journal of Consulting and Clinical Psychology, 57,* 349–357.

Zisook, S., & DeVaul, R. A. (1985). Unresolved grief. *American Journal of Psychoanalysis, 45,* 370–379.

33

A Wider View of Attachment and Exploration

Stability and Change during the Years of Immaturity

❖

KLAUS E. GROSSMANN
KARIN GROSSMANN
PETER ZIMMERMANN

Evaluating stability and change in attachment organization during infancy and childhood depends greatly on one's interpretation of attachment theory and on the particular methods one uses to assess attachment quality. In this chapter, we extend Ainsworth's argument (e.g., Ainsworth, 1985a) that exploration is an integral component of infant–parent relationships, and that security is a reflection of the way an individual balances exploration and attachment and the way his or her caregivers facilitate this balance.

We are not proposing to expand the concept of attachment per se. Instead we want to emphasize the broader functions of parent–child relationships. In our discussion of Ainsworth's concept of attachment–exploration balance, we differentiate between a wider and a narrower view of infant–caregiver relationships (Grossmann & Grossmann, 1990). The narrow view is concerned primarily with an individual's response to the real or possible loss of an attachment figure. Most research on attachment has been conducted with this view in mind and has focused on the individual's appraisals of potentially distressing situations and the regulation of emotions and behavior in response to such circumstances. In our wider view of attachment and exploration, the

organization of attachment behavior as a response to separation or loss is still very important, but we pay more attention to the full range of adaptive consequences of different attachment patterns, especially to consequences that can be understood in terms of exploration. As we will discuss, exploration plays an important role in preventing and coping with adversity. Thus, in the development of adaptive capacities, parental sensitivity to the entire range of infant emotional signals—some having to do with attachment/separation and some with exploration—is important.

In this chapter, research findings on stability and change in attachment development in infancy and childhood are reexamined with the attachment–exploration balance foremost in mind. Our focus is on the ways in which exploration is facilitated or inhibited by the quality of the attachment relationship. We also focus on the degree to which attachment assessment methods consider both (1) emotion regulation during separation or other intense distress and (2) emotion regulation during challenging exploration. We use the term "secure exploration" to indicate a pattern of exploration in which challenges are recognized, accurately assessed, and tackled realistically but not incautiously.

Attachment research is no longer exclusively focused on infancy and toddlerhood, and attachment theory never has been. With increasing age, the implications of a child's cognitive and emotional representations of caregiving and support become important. Bowlby called these representations "internal working models of self and others" (1969/1982). We will briefly consider the status of Bowlby's internal working model construct; we keep in mind, however, that ethological and behavioral systems constructs, based on observations of children in real-life environments, were the original foundations of attachment research. We discuss both behavioral systems and internal working models in relation to the measures used in attachment research. In line with Bowlby's (1988b) therapeutic goal of reorganizing maladaptive internal working models, we argue that mental exploration should be viewed as an extension of security of exploration in childhood.

In what follows, we first discuss what we mean by a "wider view" of attachment and exploration. Next we review selected studies of stability and change in, as well as sequelae of, patterns of attachment during infancy, preschool age, early school age, and later childhood/adolescence. In line with our wider perspective on attachment and exploration, when discussing research evidence for stability and change in attachment patterns, we pay special attention to the organization of emotions and behaviors along the entire attachment–exploration spectrum. That is, we emphasize exploration more than is customary in summaries of attachment research. Furthermore, we are not concerned solely with the stability of patterns of attachment as assessed in the strange situation. We are also interested in the conditions that influence quality of exploration and adaptation to reality (K. E. Grossmann & Grossmann, 1991).

A WIDER THEORETICAL CONTEXT

The Concept of Security of Exploration

Curiosity has long been recognized as conflict-engendering (Berlyne, 1960; Bronson, 1972). On the one hand, it gives rise to fascination and exploration; on the other, it can arouse fear and wariness. We consider the successful negotiation and regulation of these conflicting states to be an important issue for the wider view of the attach-

ment–exploration balance. Open-mindedness, open communication (Grossmann, Grossmann, & Schwan, 1986), and a careful but curious orientation to reality are the hallmarks of security when "security" is defined as an optimal balance between attachment and exploration. Although Bowlby conceptualized the attachment system as separate from the exploration system, he considered their functioning to be interdependent. Using the attachment figure as a secure base for exploration is a biological function of attachment.

Individual differences in quality of exploration were among the first outcomes associated with individual differences in quality of attachment to mother in infancy (Main, 1973). Quality of exploration was defined by longer periods of concentration during enthusiastic bouts of play with novel toys. The ability to concentrate during exploration, as we will show, seems to rest (1) on the ability to organize emotions and behaviors open-mindedly in response to "curious" events, and to do so "carefully"; and (2) on confidence in the attachment figure's availability and help, should this help be needed.

A secure parental base provides a child with the confidence needed for meeting the challenges of exploration. The value placed by parents—and, in a more global view, by different cultures—on playful interaction and exploratory curiosity in contrast with attachment behaviors has an important effect on personality development. Exploratory interest and enthusiasm are based on a feeling of security that reflects an anticipated positive evaluation of the environment. We propose to use the concept of "security of exploration" as an integral part of the concept of "security of attachment": Given parental presence (i.e., a potentially secure base), will a child's exploratory activity be free and playful, or will the child be compulsively attending to the toys or anxious and inattentive? Ainsworth (1985a, p. 782), in describing the function of the attachment figure as a secure base, comments as follows on the complementarity of maternal sensitivity and infant exploration:

Indeed, the experience of largely consistent maternal responsiveness that leads to secure attachment has another more indirect effect on exploratory activity; since the baby has perceived that what he does has an effect on his mother's behavior toward him, he builds up what White called "a sense of competence." . . . It is a small step to assume that this encourages an active, exploratory approach to the objects in his physical environment as well.

For the less secure child the range of the attachment–exploration balance is restricted. Exploratory activity of infants with an avoidant attachment to their mothers is restricted by too much anxiety, shown by too much attention to objects as a defensive maneuver to deactivate the attachment system. Exploratory activity of infants with an ambivalent attachment to their mothers is restricted by preoccupation with maintaining proximity to the attachment figure. This concept of "freedom to explore" and its mental companion, "freedom to evaluate experiences," can be found again in Main and Goldwyn's (in press) coding system for classifying adults' states of mind with respect to attachment. Thus freedom to explore the external and internal worlds is an important attachment-related issue throughout the lifespan.

Exploration and Internal Working Models of Attachment

Traditional attachment research beyond infancy addresses two issues: attachment behavior and attachment representations (Ainsworth, 1985b). Attachment behavior is held to characterize human beings "from the cradle to the grave" (Bowlby, 1979, p. 129). But Bowlby's concept of "internal working models of self and others" is based on the notion that an internal organization of attachment and exploration develops over the years. According to Bowlby (1979), a child whose parents are available and supportive will construct a representational model of the self as able to cope but also as worthy of help. It is the quality of help that endows the child with exploratory competence.

In his discussion of the development of attachment-related mental representations, Bowlby (1973) mentioned the possibility of multiple models, and of models' coexisting at different levels of consciousness. Bowlby (1988b) viewed psychotherapy as a set of techniques aimed at helping a person examine and rebuild dysfunctional working models. The therapist should enable the patient to "cease being a slave to old and unconscious stereotypes and to feel, to think, and to act in new ways" (Bowlby, 1988b, p. 139). Integration of attachment experiences into a coherent linguistic representation is also the key issue in classifying an adult's "current state of mind regarding attachment" with the Adult Attachment Interview (K. E. Grossmann, 1997; K. E. Grossmann & Grossmann, in press; Main & Goldwyn,

in press; see Crowell, Fraley, & Shaver, Chapter 20, and Hesse, Chapter 19, this volume). The current state of mind need not be the same as, or a direct parallel of, previous models or states of mind. Both self-initiated and therapist-initiated changes are possible.

Exploration and the Strange Situation

Before reviewing studies that have used Ainsworth's strange situation (Ainsworth, Blehar, Waters, & Wall, 1978) to assess quality of attachment as either a dependent or an independent variable, we examine this assessment procedure with our "wider," more exploration-focused perspective in mind. The organization and development of patterns of infant–mother attachment were conceptualized and carefully described by Ainsworth almost 30 years ago (Ainsworth, 1970). Ever since, her strange situation method of assessing patterns of attachment of 1-year-olds to their mothers, with its two brief separations that activate the infants' attachment system, has become the central methodology of attachment research in infancy and early childhood (Ainsworth & Wittig, 1969; for an early review, see Bretherton, 1985; for more recent reviews, see Magai & McFadden, 1995, and Solomon & George, Chapter 14, this volume). We have used the strange situation in three of our own longitudinal studies. Despite ample evidence for its validity and usefulness in predicting a host of outcomes in the social and emotional domains, our extensive use of the method has made us aware of its limitations.

Seen from our wider view, the strange situation assesses primarily the attachment side of the attachment–exploration balance. The exploration side of the balance is part of the classification system, but the quality of maternal support for exploration is only marginally noted. There is a price for the almost exclusive focus on the attachment figure as a haven of safety and a secure base. When patterns of attachment are assessed in the strange situation, the attachment figure's quality of supporting the child's interest in exploration when negative emotions arise is not part of the classification system. In discussing stability and change in, as well as outcomes of, patterns of attachment assessed in infancy in the strange situation, we address these patterns as belonging to the narrow view of attachment. Nevertheless, strategies of infants in response to separation are also examined for their ability to predict the entire range of behaviors across the attachment–exploration spectrum.

ATTACHMENT AND EXPLORATION IN THE FIRST 2 YEARS OF LIFE

Maternal Sensitivity to Attachment and Exploratory Behaviors

We wish to conceptualize maternal sensitivity as helping to organize the infant and toddler emotionally, not only in the attachment domain but also in the domain of exploration. The mobile infant is often eager to move away from the mother to explore and manipulate objects. With the attachment figure nearby, exploration can occur with a minimum of insecurity or anxiety. Some aspects of novelty, however, may frighten the infant; unsuccessful manipulations of objects may be frustrating; and the ensuing negative emotions may activate the attachment system. A sensitive attachment figure will accurately interpret the infant's negative emotional expression as a signal for help and will do something to alleviate the infant's distress while keeping him or her focused on the goal. The attachment figure's sensitivity does not interfere with the infant's concentration during play. In conflicts between curiosity and fear, the parent does not interrupt or interfere with the child's ultimate goal. The parent comforts the child while simultaneously encouraging him or her in the task at hand. Sensitive emotional support during curiosity–wariness conflicts should not be confused with distracting the infant or even with pushing the toddler toward higher achievements. Distraction can be considered insensitive because it fails to acknowledge the infant's exploratory goals. Sensitive support during exploration is characterized by acknowledging the infant's frustration and hinting toward a solution that is appropriate, given the infant's developmental level. Several studies are consistent with this interpretation of sensitivity as it applies to the attachment–exploration balance.

Research has shown that variations in the quality of infants' attachment patterns as observed in the strange situation with their mothers are predictable from maternal sensitivity during the first year (see van IJzendoorn, 1995, and Pederson & Moran, 1996). A recent multisite National Institute of Child Health and Human Development (NICHD) study of 1,153 infants' early child care experiences corroborates this observa-

tion—even for infants who attended day care during their first year of life (NICHD Early Child Care Research Network, 1997). Among many variables examined in this study, only two predicted infant security: mothers' psychological adjustment and maternal sensitivity in the home. "Maternal sensitivity in play" did not predict attachment security when other variables were controlled. On careful inspection, however, "maternal sensitivity in play" seems to have been a misnomer because that variable explicitly excluded sensitivity to infant distress signals during play. It was a composite created from scales for sensitivity to nondistress, positive regard, and intrusiveness. In studies that have included measures of maternal sensitivity to negative emotions during exploration, researchers have been able to link sensitivity during play to infant security. For example, Egeland and Farber (1984) noted the role of cooperation versus interference in mother–infant interactions. Thus maternal sensitivity to distress seems to be a major predictor of attachment security, and such sensitivity appears to be as important in the context of exploration as it is in the narrow context of attachment.

A study of mothers' and fathers' interactive behaviors in a free-play situation with their 12- or 18-month-old infants revealed a context-specific reaction pattern on the part of parents that was related to each dyad's attachment status (Grossmann, Scheuerer-Englisch, & Loher, 1991). Parents whose infants were securely attached to them (infant–mother and infant–father attachment patterns were found to be independent) interfered less with their infants' exploratory activity when their infants were content and concentrating. But when their infants signaled discontent, these parents assisted by finding new ways to facilitate exploration (e.g., offering a new toy). These parents helped their infants sustain interest in exploration by stepping in before the infant's exploration–attachment balance was tipped away from exploration toward attachment. Parents in avoidant dyads seemed to notice the same emotional expressions in their infants, but reacted differently. During their infants' concentrated exploration they often joined the infants, offered a toy, or redirected the infants' attention. As a result, these parents disrupted their infants' concentration by interfering with play, and the infants became discontented. When the infants' distress signals became evident and their exploration ceased, these parents would more often than not withdraw and wait for the infants to overcome the distress alone. This kind of interference is well and extensively described in Ainsworth's "cooperation versus interference" scale (Ainsworth, Bell, & Stayton, 1974).

Cassidy and Berlin (1994) reviewed studies suggesting a similar exploration-inhibiting pattern in ambivalent dyads. Mothers of ambivalent infants were not only less consistently available to their infants when the infants were distressed, but also interfered when their infants were exploring the environment. The exploratory behavior of the infants in these dyads was often interrupted before the infants could complete their play bouts, and exploration conflicts were not resolved in favor of continued exploration, but in favor of the mothers' own needs.

Further evidence for the wider view of attachment and exploration comes from a number of studies relating security of attachment to efficiency of infants' functioning when their curiosity and mastery motivation are challenged. Belsky, Garduque, and Hrncir (1984) related quality of play performance to attachment quality with both parents. Infants evaluated as securely attached to both parents were found to be freer to attend to the environment beyond the attachment figure when playing, and they displayed a smaller gap between their most sophisticated free play and play elicited by the experimenter. Main (1973, 1983) found 21-month-old toddlers who had been securely attached to mother in infancy to exhibit more delight in play than toddlers who were insecurely attached as infants. Secure attachment to mothers was also related to deeper engrossment in play, longer bouts of engaged episodes, and greater versatility in exploring different aspects of the toys. In a different study, toddlers who were insecurely attached to their mothers appeared less effective in their efforts to master challenging tasks, were less enthusiastic, and showed less endurance during the tasks (Matas, Arend, & Sroufe, 1978). When challenged with more difficult tool-using tasks, securely attached toddlers successfully enlisted their mothers' support in order to achieve a solution. Their mothers' support was more appropriately attuned to the needs and exploratory goals of their toddlers than the behavior of mothers in insecure dyads.

Toddlers' motivational patterns, but not their cognitive skills as assessed with developmental tests, were also found to vary with attachment quality. Toddlers with secure attachments to both parents were, at 24 months, more eager to go on

with the Bayley Scales of Infant Development (Bayley, 1969). Playful interactions between toddlers and their fathers were more harmonious and enjoyable for both if the toddlers had been classified as securely attached at 18 months (K. Grossmann & Grossmann, in press). In another study, toddlers who were securely attached to their mothers showed more adequate task-oriented problem-solving strategies than toddlers in avoidant or disorganized attachment relationships with mother (Schieche, 1995, 1996). In this study, patterned after the study by Matas et al. (1978), more securely than insecurely attached toddlers demonstrated an optimal balance between attachment and exploratory behaviors in the service of reaching their goals in difficult task situations. Their mothers had been instructed to be responsive, but not to guide the toddlers through the task. These findings support Bretherton's (1985, p. 21) proposition that "confidence in the mother's physical and psychological availability appears to lay the groundwork for autonomous exploration and problem solving, coupled with the expectation that help will be forthcoming when needed."

A Dutch intervention study, which was successful in increasing the sensitivity of low-socioeconomic-status mothers of highly irritable infants (van den Boom, 1994), was designed to increase maternal responsiveness to infants' positive as well as negative emotional expressions in attachment as well as exploratory contexts, and to discourage intrusive behavior and/or detached lack of involvement on the part of mother. The intervention greatly increased the percentage of securely attached dyads at 12 months. It also produced significant improvements in infant sociability and cognitive sophistication during exploration. (Stability data from the study are reported in a subsequent section of this chapter.)

We conclude that sensitivity to an infant's signals and communications facilitates emotion regulation in contexts in which the infant's attachment system is aroused, and in contexts in which the infant's exploratory system is aroused. Infants experiencing sensitivity from their mothers during curiosity–wariness conflicts show more effective goal-oriented exploratory behavior, in addition to demonstrating security of attachment to their mothers. This wider view of attachment security, which includes security of exploration without excluding the attachment side of the attachment–exploration balance, was also favored by Sroufe and Fleeson (1988), who proposed a holistic view of attachment relationships as encompassing the whole range of interactive contexts.

Assessing Patterns of the Attachment–Exploration Balance at Home and in the Laboratory

Ainsworth et al. (1971) described an infant attachment classification system based on the balance between attachment behavior and exploratory behavior at home (see also Ainsworth et al., 1978, p. 240 ff.). Group 1 infants showed an optimal balance of active exploration and active attachment behaviors, whereas Group 5 infants were generally passive either in their attachment behavior or in exploration. Ainsworth and colleagues used the secure-base behavior of the infant as a major criterion for their groupings, but unfortunately did not comment on the mother's specific sensitivity in keeping the infant on task in conflictual exploratory situations. This may not be immediately relevant to the attachment system per se, but it is relevant to emotional organization, adaptive functioning, and secure exploration. Ainsworth et al. characterized the intermediate groups predominantly by conflicts evident in their attachment behavior. In light of the notion that sensitivity affects the development of a sophisticated internal working model regulating current adaptations, interests, and goal orientations, effective exploratory behaviors are just as important as attachment behaviors.

In their observational study of premature and full-term infants at home with their mothers during the infants' first year and in the strange situation at 18 months, Pederson, and Moran (1996) confirmed the high concordance between maternal sensitivity and infant attachment patterns. Building on Ainsworth et al.'s (1971) home groupings, they devised a relationship classification system patterned after the subgroups of the strange situation classification system. Within the avoidant relationships, they differentiated among teaching, ignoring, and conflicted relationships. Teaching mothers were described as lacking affective sharing in response to success on cognitive tasks. Although the authors did not specifically address maternal responsiveness geared to exploration–wariness conflicts in infants, the general description of this group was "physical and emotional independence of infant and mother" (p. 917), suggesting maternal unresponsiveness in exploratory conflicts as well.

For the sample of 23 infants in Ainsworth et al.'s (1971) early study, correspondence between

home and strange situation classifications was very high. It was lower, but still quite high, in Pederson and Moran's (1996) study. For the secure groups in the latter study the concordance was 80% (*n* [B] = 40), and for the avoidant groups it was 75% (*n* [A] = 24). The identification of the ambivalent dyads in their home environment was not successful (40% for the 15 C dyads). The authors were acutely aware, however, that the laboratory assessment procedure evaluated only an infant's reaction to separation from the mother, whereas at home a wider range of interactive behaviors was assessed (Pederson & Moran, 1996).

In the strange situation classification system, exploratory behaviors enter the judgment of security only insofar as they indicate either the deactivation of the attachment system because of effective consolation, or the infant's attempt to attend to toys in an effort to control negative emotions when the attachment system is activated (Spangler & Grossmann, 1993). The strange situation classification system does not address how the attachment figure helps to organize the infant's emotions and concentration during curiosity–wariness conflicts. This may be an important addition if one wishes to extend the usefulness of the strange situation to other attachment figures besides the mother. For instance, studies on correlates of patterns of infant–father attachment suggest that the strange situation may be too limited to capture the special nature of exploration as part of an attachment relationship, which may perhaps be more important for fathers and other secondary attachment figures than for mothers (Bretherton, Golby, & Halvorsen, 1993).

Difficulties in Applying the Narrow Infant–Mother Attachment Model to the Infant–Father Relationship

The relation between sensitive, responsive care—in contrast to intrusive or disengaged care—and secure infant–mother attachment patterns at the beginning of the second year is well established. For the infant–father attachment relationship, however, other rules seem to apply. Most fathers are attachment figures for their infants, even though in most families they are not the primary caregivers and often spend relatively little time with their infants (see Parke & Tinsley, 1987, for a review of the literature concerning fathering of infants). Studies using fathers' interactive qualities, based on the notion of maternal sensitivity, as a predictor of infant–father attachment quality in the strange situation have often failed to confirm the findings obtained with mother–infant pairs.

In a longitudinal study of 113 families, Volling and Belsky (1992) found that only self-report variables such as men's recollected child-rearing histories and their involvement in household tasks distinguished between secure and insecure patterns of infant–father attachment. Of the five behavioral items listed in a precoded behavioral checklist employed during home visits to assess infant–father interaction quality, none predicted infant–father attachment patterns. Easterbrooks and Goldberg (1984) reported similar findings. Fathers' job satisfaction, parenting knowledge, and attitudes, rather than observed paternal sensitivity, were predictors of infant–father attachment quality. In our north German longitudinal study of 47 families, paternal sensitivity in father–infant interactions during home visits at 2, 6, and 10 months were rated with Ainsworth's maternal sensitivity scale (Ainsworth et al., 1978); however, none of the observed father–infant interactive behaviors was significantly related to quality of infant–father attachment at 18 months, nor was the quality of their meshing (K. E. Grossmann & Grossmann, 1991, K. Grossmann & Grossmann, in press). These diverse studies suggest that although patterns of infant–father interaction can be assessed with the same instruments as patterns of infant–mother attachment, the classifications do not imply the same origins as those documented for mother–infant pairs. Paternal sensitivity, if assessed like maternal sensitivity, predicts patterns of infant–father attachment in the strange situation only weakly or not at all.

In contrast, many father–infant interaction studies have consistently found relations between fathers' interactional sensitivity and quality of toddlers' play (Belsky et al., 1984; Easterbrooks & Goldberg, 1984; K. Grossmann & Grossmann, in press), with patterns of attachment being an intervening variable. Toddlers securely attached to their fathers demonstrated more optimal behavior patterns in problem-solving tasks and were more consistent in their task orientation, compared with toddlers who were insecurely attached to their fathers. These relations also held for toddlers of sensitive fathers (Easterbrooks & Goldberg, 1984). The quality of father–infant interaction was usually rated during a play situation. The range of infant behaviors observed, therefore, was probably more on the exploration side and less on the attachment side of the attach-

ment–exploration balance. Both studies (Easterbrooks & Goldberg, 1984; K. Grossmann & Grossmann, in press) assessed emotional supportiveness, encouragement, meshing, attentiveness, positive affect, praise, and non-intrusiveness as markers of fathers' sensitivity. These interactive qualities can also be interpreted as organizing an infant's positive and negative emotions during exploration, concentrated play, and curiosity–wariness conflicts. In these activities the toddler's attachment system is not usually aroused. It is perhaps for this reason that the strange situation seems not to be an equally valid assessment of infant–father and infant–mother attachment relationships.

The strange situation procedure was designed to assess patterns of attachment in infants younger than 18 months of age. Ainsworth (1985a) argued that a child approaching his or her second birthday will find the strange situation less stressful and will be less likely to seek proximity or contact with the mother upon reunion. Because of the lack of attachment behaviors, an infant may be classified as avoidant when he or she is merely being casual about close bodily proximity. On the other hand, joint attention to a toy or book in the service of avoidance of direct interaction may be mistaken for proximity seeking, which would be appropriate for 12-month-olds. In line with developmental advances, the older toddler is able to keep up prolonged bouts of play and his or her social skill increases, making an interpretation of the child's behavior more difficult. Thus the strange situation should be used only with infants between 12 and 18 months of age, and data regarding infant responses in the strange situation beyond that age range should be interpreted cautiously.

In the early years of attachment research, a number of studies examined the stability of infant–mother attachment patterns in the strange situation on two different occasions when infants were aged between 12 and 20 months. In three samples involving largely intact middle-class families with low-risk infants, an 80% stability rate of attachment classifications was reported (Connell, 1976; Main & Weston, 1981; Waters, 1978). This claim has recently been challenged. Belsky, Campbell, Cohn, and Moore (1996) reported rates of stability ranging from 46% to 55% for a total of 215 infant–mother pairs and 120 infant–father pairs from non-risk samples. Belsky et al. (1996) discuss a number of possible explanations, including the changing ecology of infancy over the past 10–15 years. Mangelsdorf,

Plunkett, Dedrick, McHale, and Dichtelmiller (1996) reported stability rates of patterns of attachment of 65% for full-term infants and 60% for infants of very low birthweight. Together with an infant's risk status, a family's high risk for promoting inadequate infant development has been consistently associated with unstable patterns of attachment. Little or no stability of attachment patterns was found in samples with high maternal stress in general (Lyons-Ruth, Repacholi, McLeod, & Silva, 1991), infant maltreatment (Schneider-Rosen, Braunwald, Carlson, & Cicchetti, 1985), great environmental stress on mothers (Vaughn, Egeland, Sroufe, & Waters, 1979), and relatively major changes in family circumstances, such as the onset of regular nonmaternal care (Thompson, Lamb, & Estes,) or infants' being diagnosed as highly irritable at birth (van den Boom, 1995).

A German day care study related mode of transition into day care to changes in attachment patterns in the strange situation at 12 and 21 months, which is a bit too old for the traditional procedure, according to Ainsworth (Rauh, Ziegenhain, Müller, & Wijnroks, in press). All infants who changed from a secure to an insecure attachment pattern between 12 and 21 months had experienced an abrupt mode of introduction into day care. Conversely, all infants who changed from an insecure to a secure attachment status had been introduced into day care with extensive parental support and presence. Nevertheless, as in the NICHD study, sensitive mothering was more important and overrode the effect of mode of introduction into day care. In general, stability of attachment patterns during infancy seems to vary according to risk factors, life stresses, and changing life circumstances.

For older toddlers, other methods of assessing attachment quality have been used. Waters and Deane (1985) devised an Attachment *Q*-Set (AQS) to describe the behaviors of children aged 1 to 5 years with their mothers at home in everyday situations. Security of attachment is defined in this method as the degree of congruence between a given child's profile and mostly U.S. "experts" profile for an "optimally secure" child (Vaughn & Waters, 1990). The AQS assessment of attachment security seems to measure something different from the strange situation (Solomon & George, Chapter 14, this volume) despite a number of validating studies on external variables, including some cross-cultural studies (Waters, Vaughn, Posada, & Kondo-Ikemura, 1995).

Some peculiarities of the AQS make it difficult to evaluate the resulting data. First, assessors of maternal sensitivity or quality of toddler–mother interaction at home are confined to the items of the AQS and may therefore ignore other indications of interaction quality. Second, the profile for an "optimally secure" preschool child would probably be different for a 2-year-old as compared to a 4-year-old; the "experts" did not specify the age of the child they were characterizing as "optimally secure." Perhaps for those reasons, correspondence between the resulting security scores of children and patterns of attachment in the strange situation has varied substantially. When mothers have done the ratings, correspondence is sometimes good, sometimes lacking (Mangelsdorf et al., 1996; Pederson & Moran, 1996; Stevenson-Hinde & Shouldice, 1990). Correspondence depends on the training of the mothers, as well as the range of observable behaviors at home (Teti & McGourty, 1996). In one study, prediction from strange situation classification to AQS security 7 months later was found to be satisfactory ($r = .40$), but not to AQS security 20 months later (Bretherton, Biringen, Ridgeway, Maslin, & Sherman, 1989). A review of studies using the AQS revealed that the mean AQS security score of 3-year-olds was much higher than that of 1-year-olds (Waters, Posada, Crowell, & Lay, 1994). The authors suggested that the older preschoolers were better at using their mother as a secure base, but it is just as likely that in the nonstressful home environment, secure-base behavior looks different in 1-year-olds than in 4-year-olds; an ethogram type (a full description) of preschoolers' behavior is badly lacking. Theoretically, age by itself should not affect attachment security. As the AQS seems to be affected by age and other methodological variables, we will not consider stability studies based on the AQS in this chapter.

The validity of the strange situation classification system for judging an infant as securely or insecurely attached still rests heavily on Ainsworth's observations of 23 tested infants who were also observed in their homes with their mothers. Because of this, the role of other family members as attachment figures or secure bases may have been underestimated (Schaffer & Emerson, 1964), as compared to the home ecology of infants in other cultures (K. Grossmann & Grossmann, 1991; LeVine et al., 1994; see van IJzendoorn & Sagi, Chapter 31, this volume). For a preverbal toddler, the smooth functioning of the attachment–exploration balance seems to vary with the infant's quality of attachment to the parent present. In addition, the toddler's ability to organize exploratory activity becomes more prominent from the second year on and is the basis of enculturation. The father, in his role as a facilitator of exploration, seems to play an important but certainly not an exclusive part in this process.

In summary, we view attachment quality as organizing an infant's and child's behavioral responses to anxiety, anger, and sadness. For an infant, feelings connected to separation are highly important and most salient, and for an infant under 18 months of age, quality of behavior patterns in response to separation is assessed most reliably and validly in the strange situation. With increasing age and growing cognitive skills, however, separation anxiety seems to decline, and distress due to curiosity–wariness conflicts gains importance. We propose that smooth and appropriate organization of emotions in exploratory conflicts can be interpreted as related to security of exploration. Both security of attachment and security of exploration require the coherent goal-oriented and, later, goal-corrected organization of emotions.

EMOTIONAL SECURITY IN ATTACHMENT RELATIONSHIPS AND DURING EXPLORATION FROM AGES 3 TO 5

As soon as verbal communication becomes important, children's balance of attachment and exploration behavior is bound to change dramatically. Whereas for 1-year-olds the main developmental steps are attachment and first explorations from a secure base, the important features for 2-year-olds are self-assertion and the beginnings of autonomy. Three-year-olds show positive self-evaluation, pride, shame, the beginnings of tolerance for a sibling, and enormous growth in linguistic competence. A rudimentary understanding of words that describe time periods helps them tolerate separation much longer. For 4-year-olds, gender identification and peer relationships are important; 5-year-olds are concerned with moral issues and adult rules; and 6-year-olds have to adapt to school-related activities, among (of course) many other things. Attachment development proceeds against this background of age- and culture-specific developmental tasks, conceptualized as "beyond attachment" by Dunn (1993). Research has shown that there are many links between attachment and developmental tasks, suggesting that quality of parental caregiving influences many different features of a child's personality.

Relations between Maternal Sensitive Support and Preschoolers' Adaptations in Challenging Situations

In everyday situations, learned behavioral routines are usually sufficiently adaptive. In challenging situations, however, the quality of an individual's emotional organization is revealed in the process of finding problem solutions or goals worth striving for, and keeping attention focused on that process instead of giving up because of rising emotional tension. Considered from the viewpoint of ethology, such tensions can often be observed in the form of conflict behaviors—for example, disrupting visual–motor coordination, interrupting eye contact and communication with an interaction partner, staring under the table or at the door, or manipulating objects aimlessly. Psychologically, a person's lack of, or interruption of, organized goal pursuit may indicate a breakdown of adaptive, solution-oriented, goal-corrected attention; of appropriate emotional monitoring; and of well-coordinated behavior.

Toddlerhood has been characterized as a time of dramatic changes in mother–child relationships, in which exploration and mastery of the environment normatively occur without jeopardizing the feeling of security (Lieberman, 1992). In following up her intervention study, van den Boom (1995) tested Bowlby's and Ainsworth's claim that early security fosters a continuing positive orientation in the relationship with the attachment figure, and she obtained strong confirmation of the idea. Interventions aimed at increasing maternal sensitivity during the first year (van den Boom, 1994) were associated with impressive sequelae in the lives of 2-year-olds: improvements in quality of orientation to mother, cooperation, engaging in meaningful activities, verbal interactions, and imitations of and comments about mothers' actions. At the 3-year follow-up, mothers who had received the intervention treatment offered more guidance to their children during initial encounters with peers, and their children exhibited fewer behavior problems and had more positive relationships with peers—a variable of central importance to the growth of competence in developmental adaptation to challenges (Rutter & Rutter, 1993). van den Boom (1995) noted that "appropriate regulation of negative affect seemed to belong to the mother's parenting repertoire," and that "most of the discerned effects on the quality of peer interaction were mediated by attachment history" (p. 1813). We first consider task orientation, then concentrated exploration, and finally social behavior.

Pianta and Harbers (1996) recently reviewed studies relating attachment quality or quality of mother–child interaction to measures of children's approaches to learning under naturalistic conditions (in contrast to test scores). Securely attached 5-year-olds engaged in more spontaneous reading, paid more attention to their mothers, and defied their mothers less (Bus & van IJzendoorn, 1988). Pianta and Harbers (1996) cite four studies that predicted adjustment to the requirements of formal learning in school from measures of child–mother interaction in problem-solving situations. All of these studies addressed the wider view of attachment, in the sense that security of attachment or quality of mother–child interaction seemed to go together with security of exploration into the world of learning. We ourselves have studied how the affective nature of mother–child interaction may influence a child's approaches to problem solving later in life.

Preschoolers' goal-corrected behavior and quality of emotional organization during cognitive challenges were the focus of an observational study of preschoolers confronted with a variety of tasks (Loher, 1988). Fifty 3-year-olds and their mothers were observed at home, and their mothers' quality of support was rated during their children's exploratory play, especially during "intellectually valuable experiences" (Carew, 1977, 1980). Six months later, and again 3 years later, the children were tested for their ability to concentrate on tasks that in part exceeded their abilities (Schildbach, 1992). At home, the children's exploratory activity that included intellectually valuable verbal, physical, and expressive components occurred much more frequently in the presence of their mothers than when they were alone, as Carew (1980) had already observed. Thus these young children's important experiences were mostly within the range of their mothers' influence. Maternal supportive behavior was defined as creating a warm and pleasant atmosphere and refraining from prohibitions, critical interference, and restrictions. The children's concentration during intellectually valuable play was positively related to their General Cognitive Index (GCI) on the McCarthy Scales of Children's Abilities (McCarthy, 1972) and to

mothers' IQ. However, the children's index of concentration remained positively correlated with maternal sensitive support even when GCI and IQ were statistically controlled for.

Under test conditions in the laboratory 6 months later, more negative and less playful behavior was significantly related to less warmth and less empathic maternal support at home. Children who at home had acted frequently without any recognizable goals, and who were often rejected and not well supported by their mothers, expressed fewer positive verbal self-evaluations 6 months later. Their communicative behavior (e.g., when trying to get help from the tester) was less differentiated. They expressed predominantly negative emotions, and they approached the examiner with incompetent questions, without asking for information about the task at hand. This was in clear contrast to the children from more supportive homes, whose discourse was more competently goal-oriented. Children with very poor support at home appeared rather stressed in the laboratory, as shown by their evasive and conflicted behaviors. As 3-year-olds, these children were more often rejected, less often responded to, and less often supported by their mothers at home, particularly in stressful situations.

Large differences in the organization of emotions during on-task behavior in the laboratory at 3½ years of age were predicted most strongly by maternal restrictions and lack of support in exploratory situations at home. Children who were less able to concentrate on a task in the laboratory were also frequently passive and rejected cooperation nonverbally. Children who showed unproductive evasive behavior in the laboratory had experienced very few intellectually valuable episodes at home, had already exhibited poor concentration during play at home, and were often restricted by their mothers to narrow limits. They had few opportunities for joint attention with their mothers. In contrast, children with attentive and supportive mothers in emotionally stressful home situations were significantly more competent and skilled in responding to stressful challenges in the laboratory. They often redefined challenges in a creative fashion—for instance, by changing the content of the task (e.g., building a tower or a robot instead of performing the required block designs) or by redefining the goals (e.g., declaring that the task of dressing a doll was completed even though no shoes had been put on, "because it is summer and the doll can go barefoot"). During such redefinitions, the children did not interrupt their concentration on the task or their goal-directedness.

Maternal supportive behavior at home was coded when a mother helped a child, during challenging explorations, to integrate negative emotions into uninterrupted, concentrated, playful exploratory activity, even when the child was in a relatively poor mood. This kind of maternal supportiveness, in contrast to simply entertaining the child with fun games, was positively correlated with children's ability to cope with difficult tasks (e.g., maintaining the organization of task-directed behavior). Maternal and child cognitive indices per se had only a minor influence on the children's emotional responses when a task became too difficult. The findings provide further evidence for the important role of maternal sensitivity in exploratory contexts. Sensitive mothers provide exploratory security and promote more effective concentration on novel and "curious" events that require some effort before they become familiar. Maternal sensitive support evidently helps to organize a child's emotions during exploration in the service of adaptation to various challenges. Of course, maternal sensitivity in exploratory contexts has to be tied to maternal sensitivity to the child's attachment cues, so that appropriate support as well as the secure base is available.

At 6 years, when the children were once again confronted with a task designed to be too difficult for them (given their individual intelligence scores), a continuing influence of maternal sensitivity was still observable in behavioral variables such as the children's concentration, evasive behaviors, and emotional stress symptoms (Schildbach, Loher, & Riedinger, 1995). However, maternal sensitivity in a play situation with the 6-year-olds was strongly related only to maternal sensitive supportiveness in a laboratory play situation when the children were 3½ years old, not to maternal home behavior. Still, 6-year-olds whose mothers had been more sensitive and had more efficiently reduced their 3-year-old children's exploratory conflicts in a positive emotional climate at home were more optimistic in the face of an insolvable task 3 years later. The authors differentiated between an early "spontaneous" and a later "voluntary" attentive task orientation, but they viewed both as behavioral responses to challenges in the service of coping with reality. Thus, in this study of children from 3 to 6 years of age, where only mothers but not fathers were assessed, sensitive mothers were very effective as facilitators of security of exploration in their

children. They responded sensitively to their children's needs, particularly in stressful situations, thereby enhancing their children's adaptive orientation.

Comparable results with an extension to patterns of attachment at 4½ years of age were reported by Stevenson-Hinde and Shouldice (1995) for the 78 families in their Cambridge study. The children's patterns of attachment were assessed at this age with a modified strange situation procedure (Cassidy, Marvin, & the MacArthur Working Group on Attachment, 1990). We are somewhat critical of the assessment and definition of attachment patterns at ages 3 to 5 in terms of a new kind of strange situation, because it is biased in extrapolating the attachment–exploration balance from Ainsworth's "narrow" validation procedure for 12-month-old infants to preschoolers. Again, this method does not pay special attention to management of conflictual playful exploration, nor to the child's cognitive, motivational, or emotional evaluation of the procedure. In fact, as Stevenson-Hinde and Shouldice (1995, p. 587) note, "the comings and goings involved in the seven episodes of the typical Ainsworth strange situation could not be done smoothly, since the children, unlike infants, persisted in talking to the stranger, looked puzzled when she left, and asked questions about what was going on."

These behaviors indicate age-appropriate adaptive exploratory curiosity, compatible with the wider view of attachment and exploration; however, as in the original strange situation, they are not directly addressed in the classification system. Nevertheless, a number of important validating findings were reported. At home, mothers of children classified as secure were rated higher than mothers of insecure children on positive mood, meshing, enjoyment of their children, and providing a relaxed home atmosphere. In a laboratory task, they received higher ratings for providing a sensitive framework—that is, "providing help and encouragement when needed, while allowing child to take initiative" (Stevenson-Hinde & Shouldice, 1995, p. 587). The list of maternal sensitive behaviors towards a preschooler matches very well our notion of maternal sensitive support and facilitation of security of exploration.

The children of the Cambridge sample were also observed in preschool (Turner, 1991, 1993). Preschoolers' attachment classifications were lawfully related to their reciprocal behavior patterns with adults and peers in preschool, while showing substantial interaction effects with gender. Secure children behaved and were treated in less gender-role-stereotypical ways, whereas boys with an insecure attachment to their mothers conformed more to the stereotype of an aggressive, noncompliant child, and insecure girls conformed to the stereotype of being overly compliant, helpless, and unassertive. Thus appropriate concurrent validity evidence for the preschool attachment assessment system has been provided by the Cambridge group. Another study looked at the longitudinal predictability of preschool attachment patterns from patterns of attachment at 18 months. The degree of continuity was statistically significant (Bretherton et al., 1989), but the variability was quite large.

Despite these important validating results, our stance remains critical. What is missing when one simply extrapolates the strange situation for 12-month-olds to the preschool years is an equally relevant assessment of security of exploration. It seems to us that an exclusive focus on reunion assessment beyond infancy stresses only the attachment side of the attachment–exploration balance, at the expense of behavioral, mental, and discursive exploration.

Predicting Adaptational Organization at Preschool Age from Early Attachment Classifications

Summaries of attachment-related differences in adaptation during the preschool period have been offered by, among others, Sroufe, Cooper, DeHart, and Marshall (1996); Cassidy and Berlin (1994), for the ambivalent pattern of attachment; and Belsky and Cassidy (1994). In the summary quoted just below, Magai and McFadden (1995, p. 154) point to differential outcomes for emotional organization during exploration in the play domain and in peer relationships:

> Collectively, the literature indicates that securely attached infants have longer attention spans and are more affectively positive during free play. They exhibit greater curiosity, more autonomous exploration, and have more flexible egos. They also show less frustration in problem-solving situations and are more enthusiastic. In interaction with peers they show greater social competence and in interaction with adults they are described as more compliant (Ainsworth et al., 1978). In contrast, children who are insecurely attached are more negative with peers and less compliant with teachers. They also display less empathy toward others in distress, are more likely to misperceive cartoon stimuli as having negative intentions, and are less likely to reveal their own distressed feelings when under conditions of stress. During problem-solving tasks, they are more readily frustrated, whiny, and negativistic.

We now take a closer look at the processes that seem to mediate these interrelated behavioral organizations.

The families of our north German longitudinal study (Grossmann, Grossmann, Spangler, Suess, & Unzner, 1985) were visited at home and observed in a number of interactive situations when the target children were 3 years of age. Mothers and children were asked to play a matching-to-pattern game, and the children were challenged to compete with the visitor in a tower-building task (Lütkenhaus, Grossmann, & Grossmann, 1985a, 1985b). Results of the observational analyses were related to the children's attachment classification with their mothers in the strange situation at 12 months of age. In the matching game, the most influential determinant of the children's persistence and striving for mastery was their mothers' concurrent interactive behavior (Lütkenhaus, 1983). Physical interruptions, taking the problem out of a child's hands, snippy maternal remarks, and fussing about mistakes were related to low persistence on the child's part, whereas the occurrence of joint smiles and a warm atmosphere combined with prompt helping and praise for success was associated with stronger mastery motivation. Maternal appropriate support in this game was significantly related to maternal cooperation during the first year (Lütkenhaus, 1988). Comparable to Loher's (1998) observations of mothers' interference with their children's exploratory intentions, mothers' violations of their children's sense of "self as agent" seemed to impair the children's concentration on goal-organized activities.

In a competitive game, a surprising difference—predictable from early attachment quality—emerged in the children's behavior. Each child had to stack a tower of wooden rings one by one onto a peg. The adult competitor allowed the child to win on the first and third trials, but caused the child to lose on the second trial. The children's behaviors during trial 2 (first failure) and trial 3 (second win) were compared. All children looked more at the competitor's tower during trial 2 as the upcoming failure became evident, but they reacted differently according to early attachment status. A majority of the children judged securely attached in infancy increased their building speed during the failing trial (2), but not in the second winning trial (3). The children with an early insecure attachment, whether this was avoidant or ambivalent, became nervous and less coordinated in their movements as they observed the winning competitor. Their building speed in trial 2 was lower than their speed during the other trials.

Securely attached children openly communicated their sadness upon losing while maintaining eye contact with the competitor, whereas children with an insecure attachment also showed sadness when losing, but did not show their sad faces directly to their interaction partner. Instead, they produced a "social smile" when looking at him. The formerly insecurely attached children, as a group, became less efficient at problem solving while hiding their feelings of sadness. In view of the high percentage of avoidant attachment classifications (49%) and the low percentage of secure attachments (33%) in this north German sample (Grossmann et al., 1985), the group difference is remarkable indeed. The whole group of insecurely attached infants reminds us of Cassidy and Berlin's (1994) characterization of the behavioral styles of children classified as ambivalent, in terms of immaturity and incompetent exploration.

More evidence for our wider view of attachment qualities as organizing exploration as well as attachment comes from the Regensburg longitudinal study. Between the ages of 4 and 5 years, the 39 children who attended preschool (i.e., excluding the 2 children with an ambivalent attachment to their mothers) went to 38 different preschools and 39 different classes (Suess, Grossmann, & Sroufe, 1992). Effects of early secure attachment patterns were especially evident in the amount of children's concentrated play. "Concentration" was defined as engrossment in a play theme, low distractibility, and indications of a balanced emotional state. In contrast, lack of concentration was inferred from uninvolved play and detached expressions (e.g., looking bored or daydreaming). The results showed that concentrated play (observed by raters who were unaware of children's attachment status) was more than twice as frequent in children with secure attachments to both parents in infancy than in children with insecure attachments in infancy, with quality of attachment to mother being more influential than quality of attachment to father. Unfortunately, fathers' sensitivity during play with their toddlers was not assessed in this study.

Furthermore, there was a tendency for the avoidant children to be more restless or hyperactive, and to show conflicts about play themes, play roles, and play materials, accompanied by strong signs of anger and frustration and by interruptions in the flow of play (Suess et al., 1992, p. 48). Although quality of attachment to father was not as pervasive in its effects as quality of attachment to mother, an avoidant attachment classification to both parents was strongly related to higher tension during interpersonal contacts and to odd behaviors. Conversely, secure attachment to both parents predicted more autonomous conflict resolutions, in which the children showed independence from the teacher and negotiations with the adversary to the point of agreeing on a solution and remaining friendly toward each other. Children with insecure attachments, in contrast, used more direct ways of reacting to conflicts. They tended to turn to the teacher, withdraw from the site, or displace their conflicts. In addition, they exhibited more often than securely attached children a "hostile attributional bias" (Dodge, Bates, & Pettit, 1990) in response to cartoons depicting children who intentionally or inadvertently damaged objects valued by other children, or who harmed other children directly.

Better peer relations and more competent social and emotional behavior in the peer group were found to be outcomes of early secure attachment in many studies. Sroufe, Egeland, and Carlson (in press) have offered not only a summary and review of relevant studies, but also a convincing developmental view of the process that seems to mediate the tie between parent–child and peer relationships.

Kagan (1996) has complained that an "unencumbered power of early experience" appears to be an attractive hypothesis among many contemporary psychologists. To him, "research on infant attachment represents the most contemporary form of this idea" (p. 901). In fact, however, practically all prominent theories of personality development ascribe an important influence to current environmental circumstances. Nonetheless, one challenging problem concerning the continuity and discontinuity of quality of attachment is "the degree to which an earlier pattern of adaptation may still be present even though it currently is not being expressed, and the continuing influence of early experience beyond that of current circumstances" (Sroufe, Egeland, & Kreutzer, 1990, p. 1363). The other challenge is to specify the conditions under which certain early experiences exert power over particular domains of current adaptations.

In their longitudinal study of the influence of early attachment quality on children's subsequent adaptational organization, Sroufe et al. (1990) demonstrated that absence of stability across a certain age span did not necessarily imply lack of continuity. They concentrated on "broad-band assessments of adaptation keyed to each developmental phase" (p. 1365) by combining measures. In line with our argument, Sroufe et al. (1990) observed how well a particular organization of behavior promoted development at a particular stage. Patterns of attachment to mother were assessed in the strange situation at 12 and 18 months. In this study's high-risk poverty sample, stability of attachment classifications from 12 to 18 months was only 62%, and each infant was scored "according to the number of times he or she was securely attached" (0, 1, or 2) (p. 1367).

All children who as preschoolers showed poor adaptation from 3½ to 4½ years in problem solving, self-management, and curiosity were followed longitudinally into their early school years (Sroufe et al., 1990). One group of children had been judged securely attached in infancy twice and had also shown well-balanced autonomy as toddlers; that is, they had exhibited positive adaptation in terms of attachment and exploration during their first 2 years. Children in the other group, in contrast, had shown poor adaptation during their first 2 years. In elementary school, the children with a good early adaptation were compared to the children with an early poor adaptation, given that both groups were functioning equally poorly at preschool age. At both age periods in elementary school the children with a good early adaptation received significantly higher emotional health/peer competence ratings than children with poor early adaptation, thereby showing "the greatest capacity for rebound, despite comparable (poor) adaptation in the period before school entry" (p. 1368). In general, however, cross-correlations among measures were quite low, and later assessments rather than early assessments contributed significantly more to explaining variance in elementary school competence. Qualities of attachment in infancy were, at the later age, "essentially absorbed by the combination of intermediate measures" (p. 1368).

At 10 years of age, 47 children were observed again in summer camp and rated by four highly trained counselors. The children's behavior showed an impressive stability of adaptational quality. The elementary school composite score correlated significantly with the camp criterion of quality of adaptation. Adding the infant summary attachment evaluation, however, increased the correlation significantly. Continuity depended largely on the quality and flexibility of behavioral organization in social situations involving a large variety of adaptations to structures, rules, plans, challenges, and unforeseen changes. The authors concluded that "both the total developmental history and current circumstances should be given important roles," and, most importantly for the present context, that "behavioral change per se cannot be taken as evidence for the erasure of earlier experience" (Sroufe et al., 1990, p. 1370).

We conclude this account of the stability and functions of attachment security in the preschool years by returning to our wider view of attachment and exploration. A better understanding of later adaptive competence could probably be obtained if the full range of the attachment–exploration balance in infancy as well as in the preschool years were considered. Early attachment security, measured traditionally, is able to predict a number of aspects of future socioemotional and cognitive-motivational developments in children, but not strongly. A child's emotional security to continue exploration in the face of failure or seemingly insurmountable challenges rests on a well-balanced organization of behaviors and emotions in situations of exploratory conflict. The best predictor of this aspect of security, according to our current knowledge, is sensitive and reliable parental support of the child's frequent and varied attempts to organize emotions in the direction of valued goals. A child can become familiar with many curious (i.e., novel and seemingly conflicting) aspects of new people, things, and events, with the help of parental reassurance and guidance. Parental support should be aimed at reducing emotional tension without interrupting concentrated play. At the same time, parents need to remain sensitive to the child's attachment signals, should any be expressed. In terms of Bowlby's construct of internal working models, there will be more adaptive flexibility and sophisticated adaptability to reality if attachment figures' responsiveness proceeds from meeting the child's needs for close proximity to providing developmentally appropriate, nonintrusive support of the child's attempts to organize goal-oriented emotions and behavior particularly during exploratory conflicts.

ASSESSMENT OF, AND INFLUENCES ON, PATTERNS OF ATTACHMENT DURING EARLY SCHOOL AGE

When Bowlby (1973) introduced the concept of internal working models, he emphasized that children's real experiences with attachment figures in the past and real experiences with them currently are both important for personality development all the way into adolescence. Most children are continuously cared for by their parents. The continuing effects of parental care have been suggested by a few studies (Bates, Maslin, & Frankel, 1985; Bohlin & Hagekull, in press; Londerville & Main, 1981). An intervention promoting maternal responsiveness to irritable babies during their first year showed a continuing effect via attachment quality into preschool age. "Apparently, enhancing maternal sensitive responsiveness results in a secure attachment relationship, and this secure bond then mediates the positive effects discerned later in development" (van den Boom, 1995, p. 1813). Another factor thought to promote continuity of attachment relationship quality is the parent's mental representation of attachment (Cohn, Cowan, Cowan, & Pearson, 1992; Grossmann, Fremmer-Bombik, Rudolph, & Grossmann, 1988). A wide variety of findings show that mothers' mental representations of attachment are closely related to their responsiveness during their children's childhood as well as the children's infancy (e.g., Crowell & Treboux, 1996; van IJzendoorn, 1995). Thus maternal attachment representations and behaviors continuously influence the mother–child relationship. Ainsworth commented on the stability of attachment patterns in terms of Bowlby's (1973) notion of different pathways of development: "The fact that the environment into which an infant is born tends to remain essentially the same favors continuation along the pathway of development upon which he first started" (Ainsworth, 1985a, p. 787).

Children's developmental progress makes it difficult to observe the attachment system as easily past toddlerhood as it can be observed in infancy. School children do not behave like infants, and their attachment system is not as easily activated. Indications of the quality of the child–parent attachment relationship change with age, as do attachment and caregiving behaviors (Cicchetti, Cummings, Greenberg, & Marvin, 1990; George & Solomon, 1989). During the preschool years, children develop an understanding of other people's emotions, which may lead to empathy and empathic behavior (Harris, 1994). They can infer and predict another person's plans and motives—a phase of attachment development that Bowlby called the "goal-corrected partnership." But large individual differences have been found in the use children make of that understanding. Securely attached children were observed to use their social skills and knowledge for the benefit of their relationships, by cooperating and competently managing conflict (Suess et al., 1992). Insecurely attached children were found to use their skill to the detriment of their relationships (e.g., by exploiting their peers; Troy & Sroufe, 1987). Thus relationship quality for children beyond preschool age is visible when partners in a relationship are taking into consideration what is on the other's mind—that is, engaging in a goal-corrected partnership. This aspect of a child's behavioral and emotional organization seems to be a good criterion for successful attachment organization in the preschool years. Relationship quality with specific others (e.g., best friends) will show up across the years as an outcome of attachment quality to parents.

Assessing Patterns of Attachment during Early School Age: A Critical Evaluation and Current Validity

Many studies have used a coding system for 5- to 7-year-olds based on 5 minutes of the child's reunion behavior and discourse following a 1-hour laboratory separation. The system was developed by Main and Cassidy (1988) with deliberate reference to the A-B-C system devised by Ainsworth et al. (1978) for 1-year-olds. The classification system for attachment patterns at 6 years involves looking for organizing principles that parallel those in infancy. The rating scales for interactive behaviors evaluate proximity seeking and avoidance, although the behavioral descriptions are sensitive to the fact that the behaviors of school-age children are generally more subtle than those of infants. Their discourse is interpreted as symbolizing interactive behaviors as well as mental exploration. The secure pattern at 6 is characterized by a seemingly casual but comfortable reunion: The child is oriented toward the parent, and the child responds to and elaborates on the parent's conversational leads or takes the initiative himself or herself. Avoidance at 6 is seen in failure to greet the parent or giving only an impersonal response, in the tendency of the child to orient away from the parent, or in the quality of the child's discourse (e.g., giving polite but uninformative answers). Six-year-olds are classified as ambivalent if they emphasize their dependence in response to reunion, if their attachment behaviors are heightened at the expense of their exploratory behaviors, or if they are conflicted or angry about parental leave taking (Cassidy & Berlin, 1994). Like the systems for assessing the attachment patterns of infants and preschoolers, the reunion system for 6-year-olds underemphasizes aspects of a child's security of exploration or organization of emotions and behaviors in situations that challenge his or her adaptation. This fact could make ecological validation of these patterns in the child's day-to-day behavior more difficult.

Current validity of the reunion categories for 6-year-olds was checked against the children's integration into their peer groups and their self-evaluations. Other studies focused on children's mothers' interactive behavior at home, the mothers' caregiving styles, and the mothers' attachment representations. In the south German (Regensburg) longitudinal study (Wartner, Grossmann, Fremmer-Bombik, & Suess, 1994), children were observed one year prior to their reunion assessment in their preschools (Suess et al., 1992; see the earlier discussion). Children classified as insecurely attached at age 6 with the reunion procedure were found to be less concentrated and less competent in their play and in resolving conflicts, and they attributed more hostility to other children in a projective cartoon test. Cohn's (1990) findings were convergent for boys but not for girls in the first grade. She found that boys judged secure in their reunion response received higher ratings from their peers and teachers on a scale of liking, and the teachers reported them to be more competent and to have fewer behavior problems in class than boys categorized as insecure. Cassidy (1988) compared self-evaluations of 6-year-olds to the children's current attachment patterns with their mothers. The majority of secure children described themselves with a balanced thoughtfulness, showing both a clear sense of self-worth and competence and some acknowledgment of imperfection. More insecure than secure children portrayed themselves as either perfect, or as lacking self-worth and competence. Wartner (1987), however, despite using an almost identical approach, did not find the expected correspondence between self-worth and attachment security in her German sample of 6-year-olds.

Solomon, George, and Ivins (1987) studied the quality of mother–child interaction at home with a sample of 6-year-olds and related this to the children's reunion behavior following separation. Mothers of securely attached children exhibited age-appropriate maternal behavior, but mothers of insecurely attached children displayed inappropriate matching of maternal behavior to their children's developmental needs and abilities. Mothers' internal working models of caregiving, however, were only marginally reflected in their actual interactive behavior in the home. The authors stated elsewhere, "We do not feel our observations adequately represented [a] mother's behavior in response to child stress" (George & Solomon, 1989, p. 234), perhaps because relatively little stress occurred at home. Stress, of course, best activates a child's attachment system and should elicit a mother's most relevant caregiving behavior.

In sum, the reunion paradigm for 6-year-olds assesses a significant and valid portion of a child's behavioral organization in the narrow sense—that is, the child's response to parental separation. (See also Solomon & George, Chapter 14, this volume.) However, when viewed critically from our wider perspective, this method again does not assess adaptive functioning or competence resulting from security of exploration on the basis of a goal-corrected partnership. In other words, it falls short on the side of assessing sophisticated flexibility in challenging task situations, which might be conceptualized in terms of a current internal working model of the self as competent and of the other as willing to help.

Behavior, Functioning, and Representation in Early School Age as Related to Early Patterns of Attachment

Two studies provide evidence that patterns of attachment assessed at 1 year in the strange situation and at 6 years in the reunion procedure can be highly stable for child–mother dyads. In a longitudinal study of 32 children, Main and Cassidy (1988) found an 84% concordance between the children's attachment patterns with their mothers in infancy and their reunion categories at age 6. Four classification categories were used for the reunion procedure: secure, avoidant, ambivalent, and controlling. The families were selected in a way that maximized the opportunity for finding stability of attachment patterns; families experiencing any kind of separation, divorce, or major illness were excluded. A longitudinal study in Germany replicated this finding for 40 mother–

child pairs that were unselected, except that the children were healthy at birth. A concordance of 82% was found for the four patterns of attachment. By the time the children were 6 years of age, three sets of parents had separated, but this risk factor was not associated with stability or change in the children's attachment patterns (Wartner et al., 1994).

Studies addressing the developmental sequelae or correlates of early or current attachment patterns have related qualities of mother–child attachment to a wide range of adaptational aspects of young school children's behavior. Boys who were insecurely attached to their mothers at 1 year were more likely to be identified as at risk for behavior problems at 6 years than boys who were securely attached, although the same trend did not hold for girls, and early insecure attachment of boys was predictive of behavior problems only if additional life stresses had occurred (Lewis, Feiring, McGuffog, & Jaskir, 1984). In a Swedish study (Bohlin, 1996), mothers, fathers, and teachers of 8-year-olds were asked to rate the children's prosocial orientation and social withdrawal. Children who had been insecurely attached at 15 months were functioning socially at ages 8–9 less well than children who had been classified as secure in infancy. A follow-up study of children in early day care in Germany (Jacobsen et al., 1992) found that attachment status in infancy predicted attachment status at 6 years, despite relatively high levels of stress in the families.

According to attachment theory, a child uses his or her internal working models to interpret, predict, or simulate challenging situations and their possible outcomes. This tenet of the theory has been addressed by studies that, in various ways, assess narrative representations of children's internal working models. Young children's comments about their own and their parents' behavior in imagined situations have been assessed at 6 years (Main, Kaplan, & Cassidy, 1985) and even at younger ages (Bretherton, Ridgeway, & Cassidy, 1990). Studies evaluating only children's verbal responses to separation stories found significant differences in the children's narratives and styles of answering as a function of children's attachment classifications to their mothers in infancy. The Separation Anxiety Test (SAT; Klagsbrun & Bowlby, 1976) is a preferred method for analyzing the responses of 6-year-olds to stories about mild and severe separations between a child and his or her parent. Methods of evaluating the children's verbal as well as nonverbal responses focus on behavioral and verbal cues of concern, open communication, and appropriate, realistic answers reflecting adaptive coping strategies for dealing with the depicted separations (Bohlin, 1996; K. E. Grossmann & Grossmann, 1991; Krollmann & Krappmann, 1993; Main et al., 1985; Shouldice & Stevenson-Hinde, 1992). Children who had been classified as securely attached in infancy or the preschool years communicated their negative feelings about the severe separation pictures openly, and could think of ways to cope with the imagined separations constructively, including asking for help or support from others. Their discourse style, nonverbal behavior, and attention to the pictures corroborated their verbal comments. In contrast, stereotypic head or shoulder movements, uninvolved responses ("It doesn't matter"), unrealistic coping behavior, or inability to imagine any strategy to deal with the separation situation were found significantly more often in children with early insecure attachments. In the five studies, the appropriate balance of the children's mental attachment status and exploration narratives corresponded well to their observed behaviors in the reunion situations in infancy or toddlerhood.

As with the strange situation and the reunion procedures for 6-year-olds, the various systems for analyzing children's responses to projected or role-played separations focus on a child's overt and expressed or potential response to separation and reunion in relation to the parent. However, ecologically appropriate observational studies involving responses to age-appropriate challenges, with or without the help of parents—studies identifying the salient issues of adaptation for 6-year-olds and their impact on children's personality development—are lacking. Investment in schoolwork, meeting the challenge of formal learning despite difficulties, establishing and keeping friendships despite conflicts, and finding an appropriate balance between autonomy and relatedness with the parents are important for the young school-age child and pave the way for the child's later mental health and social functioning (Rutter & Rutter, 1993). Usually more than one determinant is operating in this wide variety of developmental adaptations. Belsky, Rosenberger, and Crnic (1995) noted on the basis of extensive studies of children and families that in order "to understand how psychological and social contexts influence the development of the child–parent attachment relationship, multiple factors must be considered simultaneously" (p. 177).

In view of the many tasks of childhood (as compared with the developmental tasks of infancy), and in view of the different salience of separation from parents at different ages, it is surprising to find such impressive continuities in studies comparing the reunion patterns of 6-year-olds with their mothers to the children's patterns of attachment in infancy. We interpret this stability in line with the narrow view of attachment, together with some of the possible stabilizing factors, such as continued maternal sensitivity or perhaps mothers' relatively stable attachment representations. Referring to their reunion procedure for 6-year-olds, Main and Cassidy (1988) suggested that an assessment of a child's attachment quality to a particular parent should not rely on a single, short reunion observation; they recommended that other assessments be added, based on the child's representations of the relationship with the parent. They did this very successfully (Main et al., 1985) by assessing, in addition to reunion behavior, the children's fluency in discourse with their mothers, their responses to a family photo, and their response patterns to the SAT. However, within our wider view of attachment, it would be important to add an assessment of a child's security in organizing behaviors and emotions toward goals worth pursuing (Grossmann & Grossmann, 1993). It is most likely that the quality of mental organization reflecting exploratory security will show itself in situations that challenge supportive relationships, as well as the child's ability to adapt to changing circumstances. The open nature of the early mental organization in the preschool years will become evident upon inspection of some of our longitudinal data at 10 and 16 years of age.

Summing up our evaluation of the attachment assessments of preschool-age and young school-age children, we find an overemphasis on the narrow view of attachment. Knowing a child's response to separation from the mother does not tell us anything about the adaptive functioning of that child or the child's ability to overcome adversity. In our view, assessments of attachment quality beyond infancy should include security of mental exploration, which is evaluated predominantly through narratives. As an example, some children in Stevenson-Hinde and Shouldice's 1995 study asked about the meaning of the comings and goings of the stranger and their mothers. But this exploratory curiosity was not part of the classification procedure.

ATTACHMENT IN LATE CHILDHOOD AND ADOLESCENCE: CONTINUITIES AND CHANGES FROM INFANCY

In the preceding sections, we have reviewed the complex evidence for continuing influences of children's early patterns of attachment (as assessed in the strange situation with their mothers) on a number of aspects of adaptation during preschool and early school ages. Longitudinal attachment studies that follow children from infancy to middle childhood and beyond are still rare. We have followed two samples of children from infancy to adolescence. In the north German sample of 47 families, the children were visited repeatedly at home (K. E. Grossmann & Grossmann, 1991). For our south German sample, a series of assessments was devised for the laboratory. In this final major section of the chapter, we will summarize only results from those two studies because, as we follow the children into adolescence (and currently even into young adulthood), a simple continuity hypothesis is severely challenged. We are aware of other longitudinal studies using attachment assessments at different age points between infancy and adulthood in Israel, Minnesota, and Berkeley, but the results of those studies are just now emerging and will be reported on by the authors themselves. (For early examples, see Chapter 19, by Hesse, and Weinfield, Sroufe, Egeland, & Carlson, Chapter 4, this volume.)

Attachment and Relations with Parents and Peers at Age 10

In middle childhood, the social world widens rapidly and dramatically. The major tasks of children at this age are to find a place in the peer group, gain recognition, and establish and maintain friendships. Although children in middle childhood spend less time with their parents than preschool children do, they still see their parents as sources of nurture, emotional support, and instrumental help (Hunter & Youniss, 1982). Of course, attachment in the sense of seeking protection, help, and comfort under conditions of adversity is still a salient issue in middle childhood.

In a cross-sectional study of 9- to 12-year-old children, representations of parents as supportive, available, and trustworthy, assessed concurrently with a questionnaire and a doll-story completion task, were significantly related to the children's adjustment to the school environment. Adjustment was defined in terms of teachers' evaluations of scholastic, emotional, and behavioral adjustment, as well as peer-rated status (Granot & Mayseless, 1996). Another cross-sectional study assessed attachment-related coping styles in children from third to fifth grade (Finnegan, Hodges, & Perry, 1996). Avoidant and preoccupied coping styles were found to be related to children's adjustment in school and to peers' judgments about the children's externalizing and internalizing behavior problems. It seems that current representations of patterns of attachment as organizing feelings, perceptions, and behaviors can be assessed with various self-report measures in middle childhood, whereas assessments of behavioral patterns of attachment to parents in response to separation on the behavioral level become more difficult with increasing age.

In a follow-up of our north German longitudinal study sample, 43 of the original 49 families agreed to another home visit when the children were 10 years old. Scheuerer-Englisch (1989) conducted semistructured, open clinical interviews with the children and their parents, and concurrently observed family interactions during the entire visit. Analyses of the child and parent interviews showed that the children's current working models of their parents as supportive and sensitive were congruent with their parents' independently assessed current models of caregiving (e.g., being willing to support a child vs. ignoring or rejecting a child's needs as unjustified). A child's working model of a parent as supportive was significantly related to his or her tendency to seek parental assistance and comfort when distressed or facing problems. This finding provides empirical evidence for Bowlby's (1973) idea that a working model of supportive parents leads a child to seek parental help with adversities that are difficult to cope with alone.

Contrasting with this fairly straightforward finding concerning the children's and parents' current working models of parental supportiveness and the children's seeking of support, longitudinal analyses of various attachment variables from infancy to age 10 years revealed a mixture of continuities and discontinuities. When asked what they would do when they felt sad, angry, or worried, 10-year-olds classified as securely attached to their mothers in infancy were significantly more likely to state that they would seek help from trusted others, although not necessarily their mothers or fathers. These 10-year-olds

reported that they still enjoyed bodily tenderness more, and they were more open to the interviewer. However, their reported strategies in response to everyday problems (i.e., their coping skills) were not related to early attachment quality. And, unexpectedly, the children's representations of their mothers and/or fathers as supportive and emotionally available did not correspond to their quality of attachment in infancy. These findings suggest that the children's current working model of the parents as supportive was more strongly influenced by current experiences within the parent–child relationship than by early attachment patterns. Their parents confirmed the children's representations by describing their willingness or unwillingness to support their 10-year-old children in distressing situations. Findings from the interview were corroborated by the home visitor's rating of each family's interaction quality during the entire visit. Quality of parent–child interactions corresponded to current relationship quality as expressed in the interviews. However, a second behavioral measure—the classification of sibling interactions as adequate or hostile—was highly related to the focal child's quality of attachment to the mother during infancy (Scheuerer-Englisch, 1989).

The interview data were supplemented by findings from a videotaped family interaction task, adapted from Grotevant and Cooper (1986) and analyzed separately from all other assessments (Freitag, Belsky, Grossmann, Grossmann, & Scheuerer-Englisch, 1996). Transcripts of the parent–child conversations were scored for permeability and mutuality, connectedness, and separateness. A security-of-attachment index was composed of attachment quality in infancy, attachment representation of both parents (and in the case of the mother–child relationship) maternal sensitivity during the first year. For mother–child pairs but not for father–child pairs, this attachment index was significantly related to fewer disagreements during the task transactions and to a relative priority of connectedness over separateness. Quality of attachment to fathers in infancy was not correlated with any of the interview or conversational measures.

Quality of peer relations has been found to be highly predictive of later adjustment (Rutter & Rutter, 1993). Therefore, it is particularly interesting to find cross-culturally converging evidence for influences of attachment experiences on peer relationships. Early and current influences on quality of peer integration were demonstrated by Sroufe et al. (in press). Children with a secure attachment to their mothers in infancy described themselves, 9 years later, and were described by their parents, as better integrated with their school peers. They talked about their best friends in terms of loyalty, mutual support, and preference for each other's company. Similar results were reported by Elicker, Englund, and Sroufe (1992) for 11-year-olds. A composite attachment score based on assessments during the first 2 years of life was related to behavioral differences in 10-year-olds' adaptation to summer camp, even for children who had shown fairly poor adaptation during the preschool years (Sroufe et al., 1990).

Current as well as early parental influences on quality of peer integration were also found in our north German study (Grossmann & Scheuerer-Englisch, 1991). The ratings of quality of peer integration were taken from child as well as parent interviews. A maternal caregiving style of acceptance, and a rating of both parents as not rejecting a child's needs in everyday problem situations as assessed through the parent interviews, were associated with a higher rating of the child on peer integration. Longitudinally, a secure attachment classification to mothers in infancy was also significantly associated with quality of peer integration at 10 years. Moreover, relative priority of connectedness over separateness in the family interaction task at 10 years was related to a higher peer integration rating for the child (Freitag et al., 1996).

Our major findings from studies of 10-year-olds can be summarized as follows:

1. A history of secure attachment to the mother and the parents' current supportiveness both contributed to the quality of parent–child interactions at age 10 and to the child's peer relations.
2. Attachment history was found to be independent of 10-year-olds' current representations of their parents as emotionally available and supportive.
3. A father's sensitivity in play with his toddler predicted the child's representation of the father as emotionally available and supportive at age 10, but only if the child's parents had not separated (Grossmann et al., 1997).
4. The parents' self-reported supportiveness of a child at age 10 was not related to early patterns of attachment, but corresponded well to the child's concurrent report of parental supportiveness.

Continuity within the narrow view of attachment was also found, in that early patterns of attachment to mothers predicted the 10-year-olds' reported behaviors when feeling sad, angry, or worried. Seen from the wider view, the children's overall evaluation of their parents as supportive was at that time reflecting only their more recent experiences, which were probably not limited to attachment experiences alone.

Influences on Attachment Representation at Age 16

In adolescence, the parent–child relationship is described as changing from asymmetrical to more nearly symmetrical (Youniss & Smollar, 1985), although there is increasing evidence that parents are still seen by adolescents as an effective and important source of support (Armsden & Greenberg, 1983; Fend, 1990; Hill, 1993). Attachment organization in adolescence is usually not assessed through observation of attachment behavior, but either through questionnaires or through interviews designed to classify a person's state of mind regarding attachment (Crowell & Treboux, 1995).

Forty-four adolescents from the north German longitudinal study who had been visited at age 10 were seen at home again near their 16th birthdays (Zimmermann, 1994). The Adult Attachment Interview (AAI; George, Kaplan, & Main, 1985) was conducted, and, among other assessments, a coping questionnaire and a second extended personal interview about current relationships with peers and parents were administered. The adolescents' AAIs were scored and classified with the three methods available: The *Q*-sort method described by Kobak (1993), the Regensburg method (Grossmann et al., 1988), and the traditional method (Main & Goldwyn, in press). The three methods show significant concordance (Zimmermann, Becker-Stoll, & Fremmer-Bombik, 1997). An autonomous (i.e., secure) attachment representation was associated once again with reported positive concurrent relationships with parents; and active, socially oriented, nonavoiding coping styles. Autonomous adolescents also received higher scores on ego resiliency (in self-ratings, as well as in a combination of ratings made by a friend, both parents, and the home visitor) and presented a more positive self-concept (Zimmermann & Grossmann, 1997). An autonomous classification on the AAI was also positively related to the quality of close relationships and peer relations (Zimmermann, Scheuerer-Englisch, & Grossmann, 1996).

Longitudinally, an adolescent's attachment representation was significantly related to his or her mother's attachment representation assessed 10 years earlier, and to the number of risk factors experienced during the previous 10 years (Zimmermann, Fremmer-Bombik, Spangler, & Grossmann, 1995). The adolescents' AAI classifications, however, failed to exhibit any concordance with patterns of attachment in infancy to either parent using any of the three methods mentioned on page 779. Interestingly, a father's sensitive challenging behavior during play at age 2 was significantly related to an adolescent's autonomous attachment representation at age 16 (K. Grossmann, 1997). In contrast to our findings, two U.S. studies reported stability in patterns of attachment to mothers from infancy to young adulthood (Hamilton, 1995; Waters, Merrick, Albersheim, & Treboux, 1995). Although these are interesting results, no assessments were made between these two measurement points almost 20 years apart; therefore, little can be learned from these studies either about the nature and function of the process of attachment development, or about the processes and conditions of continuity or change of attachment.

To return to the issue of exploration and adaptation in adolescence, coping styles at age 16 revealed a strong influence of all kinds of experiences with fathers at several ages. Quality of attachment to a father during infancy, a father's sensitivity during play with his toddler, and a father's attachment representation assessed when the child was 8 years old were all related to more active and less avoiding coping styles in adolescence (Zimmermann & Grossmann, 1997). The coping styles of the 16-year-olds were not related to any of the earlier mother–child assessments, however. From the wider attachment perspective, these findings are another indication of the long-lasting influence of secure exploration, facilitated mainly by fathers, on adaptation to challenging situations.

In our south German longitudinal study of 43 families as their children progressed from 1 to 16 years of age, again no correspondence was found between patterns of attachment to mothers in infancy or at age 6 and the children's attachment representations as assessed with the AAI at age 16 (Becker-Stoll & Fremmer-Bombik, 1997). However, in videotaped adolescent–mother interactions, continuity in interactive behavioral styles was found. Adolescents' patterns of attachment in

infancy and at age 6 were significantly positively related to a behavioral style in adolescence that promoted relatedness more and inhibited autonomy less. Thus the effects of early patterns of attachment to mothers were found again in the adolescents' behavior toward their mothers, though not in their representations of attachment as reflected in their AAIs. This differentiation between behavioral responses and mental representations corroborates our differential findings for 10-year-olds.

CONCLUSION

In this chapter, we have addressed three major issues: (1) the desirability of regaining a wider view of attachment; (2) the desirability of including security of exploration in the concept of security of attachment; and (3) the stability of qualities of attachment and their consequences at different ages with respect to our interpretation of the narrow and wider views of attachment.

Attachment research has mainly followed two strategies. One has been to develop measures for children beyond infancy that assess the children's patterns of attachment behaviors, or narratives thereof, in response to separation from parents. Older children are asked in such measures for their response to feeling sad or angry, or to being worried. Such measures reflect Bowlby's idea that the crucial variable in attachment is preventing mental breakdown under conditions of adversity (Bowlby, 1991, p. 296); this is the core of the narrow view of attachment. Most studies using this strategy have demonstrated convincing and sometimes strong developmental stability in the patterns of attachment from infancy to different points in the lifespan. Our north German longitudinal study provides a differentiated view of stability: Individual differences at 10 years in response to the question what one would do when sad, angry, or worried were significantly related to patterns of attachment in infancy. Individual differences in the 10-year-olds' representation of their mothers or fathers as emotionally available, however, were related only to the mother's or father's current self-report of being supportive toward their children.

The second major strategy of attachment research has been to look for evidence of attachment-related individual differences in the quality of subsequent social relations—a strategy followed successfully by Sroufe and his coworkers (see Weinfield, Ogawa, & Sroufe, 1997, and

Weinfield et al., Chapter 4, this volume). In our review of selected attachment research spanning the years from early childhood into adolescence, we have been able to demonstrate predictive validity of patterns of attachment in infancy in relation to certain adaptational qualities in childhood, and the strength of some of the predicted findings has been impressive. Stronger continuity may perhaps be hoped for by those who judge the value of attachment research in terms of its predictive power from infancy.

That hope creates a paradox, however, because it would necessarily require a strong determinism, which would be (at least on the surface) detrimental to the changing demands of current adaptations and to the benefits of supportive current relationships. If, on the other hand, no continuities in adaptational qualities were found, then early attachment experiences would be practically irrelevant for later psychological challenges. Attachment theory assumes both continuity of adaptive qualities and opportunities for change, but the likelihood of change is believed to diminish with age (Ainsworth, 1990). Nonetheless, the theory was originally formulated with the goal of understanding change and thereby improving therapeutic interventions, which are viewed as correcting deviant developmental pathways (Bowlby, 1988a). Attachment theory, like psychoanalytic theory more generally, does place special importance on infancy, but the emphasis is not exclusive or decisive. According to Bowlby (1973), "The period during which attachment behavior is readily activated, namely from six months to about five years, is also the most sensitive in regard to the development of expectations of the availability of attachment figures" (p. 202)—and, we might add, their willingness and ability to serve as supporters of exploration. Nevertheless, "sensitivity in this regard persists during the decade after the fifth birthday albeit in a steadily diminishing degree as the years of childhood pass" (Bowlby, 1973, p. 203). As for the predictive validity of the strange situation, Bowlby (1969/1982) cautioned that "too much of prognostic significance must not be read into the statement that at the first birthday a couple is likely to have established a characteristic pattern of action. All that it means is that for most couples a pattern that is likely to persist is by that time present" (p. 343).

We propose including the concept of security of exploration in the concept of security of attachment, because we see adaptation by means of exploration as the biological function of attachment. Attachment development builds on the propensity of infants to attach themselves to their caretakers, usually their parents, and on the propensity of parents to invest in the physical and psychological security of their infants. An infant's attachment system, together with a parent's caregiving system, provides the most important platform for the child's psychological freedom to be curious and explore the world.

In general, secure children show more concentrated exploration of novel stimuli and more focused attention during tasks. Secure attachment provides the best-known psychological precondition for tension-free, playful exploration. Thus, when their adaptation is challenged, secure children can flexibly explore possible solutions or perspectives while retaining a secure feeling during exploration, and if their competence is depleted, they can rely on and summon social resources. We have called this a "wider view of attachment," in which the freedom to explore in the face of adversity and the freedom to call for and accept help are both necessary and important aspects of security.

A developmental model is still lacking that can explain how early preverbal attachment and exploration experiences are integrated and extended by cognitive and linguistic representations. What, besides general cognitive advances, influences the shift from goal-directed behavior to goal-corrected partnerships in acting and thinking? We think that the role of talking about the child's emotionally relevant experiences plays an important if not an essential role (K. E. Grossmann, 1997; K. E. Grossmann & Grossmann, 1998; Nelson, 1996). Bowlby (1988), in a chapter entitled "On Knowing What You Are Not Supposed to Know and Feeling What You Are Not Supposed to Feel," emphasized the narrative silence in some families concerning children's adverse experiences with their parents. In a recent series of studies on security of attachment and the development of social cognition, Meins (1997) looked at a mother's speech to an infant as a predictor of infant attachment security. In talking to the infant or about the infant, if the mother used language indicating that she could see things from the baby's perspective (which is part of Ainsworth's definition of sensitivity and cooperation), the "mind-mindedness" of her discourse strongly predicted security of infant attachment in the strange situation.

The organization of attachment to parental figures in infancy is only the very beginning of an individual life story. Its transformation into secure exploration, narrative representation, and social cognition paves the way for development toward a more or less adjusted adulthood. Just as children deprived of secure attachment are likely to develop into emotionally fragile adults despite support during exploration, children deprived of security of exploration may develop into psychologically restricted adults despite ample emotional closeness and warmth. In view of currently available research results, continuity can be expected to occur in the narrow sense when experiences with attachment figures remain stable. The outcome of attachment experiences within the wider view of attachment will depend on the quality of emotional and organizing support in attachment and exploration. Future research must address stability as well as change of response patterns under conditions of adversity in both directions: (1) seeking comfort in the service of psychological security, and (2) seeking help from others in the service of adaptive new internal working models if that is demanded by reality.

REFERENCES

Ainsworth, M. D. S. (1970). Attachment, exploration, and separation: Illustrated by the behavior of one-year-olds in a strange situation. *Child Development, 41,* 49–67.

Ainsworth, M. D. S. (1985a). Patterns of infant–mother attachment: Antecedents and effects on development. *Bulletin of the New York Academy of Medicine, 61,* 771–791.

Ainsworth, M. D. S. (1985b). Attachment across the life span. *Bulletin of the New York Academy of Medicine, 61,* 792–812.

Ainsworth, M. D. S. (1990). Some considerations regarding theory and assessment relevant to attachment beyond infancy. In M. T. Greenberg, D. Cicchetti, & E. M. Cummings (Eds.), *Attachment in the preschool years: Theory, research, and intervention* (pp. 463–488). Chicago: University of Chicago Press.

Ainsworth, M. D. S., Bell, S. M., & Stayton, D. J. (1971). Individual differences in strange situation behavior of one-year olds. In H. R. Schaffer (Ed.), *The origins of human relations* (pp. 17–57). London: Academic Press.

Ainsworth, M. D. S., Bell, S. M., & Stayton, D. J. (1974). Infant–mother attachment and social development: "Socialization" as a product of reciprocal responsiveness to signals. In P. M. Richards (Ed.), *The integration of a child into a social world* (pp. 99–135). Cambridge, UK: Cambridge University Press.

Ainsworth, M. D. S., Blehar, M. C., Waters, E., & Wall, S. (1978). *Patterns of attachment: A psychological study of the strange situation.* Hillsdale, NJ: Erlbaum.

Ainsworth, M. D. S., & Wittig, B. A. (1969). Attachment and the exploratory behavior of one-year-olds in a strange situation. In B. M. Foss (Ed.), *Determinants of infant behavior* (Vol. 4, pp. 113–136). London: Methuen.

Armsden, G. C., & Greenberg, M.T. (1987). The inventory of parent and peer attachment: Individual differences and their relationships to psychological well-being in adolescence. *Journal of Youth and Adolescence, 16,* 427–454.

Bates, J. E., Maslin, C. A., & Frankel, K. A. (1985). Attachment security, mother–child interaction, and temperament as predictors of behavior-problem ratings at age three years. In I. Bretherton & E. Waters (Eds.), Growing points of attachment theory and research. *Monographs of the Society for Research in Child Development, 50*(1–2), Serial No. 209, 167–193.

Bayley, N. (1969). *Bayley scales of infant development.* New York: Psychological Corporation.

Becker-Stoll, F., & Fremmer-Bombik, E. (1997). *Adolescent–mother interaction and attachment: A longitudinal study.* Poster presented at the biennial meeting of Society for Research in Child Development, Washington, DC.

Belsky, J., Campbell, S. B., Cohn, J. F., & Moore, G. (1996). Instability of infant–parent attachment security. *Developmental Psychology, 32,* 921–924.

Belsky, J., & Cassidy, J. (1994). Attachment: Theory and evidence. In M. Rutter, D. Hay, & S. Baron-Cohen (Eds.), *Developmental principles and clinical issues in psychology and psychiatry* (pp. 373–402). Oxford: Blackwell.

Belsky, J., Garduque, l., & Hrncir, E. (1984). Assessing performance, competence, and executive capacity in infant play: Relations to home environment and security of attachment. *Developmental Psychology, 20,* 406–417.

Belsky, J., Rosenberger, K., & Crnic, K. (1995). The origins of attachment security: "Classical" and contextual determinants. In S. Goldberg, R. Muir, & J. Kerr (Eds.), *Attachment theory: Social, developmental, and clinical perspectives* (pp. 153–183). Hillsdale, NJ: Analytic Press.

Berlyne, D. E. (1960). *Conflict, arousal, and curiosity.* New York: McGraw-Hill.

Bohlin, G. (1996). *Attachment, separation anxiety, and social competence in Swedish children.* Poster presented at the meeting of the International Society for the Study of Behavioral Development, Québec City, Québec, Canada.

Bohlin, G., & Hagekull, B. (in press). Behavior problems in Swedish 4–year-olds: The importance of maternal sensitivity and social context. In P. M. Crittenden (Ed.), *The organization of attachment relationships: Maturation, culture, and context.* Cambridge, England: Cambridge University Press.

Bowlby, J. (1969/1982). *Attachment and loss: Vol. 1. Attachment* (2nd ed.). New York: Basic Books.

Bowlby, J. (1973). *Attachment and loss: Vol. 2. Separation: Anxiety and anger.* New York: Basic Books.

Bowlby, J. (1979). *The making and breaking of affectional bonds.* London: Tavistock.

Bowlby, J. (1980). *Attachment and loss: Vol. 3. Loss: Sadness and depression.* New York: Basic Books.

Bowlby, J. (1988a). Developmental psychiatry comes of age. *American Journal of Psychiatry, 145,* 1–10.

Bowlby, J. (1988b). *A secure base: Clinical applications of attachment theory.* London: Tavistock/Routledge.

Bowlby, J. (1991). Postscript. In C. M. Parkes, J. Stevenson-Hinde, & P. Marris (Eds.), *Attachment across the life cycle* (pp. 293–297). London: Tavistock/Routledge.

Bretherton, I. (1985). Attachment theory: Retrospect and prospect. In I. Bretherton & E. Waters (Eds.), Growing points of attachment theory and research. *Monographs of the Society for Research in Child Development, 50*(1–2), Serial No. 209), 3–35.

Bretherton, I., Biringen, Z., Ridgeway, D., Maslin, M., & Sherman, M. (1989). Attachment: The parental perspective. *Infant Mental Health Journal, 10,* 202–220.

Bretherton, I., Golby, B., & Halvorsen, C. (1993). *Fathers as attachment and caregiving figures.* Paper presented at the biennial meeting of the Society for Research in Child Development, New Orleans, LA.

Bretherton, I., Ridgeway, D., & Cassidy, J. (1990). The role of internal working models in attachment relationships: Can it be assessed in 3–year-olds? In M. T. Greenberg, D. Cicchetti, & E. M. Cummings (Eds.), *Attachment during the preschool years: Theory, research, and intervention* (pp. 273–308). Chicago: University of Chicago Press.

Bronson, G. W. (1972). Infants' reactions to unfamiliar persons and novel objects. *Monographs of the Society for Research in Child Development, 37* (Serial No. 148).

Bus, A. G., & van IJzendoorn, M. H. (1988). Mother–child interaction, attachment, and emergent literacy: A cross-sectional study. *Child Development, 59,* 1262–1272.

Carew, J. (1977). Die Vorhersage der Intelligenz auf der Grundlage kindlicher Alltagserfahrungen [Prediction of intelligence on the basis of children's everyday experiences]. In K. E. Grossmann (Ed.), *Entwicklung der Lernfähigkeit in der sozialen Umwelt [Development of learning ability in the social environment]* (pp. 108–144). München: Kindler Verlag.

Carew, J. (1980). Experience and the development of intelligence in children at home and in day care. *Monographs of the Society for Research in Child Development, 45*(6–9, Serial No. 187).

Cassidy, J. (1988). Child–mother attachment and the self in six-year-olds. *Child Development, 59,* 121–134.

Cassidy, J., & Berlin, L. J. (1994). The insecure/ambivalent pattern of attachment: Theory and research. *Child Development, 65,* 971–991.

Cassidy, J., Marvin, R., & the MacArthur Working Group on Attachment. (1990). *Attachment organization in three- and four-year-olds: Coding guidelines.* Unpublished manuscript, Pennsylvania State University.

Cicchetti, D., Cummings, E. M., Greenberg, M. T., & Marvin, R. S. (1990). An organizational perspective on attachment beyond infancy. In M. T. Greenberg, D. Cicchetti, & E. M. Cummings (Eds.), *Attachment in the preschool years: Theory, research, and intervention* (pp. 3–49). Chicago: University of Chicago Press.

Cohn, D. A. (1990). Child–mother attachment of six-year-olds and social competence in school. *Child Development, 61,* 152–162.

Cohn, D. A., Cowan, P. A., Cowan, C. P., & Pearson, J. (1992). Mothers' and fathers' working models of childhood attachment relationships, parenting styles, and child behavior. *Development and Psychopathology, 4,* 417–431.

Connell, D. B. (1976). *Individual differences in attachment behavior: Long-term stability and relationships to language development.* Unpublished doctoral dissertation, Syracuse University.

Crowell, J. A., & Treboux, D. (1995). A review of adult attachment measures: Implications for theory and research. *Social Development, 4,* 294–327.

Dodge, K. A., Bates, J. E., & Pettit, G. S. (1990). Mechanisms in the cycle of violence. *Science, 250,* 1678–1683.

Dunn, J. (1993). *Young children's close relationships: Beyond attachment.* Newbury Park, CA: Sage.

Easterbrooks, M. A., & Goldberg, W. A. (1984). Toddler development in the family: Impact of father involvement and parenting characteristics. *Child Development, 55,* 740–752.

Egeland, B., & Farber, E. (1984). Infant–mother attachment: Factors related to its development and changes over time. *Child Development, 55,* 753–771.

Elicker, J., Englund, M., & Sroufe, L. A. (1992). Predicting peer competence and peer relationships in childhood from early parent–child relationships. In R. Parke & G. Ladd (Eds.), *Family–peer relationships: Modes of linkage* (pp. 71–106). Hillsdale, NJ: Erlbaum.

Fend, H. (1990). Ego-strength development and pattern of social relationships. In H. Bosma & S. Jackson (Eds.), *Coping and self-concept in adolescence* (pp. 92–111). Berlin: Springer.

Finnegan, R. A., Hodges, E. V. E., & Perry, D. C. (1996). Preoccupied and avoidant coping during middle childhood. *Child Development, 67,* 1318–1328.

Freitag, M. K., Belsky, J., Grossmann, K., Grossmann, K. E., & Scheuerer-Englisch, H. (1996). Continuity in parent–child relationships from infancy to middle childhood and relations with friendship competence. *Child Development, 67,* 1437–1454.

George, C., Kaplan, N., & Main, M. (1985). *Adult attachment interview.* Unpublished manuscript, University of California at Berkeley.

George, C., & Solomon, J. (1989). Internal working models of caregiving and security of attachment at age six. *Infant Mental Health Journal, 10,* 222–237.

Granot, D., & Mayseless, O. (1996). *The relation between attachment patterns and adaptive functioning in the school environment amongst children in middle childhood.* Poster presented at the meeting of the International Society for Research in *Child Development,* Québec City, Québec, Canada.

Grossmann, K. (1984). *Zweijährige Kinder im Zusammenspiel mit ihren Müttern, Vätern, einer fremden Erwachsenen und in einer Ueberraschungssituation: Beobachtungen aus bindungs- und kompetenztheoretischer Sicht [Two-year-olds in interaction with their mothers, fathers, a stranger and in a surprise situation: Observations from an attachment and a competence point of view].* Unpublished doctoral dissertation, University of Regensburg, Regensburg, Germany.

Grossmann, K. (1997). *Infant–father attachment relationship: Sensitive challenges during play with toddler is the pivotal feature.* Poster presented at the biennial meeting of the Society for Research in Child Development, Washington, DC.

Grossmann, K., Fremmer-Bombik, E., Rudolph, J., & Grossmann, K. E. (1988). Maternal attachment representations as related to patterns of infant–mother attachment and maternal care during the first year. In R. A. Hinde & J. Stevenson-Hinde (Eds.), *Relationships within families* (pp. 241–260). Oxford: Clarendon Press.

Grossmann, K., & Grossmann, K. E. (1991). Newborn behavior, early parenting quality and later toddler–parent relationships in a group of German infants. In J. K. Nugent, B. M. Lester & T. B. Brazelton (Eds.), *The cultural context of infancy* (Vol. II, pp. 3–38). Norwood, NJ: Ablex.

Grossmann, K., & Grossmann, K. E. (in press). Parents and toddlers at play: Evidence for separate qualitative functioning of the play and the attachment system. In P. M. Crittenden (Ed.), *The organization of attachment relationships: Maturation, culture, and context.* Cambridge, England: Cambridge University Press.

Grossmann, K., Grossmann, K. E., Fremmer-Bombik, E., Kindler, H., Scheuerer-Englisch, H., & Zimmermann, P. (1998). *Child–father attachment relationship: Longitudinal impact of sensitive challenging behavior during play with the toddler versus patterns of infant–father attachment in the strange situation.* Manuscript in preparation.

Grossmann, K., Grossmann, K. E., Spangler, G., Suess, G., &

Unzner, L. (1985). Maternal sensitivity and newborns' orientation responses as related to quality of attachment in northern Germany. In I. Bretherton & E. Waters (Eds.), Growing points in attachment theory and research. *Monographs of the Society for Research in Child Development, 50*(1–2, Serial No. 209), 233–256.

Grossmann, K. E. (1997). Bindungserinnerungen und adaptive Perspektiven [Memories of attachment and adaptive perspectives]. In G. Lüer & U. Lass (Eds.), *Erinnern und Behalten. Wege zur Erforschung des menschlichen Gedächtnisses [Memory and recollection: Ways to study human memory]* (pp. 321–337). Göttingen, Germany: Vandenhoeck & Ruprecht.

Grossmann, K. E. & Grossmann, K. (1990). The wider concept of attachment in cross-cultural research. *Human Development, 33,* 31–47.

Grossmann, K. E., & Grossmann, K. (1991). Attachment quality as an organizer of emotional and behavioral responses in a longitudinal perspective. In C. M. Parkes, J. Stevenson-Hinde, & P. Marris (Eds.), *Attachment across the life cycle* (pp. 93–114). London: Tavistock/Routledge.

Grossmann, K. E., & Grossmann, K. (1993). Emotional organization and concentration on reality in a life course perspective. *International Journal of Educational Research, 17,* 541–554.

Grossmann, K. E., & Grossmann, K. (1998). Développement de l'attachement et adaptation psychologique du berceau au tombeau [The development of attachment and psychological adaptation from the cradle to the grave]. *Enfance, 3,* 44–68.

Grossmann, K. E., Grossmann, K., & Schwan, A. (1986). Capturing the wider view of attachment: A reanalysis of Ainsworth's strange situation. In C. E. Izard & P. B. Read (Eds.), *Measuring emotions in infants and children* (Vol. 2, pp. 124–171). New York: Cambridge University Press.

Grossmann, K. E., & Scheuerer-Englisch, H. (1991). *Perceived parental support, emotional responsivity, peer relations and interview behavior in 10–year-olds as related to attachment history.* Paper presented at the meeting of the International Society for the Study of Behavioral Development, Minneapolis, MN.

Grossmann, K. E., Scheuerer-Englisch, H., & Loher, I. (1991). Die Entwicklung emotionaler Organisation und ihre Beziehung zum intelligenten Handeln [The development of emotional organization and its relationship to intelligent behavior]. In F. J. Mönks & G. Lehwald (Eds.), *Neugier, Erkundung und Begabung bei Kleinkindern [Curiosity, exploration, and talent in young children]* (pp. 66–76). München: Ernst Reinhardt Verlag.

Grotevant, H., & Cooper, C.R. (1986). Individuation in family relationships. *Human Development, 29,* 82–100.

Hamilton, C. E. (1995). *Continuity and discontinuity of attachment from infancy through adolescence.* Paper presented at the biennial meeting of the Society for Research in Child Development, Indianapolis, IN.

Harris, P. L. (1994). The child's understanding of emotion: Developmental change and the family environment. *Journal of Child Psychology and Psychiatry, 35,* 3–28.

Hill, P. (1993). Recent advances of selected aspects of adolescent development. *Journal of Child Psychology and Psychiatry, 34,* 69–99.

Hunter, F. T., & Youniss, J. (1982). Changes in functions of three relations during adolescence. *Developmental Psychology, 18,* 806–811.

Jacobsen, T., Ziegenhain, U., Müller, B., Rottmann, U., Hofmann, V., & Edelstein, W. (1992). *Predicting stability of mother–child attachment patterns in day-care children from infancy to age six.* Poster presented at the 5th World Congress of the World Association of Infant Psychiatry and Allied Disciplines, Chicago.

Kagan, J. (1996). Three pleasing ideas. *American Psychologist, 51,* 901–908.

Klagsbrun, M., & Bowlby, J. (1976). Responses to separation from parents: A clinical test for young children. *British Journal of Projective Psychology, 21,* 7–21.

Kobak, R. R. (1993). *The Attachment Q-Sort.* Unpublished manuscript, University of Delaware.

Krollmann, M., & Krappmann, L. (1993). *Bindung und Gleichaltrigenbeziehungen in der mittleren Kindheit [Attachment and peer relationships in middle childhood].* Poster presented at the 11th Meeting of the German Psychological Society, Osnabrück, Germany.

LeVine, R. A., Dixon, S., Le Vine, S., Richman, A., Leiderman, P. H., Keefer, C. H., & Brazelton, T. B. (1994). *Child care and culture: Lessons from Africa.* Cambridge, England: Cambridge University Press.

Lewis, M., Feiring, C., McGuffog, C., & Jaskir, J. (1984). Predicting psychopathology in six-year-olds from early social relations. *Child Development, 55,* 123–136.

Lieberman, A. F. (1992). Infant–parent psychotherapy with toddlers. *Development and Psychopathology, 4,* 559–574.

Loher, I. (1988). *Intellektuelle und soziale Erfahrungen im vierten Lebensjahr und ihre Beziehung zur Kompetenz im Alltag und in einer Belastungssituation [Intellectual and social experience in 4-year-old children and its relationship to everyday competence and in a challenging situation].* Unpublished doctoral dissertation, University of Regensburg, Regensburg, Germany.

Londerville, S., & Main, M. (1981). Security of attachment, compliance and maternal training methods in the second year of life. *Developmental Psychology, 17,* 289–299.

Lütkenhaus, P. (1983). *Forschungsbericht: Reaktionen von 3-Jährigen auf ihre Handlungsresultate und deren Bedeutung für ihre Handlungsregulation [Research report: Reactions of 3-year-olds to their action results and its implications for action regulation].* Unpublished manuscript, University of Regensburg, Regensburg, Germany.

Lütkenhaus, P. (1988). *Maternal teaching behavior and emotional support: Different relations to the attachment system and different effects on preschoolers' persistence and sense of competence.* Paper presented at the 3rd European Conference on Developmental Psychology, Budapest, Hungary.

Lütkenhaus, P., Grossmann, K. E., & Grossmann, K. (1985a). Transactional influence of infants' orienting ability and maternal cooperation on competition in three-year-old children. *International Journal of Behavioral Development, 8,* 257–272.

Lütkenhaus, P., Grossmann, K. E., & Grossmann, K. (1985b). Infant–mother attachment at twelve months and style of interaction with a stranger at the age of three years. *Child Development, 56,* 1538–1542.

Lyons-Ruth, K., Repacholi, B., McLeod, S., & Silva, E. (1991). Disorganized attachment behavior in infancy: Short-term stability, maternal and infant correlates, and risk-related subtypes. *Development and Psychopathology, 3,* 377–396.

Magai, C., & Mc Fadden, S. (1995). *The role of emotions in social and personality development: History, theory and research.* New York: Plenum Press.

Main, M. (1973). *Play, exploration, and competence as related to child-adult attachment.* Unpublished doctoral dissertation, Johns Hopkins University.

Main, M. (1983). Exploration, play, and cognitive functioning related to infant–mother attachment. *Infant Behavior and Development, 6,* 167–174.

Main, M., & Cassidy, J. (1988). Categories of response to reunion with the parent at age six: Predictable from infant attachment classification and stable over a one-month period. *Developmental Psychology, 24,* 415–426.

Main, M., & Goldwyn, R. (in press). In M. Main (Ed.), *Systems for assessing attachment organization through discourse, behavior, and drawings.* Cambridge, England: Cambridge University Press.

Main, M., Kaplan, N., & Cassidy, J. (1985). Security in infancy, childhood, and adulthood: A move to the level of representation. In I. Bretherton & E. Waters (Eds.), Growing points in attachment theory and research. *Monographs of the Society for Research in Child Development, 50*(1–2, Serial No. 209), 66–104.

Main, M., & Weston, D. R. (1981). The quality of the toddler's relationship to mother and to father: Related to conflict behavior and the readiness to establish new relationships. *Child Development, 52,* 932–940.

Mangelsdorf, S. C., Plunkett, J. W., Dedrick, C. F., McHale, J. L., & Dichtelmiller, M. (1996). Attachment security in very low birthweight infants. *Developmental Psychology, 32,* 914–920.

Matas, L., Arend, R., & Sroufe, L. A. (1978). Continuity of adaptation in the second year: The relationship between quality of attachment and later competence. *Child Development, 49,* 547–556.

McCarthy, M. (1972). *McCarthy scales of children's abilities.* New York: Psychological Corporation.

Meins, E. (1997). *Security of attachment and social development of cognition.* Hove, England: Psychology Press.

Nelson, K. (1996). *Language in cognitive development.* Cambridge, England: Cambridge University Press.

National Institute of Child Health and Human Development (NICHD) Early Child Care Research Network. (1997). The effects of infant child care on infant–mother attachment security: Results of the NICHD study of early childcare. *Child Development, 68,* 860–879.

Parke, R. D., & Tinsley, B. J. (1987). Family interaction in infancy. In J. D. Osofsky (Ed.), *Handbook of infant development* (2nd ed., pp. 579–641). New York: Wiley.

Pederson, D. R., & Moran, G. (1996). Expressions of the attachment relationship outside of the strange situation. *Child Development, 67,* 915–927.

Pianta, R. C., & Harbers, K. L. (1996). Observing mother and child behavior in a problem-solving situation at school entry: Relations with academic achievement. *Journal of School Psychology, 34,* 307–322.

Rauh, H., Ziegenhain, U., Müller, B., & Wijnroks, L. (in press). Stability and change in infant–mother attachment in the second year of life: Relations to parenting quality and varying degrees of daycare experience. In P. M. Crittenden (Ed.), *The organization of attachment relationships: Maturation, culture, and context.* Cambridge, England: Cambridge University Press.

Rutter, M., & Rutter, M. (1993). *Developing minds.* New York: Basic Books.

Schaffer, R., & Emerson, P. E. (1964). The development of social attachments in infancy. *Monographs of the Society for Research in Child Development, 29*(3, Serial No. 94).

Scheuerer-Englisch, H. (1989). *Das Bild der Vertrauensbeziehung bei zehnjährigen Kindern und ihren Eltern: Bindungsbeziehungen in längsschnittlicher und aktueller Sicht [Representations of trust-relationships in ten-year-olds and their parents: Attachment relationships in longi-*

tudinal and present perspectives]. Unpublished doctoral dissertation, University of Regensburg, Regensburg, Germany.

Schieche, M. (1995, September). *Psychobiologie und Verhaltensorganisation bei Zweijährigen: Kindliche Verhaltensstrategien, Bindungssicherheit und adrenocorticale bzw. immunologische Regulation in Anforderungssituationen [Psychology and behavioral organization in 2-year-olds: Toddler's behavioral strategies, attachment security, and adrenocortical and/or immunological regulation in challenging situations].* Paper presented at the 12th Meeting of the German Developmental Psychology Section, Leipzig, Germany.

Schieche, M. (1996). *Exploration und physiologische Reaktionen bei zweijährigen Kindern mit unterschiedlichen Bindungserfahrungen [Exploration and physiological reactions of two-year-olds with different attachment histories].* Unpublished Doctoral Dissertation, University of Regensburg, Regensburg, Germany.

Schildbach, B. (1992). *Die Bedeutung emotionaler Unterstützung bei der Bewältigung von intellektuellen Aufgaben [The meaning og emotional support in coping with intellectual tasks].* Unpublished doctoral dissertation, University of Regensburg, Regensburg, Germany.

Schildbach, B., Loher, I., & Riedinger, N. (1995). Die Bedeutung emotionaler Uterstützung bei der Bewältigung von intellektuellen Anforderungen [The meaning of emotional support in coping with intellectual challenges]. In G. Spangler & P. Zimmermann (Eds.), *Die Bindungstheorie. Grundlagen, Forschung und Anwendung [Attachment theory: Foundations, research, and application* (pp. 249–264). Stuttgart: Klett-Cotta.

Schneider-Rosen, K., Braunwald, K. G., Carlson, V., & Cicchetti, D. (1985). Current perspectives in attachment theory: Illustration from the study of maltreated infants. In I. Bretherton & E. Waters (Eds.), Growing points in attachment theory and research. *Monographs of the Society for Research in Child Development, 50*(1–2, Serial No. 209), 194–210.

Shouldice, A., & Stevenson-Hinde, J. (1992). Coping with security distress: The Separation Anxiety Test and attachment classification at 4.5 years. *Journal of Child Psychology and Psychiatry, 33,* 164–171.

Solomon, J., George, C., & Ivins, B. (1987). *Mother–child interaction at home and security of attachment at age six.* Paper presented at the biennial meeting of the Society for Research in Child Development, Baltimore.

Spangler, G., & Grossmann, K. E. (1993). Biobehavioral organization in securely and insecurely attached infants. *Child Development, 64,* 1439–1450.

Sroufe, L. A., Cooper, R. G., DeHart, G. B., & Marshall, M. E. (1996). *Child development: Its nature and course* (3rd ed.). New York: McGraw-Hill.

Sroufe, L. A., Egeland, B., & Carlson, E. A. (Eds.). (1998). One social world: The integrated development of parent–child and peer-relationships. In *Relationships as developmental context: The 29th Minnesota Symposium on Child Psychology.* Hillsdale, NJ: Erlbaum.

Sroufe, L. A., Egeland, B., & Kreutzer, T. (1990). The fate of early experience following developmental change: Longitudinal approaches to individual adaptation in childhood. *Child Development, 61,* 1363–1373.

Sroufe, L. A., & Fleeson, J. (1988). The coherence of family relationships. In R. Hinde & J. Stevenson-Hinde (Eds.), *Relationships within families* (pp. 27–47). Oxford: Clarendon Press.

Stevenson-Hinde, J., & Shouldice, A. (1990). Fear and attachment in 2.5-year-olds. *British Journal of Developmental Psychology, 8,* 319–333.

Stevenson-Hinde, J., & Shouldice, A. (1995). Maternal interactions and self-reports related to attachment classifications at 4.5 years. *Child Development, 66,* 583–596.

Suess, G., Grossmann, K. E., & Sroufe, L. A. (1992). Effects of infant attachment to mother and father on quality of adaptation in preschool: From dyadic to individual organization of self. *International Journal of Behavioral Development, 15,* 43–65.

Teti, D. M., & McGourty, S. (1996). Using mothers versus trained observers in assessing children's secure base behavior: Theoretical and methodological considerations. *Child Development, 67,* 597–605.

Thompson, R. A., Lamb, M. E., & Estes, D. (!982). Stability of infant–mother attachment and its relationship to changing life circumstances in an unselected middle-class sample. *Child Development, 50,* 971–975.

Troy, M., & Sroufe, L. A. (1987). Victimization among preschoolers: The role of attachment relationship history. *Journal of the American Academy of Child Psychiatry, 26,* 166–172.

Turner, P. J. (1991). Relations between attachment, gender, and behavior with peers in preschool. *Child Development, 62,* 1457–1488.

Turner, P. J. (1993). Attachment to mother and behavior with adults in preschool. *British Journal of Developmental Psychology, 11,* 75–89.

van den Boom, D. C. (1994). The influence of temperament and mothering on attachment and exploration: An experimental manipulation of sensitive responsiveness among lower-class mothers with irritable infants. *Child Development, 65,* 1457–1477.

van den Boom, D. C. (1995). Do first-year intervention effects endure?: Follow-up during toddlerhood of a sample of Dutch irritable infants. *Child Development, 66,* 1798–1816.

van IJzendoorn, M. H. (1995). Adult attachment representations, parental responsiveness, and infant attachment: A meta-analysis on the predictive value of the Adult Attachment Interview. *Psychological Bulletin, 117,* 387–403.

Vaughn, B., Egeland, B., Sroufe, L. A., & Waters, E. (1979). Individual differences in infant–mother attachment at twelve and eighteen months: Stability and change in families under stress. *Child Development, 50,* 971–975.

Vaughn, B. E., & Waters, E. (1990). Attachment behavior at home and in the laboratory: Q-sort observations and strange situation classifications of one-year-olds. *Child Development, 61,* 1865–1873.

Volling, B. L., & Belsky, J. (1992). Infant, father, and marital antecedents of infant–father attachment security in dual-earner and single-earner families. *International Journal of Behavioral Development, 15,* 83–100.

Wartner, U. (1987). *Attachment in infancy and at age six, and children's self-concept: A follow-up of a German longitudinal study.* Unpublished doctoral dissertation, University of Virginia.

Wartner, U., Grossmann, K., Fremmer-Bombik, E., & Suess, G. (1994). Attachment patterns at age six in south Germany: Predictability from infancy and implications for preschool behavior. *Child Development, 65,* 1014–1027.

Waters, E., & Deane, K. E. (1985). Defining and assessing individual differences in attachment relationships: Q-methodology and the organization of behavior in infancy and early childhood. In I. Bretherton & E. Waters (Eds.), Growing points of attachment theory and research *Monographs of the Society for Research in Child Development, 50*(1–2, Serial No. 209), 41–65.

Waters, E., Merrick, S. K., Albersheim, L., & Treboux, D. (1995). *Attachment security from infancy to early adulthood: A 20-year longitudinal study.* Paper presented at the biennial meeting of the Society for Research in Child Development, Indianapolis, IN.

Waters, E., Posada, G., Crowell, J. A., & Lay, K. L. (1994). The development of attachment: From control systems to working models. *Psychiatry, 57,* 32–42.

Waters, E., Vaughn, B. E., Posada, G., & Kondo-Ikemura, K. (Eds.). (1995). Caregiving, cultural, and cognitive perspectives on secure-base behavior and working models: New growing points of attachment theory and research. *Monographs of the Society for Research in Child Development, 60*(2–3, Serial No 244).

Waters, J. (1978). The reliability and stability of individual differences in infant–mother attachment. *Child Development, 49,* 483–494.

Weinfield, N. S., Ogawa, J. R., & Sroufe, L. A. (1997). Early attachment as a pathway to adolescent peer competence. *Journal of Research on Adolescence, 7,* 241–265.

Youniss, J., & Smollar, J. (1985). *Adolescent relations with mothers, fathers, and friends.* Chicago: University of Chicago Press.

Zimmermann, P. (1994). *Bindung im Jugendalter: Entwicklung und Umgang mit aktuellen Anforderungen [Attachment in adolescence: Development while coping with actual challenges].* Unpublished doctural dissertation, University of Regensburg, Regensburg, Germany.

Zimmermann, P., Becker-Stoll, F., & Fremmer-Bombik, E. (1997). Erfassung der Bindungsrepräsentation mit dem Adult Attachment Interview: Ein Methodenvegleich [Assessment of attachment representation with the Adult Attachment Interview: A comparison of methods]. *Kindheit und Entwicklung, 6*(3), 173–182.

Zimmermann, P., Fremmer-Bombik, E., Spangler, G., & Grossmann, K. E. (1995). *Attachment in adolescence: A longitudinal perspective.* Poster presented at the biennial meeting of the Society for Research in Child Development, Indianapolis, IN.

Zimmermann, P., & Grossmann, K. E. (1997). Attachment and adaptation in adolescence. In W. Koops, J. B. Hoeksma, & D. C. van den Boom (Eds.), *Development of interaction and attachment: Traditional and non-traditional approaches* (pp. 281–282). Amsterdam: North-Holland.

Zimmermann, P., Scheuerer-Englisch, H., & Grossmann, K. E. (1996, May). *Social relationships in adolescence: Continuity and transformations.* Paper presented at the 5th Biennal Conference of the European Association for Research on Adolescence, Liege, Belgium.

34

Affect, Imagery, and Attachment

Working Models of Interpersonal Affect and the Socialization of Emotion

❖

CAROL MAGAI

Some years before John Bowlby enunciated the full scope of attachment theory, Silvan Tomkins produced the first two of four volumes setting forth another expansive and original theory: affect theory, which he envisioned as an overarching theory of the human being. It is interesting that the two theories have a certain degree of commonality with respect to the importance of emotions and feeling—a much neglected aspect of human psychology during the first 70 years of the century. The theories share other characteristics as well, but they are also distinctly different, as we will see.

Although Bowlby and Tomkins were contemporaries with closely overlapping lifespans, there is little evidence that they read or were influenced by each other's work or the work of each other's colleagues. Perhaps this is because Tomkins's work had more influence in the field of adult personality research, whereas Bowlby's influence was felt more acutely in the fields of developmental psychology and infancy. However, as Bowlby's theory has been extended to the field of adult development within recent years, the complementarity of attachment and affect theory becomes ever more apparent. In this chapter I review the fundamental constructs of each theory, examine recent research in which the two fields seem to be converging, and propose future work that should further the integration of these two important models of human development. As

I have argued elsewhere (Magai & McFadden, 1995), a truly integrative theory of personality development will need to take into account attachment theory's insistence on the importance of the bond between parent and child in psychological development, as well as Tomkins's more differentiated, emotion-specific view of personality development.

COMPARISON OF ATTACHMENT AND AFFECT THEORY CONSTRUCTS

Table 34.1 displays some of the key constructs of each of the two theories under consideration. In Tomkins's theory, emotions are primarily, though not exclusively, facial behaviors. At his 1990 plenary address at the International Society for Research on Emotions, he designated affect studies as the field of "inverse archeology." He explained that emotion is not something that one has to dig for; instead, it is literally "skin deep" (i.e., located in and on the skin of the face). Like the "other" archeology, however, affect studies require certain tools to divine their mysteries—knowledge of "affect runes," if you will. Tomkins believed that the face provides some of the most important clues to decoding the affective life, and he spent a substantial part of his academic career studying and writing about facial expres-

TABLE 34.1. Theories of Human Development

Aspects	Affect theory	Attachment theory
Emotions	Facial expressions and other affective behaviors	Signals
Experiential component	Differentiated affective experience	Feelings of security and insecurity
Basic human goals	Maximizing positive affect Minimizing negative affect Minimizing affect inhibition Means–ends power	Attachment Exploration
Affect regulation Attentional processes	Ideoaffective organizations (filters, amplifiers)	Hypervigilance Deactivating strategies
Cognitive templates	Scripts/imagery	Internal working models
Relationships	Emotion socialization	Attachment styles

sions and their meaning (Tomkins, 1962, 1963, 1975, 1991, 1993; Tomkins & McCarter, 1969).

Bowlby (1969/1982, 1973, 1980) believed that the face provides some signals of consequence in early development, but that these are part of a set of "attachment signals" (e.g., smiles and cries of distress, clinging behavior, tracking with the eyes)—signals that serve to keep a caregiver in close proximity and that help guarantee a child's survival. Behavioral signals, therefore, are mediators of an important developmental process: becoming attached to a human protector. Tomkins, in contrast, viewed emotion signals not as mediators of something important, but as "the main event."

Among other things, Tomkins believed that affective experience derives from feedback from changes in the temperature of the skin as patterned emotional expressions play across it. Affective experience is discrete and differentiated, corresponding to a limited number of basic or primary emotions with facial analogues. These facial expressions are observable in the opening months of life. The feelings that are most central in Bowlby's theory are those revolving around felt security and insecurity, which are natural products of attachment strivings and their consequent satisfaction or frustration. Bowlby was not particularly concerned with differentiated emotional experience or expression.

The models of human goal-related behavior that Tomkins and Bowlby promulgated departed radically from the Hullian and Freudian drive reduction models of their day. For Tomkins, the basic goals of human existence are fourfold: to

maximize positive affect, to minimize negative affect, to minimize affect inhibition, and to have the power to maximize the other goals. Differences in individual development lead to different ways in which the goals are elaborated and to various degrees of success in achieving the goals. For Bowlby, there are two basic and organizing goals linked to biobehavioral systems—namely, attachment and exploration. Optimally, these two goals can both be achieved in development and be maintained in balance; however, nonoptimal developments also occur, constraining or warping the outcome of attachment and exploration.

In terms of affect regulation, both theorists recognized that attentional processes and cognitive strategies are drawn into play in modulating the impact of sensory–affective stimulation. In the course of development, according to Tomkins, certain frequently experienced affects become structuralized in the personality in the form of "ideoaffective organizations." These organizations then serve as filters and amplifiers of incoming sensory information. Ideoaffective organizations are closely linked to "scripts," which are rules and strategies for ordering, interpreting, evaluating, predicting, and controlling affectively laden scenes or events.

In Bowlby's system, early experiences with parental responses to negative affect can come to shape a child's attentional processes. Two attentional strategies, deactivation and hypervigilance, are associated with "avoidant" and "ambivalent" (or preoccupied) styles of attachment, respectively. The deactivating strategy operates so as to ward off experiences of distress and/or to preclude the activation of overt distress (although, as Dozier & Kobak [1992] have shown, negative emotion may remain active at a nonconscious level). The hypervigilant strategy serves to maximize the detection of sources of interpersonal distress. These patterns of affect regulation are deeply embedded in early relational experiences, though carried forward in time through the development and internalization of "working models." These internal working models of self and other form the template for ways to negotiate the interpersonal transactions of everyday life, and thus to some extent resemble Tomkins's scripts.

Finally, let us consider the role of relationships in attachment theory and in affect theory. In attachment theory, relationships are pivotal and constitute the sine qua non of development. In affect theory, relationships tend to be embedded in the constructs of emotion socialization. Although some emotional development is based on self-regulatory principles, Tomkins recognized that parents play a powerful role in the child's acquisition of emotion skills and idiosyncratic patterns of affect regulation. Tomkins suggested that parents transmit their own biases or preferential affect patterns through their articulation of ideologies about affect, the affective behavior they themselves display, and the actual manner in which they respond to their child's affect.

In summary, both theories have restored emotion to the psychology of human development, albeit with different emphases. Bowlby's theory deals with affect on a more global, undifferentiated level, and strongly emphasizes the dyadic nature of individual development and its mental complement, internal working models. Tomkins's theory, in contrast, offers a virtuoso description of the complexities of individual differences in personality, indicating that specific affects are at the core of particular personality patterns. Volume 3 of Tomkins's four-volume work, *Affect, Imagery, Consciousness* (Tomkins, 1991), specifies literally hundreds of different scripts that the human psyche can give rise to—but the specifics of each developmental history and dynamic affect pattern are not elaborated. In a collection of selected writings by Tomkins, a number of commentators note that psychology has been slow to awaken to this most eloquent and complex theory, because it is almost too rich and dense to be assimilated readily (Demos, 1995).

In recent times, others have begun to define personality in a more differentiated manner by focusing on a limited number of affect-related traits. Costa and McCrae's (1996) five-factor model specifies five broad traits with subordinate emotion facets. Tellegen (1985) proposed a model of personality that identifies primary personality dimensions in terms of affective experience; research has tended to support the separability of various negative emotions (Watson & Clark, 1992). However, there is little in either the five-factor model or Tellegen's model that relates to developmental theory or interpersonal process.

In our own research, my colleagues and I have demonstrated that trait emotion is an organizing factor in expressive behavior (Malatesta, Fiore, & Messina, 1987), information processing (Magai, Distel, & Liker, 1995), and interpersonal relationships (Magai, 1996; Malatesta-Magai & Dorval, 1992), thereby transecting various domains of the personality (Tomkins, 1962). Moreover, we have shown that trait emotion biases are largely forged within early relational experiences (Malatesta, 1990). We have also emphasized that emotion traits can be manifested by either their presence or absence as significant features of personality (Magai & McFadden, 1995; Malatesta & Wilson, 1988). To our minds, these emotion traits or biases reflect styles of emotion regulation that have as their goal the maintenance, reduction, or amplification of particular affective experiences. Though these patterns have their roots in early dyadic experiences, I argue later that emotional dispositions are not reducible to attachment patterns, though they often seem linked to them. This is because emotion traits and attachment styles are both grounded in early relational experiences of an affective nature. In fact, there is a growing recognition in the developmental field at large that attachment patterns have an inherently affective component, and that emotional dispositions can be understood as emerging from particular relational experiences. It is to this literature that I now turn.

MODERN DEVELOPMENTAL AND PERSONALITY PSYCHOLOGY: THE EMOTION–ATTACHMENT INTERFACE

In recent times, attachment researchers and affect researchers have come to converge on several common terrains. In this section, I consider two of the more developmentally interesting areas: affect regulation and interpretive biases.

Affect Regulation

Although there is a growing literature on affect regulation, it exhibits little evidence of a unifying theme or an encompassing definition. Thompson's (1994) definition of "emotion regulation" is helpful here: ". . . emotion regulation encompasses not only acquired strategies of emotion self-management but also the variety of external influences by means of which emotion is regulated" (p. 28). External influences include the behaviors of social agents—the modulatory influences of caregivers in infancy (Malatesta & Haviland, 1982), or the empathic, supportive, or humoring responses of social partners in adulthood (Magai, Cohen, Gomberg, Malatesta, & Culver, 1996). Other sources of external mood regulation are drugs, such as cigarettes and alcohol (Cooper, Frone, Russell, & Mudar, 1995). Perhaps the most acutely influential of social inputs are those inhering in attachment relationships (Cassidy, 1994).

Converging opinion and evidence now indicate that styles of affect regulation are both temperamentally and environmentally shaped (Cicchetti, 1996; Fox, 1994). In terms of environmental contributions, individual styles of emotion regulation are rooted in the process of early dyadic interchanges and have representational sequelae (Cassidy, 1994; Derryberry & Reed, 1996; Schore, 1996; Thompson, 1994). Moreover, Derryberry and Reed (1996) suggest that regulatory processes not only give rise to representations, but also subsequently contribute greatly to the capacity for self-regulation. Cassidy's (1994) review of the literature on attachment and emotion regulation found that the two major styles of insecure attachment are linked to differential patterns of emotion inhibition or enhancement. Avoidant attachment, which is associated with a deactivating attentional strategy, is also accompanied by affect inhibition or minimization. Ambivalent attachment, which is associated with hypervigilance, is accompanied by affect enhancement or heightening.

Given the descriptions above of the two different patterns of emotion expression, and given Tomkins's four primary goals, one might wonder about the long-range consequences of these patterns in the context of adult relationships, because there are both individual and relational consequences of affect inhibition and expression.

Tomkins stipulated that humans have a fundamental need to reduce affect inhibition, and that constricted affect results in "affect hunger" or the need to express affect. This suggests the possibility of uneven expression of emotion which is sometimes contained and sometimes given to eruption. Indeed, this is one of the features of the Type A behavior pattern, which is associated with heart disease. The literature indicates that this behavior pattern is characterized by constricted negative affect—specifically, constricted anger expression (Malatesta-Magai, Jones, Shepard, & Culver, 1992). It also involves fast, propulsive, and "explosive" speech (i.e., speech patterns that lurch in volume and tone in an uneven pattern).

Avoidant children likewise show a kind of unevenness and unpredictability in their affective patterns. That is, whereas avoidant children demonstrate little overt affect in the strange situation paradigm, they tend to erupt in unprovoked attacks against their mothers in more familiar environments (Ainsworth, Blehar, Waters, & Wall, 1978).

If Tomkins was right about the motive to express emotion, there is an inherent emotional conflict for the avoidantly attached individual. Because of early experiences when attachment behaviors are rejected, the avoidant child learns to dampen expressive behavior so as to avoid further challenges to the attachment relationship (Main, 1981), although, as indicated above, there may be less than perfect suppression of negative affect. Styles of emotion regulation are thought to consolidate during childhood and to continue into adulthood (Sperling & Berman, 1994). At the same time that there is a stylistic preference for affect suppression, basic processes of affect motivation exert the opposing force of affect expression. Such fundamental tensions will conceivably influence two interpersonal spheres: adult romantic relationships and parent–child relationships. There are various ramifications of such a conflict.

Adult Relationships and Constricted Affect

One consequence of excessive affect inhibition is that the inhibited individual will have to rely on other people, or on mood-altering props, to help regulate affect (i.e., to exert a corrective force on the backed-up affect that wants and needs expression).

Relationship Consequences. There is some research on the relation between constricted affect and patterns of relatedness in adults, but an illustration from biography will effectively make the point.

Edward Hopper, one of America's foremost 20th-century artists, is well known for his scenes of austerity and disquieting loneliness. Prior to the recent intimate biography of him by art historian Gail Levin (1995), he had been depicted as a particularly American artist, rendering the self-contained and self-reliant spirit of "American" individualism. Hopper seems to have subscribed to the view that artists reveal their working models of self and other, for he once declared that, "broadly stated, art is one's effort to communicate to others one's emotional reaction to life and the world" (quoted in Levin, 1995, p. 438). Indeed, his art reveals a great deal about his sense of the world and even about his relationship style.

Hopper was reclusive and antisocial by nature. He married a fellow artist by the name of Jo Nivison relatively late in life, at the age of 41, and they proceeded to live a life of domestic disharmony for decades. The relationship was conflict-ridden but symbiotic.

Hopper conformed to the profile of the adult with a "dismissing" (avoidant) attachment style—lonely, self-absorbed, alienated from people, and full of contempt for others, especially women. He once sent out Christmas cards inscribed "Peace on earth, good will to men, and to hell with women," though he was not much fonder of men. Jo, on the other hand, was intense, gregarious, and obsessed with their relationship, keeping detailed diaries of their relationship over its 43-year course. Her voluminous diaries give expression to her marital preoccupations, just as Hopper's art gives graphic representation to his attachment style. His paintings invariably depict individuals seated alone in a vacant office, theater, diner, or bedroom, or in proximity with other individuals but clearly apart from them, even alienated. There are no scenes of connection, tenderness, romance, or lightheartedness.

One could argue that these two people, Jo and Hopper, needed each other for the regulation of mood. Adults with a dismissing attachment style have been described as emotionally constricted. If Tomkins was right about the human need to minimize affect inhibition, the dismissing individual requires others to stimulate emotion expression and thereby reduce affect hunger. The adult with a "preoccupied" (ambivalent) attachment style, on the other hand, has a maximizing strategy; he or she is hypervigilant to distress and

engages in heightened emotional expression. Thus, in the context of a dismissing–preoccupied relationship, the boredom of low affect can be transformed by a certain kind of partner into an exciting hell.

Interestingly enough, the literature on romantic attachment suggests that preoccupied and dismissing individuals may seek each other out. The pairing of preoccupied and dismissing people is notably more common than dismissing–dismissing and preoccupied–preoccupied pairings (Collins & Read, 1990; Kirkpatrick & Davis, 1994; Senchak & Leonard, 1992; see also Feeney, Chapter 17, this volume, for an extensive review and discussion of this literature). There is, as well, some suggestion of dismissing–preoccupied pairings in Gottman's (1993) studies of marital couples. He has described a common dysfunctional pattern involving the withdrawn, stonewalling partner (often the male) and the pursuing, angry mate (often the female).

Addictive and Preaddictive Behaviors. Adults may also engage in addictive or preaddictive behaviors to help regulate affect. They can either sedate themselves to numbness if their dysregulation takes the form of heightened affect expression—as in the case of the flamboyant American poet Anne Sexton, who abused alcohol and tranquilizers to quell her many fears and anxieties (Magai & Hunziker, in press)—or they can engage in just enough sedation to disinhibit their affect. Indeed, one way of releasing overcontrolled or backed-up affect (Tomkins, 1963) is through the disinhibiting effects of mood-altering drugs. The literature on drug abuse has long indicated that people use drugs such as alcohol to regulate painful emotions. However, recent work by Cooper et al. (1995) indicates that alcohol use serves two very different motives. One motive is to reduce negative affect, and another is to enhance positive affect. Cooper et al.'s study strongly supported the discreteness of the two motives.

With respect to attachment, although Cassidy's (1994) analysis of the affect-inhibitory style of avoidantly attached individuals emphasizes suppression of negative affect, there are indications in the literature that positive affect is also under constraint. In the context of the strange situation, avoidant children typically do not greet their mothers with joy at reunion following separation. I suspect that the premium on affect inhibition is more system-wide than previously assumed, although there may be certain emotions that receive especially close monitoring. In one of our own studies (Hoffer & Magai, 1997; Magai, 1996), we found that there was a significant negative correlation between trait joy (as assessed by the Differential Emotions Scale) and dismissing adult attachment (as assessed by Bartholomew & Horowitz's [1991] coding system applied to results of an attachment interview). However, there were no significant correlations between dismissing attachment and negative emotion, presumably because such individuals tend to play down negative affect in their self-reports. Moreover, in the same study, in which we examined personality patterns in a nonclinical sample of light, moderate, and heavy drinkers (Hoffer & Magai, 1997; Magai, 1996), we found that dismissing attachment was not only negatively associated with trait joy, but was also negatively associated with seeking social support during stress, and positively associated with drinking when excited and with experiencing an increase in happiness as a consequence of drinking. Thus it appears that individuals with a dismissing style of attachment may drink to enhance positive affect.

Other kinds of people drink to reduce negative affect, and this seems to be strongest in the case of preoccupied adult attachment. We found that preoccupied attachment was associated with low self-esteem and depression. Such a person drinks when sad, and sadness is alleviated by drinking. This would appear to make the preoccupied individual vulnerable to alcohol abuse. Indeed, we found that the degree to which people indicated a preoccupied style of attachment was significantly correlated with their drinking frequency.

In summary, the two patterns of emotion expression identified by Cassidy (1994) as associated with attachment patterns have many ramifications, some of which have been highlighted above. The effects of affect inhibition and heightened negative affect are consequential for adult close relationships and addictive behaviors. I turn now to consider the implications for parent–child relationships.

Parent–Child Relationships, Affect Inhibition, and the Role of Shame

In considering the intergenerational transmission of affect regulation patterns, Cassidy (1994) noted that dismissing adults and parents of avoidant children show the same pattern of affect constriction found in avoidant children themselves; this suggests, to me at least, that avoidant infants may learn their style of affect inhibition through direct modeling. There are other sources of affect inhibition as well, which may surface through parallel or related processes—namely, in the process of emotion socialization.

Recall that in Tomkins's system, emotion socialization is due to particular parental practices. Parents transmit their own biases not only through their behavior toward the child and the child's affect, but also via their affect ideologies—their working beliefs and attitudes about affect and its regulation.

To be more specific, Tomkins distinguished between "rewarding" and "punitive" emotion socialization practices. Rewarding socialization involves affective engagement with the child and a validation of the child's emotional experiences, both positive and negative; it also includes helping the child cope with sources of negative affect and instructing him or her in how to avoid circumstances of undue provocation. Such a parent is comfortable with his or her own affect and displays consistency in beliefs, actions, and expressive behaviors when it comes to emotions. In contrast, punitive socialization is more likely in a parent who is uncomfortable with his or her own emotions, and whose own affect regulation is distorted in some way. Such a parent tends to engage in behaviors that result in amplifying the child's negative affect rather than reducing it. The parent communicates this by escalating conflict and by failing to validate the child's feelings or to help the child cope with distress or the sources of distress. He or she also communicates negative beliefs and attitudes about specific affects, affect regulation, and affects in general, which the child cannot help absorbing. For example, a parent may teach the child that others have hostile intentions and are not to be trusted, and that the world must be screened for situations that validate this view. The parent may also be inconsistent in attitudes, actions, and expressive behavior, thus generating uncertainty in the child.

Scheff (1994) has suggested that shame is the master socializing affect because of its powerful interpersonal pull. Earlier, Tomkins (1963) noted its importance within the parent–child relationship. There are various triggers for shame. Tomkins (1963) indicated that shame is elicited in the child by the experience of defeat. Contemptuous communications by parents, including derogatory, derisory, belittling comments or tone of voice, and physical displays of disgust and contempt (Malatesta-Magai & Dorval, 1992; Tomkins, 1963), also elicit shame. Tomkins noted that the use of contempt to induce shame is one of the most common and powerful means of achieving control over social behavior; contempt also has the most negative side effects, especially in the context of child rearing, because it is so punitive, rejecting, and distancing.

A study by Gottman and his colleagues (Hooven, Gottman, & Katz, 1995; Gottman, Katz, & Hooven, 1996) appears to support the assumption that parents' critical attitudes can have damaging and far-reaching consequences. These investigators interviewed parents regarding their attitudes about emotion, and also observed mothers performing an instructional task with their preschool-age children. Parents' attitudes were coded for "self-awareness" (awareness and tolerance of their own negative emotions) and "acceptance" (accepting attitudes toward their children's expression of negative emotions). Each mother's interactive behavior with her child during the instructional task was coded for supportiveness versus derogation, which was indexed by intrusiveness, criticism, and derisive humor. Structural equation modeling, with outcome variables assessed 3 years later, supported the toxicity of derogation. Moreover, parental derogation was linked with negative attitudes about emotion expression and emotion regulation. Parental self-awareness versus lack of awareness predicted acceptance versus nonacceptance of children's emotions and supportive versus derogatory interaction styles, as well as child achievement scores 3 years later. In terms of affect theory and attachment theory, parental styles of attention and emotion regulation that are constricted in nature (low affective self-awareness) are associated with behavioral tendencies that are fundamentally shaming and lead to negative child outcomes.

In some of our own work (Magai, 1996), we found that the fearful avoidant attachment pattern identified by some investigators (Bartholomew & Horowitz, 1991) was associated with child-rearing disciplinary styles involving physical punishment and love withdrawal, which, according to Tomkins, are both elicitors of shame; notably, fearful avoidance was the only attachment style that related to facial expressions of shame. These facial expressions were elicited in an emotion induction procedure that was videotaped and subsequently coded with an objective facial affect coding system (Izard, 1979). Our findings suggest that a fearful avoidant parent, who is shame-sensitive himself or herself, may set up conditions for the intergenerational transmission of shame and insecure attachment in the child through the undue use of coercive (shaming) disciplinary practices.

In another study involving microanalytic coding, we performed an affective and sociolinguistic analysis of the interaction and speech patterns of a family that was filmed during the course of a study of language development (Malatesta-Magai & Dorval, 1992). In this particular family, consisting of a father, mother, and son, we found a predominance of shame markers in the mother. These shame signals coincided quite specifically with dismissing, critical, and derogatory gestures, looks, and comments made by both the son and father during the course of the session. Mapping this dynamic back onto the parent–child system, one can imagine the developmental impact of critical parenting over time.

Yet another example comes from pilot work that Sari Abrams and I conducted, pursuant to a study of shame and attachment patterns. Retzinger (1991) identified a set of behaviors in adults that index shame. She called these nonverbal indicators of shame "hiding behaviors." Hiding behaviors consist of all of those gestures, head movements, and body adjustments that effect a reduction of the exposure of self, including covering the face or turning it away, ducking the head, averting the body, lowering the voice, or even leaving the scene of interaction entirely. In an attempt to validate the meaning of hiding behaviors in infants, we assigned 18- to 24-month-old infants to one of two "shame induction" conditions as each infant was seated in a highchair. Tomkins (1963) suggested that mere exposure or being the focus of attention can elicit the shame/shyness response. We thus reasoned that having a mother draw attention to a child's face would prompt hiding behaviors. One shame induction condition consisted of having mothers comment on the attractive qualities of their infants' faces (flattery condition). The other consisted of having them draw attention to a smudge of dirt or food on their children's faces, all the while maintaining an affectively neutral face and tone of voice. As it turned out, the infants did not demonstrate shame or self-consciousness in the flattery condition; they merely beamed back at their mothers. By contrast, in the dirty-face condition there was a very strong negative response. Children showed a variety of hiding behaviors, including attempts to leave the scene—in the case of one child, shrinking in body posture so much that the child was in danger of slipping out of the highchair. We assume that the hiding behaviors in response to the dirty-face condition occurred despite the fact that mothers maintained a neutral face and voice, because such commentary on dirty faces in the past had been associated with a somewhat more critical delivery. It is also clear that certain kinds of shame/shyness elicitors (flattery) may take more time than others before they become effective (i.e., it takes some time to learn to respond to flattery with modest disclaimers and demurral).

Shame plays a particularly interesting role in affect socialization because it constitutes a building block for the development of emotional traits, including traits other than shame. Tomkins (1963) suggested that children learn to inhibit certain emotions when their parents or other social agents shame them for displaying those emotions. Because shame readily attaches itself to any emotion with which it is repetitively associated, children acquire affect–shame binds. The consequence of an affect–shame bind is that when the emotion that has been socialized through shaming is activated, shame is experienced and the forbidden affect is inhibited. Thus, at least according to theory, indicators of shame (averted head and gaze) can signal the presence of an inhibited emotion. We tested this thesis in the study of the Type A behavior pattern alluded to earlier (Malatesta-Magai et al., 1992), predicting that Type A individuals would display greater amounts of shame affect during emotion induction. We found that a particular pattern distinguished the classic Type A individual (a younger Type A male): anger inhibition and anger–shame blends.

In summary, the work on attachment has helped to identify distinct patterns of affect inhibition and enhancement (Cassidy, 1994). The avoidant individual appears to be characterized by inhibition of both positive and negative affect, whereas the ambivalent individual shows a pattern of heightened affect expression. Various ramifications of these patterns have been spelled out above. Moreover, one of the mechanisms by which inhibition is accomplished is through shaming, although the links between avoidant attachment and maternal shaming have not yet been established; instead, the empirical literature has focused more broadly on "insensitive" caregiving. My colleagues and I are presently exploring these links, using videotaped sessions of mother–infant play during the first 7 months of life. Here we are suggesting that a focus on specific affects may broaden our understanding of both trait emotion and attachment styles, as well

as the relation between the two. I turn now to an examination of the relations among affect, attachment, and the formation of interpretive biases.

Internal Working Models and Interpretative Biases

One of the premises of attachment theory is that as a function of their relational histories, individuals develop internal working models of self and other, which they bring to bear upon entering new relationships or in negotiating established relationships (Bowlby, 1969/1982, 1980). Secure attachment is associated with feelings of self-confidence and trust in others. A securely attached person values relationships positively and is generally prepared to relate in a positive way interpersonally, even during periods of disagreement and conflict. Insecure attachment, on the other hand, is associated with negative feelings and expectations about the self and/or others (Bartholomew & Horowitz, 1991), and thus with somewhat negative expectations about interpersonal relationships. Presumably, these internalized expectations will have consequences for the interpretation of social stimuli and the nature of the behavior that is subsequently enacted during social interchange. One way of examining internal working models (as well as Tomkins's ideoaffective scripts) is to examine information-processing biases with respect to social stimuli.

In recent research with children, interpretative/attributional biases have been linked to emotion dysregulation associated with depression and anger (Dodge, Pettit, McClaskey, & Brown, 1986; Garber, Braafladt, & Zeman, 1991). Dodge (1986) proposed five sequential processing steps that are necessary for competent behavioral responding. The first step involves attending to social cues; the second involves interpreting them. Dodge et al. (1986) were able to demonstrate that aggression-prone children tend to interpret the social intentions of others as hostile. However, to date this kind of information-processing bias has been studied only in depressed and aggressive children, although interpretational biases have been observed in other contexts.

Several findings of interest have been obtained in studies on emotion recognition—studies in which subjects are asked to identify what emotion expression is being posed by a model. The accuracy with which individuals recognize facial expressions of emotion has been found to vary as a function of personality, mood, status as a delinquent or nondelinquent adolescent, and status as an abused or nonabused child (Camras et al., 1990; McCown, Johnson, & Austin, 1985; Schiffenbauer, 1974; Tomkins & McCarter, 1965). In these studies, participants were presented with clearly articulated facial expressions of emotion conforming to universal templates. Far less work has been done on the interpretation of ambiguous expressions, despite the fact that many everyday encounters involve decoding affect at a distance, in unclear light, or in the context of very brief exposure to the expressive behavior (Coren & Russell, 1992).

One exception is a series of studies based on Emde, Osofsky, and Butterfield's (1993) IFEEL Pictures Test, a collection of 30 photographs of ambiguous infant facial expressions. The pictures were originally normed on a group of 145 mothers (mean age 29 years) of 3- to 12-month-old infants. This group and other control groups served as the reference groups for a series of studies examining biases in selected groups of individuals, including mothers at risk for child maltreatment, teenage mothers, depressed mothers, and mothers of premature infants (Emde et al., 1993). In each instance, group differences in the pattern of emotion decoding were clearly in evidence. Although Emde et al. intended the IFEEL instrument to serve as a projective test, there was little evidence that it functioned in that way, at least in the classic sense. For example, Zahn-Waxler and Wagner (1993) compared the responses of depressed and nondepressed mothers. They found that depressed mothers were more likely to see expressions of fear, and less likely to see joy; unexpectedly, the two groups did not differ on attributions of sadness. Moreover, ratings of present mood with the Profile of Mood questionnaire did not predict the mothers' biases. Although these studies are appealing, the reader is left wondering what to make of the results. Emde et al. (1993) provided no overarching theoretical framework to guide interpretation of the results, although various contributors to their volume suggested that "projection" or "denial" may have been operative. In addition, there was no attempt to view these biases as reflecting on the participants' own relational histories.

Attachment researchers have also begun to examine interpretive biases; they are being guided by the idea that interpretive biases are linked to representational models of self and other. In a longitudinal study of attachment, Main and colleagues (Cassidy, 1988; Kaplan & Main, 1985;

Main, Kaplan, & Cassidy, 1985) assessed the attachment styles of a group of children at age 1 and again at age 6. Kaplan and Main (1985) found that attachment patterns were related to the way in which children depicted their families in a drawing. Children who had been secure with their mothers in infancy depicted family members as close but not clinging to one another; the figures were individuated and displayed a range of expressions. In contrast, avoidant children depicted their family members as uniformly happy, although there were also discrepant aspects of the drawings (greater distances between members, armless figures) suggesting that the smiling faces represented masking.

Using a different sample, Cassidy (1988) examined the children's self-representations in attachment relationships using a puppet interview and story completion task. She found that avoidant children typically did not remark on interpersonal relationships and tended to depict themselves as perfect; ambivalent children showed no clear pattern of response; secure children tended to represent themselves in a positive light, but many were also able to acknowledge less than perfect aspects of themselves.

In another set of studies, Cassidy, Kirsh, Scolton, and Parke (1996) examined the relation between attachment patterns and representations of peer relationships. Children were asked to imagine that they were the child in a story in which a peer caused something negative to happen to them. They were then asked a series of questions about both children, assessing representations of feeling, motives, and subsequent behavior. In general, the studies indicated that securely attached children had more positive representations of themselves and others than insecurely attached children, especially avoidantly attached youngsters.

Zeanah et al. (1993) assessed maternal perceptions and interpretations of infant emotion by having mothers view videotapes of infants in distress. Mothers' ratings were systematically related to both mother and infant attachment patterns. Dismissing mothers (mothers of avoidant infants) rated the emotionality of the infants significantly more negatively than did autonomous (secure) mothers and mothers of resistant children; dismissing mothers also rated the infants as more negative than autonomous mothers did.

The studies described above are at the forefront of contemporary approaches to examining internal working models, and they represent an exciting new venue of investigation for attachment researchers. However, a compelling interpretation of these effects is missing; moreover, little is known about what child-rearing experiences lead to specific kinds of biases. In the remainder of this chapter, I propose some new approaches to thinking about interpretative biases, or at least approaches using a particular kind of medium: ambiguous facial expressions. Since attachment patterns are based on internal working models of relationships, ambiguous stimuli should be particularly effective in activating these models. Attributions to these ambiguous stimuli, hypothetically, should reveal something about what an individual has learned in the context of his or her primary affective relationship.

I believe that decoding biases in the perception of facial displays reflect relationship histories, though they may be separable from attachment styles. Many aspects of people's affective lives and interpersonal relations revolve around the facial affective exchanges they share with social partners during their formative years, beginning in the opening weeks and months of life. In an early study of face-to-face play between mothers and infants (Malatesta & Haviland, 1982), we coded facial expressions of emotion of the two partners on a second-by-second basis. Subsequently, using base rates obtained in that study, we estimated that infants are exposed during these interchanges to roughly 32,000 highly articulated contingent facial expressions of emotion from the third to the sixth month of life (Malatesta, 1985). In later life as well, many facets of people's affective lives are structured around expressive interchanges between social partners (Magai et al., 1996; Malatesta-Magai & Dorval, 1992). Thus it is likely that internal working models include templates or images of the rewarding or punishing face of the other. Logically, we should be able to deduce relational histories by the manner in which individuals resolve ambiguous facial expressions. Resolution of these kind of ambiguous social stimuli may be related less to classical projection (with warded-off feelings assigned to the other) than to expectational biases revealing relational histories— that is, expectations of the other's affective stance toward the self.

We tested this thesis in a recent study (Magai, 1996), pitting a projection prediction against an expectational prediction for a clinical population whose relational histories typically involve angry interchanges—namely, children with attention-deficit/hyperactivity disorder (ADHD). In this study, in which we compared ADHD children

with control children, we examined the relation between facial decoding biases and clinical status, as well as mother–child attachment and maternal emotion socialization practices. ADHD is a common disorder of childhood afflicting an estimated 5% of the population. High activity level and impulsivity often bring ADHD children into conflict with socializing agents, frequently producing angry interchanges (Barkley, Cunningham, & Karlsson, 1983; Campbell, 1973, 1975). In addition, because of attention deficits, academic work is often compromised. The combination of negative reactions from others and poor academic performance often leads to anxiety and negative self-esteem in these children (Barkley et al., 1983; Campbell, 1973, 1975). With respect to the decoding task, clinical theory would predict a projection bias favoring higher shame or fear decoding in ADHD than in normal children, since they are surfeited with these painful emotions; attachment theory would predict an expectational bias toward anger, because the probability of significant others' being angry is high in these children's experience. Our results sustained the attachment theory prediction: ADHD children attributed more anger to the ambiguous faces than control children did.

An unanticipated finding was that the ADHD children attributed less fear to the faces than control children did, which is quite the opposite of the projection thesis. One interpretation is that the tendency of ADHD children to perceive more anger in other's faces was an artifact of the reduction in available attributions caused by the higher attributions of anger; that is, the greater the number of anger attributions out of a total of 80 judgments, the fewer the remaining judgments in favor of other emotions. However, Tomkins (1963) suggested early on that the punitive socialization of an emotion should result in a kind of perceptual blindness for that emotion. Fortunately, other data from the study supported the legitimacy of this interpretation.

We also examined maternal affect socialization practices as measured by the Child's Everyday Experiences Questionnaire (Magai & McFadden, 1995). This measure contains 30 vignettes involving children's emotional experiences, corresponding to the 30 items on Izard's Differential Emotions Scale. Subjects were asked to state what they would say or do in response to each of the scenarios. Responses that would be classified as rewarding in Tomkins's system (empathy, comfort/consoling, helping) were scored here as rewarding; responses that would be classified as punitive in Tomkins's system (shaming, guilt-inducing) were coded as punitive. We predicted that mothers of ADHD children would engage in more punitive affective socialization because of the more dysregulated and out-of-bounds behavior of these children, although we had no *a priori* predictions as to which affects might be more punitively socialized.

We found that the emotion socialization practices of mothers of ADHD children were indeed more punitive, particularly in the case of fear and guilt; this may relate to the fear and guilt such children display when recounting conflicts with others that result from their dysregulated behavior. It is our interpretation that ADHD mothers' apparently negative affective responses to children experiencing guilt and anxiety represent affect expression that is incidental to the children's current affect. We suspect that multiple occasions of hearing of a child's problematic interactions with others may cause an overriding of a parent's normally tolerant and validating response to a child's affect. Nevertheless, we may presume that the responses in question have a psychologically punitive effect on children. As a matter of fact, these particular findings are quite revealing, in light of Tomkins's thesis concerning the punitive socialization of emotion and perceptual blindness with respect to selected emotions. As indicated above, ADHD children perceived significantly fewer fear faces than did non-ADHD children. They also perceived fewer guilt faces, although this effect did not reach statistical significance.

Oddly, we did not find that the attachment styles of children or their mothers distinguished the two groups of children (maternal attachment styles were assessed by Kirkpatrick & Davis's [1994] adaptation of Hazan & Shaver's [1987] attachment measure, and children's attachment styles were assessed by Lynch & Cicchetti's [1991] relatedness scale). We were somewhat surprised by this finding, but, upon reflection, attribute it to the early origins of the attachment bond. Attachments are initially formed in the first year of life, before the ADHD behavior pattern manifests itself. Also, attachment patterns tend to remain consistent over time, unless there are extremely harsh home conditions (Cicchetti, 1990). It is conceivable that the more punitive emotion socialization of mothers of ADHD children is "discounted" by the children, because they realize that their mothers' responses do not stem from intrinsically rejecting attitudes but are reactions to their own dysregulated behavior.

In any case, we learned two important things from this study. First, individual differences in facial decoding biases are linked to relational histories and reflect expectational biases. Second, attachment histories and affect histories are related but separable phenomena linked to the broader and more differentiated condition of emotion socialization.

From another recent study, it is also apparent that different projective media reflect different kinds of biases. In our study of emotion across the lifespan (Magai, 1996; Magai, Hunziker, & Mesias, in press), participants were interviewed about their relational histories, completed a facial affect decoding task (the same set of photos used in the above-described study), and wrote stories to four Thematic Apperception Test (TAT) cards. The stories were coded for attachment-related themes, and the coded data were then subjected to principal-components analysis, producing a seven-factor solution. The factor names and their highest-loading codes were as follows: (1) "negative emotion routed from consciousness" (absence of affiliation themes, absence of story resolution, atonality, absence of conflict); (2) "rejection" (rejection by a peer, conflict over affiliation, other interpersonal conflict); (3) "hostility" (violent events, overt hostility of story characters, negative story resolution); (4) "inner conflict" (intrapsychic conflict, fearful tone of story); (5) "approval seeking" (approval of an authority figure, approval from other figures, depressive story tone); (6) "issues with authority figures" (rejection by authority figures, work conflict, latent violence); and (7) "affiliation" (intimacy with a partner, characters enjoying an affiliative relationship, upbeat story tone).

Among other analyses, we correlated attachment ratings with the factor scores and decoding biases. In terms of the decoding biases, we once again failed to confirm a projective thesis. Instead, what we found was that secure attachment was positively associated with a decoding bias toward shame, fearful/avoidant attachment with a decoding bias toward anger and sadness (and negatively associated with a bias toward interest), preoccupied attachment with no particular pattern, and dismissing attachment with a decoding bias toward disgust. Once again, findings were interpretable in terms of the hypothesized child-rearing histories of adult subjects in attachment studies. The association between secure attachment and a decoding bias toward shame makes some sense, given that shame has been described by Tomkins (1963) and Kaufman

(1989) as the negative affect most closely related to positive interpersonal relationships. Shame therefore can be considered a positive decoding bias, because a social partner who experiences interpersonal shame is one who has an attachment he or she cares about (Tomkins, 1963; Kaufman, 1989).

The findings with respect to fearful avoidance are also interpretable. The early rejection and neglect that are said to characterize the experiences of the fearful avoidant individual seem well reflected in the negative correlation with interest, if we interpret this as stemming historically from parental disinterest. The positive correlation with anger may reflect experiences with harsh physical punishment, most likely conjoined with parental anger. The positive correlation with sadness may relate to parental depression; this may help explain the origins of parental rejection, neglect, and harshness, since depression is associated with sadness, fear, and anger, according to Izard (1972).

The fact that no clear pattern was found for preoccupation may reflect the inconsistency in parenting that is said to be characteristic of the rearing experiences of preoccupied individuals (Cassidy & Berlin, 1994).

Finally, the findings for dismissing attachment are also sensible. Work by Dozier and Kobak (1992) suggests that dismissing individuals have a repressive coping style characterized by the denial of negative emotion. Dismissing individuals also tend to have a limited memory for childhood experiences. The negative correlation between dismissing attachment and a decoding bias may reflect the repressive denial of anger; the positive association with a decoding bias toward disgust may reflect a disapproving parent who would tolerate no expressions of overt anger.

Taken together, these data on decoding biases seem to reflect relational histories—the rewarding or punishing face of the parent, as Tomkins (1963) originally suggested.

We also examined the relations between attachment style and TAT factor scores. Security was negatively associated with negative emotion routed from consciousness and with issues related to authority figures. Fearful avoidance was associated with approval-seeking themes; preoccupation was positively associated with affiliative themes; and dismissing attachment was positively correlated with the themes of negative emotion routed from consciousness and with inner conflict.

The general thread running through these findings is that the TAT method of tapping attachment relationships reveals areas of conflict and reflects fantasies of wish fulfillment. This contrasts with the findings from the decoding task, so the two projective tasks tell us quite different things. Story themes express conflict areas and wish fulfillment, whereas facial decoding biases reflect relational histories and continuing expectations of the rewarding or punishing face of the other. These findings, of course, require replication in future research.

To conclude this section on interpretative biases, I want to return to the issue of the discreteness of decoding biases, and to Tomkins's notion that the face provides some of the most important clues to understanding the affective life and solving some of the puzzles of personality development. To this end, I return to the study involving decoding biases of mothers and children, some of whom had ADHD. In a secondary analysis of the data, combining ADHD and control children (Magai & Siegel, 1996), we looked more closely at several aspects of the emotion socialization process and child emotion regulation. Our hope was to be able to move to a more inclusive and differentiated model of affective development—one that includes both attachment constructs and the discrete-emotions concepts of affect theory.

First, we examined the relation between dimensional ratings of mothers' attachment styles and their emotion socialization practices and decoding biases. We found that security was positively associated with a decoding bias favoring guilt and with rewarding socialization of guilt. Ambivalence was positively associated with a decoding bias toward fear and with rewarding socialization of fear. Avoidance was negatively associated with a decoding bias toward shame and was negatively associated with punitive socialization of shame. The pattern suggested here is that parents may be more rewarding and less punitive toward emotions to which they are particularly sensitized.

We also wanted to examine children's decoding biases for particular emotions and were interested in developing models for affect-specific biases. As a first step, we examined the zero-order correlations between child decoding biases and other relational and emotion socialization experiences. We then constructed regression models based on the bivariate analyses. Predictor variables were entered sequentially in blocks according to the presumption that child decoding biases would be linked to developmental processes that could be ordered as follows: attachment style, experience with maternal disciplinary practices, maternal decoding biases, and maternal emotion socialization processes. Ten regression models were tested, one for each of 10 emotions. Seven of these models were significant.

Scanning the seven regressions, we noted that there were no significant associations between child decoding biases and child or maternal attachment style scores, and few associations between these biases and maternal disciplinary style. Instead, the children's decoding biases were closely linked with maternal decoding biases and emotion socialization practices. However, the latter effects—maternal decoding biases and emotion socialization practices—were themselves linked to attachment style variables. One example will suffice: that involving children's tendency to see fear in faces. Of the several variables entered into the equation for the prediction of children's decoding bias toward fear, only maternal emotion socialization contributed significantly to the model—specifically, maternal rewarding socialization of fear, and punitive socialization of disgust. That is, the more mothers rewarded fear and punished disgust, the more likely their children were to attribute fear to others' faces. Interestingly, in the zero-order correlations the rewarding socialization of fear was positively associated with maternal ambivalence, and punitive socialization of disgust was associated with maternal decoding of sadness, which was in turn associated with maternal ambivalence. This suggested that the ambivalently attached mothers might be amplifying the anxiety of their children—which would make children more sensitive to the detection of fear. This might also explain the Zahn-Waxler and Wagner (1993) finding that depressed mothers saw more "fear" in the IFEEL Pictures Test, if these individuals shared some features of ambivalent attachment.

As we reviewed the results across the seven decoding biases in children, we detected several patterns. First, it was apparent that decoding biases involving joy, interest, and shame were positive decoding biases, in that they were associated with more positive emotion socialization practices. Decoding biases toward anger, fear, sadness, and contempt, on the other hand, were associated with more negative emotion socialization practices, and each of these biases was associated with a different set of predictor variables. We also found that children's decoding biases were not linked to maternal attachment patterns in a direct manner, and that the biases were unassociated with children's attachment patterns. However, maternal attachment styles were related to maternal decoding biases and maternal emotion socialization practices; in turn, maternal emotion socialization practices predicted children's decoding biases.

These findings suggest that the lack of a direct relation between maternal attachment styles and children's decoding biases may be obscured by the overly broad nature of the three attachment styles (or four, in the scheme described by Bartholomew & Horowitz, 1991). Although the broad categories of secure, avoidant, and ambivalent styles of attachment have demonstrated robust predictive power in a number of recent studies, the very sweep of the broad attachment style classifications that produce reliable generalizations concerning affect regulation styles and other behaviors may inadvertently mask more idiosyncratic but developmentally important patterns. Recall, however, that Ainsworth originally identified nine attachment styles, though over the years attachment study samples have in general been too small to have the power to detect such differences. In any case, it suggests that we will have to examine more carefully the assumption that attachment styles are limited to the three or four styles that have been the foci of so much contemporary attachment research, as well as the assumption that attachment styles index only broad emotion dimensions such as security and insecurity.

SUMMARY AND CONCLUDING THOUGHTS

In this chapter I have sought to encourage the further integration of research based on attachment theory and on affect theory. I have reviewed the basic constructs from each field and examined recent research that converges on common concerns—namely, affect regulation and interpretive biases. It seems clear that parental attachment style constitutes an important source of variance in parental emotion regulation styles, whether they be well-modulated, inhibitory, or escalating styles, and in parental information-processing biases related to affect. Parental influence on children's emotion regulation begins quite early in life, as we have seen in studies of face-to-face play (Cohn & Tronick, 1983; Havilant & Lelwica, 1987; Malatesta & Haviland, 1982). Parental emotion biases interact in as yet unknown ways with the basic temperamental dispositions of infants (Schore, 1996) to set the stage for children's patterns of attachment, affect regulation, and information-processing biases. In terms of affect regulation, we know that attentional strategies are linked to amplifying and inhibitory styles of emotion expression. We need to know more about particular (affect-specific) patterns of emotion inhibition and expression, and more about shame–emotion binds.

I have also summarized the findings of several recent studies from our laboratory. To recapitulate, we have found that children have distinct attributional biases when resolving ambiguous social stimuli. These biases appear to relate more to expectational biases derived from relational histories than to projection in the classic sense. Parents show attributional biases as well, and these are closely associated with their emotion socialization practices and decoding biases. The particular patterns obtained suggest that when it comes to emotion socialization of children, parents may be more rewarding and less punitive toward emotions that they are more comfortable with and less defended against, and, correspondingly, to which they are more positively sensitive.

In parents, particular qualities of relational histories (ambivalence, security, avoidance) have been found to be associated with particular patterns of decoding bias. Such decoding biases may constitute the first step in information processing and accompanying emotion regulation and dysregulation in the parents, which may then translate into specific behavioral practices with children.

In children, decoding biases have been linked more closely to immediate parental behaviors than to the attachment styles of either mothers or children. This suggests that attachment and emotion organization may have parallel and interconnecting paths, but that they are separable and independent processes. It also suggests greater diversity of emotion socialization practices within particular attachment styles. Granted, our exploratory analysis may have capitalized on chance characteristics of the sample at hand, and thus further study is warranted. Nevertheless, this research suggests a model of attachment, working models of interpersonal affect, and emotion socialization that may be clarified in future research.

The formation of emotional attachments to caregivers in the opening year of life establishes emotional dispositions that will have far-reaching consequences for the development of attentional strategies and for the regulation of affect in childhood and beyond. Emotion socialization occurs within this most important and affectively charged relationship, and individual differences in the manner in which caregivers attend to specific affects will forge distinctive emotion biases. Our developmental models should encompass all of these considerations. From a theoretical point of view, we also need to remain open to other sources of emotion socialization. Although it is frequently acknowledged that there are sources of emotion socialization outside of the parent–child relationship, these sources of variance are rarely given more than lip service in our developmental models. For example, the acceptance or scorn of other children over long periods of time constitutes a powerful source of shame socialization, as compellingly illustrated in the recent film *Welcome to the Dollhouse* and in Margaret Atwood's (1988) fascinating novel about jealousy, contempt, and spite among a small circle of friends, *Cat's Eye*. Brutal neighborhoods in which children are inducted into a culture of violence constitute another venue of affect socialization (Miller & Sperry, 1987). Indeed, our developmental models should start with what is arguably the most important relationship of all, the attachment relationship; then, however, they must broaden their bases to include other significant relational inputs and other sources of emotional learning and adaptation.

REFERENCES

Abrams, S., & Magai, C. (1996). *Pilot study of infant shame.* Unpublished manuscript, Long Island University, New York, NY.

Ainsworth, M. D. S., Blehar, M. C., Waters, E., & Wall, S. (1978). *Patterns of attachment: A psychological study of the strange situation.* Hillsdale, NJ: Erlbaum.

Atwood, M. E. (1988). *Cat's eye.* New York: Doubleday.

Barkley, R. A., Cunningham, C. E., & Karlsson, J. (1983). The speech of hyperactive children and their mothers: Comparisons with normal children and stimulant drug effects. *Journal of Learning Disabilities, 16,* 105–110.

Bartholomew, K., & Horowitz, L. M. (1991). Attachment styles among young adults: A test of a four-category model. *Journal of Personality and Social Psychology, 61,* 226–244.

Bowlby, J. (1969/1982). *Attachment and loss: Vol. 1. Attachment.* New York: Basic Books.

Bowlby, J. (1973). *Attachment and loss: Vol. 2. Separation.* New York: Basic Books.

Bowlby, J. (1980). *Attachment and loss: Vol. 3. Loss: Sadness and depression.* New York: Basic Books.

Campbell, S. B. (1973). Mother–child interaction in reflective, impulsive, and hyperactive children. *Developmental Psychology, 8,* 341–349.

Campbell, S. B. (1975). Mother–child interactions: A comparison of hyperactive learning disabled, and normal boys. *American Journal of Orthopsychiatry, 48,* 51–57.

Camras, L. A., Ribordy, S., Hill, J., Martino, S., et al. (1990). Maternal facial behavior and the recognition and production of emotional expression by maltreated and nonmaltreated children. *Developmental Psychology, 26,* 304–312.

Cassidy, J. (1988). The self as related to child–mother attachment at six. *Child Development, 59,* 121–134.

Cassidy, J. (1994). Emotion regulation: Influences of attachment relationships. In N. A. Fox (Ed.), The development of emotion regulation: Biological and behavioral considerations. *Monographs of the Society for Research in Child Development, 59*(2–3, Serial No. 240).

Cassidy, J., & Berlin, L. J. (1994). The insecure/ambivalent pattern of attachment: Theory and research. *Child Development, 65,* 971–991.

Cassidy, J., Kirsh, S. J., Scolton, K. L., & Parke, R. D. (1996). Attachment and representations of peer relationships. *Developmental Psychology, 32,* 892–904.

Cicchetti, D. (1990). The organization and coherence of socioemotional, cognitive, and representational development: Illustrations through a developmental psychopathology perspective on Down Syndrome and child maltreatment. In R. Thompson (Ed.), *Nebraska Symposium on Motivation: Vol. 36. Socioemotional development* (pp. 259–366). Lincoln: University of Nebraska Press.

Cicchetti, D. (Ed.). (1996). Regulatory processes [Special issue]. *Development and Psychopathology, Regulatory Processes, 8.*

Cohn, J. F., & Tronick, E. Z. (1983). Three-month-old infants' reaction to simulated maternal depression. *Child Development, 54,* 185–193.

Collins, N. L., & Read, S. J. (1990). Adult attachment, working models, and relationship quality in dating couples. *Journal of Personality and Social Psychology, 58,* 644–663.

Cooper, M. L., Frone, M. R., Russell, M., & Mudar, P. (1995). Drinking to regulate positive and negative emotions: A motivational model of alcohol use. *Journal of Personality and Social Psychology, 69,* 990–1005.

Coren, S., & Russell, J. A. (1992). The relative dominance of different facial expressions of emotion under conditions of perceptual ambiguity. *Cognition and Emotion, 6,* 339–356.

Costa, P. T., Jr., & McCrae, R. R. (1996). Mood and personality in adulthood. In C. Magai & S. McFadden (Eds.), *Handbook of emotion, adult development, and aging* (pp. 369–383). San Diego, CA: Academic Press.

Demos, E. V. (1995). *Exploring affect: The selected writings of Silvan S. Tomkins.* Paris: Cambridge University Press.

Derryberry, D., & Reed, M. A. (1996). Regulatory processes and the development of cognitive representations. *Development and Psychopathology, 8,* 215–234.

Dodge, K. A. (1986). A social information processing model of social competence in children. In M. Perlmutter (Ed.), *Minnesota symposia on child psychology* (Vol. 18, pp. 77–125). Hillsdale, NJ: Erlbaum.

Dodge, K. A., Pettit, G. S., McClaskey, C. L., & Brown, M. M. (1986). Social competence in children. *Monographs of the Society for Research in Child Development, 51*(2, Serial No. 213), 1–80.

Dozier, M., & Kobak, R. R. (1992). Psychophysiology and adolescent attachment interviews: Converging evidence for repressing strategies. *Child Development, 63,* 1473–1480.

Eibl-Eibesfeldt, I. (1989). *Human ethology.* New York: Aldine de Gruyter.

Emde, R. N., Osofsky, J., & Butterfield, P. M. (Eds.). (1993). *The IFEEL pictures.* Madison, CT: International Universities Press.

Fox, N. A. (Ed.). (1994). The development of emotion regulation: Biological and behavioral considerations. *Monographs of the Society for Research in Child Development, 59*(2–3, Serial No. 240).

Garber, J., Braafladt, N., & Zeman, J. (1991). The regulation of sad affect: An information-processing perspective. In J. Garber & K. Dodge (Eds.), *The development of emotion regulation and dysregulation* (pp. 208–242). Cambridge, England: Cambridge University Press.

Gottman, J. M. (1993). Studying emotion in social interaction. In M. Lewis & J. Haviland (Eds.), *Handbook of emotion* (pp. 475–488). New York: Guilford Press.

Haviland, J. M., & Lelwica, M. (1987). The induced affect response: 10-week-old infants' responses to three emotion expressions. *Developmental Psychology, 23,* 97–104.

Hazan, C., & Shaver, P. (1987). Romantic love conceptualized as an attachment process. *Journal of Personality and Social Psychology, 52,* 511–524.

Hooven, C., Gottman, J. M., & Katz, L. F. (1995). Parental meta-emotion structure predicts family and child outcomes. *Cognition and Emotion, 9,* 229–264.

Izard, C. E. (1972). *Patterns of emotions: A new analysis of anxiety and depression.* New York: Academic Press.

Izard, C. E. (1979). *The maximally discriminative facial movement coding system (MAX).* Newark: University of Delaware, Office of Instructional Technology.

Kaplan, N., & Main, M. (1985, April). *Internal representations of attachment at six years as indicated by family drawings and verbal responses to imagined separations.* Paper presented at the biennial meeting of the Society for Research in Child Development, Toronto.

Kaufman, G. (1989). *The psychology of shame: Theory and treatment of shame-based syndromes.* New York: Springer.

Kirkpatrick, L. A., & Davis, K. E. (1994). Attachment style and relationship stability: A longitudinal analysis. *Journal of Personality and Social Psychology, 66,* 502–512.

Levin, G. (1995). *Edward Hopper: An intimate biography.* New York: Knopf.

Lynch, M., & Cicchetti, D. (1991). Patterns of relatedness in maltreated and nonmaltreated children: Connections among multiple representational models. *Development and Psychopathology, 3,* 207–226.

Magai, C. (1996). *Affect, imagery, attachment.* Plenary address presented at the International Society of Research on Emotion, Toronto, Canada.

Magai, C., Cohen, C., Gomberg, D., Malatesta, C., & Culver, C. (1996). Emotion expression in late stage dementia. *International Journal of Psychogeriatrics, 8,* 383–396.

Magai, C., Distel, N., & Liker, R. (1995). Emotion socialization, attachment, and patterns of adult emotional traits. *Cognition and Emotion, 9,* 461–481.

Magai, C., & Hunziker, J. (1998). To Bedlam and part way back: Discrete emotions theory examines borderline symptoms. In W. F. Flack & J. D. Laird (Eds.), *Emotions in psychopathology: Theory and research* (pp. 380–393). New York: Oxford University Press.

Magai, C., Hunziker, J., & Mesias, W., & Culver, C. (in press). Adult attachment styles and emotional biases. *International Journal of Behavioral Development.*

Magai, C., & McFadden, S. (1995). *The role of emotion in social and personality development.* New York: Plenum Press.

Magai, C., & Siegel, H. (1996). *Children's emotion decoding biases and parental emotion socialization.* Unpublished manuscript, Long Island University.

Main, M. (1981). Avoidance in the service of attachment: A working paper. In K. Immelmann, G. W. Barlow, L. Petrinovich, & M. Main (Eds.), *Behavioral development: The Bielefeld Interdisciplinary Project.* Cambridge, England: Cambridge University Press.

Main, M., & Goldwyn, R. (1984). Predicting rejection of her infant from mother's representation of her own experience: Implications for the abused–abusing intergenerational cycle. *Child Abuse and Neglect, 8,* 203–217.

Main, M., Kaplan, N., & Cassidy, J. (1985). Security in infancy, childhood, and adulthood: A move to the level of representation. In I. Bretherton & E. Waters (Eds.), *Growing points of attachment theory and research. Monographs of the Society for Research in Child Development, 50*(1–2, Serial No. 209), 66–106.

Malatesta, C. Z. (1985). The developmental course of emotion expression in the human infant. In G. Zivin (Ed.), *Expressive development: Biological and environmental interactions* (pp. 183–220). New York: Academic Press.

Malatesta, C. Z. (1990). The role of emotion in the development and organization of personality. In R. Thompson (Ed.), *Nebraska Symposium on Motivation: Vol. 36. Socioemotional development* (pp. 1–56). Lincoln: University of Nebraska Press.

Malatesta, C. Z., Culver, C., Tesman, J., & Shepard, B. (1989). The development of emotion expression during the first two years of life. *Monographs of the Society for Research in Child Development, 54*(1–2, Serial No. 219), 1–103.

Malatesta, C. Z., Fiore, M. J., & Messina, J. (1987). Affect, personality, and facial expressive characteristics of older individuals. *Psychology and Aging, 1,* 64–69.

Malatesta, C. Z., & Haviland, J. M. (1982). Learning display rules: The socialization of emotion expression in infancy. *Child Development, 53,* 991–1003.

Malatesta, C. Z., & Lamb, C. (1987, August). *Emotion socialization during the second year.* Paper presented at the annual meeting of the American Psychological Association, New York.

Malatesta, C. Z., & Wilson, A. (1988). Emotion cognition interaction in personality development: A discrete emotions, functionalist analysis. *British Journal of Social Psychology, 27,* 91–112.

Malatesta-Magai, C. Z., & Dorval, B. (1992). Language, affect, and social order. In M. Gunnar & M. Maratsos (Eds.), *Minnesota Symposia on Child Psychology: Vol. 25. Modularity and constraints in language and cognition* (pp. 139–178). Hillsdale, NJ: Erlbaum.

Malatesta-Magai, C. Z., Jones, R., Shepard, B., & Culver, C. L. (1992). Type A behavior pattern and emotion expression in younger and older adults. *Psychology and Aging, 7,* 551–561.

McCown, W., Johnson, J., & Austin, S. (1985, June). *Inability of delinquents to recognize facial affects.* Paper presented at the British Psychological Society's International Conference on the Meaning of Faces, Cardiff, Wales.

Miller, P., & Sperry, L. (1987). The socialization of anger and aggression. *Merrill–Palmer Quarterly, 33*(1), 1–31.

Retzinger, S. M. (1991). *Violent emotions: Shame and rage in marital quarrels.* Newbury Park, CA: Sage.

Scheff, T. J. (1994). *Bloody revenge: Emotions, war, nationalism.* Boulder, CO: Westview Press.

Schiffenbauer, A. (1974). The influence of emotional state on judgments of the emotional state of others. *Journal of Personality and Social Psychology, 30,* 31–35.

Senchak, M., & Leonard, K. (1992). Attachment styles and marital adjustment among newlywed couples. *Journal of Social and Personal Relationships, 9,* 51–64.

Schore, A. N. (1996). The experience-dependent maturation of a regulatory system in the orbital prefrontal cortex and the origin of developmental psychopathology. *Development and Psychopathology, 8,* 59–88.

Sperling, M. B., & Berman, W. H. (Eds.). (1994). *Attachment in adults.* New York: Guilford Press.

Tellegen, A. (1985). Structures of mood and personality and their relevance to assessing anxiety, with an emphasis on self-report. In A. H. Tuma & J. Mason (Eds.), *Anxiety and the anxiety disorders* (pp. 681–707). Hillsdale, NJ: Erlbaum.

Thompson, R. A. (1994). Emotion regulation: A theme in search of a definition. In N. A. Fox (Ed.). *The development of emotion regulation: Biological and behavioral considerations. Monographs of the Society for Research in Child Development, 59*(2–3, Serial No. 240), 25–52.

Tomkins, S. S. (1962). *Affect, imagery, consciousness: Vol. 1. The positive affects.* New York: Springer

Tomkins, S. S. (1963). *Affect, imagery, consciousness: Vol. 2. The negative affects.* New York: Springer.

Tomkins, S. S. (1975). The phantasy behind the face. *Journal of Personality Assessment, 39,* 551–560.

Tomkins, S. S. (1990). *Reverse archeology of the emotions.* Plenary address, International Society for Research on the Emotions, New Brunswick, NJ.

Tomkins, S. S. (1991). *Affect, imagery, consciousness: Vol 3. Anger and fear.* New York: Springer.

Tomkins, S. S. (1993). *Affect, imagery, consciousness: Vol 4. Cognition. Duplication and transformation of information.* New York: Springer.

Tomkins, S. S., & McCarter, R. (1964). What and where are the primary affects?: Some evidence for a theory. *Perceptual and Motor Skills, 18,* 119–158.

Watson, D., & Clark, L. A. (1992). On traits and temperament: General and specific factors of emotional experience and their relation to the five factor model. *Journal of Personality, 60,* 441–476.

Zahn-Waxler, C., & Wagner, E. (1993). Caregivers' interpretations of infant emotions: A comparison of depressed and well mothers. In R. N. Emde, J. D. Osofsky, & P. M. Butterfield (Eds.), *The IFEEL pictures* (pp. 83–97). Madison, CT: International Universities Press.

Zeanah, C. H., Benoit, D., Barton, M., Regan, C., Hirshberg, L. M., & Lipsitt, L. (1993). Representations of attachment in mothers and their one-year old infants. *Journal of the American Academy of Child and Adolescent Psychiatry, 32,* 278–286.

35

Attachment and Religious Representations and Behavior

❖

LEE A. KIRKPATRICK

> Probably in all normal people [attachment] continues in one form or another throughout
> life and, although in many ways transformed, underlies many of our attachments to
> country, sovereign, or church.
>
> —Bowlby (1956, p. 588)

Although Bowlby's theorizing about attachment focused largely on the evolutionary origins of the attachment system and its manifestation in infant–mother relationships, he clearly believed from the beginning that the processes and dynamics of attachment have broad implications for social development and psychological functioning across the lifespan. Early forays into attachment in adulthood were led by Parkes (1972) and Weiss (1973) in their applications of attachment theory to bereavement and loneliness, respectively. Seminal papers by Hazan and Shaver (1987; Shaver, Hazan, & Bradshaw, 1988) led the way to a now-burgeoning literature on the role of attachment in adult romantic relationships (see Feeney, Chapter 17, this volume, for a review). Contemporaneously, work by Main and others (e.g., Main, Kaplan, & Cassidy, 1985) has spawned a parallel literature concerning mental representations of attachment in adulthood as they relate to parenting and to the intergenerational transmission of attachment patterns (see Hesse, Chapter 19, this volume, for a review). Researchers have also begun to explore applications of the theory to other domains of adult life, including work and career (Hazan & Shaver, 1990), fear of death (Mikulincer, Florian, & Tomacz, 1990), and coping with stressful events (Carpenter & Kirkpatrick, 1996; Simp-son, Rholes, & Nelligan, 1992) and life-threatening events (Mikulincer, Florian, & Weller, 1993). The purpose of the present chapter is to demonstrate that many aspects of religious belief and behavior can be meaningfully and usefully interpreted in terms of attachment dynamics as well.

Serious students of attachment theory are well aware of the potential dangers inherent in extending the theory beyond its valid limits. Bowlby's choice of the term "attachment" was in one sense unfortunate, because of the word's much broader meaning in everyday language: People speak colloquially of feeling "attached" to many objects and persons in their lives, from important possessions (cars, homes, a favorite pen) to social groups to sports teams to the Grateful Dead. Whether such phenomena—including patriotism, as suggested in the Bowlby quotation above—can be understood properly in terms of attachment as defined by Bowlby remains an open question, and one that should be approached with considerable skepticism. (Even the widely accepted extension of the theory to adult pair-bond relationships may be problematic and open to alternative interpretations; see Kirkpatrick, 1998a.)

Nevertheless, I wish to argue that many aspects of religious belief and behavior represent real manifestations of attachment processes in very much the same way as do infant–caregiver relationships. In fact, application of the attachment model to religious belief is in many ways more straightforward than is its application to adult romantic relationships. The latter is complicated by a number of factors, including the reciprocal nature of adult relationships with peers and the role of sexuality in romantic relationships (Weiss, 1982). Neither of these limitations is typically evident in adults' perceptions of their relationships with God, Jesus, or other supernatural figures. In some important ways, religious belief may provide a unique window into attachment processes in adulthood.

This chapter is divided into four major sections. The first section introduces the idea that God and other deities are often perceived by many as attachment figures. In the second section I argue that this observation provides more than an interesting analogy: Perceived relationships with God meet all of the defining criteria of attachment relationships and function psychologically as true attachments. The third major section examines the empirical connections between religion and individual differences in interpersonal attachments. This section is subdivided into two subsections, the first focusing on the correspondence of mental models across interpersonal and religious domains, and the second examining more dynamic processes of religious change and development across time. Finally, the fourth major section addresses some research findings and implications of the religion-as-attachment model with respect to psychological outcomes.

GOD AS AN ATTACHMENT FIGURE

Religion as Relationship

The obvious point of departure for the application of attachment theory to religion is the observation that central to monotheistic religions, particularly Christianity, is the belief in a personal God with whom believers maintain a personal, interactive relationship. When asked, "Which of the following four statements comes closest to your own view of 'faith': a set of beliefs, membership in a church or synagogue, finding meaning in life, or a relationship with God?," 51% of a national Gallup sample chose "a relationship with God" (compared to 19%, 4%, and 20% for the other alternatives, respectively). More than half of these respondents rated "growing into a

deeper relationship with God" as at least very important to them (Gallup & Jones, 1989). In a study of clergy, the most common response to the question "How does faith help you in daily life?" was "access to a loving God who is willing to help in everyday life" (Hughes, 1989). My own research has consistently revealed that two-thirds or more of both newspaper survey respondents and college students respond affirmatively to the question "Do you feel you have a personal relationship with Jesus Christ and/or God?" (e.g., Kirkpatrick & Shaver, 1992). Other scholars have also noted this relationship focus of religiosity. Stark (1965, p. 99), for example, described religious experience as a form of dyadic interaction involving "the divinity and the individual as a pair of actors involved in a social encounter." According to Greeley (1981, p. 18), "just as the story of anyone's life is the story of relationships—so each person's religious story is a story of relationships."

It is important to note that other supernatural figures may fill this role in addition to or instead of "God." In many Christian traditions, it is Jesus with whom one maintains an active day-to-day relationship, while God remains a more distant background figure. In Catholicism, Mary typically represents the "maternal functions" related to attachment (Wenegrat, 1989). Outside of Christianity, the worlds of believers are populated by a variety of gods and other deities, many of whom may function as attachment-like figures. Even in countries dominated by Eastern religions such as Hinduism and Buddhism—which Westerners tend to think of as abstract, godless philosophies—believers often focus on the more theistic components of the belief system and on personal gods imported from ancient folk religions (see Kirkpatrick, 1994, for a discussion). Throughout this chapter I refer to "God" as an attachment figure, but it should be understood that in many cases another supernatural figure may instead fill this role.

Religion and Love

A second point of departure for discussing an attachment–religion connection is the centrality of the emotion of love in religious belief systems, and especially in people's perceived relationships with God. Bumper stickers proudly announce, "I [picture of a heart] Jesus," or, conversely, "Jesus loves me," or more broadly, "God is love." The powerful emotional experiences associated with religion are often expressed "in the language of human love," particularly in the writing of mystics (Thouless, 1923, p. 132).

The process of religious conversion has been likened frequently, by both scholars and religious writers, to falling in love (James, 1902; Pratt, 1920; Thouless, 1923). On the basis of her in-depth interviews with religious converts, Ullman (1989, p. xvi) wrote:

> What I initially considered primarily a change of ideology turned out to be more akin to a falling in love. . . . [C]onversion pivots around a sudden attachment, an infatuation with a real or imagined figure which occurs on a background of great emotional turmoil. The typical convert was transformed not by a religion, but by a person. The discovery of a new truth was indistinguishable from a discovery of a new relationship, which relieved, temporarily, the upheaval of the previous life. This intense and omnipresent attachment discovered in the religious experience promised the convert everlasting guidance and love, for the object of the convert's infatuation was perceived as infallible.

(It is worth noting here that despite her use of the term "attachment," Ullman never cited Bowlby or attachment theory in her struggle to find a theoretical perspective to explain her observations!)

The "love" experienced by a worshipper in the context of a relationship with God is of course qualitatively different from that experienced in adult romantic relationships. Greeley (1990, p. 249) observes that "The usual reaction . . . to a comparison of human love with divine love is to insist that it is utterly different from sexual attraction ('not at all physical,' my students tell me)." The potential confusion here is that adult romantic relationships include (and are largely defined by) an explicitly sexual component that is missing from perceived relationships with God. (See Hazan & Zeifman, 1994, for a discussion of the relations between attachment and sexuality in adulthood.) In fact, the form of "love" experienced in the context of a relationship with God resembles much more closely the prototypical attachment of a child to his or her mother. In Greeley's (1990, p. 252) words, "The Mary Myth's powerful appeal is to be found . . . in the marvelous possibility that God loves us the way a mother loves her baby."

Images of God

The idea that God is experienced psychologically as a kind of parental figure is, of course, hardly new. Perhaps the most familiar version of this idea is Freud's (e.g., 1927/1961) characterization of God as an exalted father figure. Wenegrat (1989), however, observed that the deities of the oldest known religions were largely maternal figures, and that modern Protestantism is unusual in its lack of significant female deities. Freud himself puzzled over this fact, confessing that "I am at a loss to indicate the place of the great maternal deities who perhaps everywhere preceded the paternal deities" (quoted in Argyle & Beit-Hallahmi, 1975, p. 187).

Whether images of God more closely resemble maternal or paternal images has been a topic of much research in the psychology of religion, with decidedly mixed results. Some studies suggest that God images are more closely related to maternal than to paternal images (Godin & Hallez, 1964; Nelson, 1971; Strunk, 1959), whereas other studies suggest that God is perceived as more similar to one's preferred parent (Nelson & Jones, 1957). The most sensible conclusion from this and other research, however, seems to be that images of God combine elements of both stereotypically maternal and stereotypically paternal qualities (Vergote & Tamayo, 1981): God is neither an exalted father figure nor an exalted mother figure, but rather an exalted attachment figure.

Apart from the misleading maternal–paternal distinction, there is considerable evidence to support the notion that believers view God as a kind of exalted attachment figure. One line of suggestive evidence comes from examination of religious writing and song. Wenegrat (1989) noted the striking degree of attachment imagery in the Psalms. Similarly, Young (1926) showed that a dominant theme of Protestant hymns is the "infantile return to a powerful and loving protector who shields humankind from all harm" (as summarized by Wulff, 1991, p. 304). In a word, God seems clearly to capture the very essence of the "stronger, wiser other" that a parent represents to a child. As summarized by Kaufman (1981, p. 67), a theologian familiar with attachment theory,

> The idea of God is the idea of an absolutely adequate attachment-figure. . . . We need not debate here whether mother-imagery or father-imagery would be more to the purpose: the point is that God is thought of as a protective and caring parent who is always reliable and always available to its children when they are in need.

Factor-analytic studies of God images consistently find a large first factor laden with attachment-related descriptors. For example, Gorsuch's (1968) first major factor (labeled "benevolent deity") included such descriptors as "comforting," "loving," and "protective" and the reverse of "distant," "impersonal," and "inaccessible"; Spilka, Armatas, and Nussbaum (1964) found a large general factor that included the items "comforting," "supporting," "protective," "strong," and "helpful"; and Tamayo and Desjardins (1976) found a first factor (labeled "availability") containing such items as "who gives comfort," "a warm-hearted refuge," "always ready with open arms," "who will take loving care of me," and "who is always waiting for me." In a study of U.S. Congress members, two of the three major clusters of items (as determined by cluster analysis) discussed by the authors were "attentive-parent God" and "companion God" (Benson & Williams, 1982). In a factor analysis of diverse religious attitude and belief statements, the largest factor to emerge was labeled "nearness to God": "Persons with high loadings on this factor would tend to feel that God was very real and constantly near and accessible. These persons feel they commune with God—'walk and talk' with Him" (Broen, 1957, p. 177).

Similar results have been found in research with children. For example, common themes observed by Heller (1986) in his extensive study of children's images of God included "God, the therapist" ("an all-nurturant, loving figure"), "intimacy" (feelings of closeness to God), and "omnipresence" (God is "always there"). Interestingly, two other common themes observed by Heller seem to parallel insecure attachment patterns: "inconsistent God" and "God, the distant thing in the sky."

RELIGION AS A DYNAMIC ATTACHMENT PROCESS

The preceding section has suggested several parallels between religious belief and attachment relationships. Specifically, (1) perceived relationships with God are central to the religious belief of many people; (2) the emotional bond experienced in this relationship is a form of love akin to the infant–mother relationship; and (3) beliefs about God tend to parallel the characteristics of secure attachment figures. In this section I wish to argue, using Ainsworth's (1985) criteria for distinguishing attachments from other types of relationships, that these resemblances are more

than interesting analogies and in fact reflect genuine attachment processes.

Seeking and Maintaining Proximity to God

The biological function of the attachment behavioral system, as described by Bowlby (1969/ 1982), is the maintenance of proximity between an infant and a protective attachment figure. To achieve the objective of establishing physical proximity, infants engage in a variety of behaviors such as crying, raising arms (to be picked up), and clinging. With increasing cognitive abilities, older children are often satisfied by visual or verbal contact, or eventually by mere knowledge of an attachment figure's whereabouts (Bretherton, 1987). This latter observation opens the door to the possibility of a noncorporeal attachment figure with whom actual physical contact is impossible.

Religious beliefs provide a variety of ways of enhancing perceptions about the proximity of God. A crucial tenet of most theistic religions is that God is omnipresent; thus one is always in "proximity" to God. God is frequently described in religious literature as always being by one's side, holding one's hand, or watching over one. Nevertheless, other, more concrete cues may be valuable in enhancing perceptions of proximity to God. For example, despite the presumption of God's omnipresence, virtually all religions provide places of worship where one can go to be closer to God. In addition, a diverse array of idols and symbols—ranging from graven images to crosses on necklaces to paintings and other art forms—seem designed to continually remind the believer of God's presence.

The most important form of proximity-maintaining attachment behavior directed toward God, however, is prayer (Reed, 1978). Heiler (1932, p. 356) concluded from his classic study of prayer that a devout person who prays "believes that he speaks with a God, immediately present and personal," and that "The man who prays feels himself very close to this personal God." Among the major forms of prayer reviewed in the comprehensive psychology-of-religion text by Hood, Spilka, Hunsberger, and Gorsuch (1996, pp. 394 ff.), two seem clearly related to proximity maintenance: "contemplative" prayer ("an attempt to relate deeply to one's God") and "meditational" prayer ("concern with one's relationship to God"). In many ways prayer seems analogous to "social referencing" in young children—an intermittent checking back to make sure the attachment figure is still attentive and potentially available (Campos & Stenberg, 1981).

Finally, other religious behaviors provide interesting analogies to the proximal attachment behaviors of infants, in much the same way that the behavior of adult lovers (cuddling, kissing, talking baby talk, etc.) seems to reveal vestiges of infant–mother interactions (Shaver et al., 1988). For example, the uplifted arms and glossolalia ("speaking in tongues") commonly observed at Pentecostal services bear a striking resemblance to the image of an infant waiting to be picked up by his or her mother.

God as a Haven of Safety

A second defining criterion of attachment concerns the provision of a haven of safety, in keeping with the presumed evolutionary function of providing protection to otherwise defenseless infants. Bowlby (1969/1982) discussed three kinds of situations that activate the attachment system and thus elicit attachment behaviors: (1) frightening or alarming environmental events; (2) illness, injury, or fatigue; and (3) separation or threat of separation from attachment figures.

As Freud (1927/1961) and many others have long speculated, religion does appear to be rooted at least partly in needs for protection and felt security. There are no atheists in foxholes, as the adage goes. Hood et al. (1996, pp. 386–387) conclude that people are most likely to "turn to their gods in times of trouble and crisis," listing three general classes of potential triggers: "illness, disability, and other negative life events that cause both mental and physical distress; the anticipated or actual death of friends and relatives; and dealing with an adverse life situation." This list bears a striking resemblance to Bowlby's (1969/1982) discussion of factors postulated specifically to activate the attachment system.

There is considerable evidence to support the view that people turn to religion particularly in times of distress and crisis, and it is important to note that they turn at such times to *prayer*— which I suggest is a form of religious attachment behavior—rather than to *church* (Argyle & Beit-Hallahmi, 1975). With respect to environmental stressors, empirical research suggests that there are indeed few atheists in foxholes: Combat soldiers do pray frequently (Stouffer, 1949). Ross (1950) queried over 1,700 religious youth about why they prayed; the two reasons most frequently cited were "God listens to and answers your prayers" and "It helps you in time of stress and crisis." Pargament (1990) has outlined a variety of religious coping strategies employed in stressful situations, including such attachment-like responses as "experienced God's love and care," "realized God was trying to strengthen me," "let God solve my problems for me," and "took control over what I could and gave up the rest to God."

Several studies show prayer to be an especially common coping method for dealing with serious physical illnesses of various types (Duke, 1977; Gibbs & Achterberg-Lawlis, 1978; O'Brien, 1982). O'Brien (1982) observed in his interviews with renal-failure patients that many of them saw God as providing comfort, nurturance, and a source of personal strength for getting through this difficult time. In reference to a series of cardiac arrests, one interviewee was quoted as saying, "Each time I knew everything would be all right because I asked God to carry me through— I know that He's got His arms around me" (p. 76).

Finally, research suggests that religiousness and prayer tend to increase following the death of loved ones, and that religious beliefs are correlated positively with successful coping at these times (Haun, 1977; Loveland, 1968; Parkes, 1972). I suggest that these effects are due to two factors: (1) Loss of a loved one activates the attachment system, and thus gives rise to religious attachment behaviors such as prayer; and (2) bereaved persons may find in God a substitute or surrogate attachment figure to replace the lost interpersonal attachment.

God as a Secure Base

Another defining characteristic of an attachment is that it provides a sense of felt security and a secure base for exploration of the environment. As noted previously, religious literature is replete with references to God's being "by my side" and "watching over me." Perhaps the best-known example is from the 23rd Psalm: "Yea, though I walk through the valley of the shadow of death, I will fear no evil: for thou art with me; thy rod and thy staff, they comfort me." Elsewhere in the Psalms, God is described or addressed as "a shield for me" (3:3), "my rock, and my fortress," (18:2), and "the strength of my life" (27:1).[1]

It is easy to imagine how an attachment figure who is simultaneously omnipresent, omniscient, and omnipotent can provide the most secure of secure bases. This is precisely what led Kaufman (1981) to his previously quoted conclusion that God represents an "absolutely adequate attachment-figure." It also led Johnson (1945, p. 191), a psychologist of religion, to write:

> The emotional quality of faith is indicated in a basic confidence and security that gives one assurance. In this sense faith is the opposite of fear, anxiety, and uncertainty. Without emotional security there is no relaxation, but tension, distress, and instability. Assurance is the firm emotional undertone that enables one to have steady nerves and calm poise in the face of danger or confusion.

This description of faith bears an almost uncanny resemblance to Bowlby's (1969/1982, 1973) own descriptions of the secure base and its psychological effects.

In their zeal to study the effects of religious beliefs on behavior and cognition in the presence of stressful events, researchers unfortunately have paid far less attention to the question of how religious beliefs affect behavior and cognition in the absence of such stressors. In other words, there exists considerably less direct evidence for a secure-base function of religious beliefs than for a safe-haven function. Nevertheless, several indirect lines of research bear on the issue. Several studies show that intrinsic religiousness is positively correlated with a sense of personal competence and control (Ventis, 1995) and is associated with an active, flexible approach to problem solving (Pargament, Steele, & Tyler, 1979). Moreover, religious faith engenders a sense of optimism and hope with respect to both the long-term and the short-term future (Myers, 1992). These and similar findings suggest that at least some forms of religious beliefs foster the kind of confident, self-assured approach to life that a secure base is thought to provide.

Responses to Separation and Loss

I have noted in a previous section that religious belief and prayer increase in response to bereavement, and I have interpreted this in terms of the safe-haven function of religious attachment. However, the fourth and fifth defining criteria given by Ainsworth (1985) concern responses to separation from, or loss of, the attachment figure per se: The threat of separation causes anxiety in the attached person, and loss of the attachment figure causes grief.

Determining whether God meets these criteria is a difficult matter, because one does not become separated from, or lose a relationship with, God as one might lose a human relationship partner. God does not die, sail off to fight wars, move away, or file for divorce. The potential for true separation from God is usually seen by believers to come only in the hereafter, at which time one spends eternity either with God or separated from God. It is noteworthy, however, that in most Christian belief systems, separation from God is the very essence of hell.

The most obvious approximation to separation from or loss of God is deconversion or apostasy—that is, abandoning one's religious beliefs. It is not clear whether "losing" a relationship with God in this way can be expected to engender grief, however, as it is the believer rather than God who is deliberately choosing to abandon the relationship. Nevertheless, Wright (1987) has described this process as psychologically analogous to divorce or the dissolution of other close interpersonal relationships. Wright maintains that defectors from cults commonly experience psychological symptoms, including "separation anxiety," similar to those associated with marital separation and divorce. Perhaps a closer analogue to involuntary loss is excommunication. I am unaware of any empirical research on psychological responses to being excommunicated involuntarily from a religious institution, but the degree to which such experiences engender grief would be an intriguing topic for future research.

INDIVIDUAL DIFFERENCES IN INTERPERSONAL ATTACHMENT AND RELIGION

An important feature of attachment theory is its virtually seamless integration of a dynamic normative model featuring a control system dynamic, on the one hand, and a model of individual differences in the functioning of that system on the other. To be complete, a theory of religion as attachment must do the same. In the preceding section I have sketched the outline of a normative model within which many aspects of religious belief and behavior, and particular perceived relationships with God, function psychologically as attachment processes. In this section I turn to the topic of individual differences, which, as it turns out, leads in two different directions—both of which are supported by data from several studies.

Correspondence of Mental Models of Attachment and Religion

According to Bowlby's model, continuity of attachment patterns across time and transmission of attachment patterns across generations are traced to "internal working models" or "mental models" (Bowlby, 1973; see also Bretherton, 1985; Collins & Read, 1994; Main et al., 1985). As a consequence of repeated experience in interaction with their attachment figures, children develop beliefs and expectations about the availability and responsiveness of caregivers, and these guide future behavioral, emotional, and cognitive responses in social interactions. Moreover, these models are linked to mental models of the self—beliefs about the degree to which one sees himself or herself as worthy of love, care, and protection.

Although the level at which such mental models operate is a matter of some debate, it seems likely that people maintain in part both (1) mental models concerning attachment figures in general, and (2) mental models specific to particular relationships. Collins and Read (1994) suggest that such models are hierarchically arranged, with a top level characterized by a highly general model of self and others, a second level comprising models of parent–child relationships versus peer relationships, and so on. I suggest that for many individuals, mental models of God (or perceived relationships with God) hold an important place somewhere in this hierarchy. For example, it may be postulated that "religious relationships" comprise a third category at the second level of the Collins–Read hierarchy, next to "parent–child relationships" and "peer relationships"; under this general model may be found more specific mental models of God, Jesus, Mary, or other supernatural beings.

Whether or not various levels of attachment-relevant mental representations are arranged in this precise hierarchical structure, it seems certain that mental models of various levels of generality are interconnected to at least some degree. For example, Fox, Kimmerly, and Schafer's (1991) meta-analysis of 11 studies demonstrated a moderate correspondence between infants' styles of attachment to their mothers and to their fathers, which seems consistent with Collins and Read's (1994) hierarchical framework. That is, there is greater correspondence than would be expected if relationship-specific mental models were independent, but less than would be expected from a single, global mental model alone.

(Fox et al. interpreted their data as more consistent with the idea of generalized models than of relationship-specific models; however, their kappa coefficients fall within a moderate range consistent with a hierarchical perspective such as Collins and Read's.)

Consideration of the interrelatedness of mental models of attachment leads to a straightforward set of predictions, which I refer to as a "correspondence hypothesis": Individual differences in religious beliefs and experience should parallel individual differences in attachment styles and mental models. Individuals who possess positive or "secure" generalized mental models of self and of attachment figures may be expected to view God and other deities in similar terms. Likewise, an "avoidant" orientation toward close relationships may be expected to manifest itself in the religious realm as agnosticism or atheism, or in a view of God as remote and inaccessible. Finally, an "ambivalent" orientation may find expression in a deeply emotional, all-consuming, and "clingy" relationship to God.

Adult Attachment Style and Religious Beliefs

These predictions have now been confirmed in several studies. In a study of respondents to a survey published in a metropolitan newspaper, over 200 of whom subsequently completed a more detailed follow-up survey on religious beliefs, a colleague and I (Kirkpatrick & Shaver, 1992) cross-sectionally correlated various religion measures with the Hazan and Shaver (1987) self-report measure of adult romantic attachment style. Respondents who classified themselves as secure scored significantly higher than avoidant respondents on a variety of religion measures, including several measures of images of God (a loving God, a distant God, a controlling God) and general religious commitment; avoidant respondents were also the most likely to describe themselves as agnostic. Results for the ambivalent group, however, varied considerably across measures: These respondents resembled avoidant respondents on some variables (the image of a loving God, commitment), fell between avoidant and secure respondents on other variables (the images of a distant God and a controlling God), and resembled secure respondents on still other variables (belief in a personal God, reporting a personal relationship with God—though these last findings were not statistically significant). This complex pattern is discussed further in the next section. Interestingly, ambivalent respondents stood apart from the other two groups on one variable: They were by far the most likely to report ever having had an experience of glossolalia (speaking in tongues).

We (Kirkpatrick & Shaver, 1992) also created a measure of attachment to God on which respondents classified their relationship with God as secure (God as available and responsive), avoidant (God as distant and inaccessible), or ambivalent (God as inconsistently available and reliable). After this variable and adult attachment style were collapsed into secure–insecure dichotomies (due to small n's), secure lovers were significantly more likely to report a secure attachment to God than were insecure lovers (76.5% vs. 59.3%), although this relationship was moderated by (retrospective self-reports of) security of attachment to one's mother during childhood.

Several of these results have been replicated in two unpublished data sets collected at the University of South Carolina.[2] In a newspaper survey sample of over 400 adults, respondents reporting a secure romantic attachment style (using the Hazan–Shaver forced-choice measure) again scored higher than the two insecure groups on general religious commitment. Secure respondents (36%) were also more likely than either avoidant (22%) or ambivalent (20%) respondents to identify themselves as "evangelical Christians"—a Christian orientation that places particular emphasis on one's relationships with God and Jesus. Avoidant respondents, on the other hand, were significantly more likely than the other groups to classify themselves as atheist or agnostic. In a related study of over 100 Christian undergraduates, romantically secure respondents again scored lowest on the image of a distant God, and avoidant respondents (64%) were much less likely than secure (90%) or ambivalent (91%) respondents to report having a personal relationship with God.

Strahan (1991) has also replicated some of these findings in a sample of students at a church-affiliated college in Australia. Avoidant respondents scored significantly lower than secure or ambivalent respondents on the single-item measure "I know for sure that God cares for me" and on intrinsic religious orientation, although the latter finding held only for males. In a second sample from the same population, ambivalent respondents scored significantly lower on the image of a punitive God (although again the pattern was stronger among males). Other predicted (but nonsignificant) trends included

avoidant respondents' scoring highest on the image of a rejecting God, and secure respondents' scoring highest on the image of an available God but lowest on that of a remote God.

Models of Self versus Models of Others

Bartholomew (1990) has argued for the existence of four rather than three adult attachment styles, by distinguishing between two distinct patterns of avoidance. These four styles in Bartholomew's model result from a 2 × 2 matrix crossing positive versus negative models of self with positive versus negative models of others. "Secure" romantic attachment reflects positive models of self and others; "fearful/avoidant" attachment reflects negative models of self and others; the "preoccupied" (ambivalent) style reflects a positive model of others combined with a negative model of self; and "dismissing/avoidant" attachment reflects a negative model of others combined with a positive model of self. According to Bartholomew (1990), the avoidant style captured by the Hazan–Shaver trichotomous measure is primarily the fearful/avoidant type. This framework offers the potential for a more fine-grained analysis of the empirical relations between adult attachment and religious belief.

Using a measure (from Bartholomew & Horowitz, 1991) of this four-category classification system in a longitudinal study, I conducted cross-sectional analyses of Time 1 data from over 1,300 undergraduate students (Kirkpatrick, 1998b). Positive mental models of both self and others predicted, independently and additively, higher scores on an aggregate religiousness measure. Analysis of the religion variables separately, however, revealed differential patterns that suggest some additional insights. Specifically, models of self were most strongly related to the loving and distant images of God, whereas models of others were most strongly related to belief in a personal (vs. impersonal or nonexistent) God and belief in having a personal relationship with God (as well as a distant, but not a loving, image of God). These results replicate the previously discussed findings (Kirkpatrick & Shaver, 1992) in remarkable detail. For example, in the Kirkpatrick and Shaver (1992) study, secure respondents outscored both ambivalent (i.e., preoccupied) and avoidant (i.e., fearful/avoidant) respondents on Loving God images, paralleling precisely the main effect for model of self (but not model of others) found in the Kirkpatrick (1998b) study. Results for the other three religion variables correspond similarly across the two studies when the Bartholomew 2 × 2 framework (used in Kirkpatrick, 1998) is mapped onto the Hazan–Shaver attachment style categories (used in Kirkpatrick & Shaver, 1992).

Although these differentiated findings warrant further replication, the pattern is intriguing. Beliefs about what God is like (e.g., loving and caring vs. controlling and wrathful) appear to correlate with mental models of the self, suggesting that people who see themselves as worthy of being loved and cared for are likely to view God as loving and caring. On the other hand, beliefs about whether God is "someone" with whom one has, or possibly could have, a personal relationship are related instead to one's model of others—that is, the degree to which attachment figures are perceived to be trustworthy and reliable relationship partners, and the degree to which close relationships are highly valued and desired. I return to this distinction in a subsequent section concerning the longitudinal results from this study.

Attachment and Religion in Childhood

The research reviewed above suggests a correspondence between religious beliefs and attachment relationships in college students and other adults. The attachment model of religion presented here suggests that similar parallels should be found in children as well; in this case, beliefs about God should be related specifically to attachment to parents rather than to peers. Unfortunately, although there has been considerable research concerning the development of religious belief in children, particularly with respect to beliefs about God (e.g., Elkind, 1971; Harms, 1944; Heller, 1986), this research has focused on stage-like developmental models rather than individual differences. One exception is research by Potvin (1977), who showed in a large, national probability sample of adolescents aged 13–18 that perceived parental affection and parental control were related significantly to images of a loving God and a punishing God, respectively.

Another important exception is an unpublished doctoral dissertation by Jubis (1991), who examined several religion measures in relation to images of parents and other family variables in a sample of 74 fourth-graders at a Catholic school. Self-reported prayer in response to both "feeling scared, worried, lonely, or sad" and "when really bad things happen to you (like an accident)" were inversely correlated with a measure (derived from a life events checklist) concerning losses of/separations from attachment figures. That is, children whose parental attachments had been disrupted by losses and/or separations (e.g., divorce, death) were less likely to turn to God as an attachment figure, perhaps paralleling the previously reported finding that avoidant adults are generally less religious, and more likely to be atheists or agnostics, than secure adults. In addition, several measures of images of God—particularly a factor-analytically derived dimension labeled "considerate attentiveness" (e.g., "listens to me," "pays a lot of attention to me")—correlated positively with several dimensions of paternal and (especially) maternal images, including factors labeled "supportive reassurance," "affectionate support," and "tolerant helpfulness." These results appear to replicate the findings from adult samples regarding security of attachment and images of God.

Cross-Cultural Analysis of Parenting and Religious Belief

Additional support for the correspondence between mental models of religion and of interpersonal attachments comes from cross-cultural research on parenting styles and religious beliefs. Studies by Rohner (1975) and Lambert, Triandis, and Wolf (1959) have shown that cultures in which "accepting" (e.g., loving, nurturing) parenting styles are predominant tend to have religious belief systems characterized by benevolent deities, whereas cultures in which "rejecting" parenting styles predominate tend to believe in more malevolent deities.

Although this pattern is consistent with the individual-difference findings reported above, it is a difficult question as to whether such cross-cultural correlations reflect the same processes as do individual-difference correlations within cultures. However, other results reported by Rohner (1975) suggest that they do. For example, in societies characterized by "rejecting" parenting styles, adults and children tend to be less emotionally responsive, less emotionally stable, and less able to become involved in affectionate relationships, as well as to show more aggressive and hostile behavior. As summarized by Bretherton (1985, p. 26), these "correlates of acceptance or rejection among societies read uncannily like the sequelae of secure and insecure attachment." Taken with the appropriate grain of salt, then, these cross-cultural analyses seem to provide additional support for the idea that mental models of human attachments parallel beliefs about God and other deities. Moreover, they suggest that this model may generalize well beyond the kinds of Western Christian samples studied to date.

God as a Substitute Attachment Figure

The preceding section suggests one way in which religious beliefs appear to reflect attachment processes: Mental models of God and one's perceived relationship with God appear to parallel, at a given point in time, one's mental models of self and attachment relationships. However, consideration of the dynamics of the attachment model suggest a second and more intriguing application to religion. In this section I argue that individuals may turn to God or other supernatural beings as *substitute* or *surrogate* attachment figures. Moreover, empirical research findings concerning who does so and under what conditions are readily interpretable in terms of attachment theory.

According to Bowlby's control system model of attachment, the attachment system continually monitors internal states and external circumstances in light of the question "Is the attachment figure sufficiently near, attentive, responsive, approving, etc.?" (Hazan & Shaver, 1994, p. 3). The set point of the system is variable, depending on expectancies (mental models) concerning the attachment figure and perceived cues of environmental dangers. A negative answer to the question, according to the theory, activates a suite of potential attachment behaviors designed to restore adequate levels of proximity.

Under certain conditions, however, the individual may anticipate (based on prior experience and/or current circumstances) that efforts to achieve adequate proximity and comfort from the primary attachment figure are unlikely to be successful. It is in these cases that a search for an alternative and more adequate attachment figure seems likely to be initiated, and consequently that individuals are likely to turn to God as a substitute attachment figure. Below I suggest three kinds of such circumstances.

Severe Stress and Crisis

First, the magnitude of the stressor or the perceived degree of danger of a given situation may simply exceed the actual or perceived capabilities of a person's primary attachment figure. Although young children tend to view their parents as omnipotent, adults typically know better when it comes to their attachment relationships. Even the most securely attached individuals realize that their parents and romantic partners (or other attachment figures) are fallible and limited with respect to where they can be and what they can accomplish. An omnipotent and omnipresent deity, however, transcends these human limitations.

Adults sometimes confront adult-sized dangers and stressors for which peers are simply inadequate; no degree of proximity is sufficient to restore felt security. A clear example of such a situation is warfare. As noted in a previous section, soldiers in combat do appear to turn to God through prayer as a haven of safety. From his interviews with combat veterans, Allport (1950, p. 57) concluded: "The individual in distress craves affection and security. Sometimes a human bond will suffice, more often it will not." Of course, soldiers develop powerful attachments to their comrades under combat conditions, and attachments to individuals back home may continue to provide a source of strength, perhaps mitigating the likelihood of turning to God for strength and protection on the battlefield. As one combat veteran reported to Allport (1950, p. 56), "There were atheists in foxholes, but most of them were in love." Nevertheless, only an all-powerful deity can offer a truly safe haven once the bullets start flying.

Although warfare provides a clear (and extreme) example, other kinds of severe stressors can lead to emotional crises in which attachment figures may be perceived as inadequate. A century of research supports the claim that sudden religious conversions are most likely during times of severe emotional distress and crisis (Clark, 1929; Deutsch, 1975; Galanter, 1979; Starbuck, 1899; Ullman, 1982). According to Strickland (1924), the turning point of the conversion process involves the surrendering of oneself to God, and the placing of one's problems—and one's faith—in God's hands.

Although turning to God as a substitute attachment figure is clearly exemplified by religious conversion, another intriguing (but more speculative) example of attachment to God is the phenomenon of glossolalia. Shaver et al. (1988) noted that many behaviors exhibited by adult lovers seem to parallel closely the behaviors characteristic of infant–mother attachments, such as kissing, nuzzling, and talking "baby talk." Glossolalia similarly has been likened to infant babbling (Oates, 1967). In a study by Kildahl (1972, p. 57), "more than 85 percent of tongue-speakers had experienced a clearly defined anxiety crisis preceding their speaking in tongues." Typically this crisis involved feelings of worthlessness and powerlessness. As described by one of Kihldahl's (1972, p. 64) respondents, "I felt like a child who could only say 'Goo.'"

Unavailability or Loss of a Principal Attachment Figure

A second kind of situation in which alternative attachment figures may be sought are those in which the principal attachment figure is situationally unavailable. In warfare, of course, one's spouse or other attachment figure from home is almost certainly not physically present. Spouses must often endure temporary separations from each other, and children frequently must endure temporary separations from their parents. Should the attachment system be strongly activated during one of these times, alternative attachment figures may be sought.

A particularly important instance of unavailability of the attachment figure is the permanent loss of an attachment figure through death or other circumstances. Loss of a principal attachment figure is a particularly powerful stressor: Not only is it a stressful event in itself, but it also eliminates the availability of the person to whom one would otherwise be likely to turn for support in a stressful situation. As noted in a previous section, considerable research demonstrates the importance of religion—particularly prayer—during times of bereavement (Haun, 1977; Loveland, 1968; Parkes, 1972). When a human attachment figure is lost, a perceived relationship with God may become an appealing alternative. We (Kirkpatrick & Shaver, 1990) noted that the majority of crises reported retrospectively by the religious converts in their sample involved relationship-focused difficulties including loss of or separation from attachment figures, particularly through relationship breakups and divorce.

A rather different example of how the loss of a primary attachment figure can lead to a search for substitute attachments occurs commonly during adolescence and young adulthood. It has long been noted by religion researchers that adolescence is a period during which religious conversions are particularly likely. Many early researchers regarded conversion as primarily an adolescent phenomenon (e.g., James, 1902; Starbuck, 1899); Argyle and Beit-Hallahmi (1975, p. 59) refer to adolescence as "the age of religious awakening." It is well known, too, that cult recruiters make teenagers and young adults prima-

ry targets for their proselytizing and recruitment activities. Because adolescence represents such a unique developmental period, it is not surprising that a wide range of explanations has been advanced for the prevalence of conversion at this time. These include postulated links to puberty and sexual instincts (Coe, 1916; Thouless, 1923); the need for meaning, purpose, and sense of identity (Starbuck, 1899); and self-realization (Hood et al., 1996).

From an attachment perspective, however, it is important to note that adolescence represents a period of *transition* between principal attachment figures—usually from parents to peers. According to Weiss (1982, p. 178), relinquishing one's parents as attachment figures has a number of predictable consequences, including vulnerability to emotional loneliness, which he defines in terms of "the absence from one's internal world of an attachment figure." At such a time, adolescents may turn to God (or perhaps a charismatic religious leader) as a substitute attachment figure. The work by Hazan and Zeifman (1994) on the stepwise transition from parental to peer attachments may provide a useful model for examining the psychological dynamics of religious conversions.

Insecure Attachment History

A third kind of circumstance expected to elicit a search for substitute attachments is a history of unsatisfactory attachments. Several researchers (e.g., Ainsworth, 1985) have argued that children who fail to establish secure attachments to parents are likely to seek surrogate attachment figures, including teachers, older siblings, other relatives, or any stronger and wiser other who reliably proves to be accessible and responsive. Although Ainsworth (1985) did not include God in her list of potential surrogates, it seems reasonable to assume that God may fill this role for many people with insecure attachment histories. In a word, God may provide the kind of secure attachment relationship one never had with one's parents or other primary attachment figures.

Various studies suggest that sudden religious conversions during adulthood tend to be associated with childhood histories characterized by problematic familial and parental relationships. Deutsch (1975) interviewed 14 members of a Hindu-inspired cult and found that most reported a history of troubled parental relationships, along with feelings of inferiority and low self-esteem. In an extensive interview study of 40 converts from various religious groups and a carefully matched sample of nonconverts, Ullman (1982) found striking differences between converts and nonconverts in regard to troubled childhood relationships with both mothers and fathers.

In a study motivated explicitly by attachment theory, we (Kirkpatrick & Shaver, 1990) attempted to simulate a longitudinal design by asking newspaper-survey respondents to report retrospectively on their childhood attachments to their mothers and fathers. Respondents read descriptions of avoidant, ambivalent, and secure parent–child relationships and indicated which best described their own experience with each parent separately. No significant differences were found with respect to fathers, but avoidant attachment to mothers was strongly related to likelihood of having experienced a sudden religious conversion during adolescence (28%, vs. 1% for those reporting secure maternal attachments and 4% for those reporting ambivalent maternal attachments) or during adulthood (22%, vs. 8% and 6%, respectively). Because responses to the measures of adolescent conversion and adulthood conversion were essentially independent, combining them showed that over 44% of those reporting avoidant maternal attachments, compared with only 9% of those reporting secure and 8% of those reporting ambivalent maternal attachments, had experienced a sudden religious conversion at some point in their lives. In addition, this avoidant group displayed significantly higher levels of religious commitment, church attendance, belief in a personal (vs. pantheistic or deistic) God, and belief in having a personal relationship with God, as compared to the other two groups—though these latter results held only for subjects whose mothers were relatively nonreligious (at least in part because of ceiling effects among subjects who were raised in highly religious homes).

These conversion findings were also replicated in the unpublished South Carolina sample of college students described earlier. In these data, however, avoidant attachment to fathers proved a stronger predictor of subsequent religious conversion than avoidant attachment to mothers: Respondents reporting avoidant (vs. secure or ambivalent) attachments to their fathers during childhood were significantly more likely (30%, vs. 5% and 6%, respectively) to report also having experienced a sudden religious conversion during adolescence or adulthood. Parallel results for maternal attachment were in the same direction but nonsignificant.

All of the principal findings reported in the Kirkpatrick and Shaver (1990) study, including both the main effect for childhood attachment insecurity on adult conversion and the interaction effect of attachment security × parental religiousness on other religion variables, have been replicated recently in a Swedish sample (Granquist, 1998). The methods and measures used in this study were highly similar to those used in the Kirkpatrick and Shaver (1990) study, with the important exception that the avoidant and ambivalent categories were collapsed into a single insecure category due to insufficient sample sizes. As in the South Carolina replication, results were consistently stronger (though in the same direction) for paternal than for maternal variables.

Although the retrospective measures of childhood attachment employed in these studies were crude and the sample sizes small (particularly for the categories of insecure parental attachment), the consistency of results across the studies and with those reported by Ullman (1982) suggest that childhood attachment history plays an important part in the development of adolescent and adult religiousness. The question of the relative roles of maternal versus paternal attachments in this process, however, appears somewhat ambiguous and suggests an interesting avenue for future research.

Insecure Adult Attachment

Although early attachment history may represent a distal influence on adult religious experience, such experiences are likely to be mediated by the more proximal influences of adult attachment relationships. Adult romantic attachment style, as defined by Hazan and Shaver (1987) and others, presumably reflects a combination of long-term effects of attachment history (via relatively stable mental models) and current or recent relationship experience (Kirkpatrick & Hazan, 1994). Consideration of attachment as a dynamic system leads to the prediction that adults who find adult romantic attachments to be inadequate will be those most likely to turn to God as a substitute or surrogate attachment figure.

One source of perceived inadequacies in interpersonal attachments is the actual or perceived attentiveness and responsiveness of attachment figures. If one's partner consistently withdraws support and availability at the very time it is most needed, it seems reasonable to expect that one may seek an alternative attachment figure. Research by Simpson et al. (1992) revealed (among other findings), that while their female romantic partners anticipated a stressful laboratory task, secure men offered more support as their partners' anxiety increased, but avoidant men offered *less* support as the partners' anxiety increased. Interestingly, men's providing of support was statistically independent of their partners' level of support seeking, suggesting that such partner effects were not attributable to individual differences among the distressed women themselves. Although I am aware of no empirical research to support this speculation, it seems reasonable to expect that persons with avoidant partners may be more likely to turn to God than to their romantic partners for support and comfort when highly distressed.

The other source of potential dissatisfaction with interpersonal attachments stems from individual differences among attached persons themselves, which presumably reflect the long-term development of mental models of attachment over the lifespan. Insecurely attached adults are, more or less by definition, dissatisfied with romantic attachment relationships. Avoidant persons either fear or dismiss the importance of intimacy and closeness, whereas ambivalent persons wish for more intimacy and closeness than relationship partners are willing to provide. Romantic relationships of insecure adults are less stable across time than those of secure adults (Kirkpatrick & Davis, 1994; Kirkpatrick & Hazan, 1994), perhaps in part because avoidant persons do not work to maintain them, and ambivalent persons drive partners away with clingy, dependent behavior. One reason why God may be perceived by romantically insecure adults as an ideal attachment figure is that God presumably cannot be driven away by excessive demands for closeness, nor does God withdraw support at crucial times. A perceived relationship with God is not constrained by the "partner's" behavior in the same way that adult peer relationships are, and can be freely construed by an individual in a way that ideally meets his or her particular desires or needs.

A perceived relationship with God seems particularly well suited for individuals characterized by the ambivalent adult attachment style. People reporting this pattern express a desire to "merge" with their partners, and describe these partners as failing to meet their needs for closeness and intimacy. In addition, they are likely to say that their strong desire for closeness sometimes drives partners or potential partners away (Hazan & Shaver, 1987). Ambivalent adults are more likely than others to fall in love easily and frequently, and to experience "lovesickness," "limerence," and related states (Shaver & Hazan, 1988). The close interpersonal relationships of ambivalent adults tend to be characterized by emotional highs and lows, jealousy, conflict, and dissatisfaction (see Shaver & Hazan, 1993, for a review). As noted previously, one can be dependent on God and "merge with" God without fear of driving God away by excessive demands for closeness, attention, and intimacy.

The research literature on glossolalia suggests that something like ambivalent attachment may be associated with this extreme form of attachment behavior expressed toward God. Glossolalics do not appear to differ significantly from nonglossolalics on most indices of psychopathology (Hine, 1969; Richardson, 1973), but several studies suggest that persons who speak in tongues differ from others in terms of the quality of their interpersonal relationships. Plog (1965) found that the only component of the California Psychological Inventory on which glossolalics differed from nonglossolalics was one concerning problems in interpersonal relationships. Wood (1965) suggested that glossolalics "have an uncommon degree of uncertainty concerning interpersonal relationships" (as cited in Richardson, 1973, p. 203) and "a strong drive to feel close fellowship with others but they are uncertain that these interpersonal involvements will be satisfactory" (as cited in Richardson, 1973, p. 203). Richardson's (1973) summary of findings reported by Vivier (1960) indicated that glossolalics were more "anxious" than nonglossolalics, scored higher on a measure of neuroticism, had more initial problems in their marriages, and came from homes with more "disturbed" atmospheres.

All of these findings seem consistent with the profile of an ambivalent attachment style, and indeed we (Kirkpatrick & Shaver, 1992) found that adults reporting this romantic style were more likely to say they had spoken in tongues at least once in their lives. However, the glossolalia research is riddled with methodological problems (Richardson, 1973), and our finding is based on cross-sectional data. Proper testing of the hypothesis that insecure (especially ambivalent) adult attachment leads to an increased likelihood of turning to God as a substitute attachment figure requires a longitudinal methodology. I have recently completed two such studies, which together provide strong support for this hypothesis.

In the first of these studies (Kirkpatrick, 1997), 146 adult women who had returned a newspaper survey on attachment and other variables 4 years earlier completed a brief follow-up survey concerning changes in their lives in several domains over the 4-year intersurvey interval. (Sample sizes for men were too small to permit meaningful statistical analyses.) Included in the follow-up survey were several questions concerning changes in religious belief and practice. In analyses predicting responses to these variables at Time 2 from Time 1 romantic attachment style (as measured with the Hazan–Shaver three-paragraph item), while controlling statistically for Time 1 religious commitment, the following findings were obtained: (1) Both avoidant (38%) and ambivalent (36%) women were significantly more likely than secure women (19%) to report having "found a new relationship with God" during the intersurvey interval; and (2) ambivalent women (25%) were more likely than either avoidant (7%) or secure (9%) women to report having "had a religious experience or religious conversion" during that period. Two other variables—having been "born again" and having "spoken in tongues"—followed this latter pattern but fell short of statistical significance, due at least in part to the low base rates for these items. Other variables that were not expected to vary by attachment style, such as changing denominations or changing churches within a denomination, produced nonsignificant results.

In a second study (Kirkpatrick, 1998b), 297 undergraduate students completed identical attachment and religion measures in consecutive semesters, approximately 5 months apart. Romantic attachment style was measured with the Bartholomew and Horowitz (1991) four-category self-classification measure. As described previously, this measure permits a 2×2 analysis of attachment style in terms of positive versus negative mental models of self and others, thus offering a potential refinement and extension of the compensation hypothesis. Results indicated that respondents who reported negative models of self (preoccupied and fearful/avoidant), relative to those reporting positive self-models (secure and dismissing/avoidant), showed a significantly greater increase across time on an aggregate measure of religiosity, as well as on separate measures of the image of a loving God and belief in a personal God. This latter result neatly replicates the Kirkpatrick (1997) finding that both avoidant and ambivalent women were more like-

ly than secure women to report subsequently having "found a new relationship with God." One interpretation of this finding is that for people who view themselves as unworthy of love and care, turning to God might be enabled by certain unique characteristics of God vis-à-vis interpersonal relationships: In most religious belief systems, either God's love is unconditional—in which case one need not be "worthy" of love and care to receive it—or specific courses of action (e.g., prayers, rituals, performing "good works") are prescribed by which one can earn God's love and forgiveness.

In addition, an intriguing main effect for model of others was also observed. Individuals with *positive* models of others evinced more positive change on the aggregate religiosity measure than those with negative models of others; they also came to view God as significantly less distant and (marginally) more loving. Negative models of others are generally thought to entail beliefs that intimate relationships are undesirable and to be avoided, and that relationship partners are not to be counted upon. Perhaps it should come as no surprise that persons who devalue close relationships generally are no more inclined to seek attachments to God than to human relationship partners.

Consideration of these two (additive) main effects together suggests that persons most likely to both seek and find a secure attachment relationship with God are those with a negative model of self combined with a positive model of others—that is, those in Bartholomew's *preoccupied* and Hazan and Shaver's (1987) *ambivalent* category. Consistent with this pattern, recall that in the Kirkpatrick (1997) study, ambivalent women reported the highest rate of religious conversions and religious experiences. For people who seek and value close relationships, but who have difficulty developing and maintaining them due to fears of being unloved and/or abandoned, it is easy to see how God's unconditional (or easily earned) love may be perceived as immensely attractive, and how the experience of finding such a relationship may be emotionally powerful and deeply rewarding.

Of course, this is not to say that all religious beliefs have their source in deficient interpersonal relationships. Indeed, it seems likely that many if not most people, develop beliefs about both attachment and religion early in life and then maintain these orientations over much or all of the lifespan. When dramatic religious change does occur, however—particularly change toward belief in a personal, loving God—attachment processes may play an important role.

THE RELIGION-AS-ATTACHMENT MODEL AND PSYCHOLOGICAL OUTCOMES

To the extent that a secure base functions to prevent or reduce fear and anxiety, as argued by Bowlby (1969/1982) and others, belief in God as an attachment figure should confer certain psychological benefits. The interconnections between religion and mental health and well-being—both complex, multifaceted constructs—are immensely complex: It seems clear that religious belief and commitment can have highly positive, highly negative, or neutral effects on well-being as variously defined (see Paloutzian & Kirkpatrick, 1995, for a diverse collection of examples). Although a thorough review of this literature is well beyond the scope of the present chapter, in this brief section I wish to point to a handful of findings that seem particularly relevant to the claim that God functions psychologically as an attachment figure for many individuals.

A number of research findings suggest that religious belief is related to those aspects of psychological well-being and mental health that are most obviously predicted from an attachment perspective. For example, religious commitment correlates inversely with trait anxiety (Baker & Gorsuch, 1982; McClain, 1978), and belief in a loving deity is positively correlated with self-esteem (Benson & Spilka, 1973; Spilka, Addison, & Rosensohn, 1975). In an extensive review of the literature on religion and mental health, Batson and Ventis (1982) found genuine religious commitment (intrinsic religious orientation, or religion "as an end") to be related to "freedom from worry and guilt" and "personal competence and control," but not to other dimensions of mental health.

Other studies suggest that the particular aspects of religious belief most strongly related to psychological well-being are those consistent with the religion-as-attachment model. For example, Pollner (1989, p. 95) found in a large national sample that a dimension of religion he labeled "divine relationships" (defined as "psychological proximity of the divine other and the frequency and depth of interaction with that other") predicted psychological well-being more strongly than several other religion measures,

even when numerous background variables (including church attendance) were statistically controlled. In another large-scale national survey, Poloma and Gallup (1991) found that prayer, and particularly the "experience of God during prayer," were more strongly correlated than other religion measures with several measures of well-being. In a study of Unification Church members, Galanter (1979) reported that the two best predictors of emotional well-being were "My religious beliefs give me comfort" and "I feel a close connection to God."

A clear example of the differential relations between an attachment-relevant construct of well-being and attachment-relevant dimensions of religiosity comes from the literature on religion and loneliness. According to Weiss (1973), attachment relationships are important as a defense against a particular form of loneliness labeled "emotional isolation" (as opposed to "social isolation"). Paloutzian and Ellison (1982) found lower loneliness scores among "born-again" Christians (whose faith emphasizes a relationship with Jesus) than in "ethical" Christians (whose faith emphasizes moral and ethical teachings). In a study by Schwab and Petersen (1990), loneliness was inversely related to "belief in a helpful God" and positively related to "belief in a wrathful God," but unrelated to "mere belief in God." Recently, we (Kirkpatrick, Shillito, & Kellas, 1998) demonstrated that belief in having a personal relationship with God predicted reduced loneliness even when other measures of interpersonal social support were statistically controlled. Interestingly, however, this result held for women but not for men, suggesting (along with other recent studies; e.g., Kark et al., 1996) that gender may moderate certain relations between religion and psychological outcomes.

Research on religious conversion and glossolalia suggests that both of these experiences—interpreted here as turning to God as an attachment figure and proximal attachment behavior toward God, respectively—are associated with an improved sense of well-being. In the studies by Galanter (1979) and Ullman (1982), converts reported substantial reductions in anxiety, depression, and emotional distress subsequent to their conversions. According to Kildahl (1972), the experience of speaking in tongues led to increased feelings of confidence and security, which he attributed to glossolalics' perception of their experience as proof of being loved and protected by God.

Research on religion and coping with stress

provides considerable support for a positive role of religion in this process. Investigations by Gibbs and Achterberg-Lawlis (1978), Jenkins and Pargament (1988), Maton (1989), and Pargament et al. (1990, 1994) all provide empirical support for the assertion that certain religious variables and coping activities predict successful coping and positive psychological outcomes in dealing with stressful events ranging from health problems (of both self and close others) to the Gulf War. The importance of religion as a source of social support is particularly well documented with respect to older adults (e.g., Koenig, George, & Siegler, 1988), perhaps in part because older adults are more likely to be without, and to have experienced the loss of, significant human attachments. (See McFadden, 1995, and McFadden & Levin, 1996, for discussions of religiosity and aging.)

As part of our study of adult attachment style and religion described earlier in this chapter, we (Kirkpatrick & Shaver, 1992) included several measures of psychological well-being. Of many religion variables included in the study, only one evinced significant and strong associations with these variables: a measure of "attachment style" with respect to God. Adults who described their perceived relationship with God as secure, as opposed to avoidant or ambivalent, scored significantly and substantially lower on measures of loneliness/depression, anxiety, and physical illness (self-reported symptoms), and higher on general life satisfaction.

Unfortunately, interpretation of all of these findings is limited by several methodological problems. First, and perhaps most obvious, the causal direction of cross-sectional religion–outcome correlations remains open to question. Second, the apparently positive effects on mental health of religious conversions and experiences are based largely on retrospective accounts, and thus are subject to various well-known forms of bias in reconstructive memory processes. Third, the distinction between correspondence and compensation processes outlined in this chapter adds further to the complexities of interpreting cross-sectional religion–outcome correlations. To the extent that religious beliefs are correspondent with contemporaneous attitudes and feelings (e.g., mental models of self and others), certain forms of religiousness would be expected to correlate positively with mental health outcomes, consistent with research reviewed above. On the other hand, to the extent that religious beliefs result from anxiety, deficient interpersonal relationships, and other life difficulties (as suggested by the compensation hypothesis), religion variables might be expected to correlate *inversely* with contemporaneous outcome measures. Well-designed longitudinal research—in which religiousness, stressful life events, and mental health are all tracked simultaneously across time—will be required for more definite answers to questions about the effects of perceived attachments to God on mental health.

CONCLUSIONS

In this chapter I have attempted to marshal evidence from various sources to support the hypothesis that many aspects of religious belief and experience—particularly those related to perceived relationships with God or other supernatural figures—reflect (at least in part) the operation of psychological attachment processes. From a normative perspective, God evinces all of the defining characteristics of an attachment figure to whom people turn for a safe haven and secure base. From an individual-differences perspective, internal working models of God appear to parallel contemporaneous working models of other close interpersonal relationships, and longitudinal analyses of religious change across time support a compensatory model, according to which people with insecure childhood or adult attachments may turn to God as a substitute attachment figure. Finally, there is evidence to suggest that attachment to God may confer the kinds of psychological benefits associated with secure interpersonal attachments.

I have sketched in this chapter little more than an outline of the theory and evidence for an attachment-theoretical approach to religion; much work remains to be done. One major theoretical and empirical task concerns the integration of the correspondence and compensation models. For some individuals, religious beliefs may reflect a response to insecure interpersonal attachments; for others, religious beliefs may be established early in life, during childhoods characterized by secure attachment, and may remain fairly constant across the lifespan. This distinction raises a host of interesting empirical questions. For example, do the religious beliefs emerging from these alternative processes differ qualitatively with respect to content, structure, or function, or with respect to their effects on psychological outcomes?

A related set of questions concerns the interaction of correspondence and compensation processes within individuals across time. For example, in cases in which religious change is motivated by insecure interpersonal attachment, does one's orientation toward interpersonal attachments then change concomitantly? If so, this knowledge might provide a useful basis for the development of therapeutic strategies for dealing with relationship-related difficulties, particularly in religious populations. Conversely, do changes in interpersonal attachments lead to concomitant changes in religious belief? For example, if an individual turns to a relationship with God in response to interpersonal difficulties, does the importance of these newly found religious beliefs then recede if the quality of his or her interpersonal relationships subsequently improves? The general question of how the centrality of religious beliefs in people's lives may wax and wane in concert with, or inversely with, the ups and downs of their interpersonal relationships remains an important avenue for future research.

A third general issue to be resolved concerns the limits of attachment theory in the psychology of religion. I have deliberately restricted my discussion to aspects of religion that I believe to be psychologically grounded in the attachment system per se—specifically, beliefs about certain kinds of supernatural beings and perceived relationships with these beings. Myriad other applications of attachment constructs to religion are tempting: "attachment" to human religious leaders (pastors, cult leaders, shamans), "attachment" to religious groups (congregations, cults, denominations), and the concept of "attachment" in Buddhism, to name just a few. Although these and other religious phenomena may seem analogous to attachment in certain ways, I suspect that many reflect the operation of psychological processes and systems other than attachment. I have argued elsewhere (Kirkpatrick, in press), from the perspective of contemporary evolutionary psychology, that the attachment system is just one of numerous domain-specific psychological mechanisms that underlie the diverse range of religious phenomena. For example, relationships with human leaders may be guided largely by mechanisms concerned with issues of status, power, and prestige, rather than (or in addition to) attachment, orientation toward religious groups may involve mechanisms concerned with social exchange, or with coalition formation and maintenance.

Notwithstanding these many unanswered questions, I submit that no model of adult interpersonal relationships in general, or attachment relationships in particular, will be complete without explicit acknowledgment of the role of God and other supernatural figures in people's relationship networks. Incorporating religious beliefs into research on adult relationships may be useful in addressing vexing questions in the attachment literature concerning such issues as the content, structure, and generality of internal working models, and the dynamic processes underlying change in attachment patterns and working models across time. Moreover, consideration of the role of religion may help to shed new light on developmental processes, such as the transition from parental to peer attachments during adolescence, and responses to loss of significant attachments in (especially late) adulthood. In short, application of attachment theory to religion not only holds promise for the psychology of religion, but also may have much to offer to the study of attachment processes and individual differences across the lifespan.

ACKNOWLEDGMENT

Preparation of this chapter was facilitated by a Faculty Summer Research Grant from the College of William & Mary.

NOTES

1. All Biblical quotes are from the *King James Version.*

2. These data were collected by Lenne Deaton at the University of South Carolina in conjunction with her doctoral dissertation research on a related topic.

REFERENCES

Allport, G. W. (1950). *The individual and his religion.* New York: Macmillan.

Ainsworth, M. D. S. (1985). Attachments across the life span. *Bulletin of the New York Academy of Medicine, 61,* 792–812.

Argyle, M., & Beit-Hallahmi, B. (1975). *The social psychology of religion.* London: Routledge & Kegan Paul.

Baker, M., & Gorsuch, R. (1982). Trait anxiety and intrinsic-extrinsic religiousness. *Journal for the Scientific Study of Religion, 21,* 119–122.

Bartholomew, K. (1990). Avoidance of intimacy: An attachment perspective. *Journal of Social and Personal Relationships, 7,* 147–178.

Bartholomew, K., & Horowitz, L. M. (1991). Attachment styles in young adults: A test of a four-category model. *Journal of Personality and Social Psychology, 61,* 226–244.

Batson, C. D., & Ventis, W. L. (1982). *The religious experience: A social-psychological perspective.* New York: Oxford University Press.

Benson, P. L., & Spilka, B. (1973). God image as a function of self-esteem and locus of control. *Journal for the Scientific Study of Religion, 12,* 297–310.

Benson, P. L., & Williams, D. L. (1982). *Religion on Capitol Hill: Myths and realities.* San Francisco: Harper & Row.

Bowlby, J. (1956). The growth of independence in the young child. *Royal Society of Health Journal, 76,* 587–591.

Bowlby, J. (1969/1982). *Attachment and loss: Vol. 1. Attachment.* New York: Basic Books.

Bowlby, J. (1973). *Attachment and loss: Vol. 2. Separation.* New York: Basic Books.

Bretherton, I. (1985). Attachment theory: Retrospect and prospect. In I. Bretherton & E. Waters (Eds.), *Growing points of attachment theory and research. Monographs of the Society for Research in Child Development, 50*(1–2, Serial No. 209), 3–35.

Bretherton, I. (1987). New perspectives on attachment relations: Security, communication, and internal working models. In J. D. Osofsky (Ed.), *Handbook of infant development* (2nd ed., pp. 1061–1100). New York: Wiley.

Broen, W. E., Jr. (1957). A factor-analytic study of religious attitudes. *Journal of Abnormal and Social Psychology, 54,* 176–179.

Campos, J. J., & Stenberg, C. (1981). Perception, appraisal, and emotion: The onset of social referencing. In M. E. Lamb & L. R. Sherrod (Eds.), *Infant social cognition: Empirical and theoretical considerations* (pp. 273–314). Hillsdale, NJ: Erlbaum.

Carpenter, E. M., & Kirkpatrick, L. A. (1996). Attachment style and presence of a romantic partner as moderators of psychophysiological responses to a stressful laboratory situation. *Personal Relationships, 3,* 351–367.

Clark, E. T. (1929). *The psychology of religious awakening.* New York: Macmillan.

Coe, G. A. (1916). *Psychology of religion.* Chicago: University of Chicago Press.

Collins, N. L., & Read, S. J. (1994). Cognitive representations of attachment: The structure and function of working models. In D. Perlman & K. Bartholomew (Eds.), *Advances in personal relationships* (Vol. 5, pp. 53–90). London: Jessica Kingsley.

Deutsch, A. (1975). Observations of a sidewalk ashram. *Archives of General Psychiatry, 32,* 166–175.

Duke, E. H. (1977). *Meaning in life and acceptance of death in terminally ill patients.* Unpublished doctoral dissertation, Northwestern University.

Elkind, D. (1971). The development of religious understanding in children and adolescents. In M. Strommen (Ed.), *Research on religious development* (pp. 655–685). New York: Hawthorn.

Fox, N. A., Kimmerly, N. L., & Schafer, W. D. (1991). Attachment to mother/attachment to father: A meta-analysis. *Child Development, 62,* 210–225.

Freud, S. (1961). *The future of an illusion* (J. Strachey, Trans.). New York: Norton. (Original work published 1927).

Galanter, M. (1979). The "Moonies": A psychological study of conversion and membership in a contemporary religious sect. *American Journal of Psychiatry, 136,* 165–170.

Gallup, G., Jr., & Jones, S. (1989). *One hundred questions and answers: Religion in America.* Princeton, NJ: Princeton Religious Research Center.

Gibbs, H. W., & Achterberg-Lawlis, J. (1978). Spiritual values and death anxiety: Implications for counseling with terminal cancer patients. *Journal of Counseling Psychology, 25,* 563–569.

Godin, A., & Hallez, M. (1965). Parental images and divine paternity. In A. Godin (Ed.), *From religious experience to a religious attitude* (pp. 65–96). Chicago: Loyola University Press.

Gorsuch, R. L. (1968). The conceptualization of God as seen in adjective ratings. *Journal for the Scientific Study of Religion, 7,* 56–64.

Granquist, P. (1998). Religiousness and childhood attachment: On the question of compensation or correspondence. *Journal for the Scientific Study of Religion, 37,* 350–367.

Greeley, A. (1981). *The religious imagination.* New York: Sadlier.

Greeley, A. (1990). *The Catholic myth: The behavior and beliefs of American Catholics.* New York: Scribner.

Harms, E. (1944). The development of religious experience in children. *Journal of Sociology, 50,* 112–122.

Haun, D. L. (1977). Perception of the bereaved, clergy, and funeral directors concerning bereavement. *Dissertation Abstracts International, 37,* 6791A.

Hazan, C., & Shaver, P. (1987). Romantic love conceptualized as an attachment process. *Journal of Personality and Social Psychology, 52,* 511–524.

Hazan, C., & Shaver, P. (1990). Love and work: An attachment-theoretical perspective. *Journal of Personality and Social Psychology, 59,* 270–280.

Hazan, C., & Shaver, P. (1994). Attachment as an organizational framework for research on close relationships. *Psychological Inquiry, 5,* 1–22.

Hazan, C., & Zeifman, D. (1994). Sex and the psychological tether. In D. Perlman & K. Bartholomew (Eds.), *Advances in personal relationships* (Vol. 5, pp. 151–177). London: Jessica Kingsley.

Heiler, F. (1932). *Prayer.* New York: Oxford University Press.

Heller, D. (1986). *The children's God.* Chicago: University of Chicago Press.

Hine, V. H. (1969). Pentecostal glossolalia: Toward a functional interpretation. *Journal for the Scientific Study of Religion, 8,* 211–226.

Hood, R. W., Spilka, B., Hunsberger, B., & Gorsuch, R. (1996). *The psychology of religion: An empirical approach* (2nd Ed.). New York: Guilford Press.

Hughes, P. J. (1989). *The Australian clergy: Report from the combined churches' survey for faith and mission.* Melbourne, Australia: Acorn Press.

James, W. (1902). *The varieties of religious experience.* New York: Longmans, Green.

Jenkins, R., & Pargament, K. I. (1988). Cognitive appraisals in cancer patients. *Social Science and Medicine, 26,* 625–633.

Johnson, P. E. (1945). *Psychology of religion.* New York: Abingdon-Cokesbury.

Jubis, R. (1991). *An attachment-theoretical approach to understanding children's conceptions of God.* Unpublished doctoral dissertation, University of Denver.

Kark, J. D., Shemi, G., Friedlander, Y., Martin, O., Manor, O., & Blondheim, S. H. (1996). Does religious observance promote health?: Mortality in secular vs. religious kibbutzim in Israel. *American Journal of Public Health, 86,* 341–346.

Kaufman, G. D. (1981). *The theological imagination: Constructing the concept of God.* Philadelphia: Westminster.

Kildahl, J. P. (1972). *The psychology of speaking in tongues.* New York: Harper & Row.

Kirkpatrick, L. A. (1994). The role of attachment in religious belief and behavior. In D. Perlman & K. Bartholomew (Eds.), *Advances in personal relationships* (Vol. 5, pp. 239–265). London: Jessica Kingsley.

Kirkpatrick, L. A. (1997). A longitudinal study of changes in religious belief and behavior as a function of individual differences in adult attachment style. *Journal for the Scientific Study of Religion, 36,* 207–217.

Kirkpatrick, L. A. (1998a). Evolution, pair-bonding, and reproductive strategies: A reconceptualization of adult attachment. In J. A. Simpson & W. S. Rholes (Eds.), *Attachment theory and close relationships* (pp. 353–393). New York: Guilford Press.

Kirkpatrick, L. A. (1998b). God as a substitute attachment figure: A longitudinal study of adult attachment style and religious change in college students. *Personality and Social Psychology Bulletin, 24,* 961–973.

Kirkpatrick, L. A. (in press). Toward an evolutionary psychology of religion. *Journal of Personality.*

Kirkpatrick, L. A., & Davis, K. E. (1994). Attachment style, gender, and relationship stability: A longitudinal analysis. *Journal of Personality and Social Psychology, 66,* 502–512.

Kirkpatrick, L. A., & Hazan, C. (1994). Attachment styles and close relationships: A four-year prospective study. *Personal Relationships, 1,* 123–142.

Kirkpatrick, L. A., & Shaver, P. R. (1990). Attachment theory and religion: Childhood attachments, religious beliefs, and conversion. *Journal for the Scientific Study of Religion, 29,* 315–334.

Kirkpatrick, L. A., & Shaver, P. R. (1992). An attachment-theoretical approach to romantic love and religious belief. *Personality and Social Psychology Bulletin, 18,* 266–275.

Kirkpatrick, L. A., Shillito, D. J., & Kellas, S. L. (1998). *Loneliness, social support, and perceived relationships with God.* Unpublished manuscript, College of William and Mary.

Koenig, H. G., George, L. K., & Siegler, I. C. (1988). The use of religion and other emotion-regulating coping strategies among older adults. *Gerontologist, 28,* 303–310.

Lambert, W. W., Triandis, L. M., & Wolf, M. (1959). Some correlates of beliefs in the malevolence and benevolence of supernatural beings: A cross-societal study. *Journal of Abnormal and Social Psychology, 58,* 162–169.

Loveland, G. G. (1968). The effects of bereavement on certain religious attitudes. *Sociological Symposium, 1,* 17–27.

Main, M., Kaplan, N., & Cassidy, J. (1985). Security in infancy, childhood, and adulthood: A move to the level of representation. In I. Bretherton & E. Waters (Eds.), Growing points of attachment theory and research, *Monographs of the Society for Research in Child Development, 50*(1–2, Serial No. 209), 66–104.

Maton, K. (1989). The stress-buffering role of spiritual support: Cross-sectional and prospective investigations. *Journal for the Scientific Study of Religion, 28,* 310–323.

McClain, E. W. (1978). Personality differences between intrinsically religious and nonreligious students: A factor analytic study. *Journal of Personality Assessment, 42,* 159–166.

McFadden, S. H. (1995). Religion and well-being in aging persons in an aging society. *Journal of Social Issues, 51*(2), 161–175.

McFadden, S. H., & Levin, J. S. (1996). Religion, emotions, and health. In C. Magai & S. H. McFadden (Eds.), *Handbook of emotion, adult development, and aging* (pp. 349–365). San Diego, CA: Academic Press.

Mikulincer, M., Florian, V., & Tolmacz, R. (1990). Attachment styles and fear of personal death. *Journal of Personality and Social Psychology, 58,* 273–280.

Mikulincer, M., Florian, V., & Weller, A. (1993). Attachment styles, coping strategies, and post-traumatic psychological distress: The impact of the Gulf War in Israel. *Journal of Personality and Social Psychology, 64,* 817–826.

Myers, D. G. (1992). *The pursuit of happiness.* New York: Morrow.

Nelson, M. O. (1971). The concept of God and feelings toward parents. *Journal of Individual Psychology, 27,* 46–49.

Nelson, M. O., & Jones, E. M. (1957). An application of the Q-technique to the study of religious concepts. *Psychological Reports, 3,* 293–297.

Oates, W. E. (1967). A socio-psychological study of glossolalia. In F. Stagg, E. G. Hinson, & W. E. Oates (Eds.), *Glossolalia: Tongue speaking in biblical, historical, and psychological perspective* (pp. 76–99). New York: Abingdon.

O'Brien, M. E. (1982). Religious faith and adjustment to long-term hemodialysis. *Journal of Religion and Health, 21,* 68–80.

Paloutzian, R. F., & Ellison, C. W. (1982). Loneliness, spiritual well-being, and the quality of life. In L. A. Peplau & D. Perlman (Eds.), *Loneliness: A sourcebook of current theory, research, and therapy* (pp. 224–237). New York: Wiley.

Paloutzian, R. F, & Kirkpatrick, L. A. (Eds.). (1995). Religious influences on personal and societal well-being. [Special issue]. *Journal of Social Issues, 51*(2).

Pargament, K. I. (1990). God help me: Toward a theoretical framework of coping for the psychology of religion. *Research in the Social Scientific Study of Religion, 2,* 195–224.

Pargament, K. I., Ensing, D. S., Falgout, K., Olsen, H., Reilly, B., Van Haitsma, K., & Warren, R. (1990). God help me: I. Religious coping efforts as predictors of the outcomes to significant negative life events. *American Journal of Community Psychology, 18,* 793–824.

Pargament, K. I., Ishler, K., Dubow, E., Stanik, P., Rouiller, R., Crowe, P., Cullman, E., Albert, M., & Royster, B. J. (1994). Methods of religious coping with the Gulf War: Cross-sectional and longitudinal analyses. *Journal for the Scientific Study of Religion, 33,* 347–361.

Pargament, K. I., Steele, R. E., & Tyler, F. B. (1979). Religious participation, religious motivation, and individual psychosocial competence. *Journal for the Scientific Study of Religion, 18,* 412–419.

Parkes, C. M. (1972). *Bereavement: Studies of grief in adult life.* New York: International Universities Press.

Plog, S. (1965). UCLA conducts research on glossolalia. *Trinity, 3,* 38–39.

Poloma, M. M., & Gallup, G. H., Jr. (1991). *Varieties of prayer: A survey report.* Philadelphia: Trinity Press International.

Pollner, M. (1989). Divine relations, social relations, and well-being. *Journal of Health and Social Behavior, 30,* 92–104.

Potvin, R. H. (1977). Adolescent God images. *Review of Religious Research, 19,* 43–53.

Pratt, J. B. (1920). *The religious consciousness.* New York: Macmillan.

Reed, B. (1978). *The dynamics of religion: Process and movement in Christian churches*. London: Darton, Longman & Todd.

Richardson, J. T. (1973). Psychological interpretations of glossolalia: A reexamination of research. *Journal for the Scientific Study of Religion, 12,* 199–207.

Rohner, R. P. (1975). *They love me, they love me not*. New Haven, CT: HRAF Press.

Ross, M. G. (1950). *Religious beliefs of youth*. New York: Association Press.

Schwab, R., & Petersen, K. U. (1990). Religiousness: Its relation to loneliness, neuroticism, and subjective well-being. *Journal for the Scientific Study of Religion, 29,* 335–345.

Shaver, P. R., & Hazan, C. (1988). A biased overview of the study of love. *Journal of Social and Personal Relationships, 5,* 473–501.

Shaver, P. R., & Hazan, C. (1993). Adult romantic attachment: Theory and evidence. In D. Perlman & W. Jones (Eds.), *Advances in personal relationships* (Vol. 4, pp. 29–70). London: Jessica Kingsley.

Shaver, P. R., Hazan, C., & Bradshaw, D. (1988). Love as attachment: The integration of three behavioral systems. In R. J. Sternberg & M. Barnes (Eds.), *The psychology of love* (pp. 68–99). New Haven, CT: Yale University Press.

Simpson, J. A., Rholes, W. S., & Nelligan, J. S. (1992). Support seeking and support giving within couples in an anxiety-provoking situation: The role of attachment styles. *Journal of Personality and Social Psychology, 62,* 434–446.

Spilka, B., Addison, J., & Rosensohn, M. (1975). Parents, self, and God: A test of competing individual–religion relationships. *Review of Religious Research, 16,* 154–165.

Spilka, B., Armatas, P., & Nussbaum, J. (1964). The concept of God: A factor-analytic approach. *Review of Religious Research, 6,* 28–36.

Starbuck, E. D. (1899). *The psychology of religion*. New York: Scribner.

Stark, R. (1965). A taxonomy of religious experience. *Journal for the Scientific Study of Religion, 5,* 97–116.

Stouffer, S. A. (1949). *The American soldier: Vol. 2. Combat and its aftermath*. Princeton, NJ: Princeton University Press.

Strahan, B. (1991). *Parenting and religiosity amongst SDA tertiary students: An attachment theory approach*. Unpublished manuscript, Avondale College, Cooranbong, New South Wales, Australia.

Strickland, F. L. (1924). *Psychology of religious experience*. New York: Abingdon.

Strunk, O. (1959). Perceived relationships between parental and deity concepts. *Psychological Newsletter, 10,* 222–226.

Tamayo, A., & Desjardins, L. (1976). Belief systems and conceptual images of parents and God. *Journal of Psychology, 92,* 131–140.

Thouless, R. H. (1923). *An introduction to the psychology of religion*. New York: Macmillan.

Ullman, C. (1982). Change of mind, change of heart: Some cognitive and emotional antecedents of religious conversion. *Journal of Personality and Social Psychology, 42,* 183–192.

Ullman, C. (1989). *The transformed self: The psychology of religious conversion*. New York: Plenum Press.

Ventis, W. L. (1995). The relationships between religion and mental health. *Journal of Social Issues, 51*(2), 33–48.

Vergote, A., & Tamayo, A. (Eds.). (1981). *The parental figures and the representation of God*. The Hague: Mouton.

Vivier, L. (1960). *Glossolalia*. Unpublished master's thesis, University of Witwatersrand, Witwatersrand, South Africa.

Weiss, R. S. (1973). *Loneliness: The experience of emotional and social isolation*. Cambridge, MA: MIT Press.

Weiss, R. S. (1982). Attachment in adult life. In C. M. Parkes & J. Stevenson-Hinde (Eds.), *The place of attachment in human behavior* (pp. 171–184). New York: Basic Books.

Wenegrat, B. (1989). *The divine archetype: The sociobiology and psychology of religion*. Lexington, MA: Lexington Books.

Wood, W. W. (1965). *Culture and personality aspects of the Pentecostal Holiness religion*. The Hague: Mouton.

Wright, S. A. (1987). *Leaving cults: The dynamics of defection*. Washington, DC: Society for the Scientific Study of Religion.

Wulff, D. M. (1991). *Psychology of religion: Classic and contemporary views*. New York: Wiley.

Young, K. (1926). The psychology of hymns. *Journal of Abnormal and Social Psychology, 20,* 391–406.

36

Implications of Attachment Theory for Child Care Policies

❖

MICHAEL RUTTER
THOMAS G. O'CONNOR

Attachment theory was derived in large measure from insights gained through clinical observations of children in institutional care, as well as of children who had been separated from or who had lost one or both parents (Bowlby, 1969/1982). Indeed, the first volume in the *Attachment and Loss* trilogy sought to integrate Bowlby's own clinical observations with those of James and Joyce Robertson (1971) and others, in order to place them in a larger conceptual framework relevant to both abnormal and normal development. Thus attachment theory was initially grounded in clinical and policy concerns regarding children. The policies most relevant to children's psychological well-being have changed dramatically in the three decades following Bowlby's first seminal writings, but there continues to be a need for a strong connection between attachment theory and child care policies.

This chapter examines that connection in relation to three main themes. First, we approach it from a historical perspective: We note the features that differentiate attachment theory from other theories of development, with particular reference to the implications for child care policies. Second, we outline some important contemporary child care policy concerns that would benefit from an attachment perspective. Third, we focus on some of the key conceptual and methodological issues that need to be considered with respect to the application of attachment theory to child care policies and practice.

Throughout, we pay attention to two parallel concerns. First, we consider whether there has been something of a split between basic and applied research that may have led to conceptual confusion in attempts to apply attachment principles to practice. Second, we ask whether attachment research has taken sufficient advantage of special populations (e.g., children in residential institutions or in foster care) to address outstanding fundamental questions in attachment theory.

THE HISTORY OF ATTACHMENT THEORY AND CHILD CARE POLICIES

Distinguishing Characteristics

In order to understand the past impact of attachment theory on child care policies, it is necessary to highlight what was distinctive about its postulates when it was introduced, as compared with other theories of personality development and psychopathology (see Rutter, 1972/1981, 1995a, 1995b). First and foremost, attachment theory emphasized the importance of both continuity and sensitive responsivity in caregiving relationships as the key features of the environment of upbringing. This emphasis differed sharply from behavior theory, which focused on such features as here-and-now perceptual stimulation and reinforcement of child behaviors (see, e.g., Casler,

1968; Gewirtz, 1972), and from traditional psychoanalysis (especially Kleinian theory), which focused on internal thought processes without paying attention to the real-life experiences from which they were likely to have derived (see, e.g., Emde, 1992; King & Steiner, 1991; Stern, 1989).

Second, attachment theory replaced the general undifferentiated notion of mother love with a specific postulated mechanism by which a loving parental relationship might have effects on a child's psychological development. The essence lay in its giving primacy to a need to develop social relationships—a need that is biologically based and not environmentally determined. In this integration of a postulated biological propensity and an environmental shaping of its qualities, attachment theory was distinctive in its placing of the parent–child relationship within an ethological, cognitive, and control systems framework (Bowlby, 1969/1982). Subsequent research has broadly confirmed the key tenets of this model (Rajecki, Lamb, & Obmascher, 1978; Rutter, 1972/1981). Most crucially, it proposed that the development of selective attachments serves a purpose—namely, the provision of emotional security and protection against stress. This was a novel notion in the 1960s, and its importance lay in the proposition that attachment might thereby have implications for both broader aspects of psychological development and for psychopathology.

Third, the theory differentiated attachment from other components of relationships. In particular, empirical findings showed that anxiety intensifies attachment (in keeping with its hypothesized protective role), whereas it inhibits play. But, in its emphasis on these special qualities, attachment theory also underlined the point that attachment does not constitute the whole of relationships (an aspect that was rather overlooked later as the success of attachment theory led some uncritical enthusiasts to neglect the rest—see both Dunn, 1993, and Sroufe, 1988, for warnings on this).

Fourth, the theory provided a means of conceptualizing individual differences in the qualities of an attachment relationship—with the focus on the extent to which it provides security. Ainsworth's (1967; Ainsworth, Blehar, Waters, & Wall, 1978) development of the strange situation provided an effective operationalized measure of these postulated qualities. Although this procedure has its limitations (see Lamb, Thompson, Gardner, Charnov, & Estes, 1984), the approach has clearly paid off richly in numerous ways

(Belsky & Cassidy, 1994; Bretherton & Waters, 1985).

Fifth, particularly in its later developments (Bowlby, 1973, 1980), attachment theory was unusual in drawing heavily from cognitive psychology in specifying how hypothesized cognitive processes might play a role in carrying forward the effects of earlier relationships into later life. Research into the components of internal working models, including internal-state language and social cognition (e.g., Bretherton, 1990), has been consistent with what was proposed; however, it has to be said that the concepts remain rather too general to be readily susceptible to critical testing (Hinde, 1988). There has been substantial progress in the measurement of internal representations of relationships (see, e.g., Cassidy, Scolton, Kirsh, & Parke, 1996; Verschueren, Marcoen, & Schoefs, 1996; see also Solomon & George, Chapter 14, this volume), and the reality of their existence is well established. Moreover, there is a theoretically meaningful coherence to the patterns found. Nevertheless, Hinde's (1988) challenge that the generality of the predictions makes for difficulty in refutation has yet to be met. The need now is to move on from an acceptance that there are internal working models to testable predictions on precisely how they operate and on their effects.

As developed more fully in Bowlby's (1988) later writings, attachment theory was distinctive in espousing a lifespan approach to understanding relationship influences on personality and social development, as well as on psychopathology. Accordingly, attachment theory came to reject the notion of "critical periods" in social and personality development (although this was part of early formulations—see Bowlby, 1951, 1969/1982). Childhood experiences were hypothesized to play a key role in subsequent development, but a deterministic model was explicitly discarded and replaced with a trajectory model that emphasized risk and resilience and a probabilistic model of developmental outcomes (Bowlby, 1988).

Other concepts—notably the psychological loss associated with both separation and rejection—that are not unique to attachment theory, but they were most clearly enunciated by attachment theory and were increasingly incorporated into models of personality development and psychopathology. What was special about attachment theory in this instance is that it offered a compelling explanation for the feelings associated with the "trauma" of separation and loss—fear, anxiety, anger, sadness, and despair—and for their disruptive effects on personality development. Thus, from its first systematic formulations in the 1960s, attachment theory stood out from other theories in the ways in which it conceptualized the nature and importance of children's relationships with their caregivers.

Implications for Child Care Policies

The first main impact on child care policies clearly came from Bowlby's (1951) World Health Organization (WHO) monograph, building on his earlier book on juvenile thieves (Bowlby, 1946), rather than from attachment theory as such (although the two were closely linked in Bowlby's writings). That is, Bowlby postulated that the key damaging feature of group residential care was the lack of personalized caregiving and hence the lack of opportunity to develop selective attachments. People were shocked by the findings on children in institutions, and were persuaded by the claims that the apathy and loss of interest shown by many young children in residential institutions represented a negative reaction and not contentment. The outstanding series of films about children in hospitals, residential nurseries, and foster care made by James and Joyce Robertson in the 1950s to 1970s (see accounts by Robertson & Robertson, 1971; Rutter, 1972/1981) probably did at least as much to change attitudes and practice as did the scientific writings on attachment. The result was a virtual revolution (over the course of some years) both in the patterns of hospital care for children (Rutter, 1979) and in the use of residential nurseries as a means of caring for children experiencing a breakdown in parenting (Triseliotis & Russell, 1984; Wolkind & Rushton, 1994). Hospital policies changed to allow regular daily visiting by parents. After a period of some medical dragging of feet, visiting tended to become unrestricted, and parents were allowed (and then encouraged) to stay overnight in the hospital with their young children. Play activities and schooling within hospitals became more generally available. Children were increasingly prepared psychologically for what hospital admission entailed. Also, it became expected that even when it was necessary for children to be on specialized medical or surgical wards, pediatricians should have general responsibility for their overall care with respect to all hospital experiences other than the treatment of their illness or injury. Although it would be misleading to argue that all is as it should be everywhere, and although it is true that many of

the changes in hospital practice took place only after years of persuasion by pressure groups, the patterns of hospital care for children in the 1990s could scarcely be more different from those that prevailed in the 1950s.

The second revolution concerned the virtual abandonment of residential nurseries and orphanages as a first-choice solution for young children whose parents could no longer care for them for one reason or another (Cliffe & Berridge, 1991). Instead, there was increasing recourse to the use of long-term, as well as short-term, foster care. The U.S. House of Representatives Select Committee on Children, Youth and Families (1990) estimated that approximately 500,000 children in the United States were living in out-of-home placements in 1990. The aim, which followed from attachment theory, was to provide personalized caregiving in a family context that would allow continuity over time in relationships. Unfortunately, the practice proved much less satisfactory than the theory, as we discuss later in this chapter. Numerous studies showed a high rate of breakdown in foster placements, with consequent problems for the children (see Berridge & Cleaver, 1987; Wolkind & Rushton, 1994). The attachment focus on selective relationships that persisted over time provided an appropriate goal, but did little to deal with the numerous practical difficulties that were involved in bringing it about. Regrettably, it cannot be claimed that much progress has been made in recent years in improving this unfortunate state of affairs.

Although large orphanages providing group residential care have been largely phased out in most countries (but not all—see Chisholm, Cater, Ames, & Morison, 1995; Dontas, Maratos, Fafoutis, & Karangelis, 1985; Sloutsky, 1997; Vorria, Rutter, Wolkind, Hobsbaum, 1998-a, 1998-b), residential institutions for some children have continued to be necessary. Most differ markedly from the orphanages of the past in terms of a much more individualized, family-style pattern of care in small groups (see King, Raynes, & Tizard, 1971; Tizard & Tizard, 1971). However, the vast majority fall very far short of what attachment theory indicates is needed in terms of continuity in caregiving; an extremely high level of staff turnover is the rule. For example, Tizard (1977) reported that in the nurseries she studied, an average of 24 different caregivers had looked after the children for at least a week by the time the children reached the age of 2, and this figure had doubled by the time they reached age 5. Moreover, an emotionally detached style was usual to prevent the children from becoming distressed when a staff member had to leave.

This last feature was a carryover (less frequent today, we hope) from the initial focus in Bowlby's WHO report on the risks associated with separations as such. As a result of Bowlby's own research (Bowlby, Ainsworth, Boston, & Rosenbluth, 1956) and that of others, it became clear that separation as such was not the main risk component. Rather, the risks stemmed from the family discord, disorganization, and rejection associated with some (but far from all) types of separation. Nevertheless, the notion that separations were harmful had caught on, and for many years professional child care continued to place a greater emphasis on the dangers of losing a relationship than on a failure to gain one in the first place. The findings on residential care were also inappropriately generalized by many people to day care (see, e.g., the WHO Expert Committee on Mental Health, 1951, warning on the permanently deleterious effects of day nurseries and crèches). Curiously, the controversies over the supposed benefits or ill effects of day care continue to the present day (Clarke-Stewart, Allhusen, & Clements, 1995)—an issue to which we return.

A further area where attachment theory has had a major impact concerns decisions over child care in relation to parental divorce or separation (see Bretherton, Walsh, Lependorf, & Georgeson, 1997; Burgoyne, Ormrod, & Richards, 1987; Emery, 1988; Strauss, 1988), and in relation to applications by foster (or other social) parents to adopt children when the biological parents withdraw permission for adoption (Wolkind, 1994). Both situations pose major dilemmas in the criteria to be used in deciding what is in the children's best interests. For many years, especially in North America, traditional psychoanalysis provided the main theoretical framework put forward (see the series of books by Goldstein, Freud, & Solnit, 1973, 1979; Goldstein, Freud, Solnit, & Goldstein, 1986). Increasingly, however, attachment theory has come to replace it. Arguments by "experts" and lawyers in family courts currently tend to focus on whether the children concerned are "attached" or "bonded" to the various adults disputing who should care for the children. This terminology, of course, fails to take account of the fact that the research findings are concerned with the quality of attachment with respect to security, rather than whether there is attachment. Nevertheless, in most respects this shift has been advantageous. Instead of assuming that the biological mother should have automatic precedence, or that the quality of physical care or economic well-being should have priority, the courts now pay much more attention to the quality of caregiver–child relationships and to the importance of maintaining continuity. The disadvantage—perhaps encouraged by the categorical nature of security of attachment codings, as well as the legal propensity to deal with absolutes rather than relatives and to adopt a deterministic rather than a probabilistic stance (see Denno, 1996)—has been the tendency to put the question in a present–absent form: Either a child is, or is not, "attached" to this or that person. Over the last 20 years, family courts have shifted considerably (at least as one of us has experienced in the United Kingdom) in recognizing the need to consider risks in probabilistic terms and in appreciating that attachment relationships are more complicated than the presence–absence of secure attachment. Nevertheless, courts have not been helped by their difficulty in knowing what to do with evidence that a high proportion of apparently normal children in the general population show attachment insecurity (see Belsky & Cassidy, 1994), and by the lack of guidance from attachment theory on how to consider degrees of insecurity.

Changes in the Interface between Basic and Applied Attachment Research

As Bowlby noted in the preface to Volume 1 of *Attachment and Loss* (Bowlby, 1969/1982), social policies concerning the care of children were a driving force in the early work on attachment theory. Since then, however, despite its continuing relevance (see Schaffer, 1990), the close research connection between attachment theory and child care policies and practice seems to have loosened considerably. There was just one reference to attachment in the whole of the edited monograph *Child Development Research and Social Policy* (Stevenson & Siegel, 1984), and the recent volume *The Politics of Attachment* (Kraemer & Roberts, 1996), while emphasizing the widespread implications of attachment theory, has noted the difficulties in applying what is known to the political and social dilemmas of contemporary concern.

Five main themes appear to dominate recent research into attachment: (1) the precursors and sequelae of secure and insecure child–parent attachment relationships; (2) the nature of attachment in the postinfancy years; (3) the relations between attachment and psychopathology (including attachment patterns in high-risk samples); (4) attachment qualities in adult life; and (5) the intergenerational continuity of attachment qualities. Findings on all these themes are clearly of potential relevance for child care policies and practice, but with the single marked exception of group day care, there has been little attachment research that has been directly concerned with child care issues. That is a significant lack, if only because of the major changes over time in specific child care policies (an issue we take up later in the chapter). It is good that attachment considerations are being given close attention in the applied literature dealing with adoption and fostering (Howe, 1995; Marcus, 1991; Pardeck, 1984; Small, Kennedy, & Bender, 1991), but there is a danger of premature inferences and implications if the theoretical extrapolations to policy are not accompanied by systematic research to test what is proposed. There are periodic debates in the literature on misapplications of attachment theory to applied settings (Heinicke, 1981; McGurk, Caplan, Hennessy, & Moss, 1993), and it is evident from the literature on areas outside attachment that it is all too easy to draw wrong conclusions about causal mechanisms from both statistical associations and theory (for possible ways forward, see Rutter, 1994a, 1994b). Nevertheless, the need to consider attachment features in relation to a broad range of child care policy issues is clear from an overview of some of the issues of contemporary relevance.

SOME IMPORTANT CONTEMPORARY ATTACHMENT-RELEVANT CHILD CARE POLICY CONCERNS

In this section of the chapter, we review briefly eight main policy matters: (1) group day care; (2) adoption; (3) births following assisted reproduction; (4) foster care; (5) residential care; (6) changes in family constellations; (7) postnatal depression and psychosis; and (8) attachment disorders and attachment treatments.

Group Day Care

One of the very first policy applications of attachment notions was to group day care, when the WHO Expert Committee on Mental Health

(1951) argued that it would have permanent adverse effects. It soon became clear that this was not the case (see Zigler & Gordon, 1982). The error arose mainly because the findings with respect to children in *residential* group care had been inappropriately generalized to those in *day* care, without any direct studies of the latter group. A key reason why this happened was that the theoretical assumption in those early days postulated selective attachment that was highly focused on just *one* person—the notion of "monotropy," with the implication that this main attachment relationship differed in quality from other attachment relationships (Bowlby, 1958, 1969/1982). This led to claims that even brief separations during the day threatened the primary relationship (see WHO Expert Committee on Mental Health, 1951). Neither the assumption nor the claims on brief separations proved to be justified, and both were later dropped from attachment theory (Bowlby, 1988; Rutter, 1972/1981, 1995a). Children's attachments are indeed highly selective but several selective attachments are usual and they serve the same purpose, albeit to differing degrees. Also, it has been usual throughout history and across cultures for children to have several caregivers, although the details of patterns have varied (see van IJzendoorn & Sagi, Chapter 31, this volume; Werner, 1984). Very young children are truly stressed by separation experiences, but they readily cope with brief separations during the day when these occur in the context of relationship continuity and good-quality caregiving. The lesson, as always, is to be guided by empirical findings and to be very cautious regarding the acceptance of untested theoretical assumptions.

Nevertheless, concerns over child care did not go away, and controversies have continued up to the present day (see, e.g., Belsky, 1990; Brazelton, 1985; Clarke-Stewart et al., 1995; McCartney & Phillips, 1988; Scarr, Phillips, & McCartney, 1990; Tizard & Hughes, 1984). Their persistence has four main sources. First, there has been doubt about whether the effects of day care are the same in all circumstances. In particular, it has been suggested that there may be risks associated with extensive use of group day care in the first year of life, even if there are no ill effects in other circumstances (Belsky & Rovine, 1988). Second, given the sometimes very deprived home conditions in deteriorating inner-city areas, it has been thought that good-quality preschool care may actually be compensatory and protective (see Egeland & Hiester, 1995;

Maughan & Rutter, 1985; Woodhead, 1985). Third, there has been a growing appreciation of the methodological limitations in much of the research. Samples have often been small and selective; little account has been taken of variations in the prior home circumstances between infants receiving and not receiving group day care; and the strange situation may have a different meaning for children receiving day care (see the reviews cited above). Fourth, the overall social context of day care has changed over the last 50 years. There has been a marked rise in the employment of mothers with young children (so that some form of alternative care has been needed for a much larger segment of the child population); in response to both changing attitudes and increased longevity after completion of the child-rearing years, a greater emphasis is now placed on the careers and education of women; in many countries, there has been a growing acceptance that the state should provide free or subsidized group day care; and there have been changes in people's perception of the needs of children, so that the quality of care both in group settings and in families during the non-group-care hours may have altered.

In response to all these considerations, the National Institute of Child Health and Human Development [NICHD] in the United States has undertaken the largest ($n = 1,153$, 10 sites), most rigorous, and most systematic evaluation of day care ever undertaken (NICHD Early Child Care Research Network, 1997, 1998). The findings at the age of 15 months were informative in showing that although there were significant effects of maternal sensitivity and responsiveness on children's distress during separations from their mothers during the strange situation, there were no overall main effects of child care experience (however assessed) on attachment security. But child care was important in its interaction with family features: Infants were less likely to be secure when low maternal sensitivity/responsiveness was combined with poor-quality, or changing, child care arrangements. Those findings are limited in two key respects: The outcome extended only to the age of 15 months, and it was assessed only with the strange situation. Even so, they highlight the importance of considering children's rearing experiences as a whole, rather than focusing on day care in isolation. Other questions remain to be answered. For example, given the importance of maternal qualities for children receiving group day care, what is the influence on the children's emotional adjustment of

their security of attachment to caregivers at the day care setting and are these effects independent of the quality of the child–parent relationship (see NICHD Early Childhood Research Network, 1997, 1998)? The research undertaken so far suggests that supplementary caregiver–child attachment relationships may well be influential (see, e.g., Aviezer, van IJzendoorn, Sagi, & Schuengel, 1994; Howes, Rodning, Galluzzo, & Myers, 1988), but much still needs to be learned about the interplay among different attachment relationships (see Howes, Chapter 29, this volume). To what extent does the importance of continuity in relationships (which seems vital in the family) also apply to caregiving in day care?

Adoption

During the last few decades, there has been a radical change in patterns of adoption (Hersov, 1994). Adoptions during the period of early infancy have become quite infrequent; by contrast, the adoption of older children, often with special needs deriving from seriously adverse early experience or from the presence of physical disabilities or mental disorders, has become relatively more frequent. Intercountry adoptions, sometimes of extremely deprived children, have increased (Tizard, 1991). "Open" adoptions, involving continuing contact with the biological parents, have begun to occur; it has also become acceptable, as well as practically possible, for adult adoptees to search out their biological parents (Haimes & Timms, 1985; Samuels, 1990).

It is obvious that attachment theory predicts that many of these changes are likely to have implications for the security and pattern of attachment relationships. But there has been regrettably (and surprisingly) little research into this possibility. Moreover, little of the research has used standardized measures of attachment. In one of the very few studies that did do so, Singer, Burkowski, and Waters (1985) found no general increase in risk associated with early adoption, but an increase associated with multiple previous placements. Howe (1995) undertook an extensive clinical study (which did not include standard attachment assessment procedures) of later-adopted children. Relationship difficulties were relatively common; in particular, Howe noted a subgroup of children with a history of neglect, abuse, and/or multiple placements who had difficulty forming relationships, who displayed indiscriminate behavior towards others, and who had relatively poor developmental outcomes. Such patterns had been noted in earlier studies of institution-reared children (e.g., Provence & Lipton, 1962; Wolkind, 1974), and have also been seen in recent studies of children from very poor-quality Romanian institutions adopted into U.K. families (Keaveney & O'Connor, 1997) or Canadian families (Chisholm et al., 1995; Goldberg & Marvin, 1996; Marcovitch et al., 1997). It is important that the strange situation does not seem optimal for picking up this pattern, and that the standard ratings do not reflect the particular unusual qualities well.

Even less is known about the implications for attachment relationships of open adoption (although research into its effects on self-esteem is beginning—Wrobel, Ayers-Lopez, Grotevant, McRoy, & Friedrick, 1996) or of the search in adult life for biological parents. As with the early studies that led to the development of attachment theory, systematic research into the consequences of these far-reaching changes in patterns of adoption should be equally informative with respect to policy/practice implications and to an understanding of social development (and hence for attachment theory itself). Action research involves the twin concerns of improving services through increased knowledge and of developing knowledge through the study of innovatory practice and of naturally occurring variations in children's circumstances (Maughan & Rutter, 1985). The changing patterns of adoption provide a range of "natural experiments" that should be most informative in testing hypotheses deriving from attachment theory. Unfortunately, research so far has made very little use of these opportunities. But the atypicality of the patterns of social relationships shown by some of the children who have experienced serious early adversities, or who have had early rearing in an institution, highlights the need to look beyond standard ratings as applied to children's behavior in the strange situation. This observational procedure has had a quite remarkable degree of success, but it is not necessarily ideal or sufficient on its own in all circumstances (Lamb et al., 1984). In addition, it is highly desirable to consider social relationships outside as well as inside an attachment framework (Dunn, 1993).

Although the adoption of older children and of children with special needs is often very successful, the rate of adoption breakdown in such instances is higher than with adoptions in early infancy (Thoburn, 1993). Attachment dysfunction in the adoptive parent–child dyad is often suggested in these cases (Johnson & Fein, 1991;

Sack & Dale, 1982), but there have been few systematic studies. Accordingly, little is known about the roles of parental sensitivity and parental representations of attachment, or about the consequences of adoption breakdown experiences for subsequent attachment relationships.

Up to now, insofar as there has been research into the attachment relationships of adopted children, the main focus has been on whether late-adopted children can still develop normal selective attachments with their adopting parents (see Schaffer, 1990; Tizard, 1977). There is, however, the equally important issue of the ways in which a person's internal working model of relationships are influenced by cognitive sets as well as by actual experiences. Are adopted children's models affected by the knowledge that their social parents are not their biological parents? What is the meaning, with respect to attachment, of their "relationship" with the biological parents they have never seen? What are the implications of wanting to seek out these parents? Are the models influenced if the adoption is transracial (Phoenix & Owen, 1996; Tizard & Phoenix, 1993)?

Births Following Assisted Reproduction

The need to examine attachment issues in a broader framework of social relationships is even more apparent in relation to children born following assisted reproduction of one sort or another. An adopted child has two sets of parents to consider, but a child born following assisted reproduction may have as many as five parents from four families(!)—the egg donor, the sperm donor, the surrogate birth mother, and the two social parents known to the child as "father" and "mother." What difference, if any, does this make to how such children think about themselves and their relationships? There has been a major increase in such births as a result of technological developments such as *in vitro* fertilization, as well as the use of donor insemination and surrogate motherhood. The limited evidence on the social development of children born through these means indicates that overall they do not constitute a high-risk group (Golombok, Cook, Bish, & Murray, 1995; McMahon, Ungerer, Beaurepaire, Tennant, & Saunders, 1995; van Balen, 1996), but very little is known about the consequences, if any, for attachment. Given a normal pattern of social rearing, there is no reason to expect any generally adverse effect on relationships, but what internal model of relationships do the children have? There is a culturally well-accepted "story" about adoption, but it is by no means clear how it should be explained to a young child that the egg and/or sperm that gave rise to the child's conception came from some unknown donor. Indeed, there is not yet a consensus that a child conceived via assisted reproduction should be told about the circumstances, although given the difficulties in maintaining secrecy, it might be expected to be desirable in most cases. Attachment theory is useful in suggesting the likely importance of internal working models of relationships, but the currently available standardized methods of assessment in childhood may not be well adapted to tap the key elements.

Foster Care

Initially, as noted earlier, foster care was viewed as the remedy to the problem of providing continuity in personalized caregiving in an institutional setting. Regrettably, the reality has fallen well short of this goal; fostering breakdown and multiple foster placements are all too common (National Research Council, 1993; Wolkind & Rushton, 1994). Even in the absence of breakdown, there is some suggestion that children in foster care exhibit higher rates of emotional and behavioral disturbance than nonfostered children from similar high-risk backgrounds (Shealy, 1995). The mechanisms involved remain obscure, and it is unclear whether attachment relationships constitute the key mediating variable. A single general answer is unlikely to be found, if only because there is such heterogeneity in what is involved in foster care. At one extreme, some instances of long-term fostering differ from adoption in little more than name and legal status. In these circumstances, the children often view their family situation as having all the qualities of lifetime commitment associated with adoption (Holbrook, 1984; Raynor, 1980). At the other extreme, some fostering is deliberately planned as short-term, with the foster parents looking after a substantial number of children who rotate in and out of the family. It might seem that a closer parallel here is with group residential care, albeit in a private home setting and without the disadvantage of ever-changing caregivers. The reality, however, is different. Studies in both the United Kingdom and the United States have shown that unless children return home quickly, temporary foster care is likely to turn into long-term care

without clear plans for the future, and with a high likelihood of frequent moves (Fanshell & Shinn, 1978; Maas & Engler, 1959; Rowe & Lambert, 1973).

Attachment theory strongly suggests that these variations in patterns of foster care, and especially the moves, are likely to have implications for children's selective attachments; once more, however, a paucity of systematic research means that we lack knowledge on whether, or in what way, this is the case. Quite apart from the effects of different qualities in caregiving by foster parents, there is a need to determine the consequences of variations in long-term commitment, of changes in placement, and of foster care when a changing roster of children in the family is involved, as well as the nature of a child's relationship with his or her biological family *during* foster placements.

Residential Care

Although long-term residential care has become an unfavored option for children when family parenting has broken down, it continues to be used for some children. Research findings have been consistent in showing that children reared from early life in an institutional setting have a greatly increased rate of emotional and behavioral disturbance, including relationship difficulties (Quinton & Rutter, 1988; Small et al., 1991; Wolkind & Rushton, 1994). It has generally been assumed that a key risk is the lack of continuous personalized caregiving but it is not known that this is in fact the case. The study by Vorria et al. (1998a, 1998b) of children in Greek institutions is informative in two respects. First, unlike the usual situation in the United Kingdom and United States, there was little turnover in caregivers; despite this, the level of psychological difficulties was high. It may be inferred either that the risks lay in nonattachment features of the children's lives, or that the quality of caregiver–child relationships was more important than continuity for attachment. Second, the psychological functioning of children who did not come from discordant/disharmonious families (usually admitted because they were orphaned or because of family poverty) was much better (and in most respects not appreciably different from that of controls). The implication is that the adverse responses to an institutional rearing may be (at least partially) dependent on the conjunction with either genetic risk or adverse rearing experiences in infancy prior to admission to residential care. A longitudinal study of children admitted to institutions in very early infancy, with measures of attachment both early and later, would be informative.

Clinical experience suggests that many seriously disturbed older children and adolescents who require some form of alternative care due to family breakdown do not adapt well to fostering, and that good-quality group residential care may be a preferred option. However, there do not appear to be any systematic studies of the social development of such children in different settings to determine whether or not that is the case.

Also, there are still parts of the world (e.g., Greece) where it is not uncommon for children to be admitted to residential group care in early infancy and then to be adopted at some time in the second year of life. The situation constitutes an important "natural experiment" for studying the effect on selective attachment relationships of this transition.

Changes in Family Constellations

The last 50 years have seen far-reaching changes both in family constellations and in public attitudes toward the family (Hess, 1995; Humphrey & Humphrey, 1988). These include a massive increase in the frequency of divorce; a marked rise in nonmarital cohabitations resulting in childbirth, and a large expansion of the proportion of children who have experienced a period of rearing by a single parent, but, in parallel with the continuing high rate of remarriage, an equally great increase in the proportion living in stepfamilies. Other developments include a growing awareness of the importance of fathers as parents (Lamb, 1986; Steele, Steele, & Fonagy, 1996); a marked increase in babies born to women in their late 30s (Berryman, Thorpe, & Windridge, 1995); an increase in children born to parents of different ethnic origins (Phoenix & Owen, 1996); a rise in two-career families, with a somewhat greater sharing of parenting between the two parents (although mothers continue to take by far the larger share of responsibility—Lewis & Cooper, 1988); and an increase in the use of joint custody after divorce (Maccoby & Mnookin, 1992). In addition, there has been a growing awareness of the role of grandparents and of the attachments of grandchildren to grandparents (Kornhaber & Woodward, 1981), as well as some changes in decisions regarding their rights in

family law with respect to visitation (see Thompson, Connell, & Bridges, 1988, for an analysis of how this has come about in the absence of a clear understanding of the complex psychological issues involved).

Relatively little attachment research has focused on the implications of these major changes in the family. There has been some research on father–infant attachment (see Cox, Owen, Henderson, & Margand, 1992; Fox, Kimmerly, & Schafer, 1991; Steele et al., 1996), but it tends not to figure much in overviews of attachment (see, e.g., Belsky & Cassidy, 1994; Carlson & Sroufe, 1995). Grandparents have received even less attention, and the large research literature on divorce and stepfamilies (Amato, 1991; Booth & Dunn, 1994; Hetherington & Clingempeel, 1992) includes very little on attachment issues. This relative neglect stands in contrast to the range of other perspectives (legal, economic, and social) applied to divorce and remarriage (see, e.g., Hanson, McLanahan, & Thomson, 1996; Mahoney, 1994; McLanahan & Booth, 1989), and to the evidence of the psychopathological risks associated with divorce for psychological functioning both in childhood (Amato, 1991; Emery, 1988) and in adult life (Amato, 1996; Amato & Booth, 1991; Chase-Lansdale, Cherlin, & Kiernan, 1995; Cherlin et al., 1991). Early writings from an attachment perspective focused on parental *loss* as the key risk factor for children when parents divorced. The much lower risks associated with parental death (see, e.g., Rutter, 1971), together with the evidence of effects on children of conflict both prior to the divorce (Amato & Booth, 1996; Block, Block, & Gjerde, 1986) and after the divorce (Hanson et al., 1996), cast doubt on this implication. For a while, social scientists, especially those with feminist leanings, focused on the profound economic effects of divorce as a possible mediator of risks for the children. There is no doubt about the reality of such effects on mothers; however, the evidence that remarriage remedies the economic ill effects but does not reduce the psychopathological risks for the children (see, e.g., Hanson et al., 1996) has made this explanation implausible.

Attention has now largely shifted to the risks associated with family discord and negative parent–child relationships, but questions remain on the mechanisms involved (Fincham, Grych, & Osborne, 1994; Rutter, 1994a). In most circumstances there is an association between overall family discord and parent–child conflict (Belsky, 1984; Engfer, 1988; Rutter, 1988), but this is much less evident in stepfamilies; indeed, there may even be a trend in the opposite direction (Hetherington, 1988). It seems that specific issues of rivalry, jealousy, and displacement may be more influential than overall problems in relationships. It would be helpful to have more research on what happens to selective attachment relationships in these changing circumstances. Once more, however, if the issue is to be tackled effectively, it will be essential to look beyond attachment in order to consider family functioning, parenting, and social relationships with respect to a range of possible causal mechanisms for the increased psychopathological risks involved.

Nevertheless, there are many issues on which a specific attachment perspective is needed. For example, what happens to children's relationships with the noncustodial parent when he or she (usually he) leaves the home? To what extent is the usual decrease in contact with that parent affected by the relationship prior to the divorce, and how far are the consequences of divorce moderated by the prior relationship? To what extent can even "disorganized" attachment represent an acute response to relationship stress in otherwise securely attached children (Lyons-Ruth, Alpern, & Repacholi, 1993)? What emphasis should be placed on attachment considerations (Hodges & Tizard, 1989; Kaplan, Ridder, Hennon, & Charles, 1991), rather than on custodial arrangements or children's psychological adjustment (Maccoby & Mnookin, 1992)? What is the importance of attachment qualities (vis à vis other relationship considerations) with respect to children's responses to parental divorce and remarriage (Booth & Dunn, 1994; Hetherington & Clingempeel, 1992), and how should these be viewed within the broader context of family social systems (Stevenson-Hinde, 1991)?

Postnatal Depression and Psychosis

Researchers and clinicians have been aware for a long time that parental mental disorder involves psychiatric risks for the children, and that some of these risks are mediated through impairments in parenting (Cummings & Davies, 1994; Downey & Coyne, 1990; Rutter, 1989). In recent years, however, attention has focused particularly on the effects of postnatal mental disorder (Murray & Cooper, 1997). The focus has come about through four main routes: (1) the development of

mother-and-baby units to treat puerperal psychoses (Brockington, 1996; Kumar & Hipwell, 1994); (2) the extensive evidence that maternal depression is associated with parenting features that would seem to carry risks for the children (Rutter, 1990); (3) a few findings appearing to suggest that a mother's depression in the first year after a child's birth may lead to cognitive impairment through effects on the social interaction of the mother and baby (Hay, 1997; Hay & Kumar, 1995; Murray, 1992); and (4) the development and testing of treatments for postnatal depression that focus on mother–infant interaction (Cooper, Murray, Hooper, & West, 1996).

The development of mother-and-baby units raises the critical question of whether babies are better off remaining with their severely ill mothers in a supervised hospital setting or whether care at home with other caregivers (such as fathers or grandparents) is preferable. The wrongheaded notion that parent–child "bonding" depended on early skin-to-skin contact during an early critical period (Klaus & Kennell, 1976) has now been abandoned (Goldberg, 1983; Kennell & Klaus, 1984; Sluckin, Herbert, & Sluckin, 1983), but the importance of considering social-contextual influences on the development over time of parent–child relationships remains (Rutter & Rutter, 1993).

The associations among maternal depression, impaired parenting, and children's psychological development raise issues that go well beyond attachment, but they highlight the need to consider the possible mediating or moderating role of difficulties in selective attachment. It is particularly necessary for applied research to test alternative modes of treatment, and not to assume that theory indicates which will be most effective. Cooper and Murray's (1997) finding, in a well-planned controlled trial, that cognitive-behavioral, counseling, and psychodynamic treatments worked equally well underlines the point.

Attachment Disorders and Attachment Treatments

Other chapters of this volume deal more extensively with attachment disorders and attachment treatments (see especially Dozier, Stovall, & Albus, Chapter 22; Greenberg, Chapter 21; and Lieberman & Zeanah, Chapter 24), but it is necessary to mention a few considerations briefly here—if only because of the increased incidence of psychopathology among children experiencing the patterns of upbringing discussed in this chapter, and because of the growth of various forms of relationship therapy to treat such problems (Cicchetti, Toth, & Lynch, 1995; Lieberman, 1991; Zeanah & Emde, 1994). We highlight four main issues. First, attachment qualities have been shown to be important features of social relationships across the entire lifespan, and to play an important role in risk and protective mechanisms for a wide range of psychopathology (see Belsky & Nezworski, 1988; Rutter, 1995a, 1995b; Sameroff & Emde, 1989; Zeanah & Emde, 1994). This constitutes sufficient reason for arguing that research needs to be undertaken to delineate the processes involved and thereby the clinical implications.

Second, the same research has indicated the lack of diagnosis specificity in the effects (Cicchetti et al., 1995). Insecure attachment of one kind or another has been associated with a range of psychopathology that spans social inhibition/anxiety (Cassidy & Berlin, 1994) to conduct disorder (Greenberg & Speltz, 1988; Lyons-Ruth, 1996), suicidal behavior (Adam, Sheldon-Keller, & West, 1996), substance use/delinquency in adolescence (Allen, Hauser, & Borman-Spurrell, 1996), and personality disorders in adult life (Fonagy et al., 1996; Patrick, Hobson, Castle, Howard, & Maughan, 1994). Attachment problems are prominent in children exposed to physical abuse and neglect and to an institutional rearing (Zeanah, 1996), but they are by no means confined to these groups. If so many psychiatric disorders are associated with attachment insecurity, it ceases to have much explanatory value. The situation is parallel to that with negative life events (Brown & Harris, 1989). The all-pervasive association does not, of course, mean that attachment problems do not play a causal role, but it does point to the difficulty of deciding when disordered attachment mechanisms predominate.

Third, although the psychiatric diagnosis of "reactive attachment disorder of childhood" (with inhibited and disinhibited subtypes) has been loosely informed by attachment research findings (but not as much as it should be—Zeanah, 1996), the validity of the diagnosis remains largely untested (O'Connor, Bredenkamp, & Rutter, in press; Zeanah & Emde, 1994). Also, as Richters and Volkmar (1994) have noted, the syndromes includes many features that appear to extend beyond an abnormality in selective attachment. Indeed, Zeanah (1996) has argued that

the conditions are more maltreatment disorders than attachment disorders.

Fourth, even when there is an undoubted attachment problem, it is by no means self-evident what form treatment should take. Helpful suggestions are available (Belsky & Nezworski, 1988; Cicchetti et al., 1995), and clearly it would seem necessary to remedy both the quality and consistency of caregiving when these are deficient, but what focus (if any) should there be on the children's internal models of relationships? What role should there be for cognitive restructuring? Should the focus be on present parent–child relationships, or on the origins of difficulties in past deficiencies in caregiving, or on both? The few data on the results of attachment-based interventions are not particularly encouraging (see Zeanah & Emde, 1994), but it is far too early to draw conclusions on efficacy. There is evidence that therapeutic interventions do have an effect on parental sensitivity, but the effects on the children's attachment security are much weaker (van den Boom, 1995; van IJzendoorn, Juffer, & Duyvesteyn, 1995). It is not certain that sensitivity is the most crucial component of parenting for attachment security; the evidence indicates its relevance, but it also points to the equally influential role of other parental qualities such as mutuality, synchrony, stimulation, positive attitude and emotional support (DeWolff & van IJzendoorn, 1997). The most important constraints on the understanding of treatment, however, are (1) the uncertainty of what is needed for the children (as distinct from the parents) when their attachment problems derive from past, rather than present, experiences; and (2) the uncertainty regarding the benefits with respect to reduction in psychopathology that follow improvements in attachment security.

The parallel with posttraumatic stress disorder rings warning bells. Theory has suggested the value of debriefing as a therapeutic technique to be applied early, but the few controlled trials are all negative on the benefits (Bisson & Deahl, 1996; Hobbs, Mayou, Harrison, & Worlock, 1996; Lee, Slade, & Lygo, 1996). Research to aid the selection of appropriate treatment is essential and likely to be informative with respect to both theory and practice (Zeanah & Emde, 1994). As we have sought to emphasize throughout, the way to understand a phenomenon is to seek to change it, and the way to develop effective methods of intervention is to understand the phenomenon that requires relief (Maughan & Rutter, 1985).

CONCEPTUAL AND METHODOLOGICAL ISSUES REGARDING THE POLICY IMPLICATIONS OF ATTACHMENT THEORY

Some aspects of attachment theory have already had a direct, significant, and probably permanent impact on child care policies and practice. The need for sensitivity and responsiveness in child–caregiver relationships is now emphasized in both day care (Howes & Hamilton, 1992) and residential settings (Shealy, 1995), as well as in ordinary family circumstances. There is a general acceptance of the effects on psychological development of young children's early social experiences, of the need for individual caregiving, and of the importance of continuity in relationships. Alongside attention to attachment issues, there has also come an awareness of the importance for children's psychological development of play, communication, and interaction. Controversies over the developmental impact of social experiences within the normal range continue (Rowe, 1994; Scarr, 1992; Wachs, 1992), but there is no longer serious dispute either over the ill effects of serious adversities in parenting or over the crucial importance of family relationships within the broader range of children's experiences (Rutter, 1995a, 1995b). Moreover, there is an awareness that attachment considerations need to be applied to a wide range of both clinical and child care policy issues. What is distinctly sparse is research in applied settings to determine *how* these considerations should be applied and *which* interventions to deal with attachment difficulties should be used in prevention and treatment. Before discussing the future with respect to attachment theory and social policy, we review selectively five interdependent issues that have significant social policy potential, but that require further research in basic and applied settings: (1) the nature of ontogenetic changes in attachment relationships; (2) dyadic and individual attachment qualities; (3) the association between attachment and nonattachment components of relationships; (4) the role of attachment in psychopathology; and (5) assessment of attachment.

Ontogenetic Change

As discussed more fully in other chapters (see especially Allen & Land, Chapter 15; Crowell, Fraley, & Shaver, Chapter 20; George & Solomon, Chapter 28; Grossmann, Grossmann, & Zimmer-mann, Chapter 33; Hazan & Zeifman, Chapter 16; Marvin & Britner, Chapter 3; and Thompson, Chapter 13), attachment relationships begin in infancy but continue throughout childhood into adult life. That this is so is not in serious doubt, but numerous questions remain. Progress has come through three main innovations: (1) the development of Q-sort procedures that could be applied to extended observations in the home by either professionals or the parents themselves (Pederson & Moran, 1995; Waters & Deane, 1985; Waters, Vaughn, Posada, & Kondo-Ikemura, 1995); (2) modification of the strange situation for use with children during the postinfancy preschool years (Cassidy & Marvin with the MacArthur Working Group on Attachment, 1992); and (3) the development of interview and narrative methods of assessing attachment representations during early and middle childhood (Main, Kaplan, & Cassidy, 1985; Oppenheim & Waters, 1995). Although the evidence is still limited, research findings suggest that these different approaches are broadly tapping the same basic constructs, although they are not isomorphic (Strayer, Verissimo, Vaughn, & Howes, 1995). It is also clear that the same methods can be used with professional caregivers as well as parents—an important consideration when attachment is being studied in applied settings (Sagi et al., 1995).

So far, so good. The difficulty comes with developmental linkages from parent–child (or caregiver–child) relationships in early childhood to peer relationships in middle childhood. How are attachment qualities in close friendships shown? Follow-up studies of institution-reared children (Hodges & Tizard, 1989) and other children (Carlson & Sroufe, 1995) indicate that early difficulties in parent–child attachment may be particularly likely to lead to a lack of selectivity, commitment, and confiding in friendships. Circumstantial evidence suggests that confiding and emotional exchange may well index attachment qualities in friendships, but satisfactory means of assessing security features in such relationships have yet to be developed.

Measures of attachment qualities in adult life were pioneered by Main et al. (1985) in their development of the Adult Attachment Interview (AAI; see van IJzendoorn & Bakermans-Kranenburg, 1996, for normative data, and van IJzendoorn, 1995, for validity findings), and by Hazan and Shaver (1987) and Crowell (see Owens et al., 1995) in their development of questionnaire and interview methods for assessing attachment qualities in adults' love relationships. Hazan and Shaver (1994), in their review of research findings, have proposed that features such as a lack of self-disclosure or indiscriminate, overly intimate self-disclosure; a reluctance to commitment in relationships; and undue jealousy or feelings of loneliness reflect insecure attachment in adult relationships (see also Feeney, Chapter 17, this volume). There is no doubt about the need to use features other than responses to separation and reunion as measures of selective attachment in the years after childhood, but it remains to be determined whether qualities such as lack of self-disclosure in adult life mean the same as insecurity in infancy. The AAI also differs crucially in its focus on the person's overall thinking about attachment relationships, rather than the qualities shown or felt in any one relationship.

Dyadic and Individual Attachment Qualities

This crucial difference in the conceptualization of attachment in the AAI raises the basic issue of the connection between attachment security as a feature of a specific dyadic relationship and attachment security as a general characteristic of an individual that extends across relationships (Rutter, 1995a). Attachment theory presupposes that this transformation does indeed occur, but little is known about the processes involved. Children's relationships with key figures in their environment intercorrelate only weakly with respect to security–insecurity (Fox et al., 1991), although there is a degree of congruence (Sagi et al., 1995). Particularly in regard to children with a mix of risk and protective experiences involving multiple caregivers, it is necessary to ask how discrepant relationships are dealt with in the transformation to an individual characteristic. Does the most important relationship predominate, is there a balance between differing relationships, or does one secure relationship compensate for insecurities in others (Bretherton & Waters, 1985)?

The usual assumption in attachment theory is that the integration takes place by means of an affective–cognitive internal working model (Belsky & Cassidy, 1994; Bretherton, 1990; Carlson & Sroufe, 1995; Stern, 1985). There is no doubt that individuals from early childhood onward do indeed actively process their experiences, and theorists both within and outside an attachment framework (Kagan, 1984) agree on the importance attributed to this process. As astutely appreciated by Main et al. (1985) in their development of the AAI, individuals differ greatly in both the extent and manner of their integration of past painful experiences into their present self-concepts. It seems highly likely that these differences in processing play a key role in determining how early attachment relationships affect later relationships. Nevertheless, there is a paucity of empirical research findings on the nature and effects of such processing, and several problems have yet to be resolved.

First, at least as far as the processes in infancy are concerned, there are uncertainties over whether the cognitive competence to represent both sides of a discrepant relationship is available at that age (Dunn, 1993). There are parallel uncertainties over how these early percepts are remembered and how they link up with later thinking patterns (see Rutter, Maughan, Pickles, & Simonoff, 1998). Second, researchers have only just begun to examine the hypothesis that differences in attachment security are associated with variations in cognitive processing (Belsky, Spritz, & Crnic, 1996), and so far there is very limited evidence on the extent to which effects on personality functioning or psychopathology derive from differences in the ways in which earlier experiences are thought about, rather than from the experiences themselves (see Patrick et al., 1994). Third, as things stand now, the notion of internal working models lacks specific predictive power. Because it is so all-encompassing, it is difficult to derive refutable and testable hypotheses on its role (Hinde, 1988). It has the potential to give rise to testable hypotheses, as articles in two special issues of the *Journal of Consulting and Clinical Psychology* (1996, Vol. 64, Nos. 1 and 2) indicate, but this process is only just beginning. Fourth, it is not obvious that either the apparent effect of early rearing in an institution on later peer relationships (Hodges & Tizard, 1989), or the pattern of indiscriminate friendliness (Chisholm et al., 1995) or autistic-like patterns (Rutter, Anderson-Wood, Beckett, et al., in press) seen in some children who experienced profound deprivation in their institutional upbringing, is best explained in this way. The effects seem to stem from experiences in the period of very early childhood, and many of the children seen by Rutter et al. (in press) showed severe cognitive impairment at that age. Fifth, the research findings on the interconnections among social relationships provide strong indications of compensatory and rivalry effects (Dunn, 1988, 1993; Hinde & Stevenson-Hinde, 1988). Although these findings are far from incompatible with attachment theory, the theory does not seem to provide an adequate explanation on its own.

Attachment and Nonattachment Components of Relationships

As we have indicated, one of the crucial contributions of attachment theory was the differentiation of the security-promoting attachment features of relationships from their other qualities (Bowlby, 1969/1982). Thus parent–child relationships normally show strong attachment elements, but they also involve caregiving, disciplinary features, the shaping of social experiences, the provision of models of behavior, teaching, conversational interchanges (and hence the development of ideas), and playful interaction. There has been almost no research into the interconnections among these different elements, or into which feature carries the main risk or protective power with respect to psychopathology or later adaptive social functioning.

For example, family discord is a well-documented risk factor for conduct disturbances and antisocial behavior more generally (Emery, 1982, 1988; Rutter, 1994a). But by what mechanism does it operate? Does the risk lie in the attachment insecurity brought about by recurrent hostile interchanges, or in the low esteem engendered by scapegoating, or in the models of aggressive behavior, or in the lack of teaching of effective social problem-solving strategies, or in the confused but ineffective feedback on the child's behavior resulting from disorganized discipline (in which punishment is as likely to stem from the parent's negative mood as from anything that the child has done), or in the lack of systematic monitoring and supervision of the child's behavior? Moreover, when is conflict dysfunctional and when is it constructive, and how is insecure attachment linked with conflict in interpersonal relationships (Shantz & Hartup, 1992)?

The interventions for which there is evidence of efficacy with respect to either prevention or treatment have not appeared to focus on attachment qualities (McGuire, 1995). Thus, the Perry Preschool Program (Schweinhart, Barnes, & Weikart, 1993) took a broad-ranging educational approach, and reviewers have pointed to the potential of high-quality nursery provision for the prevention of delinquency (Farrington, 1995, 1996). The parent training methods pioneered by Patterson and his colleagues (Patterson, Chamberlain, & Reid, 1982; Patterson, Reid, & Dishion, 1992) and by Webster-Stratton (1996; Webster-Stratton, Hollinsworth, & Kolpacoff, 1989) similarly focus on nonattachment features. Does this mean that effective discipline and monitoring are more important than attachment relationships? Clearly that does not follow, if only because the successful interventions are all very broad-based. Effective parenting involves harmonious family interactions, responsivity to children's individual needs, and the use of praise and positive appreciation. Authoritative parenting (Baumrind, 1991; Hetherington, 1993), which seems the pattern most likely to foster adaptive psychological development in children, would seem to have much in common with the sensitive responsivity shown to promote attachment security. The truth of the matter, however, is that we lack empirical evidence on the connections between attachment and nonattachment components of relationships, and especially on the specific consequences of the different aspects of parenting. Such evidence is greatly needed and requires a coming together of contrasting parenting perspectives in order to test competing hypotheses. This may be particularly important when researchers are making cross-cultural comparisons.

The Role of Attachment in Psychopathology

As noted above, attachment insecurity has been associated with a wide range of psychiatric disorders, including (but not confined to) those associated with child care circumstances thought to create risks for attachment relationships. Accordingly, it is necessary to ask how practitioners are to differentiate the disorders in which relationship insecurity represents a key feature. Because humans are social beings, it is likely that any serious mental disorder will affect social relationships adversely, and empirical research findings indicate that that is indeed the case. It is likely that this will often involve attachment insecurity. In some cases, the insecurity will have preceded the disorder and served as a risk factor for it. In other instances, although the insecurity is not a prior cause, it will constitute such a central part of the disorder that it will warrant therapeutic attention. In yet other cases, it is likely that it will be no more than a nonspecific indicator of mental malfunction. The situation is broadly comparable to that with anxiety or depression: Both are frequently present as nonspecific symptoms in a wide range of psychiatric disorders, but they may also constitute the defining feature of specific psychopathological conditions. The need is to determine which is which.

The problem is aggravated by the very high base rate of attachment insecurity (from 30% to 50%), as assessed by the strange situation, in the general population of infants (Campos, Barrett, Lamb, Goldsmith, & Stenberg, 1983). As all reviewers of attachment findings have emphasized, insecurity is not in itself an indicator of psychopathology (Belsky & Cassidy, 1994; Belsky & Nezworski, 1988; Carlson & Sroufe, 1995). Indeed, there may even be circumstances in which secure attachment to a deviant parent is a risk factor (Radke-Yarrow et al., 1995). Furthermore, the presence of insecure attachment in association with mental disorder does not necessarily indicate that it is causally connected with it. With a base rate of nearly half the children, the association is bound to arise by chance in many instances. The development of "avoidant/ ambivalent" and "disorganized" categories (the latter term being the one that has come to be accepted) (Crittenden, 1988; Main & Solomon, 1990; Radke-Yarrow, Cummings, Kuczynski, & Chapman, 1985) has probably helped somewhat, in that these seem to be more strongly associated with psychopathology. Nevertheless, they do not pick up all cases of "pathological" insecurity, and it cannot be assumed either that these categories invariably indicate pathology.

Any judgment on the role of attachment insecurity must also take into account the possibility that the insecurity as measured may derive from a more general characteristic of negative emotionality. This has usually been conceptualized as the effect of temperament on attachment measures (Vaughn et al., 1992), but Rothbart and Bates (1998) suggest that it may be an oversimplification to view temperament as an individual characteristic and attachment as a reflection of a particular dyadic relationship. Rather, it is argued, both reflect different (but related) aspects of the ways in which children regulate affect and cope with stress. Whatever the connections in ordinary circumstances, it is likely that abnormal anxiety, maladaptive coping, or extreme stress will have a greater effect on attachment security than the vice versa.

Assessment Procedures

A distinguishing feature of attachment research has been the use of the strange situation as a standardized means of assessment. This has made it relatively straightforward to compare findings across studies, and the well-established procedure and coding scheme have undoubtedly been important in leading to generally robust findings. Nevertheless, the requirements of a very controlled situation and of detailed training in the coding methods are likely to have played a part in the limited application of this method in psychiatry, social work, and other applied settings. An unfortunate and unintended side effect has been that attachment has often been defined rather differently in these practice settings, with sometimes misleading operationalizations and confused findings (cf. Berman, 1988a, 1988b; Kelly, 1988).

Although these differences in conceptualization and measurement in applied settings, when they have occurred, make for difficulties in integrating findings between standardized attachment studies and clinical reports, there is a need for the further development of assessment procedures. Four main requirements stand out most clearly. First, codings need to be developed to pick up qualities (e.g., indiscriminate friendliness) that are not well tapped by the standard schemes. It may well be that these reflect features that are not most appropriately conceptualized as security–insecurity, but they do seem to reflect important aspects of maladaptive social development that concern intimate relationships. Second, there is a need to develop measures based on children's behavior in everyday situations rather than in the laboratory. Q-sort methods represent an important step in that direction, but they are not well adapted for use in routine practice. Third, it is necessary to find some means of quantifying, and not just categorizing, attachment features. Neither theory nor practice suggests that insecurity is a feature that does not vary in degree, and measures to reflect dimensional variations are needed. Fourth, it is necessary to be able to differentiate attachment insecurity that is a characteristic of one particular relationship from insecurity that has become a more pervasive individual characteristic of a child's social relationships. The adult measures have gone in this direction, and child measures are beginning to do so, but quite a lot remains to be accomplished.

CONCLUSIONS

In our overview of the applications of attachment theory to child care policies, it has been necessary to present more questions than answers. Regrettably, with respect to most child care issues, there has not been a substantial body of empirical research findings to review. Indeed, a major theme of the chapter has been the lack of systematic studies of attachment relationships in applied settings. Both theory and practice would benefit from a much closer integration than has taken place up to now. If this is to work well, however, attention will need to be paid to the varying manifestations of attachment as children grow older, and to the variation across different types of relationships (with a special need to consider friendships with peers). Concepts and measures will also have to deal with the differentiation of attachment security–insecurity as a feature of a particular relationship and as a general feature of a person's social functioning. The connections among attachment and nonattachment components of relationships, together with their respective power as risk or protective factors, will need to be studied. Moreover, concepts and measures will have to be developed to deal with the important clinical issue of how to decide when psychopathological disorders should be considered disturbances of attachment. Finally, attachment measures will need to be modified to meet the needs of clinicians and other practitioners, who are often concerned with children from very atypical backgrounds, and who need to make their assessments in situations far removed from the research laboratory.

The policy and practice issues relevant to child care have changed dramatically over the last half century. Such issues played a key role in the initial development of attachment theory, but the conjunction of basic and applied research, and of theory and practice, has been much less evident in recent times (with the exception of the topic of group day care). Attachment theory will continue to contribute to clinical and policy issues because it is based on a solid empirical foundation, but a greater responsivity to contemporary child care issues is required. The field well illustrates Bronfenbrenner's (1974) statement that science needs social policy.

REFERENCES

Adam, K. S., Sheldon-Keller, A. E., & West, M. (1996). Attachment organization and history of suicidal behavior in clinical adolescents. *Journal of Consulting and Clinical Psychology, 64*, 264–272.

Ainsworth, M. D. S. (1967). *Infancy in Uganda: Infant care and the growth of love.* Baltimore: Johns Hopkins University Press.

Ainsworth, M. D. S., Blehar, M., Waters, E., & Wall, S. (1978). *Patterns of attachment.* Hillsdale, NJ: Erlbaum.

Allen, J. P., Hauser, S. T., & Borman-Spurrell, E. (1996). Attachment theory as a framework for understanding sequelae of severe adolescent psychopathology: An 11-year follow-up study. *Journal of Consulting and Clinical Psychology, 64*, 254–263.

Amato, P. R. (1991). Psychological distress and recall of childhood family characteristics. *Journal of Marriage and the Family, 53*, 1011–1020.

Amato, P. R. (1996). Explaining the intergenerational transmission of divorce. *Journal of Marriage and the Family, 58*, 628–640.

Amato, P. R., & Booth, A. (1991). Consequences of parental divorce and marital unhappiness for adult well-being. *Social Forces, 69*, 895–914.

Amato, P. R., & Booth, A. (1996). A prospective study of divorce and parent–child relationships. *Journal of Marriage and the Family, 58*, 356–365.

Aviezer, O., van IJzendoorn, M. H., Sagi, A., & Schuengel, C. (1994). "Children of the dream" revisited: 70 years of collective early child care in Israeli kibbutzim. *Psychological Bulletin, 116*, 99–116.

Baumrind, D. (1991). Effective parenting during the early adolescent transition. In P. A. Cowan & E. M. Hetherington (Eds.), *Family transitions* (pp. 111–163). Hillsdale, NJ: Erlbaum.

Belsky, J. (1984). The determinants of parenting: A process model. *Child Development, 55*, 83–96.

Belsky, J. (1990). Parental and nonparental care and children's socioemotional development: A decade in review. *Journal of Marriage and the Family, 52*, 885–903.

Belsky, J., & Cassidy, J. A. (1994). Attachment: Theory and evidence. In M. Rutter & D. Hay (Eds.), *Development through life: A handbook for clinicians* (pp. 373–402). Oxford: Blackwell Scientific.

Belsky, J., & Nezworski, T. (Eds.). (1988). *Clinical implications of attachment.* Hillsdale, NJ: Erlbaum.

Belsky, J., & Rovine, M. J. (1988). Nonmaternal care in the first year of life and the security of infant–parent attachment. *Child Development, 59*, 157–167.

Belsky, J., Spritz, B., & Crnic, K. (1996). Infant attachment security and affective–cognitive information processing at age 3. *Psychological Science, 7*, 111–114.

Berman, W. H. (1988a). The role of attachment in the postdivorce experience. *Journal of Personality and Social Psychology, 54*, 496–503.

Berman, W. H. (1988b). The relationship of ex-spouse attachment to adjustment following divorce. *Journal of Family Psychology, 1*, 312–328.

Berridge, D., & Cleaver, H. (1987). *Foster home breakdown.* Oxford: Blackwell.

Berryman, J., Thorpe, K., & Windridge, K. (1995). *Older mothers: Conception, pregnancy and birth after 35.* London: Pandora/HarperCollins.

Bisson, J. I., & Deahl, M. P. (1994). Psychological debriefing and prevention of post-traumatic stress: More research is needed. *British Journal of Psychiatry, 165*, 717–720.

Block, J. H., Block, J., & Gjerde, P. F. (1986). The personality of children prior to divorce: A prospective study. *Child Development, 57*, 827–840.

Booth, A., & Dunn, J. (1994). *Stepfamilies: Who benefits and who does not?* Hillsdale, NJ: Erlbaum.

Bowlby, J. (1946). *Forty-four juvenile thieves: Their characters and home life.* London: Baillière, Tindall & Cox.

Bowlby, J. (1951). *Maternal care and mental health* (WHO

Monograph Series No. 2). Geneva: World Health Organization.

Bowlby, J. (1958). The nature of the child's tie to his mother. *International Journal of Psycho-Analysis, 39,* 350–373.

Bowlby, J. (1969/1982). *Attachment and loss: Vol. 1. Attachment.* New York: Basic Books.

Bowlby, J. (1973). *Attachment and loss: Vol. 2. Separation: Anxiety and anger.* London: Hogarth Press.

Bowlby, J. (1980). *Attachment and loss: Vol. 3. Loss: Sadness and depression.* London: Hogarth Press.

Bowlby, J. (1988). *A secure base: Clinical implications of attachment theory.* London: Routledge.

Bowlby, J., Ainsworth, M. D. S., Boston, M., & Rosenbluth, D. (1956). The effects of mother–child separation: A follow up study. *British Journal of Medical Psychology, 29,* 211.

Brazelton, T. B. (1985). *Working and caring.* New York: Basic Books.

Bretherton, I. (1990). Open communication and internal working models: their role in the development of attachment relationships. In R. A. Thompson (Ed.), *Nebraska Symposium on Motivation: Vol. 36. Socioemotional development* (pp. 57–113). Lincoln: University of Nebraska Press.

Bretherton, I., & Waters, E. (Eds.). (1985). Growing points of attachment theory and research. *Monographs of the society for research in child development, 50*(1–2, Serial No. 209).

Bretherton, I., Walsh, R., Lependorf, M., & Georgeson, H. (1997). Attachment networks in postdivorce families: The maternal perspective. In L. Atkinson & K. J. Zucker (Eds.), *Attachment and psychopathology* (pp. 97–134). New York: Guilford Press.

Brockington, I. (1996). *Motherhood and mental health.* Oxford: Oxford University Press.

Bronfenbrenner, U. (1974). *Is early intervention effective?* Bethesda, MD: Office of Child Development, U.S. Department of Health, Education and Welfare.

Brown, G., & Harris, T. (Eds.). (1989). *Life events and illness.* New York: Guilford Press.

Burgoyne, H., Ormrod, R., & Richards, M. (1987). *Divorce matters.* Harmondsworth, England: Penguin.

Campos, J. J., Barrett, K., Lamb, M. E., Goldsmith, H. H., & Stenberg, C. (1983). Socioemotional development. In P. H. Mussen (Series Ed.) & M. M. Haith & J. J. Campos (Vol. Eds.), *Handbook of child psychology: Vol. 2. Infancy and developmental psychobiology* (4th ed., pp. 783–915). New York: Wiley.

Carlson, E. A., & Sroufe, L. A. (1995). Contribution of attachment theory to developmental psychopathology. In D. Cicchetti & D. J. Cohen (Eds.), *Developmental psychopathology: Vol. 1. Theory and methods* (pp. 581–617). New York: Wiley.

Casler, L. (1968). Perceptual deprivation in institutional settings. In G. Newton & S. Levine (Eds.), *Early experience and behavior: The psychobiology of development* (pp. 573–626). Springfield, IL: Charles C Thomas.

Cassidy, J., & Berlin, L. J. (1994). The insecure/ambivalent pattern of attachment: Theory and research. *Child Development, 65,* 971–991.

Cassidy, J., & Marvin, R. S., with the MacArthur Working Group on Attachment (1992). *A system for classifying individual differences in the attachment behavior of 2½ to 4½ year-old children.* Unpublished manuscript, University of Virginia.

Cassidy, J., Scolton, K. L., Kirsh, S. J., & Parke, R. D. (1996). Attachment and representations of peer relationships. *Developmental Psychology, 32,* 892–904.

Chase-Lansdale, P. L., Cherlin, A. J., & Kiernan, K. E. (1995). The long-term effects of parental divorce on the mental health of young adults: A developmental perspective. *Child Development, 66,* 1614–1634.

Cherlin, A. J., Furstenberg, F. F., Jr., Chase-Lansdale, P. L., Kiernan, K. E., Robins, P. K., Morrison, D. R., & Teitler, J. O. (1991). Longitudinal studies of effects of divorce on children in Great Britain and the United States. *Science, 252,* 1386–1389.

Cicchetti, D., Toth, S. L., & Lynch, M. (1995). Bowlby's dream comes full circle: The application of attachment theory to risk and psychopathology. In T. H. Ollendick & R. J. Prinz (Eds.), *Advances in clinical child psychology* (Vol. 17, pp. 1–75). New York: Plenum Press.

Chisholm, K., Carter, M. C., Ames, E. W., & Morison, S. J. (1995). Attachment security and indiscriminately friendly behavior in children adopted from Romanian orphanages. *Development and Psychopathology, 7,* 283–294.

Clarke-Stewart, K. A., Allhusen, V. D., & Clements, D. C. (1995). Nonparental caregiving. In M. H. Bornstein (Ed.), *Handbook of parenting: Vol. 3. Status and social conditions of parenting* (pp. 151–176). Mahwah, NJ: Erlbaum.

Cliffe, D., & Berridge, D. (1991). *Closing children's homes: An end to residential childcare?* London: National Children's Bureau.

Cooper, P. J., & Murray, L. (1997). The impact of psychological treatments of postpartum depression on maternal mood and infant development. In L. Murray & P. J. Cooper (Eds.), *Postpartum depression and child development* (pp. 201–220). New York: Guilford Press.

Cooper, P. J., Murray, L., Hooper, R., & West, A. (1996). The development and validation of a predictive index for postpartum depression. *Psychological Medicine, 26,* 627–634.

Cox, M., Owen, M., Henderson, V., & Margand, N. (1992). Prediction of infant–father and infant–mother attachment. *Developmental Psychology, 28,* 474–483.

Crittenden, P. M. (1988). Relationships as risk. In J. Belsky & T. Nezworski (Eds.), *Clinical implications of attachment* (pp. 136–174). Hillsdale, NJ: Erlbaum.

Cummings, E. M., & Davies, P. T. (1994). Maternal depression and child development. *Journal of Child Psychology and Psychiatry, 35,* 73–112.

Denno, D. W. (1996). Legal implications of genetics and crime research. In G. R. Bock & J. A. Goode (Eds.), *Genetics of criminal and antisocial behavior* (Ciba Foundation Symposium No. 194, pp. 248–256). Chichester, England: Wiley.

DeWolff, M. S., & van IJzendoorn, M. H. (1997). Sensitivity and attachment: A meta-analysis on parental antecedents of infant attachment. *Child Development, 68,* 571–591.

Dontas, C., Maratos, O., Fafoutis, M., & Karangelis, A. (1985). Early social development in institutionally reared Greek infants: Attachment and peer interaction. In I. Bretherton & E. Waters (Eds.), Growing points of attachment theory and research. *Monographs of the Society for Research in Child Development, 50*(1–2, Serial No. 209), 136–146.

Downey, G., & Coyne, J. C. (1990). Children of depressed parents: An integrative review. *Psychological Bulletin, 108,* 50–76.

Dunn, J. (1988). *The beginnings of social understanding.* Cambridge, MA: Harvard University Press.

Dunn, J. (1993). *Young children's close relationships: Beyond attachment.* Newbury Park, CA: Sage.

Egeland, B., & Hiester, M. (1995). The long-term consequences of infant day-care and mother–infant attachment. *Child Development, 66,* 474–485.

Emde, R. N. (1992). Individual meaning and increasing complexity: Contributions of Sigmund Freud and René Spitz to developmental psychology. *Developmental Psychology, 28,* 347–359.

Emery, R. E. (1982). Interparental conflict and the children of discord and divorce. *Psychological Bulletin, 92,* 310–330.

Emery, R. E. (1988). *Marriage, divorce, and children's adjustment.* Newbury Park, CA: Sage.

Engfer, A. (1988). The interrelatedness of marriage and the mother–child relationship. In R. A. Hinde & J. Stevenson-Hinde (Eds.), *Relationships within families: Mutual influences* (pp. 104–118). Oxford: Clarendon Press.

Fanshell, D., & Shinn, E. (1978). *Children in foster care.* New York: Columbia University Press.

Farrington, D. P. (1995). The explanation and prevention of youthful offending. In J. D. Hawkins (Ed.), *Delinquency and crime: Current theories* (pp. 68–148). New York: Cambridge University Press.

Farrington, D. P. (1996). *Understanding and preventing youth crime.* York, England: Joseph Rowntree Foundation/York.

Fincham, F. D., Grych, J. H., & Osborne, L. N. (1994). Does marital conflict cause child maladjustment?: Directions and challenges for longitudinal research. *Journal of Family Psychology, 8,* 128–140.

Fonagy, P., Leigh, T., Steele, M., Steele, H., Kennedy, R., Mattoon, G., Target, M., & Gerber, A. (1996). The relation of attachment status, psychiatric classification, and response to psychotherapy. *Journal of Consulting and Clinical Psychology, 64,* 22–31.

Fox, N. A., Kimmerly, N. L., & Schafer, W. D. (1991). Attachment to mother/attachment to father: A meta-analysis. *Child Development, 62,* 210–225.

Gewirtz, J. L. (1972). Attachment, dependence, and a distinction in terms of stimulus control. In J. L. Gewirtz (Ed.), *Attachment and dependency* (pp. 139–177). Washington, DC: Winston.

Goldberg, S. (1983). Parent–infant bonding: Another look. *Child Development, 54,* 1355–1382.

Goldberg, S., & Marvin, R. S. (1996). *Child–parent attachment and indiscriminately friendly behavior toward strangers in Romanian orphans adopted into Canadian families.* Paper presented at the biennial meeting of the International Conference for Infant Studies, Providence, RI.

Goldstein, J., Freud, A., & Solnit, A. J. (1973). *Beyond the best interests of the child.* New Haven, CT: Yale University Press.

Goldstein, J., Freud, A., & Solnit, A. J. (1979). *Before the best interests of the child.* New York: Free Press.

Goldstein, J., Freud, A., Solnit, A. J., & Goldstein, S. (1986). *In the best interests of the child.* New York: Free Press.

Golombok, S., Cook, R., Bish, A., & Murray, C. (1995). Families created by the new reproductive technologies: Quality of parenting and social and emotional development of the children. *Child Development, 66,* 285–298.

Greenberg, M. T., & Speltz, M. L. (1988). Attachment and the ontogeny of conduct problems. In J. Belsky & T. Nezworski (Eds.), *Clinical implications of attachment* (pp. 177–218). Hillsdale, NJ: Erlbaum.

Haimes, E., & Timms, N. (1985). *Adoption, identity and social policy: The search for distant relatives* (Studies in Social Policy and Welfare No. 23). Aldershot, England: Gower.

Hanson, T. L., McLanahan, S. S., & Thomson, E. (1996). Double jeopardy: Parental conflict and stepfamily outcomes for children. *Journal of Marriage and the Family, 58,* 141–154.

Hay, D. F. (1997). Postpartum depression and cognitive development. In L. Murray & P. J. Cooper (Eds.), *Postpartum depression and child development* (pp. 85–110). New York: Guilford Press.

Hay, D. F., & Kumar, R. (1995). Interpreting the effects of mothers' postnatal depression on children's intelligence: A critique and reanalysis. *Child Psychiatry and Human Development, 25,* 165–181.

Hazan, C., & Shaver, P. R. (1987). Romantic love conceptualized as an attachment process. *Journal of Personality and Social Psychology, 52,* 511–524.

Hazan, C., & Shaver, P. R. (1994). Attachment as an organizational framework for research on close relationships. *Psychological Inquiry, 5,* 1–22.

Heinicke, C. M. (1981). More on nonmaternal care. *American Psychologist, 36,* 422–423.

Hersov, L. (1994). Adoption. In M. Rutter, E. Taylor, & L. Hersov (Eds.), *Child and adolescent psychiatry: Modern approaches* (3rd ed., pp. 267–282). Oxford: Blackwell Scientific.

Hess, L. E. (1995). Changing family patterns in Western Europe: Opportunity and risk factors for adolescent development. In M. Rutter & D. J. Smith (Eds.), *Psychosocial disorders in young people: Time trends and their causes* (pp. 104–193). Chichester, England: Wiley.

Hetherington, E. M. (1988). Parents, children and siblings: Six years after divorce. In R. A. Hinde & J. Stevenson-Hinde (Eds.), *Relationships within families: Mutual influences* (pp. 311–331). Oxford: Clarendon Press.

Hetherington, E. M. (1993). Overview of the Virginia Longitudinal Study of Divorce and Remarriage with a focus on early adolescence. *Journal of Family Psychology, 7,* 39–56.

Hetherington, E. M., & Clingempeel, W. G. (1992). Coping with marital transitions. *Monographs of the Society for Research in Child Development, 57*(2–3, Serial No. 227).

Hinde, R. A. (1988). Continuities and discontinuities. Conceptual issues and methodological considerations. In M. Rutter (Ed.), *Studies of psychosocial risk: The power of longitudinal data* (pp. 367–383). Cambridge, England: Cambridge University Press.

Hinde, R. A., & Stevenson-Hinde, J. (Eds.). (1988). *Relationships within families: Mutual influences.* Oxford: Clarendon Press.

Hobbs, M., Mayou, R., Harrison, B., & Worlock, P. (1996). A randomised controlled trial of psychological debriefing for victims of road traffic accidents. *British Medical Journal, 313,* 1438–1439.

Hodges, J., & Tizard, B. (1989). Social and family relationships of ex-institutional adolescents. *Journal of Child Psychology and Psychiatry, 30,* 77–97.

Holbrook, D. (1984). *Knowledge of origins: Self-esteem and family ties of long-term fostered and adopted children.* Report to the Hilden Charitable Trust, London.

Howe, D. (1995). Adoption and attachment. *Adoption and Fostering, 19,* 7–15.

Howes, C., & Hamilton, C. E. (1992). Children's relationships with caregivers: Mothers and child care teachers. *Child Development, 63,* 859–866.

Howes, C., Rodning, C., Galluzzo, D. C., & Myers, L. (1988). Attachment and child care: Relationships with mother and caregiver. *Early Childhood Research Quarterly, 3,* 403–416.

Humphrey, M., & Humphrey, H. (1988). *Families with a difference: Varieties of surrogate parenthood.* London: Routledge.

Johnson, D., & Fein, E. (1991). The concept of attachment: Applications to adoption. *Children and Youth Services Review, 13,* 397–412.

Kagan, J. (1984). *The nature of the child.* New York: Basic Books.

Kaplan, L., Ridder, A., Hennon, L., & Charles, B. (1991). Issues of split custody: Siblings separated by divorce. *Journal of Divorce and Remarriage, 16,* 253–274.

Keavency, L., & O'Connor, T. (1997, April). *The network of social relations of adoptees exposed to severe early deprivation.* Paper presented at the biennial meeting of the Society for Research in Child Development, Washington DC.

Kelly, J. B. (1988). Redefining the concept of attachment in divorce. *Journal of Family Psychology, 1,* 329–332.

Kennell, J. H., & Klaus, M. H. (1984). Mother–infant bonding: Weighing the evidence. *Developmental Review, 4,* 275–282.

King, P., & Steiner, R. (Eds.). (1991). *The Freud–Klein controversies 1941–45.* London: Routledge, in association with the Institute of Psycho-Analysis.

King, R. D., Raynes, N. V., & Tizard, J. (1971). *Patterns of residential care: Sociological studies in institutions for handicapped children.* London: Routledge & Kegan Paul.

Klaus, M. H., & Kennell, J. H. (1976). *Maternal–infant bonding: The impact of early separation or loss on family development.* St. Louis, MO: C. V. Mosby.

Kornhaber, A., & Woodward, K. L. (1981). *Grandparents/grandchildren: The vital connection.* Garden City, NY: Anchor Press/Doubleday.

Kraemer, S., & Roberts, J. (1996). *The politics of attachment: Towards a secure society.* London: Free Association Books.

Kumar, R. C., & Hipwell, A. E. (1994). Implications for the infant of maternal puerperal psychiatric disorders. In M. Rutter, E. Taylor, & L. Hersov (Eds.), *Child and adolescent psychiatry: Modern approaches* (3rd ed., pp. 759–775). Oxford: Blackwell Scientific.

Lamb, M. E. (Ed.). (1986). *The father's role: Applied perspectives.* New York: Wiley.

Lamb, M. E., Thompson, R. A., Gardner, W., Charnov, E. L., & Estes, D. (1984). Security of infantile attachment as assessed in the "strange situation": Its study and biological interpretations. *Behavioral and Brain Sciences, 7,* 127–147.

Lee, C., Slade, P., & Lygo, V. (1996). The influence of psychological debriefing on emotional adaptation in women following early miscarriage: A preliminary study. *British Journal of Medical Psychology, 69,* 47–58.

Lewis, S. N. C., & Cooper, C. L. (1988). The transition to parenthood in dual-earner couples. *Psychological Medicine, 18,* 477–486.

Lieberman, A. F. (1991). Attachment theory and infant–parent psychotherapy: Some conceptual, clinical, and research considerations. In D. Cicchetti & S. L. Toth (Eds.), *Rochester Symposium on Developmental Psychopathology: Vol. 3. Models and integrations* (pp. 261–287). Rochester, NY: University of Rochester Press.

Lyons-Ruth, K. (1996). Attachment relationships among children with aggressive behavior problems: The role of disorganized early attachment patterns. *Journal of Consulting and Clinical Psychology, 64,* 64–73.

Lyons-Ruth, K., Alpern, L., & Repacholi, B. (1993). Disor-

ganized infant attachment classification and maternal psychosocial problems as predictors of hostile–aggressive behavior in the preschool classroom. *Child Development, 64,* 572–585.

Maas, H., & Engler, R. (1959). *Children in need of parents.* New York: Columbia University Press.

Maccoby, E., & Mnookin, R. H. (1992). *Dividing the child: Social and legal dilemmas of custody.* Cambridge, MA: Harvard University Press.

Mahoney, M. N. (1994). Reformulating the legal definition of the stepparent–child relationship. In A. Booth & J. Dunn (Eds.), *Stepfamilies: Who benefits? Who does not?* (pp. 191–196). Hillsdale, NJ: Erlbaum.

Main, M., Kaplan, N., & Cassidy, J. (1985). Security in infancy, childhood and adulthood: A move to the level of representation. In I. Bretherton & E. Waters (Eds.), *Growing points of attachment theory and research. Monographs of the Society for Research in Child Development, 50*(1–2, Serial No. 209), 66–104.

Main, M., & Solomon, J. (1990). Procedures for identifying infants as disorganized/disoriented during the Ainsworth Strange Situation. In M. Greenberg, D. Cicchetti, & E. M. Cummings (Eds.), *Attachment during the preschool years: Theory, research, and intervention* (pp. 121–160). Chicago: University of Chicago Press.

Marcovitch, S., Goldberg, S., Gold, A., Washington, J., Wasson, C., Krekewich, K., & Handley-Derry, M. (1997). Determinants of behavioural problems in Romanian children adopted in Ontario. *International Journal of Behavioral Development, 20,* 17–31.

Marcus, R. F. (1991). The attachments of children in foster care. *Genetic, Social, and General Psychology Monographs, 117,* 365–394.

Maughan, B., & Rutter, M. (1985). Education: Improving practice through increasing understanding. In R. N. Rapoport (Ed.), *Children, youth, and families: The action–research relationship* (pp. 26–49). Cambridge, England: Cambridge University Press.

McCartney, K., & Phillips, D. (1988). Motherhood and child care. In B. Birns & D. Hay (Eds.), *The different faces of motherhood* (pp. 157–183). New York: Plenum Press.

McGuire, J. (1995). *What works?: Reducing offending. Guidelines from research and practice.* Chichester, England: Wiley.

McGurk, H., Caplan, M., Hennessy, E., & Moss, P. (1993). Controversy, theory, and social context in contemporary day care research. *Journal of Child Psychology and Psychiatry, 34,* 3–23.

McLanahan, S., & Booth. K. (1989). Mother only families: Problems, prospects and politics. *Journal of Marriage and the Family, 151,* 557–580.

McMahon, C. A., Ungerer, J. A., Beaurepaire, J., Tennant, C., & Saunders, D. (1995). Psychosocial outcomes for parents and children after *in vitro* fertilization: A review. *Journal of Reproductive and Infant Psychology, 13,* 1–16.

Murray, L. (1992). The impact of postnatal depression on infant development. *Journal of Child Psychology and Psychiatry, 33,* 543–561.

Murray, L., & Cooper, P. J. (Eds.). (1997). *Postpartum depression and child development.* New York: Guilford Press.

National Research Council. (1993). *Understanding child abuse and neglect.* Washington, DC: National Academy Press.

National Institute of Child Health and Human Development (NICHD) Early Child Care Research. (1997). The effects of infant child care on infant–mother attachment security:

Results of the NICHD study of early child care. *Child Development, 68,* 860–879.

National Institute of Child Health and Human Development (NICHD) Early Child Care Research Network. (1998). The effects of infant child care on infant–mother attachment security: Results of the NICHD study of early child care. *Child Development, 69,* 1145–1170.

O'Connor, T. G., Bredenkamp, D., & Rutter, M. (in press). Attachment disturbances in children exposed to early severe privation. *Infant Mental Health Journal.*

Oppenheim, D., & Waters, H. S. (1995). Narrative processes and attachment representations: Issues of development and assessment. In E. Waters, B. E. Vaughn, G. Posada, & K. Kondo-Ikemura (Eds.), Caregiving, cultural, and cognitive perspectives on secure-base behavior and working models: New growing points of attachment theory and research. *Monographs of the Society for Research in Child Development, 60*(2–3, Serial No. 244), 197–215.

Owens, G., Crowell, J. A., Pan, H., Treboux, D., O'Connor, E., & Waters, E. (1995). The prototype hypothesis and the origins of attachment working models: Adult relationships with parents and romantic partners. In E. Waters, B. E. Vaughn, G. Posada, & K. Kondo-Ikemura (Eds.), Caregiving, cultural, and cognitive perspectives on secure-base behavior and working models: New growing points of attachment theory and research. *Monographs of the Society for Research in Child Development, 60*(2–3, Serial No. 244), 216–233.

Pardeck, J. T. (1984). Multiple placement of children in foster family care: An empirical analysis. *Social Work, 29,* 506–509.

Patrick, M., Hobson, P., Castle, D., Howard, R., & Maughan, B. (1994). Personality disorder and the mental representatives of early social experience. *Development and Psychopathology, 6,* 375–388.

Patterson, G. R., Chamberlain, P., & Reid, J. R. (1982). A comparative evaluation of parent training procedures. *Behavior Therapy, 3,* 638–650.

Patterson, G. R., Reid, J. B., & Dishion, T. J. (1992). *Antisocial boys: A social interactional approach* (Vol. 4). Eugene, OR: Castalia.

Pederson, D. R., & Moran, G. (1995). A categorical description of infant–mother relationships in the home and its relation to Q-sort measures of infant–mother interaction. In E. Waters, B. E. Vaughn, G. Posada, & K. Kondo-Ikemura (Eds.), Caregiving, cultural, and cognitive perspectives on secure-base behavior and working models: New growing points of attachment theory and research. *Monographs of the Society for Research in Child Development, 60*(2–3, Serial No. 244), 111–132.

Phoenix, A., & Owen, C. (1996). From miscegenation to hybridity: Mixed relationships and mixed-parentage in profile. In B. Bernstein & J. Brannen (Eds.), *Children, research and policy* (pp. 111–135). London: Taylor & Francis.

Provence, S., & Lipton, R. C. (1962). *Infants in institutions.* New York: International Universities Press.

Quinton, D., & Rutter, M. (1988). *Parental breakdown: The making and breaking of intergenerational links.* Aldershot, England: Avebury.

Radke-Yarrow, M., Cummings, E. M., Kuczynski, L., & Chapman, M. (1985). Patterns of attachment in two and three year old normal families and families with parental depression. *Child Development, 56,* 884–893.

Radke-Yarrow, M., McCann, K., DeMulder, E., Belmont, B., Martinez, P., & Richardson, D. T. (1995). Attachment in the context of high-risk conditions. *Development and Psychopathology, 7,* 247–265.

Rajecki, D. W., Lamb, M. E., & Obmascher, P. (1978). Toward a general theory of infantile attachment: A comparative review of aspects of the social bond. *Behavioral and Brain Sciences, 1,* 417–464.

Raynor, L. (1980). *The adopted child comes of age.* London: Allen & Unwin.

Richters, M. M., & Volkmar, F. R. (1994). Case study: Reactive attachment disorder of infancy or early childhood. *Journal of the American Academy of Child and Adolescent Psychiatry, 33,* 328–332.

Robertson, J., & Robertson, J. (1971). Young children in brief separation: A fresh look. *Psychoanalytic Study of the Child, 26,* 264–315.

Rothbart, M. K., & Bates, J. E. (1998). Temperament. In W. Damon (Series Ed.) & N. Eisenberg (Vol. Ed.), *Handbook of child psychology: Vol. 3. Social, emotional, and personality development* (5th ed., pp. 105–176). New York: Wiley.

Rowe, D. C. (1994). *The limits of family influence: Genes, experience, and behavior.* New York: Guilford Press.

Rowe, J., & Lambert, L. (1973). *Children who wait.* London: Association of British Adoption Agencies.

Rutter, M. (1971). Parent–child separation: Psychological effects on the children. *Journal of Child Psychology and Psychiatry, 12,* 233–260.

Rutter, M. (1972/1981). *Maternal deprivation reassessed.* Harmondsworth, England: Penguin.

Rutter, M. (1979). Separation experiences: A new look at an old topic. *Journal of Pediatrics, 95,* 147–154.

Rutter, M. (1988). Functions and consequences of relationships: Some psychopathological considerations. In R. A. Hinde & J. Stevenson-Hinde (Eds.), *Relationships within families: Mutual influences* (pp. 332–353). Oxford: Clarendon Press.

Rutter, M. (1989). Psychiatric disorder in parents as a risk factor for children. In D. Shaffer, I. Philips, & N. B. Enzer (Eds.), with M. M. Silverman & V. Anthony (Assoc. Eds.), *Prevention of mental disorders, alcohol and other drug use in children and adolescents* (OSAP Prevention Monograph No. 2, pp. 157–189). Rockville, MD: Office for Substance Abuse Prevention, U.S. Department of Health and Human Services.

Rutter, M. (1990). Commentary: Some focus and process considerations regarding effects of parental depression on children. *Developmental Psychology, 26,* 60–67.

Rutter, M. (1994a). Family discord and conduct disorder: Cause, consequence or correlate? *Journal of Family Psychology, 8,* 170–186.

Rutter, M. (1994b). Beyond longitudinal data: Causes, consequences, changes and continuity. *Journal of Consulting and Clinical Psychology, 62,* 928–940.

Rutter, M. (1995a). Clinical implications of attachment concepts: Retrospect and prospect. *Journal of Child Psychology and Psychiatry, 36,* 549–571.

Rutter, M. (1995b). Maternal deprivation. In M. H. Bornstein (Ed.), *Handbook of parenting: Vol. 4. Applied and practical parenting* (pp. 3–31). Mahwah, NJ: Erlbaum.

Rutter, M., Anderson-Wood, L., Beckett, C., Bredenkamp, D., Castle, J., Groothues, C., Kreppner, J., Keaveney, L., Lord, C., O'Connor, T. G., & the English and Romanian Adoptees (ERA) Study Team. (in press). Quasi-autistic patterns following severe early global privation. *Journal of Child Psychology and Child Psychiatry.*

Rutter, M., Maughan, B., Pickles, A., & Simonoff, E. (1998). Retrospective recall recalled (pp. 219–243). In R. B.

Cairns & P. C. Rodkin (Eds.), *The individual in developmental research: Essays in honor of Marian Radke-Yarrow*. Thousand Oaks, CA: Sage.

Rutter, M., & Rutter, M. (1993). *Developing minds: Challenges and continuities across the lifespan*. Harmondsworth, Middlesex, England: Penguin; New York: Basic Books.

Sack, W. H., & Dale, D. D. (1982). Abuse and deprivation in failing adoptions. *Child Abuse and Neglect, 6,* 443–451.

Sagi, A., van IJzendoorn, M. H., Aviezer, O., Donnell, F., Koren-Karie, N., Joels, T., & Harel, Y. (1995). Attachments in a multiple-caregiver and multiple-infant environment: The case of the Israeli kibbutzim. In E. Waters, B. E. Vaughn, G. Posada, & K. Kondo-Ikemura (Eds.), Caregiving, cultural, and cognitive perspectives on secure-base behavior and working models: New growing points of attachment theory and research. *Monographs of the Society for Research in Child Development, 60*(2–3, Serial No. 244), 71–91.

Sameroff, A. J., & Emde, R. N. (Eds.). (1989). *Relationship disturbances in early childhood: A developmental approach*. New York: Basic Books.

Samuels, S. C. (1990). *Ideal adoption: A comprehensive guide to forming an adoptive family*. New York: Insight Books.

Scarr, S. (1992). Developmental theories for the 1990s: Development and individual differences. *Child Development, 63,* 1–19.

Scarr, S., Phillips, D., & McCartney, K. (1990). Facts, fantasies, and the future of child care in the United States. *Psychological Science, 1,* 26–35.

Schaffer, H. R. (1990). *Making decisions about children: Psychological questions and answers*. Oxford: Blackwell.

Schweinhart, L. J., Barnes, H. V., & Weikart, D. P. (1993). *Significant benefits: The High/Scope Perry Preschool study through age 27*. Ypsilanti, MI: High/Scope.

Shantz, C. U., & Hartup, W. W. (Eds.). (1992). *Conflict in child and adolescent development*. New York: Cambridge University Press.

Shealy, C. N. (1995). From *Boys Town* to *Oliver Twist*: Separating fact and fiction in welfare reform and out-of-home placement of children and youth. *American Psychologist, 50,* 565–580.

Singer, L. M., Burkowski, M., & Waters, E. (1985). Mother–infant attachment in adoptive families. *Child Development, 56,* 1543–1551.

Sloutsky, V. M. (1997). Institutional care and developmental outcomes of 6- and 7-year-old children: A contextualist perspective. *International Journal of Behavioral Development, 20,* 131–151.

Sluckin, W., Herbert, M., & Sluckin, A. (1983). *Maternal bonding*. Oxford: Blackwell Scientific.

Small, R., Kennedy, K., & Bender, B. (1991). Critical issues for practice in residential treatment: The view from within. *American Journal of Orthopsychiatry, 61,* 327–338.

Sroufe, L. A. (1988). The role of infant–caregiver attachments in development. In J. Belsky & T. Nezworski (Eds.), *Clinical implications of attachment* (pp. 18–38). Hillsdale, NJ: Erlbaum.

Steele, H., Steele, M., & Fonagy, P. (1996). Associations among attachment classifications of mothers, fathers, and their infants. *Child Development, 67,* 541–555.

Stern, D. N. (1985). *The interpersonal world of the infant: A view from psychoanalysis and developmental psychology*. New York: Basic Books.

Stern, D. N. (1989). The representation of relational patterns: Developmental considerations. In A. J. Sameroff & R. N.

Emde (Eds.), *Relationship disturbances in early childhood: A developmental approach* (pp. 52–68). New York: Basic Books.

Stevenson, H. W., & Siegel, A. E. (Eds.). (1984). *Child development research and social policy*. Chicago: University of Chicago Press.

Stevenson-Hinde, J. (1991). Temperament and attachment: An eclectic approach. In P. Bateson (Ed.), *Development and integration of behaviour* (pp. 315–329). Cambridge, England: Cambridge University Press.

Strauss, M. B. (1988). Divorced mothers. In B. Birns & D. F. Hay (Eds.), *The different faces of motherhood* (pp. 215–238). New York: Plenum Press.

Strayer, F. F., Verissimo, M., Vaughn, B. E., & Howes, C. (1995). A quantitative approach to the description and classification of primary social relationships. In E. Waters, B. E. Vaughn, G. Posada, & K. Kondo-Ikemura (Eds.), Caregiving, cultural, and cognitive perspectives on secure-base behavior and working models: New growing points of attachment theory and research. *Monographs of the Society for Research in Child Development, 60*(2–3, Serial No. 244), 49–70.

Thoburn, J. (1993). *Success and failure in permanent family placement*. Aldershot, England: Avebury.

Thompson, R. A., Connell, J. P., & Bridges, L. J. (1988). Temperament, emotion, and social interactive behavior in the Strange Situation: An analysis of attachment system functioning. *Child Development, 59,* 1102–1110.

Tizard, B. (1977). *Adoption: A second chance*. London: Open Books.

Tizard, B. (1991). Intercountry adoption: A review of the evidence. *Journal of Child Psychology and Psychiatry, 32,* 743–756.

Tizard, B., & Hughes, M. (1984). *Young children learning: Talking and thinking at home and at school*. London: Fontana.

Tizard, B., & Phoenix, A. (1993). *Black, white or mixed race?* London: Routledge.

Tizard, J., & Tizard, B. (1971). The social development of two-year-old children in residential nurseries. In J. Schaffer (Ed.), *The origins of human social relations* (pp. 147–160). London: Academic Press.

Triseliotis, J., & Russell, J. (1984). *Hard to place: The outcome of adoption and residential care*. London: Heinemann Educational.

U.S. House of Representatives Select Committee on Children, Youth and Families. (1990, January 12). *No place to call home: Discarded children in America*. Washington, DC: U.S. Government Printing Office.

van Balen, F. (1996). Child-rearing following in vitro fertilization. *Journal of Child Psychology and Psychiatry, 37,* 687–693.

van den Boom, D. C. (1995). Do first year intervention effects endure?: Follow-up during toddlerhood of a sample of Dutch irritable infants. *Child Development, 66,* 1798–1816.

van IJzendoorn, M. H. (1995). Adult attachment representations, parental responsiveness, and infant attachment: A meta-analysis on the predictive validity of the Adult Attachment Interview. *Psychological Bulletin, 116,* 387–403.

van IJzendoorn, M. H., & Bakermans-Kranenburg, M. J. (1996). Attachment representations in mothers, fathers, adolescents, and clinical groups: A meta-analytic search for normative data. *Journal of Consulting and Clinical Psychology, 64,* 8–21.

van IJzendoorn, M. H., Juffer, F., & Duyvesteyn, M. G. C.

(1995). Breaking the intergenerational cycle of insecure attachment: A review of the effects of attachment-based interventions on maternal sensitivity and infant security. *Journal of Child Psychology and Psychiatry, 36,* 225–248.

Vaughn, B. E., Stevenson-Hinde, J., Waters, E., Kotsaftis, A., Lefever, G. B., Shouldice, A., Trudel, M., & Belsky, J. (1992). Attachment security and temperament in infancy and early childhood: Some conceptual clarifications. *Developmental Psychology, 28,* 463–473.

Verschueren, K., Marcoen, A., & Schoefs, V. (1996). The internal working model of the self, attachment, and competence in five-year-olds. *Child Development, 67,* 2493–2511.

Vorria, P., Rutter, M., Pickles, A., Wolkind, S., & Hobsbaum, A. (1998-a). A comparative study of Greek children in long-term residential group care and in two-parent families: I. Social, emotional and behavioural effects. *Journal of Child Psychology and Psychiatry, 39,* 225–236.

Vorria, P., Rutter, M., Pickles, A., Wolkind, S., & Hobsbaum, A. (1998-b). A comparative study of Greek children in long-term residential group care and in two-parent families: II. Possible mediating mechanisms. *Journal of Child Psychology and Psychiatry, 39,* 237–245.

Wachs, T. D. (1992). *The nature of nurture.* Newbury Park, CA: Sage.

Waters, E., & Deane, K. E. (1985). Defining and assessing individual differences in attachment relationships: Q-methodology and the organization of behavior in infancy and early childhood. In I. Bretherton & E. Waters (Eds.), Growing points of attachment theory and research. *Monographs of the Society for Research in Child Development, 50*(1–2, Serial No. 209), 41–65.

Waters, E., Vaughn, B. E., Posada, G., & Kondo-Ikemura, K. (Eds.). (1995). Caregiving, cultural, and cognitive perspectives on secure-base behavior and working models: New growing points of attachment theory and research. *Monographs of the Society for Research in Child Development, 60*(2–3, Serial No. 244).

Webster-Stratton, C. (1996). Early intervention with videotape modeling: Programs for families of children with oppositional defiant disorder or conduct disorder. In E. H. Hibbs & P. S. Jensen (Eds.), *Psychological treatments for child and adolescent disorders: Empirically based strategies for clinical practice* (pp. 435–474). Washington, DC: American Psychological Association.

Webster-Stratton, C., Hollinsworth, T., & Kolpacoff, M. (1989). The long-term effectiveness and clinical significance of three cost-effective training programs for families with conduct-problem children. *Journal of Consulting and Clinical Psychology, 57,* 550–553.

Werner, E. E. (1984). *Child care: Kith, kin and hired hands.* Baltimore: University Park Press.

Wolkind, S. (1974). The components of "affectionless psychopathy" in institutionalized children. *Journal of Child Psychology and Psychiatry, 15,* 215–220.

Wolkind, S. (1994). Legal aspects of child care. In M. Rutter, E. Taylor, & L. Hersov (Eds.), *Child and adolescent psychiatry: Modern approaches* (3rd ed., pp. 1089–1102). Oxford: Blackwell Scientific.

Wolkind, S., & Rushton, A. (1994). Residential and foster family care. In M. Rutter, E. Taylor, & L. Hersov (Eds.), *Child and adolescent psychiatry: Modern approaches* (3rd ed., pp. 252–266). Oxford: Blackwell Scientific.

Woodhead, M. (1985). Pre-school education has long-term effects: But can they be generalised? *Oxford Review of Education, 11,* 133–155.

World Health Organization [WHO] Expert Committee on Mental Health. (1951). *Report of the second session 1951.* Geneva: WHO.

Wrobel, G. M., Ayers-Lopez, S., Grotevant, H. D., McRoy, R. G., & Friedrick, M. (1996). Openness in adoption and the level of child participation. *Child Development, 67,* 2358–2374.

Zeanah, C. H. (1996). Beyond insecurity: A reconceptualization of attachment disorders of infancy. *Journal of Consulting and Clinical Psychology, 64,* 42–52.

Zeanah, C. H., & Emde, R. N. (1994). Attachment disorders in infancy and childhood. In M. Rutter, E. Taylor, & L. Hersov (Eds.), *Child and adolescent psychiatry: Modern approaches* (3rd ed., pp. 490–504). Oxford: Blackwell Scientific.

Zigler, E. F., & Gordon, E. W. (Eds.). (1982). *Day care: Scientific and social policy issues.* Boston: Auburn House.

Epilogue
Attachment Theory
Eighteen Points with Suggestions for Future Studies

❖

MARY MAIN

Readers who have completed this long and excellent volume have undoubtedly deepened their understanding of the field, and in consequence are now well equipped for further studies and applications. This epilogue is organized around 18 central points that I often make when lecturing or teaching about attachment theory and research. Several have already been elucidated in this volume, but are listed here again simply because I have found them to be readily missed by, or to represent special points of confusion for, new audiences. Others, while of central interest to the field are, I believe, still controversial and/or indicate places where data are incomplete. Some are simply heuristic devices of my own making.

The reader will find a persistent theme among my comments and suggestions for future study. I call first for an increased effort to integrate the field of attachment as it currently stands. For example, I suggest that the discovery of "hidden regulators" in infant–mother interactions, to date confined largely to animals, should be investigated in humans as well, while interview methods of assessing attachment should be combined with self-report methods. In addition, I suggest that having identified a phenomenon as remarkably stable, closely linked to identifiable aspects of experience, and clearly predictive of both health and psychopathology as attachment is, researchers within the field should now begin to attempt to forge links with fields that are currently somewhat separated. Although I have room to focus upon only one or two of the fields now open to us, these include attention, memory, and other aspects of cognitive psychology; linguistics; and connections between both the general phenomena of attachment and individual differences in its expression on the one hand, and psychophysiology and the brain on the other. Given recent advances in cognitive and affective neuroscience, I am especially intrigued by opportunities to further our understanding of the neural circuitry underlying both attachment phenomena in general, and differences observed in its organization and disorganization.

Before embarking on the epilogue proper, I would like to add three personal notes. First, rather than serving as a review of the contents of this volume, this epilogue was begun as a separate undertaking well before the volume was completed. It does not serve as a review of the volume or its contents, which are remarkably broad. Second, although one of the primary contributions of this volume will be to provide the background necessary for integrating attachment as seen in studies of animal behavior; attachment as seen in direct observations of infants, children, and adults via either film or interview methods; and attachment as studied within the traditions of personality and social psychology, my own training and research have followed the second of these traditions. Consequently, my suggestions for future studies take that tradition as their background. I have referred insofar as I am able, however, to studies in the other traditions as well, and the reader who completes this epilogue will find many suggestions for future studies regarding individual differences in attachment organization that can be undertaken using either observational, interview, or self-report measures. Some of the ideas presented here regarding attachment formation during infancy, and attachment as related to certain systems in the brain, may also apply to adult pair-bond attachments.

Finally, a series of recommended teaching points, brief commentaries, and suggestions for future studies is by its nature a kind of informal and unfinished list. Although this epilogue has been taking shape across the past 2 years, a series of untoward events occurred to prohibit the final stages of drafting and reviewing necessary to achieving a product as polished as the other chapters in this volume. In consequence, although the manuscript has been extensively edited, there may be remaining misfortunes in wording, fact, or phrasing that would have been caught in further drafts, and that are exclusively my own.

1. *An attachment is a unique form of affectional bond; the term should not be used for affectional bonds in general.* I make this point for students and teachers of attachment, although I am aware that dictionary definitions of the term typically take the more general view. The reason for stressing a more technical use of the term is that the infant's attachment to the parent is otherwise readily confused with, for example, the parent's bond to the infant, or the toddler's developing bonds to peers. The distinguishing features of our field of study are then lost, and the child's attachment to the parental figure is seen as simply one among a host of important relationships. This is an unfortunate outcome not only for students of attachment, but also for researchers investigating other kinds of relationships. Indeed if the parent is seen as simply "attached" to the infant, we are not only technically incorrect in our description of normative caregiving relationships (the parent should not be fleeing to the infant in times of alarm), but we are simultaneously letting go of the opportunity to examine parenting and caregiving as a system in its own right.

To put the case in technical terms, as opposed to the activation of other systems involving affectional bonds, the activation of the attachment system most frequently leads to increasing proximity to a second individual selected for his or her likelihood of being able to promote the attached individual's immediate safety and survival. In the case of parents, this is not the infant, and in the case of young children, it is not normally the peer. Thus, during infancy and early childhood, the relationship between an attached individual and attachment figure(s) is necessarily asymmetrical, with the attachment figure being the infant's "solution" to potentially life-threatening circumstances of an immediate kind. In a well-functioning adult couple, we see the partners as each able to serve as a secure base for the other, and in that sense the relationship is "symmetrical." However, a temporary and important asymmetry is present by definition at those particular moments when one partner seeks the other as an attachment figure, that is, as "stronger and wiser" (Shaver, Hazan, & Bradshaw, 1988).

In case the reader thinks I am exaggerating the degree of misunderstanding that exists regarding the relations between attachment and bonding, it should be noted that entire volumes have been written confusing Bowlby's theory with the early work on mother-to-infant bonding by Klaus and Kennell (1976), and criticizing Bowlby for insisting that the mother spend the hours immediately following birth in close proximity to her infant in order to promote her attachment to it (which he proposed; e.g., Eyer, 1992; see Hrdy, 1999, for a review).

An important point related to the specificity of attachment, and of caregiving as well, is the fact that neither is believed to represent the entirety of the parent–child relationship. In revising the first volume of *Attachment and Loss,* Bowlby (1969/1982) found it critical to distinguish the attachment–caregiving components of the infant–parent relationship from other important aspects. Here he also made clear that the behavioral system seen in parents that is directly complementary to infant attachment is *caregiving,* but he emphasized that parents do many other things that also promote and support the development of their offspring. For example (this list is partially my own), they are engaged with their offspring in teaching, discipline, providing material support, serving as role models, and providing partners for play.

Commentary. Some parents are not security-giving caregivers, and may not soon become so. It therefore seems important to remind audiences that some children disadvantaged by an insecure attachment to a particular parent may be advantaged by the parent's abilities in other areas, such as those listed above.

2. *Attachments develop across an extraordinarily wide range of environments, and it is only in extremely anomalous circumstances that a child will have been raised in a way that successfully prevents the formation of an attachment (as seen, e.g., in Rumanian orphanages).* As a heuristic device, Hinde (1959) proposed a continuum of environmental influence for distinguishing genetically biased behaviors from those more strongly influenced by specific environments. Genetically biased behaviors or behavioral systems (attachment formation is one) are those that are likely to develop within a very wide range of environments; others, such as learning Nintendo, may develop only within a highly restricted range. In making his claim that attachment is an instinctively biased behavioral pattern, Bowlby pointed to the wide range of environments in which it appears—or, put another way, the relatively restricted amount of exposure to potential attachment figures that is sufficient for attachment formation. This given, we must not fail to emphasize that there is no relation between *insecure* attachment and *absence* of attachment. All infants who have had the opportunity to form an attachment are attached, whether the attachment is secure or insecure. The related fact that an infant becomes as definitively attached to a battering parent as to a sensitively responsive one (Bowlby, 1958) is astonishing to some new audiences.

Commentary. We have, happily, fewer and fewer opportunities to observe the outcomes of those highly anomalous living conditions in which children have no opportunity to form an attachment to another person throughout the first 3 years of life. (Three years is the rough cutoff point of the sensitive period for primary attachment formation proposed by Ainsworth and Bowlby.) We do know, however, that children living in extreme conditions (such as, again, the much-written-about Rumanian orphanages) are still frequently observed to suffer the dramatic difficulties in forming later specific attachments that Bowlby originally outlined. Although the behavioral outcomes for these orphans, and the associated suffering of their adoptive parents, have been described elsewhere, one of the most shocking illustrations of malignant outcomes for these children appears in brain scans comparing home-reared children with those of Rumanian orphans of the same age. Astonishingly large areas of the brain appear absent or inactive in scans

taken from these orphans. I would agree, however, with many of the writers critiquing early deprivation studies that the deprivations suffered by these children are so massive we have no way of being assured that they stem specifically from the failure to have formed an attachment.

I do not currently see how we could humanely[1] seek brain scans from Tizard and Hodges's (1978; see also Hodges & Tizard, 1989) subjects who, now young adults, were raised for their first 2 years in orphanages discouraging of attachments, but otherwise offering a relatively normal environment. Because they were not only otherwise relatively well treated, but were also adopted 1 year before the ending of the proposed "sensitive period" for forming affectional ties, however, it would seem to me more reasonable to investigate their brain development than that of the multiply deprived Rumanian orphans. This might begin to assist us in understanding the effects of early attachment-related experiences upon the brain, and (albeit admittedly in the absence of the ability to prove the null hypothesis) one preferred and happy outcome would be the absence of observable differences between these young adults and those home-reared from birth. Another (again ethically difficult) study could be undertaken investigating currently existing behavioral differences among, and gradual changes in the behavioral status of, the Rumanian orphans, in relation to developments and differences in their brains.

3. *For human infants, attachments are believed to be based on social interactions, with the infant himself or herself selecting the primary figure. These data are anecdotal, however, and both experimental work and close observation of the formation of later attachments should be undertaken.* To date, it is believed that the infant *selects* his or her first (and primary) attachment figure. From informal evidence collected by Ainsworth (1967) in Uganda, and Schaffer and Emerson (1964) in Scotland, it seems that this attachment figure is normally—but not always or inevitably—the person with whom the infant lives and who provides primary care. Human infant attachments are then said somewhat casually to be based on "social interactions" (e.g., Bowlby, 1969/1982, 1987) that have taken place with the person selected. For example, in the relatively rare cases observed in which the mother provided only physical care, while another person (even a regular, visiting nonrelative) engaged the infant only in social play, the latter was sometimes "selected" as the infant's primary figure.

Again, these observations have been informal. In a more formal, related report, Rheingold, Gewirtz, and Ross (1959) found themselves able to favorably alter the state of infants confined to orphanages through social interactions amounting to only 15 minutes per day.

An instructive set of studies were conducted by my colleague John Watson at Berkeley (e.g., Watson, 1972). Watson originally intended solely to determine the earliest age at which infants could be "operantly" conditioned, and in the service of this investigation of learning, 2-month-olds were supplied with air pillows capable of operating a mobile that spun entertainingly above each infant's head contingent upon the infant's making a head movement (Watson, 1972). In the control condition, infants were exposed to mobiles that turned for the same length of time and at similar intervals, but were "noncontingent" (i.e., not under the control of the infant's air pillow).

To Watson's astonishment, infants in the "contingent" (but not the control) condition began to exhibit what he termed "preattachment" behaviors toward the mobiles, smiling, cooing, and exhibiting generally heightened attention. The mobiles were set up over cribs in the homes, and several parents reported that the infants were so entranced with the contingently turning mobiles that they would entertain themselves with them for many hours. In anecdotal reports, one developmentally delayed infant was described as being "depressed" at the removal of the mobile, and appeared "angry" upon its return. The reader should note again that these mobiles did not behave contingently only upon occasion (as might a kindly, sociable, visiting aunt), but rather were continuous in their responsiveness.

Desiring not to interfere with the formation of an infant's later-developing attachment to more truly animate objects (namely the parents), Watson eventually terminated these experiments. In reflecting upon his findings, however, he suggested that human infants would make no mistake in "identifying" the wrong species if they used contingent responsiveness to tell them that the object of their interest was, at the least, a human being. Here we can compare the case of the baby gosling, which—although occasionally tricked by wily ethologists—is seldom mistaken in following and forming a specific attachment to the first thing it sees moving, since this is most likely to be its mother. (And, as Alison Jolly [1972], wryly put it, if a fox rather than a goose is the first thing the gosling sees moving, it may

as well follow it; it is lost anyway.) There is nothing in the human infant's environment of evolutionary adaptedness (EEA) that he or she can normally control with movements of feet, hands, legs, or head other than a human being, so the infant will be safe in identifying the species correctly. Thus Watson (1972) concluded that it might not be that infants enjoy "the game" because people play it, but rather that they enjoy (select) people because they play "the game." "Contingent social interaction" would then appear to pass at least the "species" selection test.

The next question is this: What would lead to the selection of one member of our species over another? That is, what would make a person who plays "the game" more attractive than one who fails to do so? Let me suggest that a person who has sufficient interest in an infant to engage extensively in the ridiculous smiling, cooing, head-nodding games that some of us play with infants is likely to show an appreciative investment in the same infant in other circumstances. We should note first that people who engage in more than a few seconds of this type of behavior with an infant are ones with time on their hands; that is, during these minutes they toil not, neither do they spin, hunt, or gather. To be somewhat more explicit, we can compare this proposal to a number of sociobiological interpretations advanced by Zahavi and Zahavi (1997) regarding, for instance, the exaggerated sexual characteristics observable in some species that would seem to the observer to handicap the exhibiting individual, but that are nonetheless particularly attractive to members of the opposite sex. In Zahavi and Zahavi's (1997) proposals, the animal so equipped is advertising that he (or she, of course) has survived to adulthood despite what appears to be a massive handicap, and hence, as compared to his less encumbered companions, he must be an especially tough individual. The parallel (of course, unconscious) infant calculation would be that an adult with enough extra time on his or her hands to engage in energy-consuming social interaction with the infant is an adult who is a good bet for being available to that same infant when times are rough. This problem of why the apparently "silly" adult habit of playing games with very young infants may attract the infant is of course not solved by application of the Zahavis' line of thinking, but Watson's studies nonetheless point us in an interesting direction. Note, however, that to date they focus on simple, rapid contingent responsiveness to the infant's actions; it is not clear as yet whether *positive* responsiveness is required (J. Watson, personal communication, 1977; cf. Polan & Hofer, Chapter 8, this volume).

I have now admitted the anecdotal nature of the observational evidence for "social interaction" as the prospective attachment figure's manner of attracting the infant, and have pointed to Watson's studies, in which having an aspect of their environment under their own control elicited preattachment behaviors in very young infants. What more can we do to reduce the embarrassing poverty of information in what is a critical area for our field? It is difficult to study the "requirement" for tie formation in conjunction with most home observations, because the adults involved are observed to do so many things with the infant, and an observer cannot tell which of them will have led to the infant's favoritism. This is precisely why the Ugandan and Scottish reports are anecdotal. Barring a far larger sample size, then—or a set of daily observers unethically trained to engage in far more contingent games with the infant than the parents will invent, and to do so earlier—we may be forced first to examine the formation of second attachments.

Below I will discuss some ways in which we might consider the formation of second attachments in later life. Here, however, I note that Mary Dozier has begun one such project following the formation of a new (or "second") attachment in infants and toddlers removed from their biological parents to foster homes. In conjunction with this project (still in its early stages), Dozier not only utilizes the Adult Attachment Interview (AAI) with the foster mothers, and conducts the strange situation with each (foster) mother–infant pair; she also has a daily diary kept by each foster mother, recording the infant's response to falls, frights, and separations that would ordinarily be expected to arouse attachment behavior. Dozier's expectation has been not only that the child will gradually form an attachment to the foster mother, but also that the organization of that attachment will echo the mother's AAI and will be reflected in infant strange situation behavior.

In this particular study, the children entering new homes are already toddlers, and the diaries being kept focus on critical attachment-related events, as opposed to "contingent social interactions." I have two comments to make about this study. First, Dozier is not attempting to determine *how* a new attachment becomes formed to a foster mother, but only looking for signs that it *has* formed, as seen, for example, in the toddler's

beginning to go to the foster mother in times of stress. The attachment itself could nonetheless still have been based on unrecorded social interactions. It is likely that contingent social interactions (especially in Watson's sense) are only *one* of the mechanisms of "social interaction" through which young children form attachments to particular selected figures. Others could include repeated comforting in response to situations of fright or distress in individuals who do not engage in game playing, or, less optimally, simply repeated responses to such infant experiences, whether these responses are pleasant or unpleasant.

I believe that the set of still-missing studies concerning the mechanism(s) of tie formation is critical. Because children are often taken into care at very young ages, researchers could begin similar studies with quite young children, and could compare the frequency, quality, and duration of contingent social interactions across foster mothers as a new attachment is being formed.

4. *Infant attachments and the emotions that accompany them in contemporary settings do not necessarily serve an obvious immediate survival function, but the selection pressures on ground-dwelling infant primates and hunter–gatherers are believed to have been similar to each other, and the brains of hunter–gatherer infants are unlikely to have been significantly different from ours. Therefore infants in contemporary settings often behave as though their survival were at stake in situations in which we believe them to be safe.* This begins as a fairly simple point. Often the importance of attachment behavior to survival is lost on new audiences, who note that human infants are at present seldom selected, for example, for leopard dining. While this is a reasonable initial contention, it was of course one of Bowlby's central points that we can understand the otherwise apparently "unreasonable" distress of the briefly separated contemporary infant only if we consider the likely environment in which the behavior evolved (termed by Bowlby the environment of evolutionary adaptedness, "EEA," although due to our inability to specify this early environment in detail, the use of the singular article is sometimes contested; see Hrdy, 1999). Here it is helpful to consider that behavioral and evolutionary biologists make frequent reference to the conservation of "old" systems across mammalian evolution; that attachment is one such system (see Polan & Hofer, Chapter 8, and Suomi, Chapter 9, this volume); and that the human brain is believed to differ little from those

seen in our species 30,000 years ago (Greenfield, 1997). In other words, for human hunters and gatherers, the likelihood of predation and other dangers attendant upon separation (below) were realities dealt with by the attachment behavioral system, and were no doubt accompanied by emotions similar to those the infant experiences today.

5. *The expression, nature, and duration of infant–parent attachment vary across species, and may ultimately be found to be related to differences in brain structure and chemistry. Comparative studies should increase our understanding of attachment, and some of these studies should involve brain imaging.* Although imprinting as an attachment-like phenomenon is seen in precocial birds, and although rats and other mammals exhibit aspects of attachment behavior, Suomi (1995; see also Chapter 9, this volume) has argued that attachment behavior as it is presently identified may represent a relatively recent evolutionary adaptation specific to Old World and higher primates. Thus, whereas infants of all primate species (including prosimians and New World species) are dependent on protective adult figures, among the latter contact is frequently dorsal, diversity of interactions is reduced, and striking examples of secure-base behavior may be absent. Moreover, "flight to the mother as a haven of safety," which marked attachment formation in human infants observed in Uganda (Ainsworth, 1967) and marks attachment as observed in Old World monkeys, is strikingly missing among capuchin monkeys. Thus, Suomi (Chapter 9, this volume) notes that if frightened, capuchins are as likely to seek another group member as their mothers.

Attachment thus appears to grow ever more complex and to be identified by more and more behavioral indices among the higher primates. Indeed, in Bowlby's conceptualization, the likely future intentions of the attachment figure are taken into account in planning for proximity keeping in Stage IV of human attachments (Marvin & Britner, Chapter 3, this volume)—an advanced kind of thinking believed to involve the frontal cortex. For this and many other reasons, I believe it is time for a comparative study of indices of attachment, complexity of attachment, and brain capacities across the varying species exhibiting varying forms of attachment behavior. As a simple and humorously intended example, if indeed (a) the prefrontal cortex should be taken into account in the human case, and (b) as we are aware, our prefrontal cortex exceeds that of the chim-

panzee by 29%, we should perhaps be led to the expectation that human attachment may be exactly 29% more complex than that of the chimp.

Even to begin a consideration of phylogeny with respect to attachment, we will need to address some of the delicate questions involved in anatomically and physiologically locating the phenomenon itself. Bowlby repeatedly located the attachment behavioral system within the central nervous system, but as far as I know made no reference to particular locations or particular organs. Some recent writers have enthusiastically endorsed particular organs as "the" center for human attachment, but to me, Greenfield (1997) is persuasive in arguing that whole brain areas work in parallel. The well-known simultaneous activation of two or more differing brain areas during different types of language usage (activated as an individual engages in word finding, verb generating, etc.), as revealed in recent PET studies, provides one example. In addition, Greenfield notes that resultant changes in the balance of brain chemistry and electricity may be more involved in the apparently "anatomical" effects of brain lesions than we are aware.

With reference to brain anatomy itself, Honey, Horn, Bateson, and Walpole (1995) have pointed to two brain areas involved in different aspects of imprinting and its sequelae in the chick. In looking for "before and after" changes in brain function or anatomy, investigators working with animals for which imprinting is rapid, leading to changes in orientation and behavior patterns within a matter of hours, are of course advantaged over those studying the far slower and less distinct processes involved in attachment formation in higher animals. Instructively, however, imprinting in relatively simple bird species takes place in the absence of a significant neocortex. In mammals, a review by Amini, Lewis, Lannon, and Louie (1996) indicates that the cingulate gyrus—a portion of the limbic system that is believed to be especially critical to emotional behavior and expression, and to those behavior patterns most sharply associated with survival—is implicated in attachment behavior in monkeys and in caregiving behavior in the mother rat (interestingly, the latter is not affected by removal of her neocortex). Joseph (1993) has named not only the cingulate gyrus, but also the amygdala and the septal nucleus (each found within the limbic system) in promoting "feelings of attachment." In so-called "higher" animals, the amygdala is tied to the recently evolved orbitofrontal cortex, which is in turn implicated in some of our most advanced cognitive experiences and mental operations (Wheeler, Stuss, & Tulving, 1997). Thus, whatever the emotional systems, hormones, and neurotransmitters implicated in attachment in most animals, it seems that (a) the less "emotional" brain areas capable of continuously tracking the (apparently separable) identity of an object and its location, and (b) among humans, the orbitofrontal cortex, associated with complex accessing and reflecting upon autobiographical experiences, must also be centrally involved. Thus attachment is undeniably a "system," and one that involves diverse anatomy, chemistry, and patterns of activation.

Commentary. Not all psychologists are interested in questions of phylogeny, but to me it seems that comparative studies of attachment both within and across species and phyla would be highly informative. Attachment has been the product of convergent evolution across several phyla, and we should note that some animals (e.g., chicks and rats) exhibit attachment toward another species member for only a brief time. Others (e.g., some ground-living primates) form attachments and exhibit the central features of attachment toward their initial attachment figures well past the time that they have become parents themselves, but only towards members of one sex. Finally, still others (e.g., domesticated canines) form initial early attachments to individual species members, forget these and seemingly fail to identify their attachment figures, then form critical and often life-long attachments to members of another species entirely. Life history strategies (see Belsky, Chapter 7, this volume; Chisholm, 1995) are obviously of central interest in this context, and may enhance our understanding of these widely differing appearances. Here as elsewhere (see below), we may want to compare what, for each species, appears to identify the nature of an "attachment."

A comparative study somewhat closer to home would involve comparisons of attachment behavior across the prosimians, New World and Old World monkeys, the great apes, and of course ourselves. As the reader will note from the following sections, in which I review Bowlby's contention that attachment as we know it probably evolved with ground-living, nomadic primates, here we would want to compare species that "nest" their young with those that must keep the young with them and are nomadic (a likely dividing point for the development of flight to the parent as a haven of safety). However, any such studies should also consider (a)

whether the locale of the species is confined or wide-ranging, with wide-ranging species likely to exhibit a wider variation in family systems and perhaps associated attachment; (b) the typical degree of relatedness among family members, which, if other matters are held constant, should predict the likelihood of allo-mothering; and (c) the nature of mating and reproductive systems, including the male's certainty of paternity (this should be high in titi monkeys, who travel in mated pairs, with the father serving from both behavioral and chemical indices as the infant's primary attachment figure; Mendoza & Mason, 1986).

Sarah Hrdy (personal communication, January 1999; see also Hrdy, 1999) has described humans as a "weedy" species, meaning that hunters and gatherers survived and reproduced in a variety of habitats, living in many different arrangements. Human mating systems ranged from monogamous to polygamous to informally polyandrous. Moreover, people who "gravitated away from adversity and towards opportunity" lived in matrilocal, patrilocal, or (perhaps most often) bilocal groups, depending on where resources and assistance from kin were most available. An investigation of the influence of these widely varying "family systems" on attachment and couple relations would not be out of place here, where infant strange situation behavior, AAI responses, couple attachment interviews, and self-reports of early and couple attachments would be likely to yield some intriguing findings. Perhaps no matter how variable the family systems among the few hunter–gatherer groups still available for inspection, however, infant strange situation response would no doubt still rely upon the nature of interactions with the primary caregiver(s). If so, we may credit Hrdy (1999) for simplifying our task by pointing out that among the simians, the "environment of evolutionary relevance" is always the primary parenting figure(s), and usually (with notable exceptions; see above) the infant's biological mother.

Although behavior does not normally leave a satisfactory fossil record, several approaches to furthering the understanding of attachment across these varying species are available. First, armed with well-specified information regarding attachment in a given species, we can attempt various kinds of computer modeling to see whether we can reproduce the outcomes that have already been found. In this vein, Bateson and Horn (1994) have developed a connectionist model of imprinting in the chick. Lesioning is unpleasant; happily, however, brain imaging is becoming increasingly available as a substitute, with the technical advantage of fewer confounds than are created by lesions. Simple brain imaging will now yield the metrics of brain anatomy. Although this is unlikely to tell us how the more complex brain is being used with respect to attachment, it can tell us how simple a brain can be and still produce a given set of attachment-relevant characteristics.

Perhaps the most useful comparative approaches, then, will involve brain imaging, both static (MRI) and functional or ongoing (PET, EEG, fMRI, MEG, and NIRS). Despite current limitations to each of the available techniques (see also Nelson, 1997, and Springer & Deutsch, 1998), probably the most useful comparative work in attachment will eventually involve brain imaging, including the locations of pre-to-post changes in animals forming rapid attachments; changes contingent upon separation from and reunion with the attachment figure across species; and changes contingent upon the presentation of frightening stimuli comparing species utilizing varying "solutions" to natural clues to danger. It is my understanding that it is difficult outside the great apes to find the same kind of avoidance upon reunion (avoidance as an "organized shift in attention" [see Main, 1981], rather than simple backing away or even flight) that appears in human infants. Perhaps in these higher primates we may observe indications of cortical suppression (of, e.g., the amygdala) accompanying organized avoidance.

A final method I might propose for studying phylogenetic changes in attachment behavior would be evolutionary computer simulations. (Axelrod, 1984, may provide the best-known example. In his work, a stable "tit-for-tat" strategy was found to "evolve" in "species members" across time.) In these simulations, investigators provide initial parameters for species characteristics, but may allow, for example, mutual influences among species members (represented as circles, squares, etc., on the computer screen), or may look for changes in the behavioral characteristics of species members as a function of change in a single characteristic of the "environment." It seems conceivable that one might even investigate the evolution of individual differences in attachment organization in this way, including disorganization and avoidance. With respect to tracing phylogenetic "descent," it would be interesting to look for changes in the identification of the haven of safety after making a "caching" computer species nomadic, and hence subject to early predation.

6. *The biological function served by infant attachment behavior appears to be that of gaining protection.* To impress new audiences with the importance of proximity maintenance in infancy, I stress not only Bowlby's original rationale for its incorporation within the species' repertoire—namely, protection from predators—but several other protective functions, each of which is also related to immediate survival. Bowlby probably emphasized this single protective function (protection specifically from predation) because, as the evolutionary biologist J. Crook (personal communication, 1977) explained to me, at the time of Bowlby's initial writings biologists allowed for only "one" ecological or survival pressure per species-wide behavior pattern. By the mid-1970s, however, such behaviors were also seen at times as potentially incorporated and maintained in accordance with their power to solve multiple problems involving survival and reproduction. In consequence, I suggested (Main, 1979) that the protective function served by attachment may also include protection from the elements, temperature control, feeding, and keeping up with the nomadic (ground-living) primate troop, as well as protection from injury and death stemming from attack by other troop members. Bowlby (1988) accepted these extensions regarding the biological function of attachment behavior, all of which are in fact ultimately associated with his original focus on predation (death). Separation from the forward-moving troop, like separation specifically from the attachment figure, rapidly increases the likelihood of predation; animals weakened by lack of food or water, or by exposure to the environment, are especially vulnerable to predation and other forms of death; and intraspecific aggression among primates, less recognized 30 years ago than currently, can also lead to an infant's death.

7. *For many animals, a den, burrow, or other location provides the haven of safety in times of alarm. For humans and other ground-living primates, however, only gaining access to a protective, older conspecific can serve as a solution to situations involving danger and fright.* Bowlby presented the attachment behavioral system as being closely aligned to the escape or fear system, as I will discuss again below. He also pointed out, however, that ground-living primates differ from many other mammals (for whom the mothering figure may also have considerable importance) in that the haven of safety in times of

alarm is another specific individual—that is, the attachment figure—as opposed to a den or burrow (Bowlby, 1958, 1969/1982). For many animals, then, the mother provides the food and warmth without which the infant would die, but the infant seeks a special nest, den, burrow, or other location rather than the mother herself when alarmed. For ground-living primates, in contrast, no such singular location is available, and gaining proximity to an older, protective individual or one of a small hierarchy of protective individuals is the infant's primary solution to situations of fright or alarm.[2]

Interestingly, Bowlby's observation has proven unusual. Marks (1987), who places considerable emphasis on the outcomes of frightening situations, lists flight, aggression, freezing, and other responses to fear activation (also found in Hinde, 1966), but does not mention flight to another individual as a haven of safety. Strikingly, this behavior pattern is one of the primary markers of attachment in Old World monkeys, apes, and humankind.

Commentary. In recent years, I have increasingly emphasized the importance of the attachment figure as providing the primary solution to situations of fear for human infants. I have used this concept not only in attempting to explicate the general theory, but also to provide an explanation of individual differences in attachment organization and disorganization, whether observed in infant strange situation behavior (Solomon & George, Chapter 14, this volume), representational processes (Bretherton & Munholland, Chapter 5, and Solomon & George, Chapter 14, this volume), or the AAI (Hesse, Chapter 19, this volume). I believe it may be the role of the attachment figure as the infant's solution to situations of fear that accounts in large measure for the links increasingly being uncovered between certain forms of insecure attachment and psychopathology (Dozier et al., Chapter 22; Lyons-Ruth & Jacobvitz, Chapter 23; Slade, Chapter 25; and Weinfield, Sroufe, Egeland, & Carlson, Chapter 4, this volume). Briefly, securely attached infants are viewed as having been predictably soothed or comforted following any experiences of fright or strong distress. Infants falling into the "organized" categories of insecure attachment (Main, 1990) *are not believed to have experienced the attachment figure himself or herself as frightening,* despite the fact that responsiveness has been limited or nonoptimal. For these reasons, they have been able to develop "conditional" solutions to situations of

fright. Finally, infants falling into the "disorganized" category are sharply contrasted with infants in both the secure and insecure "organized" categories of infant attachment, in that they are believed to have encountered repeated experiences of fright without solution, resulting from interactions with an attachment figure who is a source of alarm (for detailed discussions of this topic, see Hesse & Main, 1999; Main, 1995; Main & Hesse, 1990). This leaves these infants vulnerable to early behavioral disorganization, which may be accompanied by physiological and eventually by neural-structural concomitants.

8. *In my view, because of the immediacy of its tie to survival, the attachment behavioral system is best conceived as standing first in the hierarchy of infants' behavioral repertoire.* In his initial presentations of attachment theory, Bowlby (1969/1982) proposed that the attachment behavioral system is as central to species survival as the systems serving feeding and reproduction. However, while primatologists have long emphasized that without the circumstances that facilitate attachment to a caregiver, no primate infant would have been likely to survive (cf. Hrdy, 1999), the fact that maintaining proximity to protective figures is a "first" necessity is often not readily grasped.

In this light, it may be important to compare the biological function of attachment behavior to that of other behavioral systems believed to serve survival and reproductive success, in both the long and the short run. Shortly following Bowlby's early proposals regarding the attachment behavioral system, for example, Ainsworth (see Marvin & Britner, Chapter 3, this volume) noted that both exploratory and affiliative behaviors could be observed within the strange situation setting, and should be considered part of the behavioral repertoire of the infant. These systems also ultimately promote survival, as they enable the infant gradually to learn the characteristics of his or her own particular social and inanimate environment.

In this context, the comparative primacy of the attachment behavioral system is relatively obvious. While exploratory behavior clearly has favorable long-term consequences for the infant, its activation should nevertheless normally be suppressed at signs of maternal leavetaking (as is seen in strange situation studies), or even at signs of inattentiveness when mothers appear preoccupied within an unfamiliar environment (see Sorce & Emde, 1981). It is presumed that exploratory behavior is gradually suppressed in these circumstances because separation and inattentiveness represent immediate threats to infant survival.

It is relatively easy, then, to comprehend why attachment behavior must usually take precedence over exploratory and affiliative behavior. Feeding is another matter, however, and students otherwise well acquainted with attachment theory often initially presume that feeding, at least, should take precedence over attachment behavior. It requires some reflection to recognize that whereas a ground-living infant primate can go without food for many hours, less than 1 hour of separation from protective figures in the natural environment is likely to result in death (either from inter- or intraspecific attack, or from the rapid effects of dehydration or exposure). Thus the probable immediacy of mortality resulting from failure to maintain proximity to the attachment figure in unfamiliar or threatening circumstances leads proximity maintenance to stand first and foremost in the infant's behavioral hierarchy in the natural environment.

9. *Bowlby proposed that the infant is not only genetically biased to seek to maintain proximity to mothering figures, but is likewise biased to respond to certain environmental settings or changes as natural clues to (the increased likelihood of) danger—a hypothesis for which there is new support.* Bowlby (1973) proposed that primates and other animals are disposed to respond to certain situations—including, especially in the primate case, unfamiliar environments, darkness, rapid approach, sudden changes in stimulation, heights, and being alone—as natural clues to the likelihood of increased danger. None of these situations is dangerous in itself, but all are conceptualized as warning or alerting the animal and are expected to arouse fear, particularly when they are experienced in combination (as in the strange situation, which eventually leaves the infant alone in an unfamiliar setting). Ethologists had already noted the effects of species-specific clues to danger in many animals, and Rowell and Hinde (1963) had demonstrated that whereas in the presence of companions rhesus monkeys were distinctly frightened by a masked, cloaked stranger, his appearance when the monkeys were instead isolated increased fear behavior by 3- to 50-fold. With respect to human infants, Bowlby (1973) reviewed informally well-known fear responses (such as young children's apprehension of darkness), together with more formal studies (such as visual cliff experiments and studies of infant re-

sponse to "looming") that were already available at the time of writing.

In general, however, the suggestion that human beings are biased to respond to certain situations as innately dangerous is received by some audiences with skepticism. This is not surprising; when applied to environmental settings or changes that have, for a given infant, no particular logical association with pain or other malignant experience, the concept appears somewhat more Jungian than many would find comfortable. It may be useful, then, to note substantiation for one expected "natural clue to danger" among primates that Bowlby (1969/1982), according to a footnote (pp. 130–131), had found particularly frustrating due to the potential confound of learning. This is the strong tendency—noted not only among many primatologists, but also earlier by Darwin—for monkeys and apes to respond to snakes with strong fear and even panic, and for this fear to be long-lived in the absence of further exposure.

With respect to primate fears of snakes, a particularly important series of studies has been conducted by S. Mineka. Although only one can be described here, the full series is recommended for its relevance to elucidating, as well as providing cures for, disorders involving fear as a primary component. In one of her best-known studies, Mineka (1987) exposed laboratory-reared rhesus monkeys to a snake. Upon this first exposure, the monkeys showed no sign of fear of the snake. She then provided them a single exposure to a film clip of a wild rhesus monkey exhibiting fear of a snake. From that time forward, the laboratory-reared animals also showed fear of snakes. An immediate question arises as to whether the monkeys would simply have learned to fear anything that the filmed wild monkeys appeared to fear themselves—a result that would have suggested no innate fear of snakes. Mineka therefore provided some laboratory-reared monkeys with spliced films in which the wild rhesus monkey (in fact exhibiting fear of a no-longer-displayed snake) was shown exhibiting the same fearful reaction to a flower. If there were no "innate" component in the primates' fear of snakes, fear of flowers should have followed upon this exposure. The monkeys did not, however (and apparently virtually could not), learn to fear flowers. But, to repeat, following a single exposure they had learned to fear snakes.

Further, although necessarily nonexperimental, support has been provided for Bowlby's thesis by those concerned with the development of fears and phobias in children and adults. Among humans, Ohman (1993) has shown that (with some exceptions) children's and adults' fears and phobias center most frequently on stimuli likely to have been signals of increased danger in the EEA (e.g., spiders, snakes, darkness, and heights), rather than on more contemporary dangers, such as automobiles and bombs.

10. *The tie between the attachment system and the fear/escape system suggests that aspects of the brain and/or brain chemistry particularly relevant to fear experiences may provide us with one starting point for increasing our understanding not only of the attachment system itself, but also of developmental differences originating in early experiences closely combining attachment and fright.* As Bowlby noted long ago, even though flight to the parenting figure as a haven of safety when an infant is frightened marks attachment in young ground-living primates, the attachment system and the fear/escape systems are separable. This point may be clarified by considering that, given the right conditions, the activation of the fear/escape system yields many outcomes other than a search for attachment figures. For example, the frightened animal may withdraw, crouch, curl, freeze, or attack.

I have noted above that the frightened infant's tendency to seek the attachment figure(s) as a haven of safety has many implications for our understanding of individual differences in the organization (and disorganization; see Lyons-Ruth & Jacobvitz, Chapter 23, this volume) of attachment. Recently, Naomi Gribneau at Berkeley has drawn my attention to the several ways in which the amygdala is implicated in human experiences of fright, and to some studies that we might begin to conduct centrally involving this structure. Many other researchers and theorists may also be interested in the intriguing role of the amygdala when considered (to my knowledge, for the first time) in relation to human attachment.

Commentary. The amygdala is a small, almond-shaped organ located in the medial temporal lobe; as noted earlier, it is a part of the somewhat elusive "limbic" system (meaning that it will have close ties to emotions and to the immediacies of survival-related behaviors) and is located near the hippocampus, the "seat" of long-term event memories. Electrical stimulation of the amygdala in humans typically elicits feelings of fright and anxiety, and LeDoux (1996) has described the amygdala as "the key to fear learning." In addition, the amygdala plays a role in sexual behavior, aggression, and emotional memory, as well as modulating the strength and storage of emotional memories.

Strikingly, the presence of the amygdala seems to be required for the experience of fright and anxiety, and fearful facial expressions appear to be recognized in and processed by the amygdala (Adolphs, Tranel, Damasio, & Damasio, 1995). As one extreme but instructive example, Damasio's (1994) patient S. M., who lacks an amygdala, can recognize most human facial expressions *except* fear, and cannot produce a fear face even while watching herself in the mirror. Frightening sounds normally reach the amygdala directly (from the thalamus), promoting behavioral reactions twice as quickly as when the pathway includes the neocortex. Although the cortex can act to suppress reactions of fright, the connections from amygdala to the cortex are markedly stronger than those from cortex to amygdala. Corresponding, perhaps, to the role it plays in fear responses and fear recognition, the amygdala also appears to be involved in reward learning. Following lesions to the amygdala, rewarding "places" are no longer sought. To my knowledge, research on this issue to date involves only places in which food and water have been found, but some obvious experiments involving attachment could also be conducted.

In nonhuman animals, electrical stimulation of the amygdala appears to elicit notably different reactions (e.g., rage) from the fright/anxiety reactions elicited in humans.[3] In humans, the amygdala is linked to the relatively "new" orbitofrontal cortex, which has been connected to working memory, and especially to rewards and punishments. Wheeler et al. (1997) have further implicated the orbitofrontal cortex in a special, "autonoetic" form of consciousness and episodic memory, which enables the user to engage in "time travel," drawing upon the past and imagining the future as specifically connected to the self in a way that involves a unique form of subjective experiencing.

Given the set of findings just described, an examination of individual differences in both the simple metrics and the functional workings of the amygdala and orbitofrontal cortex could assist attachment researchers interested in individual differences. At the outset, I should perhaps note that with respect to the relation between fear and memory, animal researchers are in agreement that learned fear responses are conserved across the individual's life and can never be completely erased, even though their expression can be suppressed (Allman & Brothers, 1994;

LeDoux, Romanski, & Xagoraris, 1989). If it is true, then, that early experiences of fright can now provisionally be understood as conserved across the individual's lifetime, and if some individuals have repeatedly experienced "fright without solution" involving the "rewarding" attachment figure as its source, we may be especially interested in effects upon the amygdala in individuals in low-risk samples judged disorganized with one (or both) parents during infancy.

The reader may be surprised that I suggest low-risk samples as a starting point when children known to have experienced direct battering by their parents are not only usually found to be disorganized in the strange situation, but also have no doubt experienced much greater fright that has taken the attachment figure as its source. I would contend, however, that low-risk samples may provide a better, if more stringent, laboratory for assessing the effects of early experiences on the brain, because in the case of the child who is disorganized by frightened behavior resulting from mother's early loss experience (see Lyons-Ruth & Jacobvitz, Chapter 23, this volume), we are not dealing with the confounding effects of direct insult to the brain and surrounding deleterious conditions that often accompany a history of severe abuse.

In sum, in the next few years (presuming there are continuing rapid developments in available techniques and equipment), both the metrics and the functioning of the amygdala and orbitofrontal cortex could be examined in follow-up studies involving individuals categorized as disorganized/disoriented (and, of course, secure, avoidant, or resistant/ambivalent) with one or both parents in infancy. Individuals disorganized in infancy have been found the most likely both to have difficulty in solving verbally presented syllogisms (Jacobsen, Edelstein, & Hofman, 1994) and to suffer from psychopathology during adolescence (Carlson, 1998; Lyons-Ruth & Jacobvitz, Chapter 23, this volume; Ogawa, Sroufe, Weinfield, Carlson, & Egeland, 1997). My own impression for the past several years has been that disorganized attachment status interferes with working memory in stressful interpersonal circumstances. This is suggested in Jacobsen et al.'s follow-up study of Icelandic children, and is also implied by close examination of the lapses in reasoning and discourse found in unresolved/disorganized speakers within the AAI (Main & Hesse, 1992). However, even positive findings including on-line recordings of confused orbitofrontal responses to verbal problem

solving will of course yield no more than an interesting instance of cartography, and—although highly interesting to me—the import of such work for the understanding and change of human cognition, feeling, and intentionality may not exceed that of the original behavioral observations (including the strange situation and the AAI). That is, finding neurological correlates to already mapped behavioral and discourse patterns may or may not provide additional insights into mechanisms and leverage points for clinical intervention.

Although I have mentioned directly above some work involving the study of individual differences, to this point in my comments I have been focusing on the more global aspects of attachment processes, rather than the individual differences in attachment organization that have become a part of the general theory, and were first elucidated by Mary Ainsworth. In the remaining points and commentaries, I move closer to an examination of the relations between the general theory and the study of individual differences.

11. *Once formed, primary attachments are not believed to vary in terms of strength. This statement is supported in part by the fact that some infants consistently showing high levels of anxious attachment behavior in the home do not exhibit attachment behavior in the strange situation. This disjunction is not fully understood, nor do we know what assists these and other infants in inhibiting the display of attachment behavior in the stressful, unfamiliar strange situation setting.* To those believing that the infant who is attached to several individuals preserves a "hierarchy" among his or her attachment figures, Ainsworth's vigorous insistence that what "varies" among attached infants is the *organization,* not the *strength,* of the attachment presents an empirical puzzle deserving of discussion (Ainsworth, 1967; Ainsworth, Blehar, Waters, & Wall, 1978). It is, in other words, admittedly somewhat difficult to coordinate the concept of absence of variation in strength of attachment with the concept of attachment hierarchies. We can nonetheless sidestep the problem presented by "attachment hierarchies" by concentrating initially on Ainsworth's own concerns, which were the development and formation of the first and primary attachment to the mother.

Based on her observations of infant–mother dyads in both Uganda and Baltimore, Ainsworth first pointed out that no single behavioral index is sufficient for identifying an infant as attached to another individual, and in her Uganda study she listed multiple indices of a specific, focused attachment. Her position was that the formation of an attachment is a neurobiological and virtually universal phenomenon, while variations in the display of attachment behavior in attached infants are the outcome of ontogeny (the infant's history) and immediate cause (Bowlby's activators and terminators, some environmental, some internal; see Bowlby, 1969/1982).

Ainsworth also attempted to dispel the notion that we could conclude from strange situation observations that avoidant infants are "less" attached than secure infants, on the basis of absence of display of attachment behavior under stress—or that, on the other hand, resistant/ambivalent infants are "more attached" than secure infants, based on their highly persistent and more vocal display of attachment behavior. These points regarding the infants' earliest and primary attachments were backed by home observations (Ainsworth et al., 1978). First, before the Baltimore 1-year-olds were ever placed in the strange situation, they had been observed to have formed definitive attachments to their mothers, and it was *with this point established* that the variations in their response to maternal leavetaking and return in an unfamiliar environment became most striking. As Ainsworth went to some length to point out, for example, four of the six infants who showed little or no attachment behavior while undergoing the stress of separation in an unfamiliar environment displayed high levels of anxiety and distress (attachment behavior) when the mother simply moved about in the home. In contrast, secure infants who cried upon separation in the unfamiliar strange situation environment cried very little in response to minor separations in the home setting. The strange situation is thus systematically related to, and in that sense *represents,* infant home behavior, but an attached infant behaves very differently under the stress of this procedure than he or she does in the home.

It may be relevant to add that if the reader is a professional who plans to lecture about individual differences in attachment behavior in infancy using videotaped examples, it is important to make certain that the audience sees not only "absence of attachment behavior" in highly avoidant infants (absence of distress and failure of approach), but also the active nature of their avoidance. Persons exhibiting such tapes should take care to point to the intrusion of a new behavior

pattern into the infant's strange situation response, and say that it is probably via avoidance that the infant is able to inhibit distress and attachment behavior. The way in which the infant actively turns away from the parent (often fumbling for a new toy) immediately upon reunion, appears deaf to the parent's call, leans out of the parent's arms on pickup (often again to point to inanimate objects) and in extreme cases, subtly continually turns so that the back is kept to the parent should be drawn to the audience's attention (and, optimally, replayed).

Observations of this kind give the viewer an opportunity to reflect on the link that Bowlby and Ainsworth, as clinicians, made between avoidance and defensive process. Seen in toddlers subjected to stressful long-term separation, Bowlby (1969/1982) called avoidant behavior ("detachment") evidence for "repression in the making," and Ainsworth and Bell (1970) conceptualized avoidance in the strange situation as a behavioral defense against expressions not only of attachment, but also of anger.

Commentary. Why four of Ainsworth's avoidant infants appeared highly anxious and distressed regarding even their mothers' slightest moves (e.g., from living room to kitchen) in the home situation, yet showed no affect in the strange situation, remains to be explained. In the strange situation, these four infants were her most avoidant (i.e., they fit into Ainsworth's "extremely avoidant" subcategory of strange situation behavior); the remaining two avoidant infants appeared independent in the home as well as in the strange situation, and were also less avoidant. All six infants had experienced rejection of attachment behavior in the home environment; however, the four who exhibited anxious attachment in the home but extreme avoidance in the strange situation had also experienced continual interference with their activities. The remaining two less avoidant children had simply been denied access to their mothers, suggestive of mild neglect.

Scholars and clinicians interested in avoidance as a prodromal defensive process are of course fascinated by these findings. Defense is presumed to arise under stress, so we can understand how it is that attachment behavior was inhibited in anxious, rejected, and interfered-with infants, but it remains puzzling that the more moderately avoidant infants simply behaved similarly in the home and in the strange situation. I could list numerous options discussed with my students over the years, but none have been decisive. I believe, however, that this is an extremely intriguing problem, deserving further investigation by researchers who are willing to undertake extensive home observations and to learn Ainsworth's subclassifications. Over the intervening years I have heard numerous reports from the mothers of highly avoidant (A1) babies that their infants are extremely anxious regarding the most minor leavetaking (including naptimes) in the home, and are behaving unexpectedly in the strange situation. Thus it seems that this may be a solid, "real" phenomenon.

Another point of theoretical interest is whether an infant would be able to maintain avoidance without inanimate objects being made available for him or her to turn to. I (Main, 1981) have described human infant avoidance as "an organized shift in attention," and my best guess is that in a bare room avoidance would rarely be witnessed. Experiments of this kind could readily be conducted, either by repeating the strange situation procedure at 12 and again at 15 months (the second time in a bare strange situation room), or by observing the infants of mothers identified as highly dismissing in the AAI (see Hesse, Chapter 19, this volume), again in a bare environment. I can imagine that an infant might be so distressed that the mother would need to be sent back quickly, and the procedure would have to be terminated. Should it be the case that inanimate objects are needed to enable the infant to shift its attention, however, I believe we would have learned something useful about what is necessary for the maintenance of what some clinicians term "working" defense.

12. *Corrections to Bowlby's initial presentation of his theory made by both Ainsworth and Bretherton have led to widespread acceptance of the notion that, rather than being activated and terminated, the attachment system is best conceived as "continually active." With respect to the organized forms of insecure attachment, this reconceptualization suggests the necessity of continually active defensive processes, involving in some cases a refocusing or manipulation of attention.* In his early writings, Bowlby described the attachment behavioral system as being "turned on" or "turned off," depending on circumstances (as seems to be the case with some other behavioral systems, such as exploration). Both Ainsworth and Bretherton realized, however, that an inactive system would leave the infant at considerable risk; they suggested an adjustment to the theory, in which the proximity and the physical and psychological accessibility of the attachment figure were continuously monitored. Bowlby at once accepted this early modification to the theory, although whether the attachment system itself, or some higher cognitive function having immediate access to the system, should be considered responsible for continuous monitoring should perhaps be left open.[4]

The continuing activity of either the attachment system or some higher process always ready to alert the system to unfavorable internal or environmental changes is important to all philosophically inclined psychologists, not only for its implications regarding the nature and central occupations of the mind, but also as it bears on our understanding of defensive and attentional processes. As a simple example, if the system is actually "turned off" at times, then infants who ignore their mothers' absence in an unfamiliar setting and then actively avoid the mothers when reunited may be reacting naturally rather than defensively, given their histories of rejection. If instead the system is in fact still activated, then avoidance can be understood as representing an alteration in the otherwise naturally occurring output of the attachment behavioral system (Main, 1979, 1981, 1990; cf. Ainsworth & Bell, 1970; Bowlby, 1969/1982), seen in terms of an organized yet relatively inflexibile shift of attention (Main, 1990, 1995), and/or as representative of defense.

13. *Although there is general agreement that an infant or adult will have only a few attachment figures at most, many attachment theorists and researchers believe that infants form "attachment hierarchies," in which some figures are primary, others secondary, and so on. This position can also be presented in a stronger form, in which a particular figure is believed continually to take top place ("monotropy"). Together with the question of how quickly an infant can change primary attachment figures, questions surrounding monotropy and attachment hierarchies remain unsettled.* One of the major points still to be elucidated regarding the nature of human attachments is whether most individuals are operating with attachment hierarchies—that is, focusing their (often unconscious) attention most fully upon a single attachment figure, while also being cognizant of a few secondary figures as well. In its strongest form, this proposition is known as "monotropy" (the seeking of one person; see Cassidy, Chapter 1, this volume), but it is generally modified to the primary seeking of one person, with others perhaps on mental standby. This is important for our general understanding of the

human mind, because a mind that focuses primarily on one other person is by nature a different mind from one that focuses on a set.

John Watson (personal communication, 1977) has suggested that mental monotropy would be favorable to infants in times of emergency. For example, debating whom to run to while being rapidly approached by a leopard ("Let's see, *X,* presently in tree *A,* holds me nicely, but *Y,* on rock *B,* is good at grooming, and *Z,* on rock *C,* has the sweetest milk," so, um. . .") could conceivably be bad for an infant's health. Cassidy (Chapter 1, this volume) has referred to Watson's hypothesis as involving automaticity, and viewed in this light, it could certainly have advantages.

However, this question and several other closely related matters that are also of interest to general psychology remain unsettled. We need a technique for ascertaining favored persons (and, in the case where the two parents are being observed with the intent to contrast the infant's proximity seeking, a rationale that is not personally hurtful). To date many imaginative techniques have been employed, some including variations on the strange situation, with double swinging doors and parents marching in and taking leave in double step. Although in general these studies point to preference for the mother in cases where she is definitively the primary caregiver (see Colin, 1985, 1987), some further variations could be tried. These would include placing the infant at midpoint between the two parents, and presenting a semifrightening stimulus, such as the masked clown utilized in the Main and Weston (1981) study. The question here is this: Toward whom does the infant take flight? Another possibility would be to have the parents take leave at the same moment and in opposite directions (variants of this have been attempted), so that we could ask which of the parents is followed. In many of these studies (see below), it would probably be useful to conduct such procedures with the same infant (and parents) three or four times.

One puzzle currently intriguing many researchers is the apparent (albeit unproven) stronger influence that early attachment to the mother seems to have, even when the infant has been found to be insecure with the mother and secure with the father. This appeared to be the case when we assessed representational processes in our original Bay Area study (e.g., using Kaplan's version of the Separation Anxiety Test, or the Kaplan and Main drawing system). That is, a 6-year-old's *overall* family representation appeared influenced almost exclusively by the organization of his or her attachment to the mother, rather than the father, during infancy. In our current follow-up study of 45 of these subjects, secure versus insecure attachment status with the mother during infancy markedly predicts secure/autonomous versus insecure AAI status at 19 years of age. In contrast, early attachment to the father is not significantly related to AAI status. This is not because our early strange situation assessments of infant–father relations were meaningless: They were significantly related to the fathers' AAI (as they have been in many samples; see Hesse, Chapter 19, this volume; cf. Grossmann, Grossmann, & Zimmermann, Chapter 33, this volume), and they predicted father–child discourse *down to the specific level of attachment subclass* at 6 years of age (Strage & Main, 1985; Main, Kaplan, & Cassidy, 1985). In addition, in our 1985 study, the quality of an infant's attachment to the father at age 1 was predictive of enjoyment of opportunities provided in the free play setting 5 years later. However, once again, both in middle childhood and in adolescence, the offspring's *overall state of mind with respect to attachment*—as seen in the Kaplan and Main family drawings, responses to Kaplan's version of the Separation Anxiety Test, and later in the AAI—seemed to be chiefly influenced by the mother. This Bay Area study is only one instance, but speaking with other researchers has led me to believe that our results are not atypical.

Perhaps the most obvious explanation would be that the offspring has spent more time with the mother. The "time spent" argument makes sense, and led Lamb working in Sweden with families in which fathers stayed home more than was usual while mothers worked outside of the home, to expect the infants to exhibit preference for their fathers. By the measures used in two such studies, however (Frodi, Lamb, Hwang, & Frodi, 1983; Lamb, Frodi, Hwang, & Frodi, 1983), the mothers were still sharply preferred. This startling finding could be related to the emerging literature regarding an infant's earliest experiences with the mother, which involve several prenatal months of hearing her voice (and an immediate preference for her voice above others); a preference for the odor of her milk (and in some species, special identification of her amniotic fluid; note that human kin recognition seems to involve olfactory perceptions of kin-like odors and responses to her internal states via uterine experiences that have led some monkeys born to distressed mothers to be "disorganized" at birth on a monkey-appropriate version of the Brazelton neonatal assessment (Spangler & Grossmann, 1993). Each of these findings could mean that no matter how many hours a father spends with an infant after birth, provided the mother is present regularly as well (as was the case in the Swedish families studied), the mother has already become the infant's preferred attachment figure before birth.

Commentary. This hypothesis might be ruled out by conducting another study (perhaps again in Sweden), involving *adoptive* housekeeping fathers (and mothers). In this case, the fathers will have begun with less of a handicap and the mothers with less of an advantage. There are of course many alternative explanations for the findings of the Swedish studies that I have not mentioned. Perhaps, for example, mothers simply engage in more contingent face-to-face interactions with their infants than their fathers do, or perhaps they have had more parenting (babysitting and sibling-sitting) practice prior to the infant's birth.

Studies examining hierarchy of preference during infancy as compared to the (separately established) secure versus insecure organization of attachment to each parent are also of great interest. For example, in a study using the simple procedures I have suggested earlier, if an infant dashes to the mother (with whom attachment is insecure) rather than the father (with whom attachment is secure) when presented with a mildly frightening stimulus, and does so repeatedly, what are we to make of it? At present, as noted above, we seem to be finding greater influence and greater preference ascribed to the mother, even when (by inference) the infant is insecurely attached to the mother and securely attached to the father. If these results held up across samples, we might want to extend our investigations to olfactory preferences—an area pursued with some investigations at the adult level in the 1970s, but currently out of fashion (except in studies of adult romantic attraction). In studies of this kind, individuals simply attempt to identify, or indicate preferences for, T-shirts worn by selected other individuals. Would "mother preference" in cases of insecure attachment to mothers and secure attachment to fathers extend to olfactory preferences? And, indeed, are there olfactory cues associated with attachment? Similar studies examining preference could also, of course, be conducted with battering versus nonbattering parental figures.

Studies of this kind need not be confined to questions of hierarchy or preference. They can be used to provide a background for addressing puzzling aspects of the behavior of some battered and avoidant infants. Battered infants (and, in my laboratory, extremely avoidant—in technical terms, "A1"—infants) have occasionally been seen to cry at the *stranger's* leavetaking and attempt to follow her out of the room. My first personal experience of this kind occurred outside of the strange situation, when a mother–infant dyad (the infant was classified as A1) visited my office just prior to the procedure, but following a home visit I had made 1 week before. Although not a dark and stormy night, it was a dark and stormy afternoon, and there was a clap of thunder with accompanying lightning very close to the building. The infant fled crying to my lap, and, embarrassingly for both me and her mother, continued to cling to me for safety without a backward glance.

Now that the "disorganized" coding system is available, we would term this behavior, together with crying at the stranger's leavetaking, "misdirected," and the infant would be classified as disorganized (Main & Solomon, 1986, 1990). Misdirected or not, however, flight to another individual as a haven of safety is a strong index of attachment, and we might wonder how many other attachment behaviors battered or extremely avoidant infants might display to new persons. Conducting the strange situation with such infants and the (favored) new persons in place of the parents might provide useful information. These could be conducted with the favored stranger a day, a week, or a month following the original strange situation (questions of memory grow interesting here), and we could also simply conduct the strange situation with the infants of extremely dismissing mothers, with "strangers" with whom the infants have had perhaps 30 minutes of previous (pleasant) interaction.

Should the infants' strange situation behavior with a virtual stranger lead "blind" coders to call them securely attached to the new person, we would have to engage in some serious thinking regarding (a) the nature of attachment, (b) the rate at which new attachments can be formed, and (c) the validity of the strange situation when external observations have not already assured us by the multiple indices recommended by Ainsworth (1967) that the infants are attached to the individuals with whom they are being observed. If secure-appearing strange situation behavior toward relative strangers was confined to highly avoidant infants, however, we might further wonder whether the function of avoidance was indeed simply to retain behavioral organization while leaving the field open to new persons.

In an earlier theoretical paper (Main, 1981), I drew on the work of several ethologists to suggest three functions of avoidance, which are not mutually exclusive. First, following Chance (1962), avoidance might keep the infant in proximity, insofar as not looking at the social partner permitted impulses toward flight and/or aggressive behavior to remain deactivated. Second, following Tinbergen and Moynihan (1952), avoidance might keep the infant in proximity by decreasing the likelihood of the mother's withdrawing in response to eye-to-eye contact with the infant. Third, following another suggestion offered by Chance, avoidance might simply assist the infant in maintaining behavioral organization, leaving the infant's further behavioral options open. A series of thought experiments led me to slightly favor the third hypothesis. Depending, of course, upon outcome, experiments of the kind suggested here might again point to the greater viability of the third hypothesis.

14. Attachment is a lifespan phenomenon. However, we have yet to understand the formation of new attachments in adulthood; in addition, the prediction of adult from infant attachment is readily misunderstood. Attachment has traditionally been associated with infancy, and Bowlby's contention that the attachment behavioral system persists throughout life—although generally less readily activated and more easily modulated in older individuals—is occasionally met with disbelief (although, of course, not among individuals investigating romantic or couple attachment). Even clinicians can be surprised at this claim. One reason for this lack of recognition of the applicability of the principles of attachment to oneself in later phases of life may lie in the failure to explain that, for example, the active exhibition of attachment behavior and caregiving behavior in healthy adult couple functioning is less frequent and normally more subtle than in child–parent dyads, and moreover the roles are flexible and interchangeable (Shaver et al., 1988). However, many middle-aged adults will readily recognize the reemergence of attachment behavior (now often directed toward themselves as attachment figures) in their parents when ill or in threatening circumstances. In a talk she gave at the age of 77, Mary Ainsworth (1991) referred to the renewed importance of attachment figures in her life, as a function of the loss of varying kinds of strength associated with aging.

Now that some studies following attachment from infancy to early adulthood have been completed, several laboratories working with low-risk samples have reported what is widely interpreted as "stability" of attachment across this time period. Hesse (Chapter 19, this volume) has already dealt with some of the confusions that can arise from these findings insofar as the AAI is concerned, but I would like to mention several others. The study of attachment would be dull indeed if we found only that secure infants tend to become secure children, who tend then to become secure adults. In this case, aside from the "stages" in the development of attachment described by Marvin and Britner (Chapter 3, this volume), we would have no developmental theory in the field.

Instead, I would like to suggest that the findings to date are rich indeed and point to further directions for research. First, let us consider the "stability" (which is often actually *predictability*) of secure versus insecure attachment in low-risk samples, uncovered with the Main and Cassidy system for analyzing reunion behavior following a 1-hour separation at 6 years of age (Main & Cassidy, 1988). Solomon and George (Chapter 14, this volume) reviewed two studies reporting the predictability of reunion behavior at 6 years from that at 1 year. Two further studies have also reported impressive predictability from infant strange situation behavior with mothers to sixth-year attachment using the Main and Cassidy system (Ammaniti, Speranza, & Candelori, 1996; Jacobsen et al., 1994). In these studies, children disorganized with the parent as infants have typically become either controlling and punitive or controlling and caregiving, but are no longer disorganized. This is *predictability,* but I do not see how this can reasonably be called stability. First, such a child is no longer overtly disorganized; in addition, a transformation in reunion behavior has occurred, such that the child takes on the parental role.

Second, when we consider the examination of the child–parent discourse record in this same setting undertaken by Strage (Strage & Main, 1985; Main et al., 1985; see Main, 1995, for a review), we see sharp differences between previously avoidant, previously secure, and previously disorganized dyads for both mother–child and father–child pairs (too few ambivalent dyads were available for analysis). Moreover, highly significant *subclass* distinctions were identified in both the mother–child and father–child samples, such that, for example, B1 (secure, but substituting interaction across a distance for physical contact), B3 (prototypically secure), and B4 (secure, but infant mildly preoccupied with the parent) dyads were easily distinguished from this 3-minute discourse record. Is ending sentences with "isn't it?", "don't you?", or "don't you think?", which is one of the linguistic features that distinguishes conversations within B4 dyads at 6 years, really the same thing as crying and maintaining contact a bit too long, as a B4 child does in infancy? Of course, at a deep level, we might say that it is "the same thing"; there is a lingering and mildly exaggerated seeking of affirmation from the partner at both the nonverbal (infancy) and verbal (middle childhood) levels. However, failing to note that we have moved from nonverbal infant behavior to discourse by simply ascribing such findings to "continuity" undermines any attempt to understand the transformations in these phenomena across developmental periods.

Finally, let us consider the relations between secure attachment in infancy and early childhood, and secure/autonomous attachment status as assessed via the AAI in adulthood. Once more, we are facing a comparison between *nonverbal infant behavioral responses* to separation and reunion in an unfamiliar setting on the one hand, and *adult discourse* on the other—this time, specifically, the ability to be coherent and collaborative in discussions with an unfamiliar person regarding early life history and its effects. As in the case of Strage's (Strage & Main, 1985; see also Main, 1995) remarkable findings predicting discourse patterns from infant nonverbal behavior across a 5-year period, to reduce the extension of this intriguing evolution across 20 or more years to a matter of mere "stability" suggests a singularly incurious attitude. At the very least, we should be intrigued and surprised when we are able to observe predictability in the face of such a dramatic change in modalities.

In addition, however, we limit our potential grasp of the complexity of this phenomenon if we fail to carefully consider what it means that security, once identified only with reference to behavior toward other specific persons (e.g., *secure with respect to* the mother, *secure with respect to* the father), now refers to the autonomy of a person judged to be secure (secure/autonomous) in himself or herself. In adulthood as opposed to childhood, then, the individual's secure (/autonomous) mental state is no longer defined by reference to a second person.

Indeed, if during infancy security is identified with the ability to confidently seek, find, and embrace a caregiver when in frightening circumstances, whereas competent caregiving is identified with a tendency to seek, comfort, and retrieve those needing care when in frightening circumstances (this is Cassidy's definition in Chapter 1 of this volume; see also George & Solomon, Chapter 28, this volume), we can see the remarkable transformations that have taken place in an individual who was securely attached to the mother during infancy and has become secure/autonomous by adulthood. This is development, and is not what is ordinarily understood by the term "stability."

Commentary. One of the major questions plaguing attachment researchers is how the multiple, independent attachments that children form to their parents and other caregivers coalesce into a usually singular overall "state of mind with respect to attachment" in adulthood. This would not be so intriguing if the AAI were not so strongly linked to caregiving behavior toward infants (van IJzendoorn, 1995; see also Hesse, Chapter 19, this volume). Thus, without knowing that the AAI is predictive of caregiving behavior, we might simply conclude that persons with a history of differing early relationships tend to talk in terms of one of them, but behave in ways that are expressive of many. However, it appears that multiple, independent early attachments do typically coalesce into a "classifiable" state of mind with respect to attachment in adulthood, and that whatever this particular state of mind, it is predictive of a concordant and "classifiable" form of caregiving.

Researchers having access to strange situation and (ideally) later attachment assessments involving both the mothers and fathers can now begin to address this question as follows. If we presume that assessments of early attachment to both mothers and fathers are available, standard AAIs could be conducted when the subjects have reached young adulthood, and the individuals' overall state of mind with respect to attachment could be assessed. Some time later, two further AAIs could be conducted for each subject—one exclusively focused on the relation to the father, and one on the relation to the mother. One possible outcome would be that the states of mind (AAI classifications) assigned to these mother and father interviews would significantly reflect the early attachment relation as observed with each parent; in that case, researchers would have a new way of checking whether "state of mind with respect to attachment" to one parent typically dominates the corresponding state of mind for the other parent during the original (standard) interview. A second outcome could be that even in cases in which the original classifications to the two parents were divergent, the classification assigned to the mother-only AAI interview would typically be the same as that assigned to the father-only interview. In this case, we would have an entirely different picture of the way in which early relationships affect later states of mind.

Following a pioneering study of this kind, independent studies of the stability of the mother-only and father-only interviews would be in order, and in later studies the three types of interview should be balanced for order of presentation. A first study examining similarities and differences between mother-only and father-only interviews is in fact underway with adolescents in Colorado (W. Furman, personal communication, 1998).

We can also investigate the formation of new attachments in later life. I would like to propose three types of studies along these lines:

a. The formation of attachments to leaders or mentors among small groups of adolescents could be studied. Here we would want to use as much direct (filmed or nonfilmed) observation as possible, accompanied by AAIs conducted with the group leader(s) and "before and after" AAIs conducted with members of the group. In addition, direct querying regarding whom an adolescent would turn to in attachment-related circumstances (before and after joining the group) should and could be utilized.

Of course, in theory if not in practice, we could combine these techniques to study inner-city adolescents joining gangs. What has brought this type of study to mind, however, is a somewhat more uplifting possibility, which I believe is feasible if carried out with imagination and sensitivity. This proposed study is based on *Street Soldiers,* a PBS documentary by Avon Kirkland featuring the Omega Boys' Club organized by Joe Marshall, Jr. at Hunter's Point, San Francisco (Kirkland, 1996; Marshall, 1996). The aim of this program is to direct young people in this extremely troubled area away from gang participation and gang violence, toward high school and (the program has been amazingly successful) college graduation.

My own study of this film has suggested that Marshall's technique (and that of his very few colleagues) involves keeping promises to intervene as possible in any trouble in his charges' lives, as well as keeping promises to act as a "stronger and wiser" figure when simple conversation and council is called for (even late at night). This means, to begin with, that Marshall and his colleagues permit as much maintenance of proximity as is possible within reasonable limits, and that they act as a secure base as well. I was particularly struck, however, by an additional promise and point of emphasis, which was that his chief aim with respect to his charges was to *keep them safe,* and that if the program (with a little cooperation from the adolescents) failed to *keep them safe,* then it had failed. This promise obviously goes well beyond the bounds of early contingent responsiveness, but since the program is working well enough to be currently studied as a model by Congress (A. Kirkland, personal communication, 1999), it might be useful to investigate whether it works in part via the formation of a (secure) attachment to the leaders in those who have benefited. (Adolescents who have not benefited from the program are, of course, also of interest.)

b. Bowlby (1988) suggested that the therapist will optimally act as a "secure base" for the patient, assisting him or her in examining working models of past and present relationships, albeit preserving the notion that it is ultimately the patient who knows the nature of his or her experiences, impulses, and feelings. Amini et al. (1996) have further pointed out that from the patient's point of view, good therapeutic relationships come to function as attachment relationships featuring the manifestation of secure-base behavior toward the therapist, signs of missing the therapist upon separation, and flight to the therapist as a haven of safety.

In direct parallel to Dozier's "maternal diary" method, a few therapists might be willing to keep track of their patients' gradual formation of an attachment to themselves (eventually, let us hope, a secure attachment) using similar criteria. However, Amini and colleagues have further proposed that from a psychobiological point of view, psychotherapy might be conceived as a directed attachment relationship whose purpose is the revision of the implicit emotional memory of attachment. This means that we cannot get away from what is usually called "transference" using this model, and that the formation of a new attachment may initially be somewhat stormy. It would still be an interesting matter to attempt to determine whether and when the new attachment is formed.

c. Finally, the study of the formation of attachments to favored nurses or assistants on the part of cognitively competent elderly people placed in nursing homes could be of interest. This idea is not my own, but comes from a student in a large undergraduate course who viewed the film *John, 17 Months: Ten Days in Residential Care* (see Robertson & Robertson, 1967–1972). In this film, as well as in a related journal article, Robertson and Robertson (1971) suggested that John's suffering could have been considerably lessened if he had been permitted more consistent care by what appeared to be his favorite nurse. Instead, nurses were assigned to different children at different times, and John's access to his preferred "Nurse Mary" was unpredictably restricted and/or flatly denied. Already having some knowledge of nursing homes for the elderly, and informed by Bowlby that attachments can again acquire heightened significance in old age, this student asked why arrangements are not made so that elderly people are permitted repeated access to a special nurse. This could obviously constitute a humane and useful change in current social policy. Moreover, at a practical level, we might find that only a limited (but predictable) period of focused interaction and care with a particular "attachment figure" is necessary to improve the mental state of many such persons (and, of course, we could study the formation of these new attachments on the side).

15. *So far, there is no convincing evidence that behavior genetics play a role in the organized categories of infant attachment observed in the strange situation. Genetics may, however, interact with attachment in other ways; here attachment-related events producing nonshared environments, as well as genetic influences upon attachment, may be investigated.* As several chapters in this volume indicate, there is little to no evidence that the *full* patterns or categories of attachment as originally described by Mary Ainsworth (as opposed to particular aspects of behavior observable in the strange situation, such as amount of crying) are influenced by heredity (Vaughn & Bost, Chapter 10, this volume).

Similarly, in a meta-analysis that included 13 samples in an examination of possible "temperamental" contributions to disorganized/disoriented attachment, van IJzendoorn and his colleagues found no evidence for a temperamental contribution (van IJzendoorn, Schuengel, & Bakermans-Kranenburg, in press). However, many of the studies within this meta-analysis relied on parental reports of infant temperament. Two that were based instead on Brazelton neonatal examinations showed some (Spangler &

Grossmann, 1993) or else no (Carlson, 1998) predictability of disorganized attachment from the neonatal period. Of course, as Spangler and Grossmann (1993) made clear, neonatal disorganization can arise from purely environmental rather than genetic factors, such as intrauterine conditions influenced by the mother's own environment. I am inclined, however, to believe that researchers should still hold open the possibility of a small heritable component in disorganization (e.g., overall fearfulness). This is an empirical question that should continue to be examined.

With respect to the "organized" attachment categories, however—especially when considered from an evolutionary viewpoint, which includes conditional strategies for parenting (see Main, 1979, 1981, 1990; Belsky, Chapter 7, and Simpson, Chapter 6, this volume), together with the likelihood that the family might expect to encounter varying environments from year to year—the lack of major contributions from heritable or temperamental factors makes sense. Since at times parents may need to modify their caregiving strategies in the face of changing personal or ecological circumstances (Main, 1990), infants will similarly need to leave the question of attachment organization with respect to the parents open or "facultative." That an infant's attachment strategy needs to be sufficiently flexible to accommodate possible variation in parental strategy can well be imagined if we consider the consequences for an infant who, "inheriting" a resistant/ambivalent (i.e., preoccupied) behavior pattern from the father, is faced with a dismissing mother. Similarly, infants should have some ability to alter their attachment patterning over time, because, for example, a toddler who remains firmly avoidant of an initially dismissing mother may fare less well than one who is capable of switching to a "secure" strategy in the face of improving maternal circumstances and security (cf. Vaughn, Egeland, Sroufe, & Waters, 1979).

Commentary. These considerations regarding the advantages of maintaining flexibility aside, behavior genetics may well be relevant to attachment. For example, recent findings concerning "nonshared" environment puzzle some family researchers because they indicate, among other things, that psychopathology does not typically appear in all of the siblings in a particular family (Pike & Plomin, 1997). However, if we take seriously the concept of "sensitivity to initial conditions," which is central to nonlinear dynamic theories, we can readily imagine early attachment-related events that could differ for children in the same family and then be magnified across the course of development. One such event would be critical parental loss experiences within 2 years preceding or following a given child's birth. "Grandparent loss" has already been associated with schizophrenia (and is specific to the schizophrenic proband in a given family; see Walsh, 1978) and with the dissociative disorders (Liotti, 1992; forthcoming replications cited in Liotti, in press). Hesse and van IJzendoorn (1998, in press) have also found dissociative-like tendencies as assessed by Tellegen's absorption scale (Tellegen, 1982; Tellegen & Atkinson, 1974) associated with losses of this kind on the part of a subject's parents in two relatively large samples of college students.

The only mediator of this relation considered by attachment theorists to date is parental frightened/frightening behavior, associated with a parent's loss experience (see Hesse & Main, 1999; Liotti, in press; and Lyons-Ruth & Jacobvitz, Chapter 23, this volume), which is in turn associated with disorganized infant attachment. Because Carlson (1998) has recently found early disorganized attachment to be predictive of dissociative behavior as observed by teachers, dissociative symptoms as determined by the Schedule of Affective Disorders and Schizophrenia for School-Age Children, and self-reported dissociative experiences, changes in parenting behavior contingent upon loss experienced near the time of the birth of a particular child could well be an important aspect of nonshared environment. Another possibility, unrelated to this first one, would be failures in the mother's immune system associated with loss at about the time of the birth of a specific child. Loss is known to have unfavorable effects on the immune system (Ader, 1995), and viral infections are increasingly being examined for their implications for certain forms of psychopathology (Muller & Ackenheil, 1995; O'Reilly, 1994).

As I have stated elsewhere (Main, 1996), a number of interesting studies investigating the interplay of attachment and genetics have yet to be conducted. First, a variation on the usual match between the prebirth AAI and the strange situation could be sought: Adoptive mothers could be given the AAI before adoption, in order to determine whether the mother-to-infant match—heretofore considered the result of a mother's caregiving behavior as determined by her own "state of mind with respect to attachment"—is reducible to simply transmitting her genetic makeup to her infant. van Londen and her colleagues in the Netherlands (van Londen, Juffer, & van IJzendoorn, 1999) have already embarked on the first of these studies. A sufficient number of studies will need to be conducted to permit meta-analytic comparisons between results obtained with biological and adoptive mothers, and researchers conducting any such study will need to conduct a ("blind") control study to rule out laboratory-specific coding biases.[5]

Another intriguing study would involve comparing AAI correspondence in identical versus fraternal twins raised apart. In my view, genetic differences may "get their innings" with respect to attachment organization late rather than early in life, when those endowed with good looks, high intelligence, high metacognitive abilities (Main, 1991; see Fonagy & Target, 1997, for a summary of studies providing initial although not yet determining corroboration), or other special abilities may be advantaged over others. Since it appears from retrospective accounts given within the AAI that some individuals have become secure/autonomous despite highly unfavorable backgrounds, such potentially "heritable" abilities and characteristics may have been of assistance, and these adults are typically termed "earned secure" (see Hesse, Chapter 19, this volume). If some agreed-upon list of unfavorable life events is taken into account, then, identical adult twins faced with similar difficult life experiences might be expected to resemble each other more than fraternal twins on these grounds.

16. *Bowlby focused on behavioral processes enhancing the likelihood of infant survival, and he referred to these as the "outer ring" of infant protection. Currently a body of work emerging within the animal literature indicates that the "inner ring" of physiological processes guarding survival is also regulated by infant–mother interactions. Indeed, some attachment-related behaviors believed to be primarily mediated by symbolic processes in young humans now appear—at least in some animals—to be influenced by separable aspects of a mother's control over separable aspects of an infant's physiology.* Bowlby (1969/1982) proposed that an infant–mother dyad that is managing to maintain sufficient proximity to permit (safe) infant exploration in favorable situations, while allowing for rapid physical contact in unfavorable ones, could be seen as a kind of behavioral "homeostasis"—an "outer" or external ring permitting variations in behavior only within safe, albeit changing lim-

its. This outer ring was compared to the "inner" ring of physiological systems controlling, for example, blood pressure and temperature regulation, which also promote life while operating within (variable but) set limits. More recently, Hofer (1984, 1987, 1995, 1996), Kraemer (1992), Reite and Capitano (1985), and others (see Polan & Hofer, Chapter 8, this volume; see also Amini et al., 1996) have proposed that early infant–mother interactions in fact control the "inner ring" of infant protection as well.

Despite his focus on behavioral processes, even 30 years ago Bowlby (1969/1982) gave brain chemistry and hormones special roles in the activation, termination, and development of attachment behavior. His original speculations are consistent with Suomi's (Chapter 9, this volume) recent finding of rapid decrease in hypothalamic–pituitary–adrenocortical activity occasioned by ventral contact with the mother in rhesus monkeys, together with an accompanying reduction in heart rate indicative of soothing. More recent studies have found still other biochemical correlates of attachment-related experiences, with separation and loss unfavorably affecting both human and nonhuman primate immune systems (Ader, 1995). Additionally, in the last decade, oxytocin, endogenous opioids, and norepinephrine have been implicated in various kinds of affiliative behavior, including attachment behavior (Carter, Lederhandler, Izja, & Kirkpatrick, 1997; Nelson & Panksepp, 1998; Panksepp, Siviy, & Normansell, 1985). Endogenous opioids have been found to play a role in the infant's positive responses to mother's milk (Blass & Ciaramitaro, 1994), as well as infant reunion responses in the rat (Hofer, 1995), where opioid antagonists block infant settling.

In an early and still continuing set of studies, Rosenblatt (e.g., 1969, 1983) revealed an exquisite interplay among context, self-generated actions, infant-generated experiences, and hormones in mothering behavior in the rat. These elegant studies were among the first to trace interacting and regulating component processes in mothering, and provide us with a background for appreciating Hofer's (1984, 1995; Polan & Hofer, Chapter 8, this volume) findings and theorizing regarding "hidden regulators" in attachment and separation processes as seen in the infant rat. Essentially, Hofer (see also Kraemer, 1992, who is of the same opinion) concluded that Bowlby had actually *underestimated* the ultimate importance of early mother–infant interactions: In rats as well as primates (Kraemer, 1992; Reite

& Capitano, 1985; see Blass & Ciaramitaro, 1994; Carter et al., 1997; and Field, 1985, for similar discussions involving human infants), mother–infant interactions are effective not only in protecting the infant from external dangers, but also in promoting life through regulating independent internal systems (i.e., in promoting survival via preservation of internal, as well as external, homeostasis). Moreover, Hofer (1995) argued that because for some time rats had not been known to cry upon separation (the sound is ultrasonic, but is now readily recorded), their capacity for separation distress had been underestimated. Rather than being symbolically mediated, as Bowlby required as a sign of "real" (Stage III) attachment in human infants, the separation distress of the rat infant seemed simply to reflect the malignant effects of each of the independent component processes regulated by the mother's presence going awry in her absence. There are, of course, issues of semantics regarding what qualifies as "attachment" here, and while some readers might disagree, Hofer (1995; see also Polan & Hofer, Chapter 8, this volume) has dealt ably with several of the more philosophical issues.

Whatever the peculiarities of the human case, it seems unquestionable that the researchers named above have advanced our understanding of the importance of the mothering figure in guiding physiological, as well as behavioral, aspects of infant survival. Variations in mothering affect the infant's physiological systems both immediately and in the long term, as Suomi (Chapter 9, this volume) has described for peer-reared infants. One of the most compelling series of studies has been conducted by Rosenblum, Andrews, and their colleagues (Rosenblum & Andrews, 1994; Rosenblum et al., 1994), who induced inattentiveness in otherwise normal bonnet macaque mothers by varying the food supply and hence the time and effort the mothers had to devote to foraging. The long-term behavioral effects were striking: The infants of these mothers were submissive, unsuccessful in affiliative conflicts, and vulnerable to depression. As might be expected, given these behavioral outcomes, permanent alterations were found in serotonergic and noradrenergic pathways.

Amini et al. (1996) have interpreted this set of studies as indicating that

the nervous system of social mammals is constituted by a number of open homeostatic loops, which require external input from other social mammals in order for internal homeostasis to be maintained. The manner in which this input is achieved is through social contact and biobehavioral synchrony attained with attachment figures (Field, 1985). In this view, then, the attachment relationship is postulated to be a crucial organizing regulator of normal neurophysiology for social mammals.

Amini et al. further quote Kraemer (1992) as stating that "the attachment system is not only an organizing feature of basic neurophysiologic function, but the central organizing system in the brain of higher social mammals." When we combine this advance in the study of the importance of early mother–infant interactions with findings regarding the long-term effects of variations in available attention (and proximity) among *normal* monkey mother–infant dyads, as noted by Andrews, Rosenblum, and colleagues, we can expect intriguing results to emerge both from studies that look for separable "maternal" controls of differing aspects of human physiology, and from long-term physiological follow-ups to early individual differences in attachment organization.

17. *Recent work in neuroscience and psychophysiology may enable us to think somewhat more concretely about the concept of "internal working models," as well as that of "representational states." Until recently, this terminology has appeared solely conceptual and abstract. It is encouraging, however, that findings in psychophysiology and cognitive neuroscience supportive of and in principle capable of extending these and other attachment-related concepts are now becoming available. I review some of these findings and offer suggestions for future studies. Some of these focus on hemisphericity as potentially related to attachment organization, and some emphasize the striking resemblance between preoccupied (or conceivably, unresolved/preoccupied) adult attachment status and difficulties implicating the frontal lobes.*

There are so many emerging findings in psychophysiology and neuroscience of relevance to attachment theory that the task of selecting among them—especially for a person like myself who has been reading in the field only recently—is necessarily somewhat arbitrary. However, I believe that some findings presented here would have greatly interested both Bowlby and Ainsworth, and are pertinent to their concerns not only with the conceptualization of mental models and defense, but also with the likely effects of early attachment-related stress in later life. Because I am covering several diverse topics

in this section, any commentary provided follows directly upon the subsection under consideration.

a. *The emergence of self-perpetuating prototypes from simple connectionist processes.* Scientists do not agree at present on the best way of conceptualizing brain processes. For some, the concept of "mental modules" makes sense—as seen, for example, in the "theory of mind module" that Baron-Cohen and others believe to be locatable in the normal brain, and absent in autistic persons (e.g., Baron-Cohen, Tager-Flusberg, & Cohen, 1993). The "mental module" approach to brain activity has conceivable, although I believe ultimately only superficial, relations to Bowlby's concept of the internal working model.

Others endorse gentler gradients of specialization, and still others put their faith in ever-changing forms of connectionist models, which can roughly be described as continuing to follow "Hebb's rule" that cells that fire together once are increasingly likely to do so again. Although linear-sounding, the connectionist models arising from recognition of the accuracy of Hebb's proposal, and studied currently in the form of computer models, have as an emergent property (see Rumelhardt & McClelland, 1986) the spontaneous production of prototypes that acquire considerable stability. A particularly elucidating and accessible description of the consequences of the "automatic" production of prototypes by computer simulations utilizing the connectionist paradigm is found in Amini et al. (1996). Just as Bowlby had remarked that internal working models take on a self-perpetuating quality, so that we continue to see new situations in terms of our earlier but now outdated models, so these prototypes, once generated by connectionist processes, continue to operate and begin to "misinterpret" poorly fitting data even in the case of clearly nonconfirmatory evidence.

"Implicit learning" as generated in computer simulations can, then, result in a clear (prototypical) processing bias of the kind that concerned Bowlby, but again—and somewhat surprisingly—no state of higher consciousness or cortex is necessary for this emergence. Amini et al. quote Lewicki, Hill, and Czyzewska (1992) as concluding that this process of self-perpetuation is a clear example of a cognitive mechanism capable of nonconsciously generating or making up new knowledge structures that are independent of, or even inconsistent with, the objective nature of the person's environment. These prototypes, patterns, or "models" are produced by simple parallel processors. If this model of brain activity holds even in part for animal brains, then we must conclude that Bowlby was correct regarding the nature and dangers of mental models, but that the complex techniques currently used to assess them may have given us an exaggerated sense of the cognitive machinery necessary to generate them.

b. *Working memory: Empirically locatable, and perhaps temporarily incapacitated for some individuals when asked to simultaneously remember and speak about traumatic experience.* What Bowlby meant by internal working models was not "provisional, rough, approximate, or changeable" models (as many attachment researchers originally believed; see Crittenden, 1990), but rather that these models are mentally maniputable. In other words, these models permit a person to engage in forecasting manifold scenarios, imagining alternative outcomes prior to undertaking action (see Craik, below, as cited in Bretherton & Munholland, Chapter 5, this volume).

There are, of course, different ways of manipulating information and guessing or imagining how things might happen in the future, using the past as a guide. The slower of us make lists, compare lists, and stare at alternative lists for 40 minutes before deciding which action to undertake, but there is also cognitive machinery for quicker, less conscious, more automatic calculations. This aspect of what is often called "working memory" may have a direct relation to the "manipulable" aspects of the internal working model. Working memory is believed to sit at the "crossroads" of bottom-up and top-down processing systems, making high-level thinking and reasoning possible. It corresponds to the activated information in long-term memory, the information in short-term memory, and the ("executive") processes that determine which information is activated in long-term memory and retained in short-term memory. As a necessarily serial processor, working memory is associated with consciousness and is involved not only in all tasks that require some form of temporary storage, but also in the interplay between information that is stored temporarily and the larger body of stored knowledge. It is used and can be studied in the completion of arithmetic tasks and in reading, speaking, and reasoning.

Some years ago working memory was only a concept (Baddeley & Hitch, 1974), but several investigators have now located parts of the prefrontal cortex that are principal players in various aspects of working memory (e.g, visual–spatial vs. auditory working memory); moreover, single-cell recordings have been made of its operation within one location (Goldman-Rakic, 1995). When an individual is overloaded with simultaneous tasks in working memory, different brain areas are engaged; success, or simply confusion, may be the result.

Commentary. What is interesting about the locatability of working memory is that eventually we may be able to "watch" when individuals with differing attachment histories are engaged in mental tasks that seem to confuse or overwhelm them. The most obvious example consists in those parts of the AAI in which individuals are asked about experiences of loss. Here, some but not all speakers exhibit lapses in reasoning or discourse that Erik Hesse and I have tentatively interpreted as involving temporary disruptions in working memory (Main & Hesse, 1992; see also Hesse & Main, 1999). For some speakers at such times, the lost figure, the self, the relation between them, and the loss event apparently cannot be discussed in normal conversational terms (a speaker may fall silent, provide inappropriate attention to detail, or suddenly move to an inappropriate speech register—e.g., eulogistic or funereal speech). In other cases, temporary interferences in reasoning processes occur (e.g., the speaker refers to the self as having caused the death with an untoward thought, or implies that the dead person is simultaneously alive in the physical sense). We can see these discourse/reasoning lapses as the product of parallel, incompatible ideation (such as, most starkly, dead/not-dead) that distress the individual sufficiently to disrupt his or her ability to simultaneously bring information out of long-term memory and operate on it. It is probably too early to conduct noninvasive on-line recordings of these lapses, but with several brain locations now identified, we may have specific places to look. From noting which aspects of working memory are or are not activated in persons exhibiting difficulties in discussing loss experiences, together with additional brain structures (such as amygdala) that may be simultaneously activated, we may learn more than we might initially imagine. One conceivable possibility is that in persons traumatized by loss, frightening visual–spatial memories are activated simultaneously with aspects of memory required for speaking, and the system as a whole is overloaded.

c. *Semantic, episodic/autonoetic, and implicit/procedural memories: Implications for therapy and for individual differences in responses to the*

AAI. Bowlby expressed great interest in the semantic–episodic memory distinction, as discussed by Tulving (1972), among others; I (Main, 1991) have used this distinction to point to inconsistencies in the portrayal of parenting by dismissing individuals in the AAI. However, humans and other animals also have "implicit" or "procedural" memories—a third important class of memory (Shachter, 1992) that cannot be accessed through words, and that Wheeler et al. (1997) in consequence term "nonpropositional." Crittenden (see Crittenden, 1995, for an overview) was to my knowledge the first researcher to discuss the implications of this third type of memory for attachment research, pointing out that procedural (nondeclarative, implicit) memories will include sequences of interaction experienced in the home and in stressful situations (comparable to Stern's [1985], concept of repeated interactions that are generalized, or RIGS), which could be especially important for expanding our understanding of the import of early attachment experiences. Several further forms of conceptual–semantic divisions among memory systems have been devised, including declarative (explicit and speakable) and nondeclarative (roughly, implicit and procedural).

When first introduced, the distinctions among memory systems were largely speculative and theoretical. However, in several ways they have now been traced to particular structures and locations in the brain, and new ideas about the nature and meaning of these differing memory systems are continually being articulated. One of the most important reviews (and discoveries) emerged from Squire and his colleagues (e.g., Squire & Knowlton, 1995; Squire, Knowlton, & Musen, 1993), who in essence located declarative memory in the medial temporal lobe, while concluding that nondeclarative (procedural, implicit, or skill) memories involve different and varying systems. In addition, declarative and nondeclarative memories were found to be associated with neuronal activity in different hemispheres. At about the same time Nyberg et al. (1996), using PET scans, found that episodic retrieval was associated with increased blood flow in the right prefrontal cortex, usually in the absence of similar activation in the left prefrontal cortex. In their summary of this PET work, Wheeler et al. (1997) conclude that right frontal blood flow is specifically associated with instructions to think back to some specific, previous personal episode. In such circumstances, they interpret the blood flow in the right pre-frontal cortex as signifying neural correlates of the intention to become "autonoetically" (self-including, subjectively experiencing) aware of a previous experience, whether or not the experience is actually retrieved.

Commentary. Amini et al. (1996) have considered the implications of the early development of implicit (vs. explicit) memory for therapy, as indeed, in varying ways, have Crittenden, Clyman, Stern, and perhaps many others. Especially in cases where we are concerned with early attachment-related experiences (including overt trauma, but also the less dramatic effects of repeated neglect, rejection, or interference associated with the "organized" categories of early insecurity), the patients will not have explicit, declarative memories of these experiences from which they can create workable narratives. There is some structural evidence compatible with this difficulty in accessing early memories: The hippocampus, which appears critical to explicit event memories, may not be developed and connected to critical other areas within the earliest years of life. This suggestion was made by Jacobs and Nadel (1985), and according to LeDoux (1996) has yet to be contradicted. Moreover, it was followed up in a study of rats investigating the relations between the kind of tasks they could accomplish (hippocampal-dependent vs. amygdala-dependent) as they aged, and it was discovered that hippocampus-dependent tasks are learned later (Rudy & Morledge, 1994). What all this means for therapy is that for some (by no means all) patients, it may initially be more important to interact with the therapist actively enough to unlearn early procedures now residing only in implicit memories, and somewhat less important to review and reconstruct their accessible memories. In making this claim, neither Amini et al. nor I would suggest that a therapist should greet patients by holding out his or her arms at the door, but it does place an emphasis on the therapist's role in helping a patient learn new interpersonal procedures, possibly before examining explicit memories. In a recent paper, Diamond et al. (in press; see also Hesse, Chapter 19, this volume) described two borderline patients who moved from insecure to secure AAI attachment status in the course of a year's intensive treatment *in which the patients' past was not discussed.* In my understanding, their treatment followed a form of therapy devised by Otto Kernberg, which at least for the first year focuses almost exclusively on the therapist's establishing a new relationship with the patient, rather than analyzing and discussing past interactions and traumatic experiences. It is fascinating to consider the implications of this study, although of course the researchers are currently continuing forward to study a larger sample. What it seems to mean is that without discussing their attachment history (utilizing explicit memories and accompanying narratives) across the course of therapy, *patients become able to discuss that history coherently and collaboratively as a simple result of learning new (implicit) procedures for interactions in a different context.* The implications of these findings, if replicated, are far-reaching: I would not have predicted these findings in advance.

Wheeler et al.'s 1997 paper on "autonoetic" consciousness was forwarded to me by Dan Siegel (Siegel, in press), with a view to considering what he saw as its likely implications for our understanding of processes observed in the AAI. Here again we have a specialized form of consciousness that the researchers believe to be physically locatable; in this case, it is one that would be expected to be pronounced in secure/autonomous individuals, who readily "travel back" when requested to search for early memories in the course of the AAI. Another interesting possibility is that (once the equipment for conducting on-line recordings is in place) we may have an opportunity to examine whether dismissing individuals even attempt to search for early memories when so requested by the interviewer. If so, there should be increased blood flow in the right prefrontal cortex, and I would guess that in many cases there is not.

Schacter et al. (1996) have also noted physiological correlates separating the intent to recall from successful recollection. In one of their PET studies, these authors found that a memory had to be successfully retrieved, quite apart from the attempt to retrieve, for the hippocampus to show signs of activation. However, in word list learning in which words were read out loud to the subjects, veridical and "false" memories both activated the hippocampus (somewhat confusingly, at least to me). Here, the "real" memories were identified by the simultaneous activation of a structure associated with the short-term retention of auditory/phonological information. Although Schacter (1996) does not recommend that these blood flow studies are ready for court cases contesting a subject's memory, this new paradigm suggests that individual differences established using both AAI and couple attachment measures

could certainly be subjected to some interesting tests.

d. *Stress, memory, and dreaming: Excessive stress can alter brain structures involved in memory and in the patterning of sleep.* From his earliest writings forward, Bowlby was interested in the phenomenon of "repression in the making" in the form of the long-separated toddler's eventual avoidance of the mother upon reunion (e.g., following an extended hospital stay without visitation). This stressful experience resulted in "repression" of memory in some cases, in that it culminated in an apparent lack of recognition of a child's most favored person (Heinecke & Westheimer, 1966). In such cases, I would personally agree that what we are seeing—especially because it is particular to the favored parent—is best conceptualized as defense.

With respect to the AAI, repeating claims to lack memory for childhood have generally been associated with the dismissing category, which is in turn often presumed to be associated with early experiences of rejection by one or both parents. Both Bowlby (1988) and I have generally associated this insistence on lack of memory with "dynamic" processes involving repression of selected aspects of experience, and studies summarized in this volume (Hesse, Chapter 19) would seem to support this claim. However, some recent findings in cognitive neuroscience suggest that long-term stress can affect brain structures involving memory, and as I will describe later, some as yet informal studies involving our own longitudinal subjects provide tentative support. In other words, some apparent lack of recognition of a beloved figure is probably defensive in nature, as is some insistence on lack of memory, and in no way involves major unfavorable changes in the brain. Nevertheless, continuing experiences of high stress can affect the brain in adverse ways that have only recently been recognized, and this might be another route from attachment-related experience to difficulties involving memory.

As noted earlier, Jacobs and Nadel (1985) had suggested that infantile amnesia might be due to the fact that the hippocampus, the seat of explicit memory, is not yet formed. To this they had added that early traumatic experiences might not be accessible through explicit memory, and for the same reason. We have also learned recently, however, that stress hormones interfere with long-term memory, and can eventually lead to damage in brain structures critical to memory. In rats, continuing output of adrenocorticotropic hormone not only interferes with long-term memory but leaves rats unable to learn the placement of the "safe" platform in a water maze.

Nelson and Carver (1998) have recently speculated about some ways in which experience with stress very early in life can have a negative impact on neural circuits that underlie memory, and have described the effects of traumatic events on the development of the neural basis of memory. At the adult level, Bremner et al. (Bremner, 1995; Bremner, Innis, & Charney, 1996; Bremner, 1998) have reported that war veterans suffering from posttraumatic stress disorder (PTSD) have an 8% decrease in the volume of the hippocampus, compared with veterans who do not display PTSD. PTSD victims also have been reported to have difficulty in repeating stories accurately and in remembering word lists. The finding of shrinkage in the hippocampus is of course the most dramatic, and conceivably, we could ask whether it is the traumatic experience as expressed in PTSD that is responsible for the shrinkage, or whether instead people suffering from PTSD are more vulnerable than others in having a smaller hippocampus to begin with. Finally, some of these findings linking stress to difficulties with memory could be mediated by sleep difficulties, which have been found to be greater for individuals suffering from early traumatic experiences. Siegel (in press) has summarized this literature, indicating that rapid-eye-movement (REM) sleep may permit the consolidation of memories, while trauma may block such consolidation.

Commentary. If stress-related hormones have a malignant effect on memory, and—as two studies have already indicated (see Lyons-Ruth & Jacobvitz, Chapter 23, this volume)—as opposed to other infants, those classified as disorganized in the strange situation with just one parent have increased cortisol output following the strange situation procedure, one study that comes immediately to mind would be an examination of potential effects on the hippocampus in infants who are judged disorganized with one (or both) parents during infancy. Because of the trouble and expense of brain imaging procedures, I would, as always, suggest a first exploration involving questionnaires, direct memory tests, or behavior observations. Oddly enough, prior to my brief review of this literature, I had noted an intriguing insistence on lack of memory occurring at age 10 (one subject) and age 19 (several subjects) who had been disorganized rather than avoidant with the mother during in-

fancy. The subject apparently unable to remember either past or recent events at age 10 had been extremely disorganized in infancy, with an alternative ambivalent/resistant category placement rather than an avoidant one. One of the 19-year-olds who stressed the greatest absence of memory for childhood was disorganized with both parents, but alternatively secure with both as well. Thus in neither of the most striking cases does the "insistence on lack of memory" seem to stem from the expected source, i.e., from early avoidance. Rather, it is possible that in these individuals—in contrast with many of our subjects who were avoidant as infants and who now frequently insist on lack of memory for childhood—early and continuous stress may have been a contributing factor. If and when possible, these findings should be extended and subjected to further examination.

Another topic area that I believe has yet to be examined in relation to early attachment organization, current couple relationships, or the AAI is the quality of an individual's dreams and sleep. I would be surprised if no relation to attachment(s) emerged. I am thinking of many differences in individuals' sleep experiences, from sleeping well to having severe sleep disorders, disturbed REM sleep, and severe night terrors (the latter have already been associated with early trauma; see Melver, van Velsen, Lee, & Turner, 1997).

At the adult level, it would be easy to begin with simple sleep questionnaires, and it would be especially interesting to see whether one particular kind of attachment relationship predominated. Thus it could be that a current favorable pair-bond relationship overrides remaining insecurities with respect to early relationships, although for the sake of interpreting such outcomes, researchers should not be too delicate to inquire in this instance whether the person is sleeping in the same bed as the partner he or she is describing in partner interviews and/or inventories. These assessments could initially be simply added to ongoing sleep studies, and the results might be highly illuminating, setting a course for further research. Should the questionnaires yield systematic results, an initial subject pool might be drawn from people already being studied in sleep laboratories.

Another possibility is that attachment researchers interested in sleep disorders and having access to strange situation assessments could add questionnaires regarding sleep patterns to their follow-up studies. If systematic relations appear—as I think they should, given that secure infants are understood to have had repeated experiences of comfort following distress, while disorganized infants are believed to have had repeated experiences of "fright without solution"—longitudinal subjects could be assessed using one of the new techniques, which involve noninvasive home recordings and do not place as much of a burden on subjects as being observed in sleep laboratories.

e. *Some brain areas are activated when an individual is simply engaged in picturing something; others are activated when movement is being imagined. In addition, of course, both psychophysiological techniques and neuroimaging can be used to test subjects' responses to sounds or images that are directly presented. These facts readily suggest several experiments involving individual differences in attachment organization at either the child or adult level.* Springer and Deutsch (1997) have summarized the results of several studies employing PET scans in which visual imaging has resulted in activation of areas of the brain normally involved in visual perception, as well as activation associated with imagined movements. These findings are of course relatively new and extremely intriguing: It appears that it does not take "real" sight or "real" movement to activate the associated brain areas. Of course, at the physiological level, we have long been accustomed to being able to follow the results of a subject's imaginings; high steady heartbeat and rapid breathing, for example, are likely to be found associated with imagining "phobic" situations in some individuals.

Commentary. I will begin with a simple example of a finding involving children's differing responses to family photographs. While the behavioral data were collected many years ago, new studies following a similar design but incorporating the methods of psychophysiology and current cognitive neuroscience could help answer some of the still unsettled issues regarding our original findings (see below).

Main et al. (1985) presented 6-year-old subjects with polaroid photographs of themselves and their parents taken over 1 hour earlier. The family photograph was presented to the child by the examiner at the conclusion to Kaplan's (1987) version of the Separation Anxiety Test, and systematic results relating to early strange situation behavior to the mother were uncovered. Briefly, children avoidant of their mothers as infants turned the photograph backwards, refused it, or looked away from it; children secure with

their mothers in infancy pleasantly acknowledged it, then gave it back to the examiner; and children who had been disorganized became strikingly depressed, characteristically lingering over the photograph or even treating it "tenderly." In the discussion to this article, I noted that it would be important to find out what would happen if we attempted to persuade the children to behave "differently" toward the picture. Although behavior is always the first guide to such studies, my thinking at that time was that it would be ideal to have accompanying physiological measures—now perhaps including EEG, NIRS, or fMRI assessments. In one assessment, we would simply "watch" what happened physiologically or neurologically as the children behaved as they usually did with the photograph. In another, we would somehow persuade the avoidant children, who typically immediately turned the photograph away, to continue to look at it, while we explored any physiological (or brain) states or processes that they had perhaps been attempting to avoid through their actions. Similarly, we would persuade the disorganized children, who typically lingered over the photograph, to immediately place it at a distance or conceal it, looking again for any physiological or brain changes arising from this atypical form of action.

Studies of this kind need not necessarily involve photographs, although in the present state of the arts of physiological and brain assessments they have advantages, in that neither speech nor large motor movement is required. These studies are of special import, because they have the power to tell us whether specific behavior patterns are enabling a child to preserve a state of homeostasis that would otherwise be violated. Similar studies could be conducted with adults, of course, and we could easily see how adults in the varying AAI categories respond to films of approaching, crying, smiling, and retreating infants. In addition, for children as well as young people, we could examine simple reactions to presentation of the face or voice of each parent.

The possibility of eventually examining the brain correlates of "imagining" an object or a movement could also be illuminating in conjunction with the study of individual differences in attachment organization. Here again, the expense of the equipment and the procedures required to run it (and the facts that some equipment is unpleasant for subjects and some procedures are invasive) suggests that we should begin with simple behavioral observation. At Berkeley, we have videotaped a "self-visualization" task with each of our 45 longitudinal subjects, for whom we have strange situation assessments as well as AAIs. The task begins with subjects being instructed to imagine their favorite paintings, to count backward from 100, and finally (each instruction is a surprise, and the task to be undertaken or image to be visualized is given only after the subject indicates that he or she is ready) "to visualize . . . *yourself*!" Subjects are asked to tap to indicate when they have begun to obtain the image requested (self or painting); to tap again when they are "looking at it" as a steady image; and then to hold that image until we tell them to let it go (10 seconds).

To this point we have examined about 20 of our subjects, with striking results. Adolescents who were secure in infancy are generally calm and alert in response to this task; they do not smile, focus readily, and appear to hold the image as requested. Adolescents who were insecure often have an instantaneous reaction, such as (in the case of previously avoidant adolescents) a self-conscious smile or look of contempt, or (previously disorganized infants) a look of distress or confusion, or even movements suggestive of disorganization (e.g., an upward eye roll or twitching of the facial muscles). We have yet to finish the analysis of this sample; however, should behavioral responses to this simple task continue to relate systematically to early attachment organization, brain reactions and physiological reactions should also be examined. We could additionally ask subjects to "imagine" a baby, and to "imagine" approaching their mothers for an embrace, both now and as infants.

f. *Twenty years ago some scientists with interests in brain functioning suffered from what they now look back on as "dichotomania," in which the left brain was, for example, conceived of as rational and "Western," whereas the right brain was seen as emotional, intuitive, and "Eastern." No such extremism remains; paradoxically, however, findings regarding differences in the functioning of the hemispheres are continuing to be assembled. Somewhat surprisingly, considered as a whole they point to qualities in the left hemisphere that can be associated with a dismissing state of mind with respect to attachment. In theory, the right hemisphere could be associated with a preoccupied state as well. A preliminary set of investigations conducted at Berkeley almost a decade ago provided some support for this hypothesis, and continuing investigations should be undertaken.*

Let us begin with some remarks regarding the similarities in the two hemispheres of the brain, always remembering its general plasticity (see especially Merzenich—(e.g., Merzenich & deCharms, 1996)—for a series of elegant studies showing change and repair even in adult brains), as well as the fact that damage to one side, where special abilities such as language are concerned, is often gradually compensated for by the other. Moreover, the two hemispheres of the brain share the same brain stem, the same hormones, the same neurotransmitters, and the same spinal cord, and some of the most noted researchers in neurology have little or no interest in either the somewhat "silent" right half of the brain, or even the entire topic of hemisphericity. Finally, Wheeler et al. (1997) have summarized a number of studies that support their "HERA" model of retrieval and encoding. Here it appears that encoding operations preferentially engage the left side of the brain more than the right, and that retrieval processes engage the right side more than the left. As the authors state, this does not seem to fit in well with the conventional wisdom that the left hemisphere "is critical for verbal processes, whereas the right one mediates processing of visual and spatial information" (p. 342).

With that said, however, I briefly review some of the findings that remain with us. First, Davidson and Fox (1982; see also Fox & Davidson, 1986) have noted that hemispheric differences in emotional reactions to stimuli are present from birth forward (see Fox & Card, Chapter 11, this volume); moreover, left-hemisphere activation is associated with approach, positive affect, exploration, and sociability, while right-hemisphere activation is associated with withdrawal, negative affect, fear, and anxiety. Indeed, Davidson and Fox have found the right hemisphere to be implicated in reactions of anger, disgust, and fear from the beginning of life. Correspondingly, if the left hemisphere is damaged (or simply subjected to temporary deactivation in conjunction with surgical procedures) later in life, subjects not infrequently report feelings of despair, hopelessness, worry, guilt, and anger—and occasionally exhibit what are termed "catastrophic" emotional reactions.

But let us now consider the effects of *right*-hemisphere damage. In badly damaged stroke patients we sometimes see denial of disability, and insistence that the self is fine when physical paralysis is present (see Springer & Deutsch, 1997, pp. 337–338, quoting extensively from a partially paralyzed patient of the neurologist Ramachandran). In patients suffering no permanent damage, but simply have the right hemisphere temporarily deactivated, we see intriguingly parallel outcomes. The patient appears "without apprehension," and may simply exhibit flat affect. Although the findings are not equally strong in all reports, some such patients are described as smiling, laughing, and expressing a sense of well-being. The interpretations of these results are somewhat complex, and I urge the interested reader to work through the arguments and studies presented by Springer and Deutsch (1997). However, having reviewed the several hypotheses under examination, they conclude that the best working hypothesis is that the left side of the brain typically subserves positive emotions, whereas the right side typically subserves negative emotions. This conclusion is further supported by recent work (Wheeler, Davidson, & Tomarken, 1993), in which individual differences in frontal electrophysiological asymmetries (as measured by EEG) can predict reactions to emotion-inducing stimuli. Higher left-sided prefrontal activation at baseline was associated with more positive reactions to a positive film clip; higher levels of right-sided prefrontal activation were associated with a more negative emotional response to a negative film clip. Finally, subjects with greater left-sided activation were found to score highly on personality measures that reflect the tendency to minimize negative affect.

Commentary. With this summary in hand, it should be clear enough to students of infant-to-adult attachment organization that the outcomes of left-hemisphere dominance—whether observed in normal subjects (Davidson's EEG subjects), nondamaged subjects whose right hemispheres have been temporarily deactivated, or subjects suffering definitive brain damage—is consonant with a somewhat avoidant or dismissing state of mind. This is so, of course, because of the associations with the tendency to minimize negative affect, the denial of difficulties, the absence of apprehension, and the occasional descriptions of highly positive affect and well-being (mixed with somewhat contrasting descriptions of flat indifference). This sounds like the avoidant infant as observed in the strange situation, as well as like the transcript of a dismissing AAI. With respect to the influence of the right hemisphere, we can also see some similarities to infant ambivalent/resistant strange situation response patterns and to the preoccupied AAI transcript. The data are, however, somewhat less striking for the adult comparison, because preoccupied individuals are not usually as expressive of extreme distress as individuals deprived of the workings of the left hemisphere.

About 10 years ago, when working through our first efforts to develop a self-report inventory capable of capturing the AAI categories, we collected data on degree of right- or left-handedness as a crude estimate of brain dominance. Extreme right-handedness was, of course, expected to stand for left-hemisphere dominance, with extreme left-handedness standing for right-hemisphere dominance. In pursuit of this issue, we collected two very large undergraduate samples and compared their responses to our four handedness questions (the details do not matter here) with our then-existing brief scales intended to represent a "dismissing" state of mind on the one hand, and a "preoccupied" state of mind on the other.

Our results were not published, for the simple reason that we did not find our scales, as later more fully developed in collaboration with Marinus van IJzendoorn (Main et al., 1999), to be related to the AAI categories for which they were intended to stand. A search through the basement, the attic, and relevant university rooms undertaken for the purposes of this epilogue has not resulted in a successful recapture of our original printout, but I believe my memory for our results is nonetheless accurate. For both samples, the scale for the "dismissing" state of mind was impressively related to right-handedness, and for one sample, left-handedness was weakly (but, as I remember, significantly) related to left-handedness. Since that time, we have developed a far more sophisticated self-report inventory attempting to estimate brain dominance (Main, 1998; since 1989, it appears that footedness is more related to brain dominance than is handedness), and tests of this inventory against infant strange situation behavior are currently being conducted in another laboratory. However, several other promising inventories are now available (see especially Merekelbach, Marris, Horselenberg, & de Jong, 1997).

An interesting recent work by Siegel (in press) is very much concerned with the relations between attachment and hemisphericity, predicting that secure infants and adults will exhibit the greatest degrees of integration between the hemispheres (and insecure individuals the least). As this epilogue goes to press, there is already some support for Siegel's hypothesis, emerging from two independent studies. In one, reported this fall in *Neuroscience* (Anderson et al., 1998), childhood abuse was found to result in abnormal cortical development, with diminished integration between the right and left hemispheres. In turn, this diminished integration was found to be correlated with dissociative experiences. In the second, Kaplan's (1987) version of the Separation Anxiety Test was used to assess security of attachment in 5- to 7-year-old children ($n = 58$). EEG recordings showed no effects of attachment on baseline measures of frontal asymmetry. However, when the children were exposed to emotional film clips, those assessed as insecure demonstrated greater deactivation of the right-frontal region (Davis & Kraft, 1999; Davis, Goldring-Ray, & Kraft, 1998). To my knowledge, this study is the first of its kind.

The studies by Davis and Kraft are currently being replicated and extended, again using the Kaplan system of assessing attachment, and more investigations of comparable depth should soon certainly be conducted. In addition, however, the many researchers who have self-report data available on either early childhood relations (i.e., AAI-like inventories) or couple relations can readily examine this hypothesis further. It has implications for the interpretation of our existing results, as well as, of course, for the relations between brain dominance and ambivalence, avoidance, and dismissing and preoccupied states of mind.

g. *Frontal lobe damage or deficit results in characteristics (listed below) that include several of the features used to classify AAI narratives as preoccupied, although of course in the case of damage or deficit these features appear in a far more extreme form. In addition, in other studies, behavioral characteristics associated with frontal lobe deficit have been noted as preoccupied mothers attempt to engage in tasks with their young children, or respond to caregiving interviews, and individuals suffering from borderline personality disorder, which is very strongly associated with the preoccupied AAI category, have been found to have relatively small frontal lobes (with other brain areas remaining normal in size) and functional frontal lobe impairments. Neuropsychological testing associated with frontal lobe deficits should be employed with individuals in the preoccupied AAI category, together with the empirically closely associated unresolved/disorganized category. If scores suggest statistically significant—but expectably mild—frontal lobe difficulties in the essentially normal populations studied by most investigators, neuroimaging studies should be undertaken.*

Although different sections of the frontal lobes appear to specialize to an impressive extent in different functions, the effects of frontal lobe damage can also be considered at the more general level and have been listed in many articles and texts. These include the inability to use information from the environment to regulate or change behavior, resulting in task perseveration; confusion; difficulty in inhibiting irrelevant thoughts; difficulties with preserving spatial order and temporal context; problems with controlling and monitoring thoughts and memories; difficulty in imposing a structure and hierarchical organization in mental representations, particularly in free-response situations; indecisiveness; deficits in novelty detection; and difficulty in assembling a plan. I do not claim that this is the full set of signs characterizing the deficits suffered by these individuals, but in my reading of the literature, these seem to appear most frequently. It should be noted that it is not necessary to establish the presence of either a lesion or a tumor to establish that a subject has frontal lobe difficulties. Frontal lobe deficits can be detected using neuropsychological testing: The Wisconsin Card-Sorting Task is perhaps the most frequently used, but there is also a Stroop test for color interference; still another methodology has been devised very recently, which is advertised as being administratable at the bedside and as producing a "frontal lobe score" (Ettlin & Kischka, 1999).

Commentary. With the exception of "deficits in novelty detection" and "difficulty in assembling a plan" (but see below), every one of the signs of frontal lobe deficit listed above is associated with the central instructions for classifying an AAI transcript as preoccupied. First, the transcript is usually inappropriately long, with the speaker failing to permit the interviewer to regulate the length of the speaker's conversational turn, and perseverating at great length with respect to any particular question[6]. Second, the extensive discussions of parents or experiences that generally characterize these transcripts are described as confused and "neither fruitful, objective, nor incisive" (p. 167). Third, speech is frequently irrelevant to the topic at hand. Fourth, violations of appropriate temporal order appear in tendencies to bring the present into discussions regarding the past. Fifth, at times the speech of preoccupied speakers appears unmonitored (cf. "uncontrolled"), in that it can be momentarily difficult to understand. Sixth, absence of structure or hierarchical order is notable, in that preoccupied subjects are described as "caught up in memories of youth and childhood, or even in current interactions with parents" (pp. 168, 169), while being at the same time "unable to move 'above' these episodes, memories and reminiscences to an objective overview at the semantic or abstract level" (p. 168). Seventh, indecisiveness (expressed in the directions for interview classification as "oscillations") often mark these interviews as well.

As regards the indecisiveness and confusion that mark those suffering from frontal lobe deficits, we have further evidence from an independent study conducted by Carol George and Judith Solomon (1996), in which a "caregiving interview" was administered. Here, the term found most fitting to the preoccupied mothers was "uncertain," and a scale was developed that identified a preoccupied mother's mental representations as made manifest during the caregiving interview as reflecting "doubt, confusion, or vacillation in opinion regarding herself as a caregiver, the child, and their relationship" (p. 204). Similarly, in another independent study, Crowell and Feldman (1988) observed secure, dismissing, and preoccupied mothers in a problem-solving session with their preschool children. Mothers in the preoccupied group "often had difficulty giving directions and suggestions to their children, presenting the goal of the task and instructions in such a confusing and dyssynchronous manner that the children appeared overwhelmed" (p. 1283). At times, the mothers seem puzzled.

Finally, as the reader may remember (Hesse, Chapter 19, this volume), borderline personality disorder is strongly associated with the preoccupied AAI category, so that the majority of individuals suffering from this disorder are classified as preoccupied. This would mean that in investigations of borderline patients, we would probably be obtaining mostly preoccupied subjects, and frontal lobe studies involving these individuals might therefore tend to confirm the association I have suggested above. Surprisingly, at least two such studies have already been conducted. In one, borderline patients were examined for functional frontal lobe impairment and found to show elevated levels (van Reekum et al., 1996). In a second, more recent MRI study, several areas of the brain were examined in borderline patients as compared to controls; the frontal lobes (but none

of the remaining structures examined) were found to be diminished in volume (Lyoo, Kyoon, Moon, & Cho, 1988).

Here then, is a new area for investigation at the interface of attachment and cognitive neuroscience, and I would urge researchers having the requisite knowledge and/or equipment to look for this relation in normal samples. A caveat to such researchers is that many, and perhaps a majority, of preoccupied subjects (like borderline patients) are also unresolved/disorganized, so that it would be too early to attribute any results to preoccupation in itself. Researchers should thus begin with both preoccupied and unresolved/preoccupied subjects, conducting the neuropsychological tests for frontal lobe deficits that have been mentioned above. The more complex and expensive processes involving neural imaging should be conducted only if these simpler behavioral procedures show elevated scores for members of this group. In that case, although the interpretation and implications for intervention and assistance will be long in coming, it will be time to examine these individuals using current neuroscience.

18. *There are several ways of approaching the problem of assessing representational processes respecting attachment, in terms of both semantics (e.g., working models, states of mind) and methodology (e.g., interviews, observations, self-reports). For example, not all assessments may fit well with the term "internal working model." In addition, methods of assessment in adulthood include both interview and self-report measures, and in many instances these could profitably be combined. A diverse set of studies utilizing some or all of these methods is suggested.*

Most readers of this epilogue are probably already familiar with the concept of internal working models. Those who are less familiar should refer to Bretherton and Munholland's chapter in this volume. Here and elsewhere, Bretherton (e.g., Bretherton, 1985) has pointed out that Bowlby's thinking about this concept was derived from that of Craik (1943), who, taking an evolutionary perspective, proposed that organisms capable of forming complex internal working models of their environment "considerably improve their chances of survival, because the ability to construct and use mental models to evaluate the potential consequences of alternative courses of action makes for much more flexible and adaptive behavior" (Bretherton & Munholland, Chapter 5, this volume, p. 90). Craik further stated that:

If the organism carries a "small-scale model" of external reality and of its own possible actions within its head, it is able to try out various alternatives, conclude which is the best of them, react to future situations before they arise, utilize the knowledge of past events in dealing with the present and future, and in every way to react in a much fuller, safer and more competent manner to the emergencies which face it. (1943, p. 61)

Much has been made of this concept, and my colleagues and I were among the first to attempt to assess individual differences in internal working models of attachment relationships at 6 years of age and in adulthood (Main et al., 1985). The methods utilized with children included responses to Kaplan's (1987) version of the Separation Anxiety Test, an assessment that has proven highly fruitful in several studies (see Solomon & George, Chapter 14, this volume), and the analysis of children's drawings of their family (Kaplan & Main, 1986). Both of these measures can be considered to yield representational *products,* but they are not the same as the internal representations themselves, which are of course inaccessible to direct inspection. Strikingly, the Separation Anxiety Test and the family drawings were strongly related to the child's strange situation behavior to the mother in infancy, and each of these outcomes have been replicated in new samples (see Fury, Carlson, & Sroufe, 1997; Grossmann & Grossmann, 1991; Jacobsen et al., 1994, and Solomon & George, Chapter 14, this volume). The "representational product" used to assess the parent's "internal working model" of attachment was the AAI (Hesse, Chapter 19, this volume), which was found to be associated with the infant's strange situation behavior to the speaker (whether mother or father) 5 years earlier.

There were several problems with the interpretations I originally offered for the outcomes of this study. Perhaps the first was to refer to children in differing early attachment categories as having differing but singular internal working models of attachment—for example, an "avoidant" or a "resistant" working model. The problem for insecure children is not that they have a particular, singular, specifiable kind of "internal working model" of the self, the attachment figure, and the relations between them, but rather that they have multiple, contradictory models. That had been Bowlby's original point: It was drawn to my attention in a later conversation with Roger Kobak, and was discussed in my own writings at a later time (Main, 1991).

A second problem was the use of similar terminology to describe differences found among children's descriptions of, for example, what a child might do upon separation from his or her parents (Kaplan, 1987), and differences found among transcripts of AAIs. Whereas "working model" (or, in the case of insecure children, multiple, contradictory working models) appears adequate to describe the child's view of the self, the parent, and the relation between them, it hardly seems able to encompass an adult's responses to a discussion of his or her entire life history with respect to attachment, including relations with both parents, important loss experiences, and perceived effects of that history. Somewhat awkwardly, I attempted the phrase "the model of the self in overall relation to attachment." This once again meets with the problem of ignoring the multiple, contradictory models that are found in the transcripts of dismissing and preoccupied individuals (Main, 1991). In addition, it glosses over the problem that many disparate aspects of experience are being discussed at the same time.

Reflection on this error brought me eventually to the conclusion that in some circumstances application of the term "internal working model of . . ." is misleading and unwarranted. First, the phrase inevitably implies a homunculus, the possessor of the model or set of models. This again may fit a child's view of the self in relation to the parent, but it cannot really accurately describe all of the phenomena involved in an adult's hour-long discussion of his or her life history. To describe what the AAI transcript can most readily be said to represent, I eventually chose "state of mind with respect to attachment." This term had the advantage of indicating an overall state that arises or is made manifest at the time of the interview, involves no overseeing executive or homunculus, and accounts for the individual's language usage in discussing multiple experiences and persons without in any way being focused on a particular experience or person. Bowlby (1973) had also at times used the term "representational state."

Although we used and continue to use multiple measures in attempting to assess an individual's representational states or models, a third flaw in this early study was our failure to provide opportunities for the parents to give their own, more direct responses to queries regarding their early relationships through oral or written self-reports. In retrospect, we can provide some defense for this oversight. We did not then believe that direct self-reports regarding early experiences with parents and their effects would relate to a measure relying in good part on the opportunity it presented for revealing apparent contradictions, distortions, and omissions in the representation of a life history, as did the AAI. Later, we had the occasion to confirm this belief painfully for ourselves (following our own unsuccessful attempts at devising an AAI-like self-report inventory [see Hesse, Chapter 19]; others have also found self-reports regarding attachment experiences and states of mind to be unrelated to infant strange situation behavior or to the AAI). Furthermore, self-report inventories regarding couple or parent relationships show little or no relation at the categorical level to the AAI (see Hesse, Chapter 19, and Crowell, Fraley, & Shaver, Chapter 20, this volume, for reviews; for one attempt to look below the categorical level at particular coder and self-report continua, see Shaver, Belsky, & Brennan, 1999). Nonetheless, the failure to collect this data left this study incomplete and was an error.

What was missed by focusing only on subtle techniques that allow for omissions, contradictions, and distortions in the subject's "representational product," while omitting simple direct reports such as those obtained with couple inventories (see Brennan, Clark, & Shaver, 1998, and Crowell et al., Chapter 20, this volume, for reviews of self-report attachment measures)? What we missed was the opportunity to study this material in comparison with our remaining observations and data—a process I would recommend that future investigators utilizing interview and other complex methods undertake.

There are a great many arguments for increasing the "multiple-measures" approach to attachment organization by including self-report inventories in interview and observational studies (and for including interview and observational measures in self-report studies, even though, like strange situation assessments, the AAI is complex). First, couple self-report inventories, although to date entirely direct in nature, are successfully predicting behavior, memory, and psychophysiological processes, and generally in exactly those ways one would expect when using more complex and indirect measures (see Crowell et al., Chapter 20, this volume). This means that when individuals discuss their general feelings regarding relations to partners or specific feelings about a particular partner, the fairly direct, conscious claim they make about being dismissing, secure, or preoccupied is backed by data very comparable to what one would expect to ob-

tain when interview measures are used. One possible explanation for the connection between self-reports and other measures in the case of adult romantic (pair-bond) attachment is that people's understanding of their typical relationships with partners is more accessible to consciousness than their early attachment history. Another possibility (discussed by Crowell et al., Chapter 20, this volume) is that adults are able to report fairly accurately on their feelings and behavior in the context of intimate relationships, despite being unable to understand the dynamics of their own defenses. (Most self-report inventories ask about specific thoughts, feelings, and behaviors in close relationships, and about what relationship partners have said about these things, without asking subjects to use the terminology of defense—i.e., without seeking directly for abstract self-characterizations such as "dismissing," etc.).

Commentary. I would suggest that one of the most beneficial effects of this volume will be to promote integration of the now somewhat divergent domains of interview and self-report assessments of attachment. Researchers who have devised and are conducting couple attachment interviews might consistently combine them with couple self-report inventories. If, as Crowell and her colleagues (e.g., Crowell & Owens, 1996; Crowell & Waters, 1997) have already demonstrated for her version of a couple attachment interview, such interviews continue to account for considerable variance in observed couple interactions—and if, as reviewed and demonstrated here (Crowell et al., Chapter 20, this volume) and elsewhere, couple self-report inventories are also successful in accounting for considerable variance in observed couple interactions—we can benefit by examining the combined variance accounted for by inclusion of both measures, and by having the opportunity to examine the cases of mismatch between assessment procedures and the relations of mismatching cases to outcome.

I would also recommend that individuals utilizing caregiving interviews (see George & Solomon, Chapter 28, this volume, for an overview) and AAIs attempt to employ direct self-report inventories as well. Although we know that to date the existing adult attachment self-report inventories do not relate to the AAI at a categorical level, we do not know what aspects of behavior, psychophysiology, or cognitive process might be accounted for, or accounted for more fully, with the addition of self-reports. While the likelihood of predicting infant caregiving or clinical status at anything approaching the levels predicted by the AAI from self-report inventories seems small, we might, for example, be able to increase our power to predict the nature of interactions between mothers and their adult daughters, each of whom has been given the AAI. Here, as in the case of couple interactions, we are asking direct questions about currently important relationships. Finally, we are continuing our own attempts to develop the Berkeley–Leiden self-report inventory (Main, Hesse, & van IJzendoorn, 1999); when further refined, the scales in this inventory may have a somewhat stronger relation to the AAI.

Even should the various existing adult attachment inventories continue to fail to relate to the AAI, however, a series of intriguing studies remain open to us. Given large enough samples, for example, we have the possibility of examining differences among persons whose self-reports agree with, or disagree with, the classifications assigned to them by the AAI. Persons who are judged dismissing on the AAI, and also describe themselves as dismissing via paragraph choices or their responses to Likert scales, may differ in important ways from those who are judged dismissing on the AAI but describe themselves as secure. Likewise, those who are judged secure/autonomous on the AAI and also consider themselves secure in self-report inventories may differ in interesting ways from secure/autonomous individuals who describe themselves as dismissing or preoccupied.

We could conduct a number of valuable new studies with the measures that are currently available. Here I focus on those involving adults, although in many cases the same questions could be addressed using measures of attachment organization for infants or young children (e.g., I suggest "mini-cross-cultural" studies, and these could be conducted at any age level). Within the adult realm, I note where I believe there is reason to begin with a particular methodology or set of methodologies; because of space limitations, however, readers are left largely on their own to determine why a particular methodology is selected.

First, many studies have now shown that when the AAI is conducted twice with the same individual over periods ranging as widely as 2 months to 4 years, the organized categories (secure/autonomous, dismissing, and preoccupied) are stable, with stability figures ranging from about 78% to 90%. These investigations have been critical to establishing the psychometric

properties of the interview, as well as the authenticity of the underlying phenomenon. For the purposes of this presentation, I will take 80% as an estimated baseline figure. I would argue that new studies are needed to determine whether we should interpret the 20% changes as "permanent" (as I believe many of us do unconsciously), or simply as reflective of short-term changes that occur as people fluctuate across the course of a week "out of" and then "back into" a predominant category. The assumption of permanent change does not, of course, make ultimate sense, because if 20% of people change permanently in classification across each 2-month period, it would be difficult to find 80% stability across periods of a year or two (which is what in fact has been found). Thus one possibility is that—while no doubt always including some permanent changes—the 80% "stability rate" reflects in part a tendency among individuals to be only "generally" in the same mental state with respect to attachment (e.g., from Monday to Thursday, but not on Friday). The answer to this question can only be addressed by a third assessment, and ideally a fourth assessment, each time accompanied at a minimum by inventories evaluating current mood, and tracking intervening life events.

Second, many cross-national studies of attachment organization have been conducted in different European and North American countries, and van IJzendoorn and Sagi (Chapter 31, this volume) have shown that, for infant strange situation behavior at least, we have now finally begun to extend our investigations to the truly cross-cultural (e.g., including ethnic groups in Africa; see True, 1994). However, if we are interested in the relation between culture and attachment, mini-cross-cultural studies are of equal interest. There are many areas of this country in which within only a few square miles we can find wealthy new gated communities; wealthy individualized older communities; ranch, fishing, and farm communities; suburban communities; high-density blue-collar communities; high-density communities subject to violence and drugs; and communities including a number of members of the Ku Klux Klan. This list is not arbitrary—it is representative of a portion of the communities within a 15-mile radius of Berkeley. The advantages of a mini-cross-cultural study comparing attachment organization across such communities is that despite differing language usages, the same language is shared, and despite selective exposure to the mass media, there are few for whom, for example, the recent adventures of our national leader remain unknown. Although in comparing individuals living in different areas, we would want to control for socioeconomic status, the cultural *similarities* among communities provide some controls not available in comparisons of Bay Area infants with infants living in Polynesia. I would recommend beginning the mini-cross-cultural research enterprise with self-report inventories administered to as many members of the community as possible, followed up with interviews to check for similarity of distributions. Understanding the results obtained might require collaboration with a cultural anthropologist, but I believe that systematic differences are to be expected.

Third, some of the classic as well as more recent interests of personality and social psychologists could be investigated in relation to individual differences in attachment organization, and here I would suggest initial use of the AAI. The reason for selecting the AAI for the studies suggested below is that it is able to identify individuals who are in a *secure/autonomous* state of mind with respect to attachment (here the *autonomy* of such individuals is of special import—see earlier discussions in this epilogue, as well as Hesse, Chapter 19, this volume), rather than secure in their general or specific partner relationships.

a. Studies of differences in the ability to resist group pressure might be conducted. I do not suggest a rerun of studies involving prison guards or electric shock, but secure/autonomous persons might be found less likely to conform in group settings in which the remaining members of the group appear to misperceive phenomena.

b. The question of the relation between security and creativity is an old one. It fascinates many people, and it has not, to my knowledge, been satisfactorily addressed. The AAI appears to me to give us a new opportunity to approach this question, but I would not recommend that researchers simply ask interview participants to complete the various creativity self-report inventories, such as innovativeness and remote associations tests. Rather, we might simply begin by interviewing renowned artists, musicians, and writers (while, of course, preserving their anonymity). As they are lost to us, I would have predicted, for example, that the singer Marian Anderson would have been judged secure/autonomous, while the equally great singer Billie Holiday would have been judged not only unresolved/disorganized but also unclassifiable in the

terms generally used in AAI analyses (see Hesse, Chapter 19, this volume, for a discussion of the "cannot classify" category). More systematic studies could also be conducted. At Berkeley, for example, "real-life" investigations of individual differences in creativity have been undertaken for many years. Within a given field, members of the field nominate their most creative representatives, who are interviewed and studied extensively with other outstandingly successful but "less creative" members of the field. The AAI could of course be added to studies of this kind.

c. A somewhat newer interest in social psychology is "empathic accuracy" (Ickes, 1997), and here we might conceivably predict that preoccupied individuals would score best. This could be due to early parental emphasis on identifying emotional states, as well as to a long preoccupation with the moods and mental states of the parents. Perhaps instead secure/autonomous individuals would be the most accurate in reading the moods of others, but it would be pleasing to begin to discover areas in which insecure individuals stand foremost. In this particular case, however, dismissing individuals might be expected to come last.

A fourth possible area of study, as Hesse has already described (Chapter 19, this volume), is illustrated by the emerging research pioneered by Hopf and Hopf in Germany on the relation between attachment organization and political extremism (Hopf, 1993; Hopf & Hopf, 1997). These authors have compared German rightwing extremist youth with nonextremist youth, finding almost none of the former to be secure/autonomous, and the very strong majority to be dismissing on the AAI. Their study is of the greatest interest, because attitudes toward the state and toward the parents were found to be similar in certain important ways. The study should be followed up—first through careful replication, perhaps including (as I believe the Hopfs had originally intended) left-wing as well as right-wing extremists. We might predict that, as opposed to right-wing extremists believing in violence, left-wing extremists ascribing to violence might tend to be preoccupied.

Like the Hopfs, future investigators should conduct a depth analysis of the relation between the individual's "state of mind with respect to attachment" (idealizing the parents and minimizing their faults) and state of mind with respect to the state. (In the Hopfs' study, right-wing extremists idealized the state and minimized its faults.) The Hopfs' investigations of attitudes toward the state involved extensive interviews, as I believe are necessary if we are to understand how attachment and these attitudes are related. Across dismissing individuals as a whole, it is of course only a very few who are right-wing extremists, so further questions and analyses are required to identify and understand the specific qualities of this subgroup. The association between attachment classification and authoritarian extremism appears to be a solid one, however, since Hesse and van IJzendoorn (1999) found dismissing college students to be significantly higher than others on an authoritarianism scale.

Although several additional studies involving extremist political attitudes come to mind, I will mention only one. As Chappell and Davis (1998) and Pietromonaco and Carnelley (1994) have already reported, even individuals identified as insecure in couple self-report inventories typically describe themselves as preferring a secure partner. But would this be true among extremist youth? Having first asked how they identify themselves within couple relationships, we might then continue the investigation by determining whether—in contrast to the nonextremist populations previously studied—they would favor an insecure partner just as, in essence, they favor an "insecure" state or form of government.

In a fifth area of research, it is already being established (see Hesse, Chapter 19, this volume) that violent criminal offenders are insecure with respect to attachment. However, there are groups in which members perform violent acts while being culturally encouraged to treat their families with kindness (and sometimes while encouraging wives and children to ignore these violent acts). I have wondered for many years what family relations in such groups are like, and in exploring the matter I would ideally employ all of the kinds of adult measures mentioned at the outset of this section with both members of the couple. The final and perhaps most critical question would be whether infants living in such families could be secure.

Finally, and fortunately, there are more uplifting investigations to be undertaken than the ones mentioned immediately above. Among these, one of the most interesting would be to conduct AAIs with individuals who risked their lives to protect potential victims of the Holocaust. Although the events are many years in the past, and any findings would have to be interpreted with caution (50-year stability for the AAI having yet to be established), I believe that a study of this kind

would nonetheless be of import. (Unfortunately for human values, but fortunately for further research on this topic, the world presents new examples of genocide and moral heroism every year.)

Although secure/autonomous status on the AAI might be expected by most attachment researchers to be associated with moral courage, any systematic outcome would be of interest. Thus, while we expect and are finding those committing violent acts to be insecure, it could be that a substantial proportion of those engaging in outstandingly courageous acts of humanity are also insecure, and in interesting ways. If it was not primarily secure/autonomous individuals who protected the potential victims of the Holocaust at great personal risk, for example, my next best guess would be that it was unresolved individuals who were alternatively classifiable as secure (see findings at Leiden discussed by Hesse, Chapter 19, this volume; see also an intriguing interpretation by Lyons-Ruth & Jacobvitz, Chapter 23). In addition, I can imagine such actions on the part of moderately dismissing individuals determined to pursue and follow the moral course. While still in the early stages of formulation, collaborative plans to undertake a study of this kind are currently underway at Leiden and at Berkeley. This line of thinking may stimulate related ideas on the part of researchers who study the complexities of moral and immoral behavior.

CONCLUDING COMMENTS

This epilogue is an attempt to remind new audiences of some central points of attachment theory that can easily be overlooked or misunderstood, and to provide several ideas for new investigations related to some of these points. I have emphasized the necessary relation between fear and attachment for the developing child, and have pointed out that children's ties to their adult attachment figure(s), in contrast with intimate adult relationship(s), are necessarily asymmetrical. In elaborating on these 18 points, I hope I have indicated that we are currently at one of the most exciting junctures in the history of our field. We are now, or soon will be, in a position to begin mapping relations between individual differences in early attachment experiences and changes in neurochemistry and brain organization. In addition, investigation of physiological "regulators" associated with infant–caregiver interactions could have far-reaching implications for both clinical assessment and intervention. Closer to my own training and research tradition, I have suggested a variety of new applications for the AAI and noted the necessity of bringing together this research domain with the study of adult pair bonds, which are often investigated with self-report inventories. The apparently greater conscious awareness that adults have regarding contemporary versus early formative relationships is highly intriguing, and in actively combining indirect interview and direct self-report approaches, we may be able to learn more about both the formation of defenses and the way some individuals manage to minimize defensive processes.

In recasting the profound and complex issues central to psychoanalytic theory, and making them compatible with evolutionary theory, developmental biology, and the methods of empirical psychology, Bowlby and Ainsworth opened the door to a host of important research findings and clinical and social policy applications. These benefits of attachment theory should soon include an increased understanding of the mechanisms through which attachments are formed; comparative studies of attachment across animal species; studies of the relations between attachment and neuroscience; and studies of adult emotions and behavior in close relationships, morally demanding situations, and the domain of politics. Attachment researchers have a great deal to be proud of, but no shortage of hard, exciting work still to be done.

ACKNOWLEDGMENTS

This epilogue would not have been brought into existence without Phil Shaver, who spent an extraordinary ten days—often working into the early morning—reading and rereading every portion of it, and improving every portion from commas, to references, to substance. He provided invaluable feedback and encouragement, and again, the manuscript could not have been completed without him.

Sarah Hrdy, Naomi Gribneau, and John Watson read and corrected varying aspects of the text, and Jude Cassidy made many useful comments. Erik Hesse read the manuscript several times in its entirety and provided final commentary. As is said in any such set of acknowledgments, any remaining errors are my own.

NOTES

1. In some places in this epilogue, I mention possible future studies that I believe could not be humanely or ethically conducted in the form in which I have quickly described them here. I do so in the hope that other investigators may be able to develop an ethical version of these or similar studies.

2. I would not want to deny that simply jumping backward may be a better immediate solution to the problem of encountering a snake.

3. It could also be, however, that the animal and human researchers have been taking readings from somewhat different sections of the amygdala.

4. I am grateful to Dan Silver at Berkeley for elucidating this point.

5. Of course, the need for this study has been lessened by the finding (Steele, Steele, & Fonagy, 1996) that within a large London sample, the infant's strange situation behavior with each parent matched that particular parent's AAI.

6. I should note here that I believe most instances of task perseveration in subjects suffering from frontal lobe deficits are motoric rather than linguistic, but it should also be noted that the subjects with whom we work in most attachment studies do not have severe deficits; that answering the interview queries is a task; and that certainly the answer to whether perseveration extends to conversation, if not already addressed in the literature, is an interesting one.

REFERENCES

Ader, R. (1995). Psychoneuroimmunology: Interactions between the nervous system and the immune system. *Lancet, 345,* 99–102.

Adolphs, R., Tranel, D., Damasio, H., & Damasio, A. R. (1995). Fear and the human amygdala. *Journal of Neuroscience, 15,* 5879–5891.

Ainsworth, M. D. S. (1967). *Infancy in Uganda: Infant care and the growth of love.* Baltimore: Johns Hopkins University Press.

Ainsworth, M. D. S. (1991, July). *Conversation hour with Mary Ainsworth.* Discussion held at the meeting of the International Society for the Study of Behavioral Development, Minneapolis, MN.

Ainsworth, M. D. S., & Bell, S. M. (1970). Attachment, exploration, and separation: Illustrated by the behavior of one-year-olds in a strange situation. *Child Development, 41,* 49–67.

Ainsworth, M. D. S., Blehar, M. C., Waters, E., & Wall, S. (1978). *Patterns of attachment: A psychological study of the strange situation.* Hillsdale, NJ: Erlbaum.

Allman, J., & Brothers, L. (1994). Faces, fear, and the amygdala. *Nature, 372,* 613–614.

Ammaniti, M., Speranza, A. M., & Candelori, C. (1996). Stability of attachment in children and intergenerational transmission of attachment. *Psichiatria dell'Infanzia e dell'Adolescenza, 63,* 313–332.

Amini, F., Lewis, T., Lannon, R., & Louie, A. (1996). Affect, attachment, memory: Contributions towards psychobiologic integration. *Psychiatry: Interpersonal and Biological Processes, 59,* 213–239.

Anderson, C. N., Polcari, A. M., McGreenery, C. E., Mass, L. C., Renshaw, P. F., & Teicher, M. H. (1998). Enduring effects of child abuse on cortical fMRI. *Society for Neuroscience Abstracts, 24,* 432.

Axelrod, R. (1984). *The evolution of cooperation.* New York: Basic Books.

Baddeley, A., & Hitch, G. (1974). Working memory. In G. H. Bower (Ed.), *The psychology of learning and motivation* (Vol. 8, pp. 47–89). New York: Academic Press.

Baron-Cohen, S., Tager-Flusberg, H., & Cohen, D. (Eds.). (1993). *Understanding other minds: Perspectives from autism.* Oxford: Oxford University Press.

Bateson, P., & Horn, G. (1994). Imprinting and recognition memory: A neural net model. *Animal Behaviour, 48,* 695–715.

Blass, E. M., & Ciaramitaro, V. (1994). A new look at some old mechanisms in human newborns: Taste and tactile determinants of state, affect, and action. *Monographs of the Society for Research in Child Development, 59*(1, Serial No. 81).

Bowlby, J. (1958). The nature of the child's tie to its mother. *International Journal of Psycho-Analysis, 39,* 350–373.

Bowlby, J. (1969/1982). *Attachment and loss: Vol. 1. Attachment.* New York: Basic Books.

Bowlby, J. (1973). *Attachment and loss: Vol 2. Separation: Anxiety and anger.* New York: Basic Books.

Bowlby, J. (1980). *Attachment and loss: Vol. 3. Loss: Sadness and depression.* New York: Basic Books.

Bowlby, J. (1987). Attachment. In R. L. Gregory (Ed.). *The Oxford companion to the mind* (pp. 57–58). Oxford: Oxford University Press.

Bowlby, J. (1988). *A secure base.* New York: Basic Books.

Bremner, J. D. (1998). Neuroimaging of posttraumatic stress disorder. *Psychiatric Annals, 28,* 445–450.

Bremner, J. D., et al. (1995). MRI-based measurement of hippocampal volume in patients with combat-related posttraumatic stress disorder. *American Journal of Psychiatry, 152,* 973–981.

Bremner, J. D., Innis, R. B., & Charney, D. S. (1996). MRI-based measurement of hippocampal volume in patients with combat-related posttraumatic stress disorder. *American Journal of Psychiatry, 153,* 1658–1659.

Brennan, K. A., Clark, C. L., & Shaver, P. R. (1998). Self-report measurement of adult attachment: An integrative overview. In J. A. Simpson & W. S. Rholes (Eds.), *Attachment theory and close relationships* (pp. 46–76). New York: Guilford Press.

Bretherton, I. (1985). Attachment theory: Retrospect and prospect. In I. Bretherton & E. Waters (Eds.), Growing points of attachment theory and research. *Monographs of the Society for Research in Child Development, 50*(1-2, Serial No. 129), 3–38.

Carlson, E. A. (1998). A prospective longitudinal study of disorganized/disoriented attachment. *Child Development, 69,* 1970–1979.

Carter, C. S., Lederhandler, I., Izja, E., & Kirkpatrick, B. (Eds.). (1996). The integrative neurobiology of affiliation. *Annals of the New York Academy of Sciences,* Vol. 807. Neuropsychiatric Manifestations of Systemic Lupus Erythematosus. New York: New York.

Chance, M. R. A. (1962). An interpretation of some agonistic

postures: The role of "cut-off" acts and postures. *Symposium of the Zoological Society of London, 8,* 71–89.

Chappell, K. D., & Davis, K. E. (1998). Attachment, partner choice, and perceptions of romantic partners: An experimental test of the attachment-security hypothesis. *Personal Relationships, 5,* 327–342.

Chisholm, J. (1995). Life history theory and life style choice: Implications for Darwinian medicine. *Perspectives in Human Biology, 1,* 19–28.

Colin, V. L. (1985). *Hierarchies and patterns of infants' attachments to parents and day caregivers: An exploration.* Unpublished doctoral dissertation, University of Virginia.

Colin, V. L. (1987, April). *Infants' preferences between parents before and after moderate stress activates attachment behavior.* Paper presented at the meeting of the Society for Research in Child Development, Baltimore, MD.

Craik, K. (1943). *The nature of explanation.* Cambridge, England: Cambridge University Press.

Crittenden, P. M. (1990). Internal representational models of attachment relationships. *Infant Mental Health Journal, 11,* 259–277.

Crittenden, P. M. (1995). Attachment and psychopathology. In S. Goldberg, R. Muir, & J. Kerr (Eds.), *Attachment theory: Social, developmental, and clinical perspectives* (pp. 367–406). Hillsdale, NJ: Analytic Press.

Crowell, J. A., & Feldman, S. S. (1988). Mothers' internal models of relationships and children's behavioral and developmental status: A study of mother–child interaction. *Child Development, 59,* 1273–1285.

Crowell, J. A., & Owens, G. (1996). *Current Relationship Interview and scoring system.* Unpublished manuscript, State University of New York at Stony Brook.

Crowell, J. A., & Waters, E. (1997, April). *Couples' attachment representations: Stability and relation to marital behavior.* Poster presented at the biennial meeting of the Society for Research in Child Development, Washington, DC.

Damasio, A. R. (1994). *Descartes' error: Emotion, reason, and the human brain.* New York: Grosset/Putnam.

Davidson, R. J., & Fox, N. A. (1982). Asymmetrical brain activity discriminates between positive versus negative affective stimuli in human infants. *Science, 218,* 1235–1237.

Davis, K. M., & Kraft, R. H. (1999). *Attachment security and frontal asymmetry: Differences in emotion regulation strategies?* Submitted manuscript.

Davis, K. M., Goldring-Ray, S., & Kraft, R. H. (1998, May). *Attachment security and frontal asymmetry: Differences in emotion regulation strategies?* Poster presented at the 10th Annual Conference of the American Psychological Society, Washington, DC.

Diamond, D., Clarkin, J., LeVine, H., Levy, K., Foelsch, P., & Yoemans, R. (in press). Borderline conditions and attachment: A preliminary report. *Psychoanalytic Inquiry.*

Ettlin, T., & Kischka, U. (1999). Bedside frontal lobe testing: The "Frontal Lobe Score." In B. L. Miller & J. L. Cummings (Eds.), *The human frontal lobes: Functions and disorders* (pp. 233–246) . New York: The Guilford Press.

Eyer, D. (1992). *Mother-infant bonding: A scientific fiction.* New Haven, CT: Yale University Press.

Field, T. (1985). Attachment as psychobiological attunement: Being on the same wavelength. In M. Reite & T. Field (Eds.), *The psychobiology of attachment and separation* (pp. 415–454). New York: Academic Press.

Fonagy, P., & Target, M. (1997). Attachment and reflective

function: Their role in self-organization. *Development and Psychopathology, 9,* 679–700.

Fox, N. A., & Davidson, R. J. (1986). Taste-elicited changes in facial signs of emotion and the asymmetry of brain electical activity in newborns. *Neuropsychologia, 24,* 417–422.

Frodi, A. M., Lamb, M. E., Hwang, C. P., & Frodi, M. (1983). Father–mother infant interaction in traditional and non-traditional Swedish families: A longitudinal study. *Alternative Lifestyles, 5,* 142–163.

Fury, G., Carlson, E., & Sroufe, L. A. (1997). Children's representations of attachment relationships in family drawings. *Child Development, 68,* 1154–1164.

George, C., Kaplan, N., & Main, M. (1996). *Adult attachment interview protocol* (3rd ed.). Unpublished manuscript, University of California at Berkeley.

George, C., & Solomon, J. (1996). Representational models of relationships: Links between caregiving and attachment. *Infant Mental Health Journal, 17,* 198–216.

Goldman-Rakic, P. (1995). Cellular basis of working memory. *Neuron, 14,* 477–485.

Greenfield, S. A. (1997). *The human brain: A guided tour.* New York: Basic Books.

Grossmann, K. E., & Grossmann, K. (1991). Attachment quality as an organizer of emotional and behavioral responses in a longitudinal perspective. In C. M. Parkes, J. Stevenson-Hinde, & P. Marris (Eds.), *Attachment across the life cycle* (pp. 93–114). London: Tavistock/Routledge.

Heinecke, C., & Westheimer, I. (1966). *Brief separations.* New York: International Universities Press.

Hesse, E., & Main, M. (1999). Unresolved/disorganized responses to trauma in non-maltreating parents: Previously unexamined risk factor for offspring. *Psychoanalytic Inquiry, 19.*

Hesse, E., & van IJzendoorn, M. H. (1998). Parental loss of close family members and propensities towards absorption in offspring. *Developmental Science, 1,* 299–305.

Hesse, E., & van IJzendoorn, M. H. (1999). *Attachment and politics.* Unpublished manuscript, Leiden University.

Hesse, E., & van IJzendoorn, M. H. (in press). Propensities towards absorption are related to lapses in the monitoring of reasoning or discourse during the Adult Attachment Interview: A preliminary investigation. *Attachment and Human Development.*

Hinde, R. A. (1959). Behavior and speciation in birds and lower vertebrates. *Biological Review, 34,* 85–128.

Hinde, R. A. (1966). *Animal behaviour: A synthesis of ethology and comparative psychology.* New York: McGraw-Hill.

Hodges, J., & Tizard, B. (1989). Social and family relationships of ex-institutional adolescents. *Journal of Child Psychology and Psychiatry, 30,* 77–97.

Hofer, M. A. (1984). Relationships as regulators: A psychobiologic perspective on bereavement. *Psychosomatic Medicine, 46,* 183–197.

Hofer, M. A. (1987). Early social relationships: A psychobiologist's view. *Child Development, 58,* 633–647.

Hofer, M. A. (1995). Hidden regulators: Implications for a new understanding of attachment, separation, and loss. In S. Goldberg, R. Muir, & J. Kerr (Eds.), *Attachment theory: Social, developmental, and clinical perspectives* (pp. 203–232). Hillsdale, NJ: Analytic Press.

Hofer, M. A. (1996). On the nature and consequences of early loss. *Psychosomatic Medicine, 58,* 570–581.

Honey, R. C., Horn, G., Bateson, P., & Walpole, M. (1995). Functionally distinct memories for imprinting stimuli: Behavioral and neural dissociations. *Behavioral Neuroscience, 109,* 689–698.

Hopf, C. (1993). Rechtsextremismus und Beziehungserfahrungen. *Zeitschrift für Soziologie, 22,* 449–463.

Hopf, C., & Hopf, W. (1997). *Familie, Personlichkeit, Politik: Eine Einfuhrung in die politische Sozialisation [Family, personality, politics: An introduction to political socialization].* Munich: Juventa.

Hrdy, S. (1999). *Mother nature: A history of mothers, infants, and natural selection.* New York: Pantheon.

Ickes, W. (Ed.). (1997). *Empathic accuracy.* New York: Guilford Press.

Insel, T. R. (1992). Oxytocin: A neuropeptide for affiliation: Evidence from behavioral, receptor, audio-radiographic, and comparative studies. *Psychoneuroendocrinology, 17,* 3–35.

Jacobs, W. J., & Nadel, L. (1985). Stress-induced recovery of fears and phobias. *Psychological Review, 92,* 512–531.

Jacobsen, T., Edelstein, W., & Hofman, V. (1994). A longitudinal study of the relation between representations of attachment in childhood and cognitive functioning in childhood and adolescence. *Developmental Psychology, 30,* 112–124.

Jolly, A. (1972). *The evolution of primate behavior.* New York: Macmillan.

Joseph, R. (1993). *The naked neuron: Evolution and the languages of the body and the brain.* New York: Plenum Press.

Kaplan, N. (1987). *Individual differences in six-year-olds' thoughts about separation: Predicted from attachment to mother at age one.* Unpublished doctoral dissertation, University of California at Berkeley.

Kaplan, N., & Main, M. (1986). *A system for the analysis of children's family drawings in terms of attachment.* Unpublished manuscript, University of California at Berkeley.

Kirkland, A. (1996). *Street soldiers* [Film]. Berkeley, CA: New Images Productions.

Klaus, M., & Kennell, J. (1976). Parent-to-infant attachment. In D. Hull (Ed.), *Recent advances in pediatrics* (pp. 129–152). New York: Churchill Livingstone.

Kraemer, G. W. (1992). A psychobiological theory of attachment. *Behavioral and Brain Sciences, 15,* 493–541.

Lamb, M. E., Frodi, M., Hwang, C. P., & Frodi, A. M. (1983). Effects of parental involvement on infant preferences for mothers and fathers. *Child Development, 54,* 450–458.

LeDoux, J. (1996). *The emotional brain: The mysterious underpinnings of emotional life.* New York: Simon & Schuster.

LeDoux, J. E., Romanski, L., & Xagoraris, A. (1989). Indelibility of sub-cortical emotional memories. *Journal of Cognitive Neuroscience, 1,* 238–243.

Liotti, G. (1992). Disorganized/disoriented attachment in the etiology of the dissociative disorders. *Dissociation 5,* 196–204.

Liotti, G. (in press). Disorganization of attachment as a model for understanding dissociative psychopathology. In J. Solomon & C. George (Eds.), *Attachment disorganization.* New York: Guilford Press.

Lewicki, P., Hill, T., & Czyzewska, M. (1992). Non-conscious acquisition of information. *American Psychologist, 47,* 796–801.

Lyoo, I. K., Kyoon, H., Moon, H., & Cho, D. Y. (1998). A brain MRI study in subjects with borderline personality disorder. *Journal of Affective Disorders, 50,* 235–243.

Main, M. (1979). The ultimate causation of some infant attachment phenomena: Further answers, further phenomena, and further questions [Letter]. *Behavioral and Brain Sciences, 2,* 640–643.

Main, M. (1981). Avoidance in the service of attachment: A working paper. In K. Immelmann, G. Barlow, L. Petrinovich, & M. Main (Eds.), *Behavioral development: The Bielefeld interdisciplinary project* (pp. 651–693). New York: Cambridge University Press.

Main, M. (1990). Cross-cultural studies of attachment organization: Recent studies, changing methodologies, and the concept of conditional strategies. *Human Development, 33,* 48–61.

Main, M. (1991). Metacognitive knowledge, metacognitive monitoring, and singular (coherent) vs. multiple (incoherent) models of attachment: Findings and directions for future ressearch. In C. M. Parkes, J. Stevenson-Hinde, & P. Marris (Eds.), *Attachment across the life cycle* (pp. 127–159). London: Routledge.

Main, M. (1995). Attachment: Overview, with implications for clinical work. In S. Goldberg, R. Muir, & J. Kerr (Eds.), *Attachment theory: Social, developmental, and clinical perspectives* (pp. 407–474). Hillsdale, NJ: Analytic Press.

Main, M. (1996). Introduction to the special section on attachment and psychopathology: II. Overview of the field of attachment. *Journal of Consulting and Clinical Psychology, 64,* 237–243.

Main, M. (1998). *Self-report inventory for estimating hemispheric dominance: Handedness, footedness, left-looking, and right-looking.* Unpublished inventory, University of California at Berkeley.

Main, M., & Cassidy, J. (1988). Categories of response to reunion with the parent at age six: Predicted from infant attachment classifications and stable over a one-month period. *Developmental Psychology, 24,* 415–426.

Main, M., & Goldwyn, R. (1998). *Adult attachment scoring and classification system.* Unpublished manuscript, University of California at Berkeley.

Main, M., Hesse, E., & van IJzendoorn, M. H. (1999). *The Berkeley–Leiden Adult Attachment Questionnaire.* Unpublished inventory, University of California at Berkeley.

Main, M., & Hesse, E. (1990). Parents' unresolved traumatic experiences are related to infant disorganized attachment status: Is frightened and/or frightening parental behavior the linking mechanism? In M. T. Greenberg, D. Cicchetti, & E. M. Cummings (Eds.), *Attachment in the preschool years: Theory, research, and intervention* (pp. 161–182). Chicago: University of Chicago Press.

Main, M., & Hesse, E. (1992). Disorganized/disoriented infant behavior in the strange situation, lapses in the monitoring of reasoning and discourse during the parent's Adult Attachment Interview, and dissociative states. In M. Ammaniti & D. Stern (Eds.), *Attachment and psychoanalysis* (pp. 86–140). (Translated from the Italian, *Attacamento e psicoanalisi*)

Main, M., Kaplan, N., & Cassidy, J. (1985). Security in infancy, childhood, and adulthood: A move to the level of representation. In I. Bretherton & E. Waters (Eds.), *Growing points of attachment theory and research. Monographs of the Society for Research in Child Development, 50* (1–2, Serial No. 209), 66–104.

Main, M., & Solomon, J. (1986). Discovery of a new, insecure-disorganized/ disoriented attachment pattern. In T. B. Brazelton & M. W. Yogman (Eds.), *Affective development in infancy* (pp. 95–124). Norwood, NJ: Ablex.

Main, M., & Solomon, J. (1990). Procedures for identifying infants as disorganized/ disoriented during the Ainsworth

strange situation. In M. T. Greenberg, D. Cicchetti, & E. M. Cummings (Eds.), *Attachment in the preschool years: Theory, research, and intervention* (pp. 121–160). Chicago: University of Chicago Press.

Main, M., & Weston, D. R. (1981). The quality of the toddler's relationship to mother and to father: Related to conflict behavior and the readiness to establish new relationships. *Child Development, 52,* 932–940.

Marshall, J. (1996). *Street soldier.* New York: Delacorte Press.

Marks, I. (1987). *Fears, phobias, and rituals: Panic, anxiety, and their disorders.* New York: Oxford University Press.

McIvor, R. J., Van Velsen, C., Lee, D., & Turner, S. W. (1997). Theoretical models of post-traumatic stress disorder. In D. Black, M. Newman, J. Harris-Hendriks, & G. Mezey (Eds.), *Psychological trauma: A developmental approach* (pp. 54–77). London, England: Gaskell/Royal College of Psychiatrists.

Merckelbach, H. M., Murris, P., Horselenberg, R., & de Jong, P. (1997). EEG correlates of a paper-and-pencil test measuring hemisphericity. *Journal of Clinical Psychology, 53,* 739–744.

Mendoza, S. P., & Mason, W. A. (1986). Parental division of labor and differentiation of attachments in a monogamous primate (*Callicebus moloch*), *Animal Behaviour, 34,* 1336–1347.

Merzenich, M. M., & deCharms, R. C. (1996). Neural representations, experience, and change. In R. R. Llinas & P. S. Churchland (Eds.), *The mind–brain continuum: Sensory processes* (pp. 61–81). Cambridge, MA: MIT Press.

Mineka, S. (1987). A primate model of phobic fears. In H. Eysenck & I. Martin (Eds.), *Theoretical foundations of behavior therapy.* New York: Plenum Press.

Muller, N., & Ackenheil, M. (1995). The immune system and schizophrenia. In B. E. Leopard & K. Miller (Eds.), *Stress, the immune system, and psychiatry* (pp. 137–164). Chichester, England: Wiley.

Nelson, C. A. (1997). The neurobiological basis of early memory development. In C. Nelson (Ed.), *The development of memory in childhood: Studies in developmental psychology* (pp. 41–82). Hove, England: Taylor & Francis.

Nelson, C. A., & Bloom, F. E. (1997). Child development and neuroscience. *Child Development, 58,* 970–987.

Nelson, C. A., & Carver, L. J. (1998). The effects of stress and trauma on brain and memory: A view from developmental cognitive neuroscience. *Development and Psychopathology, 10,* 793–809.

Nelson, E. E., & Panksepp, J. (1998). Brain substrates of infant–mother attachment: Contributions of opioids, oxytocin, and norepinephrine. *Neuroscience and Biobehavioral Reviews, 22,* 437–452.

Nyberg, L., McIntosh, A., Cabeza, R., Habib, R., Houle, S., & Tulving, E. (1996). General and specific brain regions involved in encoding and retrieval of events: What, where, and when. *Proceedings of the National Academy of Sciences USA, 93,* 11280–11285.

Ogawa, J. R., Sroufe, L. A., Weinfield, N. S., Carlson, E. A., & Egeland, B. (1997). Development and the fragmented self: Longitudinal study of dissociative symptomatology in a nonclinical sample. *Development and Psychopathology, 9,* 855–879.

Ohman, A. (1993). Fear and anxiety as emotional phenomena: Clinical, phenomenological, evolutionary perspectives and information-processing mechanisms. In M. Lewis & J. M. Haviland (Eds.), *Handbook of emotions* (pp. 511–536). New York: Guilford.

O'Reilly, R. L. (1994). Viruses and schizophrenia. *Australian and New Zealand Journal of Psychiatry, 28,* 222–228.

Panksepp, J., Siviy, S. M., & Normansell, L. A. (1985). Brain opioids and social emotions. In M. Reite & T. Field (Eds.), *The psychobiology of attachment and separation* (3–49). New York: Academic Press.

Pietromonaco, P. R., & Carnelley, K. B. (1994). Gender and working models of attachment: Consequences for perceptions of self and romantic relationships. *Personal Relationships, 1,* 63–82.

Pike, A., & Plomin, R. (1997). A behavioural genetic perspective on close relationships. *International Journal of Behavioral Development, 21,* 647–667.

Reite, M., & Capitano, J. P. (1985). On the nature of social separation and social attachment. In M. Reite & T. Field (Eds.), *The psychobiology of attachment and separation.* New York: Academic Press.

Rheingold, H. L., Gewirtz, J. L., & Ross, H. W. (1959). Social conditioning of vocalizations in the infant. *Journal of Comparative and Physiological Psychology, 52,* 68–73.

Roberston, J., & Robertson, J. (1967–1972). *Young children in brief separations* [Film series]. London: Tavistock Institute of Human Relations.

Robertson, J., & Robertson, J. (1971). Young children in brief separation: A fresh look. *Psychoanalytic Study of the Child, 26,* 264–314.

Rosenblatt, J. S. (1969). The development of maternal responsiveness in the rat. *American Journal of Orthopsychiatry, 39,* 36–56.

Rosenblatt, J. S. (1983). Olfaction mediates developmental transition in the altricial newborn of selected species of mammals. *Developmental Psychobiology, 16,* 347–374.

Rosenblum, L. A., & Andrews, M. W. (1994). Influences of environmental demand on maternal behavior and infant development. *Acta Paediatrica,* Suppl. 397, 57–63.

Rosenblum, L. A., Coplan, J. D., Friedman, S., Bassoff, T., Gorman, J. M., & Andrews, M. W. (1994). Adverse early experiences effect noradrenergic and serotinergic functioning in adult primates. *Biological Psychiatry, 35,* 221–227.

Rowell, T. E., & Hinde, R. A. (1963). Responses of rhesus monkeys to mildly stressful situations. *Animal Behavior, 11,* 235–243.

Rudy, J. W., & Morledge, P. (1994). Ontogeny of contextual fear conditioning in rats: Implications for consolidation, infantile amnesia, and hippocampal system function. *Behavioral Neuroscience, 108,* 227–234.

Rumelhardt, D. E., & McClelland, J. L. (1986). *Parallel distributed processing: Explorations in the micro-structure of cognition.* Cambridge, MA: MIT Press.

Schacter, D. L. (1992). Implicit knowledge: New perspectives on unconscious processes. *Proceedings of the National Academy of Sciences USA, 89,* 1113–1117.

Schacter, D. L. (1996). *Searching for memory: The brain, the mind, and the past.* New York: Basic Books.

Schacter, D. L., et al. (1996). Conscious recollection and the human hippocampal formation: Evidence from positron emission tomography. *Proceedings of the National Academy of Sciences USA, 93,* 321–325.

Schacter, D., Reimane, E., Curran, T., Yun, L. S., Brandy, D., McDermott, K., & Rowdigger, H. (1996). Neuroanatomical correlates of veridical and illusory recognition memory: Evidence from PET. *Neuron, 17,* 267–274.

Schaffer, H. R., & Emerson, P. E. (1964). The development of social attachments in infancy. *Monographs of the Society for Research in Child Development, 29*(3, Serial No. 94).

Shaver, P. R., Belsky, J., & Brennan, K. A. (1999). *The Adult Attachment Interview and self-reports of romantic attachment: Associations across domains and methods.* Manuscript submitted for publication.

Shaver, P. R., Hazan, C., & Bradshaw, D. (1988). Love as attachment: The integration of three behavioral systems. In R. J. Sternberg & M. L. Barnes (Eds.), *The psychology of love* (pp. 68–99). New Haven, CT: Yale University Press.

Siegel, D. J. (in press). *The developing mind: Toward a neurobiology of interpersonal experience.* New York: The Guilford Press.

Sorce, J. F., & Emde, R. N. (1981). Mothers presence is not enough: Effect of emotional availability on infant exploration. *Developmental Psychology, 17,* 737–745.

Spangler, G., & Grossmann, K. E. (1993). Biobehavioral organization in securely and insecurely attached infants. *Child Development, 64,* 1439–1450.

Springer, S. P., & Deutsch, G. (1997). *Left brain, right brain: Perspectives from cognitive neuroscience.* (5th ed.). New York: Freeman.

Squire, L. R., Knowlton, B., & Musen, G. (1993). The structure and organization of memory. *Annual Review of Psychology, 44,* 453–495.

Squire, L. R., & Knowlton, B. J. (1995). Memory, hippocampus, and brain systems. In M. S. Gazzaniga (Ed.), *The cognitive neurosciences* (pp. 825–837). Cambridge, MA: MIT Press.

Steele, H., Steele, M., & Fonagy, P. (1996). Associations among attachment classifications of mothers, fathers, and infants: Evidence for a relationship-specific perspective. *Child Development, 2,* 541–555.

Stern, D. N. (1985). *The interpersonal world of the infant: A view from psychoanalysis and developmental psychology.* New York: Basic Books.

Strage, A., & Main, M. (1985, April). *Attachment and parent–child discourse patterns.* Paper presented at the biennial meeting of the Society for Research in Child Development, Toronto.

Suomi, S. J. (1995). Influence of attachment theory on ethological studies of biobehavioral development in nonhuman primates. In S. Goldberg, R. Muir, & J. Kerr (Eds.), *Attachment theory: Social, developmental, and clinical perspectives* (pp. 185–201). Hillsdale, NJ: Analytic Press.

Tellegen, A. (1982). *Brief manual for the Differential Personality Questionnaire.* Unpublished manuscript, University of Minnesota, Minneapolis.

Tellegen, A., & Atkinson, G. (1974). Openness to absorbing and self-altering experiences ("absorption"), a trait related to hypnotic susceptibility. *Journal of Abnormal Psychology, 83,* 268–277.

Tinbergen, N., & Moynihan, M. (1952). Head-flagging in the black-headed gull: Its function and origin. *British Birds, 45,* 19–22.

Tizard, B., & Hodges, J. (1978). The effect of early institutional rearing on the development of 8–year-old children. *Journal of Child Psychology and Psychiatry, 19,* 99–118.

Tomarken, A. J., & Davidson, R. J. (1994). Frontal brain activation in repressors and non-repressors. *Journal of Abnormal Psychology, 103,* 339–349.

True, M. M. (1994). *Mother–infant attachment in communication among the Dogan of Mali.* Unpublished doctoral dissertation, University of California at Berkeley.

Tulving, E. (1972). Episodic and semantic memory. In E. Tulving & W. Donaldson (Eds.), *Organization of memory* (pp. 381–403). New York: Academic Press.

van IJzendoorn, M. H. (1995). Adult attachment representations, parental responsiveness, and infant attachment: A meta-analysis on the predictive validity of the Adult Attachment Interview. *Psychological Bulletin, 117,* 387–403.

van IJzendoorn, M. H., Schuengel, C., & Bakermans-Kranenburg, M. J. (in press). Disorganized attachment in early childhood: Meta-analysis of precursors, concommitants, and sequelae. *Development and Psychopathology.*

van Londen, M., Juffer, F., & van IJzendoorn, M. H. (1999). *Predicting infant attachment organization from prebirth*

Adult Attachment Interviews in first-time adoptive mothers. Manuscript in preparation, Leiden University.

Vaughn, B., Egeland, B., Sroufe, A. L., & Waters, E. (1979). Individual differences in infant–mother attachment at 12 and 18 months: Stability and change in families under stress. *Child Development, 50,* 971–975.

Walsh, F. W. (1978). Concurrent grandparent death and birth of schizophrenic offspring: An intriguing finding. *Family Process, 17,* 457–463.

Watson, J. S. (1972). Smiling, cooing, and "the game." *Merrill–Palmer Quarterly, 18,* 323–339.

Wheeler, M. A., Stuss, D. T., & Tulving, E. (1997). Toward a theory of episodic memory: The frontal lobes and autonoetic consciousness. *Psychological Bulletin, 121,* 331–354.

Zahavi, A., & Zahavi, A. (1997). *The handicap principle: A missing piece of Darwin's puzzle.* New York: Oxford University Press.

Author Index

Author Index

Subject Index